Ellicott's COMMENTARY ON THE WHOLE BIBLE

A VERSE BY VERSE EXPLANATION

EDITED BY
CHARLES JOHN ELLICOTT

VOLUME VIII

Ephesians — Revelation

WIPF & STOCK · Eugene, Oregon

Wipf and Stock Publishers
199 W 8th Ave, Suite 3
Eugene, OR 97401

Ellicott's Commentary on the Whole Bible Volume VIII
Ephesians - Revelation
By Ellicott, Charles J.
ISBN 13: 978-1-4982-0143-8
Publication date 4/2/2015
Previously published by Cassell, 1897

This is a reprint of the 1959 Zondervan edition. Originally
published in 1897 by Cassell as A Bible Commentary for English Readers.

The Epistles to the Ephesians, Philippians, and Colossians

BY

THE RIGHT REV. ALFRED BARRY, D.D.

The Epistle to the Thessalonians

BY

THE REV. A. J. MASON, M.A., D.D.,

Canon of Canterbury.

The Epistles to Timothy and Titus

BY

THE VERY REV. H. D. M. SPENCE, D.D.,

Dean of Gloucester.

The Epistle to Philemon

BY

THE RIGHT REV. ALFRED BARRY, D.D.

The Epistle to the Hebrews

BY

THE REV. W. F. MOULTON, D.D.

The Epistle of St. James

BY

THE REV. E. G. PUNCHARD, D.D.,

Late Fellow of St. Augustine's College, Canterbury.

The First Epistle of St. Peter

BY

THE REV. A. J. MASON, M.A., D.D.

The Second Epistle of St. Peter

BY

THE REV. ALFRED PLUMMER, M.A., D.D.,

Late Master of University College, Durham.

The Epistles of St. John

BY

THE VEN. W. M. SINCLAIR, M.A., D.D.,

Archdeacon of London.

The Epistle of St. Jude

BY

THE REV. ALFRED PLUMMER, M.A., D.D.

The Revelation of St. John

BY

THE RIGHT REV. W. BOYD CARPENTER, D.D.,

Lord Bishop of Ripon.

CONTENTS

THE EPISTLES OF PAUL THE APOSTLE TO THE

EPHESIANS, PHILIPPIANS, AND COLOSSIANS

GENERAL INTRODUCTION

TO

THE EPISTLES OF ST. PAUL'S FIRST CAPTIVITY

THE Epistles of St. Paul's captivity—to the Ephesians, Philippians, Colossians, and Philemon—form a distinct group, distinguished by certain marked characteristics both of style and subject, in the series of the writings of the great Apostle of the Gentiles. Just as, in comparison with the Thessalonian Epistles, belonging to the second missionary journey, the four great Epistles to the Corinthians, Galatians, and Romans, written at the close of the third missionary journey, show a "second manner," with exactly that union of similarity and diversity which marks a true development of thought and circumstance—so, in comparison with this latter group, the Epistles of the Captivity present a "third manner," itself again markedly distinct from that of the Pastoral Epistles, of still later date. In those early days of Christianity events moved fast; under the living Apostolic inspiration and the rapidity of the Apostolic mission, successive years marked changes as great as would have indicated the lapse of generations in more ordinary times. When we compare the marvellous growth of the Christian Church in the thirty years (or thereabouts) of St. Paul's own Apostolate—from a small sect limited to Palestine, hardly as yet completely distinguished from the Judaic system, to a community which had its branches in every province of the Roman world, and which was obviously advancing to a world-wide dominion—we may be prepared to find obvious and important developments, both of teaching and of circumstance, even in the various periods of his Apostolic ministry.

I. The Period to which they belong.—In accordance with the great majority of commentators, ancient and modern, I take these Epistles to belong to the Roman captivity, in which the history of the Acts leaves St. Paul, and to which he was consigned about the year A.D. 61. It has, indeed, been proposed by Meyer and other German commentators to refer them to the Cæsarean captivity of Acts xxiv.—xxvi. The reasons on which this proposal is based may be seen in Meyer's edition of the "Epistle to the Ephesians" (*Introduction*, sect. 2). They prove, however, on examination, to be not only trivial, even if maintained, but in themselves uncertain, resting largely on mere supposition, and certainly incapable of standing against the powerful arguments which may be brought on the other side. These are of two kinds—general and special. Of the first kind is the whole style and tone of the Epistles, indicating a transition to an entirely different and most important sphere of missionary labour, such as could not possibly be found in the comparatively unimportant town of Cæsarea; and, moreover, the obvious expectation by the writer (see Phil. ii. 24; Philem. verse 22) of a speedy release from captivity, which would enable him to visit, not Rome and Spain, as was his intention at the time when he was taken prisoner at Jerusalem (Acts xix. 21; Rom. xv. 24, 25), but Macedonia and the Eastern churches, where at the earlier time he declared that he had "no longer any place" (Rom. xv. 23; comp. Acts xx. 25). Of the latter kind are the references found—especially in the most personal of all the Epistles, the Epistle to his beloved Church at Philippi—to the manifestation of his bonds "in the whole Prætorium" (Phil. i. 13)—a phrase which (in spite of the verbal coincidence with Acts xxiii. 35) could not well be used of his prison at Cæsarea; to the converts made from "Cæsar's household," which must surely have belonged to Rome (Phil. iv. 22); to the circumstances of his captivity, which describe with an almost technical accuracy (see Note on Eph. vi. 20) the imprisonment at Rome "in his own hired house with the soldier that kept him," and the freedom which he then had (Acts xxviii. 16, 30, 31), but which at Cæsarea, especially considering the especial object contemplated by Felix in prolonging his captivity (Acts xxiv. 26), was eminently improbable.

In accordance, also, with the general opinion, I should designate this as St. Paul's "First Roman Captivity;" though it will be, perhaps, more appropriate that the evidence for the common belief that St. Paul was set at liberty from his captivity, and that, after a period of freedom, he underwent a second imprisonment, which was only closed by his death, should be considered in relation to the PASTORAL EPISTLES. For with this belief the acceptance of these Epistles as genuine is closely, if not inseparably, connected. On the general character and circumstances of both captivities see *Excursus* (at the close of the Acts of the Apostles) *on the Later Years of St. Paul's Life.*

II. The Genuineness of these Epistles.—On this point external evidence is strong and unvarying. It will be sufficient here to notice that all were included unhesitatingly in all the catalogues and versions of St. Paul's Epistles, and placed by Eusebius (as by others before him) in the list of the New Testament books "acknowledged by all." More detailed evidence will be with more advantage given in the *Introduction* to each Epistle.

It is true that, as in the case of many other New Testament books, their genuineness has been challenged, on supposed internal evidence, even by critics who are ready to acknowledge the four Epistles of the preceding group. This adverse criticism has been advanced with different degrees of positiveness against different Epistles of this group. Thus, the Epistle to the Philippians has been but little doubted; and, indeed, the similarities to St. Paul's earlier Epistles, and especially to the Epistle to the Romans, are so striking that it requires singular perversity to discover or imagine dissonance with them. The beautiful little Epistle to Philemon, again, can hardly be said to have been questioned, except in the mere wantonness of arbitrary criticism. On the other hand, the two Epistles which bear most distinctly the peculiar impress of St. Paul's "later manner"—the Epistles to the Ephesians and the Colossians—have been far more seriously attacked on that very ground; the Epistle to the Colossians, moreover, on the supposition that it involves references to a Gnosticism of later date; and the Epistle to the Ephesians, on the supposition—which it might have been thought that an attentive study of these two Epistles would have soon shown to be untenable—that it is a mere copy and expansion of the Epistle to the Colossians. On the peculiar grounds of scepticism in each case it will be more convenient to speak in connection with each Epistle separately; but on the general question of the relation of these Epistles to the earlier group it will be best to dwell here, not merely with a view to show the hollowness of this destructive criticism, but with the more important object of sketching out the main characteristics of this group of Epistles as a whole.

Now it must be considered exactly what is the nature of the question. We have not here an anonymous document, like the Epistle to the Hebrews, as to which we have to inquire into the degree of its likeness or unlikeness to St. Paul's acknowledged Epistles. We have Epistles which not only bear his name, but present various indications marking them as his; and these Epistles are received as his at a very early date—alluded to by Clement of Rome, Ignatius, Polycarp, formally included in the Muratorian Canon about the year 170. Accordingly, they are either his genuine Epistles, or Epistles written in his name at an early period by some adherent of the "Pauline School" desiring to claim a forged authority from his great master. Now, in the case of forgery, we should expect to find substantial inferiority of power and inspiration, and possibly some discrepance of the inner reality, as contrasted with the outward form, of doctrine; but certainly no marked difference of style, no peculiar words and phrases previously unknown, no change of expressions, which had become markedly characteristic of St. Paul in the acknowledged Epistles of the earlier group. In the case of genuineness, on the other hand, we should look for substantial identity of thought and teaching, coupled with free variation of expression and style, and with indications of a development of doctrine, corresponding to progress of time, change of scene and circumstance, increase of the power of Christianity over thought and society, as exemplified in the development of the Christian Church. It is all but impossible for any careful student to doubt that it is always the latter—never the former—condition which is distinctly realised in these Epistles. This will be seen clearly on examination both of their style and of their substance.

III. The Style of the Epistles.—There is unquestionably a marked difference of style, although in various degrees—the Philippian Epistle showing such difference far less than the Epistles to the Ephesians and Colossians. Now it is not a little remarkable that the nature of this acknowledged change of style singularly corresponds with the historical change in St. Paul's circumstances. When he wrote the former Epistles he was in the full tide of his Apostolic work; at periods, moreover, of marked excitement and interest—just after the tumult at Ephesus, or on his circuit through Macedonia "round about into Illyricum," or at Corinth in the very heat of the Judaising controversy. He was then emphatically the preacher and the church-founder. His Letters, written in the intervals of his busy work, would be like fragments of his preaching, marked by the incisive earnestness, the close argument, the impressive abruptness, of a pleader for God. When he wrote these later Epistles he was in the enforced inactivity and the comparative rest of imprisonment, and this imprisonment (as, indeed, we might have expected) appears to have been to him a time of study, in those "many writings" which Festus thought at that time to have "made him mad" (Acts xxvi. 24), with such "books and parchments" round him as those which he asked for even in the greater severity of his second imprisonment (2 Tim. iv. 13). He is now not so much the worker as the thinker. The impassioned emphasis of the preacher might naturally be exchanged for the quiet, deliberate teaching of the Christian sage; sounding the lowest depths of thought; wandering, as it might seem, but with subtle links of connection, from one idea to another; rising constantly in secret meditation from truths embodied in the practical forms of earthly life, to truths as they exist above in the calm perfection of heaven. Who can doubt that this is exactly the change of style which we trace in these Epistles of the Captivity? The Epistle to the Philippians has least of it: for there his remembrance of earlier times would be strongest, and would tend most to reproduce the earlier tone of thought. But in the Colossian Epistle, written to a Church which he had never seen—knowing it, indeed, well, but only by hearsay—still more in the Epistle to the Ephesians, probably an encyclical letter, certainly approaching more nearly to the nature of abstract general teaching, this characteristic difference is most vividly marked.

It manifests itself in the appearance of many words used in no other Epistles, and these frequently words compounded with a thoughtful felicity of compressed meaning. It manifests itself in sentences which, unlike the terse and often abrupt incisiveness of his earlier Letters, flow on without grammatical break, sometimes not without grammatical harshness and obscurity, but with an unfailing connection and evolution of thought, a singular and (so to speak) philosophical completeness of doctrine, a sustained perfection of meditative and devotional beauty. It manifests itself, again, in a constant looking upward to "the heavenly places" of the Ephesian Epistle; sometimes, as in the opening of that Epistle, to the source of all Christian life in the election of the divine love; sometimes to the angelic "principalities and powers," invisibly fighting for or against that love of God in salvation; sometimes to the life of Christians "hid with Christ in God," in virtue of which we sit with Him in heaven even now; most often, perhaps, of all, to Christ in His heavenly glory, seen now by the eye of faith, ready to reveal Himself in the Epiphany of the great day. Yet, with all this difference of style, the detailed links of connection, both in word and thought, are (as the Notes on the Epistles will show) simply numberless—mostly showing similarity, not absolute identity, of expression; an independent likeness, not an artificial copyism. Above all, the general impress of the mind and character of St. Paul comes out more and more clearly as we pursue the detailed study of the Epistles. Thus, the character which paints itself in the Epistle to the Philippians is obviously the same as that which we know in the Epistles to the Corinthians, or in that yet earlier Epistle to the other Macedonian Church at Thessalonica, which presents some striking similarities in detail. But there is a greater calmness and maturity, sometimes of peacefulness, sometimes of sadness: it is the picture of an older man. Again, the notion that the teaching of the Ephesian or Colossian Epistle could possibly have come from the weaker hand of a disciple will seem fairly incredible to any who have ever glanced at the writings of Clement of Rome, of Ignatius, or of Polycarp, the scholars of St. Paul and St. John. The inspired hand of the Apostle is traceable in every line; the very change of style argues at once identity and development. It is a strong internal evidence of the Apostolic authorship; it is in itself full of deep interest and significance.

IV. The Substance of the Epistles.—Still more striking is the corresponding phenomenon in relation to substance. In the doctrine of these Epistles there is the same indication of a true development.

(1) *The Doctrine of Salvation.*—Thus, for example, it is profoundly instructive to examine the relation of these Epistles to that primary doctrine of "justification by faith" which had been the one all-important subject of the Galatian and Roman Epistles. It is touched on here with the same master hand. "By grace are ye saved through faith; and that not of yourselves: it is the gift of God: not of works, lest any man should boast" (Eph. ii. 8, 9). "That I may be found in Him, not having mine own righteousness, which is of the Law, but that which is through the faith of Christ, the righteousness which is of God by faith" (Phil. iii. 9). But it is no longer the one subject to which all else leads up. It is treated as a thing known and accepted, with a quiet calmness utterly unlike the impassioned and exhaustive earnestness of St. Paul's pleading for it in the crisis of the Judaistic controversy. The emphasis on faith is less vivid and less constant. "Salvation by grace" takes the place of "justification by faith," and leads the thoughts on from the first acceptance in Christ to the continuous work of grace, of which such acceptance is the first beginning. The Law, which before its idolaters in Galatia or at Rome was resolutely thrust down to its right secondary position, described as the servile "pedagogue to bring men" to the true Teacher, depreciated as the mere subsidiary guard of the covenant of promise, is now less often touched upon, and less unreservedly condemned. It has obviously lost the dangerous fascination with which such idolatry invested it. It is only "as contained in ordinances" that it is now viewed as a separation between Jew and Gentile, or between man and God, or considered as cancelled by "nailing it to the cross" of Christ. We feel that St. Paul is already passing on from the earnest pleading of advocacy of the freedom of the gospel to the judicial calmness which was hereafter to tell how "the law is good if a man use it lawfully" (1 Tim. i. 8). Judaism has, in great measure, at least in the Eastern churches, changed its character. St. Paul's earnest pleading for Christ as all in all has similarly changed its direction and its tone. Against new idolatries it is still necessary to fight to the death. But the old battle is substantially won; on the old field no more is needed than to maintain the victory.

(2) *The Doctrine of the Catholic Church.*—Nor is it less interesting to note how in these Epistles, and especially in the Epistle to the Ephesians, the prominence of the idea of the Kingdom of God has marvellously increased. The Galatian and Roman Epistles (as the history of the Reformation of the sixteenth century showed) are the treasure-house of the truths of personal Christianity; for the very thought of justification, dominant in them, brings each soul face to face with its own sin and its own salvation, in that supreme crisis of life and death in which it is conscious of but two existences—God and itself. These later Epistles are equally the storehouse of the less vivid, yet grander, conception of the Holy Catholic Church. The central idea is of Christ the Head, and the whole collective Christianity of the Church as His Body. He is conceived not solely or mainly as the Saviour of each individual soul, but rather as "gathering up" all humanity, or even all created being, "in Himself." The two conceptions are, of course, inseparable. In the earlier Epistles the Church is constantly recognised; in these the individual relationship to God in Christ is never for a moment ignored. But the proportion (so to speak) of the two truths is changed. What is primary in the one case is secondary in the other.

It is obvious that this is the natural order. The Christian unity is directly the unity of each soul with Christ, the Head; indirectly the unity of the various members in one Body. When the gospel of salvation first speaks, it must speak to the individual. When the grace of Christ draws all men unto Him, each individual must move along the line of his own spiritual gravitation. But when the truth has been accepted in a faith necessarily individual; when the Saviour has been found by each as the Christ who "liveth in me"—then the question arises, What are His truth and His grace to that great human society, to which we are bound by a network of unseen spiritual ties? The first and proper answer to that question is the doctrine of the Holy Catholic Church. There is a second answer, larger, but less distinct, which goes even beyond this, to contemplate our Lord as the Head of all created being. The relation, therefore, of these Epistles to the earlier group is profoundly natural, even on the consideration of the right and necessary course of idea.

But here, again, it is impossible not to trace in these Epistles a special appropriateness to this period of St. Paul's life and work. Of the three great threads of ancient civilisation—the Hebrew, the Greek, and the Roman—two had already been laid hold of by Apostolic hands, and fastened to the cross of Christ. Now, as "ambassador for Christ," although "in bonds," St. Paul had been permitted to "see Rome;" the circumstances of his imprisonment had placed him in the *Prætorium*, in the very citadel of the Imperial grandeur, and had given him access to "those of Cæsar's household." The Epistles of the former group had been written from cities where Greek thought reigned supreme—from Ephesus, from Philippi, from Corinth. These later Epistles came from the centre of Imperial Rome. Now, it is a common-place to remark that the main element of all Greek thought was the freedom and sacredness of the individual, whether in the realm of thought, or of imagination, or of action. But the mission of the Roman (as Virgil has, with a true insight, declared in well-known lines) was to teach the greatness of the community—the family, the state, the whole race of humanity; to give laws, which were to be the basis of the "law of nations;" to unite all peoples in one great empire, and, perhaps by an inevitable inference, to deify its head. It can hardly be accidental that, while the former Epistles dealt with the individual, pointing him to the true freedom and the true wisdom, which Greek philosophy sought for in vain, these Epistles should similarly face the great Roman problem, and sketch out that picture which was hereafter to be wrought into the chief masterpiece of Latin theology—the picture of "the city of God." We note in the Epistle to the Ephesians the emphatic reference to the three great social relationships, so jealously and sternly guarded by Roman law—the relations of parents and children, husbands and wives, masters and servants—as deriving a higher spiritual sacredness, above all law and convention, from the fact that they are types of the relations of man to God in the great unity in the Lord Jesus Christ. We read in the Epistle to the Philippians of the "city in heaven" —not now the "heavenly Jerusalem" of Jewish aspiration, but simply the city of which all are citizens, whether "Jew or Greek, barbarian, Scythian, bond or free." We find, both in the Ephesian and Colossian Epistles, a constant recurrence to the thought of all as "one body" or "one temple" in Jesus Christ—supplying that supreme personal relation, which changes the shadowy dream of a divine republic, where the individual is lost, to the solid reality of a well-centred Kingdom of God, preserving at once perfect individuality and perfect unity. We are reminded at every step of the "fifth empire"—"a stone cut out without hands" from the mountain of the Lord, and growing till it displaced the artificial fabrics of the kingdoms of the world, and filled the whole earth. We contrast the inevitable idolatry of the Roman emperor—remembering that, by a strange irony of circumstance, that emperor was now a Nero—with the worship of the true Son of Man and Son of God, of which all such idolatries are perverted anticipations. I pass over minor points of coincidence between idea and circumstance—such as the remarkable metaphor of the Christian armour, working out a figure previously touched by St. Paul, with an obvious detailed reference to the armour of his Roman jailor; or the adaptation of Stoic ideas and phrases in the Epistle to the Philippians, bearing (as Dr. Lightfoot has shown) peculiar resemblances to the later Stoicism of Seneca, then the leader of Roman thought. But taking only the main idea of these Epistles, and comparing it with the main principle of Roman greatness, it is impossible again not to be struck with a coincidence—which must surely be more than mere coincidence—between the teaching and the circumstances of this period of the Apostle's life.

(3) *The advanced Christology.*—There is another true development, of infinitely greater importance and deeper interest, in respect of what is called the "Christology" of these Epistles. At all times the preaching of Christianity is the preaching of "God in Christ." But attentive study of the New Testament shows that gradually, line by line, step by step, the full truth was revealed as the world was able to bear it—passing, according to the true order of teaching, from visible manifestations to invisible realities—guarding at every step the supreme truth of the unity of the Godhead, so jealously cherished by the Jew, so laxly disregarded in the elastic Polytheisms of the Gentile world. The manifestation of Christ in the Incarnation, the Atonement, the Resurrection, and Ascension, is, of course, really one. Yet at different times each of the different steps of that one manifestation appears to have assumed greater prominence in Christian teaching; and it may be noted, that as, when we dig through the strata of the earth, we uncover first what is latest, and come only at last to what is earliest in deposition, so in the realisation of gospel truth, the order of preaching is the reverse of the order of actual occurrence of the great facts of the divine manifestation. First, as is natural, came the preaching of "Christ risen;" for the Resurrection—the great miracle of miracles—was the seal of our Lord's Messiahship, declaring Him who was "of the seed of David according to the flesh" to be "the Son of God with power." As risen and exalted to the right hand of God, in fulfilment of oft-repeated ancient prophecy, He was declared to be both "Lord and Christ." Even clear-sighted heathen ignorance could declare that the great question between Christian and unbeliever was then—as, indeed, it is now—"of one Jesus who was dead, whom Paul affirmed to be alive." But then, when men were called to receive in the risen Christ remission of sins, to see in His resurrection the pledge of a spiritual resurrection for themselves here, a resurrection of body and spirit in the hereafter, came the question, How can this be? To that question the answer is found in the one truth which St. Paul declared that in his teaching at Corinth, and (we may add) in his teaching to the Galatians and Romans, he cared to know—the truth of "Jesus Christ, and Him as crucified." The Resurrection, in itself, was accepted as known; to unfold its meaning it was necessary to go back to the Atonement. Hence the great teaching of these Epistles is of Christ as the one Mediator between God and the countless souls which He has made. That mediation is described sometimes in the phrase "through Christ," bringing out the access through His atonement to the Father who sent Him; sometimes in the phrase "in Christ," dwelling not so much on our justification as on our regeneration in Him to the new life. Perhaps in the great struggle for Justification by Faith the former idea was the more prominent. In either phase, however, it is the sole and universal mediation of Christ which is the one leading conception of Apostolic teaching. But, again, the question arises, Who is He who thus is—what surely no merely created being can claim to be—a mediator between God and all human souls, in all lands and in all ages of the world? To answer that question it was needful to go back once more to "Christ Incarnate:" *i.e.*, ultimately, to Christ as He is, not in manifestation, but in His own true being, before He was pleased to stoop to earth, and since He has ascended again to His own glory in heaven. It is on this last phase of thought that the Epistles of the Captivity appear to enter, standing in this respect parallel with the Epistle to the Hebrews, leading on to the yet fuller teaching of the Epistles and Gospel of St. John.

We notice that it is always through the knowledge of His mediation that they lead us into the region of yet higher truth. St. Paul, in brief yet exhaustive description of that mediation, tells us of Christ, as One "in whom we have redemption through His blood, even the remission of sins." We notice, also, that the phrase "in Christ," rather than "through Christ," is the dominant note in these Epistles. As we have seen already in relation to justification and sanctification, so we find in relation to the objective truths corresponding to them, that it is not so much on "Christ crucified" as on "Christ living in us" that he emphatically dwells. But the especial point of transcendent importance is that he leads us on from the fact of this mediation to draw out explicitly what such mediation implies. The Philippian Epistle, simple and practical as its purpose is, recites, in the great passage of its second chapter (chap. ii. 5—11) the whole creed of our Lord's Nature and Office—the distinctive creed of Christianity. It marks the two-fold humility of His mediation for us: first, the "taking on Him the form of a servant;" next, the "humbling Himself to the death of the cross." It turns next to the corresponding exaltation of His human nature in the Mediatorial kingdom (described in 1 Cor. xv. 20—28), so that "in the name of Jesus every knee should bow." But it does more than this. It speaks of Him as being essentially "in the form," that is, in the nature, "of God," in the eternal glory of which "He stripped Himself" for us; it tells us that to Him is given "the name which is above every name"—the awful and incommunicable name of

JEHOVAH. In that deeper teaching it tells us, not of His office, but of Himself; not of His mediation, but of the divine nature which alone made such mediation possible. Again, in the Epistle to the Ephesians, starting from "the redemption in His blood, the remission of sins," the idea of our Lord's mediation is infinitely enlarged and exalted in the conception, that "in Him all things are gathered in one head, both which are in heaven and which are on earth;" that "He filleth all in all;" "ascending above all heavens," "descending into the lower parts of the earth," "that He might thus fill all things." That He is, indeed, the Head of the Church we are told again and again in various forms of expression; but He is more. In Him all created being is summed up; He is, in all that relates to it, the manifestation of God. As in the unity of the Church, so in the wider unity of all creation, we have, co-ordinate with one another, the "one Spirit," the "one Lord," the "one God and Father of all." But far even beyond this, the Epistle to the Colossians carries the same higher teaching. Standing face to face with an incipient Gnosticism, stiffened to some degree into a Jewish type, but presenting all the essential features of the Gnostic idea —of one supreme God and many emanations, all real and all imperfect, from the divine fulness—St. Paul declares explicitly all that the earlier teaching had implied with ever increasing clearness. Our Lord is not only "the firstborn of God before all creation," "in whom," "through whom," "for whom," "all things in heaven and earth, visible and invisible, were created," and in whom "all things consist." In this the Colossian Epistle would but draw out more forcibly the truth taught to the Ephesians of His relation to all created being. But what is He in Himself? St. Paul answers, "the image"—the substantial manifestation—"of the invisible God," in whom "all the fulness of the Godhead dwelleth bodily." The parallel is singularly close with the Epistle to the Hebrews, which, in similar connection with the great mediation of His one priesthood and one sacrifice, declares Him (chap i. 3) to be "the brightness of the glory of the Father, and the express image of His person" (the "substance," or *essence*, of the Godhead). There remains little beyond this to bring us to the full declaration of "the Word" who "was in the beginning," who "was with God, and was God." These Epistles of St. Paul correspond, with marvellous appropriateness, to that intermediate period, when his great evangelising work was almost done, and the time was coming for the growth of the school of deep thought on a now acknowledged Christianity, which was to surround the old age of "St. John the Divine."

(4) *The Condition and Trials of the Church.*—The examination of the substance of the Epistles would not be complete without some brief reference to the condition of the Church which they disclose.

In this view, also, we trace the same coincidence with the natural growth of events. The whole tenor of the Epistles indicates that the Church had reached a condition in which the consideration, not so much of its extension, as of its unity, became the prominent idea. With but little hyperbole, St. Paul could say that the gospel had come into "all the world" of the Roman empire. His own career of active evangelisation had been stopped; in his prison at Rome, the centre of communication with all nations, he would, no doubt, hear of the growth and the trials of other churches, as we know that he heard of Philippi and Colossæ; he looked eagerly, as from a distance, on the building up of the Temple of God, which was going on by many hands and under many conditions. The one thought and prayer of his captivity was that it should grow as one, "fitly framed and joined together," on the one foundation and in the one corner-stone. To the Philippian Church the burden of his exhortation is to unity of spirit. In the Ephesian Epistle the great central passage is that which brings out, with all the incisive emphasis of a creed, the description of the "one body" and the "one Spirit"; and the fundamental conception of the gospel, as the reconciliation of the soul to God in Jesus Christ, carries with it as a perpetual undertone, the union of Jew and Gentile in the covenant of God. Even in the Colossian Epistle, although there the main idea of the sole headship of Christ assumes a more absolute predominance, yet the great anxiety of St. Paul for Colossæ and its sister churches was that their hearts might be "knit together in love" and the "full assurance of the knowledge" of a common gospel. The whole tenor of these Epistles, standing in contrast with those of the earlier group, thus corresponds with the needs of the more advanced period of Church history.

Nor is this coincidence less evident in relation to the forms of danger, by which the progress of the Church is here seen to be menaced. The old leaven of Judaism still works in the "so-called circumcision," which now deserves, in St. Paul's eyes, only the name of "concision," or self-mutilation. But it has changed its character. The Pharisaic idolatry of the Law, as a law by obedience to which man might work out, if not his own salvation, at least his own perfection, has passed away in the East, though it lingers in the simple, unspeculative Christianity of Macedonia. Perhaps by the very extension of the Church the providence of God had clenched the victorious argument of St. Paul. A church truly catholic could hardly rest on a rigid code of law, or find the spring of a world-wide salvation anywhere, except in the grace of God accepted by faith. But now, as the Epistle to the Colossians shows, Judaism had allied itself with those wild speculations, weaving the gospel into philosophical or mystic theories of religion, which arose inevitably, when Christianity, assuming to be the religion of humanity, naturally came in contact with the various philosophies and religions of all mankind. Dr. Lightfoot has shown, with much probability, that one form in which it adapted itself to the new condition of things was the form of the old Essenic mysticism. The Epistle to the Hebrews suggests that, on the other hand, it had also fixed its faith on the ritual and sacrifice from which the Essenes shrank—doubtless as having in themselves a mystic efficacy, perhaps as enabling men to enter into the region of mystic speculation, where they might learn the secrets hidden from the mass of Christians, and revealed only to the perfect. In both forms it is seen as gradually dissolving its old rigidity and carnality, and claiming, in accordance with the spirit of the age, the title of spirituality and mystic perfection.

Still more is the progress of the times shown in this very tendency, to which Judaism so strangely and incongruously allied itself. Gnosticism, in later days, marked the attempts—sometimes serious, sometimes fantastic—to weave Christianity into systems designed to solve the insoluble problem of the relation of the infinite God, both in creation and manifestation, to His finite creatures; to fix the place to be assigned to matter and spirit in the universe; to answer the question how far evil is necessarily associated with matter; and in contemplation of the gospel itself, to determine the relation between the Old and New Covenant, and to define or explain away the mystery of the Incarnation. To what wild developments it ran is told in the true, but almost incredible, record of a subsequent chapter of Church history. But it showed itself—we may almost say that it could not but have shown itself—at the close of the Apostolic age: as soon as the gospel showed itself to be not only a divine life, but a divine philosophy, to an age radically sceptical, both in its eagerness of inquiry and its discontent with all the answers hitherto found. We find traces of it—easily read by those who have studied its after-development—in the "endless genealogies," the false asceticism, or still falser antinomianism of the later Epistles of St. Paul and St. John, in the denial that "Jesus Christ was come in the flesh," and the idea that "the Resurrection was passed already." In these Epistles of the Captivity there are similar traces, but less fully developed, especially in the Colossian Epistle. The spurious claims to spiritual "perfection;" the "deceits by vain words;" the "systematic plan of deceit" of a specious antinomianism, for which St. Paul can hardly find language of adequate condemnation; the "philosophy and vain deceit" of the traditions of men, with its mere "show of wisdom" and its "intrusion" into the regions of the invisible; the supposed emanations from the Godhead taking the angelic forms of "thrones and principalities and powers"—all these mark the first beginning of that strange progress which ran its pretentious course in later times. To this time of St. Paul's history they belong, and to no other.

Thus, as it seems every way, a careful study of the style and substance of these Epistles not only confirms the external testimony which refers them to St. Paul, but illustrates to us the course of the development of the gospel, the progress and the trials of the Church. They light up the historical darkness in which the abrupt close of the record of the Acts of the Apostles leaves us; they are full of those lessons for our own days in which the close of the Apostolic age is especially fruitful.

V. The Order of the Epistles.—That the Epistles to the Ephesians, to the Colossians, and to Philemon belong to the same time, and were sent by the same messengers, is tolerably clear. The one question is, whether the Epistle to the Philippians precedes or follows them; and this question can only be answered by probable conjecture. It is obvious, from the progress already made (Phil. i. 12—18), from the whole description of the mission and the sickness of Epaphroditus (Phil. ii. 25—30), from the anticipation of release (Phil. ii. 24), that some time must have elapsed between St. Paul's arrival at Rome and the writing of this Epistle. It has also been noticed, as at least a remarkable coincidence, that Aristarchus and St. Luke, who accompanied the Apostle to Rome (Acts xxvii. 2), are named in the Epistles to the Colossians and Philemon (Col. iv. 10, 14; Philem. verse 24), and not in the Epistle to the Philippians. But this last may be a mere coincidence; and the fact that the Philippian Epistle was not written early in the imprisonment determines nothing as to its priority or posteriority to the other Epistles. The only strong argument on the subject—which has been admirably worked out by Dr. Lightfoot in his *Introduction to the Epistle to the Philippians*, sect. ii.—is the remarkable similarity in word and style between it and the Epistle to the Romans, its position as a link between the strong individuality of the earlier teaching and the characteristic universality of the Epistles to the Ephesians and Colossians, and its dealing with trials and difficulties more nearly resembling those of an earlier time. The argument is strong, yet not necessarily conclusive; for much in all these points depends on the character, and even the geographical position, of the Church addressed. To it, however, in the absence of any solid controverting evidence, we may give considerable weight and perhaps incline, without absolute decision, to place the Philippian Epistle before the other group in the Epistles of the Captivity.

[In relation to the treatment of the Epistles of the Captivity, it seems right to acknowledge the deep obligation of the writer to the Commentaries of Ellicott, Alford, Wordsworth, Meyer, Harless, and, above all, to the admirable and exhaustive treatment by Dr. Lightfoot of the Epistles to the Philippians, Colossians, and Philemon; to Conybeare and Howson, and Lewin, for their full and learned summaries of all that illustrates the life and, in less degree, the writings of St. Paul; but perhaps not least to the *Homilies* of St. Chrysostom—simply invaluable as a commentary, venerable in its preservation of ancient tradition, critically precious as dealing with the Greek as still a living language, and yet modern in that breadth and simplicity of treatment, which contrast with the frequent mysticism of great ancient commentators. The writer desires also to add that, while he has not generally thought it desirable to confuse the reader by the enumeration of various translations and interpretations, he has yet, to the best of his ability, studied all these carefully, and has endeavoured to give in the Notes the result, rather than the process, of such study.]

INTRODUCTION

TO

THE EPISTLE OF PAUL THE APOSTLE TO THE

EPHESIANS

I. **The Date and Place of Writing.**—This Epistle, for reasons hereafter to be considered, has few detailed indications, either of the personal condition of the writer or of the circumstances of those to whom it is addressed. But one point is made perfectly clear, that it was written by St. Paul when he was the "prisoner of Jesus Christ" (chaps. iii. 1; iv. 1), suffering some special "tribulations for them," which he bade them consider as "their glory" (chap. iii. 13), and being an "ambassador for Christ in a chain" (chap. vi. 20)—the word here used being the same as in Acts xxviii. 20, and being a word almost technically describing the imprisonment "with a soldier that kept him" (Acts xxviii. 16). All these things point unmistakably to what we have spoken of in the *General Introduction* as the first Roman captivity. That captivity began about A.D. 61, and lasted, without change, for at least "two full years." In the Letter to Philemon, sent by Onesimus, who is associated with Tychicus, the bearer of this Epistle, in Col. iv. 7—9, St. Paul prays him to "prepare him a lodging" against the speedy arrival, which he then confidently expected. Hence our Epistle must be placed late in the captivity—not earlier than A.D. 63.

II. **The Church to which it is addressed.**—The Epistle has borne from time immemorial the name of the "Epistle to the Ephesians." To the Church at Ephesus most certainly, whether solely or among others, it is addressed.

EPHESUS.—Of St. Paul's preaching at Ephesus we have a detailed account in the Acts of the Apostles. At the close of his second missionary circuit he had touched at Ephesus, and "entered the synagogue" to "reason with the Jews." In spite of their entreaty, he could not then remain with them, but left Aquila and Priscilla there. From them, probably, with the aid of their convert Apollos, the Christianity of Ephesus began its actual rise. It is not, indeed, impossible that there may have been some previous preparation through the disciples of St. John the Baptist. The emphatic allusion to him and to the simply preparatory character of his work in St. Paul's sermon at Antioch in Pisidia (Acts xiii. 24, 25), seems to point to knowledge of him in Asia Minor. We know that afterwards St. Paul found some disciples at Ephesus, baptised only with St. John's baptism (Acts xix. 3); and we note that Apollos, while "knowing only the baptism of John," yet still "teaching the things of the Lord," found a ready acceptance at Ephesus (Acts xviii. 24, 25). But however this may be, the full development of the Christianity of Ephesus was made under St. Paul's charge in his third missionary circuit. His first circuit had been an extension of that Asiatic Gentile Christianity which began from Antioch; his second was notable as the first planting of European Christianity, having its chief centre at Corinth; now his head-quarters for the evangelisation of the Roman province of Asia were fixed for three years at Ephesus, a city specially fit for the welding together of Asiatic and European Christianity—for there Greek civilisation met face to face with Oriental superstition and magical pretensions, in that which was made by Rome the official metropolis of pro-consular Asia; and the strange union is curiously symbolised by the enshrining in a temple which was the world-famed masterpiece of Greek art of an idol—probably, some half-shapeless meteoric stone —"which fell down from Jupiter." The summary of his work there—his re-baptism with the miraculous gifts of the disciples of St. John Baptist; the "special miracles" wrought by his hands; the utter confusion both of Jewish exorcists and of the professors of those "curious arts" for which Ephesus was notorious; the sudden tumult, so skilfully appeased by the "town clerk," who must surely have been half a Christian—make up (in Acts xix.) one of the most vivid scenes in St. Paul's Apostolic history.

Another—not less striking, and infinitely pathetic—is drawn in Acts xx. 16—38, in the farewell visit and address of St. Paul to the Ephesian presbyters at Miletus, indicating, alike by its testimony and by its warnings, a fully-organised and widely-spread Christianity—the fruit of his three years' labour. What had been the extent of the sphere of that labour we know not. We gather, with some surprise (Col. ii. 1), that the churches of the valley of the Lycus—Laodicea, Hierapolis, Colossæ—had not been visited by him personally. Yet, whether by his own presence, or through such delegates as Epaphras (Col. i. 7), "all which dwelt in Asia had heard the word of the Lord, both Jews and Greeks" (Acts xix. 10). They might well "sorrow" and "weep sore" at the thought that they should "see his face no more."

Now, in his captivity, certainly to Ephesus, and (as we shall see hereafter) probably to the other churches of Asia, he writes this Epistle—itself a representative Epistle, almost a treatise, bearing to the doctrine of the Holy Catholic Church a relation not unlike that which the Epistle to the Romans bears to the fundamental truths of personal Christianity.

After this, in the interval between the first and second captivity, we find (see 1 Tim. i. 1; 2 Tim. i. 18) that St. Paul did revisit Ephesus at least once; that, in his deep anxiety for its welfare, he placed it under the quasi-episcopal charge of his "own son Timothy;" and that, in his last captivity, he sent Tychicus, the bearer of this Epistle, to Ephesus again (2 Tim. iv. 12), perhaps in view of the coming absence of Timothy in obedience to the Apostle's summons.

From that time Ephesus passed into the charge of St. John, as the first of the seven churches of Asia (Rev. ii. 1), commended for its steadfastness, but yet rebuked as "having fallen from its first love." Of this phase of its Christianity, and its subsequent importance in the future history of the Church, especially as the scene of the Third great Council and the previous *Latrocinium*, it would be out of place here to dwell.

THE CHURCHES OF ASIA.—But while there is no doubt that the Epistle was addressed to Ephesus, there seems very strong reason for the opinion, now held by many commentators, that it was an encyclical letter to the churches of Asia, of which Ephesus was the natural head.

The evidence of this opinion may be thus summarised:—

Direct Evidence.—Taking first the direct evidence, we observe (1) that in the opening salutation, which in the ordinary reading is addressed to "the saints which are at Ephesus, being also faithful in Christ Jesus," the words "at Ephesus" are omitted in our two oldest MSS. (the Vatican and the Sinaitic), and in both supplied by a later hand. This omission is exceptional, all other MSS. and versions inserting the words. But it agrees with two remarkable ancient testimonies. Origen, the first great Biblical critic in the early Church (A.D. 186—254), (as appears from a fragment quoted in Cramer's "Catenæ in Pauli Epistolæ," p. 102, Oxford edition, 1842), noticed that in the Ephesian Epistle alone there was the "singular inscription," "to the saints who are, being also faithful." Basil of Cæsarea (A.D. 329—379) expressly says (in his treatise against Eunomius, Book ii., c. 19), "this reading was handed down by those who have gone before us, and we ourselves have found it in the ancient MSS."

Now (2) the effect of this omission is to make the passage obscure, if not unintelligible; for the only simple rendering of the Greek would be to "the saints who are also faithful," and this would give an impossible vagueness and generality to the address. Accordingly, ancient criticism (perhaps derived from Origen in the first instance) actually faced the difficulty by giving a mystic sense to the passage. St. Basil, in the passage above quoted, explains it thus:—"But, moreover, writing to the Ephesians as to those truly united by full knowledge to HIM WHO IS, he gives them the peculiar title of the 'saints who are.'" To this interpretation, also, St. Jerome refers thus (in his Commentary on Ephesians i. 1):—"Some, with more subtlety than is necessary, hold that, according to the saying to Moses, Thus shalt thou say to the children of Israel, HE WHO IS hath sent me unto you, those who at Ephesus are holy and faithful are designated by the name of essential being, so that from HIM WHO IS these are called They who are;" and adds, with his usual strong critical good sense, "others more simply hold that the address is not to Those who are, but to Those who are at Ephesus." Certainly, nothing could show a firmer conviction that the omission of the words "at Ephesus" was necessitated by MS. authority, than the desperate attempt to meet the difficulty of rendering by this marvellous interpretation.

But (3) we also find that Marcion the heretic, by Tertullian's twice-repeated testimony (in his work against Marcion, Book v., cc. 11, 16), entitled this Epistle "The Epistle to the Laodiceans." "I omit," he says, "here notice of another Epistle, which we hold to have been written to the Ephesians, but the heretics to the Laodiceans;" and he then proceeds to refer to our Epistle. In another place:—"In the true view of the Church, we hold that Letter to have been sent to the Ephesians, not to the Laodiceans; but Marcion has made it his business to interpolate an address in it, to show that on this point also he is a most painstaking critic." Now (as Tertullian adds) the question of the address was of no doctrinal importance; accordingly, Marcion could not have been tempted in this respect to falsify or invent. He gave the address on critical grounds; and Tertullian says that he "interpolated" it, presumably where there was a blank. Epiphanius, also (320?—402), in his notice of Marcion (*adv. Hær.*, Lib. I., Tom. III., xii.), after quoting "one Lord, one faith, one baptism," &c., adds:—"For the miserable Marcion was pleased to quote this testimony, not from the Epistle to the Ephesians, but from the Epistle to the Laodiceans, which is not in the Apostle's writings." He apparently refers to an apocraphal letter, of which he says elsewhere that "Marcion received fragments;" and such a letter is noticed in the Muratorian Canon. But looking to Tertullian's clear declaration, we may, perhaps, see here a confused reminiscence of this same critical achievement of Marcion. Marcion, no doubt, was led to it by a consideration of the well-known passage in the Colossian Epistle (chap. iv. 16) speaking of the "letter from Laodicea," which he (it would seem, correctly) identified with our Epistle.

(4) Now, all these things lead plainly to one conclusion—that, while an unvarying tradition declared that the Letter was "to the Ephesians," yet there was a blank in the oldest MSS. after the words "which are," generally filled up (as in most of our later MSS.) with the words "in Ephesus;" but by Marcion, with no MS. authority, simply on grounds of critical inference, with the words "in Laodicea." That this insertion of Marcion, if intended to infer that the Letter was addressed specially to the Laodicean Church, was unwarrantable, appears obvious, from the whole stream of ancient tradition assigning the Letter to the Ephesians, and the absence of any vestige of such a reading in the existing MSS. But if the Epistle were a circular letter, of which many copies were sent at one time, it would be at least probable that blanks might be left, to be filled up in each case with the proper name of the Church; and this supposition, which has been adopted by many, would furnish a very simple explanation—indeed, the only simple explanation—of this perplexing MS. phenomenon.

Indirect Evidence.—This being the state of the case in relation to direct evidence, we naturally pass on to consider what may be gathered indirectly, either to confirm or to confute this supposition, from the Epistle itself.

Now, the study of the Epistle, as a whole, must surely convey to the mind the impression of a certain generality and abstractness of character. It approaches closely—at least, as closely as the Epistle to the Romans—to the character of a treatise, dealing, with a singular completeness, accuracy, and symmetry of handling, with a grand spiritual truth—the doctrine of the Holy Catholic Church. The very opening—strongly reminding us in form, though not in substance, of the opening of the General Epistle of St. Peter to these churches and other churches of Asia Minor (1 Pet. i. 3—7)—is a complete and exhaustive statement of the mysterious truth of the election of the whole Church, as gathered up in Christ and redeemed by Him, in the eternal counsels of God. The celebrated passage (chap. iv. 4—6) on the unity of the Church, while it is full of an almost poetic beauty, has all the fulness and precision of a creed. The practical exhortations of the Epistle are drawn, with a philosophic generality, from the fundamental conception of religious unity. Nor can we fail to notice that the Epistle is entirely destitute of any reference —such as is invariable in St. Paul's other Epistles— to the particular condition, blessings, trials, graces, or defects, of those to whom it is addressed. They are simply spoken of as "you Gentiles," in contradistinction to the children of the old covenant. The sins against which they are warned are the typical sins forbidden in the Second Table, or the sins specially rife in the heathen society of that time in general.

The comparison in this respect with the Colossian Epistle is most instructive. Everywhere the Ephesian Epistle is general and (so to speak) philosophical in treatment; while in the parallel passages the other Epistle is particular and practical. Now it so happens that in the Epistles of this period we have the Philippian, written to a Church personally known and loved, while the Colossian is addressed to a Church known perhaps well, but indirectly, and not by personal intercourse. The former Epistle is pervaded from beginning to end with the personality of the writer, as fully as the Corinthian or Galatian Epistles themselves. The latter is more distant and more general, introducing the special warnings of the second chapter with a half-apologetic reference to the deep anxiety felt "for them, and for the Laodiceans, and for those who had not seen his face in the flesh." The Church of Ephesus must have been even more intimately known and bound to St. Paul than the Church at Philippi. How near it lay to his heart we know by the pathetic beauty and yearning tenderness of his address to the elders at Miletus. An Epistle written to this Church should surely have had all the strong personality of the Philippian Epistle; yet our Epistle, on the contrary, is infinitely less direct, personal, special, than the Epistle to the Colossians. The inference, even from these general considerations, seems unmistakable—that it was not addressed to any special Church, but least of all to such a Church as Ephesus.

But there are also some indications in detail, looking in the same direction, which are referred to in the Notes on the various passages. Such, for example, is the vagueness which has been noticed in the two passages (chaps. i. 15; iii. 2), "after I *heard* of your faith in the Lord Jesus," and "*if ye have heard* of the dispensation of the grace of God given me to you-ward." It is true that the former may be explained of St. Paul's hearing of them since he had left them; and, if confirmed by the parallel case of the Colossians (Col. i. 4), may be neutralised by comparison with Philem. verse 5 ("Hearing of thy love and faith"). It is also true that in the latter case the "if" of the original is not, except in form, hypothetical, and the verb may be "heard," not "heard of." But, making all reservation, there still remains a vagueness, hardly conceivable in reference to such a Church as Ephesus, especially when we remember how St. Paul in parallel cases refers to his former preaching. (See, for example, 1 Cor. ii. 1—4; 2 Cor. i. 12—19; xi. 6—9; xiii. 2; Gal. iv. 13; Phil. iv. 9; 1 Thess. ii. 1—12; iii. 4; 2 Thess. ii. 5.) Such, again, is the generality, absolutely without parallel elsewhere, in the salutation "which is the token in every Epistle"— "Grace be to all them who love the Lord Jesus Christ in sincerity"—compared with the "Grace be with you" or "with your spirit" of the other Epistles. The conclusions, again, of the Ephesian and Colossian Epistles may be compared. I do not lay stress on the simple absence of greetings: for it has been shown (by Alford), by comparison with other Epistles, that this argument is precarious. But it is impossible not to be struck with the vague generality of the one, as compared with the fulness of detail and strong personality of the other. They coincide verbally in the quasi-official commendation of Tychicus, and in this alone.

These indications may be thought to be slight, but they all point one way, and their combined force is not to be lightly put aside.

The indirect evidence, therefore, appears strongly to confirm the supposition which alone gives any simple explanation of the MSS. phenomena. But is there any trace of such an encyclical letter? That there was an "Epistle from Laodicea" to be read by the Colossians, we know; and the context shows conclusively that this was an Epistle of St. Paul himself. Laodicea was near Colossæ, and evidently in close union with it. The special warnings of the letter addressed to the Colossian Church were probably applicable to it also, and accordingly it was to be read there. But why should Colossæ read the "Epistle from Laodicea?" Had it dealt with the peculiar needs of that sister church this would be inexplicable; but if it were what our Epistle is—general in character, and dealing with a truth not identical with the main truth of the Colossian Epistle, but supplementary to it—then the direction is intelligible at once. It is not (it will be observed) an "Epistle to the Laodiceans," but an Epistle "coming from Laodicea," which would be reached from Ephesus before Colossæ, and which, being the larger and more important town, might naturally be made the recipient of a letter intended for it and Colossæ, and perhaps Hierapolis.

It may be asked, If this be so, why have no MSS. any other address than to the "saints at Ephesus?" and why has tradition invariably called this "The Epistle to the Ephesians," and nothing else? The answer which has been often given appears to be entirely sufficient. Ephesus was, as the metropolis of Asia, the natural centre of the Apostolic ministry, and the natural leader of the Asiatic churches: standing, as in the apocalyptic epistles (Rev. i. 11), at the head of all. There the Epistle would be first read; thence it would go out to the other Asiatic churches; there it would be best treasured up, and copies of it multiplied; and through these it would be likely to become known to the European churches also. It must have been quoted by some title. What title so natural as "To the Ephesians?" The use of this title evidently preceded the insertion of the words "in Ephesus" in the text. This is natural. We remember that no extant MS., except the Vatican and Sinaitic, is earlier than the beginning of the fifth century. By that time most of the Asiatic churches had sunk into insignificance. The tradition already prevalent of the address to the Ephesians would naturally express itself by the insertion of the words, without which the context of the opening passage is hardly intelligible.

This supposition seems also to be confirmed by the occasional appropriation to Laodicea. For, though after a long interval, Laodicea comes next after Ephesus in importance in Church history. On that ground St. Paul made it the centre of the churches of the Lycus valley. On that ground, also, some claim to the Epistle, as an Epistle to the Laodiceans, may have survived till the time of Marcion. It is curious that the Muratorian Canon (A.D. 170?), after noting the Epistle to the Ephesians among St. Paul's Epistles, adds: "There is in circulation also an Epistle to the

Laodiceans . . . forged in the name of Paul, to aid the heresy of Marcion . . . which cannot be received into the Catholic Church." Now the Apocryphal *Epistle to the Laodiceans*, still extant, is clearly of later date, made up of quotations or imitations of various passages of St. Paul's Epistles, and in no way bearing on Marcionism. It may perhaps be conjectured that Marcion, not content with altering the title of our Epistle, tampered with it and mutilated it, as we know that he did in the case of other New Testament books. There may be in the Canon (as afterwards in Epiphanius) a reference to this corrupted form of our Epistle, as a separate work; and this would be a kind of survival of the designation of it as an Epistle to the Laodiceans.

On all these grounds, therefore, we must hold it at least highly probable that we have in it an encyclical letter to Ephesus and the sister churches of Asia.

III. **The Genuineness of the Epistle.**—*External Evidence.*—The external evidence, as has been already said (see *Introduction to the Epistles of the Captivity*), is strong—as strong as for any other of St. Paul's Epistles.

Among the Apostolic fathers there seem to be unquestionable allusions to passages in it: as in Clement of Rome, chap. xlvi., dwelling on "the one God, one Christ, one spirit of grace . . . one calling" (comp. Eph. iv. 4—6); and in Polycarp, chap. xii., uniting the two quotations: "Be ye angry and sin not," "Let not the sun go down upon your wrath" (comp. Eph. iv. 26, 27). In Ignatius (to the Ephesians, chap. xii.) we have a remarkable reference to the Ephesians as "fellow-mystics" with St. Paul, sharing the mystery of the gospel with him (comp. Eph. i. 9; iii. 4—9; vi. 19); and he adds of St. Paul that, "in all his letter he is mindful of you in Christ Jesus." In the "longer Greek" version of the same Epistle—interpolated at a later date—there is in chap. vi. a direct quotation, "as Paul wrote to you—one body and one Spirit" (Eph. iv. 4—6), and a clear reference to the address (Eph. i. 1) in chap. ix.

Passing on to a later date, we have the Epistle formally recognised in the Muratorian Canon (A.D. 170), apparently representing the tradition of the Church of Rome: quoted repeatedly, and in some cases unmistakably, by Irenæus in the Church of Gaul (about A.D. 130—200); quoted also by Clement of Alexandria (about A.D. 150—210), and Tertullian (A.D. 160—240), representing the opposite school of Carthage. It is found in all ancient versions; and henceforth held without doubt among the acknowledged books in the Church.

Dr. Westcott has also shown ("Canon of the New Testament," pp. 314, 323, 338) that it is quoted by the heretical and Gnostic writers—the Ophites, Basilides, Valentinus, and others. Marcion's recognition and criticism of it we have already seen.

Internal Evidence.—The doubts of its genuineness which have been advanced in our own times turn entirely on internal evidence.

(1) The differences in style and substance between these Epistles of the Captivity and the earlier Epistles of St. Paul have been already discussed. I have ventured to urge that, corresponding as they do to the time and circumstances of the captivity, marking a true and natural development of doctrine, abounding in points both of similarity and independent originality, these differences are decisive against the idea of imitation, and strongly confirmatory of Apostolic authorship. To the Epistle of the Ephesians these remarks bear a special application, for this Epistle bears most distinctly of all the marks of St. Paul's later manner. I may add, also, that in a very special degree the grandeur and profoundness of treatment, which make it one of the great typical Epistles of the New Testament, speak for themselves as to its Apostolic origin. To lose it would be to leave a strange gap in the development of Christian doctrine, and to mar the harmony of the individual and corporate elements in the Scriptural exposition of the concrete Christian life. To ascribe it to the weaker hand of a mere disciple of St. Paul might, but for actual experience, have well been thought impossible.

(2) But this Epistle in particular has been described as simply an elaborate reproduction of the Colossian Epistle, and accordingly represented as of doubtful originality. It is, of course, obvious (as will be shown in the *Introduction to the Epistle to the Colossians*) that there is a very marked similarity, sometimes in idea, sometimes in actual expression, between the two Epistles. But the more both are studied, the more it must be seen that this similarity is exactly such as belongs to contemporaneousness, and is utterly incompatible with dependence of either upon the other.

In the first place, it is found that there are sections of the Colossian Epistle to which there is nothing to correspond in the Ephesian Epistle, and that these sections are principal and not subordinate. Such are, for example, Col. i. 15—17 (on the nature of the Lord Jesus Christ), Col. ii. 8—18 (the warning against mingled Judaism and Gnosticism), and Col. iv. 9—17 (the special salutations and cautions). The absence of these in the one case, and their presence in the other, are perfectly intelligible on the theory of contemporaneousness, entirely inexplicable on the theory of dependence.

On the other hand, there are sections in the Epistle to the Ephesians of the most emphatic originality, which have no counterpart in the other Epistle. Such are the great opening on the "election of God and the gathering up of all in Christ" (Eph. i. 3—14); the sublime Apostolic prayer in Eph. iii. 14—21; the celebrated and exhaustive passage on the unity of the Church in God (Eph. iv. 4—6); the profound comparison of marriage to the union of Christ with the Church in Eph. v. 23—33; the magnificent description of the Christian armour (Eph. vi. 13—17). To these the same remark must apply: to suppose these the work of a copyist appears all but preposterous.

Next, a careful study shows repeatedly and unmistakably that these differences are not accidental; they arise from a fundamental distinction between the leading ideas in the two Epistles. The Epistle to the Ephesians is the exposition of the reality, the blessing, and the glory, of the Catholic Church as the body of Christ. The famous image of the spiritual temple (in which, perhaps, we may trace some recollection of that magnificent Temple of Artemis, "which all Asia and the world worshipped") belongs to this Epistle (chap. ii. 20—22), and has no place in the other. The passage to which all else works up as a climax is chap. iv. 4—6, on the "one Body and the one Spirit." Even the ordinary moral duties and social relations of life are treated in chaps. iv. and v. with a characteristic reference to this great principle of unity with man in Christ, which is wanting in the parallel passages of the Colossian Epistle. On the other hand, the Colossian Epistle, having to deal with an incipient Gnosticism, is specially emphatic on the sole headship and the true Godhead of Christ. Its great teaching is of Him, as "the image of the invisible God," "in whom all the fulness (the *pleroma*) of the Godhead dwells bodily" (Col. i. 15—17; ii. 3—8, 10). The passage which occupies the chief place, corresponding to the great passage on Unity in the Ephesian Epistle, is that which dwells on our life as risen with Christ, and hid in God with Him, who Himself "is our life" (Col. iii. 1—4).

But besides this, it will be seen in the Notes on various passages that, on the one hand, in detailed passages parallel to each other, the similarity is almost always mingled with clear and characteristic difference, marking an independent coincidence; and on the other, that identical expressions occur again and again in entirely different contexts, and in different degrees of prominence. These are exactly the phenomena which we may expect when two letters are written at the same time to churches neither wholly identical nor wholly dissimilar in character, and under the guidance of distinct, yet complementary, ideas. They are wholly incompatible with dependence or deliberate copyism.

On this particular subject, therefore, I cannot but draw the same conclusion as on the general subject of the Epistles of the Captivity, viz., that the indirect evidence which has been thought to weaken, will be actually found to confirm the strong external evidence for the genuineness of the Epistle.

IV. **The Contents of the Epistle.**—The general character and substance of the Epistle have been already glanced at, both in the *General Introduction* and in the preceding sections of the *Special Introduction*, and they will be found to be treated in detail in the Notes on the chief passages of the Epistle itself. Full analyses, moreover, are given in each chapter.

It will be sufficient here simply to repeat that the Epistle falls into two great sections: Doctrinal and Practical. In both the one great subject is the UNITY IN CHRIST, in some sense of all created being, in a closer sense of humanity, in the closest and most sacred sense of the Holy Catholic Church.

In the doctrinal section (chaps. i. 1—iv. 16), we find this unity noticed in the first chapter as ordained in the eternal predestination of God's love, and manifested in the actual communication to His members of the Resurrection, the Ascension, and glorification of Christ, their head. Next it is shown (in chap. ii.) how the Gentiles are called into this regenerating unity out of the deadness of their old life; and thus at once brought into the covenant of God, and so united with His chosen people of Israel, that all alike, as living stones, are built into the great Temple of God. Then (in chap. iii.), after an emphatic declaration of the newness of this mystery of grace, and of the special commission for the revelation of it entrusted to St. Paul, there follows a solemn and fervent Apostolic prayer for their knowledge of the mystery, not by human wisdom or thought, but by the indwelling light and grace of Christ. Finally, the whole is summed up in a grand passage (chap. iv. 1—16), which brings out in perfect completeness the whole doctrine of this unity first in its grounds, its means, and its conditions; next in its variety of spiritual gifts; lastly, in the oneness of the object of all, in the reproduction of the life of Christ in the individual and the Church.

The practical section (chaps. iv. 17—vi. 24) opens with an unique treatment of morality and of human relationship, as dependent upon the mysterious unity of man with man and of man with God. First (chaps. iv. 17—v. 21), that unity is made the basis of ordinary moral duties towards man, and the safeguard against the besetting sins of heathen society —bitterness, impurity, and reckless excess. Next (chaps. v. 22—vi. 9), it is shown as the secret of the sacredness of earthly relations of marriage, of fatherhood, and of mastership. In the first case this idea is worked out with a transcendent beauty and solemnity, which have beyond all else hallowed Christian marriage; in the others it is more briefly touched upon, with a view chiefly to temper and soften the sternness of a recognised authority. Finally (chap. vi. 10—24), this portion of the Epistle is wound up by a magnificent and elaborate description of the full panoply of God; and the Epistle then ends, briefly and rather vaguely, with commendation of Tychicus and a general form of salutation.

The general sketch of this wonderful Epistle will, perhaps, be best explained by the analysis here subjoined, shortened from the analyses of the various chapters.

1. Doctrinal Section.

(1) THE INTRODUCTION (chap. i):
- (*a*) *Salutation* (chap. i. 1, 2);
- (*b*) *Thanksgiving for the election of the whole Church in God's love, given through redemption by unity with Christ, shown in the calling and faith both of Jew and Gentile* (chap. i. 3—14);
- (*c*) *Prayer for their fuller knowledge of this unity with the risen and ascended Christ, the Head of the whole Church* (chap. i. 15—23).

(2) THE CALL OF THE GENTILES (chap. ii.):
- (*a*) *Out of the deadness of sin and power of Satan into the new life of the risen Christ, accepted in simple faith, wrought out in good works* (chap. ii. 1—10);
- (*b*) *Out of alienation from the covenant, into perfect unity with God's chosen people, all division being broken down, and full access given to the Father; so that Jew and Gentile alike, built on the one foundation, grow into the living Temple of God* (chap. ii. 11—22).

(3) PRAYER FOR THEIR FULLER KNOWLEDGE (chap. iii.):
- (*a*) *The mystery of the universal call, new in revelation, specially intrusted to St. Paul* (chap. iii. 1—13);
- (*b*) *Prayer for their full knowledge of it (though passing knowledge) through the indwelling of Christ, accepted in faith and love* (chap. iii. 14—19);
- (*c*) *Doxology to the Father through Christ Jesus* (chap. iii. 20, 21).

(4) FINAL SUMMARY OF DOCTRINE (chap. iv.):
- (*a*) *The unity of the Church in one Spirit, one Lord, one God and Father of all* (chap. iv. 1—6);
- (*b*) *The diversity of gifts in the glorified Christ* (chap. iv. 7—11);
- (*c*) *The unity of the purpose of all, viz., the individual and corporate regeneration* (chap. iv. 12—16).

2. Practical Section.

(1) THE NEW LIFE: *learning Christ and growing unto His image* (chap. iv. 17—24).

(2) Conquest of Sin:
(a) *The conquest of sin in general in virtue of the sense of unity with man in Christ* (chap. iv. 25—30);
(b) *Conquest of special besetting sins of malice, impurity, recklessness of excess* (chaps. iv. 31; v. 21).

(3) Regeneration of Social Relations:
(a) *The relation of husbands and wives consecrated as a type of union of Christ with His Church* (chap. v. 22, 23);
(b) *The relation of parents and children hallowed as in the Lord* (chap. vi. 1—4);
(c) *The relation of masters and servants made a brotherhood of service to one Master* (chap. vi. 5—9).

(4) Final Exhortation:
The armour of God and the fight against the powers of evil (chap. vi. 10—17).

3. Conclusion.
(a) *Special desire of their prayers for him in his captivity* (chap. vi. 18—20);
(b) *Commendation of Tychicus* (chap. vi. 21, 22);
(c) *Salutation and blessing* (chap. vi. 23, 24).

In conclusion I may add that it does not appear to me fanciful to suppose that the teaching of this Epistle has as special an applicability to our age as the teaching of the Galatian or Roman Epistles had to the sixteenth century. For in all spheres of life—the political, the social, and the ecclesiastical alike—it would seem that our prominent questions are not those of individualism, but of socialism in the true sense of the word. Society is contemplated in its corporate life; in its rights over the individual; in the great eternal principles which it truly embodies and partially represents; and, moreover, this contemplation has a breadth of scope which refuses to be confined within the limits of family, or nation, or age. Humanity itself is considered, both historically and philosophically, as only the highest element in the order of the universe, which is itself bound together in a unity of unbroken connection and continuous development. It is asked, What has Christianity to declare as a gospel to society at large, and as a key to the mysterious relation of humanity with creation, and so with Him who created it? To that question, perhaps, the answer is nowhere more truly given than in the Epistle to the Ephesians. We need a real and living unity; but it must be such as will preserve the equally sacred individuality of freedom. This Epistle presents it to us in its magnificent conception of the unity of all with God in the Lord Jesus Christ.

THE EPISTLE OF PAUL THE APOSTLE TO THE

EPHESIANS

CHAPTER I.—(1) Paul, an apostle of
Chap. i. 1, 2. Salutation. Jesus Christ by the will of
God, to the saints which
are at Ephesus, and to the faithful in

A.D. 64.

Christ Jesus: (2) grace *be* to you, and
peace, from God our Father, and *from*
the Lord Jesus Christ. (3) Blessed *be*
the God and Father of our Lord Jesus

[1. **Introduction to the Epistle** (chap. i. 1—23).

(1) SALUTATION (verses 1, 2).

(2) THANKSGIVING TO GOD FOR—

(*a*) *The election of the whole Church before the world began, by the predestinating love of the Father, to holiness, grace, and glory* (verses 3—6);

(*b*) *this election depending on Redemption, in virtue of unity with Christ as the Head of all created Being* (verses 7—10);

(*c*) *and being manifested doubly, in the calling and faith, first of the Jewish, then of the Gentile Christians* (verses 11—14).

(3) PRAYER for their fuller knowledge of the hope, glory, and spiritual reality of their inheritance, manifested in the Resurrection, Ascension, and Royalty of Christ, the Head of the Church (verses 15—23).]

(1) (1) **By the will of God.**—This phrase, used in 1 Cor. i. 1; 2 Cor. i. 1; Col. i. 1; 2 Tim. i. 1 (comp. the equivalent expression of 1 Tim. i. 1), appears to be St. Paul's ordinary designation of the source of his apostolic mission and authority; used whenever there was nothing peculiar in the occasion of the Epistle, or the circumstances of the Church to which it was addressed. It may be contrasted, on the one hand, with the more formal enunciation of his commission, addressed to the Roman Church (Rom. i. 1—5), and the indignant and emphatic abruptness of the opening of the Galatian Epistle—"an apostle not of men, neither by man, but by Jesus Christ" (Gal. i. 1). On the other hand, to the Thessalonian churches, in the Epistles written shortly after their conversion, he uses no description of himself whatever (1 Thess. i. 1; 2 Thess. i. 1); in the Epistles to the Philippians and to Titus he is simply "the servant of Jesus Christ" (Phil. i. 1; Tit. i. 1): to Philemon (for special reasons) "the prisoner of Jesus Christ." The phrase in the text stands midway between the emphasis of the one class of Epistles and the more familiar simplicity of the other.

To the saints . . . . and to the faithful in Christ Jesus.—Here, as in Col. i. 2 ("the saints and faithful brethren") the same persons are described by both epithets. They are "saints," as "called" (see Rom. i. 7; 1 Cor. i. 2) into "the communion of saints" by the grace of God; they are "faithful," as by their own act believing in Christ and holding fast that faith. The two epithets are correlative to each other. Without the call and the grace of God, men cannot believe; without the energy of faith they cannot be, in effect as well as in opportunity, "saints." Both epithets belong in capacity and profession to all members of the Church militant; and St. Paul applies them accordingly to the whole body of any church which he addresses, without hesitation or distinction. In living reality they belong only to the "Invisible Church" of the present, which shall form the "Church triumphant" of the hereafter. It has been noted that the use of the word "saints," as the regular and ordinary name of Christians, is more especially traceable in the later Epistles of St. Paul. So in his speech before Agrippa he says, "Many of the saints did I shut up in prison" (Acts xxvii. 10). The phrase, "in Christ Jesus," belongs to both the words "saints" and "faithful;" but it is here more closely connected with the latter.

Which are at Ephesus.—On these words, omitted in the oldest MSS., see the *Introduction*.

(2) **Grace be to you, and peace.**—On this, St. Paul's all but invariable salutation in every Epistle (found also in the Epistles of St. Peter, 2 John, and Apocalypse), see Note on Rom. i. 7.

(2 *a*.) In verses 3—6, the first section of the Introduction, the Epistle ascends at once into "the heavenly places," naturally catching therefrom the tone of adoration and thanksgiving. It dwells on the election of the children of God by His predestinating love—an election based on His will, designed for His glory, and carrying with it the blessings of the Spirit, through which they become holy and unblamable before Him. On the whole section comp. Rom. viii. 28—30.

(3) It may be noted, as bearing on the question of the general or special character of this Epistle, that (with the single exception of the Second Epistle to the Corinthians, which may be looked upon as virtually a continuation of the First Epistle) all St. Paul's Epistles addressed to particular churches pass at once from the salutation to refer to the particular circumstances, gifts, and needs of the Church, generally in the form of thanksgiving and prayer, sometimes (as in Gal. i. 6) in rebuke. In St. Peter's First Epistle, on the other hand, addressed to those "scattered" through many churches, we have an opening exactly similar to the opening of this Epistle.

Christ, who hath blessed us with all spiritual blessings in heavenly *places*[1] in Christ: (4) according as he hath chosen us in him before the foundation of the world, that we should be holy and without blame before him in love: (5) having predestinated us

Chap. i. 3—6. The election of the whole Church;

1 Or, things.

There is, indeed, here a thanksgiving below (verses 15—22), but it is entirely general, belonging to the whole Church.

The God and Father of our Lord Jesus Christ.—On this phrase (used in Rom. xv. 6; 2 Cor. i. 3; xi. 31; 1 Pet. i. 3) see Note on Rom. xv. 6. It is, however, to be noted here, that in the Vatican MS. the words "and Father" are omitted, and that the phrase "the God of our Lord Jesus Christ" occurs below in verse 17.

Blessed be . . . who hath blessed us with all spiritual blessings.—The frequent phrase "Blessed be God" (Luke i. 68; Rom. i. 25; ix. 5; 2 Cor. i. 3; xi. 31; 1 Pet. i. 3) is here used with an unique antithesis. We can "bless" God only in thanksgiving of heart and voice, with which He deigns to be pleased, as He "rejoices over the works of His hands." God blesses us in real and life-giving "spiritual blessing," *i.e.,* blessing of the gift of the Spirit, for which we can return nothing except thanksgiving. So in Ps. cxvi. 12, 13, the natural question of the thoughtful soul—"What shall I render unto the Lord for all His benefits towards me?"—is answered simply by the words, "I will receive the cup of salvation, and call on the name of the Lord."

Who hath blessed us . . . in heavenly places.—It should be, *who blessed us* (once for all), in the election and predestination spoken of in the next verse. If this be noted, the sense of the phrase "in heavenly places" becomes far clearer. It has been doubted whether we ought to supply the word "places" or "things" (as in John iii. 12) in rendering this phrase, which is peculiar to this Epistle, and used in it no less than five times. In three out of the other four places (chaps. i. 20; ii. 6; iii. 10) the local sense is manifest; in the fourth (chap. vi. 12) and in this it might be doubtful. But (1) it is altogether unlikely that so unique a phrase would be used in two different senses; (2) the original word for "heavenly" has most properly and most usually a local meaning; (3) the transference of the thoughts to heaven above suits especially the whole tone of this Epistle and the parallel Epistle to the Colossians; and (4) the local sense agrees best with the context here, for the Apostle is speaking of the election "before the foundation of the world" as made by the foreknowledge of God in heaven, where Christ is "in the beginning with God."

It has been noticed here that we have one of those implicit references to the Holy Trinity—the blessing from God the Father, in Christ, and by the Spirit—with which St. Paul's Epistles abound.

In Christ—*i.e.,* in the unity with Christ, which is "the life eternal," ordained for us in the foreknowledge of God, and viewed as already existing. (See the whole of John xvii., especially verses 21—24.)

(4) **According as** (*i.e., inasmuch as*) **he hath chosen us in him before the foundation of the world.**—Again it should be, *He chose us for Himself.* The eternal election of God is inseparably connected with the blessing of the Spirit. This passage stands alone in St. Paul's Epistles in its use of this word "chosen" in connection with God's eternal purpose, "before the foundation of the world"—a phrase only applied elsewhere to the eternal communion of the Son with the Father (John xvii. 24), and to the foreordaining of His sacrifice in the divine counsels (1 Pet. i. 20). The word "chosen" itself is used by our Lord of His choice of the Apostles (John vi. 70; xiii. 18; xv. 16—19); but in one case with the significant addition, "one of you is a devil," showing that the election was not final. It is similarly used in the Acts (chaps. i. 2, 24; vi. 5; xv. 7, 22, 25) of His choice or the choice of the Apostles; and once (chap. xiii. 7) of the national election of Israel. In 1 Cor. i. 27, 28 (the only other place where it is used by St. Paul), and in Jas. ii. 5 it refers to choice of men by God's calling in this world. Clearly in all these cases it is applied to the election of men to privilege by an act of God's mercy here. In this passage, on the contrary, the whole reference is to the election "in Christ," by the foreknowledge of God, of those who should hereafter be made His members. From this examination of Scriptural usage it is clear that the visible election to privilege is constantly and invariably urged upon men; the election in God's eternal counsels only dwelt upon in passages which (like this or Rom. ix., xi.) have to ascend in thought to the fountain-head of all being in God's mysterious will. It will be observed that even here it clearly refers to all members of the Church, without distinction.

That we should be holy and without blame before him.—In these words we have the object of the divine election declared, and the co-operation of the elect implied, by the inseparable connection of holiness with election. There is an instructive parallel in Col. i. 22:—"He hath reconciled you in the body of His flesh through death, to present you holy and unblamable, and unreprovable in His sight." The word "without blame," or "unblamable," is properly *without blemish;* and the word "unreprovable" more nearly corresponds to our idea of one *unblamable*—*i.e.,* one against whom no charge can be brought. Here God is said to have "chosen" us, in the other passage to have "presented" us (comp. the sacrificial use of the word in Rom. xii. 1), in Christ, to be "holy and without blemish." It seems clear that the words refer not to justification in Christ, but to sanctification in Him. They express the positive and negative aspects of holiness; the positive in the spirit of purity, the negative in the absence of spot or blemish. The key to their interpretation is to be found in the idea of Rom. viii. 29, "whom He did foreknow, He did predestinate to be *conformed to the image of His Son.*" The word "without blame" is applied to our Lord (in Heb. ix. 14; 1 Pet. i. 19) as a lamb "without blemish." To Him alone it applies perfectly; to us, in proportion to that conformity to His image. The words "before Him" refer us to God's unerring judgment as contrasted with the judgment of men, and even our own judgment on ourselves. (Comp. 1 Cor. iv. 3, 4; 1 John iii. 20, 21.)

In love.—If these words are connected with the previous verse, they must be taken with "He hath chosen us," in spite of the awkwardness of the dislocation of order. But it is best to connect them with the verse following, "Having predestinated us in love."

(5) **Having predestinated us unto the adop-**

unto the adoption of children by Jesus Christ to himself, according to the good pleasure of his will, (6) to the praise of the glory of his grace, wherein he hath made us accepted in the beloved. (7) In whom we have redemption through his blood, the forgiveness of sins, according to the riches of his grace; (8) wherein he hath abounded toward

Chap. i. 7—10. as redeemed through unity with Christ;

---

tion of children by Jesus Christ to himself.—The idea of Election depends on the union of the sense of actual difference between men, as to privilege and spiritual life, with the conviction of God's universal sovereignty. Hence, in all cases, it leads back to the idea of Predestination, that is, of the conception of the divine purpose in the mind of God, before its realisation in actual fact. On the doctrine of predestination see Rom. ix. It will suffice to note that here (1) its source is placed in God's love; (2) its meritorious cause is the mediation of the Lord Jesus Christ; (3) its result is adoption, so that He is (see Rom. viii. 29) "the firstborn of many brethren," who are conformed to His image, and redeemed by Him from bondage to sonship (Gal. iv. 5). (It is clear that the adoption here is not the final adoption of Rom. viii. 23; but the present adoption into the Christian covenant, there called "the firstfruits of the Spirit;") (4) it is in itself the expression of "the good pleasure of His will" on which all ultimately depends; and (5) its final purpose is to show forth God's glory in the gift of His grace. In a few words the whole doctrine is summed up, with that absolute completeness, so eminently characteristic of this Epistle.

According to the good pleasure of his will.—In our version, "good pleasure," there is an ambiguity, reproducing the ambiguity of the original. The word used may signify (as in Matt. xi. 26; Luke x. 21; Phil. ii. 13) simply God's free will, to which this or that "seemeth good," or (as in Luke xi. 14; Rom. x. 1; Phil. i. 15) "His good will towards us." Even the old Greek interpreters were divided upon it, and either sense will suit this passage. But the close parallel in verse 11, "according to the counsel (*deliberate purpose*) of His will," turns the balance in favour of the former rendering.

(6) **To the praise of the glory of his grace.**—That is, for the acknowledgment by all God's creatures of the gloriousness of His grace; or, in other words, for the acknowledgment that God's essential glory is best manifested in His grace—that He "declares His almighty power most chiefly in showing mercy and pity." So in Ex. xxxiii. 18, 19, to the request, "Show me Thy glory," the answer is, "I will make my *goodness* to pass before thee . . . and will be gracious to whom I will be gracious." (Comp. Ex. xxxiv. 5—7.) He is pleased to consider His glory best realised in the spectacle of souls redeemed and regenerate by His grace, and to decree that it should be thus realised for our sakes. "Wherefore would He have us praise and glorify Him? It is that our love to Him may be kindled more fervently. He desires not our service, nor our praise, nor anything else except our salvation" (Chrysostom's *First Homily* on the Ephesians).

Wherein he hath made us accepted in the beloved.—The verb here rendered "made us accepted," is the same verb used in Luke i. 28 (and nowhere else in the New Testament), where we translate "highly favoured." Etymologically it means to "bestow grace upon;" the tense here is the past tense, not the perfect. Hence the meaning is (in connection with the previous clause), "His grace, which He bestowed upon us in the Beloved"—in virtue of our unity with "His beloved Son, in whom He is well pleased" (Matt. iii. 17). This special title is given to our Lord to mark a connection with the "love" declared in the last verse to be the source of God's predestination. It is a love to all mankind, as in God's foreknowledge already made one with His beloved Son. (See John xvii. 23, 25, "Thou hast loved them, as Thou hast loved Me . . . for Thou lovedst Me before the foundation of the world.")

(2 *b.*) Verses 7—10 form the second section of this Introduction to the Epistle, linked to the former by the words, "in the Beloved." From the declaration in the former section of the source of salvation in God's love, it leads us on to the mystery of the Mediation of Jesus Christ, in Whom all Being is gathered up for redemption.

(7) **In whom we have redemption through his blood, the forgiveness of sins.**—This passage is identical in sense and expression with Col. i. 14, except that the word here used for "sins" means, properly, "separate acts of transgression," while the word there is the more general word for sin in the abstract. (In chap. ii. 1, both are used.) In both passages we have united, as correspondent to each other, the two expressions under which our Lord Himself describes His atonement—in Matt. xx. 28, as the "giving His life a ransom for many," in Matt. xxvi. 28, as "the shedding of His blood for the forgiveness of sins." These two expressions appear to be complementary to each other, rather than identical. (1) The primary idea in "redemption" is deliverance from a bondage, mostly the bondage of sin itself (see Rom. viii. 23; Tit. ii. 14; Heb. ix. 15; 1 Pet. i. 18—21); occasionally (and in this sense with a different Greek word), the bondage under sentence of punishment for sin (Gal. iii. 13; iv. 5). Into that bondage man has plunged himself; God's mercy redeems him from it at an unspeakable price (John iii. 16; Rom. vii. 24, 25). (2) The primary idea in "the forgiveness of sins through His blood" is propitiation, that is, the offering to God "a full, perfect, and sufficient sacrifice" for sin, by One who is the Head and Representative of the human race (Rom. iii. 25; 1 John ii. 2; iv. 10). So St. Paul interprets our Lord's words by the declaration that "Christ our Passover is sacrificed for us" (1 Cor. v. 7); and it is notable that exactly in His words is the Atonement designated in the earliest apostolic preaching (Acts ii. 38; v. 31; x. 43; xiii. 38; xxvi. 18). Hence the former phrase looks at the Atonement from the side of God, the latter from the side of man; both being wrought by Him who is Son of God and Son of Man at once. Together they represent the whole truth.

According to the riches of his grace.—As above, in relation to praise, stress is laid on the gloriousness of God's grace, so here, in relation to enjoyment of it, on its overflowing richness. (See chaps. ii. 7; iii. 8, 16; and Rom. iii. 24; ix. 23.)

(8) **Wherein he hath abounded toward us in all wisdom and prudence.**—It should be, *which He made to overflow to us in all wisdom*

us in all wisdom and prudence; (9) having made known unto us the mystery of his will, according to his good pleasure which he hath purposed in himself: (10) that in the dispensation of the fulness of times he might gather together in one all things in Christ, both which are in heaven,[1] and which are on earth;

1 Gr. *the heavens.*

---

and prudence—the word "overflow" having an emphasis which our word "abound" has lost, and signifying here that the richness of God's grace not only fills the soul with the blessing of salvation, but overflows into the additional gifts of "all wisdom and prudence" in us, which gifts are here dwelt upon in anticipation of the declaration of the next verse. Of these two gifts, wisdom is clearly the higher gift, signifying (as in the Old Testament) the knowledge of the true end of life, which can only come from some knowledge of the "wisdom of God," that is, the divine purpose of His dispensation. (See especially Prov. viii. 22—31.) Such knowledge is revealed to us through the "mind of Christ," who is Himself the true wisdom or "Word of God." (See 1 Cor. i. 24, 30; ii. 6—10, 16.) Hence wisdom is spoken of in connection with various other gifts, which are but partial manifestations of it. Here with "prudence," that is, wisdom in action; in Col. i. 9, with "intelligence," that is, wisdom in judgment; in 1 Cor. xii. 8, Col. ii. 3, with "knowledge," that is, wisdom in perception; in verse 17 of this chapter, with "revelation," the means by which wisdom is gained.

(9) **Having made known unto us the mystery of his will.**—In the same connection we read in 1 Cor. ii. 7, "we speak the wisdom of God in a mystery." The word "mystery" properly signifies a thing which (see chap. iii. 5; Col. i. 27) "was hid from all ages, but is now made manifest." So our Lord evidently uses it (in Matt. xiii. 11; Mark iv. 11; Luke viii. 10). For the rest, except in four passages of the Apocalypse (Rev. i. 20; x. 7; xvii. 5, 7), it is used by St. Paul alone, and by him no less than twenty-one times, of which ten belong to this Epistle and the parallel Epistle to the Colossians—always in connection with such words as "knowledge," "declaration," "dispensation." The ordinary sense of the word "mystery"—a thing of which we know that it is, though how it is we know not —is not implied in the original meaning of the word; but it is a natural derivative from it. Reason can apprehend, when revealed, that which it cannot discover; but seldom or never can it comprehend it perfectly. In this verse the mystery is declared to be accordant to the good pleasure of God's will, which (it is added) "He purposed *in Himself.*" In this seems to be implied that (see chap. iii. 19) though in some sense we can know it, yet in its fulness "it passeth knowledge."

(10) **That in the dispensation of the fulness of times.**—The connection marked in our version seems certainly erroneous. The words should be connected with the previous verse, and translated thus: *which He purposed in Himself for administration* (or *disposal*) *of the fulness of the* (*appointed*) *seasons, to gather,* &c. We note (1) that the word "dispensation" is usually applied to the action of the servants of God, as "dispensers of His mysteries." (See chap. iii. 2; 1 Cor. ix. 17; Col. i. 25.) Here, however, and in chap. iii. 10, it is applied to the disposal of all by God Himself, according to "the law which He has set Himself to do all things by." Next (2) that the word "fulness," or *completeness,* frequently used by St. Paul, is only found in connection with time in this passage, and in Gal. iv. 4 ("when the fulness of time was come"). There, however, the reference is to a point of time, marking the completion of the preparation for our Lord's coming; here, apparently, to a series of "seasons," "which the Father hath put in His own power" (Acts i. 7) for the completion of the acts of the Mediatorial kingdom described in the words following. (Comp. Matt. xvi. 3; Luke xxi. 24; 1 Thess. v. 1; 1 Tim. ii. 6; iv. 1; vi. 15; Tit. i. 3.)

That he might gather together in one all things in Christ.—In these words St. Paul strikes the great keynote of the whole Epistle, the UNITY OF ALL IN CHRIST. The expression "to gather together in one" is the same which is used in Rom. xiii. 9 (where all commandments are said to be "briefly comprehended," or *summed up,* "in the one saying, Thou shalt love thy neighbour as thyself"). Here, however, there is the additional idea that this gathering up is "for Himself." The full meaning of this expression is "to gather again under one head" things which had been originally one, but had since been separated. The best comment upon the truth here briefly summed up is found in the full exposition of the Epistle to the Colossians (Col. i. 16—20), "In Him were all things created, that are in heaven and that are in earth . . . all things were created by Him and for Him . . . and in Him all things consist. It pleased the Father that in Him should all fulness dwell, and . . . by Him to reconcile all things to Himself . . . whether things on earth or things in heaven." In Christ, as the Word of God in the beginning, all created things are considered as gathered up, through Him actually made, and in Him continuing to exist. This unity, broken by sin, under the effect of which "all creation groans" (Rom. viii. 22), is restored in the Incarnation and Atonement of the Son of God. By this, therefore, all things are again summed up in Him, and again made one in Him with the Father. In both passages St. Paul uses expressions which extend beyond humanity itself— "things in heaven and things in earth," "things visible and things invisible," "thrones and principalities and powers." In both he immediately proceeds from the grand outline of this wider unity, to draw out in detail the nearer, and to us more comprehensible, unity of all mankind in Christ. (Comp. Col. i. 18, 21.) So also writes St. John (John i. 3, 4, 12), passing from the thought that "all things were made by Him," first to the declaration, "In Him was life, and the life was the light of men," and next to the power given to those who believed on Him to become sons of God. The lesser part of this truth, setting forth the unity of all mankind in the Second Adam, forms the basis of the argument of 1 Cor. xv., that "in Christ all shall be made alive," in the course of which the existence of the Mediatorial kingdom of Christ is described, and its continuance till the final triumph, when it "shall be delivered up to God, even the Father," "that God may be all in all" (1 Cor. xv. 24, 28). In virtue of it, those who are His are partakers of His death and resurrection, His ascension, even His judgment (chap. ii. 6; Matt. xix. 28; Rom vi. 3—10; 1 Cor. vi. 2, 3; Col. iii. 1—3).

(2 *c.*) Verses 11—14 form the third part of the

Chap. i. 11—14. granted alike to Jews and Gentiles.

even in him : (11) in whom also we have
obtained an inheritance,
being predestinated according to the purpose of
him who worketh all
things after the counsel of his own will :
(12) that we should be to the praise of
his glory, who first trusted[1] in Christ.
(13) In whom ye also *trusted*, after that
ye heard the word of truth, the gospel
of your salvation : in whom also after
that ye believed, ye were sealed with

[1] Or, *hoped.*

Introduction, applying the general truth of election by God's predestination in Christ, first to the original believers (the Jews), and then to the subsequent believers (the Gentiles).

(10, 11) **Even in him : in whom also we have obtained an inheritance.**—We have here (in the repetition, "even in Him") an emphatic transition to the truth most closely concerning the Apostle and his readers. The word "we" is not here emphatic, and the statement might be a general statement applicable to all Christians; but the succeeding verse seems to limit it to the original Jewish believers—the true Israel, who (like the whole of Israel in ancient days) have become "a people of inheritance" (Deut. iv. 20; ix. 29; xxxii. 9), so succeeding to the privileges (Rom. xi. 7) which their brethren in blindness rejected. Possibly this suggests the peculiar word here (and here only) used, meaning either "we were made partakers of a lot" in God's kingdom (to which Col. i. 12, "who has made us meet for a part of the lot of the saints," closely corresponds), or "we were made His lot or inheritance;" which perhaps suits the Greek better, certainly accords better with the Old Testament idea, and gives a more emphatic sense. A third possible sense is "were chosen by lot." This is adopted by the Vulgate, supported by the only use of the word in the Septuagint (1 Sam. xiv. 41), and explained by Chrysostom and Augustine as signifying the freedom of election without human merit, while by the succeeding words it is shown not to be really by chance, but by God's secret will. But this seems quite foreign to the genius of the passage.

Being predestinated . . . that we should be to the praise of his glory.—This is an application of the general truth before declared (verses 5, 6) that the source of election is God's predestination, and the object of it the manifestation of His glory.

After the counsel of his own will.—The expression evidently denotes not only the deliberate exercise of God's will by "determinate counsel and foreknowledge" (Acts ii. 23), but also the guidance of that will by wisdom to the fulfilment of the Law Eternal of God's righteous dispensation. Hooker, in a well-known passage (*Eccl. Pol.* i. 2), quotes it as excluding the notion of an arbitrary will of God, "They err, who think that of God's will there is no reason except His will."

(12) **That we . . . who first trusted in Christ.**—That the reference here is to the first Christians, in contradistinction to the Gentiles of the next verse, is clear. But the meaning of the phrase "who first hoped" (or, more properly, *who have hoped beforehand*) is less obvious. Our version seems to interpret it simply of "believing before" the Gentiles, *i.e.*, of being the "first believers;" and this interpretation may be defended by the analogy of certain cases in which the same prefix signifying "beforehand" has this sense (*e.g.*, Acts xx. 5, 13; Rom. iii. 9; xii. 10; 1 Cor. xi. 21). But the more general analogy strongly supports the other interpretation, "who have hoped in the Christ before He came"—that is, who, taught by prophecy, entering into that vision of a great future which pervades the older Covenant, looked forward "to the hope of Israel," and "waited for the consolation of Israel;" and who accordingly in due time became, on the Day of Pentecost, the firstfruits of His salvation.

(13) **In whom ye also trusted . . . in whom also after that ye believed, ye were sealed.**—The insertion of the word "trusted" (suggested by the word "trusted" in the previous verse) is probably erroneous, nor is it easy to find any good substitute for it. It is far better to refer the whole to the one verb, "ye were sealed." The irregularity of construction (arising from the addition to "hearing" of its proper accessory of "faith," Rom. x. 17) will surprise no one who studies St. Paul's Epistles, and especially these Epistles of his Captivity, remembering that they were dictated, and in all probability read over again to the Apostle for addition or correction.

After that ye heard the word of truth, the gospel of your salvation.—There is a contrast here between the Jewish believers, looking on in hope and gladly embracing its fulfilment, and the Gentiles, who had no such hope, and who therefore waited "for the word of the truth" (the full truth, not veiled in type or symbol), the glad tidings of a present salvation. The greater emphasis laid on the latter process seems intended to impress on the Gentiles a sense of the simpler and fuller means by which they were led to Christ.

After that ye believed, ye were sealed with that holy Spirit of promise.—The order is to be noted, and compared with the experience of the Day of Pentecost (Acts ii. 38). First, the light of the gospel shines before men; next, by faith they open their eyes to see it; then they are sealed by a special gift of the Holy Spirit. Such faith is, of course, the gift of God by the Spirit; but our Lord teaches us (John xvi. 8—13) to distinguish between the pleading of the Holy Spirit with "the world" "to convince of sin, because they believe not in Christ," and the special gift of His presence in the Church and the believing soul "to guide unto all the truth." This fuller presence is the seal of the new covenant.

Ye were sealed with that holy Spirit of promise.—This word "sealed" is found in exactly the same connection in 2 Cor. i. 22. The original idea of this sealing (which, it should be observed, is not of documents, but of men) is best seen in the "sealing of the servants of God in their foreheads," in Rev. vii. 3—8. In that passage, and in the passage of Ezekiel which it recalls (Ezek. ix. 4), the sealing is simply an outward badge, to be at once a pledge and means of safety amidst the destruction coming on the earth. In like sense, circumcision appears to be called "a seal" of previously existing righteousness of faith, in Rom. iv. 11; and the conversion of the Corinthians "a seal" of St. Paul's apostleship, in 1 Cor. ix. 2. (Comp. also John iii. 33; Rom. xv. 38; 2 Tim. ii. 19.) But the word is used in a deeper sense whenever it is connected

that holy Spirit of promise, (14) which
is the earnest of our inheritance until
the redemption of the purchased pos-
session, unto the praise of his glory.
(15) Wherefore I also, after I heard of
your faith in the Lord Jesus, and
love unto all the saints,
(16) cease not to give thanks
for you, making mention of
you in my prayers; (17) that

Chap. i. 15–19. Prayer for full knowledge of this divine blessing;

with the gift of the Holy Spirit. Then it corresponds to the "circumcision not made with hands" (Rom. ii. 29; Col. ii. 11); it has the character of a sacrament, and is not a mere badge, but a true means of grace. In this connection we read first of our Lord, "Him God the Father sealed" (John vi. 27), with a clear reference to the outpouring of the Holy Spirit at His baptism (comp. John i. 33; v. 37; x. 33); next of His people (as here, in chap. iv. 30, and in 2 Cor. i. 22) as being, like Himself, baptised with the Holy Ghost. In this passage the very title given to the Spirit is significant. He is called (in the curious order of the original) "the Spirit of the Promise, the Holy One." "The promise" is clearly the promise in the Old Testament (as in Jer. xxxi. 31—34; Joel ii. 28—33) of the outpouring of the Spirit on all God's people in "the latter days." The emphatic position of the epithet "Holy One" seems to point to the effect of His indwelling in the actual sanctification of the soul thus sealed. From this passage was probably derived the ecclesiastical application of the name "seal" to the sacrament of baptism, which is undoubtedly made the seal of conversion in Acts ii. 38.

(14) **Which is the earnest of our inheritance.**—On the word "earnest" (*arrhabôn*), a precious gift, as surety for a fuller gift hereafter, see 2 Cor. i. 22. The word "inheritance" has a correspondent meaning. It is a present possession (as in Acts vii. 5), which shall be developed into a more precious future. "We are very members, incorporate in the mystical body of Christ, and also heirs through hope of His everlasting kingdom."

Until the redemption of the purchased possession.—The "redemption" here is the complete and final salvation from sin and death (as in Rom. viii. 23). The original word here rendered "purchased possession" properly means "the act of purchase or acquisition," and is so used in 1 Thess. v. 9; 2 Thess. ii. 14; Heb. x. 39. But it seems clear that it is here used (in the sense of our version) with that confusion of idea, common in English, though rare in Greek, under which the result of an action is understood instead of the action itself, so that the word "purchases" is used for "things purchased," "acquisitions" for "things acquired" and the like. The transition is marked in relation to this same word in Mal. iii. 17; 1 Pet. ii. 9, where the Israelites are spoken of as "a people for acquisition," that is, as a people acquired or purchased.

(3) In verses 15—23, this introductory chapter ends in a prayer for the enlightenment of the readers of this Epistle, that they may understand all the fulness of the blessings of the gospel. In accordance with the heavenward direction of the thought of the whole Epistle, these blessings are viewed in their future completeness of glory and power, of which the present exaltation of the risen Lord to the right hand of God, as the Lord of all creatures, and the Head of the Church His body, is the earnest and assurance.

(15) **After I heard of your faith in the Lord Jesus, and love unto all the saints.**—These words have an almost exact parallel in Col. i. 4, addressed there to a church which St. Paul had not seen, and have been quoted in support of the belief that this Epistle cannot have been addressed, properly and solely, to the well-known Ephesian Church. They are not, however, decisive, for we have a similar expression to Philemon (verse 5), St. Paul's own convert.

We may note a distinction between "faith in the Lord Jesus" and "faith towards the Lord Jesus" (like "the love towards the saints"). Comp. 2 Tim. i. 13 ("faith and love in Christ Jesus"). "Faith in Christ" is a faith which, centred in Christ, nevertheless rests through Him on the Father; recognising a "life hid with him in God" (Col. iii. 3) and a sonship of God in Christ Jesus (Gal. iii. 26). The connection of the two clauses here shows that such a faith abounds (*i.e.* overflows) unto love, first necessarily to God, so being made perfect (Gal. v. 6), but next towards all His children. For "this commandment we have from Him, that he who loveth God, love his brother also" (1 John iv. 21).

(16) **Cease not to give thanks for you, making mention of you in my prayers.**—Almost all St. Paul's Epistles are introduced by this union of thanksgiving and prayer, which is, indeed, characteristic of the right harmony of all Christian worship. (See Rom. i. 8, 9; Phil. i. 3, 4; Col. i. 3, 4; 1 Thess. i. 2, 3; 2 Tim. i. 3; Philem. verse 4.) In the Galatian Epistle the omission of both is characteristic; in the two Epistles to the Corinthians thanksgiving alone is explicit, though prayer may be implied. But the proportion of the two elements varies. Here the thanksgiving has already been offered, although in the widest generality. Accordingly all that follows is prayer. In the parallel Colossian Epistle (Col. i. 3—13), which has no corresponding preface of thanksgiving, both elements are co-ordinate, with perhaps a slight predominance of thanksgiving.

(17) **The God of our Lord Jesus Christ.**—See John xx. 17, "I ascend unto My Father and your Father; and to My God and your God." It has been noted that, while on the cross, our Lord, in the cry, "My God, why hast Thou forsaken Me?" adopted the common human language of the Psalmist, He here, after His resurrection, distinguished emphatically between His peculiar relation to God the Father and that relation in which we His members call God "our Father." St. Paul's usual phrase (see above, verse 3) is "the God and Father of our Lord Jesus Christ;" the phrase here used is unique, probably substituted for the other on account of the use of the word "Father" in the next clause. It refers, of course, entirely to our Lord's nature as the true Son of Man. In that respect God is in the full sense (which in us is interrupted by sin) His God, in whom He lived and had His being. In proportion as we are conformed to His likeness, "God is our God for ever and ever."

The Father of glory.—Better, *of the glory.* This phrase is again unique. We have, indeed, such phrases as "Father of Mercies" (2 Cor. i. 3), "Father of Lights" (Jas. i. 17); and, on the other hand, "the King of Glory" (Ps. xxviii. 5), "the God of Glory" (Acts vii. 2), "the Lord of Glory" (1 Cor. ii. 8; Jas.

the God of our Lord Jesus Christ, the
Father of glory, may give unto you the
spirit of wisdom and revelation in the
knowledge[1] of him : (18) the eyes of your
understanding being enlightened; that
ye may know what is the hope of his
calling, and what the riches of the glory
of his inheritance in the saints, (19) and
what *is* the exceeding greatness of his
power to us-ward who believe, according
to the working of his mighty power,[2]
(20) which he wrought in Christ, when
he raised him from the
dead, and set *him* at his
own right hand in the
heavenly *places*, (21) far

Chap. i. 20—23. given through the headship of Christ.

2 Gr. *of the might of his power.*

1 Or, *for the acknowledgment.*

ii. 1). In all these last instances "the glory" seems certainly to be the *Shechinah* of God's manifested presence, and in all cases but one is ascribed to our Lord. But "the Father of the glory," seems a phrase different from all these. I cannot help connecting it with the missing element in the preceding clause, and believing (with some old interpreters), in spite of the strangeness of expression, that God is here called "the Father of the glory" of the incarnate Deity in Jesus Christ (see John i. 14), called in 2 Cor. iv. 6, "the glory of God in the face (or *person*) of Jesus Christ." (See *Excursus A to St. John's Gospel: On the Doctrine of the Word;* dealing with the identification of "the Word" with the Shechinah by the Jewish interpreters). The prayer which follows connects the knowledge of the glory of our inheritance with the exaltation of our Lord in glory.

The knowledge of him.—The word here rendered "knowledge" signifies "perfect and thorough knowledge;" and the verb corresponding to it is used distinctively in this sense in Luke i. 4; 1 Cor. xiii. 12. It is employed by St. Paul more especially in his later Epistles (chap. iv. 13; Phil. i. 9; Col. i. 9, 10; ii. 2; iii. 10), dealing as they do with the deeper things of God, and assuming more of a contemplative tone. It is represented here as coming from distinct "revelation."

(18) **The eyes of your understanding.**—The true reading is *of your heart,* for which the words "of your understanding" have been substituted, so as to yield a simpler and easier expression. The heart is similarly spoken of in relation to spiritual perception in Rom. i. 21; 1 Cor. ii. 9; iv. 5; it signifies the inner man in his entirety; and the phrase here used seems to convey the all-important truth, that for the knowledge of God all the faculties of understanding, conscience, and affection must be called into energy by the gift of the light of God.

That ye may know.—The knowledge which St. Paul here desires for the Ephesians, in accordance with the whole tone of this Epistle, is a knowledge of heavenly things, only experienced in part upon earth—with an experience, however, sufficient to be an earnest of the hereafter. The succession of ideas follows the order of conversion—first, "calling;" then acceptance to "inheritance;" lastly, "inward working of divine power" in the accepted. To each the conception of looking onward is attached; to the "calling" "hope," to the "inheritance" "glory," to the "power" the exaltation of Christ (and of us with Him; see chap. ii. 6) to the right hand of God.

The hope of his calling.—(See chap. iv. 4.) That is, probably, "the thing hoped for," because promised, at our calling (as in Gal. v. 5; Col. i. 5; Tit. ii. 3; Heb. vi. 18; and perhaps 1 Tim. i. 1), for the other objects of knowledge with which it is here joined are certainly objective or external to ourselves. This hope is of the perfection of all, which we are called to enjoy really, but imperfectly, here.

The riches of the glory of his inheritance in the saints.—Comp. Col. i. 27, "the riches of the glory of this mystery . . . which is Christ in you, the hope of glory." The inheritance of God is the unity with Christ, in which lies the earnest and hope of glory. "Among the saints" is best connected with the word "inheritance," showing that our personal inheritance of Christ gives us a place in the kingdom of heaven here and hereafter.

(19) **According to the working of his mighty power.**—More correctly (see margin), *the working of the might of His strength.* The word "power" is a general word for force, which may be latent, and, in fact, often describes force which is latent, in contradistinction to the word here used for working or energy. St. Paul, therefore, adds that this power of God is not latent; it actually works "according to," that is, up to the full measure of "the might of the strength" of God—of that strength which is a part of His nature. The whole phrase forms a glorious climax, in which the Apostle accumulates words ever stronger and stronger to approach to the description of the omnipotence of the Spirit. It is a "force of exceeding greatness;" it is an ever energetic force; its only measure is the immeasurable might of the divine nature. (Comp. chap. iii. 7; Phil. iii. 21; Col. i. 29; ii. 12.)

(20) **Which he wrought in Christ.**—The reality of the work of God upon us is insured by the reality of that work upon the true Son of Man, whose members we are, in His resurrection, His ascension, His exaltation over all things at the right hand of God, and His headship of the Church. It is notable that, while it is on the spiritual meaning of the resurrection of Christ that the chief stress is laid in the earlier Epistles (as in Rom. vi. 4—11; 1 Cor. xv. 12—22, 50—57), in these later Epistles the Apostle passes on beyond this, as taken for granted (see Col. iii. 1), and dwells on "Christ in heaven," exalted far above all created things, but yet vouchsafing to be in a peculiar sense the head and life of the Church on earth. See, for example, Phil. ii. 9—11; Col. i. 14—19; and compare the pervading conception of the Apocalypse. In this advance of thought he approaches to the idea of our Lord's own great intercession (John xvii. 5 *et seq.*), constantly connecting the unity of His Church in Him with the glory which was His from all eternity, and to which He was to return—"Now, O Father, glorify Thou Me with Thine own self with the glory which I had with Thee before the world was. . . . I will that they also whom Thou hast given Me, be with Me where I am, that they may behold My glory."

(21) **Far above all principality, and power, and might, and dominion.**—The words here used are intended to include all possible forms of power, corresponding to the exhaustive enumeration in Phil. ii. 10, "of things in heaven, and things in earth, and things under the earth." The words rendered "principality and power" (more properly signifying "government and the authority committed to it") are used in Luke

above all principality, and power, and might, and dominion, and every name that is named, not only in this world, but also in that which is to come:

(22) and hath put all *things* under his feet, and gave him *to be* the head over all *things* to the church, (23) which is his body, the fulness of him that filleth all in all.

xii. 11; xx. 20; Tit. iii. 1, distinctively for earthly powers; in 1 Cor. xv. 24, generally for all created powers whatever. But St. Paul mostly employs this whole group of words, especially in the Epistles of the Captivity, with a manifest reference to angelic powers of good or evil. Thus in Rom. viii. 38 we read, of "angels, and principalities, and powers" (as in 1 Pet. iii. 22, "angels, and authorities, and powers"); in chap. iii. 10 of this Epistle, of "principalities and powers in the heavenly places;" and in chap. vi. 12, of "wrestling *not against flesh and blood*, but against principalities and powers," &c.; and in Col i. 16, of "things in heaven and earth, visible and invisible, whether they be thrones, or dominions, or principalities, or powers." It is likely that he was induced so to do by the half-Gnostic speculation on the nature and worship of angels, prevalent in the later Judaism, of which we have a specimen at Colossæ (Col. ii. 18)—in the same spirit which leads the author of the Epistle to the Hebrews to dwell so emphatically (in chaps. i. and ii.) on the infinite superiority of the Son of God to all angels. We observe that his references to these orders or aspects of the angelic hierarchy vary both in fulness and in order. (Comp., for instance, this passage with Col. i. 16.) Hence we gain no encouragement for the elaborate speculation in which men have indulged as to the right succession and relation of the hosts of heaven. In this passage the names rather point to different aspects, than to different orders, of superhuman power. The first two words signify appointed government and the authority which is committed to it; the last two the actual force and the moral force of dignity or lordship in which it is clothed. In the Colossian passage the words here placed first come last, though in the same mutual connection, and the words "dignities or lordships" is connected with the word "thrones," not here found. His purpose is, indeed, better served by this comparative vagueness: for that purpose is to exalt the majesty of our Lord over all other, whatever it may be, and whatever name it may wear.

Not only in this world, but also in that which is to come.—The word "world" is here *age*, and the antithesis is exactly that of our Lord's words in Matt. vii. 32 (see Note there). Manifestly, however, it here signifies "this life" (or *dispensation*) and "the future life," that is, the life on this side, and on the other side, of the Second Coming of Christ.

(22) **And hath put all things under his feet.**—See 1 Cor. xv. 25—28, where St. Paul deals with the quotation from Ps. viii. 6, in application to our Lord's Mediatorial kingdom. In this passage these words fill up the picture of our Lord's transcendent dignity, by the declaration of the actual subjugation of all the powers of sin and death, rising up against Him, in the spiritual war which is to go on till the appointed end. They therefore form a natural link between the description of His lordship over all created being, and of His headship over the Church, militant on earth, as well as triumphant in heaven.

And gave him to be the head over all things to the church, which is his body.—This is the first time that this celebrated phrase is used, describing Christ as the Head, and viewing the Church as a whole as His body. It is characteristic that in 1 Cor. xi. 3, Christ is called "the Head of each man," as "the man of the woman;" whereas in this Epistle Christ is the Head of the whole Church, on occasion of the same comparison (see v. 23). The consideration of all Christians as the "body of Christ" is indeed found in Rom. xii. 4; 1 Cor. xii. 12—27: but it is notable that in these passages the leading idea is, first, of the individuality of each member, and then, secondarily, of their union in one body; and in 1 Cor. xii. 21, "the head and the foot," just as much as "the eye and the hand," are simply looked upon as members. (Comp. also 1 Cor. vi. 15; x. 17.) Here, in accordance with the great doctrine of this Epistle—the unity of the whole of humanity and of the whole Church, ideally co-extensive with that humanity, with Christ—the metaphor is changed. The body is looked upon as a whole, Christ as its Head. The idea is wrought out again and again (see chaps. iv. 15, 16; v. 28; Col. i. 18; ii. 19) in these Epistles of the Captivity. It is from these that it has become a household word in all Christian theology. With some variation it is expressed also in other metaphors—the building and the corner-stone, the bride and the bridegroom. But under the title of the "Head" Christ is looked upon especially in His ruling, guiding, originating power over the Church. Probably the idea of His being the seat of its life, though not excluded, is secondary; whereas in His own figure of the vine and the branches (John xvi. 6) it is primary.

(23) **The fulness of him that filleth all in all.**—The word *pleroma*, "fulness," is used in a definite and almost technical sense in the Epistles of the Captivity, and especially in the Epistle to the Colossians, having clear reference to the speculations as to the Divine Nature and the emanations from it, already anticipating the future Gnosticism. The word itself is derived from a verb signifying, first, to "fill;" next (more frequently in the New Testament), to "fulfil" or *complete*. It is found (1) in a physical sense of the "full contents" of the baskets, in Mark vi. 43, viii. 20; and of the earth, in 1 Cor. x. 26—28; and in Matt. ix. 16, Mark ii. 21, it is applied to the patch of new cloth on an old garment. It is used next (2) of fulness, in sense of the "complete tale or number," "of time" and "seasons," in chap. i. 10, Gal. iv. 4; of the Jews and Gentiles in Rom. xi. 12, 25. In the third place (3) it is applied to the full essence, including all the attributes, of a thing or person; as of the Law (Rom. xiii. 10), and of the blessing of Christ (Rom. xv. 29). Lastly (4), in these Epistles it is applied, almost technically, to the fulness of the Divine Nature. Thus, in Col. i. 19 we have, "It pleased the Father that in Christ all the fulness"—*i.e.*, all the fulness of the Divine Nature—"should dwell;" or (to take an admissible but less probable construction) "In Him all the fulness is pleased to dwell;" and this is explained in chap. ii. 9, "In Him dwelt all the fulness of the Godhead bodily." Similarly, though less strikingly, we read in this Epistle, that those who are in Christ are said (in chaps. iii. 19; iv. 13) "to be filled up to all the fulness of God," and "to come to the measure of the stature of the fulness of Christ. In which of these last senses is the Church here said to be the "fulness of Christ?" If in any, probably in the last of all. As the individual, so the Church, by the presence "of Him who filleth up all things for Him-

CHAPTER II.

Chap. ii. 1—7. God's quickening of the spiritually dead by unity with the glorified Christ.

A.D. 64.

(1) And you *hath he quickened,* who were dead in trespasses and sins;
(2) wherein in time past ye walked according to the course of this world, according to the prince of the power of the air, the spirit that now worketh

---

self in all," comes to be "His fulness," the complete image of Him in all His glorified humanity. But it may be questioned whether it is not better to take here a different sense, corresponding to the "patch" in Matt. ix. 16, and signifying the "complement." In the original Greek of Euclid (in Book i., Prop. 4), the cognate word, *parapleroma*, is used of "the complements." In this compound word the idea is, no doubt, more unequivocally expressed. But of the simple word here employed it may be reasonably contended that, if one thing or person alone is contemplated, the *pleroma* must be the fulness of the one nature; if, as here, two are brought in, each will be the "complement" to the other—as the patch to the garment, and the garment to the patch. So here (says Chrysostom) "the complement of the Head is the Body, and the complement of the Body is the Head." Thus by a daring expression, St. Paul describes our Lord as conceiving His glorified humanity incomplete without His Church; and then, lest this should seem to derogate even for a moment from His dignity, he adds the strongest declaration of His transcendent power, "to fill up for Himself all things in all," in order to show that we are infinitely more incomplete without Him than He without us. This sense, bold as it is, certainly suits exactly the great idea of this Epistle, which differs from the parallel Colossian Epistle in this—that while both dwell emphatically on Christ the Head, and the Church as His Body, there the chief stress is laid on the true Deity of the Head, here on the glory and privileges of the Body.

II.

[2. **The unity of all in Christ** (chap. ii. 1—22).

(1)—(*a*) THE QUICKENING OF MEN FROM THE DEATH OF SIN AND BONDAGE OF SATAN, by a personal union with Christ, making them partakers of His resurrection, His ascension, His endless glory (verses 1—7).

(*b*) *All this not of themselves, but by the free grace of God,* accepted in faith and wrought out in good works (verses 8—10).

(2) HENCE THE DRAWING OF THE GENTILES OUT OF HOPELESS AND GODLESS ESTRANGEMENT TO—

(*a*) *Nearness to God in Christ* (verses 11—13):
(*b*) *Union with Israel in Christ* (verses 14—18);
(*c*) *A place, as living stones, in the great fabric of His Church* (verses 19—22).]

(1 *a.*) Verses 1—7 begin the fuller exposition of the doctrine implied in the thanksgiving and prayer of the previous chapter; starting from the individual and personal union of all with Christ, in virtue of which they partake of His spiritual life, His conquest of death, and the exaltation of His glorified humanity to heaven.

(1) **And you hath he quickened.**—*And you also.* St. Paul here begins the particular application to the Ephesians, which is the main subject of this chapter, broken off in verses 3—10, and resumed in verse 11. The words "hath He quickened" (or, properly, *did He quicken*) are supplied here from verse 5—rightly, as expressing the true sense and tending to greater clearness, but perhaps not necessarily.

Trespasses and sins.—These two words, more often used separately, are here brought together, to form a climax. The word rendered "trespass" signifies a "swerving aside and falling"; the word rendered "sins" is generally used by St. Paul in the singular to denote "sin" in the abstract, and signifies an entire "missing of the mark" of life. Hence, even in the plural, it denotes universal and positive principles of evil doing, while "trespass" rather points to failure in visible and special acts of those not necessarily out of the right way.

(2) **The course** (or, *age*) **of this world.**—Here again are united the two words often rendered by "world," the former signifying simply "the age," or appointed period of this visible universe, the latter its material and sensuous character. When we are warned against the one (as in Rom. xii. 2, "Be not conformed to this world;" see also 1 Cor. i. 20; ii. 6; 2 Tim. iv. 10), it is against the "vanity"—that is, the transitoriness and unreality—of the present life; when against the other (see Gal. iv. 3; vi. 14; Col. ii. 8—10), it is against its "pomp," its carnal, material, unspiritual splendour. Here the former life of the Ephesians is described as at once transitory and carnal.

The prince of the power of the air.—The connection of the "world" with the Evil One as its "prince" is not uncommon in Holy Scripture (see John xii. 31; xiv. 30; xvi. 11); and the "power" of this passage is exactly that which Satan claims as "committed" to him in Luke iv. 32. But the phrase "the power of the air" is unique and difficult. We note (1) that this phrase signifies not "a power over the air," but "a power dwelling in the region of the air." Now, the word "power" (see Note on chap. i. 21), both in the singular and the plural, is used in this Epistle, almost technically, of superhuman power. Here, therefore, the Evil One is described as "the prince," or *ruler,* of such superhuman power—considered here collectively as a single power, prevailing over the world, and working in the children of disobedience—in the same sense in which he is called the "prince of the devils," the individual spirits of wickedness (Matt. ix. 34; xii. 24). Next (2), Why is this spoken of as ruling "in the air"? There may possibly be allusion (as has been supposed) to the speculations of Jewish or Gentile philosophy; but it seems far more probable that the "air" is here meant simply to describe a sphere, and therefore a power, below the heaven and yet above the earth. The "air" is always opposed to the bright "ether," or to the spiritual "heaven"; the word and its derivatives carry with them the ideas of cloudiness, mist, and even darkness. Hence it is naturally used to suggest the conception of the evil power, as allowed invisibly to encompass and move above this world, yet overruled by the power of the true heaven, which it vainly strives to overcloud and hide from earth. In chap. vi. 12 the powers of evil are described with less precision of imagery, as dwelling "in heavenly places," the opposition being there only between what is human and superhuman; yet even there the "darkness" of this world is referred to, corresponding to the conception of

in the children of disobedience: (3) among whom also we all had our conversation in times past in the lusts of our flesh, fulfilling the desires[1] of the flesh and of the mind; and were by nature the children of wrath, even as others. (4) But God, who is rich in mercy, for his great love wherewith he

1 Gr. *the wills.*

cloudiness and dimness always attaching to "the air."

The spirit that now worketh in the children of disobedience.—The Greek here shows that the word "spirit" must be taken in apposition, not to "prince," as an English reader would naturally suppose, but to "power." As the individual demons when considered as working on the human spirit are called spirits—"unclean spirits" in the Gospels, "evil spirits" in Acts xix. 12 (comp. Acts xvi. 16), "deceiving spirits" in 1 Tim. iv. 1—so here the collective power of evil, considered as working in "the children of disobedience," is called "a spirit," like the "spirit of the world," in 1 Cor. ii. 12, but here even more distinctly opposed to the "Spirit of God." In reference to this spiritual power over the soul our Lord's casting out demons is described (Acts x. 28) as a deliverance of those who were "oppressed of the devil;" the apostolic work of conversion (Acts xxvi. 18) as a turning "from the power of Satan to God," and excommunication as "a deliverance to Satan" (1 Cor. v. 5; 1 Tim. i. 20); and in 2 Thess. ii. 9 exactly the same word for "inward working" is applied to the action of Satan on the soul. From this half-personal use of the word "spirit" it is easy to pass to the more abstract sense of an inner spiritual principle (as in Rom. viii. 15; xi. 8; 2 Tim. i. 7; 1 John iv. 6).

(3) **Among whom also we all . . .**—Up to this point St. Paul had addressed himself especially to the Ephesians as Gentiles: now he extends the description of alienation to "all," Jews and Gentiles alike, as formerly reckoned among the children of disobedience. It is indeed the great object of this chapter to bring out the equality and unity of both Jews and Gentiles in the Church of Christ; and this truth is naturally introduced by a statement of their former equality in alienation and sin.

In the lusts of our flesh, fulfilling the desires of the flesh and of the mind.—The parallelism of these two clauses illustrates very clearly the extended sense in which the word "flesh" is used by St. Paul, as may indeed be seen by the catalogue of the works of the flesh in Gal. v. 19, 20. For here "the flesh," in the first clause, includes both "the flesh and the mind" (or, more properly, the *thoughts*) of the second; that is, it includes both the appetites and the passions of our fleshly nature, and also the "thoughts" of the mind itself, so far as it is devoted to this visible world of sense, alienated from God, and therefore under the influence of the powers of evil. In fact, in scriptural use the sins of "the flesh," "the world," and "the devil" are not different classes of sins, but different aspects of sin, and any one of the three great enemies is made at times to represent all.

And were by nature the children of wrath, even as others (or rather, *the others*—that is, the heathen).—From this passage the phrase "children of wrath" has passed into Christian theology as an almost technical description of the unregenerate state. Hence it needs careful examination. (1) Now the phrase "children of wrath" (corresponding almost exactly to "children of a curse," in 2 Pet. ii. 14) seems borrowed from the Hebrew use in the Old Testament, by which (as in 1 Sam. xx. 30; 2 Sam. xii. 5) a "son of death" is one under sentence of death, and in Isa. lvii. 4 (the Greek translation) "children of destruction" are those doomed to perish. In this sense we have, in John xvii. 12, "the son of perdition;" and in Matt. xxiii. 15, "the son of hell." It differs, therefore, considerably from the phrase "children of disobedience" (begotten, as it were of disobedience) above. But it is notable that the word for "children" here used is a term expressing endearment and love, and is accordingly properly, and almost invariably, applied to our relation to God. When, therefore, it is used as in this passage, or, still more strikingly, in 1 John iii. 10, "children of the devil" (comp. John viii. 44), there is clearly an intention to arrest the attention by a startling and paradoxical expression. "We were children," not of God, not of His love, but "of wrath"—that is, His wrath against sin; "born (see Gal. iii. 10—22; iv. 4) under the law," and therefore "shut up under sin," and "under the curse." (2) Next, we have the phrase "by nature," which, in the true reading of the original, is interposed, as a kind of limitation or definition, between "children" and "of wrath." In the first instance it was probably suggested by the reference to Israel, who were by covenant, not by nature, the chosen people of God. Now the word "nature," applied to humanity, indicates what is common to all, as opposed to what is individual, or what is inborn, as opposed to what is acquired. But whether it refers to humanity as it was created by God, or to humanity as it has become by "fault and corruption of nature," must always be determined by the context. Here the reference is clearly to the latter. "Nature" is opposed to "grace"—that is, the nature of man as alienated from God, to the nature of man as restored to his original birthright, the "image of God," in Jesus Christ. (See Rom. v. 12—21.) The existence of an inborn sinfulness needs no revelation to make it evident to those who have eyes to see. It needs a revelation—and such a revelation the gospel gives—to declare to us that it is not man's true nature, and that what is really original is not sin, but righteousness. (3) The whole passage, therefore, describes the state of men before their call to union with Christ, as naturally "under wrath," and is well illustrated by the full description, in Rom. i. 18, ii. 16, of those on whom "the wrath of God is revealed." There man's state is depicted as having still some knowledge of God (Rom. i. 19—21), as having "the work of the law written on the heart" (Rom. ii. 14, 15), and accordingly as being still under a probation before God (Rom. ii. 6—11). Elsewhere we learn that Christ, "the Lamb slain from the foundation of the world," died for all, even "the ungodly" (Rom. v. 6—8; Rev. xiii. 1); and that none are wholly excluded from His atonement but those who "tread under foot the Son of God, and count the blood of the covenant an unholy thing" (Heb. x. 29). Hence that state is not absolutely lost or hopeless. But yet, when the comparison, as here, is with the salvation of the gospel, they are declared "children of wrath" who are "strangers to the new covenant of promise," with its two supernatural gifts of justification by faith and sanctification in the Spirit, and their condition is described, comparatively but not absolutely, as "having no hope, and without God in the world."

(4) **Rich in mercy.**—Not only merciful, but rich

loved us, (5) even when we were dead
in sins, hath quickened us together
with Christ, (by grace ye are saved;)
(6) and hath raised *us* up together, and
made *us* sit together in heavenly *places*
in Christ Jesus: (7) that in the ages to
come he might shew the exceeding
riches of his grace in *his* kindness
toward us through Christ Jesus. (8) For
by grace are ye saved through faith;

"in the multitude of mercy," as attaching even to those dead in sin (see Chrysostom on this passage). The idea of richness in grace, glory, mercy, is especially frequent in this Epistle. (See chaps. i. 7, 18; ii. 7; iii. 8, 16.)

For his great love.—Again, as in chap. i. 4, stress is laid on the love of God, before all else, as the one moving cause of salvation. (Comp. Rom. v. 8, "God commendeth His love towards us, in that, while we were yet sinners, Christ died for us.")

(5) **Even when we were dead in sins.**—These words should be connected, not with "loved us," but with "hath quickened," or rather, *quickened.* He brought life out of spiritual death.

(5, 6) The thought in these verses follows exactly the same course as in chap. i. 19, 20. There the type and earnest of the working of God's mighty power are placed in the resurrection, the ascension, the glorification of Christ Himself in His human nature. Here what is there implied is worked out—(1) All Christians are declared to be quickened (or, *risen again*) to spiritual life with Christ, according to His promise, "Because I live, ye shall live also" (John xiv. 19). (See the exact parallel in Col. ii. 13.) But there is a promise even beyond this: "I am the life: whosoever liveth and believeth in Me shall never die" (John xi. 25; comp. also v. 24; xvii. 2). Hence, even more emphatically, and in full accordance with this latter promise, we have in Col. iii. 4, "Christ who is our life;" as in 2 Cor. iv. 10, 11, "The life of Jesus is made manifest in us." What this "life eternal" is He Himself declares (John xvii. 3)—"to know the only true God and Jesus Christ, whom He has sent." (2) Next, this partaking of the life of Christ is brought out in two striking forms—as a partaking, not only of His resurrection (as in Rom. vi. 5; 1 Cor. xv. 20—22; Phil. iii. 11), but also (in a phase of thought peculiar to these Epistles) of His ascension "to the heavenly places." This is "in Christ Jesus," in virtue of a personal and individual union with Christ. It implies blessings, both present and future, or rather one blessing, of which we have the earnest now and the fulness hereafter—for the resurrection and ascension of Christ are even now the perfection and glorification of humanity in Him. (3) So far as we are really and vitally His members, such perfection and glorification are ours now, by His intercession (that is, His continued mediation for us in heaven) and by His indwelling in us by the Spirit on earth. The proof of partaking His resurrection is "newness of life," "death unto sin, and new birth unto righteousness" (Rom. vi. 5—11), which is in Col. iii. 12 expressly connected with the entrance upon unity with Christ in baptism. The proof of having "our life hid in Christ at the right hand of God," is "the setting our affection on things above" (Col. iii. 1), by which "in heart and mind we thither ascend, and with Him continually dwell." (4) These proofs are seen only in measure here. Through the change which we call death, we pass at once to a still higher stage of life, by fuller union with Christ (2 Cor. v. 6—8), and at the great day we shall have both in perfection—perfect newness of life in "likeness to Him" (1 John iii. 2), and perfect glorification in Him in that communion with God which is heaven (John xvii. 5, 10, 24). The one thing which St. Paul does not attribute to us is that which is His alone—the place "at the right hand of the Father."

(7) **In the ages to come.**—Properly, *the ages which are coming on*—the ages both of time and of eternity, looked upon in one great continuity. Here, again, the manifestation of the riches of God's grace is looked upon as His special delight, and as His chosen way of manifesting His own self to His creatures.

In his kindness.—The word "kindness" (properly, *facility,* or *readiness to serve another*) is applied to that phase of God's mercy in which it shows Him as "ready to receive, and most willing to pardon." Thus we find it in Luke vi. 35 used for His goodness "to the unthankful and evil"; in Rom. ii. 4 it is joined with "long-suffering and patience"; in Rom. xi. 22 opposed to abrupt "severity"; in Tit. iii. 4, connected with love to man, "philanthropy"; and it is also used in similar connections when attributed to man (1 Cor. xiii. 4; 2 Cor. vi. 6; Gal. v. 22; Col. iii. 12). Hence in this passage it is especially appropriate, because so much stress has been laid on the former sinfulness and godlessness of those to whom God's mercy waited to be gracious. There is a similar appropriateness in the repetition of the name of our Lord "through Christ Jesus," for this gentle patience and readiness to receive sinners was so marked a feature of His ministry that to the Pharisees it seemed an over-facility, weakly condoning sin. "Through Him," therefore, the kindness of God was both shown and given.

(1 *b.*) Verses 8—10 (taking up and working out the parenthetical "by grace ye are saved" of verse 5) form an instructive link of connection between these Epistles and those of the earlier group, especially the Epistles to the Galatians and Romans. (Comp. Phil. iii. 9.) In both there is the same doctrine of "Justification by Faith," the same denial of the merit of good works, the same connection of good works with the grace of God in us. But what is there anxiously and passionately contended for, is here briefly summarised, and calmly assumed as a thing known and allowed. Even the technical phrases—the word "justification," and the declaration of the nullity of "the Law"—are no longer used.

(8) **By grace are ye saved through faith.**—Properly, *ye have been saved;* ye were saved at first, and continue in a state of salvation. In verse 5 this thought is introduced parenthetically, naturally and irresistibly suggested by the declaration of the various steps of regeneration in Christ. St. Paul now returns to it and works it out, before passing on, in verse 11, to draw out by "wherefore" the conclusion from verses 1—7. Remembering how the Epistles were written from dictation, we may be inclined to see in this passage among others, an insertion made by the Apostle, on a revision of that already written.

The two phrases—"justification by faith" and "salvation by grace"—are popularly identified, and, indeed, are substantially identical in meaning. But the latter properly lays stress on a more advanced stage of the

and that not of yourselves: *it is* the gift of God: (9) not of works, lest any man should boast. (10) For we are his workmanship, created in Christ Jesus unto good works, which God hath before ordained[1] that we should walk in them.

Chap. ii. 8—10. Received by faith, not claimed by works.

(11) Wherefore remember, that ye *being* in time past Gentiles in the flesh, who are called Uncircumcision

Chap. ii. 11—13. The Gentiles drawn near to God in Jesus Christ.

1 Or, *prepared.*

---

process of redemption in Christ. Thus, in Rom. v. 9, 10 ("having been justified," "having been reconciled," "we shall be saved"), salvation is spoken of as following on the completed act of justification (as the release of a prisoner on his pronounced pardon); and it is described, here and elsewhere, as a continuous process—a state continuing till the final judgment. Hence to lay especial stress on salvation accords better with the whole idea of this Epistle—the continuous indwelling in Christ—than to bring out, as in the Epistle to the Romans, the one complete act of justification for His sake. It is remarkable that the expression of the truth corresponds almost verbally with the words of St. Peter at the Council of Jerusalem (Acts xv. 11), "We believe that through the grace of God we shall be (properly, *we were*) saved," except that here the original shows that the salvation is looked upon as a completed act, like justification. It is also to be noted that the use of the name "Saviour," applied both to God and to Christ, belongs entirely to the later Epistles. It is used once in this Epistle (chap. v. 23) and once in the Epistle to the Philippians (chap. iii. 20), but no less than ten times in the Pastoral Epistles of St. Paul, and five times in the Second Epistle of St. Peter. The phrase in the text is, as always in this Epistle, theologically exact. Grace is the moving cause of salvation: faith only the instrument by which it is laid hold of.

And that not of yourselves: it is the gift of God.—This attribution of all to the gift of God seems to cover the whole idea—both the gift of salvation and the gift of faith to accept it. The former part is enforced by the words "not of works," the latter by the declaration, "we (and all that is in us) are His workmanship." The word here rendered "gift" is peculiar to this passage; the word employed in Rom. v. 15, 16, vi. 23, for "free gift" (*charisma*) having been appropriated (both in the singular and plural) to special "gifts" of grace.

(9) **Not of works, lest any man should boast.**—In this verse we have the echo of the past Judaising controversy; it sums up briefly the whole argument of Rom. iii. 27—iv. 25. There is a similar reminiscence, but more distinct and detached, in Phil. iii. 2—9.

(10) **We are his workmanship.**—This verse, on the contrary, is unique and remarkable, characteristic of the idea with which this Epistle starts—the election and predestination of God, making us what we are—and applying it very strikingly, not only to the first regeneration, but even to the good works which follow it. The word rendered "workmanship" is only used elsewhere in Rom. i. 20, where it is applied to the "works" of God in creation. Probably here also it does not exclude our first creation. We are His wholly and absolutely. But the next clause shows that St. Paul refers especially to the "new creation" in Christ Jesus.

Created in Christ Jesus.—This creation, when spoken of distinctively, is the "new creation" (2 Cor. v. 17; Gal. vi. 15); as, indeed, is the case below (verse 15), "to create in Himself . . . one new man." In this passage, however, St. Paul dwells, not on distinction from the old creation, but rather on analogy to it; in both we are simply God's creatures.

Unto good works.—Properly, *on the basis* (or, *condition*) *of good works* (as in Gal. v. 13; 1 Thess. iv. 17; 2 Tim. ii. 14). The good works, in themselves future, being (as the next clause shows) contemplated as already existent in God's foreknowledge, and as an inseparable characteristic of the regenerate life.

Which God hath before ordained that we should walk in them.—There is, perhaps, in all Scripture, no stronger expression of the great mystery of God's predestination; for it is here declared in reference, not only to the original call and justification and regeneration of the soul, but also to the actual good works, in which the free-will and energy of man are most plainly exercised; and in which even here we are said not to be moved, but "to walk" by our own act. In much the same sense St. Paul, in the Epistle to the Philippians (chap. iii. 12, 13), uses the well-known paradox, "Work out your own salvation . . , for it is God that worketh in you, both to will and to do of His good pleasure." Both truths—God's preordination and man's responsible freedom—are emphasised. For the reconcilement of the two we must wait till we "know even as we are known."

(2 *a.*) Verses 11—13, resuming the thread of argument from verse 7, dwell on the drawing of the Gentiles into a personal unity with God in Christ—not, however (as before), out of the deadness of sin and bondage of Satan, but rather out of the condition of alienation from God, from His covenant and His promise, in which they stood contrasted with His chosen people.

(11) **Gentiles in the flesh**—*i.e.*, not having the bodily impress of circumcision, sealing the Jewish covenant.

Who are called Uncircumcision by that which is called the Circumcision.—The use of the phrase "called"—with a touch of the contempt implied in our phrase "the so-called"—simply implies that now Circumcision and Uncircumcision were mere names, virtually "nothing." The declaration of the nullity of circumcision as a religious distinction is often repeated, yet takes various forms. Thus, in 1 Cor. vii. 19, it is contrasted with the practical reality of obedience to God's commandments; in Gal. v. 6, with the inner reality of "faith working by love"; in Gal. vi. 15, with the divine gift of the "new creation"; in Col. iii. 11, with the spiritual unity of all in Christ. (Comp. also the whole argument of Rom. ii. 25—iv. 12.)

In the flesh made by hands.—St. Paul, however, not content with this, suggests by the addition of these last words a contrast between the false or carnal, and the true or spiritual circumcision, attributing the former to the unbelieving Jews, the latter to all Christians. This contrast is expressly announced in the other Epistles of this period. In Phil. iii. 2, 3, we read, "Beware of the concision; for we are the circumcision."

by that which is called the Circumcision
in the flesh made by hands; (12) that at
that time ye were without Christ, being
aliens from the commonwealth of Israel,
and strangers from the covenants of
promise, having no hope, and without
God in the world: (13) but now in Christ
Jesus ye who sometimes were far off
are made nigh by the blood of Christ.
(14) For he is our peace, who hath made

In Col. ii. 11, still more distinctly, in significant connection with the appointed means of entrance into the Christian covenant, and significant contrast with the effete Jewish ordinance, "In whom also ye are circumcised with the circumcision not made with hands . . . in the circumcision of Christ; buried with Him in baptism, in which also ye are risen with Him." In that true circumcision lies the distinction between the Church, which is the spiritual Israel, and the heathen world without.

(12) This verse gives a dark and terrible picture of the former heathen condition of the Ephesians, intentionally contrasted in every point with the description of Christian privilege in verses 19, 20. That condition is first summed up in one expression. They were "separate from Christ." Then from this are drawn two gloomy consequences: first (1), that they had no part in God's special covenant, "alienated from the commonwealth of Israel," and so "strangers to the (often repeated) covenants of the promise" of the Messiah; next (2), that, thus left in "the world," they had "no hope" of spiritual life and immortality, and were "godless" in thought and act. For Christ is at once the end and substance of the covenant of Israel, and the Revealer of God, and therefore of spiritual life in man, to all mankind. To be without Him is to lose both covenant and light. On (1) it is to be noted that the word used is not "aliens," but "alienated," implying—what is again and again declared to us—that the covenant with Israel, as it was held in trust for the blessing of "all families of the earth," so also was simply the true birthright of humanity, from which mankind had fallen. The first "covenant" in scripture (Gen. ix. 8—17) is with the whole of the post-diluvian race, and is expressly connected with the reality of "the image of God" in man (Gen. ix. 6). The succeeding covenants (as with Abraham, Moses, and David) all contain a promise concerning the whole race of man. Hence the Gentiles (as the utterances of prophecy showed more and more clearly while the ages rolled on) were exiles from what should have been their home; and their call into the Church of Christ was a restoration of God's wandering children. In relation to (2) it is impossible not to observe, even in the highest forms of heathen philosophy, how their comparative "godlessness"—the absence of any clear notion of a real spiritual tie of nature between God and man—made their "hope" of life and immortality, though still cherished, shadowy and uncertain, always stronger in itself than in its grounds. But St. Paul's description ought to be applied strictly, not to heathen life in its nobler and purer forms, but to the heathen life of Asia Minor in his days. What that was in moral degradation and in loss of all spiritual religion, ill compensated by the inevitable proneness to various superstitions, all contemporary literature testifies. From it came, as the Romans declared, the corruption which overspread the whole empire, and which St. Paul describes so terribly in Rom. i. 18—33.

(13) This verse speaks of the restoration of the heathen as taking place, first, "in Christ Jesus"—in virtue, that is, of union with Him through all the acts of His mediation; and next, "by the blood of Christ"—that is, through that especial act of mediation, which is emphatically an atonement for sin—such sin as St. Paul had been declaring above to be the cause of spiritual deadness. They had power now "to enter into the holiest by the blood of Jesus" (Heb. x. 19).

(2 *b.*) Verses 14—18 pass on from the description of the call of the heathen to personal union with God in Christ, to dwell on the perfect unity and equality of Jew and Gentile with each other in Him, and the access of both to the Father.

(14) **He** (*Himself*) **is our peace.**—There is clearly allusion, as to the many promises in the Old Testament of the "Prince of Peace" (Isa. ix. 5, 6, *et al.*), so still more to the "Peace of Earth" of the angelic song of Bethlehem, and to the repeated declarations of our Lord, such as, "Peace I leave with you: My peace I give unto you." Here, however, only is our Lord called not the giver of peace, but the peace itself—His own nature being the actual tie of unity between God and mankind, and between man and man. Through the whole passage thus introduced there runs a double meaning, a declaration of peace in Christ between Jew and Gentile, and between both and God; though it is not always easy to tell of any particular expression, whether it belongs to this or that branch of the meaning, or to both. It is well to compare it with the obvious parallel in Col. ii. 13, 14, where (in accordance with the whole genius of that Epistle) there is found only the latter branch of the meaning, the union of all with the Head, not the unity of the various members of the Body.

Who hath made both one, and hath broken down the middle wall of partition between us.—In this verse the former subject is begun. The reunion of Jew and Gentile is described in close connection with the breaking down of "the middle wall of the partition" (or, *hedge*). The words "between us" are not in the original, and Chrysostom interprets the partition as being, not between Jew and Gentile, but between both and God. But the former idea seems at any rate to predominate in this clause. Whether "the middle wall of the hedge" refers to the wall separating the court of the Gentiles from the Temple proper (Jos. *Ant.* xv. § 5), and by an inscription denouncing death to any alien who passed it (see Lewin's *St. Paul*, vol. ii., p. 133), or to the "hedge" set about the vineyard of the Lord (Isa. v. 2; comp. Matt. xxii. 33)—to which probably the Jewish doctors alluded when they called their ceremonial and legal subtleties "the hedge" of the Law—has been disputed. It may, however, be noted that the charge of bringing Trophimus, an Ephesian, beyond that Temple wall had been the cause of St. Paul's apprehension at Jerusalem (Acts xxi. 29), and nearly of his death. Hence the Asiatic churches might well be familar with its existence. It is also notable that this Temple-partition suits perfectly the double sense of this passage: for, while it was primarily a separation between Jew and Gentile, it was also the first of many partitions—of which the "veil

both one, and hath broken down the middle wall of partition *between us;* (15) having abolished in his flesh the enmity, *even* the law of commandments *contained* in ordinances; for to make in himself of twain one new man, *so* making peace; (16) and that he might reconcile both unto God in one body by the cross, having slain the enmity

Chap. ii. 14—18. Made one with Israel in reconciliation to God.

---

of the Temple" was the last—cutting all men off from the immediate presence of God. At our Lord's death the last of these partitions was rent in twain; how much more may that death be described as breaking down the first!

(15) The connection in the original is doubtful. The words the "enmity in His flesh" may be in apposition to the "wall of partition" in the previous verse; or, as in our version, to "the law of commandments." The general sense, however, is but little affected in either case.

Having abolished in his flesh the enmity, even the law of commandments contained in ordinances.—In this difficult passage it will be well first to examine the particular expressions. (1) The word rendered "to abolish" is the word often used by St. Paul for "to supersede by something better than itself"—translated "to make void," in Rom. iii. 31; to "bring to nought," in 1 Cor. i. 28, and (in the passive) "to fail," "to vanish away," "to be done away," in 1 Cor. xiii. 8, 9, 10. Now, of the relation of Christ to the Law, St. Paul says, in Rom. iii. 31, "Do we make void the Law? God forbid! Yea, we establish the Law." The Law, therefore, is abolished as a law "in ordinances"—that is, "in the letter"—and is established in the spirit. (2) "The law of commandments in ordinances." The word here rendered "ordinance" (*dogma*) properly means "a decree." It is used only in this sense in the New Testament (see Luke ii. 1; Acts xvi. 4; xvii. 7; Heb. xi. 23); and it signifies expressly a law imposed and accepted, not for its intrinsic righteousness, but on authority; or, as Butler expresses it (*Anal.*, Part ii., chap. 1), not a "moral," but "a positive law." In Col. ii. 14 (the parallel passage) the word is connected with a "handwriting" that is a legal "bond"; and the Colossians are reproved for subjecting themselves to "ordinances, which are but a shadow of things to come"; while "the body," the true substance, "is Christ." (See verses 16, 17, 20, 21.) (3) Hence the whole expression describes explicitly what St. Paul always implies in his proper and distinctive use of the word "law." It signifies the will of God, as expressed in formal commandments, and enforced by penalties on disobedience. The general idea, therefore, of the passage is simply that which is so often brought out in the earlier Epistles (see Rom. iii. 21—31; vii. 1—4; viii. 1—4; Gal. ii. 15—21, *et al.*), but which (as the Colossian Epistle more plainly shows) now needed to be enforced under a somewhat different form—viz., that Christ, "the end of the law," has superseded it by the free covenant of the Spirit; and that He has done this for us "in His flesh," especially by His death and resurrection. (4) But in what sense is this Law called "the enmity," which (see verse 16) was "slain" on the Cross? Probably in the double sense, which runs through the passage: first, as "an enmity," a cause of separation and hostility, between the Gentiles and those Jews whom they called "the enemies of the human race"; next, as "an enmity" a cause of alienation and condemnation, between man and God—"the commandment which was ordained to life, being found to be unto death" through the rebellion and sin of man. The former sense seems to be the leading sense here, where the idea is of "making both one"; the latter in the next verse, which speaks of "reconciling both to God," all the partitions are broken down, that all alike may have "access to the Father." Comp. Col. i. 21, "You, who were enemies in your mind, He hath reconciled;" and Heb. x. 19, "Having confidence to enter into the holy place by the blood of Jesus, by a new and living way, which He hath consecrated to us, *through the veil, that is to say His flesh.*"

For to make in himself of twain one new man, so making peace.—In this clause and the following verse the two senses, hitherto united, are now distinguished from each other. Here we have the former sense simply. In the new man "there is neither Jew nor Gentile," but "Christ is all and in all" (Col. iii. 12). This phrase, "the new man" (on which see chap. iv. 24, Col. iii. 10), is peculiar to these Epistles; corresponding, however, to the "new creature" of 2 Cor. v. 17, Gal. vi. 15; and the "newness of life" and "spirit" of Rom. vi. 4, vii. 6. Christ Himself is the "second man, the Lord from Heaven" (1 Cor. xv. 47). "As we have borne the image of the first man, of the earth, earthy," and so "in Adam die," we now "bear the image of the heavenly," and not only "shall be made alive," but already "have our life hid with Christ in God" (Col. iii. 3). He is at once "the seed of the woman" and the "seed of Abraham"; in Him, therefore, Jew and Gentile meet in a common humanity. Just in proportion to spirituality or newness of life is the sense of unity, which makes all brethren. Hence the new creation "makes peace"—here probably peace between Jew and Gentile, rather than peace with God, which belongs to the next verse.

(16) **And that he might reconcile both unto God in one body.**—In this verse the latter subject opens—the reconciliation of all to God. On the reconciliation of man to God, see the great passage 2 Cor. v. 18—21. But it should be noted that in the original the word used here and in Col. i. 20, 21 (and nowhere else) is a compound signifying not simply to "conciliate," but properly to "reconcile,"—that is to reunite those who were originally united, but afterwards separated by the sin of man. This brings out the profound idea, which so especially characterises these Epistles, of a primeval unity of all created being in Christ, marred and broken by sin, and restored by His manifestation in human flesh. Note that the passage in the Colossians (on which see Notes) has a far wider scope than this passage—"having made peace through the blood of His cross, by Him to reconcile all things to Himself; by Him (I say), whether they be things on earth or things in heaven." On the other hand, this passage characteristically still lays stress on the idea "in one body"—that is, as throughout, His mystical body, the Church—although probably the phrase is suggested here by the thought of the natural body of the Lord offered on the cross, which is clearly referred to in Col. i. 21. There is a similar connection of thought in 1 Cor. x. 16, 17. "The bread which we break, is it not the communion of the body of Christ? For we are all one bread, and one body."

thereby:[1] (17) and came and preached
peace to you which were afar off, and
to them that were nigh. (18) For through
him we both have access by one Spirit
unto the Father. (19) Now therefore ye
are no more strangers and
foreigners, but fellow-
citizens with the saints,
and of the household of
God; (20) and are built

1 Or, *in himself.*

Chap. ii. 19—22. Built into the temple of God—Christ being the corner-stone.

By the cross, having slain the enmity thereby.—In this verse (in accordance with the context) "the enmity," which by His death He "slew," is the barrier between God and man, created by sin, but brought out by the Law, as hard and rigid law, "in ordinances" of which St. Paul does not hesitate to say that "sin took occasion by it," and "by it slew" man (Rom. vii. 11). This is illustrated by the cognate, though different, metaphor of Col. ii. 14, where it is said of Christ that He "blotted out the handwriting of ordinances which was against us, which was contrary unto us, and took it out of the way, *nailing it to His cross.*" Compare also, in Gal. ii. 19, 20, the connection of spiritual "death to the Law" with our partaking of our Lord's crucifixion: "I, through the Law, am dead to the Law, that I might live unto God. *I am crucified with Christ,* nevertheless I live . . . . by the faith of the Son of God, who loved me and *gave Himself for me.*" By His death Christ has both redeemed us from sin, and also "redeemed (properly, *bought*) us from the curse of the Law" (Gal. iii. 13).

(17) **And came and preached peace.**—The word "came" certainly carries back our thoughts to our Lord's own preaching, when, after the Resurrection, He came "and stood in the midst of them, and said, Peace be unto you" (Luke xxiv. 36; John xx. 19, 21). But we note that at that very time He repeated the salutation "Peace be unto you," with the expressive addition, "As my Father hath sent Me, even so send I you," and with the charge, "Receive ye the Holy Ghost," for the future mission "to remit or retain sins." In the same connection we have in John xiv. 25—28, the promise of the Comforter, and the words "Peace I leave with you; My peace I give unto you. . . . I go away and come again to you." Hence we cannot limit His "coming" to the appearance after the Resurrection. At all times through the witness of the Holy Spirit, whether with or without the preaching of His servants (John xv. 27), He "stands at the door and knocks" (Rev. iii. 20) with the message of peace. For since the "peacemakers" are "called the children of God," He, the Son of God, must be emphatically the Peacemaker.

To you which were afar off, and to them that were nigh.—As the enmity was the enmity with God, so the peace is peace with God; but still the Apostle, having the idea of reunion between Jew and Gentile present to his mind, cannot refrain from bringing out clearly the call of both to one peace, and therefore to unity with one another. The passage is a quotation from Isa. lvii. 19.

(18) **For through him we both have access by one Spirit unto the Father.**—In this verse the two meaings again unite. In the original the order is emphatic: "Through Him we have the access, both of us in one Spirit, to the Father." The greater idea of access to God is still prominent; but the lesser idea of union with each other in that access is still traceable as an undertone. "Access" is properly "the introduction" (used also in chap. iii. 12; Rom. v. 2), a technical word of presentation to a royal presence. So says Chrysostom, "We came not of ourselves, but He brought us in." The corresponding verb is found in 1 Pet. iii. 18, "Christ also suffered for sins—the just for the unjust—that He might *bring us to God.*" It will be noted that we have here one of the implicit declarations of the doctrine of the Holy Trinity, so frequent in this Epistle. The unity of the whole Church, as united "to the Father," "through the Son," and "in the Spirit," is here summed up in one sentence, but with as much perfection and clearness as even when it is unfolded in the great passage below (chap. iv. 4—6). The ultimate source of all doctrine on the subject is necessarily in the words of the Lord Himself. (See John xiv.—xvii., especially xiv. 6, 16—18, 23—25; xv. 26; xvi. 13—15; xvii. 20, 21.) For these are the "heavenly things"; and "no man hath ascended into heaven but He that came down from heaven, even the Son of Man who is in heaven" (John iii. 12, 13).

(2 *c.*) Verses 19—22 sum up the two-fold idea of this chapter—union of the Gentiles, with God and with God's chosen people—in the metaphor of the One Temple, of which Jesus Christ is the chief cornerstone, and which, both collectively and in the individuality of each part, grows into a habitation of God.

(19) **Strangers and foreigners.**—Here the word rendered "stranger" means properly *an alien,* or foreigner; while the word translated "foreignors" signifies the resident aliens of an ancient city, who were but *half-aliens,* having free intercourse with the citizens, although no rights of citizenship. The latter word is used literally in Acts vii. 6, 29 (there rendered "sojourner"), and often in the LXX. version; perhaps metaphorically in 1 Pet. ii. 11. Such a sojourner, though in some sense less an absolute alien than the mere "stranger," was one on whom by daily contrast the sense of being an alien, excluded from power and privilege, was more forcibly impressed.

Fellowcitizens with the saints, and of the household of God.—In sense this double expression preserves the double idea running through the whole chapter. The phrase "fellowcitizens of the saints" is applied to the Gentiles, as now united with the Israel of God in one "commonwealth." (See above, verse 12.) "Members of the household of God" refers rather to the union with God, restored by the blood of Jesus Christ. (See verse 13.) As to the metaphor, the word "stranger"—that is, *alien*—seems to be opposed to "fellowcitizen"; the word "foreigner"—that is, *half-alien*—to members of the household: for the resident aliens stood opposed to the "houses," the families or clans, of the citizens—the unit in ancient law being always the family, and not the individual. The Gentiles were now brought into a "household," and that household the household of God Himself.

(20—22) In these verses there is a sudden change from a political to a physical metaphor, possibly suggested by the word "household." The metaphor itself, of the Church as "a building of God"—frequently used in the New Testament—reaches its full perfection in this passage. (1) It starts, of course, upon the foundation of the apostles and prophets, Jesus Christ himself being the chief corner *stone;* (21) in whom all the building fitly framed to-

from the words of our Lord (Matt. xvi. 18), "On this rock I will build my Church;" but in the use of it sometimes the prominent idea is of the growth by addition of individual stones, sometimes of the complex unity of the building as a whole. (2) The former idea naturally occurs first, connecting itself, indeed, with the still more personal application of the metaphor to the "edification" of the individual to be a temple of God (found, for example, in 1 Thess. v. 11; 1 Cor. viii. 1; x. 23; xiv. 4; 2 Cor. v. 1; x. 8). Thus in 1 Cor. iii. 9, from "ye are God's building," St. Paul passes at once to the building of individual character on the one foundation; in 1 Cor. xiv. 4, 5, 12, 26, the edification of the Church has reference to the effect of prophecy on individual souls; in 1 Pet. ii. 5, the emphasis is still on the building up of "living stones" upon "a living stone." (Comp. Acts xx. 32.) (3) In this Epistle the other idea—the idea of unity—is always prominent, though not exclusive of the other (as here and in chap. iv. 12—16). But that this conception of unity is less absolute than that conveyed by the metaphor of the body will be seen by noting that it differs from it in three respects; first, that it carries with it the notion of a more distinct individuality in each stone; next, that it conveys (as in the "graffing in" of Rom. xi. 17) the idea of continual growth by accretion of individual souls drawn to Christ; lastly, that it depicts the Church as having more completely a distinct, though not a separate, existence from Him who dwells in it. (On this last point compare the metaphor of the spouse of Christ in chap. v. 25—33.) Hence it is naturally worked out with greater completeness in an Epistle which has so especially for its object the evolution of the doctrine of "the one Holy Catholic Church."

(20) **Built upon the foundation of the apostles and prophets.**—In spite of much ancient and valuable authority, it seems impossible to take "the prophets" of this verse to be the prophets of the Old Testament. The order of the two words and the comparison of chaps. iii. 5 and iv. 11, appear to be decisive—to say nothing of the emphasis on the present, in contrast with the past, which runs through the whole chapter. But it is more difficult to determine in what sense "the foundation of the apostles and prophets" is used. Of the three possible senses, that (1) which makes it equivalent to "the foundation on which apostles and prophets are built," viz., Jesus Christ Himself, may be dismissed as taking away any special force from the passage, and as unsuitable to the next clause. The second (2), "the foundation laid by apostles and prophets—still, of course, Jesus Christ Himself—is rather forced, and equally fails to accord with the next clause, in which our Lord is not the foundation, but the corner-stone. The most natural interpretation (3), followed by most ancient authorities, which makes the apostles and prophets to be themselves "the foundation," has been put aside by modern commentators in the true feeling that ultimately there is but "one foundation" (1 Cor. iii. 11), and in a consequent reluctance to apply that name to any but Him. But it is clear that in this passage St. Paul deliberately varies the metaphor in relation to our Lord, making Him not the foundation, or both foundation and corner-stone, but simply the corner-stone, "binding together," according to Chrysostom's instructive remark, "both the walls and the foundations." Hence the word "foundation" seems to be applied, in a true, although secondary sense, to the apostles and prophets; just as in the celebrated passage (Matt. xvi. 18) our Lord must be held at any rate to connect St. Peter with the foundation on which the Church is built; and as in Rev. xxi. 14, "the foundations" bear "the names of the twelve apostles of the Lamb." It is true that in this last passage we have the plural instead of the singular, and that the passage itself, is not, as this is, a dogmatic passage. But these considerations are insufficient to destroy the analogy. The genius therefore of this passage itself, supported by the other cognate passages, leads us to what may be granted to be an unexpected but a perfectly intelligible expression. The apostles and prophets are the foundation; yet, of course, only as setting forth in word and grace Him, who is the corner-stone.

Jesus Christ himself being the chief corner stone.—The metaphor is drawn, of course, from Ps. cxviii. 22 (applied by our Lord to Himself in Matt. xxi. 42; Mark xii. 10; Luke xx. 17; and by St. Peter to Him in Acts iv. 11), or from Isa. xxviii. 16 (quoted with the other passage in 1 Pet. ii. 6, 7); in which last it may be noted that both the metaphors are united, and "the tried corner-stone" is also "the sure foundation." In itself it does not convey so obvious an idea of uniqueness and importance as that suggested by the "key-stone" of an arch, or the "apex-stone" of a pyramid; but it appears to mean a massive corner-stone, in which the two lines of the wall at their foundation met, by which they were bonded together, and on the perfect squareness of which the true direction of the whole walls depended, since the slightest imperfection in the corner-stone would be indefinitely multiplied along the course of the walls. The doctrine which, if taken alone, it would convey, is simply the acceptance of our Lord's perfect teaching and life, as the one determining influence both of the teaching and institutions, which are the basis of the Church, and of the superstructure in the actual life of the members of the Church itself. By such acceptance both assume symmetry and "stand four-square to all the winds that blow." (See Rev. xxi. 16.) That this is not the whole truth seems to be implied by the variation from the metaphor in the next verse.

(21) **In whom all the building fitly framed together groweth unto an holy temple in the Lord.**—There is some difficulty about the rendering "all the building." Generally the best MSS. omit the article in the original. But the sense seems to demand the rendering of the text, unless, indeed, we adopt the only other possible rendering, "in whom every act of building"—that is, every addition to the building—"is bonded to the rest, and grows," &c. The clause agrees substantially, and almost verbally with chap. iv. 16—"From whom the whole body, fitly joined (*framed*) together and compacted . . . maketh increase of the body unto the edifying (*building up*) of itself." In this latter passage the leading idea is of the close union of the body to the head, to which, indeed, the metaphor more properly applies than to the relation of the building to the corner-stone. For we note that St. Paul, apparently finding this relation too slight to express the full truth of the unity of the Church with Christ, first speaks of the whole building as compacted together *in* the corner-stone, and growing—

gether groweth unto an holy temple in the Lord: (22) in whom ye also are builded together for an habitation of God through the Spirit.

A.D. 64.

CHAPTER III.—(1) For this cause I Paul, the prisoner of Jesus Christ for you Gentiles, (2) if ye have heard of the dispensation of the grace of God which is given me to you-ward:

Chap. iii. 1—4. The especial commission to St. Paul of the mystery of the call of the Gentiles.

that is, being gradually built up—in that closely compacted union; and next, calls the temple so built up a "temple holy in the Lord" (*i.e.*, the Lord Jesus Christ), deriving, therefore, all its sacredness as a temple from a pervading unity with Him. The cornerstone is only a part, though a dominant part, of the building. Christ not only "keeps all together, whether you speak of roof, or wall, or any other part whatsoever" (Chrys.), but by contact with Himself makes the building to be a temple.

(22) **In whom ye also are builded together for an habitation of God through the Spirit.**—This verse seems primarily intended simply to emphasise the truth already enunciated (in verse 20), that the Ephesians themselves are now being made part of the Church of Christ, "being built up together in Christ." But it may also illustrate to us the character of the unity of the Church, as, primarily, a direct individual unity with Christ—each stone being itself a complete and living stone—and, secondarily and indirectly, an unity with others and with the whole. The Ephesians are said to be, not a part of the habitation of God, but themselves built into Christ for an habitation of God—"Christ dwelling in their hearts by faith," and they "therefore being filled with all the fulness of God" (chap. iii. 17—19). The addition of this clause, therefore, links the teaching of this Epistle with the earlier and more individual forms of teaching, noted on verse 20.

This verse contains, again, the declaration (as in verse 18) of the union of Christians with each Person of THE HOLY TRINITY. The soul made one with THE SON becomes a temple for the indwelling of THE FATHER in the gift of THE HOLY SPIRIT. (See John xiv. 23.)

III.

[3. **Prayer for the Further Knowledge of this Mystery** (chap. iii. 1—21).

(1) PREFATORY DECLARATION of the newness of the revelation of this mystery of the calling of the Gentiles, and of the special commission of it to St. Paul, to be manifested before men and angels, both by word and by suffering (verses 1—13).

(2) PRAYER for their full understanding of this mystery (although passing knowledge) by the indwelling of Christ, wrought in them by the gift of the Spirit, and accepted in faith and love (verses 14—19).

(3) DOXOLOGY TO THE FATHER through Christ Jesus for ever and ever (verses 20, 21).]

The chapter is in form a parenthesis of fervent prayer and thanksgiving between the doctrinal teaching of chap. ii. and the resumption and summing up of that teaching in chap. iv. 1—13. At the same time it involves much profound implicit teaching in itself.

(1) Verses 1—13 contain two subjects closely blended together. The first (carrying on what is implied in the contrast drawn out in chap. ii.) is the absolute newness of this dispensation to the Gentiles—a mystery hidden from the beginning in God, but now at last revealed. The second, an emphatic claim for St. Paul himself, "less than the least" although he is, of a special apostleship to the Gentiles, proclaiming this mystery by word and deed.

(1) **For this cause . . .**—After much discussion of the construction of this verse, there seems little doubt that the nominative, "I, Paul," must be carried on beyond the digression upon the mystery of the gospel, and his part in ministering it, which follows. The only question which can well be raised is whether the resumption takes place at verse 13, "I desire that ye faint not;" or at verse 14, "I bow my knees;" and this seems decided for the latter alternative, both by the emphatic repetition of "for this cause," and by the far greater weight and finality of the latter sentence.

The prisoner of Jesus Christ.—The phrase (repeated in chap. iv. 1; Philem. verse 9; 2 Tim. i. 8) is dwelt upon with an emphasis, explained by St. Paul's conviction that "his bonds" tended to "the furtherance of the gospel"—not merely by exciting a sympathy which might open the heart to his words, but even more (see Phil. i. 13, 14) by showing the victorious power of God's word and grace—which "is not bound"—to triumph over captivity and the danger of death. The expression itself is notable. When St. Paul calls himself the "prisoner of Jesus Christ," he represents our Lord's own will, as ordaining his captivity for His own transcendent purposes of good, making him an "ambassador in chains" (chap. vi. 20), and these "the bonds of the gospel." (See Philem. verse 13; and Acts xxviii. 20, "For the hope of Israel I am bound in this chain.") Hence in this passage St. Paul seems to speak of his captivity as a special proof of the reality of his mission, and a new step in its progress; and appeals to it accordingly, just as in the final salutation of the Colossian Epistle, "Remember my bonds." The whole idea is a striking instance of the spiritual alchemy of faith, turning all things to good—not unlike the magnificent passage (in 2 Cor. xi. 23—30) of his "glorying in his infirmities."

For you Gentiles.—This was literally true of the origin of his captivity, proceeding as it did from the jealousy of the Jews, excited by the free admission of the Gentiles to the Church; but the reference is not to be limited to this. St. Paul regards the captivity as only one incident in a mission sending him entirely to the Gentiles (Acts xxi. 21; Rom. xi. 13; Gal. ii. 9). From these words the digression of verses 2—13 starts, bringing out the reality and greatness of that mission.

(2) **If ye have heard.**—The original word rendered "if" (the same used below, chap. iv. 21, and in 2 Cor. v. 3; Gal. iii. 4; Col. i. 23) conveys, in such collocation as this, a supposition which is only a supposition in form—a half-ironical reference to a thing not doubtful. The sense is "if (that is)," or "if, as I suppose," "ye heard the dispensation," &c. The passage bears on the question whether the Epistle was an encyclical letter, or one addressed to the Ephesian Church. The argument which has been drawn from it in the former direction is not so strong as appears in the

(3) how that by revelation he made known
unto me the mystery; (as I wrote afore[1]
in few words, (4) whereby, when ye read,
ye may understand my knowledge in the
Chap. iii. 5—12. The mystery long hidden, now revealed to men and angels. mystery of Christ) (5) which
in other ages was not
made known unto the sons
of men, as it is now
revealed unto his holy apostles and
prophets by the Spirit; (6) that the
Gentiles should be fellowheirs, and of the
same body, and partakers of his promise
in Christ by the gospel: (7) whereof I
was made a minister, according to the
gift of the grace of God given unto me
by the effectual working of his power.

1 Or, *a little before.*

English; for the original implies no doubt that the readers of the Epistle had heard, and the hearing might have been not about St. Paul, but from St. Paul himself. Still, there is a vague generality about the expression, which suits well an address to the Asiatic churches generally, but could hardly have been used to a church so well known and beloved as Ephesus, where "the signs of an Apostle" had been wrought abundantly.

The dispensation of the grace of God which is given me to you-ward.—The descriptive clause, "which is given me to you-ward," is seen in the original to belong to the word "grace," not (as our version might suggest) to "dispensation." The grace of God is spoken of as given to St. Paul, not so much for his own sake, as for ministration to them of the dispensation described in the next verse. We find there that the revelation of salvation to the Gentiles was the "dispensation," that is (much as in chap. i. 10), the peculiar office in the ministration of the grace of God to the world, assigned to St. Paul by His wisdom. (Comp. 1 Cor. i. 17—24, "God sent me not to baptize, but to preach the gospel . . . We preach Christ crucified . . . unto them that are called, both Jews and Greeks, Christ the power of God and the wisdom of God.")

(3) **How that by revelation he made known unto me the mystery.**—The words "by revelation" are doubly emphatic. By revelation, not by the wisdom of man (as in 1 Cor. ii. 7—16): for "God hath revealed them to us by His Spirit." By direct revelation to St. Paul himself, as in Gal. i. 12, "not of man or by man, but by revelation of Jesus Christ," and in Rom. xvi. 25, "according to my gospel, and the preaching of Jesus Christ, according to the revelation of the mystery." (See also 2 Cor. xii. 17.) This revelation we may refer especially to the time when, after his conversion, he was "in a trance while praying in the Temple," and "saw Christ Himself," saying unto him, "Depart, for I will send thee far hence unto the Gentiles" (Acts xxii. 17—21).

As I wrote afore in few words.—The reference is to the brief notice in chap. i. 10—14, and to the further explanation in chap. ii. 11—22. Hence, in English, the idea would be more clearly expressed by "I have written above." St. Paul refers them back to these passages as embodying his "understanding," or conception, of the mystery thus revealed especially to him. The reference is one of those parenthetical remarks, which, to those remembering how St. Paul's Epistles were dictated, almost irresistibly suggest insertion on the reading over of the Epistle.

(5) **Which in other ages** (rather, *to other generations*) **was not made known unto the sons of men.**—For the general sense comp. Col. i. 27. The phrase "the sons of men" (except that it is once used in Mark iii. 28) is peculiar to the Old Testament, where it is of frequent use in the poetical books, and it is notable that in Ezekiel it is the name by which the prophet himself is constantly addressed. Hence, although it is probably wrong to restrict to the children of Israel, or to the prophets, words which by their very nature apply to all mankind, yet the phrase seems to be used with a suggestion of the contrast between the old dispensation and the new. (Comp. our Lord's words in Matt. xi. 11, "Among them that are born of women there hath not risen a greater than John the Baptist: notwithstanding he that is least in the kingdom of heaven is greater than he.")

As it is now revealed unto his holy apostles and prophets by the Spirit.—The application of the epithet "holy" to the Apostles has been thought strange as coming from one of their number; and it is worth notice that this exceptional application is certainly more appropriate to the comparatively impersonal style of an encyclical epistle. But the epithet (applied to the Old Testament prophets in Luke i. 70; Acts iii. 21; 2 Pet. iii. 2), like the frequent use of it as the substantive "saints," in application to all Christians, refers not to personal character, but to official call and privilege. In this passage it is clear that it is used thus, in emphatic contrast with "the sons of men" above, and in connection with the following words, "in the Spirit." The contrast here briefly conveyed is the same which is drawn out in 1 Cor. ii. between the "wisdom of men," and the "wisdom of God," sanctifying, and so enlightening, the Christian soul.

(6) **That the Gentiles should be fellowheirs.**—More exactly, *are fellow-heirs*, admitted already fully in God's councils, as partially in actual fact to the kingdom of God.

And of the same body, and [*fellow-*] partakers of his promise.—These three words (of which the last two are peculiar to this Epistle) evidently describe progressive steps in the work of salvation. First comes the acceptance by God to a share in the inheritance, as "heirs of God, and joint-heirs with Christ" (Rom. viii. 17); next, incorporation into the mystical body of Christ; lastly, the actual enjoyment of a share in the promise—that is, all the spiritual blessings of the covenant, called "promises" because, though real in themselves, they are only an earnest of the hereafter. At every point stress is laid on their fellowship with Israel in all these gifts. The shoots of the wild olive (Rom. xi. 17) are first chosen out, then "graffed in," and lastly "partake with the natural branches of the root and fatness of the olive tree."

In Christ by the gospel.—These words should be joined with all the three preceding. Of all the privileges of the new life, the being "in Christ" is the substance, the reception of the gospel in faith the instrument.

(7) **According to the gift of the grace of God given unto me by the effectual working of his power.**—The words "given by" should be rendered *given according to.* The working of God's power is described, not as the means, but as the measure of the gift of His grace. In fact, what is a "gift" in its source, is "effectual working" in its

(8) Unto me, who am less than the least of all saints, is this grace given, that I should preach among the Gentiles the unsearchable riches of Christ; (9) and to make all *men* see what *is* the fellowship of the mystery, which from the beginning of the world hath been hid in God, who created all things by Jesus Christ: (10) to the intent that now unto the principalities and powers in heavenly

actual nature. On the phrase "effectual working of power"—a divine force in the soul, not latent but energetic—see chap. i. 19. In the whole of this passage, however, the chief emphasis is laid, not on the spiritual power, but on the freedom of God's gift to the Apostle of this high privilege of preaching the mystery of the gospel.

(8) **Less than the least of all saints.**—Compare with this expression of deep humility the well-known passages 1 Cor. xv. 9, 10; 2 Cor. xi. 30; xii. 9—11; 1 Tim. i. 12—16. It may be noted that in each case his deep sense of unworthiness is brought out by the thought of God's especial grace and favour to him. Thus in 1 Cor. xv. 9, 10, the feeling that he is "the least of the Apostles, not meet to be called an Apostle," rises out of the contemplation of the special manifestation of the risen Lord to him as "one born out of due time;" in 2 Cor. xi. 30, xii. 9—11, "boasting" has been forced upon him, and so, having been compelled to dwell on the special work done by him, and the special revelations vouchsafed to him, he immediately adds, "though I am nothing;" in 1 Tim. i. 12—16, as also here, it is the greatness of his message of universal salvation which reminds him that he was "a persecutor and injurious," "the chief of sinners," and "less than the least of all saints." Elation in the sense of privilege—"the glorying in that which we have received," so emphatically rebuked in 1 Cor. iv. 7—is the temptation of the first superficial enthusiasm; deep sense of weakness and unworthiness, the result of second and deeper thought, contrasting the heavenly treasure with the earthen vessels which contain it (2 Cor. iv. 7). Possibly there is a "third thought," deeper still, belonging to the times of highest spiritual aspiration, which loses all idea of self, even of weakness and unworthiness, in the thought of "the strength made perfect in weakness," and the consciousness (as in Phil. iv. 12, 13) that "we can do all things through Christ that strengtheneth us." See this last brought out in peculiar fulness and freedom in 2 Cor. v. 13—vi. 10; a passage almost unique in its disclosure of spiritual experience.

The unsearchable riches of Christ.—The word "unsearchable" properly carries with it the metaphor (latent in our word "investigate") of tracking the footsteps, but not tracking them completely to their source or issue—thus gaining an evidence of a living power, but "not knowing whence it cometh or whither it goeth." In this proper sense it is used in Rom. xi. 33, "How unsearchable are His judgments, and His ways past finding out!" (as also in Job v. 9; ix. 10). Here it is used in a slightly different sense—applied to that "wealth" or fulness of Christ on which this Epistle lays such especial stress, as a wealth of truth which we can see in part but cannot wholly measure, and a wealth of grace which we can enjoy but cannot exhaust.

(9) **To make all men see.**—St. Paul speaks here first of manifestation to all men. The phrase used in the original is at once stronger and weaker than our version of it. It is stronger, for the word is, properly, *to enlighten* or illuminate—the same word used above (chap. i. 18), "the eyes of your heart being enlightened." Strictly, Christ alone is the Light of the world, "which enlightens every man" (John i. 4, 5, 9; viii. 2); but, as reflecting Him, He declared His servants to be the "light of the world." Yet it is weaker, for while we can enlighten, it is our daily sorrow that we cannot "make men see." Even He wept over Jerusalem because His light was, by wilful blindness, "hidden from their eyes" (Luke xix. 41). To "open the eyes, and turn men from darkness to light," although (as in Acts xxvi. 18) attributed in general terms to the servants of God, because naturally following on their ministry, is properly the work of the Holy Spirit, even in relation to the words of our Lord Himself (John xiv. 26).

The fellowship of the mystery.—Both MS. authority and internal evidence point here to "the *dispensation* of the mystery" as the true reading. Probably here the reference is not to the commission of the mystery to the Apostle (as in verse 2), but (as in chap. i. 10) to the law or order which God Himself has ordained for the manifestation of the truth, both to men and angels.

Who created all things by Jesus Christ.—The words "by Jesus Christ" should be omitted, probably having crept in from a gloss, and not belonging to the original. The description of God as "He who created all things," material and spiritual, is here emphatic—designed to call attention to the dispensation of the gospel as existing in the primeval purpose of the Divine Mind (comp. chap. i. 4; 1 Cor. i. 7), hidden from the beginning of the world (properly, *from the ages*) till the time of its revelation was come. The New Testament constantly dwells on this view of the Mediation of Christ, as belonging in some form to the relation of humanity to God in itself, and not merely to that relation as affected by the Fall; but nowhere with greater emphasis than in the profound and universal teaching of these Epistles.

(10) In this verse St. Paul passes on to consider the manifestation of God in Christ as brought home not only to the race of man but to the angels—"the principalities and powers in the heavenly places"—who are described (1 Pet. i. 12) as "desiring to look into" the consummation of the gospel mystery. In the same sense the Apostles, in their ministration of the gospel, are said to be a spectacle to angels and to men (1 Cor. iv. 9); and in a magnificent passage in the Epistle to the Hebrews (Heb. xii. 22), Christians are encouraged in their warfare by knowing it to go on before "the city of the living God" and "an innumerable company of angels." The angels are, therefore, represented to us as not only ministering in the Church of Christ, but learning from its existence and fortunes to know more and more of the wisdom of God. Hence we gain a glimpse of a more than world-wide purpose in the supreme manifestation of God's mercy in Christ, fulfilled towards higher orders of God's rational creatures, aiding even them in progress towards the knowledge of God in Jesus Christ, which is life eternal. (There is a notable passage on a kindred idea in Butler's *Analogy*, Part i., c. iii. § 5.) This world, itself a speck in the universe, may be—perhaps as a scene of exceptional rebellion

places might be known by the church the manifold wisdom of God, (11) according to the eternal purpose which he purposed in Christ Jesus our Lord: (12) in whom we have boldness and access with confidence by the faith of him.

(13) Wherefore I desire that ye faint not at my tribulations for you, which is your glory. (14) For this cause I bow my knees unto the Father of our Lord Jesus Christ, (15) of whom

Chap. iii. 13—19. Prayer for their full comprehension of it in Christ.

---

against God, certainly as a scene of God's infinite goodness—a lesson to other spheres of being, far beyond our conception. Possibly this view of angels as our fellow-learners in the school of Christ may have been specially dwelt upon in view of the worship of angels of which we read in Col. ii. 18; but it accords well with the wide sweep of thought characteristic of this Epistle, literally "gathering up all things in Christ."

The manifold wisdom.—The word "manifold" (properly, *many-coloured*, or *wrought in many details*) is used here (and nowhere else) for the wisdom of God, as "fulfilling itself in many ways" (the "sundry times and divers manners" of Heb. i. 1). It is manifested, therefore, in the infinite variety both of the teaching and the life of the Church—manifold, yet one, as embodying but one life, the life of Jesus Christ.

(11) **The eternal purpose.**—Properly, *the purpose of the ages;* but the sense clearly is, of the purpose of God (see chap. i. 11), conceived before the ages of His dispensation, and fulfilled through them. Hence the rendering of our version is substantially correct.

Which he purposed.—It should be, *which He wrought*, or *made*, for the word is quite distinct from the substantive "purpose," and is in itself ambiguous, capable of meaning either *ordained* or *worked out*. Either sense will suit the passage; but the latter perhaps better, since the idea is throughout of the completion and manifestation of the mystery of God's purpose in the Lord Jesus Christ.

(12) This verse returns to the idea of chap. ii. 18, as though St. Paul, after the wide sweep of thought far beyond the earth in verses 10, 11, desired, as usual, to bring his readers back to the practical and personal aspects of their Christianity.

In whom we have (*our*) **boldness and** (*our*) **access with confidence.**—"Boldness" is, properly, *boldness of speech* (as in chap. vi. 19), though used in a derivative sense for confidence and frankness generally. Probably here it is suggested in its original sense by the reference in the preceding verse to the charge of proclaiming the mystery of God, and accordingly means that boldness of thought and utterance before men and angels which Christians, in virtue of that charge, ought to assume. The "access (see chap. ii. 18) in confidence" is, on the other hand, that confidence before God, as presented to Him in the Lord Jesus Christ, which belongs to Christians as no longer servants but sons. (On this confidence see 2 Cor. iii. 4—6.) Both these gifts depend on "faith in Him:" in the one case, faith in His teaching and grace; in the other, faith in His atonement and His gift of the new life.

(13) **Wherefore I desire . . .**—The verse is parenthetical—a reflection suggested by the greatness of the trust and the littleness of the minister dwelt upon in verses 8—12, and inserted as a warning to the Ephesians not to be disheartened at the present "tribulation" of his imprisonment, as if it were a failure of his mission. (See this idea more fully worked out in Phil. i. 12—29.) "To faint" (as in 2 Cor. iv. 1, 16; Gal. vi. 9; 2 Thess. iii. 13) is "to play the coward," as "thinking it (see 1 Pet. iv. 12, 13) a strange thing" that trouble should fall on him or them. It might well seem strange, when for four years at least, at Cæsarea and Rome, the marvellous activity of St. Paul's Apostolic career was apparently cut short.

At my tribulations for you, which is your glory.—There is a peculiar beauty in the thought suggested by the words "which is your glory." The suffering, triumphantly borne and actually turned to the furtherance of the gospel, is certainly a "glory," in the proof which it gives of the power of the truth and the grace of Christ. But the more obvious idea would have been to comfort the Ephesians by the declaration that St. Paul's tribulations were to himself a cause, not of pain, but of joy and glory—as is, in fact, done in Col. i. 24, and in the celebrated passage, 2 Cor. xi. 23—31. Here, however, instead of so doing, St. Paul pursues the same line of thought as in 1 Cor. iv. 10—there half ironically, here seriously—that, while the suffering falls on himself, the glory passes to the Church, for which he suffers, and in which he is content to sink himself. Hence he bids the Ephesians find encouragement and glory for themselves, instead of a cause for "fainting," in the afflictions endured on their behalf and overcome in Christ. As he identifies himself with them, so he would have them take what might be his glory to be their own.

(2) Verses 14—19 contain a prayer, addressed with special emphasis to the Father of all, that by the strengthening grace of the Spirit and the indwelling of Christ, accepted in faith and deepened by love, they may, first, know the mystery already described in all its greatness; and, next, learn by experience the unsearchable love of Christ, as dwelling in them, and so filling them up to "the fulness of God."

(14) **Unto the Father of our Lord Jesus Christ.**—The words "of our Lord Jesus Christ" appear, by both external and internal evidence, to be an interpolation—probably from a gloss indicating (in the true spirit of the Epistle) that the universal Fatherhood here spoken of is derived from the fatherly relation to Him in whom "all things are gathered up."

(15) **Of whom the whole family in heaven and earth is named.**—The original word (*patria*) here rendered "family" is literally derived from the word "father" (*pater*). It has been proposed to render it *fatherhood*, and translate, *from whom all fatherhood whatever derives its name*—all lower fatherhood being, in fact, a shadow and derivative from the Fatherhood of God. The translation is tempting, yielding a grand sense, and one thoroughly accordant with the treatment of the earthly relationship below (chap. vi. 1—4). But the usage of the word is clearly against it; and we must render it *every family*—that is, every body of rational beings in earth or heaven united under one common fatherhood, and bearing the name (as in a family or clan) of the common ancestor. Such bodies are certainly the first germs or units of human society; what their heavenly counterparts may be, who can tell? The Apostle looks upon the fathers whose names they

the whole family in heaven and earth is named, (16) that he would grant you, according to the riches of his glory, to be strengthened with might by his Spirit in the inner man; (17) that Christ may dwell in your hearts by faith; that ye, being rooted and grounded in love, (18) may be able to comprehend with all saints what *is* the breadth, and length, and depth, and height; (19) and to know the love of Christ, which passeth knowledge, that ye might be filled with

---

delight to bear as the imperfect representatives of God, and upon the family itself, with its head, as the type in miniature of the whole society of spiritual beings united in sonship to the Father in heaven. Hence he declares that it is ultimately from Him that every family derives the name of *patria*, and by that very name bears witness to the Divine Fatherhood, on which he desires here to lay especial stress.

(16) **To be strengthened with might by his Spirit in the inner man.**—From the Father, as the source of all life and being, St. Paul passes on to the Spirit, "proceeding from the Father," as the giver of life to men. His prayer here, as in chap. i. 17, is for the gift of the Spirit, but under some difference of aspect. There the prayer is for illumination, here for strength to grasp the mystery, to be rooted in love, and be filled up to the fulness of God. Accordingly, there the inner man is represented only by the "eyes of the heart;" here (as in Rom. vii. 22; 2 Cor. iv. 16) we hear of the "inner man" in his entirety, including all faculties—intellectual, emotional, moral—which make up his spiritual nature. And St. Paul emphasises this prayer very strikingly by asking that the gift may be "according to the riches of His glory," unlimited as the illimitable glory of the Divine Nature itself. Moreover, a greater closeness of communion is clearly indicated here. For light is a gift from without; strength comes from an indwelling power, making itself perfect in weakness, and continually growing from grace to grace.

(17) **That Christ may dwell in your hearts by faith.**—What that indwelling power is he now indicates, so passing to another Person of the Holy Trinity. It is (see Col. i. 27) "Christ in you, the hope of glory." The indwelling of Christ (as here the construction of the original plainly shows) is not a consequence of the gift of the Spirit; it is identical with it, for the office of the Holy Spirit is to implant and work out in us the likeness of Christ. So in John xiv. 16—20, in immediate connection with the promise of the Comforter, we read: "I will not leave you orphaned; I will come to you." "Ye shall know that . . . ye are in me and I in you." Hence the life in the Spirit is described as "To me to live is Christ" (Phil. i. 21); "I live, yet not I, but Christ liveth in me" (Gal. ii. 20). Faith is simply the condition of that indwelling of Christ (comp. chap. ii. 8), the opening of the door to Him that He may enter in.

The prayer is here complete, all that follows being but consequent from it. In accordance with the universal law of revelation, all is *from* the Father, all is *through* the Son vouchsafing to tabernacle in our humanity, all is *by* the Spirit effecting that indwelling of Christ in each individual soul.

That ye, being rooted and grounded in love.—The phrase "ye, being," &c., stands in the original before the word "that," as a kind of link between the previous clause and this, which seems to describe the consequence of the indwelling of Christ—viz., first love, next comprehension, and finally growth into the fulness of God.

The expression "rooted and grounded" (*i.e., founded*) contains the same mixture of metaphor as in 1 Cor. iii. 9, of the tree and the building—a mixture so natural as to pass into common usage. (Comp. Col. ii. 7, "rooted and being built up in Him.") The idea implied in "rooted" is of the striking down deeper and spreading wider into the soil; in "founded" of the firm basis on which ultimately we rest. "In love:" Love is not itself the root or foundation (for this is Jesus Christ Himself), but the condition under which growth takes place. Generally that growth is upward, as in 1 Cor. viii. 1: "Knowledge puffeth up, but love buildeth up;" or, as in chap. iv. 16, where the body is said "to build itself up in love." Here that growth is downward, deeper and deeper into the communion with God in Christ, as "faith is made perfect (or, *efficient*) by love." As in relation to man, so also to God, love is at once the recognition of an existing unity between spirit and spirit, and a means—probably the only means—of making that unity energetic and deepening it continually. Hence love is the first consequence of the indwelling of Christ in the soul; and by it the soul becomes rooted and grounded in the unity, given by that indwelling, with man and God.

(18) **May be able to comprehend with all saints what is the breadth, and length, and depth, and height.**—It has been asked, Of what? Various answers have been given; but as St. Paul has obviously of set purpose omitted all definition, leaving the phrase incomplete in absolute generality, no answer can be perfectly satisfactory. The early fathers delighted to refer it to the cross, and to trace in the four dimensions of the cross a symbol of this four-fold extension of the love of God in Christ. The clause following, "to know the love of Christ," though partly explanatory of this, hardly seems to be identical or co-extensive with it. The knowledge there described is a part—perhaps the chief part, but not the whole—of the comprehension here prayed for. If anything is to be supplied, it should probably be "of the mystery"—*i.e.*, of the whole mystery on which St. Paul had been dwelling, including the predestination, the redemption, the call and union of Jews and Gentiles. The prayer is that we may know it every way, in every direction in which the soul can go forth towards God.

It may be noted that comprehension is placed after love, just as in Phil. i. 9, "I pray that your love may abound (that is, *overflow*) in knowledge and in all judgment." The spiritual order of revelation differs from that of the "wisdom of the world." It has first faith, next love, and finally knowledge, because its object is a person, not an abstract principle. That knowledge must, even here, "grow from more to more;" but St. Paul's prayer can never be perfectly realised till we "know even as we are known."

(19) **To know the love of Christ, which passeth knowledge.**—The intentional paradox of this expression is weakened if (with many interpretations) we suppose that there is opposition in kind between knowledge referred to in the two clauses: as if "to know" meant to know by faith and spiritual

all the fulness of God. (20) Now unto
Chap. iii. 20, 21. Doxology. him that is able to do exceeding abundantly above
all that we ask or think, according to
the power that worketh in us, (21) unto
him *be* glory in the church by Christ
Jesus throughout all ages, world without
end. Amen.

A.D. 64.

CHAPTER IV.—(1) I therefore, the
prisoner of the Lord,[1] Chap. iv. 1—3. Exhortation to unity.
beseech you that ye

1 Or, *in the Lord.*

---

experience, while the "knowledge," which the love of Christ "passes," is mere "human knowledge"—head-knowledge, and the like. Of such opposition there is no trace (contrast 1 Cor. ii. 6—16). In the original, the word "to know" is in a tense which expresses cognition in a particular case; hence the meaning of St. Paul's prayer seems to be that they may know from time to time, as each opportunity offers, what must in its entirety pass all human knowledge, either to discover or fully to understand, even when revealing itself; so that they may always go on from faith to faith, from knowledge to knowledge, and yet find new depths still to be fathomed. The "love of Christ" is the love which He bears to us, and which is the motive of His sacrifice for our redemption. It is known only by those who are rooted in love to Him; such love being at once the consequence of the first knowledge of His love to us (1 John iv. 19) and the condition of entering more deeply into that knowledge.

That ye might be filled with (or, rather, *up to*) **all the fulness of God.**—This clause must be taken as dependent, not merely on the clause immediately preceding, but on the whole sentence. It describes the final and glorious consequence of the indwelling of Christ in the heart, viz., the "being filled" with grace "up to the fulness of God." The meaning is more clearly seen in the fuller expression below (chap. iv. 13): "till we all come . . . to the measure of the stature of the fulness of Christ." It is simply perfect conformation to the image of Him in whom "dwells all the fulness of the Godhead bodily" (Col. ii. 9), and whose fulness is therefore the "fulness of God," manifesting all the attributes of the divine nature. The process is described in 2 Cor. iii. 18, "We all, with open face beholding as in a glass the glory of the Lord, are changed into the same image from glory to glory;" its consummation in 1 John iii. 2, "When He shall appear, we shall be like Him; for we shall see Him as He is." (Comp. Phil. iii. 20, 21.) Here it completes the climax. When Christ dwells in the heart we have first, love perfecting the faith which roots the life in Him; next, a thoughtful knowledge, entering by degrees into the unsearchable riches of His love to us; and, lastly, the filling the soul, itself weak and empty, up to the perfection of likeness to Him, so renewing and deepening through all time and eternity the image of God in our humanity.

(3) Verses 20, 21 sum up the whole in a doxology to God the Father through Christ Jesus. It may be compared with the other more solemn doxologies in the New Testament: as Rom. xvi. 25; 1 Tim. v. 15, 16; Jude, verses 24, 25; Rev. i. 6. Each has its distinctive character. Here the prevailing idea of the preceding chapters is the wonder and the mystery of God's fore-ordaining love, overflowing in the riches of His grace to those who are made one with Him and with each other in Christ Jesus. Hence, God is here described as He "who is able to do exceeding abundantly above all that we ask or think," and to do all "by His power dwelling" and working in us.

(21) **Unto him be glory in the church by** (properly, *in*) **Christ Jesus.**—In the parallelism of these clauses is implied the great idea of the Epistle—the unity of the Church in Christ. Hence all that is "in the Church" is "in Christ Jesus." The visible unity of the Church represents, as it depends on, the invisible unity with God in Him.

Throughout all ages, world without end.—The original expression is emphatic and peculiar: *to all the generations of the age of the ages;* that is, in each successive generation of that age (or, *dispensation*) which includes in itself all the ages which we can reckon or conceive. The conception represents to us each generation, as adding its own peculiar thanksgiving to the great chorus of praise which fills eternity.

IV.

[4. **Final Summary of Doctrine** (chap. iv. 1—16).

(1) THE UNITY OF THE CHURCH OF CHRIST (verses 1—6).
 (*a*) *Its ground* in the unity of the Holy Trinity;
 (*b*) *Its means* in the one baptism;
 (*c*) *Its conditions and effects* in one faith, one hope, one charity.

(2) THE DIVERSITY OF GIFTS AND OFFICES IN THE CHURCH through the mediation of her glorified Lord (verses 7—11).

(3) THE DIRECTION OF ALL TO ONE OBJECT—the individual and corporate growth of all into the likeness and image of Christ the Head (verses 12—16).]

(1) Verses 1—6, although cast in a hortatory form contain the final summary of the great doctrine of the Epistle—the UNITY OF THE CATHOLIC CHURCH—in words which have all the glowing freedom of spiritual enthusiasm, and all the clear-cut precision of a creed.

Thus (*a*) the ground of that unity is laid in that spiritual communion of each soul with the "one Spirit," the "one Lord," and the "one God and Father of all," which underlies all outward ordinance, and which no power of man can either give or take away. (*b*) The means of entering that unity is the "one baptism," ordained by Christ Himself, universal in the Christian world, capable of being ministered (though irregularly) by any Christian hand. (*c*) The graces, which in germ are conditions, and in full growth are effects, of such unity are the "one hope," the "one faith," the one "bond of peace" or charity. These last most of all depend on the "fellow-working" of man—primarily in the soul receiving them, and secondarily in all who can influence it for good and for evil.

We have here a perfect and exhaustive exposition of the unity of the Church, on which depend the other qualities of "Holiness," "Catholicity," and "Apostolicity" ascribed to it in the Creed. In other passages the essential life of the Church is attributed, now to the revelation of the Father (Matt. xvi. 17, 18), now to the indwelling presence of the Son (Matt. xxviii. 20), now to the gift of the Holy Ghost (Acts ii. 38, 39). Here all are united

walk worthy of the vocation where-
with ye are called, (2) with all lowli-
ness and meekness, with longsuffering,
forbearing one another in love; (3)
endeavouring to keep the unity of the
Spirit in the bond of peace. (4) *There
is* one body, and one Spirit,
even as ye are called in
one hope of your calling;
(5) one Lord, one faith, one baptism,

Chap. iv. 4—6. The unity of the Church.

---

in one comprehensive view. The order, however, is natural, not artificial. The exhortation to peace naturally leads to the conception of one Body, animated by the "one Spirit"; next, the remembrance of their calling leads to the "one Lord," who called them to Him in one faith and by one baptism; and all ends in the contemplation of the "one God and Father," who is not only above all and through all His creation, but specially in those who are adopted to a new sonship in Christ. (See John xiv. 22, 23.) In its completeness and depth this passage stands alone. It is interesting to compare and contrast with it the equally celebrated passage occupying the corresponding place in the Colossian Epistle (Col. iii. 1—4), and to gather from this the mingled similarity and difference in the main idea of those two Epistles—the Ephesian Epistle dwelling especially on the unity and regeneration of the whole body, the Colossian Epistle on the sole Headship and Deity of Christ.

(1) **Worthy of the vocation wherewith ye are called.**—This "being worthy of the Christian calling" may obviously show itself in any of the graces of regenerate humanity, all being features of the image of Christ. Thus in 1 Pet. i. 15 it expresses itself in "holiness" (as in the frequent phrase "called to be saints"); in Phil. i. 27—30, in steadfastness of faith. But in this passage the especial point which has been dwelt upon in their calling is the fact that they were aliens, helpless and miserable, and that they are now united in one body with the ancient people of God. Hence, naturally, the graces declared to correspond with their calling, so viewed, are the graces of humility and gentleness, teaching them to sink all thought of self in "the unity of the Spirit."

(2) **With all lowliness and meekness, with longsuffering.**—See Col. iii. 12, where the same three qualities are dwelt upon, but there introduced by "compassion and kindness." They seem to correspond almost exactly to the first, third, and fifth beatitudes of the Sermon on the Mount, in which the principle of love is wrought out in various forms (as in the other beatitudes the principle of righteousness): "Blessed are the poor in spirit;" "Blessed are the meek;" "Blessed are the merciful." The word "lowliness of mind" is used by St. Paul only in the Epistles of the Captivity (Phil. ii. 3; Col. ii. 18, 23; iii. 12) and in the address to the Ephesian presbyters (Acts xx. 19). It is, indeed, a word new coined in Christian terminology, and even the root from which it comes is mostly used by the heathen moralists in a bad sense (of meanness and slavishness), of which there is still a trace in Col. ii. 18. "Meekness" is mostly "gentleness"—"the meek and quiet spirit" (1 Pet. iii. 4)—the natural, though not the invariable, fruit of humility, winning souls by its very absence of bitter self-assertion, and so "inheriting the earth." "Longsuffering" is the manifestation of such meekness, with something of especial effort and struggle, in the bearing of injury.

(2, 3) **Forbearing one another in love . . . .**—The word rendered "endeavouring" is, in the original, a word expressing "earnestness" of thought and exertion to secure a thing not lightly obtained. (See 2 Tim. iv. 9—21; Heb. iv. 11; 2 Pet. i. 10.) It shows that St. Paul here passes from the negative aspects of love, summed up in forbearance, to the more positive and energetic enthusiasm for unity and peace. Love is in both aspects, the "uniting bond" of peace. In the parallel passage of Col. iii. 14, it is "put on over" all else, and is the uniting "bond of perfectness." In the celebrated thirteenth chapter of the First Epistle to Corinthians (verses 4—7) it is made to include "longsuffering" and "kindness," and all forms of humility and gentleness. But, if it be real, it must necessarily pass into active energy; if it is to win the final beatitude of "blessing to the peacemakers," it must "labour for peace," and "follow after the things which make for peace" (Ps. cxx. 7; Rom. xiv. 19).

The unity of the Spirit is certainly the unity given by the indwelling of the Holy Ghost. This we cannot create, for it is the gift of God; but we can "keep" it: that is, cherish it, guard it, and make it effectual by love; and all experience proves that, if we would so keep it, we need the positive earnestness of exertion against evils without and within.

(4) **There is one body, and one Spirit.**—The words "There is" are not in the original, which starts with a striking abruption, and with that terse concentration of thought and word which marks out an embryo creed.

The "one body" is the Body of Christ, "from whom it is fitly framed, joined together, and compacted," so that in every part "it grows up into Him." But this communion with God in Christ being "the life eternal," the Holy Ghost, by making it effectual alike to the Church and to the individual soul, is the "Lord and Giver of Life." Hence, His presence is spoken of as being to the body of Christ what the spirit is to the natural body—the uniting and vivifying power for all its members. Under the same idea we have (in 1 Cor. xii. 13), as a description of the first entrance into the Church of Christ, "By one Spirit are we all baptised into one body . . . and have been all made to drink into one Spirit."

Even as ye are (or rather, *were*) **called in one hope of your calling.**—The connection, though not at first obvious, is clear on consideration. Since the grace of the Holy Spirit is not only the "seal" of regeneration, but also the "earnest" (chap. i. 14) of future perfection, the mention of the one Spirit suggests naturally the "hope of our calling" (*i.e.*, the perfect unity of heaven). In this, in spite of all natural and spiritual inequalities, and in spite even of our divisions and strifes upon earth, all Christians are still actually one. Hence the communion of saints is perhaps most clearly realised in the times of high spiritual aspiration, and in the near presence of death.

(5) **One Lord, one faith.**—From the idea of "the calling," the Apostle passes naturally to Him who calls—the "one Lord"—and to the method of His calling to Himself, first, by the "one faith," and then by the "one baptism" at which profession of that one faith is made. It is on the indwelling of Christ in each heart by faith that the spiritual unity of all Christians—primarily with

(6) one God and Father of all, who *is* above
all, and through all, and in you all. (7)
But unto every one of us is given
grace according to the measure of the
gift of Christ. (8) Wherefore
he saith, When he ascended
up on high, he led captivity[1] captive, and gave gifts

Chap. iv. 7—11. The variety of gifts and functions.

[1] Or, *a multitude of captives.*

Him, secondarily with one another—depends; and that spiritual unity is "put on" in baptism (Gal. iii. 27), in which we are "buried with Him and risen again" (Col. ii. 12), growing into the likeness of His death and resurrection (Rom. vi. 3, 4, 5). Again we note that, with but few exceptions, all Christians, even in the divided condition of the Church, are still united in the "one baptism;" and if we look to such expressions of the one faith as are contained in the baptismal profession (*e.g.*, of the Apostles' Creed), it is clear that our divisions, great as they are, turn mainly on the fourth subsidiary Article on the "Holy Catholic Church," and not on the three primary Articles of the Father, the Son, and the Holy Ghost. In these the mass of Christendom has still one faith.

(6) **One God and Father of all.**—Necessarily, through the Son, we pass to the Father (as the Lord Himself invariably teaches us to do), since He is (to use the old Greek expression) "the fount of Deity." He is said to be the "Father of all." We cannot limit this universal Fatherhood; although, undoubtedly, the context shows that the immediate reference is to those who are His children by adoption in Jesus Christ. The Church is essentially Catholic, inheriting by special gift what is the birthright of all humanity; incapable of perfection till all be drawn into that closer sonship, yet having neither right nor desire to deny that outside her pale at any moment the wider Fatherhood of God extends.

Who is above all, and through all, and in you all.—The word "you" has little authority; many MSS. and commentaries have "us." But the best MSS. and authorities omit both, as probably early glosses of explanation which have crept into the text. Accordingly, the word "all" throughout must be taken, as above, as applying to all God's rational creatures, made in His image (and indeed, in a lower sense, even to all His creatures), but especially and properly to the members of Christ's Church. In the three-fold sentence many ancient and modern interpreters trace a reference to the Holy Trinity. But, strictly speaking, this cannot be, as the passage expressly points to the Father; although, in virtue of the eternal unity of the Godhead, it may be true that in the expression "through all" and "in all" we trace those manifestations of the Father which are especially made through the Son and by the Holy Spirit. Hence we must refer all properly to the ultimate conception of God the Father; as "above all" in the sovereignty of His will, since to work out "His pleasure they are and were created," and His will becomes to them the "law eternal;" as "through all" in the diffusive power of the forces—physical, moral, and spiritual—by which the world of nature, still more the world of man, most of all the society of Christians, are swayed as wholes; and "in all" by the indwelling of God in the individual for creation, sustentation, regeneration, which is the breath of life—both the physical and spiritual life. (This individuality, and the especial reference to Christians, are marked by the very natural gloss "us," or "you," in this clause.)

(2) Verses 7—11 pass from the unity of the Church to the diversity of graces and offices in its members, all being gifts of the ascended Lord, and results of that universal mediation which fills all things.

(7) **But unto every one of us is given grace.**—This verse should be rendered, *To every one of us the grace* (the one "grace of the Lord Jesus Christ") *was given*—that is, given in the Divine purpose in the regeneration of the whole body, although it has to be received and made our own, separately in each soul, and gradually in the course of life. It was and is given "according to the measure of the gift of Christ." (See below, verses 13—16.) In Him it dwells "without measure" (see John iii. 34); He gives it to each according to the measure of his capacity to receive it in faith (called in Rom. xii. 3 the "measure of faith"). Compare with this verse the fuller description of the differences of "gifts," "ministries," and "operations" in 1 Cor. xii. 4—6, in which passage there is the same general reference to the Three Persons of the Holy Trinity; but the particular reference is there to the Holy Spirit, while here it is to the Son.

(8) **Wherefore he saith.**—The reference is to Ps. lxviii.—a psalm which (as the quotation from Num. x. 35, in the first verse, shows) is a psalm celebrating some moving of the ark, traditionally (and most probably) connected with David's bringing up of the ark (2 Sam vi.) to Mount Zion. The very change from the second person to the third person shows it to be a free quotation; and this is made far more evident by the remarkable variation from the text of the original, which runs, *Thou receivedst gifts in man*—*i.e.*, probably, "among men;" and adds, "even the rebellious, that the Lord God might dwell among them"—a clause which (from verses 29—31) we may suppose to refer to the homage of the heathen to the Lord Jehovah. Now, it has been noted that the word "received" is used constantly for "receiving," or "fetching," for another (Gen. xv. 9; xviii. 5; xxvii. 13, *et al.*); and it appears that the Chaldee Targum actually has here, as a gloss: "Thou hast given gifts to the sons of men," interpreting the words, curiously enough, of Moses as a mediator between God and man. The psalm also was recognised as a Messianic psalm, foreshadowing the dwelling of "God with us" in the universal kingdom of the true Mediator. St. Paul accordingly uses it with a bold variation suiting his context. The key to this use is found in the truth enunciated of our Lord in Acts ii. 33, that "being by the right hand of God exalted, and *having received* of the Father the promise of the Holy Spirit, *He hath shed forth this.*" Our Lord, as the Head of humanity, receives only in order to give. From the means, therefore, the Apostle passes to the end.

He led captivity captive.—The modern use of these words as describing our Lord's triumph over the power of evil, hitherto triumphant over man, and so giving freedom by leading captive the power of captivity, although in itself profoundly true, is not supported by the original, in which it is simply used for "a body of captives." St. Paul's use of it here is probably best interpreted by Col. ii. 15, where it is said of the "principalities and powers"—the powers of sin and death—that "He made a show of them openly,

unto men.[a] (9) (Now that he ascended,
what is it but that he also descended
first into the lower parts of the earth?
(10) He that descended is the same also
that ascended up far above all heavens,
that he might fill [1] all things.) (11) And
he gave some, apostles; [b] and some,
prophets; and some, evangelists; and

a Ps. 68. 18.

1 Or, *fulfil.*

b 1 Cor. 12. 28.

---

triumphing over them in the cross." (See Note on this passage.)

(9, 10) These verses form a parenthesis, designed to bring out the pervading idea of this and the parallel Epistle—the Divine humanity of Christ as "filling all in all" and "gathering all things" into Himself.

(9) **The lower parts of the earth.**—This may mean either *the regions of the earth*, as "lower" than heaven, or the *regions beneath the earth.* The reasoning of the text in itself would be satisfied by the former. For St. Paul is simply arguing that the use of the phrase "ascended" from earth to heaven implies a previous corresponding descent, which must be from heaven to earth; exactly as in John iii. 13, "No man hath ascended into heaven, but He that came down from heaven." But form and usage of the phrase itself seem to point to the other meaning, which is held by almost all ancient interpreters and most moderns. It agrees with the strong expression of "filling all things," in verse 10, and is possibly suggested by the leading captive of the powers of hell and death. Though, perhaps, injurious to the strictness of the antithesis, it is quite accordant with St. Paul's manner to introduce thus a fresh idea beyond the simple idea of descent, which is sufficient for his argument: "He descended—yea, even to the realms below." For this idea is most apposite to that frequent reference to spiritual powers of evil found in this Epistle, and it may be thought to correspond by antithesis to the "far above all heavens" of the next verse.

(10) **That he might fill all things.**—Compare the description in chap. i. 23 of the Lord as "filling all in all." In both cases the reference is more particularly to the gift of the fulness of His grace, flowing from His glorified humanity to all His members. But the words are too wide for any limitation. In heaven and earth, and the realms under the earth, His presence and sovereignty extends, by whatever means and over whatever beings He wills. In Rev. v. 13, accordingly, we read the ascription by "every creature in heaven, and on the earth, and under the earth . . ., of blessing, honour, glory, and power to . . . the Lamb for ever and ever."

(11) **He gave.**—In the original "He" is emphatic—He and He alone, as the ascended Head of humanity. The word "gave," instead of the more obvious word *set*, or *appointed* (used in 1 Cor. xii. 28), is, of course, suggested by verse 8. They who are ministers of His gifts are themselves gifts from Him to the Church.

Some, apostles; and some, prophets . . .—With this passage we must compare 1 Cor. xii. 28, "God hath set some in the Church, first apostles, secondarily prophets, thirdly teachers, after that miracles, then gifts of healings," &c.; and, perhaps, Rom. xii. 6—8, "Having then gifts . . . whether prophecy . . . or ministry . . . or teaching . . . or exhortation . . .," although this last passage is less formally apposite. In all three cases there is the same general idea, first of the one body, and then of the one Spirit, guiding and animating it through various ministries. The parallel between this passage and the passage in 1 Cor. is very close; for in the latter all that follows the words "after that" may be put aside, as describing, not special offices or ministries, but special gifts. We have, therefore, in both, "first apostles, secondly prophets." Then come, in the earlier Epistle, "teachers;" and this class, in our own later Epistle, is subdivided into "evangelists" and "pastors," both being teachers—the one in conversion of those still aliens from Christ, the other in edification of those already brought into His flock.

Some, apostles.—The name "apostles" is certainly used here in its technical and restricted sense, as applying to the Twelve, whom "the Apostle" of God Himself (Heb. iii. 1) named as His Apostles (Luke vi. 13), and with whom St. Paul claims equality (see 1 Cor. ix. 1; xv. 9—11; Gal. i. 1) on the ground of his own special mission and revelation from the same Lord. It is, indeed, used in a wider sense; sometimes with words distinctly implying a derivation and human mission, as in 2 Cor. viii. 23, "apostles (or, *messengers*) of the churches;" Phil. ii. 25, "Epaphroditus, your apostle (or, *messenger*);" sometimes without such qualification, as in 2 Cor. xi. 5, 13; xii. 11, 12; 1 Thess. ii. 7; and, perhaps, Rom. xvi. 7. But such use is rare, and cannot be applied to a passage like this, which is distinctive of a special and primary class. In direct charge from the Lord, universal scope of mission, special inspiration and power of miracle, which are "the signs of an apostle" (2 Cor. xii. 12), the Apostles, properly so called, stood out in office absolutely unique and supreme. What was said of the first age of the Church is true of all ages—"of the rest durst no man join himself unto them" (Acts v. 13).

Some, prophets.—For the nature and function of prophecy in the Church, see the detailed treatment of the subject by St. Paul in 1 Cor. xiv. It is sufficient here to note (1) that from very early times the "prophets" are mentioned as a separate class (see Acts xi. 27; xv. 32; xxi. 10), distinguished from teachers (Acts xiii. 1), and that, in this Epistle especially, they are spoken of, in connection with the Apostles, as receiving the revealed mystery of the gospel (chap. iii. 5), and being (or, *laying*) "the foundation of the Church;" (2) that their office, like the Apostolate, is clearly extraordinary, distinct from the ordinary and permanent teaching of the evangelists and pastors, and, probably, best described by the two phrases so constantly applied to the prophets of the Old Testament—"the word of the Lord came to me;" "the Spirit of the Lord was upon me." As all God's extraordinary gifts and workings are closely correlated with His ordinary laws of operation, so in this case the apostolic and prophetic offices gradually melt away into the regular functions of government and teaching, belonging in all times to the ministry of the Church.

Some, evangelists; and some, pastors and teachers.—In these two phrases (corresponding to the simple word "teachers" in 1 Cor. xii. 28) we find described the two-fold office of the regular ministry of the Church—first, to preach the gospel to the heathen or the unconverted, and next, to fulfil our Lord's pastoral charge (John xxi. 15—17) of feeding and shepherding those who are already His sheep. It is clear that the same person may be invested with the two offices, as Timothy,

Chap. iv. 12—16. Devoted to the one object of edification.

some, pastors and teachers; (12) for the perfecting of the saints, for the work of the ministry, for the edifying of the body of Christ: (13) till we all come in the unity[1] of the faith, and of the knowledge of the Son of God, unto a perfect man, unto the measure of the

1 Or, *into the unity.*

---

when in pastoral charge at Ephesus, is bidden "to do the work of an evangelist" (2 Tim. iv. 5); and that in some degree the two offices must always be united, for the evangelist, like the apostle, is generally called upon to organise and "confirm the churches" (Acts xiv. 22, 23; xv. 41), and the pastor must always find men unconverted, to whom he must be an evangelist. But the two elements of duty will co-exist in different proportions in different persons. Some were then, and are now, especially called to be "evangelists"—that is, as is shown by the career of Philip, to whom the name is first given (Acts xxi. 8), to be, under the apostolic guidance, missionaries to the unconverted; others to be "pastors and teachers," feeding now with "pure milk of the word," now with "solid meat" (see 1 Cor. iii. 2, and Heb. v. 12), those already gathered into the fold, and exercising over them the pastoral authority solemnly committed by our Lord to His ministers. Yet both can discharge only under limitation the functions which in the Apostles were practically unlimited.

On the question whether this celebrated passage describes the regular orders or the functions, ordinary and extraordinary, of the ministry, we may fairly say that while no doubt the very genius of the passage points to the latter alternative, yet the ultimate appeal must be made to history. It is clear, from the nature of the case, that none could inherit the direct and universal commission from Christ held by the Apostles; it is certain historically that the supernatural gifts of prophecy and miracle passed away; it is hardly less indisputable that the two functions of evangelism and pastorate were always shared among the three orders of bishops, priests, and deacons after the close of the Apostolic age.

(3) Verses 12—16 return from diversity of functions to singleness of object—viz., the perfecting individual souls in the likeness of Christ, and so building up of the whole Church in unity with Him.

(12) **For the perfecting . . .**—The parallelism of the three clauses of our version of this verse does not exactly correspond to the original, though we notice that Chrysostom supports it, and therefore evidently saw nothing in the Greek to contradict it. The preposition (*eis*) used in the two latter clauses (which should be *unto work of ministration, unto edification of the body of Christ*) properly signifies "contact with a thing," and the preposition (*pros*) used in the first clause, "direction towards a thing." The two are often apparently interchanged; but in close juxtaposition here can hardly be intended to be identical or exactly parallel; and, if distinction is to be drawn, the former must signify immediate consequence, and the other the remoter object to which such immediate consequence is designed to minister. The construction would be greatly simplified, if inversion of the first two clauses could be allowed. For it would then run, "unto work of ministration with a view to perfecting of saints, unto building up of the body of Christ;" and so would plainly represent the two-fold operation of the ministry: first, its work in its various offices for the perfecting of individual souls; and next, its general direction to the building up of the whole body. But whether this construction be grammatically possible or not, this appears to be in any case the general sense of the passage.

The perfecting of the saints.—The word rendered "perfecting" (akin to the "perfection" of 2 Cor. xiii. 9) is derived from a root which signifies either to "mend" what is broken (as in Matt. iv. 21), or to "complete" what is unfinished (as in Luke vi. 40; Rom. ix. 22); and hence is used spiritually for to "restore" the fallen (Gal. vi. 1), or to "perfect" the imperfect Christian (Heb. xiii. 21; 1 Thess. iii. 10). Both processes are necessarily implied in that perfection of the individual saints here spoken of, and more fully described in the next verses.

The edifying of the body of Christ.—This is that part of the work of the ministry (as in preaching and ministering in public worship) which tells upon the Church or congregation as a whole. It is here represented as subsequent, perhaps as subordinate, to the individual pastoral dealing with souls. But each has his own gift. Some ministries are more blessed to the individual perfecting of the saints; others to the building up of the whole Church.

(13) **Till we all come.**—The marginal rendering is correct: *till we all arrive at the unity of the faith.* The "one faith" has been spoken of above; the full grasp of that faith by each and all is the first object of all the ministries of the Church, since by it both the individual perfection and the corporate unity begin to be secured. Such faith always goes on to knowledge, that is (as in chap. i. 17) "full knowledge" of Him in whom we have believed. So in 2 Pet. i. 17, "Add to your faith virtue" (that is, energy in well-doing), "and to virtue knowledge." This knowledge (see chap. iii. 17—19) is gained mainly through the love in which faith is made perfect.

Of the Son of God.—These words should be connected with the word "faith" (as in Gal. ii. 20) as well as "knowledge." They are probably to be considered as a distinctive phrase, designating our Lord especially as glorified and exalted to the right hand of the Father in "the glory which he had with the Father before the world was." So in Rom. i. 4, He is "declared to be the Son of God by the Resurrection;" and in Heb. iv. 14, "Jesus the Son of God" is "the High Priest ascended into the heavens." Compare also our Lord's declaration that "if any man speaks against the Son of Man it shall be forgiven him" (Matt. xii. 32) with the declaration of the certain vengeance on him who "treads under foot the Son of God" (Heb. x. 29). Note again, in St. John's First Epistle, the constant reference to the belief in and confession of Jesus as "the Son of God" as the one thing needful (chaps. iv. 15; v. 5, 10—12, 20). For on the belief not only of what He was on earth, but of what He is in heaven, all distinctive Christianity depends. If He is only "Son of Man" He cannot be the universal Saviour.

Unto a perfect (that is, *full-grown*) **man, unto the measure of the stature of the fulness of Christ.**—In these words are described the second great object of the ministries of the Church—not only the production of faith and knowledge of the Son of God, but the formation of Christ in the soul, as

stature[1] of the fulness of Christ: (14)
that we *henceforth* be no more children,
tossed to and fro, and carried about with
every wind of doctrine, by the sleight of
men, *and* cunning craftiness, whereby
they lie in wait to deceive; (15) but
speaking the truth[2] in love, may grow
up into him in all things, which is the
head, *even* Christ: (16) from whom the
whole body fitly joined together and
compacted by that which every joint
supplieth, according to the effectual
working in the measure of every part,
maketh increase of the body unto the

1 Or, *age.*

2 Or, *being sincere.*

"dwelling in the heart through faith." This image of Christ in "fulness" is the absolutely perfect humanity, showing forth the image of God. Each can partake of it only up to "the measure" which God gives him. (See verse 7.) When he so partakes of it to the utmost, he is "full-grown" (relatively, not absolutely, perfect) up to the spiritual "stature" assigned to him, although (as in the body) that stature may vary in different persons, and in none can perfectly attain to the whole "fulness" of Christ. The rendering, "stature" is preferable to *age,* as suiting better the context, though both are fully admissible under New Testament usage. On the word "fulness," see Note to chap. i. 23.

(14) **That we be no more children.**—Here the process of growth is described negatively; in the next verse positively. We are to *be no more children.* The word used here and in 1 Cor. iii. 1; xiii. 11; Gal. iv. 1, 3; Heb. v. 13 (often rendered "babes"), is a word almost always applied in a bad sense, like our word "childish"—not to the guilelessness, the trustfulness, or the humility of children, which our Lord emphatically blessed (Matt. xviii. 2—4), but to their unforeseeing and unthinking impulsiveness. The distinction is marked in 1 Cor. xiv. 20, "Be not children in understanding: howbeit, in malice be ye children, but in understanding be men." Thus, in 1 Cor. iii. 1, xiii. 11, Heb. v. 13, it describes crudeness and shallowness of conception; in Gal. iv. 1, 3, incapability of free self-direction; here, liability to disturbance and change by every external impression from without, so as to be "everything by turns and nothing long."

Tossed to and fro, and carried about with every wind of doctrine.—The metaphor is of a ship drifting at the mercy of a storm, tossed by the waves, and carried round from time to time by every blast. The word "tossed" is more properly used of the waves (compare Jas. i. 6) themselves, but the following words seem to show that here it is applied to the ship rising and falling with them. The word "doctrine," as usual, is a general word for all deliberate "teaching," whether acting on the understanding or the heart. It includes, in fact, all influence consciously exercised to a definite end.

The metaphor is then dropped, and the evil influences to which childish instability is a prey are described—first, as the "sleight," *i.e.,* the sleight of hand of the dice-thrower, describing quick, sudden deceit of detail; next (to substitute an accurate translation for the unusually paraphrastic rendering of our version), as a "craftiness devoted to the systematic plan of deceit," thus referring to deeper and subtler forms of delusion. This reference is so definite in the original, that we are tempted to believe St. Paul to have had in view some particular scheme of erroneous teaching, which had already struck root in the soil of Asia Minor. The Epistle to the Colossians shows that such false teaching had appeared itself at Colossæ; it was, perhaps, the germ of the more full-grown Gnosticism noted in the Pastoral Epistles.

(15) **But speaking the truth in love.**—It has been doubted whether the words "in love" should not be connected with "may grow up," &c., exactly as in verse 16, "maketh increase of the body . . . in love." But both order and sense seem to point to the connection given in our version. The correct rendering is, *being true in love;* including in this the "being true" to others, by speaking truly and acting honestly towards them (as in Gal. iv. 16), but including also the "being true" absolutely—that is, the loving the truth, and clinging to it at all costs. The latter element, indeed, is the one which stands here more properly in antithesis to the childish instability described in the preceding verse; as it is in itself the more important, and is, in fact, the only basis for the other.

"To thine own self be true,
And it will follow, as the night the day,
Thou canst not then be false to any man."

This "being true" is expressed in many forms. Sometimes as "being of the truth" (John xviii. 37; 1 John ii. 21; iii. 19); sometimes as "abiding in the truth" (John viii. 44), or "having the truth in us" (1 John i. 8); sometimes as "doing the truth" (John iii. 21), and "walking in the truth" (2 John, verse 4; 3 John, verse 4). In all cases it is closely connected with the idea of unity with Him who is Himself "the Truth" (John xiv. 6).

With the phrase "being true in love" we may compare the corresponding phrase of "loving in truth . . . for the truth's sake, which dwelleth in us" (2 John, verse 1; see also verse 3, and 3 John, verse 1). In both we recognise the harmony of the two great principles of individuality and unity, on which true humanity, and therefore likeness to God, depends. In the contemplation and love of truth each of us is alone; even in the speaking and doing truth towards others we have to consult only God and our own conscience, which is His voice within. In love, on the contrary, we deny and sacrifice self, merging our individual being in humanity or in God. Taking the first alone, we have a hard, almost stoical, self-concentration; taking the other alone, it may become towards man an idolatry, to which both truth and freedom are sacrificed, and even towards God may pass into a mysticism, in which all active energy is lost. Uniting both, we have the perfect humanity, at once individual and social, at once free before God and lost in God. Accordingly, it is thus that we "grow up into Him who is the Head, even Christ," who, by perfect truth and perfect love, manifested to us in His humanity all the fulness of God.

The head, even Christ.—In this name of our Lord we have the link of connection between the individual perfection and corporate unity. He is (as in 1 Cor. xi. 3) the Head of each man. He is also the Head of the whole Church.

(16) **From whom the whole body fitly joined together and compacted.**—The word rendered "fitly joined together" is the same used in chap. ii. 21, with more technical accuracy, of a building—"clamped" or "bonded together." Here the two words are applied

edifying of itself in love.[a] (17) This I say therefore, and testify in the Lord, that ye henceforth walk not as other Gentiles walk, in the vanity of their mind, (18) having the understanding darkened, being alienated from the life of God through the ignorance

Chap. iv. 17—24. Contrast of heathen and Christian life.

a Col. 2. 19.

to the union of the limbs of the body, as being "jointed," and so "brought into close contact." The latter word is used in Col. ii. 19.

By that which every joint supplieth.—A paraphrastic and inaccurate rendering. It should be, *by every contact with the supply* (of nutriment) from the head. The word employed has commonly the meaning of "joint" (as in the parallel passage, Col. ii. 19), and is so used by Greek physiologists; but its original sense is abstract—the "joining" or "touching"—and this appears the simplest here. The supply (comp. Phil. i. 19, "the supply of the Spirit") is again almost a technical word for the abundant outflow of strength and nervous energy from the head. (The corresponding verb is used in 2 Cor. ix. 10; Gal. iii. 5; Col. ii. 19; 2 Pet. i. 5, 11.) Hence the phrase seems to stand in closer connection with the "maketh increase" below than the "compacted together" above. The body grows, in every part of its complex unity, through contact with the divine supply of grace through the head.

According to the effectual working in the measure of every part.—In these words is described the method, as in the preceding word the source, of the growth. The "effectiveness" of every part "in measure" (according, that is, to its right capacity and function) is the condition of corporate growth. Such effectiveness comes from direct contact with the central energy.

Maketh increase of the body unto the edifying (*the building up*) **of itself in love.**—Here, lastly, we have the function of the body itself. It is knit together by its divine organisation; it is sustained by the supply from the head; its several parts are kept in life by that supply; but it grows as a whole and builds itself up by the uniting and vivifying power of love, which is the "bond of perfectness." (Just so St. Paul says of the individual, in 1 Cor. viii. 1, "Charity edifieth.") Truth is, no doubt, the basis of unity; but love is its vital power, at once keeping together all who are united, and drawing in those who are as yet separated.

[5. **Practical Exhortation** (chap. iv. 17—21).

(1) THE NEW LIFE; first, taught in Christ and learning Christ; and secondly, regenerate in Him to the image of God (verses 17—24).

(2) HENCE THE POWER OF CONQUEST OF SIN GENERALLY—

(*a*) *Falsehood* (verse 25);
(*b*) *Passionate anger* (verses 26, 27);
(*c*) *Dishonesty* (verse 28);
(*d*) *Foulness of word* (verses 29, 30);

(3) HENCE ITS POWER AGAINST THE SPECIAL BESETTING SINS OF—

(*a*) *Bitterness and malice*, unworthy of the love of Christ (verses 31, 32, and chap. v. 1, 2);
(*b*) *Fornication and lust*, unworthy of the light of Christ (chap. v. 3—14);
(*c*) *Recklessness* and drunken excitement (chap. v. 15—21).]

(1) In verses 17—24 we enter on the practical section of the Epistle, which, indeed, appears to begin in verse 1, but is broken in upon by the magnificent digression of the doctrinal summary of verses 4—16. It opens with a striking contrast of the past and the present—the life of the heathen in its "vanity," with the two-fold result of blindness and callousness of soul; and the Christian life, which has in learning Christ found the secret of regeneration.

(17) **This I say therefore.**—The phrase "This I say" seems to be used by St. Paul in returning (so to speak) from some lofty aspiration or profound reasoning, in which some might not be able to follow him, to a solid, practical ground, which all may tread. (See, for example, 1 Cor. xv. 50.) Here he is not content to use this phrase simply, but he enforces it by the solemnity of the adjuration "I testify" (comp. Acts xx. 26; Gal. v. 3), which properly means, "I call God to witness the truth of what I say"—a phrase found in express terms in Rom. i. 9; 2 Cor. i. 23; Phil. i. 8; 1 Thess. ii. 5. Nor was even this enough, for he adds "in the Lord"—that is, in the name, authority, and spirit of the Lord Jesus Christ Himself. The whole form is therefore one of peculiar force and solemnity.

The vanity of their mind.—In these words St. Paul describes the fundamental condition of heathenism. The "mind," that is (as in Rom. vii. 23, 25), the "inner man"—the spiritual intuition of invisible principles of truth and right, which is the true humanity—has become "subject to vanity" (Rom. viii. 20)—the vanity of which the Book of Ecclesiastes so often speaks. In losing the living conception of a living God, it has lost also the conception of the true object and perfection of human life; and so wanders on aimless, hopeless, reckless, as in a dream. With what absolute fidelity St. Paul describes the heathen world of his day, its history and its literature alike testify. Compare with the whole passage the picture drawn in Rom. i. 21—32, "They became vain in their imaginations, and their foolish heart was darkened," &c. The difference is that in the latter passage the prominent idea is mainly of "judicial blindness," sent by God as a penalty on wilful apostasy from Him, whereas here St. Paul rather dwells on self-chosen blindness and hardness of heart.

(18) **Having the understanding darkened.**—Of this vanity the first result noted is the intellectual. They are "darkened in the understanding," and so, "by the ignorance in them alienated from the life of God." The phrase "the life of God" is unique. It may, however, be interpreted by a similar phrase, the "righteousness of God" (Rom. i. 7), *i.e.*, the righteousness given by God. What the life given by God is, we know by our Lord's own words (John xvii. 3), "This is the life eternal, to know Thee the only true God, and Jesus Christ whom Thou has sent." So far as the understanding is concerned, this alienation signifies the loss of the central light of Truth in God, and with it the loss, partial or complete, of the vision of other truths in their right proportion and harmony.

But the second result is moral. St. Paul attributes the alienation from God, or (possibly, though less probably) "the ignorance which is in them," to *the hardness of their heart*—for the marginal reading is correct; the word used signifies, almost technically, "callousness"

that is in them, because of the blindness[1] of their heart:[a] (19) who being past feeling have given themselves over unto lasciviousness, to work all uncleanness with greediness. (20) But ye have not so learned Christ; (21) if so be that ye have heard him, and have been taught by him, as the truth is in Jesus: (22) that ye put off concerning the former conversation the old man,

1 Or, *hardness.*
a Rom. i. 21.

and insensibility. To make his meaning clearer still he adds, "who (or, *inasmuch as they*) being past feeling, have given themselves over to lasciviousness." There is precisely a similar current of thought (noting, however, the characteristic difference referred to above) in Rom. i. 24—32, where St. Paul draws out, as consequences of the same vanity, first lusts of uncleanness, next unnatural sin, and at last breaks out into a fearful enumeration of the signs of the reprobate mind. On this side, therefore, "the alienation from the life of God" is the loss of the grace by which He dwells in the soul, and by indwelling gives it the moral and spiritual life.

(19) **Who being past feeling . . .**—We note that St. Paul, passing lightly over the intellectual loss, dwells on the moral with intense and terrible emphasis. They are (he says) "past feeling"; or, literally, carrying on the metaphor of callousness, *they have lost the capacity of pain*—the moral pain which is the natural and healthful consequence of sin against our true natures. Consequently, losing in this their true humanity, they give themselves over to "lasciviousness." The word used here (as also in Mark vii. 22; Rom. xiii. 13; 2 Cor. xii. 21; Gal. v. 19) signifies a lust devoid of all sense of decency, recklessly and grossly animal. Hence its result is not only to work out uncleanness of every kind, but to do so "with greediness," with a reckless delight in foulness for its own sake. The union of this brutality of sensual sin with intellectual acuteness and æsthetic culture was the most horrible feature of that corrupt Greek civilisation, tainted with Oriental grossness, of which he was especially writing.

(20) **Ye have not so learned Christ.**—Better, *ye did not so learn the Christ.* To "learn Christ" is a phrase not used elsewhere; but easily interpreted by the commoner phrase to "know Christ" (see John xiv. 7, 9; 2 Cor. v. 16; Phil. iii. 10), which is still nearer to it in the original, for the word used for "to know" properly means to perceive or "come to know." It would seem that the name "the Christ" is here used emphatically, in distinction from the "Jesus" of the next verse. "To learn the Christ" is to enter into the true meaning of His office as the Anointed Priest, Prophet, and King, or, in one word, as the Mediator, in whom we as Christians escape from the guilt and bondage of the sins described above. Such learning—like the "knowing" of 2 Cor. v. 14—is not "after the flesh," by the mere hearing of the ear, but "after the Spirit," writing Christ upon the heart.

(21) **If so be that.**—The word is the same which is used in chap. iii. 2, Col. i. 23, indicating no real doubt, but only that rhetorical doubt which is strong affirmation.

Ye have heard him . . .—The true rendering here is, *ye heard Him, and were taught in Him.* St. Paul begins with the first means of knowledge, the "hearing" His voice, directly or through His ministers; and then proceeds to describe the fuller and more systematic process of "being taught," not "by Him" (as in our version), but "*in* Him," that is, in that unity with Him which embraces both teachers and taught as with an atmosphere of His presence.

As the truth is in Jesus.—Here by the name "Jesus," the personal and proper name of the Lord, St. Paul leads us on from the conception of "learning the Christ," to understand the method of that learning, in the knowledge of the "truth" in the person of Jesus Himself, who declares Himself to be the Truth (John xiv. 6). By a loving study and knowledge of His person, as set forth to us in the gospel, and brought home to us by His grace, rather than by abstract musing on the office and attributes of "the Christ," we come to learn the Christ also. The use of the simple name Jesus, so common in the Gospels, is rare indeed in the Epistles, where we constantly find the fuller description "Jesus Christ," "the Lord Jesus," "Jesus the Son of God." Wherever it occurs, it will be found to be distinctive or emphatic. This distinctiveness is most strikingly evident in Rom. viii. 11: "If the Spirit of Him who raised up Jesus from the dead dwell in you, He that raised up [the] Christ from the dead shall also quicken your mortal bodies." The "raising up of Jesus," is the historical resurrection of Jesus of Nazareth; the "raising up the Christ" points to the mysterious effect of that resurrection on those for whom He is the Mediator. Of the few other passages in which the simple name occurs, some (as Rom. iii. 26; 2 Cor. iv. 10, 11; 1 Thess. i. 10; Heb. x. 10) are mere reiterations of the name occurring above with the due title of honour; others are quasi-recitals of a creed declaring the historic Jesus (1 Cor. xii. 3; 1 Thess. iv. 14; comp. 2 Cor. xi. 4). In the Epistle to the Hebrews, where, in accordance with one main purpose of the Epistle, this usage is least rare (see chaps. ii. 9; vi. 20; vii. 22; xii. 2, 24; xiii. 12), it will be found that in all cases, either special stress is laid on the lowly and suffering humanity of the Lord, or the historic facts of His ministry on earth are referred to. The modern familiarity of use of the simple name "Jesus" has little authority in apostolic usage.

(22—24) These verses explain the substance of the teaching of verse 21. The original may be interpreted either of the teaching of a fact, "that ye did put off . . . and are being renewed," &c., or of a duty, "that ye put off . . . and be renewed." The latter is, on the whole, the more probable, although the former would yield a simpler sense. It is to be noted that the words "put off" and "put on" in the original denote a distinct and complete act; the word "be renewed," a continuous and still incomplete process. The complete act is consummated, and the continuous process begun, by the practical "learning" of Christ—that is, by growth in spiritual communion with Him.

(22) **Concerning the former conversation.**—So far, that is, as concerns the conversation or mode of life described above (verses 17—19) as the moral condition of heathenism. It is in relation to this, the corruption of the true humanity, and not in relation to the true humanity itself, that the "old man" is put off.

The phrase "the old man" (found also in Rom. vi. 6; Col. iii. 9) is here illustrated by the description following: *which is being marred in virtue of the lusts of deceit.* The word rendered "corrupt" expresses not so much pollution as disintegration and decay, much as in

which is corrupt according to the deceitful lusts; (23) and be renewed in the spirit of your mind; (24) and that ye put on the new man, which after God is created in righteousness and true holiness.[1] (25) Wherefore putting away lying,
speak every man truth with his neighbour: for we are members one of another. (26) Be ye angry, and sin not: let not the sun go down upon your wrath: (27) neither give

Chap. iv. 25—30. In respect of sins against man.

[1] Or, *holiness of truth.*

2 Cor. iv. 16; and so carries out the idea implied in the epithet "old." The unregenerate nature, subject to "the lusts of deceit"—the lusts, that is, of the spirit of delusion, blind themselves, and blinding the soul which yields to them—is gradually sinking into the spiritual decay which must become spiritual death, unless by the effort of faith, entering into the communion with Christ, it be, once for all, "put off." The various qualities of the nature thus stripped off are variously described: in Rom. xiii. 22, as the "works of darkness; in Heb. xii. 1, as simply "encumbrance;" in Jas. i. 21, as "filthiness and excess of evil;" in 1 Pet. ii. 1, as "malice, and craft, and hypocrisies, and envies." All these are the "lusts of deceit."

(23) **And be renewed in the spirit of your mind.**—The word translated "renewed" is not the same as the word "new" below. It is properly "to be made young again," and the process of recovery is described as the natural effect of putting off the decrepitude of the old man, and the decay engendered by fleshly lusts. The effect is seen in "the spirit of the mind"—that is, "in the spiritual nature of the inner man." The "spirit" of man is the mind or inner man, considered in its true relation as quickened and sustained by the Spirit of God. (See Rom. viii., and especially verse 16.) We note, in Col. ii. 18, the opposite condition of "the mind of the flesh," in those who do not "hold the Head." This spirit is spoken of as regaining its undying youth, as it were, naturally, when "the muddy vesture of decay" is cast off.

(24) **And that ye put on . . .**—But this effect of "the putting off of the old man" is at once absorbed in the stronger idea of "putting on the new man." In the "new man" here is implied not merely youthfulness, but the freshness of a higher nature (as in chap. ii. 15). To "put on the new man" is, therefore, to "put on the Lord Jesus Christ," by that divine process of which we have the beginning in Gal. iii. 27, the continuation in Rom. xiii. 14, and the completion in 1 Cor. xv. 53, 54; 2 Cor. v. 3. For He is "the new man," "the second Adam," "formed after God, in righteousness and holiness of the truth."

Holiness (used only here and in Luke i. 75) is "purity" consecrated to God in His "Holy One" (Acts ii. 27). It describes the "purity of heart" of which our Lord Himself speaks as a still higher grace, gifted with a higher reward, than even "hunger and thirst after righteousness" (Matt. v. 6, 8). "Righteousness" is goodness shown to others, to man and to God: "holiness" is goodness in itself, as it is in "the High and Holy One who inhabiteth eternity." Stress is laid upon it here in contrast with the lusts and uncleanness described above.

Truth is similarly opposed to the "deceit" of verse 22. Christ is Himself "the Truth," as being the manifestation of "the fulness of the Godhead." As the corrupting and beguiling lusts belong to the spirit of Deceit, so righteousness and holiness to the Truth.

(2) From this general description of the regeneration of the soul out of the death of sin, in the Lord Jesus Christ, St. Paul now passes on to deal with special moral duties (verses 25—30)—the casting out of falsehood, wrath, dishonesty, and impurity, which are the four typical sins forbidden in the four general Commandments of the Second Table—the Ninth, the Sixth, the Eighth, and the Seventh. But he treats all with a marked and striking peculiarity of treatment—in relation to the great principle of unity in Christ, rather than in relation to a man's own nature or his individual responsibility to God. In this treatment he shows the vivid practical application of the characteristic doctrine of this Epistle.

(25) **For we are members.**—Accordingly the reason given for "putting away lying" is that "we are members one of another." Truth is the first condition of the mutual confidence which is the basis of all unity. Hence it is the first duty of that "membership one of another," which follows from our being "one body in Christ" (Rom. xii. 5; 1 Cor. xii. 27). No doubt it is also the first duty to our own humanity, and to the God "who hateth a lie." But these views, though true in themselves, would not be relevant to St. Paul's great subject here.

(26) **Be ye angry, and sin not.**—A quotation from the LXX. version of Ps. iv. 4. Anger itself is not sin, for our Lord Himself felt it (Mark iii. 5) at the "hardness of men's hearts;" and it is again and again attributed to God Himself, in language no doubt of human accommodation, but, of course, accommodation to what is sinless in humanity. In the form of resentment, and above all of the resentment of righteous indignation, it performs (as Butler has shown in his sermon on "Resentment") a stimulating and inspiring function in the strife against evil. But it is a dangerous and exceptional weapon: and hence the exhortation "sin not," and the practical enforcement of that exhortation in the next clause.

Let not the sun go down upon your wrath.—In this command (for which a Pythagorean parallel may be found) St. Paul gives a two-fold safeguard against abuse of even righteous anger. (1) It is not to be prolonged beyond the sunset—beyond the sleep which ends the old day and leads in the freshness of the new, and which by any godly man must be prepared for in commendation of himself to God, and in prayer for His forgiveness, "as we forgive those who trespass against us." (2) It is not to be brooded over and stimulated; for the word "wrath" is properly *self-exasperation,* being similar to the "contention" of Acts xv. 30, described as alien to the spirit of love in 1 Cor. xiii. 5. It is that "nursing of wrath to keep it warm," which can be checked even by those who cannot control the first outburst, and which constantly corrupts righteous indignation into selfish personal anger, if not into malignity.

(27) **Neither give place** (*i.e., scope*) **to the devil.**—The name "Devil" is used by St. Paul only in his later Epistles (see chap. vi. 11; 1 Tim. iii. 6, 7; vi. 9; 2 Tim. ii. 26; Tit. ii. 3); in the earlier Epistles (Rom. xvi. 20; 1 Cor. v. 5; vii. 5; 2 Cor. ii. 11; xi. 14; xii.

place to the devil. (28) Let him that stole
steal no more: but rather let him labour,
working with *his* hands the thing which
is good, that he may have to give[1] to him
that needeth. (29) Let no corrupt com-
munication proceed out of your mouth,
but that which is good to the use of
edifying,[2] that it may minister grace
unto the hearers. (30) And grieve not
the holy Spirit of God, whereby ye
are sealed unto the day of redemp-
tion. (31) Let all bitterness, and
wrath, and anger, and
clamour, and evil speak-
ing, be put away from
you, with all malice:

Chap. iv. 31—v. 2. Special warning against bitterness.

1 Or, *to distribute.*

2 Or, *to edify profitably.*

7; 1 Thess. ii. 18; 2 Thess. ii. 9) we have the name "Satan," which is also found, less frequently, in the later also (1 Tim. i. 20; v. 15). The latter name simply describes him as "the enemy"; the former describes one method of his enmity (as "the Tempter" another), for it signifies "one who sets at variance," man with God, and man with man. Since this fiendish work is mostly contemplated as wrought by slander, the name is commonly taken to mean "the slanderer;" and when applied to human beings (as in 1 Tim. iii. 11; 2 Tim. iii. 3; Tit. ii. 3) it seems to convey some such meaning. But here the original sense suits the distinctive idea of the passage. In accordance with the general principle noted above, excess of wrath is forbidden, as giving opportunity to the enemy, who desires to break up unity, and "set at variance" those who should be one in Jesus Christ.

(28) **Let him that stole** (properly, *the stealer*) **steal no more . . . .**—In this verse St. Paul treats dishonesty, virtually, although less distinctly, from the same point of view as before. For he is not content with forbidding it, or even with forbidding it as fatal to society; but he directs that it be superseded by the opposite spirit of self-sacrifice, working in order to give to others what is honestly our own, as the fruit of the labour of "our own hands." In that direction there is a profound wisdom, in striking at the root of that exclusive selfishness which so often and so naturally exhibits itself in dishonesty. But we note in it also a peculiar harmony with the great doctrine of unity; for the sense of unity will always exhibit itself in working what is "good," that is, *gracious*, for the sake of "him that needs."

(29) **Let no corrupt communication . . .**—The word rendered "corrupt," is a strong word, signifying "rotten"; used in Matt. vii. 17, 18, and elsewhere in the literal sense, here alone in the metaphorical. By the corrupt word, probably, here is meant especially the foul word, which is rotten in itself, and spreads rottenness in others.

The use of edifying.—This is a mistranslation, by inversion, of a difficult expression, "the building up of the need"—that is, the supplying by suggestion of good the peculiar "need" or defect of the hearer's spiritual state. Perhaps, as before, the word "good" may be taken for *gracious* and full of sympathy, noting by the quick insight of love what each man's need is, and hastening to speak accordingly, so as to "give grace" or blessing to meet that peculiar need. The same use of the word "grace" is found in 2 Cor. i. 15 ("that ye might have a second benefit"). The same idea is found in 1 Thess. iii. 10, "to perfect that which is lacking in your faith."

Here again we have a similar treatment of moral duty. The corrupt word is forbidden, not because it defiles the speaker's own soul, and is an offence in the pure eyes of God, but because it is a sin against others, pulling down instead of building them up, and aggravating, instead of supplying, their moral defects. Like the falsehood, and wrath, and dishonesty, forbidden above, it sins against the unity of all in God.

(30) **And grieve not the holy Spirit.**—This verse refers to all the practical commands given above. The four cardinal sins forbidden are regarded as "grieving the Holy Spirit of God." In that expression, even more than in the cognate expressions of "quenching the Spirit" (1 Thess. v. 19), and "resisting the Holy Ghost" (Acts vii. 51), there is implied a personal relation to a Divine Person, capable of being "grieved" by our transgressions, partly as sins against His perfect holiness, partly as suicidal rejections of His unfailing love. In the description of this effect of sin we have the needful complement to the view hitherto taken of its effect, as marring our unity with men; for that unity is always in God, through the Holy Spirit working out in each soul the image of Christ. "There is one Body" only because "there is one Spirit." Sin vexes the one, but grieves the other.

Whereby ye are sealed.—Properly, *in whom ye were sealed.* See the fuller expression of the same truth in chap. i. 13, 14, and the Notes there. The reference to it is here emphatic. The "sealing unto the day of redemption" reminds us of the glorious consummation to which we are destined, and from which every sin is a falling off. The very thought of this perfection, with all its associations of purity and love, should shame us from sin.

This general exhortation seems fitly to close the warning against the series of typical sins, which is itself exhaustive of the general sins against men. In the passage which follows (chap. iv. 31—v. 21) St. Paul does not indeed traverse new ground, but dwells with special emphasis on some of these sins, which especially beset the society to which he wrote, viz.: (in chap. iv. 31—v. 2) bitterness, (in chap. v. 3—14) impurity, (in chap. v. 15—21) reckless excess.

(3*a*) In chap. iv. 31—v. 2, he deals with malignity, as utterly unworthy of the love of God manifested to us in Jesus Christ.

(31) **Let all bitterness.**—There is a similar enumeration in the parallel passage, Col. iii. 8; and in all such catalogues in St. Paul's Epistles, while it is vain to seek for formal and elaborate system, there is always profound method and connection of idea. Here the first symptom of the temper forbidden is "bitterness," or *sharpness*—a word seldom used, and generally in half-poetical passages (see Acts viii. 23; Rom. iii. 14; Heb. xii. 15)—that is, an acerbity of temper, ready to take offence and break out in anger. The next stage is "wrath and anger," that is, passionate outburst, and the deeper anger of which it is at once effect and cause. (Comp. Rom. ii. 8; Col. iii. 8; Rev. xix. 15.) In these the smouldering bitterness kindles into flame. The last stage is "clamour and evil speaking"—"clamour"

(32) and be ye kind one to another,[a] tenderhearted, forgiving one another, even as God for Christ's sake hath forgiven you.

CHAPTER V.—(1) Be ye therefore followers of God, as dear children;
(2) and walk in love, as Christ also hath loved us, and hath given himself for us an offering and a sacrifice to God for a sweet-smelling savour. (3) But fornication, and all uncleanness, or covetousness, let it not be once named among you, as

[a] 2 Cor. 2. 10.

A.D. 64.

Chap. v. 3—5. Special warning against lusts.

(used in this sense only here) being the loud fury of the first burst of wrath, passing into the more deliberate evil-speaking, as the temper cools down without losing its settled anger.

With all malice.—All are various exhibitions of "malice"—that is, evil mindedness or malignity—the general disposition which is the opposite of goodness, graciousness, and sympathy. (Comp. Rom. i. 29; 1 Cor. v. 8; xiv. 20; Jas. i. 21; 1 Pet. ii. 1.) By the law of human nature they rise out of this temper, and react upon it so as to intensify its bitterness. Both it generally, and they in particular, must be resisted and cast out.

(32) **Kind . . . tenderhearted.**—"Kindness" is gentleness in bearing with wrong (Luke vi. 35; Rom. xi. 22; Eph. ii. 7; 1 Pet. ii. 3). "Tenderheartedness" (see 1 Pet. iii. 8) is more positive warmth of sympathy and love. Both issue in free "forgiveness," after the model of the universal and unfailing forgiveness "of God in Christ" to us—the only model we dare to follow, suggested by our Saviour Himself in the Lord's Prayer, and expressly enjoined in Luke vi. 36. It is a forgiveness which in us, as in Him, does not imply condonation of evil, or even the withholding of needful chastisement, but which absolutely ignores self, conquers man's selfish anger, and knows no limit, even up to "seventy times seven."

V.

(1, 2) These verses are an expansion and enforcement of the last verse of chap. iv. There the forgiveness of "God in Christ" is set forth in one pregnant phrase. Here the two parts of this idea are divided; and there is put before us, first, the free universal love of God as our Father, and next, the self-sacrificing love of Christ, as the Son of God and man.

(1) **Followers of God.**—The phrase is unique and very striking; literally, *imitators of God:* and the word "therefore" implies that this imitation of God must be chiefly in His essential attribute of love. It is instructive to observe that our Lord's startling command, "Be ye therefore perfect, as your Father in heaven is perfect" (Matt. v. 48), is explained both by the context and the parallel passage in St. Luke (chap. vi. 36) to mean, "Be ye therefore merciful, as your Father in heaven is merciful." See in Hooker's *Ecc. Pol.*, i. 5, a striking passage on the imitation of God as the law of all moral progress in man. In this idea, indeed, lies the essential and distinctive principle of a religious morality as such.

As dear children.—Literally, *as children beloved* of Him. The knowledge of the love of God to us is the first source, as of our love to Him (1 John iv. 19), so also of our love to men as brethren under His fatherhood (1 John iv. 11). As being His "children," and therefore partakers of the divine nature (2 Pet. i. 4), we can imitate Him; as His "beloved children" we imitate Him most naturally in love, and especially in that form of love which we call "mercy," and which, as being ourselves sinners, we especially crave and receive from Him.

(2) **As Christ also hath loved us.**—To this idea of the "imitation of God," essential to all true religion, St. Paul now adds an exhortation to follow the example of our Lord Jesus Christ, in that especial exhibition of love by suffering and self-sacrifice, which is impossible to the Godhead in itself, but which belongs to the incarnate Son of God, and was the ultimate purpose of His incarnation. There is a similar connection of idea in John xv. 12, 13, "This is My commandment, That ye love one another, as I have loved you. Greater love hath no man than this, that a man lay down his life for his friends." The imitation of God is in free and natural beneficence; the imitation of Christ is in that power of showing mercy, which is bought by suffering and sacrifice. He not only "loved us," but "gave Himself for us."

An offering and a sacrifice to God.—The same words, "sacrifice and offering," are found in close connection in Heb. x. 5, which is a quotation from Ps. xl. 7. Comparing these with the Hebrew words which they represent, and looking also to the etymology of the Greek words themselves, we see that the word "offering" signifies simply a gift offered to God, and is applied especially, though not exclusively, to unbloody sacrifices; while the word "sacrifice" distinctly implies the shedding of blood. Each word, when used alone, has constantly a more general sense. Thus "offering" is used in Heb. x. 10, 14, 18, for the sacrifice on the cross; while "sacrifice," in Acts vii. 42, is made to translate the word commonly rendered as "offering." But when placed in juxtaposition they must be held distinctive; and hence we may conclude that our Lord made Himself "an offering" in the perfect obedience of His great humility, "coming to do God's will" (according to the prophetic anticipation of Ps. xl. 7, 8), and gave Himself a "sacrifice," when He completed that offering by shedding His blood on the cross. Both are said to be offered "for us," *i.e.*, on our behalf. We have, therefore, here a complete summary—all the more striking and characteristic because incidental—of the doctrine of the Atonement.

For a sweet-smelling savour.—The sense of this phrase is explained in Phil. iv. 18 by the addition of the words "a sacrifice acceptable, well-pleasing to God." It is the translation of an expression, frequent in the Old Testament (as in Gen. viii. 21; Ex. xxix. 18; *et al.*), signifying "a smell of acquiescence" or "satisfaction." It describes the atoning sacrifice as already accepted by God.

(3*b*) Verses 3—14 warn, with even greater fulness and emphasis, against the sins of impurity and lust, as incompatible with membership of the kingdom of heaven, as works of darkness, impossible to those who are children of light.

(3) **But fornication, and all uncleanness, or**

becometh saints; (4) neither filthiness,
nor foolish talking, nor jesting, which
are not convenient: but rather
giving of thanks. (5) For this ye
know, that no whoremonger, nor
unclean person, nor covetous man, who
is an idolater, hath any inheritance in
the kingdom of Christ and of God.
(6) Let no man deceive you with vain
words: for because of these
things cometh the wrath
of God upon the children
of disobedience.[1] (7) Be
not ye therefore partakers

Chap. v. 6—21. As a work of darkness, unworthy of Christian light.

1 Or, *unbelief.*

covetousness.—"Fornication" is closely joined (as in 2 Cor. xii. 21; Gal. v. 19; Col. iii. 5) with "uncleanness," of which general sin it is a flagrant species. It is distinguished (as also in Col. iii. 5) from "covetousness," or *greediness.* "Uncleanness" is a sin against our own body and soul (see 1 Cor. vi. 18); "covetousness" (literally, *the insatiable desire for more*) is a sin against our neighbour. At the same time, the constant connection of the two words suggests the truth which is conveyed by the union of the two kinds of "coveting" in the Tenth Commandment, viz., that the temper of selfish and unbridled concupiscence has a two-fold direction—to the covetousness of lust, and to the covetousness of avarice—the one perhaps especially a vice of youth, and the other of old age.

(4) **Neither filthiness, nor foolish talking, nor jesting.**—The word "filthiness" (unlike the "filthy communication" of the parallel passage in Col. iii. 8) is in itself a general word. But the connection with the words following, and the distinction from those going before, appear to show that St. Paul here uses it for "filthy talking." He is passing from impurity of the inward soul to impurity in outward expression. Of such foul speaking he appears to distinguish two forms. There is, first of all, "foolish talking," or the talk of "the fool," in the worst sense in which that word is used in Scripture (Matt. v. 22; xxiii. 17), as implying something worse than mere emptiness or blindness—describing the condition of the soul which has "lost its savour" (Matt. v. 13), *i.e.*, has ceased to distinguish what is right or wrong, wise or foolish, noble or base. There is then "jesting," *i.e.*, properly, the more polished "versatility," which will find occasion for wit or levity in anything, however sacred, fearing nothing so much as to be dull, and mistaking all seriousness and reserve for dulness. It is notable that in classical Greek the word is sometimes used in a good sense, as a mean between "churlishness" and "obsequiousness," but yet hovers on the border of that condemnation which Christian gravity here pronounces unhesitatingly. The former kind of foul talking is coarse and brutal; the latter refined and deadly. Of both kinds Greek and Roman literature furnish specimens only too many and too striking.

Which are not convenient.—That is, "which are out of character" in a Christian—a milder repetition (perhaps suggested by the ambiguous meaning of "jesting" noted above) of the indignant declaration in verse 3, that it "becomes not saints that these foul things should be even named among them." They pollute the Christian mind and tongue even in condemning them.

But rather giving of thanks.—The opposition is striking. "The foolish talking and jesting" aim at mirth and play of mind; St. Paul will not austerely condemn such light-heartedness, but he finds a wholesome and spiritual vent for it in the habitual expression of thankfulness to God, which proceeds from a natural and childlike cheerfulness. Exactly in the same spirit below (verses 18—20) he contrasts the excitement of drunkenness with the being "filled with the Spirit . . . giving thanks always for all things."

(5) **For this ye know.**—The true reading of the original is curiously emphatic. It runs thus: *For this ye know, knowing* . . . But, as it uses two different words, in the former clause properly "ye know" and the latter "learning to know," the sense seems to be: "For this ye know, learning it afresh so as to know it better." Whatever else is doubtful, this is certain; yet it admits of an ever growing certainty.

Covetous man, who is an idolater.—Comp. Col. iii. 5, "Covetousness, which is idolatry." Whatever becomes the chief object of our desire, so as to claim our chief fear and love, is, of course, an idol; for "ye cannot serve God and mammon." Perhaps in this metaphorical idolatry, as in the literal, there are two distinct stages, passing, however, by invisible gradations into each other—first, the resting on some visible blessing of God, as the one thing in which and for which we serve Him, and so by degrees losing Him in His own gifts; next, the absolute forgetfulness of Him, and the setting up, as is inevitable, of some other object of worship to fill the vacant throne.

Hath any inheritance in the kingdom of Christ and [of] God.—The phrase "the kingdom of Christ and God," though probably it does not in strict technicality declare the identity of "Christ" and "God," yet implies that the "kingdom of the Christ" is, as a matter of course, "the kingdom of God," for "the Christ" is by prophetic definition "Emmanuel," *i.e.*, "God with us." The unworthy Christian has indeed "an inheritance" in it, to his own awful responsibility; but in the true spiritual sense he is one "who hath not," "from whom shall be taken that which he hath" (Matt. xiii. 12).

(6) **Let no man deceive you with vain words.**—It seems likely that St. Paul has in view, not mere worldly condonation of evil or low heathen morality, but some anticipation of that Antinomian form of Gnosticism which held that the things done in the body, being evil only by the irresistible, inevitable gravitation of matter to evil, could not touch the soul. We know that in the Colossian Church there was an anticipation of the more ascetic Gnosticism (Col. ii. 21; comp. also 1 Tim. iv. 1—5). As the earlier Judaistic rigour had assumed this later form, so the earlier Antinomianism (of Rom. vi. 1) may probably have passed into the more systematic and speculative Antinomianism of the Gnostic type. (Comp. Phil. iii. 18, 19.) In this same spirit St. John, himself familiar with the life of Ephesus, writes earnestly: "Let no man deceive you; he that doeth righteousness is righteous" (1 John iii. 7). Here the Apostle warns them that it is for these sins that "the wrath of God is coming on the children of disobedience," *i.e.* (see chap. ii. 2), on the heathen; and urges the Christians not to fall back, by being "partakers with them" both of their sin and their punishment, into the gross heathen darkness out of which they had been saved.

with them. (8) For ye were sometimes
darkness, but now *are ye* light in the
Lord: walk as children of light:
(9) (for the fruit of the Spirit *is* in all
goodness and righteousness and truth;)
(10) proving what is acceptable unto
the Lord. (11) And have no fellowship
with the unfruitful works of darkness,
but rather reprove *them.* (12) For it
is a shame even to speak of those
things which are done of them in
secret. (13) But all things that are re-

(8) **Ye were sometimes darkness, but now are ye light in the Lord.**—This expression is unique, and far more emphatic than the more common phrases of "being," or "walking," "in darkness" and "in light." (See Rom. ii. 9; Col. i. 2; 1 Thess. v. 4; 1 John i. 6, 7; ii. 9, 10.) For here the outward element of light or darkness is said to pervade the inner nature of the soul. (1) Christ is the "true Light," the "Sun of Righteousness" (John i. 4—9; iii. 19; viii. 12; ix. 5; xii. 46). His servants are sometimes mere secondary lights (or "candles") (Luke xi. 33, 34, 36; John v. 35; 2 Pet. i. 19), kindled from His rays; sometimes, like the moon or planets, they are said, as reflecting His light, or as having His light in them (John xii. 35), to be actually "the light of the world" (Matt. v. 14), which, however, shines as a mere reflected light, so that "men glorify" not it, but "the Father which is in heaven" (Matt. v. 16). They thus become light, but only "in the Lord:" that is, as being made one with Him. (2) So, on the other hand, they who walk in darkness are said to be themselves darkness—new sources, so to speak, of the darkness which hates and quenches light, both to themselves and to others. "The light" which is in them "becomes darkness;" "and how great is that darkness!" (Matt. vi. 23.) As there is a natural delight in giving light, so the reprobate state is distinguished by a horrible pleasure in spreading the cloud of delusion, sin, or unbelief, by which to hide God from man.

Walk as children of light.—So our Lord teaches, "While ye have the light, believe in the light, that ye may become children of light" (John xii. 36; comp. 1 Thess. v. 5). "Children of light" are they who not only love the light, but also manifest the likeness of the one true Light, "the Father of Lights" (Jas. i. 17), being His children in Jesus Christ.

(9) **For the fruit . . .**—The true reading is, *of the Light,* for which the easier phrase, "the fruit of the Spirit," has been substituted, to the great detriment of the force and coherency of the whole passage. Light has its fruits; darkness (see verse 11) is "unfruitful." The metaphor is striking, but literally correct, inasmuch as light is the necessary condition of that vegetative life which grows and yields fruit, while darkness is the destruction, if not of life, at any rate of fruit-bearing perfection.

Goodness and righteousness and truth.—These are practical exhibitions of the "being true in love," described in chap. iv. 15 as the characteristic of the Christ-like soul. For "goodness" is love in practical benevolence, forming, in Gal. v. 22, a climax to "longsuffering" and "kindness," and, in 2 Thess. i. 11, distinguished as practical from the "faith" which underlies practice. The other two qualities, "righteousness" and "truth"—that is, probably, truthfulness—are both parts of the great principle of "being true."

(10) **Proving what is acceptable unto the Lord.**—So in Rom. xii. 2, the "proving what is the good and acceptable and perfect will of God," is the fruit of transformation "in the renewing of the mind." "To prove" is to try in each case, by the full light of God, what is accordant to His will; it is a work partly of thought, partly of practical experience; and it always implies a searching examination of heart and action by the touchstone of God's word.

(11) **Have no fellowship with the unfruitful works of darkness.**—To "have no fellowship" with such works is not to refuse to take part in them (for this surely might be taken for granted), but to keep no terms with them, to have no sympathy or indulgence or excuse for them. So the word is used, in Phil. iv. 14, of "communicating with my affliction;" and in Rev. xviii. 4, of "being partakers with the sins" of Babylon. It is through such weak or cowardly indulgence, more than the actual love of evil, that sin is suffered to prevail. Hence St. Paul adds, "rather reprove them." Our Lord Himself has declared in all such cases, "He that is not with Me is against Me."

The unfruitful works of darkness.—St. Paul has a similar antithesis in the Epistle to the Romans (chap. vi. 19—22). They who are in sin "yield their members servants to iniquity unto iniquity." Iniquity has no result but iniquity; and hence he goes on to ask, "What fruit had ye then in those things of which ye are now ashamed?" This weary fruitlessness is at once the sign and the penalty of sin, so that men have fancied it to be one chief element of the suffering of the lost. But they who are in Christ "yield their members servants to righteousness unto holiness." "They have," he says, "their fruit unto holiness" now, and "in the end the everlasting life," which is everlasting holiness. Similarly, in Gal. v. 20—22, we have "the works of the flesh," but "the fruit of the Spirit." Rarely, indeed, does Scripture speak of "evil fruit" (Matt. vii. 17; xii. 33). Generally, "to be unfruitful" is an all-sufficient condemnation: "Every branch that beareth not fruit he taketh away" (John xv. 2).

Rather reprove them.—In the word "reprove," whether in its application to the witness of the Holy Ghost (John xvi. 8), or to the witness of men (as in 1 Cor. xiv. 24; 1 Tim. v. 20; Tit. i. 9—13, *et al.*), there is described a double function—to "convince," if it may be, the sinner in himself; to "convict" him, if the other function fails, before men and angels. Both these functions St. Paul urges here. It is not enough to "have no fellowship with them." To this tacit reproof open reproof in word and deed is to be added; only in such reproof it should be remembered that it would be disgraceful "even to speak" in detail of the actual "things done in secret."

(12) **It is a shame even to speak . . .**—Comp. verse 3. Sin may be plainly indicated, and perhaps most effectually branded, without polluting the tongue by describing its actual developments. The need of St. Paul's caution is only too obvious when we read some satires and denunciations against sin, or some manuals of self-examination.

(13) **But all things that are reproved are made manifest by the light.**—This should properly be rendered, *But all things, when reproved, are illuminated by the light.* The translation "are made manifest" is indeed fully in accordance with the common usage of

proved[1] are made manifest by the light: for whatsoever doth make manifest is light. (14) Wherefore he saith, Awake thou that sleepest, and arise from the dead, and Christ shall give thee light.[a] (15) See then that ye walk circumspectly,[b]

1 Or, *discovered.*

a Isa. 60. 1.

b Col. 4. 5.

---

the word. But the whole context shows that St. Paul is here using it in what is indeed its more proper etymological sense, for "are illumined." For the mere "being made manifest" is implied in the "being reproved;" whereas he is certainly passing on here to a fresh idea, and, moreover, to one which will bear the inference of the last clause of the verse. To "reprove" after the Christian manner is to bring into the full light of Christ's truth; and the effect of this is not merely to reprove, but to illumine by the inherent power of the light. Exactly with the same distinction of sense St. John uses both words (John iii. 20, 21).

For whatsoever doth make manifest is light.—That this translation (suggested, perhaps, by the difficulty of the passage when rightly rendered) is nevertheless certainly wrong, is shown both by the usage of the original word and by the genius of the whole context. It should be, *for everything which is illuminated is light.* St. Paul here explains still more clearly what he means by illumination. It implies the catching the light and reflecting it, so as to become a new source of light. It must be noted that the subject of the sentence is not "the works of darkness," but "all things" in general. Hence the whole process is described, with almost scientific accuracy, as three-fold. First, the things, or persons, are dragged out of darkness into light; then they are illuminated; lastly, they become light in themselves and to others. There are, no doubt, exceptions to this, the right and normal process, in the case of the utterly reprobate, who have lost all power of reflecting light, and are therefore dark still in the blaze of noon; but the next verse shows that St. Paul is not contemplating these; and even these may be beacons of warning to others. The whole metaphor is more and more striking to us as modern science enlarges our knowledge of the manifold effects of light, not only to illuminate, but to change and to vivify.

(14) **Wherefore he** (or, *it*) **saith.**—This phrase is used (as also in Jas. iv. 6) in chap. iv. 8 to introduce a scriptural quotation; and the most natural completion of the elliptical expression is by the supply of the nominative, "God," or "the scripture," from the ordinary phrase of quotation or citation. But no scriptural passage can be adduced which, with the fullest allowance for the apostolic freedom of quotation, comes near enough to be a satisfactory original of this passage. The nearest is Isa. lx. 1, "Arise, shine; for thy light is come, and the glory of the Lord is risen upon thee;" and this is certainly very far off indeed. Nor is the case much helped by blending other passages (as, for example, Isa. xxvi. 19) with this. Some additional verbal coincidences may be gained, but at the expense of still greater diversity from the spirit of the passage as a whole. Hence we are driven to conclude that the quotation is not from Holy Scripture. Yet the very form shows that it is from something well known. An apocryphal quotation is imagined by some, but with no knowledge of any quotation at all resembling it. Others have supposed it a traditional saying of our Lord (like Acts xx. 35); but the form seems decisive against this. On the whole, it seems most likely that it is from some well-known Christian hymn. In the original a rhythmical character, rough, but by no means indistinct, strikes us at once. The growth of defined and formal expressions—mostly, it is true, of embryo creeds of Christian faith, as in 1 Cor. xv. 3, 4; Heb. vi. 1, 2; 1 Tim. iii. 16, in the last of which the acknowledged difficulty of etymological construction in the true reading may perhaps be best explained by the supposition of quotation—is notable in the later Epistles, and especially in the "faithful sayings" of the Pastoral Epistles. The use of some liturgical forms is traced with high probability to a very early date. The embodiment of popular faith in hymns, always natural, was peculiarly natural as adapted to the imperfect education of many early converts, and to the practice of trusting so much to memory, and so comparatively little to writing. Some such usage certainly appears to be referred to in the celebrated letter of Pliny to Trajan, the first heathen description of Christian worship.

Awake, thou that sleepest, and arise from the dead.—The word "awake" is used in our version to render two different words: one which properly means "to wake," or "be awake," or "watch," as in 1 Cor. xv. 34; 1 Thess. v. 6, 8; 2 Tim. iv. 5; 1 Pet. i. 12; iv. 7; v. 8); the other, as here, which properly means "Up!" "Rouse thyself!" preparatory to "arising" and coming forth. The exhortation in both forms is common enough (see especially the famous passage in Rom. xiii. 11—14); but the following words, "Arise from the dead," are a bold and unique exhortation. Generally we are said to be raised up from the death of sin by God, as in Rom. viii. 11, "He that raised up Christ from the dead shall quicken your mortal bodies;" or Rom. vi. 11, "Reckon yourselves to be dead unto sin, but alive unto God;" or Col. iii. 1, "If ye are risen in Christ." Here the soul is described as hearing the Saviour's call, "Come forth," and as itself rising at that call from the grave. If distinction between the two clauses is to be drawn, we may be rightly said to "awake" out of lethargy and carelessness, and to "arise" out of the deadness of sin.

Christ shall give thee light.—Properly, *Christ shall dawn upon thee.* The word is virtually the same which is used for the literal dawn in Matt. xxviii. 1, Luke xxiii. 54. The same idea is strikingly enunciated in 2 Pet. i. 19, where prophecy, looking forward to Christ, is compared to "a light shining in a dark place," "till the day dawn, and the Day-star arise in your hearts"—He, that is, who is "the bright and morning star" (Rev. xxii. 16). Christ, as the "Day-star," or as the "Sun of Righteousness," is already risen. The soul needs only to come out of the darkness of the grave, and the new rays shine down upon it, till (see verse 7) they pervade it and transfigure it into light.

(3 c.) In verses 15—21 the Apostle passes from lust and impurity to the cognate spirit of reckless levity, and the love of excitement, of which drunkenness is the commonest expression. He opposes to this the united forces of soberness and sacred enthusiasm, each tempering and yet strengthening the other.

(15) **See then that ye walk** (properly, *how ye walk*) **circumspectly.**—The word rendered "circumspectly" is properly *strictly*, or *accurately*—generally used of intellectual accuracy or thoroughness (as in Matt. ii. 8; Luke i. 3; Acts xviii. 25, 28; 1 Thess. v. 2); only here and in Acts xxvi. 5 ("the straitest sect

not as fools, but as wise, (16) redeeming the time, because the days are evil. (17) Wherefore be ye not unwise, but understanding what the will of the Lord *is.* **(18) And be not drunk with wine, wherein is excess; but be filled with the Spirit; (19) speaking to yourselves in psalms and hymns and spiritual songs,**

of our religion") of moral strictness. The idea, therefore, is not of looking round watchfully against dangers, but of "seeing," that is, being careful, "how we walk strictly;" of finding out the clear line of right, and then keeping to it strictly, so as not "to run uncertainly." In the corresponding passage in the Colossian Epistle (Col. iv. 5) a similar admonition has especial reference "to those without," and bids us have a resolute unity of aim, a distinct religious profession, amidst all the bewildering temptations of the world. Here it is more general; it bids men not to trust wholly to general rightness of heart, in which "the spirit is willing," but to be watchful over themselves, and to be a law to themselves, "because the flesh is weak."

Not as fools, but as wise.—This still further explains the "strictness," for "wisdom" is the practical knowledge of the true end and purpose of life. (See above, chap. i. 8.) He who has it not, whatever his intellectual and spiritual gifts, is "unwise."

(16) **Redeeming the time.**—Or rather, *the opportunity*, whenever it arises. The meaning of this phrase (used also in Col. iv. 5) is clearly illustrated by its use (although in a bad sense) in Dan. ii. 8, "I know that you would gain the time"—*i.e.*, catch the opportunity to escape from difficulty. To "redeem" is "to buy up for oneself"—not having essentially the idea of ransom or redemption, which attaches to the use of the word in Gal. iii. 13, iv. 5, only from the nature of the context. As applied to opportunity, it carries with it the idea, first of making sacrifice for it, then quickness in seizing it, and sagacity in using it to the utmost, whether by silence or by speech, by facing or avoiding danger, by yielding to a crisis (see Rom. xii. 11) or conquering it. The reason given that "the days are evil" must be taken in the widest sense, of all that induces temptation to swerve out of the "strictness" of the right way. The general lesson is that which is drawn by our Lord in the parable of the Unjust Steward—to apply the wisdom of the buyers and sellers of the world to the work of "the children of light."

(17) **Be ye not unwise.**—The word here is stronger than in verse 15; it is properly *senseless*, used of "the fool" (in Luke xi. 40; xii. 20; 1 Cor. xv. 36; 2 Cor. xi. 16, 19; xii. 6, 11). By it St. Paul emphasises his previous warning; then he adds the explanation that to be "wise" is to "understand what the will of the Lord is"—to know His purpose towards us and towards the world, and so to know the true purpose of our life. Hence we are told in Job xxviii. 28, that "the fear of the Lord is wisdom," or, more precisely, in Prov. ix. 10, that it is "the beginning of wisdom."

(18) **Be not drunk with wine, wherein is excess.**—From the general idea of reckless levity, St. Paul passes on to the special sin of drunkenness, as not (like gluttony) primarily a gratification of the appetite, but as a reckless pursuit of excitement at all costs—glorified as an excitement of emotion, and even of wit and intellect, in such contemporary writers as Horace, and actually confused, as in the Dionysiac or Bacchanalian frenzy, with a divine inspiration. How necessary the admonition was we see by the directions as to the choice of clergy in the Pastoral Epistles (1 Tim. iii. 28; Tit. i. 7; ii. 3); the more necessary, because (as 1 Tim. v. 23 shows) the right use of wine was recognised. Hence St. Paul emphatically brands drunkenness as "excess," a word properly signifying "recklessness"—"incapable of saving," or denying itself anything, and naturally passing through this want of self-restraint into profligacy—rightly translated "riot" in Tit. i. 6, 1 Pet. iv. 4, as the corresponding adverb is rendered "riotous living" in Luke xv. 13. For drunkenness is at once the effect and cause of utter recklessness. It is the effect of a self-abandonment, by which the sensual or passionate elements of the nature are stimulated to frenzy, while the self-controlling judgment is drugged to sleep. It is the cause of yet greater recklessness: for as these passions and appetites become jaded, they need stronger and stronger stimulants, till the whole nature, bodily and mental, is lost in delirium or stupor.

But be filled with the Spirit.—The antithesis is startling, but profoundly instructive. To the artificial and degrading excitement of drunkenness St. Paul boldly opposes the divine enthusiasm of the Spirit, one form of which was scoffingly compared to it on the Day of Pentecost (Acts ii. 13). He is not content with warning us of its ruinous excess, or urging the strictness of stern self-restraint. Drunkenness comes from an unnatural craving for excitement, stimulated by unwholesome conditions of life, physical and mental. He would satisfy the craving, so far as it is natural, by a divine enthusiasm, brighter and stronger than even duty to God and man, breaking out in thanksgiving, adoration, and love.

(19) **Speaking to yourselves in psalms and hymns and spiritual songs.**—The same words are found in Col. iii. 16, with a notable difference of application. There the idea is of teaching: "teaching and admonishing one another;" here, simply of a natural vent for emotion, especially of thanksgiving, although probably here also "to yourselves" means "to one another," and refers, perhaps, chiefly to public worship. The well-known passage in Pliny, "Carmen dicere inter se invicem," describes alternate, possibly antiphonal, singing of such sacred music. Of the various kinds of this music, the "psalms" and "hymns" are easily distinguished. The "psalm," as the word itself implies, is music with instrumental accompaniment, and can hardly fail to refer to the Old Testament psalms, familiar in Jewish worship, and as we know, used in the first instance we have of apostolic worship (Acts iv. 24). On their frequent use see 1 Cor. xiv. 26; Jas. v. 12. The "hymn" is purely vocal music, apparently of the whole company (see Matt. xxvi. 30; Acts xvi. 25), more especially directed to praise of God, and probably designating the new utterances of the Christian Church itself. But the interpretation of the "spiritual song," or "ode," is more difficult. It is often considered as inclusive of the other two (as etymologically it might well be), but the genius of the passage appears to make it co-ordinate, and so distinct from them. From the use of the word "song," or "ode," as applied to lyric poetry, it may perhaps be conjectured that it describes more varied and elaborate music, sung by one person only—a spiritual utterance of one for the whole

singing and making melody in your heart to the Lord; (20) giving thanks always for all things unto God and the Father in the name of our Lord Jesus Christ; (21) submitting yourselves one to another in the fear of God. (22) Wives, submit yourselves unto your own

Chap. v. 22—25. Duty of wives and husbands.

congregation. In a passage of Philo (ii. p. 476)—quoted by Dr. Lightfoot on Col. iii. 16—on Jewish sacred music, we read, "He who stands up sings a hymn composed in praise of God, *either having made a new one for himself*, or using an ancient one of the poets of days gone by." The Christian counterpart of this might well be the "spiritual song." To some such utterance, under the name of "psalm," St. Paul seems to allude in 1 Cor. xiv. 26, a passage dealing expressly with special spiritual gifts. "Each one of you has a psalm." Evidently it might be strictly a "hymn" or "psalm," though in common usage (as here) it would be distinguished from both.

Singing and making melody in your heart.—The word rendered "making melody" is the verb corresponding to the "psalm" above, as singing to the "song." This clause is not identical but co-ordinate with the last. That described audible and public melody; this, the secret utterance of music in the soul, whether accompanying the other or distinct from it.

(20) **Giving thanks always for all things.**—This temper of universal and pervading thankfulness is dwelt upon in the First Epistle to the Thessalonians (v. 18) as indissolubly united with unceasing joy and prayer ("Rejoice evermore; pray without ceasing; in everything give thanks.") Since thanksgiving is for what God has given us, and prayer for what we still need, both must be united in our imperfect condition here. In Col. iii. 17 it is associated with action "in the name of the Lord Jesus Christ." Here it is dealt with alone, as the basis of the praises, public and private, corporate and individual, described above. In regard to the former, St. Paul marks thanksgiving as the fundamental and invariable element of all Christian worship, clothing itself naturally in all variety of music; in regard to the latter, he describes the habitual spirit of thankfulness, prevailing alike in joy and sorrow, undisturbed even by penitent sense of sin, as the inner music of all Christian life.

Unto God and the Father in the name of our Lord Jesus Christ.—Both these expressions are emphatic. To all consciousness of God belong fear and reverence; to the belief in Him as "our Father" (see Rom. viii. 14—17; Gal. iv. 4—6) specially belong love and thanksgiving. But it is "in the name of the Lord Jesus Christ"—that is, as identified in perfect unity with Him—that we have the adoption to sonship which is the ground of such thanksgiving. So also in the same unity (see John xiv. 13; xv. 16; xvi. 23, 24) we have the ground of perfect confidence in prayer.

(21) **Submitting yourselves one to another in the fear of God.**—In grammatical construction this clause is connected with the preceding verses; in point of idea it leads on to the next section, which treats of the three-fold submission of wives to husbands, children to parents, slaves to masters. There is, however, a certain connection of idea with the preceding section also, and especially with the encouragement of a Christian enthusiasm in the last clause. The strong and frequent emphasis laid in the New Testament on subjection, whether (as in Rom. xiii. 1—7; 1 Pet. ii. 13—17) to the civil powers, or (as here, in Col. iii. 18—iv. 1, and 1 Pet. ii. 18—iii. 7) to domestic authority, or (as in 1 Thess. v. 12, 13; 2 Thess. iii. 6, 14, 15) to ecclesiastical authority, probably indicates some tendency, in the first exuberance of Christian liberty and enthusiasm, to disregard the wholesome restraints, laws, and conventions of outward life. Hence St. Paul's general caution here, prefatory to the more detailed teaching of subjection which follows.

[**5. Practical Exhortation continued** (chaps. v. 22—vi. 9).

(4) THE BEARING OF THE TRUTH OF UNITY ON THE THREE GREAT RELATIONS OF LIFE.

(*a*) *Between husbands and wives*—a relation which is a type of the unity between Christ and His Church (verses 22—33).

(*b*) *Between parents and children*—a relation hallowed as existing "in the Lord" (chap. vi. 1—4).

(*c*) *Between masters and servants*—a relation softened and deepened by common service to the one Master (chap. vi. 5—9).]

(4 *a*.) In verses 22—33 St. Paul passes from warning against special sins to consider the three great relations of life, first considered as "subjections," and so illustrating the general precept of submission in verse 21, but ultimately viewed in their reciprocity of mutual obligations and rights. First, accordingly, he dwells on the relation of marriage, declaring it to be hallowed as a type of the unity of Christ with His Church, and hence drawing the inference of the duty of free obedience in the wife, and of self-sacrificing love in the husband. This passage may be held to contain the complete and normal doctrine of the New Testament on this great question, written at a time when Christianity had already begun to exalt and purify the nuptial tie; and it is instructive to compare it with 1 Cor vii., written for "the present distress," glancing not obscurely at marriage with unbelievers, and adapted to the condition of a proverbially profligate society, as yet scarcely raised above the low heathen ideas of marriage.

(22) **Wives, submit yourselves unto your own husbands.**—The same exhortation is found in Col. iii. 18; Tit. ii. 5; 1 Pet. iii. 1—6; and besides these formal exhortations there is distinct and emphatic declaration of the 'subjection of women" in 1 Cor. xi. 3, 7, 8, 9; xiv 34, 35; 1 Tim. ii. 11, 12. Probably the sense of that fundamental equality in Christ, in which (see Gal. iii. 28) "there is neither bond nor free, there is *neither male nor female*," while it was rightly accepted as showing that there is no spiritual inferiority in woman—such as Oriental theory asserted, and even Greek and corrupt Roman practice implied—was perverted to the denial of the greater natural weakness of woman, from which subordination comes, and to the foolish and reckless disregard of all social conventions. St. Paul, as usual, brings out the simple truth of principle, sanctioning whatever is fundamental and natural in woman's subordination, and leaving the artificial enactments of law or custom to grow by degrees into accordance with it.

husbands, as unto the Lord. (23) For the
husband is the head of the wife, even
as Christ is the head of the church:
and he is the saviour of the body.
(24) Therefore as the church is subject
unto Christ, so *let* the wives *be* to their
own husbands in every thing. (25) Hus-
bands, love your wives,
even as Christ also loved
the church, and gave him-
self for it; (26) that he
might sanctify and cleanse

Chap. v. 26—33. Marriage is a type of the union of Christ with His Church.

The principle of subordination is permanent; the special regulations of it in the world or in the Church must vary as circumstances change.

As unto the Lord.—These words are explained by the next verse. In Col. iii. 18 we have the less emphatic phrase, "as it is fitting in the Lord."

(23) **For the husband is the head of the wife, even as Christ is the head of the church.**—It is instructive to compare this with the partly similar passage in 1 Cor. xi. 3. There "the head of the woman is the man," as here; but "the head of every man (individually) is Christ," considered in His human nature; and finally, "the Head of Christ," as the Son of Man, "is God." There, accordingly, "headship" is simple lordship; the woman is subject to the man, the man is subject to Christ alone; Christ as the Son is subject to the Father. Here, on the other hand, we note, first, that in accordance with the general idea of the Epistle, the headship of Christ over the Church at large takes the place of His headship over the individual; next, that from the idea of His headship so conceived is derived the further idea of a spiritual unity, involving self-sacrifice in the head, as well as obedience to the head; and, lastly, that since the very idea of unity in Christ is unity with God, there is nothing to correspond to the third clause in the former Epistle.

(23, 24) **And he is the saviour of the body. Therefore . . .**—The words "and" and "is" are wrongly inserted, and the word "therefore" is absolutely an error, evading the difficulty of the passage. It should be, *He Himself being the Saviour of the Body. But . . .* This clause, in which the words "He Himself" are emphatic, notes (as if in order to guard against too literal acceptation of the comparison) that "Christ" (and He alone) is not only Head, but "Saviour of the Body," *i.e.*, "of His body the Church," not only teaching and ruling it, but by His unity infusing into it the new life of justification and sanctification. Here no husband can be like Him, and therefore none can claim the absolute dependence of faith which is His of right. Accordingly St. Paul adds the word "But." Though "this is so," yet "still let the wives," &c.

As the church is subject unto Christ, so let the wives be to their own husbands in every thing.—The subjection of the Church of Christ is a free subjection, arising out of faith in His absolute wisdom and goodness, and of love for His unspeakable love. Hence we gather (1) that the subordination of the wife is not that of the slave, by compulsion and fear, but one which arises from and preserves freedom; next (2), that it can exist, or at any rate can endure, only on condition of superior wisdom and goodness and love in the husband; thirdly (3), that while it is like the higher subordination in kind, it cannot be equally perfect in degree—while it is real "in everything," it can be absolute in nothing. The antitype is, as usual, greater than the type.

(25) **Husbands, love your wives, even as Christ also loved the church.**—The love of Christ for His Church is such that He counts Himself incomplete without her (chap. i. 23), and raises her to be one with Himself; that He bears with her weakness and frailty; that He draws her on by the cords of love; and that He gives up Himself for her. Only so far as the husband shows the like love in perfect sympathy, in chivalrous forbearance, in abhorrence of tyranny, in willingness to self-sacrifice, has he any right to claim lordship.

And gave himself for it.—Here, as before, the antitype transcends the type. In the character of our Lord's sacrifice, as an atonement offered "for" the Church, and in the regenerating and cleansing effect of that sacrifice (see next verse), none can approach Him. The husband may be said to give himself for his wife, but it cannot be in any higher sense than as taking the chief share of the burden, and if possible the pain, of life for her. He may follow Christ in love, and in that alone. Compare St. Paul's words in Col. i. 24, "I fill up that which is behind of the afflictions of Christ for His body's sake, which is the Church" (where see Note).

(25—27) In these verses we trace, under the nuptial metaphor, a clear description of the three great stages in salvation—justification in His "giving Himself for us, sanctification in the "cleansing by water in the Word," glorification in the final "presentation" to Christ in glory. The metaphor is certainly preserved in the last two clauses, which correspond to the bath of purification of the bride, and the festal presentation of her (usually by the friend of the bridegroom, John iii. 29), in all her beauty and adornment, to her husband at his own home; perhaps even in the first also, for the husband used to give a dowry, which was held in the rude simplicity of ancient times to purchase his wife, and here that which Christ gives is the unspeakable price of His own Self. Throughout, in accordance with the whole tenor of the Epistle, it is the Church as a whole, not the individual soul, which is "the Spouse of Christ."

(26) **That he might sanctify and cleanse it . .**—The true rendering is, *that He might sanctify it, having cleansed it in the laver of the water in* [*the*] *Word.* The reference in "the laver of the water" to baptism, is even more unquestionable than in "the laver of regeneration" of Tit. iii. 5. Hence we must conclude that the phrase "in the Word" is in some way connected with that sacrament. Of the two Greek words translated "word," the one here used is that which signifies not "the word" existing as a definite thought in the mind, but "the word" as audibly spoken. It has, indeed, in the original no article, but this is probably because it had assumed so technical a sense as to resemble a proper name; and it is best connected with the phrase "having cleansed it," thus being co-ordinated, not subordinated, to the "laver of the water." Accordingly it would seem to signify all that element of baptism which is "in word"—that is, the question of faith, "the answer of a good conscience" (1 Pet. iii. 21), and, lastly, the solemn formula of baptism "in the name of the Father, and of the Son, and of the Holy Ghost." If we are to single

it with the washing of water by the
word, (27) that he might present it to him-
self a glorious church, not having spot,
or wrinkle, or any such thing; but
that it should be holy and without
blemish. (28) So ought men to love
their wives as their own bodies. He
that loveth his wife loveth himself.
(29) For no man ever yet hated his own
flesh; but nourisheth and cherisheth it,
even as the Lord the church: (30) for we
are members of his body, of his flesh,
and of his bones. (31) For this cause
shall a man leave his father and mother,

out any of these, we must surely (with Chrysostom) take the last. But it is better to embrace the whole, and so include the whole spiritual element of baptism, both the acceptance of faith on the part of man, and the grace-giving blessing of God.

To "sanctify" is here to consecrate to Himself (comp. John xvii. 17, 19) after purification. In the same connection we have in 1 Cor. vi. 11, "Ye were washed, ye were sanctified, ye were justified." In virtue of such consecration the Church visible is "holy" in idea and in capacity—the Church invisible here (which will be the Church triumphant hereafter), holy in the actual purity which becomes a consecrated nature. Of such consecration baptism is unquestionably the means; as we see in command in Matt. xxviii. 19, and in fact in Acts ii. 38, 41.

(27) **That he might present it to himself.**—The original is more emphatic—*that He might Himself present it to Himself.* This presentation belonged usually to the "paranymph," or "friend of the bridegroom, to whom St. John Baptist compares himself in John iii. 29 (where see Note); St. Paul himself assumes that office in 2 Cor. xi. 2, "I have espoused (or rather, *betrothed*) you to one husband, that I may present you as a chaste virgin to Christ." Here, however, all is of Christ. He, as Paranymph, comes down to seek and to save His Bride; He, as Bridegroom, receives her in His heavenly home.

A glorious church, not having spot, or wrinkle . . .—Properly, (*that He might present*) *the Church as glorious, not having a spot* (*i.e.*, a stain on its purity), *or a wrinkle* (*i.e.*, a defect in its beauty and freshness of life); *but that it may be holy* (not merely consecrated to holiness) *and without blemish* (as He is without blemish). On these last words see Note on chap. i. 4. They are most commonly sacrificial, corresponding (see Col. i. 22) to the sacrificial use of the word "present." Here, however, they are seen clearly to have reference to the nuptial metaphor by what goes before.

In all this we have a picture which properly belongs to the Church in glory, and which is fully drawn out under the same metaphor as Rev. xix. 7—9, xxi. 2, 9, 10; for only in it can the description be fully realised. In capacity and promise it belongs to the whole Church militant; in reality, but in imperfection, to the Church invisible on earth; in absolute perfection to the Church triumphant in heaven.

(28) **So ought men to love their wives . . .**—From this glorious digression, applying only to the divine Antitype, St. Paul comes back to the one point, in which the type may imitate it—that is, a deep and unfailing love. "So" refers to the previous verse, describing the love of Christ, not to the "as" following; otherwise the want of connection would be strangely abrupt. Moreover, from this idea of the love of Christ as the pattern, the latter part of this verse and the following verses naturally arise. Christ loves the Church as His body, a part of Himself. Hence the idea that the husband is "the head of the wife" gives place to the absolute identification of himself with his wife, as "one flesh."

He that loveth his wife loveth himself.—All right "love of our neighbour" is directed to be given to him "as to ourselves." It is to be of the same kind as the love of self—that is, first, an instinct (as of self-preservation); and next a rational and settled principle (as of reasonable self-love, seeking our own perfection, which is our happiness). Here, however, this love to our neighbour is actually identified with self-love. The wife is the husband's very self; he can no more fail to love her than to love himself, though (again to follow the example of Christ) he may love her better than himself. We may note that this identification of husband and wife is the basis of all ecclesiastical, and, in great degree, of all civil, law of Christian nations as to marriage.

(29) **His own flesh**—*i.e.*, as above (verse 28), *his own body.* There are two parts of the natural care for our own bodies; first, "to nourish" (properly, *to rear them up from childhood*, as in chap. vi. 4), and then "to cherish" (literally, *to keep them warm*), to provide all they need for health, and comfort, and life. In all that corresponds to both, the husband is to show love to the wife, not only as a self, but as a weaker self, for whom he is bound to think and to act. It may be noted in passing that the very comparison accords with the Christian idea of the body as a part of the true self, redeemed to be a temple of God; and is utterly incongruous with the Gnostic conceptions (already beginning at Colossæ, probably not unknown in other Asiatic churches) of all matter as the source of evil, and of the body as that for which the spirit should not deign to care.

(29, 30) **Even as the Lord the church: for we . . .**—Again St. Paul escapes from the type to rest on the Antitype (see verse 32). The idea of the natural rearing and cherishing the body suggests the thought of the tender care of Christ, in which He "rears up" His Church from weak infancy to full maturity in heaven, and all the while "cherishes it (comp. 1 Thess. ii. 7, spoken of His servants) as a nurse cherisheth her children," "carrying it in His bosom" (Isa. xl. 11), comforting and cheering its childlike weakness. Hence he goes back again to speak with great and special emphasis of our unity with Him.

Of his flesh, and of his bones.—Literally, *made out of His flesh and bones*—parts, that is, of His glorified body, having "flesh and bones" (Luke xxiv. 39). The expression is unique, suggested, of course, by Gen. ii. 23, "This is now bone of my bone, and flesh of my flesh," but designed to bring out in a startling emphasis the true meaning of the familiar phrase, "the members of His body." We are grafted into Him. What we grow to be is, so to speak, the product of His divine substance, proceeding from the indwelling life which gradually forms the organised limbs.

(31) **For this cause.**—In spite of much authority, it seems far simpler to consider the words "Even as the Lord . . . His bones" as parenthetical, and refer

and shall be joined unto his wife, and they two shall be one flesh. (32) This is a great mystery: but I speak concerning Christ and the church. (33) Nevertheless let every one of you in particular so love his wife even as himself; and the wife *see* that she reverence *her* husband.

A.D. 64.

CHAPTER VI.—(1) Children, obey your parents in the Lord: for this is right. (2) Honour thy father and mother; which is the first commandment with promise; (3) that it may be well with thee, and thou mayest live long on the

Chap. vi. 1—4. Duty of children and parents.

---

back to verses 28, 29. In exactly the same way our Lord quotes the same verse of Genesis (chap. ii. 24) to show the indissoluble character of the marriage tie. Here the similarity of connection with that of the original passage is even stronger. Because a man's wife is as his own body, "for this cause shall a man," &c. To connect these words with those going before is indeed possible, but somewhat too mystical even for this passage.

Shall a man leave his father . . .—The relation of parentage is one of common flesh and blood, and stands at the head of those natural relations which we do not make, but into which we are born. The relation of marriage is the most sacred of all the ties into which we are not born, and which we do make for ourselves, in accordance with a true or supposed harmony of nature. It becomes, says Holy Scripture, a relation, not of common flesh and blood, but of "one flesh." Itself originally voluntary, it supersedes all natural ties. Our Lord therefore adds, "They are no more twain, but one flesh. What God hath joined together let not man put asunder" (Matt. xix. 6). Hence it strikingly represents that unity with Christ—voluntarily initiated by Him, voluntarily accepted by us—which yet so supersedes all natural ties that it is said to oblige a man to "hate his father and mother . . . and his own life also" (Luke xiv. 26).

(32) **This is a great mystery.**—Rather, *This mystery is a great one.* The words apply to the type, as well as to the Antitype. (1) The indissoluble and paramount sacredness of marriage, as all history shows, is "a mystery"—that is (see chap. i. 9), a secret of God's law, fully revealed in Christ alone. For in heathen, and, to some extent, even in Jewish thought, marriage was a contract far less sacred than the indissoluble tie of blood; and wherever Christian principle is renounced or obscured, that ancient idea recurs in modern times. It may be noted that from the translation here of the word "mystery," by *sacramentum* in the Latin versions, the application of the word "sacrament" to marriage arose. (2) But the following words, "But I" (the word "I" being emphatic) "speak concerning Christ and the Church," show—what indeed the whole passage has already shown—that St. Paul's chief thought has passed from the type to the Antitype. He has constantly dwelt on points which suit only Christ's relation to the Church, and to that relation he has, by an irresistible gravitation of thought, been brought back again and again. (3) Yet the two cannot be separate. The type brings out some features of the Antitype which no other comparison makes clear; and history shows that the sacredness of the type in the Church has depended on this great passage—bearing, as it does, emphatic witness against the ascetic tendency to look on marriage as simply a concession to weakness, and as leading to a life necessarily lower than the celibate life.

(33) **Nevertheless.**—Although, *i.e.*, the primary and perfect application is to Christ alone, let the teaching be so far applied to marriage as that practically "the husband love his wife as himself," and "the wife reverence (properly, *fear*) the husband." This return to homely, practical duty after high and mysterious teaching is characteristic of St. Paul. (See, for example, 1 Cor. xv. 58.)

VI.

(4 *b*.) In verses 1—4 St. Paul passes from the detailed exposition of the true relation of husbands and wives, to deal with the relation of parents and children, far more cursorily and simply, but under the light of the same idea. It is to be thought of as existing "in the Lord," *i.e.*, within the unity binding all to Christ, in virtue of which the parental authority and the right freedom of the child are both hallowed.

(1) **In the Lord.**—The phrase itself, though familiar in St. Paul's writings generally, is specially frequent in the Epistles of the Captivity, where it occurs in various connections no less than twenty-one times. (See, for example, chaps. ii. 21; iii. 11; iv. 1, 17; v. 8; vi. 10, 21.) It is, in fact, a brief indication of their great subject—unity with and in Christ. Here to "obey in the Lord" is to obey under the light and grace of that unity, as already belonging both to parents and children, and transfiguring all natural relations to a diviner glory.

This is right.—Right, *i.e.*, by fundamental laws of humanity, recognised in all races and all ages, declared and sanctioned in God's commandments (verses 2, 3), which are at once both old and new "in the Lord."

(2) **The first commandment with promise.**—It is, indeed, in the Decalogue "the only commandment with promise" distinctly attached to it. But it is still the first; the Decalogue being itself the introduction to the Law, in which similar promises are repeated again and again.

(3) **That it may be well with thee . . .**—The quotation is but slightly varied from Ex. xx. 12; Deut. v. 16. But by the omission of the limiting words, "which the Lord thy God hath given thee," St. Paul at once generalises the application and determines it to the earth, and not to "the good land" of heaven. The words so interpreted are, therefore, a promise that obedience "in the Lord" to the great natural law on which society rests, shall bring with it reward on earth; just as our Lord tells us of "meekness" that it shall "inherit the earth" (Matt. v. 5), and St. Paul of "godliness" that it "has the promise of the life that now is, as well as of that which is to come" (1 Tim. iv. 8). The visible exemplification of this law is, indeed, as in all other cases, obscured by the disorder brought in by sin, and, moreover, is affected by the consideration that this life, being a discipline for heaven, must present, in the true sense of the word, "imperfection" or incompleteness, if viewed alone. But it is still a natural law, and is still accordingly fulfilled in actual experience. The promise is not to us so important as to them of old; but it is ours still.

earth. (4) And, ye fathers, provoke not your children to wrath: but bring them up in the nurture and admonition of the Lord.

Chap. vi. 5—9. Duty of servants and masters.

(5) Servants, be obedient to them that are *your* masters according to the flesh, with fear and trembling, in singleness of your heart, as unto Christ; (6) not with eyeservice, as menpleasers; but as the servants of Christ, doing the will of God from the heart; (7) with good will doing service, as to the Lord, and not to men: (8) knowing that whatsoever good thing any man

---

(4) **Provoke not your children to wrath.**—The word is the same as in chap. iv. 26. It denotes the exasperation produced by arbitrary and unsympathetic rule.

Nurture and admonition of the Lord.—In this phrase we have the two elements of education. "Nurture" is a word signifying generally "the treatment due to a child," but by usage appropriated to practical training, or teaching by discipline; while "admonition" is the "putting children in mind" by word of instruction. It may be noted that in accordance with the characteristic sternness of ancient education, both words have a tinge of severity in them. The "nurture" of this passage is the same as the "chastening" of the famous passage in Heb. xii. 4—11. (Compare the cognate verb in Luke xxiii. 16; 1 Cor. xi. 32; 2 Cor. vi. 9; 1 Tim. i. 20; Rev. iii. 19.) The "admonition" is used in Tit. iii. 10 for rebuke, and, inasmuch as it implies warning, is distinguished from teaching in Col. iii. 16. In this, as in other cases, Christianity gradually softened this stern authority of the father—so strikingly exemplified in the old Roman law—by the idea suggested in the addition of the phrase "of the Lord." The children belong not to the parent only, but to Christ, taken into His arms in baptism, and sealed as His little ones. Hence the "reverence," which Juvenal enforced in theory as due to children's natural purity, became realised in Christian practice, and gradually transformed all Christian education to greater gentleness, forbearance, and love.

(4 *c.*) In verses 5—9 the hardest form of subjection, that of slaves to masters, is dealt with, still under the same idea that both are "in Christ." The slave is the servant of Christ in obeying his master, the master is a fellow-servant with his slave to the same Divine Lord. We notice on this particular subject a remarkable emphasis, and a singular closeness of parallelism between this Epistle and the Epistle to the Colossians; probably to be accounted for by the presence of Onesimus with St. Paul at the time, which would naturally press on him some special consideration of the relation of Christianity to slavery. Accordingly St. Paul's general attitude towards slavery will be best considered in the Epistle to Philemon (which see). Here it will be sufficient to note that while the institution, unnatural as it is, is left untouched, the declaration of a common fellowship in Christ enunciates a principle absolutely incompatible with slavery, and destined to destroy it.

(5) **Your masters according to the flesh.**—This phrase (used also in Col. iii. 12) at once implies the necessary limitation of all human slavery. It can subjugate and even kill the body, but it cannot touch the spirit; and it belongs only to the visible life of this world, not to the world to come. The slave is a man in spiritual and immortal being, not a "living tool" or "chattel," as even philosophy called him.

With fear and trembling.—The phrase is a favourite one with St. Paul. (See 1 Cor. ii. 3; 2 Cor. vii. 15; Phil. ii. 12, in all which cases it is applied to the condition of man as man under the weight of solemn responsibility before God.) It recognises the "spirit of bondage unto fear" (Rom. viii. 15) necessarily belonging to all who are "under law," *i.e.*, under obedience to the will of another, as enforced upon them by compulsion; and this fear, moreover, is viewed as showing itself in "trembling" anxiety to obey. So St. Peter commands (1 Pet. ii. 18), "Servants, be subject to your masters with all fear, not only to the good and gentle, but also to the froward;" and it is to be noted that he describes the suffering herein implied as a fellowship with the sufferings of the Lord Jesus Christ (verses 21—24).

Singleness of your heart, as unto Christ.—The phrase "singleness of heart," is here used in its proper sense, from which all others (see Rom. xii. 8; 2 Cor. viii. 2; ix. 11, 13) may be derived. It means having but one aim, and that the one which we profess to have, with no duplicity of reservation or hypocrisy. Such singleness of heart cannot be given perfectly to any merely human service, because no such service has a right to our whole heart; hence St. Paul adds, "as unto Christ," bidding them look on their service as a part of the service to Him who can claim absolute devotion.

(6) **Not with eyeservice, as menpleasers.**—This verse is merely an expansion of the idea of singleness of heart. The word "eyeservice" (used here, and in Col. iii. 22) is peculiar to St. Paul, and to these passages; the word "menpleasers" is not found elsewhere in the New Testament, but is used in the LXX.; and the antithesis of "pleasing men" and "pleasing God" is not unfrequent with St. Paul. (See Gal. i. 10, 11; 1 Thess. ii. 4.) To a slave, looking on his master's authority as mere power imposed by the cruel laws of man, this "eyeservice" is found to be an all but irresistible temptation. It is only when he looks on himself as "the slave of Christ"—who Himself "took on Him the form of a slave" (Phil. ii. 7) in order to work out the will of God in a sinful world, and to redeem all men from bondage—that he can possibly serve from the heart.

(7) **With good will doing service, as to the Lord, and not to men.**—Here we ascend to a still higher quality than "singleness of heart." To do service "with good will," that is, gladly and cheerfully, "counting it joy to spend and to be spent" in the service, is really to serve, not as a slave, but as a freeman. Only so far as in the relation of slaves to masters there is, or has been, any shadow of the filial and parental relation, is this possible on merely human grounds. But St. Paul urges, in 1 Cor. vii. 22, that the slave "when called in the Lord, becomes the Lord's freeman," entering a "service which is perfect freedom." That conception, logically worked out, has ultimately destroyed slavery. Meanwhile it gave to the slave in his slavery—lightened though not yet removed—the power of service "with good will, as to the Lord."

(8) **The same shall he receive of the Lord.**—This verse clenches the previous exhortations by

doeth, the same shall he receive of the
Lord, whether *he be* bond or free. (9) And,
ye masters, do the same things unto them,
forbearing[1] threatening: knowing that
your Master also[2] is in heaven; neither
is there respect of persons with him.

[1] Or, *moderating.*

[2] Some read, *both your Master and theirs.*

(10) Finally, my brethren, be strong in
the Lord, and in the power
of his might. (11) Put
on the whole armour
of God, that ye may be
able to stand against the wiles of

Chap. vi. 10—12. Exhortation to fight the spiritual battle.

---

the inculcation of a sense of responsibility and hope. The phrase itself is emphatic—not "he shall receive the reward of his deed," but "he shall receive the deed itself," considered as a thing still living and returning on his head, both in the judgments of life and in what we rightly call the "Last Judgment" of the Great Day. A slave in the eye of the law had no rights, and therefore no responsibility or hope. St. Paul therefore bids him, as a Christian, lift his thoughts to a region in which all, bond and free alike, may hear the blessing, "Well done, good and faithful servant."

(9) **Do the same things unto them**—*i.e.*, treat them as flesh and blood like yourselves, having, as men, the same claims on you as you on them; "do unto them as ye would that they should do unto you." The parallel passage in the Colossian Epistle (chap. iv. 1) is the best comment on this, "Give unto your servants what is just and equal." "To forbear threatening," or, as in the original, "*the* threatening," which is so common, is one example of this sense of sympathy. For threatening implies at every moment compulsion and coercion from a position of tyrannical superiority; dealing with the slave as one who has in him no free energy and no sense of duty, and who must be driven like a brute-beast, not led or guided as a man.

Your Master also.—The stronger marginal reading is perhaps better, *their Master and yours.*

Respect of persons.—In this phrase the word "person" is used in its original sense (still lingering in our modern use of "person" and "personal," for "body" and "bodily,") of the *persona, i.e.,* "the mask" of outward condition, circumstance, and privilege. In this general sense our Lord (Matt. xxii. 16) is said "to regard not," and (Luke xx. 21) "to accept not" the person of man, because "He teaches the way of God *in truth.*" This sense is illustrated in different forms by the other uses of the word "respect of persons," and the corresponding verb in the New Testament. Thus in Acts x. 34, Rom. ii. 11, it is used of the distinction of privilege between Jew and Gentile, circumcision and uncircumcision; in Gal. ii. 6, of apostolic dignity in the eyes of men; in Jas. ii. 1, 9, of distinction of social rank; here and in Col. iii. 25, of the difference between the slave and the freeman. In the modern sense of "person," as signifying the real man, there is, and must be, "respect of persons" in all righteous judgment, whether of God or man.

[6. **Conclusion** (chap. vi. 10—24).

(1) Final Exhortation to put on the whole armour of God, in order to stand fast in the struggle, not against flesh and blood, but against unearthly powers of evil (verses 10—17).

(2) Special Desire of their Prayers, as for themselves and for all men, so especially for St. Paul himself (verses 18—20).

(3) Commendation of Tychicus (verses 21, 22).

(4) Closing Salutation (verses 23, 24).]

(1) In verses 10—17 St. Paul sums up his practical exhortation in that magnificent description which has ever since laid hold of Christian imagination, both in metaphor and in allegory. He paints the Christian life as a battle against spiritual powers of evil, waged in the strength of the Lord, and in the panoply of God. We trace the germ of this great passage first in St. Paul's earliest Epistle (1 Thess. v. 8, 9), and then in the later Epistle to the Romans (chap. xiii. 12). In both these cases the image is of soldiers starting from sleep at day-break to arm for the fray in the morning light. But it is characteristic of the more elaborate and thoughtful style of this Epistle, and of the circumstances under which it was written (in the watchful presence of the full-armed Roman "soldiers that kept" St. Paul), that the image there briefly touched is here worked out in full beauty of detail.

(10) **Finally, my brethren, be strong in the Lord.**—The address "my brethren" appears to be an interpolation (probably from Phil. iii. 1). Frequent as it is from St. Paul, it is not found either in this or in the Colossian Epistle.

Be strong.—Properly, *be strengthened in the inner man;* go on from strength to strength (as in Acts ix. 22; 2 Tim. ii. 1). So in Phil. iv. 13 we have the cognate expression, "Christ that strengtheneth me," in whom "I can do all things." The conception is nearly that of chap. iii. 16; except that there the idea is rather of passive strength and firmness, here of active power to fight "in the power of God's might," working in us, because it works in our Master. (Comp. chap. i. 19, 20.) It differs also from that which follows. "Christ in us" is here our life and indwelling strength; in the next verses the likeness of Christ, as manifested in various graces, is the armour "put on" for the battle.

(11) **Put on the whole armour.**—The special emphasis in this verse is on "the whole armour," or "panoply" (a word only used here and in Luke xi. 22); not mainly on its strength or its brightness, as "armour of light" (comp. Rom. xiii. 12), but on its completeness, providing against all "the wiles" and "all the fiery darts" of the Evil One, leaving no one point unguarded by a carelessness which may be fatal on all. In this it accords well with the general completeness and harmony of idea so characteristic of this Epistle.

To put on the "armour of God"—given us, that is, by God—is declared (by comparison of Rom. xiii. 12 and 14) to be to "put on the Lord Jesus Christ." Hence its completeness corresponds to the divine perfection of His true humanity. We are "to grow up unto Him in all things" (chap. iv. 15), to put on His image in all the harmony of "truth" and "righteousness," of "peace" and "faith," to receive and use His "salvation" and wield the spiritual energy of His "Word."

The wiles of the devil.—The word "wiles" (used only here and in chap. iv. 14) is an almost technical

the devil. (12) For we wrestle not
against flesh and blood, but against
principalities, against powers, against
the rulers of the darkness of this world,
against spiritual wickedness[1] in high[2]
places. (13) Wherefore take unto you
the whole armour of God, that ye may
be able to withstand in
the evil day, and hav-
ing done all,[3] to stand.
(14) Stand therefore, having
your loins girt about with truth,

3 Or, *having overcome all.*
1 Or, *wicked spirits.*
2 Or, *heavenly.*

Chap. vi.13—17. in the full perfection of the armour of God.

---

word for the stratagems of a skilful leader. It is notable that these "wiles" are ascribed to the devil, the "prince of the evil spirits" directing his hosts against the army of Christ; the actual "wrestling" of hand-to-hand struggle is with these evil spirits themselves. The word "wrestling" is, of course, not used technically, otherwise the counsel must have been (as in Heb. xii. 1) to divest oneself of all encumbrance. It is the personal grapple with the foe. Still it is possible that there may be some allusion to the "wrestling with the angel" of Gen. xxxii. 24—29, though with a wholly diverse application.

(12) **For we wrestle.**—Properly, *For our wrestling is.* That there is a struggle, a "battle of life," must be assumed at once by all who look at the world as it is; the question is whether it is against flesh and blood, or against a more unearthly power of evil.

Flesh and blood.—Or rather (as perhaps also in Heb. ii. 14), *blood and flesh.* So in John i. 13, "Not of blood, nor of the will of the flesh." In Matt. xvi. 17, 1 Cor. xv. 50, we have "flesh and blood." The sense is clearly, as the comparison of all these passages shows, "mere human power." Possibly the word "blood" is here put first to prevent even a moment's confusion with the idea of wrestling against "the flesh" as an evil power within ourselves. In many passages of this Epistle St. Paul had dwelt on the opposition of the Christian to the heathen life, and the duty of rebuking and putting to shame the works of darkness; but here he warns us that the struggle is not a struggle with the "flesh and blood" of wicked men—a struggle which may still admit of some reserve of sympathy—but a truceless war with the spiritual powers of evil themselves.

Against principalities, against powers.—See Note on chap. i. 21.

Against the rulers . . .—"Principalities" and "powers" describe simply angelic powers, whether of good or evil. But in the following clauses St. Paul defines them as powers of evil, and appears to indicate two different aspects of this evil power. The original phrase is striking and powerful, "against the world-rulers of this darkness, against the spiritual powers of wickedness in the heavenly places."

The rulers of the darkness.—Properly, *the world-rulers of this darkness.* This phrase is simply a poetical expression of the idea conveyed by the title "the prince of this world," applied to Satan in John xii. 31; xiv. 30; xvi. 11 (on which see Notes). For "this darkness" is obviously (as our version renders it, following an early gloss on the passage) "the darkness of this present world," as a world overshadowed by sin, and so kept, wholly or partially, from the light of God. The title "the prince of this world," was applied by the Jews to Satan, especially in reference to his power over the heathen, as lying outside the safety of the covenant. St. Paul applies it in a corresponding sense here to those outside the wider covenant of the gospel; just as in 1 Cor. v. 5, 1 Tim. i. 20, he speaks of excommunication from the Church as a "delivery to Satan." The spirits of evil are therefore spoken of as wielding the power which the Tempter claims for himself (in Luke iv. 6) over such souls as are still in darkness and alienation from God. This is a power real, but limited and transitory, able only to enslave those who "yield themselves" to it, and destined to be overcome; and it seems to refer especially to the concrete power of evil, exercised through physical and human agency.

Spiritual wickedness in high places.—The "spiritual powers" are not spiritual principles, but "spiritual hosts" of wickedness; and the phrase "in the heavenly places," corresponding to "the power of the air" in chap. ii. 2 (where see Note), stands obviously in antithesis to "the darkness of this world." The sense, as in all other cases, seems to be local. (See Note on chap. i. 3.) The spiritual hosts of evil are described as fighting in the region above the earth. But the meaning underlying this figure surely points to the power of evil as directly spiritual, not acting through physical and human agency, but attacking the spirit in that higher aspect, in which it contemplates heavenly things and ascends to the communion with God. As the former idea corresponds to the gross work of temptation on the high mountain, so this to the subtler spiritual temptation on the pinnacle of the temple.

(13) **In the evil day.**—Comp. chap. v. 15, "Because the days are evil." The evil day is any day of which it may be said in our Lord's words, "This is your hour, and the power of darkness" (Luke xxii. 53). In this life all days may be evil, but, except to the reprobate, none wholly evil; for out of evil "all things work together for good."

Having done all, to stand.—The rendering (see Chrysostom) "having overcome all" is tempting, but does not accord with St. Paul's use of the original word. The exhortation is first "to withstand," *i.e.*, to resist all distinct attacks; then, when in this we have "done all" that we are from time to time called to do, "to stand," *i.e.*, to plant our feet firmly on the rock, being "steadfast and unmovable" (1 Cor. xv. 58). The one conveys the idea of bravery and activity; the other of calm, well-balanced steadfastness.

(14—17) In this magnificent passage, while it would be unreasonable to look for formal and systematic exactness, it is clear that (as usual in St. Paul's most figurative passages) there runs through the whole a distinct method of idea. Thus (1) the order in which the armour in enumerated is clearly the order in which the armour of the Roman soldier was actually put on. It nearly corresponds with the invariable order in which Homer describes over and over again the arming of his heroes. First the belt and the corselet, which met and together formed the body armour; then the sandals; next the shield, and after this (for the strap of the great shield could hardly pass over the helmet) the helmet itself; then the soldier was armed, and only had to take up the sword and spear. It is curious to note that St. Paul omits the spear (the *pilum* of the

and having on the breastplate of righteousness; (15) and your feet shod with the preparation of the gospel of peace; (16) above all, taking the shield of faith, wherewith ye shall be able to quench all the fiery darts of the wicked. (17) And take the helmet of salvation, and the sword of the Spirit, which is

---

Roman soldier)—exactly that part of his equipment which, when on guard within, the soldier would not be likely to assume. (2) Again, since "to put on the armour of light" is to "put on the Lord Jesus Christ," it follows that the various parts of the defensive armour are the various parts of the image of the Lord Jesus Christ; hence they are properly His, and are through His gift appropriated by us. Thus the "righteousness" is clearly the righteousness of Christ, realised in us (comp. Phil. iii. 9); the sandals, which give firm footing, are the gospel of our peace in Him; the salvation is His salvation worked out in us. Only the sword is in no sense our own: it is the "Word of God" wielded by us, but in itself "living and powerful and sharp" (Heb. iv. 12).

(14) **Your loins girt about with truth, and having on the breastplate of righteousness.**—There is here an obvious reference to two passages of Isaiah (xi. 5; lix. 17), "Righteousness shall be the girdle of his loins," "He put on righteousness as a breastplate." Truth and righteousness are virtually identical, or, at least, inseparable. Hence they are compared to the strong belt, and the breastplate continuous with it, forming together the armour of the body. Perhaps "truth" is taken as the belt because it is the one bond both of society and of individual character. But it is in the two together that men stand "armed strong in honesty." In 1 Thess. v. 8, the metaphor is different and perhaps less exact. There the breastplate is the "breastplate of faith and love"—that which here is the shield.

(15) **Shod with the preparation of the gospel of peace.**—This passage is one which even to the Greek interpreters (see Chrysostom) was obscure. What is "the preparation of the gospel of peace"? (1) It has seemed to many natural to illustrate this phrase by the celebrated passage (Isa. lii. 7; Rom. x. 15), "How beautiful are the feet of them that preach the gospel of peace"; and to interpret, "shod in (or, *for*) preparing the way of the gospel of peace." But this is inappropriate to the whole context; for each piece of armour is a quality, and not a function. (2) Again, the word rendered "preparation," is found nowhere else in the New Testament; in the LXX. we find it used in its most obvious sense of "preparedness" or "readiness" (as in Ps. x. 17, "preparedness of heart," and Neh. ii. 3); but this sense will not suit the passage, for "readiness of the gospel of peace" is hardly intelligible, and certainly is not a quality of the soul. (3) We come therefore, at last, to a derivative and improper sense, which, however, is most frequently used in the LXX., viz., "foundation" or "base," as in Dan. xi. 7; Ezra ii. 6, and iii. 3; Zech. v. 10; Ps. lxxxviii. 14. The context certainly suggests that we should explain the word here by this last Hellenistic use, as signifying simply the "footing" or "basis." The *caligæ*, or sandals, of the Roman soldiers were heavy sandals studded with hobnails, to give a secure foothold to those who would stand firm. St. Paul identifies these with the firm "footing of the gospel of peace." Clearly the word "peace" is here emphatic. The gospel is looked upon as the declaration of "peace on earth, goodwill towards men." The firm stand on this message is the firm assurance of God's love. In this, and this alone, we stand. No doubt, this is in some sense faith, but faith of a wholly different character from the defensive faith of the next verse.

(16) **Above all.**—Properly, *over all*, or *besides all else*. The shield here is the large heavy shield covering the whole body, in which the "fiery darts"—that is, the arrows, with the points made red hot, or wrapped in with burning tow (comp. Ps. vii. 14; cxx. 4)—may fix and burn themselves out without harm. St. Paul likens it to "faith." This, however, is neither the "faith in which we stand" (2 Cor. i. 24), nor the energetic faith of Heb. xi. It is the faith of patience and endurance, the almost passive faith, trusting in God's protection and submissive to His will, on which the darts of temptation, whether from fear, or from lust, or from doubt, fall harmless. The best commentary after all, on the words is found in Christian's conflict with Apollyon in the *Pilgrim's Progress*.

(17) **And take.**—There is a break here. We are said not to put on, but to "take" (or rather, *receive*)—a word specially appropriate to "salvation."

The helmet of salvation.—The word here (as in Luke ii. 30; iii. 6; Acts xxviii. 28) rendered "salvation," is not the word commonly so rendered in the New Testament. It is, indeed, not "salvation" in the abstract, but a general expression for "that which tends to salvation." But it occurs in the LXX. version of Isa. lix. 17, which seems obviously referred to, "He put" a helmet of salvation upon his head." In 1 Thess. v. 8, where the breastplate is "of faith and love," the helmet supplies the third member of the triad of Christian graces in "*the hope* of salvation." Here the metaphor is probably somewhat different. The helmet guarding the head, the most noble and vital part, is "salvation" in the concrete—all that is of the Saviour, all that makes up our "state of salvation" by His atonement and grace—received in earnest now, hoped for in perfection hereafter.

The sword of the Spirit, which is the word of God.—In this we pass to the one offensive weapon of the Christian, "the sword of the Spirit"—*i.e.*, given by the Holy Spirit—which, like the helmet, but unlike the rest of the defensive armour, does not become a part of himself, but is absolutely of God. The passage reminds us at once of Heb. iv. 12: "The word of God is living and powerful, and sharper than any two-edged sword." But there (as in 1 Cor. xiv. 26; 2 Cor. ii. 17; Col. i. 25; 2 Tim. ii. 29) the original word is the larger and deeper word (*Logos*), signifying the truth of God in itself, and gradually leading up to the ultimate sense in which our Lord Himself is the "Word of God," revealing the Godhead to man. Accordingly the work of the Word there, is that of the "engrafted Word," "to divide asunder the soul and the spirit" within. Here, on the contrary, we have another expression (*Rhema*), signifying the Word as spoken; and St. Peter (in 1 Pet. i. 25) defines it exactly: "The word of the Lord endureth for ever; and this is the word which by the gospel is preached unto you." We cannot, of course, limit it to Holy Scripture, though we naturally remember that our Lord used the Scriptures as His only weapon in the

the word of God: (18) praying always with all prayer and supplication in the Spirit, and watching thereunto with all perseverance and supplication for all saints; (19) and for me, that utterance may be given unto me, that I may open my mouth boldly, to make known the mystery of the gospel, (20) for which I am an ambassador in bonds:[1] that therein[2] I may speak boldly, as I ought to speak. (21) But that ye also may know my affairs, *and* how I do, Tychicus, a beloved brother and faithful minister in the Lord, shall make known to you

Chap. vi. 18—20. Request for their prayers.

Chap. vi. 21, 22. Commendation of Tychicus.

1 Or, *in a chain.*

2 Or, *thereof.*

Temptation. It is the gospel of Christ, however and wherever spoken, able to put to shame and to flight the powers of evil.

(2) (18) **Praying always with all prayer and supplication.**—In this verse the metaphor gives place to direct exhortation, unless, indeed, in the word "watch" there still lingers some reference to the soldier on guard. "Prayer" is the general word for "worship," appropriated to God alone; "supplication," used also towards man, is one element of such worship—the asking what we need from God. In Phil. iv. 6 we have first the general word "prayer," and then the two chief elements of worship, "supplication with thanksgiving." It is by prayer that all the heavenly armour is put on.

In the Spirit.—That is, "in the Spirit of God" (as in verse 18). Compare the relation of prayer to the inspiration of the Holy Ghost in Rom. viii. 26, 27.

And watching thereunto with all perseverance.—These words in themselves obviously supply the other part of our Lord's command, "Watch and pray," naturally apposite to the consideration of the Christian warfare. "Perseverance" implies exertion, holding out against fatigue and difficulty. The corresponding verb is used in relation to all kinds of spiritual labour (see Acts ii. 42; vi. 4; viii. 13); but especially in connection with prayer (Acts i. 14; Rom. xii. 12; Col. iv. 2). Perhaps from this frequent connection St. Paul is induced to add to it "supplication," and this time "for all saints," so leading on to his usual request for the prayers of his brethren. For this he is willing to sacrifice some part of the perfect appropriateness of idea; since the whole picture hitherto has been of the fight, waged by each for himself (although side by side with others), in the combined power of watchfulness and prayer for God's help.

(18, 19) **And supplication for all saints; and for me.**—It is curious, and probably not accidental, that the prepositions in these two clauses are different. The first is properly "touching all saints," and the second "on behalf of me." Both are often interchanged; but there is, perhaps, here a touch of greater earnestness in the request of their prayers for himself, in especial reference to the need which is spoken of in the next words.

(19) **That utterance may be given me, that I may open my mouth . . .**—This hardly renders the original "that word may be given me in opening my mouth." The "opening the mouth"—an expression always used of solemn and deliberate utterance—seems taken for granted. What the Apostle desires them to pray for is that "word may be given him"—"the word of wisdom and the word of knowledge, by the Spirit" (1 Cor. xii. 8), according to our Lord's promise (Matt. x. 19, 20), "It shall be given you in the same hour what you shall speak; for it is not ye that speak, but the Spirit of your Father that speaketh in you." Then he adds as a consequence of this—*to make known in plainness of speech the mystery of the gospel.* For to make known a mystery in simplicity needs not only boldness to speak, but also the knowledge of the true word of God.

The mystery of the gospel.—The word "gospel" being used emphatically is, of course, the mystery of the new and universal grace of God to the Gentiles of which he speaks at large in chap. iii. 1—10. This was "made known to him;" he desires inspiration "to make it known" to others.

(20) **In bonds.**—Rightly, as in the margin, *in a chain.* The word is the same which is used in Acts xxviii. 20, "For the hope of Israel I am bound in this chain." It occurs also in Mark v. 4, Luke viii. 29, where it is distinguished from a "fetter" properly so called, as binding the feet, and therefore obviously signifies a "manacle" binding the hand. Both are included (see Luke viii. 29) in the general word "bonds." The allusion is undoubtedly to the custom of chaining the prisoner by the hand to the soldier who kept him. Thus in Acts xii. 6 we read that Peter "was sleeping between two soldiers," and therefore "bound with two manacles;" and in Acts xxi. 33 that a similar precaution was used on the first apprehension of St. Paul. Here the singular number is probably to be understood literally. St. Paul was free except for the one chain, which the soldier was responsible for holding, and perhaps did not always think it needful to hold. That chain he seems to speak of as the badge of his ambassadorial dignity. To ambassadors, indeed, it belongs to be safe from imprisonment; but it was his greater glory to wear the chain for Christ.

That therein . . .—This is simply an enforcement of the previous phrase, in "plainness of speech." The same word is used, and with the same signification of simplicity, as well as boldness, which (St. Paul here adds) alone befits his office.

(3, 4) Verses 21—24 form the conclusion of the Epistle, in commendation of Tychicus' salutation and blessing. The extreme brevity and generality of this section here—in contrast with St. Paul's practice in every other Epistle, except the Second Epistle to the Corinthians and the Epistle to the Galatians (both of which have the abruptness of indignation) and especially with the parallel Epistle to the Colossians—seem to bear on the question of the encyclical character of this Epistle.

(21) **That ye also**—*i.e.*, ye as well as others. There is evidently an allusion to Tychicus' similar mission to Colossæ; and we may, perhaps, also trace some indication of a generality of scope in this Epistle.

Tychicus is first mentioned with Trophimus in Acts xx. 4, as being "of Asia," and accompanying St. Paul on his last journey from Corinth to Asia, although he is not, like Trophimus, actually named as with the Apostle at Jerusalem. It is highly probable that he was one of the "messengers of the churches" spoken of in 2 Cor. viii. 18—23, as sent to bear the alms to Jerusalem. We now find him again with

all things: (22) whom I have sent unto
you for the same purpose, that ye might
know our affairs, and *that* he might
comfort your hearts. (23)
Peace *be* to the brethren,
and love with faith, from
God the Father and the Lord Jesus
Christ. (24) Grace *be* with all them that
love our Lord Jesus Christ in sincerity.[1]
Amen.

Chap. vi. 23, 24. Concluding blessing.

¶ Written from Rome unto the Ephesians by Tychicus.

[1] Or, *with incorruption.*

St. Paul, and made by him the bearer of this Epistle and the Epistle to the Colossians. Lastly, he is alluded to as still his companion in the interval between the first and second captivity (Tit. iii. 2), and in the second captivity is despatched once more to Ephesus (2 Tim. iv. 12). It is evident that he well deserved the title of a "faithful minister" to the Apostle; and we note (in 2 Tim. iv. 11, 12) that the command to bring Mark, as being "profitable for ministration," is immediately connected with the remark, "Tychicus have I sent to Ephesus."

A faithful minister.—The word "minister" is *diaconus*; but there is no reason to think that it is used technically to describe Tychicus as a deacon. In the Colossian Epistle the words "and fellowservant" are added, showing clearly that the word "minister" refers only to ministration to St. Paul.

(22) **Whom I have sent unto you.**—This verse corresponds word for word with Col. iv. 8, being a quasi-official statement of Tychicus' commission. The words "that he might comfort (or, *encourage*) your hearts," although they might apply generally to all messengers from an Apostle, may probably be best explained by reference to the tone of the Epistle to the Philippians—in which St. Paul shows so much affectionate anxiety lest his converts should be disheartened by his continued imprisonment—and to the exhortation in this Epistle not "to faint at his tribulations for them" (chap. iii. 13).

(23) **Peace be to the brethren . . .**—In the conclusion of the Epistle, as at the beginning, St. Paul gives the double benediction, "Peace and grace be with you all." But it is impossible not to notice the difference between the generality of the terms here used ("the brethren," and "all who love the Lord Jesus Christ") and the personal "you" of all the other Epistles—a difference which would be inexplicable if this Epistle were addressed to the well-known and loved Church of Ephesus alone.

Peace seems especially dwelt upon in the Epistles of the Captivity, of which the Epistle to Philippi contains (in chap. iv. 7) the fullest description of the "peace of God which passeth all understanding." It is naturally connected here with love (as in 2 Cor. xiii. 11; Col. iii. 15, 16)—a "love with faith," "making perfect" (as in Gal. v. 6) the faith which St. Paul takes for granted as being in them. For peace is first with God, in the thankful receiving of His mercy; from this naturally arises "love with faith" towards Him; and out of this, again, peace and love towards men, in the conviction that, "if God so loved us, we ought also to love one another" (1 John iv. 11). All these are gifts from "God the Father and the Lord Jesus Christ."

(24) **Grace be with all them . . .**—The salutation, "Grace be with you," in various forms, is, as St. Paul himself says in 2 Thess. iii. 17, "the token," or characteristic signature, in every one of his Epistles, written with his own hand. It may be noted that it is not found in the Epistles of St. James, St. Peter, St. Jude and St. John, and that it is found in the Epistle to the Hebrews. Here, however, it is at once general and conditional, "to all them who love the Lord Jesus Christ." So in 1 Cor. xvi. 22, "If any man love not the Lord Jesus Christ, let him be anathema."

In sincerity.—The original is far stronger, "in *incorruptibility*," a word usually applied to the immortality of heaven (as in Rom. ii. 7; 1 Cor. xv. 42, 50, 53, 54; 2 Tim. i. 10); only here and in Tit. ii. 7, applied to human character on earth. Here it evidently means "with a love immortal and imperishable," incapable either of corruption or of decay, a foretaste of the eternal communion in heaven.

INTRODUCTION

TO

THE EPISTLE OF PAUL THE APOSTLE TO THE

PHILIPPIANS

I. Time, Place, and Occasion of the Epistle.— The indications of the time and place of this Epistle are unusually clear. It is written by St. Paul "in bonds" (chap. i. 7—13); in the *Prætorium* (chap. i. 13), that is, under the charge of the Prætorian guard; it sends greeting from the "saints of Cæsar's household" (chap. iv. 21); it expresses an expectation of some crisis in his imprisonment (chap. i. 20—26), and a confident hope of re-visiting Philippi (chap. i. 26; ii. 24). All these indications place it in the Roman imprisonment of St. Paul—which we know (Acts xxviii. 30) to have lasted without trial or release for "two whole years," and which certainly began about A.D. 61. The date of the Epistle must therefore be fixed about the year A.D. 62 or 63.

Nor is the occasion of the Epistle less obvious. The Church at Philippi now, as at an earlier time (chap. iv. 10—19), had sent contributions to St. Paul's necessities, under the distress and destitution of imprisonment, when he was unable to maintain himself by the labour of his own hands, as he had formerly done at Thessalonica, Corinth, and Ephesus. Epaphroditus, their messenger, through his affectionate exertions on St. Paul's behalf, had fallen into dangerous illness, and on his convalescence had been seized with home-sickness, aggravated by the uneasiness of knowing that his danger had been reported to his friends at home (chap. ii. 25—30). St. Paul, therefore, sent him back with this Letter, the immediate object of which was to convey his thanks and blessing for the generosity of the Philippians, and to commend warmly the devotion of Epaphroditus, which had been in great degree the cause of his illness.

II. The Church to which it was written.— Of the first preaching at Philippi we have a full and graphic account in Acts xvi., where a description of the history and character of the city itself will be found in the Notes. The preaching began, as usual, from a Jewish centre, but this was only a *proseuche*, or oratory (Acts xvi. 13)—not, as at Thessalonica, a synagogue (Acts xvii. 1); and the whole history shows no indication of any strong Jewish influence. The first convert named is Lydia, an Asiatic of Thyatira, not a Jewess, but "one who worshipped God"—a "proselyte of the gate." The first opposition came not from the Jews, as at Thessalonica (Acts xvii. 5, 6, 13), but from the masters of the "damsel possessed with a spirit of divination," simply because by the exorcism of the Apostle the "hope of their gain was gone." The accusation levelled against St. Paul and his companion was one which was intimately connected with the peculiar position of Philippi as a Roman colony—a fragment (as it were) of the imperial city itself. We note, indeed, that at this very time (Acts xviii. 2) "Claudius had commanded all Jews to depart from Rome," and it is at least probable that this decree of banishment might extend to the Roman colonies, as distinguished from the ordinary provincial cities. Accordingly, in the accusation itself stress was laid on the fact that the accused were "Jews," and the charge was that they preached a *religio illicita*, involving customs which it was "not lawful for the Philippians to receive, being Romans" (Acts xvi. 21). The Church was therefore, mainly a Gentile Church—the firstfruits of European Christianity—and its attachment to the Apostle of the Gentiles was especially strong and fervent. The Philippians alone, it appears, offered—certainly from them alone St. Paul consented to receive—those contributions to his necessities, which elsewhere (see Acts xx. 33—35; 2 Cor. xi. 7—12; 1 Thess. ii. 9; 2 Thess. iii. 8) he thought it best to refuse for the gospel's sake.

The foundation of the Church had been laid amidst a persecution, in which the Roman magistrates, with a characteristic dislike of all foreign superstitions likely to lead to uproar, and a characteristic disregard of justice towards two or three obscure Jews, simply played into the hands of mob violence. The step which St. Paul afterwards took of asserting his citizenship and forcing the magistrates to confess their wrong-doing (Acts xvi. 37, 38) looks like a precaution to render the recurrence of arbitrary persecution less likely after his departure. But we gather from this Epistle (chap. i. 27—30) that the Church had still, like the sister Church at Thessalonica (1 Thess. i. 6; ii. 14) and the other Macedonian churches (2 Cor. viii. 2), to undergo "the same conflict" of suffering from "their adversaries," "which they had seen in him." It grew up under the bracing air of trial, with a peculiar steadfastness, warm-heartedness, and simplicity, apparently unvexed by the speculative waywardness of Corinth or the wild heresies of Ephesus or Colossæ. Again like the Thessalonian Church, its dangers were mainly practical (see chap. iii.); the Judaising influence was probably foreign and not very formidable; the tendencies to Antinomian profligacy (chap. iii. 17—21), to some division by party spirit (chaps. ii 1—4; iv. 2, 3), to occasional despondency under trial (chap. i. 28), hardly appear to have affected the Church widely or seriously. In its condition, accordingly, St. Paul could rejoice almost without reserve of sorrow or anxiety.

Of St. Paul's subsequent visits to Philippi we have no full record. We cannot doubt that he visited the city on his way from Ephesus to Macedonia and Greece, on the third missionary circuit (Acts xx. 3). The common tradition, exceedingly probable in itself, dates the Second Epistle to the Corinthians from Philippi on that occasion. We know (Acts xx. 6) that it was from Philippi that he started, some months after, on his last journey to Jerusalem. At a period subsequent to this Epistle, we learn (1 Tim. i. 3) that St. Paul, apparently after a visit to Ephesus, "went into Macedonia" after his first captivity, and so, no doubt, fulfilled his hope of re-visiting this well-loved Church. After this we have no notice of the Church in history till we read of their kindly reception of Ignatius on his way to martyrdom, and study the Epistle of Polycarp to them, written shortly after, mainly practical and hortatory, and implying, with but slight reservation, a still strong and vigorous Christianity, and a constant grateful memory of the great Apostle. (See, for example, chap. i.—"I rejoiced greatly with you in our Lord Jesus Christ, because ye have adopted the imitation of true love . . . . because the firm root of your faith, celebrated from ancient times, remains even until now, and bears fruit unto the Lord Jesus Christ;" chap. iii.—"Neither I nor any like me can follow out fully the wisdom of the blessed and glorious Paul, who, when he came among you, taught accurately and durably the word of truth.") Tertullian also alludes to it (*de Præscr.* xxxvi.) as one of the churches where the "authentic letters of the Apostles"—no doubt, this Epistle itself—were read. Afterwards we have little reference to it in Church history. Like Colossæ, it sank into insignificance.

III. The Genuineness of the Epistle.—*External Evidence.*—The evidence for the genuineness of the Epistle is very strong. In all ancient catalogues, from the Muratorian Fragment (A.D. 170) downwards, in all ancient versions, beginning with the Peschito and the old Latin, it is placed among the undoubted Epistles of St. Paul. In Christian writings, before the end of the second century, knowledge of it may be distinctly traced; after that time it is quoted continually.

Thus, in the Apostolic Fathers, to say nothing of slighter indications which have been noted (as by Dr. Westcott, *Canon of the New Testament*, chap. i., and Dr. Lightfoot, in his *Introduction to this Epistle*), St. Polycarp, in his Epistle to the Philippians (chap. iii.), expressly declares that St. Paul, "when absent, wrote letters to them, by searching into which they can still be built up in the faith," and speaks of them as "praised in the beginning of his Epistle" (chap. xi.). Nor are there wanting expressions in his letter (such as the "using our citizenship worthily of Christ," "the enemies of the cross," the "rejoicing with them in the Lord," the "not running in vain," &c.) which not obscurely indicate reference to the text of our Epistle itself. Again, Dr. Lightfoot quotes from the *Testaments of the Twelve Patriarchs*, a Judæo-Christian work, dating early in the second century, certain expressions—"the form of God" and the "fashion of men" (see Phil. ii. 6), the "luminaries" of heaven (see Phil. ii. 15), and, above all, the unique phrase "the bowels (*heart*) of the Son of God" (see Phil. i. 8)—which indicate unmistakably knowledge of this Epistle.

Perhaps the earliest direct quotation of it is in the celebrated Epistles of the Churches of Lyons and Vienne (A.D. 177), on the martyrdoms in the persecution of Marcus Aurelius (Eusebius, *Ecclesiastical History*, v. 2)—where we find the great passage: "He being in the form of God, thought it not robbery to be equal with God," &c. Then, as in other cases, the habit of quotation begins in Irenæus, Clement of Alexandria, and Tertullian, and continues afterwards unbroken. Tertullian, as we have already seen, apparently speaks of the Letter as being read as an Apostolic letter in the Philippian Church; and in his controversy with Marcion (v. 20) so quotes it as to show that it had escaped the destructive criticism and arbitrary mutilation in which Marcion so constantly anticipated the critical scepticism of later times.

Internal Evidence.—But, strong as external evidence is, it is in this case far weaker than the internal, which may be said to rise almost to demonstration. The strong marks of personality which we trace in every line, the unstudied frequency of historical allusion and of undesigned coincidences with historical records, the simple and natural occasion of writing, in the reception of the offerings and the illness of Epaphroditus, the absence of all formal doctrinal or ecclesiastical purpose, the fulness and warmth of personal affection,—all are unmistakable marks of genuineness, all are fairly inconceivable on the supposition of imitation or forgery. The character of St. Paul, as unconsciously drawn in it, is unquestionably the same character which lives and glows in the Corinthian and Galatian Epistles; and yet there is in it an indescribable growth into greater calmness and gentleness, which corresponds remarkably with advance of age and change of circumstances. There are also marked similarities, both of style and expression, with the earlier Epistles, and, above all, with the Epistle to the Romans, the last of the earlier group, which will be found noted in detail on the various passages.* There is also that mingling of identity and development of idea which is notable in all the Epistles of the Captivity. But in this case, perhaps, the similarity is greater, and the diversity less, than in the other Epistles of the same period.

It is, therefore, not surprising that, even in the freest speculation of the higher criticism, there are but few examples of scepticism as to the genuineness of this Epistle.

IV. The main Substance of the Epistle.—(1) *The Picture of the Writer and the Receivers.*—The first and simplest impression made by this Epistle is the vivid portraiture which it gives us of St. Paul himself—especially in the conflict of desire for the death which is the entrance to the nearer presence of Christ, and for the longer life, which will enable him to gather a fuller harvest for Christ—in the striking union of affection and thankfulness towards the Philippians, with a dignified independence and a tone of plenary authority—in the sensitiveness to the sorrow and inactivity of imprisonment, overcome and finally absorbed into an almost unequalled fulness of joy in the Lord. Side by side with this, we are next struck with the picture which it gives us of the Macedonian Christianity at Philippi—not unlike that of Thessalonica, though, it would seem, less chequered by fanaticism or disorder, and certainly singularly accordant with the Macedonian character, as it paints itself at once speculatively inferior and practically superior to the Greek, in the pages of history. The Philippian Christianity is pre-eminently vigorous, loyal, and warm-hearted, courageous and patient, little disturbed either by speculative refinements or speculative inventions, hardly needing any warning, except against the self-assertion which is the natural excrescence of earnestness, or any exhortation, except to a deeper

* Perhaps the most notable are:—
(*a*) Phil. ii. 10, 11, compared with Rom. xiv. 11.
(*b*) Phil. iii. 10, 11, compared with Rom. vi. 5.
(*c*) Phil. iii. 19, compared with Rom. xvi. 18.
(*d*) Phil. iv. 18, compared with Rom. xii. 1.
(*e*) Phil. iii. 5, 6, compared with 2 Cor. xi. 22, Rom. xi. 1. It may be noted that in all these cases there is similarity with difference—the characteristic of independent coincidence, not of imitation.

thoughtfulness, which might "overflow into knowledge," and prove "the things which are really excellent." There is no letter of St. Paul's so absolutely free from the necessity of rebuke, and, accordingly, there is none so full of joy, in spite of all the circumstances of suffering and anxiety under which it was written.

(2) *The Condition of the Church at Rome.*—The next great subject of interest is the light thrown by this Epistle on the progress of the Church at Rome during St. Paul's imprisonment. Of his preaching to the Jews, the Asiatic Gentiles, and the Greeks, we have plain historical record in the Acts of the Apostles. That record fails us at the moment when he reaches the great centre of heathen civilisation at Rome, simply telling us that his imprisonment was not allowed to be a hindrance to his preaching, first (as always) with the Jews, then, on their rejection of the gospel, to the Gentiles who were "willing to hear it." Now, we know by the history of the Neronian persecution in Tacitus that, less than ten years after St. Paul's arrival in Rome, the Christians were already "a vast multitude," not only in the Eastern home of their religion, but in the metropolis itself. While we perceive from St. Paul's Epistle to the Romans that, before that arrival Christianity was firmly established in Rome, and suspect that the ignorance of the Jewish leaders concerning "the sect everywhere spoken against" (Acts xxviii. 22) was in great degree affected, yet we cannot but see that these ten years must have been years of rapid progress, in order to justify, even approximately, the description of the Roman historian. Naturally, we conclude that St. Paul's presence, even in his prison, must have given the chief new impulse to such progress, and inquire eagerly for any indications of his actual discharge to the Romans of the debt of gospel preaching which he had long ago acknowledged as due to them (Rom. i. 14, 15). To this inquiry almost the only answer is found in the Epistle to the Philippians.

There we learn that, as we might have expected, St. Paul's bonds "turned out" to the great "furtherance of the gospel." Wherever his prison actually was, it gave him opportunity of influence over the Prætorian guards, and all the rest of the world, civilian or military, who frequented their quarters; it gave him access, moreover, to those of Cæsar's household—that large community of the *domus Augusta* which included all varieties of occupation, character, and rank. That the earlier Christianity of Rome was largely under Jewish influence we learn from the whole argument of the Epistle to the Romans; and it has been often remarked that the names included in the long list of salutations in the last chapter show a preponderance of Greek nationality in the converts themselves. But of those who came under the spell of St. Paul's presence, probably comparatively few would be Jews, although indeed at this time, through the influence of Poppæa, the Jewish element might be more than usually prominent in Cæsar's household; and while the greater number of that household who came in contact with him would be slaves of various nationalities, still, in the higher officers and among the Prætorian soldiery, many would be of true Roman origin. Remembering the friendship of Seneca for Burrhus, the Prætorian Prefect at the time of St. Paul's arrival, and the former conduct of Gallio, Seneca's brother, towards the Apostle at Corinth, many have delighted to speculate on the probability of some direct intercourse between the Apostle of the Gentiles and the philosopher of the later and more religious Stoicism, who was then the leader of higher Roman thought. But, however this may be, and whatever may be the real weight of the apparent similarities to familiar Stoic phraseology traceable in the Epistle (see chap. iv. 11—13, and Notes thereon), those who remember the eagerness of Roman society at this time for new religions, new mysteries, and even new superstitions, from the East, will find no difficulty in believing that one who was placed, by the circumstance of his imprisonment, in the imperial court itself, might easily have produced a deep impression on men of Roman birth, perhaps of high Roman rank.

This new Christianity would therefore probably be of a type, more purely Gentile, less predominantly Oriental, than the Christianity to which the Epistle to the Romans was addressed. Of the division between the old and the new the Epistle shows traces, in the description of those who preached Christ "of good will" to St. Paul, and those who preached in "factiousness and vain-glory;" for it seems clear, from his rejoicing that "every way Christ was preached," that the division was as yet one of mere faction and party, not of the contrast of false with true doctrine, which we know that he treated with stern, uncompromising severity. (See 2 Cor. xi. 1—4; Gal. i. 6—9.) Like all such divisions, it probably marked and justified itself by some differences in religious teaching and religious life: but if these existed, they did not go down to the foundation. The time, indeed, was not far distant, when the fall of Jerusalem, and the obvious passing away of the whole Jewish dispensation, struck the final blow to the existence of Judaism in the Christian Church. In spite, therefore, of this division, it seems clear that at the time of the Philippian Epistle Christianity had advanced, and was advancing, with rapid strides. "The city which is in heaven" was already beginning to rise from its foundations in the "great Babylon of the Seven Hills," now the very type of the kingdom of the earth, destined hereafter to be, even visibly, the metropolis of Western Christianity.

(3) *The main Subjects of the Epistle.*—Turning to the teaching of the Epistle itself, the main interest centres round the great passage in the second chapter (ii. 5—11), which is the very creed of the Incarnation, Passion, and Exaltation of our Lord Jesus Christ. This has been noticed already in the *General Introduction to the Epistles of the Captivity*, and is dealt with in detail in the Notes on the passage. Here it need only be remarked that its advanced Christology is made the more striking by the occasion of its occurrence, which is, in point of form, simply incidental, in enforcement of the familiar exhortation to follow the mind of Christ Jesus in humility and self-sacrifice; and that the singular simplicity and clearness of its enunciation of truth stand to the profounder and more mysterious teaching on the same subject in the Epistle to the Colossians, much as, in later times, the simplicity of a Western creed stands to the greater subtlety of an Eastern. Next in interest, though after a long interval, is the light thrown (in chap. iii.) on the obstinate persistence in Macedonia of the old Judaising influence, elsewhere decaying or passing into new forms; and the appearance both of the pretensions to perfection (chap. iii. 12—16) and of the Antinomian recklessness (chap. iii. 17—21)—sometimes associated with these pretensions, sometimes in revolt against them—with which we are but too familiar in subsequent Church history.

(4) *Analysis of the Epistle.*—A full analysis will be found in each chapter. A shortened general sketch of these analyses we have subjoined as usual.

PHILIPPIANS.

1. The First Section (original Letter?).

(1) INTRODUCTION.

(a) *Salutation* (chap. i. 1, 2);

(b) *Thanksgiving for their "fellowship" in the work of the gospel, specially shown towards himself* (chap. i. 3—8);

(c) *Prayer for their fuller knowledge and increase of fruitfulness to the end* (chap. i. 9—11).

(2) DECLARATION OF THE POSITION AT ROME.

(a) *The progress of the gospel through his bonds, stimulating preaching of the gospel, partly in good will, partly in strife, but in any case a cause of joy* (chap. i. 12—18);

(b) *His own division of feeling, between desire to depart, and a willingness to remain for their sakes, which he knows will be realised* (chap. i. 19—26).

(3) EXHORTATION:

(a) *To steadfast boldness under persecution, now present or imminent* (chap. i. 27—30);

(b) *To unity of spirit in the humility and self-sacrifice of "the mind of Christ Jesus"* (chap. ii. 1—4).

(4) THE DOCTRINE OF CHRIST.

(a) *His humility in the Incarnation: stooping from the form of God to the form of man* (chap. ii. 5—7);

(b) *His second humility in the Passion* (chap. ii. 8);

(c) *His exaltation above all created being* (chap. ii. 9—11).

(5) ORIGINAL CONCLUSION OF THE EPISTLE.

(a) *Final exhortation to obedience, quietness, purity, joy with him in sacrifice* (chap. ii. 12—18);

(b) *Mission and commendation of Timotheus as St. Paul's forerunner* (chap. ii. 19—24);

(c) *Mission and commendation of Epaphroditus* (chap. ii. 25—30);

(d) *Final "farewell in the Lord"* (chap. iii. 1).

2. The Second Section (Postscript?).

(1) PRACTICAL WARNINGS:

(a) *Against Judaism, by the example of his own renunciation of all Jewish privilege* (chap. iii. 2—10);

(b) *Against claim of perfection, again enforced by his own example* (chap. iii. 11—16);

(c) *Against Antinomian profligacy, as unworthy of the "citizens of heaven"* (chap. iii. 17—21).

(2) EXHORTATIONS RENEWED:

(a) *To unity* (chap. iv. 1—3);

(b) *To joy, thankfulness, and peace* (chap. iv. 4—7);

(c) *To following of all good, in the fulness in which he had taught it* (chap. iv. 8, 9).

(3) ACKNOWLEDGMENT OF OFFERINGS.

(a) *Rejoicing in their renewed care for him* (chap. iv. 10—14);

(b) *Remembrance of their former liberality* (chap. iv. 15—17);

(c) *Thanks and blessing* (chap. iv. 18—20).

(4) CONCLUDING SALUTATION AND BLESSING.

THE EPISTLE OF PAUL THE APOSTLE TO THE

PHILIPPIANS

CHAPTER I.—(1) Paul and Timotheus, the servants of Jesus Christ, to all the saints in Christ Jesus which are at Philippi, with the bishops and deacons: (2) grace *be* unto you, and

Chap. i. 1, 2. Salutation.

A.D. 64.

[1. **Introduction** (chap. i. 1—11).

(1) SALUTATION (verses 1, 2).

(2) THANKSGIVING for their "fellowship in the gospel," uttered in perfect confidence and in deep personal affection (verses 3—8).

(3) PRAYER for their growth in knowledge and judgment, which may guard them from "offence," and keep them in the things that are excellent (verses 9—11).]

(1) **Paul and Timotheus, (the) servants of Jesus Christ.**—To the Philippian, as to the Thessalonian Church (see 1 Thess. i. 1; 2 Thess. i. 1), St. Paul does not think it needful to assert his apostleship; but writes, in a tone of affectionate and confident familiarity, as to those whom he could thoroughly trust. Here he and Timotheus are simply "servants" (not, as in our version, "the servants" in any position of special eminence) "of Jesus Christ"—a title of humility assumed by St. James and St. Jude (Jas. i. 1; Jude, verse 1), but nowhere else by St. Paul without the addition of some title of apostolic authority. (Comp. Rom. i. 1; Tit. i. 1.) Even in Gal. i. 10 he declares that he is "the servant of Christ," chiefly to show that he cannot and need not "please men." It is to be noted also that here, as again (with Silas) in the Thessalonian Epistles, Timotheus is joined with St. Paul almost on a footing of equality whereas in other Epistles (see 2 Cor. i. 1; Col, i. 1; Philem. verse 1), he is separated from the Apostle and distinguished as "Timotheus the brother." This is probably to be accounted for partly by the absence of all necessity for assertion of his own apostleship, partly also by the fact that (with Silas) Timotheus was St. Paul's fellow-worker in the conversion of the Macedonian Churches, and accordingly his chosen messenger to them from time to time (Acts xix. 22; xx. 5).

The saints in Christ Jesus.—The same expression is used in the salutations which commence other Epistles of this period (see Eph. i. 1; Col. i. 1): "the saints and faithful in Christ Jesus."

With the bishops and deacons.—In this passage the word "bishop" is, for the first time, used as a title, although in Acts xx. 28 ("over which the Holy Ghost hath made you overseers") it is employed as a description of duty, with a distinct reference to its etymological meaning and origin. In the Pastoral Epistles we find it similarly used (as 1 Tim. iii. 2; Tit. i. 7). There is now no question—and but for supposed ecclesiastical necessities there never could have been any question—that in Holy Scripture, as also in the First Epistle of an Apostolical Father (*St. Clement to the Corinthians*, chap. xix.), the two titles of "bishop" and "presbyter" are applied to the same persons—the latter, however, being in St. Paul's Epistles the more frequent and conventional term, while the former seems almost always used with reference to its actual meaning. The two titles are of diverse origin. The "presbyter," or "elder," is a Jewish title, so directly descended from the synagogue that the institution of the presbyterate is not, like that of the diaconate, recorded as a historical creation in the Church. The title of "bishop," or "overseer," is of heathen origin, used in classical Greek for a commissioner from head-quarters, applied in the LXX. to various secular offices (2 Kings xi. 19; 2 Chron. xxiv. 12—17; Neh. xi. 9, 14, 22; Isa. lx. 17). The former is simply a title of dignity, like the many derivations from the Latin *senior* which have passed into modern language. The latter is a title of official duty. Like the word "pastor" and "apostle," it belongs properly only to the Lord Jesus Christ, who is the "Apostle of God" (Heb. iii. 1), and "the Shepherd and Bishop of our souls" (1 Pet. ii. 25); but derivatively to His ministers, as having the oversight of His Church. This is directly shown in the application of the title to the Ephesian presbyters (Acts xx. 28; see also 1 Pet. v. 1, 2), and the idea of responsible oversight is brought out clearly in the description of the office of the "bishop" in 1 Tim. iii. 1—7. The indifferent use of the two names is made absolutely clear in Tit. i. 5—7: "Ordain elders in every city . . . if any be blameless . . . For a bishop must be blameless as a steward of God." It is only necessary to remark briefly that this identification of the two titles (of which St. Clement's Epistle is the last example) in no way weakens the significance of the undoubted historical fact of the development of what we call the Episcopate in the early part of the second century, and the overwhelming probability of its origination, under the sanction of St. John, when the representatives of the higher order of the Apostolate passed away.

The name "deacon" is also used for the first time, unless, indeed, as is probable, it is applied officially to Phœbe in Rom. xvi. 1. Although the office of the Seven, in Acts vi. 1—7, is undoubtedly the germ of the diaconate, and although the cognate words ("ministration" and "serve") are used in connection with them (see verses 1, 2), yet the actual title of deacons is nowhere given to them.

This mention of the ministers as distinct from the Church in salutation is unique. It has been conjectured, with great probability, that in the Letter of

peace, from God our Father, and *from*
the Lord Jesus Christ. (3) I thank my
God upon every remem-
brance[1] of you, (4) always
in every prayer of mine
for you all making re-
quest with joy, (5) for your fellowship
in the gospel from the first day until
now; (6) being confident of this very
thing, that he which hath begun a
good work in you will perform *it*[2]
until the day of Jesus Christ. (7) Even
as it is meet for me to think this
of you all, because I have you in
my heart;[3] inasmuch as both in my
bonds, and in the defence and confirma-

Chap. i. 3—8. Thanksgiving for their fellowship in the gospel.

1 Or, *mention.*

2 Or, *will finish it.*

3 Or, *you have me in your heart.*

---

the Philippian Church, which no doubt accompanied the mission of alms by Epaphroditus, the presbyters and deacons were so distinguished; as in the letter of the Council at Jerusalem, according to the ordinary reading of Acts xv. 23 ("the apostles and elders and brethren"). Some ancient authorities held that Epaphroditus was "the apostle" (or what we should call the bishop) of the Church at Philippi, and that he is not named here simply because he was with St. Paul: so that in the Philippian Church the three orders were already represented. (But on this see chap. ii. 25.)

(3–8) In these verses St. Paul strikes that keynote of joy and confidence, which is dominant throughout the whole Epistle, and which is singularly remarkable when we remember that it was written in captivity, in enforced absence from the familiar and well-loved scenes of his apostolic labour, and with the knowledge of faction and jealousy, taking advantage of that absence. The words "joy" and "rejoice" occur no less than thirteen times in this short Epistle; they express what his own feeling is, and what he desires that theirs should be.

(3, 4) **I thank my God . . .**—These verses more accurately rendered will run thus: *I thank my God upon all my remembrance of you at all times, in every prayer of mine for you all, uttering that prayer with joy—i.e.,* with joyful confidence. The sense, however, is not materially altered. The emphatic earnestness of thanksgiving is seen in the reiteration which runs through the passage, and its absolute universality of scope is no less clearly marked. The closest parallel is again in the Epistles to the Thessalonians (see 1 Thess. i. 2; 2 Thess. ii. 3), although in every Epistle, except the Epistle to the Galatians, there is an opening of thanksgiving.

(5) **For your fellowship in the gospel.**—More properly, *towards the gospel,* or, *as affecting the gospel.* The construction is illustrated by the more limited use of the same Greek word (as in Rom. xv. 26; 2 Cor. ix. 13) in the sense of "contribution"; in which case the word "towards" introduces the objects of the almsgiving there specified. Accordingly St. Paul must be taken here to mean the fellow-working of the Philippians in the ministry of the gospel, of which he speaks still more distinctly in verse 7. That fellow-working had been shown (see chap. iv. 15) even "in the beginning of the gospel," by a contribution to St. Paul's needs—not perhaps his personal needs only—which from them, and (so far as we know) from them only, he consented to accept.

(6) **That he who hath begun** (or rather, *who began*) **a good work in you will also** (see margin) **finish it.**—The ground of St. Paul's confidence in their perseverance is the belief that it was God's grace which began the good work in them, and that, not being resisted (as was obvious by their enthusiasm for good), He would complete what He had begun. In his view, God's grace is the beginning and the end; man's co-operation lies in the intermediate process linking both together. This is made still plainer in chap. ii. 12, 13.

The day of Jesus Christ.—So also in chaps. i. 10, ii. 16, "the day of Christ;" and in 1 Cor. i. 8, "the day of our Lord Jesus Christ;" in all other Epistles "the day of our Lord" (as in 1 Cor. v. 5; 2 Cor. i. 14; 1 Thess. v. 2; 2 Thess. ii. 2); or, still more commonly, both in Gospels and Epistles, "that day." As is usual in the Epistles, the day of the Lord is spoken of as if it were near at hand. St. Paul, in the Second Epistle to the Thessalonians (chap. ii. 2, *et seq.*), declines to pronounce that it is near; yet does not say that it is far away, and only teaches that there is much to be done, even in the development of Anti-Christian power, before it does come. It is of course clear that, in respect of the confidence here expressed, it makes no difference whether it be near or far away. The reality of the judgment as final and complete is the one point important; "the times and seasons" matter not to us.

(7) **It is meet.**—Rather, *it is but right,* or *just; it is but your due.*

To think this of you all.—Rather, *to be in this mind; to have this feeling on behalf of you all.* The word here rendered "to think" is used with especial frequency in this Epistle (see chaps. ii. 2, 5; iii. 15, 19; iv. 2, 10), as also in the Epistle to the Romans (chaps. viii. 5; xi. 20; xii. 3, 16; xiv. 16; xv. 5). It is variously rendered; but it always refers, not to a single definite opinion, but to an habitual conviction or feeling.

I have you in my heart.—This (and not the marginal reading) is to be taken. The original is, grammatically speaking, ambiguous, but both the order and the context are decisive. Compare, for the sense, 2 Cor. iii. 2, "Ye are our epistle, written in our hearts."

Both in my bonds, and in the defence and confirmation of the gospel.—These words are certainly to be connected, as in our version. St. Paul unites his bonds with "the defence and confirmation of the gospel"—that is, with his pleading for it against objections, and establishment of it by positive teaching—on the ground stated in verses 12, 13, that these, his bonds, had tended "to the furtherance of the gospel." He accepts the help sent him by the Philippians, in which they had (see chap. iv. 14) "communicated" (in the original the word used is the same as here) "with his affliction," as a means of fellowship with him in the whole of this work of evangelisation. It is true that in verse 30 he speaks of the Philippians as having themselves to undergo "the same conflict" as his own; but the expression "in my bonds, &c.," can hardly be satisfied simply by this kind of fellowship.

Ye all are partakers of my grace.—Here, on the contrary, the marginal reading is preferable. *Ye are all partakers with me of the grace—i.e.,* of the

tion of the gospel, ye all are partakers
of my grace.[1] (8) For God is my record,
how greatly I long after you all in
the bowels of Jesus Christ. (9) And this
I pray, that your love may abound yet
more and more in knowledge and *in* all
judgment;[2] (10) that ye may approve[3]
things that are excellent;[4]
that ye may be sincere and
without offence till the
day of Christ; (11) being
filled with the fruits of righteousness,

[2] Or, *sense.*
[3] Or, *try.*
[1] Or, *partakers with me of grace.*
[4] Or, *differ.*

Chap. i. 9—11. Prayer for their fuller knowledge and steadfastness.

---

privilege described in Eph. iii. 8. "Unto me, who am less than the least of all saints, is this grace given, that I should preach among the Gentiles the unsearchable riches of Christ." See below, verse 29; "To you it is given"—that is (in the original), "given as a grace"—not only to believe on Him, but also to suffer for His sake."

(8) **God is my record.**—We have a similar adjuration in Rom. i. 9; 2 Cor. i. 23; 1 Thess. ii. 5, 10. These instances show in what sense St. Paul interpreted such commands as the "swear not at all" of Matt. v. 34.

In the bowels of Jesus Christ.—The use of the word, which we translate (not very happily or correctly) by "bowels," is common with St. Paul. (See 2 Cor. vi. 12; vii. 15; Col. iii. 12; Philem. verses 7, 12, 20.) It corresponds to our use of "heart" as the seat of affection—the word "heart" itself in the New Testament being employed, in a wider sense, to signify the whole inner man. (See Eph. i. 18: "the eyes of your heart being enlightened," and Note there.) But the phrase here is striking and even startling. "I long after you" (says St. Paul) "in the heart of Jesus Christ." He can say (as in Gal. ii. 20), "I live, yet not I, but Christ liveth in me." Hence the deep yearning of love which he feels for them he knows to be an emanation, faint indeed, but true, from the "heart of Jesus Christ" dwelling in him.

(9, 10) If we study carefully the opening thanksgivings and prayers of St. Paul's Epistles, we may note that he always thanks God for what is strong in the Church to which he writes, and prays God for the supply of that in which it is weak. Here he thanks God for the characteristic enthusiasm and large-heartedness of the Philippians; he prays for their advance in knowledge, perception, judgment — the more intellectual and thoughtful side of the Christian character—in which they, and perhaps the Macedonian Churches generally, were less conspicuous. In the opposite case of the Corinthian Church (see 1 Cor. i. 4—10), he thanks God for their richness in all utterance and all knowledge, but he bids them "wait" for Him who shall "establish them as blameless," and exhorts them to unity and humility.

(9—11) In this sentence, the original shows that there is not the three-fold parallelism which our version would suggest. St. Paul's immediate prayer is that "their love may abound in knowledge and all judgment." To this is subjoined, as an immediate consequence, "the proving the things that are excellent." The final result of the knowledge and judgment so applied, is "that they may be sincere and without offence."

(9) **That your love may abound more and more in knowledge.**—The original verb here signifies to "overflow," a sense which our word "abound" properly has, but has in general usage partially lost; and St. Paul's meaning clearly is that love shall not only primarily fill the heart, but "overflow" in secondary influence on the spiritual understanding. (1) The "knowledge" here spoken of is the knowledge gradually rising to perfection, so constantly alluded to in these Epistles. (See Eph. i. 17, and Note there.) Since it is clearly a personal knowledge of God in Christ, it may be gained, under His inspiration, by one of many processes, by thought, by practice, by love, by devotion, or, perhaps more properly, by some or all of these combined. Here St. Paul singles out the way of love—the enthusiasm of love to God and man which he knew that the Philippians had—and prays that it may overflow from the emotional to the intellectual element of their nature, and become, as we constantly see that it does become in simple and loving characters, a means of spiritual insight, in "knowledge and all judgment," or rather, *all perception.* (2) The word "perception" properly applies to the senses, and seems here to signify the insight which recognises a truth as the eye recognises an object. In the same sense (Heb. v. 14) Holy Scripture speaks of those who "by use have *their senses* exercised to discern good and evil." In fact, the "perception" here spoken of differs from knowledge in dealing not with general principles, but with concrete examples and questions. (3) Accordingly he connects with it, as a direct consequence, the power of "approving" or "testing" the things that are excellent. Now the word here translated "excellent" carries with it the idea of distinctive and relative excellence, conspicuous amidst what is either evil or defective. To "test" is obviously first to distinguish what is the best, and then by trial to prove its absolute goodness. Clearly the process may be applied either speculatively to truths or practically to duties. In Rom. ii. 18, where exactly the same phrase is used, the latter application is made.

(10) **That ye may be sincere and without offence.**—This St. Paul contemplates as the result of thoughtful and discriminating judgment. The word "sincere" (used only here and in 2 Pet. i. 3), and the corresponding substantive, "sincerity" (1 Cor. v. 8; 2 Cor. i. 12; ii. 17), although there is some uncertainty as to their derivation, undoubtedly signify purity tested and found clear of all base admixtures. The word "without offence" is used in Acts xxiv. 16 ("a conscience void of offence") for that which is free from the stumbling of error; and in 1 Cor. x. 32 ("giving none offence") for that at which none will stumble. The latter sense (nearly equivalent to the "unreprovable" of Col. i. 22) better suits this passage. For "sincere" describes the positive aspect of purity; "without offence" the more negative aspect, in which it is found to present no excuse for fault-finding or scandal. It is, therefore, the "sincerity," not of unconscious innocence, but of well-tried and thoughtful purity, proof even against suspicion, which St. Paul describes as the perfect fruit of love "overflowing in knowledge."

(11) **The fruits of righteousness** is an Old Testament phrase (see Prov. xi. 30; Amos vi. 12), used also in Jas. iii. 18; Heb. xii. 11. It may mean (as in these last two passages) "righteousness as a result," or (in

which are by Jesus Christ, unto the
glory and praise of God.
(12) But I would ye should
understand, brethren, that
the things *which* hap-
pened unto me have fallen
out rather unto the furtherance of
the gospel; (13) so that my bonds in
Christ[1] are manifest in all the palace,[2]
and in all other *places;*[3] (14) and many of
the brethren in the Lord, waxing confi-
dent by my bonds, are much more bold

Chap. i. 12—18. Description of the progress of the gospel at Rome, and his joy thereat.

1 Or, *for Christ.*
2 Or, *Cæsar's court.*
3 Or, *to all others.*

---

the common sense of "fruit") the "result of righteousness." As the participle is properly "having been filled," thus referring, not to the future day of Christ, but to the whole time which that day shall complete, the former sense seems preferable. The righteousness which is "through Jesus Christ," "not" (as St. Paul says below, chap. iii. 9) "our own righteousness, which is of the Law, but that which is through the faith of Christ, the righteousness which is of God," is clearly the likeness of Christ, and therefore in itself an all-sufficient fruit. Filled with it, we are (see Eph. iii. 19) "filled with all the fulness of God."

Unto the glory and praise of God.—(Comp Eph. i. 6, 12, 14.) In accordance with our Lord's own teaching: "Let your light so shine before men, that they may see your good works, and glorify your Father which is in heaven." (See also 1 Cor. x. 31.)

[2. Statement of St. Paul's condition at Rome (verses 12—26).

(1) THE RAPID PROGRESS OF THE GOSPEL through his bonds, and through the preaching of others, whether in strife or in goodwill (verses 12—18).

(2) HIS REJOICING THEREAT; his desire to depart and be with Christ, and his confidence, nevertheless, that he will abide in the flesh and see them again (verses 19—26).]

(12—18) In these verses St. Paul, evidently anxious that the Philippians should not "faint at his tribulations for them" (comp. Eph. iii. 13), points out that his imprisonment tended to further the gospel: first, directly, by the opportunity which it afforded him of preaching, and next, indirectly, by the stimulus which it gave to the preaching of others, whether "of envy and strife" or "of good will."

(12) **The things which happened unto me**—*viz.*, since he parted from them (see Acts xx. 6)—his arrest at Jerusalem, and the long captivity of years, first at Cæsarea, then at Rome. Nothing could have appeared to be a more fatal blow to the progress of the gospel; but St. Paul assures them that "rather" (*i.e.*, on the contrary) all these things tended to its furtherance. He had intended to see Rome (Acts xix. 21; Rom. xv. 23, 24), since his work in Greece and Asia was now over. He did visit it, although in chains; and his acquaintance with the Roman soldiers at Cæsarea probably prepared for him an opening at Rome, which he could not otherwise have found, even into Cæsar's household.

(13) **My bonds in Christ are manifest.**—Properly, *My bonds are made manifest as in Christ*—*i.e.*, my captivity is understood as being a part of my Christian life and work, and so becomes a starting-point for the preaching of the gospel. So St. Paul made it to the Jews (Acts xxviii. 20), "For the hope of Israel am I bound in this chain." (Comp. Eph. vi. 20, "I am an ambassador in bonds.")

In all the palace, and in all other places.—The word "palace" is *prætorium.* It is elsewhere used in the New Testament: first, of the palace of Pilate; in Matt. xxvii. 27, Mark xv. 16, apparently, of the soldiers' guardroom, or barrack; in John xviii. 28, 33, xix. 9, of "the hall of judgment;" and next in Acts xxiii. 35, of the "judgment hall of Herod," evidently forming a part of the palace of Felix. (It may be noted that coincidence with this last passage is the chief, and almost the sole, argument for the untenable idea that this Epistle belongs to the Cæsarean and not the Roman captivity.) Its sense here has been disputed. It has been variously interpreted as the emperor's palace, or the prætorian barrack attached to it, or the prætorian camp outside the walls. Its original meaning of "the head-quarters of a general" would lend itself well enough to any of these, as a derivative sense. The first or the second sense (which is virtually the same) is the interpretation of all ancient commentators, and suits best with the mention of "Cæsar's household" in chap. iv. 22, but not very well with the historical statement in Acts xxviii. 16—30, that St. Paul dwelt "in his own hired house," "with a soldier that kept him." The other sense suits better with this last statement, and also with the delivery of the prisoner "to the captain of the guard," *i.e.*, literally, *the commander of the camp*, or *prætorian prefect*, and perhaps with abstract probability in the case of an obscure Jewish prisoner. But the difficulty is that, although the word might be applied to any of these places, yet, as a matter of fact, it is not found to be so applied. Moreover, we notice here that the words "in all other places" are an inaccurate rendering of a phrase really meaning "to all the rest" (see marginal reading). The connection therefore seems even in itself to suggest that the "prætorium" may more properly refer to a body of men than to a place. Accordingly (following Dr. Lightfoot), since the word "prætorium" is undoubtedly used for the "prætorian guard," it seems best to take that sense here. "My bonds" (says the Apostle) "are known in all the prætorian regiments"—for the soldiers, no doubt, guarded him by turns—"and to all the rest of the world, whether of soldiers or of citizens." This would leave it an open question where St. Paul was imprisoned, only telling us that it was under prætorian surveillance.

(14) **And many** (properly, *the greater number*) **of the brethren in the Lord.**—The words "in the Lord" should be connected with "trusting," as in chap. ii. 24; Gal. v. 10; 2 Thess. iii. 4. As connected with the word "brethren," they are unmeaning; whereas St. Paul constantly uses them (especially in these Epistles), generally with a verb or verbal adjective, and always to convey some distinct idea. That the words "in my bonds" follow constitutes no difficulty. "In the Lord" expresses the ground of confidence; "in my bonds" simply the occasion and circumstances.

Waxing confident by my bonds.—There is a two-fold sense here, corresponding to the two-fold division of preachers made below. Those who preached Christ "of contention" trusted in St. Paul's captivity as giving them scope; those who preached "of good

to speak the word without fear. (15) Some
indeed preach Christ even of envy and
strife; and some also of good will:
(16) the one preach Christ of contention,
not sincerely, supposing to add affliction
to my bonds: (17) but the other of love,
knowing that I am set for the defence
of the gospel. (18) What then? not-
withstanding, every way, whether in
pretence, or in truth, Christ is preached;
and I therein do rejoice, yea, and will
rejoice. (19) For I know that this shall

---

will" found in it a striking example of evil overruled to good, and so gained from it fresh encouragement.

(15) **Of envy and strife.**—Explained below as of "contention," or, more properly (as in chap. ii. 3, and in Rom. ii. 8; 2 Cor. xii. 20; Gal. v. 20), of *factiousness*, or "party spirit." It seems impossible to doubt that this refers to the Judaising party, St. Paul's old antagonists. The whole tenor of the Epistle to the Romans shows how strong a Judaic element there was in Roman Christianity. Even in approaching Rome, we may gather from Acts xxviii. 15, that the Apostle had felt doubtful of his reception there by the Church. His formal renunciation of the obstinate Jews, and proclamation that the Gentiles would hear what they had rejected, might excite against him not only the unbelieving Jews, but the Jewish and still more the Judaising Christians. The party "of Cephas" and the party "of Paul" might be placed in strong antagonism more easily than even at Corinth.

(16) **Not sincerely.**—This version conveys an incorrect impression. The original is "not purely," *i.e.,* not with unmixed and single-minded enthusiasm for Christ. St. Paul does not impute to them hypocrisy, but an admixture of partisanship, and therefore of a narrow-minded hostility to him.

To add affliction.—The true reading, *to stir up affliction,* or *oppressive severity* (properly, *pressure,* or *galling*), perhaps suggests as most probable the meaning (adopted by Chrysostom here) of "stirring" the minds of St. Paul's jailors to an increased severity, which might prevent his preaching to all "without hindrance." The uneasiness of the Government in relation to the Jewish population at Rome is well known. The growth of a secret society (for such Christianity was held to be) among them might easily induce greater severity towards a leader of the sect. (Compare verses 19, 20, in which St. Paul states his confidence that this malignant policy would be disappointed.)

(18) The contrast of this verse with such passages as 2 Cor. xii. 4—where the Judaisers at Corinth are said to preach "another Jesus and a different gospel;" with Gal. i. 6—where their gospel is declared to be "a different gospel," and not merely a variety of the same (see Note there); and even with the emphatic warning as to Philippi, in chap. iii. 2—16, is singularly instructive. St. Paul, in the words "in pretence" and "in truth," is speaking of the motives of the preachers, not of the substance of their preaching. For the latter he cares much; for the former nothing. When (as at Corinth) the rejection of his personal authority was bound up with rejection of his apostolic doctrine, he rebukes it vehemently; when (as here) there was no such connection, it is to him a very small thing. But we may also gather from this that, whatever might be the case at Philippi, at Rome St. Paul's Epistle had done its work, and the battle of principle was won; even at Colossæ it had wholly changed its character (see Col. ii. 16—23), and its old phases had passed away. The differences between the parties at Rome were no longer fundamental, although, as so often is the case, the bitterness of division might remain. "Every way Christ was preached," and accepted as justifying through faith. This being so, St. Paul could rejoice. Even an imperfect Christianity, with something of narrowness, and perhaps of superstitious formalism, cleaving to it, was as different from the gross heathenism which it superseded, as light from darkness.

Yea, and will rejoice.—Properly, *I shall rejoice* to the end. The words lead on to the next verse, which gives the reason of this persistent rejoicing.

(19—24) In these verses, under the power of that feeling of joy of which he speaks above, St. Paul unveils to the Philippians his most sacred aspirations and convictions, and the division of feeling in his own soul between longing for rest and consciousness of work yet to be done. There is a still fuller disclosure of a similar "spiritual experience" in 2 Cor. iv. 8; v. 15. It is rare in the apostolic writings. St. Paul seems, in 2 Cor. vi. 11, almost to apologise for disclosing what is usually kept, in delicacy and reverence, for God alone.

(19) **Shall turn to my salvation.**—Or, literally, *shall issue in salvation to me.* The word "salvation" does not appear to be used here in its ordinary sense, that is, of primary or ultimate salvation from sin in Christ, but in the sense of "safety." The enemies of the Apostle thought to stir up fresh danger and difficulty for St. Paul; but the attempt (he says) will only turn out to his safety—a safety which he believes (see verses 25, 26) will be shown "in life," by his actual release and return to his beloved churches, but which, if God so wills it, will be at least equally manifested in the "death," which would bring him safe home to Christ. In either case he will be safe from all the enmity both of open sin and of malignant jealousy.

Through your prayer, and the supply of the Spirit.—This overruling of all enmity to his safety he hopes for through the intercession of the Philippian Church (comp. Philem. verse 23), and the fresh supply of grace which, through such intercession, may be given to him. For the word "supply" in this sense see Eph. iv. 15; and comp. Gal. iii. 5; Col. ii. 19.

The Spirit of Jesus Christ.—Of the application of this name to the Holy Ghost we have instances in Rom. viii. 9; 2 Cor. iii. 17; Gal. iv. 6; 1 Pet. i. 11. Of these the first is the most notable, since in two clauses of the same sentence we have first "the Spirit of God," and then "the Spirit of Christ." He who is "sent by the Father in the name of the Son" (John xiv. 26), and whose regeneration of the soul is the working out the image of Christ in it, may well be called "the Spirit of Christ." But the name has always some speciality of emphasis. Thus here, the whole conception of the passage is of Christ—"to me to live is Christ;" hence the use of this special and comparatively rare name of the Holy Ghost.

turn to my salvation through your prayer, and the supply of the Spirit of Jesus Christ,

Chap. i. 19—26. And of his own division of feeling between desires to depart and to continue.

(20) according to my earnest expectation and *my* hope, that in nothing I shall be ashamed, but *that* with all boldness, as always, *so* now also Christ shall be magnified in my body, whether *it be* by life, or by death.
(21) For to me to live *is* Christ, and to die *is* gain.
(22) But if I live in the flesh, this *is* the fruit of my labour: yet what I shall choose I wot not.
(23) For I am in a strait betwixt two, having a desire to depart, and to be with Christ;

---

(20) **My earnest expectation.**—The word is only found here and in Rom. viii. 19 (where see Note). It implies an intense and almost painful longing for some crisis, a dulness of suspense lighted up with hope. The phrase is one of the many indications that the joyful and confident tone so often noticed in this Epistle came not from the absence of yearning for the freedom and activity of apostolic life, but from the victory over such longings through faith. Whatever the crisis might be, St. Paul looked eagerly for it.

In nothing I shall be ashamed.—The phrase is elsewhere used by St. Paul with especial reference to the shame which comes from hopes disappointed and professions unfulfilled. (See 2 Cor. vii. 14; ix. 4; x. 8. Compare also the quotation from Isa. xxviii. 16 in Rom. ix. 33; 1 Pet. ii. 6.) For (he says) "hope (fulfilled) maketh not ashamed" (Rom. v. 5). So probably here; he trusts that in the hour of trial the confidence which he has felt and professed of being "able to do all things through Christ who strengtheneth him" (see chap. iv. 13) may not come to shameful failure, but may "magnify Christ in all boldness of speech." There is a subtle touch of true Christian feeling in the fact that, when he speaks of the chance of failure, he uses the first person: "I shall be ashamed;" but when of triumph, it is "Christ shall be magnified" in me. If he fails, it must be through his own fault; if he triumphs, it will be through his Master's strength.

In my body, whether it be by life, or by death.—"In my body:" The phrase is, no doubt, suggested mainly by the idea of death—the death of a martyr in bodily torture or shame. There is the same connection of idea in 2 Cor. iv. 10: "always bearing about in the body the dying of the Lord Jesus, so that the life also of Jesus may be made manifest in our body." But while the word "flesh" is used in the New Testament in a bad sense, the "body" is always regarded as that in which we may "glorify God" (1 Cor. vi. 20) by word and deed. It is not merely a vesture of the soul, but a part of the true man (1 Thess. v. 23), having membership of Christ, and being the temple of the Holy Ghost (1 Cor. vi. 15—19). In this passage the whole idea is of Christ in him; hence his body is spoken of as simply the tabernacle of the indwelling presence of Christ, and devoted only to "magnify" Him.

(21) **To live is Christ.**—This, of course, means "Christ is my life," yet not in the sense that He is the source and principle of life in us, but that the whole concrete state of life is so lived in Him that it becomes a simple manifestation of His presence. The opposition in the passage is between the states of living and dying (or being dead), not between the principles of life and death. It is, therefore, in some sense distinct from the cognate passages—Col. iii. 3, 4, "Ye are dead, and your life is hid with Christ in God. . . . Christ is our life;" and Gal. ii. 20, "I live, yet not I, but Christ liveth in me." Those passages set forth the cause; this the result. If Christ be the principle of life in us, then whatever we think and say and do, exhibiting visibly that inner life, must be the manifestation of Christ.

To die is gain.—This follows from the other. Death is a new stage in the progress of union with Christ. So we read in 2 Cor. v. 6, 7, "Knowing that, whilst we are at home in the body, we are absent from the Lord . . . we are willing rather to be absent from the body, and to be present with the Lord." "To depart" (see verse 23) is, in a higher sense than can be realised here, "to be with Christ."

(22) **But if I live in the flesh . . .**—The translation of this verse in the Authorised version is inaccurate, and perhaps a gloss to soften the difficulty of the original. The exact translation is, *But if to live in the flesh this is to me a fruit of work, and what* (or, *what also*) *I shall choose I know not.* The construction is clearly broken by emotion or absorption in thought; it can only be supplied by conjecture. If (as in 2 Cor. ii. 2) the word "and," or "also," can be used to introduce the principal clause ("what then I shall choose," &c.), the construction will be correct, though harsh. If otherwise, we must suppose either that the sentence is broken at the word "work," or that the whole should run, *But what if to live in the flesh is a part of work? And what I shall choose, I know not,* &c. But though the construction is obscure, the sense is plain. St. Paul had said, "to die is gain." But the thought crosses him that to live still in the flesh, this and this only is (*i.e.*, carries with it) a fruit of apostolical labour, in souls brought to Christ or built up in Him. Accordingly what to choose he knows not. For in such a harvest there is a gain, which outweighs his own personal gain on the other side.

I am in a strait betwixt (*the*) two.—The word here used signifies "to be hemmed in," or "confined," and is generally associated with some idea of distress (as in Luke viii. 45; xix. 43), not unfrequently with the pressure of disease (Matt. iv. 24; Luke iv. 38; Acts xxviii. 8). Our Lord uses it of mental distress in Himself (Luke xii. 50): "How am I straitened till it be accomplished!" Here the sense is clear. St. Paul's mind is "hemmed in" between two opposing considerations, till it knows not which way to move, even in desire.

(23) **Having a desire . . .**—Properly, *having my own desire for departure.* The verb "depart" corresponds exactly to the substantive used in 2 Tim. iv. 6, "The time of my departure is at hand." It is itself used only here and in Luke xii. 36, "When he shall return (*break up*) from the wedding." The metaphor is drawn either from "loosing" from the shore of life, or (perhaps better) from striking tents and breaking up a camp. The body (as in 2 Cor. v. 1) is looked upon as a mere tabernacle. Each day is a march nearer home, and death is the last striking of the tent on arrival.

which is far better: (24) nevertheless to
abide in the flesh *is* more needful for
you. (25) And having this confidence, I
know that I shall abide and continue
with you all for your furtherance and
joy of faith; (26) that your rejoicing may
be more abundant in Jesus Christ for me
by my coming to you again. (27) Only
let your conversation be
as it becometh the gospel
of Christ: that whether I
come and see you, or else
be absent, I may hear of
your affairs, that ye stand

Chap. i. 27–30. Exhortation to unflinching and joyful steadfastness in suffering.

To be with Christ.—This is contemplated by St. Paul as the immediate consequence of death, even while still "out of the body," and before the great day. The state of the faithful departed is usually spoken of as one of "rest" (1 Cor. xv. 51, 52; 1 Thess. iv. 14—16; Rev. xiv. 13), although not without expectation and longing for the consummation of all things (Rev. vi. 10, 11). Such a condition of rest, and suspension of conscious exercise of spiritual energy, is, indeed, that which human reason and analogy would suggest, so far as they can suggest anything on this mysterious subject. But such passages as this seem certainly to imply that this rest is emphatically a "rest in the Lord," having an inner consciousness of communion with Christ. His "descent unto Hades," not only brings out the reality of the unseen world of souls, but also claims it as His. As on earth and in heaven, so also in the intermediate state, we are "ever with the Lord;" and that state, though not yet made perfect, is spiritually far higher than this earthly life. The original here is an emphatic double comparative, "far, far better."

(25) **I know.**—The word is not to be pressed too far. It is simply, "I feel certain;" and it is obvious to remark that in Acts xx. 25 it is used by St. Paul of a conviction (that he would "see the face" of the Ephesians "no more") which, so far as we can follow out the history, was not verified. The apostolic inspiration, like the apostolic power of miracle, was a gift relative to the apostolic work, not necessarily extending beyond it.

Abide and continue with you.—The latter verb is in the original a compound of the former, "I shall abide," and "shall abide side by side with you." It was for their sakes that it was needful for him to live. Hence to the simple idea "I shall abide," it was natural to add at once the phrase "with you," or "for you," as explaining the very object of his abiding in the flesh.

For your furtherance and joy of faith.—In these words St. Paul's presence with them is spoken of, first, as in some degree necessary for their spiritual advance; next, as being to them a gift of God for their joy and comfort, even beyond what was actually necessary. (See the next verse.)

(26) **That your rejoicing may be more abundant.**—The word translated "rejoicing" is that favourite word of St. Paul, which signifies a ground of "boasting," or exultation. It is used both of blessing beyond strict necessity, and of service beyond legal duty; in both of which there is ground for joy and thankfulness. This is, perhaps, best seen in 1 Cor. ix. 15—18, where he declares that the simple preaching of the gospel is "nothing to boast of," but that the preaching it without cost is "the boasting," of which he says that he would "rather die than that any man should make it void." (Comp. also the use of the same word in chap. ii. 16, and in Rom. iv. 2; 1 Cor. v. 6; 2 Cor. i. 14; v. 12; ix. 3.) Here, therefore, St. Paul speaks of them as having in him, and in their connection with him, a cause of boasting, or rejoicing, just as in 2 Cor. i. 14 ("We are your rejoicing, even as ye also are ours"), and declares that this will become "more abundant" by his coming to them again.

In Jesus Christ for me.—The original runs, "in Christ Jesus *in* me." The parallelism is instructive: all Christian rejoicing, or confidence, is primarily "in Christ Jesus," even if it be secondarily "in" His servants. The suggestion of this idea here softens the apparent self-consciousness of the previous words. Comp., in 2 Cor. xi., xii., his declaration of reluctance and distaste for the "boasting" of his apostolic authority and work, which was forced upon him.

By my coming to you again.—See in 1 Tim. i. 3 the evidence of the fulfilment of this confident expectation.

[**3. Exhortation** (chaps. i. 27—ii. 4).

(1) To Steadfastness and Confidence under Persecution (verses 27—30).

(2) To Unity of Spirit, based on humility and self-forgetfulness (chap. ii. 1—4).]

(27—30) In these verses St. Paul exhorts the Philippians to unanimous boldness and steadfastness, under some conflict of antagonism or persecution which threatened them at this time. Of the history of the Church at Philippi we have no historical record after the notice of St. Paul's first visit, and of the violence which he then had to endure (Acts xvi. 12—40). But in 2 Cor. vii. 5, written certainly from Macedonia, probably from Philippi, towards the close of the third missionary journey, we find St. Paul saying, "When we were come to Macedonia our flesh had no rest. Without were fightings, within were fears." (Comp. also chap. viii. 2 of the same Epistle.) It would seem, therefore, that the subsequent history of the Philippian Church corresponded only too well to the circumstances under which its Christianity first began.

(27) **Let your conversation . . .**—The original is here (as in the famous passage, chap. iii. 20), *Use your citizenship* (that is, of the kingdom of heaven) *worthily of the gospel of Christ*. The same word is employed by St. Paul in Acts xxiii. 1 ("I have walked in all good conscience before God"), with an obvious reference to his citizenship in the chosen nation of Israel. Its use in this Epistle is suggestive—both as natural to one contemplating the great imperial city, and writing to the people of a Roman colony proud of their full citizenship, and also as leading on to that great conception of the unity of the Church in earth and in heaven, which is the main subject of the Ephesian, and in some degree of the Colossian, Epistle.

In one spirit, with one mind.—Rather, *in one spirit, one soul*. The phrase "in one spirit" may refer to the spirit of man, or to the Spirit of God. If it be intended to be strictly parallel to the "one soul" (which has no separate preposition in the Greek), the former sense is manifestly suggested. If, however, the words "with one soul" be connected, as is not

fast in one spirit, with one mind striving together for the faith of the gospel;
(28) and in nothing terrified by your adversaries: which is to them an evident token of perdition, but to you of salvation, and that of God.
(29) For unto you it is given in the behalf of Christ, not only to believe on him, but also to suffer for his sake;
(30) having the same conflict which ye saw in me, and now hear *to be* in me.

A.D. 64.

CHAPTER II. — (1) If *there be* therefore any consolation in Christ, if any comfort of love, if any

Chap. ii. 1—4. Exhortation to unity of spirit in humility and sympathy.

---

unnatural, with "striving together," this suggestion falls to the ground; and the usage of this Epistle (see especially chap. ii. 1—7), and the other Epistles of the same period (Eph. ii. 18—22; iii. 5; v. 18; vi. 18; Col. i. 8), certainly favours the latter interpretation. In either case "the soul" (as in the famous three-fold division of men's nature in 1 Thess. v. 23) is that element of humanity which is the seat of emotion and passion. (Comp. the "one heart and one soul" of Acts iv. 32.) This element the Christianity of the New Testament, unlike Stoicism or asceticism, will not crush, but enlist, as it enlists the body also, in the free service of God.

Striving together for the faith.—Properly, *with the faith.* The faith of the gospel—the power of Christianity—is personified. The Philippians are to be combatants on the same side against the same foes (compare the use of the same word in chap. iv. 3). The metaphor seems drawn from the games, as is seen by the use of the simple verb in 2 Tim. ii. 8, "If a man strive . . . he is not crowned, except he strive lawfully." In the exhortation to stand fast (comp. Eph. vi. 13, 14) we have the element of passive endurance, here of active and aggressive energy.

(28) **Terrified.**—The original word is strong—*starting*, or *flinching*, like a scared animal.

Which (that is, your fearlessness) **is . .**—This fearlessness, in the absence of all earthly means of protection or victory, is a sign of a divine "strength made perfect in weakness" (2 Cor. xiii. 9)—not a complete and infallible sign (for it has often accompanied mere fanatic delusion), but a sign real as far as it goes, having its right force in harmony with others. The effect which it had on the heathen themselves is shown even by the affected contempt with which the Stoics spoke of it, as a kind of "madness," a morbid "habit," a sheer "obstinacy." (See Epictetus, iv. 7; Marc. Aurelius, *Med.* xi. 3.)

And that of God.—These words apply to the word "token," and so derivatively both to "perdition" and "salvation." The sign is of God, because the gift of spiritual strength is of God, but it may be read by both sides. Like the pillar of God's presence, it is "a cloud and darkness" to the one, but "light by night" to the other.

(29) **For** (or, *because*) **unto you it is given in the behalf of Christ.**—The force lies, first, in the phrase "it is given" (rather, *it was given*, from the beginning)—for the original signifies "it was granted as a privilege" or "favour" (as in Acts xxvii. 24; 1 Cor. ii. 12; Gal. iii. 18)—and next in the words "on behalf of Christ." The fearlessness of the Christian is a gift of God, not an inherent stoic self-sufficiency. It rests indeed upon the sense that it is a privilege to suffer (see Acts v. 41) in the cause of truth, yet still more on the belief that such suffering is for no abstract principle, but on behalf of Christ and with Christ. (See chap. ii. 17, 18.)

Not only to believe . . .—The original shows that St. Paul speaks as if he originally intended simply to say "it is given on behalf of Christ to suffer." But to show whence the impulse of that brave willingness to suffer proceeds, he inserts "not only to believe on Him," and then finishes the sentence, "but on His behalf to suffer."

(30) **Having the same conflict, which ye saw in me.**—The allusion is, of course, to the lawless scourging and imprisonment of Acts xvi. 22—24. How deeply this outrage impressed itself on the Apostle's own mind we see, both by his conduct to the magistrates at the moment, and also by the allusion in 1 Thess. ii. 2, to the time, when "we had suffered before and were shamefully entreated, as ye know, at Philippi." Here he uses the remembrance to suggest to the Philippians that their struggle was only the same which he had borne, and borne successfully. Similarly in 2 Tim. iii. 10 (going back on the eve of death to the very beginning of his ministry to the Gentiles) he reminds Timothy of the persecutions "at Antioch, at Iconium, at Lystra—what persecutions I endured, but out of them all the Lord delivered me."

II.

(1—4) In this section the hint given above, in the allusion to "one spirit" and "one soul," is expanded into a direct exhortation to unity of spirit, as shown both by absence of self-assertion and by presence of a genial sympathy.

(1) **If there be therefore any consolation . . .**—In the four-fold division of this verse we trace, first, a reference to unity with Christ, and to a spiritual effect following from it; next, a similar reference to communion with the Holy Ghost, and a corresponding spiritual result. (1) "Consolation" is properly *encouragement*—the stirring up of spiritual activity—ascribed in Acts ix. 31 to the action of the Holy Spirit, but here viewed as a practical manifestation of the life flowing from union with Christ. Out of it comes naturally the "comfort of love," that is, as always, the deep and thankful sense of comfort in His love, overflowing into comfort, lovingly given to our brethren. On this "encouragement" in Christ, both received and given out to others, St. Paul dwells at length (2 Cor. i. 3—7). (2) Next, he speaks of "communion of the Spirit" (the very word used in 2 Cor. xiii. 13), by which, indeed, we are brought into that unity with Christ; and of this, still keeping to the main idea of love, he makes the manifestation to be in "bowels and mercies"—that is, both in strong affection, and in that peculiar form of affection which is directed towards suffering, viz., compassion or pity. The whole passage (like chap. iv. 8, 9) is full of a grave and persuasive eloquence characteristic of this Epistle. No absolute distinction is to be drawn between the two elements of the sentence; but it may be noted that

fellowship of the Spirit, if any bowels
and mercies, (2) fulfil ye my joy, that ye
be likeminded, having the same love,
being of one accord, of one mind. (3) *Let*
nothing *be done* through strife or vain-
glory; but in lowliness of mind let each
esteem other better than themselves.
(4) Look not every man on his own things,
but every man also on the
things of others. (5) Let
this mind be in you, which
was also in Christ Jesus:
(6) who, being in the form
of God, thought it not

Chap. ii. 5—11. The two-fold humility and the corresponding exaltation of the Lord Jesus Christ.

---

the "consolation in Christ" is exhibited in the action which visibly follows His divine example, "the communion with the Holy Spirit" is shown by the inner emotion, not seen, but felt.

(2) **That ye be likeminded, having the same love, being of one accord, of one mind.**—In this verse there is again a four-fold division; but of a different kind. St. Paul begins with the exhortation not uncommon from him, to be likeminded," that is, to have true sympathy (as in Rom. xii. 16; xv. 5; 2 Cor. xiii. 11; also chap. iii. 16; iv. 2); which he naturally strengthens by the addition of "having the same love" (that is, a mutual love), to show that the sympathy is to be one not only of mind but of heart. But this does not satisfy him: he rises to the further exhortation to perfect "union of soul" (which is the proper rendering for "being of one accord") in which they shall not only be likeminded, but (in a phrase peculiar to this passage) be actually "of one mind," living in one another, each sinking his individuality in the enthusiasm of a common love.

(3) This verse expresses the negative result of this unity of soul—that nothing will be done in "strife," that is, *factiousness* (the word used in chap. i. 17), or "vainglory"—nothing, that is, with the desire either of personal influence or of personal glory. "For," he adds, "each will esteem other better than himself," or, rather, will hold that his neighbour is worthy of higher consideration and a higher place of dignity than himself (comp. the use of the word in Rom. xiii. 1; 1 Pet. ii. 13, of temporal dignity); for the idea is of the ascription to others, not of moral superiority, but of higher place and honour. Self-assertion will be entirely overborne. So he teaches us elsewhere that "charity vaunteth not itself, is not puffed up, doth not behave itself unseemly, seeketh not her own" (1 Cor. xiii. 4, 5).

(4) **Look not every man on his own things.**—This verse similarly describes the positive effect of this "being of one mind" as consisting in power of understanding and sympathy towards "the things of others"—not merely the interests, but also the ideas and feelings of others. To "look upon" here is something more than "to seek" (as in verse 21). It expresses that insight into the thoughts, hopes, aspirations of others, which only a self-forgetting love can give, as well as the care to consider their welfare and happiness. Yet by the word "also" we see that St. Paul does not, in the spirit of some forms of modern transcendentalism, denounce all self-consciousness and self-love, as in a bad sense "selfish." For man is individual as well as social; he can subordinate "his own things" to "the things of others," but cannot ignore them.

[4. **The Doctrine of the Great Humility of Christ** (verses 5—11).

(1) THE VOLUNTARY HUMILIATION OF THE LORD, first in His incarnation, next in His passion (verses 5—8).

(2) THE CORRESPONDING EXALTATION OF HIS HUMANITY, to bear "the Name above every name," which all creation must adore (verses 9—11).]

(5–8) From a practical introduction, in the familiar exhortation to follow the example of our Lord, St. Paul passes on to what is, perhaps, the most complete and formal statement in all his Epistles of the doctrine of His "great humility." In this he marks out, first, the Incarnation, in which, "being in the form of God, He took on Him the form of a servant," assuming a sinless but finite humanity; and next, the Passion, which was made needful by the sins of men, and in which His human nature was humiliated to the shame and agony of the cross. Inseparable in themselves, these two great acts of His self-sacrificing love must be distinguished. Ancient speculation delighted to suggest that the first might have been, even if humanity had remained sinless, while the second was added because of the fall and its consequences. Such speculations are, indeed, thoroughly precarious and unsubstantial—for we cannot ask what might have been in a different dispensation from our own; and, moreover, we read of our Lord as "the Lamb slain from the foundation of the world" (Rev. xiii. 8; see also 1 Pet. i. 19)—but they at least point to a true distinction. As "the Word of God" manifested in the Incarnation, our Lord is the treasure of all humanity as such; as the Saviour through death, He is the especial treasure of us as sinners.

(6) **Being in the form of God.**—(1) The word "being" is here the more emphatic of the two words so translated, which lays stress on the reality of existence (as in Acts xvi. 20; xvii. 28; 1 Cor. xi. 7; Gal. ii. 14). Hence it calls attention to the essential being of Christ, corresponding to the idea embodied in the name Jehovah, and thus implying what is more fully expressed in John i. 1. (2) The word "form" (which, except for a casual use in Mark xvi. 12, is found only in this passage of the New Testament) is to be carefully distinguished from "fashion." There can be no doubt that in classical Greek it describes the actual specific character, which (like the structure of a material substance) makes each being what it is; and this same idea is always conveyed in the New Testament by the compound words in which the root "form" is found (Rom. viii. 29; xii. 2; 2 Cor. iii. 18; Gal. iv. 19). (3) On the other hand, the word "fashion," as in 1 Cor. vii. 31 ("the fashion of this world passeth away"), denotes the mere outward appearance (which we frequently designate as "form"), as will be seen also in its compounds (2 Cor. xi. 13, 14; 1 Pet. i. 14). The two words are seen in juxtaposition in Rom. xii. 2; Phil. iii. 21 (where see Notes). Hence, in this passage the "being in the form of God," describes our Lord's essential, and therefore eternal, being in the true nature of God; while the "taking on Him the form of a servant" similarly

robbery to be equal with God: (7) but made himself of no reputation, and took upon him the form of a servant, and was made in the likeness[1] of men: (8) and being found in fashion as a man, he humbled himself, and became obedient unto death, even the death of the cross. (9) Wherefore God also hath highly exalted him, and given him a name which is above

1 Or, *habit.*

---

refers to His voluntary assumption of the true nature of man.

It should be noticed that, whereas in St. Paul's earlier Epistles, in which he cared not "to know anything save Jesus Christ," and "Him as crucified," the main idea is always of our Lord as the mediator between man and God, yet in the later Epistles (as here, and in Eph. i. 10, 20—23; Col. i. 15—19; ii. 9—11; to which we may add Heb. i. 2—4) stress is laid, sometimes (as in Eph. i. 10), on His gathering all things in heaven and earth unto Himself; sometimes, even more explicitly, on His partaking of the divine nature, and (as in Col. i. 17) of His possessing the divine attribute of creation. All this naturally leads up to the great declaration of His true and perfect Godhead in John i. 1—13.

Thought it not robbery to be equal with God.—There are two main interpretations of this passage; first, the interpretation given in our version, which makes it simply an explanation and enforcement of the words "being in the form of God"; secondly, the translation *thought it not a prize to be grasped at to be equal with God*, which begins in it the statement of our Lord's voluntary self-humiliation, to be completed in the words, "but emptied Himself of glory." The former preserves the literal translation of the original word "robbery;" the latter, in accordance with a not uncommon usage, makes it equivalent to "the thing snatched at," and if this be allowed, has abundant examples in other writings to support the meaning thus given to the whole phrase. Either interpretation yields good sense and sound doctrine; neither does violence to the general context. But the latter is to be preferred; first (1) because it suits better the idea of the passage, which is to emphasise the reality of our Lord's humility, and preserves the opposition implied in the "but" following; (2) because it has the great preponderance of the ancient Greek interpreters in its favour; (3) because it can, on the whole, appeal more confidently to ordinary usage of the phrase. The sense is that, being in the form of God, and therefore having equality with God, He set no store on that equality, as a glory to Himself, compared with the power of giving salvation to all men, which He is pleased to consider a new joy and glory.

(7) **But made himself . . .**—This verse needs more exact translation. It should be, *But emptied* (or, *stripped*) *Himself of His glory by having taken on Him the form of a slave and having been made* (or, *born*) *in likeness of men.* The "glory" is the "glory which He had with the Father before the world was" (John xvii. 5; comp. chap. i. 14), clearly corresponding to the *Shechinah* of the Divine Presence. Of this He stripped Himself in the Incarnation, taking on Him the "form (or, *nature*) of a servant" of God. He resumed it for a moment in the Transfiguration; He was crowned with it anew at the Ascension.

Made in the likeness of man.—This clause, at first sight, seems to weaken the previous clause, for it does not distinctly express our Lord's true humanity. But we note that the phrase is "the likeness of men," *i.e.,* of men in general, men as they actually are. Hence the key to the meaning is to be found in such passages as Rom. viii. 3, God sent His own Son in "the likeness of sinful flesh;" or Heb. ii. 17; iv. 15, "It behoved Him to be made like unto His brethren," "in all points tempted like as we are, yet without sin." It would have been an infinite humiliation to have assumed humanity, even in unique and visible glory; but our Lord went beyond this, by deigning to seem like other men in all things, one only of the multitude, and that, too, in a station, which confused Him with the commoner types of mankind. The truth of His humanity is expressed in the phrase "form of a servant;" its unique and ideal character is glanced at when it is said to have worn only the "likeness of men."

(8) **And being found . . .**—This should be, *And after having been found* (or, *recognised*) *in fashion as a man, He* [*then*] *humbled Himself, having become obedient even to death.* "After having been found," &c., clearly refers to the manifestation of Himself to the world in all the weakness of humanity: the "outward fashion" was all that men could see; and in it they found "no form or comeliness," or "beauty, that they should desire Him" (Isa. liii. 2, 3). From this St. Paul proceeds to the last act of His self-humiliation in death: "He became obedient," that is, to God's will, "even up to death." His death is not here regarded as an atonement, for in that light it could be no pattern to us; but as the completion of the obedience of His life. (See Rom. v. 19.) Of that life as a whole He said, "I came down from heaven, not to do My own will, but the will of Him that sent Me" (John vi. 38); and the doing that will (see Heb. x. 9, 10) ended in "the offering of the body of Jesus Christ once for all." In this light His death is the perfection of the suffering which, in consequence of the power of sin in the world, must be faced in doing the will of God (see 2 Tim. iii. 12); in this light we can follow it, and even "fill up what is lacking of the sufferings of Christ" (Col. i. 24).

Even the death of the cross.—Properly, *and that too, the death of the cross*; emphasising its peculiar shame and humiliation as an "accursed" death. (See Gal. iii. 13.)

(9) **Wherefore God also hath highly exalted him.**—The exaltation, like the humiliation, belongs to Him, as Son of Man; for He was "lifted up," as on the cross, so in the Ascension. It raises Him to the throne of the Mediatorial kingdom, on which He entered by the Ascension, sitting at the right hand of God till He has put all enemies under His feet, and then ready "to deliver up the kingdom to the Father, that God may be all in all." (See 1 Cor. xv. 24—28.) For it is the "Son of Man" who "cometh in the clouds of heaven" (Dan. vii. 13; Matt. xxvi. 64), and has "authority to execute judgment" (John v. 27).

Hath given him a name.—Or, rather, *the Name above every name.* "The Name" (for this seems to be the best reading) is clearly "the Name" of God. It is properly the name Jehovah, held in the extremest literal reverence by the Jews, and it came to signify (almost like "the Word") the revelation of the presence of God. See Rev. xix. 12, 13, where "the name which no man knew but Himself" is the "Word of God."

every name: (10) that at the name of
Jesus every knee should bow, of
things in heaven, and *things* in earth,
and *things* under the earth; (11) and
that every tongue should confess that
Jesus Christ *is* Lord, to the glory of
God the Father. (12) Wherefore, my
beloved, as ye have always obeyed, not
as in my presence only,
but now much more in my
absence, work out your
own salvation with fear
and trembling. (13) For it is
God which worketh in you

Chap. ii. 12–18. Exhortation to work out their salvation under God's grace, in earnestness, peace, and purity.

This is, indeed, made clear by the following verse; for the adoration there described is in the original passage (Isa. xlv. 23; comp. Rom. xiv. 11), claimed as the sole due of God Himself. The name JESUS, "Jehovah the Saviour" (like "Jehovah our Righteousness," in Jer. xxiii. 6), does contain, as an integral element, the incommunicable name of God, while the addition of "Saviour" points to the true humanity. Therefore in that Name, of Him who is at once God and Man, "every knee is to bow" with direct worship to Him.

(10) **At** (properly, *in*) **the name of Jesus every knee should bow.**—This is an instance of the significant practice, by which passages of the Old Testament speaking of God are, as a matter of course, applied in the New to our Lord Jesus Christ. "In the Name" is the phrase constantly used for worship of God. "I will lift up my hands in Thy Name" (Ps. lxiii. 4). It denotes worship to Christ, not through Him.

Of things in heaven, and things in earth, and things under the earth.—For "things" we may better substitute *beings*, for the reference is properly to personal beings; although in some sense "All the works of the Lord bless the Lord, praise Him and magnify Him for ever." (Comp. here Rev. v. 13, "Every creature which is in heaven, and on the earth, and under the earth . . . heard I saying, Blessing, and honour, and glory, and power be unto Him that sitteth upon the throne, and to the Lamb for ever and ever." See also Eph. i. 20, 21, and Notes there.)

(11) **That Jesus Christ is Lord.**—The word "Lord" is the word constantly used in the LXX. to translate, though inadequately, the name Jehovah. The context would suggest that meaning here, for the worship paid is obviously the worship done to God. But, though less perfectly, the acknowledgment of universal lordship and majesty (such as He claimed in Matt. xxviii. 18—20) would satisfy the necessities of the passage. For, after all, to what created being can it be due? (On this confession of Jesus as Lord, see Acts ii. 36; Rom. x. 9.)

To the glory of God the Father.—The acknowledgment of the glory of Christ is the acknowledgment of the glory of the Father, as the Source of Deity, manifested perfectly in Him. (See John i. 18; xiv. 9). Note in John v. 19—30, our Lord's repeated profession that His work on earth was to manifest the Father; in chap. xvii. 4, His declaration that He had so done; and in chap. xvii. 24, the truth that His glory is the glory given of the Father.

[5. **Exhortation and Commendation** (verses 12—30).

(1) EXHORTATION TO WORK OUT THEIR SALVATION through the inworking of God, and so to be lights in the world, and the glory of the Apostle, even in the hour of martyrdom (verses 12—18).

(2) ST. PAUL'S INTENTION TO SEND TIMOTHY, AND HOPE TO COME HIMSELF SHORTLY (verses 19—24).

(3) PRESENT MISSION OF EPAPHRODITUS, now recovered from his late sickness, and strong commendation of his zeal (verses 25—30).]

(12—18) By the word "wherefore" St. Paul connects this exhortation with the great passage above. For the main idea is here of the presence of God in them, working out glory through a condition of humiliation, on condition of their fellow-working with Him; so that they shall appear as the "sons of God" and as "lights in the world." In all this there is clearly the imperfect but true likeness of the indwelling of Godhead in our Lord's humanity, exalting it through the two-fold humiliation to the unspeakable glory.

(12) **As ye have always obeyed.**—It is notable that this Epistle is the only one which contains no direct rebuke. The Philippian Church has the glory of having "always obeyed," not (like the Galatian Church) "as in his presence only, but now much more in his absence." This "obedience" was to the will of God as set forth by him. In referring to it, there is an allusion to the "obedience" of Christ (in verse 8); hence their obedience includes also that willingness to suffer which He Himself has shown. (See chap. i. 29, 30.) To this, perhaps, there is a further allusion in the "fear and trembling" spoken of below. (See 2 Cor. vii. 15; Eph. vi. 5.)

Work out your own salvation.—To "work out" is (as in Eph. vi. 13) to carry out to completion what is begun. This is the function of man, as fellow-worker with God, first in his own soul, and then among his brethren. God is the "beginner and perfecter" of every "good work" (see chap. i. 6); man's co-operation is secondary and intermediate.

(13) **For it is God which worketh in you both to will and to do.**—In this famous paradox St. Paul calls on men to work by their own will, just because only God can grant them power both to will and to do. The origination of all in God, and the free action (which is in some sense origination) of man, are both truths recognised by our deepest consciousness, but to our logic irreconcilable. In one passage only (Rom. ix. 14—24) does St. Paul touch, and that slightly and suggestively, on their reconcilement: generally Holy Scripture—in this confirming human reason—brings out each vividly and profoundly in turn, and leaves the problem of their reconcilement untouched. Here the paradoxical form of the sentence forces on the mind the recognition of the co-existence of both. If that recognition be accepted, the force of the reasoning is clear. The only encouragement to work, in a being weak and finite like man, is the conviction that the Almighty power is working in him, both as to will and deed.

The word "worketh in you" is constantly applied to the divine operation in the soul (see 1 Cor. xii. 6, 11; Gal. ii. 8; Eph. i. 11, 20; ii. 2); rarely, as here (in the word rendered "to do") to the action of men. It must necessarily extend to the will as well as the action; otherwise

both to will and to do of *his* good
pleasure. (14) Do all things without
murmurings and disputings: (15) that
ye may be blameless and harmless,[1] the
sons of God, without rebuke, in the
midst of a crooked and perverse nation,
among whom ye shine[2] as lights in the
world; (16) holding forth the word of
life; that I may rejoice in the day of
Christ, that I have not run in vain,
neither laboured in vain. (17) Yea, and
if I be offered[3] upon the sacrifice and

[2] Or, *shine ye.*

[1] Or, *sincere.*

[3] Gr. *poured forth.*

God would not be sovereign in the inner realm of mind (as, indeed, Stoic philosophy denied that He was). We are familiar with the influence of one created will over another—an influence real, though limited, yet in no sense compulsive. From this experience we may catch a faint glimpse of the inner working of the Spirit of God on the spirit of man. Hence, while we cannot even conceive the existence of freedom under an unbending impersonal law or force, the harmony of our will with a Supreme Personal Will is mysterious, indeed, but not inconceivable.

Of his good pleasure.—Literally, *on behalf of His good pleasure;* that is, in harmony with it. On the double sense of "good pleasure" see Note on Eph. i. 5. Here, probably, the meaning is His "gracious will" for our salvation.

(14) **Without murmurings and disputings.**—St. Paul seems purposely to leave this precept in perfect generality, so as to apply to their relations both to God and man. We observe, however, that the word "disputings" is mostly used of objections and cavils in word (see Matt. xv. 19; Luke v. 22; vi. 8; Rom. i. 21; xiv. 1); although in Luke ix. 47, xxiv. 38, and perhaps 1 Tim. ii. 8, it is applied to the inner strife of the heart. In either case it seems mainly to indicate intellectual questionings. Similarly, the word "murmuring" is used of outward wranglings of discontent (Matt. xx. 11; Luke v. 30; John vi. 41, 43, 61; vii. 12; Acts vi. 1; 1 Cor. x. 10; 1 Pet. iv. 9), proceeding not so much from the mind, as from the heart. The object, moreover, contemplated in verse 15 is chiefly good example before men. Hence the primary reference would seem to be to their relation towards men, in spite of the close connection with the preceding verse. Nor can we forget that it is on unity among themselves that the main stress of the exhortation of this chapter turns. Of course it is obvious that the disposition rebuked is sure to show itself in both relations; and that, if checked in one, the check will react on the other.

(15) **Blameless and harmless.**—"Blameless" as to external law and judgment (as in Luke i. 6; 1 Thess. ii. 10); "harmless" in internal purity and simplicity (as in Matt. x. 16, "harmless as doves;" and Rom. xvi. 19).

The sons of God, without rebuke.—The word "without rebuke" is, according to the best MSS., the same as that which is used in Eph. i. 4 (where see Note), and elsewhere, to signify "unblemished." The whole passage seems certainly a reminiscence of Deut. xxxii. 5, as it runs in the Greek version, speaking of the Israelites as "no children of God, full of blemish, a crooked and perverse generation." The word "crooked" is similarly applied to the unbelieving Jews by St. Peter in Acts ii. 40, and the epithet "faithless and perverse generation" used by our Lord in Matt. xvii. 17; Luke ix. 41.

Lights.—Properly, *luminaries;* so used in the Old Testament, and probably in Rev. xxi. 11. Christians are as the lesser lights of heaven, dim in comparison with the Sun of Righteousness, perhaps shining by His reflected light, and seen only in the night of this life, till He shall rise on us again in the "day of Christ" spoken of in the next verse. The word, therefore, stands half-way between "light" itself, as in Matt. v. 14, and the merely artificial "light" (or, *candle*) of John v. 35.

(16) **Holding forth the word of life.**—This translation seems correct, and the reference is to the comparison above. There may, indeed, be (as has been supposed) a reference, involving a change of metaphor, to the holding forth of a torch, for guidance, or for transmission, as in the celebrated torch race of ancient times. But this supposed change of metaphor is unnecessary. The "luminaries" hold forth their light to men, and that light is the "word of life." Note the same connection in John i. 4, "In Him was life, and the life was the light of men."

The word of life.—The phrase "the word of life" is remarkable. Here it signifies, of course, the gospel of Christ. But the gradual progress of this expression should be noted. Of Him His disciples declared that He "has the words" (*i.e.*, the expressed words; see Note on Eph. vi. 17) "of eternal life" (John vi. 68); He Himself goes further, and declares that His words are themselves spirit and life (John vi. 63); here the gospel, as giving that knowledge of God and of Jesus Christ which is "eternal life" (John xvii. 3), is a "word of life;" and all these lead up to the final declaration that He Himself is "the Word of life" (1 John i. 1).

Run in vain, neither laboured in vain.—St. Paul's usual metaphor includes the "race" and the "struggle" of wrestling or boxing (as in 1 Cor. ix. 24—26; 2 Tim. iv. 7). In Gal. ii. 2 he speaks only of the "running in vain." Here, perhaps, the more general word "labour" (united in Col. i. 29 with the word "struggling") may be taken to express at any rate that element of endurance and watchfulness which the struggle in the arena represents.

(17) **If I be offered upon the sacrifice and service of your faith.**—The striking metaphor of the original is here imperfectly represented. It is, *If I am being poured out*—if my life-blood is poured out—*over the sacrifice and religious ministration of your faith.* The same word is used in 2 Tim. iv. 6, where our version has, "I am now ready to be offered." The allusion is to the practice of pouring out libations or drink-offerings (usually of wine) over sacrifices, both Jewish and heathen. Such libation was held to be a subsidiary or preparatory element of the sacrifice. In that light St. Paul regards his own possible martyrdom, not so much as having a purpose and value in itself, but rather as conducing to the self-sacrifice of the Philippians by faith—a sacrifice apparently contemplated as likely to be offered in life rather than by death.

The sacrifice and service of your faith.—The word here rendered "service," with its kindred words, properly means any service rendered by an individual for the community; and it retains something of this meaning in 2 Cor. ix. 12, where it is applied to the collection and transmission of alms to Jerusalem (comp. Rom.

service of your faith, I joy, and rejoice
with you all. (18) For the same cause
also do ye joy, and rejoice with me.
(19) But[1] I trust in the Lord Jesus to
send Timotheus shortly unto you, that
I also may be of good comfort, when I
know your state. (20) For I have no
man likeminded,[2] who will naturally
care for your state. (21) For
all seek their own, not
the things which are
Jesus Christ's. (22) But
ye know the proof of him,
that, as a son with the

Chap. ii. 19—23. Mission of Timothy as St. Paul's forerunner, and commendation of him to them.

[2] Or, *so dear unto me.*

[1] Or, *Moreover.*

---

xv. 27; and see below, chap. ii. 25, 30), and in Rom. xiii. 6 and Heb. i. 7, where "the powers that be" and the angels are respectively called "ministers of God." But the great preponderance of New Testament usage appropriates it to priestly service (see Luke i. 23; Rom. xv. 16; Heb. viii. 2, 6; ix. 21; x. 11), which is obviously its sense here. The simplest interpretation of the whole passage would be to consider the Philippians merely as priests, and to suppose "sacrifice" to describe the chief function, and "ministration" the general function, of their priesthood. But the word "sacrifice," though it might etymologically mean the act of sacrifice, has universally in the New Testament the sense, not of the act, but of the thing sacrificed. Accordingly, here it would seem that, following afar off the example of the great high priest, the Christian is described as at once sacrifice and priest, "offering" (see Rom. xii. 1) "his own body as a living sacrifice, holy, acceptable to God," and with it the "sacrifice of praise" and the "sacrifice of doing good and communicating" (Heb. xiii. 15, 16, and below, chap. iv. 18). This union of sacrifice and ministration, being the work "of faith," is in St. Paul's view the thing really precious; his own death the mere preparation for it, in which he rejoices "to spend and be spent" for them.

I joy, and rejoice with you all.—That is, *I joy, and that in sympathy with you.* First, "I joy" absolutely, in the feeling that "to depart and be with Christ," following Him in His own way of suffering, is far better. Next, "I joy in sympathy with you," in the sense of community of sacrifice, and brotherhood in suffering, for the sake of the one Lord. The emphasis laid on the latter clause harmonises with the old proverb, that sorrow is halved, and joy doubled, when it is shared with others.

(18) **Do ye joy . . .**—The Epistle lays great stress on joy, not only as a privilege, but as a duty, following from Christian faith and proving its reality. Joy is in itself natural in the first thoughts of childhood and youth; it is apt to be chequered or even destroyed by the second thoughts of fuller experience of life, as darkened by suffering, sin, and death; but in the third and deepest thoughts of the Christian, recognising these darker elements of life, but knowing that they were not in the beginning, and shall not be in the end, joy comes back, solemnised but deepened into thankfulness. A Christianity which has no power to rejoice, either in flashes of joy amidst tribulation, or, better still, in the calm steady light of cheerfulness, may be true, but is imperfect. It has not yet entered into the promise given by our Lord Himself of the "joy which no man taketh from us" (John xvi. 22).

(19—24) St. Paul takes occasion of a promise to send Timothy shortly, to give an emphatic commendation of him, and adds a hope that he may soon come to Philippi himself.

(19) We note that here Timothy is spoken of in the third person; hence, though he is joined with St. Paul in the salutation (see chap. i. 1), the Epistle is the Apostle's, and his alone. The same is the case in the First Epistle to the Thessalonians (comp. chap. i. 1 with chap. iii. 2, 6).

That I also may be of good comfort.—The words express some anxiety, but greater confidence, as to the news which Timothy on returning was likely to bring. We have instances of a similar but far stronger anxiety of affection in 2 Cor. ii. 13; vii. 6, 7, and 1 Thess. iii. 1—9. In regard to the Philippians it might exist in detail, but was swallowed up in confidence on all main points.

(20) **For I have no man likeminded.**—That is, probably, *like-minded with myself.* St. Paul calls Timothy his "genuine (or, *true*) son in the faith" (1 Tim. i. 2), a son who in spirit and affection was like his father. The word "naturally" in this verse is the same word, and should be translated *genuinely,* without either counterfeit or duplicity of aim; and the word "care" implies something of the same absorbing anxiety which is expressed on St. Paul's part in this passage.

(21) **For all seek their own, not the things which are Jesus Christ's.**—Compare our Lord's words, "Ye shall be scattered every man to his own (things), and shall leave Me alone" (John xvi. 32). St. Paul's declaration is startling; for he had certainly some "brethren with him" (chap. iv. 21). But the scanty notice of them in the close of this Epistle contrasts strongly with the detailed and affectionate mention of his companions by name in Col. iv. 7—14; Philem. verses 23, 24. It would seem as if at this time he was either separated accidentally from his most trusty disciples, or that there had been a temporary falling away from him, in some degree like that which he describes with so much sadness in 2 Tim. iv. 9, 10, 16. His words need not be taken as accusing all of absolute selfishness and unfaithfulness, but they are nevertheless startling enough.

(22) **The proof of him.**—The allusion is justified by their intimate personal knowledge. Timothy was at Philippi with St. Paul on his first visit (Acts xvi. 12—40); we find him sent to Thessalonica shortly after (1 Thess. iii. 2), and he probably then paid a second visit to Philippi; from Ephesus (Acts xix. 22) he is sent again to Macedonia; and with St. Paul on the way to Jerusalem he was at Philippi once more (Acts xx. 4—6).

As a son with the father.—The original construction is curiously broken here. It runs, *As a son to a father*—as though St. Paul was going to speak of Timothy's dutiful ministration and following of his example; but then the sentence changes, in a characteristic humility, and makes Timothy and himself merely fellow-servants—*he served with me in the gospel.* If we may judge of Timothy's character from the general character of St. Paul's directions to him in the Pastoral Epistles, and especially the significant exhortation, "Let no man despise thy youth, (1 Tim. iv. 12), it would seem to have been gentle and warm-hearted rather than commanding. Hence,

father, he hath served with me in the
gospel. (23) Him therefore I hope to
send presently, so soon as I shall see
how it will go with me. (24) But I trust
in the Lord that I also myself shall
come shortly. (25) Yet I supposed it
necessary to send to you
Epaphroditus, my brother,
and companion in labour,
and fellowsoldier, but your
messenger, and he that ministered to
my wants. (26) For he longed after
you all, and was full of heaviness,
because that ye had heard that he
had been sick. (27) For indeed he
was sick nigh unto death: but God
had mercy on him; and not on him
only, but on me also, lest I should
have sorrow upon sorrow. (28) I
sent him therefore the more carefully,

Chap. ii. 25—30. Mission and commendation of Epaphroditus.

---

perhaps, the necessity for this singularly emphatic commendation of him. (Comp. 1 Cor. xvi. 10, "If Timotheus come, see that he be with you without fear.")

(23) **How it will go with me.**—An explanatory paraphrase, though probably correct, of the original, *the things concerning me.* Probably some crisis in the imprisonment was at hand, with which the expectation of release implied in the next verse was connected.

(24) **But I trust . . .**—Compare Philem. verse 22, "Prepare me a lodging, for I trust that through your prayers I shall be given to you," where the expectation seems even more immediate. The interval between the Letters is unknown. The received belief of St. Paul's release, and subsequent re-imprisonment (resting on unvarying tradition, and on the evidence of the Pastoral Epistles), supposes this expectation to have been fulfilled in due time.

In the Lord.—So above, verse 19. The expression, connected in both cases with matters of practical life and even of detail, is one which (like "the bowels of Jesus Christ" in chap. i. 8) belongs to the consciousness of a life so absorbed in Christ, that it cannot think or live in hope except "in the Lord." But it carries with it, perhaps, also the idea suggested by St. James (chap. iv. 15) "If the Lord will, we shall do this or that." Just so far as a hope or prayer is really "in the Lord," it will be accordant with the Divine will, and will therefore be realised.

Verses 25—30 contain the immediate mission and commendation of Epaphroditus, who had been sent from Philippi with supplies, had fallen sick, and now in convalescence was longing for home, and fearful lest the report of his sickness should cause them anxiety.

(25) **Epaphroditus.**—The name was often shortened into Epaphras. But it was a common name; hence any identification with the Epaphras of Col. i. 7; iv. 12; Philem. verse 23, is, to say the least, extremely precarious. It is hardly likely that one who was a native Colossian would be a resident and chosen messenger of Philippi. The three titles here given him are closely joined together in the original, and form a kind of climax—"brother" in a common Christianity, "fellow-worker" in the service of Christ, "fellow-soldier" in the "hardness" of daring and suffering, which the warfare of the Cross implies. (See 2 Tim. ii. 3, 4.)

Your messenger.—The original word is *apostle;* and by some interpreters, ancient and modern, it has been thought that it is intended here to designate the chief pastor—or, in the modern sense, the bishop—of the Philippian Church (as probably is the case with the "angels" of the churches in the Apocalypse); and the word "your" is then explained in the same sense as the words "of the Gentiles" in Rom. xi. 13. But this is very unlikely, (1) because there seems to be no example to confirm the statement that the chief pastor of a church was ever called its "apostle;" (2) because the character of the apostolate, being general and evangelistic, was very different from that of the local and pastoral episcopate; (3) because in this passage the word is inseparably connected with the following "and minister to my needs," showing the latter phrase to be explanatory of the previous word; (4) because the style of commendation in verse 29 is hardly suitable as applied to one whose office alone should have commanded respect. Our version is, therefore, correct in rendering it "messenger," just as in 2 Cor. viii. 23 ("the messengers of the churches"), where there is a similar reference to the transmission of alms.

(26) **For he longed after you all . . . .**—The two clauses of the verse are distinct from each other. St. Paul's first reason for sending Epaphroditus was in itself a sufficient one, that in his convalescence he yearned for home, and needed a change thither. The original is strong, *because he was continually longing* (see chap. i. 8; iv. 1) *for you all.* But besides this he was "full of heaviness," or more properly, *distressed and uneasy,* because of the effect which the news of his apparently fatal illness might cause at home.

(27) **God had mercy on him . . . and on me also.**—The passage, over and above its interest as an example of the strong personal affection which belonged to St. Paul's nature, and harmonised with his wide scope of Christian love, is notable as showing clearly that the Apostle's power of miracle, great as it was, was not his own, to use at his own will. When it was needed to be "the sign of an Apostle" (2 Cor. xiii. 12) it was given; and at special times, as at Ephesus, it was given in "special" fulness (Acts xix. 11). As we note, both in the Old Testament and in the New, special epochs of miracles in the history of the Church; so it would seem there were special occasions on which miracle came out prominently in the Apostle's preaching. We may, perhaps, infer from certain points in the descriptions of the healing of the cripple at the Beautiful Gate (Acts iii. 4), and at Lystra (Acts xiv. 8) that some spiritual intimation warned them when the hour of miracle was come. But an Apostle could not, as our Lord would not, work miracles for his own needs. Thus in this case, deeply as he sorrowed for Epaphroditus, there is no hint of his exercising that power on his behalf. He could only pray that God would have mercy on him, and thank God when that prayer was heard.

Sorrow upon sorrow.—That is, probably, upon the sorrow of captivity the sorrow of losing one who had (see verse 30) risked his life in the ardour of service to the captive.

(28) **I sent him therefore the more carefully.**—That is, *I was the more earnest and anxious to send him.* In any case the Apostle would have been

that, when ye see him again, ye may rejoice, and that I may be the less sorrowful. (29) Receive him therefore in the Lord with all gladness; and hold such in reputation:[1] (30) because for the work of Christ he was nigh unto death, not regarding his life, to supply your lack of service toward me.

A.D. 64.

1 Or, *honour such.*

CHAPTER III.—(1) Finally, my brethren, rejoice in the Lord. To write the same things to you, to me indeed

Chap. iii. 1. Original conclusion.

---

desirous to express his thanks and send news by Epaphroditus. But the circumstances of his illness increased that desire to greater earnestness.

I may be the less sorrowful.—There is a peculiar pathos in this expression, as contrasted with the completeness of joy described above in verses 17, 18. Epaphroditus recovery and safe return would take away the "sorrow upon sorrow;" but the old sorrow of captivity, enforced inactivity, and anxiety for the condition of the gospel, would remain. The expression of perfect joy belongs to the "spirit which was willing" indeed; the hint of an unspoken sorrow marks the weakness of the flesh.

(30) **Not regarding his life.**—According to the true reading, the sense is "having hazarded his life"; literally, *having gambled with his life,* not merely having staked it, but staked it recklessly. It is possible that (as Bishop Wordsworth suggests) there may be allusion to the caution money, staked in a cause to show that it was not frivolous and vexatious, and forfeited in case of loss; and that Epaphroditus, risking his life through over-exertion in the cause of St. Paul, as a prisoner awaiting trial, is therefore said to have *gambled with his life.* This would give a special appropriateness to the allusion. But it is, perhaps, too artificial, and the figure is in itself intelligible and striking.

To supply your lack of service.—There is not in the original the touch of reproach which our version may seem to imply. Epaphroditus' presence and activity are said to have "filled up the one thing wanting" to make the service of the Philippians effective for its purpose.

III.

[**6. Original Conclusion of the Epistle** (chap. iii. 1).

"Finally Brethren, Farewell in the Lord."]

(1) **Finally.**—The same word is used in 2 Cor. xiii. 11; Eph. vi. 10; 2 Thess. iii. 1 (as also in this Epistle, chap. iv. 8), to usher in the conclusion. Here, on the contrary, it stands nearly in the middle of the Epistle. Moreover, the commendation above of Timothy and Epaphroditus is exactly that which, according to St. Paul's custom, would mark the final sentences of the whole. Again, the words "rejoice in the Lord" may, according to the common usage of the time (although certainly that usage is not adopted in other Letters of St. Paul), not improbably signify *farewell in the Lord;* and even if not used in this formal and conventional sense, yet certainly hold the position of final good wishes, which that sense implies. The resumption of them in chap. iv. 4, where the actual conclusion now begins, is striking. It seems, therefore, highly probable, that in this place the Letter was originally drawing to an end, and that some news was at that moment brought which induced the Apostle to add a second part, couched in language of equal affection, but of greater anxiety and more emphatic warning. Of such a break, and resumption with a far more complete change of style, we have a notable instance at the beginning of the tenth chapter of the Second Epistle to the Corinthians; as also of the addition of postscript after postscript in the last chapter of the Epistle to the Romans.

[**7. Words of Warning** (chaps. iii. 1—iv. 3).

(1) Against the Judaisers.

(*a*) *Warning against confidence "in the flesh,"* illustrated by his own renunciation of all Jewish privileges and hopes, in order to have "the righteousness of Christ" (verses 1—9).

(*b*) *Warning against confidence in perfection as already attained,* again illustrated by his own sense of imperfection and hope of continual progress (verses 10—16).

(2) Against the Antinomian Party.

Contrast of the sensual and corrupt life of the flesh with the spirituality and hope of future perfection which become citizens of heaven (verses 17—21).

(3) Against all tendency to Schism (chap. iv. 1—3).

To write the same things to you.—These words may refer to what goes before, in which case the reference must be to "rejoice in the Lord." Now, it is true that this is the burden of the Epistle; but this interpretation suits ill the following words, "for you it is safe," which obviously refer to some warning against danger or temptation. Hence it is far better to refer them to the abrupt and incisive warnings that follow.

These, then, are said to be a repetition; but of what? Hardly of the former part of this Epistle, for it is difficult there to find anything corresponding to them. If not, then it must be of St. Paul's previous teaching, by word or by letter. For the use here of the word "to write," though it suits better the idea of former communication by writing, cannot exclude oral teaching. That there was more than one Epistle to Philippi has been inferred (probably, but not certainly) from an expression in Polycarp's letter to the Philippians (sect. 3), speaking of "the Epistles" of St. Paul to them. It is not in itself unlikely that another Epistle should have been written; nor have we any right to argue decisively against it, on the ground that no such Epistle is found in the canon of Scripture. But however this may be, it seems natural to refer to St. Paul's former teaching as a whole. Now, when St. Paul first preached at Philippi, he had not long before carried to Antioch the decree of the council against the contention of "them of the circumcision;" and, as it was addressed to the churches "of Syria and Cilicia," he can hardly have failed to communicate it, when he passed through both regions "confirming the churches" (Acts xv. 41). At Thessalonica, not long after, the jealousy of the Jews at his preaching the freedom of the gospel drove him from the city (Acts

is not grievous, but for you *it is* safe.

Chap. iii. 2–11. Warning against Judaising self-confidence, contrasted with the self-abandonment of faith.

(2) Beware of dogs, beware of evil workers, beware of the concision. (3) For we are the circumcision, which worship God in the spirit, and rejoice in Christ Jesus, and have no confidence in the flesh. (4) Though I might also have confidence in the flesh. If any other man thinketh that he hath whereof he might trust in the flesh, I more: (5) circumcised the eighth day, of the stock of Israel, *of* the tribe of Benjamin, an Hebrew of the Hebrews; as touching the law, a

---

xvii. 5). When he came to Macedonia on his next journey, the Second Epistle to the Corinthians, written there and probably at Philippi, marks the first outburst of the Judaising controversy; and when he returned to Philippi, on his way back, he had just written the Epistles to the Galatians and Romans, which deal exhaustively with the whole question. Nothing is more likely than that his teaching at Philippi had largely dealt with the warning against the Judaisers. What, then, more natural than to introduce a new warning on the subject—shown to be necessary by news received—with the courteous half-apology, "To write the same things to you, to me is not grievous (or, *tedious*) but for you it is safe," making assurance doubly sure?

(2) **Beware of (*the*) dogs.**—In Rev. xxii. 15 "the dogs" excluded from the heavenly Jerusalem seem to be those who are impure. In that sense the Jews applied the word to the heathen, as our Lord, for a moment appearing to follow the Jewish usage, does to the Syro-Phœnician woman in Matt. xv. 26. But here the context appropriates the word to the Judaising party, who claimed special purity, ceremonial and moral, and who probably were not characterised by peculiar impurity—such as, indeed, below (verses 17—21) would seem rather to attach to the Antinomian party, probably the extreme on the other side. Chrysostom's hint that the Apostle means to retort the name upon them, as now by their own wilful apostasy occupying the place outside the spiritual Israel which once belonged to the despised Gentiles, is probably right. Yet perhaps there may be some allusion to the dogs, not as unclean, but as, especially in their half-wild state in the East, snarling and savage, driving off as interlopers all who approach what they consider their ground. Nothing could better describe the narrow Judaising spirit.

Of evil workers.—Comp. 2 Cor. xi. 13, describing the Judaisers as "deceitful workers." Here the idea is of their energy in work, but work for evil.

The concision.—By an ironical play upon words St. Paul declares his refusal to call the circumcision, on which the Judaisers prided themselves, by that time-honoured name; for "we," he says, "are the true circumcision," the true Israel of the new covenant. In Eph. ii. 11 (where see Note) he had denoted it as the "so-called circumcision in the flesh made by hands." Here he speaks more strongly, and calls it a "concision," a mere outward mutilation, no longer, as it had been, a "seal" of the covenant (Rom. iv. 11). There is a still more startling attack on the advocates of circumcision in Gal. v. 12 (where see Note).

(3) **We are the circumcision.**—So in Col. ii. 11, 12, evidently alluding to baptism as the spiritual circumcision, he says, "In whom ye were circumcised with the circumcision made without hands." Comp. Rom. ii. 20, "Circumcision is that of the heart, in the spirit, and not in the letter;" and passages of a similar character in the Old Testament, such as Deut. x. 16, "Circumcise therefore the foreskin of your hearts;" chap. xxx. 6, "The Lord God will circumcise thine heart." Hence the spirit of St. Stephen's reproach, "Ye uncircumcised in heart and ears" (Acts vii. 51).

Which worship God in the spirit . . .—The true reading here is, *who worship by the Spirit of God*, the word "worship," or *service*, being that which is almost technically applied to the worship of the Israelites as God's chosen people (Acts xxvi. 7; Rom. ix. 4; Heb. ix. 1, 6), and which, with the addition of the epithet "reasonable," is claimed for the Christian devotion to God in Christ (see Rom. xii. 1). Such "worship by the Spirit of God" St. Paul describes in detail in Rom. viii., especially in verses 26, 27.

And rejoice (or rather, *glory*) **in Christ Jesus.**—Comp. Rom. xv. 17, "I have therefore whereof I may glory in the Lord Jesus Christ," and the Old Testament quotation (from Jer. ix. 23, 24) twice applied to our Lord, "He that glorieth, let him glory in the Lord" (1 Cor. i. 31; 2 Cor. x. 17). In Gal. vi. 14 we have a still more distinctive expression, "God forbid that I should glory, save in the cross of our Lord Jesus Christ." To glory in Christ is something more than even to believe and to trust in Him; it expresses a deep sense of privilege, both in present thankfulness and in future hope.

In the flesh.—The phrase is used here, as not unfrequently, for the present and visible world, to which we are linked by our flesh (see John viii. 15, "to judge after the flesh;" 2 Cor. v. 16, "to know Christ after the flesh," &c.) We have an equivalent phrase in an earlier passage, which is throughout parallel to this (2 Cor. xi. 18), "Many glory after the flesh." The particular form of expression is probably suggested by the constant reference to the circumcision, which is literally "*in* the flesh."

(5, 6) The comparison with the celebrated passage in 2 Cor. xi. 18—23 is striking, in respect not only of similarity of substance, but of the change of tone from the indignant and impassioned abruptness of the earlier Epistle to the calm impressiveness of this. The first belongs to the crisis of the struggle, the other to its close. We have also a parallel, though less complete, in Rom. xi. 1, "I also am an Israelite, of the stock of Abraham, of the tribe of Benjamin."

(5) **Circumcised the eighth day**—*i.e.*, a Jew born, not a proselyte.

Of the stock of Israel—*i.e.*, emphatically, a true scion of the covenanted stock, the royal race of the "Prince of God."

Of the tribe of Benjamin—*i.e.*, the tribe of the first king, whose name the Apostle bore; the tribe to whom belonged the holy city; the one tribe faithful to the house of Judah in the apostasy of the rest.

An Hebrew of the Hebrews.—Properly, *a Hebrew descended from Hebrews.* The Hebrew Jew,

Pharisee; (6) concerning zeal, persecuting the church; touching the righteousness which is in the law, blameless. (7) But what things were gain to me, those I counted loss for Christ. (8) Yea doubtless, and I count all things *but* loss for the excellency of the knowledge of Christ Jesus my Lord: for whom I have suffered the loss of all things, and do count them *but* dung, that I may win Christ, (9) and be found in him, not having mine own righteousness, which

---

who retained, wherever born, the old tongue, education, and customs of his fathers, held himself superior to the Grecian or Hellenist, who had to assimilate himself, as to the language, so to the thoughts and habits, of the heathen around him. St. Paul united the advantages both of the true Hebrew, brought up at the feet of Gamaliel, and of the Hellenist of Tarsus, familiar with Greek language, literature, and thought. Compare his own words to his countrymen from the steps of the Temple as illustrating the whole passage: "I verily am a Jew, born in Tarsus, a city in Cilicia, yet brought up in this city at the feet of Gamaliel, and taught according to the perfect manner of the law of the fathers, and was zealous before God . . . and I persecuted this way unto the death" (Acts xxii. 3, 4).

As touching the law, a Pharisee.—Comp. Acts xxiii. 6, "I am a Pharisee, and the son of Pharisees;" and xxvi. 5, "according to the straitest sect of our religion I lived a Pharisee." In these words St. Paul passes from his inherited Judaic privileges, to the intense Judaism of his own personal life.

(6) **Concerning zeal, persecuting the church.**—The word "zeal" (as in Acts xxii. 3) is probably used almost technically to describe his adhesion to the principles of the "Zealots," who, following the example of Phinehas, were for "executing judgment" at once on all heathens as traitors, ready alike to slay or to be slain for the Law. He shows how in this he departed from the teaching of Gamaliel, when he was "exceedingly mad against" the Christians, and "persecuted them even unto strange cities."

Touching the righteousness which is in the law, blameless.—The "righteousness in Law," which our Lord called "the righteousness of the scribes and Pharisees" (Matt. v. 20), is the righteousness according to rule, in which a man, like the rich young ruler, might think himself "blameless," and even hope to go beyond it in "counsels of perfection"—not the righteousness according to principle, which can never fulfil or satisfy itself. While St. Paul confined himself to the lower form of righteousness, he could feel himself "blameless;" but when he began to discern this higher righteousness in the Law, then he felt the terrible condemnation of the Law, on which he dwells so emphatically in Rom. vii. 7—12.

(7) **I counted loss . . .**—Not merely worthless, but worse than worthless; because preventing the sense of spiritual need and helplessness which should bring to Christ, and so, while "gaining all the world," tending to the "loss of his own soul." St. Paul first applies this declaration to the Jewish privilege and dignity of which he had spoken. Then, not content with this, he extends it to "all things" which were his to sacrifice for Christ.

(8) **For the excellency of the knowledge.**—The word "excellency" is here strictly used to indicate (as in 2 Cor. iii. 9, 10, 11) that the knowledge of Christ so surpasses all other knowledge, and, indeed, all other blessings whatever, as to make them less than nothing. As Chrysostom says here, "When the sun hath appeared, it is loss to sit by a candle." The light of the candle in the sunlight actually casts a shadow. How that knowledge is gained we learn in Eph. iii. 17, 18, "That Christ may dwell in your hearts by faith: that ye, being rooted and grounded in love, may . . . know the love of Christ, which passeth knowledge."

Dung.—The word appears to mean "refuse" of any kind. The sense adopted in our version is common. Dr. Lightfoot, however, quotes instances of its use for the fragments from a feast, and remarks on the old derivation of the word from that which is "thrown to dogs," which, however etymologically questionable, shows the idea attached to the word. This use would suit well enough with the ideas suggested by the retort of the name "dogs" on the Judaisers.

I suffered the loss of all things.—There seems to be here a play on words. These things were (he has said) loss; he suffered the loss of them: and the loss of a loss is a "gain."

That I may win (properly, *gain*) **Christ, and be found in him.**—The line of thought in these two clauses is like that of Gal. iv. 9, "Now that ye have known God, or rather are known of God." The first idea suggested by the context is that of "gaining Christ," finding Him and laying hold of Him by faith; but this, if taken alone, is unsatisfactory, as resting too much on the action of man. Hence St. Paul adds, and "be found (of God) in Him," drawn into union with Him by the grace of God, so that we may "dwell in Him, and He in us," and be "found" abiding in Him in each day of God's visitation.

(9) **Not having mine own righteousness, which is of the law.**—This is not the same as "righteousness in the Law," that is, defined by law. It is a righteousness resulting from the works of the Law (Gal. ii. 16), earned by an obedience to the Law, which is "mine own"—"not of grace, but of debt" (Rom. iv. 4)—such as St. Paul declares (in Rom. x. 3—6) to have been blindly sought by Israel, which he there defines as "life by doing the things of the Law." We have here, and in the following words, a remarkable link of connection with the earlier Epistles of the Judaising controversy, corresponding to Eph. ii. 8—10, but cast more nearly in the ancient mould. Yet it is, after all, only the last echo of the old controversy, which we trace so clearly in the Galatian and Roman Epistles. The battle is now virtually won, and it only needs to complete the victory.

But . . . the righteousness which is of God by (*on condition of*) **faith.**—This verse is notable, as describing the true righteousness; first imperfectly, as coming "through faith of Jesus Christ," a description which discloses to us only its means, and not its origin; next, completely, as "a righteousness coming from God on the sole condition of faith"—faith being here viewed not as the means, but as the condition, of receiving the divine gift (as in Acts iii. 16). It may be noted that in the Epistle to the Romans, we have righteousness "through faith," "from faith," "of faith;" for there it was needful to bring out in various forms the importance of faith. Here, now that the

is of the law, but that which is through
the faith of Christ, the righteousness
which is of God by faith: (10) that I may
know him, and the power of his resur-
rection, and the fellowship of his suffer-
ings, being made conformable unto his
death; (11) if by any means I might
attain unto the resurrection of the dead.
(12) Not as though I had already attained,
either were already perfect:
but I follow after, if that
I may apprehend that for
which also I am appre-
hended of Christ Jesus.
(13) Brethren, I count not myself to
have apprehended: but *this* one thing

Chap. iii. 12—16. Disclaimer for himself of any Christian perfection already attained.

urgent necessity has passed, we have the stress laid simply on the opposition of the gift of God through Christ to the merit of the works of the Law; and faith occupies a less prominent, though not less indispensable, position. (See Eph. ii. 8—10, and Note thereon.)

(10) Inseparably connected with the possession of this "righteousness of God" is the knowledge of Christ, or more exactly, the gaining the knowledge of Christ (see verse 8), by conformity both to His suffering and death, and also to His resurrection. This "conformity to the image of Christ" (Rom. viii. 29, 30)—with which compare the having "Christ formed within us" of Gal. iv. 19)—is made by St. Paul the substance of the gracious predestination of God, preceding the call, the justification, the glorification, which mark the various epochs of Christian life.

(10, 11) The order of these verses is notable and instructive. (1) First comes the knowledge of "the power of the Resurrection." What this is we see by examining it as historically the main subject of the first apostolic preaching. There it is considered, as in St. Peter's first sermons, as giving the earnest of "forgiveness," or "blotting out of sins," and the "gift of the Holy Ghost" (Acts ii. 38; iii. 13, 26), or, as St. Paul expresses it, of "justification from all things" (Acts xiii. 38, 39). This same idea is wrought out fully in his Epistles. Thus, for example, without it (1 Cor. xv. 17) "we are still in our sins." It is the pledge of our justification (Rom. v. 1), and the means of our being "alive unto God" (Rom. vi. 11). Hence "the power," or *efficacy*, "of His resurrection" is the justification, and regeneration inseparable from it, which lie at the entrance of Christian life. (2) Next comes the "partaking of His sufferings" and "conformity to His death," which are the "taking up the cross, and following Him," in the obedience even unto death. This "fellowship of sufferings," coming partly from the sin of others, partly from our own, is the constant theme of the New Testament. (See 1 Pet. iv. 13; Rom. viii. 17; 2 Cor. i. 5; Col. i. 24; 2 Tim. ii. 11.) The "conformity to His death" is the completion of the death unto sin, described as "mortification" of sin (Col. iii. 5); "as bearing about in the body the dying (or, properly, *mortification*) of the Lord Jesus" (2 Cor. iv. 10); or more frequently as being "crucified with Christ," "the world to us and we to the world" (Gal. ii. 20; v. 24; vi. 14). (3) Lastly comes the "attainment to the resurrection of the dead," properly, "the resurrection *from* the dead," which is (see Luke xx. 35) the resurrection unto life and the glorification in Him, so nobly described below (verses 20, 21). "If we have been planted together in the likeness of His death, we shall be also in the likeness of His resurrection" (Rom. vi. 5). For of our resurrection (see 1 Cor. xv. 12—23) His resurrection is not only the pledge, but the earnest. Note how in 1 Thess. iv. 14—18, and 1 Cor. xv. 51—57, the whole description is only of the resurrection unto life, and compare the first resurrection of Rev. xx. 6. This is the completion of all; St. Paul dared not as yet anticipate it with the confidence which hereafter soothed his dying hour (2 Tim. iv. 7, 8).

Verses 12—16 lead us from the warning against trust in human merit to deprecate the supposition of a perfection here attained even in Christ. The transition is natural. The same spirit which shows itself undisguisedly in the one pretension, comes out half-concealed in the other.

(12) **Not as though . . .**—The tenses are here varied. *Not as though I ever yet attained, or have been already made perfect.* To "attain," or *receive* (probably the prize, see verse 14), is a single act; "to be perfected" a continuous process. Clearly St. Paul has no belief, either in any indefectible grasp of salvation, or in any attainment of full spiritual perfection on this side of the grave. We may note our Lord's use of the word "to be perfected" to signify His death (Luke xiii. 32), and a similar application of the word to Him in Heb. ii. 10; v. 9; also the use of the words "made perfect" to signify the condition of the glorified (Heb. xi. 40; xii. 23).

If that I may apprehend that for which also I am (rather, *was*) **apprehended of Christ Jesus.**—The metaphor throughout is of the race, in which he, like an eager runner, stretches out continually to "grasp" the prize. But (following out the same line of thought as in verses 7, 8) he is unwilling to lay too much stress on his own exertions, and so breaks in on the metaphor, by the remembrance that he himself was once grasped, at his conversion, by the saving hand of Christ, and so only put in a condition to grasp the prize. The exact translation of the words which we render "that for which," &c., is doubtful. Our version supplies an object after the verb "apprehend," whereas the cognate verb "attained" is used absolutely; and the expression as it here stands is rather cumbrous. Perhaps it would be simpler to render "inasmuch as" or "seeing that" (as in Rom. v. 12; 2 Cor. v. 4). The hope to apprehend rests on the knowledge that he had been apprehended by One "out of whose hand no man could pluck" him.

(13) **I count not myself . . .**—The "I" is emphatic, evidently in contrast with some of those who thought themselves "perfect." (See verse 15.) Not only does St. Paul refuse to count that he has ever yet "attained;" he will not allow that he is yet in a position even to grasp at the prize. (Comp. 1 Cor. ix. 27.)

Forgetting those things which are behind . . .—The precept is absolutely general, applying to past blessings, past achievements, even past sins. The ineradicable instinct of hope, which the wisdom of the world (not unreasonably if this life be all) holds to be a delusion, or at best a condescension to weakness, is

I do, forgetting those things which are behind, and reaching forth unto those things which are before,
(14) I press toward the mark for the prize of the high calling of God in Christ Jesus.
(15) Let us therefore, as many as be perfect, be thus minded: and if in any thing ye be otherwise minded, God shall reveal even this unto you.
(16) Nevertheless, whereto we have already attained, let us walk by the same rule, let us mind the same thing.
(17) Brethren, be followers together of me, and mark them which walk so as ye have us for an ensample.
(18) (For many walk, of whom I have told you often, and now

Chap. iii. 17—21. Warning against Antinomian profligacy, unworthy of the citizenship of heaven.

---

sanctioned in the gospel as an anticipation of immortality. Accordingly hope is made a rational principle, and is always declared to be, not only a privilege, but a high Christian duty, co-ordinate with faith and love (as in 1 Cor. xiii. 13; Eph. iv. 4). St. Paul does not scruple to say that, if we have it not, for the next life as well as this, we Christians are "of all men most miserable" (1 Cor. xv. 19). Hence past blessing is but an earnest of the future; past achievements of good are stepping-stones to greater things; past sins are viewed in that true repentance which differs from remorse—"the sorrow of this world which worketh death" (2 Cor. vii. 10)—in having a sure and certain hope of the final conquest of all sin. The "eternal life" in Christ is a present gift, but one test of its reality in the present is its possession of the promise of the future.

(14) **The high calling of God.**—Properly, the *calling which is above—i.e.* (much as in Col. iii. 12), "the heavenly calling,"—which is "of God," proceeding from His will, for "whom He predestinated, them He also called" (Rom. viii. 30); and is "in Christ Jesus" in virtue of the unity with Him, in which we are at once justified and sanctified.

(15) **Perfect.**—The word is apparently used with a touch of irony (as perhaps the word "spiritual" in Gal. vi. 1), in reference to those who hold themselves "to have already attained, to be already perfect." It is, indeed, mostly used of such maturity in faith and grace as may be, and ought to be, attained here (Matt. v. 48; 1 Cor. ii. 6; xiv. 20; Eph. iv. 13; Col. i. 28; iv. 12; Heb. v. 14). But, strictly speaking, this life, as St. Paul urges in 1 Cor. xiii. 10, 11, is but childhood, preparing for the full manhood, or "perfection" of the next; and his disclaimer of perfection above suggests that this higher meaning should in this passage be kept in view. The prospect of being "perfect" in indefectible faith or grace is the Christian's hope; the claim to be already "perfect" is always recurring in various forms—all natural but unwarrantable anticipations of heaven on earth. St. Paul, by a striking paradox, bids those who hold themselves perfect to prove that they are so by a consciousness of imperfection. If they have it not, he says, they have something yet to learn. "God will reveal even this unto them." The conviction of the Holy Ghost unites inseparably the "conviction of sin" and the "conviction of righteousness." The "judgment" of absolute decision between them is not yet.

(16) **Let us walk . . .**—In this verse the last words appear to be an explanatory gloss. The original runs thus: *Nevertheless—as to that to which we did attain—let us walk by the same.* The word "walk" is always used of pursuing a course deliberately chosen. (See Acts xxi. 24; Rom. iv. 12; Gal. v. 25.) The nearest parallel (from which the gloss is partly taken) is Gal. vi. 16, "As many as walk by this rule, peace be upon them." In this passage there seems to be the same double reference which has pervaded all St. Paul's practical teaching. He is anxious for two things—that they should keep on in one course, and that all should keep on together. In both senses he addresses the "perfect;" he will have them understand that they have attained only one thing—to be in the right path, and that it is for them to continue in it; he also bids them refrain from setting themselves up above "the imperfect;" for the very fact of division would mark them as still "carnal," mere "babes in Christ" (1 Cor. iii. 1—4).

(17—21) In these verses St. Paul turns from the party of Pharisaic perfection to the opposite party of Antinomian profligacy, claiming, no doubt, to walk in the way of Christian liberty which he preached. The coexistence of these two parties was, it may be remarked, a feature of the Gnosticism already beginning to show itself in the Church. He deals with this perversion of liberty into licentiousness in exactly the same spirit as in Rom. vi., but with greater brevity; with less of argument and more of grave condemnation. It stands, indeed, he says, self-condemned, by the very fact of our present citizenship in heaven, and our growth towards the future perfection of likeness to Christ in glory.

(17) **Followers together of me.**—The word is peculiar. It signifies *unite in following me.* In accordance with the genius of the whole Epistle, St. Paul offers his example as a help not only to rectitude but to unity. For the simple phrase "followers of me," see 1 Cor. iv. 16; xi. 1; 1 Thess. i. 6; 2 Thess. iii. 9. In 1 Cor. xi. 1, a passage dealing with the right restraints of Christian liberty, we have the ground on which the exhortation is based, "Be ye followers of me, *even as I also am of Christ.*" In that consciousness, knowing the peculiar power of example, both for teaching and for encouragement, St. Paul will not allow even humility to prevent his bringing it to bear upon them. Yet even then we note how gladly he escapes from "followers *of me*" to the "having *us* for an example."

(18) **Even weeping.**—The especial sorrow, we cannot doubt, lay in this, that the Antinomian profligacy sheltered itself under his own preaching of liberty and of the superiority of the Spirit to the Law.

The enemies of the cross of Christ.—Here again (as in the application of the epithet "dogs" in verse 2) St. Paul seems to retort on those whom he rebuked a name which they may probably have given to their opponents. The Judaising tenets were, indeed, in a true sense, an enmity to that cross, which was "to the Jews a stumbling-block," because, as St. Paul shows at large in the Galatian and Roman Epistles, they trenched upon faith in the all-sufficient atonement, and so (as he expresses it with startling emphasis) made Christ to "be dead in vain." But the doctrine of the

tell you even weeping, *that they are* the enemies of the cross of Christ: (19) whose end *is* destruction, whose God *is their* belly, and *whose* glory *is* in their shame, who mind earthly things.) (20) For our conversation is in heaven; from whence also we look for the Saviour, the Lord Jesus Christ: (21) who shall change our

Cross has two parts, distinct, yet inseparable. There is the cross which He alone bore for us, of which it is our comfort to know that we need only believe in it, and cannot share it. There is also the cross which we are "to take up and follow Him" (Matt. x. 38; xvi. 24), in the "fellowship of His sufferings and conformity to His death," described above (verses 10, 11). St. Paul unites both in the striking passage which closes his Galatian Epistle (vi. 14). He says, "God forbid that I should glory, save in the cross of the Lord Jesus Christ!" but he adds, "whereby the world is crucified unto me, and I to the world." Under cover, perhaps, of absolute acceptance of the one form of this great doctrine, the Antinomian party, "continuing in sin that grace might abound," were, in respect of the other, "enemies of the cross of Christ."

(19) **Whose end is destruction . . . .**—The intense severity of this verse is only paralleled by such passages as 2 Tim. ii. 1—5; 2 Pet. ii. 12—22; Jude, verses 4, 8, 12, 13. All express the burning indignation of a true servant of Christ against those who "turn the grace of God into lasciviousness," and "after escaping the pollutions of the world through the knowledge of the Lord and Saviour Jesus Christ, are again entangled therein and overcome."

Whose God is their belly.—A stronger reiteration of Rom. xvi. 18, "They serve not our Lord Jesus Christ, but their own belly." Note the emphasis laid on "feasting and rioting" in 2 Pet. ii. 13; Jude, verse 12.

Whose glory is in their shame.—As the preceding clause refers chiefly to self-indulgence, so this to impurity. Comp. Eph. v. 12, "It is a shame even to speak of those things which are done of them in secret." "To glory in their shame"—to boast, as a mark of spirituality, the unbridled license which is to all pure spirits a shame—is the hopeless condition of the reprobate, who "not only do these things, but have pleasure in those who do them" (Rom. i. 32).

Who mind earthly things.—This last phrase, which in itself might seem hardly strong enough for a climax to a passage so terribly emphatic, may perhaps be designed to bring out by contrast the glorious passage which follows. But it clearly marks the opposition between the high pretension to enlightened spirituality and the gross carnal temper which it covers, grovelling (so to speak) on earth, incapable of rising to heaven.

(20) **Our conversation.**—The original may signify either "our city" or "our citizenship" is in heaven. But both the grammatical form and the ordinary usage of the word (not elsewhere found in the New Testament) point to the former sense; which is also far better accordant with the general wording of the passage. For the word "is" is the emphatic word, which signifies "actually exists"; and the reference to the appearance of the Lord Jesus Christ is obviously suggested by the thought that with it will also come the manifestation of the "Jerusalem which is above . . . the mother of us all" (Gal. iv. 26); as in Rev. xxi. 2, "I saw the holy city, the new Jerusalem, coming down from heaven." The force of the passage would, however, in either case be much the same. "Their mind is on earth; our country is in heaven," and to it our affections cling, even during our earthly pilgrimage. It is impossible not to remember the famous words of Plato of his *Divine Republic*, "In heaven, perhaps, the embodiment of it is stored up for any one who wills to see it, and seeing it, to claim his place therein" (*Rep.* ix., p. 592B). But the infinite difference between the shadowy republic of the philosopher, to which each has to rise, if he can, by his own spiritual power, and the well-centred "kingdom of God," is suggested by the very words that follow here. The kingdom is real, because there is a real King, who has given us a place there, who will one day be manifested to take us home. It should be noted that the city is spoken of as ours already. As all the citizens of Philippi, the Roman colony, were citizens of the far distant imperial city, so the Philippian Christians even now were citizens of the better country in heaven. (See Eph. ii. 19.)

We look for.—Properly, *we eagerly wait for.* The word is a peculiar and striking expression of longing, found also in Rom. viii. 19, 23, 25, "The earnest expectation of the creature waiteth for the manifestation of the sons of God" (where see Note).

The Saviour.—The title is emphatic in relation to the hope of perfected salvation which follows. But we note that the use of the word "Saviour" by St. Paul is peculiar to the later Epistles, and especially frequent in the Pastoral Epistles. It is found also again and again in the Second Epistle of Peter.

(21) **Who shall change . . .**—This passage needs more accurate translation. It should be, *who shall change the fashion of the body of our humiliation, to be conformed to the body of His glory.* (1) On the difference between "fashion" and "form," see chap. ii. 7, 8. The contrast here signifies that humiliation is but the outward fashion or vesture of the body; the likeness to Christ is, and will be seen to be, its essential and characteristic nature. This "humiliation" marks our condition in this life, as fallen from our true humanity under the bondage of sin and death. The body is not really "vile," though it is fallen and degraded. (2) "His glory" is His glorified human nature, as it was after the Resurrection, as it is now in His ascended majesty, as it shall be seen at His second coming. What it is and will be we gather from the sublime descriptions of Rev. i. 13—16; xix. 12—16; xx. 11. What is here briefly described as change to conformity with that glory is worked out in 1 Cor. xv. 42—44, 53, 54, into the contrast between corruption and incorruption, dishonour and glory, weakness and power, the natural (animal) body and the spiritual body. In 2 Cor. iii. 18, iv. 16, we read of the beginning of glorification in the spirit here; in 2 Cor. iv. 17, 18, v. 1—4, of the completion of "the exceeding weight of glory" in the hereafter, as glorifying also "our house which is in heaven. St. John describes that glorification with brief emphatic solemnity, "We shall be like Him, for we shall see Him as He is," and draws out explicitly the moral which St. Paul here implies, "Every man that hath this hope purifieth himself, even as He is pure."

According to the working . . .—Properly, *in virtue of the effectual working of His power to subject*

vile body, that it may be fashioned like unto his glorious body, according to the working whereby he is able even to subdue all things unto himself.

CHAPTER IV.—(1) Therefore, my brethren dearly beloved and longed for, my joy and crown, so stand fast in the Lord, *my* dearly beloved. (2) I beseech Euodias, and beseech Syntyche, that they be of the same mind in the Lord. (3) And I intreat thee also, true yokefellow, help those women which laboured with me in the gospel, with Clement also, and *with*

A.D. 64.

Chap. iv. 1—3. Renewed exhortation, first, to unity.

---

all things to Himself. Comp. Eph. i. 19; iii. 7, and Notes there. Here, as there, St. Paul speaks of His power as not dormant or existing in mere capacity, but as energetic in working, unhasting and unresting. Here briefly, as more fully in the celebrated passage of the First Epistle to the Corinthians (chap. xv. 24—28) he describes it as "subduing all things unto Himself," till the consummation of this universal conquest in the Last Judgment and the delivery of "the kingdom to God, even the Father . . . that God may be all in all." Of that power the primary exhibition, in which He is pleased to delight, is in salvation, gradually preparing His own for heaven; the secondary exhibition, undertaken under a moral necessity, is in retributive judgment. It is of the former only that St. Paul speaks here, as it shall be made perfect in the resurrection unto eternal life.

IV.

[8. **Conclusion of the Epistle** (chap. iv. 1—23).

FINAL EXHORTATION—

(*a*) *To unity*, with especial mention of Euodia, Syntyche, and others (verses 1—3).

(*b*) *To joy*, confident in the power of prayer, and resting in the peace of God (verses 4—7).

(*c*) *To conformity with all that is good* after the apostolic model (verses 8—9).

THANKS FOR THE PHILIPPIAN OFFERINGS.

(*a*) *Declaration that he could not claim them of necessity* (verses 10—13).

(*b*) *Grateful remembrance of their former liberality* (verses 14—17).

(*c*) *Blessing on their present sacrifice* offered through *him* to God (verses 18—20).

GREETING AND BLESSING (verses 21—23).]

(1) **Therefore.**—By this word, just as at the conclusion of the description of the "depth of the riches of the wisdom of God" (in Rom. xi. 33—36), or of the glorious climax of the doctrine of the resurrection (in 1 Cor. xv. 50—57), St. Paul makes the vision of future glory to be an inspiring force, giving life to the sober, practical duties of the present time. For the faith, which is the root of good works, is not only "the evidence of things not seen," although already existing as spiritual realities, but also "the substantiation of things hoped for" (Heb. xi. 1).

Dearly beloved and longed for . . .—The peculiar affectionateness of this verse is notable. It is curiously coincident with the words addressed years before to Thessalonica (1 Thess. ii. 19), "What is our hope and joy and crown of rejoicing? Are not ye in the presence of our Lord Jesus Christ . . ? Ye are our glory and our joy." But it has just the addition natural to the yearnings of captivity: they are "longed for," and that (see chap. i. 8) "in the heart of Jesus Christ." The "crown" is here the garland, the sign of victory in the apostolic race and struggle of which he had spoken above (chap. iii. 12—14). The crown of glory, of righteousness, and of life, is usually described as future (see 2 Tim. iv. 8; Jas. i. 12; 1 Pet. v. 4; Rev. ii. 10), and this is the case in the Thessalonian Epistle. Here, without excluding that completer sense, the reference is also to the present. The Philippians are St. Paul's crown, as the Corinthians are his "seal" (1 Cor. ix. 2)—at once the proof of His apostolic mission and the reward of his apostolic labour. In both aspects the present is the earnest of the future.

(2) **Euodias.**—The name should be *Euodia*, as is seen by verse 3. Of Euodia and Syntyche nothing is known. Many strange attempts have been made to find symbolism in these names. Evidently they were women of note, leaders at Philippi, where, we may remember, the gospel was first preached to women (Acts xvi. 13), and the church first formed in a woman's house (Acts xvi. 14, 40). We may note the many female names—Phœbe, Priscilla, Mary, Tryphena, Tryphosa, Persis, Julia, the mother of Rufus, the sister of Nereus—in the long list of greetings to the Church of Rome (Rom. xvi.).

(3) **I intreat.**—This rendering is too strong. It is, *I ask*, or *request*. The word means properly, to ask a question; secondarily, to make a request on equal terms, as of right. Hence never used (except, perhaps, in 1 John v. 16) of prayer from us to God.

True yokefellow.—This obscure phrase has greatly exercised conjecture. (1) It is curious historically to note the opinion, as old as Clement of Alexandria, that St. Paul referred to his own wife; but the opinion is clearly untenable in the face of 1 Cor. vii. 8; ix. 5. (2) The word is never elsewhere applied by St. Paul to a fellow-Christian, and must denote some peculiar fellowship. Many guesses as to its meaning have been made. Some refer it to St. Luke, who seems to be in the history closely connected with Philippi; others to Lydia, the first-fruits of the gospel in that city. Perhaps the most likely supposition is that it may refer to Epaphroditus, the bearer, perhaps the amanuensis, of the Epistle, who had certainly come to help St. Paul to bear his yoke of suffering, and in whose case the sudden address in the second person would cause no ambiguity. (3) But a not improbable conjecture is that the word is a proper name—"Syzygus"—a name, it is true, not actually known—and that the word "true" (properly, *genuine*) means "Syzygus, rightly so-called." It is obvious to compare the play on the name "Onesimus," in Philem. verse 11.

Those women . . .—It should be, *help them* (Euodia and Syntyche), *inasmuch as they laboured with me.* The word "laboured" signifies "joined with me in my struggle," and probably refers to something more than ordinary labour, in the critical times of suffering at Philippi.

other my fellowlabourers, whose names
are in the book of life.
(4) Rejoice in the Lord
alway: *and* again I say,
Rejoice. (5) Let your mo-
deration be known unto all
men. The Lord *is* at hand.

Chap. iv. 4—7. next, to joy, resting on the confidence of prayer and hope of the peace of God;

(6) Be careful for nothing; but in every
thing by prayer and supplication
with thanksgiving, let your requests
be made known unto God. (7) And
the peace of God, which passeth all
understanding, shall keep your hearts
and minds through Christ Jesus.

Clement.—From the time of Origen downwards this Clement has been identified with the famous Clement, bishop of Rome, and author of the well-known *Epistle to the Church at Corinth*, of whom Irenæus expressly says that he had seen and been in company with "the blessed Apostles," and who in his Epistle refers emphatically to the examples both of St. Peter and St. Paul, as belonging to the times "very near at hand;" but dwells especially on St. Paul, "as seven times a prisoner in chains, exiled, stoned," "a herald of the gospel in the East and the West," "a teacher of righteousness to the whole world," and one who "penetrated to the farthest border of the West." (See his *Epistle*, chap. v.)

The fact that he was at this time working at Philippi—considering that Philippi, as a Roman colony, was virtually a part of Rome—is no objection to this identification; nor is the chronology decisive against it, though it would make Clement an old man when he wrote his Epistle. The identification may stand as not improbable, while the commonness of the name Clemens makes it far from certain.

Whose names are in the book of life.—For "the Book of Life," see Dan. xii. 1; Rev. iii. 5; xiii. 8; xvii. 8; xx. 12; xxi. 27. From that Book the name may be blotted out now (Rev. iii. 5; comp. Ex. xxxii. 33) till the end fixes it for ever. There is (as has been always noticed) a peculiar beauty in the allusion here. The Apostle does not mention his fellow-labourers by name, but it matters not; the names are written before God in the Book of Life. If they continue in His service, those names shall shine out hereafter, when the great names of the earth fade into nothingness.

(4—7) St. Paul returns once more to the exhortation to joy so characteristic of this Epistle. But it is a joy in the sense of the Lord's being at hand. Hence it turns at once to thanksgiving and prayer, and finally is calmed and deepened into peace.

(4) **Rejoice in the Lord . . . and again I say, Rejoice.**—The original word is the word always used in classical Greek (see the corresponding word in Latin) for "farewell" (*i.e.*, "Joy be with you!"), and this verse is obviously a resumption of chap. iii. 1, after the digression of warning. But the emphasis laid on it here, coupled with the constant references to joy in the Epistle, show that St. Paul designed to call attention to its strict meaning, and to enforce, again and again, the Christian duty of joy. It is, of course, a "joy in the Lord:" for only in the Lord is joy possible to any thoughtful mind or feeling heart in such a world as this.

(5) **Your moderation.**—The word here rendered "moderation," properly denotes a sense of what is seemly, or equitable, as distinct from what is required by strict duty or formal law. Such distinction the world recognises when it speaks of what is enjoined, not so much by duty as by "good taste, or "right feeling," or (with some peculiarity of application) by "chivalrous" feeling, or the "spirit of a gentleman." Here it denotes the general sense of what is seemly in a Christian tone of character. In 2 Cor. x. 1 (where it is translated "gentleness") it is ascribed emphatically to our Lord Himself. But the usage of the New Testament appropriates it especially to the "sweet reasonableness" which "gentleness" may well designate. Thus, in Acts xxiv. 4 it clearly signifies patience, or forbearance; in 2 Cor. x. 1 it is associated with meekness; in 1 Tim. iii. 3, Tit. iii. 2, with peaceableness; in 1 Pet. ii. 8, with kindness; in Jas. iii. 17 the word "gentle" is placed between "peaceable" and "easy to be entreated" (or rather, *persuaded*). This spirit is, no doubt, "moderation;" but it is something more. It may refer here both to the exhortation to unity in verses 1—3, and to the exhortation to joy immediately preceding. It would help the one and chasten the other.

The Lord is at hand.—A translation of the Syriac "Maran-atha" of 1 Cor. xvi. 22—obviously a Christian watchword, probably referring to the Second Advent as near at hand; although, of course, not excluding the larger idea of that presence of Christ in His Church of which that Second Advent is the consummation.

(6) **Be careful for nothing.**—An exact repetition of our Lord's command, "Take no thought" (in Matt. vi. 25, 34). The prohibition is of that painful anxiety which is inevitable in all who feel themselves alone in mere self-dependence amidst the difficulties and dangers of life. It is possible to sink below this anxiety in mere levity and thoughtlessness; it is possible to rise above it by "casting our care on Him who careth for us," and knowing that we are simply "fellow-workers with Him" (1 Pet. v. 7; 2 Cor. vi. 1). Hence the Apostle passes on at once to speak of the trustfulness of prayer.

Prayer and supplication with thanksgiving.—By "prayer" is meant worship generally, so called (as in common parlance now) because in this state of imperfection prayer must be its leading element, as praise will be in the perfection of the future. (See Acts ii. 42, where "the prayers" are among the essential marks of church membership.) To this general word is subjoined the distinction of the two great elements of worship, "supplication with thanksgiving." The very expression, however, shows that, though distinct, they are inseparable. (See Eph. vi. 18, and Note there.) Both words "prayer" and "supplication" have the article in the original, and may probably refer to the recognised worship of the Church.

(7) **The peace of God**—*i.e.* (like the "righteousness of God," "the life of God"), the peace which God gives to every soul which rests on Him in prayer. It is peace—the sense of unity in the largest sense—the "peace on earth" proclaimed at our Lord's birth, left as His last legacy to His disciples, and pronounced at His first coming back to them from the grave (Luke ii. 14; John xiv. 27). Hence it includes peace with God, peace with men, peace with self. It keeps—that is, watches over with the watchfulness that "neither

Chap. iv. 8—9. lastly, to steadfastness in all the perfect goodness of the gospel, preached to them.

(8) Finally, brethren, whatsoever things
are true, whatsoever things
are honest,[1] whatsoever
things *are* just, whatsoever things *are* pure, whatsoever things *are* lovely,
whatsoever things *are* of
good report; if *there be* any virtue, and
if *there be* any praise, think on these
things. (9) Those things, which ye have
both learned, and received, and heard,
and seen in me, do: and the God of
peace shall be with you. (10) But I re-
joiced in the Lord greatly,
that now at the last your
care of me hath flourished
again;[2] wherein ye were
also careful, but ye lacked
opportunity. (11) Not that I speak
in respect of want: for I have learned,

Chap. iv. 10—14. Thanks and commendation for their liberality to him.

1 Or, *venerable.*

2 Or, *is revived.*

---

slumbers nor sleeps"—both "the hearts and minds" (or, more properly, *the souls and the thoughts formed in them*), guarding our whole spiritual action, both in its source and its developments. It is "through Christ Jesus," for "He is our peace (Eph. ii. 14), as "making all one," and "reconciling all to God." The comprehensiveness and beauty of the passage has naturally made it (with the characteristic change from the "shall" of promise to the "may" of benediction) the closing blessing of our most solemn church service of "Holy Communion" with God and man.

(8, 9) Here, repeating the word "Finally," the Apostle again draws to a conclusion, in a comprehensive exhortation to stand fast in all that is good on the foundation which he had laid in the name of Christ. The exhortation is marked by the reiteration of affectionate earnestness, in which, however, we may (as always) trace an underlying method. In each pair of epithets there seems to be reference both to an inner reality and to the outward development, by which it is at once manifested and perfected. In both St. Paul would have them grow up to perfection.

(8) **True . . . honest** (better, *venerable;* see margin).—Truth is the inherent likeness to God, who is Truth. Whatever is true in itself is also "venerable"—*i.e.*, as the original word, usually rendered "grave" (as in 1 Tim. iii. 8, 11; Tit. ii. 2) etymologically signifies, it claims a share of the reverence due primarily to God; it has in it a certain majesty commanding worship.

Just . . . pure.—"Just" is (as St. Paul's habitual usage of "justify" shows) righteous in act and word, as tested by the declared will of man or God. "Pure" is righteous in essence, in the thought, which cannot be thus tested—showing itself in what is just and indeed perfected thereby, but in itself something holier still.

Lovely . . . of good report.—Both words are peculiar to this passage: in both we pass from truth and righteousness to love. "Lovely" is that which deserves love. The phrase "of good report" represents a Greek word which is commonly used for "fair-sounding," or "auspicious" and "acceptable." It is therefore the outward expression of what is "lovely," winning the acceptance which loveliness deserves.

If there be any virtue, and . . . praise.—Still there is the same antithesis—"virtue" is the inherent quality; "praise" is virtue's due. But the word "virtue," so frequent in human morality, is hardly ever used in Scripture. In fact, the only other case of application to man is in 2 Pet. i. 5, where it stands between "faith" and "knowledge," and seems specially to signify the energy of practice by which faith grows into knowledge. The reason of this is clear. To the very name of "virtue" clings the idea of self-reliance—such self-reliance as the Stoic philosophy (then the only dominant system of Roman opinion which had any nobleness in it) made its essential characteristic; and that idea is, of course, foreign to the whole conception of Christian morality. The occurrence, therefore, here of an appeal to "virtue" and to "praise" seems strange. We notice, however, that it is introduced by a new phrase of mere hypothesis ("if there be," &c.), which may be taken to mark it as an outlying consideration, occupying a less firm and important ground. Probably, therefore, it is an appeal to the lower conceptions of the society, so characteristically Roman, around them: "Nay, even if there be any truth in the virtue and praise of mere human morality," &c.

(9) **Ye have both learned, and received.**—The reference is here to St. Paul's teaching, which he "delivered" to them (see 1 Cor. xv. 1—3; Gal. i. 12) as a message, "received" by revelation of God, and which they "received" accordingly.

Heard, and seen in me.—Here the reference is to his example, as subsidiary to his teaching and confirmatory of its truth.

The God of peace.—The inversion (compared with verse 7) is striking. To have the "peace of God" with us is much; to have "the God of Peace" Himself with us is more. With this promise the Letter itself ends. What follows is but postscript.

(10—20) These verses form a singularly graceful and dignified postscript, acknowledging the offerings of the Philippians sent by Epaphroditus, in a tone mingling apostolic commendation and blessing with a true brotherly thankfulness.

(10) **Now at the last.**—There is in these words an expression of some hitherto disappointed expectation, not wholly unlike the stronger expression of wounded feeling in 2 Tim. iv. 9, 10, 16. At Cæsarea St. Paul would have been necessarily cut off from the European churches; at Rome, the metropolis of universal concourse, he may have expected some earlier communication. But, fearing to wound the Philippians by even the semblance of reproof, in their case undeserved, he adds at once, "In which ye were also careful (before), but ye lacked opportunity." Epaphroditus would seem to have arrived early, almost as soon as St. Paul's arrival at Rome gave them the opportunity which they previously lacked.

(11) **I have learned.**—The "I" is here emphatic. There is evident reference to the habit peculiar to St. Paul, and made by him his especial "glory" (1 Cor. ix. 14), of refusing that maintenance from the churches which was his of right. Compare his words to the Ephesian presbyters, "I have coveted no man's silver, or gold, or apparel. Yea, ye yourselves know, that these hands have ministered unto my necessities" (Acts xx 33, 34).

in whatsoever state I am, *therewith* to be content. (12) I know both how to be abased, and I know how to abound: every where and in all things I am instructed both to be full and to be hungry, both to abound and to suffer need. (13) I can do all things through Christ which strengtheneth me. (14) Notwithstanding ye have well done, that ye did communicate with my affliction. (15) Now ye Philippians know also, that in the beginning of the gospel, when I departed from Macedonia, no church communicated with me as concerning giving and receiving, but ye only. (16) For even in Thessalonica ye sent

Chap. iv. 15—18. as worthy of their former generosity, and blessed in God's name.

Content.—The word (like the corresponding substantive in 2 Cor. ix. 8; 1 Tim. vi. 6) properly means, *self-sufficing*. Such self-sufficiency was the especial characteristic claimed by the Stoics for the ideal wise man of their philosophy—a characteristic full of nobleness, so far as it involved the sitting loose to all the things of the world, but inhuman in relation to human affections, and virtually atheistic if it described the attitude of the soul towards the Supreme Power. Only in the first relation does St. Paul claim it here. It is difficult not to suppose that he does so with some reference to a philosophy so essentially Roman in practical development.

(12) **Every where and in all things.**—The original has no such distinction of the two words. It is, *in all and everything;* in life as a whole, and in all its separate incidents.

I am instructed.—The word again is a peculiar and almost technical word. It is, *I have been instructed; I have learnt the secret*—a phrase properly applied to men admitted into such mysteries as the Eleusinian, enshrining a secret unknown except to the initiated; secondarily, as the context would seem to suggest, to those who entered the inner circle of an exclusive philosophy, learning there what the common herd could neither understand nor care for. A Stoic might well have used these words. There is even a touch of the Stoical contempt in the word "to be full," which properly applies to cattle, though frequently used of men in the New Testament. Perhaps, like all ascetics, they mostly knew how "to suffer need," better than how "to abound." But a Marcus Aurelius might have boldly claimed the knowledge of both.

(13) **I can do all things.**—Properly, *I have strength in all things*, rather (according to the context) to bear than to do. But the universal extension of the maxim beyond the immediate occasion and context is not inadmissible. It represents the ultimate and ideal consciousness of the Christian. The first thing needful is to throw off mere self-sufficiency, to know our weakness and sin, and accept the salvation of God's free grace in Christ; the next, to find the "strength made perfect in weakness," and in that to be strong.

Through Christ which strengtheneth me.—The word "Christ" is not found in the best MSS.; it is a gloss, perhaps suggested by 1 Tim. i. 12, where we have exactly the same phrase, "Christ Jesus, our Lord, who hath enabled me." The same word is used in Eph. vi. 10, "Be strong (*strengthened within*) in the Lord." In this sentence we have the world-wide distinction between the Stoic and the Christian. Each teaches respect for the higher humanity in the soul; but to the one that humanity is our own, to the other it is "the Christ within," dwelling in the heart, regenerating and conforming it to Himself. The words of St. Paul are but a practical corollary to the higher truth (comp. chap. i. 21) "To me to live is Christ." In this consciousness alone is any thoughtful teaching of "self-reverence, self-knowledge, self-distrust," intelligible and coherent.

(14) **Ye have well done.**—Properly, *Ye did well*, in sending the offerings. In this, says St. Paul, they "did communicate with his affliction," that is (see chap. i. 7), they made it their own, helping him to bear it, by sympathy and sacrifice for his sake. The whole is an illustration of his own words (Acts xx. 35), "It is blessed to receive" what is lovingly given; but it is "rather blessed to give." He had the lower blessedness, they the higher; and he rejoiced that it was so.

(15) **Now ye Philippians know also.**—Properly, *But ye also yourselves know*. The mention of the proper name is always emphatic (comp. 2 Cor. vi. 11); here it evidently marks the dignity of their exclusive position of benefaction.

In the beginning of the gospel.—At the beginning (that is) of the gospel to them and their sister churches in Macedonia. The time referred to is his leaving Macedonia for Athens and Corinth (Acts xvii. 14). At Corinth we know that he received offerings from Macedonia: "That which was lacking to me the brethren who came (*when they came*) from Macedonia supplied" (2 Cor. xi. 9). His language to the Thessalonian Church (1 Thess. ii. 9; 2 Thess. iii. 8) precludes all idea that any part of this contribution was from Thessalonica; we learn here that it was from no other Church than Philippi. It is probably to this gift that reference is made; though it is of course possible that some contribution may have reached him at the time of his actual departure in haste after the persecution at Berœa.

Communicated with me as concerning . . .—The metaphor here is drawn from commercial transaction. Literally the passage runs, *had dealings with me on account of giving and receiving;* "opened (so to speak) an account with me," not of debit and credit, but "of free giving and receiving." There is possibly an allusion (as Chrysostom suggests) to the idea embodied in 1 Cor. ix. 11, "If we have sown unto you spiritual things, is it a great matter if we shall reap your carnal things?" (Comp. Rom. xv. 27.) In the one respect he had all to give, and they to receive; in the other the relations were reversed. But if there be such allusion, it is kept in the background. The prominent idea is of the Philippians, and of them alone, as givers.

(16) **Even in Thessalonica.**—Not only after he left Macedonia, but even before that time, when he had just passed from Philippi to Thessalonica. At Thessalonica, as at Corinth—both very rich and luxurious communities—he refused maintenance, and lived mainly by the labour of his own hands (1 Thess. ii. 9; 2 Thess. iii. 8). But it appears from this passage that even then he received "once and again" (that is, occasionally, "once or twice") some aid from Philippi "to supply his need"—that is (as in all right exercise of liberality), to supplement, and not to supersede, his own resources.

once and again unto my necessity.
(17) Not because I desire a gift: but I
desire fruit that may abound to your
account. (18) But I have all,[1] and
abound: I am full, having received of
Epaphroditus the things *which were*
sent from you, an odour of a sweet smell,
a sacrifice acceptable, wellpleasing to
God. (19) But my God shall supply all
your need according to his riches in
glory by Christ Jesus. (20) Now unto
God and our Father *be* glory for ever
and ever. Amen. (21) Salute every
saint in Christ Jesus. The
brethren which are with
me greet you. (22) All
the saints salute you,
chiefly they that are of Cæsar's house-

Chap. iv. 21—23. Concluding salutations and blessing.

1 Or, *I have received all.*

---

(17) **Fruit that may abound** (rather, *abounds*) **to your account.**—The metaphor is still kept, hardly disturbed by the introduction of the word "fruit," since this is so constantly used in the sense of "recompense" that it readily lends itself to pecuniary associations. There is, says St. Paul, "the fruit" of reward, which "is over" as a surplus, or rather a balance, "placed to their account." Their gift is a token of love and gratitude to him; but, as Christian almsgiving, it is something more, and what that something more is will be seen hereafter, when all accounts shall be finally taken. The idea is not unlike that of Prov. xix. 17, "He that hath pity on the poor lendeth unto the Lord; and behold, what he layeth out it shall be paid him again."

(18) **I have all, and abound.**—The original is stronger, *I have all to the full* (as in Matt. vi. 2, 5, 16), *and more than to the full.* "I have all, and more than all, I need." Yet not content with this, he adds, "I am full," thoroughly complete in all things. The exuberance of courtesy and gratitude is strongly marked.

An odour of a sweet smell.—See Eph. v. 2, and Note there. Here St. Paul adds at once an explanation of the meaning of this metaphorical phrase, in the words, "a sacrifice acceptable, well-pleasing to God." Comp. Rom. xii. 2, "a sacrifice holy, acceptable to God." The word "sacrifice" used in both cases is the one which properly signifies a "bloody sacrifice," and in relation to such sacrifices the idea of propitiation naturally occurs to our minds; since we know that "without shedding of blood is no remission." But it is clear that here it belongs to the class of Eucharistic or free-will offerings; for it is simply an offering made freely, in grateful love to God and man; and exactly in this sense we find, in Heb. xiii. 16 (in close connection with "we have an altar"), "To do good, and to communicate forget not; for with such sacrifices God is well pleased." In the Epistle to the Romans it is, on the other hand, used for that which the burnt offering typified—the absolute self-dedication of the sacrificer, body and soul, to God. (See Note on Rom. xii. 2.) To 1 Pet. ii. 5, where all Christians are called "a holy priesthood to offer up spiritual sacrifices acceptable to God in Jesus Christ," both senses may be fairly applied. It may be noted that most superstitions in the Church as to the spiritual value of either of these forms of sacrifice, have come from confusion between them and the true or propitiatory sacrifice.

(19) **My God.**—The expression is emphatic. St. Paul had accepted the offerings as made, not to himself, but to the God whose minister he was. Hence he adds, "my God"—the God, whom ye serve in serving me.

All your need.—Properly, *every need of yours,* spiritual and temporal.

In glory.—We have already noticed the constant reference to "glory" in the Epistles of the Captivity. Where the word relates to God in Himself, His "glory" is His true nature as manifested to His creatures; where it refers to man, "glory" is the perfection of man's nature in the communion with God in Heaven. Here the latter sense is obviously to be taken. The "supplying of every need out of the riches" of God's love can only have its consummation in the "glory" of the future. That it is "in Christ Jesus" is a matter of course; for He is to "change even our body of humiliation to be fashioned like unto the body of His glory" (chap. iii. 21).

(20) **Now unto God and our Father . . .**—The doxology of this verse seems suggested by the very use of "glory" in the previous verse. "Glory" may be derivatively the privilege of man; but "*the* glory" (for the original has the article here)—the essential and incommunicable glory—must be ascribed to God alone. Whether we supply here the word "is" or "be" matters not. His it is; to Him let it be ascribed. Such doxologies are common with St. Paul (see Rom. xvi. 27; Gal. i. 5; Eph. iii. 21; 1 Tim. i. 17; 2 Tim. iv. 18); always with the addition of "for ever and ever," or literally, *for the ages of the ages,* throughout every age till time shall be no more; always in close connection with some declaration, not so much of the majesty, as of the wisdom, and still more the goodness, of the Father.

Verses 21—23 contain the salutation and blessing. The salutation is very brief, as compared, for example, with the corresponding passage in the Colossian Epistle (chap. iv. 10—15), naming none, either of those saluted or those joining with St. Paul in the salutation. The omission in the latter case may perhaps be accounted for by the words above (chap. ii. 20, 21), in which, with the single exception of Timotheus, St. Paul declares dissatisfaction with those near him, because "all seek their own, and not the things which are Jesus Christ's.

(21) **The brethren, which are with me.**—The list of those who were with St. Paul at one time or another during his imprisonment may be gathered from the Epistles to the Colossians (chap. iv. 10—15) and Philemon (verses 23, 24); where see Notes. How many of these where with him at this particular time we cannot tell. They are distinguished from "all the saints"—the body of the Church in general.

(22) **Of Cæsar's household.**—The "household of Cæsar" included a multitude of persons of all ages and ranks and occupations. Dr. Lightfoot, in a very interesting excursus on this verse, remarking that these Christians of Cæsar's household are alluded to as if well known to the Philippians, has examined the various names mentioned in Rom. xvi. (three years before this time), and finds many of them identical with names actually found in sepulchral inscriptions, as

hold. (23) The grace of our Lord Jesus
Christ *be* with you all. Amen.

¶ It was written to the Philippians from Rome by Epaphroditus.

belonging to members of the "domus Augusta," or imperial household. These were earlier converts; but, wherever St. Paul's prison was, he can hardly have failed to gain through the prætorians some communication with the household of the emperor, whose body-guard they were; and the allusion here seems to show that for some reason these Christians of Cæsar's household were in an especial familiarity of intercourse with him. Probably, therefore, he had added from that household new converts to Christ; and he mentions this here, as he had before spoken of his bonds being made manifest in the "prætorium" (chap. i. 13), in order to show the Philippians that his very imprisonment had given special opportunity for the spread of the gospel.

(23) **The grace of our Lord Jesus Christ be with you all.**—The true reading is, *be with your spirit* (as in Gal. vi. 18; Philem. verse 25; 2 Tim iv. 22). The reading of our version is the more ordinary form of salutation. In one form or another it is "the token in every Epistle" (2 Thess. iii. 17). The grace given by the Spirit of God is received in "the spirit" of man, but in order that the whole man, "body, soul, and spirit, be preserved blameless to the coming of the Lord Jesus" (1 Thess. v. 23).

INTRODUCTION

TO

THE EPISTLE OF PAUL THE APOSTLE TO THE

COLOSSIANS

I. The Time, Place, and Occasion of Writing.—There are in this Epistle indications of the time and place of writing similar to those already noticed in the Epistles to the Ephesians and Philippians. It is written in prison: for St. Paul bids the Colossians "remember his bonds" (chap. iv. 18), and designates Aristarchus as his "fellow-prisoner" (chap. iv. 10). Like the Epistle to the Ephesians, it is sent by Tychicus, with precisely the same official commendation of him as in that Epistle (chap. iv. 7, 8; comp. Eph. vi. 21, 22); but with him is joined Onesimus, the Colossian slave, the bearer of the Epistle to Philemon. The persons named in the concluding salutations (chap. iv. 7—14)—Aristarchus, Marcus, Epaphras, Luke, Demas, and "Jesus, called Justus"—are all, except the last, named in the corresponding part of the Epistle to Philemon (verses 23, 24); two of them, Aristarchus and St. Luke, are known to have accompanied the Apostle on his voyage, as a captive, to Rome (Acts xxvii. 2): and another, Tychicus, to have been his companion on the journey to Jerusalem, which preceded the beginning of that captivity at Cæsarea (Acts xx. 4). A direction is given to forward this Epistle to Laodicea, and to obtain and read a letter from Laodicea (chap. iv. 16), which (as will be seen by the Note on the passage) is, in all probability, our Epistle to the Ephesians—an Epistle (see the *Introduction* to it) addressed, indeed, primarily to Ephesus, but apparently also an Encyclical Letter to the sister Churches of Asia. All these indications point to one conclusion—not only that the Epistle is one of the Epistles of the Roman captivity (about A.D. 61—63), but that it is a twin Epistle with the Epistle to the Ephesians, sent at the same time and by the same hand, and designed to be interchanged with it in the Churches of Colossæ and Laodicea. These indications are confirmed most decisively by the substance of the Epistle itself, which (as will be seen below) presents, on the one hand, the most striking similarities to the Epistle to the Ephesians, and, on the other, differences almost equally striking and characteristic—thus contradicting all theories of derivation of one from the other, and supporting very strongly the idea of independent contemporaneousness and coincidence of thought.

The occasion of writing seems evidently to have been a visit to the Apostle from Epaphras, the first preacher of the gospel at Colossæ, and the profound anxiety caused both to him and to St. Paul (chaps. ii. 1; iv. 12, 13) by the news which he brought of the rise among the Colossians (and probably the Christians of Laodicea and Hierapolis also) of a peculiar form of error, half Jewish, half Gnostic, which threatened to beguile them from the simplicity of the gospel into certain curious mazes of speculation as to the Godhead and the outgrowth of various emanations from it: to create a separation between those who believed themselves perfect in this higher knowledge and the mass of their brethren: and, above all, to obscure or obliterate the sole divine mediation of the Lord Jesus Christ. To warn them against these forms of error—the last development of the Judaism which had been so formidable an enemy in time past, and the first anticipation of an intellectual and spiritual bewilderment which was to be still more formidable in the future—St. Paul writes this Letter. The Colossian Church was indeed to receive a copy from Laodicea of our Epistle to the Ephesians; but in an Encyclical Letter this peculiar form of heresy could not well be touched upon. Epaphras was for the present to continue at Rome, and (see Philem. verse 24) to share St. Paul's imprisonment. Mark, the nephew of Barnabas, then with St. Paul, was perhaps coming to Colossæ (chap. iv. 10), but not yet. Accordingly, by Tychicus, the bearer of the Encyclical Letter, and Onesimus, a fugitive Colossian slave, whom the Apostle was about to send back to Philemon, his master, this Letter is despatched. Partly it repeats and enforces the teaching of the other Epistle, but regards these common truths from a different point of view, designed tacitly to correct the errors rife at Colossæ; partly it deals directly with those errors themselves, imploring the Colossians to break through the delusions of their new "philosophy and vain deceit," and to return to the simplicity of the gospel, in which they had all been one in the one mediation of the Lord Jesus Christ.

II. The Church to which it is addressed.—The Church of Colossæ, unlike the Churches of Ephesus and Philippi, finds no record in the Acts of the Apostles; for, although this city is not very far from Ephesus, we gather that it was not one of the churches founded or previously visited by St. Paul personally (chap. ii. 1; comp. chap. i. 4). But it appears, from what is apparently the true reading of chap. i. 7, that Epaphras, named as its first evangelist, and still, to some extent, in charge of it and the neighbouring Churches of Laodicea and Hierapolis (chap. iv. 12, 13), was not only a fellow-servant, but a representative of St. Paul in his mission to Colossæ. We can, therefore, hardly be wrong in referring the conversion of the Colossians to the time of St. Paul's three years' stay at Ephesus, during which we are expressly told that "all they which dwelt in Asia heard the word of the Lord, both Jews and Greeks" (Acts xix. 10), and supposing that indirectly through Epaphras the Christianity of the Colossians was due to the influence of that great

Apostolic preaching under which "the word of God grew mightily and prevailed." We find also that St. Paul had intimate personal acquaintance, and what he calls emphatically "partnership," with Philemon (see Philem. verse 17), apparently a leading member of the Church at Colossæ. It is not unlikely that through him also the Apostle had been able to influence the foundation or growth of that Church. These circumstances explain the style and tone of this Letter, which seems to stand midway between the personal familiarity and unhesitating authority of such Epistles as the Epistles to the Thessalonians, Corinthians, Galatians, and Philippians, addressed to churches founded directly by St. Paul, and the courteous reserve of the Epistle to the Romans, addressed to a Church over which he could claim none of the authority of a founder. This is, perhaps, especially notable in chap. ii., where St. Paul prefaces his definite and authoritative denunciation of the peculiar errors besetting the Colossian Church with the half-apologetic introduction: "I would that ye know what great conflict I have for you, and for them at Laodicea, and for as many as have not seen my face in the flesh."

The position and history of Colossæ are admirably described by Dr. Lightfoot in his *Introduction* to this Epistle, sect. 1. It lay in the valley of the Lycus, a tributary of the Mæander, near Laodicea and Hierapolis. These two cities stand face to face, about six miles from each other on opposite sides of the valley, and ten or twelve miles further up, on the river itself, lies Colossæ, so that any one approaching it from Ephesus or from the sea-coast would pass by Laodicea. The three cities thus form a group, so that they might naturally receive the gospel at the same time, and the Christian communities in them might easily be under the same general charge. They seem to have been politically united under the Roman Government, and to have been distinguished by a common trade; like Thyatira, they were known for their manufacture of dyes, especially purple dyes, and derived considerable wealth therefrom. Colossæ had been once a place of importance. It is described by Herodotus (chap. vii. 20) as being, at the time of Xerxes' invasion of Greece, "a great city of Phrygia," the site of which is marked by a subterranean disappearance of the river Lycus; and by Xenophon (*Anab.* i. 2, § 6), about a century later, as "a city great and prosperous." But at the time at which this Epistle was written Colossæ was of far less note than the wealthy Laodicea, the metropolis of the district, or Hierapolis, well known as a place of resort for medicinal baths, and consecrated both to the Greek Apollo and the Phrygian Cybele. In the Apocalyptic letters to the Seven Churches of Asia it finds no mention, being probably looked upon as a dependency of the proud and wealthy Church of Laodicea. After the Apostolic age, while Laodicea and, in less degree, Hierapolis are well-known, Colossæ sinks into utter insignificance. It may possibly have been laid in ruins by one of the earthquakes which are known to have been common in these regions. Comparatively few remains of it are now found, and the very orthography of the name (*Colossæ*, or *Colassæ*) has, it appears, been matter of dispute. It is notable that a Church so much honoured and cared for by St. Paul should have had hereafter so obscure and so adverse a future.*

III. The Genuineness of the Epistle.—*External Evidence.*—Speaking generally, the condition of the external evidence is much the same with this as with the other two Epistles. It is included unhesitatingly in all canons, from the Muratorian Canon (A.D. 170?) downwards, and in all versions, beginning with the Peschito and the Old Latin in the second century. Quotations or references to it have not, however, been traced in any of the Apostolic fathers. The first distinct allusion to it is in Justin Martyr (A.D. 110—170?), who says (*Apol.* i. 46, ii. 6; *Dial. c. Tryph.* c. 100):—"We were taught that Christ is the first-born of God;" "We have acknowledged Him as the first-born of God, and before all creatures;" "Through Him God set all things in order." (Comp. chap. i. 15—17.) The next is Theophilus of Antioch, who died about A.D. 180:—"God begat the Word, the first-born before all creation." After this, in Irenæus, Clement of Alexandria, and Tertullian, direct quotation begins, and continues uninterruptedly in all Christian writings. (See Westcott, *Canon of the New Testament.*) The external evidence is therefore strong. Never until these later days of arbitrary criticism has the genuineness of the Epistle been questioned.

Internal Evidence.—This Epistle, far more than the Epistle to the Philippians, perhaps a little less than the Epistle to the Ephesians, bears traces of what I have ventured to call St. Paul's "third manner." To the correspondence of the change, both in style and substance, traceable in these Epistles, to the alteration of St. Paul's circumstances, and the natural development of the gospel and of the Church, I have already referred in the *General Introduction to the Epistles of the Captivity*, and given reasons for maintaining that this change, which has been often made an argument against the genuineness of these Epistles, presents to us phenomena inexplicable on any supposition of imitation or forgery, but perfectly intelligible if we accept the Apostolic authorship.

Some critics, however—of whom Dr. Holtzmann (in his *Kritik der Epheser- und Kolosser- briefe*) may be taken as the chief representative—insist on tracing extensive interpolations (almost amounting to a virtual reconstruction) in what they believe themselves able to discover as the originals both of this Epistle and the Epistle to the Ephesians. Except so far as these hypotheses depend on the supposed traces of a later Gnosticism in both Epistles, but especially in this (on which see *Excursus* at the close of this Epistle), they seem to resolve themselves into the idea that every passage bearing strong similarity to the teaching of St. Peter and St. John must have been altered or interpolated with a view to accommodation. Without any substantial historical evidence, ignoring both the probabilities of the case and the indirect evidence of Holy Scripture, and disregarding the utter absence of any support whatever in the witness of Christian antiquity, they assume an absolute antagonism between St. Paul and the Apostles of the Circumcision, and pronounce every indication of an underlying unity, and a true development of common doctrine, which contradicts this assumption, to be a mark of interpolation or falsification by a later hand. With the rejection of this arbitrary assumption, the greater part of the ingeniously-constructed fabric of destructive criticism falls to the ground.

But, indeed, it appears difficult to conceive how any one attentively studying either of these Epistles, without any preconceived hypothesis, can fail to recognise the internal consistency and unity—all the more striking

* Views of the country near the supposed site of Colossæ, and of the ruins of Laodicea and Hierapolis, are given in Lewin's *St. Paul*, Vol. II., pp. 357—360.

because indicating a free method, as distinct from a well-squared artificial system—which runs through the whole, and makes the theory of interpolation even more improbable than the theory of imitation or forgery. Nothing, for example, is more notable in this Epistle than the substantial unity, under marked difference of form, which connects the positive statement of doctrine in the first chapter (verses 14—23) with the polemical re-statement in the second chapter. In the former we trace anticipation of the latter, and (so to speak) preparation for the more explicit development of the attack on doctrinal error; in the latter, the very repetitions, with variations, of passages in the first chapter are indicative of a free treatment of the truths previously dealt with by the same hand, and are utterly unlike the tame reproductions or artificial modifications of a mere copyist. The remarkable indications, again, of the co-existence of similarity and distinctness between this Epistle and the Epistle to the Ephesians (noticed in the *Introduction* to that Epistle), as they preclude the theory of dependence or imitation in either, so are equally fatal to the idea of an artificial interpolation and reconstruction by later hands. They indicate at every point a free, almost unconscious, coincidence, omitting or preserving the parallelisms of idea and expression by a kind of natural selection. They mark a likeness of living organic growths, not of artificial and heterogeneous fabrics. Nor should we omit to notice the sustained power of these Epistles, differing as to the peculiar style of each, but equally conspicuous in both. The Epistle to the Ephesians has about it a certain calm and almost mystic eloquence, a beauty of meditative completeness of idea, unbroken by necessities of special teaching or special warning, which well suits a general Apostolic message to Christians as Christians, in which we seem almost to hear the utterance of an inspired mind, simply contemplating the divine truth in the knowledge of Jesus Christ, and speaking out, so far as they can be spoken, the thoughts which it stirs within—conscious of God and itself, only half conscious of those to whom the utterance is addressed. In the Epistle to the Colossians, on the other hand, we find a far greater abruptness, force, and earnestness. The free course of the Apostolic thought, which occasionally, perhaps, rises to an even greater height, is, on the whole, checked and modified by the constant remembrance of pressing needs and pressing dangers—accordingly developing some elements and leaving others comparatively undeveloped: and so, while perhaps increasing intensity, certainly interfering to some extent with the majestic symmetry of the universal revelation. Each Epistle has its marked characteristics; and these, unquestionably, so run through the whole as to destroy even any show of plausibility in the theory of interpolation.

The supposed anachronisms in the references to what afterwards became peculiarities of the Gnostic system will be treated of in the *Excursus* (at the close of the Epistle) *on the Relation of the Epistle to Gnosticism.* Here it will be sufficient to say that, on more attentive examination, not only do the supposed objections to the genuineness of the Epistle disappear, but the phenomena of the "philosophy and vain deceit" touched upon in this Epistle, when compared with the opinions either of the past or of the future, accord so remarkably with the characteristics of the period to which the Epistle claims to belong, as to add a fresh confirmation of the conclusions already derived from a consideration of the external evidence, and by the study of the coherence and vigour of the Epistle itself.

In this case, therefore, as in the others, we may unhesitatingly dismiss the questions which have been ingeniously raised, and with undisturbed confidence draw from the Epistle the rich treasures of Apostolic teaching.

IV. The main Substance of the Epistle.—In considering the substance of the Epistle, we must distinguish between the large amount of matter common to it with the Epistle to the Ephesians and the portion which is peculiar to this Epistle alone.

In regard of the common matter, it may be said generally that it is found treated with a greater width of scope and completeness of handling in the Epistle to the Ephesians. It is best studied there in the first instance (see, accordingly, the *Introduction* and *Analysis* of that Epistle), and then illustrated by comparison and contrast with the corresponding passages in this Epistle. It will be seen (as is explained in the Notes on various passages) that this illustration is at every point full of suggestiveness and variety. Literal identities are exceedingly rare; in almost every set of parallel passages the treatment in the two Epistles presents some points of characteristic variety, either in expression or in meaning. Speaking generally, this variety depends on two causes. The first turns on the speciality of the Epistle, addressed to a single Church, thoroughly, though indirectly, known to St. Paul, and the generality of the other, approaching nearly to the character of a treatise rather than a letter. The second and the more important cause of this variety is the subtle adaptation even of details to the characteristic doctrines which stand out in the two Epistles respectively.

This last consideration leads on naturally to the examination of the portions of the Epistle to which there is nothing to correspond in the Ephesian Epistle.

(*a*) We have the passages in the first and last chapters which refer to the foundation of the Colossian Church by Epaphras, the declaration to them of the "truth of the gospel," and the practical fruitfulness of that teaching (chap. i. 6—11); next, to the deep anxiety felt by Epaphras and St. Paul himself for their steadfastness in the simple truths of the gospel, against the speculations of a wild philosophy and the allurements of a mystic perfection in practice (chaps. i. 23, 24; ii. 1—4, 8—10, 16—23; iv. 12, 13); lastly, the particularity and strong personality of the salutations, directions, and blessing at the close of this Epistle (chap. iv. 7—18), singularly contrasting with the brief generality of the other (Eph. vi. 21—24). All these correspond to the former of the causes above named. They mark the difference between a special and an Encyclical Epistle.

(*b*) Of infinitely greater moment is the special prominence which is given in this Epistle to the doctrine of the sole Headship of Christ. The references to the Church as His body, though not unfrequent, are brief, secondary, unemphatic; and thus stand in marked contrast with the vivid and magnificent descriptions in the Ephesian Epistle of the predestination and election of the whole body of the Church in the eternal counsels "of the heavenly places" (Eph. i. 3—14): of the union of Jew and Gentile in the divine "commonwealth," all divisions being broken down which separated each from the other and both from God (chap. ii. 11—18): of the great Temple, "built on the foundation of the apostles and prophets, Jesus Christ being the chief corner-stone" (chap. ii. 19—24): of the "one body" and "the one Spirit," the "one Lord, the one God and Father of all" (chap. iv. 4—10). It is especially notable that to the last-named passage, which is the climax of the doctrinal teaching of the Ephesian Epistle, there corresponds in this the equally celebrated but wholly different passage (Col. iii. 1—4), which addresses the Colossians as "risen with Christ," having their "life hid with Him in God," looking for the time "when He who is their life shall appear, and they with Him in glory." The reason of the distinction is made clear at once by the indications of the presence at Colossæ of a tendency to vain speculations, to obsolete Jewish forms, and to half idolatrous superstitions, all of which alike prevented them from "holding the Head," from "being dead with Christ" to the rudiments of the world, from being "risen with Him" to a communion with heaven (chap ii. 8—23). Accordingly, the sole Headship of Christ is dwelt upon—first positively, (chap. i. 18—20), next polemically, in warning against error (chap. ii. 8, 16, 18). Both passages are peculiar to this Epistle, as compared with the Epistle to the Ephesians. They deal with a subject on which the needs of Colossæ and its sister Churches forced St. Paul to lay very special emphasis.

(c) But this emphasis does but bring out with greater force what may be found elsewhere. The great characteristic feature of this Epistle is the declaration of the nature of Christ in Himself as the "image of the invisible God;" "firstborn before all creation;" "by whom," "for whom," "in whom," "all beings were created in heaven and earth" and "all things consist;" "in whom dwells all the fulness of the Godhead bodily" (chaps. i. 15—17, 19; ii. 9). In this the Epistle may be compared with the Epistle to the Philippians (chap. ii. 6, 7). But the simple declaration there made of Christ as "being in the form of God" is here worked out into a magnificent elaboration, ascribing to Him the "fulness of Godhead" and the essential divine attributes of universal creation. It may be even more closely compared with the Epistle to the Hebrews, which not only describes Him as "the express image of the essence of Godhead," but with an emphasis which reminds us of the Judaistic angel-worship condemned in this Epistle, exalts His absolute superiority over all who, however glorious, are but creatures of God and ministering spirits (Heb. i. 1; ii. 4). It is evident, again, that it anticipates, yet with characteristic difference of expression, the doctrine of the "Word of God" taught by St. John, and the ascription to Him of essential eternity and Godhead, and both of physical and spiritual creation (John i. 1—5, 14). It is this which gives to our Epistle an unique doctrinal significance and value. Called out by one of the changeful phases of a pretentious, but transitory error, it remains to us an imperishable treasure. We cannot doubt that till the end of time it will have fresh force of special application, as ancient forms of error recur with more or less of variety of outward aspect, and in their constant changes, developments, and antagonisms, stand in significant contrast with the unchanging gospel.

V. Analysis of the Epistle.—To this general description is subjoined, as before, an analysis of the Epistle, shortened from the analyses in the various chapters.

1. Doctrinal Section.

(1) SALUTATION (chap. i. 1, 2).

(a) *Thanksgiving for their faith, love, and hope, the worthy fruits of the truth of the gospel taught by Epaphras* (chap. i. 3—8);

(b) *Prayer for their fuller knowledge, fruitfulness, and patience* (chap. i. 9—12).

(2) THE DOCTRINE OF CHRIST (stated positively).

(a) *His mediation in the forgiveness of sins* (chap. i. 13, 14);

(b) *His divine nature as the image of God and the Creator of all things* (chap. i. 15—17);

(c) *His Headship over the Church and over all created being* (chap. i. 18—20);

(d) *Special application of His mediation to the Colossians, and declaration of the commission of the preaching of this mystery to St. Paul himself* (chap. i. 21—29).

(3) THE DOCTRINE OF CHRIST (stated polemically).

(a) *Declaration of St. Paul's anxiety for them that they should remain rooted and stablished in the old truth of the gospel* (chap. ii. 1—7);

(b) *Warning against speculative error, denying or obscuring the truth*—

(α) Of Christ's true Godhead;

(β) Of the regeneration of spiritual circumcision in Him;

(γ) Of His sole atonement and triumph over the powers of evil (chap. ii. 8—15).

(c) *Warning against practical superstition*—

(α) Of trust in obsolete Jewish ordinances and mystic asceticism;

(β) Of superstitious worship of angels trenching on the sole Headship of Christ (chap. ii. 16—19).

(d) *Exhortation to be*—

(α) Dead with Christ to the rudiments of the world;

(β) Risen with Christ to the communion with God in heaven (chaps. ii. 20—iii. 4).

2. Practical Section.

(1) GENERAL EXHORTATION—

(a) *To mortification of the flesh in all the sins of the old unregenerate nature* (chap. iii. 5—9);

(b) *To putting on the new man in all the graces of the image of Christ, receiving the peace of God and doing all to His glory* (chap. iii. 10—17).

(2) SPECIAL DUTIES OF HUMAN RELATIONSHIP—

(a) *Wives and husbands* (chap. iii. 18, 19);

(b) *Children and parents* (chap. iii. 20, 21);

(c) *Slaves and masters* (chap. iii. 22—iv. 1).

(3) CONCLUSION.

(a) *Exhortation to prayer and watchfulness* (chap. iv. 2—6);

(b) *Mission of Tychicus and Onesimus* (chap. iv. 7—9);

(c) *Salutations from St. Paul's companions* (chap. iv. 10—14);

(d) *Charge to exchange Epistles with Laodicea* (chap. iv. 15—17);

(e) *Final salutation* (chap. iv. 18).

VI. Comparison with Epistle to the Ephesians.—To this outline of the Epistle may also be added a tabular comparison with the Epistle to the Ephesians, noting the general lines of parallelism and peculiarity.

EPHESIANS AND COLOSSIANS.

[In this Table whatever is common to the two Epistles is printed in ordinary type, and whatever is peculiar to each in italics.]

EPISTLE TO THE EPHESIANS.	EPISTLE TO THE COLOSSIANS.
1. Doctrinal Section.	**1. Doctrinal Section.**
1. (*a*) Salutation (chap. i. 1, 2).	1. (*a*) Salutation (chap. i. 1, 2).
(*b*) *Doxology and thanksgiving for the divine election* (chap. i. 3—6).	
(*c*) Prayer and thanksgiving for them (chap. i. 15—18).	(*b*) Prayer and thanksgiving for them (chap. i. 3—5, 9—12).
	(*c*) *Special reference to the teaching of Epaphras and its effect* (chap. i. 6—8).
2. (*a*) Declaration of the "gathering up of all in Christ," of His universal mediation for Jew and Gentile, and His headship over the Church, which is His Body, "the fulness of Him who filleth all in all" (chap. i. 7—14, 19—23).	2. (*a*) Declaration of the universal mediation of Christ, and His headship over the Church *and over all created being* (chap. i. 13, 14, 18—22).
(*b*) *Fuller declaration of the union of Jew and Gentile in one covenant and temple, on sole condition of faith in Christ* (chap. ii. 1—20).	(*b*) *Declaration of the true Godhead and creative power of Christ* (chap. i. 15—17).
(*c*) The commission to St. Paul of the mystery *of the calling in of the Gentiles*, once hidden, now revealed to men and angels (chap. iii. 1—13).	(*c*) The commission to St. Paul of the preaching of the mystery once hidden, now revealed, "*which is Christ in you the hope of glory*" (chap. i. 23—29).
(*d*) *Prayer that they may know that which passeth knowledge, by the indwelling of Christ, and be filled to the fulness of God* (chap. iii. 14—21).	(*d*) *Special warnings against peculiar forms of speculative error and practical superstition, drawing them from Christ, and obscuring His sole mediation and true Godhead* (chap. ii. 1—23).
3. SUMMARY OF DOCTRINE: (*a*) *The unity of the Church in God;* (*b*) *The diversity of gifts;* (*c*) *The one object of all—personal and corporate edification* (chap. iv. 1—16).	3. SUMMARY OF DOCTRINE: *The unity of the soul with Christ, in which it is risen and exalted to heaven in Him* (chap. iii. 1—8; comp. Eph. ii. 5, 6).
2. Practical Section.	**2. Practical Section.**
1. (*a*) General exhortation to put off the old man and put on the new, *by learning Christ and being taught in Christ* (chap. iv. 17—24).	1. (*a*) General exhortation to *mortify our earthly members*, to put off the old man and put on the new (chap. iii. 5—11).
(*b*) Warning against various sins, *as breaking unity with man* (chap. iv. 25—30).	(*b*) Warning against various sins, *as unworthy of "the elect of God"* (chap. iii. 5, 8, 9, 13—17).
(*c*) *Special warnings against bitterness, against impurity and lust, and against reckless excess and drunkenness* (chap. iv. 31—v. 21).	
2. HUMAN RELATIONSHIPS:	2. HUMAN RELATIONSHIPS:
(*a*) Wives and husbands (chap. v. 22—33). (*The sacredness of marriage as a type of the union between Christ and the Church.*)	(*a*) Wives and husbands (chap. iii. 18, 19).
(*b*) Children and parents (chap. vi. 1—4).	(*b*) Children and parents (chap. iii. 20, 21).
(*c*) Slaves and masters (chap. vi. 5—9).	(*c*) Slaves and masters (chap. iii. 22—iv. 1).
3. CONCLUSION.	3. CONCLUSION.
(*a*) *Exhortation to put on the whole armour of God* (chap. vi. 10—17).	
(*b*) Request for their prayers (chap. vi. 18—20).	(*a*) Request for their prayers (chap. iv. 2—6).
(*c*) Commendation of Tychicus (chap. vi. 21, 22).	(*b*) Commendation of Tychicus *and Onesimus* (chap. iv. 7—9).
	(*c*) *Salutations from the brethren* (chap. iv. 10—14).
	(*d*) *Message to Laodicea and Archippus, and direction as to the Letter from Laodicea* (chap. iv. 15—17).
(*d*) "Peace be to the brethren." "Grace be with all them who love our Lord Jesus Christ in sincerity" (chap. vi. 23, 24).	(*e*) "Remember my bonds. Grace be with you" (chap. iv. 18).

THE EPISTLE OF PAUL THE APOSTLE TO THE

COLOSSIANS

Chap. i. 1—2. Salutation.

A.D. 64.

CHAPTER I.—(1) Paul, an apostle of
Jesus Christ by the will
of God, and Timotheus *our*
brother, (2) to the saints and faithful
brethren in Christ which are at Co-
losse: Grace *be* unto you, and peace,
from God our Father and the Lord
Jesus Christ. (3) We give thanks to
God and the Father of our Lord Jesus
Christ, praying always for
you, (4) since we heard
of your faith in Christ
Jesus, and of the love
which ye have to all the
saints, (5) for the hope which is laid
up for you in heaven, whereof ye

Chap. i. 3—8. Thanksgiving for their faith, love, and hope, in the truth of the gospel.

[1. **Introduction.**

(1) SALUTATION (verses 1, 2).

(2) THANKSGIVING, for their faith and love and hope, with an emphatic reference to the "word of the truth of the gospel" as first preached unto them in all faithfulness by Epaphras, the fellow-servant and representative of the Apostle (verses 3—8).

(3) PRAYER that they may have further knowledge, and fruitfulness in good works, being strengthened to endurance, and encouraged by the hope of heaven (verses 9—12).]

This chapter contains the main substance of the characteristic doctrine of the Epistle; to which, however, St. Paul returns in the next chapter, enforcing it with special application to the circumstances of the Colossian church, and special warning against a peculiar form of half-Judaic and half-Gnostic error. It should be compared throughout with Eph. i., ii., iii. On such comparison, we find, on the one hand, a strong general similarity both of thought and expression; on the other hand, a marked difference in the subject to which main prominence is given. The first glance discovers that both Epistles dwell emphatically on Christ the Head, and the unity of all as one Body in Him. But a more thoughtful consideration will show that in this Epistle the main stress is on the headship of Christ; in the Ephesian Epistle, on the unity and glory of the Church as His body.

(1) **Timotheus our brother.**—Except in the mention of Timotheus (as in the other Epistles of the captivity; see Phil. i. 1; Philem. verse 1), the salutation is almost verbally coincident with the opening of the Epistle to the Ephesians (where see Note). The mention of Timotheus here, and the omission of his name there, mark the difference in character between the two Epistles. In a special Epistle like this Timotheus would be joined with St. Paul as usual. In a general Epistle to the churches of Asia, the Apostle alone could rightly speak.

(2) **From God our Father and the Lord Jesus Christ.**—The best MSS. show here, that the salutation should run simply "from God the Father," thus varying from St. Paul's otherwise universal phraseology. Such variation can hardly be accidental. Could it have been suggested to St. Paul's mind, in connection with his special desire to emphasize the true Godhead of Christ, so obvious in this Epistle, by an instinctive reluctance to use in this case any phrase, however customary with him, which might even seem to distinguish His nature from the Godhead? It is certainly notable that in the true reading of chap. ii. 2 Christ is called "the mystery of God, even the Father"—an unique and remarkable expression, which marks a preparation for the full understanding of the teaching of our Lord, "He that hath seen Me hath seen the Father" (John xiv. 9).

(3—8) In this expression of St. Paul's thanksgiving for them there is as usual a peculiar correspondence to their circumstances. They had been full of faith, love, and hope, the fruit of a true gospel preached by Epaphras; there was fear now lest they should be beguiled from it, although that fear was obviously not yet realised, as had been formerly the case with the Galatians. Hence St. Paul's emphasis on their hearing, knowing, and learning the truth, and on the faithfulness of Epaphras as a minister of Christ.

(3, 4) Comp. Eph. i. 15, 16, where there is an almost exact verbal coincidence, Whatever may be the force there of the words "having *heard* of your faith," clearly here they harmonise with many indications that the Colossian Church, though well known to St. Paul, was not known by personal knowledge.

(5) **For the hope which is laid up for you in heaven.**—The union of hope with faith and love is natural enough. Compare the fuller expression of 1 Thess. i. 3, "your work of faith, and labour of love, and patience of hope." But the place assigned to hope in this passage is notable. "For the hope" is really "on account of the hope." Hence faith and love are spoken of, not merely as leading up to hope, but as being actually kindled by it. Similarly in Eph. i. 18 we find that, while faith and love are taken for granted, there is a special prayer that they may be enlightened "to know the hope of His calling" as the one thing yet needful. The prominence given to the thought of "the heavenly places" in the Epistles of

heard before in the word of the truth
of the gospel; (6) which is come unto
you, as *it is* in all the world; and
bringeth forth fruit, as *it doth* also in
you, since the day ye heard *of it*, and
knew the grace of God in truth: (7) as
ye also learned of Epaphras our dear
fellowservant, who is for you a faithful
minister of Christ; (8) who also declared
unto us your love in the Spirit. (9) For

---

the captivity, and therefore to Christ in heaven, even more than to Christ risen, is evident to any careful student. Accordingly, the hope, which is the instinct of perfection in man, and which becomes realisation of heaven in the Christian, naturally comes out with corresponding emphasis.

Ye heard before.—That is, at their first conversion. There is an implied warning against the new doctrines, which are more fully noticed in the next chapter.

The truth of the gospel.—This expression (as in Gal. ii. 14) is emphatic. It refers to the gospel, not chiefly as a message of graciousness and mercy, but rather as a revelation of eternal truths, itself changeless as the truth it reveals. There is a corresponding emphasis, but stronger still, in St. John. (See, for example, 1 John ii. 27; v. 20; 2 John 1—4; 3 John, verses 2, 3.) The gospel was now winning its way to supremacy over civilised thought. Hence the need of warning against the sudden growth of wild speculations, contrasted with the unchanging simplicity of its main truths.

(6) **Which is come unto you . . .**—There is much variety of reading here, but the text followed by our version is certainly incorrect. The probable reading is, *which is come unto you, just as in all the world it is now bringing forth fruit and growing, as also it does in you.* In this sentence there are two lessons implied. First, the universality of the gospel, in which it stands contrasted, as with all local and national religions, whether of Judaism or of Paganism, so also with the secret doctrines of Gnostic speculation, intelligible only to the initiated few. Next, the test of its reality both by practical fruit of action, and by the spiritual growth connected therewith. In relation to the former, "faith without works" is "dead"; in relation to the other it is "imperfect," needing to be developed into maturity (Jas. ii. 20, 22). Both these lessons were evidently needed, in consequence of the appearance at Colossæ of the occult mysticism and the unpractical speculation noted in chap. ii. 8, 10, 18. But the Church itself was still faithful. Hence the last words, "as also it does in you," turning back again to Colossæ in particular, are an insertion of kindly courtesy—one of the insertions of apparent afterthought not unfrequent in St. Paul's Epistles—intended to show that the implied warning is by no means a condemnation.

(7) **Ye also learned of Epaphras.**—Of Epaphras we know nothing, except what we gather from this passage, and from chap. iv. 12; Philem. verse 23. The name is a shortened form of Epaphroditus, but it is most unlikely that he is the same as the Epaphroditus of Phil. ii. 25; iv. 18. Being, it seems, a native of Colossæ itself, he was apparently its first evangelist, and is afterwards described as feeling some responsibility for it and its neighbouring cities, Laodicea and Hierapolis (chap. iv. 13). His work could not have been transient, for under him the Colossians are said not only to have "heard," but also to have "known" (come to know perfectly) "the grace of God." St. Paul here gives emphatic testimony to his faithfulness, and to his preaching to them "in truth." That he was, then or afterwards, Bishop of Colossæ is probably a mere guess of tradition. But he may have had some such charge as that which was afterwards more formally committed to Timothy at Ephesus, and Titus in Crete. At this time, however, he remained with St. Paul (chap. iv. 12, 13), and apparently shared his captivity, for he is called (in Philem. verse 23) his "fellow-prisoner."

Who is for you a faithful minister of Christ.—(1) "For you" is, properly, *on your behalf.* This has been supposed to mean that Epaphras, like his Philippian namesake, had been a representative of the Colossian Church, in ministry to the Apostle; but this is hardly compatible with the entire absence of any personal reference in the sentence. Contrast Philem. verse 13, "that on thy behalf he might minister *to me.*" If this reading, therefore, is to stand, "on your behalf" must be taken to signify generally "for your benefit," which is doubtless the meaning of our version. (2) But there is considerable, perhaps preponderating, MS. authority for the reading "on our behalf," that is, *in our stead.* This makes Epaphras a representative, perhaps an actual messenger, of St. Paul, for the conversion of the church at Colossæ; sent probably at the time when the Apostle had his head-quarters at Ephesus, and when "all that dwelt in Asia heard the word of the Lord Jesus" (Acts xix. 10). This interpretation not only gives greater force to this passage, but explains also the attitude of authority here assumed by St. Paul toward a church which he had not seen, differing so markedly from the tone of his Epistle to the Romans in a like case.

(8) **Who also declared unto us.**—This refers to news recently brought by Epaphras to St. Paul at Rome. He had been a minister in St. Paul's stead; he now, like Timothy afterwards, visited him to give account of his deputed work.

Your love in the Spirit.—"In the Spirit" is "in the grace of the Holy Ghost"—the Spirit of love. The love here would seem to be especially love towards St. Paul, a part of the "love towards all the saints" ascribed to them above (verse 4).

(9—12) From thanksgiving St. Paul passes, as always, to pray for them. The prayer is for their full and perfect knowledge of God's will; but this is emphatically connected with practical "walking" in that will, first by fruitfulness in good work, next by showing themselves strong in Christ to endure sufferings, lastly by thankful acceptance of God's call to inheritance among the saints in light. There is a hearty recognition of the blessing of knowledge (on which the incipient Gnosticism of the day was so eloquent); but it is to be tried by the three tests of practical goodness, patience, and thankful humility.

(9) **Do not cease to pray for you.**—Comp. Eph. i. 16. "To pray" (see Eph. vi. 18; Phil. iv. 6) is the general word for "to worship"; "to desire" indicates prayer, properly so called, asking from God what is requisite and necessary for ourselves or for others.

The knowledge of his will.—The "knowledge" here spoken of is the "full knowledge," to be attained in measure here, to be made perfect in heaven. See 1 Cor. xiii. 12, "Now I know in part; but then shall I

Chap. i. 9—12. Prayer for their fuller knowledge, good works, and patient endurance.

this cause we also, since the day we heard *it*, do not cease to pray for you, and to desire that ye might be filled with the knowledge of his will in all wisdom and spiritual understanding;
(10) that ye might walk worthy of the Lord unto all pleasing, being fruitful in every good work, and increasing in the knowledge of God;
(11) strengthened with all might, according to his glorious power, unto all patience and longsuffering with joyfulness;
(12) giving thanks unto the Father, which hath made us meet to be partakers of the inheritance

---

know (perfectly) even as I am known." On this word, especially frequent in the Epistles of the captivity, see Note on Eph. i. 17. It should be noted that the knowledge here prayed for is "the knowledge *of God's will*,"—not speculation as to the nature of God, or as to emanations from Deity, or even as to the reasons of God's mysterious counsels, but knowledge of what actually is His will, both in the dispensation which is to be accepted in faith, and in the commandments to be obeyed in love. So St. Paul (in 1 Tim. i. 4, 5) contrasts with the "fables and endless genealogies" of Gnostic speculation, "the end of the commandment," "charity out of a pure heart and a good conscience, and faith unfeigned."

In all wisdom and spiritual understanding.—This "knowledge of God's will" is man's "wisdom." For "wisdom" is the knowledge of the true end of life; which is (as the Book of Ecclesiastes so tragically shows) vainly sought, if contemplated apart from God's will, but found (see Eccles. xii. 13; Job xxviii. 28; Prov. i. 7) in the "fear of the Lord" and the "keeping of His commandments." (On the relation of the supreme gift of wisdom to lesser cognate gifts, see Note on Eph. i. 8.) "Understanding" here is properly the faculty of spiritual insight or judgment, the speculative exercise of wisdom, as the "prudence" of Eph. i. 8 is the practical. Hence St. Paul subjoins the practical element at once in the next verse.

(10) **Walk worthy** (*worthily*) **of the Lord.**—Here St. Paul begins to dwell on the practical life, much in the same spirit in which, in Eph. iv. 1, he returns from the profound thought of chaps. ii. and iii. to the entreaty "to walk worthy of the vocation with which they are called." "The Lord" is here, as usual, the Lord Jesus Christ; to walk worthy of Him is to have His life reproduced in us, to follow His example, to have "the mind of Christ Jesus." The "worthiness" is, of course, relative to our capacity, not absolute.

All pleasing.—The word here used is not found elsewhere in the New Testament, but is employed in classic and Hellenistic Greek to mean "a general disposition to please"—a constant preference of the will of others before our own. It is here used with tacit reference to God, since towards Him alone can it be a safe guide of action. Otherwise it must have the bad sense which in general usage was attached to it. St. Paul emphatically disowns and condemns the temper of "men-pleasing" (see Gal. i. 10; Eph. vi. 6; Col. iii. 22; 1 Thess. ii. 4), as incompatible with being "the servant of Christ." He could, indeed, "be all things to all men" (1 Cor. ix. 22); he could bid each man "please his neighbour for his edification" (Rom. xv. 12). But the only "pleasing" to which the whole life can be conformed is (see 1 Thess. iv. 1) the consideration "how we ought to walk and to please God." Only in subordination to this can we safely act on the desire of "all pleasing" towards men.

Increasing in (or, *by*) **the knowledge of God.**—The context evidently shows that the path towards the knowledge of God here indicated is not the path of thoughtful speculation, or of meditative devotion, but the third path co-ordinate with these—the path of earnest practice, of which the watchword is, "Do and thou shalt know."

(11) **His glorious power.**—Properly, *the strength of His glory*, His glory being His manifestation of Himself in love to man. (Comp. Eph. iii. 16, "According to the riches of His glory, to be strengthened with might by His spirit in the inner man.") On this use of "the glory" of God, frequent in these Epistles, see Eph. i. 6, 12, 14, and Notes there. The prayer, however, in the Ephesian Epistle looks to "knowledge of the love of Christ" as its object; the prayer here to power of endurance of trial and suffering.

Patience and longsuffering with joyfulness.—(1) "Patience" is here "endurance," rather than what we usually call patience. It is spoken of by St. James (chap. i. 3) as the result of the bracing effect of trial, and is illustrated by the typical example of Job (Jas. v. 11). Now a glance at the Book of Job will show that, while in respect of physical trial he is resignation itself (Job i. 21; ii. 10), yet that under the spiritual trial, which is the great subject of the book, he is the reverse of what is commonly called patient. He endures and conquers, but it is not without vehement passion and spiritual struggles, occasionally verging on a repining and rebellion, of which he bitterly repents (xli. 6). (2) To this "patience," therefore, here as elsewhere (2 Tim. iii. 10), St. Paul adds "longsuffering"—a word generally connected (as in 1 Cor. xiii. 4) with the temper of gentleness and love, and coming much nearer to the description of our ordinary idea of a "patient" temper, which, in its calm sweetness and gentleness, hardly feels to the utmost such spiritual trials as vexed the righteous soul of Job. Of such longsuffering our Lord's bearing of the insults of the Condemnation and the cruelties of the Passion, when "He was led as a lamb to the slaughter," is the perfect type. (3) Yet even then St. Paul is not content without "joyfulness," in obedience to the command of our Master (Matt. v. 12), fulfilled in Himself on the cross (Heb. xii. 2). The ground of such joy, so often shown in Christian martyrdom, is given by St. Peter (1 Pet. iv. 13), "Rejoice, inasmuch as ye are partakers of Christ's sufferings, that when His glory shall be revealed, ye may be glad also with exceeding joy." Of that joy St. Paul himself was a bright example in his present captivity. (See Phil. i. 18, 19; ii. 17, 18.) The words therefore form a climax. "Patience" struggles and endures; "long-suffering" endures without a struggle; "joyfulness" endures and glories in suffering.

(12) **Giving thanks unto the Father.**—These words naturally follow the words "with joyfulness," with which, indeed, they may be grammatically connected. But the "thankfulness" here is, as the context shows, the thankfulness of humility, sensible that from the Father's love we have received all, and can but receive.

of the saints in light: (13) who hath delivered us from the power of darkness, and hath translated *us* into the kingdom of his dear Son:[1] (14) in whom we have redemption through his blood, *even* the forgiveness of sins: (15) who is the image

Chap. i. 13. Christ the Redeemer.

Chap. i. 15—17. Christ the true image of God.

1 Gr. *the Son of his love.*

Which hath made us meet.—The same word is used in 2 Cor iii. 6, "who hath made us able ministers of the new covenant," and corresponds to the word "sufficient" in St. Paul's previous question (2 Cor. ii. 16), "Who is sufficient for these things?" The reference is clearly to God's foreknowledge and call (as in Rom. viii. 29, 30), in virtue of which "we are more than conquerors," and "cannot be separated from His love in Jesus Christ our Lord."

To be partakers of the inheritance of the saints.—Literally, for *the part* (appointed to us) *of the lot of the saints.* (Comp. Eph. i. 11, where, however, the sense is slightly different). The "lot" (like the Old Testament type of the share in the land of Canaan, "the lot of their inheritance") is the place assigned to the saints primarily by the grace of God. It may have, as in the case of the type, to be fought for; but it is won not by our own arm, but by "God's hand and His arm, and the light of His countenance, because He has a favour unto us" (Ps. xliv. 3). Hence, in accordance with St. Paul's usual teaching (especially emphatic in this and the Ephesian Epistle), the whole stress is laid on God's grace, giving us our lot, and "making us meet" to accept it.

In light.—Properly, *in the light.* See Eph. iv. 8—14 —a passage dwelling on the idea of the kingdom of light, almost as strongly and exhaustively as St. John himself (1 John i. 5—7, *et al.*). "In the light" (opposed to "the power of darkness" of the next verse) is in the light of God's countenance, revealed in the face of Jesus Christ.

[**2. The Doctrine of Christ.**

(1) His Salvation and Redemption of us all (verses 13, 14).
(2) His Nature as the Image of the Invisible God, the creator and sustainer of all things heavenly and earthly (verses 15—17).
(3) His Headship of the Church (verse 18).
(4) His Mediation, reconciling all to God, first generally stated, then applied especially to the Colossians (verses 19—23).]

(13—23) In this we have the great characteristic section of this Epistle, distinguished from corresponding parts of the Epistle to the Ephesians by the explicit and emphatic stress laid upon the divine majesty of Christ. It corresponds very closely with the remarkable passage opening the Epistle to the Hebrews. In the Epistles of the preceding group, to the Corinthians, Galatians, and Romans, chief and almost exclusive prominence is given to the universal mediation of Christ, as justifying and sanctifying all the souls of men. In these Epistles (this truth being accepted) we pass on to that which such universal mediation necessitates—the conception of Christ as the Head of all created being, and as the perfect manifestation of the Godhead. The former is the key-note of the Ephesian Epistle; the latter is dominant here, although the former remains as an undertone; as also in the great passage of the Epistle to the Philippians (chap. ii. 6—11), speaking of Him as "in the form of God," and having "the Name which is above every name." The especial reason for St. Paul's emphatic assertion of the great truth here we see in the next chapter. But it is clear that it comes naturally in the order of revelation, leading up to the full doctrine of "the Word" in St. John. As the spiritual meaning of the Resurrection, the great subject of the first preaching, had to be sought in the Atonement, so the inquiry into the possibility of an universal Atonement led back to the Incarnation, and to Christ as pre-existent from "the beginning" in God.

(13, 14) We enter on this great passage, as is natural, and accordant with St. Paul's universal practice, through that living and practical truth of our redemption in Christ Jesus, which in the earlier Epistles he had taught as the one thing needful (1 Cor. ii. 2).

(13) **Who hath delivered us from the power of darkness.**—"Delivered" is "rescued," properly applied to dragging a person out of battle or the jaws of danger. "The power of darkness" (see Luke xxii. 53) is, of course, the power of evil, permitted (see Luke iv. 6) to exist, but in itself a usurped tyranny (as Chrysostom expresses it), not a true "kingdom." Salvation is, first of all, rescue from the guilt and bondage of sin, to which man has given occasion by his own choice, but which, once admitted, he cannot himself break. It is here described in its first origination from the love of the Father. "God so loved the world, that He gave His only begotten Son."

And hath translated us . . .—The word "translated" is a word properly applied to the transplanting of races, and the settlement of them in a new home. Salvation, begun by rescue, is completed by the settlement of the rescued captives in the new kingdom of Christ. The two acts, indeed, are distinct, but inseparable. Thus baptism is at once "for the remission of sins" and an "entrance into the kingdom of God."

His dear Son.—The original is far more striking and beautiful. It is, "The Son of His love," corresponding to "the beloved" of the parallel passage in the Ephesian Epistle (chap. i. 6), but perhaps going beyond it. God is love; the Son of God is, therefore, the "Son of His love," partaking of and manifesting this His essential attribute.

In whom we have . . .—This verse corresponds verbally with Eph. i. 7, where see Note. From the love of the Father, the first cause of salvation, we pass to the efficient cause in the redemption and propitiation of the Son.

Verses 15—17 pass from Christ as our Mediator to Christ as He is in Himself from all eternity, "the image of the invisible God," and as He is from the beginning of time, the creator and sustainer of all things in heaven and earth. What was before implied is now explicitly asserted; what was before emphatically asserted is now taken for granted, and made the stepping-stone to yet higher and more mysterious truth.

(15) **The image of the invisible God.**—This all-important clause needs the most careful examination.

of the invisible God, the firstborn of every creature: (16) for by him were all things created, that are in heaven, and that are in earth, visible and invisible, whether *they be* thrones, or dominions, or principalities, or powers: all things

---

We note accordingly (1) that the word "image" (like the word "form," Phil. ii. 6, 7) is used in the New Testament for real and essential embodiment, as distinguished from mere likeness. Thus in Heb. x. 1 we read, "The law, having a shadow of good things to come, and not *the very image* of the things;" we note also in Rom. i. 23 the distinction between the mere outward "likeness" and the "image" which it represented; we find in 1 Cor. xv. 49 that the "image of the earthy" and "the image of the heavenly" Adam denote actual identity of nature with both; and in 2 Cor. iii. 18 the actual work of the Spirit in the heart is described as "changing us from glory to glory" into "the image" of the glorified Christ. (2) Next we observe that although, speaking popularly, St. Paul in 1 Cor. xi. 7 calls man "the image and glory of God," yet the allusion is to Gen. i. 26, 28, where man is said, with stricter accuracy, to be made "after the image of God" (as in Eph. iv. 24, "created after God"), and this more accurate expression is used in chap. iii. 10 of this Epistle, "renewed after the image of Him that created him." Who then, or what, is the "image of God," after which man is created? St. Paul here emphatically (as in 2 Cor. iv. 4 parenthetically) answers "Christ," as the Son of God, "first-born before all creation." The same truth is conveyed in a different form, clearer (if possible) even than this, in Heb. i. 3, where "the Son" is said to be not only "the brightness of the glory of the Father," but "the express image of His Person." For the word "express image" is *character* in the original, used here (as when we speak of the alphabetical "characters") to signify the visible drawn image, and the word "Person" is *substance* or *essence*. (3) It is not to be forgotten that at this time in the Platonising Judaism of Philo, "the Word" was called the eternal "image of God." (See passages quoted in Dr. Lightfoot's note on this passage.) This expression was not peculiar to him; it was but a working out of that personification of the "wisdom of God," of which we have a magnificent example in Prov. viii. 22—30, and of which we trace the effect in the Alexandrine Book of "Wisdom" (vii. 25, 26). "Wisdom is the breath of the power of God, and a pure stream from the glory of the Most High—the brightness of the everlasting light, the unspotted mirror of the power of God, and the image of His goodness." It seems to have represented in the Jewish schools the idea complementary to the ordinary idea of the Messiah in the Jewish world. Just as St. John took up the vague idea of "the Word," and gave it a clear divine personality in Christ, so St. Paul seems to act here in relation to the other phrase, used as a description of the Word. In Christ he fixes in solid reality the floating vision of the "image of God." (4) There is an emphasis on the words "of the invisible God." Now, since the whole context shows that the reference is to the eternal pre-existence of Christ, ancient interpreters (of whom Chrysostom may be taken as the type) argued that the image of the invisible must be also invisible. But this seems opposed to the whole idea of the word "image," and to its use in the New Testament and elsewhere. The true key to this passage is in our Lord's own words in John i. 8, "No man hath seen God at any time, the only begotten Son" (here is the remarkable reading, "the only begotten God"), "who is in the bosom of the Father, He hath revealed Him." In anticipation of the future revelation of Godhead, Christ, even as pre-existent, is called "The image of the invisible God."

The firstborn of every creature (*of all creation*).—(1) *As to the sense of this clause.* The grammatical construction here will bear either the rendering of our version, or the rendering "begotten before all creation," whence comes the "begotten before all worlds" of the Nicene creed. But the whole context shows that the latter is unquestionably the true rendering. For, as has been remarked from ancient times, He is said to be "begotten" and not "created;" next, he is emphatically spoken of below as He "by whom all things were created," who is "before all things," and "in whom all things consist." (2) *As to the order of idea.* In Himself He is "the image of God" from all eternity. From this essential conception, by a natural contrast, the thought immediately passes on to distinction from, and priority to, all created being. Exactly in this same order of idea, we have in Heb. i. 2, 3, "By whom also He made the worlds . . . upholding all things by the word of His power;" and in John i. 3, "All things were made by Him, and without Him was not anything made which was made. Here St. Paul indicates this idea in the words "firstborn before all creation," and works it out in the verses following. (3) *As to the name "firstborn" itself.* It is used of the Messiah as an almost technical name (derived from Pss. ii. 7; lxxxix. 28), as is shown in Heb. i. 6, "when He bringeth the first begotten into the world." In tracing the Messianic line of promise we notice that, while the Messiah is always true man, "the seed of Abraham," "the son of David," yet on him are accumulated attributes too high for any created being (as in Isa. ix. 6). He is declared to be an "Emmanuel" God with us; and His kingdom a visible manifestation of God. Hence the idea contained in the word "firstborn" is not only sovereignty "above all the kings of the earth" (Ps. lxxxix. 28; comp. Dan. viii. 13, 14), but also likeness to God and priority to all created being. (4) *As to the union of the two clauses.* In the first we have the declaration of His eternal unity with God—all that was completely embodied in the declaration of the "Word who is God," up to which all the higher Jewish speculations had led; in the second we trace the distinctness of His Person, as the "begotten of the Father," the true Messiah of Jewish hopes, and the subordination of the co-eternal Son to the Father. The union of the two marks the assertion of Christian mystery, as against rationalising systems, of the type of Arianism on one side, of Sabellianism on the other.

(16) **For by him . . . all things were created by** (*through*) **him, and for** (*to*) **him.**—Carrying out the idea of the preceding clause with accumulated emphasis, St. Paul speaks of all creation as having taken place "by Him," "through Him," and "for Him." Now we note that in Rom. ix. 36, St. Paul, in a burst of adoration, declares of the Father that "from Him, and through Him, and to Him are all things;" and in Heb. ii. 10 the Father is spoken of as One "by whom are all things, and for whom are all things" (the word "for whom" being different from the word so rendered here, but virtually equivalent to it). Hence we observe that the Apostle here takes up a phrase belonging only to

were created by him, and for him:
(17) and he is before all things,[a] and
by him all things consist. (18) And
he is the head of the body, the
church: who is the beginning, the

a 1 Cor. 8. 6; John 1. 3.
1 Or, *among all.*

firstborn from the dead; that in
all[1] *things* he might have
the preeminence. (19) For
it pleased *the Father*
that in him should all

Chap. i. 18–20. Christ the Head of the Church and Mediator.

Godhead and usually applied to the Father, and distinctly applies it to Christ, but with the significant change of "from whom" into "in whom." The usual language of holy Scripture as to the Father is "from whom," and as to the Son "through whom," are all things. Thus we have in Heb. i. 2, "through whom He made the world;" and in John i. 3—10, "All things were made"—"the world was made"—"through Him." Here, however, St. Paul twice adds "in whom," just as he had used "in whom" of God in his sermon at Athens (Acts xvii. 28), probably conveying the idea, foreshadowed in the Old Testament description of the divine "Wisdom," that in His divine mind lay the germ of the creative design and work. and indirectly condemning by anticipation the fancy of incipient Gnosticism, that He was but an inferior emanation or agent of the Supreme God.

In heaven and . . . earth . . .—Here again there is a reiteration of earnest emphasis. "All things in heaven and earth" is the ancient phrase for all creation. Then, lest this phrase should be restricted to the sublunary sphere, he adds, "visible and invisible." Lastly, in accordance with the general tone of these Epistles, and with special reference to the worship of angels introduced into Colossæ, he dwells, like the author of the Epistle to the Hebrews, on the superiority of our Lord to all angelic natures, whether they be "thrones, or dominions, or principalities, or powers." (Comp. Eph. i 21; Phil. ii. 9, 10.)

Thrones, or dominions . . .—Compare the enumeration in Eph. i. 21. The word peculiar to this passage is "thrones," which in all the various speculations as to the hierarchy of heaven, naturally represents the first place of dignity and nearness to the Throne of God. (Comp. Rev. iv. 4, "Round about the throne four-and-twenty thrones.") But it seems difficult, if not impossible, to attach distinctive meanings to those titles, and trace out their order. If St. Paul alludes at all to the Rabbinical hierarchies, he (probably with deliberate intention) takes their titles without attending to their fanciful orders and meanings. Whatever they mean, if they mean anything, all are infinitely below the glory of Christ. (See Note on Eph. i. 21.)

(17) **He is before all things.**—The words "He is" are both emphatic. He, and He only, is; all else is created. It is impossible not to refer to the "I am" of Eternal existence, as claimed by our Lord for Himself. "Before Abraham was, I am" (John viii. 58; comp. also John i. 15). Hence the word "before" should be taken, not of supreme dignity, but of pre-existence.

By him all things consist.—That is, *hold together in unity*, obeying the primæval law of their being. In this clause is attributed to our Lord, not only the creative act, but also the constant sustaining power, "in which all lives and moves and has its being," and which, even less than the creative agency, can be supposed to be a derivative and finite power, such as that of the *Demiurgus* of Gnostic speculation.

(18–20). In these verses St. Paul returns from dwelling on the eternal nature of the Son of God to describe Him in His mediatorial office as Son of Man, becoming the "Head" of all humanity, as called into "His Body, the Church." In this he touches on a doctrine more fully developed in the Epistle to the Ephesians. (See Eph. i. 10, 20, 22; ii. 19, 21; iv. 15, 16.) But still, as has been already noted, there is in this Epistle more stress on the supreme dignity of the Head, as in the other more on the unity, and blessing, and glory of the Body. It should be observed that in this, His mediatorial office, there is throughout a mysterious analogy to His eternal sonship. In both He is "the Head," first, of universal creation, next, of the new creation in His Church; He is "the beginning," in the one case in eternity, in the other in time; He is "the firstborn," now in Eternal Sonship, now in the Resurrection making Him the new life of mankind.

(18) **He is the head.**—"He" is again emphatic. "He who is the image of God, He also is the Head." (On the title itself, see Eph. i. 22.)

The beginning.—Chrysostom reads here a kindred word, *the first-fruits.* The reading is no doubt a gloss, but an instructive one. It shows that the reference is to Christ, as being in His humanity "the first principle" of the new life to us—the "first-fruits" from the dead (1 Cor. xv. 20, 23), and "the bringer of life and immortality to light" (2 Tim. i. 10).

The firstborn from the dead.—The same title is given to Him in Rev. i. 5. In his sermon at Antioch in Pisidia (Acts xiii. 33), St. Paul quotes the passage, "Thou art my Son; this day have I begotten thee," as fulfilled in that "He raised up Jesus again." (Comp. Heb. v. 5.) In Rom. i. 3, he speaks of Christ as "declared" (or, *defined*) "to be the Son of God with power by the resurrection from the dead." The Resurrection is (so to speak) His second birth, the beginning of that exaltation, which is contrasted with His first birth on earth in great humility, and of His entrance on the glory of His mediatorial kingdom. (See Eph. i. 20—23, where the starting-point of all His exaltation is again placed in the Resurrection.)

That in all things he might . . .—Literally, *That in all things He might become pre-eminent.* The words "He might become," are opposed to the "He is" above. They refer to the exaltation of His humanity, so gloriously described in Phil. ii. 9—11. Thus absolutely in His divine nature, relatively to the mediatorial kingdom in His humanity, He is "the Alpha and Omega, the beginning and the end, the first and the last" (Rev. i. 8, 11, 17, 18).

(19) **For it pleased the Father.**—(1) The construction is doubtful. There is nothing corresponding to "the Father" in the original. Our rendering involves the supply of the nominative *God, i.e.*, "the Father," or *Christ* to the verb, so that the sentence may run, *the Father* or *Christ determined of His good pleasure that,* &c. The supply of the nominative "Christ" is easier grammatically; but it accords ill with the invariable reference of all things, both by our Lord Himself and His Apostles, ultimately to the good pleasure of the Father. Moreover, the verb is so constantly used of God that the supply of the nominative "God," though unexampled, is far from inadmissible. The simplest

fulness dwell; (20) and, having made
peace[1] through the blood of his
cross, by him to reconcile all things
unto himself; by him, *I say*, whether
they be things in earth, or things in
heaven. (21) And you, that were
sometime alienated and
enemies in *your* mind by
wicked works,[2] yet now
hath he reconciled (22) in the body
of his flesh through death, to present you holy and unblameable and
unreproveable in his sight: (23) if ye
continue in the faith grounded and
settled, and *be* not moved away from
the hope of the gospel, which ye have
heard, *and* which was preached to every
creature which is under heaven; whereof

Chap. i. 21—23. The salvation of the Colossians in Him.

1 Or, *making peace.*

2 Or, *by your mind in wicked works.*

grammatical construction would, indeed, be to take "the fulness" as the nominative, and render for *in Him all the fulness* (*of God*) *was pleased to dwell.* But the personification of "the fulness," common in Gnostic speculation, is hardly after the manner of St. Paul. Perhaps, on the whole, the rendering of our version (which is usually adopted) is to be preferred; especially as it suits better with the following verse. (2) The sense is, however, quite clear, and is enforced by chap. ii. 9, "In Him dwelleth all the fulness of the Godhead bodily." On the word "fulness" (*pleroma*), see Note on Eph. i. 23. The "fulness of the Godhead" is the essential nature, comprising all the attributes, of Godhead. The indwelling of such Deity in the humanity of Christ is the ground of all His exaltation as the "Head," "the beginning," the "firstborn from the dead," and the triumphant King, on which St. Paul had already dwelt. By it alone can He be the true Mediator between God and man.

(20) **Having made peace through the blood of his cross.**—On this verse, where St. Paul returns to the subject of the Atonement, with which he began, comp. Eph. ii. 13—18, and Notes there. In the Ephesian Epistle the treatment of the subject is fuller, and in one point more comprehensive, viz., in bringing out emphatically the unity of all, Jews and Gentiles alike, with one another, as well as their unity with Christ. But, on the other hand, this passage involves deeper and more mysterious teaching in this—that it includes in the reconciliation by the blood of Christ, not merely all humanity, but "all things, whether things on earth or things in heaven." This is, indeed, only a fuller exposition of the truth that "God was in Christ reconciling the world (the *kosmos*) to Himself" (2 Cor. v. 19); and that "the whole creation waiteth," "in constant expectation," "for the manifestation of the sons of God," and "shall be delivered from the bondage of corruption into the glorious liberty of the children of God" (Rom. viii. 19—21). But it is couched in more distinct and striking terms, opening to us a glimpse of the infinite scope, not merely of our Lord's Mediatorship, but of His Atonement, which, while it almost bewilders, yet satisfies the thoughtful understanding, and more than satisfies an adoring faith. As there seems to be a physical unity in the universe, if we may believe the guesses of science, so, says Holy Scripture, there is a moral and spiritual unity also in Jesus Christ.

Verses 21—23 apply this truth of the Mediatorial work of the Lord Jesus Christ to the especial case of the Colossians. The subject here touched is more fully worked out in Eph. ii. 1, 2, 11—18; the alienation is there described as not only from God, but from His covenanted people; the reconciliation is with God and man in one great unity.

(21) **Alienated.**—Not naturally aliens, but estranged. (See Note on Eph. ii. 12.)

By wicked works.—Properly, *in your wicked works.* The enmity of heart is not properly caused by wicked works, but shown in them, and probably intensified by reflex action through them.

(22) **In the body of his flesh.**—There seems to be some emphasis on the word "flesh:" just as in the parallel of Eph. ii. 16, the expression is "in one body," with a characteristic emphasis on the word "one," suiting the genius of the passage. The meaning is, of course, His natural body, as distinguished from His mystic Body, spoken of above (verse 18). But this is no sufficient reason for the use of this phrase, for there could be no confusion between them in this passage. Hence, without ascribing to the word "flesh" a distinctly polemical intention, we may not unnaturally suppose that there was present to St. Paul's mind the thought of the Gnosticism, which depreciated the body as evil, and which must have always inclined to the idea that "Jesus Christ had not come in the flesh" (1 John iv. 2, 3); and that the presence of this thought induced some special emphasis in his language.

Holy and unblameable and unreproveable.—See Note on Eph. i. 4. The word "to present" is used both in a sacrificial sense (as in Rom. xii. 1) and in the sense of introduction and presentation (as of a bride, see Eph. v. 27). The words, "holy and unblameable," *i.e.*, "without blemish," suit the former sense. But "unreproveable" is incongruous with it, and the parallel passage (Eph. ii. 18) speaks of "access" or introduction to the Father.

(23) **If.**—The word, as in Eph. iii. 2, iv. 21 (where see Notes), conveys a supposition hardly hypothetical—"If, as I presume;" "If, as I trust." St. Paul cannot refrain from needful warning, but he refuses to anticipate failure.

Grounded.—*Built on the foundation.* Comp. Eph. ii. 20, "built on the foundation of the Apostles and Prophets, Jesus Christ Himself being the chief corner-stone."

Settled.—The result of being so grounded. The word is used in the same sense, but without metaphorical association, in 1 Cor. xv. 58, "stedfast, unmoveable," as here "settled and not being moved."

The hope.—See Note on verse 5. Here, as there, great emphasis is laid on "hope." But here there may possibly be reference to some ideas (like those spoken of in 2 Tim. ii. 18) that "the resurrection was past already," and that the hope of a true resurrection and a real heaven was either a delusion or a metaphor.

Every creature which is under heaven.—Comp. our Lord's command, "Preach the gospel to every creature" (Mark xvi. 15). In idea and capacity the gospel is literally universal; although in actual reality such universality can only be claimed by a natural hyperbole.

I Paul am made a minister; (24) who
now rejoice in my suffer-
ings for you, and fill up
that which is behind of
the afflictions of Christ
in my flesh for his body's
sake, which is the church: (25) where-
of I am made a minister, according
to the dispensation of God which is
given to me for you, to fulfil the word
of God; [1] (26) *even* the mystery which
hath been hid from ages and from gene-
rations, but now is made manifest to his
saints: (27) to whom God would make
known what *is* the riches of the glory
of this mystery among the Gentiles;

Chap. i. 24—26. The mission of St. Paul, in suffering and preaching, to the Gentiles.

[1] Or, *fully to preach the word of God*, Rom. 15. 19.

[3. **The Mission of St. Paul.**

AS APOSTLE OF THE GENTILES, a minister of the newly revealed mystery of their salvation, testifying to all alike by suffering and by preaching, in order "to present all perfect in Christ Jesus" (verses 24—29).]

(24—29) Here (as in Eph. iii., in the same connection) St. Paul dwells on his own mission to set forth the universal gospel to the Gentiles. In the Ephesian Epistle this declaration is made a direct introduction to practical exhortation (comp. chaps. iv., v., vi.); here it leads up to the earnest remonstrance against speculative errors in chap. ii., which precedes a similar practical exhortation. In both cases he dwells on the committal to him of a special dispensation; in both he rejoices in suffering as a means of spiritual influence; in both cases he declares the one object to be the presentation of each man perfect before Christ.

(24) **Who now rejoice.**—In the true reading of the original there is no relative pronoun. The sentence starts with emphatic abruptness, "Now (at this moment) I rejoice" (just as in 2 Cor. vii. 9). In all the three Epistles of the Captivity this same rejoicing is declared in himself and urged on his brethren. In Eph. iii. 13, "I desire that ye faint not at my tribulations for you, which is your glory;" in Phil. ii. 11, "Yea, if I be offered upon the sacrifice and service of your faith, I joy, and rejoice with you all. For the same cause do ye also joy, and rejoice with me." There, as here, the rejoicing is in suffering, not in itself, not solely because it is borne with and for Christ, but also because it is for the sake of the Church. Here, however, this idea is expressed with far greater emphasis.

Fill up that which is behind of the afflictions of Christ.—The sense of this passage is at first sight startling, but it could not have been thought difficult or doubtful, had not false inferences from it tempted men to shrink from the obvious meaning. Now, (1) the "afflictions of Christ" is a phrase not used elsewhere; for "affliction" (properly, *hard and galling pressure*) is the ordinary burden of life, and is generally spoken of only as coming on His servants. But, like the common phrase "the sufferings of Christ" (2 Cor. i. 5; Phil. iii. 10; 1 Pet. iv. 15; v. 1), it must mean the afflictions which He endured. It is true, as has been thoughtfully suggested (see Chrysostom and others on the passage) that we are to count as His the afflictions of His Church; but still, even if we are to include these indirect afflictions, we cannot possibly exclude the direct. Next, (2) St. Paul expressly says (in the full force of the original) that "he fills up *instead*" of his Master, what is still left unfinished of his Master's afflictions. (See the passages quoted by Dr. Lightfoot in his note on this verse.) He declares, *i.e.*, that, succeeding to the suffering of Christ, he carries it out for the sake of His body the Church. This is, indeed, nothing but a clearer and more striking expression of the truth conveyed in 2 Cor. i. 5, "The sufferings of Christ overflow to us," so that we bear our part, in addition to the full measure which He bore; and even in the commoner expression, to be "partaker of Christ's sufferings" (Phil. iii. 10; 1 Pet. iv. 13), or "to drink of His cup and be baptised with His baptism" (Matt. xx. 22, 23). But, (3) looking to the meaning and use of the word "afflictions," we note that "the afflictions of Christ" must be His sufferings on earth considered simply as a part—though immeasurably the chief part—of the burden of humanity in a sinful world. They represent, not the Cross of Atonement, on which He alone could suffer—and in which any reader of St. Paul must find it absurd to suppose that he would claim the slightest share—but the Cross of struggle against sin even to death, which He expressly bade us "take up if we would follow Him." This He has still left "behind;" this in His strength every one of His servants bears, partly for himself, partly also for others. In the former light St. Paul says, "The world is crucified to me, and I to the world" (Gal. vi. 14); in the latter he claims it as his highest privilege "to fill up that which is behind of the afflictions of Christ for His Body which is the Church."

In my flesh for his body's sake.—There is obviously an antithesis here. St. Paul suffers in his natural body for the mystical Body of Christ.

(25) **Whereof I am made** (or, *became*) **a minister.**—Above (in verse 23) St. Paul describes himself as a "minister of the gospel," here as a "minister (or, *servant*) of the Church." Elsewhere he is always the "minister of God" and "of Christ"; here of the Church, as the Body of Christ, and so indissolubly united with Christ.

The dispensation of God.—See Eph. iii. 2—9, and Notes there. The reference is to his peculiar "Apostleship of the Gentiles."

To fulfil.—The marginal reading and reference to Rom. xv. 19 give the explanation of the word, "fully to preach the Word of God"—to be a messenger of the perfect revelation, which had now unfolded what was previously a hidden "mystery."

(26) **The mystery.**—On the Scriptural sense of the word "mystery," and its relation to the modern use of the word, see Note on Eph. i. 9. In this passage, perhaps, most of all, it is defined with perfect clearness, as "a secret long hidden, and now revealed."

(27) **To whom God would**—*i.e., God willed.* The expression is emphatic. It was of God's own pleasure, inscrutable to man. So in Eph. i. 9, we read "the mystery of His will." Note also, in Eph. i. 4—6, the repeated reference to the predestination of God in His love.

The riches of the glory.—See Eph. i. 18; iii. 16; and Notes there.

Which is Christ in you.—This mystery specially committed to St. Paul to declare is in Eph. iii. 6, defined

which is Christ in you,[1] the hope of
glory: (28) whom we preach, warning
every man, and teaching every man in
all wisdom; that we may present every
man perfect in Christ Jesus: (29) where-
unto I also labour, striving according
to his working, which worketh in me
mightily.

CHAPTER II.—(1) For I would that
ye knew what great conflict[2] I have
for you, and *for* them at Laodicea,

1 Or, *among you.*

A.D. 64.

2 Or, *fear*, or, *care.*

---

thus, "That the Gentiles should be (or, *are*) fellowheirs, and of the same body, and partakers of His promise in Christ by the gospel"; and the nature of this promise is explained below, "That Christ may dwell in your hearts by faith." Here the mystery itself is boldly defined as "Christ in you;" just as in 1 Tim. iii. 16, 17, according to one interpretation of that difficult passage, "the mystery of godliness" is Christ Himself, "who was manifest," &c. Here we have again a significant illustration of the difference between the characteristic ideas of the two Epistles. In the Ephesian Epistle the unity of all in God's covenant is first put forth, and then explained as dependent on the indwelling of Christ in the heart. Here the "Christ in you" is all in all: the unity of all men in Him is an inference, but one which the readers of the Epistle are left to draw for themselves. On the great idea itself, in the purely individual relation, see Phil. i. 21, and also Gal. ii. 20; in the more general form, see Rom. viii. 10; 2 Cor. xiii. 5; Gal. iv. 19.

The hope of (*the*) glory.—So in 1 Tim. i. 1, "The Lord Jesus Christ, which is our hope." "The glory" is the glorified state of perfection in heaven, wrapt in the communion with God, and so "changed from glory to glory." Again we note (as in verses 5, 23) the special emphasis laid on the hope of heaven. Christ is "our hope," as He is "our life," *i.e.*, the ground of our sure and certain hope of the future, as of our spiritual life in the present.

(28) **Warning every man, and teaching.**—In "warning" is implied the idea of reproof of folly or sin. (See 1 Thess. v. 14; 2 Thess. iii. 5.) "Teaching" is simply instruction—including, of course, practical exhortation—of those already warned.

Perfect.—See Eph. iv. 13; Phil. iii. 15, and Notes there. Here, however, as in 1 Cor. ii. 6, 7, the reference may be to the sense of "perfect" as "initiated in mystery." St. Paul, in opposition to the exclusive claim of "perfection" by the speculators in mystic knowledge ("falsely so called") would present "every man," learned or ignorant, "perfect before God." In this universality of privilege lies the glorious distinction between the gospel and all schools of philosophy, whether they reject or assume its name.

(29) **Whereunto I also labour.**—In this verse St. Paul passes from the plural to the singular, evidently in preparation for the strong personal remonstrance of chap. ii. 1—7.

His working . . .—See Eph. i. 12, and Note there. Perhaps, as in Gal. ii. 8 ("He that wrought effectually in Peter to the Apostleship of the Circumcision, the same was mighty in me towards the Gentiles"), there is special allusion to the grace given to him for his Apostleship of the Gentiles.

II.

[**4. Special Enforcement of Doctrinal Teaching** (chap. ii. 1—iii. 4).

(1) Exhortation to Stand Fast in the Faith, dictated by special anxiety for them and the sister churches, urging them to seek all wisdom in Christ alone, and to keep to the old simplicity of the gospel (verses 1—7).

(2) Warning against Speculative Error, turning them "to philosophy and vain deceit" from Christ.

(*a*) *For in Him dwells all the fulness of the Godhead.*

(*b*) *In Him they have the true spiritual circumcision of the New Covenant.*

(*c*) *From Him, and from Him alone, can they receive justification from sin, and the new life of grace* (verses 8—15).

(3) Warning against Practical Superstition.

(*a*) *In relation to obsolete Jewish ordinances* (verses 16—17).

(*b*) *In worship of angels, sinning against the sole Headship of Christ* (verses 18, 19).

(4) Declaration of the True Christian State.

(*a*) *As dead with Christ,* and so dead to all the vain and carnal ordinances, which have a show of wisdom but no reality (verses 20—23).

(*b*) *As risen with Christ,* and so bound to seek the things above, and have a life hid with Christ in God (chap. iii. 1—4).]

(1—7) In these verses St. Paul declares his deep anxiety for the Colossians and Laodiceans and others who had not seen his face, that they might seek, not the false, but the true knowledge, finding "the mystery of God" in Christ alone. The reason of that anxiety is found in the "beguiling and enticing words" of an incipient Gnosticism. But "though absent in the body" he rejoices in the steadfastness of their faith, and only exhorts them to continue in it, deepening and enlarging it, but never changing its essence.

(1) **What great conflict.**—The word is here repeated from the "striving" of the previous verse, which is, in the original, the cognate verb. It is the same word which is used in Phil. i. 30 ("conflict"), in 1 Thess. ii. 2 ("contention"), in 1 Tim. vi. 12, 2 Tim. iv. 7 ("the good fight of faith"). Evidently it describes the intense earnestness of the whole struggle against evil which he was undergoing for them; but perhaps, looking at chap. iv. 12, we may refer it especially to "striving in prayer" for them. It is probably dwelt upon here to show why, although unknown to them personally, he yet writes so urgently to them.

And for them at Laodicea.—Comp. chap. iv. 13, "For you, and for them that are in Laodicea, and for them in Hierapolis." These three cities lay near together in the valley of Lycus, a tributary of the Mæander; probably they were converted at one time, and are evidently regarded as forming one Christian community, for which Epaphras, the evangelist of Colossæ, felt himself responsible. Colossæ and Laodicea are actually directed to exchange the apostolic

and *for* as many as have not seen my
Chap. ii. 1—4. St. Paul's anxiety for the Colossians and the sister churches. face in the flesh; (2) that their hearts might be comforted, being knit together in love, and unto all riches of the full assurance of understanding, to the acknowledgement of the mystery of God, and of the Father, and of Christ;
(3) in whom [1] are hid all the treasures of wisdom and knowledge.
(4) And this I say, lest any man should beguile you with enticing words.
(5) For though I

1 Or, *Wherein.*

Letters sent to them (see chap. iv. 16, and Note there), and to read both alike in the churches. (See Dr. Lightfoot's admirable description of "The Churches of the Lycus," prefixed to his commentary on this Epistle.) Of Laodicea, the greatest and richest of the three cities, we have no further notice in Scripture, except that stern apocalyptic letter (Rev. iii. 14—22), which has made its name proverbial for spiritual lukewarmness and presumptuous self-reliance. It has been noticed that in this Letter our Lord is called "the beginning of the creation of God." (See chap. i. 15—18 of this Epistle.) Of Colossæ and Hierapolis we read only in this Epistle. It is notable (see Dr. Lightfoot's Essay) that while Hierapolis and Laodicea play a prominent part in the subsequent history of Christianity in Asia Minor, Colossæ never attains importance, and has left but "few and meagre" remains, compared with the magnificent ruins of the other cities.

As many as have not seen my face.—This description doubtless indicates Hierapolis; but the whole context shows that it also includes Colossæ. If the reading taken in chap. i. 7 is correct, Epaphras had been commissioned by St. Paul, and thus, indirectly, the Apostle might be held to be the founder of Colossæ. Accordingly this Letter stands, so to speak, midway between the unreserved familiarity of the Epistles to Corinth or Philippi, and the more formal reserve of the Epistle to the Romans.

(2) **Comforted**—*i.e., encouraged,* or *strengthened,* both to stand fast and to advance in the faith.

Knit together.—The word here used has two senses; first, "to bring, or knit, together" (as in verse 19, and Eph. iv. 16); next, "to carry with us" in argument—*i.e.,* to "instruct," or "convince" (as in Acts ix. 22; xvi. 10; 1 Cor. ii. 16). Either would give good sense here; but the usage in this and the Ephesian Epistle, and the addition of the words "in love," are decisive for the former sense.

And unto . . . the full assurance of understanding (or, rather, *intelligence,* as in chap. i. 9).—The idea of the passage is precisely that of Phil. i. 9, "I pray that your love may abound (or, *overflow*) more and more in knowledge, and in all judgment (or, *perception*)." St. Paul bids them seek the fulness of intelligence which they were taught to crave for, not through the rashness of speculation, but through the insight of love. So in Eph. iii. 17—19 he prays that "being rooted and grounded in love, they may know . . . that which passeth knowledge;" for Christian knowledge is the knowledge of a personal Saviour, and n all personal knowledge he knows best who loves best.

The acknowledgement . . .—This clause—which explains what the "fulness of intelligence" is—is altogether obscured in our version. It should be rendered, *to the full knowledge of the mystery of God, which is Christ.* Above we read (chap. i. 27), "this mystery, which is Christ in you." There Christ, as indwelling in man, is the mystery which alone solves the problem of humanity—what it is, and whither it tends. Here Christ is the "mystery of God"—*i.e.* (according to the Scriptural meaning of the word "mystery"), He in whom the inscrutable nature of God, rich in the "hidden treasure of wisdom and knowledge," is revealed to us. The name again leads up to the doctrine of "the Word of God."

(3) **In whom are hid all the treasures.**—The order of the original is curious: "in whom are all the treasures of wisdom and knowledge, as hidden treasures." The word "hidden" (*apocryphi*) is an almost technical word for secret teaching given only to the initiated; used originally as a term of honour (as the participle of the kindred verb is used in 1 Cor. ii. 7, 8, "the wisdom of God in mystery, even the hidden wisdom . . . which none of the princes of this world knew"), afterwards, from the character of these "apocryphal" books, coming to signify spurious and heretical. St. Paul evidently takes up here a word, used by the pretenders to a special and abstruse knowledge, and applies it to the "heavenly things" which He alone knows "who is in heaven" (John iii. 12, 13). From our full comprehension they are hidden; if ever we know them, it will not be till "we know even as we are known." But the previous words show that we can have full practical apprehension of them by our knowledge of Christ, who knows them—a knowledge begun in faith, and perfected chiefly in love.

Wisdom and knowledge.—Comp. Rom. xi. 33 and 1 Cor. xii. 8 ("the word of wisdom" . . . "the word of knowledge"). On the true sense of "wisdom" and its relation to other less perfect gifts, as "prudence," "intelligence," "knowledge," see Note on Eph. i. 8. "Knowledge" is clearly the development of wisdom in spiritual perception, as "intelligence" in testing and harmonising such perception, and "prudence" in making them, so tested, the guide of life. The word "knowledge" (*gnosis*) was the word which, certainly afterwards, probably even then, was the watchword of "Gnosticism"—the unbridled and fantastic spirit of metaphysical and religious speculation then beginning to infest all Christian thought. It can hardly be accidental that St. Paul here, as elsewhere, subordinates it to the higher gift of wisdom.

(4) **Beguile you.**—"To beguile" here is *to reason into error;* and "enticing words" are words of *persuasion* rather than of reason or revelation. Both words are used by St. Paul only in this passage. It would be difficult to describe more accurately the marvellous fabrics of Gnostic speculation, each step claiming to be based on some fancied probability or metaphysical propriety, but the whole as artificial as the cycles and epicycles of the old Ptolemaic astronomy. We know these in all the elaborate monstrosity of full growth; St. Paul doubtless saw them as yet only in embryo.

(5) **Absent in the flesh.**—Comp. 1 Cor. v. 3, "I as absent in body and present in spirit."

Your order, and the stedfastness.—The word "order" is used in 1 Cor. xiv. 40; the word "stedfastness," or *solidity,* is not found elsewhere in the New Testament, though the verb from which it is derived is found in Acts iii. 7, 16, xvi. 5, and the original adjective, from which the verb is derived, in 1 Pet. v. 9, "stedfast in the faith." From the days of the ancient

be absent in the flesh, yet am I with
you in the spirit, joying
and beholding your order,
and the stedfastness of
your faith in Christ.
(6) As ye have therefore received Christ
Jesus the Lord, *so* walk ye in him:
(7) rooted and built up in him, and
stablished in the faith, as ye have been

Chap. ii. 5—7. Exhortation to keep to the old faith.

taught, abounding therein with thanks-
giving. (8) Beware lest any man spoil
you through philosophy
and vain deceit, after the
tradition of men, after the
rudiments[1] of the world,
and not after Christ. (9) For
in him dwelleth all the ful-
ness of the Godhead bodily.

Chap. ii. 8—15. Warning against false philosophy drawing them from the mediation of Christ and the new life in Him.

[1] Or, *elements.*

Greek interpreters downwards, it has been noted that both words have military associations—the one being used for discipline generally, and the other for the firm compact solidity of the phalanx; and (as in Eph. vi. 11—17) that the use of them may have been suggested by St. Paul's captivity under military guard. If both words be referred to their "faith," the Apostle obviously characterises it as having right "order" (or, *harmony*) in its various parts, and a strong "solidity" against all trials.

(6) **As ye have therefore received.**—Comp. the more emphatic language of chap. i. 5—7, 23. As in the case of the Corinthians and Galatians (2 Cor. xi. 4 and Gal. i. 6), he entreats them not to be turned aside to "another Jesus," or "another gospel, which is not another."

(7) **Rooted and built up in him.**—There is a significant change of tense in the original, *having been rooted—i.e.* (as in Eph. iii. 17), "rooted and grounded" in Him once for all, and *being built up* continually on that Foundation. (Comp. 1 Cor. iii. 9—15.) St. Paul bids them seek not only the first basis of their faith, but their continual growth, in Christ alone, by continual "strengthening in the faith" which rests in Him. We may remember that in the Gnostic teaching faith was held good for the beginner or the common herd, "knowledge" was the bright particular jewel of those who went on to perfection.

Abounding (or, *overflowing*) **therein with thanksgiving.**—The metaphor is changed. The cup of faith, filled to the full, runs over in that thanksgiving which is the expression both of faith and love.

(8—15) The general exhortation of the previous verses is now emphasised by a solemn warning against deadly speculative error. Now, (1) *the character of that error in itself* is described with apparently intentional vagueness, as "a philosophy of vain deceit," "after tradition of men," after "the rudiments of this world." Even its Judaic origin, which is made clear below (verses 16, 17), is here only hinted at in the significant allusion to Circumcision, and perhaps in the phrase "the rudiments of the world," which is also used of the Judaism of Galatia (Gal. iv. 3, 9). (2) What is brought out vividly and emphatically is *the truth which it contradicts or obscures.* First, the full indwelling Godhead of Christ and His headship over all created being; and next, as derived from this, our own "spiritual circumcision in Him, *i.e.*, the true "death unto sin and new life unto righteousness" in Him who is the One Atonement for all sin, and the One Conqueror of all the powers of evil. On the relation of the Epistle to Gnosticism see *Excursus A.*

(8) **Spoil you.**—Properly, *lead you away as a spoil,* triumph over you as a captive, and make you a slave. Comp. St. Paul's language as to the older Judaism at Corinth (2 Cor. xi. 20), "Ye suffer, if a man bring you into bondage, if a man devour you, if a man exalt himself, if a man smite you on the face."

Philosophy and vain deceit—*i.e.* (like "the knowledge falsely so called" of 1 Tim. vi. 20), a philosophy which is inseparably connected with vain deceit. The warning implied here seems to be two-fold:—(1) First, against considering Christianity primarily as a "philosophy," *i.e.*, a search for and knowledge of speculative truth, even the highest. That it involves philosophy is obvious, for it claims to solve for us the great problem of Being, in Nature, in Man, and in God. St. Paul, while he depreciates the wisdom of this world, dwells emphatically on the gospel as the "wisdom of God." (See especially 1 Cor. ii. 6—16.) In this Epistle in particular he speaks of "wisdom" again and again (chaps. i. 9, 28; ii. 3; iii. 16; iv. 6) as one great characteristic of Christian life. Nor is it less clear (as the ancient Greek commentators here earnestly remind us) that Christianity finds a place and a blessing for all true philosophy of men, and makes it, as St. Paul made it at Athens, an introduction to the higher wisdom. But Christianity is not a philosophy, but a life—not a knowledge of abstract principles, but a personal knowledge of faith and love of God in Christ. (2) Next, against accepting in philosophy the "vain deceit" of mere speculation and imagination instead of the modest, laborious investigation of facts. This is the "knowledge falsely so called"; of this it may be said (as in 1 Cor. viii. 1) that it "puffs up," and does not "build up." In ancient and modern times it has always confused brilliant theory with solid discovery, delighting especially to dissolve the great facts of the gospel into abstractions, which may float in its cloudland of imagination.

After the tradition of men.—This is the keynote of our Lord's condemnation of the old Pharisaic exclusiveness and formalism (Matt. xv. 2, 3, 6; Mark vii. 8, 9); it is equally the condemnation of the later Jewish, or half-Jewish, mysticism which St. Paul attacks here. It is hardly necessary to remark that the Apostle often claims reverence for "traditions" (1 Cor. xi. 2; 2 Thess. ii. 15; iii. 6; see also 1 Cor. xv. 3; 2 Pet. ii. 21), but they are traditions having their starting point in direct revelation of God (Gal. i. 12), and, moreover, traditions freely given to all, as being His. The "traditions of men" here condemned had their origin in human speculation, and were secretly transmitted to the initiated only.

The rudiments of the world.—See Gal. iv. 2, and Note there. This marks the chief point of contact with the earlier Judaism, in the stress still laid, perhaps with less consistency, on matters of ritual, law, ascetic observance, and the like. These are "of the world," *i.e.*, belonging to the visible sphere; and they are "rudiments," fit only for the elementary education of those who are as children, and intended simply as preparation for a higher teaching.

(9) **In him dwelleth all the fulness of the Godhead bodily.**—Here almost every word is emphatic. First, "All the fulness of the Godhead"—not a mere emanation from the Supreme Being. Next, "dwells"

(10) And ye are complete in him, which is
the head of all principality and power:
(11) in whom also ye are circumcised with
the circumcision made without hands,
in putting off the body of the sins of
the flesh by the circumcision of Christ:
(12) buried with him in baptism, wherein
also ye are risen with *him* through the
faith of the operation of God, who hath
raised him from the dead. (13) And you,
being dead in your sins and the un-
circumcision of your flesh, hath he

---

and remains for ever—not descending on Him for a time and leaving Him again. Lastly, "bodily," *i.e.*, as incarnate in His humanity. The whole is an extension and enforcement of chap. i. 19, "God was pleased that in Him all the fulness should dwell." The horror of all that was material, as having in it the seed of evil, induced denial either of the reality of our Lord's body, or of its inseparable connection with the Godhead in Him. Hence the emphasis here; as also we find (somewhat later) in St. John, "The Word was made flesh" (John i. 14); "The spirit which confesseth not that Jesus Christ is come in the flesh . . . is the spirit of antichrist" (1 John iv. 3).

On the meaning of "fulness" (*pleroma*), see chap. i. 10; Eph. i. 3; iii. 19; iv. 13. Here it is only necessary to add, that, as in the later Gnosticism, so probably in its earlier forms, the word was used for the infinite nature of the Supreme Deity, out of which all the emanations (afterwards called *Æons*) received in various degrees of imperfection, according to their capacity. Probably for that reason St. Paul uses it so emphatically here. In the same spirit, St. John declares (John i. 16), "Out of His (Christ's) fulness have all we received." It is not finite, but infinitely perfect; hence we all can draw from it, yet leave it unimpaired.

(10) **Ye are complete.**—Literally, *ye have been filled up* in His fulness, as in John i. 16. So St. Paul had prayed for the Ephesians that they might be "filled with (or rather, *up to*) all the fulness of God," and "grow into the measure of the stature of the fulness of Christ" (Eph. iii. 19; iv. 13). To partake of the divine *pleroma* is not the special privilege of the initiated; it belongs to all who are united to the Lord Jesus Christ.

Principality and power.—See chap. i. 16. His headship over all angelic natures is dwelt upon (as in Heb. i. 1—14) with obvious reference to the worshipping of angels. They are our fellowservants under the same Head. (See Rev. xxii. 8, 9.)

(11) **The circumcision made without hands.**—This abrupt introduction of the idea of circumcision would be difficult to understand, were it not for the knowledge of the enforcement of Jewish observance so strangely mixed with this "philosophy" at Colossæ. (Comp. Eph. ii. 11, "Ye who are called Uncircumcision by that which is called Circumcision in the flesh made with hands.") The phrase "made without hands" is so constantly used of heavenly realities (as in Mark xiv. 58; 2 Cor. v. 1; Heb. ix. 11, 24), as opposed to earthly symbols, that it comes to have the positive sense of "spiritual." It is defined below as "the circumcision of Christ"—that which Christ has given us in Himself—in contradistinction to the old circumcision which is now "nothing." (On the treatment of this subject in the Epistles of this period, comp. with this passage Eph. ii. 11, 12; Phil. iii. 2, 3, and see Notes there.)

In putting off the body . . .—The words "of the sins" are not found in the best MSS. They are, no doubt, an explanatory gloss to soften the harshness of the phrase "the body of the flesh." (1) What "the body of the flesh" is we see clearly by chap. iii. 9, "having put off the old man." It is, like the "body of sin" (in Rom. vi. 6) and the "body of death" (in Rom. vii. 24), the body so far as it is, in the bad sense of the word "flesh," fleshly. The body itself is not "put off:" for it is not evil; it is a part of the true man, and becomes the temple of God. It is only so far as in it the flesh rebels against the spirit, and the "old man is gradually corrupted by the lusts of deceit" (Eph. iv. 22), that it is to be "put off." (2) But why the "body of the flesh," and not the "flesh" simply? The answer is, no doubt, that which Chrysostom here gives, that the bodily circumcision was but of one member, in mere symbolism of one form of purity; the spiritual circumcision is the putting away of the whole of the power of the flesh, and that, too, not in symbol, but in reality.

(12) **Buried with him in baptism . . .**—It is very interesting to compare this passage with Rom vi. 4, "Therefore we are buried with Him in baptism unto death, that like as Christ was raised from the dead by the glory of the Father, even so we also should walk in newness of life." In the former clause both are identical. In the latter clause this Epistle is stronger. What in the earlier Epistle is the "likeness of His Resurrection" is here the participation of it, "Ye are risen with Him." Similarly, instead of the simple allusion to "Christ's being raised from the dead," we have here "through faith in the operation of God, who raised Him from the dead." Here, as in the more detailed passage of the Ephesian Epistle (chaps. i. 19—23; ii. 5—7), the "operation," the energy of "the mighty power of God," is conceived as actually working both in the Head and in the Body, so that we through it partake of the resurrection, the ascension, and the glorified majesty of Christ. The comparison shows an instructive development in this Epistle of the consequences of the unity with Christ.

This passage is also notable for the obvious contrast of baptism, as a spiritual reality, with circumcision as a symbolic form. Each is the entrance into a covenant with God; but the one into a covenant of "the letter," and the other into a covenant of "the spirit." (See the contrast between the covenants drawn out in 2 Cor. iii. 6—18; Heb. viii. 6; ix. 28.) In the earlier Epistles circumcision is contrasted with spiritual regeneration (Gal. vi. 15), as shown by various signs, such as "faith working by love" (Rom. iv. 9—12; Gal. v. 6), or "keeping the commandments of God" (1 Cor. vii. 19). Here this contrast is still as strong as ever; but baptism being (as always) looked upon as the means of such spiritual regeneration, is brought out emphatically as "the circumcision of the Spirit." As baptised into Christ, "we are the circumcision, who worship God in the Spirit" (Phil. iii. 3).

(13) **And you . . .**—Here, exactly as in Eph. ii. 1—18, there is a remarkable intermixture of the word "we" and the word "you," the former conveying the universal statement of the gospel message of mercy, the other applying it emphatically to the Gentiles, as Gentiles. The two passages should be read

quickened together with him, having forgiven you all trespasses; (14) blotting out the handwriting of ordinances that was against us, which was contrary to us, and took it out of the way, nailing it to his cross; (15) *and* having spoiled principalities and powers, he made a shew of them openly, triumphing over them

---

side by side. There is, as always, strong similarity, yet complete independence. Through the passage of the Ephesian Epistle there runs a two-fold idea, the reconcilement of Jew and Gentile to God, and the union of both in one Catholic Church. In this Epistle it is only on the reconcilement to God in Christ that stress is laid. Even the detailed expressions of the two passages illustrate each other at once by likeness and by variety.

Dead in your sins and the uncircumcision of your flesh.—See Eph. ii. 1, "You who were dead in trespasses and sins . . . who are called Uncircumcision by that which is called Circumcision in the flesh." Here the "deadness" is spoken of, as coming both from the actual power of "sins" (*transgressions*), and from the alienation from God marked by uncircumcision. In the other passage the uncircumcision is looked upon only as a name of reproach.

Hath he quickened.—It is difficult to determine what is the subject in this sentence. According to all analogy it should be "God," yet in the latter clauses (as in verses 14, 15) it must surely be "Christ." Now, when we turn to the fuller parallel passage, we see an overt change of subject. It is said (Eph. ii. 5), "God quickened us together with Christ"; "God in Christ forgave us" (Eph. iv. 32); but "Christ abolished the Law," "reconciled us to God on the cross." This suggests a similar change of subject here also, which must be at the words "and took it away," or (for the tense here is changed) "and He (Christ) hath taken it away." This, speaking grammatically, introduces an anomaly; but such anomalies are not uncommon in St. Paul, especially in passages of high spiritual teaching.

Having forgiven you . . .—There is no corresponding clause in the parallel passage; but in a different context (corresponding to chap. iii. 13 of this Epistle) we read, "forgiving one another, even as God in Christ forgave you" (Eph. iv. 32).

(14) **Blotting out the handwriting**—*i.e., canceling the bond which stood against us in its ordinances.* The "handwriting" is the bond, exacting payment or penalty in default. (Comp. Philem. verse 19, "I Paul have *written it with mine own hand;* I will repay it.") What this bond is we see by Eph. ii. 15, which speaks of "the law of commandments in ordinances," there called "the enmity slain by the cross." On the meaning of "ordinances" see Note on that passage. The metaphor, however, here is different, and especially notable as the first anticipation of those many metaphors of later theology, from Tertullian downwards, in which the idea of a debt to God, paid for us by the blood of Christ, as "a satisfaction," is brought out. The Law is a bond, "Do this and thou shalt live." "The soul that sinneth it shall die." On failure to do our part it "stands against us." But God for Christ's sake forgives our transgressions and cancels the bond. It is a striking metaphor, full of graphic expressiveness; it is misleading only when (as in some later theologies) we hold it to be not only the truth, but the whole truth, forgetting that legal and forensic metaphors can but imperfectly represent inner spiritual realities.

And took it.—Properly, *and He* (Christ) *hath taken it away.* The change of tense is significant. The act of atonement is over; its effect remains.

Nailing it to his cross.—At this point the idea of atonement comes in. Hitherto we have heard simply of free forgiveness and love of God. Now the bond is viewed, not as cancelled by a simple act of divine mercy, but as absolutely destroyed by Christ, by "nailing it to His cross." It has been supposed (as by Bishop Pearson) that there is allusion to some custom of cancelling documents by the striking of a nail through them. But the custom is doubtful, and the supposition unnecessary. Our Lord "redeemed us from the curse of the Law," by His death, "being made a curse for us" (Gal. iii. 13). St. Paul boldly speaks of that curse as a penalty standing against us, and as nailed to the cross with Himself, so to be for ever cancelled in the great declaration, "It is finished." If any more definite allusion is to be sought for, we might be inclined to refer to the "title" on the cross, probably nailed to it. Such title declared the explanation of the sufferer's death. The cancelled curse of the Law was just such an explanation of the great atoning death, and the title, declaring His mediatorial kingdom, showed the curse cancelled thereby.

(15) **Having spoiled principalities and powers . . .**—This verse is one of great difficulty. Not, indeed, in the main idea. The cross, as usual, is identified with the triumph over the powers of evil which it won. The very phrase "made a show," is cognate to the words "put Him to open shame" applied to the Crucifixion (Heb. vi. 6). The apparent triumph of the "power of darkness" over Him was His real and glorious triumph over them. The general idea is familiar to us, telling, as in the noble old hymn *Vexilla Regis*—

> "How of the Cross He made a throne
> On which He reigns, a glorious king."

His forgiveness of the penitent thief was the first act of His all-saving royalty. Accordingly, taking (as in 2 Cor. ii. 14—16) his metaphor from a Roman triumph, St. Paul represents Him as passing in triumphal majesty up the sacred way to the eternal gates, with all the powers of evil bound as captives behind His chariot before the eyes of men and angels. It is to be noted that to this clause, so characteristic of the constant dwelling on the sole glory of Christ in this Epistle, there is nothing to correspond in the parallel passage of the Epistle to the Ephesians, which dwells simply on Christ as "our peace," and as the head of the Church.

The difficulty lies in the word here translated "having spoiled." Now this translation (as old as St. Jerome's Vulgate), makes all simple and easy; but the original word certainly means "having stripped Himself"—as in chap. iii. 9, "having put off (*stripped off from ourselves*) the old man." It is a word used by St. Paul alone in the New Testament, and by him only in these two passages, the latter of which makes the sense perfectly clear. Being forced, then, to adopt this translation, we see that the words admit of two renderings. (1) First, "having stripped from Himself the principalities and powers," that is, having stripped off that condition of the earthly life which gave them a grasp or occasion against Him. But this, though adopted by many old Greek commentators (Chrysostom among the rest), seems singularly harsh in

in it.[1] (16) Let no man therefore judge
you in meat, or in drink,[2]
or in respect[3] of an holy-
day, or of the new moon,
or of the sabbath *days*:
(17) which are a shadow of
things to come; but the body *is* of

Chap. ii. 16, 17. Warning against obsolete Jewish ordinances.

Christ. (18) Let no man beguile you[4]
of your reward in a
voluntary humility[5] and
worshipping of angels, in-
truding into those things
which he hath not seen,
vainly puffed up by his fleshly mind,

Chap. ii. 18, 19. Warning against superstitious angel-worship.

1 Or, *in himself*.
2 Or, *for eating and drinking*.
3 Or, *in part*.
4 Or, *judge against you*.
5 Gr. *being a voluntary in humility*.

---

expression and far-fetched in idea, needing too much explanation to make it in any sense clear. (2) Next, "having unclothed Himself, He made a show of principalities and powers." On the whole this rendering, although not free from difficulty, on account of the apparent want of connection of the phrase "having stripped Himself" with the context, seems the easiest. For we note that a cognate word, strictly analogous, is used thus (without an object following) in 2 Cor. v. 4, "Not that we desire to unclothe ourselves, but to clothe ourselves over our earthly vesture." The context shows that the meaning there is "to put off the flesh." This is suggested still more naturally in the passage before us by the preceding phrase, "in the putting off of the body of the flesh"—a phrase there used of the flesh as evil, but found in chap. i. 22 of the natural body of Christ. Accordingly many Latin fathers (among others Augustine) rendered "stripping Himself of the flesh," and there is some trace of this as a reading or a gloss in the Greek of this passage. Perhaps, however, St. Paul purposely omitted the object after the verb, in order to show that it was by "stripping Himself of all" that He conquered by becoming a show in absolute humiliation, He made the powers of evil a show in His triumph.

(16–19) To the warning against speculative error succeeds a warning against two practical superstitions. The first is simply the trust in obsolete Jewish ordinances (the mere shadow of Christ) with which we are familiar in the earlier forms of Judaism. But the second presents much strangeness and novelty. It is the "worship of angels" in a "voluntary humility," inconsistent with the belief in an intimate and direct union with Christ our Head.

(16) **Let no man therefore judge you.**—That is, *impose his own laws upon you*. See verse 8. (Comp. Rom. xiv. 3, 10, "Why dost thou judge thy brother?" in this same connection.)

In meat, or in drink.—Or rather, *in eating and drinking*. We see by the context that the immediate reference is to the distinctions of meats under the Jewish law, now done away, because the distinction of those within and without the covenant was also done away (Acts x. 11). (Comp. on this subject the half-ironical description of Heb. ix. 10.) But a study of Rom. xiv. 2, 20, 21, written before this Epistle, and 1 Tim. iv. 3, written after it—to say nothing of the tone of this passage itself, or of the known characteristics of the later Gnosticism of the ascetic type—show that these laws about eating and drinking were not mere matters of law, but formed significant parts of a rigid mystic asceticism. Of such, St. Paul declares indignantly (Rom. xiv. 17), "The kingdom of God is not eating and drinking, but righteousness and peace and joy in the Holy Ghost."

An holyday (*feast*), **or of the new moon, or of the sabbath.**—Comp. Isa. i. 13, 14, "the new moons and sabbaths . . . the new moons and the appointed feasts My soul hateth;" also Ezek. xlv. 17; Hos. ii. 13. The "feast" would seem to be one of the great festivals; the "new moon" the monthly, and the sabbath the weekly solemnity. With this passage it is natural to compare the similar passage in Gal. iv. 10, "Ye observe days and months and times (*special seasons*) and years." But there the specially Judaic character is not so expressly marked; and, in fact, the passage has a wider meaning (like Rom. xiv. 56), showing the different position which even Christian festivals held in Apostolic days. Here it is the Jewish festivals, and they alone, which are noted. It is obvious that St. Paul gives no hint of any succession of the Lord's Day to be, in any strict sense, a "Christian Sabbath." We know, indeed, that the Jewish Sabbath itself lingered in the Church, as having a kind of sacredness, kept sometimes as a fast, sometimes as a festival. But its observance was not of obligation. No man was to "judge" others in respect of it.

(17) **Which are a shadow . . . but the body** (*the substance*) **is of Christ.**—The spirit of the passage is precisely that of the argument which runs through the Epistle to the Hebrews. "The Law had a shadow of good things to come, not the very image (or, *substance*) of the things" (Heb. x. 1). When St. Paul deals with the legal and coercive aspect of the Law, he calls it "the schoolmaster to bring us to Christ." (See Gal. iii. 24, and Note there.) When he turns to its ritual aspect, he describes it as simply foreshadowing or typifying the substance; and therefore useful before the revelation of the substance, useless or (if trusted in) worse than useless, after it. In every way "Christ is the end of the Law" (Rom. x. 4).

(18) **Beguile you of your reward.**—The original is a word used, almost technically, for an unfair judgment in the stadium, robbing the victor of his prize. The prize here (as in 1 Cor. ix. 24; Phil. iii. 14) is the heavenly reward of the Christian course. In St. Paul's exhortation there seems to be a reference back to verse 16. There he says, "Let no man arrogate judgment over you;" here, "Let no man use that arrogated judgment so as to cheat you of your prize. There is one Judge, who has right and who is righteous; look to Him alone."

In a voluntary humility and worship.—This rendering seems virtually correct, though other renderings are proposed. The original is, *willing in humility and worship*, and the phrase "willing in" is often used in the LXX. for "delighting in." Other translations are here possible, though not without some harshness. But the true sense is shown beyond all doubt to be that given in our version, by the words used below to describe the same process, "will-worship and humility."

In this passage alone in the New Testament "humility" is spoken of with something of the condemnation accorded to it in heathen morality. The reason of this is obvious and instructive. Humility is a grace, of which the very essence is unconsciousness, and which, being itself negative, cannot live, except by resting on some more positive quality, such as faith or love.

(19) and not holding the Head, from which all the body by joints and bands having nourishment ministered, and knit together, increaseth with the increase of God. (20) Wherefore if ye be dead with Christ from the rudiments [1]

[1] Or, *elements.*

Whenever it is consciously cultivated and "delighted in," it loses all its grace; it becomes either unreal, "the pride that apes humility," or it turns to abject slavishness and meanness. Of such depravations Church history is unhappily full.

Worshipping of angels.—This is closely connected with the "voluntary humility" above. The link of connection is supplied by the notice in the ancient interpreters, of the early growth of that unhappy idea, which has always lain at the root of saint-worship and angel-worship in the Church—"that we must be brought near by angels and not by Christ, for that were too high a thing for us" (Chrysostom). With this passage it is obvious to connect the emphasis laid (in Heb. i., ii.) on the absolute superiority of our Lord to all angels, who are but "ministering spirits, sent forth to minister to them who are heirs of salvation;" and the prohibition of angel-worship in Rev. xxii. 9, "See thou do it not; for I am thy fellow-servant . . . worship God."

It might seem strange that on the rigid monotheism of Judaism this incongruous creature-worship should have been engrafted. But here also the link is easily supplied. The worship of the angels of which the Essenic system bore traces, was excused on the ground that the Law had been given through the "ministration of angels" (see Acts vii. 53; Gal. iii. 19), and that the tutelary guardianship of angels had been revealed in the later prophecy. (See Dan. x. 10—21.) For this reason it was held that angels might be worshipped, probably with the same subtle distinctions between this and that kind of worship with which we are familiar in the ordinary pleas for the veneration of saints. It has been noticed that in the Council of Laodicea, held in the fourth century, several canons were passed against Judaising, and that in close connection with these it was forbidden "to leave the Church of God and go away to invoke angels"; and we are told by Theodoret (in the next century) that "oratories to St. Michael (the 'prince' of the Jewish people) were still to be seen." The "angels" in this half-Jewish system held the same intermediate position between the Divine and the human which in the ordinary Gnostic theories was held by the less personal *Æons*, or supposed emanations from the Godhead.

Intruding into those things which he hath not seen.—(1) There is a remarkable division here, both of MSS. and ancient versions and commentators, as to the insertion or omission of the negative. But the balance of MS. authority is against the negative, and certainly it is easier to suppose it to have been inserted with a view to make an easier sense, than to have been omitted if it had been originally there. (2) The general meaning, however, of the passage is tolerably clear, and, curiously enough, little affected by either alternative. It certainly refers to pretensions to supernatural knowledge by which (just as in 1 Cor. viii. 1) the mind is said to be "puffed up." We note that, even in true visions of heavenly things, there was danger lest the mind "should be exalted above measure" (2 Cor. xii. 7). Now the knowledge here pretended to is that favourite knowledge, claimed by Jewish and Christian mystics, of the secrets of the heavenly places and especially of the grades and functions of the hierarchy of heaven. St. Paul brands it as belonging to the mind, not of the spirit, but "of the flesh;" for indeed it was really superstitions, resting not on faith, but on supposed visions and supernatural manifestations. It "intruded" (or, according to another rendering, it "took its stand") upon the secrets of a region which it said that it "had seen," but which, in truth, it "had not seen." If we omit the negative, the Apostle is quoting its claims; if we insert it, he is denying their justice.

(19) **Not holding the Head.**—In this lay the fatal error. All these speculations and superstitions interfered with the direct hold of the soul on the mediation of Christ, as the Head, from whom alone, as being "the image of the invisible God," come all spiritual life and growth. Therefore they had a practical and spiritual importance.

From which all the body . . .—Comp Eph. iv. 15, 16, and see Note there. The agreement is nearly verbal, but the characteristic difference of idea, so often noted, is still traceable. There the body "maketh increase unto the building up of itself in love;" here the increase is simply "the increase of God"—the increase which God gives, and which grows into His likeness. In this passage there is also a greater scientific exactness: the "joints and bands" are the "articulations and ligaments;" the two functions thereof are the diffusion of nourishment and the knitting together of organic unity.

(20—23) In this and the succeeding section, St. Paul, starting from the idea of union with the Head, draws out the practical consequences of partaking of the death of Christ and the resurrection of Christ. In virtue of the former participation, he exhorts them to be dead to the law of outward ordinances; in virtue of the latter, to have a life hid with Christ in God.

(20) **If ye be dead with Christ.**—The whole idea of the death with Christ and resurrection with Him is summed up by St. Paul in Rom. vi. 3—9, in direct connection (as also here, see verse 12) with the entrance upon Christian life in baptism, "We are buried with Him by baptism unto death . . . we are dead with Christ . . . we are planted together in the likeness of His death . . . that like as Christ was raised from the dead by the glory of the Father, we also should walk in newness of life . . . planted together in the likeness of His resurrection . . . alive to God through Jesus Christ our Lord." The death with Christ is a death unto "the life of the flesh." But this may be (as in Rom. vi. 1, 2, 6, 7, 11) "the life of sin"; or it may be the outward and visible life "of the world." The latter is the sense to be taken here. This outward life is under "ordinances" (see verse 1), under the "rudiments of the world" (see verse 8), or, generally, "under law." Of such a life St. Paul says (in Gal. ii. 19), "I through the Law died to the Law, that I might live unto God." There (Gal. iv. 9), as here, he brands as unspiritual the subjection to the "weak and beggarly elements" of mere ordinances. Of course it is clear that in their place such ordinances have their value, both as means to an end, and as symbols of an inner reality of self-devotion. The true teaching as to these is found in our Lord's declaration to the Pharisees as to spiritual things and outward ordinances, "These things (the spiritual things) ought ye to have done, and not to leave the others (the outward observances) undone"

of the world, why, as though living in
the world, are ye subject
to ordinances, (21) (touch
not; taste not; handle
not; (22) which all are to
perish with the using);
after the commandments and doctrines
of men? (23) Which things have indeed a
shew of wisdom in will worship, and
humility, and neglecting[1] of the body;
not in any honour to the satisfying of
the flesh.

Chap. ii. 20—23. Appeal to their deadness in Christ to mere ordinances.

1 Or, *punishing*, or, *not sparing*.

A.D. 64.

CHAPTER III.—(1) If ye then be

(Matt. xxiii. 23). In later times St. Paul declared with judicial calmness, "The Law is good if a man use it lawfully" (1 Tim. i. 8). But to exalt these things to the first place was a fatal superstition, which, both in its earlier and later phases, he denounces unsparingly.

(21) **Touch not; taste not; handle not.**—The first and last of these renderings should be inverted. There is in the commands a climax of strictness. "Handle not" (the unclean thing), "taste it not," "touch it not" with one of your fingers. It will be noted that all these commands are negative, not positive. They are marked by the ordinary ascetic preference of spiritual restraint to spiritual energy.

(22) **Which all are to perish with the using.**—It has been doubted whether these words (which are literally, *all which things go to corruption*, or *destruction, in the using*) are the continuation of the ascetic ordinance, or the comment of the Apostle. But the last word—which signifies, not only "using," but "using up"—seems to decide for the latter alternative. The things are things which go to destruction and are used up. What permanent effect can they leave behind? See 1 Cor. viii. 8 (whether the words of St. Paul, or the words of the Corinthians, accepted as true by him), "Meat commendeth us not to God: for neither, if we eat, are we the better; neither, if we eat not, are we the worse." It is but an echo of our Lord's own teaching as to that which goeth into the mouth (Matt. xv. 16, 17; Mark xiii. 18, 19).

After the commandments . . .—See verse 8, and Note there. There seems to be an allusion to Isa. xxix. 13, quoted by our Lord (Matt. xv. 7, 8; Mark vii. 6, 7) in relation to these ceremonial observances.

(23) **Will worship, and humility . . .**—It seems difficult to connect these words with the merely ceremonial observances immediately above; and, in fact, they are almost an exact repetition of the description of the superstitious worship of the angels given in verse 18. "Will worship" is, indeed, nearly what we call superstition—the constant craving for objects to which we may find some excuse for paying reverence. The prefix applies in sense, though not in grammatical form, to the "humility" also; a studied humility being either a pretence or a self-degradation. But in the words "neglecting of the body" (properly, being *unsparing of it* in hardship, and generally careless of it) we pass to the ceremonial ordinances. It is more than likely that the superstition and false asceticism were connected together—the latter being the condition of the supposed spiritual insight of the former.

Which things . . . flesh.—This passage is difficult. (1) Our version translates literally, and would seem to regard the last words as simply an explanation, from the point of view of the false teachers, of "neglecting of the body," as "not honouring it for the satisfaction, or surfeiting of the flesh;" and we certainly find that the Jewish ascetics did brand the most necessary satisfaction of appetite as a "surfeiting of the flesh." But there is a fatal objection to this interpretation—that, in that case, St. Paul would leave the false pretension without a word of contradiction, which is almost incredible. Hence (2) we must regard the "not in any honour" as antithetical to "the show of wisdom." The ordinances, says St. Paul, have "a show of wisdom," but "are in no honour," *i.e.*, are "of no value." The common use of the word rendered "honour," for "price," or "pay" (see Matt. xxvii. 6; Acts vi. 34; vii. 16; xix. 19; 1 Cor. vi. 20; vii. 23; 1 Tim. v. 17), would readily lend itself to this sense. The only doubtful point (3) is the interpretation of the last words, "for the satisfying of the flesh." There seems little doubt that the phrase is used in a bad sense. Hence we must dismiss all reference to a right honouring of the body by innocent satisfaction of its needs. We have therefore to choose between two interpretations. Some interpret "of no value *against* the satisfaction of the flesh." But, though the Greek will bear this sense, it is certainly not the common sense of the preposition used; and its adoption would expose the whole phrase to the charge of ambiguity and obscurity. The other interpretation is "of no real value" (tending) "to the satisfaction of the flesh." This is abrupt, but suits well the indignant and abrupt terseness of the passage. It gives (quite after St. Paul's manner) not only a denial of the "neglecting of the body," but a retort on the false teachers of the very charge they made against their opponents. (Comp. the use of the word "dogs," in Phil. iii. 2.) It conveys a most important truth. That "extremes meet" we know well; and that there is a satisfaction of the fleshly temper (see above, verse 18) in the attempt over much to curb the flesh, the whole history of asceticism bears witness. Moreover, this interpretation alone gives a completeness of antithesis. To "the show of wisdom" it opposes the "no real value;" to the pretended "neglecting of the body" the real "satisfaction of the flesh."

III.

(1—4) As the partaking of the death of Christ taught the negative lesson of death to the Law, so the partaking of His resurrection teaches the positive lesson of the spiritual life. We observe that this celebrated passage occupies a place at the close of the doctrinal portion of the Epistle, exactly corresponding to the even greater passage on the unity of the Church in God in the Epistle to the Ephesians (iv. 1—16). It is unlike that passage, because, summing up the main teaching of this Epistle, it dwells simply on the close personal relation of all souls to God in Jesus Christ, who is at once "the image of God," and the one Mediator between God and man. It is like it (and like other passages of the Epistles of the Captivity) because it passes on from Christ risen to Christ in heaven: it takes for granted our being risen with Christ, and bids us in heart to ascend to heaven now, and look forward to the bliss of heaven in the hereafter.

(1) **If ye then be risen** (rather, *ye rose*) **with Christ.**—In these words is marked the beginning of the spiritual life, referred evidently to baptism. (See

Chap. iii. 1—4. Appeal to their resurrection with Christ to the higher spiritual life.

risen with Christ, seek those things
which are above, where
Christ sitteth on the right
hand of God. (2) Set you
affection[1] on things above,
not on things on the
earth. (3) For ye are dead, and your
life is hid with Christ in God
(4) When Christ, *who is* our life, shall
appear, then shall ye also appear with
him in glory. (5) Mortify therefore
your members which are upon the

1 Or, *mind.*

---

chap. ii. 12.) It is a "resurrection with Christ" and in Christ; as such it is dwelt upon in detail in Rom. vi. 1—14. We may note that this phrase, implying a sudden passing from death unto life, accords more exactly with the idea of adult baptism, accepted in conscious faith, and leading at once to a new life; while the later phrase, "regeneration" (Tit. iii. 5), which speaks of the soul as passing, indeed, at once into a new condition, but as having only the undeveloped germ of the new life, corresponds more closely with the idea of the infant baptism, which gradually superseded the other. Here this spiritual resurrection is taken for granted, and the Apostle goes on at once to the next stage of the spiritual life.

Christ.—The name, four times repeated, has in all cases the article prefixed to it. Evidently it used emphatically to refer to our Lord, as our Mediator—our Prophet, Priest, and King.

Seek those things which are above . . . set your affection on things above.—Here we have the spiritual life in its continuance. It is described, (1) first, as "seeking the things above"—that is, looking, and so growing, to perfection. This characteristic is dwelt upon with great fulness and beauty in Phil. iii. 12—16. (2) Next, in a still higher strain, as "setting our affection on the things above," or, more properly, *catching the spirit of the things above,* being "heavenly-minded" already—anticipating heaven, not only in hope, but in tone and temper, seeing things as God sees them, and seeing all in relation to Him. On this we may again compare the great passage in Phil. iii. 20, 21, on our "citizenship of heaven." Of such heavenly-mindedness we have, perhaps, the most perfect specimen in the calm and loving certainty of St. John's Epistles. (3) These two graces must be united In the one is the secret of growth, in the other the present earnest of perfection. Moreover, the higher grace must follow from the former; "for, where our treasure is, there will our heart be also."

Where Christ sitteth on the right hand of God.—The allusion is emphatic. Heaven is to us, in itself, a vague expression of unknown bliss. It is made definite to the Christian by the thought of Christ. in His glorified humanity, there enthroned in majesty, "preparing a place for us," and drawing us to be with Him. (Note a similar emphatic reference in Phil. iii. 21; and comp. Eph. ii. 6, "He raised us up, and made us to sit in heavenly places in Christ Jesus.")

This glorious idea of Christ in heaven, and heaven in Christ, runs through the whole book of the Revelation of St. John, from the opening Epistles to the last vision of glory.

(3) **Ye are dead.**—Properly, *ye died.* See chap. ii. 20, and Note there. The phrase here is to be taken in its whole sense, both of "death to sin" and "death to the visible world."

Your life is hid with Christ in God . . . Christ who is our life.—In these two phrases, again, we pass from a lower to a higher expression of the same truth. (1) First, "our life is hid with Christ in God." The spiritual life in man is a "hidden life, having its source in God; the full conviction of it, as distinct from the mere instinctive consciousness of it in the mind itself, comes only from the belief that it is the image of God in us, and is sustained by constant communion with Him. If God be our God at all, we must live; for "He is not the God of the dead, but of the living" (Matt. xxii. 32). It is also "hid with Christ." Our Lord's ascent to His glory in heaven is at once the pledge and the means of this our spiritual communion with God. It is "with Him" that we can "in heart and mind ascend;" it is "with Him" that we can "continually dwell." (2) But this is not all. "Christ is our life" now as well as hereafter. This is simply a summary of the two truths; "Christ liveth in me" (see Gal. ii. 20), as the source of life; and "To me to live (the actual condition of life) is Christ" (Phil. i. 21). It is but a brief expression of faith in the truth which our Lord Himself declared (John xi. 25), "I am the Life; whoso liveth and believeth in Me shall never die." (Comp. John xiv. 6.) Hence our spiritual life is not only a being "with Christ;" it is also unity with Christ in the bosom of the Father.

(4) **When Christ . . . shall appear, then shall ye also appear with him in glory.**—This describes the last stage of the spiritual life—the glorification with Christ in heaven, manifesting what now is hidden, and perfecting what exists only in germ. (Comp. 1 John iii. 1, 2, "Now are we the sons of God, and it doth not yet appear what we shall be: but we know that, when He shall appear, we shall be like Him; for we shall see Him as He is.") This same conclusion ends the corresponding passage in Phil. iii. 21.

In all these Epistles we note how constant a reference there is to the "glory of God," and to the share in it reserved for us. So we also note the especial reference to the "appearance of Christ" in the Pastoral Epistles (see 1 Tim. vi. 14; 2 Tim. i. 10; iv. 1, 8; Tit. ii. 13), and the constant revelation of it in the Apocalypse.

The whole passage forms a complete and magnificent picture of the spiritual life in Christ—the means of its beginning, the signs of its presence, and the hope of its close. It may be compared with the fuller yet hardly completer picture of Rom. viii.

[**5. Practical Exhortation, General.**

(1) NEGATIVE.—TO MORTIFY THE OLD MAN, by fleeing from—
- (*a*) *Uncleanness and lust* (verses 5—7);
- (*b*) *Wrath and malice* (verse 8);
- (*c*) *Falsehood* (verse 9).

(2) POSITIVE.—TO PUT ON THE NEW MAN, making Christ our "all in all."
- (*a*) *In love and peace, as shown in mercy, humility, patience, and forgiveness* (verses 10—15);
- (*b*) *In thanksgiving* (verse 16);
- (*c*) *In living to the glory of God* (verse 17);

(The whole of this section stands in close parallelism, frequently in verbal coincidence, with Eph. iv. 20—vi. 9. There are, however, constantly emerging indications

Chap. iii. 5—9. General warning against the sins of the unregenerate life.

earth; fornication, uncleanness, inor-
dinate affection, evil con-
cupiscence, and covetous-
ness, which is idolatry:
(6) for which things' sake
the wrath of God cometh
on the children of disobedience: (7) in the
which ye also walked some time, when
ye lived in them. (8) But now ye also
put off all these; anger, wrath, malice,
blasphemy, filthy communication out of
your mouth. (9) Lie not one to another,
seeing that ye have put off the old man
with his deeds; (10) and have put on the
new *man*, which is renewed
in knowledge after the
image of him that created
him: (11) where there is
neither Greek nor Jew,
circumcision nor uncircum-
cision, Barbarian, Scythian, bond *nor*
free: but Christ *is* all, and in all.

Chap. iii. 10—17. General exhortation to the graces of the "new man" regenerate in Christ.

---

of independence of handling. Generally speaking, the Ephesian Epistle is fuller and deeper in treatment; and, moreover, it constantly brings out, in relation both to moral duty and to the observation of the relations of life, the great characteristic doctrine of the universal unity in Christ. This Epistle, on the other hand, is briefer and more incisive, and has only slight, though clear, indications of the idea so powerfully worked out in the other Epistle.)]

Verses 5—9 contain the negative section of St. Paul's practical appeal, drawing out the consequences of the "death with Christ," in the mortification of all tendencies to impurity, malice, and falsehood. For these are the opposites to purity, love, and truth—the three great attributes of God, and therefore the three chief graces of man.

(5) **Mortify therefore your members which are upon the earth.**—The expression is doubly unique. It is the only passage where "mortification"—the killing of anything in us—is enjoined; and it is also notable, as not explicitly distinguishing between the members themselves, and the evil of which they are made the instruments. The sense is, of course, clear enough. It corresponds to the "crucifying the flesh" of Gal. v. 24; and the idea of evil, mostly expressed plainly in the word "flesh," is here hinted in the phrase "which are on the earth," that is, which are busied with earth and bind us down to the earthly life. The particular word "members" is perhaps suggested by our Lord's command to "cut off the right hand" and "pluck out the right eye" if they cause us to offend (Matt. v. 29, 30). But, as a rule, Scripture more clearly marks the distinction between the members and "the law of sin in the members" (Rom. vii. 5, 23); and we are usually bidden not to "kill our members," but to turn them from "instruments of unrighteousness" to be "instruments of righteousness unto God" (Rom. vi. 13). The fact is that this passage contains only half the truth, corresponding to the death with Christ, and not the whole truth, including also the resurrection to the new life. Accordingly, as the next verse shows, the members to be mortified are actually identified with the vices of the old man residing in them.

Fornication, uncleanness . . . covetousness, which is idolatry.—See Eph. v. 3, and Note there.

Inordinate affection, evil concupiscence.—These words are not found in the parallel passage. The word rendered "inordinate affection" is the general word for "passion" (*pathos*). It is found united to "concupiscence" in 1 Thess. iv. 5, "the lust of concupiscence." Both words here are general words, denoting the condition of soul, of which "fornication" and "covetousness" are both exemplifications. This is the condition of unrestrained passion and desire, the former word implying a passive receptiveness of impression from without, the other the positive energy of desire to seek gratification. Comp. Gal. v. 24, "the affections" (*passions*) and "lusts." Of such a temper Article IX. of the Church of England declares with singular accuracy, not that it is sin, but that it has in itself *rationem peccati*, that is, the initial principle of sin.

(7) **In the which ye also walked some time, when ye lived** (*were living*) **in them.**—The former condition of heathenism was that in which "they were living," with contagion of evil on every side. But St. Paul is not content without noting their own active participation—"ye walked in them." (Comp. Eph. iv. 17—20.)

(8) **Anger, wrath, malice, blasphemy** (*slander*—see Eph. iv. 31 and Notes there), **filthy communication.**—The word is "foul," and the context here seems to show that it refers to grossness of insult and abuse, rather than (as in the cognate word of Eph. iv. 4) to "filthiness."

(9) **Lie not one to another.**—Comp. Eph. iv. 25, and note the characteristic insertion there of a clause to which there is nothing here to correspond, "for we are members one of another."

Seeing that ye (have) put off the old man.—Comp. the fuller description of Eph. iv. 22—24.

(10—17) In these verses we have the corresponding positive exhortation, connected with the idea of resurrection with Christ, through which we put on the new man, holding Christ to be our all in all. Of the new nature there are two marks—towards man love in all its various forms, towards God thanksgiving and living to His glory.

(10) **The new man, which is** (*being*) **renewed.**—There are here the same two different words which are found in the parallel passage. (See Notes on Eph. iv. 22—24). "The new man" is here properly the *youthful man* "which is renewed," that is, to which is given a nature really fresh and new.

(11) **Where there is neither . . .**—This passage naturally suggests comparison with Gal. iii. 28. "There is neither Jew nor Greek; there is neither bond nor free; there is neither male nor female: for ye are all one in Jesus Christ." In comparing the passages (passing by the insertion here of "circumcision nor uncircumcision," which is simply explanatory of "Jew nor Greek") we notice in this—(1) The insertion of "barbarian, Scythian." This insertion is clearly intended to rebuke that pride of intellect, contemptuous of the unlearned, which lay at the root of Gnosticism.

(12) Put on therefore, as the elect of God, holy and beloved, bowels of mercies, kindness, humbleness of mind, meekness, longsuffering;
(13) forbearing one another, and forgiving one another, if any man have a quarrel[1] against any: even as Christ forgave you, so also *do* ye.
(14) And above all these things *put on* charity, which is the bond of perfectness.
(15) And let the peace of God rule in your hearts, to the which also ye are called in one body; and be ye thankful.
(16) Let the word of Christ dwell in you richly in all wisdom; teaching and admonishing one another in psalms and hymns and

1 Or, *complaint.*

The "barbarian" was simply the foreigner (comp. 1 Cor. xiv. 11); the "Scythian" was the savage, towards whom the contempt implied for the "barbarian" assumed explicitness, and reached its climax. (2) The omission of "male nor female." In the Oriental society, as in Galatia, the dignity of women needed to be asserted against supposed inferiority. In Greek or Græcised society, as at Corinth, Ephesus, and Colossæ, the new "freedom" of the gospel was apt to be abused to license; hence it was rather the "subjection" of women which needed to be suggested. (Comp. 1 Cor. xi. 3—16; xiv. 34, 35; Eph. v. 22—24; and 1 Tim. ii. 11—15.) (3) Whereas in the Galatian Epistle the stress is laid on the unity of all with one another in Christ, here (as usual) the great truth is that "Christ is all things and in all." In 1 Cor. xv. 28 we have this phrase applied to God, in contradistinction to the office of the Son in His mediatorial kingdom. Here it is in reference to that kingdom that it is used. In it Christ (see Eph. i. 23) "fills all in all;" and by His universal mediation all "life is hid with Him in God." He is all that can be needed, and that both "in all things" and "in all persons." But under both aspects the catholicity of the gospel is equally brought out; here by the direct union of all alike with Christ, there by the resulting unity of all with one another.

(12) **Elect of God.**—For the description of the election here signified see Eph. i. 4, 5, 6. The name is obviously applied to the whole Church, as "elect to privilege"; it is not opposed to "called" (as in Matt. xx. 16), but coincident with it, representing, indeed, the secret act of God's gracious will, which is openly manifested in calling. (Comp. the other instances of the word in the Epistles, Rom. viii. 33; xvi. 13; 1 Tim. v. 21; 2 Tim. ii. 10; Tit. i. 1; 1 Pet. i. 1; Rev. xvii. 14.)

Holy and beloved.—Of such election there are here two signs. The elect are "holy," consecrated to God in thought and life; and "beloved," accepted and sustained in their consecration by His love. Both epithets belong to them as conformed to the image of Christ (Rev. viii. 29); for He is "the Holy One of God" (Mark i. 24; Luke iv. 34), who "sanctifies Himself for us, that we also may be sanctified in truth" (John xvii. 19); and He is also the "Beloved," the "Son of God's love" (chap. i. 13; Matt. iii. 17; Eph. i. 16), and we are accepted in Him. The two epithets here seem intended to prepare for the two-fold exhortation following. They are "beloved," therefore they should love one another (verses 12—15); they are holy, therefore they should thank God and live to His glory (verses 16, 17).

(12, 13) Comp. Eph. iv. 2, 31; v. 1, 2. The word "tenderhearted" in those passages corresponds to the "bowels (or, *heart*) of mercies" here; "kindness" and "forgiveness," "humility," "gentleness," "forbearance," appear in both. But the enumeration here is more exact in order of idea. St. Paul starts with the natural and universal instinct of compassion or sympathy; he next dwells on "kindliness and lowliness of mind," which are closely akin, since readiness to oblige others grows naturally out of a self-neglectful humility; from these he passes to "gentleness and long-suffering" in case of injury, ready "to forbear and to forgive;" lastly, from these particulars he rises to the general spirit of "love," ruling under "the peace of God."

(13) **Even as Christ forgave you.**—The MS. authority is in favour of the word "Lord" instead of Christ; but since the name "Lord" is specially applied to Christ in these Epistles (see, for example, Eph. iv. 5) there is no real difference. In Eph. iv. 31 we have "God in Christ forgave you," because there the example of Christ, as Son of Man, is afterwards to be set forth emphatically as an example of self-sacrifice (verse 2), and hence the free mercy of forgiveness is naturally attributed to "God in Christ." Here, in accordance with the emphatic exaltation of Christ, as all in all, the simpler phrase "Christ (or, *the Lord*) forgave you" is employed.

(14) **Above all.**—Properly, *over all*—as a bond or cincture to keep all together. Love is the general principle, harmonising all the special graces named above.

The bond of perfectness.—The bond of that harmony of character which is perfection. The phrase is remarkable, apparently suggested by the claim to perfection, set up by the Gnostic teachers. They sought such perfection in knowledge peculiar to the few; St. Paul in the love which is possible to all. For as he elsewhere urges (1 Cor. viii. 1), "Knowledge puffs up, charity builds up;" knowledge gains a fancied perfection, charity a real perfection.

(15) **The peace of God.**—The true reading is *the peace of Christ*—that which He gives (John xiv. 27), that which He is (see Eph. ii. 14). The ordinary reading is, no doubt, borrowed from Phil. iv. 7. This verse forms a link between the preceding exhortation to love of man, and the following exhortation to a loving and thankful service of God. The "peace of Christ" is the sense of unity in Him, with our fellow-men and with God. We are "called to it in one Body," of which He is the Head. (Comp. the fuller treatment of this subject in Eph. ii. 14—22; where, in accordance with the whole character of that Epistle, the unity "in one Body," here only alluded to, is worked out in vividness and detail.)

(16) **The word of Christ.**—Here again the definite phrase, "the word of Christ," takes the place of the commoner phrase, "the word of the Lord," "the word of God." It is to "dwell in their hearts." Hence it is the engrafted word" (Jas. i. 21)—the truth of Christ conceived in the heart, striking root into it, and making it its dwelling-place. It will be observed how all such phrases prepare for the full conception of Him as Himself "the Word of God."

In all wisdom.—The symmetry of the original, "in all wisdom teaching . . . in grace singing," suggests the connection of the words with those following, not, as in our version, with those going before. The

spiritual songs, singing with grace in
your hearts to the Lord. (17) And what-
soever ye do in word or deed, *do* all in
the name of the Lord Jesus, giving
thanks to God and the Father by
him. (18) Wives, submit yourselves unto
your own husbands, as it is
fit in the Lord. (19) Hus-
bands, love *your* wives, and
be not bitter against them.
(20) Children, obey *your* parents in all
things: for this is well
pleasing unto the Lord.
(21) Fathers, provoke not
your children *to anger*,
lest they be discouraged. (22) Servants,
obey in all things *your*
masters according to the
flesh; not with eyeservice,
as menpleasers; but in
singleness of heart, fearing God:
(23) and whatsoever ye do, do *it* heartily,
as to the Lord, and not unto men;
(24) knowing that of the Lord ye shall
receive the reward of the inheri-
tance: for ye serve the Lord Christ.
(25) But he that doeth wrong shall
receive for the wrong which he hath
done: and there is no respect of
persons.

Chap. iii. 18, 19. Duty of wives and husbands.

Chap. iii. 20, 21. Duty of children and fathers.

Chaps. iii. 22—iv. 1. Duty of servants and masters.

---

indwelling Word of God is described as manifesting itself, first, in the wisdom of mutual teaching, next, in the grace of hearty thanksgiving.

Teaching and admonishing . . .—Here again we have at once general identity and special distinction between this and the parallel passage in Eph. v. 19, 20. There, as here, we have the "speaking to one another in psalms and hymns and spiritual songs," "the singing in the hearts to the Lord," and the spirit of "thankfulness." But there the whole is described as a consequence of "being filled with the Spirit," and, as an outburst of that spiritual enthusiasm, of which the spurious excitement of drunkenness is the morbid caricature. Here the thought starts from "the word of Christ in the soul," realised through the gift of the Spirit by all our faculties; and it divides itself accordingly into the function of teaching, which bears on the mind; "the singing in grace" of thankfulness, which comes from and goes to the heart; and the "doing all in the name of Christ," which belongs to the outer sphere of action.

Psalms and hymns.—The ascription to these of an office of "teaching and admonition" describes what is their real, though indirect, effect. In the Church, as in the world, he who "makes a people's songs" really guides their minds as well as their hearts. For good and for evil the hymns of the Christian Church have largely influenced her theology.

(17) **All in the name of the Lord Jesus.**—Comp. here the more general exhortation of 1 Cor. x. 31, "Whether ye eat or drink, or whatever ye do, do all to the glory of God." This is the first principle of all godly life. The main object of all life, speculative or practical, is declared to be, not our own happiness or perfection, not the good of our fellow-men, but the "glory of God"—the carrying out of His will, and so manifesting His moral attributes. We are taught that if we "seek this first, all the other things shall be added unto us." But here we have the principle, not only of godly life, but of Christian life. It does all "in the name of Christ," that is, as conformed to His image, and so being His representative; it looks up thankfully to God our Father, but it is through Him, "having our sonship by adoption" through His all-sufficient mediation. Its desire is, not only that God may be glorified, but that "He may be glorified through Jesus Christ" (1 Pet. iv. 11). Once more we trace here the special and emphatic purpose of the Epistle.

Chap. iii. 18—iv. 1 deals with the three great relations of life—between wives and husbands, children and parents, servants and masters. In this section we have the closest parallelism with the Epistle to the Ephesians (chaps. v. 22—vi. 9). But the treatment of the first relation is far briefer, having nothing to correspond to the grand and characteristic comparison of marriage to the union between Christ and the Church. Even in the second there is somewhat greater brevity and simplicity. The third is dwelt upon with marked coincidence of language, and at least equal emphasis. We can hardly doubt that the presence of Onesimus, the runaway slave, suggested this peculiar emphasis on the right relation between the slave and his master.

[It will only be necessary to note the few points in which this section differs notably from the parallel passage.]

[**6. Special Exhortation as to the relations of life.**

(1) THE DUTY OF WIVES AND HUSBANDS (verses 18, 19).

(2) THE DUTY OF CHILDREN AND PARENTS (verses 20, 21).

(3) THE DUTY OF SLAVES AND MASTERS (chaps. iii. 22—iv. 1).]

(18) **As it is fit in the Lord.**—For the explanation of this special fitness "in the Lord," *i.e.*, in virtue of Christian unity, see the grand description of Eph. v. 23, 24, 32, 33.

(19) **Be not bitter.**—Properly, *grow not bitter*, suffer not yourselves to be exasperated. The word is used metaphorically only in this passage, literally in Rev. viii. 11; x. 9, 10.

(21) **Provoke not . . . to anger.**—This, in the text followed by our version, is borrowed from Eph. vi. 4. The true reading is *provoke to emulation*, as in 2 Cor. ix. 2. What is forbidden is a constant and restless stimulation, "spurring the willing horse;" which will end in failure and despondency.

(22—25) Compare throughout Eph. vi. 5—9. The only peculiarity of this passage is the strong emphasis laid on "the reward of the inheritance." "The reward" is in the original, *a perfect recompense* or *requital*. The "inheritance" is exactly that which no slave could receive; only a son could be an heir (Gal. iv. 7). Hence the slave on earth is recognised as a son in heaven. He "serves the Lord," but his service is the perfect freedom of sonship.

(25) **He that doeth wrong** is clearly here the

A.D. 64.

CHAPTER IV.—(1) Masters, give
unto *your* servants that which is just
and equal; knowing that ye also have
a Master in heaven. (2) Continue in
prayer, and watch in the
same with thanksgiving;
(3) withal praying also for
us, that God would open
unto us a door of utter-
ance, to speak the mystery of Christ,
for which I am also in bonds: (4) that
I may make it manifest, as I ought
to speak. (5) Walk in wisdom toward
them that are without, redeeming the
time. (6) Let your speech *be* alway
with grace, seasoned with salt, that ye

Chap. iv. 2—6. Final exhortation to prayer and watchfulness.

may know how ye ought to answer every
man. (7) All my state shall Tychicus
declare unto you, *who is*
a beloved brother, and a
faithful minister and fel-
lowservant in the Lord:
(8) whom I have sent unto you for the
same purpose, that he might know your
estate, and comfort your hearts; (9) with
Onesimus, a faithful and beloved
brother, who is *one* of you. They shall
make known unto you all things which
are done here. (10) Aristarchus my fel-
lowprisoner saluteth you,
and Marcus, sister's son to
Barnabas, (touching whom

Chap. iv. 7—9. Commendation of Tychicus and Onesimus.

Chap. iv. 10—14. Salutation from St. Paul's fellow-workers.

---

master (see Eph. vi. 9), though, of course, the phrase cannot be limited to him.

IV.

(1) **Just and equal.**—The word "equal," or, rather, the substantive so translated, has the sense either of "equity" or "equality." The former is far commoner (especially in connection with justice), and probably all that is intended here. At the same time, the idea running through the passage is of a common fellow-service to Christ of all alike, and in chap. iii. 11 we are reminded that "in Christ Jesus there is neither bond nor free." Perhaps, therefore, St. Paul desired that his readers should remember that in some points all are literally equal before God.

[7. **Conclusion of the Epistle.**

(1) FINAL EXHORTATION to prayer (especially for St. Paul himself), and to wisdom towards those without, both in deed and in word (verses 2—6).
(2) COMMENDATION of Tychicus and Onesimus (verses 7—9).
(3) SALUTATION from Aristarchus, Marcus, Justus, Epaphras, Luke, Demas (verses 10—14).
(4) CHARGE to this Church to exchange greetings and letters with the Laodicean Church, and special charge to Archippus (verses 15—17).
(5) FINAL SALUTATION (verse 18).]

(2—4) Comp. the almost exact parallel in Eph. vi. 18—20, and see Notes there.

(3) **A door of utterance.**—Comp. a similar phrase in 1 Cor. xvi. 9; 2 Cor. ii. 12. There, however, the opened door is the door of external opportunity; here the "door of utterance" is the removal of all internal impediments to preaching.

(5) **Walk in wisdom . . . redeeming the time.**—In the parallel passage (Eph. v. 15) we have "walk strictly, not as fools, but as wise," and the limitation "towards them that are without" is omitted, although it is added that "the days are evil." The context, as will be seen by reference, is different, and the idea also somewhat different. There the "strictness" and "wisdom" are to guard against excess or recklessness within; here the "wisdom" is to watch against external dangers and make full use of external opportunities.

(6) **Seasoned with salt.**—It seems impossible not to trace here a reference to our Lord's words in Mark ix. 50, "Salt is good: but if the salt have lost his saltness, wherewith will ye season it? Have salt in yourselves." There the salt is spoken of as the preservative from corruption, and the warning against "corrupt" words in Eph. iv. 29 has been thought to point in the same direction. But the context appears certainly to suggest that the use of the salt is to teach "how to answer every man," and that this answer (like the "reason," or *defence,* of 1 Pet. iii. 15) is to be given to "those without." Probably, therefore, the "seasoning with salt" is to provide against insipidity (thus according to some extent with the classic usage of the word). Their speech is to be primarily "with grace," kindled by the true life of Christian grace in it; secondarily, however, it is to have good sense and point, so as to be effective for the inquirer or against the scoffer.

(7, 8) These verses present an almost exact verbal coincidence with Eph. vi. 21, 22, on which see Notes. In the verses, however, which follow, the particularity and detail of this Epistle stand in marked contrast with the brief generality of Eph. vi. 23, 24. Remembering that the two Epistles were sent at the same time, and that Ephesus was a church far better known than Colossæ, we cannot but regard this as supporting the idea of an encyclical character in our Epistle to the Ephesians.

(9) **Onesimus.**—See Philem. verses 10—17. The emphatic reference to him as being "faithful and beloved" like Tychicus, and "one of you" like Epaphras, is a remarkable commentary on St. Paul's exhortation as to slaves and masters in the preceding chapter.

(10) **Aristarchus my fellowprisoner.**—Apparently a Jew, one "of the circumcision." But he is "of Thessalonica," and is first named (in Acts xix. 22) as dragged with Gaius into the theatre in the tumult at Ephesus; thence he accompanied St. Paul (Acts xx. 4), at any rate as far as Asia, on his journey to Jerusalem. When, after two years' captivity, the Apostle starts from Cæsarea on his voyage to Rome, Aristarchus is again named by St. Luke as "being with us" (Acts xxvii. 2). From this fact, and from his being called here "my fellow-prisoner" (a name which there seems no adequate reason to consider as metaphorical), it would appear that, whether voluntarily or involuntarily, Aristarchus really shared his captivity. It is certainly not a little curious that in the Epistle to Philemon (verses 23, 24), sent at the same time, it is Epaphras who is called the fellow-prisoner," while Aristarchus is

ye received commandments: if he
come unto you, receive him;) (11) and
Jesus, which is called Justus, who are
of the circumcision. These only *are my*
fellow-workers unto the kingdom of God,
which have been a comfort unto me.
(12) Epaphras, who is *one* of you, a servant
of Christ, saluteth you, always labour-
ing[1] fervently for you in prayers, that
ye may stand perfect and complete[2] in
all the will of God. (13) For I bear him
record, that he hath a great zeal for
you, and them *that are* in Laodicea, and
them in Hierapolis. (14) Luke, the be-
loved physician, and Demas, greet you.
(15) Salute the brethren which are in

1 Or, *striving.*
2 Or, *filled.*

---

simply classed among the fellow-labourers." This variation is interesting to us as one of the characteristic marks of independence and genuineness in the Epistles; but it can only be accounted for by mere conjecture, such as that of their alternately sharing the Apostle's captivity.

Marcus, sister's son to Barnabas.—The notices of John Mark in the New Testament are full of interest. This is the first notice of him since the day when St. Paul rejected him from his function of "ministration," because on the former journey he had "deserted" them at Perga, and had "not gone with them to the work" (Acts xv. 38). Then he had gone with Barnabas to Cyprus, to take part in an easier work, nearer home and under the kindly guardianship of his uncle. Now the formal charge to the Colossian Church to "receive him"—a kind of "letter of commendation" (2 Cor. iii. 1)—evidently shows that they had known of him as under St. Paul's displeasure, and were now to learn that he had seen reason to restore him to his confidence. In the Epistle to Philemon Mark is named, as of course (verse 24), among his "fellow-labourers." In St. Paul's last Epistle, written almost with a dying hand (2 Tim. iv. 11), there is a touch of peculiar pathos in the charge which he, left alone in prison with his old companion St. Luke, gives to Timothy to bring Mark, as now being right serviceable for the "ministration" from which he had once rejected him. Evidently St. Paul's old rebuke had done its work, and, if Mark did join him in his last hours, he probably thanked him for nothing so much as for the loving sternness of days gone by. Before this, if (as seems likely) he is the "Marcus, my son" of 1 Pet. v. 13, he was with St. Peter, and must be identified with St. Mark the Evangelist, subsequently, as tradition has it, bishop and martyr at Alexandria.

(11) **Jesus, which is called Justus.**—The surname "Justus" is found in Acts i. 23; xviii. 7; we learn from tradition that by it, or by its equivalent, St. James, "the Lord's brother," was known. In this case it is curious that one who bore our Lord's name should also have been known by a surname which was His peculiar title, "the Just One." (See Acts xxii. 14; and comp. Luke xxiii. 47.) Of this Justus there is no other notice, not even in the Epistle to Philemon, in which all the other names recur.

Who are of the circumcision. These only . . .—The juxtaposition of the two notices seems to indicate—what is in itself likely—that the brethren who held aloof from St. Paul in "strife and envy," and whose conduct produced that sense of isolation of which he speaks so pathetically in Phil. ii. 20, were "of the circumcision." Out of them, only Aristarchus, Mark, and Justus were true fellow-workers, and as such "a comfort" to the Apostolic labourer.

(12) **Epaphras.**—See Note on chap. i. 7.

Servant of Christ.—A title assumed by St. James and St. Jude, as well as by St. Paul himself, but given by him only to Timothy (Phil. i. 1) and to Epaphras here. Of course, all Christians are "servants of Christ." But the name, as applied here, is no doubt distinctive of some peculiar character of service.

Labouring fervently.—Properly, *wrestling in agony of prayer.* (See Rom. xv. 30.)

Perfect and complete.—The word here found in the best MSS. for "complete" is used in Rom. iv. 21, xiv. 5, for "fully convinced" or "persuaded." This is probably, though not perhaps necessarily, its meaning here. In the two epithets—perfect and fully established in conviction—we may again trace, as before, reference to the pretensions of the Gnostic teachers to exclusive perfection in wisdom. St. Paul's true fellow-worker, like himself, prays that this perfection may belong to all, and that it may have its basis not in the secrets of heavenly knowledge, but in the revealed "will of God."

(13) On the natural union of Laodicea and Hierapolis with Colossæ, partly local and historical, partly, no doubt, having reference to their conversion by the same instrumentality (of Epaphras), see Note on chap. ii. 1 and *Introduction.* Epaphras is said to have great "zeal" (properly, *great labour*) of anxiety—finding vent in the wrestling in prayer noted above—for all three cities, for which he evidently still felt himself responsible. In such responsibility, as in the charges of Timothy and Titus, we see the link between the apostolate of this period and the episcopacy of the future.

(14) **Luke, the beloved physician, and Demas.**—Comp. Philem. verse 24. The original is even more emphatic, "Luke the physician, the beloved one." Demas, on the contrary, is barely named. It is impossible not to pass on in thought to the last notice of the two by St. Paul (2 Tim. iv. 10), "Demas hath forsaken me, having loved this present world . . . . only Luke is with me."

On the relation of St. Luke to St. Paul, see *Introduction to the Acts.* Here we need only remark that the emphatic mention of him as "the beloved physician" suggests the idea that it was both as physician and as friend that St. Luke, now, as in the last captivity, was with the Apostle. Though the captivity was not, according to ancient ideas, severe, it must have told upon his weak and shattered health.

(15) **The brethren which are in Laodicea.**—The comparison of this phrase with the more general "church of the Laodiceans" below has led to the idea that some special body of Christians—Dr. Lightfoot suggests a "family of Colossian Christians"—at Laodicea is here referred to. But more probably the whole of the Laodicean Christians are meant in both passages. In their individual character they are "the brethren in Laodicea;" when they are gathered to hear the Epistles they are the "Church (literally, *the Christian assembly*) of Laodicea."

And Nymphas.—There is a curious variety of reading here. Some MSS. have, as in our version, "the church in his house;" some, "in her house;" the best reading seems to be "in their house." The

Chap. iv. 15–17. Charge to the Church and to Archippus.

Laodicea, and Nymphas, and the church which is in his house. (16) And when this epistle is read among you, cause that it be read also in the church of the Laodiceans; and that ye likewise read the *epistle* from Laodicea. (17) And say to Archippus, Take heed to

second of these readings would make the name "Nympha," instead of "Nymphas," with which the form of the original hardly agrees. The last reading (from which the common reading of our version is probably a correction) must refer, in the word "their," to Nymphas and his family. Of Nymphas we know nothing, except from this passage. He is obviously a man of importance, a centre of Church life, in the Christian community at Laodicea.

The church which is in his house.—This phrase is found elsewhere only as applied to "Aquila and Priscilla" (Rom. xvi. 5; 1 Cor. xvi. 19), and to Philemon (Philem. verse 2). Of these Aquila and Priscilla are notable Christian teachers (as of Apostles, Acts xviii. 26) and confessors (Rom. xvi. 4); and Philemon is spoken of as a "beloved fellow-labourer," and one in whom "the saints are refreshed" (Philem. verses 1, 7). Hence this "church in the house" is seen to have gathered only round persons of some mark and leadership. The houses sanctified by such gatherings were the parents of the material churches of the future.

Since the word "church" means nothing more than "general assembly," it is obviously capable of definition only by the context. If undefined it is universal—the whole Catholic Church of Christ—otherwise it is civic, as is most common; or domestic, as here. Since the units of society were then the family and the city—not the country, or province—we read not of the church, but of the "churches" of Achaia, or Galatia, or Macedonia. National churches there could not be; for nations, as we understand the term, did not exist. Afterwards, when the Church was fully organised, it is well known that the ecclesiastical divisions ("parish," "diocese," &c.,) still followed the civil.

(16) **When this epistle.**—In the implied direction to read this Epistle in the Church—a direction expressly given under like circumstances to the Church at Thessalonica (1 Thess. v. 27)—we discern the method of first publication of the Apostolic Epistles; in the direction to interchange Epistles with the Laodicean Church, we trace the way in which these Epistles became more widely diffused, and recognised as authoritative in the Church at large. Thus it was that they were "canonised," *i.e.*, accepted as a part of the "canon" or rule of divine truth. The likelihood, or unlikelihood, of this public reading has an important bearing on the question of the authenticity of some of the books, which were placed among the "doubtful" by Eusebius and other ancient authorities. The fact that other books (such as our so-called Apocryphal books) were also publicly read was the cause of their being wrongly confused with the books of Holy Scripture.

The epistle from Laodicea.—The question, What was this "Epistle from Laodicea"? has given birth to a crowd of conjectures, of which an admirable and exhaustive examination will be found in Dr. Lightfoot's *Excursus* on this verse. But many of these may be at once dismissed. It seems perfectly clear, from the obvious parallelism of this Epistle from Laodicea with the Epistle to the Colossians itself, that it was a letter not from the Laodicean Church, not from any other Apostle, or Apostolic writer, but from St. Paul himself, either written at Laodicea, or (as is more likely) written to the Laodicean Church, and to be sent "from Laodicea" to Colossæ. Hence the question is narrowed to a single alternative—(1) Is it an Epistle which has been lost, or, at any rate, not found in the canon? This is, of course, possible; it cannot be necessary, as it is certainly difficult, to suppose that all St. Paul's Epistles have been preserved to us in Holy Scripture. Now, there is extant an "Epistle to the Laodiceans," circulated in the West, and known only in the Latin, although it has been thought to bear traces of translation from a Greek original. This letter (for which see *Excursus B.*) is obviously a forgery, probably not of early date, being little more than a tame compilation of phrases from St. Paul's Epistles. Putting this unhesitatingly aside, we may suppose the letter to have been lost. But this is a supposition merely arbitrary, and not to be adopted, except in default of something which has a better claim to attention. (2) Is it some other of St. Paul's known Epistles? The only letter which is noticed in our ordinary copies of the Greek Testament as written from Laodicea is the First Epistle to Timothy; but this is put out of the question, both in date and character; and, moreover, the very idea of a letter written from Laodicea at this time is negatived by St. Paul's declaration (chap. ii. 1) that the Laodiceans had not seen his face in the flesh. A fourth century tradition declares our "Epistle to the Hebrews" to have been written to the Laodiceans; but (setting aside all question of the authorship) the whole character and argument of the Epistle make this extremely unlikely. Far the most probable supposition identifies it with our "Epistle to the Ephesians." For the reasons for supposing this an encyclical letter, see *Introduction* to that Epistle. In particular it should not be forgotten that Marcion expressly calls it an "Epistle to the Laodiceans." Laodicea lay lower down the valley, and was the larger town: an encyclical letter might well be left there to be sent on to Colossæ. The two Epistles, as we have seen, have both strong likeness and marked distinction. Nothing could be more natural than that they should be interchanged, according to the direction of the text.

(17) **Say to Archippus.**—Archippus is included in the salutation of the Epistle to Philemon (verse 1) apparently as a member of his family, and is generally thought to have been his son. He held a "ministry" in the Church. The word is the same as the word "diaconate," but it is obviously used in a more general sense, precisely as in the charge to Timothy (2 Tim. iv. 5), "Make full proof of thy ministry;" and the whole tone of the passage here suggests that, like Timothy's, it was a ministry of some prominence in the Church. Tradition makes him afterwards a bishop of Laodicea; it is likely enough that he had that leadership among the presbyters, from which the episcopate was developed at the close of the Apostolic period. Whether this was at Colossæ—his father's native place—or Laodicea, cannot be gathered with any certainty from the context. The exhortation comes in close connection with Laodicea; yet, on the other hand, it seems strange to send through one church a message to a chief pastor of another. In any case this indirect transmission of a charge is curious, standing in marked contrast with

the ministry which thou hast received
in the Lord, that thou
fulfil it. (18) The salutation
by the hand of me Paul.

Chap. iv. 18. Final salutation.

Remember my bonds. Grace *be* with
you. Amen.

¶ Written from Rome to the Colossians by Tychicus and Onesimus.

---

the direct personal addresses of the Philippian Epistle (Phil. iv. 2, 3).

Which thou hast received in the Lord.—Properly, *which thou dost receive.* The probability seems to be that he received it from St. Paul, or perhaps Epaphras. The phrase is "in the Lord," not "from the Lord." Contrast Gal. i. 12, "I received it not from man, neither was I taught but by revelation of Jesus Christ."

(18) **The salutation by the hand of me Paul.**—Comp. 2 Thess. iii. 17, "The salutation by the hand of me Paul, which is the token in every Epistle." This invariable autograph salutation was "Grace be with you" in various forms, from the brevity of the text here to the fulness of 2 Cor. xiii. 15, which has become the universal Christian blessing. In different epistles it is associated with different phrases of blessing, or charge. Thus we read in 1 Cor. xvi. 22, "If any man love not the Lord Jesus Christ, let him be anathema." In the Epistle to the Galatians the autograph conclusion is expanded into a long postscript (chap. vi. 11—18). This may have been the case in the cognate conclusion (chaps. x. — xiii.) of the Second Epistle to the Corinthians, possibly from the words, "Now I Paul myself," &c. Here there is the simple and touching addition—

Remember my bonds.—In what spirit they were to be remembered we may gather from Eph. iii. 13; vi. 20; Phil. i. 13; ii. 17. St. Paul evidently does not disdain to use his captivity as an appeal for sympathy (see Philem. verse 9); but mainly he dwells on it as a "glory" both to himself and to his converts. In both these different aspects it may be that he regarded it himself, according as he looked upon it "after the flesh" in the natural feeling of humanity, or "after the spirit," in the higher power of the grace of God.

EXCURSUS ON NOTES TO COLOSSIANS

EXCURSUS A: RELATION OF THE EPISTLE TO THE COLOSSIANS TO GNOSTICISM.

It is not intended in this *Excursus* to attempt any description of the actual historical developments of those singular phases of opinion, classed roughly under the name of "Gnosticism" (on which see Neander's *Church History*, Sect. IV.), or any imitation of Dr. Lightfoot's exhaustive and scholarly investigation of the connections in detail, between the form of speculative and practical heresy denounced by St. Paul at Colossæ, and the tenets of the various Gnostic systems. For the purposes of this Commentary it will be sufficient to inquire generally—

(1) What is the fundamental principle of Gnosticism?

(2) What were the chief problems with which it dealt?

(3) How far it could, in its early stages, reasonably ally itself with the Judaic system?

(4) What was its early relation to Christianity?

(1) Gnosticism, as the name implies, is the absolute devotion to *Gnosis*, or "knowledge." It is, of course, obvious that "knowledge," as it is the natural delight of man as man, so also is sanctioned by the Apostles themselves—by none more emphatically than St. Paul, and nowhere more emphatically by him than in the Epistles of the Captivity—as one of the signs and means of the growth of the spiritual life in the image of Christ. In every one of the Epistles of this period St. Paul earnestly desires for his converts progress in knowledge. (See for example Eph. i. 17; Phil. i. 9; Col. i. 9.) It was, therefore, perfectly in accordance with Apostolic teaching that Clement of Alexandria and his school extolled the "true Gnostic," as representing some of the higher phrases of spiritual life, and reflecting in some senses, more distinctly than others, the likeness of the mind of God in Christ Jesus. But St. Paul, while he thus delights in true knowledge, also speaks (1 Tim. vi. 20) of a "knowledge falsely so called," and by this expression appears to brand with condemnation the spirit of what is commonly called Gnosticism. Where then lay the distinction between the false and the true "knowledge?"

In two points especially. First, Gnosticism exalted knowledge to an unwarranted supremacy in the Christian life. It made Christianity a philosophy, rather than a religion; as if its chief internal effect was enlightenment of the understanding rather than regeneration of the life, and its chief desire, in rising above self, was to discover abstract truths about God and man, rather than to know God Himself, with "all the heart, all the soul, and all the strength," as well as "all the mind." Thus it fatally disturbed the true harmony of the speculative, the practical, and the devotional elements of the spiritual life. Energy in practical service, and love in devotion, it considered as good enough for the mass of men, but knowledge as the one mark of "the perfect." Like all philosophies, it was aristocratic; for in work and in worship all might take their place, but only the few thinkers could "burst into the silent sea" of the higher speculation. There, by the esoteric doctrine, known only to the initiated, they believed themselves to be set apart from the ordinary Christians, for whom the exoteric or popular and imperfect teaching might suffice; and sometimes conceived that, with the higher mystic knowledge, they might gain also mysterious powers, and mysterious means of approach to a divine communion, unknown to others.

Secondly, Gnosticism also departed from the Apostolic teaching in relation to its method of knowledge. St. Paul describes, in a celebrated passage of the Epistle to the Ephesians, the process of the true knowledge of God. He prays for the Ephesians thus: "that Christ may dwell in your hearts by faith, that ye, being rooted and grounded in love, may be able to comprehend . . . and know the love of Christ which passeth knowledge, that ye might be filled with (or rather, *up to*) all the fulness of God." The order is here profoundly significant. The knowledge, being a knowledge of a Personal God, revealed to us in Jesus Christ, begins in faith—a faith which knows indeed in whom it believes, but then believes on Him, as having "the words of eternal life." It is next deepened by love, called out by the infinite love of God in Christ, naturally manifesting itself, partly in adoration, partly in active service, and by both coming to know more and more what still passes complete knowledge. Finally, even in its ultimate growth, it is still in some sense the receiving of a divine light, which pours in, and fills the soul with the revelation of God. It does not fill itself, but it "is filled up to all the fulness of God." Doubtless in all this the energy of the soul itself is implied—first to believe, then to love and to work, lastly to open itself to the divine truth: but it is throughout subordinate. If ever St. Paul allows it to be said, "Ye have known God," he adds the correction at once, "or rather are known of God." The process of Gnosticism was fundamentally different. Faith (it thought) was well for the vulgar; love, especially as shown in practice, was all they could hope to add to faith. But the Gnostic, accepting perhaps the vantage ground of ordinary gospel truth, took his stand on it, first to gaze, then to speculate, then to invent, in his own intellectual strength—now by profound thought, now by wild ingenuity of fancy, now by supposed mystic visions. As usual in such cases, he mixed up what he thought he saw with what he went on to infer by pure speculation, and turned what were simple speculations, probable or improbable, into professed discoveries of truth. Nothing is more notable in the full-grown Gnostic theories than the extraordinary luxuriance and arbitrariness of speculations, which, like the cycles and epicycles of the old Ptolemaic astronomy, stand self-condemned by their artificial ingenuity.

Now, it is clear that Gnosticism so viewed, although its full development waited for a later period, belongs in essence to all times. It arose again and again, in connection with Christianity, whenever the gospel had won its way to a position of such supremacy over actual life as to challenge speculation. This it had certainly done at the close of St. Paul's Apostolic career, in all the civilised world of Asiatic, Greek, and Roman thought; but perhaps nowhere more strikingly than in the provinces of Asia Minor, the ancient home of Greek speculation, and now the common meeting-ground of Western philosophy and Eastern mysticism, and in the famous city of Alexandria, where Greek and Jewish ideas had long been inextricably blended together. As we may trace its modern counterpart in much of the scientific and metaphysical speculation of our own day, so also it is but natural that it should emerge even in the earliest times, when the gospel confronted a highly cultivated and inquisitive civilisation. Whatever truth there may be in the old traditions that Simon Magus was the first Gnostic, it is, at least, clear that the germs of Gnosticism lay in his view of Christianity, recognising in it a mystic power and wisdom greater than his own, but ignoring its moral and spiritual regeneration of the soul.

(2) The great subjects of Gnostic speculation, under all its strange and fantastic varieties, were again the two great questions which at all times occupy the human mind. The first is speculative. What is the relation between the Infinite and the Finite, the Absolute and the Phenomenal, the First Cause and the actual Universe? The second is moral. What is the nature and origin of the Evil, both physical and moral, which forces itself upon our notice, as a disturbing element in a world essentially good and beautiful? and how can we explain its permitted antagonism to the First Cause, which is presumably good? To these two fundamental questions, belonging to all time, were added two others belonging to the centuries just before and just after the manifestation of the Lord Jesus Christ. What place is to be assigned to the Jewish dispensation in the philosophy of God and Man? What are the character and significance of the Incarnation, which is the central Christian mystery?

With regard to the first question, Gnosticism universally accepted the conception of an Eternal God, sometimes recognised, whether vividly or dimly, as a Person, sometimes looked on as a mere depth (*Bythos*) or abyss of Impersonal Being. But it insisted that, in respect of the work of Creation of the world and of humanity, in the government of the world and in the manifestation of Himself to Man, God was pleased, or was by His Nature forced, to act through inferior beings, all receiving of His *Pleroma* (or, "fulness") in different degrees of imperfection, and connected with Him in different degrees of nearness through "endless genealogies." These emanations might be regarded as personal, such as the "Angels of God," the "Word of God," the "Spirit of God"; they might be half-personal, like the *Æons* of later speculation; they might be, where Platonism was strong, even the *Ideas* or Attributes of God, gathered up in the *Logos*. But it was through these emanations that the Supreme God made and sustained the world, created man as at once material, animal (*psychic*), and spiritual, and manifested Himself to man in different ages.

Next, in relation to the Moral Problem of the Existence of Evil, Gnosticism seems to have oscillated between the idea of a direct Dualism, wherever the Persian influence predominated, and the conception of a dead-weight of resistance to the Will of God, wherever Monotheistic influence, especially Jewish influence, drove out the more pronounced conceptions of Dualism. But almost, if not quite, universally it traced the origin of evil to matter, conceived probably as eternal, certainly as independent, if not of the Supreme God, at any rate of the Creative Emanations, or of the One Being called the *Demiurgus*, or "Great Workman," to whom the Creative was in most cases assigned. Those who were, or continued to be, "material," enslaved to matter, were hopelessly evil; those who were "psychical," having, that is, the soul of emotion and lower understanding as distinct from the spirit, were in a condition of imperfection, but with hope of rising to spirituality; those who were spiritual, and they only, were free from all evil, capable of communion with the Supreme God. The first class were the world; the second the mass of the religious; the last were the possessors of the higher knowledge. On what should be the end of this condition of imperfection and conflict, there was division of opinion. But a consummation either of conquest of evil, or of absorption into the Divine *Pleroma*, was looked for by all. In the meanwhile the *Demiurgus*, or the Creative powers of the world, were regarded, sometimes as rebellious, sometimes as blinded by ignorance, sometimes as simply finite and therefore imperfect; and to these qualities in them were traced the sin, the blindness, or the imperfection of the present dispensation.

From this conception of matter as the source of evil, and therefore of the body as the evil element in our nature, followed two rival and directly antagonistic conclusions as to the appetites and passions, and the view which the spiritual man should take of them and of the objects by which they were satisfied. The nobler conclusion was, in accordance with the purer Oriental religions, and the highest Platonic philosophy, that the body was simply a hindrance, a prison-house, a dead weight, a cause of blindness or dimness to the spiritual eye; and hence was to be kept under by a rigid asceticism, mortifying all its desires, and preserving the spiritual man, as much as possible, from any contact with the material. The other—perhaps the more common, certainly the ignobler—conclusion was that the indulgence of the body could not pollute any spirit, which was sustained by the higher knowledge, and, therefore, that what common opinion held to be "a shame" was to the spiritual man "a glory," showing that the most sensual and reckless profligacy was to him a thing absolutely trivial and indifferent. It is obvious that these two rival theories would take up, and invest with a philosophical completeness, the ordinary tendencies represented by Pharisaism, on the one hand, and by Antinomianism on the other. Possibly by the natural law of reaction, the two extremes might often meet, in the same system, and even in the same individual.

A glance at these subjects will again show that Gnosticism, as in its principles, so in its chief problems, belongs to all times, and is essentially independent both of Judaism and Christianity. It was most natural that the claim of these problems to attention should assert itself in the later periods of the first century, even in reaction against the prosaic and practical systems of Stoicism and Epicureanism, then dominant in ordinary Roman thought, and, however opposed to each other, at least united in a contemptuous discouragement of all abstract speculation, especially in things divine. No home could be more congenial to such inquiries than the classic soil of philosophic speculation in Ephesus and the other cities of Asia, or the learned atmosphere of eclecticism which pervaded the Alexandrine school.

(3) But there were, as has been said above, two questions which presented themselves to the special forms of Gnosticism dominant at this period, and of these the first was of the relation of Gnostic theories to the Old Testament and the Jewish dispensation.

Now, in Judaism there was, on the one hand, much to attract the Gnostic. In it he found the one great living system of Monotheism, setting forth the absolute and infinite Godhead as the Eternal Source of being, invisible and incomprehensible to man; so infinitely above all creatures that His very Name was too sacred to be pronounced by human lips. In it he also found, or could easily develop, the doctrine of angelic intervention, in the creation and the guidance of nature, in the intercourse of God with man, even in the government of human history, and the protection both of individuals and of races. The peculiar privilege of a chosen people, easily represented as belonging to them simply through a higher knowledge, and not less easily transferred as an inheritance to a spiritual Israel of the enlightened and perfect, supplied the element of exclusiveness inherent in all Gnostic systems; and all the ordinances of ritual, of typical sacrifices, and ceremonial purity, readily lent themselves to the conception of a certain mystic consecration of the privileged, who might be a "royal priesthood," a prophetic and saintly order, before God, as distinct from "the people, who knew not the mystic law," and were "accursed." Nor would he omit to notice in the Sapiential books of the Old Testament—such as Job, Proverbs, and Ecclesiastes—the exaltation of Wisdom, as distinct from faith and holiness, to a supreme place; and he would find that round the memory of the Wise Man had grown up a whole crowd of legends of mystic lore, of supernatural insight, and of an equally supernatural power over the world of angels and of demons. So far, the Gnostic might find in the Jewish dispensation, freely handled after the manner of Alexandria, much that would give a kind of backbone of solidity to his vague and artificial speculations.

On the other hand, Gnosticism was repelled from all that element in the Jewish dispensation which is ordinarily called the "Theocracy," placing God in direct relation to the ordinary life of Israel, manifesting Him in the local sanctity of the Tabernacle or the Temple, honouring Him with physical sacrifice, setting forth His will in the clear and prosaic ordinances of the Law, dealing with all the people as a body, and as in many points equal before Him. For all this placed the Infinite Godhead in a direct, and, as it seemed to the Gnostic, an unworthy or an impossible contact, not only with man, but with that common life, that visible and tangible sphere of man's being, which he utterly despised. To some extent it could be got rid of, as at Alexandria, by allegorical interpretations, and by the impositions on the most prosaic text of mystic meanings, known only to the initiated, and handed down in secret "traditions of men." But where these failed, Gnosticism had a more sweeping remedy. It was to ascribe the whole system literally to the "disposition of angels," to attribute all that was carnal in Judaism to the inferior *Demiurgus*, perhaps imperfectly ministering the will of the Supreme God, perhaps becoming himself the God of the Jewish nation and of the Old Testament; in either case, giving a dispensation fit only in itself for the lower psychical life, needing to be sublimed by the spiritual into a hidden wisdom, "a secret treasure of wisdom and knowledge." Hereafter, when the Demiurgus came to be considered as antagonistic to the spiritual will of the Supreme God, this conception (as in the hands, for example, of Marcion) developed into an absolute hatred of Judaism, as a system entirely carnal, idolatrous, antagonistic to spiritual truth, and to the gospel so far as it was spiritual. But for this, in the first century, the time was not come. As yet, the growing power of Gnosticism treated Judaism as an ally, though perhaps in some degree a subject ally, in the victorious advance of its daring speculation.

Now, it has been shown, as with remarkable clearness by Dr. Lightfoot (in his *Introduction to the Colossian Epistle*, § 2), that some such alliance is actually traceable in the strange Jewish brotherhood of the Essenes—marked as it was (by consent of all authorities) by a rigid asceticism, "forbidding to marry, and commanding to abstain from meats;" by a denial of the resurrection of the body, as being a mere hindrance to the spiritual condition of the hereafter; by an abstinence from all sacrifices, as involving pollution, and perhaps as mere carnal ordinances; by mystic speculations as to the nature of the Godhead, and "the names of the angels," and by occasional claim of supernatural powers of magic; by the jealous preservation of secret traditions, and by a careful separation of the initiated from the mass of their fellow-Israelites.

The chosen home of the Essenes, of whom we have detailed accounts, was in Palestine, on the borders of the Dead Sea. But it is hardly likely that so remarkable a movement should have confined itself to any single locality. Certainly in Alexandria, in the tenets of the sect of the *Therapeutæ*, and in the teaching of Alexandrian Judaism, there was much of essential similarity to the Essenic system. Now, in close connection with our Epistle we notice the presence in Asia Minor of disciples of St. John Baptist, adhering, indeed, to "the way of the Lord," but knowing nothing of the "baptism of the Lord Jesus" (Acts xix. 1—7). These would come naturally from Palestine, perhaps from "the wilderness of Judæa," where John had baptised, near the chosen home of Essenism. We find, moreover, that a great Alexandrian teacher (Apollos), also "knowing only the baptism of John," had come down in the early part of the gospel to teach with singular power at Ephesus. That St. John himself, though probably quite erroneously, has been claimed as an Essene is well known. But in any case his ascetic and salutary life, his stern denunciation of the scribes and Pharisees, his very baptism of repentance, his declaration of the nullity of mere sonship of Abraham, would certainly be congenial to the Essene mind. Josephus' celebrated picture of his Essene teacher (quoted by Dr. Lightfoot, p. 161), reminds us, again and again, though with difference, of St. John Baptist himself. Certainly his disciples, when they had lost their master, clinging to his name in spite of his own warning of the transitoriness of his mission, might easily find in the Essenic system the rallying point which they needed, in order to preserve their distinctive character. Nor can we well forget the "vagabond Jews, exorcists," seeking to cast out evil spirits by the mere charm of a sacred Name of One in whom they did not believe, but a Name which they, like Simon Magus, in Samaria, recognised as having in it a supernatural power of miracle; and the mystic "books" of "curious arts" burnt publicly at Ephesus. The Essenic ideas might easily spread beyond the limits of the strict Essenic brotherhood. If once planted in the prolific soil of Asia Minor, they could hardly fail to attain a rapid development.

Now, it is certainly with a form of Judæo-Gnosticism that St. Paul has to deal in his Colossian Epistle, and one, moreover, which bears some marked similarities to the Essenic type of thought. On the one hand, he denounces the enforcement of the Jewish festivals (chap. ii. 16), and probably of the rite of circumcision (chap. ii. 11): on the other, he warns against the "traditions of men" (chap. ii. 8), containing "a philosophy and vain deceit," and alludes significantly to "the treasure, the *hidden* treasure of wisdom and knowledge." He describes, again, a "worship of angels," and an "intrusion into the things not seen," at least by the ordinary eye (chap. ii. 18, where see Note); and a rigid asceticism going beyond Pharisaic observance of the Law, and crying out at every point, "Touch not, taste not, handle not" (chap. ii. 21). Indirectly, but very emphatically, he protests against exclusive pretensions, and would present "every man as perfect before Christ" (chap. i. 22, 28). All these features belong unequivocally to Gnosticism, but to Gnosticism in its early stages, while still allied to Judaism, before it had attained to the independent luxuriance of later days. Nothing, for instance, is more striking than the reference to angelic natures, "thrones, dominions, principalities, and powers," as intervening between man and God, and the want of any vestige of allusion to the Æons of the later Gnosticism, even such as may perhaps be traced in the "oppositions" and "genealogies" of the Pastoral Epistles (1 Tim. i. 4; vi. 20; Tit. iii. 9). St. Paul uses the word *Æon* again and again (see Eph. i. 21; ii. 2, 7; iii. 9, 11, 21; Phil. iv. 20; Col. i. 26); but always in its proper sense of "age," without a shadow of the strange half-personification of the later Gnostic use. Throughout there is a distinct appropriateness to the time of the imprisonment at Rome, and just that union of similarity and dissimilarity to the later growths of Gnosticism which might be expected at this early date.

(4) But still more important and interesting is the question of the relation of Gnosticism to Christianity indicated by the Colossian Epistle. In the full-grown development of Gnosticism there were evidently two phases of this relation. In some cases the Gnostic theory, as a whole, stands out independent of Christianity, simply weaving some ideas derived from the gospel into the complexity of its comprehensive system. Such seems to have been, for example, the attitude towards Christianity of Basilides and Valentinus. In other cases, of which Marcion may be taken as a type, it identified itself in the main with Christianity, striving to mould it by free handling to its own purpose, and appealed to the Christian Scriptures, expurgated and falsified in its own peculiar sense. Moreover, in the same advanced stages Christianity was clearly distinguished by it from Judaism; "the Christ" was independent of the *Demiurgus*, the supposed author of the Jewish dispensation, and stood in far closer union with the Supreme Deity. Sometimes, as again notably in the system of Marcion, Christianity was characterised in a series of antitheses, as opposed to Judaism, and the salvation of the Christ was represented as a deliverance from the power of the God of the Jew. But a glance at the Epistle to the Colossians will show that of these things there is as yet no trace. Christianity had already broken through the narrow limits of Jewish legalism; the struggle marked in the Galatian and Roman Epistles had terminated in the complete victory of the freedom of the gospel. But, just as the Epistle to the Hebrews shows that there was still need to assert the transitoriness of the Jewish Ritual, Priesthood, and Sacrifice, so in this Epistle we observe that Jewish mysticism still claimed some dominion over the infant Church. Not till the hand of Providence had cut the knot of entanglement by the fall of Jerusalem, and the various manifestations of the bitter hostility of the Jews towards Christianity, was the dissociation complete.

In the eyes of Gnostic speculation of the East, Christianity probably as yet showed itself only as a sublimated and spiritualised Judaism, still presenting all the features which had excited sympathy, and simply crowning the hierarchy of angels by the manifestation of Him, who was emphatically "the Angel of the Lord;" while, on the other hand, it eliminated the narrowness of legalism, the carnality of ritual, and the close connection of the divine kingdom with common-place political and social life, which in Judaism had been an offence. Hence, in the phase already described at Colossæ, without throwing off its connection with Judaism, Gnosticism eagerly sought to lay hold of the new religion, to accept it in all its simplicity for the vulgar, and to mysticise it for the perfect into a higher knowledge. The error which vexed the Church at Colossæ appears still to approach it from without, much as the earlier Judaism had approached the Churches of Antioch or Galatia. Perhaps St. Paul's foreboding words at Miletus had been justified by the rise "among their own selves of men speaking perverse things to draw away disciples after them;" but the body of the Church seems still untouched, and is bidden to beware lest any man should "spoil" them, "judge" them, or "beguile them of their reward," by drawing them to this new phase of error.

It has been remarked by Neander that Cerinthus, born at Alexandria, and certainly in the days of St. John at Ephesus a propagator of his doctrine in the Churches of Asia Minor, is the Gnostic, whose system is a link between Judaism and Gnosticism proper. Certainly what can be traced as to his speculations on the function of the Angels, or of one Supreme Angel, in the Creation of the world and in the giving of the Mosaic laws, agrees well enough with the indications of the Colossian heresy. But of the distinctive points of his treatment of Christ—namely, his conception that the *Demiurgus* was ignorant of the will of the Supreme Deity, which was revealed by the Christ; his distinction between the man Jesus of Nazareth, and "the Christ," descending upon Him in the form of the dove at His baptism, and leaving Him before the Passion—we find no trace in the Colossian Epistle. The direct warnings of St. Paul refer only to the errors of the Judæo-Gnosticism. It is rather by the declaration of the positive truth of the true Godhead of the Lord Jesus Christ, His creative function, His infinite exaltation above all principality and power, and above all, the weighty declaration that in Him "all the fulness of the Godhead dwells bodily," that, as in a prophetic jealousy, he guards against the developments of Gnostic heresy in the future. We trace here a distinction from the more direct warnings even of the Pastoral Epistles—against the teaching in the Church of "other doctrines," of "fables and endless genealogies" of Gnostic emanation; the explaining away of the future resurrection; the "seducing spirits and doctrines of demons"—*i.e.*, of beings intermediate between God and man; which were united with the asceticism "forbidding to marry, and commanding to abstain from meats"; "the questions and strifes of words," and the "oppositions" (Gnostic antitheses) "of knowledge falsely so called"; the apostasy "of all which are in Asia," and the heresy "eating like a canker" into the very heart of the Church, which will no longer "endure sound doctrine."

(1 Tim. i. 3, 4; iv. 1—3; vi. 4, 20; 2 Tim. ii. 17; iv. 3). There is a still more marked distinction from the explicit warnings of St. John, protesting emphatically against the distinctive assertion of Gnostic heresy, that "Jesus Christ had not come in the flesh," and dwelling on the Incarnation of "the Word of Life," the Son, "to have whom is to have the Father," in those weighty declarations, every word of which seems charged with reference to Gnostic error. Everything shows that the heresy noted at Colossæ belongs to an earlier stage than even the Gnosticism of Cerinthus. In contemplating it, we see the last expiring struggle of Judaism, and can just trace, inextricably entwined with it, the yet deadlier error, which was hereafter to separate from it, and even to trample on it, and to advance over its dead body to the attack on the living energy of Christianity.

These considerations may suffice to mark with tolerable clearness the relation of the Epistle to Gnosticism. They certainly appear to show how entirely erroneous and inconsistent with the facts of the case is the idea, so confidently advanced, that the Epistle indicates a knowledge of full-grown Gnosticism fatal to its Apostolic origin. But they have far greater value, as enabling us better to understand its deeply interesting picture of the development, alike of Christian truth, and of the heresy, destined hereafter to assail or undermine it, in the closing years of the ministry of St. Paul.

EXCURSUS B: THE APOCRYPHAL EPISTLE TO THE LAODICEANS.

The translation of this Epistle here given is taken from the Latin (in which alone it is found), quoted by Dr. Lightfoot in the Appendix to his edition of the Epistle to the Colossians, with a conjectural rendering back into the Greek (which he thinks may have been the original) and two old English versions of the fifteenth century. He also gives a full description of the various Latin MSS., from which it appears that the earliest (the *Codex Fuldensis*) is a Vulgate New Testament of A.D. 546, in which the Epistle occurs between the Epistle to the Colossians and the First Epistle to Timothy. A glance at it will show that it is little more than a tame compilation of phrases, which, however, are taken not from the Ephesians or Colossians, but mostly from the Philippians, and that it has no bias or evidence of distinctive purpose whether for good or for evil. It certainly is not the Epistle spoken of in the Muratorian Fragment, as "in Marcionis heresim conficta." Its very simplicity induces a charitable hope that originally it may have been only "a pious imagination," made without idea of forgery, which subsequently was accepted as claiming to be a genuine Epistle of St. Paul.

It runs thus:—

"Paul an Apostle, not of men, nor through man, but through Jesus Christ, to the brethren who are in Laodicea; grace be unto you and peace, from God our Father and the Lord Jesus Christ.

"I thank Christ in all my supplications that ye are abiding in Him, and continuing steadfast in His works, waiting for the promise even unto the Day of Judgment. Neither let the vain words of some who teach beguile you, that they should turn you away from the truth of the gospel, which was preached unto you by me. And now shall God bring it to pass that they which are from me be serving to the furtherance of the truth of the gospel, and doing all goodness in the works of salvation (and) of eternal life.

"And now my bonds which I suffer in Christ are manifest; in which I am glad and rejoice; and this shall turn to my everlasting salvation, which also itself is wrought by your prayers, and the supply of the Holy Ghost, whether it be by life or by death. For to me both to live in Christ and to die is joy; and His mercy shall work out the same thing in you, that ye may have the same love, and be of one mind.

"Therefore, my dearly beloved, as ye heard in my presence with you, so hold fast and work in the fear of God, and it shall be to you unto everlasting life. For it is God which worketh in you. And do without drawing back, whatsoever ye do.

"Finally, my dearly beloved, rejoice in Christ, and beware of those who are greedy of filthy lucre. Let all your petitions be made known unto God, and be steadfast in the mind of Christ. Whatsoever things are sound, and true, and pure, and righteous, and lovely, do; and what ye have heard and received keep in your heart. And peace shall be with you.

"The saints salute you. The grace of the Lord Jesus be with your spirit. Cause this Epistle to be read to the Colossians, and that the Letter of the Colossians be read also to you."

THE EPISTLES OF PAUL THE APOSTLE TO THE
THESSALONIANS

INTRODUCTION

TO

THE FIRST EPISTLE OF PAUL THE APOSTLE TO THE

THESSALONIANS

In the earlier part of the year 52, St. Paul, in the course of his second journey, arrived at Thessalonica, the modern *Saloniki*—then, as now, one of the largest and most important cities of the Levant. The wounds which the converted gaoler of Philippi and St. Lydia had tended (Acts xvi. 33, 40) can hardly have been healed, when the Apostles Paul, Silas or Silvanus, and Timothy,* journeying rapidly through Amphipolis and Apollonia, came to found their second European Church (1 Thess. ii. 2). The Jews (who to this day form, it is believed, a moiety of the population of *Saloniki*) were massed there in great numbers, and had there "their synagogue,"—a kind of metropolitan church, contrasted with the mere *chapels* or "prayer-houses" of Philippi and other Macedonian towns. (See Note on Acts xvii. 1.) To this synagogue St. Paul repaired, and for "three Sabbath-days" reasoned, as usual, with the Jews (1) on the scriptural necessity for a suffering Messiah; (2) for a resurrection of the Messiah; and (3) on the claim of Jesus to the Messiahship. We are not informed how long the missionaries stayed at Thessalonica: probably a good deal more than the three weeks during which the preaching at the synagogue continued.† Their converts from among the Jews of the synagogue were few, though the proselytes and the ladies in connection with it joined them in large numbers.

We can draw from the Epistles, in connection with the Acts, a clear picture of the Apostles' manner of life and preaching at Thessalonica. They lodged in the house of a believing Jew of the name of Joshua, or (in the Græcised form) Jason (Acts xvii. 5; Rom. xvi. 21), but accepted nothing from him but their lodging. To *none* of the Thessalonians would they be indebted (1 Thess. ii. 9; 2 Thess. iii. 8), but maintained themselves, partly by the contributions twice forwarded to them from Philippi (Phil. iv. 16), but chiefly by hard manual labour, which occupied not the day only but extended far into the night to make up for daylight hours devoted to preaching. They were determined to be model operatives (2 Thess. iii. 9), and not merely eloquent preachers. And this was not all; besides the work of public preaching and teaching, the Apostles followed their usual method of dealing individually with the converts' souls. The Thessalonian Christians—"every one" in his turn—thus received the encouragements and warnings of their ghostly fathers (1 Thess. ii. 11). If the presbyters whom they left to carry on this work of admonition (see Notes on 1 Thess. v. 12, 14) continued it with the Apostles' zeal, they might indeed well be described as "*labouring* among them."

The preaching no doubt went on, not only on the Sabbaths, but on the week-days; for though the Acts tell us nothing of evangelistic efforts among the Gentiles, except among the "devout" (*i.e.*, the proselytes), the whole tone of the Epistles proves that the Thessalonian Church was almost wholly Gentile. Besides which, the account in the Acts of the subjects of the three sermons preached on the three successive Sabbaths does not by any means include all that we find mentioned as the staple of the Apostles' preaching there. Thus, it is clear that they had spoken strongly of the *regal* aspect of our Lord's work. The charge on which they were arraigned was the charge of proclaiming "another king" (or *emperor*, for the word is the same in Greek), "one Jesus." It was, in fact, the proclamation of what is specially distinguished as the "gospel of the kingdom" (Matt. iv. 23; ix. 35; xiii. 19; xxiv. 14; Luke viii. 1, Greek; xvi. 16), that is, not only the good news of Jesus Christ's complete empire over the individual soul, but the good news that He has organised us all into a well-disciplined Church (Rev. i. 6, Greek; comp. John xi. 52), which was to form an *imperium in imperio* within the Roman dominions. And accordingly we find the Thessalonians reminded that one of the best blessings which God had bestowed upon them was His calling them into "His kingdom" (1 Thess. ii. 12), and encouraged by the thought of God's counting them "worthy of the kingdom of God, for which they suffered" (2 Thess. i. 5). The full development of this "kingdom," at the King's return, was indeed very probably the main subject of the preaching. On this point the Thessalonians appear to have had the most accurate information (1 Thess. v. 2). St. Paul assumes that they thoroughly believed the doctrine (1 Thess. iv. 14). They not only knew the very form in which our Lord Himself had taught (see Note on 1 Thess. v. 2) the impossibility of forecasting the date, but they had been told again and again (2 Thess. ii. 5) what changes must take place before the Advent of the kingdom was to be expected. At every turn in the Epistle it is mentioned. And the moral laws of the kingdom of God had been taught in the most explicit manner (1 Thess. ii. 11), not only with regard to sins which the Gentile world permitted freely (1 Thess. iv.

* Timothy's presence is not mentioned in the Acts, but seems implied by chaps. xvi. 3, 4; xvii. 14, and made absolutely certain by the Epistle, where the "we" always includes him. Howson, nevertheless, concludes from Phil. ii. 22 that he had been left behind at Philippi.

† Several facts indicate this: The good organisation of the Thessalonian Church (though this might be partly owing to St. Timothy's subsequent visit); the fact that St. Paul had time to get regular artisan's work; the repeated contributions from Philippi that reached him there (Phil. iv. 16); the way in which St. Paul speaks of his habitual conduct among them, and of what he "used to say" (*e.g.*, 1 Thess. ii. 9, 11; 2 Thess. ii. 5).

1, 2), but also with regard to strenuous industry (2 Thess. iii. 6, 10). And as in Galatia (Acts xiv. 22) so here, the sufferings that fenced the entrance of that kingdom were fully prophesied (1 Thess. iii. 3, 4).

This teaching, delivered with all the tenderness of a nursing mother, and all the authority of a father, and all the devotion of a friend (1 Thess. ii. 7, 8, 11), yet sternly and unflatteringly (1 Thess. ii. 5), told upon the Thessalonians with great effect. The Apostles themselves were in the most exalted and confident frame of mind (1 Thess. i. 5), and their hearers, in spite of many difficulties (1 Thess. i, 6; ii. 2, 14), received with enthusiasm the instruction as proceeding from God and not from man (1 Thess. ii. 13). The difficulties, however, soon increased. The Jews grew jealous of the work going on among the Gentiles, especially among their proselytes (Acts xvii. 5), and vehemently set themselves to forbid such preaching (1 Thess. ii. 16). They stirred up the abandoned Greeks who idled in the market-place to make a riot against these disturbers of the world. The Greeks, with the passionate servility which usually marked what was called under the empire a free Greek town,* took up eagerly the cry that to preach Jesus as emperor was treason to Claudius, and began a prosecution of Jason before the politarchs. The prosecution only resulted in Jason's being bound over to keep the peace; but the irritation was so great that it was judged expedient for the Apostles to leave the city and proceed southward.

From Thessalonica St. Paul travelled to Berœa, from Berœa to Athens, and from Athens to Corinth. But though he had quitted Thessalonica, he had not forgotten his infant Church, and had not intended to be absent from it long. Twice at least (1 Thess. ii. 18) he had seriously endeavoured to make his way back, "but Satan hindered" him. The persecution of the Church had by no means been appeased (as they had hoped) by the expulsion (see Note on 1 Thess. ii. 15) of the missionaries; and St. Paul dreaded lest the temptation should have been too fiery for Christians so imperfectly taught and organised (1 Thess. iii. 10). In his extreme agony of mind for them, unable himself to travel northward, he determined, at the cost of utter loneliness in a strange and most unsympathising town (Acts xvii. 16; 1 Thess. iii. 1), to send St. Timothy to see how they fared, and to help them. To St. Paul's great relief, the younger Apostle brought back, on the whole, an excellent report. True, there were several most grave faults to be found with the Thessalonian Church, which will be best understood from the table of the Epistle's contents, but the practical St. Paul had evidently not expected even so much progress as had been made, and was overjoyed (1 Thess. iii. 8). And this Epistle —the earliest of all that are preserved of its author, perhaps the earliest book of the New Testament—contains St. Paul's comments on Timothy's report.

The question now occurs, At what point of the narrative in the Acts is the writing of this Epistle to be placed? Was it written at Athens, or at Corinth? Almost all critics agree that it was written at Corinth.† The question will be found discussed in the Notes, but it may be here stated that the difficulty consists in identifying the return of St. Timothy with his report (1 Thess. iii. 6), with the coming of Silas and Timotheus in Acts xviii. 5. The narrative of the Acts seems, at first sight, to exclude the supposition that Silas or Timothy had paid a visit to St. Paul between the time of his leaving Berœa and the time for their rejoining him at Corinth; while the words of 1 Thess. iii. 1—5 seem as urgently to require that Timothy at all events should have been with St. Paul at Athens. But on closer inspection, the Acts prove rather to favour this supposition; they tell us that St. Paul sent a peremptory and immediate summons to his two colleagues whom he had left in Macedonia (xvii. 15), which summons they probably obeyed, and if so, would no doubt reach him long before the meeting at Corinth mentioned in Acts xviii. 5; besides which, the very words, "while Paul *waited* for them at Athens," seem to imply that they *came* to that city. A few other points may be mentioned which help to fix the date. On the one hand, the letter cannot be placed *later* than the departure from Corinth, for we never read of St. Silas being with St. Paul after that time. For the same reason it must have been written some *while* before the departure from Corinth, as the Second Epistle (which equally bears Silvanus' name) was also written thence, But on the other hand, it must not be placed too early, For (1) the Thessalonian Church had had time to extend its missionary zeal over all Macedonia, and indeed over all Greece; (2) the Jewish persecutions had had time to gain crushing force and consistency; (3) errors and disorders had had time to spoil the faith and morals of the community; (4) at any rate, a few of the believers had fallen asleep, which, considering the probable numbers and nature of the members of that young Church, requires a probable lapse of some months.

The contents of the Epistle bear every sign of an early date. None of the great doctrines which are considered specially Pauline are touched upon in it, such as "faith," in its special sense, or "justification." There is no Judaic legalism to oppose, as in Galatians; St. Paul "can still point to them"—the churches of Judæa—"as examples to his converts at Thessalonica" (chap. ii. 14). There is no Gnosticism to confront, as in the Epistle to the Colossians or to St. Timothy. Again, the great prominence given to the doctrine of the Advent seems an indication of what St. Paul calls "the beginning of the gospel" (Phil. iv. 15). The earliest gospel must needs consist in teaching that CHRIST was alive from the dead, and giving each Christian a vital interest in His present life, and this cannot be effected without much preaching of the Advent.

It has already been remarked that the Thessalonian Church consisted almost wholly of Gentiles. This may be easily seen from the Epistle. There are no quotations from the Old Testament, nor arguments founded upon it. The name of Satan (1 Thess. ii. 18)

* The city of Thessalonica had been made a *libera civitas* because of the support it had given in the civil wars to the cause of Octavian and Anthony. Such cities were exempt from the interference of the provincial government, and had their own forms of administration. Thessalonica had her popular assembly, and for supreme officers certain magistrates called politarchs—a name elsewhere unknown. On the testimony given by this word to the truthfulness of the Acts, see Note on Acts xvii. 8.

† The subscription at the end of the Epistle has no weight whatever, not representing even a tradition, but being merely an uncritical inference from chap. iii. 1. The only way in which any case can be made out for the Athenian date is to suppose that the past tenses in iii. 1, 2, 5, are what is called in Greek the *epistolary aorist*, equivalent to our *present*, as *e.g.*, where St. Jude (verse 3) says, "I *gave* all diligence," "it was needful," or St. John (1 John ii. 14), "I have written," literally, *I wrote*. Thus it would mean that Timothy has just obeyed St. Paul's hasty summons, and arrived at Athens by way of Thessalonica, as (from Berœa) he naturally might. "Being no longer able to forbear, I am determined to be left at Athens alone, and I send Timothy; I send to know your faith, lest through the tempter's temptation of you our labour should prove in vain." The following verse will then mean—"Not that I seriously distrust you; for the other day when Timotheus came," &c.

is the only approach to a reference to Scriptural knowledge. The earliest revelation with which the Church is supposed to be acquainted, and which forms the canonical standard of reference, is the tradition which the Thessalonians have received from their founders by word of mouth (2 Thess. ii. 5). The Thessalonians are never credited with any experience like "turning from dead works," but, on the contrary, they had "turned to God from idols" (1 Thess. i. 9). The fierce and bitter invective against the Jews is far different in its language from what it would have been had any large proportion of the Church been but neophytes from Judaism; and, indeed, the Jews are clearly distinguished from "your own countrymen" (chap. ii. 14). The difficulty with which the young Church accepted the doctrine of the resurrection also points in that direction, as well as the dulness of conscience with regard to the sinfulness of fornication (chap. iv. 5).

The Epistle, which is entirely practical throughout, divides itself more clearly into its component sections than perhaps any other of St. Paul's Epistles. There are two main portions. The first (chaps. i., ii., iii.) is narrative and personal, designed to attach the Thessalonians more closely to the writers' persons by the ties of common memories, of imparted information, and of sympathy over the news which had been brought from Thessalonica. Attention having been thus secured, the two remaining chapters are occupied with instructions upon special points in which the Church was deficient. The contents (after the salutation) may be tabulated thus:—

I. THE NARRATIVE PORTION (chaps. i. 2—iii. 13).

A. Containing reminiscences of the apostolic *sojourn* at Thessalonica (chaps. i. 2—ii. 16).

(1) Thanksgiving for the display *of God's power and love* both in the missionaries and in the converts (chap. i. 2—10).

(2) Reminder of the missionaries' conduct there (chap. ii. 1—12).

(3) Acknowledgment of the Thessalonians' hearty response (chap. ii. 13—16).

B. Containing an account of the Apostles' (especially St. Paul's) anxieties and efforts for the Thessalonians since they left them (chaps. ii. 17—iii. 10).

Then follows a prayer for them, which connects the first portion naturally with the first subject of instruction in—

II. THE EDUCATIONAL PORTION (chaps. iv. 1—v. 28.)

(1) The necessity of abstaining from fornication (chap. iv. 1—8).

(2) The extension of sober church feeling (chap. iv. 8—12).

(3) Discussion of certain points connected with the Advent:—

(*a*) The respective part therein of the quick and the dead (chap. iv. 13—18).

(*b*) The uncertainty of its date, and consequent need of vigilance (chap. v. 1—11).

(4) Duty to the Presbyters (chap. v. 11—13), who are charged to see that orderly discipline is enforced (chap. v. 14—15).

(5) Various spiritual directions, chiefly with regard to public worship (chap. v. 16—28).

The *genuineness* of the Epistle can scarcely be said to have been ever seriously doubted. Though there are no certain patristic quotations from it, or allusions to it, earlier than the end of the second century, it has passed unchallenged (even by Marcion) until the nineteenth century. Schrader and Baur in that century argued against its Pauline authorship, alleging the absence of "Pauline" theology, contradictions to the account in Acts, marks of date which they suppose to be subsequent to the fall of Jerusalem, &c. But the internal evidence is so convincing that even such a sceptical critic as M. Renan has no hesitation in admitting both Epistles to the Thessalonians into his second class of Epistles, which he calls "Undoubted Epistles, although some objections have been made to them," and his words are as follows:—"The difficulties which certain moderns have raised against them are but those light suspicions which it is the duty of criticism to express freely, but without being stopped by them when there are more powerful reasons to draw one on. And these three Epistles (*i.e.*, 1 and 2 Thess. and Phil.) have a character of authenticity which overbears every other consideration." The attack upon the Epistles was renewed in the summer of 1877 by Holsten, in the German *Annual of Protestant Theology*, but the present writer has not seen the critique.

[The principal works which have been made use of in commenting upon these two Epistles are the Commentaries of Lünemann and his English follower Ellicott, of Hammond, and of Wordsworth, together with such works as Renan's and Howson's accounts of St. Paul, and MS. notes from lectures of Professor Lightfoot.]

THE FIRST EPISTLE OF PAUL THE APOSTLE TO THE

THESSALONIANS

A.D. 54.

CHAPTER I.—(1) Paul, and Silvanus,
and Timotheus,[a] unto the
church of the Thessalo-
nians *which is* in God the
Father and *in* the Lord Jesus Christ:
Grace *be* unto you, and peace, from God
our Father, and the Lord Jesus Christ.
(2) We give thanks to God always for
you all, making mention of you in our
prayers; (3) remembering
without ceasing your work
of faith,[b] and labour of
love, and patience of hope
in our Lord Jesus Christ,
in the sight of God and our Father;
(4) knowing, brethren beloved,[1] your

Chap. i. 1. The salutation.

Chap. i. 2—10. Thanksgiving for the success of the mission to Thessalonica.

a 2 Thess. 1. 1.

b Gal. 5. 6.

1 Or, *beloved of God, your election.*

---

(1) "The founders of the Church of Thessalonica, who have so recently left it, greet the Church in the common Father in whom they are united."

Paul, and Silvanus, and Timotheus.—There was no need to add "Apostle" to the name of Paul, in writing to a Church with which his relations were so familiar and so cordial: it is probably omitted for the same reason in the Epistle to the Philippians and in that to Philemon. Some see in the omission a mark of the early date of the letter, before St. Paul had assumed the title; others think he omits it in courtesy to his companions, to whom it could not be given. Both theories are disproved by chap. ii. 6. Silas takes precedence of Timothy (comp. Acts xvii. 14, 15; xviii. 5; 2 Thess. i. 1) as a man of higher standing. (See Acts xv. 22, and 1 Tim. iv. 12.)

In God.—Other Thessalonians were "in the world," "in darkness," "in their sins." The distinctive mark of *these* was that they were re-united to the Father of all men; and more, re-united in Christ. The words following "peace" should be struck out, not being found in the best text.

(2) "We never set ourselves to prayer without remembering your faithful activity, loving laboriousness, cheerful and persevering endurance, and thanking God for it."

We.—All three are regarded as the writers, and no doubt the sentiments of all are expressed, though the letter is St. Paul's own composition. In chap. ii. 18 he corrects himself for using "we" where it was only true of himself. It may be noticed that St. Paul never speaks of himself alone in the plural in any of the other Epistles.

To God.—None of the success is due either to the preachers or to the converts.

Always.—Not as meaning "without ceasing," but "on every occasion that reminds us of you;" the words "in our prayers" specify the happy occasions. Christians like best to be remembered then.

For you all.—"There is not one of you that we know of for whom we cannot give thanks: the whole church is what it should be."

(3) **Faith . . . love . . . hope.**—In this first of his writings, St. Paul has already fixed upon the three great *abiding* principles (1 Cor. xiii. 13) of the Christian life, and the forms in which they mainly exhibit themselves. The genitive in such phrases as "work of faith," etc., is almost equivalent to a very emphatic adjective—"faithful activity," *i.e.,* a work characterised by faith and prompted by faith, such as faith alone could have enabled you to accomplish; so "labour of love" is similarly equivalent to "loving labour," laborious toil undertaken for love's sake, and done in the spirit of love; and "patience of hope" to "hopeful endurance of trials," a steadfast endurance which is grounded upon and cheered by hope.

In our Lord.—More correctly, *of.* The words in the Greek go with all three clauses: He is the object of the faith and love, as well as of the hope. This "hope of our Lord" includes, but is not limited to, the hope of His second Advent.

In the sight of God goes closely with "remembering," and is equivalent to "in prayer."

(4) "The reason why the sight delights us is because it proves that God loves you, and has set His heart upon you."

Beloved.—The proper translation is, *knowing, brethren who have been so beloved of God, your election,* as in the margin: the Greek idiom cannot allow of the Authorised rendering. The tense of the word "beloved" represents not only God's attitude to them in the present, but the long continuance of it in the past, especially as proved by His election of them. (Comp. Rom. viii. 28, 29, 30, and 2 Thess. ii. 13.)

Election, in the language of (at any rate) St. Paul and St. Peter, seems primarily to refer to a gracious admission into religious privileges in *this* life. The word implies nothing as to the final condition of the person thus elected (see 2 Pet. i. 10, and comp. Eph. i. 4 with Eph. v. 5, 6, 7). God *elects* us to become members of the Holy Church, and *all* baptised persons are *elect,* with heaven in reversion (1 Pet. i. 2—5); but they may, according as they please, unsettle their election, or make it sure. St. Paul rejoices, because the continued possession of spiritual privileges, used or abused, is an assurance of God's continued "favour and goodness towards us." Of course, however, this observation does not much affect the mysterious doctrine of predestination. The question must still remain why

election of God. (5) For our gospel came
not unto you in word only,[a] but also
in power, and in the Holy Ghost, and
in much assurance; as ye know what
manner of men we were among you for
your sake. (6) And ye became followers
of us,[b] and of the Lord, having received
the word in much affliction, with joy of
the Holy Ghost:[c] (7) so that ye were
ensamples to all that believe in Mace-
donia and Achaia. (8) For from you
sounded out the word of the Lord not
only in Macedonia and Achaia, but
also in every place your faith to God-
ward is spread abroad; so that we
need not to speak any thing. (9) For
they themselves shew of us what
manner of entering in we had unto
you, and how ye turned to God from
idols to serve the living and true
God;[d] (10) and to wait for his Son from
heaven, whom he raised from the dead,
even Jesus, which delivered us from the
wrath to come.

a 1 Cor. 2. 4; 4. 20.

b 1 Cor. 4. 16; 11. 1; 2 Thess. 3. 7, 9.

d Acts 17. 29.

c Ps. 45. 7; Rom. 14. 17.

A.D. 54.

Chap. ii. 1—12. The Apostle's life at Thessalonica.

CHAPTER II.—(1) For
yourselves, brethren, know
our entrance in unto you,

God brings some in this life to the knowledge of His truth, and others not; but the observation, at any rate, destroys the notion of an arbitrary damnation and salvation.

(5) "If God had not set His heart upon you, we never could have been as successful among you as we were."

Our gospel came not unto you.—Or rather, *the glad tidings which we brought did not prove among you, in its action upon you.*

In word only.—Comp. 1 Cor. ii. 4; iv. 20. "It did not consist *merely* of so much eloquent instruction, but also we found we were speaking with a conscious power—indeed with all the force of the Holy Ghost—and with an overmastering conviction that we were right and should prevail." That by the "power," "assurance," etc., are meant the preachers' own, and not the people's, is proved by the next clause, "as ye know."

In the Holy Ghost.—The Greek here omits the definite article. In such cases attention is not so much called to the Blessed Person Himself, as to the exalted, inspired enthusiasm with which He fills us. The union of the divine and human spirit is so close (see 1 Cor. vi. 17) that it is often hard in the New Testament to distinguish which is meant.

As ye know sums up with an appeal to their memory: "In fact, you recollect what God made us like among you."

For your sake gives not their own purpose, but God's, carrying on the thought of the "election."

(6) **And ye became followers.**—Not so much a separate reason for believing them elected of God, because of their receptiveness, but an evidence of the power given by God to the preachers for the winning of them. "So much so, that, in spite of persecution, you became Christians with enthusiasm."

Followers.—Not "disciples," but *imitators.* The three points in which the Lord and His Apostles were imitated are then expressed—(1) meek reception (Ps. xl. 6; Isa. l. 5); (2) cost what it might; (3) rejoicing all the while (Pss. xxii. 22; xlv. 7).

In much affliction.—For examples of troubles in the early days of the Thessalonian Church, see Acts xvii. 5, 8.

Holy Ghost is used in the same way as it is in verse 5. "Joy which is the natural outcome of a spirit united with the Holy Spirit."

(7) "Your zeal was so great and sincere that you, in your turn, became a model: for even in far-away countries the tale of your conversion is told with wonder."

Ensamples.—Probably the singular should be read: the whole church became a model church.

To all that believe—*i.e., now;* not to those that *then* believed; Philippi was the only such church.

Macedonia and Achaia.—These two provinces comprised all Roman Greece. The influence of the Thessalonians spreads far beyond their own country.

(8) **For.**—"For, in fact," (supporting and exceeding the statement of verse 7 about Greece) "you form the centre from which the doctrine of Christ has rung (not *rang*) out like a trumpet through those countries; and even beyond, your faith is well known." The clauses are not quite logically balanced.

Your faith does not mean "your creed," but "the report of your extraordinary faith."

To say anything—*i.e.,* about our success at Thessalonica.

(9) **They themselves**—*i.e.,* the inhabitants of those countries. "Wherever we go we find our own story told us."

Shew.—Rather, *announce.* Both sides of the story are told: (1) of *us*—what kind of entry we made among you, explained in chap. ii. 1—12 to mean with "the word of truth, of meekness, and righteousness" (Ps. xlv. 5); (2) of *you*—how truly converted you were, as he proceeds to show further in chaps. ii. 13—iii. 13.

Living and true God.—In contrast to the lifeless and false idols. The Thessalonians had been Gentiles. Perhaps St. Paul was thinking of his own speech on Mars Hill, which had been recently uttered.

(10) **And to wait.**—The idea of the Advent is that which both here and throughout the Epistle occupies the foreground in the minds of St. Paul and his friends. These two infinitives, "to serve" and "to wait," express not so much the *intention* of the Thessalonians in turning, as the condition into which they came by turning.

Whom he raised.—Not only proves His Sonship (Rom. i. 4), but also gives a kind of explanation of the "awaiting Him *from heaven.*"

Delivered.—Better, *delivereth.*

To come.—Better, *which is already coming.* The wrath is on its way to the world, to appear with Christ from heaven (2 Thess. i. 7, 8), and He is day by day working to save us from it (Heb. vii. 25).

II.

(1) **For yourselves brethren, know.**—The writers' purpose is practical, not didactic; they therefore animate their converts with the stirring memories of their conversion. "We need not go to these foreign witnesses for the tale of how we came to you; for *you* recollect it as if it were yesterday." The "for" (as in

that it was not in vain: (2) but even
after that we had suffered before, and
were shamefully entreated, as ye know,
at Philippi,[a] we were bold in our God
to speak unto you the gospel of God
with much contention. (3) For our ex-
hortation *was* not of deceit,[b] nor of un-
cleanness, nor in guile:[c] (4) but as we
were allowed of God to be put in trust
with the gospel,[d] even so we speak; not
as pleasing men,[e] but God, which trieth
our hearts. (5) For neither at any time
used we flattering words, as ye know,
nor a cloke of covetousness; God *is*
witness: (6) nor of men sought we
glory, neither of you, nor *yet* of others,
when we might have been burden-
some,[1] as the apostles of Christ.[f]
(7) But we were gentle among you, even
as a nurse cherisheth her children:[g]

e Gal. 1. 10.
a Acts 16. 22.
b 2 Cor. 6. 8.
c 2 Cor. 4. 2.
1 Or, *used authority.*
f 1 Cor. 9. 1.
g Acts 13. 18.
d Gal. 2. 7; 1 Tim. 1. 11; Tit. 1. 3.

---

chap. i. 8) implies "for in fact," "for after all." The thought of chap. i. 5, 9 is here resumed, but with a different purpose: *there* it was to prove that the work was God's work; *here*, "to stir up their pure minds by way of remembrance."

Not in vain draws a little too much attention to the *result* of their coming. It should be, *not vain*—*i.e.*, not purposeless and idle. This may be seen from the contrast drawn in the following words.

(2) **Even after** "what was enough to have scared others" (Bengel). Such men were not likely to be "vain." The marks of their ill-treatment at Philippi were fresh upon them at Thessalonica (*as ye know*). See Acts xvi. and xvii. 1.

In our God.—These words give the ground of their boldness—"in reliance on the God whom we felt to be in union with us."

With much contention.—Rather, *in the midst of much conflict* arising from persecution.

(3) "The reason that we were able to endure so much was our consciousness of the sincerity and purity of our attention."

Exhortation.—Exhortation is an attempt to make men take a particular line of action. "*Our* efforts to get men to act as we wish," St. Paul says, "do not spring from a desire to dupe them," etc. It is a question whether "of deceit" is the right rendering, or "of error," "all a mistake." If the latter, the argument would be that of Paley's *Evidences, i.e.*, to deduce the truth of the revelation from the sufferings of its prophets. But the points raised in contrast, in verses 4—12, seem to preclude this meaning, which would be more likely to introduce some substantiation of the gospel truths, as in 2 Pet. i. 16.

Of uncleanness.—It is possible that the word only means "with impure (or *covetous*) motives;" but it probably refers to the subtle forms of temptation which often accompany spiritual work. See, for example, the Greek of 1 Tim. i. 5; also v. 1, 2; 2 Tim. iii. 4—7.

In guile.—The preposition is changed; "nor yet by the use of tricks." Not only were their motives sincere and pure, but their manner of dealing straightforward.

(4) **Were allowed.** — Rather, *have been*, and in verse 3 *is*, not "was." St. Paul is arguing from his habitual practice. "But we speak after the manner of men who remember that God Himself has tried them, and has been satisfied to entrust the gospel to them, making it our business to please, not men, but God who thus tries our hearts" (1 Cor. iv. 1, 2). The word translated "allowed" implies examining and approving (as in Luke xiv. 19; 1 Tim. iii. 10; 1 Pet. i. 7; 1 John iv. 1), and is repeated emphatically (translated "trieth"): "being examined and approved by God, we study to please Him who constantly examines and approves us, not to court those to whom we are sent." St. Paul expresses here, as elsewhere, a total disregard of men's opinions about him (1 Cor. iv. 3; Gal. i. 10).

(5) **At any time.**—Not only during the stay at Thessalonica, but neither at Thessalonica nor elsewhere, as the next verse shows. But as the Thessalonians can only be appealed to as evidence for their own experience, the writers therefore call God Himself to witness. At the same time, the absence of flattering words was a thing of which human witnesses could judge; the freedom from covetous designs was known to God alone.

Cloke of covetousness—*i.e.*, some specious pretext, under cover of which we might gain a worldly advantage; so (though the Greek word is different) 1 Pet. ii. 16, "a cloke of maliciousness."

(6) **Glory**—*i.e., recognition of our splendid position*, as in the phrase "giving glory to God," *i.e.*, "recognising Him for what He is," John v. 44. (Comp. John xii. 43; Rom. ii. 29; 1 Cor. iv. 5.)

Been burdensome.—The marginal reading is on the whole preferable. The original is, *might have been in weight*—*i.e.*, "have dealt heavily with you," in all the pomp of apostolic dignity, making people acknowledge our "glory." Although, no doubt, one means of asserting their authority would have been to claim their maintenance from the Church (comp. 1 Cor. ix. 1—6), more is meant than the mere obtaining of money.

Apostles of Christ.—The title seems here to be bestowed on St. Silas and St. Timothy just as in Acts xiv. 14 upon St. Barnabas. As *official dignity* is here the point, it cannot simply (according to the etymology of the word) mean "Christ's *missionaries*," as we speak of "the Apostle of England," &c., *i.e.*, the earliest great preacher of the gospel there. The episcopal office (which St. Timothy, at any rate, held somewhat later) may perhaps be here ranked with the apostolate. Thus, in Gal. i. 19, St. James, the Bishop of Jerusalem, wears the title, though it is scarcely probable that he was one of the Twelve. Andronicus and Junias, in Rom. xvi. 7; Epaphroditus, in Phil. ii. 25 (where it is wrongly translated "messenger," as also in 2 Cor. viii. 23), are called Apostles. In 1 Cor. xii. 28, Eph. iv. 11, probably also in Eph. ii. 20, Rev. ii. 2, the first rank in the threefold ministry of the Church seems to be meant, for the reference is to the orderly Organisation of the Society. However, in our present passage it may conceivably be stretched to mean "as an Apostle and his following." The definite article should be struck out.

(7) **Among you.**—Rather, *in the midst of you*, making the gentleness still more marked. "Her," in the Greek emphatically *her own*. The contrast is drawn between the charlatan, licentious, sophistical, fawning, greedy, vainglorious teachers, to whom Greeks were well accustomed, and the Apostles, sitting familiarly like mothers amidst a group of their own children, folding them for warmth to their bosoms. "Keep a

(8) so being affectionately desirous of you,
we were willing to have imparted unto
you, not the gospel of God only, but also
our own souls,[a] because ye were dear unto
us. (9) For ye remember, brethren, our
labour and travail: for labouring night
and day, because we would not be
chargeable unto any of you, we preached
unto you the gospel of God. (10) Ye
are witnesses, and God *also*, how holily
and justly and unblameably we behaved
ourselves among you that believe: (11) as
ye know how we exhorted and comforted and charged every one of you, as
a father *doth* his children,[b] (12) that ye
would walk worthy of God, who hath
called you unto his kingdom and glory.

Chap. ii. 13–16. The converts' acceptance of the gospel, and persecution by the Jews.

(13) For this cause also
thank we God without
ceasing, because, when ye
received the word of God
which ye heard of us, ye
received *it* not *as* the word of men, but
as it is in truth, the word of God,
which effectually worketh[c] also in you
that believe. (14) For ye, brethren,
became followers of the churches of
God which in Judæa are in Christ
Jesus: for ye also have suffered like
things of your own countrymen, even as
they *have* of the Jews: (15) who both
killed the Lord Jesus, and their own

a Rom. 9. 3.

c Acts 19. 20.

b 1 Cor. 4. 15.

---

mother's heart for men," was the advice which made Henri Perreyve's life so winning (*Méditations*, p. 87).

(8) **So** means here *even so*, confirming the simile, and is not to be taken in the sense of "therefore."

Not the gospel of God only.—The gospel was, as it were, the milk given to the young converts; but the nursing mothers were ready to let them draw their very life away, so dearly did they love them.

(9) **For.**—As in verse 1, the general principles of the foregoing verses are supported by facts which the Thessalonians will remember. If the word attaches itself to any particular phrase, it is to "impart our own souls," "we were ready to die for you; indeed, you remember how we worked ourselves almost to death."

Labour and travail—not mere synonyms here: the first describes the *kind* of work; the second, the intensity of it: "our manual labour, and how hard we worked at that."

(10) **Ye are witnesses.**—Abruptly, without conjunction, the writers add a summary description of their conduct at Thessalonica; before, they had dwelt on details, now, on the broad characteristics. As in verse 5, *God* is appealed to, because the readers could only judge of the outward propriety of their teachers' conduct; and it is a moral law that (as Aristotle says) "the righteous man is not he that does acts which in themselves are righteous, but he that does those acts in *such a mind* as befits righteous men."

Holily, of the inner, "justly," of the outer life.

Among you that believe—where (if anywhere) we might have been tempted to be lax or exorbitant.

(11) **As** (emphatic): "*we* lived holily—just (in fact) as you remember we tried to induce each one of *you* to live."

Every one.—Now they appeal to the *individual* recollection of the Thessalonians. It gives us an incidental glimpse of the apostolic method,—which was, to deal with individual souls. (Comp. Acts xx. 20, 31; Col. i. 21.) St. Chrysostom exclaims: "Fancy! not one in all that multitude passed over!" The image is changed from that of motherly tenderness to that of fatherly direction.

Comforted is here used as almost equivalent to "exhorted," or, rather, *encouraged*, when the moral aspirations were beginning to flag.

Charged.—Better, *adjured*; so Gal. v. 3.

(12) **Hath called.**—The right reading is, *was calling*, which has been altered because of the slight theological difficulty, on the analogy of Gal. i. 6, etc. The call is not simply a momentary act, but a *continual* beckoning upwards, until the privileges offered are actually attained. The Thessalonians at that time, though already by baptism members of the kingdom (Col. i. 13), were not yet so assured in their new allegiance as to be certain of reaching the full-developed *glory* of that kingdom. Note again the thought of the Advent.

(13) The first part of this chapter draws attention to the *Apostles'* part in the conversion of Thessalonica. From this point (roughly speaking) to the end of chap. iii., the action of the *converts* is the chief subject.

This verse differs from the original in several particulars of more or less importance. Literally translated, it would run thus: *And for this cause we too thank God unceasingly, that, on receiving a word of hearing at our lips of God, ye welcomed, not a word of men, but* (*as it is in truth*) *a word of God, which also*, etc.

For this cause—viz., because of the labours we went through to teach you, which we are thankful were not wasted. *We too*, as well as you. The two words rendered "received" are not the same; the first meaning merely an outward reception, the second the welcome given. The words "it" and "as" (as the italics show) do not stand in the Greek. St. Paul is not expressing so much his gratitude for the manner in which the word was greeted, as for the essential character of what was greeted.

The word of God which ye heard of us.—The same phrase as in Heb. iv. 2, which is there rendered, "the word preached." "The word might have been, so far as you knew, a mere *word spoken by us*—ordinary men—but it was in reality a word of God, and so you found when you embraced it."

You that believe.—It could have no effect without this condition. (See Heb. iv. 2.)

(14) **For ye.**—"The effectual power of this word upon you is shown in your joining the Church in spite of such difficulties."

Followers.—Better, *imitators*. The churches of Judæa are probably selected for example, not only as being the oldest and best-organised churches, but the most afflicted, both by want (Acts xi. 29; xxiv. 17; Rom. xv. 26), and (chiefly) by persecution from the "Jews."

Your own countrymen.—See Acts xvii. 8, 9. It was always the Jewish policy to persecute by means of others. Evidently the Thessalonian Church is almost entirely Gentile.

(15) **Who both killed.**—A tremendous invective against the Jews, the purpose of which is (1) to show

prophets, and have persecuted[1] us; and they please not God, and are contrary to all men: (16) forbidding us to speak to the Gentiles that they might be saved, to fill up their sins alway: for the wrath is come upon them to the uttermost.

(17) But we, brethren, being taken from you for a short time in presence, not in heart,[a] endeavoured the more abundantly to see your face with great desire. (18) Wherefore we would have come unto you, even I Paul, once and again; but Satan hindered us. (19) For what *is* our hope, or joy, or crown of rejoicing?[2] *Are* not even ye in the presence of our Lord Jesus Christ

Chaps. ii. 17—iii. 10. Hopes and fears and longings for renewal of intercourse.

1 Or, *chased us out.*

2 Or, *glorying.*

a 1 Cor. 5. 3; Col. 2. 5.

---

the deep sympathy of St. Paul with the persecuted Thessalonians, and his indignation against the persecutors; (2) to make them see still more deeply the value of their faith by the efforts made to keep it from them. Objection is often made to St. John's Gospel on the ground that no born Jew could have written of "the Jews" in the bitter way so common in that book, or viewed them so completely as a separate body from himself. This passage, in an indubitable epistle of "a Hebrew of the Hebrews," seems a satisfactory answer. The memories of St. Stephen's speech (Acts vii. 52) seem to be waking in the mind of him who was once a persecuting Jew himself.

Have persecuted.—Take the marginal version, "chased" (not "*have* chased") "us violently out of Thessalonica."

They please not God—(though to serve and please Him was the special purpose for which the nation was set apart,) "and are at cross purposes with all mankind." The historian Tacitus gives, as a characteristic of the race, "an attitude of hostility and hatred towards all others." Juvenal makes the same accusation.

(16) **Forbidding us to speak to the Gentiles.**—The Apostle indicates the special way in which their contrariety showed itself.

To fill up.—Literally, *unto the filling up.* Not exactly their *intention* in forbidding, but the end to which such conduct was steadily ("alway") tending. (Again comp. Acts vii. 51, and Matt. xxiii. 32.) St. Paul seems to mean that there may be a certain sum of wickedness which God will allow a nation, a church, a person, to complete, before cutting them off from all spiritual help; the Jews were industriously labouring to complete the sum.

For.—The Greek word is *but;* and the point is this:—"The Jews have been working up to the rounded perfection of their sin; but (they had not much left to do) the wrath burst suddenly upon them to its uttermost." The word for "is come" (which should be the simple preterite "came") is the same as that used in Matt. xii. 28, Luke xi. 20, of a sudden, unexpected apparition. "The wrath" is the wrath from which Jesus is delivering us (chap. i. 10), and it had already come upon the Jews, though its outward manifestation in the destruction of Jerusalem was not to come yet awhile. The particular moment at which St. Paul means that the wrath "came" must have been the moment of their final rejection of the Messiah.

(17) **But we, brethren.**—Now comes a change of subject: no longer the memories of the time when St. Paul was among them, but his hopes and fears about them since he left.

"But while you were being persecuted by these reprobate Jews, we, who were driven away from you, were longing to come back to see whether your faith was such an effectual working faith as to support you through it all."

Taken from you.—Literally, *bereaved from you*—*i.e.,* bereaved by being torn from you; a return to the simile of the mother (ii. 7), or father (ii. 11).

The more abundantly.—"So far were we from the proverb, 'out of sight, out of mind,' that our very absence gave us a greater yearning after your presence" (1 Cor. v. 3).

(18) **We would.**—Not merely a conditional tense, but "we were ready to come—meant to come."

Even I Paul.—Rather, *that is to say, I, Paul,* not as if it were a great thing that one like *him* should have such a wish, but showing that Silas and Timothy had not shared his intention. Why had they not? The answer shows the minute truthfulness of the Acts. Timothy, apparently, did not at first *leave* Thessalonica with St. Paul (Acts xvii. 10, where the Greek seems definitely to exclude him). Both Silas and Timothy were left at Berœa (Acts xvii. 14). It was during this period that St. Paul felt so eager a desire to return to his persecuted children. We cannot tell on what two definite occasions the desire was almost taking shape; but possibly his longing may have been stimulated by seeing his messengers start for the north, first when he sent for his two companions (Acts xvii. 15), and secondly when he despatched Timothy himself to Thessalonica (chap. iii. 2).

But Satan hindered.—How, cannot be decided; but St. Paul has no doubt that his disappointment was a direct manifestation of the work of evil, not a leading of God to stay where he was. Elsewhere he is quite as clear that the obstruction of his own plans is owing to God. (See Acts xvi. 6, 7; 1 Cor. xvi. 12, where the will spoken of is not Apollos' will, but God's.) The difficulty is to tell in each case whether God is directly saving us from a worse course, in spite of ourselves, or permitting a momentary, and yet if rightly used a disciplinary, triumph of evil.

Satan.—The Thessalonians, though originally Gentiles, had doubtless been taught enough at their conversion to recognise the word. Though it is quite clear from other passages (*e.g.,* 1 Cor. vii. 5; 2 Thess. ii. 9; 1 Tim. iii. 7) that St. Paul believed in the existence of personal fallen spirits, it cannot be positively affirmed that he *here* means anything more than a *personification* of all that is opposed to God—the hostility of wicked men, &c.

(19) "We were most anxious to come and stablish you for we should lose all our hope and joy and honours if Christ should come and we should have lost you."

Our hope—*i.e.,* the object on which our hopes are centered.

Crown of rejoicing.—Or, *of boasting;* "crown that we are proud to wear," like victors in the games For the meaning of such phrases, see Note on chap. i. 3

Even ye—(not necessarily excluding other converts) *just you, and others like you.*

In the presence.—"It is the thought of presenting you to Him that thrills us with hope, joy, pride—the

at his coming? [a] (20) For ye are our
glory and joy.

CHAPTER III.—(1) Wherefore when
we could no longer forbear, we thought
it good to be left at Athens alone;
(2) and sent Timotheus, our brother,
and minister of God, and our fellow-
labourer in the gospel of Christ, to
establish you, and to comfort you con-
cerning your faith: (3) that no man
should be moved by these afflictions:
for yourselves know that we are ap-
pointed thereunto. [b] (4) For verily, when
we were with you, we told you before
that we should suffer tribulation; [c] even
as it came to pass, and ye know. (5) For
this cause, when I could no longer for-
bear, I sent to know your faith, lest by
some means the tempter [d] have tempted

a 2 Cor. 1. 14; Phil. 4. 1.

A.D. 54.

b Acts 14. 22; 2 Tim. 3. 12.

c John 13. 19; 16. 1, 4.

d Matt. 4. 3.

---

thought of wearing such a decoration *before Him.*" (Comp. 2 Cor. xi. 2.)

III.

(1) **We could no longer forbear.**—The Greek word contains the metaphor of a vessel over-full and bursting with its contents. "We" must be understood here by the limitation of chap. ii. 18, and by the direct singular of verse 5, to mean St. Paul alone, not him and Silas.

To be left at Athens alone.—The difficulty of interpreting this passage so as to agree with Acts xvii. 15, 16; xviii. 5, is not a light one. From those passages it would appear that immediately upon reaching Athens, St. Paul sent word back to Macedonia, by the friends who had escorted him, that St. Silas and St. Timothy should join him at once; but that some delay took place, and that St. Paul had arrived at Corinth before his companions reached him; that they consequently never were with him at Athens. In that case, "to be left alone" must mean, "We resolved not to keep with us the brethren who escorted us;" and the "sent" of verse 2 will mean that he gave them a message to Timothy that he should go back to Thessalonica (presumably from Berœa), before joining St. Paul at Athens; for the *tense* of the Greek verb "to be left" absolutely necessitates an *act* of parting with some one: it cannot mean, "We were willing to endure loneliness a little longer." But such an interpretation suits ill with Acts xvii. 15; it is hard to identify an urgent message to "come with all speed" with a command to make such a *détour.* It seems, therefore, most reasonable to suppose that Silas and Timothy joined St. Paul forthwith at Athens, and were almost as soon sent back into Macedonia,—Silas to Berœa or Philippi, and Timothy to Thessalonica. This would explain St. Paul's being left *alone,* an expression which would hardly have been used had Silas remained with him at Athens, as some (misled by the word "we") have supposed; and also it explains how in Acts xviii. 5 both Timothy *and Silas* come from Macedonia to Corinth. The despatching of *Silas* from Athens is not mentioned here, simply because it had no particular interest for the Thessalonians. If the two men did not reach St. Paul at all during the time he was at Athens, after receiving so imperative a message, they must have been very slow, for a week would have allowed ample time for their journey from Berœa, and Acts xvii. 17, xviii. 1 certainly imply a much longer period of residence there. "To be left alone" was a great trial to St. Paul's affectionate nature: such a sacrifice may well impress the Thessalonians with the strength of his love for them.

(2) **Sent.**—It may possibly mean that a message was despatched to him at Berœa, ordering him to go, but is far more naturally understood if Timothy were at Athens at the time.

And minister . . .—The text here, according to the judgment of most of the best editors (though Tischendorf in his last edition has modified his opinion), is interpolated, and the verse should run: "our brother, and God's fellow-worker in the gospel of Christ." Timothy being a person so well known at Thessalonica, it is difficult to see why he should be thus particularised, unless he was the bearer of the letter, and St. Paul wished to insist upon their paying him due deference in spite of his youth.

To establish, perhaps in the sense of perfecting their organisation.

To comfort is here equivalent to "to encourage."

(3) **Moved,** or more literally, *seduced.* The very peculiar word in the original means, in the first instance, the *fawning* of an animal upon its master: then, through the intermediate sense of "wheedling," it comes to mean the gradual detachment of a person from his resolution by *any* insinuating representations, whether of flattery or (as here) of fear. The next word should be *in* or *in the midst of,* rather than "by", therefore (though both may be included) their own "afflictions" are chiefly meant, not St. Paul's.

For yourselves. —"Your previous expectation that Christianity involved the suffering of persecution ought to be enough to prevent you now from losing your faith."

We are appointed thereunto.—The "we" means all Christian people: their election into the Church must needs be an election to suffering (see marg. refs.). "No cross, no crown."

(4) **For verily, when . . .**—To appreciate the nature of the argument, see the passages referred to in the margin.

(5) **For this cause.**—"Because I knew that temptation was sure to overtake you, I sent to see whether our work still lived, and was likely to live, in spite of it."

To know your faith.—"To ascertain whether you still believed:" only the form courteously implies that the faith was certainly *there,* and St. Paul only sent to "make assurance doubly sure."

The tempter.—See Matt. iv. 3. The word and the tense in the Greek imply, not only that it is his character to tempt, but that it is his constant *occupation.*

Have tempted you . . . .—The original implies no doubt on the writer's part that the Thessalonians *had* been tempted; the only doubt was, how they had borne it. The striking out of the comma after "tempted you," and reading the clauses quickly together, will give a fair notion of the purport. It might be paraphrased, "Lest, in consequence of the temptations which the tempter brought against you, our toil should prove in vain." The "temptations" were those of persecution, and the time at which they befell, the same as in verse 4, "it came to pass."

you, and our labour be in vain.[a] (6) But
now when Timotheus came from you
unto us,[b] and brought us good tidings
of your faith and charity, and that ye
have good remembrance of us always,
desiring greatly to see us, as we also
to see you: (7) therefore, brethren, we
were comforted over you in all our
affliction and distress by your faith:
(8) for now we live, if ye stand fast in
the Lord. (9) For what thanks can we
render[c] to God again for you, for all the
joy wherewith we joy for your sakes
before our God; (10) night and day
praying exceedingly that we might see
your face,[d] and might perfect that
which is lacking in your faith?
(11) Now God himself and our Father,
and our Lord Jesus Christ,
direct[1] our way unto you.
(12) And the Lord make
you to increase and abound
in love one toward another, and toward
all *men*, even as we *do* toward you:

Chap. iii. 11–13. Prayer introductory to the instruction.

a Gal. 4. 11; Phil. 2. 16.

b Acts 18. 5.

d Rom. 15. 30, 32.

1 Or, *guide*.

c Ps. 116. 12.

---

(6) "We were in great anxiety, for fear you should have fallen away, and sent Timothy to see if all was well; but now, all anxiety is over."

Timotheus came.—According to the usual interpretation of verses 1, 2, adopted above, this will mean that Timothy had already returned from his mission to Thessalonica, as related in Acts xviii. 5, and the occasion of this present letter will be St. Paul's relief at the news brought by him.

Brought us good tidings.—An enthusiastic word, generally rendered, "preached us the gospel."

Faith and charity.—The first signifies the confidence in God which enabled them to endure ("that in all our troubles we may put our whole trust and confidence in Thy mercy"); the second, the tenderness with which they helped one another through.

Good remembrance.—Not merely "clear, vivid remembrance" (as we say, "to remember well"), but "a good, kind remembrance," as the explanation in "desiring," &c., shows. The word "good" bears the same significance in Matt. xx. 15; Rom. v. 7; 1 Pet. ii. 18. If the Thessalonians had been beginning to fall away, they would not have cared to see their teachers.

(7) **In all our affliction and distress.**—The words give no decisive indication whether the distress came from within or from without, and it is impossible to specify in what it consisted; but either way it suits very well with Acts xviii. 5—17; 1 Cor. ii. 3.

(8) **Now we live, if.**—"Now" contrasts the new life and vigour which the "gospel of their faith and charity" had infused into the Apostle, with the deadly sinking he had felt at the thought of their possible apostacy. At the same time the "if" has the half-future sense, as though St. Paul meant that the continuance of this "life" was contingent upon their continued steadfastness. Another interpretation has been suggested, according to which both the "we" and "ye" are perfectly general, and therefore interchangeable, and the sense is made to be a vague proposition, "for standing fast in the Lord is a *sine quâ non* of life"—life in the theological sense: and parts of Rom. vii. and viii. are compared. This interpretation, however, suits the Greek as little as the context.

(9) **For what thanks can we render.**—An apology for the enthusiastic expressions used in the three foregoing verses. "I may call it a gospel, a balm for all anxieties, a new life, for what mode of thanksgiving could be deemed extravagant in such a case of joy?"

Before our God.—As in chap. i. 3, the occasion on which the joy and thankfulness bursts out is "in prayer;" perhaps, in connection with *thanksgiving*, especially at the great Eucharistic Thanksgiving (1 Cor. xiv. 16), when he "stood before the Lord" in a special manner (Acts xiii. 2; comp. Lev. i. 3, 11; iii. 1, *et al.*).

(10) **See your face.**—Seeing them by proxy might satisfy for the while, but not for long. This exceeding importunate prayer is caused by the feeling that it was Satan's hindrance (chap. ii. 18), not God's will, which forbad the meeting. He would not so have prayed to go into Bithynia (Acts xvi. 7), for the essence of prayer is to conform the will to God's will.

That which is lacking in your faith.—Bishop Wordsworth points out the unflattering faithfulness of St. Paul's dealing with his converts. What the deficiencies were is unknown, but they certainly include want of knowledge of the state of the dead and concerning the Advent.

(11) **God himself and our Father.**—Better, *our God and Father Himself.* If we are to find any special person with whom the word "Himself" is intended to enforce a contrast, the contrast is probably not so much with the baffled efforts of St. Paul, as with Satan, who had hindered the journey. But the word is probably added without such specific reference: "May God Himself direct us; for in that case who could hinder?"

And our Lord . . .—An important theological passage. From the use of the *singular* in the verb "direct" (which of course the English cannot express), some divines argue in favour of the Catholic doctrine of "homoüsion," or *substantial* unity of the Son with the Father: it must not, however, be too strongly pressed, or it might otherwise lead to the false notion of a *personal* unity between Them. Nevertheless, we may admit that the prayer (or, rather, *wish*) implies the *equality* of the two Persons, and that it would have been inconceivable for a Catholic Christian to have used the verb in the plural. (See 2 Thess. ii. 17.)

(12) **And the Lord make you.**—The word *you* in the Greek is emphatic and stands first. The wish in the previous verse concerned the *writers*: "But *you* (whether we come or not) may the Lord make," &c. By "the Lord" here St. Paul seems to mean not only the Son: the word appears to be an equivalent for the name of God.

Increase and abound.—These words make the readers think first of progress and then of the state to which the progress will bring them—"Multiply you in love until you have enough and to spare of it"—and the same progress is expressed by the *objects* of the swelling charity: "So that you may not only love one another abundantly, but all mankind"—missionary efforts being the supreme work of Christian love—"such loving missionary work" (the writers go on to say) "as *ours* among *you*."

(13) to the end he may stablish your hearts unblameable in holiness before God, even our Father, at the coming of our Lord Jesus Christ with all his saints.[a]

CHAPTER IV.—(1) Furthermore then we beseech[1] you, brethren, and exhort[2] *you* by the Lord Jesus, that as ye have received of us how ye ought to walk[b] and to please God, *so* ye would abound more and more. (2) For ye know what commandments we gave you by the Lord Jesus. (3) For this is the will of God,[c] *even* your sanctification, that ye should abstain from fornication: (4) that every one of you should know how to possess his vessel[d] in sanctification and

Chap. iv. 1—8. On the duty of chastity.

b ch. 2. 12.

a ch. 4. 14.

c Rom. 12. 2; Eph. 5. 17.

1 Or, *request.*

2 Or, *beseech*

d 1 Sam. 21. 5.

---

(13) **To the end.**—A beautiful connection of thought. Perfect and settled sanctification in the eyes of God is the object in view, and the means by which it is to be attained is growing and overflowing love toward mankind. (See Col. iii. 14.) St. Paul is already thinking, probably, how he shall treat the subject of chastity in the next chapter. (See Note on chap. iv. 6.)

Before God . . . at the coming.—The hearts are to be unblamably holy before God—not only all through life, but also at the Judgment Day, when Jesus Christ is to judge us in the Father's presence. Though He has "committed all judgment unto the Son" (John v. 22), yet the judgment is His own, and the Son is the agent *by* whom He judges, just as He is the agent by whom He creates (see Acts xvii. 31): therefore in that day it is in the Father's sight rather than in the Son's (though there can be no divergence between Them) that we are to be able to clear ourselves.

With all his saints—*i.e.*, attended by them:—

"Thousand, thousand saints *attending,*
Swell the triumph of His train."

The word might possibly be stretched to include the holy angels (Deut. xxxiii. 2; Dan. iv. 13, *et al.*); but here we may more probably suppose that St. Paul is anticipating his teaching of chap. iv. 14, and besides, the Greek seems almost to indicate that these "saints" are to be assessors in the judgment—an honour to be given only to holy men. (Comp. Luke xxii. 30; John v. 28; 1 Cor. vi. 3, *et al.*)

IV.

(1) We now approach the practical portion of the Epistle. The first point on which the Thessalonians need instruction is in the matter of social purity (verses 1—8).

Furthermore hardly expresses the original. St. Paul is not adding a further injunction, for he has as yet given none. It is literally, *For the rest, then;* and serves to introduce the conclusion of the letter.

Beseech.—The marginal *request* is better, the word being one of calm and friendly asking, implying that the person so addressed will recognise the propriety of complying.

Exhort is correct, though "encourage" suits the context a little better, as assuming that they are already so acting, but not with enough heart.

By the Lord.—Better, *in the Lord.* It is not an adjuration, as in Rom. xii. 1, but states the authoritative ground of his request. "We encourage you, on the strength of our union in the Lord Jesus." (Comp. chap. i. 1.)

How ye ought to walk.—Literally, *the how.* It indicates that part of the apostolic tradition was a systematic moral code, almost as if it were the title of a well-known book. "We gave you the 'How ye ought to walk, so as to please God.'" The best texts add immediately after, "even as also ye walk."

Abound more and more.—Or, *still more.* "You *did* receive of us the rules of a holy life; you *are* living by them, and that to a very large degree; but we beg you and encourage you, on the faith of Christians, to be still more lavish in your self-denial."

(2) **For ye know.**—He calls on the Thessalonians' memory to support his statement, "ye received;" at the same time awakening their interest to catch the special point next to come, by laying stress on "*what* commandments."

By the Lord Jesus.—Not as if the Lord were the person who took the commandments from St. Paul to the Thessalonians, but the person by means of whose inspiration St. Paul was enabled to give such commandments.

(3) **For.**—The word further enforces the appeal to their memory: "Ye *know* what commandments . . . for *this* (you will recollect) is what God wants;" "a commandment given through the Lord Jesus," being, of course, identical with "God's will."

Your sanctification.—In apposition to the word *this.* The mere conversion, justification, salvation of us are not the aim of God: He would have us holy. The general idea of sanctification passes however here, as the following clauses show, into the more limited sense of purification.

Fornication.—The word is often used in late Greek for any kind of impurity, as, *e.g.*, 1 Cor. v. 1, of incest; but here it must be understood in its strict sense. To the Gentile mind, while the wickedness of adultery or incest was fully recognised, it was a novelty to be told that fornication was a "deadly sin;" hence the strange connection in which it stands in the Synodal letter to the Gentile churches (Acts xv. 20, 29; xxi. 25). This consideration also makes it easier to understand how St. Paul can praise these Gentile Thessalonians so heartily, although they need earnest correction on this vital point. It is a true instance of the sacerdotal *metriopathy* (or, *compassionate consideration*) towards the ignorant and deceived. (See Heb. v. 1, 2.)

(4) **Should know.**—The clause is simply parallel to the last, and, with it, explains the word "sanctification." The Bulgarian Father, Theophylact, says pointedly in reference to the word "to know" or "understand," "He indicates that chastity is a matter that requires self-discipline and study." (Comp. Eph. v. 17.)

To possess his vessel.—The word rendered "to possess" should rather be translated, *to procure, win, gain possession of.* The word "vessel" here has been interpreted in two ways: (1) "his wife;" (2) "his body." In favour of (1) it is argued that (while "gaining possession of one's own body" is unintelligible), "acquiring a wife of one's own" is an ordinary Greek expression; that in this context, "a vessel," or "instrument," is an expressive and natural metaphor; that the word was familiar to Hebrew speakers in that sense (*e.g.*, Ahasuerus says of Vashti, in one

honour; (5) not in the lust of con-
cupiscence, even as the Gentiles which
know not God: (6) that no *man* go
beyond and defraud[1] his brother in *any*
matter:[2] because that the Lord *is* the
avenger of all such, as we also have
forewarned you and testified. (7) For
God hath not called us unto unclean-
ness, but unto holiness. (8) He there-
fore that despiseth,[3] despiseth not man,

1 Or, *oppress*, or, *overreach*.
2 Or, *in the matter*.
3 Or, *rejecteth*.

---

of the Targums, "My vessel which I use is neither Median nor Persian, but Chaldee"); that St. Peter (1 Pet. iii. 7) uses the word of the wife. But it may be answered that this interpretation does not suit our context; first, because it would be laying an emphatic and binding veto upon celibacy, if "each one" is "to acquire a wife of his own;" secondly, because of the verb "to know," it certainly being no part of a religious man's duty "to *know how* to procure a wife;" thirdly, because the Greek cannot be translated "*a* vessel (or *wife*) of his own," but "*his own* vessel" (or *wife*)—literally, *the vessel of himself*—and to speak of "procuring" the wife who is already one's own seems unmeaning. Furthermore, although the quotations from the Targums are certainly to the point, that from St. Peter distinctly points the other way, inasmuch as the wife is called "the weaker vessel of the two," evidently meaning that the husband is also "a vessel." Thus we are driven to suppose that (2) the "vessel" is the man's own self. This usage also is well supported. In 1 Sam. xxi. 5, it is used in precisely this sense, and in the same context, as well as in 1 Pet. iii. 7. The passages, however, usually quoted in support of this interpretation from 2 Cor. iv. 7, Philo, Barnabas, Lucretius, &c., do not seem quite parallel; for there the word signifies a "vessel," in the sense of a receptacle for *containing* something; here it is rather "an instrument" or "implement" for *doing* something. Hence it approaches more nearly to the use in such phrases as Acts ix. 15, "a vessel of choice," or even (though the Greek word is different) to Rom. vi. 13. "The vessel of himself" (the "himself" being in the Greek strongly emphasised) means, not "the vessel which is his own," but "the vessel or instrument which consists of himself." Thus the body, which of course is chiefly meant here, is not dissociated from the man's personality, as in the fanciful Platonism of Philo, but almost identified with it: the Incarnation has taught us the true dignity of the body. Thus it becomes easy to understand what is meant by "knowing how to gain possession of" such an instrument as the body with its many faculties, rescuing it from its vile prostitution, and wielding it wisely for its proper uses. So the same Greek verb is used, and mistranslated in our version, in Luke xxi. 19, "In your patience possess ye your souls."

In sanctification and honour.—The circumstances *in* which—almost the means *by* which—the man may acquire and keep this skilful power over his instrument:—"*in a course* of self-purification and of self-reverence." The reverence due to the instrument is brought out in a passage of St. Peter evidently modelled upon this (1 Pet. iii. 7). (Comp. also 2 Tim. ii. 21, "an instrument for honourable purposes, and to be honourably treated, consecrated, and handy for its owner's use.")

(5) **Not in the lust of concupiscence,** for such a method of using one's faculties, such an attempt to acquire mastery of vital powers, is really to abandon them altogether to others. This notion is involved in the very word here translated "lust," which is more often rendered "passion," and implies something which *befalls* a man, something *done to* him: "Not in the helpless passivity of concupiscence" or uncontrolled desire.

The Gentiles which know not God.—Mind the punctuation. The readers of the letter were "Gentiles which *knew* God." Their brother Thessalonians are held up to them as melancholy examples of men who are trying in the wrong way to show their power over themselves. Remark that this is not one of the crimes which he alleges against Jews.

(6) **That no man.**—The form of the Greek shows that this is not exactly *parallel* with the preceding clauses, as if it ran, "this is God's will, your sanctification, for you to abstain, for you to know how to possess, for you not to go beyond," &c. It is a *final* clause, expressing the *purpose* of such continence as has just been described. Men are to be chaste and self-possessed, not only for their own salvation's sake, but in justice to their brethren. In chap. iii. 12, 13, they were to love for the sake of becoming holy; here they are to be holy for the sake of charity—a blessed action and reaction.

Defraud his brother.—The original word implies a rapacious dishonesty, of which any person is guilty who gives the rein to his lusts, especially the adulterer. The substantive formed from it is usually translated *covetousness*, and is generally thought to be used in this special sense in Eph. v. 3; Col. iii. 5. When all men are *brethren* the sin becomes worse.

In any matter should undoubtedly be *in the matter*. St. Paul chooses the phrase for delicacy's sake, both here and in 2 Cor. vii. 11.

Because that the Lord.—Again an anticipation of the Advent, for the vengeance meant is that of the Judgment Day, not the natural retribution which carnal sin brings with it. The "Lord," therefore, in this context probably means more particularly the Incarnate Son, who has a special claim upon men's bodies (1 Cor. vi. 13).

Have forewarned.—Rather, *did forewarn*. It was part of the Apostles' original teaching at Thessalonica.

(7) **For God.**—This gives the reason for stating that the Lord will take vengeance on such sins; because they are not part of the terms on which His Father called us. It should be "*did* not call." These verses 7, 8, sum up the little disquisition, returning to the principle announced in verse 3.

Unto uncleanness, but unto holiness.—The preposition translated "unto" has the same force in Gal. v. 13, "Called unto liberty," and Eph. ii. 10, "Created unto good works." It implies not so much the definite *end* to which we are invited, as the *terms* on which the invitation will still *stand;* for the call is not yet accomplished. (See Note on chap. ii. 12.) The second "unto" in the Greek is simply "in," used in the same sense as in verse 4. Paraphrase, "For God did not call us on the understanding that we might be unclean, but by the way of sanctification."

Holiness is a mistranslation for *sanctification.* The process, not the quality, is meant.

(8) "So you see that to act contumeliously in the matter is to act contumeliously not only towards your neighbour, but towards God Himself, and that, too, after He has given you a gift which should have preserved you from these corruptions."

but God, who hath also given unto us
his holy Spirit.
(9) But as touching brotherly love
ye need not that I write
unto you:[a] for ye yourselves
are taught of God[b] to
love one another. (10) And
indeed ye do it toward all the brethren
which are in all Macedonia: but we
beseech you, brethren, that ye increase
more and more; (11) and that
ye study to be quiet, and to do your
own business, and to work with your
own hands, as we commanded you;[c]

Chap. iv. 9—12. On regulating Christian fellow-feeling.

a ch. 5. 1.

b Jer. 31. 33, 34; John 6. 45; Heb. 8. 10, 11.

c 2 Thess. 3. 10.

He . . . that despiseth.—The verb means to treat as insignificant either persons or things. Here the *object* is not supplied in the first instance, in order to heighten the effect of the second clause. If we were to supply it, it would include *all* the rights which the unclean liver spurns, "the commandments which we (mere men as you thought us) gave you," the "brother" whose domestic happiness has been invaded, the unfortunate victim herself, and, finally, the "honour" due to the sinner's own body. Since it was God who ordered the relations in which we all stand to one another, contempt for these relations is contempt for Him.

Who hath also given.—Mistranslated for "who also *gave*." St. Paul is looking back to the day when he *confirmed* them; for the right reading is not "unto *us*," but "unto *you*," or more correctly "*into* you"—*i.e.*, "to enter into you, and dwell there" (John xiv. 17, and many other places). The word "holy" in the original is very emphatically put: "Who also gave His Spirit—His Holy Spirit—to enter you," thus bringing out the startling contrast between such foul lives and the holiness which befitted and was possible (Rom. vi. 14; viii. 3, 4) for men in whom the Holy Ghost, communicated by the laying on of hands, vouchsafed to dwell.

(9) **But . . .**—This forms the second subject of instruction, following naturally on the first. "We are very glad to hear of so strong a Christian feeling of brotherhood among you, and think it almost unnecessary to say anything more to you about it; still your charity is hardly *catholic* enough, nor have you exercised it with sufficient sobriety and thrift."

Brotherly love.—Not love of men at large, but of Christians in particular: in fact, pretty nearly what we call "Church feeling." It is the *natural affection* of those who feel that they are children of the same Father and the same mother (Gal. iv. 26), members of the same "household of faith" (Gal. vi. 10). In itself, it is not the most exalted of graces, being to some extent the outcome of community of interests; therefore St. Peter exhorts his readers to make it a means of obtaining the higher grace of *charity* (1 Pet. i. 22; 2 Pet. i. 7). St. Paul in this place does mean the sentiment rather than the practice, but has specially in view the exercise of liberality towards fellow-Christians. The feeling of community can only be known by acts that prove it.

Ye need not.—A sweet rhetorical figure, by which men are encouraged to the performance of a duty in which they are not perfect, by the praising of their imperfect attempts: a specimen of that "courtesy" which is a part of "brotherly love." (See 1 Pet. iii. 8.) "I" should be *we*, or *any*.

Ye yourselves.—It seems as if St. Paul had intended at first to say, "For ye yourselves know without any instruction," but suddenly inserts the *source* of their knowledge instead: "For ye yourselves are divinely taught already." This seems more natural to the context (though grammatically less easy) than to understand: "For ye yourselves (as well as we) are taught of God." (Comp., however, the references.) God's teaching here comes (though perhaps other modes are not excluded) by the direct contact with the indwelling Spirit. (See 1 John ii. 27.)

To love.—In the Greek this is not the simple infinitive after "taught;" it expresses rather the result and issue of God's teaching: "have been so schooled by God as to love one another." This love is not actually contrasted with the "brotherly kindness" above but means more.

(10) **And indeed ye do it**—*i.e.*, "love one another;" but the words seem to imply a very practical form of love. This fact justifies St. Paul in saying that the Thessalonians were so taught of God.

Toward.—Rather, *even unto*; *as far as unto*. The Thessalonians' charity has travelled already a long way from its starting-point at home, extending over all northern Greece. As Thessalonica had been the centre of evangelisation (chap. i. 8), so also of the maintenance of the Churches. The words need not necessarily (though they do probably) imply a number of missionary stations besides the three places where the Apostles had preached.

Increase more and more.—A little too emphatic: *abound* (or, *overflow*) *still more*. The words are identical with those in verse 1. The brotherly kindness of the Thessalonians did not spread over a wide enough area in merely traversing Macedonia, nor was it so unostentatious as true love should be.

(11) **And that ye study to be quiet.**—The word means more than "study;" "and that ye make it your ambition to keep quiet"—their ambition having formerly been to make a stir among the Churches. It is a strong use of the rhetorical figure called *oxymoron*, or combining words of contrary meaning in order to give force and point to the style. The warnings in this verse are not directed against *defiance* of the law of brotherly love, but against a thoroughly wrong mode of *showing* that love: the unquietness, meddlesomeness, desultoriness with which it was accompanied are not so much instances of unkindness to the brotherhood as scandals to the heathen. Hence the conjunction at the beginning of the verse has something of an adversative force: "We beg you to be even more abundantly liberal, and (yet) at the same time to agitate for perfect calmness about it." It is commonly supposed (but proof is impossible) that the unsettlement arose from belief in the nearness of the Advent.

Do your own business.—Not merely was each individual to do his own work, but the whole Church was to refrain from interfering ostentatiously with other Churches. In all languages, "to mind one's own business" signifies rather the negative idea of ceasing to meddle than the positive idea of industry.

Work with your own hands.—Apparently the Thessalonians had been so busy in organising away from home that they had had no time to see to their own industry, and so (see end of next verse) were beginning to fall into difficulties. The words "with your own hands" are supposed to indicate that most of the Thessalonian Christians were of the artisan class.

Chap. iv. 13–18. On the equality of quick and dead at Christ's Coming.

(12) that ye may walk honestly toward
them that are without,[a] and *that*
ye may have lack of
nothing.[1]
(13) But I would not
have you to be ignorant,[b]
brethren, concerning them which are
asleep, that ye sorrow not, even as
others which have no hope.[c] (14) For
if we believe that Jesus died and rose
again, even so them also which sleep
in Jesus [d] will God bring with him.

a 1 Pet. 2. 12.
c Eph. 2. 12.
1 Or, *of no man.*
d Rev. 14. 13.
b Rom. 1. 13; 11. 25; 1 Cor. 10. 1; 12. 1; 2 Cor. 1. 8.

---

(12) **Honestly.**—Not in our modern sense of the word, but "honourably," "creditably."

Toward—*i.e.,* "in reference to," "in your connection with." The heathen were certain to be watching the conduct of the members of the new religion, and it would bring down political suspicion if they were seen to be acting more like agitators for a secret society than honest citizens who worked at their handicraft and calling.

Of nothing. — Right: the marginal version is hardly consistent with the Greek. Two purposes will be fulfilled by their industry: (1) to allay heathen suspicion; (2) to be well supplied themselves. It seems as if they had been reduced to begging of other Churches in return for their own expensive charities.

(13) **But.** — We pass to the *third* clearly-marked point: the share of the Christian dead in the Coming of Christ. Possibly an association of ideas may have caused St. Paul to join these two subjects, of quietude and the Advent, so closely (see Note on verse 11). "You need have no distress about your dead: when Christ comes, they will be there too; they will come with Him, and we shall be caught up to meet them."

I would not have you to be ignorant.—The right reading is *we.* St. Paul is still speaking in the name of his companions as well as his own. The phrase is very weighty, and marks how lamentable such a piece of ignorance would be. (See references in the margin.)

Which are asleep.—The best reading is rather, *which fall asleep;* the grief renewed itself over each successive death-bed. The image of *sleep* is a mere metaphor, drawn from the outward *phenomena* of death, and is used as an *euphemism* for death; therefore no *doctrine* can be deduced with precision from it. It cannot be said (for instance) on the strength of such passages alone, that only the *body* sleeps, and not the soul; or, again, that the soul sleeps while the body remains in the grave. That the soul, or at any rate the *spirit,* still retains consciousness after dissolution is clear from other places; but when the metaphor of sleep is used, it is used of the *whole* man (*e.g.,* John xi. 11, "*Lazarus*"—not "Lazarus' body"—"sleepeth"), the explanation being either that stated above—*i.e.,* that the word is simply *picturesque,* describing the peaceful *appearance* of the dead—or that the reference is to *rest* from labour (Rev. xiv. 13). At the same time, the metaphor suggests (otherwise it would be misleading, and St. Paul would not have used it) a continued (even if partly unconscious) existence, and the possibility of a reawakening. Again, for the same reason—*i.e.,* because the word is metaphorical, not doctrinal—it cannot be limited to the *Christian* dead: when the writers need to mark specially the departed Christians they annex qualifying words, as in verse 14. Of course, on the mention of "the dead," the Thessalonians will at once think of their own brethren departed, so that there is no ambiguity.

That ye sorrow not.—The words express St. Paul's *object* in wishing them to know the truth. He wants them *not to sorrow at all* over the dead; sorrow is only fit for Gentiles who have no hope. He does not mean that they are not to sorrow *to the same degree* as those outside the Church, but that to Christians, who *have* a hope, and such a hope, death ought to have no sorrows. The Office of Burial in the Prayer-book is as joyous as the Eucharistic Office itself.

Others.—The Greek word is "the others, those who have no hope," and includes *all* who were *not* members of the Church: "That ye mourn not like the rest, which have no hope." The having no hope does not mean that there is no hope *for* them, but that *they* are not cheered by hope.

(14) **For if . . .**—A reason for thinking that if the Thessalonians knew and believed the truth, they ought not to be so miserable. The "if" implies no doubt: "if we believe (as we do), then," &c.—merely clearing the ground for a logical deduction. The writer does not care to *prove* so well-known a fact as the resurrection of Christ; he only argues from the clear faith of the Thessalonians with regard to it.

Jesus died and rose again.—Notice the human name; for though it is true that as God He raised Himself (John x. 18), *as man* He was no less dependent upon the Father than we are (Acts xvii. 31): therefore *His* resurrection is a real argument for *ours.* And the two verbs are put together because of their contrariety —"really died a human death, and yet rose again."

Even so.—The structure of the clauses is not quite regular. We should have expected either the omission of "we believe that" in the first, or the insertion of it in the second: it makes the statement of the second, however, more direct or authoritative.

Which sleep in Jesus.—Rather, *which were laid to sleep through Jesus.* The meaning of the preposition, however, is not widely different from "in." The simpler words in Rev. xiv. 13 mean "dying in full communion still with Him." Our present phrase makes Him, as it were, the *way,* or *door, by which* they journeyed to death: He *surrounded them as they sank to rest.* (Comp. John x. 9.) Additional sweetness is imparted to the phrase by the use of the metaphor of *sleep;* but it is, perhaps, too much to say, as Dean Alford does, that "falling asleep" is here contrasted with "dying," in this sense:—"Who through the power of Jesus fell asleep instead of dying"—for the word is even used of a *judicial punishment* of death in 1 Cor. xi. 30.

Will God bring with him—*i.e.,* with Jesus. In the Greek the word *God* stands in an unemphatic position—"Even so will God bring," implying that it was God also who had raised Jesus from the dead. But St. Paul is not content with saying, "Even so will God *raise* those who passed through Christ to death." The thought of the Advent is so supreme with him that he passes at once to a moment beyond resurrection. If the question be asked from *whence* God will bring the dead along with Christ, it must be answered, from Paradise, and the persons brought must be the disembodied *spirits;* for in verse 16 this coming of the Lord with the saints is the signal for the dead—*i.e.,* the *bodies*—to

(15) For this we say unto you by the
word of the Lord,[a] that we[b] which are
alive *and* remain unto the coming of
the Lord shall not prevent them which
are asleep. (16) For the Lord himself
shall descend from heaven with a shout,
with the voice of the archangel, and
with the trump of God:[c] and the dead
in Christ shall rise first: (17) then we
which are alive *and* remain shall be
caught up[d] together with them in the
clouds, to meet the Lord[e] in the air:

a 1 Kings 18. 1; 17. 18; 20. 35.
b 1 Cor. 15. 51, 52.
c Matt. 24. 31.
d Acts 8. 39; 2 Cor. 12. 4.
e Matt. 25. 6.

---

rise. It must be owned, however, that this manner of speaking is unusual. Jesus is no longer in Paradise, for the spirits to be brought thence *with Him;* and one would have expected something more like "bringing *up*" (Heb. xiii. 20), as it is always considered a *descent* into "hell" or Paradise. Because of this difficulty (which however is more in form than reality), some take the words to mean, "God will lead them by the same path with Christ"—*i.e.*, will make their whole career (including resurrection) conform with His, comparing the same verb in Rom. viii. 14; Heb. ii. 10.

(15) **By the word of the Lord.**—Literally, *in.* A most direct claim to plenary inspiration (see references). It does not mean "According to certain words which Christ spoke," nor yet "*By means* of a revelation from the Lord to me," but "*By way of* a divine revelation:" "I tell you this as a message straight from God." In what way apostles and prophets became *conscious* of supernatural inspiration we cannot tell; but elsewhere also St. Paul speaks of possessing the consciousness sometimes and not at others. (See 1 Cor. vii. 10, 12, 25, 40.) He means this declaration here to hold good of the *details,* which are such as no one would *invent* and teach with such solemnity; at the same time it must be remembered, with regard to the details, that it is the very idiom of prophecy (which St. Paul here uses) to express by material imagery spiritual facts.

We which are alive and remain.—Literally, *We, (that is) the quick, those who are left over.* There is not the least necessity for supposing from these words that St. Paul confidently *expected* the Advent before his death. Very likely he did, but it cannot be proved from this passage. Had the "we" stood alone, without the explanatory participles, it might have amounted to a proof, but not so now. His converts are strongly under the impression that *they* will be alive at the Coming, and that it will be the worse for the departed: therefore, St. Paul (becoming all things to all men) identifies himself with them—assumes that it will be as they expected—and proves the more vividly the fallacy of the Thessalonians' fears. It would have been impossible, on the contrary, for St. Paul to have said "we which are dead" without definitely abandoning the hope of seeing the Return. Besides which, St. Paul is only *picturing* to imagination the *scene* of the Advent; and for any man it is far easier to imagine himself among the quick than among the dead at that moment.

Shall not prevent—*i.e.*, "be before," "get the start of." If it were not for these words, we might have fancied that the Thessalonians had not been taught to believe in a resurrection at all; which would have been a strange departure from the usual apostolic gospel (1 Cor. xv. 1, *et seq.*). We here learn what was the exact nature of the Thessalonians' anxiety concerning the dead. They were full of excited hopes of the coming of that kingdom which had formed so prominent a part of the Apostles' preaching there (Acts xvii. 7); and were afraid that the highest glories in that kingdom would be engrossed by those who were alive to receive them; and that the dead, not being to rise till afterwards, would have less blessed privileges. This would make them not only sorry for their dead friends, but also reluctant to die themselves. The negative in this clause is very emphatic in the Greek, and throws all its force upon the verb: "We shall certainly not get the *start* of them that sleep;" *i.e.*, "if anything, we shall be *behind* them; they will rise *first.*"

(16) **For.**—A justification of the statement that we shall certainly not *prevent* the dead; therefore, the words as far as "trump of God" are logically *parenthetical;* and the proof only begins at "*They* shall rise *first: then* we shall be caught up."

With a shout.—The Greek word means a *shout of command or encouragement,* such as a captain gives to his soldiers, or a boatswain to his crew. It is not necessary to inquire *what* the command may be, or *to whom* issued, inasmuch as the word does not always imply any particular *orders;* nor *who* is represented as uttering it: the intention is only to convey the notion of the stirring noise, in the midst of which (for the original has "in," not "with") the Lord will descend. It is, however, somewhat particularised by what follows: two notes amid those sounds of mystery strike the ear—the archangel's voice, and the trump of God. Probably, therefore, the "shout of command" is uttered by the "leader of the angels;" and the trump (called "the trump of God" because used for God's purposes) is blown to summon the mustering hosts. In favour of supposing the Lord Himself to utter the cry, may be adduced John v. 25; but, on the other hand, it suits the dignity of the scene better to imagine the loud sound to come rather from one of the heralds of the great army. The preposition "in" is more effective than "with:" it calls attention to the *long* blast. (Comp. Ex. xix. 19.)

Shall rise first.—Not as meaning "shall be the first to rise," as contrasted with non-members of the Church who are to rise later; though that is a scriptural thought (Rev. xx. 5, 6), the Greek here refuses to be so explained. Rather, "the first thing will be the rising of the dead in Christ," contrasted with what follows—"*then,* and not till then, shall we be caught up." The same order is carefully observed in 1 Cor. xv. 52.

(17) **Shall be caught up.**—"Our Assumption," as Bishop Ellicott well calls it. The spiritualising of our natural bodies without death, as described in 1 Cor. xv. 50, *et seq.*, will enable us to be "caught up" equally well with, and in company with (both of which thoughts are included in "together with"), the resurgent dead. "Clouds" and "air" will be support enough for material so immaterial. Theodoret says, "He showeth the greatness of the honour: as the Master Himself was taken up upon a shining cloud, so also they that have believed in Him." The absolute equality, then, of quick and dead is proved.

To meet the Lord in the air.—St. Chrysostom says: "When the King cometh into a city, they that are honourable proceed forth to meet him, but the guilty await their judge within." The phrase "in the air" certainly does not mean "heaven." The word "air"

and so shall we ever be with the Lord.
(18) Wherefore comfort[2] one another
with these words.

CHAPTER V.—(1) But of the times
and the seasons,[a] brethren,
ye have no need that I
write unto you.[b] (2) For
yourselves know perfectly

Chap. v. 1—11. On the date of the Advent and its practical lessons.

that the day of the Lord so cometh[c] as
a thief in the night.[d] (3) For when they
shall say, Peace[e] and safety; then
sudden destruction cometh upon them,
as travail upon a woman with child;
and they shall not escape. (4) But ye,
brethren, are not in darkness, that that
day[f] should overtake you as a thief.
(5) Ye are all[g] the children of light,[h] and

c Joel 2. 1.
d Matt. 24. 43; Luke 12. 39; 2 Pet. 3. 10; Rev. 3. 3; 16. 15.
e Ezek. 13. 10.

A.D. 54.

a Dan. 2. 21; Acts 1. 7.
b ch. 4. 9.
f Rom. 13. 11, 12, 13.
g ch. 1. 2.
h Luke 16. 8; John 12. 36; Eph. 5. 8.

---

in itself properly signifies the lower, denser, grosser atmosphere, in which the powers of darkness reign (Eph. ii. 2); but here it is only used in contrast with the *ground*, and means "on the way from Heaven whence He comes," of course not to *dwell* there, but to accompany Him to His Judgment-seat on the earth.

And so.—Now that St. Paul has settled the question of disparity between the dead and the living, he does not think it necessary to describe what is immediately to follow; *that*, the Thessalonians were sure to know (see Heb. vi. 2): it only remains to say that having once rejoined the Lord, they would never be parted from Him.

(18) **Comfort one another.**—Here is a balm for the "sorrow" of verse 13. Rather, "*in* these words" than "*with*;" "Repeat these very words to one another, and you will find the comfort." What bereaved Christian has not found this true?

V.

(1) **But of the times.**—The fourth subject of instruction; the bearing of the doctrine of the Advent upon the Christian's own life. "Times and seasons" is a Hebraism, and in the original, the *second* word, not the first, is the more explicit: we should say, "About day and hour." The plural seems to mean the different periods at which men might conceive the Advent likely to come.

Ye have no need.—The next verse shows that this paragraph is not so much intended for an answer to a false theory about the time of the Advent, as practically to cure the restlessness common at Thessalonica.

(2) **Know perfectly.**—Or, *accurately*. There is something of an *oxymoron* (see Note on chap. iv. 11) here. "I need not tell you about the time, for you know to a nicety—not the hour of Christ's coming, but —the utter uncertainty respecting it." The word shows at the same time with what scrupulous care St. Paul had instructed them on this topic.

The day of the Lord.—Here "the Lord" (as usual in the New Testament) means Jesus Christ; and this day can mean nothing else than the great day of His return to judgment. The expression is taken from the Old Testament, where, of course, it does not primarily mean what we call "the Day of Judgment," but the set time which God has fixed for any great visitation. Thus in Joel ii. 1, *et seq.*, it means the time appointed for the plague of locusts; in Ezek. xiii. 5, generally, any day when God visits His people; in Joel iii. 14, the fixed time for vengeance to be taken upon the heathen for persecuting the Church; which, in Isa. ii. 12 (a passage largely influenced by recollections of Joel), seems to widen into a general day of judgment for mankind.

Cometh.—Not merely, *will come;* it is an absolute certainty that the time is on its way to come. (See Note on chap. i. 10.)

As a thief in the night—*i.e.* unexpectedly (Matt. xxiv. 43), and under cover of darkness. The frequency of the simile (see references) throws light on the words "know perfectly," making it apparent that it was the ordinary formula in which the doctrine was universally taught by the Apostles.

(3) **They.**—Quite vague and general, like the French *on*. The plural is so used frequently in St. Luke (xii. 11, 20, margin; xvi. 9, probably; xxiii. 29, 30, 31). Of course, however, no *Christian* could say so, for they are ever on the watch, so that "they" will mean "the world." The word "for" at the beginning of the verse should (according to the best MSS.) be struck out—the abruptness helps to enforce the lesson.

Peace and safety.—Carrying on the thought suggested by the word "night;" they are taking their repose in security, without dreaming of any interruption to their slumbers. Is it possible that there may here be a faint recollection of the parable related in Matt. xxv. 1—13?

Destruction cometh upon them.—Literally, *stands over them;* or *takes its stand over them; presents itself*. The present tense is used for the sake of a more vivid effect. The extreme similarity of this passage to Luke xxi. 34 (with other indications) inclines Bishop Wordsworth to think that the Thessalonians had the Gospel of St. Luke to refer to.

As travail.—A common Oriental simile to express not only suddenness, but horror also. Theodoret fairly says, "The woman with child knows that she has the child to bear, but knows not the exact time for her pangs; so we also know that the Lord of all will appear, but the moment itself we have by no means been explicitly taught." The comment, however, hardly suits this passage, as the persons on whom the destruction will thus burst are not persons who live in *any* expectation of such a judgment.

(4) **But ye.**—"Though the world (which lieth in darkness) may be surprised at the coming of the Day, you, members of the Church, living in the light, cannot be surprised." The words "in darkness" seem to be suggested by the mention of "night" in verse 2; and the chief thought (as the succeeding verses show) is that of supineness, inattention, torpor, not so much either ignorance or sin.

That day.—Literally, *the day:* so that it does not mean the Judgment Day simply as a *point of time*, but brings out its characteristic of being a *day indeed.* (Comp. 1 Cor. iii. 13.)

As a thief.—There is another reading which has two of the best MSS. and he Coptic version in its favour, and the judgment of Lachmann and Dr. Lightfoot, "As thieves." But not only is the evidence from the MSS. strongly in favour of the Received text, but the whole context shows that St. Paul was not thinking of the day as catching them at evil practices, but as catching them in inadvertence.

(5) **Ye are all.**—St. Paul recognises no exceptions, no inner distinctions, among the members of the Church: all stand alike so far as grace, privileges, and duties

the children of the day: we are not of
the night, nor of darkness. (6) Therefore
let us not sleep, as *do* others; but let
us watch and be sober.[a] (7) For they
that sleep sleep in the night; and they
that be drunken are drunken in the
night. (8) But let us, who are of the
day, be sober, putting on the breastplate
of faith and love; and for an helmet,[b]
the hope of salvation. (9) For God
hath not appointed us to wrath,[c] but to
obtain salvation[d] by our Lord Jesus
Christ, (10) who died for us, that,
whether we wake or sleep,[e] we should

b Isa. 59. 17.; Eph. 6. 17.
a 1 Pet. 5. 8.
c 1 Pet. 2. 8.
d 2 Thess. 2. 14.
e Rom. 14. 8.

---

are concerned. The following exhortation shows that it was a matter of each man's free will whether he would sustain his character as a "child of light" or not.

Children of light.—The expression is an enthusiastic Hebrew poetical turn for intimate vital connection with anything; thus, *e.g.*, "children of this world" (Luke xvi. 8; xx. 34) = "mere products of this age," with a family likeness for other worldly people; "the son of peace" (Luke x. 6) = a person with whom peace has a natural affinity, to whom the "peace" pronounced will cleave naturally. So "children of the light" are persons to whom darkness is an alien thing, whose natures have a kinship, an intuitive responsiveness for whatever may be called "light." To such persons the "light," the "day," can never come as an unwelcome, startling apparition.

We.—Notice St. Paul's courtesy again: he suddenly includes himself in his exhortation.

(6) **Let us not sleep.**—The metaphor here expresses not so much actual sin (Eph. v. 14) as carelessness in spiritual and moral things. "Let *us* not say, 'Peace and safety,' and resign ourselves to indifference about Christ's coming." St. Paul (as always) indicates that it was possible for "children of light" to be converted back into "children of darkness."

Others.—Rather, *the rest*, as in chap. iv. 13: so also Rom. xi. 7; Eph. ii. 3.

Watch and be sober.—The comparison of night now suggests to the writer another thought besides that of sloth, namely, that of dissipation. Christians are not to turn day into night by debauchery any more than by sleep.

(7) **They that sleep . . . .**—As the connection of sleep with night has already been sufficiently worked out, and is not touched upon again in verse 8, the first clause seems only to be inserted for the sake of bringing out the second, and to justify the sudden introduction of the words, "and be sober." It may thus be paraphrased: "I say, 'and be sober too,' for as they that sleep sleep in the night, so they that be drunken are drunken in the night." It is implied that the streets even of heathen Thessalonica were seldom affronted with the common English spectacle of drunken men by daylight; while among the Jews it was proof positive of sobriety to say, "It is but the third hour of the day" (Acts ii. 15). In St. Cyprian's time, Christians were known from other men because their breath smelt of wine in the early morning through attending the Blessed Sacrament (*Epistle* lxiii. 15): no heathens would have touched wine by that time.

(8) **Putting on.**—A curiously abrupt transition, suggested by the sober vigilance just advocated. The Christian must be careful to watch, not only because the Lord is coming back at some unexpected hour, but also because there are enemies all round. He is not only the *porter*, sitting up to let his Lord in at any hour when He may return from the wedding (Mark xiii. 34; Luke xii. 36), but the soldier standing sentry, liable to be surprised by the foe.

Breastplate of faith and love.—We have not to do with the Christian soldier as aggressive and going forth to conquer, which idea is developed in Eph. vi. 11 *et seq.*, but only as defensive, and protected in breast and head against sudden blows. The three "theological virtues" are the Christian's defence. (Comp. chap. i. 3; 1 Cor. xiii. 13.) The "breastplate" is a cuirass fitting close to the body, and in Ephesians this cuirass is composed of righteousness, while faith becomes the shield, and love disappears from the panoply. The "faith" here is a general trust in God's presence and goodness; the "love" is the love both of God and men. Perhaps it is unnecessary to inquire particularly why faith and love are represented as covering the body, and hope as covering the head. It seems far-fetched to consider the first two as keeping the heart, *i.e.*, the affections, from injury; the third as preserving the brain, *i.e.*, keeping us from miscalculating the dangers and so falling into despair. In the passage of Isaiah which St. Paul here imitates, the "helmet of salvation" appears to mean little more than a helmet which secures safety; but as one of the chief benefits which such armour confers is the confident hope of coming off unhurt, St. Paul fairly describes that hope itself as being a protection. In the forefront of the lost (Rev. xxi. 8) stand those who have had no "hope" or "trust."

(9) **For.**—This is not the reason for being watchful, but for being hopeful of salvation. The image of the soldier is abandoned as suddenly as it was introduced.

Hath not appointed.—Rather, *did not appoint*, referring to some mysterious moment of God's eternal counsels, when He fixed His predestination of us—whether the moment of creative thought, or of sending the gospel to us. The "wrath" is that which is to come upon the "children of wrath" at the Second Advent, as in chaps. i. 10; ii. 16. (Comp. 1 Pet. ii. 8.) We may well be confident then, for we ourselves are the only persons that can defeat God's predestinations.

To obtain salvation.—More than "obtain;" the Greek means "acquire" by one's own efforts; "earn and make our own;" being the same word as is used in 1 Tim. iii. 13 and Acts xx. 28 in the verb; and in the substantive in Eph. i. 14 (where it is translated "purchased possession"); 2 Thess. ii. 14; Heb. x. 39 (translated "saving"); and 1 Pet. ii. 9, where see Note. It will be seen that God does not predestinate men to "salvation" without laborious acquisition on *their* part, but predestinates them to occupy a position in which they will be able to "work out their own salvation" by placing them "under grace" in the Church. The very same word is used of the Christian's way of securing salvation, and of Christ's way of securing it for him (see references); both are "purchasing," "earning." But mark that the Christian can only so purchase salvation "*through* our Lord Jesus Christ:" apart from Him a man can do nothing to redeem himself, but through union with Him the believer can pay the whole price of his salvation (see *e.g.* John xv. 5).

(10) **Who died for us.**—Not a mere pious recollection of a fact which has nothing to do with the context,

live together with him. (11) Wherefore comfort[1] yourselves together, and edify one another, even as also ye do.

Chap. v. 12—15. Exhortation to discipline and unity.

(12) And we beseech you, brethren, to know[a] them which labour[b] among you, and are over you[c] in the Lord, and admonish you; (13) and to esteem them very highly in love for their work's sake. *And* be at peace among yourselves. (14) Now we exhort[2] you, brethren, warn them that are unruly,[3]

c Heb. 13. 17.
1 Or, *exhort.*
2 Or, *beseech.*
a 1 Cor. 16. 18.
b 1 Tim. 5. 17.
3 Or, *disorderly.*

---

but an account of the way by which Christ made it possible for us to set about earning salvation. What a blessed privilege a Christian's life of labour must be, if it alone—to say nothing of the "salvation" at the end—cost such a price!

Whether we wake or sleep.—The mention of Christ's death at once brings back the recollection of the Advent and the questions concerning the dead in their relation to it. The words "wake or sleep" seem distinctly suggested by the metaphor used *from verse* 2 *to verse* 8, being different in the Greek from the terms used in chap. iv., but abruptly take a much altered meaning. They here, no doubt, signify "life and death:"—"Let us arm ourselves with a brave hope of our salvation, for it will be against God's will if we should perish: He means us to save ourselves by union with Him who put an end to death for us by dying, and made all who wait for His coming to *live*, whether they be in the world's sense dead or alive."

We should live.—In sharp contrast with "who died for us." Christ's dying destroyed the power of death (Heb. ii. 14); henceforth it is only a matter of being awake or asleep; those who sleep quite as truly live, and live with Him, as we who wake (see Luke xx. 38; and compare the more developed passage in Rom. xiv. 8). The word "together" (as the Greek clearly shows) must be separated from the "with;" rather, "we should live with Him together," *i.e.*, we quick, and our brethren the dead; for St. Paul has entirely reverted from the *effect* of the Advent-doctrine upon Christian life to the subject of the last chapter—the equality of the two classes at Christ's coming. Bengel, thinking that St. Paul is still applying himself to the discussion of the *date* of the Advent (which in fact was scarcely raised), tries to make out the meaning, "That we should *there and then* live with Him."

(11) **Comfort.**—Rightly translated. St. Paul is here catching up once more the thought of chap. iv. 18. They are to comfort one another about their communion with the dead who live in Christ; but perhaps the word also involves the comfort to be imparted by the thought of predestination to earn salvation. The command to "Edify one another" certainly refers to the instruction given in verses 1—10: "Build one another up" in these settled purposes of holy living. This metaphor of building is one which St. Paul uses frequently in his later writings, and which St. Peter (who uses the same) may have adopted from his brother Apostle. St. Paul considers not only the whole Catholic Church to be a great Temple of the Spirit, the stones of which are individual souls (1 Pet. ii. 5; 1 Cor. iii. 16), but each believer is a temple too, complete in himself, or, rather, in continual process of completion (1 Cor. vi. 19).

(12) We now come to minor details of instruction, no doubt suggested by observation of manifest defects in the Thessalonian Church. These details show us still further the mixture of restless ungoverned zeal with gloomy forebodings and discontents.

To know them which labour.—A command to enter into the spirit of ecclesiastical discipline. The persons meant are not simply the hard-working laity, contrasted with the idlers of chap. iv. 11 and 2 Thess. iii. 11, but those who performed the laborious office of the priesthood, as the words subsequent show. And "knowing" them is hardly to be limited either to the sense of "recognising their position," *i.e.*, "not ignoring them," or, on the other hand, to the sense of "being on terms of familiar intercourse with them." The Greek word indicates *appreciation;* they are bidden to acquaint themselves thoroughly with the presbyter and his work, and to endeavour to understand his teaching, and to value his example. The logical connection of this verse with the preceding is that of course the main endeavours to "edify" the brethren were made by the presbytery; and the command to edify involves the command to accept edification.

Are over you in the Lord.—This is the primitive idea of the priest in the Church: he is not a member of a sacerdotal caste, ministering to an outer world, but a *superior officer* in a spiritual society consisting of nothing but priests (Rev. i. 6, where the right reading is, "Made us a kingdom of priests"). It is specially interesting to notice how much *power* is given to the presbytery in this earliest writing of the New Testament, and how carefully St. Paul seems to have organised his churches, and that at the very foundation of them. It is only "in the Lord" that the presbytery are over men, that is, in spiritual matters.

Admonish you.—The presbytery are not only organisers, managers of the corporate affairs of their Church, but also spiritual guides to give practical advice to individual Christians. These are the two senses in which they are "over you."

(13) **Very highly in love.**—The original here is difficult; but it seems best, with most good commentators, ancient and modern, to construe "in love" with "esteem," and to make "very highly" (a very enthusiastic word in the Greek) an expletive attached to "in love," implying "hold in a most extraordinary degree of love." The bond which binds the Christian community to their directors is not to be one of "recognition" and obedience only (verse 12), but of holy affection above all.

For their work's sake.—Our love is to be paid them not for any social or intellectual qualities they may have in themselves; it is the work which they have to do that should attract our sympathy. The original seems to mean that we are to love them, not only *because they do* such work, but also '*for the sake of* their work," *i.e.*, to help it forward.

Be at peace among yourselves.—Discipline to be observed towards equals, as well as superiors.

(14) **Now we exhort you, brethren.**—Rather *and* than *now.* The writers turn to the presbytery, and explain their duty in the administration of discipline to the flock. The flock will be more apt to receive the discipline when they see with what apostolic authority their pastors are armed. Several special parts of the clerical office are then enumerated.

Warn.—The same Greek word as "admonish" in verse 12, and selected for that very reason. The "unruly" or "disorderly" are those who infringe good

comfort the feebleminded, support the
weak, be patient toward all *men.* (15) See
that none render evil for evil[a] unto
any *man;* but ever follow that which
is good, both among yourselves, and to
all *men.*

b Phil. 4. 4.

a Rom. 12. 17; 1 Pet. 3. 9.
c Phil. 4. 6; Eph. 5. 20.
d ch. 4. 3.

e Luke 12. 49; 2 Tim. 1. 6.

(16) Rejoice evermore.[b] (17) Pray with-
out ceasing. (18) In every
thing give thanks:[c] for this
is the will of God in Christ[d]
Jesus concerning you.
(19) Quench not the Spirit.[e] (20) Despise

Chap. v. 16—22. Exhortations to use the Spirit aright.

---

discipline—said of soldiers who leave their ranks: here notably of those mentioned in 2 Thess. iii. 11.

Feebleminded.—Or, *fainthearted, pusillanimous.* Such persons, *e.g.,* as were overburdened with sorrow for the dead, or afraid of the persecutions, or the like.

Support the weak.—Or, *keep hold* of them, to help them on. The "weak" are not quite the same as the "feebleminded," but rather (judging from Rom. xiv. 1 *et seq.*) those who have not attained that robust common-sense and breadth of conscience which discriminates between truths and superstitions, necessities and expediencies; or who are not yet ripe enough Christians to be sure of standing in persecution.

Patient toward all men.—Church officers are not to be rendered impatient by the defects, errors, weakness, stupidity, unbelief of any one, catholic, heretic, or heathen.

(15) **See that.**—The exhortation is given to those who have the authority to *oversee* the Church (Acts xix. 28; 1 Pet. v. 2).

None render evil for evil.—Like the prohibition of fornication, abstinence from revenge is practically a new thought for Greeks, among whom feuds were frequent and undying. (Comp. Rom. i. 31; Tit. iii. 3.)

That which is good—*i.e.,* that which is *kind.* (See Note on chap. iii. 6.) This duty is to be "followed," *i.e.,* made an object to be pursued eagerly, "toward all men." There is not one standard of morals towards the brethren and another towards the world.

(16) **Rejoice evermore.**—The remaining commands are more simply spiritual, and hardly form part of the same paragraph as verses 12—15, which related to discipline; though from verses 19 *et seq.* we see that St. Paul was still addressing the Church in its corporate capacity, not only the individual members. The Christian who remains in sadness and depression really breaks a commandment: in some direction or other he mistrusts God—His power, providence, forgiveness. The command is specially good for a persecuted Church like that of Thessalonica (Matt. v. 10—12).

(17) **Pray without ceasing.**—Theophylact well says, "This shows the way to 'rejoice always'—to wit, incessant prayer and eucharist, for he that has accustomed himself to hold converse with God, and to give thanks to Him over everything that happens as happening well, will evidently have unbroken joy." Though a man cannot be incessantly praying in words, the mind may be held continuously in an attitude of prayer, even in sleep (Cant. v. 2).

(18) **In every thing give thanks.**—To the Christian who really trusts his Father's providence, and believes that his prayers are heard, every moment's occurrence will be just that which he has prayed for—the fulfilment of our Father's will. It is for this reason that thanksgiving is so inseparably joined with prayer. (See Phil. iv. 6; Col. iv. 2.)

This is the will of God—*i.e.,* that you should be always full of thanksgiving. This clause hardly enforces thanksgiving as a *duty,* "Give thanks always, for you recognise the duty of doing God's will, and this *is* His will;" but rather encourages the Thessalonians to see that thankfulness is always *possible.* "Give thanks always, for God has no wish to give you cause for sorrow: His will towards you is to fill you with thankfulness." "Towards you" seems here a more exact rendering than "concerning you."

In Christ Jesus.—This kind and loving will of God for our good was most abundantly manifested in the life and death and resurrection of Christ Jesus, and even to this day it is chiefly manifested in what Christ Jesus still is for us (*e.g.* Heb. vi. 19, 20).

(19) **Quench not the Spirit.**—The mention of prayer and thanksgiving (*eucharistia*), by which public as well as private worship is intended, leads St. Paul on to the mention of other parts of the service. The gloom and depression to which an antidote is administered in verses 16—18 had been such as almost to extinguish that fire of enthusiasm which ought to have burst out in prayers, praises, thanksgivings, and "prophecies." The "Spirit" here must not be taken too sharply to mean the Person of the Holy Ghost: the Person of the Holy Ghost may be grieved (Eph. iv. 30), expelled (Ps. li. 11), neglected (1 Tim. iv. 14), but (though His working on the individual may be stopped) *He* can never be extinguished. The word here again (as in chap. i. 5) is in that intermediate sense which expresses the *effect* of the Holy Ghost's personal working upon our spirits. He kindles in us a fire (Matt. iii. 11), that is, a consuming ardour and enthusiasm, of love to God and man; which ardour may be damped, quenched, by not giving it free air and play. Gloom (verse 16), neglect of prayer (verse 17) which is the very feeding of the flame, discontentment with the answer which God chooses to give to prayer (verse 18), will in the end reduce us to the condition in which we were before we were confirmed (Rom. viii. 9). Comp. *Ecce Homo,* p. 257 (3rd ed.):—"The Apostles in like manner became sensible that their inspiration was liable to intermissions. They regard it as possible to grieve the Divinity who resided within them, and ever to quench His influence. But neither they nor Christ even for a moment suppose that, if He should take His flight, it is possible to do without Him . . . Christianity is an enthusiasm, or it is nothing."

(20) **Despise not prophesyings.**—The highest outward or *charismatic* manifestation of this inward fire was the gift of "prophecy" (1 Cor. xii. 28; xiv. 1, 5, 39), which was an inspired and inspiring preaching. The despondency of the Thessalonians led them not only to quench the fervour of the Holy Ghost in their own bosoms, but to turn a cold and disparaging ear to the sanguine "prophets" who preached to them, the effect of which insensibility was to "quench the Spirit" by degrees in the prophets also. It is because of this double effect of gloominess, inward upon themselves, and outward upon others, that the command, "Quench not," occurs between the exhortation to thanksgiving and the warning not to despise prophecy. This seems to be the most natural way of accounting for the present warning, but there are two other main interpretations:—(1) It is said that what tempted the Thessalonians to disparage prophecy was their fascination for

not prophesyings.[a] (21) Prove all things;[b]
hold fast that which is good. (22) Abstain
from all appearance of evil.

a 1 Cor. 14. 1, &c.
b 1 Cor. 14. 29; 1 John 4. 1.
c Heb. 13. 20.

(23) And the very God of
peace[c] sanctify you wholly;
and *I pray God* your whole

Chap. v. 23—24. Prayer and assurance.

---

the more showy gift of tongues. It is true that such was the case at Corinth, and not unnaturally so; and at first sight it seems as if, in 1 Cor. xiv. 1, "spiritual gifts" were contrasted with "prophecy" as two separate classes, thus giving some ground for Bishop Wordsworth's interpretation of our present passage—viz., that verse 19 refers to the gifts of tongues, miracles, &c., in something of the same contrast with "prophecy" in verse 20 as may be found in 1 Cor. xiv. 39. But, on the other hand, it seems more likely that in 1 Cor. xiv. 1 prophecy is not contrasted with the spiritual gifts there specified as a separate class, but selected *from among* them: "It is all very well to covet spiritual gifts as a whole, but it would be better to aim more particularly at that one—prophecy—which is the greatest:" just so here, "Do not quench the Spirit, in whatever direction it may blaze up; but especially do not disparage preaching." Besides, there is nothing to prove that the Thessalonians were dazzled by the more brilliant gifts: and it accords better with the context to suppose that the fault to be corrected in them was not a light sensationalism, but a tendency to damp all ardour alike. (2) Others suppose that the Thessalonians had had experience of persons who had *abused* the gift of prophecy, and therefore were disposed to suspect and dislike prophecy altogether. This view gains support from 2 Thess. ii. 2, and also from the command in verse 21 to test, and retain only what stood the test. There is no particular ground for contradicting this view; but it is unnecessary, and does not carry on the thought so connectedly.

(21) **Prove all things.**—The right reading inserts a "but":—"I bid you pay all reverence to the cheering utterances of your prophets (comp. Acts xv. 32); but take care! put everything to the test." That the warning was needed, or would be needed soon, is shown by 2 Thess. ii. 2. It is couched in general terms (*all things*), but, of course, has special reference to all things purporting to be manifestations of the Spirit. And how were these revelations to be tested? If they were not in accordance (1) with the original tradition (2 Thess. ii. 2), (2) with the supernatural inspirations of the other prophets who sat as judges (1 Cor. xiv. 29), (3) with enlightened common sense (1 John iv. 1), they could not be "good." The word "good" here is not vague and general good in the moral sense—not the same Greek word as in verse 15—but "good" in the sense of "genuine," "answering to the proper conception of what it purports to be." The same word is used in the same sense in John x. 11.

(22) **Abstain from all appearance of evil.**—This translation cannot stand. Possibly it might be rendered "every form of evil," but the most natural version would be, "Hold yourselves aloof from every evil kind"—*i.e.*, evil kind of whatever you may be testing. The word "evil" is here used in the *moral* sense, and does not constitute an exact antithesis to the "good" of the preceding verse.

(23) **And.**—The logic of such an expression as, "Do this, and may you be happy," lies in the writer's own connection with both the command and the prayer: "I bid you abstain from every evil kind of thing, and I pray that God Himself may enable you to keep the commandment."

The very God of peace.—In more usual English, "the God of peace Himself:" the contrast is between the futile efforts after holiness of which they in themselves were capable, and the almighty power of sanctification exercised by God. This sanctification (which is the special work of the Third Person) is here ascribed to the First Person of the Holy Trinity, from whom the Holy Ghost proceeds. He is called (as in Heb. xiii. 20) the "God of peace," not in reference to any dissensions between the Thessalonians (verse 13), but because of the peace which His sanctification brings into the soul, so that it fears neither temptation's power nor persecution's rage. (Comp. the Second Collect for Evensong).

Sanctify you wholly.—Rather, *sanctify you whole.* The idea is rather that of leaving no part unsanctified, than that of doing the work completely so far as it goes: thus it serves to introduce the next sentence, which explains it.

And I pray God.—If there were need of any insertion, it should have been "*We* pray God:" Silas and Timothy are never forgotten throughout.

Spirit and soul and body.—This is St. Paul's fullest and most scientific psychology, not merely a rhetorical piling up of words without any particular meaning being assigned to them. Elsewhere, he merely divides man according to popular language, into two parts, visible and invisible, "body and spirit" (1 Cor. vi. 20; vii. 34, *et al.*); the division into "body and *soul*" he never uses. (Comp. Note on 1 Cor. ii. 14.) The "spirit" (*pneuma*) is the part by which we apprehend realities *intuitively*—*i.e.*, without reasoning upon them; with it we touch, see, serve, worship God (John iv. 23, 24; Rom. i. 9; 1 Cor. vi. 17; Rev. i. 10, *et al.*); it is the very inmost consciousness of the man (see, *e.g.*, 1 Cor. ii. 11); it is the part of him which survives death (Heb. xii. 23; 1 Pet. iii. 19; comp. Luke xxiii. 46; Acts vii. 59). The "soul" (*psyche*) includes the intellect, the affections, and the will: and it is of the very essence of the gospel to force sharply upon men the distinction between it and the *spirit* (Heb. iv. 12). Low-living men may have *soul* (*i.e.*, intellect, affection, will) in abundance, but their *spirit* falls into complete abeyance (Jude, 19); the *soul* belongs altogether to the lower nature, so that when St. Paul uses the two-fold division, "body and spirit," the *soul* is reckoned (not, probably, as Bishop Ellicott says on our present passage, as part of the *spirit*, but) as part of the *body;* and when St. Paul describes the "works of the flesh," he includes among them such distinctly *soul*-sins as "heresies" (Gal. v. 20). Sanctification preserves all these three divisions *entire*, and in their due *relation* to each other; without sanctification, the *spirit* might be overwhelmed by the other parts gaining the predominance, which would, of course, eventually be the ruin both of "soul and body in hell" (Matt. x. 28. N.B., that our Lord says nothing of the destruction of the "spirit" in hell: the question is whether He there definitely meant to *exclude* "spirit," or used "soul" popularly as including it). Where the New Testament writers *acquired* such a psychology cannot be determined, but it was probably derived from experimental knowledge of life, not from books, and all experience confirms its accuracy. Modern science tends more and more to show that "*soul*" is a function of "*body*."

Unto the coming.—A mistranslation for "*at* the coming," caused by the slight difficulty in under-

spirit and soul and body be preserved
blameless[a] unto the coming of our Lord
Jesus Christ. (24) Faithful[b] *is* he that
calleth you, who also will do *it*.

Chap. v. 25—28. Conclusion.

(25) Brethren, pray for us.
(26) Greet all the brethren
with an holy kiss.[c] (27) I charge[1] you by
the Lord that this epistle be read unto all
the holy brethren. (28) The grace of our
Lord Jesus Christ *be* with you. Amen.

¶ The first *epistle* unto the Thessalonians was written from Athens.

a ch. 3. 13.
b 2 Thess. 3. 3.
c Rom. 16. 16; 1 Cor. 16. 20; 2 Cor. 13. 12; 1 Pet. 5. 14.
1 Or, *adjure*.

---

standing the true version. The idea is not so much that of their preservation from sin during the *interval*, but rather the writers hasten in eager anticipation to the Coming itself, and hope that the Thessalonians *at* the Coming will be *found to have been preserved.* "Blameless" should have been "blamelessly."

(24) **Faithful is he.**—A reason for hoping confidently that they *will* be blamelessly preserved. God would forfeit His character for keeping His promise, if He "called," and did not enable men to obey the call. Of course He can only "do it" in case *they* continue willing to have it done. On the present tense, see Note on chap. ii. 12.

(25) **Pray for us.**—Taken in conjunction with what follows, this probably is a petition for remembrance in the great public service.

(26) **Greet all the brethren.**—It is concluded from the manner in which *some* are told to greet *all*, instead of *all* being told to greet *one another* (as in the parallel passages), that the "brethren" to whom the letter was sent specially were the priesthood of Thessalonica (comp. the next verse). If so, the "holy kiss" had hardly become the fixed Church ceremony which it afterwards was, for the practice (according to the *Apostolical Constitutions*) was for the Church members to pass the kiss from one to another, men kissing men, and women kissing women, not for all the people to be kissed in turn by the priest. This kiss, however, is no doubt intended by St. Paul to be given at a solemn assembly of the Church, *i.e.*, at the Holy Communion, which was the only fixed meeting of the Primitive Church. In the time of St. Cyril of Jerusalem, the kiss was given just before the *Sursum Corda*. It was not till the thirteenth century that the kissing of the *Pax* was substituted in the Western Church for the kissing of the brethren. This kiss was to differ from the ordinary Greek *salutation*, by being distinctly a *holy* kiss, *i.e.*, a ceremonial, religious kiss.

(27) **I charge you.**—*Adjure* is much nearer the original word, which is as solemn as can be. What is the cause of such awful solemnity? The question has never been very satisfactorily answered. It certainly seems as if the contempt of discipline and partial alienation of clergy and laity implied in verses 12, 13, might suggest to St. Paul a doubt whether his Epistle would reach *all* the Thessalonian Christians. At any rate, the adjuration marks his sense of the extreme *importance* of the letter; and perhaps the fact that this was his first pastoral letter may have made him more anxious to ensure its reception and success. It amounts to a claim to inspiration. (Comp. chap. iv. 15.) The emphasis seems to rest on the word "*all*" ("*holy*" is an interpolation). The reading is of course a public reading in the celebration of the Communion, at which we know from several early Fathers that the writings of the Apostles were read aloud. (Comp. Col. iv. 16; 2 Pet. iii. 15, 16.) Baur thought the adjuration a mark of a forger, who wished to gain authority for his cento: Bishop Wordsworth well points out, on the contrary, what a splendid guarantee for the genuineness and integrity of the Epistles this constant recitation constituted.

(28) **The grace.**—St. Paul's autograph to conclude the letter. (See 2 Thess. iii. 17, 18.)

INTRODUCTION

TO

THE SECOND EPISTLE OF PAUL THE APOSTLE TO THE

THESSALONIANS

We may confidently assert that this Epistle was written by St. Paul from Corinth during his residence there of a year-and-a-half, within a few months of the First Epistle: that is, in the year 53. Not only are all its main features so like those of the First as to suggest a very close connection in time, but it is despatched by the same apostolic group—Paul, Silvanus, and Timotheus; and, as we have remarked in the *Introduction to the First Epistle*, we have no reason to believe that Silvanus was in St. Paul's company later than the departure from Corinth in 54. It suits well with this date that the Apostle is in fear of certain "monstrous and depraved persons" (chap. iii. 2), who may well be the Jews who brought him before Gallio.

The circumstances which called forth the Letter were as follows. Since the First Epistle had been despatched St. Paul had been able to receive fresh tidings of the state of the Thessalonian Church, concerning which he was naturally anxious, as it was so young when he had been forced to leave it to itself and to God. The tidings were both good and bad. On the one hand, there was marked progress in some of the points which had before caused solicitude. St. Paul uses enthusiastic language (chap. i. 3) of the advance made in *faith* (comp. 1 Thess. iii. 10), and in individual *brotherly charity* (comp. 1 Thess. iv. 10), and also of their *steadfastness* in persecutions which were still afflicting them (chap. i. 4)—persecutions in which, apparently, both Jews and Gentiles joined. (See Note on chap. i. 8.) We may also gather, from the silence of the present Letter, that St. Paul's instructions on the state of the departed faithful had taken good effect: this being, perhaps, the special increase in *faith* mentioned above. We find, moreover, that there is no further need of warnings on the subject of purity or of submission to ecclesiastical authority. On the other hand, there were three great faults to find.

(1) The tendency to disorders and idleness, which had been censured both directly and indirectly in the former letter, had become stronger instead of receding. Some considerable number of the little Church had become mere "busybodies"—had left off work, expecting maintenance at the public expense of the community while they indulged themselves, probably, in what seemed more religious pursuits.

(2) We can trace more clearly in this Epistle than in the former the doctrinal ground on which such disorders were justified by those who were guilty of them. They nad been "shaken from their reason," and were still "in trepidation" (chap. ii. 2), from a belief that "the day of the Lord" was already upon them. Panic and exultation alike had the effect of making the Thessalonians think it not worth while to attend to the things of a doomed world.

(3) This belief had been, if not created, yet confirmed by some audacious forgeries and fictions (chap. ii. 2). Even in the First Epistle St. Paul gives signs of uneasiness, as though he were not sure of the honesty of some of his correspondents in their use of his name and writings (1 Thess. v. 27). Now it is clear that, in more than one way, persons (who might be only half conscious of their fraud) had attempted to impose on their brethren. They had pretended to a direct inspiration or angelic visitation, which had revealed to them the immediate nearness of the Advent. They had misrepresented the oral teaching given by St. Paul during his stay at Thessalonica. They had, perhaps, wrested the words of his First Epistle, which had certainly given a colourable pretext for what they now taught. More probably still, from the precaution given in chap. iii. 17, they had actually written a letter, or letters, purporting to be from the Apostle, in which the doctrine was definitely taught.

To all these three faults the writer opposes the authority of what they knew to have genuinely proceeded from himself. He has nothing to unsay. They are to "hold fast the traditions" (chap. ii. 15) which, written or unwritten, were his. (1) He reminds them not only of his example (as in the First Letter), but of his teaching levelled at their dissipated religiousness: "Withdraw yourselves from every brother that walketh disorderly, and not after the tradition which they received of us" (chap. iii. 6); "Even when we were with you, this we commanded you, that if any has no mind to work, neither let him eat" (chap. iii. 10). (2) He recalls the very definite instructions which showed that the end was not by-and-by. The Roman empire was still standing, and therefore the Man of Sin could not be revealed as yet, and therefore Christ could not be on the point of coming. "Remember ye not, that when I was yet with you, I told you these things?" (chap. ii. 5.) (3) He enforces, against their forgeries, his present Letter, even at the risk of provoking an open rebellion: "If any man obey not our word by this Epistle, note that man, and have no fellowship with him" (chap. iii. 14).

The style of the Epistle (except in the studied obscurity of the prophetic passage) is clear and easy, like that of the First; and the structure is also very simple, as will be seen from the following analysis.

and marked by the same characteristic feature as the First: *i.e.*, the *prayer* which leads on from one section of the Letter to another:—

I. THE SALUTATION (chap. i. 1, 2).

II. THE RETROSPECTIVE PORTION (chap. i. 3—12).

(*a*) Thanksgiving for progress made (chap. i. 3, 4).

(*b*) Hopes thus afforded against the Advent Day (chap. i. 5—10).

(*c*) Prayer for continuance in so happy a state (chap. i. 11, 12).

III. THE INSTRUCTIVE AND HORTATORY PORTION (chaps. ii. 1—iii. 18).

(1) *On the date of the Advent.*

(*a*) Caution against believing the Advent close at hand (chap. ii. 1—3).

(*b*) What must happen first (chap. ii. 3—10).

(*c*) Terrible fate of the apostates (chap. ii. 11, 12).

(*d*) Thanksgiving that the Thessalonians' fate is so different (chap. ii. 13, 14).

(*e*) Exhortation and prayer (chap. ii. 15—17).

(2) *On the necessity of work.*

(*a*) Request for prayers for himself, which skilfully serves to predispose the readers to obey the ensuing commands (chap. iii. 1—4).

(*b*) Prayer for the same purpose (chap. iii. 5).

(*c*) Commands to make all work, and to excommunicate the refractory (chap. iii. 6—15).

(*d*) Prayer for tranquillity (chap. iii. 16).

(*e*) Final benediction, with attention drawn to the autograph (chap. iii. 17, 18).

The genuineness of this Letter, like that of the First, is practically uncontroverted. We seem to have very early testimony to its use—St. Polycarp appearing in two places to quote it, though anonymously, according to his custom; and St. Justin, speaking of the Man of Sin in a manner which might indeed be explained by saying that that doctrine was common to the Catholic Church not special to St. Paul, but which is more simply referred to this Epistle. The objections of a few modern scholars (Baur, Schrader, &c.) are chiefly drawn from the prophecy in chap. ii., from supposed contradictions between this Epistle and the First—especially in regard to the date of the Advent; from fancied allusions to the persecution of Nero; from a mistaken notion that the doctrine of an Antichrist (which was in reality pre-Christian) was only invented by the Montanists.

Doubts have been entertained by a few critics, who acknowledged the genuineness of both, which of these Letters is the earlier in date. Ewald, the greatest of these critics, placed the Second Epistle first. It was, he thought, placed second in the Canon because, as a rule, the shorter letters in the Canon follow the longer. The arguments, however, which he adduces are scarcely worth considering, in face of the fact that in 2 Thess. ii. 15 we have an allusion to a former Epistle. All the historical portion of the First Epistle (especially 1 Thess. ii. 17; iii. 11) bears evident tokens of being the earliest communication that had passed between St. Paul and his spiritual children since he had left them.

[In preparing the following Notes the chief books consulted have been those already mentioned in 1 Thessalonians:—the patristic commentaries, especially St. Chrysostom; Hammond, Lünemann, Ellicott, and others; and the posthumous edition (which appeared too late for use in annotating the First Epistle) by the Presbyterian Professor Eadie. His notes are, however, little but a reproduction of Bishop Ellicott's, without their concentration. In the *Excursus* on the Man of Sin, I have stated my obligations to Dr. Pusey's *Lectures on Daniel.*]

THE SECOND EPISTLE OF PAUL THE APOSTLE TO THE

THESSALONIANS

A.D. 54.

Chap. i. 1, 2. The salutation.

CHAPTER I.—(1) Paul, and Silvanus,
and Timotheus,[a] unto the
church of the Thessalonians
in God our Father and the Lord Jesus
Christ: (2) grace unto you, and peace,
from God our Father and the Lord
Jesus Christ.
(3) We are bound to thank God al-
ways[b] for you, brethren, as it is meet,
because that your faith groweth ex-
ceedingly, and the charity
of every one of you all
toward each other abound-
eth; (4) so that we ourselves
glory in you in the churches of God
for your patience and faith in all your
persecutions and tribulations that ye
endure: (5) *which is* a manifest token

Chap. i. 3, 4. Thanksgiving for good news from Thessalonica.

a 1 Thess. i. 1.

b 1 Thess. i. 2.

(1) **Paul, and Silvanus, and Timotheus.**—The company which despatched the First Epistle is not yet broken up. This proves that the Second Epistle was written before the end of the second missionary journey, for after that time we do not read of Silvanus being in the company of St. Paul. The salutation is precisely the same as in the First Epistle, save for the last clause of verse 2, which is wrongly added in that place, but stands rightly here.

(3) **We are bound to thank God always for you, brethren.**—The thanksgiving is regarded as a positive *debt* incurred, which it would be a dishonesty not to pay.

Because.—This assigns the reason for saying that it was "meet," and does not merely follow after "thank God:" in which case, the words "as it is meet" would have been rather weak, as containing no more than is involved in "we are bound." The best paraphrase would be: "We *feel* the obligation to give thanks for you; and, in point of fact, it is but meet that we *should*, because," &c.

Groweth exceedingly.—An enthusiastic word in the original: "is out-growing all bounds." It is a metaphor from vegetable or animal growth. This was one of the very points about which St. Paul was anxious the last time that he had written: then there were deficiencies in their faith (1 Thess. iii. 10).

Charity.—Here, too, St. Paul remembers what he had said to them in the last Epistle, in which he had devoted a whole section to the love of the brethren "toward each other." "Of every one of you all" is a very noticeable expression, as showing the individual solicitude of the Apostles for their converts. Just as the apostolic instructions were given to each Christian privately (1 Thess. ii. 11), so news has been brought how each several Christian is progressing. The differences which had called forth such passages as 1 Thess. iii. 12, iv 6—10, v. 12—14, had apparently all ceased, and mutual love was multiplying.

(4) **So that we ourselves.**—Why was it less likely that St. Paul and his companions should thus glory in them than other friends did, or perhaps than the Thessalonians themselves? Possibly, because it seemed almost like self-praise to praise their own converts; but much more probably, because the writers had before felt and expressed misgivings on the point: this suits the thought of verse 3 better.

Glory in you in the churches of God.—Not only in thanksgiving to God (though, perhaps, outbursts of praise in the public services of "the churches" may be included), but also in talking to other men, at Corinth and elsewhere: so, in return, St. Paul "boasted" to the Thessalonians about the Corinthians (2 Cor. ix. 2).

Your patience and faith.—It was well proved that St. Paul had no more cause for misgiving, and that the tempter's tempting by persecution had not made the apostolic labours to be in vain. (See 1 Thess. iii. 5.) "Patience," in the New Testament, does not mean a meek submissiveness, but a heroic endurance. The "faith" here becomes almost equivalent to "hope," except that it introduces the *ground* of such hope: viz., confidence in the living God; it also includes the notion of *faithfulness*.

Persecutions and tribulations.—The difference between the two words is, that while "tribulation" is quite general, and implies no personal enmities, "persecution" means that a certain set of persons were organising active measures for the annoyance of the Church. Such persecution they were still "enduring" when the Letter was written.

(5) **Which is . . .**—In the fervid eloquence of the original these connecting words are omitted, and the clause added in a kind of apposition to the words "in all your persecutions;" the effect is the same as when we in English put a dash: "which ye endure—a manifest token," &c. The indication of God's righteous judgment consisted not so much in the vitality and growth of the Thessalonians' faith and love as in the very fact of their being persecuted; such persecution was an actual indication how the fair judgment of God would go in the last day. No undue stress is to be laid upon the epithet "righteous," as if it were "a token of the *righteousness of* God's judgment;" the point is only to indicate already *what* a fair judge was likely to decide.

of the righteous judgment of God,
that ye may be counted
worthy of the kingdom of
God,[a] for which ye also
suffer: (6) seeing *it is* a
righteous thing with God
to recompense tribulation
to them that trouble you; (7) and to you
who are troubled rest with us, when the
Lord Jesus shall be revealed from
heaven with his mighty angels,[1] (8) in
flaming fire taking[2] vengeance on them
that know not God, and that obey not
the gospel of our Lord Jesus Christ:[b]
(9) who shall be punished with everlast-
ing destruction from the presence of the

Chap. i. 5–10. Encouragement to bear up under persecution by the thought of coming retribution.

1 Gr. *the angels of his power.*
a Matt. 25. 34.
2 Or, *yielding.*
b Acts 6. 7; Rom. 10. 16.

That ye may be counted worthy.—This expresses the result, not of the future judgment of God, but of the patient sufferings which reveal what that judgment will be. The "counting worthy" (or rather, perhaps, the "*declaring* worthy") is, in fact, the "judgment" or sentence itself. "You suffer in such a manner that we can forecast the fair verdict of God: viz., so as to be then declared (the Greek tense points to a distinct moment of forming the estimate) fit to receive God's kingdom." The word "counted worthy" has in this place nothing to do with the theological question of merit.

The kingdom of God.—Which had formed a prominent feature of the first preaching at Thessalonica. (See *Introduction to the First Epistle to the Thessalonians.*) Are the Thessalonian Christians, then, not yet in the kingdom of God? Yes; but only as its *subjects:* hereafter they are to be counted worthy not of admission into it, but of it itself—*i.e.*, to inherit it, to become kings of it. (Comp. the parallel argument in 2 Tim. ii. 12.)

For which ye also suffer.—St. Paul is very fond of this "also" in relative clauses; it tightens the coupling between the relative and antecedent clauses, and so brings out more clearly the vital connection between suffering and reigning. They suffer "for the kingdom," not merely for the sake of winning it, but on its behalf, in defence of it, in consequence of being its citizens, to extend its dominion.

(6) **Seeing it is.**—Literally, *if so be it is fair:* a form very common in St. Paul, when he wishes to argue from some fact which he knows his readers will recognise (*e.g.*, Rom. viii. 9). "Your persecution is a clear indication what God's fair verdict will be—that He will pronounce you fit—unless indeed you deny (as you will not) that it *is* fair to recompense the persecutors with tribulation and the persecuted with rest." The context shows that St. Paul does not mean that *all* suffering deserves a requital with bliss, but he does put it as a matter of common fairness that when men have suffered for the *kingdom's* sake God should so reward them hereafter.

With God.—Such a system of requital commends itself as fair to men: is it likely to seem less fair in the eyes of God? Holy Scripture always sets forth the power of the human conscience to recognise God's principles of action: whatever is righteous for men is so for God, and *vice versâ.*

(7) **Rest with us.**—Why "with us"? It shows sympathy in their present trials, for it implies that the writers themselves had earned or were earning (see Acts xviii. 12) that rest by the like trials. The word "rest" (or *relaxation*) is the opposite of the "strain" at which the persecution kept them. Such "rest" is not to be expected in its fulness till the judgment day.

From heaven.—St. Paul seems to delight in calling attention to the quarter from which "the Lord Jesus" (the human name, to show His sympathy with trouble) will appear. (See 1 Thess. i. 10; iv. 16.)

With his mighty angels.—Literally, *with the angels of His power—i.e.*, the angels to whom His power is intrusted and by whom it is administered. The angels do not attend merely for pomp, but to execute God's purposes. (See Matt. xiii. 41, 49; xxiv. 31.)

(8) **In flaming fire.**—Most critics agree to change the punctuation here, by omitting the comma after "angels" and inserting it after "fire." The flaming fire here is not the instrument of the vengeance—*i.e.*, hell-fire—but the common pictorial attribute of the Divine Presence (Ex. iii. 2; xix. 18; Dan. vii. 9).

Taking vengeance.—The expression in the original is one which is said to be found nowhere else in Greek literature, save in Ezek. xxv. 14 (though in Hebrew there is an almost exact equivalent in Num. xxxi. 3), so that it is difficult to assign the correct meaning. It certainly does *not* mean "taking vengeance" in the sense of "taking His revenge," as though our Lord had conceived a personal grudge and were wreaking it. What it does mean would seem to be "assigning retribution:" appointing, that is, to each man what satisfaction of justice he must make. The very word for "vengeance" can only mean vengeance exacted on some one else's behalf. (Comp. 1 Thess. iv. 6, and Ps. lxxix. 10.)

On them that know not God.—According to the Greek, the word "them" should be repeated also in the next clause. The effect will then be to mark off the culprits into two classes: "them that know not," and "them that obey not." A comparison of Eph iv. 17, 18, 1 Thess. iv. 5, shows that by the first class are meant Gentiles; a comparison of Rom. x. 16, 21 (and many other passages) will show disobedience to be the characteristic of the Jews. The Greek negative particle here is one which shows that the ignorance of the one set and the disobedience of the other were just the points for which they were to be punished: therefore, of course, only those Gentiles whose ignorance was voluntary, who chose (Rom. i. 28) to be Gentiles when they might have been joined to the true God, are objects of wrath. Here, as the context shows, St. Paul is thinking chiefly of those Gentiles and Jews who actually persecuted the truth.

Obey not the gospel.—A noteworthy phrase; see the reference. The gospel, the "glad tidings," contains not only a statement of facts, but also a call to obey a law which is the outcome of the facts. Even the acceptance of evangelical promises requires a submission. (Comp. Luke xxiv. 47; Acts xi. 18; Rev. xxii. 3.) It is here called specially the gospel "of our Lord Jesus Christ," because the sin of the Jews (who constitute this class of sinners) consisted precisely in the wilful rejection of Jesus as the Christ.

(9) **Punished with everlasting destruction** specifies the "vengeance" to be taken. But the word "destruction" does not stand absolutely and alone as a synonym for "annihilation." This passage, in itself, gives us no reason to suppose that the lost will be "destroyed" in the ordinary sense of the word. They

Lord,[a] and from the glory of his power;
(10) when he shall come to be glorified
in his saints, and to be admired in all
them that believe (because our testimony
among you was believed) in that day.
(11) Wherefore also we pray always for
you, that our God would count[1] you
worthy of *this* calling, and fulfil all the
good pleasure of *his* goodness, and
the work of faith with
power: (12) that the name
of our Lord Jesus Christ
may be glorified in you,
and ye in him, according to the
grace of our God and the Lord Jesus
Christ.

a Luke 13. 28.

1 Or, vouchsafe.

Chap. i. 11, 12. Prayer, serving to introduce the practical portion.

---

are to be "destroyed *from the presence* of the Lord, and from the glory of His power"—*i.e.*, cut off from it for ever. The "presence"—or, more literally here, "*the face*—of the Lord," as well as "the glory of His power," is a metaphor from the courts of Oriental kings, where only honoured courtiers are admitted to spend their time in the immediate and familiar presence of the sovereign. Familiar contact with Christ hereafter, which will be accorded to all the saved, was God's ideal intention for the lost as well, therefore it is a positive "destruction" to be banished from it. But to the Jews, who looked for a Messiah who should keep regal state, the punishment was peculiarly appropriate. The word is used besides in 1 Cor. v. 5; 1 Thess. v. 3; 1 Tim. vi. 9. As for the word rendered "everlasting" (or *eternal*, for it is the same which is used, *e.g.*, Heb. vi. 2), it would certainly convey to St. Paul's readers the notion of *incessant duration in time*; it is, of course, only an adaptation to human language to speak of time at all in such a case, as we cannot tell what may take the place of time in the next dispensation; however, so far as the actual words go, there is nothing in these passages (Matt. xviii. 8; xxv. 41, 46; Mark iii. 29; Heb. vi. 2; Jude, verse 7) to suggest any future alteration in the state of the lost. In this, as in some other doctrines, there seem to be two distinct sets of passages, the logical reconciliation of which in our present state seems almost impossible.

(10) **When he shall come.**—Not simply a repetition of the temporal date which was mentioned in verse 7—"when the Lord," &c.—but an introduction of the contrast which will be presented "in that day" by the spectacle of the glory of the saints. Thus the penalty of verse 9 is made to appear greater, while at the same time the readers' minds are turned back to a more wholesome subject for meditation.

To be glorified in his saints.—This is not exactly the *purpose*, but the *effect* of His coming. A comparison of John xiii. 31, 32; xiv. 13; xvii. 10; 2 Thess. i. 12; shows that the saints are the objects *on* which and *by* which the glorious perfection of Christ is exhibited: to see what the saints will be exalted to "in that day" will make all observers acknowledge, not the holiness or greatness of the men, but the divine power of Him who was able so to exalt them. As the persecutors were divided into two classes to be punished, so the saved are described under two aspects: in contrast with "them that know not God" they are "saints," *i.e.*, fully consecrated to God; in contrast with "them that obey not the gospel" they are "they that believed" (for the past tense is the better reading), *i.e.*, accepted the gospel. As the profane Gentiles, looking on the saints, recognise the "glory" of the God whom they knew not, so the disobedient Jews, seeing the faithful, are aptly filled with "wonder" (Acts xiii. 41), before they perish, at the glory to be attained by obedience to the law of suffering.

Because our testimony.—Introduced to show why the writers had said specially "in all them that believed" (the past tense is employed because it looks back from the Judgment Day to the moment when the gospel was offered and the divergence between believers and unbelievers began); the reason was, because among "all them that believed" the Thessalonians would be found included.

In that day.—Added at the end to make the readers look once more (as it were) upon the wonderful sight on which the writer's prophetic eyes were raptly fixed.

(11) **Wherefore.**—Literally, *whereunto*—*i.e.*, to their being found among the blessed. The "also" serves to emphasise the "pray": we do not content ourselves with merely hoping, but we direct actual prayer to that end. The word "whereunto" seems grammatically to depend upon the word "calling"—"of the calling whereunto, we *pray* also for you always, that our God would count you worthy."

Count you worthy of this calling.—The word "this" would, perhaps, have been better left out; the "calling" of which St. Paul is thinking is the calling "in that day," such as is expressed in Matt. xxv. 34, and the act is the same as that of verse 5. But had they not been called to glory already? Yes (1 Thess. iv. 7), and had obeyed the call; and God was still calling them hourly (see Notes on 1 Thess. ii. 12; v. 24); but that was no security that they would remain worthy of that last decisive call. "Many are called, but few chosen." In the original there is some emphasis laid on the pronoun: "count *you*."

Fulfil all the good pleasure of his goodness.—Rather, *fulfil every purpose of goodness*; or, "everything which beneficence deems good." Most modern commentators take the "goodness" to be the goodness of the Thessalonians themselves, thus making the clause logically antecedent to the foregoing: "May count you worthy of His calling, and (for that purpose) fulfil every good moral aspiration you may entertain." But this seems unnecessary. The "beneficence" is used absolutely, in almost a personified sense; it is, of course, in reality, God's beneficence, but is spoken of as beneficence in the abstract. Thus the clause preserves its natural place as an explanation of the preceding: "May finally call you, and there accomplish upon your persons all that beneficence can devise."

And the work of faith with power.—This work, too, is God's work, not the work of the Thessalonians. It is used in the same sense as a like phrase in Cowper's well-known hymn—

> "Thou shalt see My glory soon,
> When *the work of grace* is done."

It means, not "perfect your faithful activity," as in 1 Thess. i. 3, but "bring to its mighty consummation the work that faith was able to effect in you." Faith, therefore, is here opposed as much to sight as to unbelief. The "beneficence" and the "power" thus exerted upon (rather than through) the Thessalonians, produces upon all spectators of the judgment, both angels and men, the effect described in the next verse.

(12) **That the name . . .**—This verse gathers up

CHAPTER II.—(1) Now we beseech you, brethren, by the coming of our Lord Jesus Christ, and *by* our gathering together unto him,[a] (2) that ye be not soon shaken in mind, or be troubled, neither by spirit, nor by word, nor by letter as from us, as that the day of Christ is at hand. (3) Let no man deceive you by any means:[b] for *that day shall not come,* except there come a falling away first,[c] and that man of sin be

Chap. ii. 1, 2. Caution against forged communications teaching the nearness of the Advent.

Chap. ii. 3—5. The Antichrist must come first.

A.D. 54.

b Matt. 24. 4.

a 1 Thess. 4. 17; Matt. 24. 31.

c 1 Tim. 4. 1.

---

what has been said in verses 8—10. Seeing the favours bestowed upon the Christians in the last day, all, the lost as well as the saved, will be forced to acknowledge the glory (*i.e.*, the divine perfection) of the Jesus whose Christship had been rejected, and the glory (*i.e.*, the true dignity) of the Christians who had been despised for their allegiance to Him. It stands to reason that Christians must share Christ's "glory" (*i.e.*, full recognition; comp. Note on 1 Thess. ii. 6) in that day, for when the lost recognise what He is, it is *ipso facto* a recognition that they were right and wise to follow Him. The words "according to the grace" belong only to "and ye in Him:" it is the gracious will (for "grace" here has hardly its strict theological sense) of God, in which Christ concurs, that we should be thus "glorified in Him."

II.

The first chapter had encouraged the Thessalonians under persecution by the thought of the *reality* of the Advent. The author has not in the least changed his opinion about the Advent since writing the First Epistle. It is still a matter of most practical comfort: "a very present help." But now, in clear tones, he warns the Thessalonians against supposing that the "end" was "by-and-by" (Luke xxi. 9). He had, in fact, taught them so from the outset, and had even then pointed out to them a sign, unaccomplished as yet, which they must see accomplished before the Advent should come.

(1) **Brethren.**—The Apostles have won a hearing for the true Advent doctrine by their sympathetic treatment of it in the former chapter; now they soften their correction of the false doctrine by using tender names.

By the coming.—Literally, *for the sake of the coming*, just as in English we adjure persons to do a thing "for God's sake." It is a stronger form of adjuration than the simple "by," inasmuch as it implies that the thing or person adjured by will suffer if the action be left unperformed. The Coming of Christ and the meeting with the beloved dead would not be so bright, so perfect, perhaps so soon, if the Thessalonians allowed themselves to be misled with regard to it.

Our gathering together.—The peculiar Greek word is the same as that used in Heb. x. 25 of the assembling to the Lord's Supper, and nowhere else, so that some have interpreted it in the same sense here. In *verb* form it is thus used in 1 Thess. iv. 17. The close connection between the two "gatherings together" may be seen in 1 Cor. xi. 26. The "our" means the meeting of the dead and the quick together.

(2) **Not soon shaken.**—The meaning would be clearer if we inserted "so" before "soon," for it does not mean vaguely that they were for the future not to be lightly shaken, but (as in Gal. i. 6) that they had already been shaken, and that in an unconscionably short time since their first teaching on the subject.

In mind.—In the original it is, *from your mind; from your reason.*

Be troubled.—The tense of the verb "be troubled" differs in the Greek from that of "be shaken"; for the "driving out of their wits" is regarded as a single act; the "agitation," or being troubled, as a chronic condition, into which there was fear of their falling. This shaking and trouble probably brought about the disorders spoken of in chap. iii. The instruments by which men had partly driven the Thessalonians out of their wits already were three:—(1) "Through spirit," *i.e.*, by pretended manifestations of the Holy Spirit's power, whether through false signs or, more probably, through "prophesyings." (See 1 Thess. v. 20—22, where the fear of some abuse of prophecy is clearly marked already.) (2) "Through word," *i.e.*, word of mouth, as opposed to the written letter next mentioned. Most modern commentators seem rightly to take the words "as from us" with this clause as well as with the next; some persons misrepresented what they had heard the Apostles say on the topic, or pretended to have been intrusted with a message from them. (3) "Through letter;" apparently forged letters, purporting to be from (or, literally, *through*) St. Paul, had been circulated. (See Note on chap. iii. 17.) "Word" and "letter" occur again in verse 15 as his ordinary means of teaching.

As that the day of Christ is at hand—*i.e.*, "to the effect that it is,"—giving the contents of the pretended revelation; for "as that" follows grammatically upon "spirit, word, letter," not upon "shaken, troubled." The word for "is at hand" implies a very close proximity indeed, the participle, in fact (like our word "instant"), being used for "present," *e.g.*, Gal. i. 4. Probably the form which the false doctrine at Thessalonica was beginning to take was that the day of the Lord had already set in, thus confusing the whole idea of a personal, visible Advent, just as, at a later period, Hymenæus and Philetus confused the true doctrine of resurrection by affirming that it was already past (2 Tim. ii. 18). St. Paul not only denies vigorously that the day is come, but proceeds in the next verse to show that the signs of its approach are not yet exhibited. The best reading gives "the day of *the Lord*," not "of Christ." (See Note on 1 Thess. v. 2.)

(3) **Let no man . . . by any means.**—"Whatever device they may adopt—spirit, letter, or what not—they are deceivers or deceived; do not be duped by them." The form of warning is a mark of St. Paul's style. (Comp. 1 Cor. iii. 18; Eph. v. 6.)

For . . . except.—The words between are rightly supplied in our version. Probably, St. Paul's first intention was to turn verse 5 differently, as, for instance: "For, except that Man of Sin, &c., ye remember that I told you the day would not come." The length of the sentence made him break off (as he often does) without regard for grammatical completeness.

A falling away.—A great change in the purpose of the sentence will be felt directly "*the*" is substituted for "a." Only one insignificant MS. omits the definite article; the same article in our version is vigorously

revealed, the son of perdition;[a] (4) who opposeth and exalteth himself above all that is called God,[b] or that is worshipped; so that he as God sitteth in

[a] John 17. 12.
[b] Dan. 11. 36.

rendered "that" before "man of sin." In both cases the purpose is by no means to utter a new, strange prophecy, or to add to the knowledge of the readers, but to remind them of careful teaching given during the first few weeks after their conversion. "That falling away" must undoubtedly imply that the persons so apostatising had formerly held (or, perhaps, still professed to hold) the Christian faith: men cannot fall from ground which they never occupied. This vast and dreadful Apostasy (see Luke xviii. 8), so clearly and prominently taught of to the ancient Church, and so mysterious to us, is further defined by the following words, as the Apocalypse or Manifestation of the Man of Sin. Of this revelation of Antichrist the same word (*apocalypsis*) is used which is often used of Christ, as, *e.g.*, chap. i. 7; Luke xvii. 30; and thrice in St. Peter; so that we may expect to recognise him when he comes as clearly as we shall recognise Christ. The conception of the Antichrist is not merely that of an opponent of the Christ, but of a rival Christ: there is a hideous parallelism between the two.

That man of sin.—It is not absolutely certain from the Greek, but the context makes it tolerably clear that the "Man of Sin" is the head and centre of the Apostasy itself, and does not form a separate movement from it. The "Man of Sin," then, will have at one time formed (or will still profess to form) part of the Christian Church, and the Apostasy will culminate in him. Thus, for instance, the requirements of the passage would not be fulfilled by (with Hammond) interpreting the Apostasy to mean the early Gnostic movement, followed up by the independent appearance of Nero as the Man of Sin. The phrase, "the Man of Sin," might, perhaps, be only a poetical personification of a movement, or of a class of men, or of a succession of men (as, *e.g.*, Ps. lxxxix. 22; Rev. ii. 20; xvii. 3); but the analogy of the parallel passages in Dan. viii. and xi. leads rather to the supposition that St. Paul looked for the coming of some actual individual man who should be the impersonation of the movement of Apostasy. The genitive (see Note on 1 Thess. i. 3) is like a forcible epithet: "A man so wicked that, bad as other men are, wickedness should be his mark by which he is distinguished from all others; a man who *belongs* to sin, in whom the ideal of sin has become realised and incarnate." What kind of sin will be most prominent in him is not expressed in the word itself; but the context points clearly to that which is, in fact, the crowning sin—spiritual pride and rebellious arrogancy (Eph. vi. 12).

The son of perdition.—The phrase which is used, in John xvii. 12, of the false Apostle; it suits well with the description of the Man of Sin, who, like Judas, will have "fallen away" from high Christian privileges: according to one popular interpretation, like Judas, from the privileges of the Apostolate itself. The expression signifies one who belongs by natural ties to perdition—who from his very birth chooses evil, and in such a sense may be said to be born to be lost (Matt. xxvi. 24; 2 Pet. ii. 12). Both his malignity and his doom are thus implied in it.

(4) **Who opposeth and exalteth himself.**—The original continues a quasi-substantival form:—"the opposer and exalter of himself"—well-known descriptions (doubtless) of the Antichrist; several of the details are drawn directly from the description of Antiochus in Dan. xi. Being merely descriptive epithets, we are not at liberty to press the present tense, and say that the Man of Sin was already thus acting at the time St. Paul wrote. The word for "the opposer," or "adversary," is a pretty close rendering of the name "Satan," and passed, in ecclesiastical Greek into a synonym for it. The acts here attributed to the Man of Sin are peculiarly Satanic. (Comp. Isa. xiv. 12—14; 2 Tim. iii. 6.) Of course, however, we must not confound Satan himself with his human minister.

Above all that is called God.—The translation here is not quite exact. The word "above" in the original is compounded with "exalteth"; it should be, *and super-exalteth*, or *exhalteth himself above measure* (2 Cor. xii. 7, where the same compound is used) *against every God so called.* Probably the clause "against every God" is to be taken *only* with "super-exalteth"; the description "who opposeth" stands absolutely: it is one characteristic of the Man of Sin to be always in opposition, and to have concord with no one. "Every God so called" includes the false gods *with* the true God (comp. 1 Cor. viii. 5): true or false, it matters not to jealous Antichrist, who would have nothing worshipped but himself. This explains the addition of the little clause, "or that is worshipped." Many things received religious homage from men without being called gods; and the original word (*sebasma*) may perhaps be designed to hint at one such worship, viz., the worship of the Augustus (*Sebastos*). It would be far-fetched, however, to see in this a direct prophecy of conflict between Antichrist and the Civil Power; although it must be admitted that even the word "gods" is *sometimes* used of secular rulers (*e.g.*, Ps. lxxxii. 1—6; John x. 34), in which sense some take it here.

So that he as God.—The words "as God" are not part of the original text, and should be struck out. In several other points, however, our version does not bring out the profanity of the act as clearly as the Greek. Literally it would be, "so as to seat *himself* in the shrine of God, showing himself off that he is God." The "himself" brings out the spontaneous arrogancy of the deed; the Man of Sin does not merely yield to servile flatterers. The "sitting" is not in the tense of habitual custom, but indicates one expressive act of taking possession. The "in" (literally, *into*) brings out the idea of actual intrusion; while the word for "temple" is not the general name for the whole group of buildings with their courts, but the sacred house itself: it is the word which would describe the Holy and Holy of Holies (see Matt. xxiii. 35; xxvii. 5, 51; Acts xvii. 4) of the Jewish temple; and probably it is the Mercy Seat that supplies the image to St. Paul's mind (Ps. xcix. 1).

The temple of God.—Though the image is drawn from the Jewish temple, we may say with some confidence that St. Paul did not expect the Antichrist as a prose fact to take his seat in that edifice. Neither is the metaphor to be pressed into a mere synonym of "the Church" (1 Cor. iii. 17). The words, so far, need not *necessarily* mean that the Man of Sin will make special claims upon the Christian community as such. Rather, the whole phrase, "taking his seat in the temple of God," is a poetical or prophetical description of usurping divine prerogatives generally: not the prerogatives

the temple of God, shewing himself that
he is God.[a] (5) Remember ye not, that,
when I was yet with you, I told you
these things? (6) And now ye know
what withholdeth[1] that he might be
revealed in his time. (7) For the
mystery of iniquity doth
already work: only he
who now letteth *will let*,
until he be taken out

[a] Rev. 13. 4.

[1] Or, *holdeth.*

Chap. ii. 6, 7. Before Antichrist comes, the Roman empire must go.

of the true God alone, but whatever prerogatives have been offered to anything "called God." Though the prophecy might be fulfilled without any symbolical act (*e.g.*, of assuming any material throne), yet the spontaneousness ("himself") and the openness ("showing himself") seem so essentially parts of the prophecy as of necessity to imply that the Man of Sin will make *formal* claim to occupy that central seat in men's minds and aspirations which is acknowledged to be due to God alone. The formal making of this claim seems to be identical with the apocalypse of the Man of Sin, the act by which he is manifested or revealed.

Shewing himself.—Or, *thus showing himself off.* It does not mean that he makes any attempt to prove that he is God; the word only carries on the pictorial representation of the Man of Sin enthroning himself upon the Mercy Seat, and by that act of session parading his pretended divinity. As has been said, the performance of a typical act is not of vital consequence to the accomplishment of the prophecy (as, *e.g.*, Zech. ix. 9 might have been truly accomplished without the literal riding of Matt. xxi. 7), though there are few great movements which do not express themselves in outward typical acts; but these words show that (unless St. Paul was mistaken) an explicit claim will be made for submission, like that of creature to Creator. Even if the "Man of Sin" only signifies a tendency, not a person, yet this "exhibition of himself as God" would hardly be satisfied by a social concession, however widespread, to a general spirit of (say) fleshly luxury or atheistic intellectualism, without the claims of these ideals being *eo nomine* put forward and consciously admitted. But it is hard to believe that anything avowedly atheistic would be spoken of as explicitly claiming or receiving divine honours. It seems, therefore, most probable that the great Apostasy will not become avowedly atheistic, but will be an apostasy (so to speak) within the Church, and that the Man of Sin, who heads that Apostasy, will make especial claim upon the Christian Church to accord consciously the very honours which she pays to the living God.

(5) **Remember ye not.**—A rebuke of the same character as Rom. vi. 3; 1 Cor. vi. 19, and, like those, levelled at ignorance of what in apostolic days were thought the six fundamental points of Christian teaching (Heb. v. 12; vi. 1, 2). The doctrine of Antichrist would naturally form part of the course on resurrection and judgment. This explains how the doctrine was enforced (1) so early in the education of the Christian churches: "while I was yet with you" (see *Introduction to the First Epistle to Thessalonians*); and (2) so emphatically and repeatedly: "my habit was to tell you these things"—for the word translated "told" is in the imperfect tense, which means more than a single action. Notice that in St. Paul's eager personal recollection of thus teaching, he for once (and nowhere else) forgets Silas and Timothy: not "we," but "I." Imagine a forger who should forge with such subtlety! Mark also how erroneous is the opinion that St. Paul in this Epistle recedes from his former teaching about the Advent and its date.

(6) **And now ye know.**—Not "now, because of what I have just said," for nothing has yet been said in the Letter from which the Thessalonians could gather what withheld the premature manifestation of the Man of Sin. The word "now" is not used exactly in a temporal sense, but as introducing another item. "You remember about Antichrist and his characteristics: very good; and now, what keeps Antichrist back? You know that too." Knowing not only that Antichrist's apocalypse must precede Christ's, but also that Antichrist could not reveal himself yet, because the way was blocked by something still (as they saw) unremoved, the Thessalonians were absurd in acting as if the day of the Lord was come.

What withholdeth.—Rather, *that which withholdeth:* they did not merely know it as a dogma, but as a familiar object. "You are perfectly acquainted with the thing which acts as a check upon the Man of Sin." Unlike the Man of Sin himself, who was a dim figure in the mysterious future, the Obstacle was present and tangible. They may have forgotten what the thing is, but St. Paul stirs their memory by telling them that they well know the thing itself. It must needs be a marked and mighty power which can prevent the development of the great Antichrist. At the same time, St. Paul's doctrine is that this marked power is destined by-and-by to be removed (verse 7). Possibly, then, St. Paul may shrink from naming it in writing, not only because he wishes to exercise the Thessalonians' memories, but also for fear the power should discover and disapprove of his prophecies. For the question what the withholding power is, see the *Excursus on the Interpretation of the Prophecy.*

That he might . . . in his time.—Or, *with a view to his being revealed at his proper moment.* Not that the withholding power is conscious of such desire, but God's design is to use that power for the purpose.

(7) **For.**—Logically, the "for" belongs to the clause "he that letteth;" thus: "For, although the mystery is already at work, the wicked one will not be revealed until he that now withholds shall disappear."

The mystery of iniquity doth already work.—Both "mystery" and "iniquity" have the article in the Greek, perhaps (as in verse 3) because the phrase was well known to the Thessalonians. *Lawlessness* is a more literal rendering than "iniquity"; the same word in 1 John iii. 4 is rendered "the transgression of the law." The word "mystery" in Greek does not necessarily involve any notion of mysteriousness in our modern sense. It means a secret (which may be, in its own nature, quite simple) known to the initiated, but incapable of being known until it is divulged. Here the whole emphasis is thrown, by a very peculiar order of the Greek words, upon the word "mystery." It may be paraphrased thus:—"For *as a secret,* into which the world is not yet initiated, that lawlessness is *already* at work." Thus the word "mystery" stands in sharp contrast with the word "revealed" in verses 6, 8: the time for publishing, openly avowing, the secret is not yet come. To whom, then, is the mystery of that lawlessness now known? Not to all those who are contributing to its ultimate manifestation, for most of them are deceived by it (verse 10), and, while sharers

of the way. (8) And then shall that
Wicked be revealed, whom the Lord
shall consume with the spirit of his
mouth,[a] and shall destroy with the
brightness of his coming: (9) *even him,*
whose coming is after the working of
Satan with all power and
signs and lying wonders,
(10) and with all deceivable-
ness of unrighteousness in

Chap. ii. 9—12. Terrors of the judgment upon false Christians.

a Isa. 11. 4.

---

in the Apostasy, still believe themselves members of the Church. The mystery is known to God, and (1) to enlightened Christians like St. Paul; (2) to Satan and a few Satanic men who avow to themselves their real object in joining the movement. Though the mystery is said to work (the verb expresses an inward activity, *e.g.*, 1 Thess. ii. 13, Rom. vii. 5, like that of leaven on the lump), it is not a personal thing, not (like "Man of Sin," "that which withholdeth,") a covert description of any person or set of persons; it is solely the unavowed design which is gradually gaining influence over men's hearts: it is the same movement as the "falling away" of verse 3. In several places (*e.g.*, 2 Pet. ii. 1 *et seq.;* Jude, verse 18 *et seq.*) the coarser side of the "falling away" is spoken of, but here the "lawlessness" seems not so much to mean ordinary antinomianism as insubordination to God—rebellion.

Only he . . . .—More correctly, *Only* [*it cannot be revealed*] *until he that now withholdeth disappear from the midst.* The English version has obscured the meaning by putting "letteth," although the word is precisely the same as in verse 6—the only difference being that there it was neuter: "the thing which withholdeth;" while here it is masculine: "he." Evidently to St. Paul's mind there was a great obstructive power, which was gathered up in, and wielded by, the person so described: "he that withholdeth." How this potentate would "disappear out of our midst" St. Paul gives no hint; but obviously not by death: for, unless the power itself was to disappear with him, his successor would equally be "he that now withholdeth." We may therefore say that the prophecy would be satisfied if "he that withholdeth" proved to be a whole succession of persons; we have hardly the same right to say so of the "Lawless One."

(8) **And then.**—Then at length, when the obstructor is gone, two things shall happen: (1) the Lawless One shall be revealed, and (2) then the Lord will come and destroy him. The purpose with which St. Paul began this chapter was to show relatively the date of our Lord's Advent; but he is now so engrossed in describing the events which must precede it, that when he does mention the Advent again he does so in a parenthetical relative clause.

That Wicked.—Or, *the Lawless One.* The English version has again obscured the passage by not keeping the same word as in verse 7. The general tendency to "lawlessness" or "rebellion" will be brought to a head in the person of "the Lawless One" or "the "Rebel," just as the "obstruction" is impersonated in "the Obstructor." The publication of the "secret of rebelliousness" will be effected by the manifesto of the Rebel-in-chief. Of course, this Rebel is the same person with the Man of Sin, the change of title being due to the particularising of his sin by the word "lawlessness" in verse 7; the specification of the *time* is the only additional intelligence; all the emphasis of the sentence, therefore, rests on "And *then.*"

The Lord.—The best text adds the name Jesus, which serves more clearly to contrast Him with His rival. The word "whom" might be more pointedly paraphrased by "and him."

With the spirit of his mouth.—St. Paul is quoting roughly from Isa. xi. 4 (comp. Job iv. 9; Ps. xviii. 15; Wisd. xi. 20: "might have fallen down with one blast, . . . scattered abroad through the breath of Thy power"); and therefore we are to understand it to signify the perfect ease with which Christ will destroy Antichrist. Even when the phrase is used of speech (as it may perhaps be here), the absence of labour is the point to be noticed (*e.g.*, Ps. xxxiii. 6).

With the brightness of his coming.—Rather, *with the appearing of His presence.* Here, again, it is the mere fact of the true Christ's showing Himself, which will reduce to nothingness (such is the meaning of the Greek for "destroy") the false Christ. When they shall stand face to face there will be no possibility of delusion any more.

(9) **Even him, whose coming.**—The "even him" does not stand in the Greek; and "whose" might, again, be rendered by *for his own,* or perhaps "though his own." The purpose of the verses following is not merely to describe Antichrist more fully, but to compare word for word his coming with that which will annihilate him. Again is used of Antichrist a peculiar word consecrated to the Christ: "coming" (literally *presence*), being the word used in verse 8, as well as verse 1, and often. In spite of the sham being well got up, it will be seen to be a sham.

Is . . . with all power.—"Is:" St. Paul sees the future as present. The predicate is not "after the working," but "in all power," &c. The advent of Antichrist will be in (*i.e.*, surrounded with, accompanied by) all kinds of miracles, "according to the working of Satan:" *i.e.*, not only wrought by Satan, but up to the full capacity of Satan to work them. The word "lying" (literally, *of falsehood*) should go with all three names, "all counterfeit power and signs and wonders." The three words are piled up to heighten the terror of the description; if you press them they mean that there will be a display of power, to attest Antichrist's doctrine (signs), and to keep men spellbound in admiration of him (wonders). Antichrist, like Christ (1 Tim. vi. 15), has one to support him—Satan, instead of God; he, like Christ (Luke xxi. 25), will have his miracles—but miracles of trickery, not of truth.

(10) **And with all deceivableness.**—"Deceivableness" does not mean "readiness to *be deceived,*" but, according to old English usage, has an active meaning; the words include and expand the list just given: "in all sham power and signs and wonders, and, in fact, in every iniquitous fraud."

In them that perish.—Rather, *for them.* These are not the persons who exercise the fraud, but the objects of it. The word depends not only on "deceivableness," but on the whole sentence: "his coming (for them) is," &c. St. Paul adds the words as a consolation to "them that are saved": it will not be possible to seduce the elect (Mark xiii. 22). "They that perish" (1 Cor. i. 18; 2 Cor. ii. 15; iv. 3; comp. also Acts ii. 47) is a phrase which contains no reference whatever to the doctrine of predestination, but merely describes the class; the men who let themselves be

them that perish; because they received
not the love of the truth, that they
might be saved. (11) And for this cause
God shall send them strong delusion,
that they should believe a lie: (12) that
they all might be damned who believed
not the truth, but had pleasure in unrighteousness.

(13) But we are bound to give thanks
alway to God for you,[a]
brethren beloved of the
Lord,[b] because God hath
from the beginning chosen
you to salvation through
sanctification of the Spirit
and belief of the truth:

Chap. ii. 13—17. Contrast presented by the happy state of Thessalonian Church; exhortation; paragogic prayer.

a ch. 1. 3.

b 1 Thess. 1. 4.

---

thus duped are, as a plain matter of fact, in course of perishing.

Because.—Here does come in the question of God's decree. The phrase rendered "because" means "in requital of the fact that," which at once implies that their being duped by Antichrist's coming is a judicial visitation. (See next verse.) "They did not receive," *i.e.*, it was offered them, and they refused it; not, as Calvinism would teach, because it was not given them. The grace of *love* of the truth is offered us along with every new presentment of truth; if we are too indolent to examine whether it be truth, we are rejecting the *love* of the truth. This is a worse thing than not accepting the truth itself: if they had only aspired to know what *was* the truth they would have been saved, even if, in fact, they had been in error.

(11) **And for this cause**—*i.e.*, because they did not care whether things were true or not. This verse is not a mere repetition of verses 9 and 10. *There* we were told of external dangers which would attend Antichrist's coming for them that perish: because they had not cared for truth, therefore the presence of the Man of Sin, which could not even imperil the truth-lovers, would for them be full of special marvels and frauds by which they might be misled. *Here* is set forth the effect upon their own *selves* of refusing to accept God's gift of love of truth: God takes from them (by His natural law) their power of discerning the true from the false, and thus (as it were) actually deceives them. Every wilful sin does this double mischief: it strengthens the power of the temptation without; it weakens the power to resist within. For an illustration, see 2 Chron. xviii. 7, 22: Ahab cares only for the pleasant, not the true, and the Lord requites him by sending forth a lying spirit to entice him.

Shall send.—The Greek has *sendeth:* so "is" in verse 9: St. Paul sees it all going on before his eyes. "A strong delusion" should be "an effectual inward working of error"—no longer a mere indifference to truth, but a real influence of error upon their hearts. This inward work of error is sent "with a view to their believing *the* lie" (the Greek has the definite article)—the lie (that is) which Antichrist would have them believe. A terrible combination when God and Satan are agreed to deceive a man! Yet what an encouragement to see God using Satan for His own purposes.

(12) **That they all.**—This is God's purpose in making them believe the lie—"in order that, one and all, they might be judged." He who desireth not the death of a sinner, now is said actually to lay plans with the intention of judging him: such are the bold self-contradictions of the Bible! It must not, however, be forgotten for a moment that God did not begin to will the sinner's judgment till after He had offered him freely the love of His own blessed truth, and had been rejected. When once the sinner is incurable, the only way to vindicate truth and righteousness is by hastening on his condemnation, whatever that condemnation may mean.

Who believed not the truth . . . .—Once more the offence for which they are condemned is insisted upon. Theirs is no fancy sin. What God wanted them to believe was not some fantastical dogma, some fiction between which and the fictions of the Man of Sin there was nothing morally to choose, but the inviolable truth by which God Himself is bound. *But had pleasure in the unrighteousness* (so runs the Greek): *i.e.*, consciously gave their moral consent to the unrighteousness of verse 10, the unrighteousness which sought to impose itself upon them, and which they would never have been led into had they loved the truth.

(13) **But we are bound.**—This may be called a recurrence to the subject dropped at chap. i. 3. The pronoun is somewhat emphatic. It might have seemed more natural to have sharpened the contrast between the Thessalonian Christians and the unhappy people just mentioned by beginning "But you." It is, however, part of St. Paul's delicacy of sympathy to describe rather the effect upon himself and his two companions of *observing* that contrast. He sets himself to work the contrast out.

Beloved of the Lord.—Precisely the same phrase as in 1 Thess. i. 4, except for the substitution of "the Lord" for "God," which shows the concurrence of the Eternal Son in His Father's predestinations. As in the former passage, the tense ("who have been loved") makes the reader think of the everlasting duration of that love (Jer. xxxi. 3), and is again connected with the mystery of election.

"O love, who ere life's earliest dawn
On me thy choice hast gently laid."

Hath . . . chosen.—The Greek tense should be rendered by *chose,* referring to the definite moment (so to speak) in the divine counsels when the choice was fixed. This moment is defined as "from the beginning," *i.e.*, from the eternity preceding the origin of time, called by the same name in Gen. i. 1, John i. 1, and 1 John i. 1. It does not simply mean "from the outset," *i.e.*, from the moment of first thinking at all about you. The identical phrase is said not to occur again in St. Paul. It may be noticed that there is a striking various-reading in some of the MSS., involving the change of only one letter, which would give us (instead of "chose you from the beginning") "chose you as firstfruits." Comp. Jas. i. 18; but the reading in the text is better supported.

To salvation.—This "salvation" is in contrast with the "destruction" (chap. i. 9), "perdition" (chap. ii. 3), or "perishing" (chap. ii. 10), all of which represent the same word in the Greek. Out of the wreck of a world, God had from eternity chosen these Thessalonians to come off safely.

Through sanctification of the Spirit and belief of the truth.—This again teaches us the apostolic idea of election. It is not an absolute irreversible predestination to a particular state of happiness

(14) whereunto he called you by our gospel, to the obtaining of the glory of our Lord Jesus Christ.[a] (15) Therefore, brethren, stand fast, and hold the traditions which ye have been taught, whether by word, or our epistle.

[a] 1 Thess. 5. 9.

on which the elect is to enter after death. The "salvation" is present, begun in this life (Eph. ii. 5, 8), and carried on along fixed lines, namely, "in sanctification of spirit and belief of truth" (such is the literal rendering). The preposition "in" has here the same force as in 1 Thess. iv. 4, 7, namely, "by way of," "by a course of." If, therefore, God chose the Thessalonian Christians to salvation by a course of sanctification and belief, one thing, at any rate, is clear: that if any of them should leave that course, and fall into the errors and sins denounced in the foregoing verses, then, in the Apostle's mind, they would have forfeited their salvation, in spite of God's choice of them. Consequently, we are forced to one of two theories: either that the man has no free will at all, the moral character of his actions depending as entirely upon God as his final destiny; or else, that the man is free, and that God singles him out to enjoy special opportunities of sanctification and of correct belief, which the man may accept or reject as he pleases. The first of these theories lies open to the question, why, if God is responsible for the moral character of the actions of His elect and for their belief, He does not sanctify them at once and completely, and make each one infallible in doctrine; but, in any case, lax morality or creed is as incompatible with the hope of a Calvinist as with that of an orthodox Christian. "Sanctification of spirit" seems to mean "spiritual sanctification:" an inward process, not merely outward change of conduct. This is, of course, wrought by the action of the Holy Spirit upon our spirits; but the omission of the definite article in the Greek is difficult to explain if the "spirit" mentioned be other than the spirit acted upon. "Belief of truth" is opposed to "believing the lie," of verse 11: acceptation of facts as they are, especially the deep facts of revelation, is always the great means of sanctification in Holy Scripture (John xvii. 17).

(14) **Whereunto.**—From the neuter gender of the relative in the Greek we see that the antecedent in St. Paul's mind is not exactly "belief of truth," nor exactly "sanctification of spirit," nor yet exactly "salvation," but the general state of life which is compounded of these three notions—"to which thing He called you." The election or choice takes place in eternity (verse 13); the call at that point of time when the men first hear the gospel. (See Rom. viii. 30.)

By our gospel—*i.e.*, of course, "by our bringing you the happy message"—the historical delivery of the message is dwelt on rather than its contents.

To the obtaining of the glory of our Lord.—Almost all the ancient commentators render it, "for obtaining of glory to our Lord;" and St. Chrysostom says, beautifully: "No small thing this either, if Christ esteems our salvation His glory. It is, indeed, a glory to the lover of men that the number of those who are being saved should be large." But this version is not so easy grammatically as our own, nor does it suit so well with the context. St. Paul is encouraging his readers with the same thought of their destiny which he has put forward in chap. i. 11, 12—the identity of the joy of the Redeemer and the redeemed (Matt. xxv. 23). It is well to be observed that God did not call them straight "to the glory of our Lord," but "to the obtaining" of the same. This "obtaining" does not mean an otiose receiving of glory in the last day, but a laborious course of "earning" or "purchasing" it during this life. The word is the same as that used in 1 Thess. v. 9, where see Note.

(15) **Therefore, brethren, stand fast.**—Such an exhortation is, in itself, conclusive against a theory of irreversible predestination. "Because God chose you from eternity, and called you in time, therefore stand your ground." If it were impossible for them to quit their ground, it would be needless to exhort them to maintain it. If it were possible for them to quit their ground, and yet be as well off after all, it would be needless also. At the same time, the "therefore" draws a conclusion, not from verse 14 alone, but sums up the whole disquisition of the chapter: "Now that you are reminded of the true Advent doctrine."

Hold the traditions.—The very same word as in Mark vii. 3, 4, 8, "holding the tradition of the elders;" also in the same metaphorical sense in Col. ii. 19; Rev. ii. 13. The action expressed is a vigorous and pertinacious grasp, as (for instance) of the lame man clutching the Apostles in Acts iii. 11. St. Chrysostom remarks: "It is plain from hence that they used not to deliver all their tradition by letter, but much without writing besides, and that both are equally worthy of belief. Therefore, let us consider the Church's tradition worthy of belief. It is tradition: ask no further questions." What were these "traditions" which it was so essential to keep? The context shows that the particular traditions which were most consciously in St. Paul's mind at the moment, were his eschatological teachings, given to them while he was among them—the lore of which he has been briefly reminding them in this chapter (verses 5, 6): for the exhortation is practically a resumption of that given in verses 2, 3. "Instead of being seduced by the forgers of prophecies or of communications from us, remember the careful instructions we gave you once for all." At the same time, he speaks generally, and we must not limit his words to that particular tradition. *Whatever* can be traced to apostolic origin is of the essence of the faith. They are to "hold tenaciously" *all* his traditions, and these would include instructions doctrinal (as 1 Cor. xv. 3; Jude, verse 3), ceremonial (1 Cor. xi. 2, 23), and moral (chap. iii. 6; 2 Pet. ii. 21). As a matter of controversy, it is not so remarkable that he should exhort his converts to cling to his own oral teaching ("whether by word") as that he should at so early a period call their special attention to what was gradually to supplant (at least, in doctrinal matters) all independent unwritten tradition —the Holy Scripture ("our Epistle"). St. Paul can speak on occasion as contemptuously of the "traditions of men" as our Lord did (Col. ii. 8). Of course, it depends entirely on the individual character of any tradition whether, and to what extent, it is to be "held" or condemned as "human." In the Church no mutually contradictory traditions can be held together; and therefore any tradition "by word" which is in disagreement with the written tradition (*i.e.*, Scripture) stands necessarily condemned.

By word, or our epistle.—The "our" belongs to both: "whether by word or epistle of ours." Unless St. Paul had written them some other letter, now lost, this proves that the "First" Epistle was in reality the earlier written. "Have been taught" should be "*were* taught"—the historic tense.

(16) Now our Lord Jesus Christ himself,
and God, even our Father, which hath
loved us, and hath given *us* everlasting
consolation and good hope through
grace, (17) comfort your hearts, and
stablish you in every good word and
work.

A.D. 54.

1 Gr. *may run.*

2 Gr. *absurd.*

CHAPTER III.—(1) Finally, brethren,
pray for us, that the word
of the Lord may have *free*
course,[1] and be glorified,
even as *it is* with you: (2) and that
we may be delivered from unreasonable[2]
and wicked men: for all *men* have not

Chap. iii. 1–3. Request for prayer.

---

(16) **Now.**—Better, *And,* connecting closely the prayer with the exhortation, just as in 1 Thess. v. 23. "Again," says St. Chrysostom, "prayer after advice: this is to help in earnest." The word "Himself," as in the passage cited, contrasts the Almighty power of our Lord with the partial instructions and feeble help which even Apostles could give, and with the impotence of the Thessalonian Christians to stand firm in their own strength.

Our Lord Jesus Christ himself, and God, even our Father.—The order of mention is unusual. (See, however, 2 Cor. xiii. 3.) It is not designedly meant to show the equality of the Blessed Persons, which is done only incidentally by the fact that the same aspiration is directed to both. Probably, in fact, the names are arranged to form a climax: St. Paul having spoken first of the Person whose work on the heart is the more immediate, and then jealously watching lest he should in any way make the Eternal Father seem less deeply interested in our welfare than the Son is. All primitive devotion and doctrine are markedly opposed to the tendency to rest in the Mediator without a real lively faith in the Father who sent Him.

Which hath loved us.—Love to us is *specially* (so fearfully wrong is much of the popular language about the Atonement) the characteristic of the *Father.* (See, for instance, John iii. 16; xvii. 23; 2 Cor. xiii. 3; Eph. ii. 4; 1 John iv. 10.) It is in the thought of this tender love of God to us that the writer adds immediately the endearing title "*Our* Father." This love seems to be mentioned here as being the ground on which the writer rests his hope for the fulfilment of his prayer. It should literally be translated, *which loved us, and gave*—the moment being apparently (as in John iii. 16) the moment of providing the Atonement for our sins.

Everlasting consolation.—This means "an ever present source of comfort," of which no persecution can rob us. This giving of comfort is the proof or explanation of the statement that He "loved us," and refers to the same act. Our unfailing comfort lies in the thought of God's love exemplified in the Incarnation of His Son.

Good hope through grace.—These words must be closely joined. God gave us not only a consolation under present trials, but a sweet prospect in the future; but this sweet prospect belongs to us only "*in* grace" (the literal version). All our hope is based on the continuance of the spiritual strength imparted by the Father through the Son and the Spirit. The qualifying words "in grace" are added to "hope" in just the same way as the words "in sanctification" are added to "salvation" in verse 13.

(17) **Comfort your hearts . . .**—"Comfort," in reference to the "unending comfort" of verse 16; and "stablish," in reference to the "good hope in grace." The "heart" needs comfort as the seat of emotions. "In every good word and work" (it should be, *work and word*) means in the maintenance of every good doctrine (as opposed to the false teaching which had got abroad about the Advent, and to the lies of the Apostasy), and in the performance of every good practice (as opposed to the lawlessness of the Apostasy, and to the disorderly conduct of which the next chapter treats: for here, as in 1 Thess. iii. 13, the prayer forms an introduction of the next subject). The singular number of the verbs "comfort" and "stablish" (which, of course, does not appear in the English), may perhaps be explained as in 1 Thess. iii. 12, where see Note, though it is not necessary so to understand it, inasmuch as the intervening relative (in the Greek, participial) clauses have turned the whole attention to the Father, who may be considered exclusively as the grammatical subject of the verbs. It would, however, have been painful to orthodox ears, however justifiable doctrinally, to have used a plural verb. It is by these little incidental touches, still more than by express doctrinal statements, that we learn what was the real belief of the Apostles concerning the Divinity of Christ; and we may say the same with regard to many other great doctrines.

III.

(1) **Finally.**—The practical portion is introduced in the same manner as in the First Epistle (chap. iv. 1), "for the rest," "as to what I have yet to say."

Pray for us.—St. Chrysostom remarks: "Himself had prayed for them; now he asks them to pray for him." How much of a Christian teacher's power, increasing as time goes on, comes from the accumulation of intercession from his spiritual children! St. Paul leaves people praying for him everywhere (Rom. xv. 30; 2 Cor. i. 11; Eph. vi. 18, 19; Col. iv. 3; 1 Thess. v. 25; comp. Heb. xiii. 18). In all these cases the request is for active help in his work of evangelising: "not that he may fall into no danger," says St. Chrysostom, "for that he was appointed unto." (Comp. 2 Tim. ii. 9.) "That" stands for "in order that," and does not introduce merely the subject of the prayer.

May have free course.—Quite literally, as in the margin, *may run along.* Speed and security are contained in this idea: no hesitation about the next turn, no anxious picking of the way, and no opposition from devils and bad men. Bengel compares Ps. cxlvii. 15.

And be glorified.—The word does not mean merely "obtain applause," "win distinction," as a successful runner; it always implies the recognition or acknowledgment of inherent admirable qualities. (See Notes on chap. i. 12; 1 Thess. ii. 6.)

Even as it is with you.—Such praise would flush the Thessalonians to pray for him with greater fervour and assurance. "With you" means, in the Greek, "in your direction," "on turning to you:" people had only to look at Thessalonica, and they were forced to recognise the character of the gospel.

(2) **And that we may be delivered.**—Compare Rom. xv. 31. This clause is an amplification of the word "may run along:" the impediments to the

faith. (3) But the Lord is faithful,[a]
who shall stablish you, and keep *you*
from evil. (4) And we have confidence
in the Lord touching you,[b] that ye
both do and will do the things
which we command you. (5) And the
Lord direct your hearts
into the love of God, and
into the patient waiting
for Christ.[1]

a 1 Thess. 5. 24.

b Gal. 5. 10.

1 Or, *the patience of Christ.*

Chap. iii. 4, 5. Expression of confidence, and preparatory prayer.

gospel progress were (except that all were overruled for good) such persecutions as these. St. Paul gives thanks for such deliverances in 2 Cor. i. 10; 2 Tim. iii. 11; iv. 17. Perhaps (as St. Chrysostom suggests) one reason for here inviting their prayers for himself was to nerve the Thessalonians by the sense that they were not the only people in the world in danger.

From unreasonable and wicked men.—The curious word rendered "unreasonable" is rendered "amiss" in Luke xxiii. 41, "wickedness" in Acts xxv. 5, "harm" in Acts xxviii. 6, occurring nowhere else in the New Testament. It properly means something "misplaced" hence "extravagant," "monstrous." Thus the dying robber says that our Lord had done "nothing so monstrous" as to deserve crucifixion; Festus ironically invites the priests to a serious journey to St. Paul's trial, "if there be something so monstrous in him;" the Maltese barbarians "saw that nothing so monstrous happened to him after all." So St. Paul wishes the Thessalonians to pray for his deliverance "from these monstrous and depraved people." He is evidently meaning some particular foes whom he fears, for the original has the definite article. Who, then, are "these monstrous persons?" If we turn to Acts xviii. 6, 9, 12, and observe the circumstances in which the letter was written, we can hardly doubt that they are the unbelieving Jews of Corinth. From these Jews he was, though narrowly, delivered. It was, perhaps, in direct answer to the prayers for which St. Paul here asks that he received the vision and assurances of our Lord, and that Gallio was moved to quash so abruptly the proceedings of the Jews.

For all men have not faith.—This clause gives the reason for the alarm implied in the last clause: "Do not be surprised at my needing help against bad men; for you know that it is not every one that believes." There is something a little scornful and embittered in the expression (recalling the invective against the same people in 1 Thess. ii. 15, 16), for it suggests the thought that nothing better was to be expected from such a set of unconverted Jews. Tacitly, also, the unbelieving Corinthians are contrasted with the Thessalonians who had so readily embraced the truth. It may, however, be doubted whether this sentence is not an instance of a common Hebrew idiom, occurring more than twenty times in the Greek Testament, by which the combination of "all" and "not" amounts to "not any." Thus, "all flesh shall not be justified," in Rom. iii. 20, is rendered "no flesh shall be justified;" "they are not all of us," in 1 John ii. 19, means "not one of them is of us." So here it may be, "for there is not one of them that believes;" and so also, again speaking of the Jews, in Rom. x. 16, "they did not all obey" may mean "none of them obeyed"—a rhetorical exaggeration, which the writer proceeds to justify by the exhaustive question from Isaiah.

(3) **But the Lord is faithful.**—It must not be thought from this that the word "faith" in the previous verse meant "fidelity." St. Paul, after his favourite manner, is playing upon two meanings of the word: "But whether men have faith or not, the Lord is faithful." There is the same play of words in Rom. iii. 3. "The Lord" seems here to be used, as was said on 1 Thess. iii. 12, without distinct reference to one Person of the Holy Trinity rather than another. This characteristic of God is named because God stands pledged to all who believe in Him.

Who shall stablish you.—How soon St. Paul reverts from his own needs to theirs! He does not continue, as we should expect, with "who will preserve *us*."

Keep you from evil.—Rather (probably), *from the Evil One*, as in the Lord's Prayer. Possibly, the word is used not without a reference to the word rendered "wicked" in verse 2, with which in the Greek it is identical.

(4) **We have confidence in the Lord touching you.**—Rather, *We rely upon you in the Lord:* the clause forms the counterpart to the last verse. St. Chrysostom's whole comment is worth transcription:—"God, saith he, is faithful, and having promised to save, save He assuredly will, but *as* He promised. And how did He promise? If we would be agreeable, and would hear Him; not unconditionally, nor while we remain inactive like stocks and stones. Yet, well has he added his, 'We rely *in the Lord:*' that is, 'We trust to His love of men.' Once more he takes them down, ascribing the whole matter to that quarter; for had he said 'We trust to you,' it would have been a great compliment indeed, but would not have taught them to ascribe all to God; and had he said We rely on the Lord that He will keep you,' without adding 'upon you,' and 'that ye both do and will do what things we command,' he would have made them less active by casting the whole upon the power of God." (See the passage of Galatians referred to in the margin.)

Both do and will do.—The emphasis of the sentence is on the future tense, the commendation of the present being only intended to do away the rebuke which might have been conveyed by the future alone. How careful St. Paul is not to wound susceptibilities, though he never "pleases men"! (See, for instance, Notes on 1 Thess. iv. 1, 9, 10; v. 11.) This expression of confidence is a happy rhetorical means of preparing readers for the commands which are to follow.

(5) **The Lord.**—See Note on verse 3. The Person of the Blessed Trinity to whom this guidance immediately belongs is the Holy Ghost. So far, the Greek expositors are right who are agreed to consider this a proof of the Holy Ghost's divinity. Their right conclusion is, however, drawn from wrong premisses, for the name is not here to be taken as consciously intending Him. The ground for their supposition is that the names "God" and "Christ" occur immediately after, and not (as we might expect) "His" or "for Him." But in 1 Thess. iii. 12, 13, there occurs precisely the same arrangement of the three words: the Greek equivalent for the sacred Hebrew Name standing first, and then, for clearness' sake, being explained by the personal titles, "God our Father," "our Lord Jesus Christ."

Direct your hearts into the love of God.—This prayer in itself implies that they had not yet

Chap. iii. 6–16. Instructions how to deal with idlers and agitators.

(6) Now we command you, brethren,
in the name of our Lord
Jesus Christ, that ye with-
draw yourselves from every
brother that walketh dis-
orderly, and not after the tradition
which he received of us. (7) For
yourselves know how ye ought[a]
to follow us:[b] for we behaved
not ourselves disorderly among you;[c]

a 1 Thess. 4. 1.
b 1 Thess. 1. 6.
c 1 Thess. 2. 10.

---

reached the point which St. Paul would have them reach, and were perhaps not taking the directest course. The same word is used in Luke i. 79; 1 Thess. iii. 11. The "love of God" here meant is that practical love which consists in keeping the commandments (John xiv. 21), as may be seen from the context:—"I am sure that the Lord will strengthen you, and that you are doing and will continue to do as you are bidden: may God help you to the obedience of true love, and to such perseverance in obedience as was shown by Christ; and it is in this hope that we bid you take steps to repress the disorders which are prevalent among you."

The patient waiting for Christ.—This rendering is so beautiful in itself, and so well in keeping with the leading thoughts of these two Epistles, that it is painful to be forced to reject it. But the only rendering which is possible is, *Christ's patience;* and the simplest meaning of that phrase is "the endurance which characterises Christ," the genitive being, as in 1 Thess. i. 3, almost a descriptive adjective, "Christ-like," "Christian endurance." This "patience" includes both the thought of bearing up under their present persecutions and also the thought of "patient continuance in well doing," as opposed to the fitful restlessness which had begun to prey upon the Thessalonian Church.

(6) **We command you.**—The practical conclusion of the letter. These words take up the expression in verse 4, "Ye will do the things which (at any time) we command you; now the thing which we command you is this."

In the name of our Lord.—To do anything in a person's name seems to mean, in the first instance, the actual pronouncing of the name in the performance of the action—to do it name on lip, just as to "come in a rod" (1 Cor. iv. 21) literally means *rod in hand.* Thus, miracles are commonly said to be performed "in the name of the Lord," viz., with the audible repetition of His name (for instance, Matt. vii. 22, Mark xvi. 17; Luke x. 17); and for examples of the way in which the name was literally so used, we may refer to Acts iii. 6; ix. 34; xix. 13—in the last case the name being employed as a mere incantation or charm. See also Phil. ii. 10, where, as the adoration paid to Jesus Himself is the point, the phrase must mean, "mentioning the name of Jesus, every knee shall bow." From this mention of the name in performing an action, our phrase assumes, at any rate, two distinct meanings: (1) As in Col. iii. 17, it implies an invocation or attestation of the person named, or a recognition of his presence and interest in the matter, in which sense it has passed into the common language of Christianity, into legal formulas, &c. (2) Here, and usually, it means a claim to the *authority* of the person named—to act officially as his representative with full powers. (See Notes on John xiv. 13, 26.) Thus the prophets spoke "in the name of the Lord"—*i.e.,* as His authoritative exponents (Jas. v. 10); St. Paul commands (Acts xvi. 18), and retains a man's sins (1 Cor. iv. 5) "in the name of the Lord"—*i.e.,* as His official spokesman or ambassador; the priests are to administer the unction of the sick with like authority (Jas. v. 14, 15). So here, the Thessalonians are not to think that in disobeying St. Paul's injunctions they are rebelling against a mere human authority; Christ Himself speaks to them through St. Paul's lips. Yet, commanding with all this tremendous authority, they are still but "brethren" (Matt. xxiii. 8).

Withdraw yourselves.—The striking word here used is (in its simple form) only found besides in 2 Cor. viii. 20: "avoiding this." In a still more striking compound, it occurs in Acts xx. 20, 27; Gal. ii. 12; Heb. x. 38. It is a metaphor from the language of strategy: a cautious general shrinking from an encounter and timidly drawing off under cover. Perhaps we might illustrate it by the familiar English "*fight shy of* every brother." A social excommunication rather than ecclesiastical seems chiefly meant, though the latter might perhaps be involved.

From every brother—*i.e.,* every Christian. It was impossible to be so strict about the outside world. (Comp. 1 Cor. v. 10, 11.) The man still remains a "brother" (verse 15).

Disorderly.—The word is rendered "unruly" in 1 Thess. v. 14, and is possibly suggested by the military metaphor above. It means properly "out of rank." The kind of irregularity which is meant is made clear by verses 10, 11. The worthy Bengel quaintly makes this an opportunity for denouncing the Mendicant Orders: "An order of mendicants, then, is not an order; if the Thessalonians had bound themselves to it by a vow, what would St. Paul have said?"

The tradition.—See Note on chap. ii. 15. The word must imply systematic and definite teaching; and we see here again that a clear code of ethics was part of the apostolic catechism. (See Note on 1 Thess. iv. 1.)

He received.—The best rendering is, *which they received*—*i.e.,* all the brethren who walked disorderly. The word "receive" is the regular correlative to "tradition" or "deliver." (See, *e.g.,* Mark vii. 4; 1 Cor. xi. 23; Gal. i. 9; Col. ii. 6.)

(7) **For** justifies the assertion that they *had* received a better teaching. (Comp. 1 Thess. ii. 1; iv. 9; v. 2.)

To follow us.—The word, of course, means "to imitate"; and the rather compressed expression seems to stand for something fuller, such as, "Yourselves know how you ought to live, for you have but to imitate us: you recollect not only a tradition, but an example." This is better than (with St. Chrysostom) to make the whole "tradition" consist of example without precept, however such an interpretation might simplify the logic.

For (or *because*).—Historical justification of the statement that their example was a trustworthy model, in this particular, at any rate: see the same use of "for" in 1 Thess. ii. 9, "for labouring," &c.; iv. 3. It is perhaps simpler, however, to translate the word "that," instead of "for": "You know perfectly how to live—how to imitate our example—that we never," &c. Then follows a description of the Apostles' conduct at Thessalonica similar to that in the First Epistle, thus giving us a clearer understanding why they dwelt so long and so passionately upon the topic *there*—namely, in order by force of tacit contrast to shame the disorderly brethren into imitation.

(8) neither did we eat any man's bread
for nought; but wrought with labour
and travail night and day, that we
might not be chargeable to any of
you:[a] (9) not because we have not
power,[b] but to make ourselves an
ensample unto you to follow us.
(10) For even when we were with
you, this we commanded you, that if
any would not work, neither should he
eat. (11) For we hear that there are
some which walk among you disorderly,

a 1 Thess. 2. 9.
b 1 Thess. 2. 6.

---

(8) **Neither.**—They might have thought it possible to live on others without incurring so serious a charge as "disorderliness."

Eat any man's bread.—Still more literally, *eat bread from any man—i.e.,* "from any man's table." St. Paul always becomes picturesque and vivid in a passage of this kind, and generally Hebraistic ("eat bread," 2 Sam. ix. 7, and often). "For nought" is literally *at a gift.* There is a flavour of scorn in St. Paul's disclaimer of such a parasite's life.

Wrought.—In the original it is the participle, "working," which better suits the rapid flow of the sentences. The order also is slightly more forcible: "We ate bread from no man's table at a gift, but in toil and travail, all night and day labouring that we," &c. To "be chargeable" means more than "to make you pay": it contains the notion of *burdensome* expense.

(9) **Power.**—Rather, *authority,* which is power *plus* legitimacy. How jealously St. Paul guards the rights of the Apostolate! not for himself, but for the brethren of the Lord and Cephas (1 Cor. ix. 5), perhaps for Silas and Timothy (1 Thess. ii. 6, Note), and for futurity. The unbounded claims of spiritual fatherhood seem copied from the Roman law of *patria potestas.* (Comp. Philem. verses 8, 19.)

To make.—Literally, *in order that we might give.* It was not without thought and design that they had adopted the plan.

An ensample.—The same word as in 1 Thess. i. 7. Literally, *a model.* The argument is a strong *à fortiori.* Whatever reason these Thessalonians might have for giving up work, St. Paul had the same, and more. He looked for the Advent, as they did; he spent his time in going about among the brethren, as they did; and over and above, he had the apostolic right to maintenance, which they had not. Why should not he have left off work, if they could justify themselves in so doing? If he thought right to work, *à fortiori,* it must be their duty to work too.

(10) **For even.**—The sequence of thought is a little difficult, but it seems best to regard this "for" as connecting its sentence, not with verse 9, but rather with verse 6. It does not give the reason why St. Paul and his companions worked: "because we strictly enjoined you to work, and therefore could not be idle ourselves." Rather, it justifies the reiteration of the command: "We do not hesitate to command you now to repress this disorderly conduct, so contrary to the example set you; for, in fact, when we were with you we used to lay down this law." So Theodoret takes it: "It is no new thing that we write to you."

We commanded.—The tense in the original is that of constant re-assertion, which brings out once more the thorough grounding which the Apostles gave at once to their converts. (See Note on verse 6: "the tradition;" also the Note on chap. ii. 5.) The same definite precept is referred to in 1 Thess. iv. 11.

If any would not work.—The word "would" stands for "is not willing," "refuses." To any weakness or incapacity for work, except in himself, St. Paul would be very tender; the vice consists in the defective *will.* The canon (in the original) is laid down in the pointed form of some old Roman law like those of the Twelve Tables: "If any man choose not to work, neither let him eat." It does not mean, "let him leave off eating," putting it to the man's own conscience to see the necessary connection between the two things (Gen. iii. 19); but, "let him not be fed." The Thessalonians are not to be misled into a false charity: giving food in Christ's name to persons who are capable of working and able to get work, and are too indolent to do so. The support which is here forbidden to be given to these disorderly persons might come either direct from the private liberality of individuals, or from some collected church fund administered by the deacons. It does not seem at all impossible that this Thessalonian Church, which St. Paul himself declares to have taken the churches of Judæa for a model (1 Thess. ii. 14), may have copied its model in adopting some form of communism, or, at any rate, some extensive use of the *agapè* which we see to have been in use at Corinth, established by the Apostle at the very time of writing this Letter (1 Cor. xi. 21). Such a supposition would give much more point to St. Paul's canon, as well as to other phrases in both these Epistles, and would enable us to understand better how this discipline could be actively enforced. That the ordinary *agapè* was a matter of considerable importance to the poorer classes is evident from 1 Cor. xi. 22.

(11) **For we hear.**—Explaining how St. Paul came to speak upon the topic at all. Hitherto he has only been giving directions, without saying why. News had been brought back, no doubt, by the bearers of the First Epistle.

Walk among you disorderly.—A verbal repetition of verse 6. It is not quite the same as "some among you which walk disorderly," for the words "among you" represent the vague and various *directions* taken by those aimless feet, going about from house to house, workshop to workshop.

Working not at all, but are busybodies.—This is what the disorderliness consists in, as we should have seen from verse 10. There is a scornful play of words here in the Greek which is lost sight of in the English: the word for "busybodies" being merely a compound form of the word "working." Quite literally, the compound means "working enough and to spare," "being overbusy," "overdoing;" then, as a man cannot possibly overdo what it is his own duty to do, it comes to signify (1) doing *useless* things, things which concern no one, and might as well be left alone as, for instance, magic, which is described by this word in Acts xix. 19; or natural science, which is so described in the Athenians' accusation of Socrates! (2) Meddling with matters which do not concern the doer, but do concern other people: so used in 1 Tim. v. 13. Prof. Lightfoot suggests (*On a Fresh Revision,* p. 59; comp. p. xviii., 2nd ed.) that the play can be kept up through the words "business" and "busy": we might perhaps say, "not being business men, but busybodies." But which of the two notions mentioned above is to be considered most prominent here we cannot tell for

working not at all, but are busybodies.
(12) Now them that are such we command and exhort by our Lord Jesus Christ, that with quietness they work, and eat their own bread.
(13) But ye, brethren, be not weary[1] in well doing.
(14) And if any man obey not our word[2] by this epistle, note that man, and have no company with him, that he may be ashamed.
(15) Yet count *him* not as an

[1] Or, *faint not.*

[2] Or, *signify that man by an epistle.*

certain. (*a*) The Thessalonians do not seem to have been much carried away by the first class of danger—idle speculations, such as those of the Colossian or Ephesian Churches. Yet we cannot altogether exclude this meaning here. St. Paul's readers had been over-busy in theorising about the position of the departed at Christ's coming (1 Thess. iv. 15, Note), and had been so eager over their idle doctrines of the Advent as to falsify, if not actually to forge, communications from St. Paul (chap. ii. 2). Such false inquisitiveness and gossiping discussions might well be described by the Greek word with which we are dealing. (*b*) Everything, however, points to a more practical form of the same disposition to mask idleness under cloak of work; feverish excitement, which leads men to meddle and interfere with others, perhaps to spend time in "religious" work which ought not to have been spared from every-day duties. (See 1 Thess. iv. 11, 12, and Notes.) There is nothing to show definitely how this busy idleness arose, but it may very probably be the shaken and troubled condition of mind spoken of in chap. ii. 2.

(12) **We command.**—The fourth time the severe word is used in this very chapter. Perhaps "we order" might convey the meaning still more sharply. But immediately, lest severity provoke rebellion, he adds, "and we beseech," alleging also the grounds on which he rests his appeal: "*in* our Lord"—*i.e.*, "on the strength of our union in the Body of Christ." (Comp. 1 Thess. iv. 1.)

That with quietness they work.—The opposites of bustling, and of idleness.

Eat their own bread.—Not other people's. This passage tempts us to take the marginal version in 1 Thess. iv. 12: "have need of no man." The phrase is not fatal to the idea of there being a communism established. The bread would still be "their own"—*i.e.*, they would have a right to it, supposing it had been earned for the community by hard work: otherwise, communism or no communism, the bread was stolen. The commentators aptly compare a rabbinical saying: "When a man eats his own bread he is composed and tranquil in mind; but if he be eating the bread of his parents or children, much more that of strangers, his mind is less tranquil."

(13) **But ye, brethren.**—The last verse was addressed to all those whose consciences would prick them on hearing it read at the Eucharist. Now the writer turns to the orderly brethren, as quite a distinct class. The rhetorical effect of this quick apostrophe would be the same as in the well-known story of Napoleon addressing the rioters, and requesting the gentlemen to separate themselves from the *canaille.* The distinction is so invidious that every one would hasten to join the ranks of the respectable.

Be not weary in well doing.—This is an exhortation to "the patience of Christ," for which the Apostle had prayed. The phrase takes for granted that they had been hitherto engaged in "well doing"—*i.e.*, in acting honourably, "walking honestly towards them that are without" (1 Thess. iv. 12); and St. Paul is anxious to preserve them from "fainting" (as the word is translated in Gal. vi. 9), and so slipping into the like idleness and bringing scandal upon the Church.

(14) **And if any man.**—An appeal to the right-minded, not only to persevere themselves, but to join with the overseers of their Church in enforcing discipline, as in 1 Thess. v. 12—15.

By this epistle.—Rightly rendered. The marginal version, "by *an* Epistle," is impossible, for in the Greek the definite article appears. It might, if the context suited, be attached to the following clause, instead of the foregoing, and translated, "by means of the Epistle signify that man," meaning "in your answer." But there is nothing to show that St. Paul was expecting any answer; and, for another thing, he has given them full directions for dealing with the case themselves, so that it would be superfluous to send the particulars to St. Paul. For several other weighty reasons it is best to attach the words to the hypothetical clause; and the sense will be, "There can be no excuse now. It was possible to forget or misinterpret our verbal tradition, painstaking and definite though it was; possible also to ignore the example which we set; but now you have it in black and white, and the man who does not submit to our directions in this form must be visited severely." There are at least three places besides this in St. Paul's writings where "the Epistle" stands absolutely for "the present Epistle," viz., Rom. xvi. 22; Col. iv. 16; 1 Thess. v. 27; possibly a fourth might be added, 1 Cor. v. 9; only once in a very clear context it refers to a former Letter (2 Cor. vii. 8).

Note that man.—The reflexive voice of the verb implies *mutual* warning against him: "*Agree* to set a mark upon him, to make a marked man of him." The notion is that of making him easily recognisable, so that no Christian should "have company" with him unawares. (Comp. Gen. iv. 15.) The word and the thought in Rom. xvi. 17 are slightly different. The best text goes on abruptly, without conjunction: "Note that man; have no company with him." This social extrusion from good men's conversation, not to speak of the Sacraments, would, to a Christian in a heathen city, be indeed a delivering to Satan, a thrusting into outer darkness.

That he may be ashamed—*i.e.*, put to shame. Comp. 1 Cor. vi. 5; xv. 34; Tit. ii. 8; and (for the end to be served by this shame) the first clause of the Commination of Sinners.

(15) **Yet.**—The original is simply *And,* which is much more beautiful, implying that this very withdrawal from brotherly intercourse was an act of brotherly kindness.

An enemy.—In the private, not the public, sense. "Do not think of him as one with whom you must be *at feud,* to be thwarted and humbled on every occasion." St. Chrysostom exclaims, "How soon the father's heart breaks down!"

Admonish him as a brother.—How was this to be done without "having company" with him? Perhaps the presbyters, to whom the work of "admonishing," or "warning," specially belonged (see 1 Thess. v. 12, 14), were to visit them in private with that object. Or possibly, the admonition was to consist in the act of separation, and not in verbal reproof at all.

enemy, but admonish *him* as a brother.
(16) Now the Lord of peace himself give
you peace always by all means. The
Lord *be* with you all.
(17) The salutation of Paul with
mine own hand, which is the token in
every epistle: so I write.
(18) The grace of our Lord
Jesus Christ *be* with you
all. Amen.

Chap. iii. 17, 18. Caution against forgeries, and valediction.

¶ The second *epistle* to the Thessalonians was written from Athens.

---

(16) **Now.**—Rather, *And,* or *But.* The prayer is joined to the exhortations, as in chap. ii. 16 and elsewhere, and of course bears upon the subject of them.

The Lord of peace.—We had "the God of peace" at the close of the last Epistle (v. 23, where see the Note). The "peace" prayed for here has perhaps a more immediate reference to external matters than in the parallel passage. St. Chrysostom suggests the danger of quarrels breaking out owing to the administration of the prescribed discipline. And the conduct of these restless busybodies was in itself destructive of peace, both for their own souls and for the community. But the words "by all means," or, more literally, *in every shape and form,* show that the Apostle is extending his glance over all the subjects mentioned in the Epistle now finished: "Peace all throughout in every form," through all persecutions and from all persecutions; through the terrors of the reign of Antichrist and through the Judgment Day; peace among themselves, in their own hearts, with God.

The Lord be with you all.—Another way of expressing the prayer for peace; for where He enters He says, "Peace be unto you." The word "all" is strongly emphasised, catching up the "always" and "in all forms." St. Paul has spoken with strong censure of some; but he wishes to show that he bears no ill-will to any; and to leave off by blessing all, as he began by giving thanks for all (chap. i. 3).

(17) **The salutation.**—At this point St. Paul takes the pen out of his secretary's hand, and adds the closing words himself. The actual salutation does not begin until the benediction of the 18th verse, to which this 17th is intended to attract attention.

Which.—Namely, the autograph addition of a salutation, or valedictory prayer, not the special words in which it was couched.

The token.—Rather, *a token*—a mark, that is, by which to tell an authentic Epistle of his from those forged letters with which false brethren had troubled the Thessalonian Church (chap. ii. 2). At first sight, it seems to us too audacious for any one to have conceived the thought of writing a letter under the name of St. Paul; but, on the other hand, we must recollect several points. (1) St. Paul's genuine First Epistle, in spite of its claim to inspiration (iv. 15), could not yet have acquired in the eyes of the Thessalonians the sanctity it wears for us; they had no notion of such a thing as Holy Scriptures, and even if they had, St. Paul was a familiar figure, a mechanic who had just left them, not yet invested with the heroic halo. (2) Such literary forgeries were not uncommon in that age, and scarcely considered reprehensible, unless they were framed to inculcate with authority some heretical teaching. Apocryphal Gospels soon after abounded, under false titles, and works fathered upon St. Clement and other great Church teachers. (3) There need not always have been a direct intention to deceive the readers as to the authorship, but the renowned name acted as a tempting advertisement for the work, and the theories thus shot forth hit their mark; whether the real authorship were discovered or not mattered little in comparison. Such points must be borne in mind before we accept as genuine any of the early Christian writings.

In every epistle.—That is, naturally, "in every Epistle which I write." It cannot be narrowly restricted to mean, "in every Epistle which I shall for the future write to you Thessalonians," though that is, of course, the practical significance. Nor does it imply a formed design of writing other Epistles to other churches. It seems necessary to suppose that St. Paul had already made a practice of concluding Letters with his autograph, though only one Letter of his is now extant of an earlier date than our present Epistle. There is no reason whatever to suppose that all the Letters ever written by St. Paul have been preserved to us (see Dr. Lightfoot's *Philippians,* p. 136, *et seq.*), any more than all the sayings and acts of Jesus Christ (John xxi. 25); and even when he wrote his First Epistle to Thessalonica he had seen the necessity of giving careful directions about his Letters (1 Thess. v. 27), and of rousing his correspondents to a reasonable scepticism (*ibid.* v. 21). The same solicitude re-appears in 1 Cor. xvi. 21; Gal. vi. 11. And the rule which St. Paul had already made he always observed, so far as we can test; for all his extant Epistles, as Bishop Wordsworth points out on 1 Thess. v. 28, contain his "salutation" at the end.

So I write.—"Such is my handwriting." It need not mean that the Thessalonians hitherto were unacquainted with his hand; he only calls their attention closely to it. The great bold handwriting (comp. Gal. vi. 11) would not easily be mistaken.

(18) **The grace.**—This is his "salutation." The Greek secular salutation, at greeting and parting alike, was *chaire* (literally, *rejoice*); so St. Paul, alike at beginning and ending, uses a word of kindred origin, *charis* ("grace"). Observe the word "all" again, as in verse 16. St. Chrysostom's beautiful comment may well be given: "What he calls his 'salutation' is the prayer, showing that the whole business they were then about was spiritual; and even when he must give a salutation, there must go some benefit along with it, and it must be a prayer, not a mere symbol of friendship. 'Twas with this he would begin, and with this he would end, fencing round that which he said with mighty walls on either side; and safe were the foundations he laid, and safe the conclusion that he laid thereon. 'Grace to you,' he cries, 'and peace'; and once more, ['Peace always' and] 'the grace of our Lord Jesus Christ be with you all.—Amen.'"

EXCURSUS ON NOTES TO II. THESSALONIANS

EXCURSUS ON THE INTERPRETATION OF THE PROPHECY, 2 THESS. II. 3—12.

In order to deal fairly with this difficult passage, it will be necessary sternly to exclude from our view all other passages of the New Testament which speak of a final manifestation of evil, and, reviewing the words simply as they stand, to consider *what St. Paul himself meant* when he so assiduously (verse 5, Note) taught the Thessalonian Church on the subject, and *what the Thessalonian Church was likely to gather* from his Letter. For though such a passage as Heb. vi. 2 shows that the whole Apostolic Church was definitely at one in the eschatological instruction given to its converts at a very early stage of their Christian life; and though the language of 1 Tim. iv. 1; Jas. v. 3—7; 2 Pet. iii. 1, 2; 1 John ii. 18; iv. 3; Jude, verse 17 (not to mention the Apocalypse)—passages representing the most different schools of thought in the early Church—fully bring out this agreement, so that Christians may fairly use those passages to explain each other, yet, on the other hand, we need to put ourselves in the position of the young Church of Thessalonica, which was expected by St. Paul to make out the significant hints of his Letter with no other help than the recollection of his oral teaching and the observation of events. We, therefore, ought to be able in like manner to catch the same significant hints by a like knowledge of the then history of the world, and of the sources from which St. Paul was likely to draw his doctrine of the "Last Things."

I. **Sources of the Apostolic Doctrine of the Last Things.**—The prophecy of St. Paul does not appear *to* be—at least, exclusively—the result of a direct internal revelation of the Spirit. Such direct revelations were, when necessary, made to him, and we have seen him claim that kind of inspiration in 1 Thess. iv. 15. But God's ordinary way of making prophets seems to be different. He gives to those who are willing to see an extraordinary insight into the things which lie before the most ordinary eyes; He throws light upon the meaning of occurrences, or of words, which are familiar to every one externally (see Maurice's *Prophets and Kings*, pp. 141—145). Even for doctrines like those of the true divinity or the true humanity of our Lord, or of the indwelling of the Spirit, or the Church's mission, the Apostles do not rest solely on direct revelation made to their own consciences, but rather dwell on the significance of historical facts (*e.g.*, Rom. i. 4; 2 Pet. i. 17), or, still more frequently and strongly, on the interpretation of Old Testament Scriptures (*e.g.*, Heb. i. 8; ii. 12, 13; 2 Pet. i. 19). If, therefore, we can find material in the Old Testament which, taken in conjunction with our Lord's own words, could have supplied St. Paul—or rather, the catholic consent of the early Church—with the doctrine of the Last Things as we find it stated in the apostolic writings, we shall be justified in using those Old Testament materials in the explanation of the New.

II. **The Book of Daniel.**—Such materials we find, not only in the general threatenings of Joel, Zechariah (chap. xiv.), and Malachi, but most clear and definite in the Book of Daniel. Into the question of the date of that book it is not necessary here to inquire. It suffices for the present purpose to know that it was much older than St. Paul's time, and was accepted as prophetic in the ordinary sense. In fact, there was, probably, no other book of the Old Testament which received so much attention among the Jews in the apostolic age (Westcott, in Smith's *Dict. Bible*, Art. "Daniel"). It was regarded with full reverence as an inspired revelation; and our Lord Himself (according to Matt. xxiv. 15 and Mark xiii. 14) either drew from it (humanly speaking) His own doctrine of the Last Things, or at least used it emphatically for His disciples' benefit as a corroboration. The taste for apocalyptic literature was at this time very strong, and the prophecies of Daniel attracted especial attention, inasmuch as the simplest interpretation of some of the most explicit of them pointed unmistakably to the time then present. Tacitus (*Hist.* v. 13) and Suetonius (*Vesp.* chap. 4), as is well known, speak of the certainty felt through the whole East, *about that time*, that universal empire was on the point of passing into the hands of men of Jewish origin. This belief, says Tacitus, was "contained in the antient literature of the priests"—*i.e.*, in the Scriptures, kept and expounded by them; and there can be no doubt that first and foremost of those Scriptures (for this purpose) stood the Book of Daniel. For every reason, then, we may well try to find what a believing Jew of the apostolic age would make out of the visions of Daniel, in order to throw light on this passage of St. Paul.

III. **The Five Monarchies.**—Now, in the Book of Daniel there are four main predictions of what was then the future history of the world. These predictions are contained in chaps. ii., vii., viii., and xi. The first two visions, vouchsafed to Nebuchadnezzar and to Daniel respectively, both describe Five Monarchies, which were successively to arise and flourish in the world. Amidst a good deal which is matter of controversy, three facts remain agreed upon by all: first, that the Five Monarchies of the one vision are intended to correspond to the Five Monarchies of the other, each to each; secondly, that the earliest of these five represents the Babylonian empire, then standing, with Nebuchadnezzar at its head; thirdly, that the last of the series portrays the establishment of the Theocracy in its full development—that is, the "Kingdom of God" (which had been the main subject of St. Paul's preaching at Thessalonica), or the visible government of the world by the Christ.

IV. **The Fourth Monarchy.**—But the question which most directly concerns us now is how to identify the Fourth of these monarchies. In Nebuchadnezzar's vision it was to be "in the days of these kings"—*i.e.*, the kings of the Fourth Monarchy, while the Fourth

Monarchy was still standing—that the Kingdom of Heaven was to come (Dan. ii. 44). In Daniel's vision this Fourth Monarchy (or rather, its continuation and development) was to exist side by side with the saints of the Most High, and between them and *one* outgrowth of the Fourth Monarchy a struggle was to take place before the final establishment of the Kingdom of the Saints (chap. vii. 25). What, then, was this Fourth Monarchy intended by the Seer (or by "the Spirit of the Christ," 1 Pet. i. 11) to represent? Or, to be still more practical, What was in St. Paul's own day, among his own countrymen, the *received interpretation* of this part of Daniel's prophecy? The question is not hard to answer. With irrefragable clearness Dr. Pusey has proved, in the second of his *Lectures on Daniel the Prophet*, the plausibility and minuteness with which the words concerning the Second and Third Monarchies may respectively be applied to the Medo-Persian and the Macedonian empires; and if even *this* point be established, there can be no hesitation in naming the Fourth. It can only be the empire of Rome. But Dr. Pusey shows, with the same force, how applicable the description itself is to the Roman empire. Whether, however, this interpretation has any ground in the original intention of the Prophet, or of Him who, we believe, spoke by him, is for our present purpose a matter of secondary importance. We have already mentioned an unimpeachable piece of evidence furnished by two great Roman historians. It was in their days a "long-established and uniform belief," entertained not in Judæa only, but "in the whole of the East," and drawn from the Jewish literature, that a great Jewish empire was destined to appear. But that is not all. Such a belief might have been drawn from Numbers or Isaiah. But Suetonius adds, *Eo tempore*, "at that time;" Tacitus adds, *Eo ipso tempore*, "at that very time." From what Jewish literature could the *date* have been made out, except from the calculation of the Seventy Weeks in Daniel? And as the same prophecy spoke of a world-wide empire, *in the days of* whose *kings* this new Jewish power was to arise, that same "long-established and uniform belief" must have recognised in the Roman empire the Fourth Monarchy which was to be shattered by it. Hence, doubtless, the hopefulness with which insurgent leaders one after another rose in rebellion against the Roman arms. It was not only that they themselves were the Lord's own people. Was not this vast system, "dreadful and terrible, and strong exceedingly," definitely doomed in Scripture to utter extinction before their arms? But we have, besides, a less indirect testimony than the foregoing. The Jew Josephus (*Ant.* x. 11, § 7) speaks at length of the prophecies of Daniel, and how he himself was watching their gradual verification. After mentioning the prophecy about Antiochus Epiphanes and its complete fulfilment, he adds: "In the very same manner Daniel also wrote concerning the empire of the Romans, and that our country should be made desolate by them." He then passes on to speak of the comfort afforded by seeing so plainly the Providence of God, with true Jewish irony not disclosing that his comfort lay in the promised revenge upon Rome as well as upon Antiochus. In another place (*Ant.* x. 10, § 4) he is recording the vision in the second chapter of Daniel, and after describing the universal dominion of the Iron Kingdom, he proceeds: "Daniel also declared the meaning of the Stone to the king, but this I do not think proper to relate, as I have undertaken to describe things past and present, not things that are future. Yet if any one be so very desirous of knowing truth as not to waive such curious points, and cannot refrain his desire to understand the uncertain future, and whether or no it will come to pass, let him give heed to read the Book of Daniel, which he will find among the Holy Scriptures." No doubt can be entertained that this writer understood the Fourth Monarchy to be the Roman empire, and did not wish to be suspected of encouraging sedition by speaking openly of its predicted downfall. This, then, was the common interpretation which St. Paul must have learned from a child: that Daniel's Fourth Monarchy, which was to break up before the Kingdom of God, was the Roman empire.

V. The Fifth Monarchy.—We may then assume that St. Paul believed Daniel to foretell the coming of the Kingdom of God *in the days of* the *kings* of the Roman empire. In one sense, indeed, the prophecy was already fulfilled. The Kingdom was already come. Heralded by the Baptist (Matt. iii. 2, *et seq.*), and expounded by our Lord (Matt. ix. 35, *et seq.*), it had been established by the Resurrection, the Ascension, and the Mission of the Holy Ghost, while the Roman empire actually stood (Ps. ii.; comp. Acts iv. 25; v. 31; xiii. 33). St. John regards the world as already virtually subdued in his own lifetime (1 John v. 4. Note). But the Church as at present constituted does not answer completely to Daniel's prophecy of the Kingdom of the Saints. To the Christian there are two comings of the Kingdom, not only one. In the Prophets the two are fused into one. We may almost say the same of the words of Christ Himself. Even the apostolic writers do not separate the two so sharply as God has historically taught subsequent ages of the Church to separate them. The early Church lived in a daily expectation of the return of Christ. For them, therefore, there was no difficulty in interpreting Daniel's prophecies as applying at the same moment to the First and Second Advent. It would not be unfair, therefore, to assume that St. Paul expected the Second Advent to take place, as the First had done, "in the days of these kings" of the Fourth or Roman Monarchy.

VI. What withholdeth.—Turning now to the statement of St. Paul, we see that he is cautioning the Thessalonians not to expect the Second Coming of Christ immediately, because, as they can see, a certain great power is still in the world, which (as they have been carefully taught) must be removed before the way for Christ's return is open. This great power—with the aspect of which his readers are perfectly familiar, though they may have forgotten its significance ("Ye know *that which* withholdeth")—is summed up in a person who wields it. This person is "he which withholdeth." His removal "out of the midst" is still a matter of futurity, yet assuredly destined to take place; and the date, though unknown to men, is fixed. The great opponent, who cannot develop so long as "he that withholdeth" remains, is to be revealed "in his time"—*i.e.*, at the time which Divine Providence has assigned to him. It seems impossible to doubt that this great opponent is the same as the "Little Horn" of Daniel (whose "time" is very definitely marked out in Dan. vii. 25), and that the power which withholds his development is the Fourth Monarchy of Daniel, and, therefore, the Roman empire. A few considerations will make the latter point clearer:—

(1) There was only one power in the world at that time, represented by a single person, in "the midst," before all eyes, of sufficient importance to restrain the development of Antichrist. It was the Roman empire and the Roman emperor.

(2) The word rendered "withholdeth," or "letteth,"

does not necessarily imply that the obstruction *actively*, *consciously*, or *designedly* obstructs the way. His *presence* in the midst is quite sufficient for the requirements of the word. Indeed, it would, perhaps, not be necessary that Antichrist's delay should even be directly *caused* by the obstruction; St. Paul might only mean that *in prophecy* the one thing was destined to come first, and that, therefore, so long as the first thing existed, it (in a manner) kept the second back. Now if Antichrist be the Little Horn of Daniel, and the obstruction the Fourth Monarchy, we get exactly what we want; for (unless the prophecy is to be falsified) before the Little Horn can spring up the Fourth Monarchy must have so totally changed its appearance as to have passed into ten simultaneous kingdoms: therefore, so long as the solid empire stood it was a sign that Antichrist must wait.

(3) Notice the extreme reserve with which St. Paul begins to speak on the subject. He does not teach, but prefers appealing to their memory of words already spoken: "Remember ye not?" His clauses become intricate and ungrammatical—in strange contrast with the simple structure which characterises these two Epistles. He names nothing, only hints. Nor can we account for this sudden ambiguity by saying that St. Paul is adopting the prophetic style; for his purpose is entirely practical, and he wishes not to awe his readers, but to recall to them plain facts which they knew and ignored. Now recollect the similar reticence of Josephus in speaking of the destiny of the Roman empire when it comes in contact with the Messianic Kingdom, and it will be felt almost impossible to doubt the truth of St. Chrysostom's shrewd observations: "A man may naturally seek to know what 'that *which letteth*' is; and after that, what possible reason St. Paul had for putting it so indistinctly. What, then, is 'that which letteth'—*i.e.*, hindereth—him from being revealed? Some say the grace of the Spirit, others the Roman empire. Among the latter I class myself. Why so? Because, had he meant to say 'the Spirit,' he would not have said it indistinctly, but straight out; that now he is restrained by the grace of the Spirit, *i.e.*, the supernatural gifts [presumably that of discerning of spirits in particular; comp. 1 John iv. 1—3]. Otherwise, Antichrist ought to have presented himself ere now, if he were to present himself at the failure of those gifts; for, as a matter of fact, they have long failed. But seeing that he says this of the Roman empire, he naturally put it enigmatically and very obscurely, for he had no wish to subject himself to unnecessary hostilities and unprofitable perils. For had he said that shortly after the Roman empire would be dissolved, they would soon have transfixed him for a miscreant, and all the believers with him, as living and fighting for this end." Was it not, indeed, for expounding this very prophecy that he had fled for his life from Thessalonica? "These all do contrary to the decrees of Cæsar, saying that there is another emperor, Jesus." Does not the history give startling point to his question, "*Remember ye not* that when I was with you I told you these things"?

VII. The Man of Sin.—We have stated our belief that "the Man of Sin" is not only to be identified with Daniel's "Little Horn," but that St. Paul consciously drew the doctrine from that passage. But it may be objected that some of the words in which St. Paul most narrowly describes him are taken, not from the description of the Little Horn in chap. vii., but from that of the Little Horn of chap. viii. 5, which represents quite a different person, viz., Antiochus Epiphanes.* It might be thought, therefore, that St. Paul was only borrowing Daniel's language, and not adopting his prophecy. The answer is, that even those prophecies of Antiochus in many points do not suit Antiochus at all; and not only so, but the Jewish expositors themselves held that Antiochus had not exhausted the meaning of the prophecy. They themselves *applied it to some Antichrist*, whose coming should precede, and be defeated by the Christ's. Even in St. Jerome's time, "From this place onwards" (he is commenting on Dan. xi. 36) "the Jews think that Antichrist is spoken of, that, after the *little help* (verse 34) of Julian, a king shall arise who shall do according to his own will, and lift himself up against all which is called God, and speak great things against the God of gods, so that he shall sit in the Temple of God and make himself god, and his will be performed, until the wrath of God be fulfilled: for in him shall the end be. Which we, too, understand of Antichrist." Thus, according to the current explanation of the Jews, Antiochus was looked upon *as a type* of the Antichrist, whom they expected to arise (in fulfilment of Dan. vii. 8) at the overthrow of the Roman empire, whose coming was to precede the Christ's. The only change made by the Christian Church is to apply to the *Second* Advent a prophecy which the Jews applied to the one Advent which they recognised. It is impossible not to do so when, in Dan. xii. 2, we have the Resurrection made to follow close upon the development of this Antiochus-Antichrist. So far, then, as St. Paul's *date* is concerned, the doctrine is drawn from chaps. ii. and vii.; traits of *character* are added (in accordance with Jewish interpretation) from chaps. viii. and xi.

VIII. St. Paul's probable Personal Expectation.—Dr. Lightfoot argues, with great probability (Smith's *Dict. Bible*, Art. "II. Thessalonians"), that, as a personal matter, St. Paul expected to witness in his own day the development of the Antichrist (whose "secret working" was already visible to him), and that he saw in the Jews the makings of the foe to be revealed. Theirs was the apostasy—professing to cleave to God and to Moses, but "departing from the living God, through an evil heart of unbelief," and "making the word of God to be of none effect through their traditions." Theirs was the lawlessness—setting the will of God at naught in the self-willed assertion of their privilege as the chosen people, and using the most unscrupulous means of checking those who preached the more liberal gospel of St. Paul. And if to St. Paul the final Antichrist was represented by the Jews, the Roman Government, which had so often befriended him, might well be called the withholder or restrainer. If such was the personal expectatien of St. Paul, it was, indeed, literally frustrated; but if the Judaic spirit, of exclusive arrogance, carnal reliance on spiritual promises, innovating tradition, should pass into the Christian Church, and there develop largely, St. Paul's expectation would not be so far wrong.

IX. The Development of the Horns.—The question naturally arises whether the prophecy has not been falsified. The Roman empire has disappeared, and Antichrist is not yet revealed. We do not need to answer with some interpreters that Roman law still rules the world. A closer observation of the two passages of Daniel already mentioned would in itself suggest the true answer. In Nebuchadnezzar's vision, indeed, the Roman empire simply comes into collision

* See Dan. viii. 11, 12, 23–25, and more particularly chap. xi. 36, 37.

with the Catholic Church, and falls before it. There is no hint of a protracted struggle between them. The long duration of the Roman empire is *perhaps* suggested by the words, "Thou *wast gazing* until that a stone" (Dan. ii. 34); the division into the Eastern and Western empires *may* be symbolised by the two legs of the colossal figure; the ten toes *may* bear the same interpretation as the ten horns of the later vision: these points, however, are not the most obvious or prominent points of the dream. But in Daniel's vision all is quite different. There, the final triumph of the Church is won only after a long struggle, and that struggle is *not* with the Roman empire itself. Though the Beast which symbolises the Roman empire is said to continue throughout (Dan. vii. 11), it is only in the same sense, apparently, as the three other Beasts are said to have their lives prolonged (verse 12). The empire itself has altogether changed its form, and developed into ten kingdoms, *among* which, yet *after* which (verses 8, 24), an eleventh has arisen, dissimilar from the other kingdoms, and uprooting some of them. With this power it is that the struggle which ends in the Church's final victory takes place, and not with the old imperial power of Rome. If, therefore, the dream of Nebuchadnezzar may be said to have been fulfilled in the first coming of Christ, *in the days of* the Roman emperors, the vision of Daniel must wait for its fulfilment until the Roman empire has passed away into an even more different form than it has at present reached.

X. Characteristics of Antichrist.—(1) He is a human being. The title "Man of Sin" excludes *Satan*, as Chrysostom remarks: Satan acts *through* the man (1 Thess. ii. 9) to the full extent of his power—"enters into him," as he entered into an earlier "Son of Perdition"—but does not destroy his humanity.

(2) He is a single person. This, too, is involved in the phrase "Man of Sin," especially when followed by the "Son of Perdition." It is not to be denied that poetically the first title, at any rate, might be a personification of a movement, or (as the "kings" in Daniel mean "kingdoms") the title of a wicked power, the head of which might even be more innocent than his subjects. But not only is it simpler to understand the phrases themselves (especially the second) of a single person, but the sharp dramatic contrast between the Christ and the Antichrist seems to require a personal exhibition of evil. The Antichrist is to have a *coming* (verse 9) and a *manifestation* (verse 3), so as to be instantly recognised, and will display himself by significant acts (verse 4), which all require a person. Besides, the types of him—Antiochus, Caligula, Nero, &c.—could hardly be said, according to Scriptural analogy, to be "fulfilled" in a mere headless movement. The application of the name "Man of Sin" to any *succession* of men (as, for instance, all the Popes of Rome) is peremptorily forbidden by the fact that the detection and destruction of the Man of Sin by the Advent of Christ follows immediately upon his manifestation of himself.

(3) This person, though single, heads a movement. He is the captain of "*the* Apostasy." He has a large and devoted following (verse 10). Indeed, though his dominion is "diverse" from other kingdoms, yet he is almost called a king in Dan. vii. 24: the word, however, is (perhaps) carefully avoided. The diversity between his monarchy and theirs might, for instance, consist in its not being, like theirs, territorial or dynastic; it might be a spiritual or an intellectual dominion, interpenetrating the territorial kingdoms.

(4) The movement of Antichrist is not atheistic. The Man of Sin super-exalts himself, indeed, against every God, true or false, but it is not by denial of the Divine existence. On the contrary, he claims himself to be the true God, and exacts the homage due to the true God; thereby acknowledging the existence and working of God, which he avers to have become his own.

(5) The antichristian movement does not even break openly with the Catholic Church. It is an "apostasy," indeed, but the same Greek word is used in Heb. iii. 12, and in 1 Tim. iv. 1, in neither of which cases will it suit the context to understand the word of an outward leaving of the Christian Church. The persons must at any rate *have been* Christians, or they could not be apostates. And the apostasy is all the more terrible if, while the forms of the Church are kept to, there is a departure from the inward spirit. And in this case several points seem to indicate an apostasy within the Church. In the first place, as we have seen above, the movement is distinctly not an atheistic movement, like the German Socialism. Then, the act of session in the "Temple of God" cannot mean anything else than an attempt to exact divine homage from the Christian Church, which, of course, could only be hoped for through adopting Christian forms. The account of the Satanic miracles which the Man of Sin will work in attestation of his claim shows that the persons who follow him are duped into believing that he actually *is* the Lord. An atheistic materialism would deny miracles altogether. Now we may venture to say that, even if St. Paul had not (as Bishop Wordsworth supposes) St. Luke's Gospel in his hands, yet he was familiar with the eschatological discourses of our Lord contained in the Synoptic Gospels. In these (which so frequently use the language of the Book of Daniel) our Lord holds up as the greatest terror of the last days, the constant danger, waiting even upon the "elect," of being seduced into mistaking certain pretenders for *Himself*. An Antichrist (in its full meaning) expresses more than an *opponent* of Christ; like the compound Anti-Pope, it implies a rival claimant to the honours which he himself acknowledges to be due only to Jesus Christ. Antichrist pretends to be actually Jesus. Such pretensions would, of course, be meaningless and ridiculous to *all except* believers in Jesus Christ and His Church. (See Matt. xxiv. 4, 5, 10—12, 23, 26, and the parallel passages in Mark and Luke.) The same would even appear, on close inspection, to be the teaching of the Book of Daniel itself. The Church is "given into his hand" (chap. vii. 25), a much more powerful expression, supposing the Church to be constitutionally bound to him, and not accidentally subject as to a Decius or a Galerius.

(6) Daniel's Antichrist is characterised by ecclesiastical *innovation*. "He shall wear out the saints of the Most High, and think to change times and laws" (Dan. vii. 25)—not to stamp Christianity out altogether, but arbitrarily to alter the Church's *worship* (see Pusey, p. 81) and traditional *constitution*. The same departure from primitive tradition characterises him in chap. xi. 37: "Neither shall he regard the God of his fathers: a God whom his fathers knew not shall he honour." The constant interpretation of "new gods" among the primitive Fathers is "new doctrines": for, as a matter of fact, whatever materially alters our conception of God may be said to make us worship a different Being: the God of the extreme Calvinist, for instance, who creates millions of immortal beings for the express purpose of being glorified by their endless pains, can hardly be called the same as the Father of our Lord

Jesus Christ. And this arbitrary innovation is, in fact, the very feature which St. Paul selects. It is the "lawlessness" or "rebellion" which marks both his movement (2 Thess. ii. 7) and himself (*ib.* verse 8)—which lawlessness, or self-will, is perfectly compatible with exaggerated external reverence for laws and discipline, as is proved by Dr. Lightfoot, who thinks that St. Paul had the Jews specially in mind (Smith's *Bible Dict.*, Art. "II. Thessalonians"). Other more obvious kinds of "sin" can hardly be said to characterise the Man of Sin; for (not to mention 1 Tim. iv. 1, which refers expressly to Daniel) in Dan. xi. 37 he is given an *ascetic* character. This spirit of innovation within the Church, implying as it does that his fiat is as good as God's, which finally leads him to claim divine honours from the Church, is his characteristic sin.

(7) It may be added that the teaching of the Apocalypse is evidently drawn from Daniel, thereby corroborating our belief that St. Paul's is also, and that such an interpretation as is here suggested has almost the catholic consent of the early Fathers, who almost all teach that the fall of the Roman empire will usher in the Antichrist, and that the Antichrist will be professedly Christian. Their testimony is valuable, inasmuch as some of them seem not merely to be offering an exegesis of particular texts of Scripture, but recording a primitive tradition coeval with the New Testament.

XI. Identification of the Man of Sin.—It is not solely a Protestant interpretation, but one which indirectly derives more or less support from several eminent names in past ages in communion with the Roman See (for instance, St. Gregory the Great, and Robert Grosseteste), that the final Antichrist will be *a* Bishop of Rome. And the present writer does not hesitate to assert his conviction that no other interpretation will so well suit all the requirements of the case. This is by no means the same as the vulgar doctrine that *the* Pope—*i.e.*, any and every Pope—is the Man of Sin. The Man of Sin has not yet made his appearance. But the diversity and yet resemblance between his kingdom and the kingdoms of the world; the firm hand over the Church; the claims made upon her homage; the unrecognised movement of rebellion against God while still He is outwardly acknowledged (the "mystery of lawlessness"); the restless innovation upon the Church's apostolic traditions; the uncompromising self-assertion: all these are traits which seem to indicate a future Roman pontiff, more clearly than any other power which we could at present point to,—and this, without having recourse to those more superficial coincidences which may be found in the Notes of Bishop Wordsworth's Greek Testament, or Dr. Eadie's Commentary on these Epistles. To those who are familiar with the way in which modern Roman dogmas have been formed—exaggerations, at first condemned, becoming more and more popular, till they acquired the consistency of general tradition, and were then stamped with authoritative sanction—and who now watch the same process at work in the popular theology of Italy and France, there would be nothing surprising in the literal fulfilment of the prophecies of Antichrist in some future Pope. Already one Divine attribute has been definitely claimed by and conceded to the occupant of the Roman See, in defiance of primitive tradition, and yet so plausibly as to suggest rather an implicit faith in God than an explicit denial of Him. Comparisons *ex aequo* between the Life and Passion of our Lord and that of Pius the Ninth formed a large proportion of the spiritual diet of foreign Papists towards the close of his pontificate. Even eminent prelates of the Roman obedience are reported not to have scrupled already to use of the Papacy such phrases as "Third Incarnation of the Deity"; and it would be only following analogies of "development," if, in process of time, these last exaggerations also should be formulated into dogma, as has been the case with the dogma of Infallibility, and some Pope to come should in some way claim to be actually identified with Jesus Christ.

THE PASTORAL EPISTLES OF ST. PAUL

"In the 'Acts of the Apostles' Luke relates to Theophilus events of which he was an eye-witness, ... but [omits] the journey of Paul from Rome to Spain.

. . . .

"An Epistle to Titus, and two to Timothy, which, though written only from personal feeling and affection, are still hallowed in the respect of the Catholic Church, and in the arrangement of ecclesiastical discipline."

(From the Muratorian Fragment on the Canon discovered in the Ambrosian Library at Milan, and supposed to have been written not later than A.D. 170.)

THE PASTORAL EPISTLES OF ST. PAUL

I. **Their Nature.**—The two Letters of St. Paul to Timothy and the one Letter to Titus, usually known as the Pastoral Epistles, differ from the other Epistles of the Apostle, being addressed to individuals, and not to churches. [There is another private Epistle of St. Paul, addressed to one Philemon, consisting only of a few lines, exclusively confined to the relations which should subsist between a Christian master and a Christian slave.]

These divinely inspired compositions were written for the guidance of two younger men, disciples and intimate friends of the elder Apostle. To these, Timothy and Titus, St. Paul had entrusted the government and supervision of two important churches—Ephesus and Crete. Of one of these churches, that of Ephesus, St. Paul was probably the founder, and from his long residence in the city, we may reasonably conclude that the Ephesian congregations had been built up mainly under his teaching and influence; the circumstances of the church of Crete will be discussed more particularly in the brief special *Introduction to the Epistle to Titus*. Over the Ephesian community, especially dear to St. Paul from his close and intimate relation with Ephesus, the Apostle placed the disciple he knew and perhaps loved the best, the pupil whom he had personally trained from early youth. Of all St. Paul's friends there was none so close to him as the one he had for so many years watched over and educated in the faith as his own adopted son. The two Letters to Timothy contain the master's last charge, his dying wishes to the son of his love, who knew so well his mind, his every thought and aspiration. We may well conceive that almost every thought in these Letters, every charge, every exhortation, was a reminiscence of some bit of public teaching well known to Timothy, of some solemn conversation between the master and the pupil, of some grave council in which St. Paul and his trusted pupil and friend had shared. The two Letters were the old master's last words, and as the master wrote, or, more probably, dictated them, he was conscious of this, and strove to compress into the necessary short compass of a brief Epistle a summary of what he had already put forth as his teaching on the question of church doctrine, church order, and church life. This is the reason why the charges concerning the life to be led are so repeated, but at the same time so brief; why the directions respecting church order are so concise; why the doctrinal statements are simply urged, and never, as was his old custom in some Epistles, argued out and discussed. "We see here," as one has eloquently described it, "rather the succession of brilliant sparks than the steady flame; burning words indeed, and deep pathos, but not the flower of his firmness, as in his discipline of the Galatians—not the noon of his bright warm eloquence, as in the inimitable psalm of love" (1 Cor. xiii.).

Many of the more doctrinal statements in these Pastoral Epistles are something more than "memories" of past conversations, past deliberations—more than reminders of former teaching—they are evidently current and well-known sayings among the Christians of the years A.D. 65—67. Now they are a well-loved line or lines of a hymn to the Father, as in the First Epistle, chap. vi. 15, 16; now a verse from a metrical creed sung by these believers of the first days, as in chap. iii. 16 of the same Epistle, where the principal events of the divine and human life of Christ, so far as that life was connected with man, are set forth; or, they are evidently well-known sayings which had become watchwords of the rapidly growing Church of Christ, introduced by the striking formula "faithful is the saying." There are no less than five of these in the Pastoral Epistles. All these are woven into the tapestry of the writings, and contain many a word, many an expression not found in any other of the known Epistles of St. Paul; and it is to the presence of these evident quotations from hymn, or creed, or sacred utterances of the faith, that these last Letters of St. Paul owe many of those peculiarities of thought and of expression which have suggested to the critical minds of so many scholars of our own thoughtful age the question—were these Epistles really the work of the great Apostle of the Gentiles?

II. **Their Authenticity.**—For seventeen centuries the Pastoral Epistles were believed to have been written by St. Paul, and in all the churches were received among the divinely inspired Scriptures of the New Testament. In the nineteenth century, for certain reasons specified below, their authenticity was first called in question by a school of German criticism.

From the very earliest times we find constant references to these Pastoral Letters of St. Paul. Although there are no exact quotations in those few fragments we possess of the writings of men contemporary with or immediately succeeding the Apostles, still the language of Clement of Rome, Polycarp of Smyrna, and Ignatius of Antioch (all three living and writing in the first century), seems to show their familiarity with the language and thought of these Epistles.

Unquestioned references to one or other of these Letters are found in Irenæus (second century), Tertullian (second century), Clement of Alexandria (second century), Theophilus of Antioch (second century). Eusebius (A.D. 320) without question includes the three Epistles in his catalogue, among the universally confessed canonical writings. In addition to this, in the famous Fragment on the Canon of Scripture edited by Muratori, generally ascribed to the latter half of the second century, we find these "three" classed among the Epistles of St. Paul.

They are also contained in the Peschito-Syriac version of the New Testament, which was made in the second century. There never, indeed, seems to have been the slightest doubt in the early Christian Church that the

Pastoral Epistles were canonical, and written by St. Paul. The only doubter, in fact, seems to have been the famous Gnostic heretic Marcion (second century), who for doctrinal reasons omitted these writings from his canon. But Marcion arbitrarily made up his own volume of Scripture, excluding what was distinctly adverse to his peculiar system. He admitted into his "canon" only ten of St. Paul's Epistles and a mutilated Gospel of St. Luke, omitting all the rest of the New Testament writings.

We possess a continuous chain of historical evidence for the authenticity of these writings from the earliest times. We can, then, aver that from the very days of the Apostles down to the beginning of the nineteenth century, the two Epistles to Timothy and the one to Titus were received in all the churches as undoubted writings of St. Paul, and were reverenced as Holy Scripture. The school of critics to which allusion has been made above has sought to undermine this testimony, stretching over one thousand seven hundred years, by arguments drawn from the contents of these three Epistles.

The following are the main points they have endeavoured to establish:—

(1) A number of words and phrases are found in these Letters which never occur in any other of St. Paul's writings.

(2) An ecclesiastical organisation of a period long subsequent to St. Paul's time apparently existed when these Pastoral Epistles were written.

(3) Heresies of a date later than the period included in the lifetime of St. Paul are combated in the three Letters.

(4) In the lifetime of the Apostle no period can be found which would suit the circumstances under which it is evident these Letters were composed.

We will reply to these arguments very briefly:—

(1) As regards the unusual words and phrases, it must be borne in mind that the Epistles or groups of Epistles of St. Paul were composed under very different circumstances, and for varied purposes, and with long intervals of time between the several writings. To a certain extent, in each Epistle or group of Epistles we should expect to find its own peculiar vocabulary: and this we find, for the number of verbal peculiarities in the group of Letters we are now considering does not appear to be greater than that existing in other undoubted Letters of the Apostle. Prof. Van Oosterzee, of Utrecht (*Die Pastoralbriefe*, 3rd edit. 1874), computes the number of these peculiar words in the three Epistles at one hundred and eighty-eight, while in the Epistles to the Philippians, Ephesians, and Colossians he reckons one hundred and ninety-four of these verbal peculiarities not elsewhere found.

But while verbal peculiarities in this group of Epistles do not appear more numerous than in other special groups of writings by the same hand, there are peculiar circumstances connected with these Letters to Timothy and Titus, which would of themselves fairly have explained a much greater divergence from the customary style and usual expressions than we actually find.

Here, and here only—with the exception of the little Letter to Philemon—is he writing to dear friends, not to churches. The official character of the communication is in great measure here lost sight of. The chief pastor is addressed, rather than the flock; and the chief pastor in each case is the pupil and intimate associate of the writer. Surely different expressions might be reasonably looked for in such Letters as these.

Again, we might fairly expect that in this last period of the Apostle's long life his theological vocabulary would have become materially enlarged. This would account for his use of certain new words when he wished to express or reiterate perhaps old thoughts.

It should be remembered, too, that he was in these Epistles combating new forms of heresy which were rapidly developing themselves in the various growing Christian communities. What more likely than that the old master, the wise and divinely inspired teacher, should have appropriated some of the favourite sayings of his opponents, the false teachers of Ephesus and the Asian cities—should have "borrowed" from these unhappy men their own words, thus rescuing them from the perversions which false philosophy had begun to make of them?

We have already, in the first section of this short *Introduction*, suggested a probable explanation of the repeated use of the formulary "faithful is the saying," and of other divine sayings which had apparently grown into customary use in the Church.

On the other hand, would not a forger who was desirous to introduce for a particular purpose a writing, or writings, into the Church, under the venerated name of St. Paul, have been specially careful not to introduce into his composition any word or expression foreign to the Apostle's most common and best known terminology?

(2) The ecclesiastical organisation to which reference is made in these Pastoral Epistles is, after all, of the simplest description. The forms of the government or the Jewish synagogue, only slightly modified to suit the exigencies of the mixed Jewish and Gentile congregations of Christians, are evidently all that existed at the time when St. Paul wrote to Timothy and Titus.

The only marked innovation is that provision which was being made in all the churches for women's work —a provision rendered necessary from the new position which women, under the teaching of our Lord and His disciples, were henceforth to occupy in the work and life of the world. (This great and important question is treated of at some length in the commentary on the Pastoral Epistles which follows.) And even of this female organisation we see the germs in such notices as in Acts vi. 1; ix. 36—41; xxi. 9; and in the life and work of one like Lydia (Acts xvi. 14), or Priscilla (Acts xviii. 2 and 26), &c.

The presbyterate, not merely in name, but also in the matter of the functions assigned to the office, was clearly adopted from the synagogue, of course with such changes and modifications as the new and growing society required.

The diaconate also, in some way, appears to have been derived from Jewish precedents. The very name, "Levites," by which these inferior ministers of the Church were often called, points to the origin of the "order." Thus Jerome (*Ep.* 27) distinguishes them from the presbyters, speaking of the deacons as "the countless number of Levites." So, too, Salvian, A.D. 450, writes of the deacons, calling them "Levites." Frequently in the Councils the term "Levite" is used as the peculiar title of the deacon.

But the diaconate—which, although probably originally a copy of a Jewish order of ministers in the public services connected with worship and religious instruction, still may be looked on as an order especially belonging to the Christian Church—existed long before "the last days" of St. Paul. Indeed, it is traceable back to the very first years of the existence of the little Jerusalem community of believers in Jesus of Nazareth.

See Acts vi. 2—6, where the famous Seven are appointed by the Twelve Apostles—*diaconein trapezais*, "to serve tables."

The functions of the "deacons of Ephesus" alluded to by St. Paul were certainly not very different from the duties apparently performed by the "Seven" of Acts vi. See, especially verses 3, 8, 9, 10, where these solemnly ordained ones assisted the Apostle in almsgiving, in the general regulation of the Church's charities, and also appear to have preached and taught publicly.

But there is one argument for the extreme antiquity of these Epistles derived exclusively from internal evidence supplied by the Epistles themselves.

At the very commencement of the second century it is an acknowledged fact that the *episcopal* office was firmly and widely established. But *these* Letters were written before any sign of episcopal government had appeared in Gentile Christendom. In the Pastoral Epistles the Greek words rendered "bishop" and "presbyter" (*episcopos, presbyteros*) are applied indifferently to the same person. (See Note on 1 Tim. iii. 1.)

Too great stress can hardly be laid on the vast difference which existed between the ecclesiastical organisation presented in the Pastoral Epistles and that revealed to us in the Letters of Ignatius, written at the very commencement of the second century, even if we only admit as genuine the shorter form of the version of the Ignatian Epistles, or the still briefer recension of the three Syriac Letters edited by Dr. Cureton.

No candid critic would surely suggest for so vast a development in ecclesiastical organisation a less period than thirty to forty years, placing the Ignatian Epistles in the early part of the second century. This would give as the date of the so-called Pastoral Letters, the last year of St. Paul's life.

(3) Heresies of a later date appear to be combated in these writings. But the false teachers referred to here were evidently *Judaistic* in their teaching (see for instance 1 Tim. i. 7; iv. 3; Titus i. 10—14; iii. 9), while the Gnostic teachers of the next century were strongly *anti*-Judaistic. This state of things was no doubt brought about by the destruction of Jerusalem and the Temple, and the total ruin of the Jewish national system, in the year of our Lord 70.

In these Epistles we have allusion to schools of heresies widely differing from those which opposed the Catholic Church in the second century. Here we find the seeds, but only the seeds, of the famous Gnostic teaching. Dean Alford (*Prolegomena to the Pastoral Epistles*) has well, though roughly, painted the development of heresy in the early days of Christianity. In the first years, the principal enemies within the church were "Judaising Christians," these are alluded to in St. Paul's earlier Epistles. "The false teachers against whom Timothy and Titus were warned seemed to hold a position intermediate to the Apostle's former Judaising adversaries and the subsequent Gnostic heretics."

The general characteristics of the heresies spoken of in the Pastoral Epistles would certainly *not* appear to belong to a period subsequent to the fall of Jerusalem (A.D. 70).

(4) As regards the last objection,—to the critics who seriously propose to throw doubt on the authenticity of these Epistles, alleging that it is impossible to assign during the lifetime of St. Paul, as related in the Acts, a period which would suit the peculiar circumstances under which it was evident that these writings were composed, we reply that St. Paul lived and worked *after* the captivity related in the last chapter of the Acts; for the unanimous testimony of the primitive Church tells us that the appeal of St. Paul to Cæsar (Acts xxv. 11) terminated successfully, that after the imprisonment related in the last chapter of the Acts, he was liberated A.D. 63, and that he spent some time (A.D. 63 to A.D. 65—66) in freedom before he was again arrested and condemned.

The principal evidences for this are found in the Epistle of Clement, Bishop of Rome, the disciple of St. Paul (Phil. iv. 3), to the Romans, written in the last year of the first century. "He, Paul, had gone to *the extremity of the west* before his martyrdom." In a Roman writer the "extremity of the west" could only signify "Spain," and we know in that portion of his life related in the Acts he had never journeyed further west than Italy. In the fragments of the Canon called Muratori's, written about A.D. 170, we read in the account of the Acts of the Apostles, "Luke relates to Theophilus events of which he was an eyewitness, as also in a separate place [Luke xxii. 31—33] he evidently declares the martyrdom of Peter, but [omits] the journey of St. Paul to Spain." Eusebius (*H. E.* ii. 22—A.D. 320) writes, "After defending himself successfully it is currently reported that the Apostle again went forth to proclaim the gospel, and afterwards came to Rome a second time, and was martyred under Nero."

St. Chrysostom (A.D. 398) mentions as an undoubted historical fact, "that St. Paul after his residence in Rome departed to Spain." St. Jerome (A.D. 390) also relates, "that St. Paul was dismissed by Nero that he might preach Christ's gospel in the West."

Thus in the Catholic Church in the East and West during the three hundred years which succeeded the death of St. Paul, a unanimous tradition was current that the great Apostle's labours were continued for a period extending over two or three years after his liberation from that Roman imprisonment related in Acts xxviii. During this renewed season of activity, probably in the last year or fifteen months, the Epistles to Timothy and Titus were written.

The last of the three Letters, the Second Epistle to Timothy, was no doubt written within a few weeks at most of the glorious end. We see, then, that internal evidence, when carefully sifted, instead of contradicting, supports, with a weighty mass of independent testimony, the unanimous tradition of the ancient Church which, with one voice, proceeding from the East as well as from the West, pronounced the Pastoral Epistles canonical, receiving them as the word of the Holy Spirit communicated through the Apostle Paul.

INTRODUCTION

TO

THE FIRST EPISTLE OF PAUL THE APOSTLE TO

TIMOTHY

I. Timothy.—Timothy was a native of the province of Lycaonia in Asia Minor—most probably of Lystra, a small town some thirty miles to the south of Iconium, the modern *Konieh*. His father was a pagan, but his mother and grandmother, Lois and Eunice, were Jewesses, evidently devout and earnest in the practice of the religion of their forefathers. They became Christians, apparently, at the time of St. Paul's first visit to Asia Minor in company with Barnabas (A.D. 46), (Acts xiv.; 2 Tim. i. 5; iii. 15).

From Lois and Eunice Timothy no doubt learned the rudiments of the faith of the Lord Jesus. Some five years later, in company with Silas (A.D. 51), St. Paul paid a second visit to Asia Minor. Moved probably by the devotion and earnestness of the young son of Eunice, and seeing in him the promise of a loving and heroic life, St. Paul took Timothy in the place of Mark, whose heart had failed him in the presence of so many difficulties and dangers. From this time (A.D. 51) Timothy's life was closely associated with that of his master.

He was with the Gentile Apostle in Macedonia and Corinth (A.D. 52—53), (Acts xvii. 14; xviii. 5; 1 Thess. i. 1); with him at Ephesus, whence he was sent on a special mission to Corinth (A.D. 55—56), (1 Cor. iv. 17; xvi. 10); with him when he wrote from Macedonia the Second Corinthian Letter (2 Cor. i. 1); with him at Corinth when he wrote to the Roman Church (A.D. 57), (Rom. xvi. 21); with him when he was returning to Asia, where he was arrested prior to the long captivity at Cæsarea and Rome (A.D. 57—58), (Acts xx. 4). We find him again specially mentioned as the Apostle's companion during that long Roman imprisonment (A.D. 61—63). (See the Epistles written at that period—Col. i. 1; Philem. verse 1; Phil. i. 1.)

After the Apostle's release from his first great captivity (A.D. 63), (see *General Introduction to the Pastoral Epistles*), Timothy, still St. Paul's companion (1 Tim. i. 3), was left in charge of the Ephesian Church (probably about A.D. 64). While fulfilling this work he received the two Epistles of St. Paul (A.D. 64—65) which bear his name. In the Epistle to the Hebrews (xiii. 23) Timothy is alluded to as having been imprisoned and again liberated. This solitary notice, however, throws but little light on the life of the Apostle's famous disciple, except that it seems to tell us that the pupil's life was full of hardship and danger, as was the master's, and that the younger man had well learned the lesson of St. Paul, who bade him with his dying breath (2 Tim. ii. 3) "endure hardness as a good soldier of Jesus Christ."

Nicephorus and the ancient martyrologies tell us that Timothy died by martyrdom under the Emperor Domitian some time before A.D. 96. Baronius, however, puts his martyr death a little later—A.D. 109—when the Emperor Trajan was reigning.

The accompanying table will assist the reader in following the life of Timothy:—

A.D.	Roman Emperor Reigning.	——
46	Claudius.	First meeting between Paul and Timothy, still a child, at Lystra—probably in the house of Eunice and Lois.
51		Paul and Silas take Timothy with them from Lystra.
52		Timothy accompanies Paul in his journey through Macedonia.
53		Timothy is with Paul at Corinth.
54—56	Nero.	Timothy is with Paul at Ephesus.
57		Timothy is with Paul at Corinth. Paul writes Epistle to Romans.
58		Timothy is with Paul in the journey from Corinth to Asia.
62—63		Timothy is with Paul during the Roman imprisonment.
64		Paul leaves Timothy at Ephesus.
65—66		Timothy receives the two Epistles from Paul.
Not later than 96	Domitian.	Alleged martyrdom of Timothy.
Or, according to Baronius, 109	Trajan.	Alleged martyrdom.

II. Date of the Epistle.—The First Epistle to Timothy was written apparently in the year 65—66, while the Apostle was passing through Macedonia, after a probable journey into Spain and a return to Ephesus, at which city he had left Timothy in charge of the church.

III. General Contents of the Epistle.—No systematic arrangement is followed in this Epistle. Its contents may be roughly divided into six general divisions, coinciding with the six chapters:—

1.—St. Paul reminds Timothy of his especial commission at Ephesus—the repression of a school of false teachers which threatened to subvert the church.

This leads to a brief review of the Apostle's own past history (chap. i.).

2.—The second division is occupied with directions respecting the public worship of Christians, and the parts which each sex should take in public prayer (chap. ii.).

3.—Treats of the office-bearers in the church—bishops (or, *elders*), deacons, and deaconesses (chap. iii.).

4.—Again St. Paul refers to Timothy's commission in respect to false teachers. He dwells upon the deceptive teaching of asceticism, showing the dangers which accompanied such doctrine. The practical godly life of Timothy and his staff would, after all, be the best antidote to the poison disseminated by these unreal, untrue men (chap. iv.).

5.—Treats (*a*) of the behaviour of the church officials to the flock of Christ; (*b*) of the public charities of the Church in connection with destitute and helpless women; (*c*) of a certain order of presbyteral or *elder* widows, which, in connection with these charities, might be developed in such a Christian community as Ephesus; (*d*) rules for Timothy, as chief presbyter, respecting ordination and selection of colleagues in the ministry, &c. (chap. v.).

6.—A few plain comments on the great social question of slavery. How Christian slaves were to behave in their condition. The false teachers must be sternly combated in their teaching on this point. Timothy is warned with solemn earnestness against covetousness. This, St. Paul argues, was the root of all false teaching (chap. vi.).

One golden thread seems to run through this, and, it may be said, through the other two Pastoral Letters. St. Paul's earnestness in these last days of his life seems rather to expend itself in exhortations to Christian men and women to live a good, pure, self-denying life. Doctrine, in these last words of the noble, generous toiler for the Lord, retreats a little into the background. It is true that he reiterates in several places the grounds of a Christian's belief—that he rehearses in plain and evidently well-known phrases the great articles of the Christian faith; but his last words dwell rather on life than on theology. The errors of the false teachers whose deadly influence Timothy was to counteract belonged rather to an evil life than to a false belief. The pure and saintly conduct, the pattern home life—these things, Timothy and his colleagues must remember, were the surest antidote against the poisonous teaching and the selfish practice of the enemies of the Lord Jesus.

THE FIRST EPISTLE OF PAUL THE APOSTLE TO

TIMOTHY

CHAPTER I.—(1) Paul, an apostle of
Chap. i. 1, 2. The salutation. Jesus Christ by the commandment of God our
Saviour, and Lord Jesus Christ, *which*
is our hope; (2) unto Timothy, *my* own
son in the faith: Grace, mercy, *and*
peace, from God our Father and Jesus

A.D. 65.

Christ our Lord. (3) As I besought thee
to abide still at Ephesus, when I went into Macedonia, that thou mightest charge some that they teach no other doctrine, Chap. i. 3—11. Timothy is urged to repress teachers of strange doctrines.
(4) neither give heed to fables and end-

(1) **Paul, an apostle of Jesus Christ.**—The letter to Timothy, though addressed to a very dear and intimate friend, was sent with a two-fold purpose. It was an affectionate reminder from his old master, "Paul the Aged," to his disciple to be steadfast in the midst of the many perils to which one in the position of Timothy would be exposed in the city of Ephesus; but it was also an official command to resist a powerful school of false teaching which had arisen in the midst of that Ephesian Church over which Timothy was then presiding. So St. Paul prefaces his letter by designating himself an Apostle according to the commandment of God. The commandment especially referred to is to be found in Acts xiii. 2: Separate me Barnabas and Saul for the work whereunto I have called them.

God our Saviour.—This designation is peculiar to the Pastoral Epistles, but frequently occurs in the Septuagint. It is fitly ascribed to the first Person of the blessed Trinity in reference to His redeeming love in Christ.

Lord Jesus Christ, which is our hope.—The words "which is," printed in italics in the English version, are better left out: *Jesus Christ, our hope.* As St. Paul felt the end of his course approaching, he loved to dwell on the thought of Jesus—to whom, during so many weary years, he had longed to depart and be with—as his hope, *his one glorious hope.* The same expression is found in the *Epistles* of Ignatius.

(2) **My own son in the faith.**—Timothy was St. Paul's very own son. No fleshly relationship existed between the two, but a closer and far dearer connection. St. Paul had taken him while yet a very young man to be his companion and fellow-labourer (Acts xvi. 3). He told the Philippian Church he had no one like-minded (with Timothy) who would care for their affairs. He wrote to the Corinthians how Timothy was his beloved and faithful son in the Lord, who would put them in remembrance of his ways in Christ.

Mercy.—Between the usual salutation "grace and peace," in these Pastoral Epistles, he introduces "mercy." The nearness of death, the weakness of old age, the dangers, ever increasing, which crowded round Paul, seem to have called forth from him deeper expressions of love and tender pity. Jesus Christ, his "hope," burned before him, a guiding star ever brighter and clearer; and the "mercy" of God, which the old man felt he had obtained, he longed to share with others.

(3) **That thou mightest charge some.**—Some time *after* the first imprisonment at Rome, and consequently beyond the period included by St. Luke in the Acts, St. Paul must have left Timothy behind at Ephesus while he pursued his journey towards Macedonia, and given him the solemn charge here referred to. The false teachers who are disturbing the Church at Ephesus are not named. There is, perhaps, a ring of contempt in the expression "some," but it seems more probable that the names were designedly omitted in this letter, which was intended to be a public document. The chief superintendent of the Ephesian community, doubtless, knew too well who were the mistaken men referred to.

That they teach no other doctrine.—"Other" —*i.e.*, other than the truth. When the Apostle and his disciple Timothy re-visited Ephesus, after the long Cæsarean and Roman imprisonment, they found the Church there distracted with questions raised by Jewish teachers. The curious and hair-splitting interpretation of the Mosaic law, the teaching concerning the tithing of mint and anise and cummin, which in the days of Jesus of Nazareth had paralysed all real spiritual life in Jerusalem, had found its way during the Apostle's long enforced absence into the restless, ever-changing congregations at Ephesus.

Dangerous controversies, disputings concerning old prophecies, mingled with modern traditions, occupied the attention of many of the Christian teachers. They preferred to talk about theology rather than try to live the life which men like St. Paul had told them that followers of Jesus must live if they would be His servants indeed.

Unless these deadening influences were removed, the faith of the Ephesian Church threatened to become utterly impractical. The *doctrine* these restless men were teaching, and which St. Paul so bitterly condemns, seems to have been no settled form of heresy, but a profitless teaching, arising mainly, if not entirely, from Jewish sources.

(4) **Neither give heed to fables.**—These fables were, no doubt, purely Rabbinical. It was said in the Jewish schools that an oral Law had been given on

less genealogies, which minister questions, rather than godly edifying which is in faith: *so do.* (5) Now the end of the commandment is charity out of a pure heart, and *of* a good conscience, and *of* faith unfeigned: (6) from which

Sinai, and that this Law, a succession of teachers, from the time of Moses, had handed down. This "Law that is upon the lip," as it was termed, was further illustrated and enlarged by the sayings and comments of the more famous Jewish Rabbis, and in the time of our Lord constituted a supplement to the written Law in the Pentateuch. For centuries this supplementary code was preserved by memory or in secret rolls, and doubtless was constantly receiving additions. It contained, along with many wild and improbable legendary histories, some wise teachings. This strange collection of tradition and comment was committed to writing in the second century by Rabbi Jehuda, under the general name of the Mishna, or repetition (of the Law). Round this compilation a complement of discussions (the Gemara) was gradually formed, and was completed at Babylon somewhere about the end of the fifth century of our era. These works—the Mishna and the Gemara, together with a second Gemara, formed somewhat earlier in Palestine—are generally known as the Talmud. The influence of some of these traditions is alluded to by our Lord (Matt. xv. 3).

Endless genealogies.—Genealogies in their proper sense, as found in the Book of the Pentateuch, and to which wild allegorical interpretations had been assigned. Such purely fanciful meanings had been already developed by Philo, whose religious writings were becoming at this time known and popular in many of the Jewish schools. Such teaching, if allowed in the Christian churches, St. Paul saw would effectually put a stop to the growth of Gentile Christendom. It would inculcate an undue and exaggerated, and, for the ordinary Gentile convert, an impossible reverence for Jewish forms and ceremonies; it would separate the Jewish and Gentile converts into two classes—placing the favoured Jew in an altogether different position from the outcast Gentile.

In the Gentile churches founded by the Apostles, for some years a life and death struggle went on between the pupils of St. Paul and his fellow Apostles and the disciples of the Rabbinical schools. In these earnest warnings of his Pastoral Epistles the great Apostle of Gentile Christianity shows us, how clearly he foresaw that if these Jewish fables and the comments of the older Jewish teachers were allowed to enter into the training of the new-formed congregations, the Church of Christ would shrink, in no long space of time, into the narrow and exclusive limits of a Jewish sect. "Judaism," writes the anonymous author of *Paul of Tarsus,* "was the cradle of Christianity, and Judaism very nearly became its grave."

Which minister questions.—Disputings, questions of mere controversy, inquiries, which could not possibly have any bearing on practical life.

Rather than godly edifying which is in faith.—The rendering of the reading in the more ancient authorities would be: *rather than the dispensation of God which is in faith;* or, in other words, the introduction into Church teaching of these Jewish myths—these traditions of the elders, these fanciful genealogies—would be much more likely to produce bitter and profitless controversy than to minister to God's scheme of salvation, designed by God, and proclaimed by His Apostles.

So do.—The Apostle, in verse 3, begins this sentence of earnest exhortation, but in his fervour forgets to conclude it. The closing words would naturally come in here: "For remember how I besought thee when I left thee behind at Ephesus, when I went on to Macedonia, to discourage and firmly repress all vain teaching, which only leads to useless controversy, *so I do now;*" or, so I repeat to you now. (This is better and more forcible than the words supplied in the English version: "so do.")

(5) **Now the end.**—The Greek word should be translated *But the end.* Though Timothy must resist and oppose these false teachers with all courage and firmness, still he must not forget what was the real end, the aim, the purpose of all Christian teaching, which, the Apostle reminds him, is Love.

Of the commandment.—There is no reference here to the famous commandments of the Law of Moses. "Commandment" may be paraphrased in this place by "practical teaching."

With the false teachers' sickly "fables," which only led to disputing, St. Paul contrasts that "healthy practical teaching," the end and aim of which was love, or charity.

Charity.—That love, or broad, comprehensive charity, towards men, so nobly described in 1 Cor. xiii.

Out of a pure heart, and of a good conscience, and of faith unfeigned.—This broad, all-embracing love, or charity, emanates only from "a pure heart:" *i.e.,* a heart free from selfish desires and evil passions. The "pure in heart" alone, said the Lord, in the sermon on the mount (Matt. v. 8), shall enjoy the beatific vision of God.

And of a good conscience.—This "charity" must also spring from a conscience unburthened of its load of guilt, from a conscience sprinkled with the precious blood, and so reconciled to God.

And of faith unfeigned.—And, lastly, the root of this "charity"—the end and aim of the practical teaching of the gospel preached by the Apostles—must be sought in "a faith unfeigned," in a faith that consists in something more than in a few high-sounding words, which lay claim to a sure confidence that is not felt. The "unfeigned faith" of St. Paul is a faith rich in works rather than in words.

Without this faith, so real that its fruits are ever manifest, there can be no good conscience; without this conscience, washed by the precious blood, there can be no pure heart.

The error of the teachers of whom Timothy was warned, we see from the next verse, consisted not so much in false doctrines as in an utter neglect of inculcating the necessity of a pure, self-denying life. They preferred curious questions and speculative inquiries to the grave, simple gospel teaching which led men to live an earnest, loving life.

(6) **From which some having swerved have turned aside.**—This sentence is rendered more accurately: *From which some, having gone wide in aim, have turned themselves aside.* These words seem to tell us that these teachers had once been in the right direction, but had not kept in it; indeed, from the whole tenor of St. Paul's directions to Timothy it is clear that these persons not only had been, but were still, reckoned among the Christian congregations of

some having swerved [1] have turned aside
unto vain jangling; (7) desiring to be
teachers of the law; understanding
neither what they say, nor whereof they
affirm. (8) But we know that the law
is good. if a man use it lawfully;
(9) knowing this, that the law is not
made for a righteous man, but for the
lawless and disobedient, for the ungodly
and for sinners, for unholy and profane,
for murderers of fathers and murderers
of mothers, for manslayers, (10) for

[1] Or, *not aiming at.*

the Ephesian Church. The presiding presbyter appointed by St. Paul could have exercised no possible authority over any not reckoned in the Church's pale.

Unto vain jangling.—These men, having missed the true aim of the commandment, have now turned themselves to vain, empty talking, which could lead to nothing except wranglings and angry disputations.

(7) **Desiring to be teachers of the law.**—"Desiring," though they really were not. They coveted the respect and influence which was ever paid to the acknowledged teachers of the Law of Moses; but these men utterly failed to understand the real spiritual meaning of that Law which they pretended to teach. Similar pretenders in a neighbouring Church, some years later, received from another Apostle—St. John—a stern rebuke for such pretensions. "I know," wrote St. John to the Christians of Smyrna, "the blasphemy of them which say they are Jews, and are not, but are the synagogue of Satan" (Rev. ii. 9).

Understanding neither what they say, nor whereof they affirm.—A wise teacher must understand what he teaches, and must, at the same time, be clear in his own mind that what he teaches is true.

The false teachers are here charged (1) with not understanding the wild fables and traditions upon which their teaching was based, and (2) with not comprehending the things whereof they make their assertions: that is, they had no real belief in those great truths which really underlie that Law with which they were meddling.

(8) **But we know.**—Better, *Now we know*: a strong expression of his knowledge, learned in the school of the Holy Ghost. He spoke with the conscious authority of an Apostle, confident of the truth of what he preached and taught.

That the law is good, if a man use it lawfully.—"The Law is good," St. Paul declared with apostolic authoritative knowledge, "should a man—*i.e.*, a teacher of the Law—make use of it lawfully; if he should use it so as to make men conscious of their sins, conscious that of themselves they deserve no mercy, only punishment." To press this sorrowful knowledge was the Law's true work upon men. It was never intended to supply materials for casuistry and idle, profitless arguments. It was never meant as a system out of which man might draw material for self-deception. It was never meant as a system through which a man might imagine that by a compliance, more or less rigid, with its outer ritual he was satisfying all the higher requirements of justice and truth.

(9) **Knowing this.**—The teacher of the Law, being aware of this great truth, now to be detailed—viz.:—

That the law is not made for a righteous man.—The stern Mosaic Law was enacted centuries before the Messiah Jesus had given to men His new Law. The Law of Moses was not, then, enacted for a "righteous man"—that is, for a Christian in the true sense of the word, who has sought and found justification by faith in Jesus, and who, sanctified by the Holy Ghost, is living a new life. In other words, the "teacher," Paul says, must teach the flock of Ephesus (1) the true use of the *prohibitions* of the Law, viz., that they served to convince a man of his hopeless condition; they showed him he was a slave to sin, from which wretched bondage, the Law, which made him bitterly conscious of his condition, gave him no assistance to free himself; (2) the "teacher" was to press home to the people that the Law, good though it was, if used as a means to open men's eyes to see their true condition, was not made for *them* if they were reckoned among the righteous—that is, if they had found acceptance in the Redeemer. In the case of these justified and sanctified ones the moral law was written in their hearts and was embodied in their lives.

But for the lawless.—Now the Law was not made for the holy and humble men of heart, whom St. Paul trusted formed the main body of the congregation of believers in Ephesus, and in every city where men and women were found who called on the name of the Lord Jesus, and who struggled to follow their dear Master's footsteps. It was made centuries before Jesus of Nazareth walked on earth, as a great protest against the every-day vices which dishonoured Israel in common with the rest of mankind. The terrible enumeration of sins and sinners in these 9th and 10th verses, while following the order of the ancient Tables of Sinai, seems to allude pointedly to the vices especially prevalent in that day in the great centres of the Roman empire.

And disobedient.—More accurately rendered, *unruly*, or *insubordinate*.

For the ungodly and for sinners.—These four terms with which the Apostle opens his sad list of those for whom the Law was enacted, generally denote those who care nothing for human law, and who despise all obedience; who to their careless neglect for all constituted authorities, unite irreligion and contempt for all sacred things.

For unholy and profane.—The persons designated in these terms are those wanting in inner purity—men who scoff at holiness of life and character in its deepest sense. These six classes may be assumed in general terms to include the prohibitions of the first four Commandments (the First Table, as it is termed), where sins against God are especially dwelt upon. The sins against man, which form the subject of the prohibitions of the Second Table (Commandments Five to Ten), are included in the following enumeration of wrong-doers.

For murderers of fathers and murderers of mothers.—The original Greek expressions here require the milder rendering, *smiters of fathers and smiters of mothers*, and refer to persons of various ages who refuse all reverence, even all kindly treatment, to their parents. The words of the Fifth Commandment exactly explain this unnatural conduct.

(10) **For menstealers.**—After enumerating the transgressors of the Sixth and Seventh Commandments against murder and adultery, St. Paul speaks of a class well known in the Roman world of his day—perhaps the worst class of offenders against the Eighth Commandment—the "slave-dealers."

For liars, for perjured persons.—In these

whoremongers, for them that defile
themselves with mankind, for men-
stealers, for liars, for perjured persons,
and if there be any other thing that is
contrary to sound doctrine; (11) ac-
cording to the glorious gospel of the
blessed God, which was committed to
my trust. (12) And I thank Christ Jesus
our Lord, who hath enabled
me, for that he counted me
faithful, putting me into the
ministry; (13) who was be-
fore a blasphemer, and a persecutor, and
injurious: but I obtained mercy, because

Chap. i. 12—20. Paul's thanks for his own conversion and commission.

---

inclusive terms St. Paul apparently reckons all who break the solemn Ninth charge given on Sinai, which forbade false witness against a neighbour. Among the sins which especially excite the hot wrath of the first inspired teachers of Christianity, "want of truth" appears singularly prominent. One after the other of the Apostles, in different language, express their deep abhorrence of this too common sin, which, in St. John's fervid words, will suffice to exclude from the city of the blessed (Rev. xxii. 15).

And if there be any other thing that is contrary to sound doctrine.—In this broad and general summary, with which St. Paul concludes his dreadful catalogue, the prohibition of the Tenth Commandment against "covetousness" is doubtless included. In the words "sound doctrine"—an expression peculiar to this group of Epistles—a sharp contrast is suggested to the "sickly and unhealthy" teaching of the false teachers, with their foolish legends and allegories—a teaching which suggested controversy and useless disputes, and had no practical influence at all upon *life.*

(11) **According to the glorious gospel.**—All that St. Paul had been saying concerning the Law—its true work and its only work—was no mere arbitrary conception of his own; it was simply a repetition of the teaching of the gospel which his Master had intrusted to him, the gospel which taught so clearly that the Law was for the condemnation of sinners—that it was for those alone who do not accept the easy yoke and the light burden of the Lord Jesus.

Of the blessed God.—The whole sentence is more accurately translated, *according to the gospel of the glory of the blessed God.* (Comp. 2 Cor. iv. 4.) "The glory of the blessed God," whether as shown in the sufferings of Christ or in the riches of His great mercy, is that which is contained in and revealed by the gospel; in other words, the "contents" of the gospel is the glory and majesty of God. God is called here "blessed," not only on account of His eternal and changeless perfection, but also on account of His blessed gift of forgiveness, offered to all sinners who accept His gospel of love.

Which was committed to my trust.—This precious deposit, this "trust," the gospel of the glory of God, was perhaps, in St. Paul's eyes, his truest title to honour. When we inquire more closely what was exactly meant by "the gospel committed to his trust," something more definite seems to be required than the general answer that he was a minister of the Church, intrusted with the proclamation of his Master's blessed message. If this were all, St. Paul's loved title to honour would have been by no means peculiar to him, but would have been shared by many another in that great company of prophets, teachers, and evangelists of the Church of the first days. St. Paul rather seems to have gloried in some peculiar and most precious trust. Was it not possibly in that Gospel of "Luke," which some of the most venerated of the fathers tell us St. Paul was accustomed to mention as the Gospel written by him? (Irenæus, Origen, Jerome.) It was, perhaps, this blessed privilege of having been judged worthy to compile, under the direction of the Holy Ghost—or, at all events, largely to furnish materials for—one of the precious records of his adorable Master's earthly life and work and suffering which St. Paul loved to tell of as his proudest title to honour.

To his own disciples—as well as to those who disputed his apostolic authority—he would now and again refer to this, the highest of all honours bestowed on him by his Master; but there the boasting of the holy and humble man of God ended. Though the blessed evangelist St. Paul knew his work was for all the ages, the true humility of the noble servant of Jesus appears in the substitution of "Luke" for "St. Paul"—the scribe's name in place of that of the real author.

(12) **And I thank Christ Jesus our Lord, who hath enabled me.**—Better rendered, *who hath given me strength within.* The ancient authorities here are divided; the majority omit the first word of the verse, the connecting "and." With or without this word, the sense is much the same; for on the words, "the gospel . . . committed to my trust," the Apostle pauses, overwhelmed with the flood of grateful memories which such a thought let loose. "How I thank God," wrote St. Paul, "who hath strengthened me within, with this power to bear witness to my Master!—*me* of all persons, who was once a blasphemer of His royal name! What an example I—your teacher, the founder of this Church of Ephesus—am of the transforming grace of the gospel—of its sweet, mighty power to forgive sins." It was the thought of the great love, passing understanding, of the tender, pitiful mercy which suffered so wondrous a trust to be committed to the charge of such a sinner, that called forth the ejaculation of deep thankfulness we read in the twelfth and following verses.

If we ask more particularly respecting the exact way in which Jesus Christ "enabled," or "strengthened St. Paul within," we must think of his strange power of winning men to his Master's side; we must remember his miraculous gifts over disease and even death; and last, but not least, that strength of endurance, that brave, sweet patience which made his life of suffering borne for Christ so beautiful, so touching, an example for men.

For that he counted me faithful.—The All-seeing, knowing from the beginning that St. Paul would continue steadfast and true, selected him as "His chosen vessel" to bear His name and the glad news of His salvation into many lands.

It is observable, however, that *this very faithfulness, this unflinching steadfastness,* which seems to have been the reason why the Lord chose him for his great work, St. Paul, in a well-known and remarkable passage, refers to as a gift of grace which he had obtained in mercy of the Lord (1 Cor. vii. 25).

(13) **Who was before a blasphemer, and a persecutor, and injurious.**—In these words of bitter self-accusation, St. Paul sums up the characteristic

I did *it* ignorantly in unbelief. (14) And the grace of our Lord was exceeding abundant with faith and love which is in Christ Jesus. (15) This *is* a faithful saying, and worthy of all acceptation, that Christ Jesus came into the world

---

features of his brilliant career as a young Pharisee leader, as a popular Jewish patriot. The *object* of his intense hatred and of his burning antagonism during these never-to-be-forgotten days was *that very Lord*, from whom later he had received such unspeakable gifts. He knew he had been "a blasphemer" of that dear Master in the truest sense of the terrible word, since, as it has been well said, that: "He who had seen Stephen die for Christ, and after this did not cease to pant like a wild beast for the blood of the Church, must have known that he had not been guilty of simply reviling men but of blaspheming God." And "a persecutor," for, to quote his own words at Jerusalem (Acts xxii. 4): "I persecuted this way unto the death, binding and delivering into prisons both men and women." (Comp., too, Acts xxv. 11: "I compelled them to blaspheme.") And "injurious" (or, more accurately rendered, *a doer of outrage*), as he must well have remembered the events referred to in the history of the Acts (ix. 1) in the words: "Saul, yet breathing out threatenings and slaughter against the disciples of the Lord."

But I obtained mercy.—The Apostle, his heart overflowing with love and gratitude, contrasts his Master's mercy with his own want of it; the "mercy" shown to him consisting in something very different to simple forgiveness of a great wrong. In St. Paul's case the pardon was crowned by many a noble gift bestowed by that pitiful King whom he had so cruelly wronged.

Because I did it ignorantly in unbelief.—This is one of the passages which throws a gleam of light on some of the hard questions which perplex us when we meditate on the principles of the final judgment. Very little is told us as to the doom of those who have not heard, or else have failed to understand, the message of Christ. Still, from even such scanty teaching as is contained in the words we are now considering, and in such passages as Matt. xii. 31, 32; Luke xxiii. 34, we gather that there is an ignorance which at least greatly modifies the guilt of unbelief; we learn at least this much—*such a sinner is not out of the pale of the operation of divine mercy* But in spite of these hints—for they are little more—of the almost limitless area of the divine mercy, great care must be taken not to press overmuch these blessed intimations of the *possibility* of a mercy far more extended than the usual interpretation of the inspired utterances would lead us to expect; for, after all, the words and teaching of the merciful Redeemer Himself (Luke xii. 48) seem to point to a mitigation of punishment, rather than to a complete forgiveness, of sins committed under circumstances of perhaps partial ignorance. "He that knew not, and did commit things worthy of stripes, shall be beaten with few stripes."

(14) **And the grace of our Lord was exceeding abundant.**—The thought of his Master's great love to one who once reviled Him so bitterly, and who had spent his strength in trying to undo His servants' work, seems to have pressed with overwhelming force on St. Paul, who struggled to find words which should express how deeply he felt the loving tenderness which had transformed the cruel persecutor into the favoured Apostle. The Greek word translated "was exceeding abundant" is very rare, and possesses a superlative force.

With faith and love.—He sums up the divine mercy showed to him in the three words: grace, faith, and love. Grace, the unspeakable gift of God to him; faith and love, the results of the exceeding abundant gift of grace.

Faith: not merely a childlike trust in Christ, but a belief which accepted Christ as the hope of an otherwise hopeless world; and love, which includes love to man as well as love to God, a strange contrast to his former cruelty and hatred; for, instead of blaspheming, *now* he believed on Him whom he once reviled, and instead of persecuting the followers of Jesus, *now*, in his great love for them, he spent himself. Then, overwhelmed with joy and thankfulness that he, the enemy of God, had obtained the mercy and love of God, and conscious, from his own sweet and bitter experiences, what that mercy of God bestowed on a sinner signified, he gave utterance to one of those bright watchwords of the faith, with which the Christians of the first days used to comfort and encourage one another, and which, perhaps, better than any other words, gave expression to the burning thoughts which rose up from his grateful heart.

(15) **This is a faithful saying, and worthy of all acceptation.**—This striking formula in the New Testament, found only in the Pastoral Epistles, here and in chap. iii. 1; iv. 9; 2 Tim. ii. 11; Titus iii. 8; and the somewhat similar expression, "these sayings [*words*] are faithful and true," Rev. xxi. 5; xxii. 6, were formulas expressing weighty and memorable truths, well known and often repeated by the brotherhood of Christians in the first ages of the faith. They were, no doubt, rehearsed constantly in the assemblies, till they became well-known watchwords in the various churches scattered over the Mediterranean-washed provinces of the Roman empire; and in these "sayings" we see, perhaps, the germs of the great creeds of Christianity. [1 Tim. iii. 1, perhaps, as usually understood, hardly falls under this category of "watchwords of the faith," unless St. Chrysostom's interpretation of the text be followed, which refers "the faithful saying" to the solemn truths which immediately preceded it in chap. ii.]

That Christ Jesus came into the world.—This is an unmistakable allusion to the pre-existence of Christ. He came into the world, leaving the glory which he had with the Father before the world was (see John xvi. 28; xvii. 5; Eph. i. 3, 4). And the purpose for which he came into the world is stated distinctly in the next sentence.

To save sinners.—There are no details given respecting this salvation. The "sinners" here mentioned is a broad, inclusive term. It includes, besides Jews, the outcasts of the Gentiles without hope and without God—*all the lost*, irrespective of race or time. In the Lord's own blessed words: "The Son of Man was come to seek and to save that which was lost" (Luke xix. 10).

Of whom I am chief.—The intense humility of the strange, beautiful character of the Gentile Apostle prompted this bitter expression. St. Paul, it has been well said, knew his own sins by experience, and every other man's *per speculationem.* In another place a

to save sinners; of whom I am chief.
(16) Howbeit for this cause I obtained
mercy, that in me first Jesus Christ
might shew forth all longsuffering, for
a pattern to them which should hereafter believe on him to life everlasting.
(17) Now unto the King eternal, immortal, invisible, the only wise God, *be* honour and glory for ever and ever.
Amen. (18) This charge I commit unto
thee, son Timothy, according to the prophecies which went before on thee,

---

similar feeling leads him to style himself as "less than the least of all saints" (Eph. iii. 8). He had been in time past so bitter an enemy of the Lord that no preaching of the disciples was effectual to work his conversion. In his case, to overcome his intense hatred of the Name, it needed a special appearance of the Risen One.

(16) **Howbeit for this cause I obtained mercy.**—In spite of this deep consciousness of his guilt, faith and confidence in his own salvation seem never to have wavered. He speaks of *this* with all certainty, and proceeds to tell us with great clearness why Christ saved him, the chief of sinners.

That in me first Jesus Christ might shew forth all longsuffering.—If Christ could show mercy to him, surely in after times the greatest of sinners need never doubt the Redeemer's power and will to save. St. Paul's conversion foretold many a patient waiting on the part of the Lord, much long-suffering, which would never hurry to punish His enemies, but which would tarry long, in the hope of the sinner repenting while it was yet time.

For a pattern to them which should hereafter believe on him.—Men were to learn that such conversions as his were to be looked forward to as no uncommon occurrences—conversion of blasphemers, of persecutors, whom the Lord would tarry long for, till they, too, coming to the knowledge of the truth, should acknowledge Him. Thus to *all* sinners was St. Paul a pattern—an example of the Lord's long-suffering, of His patient waiting. His gracious Master had dealt with him like a king, who, when judging the case of a rebel city, pardons the chief rebel. If God would redeem Saul the persecutor, none need despair of finding mercy.

To life everlasting.—And the goal—which lay before these poor redeemed sinners, who, like St. Paul, in faith and loving trust in Jesus had found peace and acceptance—was eternal life.

(17) **Now unto the King.**—The wonderful chain of thoughts (verses 12—16) which so well illustrate the great assertion of verse 15—"that Jesus Christ came into the world to save sinners"—St. Paul closes with a noble ascription of praise and thankfulness to the great God.

This doxology is addressed to no one Person of the ever blessed Trinity, but is—as has been said with great truth—"a grand testimony to the monotheism of St. Paul: the Godhead, the Trinity of his worship, is a sublime unity. To this Eternal, Incorruptible One be glory and honour unto the ages of the ages. Amen."

Eternal.—More accurately rendered, (*to the King*) *of the ages.* The King of the Ages is the sovereign dispenser and disposer of the ages of the world. There is no reference at all here to the Gnostic æons.

Immortal (or *incorruptible*).—This epithet and the following one—"invisible"—are connected with "God," not, with the preceding clause, "to the King of the Ages." God is immortal, in contrast with the beings of earth, and—

Invisible, in contrast with the visible creation.

The only wise God.—*The only God,* the most ancient authorities omitting "wise." "Only," as in chap. vi. 15: "the blessed and only potentate." "The only God," a contrast to the multitude of created spirits, angels, principalities, powers, &c. (See 1 Cor viii. 5, 6.)

For ever and ever.—Literally, *to the ages of the ages,* to all eternity—a Hebraistic expression for a duration of time superlatively (infinitely) long.

(18) **This charge I commit unto thee, son Timothy.**—The nature of the charge which he committed to Timothy must be gathered from the solemn words and thoughts of the foregoing passage—verses 15, 16. The sum of it was that men should put their whole trust in Him who came into the world to save sinners, and who alone was able to lead them into everlasting life. There is something very solemn in St. Paul's pressing home this charge to Timothy, and invoking the memory of the prophecies which went before on him. The charge was the last precious heritage, the priceless treasure which the old master, feeling that for him the end was not far distant, would leave to his favourite disciple—his own dear son in the faith. Anxious above measure for the loved group of Asian churches, of which Ephesus was the centre, foreseeing that the present perils and dangers from within and without would rapidly close round the congregations, and placing his greatest earthly hope on the steadfastness and knowledge of his own dear disciple whom he had left there as a shepherd to the sheep, he charges his son Timothy, by the memory of those strange prophetic utterances which, years before, had been made over him (Acts xvii. 1, 2) in Lystra or Derbe, and which, perhaps, had first induced him to choose the young son of Eunice as his friend and companion, to hold fast the blessed doctrine which taught men to put their whole trust in Jesus Christ.

According to the prophecies which went before on thee.—These prophetic utterances seem to have been not unfrequent in the days of the Apostles, and were among the precious gifts which enriched and encouraged the Church of the first days. We read of them at Jerusalem (Acts xi. 27, 28), at Antioch (Acts xiii. 1, 2), at Corinth (1 Cor. xiv.), at Cæsarea (Acts xxi. 8—10).

In the case of Timothy they appear to have been far-seeing glances into the life and the work and the teaching of the future Christian leader; here the last named—the doctrine and teaching—is especially referred to. The prophecies in question were uttered, no doubt, over him at his ordination, and, possibly, some of them at his baptism.

That thou by them mightest war a good warfare.—Better rendered, *that thou in them,* &c. St. Paul committed the sacred charge to Timothy concerning the faith in full confidence that, in accordance with those well-remembered glorious predictions which had been made foretelling his future zeal and success in the promulgation of the gospel, that in these—accoutred in these as his spiritual protection and

that thou by them mightest war a good
warfare; (19) holding faith, and a good
conscience; which some having put
away concerning faith have made ship-
wreck: (20) of whom is Hymenæus and
Alexander; whom I have delivered unto
Satan, that they may learn not to
blaspheme.

CHAPTER II.—(1) I exhort[1] there-
fore, that, first of all, supplications,
prayers, intercessions, *and* giving of

A.D. 65.

1 Or, *desire*.

---

armour—Timothy would wage his warfare against sin and evil.

St. Paul's words in this verse may be thus paraphrased: I give this charge to you, son Timothy, in accordance with those well-remembered predictions respecting your future steadfastness in doctrine and in life. I remind you now of them. Do not disappoint these grand hopes—these prophecies of your future—but bear them ever in your mind. Equip yourself in them as your spiritual armour, and so armed, fight your Master's fight against sin and evil—eine gute Ritterschaft, according to Luther.

The war imagery here used St. Paul employs again and again: *the* good warfare. (Comp. chap. vi. 12.) To the old, tried Apostle a Christian's life is a warfare in the truest sense of the word: to every believer it is a weary, painful campaign. In the case of the professed teachers a sleepless vigilance was especially demanded.

(19) **Holding faith, and a good conscience.**—Again, as in verse 5, the Apostle joins "faith" and "the conscience undefiled." In the mind of St. Paul, "want of faith" was no mere refusal to accept a definite religious dogma, but was ever closely connected with impurity and the love of sin. If a man dares to do wilful violence to his better nature he must not presume to dream of *faith* saving him. The thought expressed by another inspired teacher seems to run constantly in the mind of St. Paul: "The devils also *believe* and tremble."

Which some.—"Some." A quiet reference here is made to those false teachers who seem to have been doing such evil work at Ephesus among the Christian believers, and against whom Timothy is so urgently warned to be on his guard in the 6th and following verses of the chapter.

Having put away.—The simile in St. Paul's mind is a nautical one. The "good conscience" represents the ballast, or cargo, of the ship. When this is put away—tossed overboard—the vessel becomes unmanageable and is tossed about, the plaything of the waves, and in the end is wrecked.

(20) **Of whom is Hymenæus and Alexander.**—Here the Apostle names two, as examples of the utter shipwreck of all true faith—persons evidently well known to Timothy and the members of the Church at Ephesus. Hymenæus is probably identical with the heretic of that name, charged, in the Second Epistle to Timothy, with teaching that the resurrection was already passed, thus undermining the great hope which Christian faith so firmly laid hold of. In the second letter to the Presbyter presiding over the Ephesian congregations the fundamental error was specified on account of which this Hymenæus was excommunicated.

Alexander.—It would be unsafe positively to identify this person with the personal adversary of St. Paul alluded to in the Second Epistle, iv. 14, there spoken of as "Alexander the coppersmith," or with the Alexander mentioned in Acts xix. 33. The name was a very common one. Of the Alexander of Acts xix. 33 we know nothing; from the circumstances in connection with which he is there mentioned, which took place some ten years before this Epistle was written, he seems to have been a Jew.

Whom I have delivered unto Satan.—In this fearful formula the offender is delivered over to Satan, the evil one. It is a solemn excommunication or expulsion from the Church, accompanied with the infliction of bodily disease or death. In ordinary cases, the offender was quietly expelled from the Christian society. But an Apostle, and only an Apostle, seems to have possessed the awful powers of inflicting bodily suffering in the forms of disease and death. Certain special instances of the exercise of these tremendous powers are recorded in the cases of Ananias and Sapphira, Elymas, the incestuous person at Corinth, and the men here alluded to. The fear of Simon Magus, related in Acts viii. 24, seems to have been aroused by his evident expectation that this well-known apostolic power would be put in force in his case. It is, however, noticeable that this punishment was not necessarily, in the case of disease, an irrevocable sentence. The true end and purpose of this, as of all divine punishments, was not revenge for the sin, but the ultimate recovery of the sinner.

II.

(1) **I exhort therefore.**—Now Timothy was to begin to carry out his master St. Paul's great charge—the charge which bade him teach all men to put their entire, their perfect, trust in the Saviour of sinners—by instructing the Church of Ephesus, in the first place, to pray constantly for all sorts and conditions of men. The detailed injunctions *how* the charge was to be carried out are introduced by the Greek particle *oun,* translated in our version by "therefore;" it may be paraphrased thus: "In pursuance of my great charge, I proceed by special details; in the first place, let prayers *for all* be offered by the congregation."

Supplications, prayers, intercessions, and giving of thanks.—Many attempts, some of them not very happy ones, have been made by grammarians and commentators to distinguish between these terms, each of which denotes prayer. On the whole, it may be assumed that the Greek word translated "supplications" signifies a request for particular benefits, and is a special form of the more general word rendered "prayers." The third expression in the English version translated "intercessions" suggests a closer and more intimate communion with God on the part of the one praying. It speaks of drawing near God, of entering into free, familiar speech with Him. The Greek word suggests prayer in its most individual, urgent form. The fourth term, "giving of thanks," expresses that which ought never to be absent from any of our devotions, gratitude for past mercies. Archbishop Trench remarks how this peculiar form of prayer will subsist in heaven when, in the very nature of things, all other forms of prayer will have ceased in the entire fruition of the things prayed for, for then only will the redeemed know how much they owe to their Lord. The word *eucharist* is derived from

Chap. ii. 1—8. General direction respecting public prayer.

thanks, be made for all men; (2) for kings, and *for* all that are in authority;[1] that we may lead a quiet and peaceable life in all godliness and honesty. (3) For this *is* good and acceptable in the sight of God our Saviour; (4) who will have all men to be saved, and to come unto

[1] Or, *eminent place.*

the Greek word used in this place—*eucharistia*—for in the Holy Communion the Church embodies its highest act of thanksgiving for the highest benefits received.

For all men.—Professor Reynolds well comments on the hardness of the task set us here—"It is difficult for us always to love all men, to think of all men as equally dear to God, or to regard all men as equally capable of being blessed. Timothy, after reading this letter, probably walked along the marble colonnade of the great temple of Artemis, or heard the hum of some twenty thousand Asiatic Greeks crowded in the vast theatre to witness the gladiatorial fight, or encountered a procession of Bacchantes, or turned into the synagogue on the side of the Coresias and saw the averted looks, and felt the bitter hatred of some old friends. We, with some knowledge of the modern world, have to look into the 'hells' upon earth; to survey the gold-fields and battle-fields; the African slave-hunts; the throngs and saloons of Pekin, Calcutta, and Paris; the monasteries of Tibet; and make prayers, petitions, intercessions, and thanksgivings, too, on behalf of all men. In the beginning of the Gospel, Timothy received this quiet injunction from the Apostle Paul. Now the once whispered word peals like the voice of many waters and mighty thunderings over the whole Church of God."

(2) **For kings, and for all that are in authority.**—Without any special reference to the Roman emperors, the expression simply directs that prayer should be offered in all Christian congregations for the supreme authorities of the Roman empire, and especially of that particular province in which the church, where the prayer was offered, happened to be situate. Josephus especially mentions how a refusal on the part of the Jews to pray for Roman magistrates led to the great war with the empire which ended in their destruction as a separate nation.

A well-known passage in the *Apology* of Tertullian, written about a century and a quarter after St. Paul sent his first letter to Timothy, shows how well and carefully this charge of the great teacher, written to the Church in Ephesus, was kept in distant Carthage:—"We Christians . . . . do intercede for all the emperors that their lives may be prolonged, their government be secured to them, that their families may be preserved in safety, their senates faithful to them, their armies brave, their people honest, and that the whole empire may be at peace, and for whatever other things are desired by the people or the Cæsar."

Early in the second century, Polycarp of Smyrna bears similar testimony to this practice in the early Church of praying publicly for their heathen rulers:—"Pray for all the saints; pray, too, for all kings and powers and rulers, and for your persecutors, and those that hate you, and for your cruel enemies."

That we may lead a quiet and peaceable life.—What now is the special object of this prayer for those in high authority and power? First, that through *their* wise rule the Christians might enjoy peace; and, second, that the temper of the people who prayed thus for the ruling powers might be so affected by the constant repetition of such prayers: that all thoughts of revolt and resistance would be gradually stamped out.

St. Paul knew whom he was addressing. The Christian congregations of his age were largely made up of Jews. An intense longing to throw off the yoke of Rome pervaded the whole nation. The terrible events of the year 70 (only four or five years at most from the time of writing this Epistle) show how deep-seated was their hatred of the stranger. No Christian, however, was implicated in that fatal rebellion; so thoroughly had the teaching of St. Paul and his fellow Apostles done its work among the Jewish followers of the Crucified.

In all godliness and honesty.—The word rendered "honesty" is better translated *gravity*, or decorum. These words are only used by St. Paul in his Pastoral Epistles, where "godliness" occurs nine times, and "gravity" three times. The sphere, so to speak, in which St. Paul's ideal Christian must walk during his quiet, unobtrusive pilgrimage, was reverence and decorum.

(3) **For this is good and acceptable.**—That prayer be offered for all sorts and conditions of men is good and acceptable before God.

In the sight of God our Saviour.—Here, as in chap. i. 1, this title of "Saviour" is given to the Father, and is in this place singularly applicable, as it immediately precedes the famous statement of the next verse, respecting the boundless mercy of the Eternal.

(4) **Who will have all men to be saved, and to come unto the knowledge of the truth.**—Here St. Paul gives some explanation of his exhortation, that "the congregation should pray for all men." Our prayers after all—for those far off, as well as for those near—will be in strict harmony with the will of God. "Imitate God," writes St. Chrysostom; "if He wills that all men should be saved, it is surely natural that prayer should be offered for all; if *He* willed that all should be saved, do *thou* will it now; and if in earnest thou willest it, then pray."

One or two points must ever be held in mind when this great statement of St. Paul's is used as a proof of "Universal Redemption." We must remember the position it occupies in the argument, it being only introduced as a reason for the exhortation to pray for all. Then the words must be looked at very carefully. God's will is not to save (*sōsai*) all—if *that* had been His sovereign will He *would* have saved all; but His will is that all should be saved—all should come to the knowledge of the truth; not to the knowledge of the mere theoretical, but of the practical and saving truth as revealed in the gospel. "In other words, through the sacrifice and the death of Christ *all* are rendered capable of salvation (*salvabiles*); that some are indisputably not saved, is not due to any outward circumscription or inefficacy of the divine will, but to man's rejection of the special means of salvation which God has been pleased to appoint, and to which it is His divine will that man's salvation should be limited. Redemption is universal, yet conditional—all *may* be saved, yet all *will* not be saved, because all will not conform to God's appointed condition."—*Bishop Ellicott.*

the knowledge of the truth. (5) For
there is one God, and one mediator
between God and men, the man Christ
Jesus; (6) who gave himself a ransom
for all, to be testified[1] in due time.

(7) Whereunto I am ordained a preacher,
and an apostle, (I speak the truth in
Christ, *and* lie not;) a teacher of the
Gentiles in faith and verity. (8) I will
therefore that men pray every where,

1 Or, *a testimony.*

(5) **For there is one God, and one mediator between God and men, the man Christ Jesus.**—"*For.*" This gives the reason why it is good and well-pleasing in the sight of God that Christians should pray for all—for there is one Saviour, God the Father, who wills that all should be saved, and there is one Mediator, Christ Jesus, who has given Himself as ransom for all. Surely then, to us who call ourselves by the name of Christ, the fate of the heathen who as yet know not Christ cannot be a matter of indifference. We must in our praise and prayer include these strangers whom the Father wills should come to Him, for whose sake the Son has given his life.

The man Christ Jesus.—St. Paul with special emphasis speaks of the "one Mediator between God and man" as "the man Christ Jesus," no doubt wishing to bring into prominence the true humanity of the Lord. It is also a silent refutation of the docetic errors of some of the false teachers, of whose doctrines Timothy was to beware. These would have persuaded men that the Christ Jesus who was nailed to the cross was no man, but simply a phantom.

The human nature of Christ is also specially mentioned because in this state He performed His office as Mediator. In the statement of the next verse we find another reason for St. Paul's allusion here to the fact of the Mediator being a man. The Messiah must have taken the human nature upon Him before He could have suffered that death which was the ransom of all. Again, the human nature of the Mediator is brought forward to show that the mediatorial office extended over the *whole* human race—a grand thought, expressed in the following words—"who gave Himself a ransom for all."

(6) **Who gave himself a ransom for all.**—The declaration (of verse 5) that there was one God for fallen man would have been scarcely a joyful proclamation had it not been immediately followed by the announcement that between that one God and sinning man there was a mediator. Now (in verse 6) we have in a few words the inspired description of the manner in which the Mediator performed His office and work; of His own free sovereign will; He yielded up Himself to death as the price of the redemption of all mankind—His life in exchange for their forfeited lives.

St. Paul's teaching here is very definite, and is utterly irreconcilable with much of the popular (so-called) theology of the day, which rejects this great Christian doctrine, so clearly taught here by St. Paul, of a "*satisfactio vicaria.*" This teaching asserts, that without pleading the death of Christ, we may, if we please, approach and find access to the Father, and such teaching as this passage shows is irreconcilable with gospel truth.

To be testified in due time.—Better rendered, "*witness of which was to be borne in its own times.* The meaning of the words is, "Jesus Christ in the eternal counsels, gave Himself to death as the price of the redemption of fallen man; at the appointed and fitting season He endured this death—this death was the witness to the truth of the tremendous offering made in the counsels of the eternal and ever-blessed Trinity. So St. Chrysostom, who asserts that "the witness to be borne" was given in the death and suffering of the Lord.

(7) **Whereunto I am ordained a preacher, and an apostle . . .**—Whereunto, or "for which witness." To announce which witness—the witness being the suffering and the death of Christ—St. Paul was ordained an Apostle—the reference being entirely to what preceded.

I speak the truth . . . and lie not.—The warmth with which St. Paul here asserted his divinely conferred commission as preacher and Apostle, was not called out by any desire on his part to seize an occasion of asserting in the presence of his enemies, the false heretical teachers of Ephesus, his especial rank and prerogatives as an Apostle chosen and commissioned by the Most High. These fiery and earnest words had no private reference to *him*, St. Paul, or to *his* especial claims to be heard, but were uttered solely in view of the surpassing magnitude of the message with which he was charged—solely to bear a weighty and imposing testimony to the truth of his assertion, which so many were ready and eager to dispute—the assertion that the gospel of Jesus Christ was a message of glad tidings, was an offer of salvation, not to a *people*, but to a *world.*

A teacher of the Gentiles. — This specifies more clearly the especial duties of his apostleship, not perhaps without some reference to the peculiar fitness which marked him out as the declarer of the divine will in respect to this gracious offer of redemption to the isles of the scattered countless Gentiles.

In faith and verity.—Better rendered, *in faith and truth.* These words specify the sphere in which the Apostle performed his great mission. The first, "in faith," refers to St. Paul's own personal faith in Jesus—the grand motive power of his life and work; the second, "in truth," refers to the truth of Christianity—to the well-known facts of the gospel story. Or, in other words, St. Paul carried on his ceaseless labours, *within* gathering fresh and ever fresh strength from the exhaustless spring of his own loving, mighty faith in Jesus, and *without* appealing to the generally well-known incidents of the life, death, and resurrection of Jesus, the truth of which all might test. In those days there were even many *eye-witnesses* of the Passion still living.

(8) **I will therefore.**—The Apostle here again turns to the subject of "public prayer," now giving directions respecting the persons who should offer their prayers, and also telling them how these public requests to God should be made. "I will therefore" expresses on St. Paul's part no mere wish or desire, but it is the expression of his solemn apostolical authority. It might be rendered, *I desire therefore.*

That men pray every where . . .—Better rendered, *in every place.* The greater liberty which women, under the teaching of Christ, had enjoyed; the new position they occupied in the Christian commonwealth; the distinguished services many of them had been permitted to accomplish in the Master's service—in such instances as the Marys, Dorcas, Priscilla, Lydia,

lifting up holy hands, without wrath and doubting. (9) In like manner also, that women adorn themselves in modest apparel, with shamefacedness and sobriety; not with broided[1] hair, or gold, or pearls, or costly array; (10) but (which becometh women professing godliness) with good works. (11) Let the woman learn in silence with all subjection. (12) But I suffer not a woman to teach, nor to usurp authority over the

Chap. ii. 8–15. Of the part to be taken by the sexes in public prayer.

1 Or, *plaited.*

---

and others—had no doubt contributed to a certain self-assertion on the part of female converts in the Ephesian congregations, which threatened grave disorders in the conduct of divine worship. St. Paul, in his directions respecting divine service in the Christian assemblies, follows the custom here of the Jewish synagogue, where women were forbidden to speak. Men, said St. Paul, in every place where a congregation in the name of Christ was gathered together, were to be the offerers of prayer. The word "everywhere" seems a memory of the Lord's words to the woman of Samaria, "Believe me, the hour cometh when ye shall neither in this mountain, nor yet at Jerusalem, worship the Father."

Lifting up holy hands.—It was the Jewish practice, not only in taking a solemn oath—or in blessing—but also in prayer, to lift up the hands—Compare Psalm xxviii. 2; lxiii. 4. This seems to have been generally adopted by the early Christians as the attitude in prayer. See Clem. Rom., *To the Corinthians*, chap. xxix. "*Holy hands*;" see Psalm xxiv. 4; xxvi. 6; "holy"—that is, unstained with wanton sins.

Without wrath and doubting.—Here allusion is doubtless made to religious disputes and contentions among the believers themselves—"doubting" is better translated by *disputing*. These angry feelings can have no place in the heart of one who really prays, whether in public or in private.

(9) **In like manner also, that women.**—The Apostle continues his official injunctions in reference to public prayer. "Likewise," he goes on to say, "I desire that women, when they pray"—women also in the congregation had their duties as well as the men—while the latter were directed to conduct and lead the public prayer, the women who worshipped with them were enjoined, as their part of the solemn service, to be present, adorned with neatness of apparel and modesty of demeanour, and the holy reputation of kind deeds.

Adorn themselves in modest apparel.—This direction to Christian women was not intended to apply to their ordinary dress in the world, but simply explained to the sisters of the Ephesian flock that their place in public worship was one of quiet attention—that their reverence and adoration must be shown not by thrusting themselves forward with a view to public teaching or public praying, but by being present and taking part silently—avoiding especially in these services anything like a conspicuous dress or showy ornaments—anything, in fact, which would be likely to arouse attention, or distract the thoughts of others.

With shamefacedness and sobriety.—These expressions denote the inward feelings with which the Apostle desires the devout Christian women to come to divine service; the first signifies "the innate shrinking from anything unbecoming." The second, sobriety, includes the idea of self-restraint—the conquest over all wanton thought and desire.

Not with broided hair.—Comp. 1 Pet. iii. 3; Isa. iii. 24. "Broided:" the modern form is "braided." Some modern editions give "broidered," apparently by mistake.

Or gold.—Probably, the "gold" is supposed to be twined among the plaits of the hair. These elaborate adornments, so likely to catch the eye at divine worship, were quite inconsistent with Christian simplicity, besides being calculated to distract the attention of their fellow worshippers, male as well as female. On this question of seemly, quiet apparel, in an assembly gathered for divine worship, see the difficult verse, 1 Cor. xi. 10, where *another* and a still graver reason for modest demeanour and apparel of women is alleged—"because of the angels."

Pearls, or costly array.—Ear-rings, necklaces, bracelets, are included here; these costly ornaments were worn by the ladies of the luxurious age in which St. Paul lived, in great profusion.

(10) **But (which becometh women professing godliness) with good works.**—That is to say, "Let them adorn themselves in that which is befitting women who profess godliness—viz., in good works." The Apostle, still speaking of women's true part in public divine service—urges that their *works* should be in accord with their *words* of prayer—tells them that a woman's truest and most beautiful ornament consisted in those tender works of mercy and pity—her peculiar province—in other words, that they, like Dorcas of Joppa, whose praise is in the Book of Life, "should be full of good works and alms deeds" (Acts ix. 36).

(11) **Let the woman learn in silence.**—The thought of public ministration is still in the Apostle's mind, when he gives this injunction. The very questioning on difficult points is forbidden them at the public assembly (1 Corinth. xiv. 35). So averse was St. Paul to anything which might mar the quiet solemnity of these meetings for prayer and praise and authoritative instruction.

This prohibition to speak publicly in assemblies for prayer and praise in the case of Christian women, was renewed in the North African Church, at the Council of Carthage, held A.D. 398. The same Council, however, specially permitted women to teach those of their own sex in private; indeed, the power to teach "ignorant and rustic women" was required as one qualification in deaconesses. The employment of deaconesses as private instructors seems to have been the custom generally in the Eastern Churches.

(12) **But I suffer not a woman to teach, nor to usurp authority over the man, but to be in silence.**—The whole purpose of these weighty admonitions of the great founder of the Gentile Churches relegates Christian women to their own legitimate sphere of action and influence—the quiet of their own homes. St. Paul caught well the spirit of his Master here. He raised once and for ever the women of Christ out of the position of degradation and intellectual inferiority they had occupied in the various pagan systems of the East and West, and taught with all the weight of an Apostle—of an accredited teacher of divine wisdom—that woman was a fellow-heir with man of the glories of the kingdom,—where sex would exist no longer; but while teaching this great and elevating truth, St. Paul shows what is the only proper sphere in which woman should work, and

man, but to be in silence. (13) For Adam
was first formed, then Eve. (14) And
Adam was not deceived, but the woman
being deceived was in the transgression.
(15) Notwithstanding she shall be saved
in childbearing, if they continue in
faith and charity and holiness with
sobriety.

A.D. 65.

CHAPTER III.—(1) This *is* a true

---

in which she should exercise her influence and power; while man's work and duties lay in the busy world without, woman's work was exclusively confined to the quiet stillness of home. The Apostle then proceeds to ground these injunctions respecting the duties in public and private of the two sexes upon the original order of creation, and upon the circumstances which attended the fall.

(13) **For Adam was first formed, then Eve.**—The Holy Spirit seems often (comp. especially Gal. iii. 16 and following verses, and iv. 22 and following verses, and 1 Cor. x. 1—10) to have moved St. Paul to weave into the tapestry of his arguments and exhortations to the different churches, facts and principles drawn from Old Testament history. His early training in the great Rabbinical schools of Jerusalem had well supplied him with a vast store of this Old Testament learning.

The argument here based on priority of creation is much assisted by the additional statement of 1 Cor. xi. 9, "neither was the man created for the woman, but the woman for the man." This teaching of St. Paul's respecting the public position of woman as regards man, in which he shows that she is to hold a subordinate place—is based upon no arbitrary human speculation, but upon God's original order in creation—that divine order which first created man, and after man's creation, formed woman as his helpmeet.

(14) **And Adam was not deceived.**—Priority in creation was the ground alleged by St. Paul as the reason why the woman was never to exercise authority over man, the eldest born of God. "Adam was not deceived;" the Apostle now refers to the general basis of his direction respecting the exclusion of women from all public praying and teaching contained in verses 9—12. The argument here is a singular one—Adam and Eve both sinned, but Adam was not deceived. He sinned, quite aware all the while of the magnitude of the sin he was voluntarily committing. Eve, on the other hand, was completely, thoroughly deceived (the preposition with which the Greek verb is compounded here conveying the idea of thoroughness)—she succumbed to the serpent's deceit. Both were involved in the sin, but only one (Eve) allowed herself to be deluded. So Bengel, "*Deceptio indicat minus robur in intellectu, atque hic nervus est cur mulieri non liceat docere.*" Prof. Reynolds thus comments on the argument of the Apostle:—"This may sound to our ears a far-fetched argument, when used to discountenance female usurpation of intellectual supremacy. It was, however, a method current at the time to look for and find in the Scriptures the concrete expressions of almost all philosophical judgments. At the present day we could hardly find a more vivid illustration of the essential difference between the masculine and feminine nature. If there be this distinction between the sexes, that distinction still furnishes the basis of an argument and a reason for the advice here rendered. The catastrophe of Eden is the beacon for all generations when the sexes repeat the folly of Eve and Adam, and exchange their distinctive position and functions."

(15) **Notwithstanding she shall be saved in childbearing.**—The last words are more accurately and forcibly rendered—*through the childbearing.* With that tender and winning courtesy to which, no doubt, humanly speaking, the great missionary owes so much of his vast influence over human hearts, St. Paul, now anxious lest he had wounded with his severe words and stern precepts his Ephesian sisters in Christ, closes his charge to women with a few touching words, bright with the glorious promise they contained. Though their life duties must be different from those of men—yet for them, too, as for men, there was one glorious goal; but for them—the women of Christ—the only road to the goal was the faithful, true carrying out of the quiet home duties he had just sketched out for them. In other words, women will win the great salvation; but if they would win it, they must fulfil their destiny; they must acquiesce in all the conditions of a woman's life—in the forefront of which St. Paul places the all-important functions and duties of a mother.

This is apparently the obvious meaning of the Apostle's words—all *this* lies on the surface—but beneath all this the reverent reader can hardly fail to see another and deeper reference (the presence of the article, "through *the* childbearing," gives us the clue)—"she shall be saved by THE childbearing" (the Incarnation) by the relation in which woman stood to the Messiah, in consequence of the primal prophecy that her seed (not man's) should bruise the serpent's head (Gen. iii. 15), the peculiar function of her sex, from its relation to her Saviour, "shall be the medium of her salvation." (See Bishop Ellicott, *in loco.*)

If they continue in faith and charity and holiness with sobriety.—But let no one think that the true saintly woman, painted with such matchless skill by St. Paul, satisfies the conditions of her life by merely fulfilling the duties of a mother.

She must besides, if she would win her crown, hold fast to the Master's well-known teaching, which enjoins on all His own disciples, men as well as women, faith and love, holiness and modesty. The last word, "modesty," or *discretion,* or *sobriety* (all poor renderings of the Greek *sophrosune,* which includes, besides, the idea of a fight with and a victory over self), brings back the thoughts to the beautiful Pauline conception of a true woman, who wins her sweet and weighty power in the world by self-effacement.

III.

(1) **This is a true saying.**—There is no reason why the rendering of this formula adopted in chap. i. 15, "faithful is this saying," should be altered here. The "faithful saying" here refers to the wish for high and arduous work in the Church of Christ, and declares such a wish to be a noble one; for the office in question was a beautiful one, and honourable, and in those days meant stern and ceaseless work, grave and constant danger. It was no doubt one of the well-known sayings among the brethren of the first days, and not improbably, with the other "faithful sayings" of this group of Epistles, formed a part of their liturgy, and was woven into some of their special prayers offered in public.

Chap. iii. 1—13. The qualifications of bishops or presbyters (*elders*) 1—7), and of deacons 8—13).

saying, If a man
desire the office
of a bishop, he
desireth a good
work. (2) A bishop then must be
blameless, the husband of one wife,
vigilant, sober, of good behaviour,[1]
given to hospitality, apt to teach;

1 Or, *modest.*

Perhaps this "faithful saying" was a portion of a prayer offered not unfrequently in the public assembly, asking that volunteers might be moved by the Holy Ghost to present themselves for the then dangerous office of ordained ministers of the Word.

"Well might a man desire the office of chief pastor; it was indeed a good work;" but, in the first place, such a dignity could only be held by one possessing many qualities, then and there enumerated.

If a man desire the office of a bishop.—More accurately rendered, *If a man seeketh.* In the Pastoral Epistles the Greek words rendered "bishop" and "presbyter" or elder (*episcopos, presbuteros*), are applied indifferently to the same person, for up to this period (A.D. 65—6) no necessity had arisen in the constitution of the Church for the appointment of a *special order* of superintending presbyters. The numbers of the members of the brotherhood, though every year showing a vast increase, were still, comparatively speaking, small. St. Peter, St. Paul, St. James and St. John, and certainly the majority of the apostolic college, were still living; while, till A.D. 70, the Jerusalem congregation still acted as the central authority of the Church, and grave questions continued to be referred to the Fathers resident there.

Early in the second century, however, there is not a shadow of doubt that the episcopal office, as we understand it, was widely established. During the last thirty years, then, of the first century, this great change in Church organisation must have been effected—that is, *during the life-time of St. John.* How this was brought about is admirably stated by Professor Rothe, of Heidelberg, as quoted by Canon Lightfoot in his dissertation on the Christian ministry (*Commentary on the Epistle to the Philippians*), who, without accepting all the details suggested, still in the main agrees with the famous Heidelberg professor in his theory respecting the very early establishment of episcopacy in the Catholic Church. After painting the distractions and growing dissensions of the Church, occasioned by the jealousies between the Jewish and Gentile brethren, and the menacing apparition of the Gnostic heresy, Rothe states how, in the face of this great emergency, St. Peter, St. Paul, and St. James were carried away by death almost at the same time; while, with the overthrow of Jerusalem very shortly after, the visible centre of the Church was removed, the keystone of the fabric was withdrawn, and the whole edifice was threatened with ruin. There was a crying need for some organisation which should cement together the diverse elements of Christian society, and preserve it from disintegration. Out of this need the Catholic Church in its episcopal character arose. From notices in Eusebius, Irenæus, and Clement of Rome, Rothe (quoted by Lightfoot) concludes "that, immediately after the fall of Jerusalem, a council of the surviving Apostles and first teachers of the gospel was held to deliberate on the crisis, and to frame measures for the well-being of the Church. The centre of the system thus organised was episcopacy, which at once secured the compact and harmonious working of each individual congregation, and, as the link of communication between the separate brotherhoods, formed the whole into one undivided Catholic Church. Recommended by this high authority, the new constitution was immediately and generally adopted."

He desireth a good work.—The office of a presbyter of the Church in the days of St. Paul was a difficult and dangerous post. It involved much labour; it was full of risk; it meant a hard and severe life; yet, from the Christian's standpoint, it was a work, if faithfully performed, of all toils the most beautiful, the most honourable, the most noble. "*Negotium non otium*" comments Bengel, in his usual pithy, untranslatable way.

(2) **A bishop then must be blameless.**—Now follow the various *social* and moral characteristics of the appointed and recognised officers of the Christian Church—the presbyters or bishops, and the junior ministers, the deacons. The second chapter had treated of the duties of *congregations collectively* in the matter of public prayer; the third chapter speaks of the special character and qualities necessary for the *rulers* of these congregations. These "elders" must, in the first place, be men whose character is unimpeachable—men who stand high in public estimation, known for their pure life and spotless integrity. Not only must believers reverence the character of the superintending and ruling elders of their community, but even those outside the brotherhood of Christ must respect the life and conversation of these prominent and conspicuous members of a society which, from the nature of things, would be sure to provoke distrust and jealousy.

The husband of one wife.—The general opinion of the most ancient writers—the decisions of Church councils when the question seems to have been placed before them—the custom of the great Greek Church, which, while permitting a single nuptial, still regarded the repetition of the marriage relation as a disqualification for the higher grade of the episcopate—tell us in general terms that the opinion of the Church from the earliest times interprets this saying of St. Paul as a declaration against second marriages in the case of those seeking the office of presbyter or deacon. The Greek Church evidently accepts this interpretation, though it relaxes the rule in the case of the inferior orders.

There seems, however, good reason for doubting the accuracy of this popular interpretation, which appears, by thus casting a reproach upon second marriages, to urge a spirit of asceticism on all Christian society, very foreign to St. Paul's usual teaching, which was content with gently inculcating a higher and a purer life as alone in accordance with the mind of his pitiful and loving Master. It was only by slow degrees that he hoped to raise the tone of society and public opinion in this world.

Inspired Christian teaching was careful not to distract the everyday life of men and women by insisting on sudden and violent changes. The behaviour of the great Christian teachers in the matter of that terrible and universal practice of slavery should be especially noted.

When we ask, What then did St. Paul mean by these words? we must picture to ourselves the state of society in the empire at the time when the Apostle

(3) not given to wine,[1] no striker, not greedy of filthy lucre; but patient, not a brawler, not covetous; (4) one that ruleth well his own house, having his children in subjection with all gravity;
(5) (for if a man know not how to rule

1 Or, *Not ready to quarrel, and offer wrong, as one in wine.*

wrote to Timothy. An inundation of Eastern luxury and Eastern morals had submerged all the old Roman habits of austere simplicity. The long civil war and the subsequent license of the empire had degraded the character of the people. The period when St. Paul wrote was especially marked by an extreme depravity. A great and general indisposition towards *marriage* at all, and the orderly restraints of home and family life, had become so marked a feature in Roman society, that we find Augustus positively enacting laws against celibacy. Another cause which helped to undermine the stability of home life and those family ties which ought to be deemed so sacred, was the ease and frequency of divorce, which Seneca, who may be considered almost as the contemporary of St. Paul, alludes to as incidents no longer looked upon as shameful in Rome. He even, in his indignation at the laxity of the morals of his day, cites cases of women who reckoned their years rather by their husbands than by the consuls. Martial writes of a woman who had arrived at her tenth husband. Juvenal speaks of one who, in five years, had had eight husbands. Among the Jews we know *polygamy* was then prevalent. St. Paul, fully conscious of this low and debased moral tone which then pervaded all society in the empire, *in these few words* condemned all illicit relations between the sexes, and directed that in choosing persons to fill holy offices in the congregations of Christians, those should be selected who had married and remained faithful to the wife of their choice, whose life and practice would thus serve as an example to the flock, and to whose homes men might point as the pattern which Jesus loved, while the heathen world around them would see that the hated and despised Christians not only loved and honoured, but *lived* that pure home life their own great moralists pressed so earnestly upon them, but in vain. This direction, which requires that those to be selected to fill holy offices should be known for their purity in their family relations, of course does not exclude—should any such offer themselves—those men who, while contracting no marriage ties, still were known to lead upright, moral lives.

Vigilant.—The Greek word here is more accurately rendered *sober.* The presbyter or elder should be sober-minded, self-restrained, temperate (not merely in wine, but in all things).

Sober.—Better rendered, *discreet.*

Of good behaviour.—Rather, *orderly.* This word refers to outward conduct, to behaviour in public.

The Christian office-bearer must not only be wise and self-restrained in himself, but his outward bearing must in all respects correspond to his inner life.

Given to hospitality.—In the early days of Christianity, when Christians travelling from one place to another, were in the habit, when it was possible, of resorting to the houses of their brethren in the faith, to avoid consorting with idolaters in the public inns. It was of no slight importance that the presiding elders in a congregation should be men who loved to entertain strangers and others, from whom nothing could be expected in return.

Apt to teach.—The elder should possess something more than a willingness, or glad readiness, to teach the less instructed the mysteries of the faith. He ought also to have the far rarer qualification of a power to impart knowledge to others. Zeal is not by any means the only, or even the principal, qualification to be sought for in a minister of the Word.

(3) **Not given to wine.**—Drunkenness is scarcely alluded to here. It is rather a warning against choosing for the sacred office one given to frequenting noisy banquets, where wild and imprudent words are often spoken.

No striker.—Probably something more than merely brawling and fighting may here be included. Not only must the pattern minister of the Lord never smite his brother believer, but he must also never wound his soul with cutting, unkind words.

Not greedy of filthy lucre.—The Greek word thus translated does not occur in the older MSS. in this place.

But patient.—God's minister must be considerate toward the prejudices of others, forbearing, and gentle.

Not a brawler.—Better rendered, *not contentious.* He must not be easily vexed; but must exercise a steady command over his temper, avoiding all wordy strife.

Not covetous.—Literally, *not a lover of money.* The disinterested minister, who cares nothing for money for money's sake, would ever stand out in all societies a strangely attractive figure.

(4) **One that ruleth well his own house.**—Paul here again turns to the vein of thought first struck in verse 2: The life of the officer in the Church of God must be a pattern life for those without, as well as for those within the Church's fold, to copy and imitate. He must be pre-eminent in nobility of life and aims; but the life and the aims must belong to ordinary every-day life. His high standard must be no inimitable one; the example must be one that all honest men may follow and copy, if they will. So, first of all (verse 2), the Apostle places among the qualities necessary for a governing elder in the Church, the pure home life of the husband; then, after enumerating other points to be sought for in the character of one chosen to rule in the congregation, Paul comes back to this central idea, *the home life of the Church official;* that home life must present the spectacle of a well-ordered household. This will be at least a good test of a man's fitness to rule the large family gathered together in the form of a congregation, if his own home is gently yet firmly ruled; the wife, a pattern Christian lady; the children growing up in the nurture and admonition of the Lord.

Having his children in subjection with all gravity.—The Greek word rendered "gravity" occurs in chap. ii. 2, where it is translated in the authorised version, not very happily, by "honesty." The word employed in the original Greek denotes that decorum, that propriety of demeanour, which belongs especially to the pure and chaste, and seems to urge that a peculiar reverence and an especial decorum shall be aimed at in all relations with the young. *Maxima debetur pueris reverentia.* The *child life* in the families of these ministers of Christ's religion must, too, be an example to countless other homes.

(5) **For if a man know not how to rule his own house, how shall he take care of the church of God?**—The well-ordered household, the decent, modest behaviour, the reverent, affectionate relations between parents and children, between the

his own house, how shall he take care
of the church of God?) (6) not a
novice,[1] lest being lifted up with pride
he fall into the condemnation of the
devil. (7) Moreover he must have a
good report of them which are without;
lest he fall into reproach and the snare
of the devil. (8) Likewise *must* the
deacons *be* grave, not doubletongued,
not given to much wine, not greedy of

[1] Or, *one newly come to the faith.*

---

master and the dependents—these things are to be the test of a man's fitness for holding high office in the public community of believers, for, as Theodoret observes, if a man cannot rule decorously a small community (such as a family), how shall he be judged a fit person to be entrusted with administration in a broader sphere—with duties which have to do with divine things?

(6) **Not a novice.**—In the Church of Ephesus, which, when Paul wrote these charges to Timothy, had been established some years, the chief pastor would have for the church office an ample choice of disciples of some considerable standing and experience. The word "novice" here refers rather to want of experience and standing in the Christian brotherhood than to "youth." Timothy himself, to whom St. Paul was writing, and whom the Apostle had placed over this church, was at the time, comparatively speaking, still a man young in years, although old in trials and in Christian experiences.

Lest being lifted up with pride he fall into the condemnation of the devil.—The Greek word rendered here "being lifted up," would be more happily Englished by *being clouded* or *deluded.* It marks the pride or vanity engendered by the finding himself in a position of authority for which no previous training and experience had fitted him. Such a "novice" would be in imminent danger of falling into the judgment passed by God upon the devil, whose fall was owing to the same blinding effect of pride.

(7) **Moreover he must have a good report of them which are without.**—The man to be chosen as a responsible office-bearer in the Church, should be one possessing a stainless reputation for integrity and honour with the world outside the Church's pale; he should be one regarded by the world at large as having led a self-restrained, decorous life—a life free from those disorders and licentious practices which worldly men, even while themselves indulging in them, are the first to condemn in others.

Lest he fall into reproach and the snare of the devil.—For such a one, bringing with him into the new society his unhappy reputation, earned in the old thoughtless days—if placed in the new society in a prominent position of authority—would draw down upon himself and the brotherhood over whom he presided many a reproach, many a sneer. Those who once knew him among other associations living a very different life, would be only too ready to attack the blameless character of the congregation, through the stained and scarred reputation of their minister. The temptation to fall away and deny his Lord in such a case, would be overwhelming. The man might be in earnest, might be wishful to lead a new and better life, but the risk that one with such connections, with such memories of old days, would of necessity run, must be very great. Weakened and disheartened, such a presbyter would be likely to fall an easy prey into some snare skilfully laid by the Enemy, and, by his fall, cause a terrible and damaging injury to the Church of Christ. For these weighty reasons St. Paul charged Timothy to be very watchful when he chose his presiding elders, to elect only those who, in the dissolute society of Ephesus, had known how, even in old days, to preserve their good name stainless, their character unscarred.

The snare of the devil.—The teaching here of St. Paul respecting the Evil One is deserving of a special comment. What he says in verses 6, 7 is simply introduced as part of the main argument, which relates exclusively to the care to be exercised in the selection of fit persons for the sacred offices in the congregations. It is evidently not introduced as a special teaching on this mysterious subject. No disputings on this point as yet had been originated at this early period in Christian history. It lays down, however, certain broad principles which must have been the ground-work of St. Paul's belief in this now disputed question; and receiving as we do St. Paul's words in this and in his other epistles as an authoritative declaration of the mind and will of the Holy Spirit, it seems that these broad principles should have *all* weight whenever the doctrine respecting the Spirit of Evil is discussed. The lines here sketched are as follows: (1) The personality of the Evil One is distinctly affirmed. (2) This unhappy being has fallen and has been condemned, and is now able to lay snares for and to tempt men. (3) An overweening pride seems to have been the cause which led to this once mighty one's fall. (4) All idea of dualism—the old Persian belief adopted in the Manichæan heresy, and in so many other false creeds, that of two principles eternally opposed to one another—presiding respectively over the realms of light and darkness—is distinctly here repudiated by Paul, who in the course of his argument casually introduces the Evil One—the Enemy of man, as one who at some remote period rebelled, was crushed, and condemned, but to whom, in the supreme Providence of God, some terrible power over man was left.

(8) **Likewise must the deacons.**—We possess scattered and at the same time casual notices of this lower order of deacons dating from the very first days of the faith. The order clearly sprang out of the needs of the rapidly increasing church. Some two years after the Ascension (A.D. 34—35) the seven deacons were appointed to assist the Apostles as almoners of the brethren; as the Church's life developed, the functions of these primitive subordinate ecclesiastical officers were enlarged. The history of the career of Stephen and Philip supply ample evidence of this. Out of his first apostolic appointment in the year 34—35, no doubt, was developed that great inferior order in the Church, respecting which these definite rules and authoritative regulations were laid down by the Apostle Paul in his instructions to Timothy in the matter of church government and order. These primitive deacons were evidently assistants to and probably in many cases supplied the place of the presbyters. The great similarity of the directions of St. Paul respecting the qualifications to be looked for in both, implies this; still their original employment as administrators of the Church's funds and distribution of her alms remained to them. We can trace the existence of the order through and beyond the Apostle's time:—

filthy lucre; (9) holding the mystery of
the faith in a pure conscience. (10) And
let these also first be proved; then let
them use the office of a deacon, being
found blameless. (11) Even so *must their*
wives *be* grave, not slanderers, sober,

Jerusalem	...	A.D. 34—35.	Original foundation of order by the Apostles at Jerusalem. Acts iv. 1—6.
Corinth	...	A.D. 55.	1 Cor. xii. 28.
Rome	...	„ 58—9.	Rom. xii. 7.
Philippi	...	„ 63.	Phil. i. 1.
Ephesus	...	„ 66.	1 Tim. iii. 8, 13.
Asia Minor	...	„ 63—69	1 Pet. iv. 11.
———	...	„ 138—40	Justin Martyr. *Apology*, i. 65, "Those with us who are called deacons," and *Apology*, i. 67.

Corinth.—Deacons apparently alluded to under ἀντιλήψεις—"helps" (1 Cor. xii. 28). See also verse 5 of same chapter: διαιρέσεις διακονιῶν.

Rome.—εἴτε διακονίαν, ἐν τῇ διακονίᾳ. Reference lost in English translation, "or ministry, (let us wait) on our ministering" (Rom. xii. 7).

Asia Minor.—εἴ τις διακονεῖ. Reference lost in English translation, "if any man minister" (1 Pet. iv. 11).

Thus in the first half of the second century we find the order regularly and apparently universally established, constituting an acknowledged part of the Christian system of ecclesiastical government. The scattered notices of the diaconate in the New Testament, dating almost from the Ascension—over a period exceeding thirty years—show us how, out of the needs of the Church, arose this subordinate order, which was rapidly developed as the Catholic Church increased. The differences between the deacon of the Pastoral Epistles, and the deacon of the writings of Justin Martyr, are exactly what we should expect would result from the seventy years of gradual but progressive organisation under men like St. John and his disciples and the immediate successors of the Apostles.

Be grave.—St. Paul again repeats the need for this feature of character being found in the lower order of ecclesiastical officers. The reverent decorum, the quiet gravity, which never interferes with the innocent, childlike happiness (see Note on verse 4), is especially to be looked for in a deacon, who ought to show an example of every-day Christian life.

Not doubletongued.—Bengel well paraphrases it, *ad alios alia loquentes.* The deacon would have in his duties connected with the administration of the Church's alms, and also in his more directly spiritual work, much opportunity of meeting with and talking to the various families of the flock of his Master. He must be watchful, in these visits, of his words, not suiting them to the occasion, and then unsaying in one house what he had affirmed in another. Such a grave fault—not an uncommon one—would, in the long run, deeply injure his influence abroad, and would inflict a deadly wound on his own spiritual life.

Not given to much wine.—The professed minister—the advocate for the cause of the poor and needy—must show an example of the strictest sobriety, must be pointed at as one caring little for the pleasures of the table. How well and nobly the young lieutenant of St. Paul aimed at showing in himself a self-denying example to the flock, we see from chap. v. 23, when the old master deemed it requisite to warn his earnest, brave disciple from an asceticism which was positively weakening his power of work and endurance.

Not greedy of filthy lucre.—Those entrusted with the care of the Church's alms surely must be especially careful of their reputation in the matter of covetousness—among the "chosen" of Timothy there must be no Judas.

(9) **Holding the mystery of the faith in a pure conscience.**—The thought again comes to the surface—mere orthodoxy without the Christ-life was an empty, useless characteristic feature in any one; but *here* the man of God, writing to his dear son these solemn warnings respecting fit and proper persons to be chosen for their Master's work, has besides in these words another end in view. He had been dwelling with great earnestness on the *outward* characteristics which a deacon of the Church should possess—the high and stainless name—the generous respect which his old way of living had won for him among unbelievers as well as with believers; but, in addition to these things, it was absolutely necessary for one occupying such a post to know something of the deeper spiritual life—*he must hold the mystery of the faith.* Now what does St. Paul mean by the mystery? He speaks of it as "a treasure" which must be held in the casket of a pure conscience. This mystery was what was sometimes hidden, but which was now revealed by the advent of St. Paul's Master, and comprehended the truths of the redemption, the atonement, and mighty cleansing powers of the precious blood of Christ. These—the master-truths of Christianity—must the appointed teacher firmly grasp; and the true deacon, whose office it was rather *to administer* than *to preach* to the people, must also be especially careful to show that he lived the life he professed to teach; or, in St. Paul's own simile, must preserve the casket in which the precious mystery was shrined, holy and undefiled before men—*he must hold the mystery of the faith in a pure conscience.*

(10) **And let these also first be proved.**—No formal investigation, either in public before the congregation, or in private before Timothy and his fellow presbyters, is here referred to. What is most probably the meaning of the word is—the deacon should for a time perform many of the various duties on probation, to test his fitness before he was formally set apart for the holy office. So much of the work belonging to these officials of the early Church necessarily partook of a partially secular character, that such a trial of their fitness could well be made.

Then let them use the office of a deacon.—Better rendered, *let them serve as deacons,* if, after the trial, inquiry, and period of probation, they be found blameless.

(11) **Even so must their wives . . .**—The *position* of this solitary charge, respecting deacons' wives, in the midst of regulations concerning "deacons," is, of itself, almost decisive against the translation of the English version, adopted also by Luther and many others. The question naturally occurs—why are *deacon's* wives especially referred to, while nothing has been said respecting the wives of presbyters? Then, again, why should the choice of Timothy in the matter of his selection of a deacon be hampered with any special requirements in the wife of the candidate for

faithful in all things. (12) Let the
deacons be the husbands of one wife,
ruling their children and their own
houses well. (13) For they that have
used [1] the office of a deacon well purchase
to themselves a good degree, and great
boldness in the faith which is in Christ
Jesus. (14) These things write I unto
thee, hoping to come unto
thee shortly: (15) but if I
tarry long, that thou mayest
know how thou oughtest to behave thyself in the house of God, which is the
church of the living God, the pillar

Chap. iii. 14—16. What the Church really is.

1 Or, *ministered.*

---

the holy office? The literal translation of the Greek words would be, *Women in like manner must,* &c. These *women,* St. Chrysostom and most of the ancient expositors affirm, were *deaconesses.*

It is certain that there were women holding a kind of official position as deaconesses in the early Church; nor is it probable that these deaconesses were, as a class, confined to the restriction of age referred to in the direction respecting a band of widows devoted to works of mercy (chap v. 9, 10). These widows seemed to have been in the first instance a class or order apart from the ordinary deaconesses.

Phebe of Cenchrea (Rom. xvi. i.), Euodias, and Syntyche (Phil. iv. 2), probably the organisation alluded to (Acts ix. 36—41) as existing at Joppa, of which Dorcas was the chief, may be cited as instances from the New Testament of the employment of these women-servants of the Church. In the next century the Proconsul Pliny, in his famous letter to the Emperor Trajan, distinctly alludes to these Christian deaconesses, in the words, "*ancillæ quæ ministræ dicebantur.*" "In the Western Church," says Professor Reynolds, "the order did not cease to exist until the fifth century, and was continued in the Greek Church till the twelfth. The deaconess vanished into the cloister until partially revived in comparatively modern times."

Be grave.—The same word is used as in the case of the deacons. These deaconesses, too, must, with their modest behaviour, with their sweet, decorous gravity, as it has been well said, "inspire reverence having the halo of purity and sanctity about them."

Not slanderers.—A woman's most ready weapon is ever her tongue. She is, with all her noble, generous qualities, often quick-tempered, passionate, impulsive, jealous, and this weapon, always ready for attack or defence, is too often unsheathed. The professed servant of the Lord must show a high example to her sisters in self-control.

Sober.—Should be *abstemious,* even self-denying in the pleasures of the table.

Faithful in all things.—These deaconesses, from their position, would become the depositaries of many a househould secret; to those confiding in them in moments of trouble they must be true; scrupulously honest also in their distribution of alms; faithful, too, in the holy instruction they would be often called on to give in the course of their ministrations.

(12) **Let the deacons be the husbands of one wife.**—Here the exact same qualification is to be sought for as in the higher grade of presbyter. The same orderly and decorous household is required now in the case of the deacon, as was to be looked for as qualification for the presiding elder. St. Paul knew well that in the wise yet tender father, Timothy would find the firm yet generous distributor of the Church's alms, the loving and devoted friend of the poor sick.

(13) **For they that have used the office of a deacon well.**—Better rendered, *for they that have served well as deacons.* It was with good reason that the Apostle laid great stress on the many and varied qualifications necessary for one undertaking the duties of a deacon of the Church—for very great indeed was the reward reserved for the true, loyal deacon when his work was over and done (and if for the man who had performed well his work in the lower office, *à fortiori* for the one who should faithfully fulfil the yet higher duties of an elder or overseer in the Church).

Purchase to themselves a good degree.—Some scholars have suggested as a better rendering, "are acquiring (or *gaining*) to themselves a good standing. The old translation perhaps is best. Alford writes strikingly on the change of tense: "They that *have* used *are* acquiring or purchasing." The Apostle having begun by placing himself at the great day of retribution, now shifts the scene and deals with their present conduct. "Those who shall then be found to have served well, &c. . . . are now, &c."

The "good degree" they are now purchasing by earnest, patient work may refer to advancement to the higher ministries of the Church, but, more probably, has reference to their future position in the blessed life to come. This is one of the passages not unfrequent in St. Paul's Epistles, where degrees of glory among the redeemed are clearly spoken of. The plain words of St. Paul and his Master teach the people of God that although the great act of redemption alone belongs to Christ, that through His merits only men obtain salvation, still His own, will in a great measure determine, by their works and days on earth, the position they will occupy in His kingdom.

And great boldness.—The true and faithful deacons not only will in the life to come win the great reward, but *here* the result of their loyal, earnest service would be, that before *men* they would do their work with serene, fearless confidence, and would at the same time be encouraged to approach that *heavenly Father* at all times with the loving trustfulness of children.

In the faith which is in Christ Jesus.—Faith was the foundation of the "great boldness," and *the faith* rested on Jesus Christ.

(14) **These things write I unto thee.**—"These things" probably referred only to the directions respecting the special qualification to be sought for in candidates for the office of the overseers (presbyters) and deacons.

Hoping to come unto thee shortly.—The participle here has a concessive form, "though I hope," &c. "I write these special urgent directions to you, though my hope is that I shall be with you sooner than such detailed instructions presuppose."

(15) **But if I tarry long.**—St. Paul felt that dangers were pressing closer and closer—that the hoped-for visit to his loved church at Ephesus might not, probably never would be, accomplished; so these foregoing solemn directions respecting the choice of colleagues in the ministry had been written to Timothy, that, in the event of St. Paul never coming to him again, men (especially

and ground[1] of the truth. (16) And without controversy great is the mystery of godliness: God was manifest in the flesh, justified in the Spirit, seen of angels, preached unto the Gentiles, believed on in the world, received up into glory.

[1] Or, *stay.*

---

the ministers of God) should know how to conduct themselves in the congregation.

That thou mayest know how thou oughtest to behave thyself.—The words refer here not to Timothy alone, but rather to Timothy and his colleagues in their church work, concerning whom such particular directions had just been given, and should be rendered, *how men ought to behave themselves.*

In the house of God.—The image is from the Old Testament, where "the house of God" denotes, in the first place, the Temple of Jerusalem, and, in the second, the covenant-people. It is here used for the congregation of believers among whom God dwells—the true and enduring Church of living souls. Of this great spiritual temple, the corner-stone of which is Christ, the Jerusalem house on Mount Zion, with its marvellous work and its gorgeous and elaborate symbolism, was the poor, perishable, hand-wrought model.

Which is the church of the living God.—The house of God is here plainly defined to be the "Church" (or, *congregation*) "of the *living* God," who was working in its midst actively and personally, in strong contrast to that well-known graven image of the Diana of Ephesus, throned in that fair temple which glittered in its white and lifeless beauty over the roofs of the city where Timothy's charge lay.

The pillar and ground of the truth.—The imagery is here changed, and the "house of God" which the Apostle had just defined to be the Church, or congregation, belonging to the living God, and in the midst of which He was pleased to dwell, is now defined to be "the pillar and ground" (or, *basis*) "of the truth." In the first picture, the Church is painted by St. Paul as a vast congregation, with the living God dwelling in its midst: in the second, the same Church is painted as a massive pillar, holding up and displaying before men and angels *the truth*—the saving truth of the gospel. In the first picture, the thought of a great company gathered together for God to dwell among is prominent: in the second, the thought of the great redemption-truth alone comes to the front, and the Church of God is no longer viewed as a company of separate individuals, but as one massive foundation-pillar, supporting and displaying the glories of redemption.

This peculiar aspect of the Church, "the support and pillar of the truth," was dwelt upon probably by the Apostle as "defining—with indirect allusion to nascent and developing heresies—the true note, office, and vocation of the Church. . . . Were there no Church, there would be no witness, no guardian of archives, no basis, nothing whereon acknowledged truth could rest" (Ellicott).

(16) **And without controversy great is the mystery of godliness.**—"*And* is not simply copulative, but heightens the force of the predication, *Yes, confessedly great is the mystery*" (Ellicott)—for the glorious truth which the Church of God pillar-like upholds, is none other than that stupendous mystery, in other ages not made known, but then revealed—*the mystery of Christ*, in all His loving manifestations and glorious triumph. Yes, confessedly great—so great that the massive grandeur of the pillar is only in proportion to the truth it supports.

God was manifest in the flesh.—Here, in the most ancient authorities, the word "God" does not occur. We must, then, literally translate the Greek of the most famous and trustworthy MSS. as follows: *He who was manifested in the flesh.* In the later MSS., and in the great majority of the fathers who cite the passage, we certainly find *Theos* ("God"), as in the Received text. The substitution can be traced to no special doctrinal prejudice, but is owing, probably, to a well-meant correction of early scribes. At first sight, *Theos* ("God") would be a reading easier to understand, and grammatically more exact; and in the original copies, the great similitude between ΘC ("God")—the contracted form in which ΘΕΟC was written—and the relative OC ("He who"), would be likely to suggest to an officious scribe the very trifling alteration necessary for the easier and apparently more accurate word. Recent investigations have shown, however, beyond controversy that the oldest MSS., with scarcely an exception, contain the more difficult reading, OC ("He who"). The Greek pronoun thus rendered is simply a relative to an omitted but easily-inferred antecedent—viz., *Christ.* Possibly the difficulty in the construction is due to the fact of the whole verse being a fragment of an ancient Christian hymn, embodying a confession of faith, well known to, and perhaps often sung by, the faithful among the congregations of such cities as Ephesus, Corinth, and Rome—a confession embodying the grand facts of the Incarnation and the Resurrection, the preaching of the cross to, and its reception by, the Gentile world, and the present session of Christ in glory. In the original Greek the rhythmical, as well as the antithetical character, of the clauses is very striking. In the English translation they can hardly be reproduced:—

> "Who was manifested in the flesh,
> justified in the Spirit,
> seen of angels,
> was preached among the Gentiles,
> believed on in the world,
> taken up into glory."

Fragments of similar hymns to Christ are found in 2 Tim. ii. 11, and perhaps also in Eph. v. 14.

Manifest in the flesh.—When the Son of God came forth from the Father "He was manifested in the flesh;" or, in other divine words, "the Word was made flesh and dwelt among us, and we beheld His glory, the glory as of the only-begotten of the Father" (John i. 14. Comp. also 2 Tim. i. 10). The men and women of the first days of Christianity who repeated or sang such words as these, must have accepted and firmly believed the dogma of the pre-existent glory of Christ.

Justified in the Spirit.—The truth of Jesus Christ's own assertion respecting Himself, which *seemed* to be contradicted by His mortal liability to bodily weakness, and pain and suffering, and last of all to death, in the end was triumphantly vindicated or justified. Or, in other words, the claims of Jesus Christ to Divinity, put forth during His life of humiliation, were shown to be true. It was by His resurrection from the dead that Christ's lofty claims to the Godhead were justified. The Spirit, to which reference is here made, was the higher principle of spiritual life within Him—not itself the Divinity, but intimately united and associated with it. In the power of this Spirit, which he had within himself, He did take His life which He had laid down,

CHAPTER IV.—(1) Now the Spirit speaketh expressly, that in the latter times some shall depart from the faith, giving heed to seducing spirits, and doctrines of devils;

A.D. 65.

Chap. iv. 1—5. Evil attempts of false teachers to teach a useless asceticism.

---

did re-unite His soul unto His body from which He separated it when He gave up the ghost, and so did quicken and revive Himself, and thus publicly proclaimed His divine nature, His awful dignity. (Comp. Pearson, *On the Creed*, Art. V.)

Seen of angels . . .—It has been suggested that "angels" mean here nothing more than His Apostles and His own chosen messengers, by whom Jesus Christ was *seen* after His claims to Supreme power had been justified in the Spirit which had raised Him from the dead. These saw Him first, and after that carried the glad message to the distant isles of the Gentiles. But in spite of the ingenuity of such an exposition, the plain, obvious meaning of the word "angels" must be maintained, for the invariable meaning of *angelos* in the New Testament (perhaps with the exception of the earlier chapters of the Apocalypse) is never "apostle," but "angel." He was "seen of angels"—that is, Jesus Christ, after His resurrection and return to the throne at the Father's right hand, was, in His glorified humanity, visible to angels, who before had never looked on God. (Comp. Eph. iii. 10; Heb. i. 6; 1 Pet. i. 12—each of which passages bears in some way on this mysterious subject.) Theodoret and St. Chrysostom have similarly commented on this statement respecting the angels' share in the beatific vision.

Preached unto the Gentiles.—The angels now for the first time saw, and gazed on, and rejoiced in, the vision of the Godhead manifested in the glorified humanity of the Son; and what the angels gained in the beatific vision, the nations of the world obtained through the preaching of the gospel—viz., the knowledge of the endless love and the surpassing glory of Christ. This line of the ancient Christian hymn tells us that this early confession of faith was peculiarly the outcome of the Pauline churches; for in enumerating the six glories of the Redeemer-God it tells us one of these glories consisted in the preaching of His gospel to those peoples who had hitherto sat in darkness and in the shadow of death. It was the splendid fulfilment of the Isaiah prophecy respecting the coming Messiah. "It is a light thing that thou shouldest be my servant to raise up the tribes of Jacob, and to restore the preserved of Israel: I will also give thee for a light to the Gentiles" (Isa. xlix. 6).

Believed on in the world.—Different from Buddhism or even from Mahommedanism, Christianity has found acceptance among widely different nationalities. The religion of the Crucified alone among religions has a fair claim to the title of a world-religion. Its cradle was in the East, but it rapidly found a ready acceptance in the West, and in the present day it may be said not only to exist, but to exercise a vast and ever increasing influence in all the four quarters of the globe.

Received up into glory.—More accurately, *received up in glory*. These words refer evidently to the historical ascent of Christ into heaven—they declare the belief of these early churches in the fact of the Ascension as related in St. Luke's Gospel.

This fragment of the triumph-song of the early churches embraces the leading facts of the Messianic story:—

(1) The Incarnation of the Son of God.

(2) The justification in His Resurrection of the lofty claims advanced by Him during the days of His humiliation.

(3) The Epiphany of the glorified Humanity of Christ.

(*a*) To angels in the beatific vision.

(*b*) To men in the preaching of the cross.

(4) The glorious results of the great sacrifice already visible in those first suffering, struggling days of the Church.

(5) The return to heaven, and the session in power at the right hand of God—*closing* the first part of the blessed resurrection mystery, and *beginning* the glorious reign of Christ over men from His throne in heaven.

IV.

(1) **Now the Spirit speaketh expressly.**—Rather, *But the Spirit*. But (*de*) in very strong contrast to the sublime mystery of Redemption St. Paul has been speaking of as the glorious treasure contained in the Church of which Timothy and his colleagues were ministers; but in spite of that sublime truth which should occupy the thoughts and fill the hearts of Christians, men will busy themselves with other and very different things; with a spurious mock devotion, dreaming that God's mercy and love were to be purchased by mere abstinence from certain meats, or by an unnatural renunciation of the home and family life. The "words of the Spirit" here allude to a mysterious power, to a divine gift, traces of which occur again and again in the New Testament pages. Among the supernatural signs which were vouchsafed to the first generation of believers, and with very rare exceptions only to the first generation—to men and women, many, if not most, of whom had seen Jesus, and had had personal contact with Him—must be reckoned those mysterious intimations of the will of the Holy Spirit which guided and encouraged the Church of the first days. That intimation came in varied forms: to the Twelve in the form of fiery tongues (Acts ii. 1—12); to a more numerous company (Acts iv. 31); to Peter on the occasion of the conversion of Cornelius (Acts x. 10—16, 19, 20); to St. Paul on three occasions in the course of his second missionary journey (Acts xvi. 6, 7, 9, 10); through the medium of the prophet Agabus (Acts xxi. 11). St. Paul alludes to many such voices of the Spirit, and heavenly intimations, when speaking to the elders of Miletus (Acts xx. 23). One of these special revelations, made to himself, he here quotes.

In the latter times.—All those ages are here referred to which succeed the coming of the Lord. In these Paul lived, and we are still watching the slow and solemn march past of these latter ages. The errors foreseen then, have more or less affected the internal government of the Church during the eighteen hundred years which have passed since St. Paul's words were written. In no age, perhaps, have they been more ostentatiously thrust forward than in our own.

Some shall depart from the faith.—"By denying what is true, by adding what is false," says Bengel.

Giving heed to seducing spirits.—This expression must not be watered down by explanations which understand this expression as referring to false teachers. The "seducing spirits" are none other than

(2) speaking lies in hypocrisy; having their conscience seared with a hot iron; (3) forbidding to marry, *and commanding* to abstain from meats, which God hath created to be received with thanksgiving of them which believe and know the truth. (4) For every creature of God *is* good, and nothing to be refused, if it be

---

evil powers and spirits subject to Satan, and which are permitted to influence and to work in human hearts. (See Eph. ii. 2, vi. 12—passages in which these spiritual communities of wickedness and their powers over men are again alluded to by St. Paul.)

Doctrines of devils.—Doctrines and thoughts taught by, suggested by, evil spirits. The personality of these unhappy beings is clearly taught by St. Paul. Of their influence in the heathen world and their antagonism to Christ and His followers, see 1 Cor. x. 20, 21.

(2) **Speaking lies in hypocrisy.**—The Greek words here should be translated, *through the hypocrisy of men that speak lies.* The lies that these men utter, refer to their teaching that it was pleasing to the eye of the All-seeing Creator for men and women to avoid certain meats, and to abstain from marriage. Their hypocrisy consisted in their assumption of a mask of holiness, which holiness they considered was derived from their false asceticism and their abstinence from things which the Apostle proceeded to show were lawful.

Having their conscience seared with a hot iron.—Better rendered, *Branded in their own conscience as with a hot iron.* The image is drawn from the practice of branding slaves and certain criminals on their forehead with a mark. "*Qua nota turpitudinis non inusta tua vita est?*" (Cic. *Cat.* i. 6.) These men tried to teach the efficacy of a substitution of certain counsels of perfection in place of a faithful loving life. They based their teaching on wild Oriental speculations about the evil nature of all matter. They were often themselves evil-livers, who, conscious of their own stained, scarred lives, strove with a show of outward sanctity and hypocritical self-denial to beguile and to lead astray others, and in the end to make them as vile as themselves.

(3) **Forbidding to marry.**—This strange and unnatural "counsel of perfection," St. Paul, thinking and writing in the Spirit, looked forward to as a perilous delusion which would, as time went on, grow into the impious dogma of certain of the great Gnostic schools. This teaching was probably, even in those early days, creeping into the churches. The Jewish sects of Essenes and Therapeutæ had already taught that "abstinence from marriage" was meritorious. Men belonging to these sects doubtless were to be found in every populous centre where Jews congregated, and it was always in these centres of Judaism that Christianity at first found a home. St. Paul, however, saw no reason to dwell on this point at any length; the gross absurdity of such a "counsel" as a rule of life was too apparent; it was a plain contradiction of the order of Divine Providence. But the next question which presented itself in the teaching of these false ascetics, as we shall see, required more careful handling.

And commanding to abstain from meats.—Once more we must look to those famous Jewish religious communities of Egypt (the Essenes and Therapeutæ), the precursors of the great monastic systems of Christianity, as the home whence these perverted ascetic tendencies issued. These precepts too, like the counsel respecting marriage, were adopted in after years by several of the principal Gnostic sects; and it was especially those times St. Paul looked on to, although, no doubt, the seeds of their false asceticism had already been sown broadcast in the principal Christian congregations.

It has been asked why, in these solemn warnings against a false asceticism which St. Paul foresaw might and would be substituted for a really earnest God-fearing life, the question of celibacy was dismissed with one short sentence, while the apparently less-important question of abstaining from particular kinds of food was discussed with some detail. The reason is easily discoverable. The counsel to abstain from marriage was a strange and unnatural suggestion, one contrary to the plain scheme of creation. Any teaching which taught that the celibate's life was a life peculiarly pleasing to God would, at the same time, throw a slur upon all home and family life, and the Apostle felt that men's ordinary common sense would soon relegate any such strange teaching to obscurity; but with the question of abstaining from meats—that was connected with the precepts of the Mosaic law, which dealt at some length (probably from reasons connected with the public health) with these restrictions in the matter of meats.

These false teachers, while they urged such abstinence as a likely way to win God's favour, would probably base, or at all events support, their arguments by reference to certain portions of the Mosaic law, rightly understood or wrongly understood.

These points, then, might have risen into the dignity of a controverted question between the (Pauline) Gentile and the Jewish congregations. So St. Paul at once removed it to a higher platform. All food was from the hand of one Maker—nothing, then, could really be considered common or unclean without throwing a slur upon the All-Creator.

Which God hath created to be received with thanksgiving.—God's primeval intention is thus sharply contrasted with men's arbitrary restrictions. This divine intention is repeated with still greater emphasis in verse 4.

Of them which believe and know the truth.—The true "Gnostics," in St. Paul's eyes, were not those self-sufficient men who were out of their own corrupt imagination devising these strange and unnatural methods of pleasing God, but those holy, humble men of heart who *believed* on His crucified Son, and *knew* the truth of the glorious gospel.

(4) **For every creature of God is good.**—To teach that anything created was unclean would be an insult to the Creator. The very fact of its being *His* creation is enough. If made by God, then it *must* be good.

And nothing to be refused, if it be received with thanksgiving.—Every kind of food and drink may become hateful in the eyes of the all-pure God if misused, if partaken of without any sense of gratitude to the Divine giver. But nothing which can be made use of as food ought to be regarded as unclean or as polluted; every kind of food is intended for man, the only condition being that whatever is partaken of should be gratefully received by him as a gift.

received with thanksgiving: (5) for it is
sanctified by the word of God and prayer.
(6) If thou put the brethren in remembrance
of these things, thou shalt
be a good minister of Jesus Christ,
nourished up in the words of faith and
of good doctrine, whereunto thou hast
attained. (7) But refuse
profane and old wives'
fables, and exercise thyself
rather unto godliness. (8) For
bodily exercise profiteth

Chap. iv. 6—16. Timothy is to counteract such errors by teaching a practical godly life.

(5) **For it is sanctified by the word of God and prayer.**—Not only are all created things to be considered pure, and not lightly to be put aside; but in the sight of God "every creature" is holy when received as His gift with thanksgiving and with prayer—such thanksgiving-prayer containing thoughts in exact accordance with the Spirit of God revealed in Scripture. Thus all food is sanctified, not only, or even chiefly, by the common formula of a Christian grace before meat. This too often degenerates into a mere form of words—into lip-service of the most heartless form—and is too often looked upon as a kind of religious charm. The sanctification referred to by St. Paul belongs to no one prayer or grace, but to the constant habit of referring everything to God as the giver of all—to the perpetual "office" of a devout heart which, taking everything as a gift from God, the lover and the friend of man, thanks God from the heart continually.

One, if not the oldest, form of a Christian grace before meat is the one found in the Apostolic Constitutions. It is very simple and beautiful, and perhaps not too long for daily use. It runs as follows: "Blessed be Thou, O Lord, who nourisheth men from very youth up, who givest meat to all flesh; fill our hearts with joy and gladness, so that we, always enjoying a sufficiency, may abound unto every good work in Christ Jesus our Lord, through whom be ascribed to Thee glory, honour, and power unto the ages. Amen."

(6) **If thou put the brethren in remembrance of these things.**—The "things" of which he was to put the brethren in mind were those practices connected with that foolish, false asceticism alluded to in verses 3—5. Not a few, probably, in that Ephesian flock had been won over by the persuasive words of the false teachers to attribute a peculiar virtue to such practices—practices which, if persevered in, St. Paul well knew would tend to set up for imitation in the Church an unreal, unhealthy standard of life.

Thou shalt be a good minister of Jesus Christ.—A high title to honour, this, "a good minister of Jesus Christ," and one Timothy would well earn if he would set himself in all earnestness to oppose and discredit the sickly teaching of the Ascetic school.

He would by such opposition, indeed, earn the "title to honour," for St. Paul well knew how great was the danger of a comparatively young and ardent disciple like Timothy being attracted by such mistaken teachings of perfection. But "the good minister of Jesus Christ" must teach "a life" which may be led by all, not by a select few merely, of the believers on his Master. Asceticism is too often a winning and attractive school of teaching to ministers, as, at a comparatively easy price, they win a great, but at the same time thoroughly unhealthy, power over the souls of men and women who practise these austerities, which tend necessarily to remove them out of the stream of active life.

Nourished up in the words of faith and of good doctrine.—The Greek present participle rendered here "nourished up in," marks a continuous and permanent process of self-education. It might be translated "ever training thyself"—a wise and never-to-be-forgotten precept of St. Paul's, this reminder to his own dear son in the faith, Timothy—and through Timothy to all Christian ministers of every age—never to relax their efforts for self-improvement. The education of the good minister of Jesus Christ is never to be considered finished. He—the teacher of others—must ever be striving himself after a higher and a yet higher knowledge in things spiritual.

Whereunto thou hast attained.—More accurately translated, *which thou hast closely followed.* In the teaching respecting faith and practice which Timothy, as a disciple, has diligently followed out step by step—in that teaching he is to study to advance yet farther, so as to gain deeper and ever deeper knowledge of the mysteries of the kingdom.

(7) **But refuse profane and old wives' fables.**—Here Timothy—who has been previously (see verses 1—6) warned against a false asceticism, against putting an unnatural interpretation on the words of Christ, against sympathising with a teaching which would unfit men and women for practical every-day life—is now urged to guard himself against the temptation to give himself up to the favourite and apparently enticing study of the sayings of the famous Jewish Rabbis, in which every book, almost every word—in many cases the letters of the Hebrew Scriptures—were subjected to a keen but profitless investigation. In such study the spirit of the holy writers was too often lost, and only a dry and barren formalism—commands respecting the tithing of mint, and anise, and cummin—remained, while the weightier matters of the law—judgment, justice, and truth—were carefully sifted out. Round the grand old Jewish history all kind of mythical legends grew up, till for a Jewish student of the Rabbinical schools the separation of the true from the false became in many cases impossible—through all this elaborate and careful but almost profitless study. The minister of Christ was to avoid these strange and unusual interpretations, this vast fantastic collection of legends, partly true and partly false. He was to regard them as merely profane and old wives' fables, as being perfectly useless and even harmful in their bearing on practical every-day life.

And exercise thyself rather unto godliness.—Instead of these weary profitless efforts—the painful, useless asceticism on the one hand, and the endless and barren Rabbinic studies of the Law on the other—Timothy, as a good minister of Jesus Christ, was to bestow all his pains and labour to promote an active, healthy, practical piety among the congregation of believers, as we have seen in verse 6, in the words, "ever training thyself." To lead such a life required ceaseless pains and efforts, for true godliness is ever a *progressive* state. Surely exercising himself unto godliness would be a task hard enough to satisfy the most ardent, the most enthusiastic soul! The "godliness," or "piety," here alluded to, as the end toward which Timothy was to direct all his efforts, was that practical piety which influences for good, which leavens with a holy leaven all classes of society, all life, of the slave as well as of the patrician.

(8) **For bodily exercise profiteth little.**—

little:[1] but godliness is profitable unto all things, having promise of the life that now is, and of that which is to come. (9) This *is* a faithful saying and worthy of all acceptation. (10) For therefore we both labour and suffer reproach, because we trust in the living God, who is the Saviour of all men, specially of those that believe. (11) These things command

[1] Or, *for a little time.*

More accurately rendered, *bodily exercise is profitable for little.* St. Paul here, no doubt, was thinking of those bodily austerities alluded to in verse 3. The stern repression of all human passions and desires, the abstinence from all compliance with the natural impulses of the flesh—such an unnatural warfare, such an exercise, such a training of the body, no doubt in many cases would lead, in many cases certainly has led, the individual to a higher spiritual state. Such a total surrender for the one who so exercises himself is, no doubt, in a certain sense, "profitable." But then it must be remembered that this kind of victory over the flesh, in very many instances, leads to an unnatural state of mind; for the rigid ascetic has removed himself from the platform on which ordinary men and women move. His thoughts have ceased to be their thoughts, his ways are no longer their ways. For practical everyday life such an influence, always limited, is at times positively harmful, as its tendency is to depreciate that home-life and family-life, to raise and elevate which is the true object of Christian teaching. Still, the Apostle, while remembering, and in his teaching ever carrying out, the spirit of the Lord's solemn prayer to the Father, "I pray, *not* that thou shouldest take them out of the world, but that thou shouldest keep them from the evil," refrains from an *entire* condemnation of a life which received, on more than one occasion, from the lips of the Sinless One a guarded commendation (Matt. xvii. 21; xix. 12).

St. Paul, in his divinely-taught wisdom, recognises that such an austere and severe example and life, though by no means the ideal life of a Christian teacher, yet in the great world workshop of the Master might receive a blessing as "profitable for little."

But godliness is profitable unto all things.—Better, *for all things.* But while this "bodily exercise," this austere subduing of the flesh, can only weigh with a narrow and circumscribed group, St. Paul points out that the influence of "godliness is world-wide;" a godliness, not merely an inward holiness, but an operative, active piety, which, springing from an intense love for Christ, manifests itself in love for His creatures. This godliness transfigures, and illumines with its divine radiance all busy, active life—every condition, every rank, all ages. That surely is what the good minister of Jesus Christ must aim at!

Having promise of the life that now is, and of that which is to come.—For this godliness, which may and ought to enter into all states, all ages of life, promises the greatest happiness to those who struggle after it. It promises "life"—that is, the highest blessedness which the creature can enjoy in this world—as well as the rich prospect of the endless life with God in the world to come; whereas a false asceticism crushes out all the joy and gladness of this present life, and is an unreal preparation for that which is future.

(9) **This is a faithful saying and worthy of all acceptation.**—Again we have the striking formula which always calls attention to some great truth which, in the Church of the first days, had already obtained among the congregations a broad, if not a universal currency, as one of the great watchwords of the faith. Now we find one of these taken apparently from a Christian hymn, now from one of the public prayers or thanksgivings. The "faithful saying," in this instance, was that "godliness," that is, "active, living piety," is profitable for all things, seeing it has the promise of the life that now is and of that which is to come.

(10) **For therefore we both labour and suffer reproach.**—And for this end—to obtain this glorious promise, this highest blessedness *here,* that endless life with God *hereafter,* to win this glorious promise—we Christian missionaries and teachers care for no toil, however painful—shrink from no shame, however agonising.

Because we trust in the living God.—More accurately translated, *because we have our hope in the living God.* And this is why we toil and endure shame. We know that the promise made will be fulfilled, because the God on whom—as on a sure foundation—our hopes rest, is a *living* God. "Living," in strong contrast to those dumb and lifeless idols shrined in the well-known Ephesian temples.

Who is the Saviour of all men, specially of those that believe.—These words, like the assertion of chap. ii. 4, have been often pressed into the service of that school of kindly, but mistaken, interpreters, who ignore, or explain away, the plain doctrine of Holy Scripture which tells us there are those whose destruction from the presence of the Lord shall be everlasting, whose portion shall be the "second death" (2 Thess. i. 9; Rev. xxi. 8). These interpreters prefer to substitute in place of this terrible, but *repeated* declaration, their own perilous theories of universalism. Here the gracious words seem to affix a seal to the statement immediately preceding, which speaks of "the hope in the living God" as the source of all the labour and brave patience of the Lord's true servants. The *living* God is also a *loving* God, the Saviour of *all,* if they would receive Him, and, undoubtedly, the Redeemer of those who accept His love and are faithful to His holy cause.

It must be borne in mind that there were many Hebrews still in every Christian congregation, many in every church, who still clung with passionate zeal to the old loved Hebrew thought, that Messiah's work of salvation was limited to the chosen race. This and similar sayings were specially meant to set aside for ever these narrow and selfish conceptions of the Redeemer's will; were intended to show these exclusive children of Israel that Christ's work would stretch over a greater and a grander platform than ever Israel could fill; were designed to tell out to all the churches how indeed "it was a light thing that thou shouldest be my servant to raise up the tribes of Jacob, and to restore the preserved of Israel." Still, with all these guarded considerations, which serve to warn us from entertaining any hopes of a universal redemption, such a saying as this seems to point to the blessed Atonement mystery as performing a work whose consequences reach far beyond the limits of human thought, or even of sober speculation.

(11) **These things command and teach.**—

and teach. (12) Let no man despise thy youth; but be thou an example of the believers, in word, in conversation, in charity, in spirit, in faith, in purity. (13) Till I come, give attendance to reading, to exhortation to doctrine. (14) Neglect not the gift that is in thee, which was given thee

"These things"—*i.e., the real meaning* of "godliness," that practical everyday piety which, in contradistinction to the severe and strained asceticism of a limited and narrow section of society, should enter into all homes and influence all lives without distinction of class or race, age or sex. "These things" in the Church of Ephesus must form a part of the public commands and charges to the congregations, must likewise enter into private Christian teaching.

(12) **Let no man despise thy youth.**—If Timothy desired that his teaching should be listened to with respectful earnest attention, if he hoped to use a holy influence over the flock, let him be very careful that his comparative youth prove no stumbling-block. To Paul the aged, his son in the faith seemed still youthful—at this time Timothy could not have been more than forty years of age. The old master would have his young disciple supply the want of years by a gravity of life; he would have him, while fearless, at the same time modest and free from all that pretentious assumption, unhappily so often seen when the comparatively young are placed in positions of dignity and authority. Paul proceeds further to explain his solemn warning by instancing the especial points in which Timothy was to be a pattern to the other believers. These gentle words of warning, such notices as we find in chap. v. 23 and in 1 Cor. xvi. 10, 11, seem to point to the fact of there being nothing *winning* in the personal appearance of Timothy, but rather the contrary. It is deserving of comment that among the more famous of the early Christian leaders, beauty of face and form appears to have been the exception rather than the rule. This was, of course, utterly different from the old Grecian idea of gods and heroes. It was no doubt part of the counsel of God that this world-religion should owe nothing to the ordinary conditions of human success. The teaching was novel and opposed to the maxims which guided and influenced the old world. The noblest ideals proposed for Christian imitation were strange and hitherto unheard of. The very foremost preachers of the faith of Christ, as in the case of Timothy, seem to have owed nothing to those personal gifts so highly prized among Pagan nations. So the appearance of St. Paul, the greatest of the early Christian leaders, seems to have been mean and insignificant, "*ein armes dürres Männlein,*" as Luther has it. The blessed Founder of the religion is described by Tertullian, who lived in the same century with those who must have conversed with Christ's disciples, as "having no human beauty, much less any celestial splendour." Clement of Alexandria, Justin Martyr, and other very early writers, join in the same testimony. It is, however, only fair to say that on this point the view of Origen appears to have been different. The Messianic prophecies evidently looked forward to this as the will of the Most High. (See Ps. xxii. 6, 7, 15, 17; Isa. lii. 14; liii. 2—4.)

In word.—This refers to the public utterances in teaching and exhortation, but more particularly to the *words* used by Timothy in social intercourse. These, in such a life as that of the young presiding elder of the Ephesian Church, must have been of the deepest importance. The tone of his conversation was no doubt imitated by many, it would influence for good or evil the whole Christian society of that great centre. The words of men placed in such a position should ever be true and generous, helpful and encouraging, and, above all, free from slander, from all low and pitiful conceptions of others.

In conversation.—This rendering might mislead—the Greek word signifies rather "manner of life," or "conduct."

In charity.—Better rendered, *in love.* This and the following "in faith," comprehend the great graces in that inner Christian life of which the "words of the mouth," and "conduct," are the outward manifestations. He was to be the example to the flock in "love" to his neighbours, and in "faith" towards God.

The words "in spirit," which in the English version occur between "in charity," and "in faith," are found in none of the older authorities.

In purity.—Chastity of mind as well as body is here signified. The ruler of a church—among whose members evidently a school of teaching existed in which a life of stern asceticism was urged on the Christian believer as the only acceptable or even possible way of life for the servant of Christ—must be above all things watchful lest he should seem to set a careless example in the matter of morality.

(13) **Till I come, give attendance to reading.**—The words evidently imply a hope, perhaps even an expectation, on the part of St. Paul, that he would one day be enabled once more to visit the Church of Ephesus; but so long as that absence lasted, Timothy was to attend carefully to three special points in the public ministry in which he was, in the Apostle's absence, the chief officer.

The "reading" was that public reading of Scripture in the congregation—a practice borrowed from the synagogue service, when publicly the Law and the Prophets were read to the people assembled. (See Luke iv. 16; Acts xiii. 15.) In these early Christian assemblies, about the year 66—67, the question arises, Were any Scriptures read in public besides the books of the Old Testament? No certain reply can be given: it is, however, probable, even at this very early date, that one at least of the older Gospels (probably St. Mark) was already known and used in the Christian churches, and read along with the Scriptures of the old covenant. That the reading of the "Gospels" very soon became a part of the regular service in the congregations of Christians is evident from the words of Justin Martyr, *Apologia,* i. 67, written in the first half of the first century.

To exhortation, to doctrine.—These both most probably refer to the public ministry in the congregation. The first, "exhortation," particularly applies to the *feelings.* The reading of the Scriptures must be followed by an earnest practical application of their teaching to the affairs of that life in the midst of which the Christian listener was living. The word "doctrine" suggests a public teaching directed rather to the *understanding* of the hearers. The idea of exposition, or even of dogmatic teaching, seems here included.

(14) **Neglect not the gift that is in thee, which**

by prophecy, with the laying on of the hands of the presbytery.
(15) Meditate upon these things; give thyself wholly to them; that thy profiting may appear to all.[1]
(16) Take heed unto thyself, and unto the doctrine; continue in them: for in doing this thou shalt both save thyself, and them that hear thee.

CHAPTER V.—
(1) Rebuke not an

1 Or, *in all things.*
A.D. 65.

was given thee by prophecy.—Here the Apostle reminds his representative in the Ephesian congregation of his special gift of teaching and exhortation—that divine gift which had been conferred on Timothy at his solemn ordination long ago, when the young son of Eunice was designated for the post which John Mark had once held with the Apostle. It was in many respects a similar office, that which Timothy held about St. Paul, to that which in old days Elisha had held with Elijah; and, as in the case of the Hebrew prophet of the old dispensation, so here, the choice of St. Paul had been divinely guided. The very titles of the old covenant dispensation seem to have been revived in this instance of the divine selection of Timothy; for in chap. vi. 11 the older Apostle addresses his representative at Ephesus with the old prophetic title when he writes: "*Thou, O man of God,* flee these things." *Now* he solemnly calls attention to that strange, miraculous "grace" which some inspired prophet at his ordination declared was to be conferred on Timothy. The "gift" was said to be conferred, as to its certainty in the divine counsels, by such prophecy—the Holy Spirit, by the mouth of one or more of His prophets, declaring His will and intention to confer this special grace on the young companion of St. Paul.

With the laying on of the hands.—This was a symbolic action—the outward sign of an inward communication of the Holy Spirit for some spiritual office or undertaking—and was derived from the old solemn Hebrew custom. (See Num. viii. 10 in the case of the consecration of the Levites, and Num. xxvii. 18, Deut. xxxiv. 9 in the ceremony of the dedication of Joshua.)

Of the presbytery.—The brotherhood of presbyters connected with the place where the ordination of Timothy took place is here alluded to. There appears to have been such a body of elders in each particular city or district. The presbytery in this instance would seem in all probability to have belonged to the district of Lystra, Timothy's native city; but an old ecclesiastical tradition speaks of Ephesus as the place of this ordination.

(15) **Meditate upon these things.**—Better rendered, *be diligent in these things.* With these words St. Paul closes this division of his solemn directions to his chosen disciple and representative at Ephesus. He must dwell on these things and must be diligent in their practice: he must show himself active and industrious as a public teacher, and must also order his life so as to be an example to his fellow-believers.

Give thyself wholly to them; that thy profiting may appear to all.—More accurately rendered, *thy advance* (or, *thy progress*) *may be manifest to all.* To these points—his public teaching and his public example—he must give ceaseless attention, that the Christian brotherhood of the Church over which he presided should be enabled constantly to see what progress their chief pastor was making in Christian experience and life. The word we have translated "advance" or "progress" reminds Christian ministers and teachers of St. Paul's grave words to Timothy—and, through Timothy, to all occupying any position of authority in the congregations—that there must be no standing still, no resting content with knowledge already acquired, no being satisfied with the present spiritual life; there must be a restless striving after the acquirement of new stores of knowledge, ever deeper and more accurate; there must be a ceaseless endeavour to attain to a higher eminence in the spiritual life; and, if the minister or teacher would be successful, the *result* of these efforts must be manifest to the brethren with whom his lot was cast.

(16) **Take heed unto thyself, and unto the doctrine; continue in them.**—*Thy teaching* is a more accurate rendering of the original Greek word than "the doctrine." The Apostle in these words sums up the two chief pastoral requisites, and then points out the mighty consequences which will result from faithfully carrying them out. The minister of Christ must keep his attention fixed on his own demeanour and conduct, and at the same time give equally careful heed to the quality and character of his teaching. This teaching must be true and manly, and, above all, it must be faithful in doctrine; and he himself must exemplify it in word and deed. *Without* true and efficient teaching, the pure and upright life of the Christian pastor will fail to win souls for his Master; and, on the other hand, the most efficient instruction will be of no avail unless the life corresponds to the words publicly uttered.

For in doing this thou shalt both save thyself, and them that hear thee.—"Thou shalt save"—that is, in the great day of judgment; for only one meaning, and that the highest, must be given to "thou shalt save." Eternal happiness for pastor and flock is the double reward offered to the faithful servant of the Lord. In striving to save others, the minister is really caring for his own salvation.

V.

(1) **Rebuke not an elder, but intreat him as a father.**—Two-thirds of St. Paul's first Letter to Timothy have been taken up with directions, warnings, and exhortations respecting the public duties connected with the office of superintending presbyter, or bishop, of a church like that of Ephesus; from these directions in connection with the public teaching and the official life in the church, the Apostle passes on to speak of the private relations which one in Timothy's position ought to maintain with individual members of the congregation. And, first, he warns him against a misplaced zeal, which might urge him to unbefitting behaviour towards those older than himself. The enthusiastic and ardent young servant of Christ would see with sorrow and dismay the shortcomings of many an elder member of his flock, and, forgetting to make wise allowance for previous training, thought, and habits, would be likely, unwisely, and possibly unfairly, to find fault. Let him, in the cases of his elders—for the reference is rather to age than to office, as is clear from the reminder of verse 2, addressed to the "elder women"—instead of open rebuke, use respectful and affectionate entreaties, after the manner of a son, not of an official.

The younger men as brethren.—And as regards the younger Christians of Ephesus, let them not

Chap. v. 1—2. Directions respecting administering the affairs of the Church. How general reproofs were to be delivered.

elder, but intreat *him* as a father; *and* the younger men as brethren; (2) the elder women as mothers; the younger as sisters, with all purity. (3) Honour widows that are widows indeed. (4) But if any widow have children or nephews, let them learn first to shew piety[1] at home, and to requite their parents: for that is good and acceptable before God. (5) Now she that is a widow indeed, and desolate, trusteth in God, and continueth in supplications and

Chap. v. 3—8. Of the alms to be given to Christian widows.

1 Or, *kindness.*

---

be alienated by an assumption of dignity on the part of the chief presbyter of the Church. Let his relations with these younger members of the family of Christ be rather those of a brother and a friend than of a superior in rank and dignity.

(2) **The elder women as mothers.**—The same watchful care against all assumption of superiority must also be exercised in his dealings with the Christian matrons of Ephesus.

The younger as sisters, with all purity.—In the case of the younger women, St. Paul adds to his directions respecting brotherly and sisterly regard a grave word, urging upon Timothy, and all official teachers like Timothy, to add to this self-denying, loving friendship a ceaseless watchfulness in all their conversation, so as not to afford any ground for suspicion; for, above all things, the recognised teacher of Christianity must be pure. No one can read and forget the quaint words of advice of St. Jerome: "*Omnes puellas et virgines Christi, aut œqualiter ignora aut œqualiter dilige.*"

(3) **Honour widows that are widows indeed.**—The mention of the relations of a pastor to the female members of the flock suggests another train of thought. Christianity had, during the thirty years of its history, developed a perfectly new existence for women who professed the faith of Jesus of Nazareth. In the Master's new and strange (new and strange to the civilised world of that day) command—that the poor, the needy, and the sick should be succoured, that the helpless should be helped, and the comfortless comforted—a blessed calling was invented, so to speak, for Christian women. Their secluded and, in many respects, degraded life in the old world was, in great measure, owing to the fact that till Christ taught the universal duty of charity, women had no recognised public occupation in the world. The charge of the Founder of the new religion provided an endless variety of blessed, happiness-giving work for women of all ages and rank.

The novel prominence, however, of females in such great centres as Ephesus not only necessitated some organisation which should administer the alms, and generally watch over and direct the self-sacrificing labours of the female portion of the community, but also required special vigilance, on the part of the chief pastor and his assistant presbyters and deacons, to prevent the charities of the Church being misused. The widow—the desolate and destitute, the mourning widow indeed, she who is in every sense a widow and has no one to whom to look for aid—*she* always has a claim on the Church. Not merely is *she* to be honoured by a simple exhibition of respect, but she is to be assisted and supported out of the alms of the faithful.

(4) **But if any widow have children or nephews, let them learn first to shew piety at home, and to requite their parents** (or, *nephews*).—The Greek word here should be rendered *grandchildren*; the original meaning of "nephew" (*nepotes*) has disappeared. Here a warning against allowing the Church to be burdened with a burden which others ought to bear is given, in the form of a pressing reminder to the children or grandchildren of the destitute and desolate widow. It is a solemn and imperative duty for the children to afford all needful succour—a duty not to be evaded by any bearing the Christian name.

For that is good and acceptable before God.—An especial blessing is promised to those who really carry out this too often forgotten duty. (See Eph. vi. 2, 3; and also comp. Mark vii. 10, 11.)

(5) **Now she that is a widow indeed, and desolate.**—St. Paul, after mentioning this exception to the fit objects of the Church's charity and protection, again returns to this special class of helpless ones: "the widows indeed"—a class, no doubt, in those days of selfish luxury and of extreme misery and hopelessness, often utterly neglected, and not unfrequently left to starve and to perish in want and misery.

It has been asked why, in these official directions to Timothy, the question of relief of *poor Christian widows* comes so prominently forward. We find also that, in the first years which succeeded the Ascension, many *widows* in Jerusalem seemed to have been dependent on the Church for sustenance (Acts vi. 1). Now we should expect to find in the Church of Christ the same loving care which was taken in the old days, when Israel was a great nation, of these solitary and unhappy women. (Comp. Deut. xxiv. 17, where we find special laws respecting the garments of widows never to be taken in pledge. See, too, such passages as Ex. xxii. 22; Deut. xxvii. 19; Isa. i. 17; Jer. vii. 6; also Isa. x. 2; Mal. iii. 5.) Still, this hardly accounts for the statement of Acts vi. 1 and these lengthened directions to Timothy. It is more than probable that there were, especially in these Eastern cities, a very large class of these desolate and unprotected women. The practice of polygamy is accountable for this, in the first instance; and the rigid morality of the Christian teaching would place a bar to the female convert from heathenism relapsing into a life where moral restraints were utterly disregarded. The charities of the early Church, especially in Oriental cities, were, without doubt, heavily burdened with this grave and increasing charge—provision for these poor desolate women; and it was to relieve the congregations in some degree that St. Paul wrote these elaborate instructions to Timothy, warning him, as the chief minister of the Ephesian Church, against an indiscriminate charity, and at the same time providing him with a system of severe restraints to be imposed upon the assisted women.

Still, the chief pastor in Ephesus must remember that among the women of his flock there were *some* widows indeed, with neither children nor grandchildren to assist them, without friends even to cheer their desolate, widowed life. To find out and to succour these poor, sad-hearted, friendless beings, St. Paul reminds Timothy, was one of the duties of a Christian minister.

prayers night and day. (6) But she
that liveth in pleasure[1] is dead while
she liveth. (7) And these things give in
charge, that they may be blameless.
(8) But if any provide not for his own,
and specially for those of his own
house,[2] he hath denied the faith, and is
worse than an infidel. (9) Let not a

1 Or, *delicately.*
2 Or, *kindred.*

Trusteth in God.—These, without love of child or friend, cast themselves on the support of the everlasting arms. The language here used by St. Paul pictures, evidently, some loving and trustful character then living, of whom he was thinking while writing the Letter to Timothy. "*She hath* trusted and still trusts in God; she continues in prayer night and day."

And continueth in supplications and prayers night and day.—Like Anna, the daughter of Phanuel (Luke ii. 36, 37), whom some suppose St. Paul took as the model and example for these Christian widows. The meaning of these words, descriptive of a holy life, is not that the earnest and pious bereaved woman should pass her days and nights in the unrelieved monotony of constantly repeated prayers. Such a life, unpractical and useless, would never commend itself to one like St. Paul; the words simply describe the desolate one casting all her care on the Lord, and telling Him, as her only friend, of all her thoughts and actions, her words and her works.

(6) **But she that liveth in pleasure is dead while she liveth.**—This is a thoroughly Pauline thought, set forth in other language in the Roman Epistle, chap. viii. 13: "For if ye live after the flesh ye shall die." The word in the Greek rendered "she that liveth in pleasure" is very remarkable, and in the New Testament is found only in one other place (Jas. v. 5). The widow-woman who could so forget her sorrow and her duty is spoken of as a living corpse, and is sharply contrasted with her far happier sister, who, dead to the pleasures of the flesh, living a life of prayer and of self-denial, in the true sense of the word, may be spoken of as *living.* A very different estimate of *life* was held by the greatest of Greek poets, who writes thus of men giving up pleasures: "I do not consider that such a one *lives,* but I regard him as a *living corpse*" (*Antigone* of Sophocles, 1166—7, Dindorf). Comp., too, Rev. iii. 1.

(7) **And these things give in charge.**—That is to say, the duties of widows, as set forth in verse 5, together with his (St. Paul's) estimate of the gay and frivolous character painted in verse 6.

That they may be blameless.—That, whether seeking support from the public alms of the Christian community or not, the widows of the congregation should struggle after an irreproachable self-denying life, and show before men publicly *whose* servants they indeed were. In these words there seems a hint that the former life of many of these women-converts to Christianity had been very different to the life loved of Christ, and that in their new profession as Christians there was urgent need of watchfulness on their part not to give any occasion to slanderous tongues.

(8) **But if any provide not for his own.**—This repeated warning was necessary in the now rapidly widening circle of believers. Then, in those early days, as now, men and women were attempting to persuade themselves that the hopes and promises of Christians could be attained and won by a mere profession of faith, by an assent to the historical truths, by a barren reception of the doctrine of the atonement, without any practice of stern self-denial, apart from any loving consideration for others; there were evidently in that great Church of Ephesus, which St. Paul knew so well, not a few professed believers in the Crucified who, while possessed themselves of a competence, perhaps even of wealth, could calmly look on while their relations and friends languished in the deepest poverty.

And specially for those of his own house.—The circle of those for whose support and sustenance a Christian was responsible is here enlarged: not merely is the fairly prosperous man who professes to love Christ, bound to do his best for his nearest relations, such as his mother and grandmother, but St. Paul says "he must assist those of his own house," in which term relatives who are much more distant are included, and even dependents connected with the family who had fallen into poverty and distress.

He hath denied the faith.—Faith, considered as a rule of life, is practically denied by one who neglects these kindly duties and responsibilities, for "faith worketh by love" (Gal. v. 6). Faith here is considered by St. Paul, not as mere belief in the doctrine, or even in a person, but as a rule of life.

And is worse than an infidel.—The rules even of the nobler Pagan moralists forbid such heartless selfishness. For a Christian, then, deliberately to neglect such plain duties would bring shame and disgrace on the religion of the loving Christ, and, notwithstanding the name he bore, and the company in which he was enrolled, such a denier of the faith would be really worse than a heathen.

(9) **Let not a widow be taken into the number under threescore years old.**—The question respecting the assistance to be afforded to the poor and destitute widows of the great Asian Church reminded St. Paul of an organisation, consisting of widowed women, which had grown out of the needs of Christianity. He would lay down some special rules here to be observed by his friend and disciple. What, now, is this organisation commended to Timothy in these special directions? Here, and here only in the New Testament, do we find it alluded to; but the instructions in this passage are so definite, so precise, that it is impossible not to assume in the days of Timothy and of Paul, in some, if not in all the great churches, the existence of an official band of workers, consisting of widows, most carefully selected from the congregation of believers, of a somewhat advanced age, and specially distinguished for devotion—possessing, each of these, a high and stainless reputation—they were an official band of workers, a distinct order, so to speak; for these widows, formally entered on the Church's list, could not possibly represent those poor and desolate widows, friendless and destitute, spoken of above. The minimum age of sixty years would also exclude many; and the advice of St. Paul to the younger ones to marry again could never have been addressed to women wanting even many years of the requisite "sixty." Were *these* poor souls to be formally shut out from receiving the Church's alms? Again, those on the list could never be the same persons whom we hear of as deaconesses (Rom. xvi. 1, and in the Christian literature of the second century). The active duties of the office would have been utterly incompatible with the age of sixty, the minimum age at which *these* were to be

Chap. v. 9—15. Directions respecting order of Presbyteral widows.

widow be taken[1] into the number under threescore years old, having been the wife of one man, (10) well reported of for good works; if she have brought up children, if she have lodged strangers, if she have washed the saints' feet, if she have relieved the afflicted, if

1 Or, *chosen.*

---

entered on the list. We then conclude these "widows" were a distinct and most honourable order, whose duties, *presbyteral* rather than *diaconic,* apparently consisted in the exercise of superintendence over, and in the ministry of counsel and consolation to, the younger women.—That they sat unveiled in the assemblies in a separate place by the presbyters; that they received a special ordination by laying on of hands; that they wore a peculiar dress—were distinctions probably belonging to a later age.

Having been the wife of one man.—Of the conditions of enrolment in this "order," the first—that of age—has been alluded to; the second—"having been the wife of one man"—must not be understood in the strictly literal sense of the words. It is inconceivable that the hope of forming one of the highly honoured band of presbyteral women depended on the chance of the husband living until the wife had reached the age of sixty years. Had he died in her youth, or comparative youth, the Apostle's will was that the widow should marry again. (See verse 14, where St. Paul writes, "I will that the younger women marry," &c.)

The right interpretation of the words is found in some such paraphrase as, "If in her married life she had been found faithful and true." The fatal facility of divorce and the lax state of morality in Pagan society, especially in the Greek and Asiac cities, must be taken into account when we seek to illustrate and explain these directions respecting early Christian foundations.

While unhesitatingly adopting the above interpretation of the words "wife of one man," as faithfully representing the mind of St. Paul, who was legislating here, it must be remembered, for the masses of believers whose lot was cast in the busy world (see his direct command in verse 14 of this chapter, where the family life is pressed on the younger widow, and not the higher life of solitude and self-denial), still those expositors who adopt the stricter and sterner interpretation of "wife of one man"—viz., "a woman that has had *only one husband*"—have, it must be granted, a strong argument in their favour from the known honour the *univiræ* obtained in the Roman world. So Dido, in *Æn.* iv. 28, says—

> "Ille meos, primus qui me sibi junxit, amores
> Abstulit, ille habeat secum, servetque sepulchro."

Compare, too, the examples of the wives of Lucan, Drusus, and Pompey, who, on the death of their husbands, devoted the remainder of their lives to retirement and to the memory of the dead. The title *univiræ* graved on certain Roman tombs shows how this devotion was practised and esteemed. "To love a wife when living is a pleasure, to love her when dead is an act of religion," wrote Statius—

> "Uxorem vivam amare voluptas
> Defunctam religio."
> —Statius, *Sylv.* v., *in Proœmio.*

And see, for other instances, Lecky, *Hist. of European Morals*, chap. v.

But it seems highly improbable that the delicate and touching feeling, which had taken root certainly in some (alas! in only a small number) of the nobler Roman minds, influenced St. Paul, who, under the direction of the Holy Spirit, was laying down rules for a great and world-wide society, which was to include the many, not the few, chosen souls—was legislating for the masses, to whom such an expressed wish would indeed be "a counsel of perfection" rarely to be carried out; and so, without hesitation, we adopt the more practical interpretation given above.

(10) **Well reported of for good works.**—Not only must men have no evil to say of her, but she must be well known for her good works, for her kindly willingness to help the weary and heavy-laden ones of the world.

If she have brought up children.—This title to honour must be understood quite in a general sense. It must not, of course, be supposed that St. Paul deemed it necessary to exclude from the order of presbyteral widows the childless mothers. Only the candidate for admission must be well known as one who loves children, and would be ready and willing gladly to discharge any public duties to the little orphan ones of the flock who might be intrusted to her care.

If she have lodged strangers.—If, even in a comparatively humble state, she have been always mindful of the sacred rites of hospitality, a virtue perhaps even more valued in the East than in the more reserved Western countries. In the early days of the new faith, the readiness to entertain and welcome Christian strangers seems to have been an especial characteristic of believers in Jesus of Nazareth.

If she have washed the saints' feet.—Not perhaps to be understood literally, though the act of the Lord on the night before the Cross had invested this act of common hospitality with a peculiar halo of love and devotion. The woman who was to be admitted into the fellowship of this honoured order must be well known as one who had never shrunk from any act of devoted love, however painful or seemingly degrading.

If she have relieved the afflicted.—Not merely, or even chiefly, by alms, but by all kindly and sisterly encouragement: ever ready to mourn with those that mourn, deeming none too low or too degraded for her friendship, none out of the reach of her sisterly help and counsel.

If she have diligently followed every good work.—This sums up the beautiful character to be sought for in the candidates for membership in this chosen woman's band. She must be known not merely as a mother and a wife, who had well and faithfully performed the womanly duties of her home life, but men must speak of her as one who had diligently and lovingly sought out the rough places of the world, and who, with a brave and patient self-denial, with a sweet and touching self-forgetfulness, had set herself to perform those kind, good actions the Master loves so well.

In the *Shepherd of Hermas*, written about A.D. 150, some eighty years after St. Paul wrote this letter to Timothy, we have probably an example of one of these honoured widows in the person of Grapte, whose task it was to teach the widows and orphans of the Roman Church the meaning of certain prophecies. The authorship of the *Shepherd* has also been ascribed to the Hermas mentioned in Rom. xvi. 14. It belongs, how-

she have diligently followed every good
work. (11) But the younger widows
refuse: for when they have begun to
wax wanton against Christ, they will
marry; (12) having damnation, because
they have cast off their first faith.
(13) And withal they learn *to be* idle,
wandering about from house to house;
and not only idle, but tattlers also and
busybodies, speaking things which they

ever, more probably to the middle of the second century, as stated above.

The criticism which dwells on this celebrated passage, containing St. Paul's rules for admission into the order of presbyteral widows, and which finds in it subject matter belonging to a date later than the age of St. Paul and Timothy, forgets that, dating from the days when Jesus of Nazareth walked on earth, women had been enrolling themselves among His foremost followers, and had been sharing in the toils and enterprises of His most zealous disciples. We find the Marys and other holy women associated with "His own" in the days of the earthly ministry; they were foremost in the work done to the person of the sacred dead. We hear of them after the Resurrection repeatedly in the Jerusalem Church of the first days. It was the neglect of some of the Hebrew widows which led to the foundation of the deacon's order. Dorcas, before ten years of the Church's life had passed, appears to have presided over a charitable company of women at Lydda. Dorcas, no doubt, was but one out of many doing, in different centres, a similar work. Priscilla, the wife of Aquila, the wandering tent-maker of Pontus, early in St. Paul's career evidently took a leading part in organising congregations of Christians. Lydia, the purple seller of Thyatira, was prominent in developing the Philippian Church. Phebe, under the title of the Deaconess of Cenchrea, was the official bearer of St. Paul's famous letter to the Roman Church. This passage, dwelling on the growing organisation for women's work at Ephesus, tells us more, certainly, than the scattered incidental allusions of the Acts and earlier Epistles. But the words of St. Paul speak only of the natural results and development of a great movement, which, dating from the earthly days of the ministry of Christ, was destined to give women a new position among the workers of the world.

The Ephesian organisation here regulated by the Apostle is nothing more than we should expect to find after thirty or thirty-two years of female effort in the Master's cause.

(11) **But the younger widows refuse.**—The younger women—younger used in a general sense—must positively be excluded from, and held ineligible for, this presbyteral order.

This direction by no means shuts them out from participation in the alms of the Church, if they were in need and destitute; but it wisely excluded the younger women from a position and from duties which they might in their first days of grief and desolation covet, but of which, as time passed on—as experience had shown St. Paul—they not unfrequently wearied. Those who had put their hands to the plough and afterwards looked back, he proceeds to tell us, would be a hindrance to the Church's work, and in some cases might prove a subject of scandal and reproach.

For when they have begun to wax wanton against Christ.—The Apostle was looking on to the time when, the first fervour excited by grief and sorrow being past, these younger sisters in many instances would begin again to long after their old pursuits and pleasures. The Greek word rendered "wax wanton" suggests especially the idea of restiveness. They will lose—to use Jerome's well-known expression—their love for their own proper Bridegroom—Christ.

They will marry.—The sight of domestic happiness enjoyed by other women will affect them. They, too, will long in their poor hearts for home joys; they will weary for the prattle of their own little children.

How much untold misery would have been avoided—how many wasted lives would have been saved for good and useful service, had Churchmen in later times only obeyed the words and carried out the thoughts of Paul, and persistently refused, as did St. Paul and Timothy, to receive the proffered services of women still too young in years for such devoted work, but who, through a temporary pressure of sorrow, dreamed for a moment they would be able to carry out their purpose of a life-long renunciation of the world, its excitement and its joys.

St. Paul, writing under the inspiration of the Holy Spirit, saw how too often such renunciation, made under peculiar pressure of circumstances, undertaken with the hot fervour of youth, in later days would become weary and distasteful.

(12) **Having damnation.**—*Judgment,* not necessarily "damnation." The Greek word *krima* is often thus unhappily translated. The context of the passage must in all cases decide the nature of the "judgment," whether favourable or the contrary. Here it signifies that those who in after days give up a work which for their Master's sake they had undertaken, expose themselves to a searching judgment, which will thoroughly sift the reasons that induced them to forsake the begun toil, and that, if the reasons be not satisfactory, will be unfavourable, and will surely involve condemnation.

Because they have cast off their first faith.—Though, probably, no vows respecting marriage were required from those widows who devoted themselves to the Lord's service, yet virtually such a solemn enrolment partook of the nature of a life-long engagement—an engagement which, if they married again, must necessarily be given up.

Such a going back, such a giving up the higher and the more devoted life—the life of self-sacrifice, of self-abnegation—for the ordinary joys and cares of domestic life, for the useful but still every-day pursuits of ordinary men and women—such a going back, would be indeed a casting off their first faith, and such an example of backsliding could not fail to harm the cause of Christ.

(13) **And withal they learn to be idle, wandering about from house to house.**—The first fervour of their devotion and renunciation of self will have cooled, their very occupation will become a snare to them—the going about to the various dwellings for the object of consoling, instructing, assisting, would give them, now that their minds were no longer exclusively turned to religious thoughts, and their hearts were no more alone filled by Jesus, many an opportunity of wasting precious hours, of indulging in frivolous, if not in harmful, conversation; and this the Apostle seems to

ought not. (14) I will therefore that the
younger women marry, bear children,
guide the house, give none occasion to
the adversary to speak reproachfully.[1]
(15) For some are already turned aside
after Satan. (16) If any
man or woman that be-
lieveth have widows, let

Chap. v. 16. The destitute widows.

them relieve them, and let not
the church be charged; that it
may relieve them that are widows
indeed. (17) Let the
elders that rule well be
counted worthy of double
honour, especially they
who labour in the word and doctrine.

Chap. v. 17—18. Special rewards to certain Presbyters.

[1] Gr. *for their railing.*

---

have feared would be the result of these visits, and the fruit of their work, if the younger sisters were enrolled in the official list, for he speaks of such becoming "not only idle, but tattlers also and busybodies, speaking things which they ought not."

(14) **I will therefore that the younger women marry, bear children, guide the house.**—Here the Apostle deliberately expresses his *will* that in these Christian communities the younger widows should not, in the first fervour of their zeal, when borne down by sorrow, attempt anything like an ascetic life, which they would probably tire of after a season; they would thus, in the long run, instead of benefiting, positively injure the cause of Christ. St. Paul's practical mind, guided by the Spirit of God, has left us no impossible rules of perfection, no exaggerated praises of asceticism, of lofty self-denial, no passionate exhortings to a life made up entirely of self-sacrifice and of self-surrender.

He knew the ordinary man or woman was incapable of such exalted heroism, and therefore was too wise, too loving, even to recommend a life which few could live. It was not that the Master, Christ, and the greatest of his servants, St. Paul, did not themselves prize and admire the higher ideal and the nobler life—for was it not their own? Did not one attain to it, and the other die in his hero-efforts to reach it? But Master and scholar in their gospel of the world have left commands that all, not the few, can obey—have enjoined a life which all, not the few, may live.

Give none occasion to the adversary to speak reproachfully.—The reference here is not to the devil—as would at first appear probable from the direct reference in the next verse—but to the enemy of Christ—the sneering worldly man, who, jealous of a faith which he declines to receive, and envious of a life in which he will not share, is always on the look-out to discover flaws and failings in the avowed professors of a religion which he hates. (Comp. Tit. ii. 8.)

(15) **For some are already turned aside.**—It was the backsliding of these "nameless" ones, probably, which had been the immediate occasion of these directions to Timothy. Although these unhappy sisters had worked such great mischief to the cause of Christ, still St. Paul, with his tender grace and love, forbore to mention any by name. They had undertaken a task too severe for them to carry out, and had miserably failed. He spares these poor erring sisters, but directs the chief pastor of the Church at Ephesus, how to guard against such fatal results for the future.

After Satan.—They had swerved from the narrow, thorny road of self-denial which they had chosen for themselves, and perhaps dreading, after their public profession, to form afresh any legal marriage ties, had followed that downward path of sensuality which surely leads to Satan.

(16) **If any man or woman that believeth have widows, let them relieve them.**—This is not what, at first sight, it appears to be—a mere repetition of the injunction of verses 4 and 8. *There* the duties enjoined were what may be termed filial; the love, respect, and kindness to the aged was especially pressed on the younger, on the children and grandchildren of the desolate, on the master of the house or family to which the aged widow belonged. Here the reference belongs exclusively to the younger widows, who (see Note above) were, no doubt, very numerous in a great Asian Church like Ephesus; for the future of these women, often still young and totally unprovided for, St. Paul was very anxious. Until a new home was found for such, of course the Church cared for them, but this heavy burden on the Church's alms must be lightened as much as possible. It was the plain duty of relatives to care for these in their hour of destitution and sorrow. The Church would have many a one, still comparatively speaking young, utterly dependent on its scanty funds—friendless as well as homeless.

It has been asked: How is it that, considering the prominence here given to the questions (*a*) of the support of Christian widows, (*b*) of the rules respecting presbyteral widows, who evidently occupied a position of dignity and importance in the Church of the first days, no other mention of this class in the community (with the exception of Acts vi. 1 and ix. 39) appears in the whole New Testament.

This has been pressed as one of the arguments pointing to a much later date for the writing of the Epistle; but the question is, after all, readily and conclusively answered. With the exception of the short Epistle to Titus, the subject of the *internal* organisation of a church is nowhere handled. There is no room or place for such a mention in any of the more exclusively doctrinal or apologetic Epistles. In the broad field of ecclesiastical history occupied by the Acts, the two casual allusions above referred to, in the Churches of Jerusalem and Lydda, tell us of the existence of and the care for these widows in the communities of Christians, even in the earliest years of the Church's existence.

(17) **Let the elders that rule well be counted worthy of double honour, especially they who labour in the word and doctrine.**—More accurately rendered, "Let the elders (*presbyters*) who rule well." The consideration of the position and qualifications of certain ruling elder women (*the presbyteral widows*) reminded St. Paul of certain points to be impressed on Timothy connected with the rank and honour due to the more distinguished presbyters associated with him in the Ephesian congregations.

Attention should be directed here to the vast powers intrusted to the "presiding presbyter" of such a Church as Ephesus (to use the *title* of Bishop in the ecclesiastical sense would be as yet an anachronism. It probably was, however, of general use within thirty years from the date of the Epistle, certainly before the close of the century). In addition to the general office of supervisor, one in the position of Timothy evidently had the distribution of the several grades of honours

(18) For the scripture saith, Thou shalt not muzzle the ox that treadeth out the corn.[a] And, The labourer *is* worthy of his reward.[b] (19) Against an elder receive not an accusation, but before[1] two or three witnesses. (20) Them that sin rebuke before all, that others also may fear. (21) I charge *thee* before God, and the Lord Jesus Christ, and the elect angels, that thou observe these things without preferring one before another,[2] doing nothing by par-

Chap. v. 19—20. Of accused Presbyters.

Chap. v. 21—25. Solemn charge and special warnings.

a Deut. 25. 4.

b Matt. 10. 10.

1 Or, *under.*

2 Or, *without prejudice.*

---

and remuneration among the presbyteral order (verses 17 and 21). To him, as presiding elder, belonged the functions of supreme judge in all matters ecclesiastical and moral, relating to the varied officials of both sexes connected with the Church. The right of ordination which, when the Apostles and the first generation of believers had passed away, became the *exclusive* work of the bishop, is here (see verse 22) specially intrusted by an Apostle to Timothy, the chief presbyter and apostolic representative in the Church of Ephesus, in the words: "Lay hands suddenly on no man."

The elders (presbyters) to whom Timothy was to accord some special honour, were those who, in the congregations and Christian schools of so great a city as Ephesus, in addition to their many duties connected with organisation and administration, were distinguishing themselves in a marked manner by their preaching and teaching.

Among the devoted and earnest presbyters in these Asian churches, some there were, doubtless, who possessed the special gift of teaching, either in the class-room or the preacher's chair. Those who, possessing, well and faithfully exercised these invaluable gifts were to be in some way preferred by the chief minister. The "double honour" (*timè*) is a broad inclusive term, and seems to comprehend rank and position as well as remuneration—*victu et reverentiâ,* as Melancthon paraphrases the words "double honour." Timothy is here directed to confer on the more distinguished of the order of presbyters, official rank and precedence, as the reward of faithful and successful work.

(18) **For the scripture saith, Thou shalt not muzzle the ox that treadeth out the corn.**—The quotation is from Deut. xxv. 4.

The idea in the Apostle's mind, when he quoted the words of Moses, was: If, in the well-known and loved law of Israel, there was a special reminder to God's people that the *very animals* that laboured for them were not to be prevented from enjoying the fruits of their labours, surely *men* who with zeal and earnestness devoted themselves as God's servants to their fellows, should be treated with all liberality, and even dignified with especial respect and honour.

And, The labourer is worthy of his reward.—It is *possible,* though hardly likely, that St. Paul, quoting here a well-known saying of the Lord (see St. Luke x. 7), combines a quotation from a Gospel with a quotation from the Book of Deuteronomy, introducing both with the words "For the Scripture saith"—Scripture (*graphè*) being always applied by St. Paul to the writings of the Old Testament. It is best and safest to understand these words as simply quoted by St. Paul, as one of the well-remembered precious declarations of the Lord Jesus.

(19) **Against an elder receive not an accusation, but before two or three witnesses.**—By the "elder" here we must understand a presbyter—the ordained minister of the Church. St. Paul has been directing his son in the faith, and successor in the government of the chief Asian Church, carefully to watch for, and to reward by dignity and honour, the services of the more zealous and distinguished presbyters. He now tells him that the other matters, besides zeal and successful service among the Church's professed officers, will come before him when he stands at the helm of the Church. Charges—owing, possibly, to jealousy, party feeling, suspected doctrinal error—will not unfrequently be brought against a presbyter. Such an accusation is only to be received by Timothy when the evidence is perfectly clear. Every possible precaution against simply vexatious charges brought against one occupying the hard and difficult position of a presbyter, must be taken by the presiding minister. The reference is to Deut. xvii. 6.

(20) **Them that sin rebuke before all, that others also may fear.**—The Apostle here, apparently, is still referring exclusively to that order of presbyters whose more meritorious members he had directed Timothy to honour with a special honour, and towards whose accused members he instructed him how to act. He now passes to the question how to deal with these responsible officers of the Church when they were proved to be notoriously sinning. While, on the one hand, the earnest and devoted men were to be honoured with "a double honour"—while every possible *legal* precaution was to be taken in the case of those being accused—on the other hand, when proved to be men continuing in sin and error, their punishment must be as marked as in the other case was the reward. The errors and sins of teachers of the faith are far more dangerous than in those who make up the rank and file of congregations, and require a more severe and more public punishment.

It is not improbable that St. Paul was especially alluding here to false teaching—to errors of doctrine on the part of some of the Ephesian presbyters. He seems, in his parting address at Miletus to the elders (presbyters) of this very Ephesian Church, to have foreseen such a grievous falling away in the future among their company—"Also of your own selves shall men arise, speaking perverse things, to draw away disciples after them" (Acts xx. 30). Compare also the Epistle to this same Church of Ephesus (Rev. ii. 4—5). As the sin, whatever has been its nature, has been committed by men intrusted with a responsible and public charge, so the rebuke and punishment must also be in public, that the warning may then spread over the whole of the various congregations composing the Church, and thus "others also may fear."

(21) **I charge thee before God, and the Lord Jesus Christ.**—More accurately, as well as more forcibly rendered, "I *solemnly* charge thee." "Lord" must be omitted before Jesus Christ, the older authorities not containing the word. The sense of the passage remains the same. Very solemnly is Timothy adjured to carry out the varied duties of his great charge, the government of the Church of Ephesus, impartially — doing nothing hastily, ever watchful of himself. St. Paul has just pressed upon him how needful it was to exercise care in the case of an

tiality. (22) Lay hands suddenly on no man, neither be partaker of other men's sins: keep thyself pure. (23) Drink no longer water, but use a little wine for

---

accused presbyter. He must listen to no charge except several competent witnesses were produced to support the accusation. He now reminds Timothy—the chief *presbyter*—of the ever present unseen witnesses of *his* conduct (see Heb. xii. 1). In that awful presence —in sight of the throne of God, with Messiah on the right hand, and the angels, the chosen attendants and ministers of God, gathering round about the throne—would Timothy guide and rule the congregations of Christians in that famous Eastern city.

The Church of Ephesus had been built up and consolidated by the personal presence and influence of St. Paul, resident there some three years; and at the time when St. Paul wrote to Timothy it was second in numbers and in influence to none of the early groups of congregations (except, perhaps, to the Christian communities of Syrian Antioch). Placed by an Apostle as the first head of such a community, intrusted with one of the greatest and most important charges in Christendom, Timothy indeed needed to be watchful. Well might St. Paul remind him of the tremendous witnesses who would be present in *his* hour of trial.

And the elect angels.—St. Paul had been speaking of the internal organisation of the church on earth, and had been dwelling, first, on rank and order among women, and secondly, among men, especially directing that a special position of honour should be given to the more distinguished and zealous of the presbyteral order. The term "elect" here given to certain of those blessed spirits—in whose sight, as they stood and ministered before the throne of God, Timothy would rule over the charge committed to him—would seem to imply that, as on earth, so in heaven are there degrees in rank and variety in occupation. These holy ones are probably termed "elect," as especially selected by the Eternal as His messengers to the human race, as was Gabriel, who stands in the presence of God. (See Luke i. 19.) St. Paul loves to refer to the ranks and degrees of the host of heaven. (See Rom. viii. 38; Eph. i. 21; Col. i. 16.) But it is possible that these "elect angels" were those blessed spirits who "kept their first estate," and had not fallen. (See 2 Pet. ii. 4, and Jude, verse 6.)

That thou observe these things.—The "things" Timothy was to observe, as ever in the presence of so august a company of witnesses, were the varied points touched upon in the preceding verses, relating to the internal organisation of the church over which he was presiding, especially bearing in mind (for St. Paul again refers to this point) his words which bore upon judgment of presbyters—the men whose lives and conversation were to be an example to the flock.

Without preferring one before another.—More literally, *without prejudice.* He who presides over a great Christian community must be above all *party* feeling. That unhappy divisions existed in the churches, even in the lifetime of the Apostles, we have ample evidence, not only in the inspired writings, but also in the fragments we possess of the earliest Christian literature.

Doing nothing by partiality.—Although these reminding words, and those immediately preceding, were written with especial reference to the judicial inquiry Timothy would be constrained to hold in the event of any presbyter being formally accused either of a moral offence or of grave doctrinal error in his teaching, yet they must be understood in a far broader sense. The presiding elder in Ephesus must never forget that he bears rule, not only over one school of Christian thought, but over *all* men who acknowledged Jesus as Messiah and Redeemer.

(22) **Lay hands suddenly on no man.**—This command refers primarily to the solemn laying on of hands at the ordination of presbyters and deacons. It no doubt also includes the "laying on of hands" customary, apparently, even in the Apostolic age, on the absolution of penitents and their re-admission to church fellowship.

Neither be partaker of other men's sins.—By thus negligently admitting into the ministry unfit persons—by carelessly and without due caution re-admitting persons to a church fellowship, which by their evil life they had forfeited—Timothy would incur a grave responsibility, would in fact "be a partaker" in the sins and errors committed by those men, some of whom he had carelessly placed in important positions in the church, others of whom he had restored to communion before they had given sufficient evidence of their repentance. To limit, however, the reference of the command of St. Paul here to the laying on of hands in the ordination of presbyters and deacons, would imply a greater corruption in the church at that early date than is credible. Surely the number of "unfit" persons seeking the high and holy, but difficult and dangerous, posts of officers in a proscribed and hated community, would hardly by themselves have warranted such grave warning words as "Lay hands suddenly on no man, neither be partaker of other men's sins."

Keep thyself pure.—The word "pure" here has a broad and inclusive signification. It, of course, denotes the urgent necessity of one holding Timothy's high and responsible office being pure and chaste in word and deed and thought; but here it also presses on the chief presbyter of Ephesus the imperative necessity of keeping himself, by ceaseless watchfulness, pure from all reproach in the matter of selecting candidates for the ministry, or in the restoring of the lapsed sinners to church fellowship.

(23) **Drink no longer water, but use a little wine for thy stomach's sake and thine often infirmities.**—Those who argue that this Epistle was the artificial composition of an age subsequent to St. Paul's, and was written in great measure to support the hierarchical development, which, they say, showed itself only in the century after St. Paul's death, have no little difficulty in accounting for the presence of such a command as this. It can, in fact, only be explained on the supposition that the letter was, in truth, written by St. Paul to Timothy in all freedom and in all love: by the older and more experienced, to the younger and comparatively untried man: by the master to the pupil: by an old and trusted friend, accustomed to speak his whole mind, to one his inferior in years, in rank, in knowledge. No ecclesiastical forger of the second or third century would have dreamed, or, had he dreamed, would have dared to weave into the complicated tapestry of such an Epistle such a charge as "Drink no longer water, but use a little wine—considering thine often infirmities."

thy stomach's sake and thine often infirmities. (24) Some men's sins are open beforehand, going before to judgment; and some *men* they follow after. (25) Likewise also the good works *of some* are manifest beforehand; and they that are otherwise cannot be hid.

A.D. 65.

CHAPTER VI.— (1) Let as many servants as are under the yoke count their own masters worthy of all

The reminder was, no doubt, suggested by St. Paul's own words, with which he closed his solemn direction respecting Timothy's dealings with the accused presbyters, and the care to be used in the laying on of hands: "Keep thyself pure." That Timothy possessed —as did his master Paul—a feeble body, is clear from the words "thine often infirmities." He was, above all things, considering his great position in that growing church, to remember "*to keep himself pure,*" but not on that account to observe ascetical abstinence, and so to weaken uselessly the frail, perishable, perhaps ever-dying body, in which he must work that great work committed to him in the master's church. Abstinence from wine was a well-known characteristic feature of the Essene and other Jewish ascetic sects. We know there was frequent intercommunion between Alexandria and Ephesus (see Acts xviii. 24); and it has even been conjectured that Apollos, who taught publicly at Ephesus, was himself a famous Essene teacher. The practice of these grave and ascetic Jews, many of whom became Christians, no doubt affected not a little the habits and tone of thought of the Ephesian congregations. Hence the necessity of St. Paul's warning against allowing the bodily power to be weakened through abstinence and extreme asceticism.

(24) **Some men's sins are open beforehand, going before to judgment; and some men they follow after.**—The preceding verse was parenthetic, and suggested by his fears lest the effect of his direction to his son in the faith *to keep himself pure* might lead Timothy to the practice of a useless and unhealthy asceticism. St. Paul now returns and closes the subject on which he had been instructing his representative at Ephesus. He tells him, in his choice of men to fill the public positions in the Church of God—in his public inquiries into their conduct and teaching—in his inquiries respecting sinners, who, having forfeited their position as members of the community, were seeking re-admission into church fellowship, not to forget there were *two* classes of sins: the one class public and open, heralds, so to speak, of the judgment to follow. In the case of men sinning thus, the church's chief pastor would have no difficulty in determining upon his course of action. But there was another class of sins—silent and, as far as public and general knowledge went, unknown—only published after judgment had been given. To rightly estimate such characters will require much care and penetration, and *this* will be part of Timothy's work. The judgment (*krisis*) here mentioned is that of Timothy as shown in the careful selection of candidates for ordination—in determining what sinners are fit for restoration to church fellowship—in pronouncing sentence in the matter of accused presbyters.

(25) **Likewise also the good works of some are manifest beforehand; and they that are otherwise cannot be hid.**—In his difficult post Timothy might fear lest, especially in his selection of men for the Lord's service, true nobility of character might not unfrequently escape his notice and be overlooked, and that thus the best and truest might never be enrolled on the register of church officers. St. Paul bids him take courage in the thought that in many a case self-sacrifice, generosity, stern principle, will be sufficiently manifest to guide him in his choice of fit persons for the holy calling; and in those rarer cases where the higher and sweeter virtues are hidden, he may be sure that in God's good season these too *will* become known to him, in ample time for him to call them also into his Master's service.

VI.

(1) **Let as many servants as are under the yoke count their own masters worthy of all honour.**—From questions connected with the presbyters and others among the recognised ministers and officials of the church, St. Paul passes on to consider certain difficulties connected with a large and important section of the congregations to whom these presbyters were in the habit of ministering—the Christian slaves.

It was perhaps the most perplexing of all the questions Christianity had to face—this one of slavery. It entered into all grades and ranks. It was common to all peoples and nations. The very fabric of society seemed knit and bound together by this miserable institution. War and commerce were equally responsible for slavery in the Old World. To attempt to uproot it—to preach against it—to represent it in public teaching as hateful to God, shameful to man—would have been to preach and to teach rebellion and revolution in its darkest and most violent form. It was indeed the curse of the world; but the Master and His chosen servants took their own course and their own time to clear it away. Jesus Christ and His disciples, such as St. Paul and St. John, left society as they found it, uprooting no ancient landmarks, alarming no ancient prejudices, content to live in the world as it was, and to do its work as they found it—trusting, by a new and lovely example, slowly and surely to raise men to a higher level, knowing well that at last, by force of unselfishness, loving self-denial, brave patience, the old curses—such as slavery—would be driven from the world. Surely the result, so far, has not disappointed the hopes of the first teachers of Christianity.

This curse at least is disappearing fast from the face of the globe. St. Paul here is addressing, in the first place, Christian slaves of a Pagan master. Let these, if they love the Lord and would do honour to His holy teaching, in their relations to their earthly masters not presume upon their new knowledge, that with the Master in Heaven "there was no respect of persons;" that "in Jesus Christ there was neither bond nor free, for all were one in Christ." Let these not dream for an instant that Christianity was to interfere with the existing social relations, and to put master and slave on an equality on earth. Let these, by their conduct to unbelieving masters, paying them all loving respect and honour, show how the new religion was teaching them to live.

That the name of God and his doctrine be not blasphemed.—There would indeed be a grave danger of this, if the many Christian slaves, instead of

honour, that the name of God and *his*
doctrine be not blasphemed.
(2) And they that have be-
lieving masters, let them
not despise *them*, because
they are brethren; but rather do *them*
service, because they are faithful[1] and
beloved, partakers of the benefit. These
things teach and exhort. (3) If any
man teach otherwise, and
consent not to wholesome
words, *even* the words of
our Lord Jesus Christ, and
to the doctrine which is according to
godliness; (4) he is proud,[2] knowing
nothing, but doting[3] about questions

Chap. vi. 1—2. Teaching to be addressed to slaves.

Chap. vi. 3–5. Opposing doctrines held by false teachers.

1 Or, *believing.*
2 Or, *a fool.*
3 Or, *sick.*

showing increased zeal for their masters' service, should, as the result of the teaching of the new society they had joined, become morose, impatient of servitude, rebellious. Very soon in Pagan society would the name of that Redeemer they professed to love, and the beautiful doctrines He had preached, be evil spoken of, if the teaching were for one moment suspected of inculcating discontent or suggesting rebellion. An act, or course of acting, on the part of professed servants of God which gives occasion to the enemies of the Lord to blaspheme, is ever reckoned in Holy Scripture as a sin of the deepest dye. Compare Nathan's words to King David (2 Sam. xii. 14) and St. Paul's reproach to the Jews (Rom. ii. 24).

(2) **And they that have believing masters, let them not despise them, because they are brethren.**—This being in servitude to Christian masters, of course, in the days of St. Paul would happen less frequently. Let those Christian slaves who have the good fortune to serve "believing masters" allow no such thoughts as, "Shall I remain my brother's slave?" take root in the breast and poison the life-work. Let them not presume on the common brotherhood of men in Christ, on their being fellow-heirs of heaven, and on this account deem their earthly masters their equals, and so refuse them the customary respect and attention. Let them remember that, though *in heaven* there would be no respect of persons, *on earth* the old class differences were not removed.

But rather do them service, because they are faithful and beloved, partakers of the benefit.—The Greek here is better translated thus: *but the rather serve them, because believing and beloved are they who are partakers of their good service.* Let these slaves of Christians rather (or, *the more*) serve their masters zealously and loyally, because the masters who will profit by their true faithful service are themselves believers in Jesus, the beloved of God. This thought should never be absent from the heart of a Christian slave to a Christian master. "Every good piece of work I do will be a kindness shown to one who loves my Lord."

(3) **If any man teach otherwise.**—Without confining the reference strictly to what had just been taught respecting the duty of Christian slaves, there is little doubt but that some influential teaching, contrary to St. Paul's, on the subject of the behaviour and disposition of that unhappy class was in the Apostle's mind when he wrote the terrible denunciation contained in these three verses against the false teachers of Ephesus. Schismatic and heretical preachers and writers in all ages have sadly hindered the progress of true religion; but in the days of St. Paul, when the foundation-stones of the faith were being so painfully laid, there seems to have been a life-and-death contest between the teachers of the true and the false. In this passage St. Paul lays bare the secret springs of much of this anti-Christian doctrine. There is little doubt but that at Ephesus there existed then a school, professedly Christian, which taught the slave who had accepted the yoke of Christ to rebel against the yoke of any earthly lord. Hence the indignation of St. Paul. "If any man teach otherwise," different to *my* interpretation of the rule of Christ, which bids us bear all with brave patience, with loyal fortitude.

And consent not to wholesome words, even the words of our Lord Jesus Christ.—The Apostle, no doubt, was referring to well-known sayings of the Redeemer, such as "Render unto Cæsar the things that are Cæsar's," or "Blessed are the meek, for they shall inherit the earth," or "If any man will follow me, let him take up his cross daily, and follow me;" "But I say unto you, resist not evil," "Love your enemies, pray for them which despitefully use you." It was upon such sublime sayings as these—no doubt, current watchwords in all the churches—it was upon *the spirit* of the Sermon on the Mount that St. Paul based his teaching and grounded his advice to the slaves in the flock of Christ. But the false teachers, who would be Timothy's bitterest and most determined foes at Ephesus, would not consent to these "wholesome words," though they were the words of the Lord Jesus Christ.

To the doctrine which is according to godliness.—These self-willed men, in consenting not to the sublime words of Christ, at the same time refused to acquiesce in the doctrine which insisted upon a holy life: for Christian truth is inseparable from purity, single-heartedness, self-forgetfulness, brave patience.

(4) **He is proud.**—St. Paul, with righteous anger, flames out against these perverse men, who, using the name of Christ, substitute *their* short-sighted views of life for His, throw doubt and discredit upon the teaching of His chosen Apostles and servants, stir up discord, excite party spirit, barring, often hopelessly, the onward march of Christianity. The true Christian teaching is healthy, practical, capable of being carried out by all orders in the state, by every age or sex, by bond and free. The spurious Christian maxims of these men deal with subtle, useless, unpractical questions, which have no influence on ordinary life, and only tend to stir up strife and useless inquiry, and to make men discontented and rebellious. These unhappy men he first characterises as "proud:" literally, *blinded with pride.*

Knowing nothing.—Better rendered, *yet without knowing anything;* having no real conception of the office and work of Christ in the world.

But doting about questions.—While so ignorant of the higher and more practical points of Christian theology, the false teacher is "mad upon" curious and debatable questions, such as the nature of the ever-blessed Trinity; God's purposes respecting those men who know not, have not even heard of the Redeemer; and the like—problems never to be solved by us while on earth—questions, the profitless debating of which has rent asunder whole churches, and individually has broken up old friendships, and sown the seeds of bitter irreconcilable hatred.

and strifes of words, whereof cometh envy, strife, railings, evil surmisings,
(5) perverse disputings of men of corrupt minds,[1] and destitute of the truth, supposing that gain is godliness: from such withdraw thyself.
(6) But godliness with contentment is great gain.
(7) For we brought nothing into *this* world, *and it is* certain we can carry nothing out.
(8) And having food and

[1] Or, *Gallings one of another.*

Chap. vi. 6—12. Warnings against covetousness. The true teachers to flee covetousness.

And strifes of words.—Verbal disputes, barren and idle controversies about words rather than things; such wild war as also has raged, not only in the days of Timothy and of St. Paul, but all through the Christian ages, on such words as Predestination, Election, Faith, Inspiration, Person, Regeneration, &c.

St. Paul was writing, then, in the spirit of the living God, and was warning no solitary pastor and friend at Ephesus of the weeds then springing up in that fair, newly-planted vineyard of his, but was addressing the Master's servants in many vineyards and of many ages; was telling them what would meet them, what would mar and spoil their work, and in not a few cases would break their hearts with sorrow.

(5) **Perverse disputings.**—The older authorities read here a word which should be rendered "lasting or obstinate conflicts." These words close the long catalogue of the fruits of the teaching of the false masters of the new faith, and point out that the disputes engendered by these useless and unhappy controversies would be no mere temporary difficulties, but would indefinitely prolong their weary story.

Of men of corrupt minds.—More accurately rendered, *corrupted in their mind.* From their mind, over which corruption had spread, arose those mists which (verse 4) had clouded their sight with pride. The language used seems to imply that for these unhappy men a time had existed when corruption had not done its fatal work.

Destitute of the truth.—More literally, *deprived of the truth.* The truth was taken away from them: this was the immediate consequence of the corruption which had spread over their minds.

Supposing that gain is godliness.—Here the translation of the Greek words must run thus, *supposing that godliness is a source of gain.* The article before the word signifying godliness requires this rendering of the sentence. (See Tit. i. 11.) St. Paul, here adding his command to Timothy to have no dealings with these men, dismisses the subject with these few seathing words of scorn and contempt. One can imagine with what feelings of holy anger one like the noble chivalrous St. Paul would regard the conduct of men who looked upon the profession of the religion of the Crucified as a source of gain. This was by far the gravest of his public charges against these teachers of a strange and novel Christianity. We read elsewhere (1 Cor. iii. 12—15) men might go wrong in doctrine, might even teach an unpractical, useless religion, if only they were trying their poor best to build on the one foundation—Christ. Their faulty work would perish, but they would assuredly find mercy if only they were in earnest, if only they were real. But *these*, St. Paul tells Timothy and his church, were not in *earnest;* these were *unreal.* Their religion—they traded upon it. Their teaching—they taught only to win gold. There was another school of teaching—he had just been dwelling on it—the teaching which told men, even slaves, simply, lovingly to do their duty as though ever in the presence of the Lord, without any restless longing for change. This teaching would win souls to Christ, but it would never win gold, or popular applause, or gain, as the world counts gain.

From such withdraw thyself.—Most, though not all, the ancient authorities omit these words.

(6) **But godliness with contentment is great gain.**—Here the Apostle changes the subject of his letter somewhat abruptly. The monstrous thought that these wordly men dare to trade upon his dear Master's religion, dare to make out of his holy doctrine a gain—the hateful word suggests to him another danger, to which many in a congregation drawn from the population of a wealthy commercial city like Ephesus were hourly exposed. This is an admirable instance of the sudden change we often notice in the subject matter in the midst of St. Paul's Epistles, of what has been aptly termed "going off at a word." The reasoning in the writer's mind was, probably—"these false men suppose godliness will be turned into gain." Yes, though *they* were terribly mistaken, still there *is* a sense in which their miserable notion is true. True godliness is ever accompanied with perfect contentment. In this sense, godliness *does* bring along with it great gain to its possessor. "The heart," says Wiesinger, "amid every outward want, is then only truly rich when it not only wants nothing which it has not, but has that which raises it above what it has not."

(7) **For we brought nothing into this world, and it is certain we can carry nothing out.**—(Comp. Job i. 21.) Every earthly possession is only meant for this life—for the period between the hour of birth and the hour of death; we entered this world with nothing, we shall leave the world again with nothing. If we could take anything with us when death parts soul and body there would at once be an end to the "contentment" (of verse 6), for the future then would in some way be dependent on the present. This sentence is quoted by Polycarp, in his letter to the Philippians, written early in the second century. Such a reference shows that this Epistle was known and treasured in the Christian Church even at that early date.

(8) **And having food and raiment let us be therewith content.**—The Greek word rendered "let us be content" is better translated, *we shall have a sufficiency.* The argument will run thus: "All earthly possessions are only for this life; here, if we have the wherewithal to clothe us and to nourish us, we shall have enough;" if we have more than this, St. Paul goes on to show, we shall be in danger of falling into temptation.

There is no contradiction between this reading and that contained in this same Epistle (chap. iv. 1—5). There the Apostle is warning the Church against a false, unreal asceticism, which was teaching men to look upon the rich gifts of this world, its beauties and its delights, as of themselves sinful, forgetting that these fair things were God's creatures, and were given for man's use and enjoyment. Here the same great teacher is pressing home the truth that the highest good on earth was that godliness which is ever accompanied

raiment let us be therewith content.
(9) But they that will be rich fall into
temptation and a snare, and *into* many
foolish and hurtful lusts, which drown
men in destruction and perdition. (10) For
the love of money is the root of all
evil: which while some coveted after,
they have erred[1] from the faith, and
pierced themselves through with many
sorrows. (11) But thou, O man of God,
flee these things; and follow after
righteousness, godliness, faith, love,

[1] Or, *been seduced.*

---

with perfect contentment, which neither rejects nor deems evil the fair things of this life, but which, at the same time, never covets them, never longs for them. It was one thing to be rich, it was another to wish to be rich; in God's providence a man might be rich without sin, but the coveting, the longing for wealth, at once exposed him to many a grave danger both to body and soul.

(9) **But they that will be rich.**—Here St. Paul guards against the danger of his words being then or at any future time misinterpreted by any dreamy, unpractical school of asceticism, supposing that voluntary poverty was a state of life peculiarly pleasing to the Most High—the strange mistake upon which the great Mendicant orders were organised in the Middle Ages. Those who exposed themselves to the winning temptations and deadly sins he was about to speak of were not "the rich," but those who longingly plan to be rich.

Fall into temptation.—Those longing to be rich will fall into the temptation to increase their worldly goods, even at the sacrifice of principle. Some unlawful method of gratifying their passion for gain will present itself; conscientious scruples will be thrown to the winds, and they who wish to be rich will fall into the temptation. We pray so often *His* prayer, "Lead us not into temptation." In the same hour we long—perhaps even with the same breath we pray—that our worldly means may be increased, our position bettered, little thinking that the longing for an increase of riches and position will lead us into the most dangerous of all temptations!

And a snare.—A very tangle, as it has been well called, of conflicting motives—each fresh gratification of the ruling passion, perhaps excused under the plausible names of industry, home claims, praiseworthy and healthy enterprise, entangling the unhappy soul more completely.

And into many foolish and hurtful lusts.—The lusts or desires into which those who long to be rich fall, are well named "foolish," because in so many instances they are passionate desires for things utterly undesirable, the possession of which can afford neither pleasure nor advantage—such, for instance, is the love of hoarding wealth, so common to those men who have longed for and obtained riches; and "hurtful" often to the body as well as to the soul do these rich find their "longings," when gratified.

Which drown men in . . .—Better rendered, *which plunge men into . . .*

Destruction and perdition.—"Destruction" refers rather to wreck and ruin of the body, whilst "perdition" belongs rather to that more awful ruin of the eternal soul. The gratification of desires, whether these desires are centred in the lower animal passions of the table, or in the pursuit of yet baser and more selfish passions still, invariably leads to the destruction of the poor frail human body first. This premature breaking up of the earthly tabernacle is the herald and precursor of the final perdition of the immortal soul.

(10) **For the love of money is the root of all evil.**—Some would water down this strong expression by translating the Greek words by "a root of all evil," instead of "the root," making this alteration on the ground of the article not being prefixed to the Greek word rendered "root." This change, however, grammatically is unnecessary, as the article disappears before the predicate, in accordance with the well-known rule respecting subject and predicate.

St. Paul had just written (verse 9) of men being plunged into destruction and perdition—the awful consequence of yielding to those lusts into which the fatal love of riches had guided them; he now sums up the teaching contained in these words by pithily remarking, "Yes, for the love of money is the root of all evil," meaning thereby, not that every evil *necessarily must* come from "love of money," but that there is no conceivable evil which can happen to the sons and daughters of men which *may* not spring from covetousness—a love of gold and wealth.

Which while some coveted after.—There is a slight irregularity in the image here, but the sense of the expression is perfectly clear. It is, of course, *not* the "love of money," strictly speaking, which "some have coveted after," but the money itself. The thought in the writer's mind probably was—The man coveting gold longs for opportunities in which his covetousness (love of money) may find a field for exercise. Such inaccuracies in language are not uncommon in St. Paul's writings, as, for instance, Rom. viii. 24, where he writes of "hope that is seen."

They have erred from the faith.—Better rendered, *they have wandered away from the faith.* This vivid picture of some who had, for sake of a little gold, given up their first love—their faith—was evidently drawn by St. Paul from life. There were *some* in that well-known congregation at Ephesus, once faithful, now wanderers from the flock, over whom St. Paul mourned.

And pierced themselves through with many sorrows.—The language and the thoughts of Ps. xvi. 4 were in St. Paul's mind when he wrote these words—"Their sorrows shall be multiplied that hasten after another (god)." The "many sorrows" here are, no doubt, the "gnawings of conscience," which must ever and anon harass and perplex the man or woman who, for covetousness' sake, has deserted the old paths, and has wandered away from the old loved communion of Christ.

The imagery used in this tenth verse seems to be that of a man who wanders from the straight, direct path of life, to gather some poisonous, fair-seeming root growing at a distance from the right road on which he was travelling. He wanders away and plucks it; and now that he has it in his hands he finds himself pierced and wounded with its unsuspected thorns.

(11) **But thou, O man of God, flee these things.**—A commentator always speaks with great caution when he approaches in these inspired writings anything of the nature of a direct personal reference. The writers and actors in the New Testament history we have so long surrounded with a halo of reverence, that we are tempted often to forget that they were but men, exposed to temptations like us, and not unfrequently

patience, meekness. (12) Fight the good fight of faith, lay hold on eternal life, whereunto thou art also called, and hast professed a good profession before many witnesses. (13) I give thee charge in the sight of God, who quickeneth

---

succumbing to them. We owe them, indeed, a deep debt of reverence for their faithful, gallant witness —for their splendid service in laying so well the early storeys of the great Christian Temple; but we lose somewhat of the reality of the Apostolic story when in the saint we forget the man. After the very solemn, the intensely earnest warning against covetousness—that fatal love of gain and gold which seems to have been the mainspring of the life of those false teachers who were engaged in marring the noble work St. Paul had done for his Master at Ephesus—after these weighty words, the fact of St. Paul turning to Timothy, and, with the grand old covenant title Timothy knew so well, personally addressing his loved friend with "But thou, O man of God, flee these things," leads us irresistibly to the conclusion that the old Apostle was dreading for his young and comparatively untried disciple the corrupting danger of the wealth of the city in which he held so great a charge; so he warns Timothy, and, through Timothy, God's servants of all grades and powers in different ages, of the soul-destroying dangers of covetousness—"Flee these things." A glance at Timothy's present life will show how possible it was, even for a loved pupil of St. Paul—even for one of whom he once wrote, "I have no man likeminded;" and, again, "Ye know the proof of him, that, as a son with the father, he hath served with me in the gospel" (Phil. ii. 20—22)—to need so grave a reminder. Since those days, when these words were written to the Philippians, some six years had passed. His was no longer the old harassed life of danger and hazard to which, as the companion of the missionary St. Paul, he was constantly exposed. He now filled the position of an honoured teacher and leader in a rich and organised church; many and grievous were the temptations to which, in such a station, he would be exposed.

Gold and popularity, gain and ease, were to be won with the sacrifice of *apparently* so little, but with this sacrifice Timothy would cease to be the "man of God." To maintain that St. Paul was aware of any weakness *already* shown by his disciple and friend would, of course, be a baseless assertion; but that the older man dreaded for the younger these dangerous influences is clear. The term "man of God" was the common Old Testament name for "divine messengers," but under the new covenant the name seems extended to all just men faithful to the Lord Jesus. (See 2 Tim. iii. 17.) The solemn warning, then, through Timothy comes to each of His servants, "Flee *thou* from covetousness."

And follow after righteousness.—"The evil must be overcome with good" (Rom. xii. 21). The "man of God," tossing away from him all covetous longings, must press after "righteousness;" here used in a general sense, signifying "the inner life shaped after the Law of God."

Faith, love.—The two characteristic virtues of Christianity. The one may be termed the hand that lays hold of God's mercy; and the other the mainspring of the Christian's life.

Patience.—That brave patience which, for Christ's dear sake, with a smile can bear up against all sufferings.

Meekness.—The German "sanftmuth"—the meekness of heart and feeling with which a Christian acts towards his enemies. His conduct who "when he was reviled, reviled not again" best exemplifies this virtue.

(12) **Fight the good fight of faith, lay hold on eternal life.**—Then, again, with the old stirring metaphor of the Olympic contests for a prize (1 Cor. ix. 24; Phil. iii. 13, 14)—the metaphor St. Paul loved so well, and which Timothy must have heard so often from his old master's lips as he preached and taught—he bids the "man of God," rising above the pitiful struggles for things perishable and useless, fight the noble fight of faith; bids him strive to lay hold of the *real* prize—life eternal. The emphasis rests here mainly on the words "the good fight" and "eternal life." These things are placed in strong contrast with "the struggle of the covetous" and its "miserable, perishable crown." "The good fight," more closely considered, is the contest and struggle which the Christian has to maintain against the world, the flesh, and the devil. It is styled the "good fight of faith," partly because the contest is waged on behalf of, for the sake of, the faith, but still more because from faith it derives its strength and draws its courage. "Eternal life" is the prize the "man of God" must ever have before his eyes. It is the crown of life which the Judge of quick and dead will give to the "faithful unto death." (See Jas. i. 12; Rev. ii. 10.)

Whereunto thou art also called.—The "calling" here refers both to the inner and outward call to the Master's work. The inner call is the persuasion in the heart that the one vocation to which the life must be dedicated was the ministry of the word; and the outward call is the summons by St. Paul, ratified by the church in the persons of the presbyters of Lystra.

And hast professed a good profession before many witnesses.—More accurately translated, *and thou confessedst the good confession . . .* These words simply add to the foregoing clause another ground of exhortation: "Thou wast called to eternal life, and thou madest the good confession." When—has been asked—was this good confession made? Several epochs in the life of Timothy have been suggested. Were it not for the difficulty of fixing a date for so terrible an experience in Timothy's, comparatively speaking, short life, it would appear most probable that the confession was made on the occasion of some persecution or bitter trial to which he had been exposed. On the whole, however, it appears safer to refer "the good confession" to the time of his ordination. In this case the many witnesses would refer to the presbyters and others who were present at the solemn rite.

(13) **I give thee charge in the sight of God.**—Better rendered, *I charge thee in the sight of God.* If possible, with increased earnestness and a yet deeper solemnity as the letter draws to an end does St. Paul charge that young disciple—from whom he hoped so much, and yet for whom he feared so anxiously—to keep the commandment and doctrine of his Master spotless; and, so far as in him lay, to preserve that doctrine unchanged and unalloyed till the coming again of the blessed Master. So he charges him as in the tremendous presence of God.

Who quickeneth all things.—The older authorities adopt here a reading which implies, *who keepest alive,* or *preservest, all things.* The Preserver rather

Chap. vi. 13—16. Charge to preserve the doctrine of Jesus pure.

all things, and *before* Christ Jesus,
who before Pontius Pilate
witnessed a good confes-
sion;[1] (14) that thou keep
this commandment without
spot, unrebukeable, until the appearing
of our Lord Jesus Christ: (15) which in
his times he shall shew, *who is* the
blessed and only Potentate, the King
of kings, and Lord of lords; (16) who
only hath immortality, dwelling in the
light which no man can approach unto;
whom no man hath seen, nor can see:
to whom *be* honour and power ever-

1 Or, *profession.*

---

than the Creator is here brought into prominence. Timothy is exhorted to fight his good fight, ever mindful that he is in the presence of that great Being who could and would—even if Timothy's faithfulness should lead him to danger and to death—still preserve him, on earth or in Paradise.

And before Christ Jesus, who before Pontius Pilate witnessed a good confession.—Better rendered, *who before Pontius Pilate bore witness to the good confession.* The good confession which (verse 12) Timothy confessed before many witnesses, Jesus Christ, in the presence of Pilate, had already borne witness to. In other words, Jesus Christ, before Pontius Pilate, bore witness by His own solemn words, that He was the Messiah—the long-looked-for King of Israel. If the preposition which we have, with the majority of expositors, construed "before" (Pontius Pilate) have here its local meaning, the "*witness*" must be limited to the scene in the Judgment Hall—to the interview between the prisoner Jesus and the Roman governor.

Although this meaning here seems the most accurate, it is possible to understand this preposition in a *temporal*, not in a local, signification—*under* (that is, *in the days of*) Pontius Pilate—then the "witness" was borne by the Redeemer to the fact of His being "Messiah:" first, by His own solemn words; secondly, by His voluntary death. The confession was that "He, Jesus, was a King, though not of this world." (See Matt. xxvii. 11; John xviii. 36, 37, where the noble confession is detailed.) He bore His witness with a terrible death awaiting Him. It was, in some respects, a model confession for all martyrs, in so far as it was a bold confession of the truth with the sentence of death before His eyes.

(14) **That thou keep this commandment without spot, unrebukeable.**—Here St. Paul specifies what was the charge he was commending in such earnest, solemn language to his disciple and representative at Ephesus. It was that he should keep the commandment without spot, unrebukeable. The commandment was the teaching of Jesus Christ, the gospel message, *that* was to be proclaimed in all its fulness; and that this might be done effectually it was needful that the life of its preacher should be without flaw—blameless; in other words, it was absolutely requisite that the chief pastor in Ephesus should *live* the life he preached. There were those (the false teachers of whom he had been speaking, well known to Timothy) whose lives had dishonoured the glorious commandment they professed to love and teach.

Until the appearing of our Lord Jesus Christ.—The speedy return of the Lord in glory was, no doubt, looked for in the Church of the first days. The expressions of 1 Thess. iv. 15—18 evidently were written at a time when the second advent of Messiah was looked on as probably near at hand. By slow degrees—as one great teacher of the first days after the other fell asleep in Jesus, and the first generation of believers was rapidly passing away, and no fresh sign of the coming in glory was manifested—the strong expressions used in the first fervour which succeeded the Pentecost morning began to be qualified, as in this Epistle, written far on in St. Paul's life, by words which seemed to say to Timothy: "Keep the Master's commandment pure and blameless till the hour of that glorious Epiphany which your eyes will possibly behold."

(15) **Which in his times he shall shew.**—More accurately rendered, *which in his own seasons.* Here the language of fervid expectation is qualified by words which imply that in St. Paul's mind then there was no certainty about the period of the "coming of the Lord." It depended on the unknown and mysterious counsels of the Most High. The impression left upon our minds by the words of this and the preceding verse is that St. Paul had given up all hope of living himself to see the dawn of that awful day, but he deemed it more than probable that his son in the faith would live to witness it. Hence his words to him: "Keep the commandment without spot *until* the Epiphany of our Lord Jesus Christ."

Who is the blessed and only Potentate.—The stately and rhythmical doxology with which the solemn charge to Timothy is closed was not improbably taken from a hymn loved by the Ephesian Christians, and often sung in their churches; the words, then, were, likely enough, familiar to Timothy and his people, though now receiving a new and deeper meaning than before. Well might Timothy, as example to the flock of Ephesus, keep "the commandment without spot, unrebukeable"—fearlessly, even though danger and death were presented before him as the sure reward of his faithfulness—for He who in His own times should reveal (show) the Lord Jesus returning to earth in glory, was inconceivably greater and grander than any earthly potentate, king, or lord, before whose little throne Timothy might have to stand and be judged for his faithfulness to the "only Potentate, the King of kings, and Lord of lords."

Of the first of these sublime titles, God is termed "the blessed," or *the happy*, because He is the source of all blessedness and happiness; and the "only Potentate," in solemn assertion that the Christian's God was One, and that to none save to Him could this appellation "only Potentate" be applied. Possibly already in Ephesus the teachers of Gnosticism had begun their unhappy work—with their fables of the mighty æons, and their strange Eastern conception of one God the source of good, and another the source of evil.

The King of kings, and Lord of lords.—God is king over those men style kings, and lord over all men call lords here.

(16) **Who only hath immortality.**—The holy angels—the souls of men—are immortal. "But one alone, 'God,' can be said *to have immortality*," because He, unlike other immortal beings who enjoy their immortality through the will of another, derives it from His own essence.

Dwelling in the light which no man can

lasting. Amen. (17) Charge them that
are rich in this world, that
they be not highminded,
nor trust in uncertain
riches,[1] but in the living
God, who giveth us richly all things to
enjoy; (18) that they do good, that
they be rich in good works, ready to
distribute, willing[2] to communicate;
(19) laying up in store for themselves a
good foundation against the time to
come, that they may lay hold on eternal

Chap. vi. 17–19. The reminder to the rich of Ephesus.

2 Or, *sociable.*

1 Gr. *uncertainty of riches.*

---

approach unto.—This should be rendered, *dwelling in light unapproachable.* The Eternal is here pictured as dwelling in an atmosphere of light too glorious for any created beings (not only men) to approach. (See Ps. civ. 2, where the Eternal is addressed as covering himself with *light* as with a garment; see too Daniel ii. 22, where light is spoken of as dwelling with God.) The symbolism of the old covenant teaches the same truth, the unapproachable glories in which God dwells; for instance, the guarding of the bounds of Sinai in the giving of the Law; the covering of the faces of the Seraphim in the year that King Uzziah died, when Isaiah saw the divine vision; the veiled darkness of the Holy of holies in the Tabernacle and the Temple, where ever and anon the visible glory dwelt.

Whom no man hath seen, nor can see.—The Old Testament teaches the same mysterious truth—"For there shall no man see me, and live" (Ex. xxxiii. 20, and also Deut. iv. 12). John i. 18 repeats this in very plain words—"No man hath seen God at any time." The Greek word here includes all created beings. The English translation, "no man," utterly fails to reproduce the meaning of the original. (See also 1 John iv. 12.)

These last words seem to preclude the interpretation which applies the foregoing description to the Son. We have above referred this glorious doxology to the Father, as the one who, in His own times, should reveal the Lord Jesus returning to judgment.

It is, however, very noteworthy that the loftiest, the sublimest, epithets the inspired pen of Paul could frame to dignify his description of the First Person of the ever-blessed Trinity, God the Father, are used again of the Son. "The Lamb shall overcome them: for he is *Lord of lords, and King of kings*" (Rev. xvii. 14 and xix. 16; and see too Rev. i. 5).

(17) **Charge them that are rich.**—Paul had traced up the error of the false teachers—against whose work and influence he had so earnestly warned Timothy—to covetousness, to an unholy love of money; he then spoke of this unhappy covetousness—this greed of gain, *this wish to be rich*—as the root of every evil. From this fatal snare he warned the "man of God" to flee, bidding him take courage in the high service to which he was dedicated, and to be fearless of all consequences, for he served the King of kings. But in the congregations of Ephesus there were many, owing to birth or to other circumstances, already rich and powerful, already in the possession of gold and rank, in varied degrees. Before closing the letter to the chief pastor, Timothy, he must add a word of encouragement and also of special warning to these. Above all things he would have no mistake as to his meaning: the *wish to be rich* was a sure root of error and of evil, but the *being rich* was a very different thing; this class was surrounded, indeed, with special perils, but still, even "*as rich*" they might serve God faithfully. So in his charge to them he commands them not to strip themselves of their wealth, but to use it wisely, generously.

In this world.—The Greek word rendered "world" signifies, in its literal sense, *age*, and includes the period which closes with the second coming of the Lord. Now, as St. Paul had just made a reference to the probable speedy coming of the Lord in judgment in Timothy's lifetime, the words "the rich in this world" have a special signification. Very fleeting indeed will be those riches of which their possessors were so foolishly proud [be not high-minded, St. Paul urges]; these riches were a possession always terminable with life—possibly, let them bear in mind, much sooner.

Nor trust in uncertain riches.—The literal translation of the Greek here is more forcible—"nor trust in the uncertainty of riches." Uncertainty—for (1) the very duration of life, even for a day, is uncertain; and (2) the numberless accidents of life—in war, for instance, and commerce—are perpetually reminding us of the shifting nature of these earthly possessions.

But in the living God, who giveth us richly all things to enjoy.—The Greek word rendered "living" does not occur in the more ancient authorities. Its removal from the text in nowise alters the sense of the passage. The rich should set their affections and place their trust, not in these uncertain riches, but in God, the bestower of them, who wills, too, that His creatures should find pleasure in these His gifts—given to us to enjoy.

This is another of the many sayings of the old man St. Paul, in which he urges on the people of God, that their kind Master in heaven not only allows men reasonable pleasures and gratifications, but even Himself abundantly provides such for them.

(18) **That they do good, that they be rich in good works.**—These words—coming directly after the statement that the good and pleasant things of this world, which are possessed in so large a share by the "rich," are, after all, the gifts of God, who means them for our enjoyment—these words seem to point to the highest enjoyment procurable by these "rich"—the luxury of doing good, of helping others to be happy the only enjoyment that never fails, never disappoints.

Ready to distribute, willing to communicate.—In distinguishing between these words, which are nearly synonymous, the first points rather to the hand which generously *gives*, and the second to the heart which lovingly *sympathises*.

The first obeys willingly the Master's charge—"Give to him that asketh;" the second follows that loving command which bids His own to rejoice with those that rejoice, and to mourn with those that mourn.

(19) **Laying up in store for themselves a good foundation against the time to come.**—This is a concise expression, which might have been more fully worded thus—*Laying up in store for themselves a wealth of good works as a foundation*, &c. (Comp. our Lord's words in Luke xvi. 9, where the same truth is taught, and a similar promise made.)

Here a simple command, in complete accordance with the teaching of Christ, is given, and a definite consequence is attached to the obeying the command. If the "rich"—the word "rich," we must remember, is a

life. (20) O Timothy, keep that which
Chap. vi. 20, 21. The last commands to Timothy. is committed to thy trust,
avoiding profane *and* vain
babblings, and oppositions
of science falsely so called: (21) which
some professing have erred concerning
the faith. Grace *be* with thee. Amen.

¶ The first to Timothy was written from Laodicea, which is the chiefest city of Phrygia Pacatiana.

---

broad term, and in St. Paul's mind would comprehend many a one who would hesitate to apply the term in its strict sense to himself—if the "rich," or the comparatively rich, are really generous and kind with their wealth—and of this God alone can be judge—then with these perishable, fleeting riches they are laying the foundation of an everlasting habitation on the other side the veil. Bengel quaintly expresses the truth, slightly changing the metaphor—"*Mercator, naufragio salvus, thesauros domum præmissos invenit.*"

That they may lay hold on eternal life.—The older authorities here, instead of "eternal," read *truly.* The sentence will then read thus, *that they may lay hold on that which is truly life*—that is, may lay hold on that which *in truth* deserves the name "life," because the fear of death will no longer cast its gloomy shadow over it. This "laying hold on eternal life" is *the end* the wise rich Christian proposes to himself, when he orders his earthly life and administers his earthly goods, and St. Paul has just showed Timothy how this "end" is to be reached by such a man.

Such plain statements in the Book of Life as the foregoing by no means weaken the divine truth so often repeated, that men are saved only by the blood of Christ, with which they must sprinkle their sin-scarred souls. Poor men and rich men alike may try; they will find, with all their brave struggles, that of *themselves* they will never win salvation, they *cannot* redeem their souls.

But such plain statements as we have here, and in Luke xvi. 9, tell us, if we really are "of Christ's," sprinkled with His precious blood, then we must try with heart and soul, with hand and brain, to follow out such charges as we have just been discussing.

(20) **O Timothy, keep that which is committed to thy trust.**—More literally and better rendered, *O Timothy, keep the trust committed to thee.* It is a beautiful thought which sees in these few earnest closing words the very handwriting of the worn and aged Apostle St. Paul. The Epistle, no doubt dictated by the old man, was in the handwriting of some friend of St. Paul and the Church, who acted as his scribe; but, as seems to have been sometimes his habit (see especially the closing words of the Galatian Letter), the last pleading reminder was added by the hand of the Apostle himself. "O Timothy"—he writes now no longer addressing church or pastor, but his own favourite friend and pupil, the loved heir of his God-inspired traditions and maxims, which so faithfully represented the doctrine and teaching of Jesus of Nazareth—"O Timothy, keep the sacred trust committed to thy charge."

This "sacred trust," so solemnly committed as the parting charge to Timothy, was "the doctrine delivered by St. Paul to him to preach," the central point of which, we know from the Apostle's other writings, was the teaching respecting the atonement and the precious blood of Christ. There is a beautiful, though somewhat lengthened, paraphrase of the "Trust" in the *Commonitorium* of Vincentius Lirinensis, composed about A.D. 430. "What is meant," he asks, "by '*keep* the trust?' The disciple of St. Paul must keep the sound doctrine of his master safe from robbers and foes. . . . . What is meant by 'the *trust?*' Something intrusted to you to keep—not a possession you have discovered for yourself; something you have received from another—not what you have thought out for yourself. . . of this 'trust,' remember, you are nothing but the guardian. . . . What, then, is the meaning of '*keep the trust?*' It is surely nothing else than 'guard the treasure of the Catholic faith.' . . . Gold have you received; see that you hand gold on to others."

"Is there, then," asks this same wise writer "to be no progress, no development in religious teaching? Yes," he answers; "there should be a real progress, a marked development, but it must partake of the nature of a progress, not of a change. . . . Let religion in the soul follow the example of the growth of the various members which compose the body, and which, as years roll on, become ever stronger and more perfect, but which, notwithstanding their growth and developed beauty, always remain the same."

Avoiding profane and vain babblings.—The Apostle has before in this Epistle warned Timothy against these useless, profitless discussions. Anything like theological controversy and discussion seems to have been distasteful to St. Paul, as tending to augment dissension and hatred, and to exalt into an undue prominence mere words and phrases.

Oppositions of science falsely so called.—Rather, *of knowledge falsely so called.* These "oppositions" have been supposed by some to be a special allusion to some of the Gnostic theories of the opposition between the Law and the Gospel, of which peculiar school, later, Marcion was the great teacher. It is hardly likely that any *definite* Gnostic teaching had as yet been heard in Ephesus, but there is little doubt that the seeds of much of the Gnosticism of the next century were—when St. Paul wrote to Timothy—being then sown in some of the Jewish schools of Ephesus and the neighbouring cities. (Comp. the allusions to these Jewish and cabalistic schools in St. Paul's letter to the Colossian Church.) The "oppositions" here may be understood as referring generally to the theories of the false teachers, who were undermining the doctrine of St. Paul as taught by Timothy.

(21) **Which some professing have erred concerning the faith.**—In this most probably wild and visionary "knowledge" the false teachers and their hearers sought salvation and a rule of life, and miserably failed in their efforts. The result with them was, that they lost all hold on the great doctrine of Faith in a crucified Saviour.

Grace be with thee.—The ancient authorities are almost equally divided between "with thee" and "with you," the congregation. The public nature of so many of the directions and instructions contained in this Epistle account for the absence of those private greetings which we find in the Second Epistle of St. Paul to Timothy.

EXCURSUS ON NOTES TO I. TIMOTHY

ON A SUGGESTED INTERPRETATION OF CHAPTER v. 25.

IT has been suggested, with considerable ingenuity, that verse 25 belongs to, and is an introduction of, a new division of the Epistle, where the Apostle gives Timothy instructions respecting certain teachings to be addressed to different ranks in the Christian society of Ephesus. The connection with verse 24 then would be —as it is in the case of sins, so, too, it is in the case of good works. These latter are not always on the surface distinguishable. Some, of course, are manifest, but there is many a noble life the secrets of which will only come to light at the last day—"they cannot be hid" THEN. And this is too often the case with that unhappy class (the slaves), "those under the yoke," of whom the Apostle was about to speak (chap. vi. 1, 2). It is possible that St. Paul meant here to turn Timothy's attention especially to those in slavery, that he might diligently search out the noblest and most devoted, and ordain (see verse 22) them to perform sacred duties, so that each class—the slaves as well as the rich and well-born—should possess representatives among the ordained ministers. This is at least possible when we consider the vast number of slaves—not a few of them, too, possessing high culture—in the world known by St. Paul and Timothy.

In connection with, but not necessarily linked with, this thought is an interpretation of the general subject matter of the sixth chapter, which views the whole as instructions to the three broad divisions into which Christian society of the first century may be said to have been roughly divided :—

(1) SLAVES . . .	Chaps. v. 25—vi. 1—3. Instructions respecting *slaves*, who possessed nothing of their own.
	Chap. vi. 4, 5. The allusion to the false teachers, whose teaching respecting slavery was very different from his.
(2) MIDDLE CLASS.	Chap. vi. 6—16. St. Paul introduces the warning against covetousness and the wish to be rich, the special danger of *the middle class*—the free, but who were the reverse of wealthy—to which order Timothy belonged. Then followed
(3) THE RICH	Chap. vi. 17—19. Special instructions to the *rich and the highly born.*

INTRODUCTION

TO

THE SECOND EPISTLE OF PAUL THE APOSTLE TO

TIMOTHY

I. Contents of the Epistle.—Like the First Epistle, the Second Letter presents no regular plan.

1.—It commences with expression of deep love to Timothy (chap. i. 1—5);

2.—And then passes on to exhortation to a fearless and faithful discharge of his duties (chap. i. 6—14).

3.—These exhortations are interrupted by the Apostle's memory of many faithless ones, and of one faithful friend (chap. i. 15—18).

4.—The Apostle renews his exhortations to Timothy to a brave endurance, even if suffering come on him. He tells his disciple Timothy what has nerved him, Paul, to endure to the end. Then he renews his pleading, that Timothy should be careful in guarding against a religion of mere words—instancing what such a teaching might end in (chap. ii. 1—26).

5.—Again St. Paul interrupts his exhortation by writing down his sad forebodings of evil times (chap. iii. 1—9).

6.—Then he encourages his disciple by recounting his own suffering and deliverances. Timothy too must suffer, only let him remain steadfast in the faith (chap. iii. 10—17).

7.—The Apostle closes with a solemn command that his disciple should teach earnestly, for he, the old master, was at the end of his course. He would, if possible, see his dear friend once more, so he prays him to come speedily, well nigh all having deserted him. He ends with a touching reminiscence of his first trial in the Roman court of justice, and with a few greetings (chap. iv. 1—22).

This Second Epistle to Timothy has been well termed the "will or testament" of the master, addressed to his favourite disciple, and containing his last wishes, written as it was under the shadow of approaching death. It is full of light and shade; the tone of the exhortation, the warning and the encouragement constantly changing. Now the words are sad with a strange parting solemnity, now bright with the glorious sunshine of the Apostle's immortal hopes. Yet in every line of this most touching of all the Pauline writings we cannot fail to perceive something of the gloom which, owing to desertion of so many friends, had saddened that gallant, loving heart of St. Paul.

He was well-nigh quite alone, almost friendless in the midst of mortal foes, an old man, worn out with toil, weakened by illness and privation, expecting a death of agony; and yet in spite of his surroundings, in spite of his own seeming failure, in spite of his own baffled hopes, he writes to his best-loved disciple in sure confidence, that he, Timothy, will war the same warfare as his master Paul had warred; that he, Timothy, though by nature perhaps timid and shrinking, will, undeterred by dangers, sufferings, and the sad prospect of a painful death, bravely carry on the work he has seen his master do, and for the sake of which he has seen his master die. He writes to him in sure confidence that the teaching respecting the mystery of the atoning blood, the doctrine of Christ, and the life lived by Christ, the sum of the sacred deposit of the Catholic Faith committed to his charge, would be preserved intact and safe by him, and by him then handed down, when his life-work was done, to other faithful hands.

The Epistle, though ringing with a ring of hope, yet paints the future of the Church in sombre colours. The enemies would increase, and the love of many would wax cold, and in coming years the man of God would be exposed to persecution, hatred, and to cruel suffering: and yet though all this is found in this strangely touching little writing, no one who has read these dying words of St. Paul can lay the Letter down without a prayer of thanksgiving for this Epistle of immortal hope.

II. Date of the Epistle.—The Second Epistle to Timothy was written by St. Paul from Rome during his second imprisonment in that city, about the year A.D. 66. We may suppose that shortly after the writing of the First Epistle to Timothy the Apostle had been arrested at Nicopolis, "the city of victory," in Epirus (see Titus iii. 12), probably on the capital charge of being connected with the burning of Rome (A.D. 64), and after a short delay had been conveyed to Italy. The words of chap. iv. 16, refer to the first hearing of his cause, either by Nero himself, or, more probably, by the infamous Tigellinus, the Prætorian Prefect. It was no doubt shortly after this first hearing, that St. Paul, feeling that the end for him was at hand, wrote this Second Epistle to Timothy. The exact date of the martyr's passing to his rest is unknown. The last hour probably came before he looked for it, for, notwithstanding the urgent summons, no tradition speaks of Timothy again looking on the face of his beloved master.

THE SECOND EPISTLE OF PAUL THE APOSTLE TO

TIMOTHY

CHAPTER I.—(1) Paul, an apostle of
Jesus Christ by the will of
God, according to the pro-
mise of life which is in
Christ Jesus, (2) to Timothy,
my dearly beloved son: Grace, mercy,
and peace, from God the Father and

Chap. i. 1, 2. St. Paul's address and greeting to Timothy.

A.D. 66.

Christ Jesus our Lord. (3) I thank God,
whom I serve from *my*
forefathers with pure con-
science, that without ceas-
ing I have remembrance of
thee in my prayers night and day;
(4) greatly desiring to see thee, being

Chap. i. 3—5. His trust in Timothy's faith.

---

(1) **Paul, an apostle of Jesus Christ by the will of God.**—As in the Epistles to the Corinthians, the Ephesians, and Colossians, he ascribes his apostleship to the sovereign will and election of God. Apart from any merit or work of his own, God chose him for the office. He neither aspired to it nor wished for it. The reference to the Almighty will in this Epistle is singularly in harmony with the spirit of calm resignation which breathes through it. It was that sovereign will which chose him as an Apostle, which guided him all through that eventful life of his, and which brought him to the prison of the Cæsar, where, face to face with death, he wrote this last letter to his friend and disciple Timothy.

According to the promise of life which is in Christ Jesus.—The Greek word rendered "according to" should here be translated "*for* the promise of life." This preposition here denotes the object or intention of his appointment as apostle, which was to make known, to publish abroad, the promise of eternal life. Almost the first words of an Epistle, written evidently under the expectation of *death*, dwell upon the promise of *life*—the life which knows no ending—the life in Christ. The central point of all Evangelical preaching was the true, blessed life eternal, that life which, in the person of the Redeemer, was revealed to man, and which, through the Redeemer, is offered to the sinner.

(2) **To Timothy, my dearly beloved son.**—More accurately, (my) *beloved son.* The words used in the address of the First Epistle were "my own son" (γνησίῳ τέκνῳ). The change in the words was probably owing to St. Paul's feeling that, in spite of his earnest request for Timothy to come to him with all speed, these lines were in reality his *farewell* to his trusted friend and more than son, hence the loving word.

Grace, mercy, and peace . . .—See Notes on 1 Tim. i. 2.

(3) **I thank God.**—The exact reference of these words of thankfulness on the part of St. Paul has been the subject of much argument. Although the sense is a little obscured by the long parenthesis which intervenes, it seems clear that St. Paul's expression of thankfulness was for his remembrance of the unfeigned faith of Timothy and Lois and Eunice (see verse 5). The whole passage might be written thus, "I thank God, whom I serve with the devotion of my forefathers with a pure conscience (as it happens that I have thee uppermost in my thought and prayers night and day, longing to see thee, being mindful of thy tears, in order that I may be filled with joy), when I call to remembrance the unfeigned faith which is in thee, which dwelt first in thy grandmother Lois and thy mother Eunice," &c.

Whom I serve from my forefathers.—That is, with the devotion and love I have inherited as a sacred family tradition. St. Paul was here referring, not to the great forefathers of the Jewish race—Abraham, Isaac, and the patriarchs—but to the members of his own family, who, he states, were religious, faithful persons. Van Oosterzee strangely concludes: "Dass Paulus diese historische kontinuität der wahren Gottesverehrung in seinem geschlecht um so höher schätzt, da er selbst stirbt, ohne kinder zu hinterlassen!"

With pure conscience.—Literally, *in pure conscience.* The spiritual sphere in which St. Paul, as a Jew first, then as a Christian, served God. (See Notes on 1 Tim. i. 5.)

That without ceasing I have remembrance of thee.—Better rendered, *as unceasing is the remembrance which . . .* This long parenthetical sentence leads up to the point for which St. Paul was so deeply thankful to God; namely, the true faith of Timothy himself. These unstudied words tell us something of the inner life of such a one as St. Paul, how ceaselessly, unweariedly he prayed, night as well as day. The object, too, of those constant prayers of St. Paul was not St. Paul but Timothy.

(4) **Greatly desiring to see thee.**—In view of that violent death which, at this time a close prisoner, he saw was imminent, the memory, too, of the tears of his friend made him long yet more earnestly to see him once again on earth.

Being mindful of thy tears.—Shed probably by Timothy when his aged master had last taken leave of him. It is likely that the clouds of danger which were gathering thickly round St. Paul towards the close of his career had oppressed the brave-hearted Apostle with a foreboding of coming evil, and had invested the last parting with Timothy with circumstances of unusual solemnity. St. Paul had affected others besides Timothy with the same great love, so that tears

mindful of thy tears, that I may be filled
with joy; (5) when I call to remembrance
the unfeigned faith that is in thee, which
dwelt first in thy grandmother Lois,
and thy mother Eunice; and I am per-
suaded that in thee also. (6) Wherefore
I put thee in remembrance that thou
stir up the gift of God,
which is in thee by the
putting on of my hands.
(7) For God hath not given
us the spirit of fear; but of power, and of

Chap. i. 6—10. He urges him to rekindle that faith.

were shed by strong men when he bade them farewell. (See the account of the leave-taking of the Ephesian elders at Miletus, Acts xx. 37, 38—"And they all wept sore, and fell on Paul's neck, and kissed him, sorrowing most of all for the words which he spake, that they should see his face no more.")

There is no necessity for Hofmann's singular, but rather far-fetched, theory here that the tears were simply an expression for Timothy's intense sorrow at hearing of the Apostle's arrest and close imprisonment, which sorrow St. Paul was made acquainted with in a letter. The tears, according to Hofmann, were those "welche Timotheus brieflich geweint hat."

That I may be filled with joy.—When he meets Timothy again.

(5) **When I call to remembrance the unfeigned faith that is in thee.**—It is for the "unfeigned faith" which he was confident dwelt still in his dearest and best-loved companion, whom he had intrusted with the care of the Ephesian church, that he thanked God. (See verse 3.)

It is more than probable that some special instance of this unfeigned faith on the part of the chief pastor of Ephesus had come to the Apostle's knowledge, and cheered that great loving heart of his while he languished in prison.

Which dwelt first in thy grandmother Lois, and thy mother Eunice . . .—We know, in the course of his second missionary journey (Acts xvi. 1—3) St. Paul was brought into contact with this pious family at Lystra. It has been suggested that Lois, Eunice, and Timothy were kinsfolk of St. Paul, hence his intimacy with the family, and his knowledge of their faith; hence, too, perhaps, his devoted and unbroken friendship for Timothy. We are told (Acts xvi. 1) that this Eunice was a Jewess, married to a Greek. Lystra is no great distance from Tarsus—whence St. Paul came. The supposition is just possible; but it is only an ingenious thought, there being no data to support it. Of the names—Lois is the same with the more familiar Lais; Eunice is an equivalent of the Latin Victoria.

(6) **Wherefore I put thee in remembrance.**—*Wherefore* (*seeing that I am so thoroughly persuaded of thy faith*) *I am determined to put thee in remembrance* . . . It seems, from the general tenor of the Epistle, that Timothy was deeply cast down by the imprisonment of St. Paul. Timothy, as well as the martyr himself, was conscious that the end of that great and glorious career of his old master was at last come; and the heart of the younger man sank—as well it might—under the prospect of having to fight the Lord's battle at Ephesus—that famous centre of Greek culture and of Oriental luxury—against enemies without and enemies within, alone, and without the help of the great genius, the master mind, and the indomitable courage of the man who for a quarter of a century had been the guiding spirit of Gentile Christianity, and his dear and intimate friend. So St. Paul now, persuaded that faith burned in his disciple's heart with the old steady flame, but knowing, too, that he was dispirited and heavy-hearted, was minded, if possible, to cheer up the fainting heart, and to inspire it with fresh courage to fight the Master's fight when he (St. Paul) had left the scene.

That thou stir up the gift of God, which is in thee by the putting on of my hands.—The Greek word rendered "stir up" literally means *to kindle up, to fan into flame.* Chrysostom brings home the great lesson taught by this word, which belongs to all Christ's people alike, when he quotes 1 Thess. v. 19, "Quench not the Spirit;" for it is in our power both to quench this Spirit and also to fan it into flame. The "gift of God" here alluded to is that special gift of the Spirit conferred on Timothy at his ordination, and which included, in his case, powers necessary for the performance of the many and important duties to which he was in the providence of God called, especially those gifts of ruling and teaching which are necessary for the chief pastor's office. This "gift of God" was conferred through the medium of the hands laid on Timothy's head at his ordination at Lystra. In this act the presbytery at Lystra were joined with the Apostle. (See 1 Tim. iv. 14.) We know that St. Paul frequently uses for his illustrations of Christian life scenes well known among the Greek heathen nations of the Old World, such as the Greek athletic games. Is it not possible (the suggestion is Wordsworth's) that the Apostle while here charging Timothy to take care that the sacred fire of the Holy Ghost did not languish in his heart, while urging him to watch the flame, to keep it burning brightly, to fan the flame if burning dimly—is it not possible that St. Paul had in mind the solemn words of the Roman law, "Let them watch the eternal flame of the public hearth"? (Cicero, *de Legibus*, xi. 8.) The failure of the flame was regarded as an omen of dire misfortune, and the watchers, if they neglected the duty, were punished with the severest penalties.

(7) **For God hath not given us the spirit of fear.**—Or better, perhaps, *the spirit of cowardice*—that cowardice which manifests itself by a timidity and shrinking in the daily difficulties which the Christian meets with in the warfare for the kingdom of God. (Comp. John xiv. 27, and Rev. xxi. 8.) "Hath not given us," in this particular case, refers to the time when Timothy and St. Paul were admitted into the ministry. The Holy Spirit is no Spirit, be it remembered, which works cowardice in men. But the reference is also a far broader one than merely to the Holy Spirit conferred on ministers of the Lord at ordination. It is a grave reminder to Christians of every age and degree that all cowardice, all dread of danger, all shrinking from doing one's duty for fear of man's displeasure, proceeds *not* from the Spirit of God.

But of power, and of love, and of a sound mind.—Instead of rendering the Greek word by "a sound mind," it were better to substitute the translation, *self-control.* The Holy Spirit works, in those to whom it is given, power, or *strength*, to fight the fight of God, power, not only patiently to endure, but also to strike good blows for Christ—the power, for love, and of a sound mind. (8) Be not thou therefore ashamed of the testimony of our Lord, nor of me his prisoner: but be thou partaker of the afflictions of the gospel according to the power of God; (9) who hath saved us, and called *us* with an holy calling, not according to our works, but according to his own purpose and grace, which was given us in Christ Jesus before the world began, (10) but is now made manifest by the appearing of our Saviour Jesus Christ, who hath abolished death, and hath brought life and immortality to light

---

instance, of steadfastness in resisting temptation, the strong will which guides other weaker ones along the narrow way "of love." It works, too, in those to whom God gives the blessed gift, that strange, sweet love for others which leads to noble deeds of self-surrender—that love which never shrinks from a sacrifice which may benefit the friend or even the neighbour. And lastly, the Spirit works in us "self-control"—selbst-beherrschung—that power which, in the man or woman living in and mixing with the world, and exposed to its varied temptations and pleasures, is able to regulate and to keep in a wise subjection, passions, desires, impulses.

(8) **Be not thou therefore ashamed of the testimony of our Lord.**—Seeing, then—remembering, then, that God gave you and me (notice the beautiful courtesy of the old martyr waiting for death, death the *human* guerdon of his fearless life, coupling, as he has been doing, his sorrow-stricken, dispirited friend with himself, whom no danger, no failure had ever affected)—remembering, then, the spirit of power, love, and self-control given to us, do not thou be ashamed of the testimony of the Lord. This "testimony" of which Timothy was not to be ashamed, of course includes the sufferings and the shame of Christ. In these, before mocking, scornful men, must Timothy, as an example to the flock, rather glory; but "the testimony" signifies much more than what relates only to the Passion story. The Christian, instead of being ashamed of his "profession," must before the world show fearlessly that its hopes and its promises are his most precious treasure.

Nor of me his prisoner.—Nor must Timothy either then, or in days to come, be afraid of confessing before men that he had been the disciple and friend of the prisoner St. Paul, who had paid so dearly for the courage of his opinions. Nor Timothy, nor any Christian must shrink from openly espousing the unpopular cause of the Crucified, or from publicly declaring their sympathy with its hated martyrs.

But be thou partaker of the afflictions of the gospel.—More accurately rendered, *but rather suffer afflictions for the gospel.* But, on the contrary, instead of injuring the good cause by faint-hearted conduct, should Timothy rather be ready to suffer, if need be, with St. Paul, ready to bear some shame with him, ready to incur, perhaps, sore danger for the gospel's sake; and then St. Paul, emphasising his words, and strengthening with a new strength his argument and his exhortation, adds, "in accordance with the power of God"—yes, join with me in suffering, if needs be, for the gospel. Mighty and pitiful was God's power towards us; great, surely, in proportion should be *our* readiness to suffer in return, if He asks this—as He is now doing from you and me—at our hands.

According to the power of God.—What power of God? has been asked. *Not* according to the power we get from God, but according to the power which God has displayed towards us in our calling and in our marvellous salvation. In other words, God, with great power, has succoured us; surely we may be confident that He will never leave us, never desert us, but in the hour of our sorest trouble incurred for Him will help us, and will bring us safely through it. So Chrysostom, who, while asserting that suffering will be borne, but not in our strength but in God's, says, "Consider how thou hast been saved, and how thou hast been called;" inferring that He who has done so great things for man, in his calling and in his salvation, will never let him want for strength.

(9) **Who hath saved us.**—St. Paul now specifies the manner in which the power of God has been displayed towards us. This is an inclusive word, and comprehends all God's dealings with us in respect to our redemption. (See Notes on Titus iii. 5.) Again, as so frequently in these Pastoral Epistles, is the First Person of the blessed Trinity referred to as the Saviour.

Us.—Paul and Timothy, and all who believe on the name of the Lord Jesus, are included under "us."

And called us with an holy calling.—This explains the means by which God was pleased to save St. Paul and Timothy. *He* called them. He—God the Father, to whom the act of calling is regularly ascribed (Gal. i. 6); and the calling is said to be "holy," because it is a summons to share in the blessed communion of Christ (1 Cor. i. 9). There is an inner as well as an outer calling; the "outer" comes through the preaching of the word, the inner by means of the voice of the Holy Ghost in the heart.

Not according to our works, but according to his own purpose and grace.—We are told in the next clause that "the grace" was given *before the world began;* therefore "our works" could have had nothing to do with the divine purpose which was resolved on by God. As Chrysostom observes, "No one counselling with Him, but of His own purpose, the purpose originating in His own goodness." Calvin pithily remarks, "If God chose us before the creation of the world, He could not have considered the question of our works, which could have had no existence at a period when we ourselves were not." "But according to" (*in pursuance of*) "His own purposes," with emphasis on "own"—that purpose which was prompted by nothing outward, but which arose solely out of the divine goodwill, or goodness, or love. (See Eph. i. 11.) The "grace" here is almost equivalent to the "mercy" of Tit. iii. 5, "according to His mercy He saved us."

Which was given us in Christ Jesus before the world began.—This grace was "given," not "destined," to us. It was given to us, in the person of Jesus Christ, before time was, and when our Redeemer, in the fulness of time, appeared, then was it made manifest. "Before the world began"—quite literally, "before eternal times;" the meaning here is "from all eternity," before times marked by the lapse of unnumbered ages.

(10) **But is now made manifest.**—The grace, a gift given to us in Christ from all eternity, but hidden during unnumbered ages, till the fulness of

through the gospel: (11) whereunto I am appointed a preacher, and an apostle, and a teacher of the Gentiles. (12) For the which cause I also suffer these things: nevertheless I am not ashamed: for I know whom I have believed,[1] and am persuaded that he is able to keep

Chap. i. 11, 12. The Apostle Christ's herald.

1 Or, *trusted.*

time—the appointed time—arrived; the "now," when it was made manifest.

By the appearing of our Saviour Jesus Christ.—The simple act of the Incarnation by no means covers the "appearing." The "appearing" (Epiphany) here includes not only the birth, but the whole manifestation of Christ on earth, including the Passion and the Resurrection.

Who hath abolished death.—More accurately, *when he abolished*, or, *made of none effect.* The Greek word thus rendered, signifies that by the action of the Lord, death was rendered inoperative, comparatively harmless—its sting was removed. The "death" thus made of none effect has a far more extended meaning than that separation of soul and body we are in the habit of calling death. It signifies that awful punishment of sin which is best described as the exact opposite to "eternal life." The death we are acquainted with by sad experience here is only the forerunner of the death eternal. Already to the believers in Jesus this death of the body counts for nothing; the time will come when it will even exist no more.

And hath brought life and immortality to light through the gospel.—The Greek word rendered "immortality" is more accurately translated by *incorruption.* "Life" here is that true life, in its highest and completest sense, which includes the most perfect happiness—a happiness a foretaste of which is enjoyed on this side the grave; over it (this bliss) death now has no power—indeed, death is the gate, so to speak, through which we pass to its complete enjoyment. St. Paul says Christ "brought to light" life and incorruption, not only from having imparted to His own these glorious and divine attributes, but chiefly because He has displayed (or *manifested*) the life and incorruption in His own resurrection body before our very eyes. When St. Paul wrote to Timothy, we must remember, many an eye-witness of the resurrection glories still walked on earth; with these must St. Paul, and Timothy too, often have conversed. Thus it can, with all literal truth, be predicated of Jesus Christ that He brought life and incorruption out of that darkness in which, as far as men were concerned, these things lay, into the clear and bright light of day. And as the hearers of Christ and the eye-witnesses of His resurrection were, when we consider this great mass of mankind, comparatively few, the medium by which these glorious truths were made known to men was the preaching of the gospel, in which gospel the Holy Ghost had enshrined both the words and the story of Christ.

On the Greek text of this grand verse Ellicott observes that it is remarkable that "Death," being then a known and ruling power, has in the original the article, while "Life" and "Incorruption," being *then* only recently revealed and unknown powers, save to few, are written without the article.

(11) **Whereunto I am appointed a preacher . . . .**—Whereunto—that is, to preach the gospel referred to in the previous verse. (On these titles see 1 Tim. i. 12; ii. 7.) In all his deep humiliation, a solitary prisoner awaiting death, deserted by his friends, St. Paul, with solemn emphasis, rehearses the titles of dignity which, by his Master's appointment, he possessed in the Christian Church. The poor prisoner, waiting his summons to a painful death, wished his last charge to go forth with all the authority of an Apostle, adding, however, in the next verse, that his present sufferings were entailed on him, owing to this very position in the Christian community to which his Master had called him.

(12) **For the which cause I also suffer these things.**—Because he had been the teacher and apostle, had all these sufferings—the prison, the chains, the solitude, the hate of so many—come upon him. There was no need to refer to them more particularly. Timothy knew well what he was then undergoing. The reason of the Apostle's touching at all upon himself and his fortunes will appear in the next clause, when, from the depths, as it would seem, of human misfortune, he triumphantly rehearses his sure grounds of confidence. Timothy was dispirited, cast down, sorrowful. He need not be. When tempted to despair, let him think of his old master and friend, Paul the Apostle, who rejoiced in the midst of the greatest sufferings, knowing that these were the sure earthly guerdon of the most devoted work, but that there was One, in whom he believed, able and, at the same time, willing to save him for yet higher and grander things.

Nevertheless I am not ashamed.—Not ashamed of the suffering I am now enduring for the cause of the Lord. He then, by showing the grounds of his joyful hope, proceeds to show how men can rise to the same lofty heights of independence to which he had risen, whence they can look down with indifference on all human opinion and human reward and regard.

For I know whom I have believed.—Better rendered, *whom I have trusted;* yea, and still trust. "Whom" here refers to God the Father.

That which I have committed unto him.—More exactly, *my deposit.* Considerable diversity of opinion has existed among commentators of all ages as to the exact meaning which should be assigned to the words "my deposit." Let us glance back at what has gone before. St. Paul, the forsaken prisoner, looking for death, has been bidding his younger comrade *never* to let his heart sink or his spirit grow faint when oncoming dangers threaten to crush him; for, he says, you know me and my seemingly ruined fortunes and blasted hopes. Friendless and alone, you know, I am awaiting death (chap. iv. 6); and yet, in spite of all this crushing weight of sorrow, which has come on me *because I am a Christian*, yet am *I* not ashamed, for I know *whom* I have trusted—I know *His* sovereign power to whom I have committed "my deposit." *He*, I know, can keep it safe against that day. St. Paul had intrusted his deathless soul to the keeping of his Heavenly Father, and having done this, serene and joyful he waited for the end. His disciple Timothy must do the same.

"That which I have committed unto Him, my deposit," signified a most precious treasure committed by St. Paul to his God. The language and imagery was probably taken by the Apostle from one of those Hebrew Psalms he knew so well (Ps. xxxi. 5)—"Into thy

that which I have committed unto him
Chap. i. 13, 14. Hold fast sound doctrine. against that day. (13) Hold
fast the form of sound
words, which thou hast
heard of me, in faith and love which is in
Christ Jesus. (14) That good thing which
was committed unto thee keep by the
Holy Ghost which dwelleth in us. (15) This

---

hand I commend my spirit," rendered in the LXX. version (Ps. xxx. 5), "I will commit" (*parathēsomai*). In Josephus, a writer of the same age, *the soul* is especially termed a *parakatatheke*—deposit. The passage is one in which he is speaking against suicide (*B. J.* iii. 8, 5). Philo, also, who may almost be termed a contemporary of St. Paul, uses the very same expression, and also calls the soul "a deposit" (p. 499, ed. Richter). Both passages are quoted at length by Alford, who, however, comes to a slightly different conclusion.

Against that day.—The day of the coming of Christ—"that day when I (the Lord of Hosts) make up my jewels." He will keep my soul—"my deposit"—safe against that day when the crown of life will be given to all that love His appearing.

(13) **Hold fast the form of sound words, which thou hast heard of me.**—It was not sufficient for Timothy to renew his fainting courage and to brace himself up for fresh efforts; he must do something more—in his teaching he must never let those solemn formularies he had once received from him be changed. Perhaps in the heart of St. Paul lurked some dread that the new glosses and specious explanations which the school of false teachers, so often referred to in these Pastoral Epistles, chose to add to the great doctrines of Christianity would be more likely to be listened to by Timothy when the hand of his old master was cold and the heart had ceased to beat; so he urged upon him to hold fast those inspired formularies he had heard from St. Paul's lips—such, for instance, as those "faithful sayings" which come before us so often in these Epistles to Timothy and Titus.

In faith and love which is in Christ Jesus.—Timothy, in days to come, must mould and shape his teaching after the pattern of the teaching of his master St. Paul, and he must do it in that faith and love which alone comes from a life passed in communion with Christ.

The very frequent reference to the "sound, healthy words" in these Epistles by St. Paul, and from which he urges his disciples and successors never to depart, indicate to us the deep importance St. Paul and the first generation of believers attached to the very words and expressions used by the apostles and those who had been with the Lord.

False doctrines so easily might creep in, and loose forms of expression respecting great truths were an ever-present danger; a lax life, too, St. Paul knew, was the almost invariable accompaniment of false doctrine, hence these repeated exhortations of his to these representative teachers, Timothy and Titus, of the second generation of Christians, to hold fast the form of sound, healthy words—such words as these had again and again been heard from the lips of apostles and hearers of the Lord—"words which thou hast heard of me," St. Paul.

(14) **That good thing which was committed unto thee.**—"The good thing committed unto thee," or *the deposit*, differs from the "deposit" of verse 12, inasmuch as the "deposit" of verse 12 was something committed by St. Paul to God; while, on the other hand, in verse 14 a trust committed by God to Timothy is spoken of. But the Apostle, remembering the solemn meaning of the word in the first instance, uses it with especial emphasis on this second occasion. Yes, he seems to say, *God* will keep the most precious deposit you or I shall intrust to Him—our soul—safe against that day; do *thou*, in thy turn, keep safe, unharmed, the deposit He, through me, has intrusted to thee. In what God's deposit with men like Timothy and St. Paul consisted has been discussed in the Note to 1 Tim. vi. 20. "The treasure of the Catholic faith"—*that* was to be kept unchanged, unalloyed. The epithet "good," which is here applied to this most sacred trust, we find joined to "the doctrine" ("the good doctrine," 1 Tim. iv. 6), and to "the fight" ("the good fight," 1 Tim. vi. 12).

Keep by the Holy Ghost which dwelleth in us.—But this glorious deposit of the Catholic faith must be preserved, let Timothy and others holding a like position with Timothy mark well, by no human agencies. He indicates here the only means that must be employed to preserve this sacred charge safe and pure, when he bids us keep the deposit by the Holy Ghost—the Holy Ghost which, St. Paul adds, dwells in us.

It would seem that the Apostle here was warning Timothy, as the representative Christian teacher, that the sacred deposit of the Catholic faith was to be preserved by no weak compliance with the scruples of false teachers or of doubting men, by no timid accommodation, by no yielding a little here and a little there to prejudice or vanity. By no such or any other short-sighted human arts of defence was the deposit of faith to be guarded. But the Holy Ghost will keep His own, and will show His faithful teachers in every age how to hand down the lamp of holy Catholic doctrine still burning brightly, with flame undimmed, to their successors in the race of life.

(15) **This thou knowest, that all they which are in Asia be turned away from me.**—This sad desertion of friends is well known to thee. Instead of being dispirited by it, and by my arrest and close imprisonment, rather shouldest thou be stimulated to fresh and renewed exertions for the cause for which I suffer this desertion, these bonds.

All they which are in Asia.—It has been maintained by many, even by great Greek expositors such as Chrysostom, that "they which are in Asia" refers to certain Asiatic Christians who happened to be in Rome at the time of the Apostle's arrest and imprisonment. Others have even suggested that these Asiatics had gone to Rome for the purpose of bearing witness in St. Paul's favour, and finding that St. Paul's position was one of extreme danger, terrified for themselves—like others once before had been in the Christian story—lest they too should be involved in a like condemnation, forsook him and fled. But the simple and more obvious meaning is here to be preferred, and we assume as certain that the forsaking, the giving up St. Paul, took place in Asia itself. Large numbers of Christians, if not whole churches, repudiated their connection with the great father of Gentile Christianity, and possibly disobeyed some of his teaching. What, in fact, absolutely took place in Asia while St. Paul lay bound, waiting for

Chap. i. 15—18. Many have deserted me; one has stood firm.

thou knowest, that all they which are in Asia be turned away from me; of whom are Phygellus and Hermogenes. (16) The Lord give mercy unto the house of Onesiphorus; for he oft refreshed me, and was not ashamed of my chain: (17) but, when he was in Rome, he sought me out very diligently, and found *me.* (18) The Lord grant unto him that he may find mercy of the Lord in that day: and in how many things he ministered unto me at Ephesus, thou knowest very well.

---

death in Rome, had been often threatened in Corinth and in other centres. Party feeling ran high in those days, we know; and one of the most sorrowful trials the great-hearted St. Paul had to endure in the agony of his last witnessing for his Lord, was the knowledge that his name and teaching no longer was held in honour in some of those Asian churches so dear to him. The geographical term Asia is rather vague. It may—and indeed, strictly speaking, does—include Mysia, Phrygia, Lydia, Caria; but such a wide-spread defection from Pauline teaching seems improbable, and there is no tradition that anything of the kind ever took place. St. Paul probably wrote the term more in the old Homeric sense, and meant the district in the neighbourhood of the river Cayster;

"In Asian meadow by Cayster's streams."
—*Iliad* ii. 461.

Of whom are Phygellus and Hermogenes.—These names would at once suggest to Timothy the men and the congregations of "Asia" to whom St. Paul was alluding—names well known, doubtless, then, and especially to persons in the position of Timothy; but no tradition has been preserved which throws any light on the lives and actions of these traitorous friends of St. Paul.

(16) **The Lord give mercy unto the house of Onesiphorus.**—In striking contrast to those false friends who turned away from him was one, also well known to Timothy, probably an Ephesian merchant. Onesiphorus, to whose house the Apostle prays the Lord to give mercy, had, early in this last imprisonment of St. Paul, arrived in Rome on matters connected probably with business. There he heard of the arrest of that great master whom he had known well in Asia, and sought him out in his prison. There is but little doubt that when St. Paul wrote this Epistle Onesiphorus' death must have recently taken place, both from the terms of this verse—where mercy is prayed, not for him, but for his house—and also from the expression "in that day," used in verse 18. There is something strangely touching in this loving memory of "one" who, in his trouble, did *not* forsake him, but whose devotion was rather increased by his danger, and this *one* faithful friend would never be able again to show his love to the prisoner, for God had called him home.

For he oft refreshed me, and was not ashamed of my chain.—"He oft refreshed me" does not imply that he ministered only to the Apostle's bodily needs when he was in prison, though the word, no doubt, includes this. But "he refreshed" him by frequent visits, by, no doubt, much anxious forethought in the matter of St. Paul's deliverance from prison and bonds, by a noble disregard of the personal danger which he incurred by his open intimacy with a prisoner charged, as St. Paul must have been, with treason against the empire. "*He* was not ashamed of my chain." (See Acts xxviii. 20, where "the chain" of another captivity is mentioned.)

(17) **But, when he was in Rome, he sought me out very diligently, and found me.**—But, on the contrary, instead of fear—far from being ashamed—he, when he arrived in Rome, sought me out. This must have been a much more rigorous captivity than the one alluded to in the last chapter of the Acts when St. Paul dwelt in his own hired house with the soldier who guarded him. *Now* he was rigidly imprisoned, and the very place of his captivity was not, apparently, easily found.

(18) **The Lord grant unto him that he may find mercy of the Lord in that day . . .**—The Greek should be rendered here, *favour of the Lord*, instead of by "mercy of the Lord." Some commentators, who have found a difficulty in this unusual repetition of "the Lord," explain it thus: The expression, "the Lord grant," had become among Christians so completely "a formulary," that the second use of the word "Lord" was not noticed; and the prayer is thus simply equivalent to "O that he may find mercy of the Lord." It seems, however, better to keep to the strict literal meaning, and to understand the first "Lord," in the sense in which the term is always found in the Epistles of St. Paul, as a title of Christ; and the second "Lord" as used of the Father, to whom here (as in Rom. ii. 5, 16; Heb. xii. 23), judgment at the last day is ascribed.

In that day.—The Apostle can never repay now—not even with thanks—the kindness his dead friend showed him in his hour of need; so he prays that the Judge of quick and dead may remember it in the awful day of judgment. It is worthy of note how St. Paul's thoughts here pass over the interval between death and judgment. It was on that day when the great white throne would be set up that he thought of the good deeds done in the body being recompensed by the righteous Judge. No doubt the expectation of the early Christians—in which expectation certainly St. Paul shared—of the speedy coming of the Lord influenced all thinking and speaking of the intermediate state of the soul between death and judgment, and almost seems to have effaced the waiting time from their minds.

And in how many things he ministered unto me at Ephesus, thou knowest very well.—These services rendered to St. Paul at Ephesus are placed side by side with those things he had done for him at Rome, but as they are mentioned after, they perhaps refer to kind offices undertaken for the prisoner by Onesiphorus *after* his return from Rome to Ephesus. These things Timothy, the presiding pastor at Ephesus, would, of course, know in their detail better than St. Paul. The Greek word διηκόνησεν, rendered "he ministered," has given rise to the suggestion that Onesiphorus was a deacon at Ephesus. Although this is possible, still such an inference from one rather general expression is precarious.

This passage is famous from its being generally quoted among the very rare statements of the New Testament which seem to bear upon the question of the Romish doctrine of praying for the dead.

It may be well very briefly to touch on two points

A.D. 66.

CHAPTER II.—(1) Thou therefore, my son, be strong in the grace that is in Christ Jesus. (2) And the things that thou hast heard of me among[1] many witnesses, the same commit thou to faithful men, who shall be able to teach others also.

Chap. ii. 1, 2. Timothy urged to be strong and earnest.

1 Or, *by*.

which suggest themselves as to the bearing of this passage on the doctrine in question. (1) Although we here, in common with Roman Catholic interpreters and the majority of the later expositors of the Reformed Church, assume that Onesiphorus was dead when St. Paul wrote to Timothy, and that the words used had reference to St. Paul's *dead* friend, still it must be remembered that others, well worthy of being heard, writing many centuries before any doctrinal controversy on this subject arose, have held quite another opinion. Theodoret and Chrysostom (quoted by Alford) understood that Onesiphorus was with St. Paul at this time. (2) The prayer, whether it be taken as a prayer or an ejaculation, is simply the expression of an earnest desire, on the part of St. Paul, that the kind act of the *dead*—assuming, contrary to the opinion of the above quoted Fathers, that he was dead—Onesiphorus towards himself may be remembered on that day when the books are opened before the Judge of quick and dead. It, indeed, only asks—looking fairly at the context—that an act of unrequited and devoted love shown in this life may be remembered in the final judgment. Without touching upon the controversy itself, it seems only just to point out the extreme precariousness of pressing this text—the only one in the New Testament really touching on this subject, and as to the interpretation of which expositors, as we have seen, are by no means in agreement—in support of a controverted doctrine.

II.

(1) **Thou therefore, my son, be strong in the grace that is in Christ Jesus.**—St. Paul, after the reference to the faithless Asiatics and the true loyal Onesiphorus, with which he interrupted his exhortation, turns again to Timothy. Thou therefore (*oun*), my son, considering what has taken place, be strong. It is as though he said, Imitate the one loyal follower, and make up to me for the faithless conduct of so many false friends. "Thou, then, be strong," but not as men understand strength or firmness; but do thou be strong "in the grace that is in Christ Jesus"—that is, be strong in the power of that inward sanctification which enables a man to will and to do according to what God has commanded, in the power of that inward sanctification which alone proceeds from Christ, and which will never be wanting to any one who is in Christ; in other words, "Be strong in the Lord, and in the power of His might" (Eph. vi. 10).

(2) **And the things that thou hast heard of me.**—These "things" have been often understood as referring to the few great fundamental truths rehearsed by the Apostle, in the presence of the elders of the congregation, on the occasion of Timothy's solemn ordination. "The things," then, would have been something of the nature of what is contained in a creed or profession of faith. But it is better to give to "the things" which Timothy had heard of St. Paul, and which he was to deliver to other faithful men in his turn, a much broader reference, and to understand them as comprehending far more than the narrow limits of a profession of faith could possibly contain. "The things" were, no doubt, the sum of St. Paul's teaching, the general conception of Pauline theology, which Timothy, so long the Apostle's intimate and confidential friend and disciple, was to give out to another generation of believers. It was, in fact, the "Gospel of St. Luke"—"my Gospel," as we love to think St. Paul termed that matchless summary of the life and teaching of the Blessed. It was the theology shrined in such Epistles as those once written to the Romans or Ephesians in past years. These "things" again and again, in crowded congregations, before Jewish and Christian elders, before assemblies composed of idolaters, had Timothy heard that master of his, with his winning, pleading voice, tell out among "many witnesses." Those "things" Timothy, in his turn, the voice of St. Paul the Aged being hushed, was now to commit to others.

Among many witnesses.—These, according to the above interpretation, included Pagans and Jews, the rich and poor, the untaught sinners of the Gentiles and the skilled rabbi trained in the schools of Jerusalem and Alexandria.

The same commit thou to faithful men.—Not to men merely who were "believers" in Jesus Christ. This, of course, was intended, but the "faithful men" here denoted loyal, trusty souls—men who, under no temptation, would betray the charge committed to them.

Who shall be able to teach others also.—Not only must the Christian teachers to whom Timothy is to give the commission of teaching, be trustworthy men, they must also possess knowledge and the power of communicating knowledge to others. Although the divine help was to be prayed for and expected in this and all other sacred works, yet it is noticeable how St. Paul directs that no ordinary human means of securing success must be neglected. St. Paul's last charge in these Pastoral Letters of his, directed that only those shall be selected as teachers of religion whose earthly gifts were such as fitted them for the discharge of their duties. While there is nothing in this passage to support the theory of an authoritative oral teaching, existing from the days of the Apostles, in the Church—the words of St. Paul here point to the duty of the Christian soldier, not only himself to keep unchanged and safe the treasure of the Catholic faith as taught by the Apostle, but to hand down the same unimpaired and safe to other hands.

The great Christian truths were never allowed to be recklessly handled. There was a school, so to speak, of Christian theology in the time of St. Paul. His dying charge directed his best beloved disciple to make careful provision for the choice and training of teachers in the congregation. Men able as well as willing, gifted as well as zealous, should be the objects of his choice.

Some have imagined that these directions respecting the handing down the lamp of Christian truth to others were given to Timothy with a view to his leaving Ephesus—the appointed scene of his labours—for Rome, to join the imprisoned Apostle (chap. iv. 9), in which event men able as well as devoted should be left in this great centre to carry on the work of Timothy and of St. Paul. But it is far better to understand St. Paul's charge as given to Timothy, a *representative* leader of the Church of Christ, and to understand the Apostle's words as addressed to the Church of all

Chap. ii. 3–6. He is to be ready also to suffer for the gospel's sake.

(3) Thou therefore endure hardness, as
a good soldier of Jesus
Christ. (4) No man that
warreth entangleth him-
self with the affairs of
this life; that he may please him
who hath chosen him to be a
soldier. (5) And if a man also strive for
masteries, *yet* is he not crowned, except
he strive lawfully. (6) The husbandman

---

times. The runners in the Christian race must take good care before they fall out of the course that their torches, still burning, be handed on to the athletes who take their place.

(3) **Thou therefore endure hardness.**—The older authorities do not contain the Greek word rendered "thou therefore." The word translated "endure hardness" in the older authorities is compounded with a preposition, and is better and more literally rendered, *take thy share in suffering.* But Timothy must remember, if he obeys St. Paul's voice, and with steady earnestness follows St. Paul's tracks, the very same sufferings which have been the master's guerdon will be the lot of the loyal disciple. So St. Paul adds, "Take thy share of suffering," or, "Suffer hardship with me." Timothy must be prepared for this. He must look on himself as one of the pioneers of the army of the great King, as a tried veteran, as a good soldier of Jesus Christ, prepared for the dangers and trials which in those days awaited such a calling. Then, under three different pictures, the Apostle paints the duties and rewards of a Christian's life.

(4) **No man that warreth . . .**—Better rendered, *while engaged on military service,* or *serving as a soldier.* The first picture is suggested by the last simile (in verse 3). It was one very familiar to the numerous peoples dwelling under the shadow of the Roman power, this picture of the soldier concerned only in the military affairs of the great empire—the legionary wrapped up in his service, with no thought or care outside the profession of which he was so proud. None of these sworn legionaries have aught to do with buying or selling, with the Forum, or any of the many employments of civil life. So should it be with the earnest and faithful Christian; paramount and above any earthly considerations ever must rank his Master's service, his Master's commands.

The soldier of Christ should never allow himself to be entangled in any earthly business which would interfere with his duty to his own General. But while this general reference to all members of the Church lies on the outside, beneath the surface a solemn injunction may surely be read, addressed to Timothy and to others like him in after times specially engaged in the ministry of the Word and in matters connected with the government of the Church of Christ. And so the Catholic Church has generally understood this direction to Timothy as warning her ministers from engaging in secular pursuits, either connected with business or pleasure.

That he may please him who hath chosen him to be a soldier.—More accurately rendered, *who enrolled him as a soldier.* Only those soldiers who with heart and soul devote themselves to their military work win the heart of their commander. The question has been asked, What of St. Paul's own example and that of other of the early Christian teachers, such as Aquila? did not *they,* at all events from time to time, pursue a secular calling—that of tent-makers? The reply here is not a difficult one. The Jewish life in those days contemplated and even desired that its rabbis and teachers should be acquainted with, and even, if necessary, practise some handicraft. The well-known Hebrew saying, "He that teacheth not his son a trade teacheth him to be a thief," is a proof of this. In the case of these early teachers, this occasional practice of an industry or a trade brought them more directly into contact with their Jewish brethren. It was thus among the Jewish people that the Hebrew rabbi often passed imperceptibly into a Christian teacher. It must also be borne in mind that in St. Paul's case, and also in the case of the presbyters of the first and second age, especially if missionaries, it was impossible always to ensure subsistence, unless by some exertions of their own they maintained themselves. It was, too, most desirable that these pioneers of Christianity should ever be above all reproach of covetousness, or even of the suspicion that they wished for any earthly thing from their converts. That however, it was not intended that any such combination of work—at once for the Church and for the world—should be the rule of ecclesiastical order in coming days, the positive and very plain directions of 1 Cor. ix. 1—15 are decisive, and incapable of being misunderstood.

(5) **And if a man also strive for masteries.**—More accurately translated, *again, if a man strive in the games.* Another picture is drawn, and the picture is, as before, a well-known one to all the dwellers in the great cities of the empire. An athlete is chosen to represent the professed servant of Christ, one of those who, after long and careful training, contends in the public games, then so popular, so entirely a part of the life of every city—in the games of wrestling or running, or in the chariot-racing, or in the hand-to-hand contests. Again, this one—as in the case of the soldier—if he aspired to victory and success, must "endure hardness."

Except he strive lawfully.—"Lawfully"—*i.e.* according to the prescribed conditions of the contest. He must, of course, submit himself to the strict rules of the theatre where the games are held, and (for this is also included in the "lawfully") must besides—if he hopes for a prize—go through all the long and severe training and discipline necessary before engaging in such a contest. Galen uses the same phrase, in the sense of complying with the recognised rules of training as regarding diet.

(6) **The husbandman that laboureth must be first partaker of the fruits.**—Again the picture is painted from every-day life. "The husbandman that laboureth"—with an emphasis upon "that laboureth"—is the successful tiller of the ground; "the *labouring* husbandman" it is, for whom the earth brings forth her increase. It is the enduring, patient, self-sacrificing toil that is rewarded in the affairs of common life—the man that "endures hardness," whether as a soldier, or athlete, or tiller of the ground, wins the reward; and as in the world, so in religion. Further on in the Epistle the Apostle speaks of *his* having won the crown of righteousness. *He* had *endured hardness* of every conceivable kind; every affliction for the Lord's sake he had endured save death, and *that* he was expecting, and knew it could not long tarry. The teaching of

that laboureth must be first partaker of the fruits.[1] (7) Consider what I say; and the Lord give thee understanding in all things. (8) Remember that Jesus Christ of the seed of David was raised from the dead according to my gospel:
(9) wherein I suffer trouble,

Chap. ii. 7–13. What nerves St. Paul to endure.

1 Or, *The husbandman, labouring first, must be partaker of the fruits.*

St. Paul in this triple picture is—not *every* soldier wins its commander's applause, but only the veteran who devotes himself heart and soul to his profession; not *every* athlete wins the crown or prize, but only he who trains with anxious, painful care; not *every* tiller of the ground gathers the earth's fruits, but only the patient toiler. So must it be in religious life. It is not enough to *say* we are Christians, or even to *wish* to be of the brotherhood of Christ. Men must really *live* the life they say they love.

(7) **Consider what I say; and the Lord give thee understanding in all things.**—The older authorities read here *will give;* also instead of "and the Lord," the translation should be, *for the Lord.* Thus the sentence should run: *for the Lord will give thee understanding in all things.* Some difficulty has been found in explaining exactly why, when we look at the foregoing words, Timothy should be so specially charged to consider St. Paul's words here, and why the declaration respecting "understanding in all things" was made in this particular place. Theophylact suggested because the preceding exhortations were in the form of metaphors, "he spake all things in an enigmatical form:" but surely these metaphors were the reverse of obscure, and did not seem to need for their comprehension any special enlightenment; if then we refer the words of this verse exclusively to what precedes, it will be best to understand the charge of St. Paul, "Consider what I say," &c., as directing Timothy's attention to the *personal* application of each of the pictures, or metaphors. It seems, however, that the words "Consider," &c., while referring to what he *had* said, belong also to the far weightier words he was about to write in the next sentence (verse 8). He is in this chapter exhorting Timothy to be strong in the faith in the face of many troubles. He has instanced to him earthly examples to show how success, even *here,* depends on enduring perseverance, and is now passing on to set before him other and far higher inducements for him "to be strong;" and between the first set of arguments and the second he bids him "Consider what I say" (part has been said, but yet other and deeper things are to follow). God will give him power to grasp their meaning in all their depth.

(8) **Remember that Jesus Christ of the seed of David was raised from the dead.**—More accurately rendered, *Remember Jesus Christ . . . as raised* (or, *as one raised*). The words of the Greek original, "of the seed of David," come after, not before, "was raised from the dead." The translation should run thus: *Remember Jesus Christ as one raised from the dead, born of the seed of David.* Timothy was to remember, was ever to bear in mind, two great facts. They were to be the foundation stones of his whole life's work. Remembering these in the hour of his greatest trouble, he was never to be cast down, but ever to take fresh courage. And the two facts he was to remember were: that Jesus Christ, for whose sake he suffered—like him, Timothy, or like St. Paul—was born of flesh and blood, and yet He had risen from the dead. Surely, in the hour of his weakness, such a thought would be sufficient to inspire him with comfort and courage. Two facts, then, are to be ever in Timothy's mind: the Resurrection and the Incarnation of his Lord. The thought of the first mentioned, "the Resurrection," would always be reminding him of his Master's victory over death and of His present glory. The thought of the second mentioned, "born of the seed of David," "the Incarnation," would ever be whispering to him, "Yes, and the risen and glorified One sprang, too, like himself, from mortal flesh and blood." The reason of the "Incarnation" being expressed in this special manner, "born of the seed of David," was to include another truth. The "risen One" was not only born of flesh and blood, but belonged to the very race specified in those prophets so revered by Timothy and the chosen people as *the* race from which should spring the Messiah: "Behold, the days come, saith the Lord, that I will raise unto David a righteous Branch, and a King shall reign and prosper, and shall execute judgment and justice in the earth . . . and this is His name whereby He shall be called, THE LORD OUR RIGHTEOUSNESS" (Jer. xxiii. 5, 6). To raise the fainting heart of his much-tried disciple in this hour of discouragement, to supply a ground of confidence to yet unborn Christians, who in their day would be tried as Timothy was then, was the Apostle's first purpose when he pressed these thoughts on his son in the faith; but in the background, no doubt, there lay another purpose. These great comforting truths were to be maintained and taught in the presence of those false teachers who were ever ready to explain away or even to deny, *then as now,* the beginning and the end of the Son of God's life and ministry on earth—His Incarnation and His Resurrection.

According to my gospel.—This formula, for so it may be considered, occurs frequently in St. Paul's Epistles (Rom. ii. 16, and again xvi. 25, and in other places), and, with very slight variations, in 1 Tim. i. 11 and 1 Cor. xv. 1. Jerome's remark, "As often as St. Paul in his Epistles writes '*according to my Gospel,*' he refers to the volume of Luke," although received with reserve by many expositors, considering the weighty traditional evidence we possess of St. Luke's Gospel being in reality written by St. Paul, appears on the whole substantially correct.

(9) **Wherein I suffer trouble.**—Here St. Paul bids Timothy take courage, by thinking of the brave, patient example he was setting him in his Roman prison, undaunted and full of hope. "Wherein I suffer:" in which, that is, discharging my office as a preacher of the gospel, I suffer trouble.

As an evil doer.—Better rendered, *as a malefactor:* the same word used in St. Luke's Gospel for the two thieves crucified with Jesus Christ (Luke xxiii. 32, 33, 39).

Even unto bonds; but the word of God is not bound.—A prisoner in chains and, as he tells us further on in the Epistle, expecting death, and yet *he* still could write and pray and speak from his narrow prison. Surely his disciple, still free, ought to work on with undiminished spirit and zeal. Though St. Paul was in bonds, his sufferings and imprisonment had in no way weakened the power of the gospel.

as an evil doer, *even* unto bonds; but the word of God is not bound. (10) Therefore I endure all things for the elect's sakes, that they may also obtain the salvation which is in Christ Jesus with eternal glory. (11) *It is* a faithful saying, For if we be dead with *him*, we shall also live with *him:* (12) if we suffer, we

---

(10) **Therefore I endure all things for the elect's sakes.**—Better rendered, *For this cause I endure,* &c.—that is, I endure all things in order that the "word of God," which, unlike its preacher, I have just declared to be confined by no bonds—in order that that "word" may be widely spread and disseminated: for this reason do I, as a faithful soldier at my post, bear up with quiet, patient courage against suffering; and I do it for the elect's sakes, that is, for those whom, in His infinite mercy, God has been pleased to choose as His people, for those who, in His unfathomable love, are yet to be brought into the one fold. And this brave and steadfast endurance on the part of St. Paul contributed to the furtherance of God's projects for gathering these elect in this wise—(1) His endurance, his patient, gallant witness in suffering, would serve as an example to many, not only to the generation then living, but to countless men and women yet unborn; and (2) his faithful, true preaching, now that his voice was hushed, in such writings as this Epistle to Timothy, would help, through the ages to come, to draw countless others, in accordance with the divine counsels, into fellowship with Christ. The question has been often asked, whether those "elect" for whom the Apostle endured these things were, when he wrote these words, *believers.* This point has already been touched upon; it may, however, be here answered, with some certainty, that the "elect" here spoken of include both believers and unbelievers. The first—the believer—would in all ages be built up by the contemplation of the steadfastness under suffering of St. Paul; the second—the unbeliever—would be won to the faith by the divinely-inspired arguments and exhortations which the brave old man ceaselessly spoke or wrote down in prison just as when free. How could one like St. Paul, who was conscious that he himself had won the "salvation," *not patiently endure* all things, if such an endurance could help the elect to obtain that salvation which delivered those who obtained it from the misery of sin and death, and which besides—O blessed thought!—had the sure prospect of eternal glory?

(11) **For if we be dead with him, we shall also live with him.**—The last sentence ended with the words "eternal glory"—the goal, the end of the salvation which is in Christ. This it is which the Apostle will help others to win, regardless of any suffering it may cost him; then, with his mind full of the thoughts of the "eternal glory," once more he addressed himself to Timothy. "Faithful is the saying, namely, if we be dead with him," &c. It was as though he said, "Do you not remember that well-known watchword of our own faith, so often repeated among us in our solemn assemblies when the brotherhood meet together?" Many have supposed, from the rhythmical character of the clauses of verses 11, 12, 13, that this "saying" was taken from some most ancient Christian hymns, composed and used in the very earliest days of the faith; but whether or no this be the case, there is high probability that the words formed part of a liturgy in common use in the days of Timothy. If not as a hymn—which seems, on the whole, the most likely supposition—we can well conceive them as part of the tapestry of a primitive Christian liturgy, woven in like the introductory sentences in our morning and evening prayer, or like the "comfortable words" of the Communion Service. The expression "If we be dead with Him"—more accurately, *If we died with Him*—is well explained by 1 Cor. xv. 31: "I die daily." The Apostle *died* when he embraced the lot of daily death. The meaning is still further illustrated in 2 Cor. iv. 10, where we read how St. Paul and his companions were "always bearing about in the body the dying of the Lord Jesus." "He and his faithful companions (was Timothy, to whom he was then writing, to be ranked in this blessed company?) had given themselves up to a life that involved exposure to sufferings, bitter enmity, cruel persecutions, even death; but if we be thus dead with Him, what matters it? How can we fear even that last agony man can inflict on us—physical death?—for *death* with Him involves, surely, *life* with Him too: that life endless, fadeless, full of glory, we know He is now enjoying, in the possession of which I, Paul, and some of us have even seen Him, face to face, eye to eye. In that life of His we shall share; we shall be partakers in this life of His *there,* but only if we have shared in the life of suffering which was His life *here.*"

(12) **If we suffer, we shall also reign with him.**—And the faithful saying went on with this stirring declaration. How, it seems to ask, can a believer in Christ shrink from suffering, when he knows what to him will be the glorious consequences of this present suffering? The word rendered "suffer" would be better translated, *if we endure*—that is, if we bravely bear up against sufferings for His sake, and all the while work on with hand and brain for Him and for our brother as best we can. If we do this in this life, we shall, in the life to come, reign with Him—more than merely *live* with Him, as the last verse told us: we shall even "be kings with Him." (See Rom. v. 17; viii. 17; and Rev. i. 6, where Jesus Christ is especially spoken of as having made us "kings.") The promise thus woven into the faithful saying, and repeated in these several passages, of the "reign of the saints in Christ," gives us a strangely glorious hope—a marvellous onlook, concerning the active and personal work which Christ's redeemed will be intrusted with in the ages of eternity.

If we deny him, he also will deny us.—But there is another side to the words of the Blessed. While to the faithful and the believer He will grant to sit down with Him on His throne, the faithless and unbeliever will have no share in the glories of the life to come. These grave warnings are apparently addressed rather to unfaithful members of the outward and visible Church, than to the Pagan world who have never known Christ. The words, "He also will deny us," imply something of a recognition on the part of us who are denied by Him—something of an expectation on our part that He would recognise us as friends. They are evidently an echo of the Lord's own sad reply to those many who will say to Him in that day, "Lord, Lord, have we not prophesied in Thy name? . . . and then will I profess unto them, I never knew you: depart from Me, ye that work iniquity." (Matt. vii. 22, 23. See too Matt. x. 33 and Mark viii. 38.)

shall also reign with *him:* if we deny *him,* he also will deny us: (13) if we believe not, *yet* he abideth faithful: he cannot deny himself. (14) Of these things put *them* in remembrance, charging *them* before the Lord that they strive not about words to no profit, *but* to the subverting of the hearers. (15) Study to shew thyself approved unto God, a workman that needeth not to be ashamed, rightly dividing the word of truth. (16) But shun profane *and* vain babblings:

Chap. ii. 14—18 Charged to avoid disputes about mere words. The results of such vain pursuits.

(13) **If we believe not.**—Better rendered, *if we are faithless*—that is, untrue to the vows of our Christian profession. The faithlessness implies more than mere unbelief in any of the fundamental doctrines of the faith, such as the Resurrection of the Lord or His divinity.

Yet he abideth faithful: he cannot deny himself.—Those who have understood these words as containing soothing, comforting voices for the sinner, for the faithless Christian who has left his first love, are gravely mistaken. The passage is one of distinct severity—may even be termed one of the sternest in the Book of Life; for it tells how it is impossible even for the pitiful Redeemer to forgive in the future life. "He cannot deny Himself"—cannot treat the faithless as though he were faithful—cannot act as though faithfulness and faithlessness were one and the same thing. The Christian teacher, such as Timothy, and the members of his flock likewise, must remember that, sure and certain as are the promises of glory and happiness to those who love the Lord and try to live His life, so surely will fall the chastisement on all who are faithless and untrue.

With the solemn words of this "faithful saying" St. Paul closes this, the second division of his Epistle—fellowship in the sufferings of Christ *here,* on this side the grave, and fellowship in the glory of Christ *there,* on the other side the grave—the one side was the sure consequence of the other; the one could not exist without the other.

(14) **Of these things put them in remembrance.**—A new division of the Epistle begins with this 14th verse. St. Paul has been urging Timothy to be strong in endurance, to bear trouble and suffering with brave patience. He now proceeds to charge him respecting the special work he has to do; and, first he deals with his duties as a teacher of truth brought face to face with teachers of error. He prefaces his directions by bidding him, in the forefront of his teaching, "put them" (that is, those over whom he was placed: the members of his Ephesian flock) "in remembrance of these things"—namely. of those great and solemn truths set forth in verses 11—13, and which may be briefly summed up in the words: "Fellowship with Christ in suffering will be succeeded by fellowship with Christ in glory." Surely such lofty, soul-inspiring thoughts as these will form the best safeguard against the pitiful controversies and disputes about words, which were occupying the thoughts and wasting the lives of so many in Ephesus called by the name of Christ.

Charging them before the Lord.—Better rendered, *solemnly charging them before the Lord* . . . In all Timothy's solemn addresses to his flock he is, St. Paul reminds him, charging his people "before the Lord"—a very earnest, solemn thought for every public teacher, and one calculated *now,* as *then,* to deepen the life of one appointed to such an office. There was a grave danger that such empty, profitless disputes about words and expressions, which, we know, occupied the attention of many of the Ephesian so-called Christian teachers, would end in distracting the minds of the members of the several congregations, who would naturally take their tone, in matters connected with religious life, from their teacher; and thus words would soon come to be substituted for acts in the lives of those men and women called by the name of Christ in Ephesus. (See 1 Tim. vi. 4, where these "strifes of words" are mentioned among the special characteristics of the false teachers.)

But to the subverting of the hearers.—Not only are such arguments and disputes useless and profitless, but they are positively mischievous. In the long history of Christianity, St. Paul's repeated warning respecting the danger of these disputes about theological terms and expressions has been sadly verified. Such contentions serve only to unsettle the mind, only to shake true faith, only to distract the one who gives himself up to this fatal pursuit, from real, earnest, patient work for Christ.

(15) **Study to shew thyself approved unto God, a workman that needeth not to be ashamed.**—Timothy, and those in the position of Timothy, were to show themselves approved unto God, by turning others, over whom they possessed influence, from the pursuit of vain and unprofitable things. Then their work would be the work of workmen tested by trial, and would be found to have stood the test. (Comp. here 1 Cor. iii. 10—15, where the final testing of the work done by God's workmen, such as Timothy, is spoken of in very clear, heart-searching language.) His own words in the First Epistle to the Corinthians were evidently in St. Paul's mind when he wrote down this direction to Timothy.

Rightly dividing the word of truth.—Better rendered *rightly laying out the word of truth.* The Greek word translated in the English version "rightly dividing," literally signifies "cutting a straight line." It seems most correct to regard it as a metaphor from laying out a road (see Prov. iii. 6, in the LXX. rendering, where the word is so used), "or drawing a furrow, the merit of which consists in the straightness with which the work of cutting, or laying out, is performed. The word of truth is, as it were, a road which is to be laid out straightly and truly." So Ellicott. To affirm (see Alford and Huther-Meyer) that the notion of "cutting" had been gradually lost, and that the word already in the time of St. Paul signified simply "to manage rightly," "to treat truthfully without falsifying," and that the exact opposite is to corrupt or adulterate the Word of God (2 Cor. ii. 17), seems premature. (Comp. Eur. *Rhesus,* 422, ed. Dindorf.)

In the third century, Clement of Alexandria (*Stromata,* vii.), for instance, certainly uses the word in a sense in which the idea of "cutting" has been lost, when he writes *orthotomia* (a substantive) as an equivalent for *orthodoxia*—orthodoxy. It is not improbable that the use of the word here by St. Paul gave the word a fresh starting-point, and that gradually the original meaning passed out of sight.

(16) **But shun profane and vain babblings.**—

for they will increase unto more ungod-
liness. (17) And their word will eat as
doth a canker[1]: of whom is Hymenæus
and Philetus; (18) who concerning the
truth have erred, saying that the resur-
rection is past already; and overthrow
the faith of some. (19) Nevertheless the
foundation of God standeth
sure,[2] having this seal, The
Lord knoweth them that
are his. And, Let every
one that nameth the name

1 Or, *gangrene.* 2 Or, *steady.*

Chap. ii. 19. The Church of God under the figure of a foundation.

But, in strong contrast to the conduct just urged, on the workman of God, *do thou avoid* (or, *withdraw thyself from*) *vain babblings.* The word rendered "shun" is a strong one, and signifies literally, to make a circuit so as to avoid; or, as Alford paraphrases it, "the meaning seems to come from a number of persons falling back from an object of fear or loathing, and standing at a distance round it." The word is used in Titus iii. 9. On the words "profane," "vain-babblings," see 1 Tim. vi. 20.

For they will increase unto more ungodliness.—Better translated, *for they will advance unto* . . . The tendency of these useless discussions and idle disputes is to lead men into vain and profitless speculations, which end too often—as in the case, cited below, of Hymenæus and Philetus—in the most fatal doctrinal error. The close connection between grave fundamental errors in doctrine and a lax and purely selfish life is constantly alluded to by St. Paul.

(17) **And their word will eat as doth a canker.**—Better rendered, as in the margin of the English translation, *as doth a gangrene,* the usual rendering of the various English versions. "Cancer," which is adopted also by Luther—krebs—fails to express the terrible and deathly nature of the "word" of these false teachers. The life of the sufferer afflicted with cancer may be prolonged for many years; a few hours, however, is sufficient to put a term to the life of the patient attacked with "gangrene," unless the limb affected be at once cut away. To translate this Greek word here by "cancer" is to water down the original, in which St. Paul expresses his dread of the fatal influence of the words of these teachers on the lives of many of the flock of Christ. Perhaps Jerome's words, "a perverse doctrine, beginning with one, at the commencement scarcely finds two or three listeners; but little by little the cancer creeps through the body" (Jerome, in *Epist. ad Gal.*), has suggested the rendering of the English Version.

Of whom is Hymenæus and Philetus.—Of these false teachers nothing is known beyond the mention, in the First Epistle to Timothy, of Hymenæus, who, regardless of the severe action which had been taken against him (1 Tim. i. 20), was apparently still continuing in his error. Vitringa thinks they were Jews, and probably Samaritans. Their names are simply given as examples of the teachers of error to whom St. Paul was referring—famous leaders, no doubt, in their cheerless school of doctrine.

(18) **Who concerning the truth have erred.**—Or, *have erred,* or, more literally, *have missed their aim.* (See Note on 1 Tim. vi. 21.)

The resurrection of the body, grounded upon the Lord's own words (John v. 28, 29), was one of the Articles of the Christian faith upon which St. Paul especially loved to dwell. (See, for instance, his words before Felix—Acts xxiv. 15.) With this "resurrection of the body" St. Paul, prompted by the Holy Ghost, taught men that the future state of rewards and punishments was intimately bound up; the soul will be clothed with a body of glory or with a body of shame, according to the deeds done in the flesh. This doctrine appears, in very early times, to have been questioned by some in the Christian community. Then, as now, was the thought repugnant to the shrinking soul of man,—that the body in which he then lived and sinned would rise again.

Elaborated, but still scarcely disguised, the same denial of a bodily resurrection was a characteristic of the more important of the widely-spread Gnostic systems of the second and third centuries.

These early Christian followers of men like Hymenæus and Philetus had much in common with the ascetic Jewish sects of Essenes and Therapeutæ, and especially with the famous Sadducean school, which attracted then so many cultured and wealthy Jews. They opposed, to use Van Oosterzee's words, "their own sickly idealism to St. Paul's strong and healthy realism." Death and resurrection, with these early opponents of St. Paul, were terms which had only a spiritual meaning and application. As Waterland puts it, "They allegorised away the doctrine, and turned all into figures and metaphors."

Another consideration must not be lost sight of when we are considering the reasons for St. Paul's fiery indignation with this unhappy school of dreamers. In attacking, with their thinly-veiled scepticism, the great doctrine of the resurrection of the body, in pushing aside the glorious hope, they touched with their impious hands the corner-stone of all Christian belief—*the resurrection in the body of the Redeemer. This* Resurrection was indeed past already.

(19) **Nevertheless the foundation of God standeth sure.**—Better rendered, *Nevertheless God's firm foundation standeth.* Nevertheless, that is to say, though some may be shaken in faith by the unhappy teaching above referred to, yet assuredly God's firm foundation stands unshaken. "The firm foundation laid by God" is the Church of Christ, which is here termed *a foundation* laid by God, because it, the Church of Christ, is the ground-storey of the glorious Temple of the future. In other words, the Church of Christ is here considered as the foundation of a far grander building, which, in the fulness of time, will rest upon its massive work (see Eph. ii. 19—21); and this ground-storey, the corner-stone of which is Christ, "standeth" age after age, in spite of any efforts which may be made to destroy or even to shake it. The term "foundation," here used for the Church of God on earth, is remarkable, and points to a great truth: that, after all, this life is but a beginning, and that "His Church" here is but a foundation—is only the first and early storey of that glorious Church the Divine Architect has planned, and will complete in heaven.

Having this seal.—It was a custom, which dates back from the very earliest times, to inscribe upon a building or a monument an inscription which told of its origin and purpose. In some cases, as in the oldest monuments of Egypt, the engraved writing told the name of the royal or priestly builder; so in Rev. xxi. 14, we read how in the wall of the City of God there

of Christ depart from iniquity. (20) But in a great house there are not only vessels of gold and of silver, but also of wood and of earth; and some to honour, and some to dishonour. (21) If a man therefore purge himself from these, he shall be a vessel unto honour, sanctified, and meet for the

Chap. ii. 20. Good men and evil exist together.

Chap. ii. 21—26. The work of a good man.

were twelve foundations, and on them were engraved the names of the Twelve Apostles of the Lamb. On this "foundation storey," of which St. Paul was now speaking, was carved a legible inscription in two sentences—the one told of comfort and hope, reminding men God would ever know "His own;" the other told of duty, reminding men that "God's own" had no share in unrighteousness. It is called "a seal" here instead of an inscription, for a seal best conveys the idea of the solemn binding character of the writing.

The Jew was especially accustomed to see the words and promises of his God written or graven on his door-posts and on his gates. (See Deut. vi. 9; xi. 20. See, too, the words of Job xix. 24, where he would have his most solemn declaration of faith graven or sealed on a rock for ever.)

The Lord knoweth them that are his.—This was the first sentence of the inscription graven on the foundation-storey. The *words* were probably a memory of Num. xvi. 5; but the *thought* here goes far deeper. God's own people, as they read the words graven on the foundation "with an iron pen and with lead for ever," are ever reminded of their deepest, highest, truest comfort. "The Lord *knoweth* them that are His." The words may be paraphrased: "He knows His own because He loves them;" never will He cease to know them, but will keep them for ever and for ever. Compare, too, the words of the Good Shepherd (John x. 14, 27—29).

And, Let every one that nameth the name of Christ depart from iniquity.—The thought and the words are from the Old Testament. The thought is expressed in a wider and more general form in Isa. lii. 11: "Depart ye, depart ye, go ye out from thence, touch no unclean thing . . . Be ye clean, that bear the vessels of the Lord;" and for the words "nameth the name of the Lord," see Isaiah xxvi. 13. "Naming the name of Jesus" must be understood in the sense of the last clause of 1 Cor. xii. 3; in other words, this sentence of the inscription signifies that no man confessing with the *heart* that Jesus is Lord can commit iniquity deliberately—the two things are utterly incompatible. "Iniquity" here includes the teaching of those false men above alluded to, as their teaching led away from the truth, and resulted in a lax and evil way of life.

(20) **But in a great house there are not only vessels of gold and of silver.**—The Apostle goes on with the same thought of the "Church of God on earth," but he changes the imagery. He has been speaking of this Church as the "foundation-storey that cannot be moved" of a still more glorious edifice. He now, as it were, answers a question which would naturally occur to Timothy and to many a devout reader or hearer of the Epistle when they came to this part of the argument. How comes it, then, one would ask, that in this visible Church on earth are so many unworthy members? How is it that in this changeless, abiding foundation of the great Temple of the future, against which all earthly storms may beat, and yet never shake its massive storeys, so many useless crumbling stones are taken for the building?

In a great house, argues St. Paul—still thinking of the Church, but changing the foundation image for that of a great house—are always found two distinct kinds of vessels—the precious and enduring, and also the comparatively valueless and lasting for but a little while; the first kind are destined for honour, the second for dishonour. In St. Paul's mind, when he wrote these words, the natural sequel to his far-reaching and suggestive comparison of the "foundation" (verse 19) were the words of his Master, who had once compared His Church to a drag-net of wide sweep, including in its take something of every kind out of the vast sea-world. The "net"—His Church—was to gather and to hold in its meshes its great take—the good and the bad, the useful and the useless—*till the end of the world*. So St. Paul writes how in a great house there must be these varieties of vessels—some for honour, others for dishonour. By these vessels the genuine and spurious members of the Church are represented as forming two distinct classes; and in these classes different degrees of honour and dishonour besides exist—the vessels of gold and silver, the vessels of wood and of earth. To Timothy these comparisons would at once suggest the true and false teachers in his Church at Ephesus; but the reference is a far broader one, and includes *all* members of the Church of Christ. The enduring nature of the metals gold and silver are contrasted with the perishable nature of the other materials, wood and earth. The former will remain a part of the Church for ever; the latter will only endure until the end of the world.

(21) **If a man therefore purge himself from these.**—Again the reference is general, but there was a special thought for Timothy when St. Paul wrote this. If *he* would separate from all that was evil in his Church at Ephesus, then would he indeed be one of those golden vessels unto honour. The image of the great house, and its many and varied vessels, though still not quite lost sight of, is passing out of sight. This verse changes into a note of direct exhortation. The good and faithful must separate themselves from the evil and faithless. The thought of those deniers of the resurrection of the body was uppermost in St. Paul's mind. There must, as it has been well said, be no communion on the part of God's servants with impugners of fundamentals. It was imperatively necessary for Timothy—and, by implication, for all members of Christ's Church—if they aimed at becoming vessels for honour in the great Temple, to break off from all Church fellowship, from all intimate friendship, with those above referred to under the image of wooden or earthen vessels.

He shall be a vessel unto honour.—Chrysostom's note upon these words is somewhat remarkable. He points out the possibility of the vessel for dishonour becoming a vessel for honour, and the reverse; and refers to St. Paul, once an earthen vessel, who became a vessel of gold, and to the traitor Judas, who, on the other hand, from being a vessel of gold became an earthen vessel.

Meet for the master's use.—Or, *useful for the master* (of the house). "Useful," as the next sentence shows us, through those good works by means of which

master's use, *and* prepared unto every
good work. (22) Flee also youthful lusts:
but follow righteousness, faith, charity,
peace, with them that call on the Lord
out of a pure heart. (23) But foolish and
unlearned questions avoid, knowing that
they do gender strifes. (24) And the
servant of the Lord must not strive;
but be gentle unto all *men*, apt to
teach, patient,[1] (25) in meekness in-
structing those that oppose them-
selves; if God peradventure will give

1 Or, *forbearing.*

others' needs are ministered to, and the salvation of others is furthered, and the glory of God is increased.

Prepared unto every good work.—"Prepared"—that is, ready to take advantage of any opportunity which may offer itself to do a generous, noble action. So, too, Chrysostom, who would have the "vessel unto honour" ready for every emergency which would enhance the glory of the Lord—ready even for death, or (any painful) witness.

(22) **Flee also youthful lusts.**—But he who would *indeed* become a "vessel for honour" in that great house of God must do more than merely separate himself from all outward communion and friendship with men who, by their teaching and in their lives, did dishonour to the Master's religion. There was an *inner* work to be accomplished, as well as an outer and more public protest to be made. He must fight with and conquer those lusts, passions, and desires which are more peculiarly tempting to those who are still in the meridian of life. That Timothy was not now in early manhood has been already shown. He was at this time, probably, between thirty and forty years of age. These youthful lusts are by no means to be limited to those varied and fatal excesses summed up in the Seventh Commandment. A victory over these, of course, is imperatively necessary for one who would be "of use" in the house of his God: but such a one must train himself to subdue other and far more subtle lusts than are included in these. He must be watchful and stamp down all covetousness, whether of rank or gold; all longing for empty shows; all pride, conceit, readiness to take offence; all the kindred forms of love of self.

But follow righteousness, faith, charity. See Note on 1 Tim. vi. 11, where the same charge occurs.

Peace.—This last, "peace," must be joined with the words immediately following: "with them that call on the Lord," &c. The "peace" here signifies absence of contention: it is well paraphrased by, "that spiritual concord which unites together all who call upon and who love their Lord," Theodoret thus draws a distinction between "love" and "peace":—"It is possible *to love* all, and this the gospel law enjoins us in the words, 'Love your enemies:' but *to be at peace* with all is not possible." The words "out of a pure heart" contrast those holy and humble men of heart who serve God without any ulterior motive, with those false teachers who dare to make their religion a gain, a source of profit.

(23) **But foolish and unlearned questions avoid.**—The Greek word translated "unlearned" is better rendered *ignorant.* These "questions" which, as we have seen above, the false teachers, with whom Timothy was so much thrown, loved to put forward for discussion, could hardly be termed "unlearned"—much useless learning being often thrown away in these disputings of the schools—but were rather "pointless," "stupid," as well as foolish. The nature of these questions of controversy has been discussed above.

Knowing that they do gender strifes.—Knowing—as thou dost—from sad and frequent experience, what conflicts, heart-burnings, estrangements, these abstract questions between rival teachers and rival sects engendered.

(24) **And the servant of the Lord must not strive.**—Although these directions and commandments in all cases belong to God's servants of every degree and calling, yet some of them, as we should expect from the nature of the Epistle, peculiarly apply to Timothy and those like Timothy specially devoted to the ministry of the Word. And so here everything which is likely to be the cause of strife, heart-burning, or hot words, is, St. Paul urges, singularly out of place in the life of a servant of that Lord who fulfilled to the letter that Isaiah prophecy of Messiah, "He shall not strive, nor cry; neither shall any man hear His voice in the streets." (See Matt. xii. 19—20.)

But be gentle unto all men.—Quiet and kind, not only to those belonging to the brotherhood of Christ, but, as is expressly mentioned, *to all.* It is noteworthy how, in these Pastoral Epistles—which contain, so to speak, the last general directions to believers in Jesus as to life as well as doctrine of perhaps the greatest of the inspired teachers—so many careful suggestions are given for the guidance of Christians in all their relations with the great heathen world. *Conciliation* may be termed the key-note of these directions. St. Paul would press upon Timothy and his successors the great truth that it was the Master's will that the unnumbered peoples who sit in darkness and in the shadow of death should learn, by slow though sure degrees, how lovely and desirable a thing it was to be a Christian; should come at length to see clearly that Christ was, after all, the only lover and real friend of man.

Apt to teach, patient.—The Greek word is better rendered by the *forbearing* of the margin than by "patient." *Patient of wrong*, however, best gives the full force of the original. This is what the servant of God should really aim at being: the teacher rather than the controversialist—rather the patient endurer of wrong than the fomenter of dissensions and wordy strifes.

(25) **In meekness instructing those that oppose themselves.**—By "those that oppose themselves," St. Paul alludes scarcely so much to those leading teachers of false doctrine as to those led away by them. In Titus iii. 10 we read how these pronounced heretics—no doubt the teachers and leaders of the school—were, after a first and second admonition, to be shunned, were to be left to themselves. These, however, were evidently to be dealt with in a different manner. Their treatment was to be a gentle one. Nothing is here said respecting a first and second admonition only; no hint is given that these are to be shunned. They are clearly not the same as those referred to in Titus iii. 10, or above in verse 21 of this chapter, where, again, separation is definitely urged.

If God peradventure will give them repentance.—The Greek original here also carries out what was said in the Note on the last clause, and may be

them repentance to the acknowledg-
ing of the truth; (26) and *that* they
may recover[1] themselves out of the
snare of the devil, who are taken cap-
tive[2] by him at his will.

A.D. 66.

1 Gr. *awake.*

2 Gr. *taken alive.*

CHAPTER III.—(1) This know also,
that in the last days peril-
ous times shall come. (2) For
men shall be lovers of their
own selves, covetous, boasters, proud,

Chap. iii. 1—9. The vices of the last days.

---

rendered literally, *if perchance at any time God might grant to them . . .* This suggests a hope at least that at some time or other God's grace would work in these "opposing" members of the congregation a change. The "repentance" here signifies an abandonment on the part of those erring Christians of that wrong course on which they had entered, and a return to the true Church of God and to the full knowledge of the gospel truth.

(26) **That they may recover themselves.**—The literal meaning of the Greek word rendered "that they may recover themselves" is *that they may awake from drunkenness.* The English version, however, gives the meaning with great exactness. Those taken in the snare of the devil are represented as not only captives in the snare of the devil, but as also helplessly wrapped in slumber.

The deadly peril of all "captives of sin" is here well painted. These unhappy ones, before they can free themselves from the toils of the evil one, must awake from the deep slumber in which they are wrapped: in other words, must first be *conscious* of their awful danger.

Who are taken captive by him at his will.—These words have been variously interpreted by commentators. The meaning that, on the whole, seems most satisfactory, represents the captive to sin waking up from his deathly slumber and escaping the toils of the evil one, for the purpose of carrying out for the future the will of God. The rendering of the whole verse would be as follows: "*And that they may recover themselves out of the snare of the devil—being held captive by him—to do His* (God's) *will.*"

It must be remembered that the first pronoun in this sentence, "being held captive by him," referred here to the devil, and the second pronoun in the sentence, "to do *His* will," referred here to God, are represented in the Greek by two distinct words: the first by αὐτοῦ, the second by ἐκείνου.

III.

(1) **This know also.**—Better rendered, *But know this.* The Apostle had warned Timothy (chap. ii. 3—13) not to allow fear of oncoming peril and trouble to paralyse his efforts in the Master's cause, for the Lord's true servant should never lose heart, and then had proceeded (chap. ii. 14—26) to detail how these efforts of his were to be directed, showing him how his teaching should stand in contrast with that of the false teachers. St. Paul now (chap. iii. 1), having told him that although there was no reason to fear, yet warns him that grave dangers to the Church *would* surely arise, and that God's servants, like Timothy, must be prepared to combat.

In the last days.—The majority of commentators have referred "the last days" here spoken of to the period immediately preceding the second coming of the Lord—a day and an hour somewhere in the future but hidden, not merely from all men, but from the angels, and even from the Son (Mark xiii. 32).

It seems, however, more in accordance with such passages as 1 John ii. 18: "Little children, it is the last time"—where *the present,* and not an uncertain future is alluded to—to understand "the last days" as that period, probably of very long duration, extending from the days of the first coming of Messiah—in which time St. Paul lived—to the second coming of Christ in judgment. The Jewish Rabbis of the days of St. Paul were in the habit of speaking of two great periods of the world's history—"this age," and "the age to come." The former of these, "this age," including all periods up to Messiah's advent; the latter, "the age to come," including all periods subsequent to the appearance of Messiah. We find the same idea embodied later in the Talmud (treatise "Sanhedrim") 6,000 years are mentioned as the duration of the world, 2,000 years, waste or chaos, 2,000 years under the law, 2,000 years the days of Messiah." This last period, "the days of Messiah," are often alluded to by the Hebrew prophets under the expression, "in the last days"—literally, *in the end of days.* (See Isa. ii. 2; Hos. iii. 5; Mic. iv. 1.) The words of verse 5, "from such turn away," would require certainly a strained interpretation if we are to suppose that the "last days" referred to a time immediately preceding the end, or, in other words, the last period of the Christian era. The sad catalogue of vices is, alas, one with which all ages of the Church of Christ has been too well acquainted. The Christian teacher has no need to look forward to a future time of deeper iniquity, when in the Church of the living God will be found those who will deserve the dreary titles of this passage. The Church of his own age will supply him with examples of many such, for "In a great house . . . are there not only vessels of gold and silver, but also of wood, and earth, and some to honour and some to dishonour."

(2) **For men shall be lovers of their own selves.**—Hofmann and others have attempted to portion out these vices into groups. But any such effort seems artificial. A certain connection seems to exist in some part; but when pressed to preserve the groups, a strained meaning has to be given to some of the terms. It seems, therefore, best simply to understand the catalogue as representing the various more prominent vices which appeared on the surface of Christian society, and threatened the very existence of the Church, even in those early times when Timothy ruled over the congregations of Christians at Ephesus. Hofmann, however, divides the catalogue contained in verses 2—4 into three groups, consisting of five, six, and seven terms, respectively.

Lovers of their own selves.—Selfishness well heads the dreary list. It is the true root of all sin.

Covetous.—More accurately rendered, *lovers of money.* This "love of money" has been happily termed "the daughter of selfishness."

Boasters.—Those who arrogate to themselves honour which does not fairly belong to them.

Proud.—These are they who contemptuously look down on others beneath them, either in social position or wealth, or perhaps in natural gifts. The Latin, *ostentatio,* represents the vice which affects the first of these classes—"the boasters;" and *superbia,* that which affects the second class—"the proud."

blasphemers, disobedient to parents, unthankful, unholy, (3) without natural affection, trucebreakers, false accusers,[1] incontinent, fierce, despisers of those that are good, (4) traitors, heady, highminded, lovers of pleasures more than lovers of God; (5) having a form of godliness, but denying the power thereof: from such turn away. (6) For of this sort are they which creep into houses,

1 Or, *make-bates.*

Blasphemers.—The two vices just mentioned refer to man's conduct to his brother man; this alludes to his behaviour towards his God. The pride with which he looks down on his fellows develops itself into insolence in thought, if not in word, towards his God: and this is termed blasphemy.

Disobedient to parents.—The blasphemer of the Father which is in heaven is only too likely to train up little ones who, in their turn, will display a disobedience and disrespect of their earthly parents. The home life of the man who chooses not to know God in his heart will too easily reflect his evil thoughts and senseless pride.

Unthankful.—Or, *ungrateful.* The children who begin life with disobedience to their parents, with rare exceptions, are ungrateful to all others who may show them kindness in their life journey.

Unholy.—Unholy through their want of inward purity. (See 1 Tim. i. 9.)

(3) **Without natural affection.**—Careless and regardless of the welfare of those connected with them by ties of blood.

Trucebreakers.—Better rendered, *implacable.*

False-accusers.—Or, *slanderers.* (See 1 Tim. iii. 11.)

Incontinent.—Having no control over the passions.

Fierce.—Inhuman, savage, or merciless.

Despisers of those that are good.—Better rendered, *no lovers of good*—that is, hostile to every good thought and work.

(4) **Traitors.**—Or, *betrayers,* probably, as it has been suggested, of their Christian brethren. (Comp. Luke vi. 16, where this epithet is used of Judas Iscariot, "which also was the traitor;" and also Acts vii. 52, where Stephen, in his Sanhedrin speech, uses this term "betrayers" of the Jews, "of whom—the Just One—ye have been now the betrayers." In these days of Timothy, and for many a long year, to inform against the believers in Jesus of Nazareth, to give information of their places of meeting in times of persecution, was often a profitable though a despicable work.

Heady.—Better rendered, *headstrong* in words, or thoughts, or actions.

Highminded.—Better translated, *blinded by pride.* (See 1 Tim. iii. 6.)

Lovers of pleasures more than lovers of God.—Men who would make any sacrifice to procure a fleeting pleasure, and who would give nothing up in order to do honour to the eternal but invisible God. Need the ministers of the Lord tarry for the last period preceding the return of Messiah for judgment—when a still more awful iniquity shall reign—for examples of these short-sighted mortals? The sorrowful catalogue began with "love of self," that unhappy vice which excludes all love for others; it closes with that "love of pleasure" which shuts out all love of God.

(5) **Having a form of godliness, but denying the power thereof.**—Keeping up a show of observing the outward forms of religion, but renouncing its power and its influence over the heart and the life; showing openly that they neither acknowledged its guidance or wished to do so. These, by claiming the title of Christians, wearing before men the uniform of Christ, but by their lives dishonouring His name, did the gravest injury to the holy Christian cause. Another dreary catalogue of vices St. Paul gives in the Epistle to the Romans (Rom. i. 29, and following verses); but in that passage he paints the sins of Paganism. Here he describes the characteristics of a new Paganism, which went under the name of Christianity.

From such turn away.—*These,* daring to assume the sacred name, no doubt with the thought of claiming its glorious promises, without one effort to please the Master or to do honour to His name—*these* were to be openly shunned by such as Timothy. No half measures were to be adopted towards *these,* who tried to deceive their neighbours and possibly deceived themselves. The Pagan was to be courteously entreated, for in God's good time the glory of the Lord might shine, too, on those now sitting in darkness and in the shadow of death. The heretic, seduced by false men from the school of the Apostles, where the life as well as the doctrine of Jesus was taught, was to be gently instructed. Perhaps God would lead him once more home. But *these,* who, while pretending to belong to Jesus, lived the degraded life of the heathen, were to be shunned. No communion, no friendly intercourse was possible between the hypocrite and the Christian.

The command here is so definite—"from these turn away"—that any theory which would relegate the vices just enumerated to a distant future would require, as above stated, that a strained and unnatural meaning should be given to this positive direction to Timothy. The plain and obvious signification of the passage is: men committing the sins alluded to lived *then* in the Church over which Timothy presided; they were to be avoided by the chief presbyter and his brethren.

(6) **For of this sort are they which creep into houses, and lead captive silly women.**—The corrupting influence of these hypocritical professors of the religion of Jesus must have been already great, and the danger to all real vital godliness in Ephesus imminent, for Paul here specifies one of the most—perhaps *the most*—successful work of these toilers for Satan: the power they were acquiring over women. As we shall see, these unhappy men busied themselves in securing popularity among the female portion of the flock in the Ephesian Church, and the way by which they won their popularity was by supplying anodynes for the guilty consciences of these women, laden, we are told, with sins The expression, "which creep into houses," although perfectly natural, and one which, even in these Western countries, could be used with propriety to express the method in which these deceiving and perverting men make their way into households, yet, when we remember the comparative state of seclusion in which women usually lived and still live in Eastern lands, the words used by Paul acquire an increased force. Special fraud and deceit was needful for these false teachers to creep into the women's apartments in Asia. The Greek word translated "lead captive" is a peculiar one, and is only found in comparatively later Greek. It is supposed to be a word of Alexandrian or Macedonian origin. It here represents these women as wholly

and lead captive silly women laden with
sins, led away with divers lusts, (7) ever
learning, and never able to come to the
knowledge of the truth. (8) Now as
Jannes and Jambres withstood Moses,
so do these also resist the truth: men

under the influence of these bad men, to the utter destruction of all true, healthy, home life. The Greek word translated "silly women," in the Vulgate "mulierculas," is simply a diminutive, expressing contempt. There is no doubt but that the older Heresiarchs made great use of women in the propagation of their new and strange systems. They worked more easily, perhaps, on the impulsive and emotional female mind; but what has never sufficiently been taken into account is the reaction which was *then* taking place among women, so long relegated to an inferior and subordinate position, and now, by the teaching of Christ and His Apostles, raised to a position of equality with men as regards the hope of future glory. In many instances, in the first ages of Christianity, there is no doubt, but that they misunderstood their position; they claimed work they could never do, and aimed after an influence they could never exercise, and thus, no doubt, in these first feverish years many a woman fell a comparatively easy prey to these proselytisers, who, laying claim to a higher and deeper wisdom, proposed now to lead some into the knowledge of profound and hidden mysteries, now offered ease of conscience to others if they would but follow them. Irenæus, in the second century, speaks of the special power which the Valentinian Gnostic Marcus had acquired over women; and Epiphanius, in the same century, also refers to the Gnostics' deceitful influence with the female sex. Jerome, in an interesting though rhetorical passage (*Epist. ad Ctesiphontem*), cites a number of instances in which a woman shared in the baleful influence exercised by the leading masters of heresy in doctrine and laxity of life.

Simon Magus, he tells us, was accompanied by the wicked Helen. Nicolas, of Antioch, a teacher of immorality, gathered round him what Jerome calls *choros fœmineos.* Montanus is associated with the well-known names of Maximilla and Prisca. Donatus is coupled with Lucilla. Marcion, Arius, Priscillian, and other Heresiarchs, famous in the annals of the early churches, he speaks of as intimately associated with or supported by female influence.

Laden with sins, led away with divers lusts.—This gives us some insight into the source of the power which these false teachers acquired over those women of Ephesus who *in name* were Christians. They had accepted the faith of Christ, but were unable to live His life; over their passions and lusts had these no mastery. "Laden with sins," and "led away with divers lusts," these weak women fell an easy prey to men who procured them, by means of their lying doctrines, a false peace. By their words they seemed to have lulled the consciences of their female listeners to sleep. They showed them, no doubt, how in *their* school they might still be Christians and yet indulge their divers lusts.

(7) **Ever learning, and never able to come to the knowledge of the truth.**—A morbid love of novelty, and a hope to penetrate into mysteries not revealed to God's true teachers, spurred these female learners on; but "to the *full* knowledge of the truth"—for this is the more accurate rendering of the Greek word—they never reached, for by their evil life their heart was hardened. That some of these false teachers laid claim to occult arts, to a knowledge of magic and sorcery, is clear from the statement contained in the next verse, where certain sorcerers of the time of Moses are compared to them.

(8) **Now as Jannes and Jambres withstood Moses.**—To one brought up, like Timothy, by a pious Jewish mother, and who from a child knew the Holy Scriptures and all the history and ancient traditions connected with the early history of the people, such a comparison would be very striking. No child of Israel could hear the name of Moses, the loved hero of the chosen people, unmoved; and to be told that these false teachers of Ephesus stood in the same relation to him and the Church of Christ as, in old days—in the never-to-be-forgotten Egyptian episode—those famous magicians Jannes and Jambres stood to Moses, would throw for Timothy a new light on all the words and works of these wicked and ambitious men. We can well imagine the comparison being repeated in many an assembly of the faithful, long after the great Apostle's death: how St. Paul had likened these early Heresiarchs to those evil men who before Pharaoh had dared to resist God and His servant Moses. These magicians, also termed wise men and sorcerers (Ex. vii. 11—22) at the court of Pharaoh, appear as the enemies of Moses. The names "Jannes" and "Jambres," though not given in the sacred text, are preserved in the oral tradition of Israel. The names are found in the Targum of Jonathan on Ex. vii. 11; xxii. 22. These traditions relate how these men were sons of Balaam, and in the first instance were the instructors of Moses, though subsequently his enemies and opponents. One legend mentions them as perishing in the catastrophe when the waves of the Red Sea overwhelmed the armies of Egypt; another tradition speaks of their having met their death in the slaughter after the worship of the golden calf, the making of which they advised. It was their prophetic words, so say these legendary histories, which, foretelling the birth of Moses, induced Pharaoh to give this order for the destruction of the Jewish children. The later Jews distorted the names into John and Ambrose.

So do these also resist the truth.—The point of comparison between the depraved teachers of Ephesus and these Egyptian sorcerers consisted in a persistent and deadly enmity to the truth, which existed in both cases. The life of the prophet Balaam, the traditionary father of this Jannes and Jambres, supplies a vivid illustration of this malignant and persistent hatred of what is known and felt to be true. That these Ephesian heretics in like manner availed themselves, or pretended to avail themselves of occult power is just probable, though in the comparison this point is of but little moment. We know, however, that the claim at least to possess mysterious and unearthly powers was often made by covetous and worldly men in these times: as, for instance, by Simon Magus (Acts viii. 9—24), by Elymas the sorcerer, the false prophet and Jew in Cyprus (Acts xiii. 6—12). See also the episode of Acts xix. 18—20, when "many which used curious arts came to Paul and his companions, and confessed and shewed their deeds."

Men of corrupt minds.—Literally, *corrupted in their minds.* Timothy might possibly have been induced to regard these evil men, though erring in

of corrupt minds, reprobate[1] concerning
the faith. (9) But they shall proceed no
further: for their folly shall be manifest
unto all *men*, as their's also was. (10) But
thou hast fully known[2] my doctrine, man-
ner of life, purpose, faith,
longsuffering, charity, pa-
tience, (11) persecutions,

Chap. iii. 10–12. St. Paul's faith and trials.

1 Or, *of no judgment.*
2 Or, *thou hast been a diligent follower of.*

some particulars, as still of the flock of Christ, to which they belonged nominally; but he was now instructed that they were simply enemies to the truth: that it was vain to hope that they would ever come to a knowledge of the truth, for their "mind," the human spirit, the medium of communication with the Holy Spirit of God, was corrupted. There was no common ground of faith, save in the bare name of Christian, between Timothy and these men, for they, in the matter of faith, had been tried and found wanting.

(9) **But they shall proceed no further.**—After that St. Paul, with no gentle hand, had torn aside the veil which was hiding apparently from Timothy the real state of his great charge at Ephesus, and had pointed out what fearful ravages among his flock had been committed by these ambitious and evil men, the Apostle proceeds to comfort his friend and disciple with the assurance that, great though the mischief already accomplished was, still it should proceed no further. To human eyes, such a state of things as here pictured by the Apostle would appear desperate. It would seem as though a deadly and incurable cancer was eating away the whole life of the community; but Timothy need not despair: the evil would only be allowed to advance to a certain point; and since St. Paul thus wrote, the same prophecy, not only in Ephesus but in a thousand churches, has been fulfilled to the very letter. Still, the same old foes under new faces make havoc of the Church. But they never seem to advance beyond a certain point, and after all these centuries the Church is still full of faith and life, bright, too, in spite of discouragements, in spite of the perpetual presence of these treacherous, deceitful men, with promise for the future.

For their folly shall be manifest.—Men and women would be led away for a season by the plausible words of such deceivers, but one school of error after another would fall into disrepute, then into neglect, then into the silent darkness of utter oblivion (the event in numberless instances has shown the truth of this prophecy); and Timothy might take comfort, by considering what Holy Scripture had placed on record respecting the Egyptian sorcerers, *whose folly was manifest unto all men* (Ex. viii. 18, 19; ix. 11). Their folly was yet more manifest when men considered *their latter end.* (See Note above on Jannes and Jambres, verse 8.)

(10) **But thou hast fully known my doctrine.**—Literally, *But thou wert a follower of my doctrine;* thou followedst as a disciple, and thus hast fully known. The Greek word translated "fully known" (see 1 Tim. iv. 6) denotes a diligently tracing out step by step. See Luke i. 3, where the same word is rendered, in the English version: "having had perfect understanding," having traced up to their source all the events relating to the foundation of Christianity. Here St. Paul recalls to Timothy's mind what had been his—St. Paul's—life, and words, and works. No one knew the history of this life like Timothy, the pupil and the friend, who had been long trained to assist in carrying on his teacher's work after St. Paul was removed. And this appeal to Timothy's recollection of the past has two distinct purposes: (1) It was to contrast that life of St. Paul's, with which the disciple was so well acquainted, with the lives of those false men, of whom Timothy was warned so earnestly, who were poisoning the stream of Christianity at Ephesus; and (2) the memory of the master was to serve as a spur to the disciple, the heroic faith of the old man was to act as an incentive to the young teacher to suffer bravely in his turn.

With this pattern of steady faith and heroic work before his eyes, Timothy would never be able to endure the wretched mock Christianity these new teachers were labouring to introduce into the communities of the believers of Asia; he would at once separate himself and his from these evil influences.

My doctrine.—Or, *teaching,* in which the leading of a pure self-denying life was inseparably bound up with a belief in the great Christian doctrines. "*This* hast thou, my pupil from boyhood, known in all its details. Thou hast known how I taught others."

Manner of life.—"And also how I lived myself:" "my ways which be in Christ," as he once before phrased it (1 Cor. iv. 17), "my conduct."

Purpose.—"My purpose—from which you know I never swerved—of remaining true to the Gospel of my Lord and to my great life's mission to the Gentiles." (See Acts ii. 23, where the word is used in respect to others' purpose.)

Faith.—Possibly, *trust in God,* but better, St. Paul's faith or belief in the fundamental doctrines of Christianity.

Longsuffering.—Towards his many bitter adversaries, especially those among his own countrymen. In spite of all that long, unwearied, sleepless persecution, which he, the former Pharisee leader, endured at the hands of the Jews, he loved Israel to the end, with a love intense as it was changeless, loved them even to be willing for their sake to give up his eternal hopes. (See Rom. ix. 3.)

Charity.—My love, which (in his own sunny words) beareth all things, believeth all things, hopeth all things—the love which never faileth. (See 1 Cor. xiii.)

Patience.—That characteristic virtue of St. Paul, that "brave patience" which hopefully endured opposition to his favourite schemes, which cheerfully bore the most painful suffering when it came as a consequence of work in his Master's cause. This concluding word led naturally on to the brief catalogue of persecutions of the next verse.

(11) **Persecutions, afflictions.**—St. Paul adds to "persecutions" "afflictions"—for not merely were his plans thwarted, his hopes baffled, his friends alienated, through the persistent enmity of his opponents, but *bodily* suffering was inflicted on him—stoning, scourging, long and weary periods of imprisonment, were among the repeated sufferings he endured for his Master's sake. The question has been asked why, out of the pages of the closely written diary of his life's experiences, does St. Paul select the events which took place at Antioch, Iconium, and Lystra? Was there anything special in what he endured in these places? The most satisfactory answer seems to be that, with regard to the general reader or hearer of this Epistle, what happened in these places, years before, were good examples of what had often taken place

afflictions, which came unto me at Antioch, at Iconium, at Lystra; what persecutions I endured: but out of *them* all the Lord delivered me. (12) Yea, and all that will live godly in Christ Jesus shall suffer persecution. (13) But evil men and seducers shall wax worse and worse,

deceiving, and being deceived. (14) But continue thou in the things which thou hast learned and hast been assured of, knowing of whom thou hast learned *them;* (15) and that from a child thou hast known the holy scriptures,

Chap. iii. 13–15. Timothy encouraged to be steadfast.

---

since. These were among the first cities in which St. Paul preached in the course of his missionary journeys. But a deeper reason existed for the choice of these places in *his* case to whom the Epistle was originally addressed. What happened on that first journey would never be forgotten by Timothy: some of the incidents were among his first experiences with St. Paul of the work—others had taken place just before St. Paul took him as his friend and associate, and, no doubt, had been often discussed in Timothy's hearing in those anxious never-to-be-forgotten hours which preceded his choice of the calling of a missionary. Hearing of these very deeds of endurance done for the crucified Master, perhaps, not a little contributed to Timothy's resolve to emulate these acts, and to join himself closely to the heroic missionary teacher. Certainly, the memory of what happened then St. Paul knew would possess a strong and weighty influence with his disciple, even though the events themselves were only such as had been repeated often since in his long life's experience. (For details respecting what took place at Antioch, &c., see Acts xiii., xiv.)

What persecutions I endured.—Some commentators understand these words as an exclamation: "What persecution I endured!" It is, however, better simply to translate the Greek, *Such persecutions as I endured;* in other words, Thou hast been a witness of my sufferings, such [sufferings] as I endured at Antioch, Iconium, and Lystra, such persecutions as I endured, but out of them, &c. Chrysostom remarks how both these clauses supply encouragement to the harassed servant of God. The first, that St. Paul displayed a noble readiness to endure persecution; the second, that God never left him alone. It was as though he said to Timothy, "surely no danger, no trouble, however great, need appal you. You know what I have gone through, yet in all God was with me and has kept me safe. Be sure He will be with you too."

(12) **Yea, and all that will live godly.**—But St. Paul would not allow it to be thought for a moment that in the fact of his enduring persecution and suffering there was anything remarkable or singular; so he adds the words of this verse, which repeat in a peculiarly solemn way the great Christian truth that eternal glory was only to be reached by man through an avenue of sufferings. "No cross, no crown," is one of the watchwords of the faith. To the statement, "all that will live godly," it is noticeable that the Apostle adds "in Christ Jesus:" thus telling us there can be no true piety except in communion with Him. So Bengel: "Extra Jesum Christum nulla pietas." And piety, adds St. Paul, will ever suffer persecution; for the world is at enmity with the kingdom of God. "Because ye are not of the world . . . therefore the world hateth you" (John xv. 19; so, too, Matt. x. 22, 38, 39).

(13) **But evil men and seducers shall wax worse and worse.**—This verse is closely connected with the following (verse 14), to which, indeed, it serves as an introduction. Verse 14 takes up again the exhortation to Timothy begun in verse 10: "But thou hast fully known my doctrine," &c. Verse 14 takes up the thought: "Continue thou in the things which thou hast learned and been assured of, knowing of whom thou hast learned them." Here, in verse 13, these evil men and seducers (or better, perhaps, *deceivers*) are spoken of as advancing towards the worse. History has borne witness to the accuracy of these prophetic words. The false teachers known to St. Paul and Timothy developed into the leaders of the various wild and speculative Gnostic sects, whose connection with Christianity consisted alone in the name; and each succeeding age has witnessed *a development* in opposition to the truth as it is in Jesus. In this allusion to the gradual development of hostility to the truth it will hardly be out of place to instance the eighteenth Christian century, when opposition to the teaching of Jesus had reached such a pitch that, with the approval or even the applause of thousands, the most brilliant writer in Europe wrote of Christ and His religion in the well-known words, "Ecrasez l'infame!" while it was reserved for our own century—the nineteenth—to witness the rare, though we believe ephemeral popularity, among so-called Christian peoples of a work which, with honeyed phrases, and in romantic, graceful language, paints the Redeemer of man in the strange and apparently contradictory characters of a loving enthusiast and of a conscious impostor!

(14) **But continue thou in the things which thou hast learned.**—But Timothy, on the other hand, was to continue in the things he had learned. Evil teaching would become worse; the opposition to truth would, as the ages rolled on, become more intense; but Timothy and his successors must remember that there was to be no development in the fundamental doctrines of his most holy faith. He had (verse 10) fully known St. Paul's doctrine—that doctrine which St. Paul had received directly from the Holy Spirit of God.

Knowing of whom thou hast learned them.—There is some doubt whether the Greek word rendered "whom" is in the singular or plural, the older authorities being nearly equally balanced. The reading here of the singular has been adopted with the Syriac versions, Chrysostom, Augustine, and the Vulgate. The reference then is to St. Paul. If the plural were adopted, then the reference would probably be to St. Paul and Barnabas, or to some other distinguished teacher. Some commentators believe that Lois and Eunice are here alluded to, the pious mother and grandmother of Timothy. This, however, seems unlikely: for such a reminiscence, although a touching memory and one likely to appeal to his affection, would hardly be of that weighty and important character as to warrant its introduction into this solemn exhortation; besides, any reference to home and family reminiscences would be included in the next verse: "From a child thou hast known," &c.

(15) **And that from a child thou hast known the holy scriptures.**—The Greek words translated "from a child" should be rendered, *from a very child,*

which are able to make thee wise unto
salvation through faith which is in
Christ Jesus. (16) All scripture *is* given
by inspiration of God, and *is* profitable
for doctrine, for reproof, for correction,
for instruction in righteousness:
(17) that the man of God
may be perfect, throughly
furnished[1] unto all good
works.

Chap. iii. 16, 17. All knowledge must be drawn from Scripture.

1 Or, *perfected.*

---

as the word denotes that Timothy's instruction in the Holy Scriptures began at a very early and tender age.

The holy scriptures.—Literally, *the sacred writings.* The Scriptures of the Old Testament are here exclusively meant. The expression "writings" for the Scriptures is not found elsewhere in the New Testament; it is, however, used by Josephus.

Two powerful arguments have been here used by the Apostle to induce Timothy to remain steadfast to the great doctrines of faith, and neither to take anything from them or to add anything to them. The first presses upon him the *source* whence he had learned them. He, better than any one, knew *who* and *what* St. Paul was, and the position he held with his brother Apostles, as one who had been in direct communication with the Lord Himself; and the second reminded him of his own early training, under his pious mother. He appealed, as it were, to Timothy's own deep knowledge of those Old Testament Scriptures. St. Paul's disciple would know that the great Christian doctrines respecting the Messiah were all based strictly on these Old Testament writings. Timothy had a double reason for keeping to the old paths pointed out by the first generation of teachers. He knew the authority of the master who instructed him; and then, from his own early and thorough knowledge of the Scriptures of the Jews, he was able to test thoroughly whether or no his master's teaching was in accordance with those sacred documents.

Which are able to make thee wise unto salvation.—The present participle rendered by "which are able" is noticeable, being here used to express the ever-present power of the Scriptures on the human heart. The Holy Scriptures had not completed their work on Timothy when, in his boyhood, he first mastered their contents. It was still going on. "Wise unto salvation" marks the glorious end and destination of the true wisdom which is gained by a study of these sacred books. Other wisdom has a different goal. In some cases it leads to power, fame, wealth; but this wisdom leads only to one goal—salvation. The last clause—"through faith which is in Christ Jesus"—points out the only way to use these Scriptures of the old covenant so as to attain through them the goal of all true wisdom—"eternal salvation." They must be read and studied in the light of faith in Jesus Christ. "Those (Old Testament) Scriptures, he (St. Paul) granteth, were able to make him wise unto salvation;" but, he addeth, "through the faith which is in Christ" (Hooker, *Ecc. Polity,* i. 14, 4). Faith in Jesus must be the torch by the light of which these ancient prophecies and types must be read.

(16) **All scripture is given by inspiration of God.**—Although this rendering is grammatically possible, the more strictly accurate translation, and the one adopted by nearly all the oldest and most trustworthy versions (for example, the Syriac and the Vulgate), and by a great many of the principal expositors in all ages (for instance, by such teachers as Origen, Theodoret, Grotius, Luther, Meyer, Ellicott, and Alford), runs as follows: "Every scripture inspired by God is also profitable for doctrine, for reproof," &c.

The rendering followed by the English version, and which is certainly grammatically possible, by making "all Scripture" the subject, and "given by inspiration of God" the predicate, declares positively the inspiration of all the Old Testament Scriptures, for this is what the Apostle must have referred to, if we understand this verse as we have it rendered in the English version above. The New Testament at this period was certainly not all written; for instance, St. John's Gospel, St. John's Epistles, the Epistle to the Hebrews, and the Apocalypse, with several of the Catholic Epistles, probably were composed at a later date than that assigned to this letter to Timothy. St. Paul, massing together an evidently well-known number of writings under the term πᾶσα γραφή, spoke of the Jewish Scriptures, the "canon" of which was then determined.

But such a declaration of the inspiration of these writings to Timothy and to those associated with him would seem unnecessary and uncalled for. Timothy and the trained Jew of the first century would never dream of doubting the divine origin of their most prized and sacred writings. There is nothing in the verses immediately preceding which would call out such a statement. It seems, therefore, on exegetical, as well as on grammatical, considerations best to follow the interpretation of those ancient and venerable witnesses. the Syriac and Latin (Jerome's) versions, and to understand St. Paul's words here, as asserting that every inspired writing (this, it should be observed, does not exclude those recent sacred compositions which—Gospels or Epistles—he had seen or written himself, and the divine *origin* of which he well knew) is profitable for doctrine, &c. Thus he exhorted Timothy to show himself a contrast to the false teachers—ever shifting their ground and waxing worse and worse—by keeping steadily to the old teaching of doctrine and of life. *He* was not to change, not to advance, but was to remember that every inspired Scripture was profitable for doctrine and for life. It was by these writings, St. Paul would remind him, that he must test his teaching. On the way in which "inspiration of God" was understood in the Church of the first days, see *Excursus* at the end of this Epistle.

Inspiration of God.—This thought, perhaps, rather than these words, is admirably paraphrased by St. Peter: "Holy men of God spake as they were moved by the Holy Ghost" (2 Pet. i. 21). The various uses of Holy Scripture in the training of the man of God are set forth in the enumeration which closes this verse. These sacred writings must, in all ages, St. Paul would urge, be the hand-book of the Christian teacher. From it he must prove the doctrines he professes; hence, too, he must draw his reproofs for the ignorant and erring. It must be the one source whence he derives those instructions which teach the Christian how to grow in grace.

(17) **That the man of God may be perfect, throughly furnished unto all good works.**—The "man of God" here is no official designation, but simply designates the Christian generally, who is striving, with his Master's help, to live a life pleasing to God; and the "good works" have no special

CHAPTER IV.—(1) I charge *thee* therefore before God, and the Lord Jesus Christ, who shall judge the quick and the dead at his appearing and his kingdom; (2) preach the word; be instant in season, out of season; reprove, rebuke, exhort with all long-

Chap. iv. 1–4. Injunction to teach with earnestness.

A.D. 66.

reference to the labours of Timothy and his brother presbyters, but include all those generous and self-sacrificing acts to which, in these Epistles, so many references have been made.

It was in the Holy Scriptures that the true servant of the Lord, the man of God, would find defined with clearness and precision the nature of those works the Holy Spirit was pleased to call "good."

IV.

(1) **I charge thee therefore before God, and the Lord Jesus Christ.**—The parchment, or papyrus, in the prison room of St. Paul on which, probably, Luke (verse 11), the faithful friend, was writing to the Apostle's dictation, was nearly filled up. What has still to be said to the chief presbyter of the Church of Ephesus must be brief. But St. Paul would have the last words introduced by a most impressive preface. So before he sums up his directions and exhortations, he appeals to him in these stately and solemn words. The Greek word rendered "I charge (thee)," is more accurately translated by, *I solemnly charge* (*thee*), before those divine witnesses, the Eternal Father and the Blessed Son, present with me in this prison of mine in Rome, present equally with you in study-chamber or church in Asia.

Who shall judge the quick and the dead.—These words must have sounded with strange power in the ears of men like Timothy, and must have impressed them with an intense feeling of responsibility. The Apostle in his divine wisdom was charging these teachers of the Church to be faithful and zealous in their work, by the thought, which must be ever present, that *they*—either alive on the day of the Coming of the Lord, or, if they had tasted death already, raised from the dead incorruptible (comp. 1 Thess. iv. 17)—must stand before the Judge and give an account of their stewardship; on that awful morning must every man and woman render up, before the Judge who knows all and sees all, a strict account of the deeds done in the body. The looking forward to the judgment morning must surely be a spur to any faint-hearted, dispirited servant of the Lord disposed to temporise, or reluctant to face the dangers which threaten a faithful discharge of duties.

At his appearing and his kingdom.—The older authorities here—instead of the preposition "at"—read "and." The rendering then would be: "I charge thee in the sight of God and Jesus Christ, who will judge quick and dead (I charge thee) by His appearing (*epiphany*) and by His kingdom," the construction in Greek being the usual accusative of adjuration, as in Mark v. 7; Acts xix. 13. So, too, Deut. iv. 26 (LXX.): "I solemnly charge you to-day by heaven and earth." The passage, by this restoration of the ancient, and, at first sight, more difficult reading, gains, as we shall see, immeasurably in strength and power. "By his appearing," or by His manifestation or epiphany, refers, of course, to the Lord's coming a second time to judge the earth in the glory of the Father with His angels. (Matt. xvi. 27; 1 Thess. iv. 16, 17.) "And by His kingdom:" His kingdom, that kingdom is here meant which, in the words of the Nicene Creed, "shall have no end." This glorious sovereignty of Christ is to succeed what Pearson (*Creed*, Article VI., p. 529, Chevallier's edit.) calls "the modificated eternity of His mediatorship," which will end when all His enemies shall have been subdued, and He shall have delivered up the kingdom to God, even the Father. The "kingdom" here spoken of is to commence at Christ's glorious epiphany or manifestation, when "the kingdoms of the world are become the kingdoms of our Lord, and of His Christ; and He shall reign for ever and ever" (Rev. xi. 15). Timothy was conjured by the "appearing" of Christ when he would have to stand before Him and be judged; he was conjured, too, by "His kingdom," in which glorious state Timothy hoped to share, for was it not promised that His own should reign with Him? (chap. ii. 12.) There seems in this solemn ringing adjuration something which reminds us of "a faithful saying." The germs at least of one of the ancient creeds are apparent here, where allusion is made to God (the Father) and to Jesus Christ, the judge of quick and dead, to His coming again with glory and then to His kingdom.

(2) **Preach the word.**—The language of the original here is abrupt and emphatic, written evidently under strong emotion and with intense earnestness. St. Paul charged his friend and successor with awful solemnity, as we have seen, "preach," or proclaim, loudly and publicly, as a herald would announce the accession of his king. The exact opposite to what St. Paul would urge on Timothy is described by Isa. (lvi. 10), when he speaks of God's watchmen as "dumb dogs, who cannot bark, sleeping, lying down, loving to slumber."

Be instant in season, out of season.—Some difference exists between commentators respecting the exact meaning to be given to the Greek word translated "be instant." Some would give it the sense of drawing nigh to, and as it is not specified in the text to whom Timothy should draw nigh, they supply from the context "the brethren," those to whom the word is preached: "draw near to Christian assemblies." It seems, however, best to understand this rather difficult word as an injunction to Timothy to be earnest and urgent generally in the whole work of his ministry: "Press on, in season, out of season."

In season, out of season.—In other words, "For thy work, set apart no definite and fixed hours, no appointed times. Thy work must be done at all hours, at all times. Thy work has to be done not only when thou art in church, not merely in times of security and peace, but it must be carried on, in the midst of dangers, even if thou art a prisoner and in chains, even if death threaten thee."

So Chrysostom—who also uses St. Paul's words here as an urgent call to ministers to labour on in spite of discouragement and apparent failure—telling them in his own bright, eloquent way, how fountains still flow on, though no one goes to them to draw water, and rivers still run on, though no one drinks at them.

Augustine asks and answers the question to whom "in season" and to whom "out of season" refers: "in season" to those willing, "out of season" to the unwilling. This, however, only touches a portion of

suffering and doctrine. (3) For the time
will come when they will not endure
sound doctrine; but after their own lusts
shall they heap to themselves teachers,
having itching ears; (4) and they shall
turn away *their* ears from the truth,
and shall be turned unto fables. (5) But
watch thou in all things, endure afflictions, do the work of an evangelist,

Chap. iv. 5—8. The Apostle now at the end of his course.

the thought of St. Paul, who urges on God's true servants a restless, sleepless earnestness, which struggles on with the Master's work in spite of bodily weakness and discouragement, in face of dangers and the bitterest opposition.

Reprove.—Not merely those erring in doctrine, but generally those who are blameworthy: "Was tadelnswerth ist."

Rebuke.—A sharper and more severe word than the preceding. It is used by St. Jude, verse 9, in his report of the words addressed by St. Michael to the devil: "The Lord rebuke thee." It frequently occurs in the Gospels. (See, for instance, Matt. xvii. 18, "And Jesus rebuked the devil.")

Exhort.—Not only is he to remember ceaselessly to watch over the flock, and to reprove and rebuke the erring and sinners, but also with no less diligence to speak comfortable words of encouragement and hope to all, especially the dispirited and sad-hearted.

With all longsuffering and doctrine.—The word translated "doctrine" signifies, rather, *teaching.* He must reprove, rebuke, exhort, with all gentleness and patience; and in all this he must take care that "teaching"—the teaching which is right, and true, and full of hope—accompanies his rebuke and his words of comfort.

(3) **For the time will come when they will not endure sound doctrine.**—Timothy must bear in mind that things in the Church of Christ on earth will not change for the better. The great drag-net of the Church, in its wide sweep, would keep drawing into its meshes something of every kind. Errors now just apparent, he must remember, would attain more formidable dimensions. The thirst for novelties in doctrine, the desire for a teaching which, while offering peace to a troubled conscience, would yet allow the old self-indulgent life to go on as before, would increase. In full view of this development of error, in sure expectation of a future full of anxious care, Timothy and his brother teachers must indeed be wakeful, watchful, and earnest in their preaching and ministrations. And the thought that more and ever more of the so-called Christians would dislike the preaching of the "sound doctrine," as taught by the Apostle, the very knowledge of this growing unpopularity, must serve as an incentive to greater labour, more interest, and more loving activity on the part of Timothy and his companions.

But after their own lusts shall they heap to themselves teachers.—"Their own lusts:" this expression gives us some insight into the reason which led to this future apostasy of so many, concerning which St. Paul warned Timothy. "Their own lusts," which, at all risks, they would gratify, would serve to alienate them from that severe and strictly moral school of Apostolic teaching, in which the sternest morality was bound up with purity of doctrine, to which school St. Paul's pupils—men like Timothy and the presbyters of Ephesus—belonged. These worldly ones to whom St. Paul referred, reluctant to part with the hope Christianity taught, and unwilling to live the life which St. Paul and Timothy insisted upon as necessary to be lived by all those who would share in that glorious hope, sought out for themselves more indulgent teachers, who would flatter and gratify their hearers with novelties in doctrine, and would, at the same time, lay comparatively little stress on the pure and saintly life.

(4) **And they shall turn away their ears from the truth.**—This was the punishment of those who would only listen to what was pleasing to them, and which flattered instead of reproved their way of life. They became involved in the many various errors in doctrine which were then taught in the schools of the heretics, and they ended by turning away from every Christian truth. On the "fables" which they substituted for those great and eternal truths, see 1 Tim. i. 4.

(5) **But watch thou in all things.**—"But do thou," continued St. Paul, "do thou be watchful." The Greek word translated "watch thou," signifies literally, *be sober.* It has been well paraphrased, "Keep thy coolness and presence of mind, that thou be not entrapped into forgetfulness, but as one ever wakeful and ready, be on the watch." The word, as it were, sums up all those last directions of St. Paul, from chap. ii. 14, in which St. Paul charged Timothy to abstain from vain arguments and confine himself to the simple word of truth, to avoid discussions which would be likely to lead to strife, and to be patient and gentle with all—to separate himself from merely nominal Christians, and to keep steadily to the old paths in which the Apostles had walked. He was to be ever watchful in all these things.

Endure afflictions.—And in his watch must Timothy be ready to suffer. He would remember what had been said before respecting a true Christian suffering (chap. ii. 3—12), and what was the high reward purposed for such brave endurance. He would remember, too, the hard and faithful life of his master, St. Paul (chap. iii. 10—12).

Do the work of an evangelist.—The "evangelists" of the early Church seem to have been preachers of the Gospel: in the first place, assistants to the Apostles and missionaries under their direction. The especial functions of a preacher and public teacher seem always to have been allotted to Timothy, and, no doubt, a peculiar persuasive power of oratory was one of the chief gifts conferred on this eminent follower of St. Paul. In the midst of the many grave and absorbing duties of his charge of the Ephesian Church, he must be mindful not to neglect this great power which he possessed. It is here especially termed "*the work* of an evangelist," to remind him that to perform rightly this duty, needed zeal, close work, much study, thought, and prayer; and it was by worthily performing the duties of an evangelist that the many who were turning from the truth to fables, would be best won back, by hearing the great facts of the Gospel placed side by side with the fables of the false teachers.

Make full proof of thy ministry.—In other words, "Fully carry out the many duties imposed upon thee by thy great office." The office of Timothy, it should be remembered, in Ephesus, included far more than merely those of a preacher or evangelist. He was the presiding presbyter of the Church, to whom its

make full proof of[1] thy ministry.
(6) For I am now ready to be offered,
and the time of my departure is at
hand. (7) I have fought a good fight, I
have finished *my* course, I have kept
the faith: (8) henceforth there is laid up
for me a crown of righteousness,
which the Lord, the righteous judge,
shall give me at that day: and not
to me only, but unto all
them also that love his
appearing. (9) Do thy

Chap. iv. 9—13. Timothy was to come quickly.

[1] Or, *fulfil.*

government was intrusted: in fact, the many-sided life of St. Paul was now to be lived by Timothy.

(6) **For I am now ready to be offered.**—What, in the Philippian Epistle (chap. ii. 17), was alluded to as a contingency likely enough to happen here is spoken of as something which was then absolutely taking place. In his first imprisonment at Rome St. Paul looked on to a martyr's death as probable. In his second captivity at Rome he writes of the martyrdom as already beginning. The more accurate, as well as the more forcible, translation would be, *For I am already being offered.* The Greek word rendered "I am being offered," points to the drink offering of wine which, among the Jews, accompanied the sacrifice. Among the heathen this wine was commonly poured upon the burning victims—the allusion here is to St. Paul's bloody death. So convinced was he that the dread moment for him was at hand, that as he thus speaks he feels as though it was even then taking place, and sees—in his present suffering, in his harsh treatment—the beginning of that martyrdom in which his life-blood would be poured out. But he would not allow Timothy or the many Christians who revered and loved him to be dismayed by his sufferings or shocked at his painful death. He would show them, by his calm, triumphant language, that to him death was no terror, but only the appointed passage to glory. So he speaks of his life-blood being shed, under the well-known peaceful image of the wine poured out over the sacrifice, the drink offering, the sweet savour unto the Lord. (See Num. xv. 1—10; compare John xii. 24, where the Master of St. Paul, too, speaks of His approaching death of agony and shame also under a quiet, homely image.)

And the time of my departure is at hand.—"My departure:" that is, "from life," from this world to another. The moment of my death, so long looked for, is now close at hand, is all but here. The Greek word rendered "departure," among other meanings, signifies the raising of the ship's anchor and the loosing of the cables by which the vessel was hindered from proceeding on her destined voyage.

(7) **I have fought a good fight.**—More accurately, more forcibly rendered, *the good fight.* St. Paul changes the metaphor, and adopts his old favourite one, so familiar to all Gentile readers, of the athlete contending in the games. First, he speaks generally of the combatant, the charioteer, and the runner. "I have fought the good fight," leaving it undetermined what description of strife or contest was referred to. The tense of the Greek verb—the perfect—"I *have* fought," is remarkable. The struggle had been bravely sustained in the past, and was now being equally bravely sustained to the end. His claim to the crown (verse 8) was established.

I have finished my course.—Or "race," for here the image of the stadium, the Olympic race-course, was occupying the Apostle's thoughts. Again the perfect is used: "I *have* finished my course." How, asks, Chrysostom, "had he finished his course?" and answers rather rhetorically by replying that he had made the circuit of the world. The question is better answered in St. Paul's own words (Acts xx. 24), where he explains "his course," which he would finish with joy, as the ministry which he had received of the Lord Jesus.

I have kept the faith.—Here, again, the metaphor is changed, and St. Paul looks back on his lived life as on one long, painful struggle to guard the treasure of the Catholic faith inviolate and untarnished (see 1 Tim. vi. 20). And now the struggle was over, and he handed on the sacred deposit, safe. It is well to compare this passage with the words of the same Apostle in the Epistle to the Philippians (chap. iii. 12, and following verses). The same metaphors were in the Apostle's mind on both occasions; but in the first instance (in the Philippian Epistle) they were used by the anxious, careworn servant of the Lord, hoping and, at the same time, fearing what the future had in store for him and his Church; in the second (in the Epistle to Timothy) they were the expression of the triumphant conviction of the dying follower of Christ, who had so followed his loved Master in life, that he now shrank not from following the same Master in death.

(8) **A crown of righteousness.**—More accurately rendered, *the crown of righteousness.* St. Paul, after speaking calmly of death, the bitterness of which he was already tasting, looks on beyond death, and speaks of the crown which awaited him. The crown was the victory prize which the "good fight" of verse 7 had won. It is called "the crown of righteousness," it being the crown to which righteousness can lay claim—that is, the crown awarded to righteousness.

Which the Lord, the righteous judge, shall give me.—As a righteous judge will the Lord award him the crown, recognising him as one who had the prize of victory. Not improbably, the expression "the righteous judge" was written in strong contrast to that unrighteous judge who had condemned Paul, and in accordance with whose unjust sentence he would presently suffer a painful death.

At that day.—This is the third time the words "that day" are used in this Epistle (see chap. i. 12—18). The day of judgment is, of course, signified, the day when the Lord shall come again with glory.

And not to me only, but unto all them also that love his appearing.—Then St. Paul, instead of concluding this section of his letter with the glorious words telling of his serene courage and of his confidence in a crowned and immortal life, adds a gentle reminder to Timothy: *he*, too, with any others who really look for the Second Coming of the Lord, might win the same glorious crown—the sure guerdon of righteousness. The Apostle specifies here exactly the persons for whom "the crown" was reserved—those who in this life have *indeed* longed for the appearance of the Lord in judgment. None here could in very truth desire "His appearing," save His own, who love Him and struggle to live His life. Calvin well remarks: "(St. Paul) excludes from the number of the faithful those to whom Christ's coming is a source of terror."

(9) **Do thy diligence to come shortly.**—Such a request as this would—had we no other arguments

diligence to come shortly unto me:
(10) for Demas hath forsaken me, having
loved this present world, and is
departed unto Thessalonica; Crescens
to Galatia, Titus unto Dalmatia.
(11) Only Luke is with me. Take
Mark, and bring him with thee: for
he is profitable to me for the ministry.

—tell us that no forger ever wrote this Epistle. Who would ever have dreamed of putting into the letter such a request as this, *after* those solemn expressions of the last few verses, in which the Apostle spoke of himself as even *then* tasting the bitterness of death? He had been writing as though the martyr's death was so imminent that the preparations were already being made for it. This request to Timothy to come to him, *after* he had written such thoughts down, is at first sight strange, and one certainly which no forger would have appended to the writing. But though the forger would never have thought of such a summons, *St. Paul* might. He still lived, and the thought of life and the hope of life even in that brave Christ-loving heart still burned; after all, the martyrdom which seemed so close at hand *might* be delayed. Days, months, might drag on their slow, weary length, and still find the old man languishing and solitary in his chains in that dreary prison. He longed to see some of his faithful companions once more, and for the last time to bid them with his own mouth to be faithful and brave. So, as it were, hoping against hope, he dictates on the last pages of the letter, "Do thy diligence," or better, "*earnestly endeavour* to come shortly to me." His loving wish to see Timothy again appears from the words of chap. i. 4: "greatly desiring to see thee;" and again from chap. iv. 21. "Do thy diligence to come before winter." And some have seen in the expresssion, "being mindful of thy tears," in chap. i. 4 (to which we have given, however, a different interpretation), a reciprocal anxiety on the part of Timothy to see and speak again with his old master. But St. Paul, though he begged him to hasten his journey as much as possible, and still, though all seemed so dark around him, *hoped* to see him again, framed the charge of the last letter in such a way that Timothy, if when he reached Rome, should find that all was over, might know what were his master's last wishes and directions. On the natural human longing for sympathy in the supreme hour, compare our blessed Lord's words to Peter, James, and John (Matt. xxvi. 38): "My soul is exceeding sorrowful unto death: tarry ye here, *and watch with Me.*"

(10) **For Demas hath forsaken me.**—This once faithful companion of St. Paul had been with him during the first imprisonment of the Apostle at Rome (Col. iv. 14; Philem. verse 24); but now, terrified by the greater severity and the threatened fatal ending of the second imprisonment, had forsaken his old master.

Having loved this present world.—Chrysostom paraphrases as follows: "Having loved ease and safety, chose rather to live daintily at home than to suffer affliction, than to endure hardship, with me, and with me to bear these present dangers." The tradition, however, which relates that he became in after days an idol priest at Thessalonica is baseless. Demas is a shorter form, probably, for the well-known and now common Grecian name of Demetrius.

The present world (*aiōna*): that is, the present (evil) course of things.

Is departed unto Thessalonica.—From Chrysostom's words above quoted, Thessalonica was apparently the "home" of Demas. It has been supposed, however, by some, that Thessalonica was chosen by Demas as his abode when he left St. Paul because it was a great mercantile centre, and his business connections were there, and he preferred them, the rich and prosperous friends, to St. Paul, the condemned and dying prisoner. Thessalonica was, at this time, one of the great cities of the empire. It was the most populous of the Macedonian cities, and had been chosen to be the metropolis of that great province. Before the founding of Constantinople, it was evidently the capital of Greece and Illyricum, as well as of Macedonia. It was famous throughout the Middle Ages, and is celebrated by the early German poets under the abbreviated name of "Salneck," which has become the Saloniki of the Levant of our days. It is singular that the name of its patron saint, "Demetrius," martyred about A.D. 290 (identified above with Demas), whose local glory (comp. Conybeare and Howson's *St. Paul*, chap. ix.) has even eclipsed that of St. Paul, the founder of the Church, should be identical with that of the "forsaker" of St. Paul.

Crescens to Galatia.—Nothing is known of this friend of St. Paul. One tradition speaks of him as a preacher in Galatia, and another of his having founded the Church of Vienne in Gaul. There is a curious variation in some of the older authorities here, "Gallia" being read instead of Galatia. Whether Crescens, on his leaving St. Paul, went to Galatia or Gaul is, therefore, uncertain.

Titus unto Dalmatia.—Dalmatia was a province of Roman Illyricum, lying along the Adriatic. Nothing is known respecting this journey of Titus. It was, most probably, made with the Apostle's sanction.

(11) **Only Luke is with me.**—The "writer" of the Third Gospel, the Gospel which, as has been stated above, was very possibly the work of St. Paul—"my Gospel." Luke, "the beloved physician" of Col. iv. 14, of all St. Paul's companions, seems to have been most closely associated with the Apostle. Most likely this close intimacy and long-continued association was owing to the Apostle's weak and infirm health—to that dying body—the noble Paul ever bore about with him. Luke was with St. Paul, we know, in his second missionary journey, and again in his third missionary journey; he accompanied him to Asia, and then to Jerusalem; was with him during the captivity time of Cæsarea, and subsequently of Rome, the first time St. Paul was imprisoned in the capital (Acts xviii.). After St. Paul's death, Epiphanius speaks of him as preaching chiefly in Gaul; a very general tradition includes him among the martyrs of the first age of the Church. The name is probably a contraction of Lucanus. (See *Introduction to the Acts of the Apostles.*)

Take Mark, and bring him with thee: for he is profitable to me for the ministry.—"But Paul thought not good to take him with them, who departed from them . . . and went not with them to the work" (Acts xv. 38). There is something strangely touching in this message of the aged master to Timothy to bring with him on that last solemn journey one whom, some quarter of a century before, St. Paul had judged so severely, and on whose account he had separated from his old loved friend, Barnabas the Apostle. Since that hour when the young missionary's heart had failed him in Pamphylia, Mark had, by steady, earnest work, won back his place in St. Paul's heart. Barnabas, we know, when his brother Apostle rejected him, took him with

(12) And Tychicus have I sent to
Ephesus. (13) The cloke that I left at
Troas with Carpus, when thou comest,
bring *with thee*, and the books, *but* espe-
cially the parchments. (14) Alexander the
coppersmith did me much
evil: the Lord reward him
according to his works:

Chap. iv. 14—18. The Apostle's first trial.

---

him to Cyprus. After some twelve years, we find him, during the first imprisonment, with St. Paul at Rome (Col. iv. 10; Philem. verse 24). He is mentioned (1 Pet. v. 13) by the endearing term of "my son," and the unanimous traditions of the ancient Christian writers represent him as the secretary or amanuensis of St. Peter. It was his office to commit to writing the orally delivered instructions and narrations of his master. These, in some revised and arranged form, probably under the direction of Peter himself, were given to the Church under the title of St. Mark's Gospel. A later and uncertain tradition says he subsequently became first Bishop of Alexandria, and there suffered martyrdom.

For he is profitable to me for the ministry.—Profitable, according to the suggestion of Grotius, owing to Mark's knowledge of the Latin tongue. This is possible; but it is more likely that he was profitable or serviceable as an assistant who was well acquainted with the details of St. Paul's many-sided work.

(12) **And Tychicus have I sent to Ephesus.**—Instead of "and," the Greek particle here should be rendered "but Tychicus." "This 'but' appears to refer to a suppressed thought, suggested by the concluding portion of the last (11th) verse: bring Mark. I need one who is profitable (or *serviceable*) for the ministry. I had one in Tychicus, *but* he is gone" (Ellicott). Neither the period of Tychicus' journey nor its object is alluded to here. It probably took place some time, however, before the sending of this Epistle to Timothy. Tychicus was evidently one of the trusted companions of St. Paul. He had been with him, we know, on his third missionary journey, and had, during St. Paul's first Roman imprisonment, some six or seven years before, been charged with a mission by his master to Ephesus. In Eph. vi. 21 he is called a beloved brother and a faithful minister in the Lord. (See, too, Col. iv. 7, where he is spoken of in similar terms.) On the city of Ephesus, see Note on 1 Tim. i. 3. It has been, with considerable probability, suggested that Tychicus had been the bearer of the first Epistle to Timothy. Between the writing of these two letters, we know, no great interval could have elapsed.

(13) **The cloke that I left at Troas.**—The apparently trivial nature of this request in an Epistle containing such weighty matter, and also the fact of such a wish on the part of one expecting death being made at all, is at first a little puzzling. To explain this seemingly strange request, some have wished to understand by "the cloke" some garment St. Paul was in the habit of wearing when performing certain sacred functions: in other words, as a vestment; but such a supposition would be in the highest degree precarious, for nowhere in the New Testament is the slightest hint given us that any such vestment was ever used in the primitive Christian Church. It is much better to understand the words as simply requesting Timothy, on his way, to bring with him a thick cloak, or mantle, which St. Paul had left with a certain Carpus at Troas. Probably, when he left it, it was summer, and he was disinclined to burden himself in his hurried journey with any superfluous things. Winter was now coming on, and the poor aged prisoner in the cold damp prison, with few friends and scant resources, remembered and wished for his cloak. It is just such a request which the master would make of his disciple, who, knowing well the old man's frail, shattered health, would never be surprised at such a request even in an Epistle so solemn. Then too St. Paul, by his very wish here expressed, to see Timothy, as above discussed, hopes against hope that still a little while for work in the coming winter months was still before him, though he felt death was for him very near; no forger of the Epistle had dreamed of putting down such a request.

And the books.—The books were, most likely, a few choice works, some bearing on Jewish sacred history, partly exegetical and explanatory of the mysterious senses veiled under the letter of the law and the prophets, and partly historical. Others were probably heathen writings, of which we know, from his many references in his Epistles, St. Paul was a diligent student. These few choice books, it has been suggested, with high probability, St. Paul "had made a shift to get and preserve," and these, if God spared his life yet a few short months, he would have with him for reference in his prison room.

But especially the parchments.—These precious papers, above all, would St. Paul have with him. These were, most likely, common-place books, in which the Apostle—evidently always a diligent student—had written what he had observed as worthy of especial notice in the reading of either of the Scriptures of the Old Testament, or the other books bearing on Jewish or Pagan literature and history. These precious notes were probably the result of many years' reading and study. He would have them with him as long as life remained to him. (Compare on this strange but interesting verse Bp. Bull's learned and exhaustive sermon: *Works*, vol. i. p. 240, Oxford Edition, 1846.) Erasmus remarks on this request of St. Paul: "Behold the Apostle's goods or movables: a poor cloke to keep him from the weather, and a few books!"

A suggestion has been made that the words translated "Much learning doth make thee mad" (Acts xxvi. 24) should be rendered, *Thy many rolls of parchment are turning thy brain*, and that these rolls of parchment referred to by Festus as the companions of St. Paul's captivity at Cæsarea were identical with those parchments left with Carpus. The Greek words, however, are not the same in the two passages. Of this Carpus nothing is known.

(14) **Alexander the coppersmith did me much evil.**—Most probably, the same Alexander, mentioned in the First Epistle (1 Tim. i. 20) "as delivered to Satan," and not improbably identical with the Alexander "the Jew" put forward by the Jews in the Ephesian tumult (Acts xix. 33, 34).

It has been suggested that this Alexander, an influential Ephesian Jew, had done much injury to the cause of the Christians generally, and to St. Paul personally, with the imperial authorities at Rome.

The Lord reward him according to his works.—The older authorities read, "shall reward him . . ." The works referred to were the bitter injuries he had done to the cause of Christ, rather than to the Apostle himself.

(15) of whom be thou ware also; for he
hath greatly withstood our words.[1] (16) At
my first answer no man stood with me,
but all *men* forsook me: *I pray God* that
it may not be laid to their charge.
(17) Notwithstanding the Lord stood with
me, and strengthened me; that by me
the preaching might be fully known,
and *that* all the Gentiles might hear:
and I was delivered out of the mouth of

[1] Or, *our preachings.*

---

(15) **Of whom be thou ware also.**—This Alexander was evidently then at Ephesus. That he had been at Rome, and had given evidence against St. Paul, and had argued against the defence of the Apostle, is probable. "Our words" some understand as especially referring to St. Paul's defence before the imperial tribunal. If we identify him with the Alexander of Acts xix. 33, 34, then he was a Jew, one of those bitter, life-long antagonists of the Gentile Apostle who crossed his path at every step, and not improbably brought about, in the end, his death. It is an interesting suggestion which refers the connection between St. Paul and Alexander back to those days when Saul and Alexander were both reckoned as belonging to the strictest Pharisee party, determined foes to the "Nazarenes." Saul—if we adopt this supposition—became the Apostle St. Paul of the Gentiles; Alexander remained a fanatic Jew—hence the enmity.

(16) **At my first answer no man stood with me . . .**—And then, after the mention of what his *enemy* had done out of hatred to the cause of Christ, the old man passed on to speak of the conduct of his own *familiar friends* at that great public trial before—most probably—the city præfect: Præfectus Urbi, a nominee of the Emperor Nero. No one friend stood by him; no "advocate" pleaded his cause; no "procurator" (an official who performed the functions of the attorney in an English court) helped him in arranging and sifting the evidence; no "patronus" of any noble or powerful house gave him his countenance and support. The position of a well-known Christian leader accused in the year 66–67 was a critical one, and the friend who dared to stand by him would himself be in great danger. After the great fire of Rome, in A.D. 64, the Christians were looked upon as the enemies of the state, and were charged as the authors of that terrible disaster. Nero, to avert suspicion from himself, allowed the Christians to be accused and condemned as incendiaries. A great persecution, in which, as Tacitus tells, a very great multitude of the followers of Jesus perished, was the immediate result of the hateful charge. It is most probable that St. Paul, as a famous Nazarene leader, was eventually arrested as implicated in this crime, and brought to Rome. His implacable enemies among the Jews might well have been the agents who brought this about, and Alexander of the last verse was possibly principally concerned in this matter. But St. Paul, conscious of his own great peril, knew well that to stand by him now, implicated as he was in this net-work of false accusations, would be a service of the greatest danger; so he pleads for them, these weak, unnerved friends of his, who, through no ill-will to the cause, but solely from timidity, had deserted him, remembering, no doubt, his own Master, who, too, in His hour of deadly peril, had been forsaken. (See John xvi. 32, "Behold the hour cometh, yea is now come, that ye shall be scattered every man to his own, and ye shall leave Me alone.") But like his own Master, who proceeded to say, "Yet I am not alone, because the Father is with Me," so St. Paul went on to tell Timothy neither was *he* alone, for One greater than any friend on earth stood by him.

(17) **Notwithstanding the Lord stood with me, and strengthened me.**—Though men deserted him, yet One—even his Lord (Christ), who could do more for him than any friend, or advocate, or protector of earth—stood by him, and strengthened him by giving him courage and readiness.

That by me the preaching might be fully known.—More accurately rendered, *might be fully performed:* "impleatur," as the Vulgate gives it. The strength and courage which the *felt* presence of his Lord gave him, enabled him on that occasion, when alone, friendless, accused of a hateful crime before the highest earthly tribunal in the capital city of the world, to plead not only for himself but for that great cause with which he was identified. He spoke possibly for the last time publicly [we know nothing of the final trial, when he was condemned] the glad tidings of which he was the chosen herald to the Gentile world. It is probable that this great trial took place in the Forum, in one of the Pauline Basilicas—so called after L. Æmilius Paulus. It is certain it was in the presence of a crowded audience. St. Paul evidently intimates this when he tells us how he spoke "that all the Gentiles might hear." This was apparently the culminating point of St. Paul's labours—the last stone of the laborious edifice of his life's work. Had the courage of the Apostle of the Gentiles failed him on this most momentous occasion, the spirit of the sorely-tried Church of Rome had surely sunk, and that marvellous and rapid progress of the gospel in the West—which, in a little more than a hundred years, would make its influence felt in well-nigh every city and village of the empire—had been arrested.

And that all the Gentiles might hear.—Here alluding primarily to the crowded audience which had listened on this solemn occasion to St. Paul's *Apologia pro Christo;* but there is another and deeper reference to those uncounted peoples in the isles of the Gentiles, who, by St. Paul's work and words, would come to the saving knowledge of the truth as it is in Jesus.

And I was delivered out of the mouth of the lion.—Expositors have, in all ages, dwelt much on the question, "Who was to be understood under the figure of the lion?" The fathers mostly believe the Emperor Nero was here alluded to. Others have suggested that St. Paul was referring to the "lions" of the amphitheatre, from whom, at all events for the time, he had been delivered. It is, however, best to understand the expression as a figurative expression for extreme danger. His Master on that dread occasion stood by him, and gave him strength and wisdom over man to speak the words of life, and delivered him for the moment out of the imminent peril threatening him, allowing him, not only to speak his Master's words there, but also thus to write this solemn farewell charge to Timothy and the Church. That such figurative language was not unusual, compare the *Epistle of Ignatius to the Romans*, ii. 8, in which writing the prisoner describes his journey from Syria to Rome as one long "fight with wild beasts," and speaks of himself as "bound to ten leopards," thus designating his soldier guards.

the lion. (18) And the Lord shall deliver
me from every evil work, and will pre-
serve *me* unto his heavenly kingdom:
to whom *be* glory for ever and ever.
Amen. (19) Salute Prisca and Aquila,
and the household of One-
siphorus. (20) Erastus abode
at Corinth: but Trophimus have I left
at Miletum sick. (21) Do thy diligence
to come before winter. Eubulus greet-
eth thee, and Pudens, and Linus, and
Claudia, and all the brethren. (22) The
Lord Jesus Christ *be* with thy spirit.
Grace *be* with you. Amen.

Chap. iv. 19—22. Greetings.

¶ The second *epistle* unto Timotheus, ordained the first bishop of the church of the Ephesians, was written from Rome, when Paul was brought before Nero the second time.

---

(18) **And the Lord shall deliver me from every evil work . . .**—Many commentators have explained these words as the expression of St. Paul's confidence that the Lord not only had, in the late trial, strengthened His servant, and given him courage to endure, but that He would watch over him in the future which still lay before him, and would preserve him from every danger of faint-heartedness, from every risk of doing dishonour to his Master; but such an interpretation seems foreign to the *spirit* in which St. Paul was writing to Timothy. In the whole Epistle there is not one note of fear—nothing which shonld lead us to suspect that the martyr Apostle was fearful for himself. It reads—does this last letter of the great Gentile teacher—in many places like a triumphant song of death. It, therefore, appears unnatural to introduce into the closing words of the Epistle the thought of the Lord's help in the event of the Apostle's losing heart. Far better is it to supply after "every evil work" the words "*of the enemies*," and to understand the deliverance which the Lord will accomplish for him, not as a deliverance from any shrinking or timidity unworthy of an apostle of the Lord, not even as a deliverance from the martyr-death, which he knew lay before him, *but that through this very death*, the Lord Jesus would deliver him from all weariness and toil, and would bring him safe into His heavenly kingdom. (See Ps. xxiii. 4.) St. Paul before (Phil. i. 23 had expressed a longing to come to Christ through death. He then bursts into an ascription of praise to that Lord Jesus Christ whom he had loved so long and so well, and who, in all his troubles and perplexities, had never left him friendless. For a similar ascription of glory to the Second Person of the ever-blessed Trinity, see Heb. xiii. 21. (Comp. also Rom. ix. 5.)

(19) **Salute Prisca and Aquila.**—These were two of St. Paul's earliest friends after he had begun his great work for his Master. Originally of Pontus, they had taken up their abode at Rome, where Aquila exercised his trade of a tent-maker.

Driven out of Rome by the decree of Claudius, which banished the Jews from the capital, they came to Corinth, where St. Paul became acquainted with them. But they were evidently Christians when St. Paul first met them, about A.D. 51–2. We hear of them in company with St. Paul at Corinth, about A.D. 52–3 (Acts xviii. 2); at Ephesus, about A.D. 55 (1 Cor. xvi. 19); and in the year A.D. 58 St. Paul sends greetings to them at Rome (Rom. xvi. 3).

They were, evidently, among the many active and zealous teachers of the first days of the faith. That they possessed great ability as well as zeal is evident from the fact that it was from them that the eloquent and trained Alexandrian master, Apollos, learnt to be a Christian (Acts xviii. 26). In this place, and in several other passages, Prisca (or Priscilla) is named *before* her husband, Aquila. This would seem to hint that in this case the woman was the principal worker of the two in the cause of Christ. She, in fact, was one of that band of devoted holy women which the preaching of Christ and His disciples had called into existence: a representative of the great class of noble female workers which had no existence before Christ told the world what was the true position of women—until the same divine Master taught them that they, too, as well as men, had a work to work for Him here.

And the household of Onesiphorus.—St. Paul may have been aware that Onesiphorus was absent then from Ephesus; but this peculiar greeting, taken together with the words of chap. i. 16, leads us irresistibly to the conclusion that this friend of St. Paul's was dead when the Epistle was written. (See Notes on chap. i. 16.)

(29) **Erastus abode at Corinth.**—Better rendered, *remained at Corinth*. An Erastus is mentioned in Rom. xvi. 23, the "chamberlain" of Corinth, one of the Christian congregation of that city. This man was probably identical with him.

Another "Erastus" appears among those who ministered to St. Paul at Ephesus (Acts xix. 22). Him St. Paul sent on missionary work into Macedonia. There were, therefore, among St. Paul's friends two men of this name: the one a resident official personage at Corinth; the other one of that band who journeyed hither and thither for the propagation of the faith.

But Trophimus have I left at Miletum sick.—Trophimus, a Gentile Christian, who was with St. Paul on his third missionary journey, and whom the Apostle was accused of taking into the Temple at Jerusalem. It was this accusation on the part of the Jews which led to St. Paul's arrest which preceded his first long imprisonment. The event here alluded to must have taken place some time *after* the Apostle's release from the first imprisonment, A.D. 63, and, probably, in the course of his last journey, shortly before his second arrest and imprisonment at Rome, about A.D. 66.

Miletus (not "Miletum"), a seaport of Caria, about thirty miles from Ephesus, once a city of great renown, whence, it is said, eighty colonies had proceeded; but in the days of St. Paul its glories were already on the wane. It is now famous only for its vast ruined theatre. (See Acts xx. 15.)

It has been suggested that this mention of Trophimus was intended to clear him of any neglect. "Erastus," wrote the Apostle, "remained at Corinth; *but* Trophimus' reason for not coming to Rome was his sickness."

(21) **Do thy diligence to come before winter.** Probably this was added to hasten his coming. If he delayed, the season of the year would put off, perhaps hinder altogether, his voyage.

Eubulus greeteth thee.—Of this Eubulus nothing is known.

And Pudens, and Linus, and Claudia.—Of these, Linus was, no doubt, the first of the long line of Bishops of Rome. The date of his consecration corresponds with the year of St. Paul's martyrdom, A.D. 66. We know, from this greeting, he was one of the few "faithful" to his old master.

It is, perhaps, fair to assume, though of course there is no certainty of this, that the consecration of Linus to the government of the Roman Church as its first Bishop was one of the dying acts done by the Apostle Paul.

Some commentators identify the other two with "Pudens and Claudia" mentioned by Martial (*Epigrams*, iv. 13; xi. 54). Pudens was the son of a Roman senator; to Claudia, Martial gives the name of Rufina, and states she was a Briton. The dates of the Epigrams in question would agree with the identification. It is, however, *only* a supposition.

EXCURSUS ON NOTES TO II. TIMOTHY

ON THE WAY IN WHICH "INSPIRATION OF GOD" [2 Tim. iii. 16] WAS UNDERSTOOD IN THE EARLY CHRISTIAN CHURCH.

"See and ask for the old paths, where is the good way, and walk therein, and ye shall find rest for your souls."
—Jer. vi. 16.

THE question of "inspiration" is one that in the present day often is the subject of debate. In the hot and often angry controversies on this subject among us, it will be useful and interesting to see what were the opinions held by those learned and devoted men living, many of them, in the times immediately succeeding the first age of the Faith, when those walked on earth who had seen and conversed with the Lord Jesus. We will give the words of a few of the more distinguished of the early fathers of the Faith, selecting them from different centres of Christianity.

ROME.—Clement, Bishop of Rome, A.D. 70–96.

Ad Cor. Ep. i. 45.

Ad Cor. Ep. i. 47.

Our quotations begin from the very days of the Apostles. Clement, mentioned by St. Paul (Phil. iv. 3), who, as history tells us, was the second Bishop of Rome, exhorts his readers "to look carefully into the Scriptures, which are the true utterances of the Holy Spirit;" and in another place in the same writing he expressly refers to a well-known New Testament Epistle thus:—"Take up the Epistle of the blessed Paul the Apostle, what did he write to you in the beginning [that is, in the first days of the preaching] of the gospel? In truth, divinely inspired [*πνευματικῶς, divinitus inspiratus*], he wrote to you Corinthians about himself, and Cephas, and Apollos, because just then factions [party spirit] existed among you."

ASIA MINOR.—Polycarp of Smyrna, A.D. 108.

Ep. to Philippians, cap. iii.

Polycarp, Bishop of Smyrna, a disciple of St. John, in the one letter we possess of his, tells us "that neither he nor any like him is able to attain perfectly to the wisdom of the blessed and glorious Paul, who, when he was with you, before the men who were then living taught the word of truth perfectly and surely."

SYRIA.—Ignatius of Antioch, A.D. 107.

Ep. to Philad., cap. v.

Ep. to Magn., cap. viii.

Ep. to Romans, cap. iv.

"Let us love the prophets" (of the Old Testament), wrote Ignatius, Bishop of Antioch, the pupil of St. John, to the congregations of Philadelphia, "because they proclaimed the gospel, and believed in Christ, and waited for His coming, and through their faith in Him were saved." "These most divine prophets lived according to Jesus Christ," he writes to the Church of Magnesia, "being inspired by His grace." Again: "I do not command you [Romans] like Peter and Paul: they were Apostles; I am a condemned man."

EGYPT.—Barnabas of Alexandria, probably A.D. 140–160.

Ep. Barnabas, ix.

Ep. Barnabas, x. and v.

Barnabas (probably not the friend of St. Paul, but a teacher of Alexandria who lived some seventy or eighty years after St. Paul's martyrdom), in his well-known letter, speaks there of the inspiration of the Old Testament writings. Writing of Ps. xvii. 45, "The Lord saith in the prophet;" and of Ps. xxxiii. 13, "The Spirit of the Lord prophesieth;" and in another place he tells us how "the prophets received their gift from Christ and spoke of Him;" also that "Moses spake in the Spirit."

ROME & EPHESUS. Justin Martyr, A.D. 140–150.

Cohortatio ad Gentiles, 12.

Apologia, i. 44.

Apologia, i. 44, &c.; i. 40; i. 35.

Apologia, i. 36.

Cohortatio ad Gentiles, 8.

This writer, several of whose works we still possess, was a scholar and thinker of no mean order. He wrote within half a century of St. John's death. He in several places gives us his view of the inspiration of the divine writings. Referring to the Old Testament, he speaks of the history which Moses wrote by divine inspiration, while the Holy Spirit of Prophecy taught us through the instrumentality of Moses. Of David and of Isaiah he writes in similar terms (*propheta Isaias divinitus afflatus a spiritu prophetico*). His view, of the prophetic office is remarkable. "We must not suppose," he writes, "that the expressions go forth from the men who are inspired, but from the divine word which moves them." Speaking of the writers of the Old Testament, he calls them "holy men who required no eloquence, no skill in argumentative speaking, but who only needed to present themselves pure for the Divine Spirit to act upon, in order that the divine *plectrum* [an instrument, usually of gold or ivory, used for striking the lyre], coming down from heaven, acting on just men as a plectrum on a lyre or harp, might reveal to us the knowledge of divine and heavenly things."

ATHENS.—Athenagoras, A.D. 160–180.

Leg. pro Christ. 9.

This Athenian philosopher, who, while studying the Holy Scriptures with a view of refuting Christianity, was converted by the very writings he was endeavouring to bring into disrepute, writes (using the same strange, powerful metaphor which we found in the above quotation from Justin): "The prophets, while entranced . . . by the influence of the Divine Spirit, they gave utterance to what was wrought in them—the Spirit using them as instruments as a flute-player might blow a flute."

LYONS.—Irenæus, A.D. 180.

This famous writer and bishop of the early Church was connected in his early years with Polycarp, the pupil of St. John. He (to choose one out of many passages of his writings on this subject) thus writes of the Apostles:—

Contra Hœr. iii. 1.

"After that our Lord rose from the dead, and they [the Apostles] were clothed with the power of the Spirit from on high, they were filled with a perfect knowledge of all things." "The Apostles, being the disciples of truth,

Contra Hœr. iii. 5.

are beyond all falsehood, though they speak according to the capacity of their hearers, talking blindly with the blind."

Contra Hœr. ii. 28.

In another passage this Bishop of Lyons of the second century tells us, "The Scriptures are perfect, inasmuch as they were uttered by the Word of God and His Spirit."

NORTH AFRICA: CARTHAGE.—Tertullian, A.D. 200.

Tertullian, perhaps the ablest—and, had it not been for his unhappy choice in later life of a wild and perverted form of Christianity, the greatest—of the Latin fathers, calls the Holy Scriptures the "voices of God" (*voces Dei*). In another place he writes that "the four Gospels are built on the certain basis of apostolical authority, and so are inspired in a far different sense from the writings of the spiritual Christian. All the faithful, it is true, have the Spirit of God; but all are not Apostles."

Apologia, xxxi.

EGYPT: ALEXANDRIA.—Clement, master of the Catechetical School of Alexandria, A.D. 199—200.

Clement of Alexandria was master of the catechetical school of the most learned city of the world at the end of the second century, only 100 years after the death of St. John; and taught in his famous school—as did well-nigh all the early fathers of Christianity—the doctrine of the plenary inspiration of Scripture. "It was by the masters of Israel," wrote Clement, "that God led men properly to the Messiah—speaking to them in the Law, the Psalms, and the Prophets. . . The word of God, disregarding the lifeless instruments, the lyre and the harp, reduces to harmony . . . man, and through that many-voiced instrument makes melody to God, and says to man, 'Thou art my harp, my flute, my temple: my harp, from the harmony [of many notes]; my flute, from the Spirit that breatheth through thee; my temple, from the word that dwelleth in thee.' Truly of man the Lord wrought a glorious living instrument, after the fashion of His own image—one which might give every harmony of God tuneful and holy."

Pæd. i. 11.

Protr. i. 5.

ROME.—Hippolytus of Portus, A.D. 218.

Hippolytus, Bishop of Portus (one of the suburban districts of Rome), a most learned and distinguished writer of the Italian Church of the early part of the third century, a pupil of Irenæus of Lyons, in one of his treatises preserved to us, expresses himself very clearly and with singular force on this subject. Speaking of the Jewish prophets, he writes, "These blessed men . . . spake not only of the past, but also of the present and future, that they might be shown to be heralds of things to come, not for a time merely, but for all generations. . . . For these fathers, having been perfected by the Spirit of Prophecy, and worthily honoured by the Word Himself, were brought to an inner harmony like instruments; and having the Word within them to strike the notes, by Him they were moved, and announced that which God wrote. For they did not speak of their own power, be well assured, nor proclaim that which they wished themselves, but first they were rightly endowed with wisdom by the Word, and afterwards well foretaught of the future by visions, and then, when thus assured, spake that which was revealed to them by God."

De Antichristo, 2.

ALEXANDRIA.—Origen, A.D. 230.

The Church, while condemning the errors into which the great-hearted Origen fell, still reads in every age with reverence and admiration his marvellous and brilliant teaching. It will be well to close this short paper on a great subject with two or three extracts from this famous Alexandrian master, on the subject of inspiration: "The Holy Spirit inspired each of the Saints, Prophets, and Apostles. . . . The same Spirit was present in those of old times as in those who were inspired at the coming of Christ." "Christ, the Word of God, was in Moses and the prophets, and by His Spirit they spake and did all things." Again, in his work against Celsus, he writes the following wise and beautiful words:—"The true God acted on the prophets to enlighten and strengthen them, and not to cloud or to confuse their natural powers . . . . for the divine messengers, by the contact of the Holy Spirit with their soul, so to speak, gained a deeper and a clearer intuition of spiritual truth, and they then became more perfect men as well as wise seers." In one of his homilies Origen does not hesitate even to say that "there is nothing, whether in the Law or in the Prophets, in the Evangelists or in the Apostles, which does not descend from the fulness of the divine majesty."

De Principiis, lib. i. *Procemium*, 4.

De Principiis, i. *Procemium*, i.

Contr. Celsum, vii. 4.

Hom. in Jer. xxi. 2.

This gifted teacher's noble words on the way in which these God-inspired writings should be read deserve to be graven on the heart of every Christian believer: "We must read them with pure hearts, for no one can listen to the word of God . . . unless he be holy in body and spirit: . . . no one can enter into this feast with soiled garments. He who is a student of God's oracles must place himself under the teaching of God; such a one must seek their meaning by inquiry, discussion, examination, and, which is greatest, by prayer. . . . Prayer is the most necessary qualification for the understanding of divine things. . . . . If, then, we read the Bible with patience, prayer, and faith; if we ever strive after a more perfect knowledge, and yet remain content in some things to know only in part—even as prophets and apostles, saints and angels, attain not to an understanding of all things—our patience will be rewarded, our prayer answered, and our faith increased. So let us not be weary in reading the Scriptures which we do not understand, but let it be unto us according to our faith, by which we believe that *all Scripture, being inspired by God, is profitable*" (Origen, quoted by Westcott).

Hom. in Ex. xi.

Hom. in Gen. xi. 3.

De Principiis, iv. 16.

Hom. in Jos. xx.

[For many other early patristic references to the teaching of the Church of the first days on the subject of the "Inspiration of the Scriptures," the reader may consult the exhaustive paper in Westcott's *Introduction to the Study of the Gospels*, Appendix C, pp. 383—423, upon which this short *Excursus* is mainly based.]

INTRODUCTION

TO

THE EPISTLE OF PAUL TO

TITUS

I. Titus.—Among the early Christian leaders of the school of Paul, Titus, to whom one of the three Pastoral Epistles of the Gentile Apostle was addressed, must have occupied a prominent position. For some unknown reason his name never occurs in the Acts (save, perhaps, in the doubtful reference, Acts xviii. 7, on which see below); but from a few scattered notices in the Epistles of St. Paul we are able to gather some notion of the work and influence of this distinguished and able teacher of the first days.

The silence of St. Luke in the Acts with reference to one who evidently played so important a part in the days when the foundations of the Christian Church were being laid, has been the subject of much inquiry. Attempts have been made, but with little success, to identify Titus with one or other of the characters prominent in the Acts story—with Luke himself, for instance, or Silvanus (Silas). The only possible identification, however, is with the "Justus" of Acts xviii. 7, to which name, in some of the older authorities, the name "Titus" is prefixed. The circumstances, as far as we know them, connected with Justus would fit in with this identification. This Justus was, like Titus, closely connected with Corinth; and, like Titus too, was an uncircumcised Gentile, attending the Jewish services as a proselyte of the gate. That these two were identical is possible, but nothing more.

Titus was of Gentile parentage, and probably a native of Antioch—the great centre of that early *Gentile* Christianity of which St. Paul was the first teacher, and, under the Holy Ghost, the founder. Some time before A.D. 50—51 the master and scholar had come together. In that year he accompanied Barnabas and St. Paul to the council of Apostles and elders which was convened at Jerusalem to consider the question of the general obligations of the Mosaic law. The result was the drawing up of the charter of Gentile freedom from all the restraints of the Jewish law. (See Acts xv.; Gal. ii. 1—3.) From this time (A.D. 50—51) the glad tidings that Christ was indeed a Light to the Gentiles (Isa. xlix. 6) spread through Asia, North Africa, and Europe with a strange and marvellous rapidity. There is no doubt, from the scattered notices in the Epistles of St. Paul, that Titus was one of the most active agents in the promulgation of the gospel story among the peoples that had hitherto sat in darkness and in the shadow of death.

The following table will give some idea of Titus connection with St. Paul:—

DATE.	EMPEROR OF ROME.	—
Before A.D. 50—51	Claudius.	Titus meets with and is instructed by St. Paul at Antioch in the faith. (Comp. Tit. i. 4: "My own son in the faith.")
50—51		Titus accompanies St. Paul and Barnabas to the council of Apostles and elders at Jerusalem (Acts xv.; Gal. ii. 1).
54—55	Nero.	Probably with St. Paul during part of his second missionary journey. He is evidently well known to the Galatians, from the familiar reference to him in the Epistle to that Church. Perhaps he is alluded to in Gal. iii. 5.
56		With St. Paul at Ephesus. Thence sent on a special mission to Corinth, probably bearer of the First Epistle to the Corinthians (2 Cor. xii. 18).
57		With St. Paul in Macedonia (2 Cor. vii. 6—15), and perhaps with St. Paul at Corinth, if identical with Justus, according to the reading of some of the older authorities.
65—66		Titus is superintending presbyter in Crete.
66—67		At Rome with St. Paul; thence sent to Dalmatia (2 Tim. iv. 10).
		[Tradition speaks of Titus as returning from Dalmatia to Crete, where he died in extreme old age, as Archbishop of Gortyna.]

Titus, as we have seen, was a Gentile—was the one chosen by the great Apostle in very early days as the example of Christian freedom from Jewish rites and customs. At first the pupil, then the friend of St. Paul, we find him, in the brief notices in the Epistles, evidently occupying a position quite independent of, and in no wise subject to, his old master. He is St. Paul's "brother," "companion," "fellow-labourer" (2 Cor. viii. 22, 23); St. Paul's trusted and honoured friend. His missions of investigation and love, his arrangements for the famous collection for the poor saints at Jerusalem, were apparently undertaken spontaneously, rather than by the direction of a superior and elder officer of the Church. (See, for instance, 2 Cor. viii. 6, 16, 17.) Now the Acts is confessedly a very early writing, and must have been put forth not later than A.D. 62—63; would it not be very probable that, in such a work, so prominent a Gentile, who had publicly, with St. Paul's consent, held himself free from all Jewish restraints, and by his prominent example preached the perfect equality of the Gentiles in the kingdom of God—would it not be very probable that in the Acts the name and work of such a person would be omitted? The fierce hostility of a large section of the Jewish race to St. Paul on account of this very teaching of equality is well known: it probably compassed in the end his death. The gentle, loving spirit of St. Luke while telling the story of the foundation of the Christian Church with scrupulous accuracy, would be likely to avoid such passages of the early history which would tend to alienate any. (He never, for instance, hints at such scenes as the Galatian Epistle, chap. ii., relates so graphically.) This same spirit, which ever sought to win rather than to alienate, induced him, perhaps, to avoid the mention of the famous Gentile leader Titus at a period when the fierce hostility of the Christians of the Circumcision was endeavouring to compass the fall of St. Paul and the disruption of the school of Gentile Christianity.

The Holy Spirit loves to work, we know, by purely human instruments—now by the tender conciliatory pen of a Luke—now by the fiery zeal of a Paul, which refuses to recognise danger, or to acknowledge the possibility of failure.

Later on the appointment of the brilliant and successful Gentile organiser to the chief superintendence of the churches of Crete was one of singular fitness. "There was," as it has been well said, "a strange blending of races and religions" in the island which boasted the possession of the birthplace of Zeus (Jupiter), and rejoiced in the vile mysteries practised in the worship of Dionysus (Bacchus). There were many Jews we know at Crete, but the Gentile population, of course, far outnumbered them. The congregation seem to have been numerous and full of life, but disorganised and troubled with disorder, misrule, and even dishonoured with many an excess utterly at variance with their Christian profession. Who so fitted to restore order and to enforce a sterner rule in such communities as the friend of St. Paul, who had worked already so great a work among the turbulent and licentious Christians of Corinth, and had persuaded by his marvellous skill so many Gentile congregations to unite in helping with a generous liberality the pressing needs of their proud and haughty Jewish brethren who disdained them? (See the Note on chap. i. 4.)

After the year A.D. 65—66 the story of Titus is uncertain. We know he rejoined the Apostle at Rome, and left him again for Dalmatia (2 Tim. iv. 10).

Then traditionary recollections which lingered in Crete tell us how he returned from Dalmatia to the island, where he worked long and presided over the churches, and died at an advanced age. The church of Megalo-Castron, in the north of the island, was dedicated to him. In the Middle Ages, his name was still revered, and his memory honoured. The name of Titus was the watchword of the Cretans when they fought against the Venetians, who came under the standard of St. Mark. The Venetians themselves, when here, seem to have transferred to him part of that respect which elsewhere would probably have been manifested for St. Mark alone. During the celebration of several great festivals of the Church the response of the Latin clergy of Crete, after the prayer for the Doge of Venice, was, *Sancte Marce tu nos adjuva;* but after that for the Duke of Candia, *Sancte Tite tu nos adjuva* (Pashley's *Travels in Crete*, quoted by Conybeare and Howson, *St. Paul*).

II. Contents of the Epistle.—After a formal salutation and greeting St. Paul reminds Titus of his special work in Crete, viz., that the government of the various churches must be properly organised—a body of elders, or presbyters, must be ordained and set over the congregation. The qualifications of these officers are then detailed. They are for the most part of a moral nature, but these elders must also possess the power necessary for teaching and influencing such a people as were the Cretans (chap. i. 1—16). St. Paul passes on to the special kind of instruction Titus and the elders must impart to men and women of varied ages, sexes, and ranks in the Cretan churches—to aged men, to aged women, to the young of both sexes, to slaves—and then proceeds to show the reason why such instruction must be given. God's grace, he says, has appeared in the work of redemption, bringing salvation to all—old or young, free or slaves (chap. ii. 1—15). St. Paul now points out to Titus how the Christian community must conduct themselves towards the heathen world. There must be no thought of rebellion among the worshippers of the Lord Jesus. Again he enforces these solemn admonitions by an appeal to the loftiest Christian truths. He closes his Letter by reminding his friend that this practical teaching, based on gospel truth, must be the standard of instruction; no time must be wasted on useless theological questions. A few personal requests are added (chap. iii. 1—15).

THE EPISTLE OF PAUL TO
TITUS

CHAPTER I.—(1) Paul, a servant of God, and an apostle of Jesus Christ, according to the faith of God's elect, and the acknowledging of the truth which is after godliness; (2) in[1] hope of eternal life, which God, that cannot lie, promised before the world began; (3) but hath in due times manifested his word through preaching, which is committed unto me according to the commandment of God our Saviour;

Chap. i. 1—4. Apostolic address and blessing.

A.D. 65.

1 Or, *for*.

(1) **Paul, a servant of God, and an apostle of Jesus Christ.**—The titles here assumed by St. Paul in his introductory greeting are in some respects slightly different to any of his usual designations. In the other two so-called Pastoral Epistles addressed to Timothy, St. Paul simply styles himself "an Apostle of Jesus Christ." Possibly, the longer and more formal title is here adopted because his relations were hardly ever of so intimate a character with Titus as with Timothy; the latter would seem to have held the position of St. Paul's *adopted son*. (See Note below on verse 4, "To Titus.")

According to the faith of God's elect.—The English version here entirely fails to give the meaning of the Greek preposition. The rendering should be, "for (the furtherance of) the faith," or, in other words, "the object of my (Paul's) apostleship was, that through my instrumentality the chosen of God should believe." The whole question respecting these "elect," or "chosen of God," is surrounded with deep mystery; three or four guiding thoughts may, however, be safely laid down. (1) In the visible world such an *apparently* arbitrary election to special privileges, fortune, happiness, utterly irrespective, in the first instance, of individual merit, does exist. This is clear to all of us. (2) In grace we are distinctly told repeatedly that a similar election exists, and our own observation certainly coincides here with revelation. (3) Such election in no case seemingly affects our position here as free agents; surrounded with the most precious privileges, gifted with much knowledge, it is possible, as we, alas, too often see, deliberately to refuse the good and to choose the evil. (4) All such allusions to the "elect" as, for instance, the one here before us, are intended, not as a stumbling-block for the believer, but as a comfort for the faithful, struggling man of God, for it tells him how the Eternal "before the ages" had chosen him to be His servant.

And the acknowledging of the truth which is after godliness.—More accurately rendered, *and the full knowledge of the truth which is designed for godliness*, or, *which leadeth to godliness*. Here the further purpose of St. Paul's apostleship is specified. St. Paul was appointed an Apostle that through him the elect of God might believe and heed "the truth"—that truth, the knowledge of which produces as its fruit in the individual a holy, useful life.

(2) **In hope of eternal life.**—Better translated, *resting on the hope of eternal life*. The connection of the preceding clauses with these words has been well summed up: "The Apostle's calling had for its object the faith of the elect and the knowledge of the truth; and the basis on which all this rested was the hope of eternal life."

Which God, that cannot lie.—Possibly, this singular and strong expression was chosen with reference to the peculiar vice of the Cretans, over whose Church Titus was then presiding. (See verse 12: "One of themselves, even a prophet of their own, said, The Cretians are alway *liars*.")

Promised before the world began.—More accurately rendered, *from eternal ages*. (See 2 Tim. i. 9.) The promise of eternal life was the result of a divine purpose fixed from eternity.

(3) **But hath in due times.**—Or better, *but hath in his own seasons*—that is, in the fitting seasons, those fixed by Him for the manifestation.

Manifested his word.—That is, His gospel. (See Rom. xvi. 25.)

Through preaching.—Or, *in the preaching*. Paul does not shrink from calling his preaching the vehicle in which the Word or the gospel of God was to be publicly manifested, because he was conscious that he was divinely instructed in the secrets of the eternal counsels.

Which is committed unto me.—Literally, *with which I was entrusted*.

According to the commandment of God our Saviour.—The commandment came to St. Paul direct from God; we have several intimations of this. Amongst others, on the Damascus road, when the Lord appeared to him; in the Temple at Jerusalem; in the ship, during the memorable voyage which ended with shipwreck; in the visions mentioned in 2 Cor. xii. 1—9. St. Paul dwells with emphasis on the thought that *he was entrusted with* the preaching of the gospel according to the commandment of God. The work was not undertaken by him, from any will or wish of his own. "God our Saviour" in this place, as in 1 Tim. i. 1, must be understood as "God the Father." The First Person of the blessed Trinity fitly possesses the title of "our Saviour," because through the death of His dear Son He redeemed us from death and made us heirs of eternal life. The Second Person of the Trinity is likewise a possessor of the title, because He shed His blood as the price of our redemption. The epithet of "Saviour"—the title just given to the Father, in the very next verse ascribed to the "Son"—is one of the

(4) to Titus, *mine* own son after the common faith: Grace, mercy, *and* peace, from God the Father and the Lord Jesus Christ our Saviour. (5) For this cause

many indications we possess of St. Paul's belief that the Son was equal to the Father as touching His Godhead.

(4) **To Titus.**—We know comparatively little of Titus' earlier career. In the Acts he, singularly enough, is never mentioned; for what knowledge of him we possess we are entirely dependent upon a few casual allusions to him in the Epistles. This presbyter, in charge of the Cretan Church, was a Greek, the son of Gentile parents, and uncircumcised. It has been suggested, but upon very slight grounds, that his family was resident at Antioch in Syria. He owed his conversion to Christianity to St. Paul, with whom ever after he seems to have been connected by ties of intimate friendship, though he was by no means the Apostle's constant companion, as was Timothy, or Silas, or Luke. He was with St. Paul and Barnabas when they went up together to Jerusalem to plead for Gentile liberty; but in no other of the journeys of St. Paul is he directly mentioned as one of the companions of the Apostle. Only during the Apostle's long residence at Ephesus (nearly three years) Titus appears to have been, for at least part of the time, closely associated with St. Paul, and his confidant in his complicated relations with foreign churches. It is clear that during this long Ephesian residence he was drawn into close and intimate friendship with St. Paul, who then had opportunity of becoming acquainted with Titus' varied powers and evident skill in administration and in dealing with men and women.

From the several casual notices in the Second Corinthian Epistle, we gather considerable insight into the character and powers of the Gentile convert. The Church of Corinth was perhaps the largest and most wealthy of all the churches founded by St. Paul. It was soon, however, rent asunder by party divisions, and was ever distracted and disturbed by moral disorders among its members. Yet, in spite of this, the great Greek congregation of believers was full of life and zeal and earnestness, ready evidently to make the greatest sacrifices for its Master's cause. Delegated apparently by St. Paul to restore order and to introduce a severer discipline in this great and turbulent Christian centre—the example for good or for evil to so many smaller and less important churches—Titus seems to have fulfilled with rare tact, and with admirable prudence and wisdom, his difficult mission. Amongst other works, he apparently completed the collection St. Paul had set on foot in the various Gentile churches for the poor Jewish Christians at Jerusalem. His services, assisting materially to bring this famous work of charity to a successful issue, seem not to have been the least among his titles to St. Paul's friendship and high esteem. The great importance and difficult nature of this collection for the poor saints at Jerusalem are little understood or thought of now. Three weighty points connected with it deserve mention, as Titus' special task it probably was to complete and bring it to a successful issue. (1) It seems to have been the first public relief fund ever collected to help a foreign and a strange race—the first of a long line of gallant acts of self-sacrifice men have made for men for Christ's sake; but when Titus, at St. Paul's bidding, took charge of it, it was a thing unheard of in the Pagan world. Hence the many obstacles which appear to have cropped up so perpetually during the collection. (2) It was the right hand of fellowship offered by Gentile to Jew. It was the welding together, by an unprecedented act of kindness, of the two opposing and hostile elements of Christendom into one Church. (3) It was the silent yet eloquent protest of St. Paul and his school against the attempted communism of the Church of the very first days—that fatal misunderstanding of some of the Master's words which had brought ruin and poverty on the Jerusalem Christians. Titus acted as St. Paul's commissioner in the matter—which he evidently successfully completed. We know nothing of his work and employment from this period, A.D. 57, until the date of this Epistle, A.D. 65—66, early Christian history being silent respecting him. In these nine years of restless activity and burning zeal on the part of the Christian leaders, Titus, no doubt, did his part without falling short of his early promise; as we find him again, in the last years of his old master, occupying in the Christian community a post so high and responsible as that of chief presbyter of the churches of the wealthy and populous island of Crete.

Mine own son.—Alluding, no doubt, to the relation between them in religion. St. Paul converted Titus to the faith, and ever after Titus stood to St. Paul in the position of a son in the faith, without being to him what Timothy was for so long a time—his constant companion. Titus still evidently (see preceding Note) filled with St. Paul the position of one of his most trusty disciples, of one who knew the inmost thoughts of his master. The tone of the Epistle to Titus is somewhat different from St. Paul's Letter to Timothy. There was evidently a greater intimacy between St. Paul and Timothy than between the Apostle and Titus.

Grace, mercy, and peace . . .—Many of the older authorities omit "mercy." (See Notes on 1 Tim. i. 2.)

Our Saviour.—This expression is a rare one. We find it only in these Pastoral Letters. (See Note above on St. Paul's using it also of the "Father.")

(5) **For this cause left I thee in Crete.**—The "cause" is discussed below. Crete—over whose Christian population Titus had been placed by St. Paul—was a well-known large and populous island in the Mediterranean. It lies geographically further south than any of the European islands, and, roughly speaking, almost at an equal distance from each of the three Old World continents—Europe, Asia, Africa. We identify it with the Caphtor of the Old Testament (Deut. ii. 23; Jer. xlvii. 4; Amos ix. 7). In modern times it is known by us as Candia. Very early it was the scene of an advanced civilisation. In the *Odyssey* it is mentioned as possessing ninety cities; in the *Iliad* as many as one hundred. Metellus added it, B.C. 69, to the Roman dominion. In the days of Augustus it was united into one province with Cyrene. It abounded with Jews of wealth and influence; this we learn from the testimony of Philo and of Josephus. It probably received the gospel from some of those of "Crete" who we are expressly told were present when the Spirit was poured on the Apostles on the first Pentecost after the Resurrection (Acts ii. 11). The apparently flourishing state of Christianity on the island at this time was in great measure, no doubt, owing to the residence and labours among them of the Apostle St. Paul, whose work appears to have been mainly directed to preaching the gospel and to increasing the number of the converts, which, from the wording of verse 5, was evidently

Chap. i. 5—9. The duties of elders, or presbyters, in the Church.

left I thee in Crete, that thou shouldest set in order the things that are wanting,[1] and ordain elders in every city, as I had appointed thee:
(6) if any be blameless, the husband of one wife, having faithful children, not accused of riot, or unruly. (7) For a bishop must be blameless, as the steward of God; not selfwilled, not

[1] Or, *left undone.*

very great, elders (presbyters) being required in every city.

The task of organising the Church had been left for a season. We are ignorant of the circumstance which summoned the old Apostle from the scene of what seems to have been most successful labours. He left behind him one of the ablest of his disciples, Titus—a tried and well-known Christian leader of the second half of the first century—to organise the church life and to regulate the teaching of the powerful and numerous Christian community of Crete.

The Epistle addressed to Titus contains the formal credentials of his high office, stamping all his acts with the great name and authority of St. Paul; hence the careful and elaborate phraseology of the first four verses. Though addressed to one, they would have to be referred to and read often among the elders (*presbyters*) and deacons in the various churches. St. Paul wrote the Letter, we are told, when on his way to Nicopolis to winter; we believe, soon after his arrival there he was arrested and sent to Rome to die. The date of this Letter, then, would be A.D. 65 or 66, and was probably written from some place in Asia Minor—perhaps Ephesus.

That thou shouldest set in order the things that are wanting.—These words explain the "cause" of Titus' appointment in Crete. The "things that are wanting" were what St. Paul meant, no doubt, to have done himself, but was prevented by being hurried away—for *him* the end was nigh at hand. These "things" were want of church officials, lack of church government, want of cohesion between the churches of the island—in a word, there was plenty of Christian life, but no Christian organisation as yet in Crete. It was rather a number of Christian brotherhoods than one.

And ordain elders in every city.—The number of presbyters in each town or city is not specified, but is left to Titus' judgment. We know that in some churches there were certainly several of these presbyters (see Acts xiv. 23; xv. 22). The words "in every city" point to the wide extension of Christianity at that early period in Crete.

As I had appointed thee.—Or better, *as I gave thee directions.* These presbyters were to be most carefully selected, according to the special instructions Titus must remember St. Paul giving him in this important matter on some previous occasion. The more urgent of these qualifications for the presbyteral rank the Apostle now repeats for Titus' guidance.

(6) **If any be blameless.**—The candidate for the holy office must have naught laid to his charge; he must be of such a character that no one could bring a reasonable accusation against him. Blameless must be his life, spotless his name. As it has been well said, "the office of presbyter must never be allowed to cover or condone damaged reputations."

The husband of one wife.—See Notes on 1 Tim. iii. 2.

Having faithful children.— Better, *believing children.* In searching out these presbyters, whose charge would involve so many and such responsible duties, Titus must look for men of ripe age. There were even grave objections to the appointment of the comparatively young to this office. We have seen how anxious St. Paul was for Timothy, his well-known and trusted friend, on account of his want of years. Timothy must have been at least approaching forty years of age when St. Paul warned him so earnestly of his behaviour and his life, "Let no man despise thy youth." These presiding Cretan elders should be married men, with children already, so to speak, grown up.

These requirements evidently show that Christianity had been established in Crete for a very considerable period. We must remember some thirty-three years had passed since that memorable Pentecost feast of Jerusalem, when "Cretes" were among the hearers of those marvellous utterances of the Spirit. Besides the children of the candidates for the presbyter's office being professing Christians, they must also be free from all suspicion of profligacy.

Not accused of riot.—More accurately rendered, *dissoluteness.* The Greek word here rendered "riot" implies a self-indulgent or even a reckless expenditure. Such careless selfishness well-nigh always ends in profligacy. In the case of men whose duties included the superintendence of the Church's funds, it was imperatively necessary that their homes and families should be free from all suspicion of anything like that reckless waste or extravagance which in so many cases imperceptibly passes into dissoluteness and profligacy.

Or unruly.—That is, disobedient to their parents. If the presbyter was incapable of teaching his own children obedience and order, what hope was there that his influence would be of any value with his flock? All these early instructions to the master-builders whose task it was to lay the early storeys of the Christian Temple are very decisive as to the state of St. Paul's mind; and we must not forget *whence* St. Paul directly drew his wisdom. The Apostles of the Lord never seem to have thought of the Christian priesthood of the future *developing into a caste or order.* Anything more diametrically opposed to the mediæval notion of church government than the Pastoral Epistles can hardly be imagined. The writer of the Epistles to Timothy and to Titus never dreamed of building up a priestly order with views, thoughts, hopes, and joys differing from those of the ordinary worker of the world. St. Paul's presbyters were to be chosen, among other qualities, for the white and blameless lives of their families. The presbyter's home in Crete and Ephesus must supply a fair pattern for the many other Christian homes in that luxurious, dissolute age in which Titus lived.

(7) **For a bishop must be blameless.**—There is no doubt that the "bishop" here must be identified with the presbyter of verse 6. In the Pastoral Epistles written between A.D. 63—67 these terms are clearly applied indifferently to the same person. The title presbyter refers to the gravity and dignity of the office; the title bishop suggests rather the duties which belong to an elder of the church. On the question of bishops, and their position in the early Church, see Note on 1 Tim. iii. 1, where the grounds

soon angry, not given to wine,[a] no striker,
not given to filthy lucre; (8) but a lover
of hospitality, a lover of good men,[1]
sober, just, holy, temperate; (9) holding
fast the faithful word as he hath been
taught,[2] that he may be able by sound
doctrine both to exhort and to convince
the gainsayers. (10) For there are many

a 1 Tim. 3. 3.
2 Or, *in teaching.*
1 Or, *good things.*

for assuming that the episcopal order was formally introduced into church government before the end of this century, and during the lifetime of St. John, are discussed. The Christian bishop, within a quarter of a century after the death of St. Paul, assumed many of the functions and generally discharged the duties of government which were exercised by the Apostles during their lifetime. The presbyter—then writes St. Paul—seeing he is appointed an overseer or bishop (the use of the latter term bishop in the ecclesiastical sense is, however, premature), as God's steward, as a responsible administrator of the House, that is, of the Church of the Living God, ought indeed be blameless.

Not selfwilled.—He should not be one of those self-loving men who seeks to gratify his own personal ends in the first place, and in consequence is usually regardless of others.

Not soon angry.—Not soon provoked, or not irascible. He should not be one ever ready with an angry, hasty word, remembering always his Master, "who when He was reviled, reviled not again."

Not given to wine.—While the presbyter is not to be chosen on account of any stern austerities or rigid asceticism he may have practised, he must be known as one "temperate," moderate, self-denying.

No striker.—Not a brawler. No man of God—above all things, no one holding office in the church—should ever, even under sore provocation, so far forget himself as to raise his hand against his fellow.

Not given to filthy lucre.—The presbyter of the House of God must be above all dreaming of mean and paltry gains. He who is to administer the alms devoted to God must surely do it with clean hands. There is, too, another and a deeper meaning in the words. The presbyter whose mind is at all devoted to the amassing of gold is too preoccupied to be able to fix his thoughts upon those high things of God committed to his charge, among which one of his most important duties is to instruct the flock.

(8) **But a lover of hospitality.**—It has been suggested that this hospitality would be especially shown in the early centuries of Christianity, when Christians travelling from one place to another were received kindly and forwarded on their journey by their brethren; but the direction of St. Paul has that broader signification, so beautifully worded in the Epistle to the Hebrews, where we are told not to be forgetful to entertain *strangers*, for thereby some have entertained angels unawares (Heb. xiii. 2).

A lover of good men.—Although this rendering is possible, still it is better to understand the Greek word here as alluding to a virtue differing from the "hospitality" just mentioned. "A lover of good" or benevolence generally; the appellation points here to that large heart which finds room for sympathy with all that is good and noble and generous.

Sober.—Better rendered, *self-restrained.* In this expressive word (*sophrona*) *mastery of self* is especially implied—that self-command which wisely regulates pleasures and passions.

Just.—Or, *righteous.* The man who is just (*dikaios*) is one who tries strictly to perform his duties *towards men*—the duties which integrity and justice seem imperatively to ask from him in his relations with his neighbour.

Holy.—The man who is *holy* studies to be true and faithful *in his relations to God*, which duties with us largely consist in keeping pure our bodies, the temple of the Holy Spirit. While the "just" man struggles after uprightness before men, the "holy" man aims at a holy purity before God.

Temperate.—This virtue is not to be understood in the usual and more limited sense which has been already specified in "not given to wine" of the preceding verse, but signifies the being temperate—moderate in all things. The model presbyter, the ruler of a congregation of Christians, not only must be able to control his tongue, his eyes, his hands, but must show a just and wise moderation even in pressing things which of themselves are excellent. To do his Master's work efficiently, he must be able at all times to command himself—to perform that most difficult of all tasks, the tempering zeal with discretion.

(9) **Holding fast the faithful word as he hath been taught.**—More literally, *according to the teaching;* but the English version gives the sense clearly and exactly. The elder must, St. Paul says, hold fast the faithful word or saying; or, in other words, must steadily adhere to that Christian doctrine taught by St. Paul and his brother Apostles. So St. Paul pressed on Timothy, the chief presbyter of Ephesus, "to hold the pattern of sound words which thou heardest from me" (2 Tim. i. 13); and again, "But continue thou in the things which thou hast learned, and hast been assured of, knowing of whom thou hast learned them" (2 Tim. iii. 14). Here "the faithful saying," that formulary so common in the Epistles to Timothy and to Titus, and which we have generally explained as including the great Christian watchwords of the faith, echoes probably of sayings of Christ, taken up and expanded by His chosen servants, and then adopted in the various churches and woven into the tapestry of the earliest liturgies—now, possibly, after a form like the "comfortable words" of our Communion Service, now into a creed, now into a hymn, but in one shape or other thoroughly well known and loved in the different congregations—here the faithful word or saying seems to include *all* the faithful sayings, and denotes generally the teaching of St. Paul and the Apostles.

To exhort and to convince the gainsayers.—Two special purposes are specified for which the "sound doctrine" which the elder will acquire by steadfast application may be used. The first, with the sound, healthy teaching—sound, healthy, practical, compared with that sickly, morbid, and unpractical teaching of those gainsayers of whom he is going to speak—he is *to exhort* the adversaries; secondly, with the same true words he is *to confute* their arguments. Chrysostom well remarks "that he who knows not how to contend with adversaries, and is not able to demolish their arguments, is far from the teacher's chair."

(10) **For there are many unruly and vain talkers and deceivers.**—Nominally in the congregations of Christians, but in reality refusing all obedience, acting for themselves, factious, insubordinate. Titus would, alas, discover many such; these often

unruly and vain talkers and deceivers,
specially they of the circumcision: (11) whose mouths
must be stopped, who subvert whole houses, teaching things which
they ought not, for filthy lucre's sake.

Chap. i. 10—16. The Cretan character.

(12) One of themselves, *even* a prophet of
their own, said, The Cretians *are* alway
liars, evil beasts, slow bellies. (13) This
witness is true. Wherefore rebuke them
sharply, that they may be sound in the
faith; (14) not giving heed to Jewish

---

would be found to be possessed of the gift of fluent and deceptive speech, and would deceive many. Professor Reynolds characterises such restless, uneasy spirits as loquacious, restless talkers, "who *must* say something, and who have broken the peace of many a home and shattered the prosperity of many a church; the multitude of teachers who have nothing true to say is the curse of the kingdom of God."

Specially they of the circumcision.—Here St. Paul points out to Titus *where* he must look for the origin of this hostility. These unhappy men evidently did not belong to the stern and rigid Jewish party who hated with a bitter hate all the followers of the Nazarene, but were of the number of those sleepless opponents of St. Paul and his school—the Judaising Christians.

(11) **Whose mouths must be stopped, who subvert whole houses.**—The translation should run here, *seeing they subvert,* &c. There was, indeed, grave cause why these men should be put to silence; the mischief they were doing in Crete to the Christian cause was incalculable. It was no longer individuals that their poisonous teaching affected, but they were undermining the faith of whole families. For an example how Titus and his presbyters were to stop the mouths of these teachers of what was false, compare Matt. xxii. 34—46, where the Lord, by His wise, powerful, yet gentle words, first put the Sadducees to silence, and then so answered the Pharisees that "neither durst any man from that day forth ask Him any more questions."

Teaching things which they ought not, for filthy lucre's sake.—Here St. Paul goes to the root of the evil, when he shows what was the end and aim of these "teachers'" life. It was a mean and sordid ambition, after all—merely base gain. When this is the main object of a religious teacher's life, his teaching naturally accommodates itself to men's tastes. He forgets the Divine Giver of his commission, and in his thirst for the popularity which brings with it gold, his true work, as the faithful watchman of the house of Israel, is forgotten and ignored.

(12) **One of themselves, even a prophet of their own, said.**—St. Paul had spoken (verses 10, 11) in the severest terms of certain influential members of the Cretan Church; he had even alluded to their disastrous teaching ruining whole families, evidently implying that he had perceived among the Cretans a readiness to welcome a teaching which countenanced a laxer moral tone, the invariable result of perverted doctrine; and now he supports his own condemning words by a reference to a well-known Cretan poet—to one who, according to tradition, was even honoured by them as a god. The verse quoted is an hexameter, written by the famous Epimenides, of Gnossus, in Crete. He flourished some 600 years B.C., and is said to have lived to the strange age of 150 years or more. He appears to have deserved the title of prophet in its fullest sense—Plato speaking of him as a "divine man," and Cicero coupling him with the Erythæan Sibyl. The first three words were well known, and even used by Callimachus in his hymn to Zeus, "Cretans always liars." St. Paul's knowledge of the poem where the verse occurs is one of the several instances which we meet with in his writings indicating his familiarity with profane literature. The quotation, occurring as it does in the midst of an inspired writing, was the occasion of Calvin's wise, brave words, which style those who decline to avail themselves of the learning and research of profane writers as superstitious. Nothing wise and learned, he says, should be rejected, even though it proceed "ab impiis."

The Cretians are alway liars.—This terrible estimate of the national Cretan character is amply borne out by the testimony of many profane writers, such as Callimachus, Plato, Polybius, Ovid, &c. The very word "to Cretize" (*kretizein*), or to play the part of a Cretan, was invented as a word synonymous with "to deceive," "to utter a lie;" just as *corinthiazein,* "to play the part of a Corinthian," signified to commit a still darker moral offence. Some writers suggest that this despicable vice of lying was received as a bequest from the early Phœnician colonists.

Evil beasts.—These words refer to their wild, fierce nature, their ferocity, their love of cruelty.

Slow bellies.—Rather, *idle bellies.* These terms paint with sharp accuracy another of the evil characteristics of the Cretan peoples—their dull gluttony, their slothful sensuality. The words are used especially of those who, by indulging their bodily appetites, become corpulent and indolent.

(13) **This witness is true.**—St. Paul emphatically here endorses the very severe judgment which their own great prophet-poet had written on the national Cretan character. He (St. Paul) had lived long enough in their midst to be able to bear his grave testimony to the truth of Epimenides' words. He had witnessed the sad havoc in Christian life which their evil national propensities had caused.

Wherefore rebuke them sharply, that they may be sound in the faith.—Some render, *wherefore confute,* that is to say, *set them right, sharply* (*apotomōs*). The substantive *apotomia,* translated in the English version "severity," is used in the passage about the "wild olive tree" (Rom. xi. 22). As a surgeon's knife cuts away the diseased and mortifying flesh, so must the words and discipline of Titus, the Apostle's representative in Crete, sharply rebuke, and, if need be, punish the sinning members of the congregation. Not merely the false teachers—*the deceivers*—are referred to here, but also *the deceived,* those whole households mentioned in verse 11; and the object of this severity in words and acts was that the lapsed, the doctrinally and morally sick, among the Cretan Christians, should be restored to health again; and the sound state of faith and practice would, St. Paul proceeded to show, consist in "the rejection of Jewish fables and the commandments of these men."

(14) **Not giving heed to Jewish fables.**—Such as we now find embodied in the Talmud. (See Note on 1 Tim. i. 4.) The oral law and traditional

fables, and commandments of men, that
turn from the truth. (15) Unto the pure
all things *are* pure: but unto them that
are defiled and unbelieving *is* nothing
pure; but even their mind and conscience
is defiled. (16) They profess that they
know God; but in works they deny *him*,
being abominable, and disobedient, and
unto every good work reprobate.[1]

CHAPTER II.—(1) But speak thou
the things which become sound doc-

[1] Or, *void of judgment.*

A.D. 65.

---

interpretations and glosses had, to a great measure, obscured the original simple text. The Israelite of the time of St. Paul, trained in the stricter Jewish schools, was taught that the way to win the approval of the Most High was through the observance of countless ceremonies and the practice of an elaborate ritual.

And commandments of men.—The nature of these commandments we gather from the words of the next (the 15th) verse. They seem to have been on the subject of abstinence from meats and from other things created by God for the use and enjoyment of man. The directions of St. Paul here are, in spirit, in exact accordance with the Lord's teaching at Jerusalem, related in Matt. xv. 1—9. St. Paul's dread of this kind of asceticism and of the peculiar school of teaching, then so popular among the Jews, which enjoined an elaborate system of ritual and observance, which pronounced meritorious in the sight of the Eternal the practice of rites and ceremonies minute and trifling, was grounded upon a fear—too often, alas, verified—lest with the observance of the ritual, and the careful practice of the ceremonies and rites, the moral law should be lost sight of. With this school a holy life consisted rather in observing carefully a ritual, than in living justly, nobly, generously.

(15) **Unto the pure all things are pure.**—The spirit of this famous saying of St. Paul, occurring almost in the same language in the Roman Letter (chap. xiv. 20), was the groundwork of much of the Gentile Apostle's teaching. The words of the Lord Jesus above referred to (Matt. xv. 2 and 11) contain the same grand truth. "All things" include much besides mere food —in a word, include all acts connected with every-day life which in themselves are neither right nor wrong, neither good nor evil, but which derive their colouring of good or evil solely from the doer of the act. Bengel well sums this up in his "omnia externa eis, qui intus sunt mundi, munda sunt."

But unto them that are defiled and unbelieving is nothing pure.—Here, as so often in these Pastoral Epistles, the last utterance, so to speak, of that grand life of St. Paul's, purity and sound doctrine are inseparable. Here "the defiled," "the polluted," we are told, are the unbelieving; and to these, the Apostle says, nothing is pure. Yet there is nothing in God's creation impure or evil—the evil and impurity are in the mind and heart of men; these may, and often do, defile and make impure the choicest gifts of God's creation. One word is still left to be said on the teaching of this memorable verse. *Who* are the pure to whom all things are pure? Only those in this world who have sought cleansing by faith in the precious blood of Christ.

But even their mind and conscience is defiled.—Here St. Paul defines exactly the sphere over which the moral defilement of these hapless ones, who belong to the Christian company, alas, only in name, extends—the mind and conscience. The first of these—*the mind*—is the willing as well as the thinking part of man, as it has been well defined the human spirit (*pneuma*) in one of its aspects, not simply *quatenus cogitat et intelligit*, but also *quatenus vult.* Defilement of this mind (*nous*) means that the thoughts, wishes, purposes, activities, are all stained and debased. The second of these—the conscience (*suneidēsis*)—is the moral consciousness within, that which is ever bringing up the memory of the past, with its omissions and commissions, its errors, its cruel, heartless unkindness, its selfish disregard of others. When *this* is defiled, then this last safeguard of the soul is broken down. The man and woman of the defiled conscience is *self-satisfied*, hard, impenitent to the last.

(16) **They profess that they know God; but in works they deny him.**—These bitter foes to the truth, Titus must remember, will present themselves under the guise of friends. They will rank themselves in the Christian company openly, with their lips confessing God, but in their way of life, in their acts, practically denying the very things they were so careful to affirm with their lips; in other words, taking back, withdrawing, the solemn declaration of faith they had been making.

Being abominable.—This is the only place where this strong expression is used in the New Testament. It signifies that the life and actions of these men, who professed to be His servants, had made them hateful in the sight of God.

And disobedient.—Rebellious and opposed to all law and order would Titus find them.

And unto every good work reprobate.—As a consequence of their hypocritical, selfish, defiled life, these men, when any good and noble work had to be done, were simply useless, worthless; and to teachers of this kind were many of the Cretan believers content to go for instruction in Christian doctrine and practice.

II.

(1) **But speak thou the things which become sound doctrine.**—To introduce a regular organisation and the principle of a central church government into the numerous but scattered Christian congregations in Crete was Titus' first work. The second and equally weighty mission the Apostle Paul charged him to execute was the refutation of a school of professed Christian teachers, who were promulgating doctrines at variance with the teaching of St. Paul and his brother Apostles, and were also, by their example and lives, fatally lowering the tone of Christian life. It was to the latter point—the evil *moral* influence of these teachers—that the attention of Titus was especially directed. False doctrinal teaching was bringing forth already its sure fruit, in the form of a life utterly unlike the pattern life of the Master. In contrast to this erroneous and misleading teaching, Titus is directed to exhort the varied ages, the different sexes, the bond and the free, to live lives which will bring no dishonour upon their Christian profession. The strictly practical nature of these charges is remarkable. Before touching upon doctrine, he presses home to these various ages and ranks the necessity of a quiet, useful life. The "sound doctrine" by which Titus was bidden to regulate his teaching is an expression peculiar to these Pastoral

trine: (2) that the aged men be sober,[1] grave, temperate, sound in faith, in charity, in patience. (3) The aged women likewise, that *they be* in behaviour as becometh holiness,[2] not false accusers,[3] not given to much wine, teachers of good things; (4) that they may teach the young women to be sober,[4] to love their husbands, to love their

Chap. ii. 1—5. Charges to private members of the Church;

1 Or, *vigilant.*
2 Or, *holy women.*
3 Or, *make-bates.*
4 Or, *wise.*

Epistles (see Note on 1 Tim. i. 10), and stands in clear contrast to the sickly, unhealthy teaching, fanciful and false, of the misleading teachers of Crete.

(2) **That the aged men.**—Not presbyters, or elders, in an official sense, but simply the "old men" in the congregations.

Be sober.—In a more extended sense than the bare literal meaning of the word would give. Let the elder men be "thoughtful," in contrast with the thoughtlessness of careless youth.

Grave.—And quietly earnest, in contrast with all passion and undue excitability.

Temperate.—*Discreet*, or *self-restrained*, would be a better rendering for the Greek word.

Sound in faith, in charity, in patience.—Here Paul the aged sums up for the aged men of Crete in these three words, so well known by all his devoted hearers then, by all the devout students of his theology in subsequent ages, the great principles out of which the true saint life springs—faith, love, patience. In the famous Pauline trilogy of virtues, in this place, "patience" takes the place of hope, because this brave patience, this enduring fortitude, especially becomes the old man waiting for death. In respect to these "three" they must be healthy, sound. The faith must not be adulterated with superstitions—the love must be chivalrous, not sentimental. It must be no partisan feeling, but a tender affection, broad and inclusive, as was St. Paul's and his Master Christ's. The patience must be no mere tame acquiescence in what seems to be the inevitable, but must be brave, enduring, suffering—if suffering comes—for the Lord's sake with a smile on the lips. "Not without reason," writes Calvin, "does St. Paul include in these three the sum of Christian perfections." It is with "faith" that we worship God—no prayer, no work of piety, can be severed from "faith." "Love" spreads its wings over all our duties to our neighbour; and "patience" must ever go hand in hand with both "faith" and "love." Without "patience" could "faith" hardly endure; and the affronts and unkindnesses of the world would, without this high virtue of patience, soon deaden and even destroy "love."

(3) **The aged women likewise.**—St. Paul, faithful to what had now become one of the guiding principles of Christianity, the equal position of women in the city of God, fellow-heirs with men in the citizenship of the city which hath foundations, proceeds to remind the elder women of Crete of their own high duties in the company of believers. They now—the women—must remember that the position which Christ and His disciples had claimed for them in the world was not without its grave responsibilities. These aged women of the flock, like the elders just exhorted, had also much to do for Christ.

That they be in behaviour as becometh holiness.—That is, *that they should show themselves as it becometh holiness*; or, more literally, *in demeanour reverend.* The Greek word rendered "in behaviour," or "in demeanour," includes dress, appearance, conversation, manner; includes an outward deportment dependent on something more internal. The elder Christian woman in her whole bearing should exhibit a certain dignity of sacred demeanour; there should be something in her general appearance, in her dress, in her speech, in her every-day behaviour, which the younger and more thoughtless sister could respect and reverence—an ideal she might hope one day, if the Master spared her so long, herself to reach. For an admirable gloss on these words, see 1 Tim. ii. 9, 10.

Not false accusers.—Or better, perhaps, *not slanderers.* St. Paul knew well how easily old age yields itself to this temptation. Old age is at times intolerant, censorious, even bitter, forgetful especially of the days of youth; but Christ's aged saints must use their voice for better things than these.

Not given to much wine.—This warning was probably called for, owing to the evil habits and customs of the Cretans.

Teachers of good things.—Or, *teachers of what is good.* Beza's rendering, "mistresses of honour" (*honestatis magistræ*), is singular and expressive. This does not mean that these aged women should occupy the place of public instructresses, but that they should, by here and there speaking a kind warning word, and, better still, by the golden silence of a useful honoured life, teach their younger sisters lessons of truth and faith and love.

(4) **That they may teach the young women to be sober.**—Better rendered, simply, *that they may teach* (or *school*) *the young women*, omitting the words "to be sober." In Ephesus the representative of the Apostle was directed himself to exhort the younger women; very likely the same charge being given here to the aged women of the congregations was owing to the state of the Cretan Christian, which called not only for more practical and homely, but also for more individual, exhortations. So here this special work was left for the elder women among the faithful to carry out. Such a reformation, not only in the discipline of the Church, but also in the individual life and conversation, as St. Paul desired to see in Crete, would never be brought about by a sermon, or even by many sermons, however eloquent and earnest, from Titus. It would be a matter requiring long time and patience, and would, as observed above, rather follow as the result of patient individual effort and holy example.

To love their husbands, to love their children.—There was evidently in Crete a feverish longing for excitement, for novelty in religious teaching; hence the demand for, and consequent supply of, the "fables" and "commandments of men" spoken of in chap. i. 14. Women as well as men preferred rather to *do* something for religion and for God, and thus to wipe out past transgressions, and perhaps to purchase the liberty of future licence. They preferred the rigid and often difficult observance of the elaborate ritual, "the tithing of the mint, and anise, and cummin," to quietly and reverently "doing their Father's business." St. Paul's method of correcting this false and unhealthy view of religion was to recall women as well as men to the steady, faithful performance of those quiet every-day duties to which God had, in His providence, called them. The first duty of these younger women, St. Paul

children, (5) *to be* discreet, chaste, keepers
at home, good, obedient to their own
husbands, that the word of God be not
blasphemed. (6) Young men likewise
exhort to be sober minded.[1] (7) In all
things shewing thyself a pattern of good
works: in doctrine *shew-*
ing uncorruptness, gravity,
sincerity, (8) sound speech, that cannot
be condemned; that he that is of the

Chap. ii. 6–8. to young men.

1 Or, *discreet.*

---

tells Titus, and which he would have their elder sisters impress on them, was the great home duty of loving their husbands and children. While St. Paul would never have the women of Christ forget their new and precious privileges in the present, their glorious hopes in the future, yet here on earth he would never let them desert, or even for a moment forget, their first and chiefest duties. Their work, let them remember, lay not abroad in the busy world. Their first duty was *to make home life beautiful* by the love of husband and child—that great love which ever teaches forgetfulness of self.

(5) **To be discreet.**—See Note in verse 2 of this chapter.

Chaste.—Not only in act, but also in look, in speech, in thought, even in dress.

Keepers at home.—The older authorities here, instead of "keepers at home" (*domum custodientes, domus curam habentes*), read *workers at home;* the Greek word is not found elsewhere. The sense of the passage is, however, little changed by the alteration. The meaning is clear, "Domi mansit lanam fecit." Home duties, cares, pleasures, sacrifices of self—these God-appointed duties ought to fill the mind and the heart of the young wife. There should be no desire, no attempt, to go round to the other houses, and so contracting idle, gossiping habits. Hofmann thus sums up these directions to the young Christian women of Crete, "Gute Hausfrauen will der Apostel haben."

Good.—Gracious, kind, thoughtful to others, especially to inferiors.

Obedient to their own husbands.—More accurately, *submitting themselves to their own husbands.* Women who really love their Master Christ should take care that, as far as in them lay, the law of subordination in the family to its rightful head should be strictly carried out. In a Church like that of Crete, made out of divided houses often, where the Christian wife was married to a Pagan husband, such a charge as this was especially needful.

That the word of God be not blasphemed.—These words refer to all the exhortations from verse 2 onwards, but more particularly to those clauses enforcing home duties immediately preceding. There was, of course, the fear that wives, carried away by religious fervour, might neglect the plainer every-day duties for the seemingly loftier and more self-denying occupations included under the head of religious works. Such failure in every-day tasks would, of course, be bitterly charged on the religion of Christ, and the gospel would run the danger of being evil-spoken of, even in other than purely Pagan circles. But the reference extends over a broader area than that occupied by Christian mistresses of households. All, of every rank and age, who think they love the Lord Jesus should remember that the "enemy" is ever watching their words and works; never should they who wear the colours of the great King forget the charge of the King's son, "Let your light so shine before men that they may see your good works, and glorify your Father which is in heaven."

(6) **Young men likewise exhort to be sober minded.**—The task of influencing the young men belongs especially to Titus. Among them, in respect to age, he still must be reckoned; as regarded their peculiar temptations, none could be found so fit as the still young Christian disciple of St. Paul (he was probably about forty years of age when he was placed over the Cretan Church) to set out vividly before them both the peril and the only means of guarding against it. Brought up in a Pagan home, not improbably in the luxurious and wicked Syrian Antioch, drawn to the Master's side in the fresh dawn of manhood, tried in many a difficult task and found faithful, the words of Titus, exhorting the youth of Crete to be sober-minded, or self-restrained, would be likely to have great weight. In this word, which urged self-restraint, a young man's duty is briefly comprehended. No task, the wise Chrysostom tells us, is after all so hard and difficult for youth, as obtaining the mastery over oneself in the matter of harmful pleasures. The Apostle gives but few special directions here for his disciple's guidance, for he is going to tell him how he will best win these young men to the side of Christ. It will be, he proceeds to show him, most effectually done by the sight of the example of his own manly, self-restrained religious life.

(7) **In all things shewing thyself a pattern of good works.**—Here St. Paul shows Titus that his especial work is the instruction of no one peculiar class or order, or age or sex, but that he is so to fashion his whole life that it may afford a "pattern" to all—men and women, bond as well as free; in all things a ceaseless activity was prescribed to the superintending presbyter in Crete. In everything that was earnest and true, Titus ought to be the one showing an example to the rest; in peaceful, quiet days, as in times of danger and threatening, he must set the pattern—now of useful labour and toil—now of brave, patient endurance for the Lord's sake.

In doctrine shewing uncorruptness, gravity, sincerity.—The older authorities omit "sincerity." Neither of the terms "uncorruptness" and "gravity" refers to the subject-matter of the "doctrine" or "teaching," but to the bearing and behaviour of the "teacher." While he occupies the place of a teacher, Titus must show in his life and conversation "uncorruptness"—*apthoria*, the word found in the older authorities, the meaning of which differs very slightly from the word *adiapthoria*, found in the received text. He must, in all those points of his life which are connected with his teaching, show a purity (*chastity*) and freedom from all interested motives; he must be above seeking for popular applause; but besides this "uncorruptness," in everything touching public instruction he must aim at a certain "gravity," not only in his public delivery of sermons and lectures, but also in his general private intercourse with his flock. He must, in a word, never forget he is the chief teacher in the Church of Crete of his Master's religion.

(8) **Sound speech, that cannot be condemned.**—The substance of Titus' teaching, whether in the more private intercourse with individuals or in his preaching in the Christian gatherings, must

contrary part may be ashamed, having
no evil thing to say of you. (9) *Exhort*
servants to be obedient
unto their own masters,
and to please *them* well in
all *things;* not answering again;[1] (10) not
purloining, but shewing all good fidelity;
that they may adorn the doctrine of
God our Saviour in all things. (11) For
the grace of God that
bringeth salvation hath
appeared to all men,[2]

Chap. ii. 9, 10. to Christian slaves.

Chap. ii. 11—15. Reason for these charges.

1 Or, *gainsaying.*
2 Or, *that bringeth salvation to all men, hath appeared.*

---

be healthy, practical, manly, in contrast to the sickly, morbid, fanciful instruction the false teachers of Crete were in the habit of giving. His words, too, must be well weighed and thoughtful, as well as earnest and impassioned; they must be such as would expose him neither to contempt nor to the charge of presumption. Between the lines of the exhortation of the 7th and 8th verses we can read the anxiety of the Apostle that his representative in Crete should take all possible care that the matter of his teaching and preaching was studied and prepared with all the attention and thought so important a duty demanded. He should remember, too, that the *words* as well as the *works* of the Christian teacher will be subject to a sharp and often hostile criticism. These warnings and reminders of St. Paul, it should be borne in mind, belong to all ages of the faith.

That he that is of the contrary part may be ashamed, having no evil thing to say of you.—The older authorities, with one exception, read "of us," instead of "of you." If Titus fairly carries out the exhortation of the last two verses, then the enemy, either the false teacher or the Pagan opponent of Christianity, confounded by the pure, self-sacrificing, earnest life, overcome by the well-weighed, thoughtful utterance of great truths, by the impassioned exhortation to men and women to lead noble, honest lives, will surely be ashamed of his bitter opposition, when he finds neither in the life nor in the teaching anything which he can fairly criticise as "bad." As the better supported reading, "of us," associates St. Paul and others with Titus, the evil thing which might have been said of Titus in reality would be spoken against St. Paul and the elder Apostles.

(9) **Exhort servants to be obedient unto their own masters.**—The accurate translation here is *bond servants.* The words in this and the following verse, it must be remembered, are addressed to "slaves." With some special reference to the peculiar circumstances of the Church in Crete, St. Paul had been giving general directions to his representative (verses 1—8) respecting instruction and advice he considered it expedient should be given to the varied orders and ages of professing Christians in the island. These directions were arranged with respect to "age" and "sex." He now turns to the question of the instruction of another large class, among whom were to be found many Christians—"the slaves." These he masses together under one head. Not improbably these "words" to be addressed particularly to slaves were called out by some particular instances of insubordination and of impatience under their unhappy condition among the Cretan slaves. Indeed, the repeated warnings to this unfortunate and oppressed class (see Eph. vi. 5; Col. iii. 22; 1 Tim. vi. 1) tell us that among the difficulties which Christianity had to surmount in its early years was the hard task of persuading "the slave" that the divine Master who promised him a home, if he were faithful and true, among the many mansions of His Father, meant not that the existing relations of society should be then changed, or its complex framework disturbed. St. Paul knew it was a hard matter to persuade the bondman, fellow-heir of heaven with the freeman, to acquiesce patiently in his present condition of misery and servitude. Hence these repeated charges to this class. These poor sufferers were to obey cheerfully, readily, as the next clause told them.

And to please them well in all things; not answering again.—The last words are better translated *not gainsaying;* the Vulgate has *contradicentes.* It signifies that they should obey cheerfully, willingly, without sullenness; not thwarting or setting themselves against their masters' plans or desires or orders; and the Apostle, in verse 10, gives them a noble inducement for this brave, sweet patience he would have so earnestly pressed upon them. Such conduct on their part, he tells them, would serve greatly to help the Master's cause; it would prepossess many hostile minds in favour of a religion which could so powerfully influence even the slave. Chrysostom comments thus: "Greeks form their estimate of doctrines not from the doctrine itself, but from the actions and the life" (of those who profess the doctrine).

(10) **Not purloining, but shewing all good fidelity.**—It must be remembered that many of the slaves in the Roman empire were employed in other duties besides those connected with the house or on the farm. Some were entrusted with shops, and these being left often quite to themselves, of course great opportunities for dishonesty and fraud were constantly present. Others received an elaborate training, and as artists, or even physicians, worked in part for their masters. A slave in the days of St. Paul had a hundred ways of showing to his owner this true and genuine fidelity, opposed to mere assumed surface obedience and service.

That they may adorn the doctrine of God our Saviour in all things.—A slave cheerfully accepting his hard yoke, and striving with hand and brain to please and advance the interest of his earthly master only for the dear love of Christ, must have been in those days of cynical *self*-love a silent, yet a most powerful preacher of a gospel which could so mould and elevate a character so degraded. Calvin remarks that it is indeed noteworthy how God deigns to receive an adornment from slaves, whose condition was so mean and abject that scarcely were they considered to rank among men at all; "they were ranked as 'possessions,' just like cattle or horses." Professor Reynolds very happily remarks here: "This teaching of St. Paul is in harmony with the words of the Lord Jesus—out of the mouths of babes and sucklings hast thou perfected praise. God gets His highest praise from the lips of little children, His robes of glory from the faithfulness, honour, and simplicity of born slaves."

(11) **For the grace of God that bringeth salvation hath appeared to all men.**—More accurately translated, *For the grace of God hath appeared, bringing salvation to all men.* "For" gives the ground, the base upon which the practical exhortations to freemen as well as to bond-servants, contained in verses 1—10, rest. These words might be paraphrased

(12) teaching us that, denying ungodliness
and worldly lusts, we should live soberly,
righteously, and godly, in this present
world; (13) looking for that blessed hope,
and the glorious appearing of the great
God and our Saviour Jesus Christ;

thus: "Yes, exhort all classes and orders, every age of life, each sex, bond as well as free, to struggle after pure, good, righteous lives, for I tell you, in very truth, like a sun on a darkened world has the grace of God arisen with salvation in its beams." Compare the grand Isaiah passage, "Arise, shine; for thy light is come, and the glory of the Lord is risen upon thee" (Isa. lx. 1); and also the words of Malachi (iv. 2), "Unto you that fear my name shall the Sun of righteousness arise with healing in his wings." (See, too, Isa. ix. 2.) The thought of these passages was not improbably in St. Paul's view while he wrote the words to Titus telling him to exhort his flock, for God's grace had appeared to all men. The Greek word translated "appeared" occurs in Luke i. 79 and Acts xxvii. 20—both writings closely connected with St. Paul, if not in great part written by him—and in each of these passages it is used to express the shining of the sun. The "grace of God" here spoken of is that divine favour to and love for men upon which the whole work of redemption was based, the object of which redemption was the ultimate restoration of man. The epiphany, or manifestation of this grace to the world, *commenced* with the incarnation of our Lord; but the reference here must not be limited to that or to any *one* event in the blessed Life. The expression "bringing salvation to all men" is another of those hard sayings which have been pressed into the service of that kindly but erring school of expositors which shuts its eyes to the contemplation of the many unmistakable sayings which warn the impenitent and hardened sinner of the sad doom of eternal death. The "grace" *alone* brings salvation to all men—in other words, it is that grace of God whereby alone it is possible for mankind to be saved. The expression by no means asserts that all men *will* be saved by it, but that it is the *only* means by which salvation is possible.

(12) **Teaching us.**—Literally, *disciplining us*; educating us by life's sad experiences. God's grace is in truth a stern discipline of self-denial and training for higher things.

Denying ungodliness and worldly lusts.—More accurately, *to the intent that, having denied, &c.* The object of the loving discipline of our Father in heaven is that we, having done with those things in life which are offensive or dishonourable to God, having put aside as worthless all inordinate desires for the things of this world—all those things which exclusively belong to this life and have nothing to do with the life to come—having denied all this, that we should live as righteous men the remainder of our lives here.

We should live soberly, righteously, and godly.—In these three terms the blessed life our Lord would have His own to lead on earth is summed up—to ourselves, to our neighbour, and to our God. The first, "soberly," to ourselves—wisely and temperately, keeping ever a mastery over our passions; the second, "righteously"—justly and honourably, having due regard to our duty towards our neighbour; the third, "godly"—piously, ever remembering to live as in the presence of the Eternal.

In this present world.—Or, *in the present course of things.* The Apostle adds these words to his summary of the life Christians should lead, to remind them that the present world was but a transitory, passing scene after all, and that there was another and a different "course of things" at hand; and this leads him on to another point. The manifestation of the "grace of God," in the first coming of the Lord *in humiliation* (verse 11), teaches us to live our lives in expectation of the second manifestation of His glory in His second coming *in power* (verse 13). We must—in this great passage contained in verses 11 to 14—bear in mind that there is a two-fold epiphany spoken of: the one, the manifestation of the "grace of God"—*that is past* (it was the first coming and the earthly life of Christ); the other, the manifestation of the "glory of God"—*that is to come.* It will be shown in the second advent when the Lord comes in glory with His holy angels; and the first epiphany (*manifestation*) in humiliation is an ever-present reminder to us to live in continued expectation of the second in glory.

(13) **Looking for that blessed hope, and the glorious appearing.**—The Greek should here be rendered, *looking for the blessed hope and manifestation of the glory.* And that holy life, just urged on the believer, of quiet self-restraint, of love to others, of piety towards God, must be lit up by a blessed hope, by a hope which is far more than a hope; that holy life of the faithful must be a continued waiting for a blessed hope—"the hope laid up for us in heaven" (Col. i. 5). It may be asked, What *is* this hope? We answer, it is "the hope of glory" which we shall share with the Son of God, when we behold Him as He is. So for us the hope of glory is intimately bound up with the second coming of the Lord. Then the life of the lover of the Lord must be one continued looking for, waiting for, the coming of the Lord in glory—must be a looking for that hour when we shall see in all His divine majesty, Him who redeemed us. In that life and light, in that majesty and glory, His own will share.

Of the great God and our Saviour Jesus Christ.—The translation here should run, *of our great God and Saviour Jesus Christ.* From the English version, it would seem that Paul's idea was that the Christian should live waiting for the glorious appearing of the great God, accompanied with our Lord Jesus Christ. The rendering we have adopted, on what seems conclusive grounds, speaks of a Christian life, as a life ever looking for the glorious appearing of our great God and Saviour Jesus Christ.

In this sublime passage the glory of the only begotten Son *alone* finds mention. Taken thus, it is a studied declaration of the divinity of the Eternal Son, who is here styled "our great God and Saviour." Reasoning merely on grammatical principles, either translation would be possible, only even then there is a presumption in favour of the translation we have adopted. (See Ellicott's Note on this verse.) But other considerations are by no means so nearly equally balanced. The word "manifestation" (*epiphany*), the central thought of the sentence, is employed by St. Paul in his Epistles five times, and in every one of them to describe the manifestation of *Christ*, and in four of them to designate the future manifestation of His coming in glory, as here. The term epiphany is *never* applied to the Father.

Again, the *whole of the context* of the passage

(14) who gave himself for us, that he
might redeem us from all iniquity, and
purify unto himself a peculiar people,
zealous of good works. (15) These things
speak, and exhort, and rebuke with all
authority. Let no man despise thee.

A.D. 65.

CHAPTER III.—(1) Put them in mind

specially relates to the "Son of God." The introduction of the epiphany "of *the Father*" would be a thought not merely strange to the whole New Testament, but would bring quite a new idea into this statement, which sets forth so sublimely the epiphany of *Christ* as the ground of the Christian's hope—an idea, too, no sooner suggested than dropped, for the passage goes on to speak only of the Son. Perhaps, however, the weightiest argument that can be adduced is the consensus of the Greek orthodox fathers, who, with scarcely an exception, concur in the interpretation which understands the expression "of our great God" as used of Jesus Christ. To select two examples out of the long chain of fathers reaching from the apostolic age who have thus understood this text: "St. Paul here calls Christ the great God, and thus rebukes the heretical blasphemy which denies His Godhead" (Theodoret). "What can those persons say," asks Chrysostom, referring to this passage, "who allege that the Son is inferior to the Father?" (See Wordsworth's Note here.)

(14) **Who gave himself for us.**—(See Gal. i. 4; Eph. v. 25.) These words take up the thought expressed in the term "Saviour" of the last verse. "Himself," His whole self, as has been well said, "the greatest gift ever given;" "for us," that is, on our behalf.

That he might redeem us from all iniquity.—That He for us might pay a ransom, the ransom being His precious blood. Our Saviour, by the payment of this tremendous ransom—O deepest and most unfathomable of all mysteries!—released us from everything which is opposed to God's blessed will. Here the mighty ransom is spoken of as freeing us from the bondage of lawlessness; elsewhere in the divine books the same ransom is described as delivering us from the penalties of this same breaking the divine law—"alles was der ordnung Gottes widerstreitet" (Hofmann, *Commentary on Titus*).

And purify unto himself a peculiar people.—The expression "a peculiar people" is taken from the LXX. translation of the Hebrew Scriptures, where the words occur several times (see Ex. xix. 5; Deut. xiv. 2); the idea is also purely an Old Testament one. Just as Jehovah wished to establish a people which should belong to Him ("peculiarly His," "His very own"), submitting to His laws, in contrast to the rest of mankind, lawless, idolatrous—so Jesus would set apart and purify for Himself a people, which for His sake should devote itself to God, in contrast to the rest of humanity sunk in selfish sins. As Israel of old lived under the constant impression that they would again behold the visible glory of the Eternal, so His people now should live as men waiting for a second manifestation of *His* glory.

Zealous of good works.—The man who hopes to see the epiphany of Jesus his Lord and Love in glory will struggle zealously with hand and brain to live his life in such a manner that he may meet his Lord, when He comes in glory, with joy. It was a people composed of such "zealots" of goodness, of men longing for His sake to do their utmost for His cause, that our great God and Saviour wished to purify unto Himself.

(15) **These things speak, and exhort, and rebuke with all authority.**—These words are the conclusion of this part of the Letter of St. Paul to Titus. A new division of the Epistle begins immediately after this verse with the third chapter. He is to speak the words—many of them sharp and bitter—told him by St. Paul; he is to remember now to exhort, now to rebuke, and all this "with authority," as chief pastor of the flock of Crete formally commissioned and appointed.

Let no man despise thee.—"Speak," wrote the brave-hearted old man Paul, "speak with decision, and rebuke and punish if need be with vigour, remembering the dark character of the people with whom you have to do." And perhaps in the background of this stirring admonition of the aged master to his disciple, placed in so difficult and responsible a position, there is the anxious warning again: Yes, but show all diligence too in your own words and doings, so that every word of thine may have its full weight, that none may despise thee on account of thine own life.

III.

(1) **Put them in mind to be subject to principalities and powers.**—Very careful and searching have been the Apostle's charges to Titus respecting the teachers of the *Church*, their doctrine and their life; very particular have been his directions, his warnings, and exhortations to men and women of different ages on the subject of their *home* life. But, with the exception of a slight digression in the case of a slave to a Pagan master, his words had been written with a reference generally to Christian life among *Christians*. But there was then a great life outside the little Christian world; how were the people of Christ to regulate their behaviour in their dealings with the vast Pagan world outside? St. Paul goes to the root of the matter at once when he says, "Put them in mind," &c. Very needful in Crete was such a reminder respecting obedience. The island had, when St. Paul wrote to Titus, been some century and a quarter under Roman rule. Their previous government had been democratic; and historians, like Polybius, who have written of Crete, have dwelt particularly on the turbulent and factious spirit which animated their people; added to which, the many Jews who we know formed a very large part of the Christian Church there, always impatient of a foreign yoke, would in such an atmosphere of excitement be especially eager to assert their right to be free from the hated rule of Rome.

The Greek words translated "principalities and powers" are better rendered here by "rulers and authorities," as the word "principalities" is used occasionally in the English version for an "order of angels." The terms include all constituted governors and officials, Roman and otherwise, in the island.

To obey magistrates.—Taken absolutely, *to obey the temporal power.* Our Lord's words were the model for all teaching in this division of Christian ethics. One great teacher after the other, in the same spirit, in varied language, urges upon the people of Christ a reverence and submission to all legally constituted authority in the state. This devoted Christian loyalty, to be subject to principalities and powers, to obey magistrates, to be ready to every good work, (2) to speak evil of no man, to be no brawlers, *but* gentle, shewing all meekness unto all men. (3) For we ourselves also were sometimes foolish, disobedient, deceived, serving divers lusts and pleasures, living in malice and envy, hateful, *and* hating one another. (4) But after that the kindness and love[1] of God our Saviour

Chap. iii. 1—7. The attitude of Christians towards Pagans.

1 Or, *pity*.

no bitter opposition in after years to their tenets could chill, no cruel persecution of individuals lessen. Augustine, writes Professor Reynolds, could boast that when Julian asked Christians to sacrifice and offer incense to the gods they, at all hazards, sternly refused; but when he summoned them to fight for the empire they rushed to the front. "They distinguished between their Eternal Lord and their earthly ruler, and yet they yielded obedience to their earthly ruler for the sake of their Eternal Lord." Least of any should we expect St. Paul to write such words, so loyal and faithful to Rome. He had found, indeed, little cause in his chequered, troubled life to be grateful personally to the Empire; with ears too ready had Rome ever listened to the cruel "informations" laid against him by his implacable Jewish enemies; she had imprisoned him, fettered him, hindered his work, and threatened his life; and when he was writing these deathless words of his, urging upon his devoted flock a loyalty changeless and true, for him the supreme vengeance of Rome was close at hand.

To be ready to every good work.—Ready cheerfully to aid all lawful authority, municipal and otherwise, in their public works undertaken for city or state. The flock of Titus must remember that the true Christian ought to be known as a good citizen and a devoted patriot.

(2) **To speak evil of no man.**—These commands of St. Paul to the Church of Crete breathe throughout the spirit of Christ, who "when He was reviled, reviled not again;" who said "Love your enemies, do good to them that hate you, and pray for them which despitefully use you and persecute you." The Christian in the days of St. Paul, and for "many days" after St. Paul had borne that gallant witness of his outside the gates of Rome, would indeed often be called in sad earnestness to put in practice these charges of the Apostle. In days of persecution, in times of suspicion, when the Christian profession exposed men to hatred and to sore danger, when all men spoke evil of them, these words of St. Paul were remembered and acted upon, and not only in Crete.

To be no brawlers, but gentle, shewing all meekness unto all men.—Or better, *not contentious, but,* &c. These characteristics were not common virtues in Crete, then the resort and mart of so many different nationalities. Its singular situation in the Mediterranean, midway between Europe, Africa, and Asia, has been noticed, as have been the dispositions and vices of the inhabitants. Surely, St. Paul urges, the professed followers of the Crucified among the Cretans should aim at a nobler standard of life than was common among these rough and often selfish traders. These things charged here by St. Paul were new virtues to men. They are held up to admiration by no heathen moralists. The meekness signifies kindly forbearance. This Christian feeling, which looks lovingly on all sorts and conditions of men, on the stranger and the outcast, even on the vilest sinner, is especially enjoined here. It is the same sweet spirit of love which desires, in 1 Tim. ii. 1, that prayer and supplication be made in the public Christian assembly *for all men.*

(3) **For we ourselves also were sometimes foolish, disobedient, deceived.**—Better rendered, *For we were once ourselves foolish, disobedient, going astray.* Surely, the Apostle argues, *Christians* can never refuse obedience to one in authority, or decline to be meek, courteous, kind, and forbearing to their neighbours, because, forsooth, they deem the magistrate in authority or their neighbours idolators, and therefore outside the pale of *God's* mercy and *their* courtesy; for remember, writes St. Paul, *we* were once (not so long ago) ourselves in their condition. *We* once needed mercy ourselves. This strong appeal to Christians, by the memory of their past, by the memory of what *they* once were, must have gone home to one like Titus, himself of a Gentile family, and most probably nurtured in idolatry. It would, no doubt, be repeated with strange, touching earnestness, would this argument of St. Paul by Titus when he spoke to the assembly of the Cretan Christians. *We* were once ourselves "foolish," that is, without understanding what was true; and "disobedient," that is, unwilling, indisposed, to do what was right; "deceived," or rather going astray (*errantes*), wandering away from the narrow road which leads to life.

Serving divers lusts and pleasures.—This is the service we served in the old past days of our sin and shame, while we were "disobedient" to what was right and pure. We were obedient to, we were "serving" as slaves, many an impure lust, many a wrongful pleasure—for the lusts and pleasures to which St. Paul referred were those of the people with whom for the moment the Apostle was classing himself. The pleasures of these partly Greek, partly Asiatic peoples consisted, indeed, in the wanton satisfaction of the lusts of the flesh; their shameless revellings were scarcely covered with their thin and flimsy veil of beauty and false refinement.

Living in malice and envy, hateful, and hating one another.—These pleasure-loving, lust-indulging ones envied each one his neighbour the good things he possessed; and thus we—for *we*, remember, were once of this number—once spent our lives in this atmosphere of hate, hating others with a jealous dislike, hated ourselves for the same reasons. Shall we then—once like them—now refuse all sympathy to these poor souls still left in ignorance and sin?

(4) **But after that the kindness and love of God our Saviour toward man appeared.**—Another thought now wells up in the Apostle's mind. We of ourselves should never have become changed men, had not the kindness of God and His divine love for men shown itself. We, indeed, have no ground for self-exaltation, no excuse for haughty treatment of others, either in thought or action; for if we now live other and purer lives than they live, our change to better and higher things was owing to no desert or merit of ours, but solely to the mercy and the love of God. The changed life is here solely attributed to the manifestation to man of the kindness and love of God

toward man appeared, (5) not by works of righteousness which we have done, but according to his mercy he saved us, by the washing of regeneration, and renewing of the Holy Ghost; (6) which he shed on us abundantly[1] through

1 Gr. *richly.*

our Saviour. Here God our Saviour, as in 1 Tim. i. 1, and in several other passages in the Pastoral Epistles, must be understood as "God the Father;" the "kindness" differs from the "love towards man." The first signifies generally that divine, measureless, all-comprehensive love which we know is the glorious attribute of God. The second expression tells of the special love which the Almighty has for man, and which has been so marvellously shown in the sacrifice and death of the Son of God for us. The two words—the measureless, divine love which embraces all creation, and the special love of God for man—taken together, make up the one idea expressed by the "grace that bringeth salvation," of chap. ii. 11 of this Epistle. In the rare word *philanthropia,* the "love of God toward man," a quiet but very solemn reminder is given to those "Christians" who would have no dealings with their less pure heathen neighbours. The word applied here to God tells them to love men, even the enemies of their holy religion; they are to obey the heathen magistrate, and to think kindly of and to act courteously towards their heathen neighbour, because God has loved men—all men. Here are they to be imitators of the divine pity, copyists of the divine love.

(5) **Not by works of righteousness.**—This by no means asserts that such works ever had been done, and then produced, as it were, before the bar of God, and weighed and found insufficient; but it simply maintains that to *win* salvation such *must* be done. Sad experience, more forcibly than any theological assertion, has demonstrated to us all the utter impossibility of any of us, even the holiest, ever, even for one day, doing the works of a purely righteous man.

But according to his mercy.—As there was nothing in us which called for such a salvation, as there were no acts of ours which deserved reward, His gift of salvation, which includes (verse 7) eternal life, was owing entirely to His divine love which saw and pitied our misery, our endless suffering. Out of this hopeless state the eternal pity lifted us, and put us into a state of salvation. The next clause specifies the outward and visible sign of the salvation our loving God was pleased to ordain in His Church, namely, "baptism;" but here great care must be taken properly to understand what St. Paul meant by this baptism, to which he attributed so great power. In St. Paul's mind it was no mere observance, but was a sacrament, in which all that was inward properly and completely accompanied all that was outward. In another place the Apostle has grandly paraphrased his words here. In the Galatian Letter (chap. iii. 27) he writes how "that as many as were baptised into Christ have put on Christ," that is, have entered into vital union with Him—a blessed state, which most surely leads to life eternal, if the baptised only remain faithful.

By the washing of regeneration, and renewing of the Holy Ghost.—Seeing, then, that God *has* saved us by His own act, independently of any work of ours, we ask, How has He effected this? The words we are here considering give the answer to the question. The Greek should be rendered, "by the laver of regeneration," &c. Then, by means of the laver of regeneration, &c., has God put us into a state of salvation. In other words, He has effected this by means of "baptism" (for the laver here can only signify the baptismal font, and is called the laver of regeneration because it is the vessel consecrated to the use of that sacrament), whereby, in its completeness as a sacrament, the new life in Christ is conveyed. Baptism, then, is the means through which we receive the saving grace of Christ; in its laver we are born again to a new life, in it we receive strength through the Holy Ghost constantly to renew and to develop this new life, *for it is not only the laver of regeneration but also of renovation by the Holy Spirit.* But baptism is here understood in all its completion—the outward visible sign accompanied with the inward spiritual grace. In the case of one who is come to years of understanding seeking baptism, repentance and faith in the promises of God are absolutely required. In the case of infants, who have also from the very earliest times been, through this same laver, enrolled in the communion of Christians, the same profession is required, only they make it by their sureties, and directly that they have come to years of discretion they solemnly and publicly assent to what had been already affirmed in their name. Thus, by means of the laver of regeneration, &c., or, in other words, by baptism *in all its completion*—the outward act being accompanied with the inward faith—He saved us, that is, put us into a state of salvation. Of the difference between "regeneration" and "renovation," the first, "regeneration," is well explained in the words of the collect for Christmas Day, which speaks of the "regenerated" as "made God's children by adoption and grace." The second, "renovation," the same collect goes on to speak of, when it prays that "the regenerated" "may daily be renewed by the Holy Spirit." The first, "regeneration," is spoken of by St. John in his words, "Ye must be born again" (John iii. 7); the second is alluded to by St. Paul when he wrote, "the inward man is renewed day by day" (2 Cor. iv. 16).

(6) **Which he shed on us abundantly through Jesus Christ our Saviour.**—In other words, *which*—namely, the Holy Ghost—*the Father poured abundantly on us through Jesus Christ our Saviour.* The argument continues thus: He (God) saved us first by the laver of regeneration and of renewal of the Holy Ghost, which God—he proceeds to say—shed (or *poured out*) abundantly on us, and this constant renewal of the Holy Ghost poured out on the heart of each individual believer was owing to the mediation of Jesus Christ, without whose blessed atonement this effusion of the Holy Spirit never had taken place. In this verse the several operations of each of the Persons of the blessed Trinity are clearly set forth.

It is the Father who is ever pouring out upon us the Holy Ghost. It is owing to the Son's atonement and intercession that this blessed outpouring takes place at all. It is the Holy Ghost poured out on us abundantly who builds us up in the new life, and trains us for the glories of eternity. Here the "Son" is given the same title of "Saviour," which, in the preceding verse (5), was applied to the "Father." The appellation belongs to both the First and Second Persons of the blessed Trinity, inasmuch as the Father may be said to have been the architect of our salvation, while the Son was its builder.

Jesus Christ our Saviour; (7) that being
justified by his grace, we should be
made heirs according to the hope of
eternal life. (8) *This is* a
faithful saying, and these
things I will that thou

Chap. iii. 8—11. Good works enjoined.

affirm constantly, that they which have
believed in God might be careful to maintain
good works. These things are good
and profitable unto men. (9) But avoid
foolish questions, and genealogies, and
contentions, and strivings about the

---

(7) **That being justified by his grace, we should be made heirs according to the hope of eternal life.**—Here appears the glorious design of God's salvation. We were in a hopeless and lost state, from which God's love for man saved us by the laver of regeneration and renovation; and this was the end for which He saved us—*that we should be heirs of eternal life.* "Being justified," that is, freed from the future punishment and consequences of sin, and received into the favour and friendship of God, which favour and friendship had been, through sin, forfeited. "By His grace," by the favour and kindness of God the Father are we restored to His love and friendship. "Heirs," see Rom. viii. 17, where this thought of our heirship of heaven is enlarged. "According to the hope of eternal life;" this life eternal is still for us in the future, though ever present in respect of hope; children of God we indeed are, and sharers in many a good gift of our Father, but eternal life, *that* glorious inheritance, is still in the far future, and as yet can only be enjoyed by us in hope, but it is a sure hope—eternal life—the hope of which is the mainspring of all Christian work and activity—though it includes it, of course, is something far more than merely endless existence. A veil, impenetrable to mortal eye, hangs between us and the many mansions of the Father's house. "It doth not yet appear what we shall be;" we only know that then, we, in company with an innumerable host of blessed beings, shall share in the beatific vision; we only know that then "we shall ever be with the Lord;" and that with this thought and with these words are we to comfort one another. (See 1 Thess. iv. 17, 18.)

(8) **This is a faithful saying.**—Then St. Paul, having, in those few but sublime words we have been considering, painted our present happy state—happy even on earth, where the glorious promised inheritance was still only a hope—and having shown how that this blessedness was the result of no efforts of our own, but that we owe it solely to the tender love and to the divine pity of God for man—cries out, Yes, "faithful is this saying!"

And these things I will that thou affirm constantly.—I will that ever and again, in the congregation, these words of mine, woven into the tapestry of creed, or hymn of thanksgiving or supplication, be repeated by the faithful believers in the Lord, to remind them, not only of the glorious hope of eternal life, but also to bring Him to their remembrance to whom they owe this glorious heritage; and as they repeat or hear the words telling them of the wondrous mercy showed to them for no merit or desert of their own, they will the more willingly think kindly of, and act loyally with, other men still living in that deep and loathsome darkness where they once dwelt, until God, in His pity, delivered them. Hearing this "faithful saying," thought the old man St. Paul, my children in Christ will surely be disposed to be more loyal subjects, more faithful citizens, more loving neighbours, though their civil magistrates, their fellow-citizens, their neighbours, be still idolaters, living without God in the world. And there was yet another reason for the constant repetition of this "faithful saying:" men would see that they owed all their glorious Christian privileges, their present peace, their future hope, to God's free grace—that *they* had done nothing to deserve all this. Surely such a thought would spur them on to noble deeds, if it were only to show they were not wholly ungrateful. So he writes, Yes, affirm constantly this faithful saying.

That they which have believed in God might be careful to maintain good works.—But not only would St. Paul have them show their gratitude for the great mercy they had received, but he is specially anxious that they who by God's grace had been led into the Christian company should now not only quietly and unobtrusively take their part in good works, but should ever be careful to be forward in all such things; he would have Christians conspicuous in their generous zeal to forward all good and useful undertakings. "Good works" here by no means is confined to works of mercy and charity, though, of course, they include such, still they possess in this passage a far more comprehensive signification. All useful and beneficent undertakings, public as well as private, are reckoned among these "good works." As was observed before, St. Paul's ideal Christian must be a generous, public-spirited man. In the eyes of this great teacher the cloistered ascetic would have found but little favour; his hero, while ever the devoted, self-sacrificing lover of the Lord, must be known among his fellow-citizens "as careful to maintain good works."

These things are good and profitable unto men.—The accurate translation of the Greek here would be, *These are the things which are good and profitable unto men;* but the older authorities omit the article, *ta*, before *kala.* The rendering, then (omitting the article), as given in the English version, would be correct: "These things"—that is, this practical every-day teaching, which bids Christians distinguish themselves among their fellow-citizens and countrymen in all generous and useful enterprises—in all good things, whether public or private—these things, says the Apostle, are good and profitable unto men; in sharp contrast to the unpractical and useless points insisted upon in the false teaching, apparently too common in the Cretan Church, and against which Titus is earnestly warned in the next (9th) verse.

(9) **But avoid foolish questions, and genealogies.**—The "questions" and "genealogies" have been discussed above (1 Tim. i. 4). The Apostle characterises them as "foolish," because they were of an utterly unpractical nature, and consumed time and powers which were needed for other and better things. The "contentions" were disputes and wranglings which arose out of arguments advanced by different teachers upon the "questions" and "genealogies." The "strivings about the law" were, most probably, arguments suggested by disputed and intricate points connected with the law of Moses. In the Talmud we possess unnumbered instances of all these strange and curious inquiries about which men then gravely disputed and

law; for they are unprofitable and vain.
(10) A man that is an heretick after the
first and second admonition reject;
(11) knowing that he that is such is subverted, and sinneth, being condemned
of himself. (12) When I shall send
Artemas unto thee, or Tychicus, be
diligent to come unto me
to Nicopolis: for I have determined there to winter.
(13) Bring Zenas the lawyer
and Apollos on their journey

Chap. iii. 12—15. Titus will be summoned again to the Apostle.

---

wrangled, but none of which could in any way teach men how to make life more beautiful and loving, more like that fair pattern which St. Paul's Master loved. St. Paul, well versed—thanks to his early and elaborate training—in all this useless, curious lore, once and for all would expel from orthodox Christian teaching everything which seemed to bear upon this favourite Jewish theology—so called. It had, cancer-like, eaten the life out of Judaism; it should not, if he could prevent it, poison in like manner the young life of Christianity.

(10) **A man that is an heretick.**—The Greek word translated "heretick" in the New Testament occurs here only. The term "heresies" occurs twice (1 Cor. xi. 19; Gal. v. 20). In neither, however, of these passages does the word signify there a fundamental or doctrinal error. This sense belongs to a usage of later times. From the meaning of the word "heresy" in these passages of St. Paul, we are able to deduce the signification of the term "heretic" here. The "heretic" of the Church in Crete appears to have been a man who, dissatisfied with the organisation and discipline introduced by Titus into the Christian community—not improbably considering himself in some way slighted—withdrew himself from the common body, and gathering round him other discontented spirits, established what might be termed a rival Church in Crete. Although at first, perhaps, no marked erroneous teaching forms part of the practice of such schismatics, still the tendency in such small rival communities is ever more and more to distinguish between *their* teaching and that of the larger body from whom they, in the first instance, cut themselves adrift.

After the first and second admonition reject.—The Greek word rendered "reject" would be more accurately translated *shun*, or *avoid*. There was, no doubt, some self-willed factious party-leader in Crete well known to St. Paul to whom he referred here; but partly out of a loving hope that Titus would win him to his side, partly from the knowledge that this Letter was a public instruction to many a Church besides that of Crete, the disturber remained nameless. He was to be exhorted once, twice, and then if he remained contumacious he was to be left simply alone to his own devices. The community over which Titus presided in the place of Paul no longer were to know the obstinate heretic as a brother.

(11) **Knowing that he that is such is subverted, and sinneth, being condemned of himself.**—Better rendered, *is perverted and sinneth, being self-condemned.* Inasmuch as thou knowest, seeing that thy reproofs and warnings have been of none effect, that he is "thoroughly perverted"—the expression is a very strong one, and signifies literally *hath been turned inside out.* The same verb is used in the LXX. translation of Deut. xxxii. 20, the "*very froward* generation" of the English version—having been warned once and again, he is without the excuse of ignorance, but sins on in the full consciousness of his wilful and seditious life. His perverse conduct in stirring up party-feeling in the Church publicly convicts him of doing the very wrong which in general he professes to condemn. With these words the public or official portion of the Letter to the presiding presbyter in Crete closes. Paul had begun with directions how the church life of the island—up to this period apparently devoid of organisation—was to be arranged; he concludes with instructions how to deal with any who presumed to set themselves in opposition to his plans for the government of the community. The central portion of the letter is occupied in discussing how Christian doctrine is to influence the lives of those accepting it, and especially it treats of the conduct of Christians towards the Pagan world, with whom they will necessarily be brought in contact.

(12) **When I shall send Artemas unto thee, or Tychicus, be diligent to come unto me.**—But Titus is here reminded—perhaps with *some* reference to the question of the treatment of the factious or heretic persons just alluded to—that he is only the temporary ruler of the Cretan Church, on a special commission of the great missionary Apostle. Not improbably one of these two was intended to supply the place of Titus when this favourite and trusted assistant of St. Paul was recalled to his master's side. Of Artemas nothing certainly is known. Tradition, however, makes him subsequently Bishop of Lystra. Tychicus is mentioned in five of the New Testament writings—in Acts xx. 4; Col. iv. 7; 2 Tim. iv. 12; and here. He seems to have been one of the most esteemed of St. Paul's friends. He speaks of him as a beloved brother, a faithful minister and fellow-servant in the Lord; and the importance of the missions with which he was entrusted by his master to distant churches shows us how high this disciple stood in the opinion of St. Paul.

To Nicopolis: for I have determined there to winter.—There are several cities bearing this name—in Cilicia, in Thrace, and in Epirus; and considerable doubt prevails as to which the Apostle has been referring. On the whole, the Nicopolis in Epirus seems the most likely spot for the Apostle to have fixed on. This city was built by Augustus after the battle of Actium, whence it derived its name, "the City of Victory."

(13) **Bring Zenas the lawyer.**—A name contracted, as it seems, from Zenodorus. The term "lawyer" might possibly indicate that this friend of Paul's was a Roman jurist, but it is more likely that the law in which he was an expert was that of Moses. Hippolytus numbers him among the seventy disciples, and relates how in after years he was Bishop of Diospolis. He is never mentioned by name in the New Testament, except in this place.

And Apollos.—This famous teacher appears often in the New Testament records, in the Acts and several of the Epistles. A distinguished Alexandrian scholar and a disciple of John the Baptist, he was converted to Christianity by the agency of the devoted Priscilla and Aquila, the tent-makers. He became the friend and intimate associate of St. Paul, and might, had he chosen, have rivalled or even superseded St. Paul in his supreme authority over the churches planted along the Mediter-

diligently, that nothing be wanting unto them. (14) And let our's also learn to maintain good works[1] for necessary uses, that they be not unfruitful. (15) All that are with me salute thee. Greet them that love us in the faith. Grace *be* with you all. Amen.

1 Or, *profess honest trades.*

¶ It was written to Titus, ordained the first bishop of the church of the Cretians, from Nicopolis of Macedonia.

---

ranean sea-board. But Apollos seems resolutely to have declined any such rivalry, and to have lived ever as the loyal and devoted friend of the great Apostle; who, however, always seems to have treated the learned and eloquent Alexandrian as an equal power in the Church of Christ, classing Apollos with St. Peter and himself. Luther's well-known suggestion that Apollos was the unknown writer of the Epistle to the Hebrews —"auctor Epistolæ ad Hebræos . . . ut ego arbitror Apollo"—the authorship (though not the canonicity) of which has been a disputed point as far back as the days of Origen, in the first half of the third century—has been adopted, though, of course, with much reserve, by many. Attention has been called to the somewhat remarkable fact that the names of these three friends of St. Paul, who were classed among his most faithful adherents in this almost the last Epistle he wrote, were derived from three of the most famous heathen deities—Zenas from Zeus; Artemas from Artemis, the famous tutelary goddess of Ephesus; Apollos from the well-known sun-god.

(14) **And let our's also learn to maintain good works for necessary uses.**—"Ours," that is, those who with St. Paul and Titus in Crete called upon the name of Jesus. A last reminder to the brethren, whom with a loving thought he calls "ours," constantly to practise good and beneficent works. In the expression "let ours also learn," it would seem as though St. Paul would have Christians *trained* to the wise and thoughtful performance of works of mercy and charity.

It was with such injunctions as these that men like St. Paul and St. James laid the foundation storeys of those great Christian works of charity—all undreamed of before the Resurrection morning—but which have been for eighteen centuries in all lands, the glory of the religion of Jesus—one grand result of the Master's presence with us on earth, which even His bitterest enemies admire with a grudging admiration.

In the short compass of these Pastoral Epistles, in all only thirteen chapters, we have no less than *eight* special reminders to be earnest and zealous in good works. There was evidently a dread in St. Paul's mind that some of those who *professed* a love of Jesus, and *said* that they longed after the great salvation, would content themselves with a dreamy acquiescence in the great truths, while the life remained unaltered. It is noteworthy that these Epistles, containing so many urgent exhortations *to work* for Christ, were St. Paul's last inspired utterances. The passages in question are chaps. i. 16; ii. 7, 14; iii. 14; 1 Tim. ii. 10; v. 10; vi. 18; 2 Tim. ii. 21.

(15) **All that are with me salute thee.**—It is uncertain where Paul was when he wrote this letter. "All that are with me" include those with him, journeying in his company. They are not named, because the individuals composing the immediate following of St. Paul would be likely to be well known to Titus.

Greet them that love us in the faith.—An inclusive greeting, embracing each member of the Cretan Church whose love to him (St. Paul) was based upon the common faith in the Lord Jesus. Greet all who love me, as the earnest preacher of their faith and mine.

Amen.—The greater number of the ancient authorities omit "Amen."

INTRODUCTION

TO

THE EPISTLE OF PAUL TO

PHILEMON

I. The Date, Place, and Occasion of the Epistle.—These are all perfectly clear. The Epistle is of the same date as the Epistle to the Colossians, sent by Onesimus, who was one of the bearers of that Epistle (Col. iv. 9); dwelling emphatically on St. Paul's imprisonment (verses 1, 9), looking forward confidently to a speedy release and a return to Asia (verse 22). Even the salutations, with one exception, are the same in both (verses 23, 24, comp. with Col. iv. 10—14). It is written to intercede with Philemon for Onesimus, his slave—formerly "unprofitable," a runaway, and probably a thief, but now converted to a new life by St. Paul at Rome, and after his conversion becoming at once "profitable" to St. Paul for ministration in his captivity, and likely to be profitable also to his old master, to whom, accordingly, St. Paul sends him back, with this letter of intercession.

II. The Persons to whom it is addressed.—All we know of Philemon is gathered from this Epistle. It is nowhere actually said he was a Colossian; but this is inferred from the fact that Onesimus, his slave, is described as of Colossæ (Col. iv. 9). It is clear that he was St. Paul's convert; but, as the Apostle had not visited Colossæ (Col. ii. 1), we may probably conjecture that he had been brought under his influence during his long stay at Ephesus. Possibly, like Epaphras (Col. i. 7), he had been, under St. Paul's auspices, an evangelist of his native place. For he is evidently a man of mark; "the Church" gathers "in his house;" he is able, by his love, "to refresh the hearts of the saints," probably by temporal as well as spiritual gifts; to him St. Paul entrusts the charge of preparing a lodging for his hoped-for visit, and describes that visit as "being granted," "through his prayers," to him and his. We note also that the Apostle treats him as almost an equal—as a "brother" (not "a son"), as "a fellow-labourer," and as a "partner."

This last phrase—used distinctively, and without any words of limitation to some particular work—is unique. It occurs in close connection with the promise on St. Paul's part to take upon himself the pecuniary responsibility of any default of Onesimus—a promise emphasised by the writing of a bond of obligation in legal form. Accordingly, it has been supposed that Philemon was St. Paul's partner in the "tent-making" by which he maintained himself with Aquila and Priscilla—first, certainly, at Corinth (Acts xviii. 3), and afterwards, as it appears (Acts xx. 35), at Ephesus; that he may have still had in his hands some of the money earned by that common labour, and that from this St. Paul offers to discharge the obligation taken upon himself for Onesimus. The supposition is ingenious, and certainly quite possible; but it revolts against all our conceptions of St. Paul's character to suppose that he would work beyond what was actually necessary for maintenance, so as to accumulate money, and keep a regular debtor and creditor account with Philemon. Nor is it easy to see why, if this was so, he should have so urgently needed in prison the supplies sent from Philippi (Phil. iv. 10—13). Accordingly, it seems better to refer the "partnership" or "communion" (see verse 6 of the Epistle) principally, if not exclusively, to some united work of evangelisation or beneficence (possibly devised during the common labour at Ephesus) for the Churches of Asia, and especially for the Church of Colossæ. Ecclesiastical tradition, as usual, makes Philemon the Bishop of Colossæ in the hereafter.

Of Apphia we know nothing, except that tradition, and the style in which the Epistle mentions her, both support the idea that she was Philemon's wife. Archippus, a minister of the Church, either of Colossæ or Laodicea (see Note on Col. iv. 7), is on the same ground supposed to have been his son. The tone of the whole Epistle gives the impression of some wealth and dignity in the family, nobly used for the relief of necessity and the knitting closer of the bonds of Christian unity.

III. The Genuineness of the Epistle.—It is notable that, unlike the other two personal Epistles—the Second and the Third of St. John, if, indeed, the Second be really personal—this Epistle found its place in all catalogues, from the Muratorian Canon downwards, and in all the ancient versions. We might have supposed that, in respect of such reception, it would have suffered from the improbability of any public reading in the Church, from the want of adaptability to theological or ecclesiastical uses, and from the idea which seems to have prevailed—which is noticed by St. Chrysostom on the Epistle, and which St. Jerome in his preface to the Epistle (vol. vii., p. 742, ed. Vallarsii, 1737) refutes with his usual strong sense and trenchancy—that the occasion and the substance of the Epistle were too low for the Apostolic inspiration. "They will have it," St. Jerome says, "either that the Epistle which is addressed to Philemon is not St. Paul's, or that, even if it be his, it has nothing in it tending to our edification; and that by many of the ancients it was rejected, since it was written for the purpose merely of commendation, not of instruction.' But this kind of criticism did not prevail against the common acceptance of its authenticity. Even Marcion did not tamper with it, as Tertullian (*adv. Marc.* v. 42) and St. Jerome expressly declare. Origen, the great critic of the East, as St. Jerome of the West, quotes it without hesitation. In the Church generally it remained unshaken as one of the Epistles accepted by all.

In the larger criticism of modern times the very reasons which induced doubt in the fourth and fifth centuries will be accepted as the strongest internal evidence of its genuineness. The utter improbability of the forging of such an Epistle, which admits of no controversial or directly theological use, the exquisite beauty and naturalness of the whole style, even the vivid picture which it gives of an ancient Christian family—all have been felt to preclude any except the most wanton scepticism as to its genuineness. It is hard to conceive how any one can read it without feeling that we have in it a picture of the Apostle of the Gentiles, which we could ill afford to lose, but which no hand, except his own, would have ever ventured to paint.

IV. The Substance of the Epistle.—The great interest of this Epistle is two-fold—(1) in its personal relation to St. Paul's life and character, and (2) in the light which it throws on the attitude of the gospel towards slavery.

(1) It is the only strictly private Letter of St. Paul —the one survivor, we may suppose, of very many—preserved to us in the Canon of Holy Scripture. For all the other Epistles are either Letters to the Churches, or Pastoral Epistles of authoritative direction. Accordingly it exhibits the Apostle in a new light. He throws off, as far as possible, his Apostolic dignity, and his fatherly authority over his converts. He speaks simply as Christian to Christian. He speaks, therefore, with that peculiar grace of humility and courtesy, which has, under the reign of Christianity, developed the spirit of chivalry, and what is called "the character of a gentleman"—certainly very little known in the old Greek and Roman civilisations—while yet in its graceful flexibility and vivacity it stands contrasted with the more impassive Oriental stateliness. It has been customary and natural to compare with it a celebrated letter of the younger Pliny on a like occasion (*Ep.* ix. 21, quoted in Dr. Lightfoot's *Introduction*). But in Pliny himself there was a tone of feeling differing very much from the more ancient Roman character, approaching more nearly to the modern type. It would be curious to inquire, whether in this tone of character, as in the actual tenets of the later Stoicism, there might not be some unknown and indirect influence of the Christianity, which as yet would have been probably despised. Nor will the comparison for a moment place even the highly accomplished and cultivated Roman on a level with the Jewish tentmaker of Tarsus.

There is to us a vivid interest in the glimpse thus given into the private and personal life of St. Paul. We note, for example, the difference of tone—the greater pathos and the less unqualified rejoicing—in which he speaks of his captivity. We observe the gladness with which, when he rightly may, he throws off the isolation of authority, and descends into the familiarity of equal intercourse, lingering with an obvious delight in the very word "brother," which breathes the very spirit of freedom and equality. We see how, under the Apostolic mission, as under the Apostolic inspiration, free play of personal character and of familiar companionship could still live and flourish. We seem to know St. Paul better, even as an Apostle, because we are allowed to see him when he chooses not to be an Apostle, but a "partner," and, moreover, "such an one as Paul the aged, and the prisoner of Jesus Christ." But, even beyond this, we may fairly draw from this Epistle a priceless lesson, as to the place which true courtesy and delicacy occupy in Christian character, and especially as to their entire compatibility with high Apostolic enthusiasm, with a keen insight into realities as distinct from forms, and with the greatest possible plainness of speech in due season. We feel, as we read, how little it accords with the idea that Christian men and Christian ministers "have nothing to do with being gentlemen." We understand how true courtesy, as distinct from artificial and technical culture of manners, is the natural outgrowth of the "lowliness of mind" in which "each esteems other better than himself," and of the sympathy of love which "looks not only upon our own things," but, even in greater degree, "upon the things of others."

(2) But of far greater interest still is the illustration of the attitude assumed in the New Testament, and in the early Church, towards the monstrous institution of slavery.

How deeply that institution of slavery was engrained in all the history of antiquity, both Eastern and Western, we know well. Nor will this surprise any one who remembers that inequality—physical, mental, and spiritual—is, quite as truly as equality, the law of human life. Service and lordship, in some sense, there must always be; and it is absurd to deny that this law is, because we wish that it were not, or perhaps think that it ought not to be. But equality is the law of the primary qualities and rights of human nature; inequality only of the secondary qualities and rights. If this relation be reversed in practice, we pass from what is natural to that which, however frequent, is yet fatally unnatural. Slavery is just such a reversal. Because one race is stronger, abler, more commanding, more civilised than another, this is made a ground for crushing out, in the weaker race, all the essential attributes of humanity. Primarily by the unnatural agency of war, secondarily by systematised organisation in peace, the slave is made to cease to be a man: he is treated simply as a brute beast of somewhat higher organisation and usefulness than his fellows, or even "as a living chattel or machine"—having no rights whatever, except those which humanity may teach towards the lower creatures, or expediency enforce in relation to the machinery of the prosperity and progress of the master. Since, in some sense, freedom of action and cultivation bring out natural inequalities more and more strikingly, slavery, in the absence of some counterbalancing power, rather advanced than receded with the progress of heathen civilisation. Under the Roman empire, depending mainly on organised force rather than on intellectual cultivation, it presented this characteristic and intolerable incongruity, that it held in bondage men at least as noble in race as their conquerors, men even more highly cultivated, and heirs of more ancient civilisations.

That the Old Testament should recognise the existence of slavery, especially in inferior and degraded races, was only to be expected. That slavery under the patriarchal simplicity should have been lighter than under the higher civilisation of the nation of Israel, though at first sight startling, is yet, on more careful thought, seen to be natural. That the Mosaic law should attempt only to mitigate the irresponsible despotism of the master, and that in this respect it should make a marked distinction between the Israelite and the foreigner, is thoroughly accordant with our Lord's declaration, that it was made "for the hardness of men's hearts," and with the exclusiveness of privilege which it claimed in all things for the chosen race. Slavery, accordingly, continued in the Jewish people, though—thanks to those mitigations of the Law, to the protest against oppression and cruelty so familiar to us in prophecy, and to the very influence of a spiritual religion, wherever this was really accepted—it was actually very far milder than under Greece or Rome. Still it did exist. Nor will this surprise those who have duly weighed—what advocates and opponents of slavery, in dealing with the Old Testament, have constantly failed to weigh—the essentially imperfect and preparatory character of the Jewish covenant.

But what line would Christianity take? Nothing, of course, could be clearer than that it was radically opposed in principle to the whole conception and practice of slavery. For it brought out the fundamental equality or brotherhood of all, in the regenerate human nature, in which "there was neither Jew nor Greek, barbarian, Scythian, bond nor free." It devoted itself with a very special earnestness to redress all existing inequalities, by exalting the humble, by glorifying weakness, by restraining the self-assertion of strength. Above all, it consecrated that brotherhood in Jesus Christ; its whole conception of the spiritual life consisted in the union of each individual soul with God in Christ, so giving to individuality a sacredness utterly incompatible with the very possibility of absolute despotism of one Christian man over another. But of carrying out the principle there were two ways. One was, so to speak, "of law," embodying it at once in a declaration of freedom, abrogating all slavery within the Christian Church, protesting against it, as against all moral evils, in the world at large. The other was "of the Spirit," proclaiming the great truth of brotherhood in Christ and sonship of God, and then leaving it gradually to mould to itself all institutions of society, and to eradicate whatever in them was against God's fundamental law, reasserted in the word of Jesus Christ. Now of these two ways it is not hard to see that to adopt the former way would have been to revolutionise suddenly the whole of society, to preach (though unwillingly) a servile war, and to arm all existing governments by the very instinct of self-preservation against the infant Church, which, even as it was, excited their suspicion and alarm. Independently of all thought of consequences, we could not but anticipate that by its very nature Christianity would take the way of the Spirit, rather than the Law. But there can be no doubt that, historically, this was the way which it did take without hesitation or reserve. The principle laid down broadly by St. Paul (1 Cor. vii. 20—24) was that "every man should abide" in the outward condition "in which he was called," only "with God," in the new spiritual unity with God sealed to him in the blood of Jesus Christ. He applied that principle to the cases of circumcision and uncircumcision, marriage and celibacy; he did not shrink from applying it for the Christian community to the case of submission to "the powers that be," even to death, and for the individual to the crucial and extreme case of slavery and freedom. However we may interpret his words in 1 Cor. vii. 21 (where see Note), they clearly imply that to one who is at once "the Lord's freeman" and "Christ's slave" the outward condition matters comparatively little. It may be that in this case, as in the case of marriage, St. Paul was partly influenced by the consideration that "the time was short." Yet his teaching really depended, not on this expectation, but on the fundamental principle and method of Christianity. The declaration, "Not now a slave but a brother," a "brother beloved," and "a brother beloved in the Lord," brought the forces of human duty and human affection, under the inspiration of religious faith, to bear on the prison-house of slavery. Deeply founded as its walls were, and cemented by the use of centuries, they could not but fall under the combined attack of these three irresistible powers.

Meanwhile the gospel set itself to two immediate works. First, to raise the self-respect of the slave, to comfort his sorrow, to nerve him to bear the hardships of his cruel lot. This it did sometimes by glorifying suffering, in the bold declaration to the slave that his suffering, whatever it was, was a brotherhood in the suffering of the Lord Jesus Christ, who Himself "took upon Him the form of a slave," and "suffering for us left an ensample," in which even the helpless and despised slave could "follow His steps" (1 Pet. ii. 18—25). Sometimes, on the other hand, by setting forth to him the spiritual freedom, which no "master after the flesh" could take away, and by declaring that all service was ultimately a service to the Lord, to be rendered not only "from the heart," but "of good will," and rewarded here and hereafter with the heavenly prize (Eph. vi. 5—8; Col. iii. 22—25). Under both these convictions it taught the slave still to be patient under "subjection," till the end should come. Next, Christianity turned to the masters. It bade them remember their responsibility to the same Master in heaven, under whom their slaves served, and who would certainly make, in His strict retribution, no "respect of persons;" it claimed that they should "do the same things" to their slaves, recognising a mutual duty, and giving them all that was "just and equal," due to the indefeasible rights of humanity; above all that they should recognise in them a common brotherhood in Christ.

Now this is precisely the line which St. Paul pursues in respect of Onesimus. He, the runaway slave of Philemon, apparently an idler and a thief, had made his way to Rome, "the sink," as its writers bitterly complained, "of the civilised world." There St. Paul had somehow found him, and had regenerated the true humanity which had been degraded in him. He had found him a dear son; he had felt the comfort of his affectionate ministration. How deeply this had impressed on his mind the whole question of slaves and masters we see by the strong emphasis, marked by almost verbal coincidence, with which, in the Ephesian and Colossian Epistles, he dwells on the subject generally. But, coming to the particular case, he bids Onesimus acknowledge the mastership of Philemon, and go back to submit to him, and to offer atonement for his past misdeeds and flight. He will not even interpose by authority, or, by keeping Onesimus at Rome, put any constraint on Philemon's freedom to use his legal power. But he shows, by his own example, that the slave is to be treated as a son. He sends him back, not as a slave, but as "a brother beloved in the Lord." He "knew that Philemon would do even more than he said." He may have looked forward in prophetic foresight to the time when the whole Christian community, like Philemon, should draw the inference, unspoken but irresistible, and set absolutely free those who were not slaves, but brethren.

That expectation has been realised. It is remarkable that from very early days the iron cruelty of this Roman slave law began to give way. We may allow much in this respect to the growing dominion of universal law, and to the influence of the nobler philosophies; but we may be permitted to doubt whether the unacknowledged principles of Christianity were not already leavening public opinion, and beginning to make the change even in law, which was afterwards seen in the codes of Christian emperors. But one thing is certain historically, that in the abolition, certainly of ancient serfship in Europe, and perhaps of modern serfship in Russia, in the prohibition of the slave trade, in the great sacrifices for emancipation made by England in the last generation, and the United States of America in this, it was Christianity, and not simple philanthropy, which actually did the beneficent work. The battle was the battle of humanity; but it was fought under the banner of the Cross. Even while we wonder that the victory should have been so long in coming, we must confess that it has been won; and against all forms of mitigated slavery in modern society, experience certainly warns us to trust, not to the sense of common interest, the conviction of mutual duty, or even the enthusiasm of philanthropy, but to the faith which recognises in the poorest and the weakest, even in the idler and the sinner, "a brother beloved in the Lord."

THE EPISTLE OF PAUL TO

PHILEMON

A.D. 64.

Verses 1 — 3. Salutation.

(1) **PAUL**, a prisoner of Jesus Christ,
and Timothy *our* brother,
unto Philemon our dearly
beloved, and fellowla-
bourer, (2) and to *our* beloved Apphia,
and Archippus our fellowsoldier, and to
the church in thy house: (3) grace to
you, and peace, from God our Father
and the Lord Jesus Christ. (4) I thank
my God, making mention
of thee always in my
prayers, (5) hearing of thy
love and faith, which thou
hast toward the Lord

Verses 4 — 7. Thanksgiving for Philemon's love and for the comfort derived therefrom.

[This Epistle divides itself naturally into—

(1) Salutation to Philemon and his house (verses 1—3).

(2) Thanksgiving for their faith and love (verses 4—7).

(3) Intercession for Onesimus, as now the Apostle's "son" in the faith, and "the brother," not slave, of his master Philemon, with promise to make good any default of his in times past (verses 8—20).

(4) Conclusion, expressing St. Paul's confidence in Philemon, his hope of visiting them, and final salutation (verses 21—25).]

(1) **A prisoner of Jesus Christ.**—It is interesting to note the substitution of the name "prisoner," appealing to sympathy, for the usual title of "Apostle," embodying a claim to authority. In the other Epistles of this period (see Eph. iii. 1—13; iv. 1; vi. 20; Phil. i. 12—20; Col. iv. 18) the Apostle's captivity is dwelt upon mainly as a ground of glory and thankfulness, only secondarily as a cause for sympathy. Here, on the contrary, in this personal Epistle, and in accordance with St. Paul's courteous determination "not to command, but for love's sake to entreat," the latter aspect assumes an almost exclusive prominence.

Timothy.—Comp. Phil. i. 1; Col. i. 1. Here, as in the other Epistles, the salutation includes Timothy, as desiring to imply in him, St. Paul's "own son in the faith," a closeness of connection and sympathy with the Apostle not found in others. But in all cases, and especially in this, the Letter is emphatically the Letter of St. Paul alone.

Philemon.—See *Introduction.*

(2) **Apphia.**—The name is usually taken to be the Roman name *Appia.* But the occurrence of such a name in a Græco-Asiatic family, though of course possible, is perhaps improbable; and Dr. Lightfoot has shown that it occurs in the form *Apphia* in many Phrygian inscriptions, and may therefore be naturally supposed to be a native name. There seems little doubt that Apphia was Philemon's wife, like himself "the beloved," though not the "fellow-labourer" or "partner" of St. Paul.

Archippus our fellowsoldier.—From this mention of Archippus we may certainly conclude that he was a member of Philemon's family; the ordinary conjecture makes him his son. The name "fellow-soldier," applied elsewhere only to Epaphroditus (Phil. ii. 25), as the name "soldier of Jesus Christ" to Timothy (2 Tim. ii. 3), appears to denote ministerial office in Archippus, which agrees with the charge to him in Col. iv. 18 to "take heed to his ministry and fulfil it."

Church in thy house.—See Note on Col. iv. 15. The specially domestic and personal character of the Epistle need not induce any limitation of the phrase to Philemon's own family. As the joining of Timothy's name in giving the salutation did not prevent the Letter from being St. Paul's only, so the joining the Church in the house in the receiving of the salutation does not prevent its being addressed only to Philemon and his family, who were, like himself, interested in Onesimus.

(4) **I thank my God . . .**—Note the almost exact verbal coincidence with the salutations in Eph. i. 15, 16; Phil. i. 3, 4; Col. i. 3, 4, with, however, the natural distinction that this is briefer and simpler in style.

(5) **Thy love and faith, which thou hast toward the Lord Jesus, and toward all saints.**—This description of a faith directed not only to the Lord Jesus, but to all the saints, has perplexed commentators, and called out various explanations. (1) One is that "faith" here (as in Rom. iii. 3; Gal. v. 22) is simply fidelity; but this can hardly be accepted as an explanation of so well-known and almost technical a phrase as "faith toward the Lord Jesus Christ." (2) Another, noting the distinction in the original between the two prepositions here—the former (*pros*) signifying direction towards, and the latter (*eis*) actual contact with, its object—explains the phrase as signifying "the faith which has as its object the Lord Jesus Christ, but which shows itself practically towards all saints." But this, even if the word "hast" will bear this gloss, seems too artificial for such a Letter as this. (3) The comparison with the contemporaneous Letter to the Colossians—where we read, "your faith in the Lord Jesus, and your love toward all the saints" (Col. i. 4)—seems to clear up the matter. We have here an equivalent phrase, in which, however (by what the grammarians called *chiasmus*), the extremes and means correspond to each other. The idea which runs through the Letter is Philemon's "love to the saints." In writing of that love St. Paul cannot refrain from

Jesus, and toward all saints; (6) that
the communication of thy faith may
become effectual by the acknowledg-
ing of every good thing which is
in you in Christ Jesus. (7) For we have
great joy and consolation in thy love,
because the bowels of the saints are
refreshed by thee, brother. (8) Where-
fore, though I might be
much bold in Christ to en-
join thee that which is con-
venient, (9) yet for love's sake I rather
beseech *thee*, being such an one as Paul
the aged, and now also a prisoner of

Verses 8—14. Intercession for Onesimus.

---

referring it to its true origin—the faith towards the Lord Jesus Christ. Hence the broken phrase. The sense seems therefore to be that which in some MSS. has been brought out by a natural correction, "thy faith towards the Lord Jesus, and thy love to all the saints."

(6) **That the communication of thy faith . . .** —The general idea of St. Paul's prayer for Philemon is clear—that his "faith may become effectual," *i.e.*, energetic and perfected, "in full knowledge." This is exactly the prayer which, in different forms and degrees of emphasis, opens all the Epistles of the Captivity. (See Eph. i. 17; Phil. i. 9; Col. i. 9.) It describes the true order of Christian life, so fully and beautifully drawn out in Eph. iii. 17—19, beginning in faith, deepened by love, and so growing to knowledge.

But it may be asked, "Why the *communication of* thy faith?" (1) The phrase is unique, but the word rendered "communication" is the well-known word generally rendered "communion," or "fellowship," except where (as in Rom. xv. 26; 2 Cor. viii. 4; ix. 13; Heb. xiii. 16) it is used technically and derivatively of "the communication" of almsgiving. The phrase, therefore, should probably be rendered the "communion of thy faith," *i.e.*, "thy fellowship in faith." (2) But, again, the question arises, "With whom is this fellowship? With God or man?" The answer probably is, "With both." Perhaps for growth in divine knowledge the communion need only be with God. But we observe that the knowledge is not merely "of every good thing," *i.e.*, of all that is of God, but of "every good thing which is in you (or, better, *in us*) towards Christ Jesus." It is, therefore, the knowledge of good—that is, of God's gift—as dwelling in man by the unity which binds all to Christ Jesus. (3) Now for knowledge of this, fellowship with man is needed, as well as fellowship with God. The soul which dwells alone with God, even in the holiest seclusion, knows what is good in the abstract, but not what is good in man in the concrete reality. But Philemon's house was a centre of Christian life. St. Paul might, therefore, well speak of this his two-fold "fellowship in faith," and pray that it might grow into full knowledge at once of God and of man as in Him. (4) That all such growth must be "towards Christ Jesus," dependent on unity with Him and serving to deepen such unity, is the characteristic doctrine of all this group of Epistles, especially of the Colossian Epistle, of which Onesimus was one of the bearers.

(7) **The bowels of the saints are refreshed by thee.**—The same idea is here carried on. St. Paul declares his special joy to have been that "the bowels (*i.e., the hearts*) of the saints, have been refreshed through thee." The word "refresh" is the very word used by our Lord in His gracious promise: "Come unto me all ye that travail and are heavy laden, and I will *refresh you*" (Matt. xi. 28). It is ultimately in Him that the hearts of the saints are refreshed. But in this case it was through the instrumentality of Philemon, by "the communion of faith," to which his active love was the means of welcoming them, and in which they had fellowship in Christ, both with the Father and with His children. (Comp. 1 John i. 3.) St. Paul uses the word "refresh" not unfrequently to express the relief and rest given by Christian fellowship on earth. (See below, verse 20; and comp. 1 Cor. xvi. 18; 2 Cor. vii. 13.) We find it in the Apocalypse applied to the rest with Christ in heaven (Rev. vi. 11; xiv. 13).

Brother.—The name is given to Philemon here and in verse 20 with a marked emphasis of affection, evidently implying some special intimacy of friendship, not apparently at Colossæ (for see Col. ii. 1); but perhaps at Ephesus, during St. Paul's long stay there. Probably Philemon (whose son Archippus is supposed to have been) was St. Paul's equal in age, and although actually his convert is not addressed (as usual) as his "son in the faith." In this place, moreover, the title "brother" has a peculiar appropriateness: for the Apostle has been speaking of the love of Philemon, which made him a brother indeed to all in the family of Christ.

(8—20) Here St. Paul enters on the main subject of his Letter—the recommendation to Philemon of his runaway slave, Onesimus. All thoughtful readers of the Epistle must recognise in this a peculiar courtesy and delicacy of tone, through which an affectionate earnestness shows itself, and an authority all the greater because it is not asserted in command. The substance is equally notable in its bearing on slavery. Onesimus is doubly welcomed into the Christian family. He is St. Paul's son in the faith: he is to Philemon a brother beloved in the Lord. In that recognition is the truth to which, both in theory and in practice, we may look as being the destruction of slavery.

(8, 9) **Wherefore . . . for love's sake . . .**—Still the same idea runs on. Philemon's love, shown in Christian fellowship, is in the Apostle's mind; "therefore," he adds, "for love's sake"—speaking in the spirit of love, to which he knew there would be a ready response—he will not command, as an Apostle, what is "convenient," *i.e., seemly*, in a Christian (comp. Eph. v. 14; Col. iii. 18), but will "entreat" as a brother.

(9) **Paul the aged, and now also a prisoner of Jesus Christ.**—At this time St. Paul must have been between fifty and sixty, and after a life of unexampled labour and suffering he might well call himself "aged," not, perhaps, in comparison with Philemon, but in relation to his need of ministry from his "son" Onesimus. It has been suggested by Dr. Lightfoot that we should read here (by a slight change, or without any change, in the original), *the ambassador, and also the prisoner, of Jesus Christ*. The parallel with Eph. vi. 20—"for which I am an ambassador in bonds"—and, indeed, with the tone in which St. Paul in the other Epistles speaks of his captivity as his glory, is tempting. But the change seems to take much from the peculiar beauty and pathos of the passage; which from its appeal to love, rather than to authority, suits especially with the thought, not of the glory of ambassadorship for Christ, but of the weakness of an old age suffering in chains.

Jesus Christ. (10) I beseech thee for my son Onesimus, whom I have begotten in my bonds: (11) which in time past was to thee unprofitable, but now profitable to thee and to me: (12) whom I have sent again: thou therefore receive him, that is, mine own bowels: (13) whom I would have retained with me, that in thy stead he might have ministered unto me in the bonds of the gospel: (14) but without thy mind would I do nothing; that thy benefit should not be as it were of necessity, but willingly. (15) For perhaps he therefore departed for a season, that thou shouldest receive him for ever; (16) not now as a servant, but above a servant, a brother beloved, specially to me, but how much more unto thee, both in the flesh, and in the Lord? (17) If thou count me therefore a partner,

Verses 15—20. Prayer that Philemon will accept him for St. Paul's sake.

(10) **My son.**—Properly, *my own child, whom I have begotten in my bonds, Onesimus.* The name is withheld, till Philemon's interest is doubly engaged, for one who is the Apostle's "own child" (a name of endearment given elsewhere only to Timothy and Titus), and for one who was begotten under the hardships and hindrances of imprisonment. At last the name is given, and even then comes, in the same breath, the declaration of the change in him from past uselessness to present usefulness, both to the Apostle and to his former master.

Onesimus.—Of Onesimus we know absolutely nothing, except what we read here and in Col. iv. 9. Tradition, of course, is busy with his name, and makes him Bishop of Berœa, in Macedonia, or identifies him with the Onesimus, Bishop of Ephesus, mentioned in the Ignatian *Epistle to the Ephesians* (chap. i. 2—6). The name was a common one, especially among slaves.

(11) **In time past . . . unprofitable, but now profitable.**—The name *Onesimus* means "useful," or "profitable," though derived from a different root from the words here used. It is hardly possible not to see in this passage a play on words, though (curiously enough) this is not noticed by the old Greek commentators. St. Paul seems to say, "He belied his name in days past; he will more than deserve it now."

To thee and to me.—St. Paul says "to thee," for he was sending back Onesimus. He adds "to me," in affectionate notice of his kindly ministrations already rendered to his spiritual father.

(12) **Thou therefore receive him.**—The word "receive" is not in the best MSS. It is supplied here from verse 17 (apparently rightly in respect of sense) to fill up a broken construction in the original.

Mine own bowels—*i.e., my own heart,* dear to me as my own soul. There is, indeed, an usage of the word which applies it to children as begotten of our own body. But this is hardly St. Paul's usage (see 2 Cor. vi. 12; Phil. i. 8; ii. 1; Col. iii. 12; and verses 7 and 20 of this Epistle), though it suits very well with the phrase "whom I have begotten" above.

(13) **Whom I would have retained.**—In the original we have here a graceful distinction in two points between the two clauses. The verb in the first clause is "to wish;" in the second "to will." The tense in the first clause is the imperfect: "I was wishing," or "prepared to wish" (just as in Acts xxv. 22; and, in the case of a cognate verb, Rom. ix. 3), implying, perhaps, a suppressed condition; in the second it is the past definite: "I willed," or "determined" finally.

In thy stead.—Here, again, there is a certain delicacy of suggestion. A slave was his master's property; he could act only on his master's behalf and by his consent. St. Paul is sure that Philemon's love for him would have gladly given that consent, and so made Onesimus an instrument of willing service to St. Paul.

(14) **That thy benefit should not be . . .**—The benefit derived from the service of Onesimus St. Paul acknowledges as coming from Philemon, because given with his consent. He will not keep Onesimus and ask that consent by letter, lest it should be "as it were of necessity:" *i.e.,* lest it should wear even the semblance of constraint.

(15) **For perhaps he therefore departed** (or, *was parted*).—This is a further reason for sending Onesimus back. St. Paul now touches on Onesimus' "being parted" from Philemon, using a phrase not only (as has been noted) euphemistic, but also one which suggested that his running away was, however unconsciously, overruled by a higher hand. God, in His wisdom, "parted" him from Philemon "for a season, that he might receive him for ever." The phrase "for ever" is the word always used for "eternal." The contrast with "for a season" might be satisfied here by the merely relative sense of "perpetual" or "life-long service;" but, considering that the phrase is used in direct reference to the brotherhood of the Communion of Saints, it is better to take it in its absolute sense, of fellowship in the life eternal.

(16) **Not now as a servant, but . . . a brother beloved . . . in the Lord.**—In these words we have at last the principle which is absolutely destructive of the condition of slavery—a condition which is the exaggeration of natural inferiority to the effacement of the deeper natural equality. (1) The slave—the "living chattel" of inhuman laws and philosophies—is first "a brother," united to his master by natural ties of ultimate equality, having, therefore, both duties and rights. (2) But he is also a "brother beloved." These natural ties are not only strengthened by duty, but made living ties by the love which delights indeed to respect the rights of others, but is not content without willingness to sacrifice even our own rights to them. (3) Above all, this is "in the Lord." The slave is bought by Christ's blood, made a son of God, and therefore a brother to all who are members of the family of God. To reject and to outrage him is a rejection and outrage towards Christ. Compare St. Peter's striking comparison of the sufferings of the slave to the passion of the Divine Sufferer (1 Pet. ii. 18—24). They suffer with Him, and He suffers in them. It has been proved historically that only by the aid of this last and highest conception has the brotherhood of love—too slowly, indeed, but yet surely—assumed reality. (See *Introduction.*)

Specially to me, but how much more unto thee?—St. Paul first emphasises his own love for Onesimus, which, indeed, breathes in every line of the Epistle; but then goes on to infer in Philemon a yet greater affection—a natural love towards the nursling of his house, a spiritual love towards the brother "in the Lord," lost and found again.

(17) **A partner.**—The title is peculiar. In the singular

receive him as myself. (18) If he hath
wronged thee, or oweth *thee* ought, put
that on mine account; (19) I Paul have
written *it* with mine own hand, I will
repay *it:* albeit I do not say to thee
how thou owest unto me even thine
own self besides. (20) Yea, brother, let
me have joy of thee in the Lord: re-
fresh my bowels in the
Lord. (21) Having confi-
dence in thy obedience I
wrote unto thee, knowing that thou wilt
also do more than I say. (22) But withal
prepare me also a lodging: for I trust
that through your prayers I shall be
given unto you. (23) There salute thee
Epaphras, my fellowprisoner in Christ
Jesus; (24) Marcus, Aristarchus, Demas,
Lucas, my fellowlabourers. (25) The
grace of our Lord Jesus Christ *be* with
your spirit. Amen.

Verses 21—25. Salutation and conclusion.

¶ Written from Rome to Philemon, by Onesimus a servant.

---

number (in which it is naturally more distinctive) and in absolute use, unconnected with explanatory words (such as we read in 1 Pet. v. 1), it is nowhere else found, except in 2 Cor. viii. 23, where Titus is called St. Paul's "partner and fellowhelper;" and even there the context defines the partnership as relating to the collection and ministration of alms. Here it can hardly refer to general Christian fellowship, which would require some such words as "in Christ," or "in the Spirit," and would not fully justify the strong personal appeal of the passage. It must indicate some peculiar bond of fellowship between St. Paul and Philemon. Philemon was his convert (see verse 19); yet we notice that he writes to him not as a son, but as a brother. Evidently he was a leader in the Church at Colossæ. Tradition, as usual, makes him its bishop. He must have been St. Paul's partner in some common work or special communion of familiarity. (See *Introduction*, sect. 2.)

(18) **If he hath wronged thee.**—Properly, *If he wronged thee*, evidently referring to the time of Onesimus' escape. "If he oweth thee ought" is similarly, in all probability, an allusion to some theft at the same time, couched in a hypothetical form, but implying no doubt as to the fact.

Put that on mine account.—Comp. a similar commercial metaphor in Phil. iv. 15—17, and see Note there. It is strangely out of character with the whole tone of the Apostolic life to imagine (as some commentators have done) a regular debtor and creditor account between Philemon and St. Paul.

(19) **I Paul have written it with mine own hand.**—St. Paul actually introduces here a regular bond couched in legal form, written (as, perhaps, the whole Letter was written) with his own hand. In so doing he still continues the idea of the preceding verse; but the following words show that, though willing to stand to his bond, he knew Philemon too well to suppose that he would accept it.

It is clear from this passage that the Apostle had money which he could rightly call his own. At Ephesus, where he probably first knew Philemon, it would probably be earned in the work with Aquila and Priscilla, as at Corinth, and it is possible that some of it might still remain. In Rome now, it could hardly be from any other source than the offerings from the Church at Philippi. They were given him freely; he might fairly spend them on his own "son in the faith."

Albeit I do not say to thee . . .—Literally, *not to say to thee.* Here St. Paul escapes from the business-like promise of the last verse to the freer atmosphere of spiritual relations. He knew that this promise it was right for him to offer, but wrong for Philemon to accept. Philemon owed his own self—his new self in Christ—to the Apostle. In that was a debt which he could not repay, but would rejoice even in this smaller matter to acknowledge.

(20) **Let me have joy of thee.**—Properly, *may I have pleasure*, or *profit, from thee:* a phrase used especially of the mingled pleasure and help derived from children. (See Dr. Lightfoot's Note on this passage.) The word "I" is emphatic. St. Paul puts himself forward to plead for Onesimus, what he himself could not plead. Nor can it be accidental that the word "profit" is the root of the name *Onesimus.* St. Paul says, in effect, "May I find thee (as I have found him) a true Onesimus."

Verses 21—25 contain the conclusion of the Epistle—hope to visit Philemon soon, salutation, and blessing.

(21) **Confidence in thy obedience.**—It is curious to notice how, in this conclusion, St. Paul seems to glide, as it were insensibly, out of the tone of entreaty as to an equal, into the authority of a superior. The word "obedience" is found in 2 Cor. vii. 15, there in connection with "fear and trembling." He preferred to appeal to Philemon's love; he knew that in any case he could rely on his deference.

Do more than I say.—This can hardly refer to anything except the manumission of Onesimus, and possibly his being sent back again to St. Paul. Exactly in this way Christianity was to work out the release of the slave—not by command, but by free and natural inference from its emphatic declaration of his true brotherhood in Christ.

(22) **A lodging.**—The word often signifies "hospitality" generally, which Philemon might naturally offer in his own house, but which St. Paul would not suggest or ask.

I shall be given unto you.—Literally, *as a favour* from supreme authority. Comp. the technical and forensic use of the word in Acts iii. 14; xxv. 11: for good in one case, in the other for evil. If he was so "granted," it would be by Cæsar instrumentally, by God's overruling will ultimately. The passage, like Phil. ii. 24, but even more definitely, expresses St. Paul's expectation of a release which might enable him to visit the East again. It is curious that there is no similar allusion in the Colossian Epistle, sent with this.

(23) **My fellowprisoner.**—Comp. Col. iv. 10, and see Note there. The salutations here correspond exactly in substance (though more condensed in style) with that passage, except that "Jesus, called Justus" (probably unknown to Philemon) is here omitted.

(25) **The grace . . .**—This form of St. Paul's usual blessing is found also in Gal. vi. 18; Phil. iv. 23; 2 Tim. iv. 22. We notice by the word "your" that, like the opening salutation, it is addressed to all Philemon's family and "the church in his house."

THE EPISTLE OF PAUL THE APOSTLE TO THE

HEBREWS

INTRODUCTION

TO

THE EPISTLE OF PAUL THE APOSTLE TO THE

HEBREWS

As the Epistle to the Hebrews is presented to the reader in our English Bibles, various questions which beset many other books of the New Testament appear to have no place. It is entitled "The Epistle of Paul the Apostle to the Hebrews"; and from the subscription we learn that it was written in Italy and sent to its readers by the hand of Timothy. It is hardly necessary to say that, whether these statements have or have not a foundation in fact, they are wholly destitute of authority here; for no ancient manuscript adds to the Epistle anything beyond the simple words "To the Hebrews," and even this inscription can scarcely have been affixed by the writer himself. Within the few pages at our disposal we can do little more than present a summary of the ancient evidence on the points in question and the chief results of modern investigation.

I. Ancient Testimonies. Canonicity.—That the Epistle was known and read before the close of the first century is beyond doubt. The earliest Christian writing beyond the limits of the New Testament is the Epistle addressed to the Church of Corinth (about A.D. 95), by Clement, writing in the name of the Roman Church. This Letter contains no express quotation from any Book of the New Testament, and one only (the First Epistle of St. Paul to the same Church) is mentioned by name. In several places, however, words from some of St. Paul's Epistles are interwoven with the text without formal introduction. In exactly the same manner, but to a greater extent, does Clement make use of the Epistle to the Hebrews, as the following quotation (from chap. xxxvi.) will show: "Through Him the Lord willed that we should taste the immortal knowledge; who, being the brightness (or, *effulgence*) of His majesty, is so much greater than angels as He hath inherited a more excellent name. For it is thus written: He who maketh His angels winds (or, *spirits*), and His ministers a flame of fire. But in regard to His Son thus said the Lord: Thou art My Son, I have this day begotten Thee. Ask of Me, and I will give Thee nations as Thine inheritance, and as Thy possession the ends of the earth. And again He saith unto Him: Sit at My right hand, until I have made Thine enemies a footstool of Thy feet."

This passage does not stand alone; but of itself it is sufficient to prove that the Epistle was well known to the Roman Church at this early date. The traces of the Epistle in the second century are clear, but not numerous until we reach its closing years. Quotations present themselves in the Homily which is commonly called Clement's Second Epistle, written at Corinth or Rome about A.D. 140; in writings of Justin Martyr (A.D. 145), Pinytus of Crete (A.D. 170), Theophilus, Bishop of Antioch (A.D. 180). It is also important to note that the Epistle was one of the twenty-two books included in the Syriac version of the New Testament, the date of which is probably not later than A.D. 150 That Marcion should have rejected the Epistle, and that it is passed over in the Muratorian Fragment (probably written at Rome about A.D. 170) are points of little consequence; for Marcion is known to have rejected whatever conflicted with his system of doctrine, and the Latin document has not come down to us complete.

One testimony belonging to the close of the second or the beginning of the third century is of great interest and importance. It is found in one of the works of Clement, who succeeded Pantænus as head of the catechetical school of Alexandria, about A.D. 190. The work itself survives in fragments only; but the following passage is preserved by Eusebius (*Eccles. History*, vi. 14): "And in his *Outlines* to speak generally, he (Clement) has given brief expositions of all canonical Scripture, not even passing by the disputed books—I mean the Epistle of Jude and the rest of the Catholic Epistles, the Epistle of Barnabas and the so-called Apocalypse of Peter. And moreover, he says that the Epistle to the Hebrews was Paul's, but had been written to the Hebrews in the Hebrew language, and that Luke, having with great care translated it, published it for the Greeks; hence this Epistle and the Acts are found to have the same colouring of style and diction. He remarks that the Epistle does not begin with 'Paul an Apostle,' and with reason; for (he says), writing to Hebrews, men who had become prejudiced against him and were suspicious of him, he acted very wisely in not repelling them at the outset by giving his name. Then a little below he adds: And as the blessed presbyter before now used to say, since the Lord, as Apostle of the Almighty, was sent to Hebrews, Paul through modesty, as having been sent to Gentiles, does not inscribe himself Apostle of Hebrews, because of the honour belonging to the Lord, and also because he went beyond his bounds in addressing Hebrews also, when he was herald and Apostle of Gentiles."

We can hardly doubt that by "the blessed presbyter' is meant Pantænus, whom Clement held in the highest esteem. "Thus" (as Dr. Westcott observes) "the tradition is carried up almost to the Apostolic age." It will be seen that with a strong affirmation of the Pauline authorship of the Epistle is joined a distinct recognition of its unlikeness to the other writings of the Apostle. Of much greater importance is the testimony of Origen. Many passages from his writings might be quoted in which he speaks of the Epistle as St. Paul's, and many more in which he appeals to it as to other portions of the New Testament, without any reference to authorship. In one of his latest works, however, *Homilies on the Hebrews* (written between A.D. 245 and 253), we have the complete expression of his views. The Homilies are not preserved to us, but the passage is given by Eusebius in his *Eccles. History* (vi. 25), and is as follows: "That the style of the

Epistle which bears the superscription *To the Hebrews* does not exhibit the Apostle's plainness in speech (though he confessed himself to be plain in his speech, that is, in his diction), but that the Epistle is more Grecian in its composition, every one who knows how to judge of differences of diction would acknowledge. And again, that the thoughts of the Epistle are wonderful, and not inferior to the acknowledged writings of the Apostle, this, too, every one who gives attention to the reading of the Apostle's words would allow to be true." To this, after other remarks, he adds: "But if I were to give my own opinion, I should say that the thoughts belong to the Apostle, but the diction and the composition to some one who wrote from memory the Apostle's teaching, and who, as it were, commented on that which had been said by his teacher. If then any church holds this Epistle to be Paul's, let it be approved even for this. For not without reason have the men of olden time handed it down as Paul's. But as to the question who wrote the Epistle, the truth is known by God (only); but the account which has reached us is a statement by some that Clement who became Bishop of Rome was the writer, by others that it was Luke, who wrote the Gospel and the Acts."

The influence of Origen would naturally be great in removing doubts as to the acceptance of the Epistle. Whilst the more thoughtful would learn from him to distinguish between directly apostolic authorship and canonicity, the effect of his opinion and example on the many would be to strengthen the belief that the Epistle should be accounted St. Paul's. From this time onwards the Church of Alexandria, as represented by a succession of writers, seems to have held the Pauline authorship as a matter free from doubt.

It is otherwise with the Latin writers of North Africa. Tertullian (about A.D. 200), indeed, once quotes some verses of chapter vi., but assigns them to the *Epistle of Barnabas to the Hebrews;* an Epistle which, he says, deserves more respect than the *Shepherd* of Hermas, as being written by a man who learnt from Apostles and taught with Apostles. No other certain quotation from the Epistle presents itself in Latin writers for many years. At the close of the third century it would seem, as far as we may judge from extant Christian literature, that the Epistle was known and received by the Churches of Alexandria, Syria, Rome, and Asia Minor, and that in Alexandria and Syria it was regarded as a work of St. Paul. Writing before A.D. 326, Eusebius expressly mentions the Church of Rome as rejecting the Pauline authorship of the Epistle. It is not necessary to give any express quotations from writers of the fourth century. By this time the doubts respecting the Epistle are confined to the Western Churches: in Syria, Palestine, Asia Minor, Alexandria, Constantinople, the Pauline authorship appears to have been universally admitted. The influence of Jerome and Augustine ultimately prevailed in the West: neither of these eminent Fathers appears really to have regarded the Epistle as St. Paul's, but they agree in the expression of a strong conviction of its canonical authority.

The object of this summary of ancient evidence has been to show how the Epistle won its way to universal acknowledgment as a part of sacred Scripture, and at the same time to present the chief testimonies of the early Church on the other important questions which concern the Book. It cannot be thought surprising that for a time many should evince hesitation in regard to such a document as this—anonymous, peculiar in character, and addressed to a special and limited circle of readers. The doubts have in later times had little power. Their effect may, for the most part, be traced in a varying estimate of the importance of the Book as compared with the undoubted writings of St. Paul.

II. **Authorship.**—In regard to the authorship of the Epistle, the most important ancient testimonies have been cited already; and in them we find more or less clearly stated almost all the possible solutions of the problem. The character of the Epistle is beyond all question Paul-like (if we may so speak, to avoid the ambiguity of "Pauline"). If then it is not to be ascribed directly to St. Paul, we must suppose either (1) that it is a translation from a Hebrew original written by him; or (2) that, whilst the substance of the Epistle is his, the diction and style belong to one of his companions, who, for some unexplained cause, put the Apostle's thoughts into form; or (3) that the Epistle was written by a friend or disciple of St. Paul. Each of the four hypotheses may, as we have said, claim the evidence of early writers; but it is a matter of extreme difficulty rightly to estimate the value of this evidence. That the Epistle was *directly* written by St. Paul is an opinion of which we have no distinct evidence earlier than the third century. Even then the language used on the subject is not perfectly clear; for Origen's example proves that the quotation of the Epistle under St. Paul's name may mean nothing more than a recognition that its substance and teaching are his. If Origen had influence in producing the later consensus of opinion as to the authorship, that opinion may fairly be judged of (to a considerable extent) by reference to Origen's own explanation of the sense in which he ascribed the Epistle to St. Paul. At all events, his plain statement of the case as it presented itself in his day seems distinctly to prove that there existed no such clear and authoritative tradition in favour of the Pauline authorship as might claim our submission, upon the ordinary principles of literary criticism. To internal evidence Origen makes appeal: to the same test of internal evidence we believe the case must now be brought. Similar observations apply to the other hypotheses. Each of these appears earlier in existing documents than that of which we have been speaking. The opinion expressed by Clement, that the Greek Epistle is a translation, was probably derived by him from Pantænus: the traditions mentioned by Origen cannot be of later date; and Tertullian's reference to Barnabas carries back the last hypothesis to the close of the second century. But again it is impossible to say whether the ancient testimonies present independent evidence, or are no more than conjectures to explain the patent facts. At all events, the variance in the traditions may leave our judgment free, especially as we can plainly perceive in what way the traditions might very possibly arise.

If we now proceed to test each of the hypotheses that have been mentioned by the testimony which the Epistle gives respecting itself, the first question to be decided is, Have we the Epistle in its original form? If the opinion quoted by Clement is correct—that the Greek document before us is a translation—our right to argue from its characteristics will be materially affected. This opinion has not lacked advocates, and has been recently maintained in an able but very disappointing work by Dr. Biesenthal. We have no space here for the discussion of such a question, and can only express in a word or two the results to which the evidence before us leads. We do not hesitate to say that the hypothesis appears absolutely untenable: for one difficulty which it removes, it introduces many more.

Dr. Biesenthal's own treatment of various passages is sufficient to show that those who regard the Epistle as translated from a Hebrew original must necessarily regard it as a translation that is often inaccurate, and needs the correction of the commentator. Few will be prepared to surrender the Epistle to such treatment, unless under constraint of argument immeasurably stronger than any yet adduced.

Our inquiry therefore is limited to the Greek Epistle as it stands. The questions at issue are very simple. What is there, either in the substance or in the diction of the Epistle, that may lead us to ascribe it to St. Paul? What peculiarities of thought or language separate it from his writings? In its general arrangement and plan the Epistle to the Hebrews cannot but remind us of St. Paul. It is true there is no opening salutation, or direct address, such as is found in all St. Paul's Epistles. These Epistles, however, differ greatly amongst themselves in this respect. Thus, in writing to the Galatians, the Apostle is impatient of anything that may detain him from the great topics on which he is to speak; and it is possible to imagine reasons which might lead him to avoid all mention of the Church addressed, and even to keep back his own name. But, waiving this, we recognise at once the familiar plan: first the discussion of dogmatic truth; then the earnest exhortation based on the doctrine thus presented; and, lastly, the salutations, interwoven with personal notices, with doxology and prayer. The main outlines of theological teaching are in close accord with St. Paul's Epistles: chaps. ii. and v., for example, as strikingly recall Phil. ii. as does chap. xiii. the closing chapter in the Epistle to the Romans. Other points of special resemblance will easily suggest themselves, such as the relation of the writer to those whom he addresses (chap. xiii. 18, 19, &c.), the mode in which he refers to Timothy (verse 23), his Pauline illustrations (see Notes on chaps. v. 12, 13; xii. 1—4), his choice of Old Testament passages. Under the last head may be specially mentioned the quotation of Ps. viii. (1 Cor. xv. 25—28) and Deut. xxxiii. 30 (Rom. xii. 19); see the Notes on chaps. ii. 6; x. 30. It is not necessary to go into further detail in proof of a position allowed by all, that (as has been already said) the Epistle, whether by St. Paul or not, is Paul-like in the general character of its teaching and in many of its special features.

It is of much greater moment to examine those passages of the Epistle and those peculiarities of teaching or language which have been adduced as inconsistent with the Pauline authorship. Resemblance may be accounted for more readily than points of difference; for a disciple of St. Paul would hardly fail to exhibit many of the traits characteristic of such a master. Here, it will be seen, the distinction between style and subject matter must be carefully observed. If this Epistle could be proved to differ in diction only from the acknowledged writings of St. Paul, some theory of mediate authorship (similar to that mentioned by Origen) would be very possible; if the discordances lie deeper, no such theory can be maintained.

When an argument must rest on characteristics of Greek diction and style, it is very probable that different conclusions may be reached by different readers. This question, again, cannot be examined here in any detail. The writer can only state the impression made upon his own mind by the original text, and especially by the careful study pursued for the purpose of this Commentary. From point to point the general likeness of the Epistle to St. Paul's writings came out more and more plainly: on the other hand arose a continually increasing wonder that the Greek sentences and periods should ever have been attributed to that Apostle's hand. We have before us Epistles belonging to every period during the last thirteen or fourteen years of St. Paul's life, written under widely different circumstances,—some during the enforced leisure of imprisonment, others amid active labour. We can trace differences of style resulting both from the time of writing and from the circumstances which called forth the Epistles; but these differences lie within a comparatively narrow compass. At whatever date St. Paul might be supposed to have written this Epistle, we can compare it with some other of his writings belonging nearly to the same period; and the differences of language and style presented by the two documents are, we are persuaded, far greater than those presented by the most dissimilar of the thirteen Epistles. Stress has been laid on the unique character of this Epistle, as the only one addressed to Hebrews by the Apostle of the Gentiles: but it has been well asked why St. Paul should adopt a more finished Greek style in addressing Jews than when writing to the Greeks of Corinth. For ourselves we must express our decided conviction that, whatever may be the relation of the Epistle to St. Paul, the composition of the Greek was certainly not his.

The remaining points of difference which (it is alleged) separate this Epistle from St. Paul's writings may be ranged under the following heads:—(1) statements of fact which we cannot suppose to have proceeded from the Apostle; (2) divergence in doctrinal view; (3) peculiarities in the use of the Old Testament; (4) the use made of Alexandrian writers.

(1) The most important passage is chap. ii. 3: "which (salvation) at the first began to be spoken by the Lord, and was confirmed unto us by them that heard." In these words the writer appears distinctly to sever himself from those who had directly received the word from the Lord. It is urged that he is here associating himself with his readers, as when in chap. iv. 1 he writes "Let *us* therefore fear;" see also chaps. x. 24, 25, 26; xii. 1, *et al.* We will not venture to say that an Apostle *could* not have thus written; but, bearing in mind the necessity which lay upon St. Paul to defend his apostolic position, and the claim which he consistently makes to have received his teaching by direct revelation (Gal. i. 1, 11, 12, *et al.*), we must hold it extremely improbable that he should use words that might even appear to represent him as only a disciple of the Apostles. On the other passages which have been brought into this controversy a very different judgment must be passed. It is alleged that in the description of the Temple furniture (chap. ix.) the writer falls into mistakes, asserting that the altar of incense (or, *the golden censer*) was placed in the Holy of Holies, that the ark contained the pot of manna and Aaron's rod, and that even in his own day the Most Holy Place into which the high priest entered year by year still contained the cherubim and the ark of the covenant. If the writer has indeed fallen into these mistakes we may safely say that he is not St. Paul. But, as the Notes on chap. ix. 2—6 will show, we hold that there is no real reason for impugning the accuracy of his words. No part of his description relates to the Temple services or furniture: he is occupied throughout with the injunctions of the Mosaic law and the arrangements of the Tabernacle. Even the association of the altar of incense with the Most Holy Place may be very easily explained. If the view we have taken is correct, this argument against the Pauline authorship must fall to the ground. It is not necessary, therefore, to do

more than mention the ingenious attempt of Wieseler to show that in the descriptions of chap. ix. the writer had in mind, not the Tabernacle or the Temple of Jerusalem, but the temple built by Onias at Leontopolis in Lower Egypt (about B.C. 170).

(2) The alleged differences of doctrinal statement are of three kinds. Of St. Paul's favourite topics some are absent from this Epistle, some are treated in a different manner: and, again, certain themes here brought into prominence are not noticed in the Epistles of St. Paul. Thus we find only one passage in this Epistle in which the Resurrection of our Lord, ever a prominent topic with St. Paul, is mentioned (see chap. xiii. 20); the law, faith, righteousness, are looked at from a different point of view; the prominence here given to the High-priesthood of Jesus is foreign to St. Paul's Epistles. It would require a volume duly to examine the various particulars adduced under this head; for the real question is not whether the teaching is *opposed* to St. Paul's, but whether the various themes are treated in the manner characteristic of the Apostle. We do not believe that the most careful examination will detect any real discord between the dogmatic teaching of this Epistle and that of St. Paul; but the peculiarities in selection of topics and in mode of treatment are sufficient (even when all allowance has been made for the special position and aim of the Epistle) to suggest that, if St. Paul "laid the foundation," it is another who "buildeth thereon," "according to the grace of God which is given unto" him (1 Cor. iii. 10). The resemblances in teaching may show the presence of the Apostle, but the new colouring and arrangement prove that he is present only in the person of a disciple on whom his master's mantle has fallen, and who is taught by the same Spirit.

(3) A similar conclusion is suggested by a review of the arguments that are founded on the difference in the use of the Old Testament. It need hardly be said that in the Epistle before us this subject is of the greatest consequence, for "the whole argument of the Epistle depends on the reality of the spiritual meaning of the Old Testament." But the essential principle involved is found as truly in St. Paul (see 1 Cor. x.; 2 Cor. iii.; Gal. iv.; Eph. v. *et al.*). The New Testament is not divided against itself in its recognition of the Old. As has been truly said,* "The authority of Christ Himself encourages us to search for a deep and spiritual meaning under the ordinary words of Scripture, which, however, cannot be gained by any arbitrary allegorising, but only by following out patiently the course of God's dealings with man." But again when we come to details we find marks of divergence from St. Paul. In the Epistle to the Hebrews the word of Scripture is almost always quoted as the direct utterance of God ("He saith," "He hath said"), whereas St. Paul commonly uses the formula "It is written" or "The Scripture saith." The latter mode of introduction, which occurs about thirty times in the Pauline Epistles, is not once used in this; and, on the other hand, such examples as Eph. iv. 8 are very rare in St. Paul. The quotations in this Epistle, again, are commonly taken directly from the LXX., even when it differs from the Hebrew; and for the most part agree with that text which is preserved to us in the Alexandrian manuscript: St. Paul shows more acquaintance with the Hebrew. In each of these arguments (the former especially) there is force. The latter, however, has been pressed unduly; for an examination of the quotations, as they stand in the best text of the Epistle, will show not a few departures from the Greek version, and there are not wanting tokens of the writer's acquaintance either with the Hebrew original or with a more accurate translation of some passages than the LXX. affords.

(4) One distinguishing peculiarity of this Epistle is found in the many remarkable coincidences both of thought and of expression with the writings of Philo of Alexandria. One or two examples are quoted in the notes; but nothing short of a collection of all the points of similarity, as presented in the Greek text, will show this characteristic of the Epistle in its proper light. Both St. Paul and St. John exhibit acquaintance with the Alexandrian philosophy, but it has left comparatively slight traces in their writings. The resemblance in language in many passages of this Epistle is all the more remarkable because of the fundamental differences in doctrine between the Christian teacher and the Alexandrian philosopher. Another point of interest can only be briefly mentioned, —the many words and phrases common to this Epistle and the Book of Wisdom. The reader is referred to the remarkably interesting papers by Professor Plumptre in vol. i. of *The Expositor*, on "The Writings of Apollos."

On a review of the whole case, there is only one conclusion that appears possible—that the Epistle was written by one who had stood in a close relation with St. Paul, but not by St. Paul himself. It will be readily understood that the arguments given above are not adduced as being of equal weight: some are only confirmatory, and might not have very much force if they stood alone; but all point with more or less distinctness to the conclusion which has been stated. Farther than this we cannot go with certainty; and it is perhaps wisest to rest satisfied with this negative result. If we turn to the positive side, we have little to guide our judgment. Three names only seem to be mentioned by early writers—those of Barnabas, Clement of Rome, and St. Luke. The Epistle is quoted by Tertullian, as we have seen, as a work of Barnabas; and two later Latin writers, Philastrius and Jerome, mention the same tradition. In one passage Jerome says that very many (perhaps meaning many of the Greek ecclesiastical writers) assign the Epistle to Barnabas or Clement; in another he mentions Tertullian alone as an authority for this, and seems to attach no special importance to the opinion. It would seem that the tradition was very limited: it is especially noteworthy that the name of Barnabas is not found in the passages quoted from Origen. We know too little of Barnabas to judge for ourselves of the intrinsic probability of the hypothesis: the so-called internal arguments which have been adduced by some are of no worth. The Epistle which bears the name of Barnabas belongs, in all probability, to the beginning of the second century, and has no connection with the companion of St. Paul. That Epistle, therefore (which presents a remarkable contrast to the teaching of the Epistle to the Hebrews; see Westcott *On the Canon*, pp. 43—45) yields no evidence in the present inquiry.

In regard to Clement we can speak with more confidence, as we possess one Epistle which is certainly from his hand. That document contains passages belonging to our Epistle, but they are no doubt quotations from it, and the general style and character of Clement's Letter forbid us to ascribe the two works to the same writer. Much more favour has in recent times been shown to the other tradition which Origen records—that the Epistle was written by St. Luke

* Westcott, *Introduction to the Gospels*, p. 412.

The resemblances of language between this Epistle and St. Luke's writings are numerous and striking; but with all this there is great dissimilarity of style. The difference between a Letter such as this and historical or biographical memoirs must indeed be taken into account; but even when allowance has been made for this, it is difficult to receive the writer of the Acts as the author of our Epistle. Another consideration also is of weight. We can hardly doubt that we have before us here the work of a Jew; but St. Paul's words in Col. iv. 11, 14. imply that St. Luke was of Gentile birth.

The subject is not one for confident assertion; but we strongly doubt whether the Epistle can be ascribed to any of those suggested by ancient writers. One other hypothesis must be mentioned, which has commanded the adhesion of many of the ablest writers of recent times. Luther was the first to express (in his *Commentary on Genesis*) an opinion that the Epistle to the Hebrews was the work of Apollos. Some will maintain that conjecture is inadmissible, but certainly all the conditions of the problem appear to be satisfied by this conjecture. The record of St. Luke in Acts xviii. 24—28, xix. 1, supplemented by St. Paul's references in 1 Corinthians, might seem to have been expressly designed to show the special fitness of Apollos for writing such an Epistle as this. Our limits will not allow us to enter into further detail, but the reader will find all the particulars admirably stated in the Notes on the verses in the Acts. If it be not unbecoming to go beyond the words of Origen on such a subject as this, and to favour an hypothesis for which no express evidence can be adduced from ancient times, we can have no hesitation in joining those who hold that it is the Jew of Alexandria, "mighty in the Scriptures," "fervent in spirit," the honoured associate of St. Paul, who here carries on the work which he began in Achaia, when "he mightily convinced the Jews, showing by the Scriptures that Jesus was Christ."

III. **Readers.**—The inquiry as to the original readers of the Epistle is even more difficult. It may be assumed with confidence that the present title of the Epistle is not that which it originally bore. There has sometimes been a disposition to deny the propriety of the name Epistle; and it has been thought that the peculiarity of the opening verses, containing, as they do, neither address nor author's name, may be most easily explained on the supposition that the work is a homily or general treatise. But a very slight examination will prove that such a theory has no foundation. The closing verses show that a particular community is directly addressed, a community well known to the writer, whose affection the writer knew himself to possess, though some individuals may have distrusted him and misjudged his acts and motives. He complains of their declension in Christian knowledge, and points out its cause (chap. v.); thankfully recognises their generous love to the brethren (chaps. vi., x.); and urges them to be true to their own past history (chap. x.). He cannot but have known that the trials and necessities of many other communities were very similar; but, like St. Paul, he addresses the wider only through the narrower circle. The immediate impulse was given by the news he had received respecting brethren for whom he himself had laboured, and over whose welfare he was bound diligently to watch. The Epistle needed no express inscription to make the first readers understand from whom it came and to whom it was sent; and it is not impossible that (as Ewald suggests) the watchfulness of enemies may have rendered some concealment a matter of prudence. The absence of the writer's name has been considered confirmatory of the belief that Apollos wrote the Epistle. In one church, as we know, rival factions had arisen, some saying, "I am of Paul," others "I am of Apollos;" and the incident recorded in 1 Cor. xvi. 12 seems to point to the regret of Apollos that his name should have been so used. Such a feeling may have continued to operate and have led to this partial withdrawal of himself from view. (See Alford's *Gk. Test.*, vol. iv. pp. 60, 61.)

It is very plain that the Epistle is addressed to Jewish Christians, and its present name was probably given when the Epistle had passed into more general use, in order to make its destination clear. In the New Testament the name Hebrew is strictly opposed to Hellenist or Grecian Jew (Acts vi. 1), and denotes one who adhered to the Hebrew language and usages; there would therefore be some inconsistency between the name and the language of the Epistle, if the title proceeded from the writer himself. Again we are in the main thrown back on internal evidence; but in this case the materials before us are very scanty, when doubtful or irrelevant passages have been set aside. One verse of the Epistle, and one only, contains any note of place: "They of Italy salute you" (chap. xiii. 24). Unfortunately these words admit of two opposite interpretations. Either the author is himself in Italy, and sends to the Hebrew Christians whom he addresses the salutations of an Italian church; or, writing to Italy, he transmits the message which those "of Italy" who are now with him send to their fellow-Christians at home. Between these two interpretations it seems impossible to decide with any confidence; though, in itself, the latter might be the more probable. Perhaps the only other indication that we possess is the manifest destination of the Epistle for a community of Jewish Christians, exposed to peculiar danger from the solicitations and the persecutions of the unbelieving Jews. Such a community would most naturally be found in Palestine, and accordingly the prevalent opinion has been that the Epistle was first sent to Jerusalem, or to some neighbouring town. The words of chap. ii. 3 are perhaps less suitable to Jerusalem—a city in which there would still be living many who had heard the word from the Lord Himself. In chap. vi. 10 the writer speaks of a ministration to the saints which at once recalls the efforts of St. Paul and others to send help to the Christians of Jerusalem, who were oppressed by poverty. This passage *may* imply that the readers of the Epistle had engaged in that particular labour of love, but it cannot be proved that the meaning is not perfectly general. The language of chap. x. 32—34 decides nothing, if the first member of verse 33 be understood figuratively (see Note); verse 34, which has been urged in regard to the question of authorship, loses all such significance when the true reading is restored. From chap. xii. 4 has usually been drawn the inference that no members of the Church had suffered martyrdom: even here, however, it is improbable that any such allusion is intended (see Note). On the whole, it is difficult to resist the impression that the writer addresses some Church in Palestine, though Jerusalem itself may be excluded by chap. ii. 3. The readers seem to have lived under the shadow of Jewish power and influence, where opposition to Christianity was most bitter, the temptation to unfaithfulness greatest, the abjuration required of the apostate most complete. The exhortation of chap. xiii. 13, the warning of chap. x. 25, the remarkable appropriation of Old Testament promises and threatenings which we find in chap. x. 27, 28, 30, would fall with wonderful force on the ears of men in whose very presence the spirit of Judaism was exerting all its power. That there are still difficulties must be felt by all. We should not have expected that a Letter addressed to such a Church would be written in Greek, or that the writer's appeal would be to the Greek translation of the Old Testament; but the phenomena which other books of the New Testament display forbid us to regard these difficulties as decisive. It is not possible here to enumerate the other opinions which have been maintained. The reader will find an able argument in favour of Rome in Alford's *Prolegomena* to *Gk. Test.*, vol. iv.: others have argued the claims of Alexandria.*

IV. **Date.**— There is very little to guide us as to the time when the Epistle was written. The present tenses of chap. ix. 2—9 are often understood as implying that the Temple service still continued; but there is strong reason for explaining the verses otherwise (see Notes). On the other hand, the general complexion of the Epistle is such as to convince us that it was written before the destruction of Jerusalem. Of the imprisonment of Timothy (chap. xiii. 23) we know nothing from any other source. It has often been supposed that he shared St. Paul's imprisonment in Rome (see the *Introduction to* 2 *Timothy*). The date of the martyrdom of St. Paul is, however, uncertain; and it does not seem possible to say more than that our Epistle was probably written some three or four years before Jerusalem fell—in other words, about A.D. 66.

V. **Object and Contents.**—The discussion of the very important external questions which connect themselves with this Epistle has left us but little space for a notice of its internal character. In the Notes, however, on account of the peculiar difficulties which this Epistle presents, we have sacrificed all other considerations to the desire of exhibiting, as exactly as possible, the connection and course of thought. It is, therefore, less necessary to attempt a complete analysis here. The Christians addressed were in imminent danger of apostasy. The danger was occasioned partly by seductions from without, partly by weakness within. Even when the fabric of Jewish power was falling, the influence of its past history, its glorious treasure of promise, its unique associations, retained a wonderful power. As we look back on the years preceding the fall of Jerusalem the case of the people may seem to us hopeless; but the confidence of the nation was unbroken, and even at that period we note outbursts of national pride and enthusiastic hope. Bitter hate and contempt for Christianity on the one hand, and the attraction of their ancestral worship and ritual on the other, had apparently won a victory over the constancy of some Christians belonging to this Hebrew community. Where open opposition had not prevailed, the tone of Christian faith had been lowered. The special temptation of these Christians seems to have been towards a loss of interest in the higher Christian truths, and a union of elementary Christian teaching with that to which they had been accustomed as Jews. The arguments of the first and other chapters show that they held the foundation truths; the expostulation of the fifth and sixth chapters proves that the full significance of the doctrine they held was not understood, and that the doctrine was near to losing its power. In no Epistle, perhaps, do we find a more carefully sustained argument; of none can be said as truly that the whole Epistle is a "word of exhortation."

The design of the writer is to show the superiority of Christianity to Judaism. He in whom God has in these last days revealed Himself to man is His Son, to whom the Scriptures themselves bear witness as exalted above the highest of created beings, the angels, who are but ministers of God (chap. i.). The law was given through angels: salvation has now come through the Son, who, though Lord of the world to come, the Heir and Fulfiller of God's highest promises to man, submitted to suffering and death—not of necessity, but that He might by His atonement deliver man from sin and death, and might become a true High Priest for man (chap. ii.). As the faithful Apostle and High Priest He is exalted above God's most favoured servants upon earth, even above Moses (chap. iii. 1—6).

This is the first division of the argument, designed to establish the supremacy of the revelation given through the Son of God, and to remove "the offence of the cross." Next follows a powerful section of exhortation and warning. Do not imitate the unfaithfulness through which Israel failed to enter into the true rest of God (chaps. iii. 7—iv. 16).

The second portion of the Epistle (extending to chap. x. 18) is occupied with the Priesthood of Christ. Once only is the current of the argument interrupted. After the first introduction of a prophecy which will form the theme of later chapters, the writer pauses to bring into relief the carelessness which his readers have shown, and the peril they have incurred; the result is to give most powerful effect to the argument for which he is preparing them (chap. v. 11—vi. 20). Jesus made perfect through suffering (chap. v. 1—10) has been declared by God High Priest after the order of Melchizedek; by this declaration the Aaronic priesthood is abolished, giving place to a priesthood which abides continually, through which all that the former priesthood sought in vain to attain is made sure to man for ever (chap. vii.). This High Priest, seated at God's right hand, is Minister in the heavenly sanctuary, Mediator of the New Covenant (chap. viii.); and in Him all the types of the first covenant are fulfilled, for by His one offering of Himself He has put away sin, and established the new covenant in which sin is pardoned and man sanctified (chaps. ix., x. 1—18).

The remainder of the Epistle is in the main directly hortatory. These being our privileges, let us not by unfaithfulness fall short of them, for terrible is the doom of the unfaithful, and glorious the reward of Faith (chap. x. 19—39), which from the beginning has led God's servants on to victory, and of which Jesus is the Author and the Perfecter (chaps. xi.—xii. 4). Chapters xii. and xiii. continue the exhortations of the earlier chapters, but in a higher strain.

We cannot conceive of any argument by which the end contemplated could be more effectually accomplished, and men more powerfully turned from "the offence of the cross" to glorying in Christ Jesus. The value which the Epistle has for us and the extent of its influence on our theology it would be hard to overestimate. Its peculiar importance lies in the exposition which it gives of the earlier revelation, showing the meaning of the types and arrangements of the former dispensation, and their perfect fulfilment in our Lord, and in its witness to the power and abiding significance of the divine word.

* Prof. Plumptre's hypothesis that those addressed are Christian ascetics of (or connected with) Alexandria is worked out by him in a very interesting manner (see *Expos.* i. 428—432), but does not appear to suit the facts of the Epistle as well as the view defended above.

THE EPISTLE OF PAUL THE APOSTLE TO THE

HEBREWS

Chap. i. 1—14. He in whom God has now spoken to man is Son of God, exalted above all angels.

CHAPTER I.—

A.D. 64.

(1) God, who at sundry times and in divers manners spake in time past unto the fathers by the prophets, (2) hath in these last days spoken unto us by *his* Son, whom he hath appointed heir of all things, by

---

(1–14) He in whom God has at last revealed Himself to man is Son of God, exalted above all angels.

(1) **God, who at sundry times . . . .**—The fine arrangement of the words in the Authorised version fails, it must be confessed, to convey the emphasis which is designed in the original. The writer's object is to place the former revelation over against that which has now been given; and the remarkable words with which the chapter opens (and which might not inaptly serve as the motto of the whole Epistle) strike the first note of contrast. If we may imitate the artistic arrangement of the Greek, the verse will run thus, "In many portions and in many ways God having of old spoken unto the fathers in the prophets." To the fathers of the Jewish people (comp. Rom. ix. 5) God's word was given part by part, and in divers manners. It came in the revelations of the patriarchal age, in the successive portions of Holy Writ: various truths were successively unveiled through the varying ministry of law, and of prophecy, and of promise ever growing clearer through the teaching of experience and history. At one time the word came in direct precept, at another in typical ordinance or act, at another in parable or psalm. The word thus dealt out in fragments and variously imparted was God's word, for the revealing Spirit of God was "in the prophets" (2 Cor. xiii. 3). We must not unduly limit the application of "prophet"; besides those to whom the name is directly given, there were many who were representatives of God to His people, and interpreters of His will. (Comp. Num. xi. 26, 29; Ps. cv. 15.)

(2) **Hath in these last days . . .**—Better, *at the end of these days spake unto us in a Son.* The thought common to the two verses is "God hath spoken to man"; in all other respects the past and the present stand contrasted. The manifold successive partial disclosures of God's will have given place to one revelation, complete and final; for He who spake in the prophets hath now spoken "in a Son." The whole stress lies on these last words. The rendering "a Son" may at first cause surprise, but it is absolutely needed; not, "*Who* is the Revealer?" but, "*What* is He?" is the question answered in these words. The writer does not speak of *a Son* in the sense of one out of many; the very contrast with the prophets (who in the lower sense were amongst God's sons) would be sufficient to prove this, but the words which follow, and the whole contents of this chapter are designed to show the supreme dignity of Him who is God's latest Representative on earth. The prophet's commission extended no farther than the special message of his words and life; "a Son" spoke with His Father's authority, with complete knowledge of His will and purpose. It is impossible to read these first lines (in which the whole argument of the Epistle is enfolded) without recalling the prologue of the fourth Gospel. The name "Word" is not mentioned here, and the highest level of St. John's teaching is not reached; but the idea which "the Word" expresses, and the thought of the Only Begotten as declaring and interpreting the Father (John i. 18; also John xiv. 10, 24) are present throughout. There is something unusual in the words, "at the end of these days." St. Peter speaks of the manifestation of Christ "at the end of the times" (1 Pet. i. 20); and both in the Old Testament and in the New we not unfrequently read "at the end (or, *in the last*) of the days." (See 2 Pet. iii. 3; Jude, verse 18; Num. xxiv. 14; Dan. x. 14, &c.) The peculiarity of the expression here lies in "*these* days." The ages preceding and following the appearance of Messiah are in Jewish writers known as "this world" (or, *age*) and the "coming world" (or, *age*); the "days of Messiah" seem to have been classed sometimes with the former, sometimes with the latter period; but "the end of these days" would be understood by every Jewish reader to denote the time of His appearing.

Whom he hath appointed.—Better, *whom He appointed:* in the divine counsels He was constituted "Heir of all things." The clauses which follow describe the successive steps in the accomplishment of this purpose. The words have often been understood as referring to the Son's essential Lordship: as Eternal Son He is and must be Heir of all. But this explanation is less consistent with the word "appointed," with the strict significance of "Heir," and with the development of the thought in the following verses; and it is on all grounds more probable that in these words is expressed the great theme of the Epistle, the consummation of all things in the Christ.

By whom.—Rather, *through whom.* So in John i. 3 we read that all things came into being through the Word; and in Col. i. 16, "All things have been created through Him." In this manner Philo repeatedly describes the creative work of the *Logos.* Here, however, "this mediatorial function has entirely changed its character. To the Alexandrian Jew it was the work of a passive tool or instrument; but to the Christian Apostle it represented a co-operating agent" (Lightfoot on Col. i. 16).

whom also he made the worlds; (3) who being the brightness[a] of *his* glory, and the express image of his person, and upholding all things by the word of his power, when he had by himself purged our sins, sat down on the right hand of the Majesty on high; (4) being made so much better than the angels, as he hath by inheritance obtained a more excellent name than they. (5) For unto which of the angels said he at any time, Thou art my Son, this day have I begotten

a Wis. 7. 26.

The worlds.—A word of very common occurrence in the New Testament as a designation of *time* occurs in two passages of this Epistle (here and in chap. xi. 3) where the context shows more than "age" to be intended. Under time is included the work that is done in time, so that "the ages" here must be (to quote Delitzsch's words) "the immeasurable content of immeasurable time." "Also" may seem an unnecessary addition, but (almost in the sense *accordingly*) it points to creation as the first step towards the fulfilment of the design expressed in the preceding clause.

(3) **Who being the brightness . . .**—*Who being the effulgence of His glory and the exact image of His substance.* The first figure is familiar to us in the words of the Nicene Creed (themselves derived from this verse and a commentary upon it), "God of God, *Light of Light*, Very God of Very God." Again striking parallels to the language present themselves in Philo, who speaks of the spirit breathed into man at his creation as an "effulgence of the Blessed and Thrice-blessed Nature"; and in the well-known passage of the Book of Wisdom, "She (Wisdom) is the effulgence of the everlasting light, the unspotted mirror of the power of God, and the image of His goodness" (Wisd. vii. 26). In the Old Testament the token of the divine presence is the Shechinah, the "cloud of glory" (called "the glory" in Rom. ix. 4; comp. chap. ix. 5 in this Epistle); here it is the divine nature itself that is denoted by the "glory." Of the relation between this word and that which follows ("substance") it is difficult to speak, as the conceptions necessarily transcend human language; but we may perhaps say (remembering that all such terms are but figurative) that the latter word is internal and the former external,—the latter the essence in itself, the former its manifestation. Thus the "Son" in His relation to "God" is represented here by light beaming forth from light, and by exact impress—the perfect image produced by stamp or seal. These designations, relating to the essential nature of the Son, have no limitation to time; the participle "being" must be understood (comp. Phil. ii. 6; John i. 1) of eternal, continuous existence. The word "person" is an unfortunate mistranslation in this place. Most of the earlier English versions have "substance," *person* being first introduced in the Genevan Testament in deference to Beza.

By the word.—The thought seems suggested by Gen. i. (Ps. xxxiii. 9); the spoken word was the expression of His power. What is said above of "being" applies to "upholding," except that the latter implies a previous creative act.

When he had by himself purged our sins.—The older MSS. omit "by Himself" and "our," so that the words must be rendered, *when He had made purification of sins.* At first the change may seem a loss; but it is easily seen that the simpler statement is more majestic, and also more suitable in this place; the more complete explanation of the truth belongs to a later stage (chap. ix.). To "make purification of sins" is an unusual phrase (comp. Matt. viii. 3, "his leprosy was cleansed"), meaning, to make purification by the removal of sins (John i. 29; 1 John iii. 5; 2 Pet. i. 9).

Sat down on the right hand of the Majesty on high.—See chap. viii. 1; xii. 2; Matt. xxvi. 64; Mark xiv. 62; also verse 13, and chap. x. 12. This figure, which we meet with more than twenty times in the New Testament, is throughout derived from the first words of Ps. cx., which are descriptive of the exaltation of the Messiah. Jehovah's investiture of the Son of Man with unlimited dominion (Dan. vii. 14) and supreme dignity (Eph. i. 20, 21); the Saviour's rest after the accomplishment of His work on earth (chap. viii. 1); His waiting for the complete and final subjection of His enemies, are the ideas signified. On the Psalm see below (verse 13).

(4) **Being made.**—Better, *having become.* These words must be closely joined with the last clause of verse 3; they speak, not of the glory which was ever His, but of that which *became* His after He had "made purification of sins."

Better.—That is, *greater.* We may discern a twofold reason for the comparison; having become "greater than the angels," our Lord is exalted above the highest of created beings (see Eph. i. 21; Phil. ii. 9), and above those through whom God had in former time declared His law (chap. ii. 2).

Name.—The verses which follow show that we are to understand by this all the dignity and glory contained in the name SON OF GOD. Not that this name first belonged to Him as *exalted Mediator*; but the glory which "became" His (verses 3, 4) is proportionate to and consonant with the name which is His by essential right (verse 2).

That this name and dignity belong to Jesus Christ (as yet unnamed, but confessedly the subject of the preceding verses) is now to be established by the testimony of Scripture. Two important questions have been asked:—(1) Does the writer adduce these quotations as strictly demonstrative? (2) If so, on what assumption does their relevancy rest? It is evident that the whole argument is addressed to men who believed that the Christ had appeared in the person of Jesus. Of the passages here cited some were already, by universal consent, applied to the Messiah. As to the others, it was sufficient if the trained and thoughtful reader could recognise the accuracy of such an application when once suggested. That in no case is there mere "accommodation" or illustration will, it is hoped, be made clear. On the other hand, the writer's object is less to convince his readers of some *new* truth than to draw attention to what the well-known passages really contain and express.

(5) **For unto which of the angels . . . .**—"God has spoken of the Messiah as His Son, a title which no angel ever receives from Him." That the appellation "sons of God" may be used in an inferior sense, and that thus angels may be so designated (Job i. 6; xxxviii. 7), does not affect this argument; for every reader must perceive that in these quotations "Son" is used of One, and in a sense that is unique

thee? And again, I will be to him a
Father, and he shall be to me a Son?
(6) And again, when he bringeth in the
firstbegotten into the world, he saith,
And let all the angels of God worship
him. (7) And of the angels he saith,

The two quotations are taken from Ps. ii. 7 and 2 Sam. vii. 14. It seems probable that the second Psalm was written by David during the troublous times of 2 Sam. viii.—x., in the fresh recollection of the promises of which we read in 2 Sam. vii. In the midst of the rebellious conspiracies of kings and nations is heard Jehovah's word, "Yet have I set my King upon my holy hill of Zion" (Ps. ii. 6). In verse 7 the Anointed King declares the divine decree, "The Lord hath said unto me, Thou art my Son; this day have I begotten Thee;" and the following verses describe the kingly dominion of the Son. The clearest comments on verse 7 are supplied by 2 Sam. vii. 12—14, and especially by Ps. lxxxix. Verse 27 of the last-named Psalm, "I will make him my firstborn, higher than the kings of the earth," shows plainly that in their first meaning—that which relates to the royal rule of David or David's son—the words "I have this day begotten thee" signify "I have this day established thee as my chosen king, and thus constituted thee my son;" for to the first-born belongs natural, though derived, rule over the kingdom of his father. At what period the people in general, guided by prophetic teaching and the discipline of history (see below), learnt in how secondary a sense such words could be used of any human king, we do not know; but we have clear evidence, both from the New Testament (chap. v. 5; Acts iv. 25—27; xiii. 33; Rev. ii. 27) and from Jewish tradition, that the second Psalm was understood to be a distinct prophecy of the Messiah; indeed, this very name "Messiah" and the appellation "Son of God" (see John i. 34, 49) may be traced to this Psalm. The declarations of verses 6, 7, are typical of the enthronement of the Messiah. St. Paul (Acts xiii. 33) refers the words here quoted to the period of the Resurrection. With this the language used above (verse 4) perfectly agrees. As, however, in that verse the exaltation of the Christ is declared to correspond to that *essential* dignity which lay in the name Son, a name which in this very context bears its highest sense (verses 1—3), we are constrained to regard the "day" of the Resurrection as itself typical, and to believe that "this day" also pointed to the "eternal Now"—to what Origen (on John i. 1) speaks of as "the day which is co-extensive with the unbegotten and everlasting life of God."

The second passage, which seems to have been the basis of the words we have just considered, occurs in the course of the divine promise that David's seed shall be established in his kingdom, and that David's throne shall be established for ever: the seed of David shall be received as God's Son. With the words here quoted are closely joined others which plainly prove that verse 14 is not a simple and direct prophecy of Christ, but in the first instance belonged to an earthly ruler. Through the teaching of successive disappointments, each "son of David" failing to realise the hopes excited by the promise, the nation was led to look to the future King, and at once to remove from the prophecy the purely earthly limitations and to discern a higher meaning in the promise of divine sonship.

(6) **And again.**—There seems little doubt that the true translation is, *And when He again leadeth* (literally, *shall have led*) *the Firstborn into the world He saith.* The position of "again" (in the Greek) shows that it does not indicate a new step in the argument, but must be joined with "leadeth." The speaker ("He saith") is God, speaking in the word of Scripture; in this Epistle quotations from the Old Testament are usually thus introduced. The quotation involves some difficulty. It cannot be *directly* taken from Ps. xcvii. 7, "worship Him, all His angels;" for the citations from the Greek Bible in this Epistle are usually so exact that we cannot believe the writer would have so altered the form of the sentence now before us. In Deut. xxxii. 43, however, we find words identical with those of the text in most copies of the LXX.; but there is nothing answering to them in the Hebrew, and there is no sufficient reason for supposing that the clause has dropped out of the Hebrew text. There are similarities (both of subject and of diction) between the Psalm and the last section of the Song of Moses, which make it easy to see how the words could find their way into the Song. The Psalm belongs to a cycle (Pss. xciii., xcv.—xcix.) whose theme is the triumphant announcement of the coming of God's kingdom, by which was denoted (as the readers of the Epistle knew) the kingdom of Christ. In the divine plan the predicted Theophany was coincident with the fulfilment of the Messianic hope. In both Psalm and Song we read of the judgment exercised and the vengeance inflicted by the enthroned King. (Comp. Ps. ii. 9.) This agreement in tone and subject renders less important the question whether the Hebrew original of the Song really contained the words. The thought was familiar from Scripture, and in this very connection. When the Messiah, reigning as the Firstborn of God (see verse 5), shall appear for judgment—that is, when God leadeth a second time His Firstborn into "the world of men" (see chap. ii. 5), that He may receive full possession of His inheritance—He saith, And let all angels of God worship Him. The word here rendered "leadeth in" is in frequent use for the introduction of Israel (typically God's "firstborn," Ex. iv. 22) into the land of Canaan. It should, perhaps, be noted that, though in Ps. xcvii. 7 "angels" may not be perfectly exact as a rendering of the Hebrew *Elohim*, the verse so distinctly expresses the homage done to the King by superhuman powers, that its fitness for the argument here is obvious.

(7) **Spirits.**—Better, *winds.* It is very difficult to assign any clear meaning to the ordinary rendering,—unless, indeed, we were to adopt the very strange opinion of many of the earlier commentators, that the stress is laid on "maketh" in the sense of "createth." The parallelism in these two lines of Hebrew poetry is complete, "angels" answering to "ministers," "winds" to "a flame of fire." The meaning appears to be that God, employing His messengers for His varied purposes, sends them forth in what manner He may please, clothing them with the appearance of the resistless wind or the devouring fire. (We may contrast 1 Kings xix. 11, 12.) The force of the passage lies in the vividness with which it presents the thought of the Most High served by angels who "at His bidding speed," untiring as the wind, subtle as the fire. We feel much more distinctly than we can put into words the infinite contrast between such ministers and the Son seated at the right hand of God. The quotation is taken from Ps. civ. 4, without any variation in the Greek. Whether this translation faithfully represents

Who maketh his angels spirits, and his
ministers a flame of fire. (8) But unto
the Son *he saith*, Thy throne, O God,
is for ever and ever: a sceptre of
righteousness [1] *is* the sceptre of thy
kingdom. (9) Thou hast loved righteous-
ness, and hated iniquity; therefore God,
even thy God, hath anointed thee with
the oil of gladness above thy fellows.
(10) And, Thou, Lord, in the beginning
hast laid the foundation of the earth;[a]
and the heavens are the works of thine

1 Gr. *rightness*, or, *straightness*.
a Ps. 102. 25.

---

the original is a question that has been warmly discussed. Not that there is any doubt that such a rendering of the Hebrew is in itself natural; but it is often alleged that the context requires an inversion of the words, *Who maketh winds His messengers, flaming fire His ministers.* The point cannot be examined here; we will only express a decided opinion that the translation defended above not only expresses the meaning of the Hebrew, but perfectly accords with the context of the Psalm.

(8) **Unto.**—Rather, *of.* The connection with verse 7 is so close ("Whereas of the angels He saith . . . of the Son He saith"), that we must not vary the rendering of the preposition. The passage which follows is taken from Ps. xlv. 6, 7. As the words stand in the ordinary Greek text, they agree exactly with the LXX.; but certain alterations of reading are required by the best evidence. After the words "for ever and ever" *and* must be restored, and in the following clause *the* and *a* must change places. The latter change is of moment only as it affects the former. Were the words in all other respects cited with perfect exactness, the introduction of *and* would probably indicate that the writer intended to split up the quotation into two parts, each significant for his purpose. (Comp. chap. ii. 13.) As, however, we note other minor changes, the insertion of the connecting word is probably accidental. A third reading is of much greater importance. At the close of the verse the two oldest of our Greek MSS. agree in reading "His kingdom:" to this we will return afterwards.

We have every reason to believe that the application of Ps. xlv. which is here made was fully received by the ancient Jews; thus in the Targum on the Psalm verse 7 is taken as a direct address to the King Messiah. Hence the readers of this Epistle would at once recognise the argument which the words contain. It is strongly maintained by some that the Psalm (like Ps. cx., see below, on verse 13) is altogether prophetic, the promised Messiah *alone* being in the Psalmist's thought. There appear to be insuperable objections to this view, from particular expressions used (in the later verses especially), and from the general structure and colouring of the Psalm. It is in every way more probable that the second Psalm (see Note on verse 5), rather than Ps. cx., represents the class to which Ps. xlv. belongs. Originally writing in celebration of the marriage of a king of David's line (we know not whom, but many of the arguments urged against the possible reference to Solomon have no great weight), the inspired Psalmist uses words which bear their full meaning only when applied to that Son of David of whose kingdom there shall be no end. The promises made to David (2 Sam. vii.) are before the writer's mind in the first verses of the Psalm. The king appointed by God is His representative to God's people; his cause is that of truth and righteousness; his dominion will continually advance. It is at this moment that, with the promise of a divine sonship (Ps. ii.) in his thought, he suddenly addresses the king as Elohim (verse 7), a divine king who receives from God the reward of righteousness (verse 8). There are in the Old Testament examples of the use of Elohim which diminish the difficulty of its application to an earthly king (such as Ps. lxxxii. 1; xcv. 3; 1 Sam. xxviii. 13; Ex. vii. 1); but it must still be acknowledged that the passage stands alone. This difficulty, however, relates only to the primary application. As the higher and true reference of the words became revealed, all earthly limitations disappeared; the Christian readers of the Psalm recognised in the Messiah of whom it speaks a King who is God.

The reading "His kingdom" has seemed to require a different rendering of the words in the first part of the verse: *God is Thy throne for ever and ever.* This rendering, however, will suit either reading of the Greek, and is equally admissible as a rendering of the Hebrew. Nor is it really inconsistent with the position in which the verse here stands: in contrast with the ministry of angels is set, on this view, not indeed a direct address to the Son as God, but the sovereign rule which the Son receives from God. The objections raised against it are: (1) such an expression as "God is Thy throne" is contrary to the analogy of Scripture language; (2) the ordinary rendering has the support of almost all ancient authority, Jewish writers and ancient versions being apparently united in its favour. The former argument is not very strong in face of Ps. xc. 1, and similar passages; but the latter is so weighty that we hesitate to accept the change, helpful as it would be in making clear the original and typical reference of verse 7. It should be said that the reading "His kingdom" is not inconsistent with the ordinary translation of the preceding words; for a sudden transition from "*Thy* throne, O God" to "*His* kingdom" is in full accordance with the usage of Hebrew poetry. (See Pss. xliii. 4; lxvii. 5, 6; civ. 4—6, *et al.*) There are other renderings which would require discussion if we were concerned with the Hebrew text of the Psalm: the two given above are the only possible translations of the Greek.

A sceptre . . .—Rather, *the sceptre of uprightness is a sceptre of Thy* (or, *His*) *kingdom.* Righteousness itself (so to speak, the very ideal of righteous government) bears sway in Thy kingdom.

(9) The King by divine election has been exalted by divine reward. (Comp. chap. ii. 9, and Phil. ii. 9, 10.)

Therefore God.—It is possible, but not probable, that the words, both here and in the Psalm, should be rendered, *Therefore, O God, Thy God hath anointed Thee.*

Thy fellows.—In the first application, probably, these words point to other earthly kings. (Comp. Ps. lxxxix. 27.) Hence Eph. i. 21 will be the best commentary upon them in their higher meaning.

(10) **And.**—Verses 10—12 are by this word linked with verse 8, as presenting the second part of the contrast between angels and the Son. As there we read of a divine sovereignty, so here of the work of creation, the power to change all created things, the divine attribute of changeless existence. This quotation from Ps. cii. 25—27 agrees almost exactly with the text of the LXX. as we have it in the Alexandrian MS., except

hands: (11) they shall perish;[a] but thou
remainest; and they all shall wax old
as doth a garment; (12) and as a vesture
shalt thou fold them up, and they shall
be changed: but thou art the same,
and thy years shall not fail. (13) But
to which of the angels said he at any
time, Sit on my right hand, until I
make thine enemies thy footstool?[b]
(14) Are they not all ministering spirits,
sent forth to minister for them who
shall be heirs of salvation?

a Isa. 34. 4.

A.D. 64.

b Ps. 110. 1; Matt. 22. 44.

1 Gr. *run out as leaking vessels.*

CHAPTER II.—(1) Therefore we
ought to give the more
earnest heed to the things
which we have heard, lest
at any time we should let
them slip.[1] (2) For if the word spoken by
angels was stedfast, and every transgres-

Chap. ii. 1—4. Peril of disobedience to His word.

---

that the words "as a garment" (not found in the Psalm) must here (verse 12) be added, according to our best authorities. The only point of any difficulty in these verses is that the writer discovers a testimony to the supremacy of the Son in words which, as they stand in the Psalm, would appear to be directly addressed to God as Creator. If, however, the Psalm be examined, it will be found (see verses 13—16) to contain the expression of hopes which in reality were inseparably united with the fulfilment of the Messianic promise. "The Lord shall appear to build up Zion:" this is the Psalmist's theme, and it is to the same Lord that he addresses the words which are quoted here. As in Jesus the Christian Jew saw Him who fulfilled all these promises of God to His people, the application of the words of adoration to the same Lord would at once be recognised as true.

(11) **And they all . . .**—Both the earth and the heavens: see Isa. xxxiv. 4, "The heavens shall be rolled together as a scroll;" and Isa. li. 6, "The earth shall wax old like a garment."

(12) **And as a vesture . . .**—Rather (see verse 10), *And as a mantle shalt Thou roll them up; as a garment shall they also be changed.* The course of thought is easily traced: as the garment which has grown old is rolled up and changed, so the former heavens and earth shall give place to the new heavens and the new earth.

(13) **But to which of the angels.**—The final appeal is made to that Psalm which more frequently than any other is quoted in reference to Christ, and which we have already seen to be the source of all the New Testament references to the Saviour's session at the right hand of God. It is not necessary to say much here respecting Ps. cx., to which so many allusions will be made in the course of this Epistle. That it was regularly understood by the Jews of our Lord's time to be a Messianic Psalm is clear both from Matt. xxii. 43, 44, and from the independent notices which we possess. Most probably, it stands alone amongst the Psalms as being simply prophetic: the words of verse 1 have never been addressed either to angels or to an earthly king. On the special words of the quotation see verse 3.

Said he at any time.—Better, *hath He ever said.*

Until I make . . .—Literally, *until I shall have made Thine enemies a footstool of Thy feet.*

(14) **Are they not all ministering spirits?**—In this verse and the preceding is repeated the contrast of verses 7—9, in reversed order. The words "ministering spirits" at once recall the "ministers" and "winds" (expressed in Greek and Hebrew by the same word as "spirits") spoken of in verse 7. In the LXX. this word "minister" is usually applied to those who stood before God in His earthly sanctuary: so here it is fitly used of the nobler offices of the unseen world. To the English reader it may seem that those who in verse 7 are *God's ministers* are here represented as servants of *man.* It is not really so, for the words properly mean, . . . *sent forth* (that is, *continually* sent forth) *to do service* (to God), *for the sake of them who are to inherit salvation.* "Inherit" is a prelude of chap. ii. 10. The last word, "salvation," expresses the divine purpose indicated by all the prophecies that have passed under review. The chapter has been occupied with promises of the Christ: the last word brings before us Jesus, the Saviour.

II.

(1—4) These verses must be closely joined with the first chapter. Before advancing to the next step in his argument, the writer pauses to enforce the duty which results from what has been already established. But (as in chap. iv. 14—16) the exhortation does not interrupt the thought, but rather serves as a connecting link. (See Note on verse 5.)

(1) **Therefore we ought to give the more earnest heed to the things which we have heard.**—Better, *to the things heard;* for this expression contains the complement of the thought of chap. i. 1. Both "speak" and "hear" are words which carry weighty emphasis in this Epistle. (See chap. i. 1; ii. 2; xii. 25; iii. 5, 7; iv. 2, *et al.*) Because of the supreme dignity of Him in whom at the last God speaks, men are bound to give the more earnest heed to the words spoken, whether heard by them from the Lord Himself or (as in this case, verse 3) from His servants.

Lest at any time we should let them slip.—This translation (first introduced by the Genevan Bible of 1560) substantially gives the sense, but inverts the figure presented in the Greek. The words must be rendered, *lest possibly we drift away* (Wiclif, "lest peraventure we fleten awey"). It is the man that is in danger of being carried along by the current: unless the mind be held closely to the words that God has spoken, it must drift away from them, and from the salvation which they promise. There seems no foundation for the rendering of the margin, first given in the Genevan Testament of 1557.

(2) **The word spoken by angels.**—Or rather, *through angels* (comp. chap. i. 2): the word was God's, but angels were the medium through which it was given to men. In accordance with the tone of the whole passage (in which the thought is not the reward of obedience, but the peril of neglect of duty), "the word" must denote divine *commands* delivered by angels, and—as the close parallel presented by chap. x. 28, 29, seems to prove—especially the commands of the Mosaic law. Hence this verse must be joined to the other passages (Acts vii. 53; Gal. iii. 19; comp. also Acts vii. 38) which bring into relief the ministration of angels in the giving of the Law; and the nature of the

sion and disobedience received a just recompence of reward; (3) how shall we escape, if we neglect so great salvation; which at the first began to be spoken by the Lord, and was confirmed unto us by them that heard *him;* (4) God also bearing *them* witness, both with signs and wonders, and with divers miracles, and gifts [1] of the Holy Ghost, according to his own will?

(5) For unto the angels hath he not put in subjection the world to come,

1 Or, *distributions.*

---

argument of this Epistle gives special importance to the subject here. The only passage in the Pentateuch which can be quoted in illustration is Deut. xxxiii. 2: "The Lord came from Sinai . . . . He came from amid myriads of holy ones." The Greek version (introducing a double rendering of the Hebrew) adds, "at His right hand were angels with Him;" and two of the Targums likewise speak of the "myriads of holy angels." Ps. lxviii. 17 is difficult and obscure, but very possibly agrees with the passage just quoted in referring to angels as the attendants of Jehovah on the mount. Nowhere in the Old Testament is the thought carried beyond this point; but there are a few passages in Jewish writers which clearly show that such a ministration of angels as is here spoken of was a tenet of Jewish belief in the apostolic age. Philo, after saying that the angels have their name from reporting the commands of the Father to His children, and the wants of the children to the Father, adds: "We are unable to contain His exceeding and unalloyed benefits, if He Himself proffers them to us without employing others as His ministers." Much more important are the words of Josephus (*Ant.* xv. 5, § 3), who introduces Herod as reminding the Jews that the noblest of the ordinances and the holiest of the things contained in the laws had been learnt by them from God through angels. Jewish writers quoted by Wetstein speak of the "angels of service" whom Moses had known from the time of the giving of the law; and, moreover, of the angel who, when Moses had through terror forgotten all that he had been taught during the forty days, delivered the law to him again. Such speculations are of interest as showing the place which this tenet held in Jewish doctrine and belief. Here and in Gal. iii. 19 (see Note there) this mediation of angels is adduced as a mark of the inferiority of the law; in Acts vii. 53, where no such comparison is made, the contrast implied is between angels and men as givers of a law.

Was stedfast.—Rather, *proved steadfast* or *sure;* evidence of this was given by the punishment which overtook the transgressor, whether inflicted by the direct visitation of God or by human hands faithfully executing the divine will. Of the two words well rendered *transgression* and *disobedience,* the one points especially to the infraction of a positive precept, the other is more general: the former relates more commonly to "thou shalt not;" the latter rather to "thou shalt." The two words are here united, that every violation of the command may be included. The use of reward in a neutral or unfavourable sense (2 Pet. ii. 13; Ps. xciv. 2, *et al.*) is not uncommon in our older writers. (Comp. "the reward of a villain," in Shakespeare.)

(3) **How shall we escape?**—In a different context these words might naturally mean, "How shall we, transgressors of the law, escape from the penalty it threatens, if we neglect the one means of deliverance now offered us?" (Comp. Gal. iii. 13; iv. 5.) Here, however, are placed in contrast the command and threatening which came through angels and the salvation "spoken through the Lord"; while the one "word" is thus wholly unlike the other in substance and in form of proclamation, each is a *law,* in that neglect is visited with penalty. On the intrinsic greatness of the salvation the writer does not dwell; it is implied in the unique dignity and commission of Him through whom it was given.

Which at the first began to be spoken.—Better, *which having at the first been spoken through the Lord, was made sure unto us by them that heard.* "Through the Lord" (comp. chap. i. 2) was spoken this word of God which brought salvation. In two other passages Jesus receives the name "our Lord" (chap. vii. 14; xiii. 20), but nowhere else in this Epistle (unless perhaps in chap. xii. 14) is He spoken of as "the Lord"; the dignity of the title here heightens the contrast. "By them that heard" the word from Him, the writer says, it "was made sure" (not *confirmed,* as if *stronger* attestation were the meaning intended) "unto us." It is evident that the writer here classes himself with those who had not immediately heard the word from Jesus. Such language as this stands in striking contrast with St. Paul's claim, repeatedly maintained, to have received his doctrine directly from the Lord Himself (Gal. i. 12; 1 Cor. ix. 1, *et al.*).

(4) **God also bearing them witness.**—That is, *bearing witness with them to* the truth they preached. Mark xvi. 20 is a striking parallel; see also Acts iv. 30. The divine attestation was given by miracles and by "gifts" (literally, *distributions,* as in the margin; see 1 Cor. xii. 11) "of the Holy Ghost." We have here, as in Acts ii. 22 and 2 Cor. xii. 12 (see the Notes), the full threefold description of miracles, as "signs" and "wonders" and "powers"; as wonderful works that are wrought by divine power, and are thus signs of the divine presence and symbols of a corresponding spiritual work. The words here used are illustrated especially by 2 Cor. xii. 12, in its reference to miracles as attesting the apostolic preaching. But yet "greater works" (John xiv. 12) were wrought by the messengers of Christ, in that through them were bestowed the gifts of the Spirit. The last words, "according to His will," bring us back to the first words of the section (chap. i. 1); as it is God who speaks to men in His Son, it is He who works with those who proclaim the word that they have heard, attesting their message by gifts according to His will.

(5–18) It was needful that Jesus, as Author of salvation to man, should in all points be made like to those whom He saves, and in their likeness suffer and die; thus He becomes for them a merciful and faithful High Priest.

(5) **For.**—There is a very clear connection between this verse and chap. i. 14. "Angels are but ministering spirits, serving God in the cause of those who shall inherit salvation; *for* not to angels is the world to come made subject." But the connection with verses 2, 3, is equally important: "the salvation that is now given has been proclaimed not by angels but by the Lord, and it is God Himself who works with the messengers of the

whereof we speak. (6) But one in a cer-
tain place testified, say-
ing, What is man, that
thou art mindful of him?
or the son of man, that
thou visitest him?[a] (7)
Thou madest him a little
lower than[1] the angels;
thou crownedst him with glory and
honour, and didst set him over the
works of thy hands: (8) thou hast put
all things in subjection under his
feet. For in that he put all in sub-
jection under him, he left nothing *that*
is not put under him. But now we
see not yet all things put under him.
(9) But we see Jesus, who was made a
little lower than the angels for[2] the

Chap. ii. 5—18. The sufferings of Jesus were necessary, that He might become for man Author of Salvation, a true High Priest.

a Ps. 8. 4.

1 Or, *a little while inferior to.*

2 Or, *by.*

Lord; *for* not unto angels," &c. The word "salvation" binds together this section and the first. (See chap. i. 14; ii. 2; ii. 10.)

Hath he not put in subjection.—Better, *did He subject;* for the reference is to the passage quoted in the following verses, which is already in the writer's thought. "He:" God, speaking in the prophetic Scripture.

The world to come.—The same expression occurs in the English version of chap. vi. 5, but in the Greek "world" is represented by entirely different words. Here, as in chap. i. 6, the meaning is "inhabited earth," "world of man"; there, the word properly relates to time, "age." Is "the world *to come*" still future, or is it here looked at from the Old Testament point of view? (See chap. i. 2.) The following verses (especially verse 9) make it clear that the period referred to is that which succeeds the exaltation of Christ. We ourselves cannot but markedly distinguish the present stage of Messiah's kingdom from the future; but in the perspective of prophecy the two were blended. The thought of this kingdom amongst men has been present from the first verses of the Epistle onwards; hence, "whereof we speak."

(6) **But one in a certain place.**—Better, *somewhere.* The expression is perfectly indefinite (comp. chap. iv. 4). As a rule, the words of Scripture are in this Epistle quoted as God's own utterances; and though the nature of the quotation (which is an address to God) made this impossible here, the writer seems gladly to avoid the mention of the human prophet, perhaps as distracting the thought from the divine prophecy. This studious indefiniteness in citation is common in Philo, and sometimes occurs where he cannot possibly have been in doubt as to the source of his quotation.

Testified.—That is, in Biblical usage, *solemnly declared:* the words are no light exclamation of wonder. The quotation which follows (from Ps. viii. 4—6) agrees verbally with the LXX. version. The only point of doubt is whether the last clause of verse 7 was included in the quotation, as in some very good ancient authorities it is absent from the text. The weight of external evidence is certainly in its favour; but it is easier to see how a scribe may have introduced the clause through his familiarity with the Psalm than to explain its omission if it stood in the original text of this Epistle. The Greek translation here faithfully represents the Hebrew, except in one point. For "a little lower than the angels," the Hebrew text has "a little less than God." The change (which is similar to that noticed in chap. i. 6) was probably introduced by the translators on a principle which we may often trace in their work—a wish to tone down expressions relating to the Deity which seemed strong or bold. In quoting the passage the writer does not depart from the rendering most familiar to the readers of the Greek Bible; but, though the clause in its altered form accords well with what had preceded the quotation, and, so to speak, more completely interweaves the words of the Psalm with the context in which they are here placed, yet no stress is laid on "angels." The argument of this section would not be affected materially if the true rendering of the Hebrew were restored. The eighth Psalm is an expression of amazement that God, who has "set His glory upon the heavens," should deign to remember man. Not only is He "mindful of man," but He has made him but "little less than God," "crowned him with honour," given him "dominion over" all His works. The original blessing pronounced on man (Gen. i. 28) is clearly in the Psalmist's thought, and suggests his words. The language which here precedes (verse 5) and follows (verse 8) shows that the last clause ("thou didst subject all things under his feet") bears the stress of the quotation. (That the same words are the groundwork of 1 Cor. xv. 24—28 is one of the most interesting coincidences between this Epistle and St. Paul.) It is easy to see, therefore, for what purpose these verses are here adduced. Not to angels is "the world to come" subjected: in the Scripture there are found words declaring that a divine decree has subjected all things to *man.* How the thought is combined with the argument of the whole passage will be seen in verse 9. A question at once arises: Did the meaning here assigned to the Psalm exist in David's thought? If not, on what principle does this application rest? David had in mind the words of the primal blessing, and probably did not himself think of more than those words seemed to imply. But the complete meaning of God's words can be learnt only when they are fulfilled in history. To Him who speaks in Scripture the material dominion was the symbol of a higher and a universal rule, to be fulfilled in the Son of Man when the fulness of time should come The Psalm is not directly Messianic,—it relates to man; but it is through the Man Christ Jesus that it receives its complete fulfilment for mankind.

(8) **Thou hast put . . .**—There is in the Greek a studious repetition of the leading word, which should not be lost in translation: "Thou didst subject all things under his feet. For in subjecting all things to him, He left nothing unsubjected to him. But now we see not yet all things subjected to him."

For in that . . .—The assertion of verse 5 is established by this Scripture; for if God has thus declared *all things* subject to man, there is nothing that did not fall under his rule. "*Did* not," in the divine purpose; but this purpose is not yet fulfilled in regard to the race of man.

(9) **But we see Jesus . . .**—Rather, *But we see Him who has been made a little lower than angels, Jesus, because of the suffering of death crowned with glory and honour.* There is One in whom the divine

suffering of death, crowned with glory
and honour; that he by the grace of
God should taste death for every man.
(10) For it became him, for whom *are* all
things, and by whom *are* all things, in
bringing many sons unto glory, to make
the captain of their salvation perfect
through sufferings. (11) For both he
that sanctifieth and they who are sanc-
tified *are* all of one: for which cause he

---

purpose is fulfilled in all its parts. He was made a little (the rendering of the margin, "a little while," is much less probable) lower than angels, and He is crowned with glory. In one point we note an apparent departure from the sense of the Psalm, since words ("a little lower") which there denote dignity here denote humiliation. This difference is not essential; in each case it is the position of man that is signified, and our Lord's assumption of human nature must in any case be spoken of as a descent to a lower sphere. There is peculiar fitness in the use of the human name, Jesus, for Him in whom the Psalmist's words concerning man are literally fulfilled. It is noteworthy that we do not read, "We see all things put in subjection unto Jesus"—this would conflict with the truth stated in chap. x. 13: other words of the Psalm are substituted, which do not imply that the complete actual subjection is already accomplished. This exaltation of One is not a substitute for, but involves (Rom. viii. 17, 29, *et al.*), and renders possible, the exaltation of the many. This is clear from the "not yet" of verse 8; and the same truth is brought out in a different form at the close of this verse. In the midst of this application of the words of Scripture to Jesus, the writer introduces his first reference to His death. The offence of the cross (Gal. v. 11) was an ever-active force among Jews; this is present to the writer's mind throughout the Epistle. The words thus suddenly brought in here, reminding us that the exaltation of Christ was a reward for His obedience unto death (another echo of St. Paul—Phil. ii. 9, 10; see also chap. xii. 2), prepare for the more detailed teaching of the following verses—10, 14, 15, 17.

There is an apparent difficulty in the position of the last clause of the verse, "that He should taste death for every man." We cannot doubt that these words depend on those which immediately precede; and yet how can it be said that Jesus has been crowned with glory in order that He may "taste death for every man"? Almost all difficulty is removed if we consider that (to use Dean Alford's words) "it is on the triumphant issue of His sufferings that their efficacy depends." But it is impossible for the Christian to separate, even in thought, the one from the other—the sufferings from the certain triumph. We might, perhaps, say that it is only by a misuse of human analogies that we separate them even in *time*: in the Gospel of St. John, at all events (if not in this very Epistle—see verse 14), we are taught that *in His crucifixion* Jesus is exalted. This clause, then, brings us back to the thought of the glory reserved for man: through death the fulfilment of God's purpose might seem to be frustrated; through the death of Jesus on behalf of every man (1 Pet. iii. 18) it is fulfilled. The outline presented here is filled up in later chapters; there we shall read that man's inheritance was forfeited through sin, and that only through the virtue of a death which made atonement for sin is the promise again made sure (chap. ix. 15, 16, 28). To "taste death" is a familiar Hebraism. If it has any special significance here, it would seem less natural to see (with Chrysostom) a reference to the short duration of our Saviour's death, than to understand the words as pointing to the actual taste of all the bitterness of death. (Comp. chap. vi. 4, 5.)

One various reading it is impossible to pass by, though it is preserved in but two of our Greek MSS., and these of no early date. For "by the grace of God" many (apparently most) copies of the Epistle that were known to Origen read "apart from God." This reading was followed by others of the Fathers, and found its way into some manuscripts of early versions. The Nestorians gladly accepted words which to them seemed to teach that in suffering the man Jesus was apart from God. Origen and others understood the words differently, as meaning, *taste death for every being except God.* (Comp. 1 Cor. xv. 27.) A reading so widely known, which in later times has been favoured by as eminent a critic as Bengel, demanded notice, though it is almost certainly incorrect. No interpretation which the words admit yields a probable sense; on the other hand, the reference to "the grace of God" is full of significance. (See verses 4 and 10.)

(10) **For.**—What seemed to Jews incredible, that the Christ should die, was ordained "by the grace of God." For thus to make sufferings the path to His kingdom was worthy of God, for whose glory and through whose power all things exist; who as Creator commands all agencies, and who cannot but do that which will subserve His glory. If the means at which men wondered were chosen by God, no one may doubt their supreme fitness for the end. In what this fitness consisted the following words partially explain.

In bringing.—It is doubtful whether the Greek word should not be rendered, *having brought.* With this translation we must certainly explain the words on the same principle as the past tenses of verses 7 and 8. As in the divine counsels all things *were* subjected to man, with the same propriety it may be said that God *had* brought many sons to glory when the Saviour suffered and died.

Many sons.—The new thought here introduced is of great importance in the argument. The divine purpose is to bring many sons (comp. chap. i. 14) unto glory—the glory already spoken of as reserved for man—through His Son, who has Himself received this glory that He may make it theirs.

Captain.—This word occurs in three other places. In Acts v. 31 it bears its original meaning, "Leader" ("a Leader and a Saviour"); in chap. xii. 2 and Acts iii. 15 the idea of "leading the way" has passed into that of origination. In the present case, also, *Author* is the best rendering; but in a context which so distinctly presents our Lord as taking on Himself the conditions of man's lot, and so passing into the glory which He wins for man, the primary thought of *leading* must not be entirely set aside. It is as the Author of salvation that He is made perfect through sufferings. Three aspects of this truth are presented in the Epistle. By His suffering unto death He "bare the sins of many" (verse 9, chap. ix. 28); He offered the sacrifice of a perfect obedience (chap. v. 8); He was enabled to be a perfect representative of man. This last thought pervades the remaining verses of the chapter.

(11) **For both he that sanctifieth . . .**—The

is not ashamed to call them brethren,
(12) saying, I will declare thy name unto
my brethren, in the midst of the church
will I sing praise unto thee. (13) And
again, I will put my trust in him.[a] And
again, Behold I and the children which
God hath given me.[b] (14) Forasmuch
then as the children are partakers of
flesh and blood, he also himself likewise
took part of the same; that through
death he might destroy him that had
the power of death, that is, the devil;

b Isa. 8. 18.

a Ps. 18. 2.

---

special meaning of "sanctify" in this Epistle (chaps. ix. 13; x. 10, 14, 29; xiii. 12) seems to be, *bringing into fellowship with God*, the Holy One. "They who are sanctified"—literally, *are being sanctified* (comp. Acts ii. 47; 1 Cor. i. 18)—are those whom the Captain of their salvation, in fulfilment of the Father's purpose (verse 10), is leading unto glory. The thoughts of the last verse, therefore, are repeated here, with a change of figure; and again (as in verse 9) we note the brief reference to a subject which will be prominent in later chapters; see especially chap. xiii. 12.

Are all of one.—Of one Father. This is the connecting link between verse 11 and verse 10, which speaks of the "many *sons*" and their Saviour. Though His sonship is unique and infinitely exalted, He is not ashamed to own them as brethren.

(12) **I will declare thy name . . . .**—The quotation is taken (with very slight variation) from the 22nd verse of Ps. xxii.—a Psalm remarkable for its close connection with the narratives of the Passion of our Lord. Whether the inscription which speaks of David as author is correct, or whether (from the difficulty of discovering any period in David's history to which the expressions used can apply) we consider the Psalm to have been written after the Captivity, there can be no doubt of its Messianic character. Some would class this Psalm with Ps. cx. (see Note on chap. i. 13), as simply and directly prophetic, having no historic foreground; but the language of some of the verses is so definite and peculiar that we must certainly regard it as descriptive of actual experience, and must rather regard the Psalm (comp. chap. i. 8, 9) as typically prophetic of Christ. Each division of this verse is in point as a quotation. (1) Those to whom the Messiah will declare God's name He speaks of as "brethren;" (2) not alone, but in the "church" (or rather, in a *congregation* of God's people; see Ps. xxii. 22) will He sing the praise of God. The latter thought—community with men, as attested by a like relation to God—is brought out with still greater prominence in verse 13.

(13) **I will put my trust in him . . . Behold I and the children . . .**—Of the two passages cited in this verse, the latter is certainly from Isa. viii. 18; and though the former might be derived from 2 Sam. xxii. 3 or Isa. xii. 2, yet, as the words are also found in the same chapter of Isaiah (viii. 17), we may with certainty consider this the source of the quotation. That the section of Isaiah's prophecies to which chap. viii. belongs is directly Messianic, is a fact that must be kept in mind; but the stress of the quotation cannot be laid on this. The prophet, as the representative of God to the people, has given utterance to the divine message: in these words, however, "I will put my trust" (better, "I will *have* my trust," for continuous confidence is what the words denote) "in Him," he retires into the same position with the people whom he has addressed; their relation towards God's word and the hope it inspires must be his also. This two-fold position of the prophet symbolised the two-fold nature of Him of whom every prophet was a type. (In Isa. viii. 17, the Authorised version, "I will look for Him," is nearer to the strict meaning of the original; but the difference is of little moment.)

The second passage is free from difficulty up to a certain point. In Isa. vii. and viii. we not only read of the word of God sent by Isaiah, but also find his sons associated with him in his message to the people. The warning of judgment and the promise are, so to speak, held up before the people inscribed in the symbolic names borne by the sons, Maher-shalal-hash-baz ("Speed the spoil, hastens the prey") and Shear-jashub ("A remnant shall return;" see Isa. vii. 3; x. 21), and by Isaiah himself ("Salvation of Jehovah"). "Behold I," he says, "and the children whom the Lord hath given me, are for signs and for wonders in Israel from the Lord of hosts." By God's own appointment, the children whom God gave him, though themselves no prophets, were joined with himself in the relation of prophets to the people, and were representatives of those whom God, who "hideth His face from the house of Jacob" (Isa. viii. 17), will save. As in the former passage Isaiah is taken as representing Christ, so here those who, being of the same blood, are joined with him in his work and in the promise of salvation, represent those whom the Son calls "brethren." The difficulty is that, whereas the original passage speaks of "the children" *of the prophet*, the meaning here must be *children of God*, given by Him to the Son. But no type can answer in every respect to that which it represents. The association of Jesus with His people contains three elements of thought—His essential superiority, His sharing the same nature with His people, His brotherhood with them. The first two thoughts are truly represented in this Old Testament figure; the last no figure could at the same time set forth. And though verses 12 and 13 are directly connected with the word "brethren," yet, as the next verse shows, the most important constituent of the thought is community of nature. It should be observed that in these two verses the citations are not so distinctly adduced by way of *proof* as are those of the first chapter.

(14) **Forasmuch then . . .**—The two members of this verse directly recall the thoughts of verses 10 and 9. (1) It was the will of God that salvation should be won by the Son for sons; (2) this salvation could only be won by means of death.

The children.—Said with reference to verse 13.

Flesh and blood.—Literally, *blood and flesh*, the familiar order of the words being departed from here and in Eph. vi. 12. This designation of human nature on its material side is found four times in the New Testament, and is extremely common in Jewish writers.

The emphasis of the following statement is noteworthy: "He Himself also in like manner took part of the same things." His assumption of our nature had for its object suffering and death.

Destroy him.—Rather, *bring him to nought;* annul his power. The comment on these words will be found in chap. ix. 15, 26; for it was as the lord of sin, which was the cause (Rom. v. 12) and the sting (1 Cor. xv. 56) of death, that the devil held dominion over death (or, as the words might mean, wielded the power

(15) and deliver them who through fear
of death were all their lifetime subject
to bondage. (16) For verily he took not
on *him the nature of* angels; but he
took on *him* the seed of Abraham.[1]
(17) Wherefore in all things it behoved
him to be made like unto *his* brethren,
that he might be a merciful and faithful
high priest in things *pertaining* to God,
to make reconciliation for the sins of
the people. (18) For in that he himself
hath suffered being tempted,
he is able to succour them that are
tempted.

1 Gr. *he taketh not hold of angels, but of the seed of Abraham he taketh hold.*

---

possessed by death). (Comp. 2 Tim. i. 10; 1 John iii. 8; also Rev. i. 18.) Combined with this is the thought which runs through this chapter—the assimilation of the Redeemer to the redeemed in the conditions of His earthly life. By meeting death Himself, He vanquishes and destroys death for them.

(15) **Deliver them who through fear of death . . . .**—This verse brings into relief the former misery and the present freedom. We may well suppose these words to have been prompted by the intense sympathy of the writer with the persecuted and tempted Christians whom he addresses. He writes throughout as one who never forgets their need of sympathetic help, and who knows well the power of the motives, the allurements and the threats, employed to lead them into apostasy. The crushing power of the "fear of death" over those who had not grasped the truth that, in Christ, life and immortality are brought to light, perhaps no thought of ours can reach.

(16) **He took not on him the nature of angels.**—The rendering of the margin approaches very nearly the true meaning of the verse; whereas the text (in which the Authorised version differs from all our earlier translations) introduces confusion into the argument. Having spoken in verse 14 of our Lord's assumption of human nature, the writer in these words assigns the reason: "For surely it is not of angels that He taketh hold, but He taketh hold of the seed of Abraham." Though the words "take hold," which occur twice in the verse, probably cannot directly signify "help" (as is often maintained), they distinctly suggest laying hold for the sake of giving help; and a beautiful illustration may be found in some of the Gospel narratives of our Lord's works of healing (Mark viii. 23; Luke xiv. 4). It is probable that the language used here is derived from the Old Testament. In chap. viii. 9, a quotation from Jer. xxxi., we read, "In the day when I took them by the hand to lead them out of the land of Egypt." Isa. xli. 8, 9, however, is perhaps a still closer parallel (for the word used in the Greek version is very similar, and no doubt expresses the same meaning): "Thou Israel, my servant, Jacob whom I have chosen, the seed of Abraham my friend; thou of whom I have taken hold from the ends of the earth." If the writer had these verses in his thought, it is hardly necessary to inquire why he chooses the expression "seed of Abraham," instead of one of (apparently) wider meaning, such as verses 7, 8, might seem to require. But even apart from this passage of Isaiah, and the natural fitness of such a phrase in words addressed to Jews, we may doubt if any other language would have been equally expressive. For as to the *means*, it was by becoming a child of Abraham that the Saviour "took hold of" our race to raise it up; and as to the *purpose*, St. Paul teaches us that "the seed of Abraham" includes all who inherit Abraham's faith.

(17) **Wherefore.**—Since it is "the seed of Abraham," His brethren, that He would help.

In all things.—These words must be taken with "made like." In all respects (the single exception does not come into notice here, see chap. iv. 15) He must be made like to "the brethren" (a reference to verse 12): like them, He must be liable to, and must suffer, temptation, sorrow, pain, death.

That he might be.—Rather, *that He might prove*, or *become* (the words imply what is more fully expressed in chap. v. 8), *a compassionate and faithful High Priest*. The high priest was the representative of men to God; without such likeness (see chap. v. 1, 2) He could be no true High Priest for man. The order of the Greek words throws an emphasis on "compassionate" which is in full harmony with what we have seen to be the pervading tone of the chapter. One who has not so understood the infirmities of his brethren as to be "compassionate," cannot be their "faithful" representative before God. But the word "faithful" is still more closely connected with the following words. If through the power of sympathy which the Saviour has gained "by sufferings" He becomes "compassionate" as our High Priest, it is through "the suffering of death" (verse 9) that He proves Himself "the faithful High Priest in things pertaining to God, to make reconciliation (or rather, *propitiation*) for the sins of the people." The word "high priest," hereafter to be so prominent in the Epistle, is brought in somewhat suddenly, but several expressions in this chapter (see also chap. i. 3) have prepared for and led up to the crowning thought here brought before us. The characteristic function of the high priest was his presentation of the sacrifice on the Day of Atonement, that expiation might be made for the sins of the whole people, that the displeasure of God might not rest on the nation on account of sin. (Comp. verse 11.) The words rendered "propitiate" and "propitiation" are not of frequent occurrence in the New Testament (Luke xviii. 13; 1 John ii. 2; iv. 10—see also Rom. iii. 25), but are very often found in the LXX. The subject receives its full treatment in chaps. ix. and x.

(18) **For.**—The necessity of being "in all things made like to His brethren" has been shown from the nature of the case; it is now illustrated from the result. The "brethren" and the "people" of verse 17 are here "the tempted." Through the temptations arose those sins of the people for which He makes propitiation. In His having been tempted lies His special ability to help the tempted, by His sympathy, by His knowledge of the help that is needed, by the position of High Priest which He has gained through suffering. It is difficult to decide between two translations of the first words of the verse: (1) "*In that* He Himself," (2) "*Wherein* He Himself hath suffered being tempted." The former is simpler, but, perhaps, less natural as a rendering of the Greek. The latter may indeed at first seem to set a bound to our Lord's ability to help, but with the recollection of the infinitude of His life (comp. John xxi. 25) all such limitation disappears.

Chap. iii. 1—6. Consider our High Priest, who, as the faithful Son over God's house, is exalted above Moses, the servant.

A.D. 64.

CHAPTER III.—(1) Wherefore, holy
brethren, partakers of the
heavenly calling, consider
the Apostle and High
Priest of our profession,
Christ Jesus; (2) who was
faithful to him that appointed[1] him, as also
Moses *was faithful* in all his house.
(3) For this *man* was counted worthy of
more glory than Moses, inasmuch as he
who hath builded the house hath more
honour than the house. (4) For every
house is builded by some *man;* but he
that built all things *is* God. (5) And
Moses verily *was* faithful in all his

1 Gr. *made*, 1 Sam. 12. 6.

III.

(iii. 1—iv. 13) Having, therefore, this High Priest over the house of God—a faithful Son exalted above Moses the faithful servant—let us by faithfulness make sure our calling to be God's sons; that we may not, like those who through their disobedience in the wilderness provoked the Lord, be excluded from the promised rest.

(1) **Wherefore.**—The address which here begins (the first direct address in the Epistle) bears the same relation to all that has preceded, as chap. ii. 1—4 bears to the first chapter. In particular, the contents of the second chapter are gathered up in this verse, almost every word of which recalls some previous statement or result.

Holy brethren.—United in one brotherhood in virtue of a common sonship (chap. ii. 10) and of a common brotherhood (chap. ii. 11) with Jesus, Him "that sanctifieth" (chap. ii. 11).

Partakers.—Through Him who "took part" of our earthly nature (chap. ii. 14) we are partakers of a "heavenly calling" (chap. ii. 10) as God's sons.

The Apostle and High Priest of our profession, Christ Jesus.—The best MSS. omit "Christ"; and it is impossible not to feel how fitly the personal name "Jesus" is used after the later verses of chap. ii. Here only is the name Apostle directly given to our Lord; but the thought is present in chap. ii. 3, and in the many passages in which Jesus designates Himself as the Sent of God, using the word from which *Apostle* is derived (John iii. 17; v. 36, *et al.;* especially John xvii. 18; xx. 21). There is very little difference between *Apostle* and *Prophet,* thus applied; but the one brings into relief the mission, the other the office and position. Each presents a thought complementary of that contained in high priest: "as Apostle Jesus pleads the cause of God with us; as High Priest He pleads our cause with God" (Bengel). The next verse renders it probable that the two terms contain a reference to the special mission of Moses and the priesthood of Aaron; our Christian confession looks to *One* mediator.

(2) **Who was.**—Rather, *as being;* or *that He was.* Not merely, *fix your thought on Jesus;* but also (and especially), *think of Him as faithful* to God (chap. ii. 17).

Appointed him.—Literally, *made Him,* an expression which some ancient (Ambrose and other Latin fathers,—apparently also Athanasius) and many modern writers have understood as relating to the creation of the human nature of our Lord. It is probable, however, that 1 Sam. xii. 6 is in the writer's mind. "It is the Lord that made Moses and Aaron, and that brought your fathers up out of the land of Egypt." As there Samuel speaks of the raising up of Moses and Aaron, constituted by God deliverers of the people; so here our thought must rest on Him who constituted Jesus "Apostle and High Priest."

As also Moses.—These words, which give the key to the following verses, are quoted from Num. xii. 7, where Moses is placed in contrast with prophets in Israel to whom the Lord will make Himself known by vision or dream. "My servant Moses is not so, who is faithful in all mine house. With him will I speak mouth to mouth." The "house" or household is God's people Israel. To others will God reveal Himself in various ways in regard to the many parts of the house, the many concerns of the household. Throughout the whole house Moses was the recipient of the divine commands, and was faithful—"faithful" (as one of the Targums paraphrases), "as chief of the chiefs of my court."

(3) **For this man was counted.**—Rather, *For He hath been accounted,* by God, who hath crowned Him with glory and honour (chap. ii. 9). In this reward lies contained the proof that He was faithful. This is probably the connection of thought; others join this verse with the first: "Consider Him . . . for He hath received higher glory than Moses."

Inasmuch as.—That is, *in proportion as:* the glory attained by Jesus exceeds the glory of Moses, as the honour due to the builder of the house exceeds that possessed by the house itself. It is not said that Jesus is the Builder; but the relation in which He stands to the Builder of the house is compared with that of Moses to the house. (See verses 5, 6.) "Builded" is not a happy word here (especially if we consider the sense in which "house" is used), but it is not easy to find a suitable rendering. The meaning is, He who prepared or formed the house, with all its necessary parts and arrangements.

(4) **For every house is builded by some man.**—Rather, *by some one:* the thought of the house leads at once to the thought of the builder of it. The meaning of the several parts of this verse is very simple; but it is not easy to follow the reasoning with certainty. The second clause seems to be a condensed expression of this thought: "But He that built this house is He that built all things, God." "Moses is possessed of lesser glory than the Apostle of our confession, as the house stands below its maker in honour. For this house, like every other, has its maker:—it is He who made all things, even God.

(5) **As a servant.**—What was before implied is now clearly expressed. Verse 3 associated Moses with the house, Jesus with Him who builded it; of what nature this relation was, is stated in this verse and the next. Moses was "in God's house;" however exalted his position, he was in the house as a servant. The Greek word used here does not occur elsewhere in the New Testament, but is taken from the LXX. version of Num. xii. 7. There is nothing special in the Hebrew word in that place, but the translators seem to have felt that "bond-servant" was less suitable in such a context than "attendant" or "minister." The object of his service was that he might bear "testimony of the things that should hereafter be spoken." Are we to understand by these the divine commands that would from time to time be given to Moses? If so, then the statement "Moses was faithful" must be regarded as a pure quotation, equivalent to "Moses was at that time

house, as a servant, for a testimony of
those things which were to be spoken
after; (6) but Christ as a son over his
own house; whose house are we, if we
hold fast the confidence and the rejoic-
ing of the hope firm unto the end.
(7) Wherefore (as the Holy Ghost
saith, To day if ye will
hear his voice,[a] (8) harden
not your hearts, as in the
provocation, in the day of
temptation in the wilder-
ness: (9) when your fathers
tempted me, proved me,

a Ps. 95. 7.

Chaps. iii. 7—iv. 13. Let us not through unfaithfulness fail of the promise, as unfaithful Israel was excluded from God's rest.

declared faithful." This does not seem probable. If, however, the words of Num. xii. 7 are taken as descriptive of the whole life of Moses, his "witness" must relate to the things spoken "in these last days;" of these, by his writings, his acts, his life, Moses bore constant witness. (See verse 2; chaps. viii. 5; ix. 19; xi. 26; John v. 46, *et al.*) The latter interpretation is confirmed by verse 6, in which the name given to our Lord is not Jesus, as in verse 1, but *Christ.*

(6) **But Christ as a son over his own house.**—Rather, *over His house.* Throughout this passage (verses 2, 5, 6) "His house" must be taken in the sense of the quotation, as the house of God. Whereas Moses was faithful as a servant in this house of God, Christ was faithful as a son set over His Father's house. The antithesis is complete: the one is a servant for witness, the other a Son having a natural right to rule. The concluding words in verse 5 have no formal answer here, but the contrast is not the less distinctly expressed. The name Christ (which here occurs for the first time) is in this Epistle never a mere name: it contains implicitly the thought that all that to which Moses bore witness has reached its fulfilment now. Christ has come: God's house, formerly typified by Israel, is now manifested as it really is, containing all "sons" whom God leads to glory (chap. ii. 10). The terms applied by constant usage to the one nation are thus successively enlarged: the "seed of Abraham" (chap. ii. 16), "the people" (chap. ii. 17), the "house of God" (see chap. x. 21).

If we hold fast the confidence.—Better, *If we hold the boldness and the glorying of our hope firm unto the end.* Faithful to his practical purpose, the writer adds to the words "whose house are we" the indispensable condition. The "house" exists ("are we"), to it belong all who possess the Christian "hope;" but for assured and final appropriation of the promise there must be steadfastness "unto the end." This exhortation differs from that in chap. ii. 1—4, in that it more distinctly implies that those who are addressed have a possession which they may lose. The Christian "hope," that aspect of faith which is turned towards the future, is naturally often in the writer's thoughts. The words associated are very striking: hope gives us boldness (see 2 Cor. iii. 12), and of this hope we make our boast. "Boldness" is spoken of again (in chaps. iv. 16; x. 19, 35): properly meaning "freedom of speech," it denotes the confident, bold feelings and demeanour which connect themselves with the free utterance of thought.

(7) **Wherefore.**—Since without steadfastness all will be lost. With the words introducing the quotation compare chaps. ix. 8; x. 15.

Whether the marks of parenthesis here introduced in our ordinary Bibles (not inserted by the translators of 1611) express the true connection of the verses is a question very hard to decide, and one that does not admit of full discussion here. It is very possible that the writer (like St. Paul in Rom. xv. 3, 21; 1 Cor. i. 31) may have merged his own exhortation in that which the quotation supplies (verse 8); and the objection that verse 12 would naturally in that case have been introduced by some connective word is shown to be groundless by such passages as chaps. viii. 13; x. 23; xii. 7, 25. On the other hand, if we connect "Wherefore," in this verse, with "Take heed" in verse 12, we have greater regularity of structure—a strong argument in this Epistle. It seems unlikely, moreover, that the writer (whose tenderness of tone and sympathy are so manifest in his words of warning) would at this stage adopt as his own the stringent and general exhortation, "harden not your hearts:" the spirit of verse 12 ("lest *haply* there *shall be* in *any one* of you") is altogether different. On the whole, therefore, it seems best to consider verses 7 ("To-day . . .") to 11 (". . . my rest") as a pure quotation, enforcing the warning that follows.

Psalm xcv., the latter part of which (verses 7—11) is here cited, is in the LXX. ascribed to David, but is probably of later date. (As to chap. iv. 7, see the Note.) In most important respects the words of the quotation agree with the Greek version, and with the Hebrew text. The chief exceptions will be noted as they occur.

To day if ye will hear his voice.—Rather, *To-day if ye shall hear* (literally, *shall have heard*) *His voice.* The Greek will not allow the sense in which the words are naturally taken by the English reader, "if ye are willing to hear." The meaning of the Hebrew words is either—(1) "To-day, oh that ye would hearken to (that is, *obey*) His voice!" or, (2) "To-day if ye hearken to His voice." The "voice" is that which speaks in the following verses. As the words stand before us, the Psalmist does not formally complete the sentence here commenced ("if ye shall hear . . ."). He introduces the divine words of warning, but adds none in his own person. The entreaty "Harden not your hearts" is at once the utterance of the divine voice and the expression of his own urgent prayer. Other passages in which the hardening of the heart is spoken of as the work of man himself are Ex. ix. 34; 1 Sam. vi. 6; Prov. xxviii. 14.

(8) **In the day of temptation.**—Better, *like the day of the temptation.* As in the LXX., so here, two words which in the Hebrew are proper names ("as at Meribah, and as in the day of Massah") are translated according to their intrinsic meaning. (For the former see Ex. xvii. 7; Num. xx. 13; and for the latter Ex. xvii. 7.) We may believe that these places are here chosen for reference partly on account of their significant names; but it is noteworthy that the rebellions recorded in the names belonged to the beginning and to the close of the years of wandering.

(9) According to our best MSS. this verse will run thus: *Where* (or, *wherewith*) *your fathers tempted by trial, and saw My works forty years.* The meaning of the Hebrew (with which the LXX. very nearly agrees) is: "Where your fathers tempted Me, proved Me; also saw My work." The change of reading is more interesting than important, as the sense is not materially different. Both here and in the original passage it

and saw my works forty years.
(10) Wherefore I was grieved with that
generation, and said, They do alway
err in *their* heart; and they have not
known my ways. (11) So I sware in
my wrath, They shall not enter[1] into
my rest.) (12) Take heed, brethren, lest
there be in any of you an evil heart of
unbelief, in departing from the living
God. (13) But exhort one another daily,
while it is called To day; lest any of
you be hardened through the deceit-
fulness of sin. (14) For we are made
partakers of Christ, if we hold the be-
ginning of our confidence stedfast unto
the end; (15) while it is said, To day if
ye will hear his voice, harden not your
hearts, as in the provocation. (16) For
some, when they had heard, did pro-
voke: howbeit not all that came out

1 Gr. *If they shall enter.*

---

seems probable that the "work," or "works," should be understood of the divine judgments which the disobedient people "saw" and bore during forty years. In the Psalm (and apparently in verse 17 of this chapter) the mention of the forty years connects itself with the words which follow; but here with the provocations of the people and their punishment. It is held by many that in this period of forty years is contained a reference to the time that intervened between our Saviour's earthly ministry and the destruction of Jerusalem; and a Jewish tradition is quoted which assigns to "the days of Messiah" a duration of forty years.

(10) **I was grieved with that generation.**—Rather, *I was angry with this generation.* The Hebrew is very strong: "I loathed a (whole) generation." The first word, "Wherefore," is not found in the Psalm, but is added to make the connection more distinct.

And they have not known my ways.—Better, *yet they took not knowledge of My ways.* Although throughout the forty years He had shown to them their disobedience and His displeasure, yet the warning and discipline were fruitless. They gained no knowledge of His ways. It is very important to observe this explicit reference to the *close,* as well as the beginning of the forty years. (See verse 8.)

(11) **So.**—Rather, *as* (chap. iv. 3). It is with these as it was with their fathers, the generations that came out of Egypt, unto whom God sware, "They shall not enter into My rest" (Num. xiv. 21—24). The form in which these words appear below (chap. iv. 3, 5) in the Authorised version, "If they shall enter into my rest," is an imitation of the original construction. See Num. xiv. 23, where "they shall not see" is, as the margin shows, expressed in Hebrew by "if they (shall) see" the land.

Into my rest.—Into the land where Jehovah shall give rest to His people and shall dwell with them. (See Deut. xii. 9; 1 Kings viii. 56; Ps. cxxxii. 14; Isa. lxvi. 1; 1 Chron. vi. 31; 2 Chron. vi. 41.)

(12) **Lest there be in any of you.**—Better, *lest haply there shall be in any one of you.* (See above, on verse 7.)

In departing.—Better, *in falling away from a Living God.* The heart of unbelief will manifest its evil in apostasy. The Greek word *apistia* stands in direct contrast to "faithful" (*pistos*), verse 2, and combines the ideas of "unbelief" and "faithlessness." He whose words they have heard is a living God, ever watchful in warning and entreaty (verse 8), but also in the sure punishment of the faithless (verse 11; chap. x. 31).

(13) **While it is called To day.**—Literally, *as long as the "to-day" is called* (to you), *lest any one of you be hardened by deceit of sin.* As long as they heard the word of God speaking in the Scripture, "To-day if ye shall hear," so long is the way of obedience open to them. Sin is here personified as the Deceiver (Rom. vii. 11), alluring from God by the offer of "pleasures" (chap. xi. 25), or persuading that forbearance and "respite" (Ex. viii. 15; Eccles. viii. 11) imply the absence of a Living God.

(14) **For.**—Take heed (verse 12) lest there be anything that may lead astray, *for we have become partakers of the Christ if* (and only if) *we hold the beginning of our confidence firm unto the end.* In verse 6, since Israel had been spoken of as God's house, the Christian hope finds expression in "whose house are we." Here the comparison with Israel journeying to the land of promise suggests another figure, and all blessing is summed up in becoming "partakers of the Christ," foretold and expected as the Fulfiller of all promises. Two different words in the two verses are rendered "confidence" in the Authorised version. The former, as we have seen (verse 6), is "boldness;" the latter (here used) is applied to men who make a firm stand when attacked, who stand firmly under pressure. In the first energy of the new life such firm constancy had been shown by them (chap. x. 32—34); but would it be maintained "unto the end"?

(15) **If ye will hear.**—Rather, as before (verse 7), *if ye shall hear.* The true connection of this verse is not easily decided. By many it is held that the words should be joined with what follows, and commence a new paragraph; but this does not seem probable. Either verse 14 is parenthetical, so that this verse emphasises the reference to "to-day" in verse 13; or the thought of the writer is that we must "hold fast the beginning of our confidence" *in the presence of* this divine warning—whilst day by day these words are addressed to us anew.

(16) **For.**—The connecting link is the thought of "the provocation." A slight change in the accentuation of the first Greek word effects a complete change in the sense: *For who when they had heard did provoke? Nay, was it not all that came out of Egypt through Moses?* Those who were disobedient were the people whom God, through Moses, had but now delivered from bondage! The two exceptions (Num. xiv. 30) are left out of account in the presence of the multitude of rebels. There can be little doubt that the above translation (now generally received) presents the true meaning of the verse. It will be remembered that the oldest MSS. give no evidence on such points as accentuation, and therefore leave our judgment free. In modern times Bengel was the first to point out the true form of the Greek word; but one of the ancient versions (the Peschito-Syriac), and at least three of the Greek Fathers, are found to give the same interpretation. It will be seen at once that, with this arrangement of the words, the present verse is similar in structure to the two following.

of Egypt by Moses. (17) But with
whom was he grieved forty years? *was
it* not with them that had sinned,
whose carcases fell in the wilderness?
(18) And to whom sware he that they
should not enter into his rest, but to
them that believed not? (19) So we see
that they could not enter in because of
unbelief.

A.D. 64.

CHAPTER IV.—(1) Let us therefore
fear, lest, a promise being left *us* of
entering into his rest, any of you should
seem to come short of it. (2) For unto
us was the gospel preached, as well as
unto them: but the word preached[1]
did not profit them, not being mixed
with faith in[2] them that heard *it*.
(3) For we which have believed do enter

1 Gr. *the word of hearing.*

2 Or, *because they were not united by faith to.*

(17) **But.**—Better, *And with whom was He angry forty years?*

Whose carcases.—Literally, *limbs*. The word is taken from the Greek version of Num. xiv. 29; and seems intended to convey the thought of bodies falling *limb from limb* in the wilderness.

(18) **That believed not.**—Rather, *that disobeyed*. Every part of the solemn sentences of the Psalm is applied to the reader's conscience, that the effect of the whole warning may be deepened: the nature of the transgression is thus brought out with the strongest emphasis. Those with whom God was angry had provoked God (verse 16), had sinned (verse 17), had been disobedient, had refused to believe His word (verse 19). The action of the Israelites (Num. xiv.) involved at once disobedience to God's command that they should advance to the conquest of the land, and want of faith in the promise which made victory sure.

(19) **So we see.**—Rather, *And we see*. It is not the general conclusion that is here expressed; but, as in verse 18 we read of the *oath* of exclusion, this verse records the *fact*, and also states the cause under an aspect which is most suitable for the exhortation which is in the writer's thought. There is force in "could not enter":—not only disobedience, but cowardice and weakness, sprang from "unbelief."

IV.

This chapter is manifestly a continuation of the last, and should not have been detached from it. As with the exhortation of chap. iii. 12, 13, are interwoven some of the early words of the quotation from Ps. xcv., so here the later thoughts of the same passage are taken up and applied.

(1) **Let us therefore fear.**—The emphasis rests upon "fear," not upon "us." It is noteworthy that the writer begins with "Let us," though about to write "lest any of *you;*" he will have gained his object if he brings his readers to share his fear.

Lest, a promise being left us.—Rather, *lest haply, a promise being* (still) *left*. No word must be inserted here that can diminish the generality of the words; in the sequel the statement will be repeated with all possible clearness. Here it is simply said that such a promise remains unexhausted, waiting for complete fulfilment. No Hebrew Christian would doubt this. As in chap. i., the writer's aim is not to establish a truth absolutely new, but to show that in this and in that Scripture a received truth lies contained. Most of our earlier versions (following Luther and Erasmus) give to this clause a different turn, which cannot be correct: "Lest any of you by forsaking the promise of entering in His rest."

Any of you should seem to come short of it.—Rather, *any one of you should be accounted to have come short of it*. The difficulty here lies in the words rendered "seem" or "be accounted." It appears impossible that the meaning can be "should *even* seem," or "should think himself," or "should show himself," to have failed. It may be that the writer avoids positive and direct language in speaking of what lies beyond mortal ken, and therefore reverently says "should seem to have come short of it." It is more probable that he is influenced by the figure contained in the next word, the *falling short of* a mark; and is thus led to refer to the judge who witnesses and declares the failure,—"Lest any one . . . be held (or, *be adjudged*) to have come short of" the promise.

(2) **For unto us was.**—Rather, *for we have had glad tidings preached unto us, even as they had*. The object of these words is to support verse 1, "a promise being left." How fitly the good news of the promise might, alike in their case and in ours, be designated by the same word as the "gospel," will afterwards appear.

The word preached.—Literally, *the word of hearing, i.e.*, the word which was heard (1 Thess. ii. 13). But this does not mean the word heard *by them*. As in Isa. liii. 1 (where the same word is found in the Greek version) the meaning is "our message," "that which we have heard from God," so here the words signify what was heard by those who declared the promise to the people, especially the message which Moses received from God.

Not being mixed with faith.—A change of reading in the Greek, which rests on the strongest authority, compels us to connect these words, not with the message, but with the people: "since they had not been united (literally, *mingled*) by faith with them that heard." That the word of Moses and those associated with him in declaring God's promise (perhaps Aaron, Joshua, Caleb) might benefit the people, speakers and hearers must be united by the bond of faith. Here the margin of the Authorised version preserves the true text, following the Vulgate and the earliest of the printed Greek Testaments (the Complutensian).

(3) **For we which have believed.**—The emphasis is two-fold, resting both on "believed" and on "we enter." The former looks back to verse 2, "by faith"—"*for* it is we who believed that enter." . . . The latter looks forward to the remainder of the verse, the purport of which is that the rest exists, and that "entering into the rest" may still be spoken of.

As I have sworn . . .—Rather (as above), *as I sware in My wrath, They shall not enter into My rest*. (See chap. iii. 11.) If in the Scripture (Ps. xcv. 8) God warns men of a later age not to imitate the guilt of those whom He excluded from His rest, it follows (see below on verse 10) that the time for entering into the rest of God was not then past and gone.

Although the works were finished from the foundation of the world.—And therefore the rest into which God will enter with His redeemed people is not that which succeeded the works of creation. This

into rest, as he said, As I have sworn in
my wrath, if they shall enter into my
rest: although the works were finished
from the foundation of the world. (4) For
he spake in a certain place of the seventh
day on this wise, And God did rest the
seventh day from all his works. (5) And
in this *place* again, If they shall enter
into my rest. (6) Seeing therefore it re-
maineth that some must enter therein,
and they to whom it was first preached[1]
entered not in because of unbelief:
(7) again, he limiteth a certain day,
saying in David, To day, after so long
a time; as it is said, To day if ye
will hear his voice, harden not your
hearts. (8) For if Jesus[2] had given
them rest, then would he not afterward
have spoken of another day. (9) There
remaineth therefore a rest[3] to the people
of God. (10) For he that is entered into
his rest, he also hath ceased from his

2 That is, *Joshua.*

3 Or, *keeping of a sabbath.*

1 Or, *the gospel was first preached.*

---

caution is added because the words used by the Psalmist (Ps. xcv. 11) are derived from Gen. ii. 2, 3; though the same words are used, yet, we are reminded, the thought is widely different. The next two verses simply expand and support the thought contained in this: "For whereas we read in one Scripture that God 'rested' on the seventh day, another records His sentence on the disobedient people, 'They *shall not* enter into My rest.'"

(4) **For he spake in a certain place.**—Better, *For he hath spoken somewhere,* another example of indefiniteness of citation. (See Note on chap. ii. 6.)

(6) The substance of the preceding verses may be thus expressed: There is a rest of God, into which some are to enter with God,—a rest not yet entered at the time of the wandering in the wilderness, and therefore not that which followed the work of creation,—a rest from which some were excluded because of unbelief. These five particulars are repeated in substance in the present verse: "Seeing, therefore, it is (still) left that some should enter in, and they to whom formerly glad tidings were declared entered not in because of disobedience, He again," &c. "Disobedience"—though verse 2 speaks of *unbelief* as the cause: see Note on chap. iii. 18. In John iii. 36, the transition from "believeth" to "obeyeth" is equally striking.

(7) **Again, he limiteth.**—Better, *He again marketh out* (or, *defineth*). The next step taken (see the last Note) is to point out that, long after the occupation of Canaan, the Psalmist—God speaking in the Psalm—says "To-day," in pleading with Israel. The implied meaning is as if He said, "Harden not your hearts to-day, lest I swear unto you also, Ye shall not enter into My rest."

In David.—Probably this is equivalent to saying, *In the Book of Psalms.* In the LXX., however, Ps. xcv. is ascribed to David.

After so long a time.—The period intervening between the divine sentence on the rebels in the wilderness (Num. xiv.) and the time of the Psalmist.

As it is said.—The best MSS. read, *as it hath been before said.*

(8) For, had the promise been fulfilled in Joshua's conquest, the Psalm (God in the Psalm) would not be speaking of another day, saying "To-day" (verse 7). (In one other place in the New Testament the Greek form of the name of Joshua is preserved. See the Note on Acts vii. 45.)

(9) **There remaineth therefore.**—Or, *therefore there is* (still) *left:* the word is the same as in verse 6. It is tacitly assumed that no subsequent fulfilment has altered the relation of the promise. Few things in the Epistle are more striking than the constant presentation of the thought that Scripture language is *permanent* and at all times *present.* The implied promise, therefore, repeated whenever the "to-day" is heard, must have its fulfilment. The rescued people of Israel did indeed find a rest in Canaan: the true redeemed "people of God" shall rest with God.

A rest.—As the margin points out, the word is suddenly changed. As the rest promised to God's people is a rest with God, it is to them "a sabbath-rest." So one of the treatises of the Mishna speaks of Ps. xcii. as a "Psalm for the time to come, for the day which is all Sabbath, the rest belonging to the life eternal."

(10) **Into his rest.**—That is, *into God's rest.*

Hath ceased.—Rather, *hath rested from his works as God did from His own* (works). This verse is added to explain and justify the reference to a "sabbath" in verse 9. Man's sabbath-rest begins when he enters into God's rest (Gen. ii. 2); as that was the goal of the creative work, so to the people of God this rest is the goal of their life of "works."

As the whole argument is reviewed, the question may naturally be asked, To what extent is this wide meaning present in the Psalm itself? Where must the line be drawn between the direct teaching of the words and the application here made? The apparent expansion of the meaning of the Psalm relates to verse 11 alone. There, in the first instance, an historical fact is mentioned—the exclusion of the rebels from the promised land. But though the mention of the oath of God is derived from Num. xiv. 28—30, the language of the historian is significantly changed; for "ye shall not come into the land," we read, "they shall not enter into My rest." True, the land could be spoken of as their "rest and inheritance" (Deut. xii. 9); but the language which the Psalmist chooses is at all events susceptible of a much higher and wider meaning, and (as some of the passages quoted in the Note on chap. iii. 11 serve to prove) may have been used in this extended sense long before the Psalmist's age. That verse 8, when placed by the side of verse 11, shows the higher meaning of the words to have been in the Psalmist's thought, and implies that the offer of admission to the rest of God was still made, it seems unreasonable to doubt. As the people learnt through ages of experience and training (see chap. i. 5) to discern the deeper and more spiritual meaning that lay in the promises of the King and the Son of David, so was it with other promises which at first might seem to have no more than a temporal significance. If these considerations are well founded, it follows that we have no right to look on the argument of this section as an 'accommodation" or a mere application of Scripture: the Christian preacher does but fill up the outline which the prophet had drawn.

own works, as God *did* from his. (11) Let
us labour therefore to enter into that
rest, lest any man fall after the same
example of unbelief.[1] (12) For the word
of God *is* quick, and powerful, and
sharper than any twoedged sword,
piercing even to the dividing asunder
of soul and spirit, and of the joints
and marrow, and *is* a discerner of the
thoughts and intents of the heart.
(13) Neither is there any creature that is
not manifest in his sight: but all things
are naked and opened unto the eyes of
him with whom we have to do.
(14) Seeing then that we have a great
high priest, that is passed into the

1 Or, *disobedience.*

---

(11) **Labour.**—Rather, *give diligence, strive earnestly.* It is the necessity of watchful and constant faithfulness that is enforced. Hence the words that follow: "Lest any one fall into (or, *after*) the same example of disobedience" (verse 6; chap. iii. 18).

(12) As in chap. iii. 12 the warning against the "evil heart of unbelief" is solemnly enforced by the mention of the "Living God," so here, in pointing to the peril of disobedience, it is to the living power of the word of God that the writer makes appeal. But in what sense? Does he bring before us again the word of Scripture, or the divine Word Himself? Outside the writings of St. John there is no passage in the New Testament in which the word of God is as clearly invested with personal attributes as here. The word is "quick" (that is, *living*), "powerful" (or, *active—mighty in operation*, as most of our versions render the word), "able to discern the thoughts of the heart." Philo, whose writings are pervaded by the doctrine of the divine Word (see the Note appended to St. John's Gospel in Vol. I. of this *Commentary*, p. 553), in certain passages makes use of expressions so remarkably resembling some that are before us in this verse that we cannot suppose the coincidence accidental. Thus, in an allegorical explanation of Gen. xv. 10, he speaks of the sacred and divine Word as cutting through all things, dividing all perceptible objects, and penetrating even to those called indivisible, separating the different parts of the soul. But though these and the many other resemblances that are adduced may prove the writer's familiarity with the Alexandrian philosophy, they are wholly insufficient to show an adoption of Philo's doctrinal system (if system it could be called) in regard to the divine Word, or to rule the interpretation of the single passage in this Epistle in which an allusion to that system could be traced. Nor is the first-mentioned argument conclusive. There certainly is personification here, and in part the language used would, if it stood alone, even suggest the presence of a divine Person; but it is not easy to believe that in the New Testament the words "sharper than a twoedged sword" would be directly applied to the Son of God. In this Epistle, moreover (and even in this context, verse 2), reference is repeatedly made to the word of God in revelation, without a trace of any other meaning. The key to the language of this verse, so far as it is exceptional, is found in that characteristic of the Epistle to which reference has been already made —the habitual thought of Scripture as a *direct* divine utterance. The transition from such a conception to those of this verse was very easy; and we need not feel surprise if with expressions which are naturally applied to the utterance are joined others which lead the thought to God as Speaker. It is, therefore, the whole word of God that is brought before us—mainly the word of threatening and judgment, but also (comp. verse 2 and the last member of this verse) the word of promise.

Piercing even to the dividing asunder . . .—Rather, *and piercing even to the dividing of soul and spirit, both joints and marrow.* For the comparison of God's word to a sword see Isa. xlix. 2; Eph. vi. 17; (Rev. i. 16); comp. also Wisd. xviii. 15, 16, "Thine Almighty word leapt down from heaven out of Thy royal throne . . . and brought Thine unfeigned commandment as a sharp sword, and standing up filled all things with death." The keen two-edged sword penetrates even to dividing soul and spirit (not soul *from* spirit), with unfailing stroke severing bone from bone and piercing the very marrow. The latter words, by a very natural metaphor, are transferred from the material frame to the soul and spirit.

And is a discerner . . .—Is quick to discern, able to judge, the thoughts (reflections, conceptions, intents) of the heart. Man's word may be lifeless, without power to discriminate, to adapt itself to a changed state or varying circumstances, to enforce itself: the Spirit of God is never absent from His word.

(13) **In his sight.**—Still the proper subject is "the word of God"; but, as explained above, it has assumed the meaning, *God speaking and present in His word.* Touched by this word, every creature "returns of force to its own likeness"—shows itself as it is.

Opened.—Better, *exposed, laid bare.* The Greek word is peculiar (literally meaning, *to take by the neck*), and it seems impossible to determine with certainty the exact metaphor which it here presents. It is usually applied to a wrestler who by dragging back the neck overthrows his adversary: and "prostrate" has been suggested as the meaning here. Another explanation refers the word to the drawing back of a criminal's head, so as to expose his face to public gaze; but, though we read of such a custom in Latin authors, we have no proof that the Greek word was used in this sense. There seems no good reason for supposing any allusion to a sacrificial victim with head thrown back (slain, or ready to be slain).

Unto the eyes of him . . .—Rather, *unto His eyes: with Whom* (or, *and with Him*) *we have to do.* The last solemn words recall the connection of the whole passage. No thought of unbelief or disobedience escapes His eye: the first beginnings of apostasy are manifest before Him.

Verses 14—16 are the link connecting all the preceding part of the Epistle with the next great section, chaps. v.—x. 18. Following the example of Luther, Tyndale and Coverdale begin the fifth chapter here; but the connection of the three verses with what precedes is too close to justify this.

(14) All the chief points of the earlier chapters are brought together in this verse and the next:—the High Priest (chaps. ii. 17; iii. 1); His exaltation (chaps. i. 3, 4, 13; ii. 9); His divine Sonship (chaps. i.; iii. 6); His compassion towards the brethren whose lot He came to share (chap. ii. 11—18).

heavens, Jesus the Son of God, let us hold fast *our* profession. (15) For we have not an high priest which cannot be touched with the feeling of our infirmities; but was in all points tempted like as *we are, yet* without sin. (16) Let us therefore come boldly unto the throne of grace, that we may obtain mercy, and find grace to help in time of need.

Chap. iv. 14—16. Having a merciful High Priest, let us through Him draw nigh to God.

A.D. 64.

1 Or, *can reasonably bear with.*

CHAPTER V.—(1) For every high priest taken from among men is ordained for men in things *pertaining* to God, that he may offer both gifts and sacrifices for sins: (2) who can have compassion on[1] the ignorant, and on them that are out of the way; for that he himself also is compassed with infirmity. (3) And

Chap. v. 1—10. The idea of High-priesthood fulfilled in Christ, perfected through sufferings, and declared by God High Priest for ever.

That is passed into the heavens.—Rather, *that hath passed through the heavens.* As the high priest passed through the Holy Place to enter the Holy of Holies, Jesus "ascended up far above all heavens," and sat at the right hand of God. This thought is developed in chaps. viii.—x.

Our profession.—See chap. iii. 1.

(15) We cannot but note again how the power of the exhortation (especially to those immediately addressed) lay in the combination of the two thoughts—the greatness and the tender compassion of the High Priest of our confession. The two are united in the words of verse 16, "the *throne* of *grace*." (Comp. chap. viii. 1.) The beautiful rendering, "touched with the feeling of our infirmities," is due to the Genevan Testament of 1557.

But was in all points . . .—Better, *but One that hath in all points been tempted in like manner, apart from sin.* These words show the nature and the limits of this sympathy of Christ. He suffers with His people, not merely showing compassion to those who are suffering and tempted, but taking to Himself a joint feeling of their weaknesses. He can do this because He has passed through trial, has Himself been tempted. In speaking of "weaknesses" the writer uses a word applicable both to the people and to their Lord, who was "crucified through weakness" (2 Cor. xiii. 4). Its meaning must not be limited to the region of pain and bodily suffering: whatever belongs to the necessary limitations of that human nature which He assumed is included. As He learned His obedience from sufferings (chap. v. 8), He gained His knowledge of the help we need in that "Himself took our weaknesses" (Matt. viii. 17), and was Himself tempted in like manner, save that in Him sin had no place (chap. vii. 26). These last words supply the limit to the thought of weakness and temptation as applied to our High Priest. Not only was the temptation fruitless in *leading to* sin (this is implied here, but only as a part or a result of another truth), but in the widest sense He could say, "The prince of this world cometh and hath nothing in Me" (John xiv. 30). "Was tempted in all points in like manner," are words which must not be over-pressed; but the essential principles of temptation may be traced in those with which Jesus was assailed. (Comp. John xxi. 25.)

(16) **Obtain mercy.**—The real meaning is, *receive compassion* (chap. ii. 17) in our weakness and trials. The thought of obtaining *mercy* for guilt is not in these words, taken by themselves; but "grace" meets every need. If the last verse brought evidence that our High Priest has perfect knowledge of the help required, this gives the assurance that the help shall be given as needed, and in the time of need.

V.

With this chapter begins the longest and most important division of the Epistle, extending (with one break, chaps. v. 11—vi. 20) as far as chap. x. 18. The general subject is the nature of the High Priesthood of our Lord.

Verses 1—10 link themselves with the last words of the fourth chapter. The thoughts which have been briefly expressed in verses 14, 15, and on which verse 16 rests, are resumed, and in this section fully developed. Hence chap. iv. 16 is connected both with what precedes (by "therefore") and with the present chapter (by "For"): "For as every human high priest shares the nature of those on behalf of whom he appears before God, and thus can be compassionate towards them, and, moreover, can only receive his appointment from God; so Christ is God-appointed, He has learnt His obedience through sufferings, and, thus made perfect, is declared by God High Priest for ever."

(1) **Taken.**—Rather, *being taken, since he is taken,* from among men.

Gifts and sacrifices.—The former is in itself perfectly general; but when thus contrasted with "sacrifices" it denotes the "unbloody offerings" of the Law. On the Day of Atonement (which, as we shall see, is almost always in the writer's thoughts as he refers to the functions of the high priest) the "offerings" would consist of the incense and of the "meat-offerings" connected with the burnt-sacrifices for the day. On that day all offerings, as well as all sacrifices, had relation to "sins."

(2) **Who can have compassion.**—Rather, *as one who can deal gently with* (or, more strictly, *feel gently towards*) *the ignorant and erring, because . . .* Either apathy or undue severity in regard to transgression would disqualify this representative of men to God. It cannot be said that sin is mildly designated here, since the words so closely resemble those which occur in chap. iii. 10; still the language is so chosen as to exclude sinning "with a high hand."

(3) To be closely joined with verse 2: "Is compassed with infirmity, and by reason thereof is bound . . ." The law of the Day of Atonement required a sin-offering of a bullock and a burnt-offering of a ram for the high priest himself, and for the congregation a sin-offering of two he-goats and a burnt-offering of a ram. Over his own sin-offering the high priest made confession of sins, first for himself and his household, then for the priests; over the goat sent into the wilderness the sins of the people were confessed.

by reason hereof he ought, as for
the people, so also for himself, to
offer for sins. (4) And no man taketh
this honour unto himself, but he that
is called of God, as *was* Aaron. (5) So
also Christ glorified not himself to be
made an high priest; but he that said
unto him, Thou art my Son, to day
have I begotten thee. (6) As he saith
also in another *place*, Thou *art* a priest
for ever after the order of Melchisedec.
(7) Who in the days of his flesh, when he
had offered up prayers and supplications
with strong crying and tears unto him
that was able to save him from death,
and was heard in that he feared;[1]
(8) though he were a Son, yet learned
he obedience by the things which he
suffered; (9) and being made perfect, he
became the author of eternal salvation

[1] Or, *for his piety.*

(4) **But he that is called.**—The true reading requires, *when he is called.* "Not unto himself doth any man take the honour, but when . . ."

(5) **Christ.**—Better, *the Christ.* (See chap. iii. 14.) It is important to note that in passages of the Pentateuch where the high priest receives a special designation (usually "the priest" is sufficiently distinctive) his title is almost always "the anointed priest." Hence in the one designation, "the Christ," are united the two testimonies of Scripture which follow. He is the Anointed King (Ps. ii. 7), addressed by Jehovah as His Son (see Notes on chap. i. 2, 4, 5); by the same Jehovah He is addressed as Priest for ever after the order of one who was both priest and king (Ps. cx. 4).

(6) **Thou art a priest for ever . . .**—On Ps. cx. see the Note on chap. i. 13. The fourth verse, here quoted, is the kernel of the Psalm, and supplies the theme for a large portion of this Epistle, especially chap. vii. As the promise of 2 Sam. vii. was the prelude to the revelation of the second Psalm, the divine declaration recorded in Ex. xix. 6 may have prepared the way for the promise of Ps. cx. 4. The king of Israel was the type of the Son of David; and in the consecrated people, who, had they been faithful, would have remained the representatives of all nations before God, was dimly foreshadowed the Anointed Priest.

(7, 8) **Who in the days of his flesh . . .**—It will be observed that, of the two essential conditions mentioned in verse 2 and verse 4, the latter is first taken up in its application to Christ (verses 5, 6). This verse and the next correspond to the general thought of verses 1, 2, so far as it is applicable to "Him who knew no sin."

The following rendering will, it is believed, best show the meaning of these two important verses, and the connection of the several parts: *Who, in the days of His flesh, having with a strong cry and tears offered up prayers and supplications unto Him that was able to save Him out of death, and having been heard for His reverent fear, though He was a son, yet learned obedience by the things which He suffered.* The most noticeable change of rendering occurs at the close of the seventh verse; here the interpretation given by all the Greek Fathers, followed in most of our English versions (and in the margin of the Authorised itself), certainly deserves the preference over that which, through the influence of Calvin and Beza, found its way into the Genevan Testament, and hence into the Bishops' Bible and the translation of 1611. The word rendered "reverent fear" occurs in but one other place in the New Testament (chap. xii. 28); but the kindred verb and adjective are found in chap. xi. 7; Luke ii. 25; Acts ii. 5; viii. 2. It properly denotes, not terror, but a cautious foreseeing fear, opposed alike to rashness and to cowardice: the adjective, which is always rendered "devout," is fully explained in the Notes on Acts ii. 5. No word could be more suitable where the relation of the Son of Man to His "God and Father" is expressed; and it would be very difficult to find any other word which should be suitable to this relation and yet contain no implication of sin to be acknowledged with humility and shame. The object of the "prayers and supplications" thus heard and answered is implied in the words "unto Him that was able to save Him *out of death.*" Not "from death:" the Greek words may have that meaning, but it is not their most natural sense, as a comparison of other passages would show. The prayer, we are persuaded, was not that death might be averted, but that there might be granted deliverance out of death. This prayer was answered: His death was the beginning of His glory (chap. ii. 9). It may indeed be asked, Could such a prayer be offered by One who knew "the glory that should follow" His sufferings? In a matter so far beyond our reasoning it is most reverent to point to the mystery of another prayer (Matt. xxvi. 39) offered by Him who had often taught His disciples that He *must* be put to death (Matt. xvi. 21). Mark the striking correspondence between the petition thus understood and St. Peter's quotation of Ps. xvi. 10 (Acts ii. 24). Some of the expressions in this verse would lead us to believe that the writer's thought is resting on the Agony in the Garden; but the "strong cry" brings before us the Crucifixion (Matt. xxvii. 46, 50), and the words of Ps. xxii. 1 lie very near the thought of this verse. It does not seem necessary to decide—we may doubt whether it is possible, and whether both should not be included. The opening words, "in the days of His flesh" (comp. chap. ii. 14; John i. 14; 1 Pet. iii. 18), would certainly seem to favour this latter view. The word "offered" must not be lightly passed over. Of frequent occurrence in this Epistle, in every case except one (which is not at all in point) it has a sacrificial sense; it seems certain, therefore, that these prayers—a token of His suffering, an example of His reverent fear—are included in the sacrifice which comprised His whole life and death.

(8) **Though he were a Son.**—These words may be connected with what precedes (implying that He was heard for His reverent fear, not because, in the preeminent sense, He was God's Son); but they are still more closely joined with the following sentence, "Though He was a Son, He *learnt* His obedience by the things which He suffered." "The disposition of obedience Jesus possessed before He suffered, but the proof that this disposition existed must be shown in deed; this progress from the disposition to the deed of obedience is a practical learning of the virtue of obedience" (Lünemann). The suffering recorded in verse 7 is regarded as the culmination of His life of suffering.

(9) **And being . . .**—Rather, *and having been made perfect.* This was the mode in which He who "glorified Him to be made High Priest" (verse 5) led Him into the possession of this office. The thought of this verse and the last is closely analogous to chap. ii. 9, 10 (see Notes), and to Phil. ii. 6—13. The transition from the

unto all them that obey him; (10) called
of God an high priest after the order of
Melchisedec.
(11) Of whom we have many things
to say, and hard to be
uttered, seeing ye are dull
of hearing. (12) For when
for the time ye ought
to be teachers, ye have
need that one teach you again which
be the first principles of the oracles
of God; and are become such as
have need of milk, and not of strong
meat. (13) For every one that useth
milk *is* unskilful[1] in the word of
righteousness: for he is a babe.
(14) But strong meat belongeth to them
that are of full age,[2] *even* those who
by reason of use[3] have their senses
exercised to discern both good and
evil.

CHAPTER VI.—(1) Therefore leaving
the principles of the doctrine of Christ,[4]
let us go on unto perfection; not laying
again the foundation of repentance from

Chap. v. 11—vi. 8. Complaint of the declension of his readers' earnest warning.

A.D. 64.

1 Gr. *hath no experience.*

2 Or, *perfect.*

3 Or, *of an habit,* or, *perfection.*

4 Or, *the word of the beginning of Christ.*

---

obedience manifested by our Lord to that which must be rendered by all who seek from Him salvation, strikingly recalls verses 8 and 12 of the last-named chapter. He presents to all the model of the obedience to be rendered to Him, and through Him to the Father. "Eternal" salvation,—for He is a priest "*for ever*" (verse 6). On the connection of "salvation" with His priesthood, see the Note on chap. vii. 25.

(10) **Called.**—Rather, *addressed.* The divine words are, "Thou art a priest for ever." In the quotation from the Psalm, "priest" is now altered into "High Priest." The purport remains the same; or, rather, it is by this change of word that the meaning of the Psalm is fully expressed. This repetition of the words of verse 6 at the close of the paragraph is singularly impressive.

At this point the course of the argument is interrupted by a long digression (chaps. v. 11—vi. 20), to which the writer is led by reflection on the inability of his readers to receive the teaching which befits their Christian standing. If, however, we remember the practical aim that is predominant in the Epistle, we can hardly call this a digression, so powerfully is every portion of it made subservient to one great purpose.

(11) **Of whom.**—Or, *of which* (subject), "Christ made High Priest after the order of Melchizedek."

Hard to be uttered.—Rather, *hard of interpretation, seeing ye have become sluggish in hearing.* Their faculty of "hearing" had once been acute, and then few words and little explanation, even on such a subject as this, would have sufficed; now there has come upon them a lack of interest, and with this a want of power.

(12) **For the time.**—Taking into account the time that had elapsed since they became Christians.

Ye have need.—Literally, *ye have need that some one teach you again the rudiments of the beginning of the oracles of God* (Acts vii. 38; Rom. iii. 2; 1 Pet. iv. 11). These first rudiments, which they need to learn again (but which he himself is not about to teach), it may seem natural to identify with what the writer in chap. vi. 1 calls "the doctrine of the first principles of Christ." If, however, we examine the usage of the New Testament, of Philo, and of other writers, we shall find good reason for regarding "the oracles of God" as synonymous with the Scriptures of the Old Testament. (See verse 13.)

Of strong meat.—Better, *of solid food.* (See 1 Cor. iii. 2.)

(13) The change of expression from *having need of milk* to *partaking of milk* (that is, making it the *sole* food) is significant. Those who are addressed had lost interest in the deeper truths of Christianity, those truths which alone expressed and explained its proper nature. Their temptation apparently was towards mingling a rudimentary Christian doctrine with the teaching of the synagogue. Yielding to this they would lose all real knowledge of the very elements of Christian truth, and with this all true knowledge of the Old Testament itself. The connection between this verse and the last may probably be, *Ye have come to need milk, for —making it by choice your sole food—ye stand self-confessed as babes.*

Unskilful.—Rather, *without experience.* The "word of righteousness" evidently must signify complete, properly-developed Christian teaching. The only question is, Why is this particular designation chosen? In the Epistle to the Romans such a description would be natural (see especially Rom. i. 17; ix. 31); but "righteousness" is not the direct and manifest subject of this Epistle. Still, the expressions of which the writer makes use in chaps. x. 38 and xi. 7, together with the general similarity between his teaching and St. Paul's, go very far towards explaining his choice of this special expression as descriptive of the religion of Christ. In like manner another phrase, "law of liberty," is characteristic of St. James.

(14) **Strong meat.**—"Solid food belongs to full-grown men." If they occupied themselves with the rudiments alone, their spiritual senses could not be trained by use (or, *habit*) in distinguishing between good and evil, truth and falsehood, in the various systems of teaching which men offered as the doctrine of Christ.

VI.

(1) **Therefore.**—Since "for the time ye ought to be teachers," but have so perilously sunk down into the lower state of Christian knowledge and experience.

The principles of the doctrine.—Rather, *the doctrine of the first principles.* The margin gives the literal meaning of the Greek, *the word of the beginning.* Comp. chap. v. 12, "the rudiments of the first principles of the oracles of God."

Let us go on.—Better, *let us press onwards unto perfection.* There is an urgency in the words which is missed by the ordinary rendering. The word "perfection" (*teleiotes*) answers to that rendered "full grown" (*teleios*) in the preceding verse, and expresses maturity, fulness of growth. There the contrast is with "babes," and the whole context relates to Christian instruction—the elementary and the complete. The

dead works, and of faith toward God,
(2) of the doctrine of baptisms, and of laying on of hands, and of resurrection of the dead, and of eternal judgment.

closeness of the connection would seem to show that the same meaning must be intended here also: "Let us—I, as your teacher, leading you on with me—press on to maturity of Christian knowledge." But if what precedes makes this reference clear, the following verses show not less clearly that teaching and learning are not alone in the writer's thoughts. The relation between verses 3 and 4 proves that, as is natural, he assumes a necessary union between learning and practice: indeed, the connection between immaturity of apprehension of Christian truth and the danger of apostasy is a thought present throughout the Epistle. Hence, though the direct meaning of "leaving the doctrine of the beginning" is *ceasing to speak of* elementary truths, there is included the further thought of passing away from that region of spiritual life to which those must belong who choose the "milk" of the Christian word as their sole sustenance.

Not laying again the foundation.—Better, *a foundation.* There can be no doubt that the particulars which follow are intended to illustrate the nature of the elementary teaching which will not be taken up in this Epistle. It will be observed (1) that there is no disparagement of these subjects of teaching. They belong to the foundation; but neither teachers nor learners must occupy themselves with laying a foundation again and again. (2) That the subjects here specified are not in themselves distinctively Christian. One and all they belonged to the ancient faith, though each one became more or less completely transformed when Jesus was received as the Messiah. Hence these were literally first principles to the Hebrew Christian,—amongst the truths first taught and most readily received. We have many indications, both within and without the pages of the New Testament, that the tendency of Jewish converts was to rest satisfied with this class of truths.

Repentance from dead works.— Of "dead works" we read again in chap. ix. 14, "shall purge our conscience from dead works to serve the living God" (see Note). The meaning cannot be "works that bring death," as some have supposed; rather, works in which there is no principle of life, wrought by those who are "alienated from the life of God" (Eph. iv. 18), in whom there is not the spirit of "life in Christ Jesus." The law, indeed, promised that the man who should do "its statutes and judgments" should find life in them (Lev. xviii. 5, quoted in Gal. iii. 12); but even these works are "dead," for no man can show more than partial obedience, and the law exacts the whole. The first step toward Christianity involved the acknowledgment of this truth, and the separation by repentance from all "dead works." On the importance assigned to repentance in the Jewish creed little need be said. The teaching of the prophets (Ezek. xviii., *et al.*) is faithfully reflected in the sayings preserved in the Talmud: "The perfection of wisdom is repentance;" "Repentance obtains a respite until the Day of Atonement completes the atonement;" "Without repentance the world could not stand."

Faith toward God.— Rather, *faith upon God.* (Comp. Acts xvi. 31; Rom. iv. 5.) The Hebrew doctrine of faith connected itself closely with a cardinal passage of prophecy (Habak. ii. 4), "the just shall live by his faith;" and there is a Jewish saying that on this one precept rest "all the six hundred and thirteen commandments of the Law." (See the Note on chap. x. 38, and the *Excursus* on Rom. i. 17, Vol. II., p. 274.) This faith became new and living when the Jew believed in God *through Jesus the Christ* (John xiv. 1; 1 Pet. i. 21). It is hardly necessary to say that it is of repentance and faith as a foundation, not as belonging to later Christian experience, that the writer speaks.

(2) **Of the doctrine of baptisms.**—The meaning of these words has been much controverted. The order of the Greek has been thought to require the rendering *baptisms of doctrine* (or, *teaching*); and it has been believed that the writer in this manner seeks to characterise Christian baptism as contrasted with the Jewish lustrations. Matt. xxviii. 19, "baptising them . . . teaching them," is often quoted in favour of this view. The whole question of baptism amongst the Jews of the Apostolic age is full of difficulty, since the first references to the rite in connection with proselytes belong to a much later date. But, waiving this, we must surely regard it as most unlikely that the baptism specifically Christian would be marked as "baptism *of teaching.*" Teaching would rather be the point of resemblance than the point of contrast between the Jewish and the Christian rite. We must, therefore, adhere to the ordinary view. The word *doctrine,* or *teaching,* seems to be introduced in order to avoid the ambiguity which would lie in the words, "a foundation of repentance, faith, baptism," &c.; not a doctrine, but the repetition of a rite might seem to be intended. But what are we to understand by teaching regarding *baptisms?* Both the word itself and the use of the plural are remarkable. The word (which is not the ordinary term *baptisma,* but *baptismus*) occurs in chap. ix. 10, Mark vii. 4, in the plural, and in Col. ii. 12 in the singular; in the last of these passages it denotes Christian baptism, but in the others the ceremonial *washings* of the Jews. We must not forget the importance which of right belonged to these washings in the Levitical law, as one of the appointed modes of removing that uncleanness which excluded from every sacred place. The baptism of John attached itself to passages in the Scriptures in which this symbol was taken up by the prophets with profound spiritual application (Ezek. xxxvi., *et al.*). Both John's baptism and that of Christ, therefore, would, from the Hebrew point of view, be "washings"; and the teaching which every new convert must receive would include instruction on the symbolical purifications of the Old Covenant and the New. (See the very interesting Notes in Vol. II. on Acts xviii. 24, 25; xix. 4.)

And of laying on of hands.—This ceremony is repeatedly mentioned in the Old Testament, and also in the New. Besides the sacrificial use of the symbol, we find imposition of hands connected with blessing (Gen. xlviii. 14; Matt. xix. 13, *et al.*); with works of healing (2 Kings v. 11; Mark viii. 23; xvi. 18, *et al.*); with ordination (Num. xxvii. 18; Deut. xxxiv. 9; 1 Tim. iv. 14, *et al.*); and with the gift of the Holy Spirit (Acts viii. 17; xix. 6). In every case the figure denotes either a transfer, or the communication of a gift from (or through the medium of) the person who lays his hands upon another. Neither transfer of guilt, nor blessing, nor miracle can be in point here; nor is it conceivable that ordination could be referred to in such a context. As the passages quoted from the Acts of the Apostles

(3) And this will we do, if God permit.
(4) For *it is* impossible for those who
were once enlightened, and have tasted
of the heavenly gift, and were made
partakers of the Holy Ghost, (5) and
have tasted the good word of God, and
the powers of the world to come, (6) if
they shall fall away, to renew them

---

agree with this in closely connecting the rite with baptism, we can have little doubt that the meaning in all is substantially the same. The believers in Samaria had been baptised by Philip; when Peter and John came, they "prayed for them that they might receive the Holy Ghost; then laid they their hands on them, and they received the Holy Ghost." In the second case, which in other respects is similar (whether Paul himself baptised, or not, we are not informed), there is reference to the special gifts of the Holy Ghost which were bestowed: "they spake with tongues and prophesied." There seems no reason for believing that there was a designed connection between the imposition of hands and the bestowal of *miraculous* powers; such imposition was rather the recognised symbol of the gift of the Holy Spirit to those who were baptised in the name of the Lord Jesus, in whatever manner the Spirit might be pleased to work in those who received His influence. The early Church naturally retained the rite, making it the complement or adjunct of baptism; whilst the one symbolised the putting away of sin, the other was the emblem of the reception of new spiritual life. Historical testimonies extend as far back as Tertullian (A.D. 200): "Then the hand is laid on, calling for and inviting the Holy Spirit." To trace the relation between this imposition of hands and the later practice of confirmation would lead us beyond our limits.

The two points which remain do not require an extended notice. We know (Acts xxiii. 8) that, though the Sadducees denied that there was any resurrection of the dead (and the Alexandrian philosophy seems to have held only the immortality of the soul), yet by the most influential amongst Jewish teachers this doctrine was held and enforced, as indeed it was plainly taught in their Scriptures (Dan. xii. 2). On the nature and extent of the resurrection—whether it would be universal, and whether it would precede or follow the Messianic age—varying opinions prevailed. Nor were the Pharisees less clear in their teaching of a future "judgment," the reward of which should be "eternal" bliss for the godly, punishment for the sinners in Israel and for Israel's enemies. These doctrines, then, would place no obstacles in the way of a convert to the Christian faith. Instead of vagueness and discordant opinion he now received a clear statement of truth: the Messiah, Jesus, in whom he has placed his trust, will judge the world; and of this God has given a pledge "in that He hath raised Him from the dead" (Acts xvii. 31). It is noteworthy that, of the four particulars which are mentioned after repentance and faith, two relate to the commencement and two to "the last things" of the Christian life.

(3) **And this will we do, if God permit.**—There may be some with whom it will be impossible for him thus to press on to maturity of teaching and of Christian experience. There is a case excepted by God Himself from all efforts of the Christian teacher; in this case, though nothing can avail except the laying of a new foundation of repentance, God has appointed no agencies by which such foundation can be laid.

(4) **For it is impossible for those . . .**—The connection of thought has been already explained (verse 3); the general meaning will be examined below (verse 6). It will be seen that the greater part of this long sentence is dependent on the word "renew" in verse 6, "It is impossible to renew again unto repentance those who were once," &c.

Those who were once enlightened.—This metaphor is introduced again in chap. x. 32; neither there nor here does the context contain any notice or expansion of the figure. In that passage, however, it is applied generally to all who are addressed, and includes everything that was involved in the reception of the Christian faith. This inclusive application of the term (familiar from prophecy, from our Lord's own words, from Apostolic usage; see Acts xxvi. 18; Eph. i. 18; 1 Pet. ii. 9) throws light on the construction of the verse before us. As the words stand in the Authorised version, "enlightened" is but the first term of a series; but it is far more probable that the clauses which follow should be regarded as explanatory of the enlightenment itself: ". . . those who were once enlightened, having both tasted . . . and been made partakers . . . and tasted . . ."

Tasted of the heavenly gift.—On the first word, see the Note on chap. ii. 9. From the clear parallelism which exists between these verses and chap. ii. 3—5 we may infer that the "salvation" offered in the gospel (chap. ii. 3) is intended by this "gift." It is a gift which belongs to heaven (comp. chap. i. 14), bestowed by Him from whom has come the "heavenly calling" (chaps. iii. 1; ii. 10). The following words at once recall chap. ii. 4, "gifts (*distributions*) of the Holy Ghost."

(5) **Tasted the good word of God.**—There is a change of construction in the Greek which suggests that the words rather mean, *tasted that God's word is good*,—tasted the excellence of God's word, and of the powers, &c. God's word was "spoken through the Lord" (chap. ii. 3); the Hebrew Christians had heard and received this word, and had proved for themselves its excellence. (Comp. 1 Pet. ii. 3.)

Powers of the world to come.—Literally, *powers of a coming* (or, *future*) *age*. As has been before remarked, the last word is different from that which we find in chap. ii. 5, the one relating to time, the other to the world as inhabited by man. Perhaps we may say that this is the only difference; the same *future* is contemplated in both places, namely, the age of the Messianic reign. We have seen (see chap. i. 2) that in the earliest days of the Church little account was taken of the period separating the pre-Christian age from that of the full manifestation of the kingdom of God; the "powers" received from God by those who believed (chap. ii. 4) belonged to no earthly state, but were as truly anticipations of a future age of glory as was the "heavenly gift" an anticipation of the "heavenly fatherland" (chap. xi. 16).

(6) **If they shall fall away.**—Rather, *and* (*then*) *fell away*. There is no doubt that the ordinary translation is altogether incorrect, the Greek admitting of one rendering only. At the same time, the suspicion sometimes expressed that this is one of the (very few) instances in which our translators have been misled by dogmatic bias seems altogether unfounded. On tracing back the translation we find it due, not to the Genevan versions, in which the influence of Calvin and Beza is predominant, but to Erasmus, Luther, and Tyndale.

again unto repentance; seeing they crucify to themselves the Son of God afresh, and put *him* to an open shame.
(7) For the earth which drinketh in the rain that cometh oft upon it, and bringeth forth herbs meet for them by[1] whom it is dressed, receiveth blessing from God:
(8) but that which beareth thorns and briars *is* rejected, and *is* nigh unto cursing; whose end *is* to be burned.
(9) But, beloved, we are persuaded better things of you, and things that accompany salvation, though we thus speak.
(10) For God *is* not unrighteous to forget your work and labour of love,

Chap. vi. 9—12. His hope of better things.

1 Or, *for.*

The contrast with the preceding description is presented in the fewest possible words. The successive clauses have shown that all the marks of the divine working in and with His word (chap. ii. 4) have been found in these men, who, notwithstanding, "fell away."

To renew them again.—A second time to make "the old" into a "new man." In this place "renew" is distinctly used in reference to the action of man. Similarly, by the side of 1 Pet. i. 3, "God . . . who hath begotten us," we may set St. Paul's words to the Corinthians, "In Christ Jesus I have begotten you;" so also St. Paul can say, "Let us cleanse ourselves from all filthiness of the flesh and spirit;" and St. James can speak of a man's saving a soul from death. In these and the many other examples of a similar kind there is no thought of human power acting by itself, but of the human appropriation of divine power, in accordance with the laws of the kingdom of God. The verse before us is often read as an assertion that men who have thus fallen *cannot be renewed;* and therefore it is the more necessary to lay stress on the simple meaning of the words, as relating neither to the absolute power of God, nor to the efforts of the Christian teacher in unassisted human strength, but to the economy of God's spiritual kingdom, in which Christ's servants achieve every great result by claiming and obtaining the "fellow-working" of their Lord.

Seeing they crucify.—The apostasy was indicated by a single word; these added clauses describe the depth of the fall, whilst they explain the futility of all effort towards recovering the fallen. Both the writer and his readers knew well what was involved in "falling away" in such a case as this. To go back to Judaism implied an acceptance of all that Jews had said and done against the Son of God, a return to the bitter hate cherished by the falling nation against the Crucified, a repetition in spirit of all that Pharisees had done, and without the palliation of ignorance; for the highest evidence for Christianity—that of true and deep Christian experience—had been given to them. Again, the words used clearly describe a continuing state. Not the punishment for a past act, but the hopelessness of an existing state, is brought before us here. It is therefore of those who, with a distinct conviction of the divine mission of Jesus, have deliberately joined His foes, unite in denouncing Him as a "deceiver" (Matt. xxvii. 63), rejoice in His shame, and thus "for themselves crucify a second time the Son of God," that the writer says, "It is impossible to renew them again unto repentance."

That this impossibility relates to the action of man is shown very clearly by the writer's words in verse 3, "This will we do if God permit; . . . . *for* it is impossible." He is ready to lead his readers on with him—unless, indeed, he is addressing any whom no man can thus lead. In that case the means which God has appointed have no application; such wilful and persistent hardening of heart must be left with Him.

The perplexity and trouble of mind to which these verses have given rise will furnish an apology for the length of these remarks. It is a true Christian instinct that has protested against the misuse of this passage by men who have doubted whether those who, after receiving the knowledge of the truth, fall under temptation, can again receive forgiveness; but the difficulty has been met by hazardous expedients. Some have denied that verses 4 and 5 necessarily describe real Christian experience. By others it has been held that "impossible" was not intended to express more than the great difficulty of the attempt; others, again, have believed that in verse 6 the writer brings before us a supposed case only, one that cannot really occur. The passage, together with chap. x. 26—29, Matt. xii. 32, 1 John v. 16 (see the Notes), occupied an important place in early controversies, as those of the Montanists and Novatians, who refused absolution to those who, after baptism—or, in the language of the early Church, after "illumination" (verse 4)—fell into heinous sin.

(7) **For the earth.**—Rather, *For land which has drunk in.* Land which not only receives but also drinks in abundance of rain (Deut. xi. 11), in such a climate as is here thought of, must either "bring forth herbage" or be condemned as irretrievably barren.

By whom it is dressed.—Rather, *for whom it is also tilled.* This clause is added to show that nothing is wanting on the part of the owner or of the tillers of the land.

Receiveth blessing from God.—Receives as a reward a share in the blessing which God pronounces on the fruitful earth, resulting in increased fertility (Gen. xxvii. 27; xlix. 25; Deut. xxxiii. 13). In the application of the parable, God is the owner of the land, men the tillers; men also are "God's field" (1 Cor. iii. 9), who bring forth fruit unto God.

(8) **But that which beareth.**—Rather, *But if it bear thorns and briars it is rejected.* We are told that the presence of briars (*i.e.,* caltrops) is a sure evidence of a poor soil, on which labour will be wasted. The words are partially a quotation from Gen. iii. 18. The change of translation here is important; if that very land, which has drunk in the abundant rain and has received careful culture still prove unfruitful, it is rejected. Man can do no more; and the curse of God is "near"; its end is "for burning." The explanation of the last words is probably found in Deut. xxix. 23, which speaks of the land of Sodom which God overthrew, which "is brimstone and salt and burning." The connection between these two verses and the preceding passages is obvious. In the case of the apostates there described, man is helpless; God's curse is near. But, as Chrysostom says, in this very word there is mercy; "the end" is not yet come.

(9) **Better things.**—Literally, *the better things;* that is, the alternative spoken of in verse 7. He has not written in despair, but for warning only; believing that to them belongs, not the state which is "nigh unto a curse," but that which borders on salvation (chap. v. 9).

(10) In expressing the ground of his hope he does

which ye have shewed toward his name,
in that ye have ministered to the saints,
and do minister. (11) And we desire that
every one of you do shew the same
diligence to the full assurance of hope
unto the end: (12) that ye be not sloth-
ful, but followers of them who through
faith and patience inherit the promises.

Chap. vi. 13—20. Encouragement. The promise and oath of God.

(13) For when God made
promise to Abraham, be-
cause he could swear by
no greater, he sware by
himself, (14) saying, Surely blessing I will
bless thee, and multiplying I will multi-
ply thee. (15) And so, after he had patiently
endured, he obtained the promise. (16) For
men verily swear by the greater: and an
oath for confirmation *is* to them an end
of all strife. (17) Wherein God, willing
more abundantly to shew unto the heirs
of promise the immutability of his coun-
sel, confirmed *it* by an oath:[1] (18) that by
two immutable things, in which *it was*
impossible for God to lie, we might have
a strong consolation, who have fled for
refuge to lay hold upon the hope set

[1] Gr. *interposed himself by an oath.*

---

not directly say, "For I have heard of your fruitfulness;" he implies this, and then, in accordance with the parable of verse 7, he declares that God will surely bestow the promised reward. Herein lies his hope. Man's work cannot in itself merit reward from God, but (1 John i. 9) the righteous God cannot neglect His own promise and law that such works shall receive reward.

Your work and labour of love.—The best MSS. omit "labour"; so that the words run thus: *to forget your work, and the love which ye showed toward His name.* The "fruit" consisted in brotherly love, but it was offered *unto God* (verse 7); the bond of brotherhood was the joint relation to "His name" (chap. ii. 10). With the last words compare Rom. xv. 26, 31.

(11) **Full assurance.**—Rather, *fulness* (full productiveness) *of hope* (chap. x. 22). His desire is that the zeal which they have manifested in works of love may be directed toward the attainment of the full harvest of Christian hope—may be shown until the very end (chap. iii. 6, 14).

(12) **That ye be not slothful.**—Rather, *that ye become not sluggish.* The same word is used as in chap. v. 11, there applied to apprehension of truth, here to the Christian hope and life; if the truth be not welcomed, there will be no vigour in the life.

Followers.—Better, *imitators.* (Comp. chap. xiii. 7; 1 Cor. xi. 1, *et al.*). They are not the first to whom "hope" has been given, and who have needed zeal that they might not fail of their hope. As in chap. xi. the writer appeals to precursors of *faith*, so here of *hope*; to men who, having lived in hope, passed to the actual possession of the promised blessings by means of faith (which accepted and clung to the promise) and patience. The last word is not that which occurs in the similar exhortation in chap. x. 36. That is a brave endurance; this is the word usually rendered "long-suffering," which here and in Jas. v. 7 signifies *patient waiting.*

(13) The connection seems to be this: "You, like them, have promises—promises to which God has given all possible certainty; you, like them, can attain the fulfilment only through faith and patient waiting."

For when God made promise.—It is better to follow the words literally, *For when to Abraham God had made promise.* Abraham is chosen for special mention as the most illustrious example of those who "inherit the promises" (comp. John viii. 58); also because (1) the assurance given to him was confirmed by oath; and (2) in it lay included the promise of the Christ. The promises made to Abraham were essentially one, with various parts progressively fulfilled. It seems likely that, though the next verse is quoted *from* Gen. xxii. 17, the writer also has in mind ("*had* promised") Gen. xii. 3, and especially Gen. xv.

(14) **Saying.**—The words of the oath itself, "By myself have I sworn, saith the Lord" (Gen. xxii. 16), are not repeated, because they are almost identical with the writer's own words introducing the citation (verse 13). It will be observed that one change is made—in the last word; for in Genesis we read, "I will multiply *thy seed.*" The alteration may be made for brevity, as the quotation is abridged; but it will be seen that the effect of it is to direct greater attention to the first words, and to fix the thought on the blessing promised to Abraham himself.

(15) **And so, after he had patiently endured.**—Better, *and thus* (thus being in possession of the promise and the oath of God), *having patiently waited* (verse 12) *he obtained the promise*—the promised gift. Though some portions of the promise received a partial accomplishment during Abraham's life, it is not this that the writer has in view. (See verse 12, and chap. xi. 13.)

(16) **And an oath for confirmation.**—Rather, *and of every dispute in their case the oath is an end* (is final) *to settle the matter.*

(17) **Wherein.**—Since this is the case.

Of promise.—Rather, *of the promise.* The promise made to Abraham was substantially and really (see verse 13) that which embraced all Messianic hope; of this promise not Abraham's sons only, but all "they which are of faith" (Gal. iii. 7, 29), Abraham's spiritual seed, are the heirs. In an Epistle so distinctly Pauline there can be no doubt as to this interpretation.

Confirmed it by an oath.—Literally, *mediated with an oath.* When a man confirms a promise or declaration to another by solemn appeal to God, between the two God is Mediator. Condescending to man's weakness, that the certainty may be "more abundant," God thus confirms His word, at once the Promiser and the Mediator: God the Promiser (if we may so speak) makes appeal to God the Hearer and Witness of the oath. We cannot doubt, as we read this whole passage, that there is a special reason for the emphasis thus laid on God's *oath* to Abraham. The writer dwells on this confirmation of the divine word of promise, not merely because it is the first recorded in sacred history, but because he has in thought the declaration of Ps. cx. 4. To this as yet he makes no reference; though he has quoted from the verse repeatedly, it has been without mention of the divine oath: but throughout the section before us he is preparing the way for his later argument in chap. vii. 21.

(18) **Two immutable things.**—The promise and the oath.

before us: (19) which *hope* we have as an anchor of the soul, both sure and stedfast, and which entereth into that within the veil; (20) whither the forerunner is for us entered, *even* Jesus, made an high priest for ever after the order of Melchisedec.

CHAPTER VII.—(1) For this Melchisedec, king of Salem, priest of the most high God, who met Abraham returning from the slaughter of the kings, and blessed him; (2) to whom also Abraham gave a tenth part of all; first being by interpretation King of righteousness, and after that also King of Salem, which is, King of peace; (3) without father, without mother,

A.D. 64.

Chap. vii. 1—28. Jesus High Priest after the order of Melchizedek.

Consolation.—Rather, *encouragement.* For us, rather than for Abraham alone, was the encouragement designed; for us, who (as men in danger of their lives flee to the sanctuary) "fled for refuge to lay hold upon the hope set before us" in the promise. Up to this point we read of what God has done; here of what must be done by man. The *laying hold* expresses the "faith," and implies the "patient waiting" (verse 12); by it we become true "heirs of the promise" (verse 17).

(19) **Which hope we have as an anchor of the soul.**—A beautiful image, introduced for a moment only to set forth the security of the soul, though tossed by the waves of trouble. This symbol of hope, so familiar to us in Christian art, is not mentioned in the Old Testament, but is found in Greek proverbial sayings, and (it is said) appears on ancient coins.

Both sure and stedfast.—These words and the following *may*, indeed, form part of the figure; but more probably relate to the hope itself—a hope unfailing, firm, which entereth where no human sight can follow, even into the Most Holy Place, into heaven itself. The hope becomes personified, that the reader's thought may be led to Him who is Himself our hope.

(20) **Whither the forerunner.**—Rather, *Whither, as forerunner, Jesus entered for us, having become High Priest after the order of Melchizedek for ever.* The Jewish high priest entered the Holiest Place by himself—a representative but not a leader. Jesus has entered the true sanctuary (chap. ix. 24) that He may give His people entrance there (chap. x. 19; John xiv. 2, 3). With this renewed mention of the great high-priestly act (chap. iv. 14), the writer returns to the words of Scripture on which he was about to dwell (chap. v. 10), when the painful thought of the unpreparedness of his readers for higher Christian teaching forced itself upon his mind. In this verse the order of the words taken from the Psalm is changed; in the last words "for ever" is declared with unequalled impressiveness the permanence of our Christian hope.

VII.

Jesus the High Priest after the Order of Melchizedek.

(1) **For this Melchisedec.**—The sentence is completed in the last words of verse 3, . . . "abideth a priest continually;" the connection with the last chapter, therefore, is very clear. Of Melchizedek we know nothing beyond what we learn from the brief narrative of Gen. xiv. A Jewish legend, preserved in the later Targums on the Pentateuch, but not in the Targum of Onkelos, identifies him with the patriarch Shem; and many conjectures of a later date (stimulated by the remarkable language of these verses) have been far wilder in their extravagance. It may be that the result of these speculations has been to invest this chapter with a mystery which does not belong to it. The object of the writer is, in reality, very simple—to deal with the question, What is the import of the divine utterance that David's Lord is a "Priest for ever after the order of Melchizedek"? Not to take up the history of Melchizedek and allegorise each part, but to point out the full meaning of the comparison made in the prophecy, which declares the priesthood of the future King to be "after the order of Melchizedek—*i.e.,* to be such as the priesthood of Melchizedek typically set forth. The first part of this sentence (verses 1 and 2, as far as " . . . tenth part of all") enumerates the known facts of the history of Melchizedek; the following clauses are occupied with the interpretation of the history, and with inferences from it. Of the facts recorded in Genesis none are passed over, except the gift of bread and wine; the blessing also is mentioned in general terms only. The language of the LXX. is, as a rule, closely followed throughout.

King of Salem.—Jewish tradition affirms strongly that this Salem occupied the site on which Jerusalem afterwards stood; and certainly Salem is a poetic name of Jerusalem (Ps. lxxvi. 2). This tradition, found in Josephus and in the earliest of the Targums, agrees well with the circumstances of the narrative as far as we can follow them, and seems to deserve acceptance. Jerome maintained that Salem was situated near Scythopolis, where in his day were pointed out ruins of "Melchizedek's palace." Another tradition (probably of Samaritan origin) makes Mount Gerizim the place of meeting, in which case the city of Melchizedek would probably be near Shechem.

The most high God.—A title characteristic of the narrative (Gen. xiv. 18—20, 22). Melchizedek is the first who in Scripture is spoken of as priest, and the name is given without explanation. As in the earliest times this office was held by the head of a family (Job i.), it is not remarkable to find a union of regal and sacerdotal functions in the same man.

Returning from the slaughter.—Rather, *from the smiting,* or *defeat.* According to the narrative in Genesis the meeting took place "after Abraham had returned" from the defeat of the king; but probably the meaning does not differ from that here given.

(2) **Gave a tenth part.**—Literally, *divided a tenth.* This point is fully treated of in verses 4—9.

King of righteousness.—Josephus notes the significance of this name: "The first founder of Jerusalem was a chief of the Canaanites, who in our tongue is called Righteous King; for indeed such he was." Philo also interprets King of Salem as "King of Peace." The special interest of these titles for the writer lies in the application to Jesus the Messiah. (See chap. i. 8, 9; Isa. ix. 6, 7; xxxii. 1; Jer. xxiii. 5, 6; Zech. ix. 9; Eph. ii. 14.) On this, as obvious to every Christian reader, he does not further dwell.

(3) **Without father, without mother, without descent.**—The last words. "without descent" (or rather, *without genealogy*), throw light on the meaning

without descent,[1] having neither begin-
ning of days, nor end of life; but made
like unto the Son of God; abideth a
priest continually. (4) Now consider
how great this man *was,* unto whom
even the patriarch Abraham gave the
tenth of the spoils. (5) And verily they
that are of the sons of Levi, who receive
the office of the priesthood, have a com-
mandment to take tithes of the people
according to the law, that is, of their
brethren, though they come out of the
loins of Abraham: (6) but he whose
descent[2] is not counted from them re-
ceived tithes of Abraham, and blessed
him that had the promises. (7) And
without all contradiction the less is
blessed of the better. (8) And here men
that die receive tithes; but there he
receiveth them, of whom it is witnessed

1 Gr. *without pedigree.*

2 Or, *pedigree.*

---

of those which precede. Not because we find no mention of the parents of Melchizedek is he thus spoken of as fatherless and motherless, but because he is suddenly introduced as priest, without any token whatever that he held the office by right of genealogy, the only claim familiar to Hebrew readers. It is not necessary to adduce proof of the care with which inquiry was made into the parentage of the Jewish priests (Neh. vii. 64): in their marriages they were subject to strict restraints (Lev. xxi. 13, 14); their statement of pedigree (in which was given the name not of father only, but also of every mother) must be complete, ascending to Aaron, and containing no doubtful link. He who is a priest "like Melchizedek" holds a priesthood that rests on no such rights or claims. The words that follow are of similar character. No commencement and no close of priestly position or function are recorded in the sacred history. As the Scripture is silent as to his reception of the office, so also as to any transmission of it to another. In these respects "made like (as a divinely ordained type) unto the Son of God," he bears perpetually the character of priest.

There have from the first been many who have been dissatisfied with such an explanation of these remarkable words, and have understood them to ascribe to Melchizedek a mysterious and superhuman existence and character. It has been maintained that he was the Son of God Himself, or the Holy Spirit—an angel or a Power of God. The last tenet was the distinguishing mark of a sect bearing the name of Melchizedekians in the third century. The feeling that the most startling of the expressions here used must surely be intended to point to more than the *silence* of Scripture on certain points, is not at all unnatural; but perhaps it is not too much to say that every such difficulty is removed by the consideration that here the writer is simply analysing the thought of the inspired Psalmist. Such an oracle as that of Ps. cx. 4 must yield up to him its full significance. The divine words are not to be measured by the meaning which man may at first assign to them. The true import of the prophecy which declared that the future priesthood would bear the likeness of Melchizedek's can only be known when all the characteristics of that priesthood have been traced. The narrative of Genesis was the basis of the prophecy; all that the history presented was taken up in the Psalm.

(4) **How great this man was.**—Better, *is:* the greatness abides, set forth in the words of Scripture. In the rest of the verse (where the best MSS. omit the word "even") it is well to follow the literal rendering, *unto whom Abraham gave a tenth out of the chief spoils—(Abraham) the patriarch.* "He gave him tithes of all" (Gen. xiv. 20), but the tenth was selected from the choicest part of the spoils. "Patriarch" is a word used in the LXX. (in Chronicles only) for the head of a family or chief of a clan. In the New Testament it is used of David in Acts ii. 29, and twice in Acts vii. of Jacob's sons.

The next verse deals with the same subject, but under a new aspect. Here the thought is, Melchizedek received tithes even from Abraham the patriarch; there, He has been thus honoured, though no enactment of law invested him with superior rights.

(5) **They that are of the sons.**—Rather, *those of the sons of Levi that receive,* &c. There is an apparent difficulty here. The priests, it is urged, did not receive tithes from the people; the tithe was paid to the Levites, and but the tenth part of this tithe fell to the lot of the priests. Two considerations seem entirely to remove this difficulty. (1) The question is not one of emolument, but of position. The authority to exact tithes was in strictness vested in the priests, the supreme guardians of the laws relating to all religious duties and observances, and the Levites were but their assistants. That the priests received for their own use but a part of the tribute paid by the nation is a matter of no moment here. (2) The Levites themselves paid tithes to the priests, who therefore stood alone in receiving tithes but paying none. It is the positive ordinance of the law, and nothing but this, that raises brethren above brethren, and gives to the priest this claim upon men who would otherwise be on an equality with himself through common descent from Abraham.

(6) **Whose descent.** — Better, *whose genealogy* (verse 3).

Received tithes.—Rather, *hath taken tithes of Abraham, and hath blessed him that hath the promises.* In Melchizedek we see a man who, though no law gave him pre-eminence, takes tithes of Abraham, and therefore appears in Scripture as holding a position of inherent and acknowledged superiority. This superiority is not dwelt upon, for the same thought will be presented still more strikingly in connection with the *blessing* (verse 8). "Hath taken tithes," "hath blessed:" here, as in many other passages, the writer refers to facts recorded in Scripture not as belonging to the past, but as they now stand before us in the unchanging and ever present word of God.

(7) **And without all contradiction.**—Better, *but without any dispute.* Two parts of the argument are specified in this verse and verse 6. Melchizedek has blessed Abraham; but certainly (in every such act of blessing as is here contemplated) it is the less that is blessed by the greater. The conclusion, that Melchizedek in this act appears as Abraham's superior, it did not seem necessary to express.

(8) "Here," under the Levitical economy, dying men receive the various tithes. Men enter by birth into a state with which this right is associated, and by death again pass out of it. No special significance, therefore, attaches to the men themselves. "There," in the history

that he liveth. (9) And as I may so
say, Levi also, who receiveth tithes,
payed tithes in Abraham. (10) For he
was yet in the loins of his father, when
Melchisedec met him. (11) If therefore
perfection were by the Levitical priesthood, (for under it the people received the law,) what further need *was there* that another priest should rise after the order of Melchisedec, and not be called after the order of Aaron? (12) For the
priesthood being changed, there is made of necessity a change also of the law.
(13) For he of whom these things are spoken pertaineth to another tribe, of which no man gave attendance at the altar. (14) For *it is* evident that our Lord sprang out of Juda; of which tribe Moses spake nothing concerning priesthood. (15) And it is yet far more evident: for that after the similitude of Melchisedec there ariseth another priest, (16) who is made, not after the law of a carnal commandment, but after

---

now considered, one (receives tithes) of whom the Scripture simply witnesses that he lives. The narrative of Genesis gives no other basis for his priesthood than the mere fact of his life. What he holds, he holds by *personal* right.

(9) **And as I may so say.**—Or, *so to speak:* an apologetic mode of introducing an expression which might seem strange. In the thought itself there is no real difficulty, if we are careful to take into account the principle which prevailed throughout, that pre-eminence depended upon descent alone. Had Judah possessed an inherent superiority over his brother Levi, the descendants of Judah (in such a system as is here before us) might have claimed the like pre-eminence over the descendants of Levi. "Through Abraham even Levi, who receiveth tithes, hath payed tithes." The descendants of Abraham cannot but occupy a lower position in presence of one who appears as Abraham's superior.

(11) The connection of thought may be given thus:—It has been shown that the position of Melchizedek towards Abraham involves of necessity his superiority to Abraham, to Levi also and his descendants, so that "the order of Melchizedek" is altogether different from, and higher than, "the order of Aaron." This being so, how could this other priesthood take the place of the Levitical if this latter had answered its full purpose?

Perfection.—Literally, *the making perfect*—the full accomplishment of the essential aim of priesthood, in bringing men "near to God."

Received.—The better reading is *hath received.*—The object of this parenthesis is to point out the intimate relation between the Law and the priesthood: "I speak of the Levitical priesthood, for it is on the basis of this that the Law given to the people rests."

Another priest.—That is (as the Greek implies), *a priest of a different kind* (verses 13, 15). The question is equivalent to a strong denial: there could be no such need.

(12) This verse connects itself with the parenthesis in verse 11. "For if the priesthood is changed there takes place also of necessity a change of law." It is no light matter to speak of the order of Aaron as set aside: this carries with it a change of law.

(13) In verse 11 the "other priest" is spoken of as not connected with Aaron; verse 12 is interposed to show the serious significance of such a fact; here the assertion of verse 11 is substantiated—not, however, from the words of the Psalm, but from their fulfilment in Jesus.

Pertaineth.—Literally, *hath partaken of:* the same word is used in chap. ii. 14, "He also . . . . took part of the same."

Another tribe, of which no man gave . . .—Better, *a different tribe, from which no man hath given attendance at the altar.* In comparison with Levi every tribe was not merely "another," but essentially, in regard to the subject before us "a *different* tribe."

(14) **Evident.**—That is to say, manifest before the eyes of all.

Sprang.—Better, *hath arisen out of Judah.* In every other place in the New Testament this word is applied to the rising of the sun, the light, the day-star (2 Pet. i. 19), or the clouds (Luke xii. 54); and in the prophecies of Num. xxiv. 17 and Mal. iv. 2 the same word is used. On the other hand, the word also denotes the springing up of plants (Isa. xliv. 4; Ezek. xvii. 6), and a word closely connected with it occurs in the LXX. in the Messianic prophecy of "the Branch" (Jer. xxiii. 5; Zech. iii. 8). The latter meaning seems much more suitable here.

(15, 16) **And it is.**—That which is "yet far more evident" is the proposition of the preceding verses, viz., the failure of the Levitical priesthood to bring "perfection" (verse 11), a failure placed beyond doubt by the change of priesthood (verses 13, 14). "And what we are speaking of is yet more abundantly evident if after the likeness of Melchizedek there ariseth a different priest, who hath been made (priest) not according to a law of a carnal commandment, but according to power of indissoluble life." Hitherto, in verses 12—14, the thought has rested on what is *given up,*—viz., the priesthood of Aaron, set aside by the words of prophecy (Ps. cx. 4); and so far as these three verses are concerned, nothing more might be intended than the transference of the priesthood to *another line of men.* Far more striking will the proof appear, when we look on the other side, and observe what is *brought in*—a priesthood like Melchizedek's, resting not on mere positive enactment, but assumed by inherent power, by right of "life" (verse 8).

(16) **A carnal commandment.**—Literally (according to the true reading of the Greek), *a commandment of flesh:* one that is limited to the sphere of man's nature of flesh. As such, it is bound up with distinctions of race and tribe and family; it is limited by human infirmity and the changes wrought by sickness and death; what it accomplishes is the purifying of the flesh; in its own nature it is temporary, and may be set aside. (See chap. ix. 10, 13.) In contrast to the enactment is placed an essential right, possessed by Him of whom Melchizedek was the type: in contrast to all that is temporary and limited is placed an indissoluble life. Because He lives—in virtue of what He *is*—He is Priest: in virtue of an *endless* life He is priest *for ever.*

the power of an endless life. (17) For he
testifieth, Thou *art* a priest for ever
after the order of Melchisedec. (18) For
there is verily a disannulling of the
commandment going before for the
weakness and unprofitableness thereof.
(19) For the law made nothing perfect,
but the bringing in[1] of a better hope
did; by the which we draw nigh unto
God. (20) And inasmuch as not without
an oath *he was made priest:* (21) (for
those priests were made without an
oath;[2] but this with an oath by him
that said unto him, The Lord sware and
will not repent, Thou *art* a priest for ever
after the order of Melchisedec:[a]) (22) by

2 Or, *without swearing of an oath.*

a Ps. 110. 4.

1 Or, *but it was the bringing in.*

---

(17) **For he testifieth.**—A slight change of reading makes the sense clearer: "For witness is borne to him"—as to this "power" of indissoluble life—in the words of the prophecy itself.

(18, 19) The intimate connection between these two verses is obscured by the ordinary translation. They point out with greater fulness and clearness what is involved in the statement of verse 16. "For there is an annulling of a preceding commandment, because of its weakness and unprofitableness (for the Law made nothing perfect), and a bringing in thereupon of a better hope, by which we draw nigh unto God." (It must be borne in mind throughout that by the "commandment" is meant the ordinance *which created the Levitical priesthood,* not the Law in general.) That Jesus was not made Priest according to a law of a carnal commandment (verse 16) involves the annulling of that commandment; in His becoming Priest according to a power of indissoluble life is involved the introduction of a better hope. This is the general meaning, but each division of the thought is expanded. The appointment of a different priest by the very authority on which the former commandment rested, the divine decree, showed that commandment to be of force no longer: as we have already seen (verse 11), this is because the commandment is weak and unprofitable—because the priesthood it creates cannot attain the end of its institution, which is to bring men into fellowship with God. The parenthesis, "for the Law made nothing perfect," points out that the weakness just spoken of corresponds to that imperfection which confessedly belongs to the earlier dispensation: even the Jew (who would have accounted a change of priestly line impossible) expected perfection only when Messiah should have appeared. When the earlier commandment is annulled, in its place there is brought in a better hope. The "better hope" stands connected with the "better covenant" (verse 22) and the "better promises" (chap. viii. 6). "And by this (better hope) we draw nigh unto God." The end of the priesthood therefore is attained. (See verse 11.) In the Law (Lev. x. 3) the priests are "those who come nigh unto God," that is, in the service of the sanctuary: with a nobler meaning this name shall now belong to all God's people.

(20) This and the next two verses constitute one sentence, the third verse answering to the first, and verse 21 being parenthetical. Hitherto no reference has been made to the remarkable opening of Ps. cx. 4, so often quoted: these three verses are occupied with the thought of the oath—or rather (for a very uncommon word is used, one that answers well to the importance of the thought) the "swearing of an oath." This is a further illustration of the words of verse 15, "a different priest."

He was made priest.—Some supplement is needed to give clearness to the English sentence; but one of general meaning, such as "all this was done," will best answer the purpose.

(21) **For those priests.**—Rather, *For they indeed have been made priests without an oath.*

By him that said unto him.—Better, *by* (or, *through*) *Him that saith of Him.* The last five words of the verse are absent from the best authorities: they were not needed for this part of the argument, and are therefore omitted from the quotation. All that has been said in chap vi. (verses 13—18) on confirmation by oath must be brought in here (see Notes on chap. vi. 16, 17): the words of the Psalm are really words of promise, and the "more abundant encouragement" is given us by means of the oath that shall never be reversed.

(22) **By so much was Jesus made.**—Better, *by so much also hath Jesus become surety of a better covenant.* The form of the sentence recalls chap. i. 4. As the priest whose appointment is confirmed by the oath of God is raised above all former priests, in the same proportion is the covenant of which Jesus is surety higher, better, than the former covenant. For the "better hope" of verse 19 we now read "better covenant"; the new idea is not different in substance, but is more definite and clear. The very promise of the "other priest" brought with it a "better hope"; the recollection of the divine oath is fitly succeeded by the mention of a "covenant."

This is the first occurrence in this Epistle of a very interesting word (*diathēkē*) which hereafter will occupy an important place in the argument. Throughout the Greek translation of the Old Testament it is used to represent a Hebrew word which is (more than 200 times) rightly rendered *covenant* in our version; and, like the Hebrew word, it is applied both to mutual agreements between man and man, and to "covenants" or engagements into which God enters in regard to man. In classical writers *diathēkē* commonly denotes a *testament;* and hence in the old Latin translation of the Scriptures *testamentum* became the common rendering of the word. As, however, this rendering is very often found where it is impossible to think of such a meaning as *will* (for example, in Ps. lxxxiii. 5, where no one will suppose the Psalmist to say that the enemies of God "have arranged a *testament* against Him"), it is plain that the Latin *testamentum* was used with an extended meaning, answering to the wide application of the Greek word. St. Paul's designation of the Jewish Scriptures as "the Old Covenant" (2 Cor. iii. 14) thus became familiarly known as *The Old Testament.* In the New Testament the Authorised version more commonly presents the better rendering; but, through the influence of the Latin, *testament* is retained in several places—viz., in the various accounts of the institution of the Lord's Supper; in 2 Cor. iii. 6, 14; in Rev. xi. 19 ("the ark of His testament," a very strange translation); in the present verse; and especially in the very important passage, chap. ix. 15—20. There is a very general agreement of opinion that "covenant" must be the true meaning in all passages of the New Testament except the one last mentioned; and even in

so much was Jesus made a surety
of a better testament. (23) And they
truly were many priests, because they
were not suffered to continue by reason
of death: (24) but this *man*, because he
continueth ever, hath an unchangeable
priesthood.[1] (25) Wherefore he is able
also to save them to the uttermost[2]
that come unto God by him, seeing he
ever liveth to make intercession for
them. (26) For such an high priest be-
came us, *who is* holy, harmless, unde-
filed, separate from sinners, and made
higher than the heavens; (27) who need-
eth not daily, as those high priests, to
offer up sacrifice, first for his own sins,

1 Or, *which passeth not from one to another.*
2 Or, *evermore.*

that place there are strong reasons for retaining the same rendering. (See the Note on chap ix. 15.) In this verse, at all events, we cannot doubt that the writer is thinking of a covenant. (See chap. viii. 6, 8.) Here only is Jesus spoken of as Surety, elsewhere as Mediator (chaps. viii. 6; ix. 15; xii. 24). As through the Son of Man the covenant becomes established, so in Him it remains secure; the words addressed by God to Him as Priest and King contain the pledge of its validity and permanence.

(23) **Were many priests.**—Rather, *have been made priests many* (*i.e.*, in large numbers), *because by death they were prevented from continuing.* (Comp. verse 8, where the thought is somewhat similar.)

(24) **But this man.**—Better, *But He, because He remaineth for ever, hath His priesthood inviolable* (or, *unchangeable*). The former ordinance related to a race, and the individuals were ever passing away; since His life is "indissoluble" (verse 16), none can trespass on His right and invade His priesthood. The rendering of the margin, "that passeth not from one to another," expresses nearly the same thought; but it is very doubtful whether the Greek will bear this meaning.

(25) **Wherefore.**—Since His priesthood is inviolable, His power of saving is *complete.* The association of the thought of "salvation" with the priesthood recalls chap. v. 9, 10; as indeed several points in the later verses of this chapter show that the writer's thought is resting on the first section of chap. v. In His supplication unto God, "who was able to save Him out of death," He was heard; this was the type—and more than the type (see the Note on chap. v. 7)—of the eternal salvation of which He, when made perfect, becomes the Author. The connecting link between the priestly office and "salvation" appears, therefore, to be the prevalent intercession of which this verse speaks—an intercession which implies all that has preceded in His priestly ministration. (See chap. ix. 12, 24.)

That come unto God by him.— Better, *that approach through Him to God.* See chap. x. 19—22, where full expression is given to the thought here briefly indicated. He leads and represents His people, and is the medium of their approach to God.

To make intercession for them.—The word occurs in Rom. viii. 34 in reference to Christ; in Rom. viii. 27 it is applied to the intercession of the Holy Spirit. The thought meets us in chap. ix. 24; John xiv. 16; 1 John ii. 2. With the high priest's confession of the sins of the people on the Day of Atonement was joined fervent intercession on their behalf; this intercession was also symbolised in the offering of the incense.

Verses 26—28 look back on all that has preceded, since the beginning of the fifth chapter, and prepare the way for the subsequent sections. The type afforded by Melchizedek has yielded its lessons, and to this there is no further reference. The mention of the *high priest* (chap. vi. 20, taking up chap. v. 10) is resumed. The unique special teaching of Ps. cx. 4 was far from bringing out the full significance of the priesthood of Jesus; for the sacred history does not connect Melchizedek with any of the most prominent high-priestly functions, or with any temple or place of ministration. The abrogation of the Levitical priesthood and the infinite elevation of the "other Priest" above those of the order of Aaron have been so clearly set forth that it is possible henceforth to concentrate attention on the types and lessons furnished by the Jewish ritual itself. Hence there is the closest connection (as has been already mentioned) between these verses and chap. v. 1—5.

(26) **For such an high priest.**—Better, *For such a one also became us as* (*our*) *High Priest.* Such a priest as has been portrayed was the High Priest that befitted us—no one less exalted could have met our necessities. The added words carry the description farther still. The thought of high priest immediately brings to mind the annual Day of Atonement, to which belonged the characteristic ministration of the high priest. As we read the following words we cannot doubt their direct reference to the ceremonial observances of that day.

Holy.—Not the word of chap. iii. 1, but a word seldom used in the New Testament (except in quotations), though of frequent occurrence in the LXX. (as in Deut. xxxiii. 8; Pss. iv. 3; xvi. 10; cxxxii. 9, 16): the idea contained is that of *holy purity.* The next word may denote either freedom from malice or evil, or freedom from guile (Rom. xvi. 18); the former meaning is more likely here. The three words, denoting personal purity and innocence and freedom from all pollution of sin, present the idea of which the ceremonial purity of the high priest was the type. Seven days before the Day of Atonement the high priest left his house and took up his abode in the Temple, that, thus separated from men and things unclean, he might when the day arrived be found free from all defilement; five washings and ten purifications were required of him on the day itself.

Separate from sinners.—These words may be understood in two ways—as connecting themselves either with what goes before or with the following words. If they extend the idea expressed by "undefiled," they point to the perfect sinlessness of our Lord, who lived amongst sinners and yet was ever separated from their sin—not needing external separation to preserve Him from pollution. If this member is to be joined with the following, it points to the complete severance which now exists: our exalted Lord is for ever removed from a life in the midst of transgressors. The latter view receives some support from chap. ix. 28, but is on other grounds less probable. With the concluding words comp. chaps. iv. 14; viii. 1; Eph. iv. 10.

(27) This verse carries on the description, presenting what follows from this purity and sinlessness.

and then for the people's: for this he did once, when he offered up himself. (28) For the law maketh men high priests which have infirmity; but the word of the oath, which was since the law, *maketh* the Son, who is consecrated[1] for evermore.

[1] Gr. *perfected.*

A.D. 64.

CHAPTER VIII. — (1) Now of the things which we have spoken *this is* the

---

As those high priests.—The high priest's offering up sacrifices first for himself and then for the people constituted a chief part of his duty upon the Day of Atonement. (See chap. v. 3.) The *annual* recurrence of that day is distinctly referred to more than once in this Epistle (see chaps. ix. 25; x. 1, 3): hence the words now before us, which seem to imply *daily* sacrifices thus offered by the high priests, have given rise to much discussion. Neither the morning and evening sacrifices nor the daily meat-offering of the high priest could have been spoken of in the terms here used, which in their natural meaning suit the ritual of the Day of Atonement, and that alone. It is true—and passages of Philo and the Talmud are appositely quoted to illustrate the fact—that, as the high priest was represented by all other priests, their actions were counted as his; but it seems impossible to think that the words have no more significance than this. Either we must take "daily" as equivalent to "day by day" (as the Jews were accustomed to speak of the Day of Atonement as "the day"),—which will give us the meaning, "on each recurrence of this sacred day;" or we must connect the word, not with the Jewish high priests, but with Jesus alone. The order of the Greek would of itself suggest this latter arrangement of the words. If it is correct, the choice of the word "daily" presents but little difficulty. There could be no question of *years* in regard to the ministration of the Lord Jesus in the heavenly sanctuary; and "daily" was perhaps the most natural word in such a case, when the frequently stated repetition of a sacrifice was the thought to be expressed.

For this he did once.—Rather, *once for all.* These words and those that follow, "when He offered up Himself," are best understood as a parenthesis. The truth stated in the former part of the verse, that Jesus needeth not, like the high priests, to offer up sacrifices, first for His own sins and then "for those of the people," finds its explanation in verse 28, "For the Law," &c. But, having introduced the thought of a sacrifice for the sins of the people—a thought not yet expressly mentioned in any part of the Epistle in connection with Jesus, though virtually presented, as we have seen, in many earlier words—the writer will not pass on without the most emphatic statement that such a sacrifice was offered, once for all, in the sacrifice of Himself.

(28) **For the law maketh men high priests which have infirmity . . .**—Better, *For the Law appointeth men high priests, (men) having infirmity; but the word of the oath, which was after the Law, appointeth a Son, who hath been perfected for ever.* On "the word of the oath" see verses 20, 21. Coming "after the Law," it revoked the commandment (verse 18), and was not revoked by it. ("A Son," see chaps. i. 3; v. 8. "Perfected," see chaps. ii. 10; v. 10.) We are not to understand that Jesus was first "perfected" and then appointed as High Priest: this would contradict what has just been taught (verse 27), for it was as High Priest that He offered the sacrifice of Himself. In these closing words are united the two cardinal predictions of Ps. ii., cx. (comp. chap. v. 5, 6): Thou art My Son," "Thou art a Priest for ever."

VIII.

The mode in which this chapter is introduced shows that, in the writer's own arrangement, a new division of the argument begins here. On examination we shall find that there is a clear difference between the topics discussed before and after this point; though it was hardly possible, and certainly was not the intention of the writer, strictly to maintain this distinction in every particular. Hitherto the personal characteristics of the High Priest have occupied the chief place: from this point to chap. x. 18 it is His ministration that is brought before us. Chap. v. 1—10 sets forth whatever there is of similarity between Jesus and the high priests of the Law: the principal subject of chap. vii. is the contrast between the priest of whom Ps. cx. speaks and all others, in respect of dignity (verses 4—7, 9, 10), right of priesthood (verses 8, 16), mode of appointment (verses 20—22), duration of office (verses 23—25), and freedom from sin (verses 26—28). Interwoven with this contrast is another—between the former dispensation, which has failed to attain its purpose, and the new covenant and better hope (verses 11. 18, 19, 22). The same kind of comparison is continued in the rest of the section, and not between the high priests only, but also between the covenants to which their ministry belongs. First the writer dwells on the place in which the high priest ministers (chaps. viii. 1—5; ix. 1—5), then on his ministration, and especially the sacrifice which he presents (chaps. viii. 6; ix. 6—x. 18). In chaps. viii. 7—13 (ix. 15—19), x. 15—17, is introduced the thought of the contrasted covenants.

(1) **Now of the things . . .**—Better, *Now in the things which we are saying* (literally, *which are being said*) *this is the chief point.* Opinion has been much divided as to the meaning of the first Greek word, whether it should be taken as "summary" or as "chief point," each of these meanings being well supported by the usage of the language. The words joined with it, "in the things which we are saying," would lead us to prefer the second rendering; and when the course of the argument is traced we find it difficult to believe that the writer could express a *summary* of his thought in such words as those which follow.

Who is set.—Better, *who sat down.* Twice before have the words of Ps. cx. 1 been thus referred to Jesus (chap. i. 3, 13), but their full significance in regard to the present subject has yet to be brought out. When in chap. vii. 26 we read, "such an high priest became us," we must look to what precedes for the explanation —"such a one" as has already been portrayed. Here the case is different, and the meaning of "such" is found in the description which the following words contain. The last verse of chap. vii. united the two predictions which pointed to Jesus as Priest and King, and the same thought is contained here, expressed in language which at once recalls chap. i. 3. A later passage (chap. x. 11, 12) will show that the words "sat down" have yet further significance, involving a contrast to the continued and ever incomplete services of those who "stood before God" in His earthly sanctuary.

sum: We have such an high priest, who is set on the right hand of the throne of the Majesty in the heavens; (2) a minister of the sanctuary,[1] and of the true tabernacle, which the Lord pitched, and not man. (3) For every high priest is ordained to offer gifts and sacrifices: wherefore *it is* of necessity that this man have somewhat also to offer. (4) For if he were on earth, he should not be a priest, seeing that there are priests[2] that offer gifts according to the law: (5) who serve unto the example and shadow of heavenly things, as Moses was admonished of God when he was about to make the tabernacle: for, See, saith he, *that* thou make all things according to the pattern shewed to thee

Chap. viii.—Christ High Priest in the heavenly sanctuary, and Mediator of a new covenant.

1 Or, *of holy things.*

2 Or, *they are priests.*

The next verse must be closely joined with this, for the contrast just spoken of does not imply that He no longer "ministers" on behalf of men (see chaps. vii. 25; ix. 24); on the contrary, it is as "a minister" of the sanctuary that He sat down on the right hand of God.

(2) **Of the sanctuary.**—The word here rendered "minister" (see chap. i. 7, 14) is very commonly used in the LXX. for the officiating priest. It is difficult, however, to decide on the meaning of the words here joined with it—whether they denote holy things or holy place; if the latter, what is the distinction between this holy place and "the true tabernacle"? The ordinary usage of the Epistle would suggest "holy place," and perhaps the occurrence of both expressions in chap. ix. 11, 12 (where there is no doubt as to the translation) is sufficient to remove any hesitation here. The "sanctuary," therefore, will probably be the heavenly counterpart of the Holiest Place; the "true (or, *real*) Tabernacle," the counterpart of the sacred Tent of Moses, containing both the Holy Place and the Holiest of all (chap. ix. 2—4). It is not certain that in this place we need go beyond this point, though in chap. ix. 12 the more developed thought may require a closer interpretation. The Holy of Holies is the place of God's immediate presence; the Tabernacle, that of God's appointed service. The latter is expressly mentioned here because special reference is to be made to its typical representation upon earth; this is shown by the following words, which point to Ex. xxxiii. 7. The word rendered "true" (which occurs again in chaps. ix. 24; x. 22) is full of interest, denoting that which is contrasted with everything shadowy or imperfect or merely typical; it is a word especially characteristic of the Gospel of St. John. (See Note on John i. 9.)

(3) This verse and the three following confirm and illustrate the importance of the statement just made. The general course of thought appears to be as follows:—That which stands "at the head" of what we are saying, and gives completeness to the whole, is, that we have a High Priest who ministers in heaven itself (verses 1, 2). For, whereas the very conception of high-priestly duty would, were He on earth, exclude Him from being a priest at all (verses 3, 4), like those who "serve a copy of the heavenly things" (verse 5), He in heaven holds and exercises that more excellent ministry of which their service was a shadow and a type (verse 6).

That this man have . . .—Better, *that this High Priest also have somewhat to offer.* If these words refer to the continued ministration in the heavenly sanctuary, the explanation is found in chap. ix. 24; but the meaning may simply be that every high priest, and therefore the Lord Jesus, must have some sacrifice to present to God, this being (chap. v. 1) the very object of his appointment to the office.

(4) **For if he were . . .**—The oldest Greek MSS. and two important versions read, "If then He were"; and two other changes in the text of this verse also rest on high authority. In its correct form the verse will stand thus: *If then He were on earth, He would not even be a priest* (that is, He would not be a priest at all), *seeing there are those who according to law offer the gifts.* The argument somewhat resembles that of chap. vii. 13, 14; there, however, the impediment is that of tribe; here the thought is that the place is preoccupied by men who by express command are bringing the gifts unto God.

(5) **Who serve unto . . .**—Better, *men who serve a copy and shadow of the heavenly things.* So in chap. xiii. 10 we read of those who "serve the tabernacle." On the connection of thought, see verse 3. "Copy," not in the sense of perfect resemblance, but rather a *token* suggesting and designed to suggest the original. (See Note on chap. ix. 23, where the same word is used.) "Shadow," as the shadow has no substance or independent existence, but represents only the outline of an object. (Comp. chap. x. 1, where "shadow" is contrasted with "the very image"; and Col. ii. 17, where it is opposed to "the body.") We must not confound these words, "token" and "shadow," with "the pattern" mentioned in Ex. xxv. 40, quoted later in this verse. The "heavenly things" are "the sanctuary" and "the tabernacle" of verse 2, the realities to which the true earthly tabernacle corresponded; their nature can be understood only when Christ has come as High Priest of the good things to come. (See chaps. ix. 11; x. 1.) That every part of God's earthly house might be a fitting emblem of spiritual truth to be afterwards revealed, Moses was charged in all respects to follow the pattern which had been shown him in the mount (Ex. xxv. 40). Jewish tradition understood these words to imply the presentation of a heavenly tabernacle to the sight of Moses, as a model to be imitated with exactness; and Stephen's words in Acts vii. 44, "according to the pattern" (the same word is here used) "which he had seen," convey the same meaning. In itself, Ex. xxv. 40, when compared with verse 9 in the same chapter, does not necessarily involve a visible representation. But whether we think of a pattern shown in vision, or merely of explicit direction received by Moses, the meaning of "the heavenly things" remains the same. The view here presented of the Jewish tabernacle involves no depreciation, except in comparison with "the good things to come." It was only *a shadow*; but it rises above all temples and symbols of man's art and device as being a shadow *of the heavenly things.*

Was admonished of God.—The words "of God" are not in the text, but are implied in "admonished." (See the Note on Luke ii. 26.) "Hath been admonished:" another example of the writer's characteristic mode of regarding Scripture (chap. iv. 9).

in the mount. (6) But now hath he
obtained a more excellent ministry, by
how much also he is the mediator of a
better covenant,[1] which was established
upon better promises. (7) For if that
first *covenant* had been faultless, then
should no place have been sought for
the second. (8) For finding fault with
them, he saith, Behold, the days come,
saith the Lord, when I will make a new
covenant with the house of Israel and
with the house of Judah: (9) not according to the covenant that I made
with their fathers in the day when I
took them by the hand to lead them
out of the land of Egypt; because they
continued not in my covenant, and I
regarded them not, saith the Lord.
(10) For this *is* the covenant that I will
make with the house of Israel after
those days, saith the Lord; I will put[2]
my laws into their mind,[a] and write
them in[3] their hearts: and I will be to
them a God, and they shall be to me a
people: (11) and they shall not teach
every man his neighbour, and every
man his brother, saying, Know the
Lord: for all shall know me, from
the least to the greatest. (12) For I will
be merciful to their unrighteousness,

1 Or, *testament*.

2 Gr. *give*.

a Jer. 31. 33.

3 Or, *upon*.

---

(6) **But now.**—That is, as the case really is. (See verse 3.) We have here another of those proportional statements commented on in chaps. i. 4; iii. 3; vii. 22. The last of these passages is closely akin to this. There we read that by how much the Priest appointed by the divine oath is raised above all other priests, by so much is His covenant better than theirs. Here, that as He is Mediator of a better covenant, in the same proportion does His ministry excel that of priests on earth.

Which was established.—Better, *one that hath been ordained.* The verb, properly meaning "to legislate," has already occurred in chap. vii. 11, "the people hath received the Law" (literally, *hath been legislated for*). Here, then, a word which properly refers to the passing of a law is applied to a covenant. The explanation must be sought in the special nature of the covenants of God with man (see chap. vii. 22), which are not compacts between equals, but arrangements offered by the divine goodness, and made dependent upon conditions. Hence such a covenant may be spoken of as ordained, enacted, on the basis of promise. On the promises (see verses 8—12) which are given by God is based the "covenant" which becomes the law of His kingdom and the declaration of His procedure. The man who accepts the promises by entering into the conditions laid down is dealt with according to this law. Here, Jesus is the "Mediator," in chap. vii. 22 (see Note) the "Surety," of the better covenant. The idea is expanded below in chap. ix. 15—18. On the tacit comparison with Moses, as mediator of the first covenant, see Note on Gal. iii. 19.

(7) **For the second.**—Rather, *for a second.* This verse connects itself with the words "a better covenant" in verse 6. The form of expression used clearly points to the intended inference—that covenant *was* faulty, and a place was sought for a second; this makes plain the connection with verse 8. The failure of the first covenant was manifest (chap. vii. 11, 18) to God, who, whilst the first still existed, "sought" and found place for a second.

(8) **Finding fault with them.**—Not, "with it," but with those through whom the covenant had failed. The following quotation (verses 8—12) is taken from Jer. xxxi. 31—34. It is the crowning point of that collection of prophecies which is brought together in chaps. xxx.—xxxiii., descriptive of the hope and salvation of Israel. The characteristics of the prophecy and its significance in this place will be noticed below (verse 12). The quotation agrees in the main with the LXX. (and, except in verse 11, with the text contained in the Alexandrian MS.), and in one clause only fails to represent the meaning of the Hebrew original. The only point requiring notice in this verse is the substitution of "I will accomplish" for "I will make." The new word closely answers to that which was used in verse 6, "ordained." (See the Note.)

(9) **Not according to the covenant.**—The difference is declared below (verses 10—12). "In the day when" they were led forth out of Egypt the token of God's covenant was the deliverance itself. At Sinai, Ex. xxiv. 7, 8 (see chap. ix. 18—22), the "book of the covenant" was read, and "the blood of the covenant" was "sprinkled on the people," who had promised obedience to all the words that the Lord had said.

And I regarded them not.—It is here that the translation departs from the Hebrew, which, as is now generally believed, is faithfully represented in our Authorised version: "although I was an husband unto them" (that is, had the authority of a husband). The quotation here follows the LXX. without change.

(10) **I will make.**—Literally, *I will covenant*—not the same word as in verse 8.

Israel.—Formerly (verse 8), Israel and Judah. When the reunion of the nation had once been signified, "Israel" could stand alone as the name of the one people.

I will put.—Better, *putting my laws into their mind, I will also write them on their heart.* In the former clause the Hebrew has, "I will put my law in their inward parts;" the law shall be *within* them, not an external code. In the latter, the "fleshy tablets of the heart" are contrasted with "the tables of the Law." This is the first of the "better promises."

(11) **His neighbour.**—Rather, *his fellow-citizen,* according to the best reading. The second promise is the universality of the knowledge of God. The divine teaching shall not only be internal, but for this very reason shall extend to all.

(12) **Merciful.**—Literally, *propitious.* On the kindred word "make propitiation," see chap. ii. 17.

To their unrighteousness.—Rather, *to their unrighteousnesses, and their sins will I remember no more.* The words "and their iniquities" are omitted by the best authorities. Here is given the third and chief promise: the characteristic of the new covenant is the full pardon of sin.

Of this new covenant, "ordained" on the three promises of an inward revelation, universal knowledge of God, and free pardon of sin, Jesus is the Mediator.

and their sins and their iniquities will I
remember no more. (13) In that he
saith, A new *covenant*, he hath made
the first old. Now that which decayeth
and waxeth old *is* ready to vanish away.

CHAPTER IX.—(1) Then verily the
first *covenant* had also ordinances[1] of

A.D. 64.

[2] Or, *holy*.
[1] Or, *ceremonies*.

divine service, and a worldly sanc-
tuary. (2) For there was
a tabernacle made; the
first, wherein *was* the
candlestick, and the table,
and the shewbread; which is called
the sanctuary.[2] (3) And after the
second veil, the tabernacle which is

Chap. ix. 1—10. The first covenant: its tabernacle and ordinances.

How this is to be understood the writer himself will teach, for all these promises are present (virtually or formally) in the last portion of his argument (chap. x. 14—18). In part they belong to the new covenant from the beginning. The pardon is spoken of not as a gift to individuals, but rather as from the first a characteristic of the covenant (chaps. ix. 26; x. 18). The first promise is seen in the gift of the Holy Spirit, and in the teaching represented by the Sermon on the Mount, in which inward principles of life take the place of many an outward rule. The second waits for full accomplishment, but is seen in the abolition of distinctions between nation and nation, and the common influence of the Holy Spirit.

This subject has presented difficulties, because it has been forgotten that this Scripture speaks of no sudden change in man's relation to God. The essential promises of the new covenant were not unknown under the old. "Thy law is within my heart" is the saying of one Psalmist; "Thou forgavest the iniquity of my sin," of another. But in regard to the nation there was failure. The rites of the Law did not lead to the perception of spiritual truths; ordinances which were intended to teach the divine intolerance of sin became mere ceremonies; external sanctions did not preserve the nation in true obedience to God's law. To all, the former covenant (like the first Tabernacle, chap. ix. 9) was a parable, explained only when the new covenant (which was in truth *before* the old, Gal. iii. 17) was "ordained."

(13) **In that he saith . . .**—Rather, *In saying "new" He hath made the first old: now that which groweth old and is failing for age is nigh unto vanishing away.* The very language of the prophet contains a declaration of the speedy dissolution of the former covenant. If "nigh unto vanishing" at the time when Jeremiah wrote, well might it now be believed to have passed away.

IX.

(1) The subject commenced in the last chapter (verses 1—6) is continued here. The mention of the "more excellent ministry" led to the description of the new covenant with which it is united (verses 6—13). This verse, then, attaches itself to the fifth and sixth verses of chap. viii. "Even the first (covenant), then, had ordinances of divine service and its sanctuary, of this world." The "service" is spoken of again in verse 6; the "ordinances" in verse 10, where they are called "carnal." Very similar is the language here, for the words so emphatically standing at the close of the verse are probably descriptive not of the "sanctuary" only, but also of the "ordinances." Both place and ministrations belonged to *this world*, and thus stand in contrast with "the heavenly things," of which the Tabernacle was a token and shadow. (See Note on chap. viii. 5.) The ordinary Greek text (here following the first printed Greek Testament) has "the first Tabernacle," and this reading was followed by Tyndale and Coverdale. All ancient MSS. omit the word; and, as in a long succession of verses "covenant" has been the leading thought, the rendering of the Authorised version is certainly correct.

(2) **Tabernacle.**—It must be carefully observed that the Epistle throughout refers to the Tabernacle, and not once to the Temples which succeeded it. Though they were formed on the same general model, their very nature and design necessitated changes of plan and detail which unfitted them for the writer's argument here. So far as the Temple was a copy of the Tabernacle, and so far only, was it made "after the pattern" that Moses had seen; and so far only was its symbolism of divine and not human origin.

The first, wherein was . . .—In verse 6, when the writer passes from place to ministration, he uses the present tense, although it is of the Tabernacle that he is speaking. The explanation is that which has come before us again and again: the arrangements prescribed in Scripture are to him ever present, abiding from age to age in that unchanging word. Hence probably we should here read *are* instead of "were." The golden candlestick, the table, and the showbread *are* in the Holy Place as it is described in the Law. With the symbolical meaning of the furniture of the Holy Place we are not here concerned. The writer contents himself with words which plainly imply that none of the parts and arrangements of the Tabernacle were without significance. On the golden candlestick (more strictly, *lampstand*) see Ex. xxv. 31—37, and on the ten candlesticks of the Temple of Solomon, 1 Kings vii. 49; on the table and the showbread, Ex. xxv. 23—30; Lev. xxiv. 5—9 (1 Kings vii. 48; 2 Chron. iv. 8). It is somewhat remarkable that the table should here be so distinctly mentioned, for usually (both in the Bible and in Jewish tradition) no special importance appears to be assigned to it apart from the offering which was placed thereon. (Comp., however, Lev. xxiv. 6; 2 Chron. xiii. 11; Mal. i. 7, 12.) This offering is in Hebrew called "bread of the face"—*i.e.*, bread of the (divine) Presence; in Matt. xii. 4, Luke vi. 4, "loaves of the setting forth;" here "the setting forth of the loaves."

Sanctuary.—Or, *holy place.* The same word is applied to the Holy of Holies in chaps. viii. 2; ix. 8, 12, 24, 25; x. 19; and probably in xiii. 11. This verse and the next give the proper names of the two parts of the Tabernacle, which must be used when the one is to be distinguished from the other. Where there is no risk of mistake the simpler designation is sufficient. (See Lev. xvi. 2, 17, 20.) It will be observed that here and in verses 3, 6, 7, these divisions are spoken of as if two distinct Tabernacles.

(3) **The tabernacle.**—Rather, *a tabernacle which is called the Holy of Holies.* This literal translation of a Hebrew expression for "most holy" does not occur in the Bible, but has become familiar through the Latin *sanctum sanctorum.* The inner chamber of the Tabernacle is in a few passages only mentioned separately in the Pentateuch as the "Most Holy Place"

called the Holiest of all; (4) which
had the golden censer, and the ark
of the covenant overlaid round about
with gold, wherein *was* the golden pot
that had manna, and Aaron's rod that
budded, and the tables of the covenant;
(5) and over it the cherubims of glory
shadowing the mercyseat; of which we

(Ex. xxvi. 33, 34), or "the Holy Place" (Lev. xvi. 2, *et al.*). In the description of the Temple a different word is employed, always rendered "oracle" (1 Kings vi. 16, *et al.*). The veil separating the two divisions (described in Ex. xxvi. 31; xxxvi. 35) is here called the second veil, by way of distinction from the "hanging for the door" of the Tabernacle (Ex. xxvi. 36; xxxvi. 37).

(4) **Having a golden censer.**—Or, *having a golden altar of incense.* Hardly any passage in the Epistle has given rise to more controversy than this; and even now opinions are greatly divided. The question raised does not merely concern the interpretation of a single verse, but has been brought into prominence in all recent discussions as to the authorship of the Epistle. It will be possible to notice all important points in the controversy without entering into any discussion of the Greek, for it is allowed on both sides that the word here used—*thumiaterion* (which simply means an instrument or a place connected with the offering of incense)—will admit of either rendering. The usage of the LXX., in most cases peculiarly helpful in this Epistle, throws little light on the matter; for this word is entirely absent from the descriptions in the Pentateuch, and occurs twice only in later books (Ezek. viii. 11; 2 Chron. xxvi. 19—both times for "censer"). The Pentateuch, indeed, makes no mention of a special censer for the use of the high priest on the Day of Atonement (Lev. xvi. 12); but, as we learn from the Mishna, the later law not only prescribed a censer of gold, but laid stress on the particular kind of gold. On the other hand, in Philo and Josephus the word here used is the regular designation of the *altar of incense.* That altar, it is true, was not of gold, only overlaid with gold; but as one of its names in common use was "the golden altar" (Ex. xl. 5, *et al.*) this point is of no moment. If we look at internal probabilities, it is hard to decide which would be more surprising—the special mention of the censer (by the side of the ark and the cherubim) in this description of the Most Holy Place, or the absence of all notice of the incense-altar, which held so important a place in connection with the ceremonies of the Day of Atonement. Hence, though "censer" has (mainly through the influence of the Vulgate) been the more familiar rendering, the most eminent modern commentators have, with some marked exceptions, adopted the other view. Probably there would be little difference of opinion on the question, were it not that the words here used seem to assign to the altar of incense a place *within the veil.* As, however, there are the strongest reasons for believing that the golden censer was not kept in the Holiest Place, this difficulty applies almost equally to both interpretations. At first sight the difficulty is very great. The incense-altar and the ark are coupled together, and the word which describes their relation to the Holiest Place is that which, a little later in this verse, distinctly signifies "containing." So weighty is this consideration that many have been unable to avoid the conclusion that the writer has erred in this matter of detail; and various suppositions have been resorted to in explanation of his mistake. (See *Introduction.*) But, to take the lowest ground, surely ignorance on such a point is inconceivable. Not only are the notices in Exodus perfectly plain, but passages in Philo and Josephus show how customary in the writer's own age it was to speak of the three sacred objects in the Holy Place—the candlestick, the table, and the golden altar. There must exist some special reason for this connection of the altar with the Most Holy Place—a connection which (we may well believe) would have been otherwise expressed had the writer held it possible that readers, familiar with the facts, could regard his language as even ambiguous. Such a reason will be found to be suggested by the language of the Pentateuch, and by the ceremonial of the Day of Atonement. In Ex. xxx. 6, Moses receives special injunction to place the altar of incense "before the veil that is by the ark of the testimony, before the mercy seat that is over the testimony;" similarly in Ex. xl. 5. The purification of this altar is most expressly associated with the purification of the Holiest Place on the Day of Atonement: this stands out in strong relief both in the Pentateuch (see Ex. xxx. 10; Lev. xvi. 18) and in the Mishna. The typical significance of the altar of incense (comp. Rev. viii. 3, 4; ix. 13) we might also show to be in full harmony with the thought here presented. There is, however, one passage in the Old Testament (1 Kings vi. 22) which appears to give direct expression to what these other passages imply; for there the true translation must be, "also *the whole altar that belongeth to the oracle* he overlaid with gold."*

Ark of the covenant (Num. x. 33; Deut. xxxi. 26, *et al.*), often called "the ark of the testimony," *i.e.*, the ark containing the tables of the Ten Commandments, which were the symbol of the covenant of God with the people. (See Ex. xxv. 10—16.)

Wherein was . . .—Rather, *wherein are* (see verse 2) *a golden pot having the manna,* &c. In Ex. xvi. 33, 34, and Num. xvii. 10, 11, the pot containing "an omer of manna" and also Aaron's rod are said to have been laid up "before the testimony." This is often understood as meaning "before the ark of the testimony;" but it is as natural to suppose that these memorials were placed inside the ark, in front of the tables. 1 Kings viii. 9 clearly suggests that the ark had at one time contained more than the tables of stone, and so it has been understood by Jewish commentators. There is no mention of a "golden" vessel in the Hebrew of Ex. xvi. 33; the word is added in the LXX. It will be observed that this epithet is mentioned three times in the verse: such splendour was natural in the sanctuary "of this world" (verse 1).

(5) **Cherubims of glory.**—See Ex. xxv. 18—22; xxix. 43; Num. vii. 89; Ezek. x. 19, 20. As these passages will show, the reference is to the glory which appeared above the mercy seat. (See Note on chap. i. 3.) This is the only express mention of the cherubim in the New Testament; but see the Notes on Rev. iv. 6, *et seq.*

The mercy seat (literally, *the propitiatory*) is the rendering adopted in the LXX. for the Hebrew *Capporeth,* signifying the golden covering of the ark (Ex. xxv. 17). Whether the Hebrew word properly

* Some interesting remarks on this passage will be found in a paper by Dr. Milligan in the *Bible Educator* (vol. iii., p. 230). His suggestion is that the writer, having in mind the Day of Atonement, sees the Tabernacle with its inner veil withdrawn.

cannot now speak particularly.
(6) Now when these things were thus ordained, the priests went always into the first tabernacle, accomplishing the service *of God.*
(7) But into the second *went* the high priest alone once every year, not without blood, which he offered for himself, and *for* the errors of the people:
(8) the Holy Ghost this signifying, that the way into the holiest of all was not yet made manifest, while as the first tabernacle was yet standing:
(9) which *was* a figure for the time then present, in which were offered both gifts and sacrifices, that could not make him that did the service perfect, as pertaining to the conscience;
(10) *which stood* only in meats and drinks, and divers washings, and carnal ordinances,[1] imposed *on them* until the time of reformation.

[1] Or, *rites,* or, *ceremonies.*

---

denotes *covering* or bears the meaning which is expressed by the Greek translation, is a disputed question, into which we cannot here enter. The act of expiation with which the Greek name at all events stands connected is that of Lev. xvi. 10—14. It is noteworthy that in 1 Chron. xxviii. 11 the Most Holy Place itself is called "the house of the mercy seat." (See the Note on Rom. iii. 25.)

Of which—viz., all things that the Holy Place and the Holy of Holies contained.

Particularly—*i.e.*, severally, one by one.

(6) **Now when these thing were thus ordained . . .**—Better, *And when these things have been thus prepared, into the first tabernacle the priests enter continually, accomplishing the services.* As has been already observed (verse 2), the present tense is used throughout these verses (6—10), not because the writer refers to the services as still continuing, but because he is still tracing the ordinance of Scripture. It is of the Tabernacle alone that he speaks. The words of verse 4 would have been entirely incorrect in regard to the temple of his day, in which the Most Holy Place was empty.

The service.—Comp. Ex. xxx. 7, 8; Lev. xxiv. 1—8.

(7) **Went . . . offered.**—Rather, *entereth . . . offereth.*

Errors.—Literally, *ignorances.* (See chaps. v. 2, 3; vii. 27.) By "once in the year" we must of course understand on one day of the year, viz., the tenth day of Tisri. On that day, according to Lev. xvi., it was the duty of the high priest to enter the Holy of Holies twice: (1) with the incense and with the blood of the bullock, his own sin-offering (Lev. xvi. 12—14); (2) with the blood of the same bullock and that of the goat, the sin-offering for the people (verses 15—19). In the ritual described in the tract "Joma" of the Talmud, he is said to enter four times; the first ministration being separated into its two parts (offering incense, sprinkling the blood of the bullock), and a fourth entering (to bring out the censer) being added.

(8) **That the way into the holiest of all was not yet made manifest.**—Rather, *that the way into the sanctuary has not yet been made manifest.* By "sanctuary," or "holy place," is here meant the Holy of Holies; not, however, as existing upon earth, in type and figure, but in the sense of chaps. viii. 2 and ix. 24. These external arrangements show that the way into the Holy Place (of the Tabernacle) is not open: by this the Holy Spirit, whose word we are reading whenever we trace the injunctions of the Law, teaches this lesson, that the way into God's immediate presence is not yet manifest.

While as the first tabernacle was yet standing.—Rather, *while the first tabernacle yet has place* (or, *standing*), *i.e.*, whilst there exists such a distinction as that between "the first Tabernacle" (verse 6), and "the second." It is impossible to understand "the first Tabernacle" in any other sense than that which it bears in the early part of the sentence—the Holy Place as distinguished from the Holiest of all. This outer Tabernacle, however, may be looked at from different points of view. On the one hand, it was the place from which (as well as from the inner sanctuary) the people generally were excluded; and on the other, it was the place beyond which the ministration of the priests in general might not extend. It is the latter that corresponds to the thought of this verse. The contrast between the body of priests and the people hardly meets us once in the whole Epistle, except in a very small number of general statements (chaps. vii. 14; viii. 4; ix. 6); the only contrast is between the one Priest or High Priest and all who approach unto God through Him. Not the Jewish economy, but that to which it pointed, is the subject of the writer's thoughts: Christ's people are now the priests, who offer through Him their constant sacrifice. (See chaps. xii. 28; xiii. 10, 13, 15.) Those who ministered in "the first Tabernacle" (who are looked upon merely as substitutes for the people, performing the "services" in their place, and as their representatives) were excluded, not from entrance only, but even from sight of the place of God's presence. What was thereby "signified" we have already seen.

(9) **Which was a figure . . .**—Rather, *Which is a parable unto the time present, according to which* (parable) *are offered both gifts and sacrifices, which cannot perfect, as to the conscience, him that doeth the service.* The general meaning may be given thus: this "first Tabernacle" (*i.e.*, the existence of an outer as distinguished from an inner sanctuary) is a parable for the period connected with it (literally, "for the season that stands near it," *the adjacent period*, so to speak); and in full accordance with the parabolic character of the first Tabernacle (see verse 8) is the presentation of offerings which have no power to accomplish the perfect end of worship in the case of any worshipper. The priests offered sacrifices to God, but were limited to the outer sanctuary, which was not the place of God's manifested presence; a fit symbol this of offerings which cannot purify the conscience (see verse 14; chap. x. 1). The above rendering follows the best reading of the Greek; in the ordinary text the relative "which," in the second clause, refers to "the time," not to "the first Tabernacle."

(10) **Which stood only in . . .**—Better, *only joined with meats and drinks and divers washings,—carnal ordinances, imposed until a time of reformation.* Here again the best authorities correct the received Greek text, omitting "and" before the word "carnal," and so altering the next word as to make it descriptive of the "gifts and sacrifices" mentioned in verse 9. These sacrifices—looked at in themselves, as powerless

Chap. ix. 11—18. These types fulfilled in Christ.

(11) But Christ being come an high priest of good things to come, by a greater and more perfect tabernacle, not made with hands, that is to say, not of this building, (12) neither by the blood of goats and calves, but by his own blood he entered in once into the holy place, having obtained eternal redemption

to attain the end designed (chap. x. 1, 4)—are mere appendages of such regulations as deal with meats and drinks and washings. The character of this latter class of ordinances no one could mistake; and what the writer here says is that these powerless sacrifices belong to the same line of things. On the "washings" see Note on chap. vi. 2. The preceding words would most naturally refer to meats, &c., of which men were *required to partake* (as Ex. xii.; Lev. vii. 15, *et al.*); but no doubt include the various restrictions and distinctions of the ceremonial law (Lev. xi.; Num. vi., *et al.*). All these are "ordinances of flesh," ordinances which relate to the outward state of things only; closely connected with the maintenance of external privileges and relations, but (in themselves) nothing more. "Imposed," comp. Acts xv. 10: "reformation," chap. viii. 7—12.

(11, 12) The changes of translation required in these verses are not considerable in themselves, but important for the sake of bringing out the unity of the sentence and the connection of its parts. *But Christ having come a High Priest of the good things to come* (or, *the good things that are come*, see below), *through the greater and more perfect Tabernacle, not made with hands, that is to say, not of this creation, also not through blood of goats and calves, but through His own blood, entered once for all into the Holy Place, having won eternal redemption.* With verse 11 begins the contrast to the first verse. In that we read of the first covenant as possessing ordinances of service and its holy place—both, however, "of this world," and the following verses describe the sanctuary itself (1—5) and the ordinances (6—10). Now, the Mediator of the New Covenant (chap. viii. 6), "Christ," whose name brings with it the thought of the satisfaction of all hope and fulfilment of all promises, has appeared as High Priest; and entering into the true Holy of Holies has accomplished once for all what the earlier ministrations typified. This is the main thought; but in few verses do the single words require more careful study. The various-reading mentioned above, "the good things that are come," is very interesting. It is not supported by a large number of authorities, but amongst them are the Vatican MS. (whose guidance, it may be remarked, we shall soon lose, as the ancient text breaks off suddenly in the middle of a word in verse 14), the Claromontane MS., and two Syriac versions. One strong argument in its favour presents itself on a comparison with chap. x. 1 (where there is no doubt about the reading), "the good things to come." A scribe who had in mind those words, confirmed by the repeated occurrence of a similar thought in different parts of the Epistle (chaps. ii. 5; vi. 5), might easily substitute them for words expressing a less familiar thought. The two phrases differ more in form than in reality. In one we look at the new order of things, which is never to pass away, as already introduced by Christ (see Note on chap. i. 2); and in the other the same new order is thought of as future to those who waited through long ages for "the Christ," and in its consummation still future to ourselves (chap. vi. 5). The form of expression reminds us of chap. iii. 1, where Jesus is called the High Priest of our confession (compare also Mal. iii. 1, "the Messenger of the covenant"): He is associated with "the good things" as having brought them in, as Mediator of the covenant to which they belong.

Through (or, *by means of*) the more perfect Tabernacle, through (or, *by means of*) His own blood, Christ entered into the Holy Place. The two-fold reference to the type is very plain. It was by passing through "the first Tabernacle" that the high priest reached the Holiest Place; it was by means of the blood of the sin-offering that he was enabled to enter into that place of God's presence (verse 7). But what in the antitype answers to this Tabernacle? The expression of chap. iv. 14, perhaps, first presents itself to the mind: if, however, we were right in understanding the words "that has passed through the heavens" as descriptive of our Lord's ascension far above all heavens (Eph. iv. 10), it seems evident that this verse is no real parallel. In chap. x. 20 the thought is somewhat different, but yet sufficiently akin to be suggestive in regard to these words. There the veil is spoken of as symbolising "the flesh" of our Lord. Here we have in all probability an extension of the same thought, "the more perfect Tabernacle" being the human nature of our Lord. We think at once of a number of passages presenting the same idea: "The Word was made flesh and made His tabernacle among us" (John i. 14); "He spake of the temple of His body (John ii. 19); "The Father that dwelleth in Me" (John xiv. 10); "In Him dwelleth all the fulness of the Godhead bodily" (Col. ii. 9). As in Him God gave to the world the first true revelation of Himself (chap. i. 2), God's dwelling-place amongst His people was a type of the Incarnate Word. The symbolism of the present verse compels us to think of the first and second Tabernacles as separate. It was otherwise in chap. viii. 2, a verse which can only receive its proper explanation when the words now before us are considered. There the reference is to the High Priest who has already entered the Holiest Place and has "sat down at the right hand" of God. The distinction of outer and inner sanctuary has disappeared; and, carrying out more fully the thought of the passages quoted above, we may say that, as "the sanctuary" of chap. viii. 2 symbolises the place of God's immediate presence, "the true Tabernacle" represents the place of His continued and unceasing revelation of Himself to man, "in Christ." There is no difficulty now in explaining the epithets, "greater," "more perfect," "not of this creation." By means of this assumption of human nature He received power to become High Priest, power also to become Himself the sin-offering. Once before only in the Epistle have we read of this two-fold relation of our Lord to the sacrificial act. There it is mentioned parenthetically (chap. vii. 26) and by anticipation, here it is the leading thought (verses 14, 26, 28; chap. x. 10, *et al.*). The efficacy of this offering is taken up again in verses 13, 14; the entering into the Holiest Place, in the latter part of the chapter. A new thought is introduced in the last words of this verse, "having won eternal *redemption.*" Through the sacrifice atonement has been made and sin expiated: the blessing won, which in chap. v. 9 is called eternal salvation (see

for us. (13) For if the blood of bulls
and of goats, and the ashes of an
heifer sprinkling the unclean, sanc-
tifieth to the purifying of the flesh:
(14) how much more shall the blood of
Christ, who through the eternal Spirit
offered himself without spot to God,[1]
purge your conscience from dead works
to serve the living God? (15) And for
this cause he is the mediator of the new
testament, that by means of death, for
the redemption of the transgressions

1 Or, *fault.*

Note on chap. vii. 25), is here "eternal redemption." The latter figure enlarges the former by the additional thought of the payment of a price. The deliverance of man from God's wrath and the penalty of sin, which Jesus effected by means of the offering of Himself, is the "eternal redemption which He won" (see verse 14, and Eph. i. 7). The words, "for us," are not in the text: they are too intimately present in the whole thought to need direct expression.

(13) **For if the blood of bulls and of goats.**—This verse connects itself with the last words of verse 12, "having won eternal redemption," showing why our hope may rise so high. The sacrifice is mentioned here in words slightly different from those of verse 11; but in each case the writer's thought is resting on the sin offering of the Day of Atonement, a bullock for the high priest himself, a goat for the people. (There is no distinct reference in this Epistle to the "scapegoat" sent into the wilderness.)

And the ashes of an heifer.—The nineteenth chapter of Numbers is wholly occupied with the remarkable institution here referred to. A red heifer without spot was slain and wholly burnt, "with cedar-wood and hyssop and scarlet," and the ashes were laid up in a clean place without the camp. "And for the unclean they shall take of the ashes of the burning of the sin-offering, and running water shall be put thereto in a vessel: and a clean person shall take hyssop and dip it in the water and sprinkle . . . . upon the unclean" (verses 17—19). The "unclean" are those that have been defiled by touching the dead body of a man, or by being in any way brought into connection with death. It is said that on the third and seventh days of the high priest's week of preparation for the Day of Atonement (see Note on chap. vii. 26), he was sprinkled with this water of purification, lest he should inadvertently have contracted such defilement.

Sanctifieth to the purifying of the flesh.—Better, *sanctify unto the cleanness of the flesh.* As we have seen already (verse 10), the writer is looking at the intrinsic character of the sacrifices (chap. x. 4) and rites of purification, apart from their importance as marks of obedience or their value to those who were able to discern their spiritual lessons. They could not cleanse the conscience (verse 9); but they could and did remove what the Law accounted "uncleanness," and disabilities connected with the outward life and religious worship of the commonwealth.

(14) **Through the eternal Spirit.**—Better, *through an eternal Spirit;* for in a passage of so much difficulty it is important to preserve the exact rendering of the Greek, and the arguments usually adduced seem insufficient to justify the ordinary translation. By most readers of the Authorised version, probably, these words are understood as referring to the Holy Spirit, whose influence continually rested on "the Anointed One of God" (Acts x. 38). For this opinion there seems to be no foundation in the usage of the New Testament, and it is not indicated by anything in the context. The explanation of the words must rather be sought in the nature of our Lord, or in some attribute of that nature. There are a few passages, mainly in the Epistles of St. Paul, in which language somewhat similar is employed in regard to the spirit (*pneuma*) of our Lord. The most remarkable of these are Rom. i. 4, where "spirit of holiness" is placed in contrast with "flesh;" and 1 Tim. iii. 16, "in spirit." On the latter Bishop Ellicott writes: "*in spirit,* in the higher sphere of His divine life: the *pneuma* of Christ is not here the Holy Spirit, but *the higher principle of* spiritual life, which was not the Divinity (this would be an Apollinarian assertion), but especially and intimately united with it." (Another passage of great interest is 1 Pet. iii. 18.) The attribute "eternal" is explained by chap. vii. 18, 19, "according to power of indissoluble life (He hath become priest), for of Him it is testified, Thou art a priest for ever." Through this spirit, a spirit of holiness, a spirit of indissoluble life, He offered Himself to God. This made such a self-offering possible; this gave to the offering infinite worth. In the words which stand in contrast with these (verse 13) we read of the death of animals which had no power over their own transient life: He who was typified in every high priest and in every victim, "through an eternal spirit," of Himself laid down His life (John x. 18), offering Himself to God in the moment and article of death,—offered Himself in His constant presence in the Holiest Place (verse 24).

Without spot.—The word here used is frequently applied in the LXX. to the victims "without blemish" that were offered in sacrifice. The sinlessness of Jesus is expressed under the same metaphor in 1 Pet. i. 19.

Purge your conscience from dead works to serve the living God.—Better, *cleanse our conscience from dead works to serve a Living God.* The word "cleanse" is akin to "cleanness" in verse 13. Authorities are divided between "our" and "your"; but the former is probably the better reading. Once before, in chap. vi. 1, the writer has spoken of "dead works." (See the Note.) It is here, however, that the significance most fully appears; for we cannot doubt that there exists a reference to the purification made necessary by all contact with death. (See verse 13.) Since the works are dead because they had no share in true life, which is the life of God, the last words bring before us the thought of a Living God (chap. iii. 12). This thought also stands connected with "*eternal* Spirit," for those who are cleansed through the offering of Christ shall share His relation to the Living God. The contrast is in every respect complete. From the whole number of Jewish rites had been selected (verse 13) the two which most fully represented the purification from sin and from pollution through death, in order that this completeness of antithesis might be attained. It is not necessary to trace the details of the contrast. In each and in all we read the "How much more!"

(15) **And for this cause.**—Or, *And because of this.* This verse looks back to the great truth of verses 11, 12, which the last two verses have served to confirm and place in bolder relief. "Christ through His own blood entered once for all into the Holy Place, having won eternal redemption; and by reason of this He is the

that were under the first testament, they which are called might receive the promise of eternal inheritance. (16) For where a testament *is*, there must also of necessity be[1] the death of the testator. (17) For a testament *is* of force after men are dead: otherwise it is of no strength at all while the testator

[1] Cr, *be brought in.*

Mediator of a covenant, a new covenant, in order that they who have been called may receive the promise of the eternal inheritance." For "the new testament" we must certainly read *a new covenant:* whatever may be thought of the following group of verses, the rendering *testament* has no place here. The leading thought of chap. viii. is the establishment of a new covenant, and the former covenant has been referred to three times in this very chapter (verses 1, 4).

That by means of death.—Rather, *that, death having taken place for redemption from the transgressions, &c.* The first covenant had been broken by "transgressions:" unless there be redemption from these—that is, from the bondage of penalty which has resulted from these—there can be no promise and no new covenant. In respect of this bondage, this penalty, the death of Christ was a ransom—an offering to God looked at in the light of a payment in the place of debt, service, or penalty due. When debt and payment are changed into the corresponding ideas of sin and punishment, the *ransom* gives place to the *sin-offering*, of which the principle was the acknowledgment of death deserved, and the vicarious suffering of death. So far our thought has rested on the removal of the results of the past. The covenant and the promise relate to the establishment of the better future. Death was necessary alike for both. The offering of Christ's life (Matt. xx. 28) was a ransom or an offering for sin; it was also a sacrifice inaugurating a new covenant, which contained the promise of the eternal inheritance. See verses 16—18; also Gal. iii. 13, 14, where the thought is very similar.

They which are called.—More clearly, *they that have been called.* (See Acts ii. 39; Rom. i. 6, 7; 2 Thess. ii. 13, 14.) In chap. iii. 1 we have a similar expression, "partakers of a heavenly calling:" there also the idea of sonship (chap. ii. 10), with its right of "inheritance," is certainly present.

(16) **Testament.**—As has been already pointed out, the greatest difference of opinion has existed in regard to the meaning of the Greek word *diathēkē* in this passage. (See Note on chap. vii. 22.) It will be seen at once that the interpretation of this verse and the next entirely depends on that one question. If "testament" is the correct meaning of the Greek word, the general sense of the verses is well given in the Authorised version. A few commentators even agree with that version in carrying back the idea of testament into verse 15, although in the other two places in which the word is joined with "Mediator" (chaps. viii. 6; xii. 24) they adhere to the ordinary rendering, "covenant." By most, however, it is held that a new thought is introduced in the present verse. The writer, it is urged, having spoken of a promise of an *inheritance*, (verse 15), and a promise that cannot be made valid unless death take place, avails himself of the illustration which a second (and very common) meaning of the leading word affords; and though a covenant has hitherto been in his thoughts, he adds interest and force to his argument by calling up the analogy of a testament or will. It is further urged that this procedure will not seem unnatural if we reflect that the *diathēkē* between God and man is never exactly expressed by *covenant*, since it is not of the nature of a mutual compact between equals. (See chap. vii. 22.) The position is chiefly defended by two arguments:—(1) verse 16, being a general maxim, gives no intelligible sense in regard to a covenant, but is easy and natural as applied to a will. (2) A Greek word used in verse 17, where the literal translation is "over (the) dead," cannot be used of sacrifices of slain animals, but of men only. This, we believe, is a fair statement of the case on the one side; and it may be fully acknowledged that, if verses 16, 17 stood alone, and if they were written of Gentile rather than Jewish usage, the case would be very strong. As it is, we are compelled to believe that the difficulties which this interpretation brings with it are beyond comparison more serious than those which it removes. (1) There is no doubt that in the overwhelming majority of New Testament passages the meaning *covenant* must be assigned. By many high authorities these verses are considered to contain the *only* exception. (2) In the LXX. the word is extremely common, both for the covenants of God and for compacts between man and man. (See Note on chap. vii. 22). (3) The application of *diathēkē* in this Epistle rests on the basis of the Old Testament usage, the key passage being Jer. xxxi. 31—34, quoted at length in chap. viii. With that quotation this passage is linked by the association of *diathēkē* with Mediator in verse 15 and chap. viii. 6, and with "the first" in verse 15 and in chaps. viii. 13 and ix. 1. (4) In the verses which follow this passage the meaning *covenant* must certainly return, as a comparison of verse 20 with the verse of Exodus which it quotes (chap. xxiv. 8) will show. (5) It is true that the idea of "death" has appeared in verse 15, but it is the death *of a sin-offering;* and there is no natural or easy transition of thought from an expiatory death to the death of a testator. And yet the words which introduce verses 16 and 18 ("For" and "Wherefore") show that we are following the course of an *argument.* (6) Though to us verse 16 may present a very familiar thought, we must not forget that to Jews dispositions by will were almost altogether unknown. Were it granted that a writer might for illustration avail himself of a second meaning which a word he is using might happen to bear, this liberty would only be taken if by that means *familiar* associations could be reached, and the argument or exhortation could be thus urged home. In an Epistle steeped in Jewish thought such a transition as that suggested would be inexplicable. There are other considerations of some weight which might be added; but these seem sufficient to prove that, even if the difficulties of interpretation should prove serious, we must not seek to remove them by wavering in our rendering of *diathēkē* in these verses. We believe, therefore, that the true translation of verses 16, 17, must be the following:—*For where a covenant is, there must of necessity be brought in the death of the covenanter. For a covenant is of force when there hath been death* (literally, *over* the *dead*)*; for hath it ever any strength while the covenanter liveth?* In verse 15 we have seen the two-fold reference of the death of Jesus, to the past and to the future. As High Priest He has offered Himself as a sin-offering to cleanse the conscience from dead works; the same offering is also looked on as a ransom redeeming from

liveth. (18) Whereupon neither the first *testament* was dedicated[1] without blood. (19) For when Moses had spoken every precept to all the people according to the law, he took the blood of calves and of goats, with water, and scarlet[2] wool, and hyssop, and sprinkled both the book, and all the people, (20) saying, This *is* the blood of the testament which God hath enjoined unto you. (21) More-

2 Or, *purple.*
1 Or, *purified.*

the penalty of past transgressions; and, still by means of His death, He has, as Mediator, established a new covenant. We are reminded at once of the words of Jesus Himself, "This cup is the new covenant *in My blood*" (1 Cor. xi. 25). It is this very thought which the writer proceeds to develop: a covenant cannot be established without death—cannot exist at all. That amongst Jews and Greeks and Romans alike covenants were confirmed by sacrifice we need not pause to prove; of this usage we have the earliest example in Gen. xv. In such sacrifices, again, there is "brought in," or *assumed* the death of him who makes the covenant. There will not, perhaps, be much difficulty in accepting this as a maxim. The conflict of opinion really begins when we ask *in what manner* this is assumed. The usual answer is, that the death of victims is emblematic of the punishment which the contracting parties imprecated on themselves if they should break their compact. It may have been so amongst the Greeks and Romans, though this is doubtful.* Amongst the Jews, however, the analogy of their general sacrificial system, in which the victim represented the offerer, renders such an explanation very improbable. As to the precise idea implied in this representation, it is not easy to speak with certainty. It has been defined in two opposite ways. In the death of the victim each contracting party may be supposed to die either as to the *future,* in respect of any power of altering the compact (the covenant shall be as safe from violation through change of intention as if the covenanter were removed by death); or as to the *past,* to the former state of enmity each is now dead. It is not necessary for our argument to decide such a question as this. The only material points are, that a covenant must be established over sacrifices, and that in such a sacrifice "the death of him that made the covenant" must in some manner be "brought in" or assumed. There remains only the application to the particular covenant here spoken of. If this be taken as made between God and man, the sacrificial death of Jesus in man's stead ratified the covenant for ever, the former state of separation being brought to an end in "the reconciliation" of the gospel. The peculiar character of verse 15, however (see above), seems rather to suggest that, as Jesus is set forth as High Priest and sacrifice, so He is both the Author of the covenant and the sacrifice which gives to it validity. In this case we see represented in His sacrifice the death of each "covenanter." (The transition from "Mediator" to Giver of the covenant is not greater than that which the other interpretation requires—a transition from a mediator of a testament to a testator.) There are minor points relating to details in the Greek which cannot be dealt with here. Of the two arguments quoted above, the former has, we hope, been fully met; though (it may be said in passing) it would be easier to give up verse 16 as a *general* maxim, and to regard it as applying only to a covenant between God and *sinful* man, than to divorce the whole passage from the context by changing "covenant" into "will." One point of interest must not be omitted. There are coincidences of expression with Ps. l. 5 which make it very probable that that Psalm, memorable in the development of the teaching of the Old Testament, was distinctly in the writer's mind. This comparison is also of use in the explanation of some expressions in the original of these two verses.

(18) **Whereupon.**—Better, *Wherefore not even has the first* (*covenant*) *been dedicated* (or, *inaugurated*) *without blood.* (See Ex. xxiv. 6—8.)

(19) **Every precept.**—Or, *commandment.* See Ex. xxiv. 3; where we read that Moses "told the people all the words of the Lord, and all the judgments." These he wrote in a book (verse 4), and this "book of the covenant" (verse 7) he "read in the audience of the people." The contents would probably be the Ten Commandments, and the laws of Ex. xx. 22—xxiii. 33.

Of calves and of goats.—In Exodus (verse 5) we read of "burnt offerings" and of "peace offerings of oxen." The "goats" may be included in the burnt offerings; for though Jewish tradition held that a goat was never sacrificed as a burnt offering, Lev. i. 10 is clear on the other side. It is possible that "the calves and the goats" may be only a general expression for "the sacrificial victims." (See verse 12.)

With water, and scarlet wool, and hyssop.—In Ex. xxiv. there is no mention of these details, but similar notices are found in other parts of the Pentateuch, where the ceremony of sprinkling for purification is described (Ex. xii. 22; Lev. xiv. 4, 6; and Num. xix. 6, 17, 18). The water (itself an emblem and means of cleansing) was designed to prevent the coagulation of the blood, and to increase the quantity of the purifying fluid. The "scarlet wool" may have been used to bind the hyssop to the stick of cedar-wood, which was the instrument of sprinkling. The precise notices in the Law forbid us to doubt that each of these substances had a definite symbolical meaning, but to us the subject is involved in obscurity.

Both the book and all the people.—The Greek is more emphatic: *both the book itself and all the people.* The latter fact alone is mentioned in Exodus (verse 8). The sprinkling of the book of the covenant may be regarded from two points of view. It may depend either on the same principle as the (later) sprinkling of the Tabernacle (verse 22), and the "reconciling" of the Tabernacle and the Holy Place (Lev. xvi. 20) on the Day of Atonement; or on the symbolism of the covenant as noticed above (verses 15—17). In the latter case we must suppose that, as the blood was divided into two portions (Ex. xxiv. 6) in token of the two parties to the covenant, and part "cast upon the altar," the book of the covenant was associated with the altar as representing the presence of Jehovah.

(20) **The testament which God hath enjoined unto you.**—Better, *the covenant which God commanded in regard to you.* "Commanded," see chap. viii. 6: in the LXX. the word is "covenanted."

(21) **He sprinkled with blood.**—Rather, *he sprinkled in like manner with the blood.* It is singular that the word rendered "in like manner" (found

* See Mr. Wratislaw's very interesting note in his "Notes and Dissertations," pp. 155, 156. The whole subject is very carefully treated in an admirable pamphlet by Professor Forbes, of Aberdeen.

over he sprinkled with blood both the tabernacle, and all the vessels of the ministry. (22) And almost all things are by the law purged with blood; and without shedding of blood is no remission. (23) *It was* therefore necessary that the patterns of things in the heavens should be purified with these; but the heavenly things themselves with better sacrifices than these. (24) For Christ is not entered into the holy places made with hands, *which are* the figures of the true; but into heaven itself, now to appear in the presence of

---

in the Bishops' Bible, "likewise," and in other versions) should have been overlooked in the Authorised version. The incident here mentioned belongs, of course, to a later date. It is not expressly recorded in Scripture, but is related by Josephus (*Ant.* iii. 8, § 6); and, apart from internal probability, might almost be concluded from the narrative of the Pentateuch itself. In Ex. xl. 9—15 we read of the divine injunction that Moses should put the anointing oil not only upon Aaron and his sons, their garments, and the altar, but also upon the Tabernacle and its vessels. In Lev. viii. 10—12 is recorded the fulfilment of this command; but in the later verses of the same chapter we read that the altar was sprinkled with the blood of the sin-offering (verse 15), and that Moses sprinkled Aaron and his sons and their garments with "the anointing oil and the blood which was upon the altar." Manifestly we may infer that the Tabernacle and its vessels were included in the latter ceremony. Whatever was connected with the covenant which God made with His people must be sprinkled with the blood, which at once typified purification (verses 14, 24), and ratified the covenant (verses 15, 17).

(22) **And almost all things.**—The meaning of the word "almost," as it stands in the Greek, is rather, "One may almost lay down the rule," "One may almost say." What follows, in both parts of the verse, is a general saying, modified by these introductory words. *And one may almost say—according to the Law, all things are cleansed in blood, and apart from the shedding of blood there is no forgiveness.* To the first rule an exception is found in the various purifications by water or by fire (see Num. xxxi. 22—24); to the second in the remarkable law of Lev. v. 11—13. The expression "*in* blood" is used because sprinkling with the blood of the slain victim was in figure a surrounding with, or inclusion within, the purifying element. On "cleansed" (chap. i. 3) the best comment is found in Lev. xvi. 19, 30; on "forgiveness," in the words which in Lev. iv. are repeatedly (verses, 20, 26, 31, 35) used of the effect of the sin offering, "it shall be forgiven him." The second clause of the verse is founded on Lev. xvii. 11. By "shedding of blood" we must probably understand the slaying of the animal, rather than the pouring out of the blood by the altar (Lev. iv. 34, *et al.*) With these words compare Luke xxii. 20.

(23) **The patterns of things in the heavens.**—Rather, *the tokens* (chap. viii. 5) *of the things in the heavens.* In the first part of the verse a conclusion is drawn from the sacred history, which related the accomplishment of the divine will, and showed therefore what was "necessary." But the real stress lies on the second part. The whole may be paraphrased thus: "Whilst then it is necessary that what are but tokens of the things in the heavens should be cleansed with these things, it is necessary that the heavenly things themselves should be cleansed with better sacrifices than these." The meaning of "these things" might perhaps be found in verse 19 (the various instruments of purification), or in verse 13 (the two sin offerings there spoken of); but, from the prominence given to *repetition* in the following verses, the plural seems rather to mean with these sacrifices repeated from time to time. The common thought in the two parts of the verse appears to be (as in verse 21) that everything relating to the covenant of God with sinful man must be brought under the symbol of expiation, without which he can have no part in that covenant. The "heavenly things" are not defiled by sin; but the true heavenly sanctuary cannot be entered by man, the new fellowship between God and man "in heavenly places" cannot be inaugurated, till the heavenly things themselves have been brought into association with the One atoning sacrifice for man.

Better sacrifices.—Here again the use of the plural is remarkable. It seems to arise from the studious generality in the terms of this verse. To "these things" the natural antithesis is "better sacrifices." That in the ministry of the true High Priest there was a presentation of but *one* sacrifice is not assumed here, because it is to be strongly brought out below (verses 25, 26).

(24) **For Christ is not entered.**—Better, *For Christ did not enter into a holy place made with hands, of like pattern to the true* (or, *real*) *holy place.* In the second part of verse 23 the two thoughts were the "heavenly things themselves" and "better sacrifices." Of these the first is taken up here; the second in verses 25, 26. That verse was general: this sets forth the actual fact. "For the sanctuary into which Christ entered is not a copy or a token of the things in the heavens, but heaven itself." "Of like pattern," see chap. viii. 5; "the true," chap. viii. 2; "into heaven itself," chap. viii. 1.

Now to appear in the presence of God for us.—Better, *now to be made manifest before the face of God for us.* We cannot doubt that these words continue the contrast between the true High Priest and the high priest on earth. On the Day of Atonement the high priest came before what was but a symbol of the Divine Presence; he caused the Holiest Place to be filled with the smoke of the incense before he entered with the blood of the offering. He did not dare to delay his return, even by prolonging his prayer, lest he should "excite terror in Israel." In the heavenly sanctuary the High Priest is made manifest before the face of God. (Comp. Ex. xxxiii. 20.) Three different words in these verses (24, 26, 28) are in the Authorised version rendered by the same word "appear": "to make manifest," "to manifest," "to appear," may serve as renderings which shall keep in mind the difference of the words. The form of the Greek verb might seem to imply a single appearance only; by the added word "now" the writer corrects, or rather enlarges, the thought, and shows that the true meaning is a manifestation which is both one and unceasing. With emphasis he places at the close the words which indicate "the people" whose High Priest He has become. As in chap. viii. 1 his language was "*we* have such a High Priest," and in chap. ix. 14, "shall purge

God for us: (25) nor yet that he should
offer himself often, as the high priest
entereth into the holy place every year
with blood of others; (26) for then must
he often have suffered since the foundation of the world: but now once in the
end of the world hath he appeared to
put away sin by the sacrifice of himself.
(27) And as it is appointed unto men
once to die, but after this the judgment: (28) so Christ was once offered to
bear the sins of many; and unto them
that look for him shall he appear the
second time without sin unto salvation.

---

our conscience;" so here, it is on *our* behalf that Christ is manifested unto God.

(25) **Nor yet that he should**—*i.e., Nor yet* (*did He enter into heaven*) *that He may offer Himself often.* The connection has been pointed out already in the last Note. The "offering" which is here in thought does not correspond to the actual sacrifice of the sin-offerings on the Day of Atonement, but to the presentation of the blood in the Holiest Place. In this really consisted the presentation of that sacrifice to God. That this is the meaning here is shown by the contrast in the latter part of the verse, where we read of the high priest's entering the Holy Place (*i.e.*, the Holy of Holies; see Note on verse 2) "with blood not his own," and by the argument of verse 26.

(26) **For then must he often have suffered.**—The repeated presentation of Himself to God must imply, as a necessary condition, a repeated "suffering" of death; as the high priest's offering of the blood of expiation in the Holiest Place implied the previous sacrifice of the victim. The writer's point of view is the time when "Christ entered into heaven itself." In speaking of the repeated "suffering" (Luke xxiv. 26, 46, *et al.*), he marks the limits within which it must lie, reaching back to the "foundation of the world." The expression in the second part of the verse is the converse of this: looking forward from the "foundation of the world," through all the successive periods of human history until the Incarnation, he writes, "Now once at the end of the world"—"at the consummation of the ages"—hath Christ "been manifested." The words "consummation of the age" occur five times in St. Matthew's Gospel—chaps. xiii. 39, 40, 49; xxiv. 3; xxviii. 20. (See the Notes.) The phrase here is more expressive still. The history of all preceding ages was a preparation for the manifestation of the Christ ("who verily was fore-ordained before the foundation of the world, but was manifest in these last times" (literally, *at the end of the times*), 1 Pet. i. 20; all subsequent history develops the results of that manifestation. A similar thought is contained in St. Paul's words "the fulness of the seasons" (Eph. i. 10), "the fulness of the time" (Gal. iv. 4). (See further the Note on chap. i. 2.)

To put away sin by the sacrifice of Himself.—Literally, *for the annulling of sin through His sacrifice.* The word which in chap. vii. 18 was used for the abrogation of the command relating to the line of earthly priests, is here applied to the destruction of the power and abolition of the results of sin. As in the manifestation before the face of God we see the proof that the goal which the human high priest failed to reach had been attained, so these words proclaim full deliverance from guilt and penalty, and from the hold of sin itself—a deliverance which the sin-offering could but express in figure.

(27) **And as it is appointed . . .**—More literally, *And as there is laid up for men once to die, and after this judgment.* Man's life and works on earth end with death: what remains is the result of this life and these works, as determined by God's "judgment." Man does not return to die a second time. That some few have twice passed through death does not affect the general law. The emphatic word "once" and the special design of the verse are explained by the words which follow.

(28) **So Christ was once offered.**—The ordinary translation, dividing the verse into two similar portions, fails to show where the emphasis really lies. The two members of the verse correspond to each other, point by point, with remarkable distinctness; but the first is clearly subordinated to the second. "So the Christ also, having been once offered that He might bear the sins of many, shall appear a second time apart from sin to them that wait for Him unto salvation." It is important to notice that, not only is there perfect parallelism between the two members of this verse, but there is a similar relation between this verse as a whole and verse 27. In that were presented two cardinal points of the history of sinful man; in this the main outlines of the Redeemer's work. Each verse deals first with the present world, and secondly with "the last things." The two verses, taken together, are connected with the preceding argument by the word "once." Christ will not "suffer" often. He has been manifested once, to accomplish by one act the "annulling" of sin (verse 26). And this is in harmony with the lot of man, who must die once, and but once (verses 27, 28). But what is the exact nature of this correspondence? Do the words simply mean that, as the Christ was man, so it was laid up for Him to die but once? Or may the connection of thought be expressed thus?—The work of redemption is so ordered as to correspond to the course of man's history: as man must die once, and what remains is the judgment which he must abide, so the Christ has died once, and what remains is His return for judgment—a judgment which He Himself administers, giving salvation to His people. We will not venture to say that the former thought is absent from the words (which are sufficiently general to include both), but certainly the second is the more important. If now we return to verse 28, it will be seen that the words "having been once offered" in the first member are answered by "shall appear" in the second; "to bear sins," by "apart from sin . . . unto salvation;" and "of many," by "to them that wait for Him." In verses 14, 25, the writer spoke of Christ as offering Himself, here as "having been offered;" so in Eph. v. 2 we read that He "delivered Himself up for us," but in Rom. viii. 32 that God "delivered Him up for us all," and in Rom. iv. 25, "who was delivered up for our offences." The words which follow are taken (with a slight change) from Isa. liii. 12, "and He bare the sin of many." These words clearly involve sacrificial imagery. What is signified is not directly the *removal* of sin (as in the different words of John i. 29); but, as on the animal to be slain the sins of the offerer were in figure laid, and the death which followed signified the death which the offerer had deserved, so, with an infinite extension

CHAPTER X. — (1) For the law having a shadow of good things to come, *and* not the very image of the things, can never with those sacrifices which they offered year by year continually make the comers thereunto perfect. (2) For then would they not have ceased to be offered? because that the worshippers once purged should have had no more conscience of sins. (3) But in those *sacrifices there is* a remembrance again *made* of sins every year. (4) For *it is* not possible that the blood of bulls and of goats should take

Chap. x. 1—18. The repeated sacrifices of the Law. The One Sacrifice which takes away sin.

A.D. 64.

of meaning, are the words here applied. It is certainly no mere accident that the writer, thus availing himself of the prophet's words, speaks of *the Christ.* In contrast with the one Sufferer are the "many" whose sins are borne (comp. chap. ii. 10; Matt. xxvi. 28). When the Christ shall appear the second time, it shall be "apart from sin"—no longer bearing sin, but "separate from sinners" (chap. vii. 26). Of the judgment which He shall pass upon "the adversaries" (chap. x. 27) this verse does not speak, but only of His appearing to His own people, who "wait for Him." This expressive word, again and again used by St. Paul (see Note on Rom. viii. 19) to describe the attitude of Christ's people upon earth towards their Lord (Phil. iii. 20; 1 Cor. i. 7) and His salvation (Rom. viii. 23, 25), is here applied to *all* who love His appearing. By these "He shall be seen" as He is (1 John iii. 2). The last words "unto salvation" declare the purpose of His appearing, in a form which at once recalls the teaching of earlier verses in the Epistle (chap. v. 9; vii. 26), and especially verse 12 of this chapter, and which brings to mind the name of Him for whom we wait, the Saviour (Phil. iii. 20).

X.

The latter part of the ninth chapter was an expansion of verses 11, 12. In particular, verses 23—28 have been occupied with the theme, "Christ entered once for all into the Holy Place, having won eternal redemption." The repeated offerings presented by the high priests have been contrasted with the sacrifice which He has offered. To this thought the opening verses of this chapter attach themselves, explaining more fully the inefficacy of the one, the power and virtue of the other. Gradually the main thoughts of the preceding chapters are gathered up, and the last and chief division of the argument of the Epistle is brought to a close in verse 18.

(1) **A Shadow of good things to come.**—These words have already come before us; the "shadow" in chap. viii. 5, and "the good things to come" in the ordinary reading of chap. ix. 11.

Not the very image.—The antithesis is hardly what we should have expected. The word "image" is indeed consistent with the very closest and most perfect likeness; but why is the contrast to "shadow" expressed by a word which cannot denote more than likeness, and not by a reference to the things themselves? The answer would seem to be that, from the very nature of the "good things to come," the law could not be conceived of as having the things themselves; but had it possessed "the very image" of them, a representation so perfect might have been found to bring with it equal efficacy.

Can never with those sacrifices.—It is difficult to ascertain the exact Greek text in the latter half of this verse. With the ordinary reading the general construction of the sentence is that which the Authorised version represents, "For the law . . . can never . . . make perfect." The better MSS., however, read "they can," a change which introduces some irregularity of construction: the pronoun "they" must probably in this case be understood of the priests. The order of the Greek is also very peculiar. Two translations of the verse (with the changed reading) may be given: (1) "They can never with the same sacrifices year by year which they offer continually make them that draw nigh perfect." (2) "They can never year by year, by the same sacrifices which they offer continually, make them that draw nigh perfect." The difference between the two renderings will be easily seen. The former makes the whole sentence to relate to the annual sacrifice on the Day of Atonement, and gives to "continually" almost the same meaning as "year by year." The meaning of the latter is that by the annual sacrifices, which are the same as those which the priests are offering for the people day by day (for the sacrifice of the Day of Atonement did not *in itself* differ from the ordinary sin offering), they cannot make the worshippers perfect. The latter translation agrees best with the original, and conveys a very striking thought. It is open, however, to a very serious objection—that it separates the verse into two incongruous parts. That annual sacrifices not different in kind from the sin offerings which were presented day by day (and which the very institution of the Day of Atonement declared to be imperfect) could not bring to the worshippers what they needed, is an important argument; but it has no connection with the first words of the verse. Hence, though the Greek does not very readily yield the former translation, it is probably to be preferred. With the expression "them that draw nigh" or "approach" (to God) comp. chap. vii. 26, where the same word is used. On "make perfect" see chaps. vii. 11; ix. 9.

(2) **For then.**—Better, *otherwise.* The very repetition of the annual ceremonial was a testimony to its imperfection. The idea of repetition has been very strikingly brought out in verse 1.

Once purged.—Better, *because the worshippers, having been once cleansed, would have no more consciousness of sins.* "Worshippers," not the same word as in verse 1, but similarly used in chap. ix. 9, 14; xii. 28 (Phil. iii. 3, *et al.*): in chap. viii. 5; xiii. 10, it is applied to priestly service.

(3) **There is a remembrance.**—Better, *a remembrance of sins is made year by year.* In each of the three prayers of the high priest (see chap. v. 3) for himself and his house, for the priesthood, for the people, he made special acknowledgment of sin. "I have sinned, I and my house and the sons of Aaron: Thy people have done perversely."

(4) This verse explains those which precede. No inconsistency really belonged to these sacrifices and this ceremonial, though so often repeated; for it was impossible that any such sacrifice should really remove sin. The offering was necessary, and it answered its purpose; but it could not remove the necessity for another and a better offering.

away sins. (5) Wherefore when he cometh into the world, he saith, Sacrifice and offering thou wouldest not, but a body hast thou prepared me:[1] In burnt offerings and *sacrifices* for sin thou hast had no pleasure. (7) Then said I, Lo, I come (in the volume of the book it is written of me,) to do thy will,

[1] Or, *thou hast fitted me.*

(5) **Wherefore.**—That is, on account of this powerlessness of the sacrifices of the law.

He saith.—Christ, in the prophetic word of Scripture. Though not directly mentioned here, He has been the subject of the whole context (chap. ix. 25—28). The words which follow are a quotation from Ps. xl. 6—8, and agree substantially with the LXX., except that in verse 7 a word of some importance is omitted (see the Note there). The LXX., again, is on the whole a faithful representation of the Hebrew text: one clause only (the last in this verse) presents difficulty. Particular expressions will be noticed as they occur: the general meaning and application of the psalm must first receive attention. Like Ps. l. and li. (with some verses of Ps. lxix.), Ps. xl. is remarkable for its anticipation of the teaching of the prophets (Isa. i. 11—17; Jer. vii. 21; Hos. vi. 6; Mic. vi. 6—8; *et al.*) on one point, the inferior worth of ceremonial observances when contrasted with moral duties. It seems probable that the psalm is David's, as the inscription relates, and that its key-note is to be found in the words of Samuel to Saul (1 Sam. xv. 22): "Hath the Lord as great delight in burnt offerings and sacrifices, as in obeying (literally, *hearkening to*) the voice of the Lord? Behold, to obey (literally, *to hear*) is better than sacrifice, and to hearken than the fat of rams." The first part of the psalm is an expression of thanksgiving to God for deliverance from peril. David has learned the true mode of displaying gratitude, not by offerings of slain animals, but by the sacrifice of the will. So far does the latter excel the former, so truly is the sacrifice of will in accordance with the will of God, that the value of the legal offerings is in comparison as nothing. There is in all this no real slighting of the sacrificial ritual (see Jer. vii. 21—28), but there is a profound appreciation of the superiority of spiritual service to mere ritual observance. It can hardly be said that this quotation rests on the same principle as those of the first chapter. The psalm is certainly not Messianic, in the sense of being wholly predictive like Ps. cx., or directly typical like Ps. ii. In some respects, indeed, it resembles 2 Sam. vii. (See the Note on chap. i. 5.) As there, after words which are quoted in this Epistle in reference to Christ, we read of David's son as committing iniquity and receiving punishment; so in this psalm we read, "Mine iniquities are more than the hairs of mine head." David comes with a new perception of the true will of God, to offer Him the service in which He takes pleasure. And yet not so—for such service as he can offer is itself defective; his sins surround him yet in their results and penalties. Hence, in his understanding and his offering of himself he is a type, whilst his sinfulness and weakness render him but an imperfect type, of Him that was to come. Such passages as these constitute a distinct and very interesting division of Messianic prophecy. We may then thus trace the principle on which the psalm is here applied. Jesus came to His Father with that perfect offering of will and self which was foreshadowed in the best impulses of the best of the men of God, whose inspired utterances the Scriptures record. The words of David, but partially true of himself, are fulfilled in the Son of David. Since, then, these words describe the purpose of the Saviour's life, we can have no difficulty in understanding the introductory words, "when He cometh into the world, He saith;" or the seventh verse, where we read, "Lo, I am come to do Thy will." When David saw the true meaning of the law, he thus came before God; the purpose of Jesus, when He received the body which was the necessary instrument for human obedience, finds its full expression in these words.

Sacrifice and offering.—The corresponding Hebrew words denote the two divisions of offerings, as made with or without the shedding of blood.

But a body hast thou prepared me.—Rather, *but a body didst Thou prepare for me.* Few discrepancies between the LXX. and the Hebrew have attracted more notice than that which these words present. The words of the Psalmist are, "In sacrifice and offering Thou hast not delighted: ears hast Thou digged for me." As in Samuel's words, already referred to as containing the germ of the psalm, sacrifice is contrasted with *hearing* and with *hearkening to the voice of the Lord*, the meaning evidently is, Thou hast given me the power of hearing so as to obey. A channel of communication has been opened, through which the knowledge of God's true will can reach the heart, and excite the desire to obey. All ancient Greek versions except the LXX. more or less clearly express the literal meaning. It has been supposed that the translators of the LXX. had before them a different reading of the Hebrew text, preferable to that which is found in our present copies. This is very unlikely. Considering the general principles of their translation, we may with greater probability suppose that they designed merely to express the general meaning, avoiding a literal rendering of a Hebrew metaphor which seemed harsh and abrupt. They seem to have understood the Psalmist as acknowledging that God had given him that which would produce obedience; and to this (they thought) would correspond the preparation of a body which might be the instrument of rendering willing service. If the present context be carefully examined, we shall see that, though the writer does afterwards make reference (verse 10) to the new words here introduced, they are in no way necessary to his argument, nor does he lay on them any stress.

(6) **Burnt offerings.**—Better, *whole burnt offerings.* These (which were the symbol of complete consecration) are not mentioned in this Epistle, except in this verse and verse 8.

Thou hast had no pleasure.—Better (for conformity with the preceding clauses), *Thou hadst no pleasure.*

(7) **Lo, I come.**—Rather, *Lo, I am come*—I am here. The original meaning of the following words is not quite certain. The Hebrew admits of two renderings. (1) Then I said, Lo, I am come! in the roll of the Book it is prescribed unto me; (2) Then I said, Lo, I am come with the roll of the Book that is written concerning me. The "roll of the Book" is the roll containing the Divine Law. The next clause is quite distinct in construction: "I delight to do Thy will, O God; yea, Thy law is within my heart." The omission of the words "I delight," alters the connection of the words; but it will be seen that, though the Hebrew verses are condensed, their meaning is exactly preserved.

O God. (8) Above when he said, Sacrifice and offering and burnt offerings and *offering* for sin thou wouldest not, neither hadst pleasure *therein;* which are offered by the law; (9) Then said he, Lo, I come to do thy will, O God. He taketh away the first, that he may establish the second. (10) By the which will we are sanctified through the offering of the body of Jesus Christ once *for all.* (11) And every priest standeth daily ministering and offering oftentimes the same sacrifices, which can never take away sins: (12) but this man, after he had offered one sacrifice for sins for ever, sat down on the right

---

(8) **Above when he said.**—Better, *Whereas he saith above*; or, as we might express it, "Saying at the outset," "Setting out with saying." In the following words the best MSS. have the plural, "*Sacrifices and offerings and whole burnt offerings and* (*sacrifices*) *for sin.*" The change from singular to plural is in harmony with the thought of verses 1—4, the repetition of sacrifices.

Which are offered by the law.—Rather, *such as are offered according to law.* The change from "the law" to "law" seems intentional, as if the writer had in thought the contrast between any external law of ritual and a principle of inward obedience.

(9) **Then said he, Lo, I come.**—Rather, *then hath he said, Lo, I am come to do Thy will.* The words "O God" are not in the true text, but have been accidentally repeated from verse 7.

He taketh away the first, that he may establish the second.—It is important to inquire how this is done, first in the case of the writer of the psalm, then as the words are used of Jesus. David, perceiving that that which God seeks is the subjection of man's will, refuses to rest in the sacrifices of the law. No one will think that burnt offering or gift or sacrifice for sin was henceforth at an end for him: the confession of his iniquities (verse 12) implied a recourse to the appointed means of approach to God: even the sacrifices themselves were taken up into the service of obedience. But to the symbols shall be added the consecration and the sacrifice of praise (Ps. l. 23) which they typified. The application to the Saviour must be interpreted by this context. In making these words His own, He declares the sacrifices of the law to be in themselves without virtue; Jehovah seeks them not from Him, but, having prepared a human body for Him, seeks only the fulfilment of His will. But included in that will of God was Christ's offering of Himself for the world; and, on the other hand, it was His perfect surrender of Himself that gave completeness to that offering. His death was at once the antitype of the sacrifice for sin and the consummation of the words, "I am come to do Thy will, O God." Hence, in saying, "Lo, I am come to do Thy will" (that which God has really willed), He taketh away the sacrifices of slain animals that He may establish the doing of God's will. That such sacrifices as were formerly offered are no longer according to God's pleasure follows as an inference from this.

(10) **By the which will we are sanctified.**—Better, *In which will we have been sanctified.* In the last verse we read of that which Jesus established—the doing of the will of God. He did that will when He offered the sacrifice of His perfect obedience—"obedience as far as death" (Phil. ii. 8). In this will of God which He accomplished lies our sanctification, effected "through the offering of the body of Jesus Christ once for all." In chap. ix. 14 the efficacy of the blood of Christ to cleanse the conscience is contrasted with the power of the offerings of the law to "sanctify in regard to cleanness of the flesh:" here the real sanctification is joined with "the offering of the body of Jesus Christ." In the word "body" lies a reference to verse 8, where the body is looked on as the instrument of obedient service (comp. Rom. xii. 1); but the word "offering" still preserves its sacrificial character, and contains an allusion to the presentation of the body of the slain victim. (Comp. chap. xiii. 11). As this offering has been presented "once for all" (chaps. vii. 27; ix. 12), so "once for all" has the work of sanctification been achieved.

(11) The last was a verse of transition. Naturally following from and completing the previous argument, it leads in the words "once for all" to a new thought, or rather prepares the way for the resumption of a subject to which in an earlier chapter marked prominence was given. If the sanctifying work of the true High Priest has been accomplished "once for all," such ministry remains for Him no longer (verses 12—14). Here, then, the writer brings us back to chap. viii. 1, 2—to that which he there declared to be the crowning point of all his words.

And every priest.—Some ancient MSS. and versions read "high priest," but the ordinary text is in all probability correct. (With the other reading the work of the priests in their daily ministrations is ascribed to the high priest, whose representatives they were.) Hitherto the thought has rested almost entirely on the ceremonial of the Day of Atonement; there is therefore new significance in the contrast between Jesus and "*every* priest" in all His ministrations. On "standeth" see the Note on chap. viii. 1. The accumulation of words which point to the ceaseless repetition of the offerings of the law (verse 1) is very noteworthy. The last words point to verse 4.

(12) **But this man.**—Rather, *but He.* In the main this verse is a combination of chaps. vii. 27 (ix. 26) and viii. 1. One addition is made, in the words, "for ever." These words (which occur in three other places, chaps. vii. 3; x. 1, 14) are by many joined with what precedes, by others with the latter part of the sentence, "sat down on the right hand of God." The different editions of our Bible and Prayer Book (Epistle for Good Friday) are divided, some (including the earliest) having a comma at the word "ever," others at "sins." In most of our earlier English versions the construction adopted was shown by the arrangement of the words. Thus Tyndale has, "sat him down for ever;" and the Bishops' Bible, "is set down for ever." Coverdale (following Luther) is very clear on the other side: "when He had offered for sins one sacrifice which is of value for ever." Most modern commentators seem to adopt the latter view ("for ever sat down"), but hardly, perhaps, with sufficient reason. The analogy of verse 14 is distinctly on the other side; and the Greek phrase rendered "for ever" is more suitably applied to the offering of a sacrifice than to the thought of the following words.

hand of God; (13) from henceforth expecting till his enemies be made his footstool. (14) For by one offering he hath perfected for ever them that are sanctified. (15) *Whereof* the Holy Ghost also is a witness to us: for after that he had said before, (16) This *is* the covenant that I will make with them after those days, saith the Lord, I will put my laws into their hearts, and in their minds will I write them; (17) and their sins and iniquities will I remember no more.[a] (18) Now where remission of these *is, there is* no more offering for sin.

Chap. x. 19—39 Exhortation to steadfastness in faith and good works.

(19) Having therefore, brethren, boldness[1] to enter into the holiest by the blood of Jesus, (20) by a new and living way, which he

a Jer. 31. 33.

1 Or, *liberty.*

The contrast to verse 11 is strongly marked. The sacrificial work has been performed, and the High Priest no longer "standeth ministering." The words "sat down" (Ps. cx. 1) add to the priestly imagery that of kingly state.

(13) **Expecting.**—This word belongs to the contrast just mentioned. He does not minister and offer His sacrifice again, but waits for the promised subjection of His foes. Once before in this context (chap. ix. 28) our thought has been thus directed to the future consummation. There it consists in the second coming of Christ for the salvation of "them that wait for Him;" here it is He Himself who is "waiting," and the end is the attainment of supreme dominion. (See chap. i. 3, 13.)

(14) No repetition of His offering is needed, for by one offering He hath brought all unto "perfection," and that "for ever." In chap. vii. 11 we have read that "perfection" did not come through the Levitical priesthood or through the law (verse 19); the object of man's hopes and of all priestly service has at last been attained, since through the "great High Priest" "we draw nigh to God" (chap. vii. 19). In this is involved salvation to the uttermost (chap. vii. 25). The last word of this verse has occurred before, in chap. ii. 11. As was there explained, it literally means those who *are being sanctified*, all those who, from age to age, through faith (verse 22) receive as their own that which has been procured for all men.

(15) **Whereof.**—Better, *And the Holy Ghost also beareth witness unto us.* The Holy Ghost, speaking in Scripture (chap. iii. 7; ix. 8)—the Scripture quoted in chap. viii. 8—12—beareth witness.

After that he had said before.—Rather, *after He hath said.* The word "before" is not in the best MSS.

(16) **I will put my laws.**—Rather, *putting my laws upon their heart, upon their mind also will I write them.* The first part of the quotation (chap. viii. 8, 9, 10 in part) is omitted, and also some later lines (the last words of verse 10 and the whole of verse 11 in chap. viii.). In the remainder we notice some variations, which prove that the writer is not aiming at verbal agreement with the original passage, but is quoting the substance only. (See the Note on chap. viii. 10.)

(17) Every reader must feel that as these verses stand in the Authorised version the sense is imperfect. The words "after He hath said before" (verse 15) imply "then He saith," or similar words, at some point in the verses which follow. Our translators did not attempt to complete the sense; for the marginal note ("some copies have, *Then he saith, And their*") found in ordinary editions was added at a later date.* By many commentators it is believed that the words "saith the Lord" (verse 16) are intended as the completion of the sentence, so that no supplement is needed. This is, we think, very improbable. As it is the last part of the quotation that is taken up here, it is at the beginning of this verse that the explanatory words must come in: "*Then He saith,* And their sins and their iniquities will I remember no more." This we have seen to be the crowning promise of the new covenant of which Jesus is the Mediator. When these words were first quoted (chap. viii. 12), some important points in the argument were still untouched. Now the firm basis of the promise has been shown, for the covenant has been ratified by the death of Christ, and the blessings He has won for men are eternal (chap. ix. 15, 12).

(18) **Now where.**—Rather, *But where remission* (or *forgiveness,* see chap. ix. 22) *of these is, there is no longer offering for sin.* Here the argument reaches its triumphant close.

At this point we enter on the last great division of the Epistle (chaps. x. 19—xiii. 25), which is occupied with earnest exhortation, encouragement to perseverance alternating with solemn warning against apostasy. The first section of this main division extends to the end of this chapter.

(19) The exhortation which here begins is very similar to that of chap. iv. 14—16. Its greater fulness and expressiveness are in accordance with the development in the thought.

Therefore.—The chief thoughts taken up are those expressed in chap. ix. 11, 12. The word "boldness" has occurred in chap. iii. 6; iv. 16. (See the Notes.)

By the blood of Jesus.—Better, *in the blood of Jesus;* for the meaning probably is, "Having therefore boldness in the blood of Jesus for entering into the Holy (*i.e.,* the Holiest) Place." It is not that we enter "with the blood," as the high priest entered the Holy of Holies (chap. ix. 25): no comparison is made between Christ's people and the Jewish high priest. But as when he entered within the veil the whole people symbolically entered in with him, so do we enter with our High Priest, who "by means of His own blood" entered for us (and as our "Forerunner," chap. vi. 20) into the immediate presence of God. In that through which He entered we have our "boldness to enter."

(20) **By a new and living way.**—Better, *by the way which He dedicated* (or *inaugurated*) *for us, a new and living way.* This way was opened to us by Him; in it we follow Him. For Him, the way into the Holiest led through the veil, His flesh. As the veil concealed from the high priest the place of God's presence, which he could enter only by passing through the veil; so, although in His earthly life Jesus dwelt in the presence of God, yet as our representative He

* From Dr. Scrivener's "Cambridge Paragraph Bible" (p. xxxii.) we learn that the note was added by Dr. Paris in the Cambridge Bible of 1762. Dr. Scrivener adds: "probably from the Philoxenian Syriac version, then just becoming known."

hath consecrated[1] for us, through the veil,
that is to say, his flesh; (21) and *having*
an high priest over the house of God;
(22) let us draw near with a true heart
in full assurance of faith, having our
hearts sprinkled from an evil conscience,
and our bodies washed with pure water.
(23) Let us hold fast the profession of
our faith without wavering; (for he *is*
faithful that promised;) (24) and let us
consider one another to provoke unto
love and to good works: (25) not for-
saking the assembling of ourselves
together, as the manner of some *is;*
but exhorting *one another:* and so much
the more, as ye see the day approaching.
(26) For if we sin wilfully after that we
have received the knowledge of the

1 Or, *new made.*

could not enter the heavenly sanctuary until He had passed through and out of His life of flesh (see chap. ix. 11). There is probably a covert allusion to the rending of the Temple veil in the hour when Jesus thus passed through the rent veil of His flesh. This way is new (chap. ix. 8, 12), it is living, for in truth this "way" is living union with Christ (John xiv. 6).

(21) **An high priest.**—The Greek words properly signify a *great priest* (comp. chap. iv. 14), which is one of the names by which the high priest is frequently designated, both in the Hebrew (Lev. xxi., *et al.*), and in the LXX. It may seem strange that the writer should here make use of a new word in the place of that which has occurred so frequently. But there is strong reason for believing that the language of one of the prophecies of Zechariah (vi. 11—13) is here before his mind. In the preceding verses (12—14) he has used words which united sacerdotal and kingly imagery; and it would be remarkable if this did not lead his thought to that prophecy. On the head of Joshua, "the great priest" (Zech. vi. 11), are placed crowns of silver and gold in token of royal dignity: then follows the prediction of Him of whom Joshua was the type. "He shall build the house of the Lord: and He shall bear the glory, and shall sit and rule upon His throne; and He shall be a priest upon His throne." In the verse before us are combined several of the characteristic thoughts of that passage—the great priest, the priestly ruler, the house of God. The last-mentioned words are repeatedly used throughout the Old Testament, both in the Pentateuch and in later books, for the Tabernacle or Temple of God. In chap. iii. 6 (to which there is a manifest allusion here) the meaning is enlarged, but only so that under "the house" is also comprised the *household* of God. Here the two thoughts are combined. Into the house of God we may enter; over it Jesus rules as "the great Priest." The family of God subject to His rule includes the whole community of "the people of God" in heaven and upon earth.

(22) **Let us draw near.**—See verse 1; also chaps. iv. 16; vii. 25; xi. 6.

With a true heart.—"True," the word used in chaps. viii. 2, ix. 24, a *real*—*i.e.*, a sincere heart. As in chap. vi. we read of "full assurance," or rather, "fulness of hope," so here of *fulness of faith.* Without this there could be for us no "living way" (verse 20) for entering into the holiest place. The thought of the whole verse connects itself with the priestly character of those who are the people of God (Ex. xix. 6; Rev. i. 5, 6). It is as priests that they enter the house of God, sprinkled with the blood of atonement (chaps. xii. 24; ix. 14; Lev. viii. 30; 1 Pet. i. 2), and with all defilement washed away (Lev. viii. 6). "Sprinkled from an evil conscience:" that is, freed by means of the "sprinkling" from a conscience defiled by guilt. In the last words there is a clear allusion to baptism, as the symbol of the new life of purity (Eph. v. 26; Tit. iii. 5; 1 Pet. iii. 21).

(23) In this verse again we have the characteristic words of earlier exhortations: "hold fast" (chap. iii. 6, 14); "profession," or, rather, *confession* (chaps. iii. 1; iv. 14).

Of our faith.—This rendering, apparently found in no earlier English version, is supposed to be due to oversight on the part of our translators. The true reading is "of the hope" (chap. vi. 11, 18, 19). The two following words must be joined with "confession," "let us hold fast the confession of the (Christian) hope so that it waver not." This hope "maketh not ashamed" (Rom. v. 5), for the promise is sure.

(24) Gradually the writer passes from that which belongs to the individual (verses 19, 20) to the mutual duties of members of a community. Possibly he knew that amongst those whom he addresses there had existed "provocations" that did not tend towards brotherly love. The strict meaning may simply be—let us take note of one another, to stimulate one another to good works; but in the result, if not in the expression, is included the converse thought, "that we may ourselves be thus provoked."

(25) **As the manner of some is.**—Some members of this community, it would seem, had persuaded themselves that the relation of Judaism to Christianity, of the "synagogue" (the Greek word here used seems to allude to this technical name, and yet intentionally to avoid it) and the Church, was such as to permit them to avoid close intercourse with Christians and direct association with Christian assemblies. This neglect was the first step towards apostasy.

Exhorting.—Better, *encouraging.* (Comp. chap. xii. 12.)

The day.—See 1 Cor. iii. 13—"the day shall declare" every man's work. Elsewhere we read of "the day of the Lord" (1 Thess. v. 2); "the day of Christ" (Phil. i. 10). The words of Jesus to His disciples (Matt. xxiv.; Luke xvii.) had enabled all who were willing to hear to understand "the signs of the times." As the writer gave these warnings, the day when the Son of Man should come in His kingdom, bringing judgment upon Jerusalem (Matt. xvi. 28), was close at hand—that day which is distinctly presented to us in the New Testament as the type of His final coming.

(26) **For.**—The connecting links are the thought of the consequences to which such sinful neglect (verse 25) may lead, and the awful revelation of judgment which the final day will bring. Even more clearly than in chap. vi. 4—6 the state described is one of wilful and continued sin, which is the result and the expression of apostasy from Christ. It is not, "If we fall under temptation and commit sin;" but, "If we are sinning wilfully." The descriptive words are few as compared with those of the former passage, but they teach the same lesson. Not merely the "knowledge" but the

truth, there remaineth no more sacrifice for sins, (27) but a certain fearful looking for of judgment and fiery indignation, which shall devour the adversaries. (28) He that despised Moses' law died without mercy under two or three witnesses: (29) of how much sorer punishment, suppose ye, shall he be thought worthy, who hath trodden under foot the Son of God, and hath counted the blood of the covenant, wherewith he was sanctified, an unholy thing, and hath done despite unto the Spirit of grace? (30) For we know him that hath said, Vengeance *belongeth* unto me, I will recompense,[a] saith the Lord. And again, The Lord shall judge his people. (31) *It is* a fearful thing to fall into the hands of the living God. (32) But call to remembrance the former

[a] Deut. 32. 35; Rom. 12. 19.

"full knowledge" (Rom. i. 28) of the truth has been received by those to whom the writer here makes reference; they have been "sanctified in the blood of the covenant" (verse 29). For such "there remaineth no longer a sacrifice for sins:" that offering of Jesus which they deliberately reject has abolished all the earlier sacrifices. The observances and ceremonies of Judaism, which had been full of meaning whilst they pointed to Him that was to come, have lost all their virtue through His coming. Nay more: for such sin as this, the sin of knowing and wilful rejection of the only Sin offering, God has provided no other sacrifice. In its general significance this passage does not differ from chap. vi. 4—6. (See the Notes.)

(27) **But a certain fearful looking for.**—Better, *But a fearful awaiting of judgment, and a jealousy of fire that shall devour the adversaries.* For Christ's "waiting" servants the thought of "judgment" is lost in that of "salvation" (chap. ix. 27, 28); to these sinners nothing is left but the awaiting of judgment. The next words are a partial quotation, or an adaptation, of Isa. xxvi. 11: "Let them see (and be ashamed) the zeal for the people; yea, fire shall devour Thine adversaries." (The Greek translation gives the second clause correctly, but not the former part of the sentence.) In the prophetic imagery of the Old Testament the destruction of the enemies of Jehovah is but the other aspect of His zeal or jealousy for His people. This imagery was familiar to every Hebrew; and no words could show more powerfully than these that to forsake Christ for Judaism was (not to join, but) to *abandon* "the people of God." For such apostates there remaineth the zeal, the jealous wrath, of a devouring fire. (Comp. chap. xii. 29; Mal. iv.)

(28) **He that despised Moses' law.**—Rather, *A man that hath set at nought a law of Moses dieth without pity before two or three witnesses.* The reference is to Deut. xvii. 2—7, the last words being a direct quotation from verse 6 in that section. There the subject is apostasy from Jehovah to the worship of idols. That sin which, by the acknowledgment of all, had in ancient time robbed Israel of the name of God's people is tacitly placed by the side of the sin of those who forsake Christ. It will be seen how impressively the thought of the last verse is maintained in this.

(29) **Shall he be thought worthy.**—Better, *shall he be accounted* (or, *judged*) *worthy*, by God the Judge of all, when "the Day" shall come. In the act of apostasy the sinner trampled under foot the Son of God, treated with contempt and scorn Him to whom belongs this highest Name (chap. i. 1—4); and the principle of this act becomes the principle of the whole succeeding life. That "blood" by which the new covenant was established (chap. ix. 15—17)—the blood in which he himself had received the sanctification which the law could not give—he has esteemed an unholy thing. There is no medium between highest reverence and utter contumely in such a case: to those who did not receive Jesus as Lord He was a deceiver (Matt. xxvii. 63), and one who deserved to die.

Hath done despite.—Hath treated with outrage and insult the Spirit of whose gifts he had been partaker (chap. vi. 4), for "grace" returning arrogant scorn.

(30) **Vengeance belongeth unto me, I will recompense.**—This quotation from Deut. xxxii. 35 completely preserves the sense of the original words, "To me belongeth vengeance, and recompence," whilst departing from their form. The LXX. shows still wider divergence, neglecting entirely the emphasis which rests on the words "to *Me*." It is therefore very remarkable that this quotation is given, in exactly the same form, in Rom. xii. 19. As, however, the words "I will recompense" are found in the most ancient of the Targums (that of Onkelos) it is very possible that St. Paul may have there adopted a form already current amongst the Jews. (See Note on Rom. xii. 19.) If so, there is no difficulty in accounting for the coincidence in this place. But, even if this supposition is without foundation, and the saying in this form was first used in Rom. xii. 19, is there any real cause for wonder if a disciple of St. Paul in a single instance reproduces the Apostle's words? It should be observed that the words "saith the Lord" must be omitted from the text, according to the best authorities.

The Lord shall judge his people.—This, again, is a quotation, and from the same chapter (Deut. xxxii. 36). If the context of the original passage be examined, there will be no doubt as to the meaning of the words. As in Ps. xliii. 1, cxxxv. 14, "to judge," as here used, signifies to maintain the right of one who is exposed to wrong. "The Lord shall judge His people" (see verse 27) when He shall appear to establish their cause by taking vengeance on His enemies and theirs. With what impressive force would the quotations in this section (verses 27, 28, 30)—differing widely in form, but presenting a very striking agreement in their meaning—fall on the ears of readers familiar from childhood with the ideas and language of the Old Testament Scriptures!

(31) **The living God.**—As in chaps. iii. 12; ix. 14, the exact meaning of the writer's words is "a Living God;" and a reference to the first of these passages (and to chap. iv. 12) will show clearly what is their force in this place. There can be little doubt that Deut. xxxii., from which he has been quoting, is still in his thought. See verse 40—"I lift up my hand to heaven, and say, I live for ever."

(32) In the last six verses the writer has enforced his exhortation by an appeal to the danger of falling away and the fearful consequences of unfaithfulness. From warning he now turns to encouragement, as in chap. vi.;

days, in which, after ye were illuminated, ye endured a great fight of afflictions; (33) Partly, whilst ye were made a gazingstock both by reproaches and afflictions; and partly, whilst ye became companions of them that were so used. (34) For ye had compassion of me in my bonds, and took joyfully the spoiling of your goods, knowing in yourselves that ye have in heaven a better and an enduring substance. (35) Cast not away therefore your confidence, which hath great recompence of reward. (36) For ye have need of patience, that, after ye have done the will of God, ye might receive the promise. (37) For yet

---

and here, as there, he thankfully recalls the earlier proofs which his readers had given of their Christian constancy and love. Let them call to mind and ever keep in remembrance what the grace of God had already enabled them to endure. (Comp. 2 John 8). As Theophylact has said, he bids them imitate, not others, but themselves.

Illuminated.—Better, *enlightened.* It is important to keep the word used in the parallel verse, chap. vi. 4 (see Note).

Fight of afflictions.—Rather, *conflict of sufferings;* for the last word has in this Epistle (chap. ii. 9, 10) associations too sacred to be lost. The former word (akin to that used by St. Paul in 2 Tim. ii. 5 of the contests in the public games) recalls the intense struggles of the contending athletes; it occurs nowhere else in the New Testament. Comp. Phil. i. 27, iv. 3; (Phil. i. 30; Col. i. 29, ii. 1; 1 Tim. vi. 12; chap. xii. 1.) This struggle they had manfully endured.

(33) **Whilst ye were made a gazingstock.**—Literally, *being exposed in the theatre* (see the Notes on Acts xix. 29; 1 Cor. iv. 9; xv. 32). Here also it is probable that the word has only a figurative sense.

Whilst ye became companions.—Better, *having become sharers with them that thus lived*—that lived amidst "reproaches and afflictions." Not "companions" only had they been, but sharers of the lot of their persecuted brethren, both by sympathy and by voluntary association with their sufferings.

(34) **For ye had compassion of me in my bonds.**—Rather (according to the true reading of the Greek), *for ye had sympathy with them that were in bonds* (comp. chap. xiii. 3, "Remember them that are in bonds as bound with them"). The change of reading is very important in connection with the question of authorship. (See the *Introduction.*)

And took joyfully.—Better, *and accepted with joy the spoiling of your possessions.* In the spirit of Matt. v. 12 (Acts v. 41; 2 Cor. xii. 10), they accepted persecution not with "patience and long suffering" only, but "with joy" (Col. i. 11). The rendering "possessions" is necessary because a similar word ("substance" in the Authorised version) will immediately occur. In the last clause two remarkable changes in the Greek text are made necessary by the testimony of our best authorities. The words "in heaven" must certainly be removed; they are omitted in the oldest MSS., and are evidently an explanatory comment which has found its way into the text. For the reading, "in yourselves," there is hardly any evidence whatever. The MSS. are divided between two readings, "yourselves" and "for yourselves;" the former having also the support of the Latin and Coptic versions. There is little doubt that we must read "yourselves;" and the most probable translation will now be, *perceiving that ye have your own selves for a better possession and one that abideth.* They had been taught the meaning of the words spoken by Jesus of the man who gains the world and loses himself (Luke ix. 25), and of those who win their souls by their endurance (Luke xxi. 19); so in verse 39 the writer speaks of "the gaining of the soul." Thus trained, they could accept with joy the loss of possessions for the sake of Christ, perceiving that in Him they had received *themselves* as a possession, a better and a lasting possession. (It would be possible to render the clause, "knowing that ye yourselves have a better possession," &c.; but the parallelism of verse 39 renders it almost certain that the former view of the words is correct.)

(35) **Cast not away therefore your confidence.**—Rather, *Cast not away therefore your boldness, seeing it hath a great recompence.* To "cast away boldness" is the opposite of "holding fast the boldness of the hope" (chap. iii. 6); the one belongs to the endurance of the faithful servant (verses 32, 36), the other to the cowardice of the man who draws back (verse 38). This verse and the next are closely connected: Hold fast your boldness, seeing that to it belongs great reward; hold it fast, for "he that endureth to the end shall be saved." On the last word, "recompence," see chap. ii. 2.

(36) **Patience**—*i.e.,* brave, patient endurance (see the Note on chap. vi. 12). The general strain of the exhortation in that chapter (verses 9—20) closely resembles these verses.

That, after ye have done . . . ye might.—Better, *that, having done the will of God, ye may receive the promise.* To do the will of God (chap. xiii. 21) is the necessary condition for receiving the promised blessing and reward (see chap. xi. 39); for both "endurance" is necessary. In these words we have an echo of Matt. vii. 21, where our Lord sums up His requirements from those who call themselves His in words which express the purpose of His own life (verses 7, 9; John iv. 34).

(37) The connection is this: "Ye have need of endurance" for "the end is not yet" (Matt. xxiv. 6); ye shall "receive the promise," for the Lord shall surely come, and that soon.

A little while.—Rather, *a very little while.* The expression is remarkable and unusual; it is evidently taken from Isa. xxvi. 20—"Come my people . . . hide thyself for *a little moment* until the indignation be overpast." The subject of this passage, from which the one expressive phrase is taken, is the coming of Jehovah "to punish the inhabitants of the earth for their iniquity;" in "a little moment" shall the indignation consume His foes, then will He give deliverance to His people. Even this passing reference would serve to call up before the mind of the Hebrew readers the solemn associations of the prophecy—the promised salvation, the awful judgment.

And he that shall come will come.—Rather, *He that cometh will come and will not tarry.* In this and the next verse the writer of the Epistle takes up a passage, Habak. ii. 3, 4, which occupies a very important place in the writings of St. Paul (Rom. i. 17; Gal. iii. 11), and, as we have already seen (Note on chap. vi. 1), in the later Jewish teaching. St. Paul's citations are

a little while, and he that shall come
will come, and will not tarry. (38) Now
the just shall live by faith: but if *any
man* draw back, my soul shall have no
pleasure in him. (39) But we are not of
them who draw back unto perdition;
but of them that believe to the saving
of the soul.

A.D. 64.

CHAPTER XI.—(1) Now faith is the

limited to a few words of verse 4, "But the just shall live by faith;" here are quoted the whole of the fourth verse and part of the third. Perhaps it is too much to say that they are *quoted*, they are rather applied, for, as will be seen, the order of the clauses (see next verse) is changed, and some alterations are made in the language. It is important in this Epistle to discriminate between the instances of direct quotation from the Scripture, where the word of God is appealed to as furnishing proof, and those in which passages of the Old Testament are explained and applied (see the Note on verse 5). The words before us nearly agree with the LXX., "If he delay, wait for him, because coming he will come, and will not tarry." The subject of the sentence there is not clear; probably the translator believed that the Lord spoke thus of His own coming, or the coming of the future Deliverer. In the Hebrew all relates to the vision, "it will surely come, it will not tarry." The only difference between the LXX. and the words as they stand here consists in the substitution of "He that cometh" for "coming." Now the reference to the Deliverer and Judge is made plain. No designation of the Messiah, perhaps, was more familiar than "He that cometh" (Matt. xi. 3, *et al.*); but in is here employed with a new reference—to the second advent in place of the first. The departure from the sense of the Hebrew is not as great as may at first appear. When the prophet says "The *vision* . . . shall surely come," it is of that which the vision revealed that he speaks, *i.e.*, of the fall of the Chaldeans; but the salvation of Israel from present danger is throughout the prophets the symbol of the great deliverance (comp. chap. xii. 26 and Hagg. ii. 6). With this verse comp. verse 25; also Phil. iv. 5; Jas. v. 8; 1 Pet. iv. 7; Rev. i. 3; xxii. 20, *et al.*; and, in regard to the application of the prophecy, verses 27, 28, 30.

(38) **Now the just shall live by faith.**—The Greek text of this clause is not perfectly certain, but it is probable that the word "my" should be added, so that the translation of the verse will be as follows, *But my righteous one shall live by faith.* In the Hebrew the first part of the verse is altogether different: "Behold his soul is lifted up, it is not upright in him; but the righteous shall live in (or, *by*) his faithfulness (or, *faith*)." The first words seem to refer to the haughty Chaldean invader; the rendering of the last words is considered below. The Greek translation varies a little in different MSS.: "If one draw back, my soul hath no pleasure in him; but the righteous one shall live by my faithfulness" (or *possibly*—not probably—"by faith in me"). In the Alexandrian MSS. the last words run thus: "But my righteous one shall live by faith" (or *faithfulness*). It is clear, then, that in the passage before us the writer has taken the words as they stood in his text of the LXX., only changing the order of the clauses. Though the Hebrew word usually rendered faith in this passage occurs more than forty times in the Old Testament, in no other case has it this meaning, but almost always signifies faithfulness or truth. Here also the first meaning seems to be "by his faithfulness"; but the thought of faithful constancy to God is inseparably connected with trustful clinging to Him. Hence the accepted Jewish exposition of the passage seems to have taken the word in the sense of "faith." "My righteous one" will naturally mean "my righteous servant"—the man who will not be seduced into wickedness; he shall live by his faithful trust, for salvation and life shall be given him by God Himself. In this context the word righteous recalls verse 36, "having done the will of God."

The transposition of the two clauses makes it almost certain that the "righteous one" is the subject of both: not *if any man*, but, *if he* (the righteous one) *shrink back*. The Genevan and the Authorised stand alone amongst English versions in the former rendering.

(39) **Of them who draw back.**—Literally, *But we are not of drawing* (or *shrinking*) *back unto perdition, but of faith unto the gaining of the soul.* On the last words (which are nearly identical with those of Luke xvii. 33, though deeper in meaning) see the Note on verse 34. The exhortation thus closes with words of encouragement and hope.

XI.

This chapter is very closely connected with the last verses of chapter x. Those verses have taught the necessity of faith for the attainment of the promise. Here we read of men to whom, through their faith, the promise has been made sure.

(1) We have seen how the writer approached the subject which is the chief theme of this last division of this Epistle. The coming of the Lord, for judgment upon His adversaries, for salvation to His people, draws nigh. In the midst of dangers and judgments God's righteous servant shall live, and the ground of his life is his steadfast faith—if he shrink back, destruction will overtake him. "Our principle of action" (the writer says to his Hebrew readers) "is not shrinking back, but faith. And faith is this . . . ." It has been debated whether that which follows is a definition of what faith is, or in reality a description of what faith does. It is not a complete definition, in the sense of including all the moments of thought which are present in the word as used in the last chapter (verse 38) or in this. The "things hoped for" are not mere figments of the imagination; their basis is *the word of God.* If we keep this in mind, the words, still remaining general in their form, agree with all that has led up to them and with all that follows; and whether they be called definition or description will be of little consequence.

The exact meaning of the special terms here used it is not easy to ascertain. The word rendered "substance" has already occurred twice in the Epistle. In chap. i. 3 this was its true meaning—the essence which, so to speak, underlies, "stands under," the qualities possessed. In chap. iii. 14 the same metaphor of *standing under* is applied to steadfastness, confidence (see the Note). The former of these renderings the Authorised version—in this instance deserting the earlier translations (which for the most part have "sure confidence" or "ground") to follow the Rhemish in its rendering of the Latin *substantia*—has made familiar in the present passage. The sense which it presents, however, is not very clear;

substance[1] of things hoped for, the evi-
dence of things not seen.
(2) For by it the elders
obtained a good report.

Chap. xi. The triumphs of Faith.

(3) Through faith we understand that
the worlds were framed by the word of
God, so that things which are seen were
not made of things which do appear.

1 Or, *ground,* or, *confidence.*

and the symmetry of the verse almost compels us here to make choice of some word which denotes an act, or at all events an attitude, of the mind. Most commentators of our own day accept the second meaning explained above, "confidence" or "assurance in regard to things hoped for." To adopt Dr. Vaughan's clear explanation, "Faith is that principle, that exercise of mind and soul, which has for its object things not seen but hoped for, and which, instead of sinking under them as too ponderous, whether from their difficulty or from their uncertainty, stands firm under them—supports and sustains their pressure—in other words, is assured of, confides in and relies on them." This interpretation yields an excellent sense, and has the advantage of assigning to the Greek word a meaning which it certainly bears in an earlier chapter, and in two places of St. Paul's Epistles. On the other hand, the analogy of the second member of the verse, and a peculiarity in the Greek construction which we cannot here discuss, seem to be in favour of a third rendering of the words: "Faith is the giving substance to things hoped for." It has indeed been said that by such a translation the things hoped for are represented as being *without substance.* But this difficulty is only apparent; for *in regard to ourselves* these objects of our hope do not yet exist, since they still belong to the future (Rom. viii. 24, 25). In the second clause the word "evidence" is likely to mislead; very probably, indeed, it now fails to convey the sense intended by our translators, who here followed the rendering of the Genevan Bible (suggested by Calvin's "evidentia"). The Greek word denotes putting to the test, examining for the purpose of proof, bringing to conviction. Under this aspect faith appears as neither blindly rejecting nor blindly accepting whatever may be said about things unseen, but boldly dealing with them as if with things seen, and then unflinchingly accepting that which has stood the proof. One peculiarity of the Greek yet remains to be noticed. In the second clause the word "things" is expressed in the Greek (as in chap. vi. 18), but not in the first; we are by this means reminded of the *reality* of that which is thus spoken of as unseen. The whole verse, then, may be rendered "Now faith is the giving substance to what is hoped for, the testing of things not seen." And now passing away from the general aspect of the words to that in which they are presented by the context, we have as the meaning: Faith, holding to God's word, gives substance to what that word promises, investing the future blessings with a present existence, treating them as if already objects of sight rather than of hope. Through faith, guided by the same word, the things unseen are brought to the proof; what that word teaches, though future, or though belonging to a world beyond human sight, is received with full conviction. Thus "every genuine act of faith is the act of the whole man, not of his understanding alone, not of his affections alone, not of his will alone, but of all three in their central, aboriginal unity." And thus faith becomes "the faculty in man through which the spiritual world exercises its sway over him, and thereby enables him to overcome the world of sin and death." (Hare, *Victory of Faith.*)

(2) **For by it.**—Better, *For therein the elders had witness borne to them.* The connection seems to be this: Faith truly accomplishes all this; for it was in the exercise of such a faith that the elders gained the witness which the Scripture bears (see verses 4, 5, 39) to them and to their noble deeds. This verse, then, is added to confirm the first.

(3) **Through faith.**—Rather, *By faith,* as in the following verses. The first place is not given to "the elders," for the writer's object is to set forth the achievements of *faith.* With these, he would say, the Scripture record is filled. Even where there is no mention of this principle we must trace it in the lives of God's servants; even where there is no history of men, there is a necessity for the exercise of faith by ourselves, and the first words of Scripture teach this lesson.

That the worlds were framed.—Literally, *that the ages have been prepared.* The remarkable expression which was used in chap. i. 2 is here repeated. The complete preparation of all that the successive periods of time contain is the idea which the words present. The narrative of the first chapter of Genesis ascribes the whole creation of "the heaven and the earth" to God; and associates with "a word of God" every stage in the preparation and furnishing of the earth. (See Note on chap. i. 2.) This is the first lesson of that record. But it does not stand alone, as is taught more plainly still by the next clause.

So that things which are seen.—A slight alteration in the Greek is necessary here—"the thing seen" (or "what is seen") being the true reading. A more important point is a change in the aspect of the whole clause, which the Greek seems to require. As the English words stand, they point out the significance of the statement of Scripture respecting the creative act: we believe the writer intended rather to state the divine *purpose* in relation to that first creation and all subsequent acts that are included in the "preparing of the ages." "In order that what is seen should not have come into being out of things which appear." This is probably the true meaning of the clause. In the narrative of the first chapter of Genesis God would have us learn a lesson for the whole course of human history and development. As the visible universe did not take its being out of what was apparent, so what from time to time is seen does not arise of itself out of what is manifest to man's natural perceptions. Not only is the eternity of matter denied, but from the beginning a warning has been given against a materialistic philosophy. The first page of Scripture is designed to teach the constant presence and work of the Creator. This lesson we learn and apply by faith; and the result of its application is seen in many points of the history which follows. In that history the operation of faith is twofold. The writer's most obvious design is to call attention to the faith possessed by "the elders," and its wonderful triumphs; but it is in many cases by the same faith that we interpret the Scripture record so as to discover this to have been their guiding principle. But seldom does the Old Testament directly speak of faith, and hence the importance of this verse (which some have thought incongruous, since it retards the exhibition of the elders' faith) as throwing light on our interpretation of the teaching of God's word.

(4) By faith Abel offered unto God a more excellent sacrifice than Cain, by which he obtained witness that he was righteous, God testifying of his gifts: and by it he being dead yet speaketh.[1] (5) By faith Enoch was translated that he should not see death; and was not found, because God had translated him: for before his translation he had this testimony, that he pleased God. (6) But without faith *it is* impossible to please *him:* for he that cometh to God must believe that he is, and *that* he is a rewarder of them that diligently seek him. (7) By faith Noah, being warned of God of things not seen as yet, moved with fear,[2] prepared an ark to the saving of his house; by the which he condemned the world, and became heir of the righteousness which is by faith. (8) By faith Abraham, when he was called to

1 Or, *is yet spoken of.*

2 Or, *being wary.*

(4) **A more excellent.**—The Greek literally means that Abel's sacrifice was "more than" Cain's (comp. chap. iii. 3, "more glory"; Matt. vi. 25; Luke xi. 32, *et al.*). The word "sacrifice" (which, as is the case with very many words in this chapter, is taken directly from the LXX.) has not its special sense (see Note on chap. x. 5) in the narrative of Gen. iv.; for the offerings of the two brothers are there designated by the same name, both in the Hebrew ("offering") and in the Greek ("sacrifice"). Hence, apart from the first words, "by faith," there is nothing here said to explain the superiority of Abel's offering; though one who believes sacrifice to have been of Divine institution, and who notes the close connection between God's word and the actions of the men whose faith is here recorded, may hold it probable that Abel's obedience was manifested in his mode of approaching God.

By which he obtained witness.—Probably, "through which *faith*," but the Greek may also mean *through which sacrifice.* The witness (verse 2) is that borne by God in His acceptance of the offering (shown by some visible sign); we might also add that such a testimony to Abel is implied in the reproof of Cain (Gen. iv. 7), but the following words, "God bearing witness over" (or *in regard to*) "his gifts," show what was chiefly in the writer's thought. Such acceptance implied Abel's righteousness, and thus testified to his "faith." It is remarkable that in three out of the four places in which Abel is mentioned in the New Testament this epithet is used (Matt. xxiii. 35; 1 John iii. 12). In the later Jewish tradition (contained in the Targum of Jerusalem) the brothers are represented as types of faith and unbelief; and in verse 10, "thy brother's blood" (Hebrew, "bloods") is expanded into "the blood of the multitude of the righteous who were to arise from thy brother." In this clause the authorities for the Greek text are much divided. One reading, "he testifying over his gifts to God," has the support of the three oldest MSS., but can hardly be correct.

And by it.—Better, *and through it* (his faith). The reference is to Gen. iv. 10, "the voice of thy brother's blood crieth unto me from the ground" (see chap. xii. 24); hence, as Calvin remarks, "he was plainly numbered among God's saints, whose death is precious in His sight."

(5) **See death.**—See Luke ii. 26; Ps. lxxxix. 48 (John viii. 51).

And was not found . . . translated him.—An exact quotation from the LXX. (Gen. v. 24). The word rendered "translated" is a very simple one, denoting merely change of place; but nothing can equal the simplicity of the Hebrew, "he was not for God took him."

He had this testimony.—Better, *he hath had witness borne to him* (verses 2, 4) *that he hath been well pleasing to God.* The form of the expression shows that the writer is again speaking of the ever present word of Scripture (chap. iv. 9, &c.) That word does not record the translation of Enoch until it "hath" borne witness to him that he pleased God. The words "walked with God" are rendered in the LXX. "was well pleasing to God," and it is this rendering that is quoted here and in the next verse. The writer himself supplies the comment in the next verse, which has a very close connection with this.

(6) **But without faith.**—Better, *and apart from faith it is impossible to be "well pleasing"* (unto Him); *for he that draweth near* (chap. vii. 25; x. 1, 22) *to God must believe . . .* Thus the very statement that Enoch pleased God is an assertion that in him faith was found. No one can be the habitual worshipper of God (this is what the phrase implies) if his faith does not grasp these two truths. "Is a rewarder"—literally, *becometh a recompenser* (chap. ii. 2; x. 35); the future recompense is present to the eye of faith.

(7) **Being warned of God.**—(See chap. viii. 5.)

Moved with fear.—The marginal rendering "being wary" (or better, *taking forethought*) is preferred by some, and agrees very well with the proper meaning of the word; but it is more probable that the writer has in view that devout godly fear which the words akin to this regularly denote in the New Testament. (See the Notes on chaps. v. 7; xii. 28.) Noah's obedience to the divine warning was an evidence at once of his fear of God and of the faith which gave substance and present reality to "the things not seen as yet."

By the which.—As before (verse 4), the words "through which" are slightly ambiguous, for they may relate either to the ark or to the faith. The latter reference is more probable. His faith, shown in the building of the ark, exposed the unbelief of "the world," which would not listen to his warnings, and thereby incurred the divine condemnation. Our Lord uses "condemn" in the same sense in Matt. xii. 41, 42. By the same faith Noah "became an heir of the righteousness which is *according to faith.*" Noah is the first to receive in Scripture the name "righteous" (Gen. vi. 9). See also Ezek. xiv. 14, 20; and 2 Pet. ii. 5, "Noah, a preacher of righteousness." This righteousness is looked on as an *inheritance,* received by all who manifest the faith. In this place the righteousness is connected with faith, as in the writings of St. Paul, but with a change of figure. It is not looked on as arising out of faith (Rom. x. 6), or as resting on the condition of faith (Phil. iii. 9), or as obtained by means of faith (Rom. iii. 22), but as corresponding with faith, or answering to it. There is no important difference of thought, but the idea of a continuous inheritance answering to continuous faith is very strikingly presented here.

(8) **When he was called to go out.**—Our older versions are here better than the Authorised, bringing in the word "obeyed" after "called"—"obeyed to go out into," &c.

go out into a place which he should after receive for an inheritance, obeyed; and he went out, not knowing whither he went.
(9) By faith he sojourned in the land of promise, as *in* a strange country, dwelling in tabernacles with Isaac and Jacob, the heirs with him of the same promise:
(10) for he looked for a city which hath foundations, whose builder and maker *is* God.
(11) Through faith also Sara herself received strength to conceive seed, and was delivered of a child when she was past age, because she judged him faithful who had promised.
(12) Therefore sprang there even of one, and him as good as dead, *so* *many* as the stars of the sky in multitude, and as the sand which is by the sea shore innumerable.
(13) These all died in faith,[1] not having received the promises, but having seen them afar off, and were persuaded of *them*, and embraced *them*, and confessed that they were strangers and pilgrims on the earth.
(14) For they that say such things declare plainly that they seek a country.
(15) And truly, if they had been mindful of that *country* from whence they came out, they might have had opportunity to have returned.
(16) But now they desire a better *country*, that is, an heavenly: wherefore God is not ashamed

[1] Gr. *according to faith.*

Which he should after receive.—The English rendering may seem to imply that when "called" Abraham received the promise that the land to which he would be directed should in the future be his inheritance. It is not so (Acts vii. 5); for this promise is not found in Gen. xii. 1—3, but was bestowed when he had obeyed (Gen xii. 7). The meaning here is, "unto a place which he was to receive."

(9) **The land of promise.**—More correctly, according to the true reading, *a land of the promise:* into a land which the promise (Gen. xii. 7) made his own he came as a sojourner, and sojourned in it as in a land belonging to others, making his settled abode there in tents. The words of which this is a paraphrase are very expressive, especially those of the last clause. Abraham there "made his home once for all, well aware that it was to be his home—expecting no change in this respect all his life long—in tents," movable, shifting abodes—here to-day, there to-morrow—with (as did also in their turn) "Isaac and Jacob," the "heirs with him of the same promise." (Dr. Vaughan.)

(10) **A city which hath foundations.**—Rather, *the city which hath the foundations.* The general thought is that which we find expressed in verses 14—16. There, the strangers and pilgrims are seeking for a *country* of their own; here, the dweller in tents is waiting for the *city* that hath the foundations. All these verses clearly teach that the promise as apprehended by the patriarchs was not bounded by the gift of Canaan. Of what nature their expectations of the future life may have been we cannot tell; but this they knew, that their fellowship with God and their interest in His promises would not cease with this transient life. What they saw of earthly blessing was but the earnest of some greater gift still future, and yet present through the power of their faith. The shifting tent might be Abraham's home now, but he waited for that city which should never know change—of which alone it could be said that it hath "the foundations," and whose Architect and Maker is God. (Comp. Ps. lxxxvii. 1; Rev. xxi.)

(11) **Through faith also Sara herself.**—Rather, *By faith Sarah herself also*, or, *even Sarah herself.* This emphatic introduction of the name of Sarah may point to the unbelief which for a brief while she displayed (Gen. xviii. 12); but the words may simply mean, "Sarah also, on her part"—the joint recipient with Abraham of the divine promise, a promise in which it might at first seem that she had no part. (Comp. Gen. xvi. 1, 2.) The words "was delivered of a child" are absent from the best authorities; so that we must read, "even when she was past age." With the last words of the verse compare chap. x. 23.

(12) **The stars of the sky.**—Better, *the stars of the heaven.* (See Gen. xv. 5; xxii. 17.)

And as the sand.—"And as the sand by the sea-shore, which is innumerable" (Gen. xxii. 17). With the first words of the verse compare Rom. iv. 19.

(13) **These all died in faith.**—We must not change the order of the original. Seven verses up to this point have begun with the emphatic words "by faith." There is a change here, but not in the emphasis of this thought. We should not expect to read "*By faith* these died;" what is said is, "In accordance with faith all these died;" faith had been the support and guide of their life, and their death was in accordance with the same principle. That is, they (Abraham, Isaac, Jacob, Sarah) did not die in possession of what had been promised (verse 39), but saw at a distance the blessings of which God had spoken (verse 1).

And were persuaded of them.—These words do not belong to the true text; and the word "embraced" should be rendered "greeted," or "saluted." We read, therefore: "Not having received the promises, but having seen and greeted them from far" (Gen. xlix. 18), "and having confessed that they were strangers and sojourners upon the earth" (Gen. xlvii. 9; xxiii. 4). (Comp. 1 Chron. xxix. 15; Ps. xxxix. 12; cxix. 19, 54; also 1 Pet. i. 1; ii. 11. The verses which follow are a comment on this. For the last words, "on the earth," see verse 16.

(14) **Such things.**—"I am a stranger and a sojourner with you" (Gen. xxiii. 4). "The days of the years of my pilgrimage . . . . the life of my fathers in the days of their pilgrimage" (Gen. xlvii. 9).

Declare plainly that they seek a country.—Rather, *make it plain that they are seeking a home*, or fatherland.

(15) **They might have had.**—Rather, *they would have had opportunity to return.* All their life long they would have been able to claim again their earlier fatherland, by returning whence they came.

(16) They confess themselves but sojourners (verse 13), and thus make it plain that they are still seeking their true home (14); and yet, if they had sought nothing more than an earthly home, there is one already, which was once theirs, and to which they

to be called their God: for he hath
prepared for them a city. (17) By faith
Abraham, when he was tried, offered up
Isaac: and he that had received the
promises offered up his only begotten
son, (18) of[1] whom it was said, That in
Isaac shall thy seed be called: (19) ac-
counting that God *was* able to raise *him*
up, even from the dead; from whence
also he received him in a figure. (20) By
faith Isaac blessed Jacob and Esau con-
cerning things to come. (21) By faith
Jacob, when he was a dying, blessed
both the sons of Joseph; and wor-

1 Or, *to.*

might return (15); hence it is no earthly but a heavenly country that they desire. This is the general current of thought in these verses, presenting a very close analogy to the argument of chap. iii. 7—iv. 11; here, as there, words which otherwise might appear to have but an earthly reference are seen to have a higher and a spiritual import. In verses 8 and 9 we have before us only the land of inheritance, but in verse 10 the heavenly rest; and in verse 13 words which as read in Genesis might seem to refer to a wandering life in the land of Canaan are taken as a confession of sojourning upon *earth.* It is not necessary to suppose that the desires and yearnings of "the fathers" expressed themselves in the definite forms which later revelation has made familiar; in all that is essential the hope existed, whilst the mode of the fulfilment was unknown. Through faith the patriarchs were willing to connect their whole life and that of their children with waiting at God's bidding for the fulfilment of a promise—wandering and sojourning until God's own time should come when He would grant a home in a country of their own. And yet each of these servants of God recognised that relation to God in which lay the foundation of the promise to him to be personal and abiding. If these two thoughts be united, it will be easy to see how each one for himself would be led to regard the state of wandering in which he spent his life as an emblem of a state of earthly waiting for an enduring home; the sojourning in the land was a constant symbol of the sojourning upon earth. Hence (see the passages quoted in verse 13) the same language is used from age to age after Canaan is received as an inheritance. (Comp. chap. iv. 9; and see Ex. iii. 15, and Matt. xxii. 31, 32.)

But now.—See chap. viii. 6; the meaning is not "at this present time," but "as the case stands in truth."

Wherefore God is not ashamed.—Rather, *Wherefore God is not ashamed of them* (compare chap. ii. 11). Because of this lofty desire, or rather, because of the faith and love towards Him in which the desire was founded, and of which therefore the longing for a heavenly country was the expression, God is not ashamed of them, to be called (literally *surnamed*) their God (Gen. xvii. 7; xxvi. 24; xxviii. 13; Ex. iii. 6; *et al.*). That He is not ashamed of them He has shown, "for He prepared for them a city." Before the desire existed the home had been provided. (Comp. Matt. xxv. 34.)

(17) The patriarchs displayed their faith in the attitude of their whole life, and in their death. This has been the thought of the preceding verses; the writer now passes to the lessons taught by particular actions and events.

Tried.—Gen. xxii. 1: "God did tempt Abraham." The following word is in the Greek "*hath* offered up Isaac," and several other examples of a similar peculiarity will present themselves in this chapter. As in former cases (chaps. iv. 9; vii. 11; x. 9) the reference is to the permanent record of Scripture, in which the fact related is ever present. Abraham stands before us there as having offered his son. It will be seen that the offering is spoken of as if consummated. As regards faith the sacrifice was indeed complete; the perfect surrender of will had been made, and the hand was stretched out for the deed.

And he that had received the promises offered up.—Rather, *and he that had welcomed* (gladly accepted) *the promises was offering up.* From the figurative accomplishment of the deed the writer passes to the historical narrative; hence we read, "he . . . was (in the act of) offering." This clause and verse 18 set forth the greatness of the sacrifice (compare Gen. xxii. 2, in the literal rendering, "Take now thy son, thine only one, whom thou lovest, Isaac"); verse 19 explains the operation of his faith.

(18) **Of whom.**—That is, Isaac. But the Greek words should perhaps be rendered *to whom* (Abraham): "Even he to whom it was said." On this quotation from Gen. xxi. 12 see the Note on Rom. ix. 7.

(19) **That God was able.**—These words are better taken as the expression of a general truth—"Accounting that God is able to raise up even from the dead. The faith which tests and brings conviction of the things not seen made this reasoning possible, and gave power to act upon it even when Isaac must be slain.

From whence also.—Better, *from whence he did in a figure* (literally, *a parable*) *receive him.* As in a figure the offering was completely carried out (verse 17), so also in figure he received his son back from the dead.

(20) **Concerning things to come.**—It is probable, though not certain, that the word "even" should be inserted before "concerning"; on these words, then, the emphasis will rest. Not having regard to things present only, or things almost at hand, but looking far into the future, through the divine revelation which opened to him the meaning of the promises received by Abraham, he gave to each son the blessing designed by God (Gen. xxvii. 27—29, 39, 40). Isaac's confidence in the divine guidance of his words is especially seen in verse 33 of the chapter.

(21) **Both the sons.**—Rather, *each of the sons.* The separate character of the two blessings is thus brought out (Gen. xlviii. 14—19). (See the last Note.) In the case of the two events mentioned in this verse the order of time is reversed, probably that the blessing of Jacob may immediately follow the similar record of verse 20.

And worshipped.—The incident referred to will be found in Gen. xlvii. 31. After receiving from Joseph a promise, confirmed by oath, that he shall be buried with his fathers, "Israel bowed himself upon" (or, *worshipped towards*) "the bed's head." In the LXX. and in the Targums the words are understood as denoting an act of worship. The Greek translators have taken the last word of the Hebrew verse to denote "staff" (Gen. xxxii. 10), not "bed," the words which bear these different meanings differing very slightly in form. The whole clause is given here as

shipped, *leaning* upon the top of his
staff. (22) By faith Joseph, when he
died, made mention of[1] the departing
of the children of Israel; and gave com-
mandment concerning his bones. (23) By
faith Moses, when he was born, was hid
three months of his parents, because
they saw *he was* a proper child; and
they were not afraid of the king's com-
mandment. (24) By faith Moses, when
he was come to years, refused to be
called the son of Pharaoh's daughter;
(25) choosing rather to suffer affliction
with the people of God, than to enjoy the
pleasures of sin for a season; (26) esteem-
ing the reproach of Christ[2] greater
riches than the treasures in Egypt: for
he had respect unto the recompence of
the reward. (27) By faith he forsook
Egypt, not fearing the wrath of the

1 Or, *remembered.*

2 Or, *for Christ.*

---

it stands in the LXX., the difference between the renderings being immaterial for the purpose which the writer had in view. The quotation of the familiar words serves to recall the scene, and brings before us Israel's thankful and devout satisfaction when assured that he should rest with his fathers in the land of Canaan; by this, at the point of death, he expressed his faith in the promise by which Abraham and his seed received Canaan as their inheritance.

(22) **When he died.**—Literally, *drawing to his end.* The word is taken from Gen. l. 26; and the mention of the departure (literally, *the Exodus*) of the children of Israel is found in verses 24, 25. This example of faith in the promise and clinging to the hope which it held forth needs no comment. For the fulfilment of Joseph's dying request see Ex. xiii. 19, "Moses took the bones of Joseph with him" out of Egypt; and Josh. xxiv. 32, "And the bones of Joseph buried they in Shechem."

(23) **Because they saw he was a proper child.**—"Proper" has its now obsolete sense of *handsome, comely,* a meaning not uncommon in Shakespeare. The word used in the Greek translation of Ex. ii. 2 is preserved both in Acts vii. 20 (see the Note) and in this place. It would seem that the remarkable beauty of the infant was understood by his parents as a divine sign given for the guidance of their conduct. The next clause should probably be closely connected with this—"because they saw . . . and were not afraid of the king's commandment" (Ex. i. 16). Their reliance on the protection of God enabled them to brave the anger of the king.

(24) **Come to years**—*i.e.,* grown up, "when he was full forty years old" (Acts vii. 23). The words here used are taken from the Greek translation of Ex. ii. 11, where we first read of Moses as openly associating himself with his oppressed people. When Moses slew the Egyptian who was "smiting a Hebrew, one of his brethren," he in act "refused to be called a son of Pharaoh's daughter," and chose "to suffer affliction with the people of God." (See Ex. ii. 15.)

(25) **Choosing.**—Better, *having chosen.* His act was an expression of his deliberate choice. He joined his people because it was "the people of God." To stand aloof for the sake of ease and pleasure would for him have been apostasy from God ("sin," comp. chap. x. 26). The faith of Moses had brought "conviction of the things not seen," which "are eternal"; hence he looked not at "the things seen" which are "for a season" (2 Cor. iv. 18, where the same word is used).

(26) **The reproach of Christ.**—Better, *The reproach of the Christ.* Many explanations have been proposed of this remarkable phrase, some of which—as "reproach for Christ," "reproach similar to that which Christ endured"—cannot possibly give the true meaning. The first point to be noted is that the words are almost exactly a quotation from one of the chief of the Messianic Psalms (Ps. lxxxix. 50, 51)—"Remember, Lord, the reproach of Thy servants; how I do bear in my bosom the reproach of many peoples: wherewith Thine enemies have reproached, O Lord; wherewith they have reproached the footsteps of Thine Anointed." Here the writer in effect speaks of himself as bearing "the reproach of the Anointed" of the Lord; pleading in his name and identifying himself with his cause. "The Anointed" is the king who (see the Note on chap. i. 5) was the type of the promised Christ. Throughout the whole of their history the people of Israel were the people of the Christ. Their national existence originated in the promise to Abraham, which was a promise of the Christ; and till the fulness of time should come their mission was to prepare the way for Him. The reproach which Moses accepted by joining the people of the promise was, therefore, "the reproach of the Christ," the type of that "reproach" which in later days His people will share with Him (chap. xiii. 13). He who was to appear in the last days as the Messiah was already in the midst of Israel (John i. 10). (See Ps. lxix. 9; Col. i. 24; 1 Pet. i. 11; and the Note on 2 Cor. i. 5. Phil. iii. 7—11 furnishes a noble illustration of this whole record.)

For he had respect unto the recompence of the reward.—Rather, *for he looked unto the recompence* (chap. x. 35). He habitually "looked away" from the treasures in Egypt, and fixed his eye on the heavenly reward.

(27) **By faith he forsook Egypt.**—It is a matter of great difficulty to decide whether these words refer to the flight into Midian (Ex. ii. 15), or to the Exodus. The former view, which seems to be taken by all ancient writers and by most in modern times, is supported by the following arguments:—(1) The institution of the Passover is mentioned later in this chapter (verse 28); (2) the second departure was made at Pharaoh's urgent *request* (Ex. xii. 31); (3) "he forsook" is too personal an expression to be used of the general Exodus. On the other side it is urged with great force: (1) that, although the actual departure from Egypt followed the institution of the Passover, the "forsaking" really commenced in the demand of chap. v. 1—3, persevered in until the anger of the king was powerfully excited (chap. x. 28); (2) that, as might have been certainly foreseen, the wrath of both king and people was aroused as soon as the people had departed (Ex. xiv. 5); (3) that the flight to Midian was directly caused by fear (Ex. ii. 14, 15); (4) that the following words, "he endured, &c.," are much more applicable to the determined persistency of Moses and his repeated disappointments (Ex. v.—xii.) than to the inaction of his years of exile. On the whole the latter interpretation seems preferable. If the former be adopted, we must distinguish between the apprehension which led him

king: for he endured, as seeing him
who is invisible. (28) Through faith he
kept the passover, and the sprinkling of
blood, lest he that destroyed the first-
born should touch them. (29) By faith
they passed through the Red sea as by
dry *land:* which the Egyptians assaying
to do were drowned. (30) By faith the
walls of Jericho fell down, after they
were compassed about seven days.
(31) By faith the harlot Rahab perished
not with them that believed not,[1] when
she had received the spies with peace.
(32) And what shall I more say? for the
time would fail me to tell of Gedeon,
and *of* Barak, and *of* Samson, and *of*
Jephthae; *of* David also, and Samuel,
and *of* the prophets: (33) who through
faith subdued kingdoms, wrought right-
eousness, obtained promises, stopped
the mouths of lions, (34) quenched the
violence of fire, escaped the edge of
the sword, out of weakness were made
strong, waxed valiant in fight, turned
to flight the armies of the aliens.
(35) Women received their dead raised to
life again: and others were tortured,[a]
not accepting deliverance; that they

1 Or, *that were disobedient.*

a 2 Macc. 7. 7.

---

to seek safety in flight and the courage which enabled him to give up Egypt.

He endured.—In the presence of Pharaoh (or in the weariness of exile) he was strong and patient, as seeing the invisible King and Leader of His people.

(28) **Through faith he kept.**—Rather, *By faith he hath kept* (see verse 17). The celebration of the Passover and the sprinkling of the blood were acts of obedience, having reference to a danger as yet unseen, but present in God's word (Ex. xii. 12).

Lest he that destroyed—Better, *that the destroyer of the first-born may not touch them.* (See Ex. xii. 21, 22, 28, 29.)

(29) **Which the Egyptians assaying to do.**—Literally, *Of which the Egyptians making trial were swallowed up* (Ex. xiv., xv.). In the same "trial," but with the support of the word of God, had consisted Israel's faith. The word *land* is not in the ordinary Greek text (and hence stands in italics), but is found in the best MSS. It is with this word that the following clause ("of which . . .") connects itself.

(30) **Seven days.**—It is the persistence of Israel's obedience (in the midst, we cannot doubt, of the unmeasured contempt and ridicule of their foes) during the seven days of almost total inaction (Josh. vi.) that is here brought into relief.

(31) **That believed not.**—Rather, *that were disobedient* (see chaps. iii. 18; iv. 6, 11). To her and to her countrymen alike had come the knowledge of what the Lord had done for Israel (Josh. ii. 10). She recognised from these signs, and acknowledged, the supremacy of Jehovah (verse 11), and she cast in her lot with His servants; the men of Jericho continued in their disobedience, and perished (Josh. vi. 21). Through faith, therefore, a despised heathen woman became united with the people of God. With such an example these more detailed histories may fitly close.

(32) The sacred writer has lingered over the life and deeds of the greatest of the patriarchs and of Moses the legislator of the nation: two examples only—differing in kind from those which have preceded, and peculiarly suggestive and important—have been taken from the history of the people after the death of Moses. Enough has now been said to guide all who are willing to search the Scriptures for themselves. With a brief mention of names which would call up before the minds of his readers achievements almost as wonderful as those on which he has been dwelling, he passes from the elders who received witness from God by their faith, and (verses 33—38) speaks in general terms, but all the more distinctly, of the triumphs which faith has won.

The time would fail me.—The slight changes of text required by our best evidence give increased vividness: *For the time will fail me if I tell of Gideon, Barak, Samson, Jephthah.* To the exploits of Barak (Judg. iv., v.), Gideon (vi.—viii.), Samson (xiii.—xvi.), Jephthah (xi., xii.), there is manifest reference in the words of later verses (33, 34). There seems to be no design in this arrangement of the names. In the following clause also, "of David and Samuel and the prophets," there is a similar departure from the order of time.

(33) **Subdued kingdoms.**—Better, *overcame kingdoms.* To all the deliverers of Israel of whom we have read in verse 32 (and especially to David, 2 Sam. viii., x., xi.) these words will apply. They also "wrought righteousness," as each judge or king or prophet "executed judgment and justice unto all his people" (2 Sam. viii. 15).

Obtained promises.—Do these words mean that these men of faith won promises of future blessing (such as were vouchsafed to David and the prophets), or that promises of deliverance were fulfilled to them? There seems no reason for doubting that the writer's language may include both thoughts. The words which follow (though illustrated in the history of Samson and of David) clearly point to Daniel (chap. vi.).

(34) **The violence.**—Rather, *the power* (Daniel iii.).

Escaped the edge of the sword.—Though it would not be difficult to trace the application of this and the following clauses to the heroes of Israel celebrated in the Old Testament history (the perils of David and Elijah and the "weakness" of Samson and Hezekiah will occur to the mind of all), it seems likely that the writer's thought is resting mainly on the history of the Maccabæan times. That the following verse relates to narratives contained in the Second Book of Maccabees is generally acknowledged; and no words could more truly characterise the general contents of the First Book than those of the present verse.

(35) **Raised to life again.**—Literally, *by a resurrection.* (See 1 Kings xvii. 22, 23; 2 Kings iv. 35—37.) At this point the character of the record is changed; hitherto we have heard of the victories of faith in action, now it is of the triumph of faith over suffering that the writer speaks. Those who "escaped the edge of the sword" (verse 34) and those who "were slain with the sword" alike exemplified the power of faith.

Others were tortured.—See the account of the aged Eleazar (2 Macc. vi. 30), martyred because he would not pollute himself with swine's flesh and the "flesh taken from the sacrifice commanded by the

might obtain a better resurrection:
(36) and others had trial of *cruel* mockings
and scourgings, yea, moreover of bonds
and imprisonment: (37) they were stoned,
they were sawn asunder, were tempted,
were slain with the sword: they wandered about in sheepskins and goatskins; being destitute, afflicted, tormented;
(38) (of whom the world
was not worthy:) they wandered in
deserts, and *in* mountains, and *in*
dens and caves of the earth.
(39) And
these all, having obtained a good
report through faith, received not
the promise:
(40) God having provided[1] some better thing for us, that
they without us should not be made
perfect.

1 Or, *foreseen.*

A.D. 64.

CHAPTER XII.—
(1) Wherefore seeing we also are compassed about with so great a cloud of witnesses, let us lay aside every weight, and the sin

Chap. xii. 1—17. Let us through faith persevere to the end.

---

king." The following chapter records the martyrdom of seven brethren, who for their adherence to their law were put to death with cruel tortures. (See especially verses 9, 14, 23, 29, 36.)

Not accepting deliverance.—Literally, *not accepting the redemption, i.e.,* the deliverance offered, which must be purchased at the price of their constancy.

A better resurrection.—Better than that return to the present life which is spoken of in the first words of the verse.

(36) The language becomes more general, but still chiefly refers to the same troublous times.

Yea, moreover of bonds. — Lasting and cruel captivity, a worse fate even than "mockings and scourgings."

(37) **They were stoned.**—As Zechariah (2 Chron. xxiv. 20—22), and—according to a Jewish tradition mentioned by Tertullian and others—Jeremiah. (See Matt. xxiii. 35, 37.)

They were sawn asunder. — An ancient tradition, mentioned both by Jewish and by early Christian writers, relates that Isaiah was thus put to death by order of Manasseh. The following words, "they were tempted," are very remarkable in such a position; and many conjectures have been hazarded on the supposition that a mistake of transcription has occurred. If the text is correct, the writer is speaking of the promises and allurements by which the persecutors sought to overcome the constancy of God's servants.

Slain with the sword.—See 1 Kings xix. 1, 10; Jerem. xxvi. 23.

They wandered about.—Rather, *they went about,* as outcasts; compelled to live the life of wanderers and exiles.

Tormented.—Rather, *being destitute, afflicted, ill-treated* (*of whom the world was not worthy*), *wandering in deserts and mountains and caves and the holes of the earth.* Once more the Maccabæan persecutions seem to be chiefly in view. (See 1 Macc. ii. 28, 29; 2 Macc. v. 27; vi. 11. Comp. also 1 Sam. xxii. 1; 1 Kings xviii. 4.)

(39) **Having obtained a good report.**—Now that the history is concluded the word of verse 2 is resumed. That in such a faith as was described in verse 1 "the elders" received their witness from God, the records themselves have shown; yet "these all, having had witness borne to them through their faith, received not the promise," *i.e.,* the promised blessing. There are three passages of the Epistle which must be kept together—chap. vi. 15, "And so, having patiently waited, he (Abraham) obtained the promise;" chap. x. 36, "Ye have need of endurance, that having done the will of God ye may receive the promise;" and the present verse. To the saints of the Old Testament the promised blessing was future; they obtained it, but not within the limits of this present life. To us the promised blessing is present, revealed to us in its true nature, obtained for us once for all; for we know that eternal redemption has been won through Christ's entering for us once for all into the heavenly sanctuary (chap. ix. 12), and to us the "perfection" has come, in that through Him we "draw near to God" (chap. vii. 11, 19). That (1) the full personal appropriation of the gift is for every one of us still future, and (2) the full revelation belongs to another state of being, is true, but not inconsistent with what has been said.

(40) **For us.**—Rather, *concerning us, that without* (or, *apart from*) *us they should not be made perfect.* "Some better thing"—better than they had received (Matt. xiii. 17; 1 Pet. i. 10, 11). The design of God was that they and we may be perfected together; first in the joint reception of mature knowledge and privilege through the High-priestly work of the Lord Jesus (comp. Eph. iii. 10; 1 Pet. i. 12); and then that we with them may, when the end shall come, "have our perfect consummation and bliss both in body and soul, in the eternal and everlasting glory of God." See further the Note on chap. xii. 23.

XII.

In this chapter the writer takes up again the exhortation of chap. x. 19—39, pointing to the example of Jesus, encouraging those who are in trial, warning against sin, and especially the sin of rejecting Him who speaks to us from heaven.

(1) **Wherefore seeing we also are compassed about.**—Rather, *Therefore let us also—since we are compassed about with so great a cloud of witnesses—having put away all encumbrance and the sin . . . run with patient endurance the race that is set before us, looking,* &c. (In so difficult a verse as this we need an exactness of translation which might not otherwise be desirable.) It is plain that the chief thought is, "Let us run our race with patient endurance, looking unto Jesus the Author . . . of our faith;" so that here again we have the thought which the writer is never weary of enforcing, the need of faith and patience for all who would inherit the promises. The connection is chiefly with the last verses of chap. xi., which are, indeed, a summary of the whole chapter. The purpose of God has been that those who throughout the past ages obtained witness of Him through their faith should not reach their consummation apart from us. To that consummation, then, let us press forward. Present to us in the view of Christ's accomplished sacrifice, it is all future in regard of

which doth so easily beset *us*, and let us
run with patience the race that is set before us, (2) looking unto Jesus the author[1]
and finisher of *our* faith; who for the joy that was set before him endured the cross, despising the shame, and is set

1 Or, *beginner*.

personal attainment. As those who have preceded us reached the goal, each one for himself, by faith and patient endurance, so must we. The thought of persevering effort crowned by a recompence of reward (chaps. vi. 12, 18; x. 35—39) very naturally suggested the imagery of the public games (by this time familiar even to Jews), to which St. Paul in his Epistles so frequently alludes. (See 1 Cor. iv. 9; ix. 24—27; Phil. iii. 12—14; 1 Tim. vi. 12; 2 Tim. iv. 7, 8; comp. chap. x. 32, 33.) In these passages are called up the various associations of the great national festivals of Greece—the severe discipline of the competitors, the intenseness of the struggle, the rewards, "the righteous judge," the crowd of spectators. Most of these thoughts are present here (verses 1, 2, 4), and new points of comparison are added, so that the scene is brought vividly before our eyes. It has been often supposed that the word "witnesses" is used in the sense of *spectators* of the race. To an English reader this idea is very natural (as "witnesses" may simply mean *beholders*), but there is no such ambiguity in the Greek word (*martyres*). The Greek fathers rightly understood it to signify those who bear witness, and the chief point of doubt seems to have been whether the sense is general, or whether the word bears its later meaning—*martyrs*, who have borne testimony with their blood. Those who thus encompass us, a countless host (a "cloud" of witnesses), have had witness borne to them through their faith, and in turn stand forth as witnesses to faith, bearing testimony to its power and works. One and all they offer encouragement to us in our own contest of faith, and for this reason they are mentioned here. That the idea of the presence of spectators may be contained in the other words, "compassed about with so great a cloud," is very possible; but no interpretation must be allowed to interfere with the chief thought—that the runner's steadfast gaze is fixed on Him who has Himself traversed the course before us, and is now the Judge and Rewarder.

Every weight.—The Greek word was sometimes used by Greek writers to denote the excessive size and weight of body which the athlete sought to reduce by means of training; but may also signify the encumbrance of any burden, unnecessary clothing, and the like. It is here best taken in a general sense, as denoting anything that encumbers, and thus renders the athlete less fitted for the race. In the interpretation we might, perhaps, think of the pressure of earthly cares, were it not that the writer seems to have in mind the special dangers of the Hebrew Christians. The "divers and strange teachings" spoken of in chap. xiii. 9, in which would be included the Judaising practices which they were tempted to observe (such as St. Peter described as a "yoke" too heavy to be borne), will probably suit the figure best.

And the sin which doth so easily beset us.—The last six words are the translation of a single adjective, which does not occur elsewhere. The Greek commentators, from whom we might expect some light on the phrase, seem to be entirely reduced to conjecture. Chrysostom, for example, adopts in various places two altogether different meanings, "sin which easily (or, *completely*) surrounds us," "sin which is easily overcome." To these Theophylact adds a third, "sin through which man is easily brought into danger." The prevailing opinion amongst modern writers appears to be that the word signifies *well* (or, *easily*) *surrounding;* and that the writer is comparing sin with a garment—either a *loosely* fitting garment by which the runner becomes entangled and tripped up, or one that clings *closely* to him and thus impedes his ease of movement. This view of the meaning is taken in our earlier English versions, which either follow the Latin (Wiclif, "that standeth about us;" Rhemish, "that compasseth us"), or render the words, *the sin that hangeth on*, or, *that hangeth so fast on*. The sense is excellent, but it is very doubtful whether the Greek will admit of such a rendering. Though the exact word is not found elsewhere, there are words closely allied as to the meaning of which there is no doubt. Analogy clearly points to the signification *much admired* (literally, *well surrounded* by an admiring crowd). It is not impossible that even with this meaning the words "lay aside" or *put away* (often applied to putting off clothing) might still suggest a garment; if so, the allusion might be to a runner who refused to put off a garment which the crowd admired, though such an encumbrance must cause him to fail of the prize. It is more likely that the writer speaks of sin generally as an obstacle to the race, which must be put aside if the runner is to contend at all. If we look at the later exhortations of the Epistle, we shall find repeated mention of the reproach which the followers of Christ must bear. Even in the history of Moses (chap. xi. 26) there are words which suggest the thought. (See also chaps. x. 33; xiii. 13). So in the next verse we read of the cross of Jesus and the shame which He despised. Over against this "reproach" is set the sin which is sure to win man's favour and applause—the sin of which we have read in chap. x. 26 (comp. chap. xi. 25), which, seemingly harmless in its first approaches, will end in a "falling away from the living God." The rendering with which the Authorised version has made us familiar is full of interest, but cannot (at all events as it is commonly understood) be an expression of the sense intended. Whatever view be taken of the one peculiar word, it does not seem possible that the phrase can point to what is known as a "besetting sin," the sin which in the case of any one of us is proved to possess especial power.

(2) **Looking unto Jesus.**—As in chap. ii. 9, the description precedes the mention of the name, "Looking unto the Author and Perfecter of (our) faith, Jesus." The first word is very similar to that of chap. xi. 26; the runner looks away from all other objects and fixes his gaze on One. Jesus is not directly spoken of as the Judge (2 Tim. iv. 8); but, as the next words show, He has Himself reached the goal, and His presence marks the point at which the race will close. As the last verse spoke of our "patient endurance," this speaks of our faith, and of this Jesus is the Author and the Perfecter. The former word has occurred before, in chap. ii. 10; and here, as there, *origination* is the principal thought. There the idea of leading the way was also present; but here "Author" stands in contrast with "Perfecter," and the example of our Lord is the subject of the clause which follows. Because it is He who begins and brings to perfection our faith, we must run the race with our eye fixed upon Him:

down at the right hand of the throne of
God. (3) For consider him that endured
such contradiction of sinners against
himself, lest ye be wearied and faint in
your minds. (4) Ye have not yet re-
sisted unto blood, striving against sin.
(5) And ye have forgotten the exhorta-
tion which speaketh unto you as unto
children, My son, despise not thou the
chastening of the Lord, nor faint when
thou art rebuked of him: (6) for whom
the Lord loveth he chasteneth, and
scourgeth every son whom he receiveth.
(7) If ye endure chastening, God dealeth
with you as with sons; for what son is
he whom the father chasteneth not?
(8) But if ye be without chastisement,
whereof all are partakers, then are ye
bastards, and not sons. (9) Furthermore
we have had fathers of our flesh which
corrected *us*, and we gave *them* reverence:
shall we not much rather be in subjec-

---

in Him is the beginning, in Him the completion of the promises (2 Cor. i. 20); and in the steady and trustful dependence upon Him which this figure describes consists our faith.

Who for the joy that was set before him endured the cross.—The literal meaning is very forcible, *endured a cross, despising shame;* the shame of such a death being set over against the joy that lay before Him. Here again we have the thought of chap. ii. 9 (Phil. ii. 9, 10); the joy of His accomplished purpose (Isa. liii. 11; Matt. xxv. 21; Luke x. 21, 22) and the glory with which He was crowned (John xvii. 1; 1 Pet. i. 11) being the reward for His "obedience even unto death." The whole form of the expression (comp. especially chap. vi. 18, "the hope set before us") shows that Jesus is presented to us as an example not of endurance only, but also of faith (chap. ii. 12). On the last words of the verse see chaps. i. 3, 13; viii. 1; x. 12, 13; there is here a slight change in the Greek, which requires the rendering, *and hath sat down at the right hand of the throne of God.*

(3) The figure of the race is still continued, "For unless ye thus look unto Jesus ye will grow weary."

Consider.—Literally, *compare*; place your sufferings by the side of His.

Him that endured such contradiction.—Rather, *Him that hath endured such gainsaying from sinners against themselves.* The word "gainsaying," (chaps. vi. 16; vii. 7) is so frequently used in the LXX. for the rebelliousness of the people of Israel, that we need not here limit it to contradiction in words. The change of "Himself" into "themselves" (the reading of the oldest MSS.) is important, but it is not easy to say with what the last two words should be joined; for the meaning may be either "sinners against themselves" (comp. Num. xvi. 38), or "gainsaying against themselves." In either case the force of the words will be that the sin or the opposition manifested against Him was really against themselves, since it was for their salvation that He came upon earth. To all His other sorrows were added the pain of their ingratitude and His grief over their aggravated guilt.

And faint.—Rather, *fainting in your souls.*

(4) **Ye have not yet resisted unto blood.**—Still the general figure is retained, but for the foot-race is substituted the contest of the pugilists. In verse 1 sin was the hindrance which must be put aside; here it is the antagonist who must be subdued. It is interesting to note exactly the same transition in 1 Cor. ix. 26. (See Note.) The contest has been maintained but feebly, for no blood has flowed in their struggle with temptation and sin; they have not deserted the arena, but have shrunk from the suffering which a determined struggle would have caused. It is possible that the writer goes beyond the figure in these words, and that the price of their resistance might indeed have been their "blood."

(5) In this cowardly avoidance of trouble and persecution they have been shrinking from that chastening which every son receives from the Lord.

Which speaketh unto you.—Better, *which holds converse* (or, *reasoneth*) *with you as with sons.* The words which follow are taken from Prov. iii. 11, 12, and agree with the text of the LXX., except that for "son" we have "my son," and for "reproveth" (verse 6) "chasteneth." In the original passage Solomon is the speaker, and it is the second verse only that speaks of God's fatherly love. It may be so here also, but the exhortation of the Scripture seems to be quoted as if spoken directly by God Himself to His sons.

Despise.—Better, *think not lightly of.* In the next clause the Hebrew ("and loathe not His correction") denotes rather a spirit that rejects and chafes under divine discipline. As the words are found here, they point to losing heart and hope.

(6) **And scourgeth.**—As the words stand in our Hebrew text, the meaning is "even as a father the son in whom he delighteth." A very slight change in one word, however, will yield the sense in which the clause was understood by the Greek translators, and which is here retained. For the purpose of this quotation the difference between the two renderings is not material.

(7) **If ye endure chastening.**—The whole weight of ancient evidence is in favour of a change in the first Greek word. Two translations are then possible: (1) "It is for chastening that ye endure:" the troubles that come upon you are for discipline—are not sent in anger, but in fatherly love. (2) "Endure for chastening:" bear the trial, instead of seeking to avoid it by unworthy and dangerous concession; endure it, that it may effect its merciful purpose.

What son is he.—Or, *what son is there whom his father chasteneth not?*

(8) **Whereof all are partakers.**—Better, *whereof all* (God's children) *have been made partakers.* Were it possible that they have never known this fatherly "chastening," it must be that they are not sons whom a father acknowledges, and for whose training he has care.

(9) **Furthermore we have had fathers.**—Rather, *Furthermore we had the fathers of our flesh as chasteners* (*i.e.*, to chasten us). The thought of the former verses has been, "He chastens as a father." From likeness we here pass to contrast. The contrast drawn is between our natural parents and "the Father of spirits" (comp. Num. xvi. 22; xxvii. 16; Zech. xii. 1)—the Creator of all spirits, who is the Giver of life to all, who knows the spirit which He has made (see Ps. xciv. 9, 10) and can discipline it by His chastening.

tion unto the Father of spirits, and live?
(10) For they verily for a few days chas-
tened *us* after their own pleasure; but
he for *our* profit, that *we* might be
partakers of his holiness. (11) Now no
chastening for the present seemeth to
be joyous, but grievous: nevertheless
afterward it yieldeth the peaceable fruit
of righteousness unto them which are
exercised thereby. (12) Wherefore lift up
the hands which hang down, and the
feeble knees; (13) and make straight[1]
paths for your feet, lest that which is
lame be turned out of the way; but let
it rather be healed. (14) Follow peace
with all *men*, and holiness, without
which no man shall see the Lord:
(15) looking diligently lest any man fail
of[2] the grace of God; lest any root of
bitterness springing up trouble *you*, and

1 Or, *even.*

2 Or, *fall from.*

And live.—Since the life of the spirit subsists only in union with Him.

(10) **After their own pleasure.** — Rather, *as seemed good unto them.* The contrast is continued here between human liability to mistake and the perfect knowledge of our heavenly Father, who seeks our profit, and cannot err in the means which He employs. There is a general resemblance between this verse and the last, the "few days" corresponding to the "fathers of our flesh;" and the last clause here, "that we may be partakers of His holiness," to the words which close verse 9, "and live." To the "few days" no contrast is directly expressed in the second member of the verse; none was needed, because the last words so clearly imply the *permanence* of the result.

(11) **Now no chastening . . .**—Better (the reading being slightly changed), *All chastening seemeth for the present time to be not joyous, but grievous.* The language, so far, would seem to be perfectly general, relating to all chastening, whether human or divine. The following clause may seem to confine our thought to the latter; but, with a lower sense of "righteousness," the maxim is true of the wise discipline of earthly parents.

The peaceable fruit of righteousness.—Better, *peaceful fruit, (fruit) of righteousness, to them that have been trained thereby.* The "peaceful" fruit stands in contrast with the unrest and trouble which have preceded during the time of "chastening." But there is more than rest after conflict, for the object of the conflict is attained; the fruit consists in righteousness. (Comp. Isa. xxxii. 17; Prov. xi. 30; Jas. iii 17; Phil. i. 11.) It has been sometimes supposed that in the word "trained" the writer returns to the figure of verse 4; but this is not probable.

(12) **Wherefore.**—As in chap. x. 24, the writer passes from the thought of personal risk and duty, to speak (in verses 12—17) of that which is binding on all members of a community. "Wherefore"—since the trouble which has brought discouragement should rather call forth thankfulness—"strengthen (literally, *make straight again,* restore to a right state) the weakened hands and the palsied knees." The words are almost a reproduction of Isa. xxxv. 3, where those who have lost heart and hope (compared to men whose limbs are palsy-stricken) are encouraged by the promise of the coming of their God bringing recompense and salvation. (See chap. x. 36, 37.)

(13) **And make straight paths.**—Quoted with some slight changes from the Greek translation of Prov. iv. 26, "ponder" (or, more probably, *make even*) "the path of thy feet."

Be turned out of the way.—The difficulty in these words is concealed to some extent when they are separated from the following clause, as in the Authorised version; this separation, however, the Greek will not allow. If the words be rendered, "that what is lame may not be turned out of the way, but may rather be healed," we cannot but feel that the two members are somewhat incongruous. It is probable, therefore, that the first verb here bears the meaning which it not unfrequently has in medical writers, *be put out of joint.* Let the paths (or tracks) which you follow be straight, for crooked and uneven paths will make the limbs which are lame more helpless still; should nothing aggravate the hurt that has been received, it may soon be healed. In the application, the words are a warning against the shifting courses of men who are ready to turn aside from strict duty when persecution threatens, and seek to avert the danger by compliance with what they do not in heart approve. Whatever may be the result in the case of "the strong" (Rom. xiv. 1; 1 Cor. viii.), the example brings destruction on "the weak."

(14) **Follow peace.**—More clearly (as our word "follow" is somewhat ambiguous), *follow after peace.* There is a manifest allusion to Ps. xxxiv. 14 (quoted also in 1 Pet. iii. 11). This charge is general (Rom. xii. 18), and must not be limited to peace with fellow Christians (Rom. xiv. 19). The two admonitions of this verse were admirably suited to a period of persecution. Let all make peace their aim, yet not so as to sacrifice purity. (Comp. Jas. iii. 17.)

And holiness.—Better, *and the sanctification without which no man shall see the Lord.* In chap. ix. 28 we have the promise that "Christ . . . shall be seen" by them that wait for Him: hence it might be supposed (especially as in the next verse we read of "the grace of God") that "the Lord" is here, as in chap. ii. 3, a designation of our Saviour. As, however, this Epistle especially brings Him before us as the Sanctifier (chaps. ii. 11; xiii. 12), who leads us into the presence of God (chap. x. 19), we must rather look on these words as akin to Matt. v. 8, "Blessed are the pure in heart, for they shall see God" (Rev. xxii. 4).

(15) **Lest any man fail.**—Rather, *whether any one be falling back from the grace of God.* The defection of one member of the community brings loss and danger to the whole body. The last words of chap. x. 26 will show what is implied in this "falling back from the grace of God."

Any root of bitterness.—It is clear that Deut. xxix. 18, though not formally quoted, is before the writer's mind. In that chapter Moses had again brought before the people the covenant which, nearly forty years before, had been made and ratified "in Horeb" (see chap. ix. 18—20). With especial solemnity he sets before them the sin and terrible punishment of idolatry, "Lest there should be among you man or woman . . . whose heart turneth away this day from the Lord our God, to go and serve the gods of these nations; lest there should be among you a root that

thereby many be defiled; (16) lest there
be any fornicator, or profane person, as
Esau, who for one morsel of meat sold
his birthright. (17) For ye know how that
afterward, when he would have inherited
the blessing, he was rejected: for he
found no place of repentance,[1] though
he sought it carefully with tears.
(18) For ye are not come unto the
mount that might be touched, and that
burned with fire, nor unto blackness,
and darkness, and tempest,
(19) and the sound of a
trumpet, and the voice of
words; which *voice* they
that heard intreated that
the word should not be spoken to
them any more: (20) (for they could not
endure that which was commanded,
And if so much as a beast touch the

Chap. xii. 18—29. The terrors of Sinai. The New Covenant of Grace.

1 Or, *way to change his mind.*

---

beareth gall and wormwood." The marginal note on the last words ("poisonful herb") explains their true meaning—that which springs from the root is not merely bitter, it is also poisonous. Again, therefore (see chap. x. 27, 28, 30), the apostasy to which the Hebrew Christians were tempted is compared with the sin committed by those who by idolatry fell away from God's ancient covenant; and as one idol-worshipper in a community might bring into it a root of bitter poison, so one apostate from the Christian faith would bring trouble and defilement on the Church. In Acts viii. 23 St. Peter makes reference to the same chapter of Deuteronomy as he speaks to Simon Magus, who, above all other men, proved a root of bitter poison in the early Church.

Many.—Rather, *the many* (according to the best reading)—*i.e.*, the whole community.

(16) **Lest there be.**—Better (as in the last verse), *whether there be.* Though Jewish tradition (see, for example, the Targum of Palestine on Gen. xxv. 29) affirms that Esau was a man of impure life, it is not probable that he is so represented in this verse. Here he is mentioned as a type of "the profane," who care not for divine things, but only for the gains and pleasures of this world.

Who for one morsel of meat.—Better, *who for one meal sold his own birthright* (Gen. xxv. 29—34). We cannot suppose that the writer has in thought the material rights of the firstborn, such as his claim on pre-eminence and, possibly (see Deut. xxi. 17), on a larger share of his father's possessions. Tradition relates that, up to the time of Aaron, priestly functions were discharged by each firstborn son (comp. Num. iii. 5—12); and to the line of the firstborn would seem to belong that "blessing of Abraham" (Gen. xxviii. 4) which every one who shared Abraham's faith would earnestly desire to possess.

(17) **For ye know how that afterward . . .**—The meaning of the verse will be seen more clearly if one clause be placed in a parenthesis: "For ye know that even when he afterward desired to inherit the blessing he was rejected (for he found no place of repentance), though he sought it earnestly with tears." The blessing of Jacob related in Gen. xxvii. is here viewed (apart from all attendant circumstances) as a necessary consequence of Esau's "profane" scorn of his birthright. Notwithstanding Esau's piteous entreaty, Isaac cannot but ratify (verse 33) the blessing which he has pronounced; though his son sought the blessing earnestly with tears (verse 38), he was rejected. He "found no place of repentance;" that first act (Gen. xxv. 33) could not be recalled, but brought with it a loss which nothing could retrieve.

(It is right to add that other interpretations of the verse have been given, which seem, however, much less probable. Thus, the last clause has been understood to mean that Esau earnestly sought repentance; and the preceding words, which we have placed in a parenthesis, that he could not bring his father to a change of purpose.)

(18—29) The exhortation to faithfulness is most impressively enforced by means of a comparison between the earlier revelation and that which is given in Christ.

The mount that might be touched.—It appears certain that the word "mount" has no place in the true Greek text. Had this word been in the sentence as originally written, its absence from all our more ancient authorities would be inexplicable; whilst, on the other hand, the contrast with verse 22, and the recollection of Deut. iv. 11, from which the last words in this verse are taken, would very naturally lead a transcriber to supply this word, which he might suppose to have accidentally dropped out of the text. If, however, the writer did not make use of the word here, though the contrast of verse 22 was already before his mind, it seems certain that the word was not in his thought; and hence we have no right to introduce it in the explanation of the verse. The true translation, in all probability, is as follows: *For ye are not come unto a material* (literally, *a palpable*) *and kindled fire, and unto gloom and darkness and tempest.* The object of the writer is to set forth the terrors which accompanied the giving of the Law,—that which the awe-stricken people saw and heard. Not the mount, but the terrible fire was that which met their gaze. Thus again and again in Deuteronomy we find reference to the voice and the fire alone (chaps. iv. 33, 36; v. 4, 25, 26; xviii. 16). Shortly before "the day of the assembly" in Horeb Israel had been led by "a pillar of fire" (Ex. xiii. 21); in verse 29 of this chapter the figure of "a consuming fire" is applied to God Himself. To avoid such associations as these, and vividly to represent what then was shown to the Israelites, he speaks of "a material and kindled fire." The metaphor in "palpable" as applied to fire is hardly more remarkable than that involved in "a darkness which may be felt" (Ex. x. 21, where the word used in the LXX. is almost the same as that which we have here).

(19) See Ex. xix. 19 ("the voice of the trumpet"), Deut. iv. 12 ("the voice of the words").

Intreated.—"If we hear the voice of the Lord our God any more, then we shall die" (Deut. v. 25; Ex. xx. 19). Though God drew near to Israel, to reveal Himself, so terrible was His voice to them, so awful the penalties which fenced round their approach to Him, that they shrank back from hearing His words.

(20) There is no sufficient reason for enclosing this verse and the next in a parenthesis.

And if so much as.—Better, *If even a beast touch the mountain, it shall be stoned* (Ex. xix. 12, 13). The next clause, "or thrust through with a dart,"

mountain, it shall be stoned, or thrust through with a dart: (21) and so terrible was the sight, *that* Moses said, I exceedingly fear and quake:) (22) but ye are come unto mount Sion, and unto the city of the living God, the heavenly

---

is absent from our best authorities; and has accidentally found its way into the text from Ex. xix. 13.

(21) **And so terrible was the sight that ....**—Better, *And* (*so fearful was the appearance*) *Moses said, I exceedingly fear and tremble.* Deut. ix. 19, as it stands in the Greek translation, contains these words in part ("I exceedingly fear"); there, however, they belong to a later time, when Moses was "afraid of the anger and hot displeasure" of the Lord against the worshippers of the golden calf (Ex. xxxii.). Various Jewish traditions speak of the terror of Moses as upon Mount Sinai he beheld the wonders of the heavenly world (see chap. ii. 2); but no saying that has been preserved throws additional light on the words before us.

(22—24) "What it was to which Israel in the time of the Old Covenant drew nigh, we have now heard. Their drawing nigh was at the same time a standing afar off; the mount of the revelation might not be approached by them; the voice of God was too terrible to be borne; and yet it was only tangible material nature in which God at once manifested and concealed Himself. The true and inner communion with God had not yet been revealed: first must the Law lead to the painful consciousness that sin prevents such communion, and intensify the longing that sin may be taken out of the way. Under the New Covenant, no longer is a tangible mountain the place of a divine revelation made from afar; but heaven is thrown open, and a new supersensuous world in which God is enthroned is opened to admit us, opened through the Mediator of the New Covenant, accessible in virtue of His atoning blood" (Delitzsch).

(22) **Unto mount Sion.**—Literally (and in these difficult verses it is unusually important to follow the literal rendering of the Greek), *Ye are come unto Zion* (*the*) *mountain and city of a Living God, a heavenly Jerusalem.* The thought of a celestial city which should be the exact counterpart of the earthly Jerusalem is often dwelt upon in Jewish writings: hence the writer is using familiar words, but with a new and spiritual meaning. The same imagery has been employed in chap. xi. 10, 13—16, for this is the city "that hath the foundations, whose Architect and Maker is God." (See also Rev. xxi. 2, *et seq.*; Gal. iv. 26.) This "heavenly Jerusalem" is "Zion, mountain and city of a Living God." Mount Zion is mentioned first, because the contrast with Mount Sinai is throughout present in thought. The name recalls many passages of the Old Testament, especially of the Psalter, as far back as the time when David chose the place for the Ark of the Covenant. Here God desired to dwell (Ps. lxviii. 16); in this holy hill He set His anointed King (Ps. ii. 6). (See also Pss. xlviii. 2, 11; lxxviii. 68; cx. 2; cxxxii. 13.) Zion is not only the mount of God, His dwelling place; it is also "the city of God," whose gates the Lord loveth (Ps. lxxxvii. 2). (See Ps. xlviii. 12, 13, *et al.*) In chap. viii. 2 we find associated the place of the special manifestation of the glory of God and the resort of His worshipping people; so here the heavenly sanctuary and the city inhabited by "the ransomed of the Lord" (Isa. xxxv. 10). In Horeb Israel intreated that they might not hear the voice of "the living God" (Deut. v. 26). In this spiritual commonwealth we all "have drawn nigh" to Him.

In the first member of these three verses (22—24), therefore, there is very little that is open to question; the difficulties lie in the words which follow, "and to an innumerable company of angels, to the general assembly and church of the firstborn which are written in heaven." Four or five different arrangements of these words are allowed by the Greek, and every one of these has been adopted and defended by writers of eminence. Here the discussion must be very brief. On a careful examination of the whole passage, it seems in the highest degree probable that the writer introduces by "and" each successive member of the sentence, and that groups of words not so introduced serve as appositions, explaining what precedes them. If this be so, the arrangement of the Authorised version is not tenable. We believe that the choice must lie between two renderings: (1) "And to myriads of angels, a festal assembly and congregation of the firstborn enrolled in heaven." (2) "And to myriads, a festal assembly of angels and a congregation of the firstborn enrolled in heaven." In the first of these renderings angels are the subject throughout; in the second, "the myriads" to whom we have come nigh are divided into two companies—the festal host of angels, the church of the firstborn. Let us look at the latter interpretation first. By it the "firstborn" are sought amongst men; either those who are already inhabitants of the heavenly world, or men still living upon earth, though enrolled as citizens of heaven (Luke x. 20). Some have understood the words to relate to those who hold precedency, either in rank or in time, among men to whom God has given the name of sons; as, saints of preeminent piety, "the noble army of martyrs," the faithful under the Old Covenant, Enoch and Elijah, the Apostles, the first generations of Christians, or the believers of the later as distinguished from those of the earlier dispensation. A far more probable explanation is that which makes the word here "equivalent to *heirs of the kingdom*, all faithful Christians being *ipso facto* 'firstborn,' because all are kings" (Dr. Lightfoot on Col. i. 15). See chap. i. 6; also, "as instances of the figurative use of *firstborn* in the Old Testament, where the idea of priority of birth is overshadowed by and lost in the idea of pre-eminence," Job xviii. 13; Isa. xiv. 30. If this be the true interpretation, 1 Pet. ii. 9 unites the two thoughts which this figure suggests, "Ye are . . . a royal priesthood" (see above, verse 16); and the whole of that verse, especially as compared with Ex. iv. 22, well illustrates the position here assigned to the company of the faithful upon earth. The word which we have here rendered *congregation*, moreover, is that which is regularly applied to the Church of Christ. There is, therefore, very much to be said on behalf of this interpretation, which is in every way attractive. And yet, full of interest as is such an explanation of the special words, it seems certainly unsuitable to the passage as a whole. It is not easy to believe that the words "and to myriads" are to be taken by themselves. It is still more difficult to explain the introduction of the living Church on earth in this position—between angels and the "God of all," whilst "the spirits of just men made perfect" are mentioned later, in an association from

Jerusalem, and to an innumerable company of angels, (23) to the general assembly and church of the firstborn, which are written[1] in heaven, and to God the Judge of all, and to the spirits of just men made perfect, (24) and to Jesus the mediator of the new covenant,[2] and to the blood of sprinkling, that speaketh better things than *that of* Abel. (25) See that ye refuse not him that speaketh.

1 Or, *enrolled.*
2 Or, *testament.*

which the Church on earth cannot be severed—with "Jesus the Mediator of a new covenant and the blood of sprinkling." For these reasons especially it seems necessary to adopt the first-mentioned arrangement of the words: "ye have come near . . . to myriads of angels, a festal assembly and congregation of the firstborn enrolled in heaven." Two passages of the Old Testament seem to have been chiefly in the writer's mind (Deut. xxxiii. 2, and Dan. vii. 10); in each of these the Lord appears attended by "myriads of angels," who stand before Him and minister to Him (Ps. ciii. 20). We who by means of the "better hope draw near to God" (chap. vii. 19) are led to this "holy hill" and city, and through the hosts of "ministering spirits" into the very presence of the "God of all." The descriptive words which follow are borrowed from the history of Israel. The first (Ezek. xlvi. 11; Hos. ii. 11; ix. 5; Amos v. 21; Isa. lxvi. 10) is the general and joyous gathering for the feasts of the Lord; the second is the word used throughout for the "church in the wilderness," the "congregation" of Israel. The latter points to the united body of the servants of God, the former to the joyful gathering for His service. The second word is so commonly used of Israel and of the Christian Church that it has been denied that any other application is ever made; but there is certainly an exception in Ps. lxxxix. 7 (a Psalm which, as we have seen, was much in the writer's thoughts), "God is greatly to be feared in the congregation of the saints." How fitly angels—who in Job i. 6, ii. 1, xxxviii. 7 (comp. Ps. xxix. 1, *et al.*), are called "sons of God," are here spoken of as "firstborn," needs no explanation; they are the enrolled citizens of heaven, whose assembly we are permitted to join (Rev. v. 11; comp. Luke xx. 36).

(23) **And to God the Judge of all.**—The order of the Greek seems to require the rendering, *and to a Judge* (*who is*) *God of all.* Up to this point our thought has rested on the heavenly world and those who from the time of their creation have been its inhabitants. Men who have passed through this earthly life have no essential right to citizenship in the "heavenly Jerusalem." They come before a Judge (comp. chap. ix. 27). "The Lord shall judge His people" (chap. x. 30), severing between His servants and His foes (Mal. iii. 18; iv. 1), condemning the wicked, and receiving the righteous to His own dwelling-place. This Judge is "God of all"—of angels and of righteous souls (Wisd. iii. 1), and of Christian men who "draw nigh" to the celestial city. How characteristic of the writer and his theme is the introduction of these solemn words into the midst of this description of Christian privilege and blessing.

And to the spirits of just men made perfect.—The last verses of chap. xi. are at once called before the mind by these words. The "righteous" men have "by faith" run their course (chaps. x. 38; xi. 4, 7; Phil. iii. 12); they have obtained the promises (chaps. vi. 15; xi. 1). The analogy of Scripture forbids us to consider their present state as the full consummation; for that, these "spirits" and we who are yet "in the body" await the day of the resurrection. These words, however, do not refer to the period of the Old Covenant only; indeed they do not in strictness belong to that period at all. The spirits of the righteous servants of Christ join the same fellowship; and only when Christ was manifested does the state to which the name "perfection" is thus given seem to have begun. What was received by those "spirits of the righteous" when they saw the day of Christ, we cannot tell; but the teaching of Scripture seems to be that they were raised to some higher state of blessedness. These are the new inhabitants of the world above; they have come into the presence of God by means of the blood of sprinkling, through Jesus.

(24) **And to Jesus the mediator of the new covenant.**—Rather, *a new covenant.* There is another change in the Greek which it is not easy to express. In all other places in which we read of the New Covenant (chaps. viii. 8, 13; ix. 15; Luke xxii. 20; 1 Cor. xi. 25; 2 Cor. iii. 6) a word is used which implies newness of kind and quality; here it is a covenant which is newly made—literally "young," having all the freshness of youth in comparison with that which long since was waxing old (chap. viii. 13). Here also, if we follow the order of the original (see chaps. ii. 9; iii. 1; xii. 2, *et al.*), the description precedes, and the name "Jesus" follows, thus standing between the words which describe His covenant and those which speak of His blood.

And to the blood of sprinkling.—Rather, *and to blood of sprinkling that speaketh better* (or, *more powerfully*) *than Abel.* Jesus is Mediator of a new covenant (chaps. viii. 6; ix. 15) through the shedding of His blood (chaps. ix. 15—17; x. 29). This is "blood of sprinkling," blood which cleanseth the conscience from dead works to serve a living God (chap. ix. 14): it was typified by the blood of the covenant with which Moses sprinkled all the people (chap. ix. 19, 20). Abel being dead yet speaketh (chap. xi. 4), for his blood crieth for vengeance. This blood speaks with greater power, and speaks not for wrath but for purification and atonement. 1 John ii. 1, 2, completes the contrast: God was the Avenger of "righteous Abel," but Jesus Christ the righteous is our Advocate with the Father, and He is the propitiation for our sins.

It does not seem probable that the writer designs a detailed contrast between the several particulars of these verses and of verses 18—21. The number in each case is the same (*six*), and in the case of the first and last some analogy may be traced; but this is all that can be said with safety. If our interpretation of these verses is correct, there is no mention of the Church on earth. But can we wonder at this? It is to that living Church that the words themselves are from age to age addressed. They describe the blessed heavenly fellowship to which each servant of Christ now toiling on earth is joined: when he has run the race set before him, he will, through the blood of sprinkling and through Jesus the Mediator, reach the company of the just made perfect, and stand before the "God of all."

(25) **Refuse not.**—In verse 19 we have read that the Israelites entreated that they might no more hear the

For if they escaped not who refused
him that spake on earth, much more
shall not we *escape*, if we turn away
from him that *speaketh* from heaven:
(26) whose voice then shook the earth:
but now he hath promised, saying, Yet
once more I shake not the earth only, but
also heaven. (27) And this *word*, Yet
once more, signifieth the removing of
those things that are shaken,[1] as of
things that are made, that those things
which cannot be shaken may remain.
(28) Wherefore we receiving a kingdom
which cannot be moved, let us have[2]
grace, whereby we may serve God
acceptably with reverence and godly
fear: (29) for our God *is* a consuming
fire.

2 Or, *let us hold fast.*

1 Or, *may be shaken.*

A.D. 64.

CHAPTER XIII.—(1) Let brotherly

voice of God (literally, *deprecated* the speaking of more words). Twice in this verse the same word is used in the sense of declining to listen, with clear reference to the earlier verse.

Him that speaketh.—God speaking to us from heaven (chap. i. 1, 2). See below.

For if they escaped not who refused.—Rather (according to the better reading of the Greek), *For if they escaped not when they refused on earth Him that warned.* The terrors which accompanied the giving of the Law were designed to impress all hearts with the fearful peril of disobedience. In shrinking from the voice of Him that warned they could not escape the declaration of the Law or the terrible penalties which awaited all transgressors.

If we turn away.—Rather, *who turn away from Him that* (*warneth*) *from heaven.* The argument is similar to that of chap. ii. 2, 3, where the same word "escape" is found. He from whom they turned aside on earth is He who now speaks to us; but then His voice was heard amidst earthly terrors, now His revelation comes through His Son who is exalted in heaven. If we do not hearken to the word of life and promise that is ever coming to us from God through His Son, it will be because we deliberately "turn away," for the excuse of the panic-stricken Israelites cannot be ours. The voice that speaks on earth fell on the outward ear, but He who speaks from heaven makes His voice heard in the inner conscience; the one may fail to be heard and understood, the other will find us out, and is neglected only through stubbornness of will. Much less, then, shall we escape if we turn away from Him who warns from heaven.

(26) **Shook the earth.**—Ex. xix. 18, 19; Judg. v. 4, 5. The terrors of Sinai were, moreover, a type of a more terrible revelation of judgment, when not only shall the earth tremble, but the earth and the heaven shall be moved, and all that is transitory and mutable shall pass away. The words of Hag. ii. 6 are taken as a prophecy of this consummation. The reference of the prediction of which this forms part to the *first* coming of the Messiah is passed over; it is only as bearing upon the last days that the words are quoted here.

Now he hath promised.—This whole time of waiting is included in the "now." It is as if the words were: "now we have this promise, and are looking for its fulfilment."

I shake.—Rather (according to the better reading), *I will move* (or, *make to tremble*).

(27) This word, "Yet once more," is equivalent to *once more only;* and the words "once more only will I move the heaven and the earth" must of necessity point to the final change, which issues in the removal of all that can pass away.

Which cannot be shaken.—Literally, *which are not shaken.* The great difficulty of the verse is to ascertain on what word this clause depends. (1) If upon "removing," the sense will be: This word . . . signifieth the removing of the things made (as being created things), that the things not shaken may remain. The next verse throws light on the writer's meaning; there that which "cannot be shaken" is the kingdom which we receive: he is not speaking of that which belongs to a material creation. (2) The other view can only be briefly mentioned: This word . . . signifieth the removing of the things shaken, as of things that have been made in order that the things not shaken may remain. The idea is striking—that created things were made for the very purpose of giving place to what shall abide; but the other view seems to give the more probable meaning of the verse.

(28) **Receiving a kingdom.**—These words clearly contain a reference to Dan. vii. 18, "The saints of the Most High shall receive the kingdom." Nor can it well be doubted that the closing verses of Hag. ii. are also before the writer's mind; after verse 21, which repeats the words of verse 6, quoted above, the prophet declares the overthrow of earthly kingdoms, and continues to His servant Zerubbabel the Messianic promise. Christ has made His people kings; and when heaven and earth have passed away, they shall be found heirs of a kingdom that cannot be shaken (chap. ii. 5—9).

Let us have grace.—Many render the last word *thankfulness*, but the ordinary translation is preferable. There is for us a "throne of grace" to which we may draw near and "find grace" (chap. iv. 16). The characteristic of our Christian state is that we "have grace," and have not "fallen back from the grace of God" (verse 15). Let us continue in this state and thus be enabled to offer our priestly service unto God (chaps. ix. 14; xiii. 15).

Acceptably.—Literally, *well-pleasing.* (See chaps. xi. 5; xiii. 16.)

With reverence and godly fear.—According to the true reading of the Greek, the meaning is *with reverent fear and awe.* The former word is that which occupies so important a place in chap. v. 7. (See Note.) The tone of the whole chapter—we might rather say, the whole Epistle—is presented in this combination of "grace" and acceptable service with awe and reverent fear. The last thought connects itself closely with the following verse.

(29) A quotation from Deut. iv. 24. There these words follow a solemn warning against idolatry. This passage then belongs to the same class as chap. x. 27, 28, 30. (See the Notes.)

XIII.

This concluding chapter is chiefly occupied with special exhortations relating to Christian conduct: with these, however, are intermingled some important and characteristic references to the leading themes of the Epistle.

(1) **Brotherly love.**—Better, *The love of the brethren.* (See Rom. xii. 10, and Note; 1 Thess. iv. 9;

love continue. (2) Be not forgetful to
entertain strangers: for
thereby some have enter-
tained angels unawares.
(3) Remember them that
are in bonds, as bound with them; *and*
them which suffer adversity, as being
yourselves also in the body. (4) Marriage
is honourable in all, and the bed unde-
filed: but whoremongers and adulterers
God will judge. (5) *Let your* conversa-
tion *be* without covetousness; *and be*
content with such things as ye have:

Chap. xiii. 1—6. Exhortation to brotherly love, purity, contentment.

for he hath said, I will never leave
thee, nor forsake thee.[a] (6) So that we
may boldly say, The Lord *is* my helper,
and I will not fear what man shall do
unto me.
(7) Remember them which have
the rule[1] over you, who
have spoken unto you
the word of God: whose
faith follow, considering
the end of *their* conver-
sation. (8) Jesus Christ the same
yesterday, and to day, and for ever.

a Josh. i. 5.

1 Or, *are the guides.*

Chap. xiii. 7—17. Imitate your Christian guides. Bear Christ's reproach.

---

1 Pet. i. 22.) The love which they had shown to the Christian brotherhood is commended in chap. vi. 10 (x. 33); and yet there was some ground for fear that such affection might not "continue" (chap. x. 25).

(2) **To entertain strangers.**—Hospitality to Christian brethren at a distance from their homes is especially intended (1 Pet. iv. 9): this was one manifestation of the "love of the brethren" (verse 1). The prominence assigned to this duty in the exhortations of the Epistles of the New Testament was faithfully reflected in the practice of the early Church.

Thereby some have entertained angels unawares.—See Gen. xviii., xix. The Greek word for "angels"—*messengers*—of itself would serve to remind these Christians that, though the strangers whom they welcomed were but men, they might be special messengers of God. Clement of Rome, in his Epistle to the Corinthians (A.D. 95), appeals to the same examples (and also to Rahab): "For his faith and hospitality a son was given to Abraham in his old age. For his hospitality and godliness Lot was saved from Sodom."

(3) **As bound with them.**—Either (1) "As if ye yourselves were in bonds" (see chap. x. 33, 34; 1 Cor. xii. 26)—by true fellow-feeling make yourselves sharers in their lot; or, (2) "mindful that ye too are in bonds"—like them ye are Christ's prisoners, and their bonds are but one of the tokens of that service in which all Christians are bound. (Comp. 1 Cor. vii. 22.)

As being yourselves also in the body.—"Mindful that you, like them, still dwell in a body liable to pain, and may therefore suffer ill-treatment in the cause of Christ."

(4) **Marriage is honourable in all.**—Rather, *Let marriage be held in honour among all, and let the bed be undefiled; for fornicators and adulterers God will judge.* The precept is directed against impurity (chap. xii. 16), and also against the false asceticism of men "forbidding to marry" (1 Tim. iv. 3). The laxity of morals among Gentiles (Note on Acts xv. 20) and the prevalence of divorce amongst Jews (Matt. v. 32) explain the sudden introduction of such warnings: of these sinners the all-seeing God will be the judge. (Comp. 1 Thess. iv. 6.)

(5) In these two verses (4, 5) we have the same connection of thought as in chap. xii. 16; Col. iii. 5; Eph. v. 3. "Impurity and covetousness may be said to divide between them nearly the whole domain of human selfishness and vice" (Lightfoot on Col. iii. 5).

Conversation.—Literally, *way* of thought and life, character, disposition.

For he.—Rather, *for He Himself hath said.* As in many other places in this Epistle, the word of Scripture is regarded as directly spoken by God; but there is an emphasis here ("He Himself") which well suits the remarkable impressiveness of the words quoted, "I will in no wise let thee go; no, nor will I forsake thee." This promise of divine support and protection does not occur exactly in the same form in the Old Testament, but is clearly taken from Deut. xxxi. 6, "He will not fail thee nor forsake thee." (Comp. also Gen. xxviii. 15; Josh. i. 5; 1 Chron. xxviii. 20.) The appositeness of these words and those which follow (verse 6) will be seen if we remember the trials which the Hebrew Christians had already endured (chap. x. 32—34). It is very probable that this thought supplies the link of connection between verses 5, 6, and verse 7.

(6) **We may boldly say.**—Rather, *so that we say with courage.* The words of the quotation (Ps. cxviii. 6) should be arranged thus: "The Lord is my helper; I will not fear: what shall man do unto me?"

(7) **Which have the rule.**—Rather, *which were your leaders* (verse 17, 24; Acts xv. 22), *who spake unto you the word of God.* These spiritual guides had been removed from them by death.

Whose faith follow.—Better, *and, contemplating the end* (or, *issue*) *of their life, imitate their faith.* Their Christian life and course (Jas. iii. 13; 1 Pet. i. 15, *et al.*), had been known by the Church; they, too, have obtained a good report "by faith" (chap. xi. 2), and all who contemplate the blessed issue of such a life will be strengthened to imitate their faith. We may well suppose that some had died a martyr's death, but the writer seems carefully to avoid any direct expression of this thought; his words apply to all who have ended their course in the triumph of faith. This verse recalls a striking passage in the Book of Wisdom, chap. ii. 17—20; especially verse 17, where the ungodly say of the righteous man, "Let us see if his words be true, and let us prove what shall happen in *the end* of him."

(8) **Jesus Christ the same . . .**—Rather, *Jesus Christ is yesterday and to-day the same; yea, also for ever.* Their earlier guides have passed away (verse 7); their Lord and Saviour abides the same for ever. He who is the subject of all Christian teaching is the same, therefore (verse 9) "be not carried away by divers teachings." Thus, this verse stands connected both with what precedes and with what follows. "Yesterday" carries the thought back to the lifetime of the teachers now no more; what the Saviour was to them, that will He be to their survivors. The whole period since He "sat down on the right hand of God" (chap. x. 12, 13) is covered by this word. What He was "yesterday and to-day" He will be for ever. (See chap. i. 11, 12.)

(9) Be not carried about with divers and
strange doctrines. For *it is* a good
thing that the heart be established with
grace; not with meats, which have not
profited them that have been occupied
therein. (10) We have an altar, whereof
they have no right to eat which serve
the tabernacle. (11) For the bodies of
those beasts, whose blood is brought
into the sanctuary by the high priest
for sin, are burned without the camp.
(12) Wherefore Jesus also, that he might
sanctify the people with his own blood,
suffered without the gate. (13) Let us
go forth therefore unto him without the
camp, bearing his reproach. (14) For

---

(9) **Be not carried about.**—The better reading of the Greek gives a meaning somewhat different, *Be not carried away by divers and strange teachings.* The ordinary reading may have come in from Eph. iv. 14. The "teachings" by which they were in danger of being led astray were various, and were all foreign to the one true word. The contrasts expressed in the second part of this verse and in verses 10, 11, throw light on the nature and source of the erroneous doctrine. Its subject was not "grace," but "meats;" its promoters were connected with those who serve the Tabernacle. Hence the writer is probably speaking of doctrines and practices similar to those censured by St. Paul in Col. ii. 16—23. (See the introductory Note on Rom. xiv.; also 1 Tim. iv. 3.) In chap. ix. 10 we read of "meats and drinks" in connection with the Law of Moses; here the divers and strange teachings" must include human additions to that Law and perversions of its spirit.

With grace; not with meats.—Better, *by grace, not by meats.* Instead of being "carried away by strange teachings," let your hearts be made firm and sure by grace. As the whole system of ceremonial observance is alluded to under the one term "meats," so the blessings of the Christian faith are comprised under "grace," a word used throughout this Epistle with peculiar significance. (See especially chaps. x. 29; xii. 15, 28.) One human system of teaching will but lead on to another; grace will keep the heart firm in its loyal love to Jesus Christ, who is ever "the same" (verse 8).

Which have not profited.—Literally, *in which they that walked were not profited.* To the English reader the mode of expression must appear peculiar; in the Greek, however, there is little or no incongruity, for the word which we render "walk" is used most freely to denote a course or manner of life. Comp. Eph. ii. 10, "unto good works which God hath before ordained that we should walk in them." Here the meaning is, that those who have made these external observances the rule of their life have failed of the profit which they sought. (Comp. chap. vii. 18, 19.)

(10, 11) "We need not such profitless teaching; we already have sustenance which is 'meat indeed,' by which the heart is established." According to the Law, the priests (they who "serve the Tabernacle," see chap. viii. 5) received for themselves a greater or smaller portion of the animals offered as peace-offerings and trespass-offerings; in some cases, also, the flesh of the sin-offerings fell to their lot (Lev. iv., v., vii., xxiii.). When the high priest presented a sin-offering on his own behalf (Lev. iv. 3—12), or for the congregation (verses 13—21), he sprinkled some of the blood in the Holy Place in front of the veil; on the Day of Atonement alone was the blood taken within the veil into the Most Holy Place. In the case of these three offerings the priest received no part of the animal sacrificed; certain portions were burnt on the altar of burnt-offering, and the rest of the body was carried forth "without the camp," and wholly consumed by fire. Though the writer here speaks of animals whose blood is brought into *the Holy Place* through the high priest, as an offering for sin, it is probable that (as in chaps. v.—ix.) he has in thought the Day of Atonement only, so that here "the Holy Place" bears the sense of the "Holiest of all." (See Note on chap. ix. 2.) (It will be noted that throughout he uses the present tense; see the same Note). For us there is but one sacrifice for sin, the efficacy of which endures for ever (chap. x. 12): Jesus entering the Holiest Place for us in virtue of His own sacrifice has fulfilled the type contained in the high priest's sprinkling of the blood. But whereas those priests might not eat of their sin-offering, to us greater privilege is given; we feed on Him who was slain for us, whose flesh was for the life of the world (John vi. 51—56). We then (who are all "priests unto God") "have an altar of which," on the very principles of their Law, "they that serve the Tabernacle (see chap. viii. 5) have no right to eat." The stress is laid on the *sacrifice*, of which we eat, not upon the altar itself. If separately interpreted, the altar will be the place of sacrifice, the Cross.

(12) The sin-offering was burned *without the camp.* Jesus who in all other points fulfilled the law of atonement fulfilled it in this point also, in that He suffered "without the gate" (Matt. xxvii. 32; John xix. 20). The two expressions answer to one another, each denoting that which lay beyond the sacred precincts, outside the special dwelling-place of God's people. "The people," see chap. ii. 17; "sanctify," chaps. ii. 11; ix. 13; x. 10.

(13) The suffering "without the gate" was a symbol of His rejection by the Jews. All who would be His must share the reproach which came upon Him, who was cast out by His people and crucified (chap. xi. 26): they also must go forth "without the camp," forsaking the company of His foes. Each one must for himself make choice either of the synagogue or of the church of Christ; between the two there can be no fellowship.

(14) In this verse there seems to be a union of two thoughts: (1) We are free to go forth from the city so long held sacred, for our hopes are bound up with no abiding earthly sanctuary. (2) We may not shrink from the reproach of Christ because it will sever us from kindred and friends; for by the very profession of our faith we are "strangers and sojourners" (chap. xi. 13), seeking after the heavenly Jerusalem (chaps. xi. 10; xii. 22). How impressive are these words when read in the light of the events then unlooked for, yet so near at hand, issuing in the destruction of both Temple and city!

We seek one to come.—Rather, *we seek after that* (city) *which is to come.*

here have we no continuing city, but we
seek one to come.[a] (15) By him there-
fore let us offer the sacrifice of praise to
God continually, that is, the fruit of
our lips giving thanks to[1] his name.
(16) But to do good and to communicate
forget not: for with such sacrifices
God is well pleased. (17) Obey them
that have the rule over[2] you, and
submit yourselves: for they watch for
your souls, as they that must give

a Mic. 2. 10.

1 Gr. *confessing to.*

2 Or, *guide.*

account, that they may do it with joy,
and not with grief: for that *is* unprofit-
able for you.
(18) Pray for us: for we trust we have
a good conscience, in all
things willing to live hon-
estly. (19) But I beseech
you the rather to do this,
that I may be restored to you the sooner.
(20) Now the God of peace, that brought
again from the dead our Lord Jesus,

Chap. xiii. 18—25. Closing salutations and prayers.

---

(15) **By him.**—Better, *through Him.* Through His sacrifice, which has made atonement, we are hallowed (verse 12), and fitted for our priestly service (1 Pet. ii. 5).

Let us offer the sacrifice.—Rather, *let us offer up a sacrifice of praise continually unto God, that is, fruit of lips making confession to His name.* The sacrifice we may bring is that symbolised by the thank-offering of Lev. vii. 12—where the same word is used. (See Ps. l. 14, 23.) "We will render the fruit of our lips" is the Greek version of Hos. xiv. 2; the Hebrew text (as we have it) differs in expression but not in meaning, "We will render our lips as bullocks"—*i.e.,* as sacrifices. (Comp. Ps. cxix. 108; Isa. lvii. 19.) The fruit is borne by lips which offer thankful acknowledgment to the name of God (Ps. cxiii. 1).

(16) And yet another offering may we bring: with thankfulness to Him must be joined acts of well-doing to men; these, too, being presented as sacrifices to God.

To communicate—*i.e.,* freely to impart to others. (See Rom. xii. 13; xv. 26; 2 Cor. ix. 13; 1 Tim. vi. 18.)

(17) The present section of the chapter begins (verse 7) and ends (verse 17) with a reference to the rulers of the Church: Remember your former leaders, and imitate their faith; obey them that lead you now.

Submit yourselves.—Better, *yield* (*to them*). Besides fulfilling their injunctions, be ready to comply with their wishes and requests.

For they watch.—The Greek is emphatic: "For it is they that watch on behalf of your souls as having to give account."

That they may do it.—Be obedient and yielding to them, *that they may do this* (may watch for your souls) *with joy and not sighing* (or, *groaning*), *for this would be unprofitable for you*; if ye so live that they must watch over you with grief, this will both weaken their hands and bring on you the divine displeasure. No words could more powerfully present to members of the Church the motives for obedience to their spiritual guides; and to these guides themselves the ideal of their work and life, as men who are keeping watch for souls, either with rejoicing or with mourning (Acts xx. 31), ever mindful of the account they must give to God for the flock which He entrusted to their care (Ezek. iii. 18; xxxiii. 7; xxxiv. 10; 1 Pet. v. 4).

(18) The following verses—containing personal notices relating to the writer himself and his readers (verses 18, 19, 22, 23), a prayer on their behalf (verses 20, 21), a doxology (verse 21), and brief salutations (verses 24, 25)—present many points of resemblance to the concluding sections in some of St. Paul's Epistles. The first words, "Pray for us," are found in Col. iv. 3; 1 Thess. v. 25; 2 Thess. iii. 1. That the writer does not use the plural pronoun of himself alone appears certain from the change in verse 19; but it is not clear whether he is associating himself with the rulers of the Church (mentioned in verse 17), or with the companions in labour who were with him as he wrote.

We trust.—A change in the reading of the Greek requires the translation: *For we are persuaded that we have a good conscience, desiring in all things to conduct ourselves well.* Some prejudice against the writer, or some mistrust of his motives, must have existed in the Church; that amongst Hebrew Christians a disciple of St. Paul should be misrepresented or misunderstood, can cause us no surprise. But whatever suspicion might be cherished by a few, the next verse is proof that he knew himself to be beloved by the many.

(19) **But I beseech you.**—Rather, *And I exhort you the more* (literally, *the more abundantly*) *to do this.* All that we can certainly infer from this verse (see *Introduction*) is that the writer had formerly been associated with those whom he now addresses, and that he is at present hindered from returning to them.

(20) **Now the God of peace.**—See Rom. xv. 33; xvi. 20; 2 Cor. xiii. 11; Phil. iv. 9; 1 Thess. v. 23; 2 Thess. iii. 16. In almost all these places there is something in the context suggestive of strife or turmoil to be brought to rest by "the God of peace." Hence we may well believe that the writer here has in thought those divisions of thought and feeling which have been hinted at in verses 17—19, and which in truth were the expression of the deep-seated mental unrest which it is the object of the Epistle to remove.

Our Lord Jesus.—As in chaps. ii. 9, iii. 1, xii. 2, the name is introduced after the description, according to the order of the Greek: "Now the God of peace that brought up from the dead (Rom. x. 7) the great Shepherd of the sheep, by the blood of an eternal covenant, our Lord Jesus . . ." Two passages of the prophets have contributed to the language of this remarkable verse: (1) Isa. lxiii. 11, "Where is He that brought them up out of the sea with the shepherds of His flock?" Here the shepherds are no doubt Moses and Aaron (Ps. lxxvii. 20); the Greek translation, however, has, "Where is he that raised up out of the sea the shepherd of the sheep?" Moses, who led Israel through the sea, was brought up therefrom in safety to be the "shepherd" of his people Israel; by the same Almighty hand the great Shepherd of the sheep has been brought up from among the dead. (2) Zech. ix. 11, "As for thee also, by the blood of thy covenant I have sent forth thy prisoners out of the pit wherein is no water." In other words, "because of the blood which ratified thy covenant (Ex. xxiv. 8) I have released thy prisoners." As in the former case, the resemblance between the words in the LXX. and those here used is sufficient to convince us that the passage was in the writer's thought. In (*i.e.,* in virtue of) the blood of an

that great shepherd of the sheep, through the blood of the everlasting covenant,[1] (21) make you perfect in every good work to do his will, working[2] in you that which is well pleasing in his sight, through Jesus Christ; to whom *be* glory for ever and ever. Amen.
(22) And I beseech you, brethren, suffer the word of exhortation: for I have written a letter unto you in few words.

1 Or, *testament.*

2 Or, *doing.*

(23) Know ye that *our* brother Timothy is set at liberty; with whom, if he come shortly, I will see you. (24) Salute all them that have the rule over you, and all the saints. They of Italy salute you. (25) Grace *be* with you all. Amen.

¶ Written to the Hebrews from Italy by Timothy.

---

eternal covenant (chap. ix. 15—18) God has raised up the Lord Jesus. The covenant was ratified by His blood; the first of the blessings of the covenant, and that in which all blessing lay included, was this, that God raised Him up from the dead to be "the great Shepherd of the sheep." If these prophetic words respecting Him who brings peace to the world (Zech. ix. 10, *et al.*), were in the writer's mind, how natural is his appeal to the God of *peace.* It has been often observed that this is the only passage in the Epistle in which we read of the resurrection of our Lord apart from His ascension; elsewhere His exaltation is contemplated as one act (chap. ii. 9, *et al.*). It is not certain that we have an exception even here, for though the meaning of Rom. x. 7 is beyond doubt, the words may in this place be used with a wider meaning.

(21) **Make you perfect.**—To "make perfect" is the translation of two different words in this Epistle. In the one, which is of frequent occurrence (chaps. ii. 10; x. 1; xii. 23, *et al.*), "perfect" stands contrasted with that which is immature, which has not attained its end and aim. The other, which is used here (and in a somewhat different sense in chaps. x. 5, and xi. 3), rather conveys the thought of completeness, complete equipment or preparation.

Every good work.—The best authorities read "every good thing;" and below, substitute "us" for "you."

Working.—Literally, *doing*, or *making.* The words of Phil. ii. 12, 13, are different, but the general thought is the same. "Well pleasing" recalls chaps. xi. 5; xii. 28; verse 16. (Rom. xii. 2; Eph. v. 10.)

Through Jesus Christ.—That is, "working in us through Jesus Christ that which is well-pleasing in His sight." In verse 20 (as in chap. ii. 9) we read of the exaltation of "Jesus." Here, where the subject of thought is the lasting mediation of our High Priest, the writer introduces the complete name "Jesus Christ," thus preparing for the doxology which follows. That this ascription of praise is addressed to our Saviour (as in 2 Tim. iv. 18; Rev. i. 6; 2 Pet. iii. 18), it seems hardly possible to doubt.

Glory.—Rather, *the glory.* (See Gal. i. 5.)

(22) **And I beseech you.**—Rather, *But I exhort you, brethren, bear with the word of exhortation; for indeed it is in few words that I have written unto you.* How fitly the whole Epistle may be spoken of as an "exhortation" is obvious. (See Note on chap. v. 11.) And if we take into account the subjects with which the writer has been dealing, we shall not wonder that a Letter which might have been read to the assembled church in less than an hour should be described as brief. (Comp. 1 Pet. v. 12.)

(23) It is clear that the Hebrew Christians knew of the imprisonment of Timothy, but had not heard the news of his release. In 2 Cor. i. 1; Col. i. 1; Philem. verse 1, Timothy is spoken of as "the brother;" in 1 Thess. iii. 2, and here, as "our brother" (for the word "our" printed in italics in the Authorised version, belongs to the true text). With him, the writer adds, "if he come shortly [sooner than the date at which he himself must depart], I will see you."

(24) **That have the rule over you.**—Better, *that are your leaders:* see verses 7, 17.

They of Italy salute you.—These much discussed words are consistent with either of two hypotheses:—(1) That the writer is in Italy, and salutes "the Hebrews" in the name of the Christians of Italy: (2) That the writer is addressing a Church of Italy, and sends greeting from Christians who have their home in Italy, but are now with him. (See *Introduction.*)

(25) **Grace be with you all.**—This brief closing benediction is also found in Titus iii. 15, and, with the omission of "all," in Col. iv. 18; 1 Tim. vi. 21; 2 Tim. iv. 22.

[As in the other Epistles the subscription is destitute of authority, not being found (in the form given above) in any MS. of the Epistle earlier than the ninth century. No ancient MS. contains more than the simple notice, "To the Hebrews," except the Alexandrian, which adds "written from Rome." The mention of Rome or Italy is, no doubt, due to verse 24. It is possible also that verse 23 is the only authority for the reference to Timothy as the bearer of the Epistle: for an ancient interpretation understands that verse to speak, not of the release of Timothy from captivity, but of his departure on some official mission.]

[The works chiefly used have been the commentaries on the Epistle by Bleek, Delitzsch, Hofmann, Lünemann, Kurtz, Bengel, Ewald, Alford, Wordsworth, McCaul, and Biesenthal; Westcott *On the Canon;* Lightfoot's *Clement;* Bleek's *Einleitung in das N. T.* (by Mangold); Ewald's *Geschichte;* Davidson's two *Introductions to the New Testament;* Reuss's *History of Christian Theology;* Riehm's special work on the Doctrinal System of this Epistle; Stanley's *Sermons and Essays;* the *Commentaries on the Psalms* by Delitzsch, Perowne, Jennings and Lowe; and Carpzov's *Sacrae Exercitationes.*]

INTRODUCTION

TO

THE GENERAL EPISTLE OF

JAMES

I. The Writer.—*Questions of Identity.*—"James, a servant (literally, *a slave*) of God and the Lord Jesus Christ:" this is all the direct information to be learned from the author concerning himself. The name James was, of course, a favourite with the Jews under the more common form of Jacob, and is familiar to us in studying the books of the New Testament. We read there of:—

1. James the son of Zebedee.
2. James the son of Alphæus.
3. James "the Lord's brother."
4. James the son of Mary.
5. James "the Less" (or, "the Little").
6. James the brother of Jude.
7. James the first Bishop of Jerusalem.

Is it possible for us to decide between so many, or even feel fairly convinced that we can identify one of these as the writer of our Epistle? To reject them all, and ascribe it to another James, of whom no further mention is made, would seem to be the addition of fresh and needless difficulty to a problem already sufficiently obscure. The first claimant in the above list may be dismissed at once, from the fact of his early death. James the Great, as he is called, the brother of John, was executed by Herod Agrippa I. in A.D. 44 (Acts xii. 2), a date much too early for this Letter; and no tradition or opinion worthy of consideration has ever attributed it to him.

The next inquiry must be one of much circumspection, beset as it is with thorns of controversy: in fact, the conflict of authorities must seem well nigh hopeless to an ordinary mind. Apart from the main question, many collateral ones have arisen to embitter the dispute, and by no means the last word has been said on either side. If, then, an attempt be here made to arrive at some conclusion, it must confessedly be with much misgiving, and full admission of the almost equal arguments against our decision.

By comparing St. Paul's description concerning numbers 4 and 7 (above) in Gal. i. 19 and ii. 9—12, it is thought he must be referring to one and the same man; let that be granted, therefore, to begin with. We may identify numbers 3 and 4 by the knowledge that James the son of Mary had a brother called Joses (Matt. xxvii. 56), and so also had James "the Lord's brother" (Matt. xiii. 55); and further we may consider numbers 3 and 6 identical, because each was brother to Jude (Mark vi. 3; Jude, verse 1); James the Little, number 5, is clearly the same as the son of Mary, number 4. (Comp. Matt. xxvii. 56; Mark xv. 40; Luke xxiv. 10.) These might, it is true, be coincidences merely, and, when we remember the frequency of Hebrew names, seem insufficient for more than hypothesis; but we are arguing on probability only, and not to absolute demonstration. Thus far, then, numbers 3, 4, 5, 6, and 7, are thought to be one and the same person—the Apostle James, and he the Lord's brother; the claims of number 1 have been disposed of; those of number 2, the son of Alphæus, remain. The question, perhaps the greatest of all, is whether the process of identification can be extended further, for on this depends largely the issue of the dispute with regard to the brethren of the Lord and the perpetual virginity of His mother.

Further Consideration of "the Brethren of the Lord."—We have no need in the present instance to enter on the war-path of this theological quarrel. There seems an intentional silence in Holy Writ concerning the family of our Saviour, to teach us, perhaps, that it stood in no spiritually peculiar position nearer to Him than we may be ourselves, and to remind us of His precious words, "Whosoever shall do the will of My Father which is in heaven, the same is My brother, and sister, and mother" (Matt. xii. 48—50). Bearing this in mind, and with thoughts of peace in our heart for those who truly—and reverently—differ from us, we may soon learn the outlines of this discussion.

The terms "brother" and "brethren" meet us so often in the New Testament, as applied to Jesus Christ, that we can hardly pass them by. Do they infer the strict and actual relationship, or one merely collateral?

1. *Uterine, or Helvidian Theory.*—The advocates of the natural sense, that these men were the younger sons of Joseph and Mary, urge the plain meaning of the Greek word *adelphos*, *i.e.*, "brother," and deny its use figuratively. They point, moreover, to Matt. i. 25, and suppose from it the birth of other children in the holy family. Those who shrink from such a view are charged with sentiment, as impugners of marriage, and even with ideas more or less Manichæan concerning the impurity of matter. The German commentator Bleek, and Dean Alford and Dr. Davidson amongst ourselves, contend thus for the actual brotherhood, maintaining the theory originally propounded by Helvidius, a writer of the fourth century, answered by the great Augustine. To their first argument we may answer that in holy Scripture there are four senses of brotherhood, namely, of blood, of tribe, of nation, of friendship, and the three last of these will all apply to the case in point. As for the view based on Matt. i. 25, the words, either in the Greek tongue or our own, authorise it not. To say "he did not do such a thing until the day of his death" does not (as Bishop Pearson has observed) suggest the inference that he did it then or afterwards; and the term "first-born" by no means implies a second, even in our present use of language, under similar

circumstances. Above all, though it is confessedly no argument, there is the feeling alluded to by Pearson and others, and acquiesced in by many, that there could have been no fresh maternity on the part of

> "Her who with a sweet thanksgiving
> Took in tranquillity what God might bring;
> Blessed Him, and waited, and within her living
> Felt the arousal of a Holy Thing."

"And as after His death His body was placed in a sepulchre 'wherein never man before was laid,' so it seemed fitting that the womb consecrated by His presence should not henceforth have borne anything of man." It is right, however, that the reader should be referred to the excellent Note of Professor Plumptre on Matt. xii. 46, where the question is carefully discussed.

2. *Agnatic, or Epiphanian Theory.*—A second class of divines are in accordance with the theory of Epiphanius, who was Bishop of Salamis, in Cyprus, towards the end of the fourth century, and no mean antagonist of the Helvidians. At the head of their modern representatives, *facile princeps* for scholarship and fairness, is Canon Lightfoot. The brethren of the Lord are said to be the sons of Joseph by a former wife, *i.e.*, before his espousal of the Virgin Mary, and are rightly termed *adelphoi* accordingly. Far from being of the number of the Twelve, they were believers only after Christ's resurrection. Thus, then, are explained such texts as Matt. xii. 46, Mark iii. 31, Luke viii. 19, John vii. 5. By this supposition, James the Lord's brother must be a distinct person from James the son of Alphæus. But an objection—nay, "the one which has been hurled at the Helvidian theory with great force . . . and fatal effect"—is strangely thought by Lightfoot to be powerless against his favourite Epiphanian doctrine. It is this: our Lord on the cross commended His mother to St. John: "Behold *thy* mother," "Behold thy son" (chap. xix. 26, 27); "and from that hour," we are told, "that disciple took her unto his own home." If the Uterine theory be right, she had at least four sons living at the time. "Is it conceivable that our Lord would thus have snapped asunder the most sacred ties of natural affection?" Nor could the fact of His brethren's unbelief "override the paramount duties of filial piety;" and the objection is weakened further by our knowledge that within a few days "all alike are converted to the faith of Christ: yet she, their mother, living in the same city, and joining with them in a common worship (Acts i. 14), is consigned to the care of a stranger, of whose house she becomes henceforth an inmate." Now, all this argument, forcible and fatal as it unquestionably is to the idea of real and full relationship, is hardly less so against that of step-sons. For, seeing they were borne by a former wife, they must have been older than Jesus; and, on the death of Joseph, the eldest would certainly have become head of the family, in full dominion over the younger children and the widow herself, and with chief responsibility for their protection and welfare. The custom prevailed under Roman law as well as Jewish, and exists in the East still: being, in fact, a relic of immemorial antiquity. Nor can we conceive, for other than the weightiest reasons, such as immorality or crime, that our Lord, who came "not to destroy the Law, but to fulfil," would thus openly have set one of its firmest obligations aside. It seems clear that the widowed mother watching by the cross, and soon to be childless among women, with the sword of separation piercing to and through her own soul (Luke ii. 35), had none to care for her, except the beloved disciple into whose charge she was given by her dying Son.

3. *Collateral, or Hieronymian Theory.*—There remains one proposition more, known, from the name of its foremost champion, Jerome, as the Hieronymian theory; and this, on the whole, presents fewest difficulties to the religious mind. The sons of Alphæus (or Cleopas: the name is the same in different dialects) were the cousins of our Lord, their mother and His being sisters; and such a relationship would entirely justify the use of the word "brethren." The balance of evidence seems to the writer of these Notes to incline towards this venerable belief; and, identifying "the son of Alphæus" with "the brother of the Lord," he considers him to have been the James of the Epistle. Unless this solution of the difficulty be allowed, we are committed to the recognition of a *third* James an *Apostle*, and one so called in only a secondary sense. It is true the term was not strictly applied to the original Twelve, and therefore might have been applied to a third James as well as to a Barnabas; and we will further admit that, if James were one of the unbelieving brethren mentioned in John vii. 5, he could hardly have been the early convert enrolled by our Saviour in His apostolic band: though Bishop Wordsworth, on the contrary, thinks that he, like Peter, might have fallen away for a time. A better account for such a statement may be sought in the reflection that, although it is recorded "neither did His brethren believe in Him," there is no evidence against them *all;* and in the absence of negative proof it seems safer—at least, not inconsistent with the charity which "hopeth all things"—to think of James and Jude as happy exceptions to the family jealousy and mistrust.

Again, unless we consider the son of Alphæus the brother of our Lord, in the tribal sense of Jerome, we must admit the existence of two men, strikingly similar in life and calling, evidently related, each with a mother named Mary, and brethren Joses and Jude; and to which of these two, if they were not one and the same, can the Epistle be best ascribed?

Opinions of Theologians.—These problems, hard assuredly, seem fairly such as may best be solved by the ingenuity of ancient writers, well acquainted with contemporary ideas. The opinions of moderns, such as Lightfoot, Bleek, Alford, and Davidson, are grounded on no discovery of facts hidden from theologians who were at least as able and honest as themselves; and the old testimony has been so thoroughly sifted that, until more be brought forward, we had better remain undecided if we cannot hold a conclusion fortified by the consensus of Clement of Alexandria and John the Eloquent, in the Greek Church; Jerome and Augustine, in the Latin; Pearson, Lardner, Horne, Wordsworth, and Ellicott in our own; and by German writers, such as Lampe, Hug, Meier, and Lange.

Conclusion.—Thus we see the best ecclesiastical authority and traditions have pretty constantly assigned the authorship of the catholic Epistle to the third name on our list (above), and identified him with the second, fourth, fifth, sixth, and seventh, in accordance with what we venture to affirm is the plainest path out of the maze.

Further History of James.—So much externally; for internal evidence we have a singular agreement between the fervid abrupt style of the Letter and the character of its reputed writer, known as "the Just" by the Jews, and termed by them (in honour, not reproach) the "Camel-kneed," from his long and frequent devotions. In no way conspicuous amongst the disciples, he comes into prominence only after the Resurrection; perhaps that witness to the Lord Christ was specially needed in his case to perfect faith, and to transform the silent man of prayer into the strong and fearless leader of the infant Church.

As the first Bishop of Jerusalem we find him (Acts xv.) presiding in a solemn assembly to hear the missionary reports and to arrange for the requirements of Gentile converts. The pastoral letter (Acts xv. 24—29) may be compared with the catholic one now before us, as it was probably written by the same hand. The last Scriptural notice of James is (Acts xxi. 18) on St. Paul's final visit to the Holy City, when, again, a synod of the elders seems to have been held. A Greek Christian writer, named Hegesippus, himself a convert from Judaism, tells us more of the fate of this "bulwark" of the fold. Comparing his highly artificial account (preserved for us in the history of Eusebius: too prolix for insertion here) with the narrative in Josephus, the plain truth seems that James the Just was hurled from a pinnacle of the Temple, and finally despatched by stoning, as a believer in Jesus of Nazareth, about the year 69, immediately before the siege of Jerusalem by the Roman emperor Vespasian. Josephus (*Ant.* xx. 9) accuses the high priest Ananus, a Sadducee, of the judicial murder, and declares that the "most equitable of the citizens, and such as were the most uneasy at the breach of the laws, disliked what was done," and complained to King Agrippa and Albinus the procurator, who, in consequence, removed Ananus from his office. Many authors, ancient and modern, have been of opinion that the martyrdom of James was the "filling up of the sins of Jerusalem, and made its cup of guilt to overflow."

"Though the mills of God grind slowly, yet they grind exceeding small:
Though with patience He stands waiting, with exactness grinds He all."

II. **His Epistle.**—*To whom written.*—In the first and chief place, James unquestionably wrote to his countrymen, scattered over the whole earth, though still belonging to their twelve tribes. But in no sense can the Letter be looked upon as an appeal to unbelieving Jews, abounding as it does with references to Christian doctrines held, and Christian works to be maintained, by those who had "the faith of our Lord Jesus Christ." That the majority of its readers would be the poor and meek can hardly be doubted, if we turn to such passages as those in chap. ii. And it would seem that these struggling societies of humble Christians were in a danger more peculiar to the poor—that is, of envying and fawning upon the rich and well-to-do; forgetting that they themselves were oppressed by such, dragged before judgment-seats, and exposed to the blasphemy and contempt outpoured by unbelievers on the "Christian" name (chap. ii. 6, 7).

Style and Character.—In his denunciation of the rich defrauders, James breaks out into a fiery eloquence worthy of an ancient prophet; the tender change from rebuke of the wrongers to comfort for the wronged (chap. v. 7, 8) is unsurpassed in the whole roll of inspired utterance; and in condemnation of lust (chap. iv. 1—4), pride (chap. iv. 5—10), evil speaking (chap. iv. 11, 12), and all worldliness (chap. iv. 13—17), the fervour and righteous indignation of the Apostle show of themselves the manner of his life and death: for again, as with God's servant of old, "the land was not able to bear all his words" (Amos vii. 10).

Scope and Aim.—Nothing can be clearer and simpler than the scope and aim of this Letter; as the Sermon on the Mount compared with the rest of Matthew, so this exhortation of James the Just (or "the Wise," as the Greeks love to call him) stands forth among its fellow Epistles, a lovely gospel of good works, of Christian steadfastness and patience. Some theologians unfortunately, blinded by their own partial apprehension of one side of God's truth, have misread its chapters, and found therein an opposition to the doctrine of St. Paul. Luther even could go so far as to call the Epistle "worthless as one of straw." Happily, later criticism has vindicated the teaching of the brother of the Lord; and the plainest reader may learn for himself that Paul and James were at one, infallibly moved by the same Spirit of the living God.

State of Religious Opinion:—Judaism and Christianity.—Let us recollect a little more fully the condition of the faith among those Christians who were first converted from Judaism. With them the adherence to outward forms, the stickling for the letter of the Law, and other like barren principles, had become a belief, which displayed itself in new shapes, corresponding with their altered state of religion. "Wherever," it has been well said, "Christianity did not effect a complete change in the heart the old Jewish spirit naturally manifested itself in the professed converts." It was what our Puritan divines quaintly, but correctly, termed "the Popery of the human heart." The souls that had trusted wholly and entirely in sacrifice as a bare substitution of victims, and deliverance from an indiscriminate vengeance, now clung to faith, as a passive thing, instead. The old idol had, as it were, been torn down by these ardent disciples: a new one was upraised to the vacant niche; faith in a faith became the leading idea, and the light which was in them turned to darkness, the breath of life to death.

Affected by Oriental Theories.—But perhaps a cause of this confusion is to be found much further afield. The Jewish Church had become largely affected by the more remote Eastern thought; the captivity, while it eradicated utterly all wish for idolatry, influenced the chosen people in a strange and unlooked-for way. The power of the mystical speculations of India, more especially of the devout followers of Gōtoma Sakya Muni, now known as Buddhists, is only beginning to be rightly pondered by Christian scholars and divines. It was not the Persian systems, nor the Chaldæan, but the Hindu (and not infrequently working through, and by means of, them) which perplexed anew the Oriental mind. Here was, doubtless, the origin of the Essenes and other offshoots of Judaism; and even in the Church itself similar mischief may be traced in the varying forms of heresy which drove her almost to destruction. The ancient theory of sacrifice in India was abandoned by the Brahmans, and in its place faith was everywhere preached; the sole essential was dependence on God; implicit "reliance on Him made up for all deficiencies in other respects, whilst no attention to the forms of religion or to the rules of morality was of the slightest avail without this all-important sentiment." * Precisely the same wave of thought seems to have broken on the Jewish Church; and one not much dissimilar, we know, in later times, has changed the whole set of religious tendencies in Western Europe.

Denounced accordingly.—It seems, then, that in complete aversion from such innovations, James wrote what he did of moral righteousness, as opposed to correct belief; in other words, contending for a religion of the heart and not the lips alone; with him

* See Elphinstone's *India*, Vol. i., Book 2, chap. iv., quoting from the text-book called Bhagwat Gita.

Christianity was indeed "a life, and not a mere bundle of dead opinions." "Wilt thou know, O vain man," pleads the impassioned Apostle (chap. ii. 20, 21), "that faith without works is dead? Was not Abraham our father justified by works when he had offered Isaac?" And surely here we catch the echoes of a greater than James, who answered the Jews when they boasted to Him in the Temple, "Abraham is our father," "If ye were Abraham's children ye would do the works of Abraham" (John viii. 39). His "faith, working by love," upheld him through a desolating trial. If we look at the motive, he was justified by faith; if we look at the result, he was justified by works. No less a faith than Abraham's could have wrought thus mightily before the face of heaven, or can so take the kingdom thereof by violence still; and the theology which could discern opposition in the plain declarations of God's word herein is fit only for the dust that has buried its volumes on forgotten shelves.

"Who are we that with restless feet,
And grudging eyes unpurged and dim,
Among the earthly shadows beat,
And seek to question Him?"

Date of the Epistle.—The Epistle has been called "general"—that is, "universal"—chiefly because it was addressed to no body of believers in one place in particular. The absence of all allusion to Gentile converts fairly proves an earlier date than the circular letter preserved in Acts xv. 24—29, that is, somewhere about the year A.D. 44. And, if such be correct, we must look on this as one of the oldest writings in the canon of the New Testament.

Genuineness and Canonicity.—It does not seem to have been known at first to all the early Church, no direct quotation being found till the time of Origen, though indirect references may be traced in the Apostolic Fathers. In the lists of sacred books universally acknowledged, or the contrary, drawn up by Eusebius, Bishop of Cæsarea (in Palestine), at the beginning of the fourth century, the Epistle of James is amongst the latter—the "antilegomena," or "those spoken against," along with the Epistles of Jude, 2 Peter, and 2 and 3 John. The uncertainty was with regard to its author; little doubt ever being felt concerning its inspiration. The great Greek Fathers of the fourth century all quote it as canonical, and are supported by the Latin. Some of the divines of the Reformation, however, mistrusted it, chiefly on account of internal and doctrinal evidence; and, of course, the German rationalists have eagerly attacked the Epistle from such a ground of advantage. But it has thus far well survived the storms of controversy, and will as surely remain unharmed, to be the help and delight of the patient souls who trust still that "the coming of the Lord draweth nigh."

"Hora novissima, tempora pessima sunt, vigilemus;
Ecce minaciter imminet, Arbiter Ille supremus:
Imminet, imminet, ut mala terminet, æqua coronet,
Recta remuneret, anxia liberet, æthera donet."

So wrote Bernard of Morlaix, seven hundred years ago, with the words of James (chap. v. 8) above quoted in his heart. It were well to grave them on our own: "For yet a little while, and he that shall come will come, and will not tarry" (Heb. x. 37). The free translation appended is the familiar one, by Dr. Neale:—

"The world is very evil; the times are waxing late;
Be sober, and keep vigil; the Judge is at the gate:
The Judge that comes in mercy, the Judge that comes with might,
To terminate the evil, to diadem the right."

ANALYSIS OF CONTENTS.

THE SALUTATION (chap. i. 1).

I. Appeals on behalf of—
- (i.) 1. Patience (chap. i. 2—4).
  - 2. Prayer for wisdom: to be asked in faith (chap. i. 5—8).
  - 3. Lowly-mindedness (chap. i. 9—11).
- (ii.) α. Endurance (chap. i. 12—15).
  - β. Because of God's goodness (chap. i. 16—18).
- (iii.) 1. Meekness (chap. i. 17—21).
  - 2. Self-knowledge (chap. i. 22—25).
  - 3. Practical religion (chap. i. 26, 27).

II. Rebukes on account of—
- (i.) α. Respect for persons (chap. ii. 1—9).
  - β. Because leading to a violation of law (chap. ii. 10, 11).
- (ii.) Faith without works (chap. ii. 14—26).
  - α. Example of Abraham (chap. ii. 21—24).
  - β. Example of Rahab (chap. ii. 25).
  - γ. Summary (chap. ii. 26).
- (iii.) Censoriousness and sins of the tongue (chap. iii.).
  - α. Warnings and examples against (chap. iii. 5—12).
  - β. Exhortations to gentleness, or silence (chap. iii. 13—18).
- (iv.) 1. α. Lust (chap. iv. 1—4).
  - β. Pride (chap. iv. 5—10).
  - 2. Evil speaking (chap. iv. 11, 12).
  - 3. α. Worldliness (chap. iv. 13—17).
  - β. Trust in riches (chap. v. 1—6).

III. Conclusion.
- (i.) Exhortation to patience (chap. v. 7—11).
- (ii.) Caution against swearing (chap. v. 12).
- (iii.) Advice of divers kinds:—
  - α. 1. To the sorrowful (chap. v. 13).
    - 2. To the joyful (chap. v. 13).
    - 3. To the sick and suffering (chap. v. 14, 15).
  - β. 1. Concerning confession (chap. v. 16).
    - 2. Concerning prayer: example of Elias (chap. v. 17, 18).
    - 3. Concerning conversion (chap. v. 19, 20).

[*References.*—Much abler and fuller treatment of the subject may be read in the following books, to all of which, and to many others by way of reference, the writer of these Notes is under much obligation:—

Alford's *Greek Testament, with a Critically-revised Text.* Vol. IV. Rivingtons, 1871.

Bleek's *Introduction to the New Testament.* (Translated by Urwick.) Vol. II. T. & T. Clark, 1874.

Davidson's *Introduction to the New Testament* Vol. III. Bagster, 1851.

Horne's *Introduction to the Holy Scriptures.* Vol. IV. Twelfth Edition. By Tregelles. Longmans, 1869

Lightfoot on *St. Paul's Epistle to the Galatians: Dissertation* II., *The Brethren of the Lord.* Macmillan, 1869.

Meyrick's articles on "James" and "The General Epistle of James," in Smith's *Dictionary of the Bible.* Vol. I. Murray, 1863.

Wordsworth's *New Testament, with Introductions and Notes, The General Epistles, &c.* Rivingtons, 1872.]

THE GENERAL EPISTLE OF

JAMES

Chap. i. 1. The salutation.

A.D. cir. 60.

CHAPTER I.—(1) James, a servant
of God and of the Lord
Jesus Christ, to the twelve
tribes which are scattered abroad,
greeting.
(2) My brethren, count it all joy when

---

(1) **James, a servant** (or *slave*, or *bond-servant*) **of God and of the Lord Jesus Christ.**—Bound to Him, *i.e.*, in devotion and love. In like manner, St. Paul (Rom. i. 1, *et seq.*), St. Peter (2 Pet. i. 1), and St. Jude brother of James (verse 1), begin their Letters. The writer of this has been identified (see *Introduction, ante*, p. 352) with James the Just, first bishop of Jerusalem, the brother of our Lord.

To the twelve tribes which are scattered abroad.—Or, *to the twelve tribes in the dispersion.* To these remnants of the house of Israel, whose "casting away" (Rom. xi. 15) was leading to the "reconciling of the world;" whose "fall" had been the cause of its "riches;" "and the diminishing of them the riches of the Gentiles" (verse 12). Scattered abroad indeed they were, "a by-word among all nations" (Deut. xxviii. 37), "a curse and an astonishment" (Jer. xxix. 18) wherever the Lord had driven them. But there is something figurative, and perhaps prophetic, in the number twelve. Strictly speaking, at the time this Epistle was written, Judah and Benjamin, in great measure, were returned to the Holy Land from their captivity, though numbers of both tribes were living in various parts of the world, chiefly engaged, as at the present day, in commerce. The remaining ten had lost their tribal distinctions, and have now perished from all historical record, though it is still one of the fancies of certain writers, rather pious than learned, to discover traces of them in the aborigines of America, Polynesia, and almost everywhere else; most ethnologically improbable of all, in the Teutonic nations, and our own families thereof. But long before the destruction of Jerusalem by Titus, and even the preaching of Christianity, Jewish colonists were found in Europe as well as Asia. "Even where they suffered most, through their own turbulent disposition, or the enmity of their neighbours, they sprang again from the same undying stock, however it might be hewn by the sword or seared by the fire. Massacre seemed to have no effect in thinning their ranks, and, like their forefathers in Egypt, they still multiplied under the most cruel oppression." (See Milman's *History of the Jews*, vol. i., p. 449, *et seq.*) While the Temple stood these scattered settlements were colonies of a nation, bound together by varied ties and sympathies, but ruled in the East by a Rabbi called the Prince of the Captivity, and in the West by the Patriarch of Tiberias, who, curiously, had his seat in that Gentile city of Palestine. The fall of Jerusalem, and the end therewith of national existence, rather added to than detracted from the authority of these strange governments; the latter ceased only in the reign of the Emperor Theodosius, while the former continued, it is said, in the royal line of David, until the close of the eleventh century, after which the dominion passed wholly into the hands of the Rabbinical aristocracy, from whom it has come down to the present day. The phrase "in the dispersion" was common in the time of our Lord; the Jews wondered whether He would "go unto the dispersion amongst the Gentiles" (John vii. 35, and see Note there).

(2–27) Immediately after the salutation, and with more or less a play upon the word which we translate "greeting" ("rejoice," verse 1; "count it all joy," verse 2) there follow appeals on behalf of patience, endurance, and meekness.

(2) **Count it all joy when ye fall into divers temptations.**—Better, *Account it all joy whenever ye fall into divers temptations—i.e., trials*; but even with this more exact rendering of the text, how can we, poor frail creatures of earth, it may well be asked, feel any joy under such? Do we not pray in our Saviour's words, "Lead us not into temptation"? (See Matt. vi. 13, and Note there.) Yet a little consideration will open out the teaching of Holy Scripture very plainly. The Apostle here is following the same line of thought as that expressed in Heb. v. 14. By use (or *habit*, more properly) our senses may be exercised to the discernment of good and evil. The grace of God given to the soul is capable of growth and enlargement, like the powers of body and mind. If either be unemployed, weakness must supervene, and eventually decay and death. And just as the veteran who has proved his armour well, and learned to face habitual danger as a duty, is more trustworthy than a raw recruit, however large of limb and stout of heart, so with the Christian soldier. He must learn to "endure hardness" (2 Tim. ii. 3), and bear meekly and even gladly all the trials which are to strengthen him for the holy war. Innocence is a grace indeed, and yet there is a higher stage of the same virtue, viz., the purity which has been won by long and often bitter conflict with the thousand suggestions of evil from without, stirring up the natural impurity within. Temptation is not sin. "You cannot," says the old German divine, "prevent the birds flying over your head, but you can from making nests in your hair;" and the soul victorious over some such trying onset is by that very triumph stronger and better able to undergo the next assault. The act of virtue has, in truth, helped to build up the

ye fall into divers temptations; (3) know-
ing *this*, that the trying of
your faith worketh pa-
tience. (4) But let patience
have *her* perfect work, that
ye may be perfect and entire, wanting
nothing.

Chap. i. 2–4. An appeal on behalf of patience.

(5) If any of you lack wisdom, let him
ask of God, that giveth to
all *men* liberally, and up-
braideth not; and it shall
be given him. (6) But let
him ask in faith, nothing wavering. For
he that wavereth is like a wave of the

Chap. i. 5–8. Wisdom to be prayed for in faith.

---

habit, from which, when it is perfected, a happy life cannot fail to spring. The interpretation of our Lord's prayer is rather the cry for help to God our Father in the trial, than for actual escape from it: Lead us not, *i.e.*, where we in our free will may choose the wrong and perish. And there is a strangely sweet joy to be snatched from the most grievous temptation in the remembrance that "God is faithful, who will not suffer you to be tempted above that ye are able; but will with the temptation also make a way to escape, that ye may be able to bear it" (1 Cor. x. 13).

(3) **Knowing this, that the trying of your faith worketh patience.**—And this verse confirms our view of the preceding one; the habit of patience is to be the blessed result of all the weary effort under God's probation. James the Wise had learned it long and painfully, and he returns to his exhortation of it again, especially in chap. v. 7—11 (which see).

(4) **Let patience have her perfect work.**—Do not think the grace will come to its full beauty in an hour. Emotion and sentiment may have their place in the beginning of a Christian career, but the end thereof is not yet. Until the soul be quite unmoved by any attack of Satan, the work cannot be deemed "perfect." The doctrine is not mere quietism, much less one of apathy, but rather this, that the conscious strength of patient trust in God is able to say at all times (comp. Ps. lxiii. 8)—

"My soul hath followed hard on Thee;
Thy right hand hath upholden me."

And if in this patience we can learn to possess our souls (Luke xxi. 19) the perfect work of God will be wrought within us.

That ye may be perfect and entire (or, *complete*).—A special proof herein for religious people may be taken with regard to temper. Few trials are harder; and sweetness of disposition often melts away from physical causes, such as ill-health or fatigue. But the great test remains; and it is one which the world will ever apply with scorn to the nominally Christian, refusing to admit the claims of saintliness on the part of any whose religion is not of the household as well as the Church. The entirety and completeness of the life hidden with Christ in God (Col. iii. 3) are manifested most by self-restraint.

Wanting nothing.—The older version, "lacking," found in Tyndale, Cranmer, and the Genevan Bible seems decidedly better. Here is no wish that the faithful should be free from care, heeding nothing; but rather that their whole lives might be without fault or flaw: a perfect sacrifice, as it were, offered up to God. And this idea is confirmed by reflecting on the original meaning of the word translated "entire" above in the Authorised version=*complete, i.e.*, as an offering, with no blemish.

(5) **If any of you lack wisdom.**—The Apostle passes on to the thought of heavenly wisdom; not the knowledge of the deep things of God, but that which is able to make us wise unto our latter end (Prov. xix. 20). Few may be able, save in self-conceit, to say with Isaiah (chap. l. 4), "The Lord God hath given me the tongue of the learned;" and, on the other hand, the wisest and most gifted of men may truly be wanting in the wisdom descending from above.

Let him ask of God.—But whoever, learned or unlearned, feels in his heart the need of the knowledge of God, since to know Him "is eternal life" (John xvii. 3), "let him ask" for it in all purity of intention, simply, *i.e.*, for His honour and service, "and it shall be given him."

That giveth to all men liberally, and upbraideth not.—"Liberally" had better, perhaps, be changed to *simply*—*i.e.*, God gives fully and directly, and *reproacheth* (or, "upbraideth") not the utterance of such a prayer, in no way detracting from the graciousness of His gifts. How wide the difference from any generosity of man! "Yea," wrote Dante, in exile at Verona,

". . . thou shalt learn how salt his food, who fares
Upon another's bread,—how steep his path,
Who treadeth up and down another's stairs."

"The fool," said the wise son of Sirach, "giveth little, and upbraideth much . . ., and is hated of God and man" (Ecclus. xx. 15).

(6) **But let him ask in faith, nothing wavering.**—Surely this verse alone would redeem the Apostle from the charge of slighting the claims of faith. It is here put in the very forefront of necessity; without it all prayer is useless. And mark the addition—

Nothing wavering.—Or, *doubting nothing:* reechoing the words of our Saviour to the wondering disciples, as they gazed at the withered fig-tree on the road to Bethany (Matt. xxi. 21). This "doubting" is the halting between belief and unbelief, with inclination towards the latter. But it may be asked by some one, whence and how is an unhesitating faith to be gained? And the reply to this will solve all similar questions: faith, in its first sense, is the direct gift of God; but it must be tended and used with love and zeal, or its precious faculties will soon be gone. In the hour of some besetting thought of unbelief "the shield of faith" will "quench all the fiery darts of the wicked" (Eph. vi. 16), but that shield must be lifted up, as it were, in an act of faith. "There is no God—at least, to care for me," may be the hopeless cry, responsive to a cruel wound of the enemy. Let the battle-hymn of the Christian make quick answer, "I believe in God;" and often, with that very effort, the assault will cease for awhile. Further, let us take comfort in the thought that intellectual is not moral doubt: the unorthodox are not as the adulterous. Nevertheless, intellectual doubt may spring from an evil habit of carping criticism and self-opinion, for the foundation of which, in so far as a man himself has been either the wilful or the careless cause, he must bear the curse of its results.

For he that wavereth (or, *doubteth*) **is like a wave of the sea driven with the wind and**

sea driven with the wind and tossed.
(7) For let not that man think that he
shall receive any thing of the Lord.
(8) A double minded man *is* unstable
in all his ways.
(9) Let the brother of low degree re-
joice[1] in that he is exalted: (10) but the
rich, in that he is made
low: because as the flower
of the grass he shall pass
away. (11) For the sun is no sooner
risen with a burning heat, but it

Chap. i. 9—11. Of lowly-mindedness.

1 Or, *glory.*

---

tossed.—*Doubteth* is preferable to "wavereth"; there is no play on the Greek words, as in the English text—"wavereth" and "wave." Like storm-beaten sailors, the doubtful are "carried" up to heaven and down again to the deep; their soul melteth away because of the trouble (Ps. cvii. 26). And who can describe the terror, even of the faithful, in those hours of darkness when the face of the Lord is hidden; when, as with the disciples of old, the ship is in the midst of the sea, tossed with the bitter waves. Nevertheless, the raging wind will clear the heavens soon from clouds, and by the radiance of the peaceful moon we too may behold our Helper near—the Lord Jesus walking on the sea—and if He come into the ship the storm must cease.

(7) Once more the Apostle warns the doubtful, holding out no hope of help until the wavering mind be fixed on God.

(8) The eighth verse had better be joined with the seventh, and punctuated thus:—*Let not that man think he shall receive anything of the Lord:—double-minded, unstable in all his ways.* The reason why he can obtain nothing is because he is a man of two minds, and by consequence uncertain in his ways. The words, apparently are those of a proverb. It is useless to have, as it were, two hearts, one lifted up to God, the other turned away. "Come not unto Him with a double heart" (Ecclus. i. 28; and comp. Matt. vi. 24).

(9—11) Lowly-mindedness is the subject of the next paragraph. There is wide misapprehension of our state of trial: the poor and humble are apt to forget the honour thus vouchsafed to them, worthier in truth than the wealth of this world, which quickly fades away; and the rich and noble are often unmindful of the true source of their dignity, and that "unto whomsoever much is given, of him shall be much required" (Luke xii. 48).

(9) **Let the brother of low degree rejoice in that he is exalted** (or, better, *in his exaltation*).—There is no praise from the plain St. James for the pride which apes humility, nor the affectation which loves to be despised. If it please God to "exalt," as of old, "the humble and meek," then anew should be sung a *magnificat* to Him. The lowly-minded doubt of the Virgin Mary, "How shall this be?" (Luke i. 24), was not reproved by the angel; while the question of blunt incredulity on the part of Zacharias was severely punished (Luke i. 20), and this diverse treatment thus experienced was deserved in either case. Both doubted, yet quite differently, and she of the lower degree rejoiced most in God her Saviour for regarding the lowliness of His handmaiden (Luke i. 47, 48). Willingness thus for Christ's service, whether it be great or little, is the right condition of mind for all disciples, and specially the young, with readiness, nay gladness, for "duty in that state of life unto which it *shall* please God to call them." Pleasure will be naturally felt by most at the prospect of a rise in the world; but there are some finer spirits who fain would shrink from anything like exaltation; and to these the kindly Apostle writes that they may take heart, and not fear the greater dangers which of necessity accompany a higher call.

(10) **But the rich, in that he is made low** (or, better, *in his humiliation*).—And, on the other hand, let a change of state be a cause of joy to the rich man, hard though the effort thereto must confessedly be.

There is an antithesis between his *humiliation* and the *humility* of "the brother of low degree:" "God putteth down one, and setteth up another" (Ps. lxxv. 7). Such seems to be the primary meaning of this passage, though, doubtless, there is a more spiritual significance underlying, which would teach the poorest that he may be "rich toward God," and win from the most wealthy the acknowledgment of his deep poverty beside the Lord of all "good treasure" (Deut. xxviii. 12). "I know thy poverty," said the Spirit unto the Church in Smyrna, "but thou art rich" (Rev. ii. 9); and to the Laodiceans, "Thou sayest, I am rich . . ., but thou art poor" (Rev. iii. 17).

Because as the flower of the grass he shall pass away.—No more simple and striking simile of human instability and vanity can be found than "the grass of the field, which to-day is, and to-morrow is cast into the oven" (Matt. vi. 30); and the thought suggests a picture to the mind of the writer, which he draws with strong and yet most tender lines. Our English version misses the setting of his graceful idyl, the exquisite beauty of which can hardly be transferred from the Greek; but the following attempt is at least nearer the original:—

(11) **For the sun is no sooner risen . . .**—Translate, *the sun arose with the burning heat, and dried up the grass; and the flower thereof fell away, and the grace of its fashion perished.* The grace, the loveliness, the delicacy of its form and feature—literally, *of its face*—withered and died away. Often must the Apostle have seen such an effect of the fiery Eastern sun, scorching with its pitiless glare the rich verdure of the wilderness; and in his ear, perchance, was the cry of Isaiah (chap. xl. 6—8):—

"All flesh is grass:
And all the goodliness thereof is as the flower of the field.
The grass withereth;
The flower fadeth;
Because the Spirit of the Lord bloweth upon it:
—Surely the people is grass.
The grass withereth;
The flower fadeth;
But the Word of our God shall stand for ever."

So also (or, *thus*) **shall the rich man fade away** (or, *wither*) **in his ways.**—Not the rich brother, observe, is to fade thus, though his wealth will so pass away. The warning is rather (as in Mark x. 24) "for them that *trust* in riches." Even "the mammon of unrighteousness," well used, will make for us "friends that may receive us into everlasting habitations" (Luke xvi. 9). And he who, out of the possessions wherewith God has blessed him, "deviseth liberal things, by liberal things shall stand" (Isa. xxxii. 8). There seems, moreover, looking closely at the text, a special fitness in its exact words: for they mean that

withereth the grass, and the flower thereof falleth, and the grace of the fashion of it perisheth: so also shall the rich man fade away in his ways.

(12) Blessed *is* the man that endureth temptation: for when he is tried, he shall receive the crown of life, which the Lord hath promised to them that love him. (13) Let no man say when he is tempted, I am tempted of God: for God cannot be tempted with evil,[1] neither tempteth he any man:

Chap. i. 12—15. The blessedness of endurance under trials and temptations, and the difference between the two.

1 Or, *evils.*

---

the rich shall perish in their journeyings for the sake of gain; and to no people could the rebuke apply more sharply than to the Jews, the lenders unto "many nations" (Deut. xv. 6), the merchants and bankers of the world. Nor can "the sword of the Spirit," unsheathed from this Word of God (Eph. vi. 17), be without an edge for those of us in these latter times who err in the former ways.

(12–18) The Apostle returns to the consideration of the afflicted Christian. Such a one has a blessedness, greater infinitely than any earthly happiness, already in possession, and the promise of a future beyond all comparison.

It may be well to point out in this place that the idea of blessedness with regard to man is conveyed to us in the New Testament by a different word from that which expresses the like concerning God. The force of this may be seen in Mark xiv. 61, where the high priest asks our Lord, "Art Thou the Christ, the Son of the Blessed?" *i.e.,* the Blessed God, to show which the adjective is rightly printed with a capital letter. The word applied to God—as in Luke i. 68; Rom. i. 25; ix. 5; 2 Cor i. 3; xi. 31; Eph. i. 3; 1 Pet. i. 3—may be almost called a Christian one; at least, it is not found in much earlier writings, whereas the other term descriptive of man's blessedness (or rather, happiness) is ancient and classical. Only in one passage (1 Tim. i. 11) is there an exception to this remarkable distinction; and such may well be considered, as it is by the German critic De Wette, *un-pauline,* though on no such a single instance, or even several such, could the superstructure be built that has been raised up by those who deny the genuineness of the Pastoral Epistles.

(12) **Blessed is the man that endureth temptation.** Surely the Apostle links such blessedness with the nine Beatitudes, heard in the happy days gone by upon the Mount with Christ (Matt. v. 3—11). The words he uses in the original are the same as those which are expressed above, in our second, third, and fourth verses, by "patience" and "trials," and mean a firm endurance, steadfastness, tenacity of purpose, and quenchless enthusiasm, such as men of Teutonic blood can appreciate perhaps even better than could either Greek or Jew.

For when he is tried (literally, *proved,* or *tested, and found worthy*) **he shall receive the crown of life,** (*i.e., the life*) **which the Lord hath promised to them that love him.**—"Lord" is not found in the best MSS., but of course is required by the sense of the passage. Probably in this case, as in so many others, a little note—or "gloss," as it is called—was made on the margin of an early manuscript, and included unwittingly in the text by some later copyist.

The "pride" and "beauty" of the worldling are as "a fading flower" (Isa. xxviii. 1) under the scorching sun; but the unfading, ever-living crown is for the spiritual, the true lovers of their Lord: blessed in truth are they who thus endure the trial. "Therefore," says the Book of Wisdom (chap. v. 16), "shall they receive a glorious kingdom, and a beautiful crown from the Lord's hand." "The righteous live for evermore" (Wisd. v. 15).

(13) **Let no man say when he is tempted, I am tempted of God.**—Far be it from the true Christian either to give way to sin "that grace may abound" (Rom. vi. 1), or to suppose for one moment that God, and therefore power invincible, is drawing him from righteousness. Almost every reflection upon the nature of sin leads up to an inquiry as to its cause; and the enigma will hardly be solved in this life. The very facts of the presence of evil amongst God's creatures, and its continual attraction even for the best, have often driven men to doubt His supremacy. Sadly—how can we of charity think otherwise?—some have felt the pain, but not the purpose of the world. At times they cannot see in nature "the work of a Being at once good and omnipotent," and prefer to doubt the latter quality sooner than the former.* But this nineteenth-century conclusion is no advance beyond the dual system of the Persians, or rather, of Manes, who corrupted with his Indian fancies the faith of Zoroaster. The Manichees settled the difficulty better than our Deists by declaring the existence of a good God and a bad one; and appealed to the daily strife between virtue and vice, nay, life and death, in witness of their simple creed. Thanks to the gospel, a nobler theology is our Christian heritage, whereby we are persuaded that good will triumph at the last, and by which we are taught humility withal to own that God's ways in so permitting and overworking evil are beyond man's comprehension. And a better scepticism remains for us than that of the Theist, or Agnostic either; a disbelief more vehement that here can be the end, since in this life we experience in no sense the rewards of just and unjust to the full.

For God cannot be tempted with evil.—We can see here a good instance of the excellence of the old Geneva Bible, "the first on several occasions to seize the exact meaning of a passage which all the preceding versions had missed." Our present rendering follows the Genevan exactly, rejecting those of Wiclif, "God is not a tempter of yuell things"; Tyndale, "God tempteth not vnto evyll"; and Cranmer, "God cannot tempte vnto euyll."

Neither tempteth he any man.—The trial comes of Him, *i.e.,* the Tempter is allowed; but so far, and no further. God Himself is "unversed of evils," and no possibility of temptation remains with Him. Into the unseen splendour of His fulness no thought of wrong can enter; no foul thing wing its silent flight. It were blasphemy, perilously near that of the Pharisees (Matt. xii. 22—37) to think God's kingdom could be so divided against itself, that He, directly or indirectly, should seduce His subjects into the revolt of sin. No; if we have one golden clue by which we may feel our erring way out of the labyrinth of this lower world into the

* Specially see J. S. Mill's "Three Essays on Religion," *Nature,* p. 38.

(14) but every man is tempted, when
he is drawn away of his own lust,
and enticed. (15) Then when lust hath
conceived, it bringeth forth sin: and
sin, when it is finished, bringeth forth
death.

(16) Do not err, my beloved brethren.
(17) Every good gift and
every perfect gift is from
above, and cometh down
from the Father of lights,
with whom is no vari-

Chap. i. 16—18. An argument from God's unchangeableness.

---

belief and trust in God our Father for the life to come, it is this: trials and temptations are permitted to strengthen us—if we will—for His mightier service. And, as compulsory homage would be worthless to the loving Lord of all, voluntary must be found instead, and proved and perfected. Herein is the Christian conflict, and the secret of God's ways with man.

(14) So far the inspired Apostle has spoken of the outward part of temptation; now he lays bare the inner—for we suffer the two-fold evil. From without come the whispers of Satan, by himself or his legionaries, skilled in all that may entice and delude the unwary soul. And if the doctrine be true that to every one a guardian angel is appointed, so also would seem to be the opposite idea, that each has some demon of the pit watching him incessantly, and commissioned specially for his utter destruction. How terrible must be the skill of such assailants, experienced in the arts which have deceived mankind since the first fatal day. But there is the limit of external power in this matter; the ablest and subtlest fiend can but guess what is passing in its victim's mind, and shape its snares accordingly. God only is the discerner of hearts, and the "spirit of man which is in him" alone, with its Maker, "knoweth the things of a man" (1 Cor. ii. 11). The Holy Spirit "searcheth all things" (verse 10), and all are manifest in His sight (Heb. iv. 13), but to no less than His own omniscience. Satan, therefore, can merely act on his general knowledge of human nature, aided by particular guesses at the individual before him, whom he fain would destroy. He has learned too well the deep corruption of the heart, and knows what gaudy bait will most attract the longing and licentious eyes.

Every man is tempted when he is drawn away of (or, *by*) **his own lust, and enticed.**—Evil humanity thrills responsive as a harp played by a cunning hand; but no power of hell can force its way through the barriers which God the Holy Ghost erects around the faithful and confiding soul: only by treason of the man himself can the great enemy enter in and reign.

(15) **Then when lust have conceived . . . .**—Then come the downward steps of ruin—Lust, having conceived, bringeth forth sin; and sin, when it is finished, bringeth forth death. The image well depicts the repellent subject. The small beginning, from some vain delight or worldly lust and pleasure; next from the vile embrace, as of an harlot—sin, growing in all its rank luxuriance, until it bear and engender, horribly, of itself, its deadly child. The word of parturition is frightful in the sense it would convey, as of some monstrous deformity, a hideous progeny ten-fold more cursed than its begetter.

The one effect of sin, more especially that of the flesh here alluded to, must be Death. The act itself is mortiferous, the result inevitable; just as much so, and as naturally, as the work of poison on the body. There are antidotes for both, but they must be given in time; the door of mercy stands not always open, nor will the "fountain opened . . . for sin and uncleanness" (Zech. xiii. 1) flow on for ever. "Because," says the Wisdom of God (Prov. ii. 24—26), "I have called, and ye refused . . . I also will laugh at your calamity." "The wages of sin is death" (Rom. vi. 23), and their paymaster is the devil.

(16) **Do not err, my beloved brethren.**—Thus far James the Wise has declared what God is not, what qualities are alien to Him; but this is only a negative aspect of the truth, and he now would show the positive—namely, that God is the Author of all and every good. And this lesson he introduces with a caution to his *brethren beloved, not to err.* He is most earnest and emphatic. "Be not *ye* deceived," however much the world may wander in delusive paths. A marked change from the dreadful tenor of the last verse is here made to bright reflections on the gifts of God; and a new incentive to endurance is found in the happy thoughts of His goodness.

(17) **Every good gift and every perfect gift is from above.**—This beautiful sentence, more musical still in the Greek, is thought to be the fragment of some Christian hymn. Two words are translated by our one "gift"; the first is rather the act of giving, the second the gift itself, and the effect of both together is a climax to the statement of God's benevolence. The difference between the two is observed in the Genevan version of 1557. "There are diversities of gifts" (1 Cor. xii. 4), even as "one star differeth from another star in glory" (1 Cor. xv. 41), but "the same Spirit" is the giver of all. Where in St. John's Gospel (chap. iii. 1) we read, "Except a man be born again," the most probable meaning is "from above," expressed exactly as in the present case; and thus we know whence is the true birth of the soul.

Cometh down from the Father of lights.—Great difference of opinion is found concerning these "lights," whether the term be figurative, as of goodness or wisdom; or a reference to the mysterious Urim (Ex. xxviii. 30, *et seq.*) which flamed on the breast of Aaron; or spiritual, as of grace and glory; or material, viz., the "lights" set "in the firmament of heaven" (Gen. i. 14, 15) "when the morning stars sang together" (Job xxxviii. 7). It were not amiss to take the whole of these interpretations, for they, and perhaps others, the purport of which we as yet can barely guess, are included in this Scripture. "God," remarks Bishop Wordsworth, "is the Father of all lights—the light of the natural world, the sun, the moon, and stars, shining in the heavens; the light of reason and conscience; the light of His Law; the light of prophecy, shining in a dark place; the light of the gospel shining throughout the world; the light of apostles, confessors, martyrs, bishops, and priests, preaching that gospel to all nations; the light of the Holy Ghost shining in our hearts; the light of the heavenly city; God is the Father of them all. He is the everlasting Father of the everlasting Son, who is the Light of the world." But that the mind of the sacred writer was mainly on the lights of the material universe may be seen from his next thought.

ableness, neither shadow of turning.
(18) Of his own will begat he us with
the word of truth, that we should be
a kind of firstfruits of his creatures.
(19) Wherefore, my beloved brethren,
let every man be swift to hear, slow to
speak, slow to wrath: (20) for the wrath
of man worketh not the righteousness
of God. (21) Wherefore lay
apart all filthiness and
superfluity of naughtiness,
and receive with meekness
the engrafted word, which
is able to save your souls.

Chap. i. 19—21. Appeals therefore on behalf of meekness and steadfastness.

With whom is no variableness, neither shadow of turning.—The phraseology is almost scientific. There are changes, literally "parallaxes," of the heavenly bodies themselves, and eclipses one of another by shadows projected through space, but no such variableness with God, nor changing of faintest shade. And even further, the greatest and most marvellous of His works on high "must be dissolved" (2 Pet. iii. 11), "the sun darkened, the moon not give her light, the stars fall from heaven" (Matt. xxiv. 29), and the heavens themselves "be rolled together as a scroll" (Isa. xxxiv. 4). But if "the things which are seen are temporal, the things which are not seen are eternal" (2 Cor. iv. 18). "I am the Lord," is the burden of His latest prophet; "I change not" (Mal. iii. 6).

(18) **Of his own will begat he us with the word of truth.**—There is a greater witness to God's goodness than that which is written upon the dome of heaven, even the regeneration of man. As the old creation was "by the Word" (John i. 3, 10, *et seq.*), the new is by Him also, the Logos, the Word of Truth, and that by means of His everlasting gospel, delivered in the power of the Holy Ghost. So tenderly is this declared, that a maternal phrase is used—*God brought us forth* in the new birth; and though "a woman" may forget "the son of her womb" (Isa. xlix. 15), yet will He "never leave, nor forsake" (Heb. xiii. 5).

That we should be a kind of firstfruit of his creatures.—And why this mercy and loving-kindness? for our own sakes, or for others and for His? Surely the latter; and "if the firstfruit be holy, the lump is also holy" (Rom. xi. 16). We know "Who is the firstborn of every creature" (Col. i. 15) "the first-begotten of the dead" (Rev. i. 5), nay, "the beginning of the creation of God" (Rev. iii. 14); "and we are created in Christ Jesus" (Eph. ii. 10), become new in Him (comp. 2 Cor. v. 17; Gal. vi. 15), made the firstfruits of His redemption; and, moreover, it would seem we are the sign of the deliverance promised to the brute creation "which waiteth for the manifestation of the sons of God" (Rom. viii. 19, 21). The longing for a future perfection is shared by all created beings upon earth, and their discontent at present imperfection points to another state freed from evil (Rom. viii. 18—22). "The creature was made subject to vanity, not willingly, but by reason of Him who hath subjected the same in hope" (Rom. viii. 20). And the fruition of this hope is foreshadowed in the words above. "The very struggles," it has been well observed by Dean Howson, "which all animated beings make against pain and death show that pain and death are not a part of the proper laws of their nature, but rather a bondage imposed upon them from without; thus every groan and fear is an unconscious prophecy of liberation from the power of evil." "The creature itself also shall be delivered" is the plain assertion of St. Paul (Rom. viii. 21); comparing his with that of St. James, we must conclude that they point to all nature, animate and inanimate as well. "We look for new heavens and a new earth, wherein dwelleth righteousness" (2 Pet. iii. 13), and "there shall be no more death . . . nor any more pain" (Rev. xxi. 4).

"All creation groans and travails;
Thou, O Lord, shalt hear its groan.
For of man, and all creation,
Thou alike art Lord alone."

(19) We come now to the third subdivision of the chapter. By reason of the Divine benevolence, the Apostle urges his readers—(1) to meekness, (2) self-knowledge, (3) practical religion.

Wherefore, my beloved brethen.—There appears to be some small error in the MSS. here, but the alteration is only just worth mentioning: *ye know my brethren beloved*, seems the correct version, the very abruptness of which may serve to arrest attention. Yea, "have ye not known?" might well be asked further in the indignant language of Isaiah (chap. xl. 21; comp. Rom. v. 19).

Let every man be swift to hear, slow to speak, slow to wrath.—For all these cautions are required in the building up of the new life. "The quick speaker is the quick kindler;" and we are told later on "how great a matter a little fire kindleth" (chap. iii. 5). And what have we at all to do with wrath, much less that our whole life—as unhappily it often is—should be wasted with such bitterness? Anger, no doubt, is a wholesome tonic for some minds, and certain weaknesses; but "he that is slow to anger is better than the mighty, and he that ruleth his spirit than he that taketh a city" (Prov. xvi. 32).

(20) **For the wrath of man worketh not the righteousness of God.**—Sarcastically rings the context. Perhaps there is still a sharper point to the satire: the wrath of man does not work God's righteousness "to the full." The warning may well be sounded in the ears of Christians still, who are not less apt than Jonah of old to say quickly and in self-excuse, "I do well to be angry" (Jonah iv. 9). How many a holy work of household and parish has been and is thus hindered and destroyed; and if the golden words of the first bishop of the Church had been heeded better, there never had appeared one page of her long history blotted with the blood of a religious war.

(21) **Wherefore lay apart all filthiness and superfluity of naughtiness.**—So Peter (1 Pet. iii. 21) speaks of "the filth of the flesh." But the defilement here referred to seems general and not special, common, that is, to the whole natural man. The superabundance—the overgrowth—of evil will occupy the heart, if care be not taken to root it out; and, like the thorns in the parable of the sower (Matt. xiii. 7, *et seq.*), spring up and choke the good seed. All such a rank and poisonous crop must be gathered and laid aside, in heaps may be, for some fiery trouble to consume, that out of the dead luxuriant weeds a richer soil for virtue may be made.

Naughtiness (*ne-aughtiness*, or *nothingness*) was used in 1611, instead of the older and more correct

Chap. i. 22—25. Further caution as to the true knowledge of self.

(22) But be ye doers of the word, and
not hearers only, deceiving
your own selves. (23) For
if any be a hearer of the
word, and not a doer, he
is like unto a man behold-
ing his natural face in a glass: (24) for
he beholdeth himself, and goeth his
way, and straightway forgetteth what
manner of man he was. (25) But whoso
looketh into the perfect law of liberty,
and continueth *therein*, he being not a
forgetful hearer, but a doer of the work,
this man shall be blessed in his deed.[1]

1 Or, *doing*.

---

translation, *malice* or *maliciousness*. The badness implied in the original is much more positive than that which appears from our present version.

Receive with meekness the engrafted word. —Or, *in mildness accept ye this word of truth* (see verse 18, above), engrafted, like a good olive tree, or rather *implanted*, in you. The term is peculiar to this place, and means "innate" in its first intention. If taken so, "the innate Word" will be Christ Himself formed within us. (Comp. Gal. iv. 19.)

Able to save your souls.—In like manner Paul at Miletus commends the elders of Ephesus "to God, and to the Word of His grace, which is able to build you up, and to give you an inheritance among all them which are sanctified" (Acts xx. 32). Observe, the idea of salvation thus conveyed by the implanted word, is so potentially and not actually. Tended and cultured, it will grow into a tree of life, the fruit whereof may heal the wounds of sin; but the after-growth of this plant of God is largely in the hands of man.

We can hardly help making a brief inquiry in this place on the meaning of "soul." There are few words more vaguely used by devout persons, or which present greater difficulties to the learned, or open wider fields of speculation for the thoughtful. In common language we speak of "body and soul," meaning much the same as "body and spirit;" but theologians write more carefully of "body, soul, and spirit" (comp. 2 Thess. v. 23); and psychologists distinguish between the animal branch of their subject and the rational or intellectual (ψυχή-νοῦς). The second of these methods of division is known as the trilogy, and is of most importance to the Christian reader. By it is understood (1) the body, wholly and entirely material, of and belonging to this world; (2) the mind or reason, corporal also—that is, arising from the body, and depending in its exquisite balance upon it; (3) the true soul or spirit, the breath as it were of God, immaterial and immortal. Our bodily nature, of course, is shared with the lower creation, and the spiritual with the higher, while the intellectual is peculiar to mankind. If it be hard to draw a line between vegetable and animal, harder still is it to separate instinct from reason, the difference being of degree rather than kind. But if the one side of the mental soul—namely, the rational, be near akin to what is termed instinctive in the brute, the other, the intellectual, however it may, as it does, soar upward, yet approaches not to the angels, for the difference here is of kind and not degree. Now, strange to say, the Apostle treats not of the spirit but the natural soul. Other texts in plenty assure us that God is able to save the one; from this we may learn salvation is for both, such being the work of "the engrafted Word." Reason and intellect consecrated to divine service have an eternity before them, one of activity and not repose. The highest conception of God to the Greek mind was the Aristotelian idea of intellectual self-sufficiency and contemplation; the Oriental strives, as for ages it has striven, for extinction and nothingness; but to the Christian is given the sure and certain hope of the glorified body, the enlightened soul, the perfected spirit—three in one, and one in three—working the will and praise of its Maker and Redeemer for ever.

(22) **Doers of the word.**—Acting up to the full of their knowledge, whether gained by the spoken or the written Word of God. There is a force in the original sentence, which our own language cannot supply. The term "deceiving" is the contrary of that rendered "word," and means its corruption; the Word which is the source of knowledge and life may be so handled as to cause error and death. No acquaintance with the Bible, apart from the practice of its precepts, will avail the Christian any more than it did the Jew. "For not the hearers of the law are just before God, but the doers shall be justified" (Rom. ii. 13). Those who deceive themselves may not altogether be hypocrites; there is a subtler danger of being blind, and nevertheless exclaiming "We see." (Comp. John ix. 41.)

(23) **He is like unto a man beholding his natural face in a glass.**—The Apostle points grimly to an example of this self-deception. *He* (literally, *this*) *is like unto a man beholding his natural face in a mirror.* Not a "glass," but a mirror of polished steel, such as are still used in the East. "His natural face," or *the face of his birth*—the real appearance, that is, which the reflection of the Word of God, properly looked into, will afford the inquirer.

(24) **For he beholdeth himself . . .**—Better, *for he beheld himself and went his way, and straightway forgot what he was.* Like the simile in verse 11, this is described as an actual occurrence, seen and noted by the writer. There is a recognition of the well-known face, followed by instant and complete forgetfulness; and thus is it often with the mirror of the soul. In some striking sermon or book a man's self is made manifest to him, and the picture may be too familiar to cause aversion; but, whether or no, the impression fades from his mind as quickly as the echoes of the preacher's words. At the best the knowledge was only superficial, perhaps momentary; widely different from that which comes of a holy walk with God.

(25) **But whoso looketh . . .**—Translate, *But he who looked into the perfect law of liberty and continued therein.* The past tense is still kept to enforce the figure of the preceding verse. The earnest student of the Scriptures stoops down in humility of body and mind to learn what the will of their Author may be. He reads, as it were, upon his knees; and if he finds therein a law, it is one of liberty and not slavery, life and not death—although, as Dean Alford observes here, "not in contrast with a former law of bondage, but as viewed on the side of its being the law of the new life and birth, with all its spontaneous and free development of obedience."

Not a forgetful hearer . . .—Literally, *not a hearer of forgetfulness, but a doer of work.* Thus rendered, the words of the sentence balance each other, and comment is needless.

This man shall be blessed in his deed.—Or,

(26) If any man among you seem to be
religious, and bridleth not
his tongue, but deceiveth
his own heart, this man's
religion *is* vain. (27) Pure religion
and undefiled before God and the
Father is this, To visit the father-
less and widows in their affliction, *and*
to keep himself unspotted from the
world.

Chap. i. 26—27. Practical religion.

A.D. cir. 60.

CHAPTER II.—(1) My brethren, have

---

as in the margin, *doing*. A return perhaps in thought to the Beatitudes, and the close of that Sermon on the Mount, of which they were the opening words. The blessedness of this humbly active Christian is like that of the wise man there spoken of "which built his house upon a rock" (Matt. vii. 24, 25).

(26) But St. James has thus far dilated only on the first part of his advice in verse 19, "Let every man be swift to hear"; now he must enforce the remaining clause, "slow to speak."

If any man among you seem to be religious . . .—Better, *If any one imagine himself to be religious, not bridling his tongue, but deceiving his own heart, this man's religion is vain.* The sense of the Greek is slightly obscured by the English version. "If any man . . . seem"—*i.e.*, to himself, and not to others merely; the warning is not to the hypocrite, but the self-deceived. A Christian may have, or rather cannot help having, the feeling that he is a religious man; and so far well. But if such a one deceive his own heart, as confessedly he may, and give to those around him the proof of his self-delusion in not curbing his tongue, vain and useless is all his religious service. Just as some mistakenly suppose there can be a religion of hearing without acting, so others rest satisfied "in outward acts of worship, or exactness of ritual." "But," remarks Bishop Moberly on this passage, and his voice may win an audience where another's would not, "if a man think himself a true worshipper because he conforms to outward services, while he lets his tongue loose in untruth or unkindness or other unseemliness, he deceives himself." The first mark of true religion is gentleness of tongue, just as the contrary, blasphemy, is the most damning fault of all. Our Lord directly says, "By thy words thou shalt be justified, and by thy words thou shalt be condemned" (Matt. xii. 37). The text, however, is more a guide for self-examination than a stone to be cast at a neighbour; and "well is" it indeed for "him that hath not slipped with his tongue" (Ecclus. xxv. 8).

The Apostle returns to this subject, though from a different point of view, in chap. iii., which compare with the above. The best commentary on the whole is Bishop Butler's Sermon, No. IV., "Upon the Government of the Tongue."

(27) **Pure religion . . .**—It will be observed that by religion here is meant religious service. No one word can express this obvious interpretation of the original, taken as it must be in completion of the verse before; and certainly "religion" in its ordinary sense will not convey the right idea. Real worship, we may say, pure and undefiled, beheld and acknowledged as such in the presence of God, even the Father—mark the tender pathos of His divine relationship—is this:

To visit the fatherless (or, *orphans*) **and widows in their affliction, and to keep himself unspotted from the world.**—Here is the double proof of the perfect life of holiness, the savour whereof is as perpetual incense before the throne of God. And the help afforded to the helpless, put thus in the first place of the two requirements, will often bring about the second—namely, that spotless condition of unworldliness which marks, and will ever mark, the true servant of the Lord Jesus Christ. Deeds of benevolence may be and are often done by those who are not His; but all who truly belong to Him must live a life which praises Him continually in good works; not, it is hardly needful to say, as a cause—but rather the natural and inevitable result of love for Him, warming the heart within.

Scrupulous indeed were the "religious" contemporaries of James; they would not enter where the image of Divus Cæsar had its votive flame, while they were ceremonially clean for the keeping of their passover —"they went not into the judgment hall lest they should be defiled" (John xviii. 28). But He whom there they cruelly sought to slay had told them before, though in vain, "that which cometh out of the man, that defileth the man" (Mark vii. 20), and "nothing from without can defile him" (verse 15). What an eternal caution may be learned here against cold reliance upon ritual! What an instance, ever, under all varieties and forms, to be applied to themselves by the erring, persecuting, and deceitful sons of men! while, on the other hand, from these words of the wise Apostle we may be sure what is truest, nay, the only true service, acceptable and accepted, of the Most High—"To visit the fatherless and the widow," beholding in them a new image of Christ, the Man of Sorrows, is to show pity verily to Him; and at the last such "pure religion" will receive His own approval. "Inasmuch as ye have done it unto one of the least of these, my brethren, ye have done it unto me" (Matt. xxv. 40). Blessed be the ears attuned to catch the golden cadence, for it rings in angel voices round the soothers of the sick and sorrow-laden even now!

II.

(1) **My brethren.**—The second chapter opens with some stern rebukes for those unworthy Christians who had "men's persons in admiration," and, doubtless, that "because of advantage" to themselves. (Comp. Jude, verse 16.) The lesson is distinctly addressed to believers, and its severity appears to be caused by the Apostle's unhappy consciousness of its need. What were endurable in a heathen, or an alien, or even a Jew, ceased to be so in a professed follower of the lowly Jesus. And this seems to be a further reason for the indignant expostulation and condemnation of verse 14. Thus the whole chapter may really be considered as dealing with Faith; and it flows naturally from the foregoing thoughts upon Religion—or, as we interpreted their subject-matter, Religious Service.

Have (or, *hold*) **not the faith of our Lord Jesus Christ, the Lord of glory, with** (or, *in*) **respect of persons.**—"Ye know the grace of our Lord Jesus Christ," wrote St. Paul to the proud and wealthy men of Corinth (2 Cor. viii. 9), "that, though He was rich, yet for your sakes He became poor, that ye through His poverty might be rich;" and, with more cogent an appeal, to the Philippians (chap. ii. 4—7), "In lowli-

not the faith of our Lord Jesus Christ,
the Lord of glory, with re-
spect of persons. (2) For if
there come unto your as-
sembly[1] a man with a gold
ring, in goodly apparel, and
there come in also a poor
man in vile raiment; (3) and
ye have respect to him that weareth the
gay clothing, and say unto him, Sit
thou here in a good place;[2] and say to
the poor, Stand thou there, or sit here
under my footstool: (4) are ye not then
partial in yourselves, and are become
judges of evil thoughts? (5) Hearken,
my beloved brethren, Hath not God
chosen the poor of this world rich in
faith, and heirs of the[3] kingdom which

Chap. ii. 1—9. Rebukes on account of wrong respect for persons: with divers instances thereof.

2 Or, *well*, or, *seemly*.

1 Gr. *synagogue*.

3 Or, *that*.

---

ness of mind let each esteem other better than themselves: look not every man on his own things, but every man also on the things of others. Let this mind be in you, which was also in Christ Jesus: *Who, being in the form of God"—i.e.,* Very God, and not appearance merely—nevertheless "*thought not His equality with God a thing to be always grasped at,*" as it were some booty or prize, "*but emptied Himself*" of His glory, "*and took upon Him the shape of a slave.*" Were these central, nay initial, facts of the faith believed then; or are they now? If they were in truth, how could there be such folly and shame as "acceptance of persons" according to the dictates of fashionable society and the world? "Honour," indeed, "to whom honour" is due (Rom. xiii. 7). The Christian religion allows not that contempt for even earthly dignities—affected by some of her followers, but springing more from envy and unruliness than aught besides. True reverence and submission are in no way condemned by this scripture: but their excess and gross extreme, the preference for vulgar wealth, the adulation of success, the worship, in short, of some new golden calf.

(2) **For if there come unto your assembly** (literally, *synagogue*).—This is the only place in the New Testament where the Jewish word is used for a Christian congregation.

A man with a gold ring, in goodly apparel.—Better, *a man golden-ringed, in bright apparel.* Roman satirists had much to say upon the fops and dandies of their time, with "all their fingers laden with rings"; some, if we may trust the sneer of Martial, having six on each; and others with heavy gold or light, according to the oppressiveness of the season; no doubt, the fashions set in Rome extended to Jerusalem. "Goodly apparel" is, rather, *gorgeous*—splendid in colour or ornament; the same two words are translated "gay clothing" in the following verse.

And there come in also a poor man in vile raiment.—Squalid, even dirty, as from work and wear—the exact opposite of the idle over-dressed exquisite.

(3) **And ye have respect to him that weareth the gay clothing** (or, *bright apparel*).—Look on him, that is, because of his fine appearance, with undue respect and consideration.

And say unto him, Sit thou here in a good place (or, as margin, *well*); **and say to the poor, Stand thou there, or sit here under my footstool.**—The sidesman or elder in charge of the church finds a stall for the person of substantial presence, while anything does for the poor one; but—most considerate offer—he can stand; or, if he prefer it, sit under the great man's footstool, lower down, that is, on the floor beneath. We know Christ's words for those who loved of old "the chief seats in the synagogues" (Matt. xxiii. 6), nor can there be doubt as to their full application now. What is to be urged in excuse for the special pews in churches and chapels, hired and appropriated, furnished luxuriously, and secured by bolt and lock? If in the high places sit the men and women in goodly raiment still, while the poorly clad are crowded into side benches and corners, or beneficently told to stand and wait till room be found somewhere beneath the daintier feet,—how can there be escape from condemnation on the charge which follows?—namely this—

(4) **Are ye not then partial in yourselves, and are become judges of evil thoughts?**—Or, as the sense, fully expressed, would be: "My brethren, if you acted thus, did you not doubt in yourselves, and become by such false and unfaithful discrimination judges of and in your own evil thoughts? Did you not lose the idea of brotherhood, and become contentious as to supremacy of self and place—serving yourselves while prepared for the service of Christ? The Lord Jesus thought not His equality with God a thing ever to be grasped at, if work for man could be done by self-humiliation. Therefore, although being 'equal to the Father, as touching His Godhead,' He became 'inferior . . . as touching His Manhood.' And none may turn unmoved from that picture of sublime condescension to the petty strifes of quality and position which profane the Christian sanctuary. Most sadly true is it that in making distinctions such as these between rich and poor, we 'become of the number of those who doubt respecting their faith;' for, while it abolishes such altogether in the presence of God, we set them up of our own arrogance and pride. 'We draw nigh unto Him with our mouth, and honour Him with our lips, but our heart is far from Him; and our worship therefore vain.'" (Comp. Isa. xxix. 13; Ezek. xxxiii. 31; Matt. xv. 8—9.)

(5) **Hearken, my beloved brethren.**—With complete change of manner the Apostle writes now as if he were speaking, in brief quivering sentences, appealing to the hearts which his stronger words may not compel.

Hath not God chosen . . . ?—There is, then, an election on the part of God. It were folly to deny it But this passage, like so many others, gives the reason for that choice. "The poor of this world" are His chosen; not merely for their poverty, although it may have been the air, so to speak, in which the virtues which endeared them to Him have flourished most. And these are rich for present and for future. They know Him "now by faith," and "after this life have the fruition of His glorious Godhead." "Blessed be ye poor, for yours is the kingdom of God" (Luke vi. 20). The way thereto for them is nearer and less cumbered than for the rich, if only they fulfil the Scripture (comp. Matt. vi. 3), and be poor "in spirit:" then, indeed, are they "heirs of the kingdom which He hath promised to them that love Him." The world must always measure by its own standard, and consider

he hath promised to them that love
him? (6) But ye have despised the poor.
Do not rich men oppress you, and draw
you before the judgment seats? (7) Do
not they blaspheme that worthy name
by the which ye are called? (8) If ye
fulfil the royal law according to the scripture, Thou shalt love thy neighbour as thyself, ye do well: (9) but if ye have
respect to persons, ye commit sin, and are
convinced of the law as transgressors.
(10) For whosoever shall keep the whole
law, and yet offend in one
point, he is guilty of all.
(11) For he that said,[1] Do
not commit adultery, said
also, Do not kill. Now if
thou commit no adultery, yet if thou

Chap. ii. 10—11. The whole Law is broken by failure at one point.

[1] Or, *that law which said.*

poverty a curse, just as it looks on pain and trouble as evil. But the teaching of God, declared most eloquently in the life of His blessed Son, is the direct opposite to this. In a worship which demands of its votaries costly gifts and offerings—and every religion tends downwards to such desires—the rich man has a golden pavement to his future bliss. No wonder, therefore, that again and again the voice of the Spirit of God has pointed out the narrow way, and the eternal excellency of truth, and faith, and love, the riches easiest of acquisition by the poor.

(6) **But ye have despised the poor.**—Better, *ye dishonoured the poor man—i.e.*, when, as already mentioned (chap. ii. 2, 3), you exalted the rich unto the "good place" of your synagogue. Thus whom God had called and chosen, you refused. "It is unworthy," observes Calvin on this passage, "to cast down those whom God lifts up, and to treat them shamefully whom He vouchsafes to honour. But God honoureth the poor; therefore whoever he is that rejects them perverts the ordinance of God."

Do not rich men oppress you?—Or, *lord it over you* as a class; not assuredly that this can be said of each wealthy individual. It is the rich man, of the earth earthy, trusting in his riches (comp. Matt. x. 24), who makes them a power for evil and not for good. Here is presented the other side of the argument, used on behalf of the poor, viz., observe first how God regards them (verse 5), and next, judge their adversaries by their own behaviour.

Draw you before the judgment seats?—Better, *Do they not drag you into courts of justice?* "Hale" you, as the old English word has it. *Summum jus summa injuria*—extreme of right is extreme of wrong—a legal maxim oft exemplified. The purse-proud litigious man is the hardest to deal with, and the one who specially will grind the faces of the poor. No body of laws could on the whole be more equitable than the Roman, but their administration in the provinces was frequently in venal hands; and besides, the large fees demanded by the *juris-consulti*—"the learned in the law"—quite barred the way of the poorer suitors, such as, for the most part, were the Christians to whom this Letter was written.

(7) **Do not they blaspheme . . .**—To "blaspheme" is to hurt with the tongue, and includes all manner of evil speech; but a more exclusive use of the word is with regard to things divine, and particularly the unpardonable sin against the Holy Ghost (Matt. xii. 31). A moment's reflection will show, unhappily, that this is alluded to in the text.

That worthy name by the which ye are called?—Better, *that good, that glorious Name which was invoked* (or, *called*) *over you*—viz., at baptism. "Into the Name of the Father, and of the Son, and of the Holy Ghost" (Matt. xxviii. 19) had all been baptised who were thus addressed; but most probably the Second Person of the Trinity is referred to here. And it was the scorn and contempt visited upon His Name, which changed the mere abuse and ribaldry into a perilous likeness to the deadliest sin. Most commentators thus restrict the Name here to that of Christ. If their view be correct, the blasphemy would probably be linked with that epithet of "Christian"—then so dishonourable—coined, we are told, first in Antioch (Acts xi. 26). But there were far more insulting terms found for the poor and struggling believer—"Nazarene," "Atheist," and even worse.

(8) **If ye fulfil the royal law.**—Better paraphrased thus, *If, however, ye are fulfilling the Law, as ye imagine and profess ye are doing, the royal law, according to the Scripture, "Thou shalt love thy neighbour as thyself, ye are doing well; but . . . .* Mark the touch of irony in the defence which St. James puts into the mouths of his hearers. It were certainly a sweet proof of neighbourly affection, that exemplified in verse 3. The "royal," or "kingly law," is, of course, God's, in its highest utterance; and may be taken as an illustration of what a law really consists: viz., a command from a superior, a duty from an inferior, and a sanction or vindication of its authority. There is much confusion of thought, both scientific and theological, with regard to this; were it not so we should hear less of the "laws of nature," and divers other imaginary codes which the greatest legist of modern times has called "fustian." The sovereign law of love, thus expressed by the Apostle, is one so plain that the simplest mind may be made its interpreter; and the violation of it is at once clear to the offender.

(9) **But if ye have respect to persons . . .**—Translate, *But if ye respect persons. ye work sin, and are convicted by the Law* (*i.e.*, at the bar of conscience) *as transgressors.* The first principle has been broken, and not a mere detail. *De minimis non curat lex:* the laws of men cannot concern themselves with trifles; but the most secret soul may be proven and revealed by some little act of love, or the contrary: and such is the way of the Lord "that searcheth the hearts" (Rom. viii. 27).

(10) **For whosoever shall keep . . .**—Better, *have kept the whole Law, but shall have offended in one, has become guilty of all.* As a chain is snapped by failure of the weakest link, so the whole Law, in its harmony and completeness as beheld by God, is broken by one offence of one man; and the penalty falls, of its own natural weight and incidence, on the culprit.

(11) **For he that said . . .**—All men have favourite vices and indulgences; and most

> "Compound for sins they have a mind to
> By damning those they're not inclined to;"

forgetful that the same Lawgiver has laid His restrictions upon every sort and kind. Not that we can believe all sins are the same in their deadening effect upon the

kill, thou art become a transgressor of
the law. (12) So speak ye, and so do, as
they that shall be judged by the law
of liberty. (13) For he shall have judgment without mercy, that hath shewed
no mercy; and mercy rejoiceth[1] against
judgment.
(14) What *doth it* profit, my brethren,

1 Or, *glorieth.*

soul, or, further, in their punishment. The point which St. James urges is that sin, as sin, involves the curse of the law; and that "respect of persons," with its unloving and unlovely results, must bring its deceived possessor into condemnation before God. Just as our Lord referred the Sixth and Seventh Commandments (Matt. v. 21—32) to the first issues of the angry or lustful heart, and by no means confined them as did the Rabbinical teachers to the very act, so now in like manner the Apostle takes his stand upon the guiltiness of any breach whatever of the Law. Love is its complete fulfilment, we are well informed (Rom. xiii. 10), but in that startling briefness lies comprehended all the decalogue, with its utmost ramifications; and men of the world would find a rule of the most minute and rigid ceremony easier to be followed than this simple all-embracing one. "The *fulfilling* of the Law" is very different from the substitution of a single plain command for a difficult code; this would seem to be the mistake of many, noisily asserting their freedom from the older obligations, who do not so evidently live under the mild bondage of the new.

A curious question may be raised upon the inverted order of the Sixth and Seventh Commandments in this passage, as well as in Mark x. 19; Luke xviii. 20; Rom. xiii. 9. (Not so however, observe, in the sermon on the Mount, Matt. v. 21—27.) Professor Plumptre says they are thus placed because "standing first in the second table, the Fifth being classed by most Jewish writers as belonging to the first," and "there was, probably, a traditional order of the Tenth, varying from that at present found in the Hebrew Pentateuch." The Greek version, known as the Septuagint, supports this theory, placing "Thou shalt not commit adultery" in verse 13 of Ex. xx., and "Thou shalt not kill" in verse 15.

(12) **So speak ye, and so do.**—The writer has shown how unsuspected sins lead quickly to a violation of the Law, and in concluding this part of his Epistle he returns to the warning against an unguarded tongue, with which he commenced in chap i. 26.

The law of liberty.—The term is only found here and in chap. i. 25, and seems one of which James the Wise was peculiarly fond. What, however, did he precisely mean? Neither the ceremonial, nor the moral, most certainly; but the spiritual law of One greater than Moses. The idea, however, is in most of the New Testament writings, and particularly St. Paul's. (Comp. John viii. 32; Rom. viii. 21; 1 Cor. x. 29; 2 Cor. iii. 17; Gal. ii. 4; v. 1, 13; and 1 Pet. ii. 16.)

(13) **For he shall have judgment without mercy, that hath shewed no mercy.**—Better, *For unmerciful judgment shall be to him that wrought not mercy.* Here again are the clearest echoes of our Saviour's words (Matt. vi. 1, 2, *et seq.*), and a reference, we can hardly doubt, to His well-known parable (Matt. xviii. 21—35); and we must remember, further, that "the unforgiving temper, apart from all outward wrong, constitutes the sin of the unmerciful servant;" opportunity only being lacking for its full effect. The pitiless are usually cowards, and may well be moved by fear, if they will not by love: "I will repay, saith the Lord" (Rom. xii. 19).

Mercy rejoiceth against judgment.—There can hardly be a fitter comment on this text than that which must be present in every reader's mind—the speech of Portia in *The Merchant of Venice,*

> "The quality of mercy is not strained;" &c
> —(Act iv. scene 1.)

But let the words of the Greek, John the Golden Mouthed, be added, for their exceeding beauty also. "Mercy is dear to God, and intercedes for the sinner, and breaks his chains, and dissipates the darkness, and quenches the fire of hell, and destroys the worm, and rescues from the gnashing of teeth. To her the gates of Heaven are opened. She is the queen of virtues, and makes men like to God, for it is written, 'Be ye merciful as your Father also is merciful' (Luke vi. 36). She has silver wings like the dove, and feathers of gold, and soars aloft, and is clothed with divine glory, and stands by the throne of God; when we are in danger of being condemned she rises up and pleads for us, and covers us with her defence, and enfolds us in her wings. God loves mercy more than sacrifice" (Matt. ix. 13).

(14—26) FAITH AND WORKS.—We now enter on the most debatable ground of the Epistle; a battle-field strewn with the bones and weapons of countless adversaries. It is an easy thing to shoot "arrows, even bitter words"; and without doubt, for what seemed to be the vindication of the right, many a hard blow has been dealt on either side—so many, indeed, that quiet Christian folk have no desire to hear of more. The plain assertions of holy Scripture on this matter are enough for them; and they experience of themselves no difficulty in their interpretation.

The old story of the Knights who smote each other to the death upon the question of the gold and silver shield, each looking at it only from his own point of view, may well apply to combatants who cried so lustily for "Paul" or "James." But, now the dust of conflict has somewhat blown aside, it would be hard to prove that the Apostles themselves were ever at variance, or needed such doughty champions at all.

Truth is, they regarded the same object with a different motive, and aimed at a dissimilar result: just as in medicine, very opposite treatments are required by various sicknesses, and in the several stages of disease. The besetting error of the Jewish Christians to whom St. James appealed was that which we have traced (see *Introduction*, p. 353) to a foreign source; and, as it wandered but slowly from the furthest East, it had not yet reached the churches of Europe, at least sufficiently to constitute a danger in the mind of St. Paul. No better tonic for the enervating effect of this perverted doctrine of Faith could be found than a consideration of the nobler life of Abraham; and what example could be upheld more likely to win back the hearts of his proud descendants? And, if to point his lesson, the Apostle urged a great and stainless name, even that of the Friend of God, so with it would he join the lowly and, perhaps, aforetime dishonoured one of Rahab, that he might, as it were, plead well with all men of every degree or kind.

Chap. ii. 14—26. An excursus on Faith, and particularly on Faith without works.

though a man say he hath faith, and have not works? can faith save him? (15) If a brother or sister be naked, and destitute of daily food, (16) and one of you say unto them, Depart in peace, be *ye* warmed and filled; notwithstanding ye give them not those

---

Dean Alford, quoting with entire approbation the opinion of the German commentator De Wette, found it "impossible to say" that the ideas of Faith, Works, and Justification in the two Apostles were the same. The summary of his remarks is fairly this:—According to St. James, Faith was moral conviction, trust, and truth; and yet such a theoretical belief only that it might be held by devils. Works are not those of the Law, but an active life of practical morality and well-doing; Justification is used in a proper or moral sense, but not the higher or "forensic," as we now call it. On the other hand, St. Paul's idea of Faith presupposes self-abasement, and "consists in trust on the grace of God, revealed in the atoning death of Christ"; Works with him referred chiefly to a dependence on legal observances; Justification assumed a far wider significance, especially in his view "of the inadequacy of a good conscience to give peace and blessedness to men" (1 Cor. iv. 4), such being only to be found by faith in God, who justifies of His free grace, and looks on the accepted penitent as if he were righteous. But even this divergence, small as it is compared with that discerned by some divines, is really overstrained; for in the present Epistle the Church of every age is warned "against the delusive notion that it is enough for men to have religious emotions, to talk religious language, to have religious knowledge, and to profess religious belief, without the habitual practice of religious duties and the daily devotion of a religious life": while the letters of St. Paul do not, in this way, combat hypocrisy so much as heterodoxy. There is always the double danger, dwelt upon by Augustine somewhat after this manner:—One man will say, "I believe in God, and it will be counted to me for righteousness, therefore I will live as I like." St. James answers him by showing that "Abraham was justified by Works" (chap. ii. 21). Another says, "I will lead a good life, and keep the commandments; how can it matter precisely what I believe!" St. Paul replies that "Abraham was justified by faith" (Rom. iv.). But, if the Apostle of the Gentiles be inquired of further, he will say that, although works go not before faith, they certainly come after. (Witness his discourse on Charity, 1 Cor. xiii.) And, therefore, concludes Bishop Wordsworth, "the faith described by St. Paul is not *any* sort of faith by which we believe in God; but it is that healthful evangelical faith whose works spring from love."

Thus the divine lesson stands forth, clearly written; and he who runs may read. Faith must be embodied in acts: "faith, without acts of faith, is but a dream." "The two cannot be separated, for they are given in one by God to man, and from him go back in one to God. As by faith we behold the greatness of God, and of His eternal grace, His ineffable holiness, majesty, glory, goodness, love; so we shall know and feel the nothingness of all in ourselves—whether faith or works—save as they are the gift of God. As we probe ourselves, we learn the depth of our own evil; but, as we confess our own evil and God's good, He will take away from us the evil, and crown us with His goodness: as we own ourselves to be, of ourselves, unprofitable servants, He, owning us in His works, will say, 'Well done, good and faithful servant, enter thou into the joy of thy Lord'" (Matt. xxv. 21).

A deeply learned and interesting excursus on Faith, in its active and passive meanings, and on its Hebrew, Greek, and Latin synonyms, may be read in Bishop Lightfoot's *Notes on the Galatians*, pp. 152—162. Admitting that "so long as our range of view is confined to the apostolic writings, it seems scarcely possible to resist the impression that St. James is attacking the teaching, if not of St. Paul himself, at least of those who exaggerated and perverted it," our profoundest theologian assures us that the passage in Genesis (chap. xv. 6) was a common thesis in the Rabbinical schools, the meaning of faith being variously explained by the disputants, and diverse lessons drawn from it. The supremacy of faith, as the means of salvation, might be maintained by Gentile Apostle and Pharisaic Rabbi: but faith with the former was a very different thing from faith with the latter. With one its prominent idea was a spiritual life, with the other an orthodox creed; with the one the guiding principle was the individual conscience, with the other an external rule of ordinances; with the one faith was allied to liberty, with the other to bondage. "Thus," he says in conclusion, "it becomes a question whether St. James's protest against reliance on faith alone has any reference, direct or indirect, to St. Paul's language and teaching; whether, in fact, it is not aimed against an entirely different type of religious feeling, against the Pharisaic spirit which rested satisfied with a barren orthodoxy, fruitless in works of charity."

(14) **What doth it** (or, *is the*) **profit, my brethren, though a man say he hath faith, and have not works?**—Some allusion here is made most probably to the Shemà, the Jewish creed, "Hear, O Israel, the Lord our God is one Lord" (Deut. vi. 4). It was the daily protest of the devout Israelite in the midst of idolaters, and the words of his morning and evening of life, as well as of the ordinary day. A similar utterance of faith is held to be the test of the true believer in Islam, when the two inquiring angels put their awful questions to the departed soul. But the idea is much more ancient, for a similar confession was required of the just before Osiris, the Lord of the Egyptian Heaven.

Can faith save him?—The stern inquiry comes like a prophecy of woe upon the wretched man—saved, as he fancied, by covenant with God, and holding a bare assent and not a loving faith in Him.

(15) **But** (the word should be added, for it continues an argument) **if a brother or sister be naked, and destitute of daily food**—*i.e.*, the food for each day, not that which suffices for one, or for a present distress; the case is rather of worst and direst want, so that the heart untouched by the spectacle of such misery must be hard indeed.

(16) **And one of you say unto them, Depart in peace, be ye warmed and filled.**—Is it unlikely, knowing as we do the style of the rugged Apostle, that he was drawing other than from the life? Perhaps it was a scene in his own experience during that very famine foretold by Agabus (Acts xi. 28—30).

things which are needful to the body;
what *doth it* profit? (17) Even so faith,
if it hath not works, is dead, being
alone.[1] (18) Yea, a man may say, Thou
hast faith, and I have works: shew me
thy faith without thy works,[2] and I
will shew thee my faith by my works.
(19) Thou believest that there is one
God; thou doest well: the devils also
believe, and tremble. (20) But wilt thou
know, O vain man, that faith without
works is dead?
(21) Was not Abraham our father jus-
tified by works, when he
had offered Isaac his son
upon the altar? (22) Seest
thou[3] how faith wrought
with his works, and by works was faith
made perfect? (23) And the scripture
was fulfilled which saith, Abraham be-

Chap. ii. 21—24. Example 1: the faith of Abraham;

1 Gr. *by itself.*

2 Some copies read, *by thy works.*

3 Or, *Thou seest.*

There would, however, seem to be a worse interpretation of the words, beginning so softly with the Eastern benediction: namely, "Ye are warming and filling yourselves." It is the rebuke of cool prosperity to importunate adversity: "Why such impatience? God is one, and our Father: He will provide." No amount of faith could clothe the shivering limbs and still the hunger pangs; what greater mockery than to be taunted with texts and godly precepts, the usual outcome of a spurious and cheap benevolence.

Notwithstanding ye give them not.—The "one of you" in the beginning of the verse, then, was representative of the whole body addressed by St. James; and now by his use of the plural "ye," we see that no individual was singled out for condemnation: the offence was wider and worse.

(17) **Even so faith, if it hath not works, is dead, being alone.**—Better, like the margin, *is dead in its own self.* If to be childless among women were a curse in Israel, so to be barren among God's graces is the condemnation of faith in Christendom. And St. Paul, in substantial harmony with this assertion of his brother Apostle, declares (Rom. ii. 13) "Not the hearers of the Law are just before God, but the doers of the Law shall be justified." There had been no lack of charity under the earlier Jewish teaching; in fact, "righteousness" in many passages of Holy Writ, and in the paraphrases for the unlearned, called the Targums, was explained to be "almsgiving." But the whole system of Rabbinism seems gradually to have destroyed the spiritual life of its scholars; and amongst them now was fast spreading the doctrine of a sterile faith. In the revival of Monotheism under the sword of the prophet of Mecca, the faith of Abraham once more shone in the creed of his descendants; though, alas! the sons of Ishmael, and not Isaac the chosen: and the Muhammedans tell us still that if fasting and prayer bring the believer to the gates of Paradise, alms will let him in.

(18) **Yea, a man may say . . .**—The bearing of this verse is commonly misunderstood; its words are those of scorn, uttered probably by some enemy of the faith—Jewish or Pagan—and are another instance, like that of the unruly tongue, by which those outside the pale of Christianity may and will judge us within. Verses 18 to 22 are all the speech of this practical opponent of first century solifidianism. The English version, "Show me thy faith *without* thy works" is correct, though according to some editors (see marginal variation) it should be *by* or *from.*

The sense is obvious; and whether the speaker be Christian or no, he lays claim to faith in God, the Father of all, as the efficient cause of his good deeds.

(19) **Thou believest that there is one God; thou doest well.**—Better thus, *Thou believest that God is One; thou doest well.* He is the formal object of faith derived from knowledge, whether by sense, intuition, or demonstration; you are theologically correct, and may even declare your internal faith by external confession—well, indeed.

The devils also believe, and tremble.—They *shudder* in the belief which only assures them of their utter misery; literally, their hair stands on end with terror of the God they own. Assent, opinion, knowledge—all are thus shared by demons of the pit; call not your joint possession by the holier name of Faith. "I believe in God," "I believe in one God"—such is the voice of the Christian; and this is said in the full sense "only by those who love God, and who are not only Christians in name, but in deed and in life."

(20) **But wilt thou know, O vain man, that faith without works is dead?**—"Vain," *i.e.,* empty and useless. Some copies have a word which means idle, fruitless, workless, in place of that translated "dead"; but the sense is the same either way. "If," says Bishop Beveridge, "I see fruit growing upon a tree, I know what tree it is upon which such fruit grows. And so, if I saw how a man lives, I know how he believes. If his faith be good, his works cannot but be good too; and if his works be bad, his faith cannot but be bad too: for, wheresoever there is a justifying faith, there are also good works; and wheresoever there are no good works, there is no justifying faith." Works are the natural fruit of faith; and without them it is evident the tree is dead, perhaps at the very roots, ready to be cut down and cast into the fire.

(21) **Was not Abraham our father justified by works . . ?**—St. James now addresses his two examples from familiar history in force of his plea for active faith. The first is the marvellous devotion and trust of Abraham (Gen. xxii.) *when he offered Isaac his son upon the altar;* that boy himself the type of God's dear Son, who bore, like His meek ancestor, the sacrificial wood up the long weary road of death. Happily, the story is as well known to Christian readers as to the Jewish of old time, and may safely be left here without further comment.

(22) **Seest thou how . . ?**—Better taken simply, and not as a question, *Thou seest how,* &c.

(23) **The scripture was fulfilled.**—Namely, that earlier declaration of God (Gen. xv. 6) when the childless Abraham, with only a Syrian slave for his heir, trusted in the divine promise that his own seed should be as the number of the stars of heaven.

Abraham believed God, and it was imputed unto him for righteousness.—He proved his faith by obedience, when he freely gave back to the Giver his son, the heir of all the promise.

The Friend of God.—*Amatus a Deo*—beloved *of* Him, not the friend *to* God, nor *lover of Him,* as some have hastily imagined. It is not an exact quotation from the Hebrew Bible, though the substance thereof may be found in Isa. xli. 8. The term was traditional

lieved God,[a] and it was imputed
unto him for righteousness: and
he was called the Friend of God.
(24) Ye see then how that by works
a man is justified, and not by faith
only.
(25) Likewise also was not Rahab the
harlot justified by works,
when she had received the
messengers, and had sent
them out another way? (26) For as the
body without the spirit [1] is dead, so faith
without works is dead also.

Chap. ii. 25. Example 2: that of Rahab.

a Gen. 15. 6; Rom. 4. 3; Gal. 3. 6.
1 Or, *breath.*

A.D. cir. 60.

2 Or, *judgment.*

CHAPTER III.—(1) My brethren, be
not many masters, know-
ing that we shall receive
the greater condemnation.[2]
(2) For in many things we
offend all. If any man
offend not in word, the
same *is* a perfect man,

Chap. iii. 1—12. Warnings against censoriousness, and sins of the tongue; with examples of its venom and unruliness.

---

throughout the East, and is used by the Arabs as descriptive of the patriarch to this day.

(24) **Ye see then how that by works . . .**—Observe that St. James says a man is not justified "by faith *only*," putting the adverb in the last and most emphatic position. He never denies Justification by Faith; but that fancied one of idle, speculative, theoretic faith, with no corresponding acts of love.

(25) **Likewise also . . .**—The second example, brought forward in strange and complete contrast to Abraham, "the father of many nations," is that of Rahab, the harlot, who received and sheltered in her house at Jericho the two spies sent out from the camp of Israel (Josh. ii.). The evil name of the poor woman's unhappy trade cannot truthfully be softened down to "innkeeper," nor even "idolater."

Sent them out.—Literally, *hastened*, or *thrust them forth*, showing her haste and fear.

It may not be out of place to notice that Clement, Bishop of Rome, one of the Apostolic Fathers, in his first letter to the Corinthians, sees in the scarlet thread which Rahab bound in her window a type of our Redeemer's blood. And it is most remarkable, as showing the mercy of God, that this outcast of society was not only saved alive and brought into the fold of Israel, but became a direct ancestress of her Saviour, by marriage with Salmon, the great-great-grandfather of David (Matt. i. 5).

(26) **As the body without the spirit . . .**—A closing simile of much force, *As the body without the spirit, so faith without works.* But the term "without" is hardly strong enough to represent the Greek "apart from." Of our own human wisdom we had been rather inclined to say that works were likest to the body, and faith to the breath or animation thereof. "The Apostle's view," says Alford, "seems to be this, Faith is the body, the sum and substance of the Christian life; works (= obedience) the moving and quickening of that body, just as the spirit is the moving and quickening principle of the natural body. So that 'as the body without the spirit is dead, so faith without works is also dead.'"

III.

Chapter iii. is a division of the Epistle complete in itself, specially concerned with Sins of the Tongue. Warnings and examples are given in plenty (verses 5—12) followed by exhortations to meekness and gentleness, and the promise of "the fruit of righteousness" to the lovers of peace (verses 13—18).

(1) **Be not many masters.**—Better, *teachers*, which meaning was conveyed by "masters" when the English Bible was first published. The condemnation is of those who appoint themselves, and are as "blind leaders of the blind" (Matt. xv. 14). No man had a right to exercise the sacred functions of the appointed masters in Israel (see Note on John iii. 10), and none might take the honour of the priesthood unto himself, "but he that was called of God, as was Aaron" (Heb. v. 4). Whereas we know from our Lord's own words that the Scribes and Pharisees loved respectful "greetings in the markets, and to be called of men 'Rabbi, Rabbi'" (Matt. xxiii. 1—12). Nevertheless His disciples were not to be acknowledged thus: for "one is your Master, even Christ; and all ye are brethren." The neglect of this wholesome caution perplexed the early Church, as much as the later branches thereof. (Comp. Acts xv. 24; 1 Cor. i. 12; 1 Cor. xiv. 26; Gal. ii. 12.)

The greater condemnation.—Rather, *the greater judgment*—more strictly searching and severe. "None of us liveth to himself, and no man dieth to himself" (Rom. xiv. 7), and, if this be true of common Christian life, how deep is the responsibility incurred in the attempt to teach others! Nay—"who is sufficient for these things?" (2 Cor. ii. 6.) The test of all ministry must come at last in the day of trial and fiery inquisition of God; this and not the world's opinion will be the real approval (1 Cor. iii. 11—15). If the work of any teacher abide, his reward will be exceeding great; if it "be burned," woe to him! "He himself shall be saved, yet so as by fire," scathed by that which shall consume the rubbish he has raked together; the faith which prompted such a man shall save him, but no reward can follow useless teaching; nor can there be escape for his own soul, except he wrought honestly.

(2) **For in many things we offend all.**—Better thus, *For in many things we all offend*: not, what might be inferred, "we are an offence to all," as Matt. xxiv. 9; 1 Cor. iv. 13, *et al.* Humble, indeed, was the holy mind of James, but this confession of error uplifts him in all right appreciation, and in no way casts him down. The very human weakness of Peter, and Paul, and James, endears them to us; for so we know assuredly that they were "men of like passions" with ourselves (Acts xiv. 15), and, where they succeeded, we, by the like grace of God, may also win the crown.

If any man offend not in word, the same is a perfect man.—If *any* man: much more one who fain would teach his fellows. To "offend" means to stumble over something, and fall, and in this sense we get the exact meaning of "offending" by an unguarded allusion to a subject painful in the mind of another. "A constant governance of our speech, according to duty and reason, is a high instance, and a special argument of a thoroughly sincere and solid goodness," says Isaac Barrow; but the meekest of men failed once, and blessed indeed is he who takes heed to his ways that he sins not with his tongue (Ps. xxxix. 1).

and able also to bridle the whole
body. (3) Behold, we put bits in the
horses' mouths, that they may obey
us; and we turn about their whole
body. (4) Behold also the ships, which
though *they be* so great, and *are* driven
of fierce winds, yet are they turned about
with a very small helm, whithersoever
the governor listeth. (5) Even so the
tongue is a little member, and boasteth
great things. Behold, how great a
matter[1] a little fire kindleth! (6) And
the tongue *is* a fire, a world of iniquity:
so is the tongue among our members,
that it defileth the whole body, and
setteth on fire the course of nature;
and it is set on fire of hell.
(7) For every kind[2] of beasts, and of
birds, and of serpents, and
of things in the sea, is
tamed, and hath been
tamed of mankind:[3] (8) but

Chap. iii. 7—12. The unnatural behaviour thereof.

1 Or, *wood.*

2 Gr. *nature.*

3 Gr. *nature of man*

Able also to bridle the whole body.—Not that if the tongue be stilled all the members of the body are consequently in peace; but, because the work of ruling the one rebel is so great, that a much less corresponding effort will keep the others in subjection.

(3) **Behold.**—A more clumsy reading is insisted upon here: *but if*, instead of "behold." The supporters of such curious corrections argue that the least likely is the most so; and thus every slip of a copyist, either in grammar or spelling, becomes more sacred in their eyes than is the Received text with believers in verbal inspiration.

Three comparisons of the tongue are now introduced; the bit (verse 3), the rudder (verse 4), and a fire (verse 6): the two former to show what mastery may be gained by self-discipline, the latter to warn us of a danger which may quickly spread beyond our power to quell.

(4) **The governor**—*i.e.*, the "helmsman," from the Latin *gubernator.* The Venerable Bede, our earliest English translator, refers the ships here to an image of ourselves, and the winds to the impulses of our own minds, by which we are driven hither and thither.

St. James, remembering the storms of the Galilean lake, could well rejoice in a simile like this, although he himself may only have known the craft of an inland sea, and never have beheld "broad rivers and streams" wherein went "galley with oars and gallant ship" (Isa. xxxiii. 21). And none knew better than the brother of the Lord who was the true

"Helm of the ships that keep
Pathway along the deep."

(5) **Even so . . .**—*Thus,* like the tiny rudder of the mighty ship, whereon its course most critically depends—*the tongue is a little member;* for it "vaunts great words which bring about great acts of mischief." The verb translated *boasteth* is peculiar to this place, but occurs so often in the works of Philo that we may be almost certain St. James had read them. And many other verses of our Epistle suggests his knowledge of this famous Alexandrian Jew.

Behold, how great a matter a little fire kindleth!—It would be more in the spirit and temper of this imaginative passage to render it, "Behold, how great a *forest* a little spark kindleth!" Thus it is expressed in the Latin Vulgate; and note our own margin, "wood." The image constantly recurs in poetry, ancient and modern; and in the writer's mind there seems to have been the picture "of the wrapping of some vast forest in a flame, by the falling of a single spark," and this in illustration of the far-reaching mischief resulting from a single cause. (Comp. Ecclus. xxviii. 10.)

(6) **And the tongue is a fire.**—Better thus, *The tongue—that world of iniquity—is a fire,* to burn and destroy the fairest works of peace. *The tongue is in our members that which defileth the whole body, and setteth the world aflame, and is set on fire itself of Gehenna.* "The course of Nature" is literally the "wheel," the "orb of creation." The Jewish word for the place of torment, the accursed side of Hades, should be thus preserved: whence it was that the rich man of the parable prayed for water to cool his tongue (Luke xvi. 24).

"Speech is silver; silence, gold." But even the Christian world will not endure overmuch the godly discipline of silence. Three temptations "to smite with the tongue" are specially powerful of evil: viz., as a relief from passion, as a gratification of spite, as revenge for wrong. The first is experienced by hot-tempered folk; the second yielded to by the malicious; the third welcomed by the otherwise weak and defenceless; and all of us at times are in each of these divisions. Then, again, there are the "foolish talkings" (Eph. v. 4), and worse, the jestings at holy things, and misquotations of Scripture: all to be avoided as not becoming saints. If then we would "walk in love" we must curb the tongue; but, better still, strive to cleanse the heart, and so be quite determined that nothing shall go forth but words of meekness and affection. Nay, if we be truly Christ's, though "reviled" by the unruly tongues of others, we shall, like Him, "revile not again" (1 Pet. ii. 23). And as the whole body is the Lord's to be sanctified to Him (1 Cor. vi. 19 *et seq.*), so particularly must the tongue be kept from "evil-speaking, lying, and slandering," and used rightly for the service of God. Thus may we truly offer "the calves of our lips" (Hos. xiv. 2), more acceptable than the blood of victims slain on a thousand altars, "than all whole burnt-offerings and sacrifices" (Mark xii. 23).

(7) **For every kind of beasts . . .**—Compare the margin, and read more exactly, thus: *Every nature of beasts and birds, and creeping things, and things of the sea, is tamed, and hath been tamed, by the nature of man.* All kinds have been mastered by mankind, as promised at creation (Gen. i. 26—28). There lives no creature which may not be won by kindness and gratitude; and—

"He prayeth best who loveth best
All things both great and small;
For the dear God Who loveth us,
He made and loveth all."

The four-fold division of animal life above is curiously like and unlike that in Acts x. 17, where we read of "four-footed beasts of the earth, wild beasts, creeping things, and fowls of the air."

(8) **But the tongue can no man tame; it is an unruly** (or, *restless*) **evil, full of deadly**

the tongue can no man tame; *it*
is an unruly evil, full of deadly
poison. (9) Therewith bless we God,
even the Father; and therewith
curse we men, which are made after the
similitude of God. (10) Out of the same
mouth proceedeth blessing and cursing.
My brethren, these things ought not so
to be. (11) Doth a fountain send forth
at the same place[1] sweet *water* and
bitter? (12) Can the fig tree, my brethren,
bear olive berries? either a vine, figs?
so *can* no fountain both yield salt water
and fresh.

Chap. iii. 13—18. Exhortations towards meekness, gentleness, and peace.

(13) Who *is* a wise man and endued
with knowledge among
you? let him shew out
of a good conversation
his works with meekness
of wisdom. (14) But if ye
have bitter envying and strife in your
hearts, glory not, and lie not against

1 Or, *hole.*

---

poison.—Mortiferous, bringer of death, like a poisoned dart or arrow; and therefore most suggestive of envenomed flights at the fame of others. St. James does not mean that no one can tame his own tongue, for so he would hardly be responsible for its vagaries; and lower down it is written expressly, "these things ought not so to be." The hopeless savagery of the tongue, excelling the fury of wild beasts, must be that of the liar, the traducer, and blasphemer. (Comp. Ps. cxl.)

(9) **Therewith bless we God, even the Father.**—A strange reading of this verse in the more ancient manuscripts makes it, *Therewith bless we the Lord and Father.* And it may serve to remind us of the oneness of our God, that thus He may be termed Lord and Saviour. His worship and praise are, as explained under verse 6, the right use of the tongue; but, most inconsistently, *therewith curse we men* which have *been made in the image, after the similitude, of God.* See Ps. l. 16—23, with its final words of warning to the wicked, and praise "to him that ordereth his conversation right."

The "likeness of God" assuredly remains in the most abandoned and fallen; and to curse it is to invoke the wrath of its Creator. What then can be urged in defence of anathemas and fulminations of councils, or the mutual execrations of sects and schisms, in the light of these solemn words? "Though they curse, yet bless thou . . . and let them cover themselves with their own confusion" (Ps. cix. 28, 29).

(10) **Ought not.**—The Greek equivalent for this is only found here in the New Testament, and seems strangely weak when we reflect on the usual vehemence of the writer. Was he sadly conscious of the failure beforehand of his protest? At least, there seems no trace of satire in the sorrowful cadence of his lines, "Out of the same mouth!"

(11) **Doth a** (or, *the*) **fountain send forth** (literally, *spurt*) **at the same place** (or, *hole,* see margin) **sweet water and bitter** (*i.e., fresh water and salt*)?—A vivid picture, probably, of the mineral springs abounding in the Jordan valley, near the Dead Sea; with which might be contrasted the clear and sparkling rivulets of the north, fed by the snows of Lebanon. Nature had no confusion in her plans; and thus to pour out curse and blessing from the same lips were unnatural indeed. Or, again—

(12) **Can the fig-tree, my brethren, bear olive berries? either a vine, figs?**—Read, *Can a fig-tree bear olives, or a vine, figs?* The inquiry sounds like a memory of our Lord's, "Do men gather grapes of thorns, or figs of thistles?" (Matt. vii. 16.)

So can no fountain . . .—This, the last clause of the sentence above in the Authorised version is very confused in the original, but seems to be merely this, *Neither can salt* (water) *bring forth fresh;* or, as Wordsworth renders it, *Nor can water that is salt produce what is sweet.* And such in effect is Alford's comment: "If the mouth emit cursing, thereby making itself a brackish spring, it cannot to any purpose also emit the sweet stream of praise and good words; if it appear to do so, all must be hypocrisy and mere seeming." Every blessing is, in fact, tainted by the tongue which has uttered curses; and even "Praise is not seemly in the mouth of a sinner" (Ecclus. xv. 9).

(13) **Who is a wise man and endued with knowledge?**—Who is wise, *i.e.,* in the wisdom of God, and learned in that of man? The latter state is of knowledge natural or acquired, the former is *Sophia,* the highest heavenly wisdom, "the breath of the power of God—the brightness of the everlasting light—more beautiful than the sun, and above all the order of the stars" (Wisd. vii. 25—29). Just as the devils hold with man the lower kinds of faith, that is belief merely (chap. ii. 19), so do they share in his earthly knowledge. The self-same term as that describing it above is used by the evil spirit who answered the presumptuous sons of Sceva, "Paul I *know,*" while a different one altogether referred to the Lord Jesus (Acts xix. 15).

> "Where shall Wisdom be found,
> And where is the place of Understanding?"

was the question of Job (chap. xxviii. 12). And the LXX version marks the parallelism in the same Greek words as those used by St. James to distinguish between the two ideas.

Let him shew out of a good conversation—*i.e., right conduct.* "Conversation" has slipped from its original meaning, which exactly represented the Greek, and is often misapprehended by the English reader. Literally, "turning oneself about," it changed to "walking to and fro," and the talking while engaged in these peripatetics, and then to its limited modern use. There is to be general *good conduct,* and particular proofs of it in kindly *works in meekness of wisdom;* noble acts of a holy habit.

(14) **But if ye have bitter envying and strife in your hearts.**—Rather, it should be, *bitter zeal and party-spirit.* "Above all, no zeal" was the worldly caution of an astute French prelate. But that against which the Apostle inveighed had caused Jerusalem to run with blood, and afterwards helped in her last hour to add horror upon shame. The Zealots were really assassins, pledged to any iniquity; such were the forty men "who bound themselves under a curse, saying they would neither eat nor drink till they had killed Paul" (Acts xxiii. 12; see Note there). Some of these desperadoes unluckily escaped the swords of the Romans, and fled to the fastnesses of Mount Lebanon. They were probably the nucleus of a still more infamous society, known in the middle ages as that of the Old

the truth. (15) This wisdom descendeth not from above, but *is* earthly, sensual,[1] devilish. (16) For where envying and strife *is*, there *is* confusion[2] and every evil work. (17) But the wisdom that is from above is first pure, then peaceable, gentle, *and* easy to be intreated, full of mercy and good fruits, without partiality,[3] and without hypocrisy. (18) And the fruit of righteousness is sown in peace of them that make peace.

CHAPTER IV. — (1) From whence

3 Or, *without wrangling.*
1 Or, *natural.*
2 Gr. *tumult*, or, *unquietness.*

A.D. cir. 60.

Man of the Mountain; in fact, our word "assassin" comes from "Hassan," their first sheik. Happily for humanity they were at length exterminated by the Turks.

Glory not.—*Boast not* yourselves as partakers of this accursed zeal; behold already what ruin it is bringing on us as a nation and a Church. And it were well to take care even in these milder days of religious factions, that the strife of creeds be wholly different in kind from the old zealot feuds, and not merely in degree. Able only to rend and overthrow, party-spirit will, if it be gloried and exulted in, lay down the walls of Zion "even to the ground." But "if any man defile the temple of God, him shall God destroy" (1 Cor. iii. 17), and the words must be translated much more sternly, "If any man *destroy* . . ."

Lie not against the truth.—This is not tautology, nor a Hebraism, but of far deeper import. "What is truth?" said jesting Pilate (John xviii. 38), and, as Bacon remarks in his *Essay on Truth*, he would not stay for an answer. Probably he put a question familiar to himself, learned in a certain school of knowledge whose wise conclusion was that mankind could not tell; and the inquirer turned away, unwitting that before him stood the incarnate Truth itself. The world of unbelief repeats the careless utterance of the Roman Governor, and holds with him in its new Agnosticism; and to its self-assurance and pride of life He, Who can only be learned in the doing of His will (John vii. 17), is alike unknowable and unknown. But the words of the Apostle have a mournful significance for the ignorant of God; and a terrible one for the Christian who knows and sins against the Light. Falsehood is not the hurt of some abstract virtue, or bare rule of right and wrong, but a direct blow at the living Truth (John xiv. 6), Who suffered and still "endures such contradiction of sinners against Himself" (Heb. xii. 3). As the fault of Judas was double—personal treachery against his Friend and Master, and a wider attack on Christ, the Truth manifest in the flesh—so in a like two-fold manner we smite at once God and our brother when we speak or act a lie. All faintest shades of falsehood tend to the dark one of a fresh betrayal of the Son of Man if they be conceived against others, while if they be wrought only to shield ourselves, we are, as Montaigne observed, "brave before God, and cowards before men," who are as the dust of His feet.

(15) **This wisdom descendeth not from above . . . .**—Better thus, *This is not the wisdom coming down from above, but is earthly, natural, devilish.* This—it were profanation to call it by the holy name of Σοφία (*Sophia*), being in sharpest contrast to it, of the earth earthy; natural (as margin), or "psychical," in the second sense of the tripartite division of man—body, *soul*, and spirit—explained under chap. i. 21 (comp. Jude, verse 19, "Sensual, having not the Spirit"); and even worse, akin to the craft of devils.

(16) **For where envying and strife is, there is confusion.**—Where emulation, zeal, and rivalry exist, there also are sedition, anarchy, restless disturbance, and every villainous act. The whole state is evil, and utterly contrary to the rule of the Gospel—

> "For words and names let angry zealots fight:
> Whose life is in the wrong can ne'er be right."

(17) **But the wisdom that is from above . . .**—Whereas, in sweetest contrast to all this repulsive foulness and riot, the true *wisdom from above is first pure*, chaste as the Lamb of God, "the Word made flesh" (John i. 14), then *peaceful, gentle, and compliant*—easy to be won, *full of mercy and good fruits, impartial*, not double-minded (*non duplex*), *nor hypocritical.* Compare with this beautiful description St. Paul's list of the fruits of the Spirit, "love, joy, peace, long-suffering, gentleness, goodness, faith, meekness, temperance" (Gal. v. 22), and his discourse on Love (1 Cor. xiii.).

Truly this wisdom "cannot be gotten for gold, neither shall silver be weighed for the price thereof;" "Happy is the man that findeth her." (Read Job xxviii. 14—19, and Prov. iii. 13—18.)

(18) **And the fruit of righteousness . . .**—Better thus slightly altered: *And fruit of righteousness is sown in peace by them that make peace.* They "shall be called the children of God" (Matt. v. 9). Their fruit is hidden in the precious seed, but "the times of refreshing shall come," and the glorious plant bring forth her flower, and bear the golden fruit for the blessed ones to eat in the fadeless paradise of God. As "whatsoever a man soweth that shall he also reap" (Gal. vi. 7)—here is a harvest laid up for the righteous to enjoy for ever; and (comp. Heb. xii. 11) God's chastening of the truly penitent yields with it a like promise afterwards of "the peaceable fruit of righteousness"—so, in the tender mercy of our Saviour, "they that sow in tears shall reap in joy" (Ps. cxxvi. 6). Thus, in some words which well might mark the close of one whose "quiet spirit slowly passeth by to some more perfect peace"—

> "Peace comes at length, though life be full of pain;
> Calm in the faith of Christ I lay me down;
> Pain for His sake is peace, and loss is gain:
> For all who bear the cross shall wear the crown."

IV.

At the end of what has been considered the second portion of this Epistle, there is a last series of rebukes, suggested apparently by those already given. Chap. iv. is included in this fourth subdivision. (See *Analysis of Contents.*) The lust of the eye and the pride of life are at the root of all the wrong-doing.

(1) **From whence come wars . . ?**—More correctly thus, *Whence are wars, and whence fightings among you?* The perfect peace above, capable, moreover, in some ways, of commencement here below, dwelt upon at the close of chap. iii., has by inevitable reaction led the Apostle to speak suddenly, almost fiercely, of the existing state of things. He traces the conflict raging around him to the fount and origin of evil within.

come wars and fightings[1] among you? *come they* not hence, *even* of your lusts[2] that war in your members? (2) Ye lust, and have not: ye kill, and desire to have, and cannot obtain: ye fight and war, yet ye have not, because ye ask not. (3) Ye ask, and receive not, because ye ask amiss, that ye may consume *it* upon your lusts.[3]

Chap. iv. 1—4. Rebukes of lust and low desires.

(4) Ye adulterers and adulteresses, know ye not that the friendship of the world is enmity with God? whosoever

1 Or, *brawlings.*

2 Or, *pleasures.*

3 Or, *pleasures.*

Come they not . . .—Translate, *come they not hence, even from your lusts warring in your members?* The term is really *pleasures*, but in an evil sense, and therefore "lusts." "The desires of various sorts of pleasures are," says Bishop Moberly, "like soldiers in the devil's army, posted and picketed all over us, in the hope of winning our members, and so ourselves, back to his allegiance, which we have renounced in our baptism." St. Peter (1 Pet. ii. 11) thus writes in the same strain of "fleshly lusts, which war against the soul"; and St. Paul knew also of this bitter strife in man, if not actually in himself, and could "see another law" in his members—the natural tendency of the flesh—"warring against the law of his mind, and bringing him into captivity to the law of sin which is in his members" (Rom. vii. 23). See also Note on 2 Cor. xii. 7.

Happily the Christian philosopher understands this; and with the very cry of wretchedness, "Who shall deliver me?" can answer, "I thank God, through Jesus Christ our Lord" (Rom. vii. 24, 25). But the burden of this hateful depravity drove of old men like Lucretius to suicide rather than endurance; and its mantle of despair is on all the religions of India at the present time—matter itself being held to be evil, and eternal.

(2, 3) **Ye lust, and have not . . .**—Better thus: *Ye desire, and have not; ye kill, and envy, and cannot obtain; ye fight and make war; ye have not, because ye ask not; ye ask and receive not, because ye ask that ye may spend it on your lusts.* It is interesting to notice the sharp crisp sentences, recollecting at the same time that St. James himself fell a victim to the passions he thus assails, probably at the hands of a zealot mob. The marginal note to the second of the above paragraphs gives *envy* as an alternative reading for "kill": but this is an error. "Ye kill and play the zealot" would be still nearer the original: for, as with Jedburgh justice in the old Border wars, hanging preceded the trial, so with these factions in Jerusalem death went first, almost before the desire to deal it. Lust, envy, strife, and murder:—like the tale of human passion in all ages, the dreadful end draws on. It is written in every national epic; its elements abound in the life of each individual: the slaughter in Etzel's halls overshadows the first lines of the Nibelungen-lied; the curse of Medea hangs like a gathering cloud around Jason and his Argonauts. Is it objected (verse 3) that prayer is made but not answered? The reply is obvious; *Ye ask not* in the true sense; when ye do ask ye receive not, because God is too loving, even in His anger. Nevertheless, remember, He gave the Israelites "their desire, and sent leanness withal into their soul" (Ps. cvi. 15). "I," said He by Ezekiel (chap. xiv. 4), "will answer him that cometh to Me, according to his idols." What greater curse could fall than an eternity of avarice to the miser, of pollution to the sensual, of murder to the violent? Many a man of quiet Christian life will thank God by-and-by, when he knows even as he is known (1 Cor. xiii. 12), that not a few of his prayers were unanswered, or at least that they were not granted in the way which he had desired. Safety is only to be found in our Lord's own manner of petition, "Not my will, but Thine be done" (Luke xxii. 42). Alas! in shameful contrast to this we read of many an evil-hearted prayer offered up to the Lord our Righteousness; invocations of saints for help in unholy deeds; of angels, for acts rather befitting devils of the pit; and can hardly have the conscience to reproach the heathen for supplicating their gods in no worse a manner for no better cause.

(4) **Ye adulterers and adulteresses.**—The phrase may seem to flow naturally after the former ones, but the Received text, from which our version was made, is wrong. It should be, *ye adulteresses!* as accusing those who have broken their marriage vow to God. The sense is familiar to us from many passages in the Old Testament, in which God speaks of Israel in a similar manner, *e.g.*, Ps. lxxiii. 27; Isa. liv. 5; Jer. ii. 2; Ezek. xvi. *passim;* xxiii. 37—43; Hos. ii. 2 Again in the New Testament: Matt. xii. 39; xvi. 4; Mark viii. 38; Rev. ii. 20—22; xvii. 1, 5, 15, &c.; St. Paul's description of the church (2 Cor. xi. 2), espoused "as a chaste virgin to Christ;" and comp. 2 Pet. ii. 14, specially the margin. "God is the Lord and husband of every soul that is His;" and in her revolt from Him, and love for sin, her acts are those of an adulterous woman.

Know ye not that the friendship of the world is enmity with God?—*i.e.*, the state of being an enemy to God, not one of simpler enmity with Him. There cannot be a passive condition to the faith of Christ: "he that is not with Me is against Me" (Matt. xii. 30). Renunciation of the world, in the Christian promise, is not forsaking it when tired and clogged with its delights, but the earliest severance from it; to break this vow, or not to have made it, is to belong to the foes of God, and not merely to be out of covenant with Him. The forces of good and evil divide the land so sharply that there is no debatable ground, nor even halting-place between. And if God be just, so also is He jealous (Ex. xx. 5).

"Let us not weakly slide into the treason:
Yielding another what we owe to Him."

Whosoever therefore will be (or, *wills to be*) **a friend of the world is the enemy of God.**—The choice is open; here is no iron fate, no dread necessity: but the wrong determination of the soul constitutes it henceforth as an ally of Satan. "Woe unto you, when all men speak well of you" (Luke vi. 26), for the world, as our Lord has taught us, must "love its own" (John xv. 19). And the sooner the soldier of Christ learns to expect its animosity, the better will he give himself up to the battle. (Comp. Matt. vi. 24; Luke xvi. 13.)

therefore will be a friend of the world
is the enemy of God.
(5) Do ye think that the scripture saith
in vain, The spirit that
dwelleth in us lusteth to
envy?[1] (6) But he giveth
more grace. Wherefore
he saith, God resisteth the proud, but
giveth grace unto the humble.[a] (7) Sub-
mit yourselves therefore to God. Resist
the devil, and he will flee from you.
(8) Draw nigh to God, and he will draw
nigh to you. Cleanse *your* hands, *ye*

Chap. iv. 5—10. Condemnations of arrogance and pride.

[1] Or, *enviously?*

[a] Prov. 3. 34; 1 Pet. 5. 5.

sinners; and purify *your* hearts, *ye*
double minded. (9) Be afflicted, and
mourn, and weep: let your laughter
be turned to mourning, and *your* joy
to heaviness. (10) Humble yourselves
in the sight of the Lord, and he shall
lift you up.
(11) Speak not evil one of another,
brethren. He that speak-
eth evil of *his* brother,
and judgeth his brother,
speaketh evil of the law,
and judgeth the law: but

Chap. iv. 11, 12. Of evil speaking, and hasty judgment.

---

(5) **Do ye think . . ?**—The tone of the Apostle is changed to one of appeal, which, perhaps (but see below), may be rendered thus: *Suppose ye that the Scripture saith in vain, The* (Holy) *Spirit that dwelleth in us jealously regards us as His own?* Our Authorised version does not allow of this apparent reference to the Spirit of God indwelling His human temples (1 Cor. iii. 16; vi. 19, *et seq.*) for "lusteth to envy," or *enviously*, would imply evil and not good. It were well that the unfaithful, addressed in verse 4, should bear the general sentiment of this verse in mind, and not fancy such warnings of holy writ were uttered *emptily, in vain.*

Many commentators have been puzzled to say whence the words came which are quoted as authoritative by St. James. Surely the substance was sufficient for him, as for other inspired writers, without a slavish adherence to the form: comp. Gen. ii. 7 for the inbreathing of the Spirit, with any such chapter as Deut. xxxii. for His jealous inquisition. It must, however, be noted that a slightly varied punctuation of the verse will give quite another sense to its questioning. (See Wordsworth.) *Suppose ye that the Scripture speaketh in vain? Doth the Spirit, which took up His abode in you, lust to envy?* And defensible or not as this translation may be, at least it escapes some of the difficulties of the foregoing. (Exhaustive notes, with references to most authorities, are in Alford; or an easy summary of the matter may be read in Plumptre's *St. James.*)

(6) **But he giveth more grace**—*i.e.*, because of this very presence of the Holy Ghost within us. He, as the author and conveyer of all good gifts, in their mystic seven-fold order (Isa. xi. 2) adds to the wasted treasure, and so aids the weakest in his strife with sin, resisting the proud, lest he be led to destruction (Prov. xvi. 18), and helping the humble, lest he be "wearied and faint in his mind" (Heb. xii. 3).

God resisteth the proud . . .—Excepting "God," instead of "Lord," this is an exact quotation from the LXX. version of Prov. iii. 34, which reads in our Bibles, "Surely He scorneth the scorners, but He giveth grace unto the lowly." It is again brought forward by St. Peter (1 Pet. v. 5), and seems to have been a common saying—"a maxim of the wise that had become, as it were, a law of life."

(7) **Submit yourselves therefore to God.** (*But*) **resist the devil.**—The hardest advice of all, to a man reliant on himself, is submission to any, more especially to the Unknown. But, as a correlative to this, the Apostle shows where pride may become a stimulant for good, viz., in contest with the Evil One.

He will flee.—Or, *he shall flee.* "The Devil," says the strange old book called *The Shepherd of Hermas,* "can fight, but he cannot conquer; if, therefore, thou dost withstand him, he will flee from thee, beaten and ashamed."

The text is another proof of the personality of Satan; no amount of figures of speech could otherwise interpret it.

(8) **Draw nigh to God . . .**—God waiteth to be gracious (Isa. xxx. 18). Like the father of the prodigal son (Luke xv.), He beholds us while we are "yet a great way off," and runs, as it were, to hasten our return. He has "no pleasure in the death of him that dieth" (Ezek. xviii. 32). But who shall come "into the tabernacle of God, or rest upon His holy hill" (Ps. xv. 1), except the man "of uncorrupt life"? Surely, the penitent as well; the murderous hands "which all the perfumes of Arabia will not sweeten," the hearts polluted with the most abominable lusts, may and must be cleansed; *sinners and double-minded* (refer to chap. i. 8) though they be, and both in one, the Lord of mercy will "draw nigh" to them, if they to Him; all their "transgressions shall not be mentioned," they "shall live and not die" (Ezek. xviii. 21, 22).

(9) **Be afflicted, and mourn, and weep.**—For wretchedness, sorrow, and tears are the three steps of the homeward way to peace and God. And in proof of real conversion there must be the outward lamentation, as well as the inward contrition. Grieve, therefore, with a "godly sorrow not to be repented of" (2 Cor. vii. 10)—the remorseful anguish of a Peter, and not a Judas. Let the foolish laughter at sin, which was "as the crackling of thorns" before the avenging fire (Eccles. vii. 6), be turned to mourning; banish the joyous smile for the face cast down to heaviness, and so await the blessedness of those that mourn (Matt. v. 4), even the promised comfort of God.

(10) **Humble yourselves . . .**—Read, *Humble yourselves therefore before the Lord, and He shall lift you up.* "For thus saith the high and lofty One" (Isa. lvii. 15), "I dwell in the high and holy place, with him also that is of a contrite and humble spirit, to revive the spirit of the humble, and to revive the heart of the contrite." (Comp. 1 Pet. v. 6.) "God," says Thomas à Kempis, "protects the humble and delivers him; He loves and consoles him; He inclines Himself towards the humble man, He bestows on him exceeding grace, and after his humiliation He lifts him up to glory; He reveals his secrets to the humble, and sweetly draws and leads him to Himself."

(11) **Speak not evil . . .**—Do not "back-bite," as the same word is translated in Rom. i. 30, and

if thou judge the law, thou art not a
doer of the law, but a judge.
(12) There is one lawgiver, who is able
to save and to destroy:
who are thou that judgest
another? (13) Go to now,
ye that say, To day or to
morrow we will go into
such a city, and continue there a year,

Chap. iv. 13—17. The folly of worldliness, in our uncertain state.

and buy and sell, and get gain:[a]
(14) whereas ye know not what *shall*
be on the morrow. For what *is* your
life? It is[1] even a vapour, that ap-
peareth for a little time, and then
vanisheth away. (15) For that ye *ought*
to say, If the Lord will, we shall live,
and do this, or that. (16) But now ye
rejoice in your boastings: all such re-

a Prov. 27. 1.

1 Or, *For it is.*

---

2 Cor. xii. 20. The good reason why not is given in the graceful interjection "brothers." Omit the conjunction in the next phrase, and read as follows:—

He that speaketh evil . . .—Punctuate thus: *He that speaketh evil of his brother, judgeth his brother; speaketh evil of the law, and judgeth the law.* In this way the cumulative force of St. James's remarks is best preserved. Hearken to the echo of his Master's words. "Judge not, that ye be not judged" (Matt. vii. 1). But the apostolic condemnation is in no way meant to condone a vicious life, and leave it unalarmed and self-contented; for boldness in rebuke thereof we have the example of John the Baptist. All that he reproves is the setting up of our own tribunals, in which we are at once prosecutor, witness, law, lawgiver, and judge; not to say executioner as well. *Prœjudicium* was a merciful provision under Roman law, and often spared the innocent a lengthier aftertrial; but *prejudice*—our word taken from it—is its most unhappy opposite. Many worthy people have much sympathy with David, in their effort to hold their tongue and keep "silence, yea even from good words;" truly it is "pain and grief" to them (Ps. xxxix. 3). But "to take the law into one's own hands" is to break it, and administer inequitably.

(12) **There is one lawgiver . . . .**—Better thus: *One is the Law-giver and Judge, Who is able to save and to destroy: but thou—who art thou that judgest a neighbour?* As a king is the fountain of honour, so the ultimate source of law is God; and all judgment really is delegated by Him, just as ordinary courts represent the royal majesty: to usurp such functions is to provoke the offended sovereign—whether of earth or heaven. "It is not our part," said Bengel, "to judge, since we cannot carry out our sentence." (Comp. a parallel scripture, Rom. xiv. 4.)

Able to save and to destroy.—Life and death, salvation and utter destruction, seem to be placed in intentional contrast here. (Comp. Matt. x. 28.) The thought of annihilation meets us with awful suggestiveness, yet let us leave the mystery for awhile in happier thought—

"That nothing walks with aimless feet;
That not one life shall be destroyed,
Or cast as rubbish to the void,
When God hath made the pile complete."

(13) **Ye that say . . . .**—The Apostle would reason next with the worldly; not merely those abandoned to pleasure, but any and all absorbed in the quest of gain or advancement. The original is represented a little more closely, thus: *To-day and tomorrow we will go into this city, and spend a year there, and trade and get gain.* "Mortals think all men mortal but themselves;" yet who does not boast himself of to-morrow (Prov. xxvii. 1), in spite of a thousand proverbs; and reckon on the wondrous chance of

"That untravelled world, whose margin fades
For ever and for ever as he roams?"

(14) **Whereas ye know not . . . .**—Read, *Whereas ye know not aught of the morrow*—what, *i.e.*, the event may be. The hopeless misery of the unfaithful servant comes into mind at this; he has left the greater business to perform the less; or, it may be, said in heart, "My lord delayeth his coming," and so has begun "to smite his fellow-servants, and to eat and drink with the drunken." And lo! the thunder of the chariot wheels, the flash of the avenging sword, the "portion with the hypocrites," the "weeping and gnashing of teeth." (Read Matt. xxiv. 42—51.)

For what is your life? It is even a vapour.—The rebuke is stronger still, the home-thrust more sharp and piercing—*Ye are even a vapour:* ye yourselves, and all belonging to you; not merely life itself, for that confessedly is a breath; and many a man, acknowledging so much, counts of the morrow that he may lay up in store for other wants besides his own.

A vapour, that appeareth for a little time, and then vanisheth away (or, *disappeareth*).—There is a play upon words to mark the sad antithesis. The vision of life vanisheth as it came; and thus even a heathen poet says—

"Dust we are, and a shadow."

(Comp. Wisd. v. 9—14.)

(15) **For that ye ought to say . . . .**—Referring to verse 13, in some such a continuation of reproof as this: *Woe unto you that say,* . . . . *instead of saying, "If the Lord will"* . . . . In fact, it is a thing of the past, not of time, but completed action on the part of God—"If the Lord *have willed* it, we shall both live and do this or that." Such is far, be it noted, from Fatalism, in even its best form, as under the teaching of Islam. The sovereignty of God is acknowledged, but with it is plainly recognised the existence of man's free will, dependent, however, on the permission of the Most High for its fleeting duration and power. St. Paul speaks in similar tone of coming to Corinth, "if the Lord will" (1 Cor. iv. 19); and "God willing" (D.V.), "the reference of all the contingencies of the future to One supremely wise and loving Will, has been in all ages of Christendom the stay and strength of devout souls."

(16) **But now . . . .**—How different is the case with you, cries St. James; you actually glory and delight in your own self-confidence and presumption, and every such rejoicing is evil. The word for "boastings" is the same as that translated "the pride of life" in 1 John ii. 16—*i.e.*, its braggart boastfulness, not the innocent gladness of living. It is the trust of the "ungodly" (Ps. x. 6, "There shall no harm happen unto me"), and the mistaken confidence of even such godly men as Job (chap. xxix. 18, "I shall die in my nest"), before the Almighty instructs them by trouble, and loss, and pain.

joicing is evil. (17) Therefore to him
that knoweth to do good, and doeth *it*
not, to him it is sin.

CHAPTER V.—(1) Go to now, *ye* rich
men, weep and howl for
your miseries that shall
come upon *you*. (2) Your
riches are corrupted, and
your garments are moth-
eaten. (3) Your gold and silver is
cankered; and the rust of them shall
be a witness against you, and shall eat
your flesh as it were fire. Ye have
heaped treasure together for the last
days. (4) Behold, the hire of the labourers
who have reaped down your fields, which
is of you kept back by fraud, crieth: and
the cries of them which have reaped are
entered into the ears of the Lord of

Chap. v. 1—6. Rebukes on the love of riches, and the vain confidence therein.

A.D. cir. 60.

---

(17) **Therefore . . . .**—A difficulty presents itself in this verse—whether the application be general, or a particular comment on the words preceding. Probably both ideas are correct. We learn the converse to the evil of vainglory in life, namely, the good which may be wrought by every one. Occasions of well-doing lie in the abject at our doors, and the pleadings of pity in our very hearts. And thus it is that omission is at times worse than commission; and more souls are in jeopardy for things left undone than for things done. In "The Beautiful Legend" there is a strife between the call of duty to give out a dole of bread to the hungry, and the temptation to linger in religious ecstasy over a vision of Christ. But the true brother knew "to do good," and did it; and, returning at the end of his work, found his cell full of the radiant presence of the Lord, and heard the words of rich approval—

"Hadst thou stayed, I must have fled."

And again, in another succession of thoughts on the text, God has no need of human knowledge; no, nor of our ignorance; "and it is a sin to shut the ears to instruction: it is a duty to get knowledge, to increase in knowledge, to abound in knowledge." Nor must we rest therein, but (2 Pet. i. 6, 7) "add to knowledge temperance, patience, godliness, brotherly kindness, charity."

V.

The first six verses, condemnatory of the trust in riches, ought to follow chap. iv. 17 without a break, and thus end the proper division of the Epistle. Our present arrangement of chapter and verse here, as in so many cases, tends to confusion rather than clearness.

(1) **Go to now, ye rich.**—As in chap. iv. 3, it was "Woe to you, worldly," so now "Woe to ye rich: weep, bewailing"—literally, *howling for your miseries coming upon you*. Comp. Isa. xiii. 6; xiv. 31, and xv. 3, where (in the LXX.) the same term is used;—a picture word, imitating the cry of anguish,—peculiar to this place in the New Testament. Observe the immediate future of the misery; it is already coming. Doubtless by this was meant primarily the pillage and destruction of Jerusalem, but under that first intention many others secondary and similar are included: for all "riches certainly make themselves wings" and fly away (Prov. xxiii. 5). Calvin and others of his school fail to see in this passage an exhortation of the rich to penitence, but only a denunciation of woe upon them; in the sense, however, that all prophecy, whether evil or good, is conditional, there is sufficient room to believe that no irrevocable doom was pronounced by "a Christian Jeremiah."

(2) **Your riches are corrupted . . .**—As expanded in the eloquent gloss of Bishop Wordsworth, "Your wealth is mouldering in corruption, and your garments, stored up in vain superfluity, are become moth-eaten: although they may still glitter brightly in your eyes, and may dazzle men by their brilliance, yet they are in fact already cankered; they are loathsome in God's sight; the Divine anger has breathed upon them and blighted them; they are already withered and blasted." (Comp. Matt. vi. 19.)

(3) **Your gold and silver . . .**—In like manner, the gold and silver are said to be "cankered," or eaten up with rust. The precious metals themselves do not corrode, but the base alloy does, which has been mixed with them for worldly use and device. *The rust of them shall be a witness to you*: not merely against, but convincing yourselves in the day of judgment; and, moreover, a sign of the fire which shall consume you. So will the wages of the traitor, and the harlot, the spoil of the thief and oppressor, burn the hands which have clutched them; the memories of the wrong shiver through each guilty soul, like the liquid fires which Muhammedans say torture the veins of the damned in the halls of Eblis.

Ye have heaped . . .—Read, *Ye heaped up treasures in the last days*:—the days of grace, given you for repentance, like the years when "the long-suffering of God waited in the days of Noah" (Gen. vi. 3; 1 Pet. iii. 20), or the time during which God bore with Canaan, "till the iniquity of the Amorite" was "full" (Gen. xv. 16).

Some expositors have seen in this verse an instance of James's belief that he was "living in the last days of the world's history;" and compared his delusion with that of Paul and John (1 Thess. iv. 15, and 1 John ii. 18). But there was no mistake on the part of the inspired writers; freedom from error in their sacred office must be vindicated, or who shall sever the false gospel from the true? The simple explanation is an old one—the *potential* nearness of Christ, as it is called. In many ways He has been ever near each individual, as by affliction, or death, or judgment; but His actual return was probably nearer in the first ages of faith than in the brutality of the tenth century, or the splendid atheism of the fifteenth, or the intellectual pride of the nineteenth. His advent is helped or hindered by the state of Christendom itself: "one day is with the Lord as a thousand years, and a thousand years as one day" (2 Pet. iii. 8), there is neither past nor future in His sight; only the presence of His own determination: and nought retards Christ's Second Coming so much as the false and feeble Christianity which prays "Thy kingdom come" in frequent words, but waits not as the handmaid of her Lord, with "loins girded about and lights burning" (Luke xii. 35), "until the day dawn, and the day-star arise" (2 Pet. i. 19).

(4) **Behold, the hire of the labourers.**—Not merely the wrong of the poor, but the wages kept back

sabaoth. (5) Ye have lived in pleasure on the earth, and been wanton; ye have nourished your hearts, as in a day of slaughter. (6) Ye have condemned *and* killed the just; *and* he doth not resist you.
(7) Be patient [1] therefore, brethren,

[1] Or, *Be long patient, or, suffer with long patience.*

---

from him by the niggardly master, contrary to the merciful Jewish law (Lev. xix. 13), which permitted no delay in payment whatever (comp. Jer. xxii. 13; Mal. iii. 5). And the indignant remonstrance of the text is "a swift witness" also against the like-minded of this generation—whose God is self, whose religion political economy, and whose one great object in life is to buy in the cheapest market and sell in the dearest: as if for these ignoble purposes the Lord God had given them a brain and a soul.

The hire of the labourers . . . kept back by fraud, crieth (*out*).—A question has arisen concerning the right position of the word translated "of," or *from you*, in this clause; whether the withholden dues appeal "*from* the wronger to God," or as the Authorised version has it above, "the hire of the labourers *of* you kept back by fraud." The balance of opinion seems to be with the latter.

Are entered into the ears of the Lord of sabaoth.—"A sublime and awful picture" is in the mind of the Apostle. *The Lord of Hosts*, the name by which He is called, especially by the last of the prophets, Malachi, is seated as a judge on His throne, to hear the right; the charge is laid, the guilty called, the witnesses are heard: the cries of the wronged *have entered* into His ears:—

"The Lord of the Vineyard beholdeth afar;
The arm of His fury is bared to the war:
The day of His terrible wrath is at hand."

It is the reflection of our own Bede that St. James thus speaks (comp. Rom. ix. 29) of the Lord of Sabaoth, or *armies*, to terrify those who suppose that the poor have no helpers. (Comp. Ps. lxxii. 12.) God's majestic title is proclaimed, we may believe, by an Hebrew to Hebrews, for a warning against their darling sin of covetousness, and in hope that the vision of Isaiah (chap. vi. 1—4) would move them to consider who and what the Lord of Hosts, of angels, of cherubim, of seraphim, might be "when He maketh inquisition for blood," forgetting not the complaint of the poor" (Ps. ix. 12).

(5) **Ye have lived in pleasure.**—And what an indictment is this brought against them by the Apostle:—*Ye revelled upon earth, and wantoned; ye nourished your hearts in a day of slaughter.* The pleasure and wantonness wherein the rich had lived, the selfishness with which they had cared for their own hearts, in a time of death for others—nay, preparation of like for themselves: this is the aggravated wrong, and the inexpiable shame. In the Received text above they are accused of having "nourished their hearts *as* in a day of slaughter," the cries of the victims thus seeming an addition to their own delights; but the charge against them is heavy enough without this insertion.

As they had dealt to others, so the vengeance of God dealt with them. The Passover called together the richest Jews from all parts of the earth, and they themselves were the victims in their last sacrifice. No words can overdraw the fury of the Roman onset, under Titus, when the Temple floors ran with blood, and the roofs raged in fire till all was utter desolation.

(6) **Ye have condemned and killed the just.**—Better thus: *Ye condemned, ye slew the just*—as in the speech of Peter (Acts iii. 14, 15), or that of Stephen (Acts vii. 52). Such a reference, however, has been disallowed by some commentators as conveying too harsh an accusation against the whole Jewish people; and besides, it being unfair to forget that St. James was writing to Christian Jews, as well as to the anti-Christian. But, in a manner, all wrong and oppression tend towards the murder of the Just One, as every falsehood (see Note on chap. iii. 13) is an attack on the Truth. And far beyond this, in the present case our Lord is rightly to be considered the victim of the Jews. His blood is on them and on their children (Matt. xxvii. 25); they filled up "the measure of their fathers" (Matt. xxiii. 32), that "the blood of all the righteous" might come upon them, from Abel to Zacharias (Matt. xxiii. 35): the one crowning sin made them guilty of all. And not only is this backward participation true, but there is a forward one as well. Christ Himself was persecuted by Saul in the afflictions of His servants (Acts ix. 4, 5), and so onward ever till the martyr-roll be full.

It is of strange significance that in this verse—*ye condemned, ye slew the just*—James the Just prophetically described his own murderers. The last words, moreover, of the Scripture, simply record the behaviour of himself, as of every real witness for Christ: *He doth not resist.* No: "the servant of the Lord must not strive" (2 Tim. ii. 24) even in death; and by such meekness and resignation is best seen the likeness to the divine Master, Who "was brought as a lamb to the slaughter" (Isa. liii. 7). Comp. Wisd. ii. 10—20 for a striking parallel, on the oppression of the righteous, which would not inaptly describe *the* "just man," *the* "Son of God."

(7) **Be patient.**—The third, and last, part of the Letter commences here with these exhortations towards endurance.

Therefore—*i.e.*, because of this your deep and abiding misery, be sure God's help is nigh:—

"The darkest hour is on the verge of day."

"Out of your stony griefs" build, like Jacob of old, a house of God (Gen. xxviii. 19), whereunto you may run and find refuge. If there be wrath laid up in store for the oppressor, great is the coming peace of the oppressed.

The husbandman waiteth for the precious fruit of the earth, and hath long patience for it . . . Be ye also patient.—It becomes you, the just, to bear with the unjust till God work the end of your trial, and prove them at the same time. Again and again, through several verses (7—11), St. James repeats his advice, emphasising it with various reasons: the nearness of deliverance; the Judge standing at the gate; the example of the prophets—persecuted by men, and therefore blessed of God; the hope of those who endure—Job for example: the very faithfulness and tender mercy of the Lord, bringing all things to a perfect end. Few ideas are more startling (is a reflection of Dr. Evans) than those produced by the strange combinations in Scripture. Matters are joined there which we mostly put asunder here, speaking of

unto the coming of the Lord. Behold, the husbandman waiteth for the precious fruit of the earth, and hath long patience for it, until he receive the early and latter rain. (8) Be ye also patient; stablish your hearts: for the coming of the Lord draweth nigh. (9) Grudge not[1] one against another, brethren, lest ye be condemned: behold, the judge standeth before the door. (10) Take, my brethren, the prophets, who have spoken in the name of the Lord, for an example of suffering affliction, and of patience. (11) Behold, we count them happy which endure. Ye have heard of the patience

Chap. v. 7—11. Exhortations of patience to the afflicted, with the assurance of God's deliverance—examples of old time.

1 Or, *Groan*, or, *grieve not.*

---

them, at least, as apart. And thus we read in the Revelation (chap. i. 9) of the *kingdom and patience* of Jesus Christ. But all Christians are citizens of a patient kingdom; the King thereof is more patient, as He hath greater need of patience than His subjects, and He is patient, because He is strong. Impatience is a sign of weakness. God can afford to wait, for His time is eternity. And we can be strong in His strength, and wait also in patience. In so far as St. James's hearers were earthly minded, they could not learn this lesson; so often with ourselves we would have our wrong righted instantly, and to the full. Only one view of life can alter this, viz., the lifting of our gaze from earth to heaven, remembering that "the time is short" (1 Cor. vii. 29).

The early and latter rain.—It is, perhaps, just as well to recollect there were only two seasons of rainfall in the Holy Land, and, if long delayed, famine was a certain result. With the change of the Israelites from pastoral life to agricultural, the malignity of these dearths was lessened; but they were and are still severe. The Bible mentions many such—*e.g.*, in the days of Abraham (Gen. xii. 10), Isaac (Gen. xxvi. 1), Jacob (Gen. xlii. 2), Ruth (chap. i. 1), Samuel (2 Sam. xxi. 1), Ahab (1 Kings xviii. 2). The "early rain" fell during the autumn sowing—in October, November, and December; "the latter" in March and April. By many versions the word "rain" is omitted, but, of course, was always intended.

(8) **The coming of the Lord draweth nigh.**—Read thus, *The presence of the Lord is nigh.* For the ancient belief in the nearness of Christ's second advent, see Note above, in verse 3. The word used by the Apostle to describe its closeness is the same as that used in Matt. iii. 2, "The kingdom of heaven is *at hand.*" The afflicted are therefore to stablish, or rather *strengthen*, their hearts. If "comfort" retained its older sense, such would express the true idea. Comp. the great prophecy of Israel's consolation (Isa. xl., *et seq.*).

(9) **Grudge not.**—Say in preference, *Murmur not.* "Grudge" has curiously changed its meaning from an outward murmur to an inward feeling. It has unfortunately been retained both here and in 1 Pet. iv. 9. See also Ps. lix. 15, specially the Prayer Book version, "They will . . . *grudge* if they be not satisfied"—*i.e.*, complain and murmur.

Lest ye . . .—It is not "lest ye be condemned," but *lest ye be judged*, repeating the exact words of the original in Matt. vii. 1.

Behold, the judge standeth before the door.—Compare this scene with that depicted in Rev. iii. 20. In the one Christ lingers mercifully outside the door that "loves its hinge"; fain would He enter and abide. In the other He sounds a note of alarm; men are "waked in the night, not girding their loins for a journey, but in vague wonder at uncertain noise, who may turn again to their slumber," or in wistful listening wait in vain for the voice of mercy which shall plead with them no more for ever (Ruskin).

One of the mocking questions put to St. James by his enemies, as they hurried him to death, was, "Which is the *door* of Jesus?" And failing to receive an answer to their mind, they said, "Let us stone this James the Just!" which they did, after they had cast him over the Temple wall.

(10) **For an example.**—Another reason for endurance, *an example of affliction and patience, the prophets who spoke in the name of the Lord.* These are the bright ones in the cloud of witnesses, of whom the Epistle to the Hebrews (chap. xii. 32—38) speaks, who, like Daniel, "stopped the mouths of lions"; like Jeremiah and Elijah, "escaped the edge of the sword;" "out of weakness were made strong"; who "were stoned," like Zachariah; "sawn asunder," like Isaiah; "slain with the sword," like Urijah and John; "of whom the world was not worthy." Thus the saints of the Old Covenant are held up for honour and imitation to those of the New. James was not advocating a religion alien to that of Moses, but building again more widely "the ruins of the tabernacle which had fallen down," that "all the Gentiles might seek after the Lord." (Comp. his speech in the synod, Acts xv. 13—21.)

(11) **We count them happy which endure.**—Rather read it, *we count them blessed which endure*; or, as some critics would have it, *endured.* (See Matt. v. 11, and 1 Pet. ii. 19.) The heathen philosopher Solon called no one "happy" upon earth; but, with the mystery of pain around him, cried sadly, "Look to the end." And the sated and weary soul of Solomon had no better thought than to praise "the dead which are already dead, more than the living" (Eccles. iv. 2). How different the teaching of St. James, himself taught by the example of the suffering Christ: verily, "he that is least in the kingdom of heaven is greater than" the greatest and the wisest who know not of its light and peace (Matt. xi. 11).

The patience of Job.—The earliest notions current in the world were, doubtless, that on the whole prosperity came to those who lived morally and physically well, while adversity in body or mind followed closely on the wicked and improvident. It is easy to see how these opinions, even among the happier races who had not wandered far from God, gradually hardened into stern rules of judgment, by which each man saw in the chances and calamities of life an immediate effort of an avenging Deity. This was ages before a pious Asaph (Ps. lxxiii.) could reflect on the contradiction of experience in this matter, and be troubled at the "prosperity" of the wicked; or before the wise king could notice (Eccles. vii. 15, and viii. 14) the just man perishing "in his righteousness," and the unjust prolonging "his days in wickedness"; "the

of Job, and have seen the end of the
Lord; that the Lord is very pitiful, and
of tender mercy.
(12) But above all things, my brethren,
swear not, neither by
heaven, neither by the
earth, neither by any other
oath: but let your yea be yea; and
your nay, nay; lest ye fall into condemnation.
(13) Is any among you
afflicted? let him pray.
Is any merry? let him
sing psalms.

Chap. v. 12. Caution against swearing.

Chap. v. 13. Advice to sorrowful and joyful

fishes taken in an evil net," and "the birds caught in the snare" (Eccles. ix. 12). It was ages earlier still than the presence of that Wiser than Solomon, who spoke of the hapless "eighteen on whom the tower in Siloam fell"—"Think ye that they were sinners above all?" (Luke xiii. 4, 5). Job's friends were so certain of his misdeeds, that they would not hear his self-defence; if God tried his endurance, man surely afflicted his patience. We can hear the three in council against him, becoming more zealous as they believe themselves the defenders of God's justice. (See Job iv.—xxii.) They are shocked at Job's obstinacy, and annoyed into vehement accusation against him, because he will "hold fast" to his "integrity." It is a damning proof to them of his guilt. Not only had he been wicked, but now actually he is impious and rebellious; such conduct is not to be borne. "Is not thy wickedness great?" says Eliphaz (Job xxii. 5). Thou must have—nay, "thou hast taken a pledge from thy brother for nought, and stripped the naked of their clothing;" thou couldst not—nay, "thou hast not given water to the weary, and thou hast withholden bread from the hungry:" truly thine iniquities are infinite." Now, we know Job was innocent; God Himself bears witness to it (Job i. 8). And finally the suffering, patient, righteous man was declared to have spoken wisely: as Eliphaz, Bildad, and Zophar the contrary. They—types of a censorious piety—had conceived of God by their own faulty notions of religion, and fondly deemed they could enter into the motives of the Most High. Job for awhile had seemed to cloud his own belief with baser attributes, as (Job xvi. *et seq.*) to a God who causelessly dealt in cruelty and pain; but through such fleeting mistakes he rose at last to the full conviction of His perfect truth and justice. It might be that He gave happiness to those who sought Him; it might be He allowed them misery—as the world would call it; but this nor that had part in the matter at issue. Earthly blessings "He gives to whom He wills, or leaves to the powers of nature to distribute among those who fulfil the laws" thereof; but "to serve him and love Him is higher and better than any mundane welfare, though it be with wounded feet and bleeding forehead, or an ash-heap and filthy sores" (Froude). This was the faith to which Job attained: higher, "clearer, purer, there is not possible to man." In such like "patience" it were well for us that we should "possess our souls" (Luke xxi. 19).

And have seen the end of the Lord.—Better thus, *Ye have heard . . . see also the end of the Lord.* The reference is at once past and future: consider, *i.e.*, what God wrought in the end of trial, on the faithful of old time, like Job; learn from it how great a deliverance He will also work for you. But "if ye will not believe, surely ye shall not be established" (Isa. vii. 9). It is a mistake to understand here any allusion to the death of Christ, as if the Apostle spoke to those who witnessed it.

That the Lord is very pitiful.—St. James, in the fulness of his gratitude, seems to have coined a word for this single place. "Great-hearted" would be close to its meaning; but originally the *bowels* were thought to be the seat of the affections, and hence such terms of expression: as also in Gen. xliii. 30; 1 Kings iii. 26; Isa. lxiii. 15; Lam. i. 20; Phil. i. 8; 1 John iii. 17, *et al.*

"The Lord" here is Jehovah: under which name the Lord spake and wrought before He was made man. See Bishop Pearson *On the Creed*, in Article 2, proving the significance of κύριος, or *Lord*, as the right translation of the Hebrew *El*, *Elohim*, *Shaddai*, *Adonai*, and *Jehovah*. And compare Isa. xl. 3 with Matt. iii. 1; Mal. iii. 1 with Matt. xi. 10 and Jer. xxiii. 6.

(12) The question of the lawfulness of oaths has oftentimes perplexed alike the doctors of the Church and its simpler hearers of God's word. The text, taken as it stands, would support the views of the Essenes, and many of the Paulicians, and other ancient sectaries. With equal force it might be urged by the followers of Peter Waldo, or the Unitas Fratrum (the Moravians), or the Society of Friends.

Swear not.—The words are put quite distinctly in Greek and English—*neither by the heaven, nor by the earth.* And it sounds like special pleading, worthy of a rabbi, to hear such a divine as Huther say that "swearing by the name of God is not mentioned," nor accordingly is such an oath prohibited. "We must not imagine," he continues (and his argument had best be fairly given), "that this is included in the last member of the clause, the Apostle evidently intending by it (*i.e.*, 'neither by any other oath') to point only at certain formulæ, of which several are mentioned in Matt. v. 34—37. Had he intended to forbid swearing by the name of God he would most certainly have mentioned it expressly; for not only is it in the Law, in contradistinction to other oaths, commanded (see Deut. vi. 13; x. 20; Ps. lxiii. 11), but in the prophets is announced as a token of the future turning of men to God" (Isa. lxv. 16; Jer. xii. 16; xxiii. 7, 8). There were, we learn, many subtle distinctions in Jewish oaths; and the unlucky foreigner who trusted in an apparently firm one, too often found out his mistake. Certainly all such subterfuges are utterly condemned; and further, every word which breaks the letter or spirit of God's Third Commandment. As to the higher judicial forms of oaths, remembering that our Lord answered such before Caiaphas (Matt. xxvi. 63, 64), we can fearlessly conclude, with the 39th Article of Religion, that "a man may swear, when the magistrate requireth, in a cause of faith and charity, so it be done according to the prophet's teaching—in justice, judgment, and truth."

Let your yea be yea . . .—Your word be as your bond, needing no strengthening by any invocation of God, or holy things, "lest ye fall into *judgment*"—not "condemnation," though certainly such might follow.

(13) We now pass on to advice of different kinds—to the heavy-laden or light-hearted, to the suffering and

Chap. v. 14. 15. Counsel for the sick: the anointing with oil, and praying over them in faith.

(14) Is any sick among you? let him call for the elders of the church; and let them pray over him, anointing him with oil in the name of the Lord: (15) and the prayer of faith shall save the sick, and the Lord shall raise him up; and if he have committed sins, they shall be forgiven him.

---

afflicted. Prayer is to be the refuge of one, praise the safeguard of another; the whole life is to revolve, as it were, around the throne of God, whether in the night of grief or day of joy.

Let him pray.—No worthier comment can be found than Montgomery's hymn—

> "Prayer is the burden of a sigh,
> The falling of a tear,
> The upward glancing of an eye,
> When none but God is near."

Long petitions, or many, cannot be always made; mind and body may be too weak and ill; but ejaculations—"Arrows of the Lord's deliverance," as Augustine called them, "shot out with a sudden quickness"—these are ever in the power of the beleagured Christian. And—

> "More things are wrought by prayer
> Than this world dreams of."

Let him sing.—The word originally applied to instrumental music, the Eastern accompaniment of "psalms." Praise, like prayer, ought to be individual as well as congregational. Hymns might be used by all in their devotions, and could not fail to be a blessing; while for those who have God's great gift of music, it were surely better to sing—as the Apostle urges—than to say. There is a sadness latent in the most jubilant of earthly tunes, but not so with the heavenly; and quiring angels do not scorn to catch our humblest notes, and weave them in their endless song, if they be raised in thankfulness to Him Whom they and all creation praise.

(14) **The elders of the church**—*i.e.*, literally, *the presbyters*. The identity of "bishop" (*episcopus*) and "presbyter" in the language of the apostolic age seems conclusive. Such is the opinion of Lightfoot (*Epistle to the Philippians*, 93—97; see also his *Dissertation on the Christian Ministry*, *ibid.*, 180—267), and few may hope to gainsay it. In fact, the organisation of the early Church was much more elastic than theologians always suppose; and names and terms were applied less rigidly than the schoolmen of the Middle Ages have so stoutly declared. But, on the other hand, no man who has read the *Patres Apostolici* can deny the reality of Church government as enforced by them, nor base on their authority any defence of congregationalism or the rule of a mere presbytery. The theory of development must be maintained, though not on the lines of Dr. Newman.

(14, 15) **Anointing him with oil.**—Or, *unction*. The use of some precious and mysterious ointment, on solemn occasions, obtained in most of the ancient nations, specially the Eastern. The Jews themselves were by no means originators of the habit, although they carried it to its highest ceremonial and significance. Apart, too, from the regular performances of the rite, as upon the accession of a king, or the consecration of a high priest, it often occurred in private cases, and some striking instances are recorded in the Gospels:—the spikenard, costly and fragrant (Luke vii. 36—50), wherewith the Saviour's feet were anointed by "a woman which was a sinner;" and that, again, which Mary, of her grateful love, poured upon Him six days before His death (John xii. 3—9). These were not unusual acts, but chiefly worthy of note because of the persons concerned. It was not remarkable for women to make such offerings to a famous rabbi, but that our Lord should be so treated, carried a deeper meaning. Nor, again, was it a new ordinance with which the Apostles were first commissioned, in pursuance whereof they "anointed with oil many that were sick, and healed them" (Mark vi. 13). "Here," observes Bishop Harold Browne, "unction was evidently an outward sign, similar to that used by our Saviour, when He made clay, and put it to the blind man's eyes. It was connected with the miraculous power of healing." This connection only, this use of a known form with a diviner import, was the cause of astonishment; and clearly it was to such a practice, with simply its common intention, that St. James refers. Nor can we refrain from saying, however undesirous of controversy, that all which unction now implies to the Romanist is quite opposed to whatever force and value are given it in Holy Writ. There unction is enjoined "with the special object of recovery;" its purport was a present bodily one, and in no way applicable to the future of the soul. "The prayer of faith shall save the sick"—*i.e.*, shall *heal* him: the faithful prayer shall be that which God will answer, and so "*raise up*" the sufferer. But, it is urged, the next clause has a different force: "If he have committed sins, they shall be forgiven him." Such is only apparent in our own version, and not in the original. The grammatical sense infers that the sick man is abiding under the consequence of some committed sin, which is "presumed to have been the working cause of his present sickness." So Alford, and Bede similarly: "Many by reason of sins done in the soul are compassed by weakness: nay, even death of the body." And the former theologian again: "Among all the daring perversions of Scripture, by which the Church of Rome has defended her superstitions, there is none more patent than that of the present passage. Not without reason has the Council of Trent defended its misinterpretation with anathema; for indeed it needed that, and every other recommendation, to support it, and give it any kind of acceptance. The Apostle is treating of a matter totally distinct from the occasion and the object of extreme unction. He is enforcing the efficacy of the prayer of faith in afflictions (verse 13). Of such efficacy he adduces one special instance. In sickness let the sick man inform the elders of the church. Let them, representing the congregation of the faithful, pray over the sick man, accompanying that prayer with the symbolic and sacramental act of anointing with oil in the name of our Lord. Then the prayer of faith shall save (*heal*) the sick man, and the Lord shall bring him up out of his sickness; and even if it were occasioned by some sin, that sin shall be forgiven him. Such is the simple and undeniable sense of the Apostle, arguing for the efficacy of prayer; and such the perversion of that sense by the Church of Rome." Not that we should think this and other like cases are wholly intentional twistings of God's word. The Latin Bible is in many

Chap. v. 16. Mutual confession of faults.

(16) Confess *your* faults one to another, and pray one for another, that ye may be healed. The effectual fervent

places a faulty—though not deliberately unfaithful—rendering of the Hebrew and Greek; and half our differences with Rome arise from such misinterpretations. Allowing the beginning of mischief to have been oftentimes a wrong translation, religious opinions engendered from it, we can understand, would be hardly cast aside, more especially when advantageous to their possessors. Little by little the change of doctrine drew on, and most probably thus:—The aim of the apostolic anointing was bodily recovery, and (again we quote Bishop Browne) "this exactly corresponds with the miraculous cures of early ages; . . . so long as such . . . powers remained in the Church, it was reasonable that anointing of the sick should be retained." But these powers ceased, in the wisdom of God, after awhile; not so, however, the ceremony to which men's minds in distress had been accustomed. It was retained in affection when its true force had departed. But since no outward result remained visible, fervent and mystical teachers could not well avoid searching for the invisible; and thus the area of operations was removed from the flesh to the spirit. The words of Holy Scripture would, with a little straining, bear such a colourable translation: and so was laid the foundation of that belief now current in a great part of Christendom. The Greek Church still practices unction, but rather in memory of a venerated custom, wherein God's mercy was aforetime present; the Latin, unfortunately, is bound by its Council of Trent (*Sessio* xiv.) to believe "extreme unction to be a sacrament, instituted by Christ, conferring good, remitting sins, and comforting the infirm." Its authorised manual of devotion—*The Crown of Jesus* (p. 710)—says, "Our Lord and Saviour Jesus Christ, in His tender solicitude for those whom He has redeemed by His precious blood, has been pleased to institute another sacrament, to help us at that most important hour on which eternity depends—the hour of death. This sacrament is called Extreme Unction, or the last anointing." And further explains, "The priest, in administering this sacrament, anoints the five principal senses of the body—the eyes, the ears, the nostrils, the lips, the hands and the feet—because these have been employed during life in offending God. At each anointing he pronounces these words: 'May the Lord by this holy anointing, and by His own most tender mercy, pardon thee whatever sin thou hast committed, by thy sight, hearing,' &c. . . ." Notwithstanding this lamentable departure from right exegesis, some divines think it wise and well to reflect how far with profit the ancient ceremony could be revived; while others would rather let it slumber with the past. "When miraculous powers ceased, it was reasonable that the unction should cease also." Still more reasonable is it that even the form or memorial, however touching and beautiful, should be abandoned, rather than we should seem by it to be at one with the changed—alas! the false—teaching of that Church of man's tradition, Rome.

(16) **Confess your faults one to another.**—The meaning attributed to the words of this verse by many devout Catholics cannot be established either from the opinion of antiquity, or a critical examination of the Greek text according to modern schools. "We have," observes Alford, "*a general injunction* arising out of a circumstance necessarily to be inferred in the preceding example (verses 14, 15). There, the sin would of necessity have been confessed to the elders, before the prayer of faith could deal with it. And seeing the blessed consequences in that case 'generally,' says the Apostle, in all similar cases, and 'one to another universally, pursue the same salutary practice of confessing your sins . . .' *Confess therefore one to another*—not only to the elders (*presbyters*) in the case supposed, but to one another generally—*your transgressions, and pray for one another that ye may be healed*, in case of sickness, as above. The context here forbids any wider meaning . . . and it might appear astonishing, were it not notorious, that on this passage, among others, is built the Romish doctrine of the necessity of confessing sins to a priest."

Not that all Roman Catholic divines, indeed, have thus read the injunction. Some of the ablest and greatest have admitted "that we cannot certainly affirm sacramental confession to have been meant or spoken of in this place" (Hooker). How then did the gradual perversion take hold of men's minds? The most laborious investigation of history and theology will alone answer the question properly; and here only a brief *résumé* is possible. There can be little doubt that, strictly consonant with the apostolic charge, open confession was the custom of old. Offenders hastened to some minister of God, and in words, by which all present in the congregation might take notice of the fault, declared their guilt; convenient remedies were as publicly prescribed, and then all present joined in prayer to God. But after awhile, for many patent reasons, this plain talk about sins was rightly judged to be a cause of mischief to the young and innocent; and such confessions were relegated to a private hearing. The change was in most ways beneficial, and hardly suspected of being a step in a completely new doctrine. It needed years—centuries, in fact—to develop into the hard system of compulsory individual bondage which cost Europe untold blood and treasure to break asunder. A salutary practice in the case of some unhappy creatures, weakened by their vices into a habit of continual sin, was scarcely to be conceived as a rule thrust upon all the Christian world. Yet such it was, and "at length auricular confession, followed by absolution and satisfaction, was elevated to the full dignity of a necessary sacrament. The Council of Trent anathematises all who deny it to be truly and properly a sacrament instituted by Christ Himself, and necessary to salvation (*jure divino*); or who say that the method of confessing secretly to the priest alone . . . is alien to Christ's institution, and of human invention" (Harold Browne). Marvellous perversity of acute brains and worthy sentiment, showing only how steep is the way of error; and how for Christian as for Jew the danger of tradition is perilous indeed. "To conclude," in the words of Hooker, "we everywhere find the use of confession, especially public, allowed of, and commended by the fathers; but that extreme and rigorous necessity of auricular and private confession, which is at this day so mightily upheld by the Church of Rome, we find not. It was not then the faith and doctrine of God's Church, as of the Papacy at this present—(1) that the only remedy for sin after baptism is sacramental penitency; (2) that confession in secret is an essential part thereof; (3) that God Himself cannot now forgive sins without the priest; (4) that because

prayer of a righteous man availeth
much.
(17) Elias was a man subject to like
passions as we are, and
he prayed earnestly[1] that
it might not rain: and it
rained not on the earth by
the space of three years
and six months. (18) And he prayed
again, and the heaven gave rain,
and the earth brought forth her
fruit.

Chap. v. 17, 18. The effect of fervent prayer; the example of Elijah.

(19) Brethren, if any of you do err from
the truth, and one convert
him; (20) let him know,
that he which converteth
the sinner from the error
of his way shall save a
soul from death, and shall hide a multi-
tude of sins.

Chap. v. 19, 20. Of conversion: the blessedness of bringing home the lost.

[1] Or, *in his prayer.*

---

forgiveness at the hands of the priests must arise from confession in the offender, therefore to confess unto him is a matter of such necessity as, being not either in deed, or, at the least, in desire, performed, excludeth utterly from all pardon, and must consequently in Scripture be commanded wheresoever any promise of forgiveness is made. No, no; these opinions have youth in their countenance. Antiquity knew them not; it never thought nor dreamed of them" (*E. P.*, vi. iv. 14).

"As for private confession," says Jewel in his *Apology*, "abuses and errors set apart, we condemn it not, but leave it at liberty." Such must be the teaching of any Church which, in the epigram of Bishop Ken, "stands distinguished from all papal and puritan innovations," resting upon God's Word, and the earliest, holiest, simplest, best traditions of the Apostles of His dear Son. And if an ancient custom has become a universal practice in the Latin communion, presumed to be of sacramental virtue, scholars will tell us that the notion has never been absent altogether from any branch of the Catholic Church; and that in some shape or form, it lives in most of those societies which sprang into existence at the Reformation largely from abhorrence of the tyranny and misuse of confession.

The effectual fervent prayer . . .—Better, *The prayer of a righteous man availeth much in its working.* It moves the hand of Him Who moves the world.

> "What are men better than sheep, or goats,
> That nourish a blind life within the brain,
> If, knowing God, they lift not hands of prayer—
> Both for themselves, and those who call them friend?
> For so the whole round earth is, every way,
> Bound by gold chains about the feet of God."

In Matt. xiv. 2, and Mark vi. 14, we read of John the Baptist, that "mighty works do *show forth* themselves in him." A nearer approach to the sense would be "they work"—*energise*, if we might coin a word; and such is also the meaning of the present passage—the prayer of the just, pleading, striving fervently, hath power with God, even like Israel of old, and sha'l prevail (Gen. xxxii. 28). Some divines trace a literal force in the passage, finding in it an allusion to the Energumens of the first century (the "mediums" of that age), who were possessed by demons; that, just as these unhappy beings strove in their bondage, so equally—nay, infinitely more—should Christians "wrestle with the Lord."

(17) **Elias.**—James supplies a lacuna in the story of Elijah. In 1 Kings xvii. 1, the prophet simply and sternly tells Ahab "there shall not be dew nor rain these years, but according to my word." Further on (1 Kings xvii. 41—46) "there is a sound of abundance of rain." In our Epistle we read that Elias "prayed earnestly"—literally, *prayed in his prayer*, a Hebraistic form of emphasis (see margin). He asked for drought, and it lasted three years and a half, so that "there was a sore famine in Samaria." He prayed once more, and "the heaven was black with clouds and wind, and there was a great rain," and thus again "the Lord hearkened unto the voice of a man." Yet Elijah was no demi-god; we even learn how he shrank from his prophet's yoke, and longed to die. No one therefore may despair in his petitions but rather let his "requests be made known unto God;" for "men ought always to pray, and not to faint" (Luke xviii. 1).

It rained not on the earth.—This Orientalism need not be a snare to the most literal of readers. The punishment, because of Ahab and Jezebel, fell on their own kingdom, and not the whole world. In a similar hyperbole Obadiah told Elijah, concerning this very famine, "there is no nation, or kingdom, whither my lord hath not sent to seek thee" (1 Kings xviii. 10).

(19) **Brethren.**—*My brethren*, it rather ought to be. The last, and, to some, the dearest of the wise Apostle's remarks, is this on conversion; and it fitly closes his loving and plain-speaking Letter.

If any of you do err . . .—Better thus, *If one of you be led away from the truth, and one convert him.* It is not the wilful error, so much as the being seduced by others, who draw the unwary from their proper course, till in time they become of themselves "wandering stars, to whom is reserved the blackness of darkness for ever" (Jude, verse 13). As the leading away was an act prompted by the devil, so the bringing home is the service of God, and each will have its fit reward. The sinner is riding, as it were, headlong to destruction, when a friend lays hold upon the rein, and literally "converts" him, *i.e.*, turns him round; but, observe, the wanderer is still far from home, and many a weary league must he traverse, even with face turned and kept heavenward, before the end be neared.

(20) **Let him know.**—Or, as it rather seems to be, *Know ye:* be absolutely sure of this, in a knowledge better than all the Gnostic and Agnostic learning of the day. *He which turneth a sinner from the error of his way shall save a soul from death*—the means thereto being given him by the Saviour of all—*and shall hide a multitude of sins;* not, of course, his own, but those of the penitent, brought back by this good servant into the fold. So is it possible to be a fellow-worker with Christ (2 Cor. vi. 1), and a sharer in His work of salvation, as, in another sense, we too vicariously suffer for the sins and faults of others. (Comp. Col. i. 24, and Butler's *Analogy*, part 2, chap. v.)

What St. James was in word that also was he in deed; for he "prayed fervently" for the pardon and conversion of those who killed him. "Hold," said some of the by-standers, when the martyr sank upon the stones, "the Just is praying for you!" Stephen's prayer won Saul for the infant Church: it can hardly be that James's last breathings of pity were unanswered of God.

INTRODUCTION

TO

THE FIRST EPISTLE GENERAL OF

PETER

I. **The Author.**—The authorship of this Epistle can hardly be called a matter of question. If it be not St. Peter's own, we have no choice but to set it down as an impudent forgery. It claims directly, and in the simplest form, to be the writing of the chief Apostle of our Lord (chap. i. 1). The author asserts himself to be a "witness of the sufferings of Christ" (chap. v. 1), and yet does it so modestly and with such absence of detail as would be inconceivable in a forger acquainted with St. Peter's history. The enthusiastic and impassioned style of the Letter corresponds with the character of St. Peter as we find it recorded in history; and in several marked points not only the doctrinal statements, but even the literary style and turn of the sentences, recalls the style of St. Peter's speeches in the Acts. The fact that the Letter was written in Greek (for the adjectives alone are sufficient disproof of the theory that it is a translation from an Aramaic original) is no objection to the Petrine authorship. Galilee was a half-Greek country, studded with Greek cities; St. Peter's brother bore a Greek name. No Galilean of the middle classes (to which St. Peter evidently belonged) could have been ignorant of the language; indeed, there is sufficient evidence that Greek was as much used in Galilee as Aramaic.

It seems that no question was entertained until the nineteenth century with regard to the genuineness of the Epistle by any church, or by any individual, whether orthodox or heretical. The Epistle was, indeed, rejected by Marcion, but distinctly on the ground that it *was* St. Peter's. Origen speaks of it as one of the books whose authority had never been disputed. The Second Epistle of St. Peter, which, even if not genuine, cannot be dated later than the early part of the second century, refers back to it, and refers to it expressly as the work of St. Peter. St. Clement of Rome, writing (probably) A.D. 95, though he does not directly quote from it with marks of citation, has expressions such as "His marvellous light," and several others less marked, which seem certainly to indicate his acquaintance with it. St. Polycarp (about 115 A.D.), bishop of one of the churches to which the Epistle was addressed, within the compass of one short letter to the Philippians, cites it again and again—*e.g.*, "In whom, though ye never saw Him, ye believe, and believing ye rejoice;" "not rendering evil for evil, or railing for railing;" and many other passages. St. Polycarp's friend Papias (according to Eusebius) made use of this Epistle too, and seems to have made special comments on the connection between St. Peter and St. Mark. Besides traces of the use of it to be found in Hermas, Theophilus, and others, it is freely quoted, and by name, by Irenæus, Clement of Alexandria, Tertullian, and all subsequent writers. In fact, it would be difficult to imagine stronger external evidence in its favour. M. Renan, to take one example of an historical critic whose theology is not that of St. Peter, writes: "If, as we are happy to believe, this Epistle is really Peter's, it does honour to his good sense, his straightforwardness, and his simplicity;" and he gives many good reasons for his belief.

There is but one argument against the genuineness of the Epistle to which any weight at all can be assigned, and even this loses all its force when it is examined. "As for the eclectic and conciliatory tendencies observed in the Epistle of Peter," writes M. Renan (*Antéchrist*, p. ix.), "they constitute no objection to any but those who, like Christian Baur and his disciples, imagine the difference between Peter and Paul to have been one of absolute opposition. Had the hatred between the two parties of primitive Christianity been as profound as is thought by that school, the reconciliation would *never* have been made. Peter was not an obstinate Jew like James." Without necessarily agreeing in this description of James, we may well accept the statement that St. Peter was a man peculiarly susceptible of impressions, and (even putting out of view the two Epistles in our Canon) his admiration, and indeed his awe of St. Paul are visible to any reader of the Acts and the Epistle to the Galatians. No writer recognises them more frankly than M. Renan (*Saint Paul*, pp. 85, 86). Now, on the one hand, it is very easy to exaggerate the Pauline character of this Epistle. It contains no one doctrine, such as Justification by Faith, which is essentially bound up with the name of St. Paul. On the matter of the free admission of Gentiles into the Church (which indirectly forms a large element in this Epistle) St. Peter had made up his mind long years before he came much under the influence of St. Paul (Acts x. 34; xi. 17; xv. 11). But on the other hand, there were special reasons why, in this Epistle, all St. Peter's sympathy for his co-Apostle should come out. He was using, either as his secretary or as his letter-bearer—perhaps in both capacities—that liberal-minded Silas (chap. v. 12), who, after being chosen by the Church of Jerusalem as their own exponent to the Gentiles of Antioch, had attached himself to St. Paul, accompanied him in the most momentous of his missionary travels, and had (apparently) devoted himself to the edification and extension of those Asiatic churches which the two had founded together. St. Mark, too, dear to St. Peter as his own "son" in the faith (chap. v. 13), had been but recently again (after early misunderstandings) a chosen companion of St. Paul, and was probably not very long returned from a mission on which that Apostle had despatched him into Asia Minor (Col. iv. 10). And, moreover, all St. Peter's chivalrous nature would be aroused by the manner in which the churches of all that region, or any rate the Jewish element in them, were beginning to revolt (as at Corinth also) against their founder when his back was turned.

II. The Place, Time, and Occasion of the Epistle.—The place from which the Letter was written was, we may say without any hesitation, Rome. If this be not the case, we must understand the "Babylon" of chap. v. 13 to mean the Eastern Babylon; and it is neither very probable in itself that St. Peter should have visited that city, and there have been met by St. Silas and St. Mark, nor is there any trace of a tradition, however meagre, that he ever travelled in those parts. On the other hand, were it not for the abuse made of the fact by the supporters of the Papacy, no one would ever have questioned the universal and well-authenticated tradition which affirms that St. Peter was, along with St. Paul, co-founder of the Church of Rome. The whole subject has been, of late years, sifted to the bottom by various German and other writers, especially by Dr. Hilgenfeld in repeated articles between 1872 and 1877 in his *Zeitschrift*. Though every conceivable difference may be found between these authors respecting the dates and duration of St. Peter's sojourn at Rome, very few are so hardily sceptical as to reject altogether evidence as strong, early, and wide, as that on which we believe that Hannibal invaded Italy. This fact being then certain, the only question is whether Eusebius is right—or St. Clement of Alexandria, and even Papias, whom he appears to be quoting—in suggesting that "Babylon" in this Epistle meant Rome. *

About this there can be no difficulty. Not only is Rome so styled in the Apocalypse, and some few years later in the Jewish *Sibylline Oracles*, but M. Renan quotes passages from various Rabbinical writings where the same name occurs with the same meaning. The Jews delighted in substituting symbolical names and epithets even in plain prose speech (*e.g.*, Jerub-*besheth* for Jerub-baal, Haman the *Agagite;* St. Peter himself, if the Second Epistle be his, seems to do the same when he calls Balaam "the son of *Bosor*"); and the detestation of Rome, natural to a Jew at all times, and heightened by Christianity when once the persecution began, found vent for itself in all manner of names culled from the Old Testament, such as Nineveh and Edom, as well as Babylon.

If, then, Rome be the place from which St. Peter wrote, how can we find approximately the time? It cannot be put earlier than the year 64, for two reasons especially: (1) because it shows a deep acquaintance with the Epistle (so-named) to the Ephesians,† the date of which is 62 or 63; (2) because direct persecution had broken out against the Christians *as* Christians, and this did not take place until after the great fire at Rome in July, 64. The phenomena of the letter will not bear interpreting by the theory of simple disaffection, however deep and spiteful, of the populace against the Christians. They are liable at any moment, even away in Asia, to be called upon to give an account for their faith in the law courts (chap. iii. 15). If any of them is proved to be a Christian, he will very likely "suffer" —suffer capital punishment—for that crime (chap. iv. 16). The whole piece is burdened with persecution of a most systematic kind on every side. There is, however, one side-question which causes some difficulty. St. Paul is not mentioned as joining in the salutation to the churches which he had founded. Why so? No more probable conjecture can be made than that, shortly after writing his Epistles to the Asiatic Churches, St. Paul was tried and liberated, and made that journey into the far West on which he had long set his heart, and which St. Clement of Rome, who must have known well, says that he took. By this journey he escaped death in the outbreak of Nero's persecution; and St. Peter, arriving at Rome about the same time, finds him gone, and Silas and Mark just coming back to head-quarters from their work in Asia, with reports of division and disorder which required immediate attention. Accordingly St. Peter issues this circular letter which we have before us.

Opinions are much divided as to whether the Letter was addressed primarily to Jewish or to Gentile Christians, or to both indifferently. Either answer is beset with difficulties, but the question will be found fully discussed in the Notes on the chief passages (chap. i. 1, 14, 17, 18; ii. 9, 10; iv. 3, *et al.*), in which it will be seen that the annotator adheres to the usually received opinion that St. Peter keeps to his original intention of going to the circumcision only. The pact between the Apostles was, indeed, not of that rigid nature which would preclude the possibility of his writing to the Gentiles, even as St. Paul wrote to Jews; still, it seems more natural on the whole to suppose that he adhered to the pact. The letter is throughout exactly what the author describes it as being (chap. v. 12). He "exhorts and testifies that this is God's true grace." That is, he insists upon the Jewish Christians recognising fully that St. Paul's gospel was all that it ought to be (chap. i. 12, 25), and exhorts them to consequent unity and brotherly love. The presence of persecution both increases the temptation to fall away and also heightens the heinousness of such desertion, therefore every warning and every encouragement is pointed by the mention of sufferings and of the reward that is coming when Christ returns. The analysis of the Letter, which is somewhat hard to make, may be seen in the marginal notes.

In the preparation of the Notes, the writer has not only had the usual printed commentaries and books of reference, but every now and then has had the advantage of manuscript notes of lectures (such as will scarcely be heard in Cambridge again) by Bishop Lightfoot.

---

* The words occur in a passage describing the origin of the Gospel of St. Mark, which ends thus, "and that [St. Peter] ratified the book for the churches to study (Clement, in the sixth of his *Hypotyposes*, has put the story in our hands, and his account is substantiated also by the Bishop of Hierapolis named Papias), and that Peter mentions Mark in his former Epistle, which also they say that he composed at Rome itself, and that he means this when he calls the city in a figurative kind of way 'Babylon,' in these words, *The co-elect one in Babylon greeteth you, and Mark my son.*"—(Eus. *Hist. Eccl.* II. xv. 2.)

† Compare chap. i. 1, 2 with Eph, i. 4; chap i. 3 with Eph. i. 3; chap. i. 4, 5 with Eph. i. 11, 18; chap, i. 12 with Eph. iii. 10; chap. i. 14 with Eph. ii. 2, 3; chap. ii. 5 with Eph. ii. 20, 21, 22; chap. ii. 18 with Eph. vi. 5; chap. iii. 1 with Eph. v. 22; chap. iii. 22 with Eph. i. 20, 21; chap. iv. 3 with Eph. ii. 2; and other passages. The connection with Silvanus, and with Mark, is sufficient to explain St. Peter's close familiarity with an Epistle which had been destined (largely) for the same readers as his own. His deep knowledge of the Epistle to the Romans (which is traceable in very many passages is a strong argument in favour of the identification of "Babylon" with Rome. There are some indications also of an acquaintance with the Epistles to the Thessalonians, again perhaps through Silvanus. It is noteworthy, as showing the position which St. Peter held amidst conflicting parties, that the document which, next after the Epistles to the Romans and Ephesians, has most influenced this Letter, is the Epistle of St. James; for instance, compare chap. i. 6, 7 with Jas. i. 2, 3; chap. i. 24 with Jas. i. 10, 11; chap. iv. 8 with Jas. v. 20; chap. v. 5—9 with Jas. iv. 6—10; *et al.*

THE FIRST EPISTLE GENERAL OF

PETER

CHAPTER I.—(1) Peter, an apostle of Jesus Christ,[a] to the strangers scattered[b] throughout Pontus, Galatia, Cappadocia, Asia, and Bithynia, (2) elect according to the foreknowledge of God

Chap. i. 1, 2. The salutation.

A.D. cir. 60.

a Matt. 10. 2.
b John 7. 35; Jas. 1. 1.

The Salutation.—A comparison of this salutation with those of St. James, St. Jude, and St. John (Second and Third Epistles, and Rev. i. 4—6), will show that it is not distinctively a Pauline form of beginning a letter, but one common to all the early Christians. The same may be observed in the letters of the apostolic Fathers. And the outburst of praise immediately following is likewise a usual type.

(1) **Peter, an apostle.**—The authoritative tone of this Epistle is shown at the outset. The writer assumes his full titles; not (as in the Second Epistle) his merely human name of Simeon, nor his humble capacity of "servant," but the Rock-name which Christ had given him, and the official dignity of an "Apostle of Jesus Christ"—*i.e.*, one charged with full legatine authority from Christ (John xvii. 18; xx. 21)—a vicar of Christ to the Church, and not only a representative of the Church to Godwards. Observe also that while St. Paul constantly adds "by the will of God," or some similar phrase, by way of justifying his assumption of the title, St. Peter has no need to do more than mention it; *his* claim was never questioned. Again, though St. Silas and St. Mark are with him, they are not associated in the initial greeting, as they would probably have been by St. Paul (*e.g.*, 1 and 2 Thess. i. 1). "Apostle" though Silas was (see 1 Thess. ii. 6), and "faithful brother" to the recipients of the Letter (chap. v. 12), his support would have added but little weight to the utterances of the Rock-Apostle. And yet, with all this quiet assumption of dignity, St. Peter knows no higher title to bestow on himself than that which he held in common with the other eleven—"*an* Apostle;" not "*the* Apostle," nor "bishop of bishops," nor (which means the same thing) "servant of servants."

To the strangers scattered throughout . . .—Literally, *to the elect, sojourners of the dispersion of Pontus.* The persons for whom the Letter is destined are very clearly specified. In John vii. 35 we have "the dispersion of the Greeks," where it clearly means "those of the dispersed Jews who live among the Greeks," so here "the dispersion of Pontus," or "the Pontine dispersion," will mean "those of the dispersed Jews who live in Pontus." In Jas. i. 1 the same word is used, and, in fact, it seems to have been the recognised name for all Jews who did not live in Palestine. The word rendered by "sojourners" means people who are resident for a time among strangers: it might, for instance, describe English people who have taken houses in Paris without becoming naturalised; and, as it is here in so close a connection with geographical words, it seems forced to interpret it metaphorically (as in chap. ii. 11). Palestine, not Heaven, is the home tacitly contrasted; Pontus, not earth, is the place of sojourn. This, then, is clear, that the Apostle of the Circumcision is writing to those of the Circumcision. The addition of the words "the blood of Jesus Christ" is the only thing which shows that they are *Christian* Jews.

Pontus, Galatia . . .—The provinces which between them make up the whole, or nearly so, of what we call Asia Minor, are named in no order that can be assigned a meaning, or that indicates the quarter whence the Letter was written. Possibly the circumstances which called for the writing of the Epistle may have been most striking in Pontus. Notice that at any rate the churches of Galatia and Asia owed their origin to *St. Paul.* Of the founding of the rest we know nothing; perhaps they were founded by St. Silas: but Jewish settlers from Cappadocia and Pontus had heard St. Peter's first sermon on the Church's birthday (Acts ii. 9). A few years later and Pliny finds the whole upper shore of Asia Minor overrun and swallowed up by Christians.

(2) **Elect.**—A *true* chosen people. This word marks them off from the rest of the Jewish settlers in those parts. It is an evasion of the difficulty to say that they were elect only in the mass, as a body. The election was individual and personal. God selected these particular Hebrews out of the whole number, and made them Christians; but *what* He elected them *to* is abundantly shown in the next words. For all their election they are not certain of salvation, and their title of "elect" implies no more than the fact that God has put them into the visible Church. (See Notes on 1 Thess. i. 4, and 2 Pet. i. 10.)

According to the foreknowledge of God.—The origin of this election, the aim, and the means employed are now touched upon, and connected with the three Divine Persons respectively. (1) The origin. Their election is not accidental, nor yet something done on the spur of the moment, an afterthought of God, but "according to the foreknowledge of God the Father"—*i.e.*, in execution of His fore-arranged scheme. The word implies not simply a *perception* of the future, but the forming of a *decision.* (Comp. the same word in verse 20, and in Rom. viii. 29; xi. 2.) Though the thought is common also to St. Paul, St. Peter was familiar with it before St. Paul's conversion. (See Acts ii. 23.) (2) The means. The preconcerted scheme of God embraced not only the *choice* of these particular persons for a blessing, but the lines on which the choice

the Father,[a] through sanctification of the
Spirit,[b] unto obedience and sprinkling
of the blood of Jesus Christ:[c] Grace
unto you, and peace, be multiplied.
(3) Blessed *be* the God and Father of our
Lord Jesus Christ,[d] which
according to his abundant[1]
mercy hath begotten us
again unto a lively hope[e]
by the resurrection of

a Rom. 8. 29; 11. 2.
d 2 Cor. 11. 31; Eph. 1. 3, 17.
b 2 Thess. 2. 13.
1 Gr. *much.*
c Matt. 26. 28; Heb. 12. 24.
e Titus 3. 5, 7.

Chap. i. 3—12. Praise of God for the Gospel and its comforts and glories.

was to work itself out—"in a course of sanctification by the Spirit." The words and the thought are identical with those of 2 Thess. ii. 13, but probably so far differ in exact meaning that there "the Spirit" is the spirit sanctified, here it is the Spirit which sanctifies. (Comp. also 1 Thess. iv. 7.) We see that even the blessing of "obedience and sprinkling"—much more that of glory hereafter—is unattainable except in the path of sanctification. (3) The end. That to which God had elected them was not in the first instance the participation of the joys of the post-resurrection life, but the benefits of redemption on this side of the grave. While other "sojourners of the Pontine dispersion" were allowed to remain in the disobedience which characterised the Jews, and trusting to the efficacy of membership in the covenant people, *these* had, in accordance with God's plan, been admitted to "obedience"—*i.e.*, the reception of the gospel facts and precepts (see Note on 2 Thess. i. 8), and to the—

Sprinkling of the blood.—This important phrase must be compared with Heb. ix. 19, and xii. 24, which passages were, perhaps, suggested by it, unless, indeed, the idea had become the common property of the Church already. There is nothing in St. Paul's writings to compare with it. As the people themselves are "sprinkled," and not their houses, the reference cannot be to the Paschal sprinkling (Ex. xii. 22), but, as in Hebrews, to the scene under Mount Sinai in Ex. xxiv. 8, where, once for all, the old covenant was inaugurated by the sprinkling of the people. It was to that same scene that our Lord referred when He said of the Eucharistic cup, "This is *My* blood of the *new* covenant." Thus, "elect unto the sprinkling of the blood," seems to mean "selected for admission into the new covenant inaugurated by the sprinkling of Christ's blood." But whereas the old covenant was inaugurated by sprinkling the people *collectively* and once for all, the new is inaugurated anew and anew by *individual* application; so that the Eucharistic cup was not (according to the Quaker theory) to be drunk once for all by the Apostles then present as the representatives of the whole subsequent Church. Neither does this inauguration by sprinkling come but once for all in the individual's lifetime, but as often as the covenant is broken by his sin he comes to renew it again. Doubtless the participation of the Holy Communion is the act of "sprinkling" here before St. Peter's mind, it being the one act which betokens membership in the new covenant-people, the new Israel. Of course the application of *blood* in both covenants rests on the notion of a death-forfeit being remitted.

Of Jesus Christ.—He does not say "of the new testament," but substitutes the name of the Victim in whose blood the covenant is inaugurated—Jesus. And who is this Jesus? The Christ! The Messiah! As though Israel at Sinai had been sprinkled with the blood of Moses. What a contrast between the other Jews of Pontus, with *their* Messianic expectations, and these "elect sojourners" sprinkled with *Messiah's blood!*

Be multiplied.—This occurs again only in 2 Pet. i. 2; Jude, verse 2. (Comp. Dan. iv. 1.) It contains an exhortation to progress. There are *some* good things of which we cannot have too much.

(3–12) PANEGYRIC OF THE GOSPEL FROM A HEBREW POINT OF VIEW.—The Apostle thanks God for the resurrection of Jesus Christ. That fact is a regeneration of us, and a pledge of future glory, in view of which such afflictions as beset the Asiatic Hebrews were seen to serve a purpose, and that purpose the very "salvation" which had formed the theme of the Old Testament.

(3) **Blessed.**—A form consecrated to God alone (*e.g.*, Mark xiv. 61; Rom. ix. 5; 2 Cor. xi. 31), a completely different word from the "blessed," or *happy*, of the Beatitudes; and differing from the "blessed" of the Virgin Mary (Luke i. 28, 42) in that *this* form implies that blessing is always *due* on account of something inherent in the person, while *that* only implies that a blessing has been *received.* The idea of blessing God (literally, *speaking Him well*, Ps. c. 3) is, of course, wholly Hebrew.

Of our Lord Jesus Christ.—No longer only "the Lord God of Israel," as, *e.g.*, 1 Chron. xxix. 10; 2 Chron. vi. 4; Luke i. 68; He is now in a nearer, tenderer relation to these members of the new covenant. He is the Father of the Messiah, and yet the God whom Jesus adores (John xx. 17).

Which according to his abundant mercy.—This is the reason for which God deserves blessing from us. The word "according" never means exactly the same as "in" or "by"; here it rather shows that the particular instance was in keeping with what might have been expected, had we but known, from the "much pity" which God must have felt for creatures so forlorn. Our regeneration was no sudden capricious favour.

Hath begotten us again.—Rather, *begat us again*—the historical moment being here given as that of the resurrection of Christ. This great word, which is St. Peter's own, being only found again in verse 20, evidently contains the whole meaning of the being "born from above" or "begotten all over again" of John iii. 3, of the "fresh creation" of 2 Cor. v. 17, Gal. vi. 15, of the "regeneration" of Tit. iii. 5, of the "begotten of God" in St. John's Epistle, and (to a certain extent) of the "brought He us forth" of Jas. i. 18. It seems to indicate that, if it takes effect, it makes a complete change not only in the condition and prospects of the man, but in the man himself: such a change, for example, as would pass over an animal if it were suddenly to receive the powers of a human being. It is no metaphor when the change from the natural man to a man united with the Incarnate God is described as an act of *creation* parallel only to those of the creation of matter and force (Gen. i. 1, 2), the creation of life (Gen. i. 21), and the creation of humanity (Gen. i. 27), for, according to St. Peter's teaching, we are thus actually made "partakers of the divine nature" (2 Pet. i. 4).

Unto a lively hope.—Or, *into a living hope.* Before this regeneration there was nothing to look forward to—at best a kind of dead-alive surmise that there *might* be something beyond the weary world. But as the animal we have imagined would find himself suddenly new-begotten into a state in which he was

Jesus Christ from the dead,[a] (4) to an inheritance incorruptible, and undefiled, and that fadeth not away, reserved in heaven[b] for you,[1] (5) who are kept by the power of God through faith[c] unto salvation ready to be revealed[d] in the last time. (6) Wherein ye greatly rejoice,[e] though now for a season, if

a ch. 3. 21; Rom. 6. 4.
c Eph. 2. 8.
d Rom. 8. 18.
b Col. 1. 5.
1 Or, *for us.*
e Matt. 5. 12; Rom. 5. 3; Jas. 1. 2.

conscious of himself and of God, so *we* found ourselves new-begotten into a state of definite and most energetic expectation of whole *sæcula sæculorum*—worlds beyond worlds—of bliss before us.

By the resurrection of Jesus Christ.—Mystically speaking, the moment of our emergence into this new glow of expectation was that when the Messiah Jesus, who had been cut off, emerged from among the dead. *Then* we saw it all! St. Peter, indeed, is speaking, so far as himself was concerned, not mystically, but literally, as his history before and after the Resurrection shows. To him, and to the other Apostles, the Resurrection *was* a regeneration, and they became new beings. To subsequent Christians precisely the same effect takes place when (suddenly or gradually) the fact of the Resurrection is acknowledged and its significance realised. (See what St. Paul says, Phil. iii. 10.) Yet we must not confine the meaning of the words to the effects of this conscious realisation. St. Peter is viewing the transaction theologically, *i.e.*, from God's point of view, not phenomenally, from man's. He speaks of the begetting, not of the being born—of the Resurrection itself, not of the preaching of the Resurrection. To God, with whom, according to St. Peter, time does not exist (2 Pet. iii. 8), there is no interval between His begetting of Christ again from the dead (Acts xiii. 33; Rev. i. 5), and His begetting of us again thereby. In the mystery of our union with the Incarnate Word, His historical resurrection *did*, through baptism, in some ineffable manner, infuse into us the grace which makes new creatures of us. Archbishop Leighton says well, "Not only is it (the Resurrection) the exemplar, but the efficient cause of our new birth." (See below, chap. iii. 21, and Rom. vi. 4.)

(4) **To an inheritance.**—This is structurally parallel to and explanatory of, the clause "into a living hope." We are, as the saying is, born to an estate. This notion of an "inheritance," or property, that we have come in for, is particularly Hebrew, occurring very frequently in the Old Testament. The Pontine dispersion had lost their "inheritance" in Palestine, but there is a better in store for them.

Incorruptible, and undefiled, and that fadeth not away.—Exuberant description of the excellencies of the new Canaan. The first epithet contrasts its imperishable nature (see Rom. i. 23; 2 Tim. i. 10) with the fleeting tenure of the earthly Canaan. The second speaks of its freedom from pollutions such as desecrated the first "Holy Land." Perhaps it may specially mean that the new Holy Land will never be profaned by Gentile incursions and tyrannies. The third, and most poetical of all (which is only found besides in Wisd. vi. 12), conveys the notion of the unchanging beauty of that land—no winter in the inheritance to which the Resurrection brings us (Cant. ii. 11).

Reserved.—The perfect tense, *which hath been reserved unto you, i.e.*, either in the *temporal* sense—"kept all this while until you came," or "with a view to you." (Comp. Heb. xi. 40.) He now adds explicitly that it is no earthly, but a heavenly possession.

(5) **Who are kept.**—This explains the word "you:" "those, I mean, who are under the guardianship of God's power." Bengel says, "As the inheritance hath been preserved, so are the heirs guarded; neither shall it fail them, nor they it."

Through faith.—The Apostle is fearful lest the last words should give a false assurance. God can guard none of us, in spite of His "power," unless there be a corresponding exertion upon our part—which is here called "faith"—combining the notions of staunch fidelity and of trustfulness in spite of appearances. It is through such trustful fidelity that we are guarded.

Unto salvation.—These words "unto" arise like point beyond point in the endless vista. "Begotten *unto* an inheritance, which hath been reserved *unto* you, who are kept safe *unto* a deliverance." This salvation, spoken of again in verse 9, must not be taken in the bald sense of salvation from damnation. Indeed, the thought of the perdition of the lost does not enter at all into the passage. The salvation, or deliverance, is primarily a deliverance from all the trials and persecutions, struggles and temptations of this life—an emergence into the state of peace and rest, as we can see from the verses that follow.

Ready to be revealed in the last time.—How such an assurance helps to form the very "faith" through which the treasure is secured! That perfect state of peace, that heavenly inheritance, is not something to be prepared hereafter, but *there it is.* If only our eyes were opened, we should already see it. It is all ready, only waiting for the great moment. The tense of the word "revealed" implies the suddenness of the unveiling. It will be but the work of an instant to put aside the curtain and show the inheritance which has been kept hidden so long behind it. This, however, will not take place till the *exact* period (so the word for "time" suggests; comp. 2 Thess. ii. 6), and that period will be the last of the world's history. For such teaching the Hebrews would be well prepared by the Old Testament—for instance, comp. Dan. xii. 9, 13—and it was the earliest kind of teaching culled for converts out of the "oracles of God" (Heb. v. 12; vi. 2).

(6) **Wherein ye greatly rejoice.**—"His scope," says Leighton, "is to stir up and strengthen spiritual joy in his afflicted brethren; and therefore having set the matter of it before them in the preceding verses, he now applies it, and expressly opposes it to their distresses." There is a little doubt as to the antecedent of the word "wherein." At first sight it would seem to be "in the last time," and the thought would then be that this "last time," with all its predicted afflictions, was already begun, and that the Pontine Hebrews were fulfilling the injunction of our Lord in Luke xxi. 28, and "rejoicing" (the word is one of enthusiastic and demonstrative joy) in the near approach of their redemption. This makes good sense, but it is better to see the antecedent in "the whole complex sense of the preceding verses, concerning the hope of glory. In this thing ye rejoice, that ye are begotten again; that there is such an inheritance, and that you are made heirs of it; that it is kept for you, and you for it; that nothing can come betwixt you and it, and disappoint you of possessing and enjoying it, though there be many deserts and mountains and seas in the way, yet

need be, ye are in heaviness through manifold temptations: (7) that the trial of your faith, being much more precious than of gold that perisheth, though it be tried with fire,[a] might be found unto praise and honour and glory at the appearing of Jesus Christ:[b] (8) whom having not seen, ye love; in whom, though now ye see *him* not, yet believing,[c] ye rejoice with joy unspeakable

b Rom. 2. 10.

a Dan. 12. 10.
c 2 Thess. 1. 7, 10, 12; John 20. 29.

---

you are ascertained that you shall come safe thither." (Leighton.)

Though now for a season.—Literally, *after having been grieved in the present* (*if it must be so*) *for a little while in the midst of manifold temptations.* The Apostle takes his stand at the moment of the revelation and *looks back* upon the fast-passing present and its griefs. What the temptations were we cannot tell; but the word "manifold" shows that it was not only *one* type of temptation under which all lay alike. The chief was probably the unkind attitude of Gentile neighbours (chaps. ii. 12, 15; iii. 14—17; iv. 4, 12—19), which was the most searching "test of faith." Identical words (in the Greek) occur in Jas. i. 2, 3, so as almost to suggest a common origin—possibly to be found in Rom. v. 3.

If need be.—Or, *if it must be so.* To encourage them to bear up St. Peter throws in this phrase, so as not to take it for *granted* that they will have to suffer; he hopes it may not be so. (Comp. chap. iii. 17.)

(7) **That the trial of your faith.**—This depends grammatically on "having been grieved." The purpose of God's providence in sending the griefs is "that the trial of your faith might be found unto praise." The word "trial" here does not mean exactly the same as in the passage of St. James; in that passage it signifies the active testing of faith, *here* it has rather the meaning of the cognate word translated "assurance" in Rom. v. 4, "proof" in 2 Cor. ii. 9, Phil. ii. 22, *i.e.*, the attested worth, the genuine character. This seems necessitated by the comparison of the *trial* with the *gold* itself, as we shall see. You cannot compare an act or process with gold, but you can compare "the genuine character" brought out by the process properly enough. Besides, that which you wish to "praise" at Christ's coming is not the process by which the faith was proved, but the worth of the faith itself. "Faith" seems to mean the same as in verse 5.

Being much more precious than of gold.—There is no reason, or indeed any grammatical right, to insert the "of." It should be, *more exceedingly valuable than gold.* He does not say "your *faith* is more valuable than gold," but "your faith's *genuineness* is more valuable than gold." It is worth anything to establish the *true character* of your faith; it would be a most serious loss to leave a chance of an imputation upon your Christianity.

That perisheth, though it be tried with fire.—Rather, *which is a thing that perisheth, and yet is tried through fire.* The argument is this. Gold is a perishable thing, and comes to an end with the rest of the world, or is worn away with handling and is lost; and yet men take great pains to test it and show that it contains no dross, and do so by means of fire. How much more may we expect a fiery trial (chap. iv. 12) to test the character of our belief in the unseen Christ, when that belief is never to come to an end (1 Cor. xiii. 13), and on its freedom from alloy everything depends!

Might be found.—That is, *might clearly prove to be.* The time will come when the gold will be *inspected*, and the Judge, and all the spectators, will "find" that the testing was sufficient and the character satisfactory. "Found *unto* praise," or, *found for a praise*, is a Hebraism, meaning "found to be a matter of praise." St. Peter is fond of heaping up words of like signification. (See verse 4, and chap. v. 10.) "Praise" is the *language* that will be used about these men's faith; "honour," the *rank* in which they will be placed; "glory," the fervent *admiration* accorded to them: the three words correspond to the regions of word, act, and feeling.

At the appearing of Jesus Christ.—*Revelation* would have been better, as the word in the Greek is the same as in verse 5. This gives the date at which the trial will have done its work: it is the same as the "last time" when the "deliverance" will be revealed. Remember that all through the afflictions and assaults the men are "being guarded by the power of God." There are several words and thoughts in this whole passage which would suggest that Dan. xii. was before the mind of the Apostle more or less consciously.

(8) **Whom, having not seen.**—Said in contrast to the word "revelation" in the last verse: "whom you love already, though He is not yet revealed, so that you have not as yet seen Him." There seems to be a kind of tender pity in the words, as spoken by one who himself had seen so abundantly (Acts iv. 20; x. 41; 2 Pet. i. 16). In this and the following verse we return again from the sorrow to the joy, and to the true cause of that joy, which is only to be found in the love of Jesus Christ. There is another reading, though not so good either in sense or in authority: "whom, without *knowing* Him, ye love." Bengel remarks that this is intended for a paradox, sight and knowledge being the usual parents of love.

Ye love.—The word of calm and divinely-given attachment, in fact the usual word in the New Testament, that which Christ used in questioning the writer (John xx. 15), not the word of warm human friendship with which St. Peter then answered Him.

In whom.—To be construed, not with "ye rejoice," but with "believing." The participles give the *grounds* of the rejoicing: "because at present without seeing ye believe in Him none the less, therefore ye rejoice." The word "rejoice" takes us back to verse 6: "ye greatly rejoice, I repeat." Notice, again, the stress laid on faith: we have already had it three times mentioned. St. Peter, whose own faith gained him his name and prerogative, is, at least, as much the Apostle of faith as St. Paul is, though his conception of it, perhaps, slightly differs from St. Paul's. The definition given by the writer of the Epistle to the Hebrews (chap xi. 1) might have been, perhaps was, drawn from a study of St. Peter's writings. Our present verse gives us the leading thought of "faith" as it appears in both of these works addressed to Hebrews, viz., its being the opposite of *sight*, "the evidence of things not seen," rather than as the opposite of *works.* And the main object of both these Epistles is to keep the Hebrews from slipping back from internal to external religion, *i.e.*, to strengthen *faith.* (Comp. Heb. iii. 12.) The Apostle is full of admiration for a faith which (unlike his own) was not based on sight. (See John xx. 29—an incident which may have been in the writer's mind.)

and full of glory: (9) receiving the end
of your faith, *even* the salvation of *your*
souls.[a] (10) Of which salvation the pro-
phets[b] have enquired and searched
diligently,[c] who prophesied of the grace
that should come unto you: (11) searching

a Matt. 16. 25, 26. b Luke 1. 69, 70. c Matt. 13. 17.

Unspeakable.—The beautiful Greek word (which means "unable to find expression in words") seems to have been coined by St. Peter.

Full of glory.—Literally, *that hath been glorified; i.e.*, a joy that has reached its ideal pitch, and feels no further sense of imperfection; a signification of the word found, for instance, in Rom. viii. 30.

(9) **Receiving the end of your faith.**—The "*end* of our faith" means, the *object* to which our faith is directed, the thing we believed *for.* And "faith" catches up the "believing" of last verse, so that, in reading, the accent of the sentence falls on "end," not on "faith;" and the whole clause is added to justify the statement that we rejoice with a joy which has already attained its full perfection. The reason is, he says, because we receive already, in the present life, the object of all this trusting without sight; we need not wait till the next world to attain our glorification.

The salvation of your souls.—It might be simply, *salvation of souls*, including other men's besides our own, but the context is against it, and the absence of articles is characteristic of St. Peter. It seems at first sight not a very exalted object for our faith to work to, the deliverance, or safety, of our own souls. And yet our Lord fully recognises the instinct of the higher self-preservation as that to which the ultimate appeal must be made (Matt. xvi. 25, 26). He could give His own soul a ransom for many (Matt. xx. 28); He could save others and not Himself (Matt. xxvii. 42); St. Paul could wish himself accursed from Christ for his brethren's sake, "that they might be saved" (Rom. ix. 3; x. 1); Moses could ask to be "blotted out of the book" (Ex. xxxii. 32); and yet the fact remains, that in seeking our own welfare, in the highest sense, we are fulfilling a primal law of our being, imposed upon us by the Creator. We are bound to make that our first object, if it were only to gratify Him who has no pleasure in the death of him that dieth, even if we could possibly divest ourselves of all "selfish" interest in the matter.

> "A charge to keep I have,
> *A God to glorify;*
> A never-dying soul to save,
> And fit it for the sky."

The Buddhist longing for Nirvâna is as far as possible removed from the healthy spirit of Christianity. "Salvation" here seems to have widened its meaning since verse 5; while *there* the main thought was final deliverance from the afflictions of life, *here* the salvation is said to be received in the very midst of all these afflictions. The addition of the word "souls," appears to make the difference. For the soul, there is *present* salvation, because persecutions, &c., do not touch it, and it is *capable* of the most complete emancipation from the evils of *sin* (Matt. i. 21; Luke i. 69, 71, 75; Rom. vi. 14; vii. 24, 25.) Salvation, then, is the restoration of man to the ideal excellence from which he was fallen: it contains—here, at any rate—no allusion to "damnation" as an opposite.

(10) Now St. Peter brings his doctrine home to the hearts of his readers of the Dispersion, by showing them how scriptural it is. Surely they will not "draw back" (Heb. x. 39), but believe on to the purchasing of their souls, when they consider that all the prophets looked forward with envy to the prize now in their hands.

(10) **Of which salvation.**—The "of" stands for "concerning," "with regard to"; and the salvation which formed the subject of investigation to the prophets was the present deliverance of the believing soul from sin and gloom, as well as the salvation yet future. It is difficult not to believe that the song of Zacharias was in St. Peter's mind when he thus wrote; the theme of that song is precisely the glory of present salvation through Christ, and the fulfilment of prophecy thereby: "Blessed be the Lord God . . . who hath raised up a horn of salvation for us . . ., as He spake by the mouth of His holy prophets,—salvation from our enemies . . ., that we might serve Him without fear, in holiness and righteousness before Him all the days; and thou *too*, little child, shalt be called a prophet . . . to give knowledge of salvation unto His people."

Have enquired and searched diligently.—Rather, *did inquire;* for our present version tends to convey the notion that the prophetic writings which we now possess are the *result* of the inquiry. This would be wrong. Calvin rightly says: "When he states that the prophets inquired and examined, this refers not to their writings or teaching, but to the private longing with which each was fired." In fact, St. Peter goes on to say that the writings which the Holy Spirit impelled them to make were actually the text on which their longings were the comment: they endeavoured to understand what they themselves had written. The two Greek words give a much more lively picture than the English, of the intense eagerness of the search, and of the depth to which it penetrated. If these great prophets took such pains to understand our present salvation, we ought to take heed not to "let it slip." Precisely the same argument is used for precisely the same purpose by our Lord in Matt. xiii. 16, 17.

Who prophesied of the grace.—This is a description of the prophetic scriptures. The whole subject of the Old Testament is the bounty of God under the New; and this was what the prophets tried to realise.

The grace that should come unto you.—Perhaps the words in italics might be with advantage changed into, "the grace *in reserve* for you:" the word is the same as in verse 4. "Grace" here seems to mean little more than "favour" or "bounty," not the ordinary theological sense. The "favour" consists in our salvation.

(11) **Searching.**—This further explains the "inquired and searched" above; it particularises the object of the inquiry. They knew that they spoke "concerning a salvation," but they did not know the *details.* The present passage is perhaps the most striking in the whole New Testament in regard to the doctrine of prophetic inspiration. Assuming that the prophets did not speak simply of their own human calculation, but somehow under the influence of the Divine Spirit, we are brought to face the question, *how far* their utterances were their own, and how far suggested to them from on high. The doctrine of Montanism, which has not altogether died out of the Church yet, asserts that from first to last prophecy is superhuman; that every word and letter is forced upon the man by a power not his own, which leaves him no choice. God, and God alone, is responsible for every syllable. The human will and intelligence need not even concur in the

what, or what manner of time the Spirit[a] of Christ which was in them did signify, when it testified beforehand the sufferings of Christ,[b] and the glory

a Matt. 22. 43; 2 Pet. 1. 21.
b Isa. 53; Dan. 9. 26.

message they deliver, nor even be conscious that they are delivering it. Thus Montanus makes God to say through him: "Lo, man is as a lyre, and I am as that which strikes the chords: the man is unconscious, and I alone wake." On the other hand, some of the early opponents of Montanism went so far as to say that the inspired writers had a clear and immediate perception, a complete insight into the mysteries which they foretold,—that Isaiah, for instance, saw, as plainly as we do, Mary and Jesus in his prophecy of Immanuel. Our present verses show a doctrine between the two. The prophets find themselves impelled to say words which they are conscious of choosing and using, but which they feel to have a deeper meaning than they themselves were conscious of intending. It is clear to them (verse 12) that what they meant primarily as applying to present circumstances, was in reality being overruled by the Spirit to apply more fully to the future. But what that future was they struggled, and half in vain, to know. We may apply to them what Keble says of the Greek poets:—

"As little children lisp, and tell of Heaven,
So thoughts beyond their thoughts to those high bards were given."

What, or what manner of time.—If this be right, it must mean, "what exact or approximate date." But the simplest translation would be, *to whom, or what period, the Spirit of Christ in them was pointing.* This would give new significance to the sentence. They were aware that they were speaking of a *Messiah;* but who the man should be who would hold that office, or at what period of their history he would arise, this was what they longed to know. They foresaw a Christ, but they could not foresee Jesus; they could give to their Christ no definite position in future history. (Comp. Matt. xxii. 42; Luke iii. 15; xxiii. 35; John iii. 28; vii. 26, 41; Acts ii. 36, and often.)

The Spirit of Christ which was in them.—They are conscious of a power *within* them which is not themselves, "moving" them. And this power is described as "the Spirit of Christ." Now, observe that a change has come over St. Peter's way of speaking. Hitherto, he has always said, "Jesus Christ," his object being to keep constantly before the eyes of these Hebrews the truth which he was the first man to enunciate, viz., "*Thou* art the Christ" (Matt. xvi. 16), that *Jesus* was the person who fulfilled all that was expected of the Messiah. "Christ" is not once used by St. Peter (as it is often by St. Paul) as a proper name: it always marks the office, not the person. Therefore we may not prove by this expression two doctrines, however true they may be in themselves, which are commonly sought to be supported by it, viz., the pre-existence of our Lord, and the procession of the Holy Ghost from Him as well as from the Father. In spite of a well-quoted passage in Barnabas (chap. v.), "The prophets had the gift from Him, and prophesied of Him," it cannot here mean, "the Holy Ghost given them by our Lord Himself." Besides, it is theologically incorrect to say that Christ as the Anointed had any pre-existence, except as an indefinite hope in the minds of the Hebrews. The *Son,* the unincarnate Word, pre-existed, but it is Apollinarianism to say that *Jesus* had any existence before the Incarnation,—still more Christ, since it may be doubted whether the Incarnate Word became "Christ" until His baptism. That, at least, appears to be St. Peter's doctrine (Acts x. 38). "The Spirit of Messiah," then, at any rate when applied to the ages before Christ came, must have a different meaning. Probably not exactly "the Spirit that was to anoint and be in the Messiah," but rather, "the Messiah-spirit" or "the Messianic spirit." The prophets wondered who the man was, and where he would live, to whom this Messianic inspiration which they felt within was pointing. St. Peter himself, we repeat, was the first person who fully knew the answer.

When it testified beforehand.—A much more solemn word in the original than it looks in the English, and used by no other writer than St. Peter. It does not mean simply, "when it *bore* witness beforehand;" but "testifying" means an appeal to Heaven to mark and record the words so spoken: "when with a solemn appeal it announced beforehand." Was he not thinking of the awful appeal in Dan. xii. 7?

The sufferings of Christ.—This unduly contracts the fulness of the Greek, which reads, *the sufferings for Christ* (just as we had before "the grace for you"), *i.e.,* "these sufferings in reserve for Messiah." The Old Testament passages which may be supposed to be chiefly indicated are Isa. liii. and (still more) Dan. ix. 24—26. If it be asked how St. Peter *knew* that the prophets had these longings and doubts, we answer, that it was not only a probable *guess,* but the result of a study of Daniel, who records again and again the prophetic agony of his search into the future. Beware of treating the title "Christ" as a proper name. *Eight* out of the *ten* times that St. Peter uses the word by itself, *i.e.,* without "Jesus" or "the Lord," it is in direct connection with *suffering* (here, and in chaps. i. 19; ii. 21; iii. 18; iv. 1, 13, 14; v. 1). Conversely, he *never* speaks of the sufferings of *Jesus* Christ. That is to say, he loves to dwell upon the Passion of our Lord, not in its *personal* but its *official* aspect. The striking point is that the *Messiah* should have suffered thus. It was especially necessary to show this in any effort to retain the faith of the *Hebrews.* Comp. Luke xxiv. 26—46 (Peter present); Acts iii. 18 (Peter speaking); xvii. 3 (to Hebrews); xxvi. 23. And we can see a reason for the insistence in St. Peter's history. The very same day, apparently, when he had announced his belief that Jesus was the Messiah, he took Him to task for speaking of sufferings and shame. He never could forget the reprimand, like a sword-cut, which he received. The whole Epistle may be said to be an expansion of what Jesus said in answer (Matt. xvi. 23—27). Some commentators include in this phrase of "the sufferings in reserve for Messiah," the thought of the sufferings of the Church as well; but it seems far-fetched, especially when we see the true meaning of the word "Christ." Finally, we may add, that some would join very closely together the words for "signify" and "testifying beforehand," which would give us this sense: "examining, in reserve for *whom,* or for what period, the Spirit, with its solemn appeal beforehand, was pointing out these sufferings in reserve for Messiah." This is possible, and keeps the same sense, but it unnecessarily complicates the sentence.

And the glory that should follow.—Literally, *and the glories after them.* The plural "glories" corresponds to the plural "sufferings,"—the one as multiform

that should follow. (12) Unto whom it was revealed, that not unto themselves,[a] but unto us they did minister the things, which are now reported unto you by them that have preached the gospel unto you with the Holy Ghost sent down[b] from heaven; which things the angels desire to look into.[c]

a Dan. 10. 14.
b Acts 2. 2.
c Eph. 3. 10.

---

as the other; resurrection, ascension, reassumption of the divine glory (John xvii. 5), triumphs of Church history, restitution of all things. The sufferings and subsequent glories of the Christ form, of course, together the whole of the gospel.

(12) **Unto whom it was revealed.**—As verse 11 expanded and expounded the words "inquired and searched," so the first part of verse 12 expounds the words "prophesied of the grace in reserve for you." That is to say, the revelation here spoken of is not a special revelation sent in answer to their laborious musings, but rather the very thing which occasioned them; the perplexity consisted in feeling that God had a further meaning for their words. And the exact limits of the revelation are mentioned: they were shown that they spoke for the benefit of futurity, and no more! What a "trial of faith!" What a sublime disappointment! (Heb. xi. 40.)

Unto us.—Far the better reading is, *unto you.* It is a distinct characteristic of this Epistle, that "we," "us," "our," are so seldom used (in the best text) where they might have been expected. Where St. Paul throws in his own sympathy, and puts himself on a footing with those whom he addresses, St. Peter utters his lofty pastoral from above. There are but four places in the Epistle (chaps. i. 3; ii. 24; iii. 18; iv. 17) where he associates himself thus with his brethren, and one of those (chap. ii. 24) is really a quotation, and one (chap. iii. 18) at best a very doubtful reading. The same tendency may be observed in his speech (Acts xv. 7), where the right reading is "made choice among *you.*"

The things.—In the original simply *them;* so that a semicolon might better follow than a comma, and *which things* be put instead of "which." The most natural thing is to suppose that the pronoun represents the preceding "sufferings in reserve for Messiah and the glories after." In what sense, then, could the prophets "minister," either to themselves or to us, the sufferings and glories of Messiah? The word is one which signifies a servant bringing to his master the things which he needs—commonly used (*e.g.,* John xii. 2) of serving up a meal; and the prophets are said to *serve* the Messianic sufferings and glories to us, to wait upon us with them, to present them to our use and study and comfort. (Comp. chap. iv. 10.) When it says, however, that they ministered them "*not* to themselves but to us," we must not suppose that they derived *no* comfort from their predictions (see John viii. 56): the "not" must be taken in the same sense as in "I will have mercy and not sacrifice" (Matt. ix. 13).

Which are now reported unto you.—Rather, *which things* (*i.e.,* the gospel story) *now* (in contrast with the days of the prophets) *were* (not "are") *openly declared to you* (in all their details, in contrast with the dim and vague way in which they were seen before). Such is the force of this compound Greek verb in John iv. 25, Acts xix. 18; xx. 20, 27.

By them that have preached.—More correctly, *through those who preached;* the difference being that St. Peter is referring to the *first* bearers of the gospel to those parts, not to *all* who from that time to the date of the Letter had preached. This is a point well worth noticing. The phrase seems to show that St. Peter himself was not of the number. Perhaps half the churches which received the Letter looked to St. Paul as their founder. (See last Note on verse 1.) Here, then, we find the Rock-Apostle authoritatively setting his seal to the teaching of his junior colleague, just as he does in the Second Epistle (chap. iii. 15). It seems to imply that these Jewish Christians were beginning to feel a reaction from St. Paul's evangelical teaching; and the Apostle of the Circumcision is called in to enforce what the Apostle of the Uncircumcision had taught. The revolt of the Hebrew Christians in *Asia* from evangelical teaching appears again at a still later period (Rev. ii. 9; iii. 9). It was, perhaps, only with *Jewish* Christians that such an appeal from St. Paul to St. Peter would be made, and need not imply superiority throughout the whole Church. St. Peter's perfect concurrence with St. Paul here is a sufficient contradiction to the Tübingen theory of their irreconcilable divergence—only the Tübingen school reject the Epistle on the ground that it makes the Apostles too harmonious!

With the Holy Ghost sent down from heaven.—The magnificent phrase seems meant to contrast the *full* effusion of the Spirit now, with His limited working in the prophets (verse 11). But it contains more teaching than this. The tense of the participle "sent" is such as might without violence be rendered "sent once and for ever," "sent in a moment." Now, remember that almost undoubtedly some of the recipients of the Letter (see last Note on verse 1) were eye-witnesses of His being "sent" to St. Peter and the rest on the Day of Pentecost. St. Peter, then, here claims for St. Paul (and St. Silas perhaps) the very same inspiration with which himself was furnished. And as here he claims full inspiration for St. Paul's *preaching,* so he does afterwards for his *writing* (2 Pet. iii. 15).

Which things the angels.—The "which things" here is grammatically parallel to the "which things" of the last sentence, and therefore would mean "the sufferings of Messiah and the glories after." But logically we have to go back to the beginning of verse 10: "Do I say that *prophets,* who had the mysteries of our redemption on their lips, yet pored in vain to catch the detailed meaning which you catch? Nay; angels (not "*the* angels"), who were present at every detail, and bore an active part in it all (see Matt. i. 20; iv. 11; xxviii. 2; Luke i. 26; ii. 9; xxii. 43; John i. 52),—*angels,* of whom He '*was seen*' (1 Tim. iii. 16),—covet now to exchange places with you that they may gaze into the mystery." The word which has here shrunk into our word "to look into," means really, *to bend aside to see.* In its literal sense it occurs in John xx. 5, 11, and in Luke xxiv. 12 (a verse not found in the best text), of people standing at the side of the cave so as not to get in their own light, and stooping sideways to peer in. Metaphorically it is used in Jas. i. 25, where see Note. It seems to mean a strained attention to something which has caught your eye somewhat out of your usual line of sight. Here then, the intention is to show that we are in a better position to understand the mysteries of redemption, not only than prophets, but also than angels; and they covet to stoop from their

Chap. i. 13—25. Exhortation to live like regenerate persons.

(13) Wherefore gird up the loins [a] of your mind, be sober, and hope [b] to the end [1] for the grace [c] that is to be brought unto you at the revelation of Jesus Christ; (14) as obedient children, not fashioning [d] yourselves according to the former lusts [e] in your ignorance: [f]

a Luke 12. 35. b verse 3. 1 Gr. *perfectly*. d Rom. 12. 2. c verse 10. e ch. 4. 3. f ch. 2. 9.

---

own point of view to ours. And why so? Not because of the inherent mysteriousness of the union of the two natures in Christ, for of that they are as intelligent as we, or more so; but because they are incapable of fully understanding *human* nature, flesh and blood, with its temptations and pains, its need of a Saviour. In Francia's great picture, the two angels kneel by weeping Mary and dead Christ without a trace of grief on their countenances. The Son of God Himself only became capable of entering into our infirmities through becoming flesh, and experiencing the same (Heb. ii. 16, 18; iv. 15). Several passages show us that the tragedy of human history is by no means enacted only for the benefit of the actors, but as a lesson (possibly, as Archbishop Whately pointed out, only a single *illustration* out of many in one lesson) for the instruction of unfallen spirits (1 Cor. iv. 9; Eph. iii. 10; 1 Tim. iii. 16). Our present passage has impressed itself on Christian lyrics as much, perhaps, as any in the New Testament. Charles Wesley well strikes the meaning in many of his poems: as—

> "Ask the Father's Wisdom how,
> Him that did the means ordain;
> Angels round our altars *bow*
> To search it out in vain;"

or again—

> "Angels in *fixt amazement*
> Around our altars hover,
> With *eager gaze* adore the grace
> Of our Eternal Lover."

Though very possibly the divine intention of the cherubim over the mercy-seat (Ex. xxv. 20) may have been to symbolise that which is here said, yet it is not to be thought that St. Peter was consciously thinking of the symbol.

(13–25) General Application of the Foregoing.—This salvation being so magnificent, the Asiatic Hebrews must cling to it tenaciously, in holiness, in reverence caused by consideration of the cost of it, and in charity: the gospel they have received cannot be improved upon.

(13) **Gird up the loins of your mind.**—A metaphor from persons gathering up the flowing Oriental dress (which had been let down for repose), so as to be ready for energetic action (*e.g.*, 1 Kings xviii. 46, for running; Job xxxviii. 3, for arguing). What exact kind of action St. Peter meant them here to prepare for we need not inquire. A "mind," rather than "soul" or "heart," seems to bespeak *practical intelligence.* Thus when the *Galatians*, too, began to fall from evangelical to Judaic religion St. Paul calls them "senseless" (Gal. iii. 1).

Be sober.—Not in the literal sense, but with the same notion of alertness as in "gird up"; sobriety and wakefulness are often combined (*e.g.*, chap. v. 8; 1 Thess. v. 6).

Hope to the end.—Literally, *hope perfectly*, or, *thoroughly*, or, *with completeness.* "Indeed this hope," says Leighton, "is perfect in *continuance*, it is a *hope unto the end*, because it is perfect in its *nature*." The chief thought, however, is that the hope should not be half-hearted, dispirited. St. Peter brings us back to what he began with, that ours is a *living* hope. The exhortation is exactly of the same nature as that which pervades the Epistle to the Hebrews (see, for instance, Heb. iii. 6, 14; vi. 11), and for the same reason—*i.e.*, that spiritual sloth, combined with fear of man, was beginning to turn these Jewish Christians back to dead works. "Hope on," in these passages, is tantamount to "remain Christians."

For the grace.—Not exactly "hope *for* the grace," *i.e.*, expect confidently that it will come: rather, "hope *upon* the grace," as in 1 Tim. v. 5, the only other place where the same construction is used, and where it is rendered "*trusteth in* God." Here, therefore, it is, "confidently hope (for salvation, glory, &c.) on the strength of the grace." The grace is the same as in verse 10.

That is to be brought.—"If we will render it strictly, it is, *That is a-bringing to you.* That blessedness, that consummation of grace, the saints are hastening forward to, walking on in their way, wheresoever it lies indifferently, through honour and dishonour, through evil report and good report. And as they are hastening to it, it is hastening to them in the course of time; every day brings it nearer to them than before; and notwithstanding all difficulties and dangers in the way, they that have their eye and their hopes upon it shall arrive at it, and it shall be brought safe to their hand; all the malice of men and devils shall not be able to cut them short of this *grace that is a-bringing* to them against the revelation of Jesus Christ" (Leighton). On the tense, see also Note on 1 Thess. i. 10. Notice also that it is now the *personal Name*, not the official title. St. Peter is enforcing the gospel as we know it; we no longer "search unto *whom*" the title of the Messiah belongs.

(14) **As obedient children.**—Literally, *as children of obedience*—children, *i.e.*, in the sense of relationship, not of age. It is characteristic of the writer to keep one thought underlying many digressions, and so here, the appeal to them as "children" is based on the "begotten again" of verse 3, and "inheritance" of verse 4; it comes up again in verse 17, "the Father"; in verse 22, "the brethren"; and again in verse 23, "begotten again." The usual characteristic of Jews in the New Testament is *disobedience.* (See Note on 2 Thess. i. 8.) The "as" means "in keeping with your character of," just as we say in common English, "Do so *like* obedient children."

Not fashioning yourselves according to.—This rare verb is the same as is translated "be not conformed," in Rom xii. 2, from which some think it is borrowed. The expression is a little confused, the lusts themselves being spoken of as a model not to be copied, where we should rather have expected "not being conformed to your former selves."

The former lusts in your ignorance—*i.e.*, which you indulged before you came to know the gospel truth—of course implying also that the ignorance was the mother of the lusts. The same assumption is made here which we shall find again below in chap. ii. 9, and still more in chap. iv. 3, that the recipients of this Letter had lived in ignorance and in vice up to a certain point of their lives. And it is contended, with much plausibility, that both accusations show the

(15) but as he which hath called you is
holy, so be ye holy in all manner of
conversation; (16) because it is written,[a]
Be ye holy; for I am holy. (17) And if
ye call on the Father,[b] who without
respect of persons judgeth according to
every man's work, pass the time of your
sojourning *here* in fear:[c] (18) forasmuch
as ye know that ye were not redeemed
with corruptible things, *as* silver and
gold, from your vain[d] conversation *re-
ceived* by tradition from your fathers;

c Mal. 1. 6.
a Lev. 11. 44; Matt. 5. 48.
b Luke 11. 2.
d Mark 7. 7.

---

recipients of the letter to be of Gentile and not of Jewish origin. It is true that lusts of the flesh are not usually laid to the charge of the Jews, as they are of the Gentiles. (See, for instance, 1 Thess. iv. 5; Eph. iv. 17.) It is also true that the ignorance with which the Jews are charged (for instance, Acts iii. 17; Rom. x. 3; 1 Tim. i. 13) has quite a different tendency from this. But it may be answered that such details are of little weight in comparison with the direct evidence of the first verse, and the indirect evidence of the whole tone of the Letter; also that, putting out of sight expressions of St. Paul's which have nothing to do with St. Peter, "ignorance" is surely not an unnatural word to represent the contrast between the state of unregenerate Jews and the same persons when they have attained to knowledge higher than that of prophets or of angels; that even Jews were men of flesh and blood, and therefore not exempt from the temptations of the flesh, from which mere legalism was quite insufficient to protect them (see Rom. vii. 8, "sin through the commandment wrought in me *every lust*); that in Heb. v. 2, and ix. 7, Jewish people are supposed to have need of a high priest to bear with and atone for their "ignorance" and "ignorances;" that the same writer contemplates the possibility of "many" of his Hebrews being "defiled" through fleshly sin (Heb. xii. 15, 16), and deems it necessary to urge strongly the sanctions of marriage (Heb. xiii. 4).

(15) **But as he which hath called you is holy.**—More correctly, *But according to* (or, *after, i.e.*, in the likeness of: see Eph. iv. 24, "after God") *the Holy One who called you.* The "calling" is mentioned because of the obligation it imposes upon us. Bengel notices how fond St. Peter is of the words "call," "calling." (See chaps. ii. 9, 21; iii. 9; v. 10; 2 Pet. i. 3, 10.) The "call" here seems to mean specially the call to be *children* of God.

So be ye holy.—Perhaps the imperative would come out stronger thus, *Do ye also show yourselves holy in every part of your conduct.* Leighton says, "He hath severed you from the mass of the profane world, and picked you out to be jewels for Himself; He hath set you apart for this end, that you may be holy to Him, as the Hebrew word that signifies 'holiness' imports 'setting apart,' or fitting for a peculiar use; be not then untrue to His design. It is *sacrilege* for you to dispose of yourselves after the impure manner of the world, and to apply yourself to any profane use, whom God hath consecrated to Himself."

(16) **Be ye holy; for I am holy.**—The better reading here is, *Ye shall be holy;* it is still, however, a command, not a promise—except that all God's commands are promises. The command comes some five or six times in the Book of Leviticus, addressed not only to the Levites, but to all the people. It would, therefore, apply twice over to the recipients of this letter by virtue of their twofold consecration, in the old and in the new Israel.

(17) **And if.**—The "if" casts no doubt, but, on the contrary, serves to bring out the necessary logical connection between invoking the Father—and such a Father—and fear. (See Note on 1 Thess. iv. 14.)

Ye call on the Father.—We might paraphrase by "if you use the Lord's Prayer." (Refer again to verses 3, 14.) The word seems not only to mean "if you *appeal* to the Father," but "if you appeal to the Father by the *title* of Father." (Comp. Rom. viii. 15; Gal. iv. 6.)

Who without respect of persons judgeth.—This "judgeth," or *decideth,* refers not only to the great judgment of the last day, but is used in reference to the word "if ye *call upon* the Father." That word has a forensic sense (in which it is used in Acts xxv. 11) of lodging an *appeal,* and every time we lodge our appeal to the Father on the ground of His Fatherhood, He decides the case, but decides it without favour—makes no allowance to our wrong doing on the ground of being His regenerate children, and certainly none on the ground of being of the Hebrew race. That this last notion finds place here we may see from St. Peter's words in Acts x. 34, 35. He decides "according to every man's work"—*i.e.*, upon the individual merits of the case before Him. The man's "work" (not "works") embraces all his conduct in the lump, as a single performance, which is either good on the whole or bad on the whole.

Pass the time . . . in fear.—The word for "pass" really is the same as the "conversation" of verse 15, and is intended to take our thought back to it: "As obedient children, be holy in every part of your conduct; and if you wish for favour from the Father, see that that conduct is characterised by *fear.*" "This fear," says Archbishop Leighton, "is not cowardice (nor superstition, we may add); it drowns all lower fears, and begets true fortitude; the righteous dare do anything but offend God. Moses was bold and fearless in dealing with a proud and wicked king, but when God appeared he said (as the Apostle informs us), 'I exceedingly fear and quake.'" This extract well contrasts with the meaning which some would apparently thrust into the word "fear," as though it meant that the position of the Christians, as "aliens" in the midst of a hostile world, required a timid attitude towards man. The "fear" of the *Father* may be seen in the first two clauses of the Lord's Prayer itself.

Your sojourning.—See on verse 1, "strangers." Because the word is metaphorical here and in chap. ii. 11, is no reason why the similar word should be so there, in quite a different context. The expression here sets a limit for the discipline of fear, and at the same time suggests a reason for it—children though they are, they are not yet entered on their "inheritance" (verse 4), and have to secure it.

(18) **Forasmuch as ye know.**—This correctly paraphrases the simple original *knowing.* Security, which is the opposite of the fear of the Father, is incompatible with knowing by whose and what anguish alone the inheritance could be purchased for us.

Corruptible things.—St. Peter's contempt for "silver and gold" is shown early in his history (Acts iii. 6; comp. chap. iii. 4). Gold and silver will come

(19) but with the precious blood of Christ, as of a lamb[a] without blemish and without spot: (20) who verily was foreordained before the foundation of

a Isa. 53. 7; John 1. 29; Rev. 5. 6.

to an end with everything else that is material. Observe that, by contrast, the "blood of Christ" is implied to be *not* corruptible; and that, not because of the miraculous incorruption of Jesus Christ's flesh, but because the "blood of Christ" of which the Apostle here speaks is *not material.* The natural blood of Jesus was only the sign and sacrament of that by which He truly and inwardly redeemed the world. (See Isa. liii. 12, "He poured out *His soul* unto death," and Heb. x. 9, 10.)

Redeemed . . from your vain conversation.—We have to notice (1) what the "redemption" means, and (2) what the readers were redeemed from. Now (1) the word "redeem" is the same which is used in Luke xxiv. 21 ("We used to hope that *He* was the person destined to redeem Israel"), and in Titus ii. 14 ("Gave Himself for us, that He might redeem us from all iniquity"), and nowhere else. The substantive appears in Luke i. 68; ii. 38; Heb. ix. 12, to represent the *action* of redeeming; and in Acts vii. 35, of Moses, to represent the *person* who effects such a redemption. Properly it means to ransom a person, to get them out of slavery or captivity by paying a ransom (Matt. xx. 28; Mark x. 45; comp. 1 Tim. ii. 6). The notion of an actual ransom paid, however, was apt to slip away, as in the case of Moses just quoted, who certainly gave nothing of the nature of an equivalent to Pharaoh for the loss of his serfs. So that here, as in all passages relating to the Atonement, we must be very careful not to press the metaphor, or to consider it as more than a metaphor. The leading notion here is not that of paying an equivalent, but to call closer attention to the state in which the readers were before. It was a servitude like that of Egypt, or a captivity like that of Babylon, from which they needed a "ransomer" like Moses or Zerubbabel. What then was that condition? (2) St. Peter describes it as a "vain conversation traditional from the fathers." The word "conversation" again catches up verses 15, 17, "be holy in your conduct; let it be a conduct of fear; for your old vain conduct needed a terrible ransom before you could be set at liberty from it." The question is, whether a Gentile or Jewish mode of life is intended. If it meant merely as regards religious worship, it would suit either way, for it was of the essence of Roman state "religion" that it should be the same from generation to generation. (See Acts xxiv. 14.) But "conversation" or "manner of life" is far too wide a word to be thus limited, and at the same time the word "tradition" implies (in the New Testament) something sedulously taught, purposely handed down from father to son as an heirloom, so that it could not be applied to the careless, sensual life of Gentiles, learned by example only. On the other hand, among the Jews "tradition" entered into the minutest details of daily life or "conversation." (See Mark vii. 3, 4—the Petrine Gospel.) It was a matter of serious "tradition" how a cup was to be washed. "Vain" (*i.e.*, frivolous) seems not an unnatural epithet to apply to such a mode of life, especially to one who had heard Mark vii. 7. It would seem, then, that the readers of this Letter were certainly Jews by birth. But would the Apostle of the Circumcision, the supposed head of the legal party in the Church, dare to call Judaism a "vain conversation," to stigmatise it (the single compound adjective in the Greek has a contemptuous ring) as "imposed by tradition of the fathers," and to imply that it was like an Egyptian bondage? We have only to turn to Acts xv. 10, and we find him uttering precisely the same sentiments, and calling Judaism a slavish "yoke," which was not only so bad for Gentiles that to impose it upon them was to tempt God, but also was secretly or openly felt intolerable by himself, by all the Jews there present, and even by the fathers who had imposed it. Judaism itself, then, in the form it had then assumed, was one of the foes and oppressors from which Christ came to "ransom" and "save" His people. (See Notes on verses 9, 10, and comp. Acts xiii. 39.)

(19) **With the precious blood of Christ.**—"Precious" means, not "much prized by us," but *costly*, precious in itself; opposed to the perishableness of gold and silver. Notice that it is not "Jesus," but "Christ," *i.e.*, the Messiah. No price short of the "blood," *i.e.*, the death, of the Messiah could free the Jews from the thraldom of their "vain conversation." (Comp. verse 2 and Note.) How Christ's death freed them from it is not explained here; but we may give a twofold explanation, as we did of His resurrection being our regeneration, in verse 3. Historically it did so, because when they came to realise that their Messiah could only reach His glories through suffering it gave them a new insight into the whole meaning of the system under which they had been brought up. It did also, however, doubtless, in a more mysterious way, such as we cannot imagine, procure in God's sight their emancipation; and the following verses show that again St. Peter is thinking more of the theological than of the phenomenal side of the occurrence.

As of a lamb without blemish and without spot.—We might roughly paraphrase it by, "as of a sacrificial victim, to the sufficiency of whose offering no exception can be taken." The word "as" shows that in St. Peter's mind the notion of a "sacrifice," in reference to the atonement, was only a simile, or metaphor, just as it was with the notion of "ransom." Once more observe that the sacrifice was offered to effect a redemption which for the readers had already taken place. (Comp. Heb. ix. 14.) The primary thought in mentioning a "lamb" is, of course, that of sacrifice; but when we come to consider why that particular sacrificial animal was named rather than another, it is, no doubt, for two reasons. First, because of the whiteness, the helplessness, the youth, the innocence, and patience, which make it a natural symbol of our Lord. (Comp. *Ecce Homo*, p. 6, ed. 3.) The second reason is to be found in St. Peter's own life. The first thing that we know in his history was a putting together of those two words—Messiah, and the Lamb (John i. 36, 40, 41). Neither he nor St. John (see Rev. v. 6, *et al.*) ever forgot that cry of the Baptist. They, no doubt, understood that cry to refer, not primarily to the Paschal, or any other sacrifice, but to Isa. liii. 7, and perhaps to Gen. xxii. 8. A word in the next verse will make it clearer that St. Peter really had the Baptist consciously before his mind when he thus wrote.

(20) **Who verily was foreordained.**—There is a sharp contrast intended between the two clauses of this verse, and in the Greek the tenses are different. "Who *had been foreknown*, indeed, before the foundation of the world, but for your benefit *was* (*only*)

the world,[a] but was manifest [b] in these last times for you, (21) who by him do believe in God, that raised him up from the dead, and gave him glory; that your faith and hope might be in God. (22) Seeing ye have purified your souls in obeying the truth through the Spirit unto unfeigned love of the

a Acts 2. 23; Rev. 13. 8.
b John 1. 31.

pointed out at the end of the times." St. Peter is returning once more to the great argument of verses 10—12, "Do not treat your share in the gospel liberation as if it were, at best, a piece of good luck, and so learn to despise it. Neither think of it as if Paul and Silvanus were preaching to you a novel invention at discord with the spirit of the old covenant, under which you were bred. God knew from all eternity who was to be His Messiah and His Lamb, but for your sakes the particular and personal declaration of Him was reserved till now. For you has been kept the revelation of a secret which underlay the whole Old Testament system." The grammatical antecedent of the relative "who verily" is not "lamb," but "Christ;" and the word for "foreordained" is, literally, *foreknown*, only as in verse 2 (see Note), with the additional notion of coming to a decision. We see that St. Peter's doctrine has not changed since the great day of Pentecost (Acts ii. 23). The foreknowledge (as that passage would show) includes not only the knowledge and decision that Jesus should be the Christ, but that the Christ's history should be what it was; and this seems to involve not only the doctrine that the Incarnation was no mere episode, consequent upon the Fall of man, but also the doctrine that, "before the foundation of the world," God had foreknown, and predecided to allow, the Fall itself. The same doctrine seems to be involved in Rev. xiii. 8, but only indirectly, because there the words "from the foundation of the world," are to be attached, not to the word "slain," but to the word "written."

Was manifest.—Better, *was manifested, i.e.*, unambiguously shown, pointed out. The context shows that it does not simply mean the visible life of the Incarnate Word among men, as in 1 Tim. iii. 16; 1 John iii. 5; but that the Messiah and Lamb of God was pointed out as being identical with the Man Jesus. And this was the work of John the Baptist, to say of the particular Person whom he saw walking by Jordan, "*Behold* the Lamb." So St. John Baptist himself described his mission: "The whole purpose of my coming was that He might be *manifested*, singled out and shown to Israel," as the Person round whom all their Messianic hopes were gathered (John i. 31).

In these last times—*i.e.*, not merely "in modern times," "lately," but "at the end of the times," showing St. Peter's belief that the end of the world was not far distant. (Comp. once more Dan. xii. 4, 9, 13.) Almost exactly the same phrase is used in Heb. i. 2; 2 Pet. iii. 3.

(21) **Who by him do believe in God.**—The sentence is joined on to the foregoing verse just as in verse 5, "Who are kept." The "who" might be rendered by "and you;" and the clause adds a kind of proof of the foregoing statement, drawn from the result of God's manifestation of Christ to them. "This Christian doctrine is no innovation, nothing to lead you away from the God of our fathers. That same God had had the scheme in His thoughts from the beginning, and it is in that same God that you have been led thereby to believe." There is a better supported and more forcible reading, *Who through Him are faithful towards God*, which combines the ideas of believing, *i.e.*, putting the whole trust in God, and of loyal inward observance of Him. And if any one asks whether it be possible to say that Hebrew men only came to believe in God through the revelation of Christ, we must answer by pointing to the whole scope of the Epistle to the Hebrews, and especially to Heb. iii. 12, where it is not faith in Christ, but faith in a living God, which they are warned not to abandon; and to Heb. vi. 1, where faith toward God is part of the "word of the beginning of *Christ*."

That raised him up.—These clauses give the historical facts which had led them, "through Christ," to a living faith in God. Though the thought is common with St. Paul (*e.g.*, Rom. i. 2—4), St. Peter was familiar with it years before St. Paul's conversion. See this in Acts ii. 23, 24; and verses 33—36 of the same chapter will show what he means by "gave Him glory"—not to be confined to the Ascension, though that is the prominent thought; the glory was already partly given in the Resurrection. Comp. John xvii. 1, where there is the same reciprocal glorification of the Father and the Son, as here.

That your faith . . . might . . .—An inexact rendering which obscures the connection. Literally it is, *so that your faith and hope is in* (or, *toward*) *God*; that is to say, "Your faith and hope does not stop short in Jesus." Hammond seems to be quite right in paraphrasing, "Who by believing on Him (Jesus Christ) are far from departing from the God of Israel, but do, indeed, the more firmly believe and depend on Him as that omnipotent God who hath raised Christ from the dead." The co-equal Son is less than the Father (John xiv. 28); and we should terribly mistake the meaning of the gospel were we content to rest in the love of Christ Himself without accepting His revelation of the Father. This is the "living hope" of verse 3, brought about by Christ's resurrection. Some of the German commentators translate, "So that your faith may be also hope in God;" which has nothing ungrammatical in it, but does not suit the context so well.

(22) **Purified your souls in obeying.**—Bengel well points us to 2 Pet. i. 5—7, where, in like manner, St. Peter delights to exhibit gradations of grace. "Obeying the truth" here will correspond to "knowledge" there, with its immediate consequences of "self-mastery," "endurance," and "reverence;" after which we pass on to "love of the brethren," and thence, as to a higher grace, to "love" or "charity." On this last point see Note on 1 Thess. iv. 9. Perhaps the literal "in the obedience of the truth" (*i.e.*, the Christian gospel) does not exactly coincide with "obeying the truth," as implying rather "the obedience (to God) which the truth (*i.e.*, the knowledge of the truth) demands." Truth has a claim, not only to be accepted intellectually, as truth, but to alter moral conduct in accordance (comp. John xvii. 17): a doctrine which lies at the bottom of the Socratic maxim, "Virtue is knowledge." That Socratic maxim, however, does not sufficiently take into account the inertness of the will to act on principle; and no doubt it was under some such instinct that some copyist first added as a gloss the words (not found in the original text) "through the Spirit." The first effect of such knowledge of the truth, under the Spirit's influence, is to "purify" the soul of selfish aims, and

brethren, *see that ye* love one another
with a pure heart fervently: (23) being
born again, not of corruptible seed, but
of incorruptible,[a] by the word[b] of God,
which liveth[c] and abideth for ever.
(24) For[1] all flesh *is* as grass, and all the

a John 1. 13.
b Heb. 4. 12.
c Isa. 40. 6, 7, 8.
1 Or, *For that.*

to give it that "altruism" (as they call it now), or desire for the benefit of the community rather than self, which is here described as "love of the brethren." (See Notes on 1 Thess. iii. 13, and iv. 6.)

Unfeigned love of the brethren.—The epithet "unfeigned," in itself, would suggest that St. Peter was uneasy about the depth of their brotherly kindness. And the brotherly kindness is here, as usual, attachment to other members of the Church, special point being added to the word here because of the notion of regeneration running through the whole passage. (See verse 14.) Is it not possible that some coolness had arisen between the Jewish and Gentile members of the Church, and that St. Peter finds it necessary to remind the former that they are truly brethren, sons of one Father, and that they ought not only unaffectedly to have done with all jealousy of the Gentile members, but to be far beyond that, loving one another "from the heart (the word 'pure' is not part of the original text, and interrupts the run of the sentence) strenuously?"

(23) **Being born again.**—Rather, *Having been begotten again.* It is not part of the exhortation, as though they had still to be thus begotten, but assigns the moral grounds for the exhortation. It is logically parallel with "seeing ye have purified," and might be rendered, *seeing that ye have been begotten again.* For the meaning of the word, refer back to verse 3.

Not of corruptible seed.—That is, *not of the seed of Abraham, but of the seed of God.* This is the argument: "You must learn not to be selfish, or arrogant, as being of the chosen race, but to have a true brotherly feeling and earnest love for the Gentile converts, and for those who, like St. Paul, are specially working for the Gentiles, because your inheritance of the promised 'salvation' is grounded, not on your Abrahamic descent, but on your spiritual regeneration, in which matter the Gentile converts are your equals." That this was the doctrine of St. Peter is certain from his speech at the Council of Jerusalem, "God put no difference between us and them, having purified their hearts by faith;" and again, "It is only through the favour of the Lord Jesus that we hope to be saved, in precisely the same manner as they" (Acts xv. 9, 11). (Comp., for the argument, 1 John v. 1.)

By the word of God.—"Seed," in the beginning of the clause, is more literally the act of *sowing,* or *engendering,* which sowing is carried on "through the living and abiding word of God," this "word of God" being the actual seed sown. The "seed" of all existence is the spoken Word of God, the expressed will and meaning of creative thought (Ps. xxxiii. 6); and so here, even when spoken mediately, through the lips of men (as explained in verse 25), it is that which begets men afresh. God creates afresh, though men speak the creative word for Him, just as "it is He that hath made us," although He does so through natural laws and human powers. The "Word of God" here is, no doubt, the preaching of the gospel, but especially, as it would seem, the preaching of the Resurrection (verse 3), or of the sufferings and glories of Messiah (verse 12), the "truth" of the last verse. The part taken by "the Word" in the sacrament of regeneration may be seen again in Eph. v. 26 and Jas. i. 18; in connection with the other sacrament we may also refer to John vi. 63. "Incorruptible" (*i.e., imperishable;* see verses 4, 18) finds a more energetic paraphrase here in "living and abiding" (the words "for ever" not being part of the true text). The former epithet is a favourite with St. Peter (verse 3, chap. ii. 4, 5), and is perhaps borrowed from this place by the author to the Hebrews, in connection with the "word of God" (Heb. iv. 12). The epithets serve to prepare the way for the quotation.

(24) **For all flesh is as grass.**—The citation is from Isa. xl. 6—8, and varies between the Hebrew and the LXX. in the kind of way which shows that the writer was familiar with both. But the passage is by no means quoted only to support the assertion, in itself ordinary enough, that the Word of the Lord abideth for ever. It is always impossible to grasp the meaning of an Old Testament quotation in the mouth of a Hebrew without taking into account the context of the original. Nothing is commoner than to omit purposely the very words which contain the whole point of the quotation. Now these sentences in Isaiah stand in the forefront of the herald's proclamation of the return of God to Sion, always interpreted of the establishment of the Messianic kingdom. This proclamation of the Messianic kingdom comprises words which St. Peter has purposely omitted, and they contain the point of the quotation. The omitted words are, "the Spirit of the Lord bloweth upon it: surely *the people*"—*i.e.,* Israel—"is grass." Immediately before our quotation went the words, "the glory of the Lord shall be revealed, and *all flesh* shall see it together;" statements which so shocked the LXX. translator that he entirely omitted verse 7, and changed the previous verse so as to make *some* difference between Jew and Gentile (as Godet points out on Luke iii. 6), into "the glory of the Lord shall be revealed," *i.e.,* to Israel, "and all flesh shall see *the salvation* of God." The comment of Bishop Lowth on the original passage will well bring out what St. Peter means here: "What is the import of [the proclamation]? that the people, the flesh, is of a vain temporary nature; that all its glory fadeth, and is soon gone; but that the Word of God endureth for ever. What is this but a plain opposition of the flesh to the Spirit; of the carnal Israel to the spiritual; of the temporary Mosaic economy to the eternal Christian dispensation?" Here, then, St. Peter is quoting one of the greatest of Messianic prophecies; and his Hebrew readers would at once understand the Hebrew method of the quotation, and see that he was calling attention to the absolute equality of Jew and Gentile there proclaimed. Generation of the corruptible seed, physical descent from Abraham, was "the glory of the flesh" (observe that according to the best text St. Peter does *not* follow the LXX., and insert "of man," but follows the Hebrew, and says "all the glory thereof," *i.e.,* of the flesh). On this "the *Spirit* of the Lord" had breathed (Ps. civ. 30); and the merely fleshly glory had withered like grass. But "the word of our God," which, mark well, St. Peter purposely changes into "the Word of the Lord," *i.e., of Jesus Christ,* incidentally showing his Hebrew readers that he believed Jesus Christ to *be* "our God"—this "abideth for ever." The engendering by *this* is imperishable, *i.e.,* involves a privilege which is not, like that of the Jewish blood, transitory: it will never

glory of man as the flower of grass.
The grass withereth, and the flower
thereof falleth away: (25) but the word
of the Lord endureth for ever. And
this is the word which by the gospel is
preached unto you.

CHAPTER II.—(1) Wherefore laying
aside[a] all malice, and all guile, and
hypocrisies,[b] and envies,
and all evil speakings,
(2) as newborn babes, de-
sire the sincere milk[c] of
the word, that ye may
grow thereby: (3) if so be ye have
tasted that the Lord *is* gracious.[d]

Chap. ii. 1—10. The idea of the New Israel as seen in prophecy to be realised by them.

a Eph. 4. 22; Col. 3. 8; Jas. 1. 21.
b ch. 1. 22.
c 1 Cor. 3. 2; Heb. 5. 12.
A.D. cir. 60.
d Ps. 34. 8.

---

become a matter of indifference whether we have been engendered with this, as is the case now (Gal. vi. 15) with regard to the "corruptible seed;" no further revelation will ever level up the unregenerate to be the equals of the regenerate. And in this regeneration "all flesh" share alike. The teaching of the Baptist, who fulfilled this prophecy, is here again apparent. (See Matt. iii. 9.)

(25) **The word which by the gospel is preached.**—An incorrect rendering of the original tense. It literally runs, *And this is the word which was preached unto you.* The whole magnificent peroration of this paragraph, as of the last, leads up to this: that, in the opinion of St. Peter, the Gospel, as delivered by St. Paul and his followers—the Gospel of equality, or rather of unity between Jew and Gentile in Jesus Christ—was the living and supreme abiding revelation of the will of God! Well may the Tübingen school wish to disprove the genuineness of this Epistle!

II.

(1–10) Exhortation to realise the Idea of the New Israel.—The Apostle bids them put away all elements of disunion, and to combine into a new Temple founded on Jesus as the Christ, and into a new hierarchy and theocracy.

(1) **Wherefore.**—That is, Because the Pauline teaching is correct which brings the Gentiles up to the same level with the Jews. It may be observed that this newly enunciated principle is called by St. Peter in the previous verse of the last chapter, a "gospel," or piece of *good* news, for all parties.

Laying aside.—This implies that before they had been *wrapped up* in these sins. There had been "malice" (*i.e.*, ill will put into action) on the part of these Hebrew Christians against their Gentile brethren, and "guile," and "hypocrisies," and "jealousies," which are all instances of concealed malice. Of these three, the first plots, the second pretends not to plot, and the third rejoices to think of the plot succeeding. The word for "all evil speakings" is literally, *all talkings down*—this is "malice" in *word*. Archbishop Leighton well says, "The Apostles sometimes name some of these evils, and sometimes other of them; but they are inseparable, all one garment, and all comprehended under that one word (Eph. iv. 22), 'the old man,' which the Apostle there exhorts to put off; and here it is pressed as a necessary evidence of this new birth, and furtherance of their spiritual growth, that these base habits be thrown away, ragged filthy habits, unbeseeming the children of God." All these vices (natural vices to the Jewish mind) are contrasted with the "unfeigned (literally, *un-hypocritical*) brotherly kindness" of chap. i. 22.

(2) **As newborn babes.**—The word "newborn" is, of course, newly, lately born, not born anew, although the birth meant is the new birth of chap. i. 23. They are said to be still but newborn because they are still so far from maturity in Christ, as these sins testified. The metaphor is said to be not uncommon in Rabbinical writers to denote proselytes. St. Peter would, therefore, be describing Jews who had newly received the word of God, as *proselytes* of the new Israel. "As" means "in keeping with your character of." (Comp. chap. i. 14.)

Desire the sincere milk.—The word for "desire" here is a strong word—*get an appetite for it.* Bengel is perhaps right when he says on "newborn babes," "It is their only occupation, so strong is their desire for it." St. Peter here again seems to lend a thought to the writer to the Hebrews (Heb. v. 12—14). In both places Jewish Christians are beginning to rebel against the Gospel instructions, and in both places they are warned that they have not yet outgrown the need of the very simplest elements of the Gospel. The epithet "sincere" should have been rendered *guileless*, as it contains a contrast with "guile" in the verse before; perhaps the intention of the epithet may be to rebuke the attempt to deal deceitfully with the Old Testament Scriptures after the example of the Septuagint passage quoted above.

Of the word.—This translation of the original adjective cannot possibly be right. The only other place in the New Testament where it is used, Rom. xii. 1, will show clearly enough its meaning here. There it is rendered "your *reasonable* service"—*i.e.*, not "the service which may be reasonably expected of you," but "the ritual worship which is performed by the reason, not by the body." So here, "the reasonable guileless milk" will mean "the guileless milk which is sucked in, not by the lips, but by the reason." The metaphor of milk (though used by St. Paul, 1 Cor. iii. 2) was not so hackneyed as now; and the Apostle wished to soften it a little, and explain it by calling it "mental milk," just as (so Huther points out) he explained the metaphor in chap. i. 13, by adding "of your mind." It is needless to add that the "mental milk" would, as a matter of fact, be "the milk of the word," and that the Apostle is pressing his readers to cling with ardent attachment to the evangelical religion taught them by the Pauline party.

That ye may grow thereby.—All the best manuscripts and versions add "unto salvation," which may confidently be adopted into the text. "Grow" is, of course, said in reference to the infant state of the converts as yet, and the maturity set before them (children long to be grown up) is spoken of as "salvation." When we compare this with chap. i. 18, we see that the perfect emancipation from Jewish superstitions is a main part of the "salvation" to which they are to grow up.

(3) **If so be ye have tasted.**—The "if so be," as elsewhere (2 Thess. i. 6, Note), constitutes a strong appeal to the readers to say whether it were not so. St. Peter confidently reckons that it is so. It should rather be *ye tasted*, looking back to a quite past time, probably that of the first conversion, when the

(4) To whom coming, *as unto* a living stone, disallowed indeed of men,[a] but chosen of God, *and* precious, (5) ye also, as lively stones, are [1] built up a spiritual house,[b]

a Ps. 118. 22.
1 Or, *be ye built.*
b 1 Cor. 3. 9; Eph. 2. 21.

taste of spiritual things is the most delicious. How sad to be past the relish for evangelical truth! The quotation, or rather adaptation, from Ps. xxxiv. 8 is, no doubt, suggested by the metaphor of "milk." A curious little point about our translation here is that the word "gracious" has been adopted to suit the Prayer Book version of the Psalm. It is scarcely suitable to the Greek word, which, originally signifying "usable," "serviceable," passes on to be used of anything mild and pleasant, as, for instance, in Luke v. 39, of the mellowness of old wine. Here, therefore, the word seems to be peculiarly used with reference to the sense of taste. A more important point, doctrinally, is that St. Peter is here applying to Jesus Christ (as the next verse shows) a passage which otherwise we might not have thought of applying to Him in particular. It gives quite a new complexion to the 34th Psalm, when we see that in St. Peter's view the Psalmist was speaking prophetically of our Lord. We shall find him quoting the same Psalm in the same sense again in chap. iii. 10.

(4) **To whom coming.**—The word used is that which gives rise to the name of a "proselyte." (Comp. Note on verse 2.) It is also strangely used in something of the same sense in 1 Tim. vi. 3. "Joining Him therefore as proselytes." Not that St. Peter has any notion of a mere external accession. The Apostolic writers do not contemplate the possibility of a difference between the visible and invisible Church. From this point the regeneration-idea, which coloured the whole of the preceding portion of the Epistle, suddenly disappears. The thought is no longer that of a spiritual seed instead of a carnal seed, but of a spiritual Temple instead of the stone temple at Jerusalem.

A living stone.—The very structure and order of the sentence puts Jesus Christ first. Foundation first, building afterwards. It is a pity to insert "as unto" with our version; it takes off from the striking, attracting effect of the sudden metaphor. St. Peter is fond of explaining his metaphors—*e.g.*, "inheritance . . . in heaven," "tested genuineness . . . more precious than of gold," "gird up . . . loins of your minds:" so here, "living stone." It is more than doubtful whether St. Peter, in what follows, had before his mind the giving of his own surname. The word which he here uses is neither *petros*, nor *petra*, but *lithos;* and indeed the whole idea of the relative position of the Church to the *petra* and to the *lithos* is quite different. Neither *petros* nor *petra* could possibly be used of the squared wrought stone, but represent the native rocky unhewn substratum—part, or whole—which pre-exists before any building is begun, even before the "chief corner-stone" would be placed. (Comp. Matt. vii. 24.) Here, therefore, the idea is quite different: the substratum is not thought of at all; and Jesus Christ is a carefully selected and hewn stone (*lithos*), specially laid as the first act in the work of building. The only thing, therefore, which is, in fact, common to the two passages is the simple thought of the Christian Church being like a building. Our present verse gives us no direct help towards finding how St. Peter understood the famous name-passage. All we can say for certain is that he did not so interpret it as to suppose an official connection with his own person to be the one essential of the true Church, or else in again using the metaphor of building the Church (though in a different connection) he could hardly have omitted all mention of himself. He is, apparently, thinking only of the Messianic interpretation of Old Testament sayings as expounded by our Lord—the "unsophisticated milk of the word" of verse 2.

Disallowed indeed of men.—A direct reference to the passage (Ps. cxviii. 22), which is quoted below in verse 7. It here says "men," rather than "builders," in order to contrast them more forcibly with God. The word "disallowed," or "rejected," implies a form of trial or probation which comes to an unsatisfactory conclusion. The human builders examine the stone, inspect all its qualifications, and find it unsuited to the edifice which *they* have in hand, and refuse it not only the place of honour, but any place at all, in their architecture. St. Peter wishes to bring out strongly the absolute opposition between God and the Jews.

But chosen of God, and precious.—Literally, *but with God elect, honoured.* This is a direct allusion to the passage, Isa. xxviii. 16, which is quoted in verse 6. While the human builders saw the qualities of the stone, and rejected it because of its not fitting in with their ideal, on the other hand, "with God," *i.e.*, in God's counsel and plan, it was "elect," *i.e.*, choice had been laid upon it, it had been selected for God's building purposes; and not only "elect" (for this might be equally said of all the "living stones;" see chap. i. 2, where the word has precisely the same meaning), but also "honoured," which is further explained to mean, singled out for the place of honour, *i.e.*, for that of corner-stone. The designation of this stone as "elect," brings out again what we have had in chap. i. 11, 20, viz., the eternal predestination of Jesus to the Messiahship.

(5) **Ye also, as lively stones, are built up.**—This is true enough: they *were* in process of building up; but it suits the hortatory character of the whole Epistle better to take it (the one is as grammatical as the other) in the *imperative* sense: *Be ye also as living stones built up.* The rendering "lively," instead of "living," as in verse 4, is arbitrary, the Greek being precisely the same, and the intention being to show the complete conformation of the believers to Him who is the type and model for humanity. "Built up," too, only expresses a part of the Greek word, which implies "built up *upon* Him."

A spiritual house.—The epithet is supplied, just as in "*living* stone," to make it abundantly clear that the language is figurative. In the first three verses of the chapter these Hebrew Christians were treated *individually*, as so many babes, to grow up into an ideal *freedom of soul:* here they are treated *collectively* (of course, along with the Gentile Christians), as so many stones, incomplete and unmeaning in themselves, by arrangement and cemented union to rise into an ideal *house of God.* St. Peter does not distinctly say that the "house" is a temple (for the word "spiritual" is only the opposite of "material"), but the context makes it plain that such is the case. The temple is, however, regarded not in its capacity of a place for *worship* so much as a place for Divine *inhabitation.* "The spiritual house," says Leighton truly, "is the palace of the Great King. The Hebrew word for *palace* and *temple* is one." And the reason for introducing this figure

an holy priesthood,[a] to offer up spiritual sacrifices, acceptable to God by Jesus Christ. (6) Wherefore also it is contained in the scripture,[b] Behold, I lay in Sion

a Isa. 61. 6; 66. 21.
b Isa. 28. 16.

seems to be, to console the Hebrews for their vanishing privileges in the temple at Jerusalem. They are being taught to recognise that they themselves, in their union with one another, and with Jesus Christ, are the true abode of the Most High. The Christian substitution of something else in lieu of the Jerusalem Temple was one of the greatest stumbling-blocks to the Hebrews from the very first. (See Mark xiv. 58; John ii. 21; Acts vii. 48; xxi. 28; compare also Heb. ix. 8, 11.) All history is the process of building up a "spiritual palace" out of a regenerate humanity, in order that, in the end, the *Father Himself* may occupy it. This follows from the fact that the Incarnate *Son* is described as a *part* of the Temple. Even through the Incarnation—at least so far as it has as yet taken effect—creation has not become so completely pervaded and filled with the Deity as it is destined to be when the "palace" is finished. (See 1 Cor. xv. 28.) The idea of the Eternal Son occupying such a relation to the Father on the one hand, and to humanity and creation on the other hand, is really the same as when He is called (by an entirely different metaphor) the "first-born of all creation" (Col. i. 15).

An holy priesthood.—"Being *living* stones," says Bengel, "they can be priests as well." They not only *compose* the Temple, but minister in it. By becoming Christians they are cut off from neither Temple nor hierarchy, nor sacrifice; all are at hand, and they themselves are all. The old priesthood, like the old Temple, has "had its day, and ceased to be." Mark, though, that the Apostle is not dwelling on the individual priesthood of each (though that is involved), but on the hierarchical order of the whole company of Christians: they are an organised body or college of priests, a new seed of Aaron or Levi. (See Isa. lxvi. 21.) The very word implies that all Christians have not an equal *degree* of priesthood. And this new priesthood, like the old, is no profane intruding priesthood like that of Core (Jude 11), but "holy"—*i.e.*, consecrated, validly admitted to its work. The way in which this new metaphor is suddenly introduced,—"to *whom* coming, be built up *upon Him* . . . to be an holy priesthood," implies that Jesus Christ is the High Priest quite as much as it implies His being Corner Stone. The Incarnate Son heads the adoration offered to the Father by creation, just as He binds creation into a palace for the Father's indwelling.

To offer up spiritual sacrifices.—The new priesthood is not merely nominal; it is no sinecure. None is a priest who does not offer sacrifices (Heb. viii. 3). But the sacrifices of the new hierarchy are "spiritual,"—*i.e.*, not material, not sacrifices of bulls and goats and lambs. What, then, do the sacrifices consist of? If our priesthood is modelled on that of Jesus Christ, as is here implied, it consists mainly (Calvin points this out) of the sacrifice of *self*, of the *will*; then, in a minor degree, of words and acts of worship, thanks and praise. (See Heb. xiii. 10—16.) But in order to constitute a true priesthood and true sacrifices after the model of Jesus Christ, these sacrifices are offered up on behalf of others. (See Heb. v. 1, and 1 John iii. 16.) The first notion of the priesthood of all believers is not that of a mediatorial system being abolished, but of the mediatorial system being extended: whereas, before, only Aaron's sons were recognised as mediators and intercessors, now all Israel, all the spiritual Israel, all men everywhere are called to be mediators and intercessors between each other and God.

By (or, *through*) **Jesus Christ.**—The *name* again, not the title only. We all help one another to present one another's prayers and praises, which pass through the lips of many priests; but for them to be acceptable, they must be presented finally through the lips of the Great High Priest. He, in His perfect sympathy with all men, must make the sacrifice His own. We must unite our sacrifices with His—the Advocate with the Father, the Propitiation for our sins—or our sacrifice will be as irregular and offensive as though some Canaanite should have taken upon himself to intrude into the Holy of Holies on Atonement Day. (See Heb. x. 19—25, especially verse 21.)

(6) **Wherefore also.**—The mention of Jesus Christ brings the writer back again to his theme, viz., that the whole system to which his readers belong has undergone a radical change, and is based on Jesus and His fulfilment of the sufferings and glories of the Messiah. The right reading here is not "wherefore also," but *because*—*i.e.*, the quotations are introduced in the same way as in chap. i. 16 and 24, as justifying the foregoing expressions.

It is contained in the scripture.—In the original the phrase is a curious one. "The scripture" never means the Old Testament as a whole, which would be called "the Scriptures," but is always the particular book or passage of the Old Testament. Literally, then, our present phrase runs, *because it encloses* or *contains in that passage*. Thus attention is drawn to the context of the quotation, and in this context we shall again find what made St. Peter quote the text.

Behold, I lay.—The sentence is taken from Isa. xxviii. 16, and, like the last, is adapted to the occasion out of both Hebrew and LXX. Gesenius on that passage gives evidence to show that the early Jewish explanation, current in our Lord's time, referred it to the Messiah; the later Rabbinical expositors, probably by way of opposition to the Christians, explained it to mean Hezekiah. In order to gain a clear conception of St. Peter's aim in the quotation, it is necessary to glance over the whole section contained in the 28th and 29th chapters of Isaiah. "The prophecy here cited," says Archbishop Leighton, "if we look upon it in its own place, we shall find inserted in the middle of a very sad denunciation of judgment against the Jews." Besides our present text, which is quoted also in Rom. ix. 33, our Lord's prophecy of the destruction of Jerusalem is an amplification of Isa. xxix. 3, 4; His sharp censure of the corrupt traditions which had superseded the law of God (Matt. xv. 7—9) is taken from Isa. xxix. 13; St. Paul's image of the potter changing his purpose with the lump of clay (Rom. ix. 21), comes from Isa. xxix. 16. Like one bright spot in the sad picture appears our verse, but only as serving to heighten the general gloom. St. Peter's quotation here, therefore, calling attention as it does to the context, is at least as much intended to show his Hebrew readers the sweeping away of the carnal Israel as to encourage them in their Christian allegiance. In the original passage the sure foundation is contrasted with the refuge of lies which the Jewish rulers had constructed for themselves against Assyria, "scorning"

a chief corner stone, elect, precious: and he that believeth on him shall not be confounded. (7) Unto you therefore which believe *he is* precious:[1] but unto them which be disobedient, the stone which the builders disallowed, the same

[1] Or, *an honour.*

---

this sure foundation as a piece of antiquated and unpractical religionism. Nägelsbach (in his new commentary on Isaiah) seems to be right in interpreting the "refuge of lies" to mean the diplomatic skill with which Ahaz and the Jewish authorities flattered themselves their treaty with Egypt was drawn up, and the "sure foundation" opposed to it is primarily God's plighted promise to the house of David, in which all who trusted would have no cause for flight. In the Messianic fulfilment, those promises are all summed up in the one person of Jesus Christ (Acts xiii. 33; 2 Cor. i. 20); and the "refuge of lies" in which the Jewish rulers had trusted was the wicked policy by which they had tried to secure their "place and nation" against the Romans (John xi. 48).

In Sion.—In Isaiah it means that the people have not to look for any distant external aid, such as that of Pharaoh: all that they need is to be found in the city of David itself. Here, it seems to impress upon the Hebrew Christians that they are not abandoning their position as Hebrews by attaching themselves to Jesus Christ. It is they who are really clinging to Sion when the other Jews are abandoning her.

Shall not be confounded (or, *ashamed*).—Our version of Isaiah translates the Hebrew original by the unintelligible "shall not make haste." It really means, *shall not flee.* While all the Jewish rulers, who had turned faithless and trusted in their *finesse* with Egypt, would have to flee from the face of the Assyrians, those who preserved their faith in God would be able to stand their ground. This, of course, did not come literally true in the first instance, where a common temporal overthrow came upon faithful and faithless alike, from Babylon, though not from Assyria. In the Messianic fulfilment, however, the faith or unbelief of the individual makes all the difference to him: the overthrow of the many does not affect the few. St. Peter adds to "believe" the words "on Him" or "on it," which are found in neither the Hebrew nor the Greek of Isaiah, such an addition being quite in keeping with the Rabbinic method of quotation, which frequently alters words (comp. Matt. ii. 6) to bring out the concealed intention more fully. The general quality of "faith" of which the prophet spoke, *i.e.*, reliance on the promises of God, becomes faith in Him in whom the promises are fulfilled. For a like cause St. Peter prefers the LXX. "be ashamed" to the Hebrew "flee away," there being (except at the Fall of Jerusalem) no opportunity for actual flight. It comes to the same thing in the end: "shall not find his confidence misplaced."

(7) **He is precious.**—Rather, *Unto you therefore, the believers, belongs the honour.* So said in reference to His being called "a stone elect, *honoured,*" taken in conjunction with "shall not be ashamed." Both the Hebrew and the Greek word rendered "precious" may with equal propriety be translated "honoured," and this contrasts better with the "shame" just spoken of. Thus Dr. Lightfoot takes it. The argument is this: "God has selected Jesus for special honour, and has promised that all who trust in Him, instead of scorning Him like the Jewish rulers, shall have no cause to blush. Now *you do* trust in Him, therefore to you belongs the promise, and the honour bestowed by God on Him reflects on you. You, like Him, are made parts of the divine imperishable architecture."

Unto them which be disobedient.—The better reading is, *Unto them which disbelieve*; the other word being an importation from verse 8. The true reading better preserves the contrast with "you that believe."

The stone which the builders disallowed.—We should perhaps have rather expected the sentence to run more like this: "To you which believe belongs the honour, but to those who disbelieve belongs the shame from which you are secured." But instead, the Apostle stops short, and inserts (by a quotation) the historical fact which *brought* the shame, viz., the disappointment of their own design, and the glorious completion of that which they opposed. The words which follow are quoted directly from the LXX., and properly represent the Hebrew. Almost all the best modern critics consider the Psalm from which this verse is cited to be a late Psalm, written subsequent to the return from Babylon, in which case it is most probable that the composer was directly thinking of the prophecy of Isaiah above quoted. The Messianic interpretation of the Psalm would be no novelty to the Hebrews who received this Epistle (see Matt. xxi. 9), though probably they had not perceived it in its fulness. In its first application the passage seems to mean as follows: The speaker is Israel, taken as a single person. He has been a despised captive. The great builders of the world—the Babylonian and Persian empires—had recognised no greatness in him, and had no intention of advancing him; they were engaged in aggrandisement of self alone. Yet, after all, Israel is firmly planted once more in Sion, to be the first stone of a new structure, a new empire. Thus this interpretation at once suggests the admission of the Gentiles, humanity at large, into the architecture. Israel is the corner-stone, but corner-stones are not laid to be left unbuilt upon. In the fulfilment Christ takes the place of Israel, as is the case with Isa. liii. The builders are the rulers of the Jews. In Acts iv. 11 our author had called the Sanhedrin to their face, "you builders." They, like the kings of Babylon, had been intent on building a fabric of their own, and had despised Jesus, yet, without any intention of so doing, had been the means of advancing Him (Acts iv. 27, 28). He had been made the basis of a new spiritual structure, in which faith, not fleshly lineage, was the cement and bond; and the believing Israelites, united to Him in both ways, shared the honour of being corner-stone. A further point is given to the quotation if we suppose, with Hengstenberg, Delitzsch, and others, that the remembrance of Isaiah's prophecy of the "corner-stone" was suggested to the original Psalmist by the works of the Second Temple, then begun, advancing, or fresh completed. It will then fit in more perfectly with the description of the "spiritual house." Leighton well points out how sore a trial it was to the faith of Jewish Christians to see that their own chosen people, even the most learned of them, rejected Christ, and adds, "That they may know this makes nothing against Him, nor ought to invalidate their faith at all, but rather testifies with Christ, and so serves to confirm them in believing, the Apostle makes use of those prophetical scriptures that foretell the unbelief and contempt with which the most would entertain Christ."

is made the head of the corner,[a] (8) and
a stone of stumbling, and a rock of
offence,[b] *even to them* which stumble at
the word, being disobedient: whereunto
also they were appointed.[c] (9) But ye
are a chosen generation,[d] a royal priest-
hood,[e] an holy nation, a peculiar
people; [1] [f] that ye should shew forth

a Ps. 118. 22; Matt. 21. 42; Acts 4. 11.
b Isa. 8. 14.
c 1 Thess. 5. 9.
d Deut. 10. 15.
e Ex. 19. 6.
1 Or, *a purchased people.*
f Deut. 14. 2.

---

(8) **And a stone of stumbling and a rock of offence.**—Another quotation, no doubt suggested by the word "a stone," but conveying a totally different metaphor. Here there is no thought whatever of the stone as a material for building; the thought is that of a mass of rock on the road, on which the terror-stricken fugitives stumble and fall. The words are taken from Isa. viii. 14, and are translated directly from the Hebrew. The LXX. not only makes nonsense, but can again be hardly acquitted of "guile" (verse 1) in its endeavour to make out the best possible case for Israel by deliberately inserting the word "not" twice over. We shall find St. Peter in chap. iii. 14 quoting the verses which immediately precede our present citation, and again the point lies in the context. The words are no mere phrase hastily caught up to serve the turn. They come out of the great Immanuel section of Isaiah, and immediately involve, like the quotation in verse 6, the sharp contrast between the Jews who trust in Immanuel (the presence of God with Israel) and the Jews who do not, but rely on "confederacies." To the one party, the Lord of Hosts will be "for a sanctuary;" but to the other party, who are described as "both houses of Israel," and specially as the "inhabitant of Jerusalem," He will be "for a stone of striking, and for a rock of stumbling over," and also "for a snare." The "sanctuary" does not seem to mean a temple (though this would connect it with the preceding words of St. Peter), but rather such a "sanctuary" as that of Bethel (Gen. xxviii. 18), a consecrated stone to which a man might flee as an asylum. In the flight of terror before the face of the Assyrians the very stone which afforded right of sanctuary to those who recognised and trusted it, was a vexatious and dangerous obstacle, a trap full in the way to those who did not. Once more, therefore, the Hebrews of the Dispersion, in separating themselves from "both houses of Israel" and the "inhabitant of Jerusalem," were obeying the warnings of the Immanuel prophecy, which every Hebrew recognised as Messianic. Though the coupling of these passages of the Old Testament together certainly seems to show traces of the influence of St. Paul (comp. Rom. ix. 32, 33), yet St. Peter must have been present and heard "the Lord of Hosts" Himself put them together (Luke xx. 17, 18), and probably St. Paul's use of the passages is itself to be traced back to the same origin.

Stumble at the word, being disobedient.—It seems better to arrange the words otherwise: *which stumble, being disobedient to the word.* The participle thus explains the verb. "'A stone of stumbling' He is to them; and the manner of the stumbling is in being disobedient to the gospel preaching" (Leighton).

Whereunto also they were appointed—*i.e.,* unto stumbling. The present commentator believes that when St. Peter says that these unhappy Jews were appointed to stumble, he primarily means that the clear prophecies of the Old Testament which he has quoted marked them for such a destiny. It was no unforeseen, accidental consequence of the gospel. It had never been expected that all who heard the gospel would accept it. Those who stumbled by disbelief were marked out in prophecy as men who would stumble. Thus the introduction of the statement here has the direct practical purpose of confirming the faith of the readers by showing the verification of the prophecy. Still, in fairness, we must not shirk the further question which undoubtedly comes in at this point. Even though the moment of their appointment to stumble was that of the utterance of the prophecy, it cannot be denied that, in a certain sense, it was God Himself who appointed them to stumble. It will be observed, however, from the outset, that our present passage casts not a glance at the condition of the stumbling Jews *after death.* With this caution, we may say that God puts men sometimes into positions where, during this life, they almost inevitably reject the truth. This is implied in the very doctrine of election—*e.g.,* in 2 Thess. ii. 13, where, if God selects one man out of the hundred to a present salvation through belief of truth, it seems to follow logically that the ninety and nine are appointed to have no share in that salvation, so far as this life is concerned, through disbelief of truth. These things remain as a trial of faith. It suffices that we know for certain that God is Love. He has "brought us forth at His own option by the word of truth, that we should be a kind of firstfruits of His creatures" (Jas. i. 18). We have but to prize more highly our own present salvation, and to trust His love for that fuller harvest of which we are but the firstfruits. In some way even their stumbling will ultimately prove His love, to them as well as to us.

(9) **But ye.**—Like St. Paul in 2 Thess. ii. 13, St. Peter turns with an outburst of triumph to the happier and more practical and attractive theme. All the most splendid titles of the old Israel belong in a fuller sense to these Hebrews who have joined the new Israel. In verse 5 they are bidden to aim at being what here they are said to be. (Comp. Col. iii. 3, 5.)

A chosen generation.—Better, *a chosen,* or *elect race.* As originally the clan of Abraham was selected from among "all the families of the earth" (Amos iii. 2), so out of the clan of Abraham after the flesh were these men selected to be a new clan, or race. They are not merely individuals selected one by one and left in isolation, but a tribe consolidated, only the bond henceforth is not merely one of common physical descent.

A royal priesthood, an holy nation.—These words are a direct quotation from Ex. xix. 6, according to the LXX. version. The Hebrew has "a kingdom of priests," as in Rev. i. 6 (according to the best reading); which would mean, God's organised empire, every member of which is a priest. Nor is the thought far different here. The word "royal" does not seem intended to imply that every Christian is a king, or of royal birth (though that, of course, may be shown from elsewhere), but describes his *belonging* to the King as we might speak of the royal apartments, the royal borough, the royal establishment, or even of the royal servants. The substitution, therefore, of "royal priesthood" for "kingdom of priests" brings out more clearly the personal relation to the Personal King. But if the writer had said "royal priests," the notion of organisation would have slipped out of sight altogether. By way of compensation, therefore, it is restored in the substitution of "priesthood" (see Note on verse 5) instead of "priests." This, and the next phrase, "an holy (*i.e.,* consecrated)

the praises [1] of him who hath called you out of darkness into his marvellous light: (10) which in time past *were* not a people,[a] but *are* now the

[1] Or, *virtues.*

[a] Hos. 2. 23; Rom. 9. 26.

nation," describe the whole Israelite nation as they stood beneath Mount Sinai. This must be taken into consideration in dealing with the doctrine of the Christian ministry. The sacerdotal office was as common to all Israelites under the Law as it is to all the new Israel under the Gospel.

A peculiar people.—This curious phrase is literally, *a people for a special reservation.* It is, no doubt, intended to represent Ex. xix. 5, though it differs both from the Greek and the Hebrew, the variation being due to a recollection of the Greek of two other passages of the Old Testament (Isa. xliii. 21; Mal. iii. 17). The word rendered "peculiar" means properly "making over and above," and would be represented in Latin by the word *peculium,* which means a man's private pocket-money, as, for instance, the money a slave could make by working over hours, or such as a wife might have apart from her husband. When children speak of a thing being their "very own" it exactly expresses what we have here. From this sense of "making over and above," by working out of hours, the word comes in other places to mean "earning by hard work," in such a way as to establish peculiar rights of property over the thing earned. So in Acts xx. 28, where St. Paul is probably thinking of the passage of Isaiah above referred to, both the hard earning and the special possession are intended: "the Church of God, which He won so hard for His very own, by His own blood." Here, perhaps, the thought of "earning" is less obvious, and it means "a people to be His very own." Comp. 1 Thess. v. 9, and Eph. i. 7, where (according to Dr. Lightfoot) it means "for a redemption which consists of taking possession of us for His own."

That ye should shew forth the praises.—This is an adaptation, though not exactly according to the LXX., of Isa. xliii. 21, which passage is brought to St. Peter's mind by the word rendered "peculiar." The word "praises" is put here in accordance with the English version there. The Greek means "virtues," or "powers," or "excellencies," a rare word in the New Testament (see 2 Pet. i. 3). And the word for "shew forth," which is nowhere else found in the New Testament, means by rights "to proclaim to those without what has taken place within." This strict signification is very suitable here. St. Peter says that God has taken us for a people peculiarly near to Him, and the purpose is, not that we may stand within His courts and praise Him, but that we may carry to others the tidings of what we have been admitted to see. This was the true function of the old Israel, "Do My *prophets* no harm" (Ps. cv. 15). They were not elect for their own sake, but to act as God's exponents to the world. This function they abdicated by their selfish exclusiveness, and it has descended to the new Israel. St. Peter and St. Paul are at one.

Of him who hath called you out of darkness.—This is to be understood of the Father, not of Christ. For one thing, the act of calling is almost always ascribed in the New Testament to God Himself; and for another thing, it is probable that St. Peter regards our Lord as Head of this "people of God," just as He is corner-stone of the Temple, and High Priest of the hierarchy. The act of calling (literally it is, *who called,* not "who *hath* called") was that of sending the preachers of the gospel to them, *i.e.,* St. Paul and his followers (comp. chap. i. 12, 25). Here again, then, we have St. Peter speaking in praise of St. Paul's mission, and, indeed, speaking in the same tones of unbounded admiration: "His marvellous light." But could Hebrew Christians be said to have gone through so great a change in becoming believers? Had they been in "darkness?" We may answer that St. Peter's use of the word "marvellous" is no affectation of sympathy. He himself found the change to be what he here describes, therefore there is no difficulty in supposing that other Hebrews should have found it so too. Besides which, the state of the Jews immediately before Christ and without Him is often described as "darkness." (See Matt. iv. 16; Luke i. 79.) This very passage is quoted a few years later by St. Clement of Rome (chap. xxxvi.), as applying to himself among others, and Dr. Lightfoot has clearly established that St. Clement was a Jew.

(10) **Which in time past were not a people.**—Here at last, say some, we have a distinct proof that the Epistle was written to the Gentiles only, or, at least, to churches which contained a very small proportion of Jews. Such, however, is by no means the case; in fact, the opposite. We have here an emphasised adaptation of Hos. ii. 23, "And I will have mercy upon Lo-ruhamah, and I will say to Lo-ammi, 'Thou art Ammi,' *i.e.,* My people." Now who were Lo-ruhamah and Lo-ammi? Types of Israel left unpitied, and rejected from their covenant with God. And this unpitied and rejected Israel, after being "scattered," or *sown,* all over the earth, was to be restored again to favour, together with the increment of the Gentiles who joined it as the result of the "sowing." St. Peter means, then, that in his Hebrew readers and the brethren from among the Gentiles, who by the gospel of St. Paul had adhered to them, this promise given by Hosea had found its fulfilment. But, as usual, the quotation demands a more searching scrutiny of the context from which it is taken. The name *Diaspora,* or Dispersion, by which St. Peter, in chap. i. 1, designates those to whom he writes, was applied to themselves by the Jews in direct allusion (as seems probable) to the name Jezreel, or *God will scatter,* in Hos. i. 4. Now mark that St. Peter does not say "which in time past were not God's people," but "were not *a* people." This was the effect of the dispersion, or "scattering." Though each Jew of the dispersion retained, and still retains, in isolation, his national characteristics and aspirations, yet their unity—that which made them a "people"—was, and is, for the time broken. The Hebrews had not only ceased to be in covenant as "God's people," but had ceased to be "a people" at all. But in Christ, that very "scattering" becomes a "sowing" (Hos. ii. 23), for the name Jezreel means both equally; their very dispersion becomes the means of their multiplication by union with the Gentiles in Christ, and thus spiritually they recover the lost unity, and become once more a solid and well-governed confederation, *i.e.,* "a people," and that "the people of God." (See John xi. 52, and Dr. Pusey's notes on Hosea.) It is a mistake to take St. Paul's quotation of this passage in Rom. ix. 26, as if it referred solely to the Gentiles; for he expressly affirms that the title "My people" belongs to neither section exclusively, but to both in reunion—"us whom He called, *not only* of the Jews, but *also* of the Gentiles."

people of God: which had not ob-
tained mercy, but now have obtained
mercy.
(11) Dearly beloved, I beseech *you* as
strangers[a] and pilgrims, abstain from
fleshly lusts, which war
against the soul;[b] (12) having
your conversation honest
among the Gentiles: that,
whereas[1] they speak against you as

b Rom. 7. 23; Jas. 4. 1.

a ch. 1. 17.

1 Or, *wherein.*

Chap. ii. 11—25. The present crisis needs vigilant purity of life.

PRUDENTIAL RULES OF CONDUCT IN VIEW OF THE HOSTILE ATTITUDE OF THE HEATHEN.—As slanders against the Christian name are rife, and bringing practical persecution on the Church, they are exhorted to extreme care about their conduct, especially in regard (1) to purity, and (2) to due subordination, whether as subjects to the officers of state, or as slaves to their masters, or as wives to their husbands (chaps. ii. 11—iii. 12.)

(11) **Dearly beloved.**—"Affectionate and pressing exhortation," says Bengel. "That which is known to come from love," says Leighton, "cannot readily but be so received too, and it is thus expressed for that very purpose, that the request may be the more welcome. *Beloved,* it is the advice of a friend, one that truly loves you, and aims at nothing but your good; it is because I love you that I intreat you, and intreat you, as you love yourselves, to abstain from fleshly lusts."

As strangers and pilgrims.—The exhortation will be felt with the more force if we turn to the Psalm from which St. Peter draws the phrase (Ps. xxxix. 12, LXX.). The words, especially when compared with that Psalm, prepare for the description of distress which is to follow. (Comp. also Ps. cxix. 19.) The word "pilgrim" (which comes to us through the French form *pèlerin,* from the Latin *peregrinus*) does not originally, or in this place, mean one *on a pilgrimage.* It implies no journeying, but simply residence in a foreign country. Here it represents the same Greek word which is rendered "strangers" in chap. i. 1, but is used in a metaphorical and not literal sense. Though no longer "scattered," but gathered mercifully once more into "a people," they were still far from home—unprotected residents in an alien and hostile world, which scrutinised their conduct and was anxious for an opportunity to get rid of them.

Abstain from fleshly lusts.—First prudential rule. Although *all* bad desires might be described as fleshly, the word seems here to mean what we usually understand by it, the lusts which lead to drunkenness, gluttony, and uncleanness. And though such sins are usually characteristic of the Gentile, not of the Jew, yet see our Note on chap. i. 14. Jews were not impeccable in such matters, and here the Apostle has a special reason for insisting on the observance of the seventh commandment. It may even be said that his mode of insistence recognises that his readers usually do observe it. He appeals to them as "Israelites from home" to be on their guard in such matters, as Leonidas might exhort Spartans going into battle not to flinch, or Nelson tell English sailors that "England expects every man to do his duty." There was special reason for these Hebrew Christians to be more than ever vigilant, because (see Note on next verse) of the calumnies which the heathen were beginning to circulate about the Christians.

Which war against the soul.—This clause is no specifying of the particular fleshly lusts to be guarded against, as though there were some of them which did *not* war against the soul; but it is a description of the way in which all fleshly lusts alike act. It means not merely a general antagonism between soul and body, but that the lusts are *on active service,* engaged in a definite campaign against the immortal part of the man. St. Peter has probably forgotten for the moment his metaphor of strangers and sojourners, and we are not to put the two things together too closely, as though their position of strangers rendered them more liable to the attack of the hostile lusts. "Abstain" cannot mean merely "be on your guard against." It runs rather thus: "You Christian Jews are dwelling as sojourners in the midst of jealous Gentile foreigners, and must, therefore, be particularly observant of moral conduct; for though I know that you usually are so, yet the fleshly appetites are actively engaged against your soul all the time; and if you should in any degree let them get the better of you, the heathen neighbours will at once take advantage of you." As the expression might have been drawn equally well from St. Paul or from St. James, it is perhaps the easiest thing to suppose that (like the metaphors of building or of giving milk) it was part of the common property of Christians, and not consciously traceable to any originator.

(12) **Conversation.**—A favourite word with St. Peter, occurring (substantive and verb) seven times in this Epistle, and thrice in the second—*i.e.,* as often as in all the other New Testament writings put together. It means the visible conduct of the daily walk in life. This, as among Gentiles—*i.e.,* heathen (the words are synonymous, though St. Paul generally says "those without" when he means heathen as opposed to Christian)—is to be "honest." We have no word adequate to represent this charming adjective. It is rendered "good" immediately below and in John x. 11 ("the *Good* Shepherd"), "worthy" in James ii. 7, "goodly" in Luke xxi. 5. But it is the ordinary Greek word for "beautiful," and implies the attractiveness of the sight, the satisfaction afforded by an approach to ideal excellence.

That whereas.—The marginal version is more literal, and in sense perhaps preferable, "wherein." It means that the very fact of the heathen having slandered them will make their testimony "in the day of visitation" all the more striking, as (by way of illustration) the doubts of St. Thomas tend to "the more confirmation of the faith." So in Rom. ii. 1, "wherein thou judgest another, thou condemnest thyself;" or Heb. ii. 18 (lit.), "*wherein* He Himself hath suffered, being tempted."

They speak against you as evildoers.—A significant phrase. St. Peter asserts distinctly that calumnies were really rife, about some particulars of the Christian morality, at the time that this letter was written. It is a mark of a late date, for at first the Christians had not attracted sufficient notice, as a body, to be talked of either in praise or blame. The heathen at first regarded them as merely a Jewish sect (Acts xviii. 15; xxv. 18—20), and as such they received from the Roman Government a contemptuous toleration. The first state recognition of Christianity as a separate religion, with characteristics of its own, was the *Persecution of Nero* in the year 64. Now, it so happens that we have almost contemporary heathen documents which bring out the force of this passage.

evildoers,[a] they may by *your* good
works, which they shall behold, glorify
God[b] in the day of visitation. (13) Submit
yourselves to every ordinance of man for
the Lord's sake:[c] whether it be to the
king, as supreme; (14) or
unto governors, as unto
them that are sent by him

Subjection to authority.

a ch. 3. 16.
c Rom. 13. 1.
b Matt. 5. 16.

Suetonius, in his life of Nero (chap. 16), calls the Christians by the very name St. Peter uses, "the Christians, a kind of men of a new and *malefic* superstition." Only about forty years later, we have Pliny's famous letter to Trajan, written actually from the country in which St. Peter's correspondents lived, and referring to some of the very persons (probably) who received the Epistle as having apostatised at the time of the persecution under Nero; in which letter Pliny asks whether it is the profession of being a Christian which is itself to be punished, or "the crimes which attach to that profession!" The Apologists of the second century are full of refutations of the lies current about the immorality of the Christian assemblies. The Christians were a secret society, and held their meetings before daylight; and the heathen, partly from natural suspicion, partly from consciousness of what passed in their own secret religious festivals, imagined all kinds of horrors in connection with our mysteries. From what transpired about the Lord's Supper, they believed that the Christians used to kill children and drink their blood and eat their flesh. Here, however, the context points to a different scandal. They are warned against the *fleshly lusts,* in order that the heathen may find that the Christians' great glory lies in the very point wherein they are slandered. "Evildoers," therefore, must mean chiefly offences on that score. It is historically certain that such charges against Christian purity were extremely common. Even as late as the persecution under Maximin II., in the year 312, it was reported that these meetings before light were a school for the vilest of arts.

By your good works which they shall behold.—More literally, *they may, in consequence of your beautiful works, being eye-witnesses thereof.*—The "good works" are not what are commonly so called—*i.e.*, acts of benevolence, &c. Rather, their "works" are contrasted with the current report, and mean scarcely more than the "conversation" mentioned already. The present passage is, no doubt, a reminiscence of Matt. v. 16, where the word has the same force.

Glorify God in the day of visitation.—This "glorification" of God will be like that of Achan in the book of Joshua (chap. vii. 19), an acknowledgment how far they had been from the glorious truth. Some commentators understand the day of visitation to mean the day when the heathen themselves come really to look into the matter. This is possible; and it came true when Pliny tortured the Christian deaconesses and acquitted the poor fanatics, as he thought them, of all immoral practices. But from the ordinary use of the words, it would more naturally mean the day when God visits. And this will not mean only the great last day, but on whatever occasion God brings matters to a crisis. The visitation is a visitation of the Christians and the heathen alike, and it brings both grace and vengeance, according as men choose to receive it. (See Luke xix. 44, and comp. Luke i. 78.)

(13) **To every ordinance of man.**—Second prudential rule, subordination. Literally, *to every human creation, i.e.,* to every office or authority which men have established. It is not only to ordinances of directly Divine institution that we are to submit. Mind that he does not say we are to submit to every *law* that men may pass. This passage is most directly modelled on Rom. xiii. 1, *et seq.*, where the reason assigned for submission is the same as that in John xix. 11, viz., that ultimately the authority proceeds from God Himself. Here, however, the thought is quite different. They are to submit, but not because of the original source from which the authority flows, but because of the practical consequences of not submitting. It must be done "for the Lord's" (*i.e.*, Jesus Christ's) "sake," *i.e.*, in order not to bring discredit upon His teaching, and persecution upon His Church. This difference of treatment, in the midst of so much resemblance, shows that at the date of St. Peter's letter there was much more immediate cause for laying stress on political subordination. St. Paul, writing *to* the Roman Church, urges submission to Claudius, because the Roman Jews (among whom the Christians were reckoned) were often in trouble and expelled from the city of Rome (Acts xviii. 2); St. Peter, writing in all probability *from* the Roman Church, urges submission to Nero and the provincial governors because "ignorant and foolish men" were beginning to misrepresent the Christian Church as a kind of Internationalist or Socialist conspiracy.

The king, as supreme.—First division of second prudential rule: subordination political. Of course it means the emperor. The name "king," though detested in Latin, was used without scruple by the provincial Greeks to express the sovereignty of the Cæsars. When he is described here as "supreme," it is not intended (as our English version would convey) to contrast his supreme power with the inferior power of the "governors;" the word is only the same which is rendered "higher" in Rom. xiii. 1. Huther rightly says, "The emperor was in the Roman Empire not merely the highest, but actually the only ruler; all other magistrates were but the instruments by which he exercised his sway." Of course all Asia Minor, to which St. Peter was writing, was in the Roman Empire; the language would have been different had the letter been addressed to, or perhaps had it even been written from, the geographical Babylon.

(14) **Governors, as unto them that are sent by him.**—This word will include *legati*, proconsuls, proprætors, procurators, all officers entrusted with the administration of provinces. Of course the person "by" whom they are here said to be (from time to time) "sent" is Cæsar, not "the Lord." The persons to whom the letter is addressed would have very little to do with Cæsar himself directly, their submission would be chiefly shown to the lieutenants. Yet how personal was the Imperial government, even in details, is shown in Pliny's letters; the very letter before that in which he asks how to deal with the Christians of Bithynia requests Trajan's leave to cover in an unhealthy beck in the town of Amastris.

For the punishment of evildoers.—St. Peter credits Roman imperialism (rightly in the main) with having as its aim the promotion of moral behaviour among its subjects. The word for "punishment" is that which is translated "vengeance" in 2 Thess. i. 8, and implies forcing the malefactors to make satisfaction to those whom they had wronged, the "avenger" being, of course, quite disinterested. The "praise"

for the punishment of evildoers, and for
the praise of them that do well. (15) For
so is the will of God, that with well doing
ye may put to silence the ignorance of
foolish men: (16) as free, and not using[1]
your liberty for a cloke of maliciousness,[a]
but as the servants of God. (17) Honour[2]
all *men*. Love the brotherhood. Fear

1 Gr. *having*.
a Gal. 5. 13.
2 Or, *Esteem*.

---

which here, as in Rom. xiii. 3, is said to have been bestowed by the government on welldoers, must mean the solid praise of preferments, which is hardly so marked a feature of government as the foregoing. Be it observed that neither St. Peter nor St. Paul lay down any exceptions to the rule of complete obedience. They refuse to contemplate, at least to formulate, the occasions when disobedience may be necessary. Obedience is the first thing to learn, and when they have learnt it, they will know of themselves when to disobey. St. Peter himself stands to all time as the type of magnificent disobedience (Acts iv. 19).

(15) **For so is the will of God.**—This refers to the command contained in the last two verses, which then is further explained by the clause which follows, "that with well-doing." See a very similar construction in 1 Thess. iv. 3. The "well-doing" of this and the last verse bears the most general sense of good conduct, not the special sense noticed on the "fair works" and "fair life" of verse 12.

Put to silence the ignorance of foolish men.—A very contemptuous expression, the word for "put to silence" being the same as in 1 Cor. ix. 9; 1 Tim. v. 18, to "muzzle" or "gag," implying that there is something of the animal about these "foolish men." The same contempt appears in each word of the clause, even down to "men," which might be rendered "people" or "creatures." The word for "ignorance" implies a stolid and wilful ignorance, and is so used by heathen authors, as well as very markedly in the only other place in the New Testament, 1 Cor. xv. 34. "Foolish," too, contains moral reprobation, Luke xi. 40; xii. 20; 1 Cor. xv. 36, suggesting *thoughtlessness* rather than *senselessness*. The definite article is also used in the Greek (as in 2 Thess. iii. 2), and again seems to indicate that St. Peter had some particular enemies in view who had brought the charges. This accusation was evidently one of a *political* nature; and, indeed, history shows us that the hostility of the empire to the faith was entirely based on the corporate nature of the Christian religion. They would not have minded the *cultus*, but they could not tolerate the *Church*. Pliny distinctly says in his letter to Trajan, that it was in consequence of Trajan's issuing an order against *hetœriœ* or societies, that he was led to contend with the Christians in Bithynia.

(16) **As free.**—This points at once to what was the gist of the accusation. The Christian took up a position of complete independence within, and professed himself in a certain sense to be above the laws, by virtue of being a member of Christ's kingdom. This position of independence the heathen state resented, and looked upon the Christian Church as a dangerous organisation. Here, therefore, St. Peter both insists upon, and defines that independent position. "This the Apostle adds," says Leighton, "lest any should so far mistake the nature of their Christian liberty as to dream of an exemption from obedience either to God or to man for His sake, and according to His appointment. Their freedom he grants, but would have them understand aright what it is."

And not using.—The word "as" in the Greek attaches better to the participle instead of to the word "cloke," so that the sentence will run, *As free* (*i.e.*, as men who are *really* free), *and not as using freedom for a curtain of vice*. In this way the true and the false freedom are more forcibly contrasted.

For a cloke of maliciousness.—The uncommon word here used means any kind of covering, but not in the sense of a garment, so that we must not insist on the metaphor of the word "cloke." The same Greek word is used in Ex. xxvi. 14 to express the *second* covering of the tabernacle there mentioned, *i.e.*, the uppermost, outermost covering. Grimm quotes a fragment of the comic poet Menander, "Wealth is a covering of many a bad thing;" this helps us to see that what St. Peter means is not ordinary hypocrisy. The man does not profess to be better than he is, but loudly asserts that he is not a slave. Men admire such freedom of speech, and excuse his vices just because of their openness.

But as the servants of God.—Such freedom as has been mentioned is no freedom. It is moral slavery. The only true freedom lies in being "servants" (or rather *slaves*) "of God," whose will it is that you should be good subjects (verses 13 and 15). For a slightly different turn of thought, see Gal. v. 13.

(17) **Honour all men.**—"These words have very briefly, and yet not obscured by briefness, but withal very plainly, the sum of our duty towards God and men; to men, both in general, *honour all men*, and in special relations, in their Christian or religious relations, *love the brotherhood;* and in a chief civil relation, *honour the king*. And our whole duty to God, comprised under the name of His *fear*, is set in the middle betwixt these, as the common spring of all duty to men, and of all due observance of it, and the sovereign rule by which it is to be regulated" (Leighton). St. Paul had said that this honour was to be paid to those to whom it was due; St. Peter says that this includes all men; there is not one who can be entirely despised, not one who has quite lost the likeness of Christ; Jews are not at liberty to despise even the idolatrous Gentiles.

Love the brotherhood.—See chap. v. 9, and Note on chap. i. 22. The brotherhood means, of course, all Christian men, who (mystically even now that the Church is divided, but then actually) formed a single confraternity. "All men," Christian or heathen, are to be "honoured," but there is a special sense in which love is only possible between fellow-Christians. For the converse proposition, see Matt. v. 44.

Fear God.—This enforces reverence for every law and ordinance of God, and therefore serves fitly to introduce the next precept. Rebellion against Nero is rebellion against God (Rom. xiii. 2. Bengel compares Prov. xxiv. 21).

Honour the king.—This is the climax. Logically, the foregoing commands have only been inserted for the purpose of bringing out this last more clearly. This was the point on which the Christian religion was assailed, and the putting the readers through their catechism (as it were) of duties in other respects awakes their conscience to receive this precept. Verses 13—16 have insisted on the duty of political submission, and then the writer steps back, so to speak, for a final thrust: "so—as to all men you must pay

God. Honour the king. (18) Servants, *be* subject to *your* masters with all fear;[a] not only to the good and gentle, but also to the froward. (19) For this *is* thankworthy, if a man for conscience toward God endure grief, suffering wrongfully. (20) For what glory *is it*, if, when ye be buffeted for your faults, ye shall take it patiently? but if, when ye do well, and suffer *for it*, ye take it

[a] Rom. 13. 7.

reverence; as to the Christians, love; as to God, fear—so to the emperor you must pay constant reverence." It is hardly right to say with Bengel that this paragraph is specially written because of the usual disaffection of Jews towards the Roman government; rather it is called for (like the warning of verses 11, 12), not by any special temptation within them, but by the particular circumstances of the time, *i.e.*, the calumnies that were afloat against Christians.

(18) **Servants**—Second division of the second prudential rule: subordination social. This word is not the same as is used by St. Paul—*e.g.*, Eph. vi. 5; Col. iii. 22—but is used only besides in Luke xvi. 13; Acts x. 7; Rom. xiv. 4. It brings forward the *family* or *household* relation of servant or slave to master, and not (as does the common word used in verse 16) the mere fact of *ownership*. We need not be surprised at directions for household servants, or slaves, in a letter addressed to *Jewish* Christians, for there were large numbers of Hebrews in this position both now and later; St. Clement, for example, was probably both.

Be subject.—Rather, *being subject*, or *submitting yourselves*. The participle joins this clause loosely to the "submit yourselves" of verse 13, where the word is the same. (Comp. chap. iii. 1.)

With all fear.—"All" implies everything which goes to make up true fear, every kind of fear; and the "fear" (as when we speak of the fear of God) is not intended to mean any unmanly cowardice, dread of punishment, or such terror as is involved in having secrets which one dreads to have divulged. One commentator well defines it as "the shrinking from transgressing the master's will, based on the consciousness of one's own inferiority."

Masters.—This is the word which properly corresponds to the word by which the "servants" are described, not merely "owners," as in Eph. vi. 5; Col. iii. 22.

The froward.—Literally, *the crooked*. Its meaning is made clear by the contrasted adjectives, "good," *i.e.*, kindly, considerate; and "gentle," or, rather, reasonable, not disposed to take too stern a view of matters. A "froward" master, then, is one with a warped nature, who is unreasonably exacting, capricious, and cross-grained; in fact, one who will deal with his servants in the manner spoken of in the following verses.

(19) **For this is thankworthy.**—"This," viz., what goes before, which is further explained in what follows. Quite literally it is, *for this is grace*, or else (for, like *grâce* in French, the word has the double signification) *this is thanks*. The passage has some little importance in controversy, as some of the older Roman Catholic divines pressed it into the service of the supererogation theory. "This is grace," they said, means "this *deserves* grace as its reward." It is needless to point out how shallow a view of *duty* is implied in the thought that it was *more* than duty to be thus submissive. Still taking the first translation, others would interpret, "this is a mark of grace"—*i.e.*, shows that you are Christians indeed; or, "this is a gift of grace"—*i.e.*, a supernatural and heroic virtue, such as must have come from God, and not from you." These two interpretations make good sense in themselves, but they seem not to suit the context ("what *glory* is it") quite so well as our authorised rendering, and they ignore the sayings of our Lord, which must certainly have been in St. Peter's mind, recorded in Luke vi. 27—35, especially verses 32—34, and again in Luke xvii. 9. The thought is that where duty is both obvious and easy (as is the case with good masters), people do not lavish gratitude for the performance of it. The best of masters hardly feels grateful to the best of servants for *doing* his duty, though he will be grateful for the spirit and manner in which it is done. Here the "thanks" are put quite generally, as in the first passage in St. Luke: "this is a matter for thanks." It does not say as yet who is to pay the thanks, and we may naturally conclude that the master so served, and all who are cognisant of the service, are the persons meant.

For conscience toward God endure grief, suffering wrongfully.—This does not mean "if a man is afflicted for his religion's sake." Rather, *the conscience towards God*, or, perhaps, rather, *consciousness of God*, is thrown in to guard against any false theory that patience *by itself* is a thankworthy thing. However unjust the man's treatment may be, and however little he may resent it in act, it is not thankworthy unless his resignation be grounded on consciousness of God's presence. A resignation which comes from stolid want of feeling, or stoical fatalism, or from the sense that it is no good to seek redress—such resignation is sinfully defective. The two necessary qualifications, before patience can become in any sense meritorious, are (1) that the suffering should be *undeserved*, (2) that the man should recognise in it the hand of God.

(20) **For what glory is it.**—A poetical and pagan-sounding word, not elsewhere found in the New Testament; in the Old Testament it corresponds to the word "fame," in Job xxviii. 22. The sense may be said to be slightly humorous. "If you make a blunder" (such is the meaning of "fault" here—it might include such things as the breaking of dishes), "and receive a buffet for it" (or a box on the ear—a common punishment of slaves for trifling faults), "and bear it with fortitude" (the *meekness* of patience has no place in the word), "do you expect to be made the subject of an heroic or dithyrambic poem, to have your name resounded through the world and immortalised among posterity?" The "for" at the beginning of the clause explains why the writer added "suffering *wrongfully*" at the end of the last.

When ye do well, and suffer for it.—It is a pity that the translators have limited St. Peter's meaning by the insertion of the last two words. It is unnecessary to understand the suffering to be directly *provoked* by the well-doing. It would have done just as well to say, "when ye do well, and yet are ill-treated." The "froward" master makes his servants suffer without thinking what he makes them suffer for.

This is acceptable with God.—Timidity about St. Peter's theology has caused a difference between the rendering of the same word in two consecutive

patiently, this *is* acceptable[1] with God.
(21) For even hereunto were ye called:
because Christ also suffered for us,[2]
leaving us an example, that ye should
follow his steps: (22) who did no sin,[a]
neither was guile found in his mouth:[b]
(23) who, when he was reviled,[c] reviled not
again;[d] when he suffered, he threatened

1 Or, *thank.* a John 8. 46. b Isa. 53. 9.
2 Some read, *for you.* c ch. 3. 9. d Isa. 53. 7.

---

verses. It should be translated "thankworthy" here as well as above, and must be taken in precisely the same sense. Observe that the Apostle does not continue, "this *is* glory," as we might have expected; a Christian is not supposed to care for such trash as fame. But a Christian may well care to win the *thanks of God!* And such endurance of griefs for God's sake is now distinctly said to be "thankworthy with God"—*i.e.*, from God's point of view. See 2 Thess. i. 6, where, as here, it is assumed that the moral law is identical for God and for us, and that His principles and impulses of action are the same as those which He has implanted in us. "He will thank a man for it," says Archbishop Leighton, not a divine to favour the doctrine of human merit, but too honest a scholar to shrink from the meaning of words. Many things are strictly duty, and yet we do not expect to find them done, and are proportionably grateful when we see that they are done. And shall we, for the sake of a doctrinal thesis like that, "that man can deserve nothing at the hand of God," deny to God the possibility of enjoying one of the happiest exercises of love, the sense of gratitude?

(21) **For even hereunto were ye called.**—Namely, to the combination of suffering and well-doing. To this they "were called" by the Gospel which St. Paul had preached to them; it ought not to be a surprise to them when it comes. (See chap. iv. 12.) It was a special point in St. Paul's preaching to forewarn fairly of the tribulations attending all who wished to enter the kingdom of God. Comp. 1 Thess. iii. 3, 4, and Acts xiv. 22, which latter passage refers to preaching in the very homes of some of the recipients of this Epistle.

Because.—This justifies the last assertion. It appeared on the very face of the gospel message that we should all (slave and freeman alike) have to do well, and at the same time suffer, because the gospel told us that it was so with Him, the subject of the gospel. Notice what a fine assumption lies in this "because"—viz., that Christ's experience must needs be that of every Christian.

Christ also suffered.—It is to be carefully observed again that he does not say "*Jesus* suffered;" the whole point is that these Hebrew Christians have given in their adhesion to a *suffering Messiah.* (See Note on chap. i. 11.) And the true reading immediately after is "for *you,* leaving *you* an example, that ye should follow His steps;" not, of course, that St. Peter exempts himself from the need of the atonement or the obligation of following Christ's steps, but because it is his accustomed style to give a charge (as it were) rather than to throw himself in with those whom he addresses. (See Note on chap. i. 12.) There is one important point to be observed. Christ is said to have suffered "*for* you," but this does not mean "in your *stead,*" but "on your behalf, for your good." Christ's atonement for us is not represented in this passage as *vicarious.* He did not, according to St. Peter's teaching, die as a *substitute* for us, any more than He *rose again* as our substitute. So far as the words themselves go, the death of the Messiah "for us" might have been such a death as that of the hero who, in the battle of Murgarten, gathered the Austrian spears like a sheaf into his own bosom, "*for*" his fellow-patriots, clearing the way for them to follow. The addition "for you" conveys the thought that in gratitude we ought to suffer with, or even for, Him.

Leaving us (*you*) **an example.**—This clause seems added as a kind of explanation of the abrupt "because" just before. "You were called to suffering, I said, *because* Christ, too, suffered; for in so suffering He left ("as something to *survive* Him" is implied in the word) an example to *you.*" (This last "you" stands very emphatically in the Greek). The curious word for "example," nowhere else used in the New Testament, means primarily the "copy" given to a child to write from, or a "plan" suggested for carrying out in detail, a sketch to be filled in. It is used in this literal sense in 2 Macc. ii. 28, 29, and in the metaphorical sense it occurs repeatedly in the Epistle of St. Clement; in one passage (chap. xvi.) apparently with a reminiscence of this place, for the author has been quoting the passage of Isaiah to which we shall come presently, and then adds, "See then, beloved sirs, what is the copy which has been set us; for if the Lord was so lowly-minded, what shall we do who through Him have come under the yoke of His grace?" The leaving us of this copy was one of the benefits of His passion implied in "suffered *for you.*"

Follow his steps.—In all probability St. Peter used the word rendered "example" without any sense of its containing a metaphor, or else it would accord badly with the metaphor here. The word for "follow" is a strengthened form, and in 1 Tim. v. 10 is rendered "diligently follow;" in verse 24 of the same chapter it is "follow after"—*i.e.*, "dog;" the only other place being Mark xvi. 20. It means (as in 1 Tim. v. 24) rather "to follow up," made still more vivid by the addition of "His steps" (Rom. iv. 12; 2 Cor. xii. 18). St. Peter could remember the day when he was called to follow, and he did so literally (Matt. iv. 19; John xxi. 19); but the Pontine Christians, who had believed without having seen (chap. i. 8), could only "follow Him up" by the footprints which He had left.

(22) **Who did no sin.**—This verse is not to be taken by itself, but in the closest conjunction with the following. It is not the sinlessness of Christ by itself that is here set as an example before the servants, but His sinlessness in combination with His ill-treatment, or rather, His meekness under the combination. St. Peter again adapts the words of Isaiah (chap. liii. 9) to his purpose. The word there was one of violent transgression; St. Peter substitutes the simple word which he had used in verse 20, "fault"—"who never made a fault"—such as household servants were often committing—"neither was guile found in His mouth"—again referring to what was common with servants—petty acts of dishonesty, and petty deceits to screen themselves from punishment. One thing which lends special point to the allusion to Isaiah's prophecy is that Israel is in that passage spoken of under the title of God's "servant," a thought familiar to St. Peter long ago in connection with Christ. (See Note on Acts iii. 13.)

(23) **Who, when he was reviled.**—This "who" might be rendered by *and yet He.* Conscious though He was of being blameless (John viii. 46), it did not

not; but committed *himself* [1] to him that judgeth righteously: (24) who his own self bare our sins [a] in his own body on [2] the tree, that we, being dead

1 Or, *committed his cause.*
a Isa. 53. 11, 12; Heb. 9. 28.
2 Or, *to.*

make Him retaliate upon His accusers by counter-accusations, true though these might have been. The word here translated "revile" is the same which re-appears in chap. iii. 9 as "railing," and a sample of what it means is given in John ix. 28. The servants would be particularly liable to be thus abused, and instances are not wanting in the comic poets where they lose their self-control under it, and openly rate their owners in return. The "suffering," on the other hand, implies actual bodily maltreatment, "buffeting" (verse 20) and the like, to which the slaves could not answer directly by striking in return, but would sometimes take their revenge by "threats" of what they would do—run away, or burn the house, or poison the food, or do little acts of spite. Instances of our Lord's silence or meekness under "reviling" may be seen in John vii. 20; viii. 40; Matt. xii. 24, as well as in the accounts of the Passion. There are no recorded instances, until the last day of His life, of His "suffering" in the sense here intended; but the tense of the verbs "reviled," "threatened," "committed," shows that the writer was not thinking exclusively of any one occasion, but of our Lord's constant habit, though naturally there would be uppermost in St. Peter's mind the hours while he stood warming himself at Caiaphas' fire, with the denial on his lips, and saw the Messiah blindfold and buffeted. He is also thinking of Isa. liii. 7.

But committed himself.—This was His only form of revenge. As the Greek does not express the grammatical object of the verb, it is better not to supply one so definite as "Himself" or "His cause," rather, "but would leave it to Him that judgeth righteously." M. Renan (*Antéchrist*, p. 117) says that this passage "requires it to be understood that the incident of Jesus praying for His murderers was not known by Peter;" and other critics have held the same view. But (1) St. Peter, as we have said, is speaking of what was the *constant habit* of Jesus, not of what He did on the day of His crucifixion only. (2) The word does not necessarily imply any act or word of direct appeal to God to judge between His murderers and Him; on the contrary, the leading thought is that of "passing the matter over" to God (comp. Rom. xii. 19), by simply refusing to take any action in self-defence. (3) It would have been unlike the usual method of the Epistles to make direct reference to any of the minor details of our Lord's history. (4) Such a reference here would be beyond the point, for St. Peter said nothing in verse 19 about *praying* for the bad masters, and here he is only justifying by Christ's example the position he had laid down there.

To him that judgeth righteously.—God is described in the aspect which is most reassuring to men who are suffering unjustly (2 Thess. i. 5). This looks back to that "consciousness of God" spoken of in verse 19. There is a curious various reading which is adopted by the Vulgate, though without any solid authority, and evidently a mere blunder, the interpretation of which we may leave to those who are committed to it: "He gave Himself over to him (or, to one) who judgeth unrighteously." St. Cyprian seems to have understood it of our Lord's voluntary self-surrender to Pilate.

(24) **Who his own self.**—This verse, like the "for you" in verse 21, is intended to make the readers feel the claims of gratitude, not to set before them another point in which Christ was to be imitated. But at the same time it serves to enforce still more strongly the two points already mentioned—*i.e.*, sinlessness and suffering. So far was Christ from "doing sins," that He actually His own self bore ours, and in so doing endured the extremity of anguish "in His own body," so that He could sympathise with the corporal chastisements of these poor servants; and "on the tree," too, the wicked slave's death.

Bare our sins . . . on the tree.—This brings us face to face with a great mystery; and to add to the difficulty of the interpretation, almost each word is capable of being taken in several different ways. Most modern scholars are agreed to reject "*on* the tree," in favour of the marginal "to," the proper meaning of the Greek preposition, when connected (as here) with the accusative, being what is expressed in colloquial English by the useful compound "*on-to* the tree." It is, however, not obligatory to see motion consciously intended in this preposition and accusative everywhere. It is used, for instance, Mark iv. 38, of sleeping *on* the pillow; in 2 Cor. iii. 15, of the veil resting *upon* their hearts; in Rev. iv. 4, of the elders sitting *upon* their thrones. This word, then, will give us but little help to discover the meaning of the word translated "bare." (1) That verb means literally "to carry or take up," and is used thus in Matt. xvii. 1, Mark ix. 2, of taking the disciples up the Mount of Transfiguration; and in Luke xxiv. 51, of Jesus being carried up into heaven: therefore Hammond, Grimm, and others would here understand it to be, "He carried our sins up with Him on-to the tree," there to expiate them by His death. (2) A much commoner meaning of the word is that which it bears in verse 5, "to offer up" (so also in Heb. vii. 27; xiii. 15; Jas. ii. 21). The substantive formed from it (*Anaphora*) is still the liturgical term for the sacrificial section of the Eucharistic service. This interpretation is somewhat tempting, because the very preposition here used, with the very same case, appears in Jas. ii. 21, and frequently in the Old Testament, together with our present verb, for "to offer up *upon* the altar." In this way it would be, "He offered up our sins in His own body *on the altar of* the cross." So Luther and others take it. This would be perfect, were it not for the strangeness of regarding the sins themselves as a sacrifice to be offered on the altar. The only way to make sense of it in that case would be to join very closely "our sins in His own body"—*i.e.*, as contained and gathered up in His own sinless body, which might come to nearly the same thing as saying that He "offered up His own body laden with our sins" upon that altar. (3) Both these renderings, however, pass over the fact that St. Peter is referring to Isa. liii. In the English version of that chapter, "hath borne," "shall bear," "bare," appears in verses 4, 11, and 12, indifferently; but the Hebrew is not the same in each case, for in verse 11 the word for "shall bear" is identical with that rightly rendered "carry" in verse 4, and has not the same signification as that which appears as "to bear" in verses 4 and 12. The difference between these two Hebrew roots seems to be that the verb *sabal* in verse 11 means "to carry," as a porter carries a load, or as our Lord carried His cross; while the verb *nasa'*, used in verses 4 and 12, means rather "to lift or raise,"

to sins, should live unto righteousness:[a] by whose stripes ye were healed.[b] (25) For ye were as sheep going astray;[c] but are now returned unto the Shepherd[d] and Bishop of your souls.

c Isa. 53. 6.
a Col. 1. 22.
d ch. 5. 4; Heb. 13. 20.
b Isa. 53. 5.

which might, of course, be the action preparatory to that other of "carrying." Now, the Greek word which we have here undoubtedly better represents *nasa'* than *sabal*, but the question is complicated by the fact that the LXX. uses it to express both alike in verses 11 and 12, observing at the same time the distinction between "iniquities" and "sin," while in verse 4 (where again it reads "our sins" instead of "our griefs") it adopts a simpler verb; and St. Peter's language here seems to be affected by all three passages. The expression "our sins" (which comes in so strangely with the use of "you" all round) seems a reminiscence of verse 4 (LXX.). The order in which the words occur is precisely the order of verse 11, and the tense points to verse 12, as well as the parallel use in Heb. ix. 28, where the presence of the words "of many" proves that the writer was thinking of verse 12. We cannot say for certain, then, whether St. Peter meant to represent *nasa'* or *sabal*. We have some clue, however, to the way in which the Greek word was used, by finding it in Num. xiv. 33, where the "whoredoms" of the fathers are said to be "borne" by their children (the Hebrew there being *nasa'*). Many instances in classical Greek lead to the conclusion that in such cases it implies something being *laid* or *inflicted* from without upon the person who "bears." Thus, in Num. xiv. 33, it will be, "your children will *have to* bear your whoredoms," or, "will have laid upon them your whoredoms." In Heb. ix. 28 it will be, "Christ was once for all presented (at the altar), to have the sins of many laid upon Him." Here it will be, "Who His own self had our sins laid upon His body on the tree." Then comes a further question. The persons who hold the substitute theory of the Atonement assert that "our sins" here stands for "the *punishment* of our sins." This is, however, to use violence with words; we might with as good reason translate verse 22, "Who did, or performed, no punishment for sin." St. Peter asserts that Christ, in His boundless sympathy with fallen man, in His union with all mankind through the Incarnation whereby He became the second Adam, actually took, as His own, our sins, as well as everything else belonging to us. He was so identified with us, that in the great Psalm of the Messianic sacrifice, He calls them "My sins" (Ps. xl. 12), sinless as He was. (See St. Matthew's interpretation of the same thought, chap. viii. 17.)

That we being dead.—Just as the former part of this verse is an expansion of "Christ suffered for us," so the latter part is an expansion of "that ye should follow His steps." The "we," however, is too emphatically placed in the English. To St. Peter, the thought of our union with Christ is so natural, that he slips easily over it, and passes on to the particular point of union which he has in view. "He bore our sins on the tree, in order that, having thus become 'lost' to those sins, we might live to righteousness." The words present, perhaps, a closer parallel to Col. i. 22 than to any other passage; but comp. also Rom. vi. 2, 8, 11, and 2 Cor. v. 14, and Notes. St. Peter's word for "dying" in this place is not elsewhere found in the New Testament, and is originally an euphemism for death; literally, *to be missing*—*i.e.*, when sin comes to seek its old servants it finds them gone.

With whose stripes ye were healed.—Observe how soon St. Peter reverts to the second person, even though he has to change the text he is quoting. Another mark of his style may well be noticed here, viz., his fondness for a number of co-ordinate relative sentences. (See chap. i. 8, 12; 2 Pet. ii. 1, 2, 3; and his speeches, Acts iii. 13, 15; iv. 10; x. 38, 39.) He is especially fond of finishing off a long sentence with a short relative clause, as here. Comp., for instance, verse 8, 2 Pet. ii. 17, also Acts iv. 12, where it would be more correct to translate, "Neither is the salvation in any other, for, indeed, there is no second name under heaven which is *the appointed* name among men; *in whom* we *must* be saved"—*i.e.*, if we are saved at all. The purpose of the little clause seems to be once more to make the good and ill-used servants feel, when the weals were smarting on their backs, that the Righteous Servant of Jehovah had borne the same, and that it had served a beneficial purpose, as they knew to their everlasting gratitude. Of course the "stripes" (in the original singular number, and literally *weal*) do not refer *merely* to the scourging. The words form a paradox.

(25) **For ye were as sheep going astray.**—The right reading does not attach "going astray" to "sheep," but as predicate of the sentence, "ye were going astray like sheep." The "for" introduces an explanation of how they came to be in need of "healing." "I may well say that ye were healed; for Israelites though you are, your consciences and memories tell you that you were as far gone in wilful error as any Gentiles, and needed as complete a conversion." (Comp. verse 10.) Jew and Gentile take different ways, but both alike fulfil the prophecy, "every man to his own way." The two metaphors, of healing and going astray, do not match very well, but the fact that both are quotations from Isa. liii. makes their disagreement less harsh. We must notice how deeply that prophecy (the interpretation of which was probably learned from the Baptist) had sunk into St. Peter's mind. (See chap. i. 19.)

But are now returned.—The tense of the original verb points to the actual historical time at which it took place, rather than the position now occupied, "but now ye returned." The word "now" is used in the same way in verse 10, where literally it is, "but now *did* obtain mercy." "Returned" does not in the Greek imply that they had at first been under the Shepherd's care and had left Him. The word is that which is often rendered "were converted," and only indicates that they turned round and moved in a contrary direction.

The shepherd and bishop of your souls.—Undoubtedly this means Christ. The first of the two titles is of course suggested by the simile of the sheep. The image is so natural and so frequent, that we cannot say for certain that it proves St. Peter's acquaintance with the parable of the Good Shepherd in John x. More probably, perhaps, he is thinking of Ps. xxiii. 3, "He converted *my soul*" (LXX.), where "the Lord," as usual, may be taken to mean the Son of God rather than the Father; or else of Ez. xxxiv. 11, 16, where the words rendered "seek them out" in our version is represented in the LXX. by that from which the name of a "bishop" is derived. (Comp. Ezek. xxxiv. 23; xxxvii. 24; also Isa. xl. 11, which last citation comes from a passage which has been in St. Peter's mind

Chap. iii. 1—6. Subjection of wives to husbands.

A.D. cir. 60.

CHAPTER III.—(1) Likewise, ye wives, *be* in subjection to your own husbands;[a] that, if any obey not the word, they also may without the word be won by the conversation of the wives; (2) while they behold your chaste conversation *coupled* with fear.

a Eph. 5. 22; Col. 3. 18; Tit. 2. 5.

---

just before, chap. i. 24.) It is hardly necessary to add that to the Hebrew mind the thought of superintendence and ruling, not that of giving food, was uppermost when they spoke of shepherds, and that the pastors spoken of in the Old Testament are not the priests or givers of spiritual nutriment, but the kings and princes. Thus it will here be nearly synonymous with the second title of bishop. This name suggests in the first instance not so much overseeing as *visiting* —*i.e.*, going carefully into the different cases brought under the officer's notice. (Comp. chap. v. 2, 4, and Acts xx. 28.) Both words were already familiar as ecclesiastical words already, and as such were especially appropriate to Christ, the Head of the Church; but as they had not yet become stereotyped in that sense, the writer adds, "of your souls," to show that it was not an outward sovereignty and protectorate which the Messiah had assumed over them. "Soul" is a word of which St. Peter is fond (chaps. i. 9, 22; ii. 11; iv. 19; 2 Pet. ii. 8), but which is, perhaps, never used by St. Paul in this sense. It is to be remarked how St. Peter works almost every section of the Epistle round, so as to end with some encouragement to the readers to cling to Jesus as the Messiah, and to their Christian state, from which they were in danger of receding into Judaism. He makes even the special exhortations lead up to that which is the main exhortation of the Letter.

III.

(1) **Likewise ye wives . . .**—Third division of second prudential rule: subordination conjugal. Here, again, the form in the original is participial, joining this injunction on to chap. ii. 13, 18, where the word is the same in Greek, "wives, in the same way submitting yourselves." Whether this imposes for all time upon Christian wives as complete a submission towards their husbands as is here enjoined might perhaps be questioned, because the special reason for the command in this place was to allay suspicions engendered by the boldness with which Christianity proclaimed the freedom of the individual. St. Peter has just been giving injunctions for absolute submission, even to injustice, on the part of slaves; and the progress of Christianity has abolished slavery altogether. The measure of the Christian wife's submission may safely be left to her own enlightened conscience, guided by other passages of the New Testament not written, like this, for a special emergency.

Your own husbands.—This does not order submission to the husband in contrast to submission to other directors, but rather gives a *reason* for obedience. "The Christian wife that hath love to God," says Leighton, "though her husband be not so comely, or so wise, or any way so amiable, as many others, yet because he is her *own husband,* and because of the Lord's command in the general, and His providence in the particular disposal of His own, therefore she loves and obeys."

That if any obey not the word.—Rather, *in order that even supposing some* (*at present*) *disobey the word.* "The word" is, of course, the Gospel, the declaration of the fulfilment of the prophecies in Jesus. And those who "disobey the word" are, according to constant usage, the Jews. The present verb is used of the Jews in Acts xiv. 2; xvii. 5; xix. 9; Rom. x. 21; xi. 31; xv. 31, besides St. Peter's own use in chap. ii. 8; iv. 17. The only places where it is distinctly used of others are Rom. ii. 8 (of Jew and Gentile together), Rom. xi. 30 (where the Gentiles are compared with the Jews), Heb. iii. 18 (of the Israelites in the wilderness), Heb. xi. 31 (of the men of Jericho), 1 Pet. iii. 20 (of the refractory antediluvians). In any case it must mean a wilful refusal to submit to the Word, in spite of being intellectually convinced. (See especially chap. ii. 8.) For every reason, therefore, it is more probable that the case here supposed is that of Hebrew (Christian) women, married to men of their own race who reject the gospel.

They also may . . .—The order here is not so neat as in the original, and it spoils the point to insert the definite article before "word." It should run, *In order that . . . through their wives' conversation, without a word, they may* (literally, *shall*) *be gained.* There is something almost playful in the substitution of "their wives" instead of "you," and in the "without a word" contrasted with "the word" before. St. Peter seems to enjoy laying the little innocent plot. He was himself, as the Prayer Book reminds us, a married man. And what he means here, is not that those who have resisted the public preaching in the synagogues, should even without that public preaching be won; rather, that though the gospel as uttered verbally only provokes them to opposition, the gospel as submissively *acted* by their wives, without a word said on the matter, ought to convert them. "This model of submission and humility," says M. Renan, meaning the Lamb of God, "is made by Peter the law for all classes of Christian society. The wife above all, without setting up for a preacher (*sans faire la prêcheuse*), ought, by the discreet charm of her piety, to be the great missionary of the faith." The word rendered "won" keeps up the playfulness of that which goes before; it means "to turn a profit," and there is just enough of *ruse* in it to make the enforcement of submission to a husband of opposed religious views seem an enticing little speculation. The tense of the original verb indicates that the scheme is certain to succeed. (Comp. Matt. xviii. 15; 1 Cor. ix. 19, 20.) Archbishop Leighton points out that in Hebrew the name of the book of "Ecclesiastes; or, the Preacher," is a feminine, and the same is the case in Ps. lxviii. 11, and elsewhere.

(2) **While they behold . . .**—The same curious word as in chap. ii. 12, and the tense, which is ill-represented by "while they behold," sets us at the moment of the triumph of the wife's conduct, literally, *having kept,* or *when they have kept an eye on your chaste conversation.* The husband is jealously on the watch to see what his wife does who has embraced these foolish notions; at last he breaks down. Jesus must be the Messiah, or his wife could not have been so chaste! The adjective "chaste" is here to be taken in a large sense; it is the same which enters into the verb translated "purify" in chap. i. 22, and it is implied that the "fear" (*i.e.*, of the husband; comp. Note on chap. ii. 18) has been an incentive to this sweet virtue; "your life so immaculate in fear," or even almost "so timidly

(3) Whose adorning let it not be that outward *adorning* of plaiting the hair, and of wearing of gold, or of putting on of apparel;[a] (4) but *let it be* the hidden man of the heart, in that which is not corruptible, *even the ornament* of a meek and quiet spirit, which is in the sight of God of great price. (5) For after this manner in the old time the holy women also, who trusted in God, adorned them-

a 1 Tim. 2. 9.

pure." Leighton says, "It is a delicate, timorous grace, afraid of the least air, or shadow of anything that hath but a resemblance of wronging it, in carriage or speech, or apparel, as follows in the third and fourth verses."

(3) **Whose adorning let it not be . . . .**—The passage shows that the Asiatic Christians were not all of the poorer classes. Many of the wealthy Jewesses had joined them. The wealth of the Ephesian Christians about this time may be gathered from 1 Tim. ii. 9, and of the Laodiceans from Rev. iii. 17. Two things are to be noted about the advice here given. (1) It is not intended directly as a corrective of vanity. St. Peter is not bidding them beware of love of dress, although (as Bengel points out) the three words of "plaiting," "wearing" (literally, *putting round oneself*), and "putting on," are intended to convey the notion of elaborate processes in which time is wasted. But the main thought is, How are the husbands to be attracted? Not, says St. Peter, by any external prettiness of adornment, but by inward graces. (2) The Apostle is not *forbidding* the use of gold, &c. Leighton (himself something of a precisian) says, "All regard of comeliness and ornament in apparel is not unlawful, nor doth the Apostle's expression here, rightly considered, fasten that upon the adorning he here speaks of. He doth no more universally condemn the use of gold for ornament than he doth any other comely raiment, which here he means by that general word of *putting on of apparel*, for his 'not' is comparative; *not this adorning, but the ornament of a meek spirit*, that rather, and as much more comely and precious; as that known expression (Hos. vi. 6), '*I will have mercy, and not sacrifice.*'" At the same time he is, of course, speaking of these things with studied contempt; and we may be sure he would have spoken with abhorrence of any adorning which partook of the nature of lying. Even in one of Xenophon's works there is a charming passage where an Athenian gentleman expostulates with his wife on the folly of hoping to attract him by wearing high-heeled shoes and painting her face with rouge and white.

(4) **But let it be . . .**—The connection of the clauses is somewhat difficult, but is made more so by our translation of verse 3. Literally it would run, *of whom let it not be*, or, *to whom let there not belong the outward adorning, but the hidden man of the heart.* If we adopt the translation in the Authorised Version, it makes "the hidden man" an ornament to be worn in preference to the gold and braided hair, which would be both illogical, and dishonouring to "the hidden man." What St. Peter says is, "Do not rely, for winning your husbands, upon ornamentation (which is but external), but upon character."

The hidden man of the heart.—Not equivalent to St. Paul's expression, "the *new* man" (Eph. iv. 24), but simply *the inner self, the true self—i.e.*, the genuine moral character. It is more like St. Paul's phrase, "the inward man," and may, perhaps, have been adapted from it. (Comp. Rom. vii. 22; 2 Cor. iv. 16; Eph. iii. 16.) According to his custom, St. Peter explains by adding the genitive, "of the heart." (Comp. chap. i. 13.) At the same time, the choice of that particular word, rather than "soul" or "mind," gives warmth and affection to what might otherwise seem a bare moral or metaphysical conception.

In that which is not corruptible.—The sense is somewhat obscured by our insertion of "even the ornament." Had it been "even *in* the ornament," it would have been clearer, though not right even then. It is literally, *in the imperishableness of the meek and quiet spirit*, contrasting the abiding beauty of character with the "perishable" or "contemptible" nature of the ornaments just spoken of. So in chap. i. 18, he spoke of "silver and gold" as "perishable." The same kind of phrase is used by St. Paul in 1 Tim. vi. 17, "trust in the uncertainty of riches"—*i.e.*, in riches which are but uncertain things. So here, "in the imperishableness of the meek spirit" means *in the meek spirit, which is not* (*like gold*) *a perishable thing.* Yet the preposition "in" must not be taken as equivalent to "dressed in," "adorned with;" the "meek and quiet spirit" is not a mere *decoration* of the "hidden man." Neither, on the other hand, is it quite "consisting in," as though "hidden man" and "meek spirit" were identical; for "the hidden man of the heart" would be bad in bad men, and good in good: see, for instance, our Lord displaying the hidden man of the Pharisee's heart (Matt. xxiii. 28). It is rather the particular *mode* in which St. Peter wishes the inward character to exhibit itself. We might paraphrase the whole thus:—"Let it not be with you a matter of external ornamentation—elaborate processes, and costly, but perishable, decorations—but let it be a matter of the heart, the character, the true self, manifesting itself in a constant tone of unassuming and imperturbable sweetness—an imperishable attraction." The word "spirit" here is used, not in its strict metaphysical sense, but in the sense of a mood or general tenour and complexion of life; as, for instance, in Luke ix. 55 (perhaps), 1 Cor. iv. 21, Gal. vi. 1, and elsewhere. St. Peter assures us in this passage that moral characteristics gained in this life remain our characteristics in the next.

Which is in the sight of God of great price.—The antecedent to "which" has been variously taken. Is it "the meek and quiet *spirit?*" Is it "the *imperishableness* of the meek and quiet spirit?" Or is it "the hidden man of the heart exhibiting itself in such a spirit?" Each has something to be said for it, but the last seems nearest to the truth. The thing which is valuable in the eyes of God is the *having* such an inward character. Thus we might put a stronger stop at the word "spirit;" and this relative clause will be another instance of St. Peter's favourite mode of speech noticed on chap. ii. 24. Such a possession will be not only attractive to the husband for the time, but has a permanent value as being esteemed by God.

(5) **For after this manner.**—Here we have not only the ground of the foregoing precepts, but also of the assurance that God sets a value on such embellishments. It had been accepted by Him in the holy women of old who hoped in Him, and would be accepted again. "The Apostle enforces his doctrine by example," says Leighton: "the most compendious way of teaching." By "holy women" he means, not only

selves, being in subjection unto their own husbands: (6) even as Sara obeyed Abraham, calling him lord:[a] whose daughters[1] ye are, as long as ye do well, and are not afraid[b] with any amazement. (7) Likewise, ye husbands, dwell with *them*[c] according to knowledge, giving honour[d] unto the wife, as unto the weaker vessel,

c 1 Cor. 7. 12.
a Gen. 18. 12.
1 Gr. *children.*
d 1 Thess. 4. 4.
b Prov. 3. 25.

Chap. iii. 7. Corresponding duty of husbands.

---

holy in character, but "sainted"—consecrated by their memories being recorded for our reverence in Holy Writ.

Who trusted in God.—It is a great pity that "trusted" should have been substituted for the original "hoped." The position of Sara and the holy women of the Old Testament was one of *expectancy*, of looking *forward* to the fulfilment of a promise; and the description of them as such is intended to make the readers of the letter feel the difference of *their* position. To *them* the promise to Sara was accomplished. The expression contains a reference to the mention of God in the last verse.

Adorned themselves, being in subjection.—The imperfect tense of the verb means "*used* to adorn themselves." They took daily pains thus to adorn themselves, and spent, perhaps, as long in the process as the other ladies over their toilette. The participle which is added explains more fully the "after this manner." Their subjection was their ornament.

(6) **Even as Sara.**—A definite example of the general fact just alleged. St. Peter seems rather to have argued from what every one would feel *must* have been the case than from explicit records. Sara's usual subjection is clearly seen in the one instance to which St. Peter refers (Gen. xviii. 12), where Sara, though not addressing Abraham, but speaking to herself, calls him "my lord." People show their usual habits of mind more freely in speaking to themselves.

Whose daughters ye are.—A very misleading version, following the Vulgate. What St. Peter says is, *whose children ye became*, or *were made*. There was a definite period in their past lives at which they came to be—what they were not before—children of Sara. Have we not here, therefore, a distinct proof that these readers of the Epistle were Gentiles and not Jewesses? Not so. The phrase, "which hoped in God," pointing as it does to the coming of the Messiah, prepares us to understand how these Hebrew women *became* Sara's children. It was only by entering into her hope and attaching themselves to Jesus Christ, for whose coming she had looked. St. Peter has already been insisting on the nothingness of the fleshly descent, the "corruptible seed." As has been pointed out on chap. i. 24, this doctrine was not first taught by St. Paul, for St. Peter had heard it from the Baptist (Matt. iii. 9) and from our Lord Himself (John viii. 39). Whether persons were naturally Jews or Gentiles, they could not be children of Abraham without voluntarily becoming so by embracing his principles—*i.e.*, by becoming Christians. The participial clauses which follow will need no change of translation, for they express not the act or process by which these ladies *became* children of Sara, but the condition on which they would *remain* her children. A very similar passage occurs in Heb. iii. 14: "We have become partakers of the Christ, if (for the future) we hold," &c. (Comp. also 1 Thess. iii. 8; Heb. iii. 6.)

Do well.—See chap. ii. 12, 15, 20. The word means, of course, general good behaviour, especially in all wifely duties. As this is a condition of remaining Sara's children, it is implied that it was a characteristic of Sara. Some critics would even put in a parenthesis all the words from "even as" to "ye are," and attach these participles (as they are in the Greek) to the last clause in verse 5, thus: "adorned themselves, being in subjection to their own husbands (as Sara, for instance . . . whose daughters ye were made), doing well, and not being afraid," &c. This is, however, somewhat cumbrous, and leaves the clause "whose daughters ye became" a little too bald.

Are not afraid with any amazement.—Though this translation is grammatically possible, it does not make such good sense as to translate, *are not afraid of any alarm.* It is, in fact, a quotation from or allusion to Prov. iii. 25, as Bengel points out, where "Be not afraid of sudden fear" is rendered in the LXX. by these same peculiar words. The "Wisdom" in that passage, which brings the calmness with it, is Christ, and it is Christ who must be understood in verse 26: "the Lord shall be thy confidence." To be afraid of sudden alarms and panics argues a lack of trust in God's providence and power, and would, therefore, be unbecoming the daughters of Sara, who "hoped in God." The "alarms" which they naturally might fear are, of course, quite general, but especially here, we may suppose, dread of what their unbelieving husbands might do to them. (Comp. verse 13 *et seq.*)

(7) **Likewise, ye husbands.**—The subjection is not to be all one-sided, though the husband's subjection to the wife will be of a different kind from the wife's to him. We are hardly to take this as a separate paragraph from the foregoing, but rather as a corollary added to it, to correct a false impression that might otherwise have been conveyed.

Dwell.—Rather, *dwelling.* The participle is attached to the previous sentences, just as in chaps. ii. 16, 18, iii. 1; but St. Peter does not like to say to the husbands "submitting yourselves" (though it is implied in the "likewise"), and conveys the deference which the husbands are to pay under other terms: such as "according to knowledge," "giving honour."

With them.—The whole order of the sentences needs re-arrangement as follows: *Ye husbands, likewise, dwelling according to knowledge, as with a weaker vessel, with what is female, apportioning honour as to joint heirs also of a grace of life.* In order to understand this very hard passage, we must remember what is St. Peter's object all throughout these instructions, viz., to commend Christianity to jealous watchers without. Here, therefore, we may well suppose that he is thinking chiefly of the case of believing husbands (Jewish) married to unbelieving wives (Jewish also), thus presenting the counter-picture to that of verse 1. And the first thing is that they are to "dwell with" these wives, not to divorce them, nor to cease from conjugal cohabitation with them; such harshness would lend very little attractiveness to the Christian religion among the Jewish homes to which the divorced wife would turn. (See 1 Cor. vii. 12 *et seq.*—a passage which must almost have been in St. Peter's mind.)

According to knowledge.—This phrase, which is like an adverb, such as "scientifically, intelligently." means that the husband is to study to enter into the whole bearings of the case, to take everything into account. Husband and wife will not get on together

and as being heirs together of the grace of life; that your prayers be not hindered.

Chap. iii. 8—12 Mutual duties of all.

(8) Finally, *be ye* all of one mind, having compassion one of another, love[1]

1 Or, *loving to the brethren.*

smoothly at haphazard, without pains taken to *understand* the situation. (See 1 Thess. iv. 4; "you should *know.*")

Unto the wife, as unto the weaker vessel.—Or rather, as we now take it, *as with a weaker vessel, with what is female.* This explains the saying "according to knowledge." The thing which the husband is specially to understand and take into account is that he is dealing with a thing less strong than himself. The whole of chivalry is in these words, and St. Peter (next after Christ) may be considered the founder of it. Weakness itself, by being weakness, has a claim upon the strong man's deference and self-submission. The weakness here ascribed to the female sex is primarily that of the body, as we shall see when we consider the word "vessel," though it may, perhaps, indicate frailty in other respects as well. If the word "vessel" is to be here a description of a "wife," as some contend on 1 Thess. iv. 4, in a sense in which it does not equally describe a husband, it is difficult to see with what the vessel is compared and pronounced weaker. "Dwell with the female as with a more delicate vessel or instrument" than what? If we answer "than yourselves," it becomes clear that the husbands are, by implication, *less* delicate *vessels.* And this is the case. In the Note on 1 Thess. iv. 4, it has been shown that the word "vessel" (whether as receptacle or as instrument) is a description of the *body,* or rather of the *self* as manifested in the body. The word in itself may be used to describe anything made to be serviceable—machinery, tackle and gear, pots and pans, and, in fact, any kind of apparatus or implement—and here it might be very fairly rendered, "as with a weaker thing or object." That which is translated "the wife" is really a neuter adjective, and it is a question whether we are to supply with it the noun "vessel"—"with the female [vessel] as with a vessel which is weaker"—or whether it is to stand absolutely, "the female," as we say "the good," "the evil"—*i.e.,* "that which is female." The latter seems, on the whole, simpler and more forcible, as calling closer attention to the fact of weakness being inherent in the sex.

Giving honour.—The word for "giving" implies rendering a portion which is *due.* And what is here called "honour" is not to be understood only of the wife's maintenance (as some say), though such is probably the interpretation of the word in 1 Tim. v. 17, and comp. Ex. xxi. 10; nor is the wife only to be honoured by being consulted in affairs of moment and put in charge of the household. The "honour" to be accorded to wives "as to joint heirs of a grace of life" is the same kind of "honour" as St. Paul, in 1 Thess. iv. 4, says must be accorded to oneself. Indeed, from the juxtaposition of three significant words there, we can hardly escape the conclusion that St. Peter was remembering that passage of St. Paul, "that every one of you should *know* how to obtain possession of the *vessel* of himself in sanctification and *honour.*" It is that chaste respect for the wife which is meant in the Prayer Book by the phrase, "With my body I thee worship." It means that the husband must not dare to take any *liberties* with his wife. Would the Christian husband be likely to approve his religion to the unbelieving wife if she found that he took a coarse view of the conjugal tie?

And as being heirs together of the grace of life.—There is here a very intricate question of readings, on which it depends whether the "heirs" are to be nominative or dative, the husbands or the wives. The present annotator prefers, on the whole, to follow Tischendorf, and read the dative, "paying respect as to persons who are also joint heirs (*i.e.,* with you) of a grace of life." Happily, it comes to much the same thing, the only difference being that in the one case deference is paid to the wife on the ground of her possessing a joint dignity with the husband, and in the other case on the ground that the husband does not possess his dignity except conjointly with the wife. That dignity which they conjointly "inherit"—*i.e.,* possess as a gift from God—is called "the grace (or perhaps, a grace) of life." This is generally interpreted to mean, "the gracious gift of everlasting life." Undoubtedly, "life" is often used absolutely in the New Testament to mean eternal life—*e.g.,* Matt. xviii. 8; and it gives a very intelligible sense, that the husband should reverence the wife as being equally with himself an everlasting soul. But this neither gives sufficient force to the *conjoint* nature of the possession, nor does it take into account the possibility of such a case as, in fact, we suppose to be here intended, viz., of a believing husband and unbelieving wife. Although, in a sense, "the unbelieving wife is sanctified by the husband" (1 Cor. vii. 14), yet not in such a sense as for them to be called conjoint possessors of eternal life. It seems best, therefore, to suppose that the "grace (or dower) of life" which husband and wife hold, not only in common, but *conjointly,* is life in the *natural* sense. This "grace," this mysterious and divine gift—not apart from one another, but conjointly—they are privileged by the Creator's primeval benediction (Gen. i. 28) to transmit. They have the power (no Archangel has the like) to bring human beings into existence. And in consideration that such is the dignity and the intention of marriage, a man may well be called upon to revere his partner in the great prerogative.

That your prayers be not hindered—*i.e.,* the husbands' prayers, not necessarily their prayers *with* their wives. It is easy to feel how the consciousness of having treated a wife with less awe than is indicated by the foregoing words would clog the man's prayers, whether for himself or for his wife's conversion—the latter being, probably, what St. Peter chiefly meant. Very likely he had in view what St. Paul writes in 1 Cor. vii. 5.

(8) **Finally, be ye all.**—A return from the special to the general. St. Peter has not, however, forgotten the *purpose* with which the former rules were given; his thought is still how to produce a right impression on the unbelieving world, although some of these injunctions touch only *internal* relations between members of the Church. "By this shall *all men,*" says our Lord, "know that ye are my disciples, if ye have love *one to another*" (John xiii. 35); and, again, "That *they* all may be *one* . . . that the *world* may believe that thou hast sent me" (John xvii. 21). Accordingly, this verse, like verses 1 and 7, is attached to chap. ii. 13, and should be translated, *Finally, being all.*

Of one mind.—Or, *unanimous.* Though the Greek word does not occur elsewhere in the New Testament,

as brethren, *be* pitiful, *be* courteous:
(9) not rendering evil for evil, or railing
for railing: but contrariwise blessing;
knowing that ye are thereunto called,
that ye should inherit a blessing. (10) For
he[a] that will love life, and see good
days, let him refrain his tongue from
evil, and his lips that they speak no
guile: (11) let him eschew evil, and do
good; let him seek peace, and ensue it.

a Ps. 34. 12, &c.

---

the duty is enjoined often, *e.g.*, Rom. xii. 16; 2 Cor. xiii. 11; Phil. ii. 2. It involves an agreement not only in doctrine but in practical aims, the affections of all being in the same direction. This unanimity requires *expression* to be conscious, and therefore it strikes at the root of the reserve by which Christian people do not open out their hearts to each other in the matter of religion. Such unity of mind is no product of indifference, which Leighton describes as "not a knitting together, but a freezing together, as cold congregates all bodies how heterogeneous soever, sticks, stones, and water."

Having compassion one of another.—Literally, *sympathetic.* The word "compassion" has lost the meaning which it once had, and signifies little more than pity. Here the command includes the "rejoicing with them that do rejoice," as much as the "weeping with them that weep" (Rom. xii. 26). The same word only occurs again in Heb. iv. 15; x. 34.

Love as brethren.—Again a single adjective, *fraternal*, or, loving the brethren. For the meaning see chap. i. 22, Notes.

Be pitiful.—Rather (omitting the word "be"), *tender-hearted.* So it is translated in Eph. iv. 32, the only other place where it occurs. It differs from "sympathetic" in being limited to yearnings over the afflicted. Strangely enough, in profane Greek, the word is only found to mean "*strong*-hearted."

Be courteous.—The injunction is so charming, and so appropriate in the mouth of St. Peter, that one is almost loth to correct the reading, and substitute (undoubtedly the right word) *humble-minded.* This adjective brings us back to that mutual *subjection* and complaisance which is the main subject of all these rules. Comp. also chap. v. 5.

(9) **Not rendering.**—So far St. Peter has been speaking of *internal* conduct. The two last adjectives, however, lead gradually into the wider field of conduct, and probably now he is thinking solely of relation to the adverse world. Among the Christians surely there would be no "evil" or "railing" to *provoke* a retort! "Evil," in act; "railing," in word. (See chap. ii. 23, and Rom. xii. 17.)

But contrariwise blessing.—No doubt a reminiscence of the Sermon on the Mount (Matt. v. 44). The word "blessing" here is not substantive, but a participle, opposed to "rendering:" "not rendering them evil or railing, but on the contrary blessing them." Though the word is chosen as the exact opposite of the bad *language* used against the Christians, "blessing" may perhaps involve the opposite of unkind *action* as well. It is used for the conferring of *benefits*: (1) spiritual, in Acts iii. 26; Gal. iii. 8; (2) material, in 2 Cor. ix. 5. (Comp. 2 Kings v. 15; Joel ii. 14; Hag. ii. 19.)

Knowing that ye are hereunto called.—Comp. chap. ii. 21. It should be, *were called*, viz., when St. Paul and others first preached to you. What, then, does he mean that they were called to? to the foregoing, or to the following? to blessing instead of rendering evil and railing? or to receive a blessing? The comparison of chap. ii. 21 seems to support the former, for there the "hereunto" points to what preceded. The argument will then be precisely the same as in that passage: "You ought not now to shrink from so hard a duty, for you were given clearly to understand, when you were admitted into Christianity, that you would have to act thus."

That ye should inherit a blessing.—Rather, *in order that ye may inherit a blessing.* God had a purpose in calling them to so hard a task, and in now requiring of them the fulfilment of it; and that purpose is that they may receive a blessing. They must not think it an arbitrary hardship, or a restriction which will not in the end be found gainful to themselves. God's full and eternal blessing is only to be obtained through such a course of self-suppression and of love even to those who hate us. The argument thus becomes more forcible, and the question which follows more appropriate, than if we adopt the other view, viz., "Bless, instead of retorting, for it is more suitable for men who are expecting to be blessed."

(10) **For.**—St. Peter will show that he is not going beyond his book when he says that the blessing is only to be obtained by those who bless.

He that will love life.—The "will" here is not merely the future tense, but "he that hath a mind to love life." St. Peter's quotation, from Ps. xxxiv. 12—16, is not exact, according to either Septuagint or Hebrew, but the divergence is probably not due to a confusion of memory, but (as often) designed to bring out an additional significance. The Psalmist had asked merely, "What man is he that lusteth to *live?*" and he promises merely long life to self-restraint. The Apostle asks, Who cares to have a life *worth having*, a life which makes a man *glad to live?* This is the "blessing" spoken of in verse 9—not simply everlasting life, but a life of unruffled happiness. (Comp. Ps. cxxxiii. 3.) This healthy enjoyment of life, the opposite of a morbid craving for death (see Eccles. ii. 17), is implied to be competent for any person to attain who "wills."

"Serene will be our days, and bright,
And happy will our nature be,
When love is an unerring light,
And joy its own security."

See good days.—"See" in the same sense as—*e.g.*, Ps. xxvii. 13; John iii. 3; Heb. xi. 5—for to "experience"—consciously to enjoy or to suffer, as the case may be.

Let him refrain.—Literally, *let him stop.* The evil word is on the very tip of his tongue.

No guile.—"Guile" is often used, in a very wide sense, of almost anything wrong (see chap. ii. 22); but here, probably, the distinction is that "evil" means open railing and bitter speech, while "guile" may mean the words which are "softer than butter, having war in his heart" (Ps. lv. 21).

(11) **Let him eschew evil.**—Literally, *swerve out of the way from evil.* The two former clauses dealt with the domain of *word;* these two with the domain of *action.* It suits St. Peter's intention better to take the verse, not as an exhortation to virtue in general, but as an instruction how to behave under provocation

(12) For the eyes of the Lord *are* over
the righteous, and his ears *are open*
unto their prayers: but the face of
the Lord *is* against[1] them that do
evil.
(13) And who *is* he that will harm you,
if ye be followers of that
which is good? (14) But and
if ye suffer for righteous-
ness' sake, happy *are ye*:
and be not afraid[a] of their
terror, neither be troubled;

1 Gr. *upon*.
a Is. 8. 12, 13.

Chaps. iii. 13—iv. 6. Consciousness of integrity is the secret of a happy life, and the secret of Christ's triumphs.

and in danger. The "good" which the man is to do is what is *kind*, not merely what is virtuous; and so, by contrast, the "evil" to be eschewed probably means chiefly what is *malicious*.

Seek peace, and ensue it.—"As much as in *you* lieth," says St. Paul, "live peaceably with all men." It is to be a matter of diligent *search;* and if it seems to flee away it is to be "ensued"—*i.e.*, pursued. The active practical measures here prescribed confirm the surmise that "blessing" in verse 8 covered more ground than benedictory prayers.

(12) **For.**—Or, *Because.* In the Psalm there is no such connecting particle, but it is involved in the juxtaposition. The sense that the Lord's eyes are over you is a sufficient reason for self-restraint under provocation: especially, perhaps, when we see that by "the Lord" St. Peter understands Jesus Christ. That this is the case is clear from his use of the same Psalm in chap. ii. 3. If Christ, the model of meekness under persecution (chap. ii. 23), is watching, we not only *need* no passionate self-defence, but should be ashamed to use it. Was St. Peter thinking how once, while he himself was cursing and swearing at those who accused him of being a Christian, he felt the eyes of the Lord turn upon him? The thought of His eyes being over us is chiefly that of guardianship.

Open unto their prayers.—Rather, *are towards their prayer—i.e.*, directed towards it. Here, as in chap. ii. 3, the Prayer Book version has influenced our translation.

Against them that do evil.—There is no difference in the Greek between this preposition and that just rendered "over." *But the countenance of the Lord is over them that do evil things.* He *marks* what they are doing. This is sufficient comfort when men injure us (chap. ii. 23); sufficient warning not to injure in return. It is instructive now to turn and see the circumstances in which this lovely Psalm was composed. The moment was one of David's extremest peril among an infuriated heathen population. The danger and dread he was in are shown in Ps. lvi. Yet nothing can be brighter and more serene than Ps. xxxiv. He had obtained life and days; and it was all through confidence in God on the one hand, and inoffensive self-submission on the other. Had he used violence—"shown spirit," as we say—like the "young lions," he would have come worse off. It seems to be for this cause that St. Peter deemed the Psalm so appropriate to his readers, misjudged and suspiciously watched (Ps. lvi. 5, 6) by unbelievers, who only waited the opportunity to shed their blood (*ibid.* 1, 2). But the striking change is that, whereas David's trust in Jehovah was a trust simply in the Eternal Being without distinction of Persons, St. Peter bids the Hebrews of Asia read that Psalm into an act of faith in Jesus. We shall see the same thing in verse 15, as we saw it in chap. ii. 3. The force of the change will be felt by any one who reads through that Psalm, substituting (like the Rheims version) "our Lord" for "the Lord."

(13–iv. 6) EXHORTATION TO KEEP A PURE CONSCIENCE.—It is the only charm against persecution. It is like Christ to suffer with a good conscience; and He had His reward for it, in bringing us, and even the spirits of men who had died impenitent, to God thereby. It is the very meaning of the baptism by which He saves us. To feel its beauty and safety, we have but to consider the ugliness and danger of our former life.

(13) **And who is he that shall harm you?**—There is always a ring of scornful assurance in an interrogative introduced by "and:" "And who, pray?"

If ye be followers.—Rather, *if ye make yourselves zealots.* The phrase looks on into the future; not merely "if at present ye be." And the word which means "follower" (*i.e.*, imitator) is here a false reading for *zelotes*, the name by which St. Peter's lesser namesake among the Apostles was known, probably because of his enthusiastic attachment to the old or to the new Law. The same *zelotes* is found in Tit. ii. 14 and elsewhere. The translation, "of Him which is good," is perfectly possible, but does not quite so well suit the context. Some writers (Leighton among them) take the verse to mean, or at least to include, that when men see the goodness and loving-kindness of our lives they will not be *disposed* to hurt us. This thought is, however, foreign to the passage. It means that men and devils may try their worst, as they did on Christ, and cannot harm us.

(14) **But and if ye suffer.**—The old-fashioned phrase would read more intelligibly thus: *Nay, if ye should even suffer.* So far are men's attempts to "harm" us (by acts of malice to property or good name, &c.) from really injuring us, that even if it should come to be a matter of "suffering" we are to be congratulated. What he means by this "suffering," which is so much more than being "harmed," may be seen from chaps. ii. 21; iii. 17; iv. 1, 15. He means the horrors of capital punishment. He does not speak of this as something that was already occurring, nor as though it were something immediately and certainly impending, but as a case well supposable. There had then as yet been no martyrdoms in Asia. The letter is therefore earlier in date than the Apocalypse (Rev. ii. 13). It is a noticeable point that in all St. Paul's Epistles the word "to suffer" occurs but seven times, and nowhere twice in the same Epistle; whereas it comes twelve times in this one short Letter of St. Peter.

For righteousness' sake.—Like the "suffering wrongfully" of chap. ii. 19. It is not *as* suffering that it is valuable.

Happy are ye.—Quite the right word: yet the use of it obscures the obvious reference to the Sermon on the Mount (Matt. v. 10). The reference to it is all the clearer in the Greek from the significant way in which St. Peter leaves his sentence incomplete, merely giving the catchword of the beatitude. We might represent it to ourselves by putting "Blessed" in inverted commas, and a dash after it. He makes sure his readers will catch the allusion. There is no part of our Lord's discourses which seems (from the traces in

(15) but sanctify the Lord God in your hearts: and *be* ready always to *give* an answer to every man that asketh you a reason of the hope that is in you with

the earliest Christian literature) to have taken so rapid and firm a hold on the Christian conscience as the Sermon on the Mount.

Be not afraid of their terror.—Here the translators might with advantage have kept the same word, and said (as in the original passage from which St. Peter is quoting, Isa. viii. 12), *Fear ye not their fear—i.e.*, the thing which makes them fear; do not regard with dread the same object as they do. In the original, the persons whose fears Isaiah and the faithful Jews are not to fear are those who were in dread of Syria and Israel. Here the persons are not named; but, of course, according to this interpretation, "they" cannot be the enemies who try to harm the Christians, but, if any one, those of the Christians who, for fear of man, were beginning to abandon Christianity. The intention, however, is not to press this clause for its own sake, but to throw greater force upon the clause which begins the next verse. It argues carelessness about the passage in Isaiah to interpret, "Be not afraid of the fear which your foes strike into you."

(15) **But sanctify the Lord God in your hearts.**—The tense of this and the two preceding imperatives shows that St. Peter meant this for advice to be acted upon at the moment of being called on to suffer. The passage, as it stands in Isaiah, runs literally, "Jehovah Sabaoth, Him shall ye sanctify, and He (shall be) your fear, and He your dread." It becomes, therefore, very striking when we find that, without a shadow of doubt, the right reading here is, *But sanctify the Lord the Christ in your hearts.* How is it possible, except on the supposition that the Catholic doctrine is really a statement of fact, that a Jew like St. Peter should ever have come to apply to a Man whom he had known familiarly, a Man who had served him at table and had washed his feet, the words which Isaiah had said about the "Lord of Hosts?" This passage immediately precedes that which was quoted in chap. ii. 8, and (like that) is not caught up at random, but as coming in the great Immanuel passage. That presence of God which was the palladium of Israel in the days of Hezekiah has found fulfilment in "the Christ" now given. But what is meant by "sanctifying" Him? The phrase is not elsewhere used in the New Testament, except in the Lord's Prayer; but in the Old Testament see Lev. x. 3; Isa. xxix. 23; Ezek. xxxviii. 23. As to "glorify" God means (in word and deed) to recognise His glorious perfections; as to "magnify" Him means to recognise His greatness; as to "justify" Him means to recognise His inherent justice; so to "sanctify" Him means to recognise, in word and deed, His full holiness, and therefore to treat Him with due awe. This not only substitutes the fear of God for the fear of man (since they mutually exclude each other), but enforces purity of life, thus catching up again "that which is good" and "for righteousness' sake." This, adds St. Peter, is to be done "in your hearts." This does not mean simply "*with* your hearts," or "*from* your hearts" (*i.e.*, inwardly, or, with all sincerity and devotion), but it signifies the local habitation *where* the Christ is to be thus recognised. That is to say: St. Peter, like St. Paul (Eph. iii. 17), acknowledges an *indwelling* of Christ in the hearts of the faithful; and this indwelling not merely subjective, consisting of their constant recollection of him, but real and objective: there He is, as in a shrine, and they must pay due reverence to His presence. The Apostle does, in fact, in those words "in your hearts," purposely call attention to the difference between Isaiah's use of the name Immanuel and the Christian meaning of it. To Isaiah, God dwelt in the midst of a people in its corporate capacity; St. Peter knew that, through the Incarnation, each individual Christian has God in him, united with him.

And be.—The better reading omits the connecting particle, so that we should put "being" instead of "and be."

Ready always to give an answer.—This is the consequence of sanctifying Christ within by the worship of a pure life, that no moment, no questioner finds us unprepared to speak with freedom of our hope in Him. The word for "answer" here is *apologia*, an apology; not, of course, in the modern sense of an *excuse*, but a defence, the reply of an accused person, like the well-known *Apologia Socratis*, or the great modern *Apologia pro Vita Sua*, or the works from which Tertullian, Athenagoras, St. Justin, and others are called "The Apologists." It does not mean that every person is bound to be able to state intellectually the nature and grounds of the Christian creed, though such a duty may, perhaps, be fairly *deduced* from the text. It does not say that every Christian ought to know why he is a Christian, but that every Christian's own life ought to be so free from taint, so conscious of Christ enshrined within, as to cause him no misgiving in defending the faith from the calumnies (see chap. ii. 12) brought against it. The constant readiness, or freedom from encumbrance of sin, is the main point, "which intimates," says Leighton, "it was not always to be *done* to every one, but we, being *ready* to do, are to consider when, and to whom, and how far." Consciousness of impurity of life shuts a man's mouth from defending Christian morality.

That asketh you a reason.—Rather, *that demandeth of you an account.* It does not mean inquirers about Christian doctrine, but those who call Christians to account for their profession of the Gospel hopes. Though it must not be exclusively so taken, St. Peter evidently means chiefly the being called into the law court to give account. Probably he is thinking of our Lord's charge to himself and his co-apostles, in St. Luke xii. 11. (Comp. Matt. x. 5, 16, 19.)

Of the hope that is in you.—More literally, *with regard to the hope that is in you*: *i.e.*, with regard to the Christianity in which you share. It is, of course, quite a modern application to the text to see in this anything of the individual assurance of salvation. However fairly it may be argued that a Christian ought to know why he, personally, expects to be saved, it is not the thought of St. Peter here. Christianity is here called a hope, rather than a faith, as in Acts xxviii. 20, Col. i. 23, because, especially in times of persecution, so much of our creed has a future tinge.

With meekness and fear.—There ought certainly to be added a warning *But* before these words. The readiness of the Christian's defence of himself and the Church from all moral aspersions is not to be marred by any self-exaltation or improper confidence. Archbishop Leighton says, "Not, therefore, blustering and flying out into invectives because he hath the better on it against any man that questions him touching this hope, as some think themselves certainly authorised to use rough speech because they plead for meekness[a] and fear:[1] (16) having a good conscience; that, whereas they speak evil of you, as of evildoers, they may be ashamed that falsely accuse your good conversation in Christ. (17) For *it is* better, if the will of God be so, that ye suffer for well doing, than for evil doing. (18) For Christ also hath once suffered for sins, the just for the unjust, that he might bring us to God,[b]

a 2 Tim. 2. 25.
1 Or, *reverence*.
b 2 Cor. 5. 18.

truth. On the contrary, so much the rather study meekness, for the glory and advantage of the truth." The "fear" will be, in large measure, a dread of overstepping the bounds of truth or modesty in speaking of the Christian morals. The Acts of the Martyrs, with all their splendour, too often show how St. Peter's cautious *But* was needed.

(16) **Having a good conscience.**—This strikes the key-note of the paragraph. How vigorously St. Peter repeats it! "Zealous for that which is good," "for righteousness' sake," "*sanctify* the Lord," "with meekness and fear," "a good conscience," "your good conversation."

Whereas.—The word means precisely the same as in chap. ii. 12, where see Note.

They speak evil of you, as of evil doers.—Tischendorf follows one of the best manuscripts and the Peschito-Syriac version in reading *whereas ye are evil spoken of.* It is easy to see how the ordinary reading would come in, from the similarity of chap. ii. 12; and we may pretty confidently adopt the emendation. In any case, the words "as of evil doers" should be removed.

They may be ashamed (or, *confounded*).—When? St. Peter is evidently thinking of the Christian at the bar of the curator or pro-consul, and the mortification of the *delator*, or spy, who had given information against him.

Falsely accuse.—Literally, *insult*, that is, "odiously calumniate." The word occurs again only in Luke vi. 28.

In Christ.—This is the nearest approach in St. Peter to a use of this word as a proper name. Still, it is not so. Other Hebrews, he reminds them in this word, were safe from persecution only by rejecting the national hope of a Messiah. It is simply because these men are "in Christ" that the heathens (perhaps also their fellow Jews) insult their conversation. The phrase "in Christ," *i.e.*, as members of the Church, occurs again in chap. v. 10, 14, and the thought is common enough in St. John (*e.g.* 1 John v. 20), but it does not come in 2 Peter, nor in Hebrews, St. James, or St. Jude. Of course, St. Paul's writings teem with it. It contains the converse side of the Incarnation doctrine to that involved in verse 15; we not only have the whole Christ dwelling in us, but He embraces us all; "Ye in me, and I in you" (John xiv. 20).

(17) **For it is better.**—There is a kind of ironical suppression in this comparison.

If the will of God be so.—A strikingly reverent phrase in the original, *If the will of God should will it.* This is, of course, to be taken only with the word "suffer," which itself means, as in verse 14, to suffer *capitally*. St. Peter is thinking of the legal process of verses 15, 16, coming to a verdict of "guilty." He was himself daily expecting such a death.

For well doing.—Better, perhaps, *as well doers.* It does not necessarily mean, in the Greek, that the well doing was the *reason* of the suffering, but simply that it accompanied it.

(18) **For Christ also.**—This gives a reason for thinking it no such formidable thing to suffer when one is innocent. It has been tried before, and the precedent is encouraging. "It is," says Archbishop Leighton, "some known ease to the mind, in any distress, to look upon examples of the like or greater distress in present or former times . . . As the example and company of the saints in suffering is very considerable, so that of Christ is more than any other, yea, than all the rest together." If King Messiah (note that he does not call Him Jesus) could endure to be cut off (but not for Himself), was it for any one who clung to the promises to shrink from the like test?

Hath once suffered.—Even if we retain the verb, it should be *suffered*, not "hath suffered," it is all past now; but much the better reading is *died*, which leaves no doubt about the meaning of "suffering" in verse 17. And this He did "once." In this significant word St. Peter strikes out the main argument of a great portion of the Epistle to the Hebrews (Heb. vii. 27; ix. 27; x. 10). The thought that Christ suffered or died "once" conveys comfort to these Christians for several reasons: (1) because His death has, once for all, taken all terror from an innocent death; (2) because no Christian will have to die more than one death; (3) because one death, so soon over for ever, contains the further idea of happiness and peace beyond. The word "to die" in Greek is often used in a penal sense—"to be put to death"—and is to be so taken here.

For sins.—When the Apostle says "Christ *also*," he raises a comparison between Christ and the Christian martyr. Now the parallel does not merely consist in the fact that both "suffer" or are put to death. Both are put to death but once. Both are put to death innocent: the martyr "while well-doing," Christ acknowledged to be "just." But this does not exhaust the likeness. The Messiah is said to be put to death "for sins." Now this expression "for sins" (literally, *in connection with sins*) is that which is used to mean "as a sin-offering." (See Rom. viii. 3; Gal. i. 4; Heb. x. 6, 8, 18, 26; xiii. 11; 1 John ii. 2; iv. 10.) If, therefore, "Christ *also* was put to death as a sin-offering," it is implied that, in a sense, the Christian martyr is also a sin-offering, and (though in an infinitely lower degree) dies, like Him, "just for unjust." This is a fresh encouragement to St. Peter's first readers to meet death bravely. In what sense they can be sacrifices for other men's sins we shall consider presently.

The just for the unjust.—That preposition "for" contains a volume of theology. Though it is not so weak a word as the one which occurs in the phrase "for sins," it does not express the notion of *substitution.* (Comp. Note on chap. ii. 21.) It is simply "on behalf of." As a substitute for the unjust, we make bold to say that (according to Holy Scripture, and the primitive fathers, and the conscience of man) neither the martyrs nor Christ Himself could have made atonement; "on behalf of" other men, the martyrs could very easily be said to die. It is, perhaps, a pity that the definite article has been inserted in our version. Though, of course, our Lord is the only human being who can in strictness be called just,

being put to death in the flesh, but | quickened by the Spirit: (19) by which

St. Peter means the word here to cover others besides Him; "Christ *also* died, a just man on behalf of unjust men."

That he might bring us to God.—Or, better, *bring you;* though it cannot be stated peremptorily in this case that such is the reading. (See Note on chap. i. 12.) The substantive derived from this verb appears as "access" in Rom. v. 2; Eph. ii. 18; iii. 12. A most important doctrinal passage. St. Peter says not a word about the Atonement in its effect upon the mind of the Father towards man. Though there is, no doubt, some deep truth in the phrase which occurs in the second of the Thirty-nine Articles—"suffered . . . to reconcile His Father to us"—it is a side on which the New Testament writers do not much dwell. It is too high a mystery for our minds to reach. The phrase is itself not Scriptural. The New Testament, as has been well pointed out, never even speaks of the reconciliation as *mutual.* The quarrel is treated as one-sided, so far, at least, as in connection with the Atonement. When, then, our Lord was put to death as a sacrifice for sins—a righteous man on behalf of unrighteous men—St. Peter explains these terms by the expression "in order that He might bring you to God," not "in order that He might bring God to you." The voluntary death of a righteous man upon the cross, in the calm calculation that nothing else would so attract sinful men to Himself, and thus to the Father who sent Him (John xii. 32—this is the aspect of the Atonement which St. Peter sets forth. Perhaps on another occasion he might have set forth a different aspect; but now he is still thinking of the effect of Christian conduct upon the outer world, and his object is to make the Christians feel that they too can, in their measure, bring the unjust, the persecuting heathens and Jews, to God by innocent and voluntary deaths. Thus their deaths are carrying on the work of reconciliation; and what Christ did for them ("died for you") they do for others. Well then may they be called blessed when they suffer (verse 14).

Being put to death in the flesh, but quickened by the Spirit.—The interpreters of this sentence may be classified in two groups, according as they understand the fact referred to in the second clause to be (1) the resurrection of Christ, or (2) something which took place between His death and His resurrection. Now, if we could accept the translation in the English Bible, "by the Spirit," it would be pretty obvious to accept (1); and we should point to such passages as Rom. i. 4, viii. 11, to show that the resurrection of Christ was due to the action of the Holy Ghost. It would not be possible to follow Oecumenius, Calvin, Beza, and Leighton, in taking "the flesh" to mean generally the human nature of Christ, and "the Spirit" by which He was quickened to mean His own divine nature; for Christ has a human spirit as truly as a human body and soul, and it would be heresy to call His divine nature His spirit, as though it occupied in Him the position which is occupied in men by the human spirit. But, as a matter of fact, we cannot translate it "quickened *by* the Spirit." It is literally, *killed indeed in flesh, but quickened in spirit.* Now, how can "quickened in spirit" be a description of the Resurrection? It cannot be answered (with Huther) that the "spirit" here means the resurrection body; for though that is indeed a spiritual body, yet it is playing fast and loose with words to identify "spirit" and "spiritual body." If the resurrection body be only spirit, where is the resurrection? Neither would the antithesis be correct between "flesh" and "spirit," if by "spirit" is meant the new form of body given at the Resurrection. Or, again, taking "spirit" in its true sense of the inward incorporeal self, could the Resurrection be described as a quickening of it? True, the spirit itself will *gain* in some way by its re-incorporation (2 Cor. v. 4); but as the spirit has been alive all along, but the flesh has been dead, the contrast would be very forced to express death and resurrection by "killed in flesh, but quickened in spirit," instead of saying rather "killed in flesh, but soon quickened in the same." Thus we are driven to (2). As a matter of fact, there is nothing in the words to suggest an interval between the quickening and the killing. They both are parts of the same act, and both are used to explain the word "died." It is a kind of apology for having used the word death at all (for we have seen that St. Peter's object is to help the future martyrs to despise death, verse 14): "Died, do I say? yes, killed in flesh, it is true, but actually quickened to fresh energies in spirit by that very act of death." (Comp. our Lord's charge to the Twelve, Matt. x. 28.) But how can His death be said to have been a quickening of His human spirit? Some take the word to mean simply "preserved alive," a word almost identical, being used apparently in that sense in Luke xvii. 33, Acts vii. 19. The notion, however, would be too weak here; some energetic action seems required to balance "being killed." That St. Peter is speaking of something not altogether peculiar to Christ, but common to men, may still be inferred from his saying "Christ *also.*" The doctrine, then, seems to be (as Bengel and others say) that the spirit, set free from the body, immediately receives new life, as it were, thereby. To purely spiritual realities it becomes alive in a manner which was impossible while it was united to the flesh. The new powers are exemplified in what follows immediately. So long as Christ, so long as any man, is alive in the flesh, he cannot hold converse with spirits as such; but the moment death severs flesh and spirit the spirit can deal with other spirits, which Christ proceeded forthwith to do.

(19) **By which.**—If "by the Spirit" had been right in the former verse, this translation might have stood here, though the word is literally *in;* for "in" is often used to mean "in the power of," "on the strength of:" *e.g.,* Rom. viii. 15. But as that former rendering is untenable, we must here keep strictly to *in which—i.e.,* in spirit. This might mean either of two things: (1) "spiritually speaking," "so far as thought and sympathy goes," as, for instance, 1 Cor. v. 3, Col. ii. 5; or else (2) "in spirit," as opposed to "in the body"—*i.e.,* "out of the body" (2 Cor. xii. 2; comp. Rev. i. 10), as a disembodied spirit. We adopt the latter rendering without hesitation, for reasons which will be clearer in the next Note.

He went and preached unto the spirits in prison.—There are two main ways of interpreting this mysterious passage. (1) The spirits are understood as being *now* in prison, in consequence of having rejected His preaching to them while they were still on earth. According to this interpretation—which has the support of such names as Pearson, Hammond, Barrow, and Leighton (though he afterwards modified his opinion), among ourselves, besides divers great theologians of other countries, including St. Thomas Aquinas on the

also he went and preached[a] unto the spirits in prison;[b] (20) which sometime were disobedient, when once the longsuffering of God waited in the days of Noah, while the ark was a preparing, wherein few, that is, eight souls were

a ch. 4. 6.
b 2 Pet. 2. 4.

one hand and Beza on the other—it was "in spirit," *i.e.*, mystically speaking, our Lord Himself who, in and through the person of Noah, preached repentance to the old world. Thus the passage is altogether dissociated from the doctrine of the descent into hell; and the sense (though not the Greek) would be better expressed by writing, *He had gone and preached unto the spirits* (*now*) *in prison.* In this case, however, it is difficult to see the purpose of the digression, or what could have brought the subject into St. Peter's mind. (2) The second interpretation—which is that of (practically) all the Fathers, and of Calvin, Luther (finally), Bellarmine, Bengel, and of most modern scholars—refers the passage to what our Lord did while His body was dead. This is the most natural construction to put upon the words "in which also" (*i.e.*, in spirit). It thus gives point to the saying that He was "quickened in spirit," which would otherwise be left very meaningless. The "spirits" here will thus correspond with "in spirit" there. It is the only way to assign any intelligible meaning to the words "He went and" to suppose that He "went" straight from His quickening in spirit—*i.e.*, from His death. It is far the most natural thing to suppose that the spirits *were* in prison at the time when Christ went and preached to them. We take it, then, to mean that, directly Christ's human spirit was disengaged from the body, He gave proof of the new powers of purely spiritual action thus acquired by going off to the place, or state, in which other disembodied spirits were (who would have been incapable of receiving direct impressions from Him had He not Himself been in the purely spiritual condition), and conveyed to them certain tidings: He "preached" unto them. What was the substance of this preaching we are not here told, the word itself (which is not the same as, *e.g.*, in chap. i. 25) only means to publish or proclaim like a crier or herald; and as the spirits are said to have been disobedient and in prison, some have thought that Christ went to proclaim to them the certainty of their damnation! The notion has but to be mentioned to be rejected with horror; but it may be pointed out also that in chap. iv. 6, which refers back to this passage, it is distinctly called a "gospel;" and it would be too grim to call that a gospel which (in Calvin's words) "made it more clear and patent to them that they were shut out from all salvation!" He brought *good* tidings, therefore, of some kind to the "prison" and the spirits in it. And this "prison" must not be understood (with Bp. Browne, *Articles*, p. 95) as merely "a place of safe keeping," where good spirits might be as well as bad, though etymologically this is imaginable. The word occurs thirty-eight times in the New Testament in the undoubted sense of a "prison," and not once in that of a place of protection, though twice (Rev. xviii. 2) it is used in the derived sense of "a cage."

(20) **Which sometime were disobedient.**—The absence of the definite article here in the Greek (contrary to St. Peter's usage in participial sentences—*e.g.*, chap. i. 5, 7, 10, 17) makes it possible to think that the spirits mentioned in this verse are not co-extensive with those in prison. It is, literally, *to men who once upon a time were disobedient.* Our Lord preached to the whole class of spirits in prison, of all times and races; and then, to magnify the bounty of this act, St. Peter instances a particular group of them, who were the most marked criminals of any, and whose case suggested a useful application. He has a reason for using the word "disobedient." It would not describe *all* sinners, but those who had heard and been convinced by the word of God, but refused to accept it. (See Note on verse 2.) This was the case with those to whom Noah preached (2 Pet. ii. 5); and, in spite of their "disobedience," Christ, after His innocent and sacrificial death, went in spirit and preached a gospel to them. Now, let it be recollected that St. Peter's object through the whole of this section is to encourage the Hebrew Christians to be ready, through a good conscience, for a brave martyrdom, if need be. They are to think how their deaths, like Christ's, may bring their persecutors to God. Nay—he seems to imply—their very spirits going forth into the world of spirits may conceivably carry a gospel of some kind even to Hebrew relatives who have passed away, like those Antediluvians, in the "disobedience" which was characteristic of the Jews. St. Clement of Alexandria, who derives the notion from the *Shepherd* of Hermas, gives his belief that the Apostles also, when they died, preached to those who had died before them; and though there is little that throws light on our occupation in the intermediate state, it can hardly be pronounced impossible for some spirits to be allowed to follow Christ's example there by preaching to spirits in prison. Many expositors, afraid of the consequences of admitting that there could be a possible gospel for men who died impenitent, have supposed that the imprisoned spirits to whom Christ went were the less wicked people destroyed by the Flood; others that they were those who had some motions of penitence when the rain began to fall; but these ideas are foreign to the text, which only tells us that they "were disobedient," and adds nothing to extenuate their crime. They are a typical instance of men who died "as evil doers" (verse 17).

When once the longsuffering of God waited.—The word "once" has no business in the text, originating only in an ingenious but unnecessary guess of Erasmus. The clause serves to heighten the guilt of the poor sinners to whom Christ preached in prison. Not only did they die a judicial death for their extreme sensuality (Gen. vi. 3, 11), not only did they disobey an isolated call to repentance from Noah, but continuously, through all the time of the building of the ark (traditionally 120 years), they went on refusing to listen. Sodom and Gomorrah were destroyed without a preacher to warn them, the Canaanites were annihilated without an offer of repentance, but these abandoned Antediluvians sinned in spite of the long ministry of Noah, and died impenitent. Both their wickedness and God's longsuffering with them were embodied in Hebrew proverbs, which St. Peter's readers would know, and yet Christ had a gospel for them.

While the ark.—Better, *while an ark.* It does not merely describe the period of the disobedience, but rather changes the thought altogether. We now turn from the destruction of the majority to the salvation of the few.

Wherein.—Literally, *whereinto—i.e.*, by getting into which.

Few, that is, eight souls were saved.—The mention of disobedience calls up to the Apostle's mind

saved by water. (21) The like figure whereunto *even* baptism doth also now save[a] us (not the putting away of the filth of the flesh, but the answer of a

a Tit. 3. 5.

at once the vast number of Hebrews who rejected the gospel of Christ. As in chap. ii. 4 *et seq.*, so here, he stablishes the readers against the thought, "Can I be right and all these people wrong?" by showing that from the beginning it was always a small number who accepted salvation, and they should naturally expect it to be so now. It is better to be one of the eight in the ark than of the many disobedient in the water.

By water.—Or, *through water.* The very water which drowned the disobedient was the instrument of saving to those who believed, for it floated their ark. It cannot be denied that this is a little forced. So, in the same way, in chap. ii. 8, the same stone is to some a sanctuary, to some a stumbling-block. This pregnant word "water" leads on to the next thought.

(21) **The like figure whereunto even baptism doth also now save us.**—There are two undoubted false readings in this sentence which must be cleared away before we can consider the meaning. First, the word "whereunto" is a mistake for the more difficult *which;* and second, it should be *you,* not "us." We may then translate, either, *Which baptism also, in antitype, doth now save you,* or else, *Which* (*water*) *also, in antitype, now saveth you—baptism.* The first is less likely, both from the order of the words in Greek, and also because of the difficulty of calling the Flood point-blank a baptism. According to the second translation, the water through which Noah was saved is said in the present day ("now," as opposed to "in the days of Noe") to save *us* (the "you" is emphatic). It does so, in the same sense as we might say, for instance, that the sprinkling of the paschal blood saves us: that is to say, it foreshadowed something which does as a fact save us. This St. Peter expresses by the adjective which may be rendered "in antitype." The thing it represented is Christian baptism. Where, then, lies the likeness between the two? Not merely in the identity of the element water, which serves but to arrest the fancy, and make one think of the deeper resemblance. One obvious point is that the number of persons accepting the proffered salvation at the present crisis is, as in the days of Noe, very small compared with those who reject it. The main thought, however, is not of the Christians, as a body or family (like Noe's), being saved while others are lost. For each individual by himself there is a meaning in his baptism which is prefigured by the Flood; and the explanation of baptism which follows, and the opening of the next chapter, show that the Apostle was thinking chiefly of this individual application. As the passage of Israel through the Red Sea is described as a baptism (1 Cor. x. 2) because it marked their transition from the state of bondage to a new national life, and left their enemies destroyed in the water, so Noe's safe passage through the Flood is a type of baptism, because it was a regeneration of humanity, it was a destruction of the carnal, sensual element (Gen. vi. 3 "he also is *flesh*"), it washed the human race from its pollutions, and man rose to a new and more spiritual existence for the time being, with the bow for a sign of a perpetual covenant made. So baptism is a destruction and death to the flesh, but a new life to the spirit. It must be observed how carefully St. Peter expresses the *permanent* effect of baptism by the present tense "saveth:" not "saved you," nor "hath saved you;" it is a living and ever-present fact, the "*everlasting* benediction of His heavenly washing;" it washes the neophyte not from past sins only, but from those which he afterwards commits, if only he still repents and believes.

Not the putting away of the filth of the flesh.—The Apostle is not cautioning his readers against the thought that baptism acted *ex opere operato,* as a charm, but he is telling them, on the contrary, that it is no external rite. He was writing to Jews, who were very familiar with ceremonial washings, or "baptisings," which, though they *symbolised* a cleansing from sin, really *effected* nothing but to make the skin less dirty.

But the answer of a good conscience toward God.—An expression which has caused almost as much difficulty as any in the New Testament. The difficulty lay especially in two points: first, that the context was so involved as to give little indication what to *expect;* secondly, that the Greek word (*eperôtêma*) which is here rendered "answer" is so seldom found, and might easily take such various shades of meaning. (1) Touching the word itself, we may at once reject the translation "answer," for it could only mean an "answer" in that sense in which "question" and "answer" are identical, both of them being "the thing asked," the subject matter of both being the same; but so cumbersome a sense is not in keeping here. (2) Next we may consider the attractive theory that it means a "contract." The form in which a contract was made was as follows: N says to M, "Dost thou promise?" and M answers, "I promise." Now, in Byzantine Law-Greek such a contract is known as an *eperôtêma,* or "questionment," from the question with which proceedings began. And, as a matter of fact, the baptismal covenant has undoubtedly been entered upon from the earliest times with just such questions and answers. Tertullian speaks of this (*De Corona,* chap. iii.) as an ancient custom in the end of the second century. There are, however, three serious objections: first, that "the contract of a good conscience" is a somewhat vague and imperfect phrase, and far more difficult in Greek than in English; secondly, that there is no trace of the legal term *eperôtêma* until centuries after the date of St. Peter, or of Tertullian either; thirdly, that had *eperôtêma* been a recognised term for a "contract" in St. Peter's time, we should have been certain to find this explanation in some of the Greek Fathers. (3) The usual meaning of the verb would lead us towards a less unsatisfactory conclusion. *Eperôtân* is "to put a question" for further information's sake. And we may remark that the order of the Greek would strongly suggest that the words "toward God" should be attached (in spite of the analogy of Acts xxiv. 16) not to "good conscience," but to the word *eperôtêma.* Now, there is a constant use of the verb *eperôtân* in the Old Testament in connection with the name of God. In Josh. ix. 14, Judg. i. 1, xviii. 5, and many other places, it means "to consult God," "to inquire of the Lord," to seek to Him for direction. Or, with a slightly different turn, it is used, as in Isa. xix. 3, lxv. 1, for "to inquire after God," in which sense it finds its way into the New Testament in Rom. x. 20. Thus baptism would be said to be, "not the flesh's putting away of dirt (for so it might be turned, though it is somewhat forced), but a good conscience's inquiry at the hands of God," or "a good conscience's inquiry after God." Observe that if the "good conscience" is

good conscience toward God,) by the
resurrection of Jesus Christ:[a] (22) who is
gone into heaven, and is on the right
hand of God; angels and authorities
and powers being made subject unto
him.[b]

a ch. 1. 3; Rom. 6. 4.
b Eph. 1. 21.

the agent in this transaction, as here expressed, St. Peter would recognise (as in Luke viii. 15) the man's happy state of soul *before* baptism, and baptism would be the mode of his further approach to God. That this is good doctrine cannot be denied. (4) There is, however, another version for which a still better case can be made out: viz., "demand." It is true that the verb *eperôtân* more frequently means "to ask" a question than "to ask" a boon, expecting a verbal response rather than a practical one; but it is once used in the New Testament in the latter sense (Matt. xvi. 1), and in the Old Testament also (as Ps. cxxxvii. 3). And the only other instance of the word *eperôtêma* in inspired literature makes for this view. This occurs in Dan. iv. 17, where the English has "demand," and the Latin *petitio.* There is, indeed, almost as much difficulty in ascertaining the exact sense there as here; but, on the whole, it seems to mean the "demand" for Nebuchadnezzar's degradation. This was evidently the meaning assigned to our present passage by the anonymous Father in the Catena, for, wrongly joining the words "through the resurrection" with *eperôtêma,* he says: "It teacheth also how we *beseech* of Him; and how? by confessing the resurrection of the Lord." Taking, then, the rendering "demand," a further question arises: Does St. Peter mean that baptism is the demand (made by God or the Church upon the man) *for* a good conscience towards God? or the demand *made by* a good conscience upon God, without specifying the demand? or finally, the demand upon God (made by the man) *for* a good conscience? Of these the second seems the weakest, because it leaves the nature of the demand so open, and because the notion of a good conscience *previous* to baptism is less suited to the context. The first would indeed give a vigorous sense. St. Peter would then be saying, "Have a good conscience (verse 16), for, besides all else, it is your baptismal obligation, and in defiling conscience you forfeit your baptismal salvation;" but it labours under the defect of connecting "toward God" with "conscience" instead of with "demand," and it is imperfect, moreover, in not demanding a good conscience toward men as well as toward God. The last seems both the clearest in itself, the best antithesis to the balancing clause, and the most in keeping with the context. It will then be: "Noah's flood, in antitype, to this day saves you—that is to say, baptism, which is no cleansing of the skin from dirt, but an application to God for a clear conscience." A "good conscience," in this case, will not mean an honest frame of mind, but a consciousness of having nothing against you, such as would come to even the chief of sinners from the baptismal remission of sins. "Conscience" is used in this retrospective sense four times in Hebrews (chaps. ix. 9, 14, and x. 2, 22); and, indeed, in verse 16 it meant "having nothing on your mind because of the past," rather than "being sure that you *mean* well." And how well this suits the context! The Apostle, from chap. iii. 13 to chap. iv. 6, is uttering the praises of a clear conscience, and warning from everything that could defile it. "With this," he says, "you cannot be harmed; with this, you will be always ready to defend the faith when called to account. It was because He had this that Christ was able to atone for you and bring you to God, and to conduct His mission to the dead, and to give by His resurrection an efficacy to your baptism; and that baptism itself only saves you by the fact that in it you ask and receive the cleansing of the conscience."

By the resurrection.—Rightly joined in our version with "doth save." Baptism derives all its sacramental efficacy from the fact that Christ has, by the Resurrection, introduced into the world a new kind of life, which in baptism is imparted to the believer. The doctrine here approaches still nearer to that of Rom. vi. than to that of chap. i. 3. In the first chapter, the Resurrection of Christ was said to be the means and the moment of our regeneration, but baptism (though of course implied) was not mentioned, nor the death to sin. But here, as in Romans, these two take a prominent place. As humanity died to the flesh in the bad Antediluvians, and rose again, washed clean, in Noe, so to the believer there was in baptism a death to the flesh, and he rose again, with a conscience washed clean through the union thereby effected with the crucified and risen Christ. Note, again, that when the Apostle speaks of glories he uses the name of Jesus: when of sufferings, it is the title of Christ.

(22) **Who is gone into heaven, and is on the right hand of God.**—This verse (which partakes of the character of a doxology) serves two purposes. First, it carries on the history of Jesus Christ. How carefully, in spite of what seem at first irrelevant digressions, St. Peter holds his threads. Christ's passion and death, activity among the dead, resurrection from among them, ascension into heaven, perpetual session in glory, follow one another in due order. The second purpose of the clause runs parallel to the first. St. Peter is teaching the entire conformity of the believer to the Lord. If the believer will but retain his good conscience, he may hope for a precisely similar experience. The Latin and several other good versions, together with several Latin Fathers, add a curious sentence after the words "on the right hand of God," which runs: *swallowing up death, that we might be made heirs of eternal life;* but there is no sufficient authority for the sentence. The first notion of being "on the right hand of God," taken, probably, from Ps. cx. 1, seems to be that of occupying the highest post of honour possible, next after that of God—*i.e.*, the Father—Himself It is not necessary here to consider what else may be implied in the phrase as to the conditions of our Lord's human existence; but when we compare St. Paul's statement, in Eph. iv. 10, about His now "filling all things," we feel that these pictorial words, such as "heaven" and "right hand of God," are intended to convey the notion that His humanity is now entirely *without* conditions, though still retaining all that is truly essential to humanity. It may be observed that, assuming (as even most sceptical critics do) the genuineness of this Epistle, we have here at first hand the deliberate evidence of one who had been perfectly familiar with Jesus Christ as man with man. By what stretch of imagination can we suppose that such a person could ever have invented, or have accepted from others this mode of speaking about his former Teacher, had he not been conscious of the resurrection and ascension of Jesus as simply historical facts, of the same order as the fact of His death?

Angels and authorities and powers being made subject unto him.—There can be no doubt

CHAPTER IV.—(1) Forasmuch then
as Christ hath suffered for us in the
flesh,[a] arm yourselves likewise with the
same mind: for he that hath suffered
in the flesh hath ceased from sin;[b]
(2) that he no longer should live the
rest of *his* time in the flesh to the lusts
of men, but to the will of God. (3) For
the time past of *our* life may suffice us
to have wrought the will of the Gentiles,

A.D. cir. 60.

a ch. 3. 18.

b Rom. 6. 7.

---

that this whole verse is coloured by recollection of the circular letter which St. Paul had sent to the Churches of Asia, which we call the Epistle to the Ephesians. Perhaps the heresy which St. Paul lamented in that Epistle may still have lingered in existence, in cabalistic Jewish circles, among those same Churches when St. Peter thus wrote to them. He may, for the moment, be glancing away from his faint-hearted Hebrew brethren, who, in fear of persecution, were slinking back into Judaism, and turning rather to those Gnosticising Jews who began to abound in Asia, who made "genealogies" of æons, and gave Christ a place among them. In favour of such an opinion one might appeal to the vivid picture of licentiousness in the next chapter, and the development of the same, manifestly under Gnostic influence, in the Second Epistle and in the Apocalypse. From the expression "being made subject," or, literally, *having been subdued* (or, *subjected*)," we may infer that St. Peter meant *evil* spirits, this being a crowning *triumph* of Christ, and not only a mark of His *exaltation*. We need not think that St. Peter, any more than St. Paul, is distinctly teaching that there *are* such grades of spiritual beings; he is probably only borrowing the titles from the heretics glanced at, and saying that, whatever unseen powers there are, whatever they may be called, they are now subdued to Christ.

IV.

(1) **Forasmuch then . . .**—Literally, a participial phrase: *Christ, then, having suffered in* (or, *to*) *the flesh*—*i.e.*, so far as the flesh is concerned. The reference is to the words "killed in (or, *to*) the flesh" in chap. iii. 18, to which the word "then" takes us back. It is difficult to decide about the right of the words "for us" to stand in the text. Tischendorf and Lachmann strike them out, and they are probably right in doing so. The authority for the reading "for you" is nearly as strong; but in fact neither is wanted here, as the point is not the atoning character of Christ's death, but the death itself.

Arm yourselves likewise with the same mind.—Or rather, *with the same conception.* It does not mean merely "put yourselves into the same disposition:" that is, "resolve to die with Him." Though the word which is here rendered "mind" may possibly bear the meaning "intent" assigned to it in Heb. iv. 12 (the only other place in the New Testament where it occurs), the more natural and common sense is that of *conception, notion, view.* Christ is therefore said to have been "armed" with a particular "conception" or "view," which He found to be sufficient shield in the day of suffering; and we are exhorted to try the same defensive armour. The "view" which Christ found so efficacious was the view He took of the "suffering" itself. What that view was is forthwith explained.

For he that hath suffered in the flesh . . .—Rather, *that he that hath suffered to the flesh is at rest from sin.* This is the "view" which we are to take. The thought is probably derived from Rom. vi. 7. The death of the body puts a stop (at any rate, for the redeemed) to any further possibility of sin. Welcome, death! A slight difficulty is caused by the implied fact that Christ, too, in dying "ceased from sin." But the Greek word for "hath ceased" literally means *hath been caused to rest,* St. Peter using expressly (for the only time in the New Testament) that part of the verb which does not mean a voluntary cessation from what one was doing before, but a pause imposed from without. And that Christ looked upon His death as a boon of rest from sin (it does not say from *sinning*) is not only a true and impressive thought, but is fully justified by Rom. vi. 10, "He died unto sin," and even by His cry, "It is finished." Whatever harshness there is in the thought is much softened by the fact that St. Peter names it as the view *we* are to take, not *directly* as the view *He* took; so that it admits of some adjustment when applied to *Him.*

(2) **That he no longer.**—The Greek admits at least equally of the translation, *That ye no longer.* Thus, this second verse will attach itself, not to the clause "that he that hath suffered," but to the clause "arm yourselves." And unless this be understood, we become involved in the difficulty that whereas, up to this very point, St. Peter has been urging the future martyrs, by the example of Christ, to face the death of the body bravely, he would now be sliding confusedly into treating of the baptismal death to sin, and indeed actually saying that a martyr's death was a step to leading the rest of the life on earth becomingly! But if we attach verse 2 to the clause "arm yourselves," it runs, without any confusion, thus: "As Christ suffered to the flesh without shrinking, take for your protection and support the same thought which proved a protection and support to Him—viz., that to be rid of sin for ever was the greatest of all possible blessings, and that this is only attainable through the bodily death; and the result of embracing this thought will be, that for the rest of your lives on earth (so soon, perhaps, to be cut violently short) you may no longer live to men's lusts, but to God's will."

(3) **For the time past of our life.**—There are two words in the English here which do not stand in the true text, and sadly impede the sense. They are "of our life," and "us." The first is added by some scribe to point the contrast with "the rest of his time." The second—which should be "you," if anything at all—is simply put to fill the gap after the word "suffice." If "our life" and "us" were right, we should have St. Peter, quite unlike his wont, identifying himself with the bad life here described, as though he himself had shared in it.

May suffice.—It is the same word as in Matt. vi. 34; x. 25, and would be, literally, *For sufficient is the past.* There is an irony in the word similar to that in chap. iii. 17, "it is better."

To have wrought.—Rather, *to have perpetrated.* The Greek word denotes the accomplishment of a *criminal* purpose, as in Rom. ii. 9; 1 Cor. v. 3; and one passage more horrid still.

The will of the Gentiles.—Just as, in verse 2, there was a contrast between man's manifold and conflicting lusts and God's unity of will, so there is a

when we walked in lasciviousness, lusts, excess of wine, revellings, banquetings, and abominable idolatries: (4) wherein they think it strange that ye run not

contrast now between God's "will" and (for the Greek word is quite different) the heathen's "wish." "To have perpetrated the heathen's wish" means to have done the bad things which the heathen wanted them to be guilty of. The heathen were fain to catch them at malpractices. (See Note on chap. ii. 12, and the word "speaking evil" below.)

When we walked.—A participle in Greek, which gives no support to the use of "we," but means simply *having proceeded.* Thus it does not directly state that they *had* so proceeded, for the participle explains the foregoing verb: "The past is sufficient to have done what the heathen want you to have done—viz., to have walked."

Lasciviousness.—It should be plural, expressing the repeated acts of sin. The word in Greek means any outrageous debauchery, so that it may be said to include all the words that follow.

Excess of wine, in like manner, should be plural. It is a contemptuous word (*wine-swillings*), and differs from the word translated "banquetings" below, because the latter is more refined, and also implies company, which the first need not. The "revellings" might mean any roystering parties, but contains more of the notion of making a pretext of a *meal* than "banquetings," which consist solely of drinking.

Abominable idolatries.—It is not *as* idolatries that they are called abominable, but because of the abominable adjuncts of the idol-festivals. This clause is the main support of those who think that the Letter was written to converts from heathenism and not from Judaism. How, it is urged, could St. Peter have said to persons who had been brought up as Jews, "The time past is long enough for you to have proceeded in abominable idolatries"? The argument is most convincing as it stands. If they had been living in idolatry, it is incredible that they were of Hebrew race: if they were of Hebrew race, it is incredible that they should have lived in idolatry. But, as a matter of fact, St. Peter does not say that they ever *had* lived in those sins. Quite on the contrary, he says, in verse 4, that the heathen found, to their surprise, that the Christians would *not* go with them in these things; and that, finding it to be so, they "blasphemed" or slandered them in this very respect. It may, perhaps, be answered that the Apostle is alluding to a period *long* past, and contrasting it with the present which so puzzled the Gentiles. But there is no ground for taking "the time past" to mean the time up to the date of their conversion to Christianity. It is simply "your past time" (*i.e.*, the whole up to the date of the Letter), in contrast with "the rest of your time" (verse 2, literally, *your remaining time*), *i.e.*, the whole subsequent to the date of the Letter; so that it cannot mean, "The heathen think it strange that you do not join their profligate courses as you used in old days," in which case we should naturally have expected him to say, "They think it strange that ye *no longer* run with them." Besides, it seems plain, from verse 2, that, whatever may be meant by "perpetrating the wish of the Gentiles," it was still a *present* danger when St. Peter wrote, or there would be little point in mentioning it at all. But if he means that, up to the date of the Letter, some of the recipients of it had been living in "abominable idolatries," how could he continue that the Gentiles were astonished that they did *not* do so? for if the idolatries meant were the heathen's own idolatries, the heathen would have been aware of their joining them, and it would have been no "slander" to say so. The conclusion is, that neither before nor after their conversion had they been really proceeding thus. St. Peter is, in fact, only putting in words the slander of the Gentiles, at which he had hinted in chap. ii. 12—15; iii. 16. "For the *future,*" says he, "live to the will of God, not to the lusts of men. The *past* is long enough (without invading the future) to have perpetrated what the heathen want you to have perpetrated—viz., to have been proceeding in debaucheries and abominable idolatries—slandering you in that very point wherein they are puzzled if you do not run with them to the same excess of riot." As an historical fact, these are the very calumnies which we find to have been brought against the early Christians—idolatries and all. The filthy idolatry ascribed to the Christians by the heathen may be found recorded in Tertullian's *Apology*, and (so it is said) on the walls of Pompeii. But what, then, does St. Peter mean when he says that the past is sufficient to have perpetrated what the heathen wanted? It certainly implies that some of them had, even since their conversion, been doing what the malicious heathen would be glad to see them do. But we have already noticed that he is speaking ironically in using the word "sufficient," and the irony continues through the rest of the clause. "Some of you have been living, up to the present time, more or less to human lusts (verse 2). You have done so quite long enough now. You have quite sufficiently gratified the Gentiles, who long to prove that you are no better than themselves." The argument is like that which Nestor, in Homer, addresses to the wrangling Greek captains:—

> "Sure Priam would rejoice, and Priam's sons,
> Could they but learn this feud betwixt you twain."

We may observe, further, that all through the Epistle St. Peter appears to have dread of a doctrine which was fast beginning to rise among the Asiatic Christians—that such sins as fornication and idolatry, being but bodily, were venial, especially in time of persecution. (See chaps. i. 14, 15; ii. 11; v. 8.) Such pernicious doctrine was probably founded on a "wresting" of St. Paul's teaching (2 Pet. iii. 16) on eating things offered to idols; from which it was concluded that the accompanying impurities were innocent likewise. This doctrine becomes very prominent in the Second Epistle; and in the Apocalypse there is even some reason to connect it specially with the Jewish element in the Church. (Comp. together 2 Pet. ii. 15; Rev. ii. 6, 14, 15, with Rev. ii. 9.)

(4) **Wherein they think it strange.**—The word "wherein" is used in exactly the same sense as in chap. ii. 12; that is to say, it does not directly point back to the list of sins just named, but the grammatical antecedent is to be supplied in the participial clause which follows, thus: "In a particular where they cannot imagine your *not* being as bad as themselves, slanderously affirming that you *are.*" The only difficulty involved in this view is one which does not show in the English, viz., that the participle is attracted into the nominative case by the influence of the finite verb, instead of being (as it strictly should) in the genitive, agreeing with "of the Gentiles." But we have seen before that St. Peter deals very freely with participles

with *them* to the same excess of riot, speaking evil of *you:* (5) who shall give account to him that is ready to judge the quick and the dead.[a] (6) For for this cause was the gospel preached also to them that are dead,[b] that they might

a 2 Tim. 4. 1.

b ch. 3. 19.

in the nominative case. (See chap. ii. 12, where "having" is nominative, though in strictness it should be accusative, agreeing with "you, as strangers and pilgrims;" comp. also ii. 18; iii. 1, 7, 9, 15, 16.) Like instances are not wanting in classical Greek.

(5) **Who shall give account.**—Perhaps said with a reference to chap. iii. 15, where these very persons call the Christians to give "account" (the Greek word is the same). The side-purpose of the clause (as in the similar threat, chap. ii. 8) is to warn the readers against sharing their fate by sharing their sins.

To him that is ready to judge.—This carries on the history of Jesus Christ a step further still. The last thing was His sitting on the right hand of God. This is the order of the Apostles' Creed. Bengel wisely remarks: "The Apostles, when they are not expressly treating of the date of Christ's advent, set forth that advent to their longing and devotion as close at hand. Hence Peter includes the slanderers of his day among the *living,* as just about to be judged."

(6) **For for this cause was the gospel preached also to them that are dead.**—This version is misleading, and seems indeed to be one of those rare cases where the original has been expanded by the translators for doctrinal ends. The Greek is simply, *For for this end was the gospel preached to the dead also,* or, still more literally, *to dead men also.* No one with an un-preoccupied mind could doubt, taking this clause by itself, that the persons to whom this preaching was made were dead at the time of being preached to. If this is the case, then, pretty obviously, St. Peter is carrying us back to his teaching of chap. iii. 19, and is explaining further the purpose of Christ's descent into hell.

That they might be judged according to men in the flesh, but live according to God in the spirit.—In order to obtain a clear notion of this hard saying, it will be necessary once more to survey the course of the whole passage. "It is better," the Apostle said, "to suffer in well-doing than in evil-doing." They must take their choice, that is, which kind of suffering they would have. It was not indeed certain that in case they chose to do *well* they would suffer for it; and if they *did,* there was the history of Christ to encourage them. But in case they chose to be evil-doers, it was certain that they would suffer. "And you had better," he says, "suffer in well-doing than in evil-doing." He then gives an instance of persons who suffered in evil-doing—the fleshly Antediluvians, whom God cut short in their crimes by the Flood, and to whom Christ went to preach in their prison-house. He then exhorts his readers—some of whom had, for one reason or another, been allowing themselves to fall into antinomian ways—not to live any longer to the flesh, not to make true the slanders of the heathen, who tried to make out that the Christians were as bad livers as themselves; for such evil-doers were doomed to speedy suffering; those heathens would soon be called to account by Him who was ready to judge quick and dead alike; "for," he adds, "the object of that preaching to the dead also was that they may be judged according to men in flesh, but may live according to God in spirit." (1) The first question is, What does the Apostle mean to substantiate by this last verse, "*for* for this cause?" Not the fact that Christ will judge the dead as well as the quick, for that would have no practical bearing upon the readers. Not the fact that Christ was now *ready* for judgment; for although He will certainly not come until the dead as well as the quick are in a position to be judged, yet we should then have expected something more like, "The reason why the dead were preached to was that the judgment might no longer be put off;" instead of which, the whole point of the verse is the particular destiny in reserve for those dead, which destiny was the intention and result of Christ's preaching the gospel to them. It must, therefore, be a further reason for warning the Christians not to live lives of evil-doing like the contemporaries of Noah or their own heathen contemporaries. If it be necessary to attach the word "for" to any particular words, we may perhaps attach it to the words "they shall give account;" and verse 6 would hint at the kind of account they would have to give, as "giving account" implies the settlement which follows. (2) But if verse 6 clenches the warning to the Christians not to become antinomian, then we must understand the destiny of these dead to whom Christ preached to be not the brightest, after all. This brings us to consider what is meant by their being "judged in flesh" (*i.e.,* as in verse 1, so far as flesh is concerned). In the previous verse, Christ is said to be quite ready to "judge" quick and dead. The context makes us feel that St. Peter is not picturing to himself that scene as one of calm forensic investigation, with "opened books" or the like. His idea of this judgment is rather of a "judgment" such as took place in the days of Noe, a great *crisis* (the Greek word for "judgment") or world-wide catastrophe, which, of course, cannot harm the just, but only the unjust. He shows the same conception of the Judgment, and illustrates it by Noe's Flood, in 2 Pet. ii. 5—9, and iii. 6, 7. Now "judgment" is a neutral word, which, in Scripture, takes its colour from the surroundings, so that it sometimes is a thing to be longed for (*e.g.,* Ps. xliii. 1, lxxii. 2; Heb. x. 30); at other times a thing to be dreaded, as here. Though we do not limit the "quick and dead" here to mean the *wicked* quick and dead, yet they are evidently uppermost in St. Peter's mind, so that there is scarcely any conscious change in the meaning of the word "judged" when we pass from verse 5 to verse 6. It there means certainly a judicial punishment, or even judicial destruction. While the word often denotes a condemnation (as in English we say "to sentence")—for example, in John xvi. 1, 2; Thess. ii. 12; Rev. xix. 2—it seems to have the further notion of a judicial *death* in 1 Cor. xi. 31, 32: "Had we been in the habit of discerning ourselves, we should not have been subject to these repeated judgments (weakness, sickness, death—verse 30); but now these judgments are a discipline from our Lord, to save us from being condemned with the world." And that judicial *destruction* to the flesh is what St. Peter means, he proves by contrasting "but may *live* in spirit" rather than "be saved" or "justified." (3) It is next to be considered what date we are to fix for this judgment of the flesh. Was it previous to Christ's preaching the gospel to them in hell, or was it to be subsequent? Taking the former line, we should be able to paraphrase, "His object was, that though in flesh they had been judged, having been judicially destroyed by the Flood,

be judged according to men in the
flesh, but live according to God in the
spirit.[a]
(7) But the end of all things is at hand:
be ye therefore sober, and
watch unto prayer. (8) And
above all things have fer-
vent charity among your-

a 1 Cor. 5. 5.

Chap. iv. 7—11. Need of charity, hospitality, and bounty.

they yet might live hereafter in spirit." But, besides other difficulties, it is far more than doubtful whether it is Greek to infuse a *past* sense into the subjunctive mood here used: *i.e.*, to render this, "it was preached in order that they *might have been* judged." Had we the words by themselves, and no preconceived theology to hinder us, we should undoubtedly translate, "To this end was the gospel preached to dead men too: viz., in order that they *may be* judged indeed according to men so far as they are flesh, but may live according to God so far as they are spirit." The judgment spoken of would not be their death beneath the waves of Noe, but something still future; and this view would be confirmed by reading what St. Peter says of them, and of the angels who (in all probability) sinned with them, in the passages of the Second Epistle above referred to. How, then, will they be hereafter condemned to a judicial destruction of the flesh, but a merciful preservation of the spirit? The answer, though it seems inevitable to the present writer, must be given with trembling, and in deference to the judgment of the Church, the collective Christian consciousness, whenever that shall be expressed upon the point. A close parallel may be found in 1 Cor. v. 5. There St. Paul judges to deliver to Satan (is he the warder of the "prison" where such spirits are confined?) a person who has foully sinned in the flesh, "for annihilation of the flesh, that the spirit may be saved in the day of the Lord Jesus." That in that place it does not mean a temporal judgment upon the bodily life (such as was passed upon the Antediluvians or the profaners of the Eucharist at Corinth) is clear, from the fact that excommunication was *not* attended with temporal death. That it does not mean voluntary self-mortification of the flesh in this world seems clear (among other considerations) by comparison of our present passage, for the opportunity for self-mortification in the flesh was long past for the spirits to whom Christ preached. Now why, in these two cases, do the writers take pains to point the antithesis between "flesh" and "spirit," if, after all, the flesh is to share the mercy shown to the spirit? The antithesis becomes a false one. Why did not St. Paul say, "To deliver such an one to Satan for the destruction of the flesh, that he may be saved in the day of the Lord Jesus?" and St. Peter, "For this cause was the gospel preached to the dead also, that though judged indeed in flesh, they might, after all, live according to God?" And what is the point of this dread warning, if in the end these Antediluvians attain to the same bliss, "both in body and soul," as other men? There is a whole set of passages which seems to teach that resurrection—*i.e.*, the permanent restitution of life to the body—is a gift which does not belong to all. To those who eat Christ's flesh, He promises, "I will raise him up at the last day" (John vi. 54). St. Paul suffers the loss of all things, "if by any means he may attain to the resurrection of the dead" (Phil. iii. 11; comp. 2 Cor. v. 3, 4). Our Lord bids the Apostles "fear Him [it is doubtful whether he means God, or Satan, who acts by God's permission] who is able to destroy both soul [He does not say 'spirit'] and body in hell." So it would be the simplest explanation of our present text if we might believe that these Antediluvians were to be deprived of resurrection of the flesh which they had so foully corrupted, but in God's mercy, through accepting the gospel preached to them by Christ after their death, were to be allowed a purely spiritual existence. They would thus be sentenced "according to men," *i.e.*, from a human point of view: they would be unable to take their place again among the glorified human species in a human life; but still they would be alive "according to God," from God's point of view—a divine life, but "in the spirit" only. It was a gospel that Christ preached to them, for without it they would not have come to "live according to God" at all. Yet, on the other hand, it was a warning to the Christians. When it says "the gospel was preached to the dead *also*," it implies a similar preaching to others, viz., to the heathen who were to "give account," and that the result of the preaching would be the same. Those heathen who through ignorance lived corrupt lives all around, might possibly, in the intermediate state, hope to receive a gospel which would enable a bare half of their humanity to live according to God hereafter. It could not avert the destruction of their flesh. What, then, could be the hope of a Christian, one who had heard and embraced the gospel in this life, and had then surrendered himself to the same corruptions as the Gentiles?

(7—11) DUTY OF BENEVOLENCE WITHIN THE CHURCH IN VIEW OF THE ADVENT.—The end of the world is not far off; let it find you not only sober, but (above all else) exerting an intense charity within the Church, by hospitality and generosity, in these as much as in spiritual ministrations seeking not your own glory, but God's.

(7) **The end of all things is at hand.**—Or, *hath come nigh*; the same word (for instance) as in Matt. iv. 17; xxvi. 46. It is but a repetition in other words of verse 5, inserted again to give weight to all the exhortations which follow. Probably, if St. Peter had thought the world would stand twenty centuries more, he would have expressed himself differently; yet see 2 Pet. iii. 4—10.

Be ye therefore sober, and watch unto prayer.—These words sum up the cautions given in verses 1—6, before passing on to the next subject. The first verb includes more than sobriety, and means the keeping a check upon all the desires. The usual notion of sobriety is more exactly conveyed in the word rendered "watch," which is the same as in chap. i. 13 and chap. v. 8. "Unto prayer" is a slip for *unto prayers*; the difference is that it does not mean that we are to be always in frame to pray, but that actual prayers should be always on our lips: every incident in life should suggest them. They would be especially necessary if any moment might see the end of the world. The tense of the imperatives in the Greek carries out the notion that the persons addressed had slipped into a careless state, from which they needed an arousal.

(8) **And above all things have fervent charity among yourselves.**—The original is far more vigorous: *But before all things keeping intense your charity towards yourselves.* St. Peter assumes that the charity is there, but insists on its not being suffered to flag in outward expression. (Comp. the same word

selves: for charity shall[1] cover the multitude of sins. (9) Use hospitality one to another without grudging. (10) As every man hath received the gift,[a] *even so* minister the same one to another, as good stewards of the manifold grace of God. (11) If any man speak, *let him speak* as the oracles of God; if any man minister, *let him do it* as of the ability which God giveth:[b] that God in all

1 Or, *will.*

a Rom. 12. 6—8.

b 1 Cor. 4. 7.

in chap. i. 22; also in Luke xxii. 44; Acts xii. 5; xxvi. 7.)

Shall cover.—Properly, neither "shall" nor "will," the right reading being present, *covereth.* The words are usually said to be a quotation from Prov. x. 12, "Hatred stirreth up strifes, but love covereth all sins;" but they are widely different from the LXX. in that passage, and also vary from the Hebrew; and as precisely the same variation occurs in Jas. v. 20, it seems more probable either that St. Peter had the passage of St. James consciously in his mind, or that the proverb was current and familiar to both writers in the form, "Love covereth a multitude of sins." It is, therefore, unsafe to argue from the exact shade of meaning which the words bear in Prov. x. 12. To "cover," in Hebrew, often means to "forgive," the idea being that of an offensive object which you bury or hide by putting something else over it; see, for examples, Ps. xxxii. 1; lxxxv. 2; and the place in Proverbs seems to mean that whereas a bitter enemy will rake up every old grudge again and again, one who loves will not allow even himself to see the wrongs done to him by a friend. If this sense be accepted here, it will imply that the Christians in Asia had a good deal to put up with from each other; but even so, the argument seems a little strained: "Keep your charity at its full stretch, *because* charity forgives, however many the wrongs may be." It far better suits the context to take the proverb in the same sense as in St. James, without any reference to the Old Testament passage. In St. James it is usually taken to mean, "He shall save (the convert's) soul from death, and shall cover (*i.e.*, procure for him the pardon of) a multitude of sins;" but as the true reading there is "*his* soul," it is more natural to suppose that St. James is holding up, as the reward of converting the sinner, that the person who does so shall save his *own* soul, and procure for *himself* the pardon of a multitude of sins. So here it seems obvious that St. Peter is urging charity as something which will be found advantageous when the "end of all things" comes; and the advantage he mentions is, "because charity covereth a multitude of sins:" *i.e.*, the exercise of this grace makes up for a great many other shortcomings in the man. A very good case might be made out for a doctrine of Justification by Love.

(9) **Use hospitality.**—It is a great pity that again (as in chap. iii. 8, and elsewhere) the participial clauses are broken up in our version into separate injunctions. Here it is, properly, *being hospitable.* This is the first form of charity—receiving Christians who came from other towns (comp. 3 John, verses 5, 6). See how such hospitality covers (to the surprise of the bestowers) a multitude of sins in Matt. xxv. 35—38.

Without grudging.—That is, *without murmuring.* How frequently Christian hospitality is marred by grumbling at the expense and the trouble which it costs!

(10) **As every man hath received the gift.**—There is no definite article in the Greek, which might be rendered, *According as every man was gifted.* They are reminded, as in 1 Cor. iv. 7, that the gift was *received,* and for the same purpose. At what period these gifts were received it is hard to say, as in some instances the gift was of a spiritual nature, in others of a temporal nature. Each, however, has a gift of *some* kind for the benefit of the community.

Even so minister.—In the original, *ministering.* It is still an exhibition of the "intense charity" of verse 8. The verb is the same as in chap. i. 12, where see Note.

As good stewards.—No one receives these gifts, spiritual or temporal, as his own; he is but a "steward," and when he offers them to the Church it is not as a benefactor, but as a servant, "ministering."

Of the manifold grace of God.—"Grace" is here used, not in its theological sense, but, as in chap. iii. 7, in the sense of bountiful giving; and the beautiful word rendered "manifold" brings out the subtle and picturesque *variety* with which God arranges and distributes His bounty. But the emphatic word of the sentence is "of God."

(11) **If any man speak.**—St. Peter proceeds to speak of two particular forms taken by this "manifold grace of God;" (1) the power to speak; (2) the power to minister. The speaking is, of course, public preaching in the Church; and the man who does so is to do it "as oracles of God." The article is not added in the Greek, so that it must not be pressed to mean "speaking on the model, or in accordance with the doctrines of, the Old Testament." Rather, the emphatic word is "of God;" and the Apostle means that the preacher is not to trust to his own natural powers and wit, or to seek applause for himself, but to act as one possessed of powers not his own; to speak only that which God inspires him to speak. This clause must not be taken as being in this place complete in itself. It is apparently only introduced to give point to what follows, the intention of the whole paragraph being to enforce liberality. It is easy to recognise in *spiritual* things the principle of God being all in all; and St. Peter bids them apply the same principle to material gifts. "Recollect that *whatever* you possess, you possess from God in trust for the Church. Just as the man who preaches is to preach as a mere mouthpiece of God, so the man who gives must consider himself as being but God's dispenser, that in this, too, God may have all the glory." For the same kind of rhetorical effect, see chap. ii. 17, last Note.

If any man minister.—This does not mean "ministering" in the congregation, or spiritual ministrations of any sort, but giving the good things of this life for the benefit of the poor. The word rendered "ability" not unfrequently expresses (like our word "resources") a sufficiency of wealth; and the word which appears as "giveth" is the same which is used of supplying material blessings in 2 Cor. ix. 10. In a compound form, the same verb occurs in Gal. iii. 5, Col. ii. 19, 2 Pet. i. 5—11; and the substantive in Eph. iv. 16, Phil. i. 19. The original classical meaning of the word is to pay the expenses of putting a play on the stage, which at Athens was a public burden borne by the wealthier citizens in turn, like the shrievalty of an English county. Thus the wealthy Christian who

things may be glorified through Jesus Christ, to whom be praise and dominion for ever and ever. Amen.

(12) Beloved, think it not strange concerning the fiery trial which is to try you, as though some strange thing happened unto you: (13) but

Chap. iv. 12—19. Encouragement against the evil days to come.

rejoice,[a] inasmuch as ye are partakers of Christ's sufferings; that, when his glory shall be revealed, ye may be glad also with exceeding joy. (14) If ye be reproached for the name of Christ, happy *are ye;*[b] for the spirit of glory and of God resteth upon you: on their part he is evil spoken of, but on your part he is glorified.

a Jas. 1. 2.

b Matt. 5. 11.

---

supports the Church and relieves all the poor is not really the Church's patron: he is a responsible manager; but the paymaster is God.

That God in all things may be glorified.—How clearly St. Peter works it out: "the manifold grace of *God,*" "as oracles of *God,*" "out of the resources of which *God* is paymaster," "that *God* in all things may be glorified." The "all things" means emphatically that in these money matters as much as in the spiritual works God's honour is concerned. For a most touching expansion of this text, see the Epistle of St. Theonas, Patriarch of Alexandria, to the High Chamberlain of the Emperor Diocletian, an English translation of which may be seen in *The Persecution of Diocletian,* by the same hand as these Notes.

Through Jesus Christ.—They see and feel that, had it not been for Jesus Christ, these rich men would not have been so liberal; and when they thus thank Him for it, they are in effect thanking God.

To whom.—That is, to God, rather than to Jesus Christ. And it should be, "to whom *is,*" or *belongs,* rather than "to whom *be,*" and "*the* glory and *the* dominion," not "glory and dominion."

(12–19) Exhortation to Courage and Steadfastness in Persecution.—All ought to be prepared for persecution. It is a blessed and glorious thing to have to bear it. A criminal's death and a Christian martyrdom are the exact opposites of each other. Vengeance is speedily coming.

(12) **Beloved.**—See Note on chap. ii. 11.

Think it not strange.—The same word as in verse 4. It means, literally, to feel like people in a strange country, lost and bewildered. It is further explained by the clause "as though some strange thing were (by bad luck) happening unto you." These Hebrew Christians felt at first it was not what was to be expected, that those who attached themselves to the Messiah should have a life of sorrow and persecution in the world.

The fiery trial which is to try you.—This rendering is not only slovenly, but conveys a false impression, for the fiery trial was not future, but actually present. Literally it runs, *Be not bewildered at the conflagration among you taking place for a trial to you.* Already, then, the Asiatic Christians are enduring a fierce persecution. The word which describes it is only found besides in Rev. xviii. 9, 18, "burning." (Comp. chap. i. 7.)

(13) **But rejoice.**—The opposite of being bewildered at it, for "rejoicing" in it implies a *recognition* of its character and purpose. The word rendered "inasmuch as" (which occurs also in 2 Cor. viii. 12) seems to mean, "in proportion as:" "the more nearly you are made to share Christ's sufferings the more you should rejoice." In the *Acts of St. Probus* (a Cappadocian), when, after many other tortures, the judge ordered them to heat some nails and run them through his hands, the martyr exclaims, "Glory to Thee, Lord Jesu Christ, who hast even deigned to let my *hands be pierced* for Thy name's sake!"

Christ's sufferings.—Rather, *the sufferings of the Christ.* (Comp. Note on chap. i. 11.)

That—*i.e.,* "in order that." This is to be attached to "think it not strange, but rejoice"—"in order that at the revelation of His glory also (as now, in the sharing of His sufferings) ye may rejoice (the word is the same), exulting." Such a recognition of the meaning of suffering, such a rejoicing in suffering now, is a sure means to rejoicing in glory also hereafter.

(14) **If ye be reproached.**—The form of speech denotes that they *were* so reproached.

For the name of Christ.—Literally, "*in* the name of Christ," *i.e.,* on the score of being Christians only. (Comp. verse 16.) Again, see how St. Peter presses the Messianic title: surely they will not abandon the hopes of Israel!

The spirit of glory and of God resteth upon you.—He is called the "Spirit of glory" here in the same way as He is called the "Spirit of truth" John xiv. 17), the "Spirit of holiness" (Rom i. 4), the "Spirit of grace" (Heb. x. 29), &c. It expresses that glory—*i.e.,* the triumphant manifestation of perfections—is His *gift* and His distinguishing sign and the atmosphere in which He lives. "Glory" stands in contrast with "reproach." And lest it should be doubted who was meant by the splendid phrase, the Apostle adds, "and of God." All "glory" is His, and therefore the Spirit which is the "Spirit of glory" can be no other than the "Spirit of God;" but as God Himself is greater than His own glory, the words form a climax, and it means more to call Him the "Spirit of God" than to call Him the "Spirit of glory." And this Spirit "resteth" upon the persecuted Christians. It means far more than "remaineth" or "abideth." It expresses the complete repose and satisfaction with which the Spirit of glory abides on men who have the hearts of martyrs. "This shall be My rest for ever: here will I dwell, for I have a delight therein." It is the word which is used of the quiet retreat which our Lord took after John's death (Mark vi. 31); of the calm relief which He offers to the weary souls who come to Him (Matt. xi. 28, 29); of the repose of the blessed dead after the work of life is over (Rev. vi. 11; xiv. 13). In the Old Testament it is used of the Spirit in Num. xi. 25, and 2 Kings ii. 15; but, above all, in Isa. xi. 2, which was probably in St. Peter's mind. And the argument is, that reproach for the name of the Christ is a proof of glory in reserve, or rather, already belonging to the man. Perhaps St. Peter intentionally hints (in speaking of the "Spirit") that all who make themselves partakers of Christ's reproach are made partakers of His chrism.

On their part.—These words, to the end of the verse, are an undoubted interpolation, though of very early date, appearing even in St. Cyprian's works. The clause would bring out the different view taken by believers and unbelievers of the martyr-spirit. Pliny

(15) But let none of you suffer as a murderer, or *as* a thief, or *as* an evildoer, or as a busybody[a] in other men's matters.
(16) Yet if *any man suffer* as a Christian, let him not be ashamed; but let him glorify God on this behalf. (17) For the time *is come* that judgment must begin at the house of God:[b] and if *it* first *begin* at us, what shall the end *be* of them that obey not the gospel of God?

a 2 Thess. 3. 11.
b Ezek. 9. 6.

says in his letter that, whatever Christianity itself may be, there can be no doubt such *obstinacy* ought to be punished. Marcus Aurelius speaks with contempt of the spirit in which Christians suffered themselves to be put to death as mere self-will, unlike the philosophical grace of the Stoics. Gibbon speaks of the "pious obstinacy" of St. Felix of Tibiura.

(15) **But let none of you.**—The Greek takes exactly the opposite turn: "*for* let none of you suffer." The connection is a little difficult, but it seems to be this: "I say advisedly that you are happy, and that the Spirit of glory reposes on you who die for the faith; for I am sure that you will not try to deceive yourselves and others by pretending to die as martyrs, when in reality you are dying as criminals." In order to understand this caution, we must recollect how largely the first converts were drawn from actually criminal classes, and how easily they were admitted. In the persecution of Diocletian, Mensurius of Carthage found it necessary to expose those who drew persecution upon themselves to cloke their crimes under pretence of Christian faith. "Some," he says, "are criminals, some debtors, who take the opportunity of persecution to be rid of so burdensome a life, thinking to atone for and wash off their misdeeds thereby." It is conceivable that St. Peter may have had some such danger in view.

As a murderer, or as a thief, or as an evildoer.—The insertion of "as" in the two latter cases obliterates the distinction between the class composed of these three words, and that which follows. It should be, *as a murderer, or thief, or evildoer.* When Pliny came to govern these men, a little later, he found that on a fixed day they met together before daylight, "and bound themselves by a sacramental oath, not to any crime, but that they would not do or see done any thefts, any robberies, any adulteries; that they would break no promises, and would repudiate no liabilities when called upon." These words will partly explain the general term "evildoer." (See also chaps. ii. 12, 14; iii. 16.)

Or as a busybody in other men's matters.—M. Renan writes (*Antéchrist*, p. 42):—"Others, through excess of zeal, declaimed aloud against the pagans, and cast their vices in their teeth. Their more sensible brethren humorously called them 'bishops,' or 'overseers of those who are without.'" Such is, indeed, the meaning of the droll word which St. Peter here gives: except that, instead of "bishops of those without," it means "bishops of other men's matters." It denotes those prying and self-important people who fancy they can set everything to rights, and that everybody they come across is under their personal jurisdiction. Such persons would tend to make Christianity unpopular among the unbelievers, and, in case of persecution, would be the first to "suffer" (*i.e.*, to be picked out for *martyrdom*; see Note on chap. iii. 14); and while flattering themselves for the boldness with which they had spoken out, they would incur St. Peter's censure, and their martyrdom would be reckoned no martyrdom by the Church. "Cruel mishaps," continues M. Renan, "befell them; and the wise directors of the community, so far from extolling them, told them pretty plainly that it did but serve them right."

(16) **Yet if any man suffer as a Christian.**—St. Peter purposely uses the name which was a name of derision among the heathens. It is not, as yet, one by which the believers would usually describe *themselves.* It only occurs twice besides in the New Testament—in Acts xi. 26, where we are told of the invention of the nickname (see Note there), and in Acts xxvi. 28, where Agrippa catches it up with the insolent scorn with which a brutal justice would have used the word "Methodist" a century ago. So contemptible was the name that, as M. Renan says (p. 37), "Well-bred people avoided pronouncing the name, or, when forced to do so, made a kind of apology." Tacitus, for instance, says: "Those who were *vulgarly* known by the name of Christians." In fact, it is quite an open question whether we ought not here (as well as in the two places of Acts above cited) to read the nickname in its barbarous form: *Chrestian.* The Sinaitic manuscript has that form, and the Vatican has the form *Chreistian;* and it is much harder to suppose that a scribe who commonly called himself a *Christian* would intentionally alter it into this strange form than to suppose that one who did not understand the irony of saying a *Chrestian* should have written the word with which he was so familiar.

Let him not be ashamed.—Although the name sounds worse to the world than "murderer," or "thief," or "malefactor."

On this behalf.—This is a possible rendering, but it is more pointed to translate literally, *but let him glorify God in this name—i.e.,* make even this name of ridicule the ground of an act of glory to God.

(17) **For the time is come.**—The "for" (literally, *because*) seems to substantiate the whole of the former part of the section, from verse 12 onwards, but with special reference to the injunction to glorify God on the ground of bearing the name of Christians, upon which it follows in much the same way as "*for* the spirit of glory" followed upon "if ye be reproached . . . happy are ye." The judgment is just about to begin, and all those who bear the name of Christians may well be thankful that they do.

That judgment.—It should be, *that the judgment —i.e.,* the great judgment which we all expect. The word "begin," however, shows that in St. Peter's mind it would be a long process; and he probably does not distinguish in his mind between the "burning which is befalling for a trial" and the final judgment, except that that "burning" is but the beginning. (Comp. verse 5.)

Begin at the house of God.—The phrase contains an obvious reference to Ezek. ix. 6 (comp. also Jer. xxv. 29). Who are meant by the "house of God" is clear, not only from such passages as chap. ii. 5; 1 Cor. iii. 16; 2 Thess. ii. 4, but also from the immediate addition, "and if first *at us.*" We who are *Chrestiani,* who bear the mark of the Christ's shame upon our foreheads, and are not ashamed of it, are quite safe in this judgment: "come not near any man upon whom is the mark." The sense is a little closely

(18) And if the righteous scarcely be
saved, where shall the ungodly and the
sinner appear? [a] (19) Wherefore let them
that suffer according to the will of God

a Prov. 11. 31.

---

packed. It seems as if St. Peter meant at first only to say, "Thank God that you *are* 'Christians,' for the judgment is just about to begin," as something which only concerns the unbelievers; then, as an afterthought, he adds, "and begin, too, at the house of God," by way of making the believers also feel the need of care.

And if it first begin at us, what shall the end be . . .?—It is more expressive to omit, with St. Peter, the verb "begin": *and if first at us.* The argument is: "If we, who are the very household of God, must undergo this searching investigation first, what will happen, as the judgment nears its climax, to those who," &c.? When he says "*the end* of those that obey not," he does not mean exactly "the final doom of those that obey not," as contrasted with "the end" of those that obey, or as contrasted with their own earlier opportunities: rather, "the end" is the end of the great process of judgment, as contrasted with the "beginning first at us." The judging of the house of God has now gone on for eighteen hundred years, but it has not yet touched those who are without.

That obey not the gospel of God?—Rather, *that disobey the gospel of God?* The word is the same which we have noticed several times (see Note on chap. iii. 1) as being peculiarly applied to the Jews. Now the object of this mysterious threat (which is made more terrible by being thrown into the form of a question) is not only to solace the persecuted by the thought of God being their avenger, but to warn them against slipping into the position of those thus threatened. The recipients of the Letter, we must recollect, were Jewish Christians, who were in a two-fold danger—either of relapsing sullenly into Judaism, or of plunging into heathen excesses, like the Nicolaitan school, under the notion that such things could not hurt the spiritually-minded. To meet these two forms of danger, the Apostle hints darkly at the punishment of the two classes in this phrase and in the verse following, precisely as St. Paul, in 2 Thess. i. 8 (see Note there), divides the wicked to be punished into Jew and Gentile, or, in Rom. ii. 9, still more particularly. And that he is thinking specially of unbelieving *Jews* in this place appears from the context in Ezek. ix. 6 (especially verse 9), where the separation to be effected is not between Jew and Gentile, but between Jew and Jew—those "that sigh and that cry for all the abominations" committed by Israel, and those that commit the abominations. As Bengel remarks, "The persecution of Nero was but a few years before the catastrophe of the Jews."

(18) **And if the righteous scarcely be saved.**—This is a literal quotation, word for word, of Prov. xi. 31, according to the LXX. The quotation proves to us St. Peter's perfect familiarity with both the Hebrew original and the Greek version. We have seen how he rejects the LXX. version when it does not suit his meaning (*e.g.,* chap. ii. 8): here it suits him (though it differs from the Hebrew), and he accepts it. The "righteous" man here means, apparently, as Leighton says, "he that endeavours to walk uprightly in the ways of God," rather than the man who is then declared finally justified. The fact that they are "scarcely" saved "imports not," according to Leighton, "any uncertainty or hazard in the thing itself to the end, in respect of the purpose and performance of God, but only the great difficulties and hard encounters in the way." This is only partly true. The Apostle is rather thinking of the final judgment than of the life of trial; and he means that there was but little margin left: a very few more falls, a few more refusals to follow the calls of grace, and they would have been lost. Doubtless, when the best of us looks back, in the light of the last day, upon all that he has been through, he will be amazed that he ever could be saved at all. Yet Bengel well calls us to see the other side of the picture in 2 Pet. i. 11.

The ungodly and the sinner.—This is the Gentile character. "Ungodly" denotes open irreligion—contempt of God and all that belongs to His worship. "Sinner" goes more to the moral side of the nature, pointing most of all to sins of the flesh. (Comp., for instance, Luke vii. 37.) "Sinners" was almost a synonym for "Gentiles." (See, *e.g.,* Luke vi. 32; xxiv. 7; Gal. ii. 15.) The question "Where shall he appear?" imagines some scene such as that of Matt. xxv. 32: "Where shall we see him? where will he have to stand?"

(19) **Wherefore.**—Because the beginning of the judgment—the judgment of the Christians—is so light in comparison with the fearful end when it lights on the disobedient and wicked.

Let them that suffer according to the will of God.—Our version omits an important little word: *Let them that suffer also* (or, *Let even them that suffer*) *according to the will of God.* The stress is on "suffer"—*i.e.,* be put to death. And the clause, "according to the will of God," seems not intended to mean "in a godly and unblameable manner," as opposed to the "suffering as a murderer" (verse 15); rather, it brings out that such a death is no accident, no sudden calamity, but in strict accordance with God's prearranged design. (Comp. chap. iii. 17: "if the will of God will it.") Thus it harmonises with the following: "faithful Creator," "commit their souls."

Commit the keeping of their souls.—The beautiful verb rendered "commit the keeping of" is a technical term for *depositing* a deed, or sum of money, or other valuable, with any one in trust. In the literal sense it occurs in Luke xii. 48; 2 Tim. i. 12: in a metaphorical sense, of *doctrines* committed in trust to the safe keeping of the Episcopate, in 1 Tim. i. 18; vi. 20; 2 Tim. i. 14; ii. 2: of leaving *persons* whom you love in trust, in Acts xiv. 23; xx. 32. But the words which St. Peter probably has ringing in his ears when he thus writes are the words of our Lord on the cross (where the same verb is used): "Father, into Thy hands I commend My spirit" (Luke xxiii. 46). "Their souls" might, perhaps, with still more propriety, be here translated *their lives.* The connection will then be: "Consider the mildness of these trials compared with the terrors overhanging the sinful. Even if the worst should come to the worst, and you must die a martyr's death, it is but the execution of God's plan for you. View your life as a deposit: lay it confidently in His hands, to be returned to you again when the time comes: and you will find Him faithful to what a Creator ought to be."

A faithful Creator.—The word "faithful" is used in reference to the "deposit" placed in His hands; and the title "Creator" seems to be chosen here rather than "Father," or the like, because creation of the soul

commit the keeping of their souls[a] *to him* in well doing, as unto a faithful Creator.

a Ps. 31. 5; Luke 23. 46.

CHAPTER V.—(1) The elders which are among you I exhort, who am also an elder, and a witness of the sufferings of Christ, and also a partaker of the glory that shall be revealed: (2) feed the flock of God which is among you,[1] taking the oversight *thereof*, not by constraint, but willingly; not for filthy

A.D. cir. 60.

1 Or, *as much as in you is.*

Chap. v. 1—14. General exhortations and conclusion.

---

includes not only the giving of its existence but the shaping of its destiny. "The will of God," in accordance with which they "suffer," is part of the act of creation. The noble expression, however, contains the idea that the act of creation imposes duties and responsibilities upon the Creator. It is conceivable that some powerful being (not our God) might create, and be careless of the happiness or of the moral welfare or of the mutual relations of his creatures. Such a creator would be "unfaithful:" we should have a right to expect differently of him. But God is a "faithful Creator." "Though He slay me, yet will I trust Him."

In well doing.—In the Greek these words come emphatically last. (Comp. chap. iii. 17.)

V.

(1–11) FURTHER EXHORTATIONS SUGGESTED BY THE CRISIS.—The officers of the community are not to flinch from the duties imposed upon them, nor yet to perform them in any spirit of self-assertion. The laity, on the other hand, are to observe discipline. Indeed, mutual submission is the only safe-guard in the face of a common danger. An unbroken front must be presented, and the sense of brotherhood fostered.

(1) **The elders which are among you . . .**—The best text preserves the word "therefore" after "elders." In view, that is, of these hopes and threats, of the present persecution, and of the coming judgment, St. Peter gives his solemn charge to those who shared with him the responsibility of office in the Church. The word rendered "exhort" is that common New Testament word (*parakalô*), which we miss in English, including encouragement and entreaty, and even consolation, as well as exhortation. (See, *e.g.*, Acts iv. 36.) The whole of this Epistle is an example of such *paraclesis*.

Who am also an elder.—St. Peter is giving no irresponsible advice. He knows by experience the dangers which beset the office. The head Christian of the world, and writing from the thick of the persecution already begun in Rome, the Asiatic elders cannot set his advice down as that of some easy layman who is untouched by the difficulty. It can hardly be said, therefore, that this is an example of St. Peter's *humility*, as though he recognised in himself no higher office than that of these presbyters. The effect is, on the contrary, to make the recipients of the Letter feel that he is using a strong argument *à fortiori*.

And a witness of the sufferings of Christ.—The Greek word calls attention, not so much to the fact of his having been a *spectator*, an *eye*-witness, but rather to the fact of his bearing *testimony* to the sufferings. Here again, too, it is in Greek "the sufferings of *the* Christ." (See Note on chap. i. 11.) Not only did St. Peter know, by bearing office himself, what the dangers of office were, but he was able to testify how the Messiah Himself, the Apostle and High Priest of our profession, had suffered, from which it was natural to conclude that all Christians also were destined to suffer.

And also a partaker of the glory . . .—This splendid assurance follows naturally from being a witness of the sufferings of the Christ. "I am in as much danger as any of you," the Apostle says, "but I can testify that the Christ Himself suffered thus, and therefore I know that we who suffer with Him are even now partakers of the glory, though a veil at present hides it." St. Peter insists in the same way on our *present* possession of what will not be *shown* us for a time in chap. i. 5.

(2) **Feed the flock of God which is among you.**—By the word "feed" here is meant, not merely the giving of pasture, but the whole government. It is the verb used in John xxi. 16, not that in the 15th and 17th verses. There can be hardly any doubt that St. Peter was thinking of that scene when he issued these directions. Our Lord had committed into his hands all His sheep and lambs, without restriction of age or country, to be fed and shepherded; and now the time was approaching when he would have to "put off this tabernacle" (2 Pet. i. 14), and he here takes order that "after his decease" the charge committed to him may be fulfilled. He still shepherds the flock by proxy. Two other points must be mentioned, which bring this passage into connection with the charge given by St. Paul to the Ephesian elders (Acts xx. 28), which was very probably known to St. Peter. (1) St. Peter calls it "the flock *of God*." Textual critics are much divided on the reading in Acts xx. 28, but, on the whole, the Received reading seems the best supported: "the Church of God which He hath purchased with His own blood." At the same time, St. Peter is in remembrance how Christ had said, "Feed *My* sheep." It may be fairly thought, therefore, when we see St. Peter's own theology in chaps. i. 25, ii. 3, iii. 15, that when he writes, "Feed the flock *of God*," his thoughts turn to the Second Person of the Holy Trinity rather than to the First. (2) Hooker well points out, on Acts xx. 28, the *unity* of the flock. Though there were many elders in Ephesus, there was but one flock they fed between them. So now, all over Asia Minor, it was but one flock. St. Peter, to whom the flock throughout the whole world was committed, saw it as a whole, but the elders to whom he writes had only to look to that part of the one flock which was "among them." The marginal rendering is against the order of the Greek words, and does not suit the context so well when the context is rightly understood.

Taking the oversight thereof.—It is exceedingly doubtful whether these words form part of the original text or not. If they do, the translation unduly limits the meaning, which would be better expressed by "maintaining (or, *exercising*) the oversight," or "performing the duties of bishops," for he is addressing men who were already ordained. By this time the word "bishop" had not become a fixed title of one special office, though the office itself was in existence.

Not by constraint, but willingly.—Why should this exhortation be given so prominently? It is hardly to be thought that St. Peter had in view the humility which led men to adopt such strange methods of

lucre, but of a ready mind; (3) neither as being lords [1] over *God's* heritage, but being ensamples to the flock. (4) And when the chief Shepherd shall appear, ye shall receive a crown of glory that fadeth not away. (5) Likewise, ye younger, submit yourselves unto the elder. Yea, all *of you* be subject one to another, and be clothed with humility: for God resisteth the proud, and giveth grace to the

1 Or, *overruling.*

avoiding the responsibility of the priesthood as we find resorted to by Chrysostom and Ambrose. Much more probably he is thinking of the actual *danger* to life and property of being "ringleaders of the sect" (Acts xxiv. 5), which would lead cowardly bishops to throw up their office. He is not treating of the motives which should lead a man to accept the position. He speaks to persons who already *hold* the office, and urges them not to leave the flock, like hirelings, when they see the persecution coming on. Several of the best authorities add, "but willingly, according to God." It was God, that is, who put them in that station, and they must not need the compulsion of their laity, or of the rest of the episcopate, or of the Apostles, to keep them at their post.

Not for filthy lucre, but of a ready mind.—The opposite vice to that on which he has just passed sentence. Some, who had no fears, might be tempted to retain the office by the good salary which the Church gave, or might threaten to resign if their salaries were not raised in proportion to their risk. The "ready mind," of which the Apostle speaks, means the love of the work itself, which should be the sole motive in seeking, or performing, the gospel ministry.

(3) **Neither as being lords.**—Rather, *nor yet as lording it.* The English version is somewhat too strict for the Greek and for the sense. There is a sense in which the heads of the Church are, and ought to be, lords and princes over the rest; but this is very different from "lording it," acting tyrannically, forgetting the constitutional rights of their subjects.

Over God's heritage.—Quite literally, *Over the lots.* The word first of all means (as in Matt. xxvii. 35 or Acts i. 26) the actual scrap of paper or wood that was tossed. Then it comes to mean (like the word "lot" in the language of auctions) the piece of property that falls by lot to any one's share. Then all notion of *chance* disappears, and it comes to mean the portion assigned to any one. So St. Peter says that Simon Magus has "no share nor lot in this thing" (Acts viii. 21). In Acts xxvi. 18, Col. i. 12, the same word is rendered "inheritance." In Acts xvii. 4, our version endeavours, not very successfully, through the Latin word "consorted," to keep up the underlying notion of the Greek, which literally is "were *allotted* to Paul and Silas." Here, therefore, we must understand "the lots," over which the clergy are not to lord it, to be the different congregations, districts, parishes, dioceses, which had been allotted to them. At the same time it does not at all imply that any process like drawing of lots had been resorted to in their appointment, as is seen from Acts xvii. 4, just cited. It will be seen that our version is misleading in substituting singular for plural, and in inserting the word "God's." The whole flock is God's (verse 2), purchased with His own blood; but the "allotments" are the portions assigned by Him to the different clergy. It is some consolation to see, when we groan under the lives and characters of some church officers now, that even in the Apostles' days cowardice, greed, and self-assertion were not unknown.

Ensamples to the flock.—The best way of becoming a real prince and lord over men is to show them by example what they ought to do, like Chaucer's Parson, who—

> "Cristes lore and hys Apostlis twelve
> He taught, but fyrst hee practys'd it himselve."

Leighton well quotes from Nazianzen: "Either teach not, or teach by living."

(4) **And when the chief Shepherd shall appear.**—Or, *And at the chief Shepherd's appearing.* The "and" treats it as a simple natural consequence of acting as just indicated. The beautiful word for "chief Shepherd" seems to have been invented by St. Peter, and it has been apparently imitated in Heb. xiii. 20. How could an office be more honoured than by speaking of Christ as the chief bearer of that office?

A crown of glory that fadeth not away.—It might perhaps be more closely, though less beautifully, represented by *the glorious crown of amaranth,* or *the amaranthine crown of glory.* Amaranth is the name of a flower which, like our immortelles, does not lose its colour or form. St. Peter immediately adds "of glory," lest we should think too literally of the wreath of immortelles.

(5) **Likewise, ye younger.**—Self-submission has been, at least tacitly, inculcated upon the pastors in verse 3; so the writer can say "likewise" in turning to the rest. In comparison with the presbyters or elders, the lay people are styled "younger," or "juniors;" although in point of natural age, or of baptismal seniority, they might be the older. So our Lord addresses His disciples (according to the rabbinical fashion) as "children," though there is good reason to suppose that several were older than Himself; and St. Paul, in the same way, called all the Corinthian Christians his "sons." This seems to be the most natural interpretation of the word; for it was undoubtedly in respect of the supposed juniority of the whole of the lay people that their rulers received the name of "presbyters." Otherwise there is nothing against the interpretation which makes "ye younger" to be an address to those who held inferior offices in the Church, such as deacons, catechists, readers, and the like (Acts v. 6, 10). The danger of any insubordination of the laity or inferior clergy against the priesthood at such a crisis was very obvious.

Yea, all of you.—Here the true text strikes out the words "be subject and," so that the clause will run, *Yea, all of you be clothed with humility one to another.* Not only mutual complaisance between rulers on the one hand and ruled on the other, but clergy to clergy and laity to laity are to behave with the same self-suppression.

Be clothed with humility.—The Greek verb is a rare and curious one. It means properly, "tie yourselves up in humility." Humility is to be gathered tight round about us like a cloak, and *tied up* so that the wind may not blow it back, nor the rain beat inside it. But there is a still further and more delicate shade of meaning in the word. There was a peculiar kind of cape, well known by a name taken from this verb (we might call it a "tie-up"), and this kind of cape was worn by slaves, and by no others. It was a badge of servitude. Thus St. Peter bids them all gird them-

humble. (6) Humble yourselves there-
fore under the mighty hand of God, that
he may exalt you in due time: (7) casting
all your care upon him; for he careth
for you. (8) Be sober, be vigilant;
because your adversary the devil, as a
roaring lion, walketh about, seeking
whom he may devour: (9) whom resist
stedfast in the faith, knowing that the
same afflictions are accomplished in your
brethren that are in the world. (10) But
the God of all grace, who hath called us
unto his eternal glory by Christ Jesus,
after that ye have suffered a while, make

---

selves for one another in a slave's "tie-up" of humility. None are to be masters in the Church of Christ. And the humility is to be the very first thing noticed about them, their outward mark and sign.

For God resisteth the proud.—The exhortation to mutual self-submission is reinforced by a quotation of a well-known proverb. The proverb is based on the LXX. translation of Prov. iii. 34; but as it differs somewhat from both the Hebrew and the Greek of that passage, and is found word for word in Jas. iv. 6, we may probably give the same account of it as of the other proverb quoted in chap. iv. 8, where see Note. A sad calamity for Christians under persecution, suddenly to find God Himself in array on the enemy's side! (such is the meaning of "resisteth"); and this is what they *would* find, if they went against discipline. On the other hand, if they were submissive, He would bestow "grace" upon them; here again, perhaps, not in the strict theological sense, but in that of "favour."

(6) **Humble yourselves therefore.**—This, too, looks an amplification of a proverb, when we compare it with Jas. iv. 10. The humility here recommended is not merely a submissive bearing of the strokes which it pleased God to let fall upon them, but it was to be shown, as we see in the former verse, in their bearing toward one another. And "the mighty hand of God" is not to be regarded as that which is chastising them, but as the protecting shelter which they are humbly to seek.

In due time.—St. Peter probably means, in the day of judgment, which seemed so instant.

(7) **Casting all your care upon him.**—An adaptation of Ps. lv. 22, according to the LXX. Anxiety implies not only some distrust of God's providence, but also some kind of belief that we may be able to manage better for ourselves; therefore here, as in the Sermon on the Mount, we are exhorted, especially in time of danger, simply to do what we know we ought to do, and to be unheeding about the rest.

> "Lord, it belongs not to my care
> Whether I die or live."

The confidence cannot be misplaced, for God is not forgetful of us. The play of words in the English does not represent anything in the original, where the two words for "care" are quite different.

(8) **Be sober, be vigilant.**—Single words in the Greek, and in the tense which bespeaks *immediate* attention. The best text omits the following "because." These are the sudden cries of warning of a shepherd who spies the lion prowling round the flock in the darkness, while the guardians of the flock lie drowsy and secure.

As a roaring lion.—The epithet is not only added to lend terror to the description, but the roaring implies hunger and determination.

Walketh about.—Comp. Job i. 7; ii. 2. St. Peter, however, is not calling attention to the fact that Satan is *always* prowling about, but he warns the sleeping shepherds that he is especially doing so *now*. This season of persecution was just his time for picking off one here and another there.

Seeking whom he may devour.—Perhaps still more expressive to say, "seeking *which* he may devour." Satan is eyeing all the Christians in turn to see which he has the best chance of, not merely stalking forth vaguely to look for prey.

(9) **Whom resist stedfast in the faith.**—The expression is somewhat more picturesque in the Greek than in the English. "Stand and face him," instead of running away from posts of duty (verse 2), or lying still and letting things take their course (verse 8). And the words for "stedfast in the faith" seem to mean not only that each individual is to stand firm, but that they are to present all together a solid front to the lion.

Knowing that the same afflictions are accomplished in your brethren that are in the world.—The phraseology of the original is very strange. The *sameness* of the sufferings is brought out by an expression which literally runs "the same things in the way of sufferings;" the fraternal unity, by the use of the same abstract word which we had in chap. ii. 17. The verb rendered "to accomplish" sometimes denotes execution or infliction. So the whole will run, *knowing that the very same things in the way of sufferings are being inflicted upon your brotherhood which is in the world.* "There is one thing," says Archbishop Leighton, "that much troubles the patience and weakens the faith of some Christians; they are ready to think there is none, yea, there was never any beloved of God in such a condition as theirs. Therefore the Apostle St. Paul breaks this conceit (1 Cor. x. 13), 'no temptation hath taken you but such as is common to man:' and here is the same truth, 'the same afflictions are accomplished in your brethren.' This is the truth, and, taken altogether, is a most comfortable truth; the whole brotherhood go in this way, and our eldest Brother went first." The addition, "that are in the world," points the suffering Christians indirectly to solace themselves with the thought of that portion of the brotherhood which has got beyond the infliction. It would be possible to translate, though somewhat far-fetched in point of thought, "knowing that the same sufferings (or, *the identity of the sufferings*) is completed by your brotherhood in the world"—*i.e.*, finds a consummation in making closer the bonds of brotherhood between you.

(10) **Who hath called us unto his eternal glory.**—The true reading is, *who called you*, not "us." The moment of the call was that when St. Paul and the others first preached there. (See chap. i. 12, 25, and Notes.) The God who *now* bestows all *grace*, by the giving of that grace calls us into glory.

> "The men of grace have found
> Glory begun below."

By Christ Jesus.—On the whole it seems best, with Tischendorf, to drop the name of Jesus out of the text: the title "Christ" will then stand between

you perfect, stablish, strengthen, settle
you. (11) To him *be* glory and dominion
for ever and ever. Amen. (12) By
Silvanus, a faithful brother unto you,
as I suppose, I have written briefly,
exhorting, and testifying that this is
the true grace of God wherein ye
stand. (13) The *church that is* at

"the eternal glory," which we possess "in Him" (not "*by* Christ Jesus," as our version has it, but *by virtue of our union with the Christ*), and the immediate mention of suffering. In Him the two are drawn inseparably together.

Suffered a while.—The Greek says distinctly, "a *little* while," as in chap. i. 6. All time is short in comparison of what comes after. The original looks as if St. Peter meant not only "*after* that ye have suffered," but also "by the fact of your having suffered."

Make you perfect.—Strictly these are futures, "*shall* (or, *will*) *make you perfect*," &c. This verb occurs again in 1 Thess. iii. 10, and elsewhere. It implies the reduction to order and fitness for work of what is disordered or broken. The others, which are all very similar in meaning, are heaped up after St. Peter's manner. Bengel thus explains them: "Make you perfect, that there remain no defect in you. Stablish, that nothing shake you. Strengthen, that you may overcome all force brought against you." The word for "to settle" means "to found," to give a solid foundation. All this is to take place at the close of the short spell of suffering which is the means to it. St. Peter seems, therefore, to contemplate the passing off of the persecution before the end of the world; for these verbs could hardly be so naturally used to express our education in the world to come.

(11) **To him be glory.**—"The Apostle," says Leighton, "having added prayer to his doctrine, adds here, you see, praise to his prayer." This is the true consolation in trouble, to extol the power of God. If His be the dominion, and He have called us to His glory, then what can we fear?

(12–14) CONCLUDING GREETING.—You will trust the bearer of this Letter, and abide steadfastly in the faith which he has taught you. The exiled Israel in this wicked capital feels for you. Love and peace be among you.

(12) **By Silvanus, a faithful brother unto you, as I suppose.**—There is not any reason for doubting that this is the same as the Silas of the Acts and the Silvanus of 2 Cor. i. 19; 1 Thess. i. 1; 2 Thess. i. 1. It is not a common name, and nothing would suggest the doubt, except the acceptance *à priori* of the Tübingen theory, that the feud between St. Peter and St. Paul was so deadly as to preclude the possibility of the first giving his patronage to a friend of the second. We have already seen repeatedly how false that theory is. That the bearer of this Letter was a personage of great consideration, may be seen from the fact that St. Peter speaks of him as well known throughout the whole Hebrew population of Asia Minor. In the original the testimony is still more marked than in our version, as it has the definite article, "*the*, or *that*, faithful brother unto you." Silas being of the circumcision himself (Acts xv. 22), St. Peter can without any risk, writing to the Jews, call him "brother." And since there was probably some disaffection towards him among the Jewish Christians, for the way in which he had sided with St. Paul, St. Peter, the Apostle of the circumcision, adds it as his own personal conviction that Silas was no false brother to the Hebrew Christians, by saying, "as I reckon." The words "as I suppose" (or, rather, *as I reckon*) do not imply any uncertainty on St. Peter's part, nor even that St. Peter's knowledge of Silas was less intimate than that of the persons to whom he writes. It means, rather, the most complete confidence in Silas, which the writer is not at all ashamed to declare—"that faithful brother unto you, in my estimation, if my conviction is worth anything." This only shows that St. Peter had not altered his opinion either of Silas or of the relative positions of Jew and Gentile in the Church, since that great council in which he took so prominent a part, when Silas was selected, no doubt because of his uniting liberal views with steadfast allegiance to the Law, to bear the apostolic mandates to the Gentile metropolis of Antioch. The same qualifications which fitted him for that work, would now again serve him in good stead to bear to the Jews of Asia Minor St. Peter's countersignature to the doctrine of St. Paul. At the same time the expression, "that faithful brother unto you," indicates that St. Silas had been himself working in Asia Minor. Of his history nothing is recorded subsequent to his labours with St. Paul at Corinth (Acts xviii. 5; 2 Cor. i. 19); but putting together the fact that he is not included in the list of St. Paul's companions in Acts xx. 4, with what is implied by this present passage, we might naturally infer that he was left at Ephesus, and devoted himself to the evangelisation of the Asiatic provinces.

Briefly.—So Heb. xiii. 22. The writer hints that if this present Letter is not enough to effect its purpose, it is not because there is any lack of matter or weakness of conviction. (See also John xx. 25.)

Exhorting, and testifying that this is the true grace of God wherein ye stand.—These words give St. Peter's own account of the object and contents of the Epistle. The "exhortation" involves all that was mentioned in the Note on verse 1. The word for "testifying" has a little further force than appears in our version; it is "bearing witness *thereto*." The fact had been *alleged* by others; St. Peter comes in as evidence to its truth. Literally it would run: "that this is true grace (or, *a true grace*) of God"; *i.e.*, that the position which they now occupy, through the preaching of the gospel, is indeed one which the favour of God had brought them into: it was no fictitious grace, no robbing of them under pretence of bringing them glad tidings. When he says "this," he seems to mean "this of which I have spoken," "this which has formed the subject of my Letter." And the best text pursues; "wherein stand ye," or "whereupon take up your stand." Thus the very sentence itself would contain the two elements of the Letter—"exhorting" as well as "testifying." Nothing is to drive them or entice them from the ground which the Pauline preachers have marked out for them.

(13) **The church . . . . elected together with you.**—In the original it simply stands "the co-elect one [fem. sing.] in Babylon." Some, therefore, seeing immediately after, "Marcus, my son," and knowing that St. Peter was a married man (Matt. viii. 14, 1 Cor. ix. 5), have thought that this "co-elect one" was St. Peter's wife. But (1) it is highly improbable that St. Mark was in that sense "son" to St. Peter; (2) quite as improbable that she would have been put so

Babylon, elected together with *you*, saluteth you; and *so doth* Marcus my son. (14) Greet ye one another with a kiss of charity. Peace *be* with you all that are in Christ Jesus. Amen.

---

prominently forward in such an Epistle; (3) the word "co-elect" evidently refers back to chap. i. 2, and means "co-elect with *you*," not "with me." It was becoming a not infrequent mode of designating a church, to personify it under a female title (see 2 John, verses 1, 4, 5, 13); and it seems therefore much more natural to suppose that the salutation is from this church of "Babylon" to her sister churches in the provinces of Asia Minor. The modesty with which this church at "Babylon" is spoken of, as being only one of many "co-elect" ones is noteworthy. She does not claim such a position among churches as (*e.g.*) in Cant. vi. 8, 9.

That is at Babylon.—Three places have claimed to be understood under this name: (1) A little place called Babylon in Egypt, which has nothing to plead for itself except the unlikelihood of St. Peter ever being at the Oriental Babylon, coupled with the difficulty of supposing that the name is used quite figuratively. Perhaps, also, we should mention the traditional connection of St. Mark with Egypt. No one now, however, maintains this view. (2) The literal Babylon in the East. This has for itself the simple way in which St. Peter uses the word without any circumlocution. But it has nothing else for it, to set against all the overwhelming arguments in favour of the third claimant; besides which we learn from Josephus of a great expulsion of Jews from the Oriental Babylon a few years before this date: these Jews might of course, however, have gathered there again, as they did at Rome, in spite of frequent expulsions. (3) It may be called the established interpretation that the place meant is Rome. We never hear of St. Peter being in the East, and the thing in itself is improbable, whereas nothing but Protestant prejudice can stand against the historical evidence that St. Peter sojourned and died at Rome. Whatever theological consequences may flow from it, it is as certain that St. Peter was at Rome as that St. John was at Ephesus. Everything in the Letter also points to such a state of things as was to be found at Rome about the date when we believe the Letter to have been written. It is objected that St. Peter would not gravely speak of Rome under a fanciful name when dating a letter; but the symbolism in the name is quite in keeping with the context. St. Peter has just *personified* the church of the place from which he writes, which seems quite as unprosaic a use of language as to call Rome "Babylon." And it seems pretty clear that the name was quite intelligible to Jewish readers, for whom it was intended. The Apocalypse (xvii. 18) is not the only place where Rome is found spoken of under this title. One of the first of living Hebraists (who will not allow his name to be mentioned) told the present writer that no Hebrew of St. Peter's day would have had need to think twice what city was meant when "Babylon" was mentioned. And on the mention of the name, all the prophecies of the vengeance to be taken on the city which had desolated the Holy Land would rush with consolation into the mind of the readers, and they would feel that St. Peter, though supporting St. Paul, was still in full sympathy with themselves. Finally, as M. Renan suggests, there were reasons of prudence for not speaking too plainly about the presence of a large Christian society in Rome. The police were still more vigilant now than when St. Paul wrote in guarded language about the Roman empire to the Thessalonians. (See *Excursus on the Man of Sin*, after 2 Thess.) It might provoke hostilities if the Epistle fell into the hands of a *delator*, with names and places too clearly given.

Marcus, my son.—The particular word here used does not occur elsewhere of spiritual relationship, but the other thought is very improbable. We should have heard of it in other places had St. Mark been his son in the flesh. (See Acts xii. 12.) St. Mark was, of course, well known in Asia Minor (Acts xii. 25; Col. iv. 10; 2 Tim. iv. 11).

(14) **Kiss of charity.**—Not only does he wish them to receive the greetings of the Roman Church, but to display their brotherly love to each other as well. On the kiss of charity, see 1 Thess. v. 26. The "peace" which he wishes to them includes, though it is not limited to, peace amongst themselves.

INTRODUCTION

TO

THE SECOND EPISTLE GENERAL OF

PETER

I. The Authorship.—The question of the authenticity of our Epistle is one of well-known difficulty. The objections to its genuineness are more serious than those against any other book in the New Testament, and yet are not so conclusive as by any means to have silenced those who defend the authenticity. Before proceeding to a consideration of the arguments on each side, two remarks seem to be necessary.

(1.) The Epistle must stand or fall as a whole. It is impossible to reject passages which appear to be open to objection and retain the rest. The thought is eminently consecutive throughout, the style is uniform, and the writer frequently glances back at what he has said before or anticipates what is coming. The network of connected ideas which thus pervades the whole cannot be severed otherwise than violently. Moreover, the singular want of agreement among those who advocate an expurgated edition as to what portions should be struck out and what not, is another reason for refusing to disintegrate the Epistle. Thus, Grotius thinks that the words "Peter" and "Apostle," in chap. i. 1, and verses i. 18 and iii. 15, 16, are interpolations. Bertholt would retain chaps. i. and iii., rejecting chap. ii. Lange (in *Herzog*) would reject all that lies between chaps. i. 19 and iii. 3, *i.e.*, from the words "knowing this first" in chap. i. 20 to the same words in chap. iii. 3. Ullmann surrenders all but chap. i. Bunsen retains nothing but the first eleven verses and the doxology.

(2.) It is inexpedient to encumber the discussion with an attempted *reductio ad horribile* of one of the alternatives. A court must not concern itself with the consequences of finding the prisoner guilty. Let us, therefore, at once set aside all such notions as this; that if the Epistle is not by St. Peter, "the Church, which for more than fourteen centuries has received it, has been imposed upon by what must, in that case, be regarded as a Satanic device." Satan forging the Second Epistle of St. Peter would indeed be Satan casting out Satan. Or, again, "If any book which she reads as the Word of God is not the Word of God, but the work of an impostor, then—with reverence be it said—Christ's promise to His Church has failed, and the Holy Spirit has not been given to guide her into all truth . . . The testimony of the universal Church of Christ, declaring that the Epistles which we receive as such are Epistles of St. Peter and are the Word of God, is not her testimony only—it is the testimony of Christ." Every true Christian will sympathise with the zeal for God's Word which is conspicuous in these passages; but it will be well to keep apart two questions which they combine and almost confuse—(*a*) Is this Second Epistle the work of St. Peter? (*b*) Is it part of the Word of God? The second question is here taken for granted. The Church answered it in the affirmative fifteen hundred years ago, and it is no part of the present work to question the decision. Only the first question will be discussed; and to attempt to settle *it* by considerations such as the passages just quoted suggest, is neither just, nor wise, nor in the deepest sense reverent. It is not just; for how can we give a fair hearing to adverse evidence if we approach it in a spirit which compels us to regard it as false or misleading? It is not wise; for what will be our position if, after all, the adverse evidence is too strong for even our pre-judgment? It is not reverent; for it virtually assumes that the Almighty *cannot* exalt an Epistle put forth under a pretended name to the dignity of being His Word; and that He who spoke to His chosen people by the lips of impure Balaam cannot speak to us by the writings of one who may have ill-advisedly assumed the pen of an Apostle. Hos. i. 2, 3 and iii. 1, 2 may warn us to be on our guard against pronouncing hastily beforehand as to what means and instruments it is or is not possible for God to employ for the instruction of His people.

These remarks are not made with a view to surrendering the authenticity of the Epistle as a thing of no moment, but only that we may be able to weigh the evidence with calmness. The question of the genuineness of the Epistle is one of immense interest and no small importance; but there is no terrible alternative before us. If, after all, we have to admit that the Epistle is possibly, or probably or certainly not the work of St. Peter, the spiritual value of the contents, both in themselves and in having received the stamp of the Church as canonical, will remain absolutely unchanged; although, possibly, our own views of God's providence in relation to the canon of Scripture may require re-consideration and re-adjustment. This, however, is but the common experience both of the individual and of the race. Men's views of God's dealings with them are ever needing re-adjustment, as He hides and manifests Himself in history; for His ways are not as our ways, nor His thoughts as our thoughts.

The objections to the genuineness of the Epistle are of four kinds: being drawn (*a*) from the history of the Epistle; (*b*) from its contents in relation to the First Epistle; (*c*) from the contents considered in themselves; (*d*) from the same in relation to the Epistle of St. Jude.

In each case it will be most convenient to state the adverse facts first, and then what may be said on the other side.

(*a*) *External Evidence: The History of the Epistle.*—Among the earliest writers there is a remarkable silence with regard to this Epistle. There is no mention of it, and no *certain* quotation from it or allusion to it, in either the first or second century. Neither the Apostolic Fathers nor Justin Martyr nor Irenæus yield anything that can be relied upon as a reference. It is probable that Irenæus did not know of its existence; it is almost certain that neither Tertullian nor Cyprian did. About Clement of Alexandria there is some doubt, owing to inconsistent statements of Eusebius and Cassiodorus. But seeing that in the large amount of Clement's writings now extant there is only one possible, and not one probable, reference to it, and that, in quoting 1 Peter, he writes, "Peter *in his Epistle* says," the probability is that he did not know it. The Muratorian Fragment (*circ.* A.D. 170) omits it. It is wanting in the Peschito or old Syriac version (and St. Peter was personally known in Syria, especially at Antioch), and also in the old Latin version which preceded the Vulgate. Thus we are brought quite into the third century without any sure trace of the Epistle.

Origen certainly knew it. In those of his works which exist only in the Latin translation of Rufinus he quotes it as the work of St. Peter. But Rufinus is not a trustworthy translator; and Origen, in works of which the original Greek is still extant, either expresses a doubt about it or rejects it by implication, as Clement of Alexandria does. Eusebius certainly rejected it; Chrysostom, Theodore, and Theodoret probably did so; and we learn from Didymus, Jerome's preceptor, that doubts about it still survived late in the fourth century, though he seems to have overcome them in himself. At the Reformation these doubts revived again, and have never subsided since. At the present time, a large number of the best critics consider the Epistle suspicious or spurious.

On the other hand, there are *possible* allusions to it in Clement of Rome, Polycarp, Hermas, Justin Martyr, Melito, Theophilus, and Hippolytus: and some even among adverse critics consider those in the *Shepherd* of Hermas (*circ.* A.D. 140) to be certain. Specimens of these possible allusions will be found in the Notes on passages which they resemble:—Clement, ii. 5; iii. 4; Polycarp, iii. 4; Hermas, ii. 13, 15, 20; iii. 5; Justin Martyr, ii. 1, iii. 8; Melito, iii. 5—7; Theophilus, i. 19, 21; Hippolytus, i. 21. The first *certain* reference to the Epistle as by St. Peter is in a Latin translation of a letter by Origen's pupil, Firmilian of Cæsarea, to Cyprian (A.D. 256). Athanasius, Cyril of Jerusalem, Basil, Gregory Nazianzen, Jerome, Rufinus, and Augustine accepted it, although they knew that it had been much suspected; and they, of course, had evidence which has not come down to us. The Councils of Laodicea (*circ.* A.D. 360) and of Hippo (A.D. 393) formally included it in the Canon, decisions which have never been reversed. Its omission from the Muratorian Fragment is somewhat weakened by the fact that 1 Peter (about which there is no doubt) is omitted also; and, as a set-off to its omission from the Peschito, we have the fact that Ephrem Syrus seems to have accepted it.

Thus the adverse external evidence, serious though it is, is anything but conclusive. It can easily be explained. Communication between the churches was fitful and irregular, sometimes slow, sometimes very rapid. Accidents might favour the circulation of the First Epistle and delay that of the Second. The very fact of its being the first Letter from the pen of the chief Apostle would promote the spread of the First Epistle; and as it was known to have been written only a few years before the death of St. Peter, this would make a second Letter within so short an interval a little improbable. The marked difference of style and language between the two Letters, which Jerome tells us had attracted notice, would increase the distrust. The amount of apocryphal literature which began to appear at a very early date, and flooded the Church in the second and third centuries, made all churches very suspicious about unknown writings; and several of these apocryphal books bore the name of St. Peter. Every year that the arrival of the Epistle at any particular church was delayed would make its acceptance by that church less probable. The fate of the Fourth Gospel, on account of its appearing after the others had obtained full possession of the field, is an illustration of similar causes and effects. When we remember that many narratives of Christ's life (Luke i. 1, Note) and some letters of St. Paul have entirely perished, we need not be surprised that a short Epistle like this, containing little that ordinary Christians did not know, should have remained for more than a century quite unknown to many churches and suspected by others. If the external evidence were all, we might admit that the general and authoritative reception of the Epistle in the fourth century, *after* such full doubt and debate, is more than sufficient for us.

(*b*) *Internal Evidence: The Contents of the Second Epistle in relation to the First.*—Very formidable lists of points of difference between the two Epistles have been drawn up, but recent adverse critics have ceased to urge many of these supposed differences; we may, therefore, content ourselves with some of the most telling of such arguments as specimens. (α) 1 Peter uses Old Testament phraseology, and quotes Old Testament writers; 2 Peter, with two doubtful exceptions (chaps. ii. 22; iii. 8), does neither. (β) 1 Peter is mainly about suffering persecution; 2 Peter is mainly about heresy. (γ) 1 Peter speaks of the Death, Resurrection, and Ascension of Christ; 2 Peter mentions none of them. (δ) 1 Peter represents the return of Christ as near (chap. iv. 7), and calls it a "revelation" (chaps. i. 7, 13; iv. 13); 2 Peter represents it as possibly distant (chap. iii. 15), and calls it "coming" (chaps. i. 16; iii. 4, 12). (ε) 1 Peter calls our Lord simply "Christ" or "Jesus Christ;" 2 Peter always adds "Saviour" (five times; and the word does not occur once in 1 Peter), or "Lord," or both. (ζ) 1 Peter insists on *faith;* 2 Peter on *knowledge.* (η) The Greek of 1 Peter is smooth, with easily-moving sentences, simply connected; that of 2 Peter is rough, with heavily-moving sentences, of which the construction is often harsh and, when prolonged, broken.

To these and similar arguments it may be replied that considerable differences between the two Epistles are admitted, but they may easily be exaggerated. Of the above, some are not strictly true; in particular, (α) and (ε), others tell rather in favour of the genuineness of 2 Peter. Why should a second letter, written soon after the first, on a very different subject, repeat the topics of the first, or even use much of its phraseology? Encouragement under persecution and denunciation of corrupt doctrine and conduct require very different language. Great similarity of expression under such very different circumstances would have looked like the careful imitation of a forger. Jerome's suggestion, that St. Peter used different "interpreters" in the two Epistles to put his thoughts into Greek, is a possible solution of many differences; but it is not likely that St. Peter, though originally an illiterate fisherman, was still, at the end of a long and active life, unable to write the Greek of either Epistle; and both of them show traces of a writer not perfectly at home in the language. King's theory, that 2 Peter is a translation from an Aramaic original, is another possible solution. But neither theory is needed. Both Epistles are too short to supply satisfactory materials for an argument of this kind; and neither of them exhibit any such marked characteristics as those found in the writings of St. Luke or St. Paul or St. John. An anonymous pamphlet on any subject by Carlyle or Victor Hugo would probably be assigned to the right author at once; but most writers, even if known by many books, have no such marked style as would betray them in a few pages on a special subject: and here we are arguing as to the authorship of a tract of four pages from a tract of six pages on a different subject. In such a case, similarities, which cannot easily be the result of imitation, are stronger evidence of identity of authorship than dissimilarities are of non-identity. Difference of mood, of subject, of surroundings, would probably account for all the dissimilarities, did we but know all the facts. The First Epistle would seem to have been written with much thought and care, as by one who felt a delicacy about intruding himself upon communities which St. Paul had almost made his own. Hence the earnest, gentle dignity of the Epistle, which makes one think how age must have tamed the spirit of the impetuous Apostle. But in the Second Letter, written probably under pressure, we see that the old vehemence is still there. There is a slight indication of it in the way in which he goes at once to the point (chap. i. 3—5); as he nears the evil which has so excited his fear and indignation, the construction becomes broken (chap. i. 17); and when he is in the full torrent of his invective, feeling seems almost to choke his utterance. Hence the rugged Greek, from which at times we can scarcely extricate the construction; hence, too, the repetitions, which some have thought a sign of inferiority. They are the natural results of emotion struggling to express itself in a language with which it is not perfectly familiar. Similar harsh constructions and tautological repetitions may be found in some of St. Peter's speeches as recorded in the Acts (chaps. i. 21, 22; iii. 13—16, 26; iv. 9; x. 36—40).

Against the admitted differences may be set some very real coincidences, both in thought and language, between the two Epistles. These also may be exaggerated and their force over-estimated; but when soberly treated they are a valuable contribution to the evidence. Obvious similarities of language are of no great moment (see Notes on chaps. i. 14, 16; ii. 7); for it is admitted by all that the writer of the Second Letter knew the First. But subtle coincidences of thought, lying almost beyond the reach of the conscious imitator, are worth considering. (See on chaps. i. 3, 5, 7; ii. 18, 19.) The traces of St. Paul's phraseology, which have been urged against the originality of 2 Peter, may, from this point of view, be counted in its favour, for such traces are very strong in the First Epistle.

The arguments, therefore, to be drawn from a comparison of the two Letters do not give much support to those who impugn the genuineness of the Second Epistle. A patient consideration of the facts may lead some to the conclusion that, considering the brevity of both Letters and the different purpose of each, the amount of agreement, both on and below the surface, throws the balance in favour of both being the product of one mind. The assertion that had the Second Epistle not claimed to be by St. Peter no one would ever have dreamed of assigning it to him, is easily made and not easily refuted; but study of the phenomena will lead to its being doubted.

(c) *Internal Evidence: The Contents of the Epistle considered in themselves.*—It is in this section of the argument that far the most serious objections to the authenticity occur. The following have been urged:—(α) It is unlike the simple, practical spirit of St. Peter to enlarge upon the manner of the creation and of the destruction of the world (chap. iii. 5—7, 10—12). (β) It is unlike an Apostle to appeal to "the commandment of your Apostles" (chap. iii. 2). (γ) The interchange of future and present tenses (chaps. ii. 1, 2, 3, 10, 12, 13; iii. 3, 5) looks like a later writer trying to write like a prophet in an earlier age, and at times forgetting his assumed position. (δ) Ideas belonging to an age later than that of the Apostles are introduced. Of this there are four marked instances—(1) The expression "the *holy* mount" (chap. i. 18) betrays an age which professes to know where the Transfiguration took place (of which the Gospels tell us nothing), and which has a taste for miracles. (2) No such argument as that urged by the scoffers (chap. iii. 4) would be possible in St. Peter's lifetime; it implies that at least the first generation of Christians has died out. (3) 2 Peter is addressed (chap. i. 1) to all Gentile Christians, and at the same time (chap. iii. 1) to the same readers as those of 1 Peter, which is addressed (chap. i. 1) to particular churches, *i.e.*, the post-Apostolic idea that the letters of Apostles are the common property of all Christians is implied. (4) St. Paul's writings are spoken of as equivalent to Scripture (chap. iii. 16).

Let us take these objections in order. (α) That St. Peter should enlarge upon the details of the creation and of the destruction of the world is not more strange than that he should enlarge upon "the spirits in prison" (1 Pet. iii. 19, 20; iv. 6). It would almost seem as if such mysterious subjects had an attraction for him (1 Pet. i. 12). At least it is more reasonable to suppose this, seeing that there are some facts to support us, than to settle precariously what "the simple, practical spirit of St. Peter" would or would not be likely to enlarge upon. (β) Let us grant that an Apostle is often content with insisting on his own authority: this is no proof that he would never appeal to the authority of another Apostle. In 2 Peter the writer has more than once stated his personal claim to be heard (chap. i. 1, 18), and is then willing to sink his own authority in that of the Apostolic body, nay, is anxious to do so; for, as in the First Epistle, he still feels a delicacy about addressing congregations which, in the first instance, belonged to the Apostle of the Gentiles, and so he not only appeals to that Apostle's commandment, but points out that his commandment is at the same time that of Jesus Christ. In Eph. iii. 5 St. Paul makes a similar appeal to the authority of others; and it may warn us to be cautious in arguing as to what an Apostle would be sure to do in certain cases when we find this passage used to cast doubt on the Apostolic origin of such an Epistle as that to the Ephesians. (γ) This plausible argument will not bear close inspection. The evils which the writer foretells are already present in the germ. Moreover, the prophetic present as equivalent to a future is very common in prophecies; the future is so confidently realised that it is spoken of as present. In similar prophecies in the New Testament there is a similar mixture of future and present (2 Thess. ii. 3, 7; 2 Tim. iii. 1, 2, 8). (δ) We come now to the most weighty group of objections. (1) The expression "the holy mount" does not imply that the mount is known; and the theory that it does is reduced to an absurdity when it is further urged that "the holy mount," as applied to a known spot, must mean Mount Zion. Would any sane Christian, whether of the first or of the second century, represent the Transfiguration as taking place on Mount Zion? "*The* mount" simply means the one spoken of in the Gospels in connexion with this event. Nor does the epithet "holy" indicate a miracle-loving age. Any Jew would naturally use it of a spot where the glory of the Lord had been revealed (Ex. iii. 5; Josh. v. 15). (2) The force of this argument is not so great as at first sight appears. In the Epistle of Clement of Rome (A.D. 95—100) the same scoffing argument is quoted as condemned by "Scripture" (chap. xxiii.). The "Scripture" is probably not 2 Peter. But we here have proof that this scoffing objection was old enough to have been *written against* before A.D. 95. The kindred error of Hymenæus and Philetus was in existence in St. Paul's lifetime. Besides which, it is not certain that "since the fathers fell asleep" refers to Christians at all. (See Notes on chap. iii. 4.) The argument may be a piece of Sadducism, which had found its way into the Christian Church; the tone of it is not unlike that in Mark xii. 23. (3) The premises here are too vague for so definite a conclusion. To state the premises fairly we must say 2 Peter is addressed *in the main* to all Gentile Christians, and also *in the main* to the same readers as 1 Peter, which is addressed *mainly* to five or six different churches. From such indefinite data no very clean-cut and decided result can be obtained. Moreover, it is open to question whether the idea that the letters of Apostles are the common property of Christians was not in existence in the Apostolic age. The phenomena of the text of the last two chapters of Romans (see Notes there) tend to show that this idea was beginning to arise some years before the traditional date of St. Peter's death. The Epistle to the Ephesians would lead us in the same direction. So that it is doubtful (*a*) whether the idea is implied in 2 Peter; (*b*) whether it was not in existence in St. Peter's lifetime. (4) No objection, probably, has had more effect than this. "The other Scriptures," it is urged, may mean either Old Testament or New Testament writings; in either case, we are face to face with a writer later than the Apostolic age. If Old Testament Scriptures are meant, it is incredible that St. Peter would place Epistles of St. Paul side by side with them as "Scripture." If New Testament Scriptures are meant, this indicates a date at which certain Christian writings had begun to be considered equal in authority to the Old Testament, and this date is later than the death of St. Peter. In the Notes (chap. iii. 16) it is shown that probably not Old Testament, but Christian, writings are meant; not any definite *collection* of writings, but certain well-known documents other than the Epistles of St. Paul just mentioned. We must remember that the Greek words for "other" are sometimes used loosely, and rather illogically, without the two individuals, or two classes, being exactly alike (comp. Luke x. 1; xxiii. 32; John xiv. 16); so that we cannot be sure that the writer means to place these Epistles of St. Paul on precisely the same level with "the other Scriptures." And that "Scripture" was used in the first century as rather a comprehensive term is shown by the passage from Clement of Rome alluded to above, where he quotes (chap. xxiii.) as "Scripture" a passage not found either in the Old or New Testaments. Again, the high authority claimed by Apostles for their own words makes this passage, although unique in the New Testament, quite intelligible. (Comp. Acts xv. 28; 1 Cor. v. 3, 4; 1 Thess. ii. 13.) Perhaps the nearest parallel is 1 Pet. i. 12, where evangelists are placed on the same level with the Old Testament prophets, a very remarkable coincidence between the two Epistles. One more consideration must be urged. The date of St. Peter's death is not certain, and the traditional date may be too early. Several of the objections just considered would be still further weakened if St. Peter's death took place not in the third, but in the fourth quarter of the century.

But besides answering objections, we may observe—(1) that the writer professes to be Simon Peter (chap. i. 1), one whose death Christ foretold (chap. i. 14), a witness of the Transfiguration (chap. i. 16—18), and the writer of the First Epistle (chap. iii. 1); (2) that he speaks with authority (chap. i. 12, 13, 15, 16), yet is not afraid to admit the high authority of prophecy (chap. i. 19); (3) that there is some trace of the conciliatory position between Jewish and Gentile converts which St. Peter occupied between the rigour of St. James and the liberty of St. Paul (chaps. i. 1, 2; iii. 15); (4) that the expression "our beloved brother Paul," so unlike the way in which Clement of Rome, Ignatius, Polycarp, and Clement of Alexandria speak of St. Paul (see Note on chap. iii. 15), is a strong mark of an Apostolic author—a writer of the second century would scarcely find his way back to this; (5) that some striking coincidences between thoughts and expressions in this Epistle and passages in St. Peter's speeches as reported in the Acts exist, and will be pointed out in the Notes. (See Notes on chaps. i. 1; iii. 12.)

On the other hand, no weight can be allowed to the argument that "all motive for forgery is absent." It is quite true that "this Epistle does not support any hierarchical pretensions nor bear upon any of the controversies of a later age." But a motive quite sufficient can be found, viz., to put down with the authority of an Apostle an alarming corruption, both in doctrine and conduct. This motive might have induced excellent men in the primitive Church to write in the name of St. Peter, and the moral sense of the community would not have condemned them. Such personations, purely in the interests of religion and virtue, are neither impossible nor unknown; and the very words "forgery" and "impostor," in reference to such acts and agents in primitive times, are fallacious. We must beware of transferring our own ideas of literary morality to an age in which they were absolutely non-existent.

(*d*) *Internal Evidence: The Contents of the Epistle in relation to the Epistle of St. Jude.*—This subject is discussed in the *Introduction to Jude*. The conclusion there arrived at is that the priority of neither Epistle can be proved, but that the balance inclines decidedly towards the priority of 2 Peter. If the priority of Jude should ever be demonstrated, then we have still more reason for placing the date of St. Peter's death later than A.D. 67 or 68, unless the authenticity of 2 Peter is admitted to be more than doubtful.

The conclusion, then, to which this long discussion leads us is this—the objections to the Epistle are such that, had the duty of fixing the Canon of the New Testament fallen on us, we should scarcely have ventured, on the existing evidence, to include the Epistle; they are not such as to warrant us in reversing the decision of the fourth century, which had evidence that we have not. If modern criticism be the court of appeal to which the judgment of the fourth century is referred, as it has not sufficient reasons for reversing that judgment it can only confirm it. Additional evidence may yet be forthcoming. A Hebrew or Greek text of the *Book of Enoch* might settle the relation between 2 Peter and Jude beyond dispute; and this would clear the way not a little. Meanwhile, we accept the authenticity of the Epistle as, to say the very least, *quite the best working hypothesis*.

II. The Place and Time.—The suggestions as to the place where the Epistle was written are mere conjectures; we have no evidence of any value. As to the date, any time after the writing of the First Epistle may be right; probably not long before the Apostle's martyrdom. The fact that the destruction of Jerusalem is not mentioned is reason for believing that it had not taken place when the letter was written. If it be said that a writer personating St. Peter would have avoided so obvious a blunder, we may reply (1) that these are just the pitfalls into which literary personators in an early age fall; (2) that it is not certain that it would have been a blunder—St. Peter may have been living A.D. 70; (3) that the destruction of Jerusalem would have served the purpose of the letter so well, as an argument (more strong than the Transfiguration) for Christ's return to judgment, as a fulfilment of prophecy on this subject, and as a signal instance of divine vengeance, that no explanation of its omission is so satisfactory as that it had not yet taken place.

III. Object and Contents.—The object of the Epistle is twofold: (1) warning against the seductions of false doctrine and the licentiousness akin to it; (2) exhortation to increase in the grace and knowledge of our Lord Jesus Christ. The basis for both is the same—the certainty of Christ's return to judgment. With true tact, the writer begins and ends with exhortation and encouragement; the warning and denunciation lie in between, and strongly as the latter are worded, terrible as are the metaphors and illustrations employed, even here the gentleness and tenderness of one who knew from experience what tenderness could do for those who had gone the length of "denying even the Master that bought them" (2 Pet. ii. 1; Luke xxii. 61) continually come to the surface, and break the flood of vehement denunciation (chaps. ii. 5, 7—9; iii. 1, 2).

The plan of the contents is easily recognised, and the transitions from one division to another are so natural, that (as remarked at the outset) it is impossible to strike out any portion as spurious and retain the rest.

I.—Introductory.

Address and greeting (chap. i. 1, 2).

II.—Hortatory and Argumentative.

(1) Exhortation to increase in spiritual graces, in order to gain eternal life at Christ's coming (chap. i. 3—11).

(2) Transition to the argumentative part; the purpose of this Epistle stated (chap. i. 12—15).

(3) Basis of the exhortation—the certainty of Christ's coming, which is proved:

(*a*) By the Transfiguration, which was an anticipation of it (chap. i. 16—18).

(*b*) By the utterances of prophets, who have predicted it (chap. i. 19—21).

III.—Warning.

(1) *First Prediction*: false teachers shall have great success and certain ruin (chap. ii. 1—10); their impious practices described (chap. ii. 10—22).

(2) Transition to the second prediction; the purpose of both Epistles stated (chap. iii. 1, 2).

(3) *Second Prediction*: scoffers shall throw doubt on Christ's return (chap. iii. 3, 4); their argument refuted (chap. iii. 5—9).

(4) Basis of the warning—the certainty of Christ's coming (chap. iii. 10).

IV.—Hortatory.

(1) Concluding exhortations (chap. iii. 11—18);

(2) Doxology (chap. iii. 18).

IV. The False Teachers and the Scoffers.—We are probably to regard these as in the main identical; but in spite of the vigorous language in which they are described, it is difficult to say what particular heresy is indicated. As in many of the Old Testament prophecies, the picture is painted in strong, lurid colours; but the outlines are not sufficiently defined to enable us to specify any distinctive characteristics. The spirit of heresy, capable of developing into endless varieties, rather than any one of the varieties themselves, is placed before us. Cavilling, pride, irreverence, impatience of restraints, impatience of mysteries—these form the corrupt atmosphere in which heresies are generated, and these are just the qualities that are depicted here. The indefiniteness of the description has been pointed out by critics on both sides of the question of authenticity. It is a strong argument in favour of an early date for this Epistle. A writer of the second century, with the full-blown Gnosticism of Basilides, Carpocrates, Valentinus, and Marcion around him, could scarcely have divested himself of his experience, and given us, not the details of what he saw and heard, but the germs that had developed into these after a growth of half a century. Historic divination, by means of which the essentials of an earlier age are discovered and separated from what is merely accidental—historic imagination, by means of which these essentials are put together in a life-like picture—are powers of modern growth. The divination of the second century was exercised on the future, not on the past; its imagination on the possibilities of the unseen world, not on the realities of the world of sense. The disagreement of critics as to the time in the second century at which the letter was probably written makes us all the more disposed to doubt whether the second century is right at all. Bleek suggests A.D. 100—150; Mayerhoff, *circ.* A.D. 150; Davidson, *circ.* 170; Schwegler and Semler, A.D. 190—200.

The view here taken of the false teachers and scoffers, that they are the forerunners of the Antinomian heretics of the second century, is confirmed when we turn to St. Paul's Epistles. There we find indications of these evils at a slightly earlier stage. We see him contending against corrupt practices, which were on their road to being established, inasmuch as some tried to justify them on principles which were a caricature of his own teaching. His Christian liberty is stretched to cover the detestable maxim, "Let us do evil that good may come," participation in idolatrous feasts, incestuous marriages, intemperance at love-feasts, &c. (Rom. iii. 8; 1 Cor., *passim*). A self satisfied knowledge is intruding itself (1 Cor. viii. 1—4). The resurrection of the dead is being denied (1 Cor. xv. 12; 2 Tim. ii. 18). In 2 Peter the corrupt practices and the corrupt principles are more definitely combined. St. Peter predicts that still greater abominations than those against which St. Paul wrote will not only be justified, but taught upon principle. Going beyond those who denied the resurrection, men will mock at the coming of Christ and the day of judgment. Thus the false teachers of 2 Peter are just a step nearer to the systematised Antinomianism of the second century than the evil-doers denounced by St. Paul. St. Jude shows us in active operation the mischief of which St. Paul and St. Peter had seen the beginning and foretold the development. Tertullian, Irenæus, and Hippolytus tell us to what hideous proportions and fantastic variety the development eventually progressed.

It is well known that the framers of our Authorised version, while on the whole making an enormous advance on previous English versions, sometimes went back. In some instances the changes they made in the translations on which they worked were the reverse of improvements. Perhaps no portion of the New Testament is more full of cases of this kind than the Second Epistle of St. Peter. In a large number of such cases it will be found that the earlier versions which are superior to the Authorised version are Wiclif's and the Rhemish; and not unfrequently that the version which has led our translators astray is the Genevan. None of these three versions were among those which the translators were instructed to use; and of Wiclif's they probably made very little use; of the other two they made a great deal of use. Wiclif's version and the Rhemish were made from the Latin Vulgate, not from the Greek: so that we have what at first sight seems to be a startling fact, that versions made from a Latin translation are often superior to the best version made from the Greek. The explanation is simple. The Vulgate is a good Latin translation of excellent Greek texts; our version is a good English translation of very defective Greek texts. "The errors in the text of our English Testament inherited from them are considerably more important than the existing errors of translation" (Westcott). The late Dr. Routh, when asked what commentary he considered to be on the whole the best, is said to have answered "The Vulgate." The facts just noticed are a striking illustration of his meaning. In the Notes the renderings of previous versions will often be given, where our translators seem to have adopted an inferior rendering.

[In writing the Introduction and Notes for this Epistle, use has been made of the Commentaries of Alford, Bengel, Brückner's edition of De Wette, Hofmann, Huther, Reuss, Schott, and Wordsworth, together with the Introductions of Bleek and Davidson, and the articles in Smith and Herzog. A much better use might have been made of them had time permitted. But it is only just to the editor and the reader to say, that the commentator on 2 Peter and Jude was asked to undertake the work at very short notice, and to complete it within a very short time. If he is found to have undertaken a task beyond his strength, he must plead in excuse the attraction which the work had for him, and the wish to render help to a far abler but over-worked contributor to this Commentary].

THE SECOND EPISTLE GENERAL OF

PETER

Chap. i. 1, 2. Greeting.

A.D. 66.

CHAPTER I.—(1) Simon Peter, a servant and an apostle of Jesus Christ, to them that have obtained like precious faith with us through the righteousness of God and our Saviour Jesus Christ:

---

(1) **Simon Peter.**—The marginal reading "Symeon" is to be preferred. "Simon" has probably been substituted as being more usual. The Geneva Bible, which our translators unfortunately sometimes follow when it is *misleading*, has "Simeon." "Symeon," of St. Peter, occurs elsewhere only Acts xv. 14, in a speech of the strongly Jewish St. James. As being the more Jewish form of the name, it points to a Jewish Christian as the author; and as being unusual, it shows that the writer, if not the Apostle, is no slavish imitator. As coming from St. Peter, the Apostle of the circumcision, it is natural enough. The differences between this opening and that of 1 Peter are instructive. There, as approaching communities which might seem to belong to St. Paul, he carefully suppresses everything personal; he calls himself merely "Peter," the name which Christ Himself had given him along with his high commission (Matt. xvi. 18), and "Apostle," the title which stated his commission. Here, as coming a second time to those who now know him better (both through his former Epistle and through Silvanus), he adds personal designations. There, as if not venturing to depart greatly from his own peculiar field, he addresses himself mainly to the Jewish converts. Here, with more boldness, the natural result of increased familiarity, he addresses Gentile converts chiefly. (See Note on 1 Pet. i. 1.)

A servant and an apostle.—De Wette suspects a combination of 1 Pet. i. 1 with Jude, verse 1. The coincidence is too slight to argue upon. (See Rom. i. 1 and Note on Jude, verse 1.) The amount of similarity between the opening verses of Jude and those of this Epistle is too small for any conclusions as to the dependence of one on the other. Although the word for "servant" strictly means *slave*, the English version is quite correct. (See on Rom. i. 1.)

To them that have obtained.—The Greek word implies that they have not won it or earned it for themselves, but that it has been allotted to them. Comp. Acts i. 17, where the same word (rare in the New Testament) occurs *in a speech of St. Peter*. (See Note on "godliness," verse 3.) Another coincidence to be noticed is the way in which St. Peter speaks of the Gentile Christians (Acts. xi. 17) when charged with having visited "men uncircumcised," and again (Acts xv. 8—11) at the Council of Jerusalem; both remarkable parallels to this.

Like precious faith with us.—Not that all had an equal amount of faith, which would scarcely be possible; nor that their faith gave all an equal right to salvation, which the Greek could scarcely mean; but that all believed the same precious mysteries. (Comp. 1 Pet. i. 7.) It is delicately implied that "we as well as you have had it allotted to us; it is no credit to us; we are not superior to you." "Us" may mean either the Apostles, or (more probably) the first Christians, as distinct from those converted later, *i.e.*, Jewish as distinct from Gentile Christians. This shows that Gentile converts are chiefly addressed in this Epistle, as Jewish in the First Epistle. Gentiles would be more likely to be doubters respecting Christ's return to judgment, than Jews well acquainted with Hebrew prophecies on the subject. Gentiles also would be more likely than Jews to fall into the excesses denounced in the second chapter, which bear a strong resemblance to the catalogue of heathen vices given by St. Paul in Rom. i. The idea that Christians are the antitype of the chosen people is prominent in St. Peter's writings. (Comp. chap. ii. 1, and 1 Pet. i. 10.) Note that no particular churches are mentioned. The Second Epistle is more "general" or "catholic" in its address than the First. Here again we have a mark of independence. A writer personating St. Peter, and referring to the former Letter (chap. iii. 1), would probably have taken care to make the address of the second letter tally exactly with that of the first.

Through the righteousness.—Better, *in the righteousness*. So Wiclif, Tyndale, and Rheims version. "Righteousness" is variously explained. Perhaps the best interpretation is "fairness, justice." He has no respect of persons, and hence has given to all Christians, early or late, Jew or Gentile, a "like precious faith."

Of God and our Saviour Jesus Christ.—Better, *of our God and* (*our*) *Saviour Jesus Christ*. Here, as in Titus ii. 13 (comp. 2 Thess. i. 12), we are somewhat in doubt as to whether we have one or two Persons of the Trinity mentioned. Rigid grammar would incline us to make "God" and "Saviour" both apply to Christ. But rigid grammar alone is not always the safest guide in interpreting Scripture. The very next verse, independently of other considerations, seems to determine that both the Father and the Son are here mentioned. The mode of expression which causes doubt on the subject, perhaps indicates the writer's perfect belief in the oneness of the Father with the Son. The addition of "Saviour" to the name of Jesus Christ is very frequent in this Epistle (verse 11, chaps. ii. 20; iii. 18; comp. chap. iii. 2). It shows how completely "Jesus" had become a proper name, the exact signification of which was becoming obscured. "Saviour" does not occur in 1 Pet., but the cognate "salvation" does (chaps. i. 5, 9, 10; ii. 2). Both words point onwards to safety from perdition at the last. (Comp. St. Peter's speech, Acts v. 31.)

(2) grace and peace be multiplied unto
you through the knowledge of God, and
of Jesus our Lord, (3) according as his
divine power hath given
unto us all things that
pertain unto life and godli-
ness, through the knowledge of him that
hath called us to [1] glory and virtue:
(4) whereby are given unto us exceeding
great and precious promises: that by
these ye might be partakers of the
divine nature, having escaped the cor-

Chap. i. 3—11. Exhortation to progress in spiritual graces.

[1] Or, *by*.

---

(2) **Grace and peace be multiplied unto you.**—Identical with the last clause of 1 Pet. i. 2, and with no other greeting in any Epistle. What follows here is peculiar to this Epistle, which begins and ends with grace and knowledge. (Comp. chap. iii. 18.)

Through the knowledge.—Better, as before, *in.* The preposition indicates the sphere or element in which the action takes place, or the aspect in which it is contemplated. Tyndale and the Rhemish version have "in." "Knowledge" is not quite strong enough. In the original we have a compound word, which implies fuller, riper, more minute knowledge. But any of these expressions would be a little too strong, as the simple word is a little too weak. The same compound recurs verse 3. It is rare in St. Paul's earlier letters, but is more common in the later ones. This fact, coupled with its appearance here, agrees well with the more contemplative aspect in which the Gospel began gradually to be presented; a change which finds its fullest expression in the transition from the first three Gospels to the fourth. The word is introduced here with telling emphasis; "in the fuller knowledge of God" anticipates the attack that is coming upon the godless speculations of the "false teachers" in chap. ii.

And of Jesus our Lord.—Deliberately added. These false teachers "denied the Lord that bought them" (chap. ii. 1), and promised all kinds of high-sounding benefits to their followers (chap. ii. 18). The Apostle assures his readers that only in fuller knowledge of their Lord can grace and peace be multiplied to them. The combination "Jesus our Lord" is unusual; elsewhere only Rom. iv. 24. Another small indication of independence (see first Note). There should be a full-stop at "Lord;" so Tyndale, Cranmer, and Geneva.

(3—11) Exhortation to progress in spiritual graces in order to win eternal life at Christ's coming. God has given us all we need for salvation; let us profit by it, and show ourselves worthy of it.

(3) **According as.**—Better, *seeing that.* This must not be made to depend on verse 2. In the canonical Epistles the address does not go beyond the blessing. Galatians is the only exception; there a relative clause is added to the blessing; but this is solemnly brought to a close with a doxology, so that the exception is one that almost proves the rule. In Hebrews, James, 1 and 3 John, there is no opening blessing; the remark holds good of all the rest. Verses 3 and 4 are a brief introduction to the direct exhortations contained 5—11. The eagerness with which the writer goes direct to his subject is characteristic of St. Peter's temper.

His divine power.—The pronoun refers to "Jesus our Lord." The adjective occurs in the New Testament in these two verses (3 and 4) only; elsewhere we have the genitive case, "of God," "of the Lord," "of the Father," and the like.

All things that pertain unto.—All that are necessary for the attainment of. He does not give life and godliness in maturity, but supplies us with the means of winning them for ourselves. "All" is emphatic; nothing that is requisite is grudged us, and nothing is our own, it is all the gift of God.

Godliness.—The Greek word occurs Acts iii. 12, in a speech of St. Peter, and four times in this Epistle; elsewhere only in those to Timothy and Titus. It belongs to the phraseology of the later books of the New Testament. "Godliness" is the realisation of God's abiding presence, the fruits of which are reverence and trust: "Thou God seest me;" "I have set God always before me, therefore I cannot fall." It is introduced here, perhaps, in opposition to the godlessness and irreverence of the false teachers. (Comp. 2 Tim. iii. 5.)

Through the knowledge.—Through learning to know God as One who has called us to salvation. (Comp. verse 2.)

To glory and virtue.—Rather, *by glory and virtue;* or perhaps, *by His own glory and virtue,* according to another reading. "To" cannot be correct, whichever of the various readings is the right one. Tyndale, Cranmer, and Rheims have "by;" the error comes from Geneva, which has "unto." "Glory" points to the majesty of God, "virtue" to His activity. "Virtue" as applied to God is unusual, but occurs 1 Pet. ii. 9 (see Note there), a coincidence to be noted. The word is rendered there "praises," but "virtues" is given in the margin. The whole verse is strikingly parallel to this one, though very differently expressed.

(4) **Whereby.**—By God's "glory and virtue;" not by "all things that pertain unto life and godliness," although the latter is possible, and is preferred by some.

Are given unto us.—Better, *He hath given unto us,* viz., He who called us, God. Wiclif, "He gaf;" Rheims, "He hath given."

Promises.—The Greek word occurs here and in chap. iii. 13 only. Its termination indicates the things promised rather than the act of promising. They are "exceeding great," or rather "the greatest," because they contain an earnest of the completion and perfection of the Christian life; they are very "precious," because this earnest is in itself something real, and not mere empty words. Not the promises of the Old Testament are meant, that Christ should come; but those of the New Testament, that Christ should come again. The certainty of Christ's return to reward the righteous and punish the wicked is one of the main subjects of the Epistle.

That by these.—"These" is variously referred (1) to "all things that pertain unto life and godliness," (2) to "glory and virtue," (3) to "promises." The last is most likely, the second least likely to be right. The hope expressed in this verse, and again iii. 13, is distinctly parallel to that in 1 Pet. i. 4.

Ye might be partakers.—Better, *become partakers.* Rheims, "be made." This idea of close relationship to God and escape from corruption is found in 1 Pet. i. 23. The change from the first person plural to the second is easy enough both in Greek and English: by it what is true of all Christians is applied specially to those whom the writer is addressing. We have a similar change in 1 Pet. i. 3, 4; ii. 21, 24.

ruption that is in the world through lust. (5) And beside this, giving all diligence, add to your faith virtue; and to virtue knowledge; (6) and to knowledge temperance; and to temperance patience; and to patience godliness; (7) and to godliness brotherly kindness; and to brotherly kindness charity.

Through lust.—Rather (as in verses 1, 2, 13; chap. ii. 3) *in lust.* It is in lust that the corruption has its root. (Comp. 1 Pet. i. 22.) The word "escaped" indicates that "*bondage* of corruption" (Rom. viii. 21) from which even the Christian is not wholly free, so long as he is in the body; and in which others are hopelessly held. A comparison of this last clause with chap. iii. 13 will confirm us in the view that "by these" refers to the "promises." We see there what the things promised are. Instead of merely "having escaped" evil, "we, *according to His promise,* look for" better things; for, from "the corruption that is in the world in lust" we turn to "new heavens and a new earth, wherein dwelleth righteousness." There should be no full-stop at the end of this verse; the sentence continues unbroken from the beginning of verse 3 to the end of verse 7.

(5) **And beside this.**—Rather, *and for this very reason.* The Authorised version is quite indefensible, and is the more to be regretted because it obscures a parallel between this and 1 Peter. There also we are exhorted to regulate our conduct by God's (1 Pet. i. 15; ii. 1, 5). [In the Notes on verses 5—8 use has been made of addresses *On some Traits in the Christian Character.* Camb. 1876.]

Giving all diligence.—Literally, *bringing in all diligence to the side of* God's gifts and promises; making your contribution in answer to His. He has made all things possible for you; but they are not yet done, and you must labour diligently to realise the glorious possibilities opened out to you.

Add to your faith virtue.—Rather, *in your faith supply virtue.* The error comes from Geneva; all other English versions are right. The interesting word inadequately translated "add" occurs again in verse 11, and elsewhere only in 2 Cor. ix. 10; Gal. iii. 5; Col. ii. 19. Everywhere but here it is translated "minister." Sufficient explanation of the word will be found in Notes on 2 Cor. ix. 10 and Gal. iii. 5. The notion of rendering a service that is expected of one in virtue of one's position fits in admirably here. God *gives;* His blessings and promises come from His free undeserved bounty; man *renders, supplies, furnishes.* that which, considering the benefits which he has received, is fairly required of him. Note that we are not told to supply faith; that comes from God (Eph. ii. 8), and the Apostle assumes that his readers possess it. "Virtue" is that which is recognised by all men as excellent; the excellence of man as man. Heathen moralists had drawn a noble picture of what man ought to be; the gospel gave the command to realise a yet nobler ideal, and also gave the power by which it could be realised.

And to virtue knowledge.—As before, *and in your virtue* [*supply*] *knowledge—i.e.,* in the virtue which each of you possesses. Virtue for each individual is the excellence corresponding to the talents committed to him. The word for "knowledge" here is not the compound used in verses 2 and 3, but the simple substantive. It means, therefore, knowledge that still admits of growth, not yet ripe or complete. It is worth noting that the word for *absolute* knowledge, *epistêmê,* does not occur in the New Testament. By "knowledge" here is probably meant spiritual discernment as to what is right and what is wrong in all things; the right object, the right way, the right time.

(6) **And to knowledge temperance; and to temperance patience; and to patience godliness.** — *And in your knowledge* [*supply*] *self-control, and in your self-control, patience, and in your patience, godliness.* In other words, your discerning between good and evil must lead to avoiding the evil and choosing the good—*i.e.,* to the control of your own lawless propensities; and in restraining these you must endure difficulties patiently; and your patience must not be the stolid defiance of the savage, or the self-reliant and self-satisfied endurance of the Stoic, but a humble and loving trust in God. Virtue and knowledge are energetic and progressive; they are exercised in developing the powers implanted in us. Self-control and patience are restrictive and disciplinary; they are exercised in checking and regulating the conflicting claims of many co-existing powers, so as to reduce all to harmony. There is special point in "self-control" being placed as the consequence of "knowledge." The false teachers would insist that knowledge led to liberty, which with them meant emancipation from all control whatever. Self-mastery is to the world at large the opposite of liberty; to the Christian it is another name for it—that service which is perfect freedom. Patience to the world is to accept loss and suffering; to the Christian it is to win the best of prizes—"in your patience ye shall win your souls."

(7) **And to godliness brotherly kindness; and to brotherly kindness charity.**—*And in your godliness* [*supply*] *love of the brethren, and in your love of the brethren, charity.* In other words, your godliness must not be selfish and solitary, but social and Christian; for he who loveth God must love his brother also (1 John iv. 20, 21). And though "charity begins at home" with "them who are of the household of faith," it must not end there, but reach out to all men, whether Christians or not. (Comp. 1 Thess. iii. 12; Gal. vi. 10.) The translation "brotherly kindness" is a little to be regretted; it obscures the exact meaning of the word, and also the fact that the very same word is used in 1 Pet. i. 22. "Love of the brethren" means love of Christians as such, as members of the same great family, as God's adopted children. "Charity" means love of men as such, as creatures made in the likeness of God, as souls for which Christ died. The word for "charity" is emphatically Christian love; not mere natural benevolence.

Each in this noble chain of virtues prepares the way for the next, and is supplemented and perfected by it. It begins with faith, and it ends (like St. Paul's list of virtues, Col. iii. 12—14) with charity. But we must not insist too strongly upon the order in the series, as being either logically or chronologically necessary. It is a natural order that is here given, but not the only one. These three verses are the First Epistle condensed. Each one of the virtues mentioned here is represented quite distinctly in 1 Peter: virtue, i. 13; knowledge, iii. 15; self-control, i. 14; ii. 11; patience, i. 6; ii. 21; godliness, i. 15, 16; iii. 4; love of the brethren, i. 22; iii. 8; charity, iv. 8. The list of virtues given in the *Epistle of Barnabas* ii. runs thus: —*Faith,* fear, *patience,* long-suffering, *temperance,* wisdom, prudence, science, *knowledge.* The very slight

(8) For if these things be in you, and
abound, they make *you that ye shall*
neither *be* barren nor unfruitful in the
knowledge of our Lord Jesus Christ.
(9) But he that lacketh these things is
blind, and cannot see afar off, and hath
forgotten that he was purged from
his old sins. (10) Wherefore the rather,
brethren, give diligence to make your
calling and election sure: for if ye
do these things, ye shall never fall:
(11) for so an entrance shall be minis-

---

amount of similarity affords no ground for supposing that the writer was acquainted with 2 Peter.

(8) **For if these things be in you.**—First reason for the preceding exhortation—the benefit of having these graces. The original of "be in you" is a strong expression, implying permanent and not mere momentary existence.

And abound.—Strictly, *and multiply* or *increase.* (Comp. Rom. v. 20, and Note there; vi. 1; 2 Thess. i. 3, where the same inadequate translation occurs in the Authorised version.)

Neither be barren nor unfruitful.—Better, *not idle nor yet unfruitful.* Cranmer, Tyndale, and Geneva all have "ydle." The Greek word literally means "without work"—*i.e.*, doing nothing, as "unfruitful" means producing nothing. "That ye shall be" is not in the Greek, and is not needed. The two adjectives "idle" and "unfruitful" exactly correspond to the two verbs "be in you" and "increase." If these things be in you, you will be morally active; if they increase, you will be morally productive.

In the knowledge.—Rather, *unto the knowledge;* the fuller, more advanced knowledge of verses 2, 3, and chap. ii. 20. This is the goal towards which all these virtues tend, the fruit which they tend to produce—the perfect knowledge of Christ. Those who are the most like Christ in their lives have the fullest knowledge of Him in this world, a knowledge to be perfected in the next world, when, purified from sin, "we shall see Him as He is." This clause, without the negatives, accurately describes the condition of the false teachers whom the Apostle has in view. They were both "idle and unfruitful unto the knowledge of our Lord Jesus Christ." They neither did nor produced anything that in any degree advanced such knowledge either in themselves or others. The list of virtues just commended (verses 5—7) constitutes a solemn indictment against them. Practical infidelity leading to vicious conduct; a hollow and pretentious philosophy leading to libertinism; an impatience of control leading to utter godlessness; a selfish indifference to the claims of those nearest to them ending in absolute heartlessness towards all men—such is the charge brought against them, by implication here, directly in chap. ii.

(9) **But he that lacketh.**—Rather, *for he that lacketh.* Geneva and Rheims have "for." The "for" introduces the second reason for the exhortation to furnish forth all these graces—viz., the evil of not having them. The Greek implies absence of possession in any degree, not merely absence of permanent possession. (See first Note on verse 8.)

Is blind.—We might have expected "will be idle and unfruitful, &c.," but the writer is not content with merely emphasizing what has just been said, after the manner of St. John (*e.g.*, chap. i. 3; 1 John i. 5; ii. 4, 27, 28; iv. 2, 3, 6); he puts the case in a new way, with a new metaphor equally applicable to the subject of knowledge. Note that he does not say "*will* be blind," but "*is* blind." The very fact of his possessing none of these graces shows that he has no eye for them.

Cannot see afar off.—The Greek word means literally *closing the eyes;* and the point seems to be, not wilful shutting of the eyes (those who *won't* see), but involuntary and partial closing, as in the case of *short-sighted* people; in a spiritual sense, those who have only a very hazy apprehension of the objects of belief and of the bearing which their beliefs should have on their conduct. There is, therefore, no anti-climax, a weak expression following a strong one, but a simple explanation, a more definite term following a general one; it explains what kind of blindness is meant. The special kind of short-sightedness here indicated is that of one who just sees that he is a member of a Christian community, but perceives neither the kind of life that one who has been purged from heathen enormities is bound to lead, nor the kind of life which alone can win an entrance into Christ's kingdom. The short-sightedness of not being able to see beyond this present world is probably not expressed here.

And hath forgotten.—Literally, *having received* or *incurred forgetfulness*—a unique expression in the New Testament. The phrase does not necessarily imply that the forgetfulness is voluntary; it is the inevitable result of wilful neglect—the neglect to cultivate Christian virtues. The forgetfulness is not the cause of the shortsightedness, but a phase of it.

His old sins.—Those committed before he was "purged" in baptism (1 Cor. vi. 11; Eph. v. 26; 1 Pet. iii. 21).

(10) **Wherefore the rather.**—Exhortation resumed, with still more earnestness, for the reasons just stated in verses 8 and 9. The direct address, "brethren," is a mark of this increased earnestness, and also assures those addressed that they are not included among the mere nominal Christians described in the preceding verse.

Give diligence.—Recalling "bringing all diligence" in verse 5.

Calling and election.—By God into the kingdom of heaven. "Calling" and "election" are two aspects of the same fact, "calling" referring to God's invitation, "election" to the distinction which this invitation makes between those who are called and those who are not. "Election" is one of St. Paul's words. One of the best MSS. and several versions insert "by means of your works," which gives the right sense, although the words are wanting in authority. It is by following the injunctions given (verses 5—7) that our election is made secure. God calls us to salvation (verse 3), selects us from the heathen; it is for each one of us to respond to the call, and thus ratify His choice.

If ye do these things.—Showing that the making sure of our election is not a single act, but multiform, viz., the furnishing the graces commended (verses 5—7).

Never fall.—The same word is translated "offend" (Jas. ii. 10; iii. 2); and "stumble" (Rom. xi. 11). It means to knock one's foot and stumble. The man who has acquired these graces has his path freed from many stumbling-blocks, and his vision cleared to see and avoid the rest.

(11) **An entrance shall be ministered unto you.**—"Ministered" is the passive of the same verb that is translated "add" in verse 5, and is probably

tered unto you abundantly into the
everlasting kingdom of our Lord and
Saviour Jesus Christ. (12) Wherefore
Chap. i. 12—15. Transition from exhortation to argument. I will not be negligent
to put you always in
remembrance of these
things, though ye know
them, and be established in the present
truth. (13) Yea, I think it meet, as
long as I am in this tabernacle, to
stir you up by putting *you* in remem-
brance; (14) knowing that shortly I
must put off *this* my tabernacle, even
as our Lord Jesus Christ hath shewed
a John xxi. 18. me.[a] (15) Moreover I will endeavour that
ye may be able after my decease to have
these things always in remembrance.
(16) For we have not followed cunningly

---

chosen to answer to verse 5. "Supply these graces, and an entrance into the kingdom shall be abundantly supplied to you"—"abundantly," *i.e.*, with a warm welcome, as to a son coming home in triumph; not a bare grudging admission, as to a stranger.

Thus ends the first main section of the Epistle, which contains the substance of the whole. Its gentle earnestness and obvious harmony with the First Epistle have made some critics ready to admit its genuineness, who throw doubt on much of the rest. But if it stands it carries with it all the rest. Change of style is amply accounted for by change to a new and exciting subject; and the links between the parts are too strong to be severed by any such considerations. (See opening observations in the *Introduction.*)

The first sections of the two Epistles should be carefully compared. In both we find these thoughts pervading the opening exhortation: Be earnest, be active; for (1) so much has been done for you, and (2) there is such a rich reward in store for you. (Comp. especially the conclusions of the two sections, 1 Pet. i. 13 with 2 Pet. i. 10, 11.)

(12—15) Transition from the exhortation just concluded to the argument that follows, closely and naturally connected with both.

(12) **I will not be negligent.**—According to the right reading, *I shall be sure to;* because on your doing these things depends your entrance into Christ's kingdom.

Though ye know them.—We find the same affectionate delicacy in Rom. xv. 14, 15 (see Notes there); 1 John ii. 21; Jude, verse 5.

And be established in the present truth.—Comp. "This is the true grace of God wherein ye stand" (1 Pet. v. 12), to which it is not impossible that this verse refers; the "always" here looks like a half apology for what his readers might think needless repetition. "The present truth" is an instance of a translation being misleading through its very literalness. The three Greek words are exactly represented, but the sense is misrepresented. The meaning is, not the truth that we are now discussing, the truth before us, but the truth of the gospel that is come unto you (Col. i. 5, 6), and is present with you: "the faith once for all delivered unto the saints" (Jude, verse 3).

(13) **Yea, I think it meet.**—Better, *But I think it right.* So Rheims; Tyndale and Cranmer have "notwithstanding." The meaning is, "but (so far from my writing being unnecessary) I think it right," &c.

In this tabernacle.—The comparison of the human body to a dwelling is common in all literatures, and the temporary nature of a tent makes it specially appropriate. (Comp. 2 Cor. v. 1.)

By putting you in remembrance.—Better, *in putting you.* The stirring up consists *in* the reminding. (See verses 1, 2, 4; also chap. iii. 1, where the same phrase occurs.)

(14) **Knowing that shortly I must put off this my tabernacle.**—This is rather wide of the mark. Among English versions Wiclif alone is right. The meaning is, *Knowing as I do that the putting off of my tabernacle will be done swiftly* (comp. chap. ii. 1)—*i.e.*, will soon be over when it once begins. The point is, not that the writer believes himself to be near his end, but that his end would be such as to allow of no death-bed exhortations; what he has to say must be said in good time, for Christ had told him that his death would be a violent one (John xxi. 18). Some of those who have taken the passage in the sense of the Authorised version have supposed a special revelation to be implied in the last half of the verse. But without any revelation an old man might know that his end must soon come; and Christ had already told him that it should come when he began to be old. "The putting off of my tabernacle" involves rather a mixture of metaphors; we have a similar mixture in Col. v. 1—4. The word for "putting off" occurs nowhere but here and 1 Pet. iii. 21; but the coincidence is not one on which much stress can be laid.

Hath shewed me.—More strictly, *shewed me.* The substitution of perfect for aorist is here objectionable, as it obscures the reference to a definite moment in the Apostle's life. If the reference were to John xxi. 18, this would be at once fatal to the authenticity of our Epistle; for of course no part of St. John's Gospel, and least of all the last chapter, was written during the life of St. Peter. But if the reference be to the event *narrated* in John xxi. 18, then that narrative confirms what is said here, this being a prior and independent allusion to the same occurrence. In this case we have strong evidence of the authenticity of St. Peter.

(15) **Moreover I will endeavour.**—The verse requires re-arranging. "Always" (or better, *at all times*) belongs to "may be able," not to "have in remembrance;" and perhaps "moreover" is not quite right. Better, *But I will endeavour that ye may at all times also* (as well as now) *have it in your power after my decease to remember these things.* To what does this declaration point? The simplest answer is, to his writing this letter, which they might keep and read whenever they liked. (Comp. verse 13.) Other suggestions are—to his having copies of this letter distributed; or, writing other letters; or, instructing St. Mark to write his Gospel; or, commissioning "faithful men" to teach these things. There seems to be nothing either for or against these conjectures. It is a coincidence worth noting that, with the Transfiguration in his mind (verses 16—18), he uses, in close succession, two words connected in St. Luke's account of the Transfiguration (Luke ix. 31, 33)—"decease" and "tabernacle."

(16—21) The certainty of Christ's coming again is the basis of these exhortations; and that certainty is proved (1) by the Transfiguration, which was an

devised fables, when we made known unto you the power and coming of our Lord Jesus Christ, but were eyewitnesses of his majesty.
(17) For he received from God the Father honour and glory, when there came such a voice to him from the excellent glory, This is my beloved Son, in whom I am well pleased.
(18) And this voice which came from heaven we heard, when we were

Chap. i. 16—21. The certainty of Christ's coming the basis of these exhortations.

anticipation of His coming again in glory; (2) by the utterances of the prophets who predicted it.

(16) **For we have not followed.**—More literally, *For we did not follow,* or, *It was not by following out, &c., that.* "For" introduces the reason for "I will endeavour" above. The word for "follow," or "follow out," occurs again in chap. ii. 2, 15, and nowhere else in the New Testament.

Cunningly devised fables.—We cannot be sure that any in particular are meant, whether heathen, Jewish, or Christian; the negative makes the statement quite general. Various things, however, have been suggested as possibly indicated—heathen mythology, Jewish theosophy, Gnostic systems (as yet quite in their infancy in Simon Magus, St. Peter's adversary), and Apocryphal Gospels. Probably some elements in the doctrine of the false teachers are alluded to; something analogous to the "feigned words" of chap. ii. 3. There is reason for believing that the particular elements in their teaching thus incidentally condemned were of *Jewish* origin. If this conjecture be correct, then St. Peter is here dealing with errors similar to those condemned by St. Paul (1 Tim. i. 4; 2 Tim. iv. 4; Tit. i. 14—the only other passages in which the word "fables" occurs). And in this case much light is thrown on some of the marked peculiarities of this Epistle and that of St. Jude, viz., the fondness of both writers for the oldest, and sometimes the most obscure, passages of Old Testament history, as well as for some strange portions of uncanonical and apocryphal tradition. They were fighting these seducers with their own weapons; difficult passages of Scripture and tradition, which these men had worked up into a system of pernicious mysticism, St. Peter and St. Jude proved to be altogether of a different meaning, and to tell against the very doctrines that they were employed to support.

When we made known unto you.—It is difficult to determine to what this refers. It is erroneous to suppose that the phrase necessarily implies personal communication by word of mouth. In the First Epistle the Apostle wrote to congregations not personally acquainted with him; and we have no reason for assuming that he had visited them since. "When we made known" may possibly refer to the First Epistle, against which supposition the plural "we" is not conclusive. Or a written Gospel—and, if so, the one with which St. Peter is commonly connected, viz., that of St. Mark—may be in the Apostle's mind. But the simplest explanation is that he refers to the Apostolic teaching generally.

The power and coming.—The *power* conferred upon Christ after being glorified in His passion and resurrection, and his *coming* again to judgment. (Comp. chap. iii. 4; Matt. xxiv. 3, 27; 1 Cor. xv. 23; &c., &c., where the same Greek word is used.) In this power He will come again. His first coming at the Incarnation would neither be the usual meaning of the word nor would suit the context.

But were eyewitnesses.—More literally, *but by having been made eye-witnesses.* "It was not by following fables that we made known to you His power and coming, but by having been admitted eye-witnesses." The word for "eye-witness" is sometimes a technical term for one who was admitted to the highest grade of initiation in the Eleusinian mysteries. This meaning would be very applicable here; but it may be doubted whether St. Peter would be familiar with this use of the word. It occurs nowhere else in the New Testament. The kindred verb, "to be an eye-witness," occurs in 1 Pet. ii. 12; iii. 2, and nowhere else—a coincidence worth noting. The words of another witness of the Transfiguration, "And we beheld His glory," &c. (John i. 14), should be compared with the passage before us.

Of his majesty.—At the Transfiguration, which was a foretaste and an earnest of the glory of His second coming. This is St. Peter's view of it; and that it is the correct one is perhaps shown by the Gospels themselves. All three accounts of the Transfiguration are preceded by the declaration, "Verily I say unto you, there be some standing here, which shall not taste of death, till they see the Son of man coming in his kingdom," or similar words (Matt. xvi. 28; Mark ix. 1; Luke ix. 27). Apparently the Transfiguration was regarded by Christ Himself as in *some* sense the coming of the Son of man.

(17) **For he received.**—Literally, *For having received.* The sentence is unfinished, owing to the long dependent clause, "when there came . . . well pleased." The natural ending would be, "He had us as His attendants to hear it," or something of that kind.

Honour and glory.—Both refer to the voice from heaven. To make "honour" refer to the voice, and "glory" to the light shining from Christ's body, about which nothing has been said, is forced and unnatural.

When there came such a voice to him.—Better, *in that a voice was borne to Him speaking thus.* The expression "a voice was borne to Him" is peculiar, and occurs nowhere else. The Greek for "the grace that is to be brought to you" (1 Pet. i. 13) is parallel to it, and is another small coincidence worth noting. Note also that the writer has not slavishly followed any of the three accounts of the Transfiguration, which a forger might be expected to do. A genuine witness, knowing that he is on firm ground, can afford to take his own line; a "claimant" must carefully learn and follow the lines of others.

From the excellent glory.—Rather, *by the excellent glory*—another unique expression. The preposition "by" almost compels us to reject the interpretation that either the bright cloud or heaven itself is meant. It is rather a periphrasis for God. In Deut. xxxiii. 26, God is called by the LXX., "the Excellent of the sky."

This is my beloved Son, . . .—The Greek is almost the same as in St. Matthew's account (chap. xvii. 5); but "hear him" is omitted, and for "in Whom" we here have, "unto Whom" which can scarcely be brought into the English sentence. The meaning is "*unto Whom* my good pleasure came and on Whom it abides." (Comp. Matt. xii. 18, and Clem., *Hom.* III. liii.)

(18) **And this voice which came from heaven we heard.**—Rather, *And this voice we heard borne from heaven*: We were ear-witnesses of the voice

with him in the holy mount. (19) We have also a more sure word of prophecy; whereunto ye do well that ye take heed, as unto a light that shineth in a dark place, until the day dawn, and the day star arise in your hearts: (20) knowing this first, that no prophecy of the scripture is of any private interpretation.

---

coming from heaven, as we were eye-witnesses of His majesty. It was no vision, it was no hallucination. We all heard, and we all saw; so that I have the highest authority for what I would now impress upon you. A voice which I myself heard borne from heaven to earth, in the midst of glory which I myself saw, foretelling the glory that is yet to come.

In the holy mount.—It is, perhaps, not even "partly right" to say that the epithet "holy" indicates a view of the event later than that of the Evangelists, and points to a miracle-loving age. Rather, it indicates a view many centuries older than the Evangelists—that wherever God had specially manifested Himself was "holy ground" (Ex. iii. 5; Josh. v. 15. Comp. Gen. xxviii. 16, 17; Ex. xix. 12; Acts vii. 33.) The expression would be natural to any Jew speaking of the Transfiguration. (See *Introduction*, I. c.)

(19) **We have also a more sure word of prophecy.**—Rather, *And we have the prophetic word more sure* (so Rheims alone); or, *And we have, as something more sure, the prophetic word*, as a second proof of the truth of my teaching respecting Christ's coming. The expression, "the prophetic word," occurs nowhere else in the New Testament. "The Scripture" given below (Note on chap. iii. 4), as quoted by Clement of Rome, is quoted again in the so-called Second Epistle of Clement (chap. xi.) as "the prophetic word." The quotation in both cases is probably from some uncanonical book of prophecies. Here the expression means the whole body of prophecy respecting the subject in hand; but the meaning of the whole sentence is not quite clear. It may mean (i.) that the Transfiguration has made prophecies more sure, for we who were there have thus witnessed their fulfilment. In this case, however, we should have expected something more than "and" to introduce the statement, such as "and hence," "and thus," "whereby," &c. Or it may mean (ii.) that in the prophetic word we have something more sure than the voice from heaven. Here a simple "and" is natural enough; and the *word* of prophecy is suitably compared with the *voice* from heaven. But how can the word of prophets be more sure than the voice of God? In itself it cannot be so; but it may be so regarded (1) in reference to those who did not hear, but only heard of, the voice from heaven; (2) in reference to the subject in hand. (1) For the readers of this Epistle the many utterances of a long line of prophets, expounded by a school of teachers only second to the prophets themselves, might easily be "more sure" evidence than the narrative of a single writer; and "if they heard not Moses and the prophets, neither would they be persuaded" by the report of a voice from heaven. (2) The Transfiguration, though an earnest of Christ's future glory, was not so clear a promise of it as the express words of prophecy. If this latter interpretation be right, we have another mark of authenticity. A forger would be likely to magnify his own advantage in hearing the voice from heaven over the ordinary proofs open to every one. In any case, the coincidence with 1 Pet. i. 10—12 must not be overlooked. (Comp. also St. Peter's speech, Acts iii. 20, 21).

Whereunto ye do well that ye take heed.—Or, *and ye do well in giving heed to it*—a gentle mode of exhortation, by assuming that the thing urged is being done. The exhortation is quite in harmony with 1 Pet. i. 10. We have a similar construction in 2 Pet. ii. 10, "Do not tremble in speaking evil."

A light that shineth.—Better, *a lamp that shineth.* Prophecy, like the Baptist, is a "lamp that is lighted and shineth," preparatory to the Light. (See Note on John v. 35.) Theophilus, Bishop of Antioch, *circ.* A.D. 170, has (*Autolycus* II. xiii.) "His word, *shining as a lamp* in a chamber;" too slight a parallel to this passage to be relied upon as evidence that Theophilus knew our Epistle. (See below, second Note on verse 21.)

In a dark place.—This translation is somewhat doubtful. The word rendered "dark" occurs here only in the New Testament, and its usual meaning is "dry." From "dry" we pass easily through "rough" to "dirty," meanings which the word has elsewhere (comp. the Latin *squalidus*); but the passage from "dirty" to "dark" is less easy, and there is lack of authority for it. "In a *waste* place" would perhaps be safer; and the image would then be that prophecy is like camp-fires in the desert, which may keep one from going utterly astray, till sunrise frees one from difficulty. The "waste place" is either the wilderness of this world or the tangled life of the imperfect Christian.

Until the day dawn.—Literally, *until the day beam through* the gloom. Here, again, the meaning may be two-fold: (1) Christ's return in glory to illumine the wilderness of this world, to clear off its obscurities, and show the way through its mazes; or (2) the clearer vision of the purified Christian, whose eye is single and his whole body full of light. (Comp. 1 John ii. 8.) No comma at dawn; "in your hearts" belongs to *both* "dawn" and "arise," if to either.

And the day star arise.—An amplification of "until the day dawn." "Day star" occurs nowhere else in the New Testament. Christ calls Himself "the bright morning star" (Rev. xxii. 16).

In your hearts.—It is difficult to determine to what these words belong. The Greek admits of three constructions: (1) with "take heed"; (2) with "dawn" and "arise"; (3) with "knowing this first." The last is not probable. Perhaps "and ye do well in giving heed to it in your hearts" is best—*i.e.*, let it influence your lives, not receive a mere intellectual attention.

(20) **Knowing this first.**—The participle belongs to "take heed" in verse 19. "First" means "first of all" (1 Tim. ii. 1), not "before I tell you." In studying prophecy this is the first thing to be borne in mind.

Is of any private interpretation.—Better, *comes to be*, or *becomes of private interpretation.* The word rendered "interpretation" occurs nowhere else in the New Testament; but the cognate verb occurs in Mark iv. 34, where it is translated "expound." (See Note there.) There can be little doubt that "interpretation," or "solution," is the right rendering here, although others have been suggested. The main question however, is the meaning of the word rendered "private," which may also mean "its own." Hence three explanations are possible. The term may refer (1) to the recipients of the prophecies—that we may not expound prophecy according to our own fancy; or (2) to the utterers of the prophecies—that the prophets had not

(21) For the prophecy came not in old
time[1] by the will of man: but holy men
of God spake *as they were* moved by the
Holy Ghost.

CHAPTER II.—(1) But there were
false prophets also among the people,
even as there shall be false
teachers among you, who
privily shall bring in damnable
heresies, even denying
the Lord that bought them, and

[1] Or, *at any time.*

A.D. 66.

Chap. ii. 1–3. First prediction: False teachers shall arise.

---

the power of expounding their own prophecies; or (3) to the prophecies themselves—that no prophecy comes to be of its own interpretation, *i.e.*, no prophecy explains itself. The guide to the right explanation is verse 21, which gives the reason *why* "no prophecy of the scripture," &c. This consideration excludes (3); for verse 21 yields no sense as showing why prophecy does not interpret itself. Either of the other two explanations may be right. (1) If prophecy came "by the will of man," then it might be interpreted according to man's fancy. But it did not so come; consequently the interpretation must be sought elsewhere—viz., at the same source from which the prophecy itself proceeded. (2) If the prophets spoke just as they pleased, they would be the best exponents of what they meant. But they spoke under divine influence, and therefore need not know the import of their own words. Prophecy must be explained by prophecy and by history, not by the individual prophet. The whole body of prophecy, "the prophetic word" (verse 19), is our lamp in the wilderness, not the private *dicta* of any one seer. In modern phraseology, interpretation must be comparative and scientific. This view is strengthened by comparing 1 Pet. i. 10—12, where it is stated that the prophets did not know how or when their own predictions would be fulfilled. Possibly this passage is meant to refer to 1 Pet. i. 10—12, and if so, we have a mark of genuineness; a forger would have made the reference more clear. If the coincidence is accidental, this also points in the same direction; in any case, the coincidence is worth noting.

(21) **For the prophecy came not in old time.**—Rather, *For prophecy was never sent*, or *brought*. Wiclif and Rheims alone have "brought"; all the rest "came." The verb is the same as that used of the voice from heaven (verses 17 and 18), and also in this verse for "moved," so that there is a telling antithesis, difficult to preserve in English. Prophecy was not brought in by men; but men were brought to utter it by the Spirit. (Comp. 2 John, verse 10.) The rendering in the margin is right—"not *at any time*," rather than "not *in old time*." "Not at any time" = "never," which both Tyndale and Cranmer have; Wiclif has "not ony time." The erroneous "in old time" comes from Geneva.

But holy men of God . . .—The Greek is uncertain. A reading of very high authority would give us, *But men spoke from God moved by the Holy Ghost.* This is probably to be preferred. Men spoke not out of their own hearts, but as commissioned by God; not "by the will of man," but under the influence of the Holy Spirit. (Comp. St. Peter's speech at the election of Matthias, and again in Solomon's Porch, Acts i. 16; iii. 18.) The word for "moved" is a strong one, meaning "borne along," as a ship before the wind (Acts xxvii. 16,17). Theophilus of Antioch (*Autolycus*, II. ix.) writes "men of God, moved (or, *filled*) by the Holy Ghost, and becoming prophets, inspired and made wise by God Himself, became taught of God." Here, again, the parallel is too slight to be relied on as evidence that Theophilus was acquainted with this Epistle. (See above, third Note on verse 19.) The same may be said of a passage in Hippolytus (*Antichrist*, ii.), "These fathers were furnished with the Spirit and largely honoured by the Word Himself . . . . and when moved by Him the Prophets announced what God willed. For they spake not of their own power, neither did they declare what pleased themselves, &c. &c."

Some have fancied that these last three verses (19—21) savour of Montanism, and are evidence of the late origin of the Epistle. But what is said here of the gift of prophecy is not more than we find elsewhere in the New Testament (Matt. i. 22; ii. 15; Acts i. 16; iii. 18); and in the Old Testament (Num. xi. 17, 25, 29; 1 Sam. x. 6, 10; xix. 20, 23; Jer. i. 5—7). Montanists used much stronger language, as readers of Tertullian know. With them prophecy was ecstasy and frenzy; prophets ceased to be men—their reason left them, and they became mere instruments on which the Spirit played. The wording of these verses points to an age previous to Montanism. A Montanist would have said more; an opponent of Montanism would have guarded himself against Montanist misconstruction.

II.

By a perfectly natural transition, we pass to an entirely different subject—from exhortation to show forth Christian graces to a warning against corrupt doctrine. True prophets (chap. i. 21) suggest false prophets, and false prophets suggest false teachers. On the character of the false teachers here attacked see *Introduction*, IV. There are several prophecies in the New Testament similar to the one contained in this and the next chapter (Acts xx. 28—31; 2 Thess. ii. 3—7; 1 Tim. iv. 1—7; 2 Tim. iii. 1—9; iv. 3, 4; comp. 1 John ii. 18; iv. 3). Those in 2 Thess. and 2 Tim. iii. are specially worthy of comparison, as containing, like the present chapter, a mixture of future and present. (See *Introduction*, I. *c*, *γ*.) The fervour and impetuosity with which the writer attacks the evil before him are thoroughly in harmony with St. Peter's character. (Comp. Notes on Jude throughout.)

FIRST PREDICTION: False teachers shall have great success and certain ruin (verses 1—10).

(1) **But there were false prophets also.**—To bring out the contrast between true and false prophets more strongly, the clause that in meaning is secondary has been made primary in form. The *meaning* is, "There shall be false teachers among you, as there were false prophets among the Jews;" the *form* is, "But (in contrast to the true prophets just mentioned) there were false prophets as well, even as," &c.

Shall be false teachers among you.—We must add "also." With this view of Christians as the antitype of the chosen people comp. 1 Pet. ii. 9. The word for "false teachers" occurs here only. It is probably analogous to "false witnesses," and means those who teach what is false, rather than to "false Christs," in which case it would mean pretending to be teachers when they are not. "False prophets" has both meanings—sham prophets and prophesying lies. Justin Martyr, about A.D. 145 (*Trypho*, lxxxii.), has "Just as there were false prophets contemporaneous with your holy prophets" (he is addressing a Jew), "so are there

bring upon themselves swift destruction.
(2) And many shall follow their pernicious[1]
ways; by reason of whom the way of
truth shall be evil spoken of. (3) And
through covetousness shall they with
feigned words make merchandise of
you: whose judgment now of a long
time lingereth not, and their damnation

[1] Or, *lascivious ways*, as some copies read.

now many false teachers amongst us." Another possible reference to this Epistle in Justin is given below on chap. iii. 8. As they occur close together, they seem to render it probable that Justin knew our Epistle. "There shall be false teachers among you, who privily shall bring in heresies of destruction," is quoted in a homily attributed, on doubtful authority, to Hippolytus. (See below, on chap. iii. 3.)

Privily shall bring in.—Comp. Jude, verse 4, and Gal. ii. 4; and see Notes in both places. Comp. also the *Shepherd* of Hermas, *Sim.* VIII. vi. 5.

Damnable heresies.—Rather, *parties* (*full*) *of destruction* (Phil. i. 28), "whose end is destruction" (Phil. iii. 19). Wiclif and Rheims have "sects of perdition." "Damnable heresies" comes from Geneva—altogether a change for the worse. The Greek word *hairesis* is sometimes translated "sect" in our version (Acts v. 17; xv. 5; xxiv. 5), sometimes "heresy" (Acts xxiv. 14; 1 Cor. xi. 19; Gal. v. 20). Neither word gives quite the true meaning of the term in the New Testament, where it points rather to divisions than doctrines, and always to parties inside the Church, not to sects that have separated from it. The Greek word for "destruction" occurs six times in this short Epistle, according to the inferior texts used by our translators (in the best texts five times), and is rendered by them in no less than five different ways: "damnable" and "destruction" in this verse; "pernicious ways," verse 2; "damnation," verse 3; "perdition," chap. iii. 7; "destruction," chap. iii. 16.

Even denying the Lord that bought them.—Better, *denying even the Master that bought them.* (See Note on Jude, verse 4.) The phrase is remarkable as coming from one who himself denied his Master. Would a forger have ventured to make St. Peter write thus?

This text is conclusive against Calvinistic doctrines of partial redemption; the Apostle declares that these impious false teachers were redeemed by Jesus Christ. (Comp. 1 Pet. i. 18.)

And bring upon themselves.—More literally, *bringing upon themselves.* The two participles, "denying" and "bringing," without any conjunction to connect them, are awkward, and show that the writer's strong feeling is already beginning to ruffle the smoothness of his language.

Swift destruction—*i.e.*, coming suddenly and unexpectedly, so as to preclude escape; not necessarily coming *soon.* (See first Note on chap. i. 14.) The reference, probably, is to Christ's sudden return to judgment (chap. iii. 10), scoffing at which was one of the ways in which they "denied their Master." By their lives they denied that He had "bought them." He had bought them for His service, and they served their own lusts.

(2) **Many shall follow their pernicious ways.**—"Pernicious ways" is a translation of the plural of the word just rendered "destruction." (See fourth Note on verse 1.) But here the reading is undoubtedly wrong. The margin has the right reading—*lascivious ways* (or better, *wanton ways*)—being the plural of the word translated "wantonness" in verse 18. Wiclif has "lecheries;" Rheims "riotousnesses."

The connexion between false doctrine and licentiousness was often real, and is so still in some cases—*e.g.*, Mormonism. But it was often asserted and believed without foundation. Impurity was the common charge to bring against those of a different creed, whether between heathen and Christian or between different divisions of Christians.

By reason of whom.—The many who are led astray are meant, rather than the original seducers. (Comp. Rom. ii. 24.)

The way of truth.—(See Note on Acts ix. 2.) "The way of truth" occurs in Clement of Alexandria (*Cohort. ad Gentes*, x.), the only near approach to anything in 2 Peter in all the writings of his that have come down to us. This is strong evidence that he did not know the Epistle, especially as references are frequent to 1 Peter, which is sometimes quoted thus: "Peter in his Epistle says" (*Strom.* IV. xx.).

Shall be evil spoken of.—By the heathen, who will judge of the way of truth by the evil lives of the many who have really been seduced from it, though they profess still to follow it. In the homily commonly called the *Second Epistle of Clement* (xiii.) there is a remarkable amplification of this statement. Our Epistle was probably known to the writer of the homily, who to a considerable extent preaches against similar evils.

(3) **And through covetousness.**—Better, *In covetousness.* This is the atmosphere in which they live. (See Notes on verse 18 and chap. i. 1, 2, 4, 13.) Wiclif and Rheims have "in." Simon Magus offering St. Peter money, which no doubt he was accustomed to take himself for his teaching, may illustrate this (Acts viii. 18; comp. 1 Tim. vi. 5; Tit. i. 10, 11). These false teachers, like the Greek Sophists, taught for money. A bombastic mysticism, promising to reveal secrets about the unseen world and the future, was a very lucrative profession in the last days of Paganism, and it passed over to Christianity as an element in various heresies. (Comp. the *Shepherd* of Hermas, *Sim.* IX. xix. 3.)

Make merchandise of you.—The verb means literally *to travel*, especially as a merchant on business; and hence "to be a merchant," "to trade," and, with an accusative, "to deal in," "make merchandise of." (Comp. our commercial phrase, "to *travel* in" such and such goods.) It may also mean simply "to gain," or "gain over," which would make good sense here; but our version is perhaps better. The word occurs elsewhere only in Jas. iv. 13. "With feigned words" possibly refers back to "cunningly devised fables" (chap. i. 16).

Lingereth not.—Literally, *is not idle*, the cognate verb of the adjective in chap. i. 8. Their sentence has long since been pronounced, is working, and in due time will strike them. We have a similar thought in 1 Pet. iv. 17.

Their damnation slumbereth not.—Better, *their destruction.* (See fourth Note on verse 1.) Wiclif and Rheims have "perdition." The destruction involved in the judgment pronounced by God is awake and on its way to overtake them. The word for "slumbereth" occurs in Matt. xxv. 5 only.

We now pass on to see how it is that this judgment "*of a long time*" has been working. It was pronounced

slumbereth not. (4) For if God spared not the angels that sinned, but cast *them* down to hell, and delivered *them* into chains of darkness, to be reserved unto judgment; (5) and spared not the old world, but saved Noah the eighth *person*, a preacher of righteousness, bringing in the flood upon the world of the ungodly; (6) and turning the cities of Sodom and Gomorrha into ashes condemned *them* with an overthrow, making *them* an ensample unto those that after should live ungodly; (7) and delivered just Lot, vexed with the filthy conversation of the wicked:

Chap. ii. 4—10. Their certain ruin.

---

against all sinners, such as they are, from the first beginning of the world.

(4—8) Three instances of divine vengeance, proving that great wickedness never goes unpunished.

(4) **For if God.**—The sentence has no proper conclusion. The third instance of God's vengeance is so prolonged by the addition respecting Lot, that the apodosis is wanting, the writer in his eagerness having lost the thread of the construction. The three instances here are in chronological order (wanton angels, Flood, Sodom and Gomorrha), while those in Jude are not (unbelievers in the wilderness, impure angels, Sodom and Gomorrha). Both arrangements are natural—this as being chronological, that of St. Jude for reasons stated in the Notes there. (See on verse 5.)

The angels that sinned.—Better, *the angels for their sin:* it gives the reason why they were not spared, and points to some definite sin. What sin is meant? Not that which preceded the history of the human race, commonly called the fall of the angels—of that there is no record in the Old Testament; and, moreover, it affords no close analogy to the conduct of the false teachers. St. Jude is somewhat more explicit (Jude, verse 6); he says it was for not keeping their own dignity—for deserting their proper home; and the reference, both there and here, is either to a common interpretation of Gen. vi. 2 (that by "the sons of God" are meant "angels"), or, more probably, to distinct and frequent statements in the *Book of Enoch*, that certain angels sinned by having intercourse with women—*e.g.*, chaps. vii. 1, 2; cv. 13 (Lawrence's translation). Not improbably these false teachers made use of this book, and possibly of these passages, in their corrupt teaching. Hence St. Peter uses it as an *argumentum ad hominem* against them, and St. Jude, recognising the allusion, adopts it and makes it more plain; or both writers, knowing the *Book of Enoch* well, and calculating on their readers knowing it also, used it to illustrate their arguments and exhortations, just as St. Paul uses the Jewish belief of the rock following the Israelites. (See Note on 1 Cor. x. 4.)

Cast them down to hell.—The Greek word occurs nowhere else, but its meaning is plain—*to cast down to Tartarus;* and though "Tartarus" occurs neither in the Old nor in the New Testament, it probably is the same as Gehenna. (See Note on Matt. v. 22.)

Into chains of darkness.—Critical reasons seem to require us to substitute *dens*, or *caves*, for "chains." The Greek words for "chains" and for "caves" here are almost exactly alike; and "caves" may have been altered into "chains" in order to bring this passage into closer harmony with Jude, verse 6, although the word used by St. Jude for "chains" is different. (See Note there.) If "chains of darkness" be retained, comp. Wisd. xvii. 17. There still remains the doubt whether "into chains of darkness" should go with "delivered" or with "cast down into hell." The former arrangement seems the better.

(5) **And spared not the old world.**—The fact that the Flood is taken as the second instance of divine vengeance gives us no clue as to the source of the first instance. In the *Book of Enoch* the Flood follows closely upon the sin of the angels, as in Gen. vi. upon that of the sons of God, so that in either case the first instance would naturally suggest the second.

Noah the eighth person.—According to a common Greek idiom, this means *Noah and seven others;* and the point of it is that the punishment must have been signal indeed if only eight persons out of a whole world escaped. The coincidence with 1 Pet. iii. 20 must not pass unobserved, especially as there the mention of "spirits in prison" immediately precedes, just as here, the angels in "caves of darkness." The suggestion that eight is here a mystical number (the sabbatical seven and one over) is quite gratuitous; as also that "eighth" may mean eighth from Enos, which would be utterly pointless, there being neither mention of Enos nor the faintest allusion to him. (Comp. Clement I. vii. 6; ix. 4; and see Note on verse 9.)

Bringing in the flood upon the world.—"In" should be omitted. The phrase is exactly parallel to "bring upon themselves swift destruction" in verse 1. The word for "bring" is the same in both cases.

(6) **And turning . . . .**—The construction still depends upon the "if" in verse 4. (See Note on Jude, verse 7.)

Condemned them with an overthrow.—Or, perhaps, *to an overthrow*, like "condemn to death" in Matt. xx. 18. The very word here used for "overthrow"—*catastrophe*—is used by the LXX. of the overthrow of these cities (Gen. xix. 29); in the New Testament it occurs in 2 Tim. ii. 4 only.

An ensample unto those.—Literally, *an ensample of those*—*i.e.*, of the punishment which such sinners must expect. (Comp. "Are set forth for an example," Jude, verse 7.)

(7) **And delivered just Lot.**—Better, *righteous Lot;* it is the same adjective as occurs twice in the next verse. These repetitions of the same word, of which there are several examples in this Epistle ("destruction" thrice, chap. ii. 1—3; various repetitions, chap. iii. 10—12; "look for" thrice, chap. iii. 12—14, &c.), and which have been stigmatised as showing poverty of language, are perfectly natural in St. Peter, and not like the laboured efforts of a writer endeavouring to personate him. A person writing under strong emotion does not stop to pick his words; he uses the same word over and over again if it expresses what he means and no other word at once occurs to him. This is still more likely to be the case when a person is writing in a foreign language. The fact that such repetitions are frequent in the Second Epistle, but not in the First, is not only fully explained by the circumstances, but, as being so entirely in harmony with them, may be regarded as a mark of genuineness. "Delivered righteous Lot." Here, as in the case of the Flood (verse 5), the destruction of the guilty

(8) (for that righteous man dwelling
among them, in seeing and hearing,
vexed *his* righteous soul from day to
day with *their* unlawful deeds;) (9) the
Lord knoweth how to deliver the godly
out of temptations, and to reserve the
unjust unto the day of judgment to be
punished: (10) but chiefly them that walk
after the flesh in the lust of
uncleanness, and despise
government.[1] Presump-
tuous[a] *are they*, selfwilled,
they are not afraid to speak evil of digni-
ties. (11) Whereas angels, which are

Chap. ii. 10–22. Detailed description of the false teachers.

1 Or, *dominion.*
a Jude 8.

suggests the preservation of the innocent. Is it fanciful to think that these lights in a dark picture are characteristic of one who had himself "denied the Master who bought him," and yet had been preserved like Noah and rescued like Lot? This brighter side is wanting in Jude, so that in the strictly historical illustrations this Epistle is more full than the other (see Note on verse 15); it is where apocryphal books seem to be alluded to that St. Jude has more detail.

The filthy conversation.—Literally, *behaviour in wantonness* (comp. verses 2 and 18)—*i.e.*, licentious mode of life. The word for "conversation," or "behaviour," is a favourite one with St. Peter—six times in the First Epistle, twice in this (chap. iii. 11); elsewhere in the New Testament only five times.

Of the wicked.—Literally, *of the lawless*—a word peculiar to this Epistle; we have it again in chap. iii. 17. The word translated "abominable" in 1 Pet. iv. 3 is closely allied to it.

The judgment on Sodom and Gomorrha forms a fitting complement to that of the Flood as an instance of God's vengeance, a judgment by fire being regarded as more awful than a judgment by flood, as is more distinctly shown in chap. iii. 6, 7, where the total destruction of the world by fire is contrasted with the transformation of it wrought by the Flood.

(8) **For that righteous man.**—This epithet, here thrice given to Lot, seems at first sight to be at variance with his willingness to remain, for the sake of worldly advantages, in the midst of such wickedness. But "righteous" is a relative term; and in this case we must look at Lot both in comparison with the defective morality of the age and also with the licentiousness of those with whom he is here contrasted. Moreover, in the midst of this corruption he preserves some of the brighter features of his purer nomad life, especially that "chivalrous hospitality" (Gen. xix. 2, 3, 8) to which the author of the Epistle to the Hebrews seems to point as a model: "Be not forgetful to entertain strangers, for thereby some have entertained angels unawares" (chap. xiii. 2). Add to this the fact of God's rescuing him and his family, especially in connexion with the declaration that ten "righteous" people would have saved the whole city (Gen. xviii. 32), and his ready belief and obedience when told to leave all, and also the fact that Zoar was saved at his intercession (chap. xix. 21), and we must then admit that the epithet "righteous" as applied to Lot is by no means without warrant.

(9) **The Lord knoweth.**—This is the main sentence to which the various conditional clauses beginning verse 4 (see Note there) have been leading. But the construction is disjointed, owing to the eagerness of the writer, and the main clause does not fit on to the introductory clauses very smoothly. Even the main clause itself is interrupted by the insertion of "to deliver the godly out of temptations." What the writer *specially* wishes to prove is that "the Lord knoweth how to reserve the ungodly unto the day of judgment under punishment," as is shown by the "for" connecting verse 4 with verse 3.

To be punished.—Rather, *being punished*, or *under punishment*. They are already suffering punishment while waiting for their final doom. The error in our version is parallel to that in Acts ii. 47, where "such as should be saved" stands instead of "those who were being saved." The participle is present, not future.

The same double moral—that God will save the righteous and punish the ungodly—is drawn from the same historical instance by Clement of Rome (*Epistle to the Corinthians*, xi.): "For his hospitality and godliness Lot was saved from Sodom, when all the country round was judged by fire and brimstone; the Master having thus foreshown that He forsaketh not them who set their hope on Him, but appointeth unto punishment and torment them who swerve aside." A possible, but not a certain, reference to our Epistle. (See Note below on chap. iii. 4.)

(10) **Them that walk after the flesh.**—Less definite than Jude, verse 7. Here there is nothing about going *away* or *astray*, nor about the flesh being "other" than is allowed. This is natural; Jude's remark applying to the inhabitants of the cities of the plain in particular, this to sensual persons generally.

In the lust of uncleanness.—Better, *in the lust of pollution*—*i.e.*, the lust that causes pollution. The exact word occurs nowhere else; the same word, all but the termination, occurs in verse 20, and nowhere else.

Despise government.—(Comp. "despise dominion," Jude, verse 8.) Our version is minutely perverse. The word translated "government" here and "dominion" in Jude is one and the same in the Greek; whereas the words translated in both places "despise" are different.

Presumptuous are they.—A fresh verse should begin here; the construction is entirely changed, and a fresh start made. From "the unjust" to "government" the reference is to ungodly and sensual people in general; here we return to the false teachers in particular. *Audacious* would be more literal than "presumptuous." The word is found here only. On the change to the present tense, see *Introduction*, I., *c*, *γ*.

Speak evil of dignities.—The exact meaning of "dignities," or "glories," is not clear, either here or in Jude, verse 8. The context in both places seems to show that spiritual powers alone are intended, and that earthly powers, whether civil or ecclesiastical, are not included, much less exclusively indicated. The construction here resembles that in chap. i. 19: "Do not tremble in (or, *while*) speaking evil of dignities," like "ye do well in taking heed." These men deny the existence of, or irreverently speak slightingly of, those spiritual agencies by means of which God conducts the government of the world.

(11) **Whereas angels.**—Literally, *Where angels*—*i.e.*, in circumstances in which angels. This verse, if it

greater in power and might, bring not railing accusation against them[1] before the Lord. (12) But these, as natural brute beasts, made to be taken and destroyed, speak evil of the things that they understand not; and shall utterly perish in their own corruption; (13) and shall receive the reward of unrighteousness, *as* they that count it pleasure to riot in the day time. Spots *they are*

1 Some read, *against themselves.*

---

refers to the same incident as Jude, verse 9, seems at first sight to tell somewhat in favour of the priority of Jude; for then, only when compared with Jude, verse 9, does it become intelligible. The inference is that this is an abbreviation of Jude, rather than Jude an amplification of this. But (1) such an inference is at best only probable. The writer of this Epistle might possibly count on his readers at once understanding his allusion to a tradition that may have been well known, while St. Jude thought it best to point out the allusion more plainly. (2) It is possible that the contest alluded to is not that between Satan and Michael about the body of Moses, but that between Satan and the angel of the Lord about Joshua the high priest (Zech. iii. 1, 2). (3) It is also possible that it does not refer to any contest with Satan at all, but merely to angels not denouncing these false teachers before God, but leaving them to His judgment. If either (2) or (3) is correct, the argument for the priority of Jude falls to the ground. If (1) is right, then the argument really favours the priority of 2 Peter; for if the author of 2 Peter had Jude before him (and this is maintained by those who contend for the priority of Jude), and wished to make use of St. Jude's illustration, why should he so deface St. Jude's statement of it as to make it almost unintelligible? The reason suggested is altogether inadequate—that reverential feelings made him wish to avoid mentioning Michael's name—a name that every Jew was perfectly familiar with in the Book of Daniel.

Greater in power and might.—This is taken in two ways—either "greater than these audacious, self-willed men," which is the simpler and more natural explanation; or "greater than other angels," as if it were a periphrasis for "archangels," which is rather awkward language. But either explanation makes good sense.

Railing accusation against them.—Literally, *a railing judgment.* Wiclif has "doom," all the rest "judgment"; both superior to "accusation." "Against them," if the reference is either to the contest about the body of Moses or to Zech. iii. 1, 2, must mean against "dignities," and "dignities" must here mean *fallen* angels, who are considered still to be worthy of reverence on account of their original glory and indefectible spiritual nature. The position is, therefore, that what angels do not venture to say of devils, this, and worse than this, these audacious men dare to say of angels and other unseen powers. But "against them" may possibly mean "against the false teachers," *i.e.*, they speak evil of angels, yet the angels bring no denunciation against them, but leave all judgment to God (Deut. xxxii. 35, 36; Rom. xii. 19; Heb. x. 30). This explanation avoids the awkwardness of making "dignities" in verse 10 mean unseen powers generally, and chiefly *good* ones; while "against dignities" in this verse has to mean against *evil* powers *only.*

(12) **But these, as natural brute beasts.**—Omit "natural." This verse appears to tell strongly in favour of the priority of our Epistle. The literary form of Jude, verse 10, is so very superior; the antithesis (quite wanting here) between abusing what they cannot know and misusing what they cannot help knowing is so telling, and would be so easily remembered, that it is improbable that a writer who was willing to adopt so much would not have adopted in this respect also; and whichever writer is second, it is evident that he was willing to adopt his predecessor's material almost to any extent. On the other hand, there is nothing improbable in a writer who knew this verse improving upon it by writing Jude, verse 10. The verses, similar as they are in much of their wording, are very different in their general drift. Jude, verse 10, is simply an epigrammatic description of these ungodly men; this verse is a denunciation of final ruin against them.

Made to be taken and destroyed.—Literally, *born naturally for capture and destruction.* "Natural" comes in better here as a kind of adverb than as an additional epithet to beasts. The force of it is that these animals cannot help themselves—it is their nature to rush after what will prove their ruin; but the false teachers voluntarily seek their own destruction against nature. This verse contains one of the repetitions noticed above (see on verse 7) as characteristic of this Epistle. The word for "destruction" and "corruption" is one and the same in the Greek, the destroying being literal in the first case, moral in the second. Moreover, the word for "perish" is from the same root. "Like brutes born for capture and *destruction,* these men shall be *destroyed* in their *destruction.*" But such a translation would be misleading in English.

Shall utterly perish.—A reading of higher authority gives us, *shall even perish.*

In their own corruption.—"Own" may be omitted. Their present evil life anticipates and contains within itself the elements of their final destruction. Thus they "bring it upon themselves" (verse 1). The right division of the sentences here cannot be decided with certainty; the Apostle hurries on, in the full flood of his denunciation, without paying much attention to the precise form of his language. On the whole, it seems best to place only a comma at the end of verse 12, with a full stop or colon at "unrighteousness," and to make what follows part of the long sentence, of which the main verb is "are gone astray" in verse 15.

(13) **And shall receive.**—Literally, *about to receive* (as they are). (Comp. 1 Pet. i. 9; v. 4; see also *Epistle of Barnabas,* iv. 12.)

As they that count.—We must begin a fresh sentence, and somewhat modify the translation. "To riot" is too strong; the word means "delicate fare, dainty living, luxury," and if the exact meaning be retained, this will necessitate a change of "in the day time." For though "rioting in the day time" makes good sense—revelry even among professed pleasure-seekers being usually confined to the night (1 Thess. v. 7)—"dainty fare in the day time" does not seem to have much point. The meaning is, perhaps, "for the day," without thought for the morrow, *counting luxury for the moment a pleasure*—the doctrine of the Cyrenaics and the instinct of "brute beasts." In the *Shepherd* of Hermas (*Sim. VI.* iv. 4) there is a passage which may possibly be an echo of this: "The time of luxury and deceit is one hour, but the hours of torment

and blemishes, sporting themselves with their own deceivings while they feast with you; (14) having eyes full of adultery,[1] and that cannot cease from sin; beguiling unstable souls: an heart they have exercised with covetous practices; cursed children: (15) which have forsaken the right way, and are gone astray, following the way of Balaam *the son* of Bosor, who loved the wages of unrighteousness; (16) but was rebuked for his iniquity: the dumb ass speaking with man's voice forbad the madness of the prophet. (17) These are wells without water, clouds that are carried with a tempest; to whom the

1 Gr. *an adulteress.*

---

have the power of thirty days; if, then, a man luxuriates for one day," &c. &c. (See below on verses 15, 20; chap. iii. 5.)

Sporting themselves.—The word is a compound of the one just translated "luxury"; hence *luxuriating.* It is worth noting that the words for "spots and blemishes" exactly correspond to the words translated "without blemish and without spot" in 1 Pet. i. 19. (See below on chap. iii. 14.)

With their own deceivings.—Better, *in their deceits,* if this is the right reading. But both here and in Jude, verse 12, the reading is uncertain, authorities being divided between *agapai,* "love-feasts," and *apatai,* "deceits." In Jude the balance on purely critical grounds is decidedly in favour of "love-feasts;" here (though much less decidedly) in favour of "deceits." In Jude the context confirms the reading "love-feasts;" here the context is neutral, or slightly inclines to "love-feasts," to which "while they feast with you" must in any case refer. But if "love-feasts" be right in Jude (and this is so probable that we may almost assume it), this in itself is strong support to the same reading here. Whichever writer is prior, so strange a change from "deceits" to "love-feasts" would hardly have been made deliberately; whereas, in copying mechanically, the interchange might easily be made, the words being so similar. The change from "spots" to "rocks," if such a change has been deliberately made by either writer (see on Jude, verse 12), would not be parallel to a change between "deceits" and "love-feasts." The one is a mere variation of the metaphor, the other an alteration of the meaning. In 2 Thess. ii. 10 there is possibly an intentional play upon the similarity of these two words.

(14) **Of adultery.**—Literally, *of an adulteress.* This verse has no counterpart in Jude.

That cannot cease from sin.—Literally, *that cannot be made to cease from sin.* (Comp. attentively 1 Pet. iv. 1.) It was precisely because these men refused to "suffer in the flesh," but, on the contrary, gave the flesh all possible licence on principle, that they could not "cease from sin."

Beguiling.—Strictly, *enticing with bait.* We have the same word in verse 18, James i. 14, and nowhere else. If "deceits" be the right reading in verse 13, this clause throws some light on it. In any case, the metaphor from fishing, twice in this Epistle and only once elsewhere, may point to a fisherman of Galilee. (Comp. Matt. xvii. 27.)

With covetous practices.—Better, *in covetousness.* The word is singular, as in verse 3, according to all the best MSS. and versions.

Cursed children.—Rather, *children of malediction.* So Rheims; Wiclif has "sones of cursynge." They are devoted to execration; malediction has adopted them as its own. (Comp. "son of perdition," John xvii. 12; 2 Thess. ii. 3.)

(15) **The right way.**—(Comp. Acts xiii. 10.) In the *Shepherd* of Hermas (I. *Vis.* III. vii. 1) we have "Who have believed indeed, but through their doubting *have forsaken their true way.*" (See Notes on verses 1, 3, 13, 20; chap. iii. 5.)

Are gone astray.—The main verb of this long sentence. Here parallels with Jude begin again. In the historical incident of Balaam, as in that of Sodom and Gomorrha, our Epistle is more detailed than Jude (see on verse 7). The past tenses in this verse are quite in harmony with the view that this chapter is a genuine prediction. (Comp. Gen. xlix. 9, 15, 23, 24.) The future foretold with such confidence as to be spoken of as already past is a common form for prophecy to assume.

Balaam the son of Bosor.—Bosor seems to be a dialectical variation from Beor, arising out of peculiar Aramaic pronunciation—a slight indication that the writer was a Jew of Palestine. The resemblance between these false teachers and Balaam consisted in their running counter to God's will for their own profit, and in prostituting their office to an infamous purpose, which brought ruin on the community. He, like they, had "enticed unstable souls," and had "a heart exercised in covetousness." A comparison of this passage with Rev. ii. 14, 15, gives countenance to the view that among the false teachers thus stigmatised the Nicolaitans may be included. In Jude, verse 11, these ungodly men are compared not only to Balaam, but also to Cain and Korah. It seems more likely that St. Jude should add these two very opprobrious comparisons than that the vehement writer of this Epistle should reject material so suitable to his invective. If so, we have here another argument for the priority of our Epistle. (See on verse 12.)

(16) **But was rebuked for his iniquity.**—Literally, *But had a conviction of his own transgression*—*i.e.,* was convicted of it, or rebuked for it. His transgression was that, although as a prophet he knew the blessedness of Israel, and although God gave him leave to go only on condition of his blessing Israel, he went still cherishing a hope of being able to curse, and so winning Balak's promised reward.

The dumb ass.—Literally, *a dumb beast of burden.* The same word is rendered "ass" in Matt. xxi. 5, in the phrase "foal of an ass." In Palestine the ass was the most common beast of burden, horses being rare, so that in most cases "beast of burden" would necessarily mean "ass."

Forbad the madness.—Strictly, *hindered the madness;* and thus the trivial discrepancy which some would urge as existing between this passage and Num. xxii. disappears. It has been objected that not the ass but the angel forbad Balaam from proceeding. But it was the ass which hindered the infatuation of Balaam from hurrying him to his own destruction (Num. xxii. 33). The word for "madness" is probably chosen for the sake of alliteration with "prophet"—*prophêtou paraphronian.* It is a very rare formation, perhaps coined by the writer himself.

(17) **These are wells.**—Or, *springs;* same word as John iv. 6. These men are like dried-up watering-

mist of darkness is reserved for ever.
(18) For when they speak great swelling
words of vanity, they allure through the
lusts of the flesh, *through much* wanton-
ness, those that were clean [1] escaped
from them who live in error. (19) While
they promise them liberty, they them-
selves are the servants of corruption:
for of whom a man is overcome, of the
same is he brought in bondage. (20) For
if after they have escaped the pollutions
of the world through the knowledge of
the Lord and Saviour Jesus Christ, they
are again entangled therein, and over-

[1] Or, *for a little*, or, *a while*, as some read.

places in the desert, which entice and mock the thirsty traveller; perhaps leading him into danger also by drawing him from places where there is water. (Comp. Jer. ii. 13; xiv. 3.) The parallel passage, Jude, verses 12, 13, is much more full than the one before us, and is more like an amplification of this than this a condensation of that—*e.g.*, would a simile so admirably suitable to false guides as "wandering stars" have been neglected by the writer of our Epistle? A Hebrew word which occurs only twice in the Old Testament is translated by the LXX. in the one place (Gen. ii. 6) by the word here used for "well," and in the other (Job xxxvi. 27) by the word used in Jude, verse 12, for "cloud." Thus the same Hebrew might have produced "wells without water" here and "clouds without water" in Jude. This is one of the arguments used in favour of a Hebrew original of both these Epistles. Coincidences of this kind, which may easily be mere accidents of language, must be shown to be numerous before a solid argument can be based upon them. Moreover, we must remember that the writers in both cases were Jews, writing in Greek, while thinking probably in Hebrew, so that the same Hebrew thought might suggest a different Greek expression in the two cases. When we have deducted all that might easily be accounted for in this way, and also all that is perhaps purely accidental, from the not very numerous instances of a similar kind that have been collected, we shall not find much on which to build the hypothesis of these Epistles being translations from Hebrew originals. (See *Introduction to Jude*, II.)

Clouds that are carried with a tempest.—Better, *mists driven by the storm-wind.* Wiclif has "myistis." The words for "clouds" and "carried about" in Jude, verse 12, are quite different, so that our version creates a false impression of great similarity. The idea is not very different from that of the "wells without water." These mists promise refreshment to the thirsty soil (Gen. ii. 6), and are so flimsy that they are blown away before they do any good. So these false teachers deceived those who were thirsting for the knowledge and liberty promised them by raising hopes which they could not satisfy.

To whom the mist of darkness.—Better, *for whom the gloom of darkness.* (See Note on Jude, verse 6.) "For ever" is wanting in authority; the words have probably been inserted from the parallel passage in Jude.

(18) **Great swelling words of vanity.**—Exaggeration, unreality, boastfulness, and emptiness are expressed by this phrase. It carries on the same idea as the waterless wells and the driven mists—great pretensions and no results. The rebuke here is not unlike the warning in 1 Pet. v. 5, 6.

Allure.—Translated "beguile" in verse 14, where see Note.

Through the lusts of the flesh.—Better, *in the lusts of the flesh* (as in verse 3, and chap. i. 1, 2, 4, 13). The preposition "in" points to the sphere in which the enticement takes place; "through" should be reserved for "wantonness" (see Note on verse 2), which is the bait used to entice.

Were clean escaped.—Both verb and adverb require correction. The margin indicates the right reading for the adverb—"for a little," or better, *by a little; scarcely.* The verb should be present, not past—*those who are scarcely escaping*, viz., the "unstable souls" of verse 14. Wiclif has "scapen a litil;" Rheims "escape a litle." The word translated "scarcely" occurs nowhere else in the New Testament; that translated here "clean," and elsewhere "indeed," or "certainly," is frequent (Mark xi. 32; Luke xxiii. 47; xxiv. 34, &c. &c.). Hence the change, an unfamiliar word being, by a slight alteration, turned into a familiar one. The two Greek words are much alike.

(19) **Promise them liberty.**—A specimen of the "great swelling words"—loud, high-sounding talk about liberty. The doctrines of Simon Magus, as reported by Irenæus (I., chap. xxiii. 3) and by Hippolytus (*Refut.* VI., chap. xiv.), show us the kind of liberty that such teachers promised—being "freed from righteousness" to become "the slaves of sin."

Servants of corruption.—Better, *bond-servants*, or *slaves of corruption.* Our translators have often done well in translating the Greek word for "slave" by "servant" (see Note on chap. i. 1), but here the full force of the ignominious term should be given. Tyndale, Cranmer, and Geneva have "bond-servants;" Rheims "slaves." (Comp. "bondage of corruption," Rom. viii. 21.)

Brought in bondage.—Or, *enslaved.* We seem here to have an echo of John viii. 34 (see Notes there): "Every one who continues to commit sin is the slave of sin," words which St. Peter may have heard. Comp. Rom. vi. 16—20, which the writer may also have had in his mind. There is nothing improbable in St. Peter being well acquainted with the Epistle to the Romans during the last years of his life; the improbability would rather be in supposing that he did not know it.

(20) **For if after they have escaped the pollutions of the world.**—Applying the general statement of the preceding verse to the case of these false teachers. In the *Shepherd* of Hermas (I. *Vis.* IV. iii. 2.) "the black there is the world in which we dwell, and the fire-and-blood-colour (indicates) that this world must perish through blood and fire; but the golden part are ye *who have escaped this world.*" Another *possible* reminiscence of our Epistle. (See above on verses 1, 3, 13, 15; and below, chap. iii. 5.)

Through the knowledge.—Better, *in knowledge*, the preposition "in" pointing to that in which the escape consists. (See on verse 18, and comp. Luke i. 77.) The knowledge is of the same mature and complete kind as that spoken of in chap. i. 2, 3, 8 (where see Notes), showing that these men were well-instructed Christians.

Entangled therein, and overcome.—Or, *entangled and overcome thereby*, which, from the latter part of verse 19, seems to be the more probable construction.

come, the latter end is worse with them than the beginning. (21) For it had been better for them not to have known the way of righteousness, than, after they have known *it,* to turn from the holy commandment delivered unto them. (22) But it is happened unto them according to the true proverb, The dog *is* turned to his own vomit again; and the sow that was washed to her wallowing in the mire.

A.D. 66.

CHAPTER III.—(1) This second epistle, beloved, I now write unto you; in *both* which I stir up your pure minds by way of remembrance: (2) that ye may be mindful of

Chap. iii. 1, 2. Transition to second prediction.

The latter end is worse with them than the beginning.—Most certainly this should be made to correspond with Matt. xii. 45, of which it is almost an exact reproduction—*their last state is worse than the first.* The only difference is that the word for "is" in Matt. xii. 45 means literally "becomes," and here "has become." (Comp. the *Shepherd, Sim.* IX. xvii. 5.)

(21) **It had been better for them not to have known.**—There are many things of which the well-known lines,

"'Tis better to have loved and lost,
Than never to have loved at all,"

do not hold good. To have loved a great truth, to have loved a high principle, and after all to lose them, is what often causes the shipwreck of a life. To have loved Jesus Christ and lost Him is to make shipwreck of eternal life.

The way of righteousness.—The life of the Christian. That which from a doctrinal point of view is "the way of truth" (verse 2), from a moral point of view is "the way of righteousness." So also "the faith delivered to the saints" of Jude, verse 3, is the doctrinal equivalent of "the holy commandment delivered unto them" of this verse.

(22) **But it is happened unto them according to the true proverb.**—More literally, *There has happened to them what the true proverb says;* "but" is of very doubtful authority. The word for "proverb" is the one used elsewhere only by St. John in his Gospel, and there translated once "parable" and thrice "proverb." "Parable," or "allegory," would have been best in all four cases (John x. 6, where see Note; xvi. 25, 29). The first proverb is found, Prov. xxvi. 11, and if that be the source of the quotation, we have here an independent translation of the Hebrew, for the LXX. gives an entirely different rendering, "dog" being the only word in common to the two Greek versions. The word for "vomit" here is possibly formed by the writer himself; that for "wallowing" is also a rare word. The LXX. adds, "and becomes abominable," which has no equivalent in the existing Hebrew text; and it has been suggested that these words may misrepresent the Hebrew original of the second proverb here. But it is quite possible that both proverbs come from popular tradition, and not from Scripture at all. If, however, the Book of Proverbs be the source of the quotation, it is worth while noting that no less than four times in as many chapters does St. Peter recall passages from the Proverbs in the First Epistle (chaps. i. 7; ii. 17; iv. 8, 18). In the Greek neither proverb has a verb, as so often in such sayings—*a dog that has returned to his own vomit; a washed sow to wallowing in the mire;* just as we say "the dog in the manger," "a fool and his money."

The word for "mire," not a very common one, is used by Irenæus of the Gnostic false teachers of his day, who taught that their fine spiritual natures could no more be hurt by sensuality than gold by mire. "For in the same way as gold when plunged in mire does not lay aside its beauty, but preserves its own nature, the mire having no power to injure the gold, so they say that they, no matter what kind of material actions they may be involved in, cannot suffer any harm, nor lose their spiritual essence." (I. chap. vi. 2). But it is not probable that Irenæus knew our Epistle.

III.

(1, 2) Just as the two halves of the first main portion of the Epistle are linked together by some personal remarks respecting his reason for writing this Epistle (chap. i. 12—15), so the two predictions which form the second main portion are connected by personal remarks respecting the purpose of both his Epistles.

(1) **This second epistle, beloved, I now write.**—Rather, *This now second epistle I write, beloved;* or, *This epistle, already a second one*—implying that no very long time has elapsed since his first letter, and that this one is addressed to pretty much the same circle of readers. There is no indication that the first two chapters are one letter, and that this is the beginning of another, as has been supposed. With this use of "now," or "already," comp. John xxi. 14.

Pure minds.—The word for "pure" means literally "separated"—according to one derivation, by being sifted; according to another, by being held up to the light. Hence it comes to mean "unsullied." Here it probably means untainted by sensuality or, possibly, deceit. In Phil. i. 10, the only other place where it occurs in the New Testament, it is translated "sincere." (Comp. 1 Cor. v. 8; 2 Cor. i. 12; ii. 17.) The word for "mind" means "the faculty of moral reflection and moral understanding," which St. Peter, in his First Epistle (chap. i. 13), tells his readers to brace up and keep ready for constant use. These very two words are found together in a beautiful passage in Plato's *Phaedo,* 66A.

By way of remembrance.—We have the same expression in chap. i. 13, and the translation in both cases should be the same—*stir up in putting you in remembrance.*

(2) **By the holy prophets.**—Appealed to before in chap. i. 19. (Comp. Jude, verse 17.) The coherence of the Epistle as a whole comes out strongly in this last chapter: verse 1 recalls chap. i. 12, 13; chap. iii. 17 recalls chap. i. 10—12; chap. iii. 18 recalls chap. i. 5—8. In this verse the Apostle commends the warnings of the Old Testament and the New Testament, as to the coming of Christ, to Christians throughout all ages.

The commandment of us the apostles of the Lord.—"Of us" is, beyond all doubt, a false reading; it should be "of you," or "your." The Greek is somewhat awkward, owing to the number of genitives, but the order of the words is conclusive as to the meaning—

the words which were spoken before by
the holy prophets, and of the command-
ment of us the apostles of the Lord and
Saviour: (3) knowing this first, that
there shall come in the
last days scoffers, walking
after their own lusts, (4) and
saying, Where is the

Chap. iii. 3, 4. Second prediction. Scoffers shall arise.

promise of his coming? for since the
fathers fell asleep, all
things continue as *they*
were from the beginning
of the creation. (5) For this they
willingly are ignorant of, that by the
word of God the heavens were of old,
and the earth standing[1] out of the

Chap. iii. 3—9. Answers to the scoffers.

1 Gr. *consisting.*

---

the commandment of your Apostles (or rather) *of the Lord and Saviour.* The commandment is at once a commandment of the Apostles and of the Lord. "The Apostles of the Lord" must not be taken together, as in our version. The expression "your Apostles" may be taken as a mark of genuineness rather than of the contrary. It is at least not improbable that a true Apostle, having once stated his credentials (chap. i. 1), would sink his own personality in the group of his colleagues from a feeling of humility and of delicacy towards those whom he was addressing, especially when they owed their Christianity mainly to other Apostles than himself. It is not improbable that a writer personating an Apostle would have insisted on his assumed personality and personal authority here.

What commandment is meant? Surely not the whole Christian law; but either the command to beware of false teachers (Matt. vii. 15; xxiv. 5, 11; Mark xiii. 22; Rom. xvi. 17; Eph. v. 6; 2 Tim. iv. 3), or, more probably, what is the main subject of this Epistle, to be ready for Christ's coming (Matt. xxiv. 36—39; Mark xiii. 35—37; Luke xii. 40; 1 Thess. v. 2—4).

SECOND PREDICTION: Scoffers shall throw doubt on Christ's return.

(3) **In the last days.**—Comp. 1 Pet. i. 20; Heb. i. 2; and the parallel passage to this, Jude, verse 18. "Know this first, children, that there shall come in the last days scoffers, walking after their own lusts" is quoted in a homily attributed on doubtful authority to Hippolytus. (See above on chap. ii. 1.)

Scoffers.—The best authorities add "*in scoffing,*" intensifying the meaning by repetition (as in Eph. i. 3; Rev. xiv. 2; comp. Luke xxii. 15). There are other repetitions of this kind in the New Testament, which have been rendered by strengthening the verb in some other way (John iii. 29; Acts iv. 17; v. 28; Jas. v. 17).

(4) **Where is the promise?**—Not meaning, of course, "In what passages of Scripture is any such promise to be found?"—but, "What has come of it? where is there any accomplishment of it?" (Comp. Ps. xlii. 3; lxxix. 10; Jer. xvii. 15; Mal. ii. 17.)

Of his coming.—"His" instead of "the Lord's" indicates not merely that only one Person could be meant, but also the irreverent way in which these scoffers spoke of Him.

Since the fathers fell asleep.—What fathers are meant? Four answers have been given to this question: (1) The ancestors of the human race; (2) the patriarchs and prophets; (3) the first generation of Christians; (4) each generation of men in relation to those following. Probably nothing more definite than our remote ancestors is intended. The expression "fell asleep" is used of St. Stephen's death in Acts vii. 60 (comp. Matt. xxvii. 52; 1 Cor. vii. 39, where the word is not literally translated; xv. 6, 18, &c.). The thoroughly Christian term "cemetery" (= sleeping-place), in the sense of a place of repose for the *dead,* comes from the same Greek root.

There is a passage quoted by Clement of Rome (*circ.* A.D. 100) which seems at first sight to contain a reference to this verse: "Far be from us this Scripture where He saith, Wretched are the double-minded, who doubt in heart and say, *These things we heard in the times of our fathers also, but behold, we have grown old, and none of them has happened to us*" (*Epistle to the Corinthians,* xxiii.). But the remainder of this "Scripture," as quoted by Clement, is so utterly unlike the verse before us, that one suspects some other source. And this suspicion is confirmed when we find the same passage quoted in the so-called *Second Epistle of Clement* (xi.) as "the prophetic word." (See on chap. i. 19 and on chap. ii. 9). The differences between the two quotations are such that the pseudo-Clement appears to be quoting independently, and not merely borrowing from the true Clement. In neither case does close inspection encourage us to believe that our present verse is the source of the quotation. But the quotation by the true Clement is important as a complete refutation of the objection that "the fathers" means the first Christians, and consequently no such scoffing argument as this would be possible in the lifetime of St. Peter This very argument was not only in existence, but was condemned in a document which Clement before the close of the first century could quote as "Scripture." Comp. *Epistle of Polycarp,* chap. vii.: "Whosoever perverts the oracles of the Lord to his own lusts, and says there is neither resurrection nor judgment, he is the firstborn of Satan."

All things continue as they were.—Rather, *as they are.* The error has probably arisen from a desire to get rid of the slight difficulty of *two* dates being given: (1) from the death of "the fathers," and (2) from the beginning of the creation. The suggestion that "the fathers" are the first progenitors of the human race is another attempt to get rid of the difficulty by making the two dates virtually one and the same. But the second date is an after-thought, frequent in Thucydides, intensifying and strengthening the first. *Since the fathers fell asleep all things continue as they are*—nay, more, *since the beginning of the creation.*

This sceptical argument is used with increased force as each generation passes away. It will be at its strongest just before the fallacy of it is irrefragably exposed—on the eve of the day of judgment.

(5) **For this they willingly are ignorant of.**—Literally, *For this escapes their notice of their own will.* They voluntarily blind their eyes to this fact—at once an explanation of their argument, and *first answer* to it, drawn from the Mosaic account of the Creation.

The earth standing out of the water and in the water.—The margin is nearer the true meaning with "consisting" for "standing," and the same word is translated "consist" in Col. i. 17. The notion is that of coherence, solidarity, and order, as distinct from chaos. "Out of [the] water" indicates the material out of which the earth was made; not, as our version leads us to suppose, that out of which the earth rose,

water and in the water: (6) whereby the world that then was, being overflowed with water, perished: (7) but the heavens and the earth, which are now, by the same word are kept in store, reserved unto fire against the day of judgment and perdition of ungodly men. (8) But, beloved, be not ignorant of this one thing, that one day *is* with the Lord as a thousand years, and a thousand years as one day. (9) The Lord is not slack concerning his promise, as some men count slackness; but is longsuffering to us-ward, not willing that any should

---

like an island from the ocean. "In the water" is wrong, and again the error is probably derived from Geneva, though Tyndale has it also. We should render rather, *by means of* [*the*] *water.* In both clauses the article should perhaps be omitted—*the earth consisting out of water and through water.* (Comp. Ps. xxiv. 2; cxxxvi. 6.) In the *Clementine Homilies* (XI. xxiv.) we have the idea of all things being made by water. In the Greek "by the word of God" comes last, not first; emphasis is obtained either way. "By the word of God;" not by a fortuitous concourse of atoms, not by spontaneous generation. In the *Shepherd* of Hermas (I. *Vis.* I. iii. 4) we read, "Behold, the God of virtues (powers) . . . . by His mighty word has fixed the heaven, and laid the foundation of the earth upon the waters." (See above on ii. 1, 3, 13, 15, 20.) In an *Apology* of Melito, Bishop of Sardis, addressed to Antoninus Cæsar about A.D. 170, there is a passage bearing a considerable amount of resemblance to these verses (5—7).

(6) **Whereby.**—The meaning of this is much disputed. The original literally signifies, *by means of which things.* But what things? The context allows various alternatives: (1) These facts about the Creation; (2) the heavens and the earth; (3) the water out of which, and the water by means of which, the world was made; (4) any or all of these together with the word of God. There is good reason for preferring the second of these. Both the heavens and the earth contributed to the deluge; for then "all the fountains of the great deep were broken up, and the windows of heaven were opened" (Gen. vii. 11). The English "whereby" is as vague as the original.

The world that then was, . . . perished.—So that it is absurd to say that all things continue unchanged since the Creation. The world was so transformed by the deluge that the world previous to that catastrophe perished, chaos for the moment returned, and a new world issued from the crisis. "The world that then was, perished" is equivalent to "He spared not the old world" in chap. ii. 5.

(7) **By the same word.**—Or, as some first-rate authorities read, *by His word.* The sense in either case is that the universe is preserved for judgment by the same power that created it. "His word" here does not mean any single utterance of God or passage of Scripture, such as Isa. lxvi. 15; Dan. vii. 9, 10; Mal. iv. 1. Just as "the world that then was" was destroyed by water, so the present world is being treasured up to be destroyed by fire. Comp. Rom. ii. 5. Christ Himself, in a discourse which St. Peter heard (Mark xiii. 3), had made the Flood a type of the Judgment (Matt. xxiv. 37—39). (See below on verse 10.) "Unto fire," or "for fire," should perhaps be taken with "kept in store" rather than with "reserved."

(8) *Second Answer* to the sceptical argument: Time is the condition of man's thought and action, but not of God's. His thoughts are not as our thoughts, nor His ways as our ways; what seems delay to us is none to Him.

But, beloved, be not ignorant of this one thing.—Although these scoffers are willingly ignorant of what refutes their error, do not you be ignorant of what will lead you to the truth.

One day is with the Lord as a thousand years.—This half of the saying is quite original, and has no equivalent in Ps. xc. 4. The second half is only partially parallel to "a thousand years in Thy sight are but as yesterday, when it is past." Consequently, we cannot be sure that the Apostle had this passage from the Psalms in his mind, though it is probable enough that he had. That God can punish in one day the sins of a thousand years is a thought which is neither in the text nor in the context. What is insisted on is simply this—that distinctions of long and short time are nothing in the sight of God; delay is a purely human conception. Justin Martyr, about A.D. 145 (*Trypho.* lxxxi.), gives "the day of the Lord is as a thousand years" as a quotation, and in this form it is closer to 2 Pet. iii. 8 than to Ps. xc. 4. As another possible reference to our Epistle follows in the next chapter, it may be regarded as not improbable that Justin knew the Epistle. (See above, second Note on chap. ii. 1.) But the saying may have been a favourite one, especially with those who held Millenarian views. In the *Epistle of Barnabas* (xv. 4) we read, "For a day means with Him a thousand years, and He Himself witnesseth, saying, Behold, to-day shall be as a thousand years," where for "to-day" the *Codex Sinaiticus* reads "the day of the Lord." Irenæus has "The day of the Lord is as a thousand years" twice—(V. xxiii. 2; xxviii. 3); Hippolytus has it once (*Comm. on Daniel*, Lagarde, p. 153); Methodius once (in Photius' *Bibliotheca*, cod. 235). In no case, however, is the context at all similar to the verses before us.

(9) *Third Answer*—a practical one: Make good use of what to you seems to be delay.

The Lord is not slack.—We are in doubt whether "the Lord" means Christ or God the Father. In verse 8 "the Lord" certainly means God; and this is in favour of the same meaning here. On the other hand, "concerning His promise" naturally refers to Christ's promise that He will return. The same doubt recurs with regard to verse 15 (see Note there). By "is not slack" is meant "does not delay beyond the time appointed." There is no dilatoriness; He waits, but is never slow, is never late.

Concerning his promise.—The Greek construction is peculiar, formed on the analogy of a comparative adjective—"is not slower than his promise." (Comp. Rom. iii. 23.)

But is longsuffering.—(Comp. verse 15 and 1 Pet. iii. 20. As St. Augustine puts it, God is *patiens quia aeternus*—longsuffering because He is eternal. He who is from everlasting to everlasting can afford to wait. (Comp. the *Shepherd*, *Sim.* VIII. xi. 1.)

To us-ward.—The true reading, beyond all doubt, is *towards you.* It is specially natural here that St. Peter should not include himself among those whom he addresses; for he is writing mainly to Gentile Christians

perish, but that all should come to repentance. (10) But the day of the Lord will come as a thief in the night; in the which the heavens shall pass away with a great noise, and the elements shall melt with fervent heat, the earth also and the works that are therein shall be burned up. (11) *Seeing* then *that* all these things shall be dissolved, what manner *of persons* ought ye to be in *all* holy conversation and godliness, (12) looking for and hasting [1] unto the coming of the day of God, wherein the heavens being on fire shall be dissolved, and the elements shall

Chap. iii. 10. The certainty of Christ's coming the basis of this warning.

Chap. iii. 11–18. Concluding exhortations.

1 Or, *hasting the coming.*

(chap. i. 1), and this longsuffering of God had been conspicuous in His dealings with the Gentiles (Rom. xi. 11—36.) (See second Note on 1 Pet. i. 12.)

(10) The certainty and possible nearness of Christ's coming is the basis of the preceding warning and of the exhortations which follow.

As a thief in the night.—Suddenly and without warning. The words are an echo of Matt. xxiv. 43, a saying which St. Peter certainly heard (Mark xiii. 3), or possibly of 1 Thess. v. 2, which may easily be included in the Epistles referred to below in verse 16. The words "in the night" are here wanting in authority.

The heavens shall pass away.—Again an apparent reminiscence of the discourse in Matt. xxiv. (where comp. verse 35)—the third such reminiscence in this chapter (see preceding Note, and on verse 7). This repeated reproduction of words and ideas from one of the most impressive of Christ's discourses, which only St. Peter and three others seem to have heard, may fairly be added to the evidence in favour of the authenticity of the Epistle.

With a great noise.—Better, *with a rushing noise.* The expression occurs nowhere else in the New Testament, but some such idea as that in Isa. xxxiv. 4, Rev. vi. 14, is probably indicated—not the roar of flames or the crash of ruins, but the parting and rolling up of the heavens. (Comp. Rev. xx. 11.)

The elements shall melt with fervent heat.—The meaning of "elements" here is much disputed. (See Notes on the word in Gal. iv. 3, 9.) The difficulty of supposing fire to be destroyed by fire seems to exclude the four elements being intended; moreover, the earth is mentioned separately. Hence, some take "the elements" to mean water and air, the two remaining elements; but this is not very satisfactory. More probably, the various forms of matter in the universe are intended, without any thought of indicating what they are precisely. But seeing that Justin Martyr calls the sun, moon, and stars "heavenly elements" (*Apol.* II. v., *Trypho,* xxiii.), and that in predictions of the last day frequent mention is made of "signs in the sun, and in the moon, and in the stars" (Matt. xxiv. 29; Mark xiii. 24; Luke xxi. 25; Isa. xiii. 10; xxiv. 23; Joel ii. 31, &c.), it is possible that the heavenly bodies are meant here, all the more so, as the mention of these "elements" immediately follows that of the heavens. Bengel (perhaps with more poetry than correctness) ingeniously connects this explanation with the radical signification of the word, viz., "letters of the alphabet," "for stars in the heaven are as letters on a scroll." (Comp. Rev. vi. 14.) "Shall melt" should rather be, as in the next two verses, *shall be dissolved.* Wiclif has "dissolved," Rheims "resolved." This dissolution is the opposite of the consistency spoken of in verse 5. In verse 12 "melt" is correct, and suits the heavenly bodies better than the four elements. (Comp. *The Second Epistle of Clement,* xvi. 3.)

The earth also and the works that are therein.—Equivalent to "the earth and the fulness thereof," "works" being used in a comprehensive sense for products both of nature and art. The moral work of each individual is not meant; consequently, a reference to 1 Cor. iii. 13 is misleading. The two passages have little in common, and nothing is gained by bringing in the difficulties of the other passage here. In this passage the Apostle is stating plainly and in detail what some of the Prophets of the Old Testament had set forth in general and sometimes obscure language—that a judgment by fire is in store for the world (Isa. lxvi. 15, 16, 24; Mal. iii. 1—3; iv. 1).

Shall be burned up.—The question of readings here is one of known difficulty. One important MS. has "shall vanish away" (James iv. 14); two first-rate MSS. and other authorities have "shall be found." The later Syriac has "shall not be found," which is pretty nearly equivalent to "shall vanish away," and is sometimes given as exactly equivalent to it. "Shall be found," the reading most strongly attested, is summarily rejected by some editors as yielding no sense. The theory that it has grown out of the Latin for "shall be burned up"—*eurethesetai* out of *exurentur*—does not seem very probable. Nor is it true that it yields no sense. By placing a colon at "also," and making what follows a question, we obtain—*The elements shall be dissolved, the earth also: and shall the works that are therein be found?* Happily, nothing of importance turns on the reading; all the variations amount practically to the same thing—that the elements, the earth, and all that is in it, shall be destroyed.

(11) **Seeing then that all these things shall be dissolved.**—For "then" we ought probably to read "thus," *seeing that all these things are thus to be dissolved.* The original is present in form, but rightly translated by the future, being the prophetic present, *i.e.,* the future prophetically regarded as present.

What manner of persons.—Not so much a question as an exclamation. In any case, the sentence should run on to the end of verse 12. To put an interrogation at "to be" or at "godliness," and make what follows an answer to the question, would be stiff and frigid, and very unlike the fervour of this Epistle.

Ought ye to be.—We might fairly translate, *ought ye to be found.* The Greek implies that the state is one that has continued for some time before the day comes.

In all holy conversation and godliness.—Literally, *in holy behaviours and godlinesses.* (See Notes on chap i. 3 and chap. ii. 7.) The plurals indicate a variety of acts. They occur in this passage only.

(12) **Hasting unto.**—There is no "unto" in the Greek. The margin is probably right, *hasting the coming—i.e.,* hastening Christ's coming by holy lives, by helping to make the Gospel known to all nations (Matt.

melt with fervent heat? (13) Neverthe-
less we, according to his promise,
look for new heavens and a new
earth, wherein dwelleth righteousness.
(14) Wherefore, beloved, seeing that
ye look for such things, be diligent
that ye may be found of him in
peace, without spot, and blame-
less. (15) And account *that* the long-
suffering of our Lord *is* salvation;

xxiv. 14), so as to "accomplish the number of the elect," and by praying "Thy kingdom come." (Comp. 2 Tim. iv. 8; Rev. xxii. 20.) The thought is singularly parallel to St. Peter's speech in Solomon's Porch (Acts iii. 19—21, where see Notes); and as the thought is striking and unusual—perhaps nowhere else in the New Testament distinctly—this coincidence may fairly be admitted as a note of genuineness.

The coming of the day of God.—A phrase which occurs here only. It is doubly remarkable: (1) "coming," in the special sense indicated by the particular word used in the Greek, is elsewhere used of Christ Himself, not of the day; (2) "the day of God" is a very unusual expression.

Wherein.—Rather, *by reason of which*, either "the day" or "the coming" being meant.

Shall melt.—"Melt" is here correct, being quite a different word from that rendered "melt" in verse 10, which is the same as that here translated "be dissolved." In the so-called *Second Epistle of Clement* (chap. xvi.) we have a somewhat similar passage—"The day of judgment cometh even now *as a burning oven* (Mal. iv. 1), and [*the powers*] *of the heavens shall melt*, and all the earth as lead melting on the fire."

(13) **Nevertheless we, according to his promise.**—"Nevertheless" is too strong, and the emphasis is on "new," not on "we." *But new heavens and a new earth, wherein dwelleth righteousness, we look for, according to His promise.* (Comp. Rev. xxi. 1.) On the repetition of "look for," three times in three verses, see above on chap. ii. 7. The promise of the new heavens and new earth is given in Isa. lxv. 17; lxvi. 22. There are two words for "new" in Greek; one looks forward, "young" as opposed to "aged;" the other looks back, "fresh" as opposed to "worn out." It is the latter word that is used here and in Rev. xxi. 1, 2. Both are used in Matt. ix. 17, but the distinction is not marked in our version—"They put *new* wine into *fresh* wine-skins."

Wherein dwelleth righteousness.—Comp. Isa. lxv. 25; Rev. xxi. 27. Righteousness has its home there; is not a wanderer and changeful guest, as on earth, therefore by righteousness must ye make yourselves worthy of entering therein.

With this whole verse compare 1 Pet. i., where (verse 4) a similar thought is expressed with equal beauty, and where (verse 13) a similar conclusion is drawn from it. (See next verse.)

(14) **Be found of him in peace, without spot, and blameless.**—Rather, *Be found spotless and blameless in His sight.* "Be found of Him," *i.e.*, "by Him" (comp. chap. ii. 19), cannot stand; the construction is parallel to "be found unto you" (2 Cor. xii. 20), *i.e.*, "in your judgment," or "in your sight." The pair of epithets, "spotless and blameless," should be noticed as coinciding with 1 Pet. i. 19, and also as forming a marked contrast to the false teachers, who are called "spots and blemishes" (2 Pet ii. 13). "In peace" cannot well refer to differences between Jewish and Gentile Christians, a subject quite foreign to this Epistle. It may possibly refer to the false teachers and the discord caused by them; but more probably it has no special reference. It expresses at once the condition and the consequence of being "spotless and blameless." "There is no peace, saith my God, for the wicked."

(15) **The longsuffering of our Lord.**—Again, as in verse 9, we are in doubt as to whether God the Father or the Lord Jesus is meant. In neither case is absolute certainty obtainable; but here the balance seems decidedly in favour of the latter meaning. In verse 8 "the Lord" certainly means God, and not the Lord Jesus (comp. chap. ii. 9, 11). In verse 18 "our Lord" is expressly stated to be Jesus Christ. The two intermediate verses, 9 and 15, are open to dispute. The fact that "our" appears in this verse before "Lord," as in verse 18, inclines the balance here towards the meaning in verse 18. Moreover, had God been meant, it would have sufficed to say, "and account that *His* long-suffering is salvation." If this is correct, and "our Lord" means Jesus Christ, "then throughout this weighty passage the Lord Jesus is invested with the full attributes of Deity." Here, possibly, as also in chap. i. 1 (see Note), the expression points to the writer's entire belief in the unity of the two Persons. *Account the longsuffering of our Lord salvation* instead of accounting it to be "slackness" (verse 9); make use of it for working out your own salvation in fear and trembling, instead of criticising it.

As our beloved brother Paul.—This may possibly mean something more than that St. Paul was a fellow-Christian and a personal friend—viz., that he was a fellow-worker and brother-evangelist. More than this it cannot well mean, though some interpret it "brother-Apostle." Tychicus is twice called "beloved brother" by St. Paul (Eph. vi. 21; Col. iv. 7), and the addition of "our" here can make no such change of meaning. It is doubtful whether there is any allusion to the dispute between St. Peter and St. Paul (Gal. ii. 11), although an expression of marked affection would be quite in place as evidence that all such differences were now forgotten. In any case the familiarity and equality which the expression "our beloved brother Paul" implies should be noticed. It is in marked contrast to the way in which Clement of Rome, Ignatius, Polycarp, and Clement of Alexandria speak of St. Paul, and in this way is a decided note of genuineness. A writer of the sub-Apostolic age would not easily be able to free himself from the feeling of the age in this respect. Clement of Rome (*Corinthians*, xlvii. 1), says, "Take up the Epistle of *the blessed Paul the Apostle.*" Ignatius (*Ephesians*, xii. 2) calls him "*Paul the sanctified, the martyred, worthily called blessed.*" Polycarp (see next Note) calls him "*the blessed and glorious Paul,*" or "*the blessed Paul.*" Clement of Alexandria commonly says simply "*the Apostle,*" but sometimes "*the divine Apostle,*" or "*the noble Apostle.*" An imitator in the second century would scarcely have attained to the freedom of "our beloved brother Paul."

According to the wisdom given unto him.—Comp. 1 Cor. iii. 10; Gal. ii. 9. Polycarp, in his *Epistle to the Philippians* (chap. iii. 2), says, "Neither I nor any one else like me can equal the *wisdom* of the

even as our beloved brother Paul also according to the wisdom given unto him hath written unto you; (16) as also in all *his* epistles, speaking in them of these things; in which are some things hard to be understood, which they that are unlearned and unstable wrest, as *they do* also the

blessed and glorious Paul, who . . . *wrote letters to you,* into which if ye look diligently, &c. &c." This seems to show that St. Paul's letters had already become the common property of the churches.

Hath written unto you.—More literally, *wrote to you.* What Epistle, or Epistles, are here meant? Few points in this Epistle have been more debated. The following are some of the many answers that have been given to the question: (1) a lost Epistle; (2) Hebrews, because of chaps. ix. 26—28; x. 23—25, 37; (3) Galatians, Ephesians, Colossians, because our Epistle is supposed to be addressed to the Christians of Asia Minor; (4) Ephesians only, for the reason just stated, and because Colossians and Galatians contain little or no mention of the day of judgment; also because of Eph. iv. 30, and the encyclical character of the Epistle; (5) 1 Corinthians, because of chap. i. 7—9; (6) Romans, because of chaps. ii. 4 and ix. 22, 23; (7) 1 and 2 Thessalonians, because of 1 Thess. iv. 14—18; v. 1—11, 23, because 2 Pet. iii. 10 recalls 1 Thess. v. 2, also because "things hard to be understood" admirably describes much of 2 Thess. ii., which treats of the time of Christ's coming, the very subject here under discussion.

Of these seven theories, (1) can neither be proved nor disproved; (3) and (4) lose much of their weight when we consider that the persons addressed in 2 Peter are nowhere defined, excepting that to some extent they are identical with those addressed in 1 Peter. Of the remaining four, (7) seems to be very probable, both on account of the large amount of coincidence, and also because of the early date of those Epistles, allowing an interval of fifteen years, in which the two Epistles might easily have become well known in other churches. Still it is difficult to find a passage in them about the *longsuffering* of God, such as Rom. ii. 4; ix. 22, 23. And when we consider that Romans also appears to have been an Encyclical Letter, and was written not so very long after the Epistles to the Thessalonians; that in Rom. iii. 8 St. Paul himself tells us that he had been grossly misunderstood; that chap. ix. 3 might easily cause serious misunderstanding, and that Rom. vi. 16 seems to be recalled in 2 Pet. ii. 19—it will perhaps be thought that on the whole Romans best answers to the requirements of the context.

(16) **As also in all his epistles.**—All those known to the writer. The expression does not necessarily imply that St. Paul was dead, and that his Epistles had been collected into one volume. That each church made a collection of them as they became known to it, and that in the great centres they became known soon after they were written, are conjectures of great probability.

Speaking in them of these things—viz., of the return of Christ and of the destruction of the world. Some, however, understand the words as meaning the exhortations to holiness here given.

Some things hard to be understood.—Certainly the difficulties with which 2 Thess. ii. bristles are well described by this expression, and they relate to the very point in question—the time of Christ's coming. Moreover, scoffers could easily turn them to account by arguing that "the man of sin" had not yet appeared, and that therefore there was no likelihood of the end of the world coming just yet. But in admitting that 2 Thess. ii. is among the passages alluded to here, we are not committed to the theory that 1 and 2 Thess. are alluded to in verse 15. Many refer these words to St. Paul's doctrine of justification by faith as wrested to mean "faith without works." So, again, Eph. ii. 5, 6, and Col. ii. 12 might be wrested to mean that "the resurrection is past already" (2 Tim. ii. 18). (See Note on Rom. iii. 8 respecting perversion of his teaching.)

Unlearned and unstable.—The word for "unlearned" here is not the same as that translated "unlearned" in Acts iv. 13. (See Note there.) That signifies "without special study;" this means "without ordinary instruction." Ignorance naturally produces instability; those who have no clear principles of Christian doctrine easily fall victims to seductions of all kinds. (Comp. chap. ii. 14.)

Wrest.—Literally, *torture by means of the rack;* and hence "strain," "distort." That St. Paul's doctrine of Christian liberty, as opposed to the bondage of the Law, was seen by himself to be liable to great abuse, and had already begun to be abused, we learn from his own writings (1 Cor. vi. 12—20; Gal. v. 13—26; where see Notes. Comp. Rev. ii. 20.)

The other scriptures.—The Old Testament cannot well be meant. St. Peter would scarcely have placed the writings of a contemporary side by side with the Scriptures of the Old Testament (the canon of which had long since been closed) without some intimation of a grouping which at that time must have been novel, and probably was quite unknown. It is much more probable that Christian writings of some kind are intended, but we can only conjecture which, any of the canonical writings of the New Testament then in existence, and perhaps some that are not canonical. That an Apostle should speak of the writings of a brother-Apostle in the same *terms* as the books of the Old Testament—viz., as *Scripture*—need not surprise us, especially when we remember the large claims made by St. Paul for his own words (1 Thess. ii. 13; 2 Thess. ii. 15; Eph. iii. 3—5. Comp. Acts xv. 28; Rev. xxii. 18, 19). In 1 Pet. i. 12, Evangelists are almost made superior to the Old Testament Prophets—a statement indicating a view which harmonises well both with 2 Pet. i. 15—19 and with the view set forth here; for in chap. i. 15 he assigns to this Epistle much the same purpose as in chap. i. 19 he assigns to the Old Testament Prophets. Moreover, we have seen how Clement of Rome uses the term "Scripture" of a passage which comes from some uncanonical book (see above on verse 4). See *Introduction,* I. c. δ. 4.

Unto their own destruction.—The Greek is very emphatic as to its being "their own." (Comp. "Bring upon themselves swift destruction," chap. ii. 1.) It is their own doing—St. Paul and other writers of Scripture are not to blame; and it befits them—they will find the end they deserve. This passage gives no countenance to the Roman doctrine that all Scripture is hard to understand, and therefore not to be read by the people. All that is here said is that *some* Scripture is hard to understand, and that bad men make a bad use of the fact. The inference drawn from this by St.

other scriptures, unto their own destruc-
tion. (17) Ye therefore, beloved, seeing
ye know *these things* before, beware
lest ye also, being led away with the
error of the wicked, fall from your
own stedfastness. (18) But grow in
grace, and *in* the knowledge of our
Lord and Saviour Jesus Christ. To
him *be* glory both now and
for ever. Amen. Doxology.

Peter is not, "Do not read Scripture," nor even "Pass over what seems to be hard," but "Be on your guard against being led astray by interpretations contrary to the spirit of the gospel."

(17) **Know these things before.**—Seeing that I have forewarned you of the certain appearance, conduct, and success of these false teachers and scoffers. "Forewarned, forearmed."

Being led away with.—The Greek word occurs only thrice in the New Testament—here, Rom. xii. 16, and Gal. ii. 13. In Rom. xii. 16 its meaning is a good deal different (see Note there). In Gal. ii. 13 it has the same meaning as here; and, strangely enough, it is of Barnabas being "carried away with" the dissimulation of Peter and his associates.

The error of the wicked.—Better, *the error of the lawless* (chap. ii. 7), but not "the seduction" or "deceit of the lawless," as some would render it. It is the same word as occurs at the end of chap. ii. 18, and it implies wandering from the path, but not leading others astray. The context, not the word itself, shows that there was seduction. "The lawless" are the false teachers and scoffers.

Fall from your own stedfastness.—Referring back to chap. i. 10—12, just as verse 18 refers back to chap. i. 5—8; showing how complete is the coherence between the beginning and ending of the Epistle. (Comp. Gal. v. 4.) This "steadfastness" will be based on belief in Christ's coming, and on the hope of entering into His kingdom, and thus will be in marked contrast to the unbelief of the "unstable" in verse 16. The word for "steadfastness" occurs nowhere else.

The entire absence of directions—which St. Jude gives rather elaborately—as to how these evil men and their victims are to be treated by sound Christians is in favour of the priority of this Epistle. When evil men begin to arise, the first impulse is to avoid them and their ways, and to this course St. Peter exhorts his readers. When such men have established themselves and gained proselytes, people begin to consider how to deal with the seducers and to win back the seduced, and to these points St. Jude directs his readers.

(18) **But grow in grace, and in the knowledge of our Lord.**—Or, *But grow in the grace and in the knowledge of our Lord—i.e.*, it may mean "the grace of our Lord" as well as "the knowledge of our Lord." But the Greek is not decisive on this point; and the rendering in our version avoids the awkwardness of coupling a subjective and objective genitive together by "and." For "the grace of our Lord" must mean the grace of which He is the *giver;* while "the knowledge of our Lord" must mean the knowledge of which He is the *object*. Rom. xv. 4 and 1 Pet. i. 2 are not instances of such coupling.

The Apostle ends, as he began, by exhorting them to that sound knowledge which he sets forth as the sure basis of all Christian activity, whether the knowledge be full and mature, as in chap. i. 2, 3, 8; ii. 20 or to be acquired and increased, as in chap. i. 5 and here.

DOXOLOGY.—The Epistle comes to a most abrupt conclusion, without any personal remarks or greetings. This is so unlike the First Epistle, so unusual in Apostolic letters generally, that an imitator, and so accomplished an imitator as the writer of this Epistle must have been, would scarcely have omitted so usual and natural an addition. The addition would have been doubly natural here, for the personator (if the writer of the Epistle be such) is personating St. Peter near the end of his life, writing to congregations whom he is not likely either to see or address again. Surely the circumstances would have seemed to him to demand some words of personal greeting and tender farewell; and Acts xx. 18—35; 2 Tim. iv. 6—18, would have supplied him with models. But nothing of the kind is inserted. Assume that St. Peter himself is the writer, and then we can understand how he came to disappoint such natural expectations. His heart is too full of the fatal dangers which threaten the whole Christian community to think of himself and his personal friends. As to his death, which cannot be far off, he knows that it will come swiftly at the last, and his chief fear is lest it should come upon him before he has left on record these words of warning and exhortation (chap. i. 13—15). Therefore, at the opening he hurries to his subject at once, and presses on, without pause or break, until it is exhausted; and now that he has unburdened his heart he cares to say no more, but ends at once with a tribute of praise to the Master that bought him.

To him be glory.—Better, *to Him be the glory*—all that His creatures have to render. Whatever may be our view of verse 15, there can be no doubt that in this doxology homage is paid to Jesus Christ as true God. It is, perhaps, the earliest example of that "hymn to Christ as God" which Pliny tells Trajan the Christians were accustomed to sing before daybreak.

And for ever.—Literally, *and to the day of eternity.* The phrase is used by the LXX. in Ecclus. xviii. 10, but is found nowhere else in the New Testament. It means that day which marks the end of time and the beginning of eternity, the day which not only begins but is eternity. The expression is quite in harmony with the general drift of the chapter. "Heaven and earth shall pass away, but" "the day of God" "shall not pass away."

Amen.—Comp. Jude, verse 25. Here the word is of rather doubtful authority. Being usual in doxologies, it would be very likely to be added by a copyist.

INTRODUCTION

TO

THE FIRST EPISTLE GENERAL OF

JOHN.

I. Who was the Writer?—Three Epistles come before us in the New Testament bearing a very strong family likeness to each other and to the Fourth Gospel. They carry no superscription in their text, but "the elder," or "the old man." Whose are they? The manuscripts from which they are derived have always said "John's," and in some is added "the Apostle."

We will here consider the First. The Second and Third will be treated separately. The evidence for the First is as strong as anything could be. It was accepted as the Apostle's by the whole Church. Eusebius, the historian (born about A.D. 270), places it among the writings "universally admitted (*homologoumena*)"; and Jerome states that it received the sanction of all members of the Church. The only exceptions were such sects of heretics as would be likely to repudiate it as not harmonising with their theological errors: the Alogi, or "Unreasonables," an obscure and rather doubtful sect in the second century, who rejected St. John's Gospel and the Revelation, and therefore, probably, these three Epistles; and Marcion, in the same century, who chose such parts of the New Testament as suited him best, and altered them at pleasure.

The evidence of quotation and reference begins early. Polycarp, the disciple of St. John, became a Christian A.D. 83. In the epistle which he wrote to the Philippians, occur these words: "For every one that confesseth not that Jesus Christ is come in the flesh is antichrist." The likeness to 1 John iv. 2, 3, is marked; and it is far more probable that a loosely written letter, such as his, should embody a well-known saying of so sententious and closely worded a treatise as the First Epistle of John than the other way.

Papias, Bishop of Hierapolis, flourished in the first half of the second century. Irenæus, who was born about the end of the first century, says that he was a hearer of St. John. This is contradicted by Eusebius on the evidence of Papias' own writings (*H.E.* III. 39, 1, 2); but he wrote a work called, *An Explanation of the Oracles of the Lord*, in which he bore witness to the authenticity of Christian doctrine. The account of his work is derived from Eusebius, the historian, who says that "he used testimonies from the First Epistle of John." By balancing the name of St. John in this sentence with that of St. Peter, Eusebius evidently understood the Apostle.

About A.D. 100 was born Justin Martyr. In his time was written the anonymous epistle to Diognetus. Six of its chapters contain indisputable reminiscences of the First Epistle. The epistle of the Churches of Vienne and Lyons was written in A.D. 177. It quotes 1 John iii. 16. Carpocrates, the Gnostic, lived at Alexandria at the beginning of the second century. He tried to pervert 1 John v. 19, "The whole world lieth in the evil one." Irenæus cites three passages from the First Epistle, mentioning its author; and Eusebius mentions this piece of evidence in exactly the same manner as that from Papias. Clement of Alexandria was born about A.D. 150. Like Irenæus, he quotes passages from the First Epistle, naming the author. So Tertullian, born about the same time, Origen, and the succeeding Fathers. About A.D. 170, a Canon of the New Testament was drawn up by some teacher for the use of catechumens. This is now known by the name of Muratori, who discovered and printed it A.D. 1740. (See Tregelles' *Canon Muratorianus*, pages 1, 81—89: Oxford, 1867.) "What wonder," it says, "that St. John makes so many references to the Fourth Gospel in his Epistles, saying of himself, 'that which we have seen with our eyes, and have heard with our ears, and our hands have handled, that have we written'? for thus he professes himself not only the eye-witness, but also the hearer and the writer of all the wonders of the Lord in order." And, after cataloguing St. Paul's Epistles, it continues: "The Epistle of Jude, and the two which bear the name of John as a title, are considered General." The writer evidently means the Second and Third Epistles, which might not have been considered general from their shortness and slightness. The Peschito, or Syrian version, of about the same date, gives the same evidence as the Muratorian Canon. We have thus a consentient voice from the churches of East and West, of Syria, of Alexandria, of Africa, and of Gaul.

So strong, so clear, is the external proof. On the internal, nothing can be better than the words of Ewald. "As in the Gospel, we see here the author retire to the background, unwilling to speak of himself, and still less to support anything by the weight of his name and reputation, although the reader here meets him, not as the calm narrator, but as an epistolary writer, as exhorter and teacher, as an Apostle, and, moreover, as the only surviving Apostle. It is the same delicacy and diffidence, the same lofty calmness and composure, and especially the same truly Christian modesty, that cause him to retire to the background as an Apostle, and to say altogether so little of himself. He only desires to counsel and warn, and to remind his readers of the sublime truth they have once acquired; and the higher he stands the less he is disposed to humble 'the brethren' by his great authority and directions. But he knew who he was, and every word tells plainly that he only could thus speak, counsel, and warn. The unique consciousness which an Apostle as he grew older could carry within himself, and which he, once the favourite disciple, had in a peculiar measure; the calm superiority, clearness, and decision in thinking on Christian subjects; the rich experience of a long life, steeled in the victorious struggle with every unchristian element; and a glowing language lying concealed under this calmness, which makes us feel intuitively that it does not in vain commend to us love as the highest attainment of Christianity—all this coincides so remarkably in this Epistle, that every reader of that period, probably without any further intimation, might readily determine who he was. But where the connection required it the author intimates with manifest plainness that he stood in the nearest possible relations to Jesus (chaps. i. 1—3; iv. 16; v. 3—6), precisely as he is wont to express himself in similar circumstances in the Gospel; and all this is so artless and simple, so entirely without the faintest trace of imitation in either case, that nobody can fail to perceive that the self-same author and Apostle must have composed both writings" (Ewald, *Die Johann. Schriften*, i. 431).

No less than thirty-five passages of the Fourth Gospel are common to the First Epistle. These expressions occur in twenty-three different places, and are used in a way of which only the author of the same two treatises could be capable. Considerably more than half of the parallel places in the Gospel belong to the farewell discourses of John xii.—xvii. There the tender, loving, receptive, truthful, retentive mind of the bosom-friend had been particularly necessary; at that great crisis it had been, through the Spirit of God, particularly strong; and the more faithfully St. John had listened to his Master and reproduced Him, the deeper the impression was which the words made on his own mind, and the more likely he was to dwell on them in another work instead of on his own thoughts and words. The style may be his own both in Gospels and Epistles, modified by that of our Lord; the thoughts are the thoughts of Jesus. (See Vol. I., pp. 557 and 558.) An examination of the following parallels will illustrate this:

First Epistle of John.	Gospel of John.
Chap. i. 1, 2	Chap. i. 1, 2, 14.
„ i. 4.	„ xv. 11.
	„ xvi. 24.
„ i. 10.	„ v. 38.
„ ii. 1, 2.	„ xiv. 16.
	„ xi. 51, 52.
	„ xiii. 15, 34, 35.
„ ii. 4—6.	„ xiv. 21—24.
	„ xv. 10.
„ ii. 8.	„ xiii. 34.
„ ii. 11.	„ xii. 35.
„ ii. 23.	„ xv. 23, 24.
	„ v. 24.
„ ii. 27.	„ xiv. 26.
„ iii. 1.	„ xvii. 25.
„ iii. 8.	„ viii. 44.
„ iii. 10.	„ viii. 47.
„ iii. 13—15.	„ v. 24, 38.
	„ xv. 18, 19.
Chap. iii. 16.	Chap. xv. 12, 13.
„ iii. 22.	„ ix. 31.
	„ xvi. 23.
„ iv. 5, 6.	„ iii. 31.
	„ xv. 19.
	„ viii. 47.
„ iv. 9.	„ iii. 36.
„ iv. 16.	„ vi. 69.
„ v. 3, 4.	„ xiv. 15.
	„ xvi. 33.
„ v. 9.	„ v. 36.
„ v. 12.	„ iii. 36.
	„ xiv. 6.
„ v. 13.	„ xx. 31.
„ v. 14.	„ xiv. 13, 14.
	„ xvi. 23.

The proof that the Fourth Gospel was the work of St. John is given in the *Introduction* to that Gospel, in the first volume. On internal grounds alone, without the strong external evidence already sketched, an unbiassed mind would find it very difficult to believe that the First Epistle (and the Second and Third also) are not by the same author. Even the style and construction have an identity which could not easily be spurious or accidental. This is seen in the habit of thinking in periods the limbs of which are parallel and co-ordinate instead of progressive: the juncture of these by "and" instead of by particles, expressing consequence or movement: the peculiar use of four special particles: the general Aramaic framework of the diction: and the constant reappearance of special words and phrases. The identity of ideas in both writings is of the same character; they bear no sign of imitation, but are the free production of the same spirit. Light, life, darkness, truth, the lie, propitiation, doing righteousness, doing sin, doing lawlessness, life and death, loving and hating, love of the Father and love of the world, children of God and children of the devil, the spirit of truth and the spirit of error: all these notions underlie the thought of both Gospel and Epistle. The writer of each, too, has the same characteristics: love of the background for himself; absorbing devotion to his Lord; faithful receptiveness and faculty for sympathetic reproduction of His thoughts and spirit; pure unruffled, unfaltering movement among the very inmost facts of life and being; intense unhesitating indignation (like thunder from a clear sky) for wilful depravers of spiritual truth; and the absolute tranquillity of that certainty which comes from long conviction and demonstrable experience. So, again, the particular dogmatic notes of each are the same: the Spirit already marking off the true from false believers, and so preparing the way for the final judgment; the manifestation of the sons of God already by the presence of the Father and the Son in the Spirit; the actual present beginning of everlasting life, and the safety from future judgment; the present existence of the last hour; Christ the actual Paraclete, the Divine Spirit being another. It would, indeed, be difficult to find a more structural and penetrating identity between the works of any author whatever than there is between the Gospel and the First Epistle.

It was Scaliger (1484—1558) who first announced "the three Epistles of John are not by the Apostle of that name." The tradition mentioned by Eusebius that there was living at Ephesus at the same time as St. John a presbyter of the same name, to whom great weight was attributed because he was a hearer of our Lord, seems to have given rise to the notion that "the elder" of the three Epistles was this traditional person. Those who take this view are guilty of the fallacy that if this man existed he must have had all the characteristics of the Apostle because he had his name and was contemporary. It is far more probable that the beginning of the three Epistles gave rise among the ignorant to the tradition.

In modern times, S. G. Lange was the first who questioned the Epistle on internal grounds. His argument rests on the assumption that it is destitute of all characteristic individuality and personality; that the affinity of the Epistle to the Gospel is an imitation; that the Epistle exhibits marks of senile decay; and that if it was written after the destruction of Jerusalem mention must have been made of it in chap. ii. 18. Few sound critics will think these assumptions worth refutation. The next opponent, Bretschneider, lived to recant his doubts. The unreasonableness of Claudius, Horst, and Paulus is even more arbitrary, imaginative, and groundless than that of Lange.

The Tübingen school have a preconception of their own to support. As, according to them, there can be no miracle, so there can be no direct revelation; the beginning of Christianity must have been the natural consciousness of an individual, such as Jesus of Nazareth, developing gradually through a much longer period than the accepted Christian history; they hold that Christ only slightly modified Judaism; that in the hands of St. Peter and of St. John in the Apocalypse, His teaching took an Ebionite form, in the hands of St. Paul was adapted to the Gentile world at large; thence arose contentions, in reconciliation of which the greater part of the writings of the New Testament were composed, as party-writings without strict historical value. The Epistle is therefore treated by different members of the school as it will best suit their special theory. Köstlin and Georgii think the author of the Gospel the same as of the Epistle; Zeller supposes it possible that they may be by different hands. Baur pronounces the Epistle a weak imitation of the Gospel; Hilgenfeld a splendid product of it. Thus they contradict each other. The main arguments of Baur are five, and may be given as a specimen:—(1) Studious anxiety of the writer of the Epistle in his preface to be considered the same as the author of the Gospel; (2) vain attempt at drawing a distinction between divine and human testimony; (3) the eschatology of the Epistle more material than that of the Gospel; (4) the ideas of propitiation and Christ the interceding Paraclete more like the Epistle to the Hebrews than the Gospel; (5) the teaching wholly Montanistic, because it describes Christians as holy and sinless, mentions the anointing, and draws a distinction between venial and mortal sins. Of these it may be shortly said (1) that an imitation would have been more skilful, and that the intense consciousness of the eye-witness would necessarily produce the same line of thought when St. John was prefacing his moral treatise as when he was writing his history; (2) that the distinction runs throughout the Gospel; (3) to a candid reader the difference is impossible to discover; (4) no expression could be more sacrificial than "the Lamb of God which taketh away the sin of the world;" (5) St. John is describing the ideal, not a class: the anointing is most certainly not that in baptism, mentioned for the first time by Tertullian, but that of "pouring out the Spirit:" and there is no reference whatever to the six or seven deadly sins of Tertullian, while there is a very distinct similarity between the idea of the sin unto death and the sin against the Holy Ghost of the Gospels. Baur, in fact, as Düsterdieck says, has taken the Gnostic and Montanistic caricatures of the Apostolical teaching as if they were its type and origin.

The Epistle, then, has abundant historical evidence; the internal evidence that it is by the same hand as the Fourth Gospel is particularly strong; and the attacks of hostile critics are peculiarly arbitrary and unfounded.

II. Who were the Readers?—There is in St. Augustine's works—and he often quotes this Epistle—a solitary citation of it as written to the Parthians. Whether this was his own opinion, a mere current traditional title, or a clerical error, the designation seems to have arisen from the fact mentioned by Clement of Alexandria that the Second Epistle was sometimes called "that to the virgins" (the word in the Greek for "virgin" being *parthenos*). This title evidently became misunderstood, and may have been applied to the First Epistle in error. One critic has discovered in "that which ye heard from the beginning" a proof that the readers were the inhabitants of Judæa; another, identifying St. John's correspondent Caius with St. Paul's host at Corinth (it was one of the commonest of all classical names), fancies that they must have been Corinthians; but it was evidently written to no church in particular: probably to a circle of churches in immediate connection with St. John, such as the seven addressed in the Revelation. The warning against idolatry may not unreasonably suggest Gentile Christians, and the contrast of the knowledge of the true God in Jesus Christ, implying eternal life, with the dazzling speculations of innovating teachers, harmonises with the historical notice that St. John resided at Ephesus.

III. What were the Circumstances of the Churches?—(1) There is no allusion to persecutions. The hatred of the world, the victory over the wicked one, the victory over the world, suggest spiritual conflict rather than hostile attacks.

(2) The internal indications point rather to disunion, want of brotherly love, want of steadfastness in the fellowship of the Father and the Son, the seductions of worldliness, the snares of false brethren, the evils of a time of peace, when persecution no longer braces the sinews of faith, and warning is needed rather than consolation; or when perversion has lost the moral shock of novelty and Christian loyalty the fire of its indignation; a time full of evidence of continued spiritual vitality in old and young, but also when a recognised leader of a church can be so ambitious as to reject the authority of the last of the Apostles, and when heathen speculation rather than Jewish prejudice is beginning to corrupt Christian faith.

(3) The particular heretics combated had a Docetic tendency, not yet fully developed. Their theory was that the Son of God was a phantom, united for a time with the man Jesus. St. John's contemporary, Cerinthus, already noticed in the *Introduction* to his Gospel, held that Jesus was the son of Joseph, to whom the Logos was united from His baptism to His crucifixion. The stress laid on the true knowledge as growth in understanding what had been revealed from the beginning, points also to the beginning of Gnosticism, the system which exalted speculation into religion, buried Christianity under a heterogeneous philosophy, and

substituted intellectual athletics for faith working by love.

(4) The only division of Christians recognised is that into mature and young. All alike receive the unction of the Holy Ghost. John himself joins in the confession of sin. He lays on all the duty of trying the spirits. He makes all alike responsible directly to the Lord.

IV. Is the Writing an Epistle?—As an Encyclical Letter, it would have no special dedication nor salutations; the Epistle to the Hebrews is similarly without the one, that of St. James without the other. "I write" occurs seven times, "I have written" six, "you" thirty-six, "little children" ten, "beloved" six, "fathers" and "young men" twice each, "brethren" once. The introduction is an amplification of the ordinary epistolary address, founded on a reminiscence of the more abstract introduction to the Gospel. Bacon says: "An Epistle has more natural feeling than a treatise; more ripe development than momentary conversation." Düsterdieck says: "The whole writing rests as thoroughly on a living personal relation between the author and his readers, the application of the written exhortation is so absolutely personal, that this ground is enough to make us consider the writing as a genuine Epistle. This epistolary character belongs, moreover, to the whole keeping and character of the short writing. With all logical order there reigns in it that easy naturalness and unconstraint of statement which suits the immediate interest and hortatory tendency of an Epistle; while the strict, progressive, dialectical development, peculiar to a treatise or a homily, is held back." It may be described, then, as a circular letter of St. John to the churches connected with his ministry, embodying a succinct statement of his principal views of Christian doctrine. There is no good reason for calling it either with one critic, the "polemical," or, with another, the "practical" part of the Gospel; or "a homiletical essay, the readers being present;" or "a summary," or "a companion letter of the Gospel."

V. When was it written?—(1) As it contains no reference to persecutions, it is less likely to have been written in the time of Trajan (A.D. 98—117); probably before the end of the reign of Domitian, A.D. 96; after the reign of Nero and the destruction of Jerusalem, A.D. 70. Thus we get the period between A.D. 70 and 96. A date near 70 is less likely, because the breaking up of the Jewish world would have made some reference of the kind probable. "The last hour" is a note of spiritual, not material time.

(2) Jewish opposition no longer troubles the apostolic horizon.

(3) The life of individual churches apart from Jerusalem seems by this time the natural order of the Christian world.

(4) The heresies are the seeds of Docetism and Gnosticism: this points to the end of the first century.

(5) St. John is not mentioned in the Acts after the Jerusalem Council of A.D. 51. But he does not seem to have been at Ephesus when St. Paul took leave of the elders in A.D. 60. (See Vol. I., *Introduction to the Gospel*, p. 371.) If St. Paul died in A.D. 64, St. John can hardly have begun working at Ephesus till then. The tone of the Epistle implies a long and ripe pastoral intimacy. St. John was banished to Patmos before the end of the reign of Domitian, A.D. 96. He died after A.D. 100.

(6) It must always be a matter of opinion whether the Gospel or Epistle was written first. It may be that a comparison of John xx. 31, "These things are written that ye might believe," with 1 John v. 13, "These things have I written unto you that believe," indicates an earlier and more elementary object for the Gospel; but it cannot be pressed. It is certainly likely that the doctrinal chords struck in the Narrative should afterwards receive their fuller variations in the Exhortation. It may even be that some of the churches or their members, aroused by these solemn notes, asked St. John for a doctrinal writing.

(7) On the whole, there is no improbability in putting the date about A.D. 90.

VI. Where was it written?—On such a point as this we are left to groundless conjecture, which is useless. An old tradition mentions Ephesus.

VII. What is its Scope?—That the joy which Christians already had might not be dimmed by the world or by error, but might be crowned with completeness even in this life (1 John i. 4), and that they might realise the assurance of the actual beginning of eternal life within them.

For this purpose God is held up as Light and Love, both through Jesus Christ. By that exercise of their will, which would make them remain in Christ as they knew Him, both by hearing and by their consciences, they would enjoy the serene dignity of companionship with the Almighty Father and His Son, and so secure these two grand objects.

Christians, looked at in the ideal, cannot be wilful sinners; but when betrayed into sin, they may recover through confession and reconciliation. The proof of the Christian life must be sought in obedience to the will of God, showing itself specially in true brotherly love. The chief dangers are the world and the depravation of Christian doctrine.

The light of God is shown in the absolute distinctness from Him of everything that is evil.

The love of God is shown in that sonship of Christians which is manifested by personal righteousness. Its correlative in us is love to God, shown in pure love for one another. The purity of love is measured by the purity of faith. And that faith is irrefragably grounded in the witness of the Old Testament through the Father, culminating in the inauguration of baptism; in the witness of the New Testament through the Son, culminating in the blood of Calvary; and in the witness of the Spirit speaking through our own consciences.

Christians cannot be reminded too often that their religious life is a matter of positive, demonstrable, realised facts, to be completed by earnest continual progress. They are already in the Father and in the Son; they have eternal life begun within them; they have passed from death unto life; they have the witness of the Spirit. If they are in doubt, they can prove the truth of their life by obedience to God and love to the human family. For those in sin or error they can pray. The sight of the world and the knowledge of the Redeemer make it finally most important that they should hold to the faith in the utmost simplicity, and avoid all substitution of shadow for substance.

St. Paul writes now in a storm of argument, then in a humble strain of self-forgetful, self-abasing expostulation and entreaty; now eloquently on high abstract truths, now in exquisite descriptions, then about the homeliest and simplest duties. St. John moves in a calm sphere of certainty among the very highest, grandest, and largest of Christian truths, raising the general outlines of human life into the same atmosphere till they are illuminated and penetrated by the clear rays of Light and Love. All is simple, broad, clear, calm, sure. He writes at once with the most commanding authority, and the most loving tenderness; the profoundest wisdom, and the most touching simplicity; the most searching knowledge of the human heart and its difficulties and failures, and the most elevating and bracing courage and confidence; the gentlest affection, and the most pitiless and sternest condemnation of wilful departure from truth in practice or opinion.

It is noticeable that in a treatise on the very innermost secrets of religious life, to all Christian souls are attributed the same duties and privileges, and no mention is made of ministerial authority or responsibility; and that, though fellowship with the Father and the Son and the witness of the water and the blood are both brought into prominence, no allusion is made to sacraments.

VIII. Notes on Difficult Passages.

(1) *Propitiation.*

"He is the propitiation for our sins" (1 John ii. 2).

"Sent His Son to be the propitiation for our sins" (1 John iv. 10).

The same form is used in Luke xviii. 13: "God be merciful (*be made propitious*) to me a sinner;" and in Heb. ii. 17: "to make reconciliation for the sins of the people."

In classical Greek the verbal form means "to make a person favourable."

From these facts it is clear that Christ is regarded as making God favourable to us. The word "reconciliation" introduces another idea, and should be kept for another Greek word, which occurs in 2 Cor. v. 18, 19; Eph. ii. 16; Col. i. 20. Although God is kind to the unthankful and the evil, yet for the sake of eternal Order and Righteousness He is represented to us as unable to pass over rebellion without punishment, as a warning and a security as well as a discipline. In this sense He could not look favourably on the world until His Son had bought it back by becoming sin for us. Thus He is the sacrifice on behalf of the sins of the whole world, which enables the Father, whose name is Love, to show the full scope of His favour. Divine love then can have its perfect operation in reconciling man, or bringing him back. Expiation appeases that wrath, without which God would not be just; Reconciliation breaks down the enmity of man in his state of sin.

(2) *Brotherly love.*

The unflinching truthfulness and courage of St. John are nowhere more remarkable than in the pertinacity with which, amongst the perversions of human affection which are the blot of all societies, and were especially flagrant in the ancient world, he urges his friends to brotherly love. Love is the fulfilling of the law, the proof of union with God, the sign of having passed from death unto life, the great commandment of Christ, the outcome of birth from God, the witness of God's presence, the perfection and crown of our love to Him: the absence of it is the mark of spiritual death. It is that desire for the good of others, temporal and eternal, without which self-denial and self-sacrifice are but barren pride. Like St. Paul, it knows no man after the flesh —that is, for mere fancy, pleasure, or advantage—but is the instant recognition of merit and of God's good gifts wherever they may present themselves. Founded on faith and measured by it, it is absolutely pure and unselfish; it would lay down life itself for the good of others. And because it is that attitude of the human mind towards its fellows which is the reflex of God's mind towards us, it embraces and implies all human virtues.

(3) *The last hour* (chap. ii. 18).

This phraseology occurs first in Gen. xlix. 1, "That I may tell you that which shall befall you in the last days"; where it means "the sequel of days," "far-off times." So Num. xxiv. 14, "What this people shall do to thy people in the latter days;" Deut. iv. 30, "When all these things are come upon thee, even in the latter days;" and Deut. xxxi. 29, "Evil will befall you in the latter days."

In Isa. ii. 2, it has begun to mean the new age of the world; a vague indefinite time, during which, or before which, Messiah's kingdom would be established. "It shall come to pass that in the last days the mountain of the Lord's house shall be established." So Micah iv. 1.

In Matt. xii. 32, our Lord distinguishes between this world (or rather, *age*) and the world to come. So "this time" is contrasted with "the world to come" in Mark x. 30 and Luke xviii. 30. In our Lord's usage, then, the beginning of the kingdom of Messiah belonged to the present age, and the coming age would not be till the completion of that kingdom. So the day of resurrection and final judgment, the beginning, that is, of the coming age, is "the last day" of the present (John vi. 39, 40, 44, 54; xi. 24; xii. 48).

St. Paul also speaks of the present age and the coming, the sufferings of the present time and the glory that shall be, and of things present and things to come (Rom. viii. 38). In Tit. ii. 12, 13, those who live "in this present world" are "looking for the glorious appearing of the great God and our Saviour." He says that "in the last days" before that final period there "shall come perilous times" (2 Tim. iii. 1); and that "in the latter times some shall depart from the faith" (1 Tim. iv. 1). Although actually in this present age, yet, according to St. Paul, Christians have more or less entered on the coming age proportionally to their degrees of progress. So the present age is regarded as tainted with sin and alienated from God (Rom. xii. 2; 1 Cor. ii. 6, 8; iii. 18; 2 Cor. iv. 4; Gal. i. 4; Eph. ii. 2; 2 Tim. iv. 10). Since the first advent of Christ, he regarded the present age as beginning to draw to its close; "our admonition, upon whom the ends of the world are come" (1 Cor. x. 11).

St. Peter identified his age with the "last days" of the prophets (Acts ii. 17), and considers the date of the first advent as "in these last times" (1 Pet. i. 20). But as a few verses before (verse 5), he speaks of "salvation ready to be revealed in the last time"; and again (2 Pet. iii. 3), "There shall come in the last days scoffers" (comp. Jude, verse 18), he evidently looked to a still more definite close of the already closing age.

St. James, too, looked forward to such a period: "Ye have heaped treasure together for the last days" (Jas. v. 3). The Epistle to the Hebrews, like the first usage in St. Peter, treats the existing times as "these last days" (Heb. i. 1, 2); "now once in the end of the world hath He appeared to put away sin by the sacrifice of Himself" (Heb. ix. 26). As well as this, it looks forward to the future age of which Christians already, in varying degrees, partake: "Have tasted the powers of the world to come" (Heb. vi. 5); "Christ being come an high priest of good things to come" (Heb. ix. 11). This tasting is only a beginning, not an actuality, till the second coming (Heb. xiii. 14).

St. John, then, having, like the other Apostles, the notion that the first age was drawing to its close, and that the latter days were already upon the earth, and believing—or, at the very least, firmly hoping—that the second advent was not far off, did not hesitate, especially in view of Matt. xxiv. 22, 24, to speak of the time of his old age as "the last hour." Of the date of the second coming even the Son was to be ignorant; but at any rate, since the death of the last of the Apostles, and the closing of the Canon, there has been no change in the Christian dispensation, it has been a constant repetition of repentance, forgiveness, watching.

(4) *Antichrist.*

"As ye have heard that antichrist shall come, even now are there many antichrists" (1 John ii. 18).

"He is the antichrist, that denieth the Father and the Son" (1 John ii. 22).

"Every spirit that confesseth not that Jesus Christ is come in the flesh is not of God: and this is that spirit of antichrist, whereof ye have heard that it should come: and even now already is it in the world" (1 John iv. 3).

"For many deceivers are entered into the world, who confess not that Jesus Christ is come in the flesh. This is the deceiver and the antichrist" (2 John, verse 7).

Our Lord foretold false Christs and false prophets, who "shall show great signs and wonders: insomuch that if it were possible they shall deceive the very elect" (Matt. xxiv. 11, 24; Mark xiii. 22, 23).

St. Paul spoke of the growth of the antichristian "lie," especially in the cities of Asia Minor. "After my departing shall grievous wolves enter in among you, not sparing the flock. Also of your own selves shall men arise, speaking perverse things, to draw away disciples after them" (Acts xx. 29, 30; and 2 Tim. iii. 1—9). These would be but anticipations of that concentrated force of opposition for which St. Paul looked immediately before the second coming. "For that day shall not come, except there come a falling away first, and that man of sin be revealed, the son of perdition, who opposeth and exalteth himself above all that is called God, or that is worshipped: so that he as God sitteth in the temple of God, shewing himself that he is God . . . Then shall that Wicked be revealed, whom the Lord shall consume with the spirit of His mouth, and shall destroy with the brightness of His coming: even him, whose coming is after the working of Satan with all power and signs and lying wonders, and with all deceivableness of unrighteousness in them that perish; because they received not the love of the truth that they might be saved" (2 Thess. ii. 3—10).

St. John meant by the antichrists what St. Paul meant by the grievous wolves; the individual manifestations of "the spirit of antichrist," which St. Paul describes as "he whose coming is in them that perish." There is a difference, however, in the application of the idea, for the opposer in St. Paul's view is rather from without, St. John's principle of evil rather from within. Just as St. John noticed the same tendencies showing themselves in the same way in different individuals, and called them spirits, so in looking forward to a more formidable and final apostasy, he calls it "the spirit of antichrist," which has already declared itself in so many personal antichrists. St. Paul's "man of sin" must be of the same spiritual character, for no human being could ever be powerful and dangerous enough to answer the description.

(5) *The three witnesses* (1 John v. 7, 8).

The authority for the words, "in heaven, the Father, the Word, and the Holy Ghost, and these three are one; and there are three who bear witness in the earth," is a copy made in the sixteenth century, of Codex 173, which dates from the eleventh.

The words are wanting in all the Greek Codices, including the Codex Sinaiticus, and in all the ancient versions, including the Latin, as late as the eighth century. Since then they are found in three variations. Had they been known, they must have been quoted in the controversies about the Trinity; but they are not cited by any Greek or any of the older Latin Fathers. A quotation from Tertullian (*adv. Prax.* 25) and a parallel quotation from Cyprian (*Ep. ad Jub.*), where each is establishing the doctrine of the Trinity, refer to John x. 20, and xvi. 5; and another from Cyprian (*de Unit. Eccl.* p. 79) refers to 1 John v. 8, where the spirit, the water, and the blood, were interpreted patristically as direct symbols of the Trinity.

The words probably crept into the text gradually from Greek notes on the passage, and from the expression of Cyprian, which would be placed alongside to show how he interpreted St. John's meaning. The second place in Cyprian runs thus: "The Lord says, 'I and My Father are one'; and again, concerning the Father, and the Son, and the Holy Spirit, it is written: 'And these three are one.'"

Their first appearance is in a work ascribed to Vigilius, of Thapsus, at the close of the fifth century. They afterwards occur in Latin translations. They first appeared in print in the earliest Greek edition, the Complutensian, published A.D. 1522. (See Vol. I., p. xviii., and Dr. Scrivener's *Introduction to the Critical Study of the New Testament*, on this passage.)

Erasmus at first refused them, but at last yielded to pressure, when he heard that they were in the Codex Britannicus. But that manuscript is only of the fifteenth or sixteenth century. Stephanus, Beza, and the Textus Receptus followed his lead. Luther never translated them; in his first commentary he pronounced them spurious, in his second he commented on them. We owe them solely to the reluctant deference paid by Erasmus to unlearned current opinion. There is hardly a passage in all literature more demonstrably spurious.

On the internal evidence, after such adverse criticism, it is hardly necessary to speak, but it may be well to quote Sir Isaac Newton. After writing of the fulness and strength of the argument as it stands, without the inserted words, he says: "If you insert the testimony of the three in heaven, you spoil it, for the whole design of the Apostle being here to prove to men by witness the truth of Christ's coming, I would ask how the testimony of the 'three in heaven' makes to this purpose? If their testimony be not given to men, how does it prove to them the truth of Christ's coming? If it be, how is the testimony in heaven distinguished from that on earth? It is the same Spirit which witnesses both in heaven and in earth. If in both cases it witnesses to us men, wherein lies the difference between its witnessing in heaven and its witnessing in earth? If in the first case it does not witness to them, to whom does it witness? And to what purpose? And how does its witnessing make to the design of St. John's discourse? Let them make good sense of it who are able; for my part, I can make none." (Paraphrastic exposition.)

IX. Literature.—I am indebted chiefly to Dr. Karl Braune, *The Epistles General of John*, in Dr. J. P. Lange's series (an English Translation is published by

T. and T. Clark, Edinburgh); to Dr. H. A. Ebrard's *Die Briefe Johannes*, Königsberg, 1859 (an English translation was published by T. and T. Clark in 1860); and to Dr. Friedrich Lücke's *Commentar über die Briefe des Evangelisten Johannis*, Bonn, 1836 (an English translation was published by T. and T. Clark in 1837). Perhaps the best authority of all is Erich Haupt, *Der Erste Brief des Johannes*, Colberg, 1870; London, Williams and Norgate. There are also Dr. J. E. Huther's *Handbuch über die Drei Briefe des Apostel Johannes*, 3rd Edition, Göttingen, 1868, in Meyer; De Wette in his *Commentary on the New Testament*; and Düsterdieck's *Die Drei Johanneischen Briefe*, Göttingen, 1852—54.

Of the Greek commentaries, those of Diodorus of Tarsus and Chrysostom have been lost; a few fragments remain from Clement of Alexandria, a few more from Didymus of Alexandria. *Catenæ* have been preserved from Oecumenius, Theophylact, and two Scholiasts.

Among Latins, an *Expositio* remains by Augustine, and one by Bede. The epistle was also commented on by Erasmus, Luther, Calvin, Beza, Zwingli, and Bullinger. Calovius, Grotius, and Bengel are often quoted in modern editions.

Besides the commentaries of Wordsworth and Alford should be mentioned A. Neander's, *The First Epistle of John practically explained*, Berlin, 1851 (translated by Mrs. Conant, New York, 1853), and F. D. Maurice's, *The Epistles of John: Lectures on Christian Ethics*, Macmillan, 1867; also the able but posthumous edition of W. E. Jelf.

THE FIRST EPISTLE GENERAL OF

JOHN

CHAPTER I.—(1) That which was
Chap. i. 1—4. Exordium. from the beginning, which
we have heard, which we
have seen with our eyes, which we
have looked upon, and our hands
have handled, of the Word of life;
(2) (for the life was manifested, and we
have seen *it*, and bear witness, and
shew unto you that eternal life, which
was with the Father, and was manifested unto us;)
(3) that which we have
seen and heard declare we unto you,
that ye also may have fellowship with
us: and truly our fellowship *is* with the
Father, and with his Son Jesus Christ.
(4) And these things write we unto you,

After A.D. 90.

[1. **The Exordium** (chap. i. 1—4).

(1) Object and Purpose of the Apostolic Preaching: The setting forth of the historical Christ for the spread of human fellowship with the Father and the Son (verses 1—3).

(2) Design of the Epistle: Fulness of joy for those who should read it (verse 4).]

(1) **That which was from the beginning.**—The profound emotion, the hearty sympathy, the tender anxiety which St. John feels as he begins his counsels to his friends, mark off this introduction very distinctly from the parallel passage in the Gospel. There it was calm contemplation of the height and depth of Christ's existence; here he vehemently insists on the personal relation between the Word and those to whom He had been revealed.

As in the Gospel, he starts with the grandeur of an indefiniteness beyond which no eye can pierce: At the beginning of all that concerns us, be it world or universe or all creation, there was——that which we are announcing. "That which," not "Him who," because it is not merely the Person of Christ which he is going to declare, but also His Being, all that relates to Him, His gospel, the treasures of wisdom that lay in Him, His truth, all that could be known about Him by human ken.

The vibrating eloquence of the passage makes the construction at first sight obscure. But take "that declare we unto you" (verse 3) as the principal verb, set aside verse 2 as a parenthesis, notice the rising climax of verse 1 (heard, seen, looked upon, handled), pause at the end of verse 1 to sum up the results of this climax in the words "of (or, *that which concerns*) the Word of life," and at the beginning of verse 3 resume the thoughts interrupted by the parenthesis, and all is at once clear.

Which we have heard. — All those gracious words which proceeded out of His mouth, enough to fill countless books could they have been noted down. St. John has given us more of these than any other of the Evangelists; and their effect upon him was such that it is almost the same as if he had written down nothing at all of his own; for the thought and style of Him who had loved him more intimately than others, had moulded his own thought and style into a strikingly close resemblance. "We" includes all the eye-witnesses. (Comp. Luke i. 2.)

Which we have seen.—All that is meant by the Word of God in its fullest sense had been seen in the human Person of Jesus of Nazareth during His earthly sojourn, and especially during the three years' ministry. In a similar sense Jesus Himself said, "He that hath seen Me hath seen the Father," John xiv. 9. (Comp. chap. iv. 14; Isa. xl. 5; 2 Pet. i. 16.)

With our eyes.—This gives the same force as "the Word was made flesh;" it was an actual personal visible revelation, as opposed to the evolving of a religious system out of the inner consciousness or reflection.

Which we have looked upon.—A more deliberate and closer contemplation; for which John had special opportunities, as one of the inner three, and again as he who lay on Jesus' bosom. There is a change of tense implying emphasis on the historic fact, "which in those days we gazed upon."

And our hands have handled.—Comp. Matt. xxvi. 49; Luke xxiv. 39; John xx. 27. This and the foregoing expressions might be directed against Cerinthus and the Doketists—those that held that Christ was only a phantom.

Of the Word of life.—*All that concerns the Word of the true Life*, the Reason, or Son, or Express Image of God, in whom was inherent all life, material as well as moral or religious. (Comp. John i. 4; v. 26; xi. 25; Col. i. 16, 17; Heb. i. 3.)

(2) **For the life was manifested, and we have seen it, and bear witness, and shew unto you that eternal life, which was with the Father, and was manifested unto us.**—The parenthesis reiterates with redoubled force that the whole essence of the relation of God to man lies in the audible, visible, tangible, historical appearance of God in Jesus. After the manner of St. John, the word "life" at the end of the last sentence suggests the form of the phrasing in the new sentence: Jesus was that *Eternal Life* which was at the side of the Father, in communion with Him, in equal intercourse with Him; that Life on which all other existence, physical and spiritual, depend (1) for its license to exist, (2) for its fulfilment of the end for which it was created. (See Note on John i. 4.)

that your joy may be full. (5) This then
is the message which we
have heard of him, and
declare unto you, that God
is light, and in him is no
darkness at all. (6) If we say that we
have fellowship with him, and walk

Chaps. i. 5—ii. 28, God is Light.
Chap. i 5, The leading thought.

in darkness, we lie, and do not the
truth: (7) but if we walk
in the light, as he is in
the light, we have fellow-
ship one with another, and the blood
of Jesus Christ his Son cleanseth
us from all sin. (8) If we say that

Chap. i. 6, 7. Light excludes sin.

[2. **First Half. God is Light** (chaps. i. 5—ii. 28).

(1) STATEMENT OF THE LEADING THOUGHT (verse 5).

(2) FIRST INFERENCE: The true fellowship (verses 6, 7); the Christian must not sin.

(3) SECOND INFERENCE: Confession of sins (verses 8—10); the Christian must not conceal his sin.

(4) THIRD INFERENCE: Remedy for sins (chap. ii. 1, 2).

(5) OBEDIENCE THE SIGN OF WALKING IN LIGHT (verses 3—8).

(6) ESPECIALLY BROTHERLY LOVE (9—11).

(7) THE THINGS THEY MUST NOT LOVE IF THEY WALKED IN THE LIGHT (12—17).

(8) THE MANIFESTATIONS OF DARKNESS (18—28).

(*a*) *Signs whereby they should know the forerunners of the last time* (18—23).

(*b*) *Exhortation to continue in the light* (24—28).]

(1) (5) **This then is the message which we have heard of him, and declare unto you.**—What the Son had received from the Father, this the Apostles were to report to the world. The attention is aroused, as by the silence before the thunderstorm, to expect a central and fundamental notion of the utmost importance.

That God is light.—Here is the essence of Christian theology, the truth about the Deity as opposed to all the imperfect conceptions of Him which had embittered the minds of the wise. To the heathen, Deity had meant angry, malevolent beings, worshipped best by the secrecy of outrageous vice; to the Greeks and Romans, forces of nature transformed into superhuman men and women, powerful and impure; to the philosophers, an abstraction either moral or physical; to the Gnostics it was a remote idea, equal and contending forces of good and evil, recognisable only through less and less perfect deputies. All this John, summing up what the Old Testament and our Lord had said about the Almighty Father, sweeps away in one simple declaration of truth. Light was God's garment in Ps. civ. 2; to Ezekiel (chap. i. 2), the appearance of the likeness of the glory of the Lord was brightness; to Habakkuk (chap. iii. 3), His brightness was as the light; Christ had called the sons of God children of the light (John xii. 36), and announced Himself as the Light of the World (chap. viii. 12); in the Hebrews (chap. i. 3), Christ was the refracted ray of the Father's glory, "the express image of His person;" to James, the Almighty was the Father of all lights (chap. i. 17); to Paul, He dwells "in the light that no man can approach unto" (1 Tim. vi. 16); to St. Peter, the Christian state is an admission "into His marvellous light" (1 Pet. ii. 9). These ideas John comprehends: God is Light. Light physical, because (1) it was He who called everything first out of darkness, and (2) from whom proceeds all health and perfection; light intellectual, because (1) He is the source of all wisdom and knowledge, and (2) in His mind exist the ideals after which all things strive; light moral, because (1) His perfection shows that the difference between good and evil is not merely a question of degree, but fundamental and final, and (2) the life of Christ had exhibited that contrast sharply: once for all. Thus, on this declaration depends the whole doctrine of sin: sin is not merely imperfection; it is enmity to God. There can be no shades of progression, uniting good and evil: in Him is no darkness at all. Good and evil may be mixed in an individual: in themselves they are contrary.

(2) (6) **If we say.**—A favourite form with John, expressing sympathetic delicacy.

That we have fellowship with him . . . .—Some of the Gnostics (like the Anabaptists) said that on account of their spiritual knowledge they were free to act as they liked, without committing sin. For walking as a description of the spiritual state, compare chap. ii. 6; 2 John vi.; Rom. vi. 4, viii. 4; Eph. iv. 17; Phil. iii. 20.

Darkness would include any conscious habit which was opposed to God's example of perfection.

We lie.—We are a self-contradiction, and we know it.

And do not the truth.—The truth with St. John is as much a matter of action as of thought and word; that sphere of conduct which is in harmony with God, whose nature is Light.

(7) **As he is in the light.**—The effulgence of the atmosphere of the perfectly good, the sinlessly loving, the gloriously pure, which, created by God and proceeding from Him, is specially "His throne." At the same time, wherever such characteristics of Divine Light are found, there He is particularly present.

We have fellowship one with another, and the blood of Jesus Christ his Son cleanseth us from all sin.—The antithesis to "lying and doing not the truth," presented under the twofold aspect of (1) the brotherly result of walking with God, (2) its purifying influence. Each human being that comes near us becomes the object of our friendly sympathy; and the sacrifice of Christ has both put away the sin of the world and prevents sin from reigning in our mortal bodies; it obtains forgiveness for us, and by reminding us that it was sin that brought Jesus to the cross, has a continually purifying power over us, through the Spirit of Christ and of the Father. (See 1 Cor. vi. 11; Eph. i. 7, 19, 20; Heb. ix. 14; 1 Pet. i. 19—23.)

(3) (8) **If we say that we have no sin.**—The preceding words had reminded St. John that even mature Christians, though certainly not "walking in darkness," yet have sinful tendencies in themselves: sensuous impulses, non-spiritual inclinations, lack of self-knowledge, a lowered standard, principles and views borrowed partly from the world, wavering of will, and hence even graver faults. Not to admit this would be to mislead ourselves, and in us the power and energy of light, searching the very corners of the

we have no sin, we deceive ourselves,
and the truth is not in
us. (9) If we confess our
sins, he is faithful and just
to forgive us *our* sins, and
to cleanse us from all unrighteousness.
(10) If we say that we have not sinned, we
make him a liar, and his word is not in us.

Chap. i. 8—10. Light enforces confession to God.

After A.D. 90.

CHAPTER II.—(1) My little children,
these things write I unto
you, that ye sin not. And
if any man sin, we have
an advocate with the Father, Jesus
Christ the righteous: (2) and he is the
propitiation for our sins: and not for
our's only, but also for *the sins of* the

Chap. ii. 1, 2. The remedy for sin.

---

heart, would not be working. (See Rom. vii. 18—23; Gal. v. 17.)

(9) **If we confess our sins.**—An advance in the thought from the general "having sin." Confession to God must recognise and measure each particular fault. (Pss. xxxii. 5; li. 3; Prov. xxviii. 13; Luke xv. 21.)

He is faithful and just to forgive us our sins, and to cleanse us from all unrighteousness.—He, from the context, cannot possibly be any other than God. Here another grand progression of thought meets us: not merely "we are in the truth," but the actual and glorious result on God's side; faithful and just on account of Christ's sacrifice and our repentance. For the double notion of forgiving and cleansing, see Note on verse 7. The Romish interpreters, in their arbitrary way, limit the cleansing here to purgatory.

(10) **If we say that we have not sinned.**—The argument of the passage equally excludes the interpretation "freedom from guilt since conversion" as "innocence during the whole life." St. John is here repeating, in a more emphatic form, the thought of verse 8.

We make him a liar, and his word is not in us.—Stronger far than "we lie," or "the truth is not in us." Our foolish presumption is regarded in its worst aspect: an impiety against God, whose word, revelation, appeal to our conscience, and witness by the Spirit, are thus blasphemously contradicted. Parallel to "we do not the truth" and "the truth is not in us," the practical result here is that we cannot be regarded as having in any sense received God's revelation into our hearts.

II.

(4) The third idea that arises from the great fact that God is Light has already been suggested (chap. i. 7), but now takes its distinct place in the series. It is the doctrine of Reconciliation and Redemption. St. John does not wish them to contemplate with complacency the probability of sinning; but to remember gratefully, in spite of falls, that the Author and Restorer of Light has provided a remedy both for the offence before God, and for its effect on themselves. First comes the principle that we must not sin; second, the admission that we do sin; third, the consolation for actual sin when it is in spite of sincere zeal for sanctification.

(1) **My little children.**—Six times in the letter occurs this diminutive of tender and caressing love: chaps. ii. 12, 28; iii. 18; iv. 4; v. 21. He was aged, he felt a fatherly care for them, he was their spiritual progenitor. (Comp. Gal. iv. 9.) The thought of the shame and misery of sin melted his heart. "My child" was what he called out to the lapsed youth, according to Eusebius (*H. E.* iii. 23).

These things.—He carries them on through the former points up to the new thought.

That ye sin not.—Another side of the object of the teaching: their joy could not be full unless they were earnest against sin. And yet the most holy would not be perfect.

If any man sin.—See chap. i. 8—10.

We have an advocate with the Father, Jesus Christ the righteous.—The word here translated Advocate was translated Comforter in John xiv. 16, 25; xv. 26; xvi. 7. It has two meanings; one, as in Job xvi. 2, he who comforts, or exhorts; the other, as here, he who is appealed to—a proxy, or attorney. (Comp. Rom. viii. 26; Heb. iv. 14—16; vii. 25.) The Redeemer, the Word made flesh, and reascended with His human nature, is that part of the Deity which assures us of the ever-active vitality of divine love. If the justice of God is connected most with the Father, the mercy is pledged by the Son. He has exalted our nature, undertaken our interests, presents our prayers, and will one day be surrounded by the countless millions of His human brothers whom He has rescued, wearing the same nature as Himself. He is represented as continuing our advocate, because otherwise His work might appear a mere separate earthly manifestation; "righteous," because Christ, the only blameless example of human nature, can alone intercede for it with God (Heb. vii. 26; 1 Pet. iii. 18; John xvi. 8—10). The Armenian translation actually adds "and blameless." Augustine remarks that St. John did not set forth any apostle or saint as intercessor (here, if anywhere, he would have done so), but only Christ. "We" is not the Church corporately, but merely another instance of St. John's kindly delicacy, as in chap i. 6, &c.

(2) **And he is the propitiation for our sins.**—On the word "propitiation," see the Introduction. By the satisfaction which the voluntary sacrifice of the Saviour offered to that divine order which requires the punishment of rebellion, both for its own correction and for a universal warning, the whole Deity has been rendered propitious, His graciousness has been called out, the righteousness of Rom. iii. 16 has been set in motion, that willeth not the death of a sinner, and is higher than mere retributive justice. (Comp. chap. iv. 10; John xiv. 5, 6; 1 Cor. i. 30; 2 Cor. v. 18, 21; Heb. ii. 17, ix. 28, x. 20; 1 Pet. ii. 21—24.)

And not for ours only, but also for the sins of the whole world.—This statement must not be limited. Its scope is that Christ's redemption was offered for the whole of mankind, from Adam to the last man. Who lay hold of the redemption, must be determined on other considerations. (Comp. chap. iv. 14; John i. 29; iv. 42.) Multitudes may be saved through this redemption who never heard of Christ (Acts x. 34, 35; Rom. ii. 14, 15). St. John's object in introducing this truth here is to rebuke the arrogance of those Christians who looked down on the non-Christian world as outside the Fatherhood and mercies of God. Such an error might be seen, for example, in

Chap. ii. 3—8. Assurance through obedience.

whole world. (3) And hereby we do
know that we know him,
if we keep his command-
ments. (4) He that saith,
I know him, and keepeth
not his commandments, is a liar,
and the truth is not in him. (5) But
whoso keepeth his word, in him verily
is the love of God perfected: hereby
know we that we are in him. (6) He
that saith he abideth in him ought
himself also so to walk, even as he
walked. (7) Brethren, I write no new
commandment unto you, but an old
commandment which ye had from the
beginning. The old commandment is
the word which ye have heard from the
beginning. (8) Again, a new command-
ment I write unto you, which thing is
true in him and in you: because the

---

the heated partisanship of a Crusader or persecutor for a civilisation politically Christian against one outside his own sympathies. (Comp. Tit. iii. 2—7; Rom. xi. 17, 18.)

(5) The fourth inference from the doctrine that God is Light analyses more accurately the general expression of chap. i. 7, *walking in the light.* If Christ is, as in verses 1, 2, the Paraclete and Propitiation of the world, it becomes necessary to ascertain whether He is this to us; lest, when this salvation is offered, we condemn ourselves by rejecting it. The test is, "obedience to the commandments, especially in brotherly love."

(3) **Hereby** means, *by what follows.*

That we know him.—Rather, *have known Him* (so also in verse 4, *I have known Him*); that we have not grasped a shadow, but have been in intercourse with the living God, who reveals Himself not through speculation, but through a true inward life of man.

If we keep his commandments.— Christ's—because of the reference to John xiv. 15. "Keep" like a precious heirloom, watching them against the inroads of our lower nature. (Comp. Matt. xix. 17; xxviii. 20; 1 Tim. vi. 14.) If each man's conscience was the standard of practice, confusion would again reign in morals as it reigned in the days of the Sophists at Athens. (Compare Plato's *Republic,* Bk. ii., Jowett's translation.) A code and an example fitted for all times and all circumstances have been given by our Lord.

(4) **He that saith . . .**—In particularising the general proposition according to his custom, St. John rejects the first person plural as shocking, unreal, and artificial, and throws the blasphemy on some third person. So "is a liar" is stronger than "we lie," and "we deceive ourselves;" in such a case the lie has entered thoroughly into the man's nature.

(5) **But whoso keepeth his word.**—The revelation of the will of God, looked at as a whole.

In him verily is the love of God perfected.—St. John has before his mind an ideal of a man so filled with the Spirit that in all things he embodies the will of God; the love that such a man has for God is indeed complete. But he knows that the best of the human race can only approach such an ideal in different degrees, at a great distance; and the perfection of the love which they bear to God will vary in the same degree. (Comp. chaps. ii. 15; iii. 17; iv. 12; v. 3.) "In him verily;" rather, *Truly in him.* It is most emphatic, and refers back "the truth is not in him," in verse 4.

Hereby know we that we are in him.—Comp. verse 3 and chap. i. 6; without such a test there could be no happiness in religion. "In him" implies that we are saved by His grace, surrounded by His love, inspired by His thoughts, partakers of His nature, filled by His Spirit, the dwelling-place of the Father and the Son, with certain access to the divine throne and certain answer to prayer, heirs of the heavenly kingdom.

(6) **Ought himself also so to walk, even as he walked.**—Abiding in Him—in Christ—is an evident reference to John xv. 4—11. In the terms of verses 3—5 there is a double gradation: on the one hand, knowing Him, being in Him, remaining in Him; on the other, keeping His commandments, keeping His word, walking even as He walked. The last expression is the strongest of the latter three, as it views the Christian in action. The walk of Christ was the walk in the light (comp. chap. i. 7); divine love the secret spring developing itself in a new virtue for every variety of circumstance. In verses 7—11 brotherly love is introduced as the special manifestation of this obedience that springs from the walk in the light. At a superficial glance it might have been thought that the personal address introduced a new paragraph; it is really only like the "Verily, verily," of our Lord, breaking in to emphasize a message to be brought directly home to the hearts of the readers. The life of obedience, the walk in light, is nothing else but the life of brotherly love: "This is my commandment, that ye love one another" (John xv. 12; comp. also chap. xiii. 34, 35).

(7) **I write no new commandment unto you, but an old commandment which ye had from the beginning. The old commandment is the word which ye have heard from the beginning**—*i.e.,* "I am preparing to give you a special direction, which has been implied already by the walk in light. If you look at it from the point of view of your first entrance into Christ's kingdom it is old, because it was the chief point of His moral teaching which you then heard. If you look at its effect in you it is new, because (1) it had never been taught so forcibly and clearly before Christ; (2) you are so imperfect that you are always liable to forget it; (3) your obedience to the command can never be complete, but will always require fresh growth; (4) it can never be permanent without continual renewal by Christ's presence." "*Ye*" is therefore his present Christian audience; "*from the beginning*" implies the time of their conversion; "*the word*" is here less wide than in verse 6, and means rather Christ's teaching on this point. (Comp. 2 John, verse 5; Lev. xix., xviii. 24.)

(8) **Which thing is true in him and in you.**—The commandment might have hung in the air and remained "old," *i.e.,* confined to the definite point of time of its promulgation, had it not been embodied for ever (1) in the living example of Christ during His life on earth; (2) in His active presence and power since His resurrection; (3) in the conduct and character of His people, radically renewed by His Spirit and continually growing after His image. (Comp. chap. iii. 23; John xiii. 34.)

Because the darkness is past, and the true light now shineth.—Rather, *is passing away;*

darkness is past, and the true light
now shineth. (9) He that saith he is in
the light, and hateth his
brother, is in darkness even
until now. (10) He that
loveth his brother abideth
in the light, and there is none occasion
of stumbling[1] in him. (11) But he
that hateth his brother is in dark-
ness, and walketh in darkness, and
knoweth not whither he goeth, be-
cause that darkness hath blinded
his eyes. (12) I write unto you,
little children, because your sins are

Chap. i. 9—11. Obedience shown in brotherly love.

1 Gr. *scandal.*

---

already shineth. Here he gives the reason why he announces as new what he says is already truly realised in Christ and in process of realisation in His people. A visible change, a notable renovation, is going on; the gross darkness that covered the face of the earth is being rent away in the circle of the apostolic preaching; the life of the Lord, which gleamed forth for three-and-thirty years in the cities and on the hill-sides of Judæa and Samaria and Galilee, is now bursting far and wide into ever-increasing brightness; wondrously quick is the spread of the rays of His glory; multitudes in every known land are gathered into His kingdom. Old things are passing away as the Apostle looks round, and all things are becoming new. (Comp. John i. 4—9; Rom. xiii. 12; Eph. v. 8; 1 Thess. v. 4, 5.)

(6) Here (verses 9—11) is the chief way in which the old commandment, the new commandment, the word from the beginning, the walk in light would be manifested: brotherly love towards those with whom we have fellowship in Jesus Christ, God's Son. And as He, by being the propitiation for the sins of the whole world, had declared the universality of God's family and kingdom, so the sympathy of believers would extend in different degrees as far as the whole human race; to those first who were conscious of the same hopes as themselves; to those next who might be brought to share them; to those, perhaps, in a less degree, who in every nation feared God and worked righteousness without knowing the Saviour personally; and so on, finally, to all who did not wilfully excommunicate themselves. But the brotherly love would be chiefly amongst Christian friends, else it would be diffused into nothingness.

(9) **He that saith . . .**—The whole history of religious rancour has been a deplorable illustration of these words. Controversy for principles honestly and reasonably held is one thing: prejudice, spite, private censures and condemnations, harsh words, suspicions, jealousies, misunderstandings and misrepresentations are the chief props of the kingdom of darkness among Christian churches and nations. (Comp. John xiii. 34; xv. 12; 1 Cor. xiii. 2; 1 Pet. i. 22; 2 Pet. i. 7—9.)

Hateth means not merely the absence of love, but the presence, in ever so small a degree, of dislike or any of the feelings already described, or those kindred to them.

(10) **He that loveth.**—From the associations connected with love in poetry and romance this saying sounds strange. But all such love is tinged with passion, and the desire of satisfying some personal lack; this is the pure disinterested seeking for another's welfare, of which Christ was the great example. It is that which the modern scientific non-Christian world is trying to make its religion; but without the Christian motive, and cultivated for its own sake instead of by the working of the Spirit of God, it seems artificial and powerless.

Occasion of stumbling.—*Stumbling-block.* (Comp. Isa. viii. 14; xxviii. 16; Ps. cxix. 165; John xi. 9, 10; Rom. ix. 33; xiv. 13; 1 Cor. i. 23; 1 Pet. ii. 7.) When love such as Christ's is the ruling principle of life, then the stumbling-blocks of human nature are removed—such as impurity, pride, selfishness, anger, envy, suspicion, unsympathetic coldness, censoriousness.

(11) **But he that hateth.**—Verse 10 was an antithesis to verse 9; verse 11 is, after St. John's manner, an antithesis again to verse 10, putting the matter of verse 9 more strongly and fully, and forcibly concluding the section which describes the walk in the light.

Walketh in darkness.—This describes the acts of the man whose selfishness or other sins interfere with his love. Such are all insisting upon class distinctions; all ambitions, political, social, or personal; everything that savours of shrinking from "in honour preferring one another."

Knoweth not whither he goeth.—This refers to the "occasion of stumbling" in verse 10. He is sure to stumble; is like a blind man groping his way among pitfalls; has all the snares of human nature within him. (Comp. Isa. vi. 9 *et seq.*; Matt. xiii. 14 *et seq.*; John xii. 40; Acts xxviii. 26; 2 Cor. iv. 4.)

Hath blinded.—Just as it is we ourselves who make the gate strait and the way narrow, so it is our own fault if the darkness settles down on our eyes.

(7) THE THINGS THEY MUST NOT LOVE IF THEY WALKED IN THE LIGHT (verses 12—17).—The solemnity of the thoughts of verses 9 and 11 is too much for the warm heart of the Apostle. He cannot bear even to seem to suggest that his "dear little children" are shrouded in the gloomy horrors of moral darkness, haunted by the faithful memories of their sins, and enticed hither and thither by the malevolent spirits of evil. He will warn them with the most tender and pitiful affection against the wicked one, the world, the flesh, the follies and vanities of the human heart; but first he will show them frankly what he thinks of them, what he hopes of them, the trust he places in them, the grounds which he takes for granted in writing to them.

(12) **I write unto you, little children.**—The arrangement of these triplets should be prefaced by saying that the last "I write," in verse 13, is, according to the best reading, "I wrote," or "I have written;" and that the "little children" of verse 12 is the same word as that which he used in verse 1 for the whole class of his readers, and is therefore quite general, but that the "little children" of verse 13 is a different word, meaning children in age. So we get:—

I write.	*I wrote.*
1. All readers.	1. Children in age. [Suggested, according to the perfect simplicity of St. John's style, by the term used in the first set for his readers generally.]
2. Fathers.	2. Fathers.
3. Youths.	3. Youths.

forgiven you for his name's sake. (13) I
write unto you, fathers,
because ye have known
him *that is* from the
beginning. I write unto
you, young men, because ye have
overcome the wicked one. I write
unto you, little children, because ye
have known the Father. (14) I have
written unto you, fathers, because ye
have known him *that is* from the
beginning. I have written unto you,
young men, because ye are strong, and
the word of God abideth in you, and ye
have overcome the wicked one. (15) Love
not the world, neither the
things *that are* in the
world. If any man love
the world, the love of the Father
is not in him. (16) For all that *is*
in the world, the lust of the flesh,
and the lust of the eyes, and the

Chap. ii. 12—14. His opinion of different classes of his hearers.

Chap ii. 15—17. The things contrary to light.

Reasons.

1. Forgiveness.	1. Knowledge of the Father.
2. Knowledge of Christ.	2. Knowledge of Christ.
3. Victory.	3. Strength, perseverance, victory.

Some have thought the second triplet an explanatory note that has crept into the text; others that "I write" refers to what he is doing at the moment, "I wrote" the view they would take when they read what he had written. It seems better, however, if we allow the Gospel to have been written first, to refer "I am writing" to the Epistle; "I did write" to the Gospel.

Because your sins are forgiven you for his name's sake.—Rather, *have been forgiven.* When Christ expired on the cross, the sins of all were forgiven who should in after-time believe and carry on their repentance towards perfection. The process is realised in the soul when it wakes up to a sense of love of the Saviour through faith.

(13) **Fathers.**—The heads of families.

Him that is from the beginning.—There can be little doubt that this means the same Person as the subject of "His name's sake." (Comp. John i. 1; viii. 58; xvii. 5; Knowledge of Christ is assigned in both cases as the reason for addressing the elder members of his audience, because fully to understand the work, the doctrine, the example of Christ, is a work fitted for mature thought. (Comp. 1 Cor. iii. 1, 2.)

Young men.—They might be regarded more as still engaged in the work of settling their character, forming their habits, disciplining their inclinations, confirming the choice which all must make for themselves between good and evil. (Comp. 2 Tim. ii. 22.) St. John is not here addressing those who have failed in the struggle and not repented, but those who have got the better of such temptations, or are in process of getting it.

The wicked one.—Comp. chaps. iii. 12; v. 18; Matt. xiii. 19; Eph. vi. 16.)

(14) **Because ye have known.**—To those who have once begun to understand Christ, the topic must always be delightful and interesting.

Because ye are strong.—For the reasons mentioned before, young men have more special need of strength. (Comp. Ps. cxix. 9.) This power can only come through the presence of the message and teaching of God in their hearts, which will be brought by faith in Christ, acceptance of His redemption, and reverential study of His example. When Christ has thus dwelt in their minds, then the victory is won, and the spirits of evil can no longer entice them.

(15) **Love not the world.**—Having thus affectionately expressed his hopes about each class of them, the last of the Apostles is freer to express that warning which was suggested to his mind by the mournful picture of verse 11. If they would not walk in darkness—if they would be where the true Light shineth—then they must not love the world. What does "the world" mean? In Acts xvii. 24 it meant the universe; in John i. 9, perhaps more distinctly, the earth; in 1 John ii. 2 the sum total of mankind; in John viii. 23 that moral order, to be found in this spot of creation, which is antagonistic to God. Thus it became a phrase for all such inventions, plans, customs, thoughts, and estimates of mankind as are not in harmony with the will and purpose of God. It is ridiculous to suppose that St. John intended to condemn the love either of natural philosophy; or of the scenery of that creation which God saw to be very good, and which sin has been unable to injure; or of all mankind, who are His children. No created thing is evil in itself; the evil lies in the use which man makes of it. We must remember that our Lord said, "I am the Light of the World" (John viii. 12), so that none of the phases of the meaning of the word can be essentially evil, except where it implies man's own ungodly creations. The world which is not to be loved is the sphere of rebellion, caprice, ambition, vanity, pride, avarice, forgetfulness of God, self-pleasing, sensuous desires and interests, connivance with standards of thought and action antagonistic to the will of God. To take one example: Christ declared all Christians brothers; any respect for rank and wealth beyond a conscientious "bowing in the house of Rimmon" is a sign of the forbidden affection.

The love of the Father is the true posture of the soul towards God. If the soul is evenly balanced between love of God and of the world it is negative and colourless. If the balance incline towards the things that distract from the pure and simple walk with God, then the emotion for Him has died away; if the balance be for Him, "the expulsive power of the new affection" makes the contrary attractions insignificant and increasingly powerless.

(16) **All that is in the world.**—The essence, the kernel of this sphere showing itself in countless ways.

The lust of the flesh—*i.e.,* that proceeds from the earthly nature; all desire taking possession of the soul as a motive for thought and action which does not arise from principles in harmony with the will of God.

The lust of the eyes—*i.e.,* of which the eyes are the seat; all delight in objects living or inanimate apart from their moral and religious importance; personal beauty, for instance, considered otherwise than as an index of a Christ-like soul. (Comp. John vii. 24; viii. 15; 2 Cor. v. 16; Jas. ii. 1.) Our Lord's introspection was of moral qualities in Mark x. 21.

pride of life, is not of the Father,
but is of the world. (17) And the
world passeth away, and the lust
thereof: but he that doeth the will of
God abideth for ever. (18) Little children,
it is the last time: and
as ye have heard that
antichrist shall come, even
now are there many anti-

Chap. ii. 18—23. Signs of the forerunners of the last hour.

christs; whereby we know that it
is the last time. (19) They went out
from us, but they were not of us;
for if they had been of us, they would
no doubt have continued with us:
but *they went out*, that they might
be made manifest that they were not
all of us. (20) But ye have an unction
from the Holy One, and ye know all

The pride of life.—The Greek word is only used besides in the New Testament in Jas. iv. 16. The phrase means a boastful, ostentatious attitude in regard to the good things of this life allotted by God to be spent in His service. All living up to a supposed social position instead of as the responsible steward of undeserved bounties, is hereby condemned. Of this any social organism existing for pleasure instead of for moral or religious ends might be considered illustrative.

(17) **The world passeth away.**—No reasonable man can set his affections on what is in its very essence perishable; for the perishable must be ever disappointing, and can in no sense satisfy. It is only passion, and the madness of folly, and the contagion of accumulated examples, that influence the soul towards what can only create the agonising ache of a growing void.

And the lust thereof.—Of all the long succession of impulses excited by the world, nothing remains but the injury which they have inflicted.

But he that doeth the will of God abideth for ever.—There is no permanence but that of defeat and failure in what is in rebellion to the Supreme Author and Ruler of all things. But that which has continuously derived all its sustenance from Him, must have absorbed from Him the "bright shoots" of that "everlastingness" which is His. Everything that is good is a part of Him, and can no more fade than He can. It is by being in harmony with this undeviating tendency of righteousness to victory that real happiness discovers its own secret. (Comp. John x. 28, 29; 1 Cor. vii. 31; Jas. i. 10; 1 Pet. i. 24.)

(8) The Manifestations of Darkness (verses 18—28).

(*a*) *Signs whereby they should know the forerunners of the last time* (verses 18—23).

(*b*) *Exhortation to continue in the light* (verses 24—28).

After cheering his readers by stating the grounds of his writing, and the opinion which he has of them, he reminds them of the momentous epoch at which they are living, of the discriminating effect which it has had on mere nominal Christians, and of the signs by which such might be known, introducing, as in verse 12, a saving clause to separate his friends from the condemnatory category. The train of thought connected with "the last hour" is suggested by verse 17, "the world passeth away," and is appropriate to the treatment of the general subject of light as it brings the manifestation of its contrary.

(18) **The last time.**—Rather, *hour.* Until the visions of the Apocalypse, St. John naturally thought from Christ's words, "If he tarry till I come" (John xxi. 22), that he would see the last days before the Second Advent. Our Lord, in Matt. xxiv. 36, distinctly asserted that not even the angels knew the day and the hour; and on this subject accordingly the Apostles were evidently left to their own conjectures. St. Paul expected a speedy return (2 Thess. iv. 17); so did St. Peter (2 Pet. iii. 12—15). In the same way St. John thought that he recognised in the serious signs of his time that final period spoken of in Isa. ii. 2; Mic. iv. 1; Acts ii. 17; 1 Tim. iv. 1; 2 Tim. iii. 1; and 2 Pet. iii. 3. And it was indeed true that with the approaching death of the last living witness of the Lord's life, the new revelation was being finally closed, miraculous outpourings of the Spirit were ceasing, heresies and opponents were growing, and the lives of Christians were beginning to fade into the light of common day.

Antichrist.—See *Introduction.* Of the terrible personage or power prophesied in 2 Thess. ii. 1—12, Rev. xi., xiii., and xvii., the "liars" already mentioned in chap. i. 6, and afterwards in chaps. iv. 3, 14; are regarded as forerunners. So might Hymenæus and Philetus (2 Tim. ii. 17), Diotrephes (3 John, verse 9), the Nicolaitanes (Rev. ii. 6), or Simon Magus, Cerinthus, Ebion, any who opposed the teaching of Christ from within or without. (Comp. also Jude, verse 4.) See *Excursus* on 2 Thess. ii. 3—12.

(19) **They went out.**—The special instances in his mind were of men who had seemed to belong to the body of Christ, but were never really penetrated by His Spirit. (Comp. Matt. xiii. 3—7, 24—30, 47—50.) St. John is not pronouncing a general law that "grace is indefectible;" but in looking back on each case of apostasy he sees there must have been some element in the character not subdued to Christ. The writer of the Epistle to the Hebrews (chap. vi. 4—6) regarded it as possible for those who have been made partakers of the Holy Ghost to "fall away." They might have partaken of the Holy Ghost in some degree, and yet not have been wholly Christian. Safety lies in the continual appeal to Christ.

(20, 21) **But ye have an unction from the Holy One, and ye know all things. I have not written unto you because ye know not the truth, but because ye know it, and that no lie is of the truth.**—If the Antichrists had formerly any unction at all from Christ, the Holy One (comp. John xv. 26; 2 Cor. iii. 17, 18; Eph. iii. 16; Phil. i. 29), they must have grieved His Spirit. But St. John's hearers were still "holding the Head," and therefore had the divine instinct which "guided them into all truth." If they trusted to the Spirit in simplicity, questions of morality and religion, all that concerned the soul, would be made sufficiently plain to them. He does believe this of them; humbly he begs them not to think that he distrusts them. If he did not think that they had the eye of their understanding spiritually enlightened, he would know that there would be no response in their hearts to his words, nor interest about them in their intelligence.

things. (21) I have not written unto you
because ye know not the truth, but
because ye know it, and that no lie is
of the truth. (22) Who is a liar but he
that denieth that Jesus is the Christ?
He is antichrist, that denieth the Father
and the Son. (23) Whosoever denieth
the Son, the same hath not the Father:
[but] *he that acknowledgeth the Son hath
the Father also.* (24) Let that therefore
abide in you, which ye
have heard from the be-
ginning. If that which
ye have heard from the

Chap. ii. 24—28. Exhortation to continue in the light.

beginning shall remain in you, ye
also shall continue in the Son, and
in the Father. (25) And this is the
promise that he hath promised us,
even eternal life. (26) These *things* have
I written unto you concerning them
that seduce you. (27) But the anointing
which ye have received of him abideth
in you, and ye need not that any man
teach you: but as the same anointing
teacheth you of all things, and is truth,
and is no lie, and even as it hath taught
you, ye shall abide in him.[1] (28) And
now, little children, abide in him; that,

1 Or, *it.*

---

(22) **Who is a liar?**—Rather, *the liar,* the enemy of light above all others. St. John thrusts home his point by a lively personal reference. All who err from Christ's teaching are liars; the greatest of all, he who may be called actually Antichrist, is he who denies that the Crucified is the Son of God. Such a man, with the opportunity of seeing and believing in the light, by refusing to do so loses the knowledge of God in the impressive beauty of His relation as Father revealed in Jesus. And a God who cannot be revealed, who has no Son, who cannot be heard or seen, is at best a cold abstraction.

(23) **Whosoever denieth the Son. . . .**—The sentence in italics has good authority, and should stand as part of the text. "Acknowledging" here, as the opposite of that denial which involved such weighty consequences, implies, as Bede says, "the confession of the heart, the mouth, and the deed."

After this description of the manifestations of darkness in their midst, and of his trust in them, he winds up with some forcible practical appeals, weaving together with concentrated power ideas which have already been suggested, and introducing the most familiar associations of the Lord's teaching.

(24, 25) *As for you* (omit "therefore"), *that which ye heard from the beginning, let it remain in you. If there remain in you that which ye heard from the beginning, ye in your turn shall remain in the Son and in the Father. And this is the promise which He Himself promised to us, the life eternal.*

He turns over in his mind the question, "What shall I say to my dear children about these sad apostasies that shake the faith and darken the heart?" Well, there is nothing new to tell them; they have heard it all, only let it remain fixed and fresh in them! Then all he could wish will be theirs; they will be living and moving and having their being in the life and mind and love of the Son, the beloved Lord who has ascended, and through Him not less in the Father Almighty Himself. And the great promise which the Son made to them and to the world transcends all else, for it is of life eternal.

(24) **Let that therefore abide.**—An echo of John xv. 7.

Which ye have heard from the beginning.—Since each individual first felt the gospel brought home to his heart. Its message is always the same.

(25) **Eternal life.**—The life which cannot be measured by days and years, but is the enjoyment of the blessedness of virtue. This is a present fact, begun as soon as the believer begins to be in Christ, growing more and more unto the perfect day as he walks more closely with God, secured for ever when he enters into his rest, and perfected in the glory of heaven. (Comp. John v. 21—26; x. 10, 27, 28; xi. 25, 26; xvii. 3.) That this life, depending on knowledge of God, is begun here, does not lessen the reasonableness of its being perfected hereafter, any more than its future completion prevents its present beginning.

(26) **These things have I written.**—To remind them that he is still on the subject of the Antichrists, and to sum up what he has said about them.

(27) **But the anointing.**—He reverts to verses 20 and 21 as a favourite ground of consolation and encouragement. Anointing played a great part in the physical life of Eastern races. The climate was dry, sultry, and enervating; unguents restored freshness, elasticity, and life to the parched and feeble frame. So, like dew reviving the verdure of the hill-side, or ointment restoring the vigour of muscles and sinews, the healing, soothing, influence of the Divine Spirit breathes about the children of God, unfolds the meaning of what they have heard, brings all things to their remembrance, and guides them into all truth. They needed not the pretended discoveries of false teachers; all they wanted was the unction of God to bring home what they had heard from the beginning.

Shall abide in him.—Rather, *abide ye in Him* (imperative). These words are the conclusion to the four parallel clauses of the last half of verse 27. On the grounds that their minds were visibly alive to spiritual insight; that this insight was from God, a living power, witnessed to by the life of Christ and His Apostles, and all the phenomena of Christianity; that it was no mere human theory like the speculation of false teachers, demonstrably at variance with Christ; and, lastly, that it had already brought home to their inmost souls the priceless lessons of which they were aware, he earnestly charges them, "Abide ye in Christ!"

(28) **And now.**—As in John xvii. 5; Acts iii. 17; iv. 29; vii. 34; x. 5; xxii. 16; 2 Thess. ii. 6, these words mark a conclusion arising naturally from previous thoughts. As they have this holy anointing, and can exercise the Christian critical ability, and can see the truth, all they have to do is to let their whole being rest in the Son; this cannot be urged upon them too often, or too simply. Their safety depends on the exercise of their own will. (Comp. John xv. 1—6.)

Little children.—Tenderly, as in verse 18.

When he shall appear.—Rather, *if.* Compare verse 18 for the thought of the possible nearness of Christ's Second Advent. He passes to the first person

After A.D. 90.

when he shall appear, we may have
confidence, and not be ashamed before
him at his coming. (29) If
ye know that he is right-
eous, ye know[1] that every
one that doeth righteous-
ness is born of him.

Chaps. ii. 29—v. 12. God is Love. Chap. ii. 29. Criterion of sonship.

1 Or, *know ye.*

CHAPTER III.—(1) Behold, what
manner of love the Father
hath bestowed upon us,
that we should be called
the sons of God: therefore the world
knoweth us not, because it knew him
not. (2) Beloved, now are we the sons

Chap. iii. 1—3. Sonship the index of God's love.

---

plural, to place himself under the same experiences, laws, promises, hopes, fears, as his friends. It would be foreign to his nature to express a personal wish that he himself might not be ashamed on the score of their declension.

So ends the treatise on LIGHT. From the thought that the true fellowship excluded sin, he passed on to forbid the concealment of sin, for sin could not be altogether banished; then he spoke of the remedy for sin; then of the test of walking in the Light; so he was led to speak of the chief Christian characteristic; and then of the things to be forsworn. That led him to think of nominal Christians who had been unable to forswear them, and had therefore become enemies of Christ and beacons of warning. His friends needed no practical counsel except reminders of what they knew, and exhortations to exercise their moral choice by holding on to Christ.

[3. **Second Half. God is Love** (chaps. ii. 29—v. 12.)

(1) RIGHTEOUSNESS THE CRITERION OF DIVINE BIRTH (chap. ii. 29).
(2) THE DIVINE BIRTH THE OUTCOME OF GOD'S LOVE (chap. iii. 1—3).
(3) ITS CONSEQUENCE ON HUMAN CONDUCT (verses 4—10).
(4) BROTHERLY LOVE THE NECESSARY FLOWER OF THE DIVINE BIRTH (verses 10—18).
(5) THE GLORIOUS RESULTS OF GOD'S LOVE IN SONSHIP (verses 19—24).
 (*a*) *Assurance* (verses 19—21).
 (*b*) *Grant of requests* (verse 22).
 (*c*) *Presence of God* (verse 24).
 (*d*) *Gift of the Spirit* (verse 24).
(6) NECESSITY OF TRYING THE SPIRITS (chap. iv. 1—6).
(7) THE PERFECT LOVE THE SUREST TEST (verses 7—21).
(8) FAITH THE TEST OF LOVE (chap. v. 1—12).
 (*a*) *The power of faith* (verses 1—5).
 (*b*) *The witness of faith* (verses 6—10).
 (*c*) *The content of faith* (verses 11, 12).]

(1) RIGHTEOUSNESS THE CRITERION OF THE DIVINE BIRTH (verse 29).—In passing on to think of God in His character of Love rather than of Light (this, with several interludes, is the leading thought up to chap. v. 12), St. John is led, by the earnest exhortation of verse 28 (with which he closes the former subject), to pause for a moment on the idea of righteousness, which, as it was the main object of the earlier dispensation, so is the final cause of Christianity. This suggests to his mind the new idea, "The righteous are born of God." Wherever there was a spark of true righteousness, there was a birth from God.

(29) **He is righteous.**—St. John looks at the Father and the Son as so essentially one, that from his use of the pronoun merely it would not be clear which Person he meant. Here "born of Him," shows that he thinks of the Father, or of the Deity in its oneness; not specially of Christ.

Ye know.—Rather, *ye perceive.* A divine germ, sent by the will of God, has come into the life, and, just as the body and spirit grow in the womb, so the new man is gradually formed in the soul, not to be perfected till the future life.

III.

(2) THE DIVINE BIRTH THE OUTCOME OF GOD'S LOVE (chap. iii. 1—3).—The thought of the new birth suddenly fires the Apostle's mind with reverent amazement, in which he calls on his hearers to join. He then sketches some consequences of the Sonship:—

(*a*) *Neglect by the world, just as the world knew not Him who made them sons.*
(*b*) *The future glory in the perfected likeness.*
(*c*) *The purifying result of hope.*

Sons.—Rather, *children.* The asserted relationship is no mere empty rhetorical title. It is not only a comparison to point origin, dependence, sympathy, care, union, love; it is a fact. As our spiritual life comes from God, we have but to be conscious of it, and to claim its privileges.

(2 *a.*) It passes before St. John's mind how strange it is that the stream of the world's thought, the tide of the world's history, should be going on as they had been before Christ came. Of how small account was the old man, at Ephesus, or elsewhere, in the eyes of the wise, the powerful, the popular! Why was this? Because God, manifest in Christ, had been unintelligible to the world as such, or, if intelligible, the cause only of antagonism. As far as the children were like their Father, so far would the elements that made up their character be antagonistic to the elements that make up the character of the world. For, as far as "the world" exists at all in the moral meaning of the word, it is a mixture of qualities and tendencies which may or may not be like each other, but which all agree in being opposed to true righteousness.

(2 *b.*) We can imagine some one saying in the room where St. John was dictating, or the thought occurring to himself, "If you say we are already sons, what shall we be hereafter?" We cannot say. It is not good for us to know. At any rate, there will be the perfected sonship, the completed likeness, the unquiet and rebellious children conformed to the Father's character. (Comp. Rom. viii. 17, 18; 1 Cor. ii. 9; Gal. iv. 1; Col. iii. 3.)

(1) **Of God.**—Literally, *out of God*—a part of His holy nature. (Comp. John i. 12, 13; iii. 3, 5, 6; Rom. xii. 2; Eph. iv. 23, 24; Tit. iii. 5; 1 Pet. i. 3, 23; 2 Pet. i. 4.)

(2) **For we shall see.**—The old philosophical dogma that if knowledge could be perfect it would necessitate virtue, is true in this sense: the more we see God in

of God, and it doth not yet appear what
we shall be: but we know that, when
he shall appear, we shall be like him;
for we shall see him as he is. (3) And
every man that hath this hope in him
purifieth himself, even as he is pure.

(4) Whosoever committeth sin transgresseth also the law: for sin is the transgression of the law. (5) And ye know that he was manifested to take away our sins; and in him is no sin.

Chap. iii. 4—10. Moral effects of sonship.

---

this life (provided it is a real sight) the more like Him we must be. When we are able to see Him, by entering on the glorified life hereafter, our likeness will have grown complete, and it will never again be able to be defaced. (Comp. Ps. xvii. 15; Matt. v. 8; 1 Cor. xiii. 12; 2 Cor. iii. 18; Rev. xxii. 4.) A true knowledge must be convincing; when we are permitted to see the actual truth in God Himself, it will be impossible for any corner of the soul to remain unconvinced, unwarmed, unrenewed.

(2 c.) St. John, as usual, turns gently to the practical side of his thought. If we really hold this glorious hope of the future likeness, it cannot help having a correlative force in our present life. Such a hope must be the mother of the determination to be purified here; the resolve to be rid of all pollution in body or soul, and to struggle free from the chains of sins. The word for purifying is applied in the New Testament—

1. To wisdom (Jas. iii. 17);
2. To vows (Acts xxi. 24, 26; xxiv. 18);
3. To the Christian walk (2 Cor. vi. 6; 1 Tim. v. 22; Jas. iv. 8; 1 Pet. i. 22);
4. To chastity (2 Cor. xi. 2; 1 Tim. iv. 12; v. 2; Tit. ii. 5).

Our Lord gives a list of things that defile in Matt. xv. 18. St. John probably thought of Matt. v. 8 in thus connecting the future vision with present purity.

(3) The Consequence of the Divine Birth on Human Conduct (chap. iii. 4—10).—This paragraph is an expansion of the thought of verse 3, which was the practical conclusion of the meditation on the divine love as seen in the new birth. In thinking of the nature of righteousness, of the new birth, and of purity, the Apostle is led to dwell on their opposite, lawlessness, the synonym and essence of sin. His object being to bring purity and righteousness into relief, and to determine who are the children of God and who of the devil, he pursues the contrast by a series of antitheses, introducing, after his manner, reflections suggested by particular stages of the thought.

1st Contrast: Purity, and the act of sin regarded as lawlessness (*abstract*).
Reflection: Christ manifested to take away our sins.
2nd Contrast: Abiding in Christ, we sin not; sinning, we have neither seen nor known (*practical*).
3rd Contrast (in the form of a warning): The righteous are like God; sinners are of the devil (*hortatory*).
Reflection: Christ manifested to destroy the works of the devil.
4th Contrast: The sons of the devil sin; the sons of God keep the germ from Him, and sin not (*explanatory*).
5th Contrast: The criterion between the two sonships is doing righteousness and (a new thought in this passage) loving the brother (*the test*).

(4) **Transgresseth also the law.**—Rather, *doeth lawlessness.*

The transgression of the law.—Or, *lawlessness.* He is not thinking of the law of Moses, but defining and analysing the nature of sin in general: it is acting from caprice instead of on principle, disobeying the conscience, neglecting the will of God, rebelling against His commandments.

(5) **And ye know . . .**—The Incarnation is here mentioned with the purpose of strengthening the appeal to purity. The very object of Christ's coming was to take away our sins by atonement, and their power in us by reformation. He is Himself sinless. Those who really rest firm in Him cannot be habitual sinners, nor, on the other hand, can habitual sinners be really in Him.

To take away our sins.—See John i. 29. For the use of the word "take away," compare John xi. 48; xv. 2; xvii. 15; xix. 31, 38. The idea of sacrificial substitution was uppermost in chap. ii. 2. Here it is rather that of sanctification; but the other is not excluded. The two are always connected in St. John's mind. (Comp. chaps. i. 7; iv. 9, 10, 11.) The purpose of Christ's coming was not so much to teach a new doctrine as to produce a new life; the first was the means to the second.

And in him is no sin.—The fact that Christ is perfectly sinless is dwelt on because He is the vital element of the Christian's being, and if present in him must produce a result like Himself.

(6) **Abideth in him.**—See chap. ii. 6, 24, and John xv. 4. The whole nature must consciously repose in Christ, breathe His spiritual atmosphere, draw all nourishment from Him, have no principle of thought or action apart from Him. This intimate union is regarded as the direct consequence of Christ's manifestation, and of His sinless character as manifested.

Sinneth not.—See Rom. vii. 17. Although the Christian does not always do what is best, he does not willingly commit sin; his real self is on the side of God's law.

Whosoever sinneth.—Adopts the lawless disposition deliberately. In the moment of conscious wilful sin, any former partial sight or knowledge he may have had of Christ becomes a thing of the past, as if it were not, and proves its own inadequacy. Ignatius says, "None who professeth faith sinneth, and none who hath love hateth. They who profess themselves Christians will be manifest by what they do." (Comp. chap. ii. 19, and Matt. vii. 23.) A real saving *sight* of Christ is when our mind becomes conscious of the convincing truth, beauty, perfection, love, and power of His existence. The corresponding *knowledge* is when that sight has become experience, the soul having learnt the effect of His strengthening, purifying grace; having proved the happiness of spiritual intercourse with Him; and having meditated continually on the records of the sayings and doings of His earthly manifestation. There may be here a reference to the Gnostics, who said that their "knowledge" was so great that they had no need to work righteousness: grace would be enough, without works.

(6) Whosoever abideth in him sinneth
not: whosoever sinneth hath not seen
him, neither known him. (7) Little
children, let no man deceive you: he
that doeth righteousness is righteous,
even as he is righteous. (8) He that
committeth sin is of the devil; for the
devil sinneth from the beginning. For
this purpose the Son of God was mani-
fested, that he might destroy the works
of the devil. (9) Whosoever is born of
God doth not commit sin; for his seed
remaineth in him: and he cannot sin,
because he is born of God. (10) In this
the children of God are
manifest, and the children
of the devil: whosoever
doeth not righteousness is not of God,
neither he that loveth not his brother.
(11) For this is the message[1] that ye

Chap. iii. 10—18. Sonship shown in brotherly love.

[1] Or, *commandment.*

(7, 8) By the solemn appeal, "My little children," the practical contrast of verse 7 is introduced in the form of a warning in verses 7 and 8. The words "is of the devil," in the second branch of the antithesis, show that the words "is righteous, even as he is righteous," are meant to claim for the true Christian a likeness of nature to Christ. Although there is no allusion to it here, the teaching of the Epistle to the Romans shows that the eternal righteousness of Christ may be an object of faith, even though His name and earthly manifestation be unknown.

(8) **Of the devil.**—See on John viii. 44. Not that the devil has created the sinner, but that the sinner has allowed him to generate his evil nature, until gradually the whole nature may have become evil, and therefore generated by the devil, to the exclusion of any elements of goodness. By making the devil the antithesis to Christ, St. John insists as strongly as it would be possible for him to insist on the moral importance of remembering the existence and kingdom of an allowed power of evil. The work of the Messiah cannot be fully understood without acknowledging this fact of human consciousness.

For the devil sinneth from the beginning.—"For" states the reason why sinners are of the devil. By "from the beginning," therefore, we understand, not the date of the devil's existence, or of the creation of the earth and solar system, or of human history, or of the devil's fall, but the beginning of human sin. As soon as human sin began, then the devil was at work and claiming his parentage.

The Son of God was manifested.—The devil is not honoured by being placed over against the whole Almighty Deity, but is regarded as the special antagonist of the Son. (Compare verse 5.) In taking away our sins Christ would be destroying the works of the devil, which are every possible variety of sin. The consequences of sin—affliction, death, condemnation—are rather the wholesome discipline of God.

Verse 9 repeats, in a more perfect form of contrast to verse 8, the thought of verse 7. (Comp. chaps. ii. 29, and iii. 6.) We have seen that the birth of the new nature is not complete till we enter into our rest; so also the freedom from sin is progressive. *His seed* is the Holy Spirit: that influence proceeding from God, imbued with divine vitality, regenerating, renewing, refreshing, causing the nature of holiness to spring, to grow, to bloom, to bear fruit. The result is the same whether the metaphor is regarded as animal or vegetable. The Christian does not say, "I have the seed of God within me, so I need not mind if I am betrayed into sin." That would alone be enough to prove that the seed of God is not there. If he is betrayed into sin, he trembles lest the seed of God should not be there. He struggles to free his permanent will from all participation in what was wrong. He claims the help of the Spirit in his struggle; and his sincerity shows that it was a genuine *bonâ fide* betrayal, not a pre-conceived moral choice. "Sinneth not," therefore, looks rather to the Christian's course as a whole. "He cannot sin," means that if he is really born of God it is an impossibility for him deliberately to choose evil. If he deliberately chooses evil he is not born of God. "A child of God in this conflict receives indeed wounds daily, but never throws away his arms or makes peace with his deadly foe" (Luther).

Verse 10 sums up the matter in a terse distinction: all mankind are either children of God or children of the devil—they who try to do good, and they who deliberately and consciously choose evil. It is not even for an Apostle to judge which man belongs to which class; at any rate, the true Christian can never be a wilful rebel. And here, as the importance of brotherly love is so constantly before his mind, St. John allows the note which he struck in chap. ii. 9 to enter again into the melody of his thoughts. Brotherly love, the most prominent part of Christian righteousness, may well be mentioned in the contrast between sin and holiness, as it is the most comprehensive of all virtues.

(4) Brotherly Love the necessary flower of the Divine Love in the Divine Birth (chap. iii. 11—18).—In verse 10 St. John showed the necessary connection between righteousness and love; there is no contradiction between the two: the one is necessary to the other. Justice will become sternness without love; love will be weakness without justice. The two thoughts are introduced and connected in both halves of the Epistles. (See chap. ii. 3—11.) Here the duty of love is still more strongly insisted on, as the general subject is the love of God, as in the first half of the Epistle it was the light of God. We have (*a*) the command or message of Christ; then (*b*) the contrast of Cain; then (*c*) the similar conduct of the world (a thought which had occurred before, in verse 1); then (*d*) the comfort of the connection between love and life, as contrasted with hatred and death; then (*e*) the identification of the hater with the murderer, and the impossibility of associating the idea of eternal life with the destroyer of temporal life; then (*f*) the example of God's love in the death of the Son, urging us even to the same extremity of self-sacrifice; then, (*g*) as a minor premiss, the thought thrust home, for a practical conclusion, that the smaller self-sacrifice of daily assistance to others is an essential to the Christian life.

(4 *a.*) (11) **For** states the reason why brotherly love was added to righteousness at the end of the last paragraph: because it was the earliest and most prominent feature of Christianity presented to them.

heard from the beginning, that we
should love one another. (12) Not as
Cain, *who* was of that wicked one, and
slew his brother. And wherefore slew he
him? Because his own works were evil,
and his brother's righteous. (13) Marvel
not, my brethren, if the world hate you.
(14) We know that we have passed from
death unto life, because we love the
brethren. He that loveth not *his*
brother abideth in death. (15) Whoso-
ever hateth his brother is a murderer:
and ye know that no murderer hath
eternal life abiding in him. (16) Hereby
perceive we the love *of God*, because he
laid down his life for us: and we ought
to lay down *our* lives for the brethren.
(17) But whoso hath this world's good,
and seeth his brother have need, and
shutteth up his bowels *of compassion*
from him, how dwelleth the love of God
in him? (18) My little children, let us
not love in word, neither in tongue;
but in deed and in truth. (19) And

Love one another.—The injunction is perfectly general, without the restrictions of society; wherever Christian love is due, there it must immediately be paid. (Comp. 1 Pet. i. 22.)

(4 *b.*) (12) **Not as Cain, who was of that . . .**—Rather, *Not as Cain was of that . . .;* an abrupt conversational form. (Comp. John vi. 58.) Cain is introduced as the prototype of envy, jealousy, and the inward hatred which the evil feel at the good.

(4 *c.*) (13) The conduct of the world to Christians is of a piece with this invariable characteristic of those who are in darkness, exemplified in Cain. (Comp. John xv. 18, 19; xvii. 14; 2 Tim. iii. 12.)

Marvel not is equivalent to "Be not dismayed; be of good courage."

(4 *d.*) (14) This is a characteristic instance of St. John's logic. From the terseness and pregnancy of his style, he does not give all the steps of an argument, but frequently turns it upside down, in order more speedily to bring out a forcible spiritual truth. But for this he would have written, "We love the brethren, because we have passed from death unto life; but he that abideth in death loveth not." But wishing to put these ideas in the form of a direct encouragement, in face of a hating world, he puts the reason as the conclusion, and the conclusion as the reason. This unexpected turn rivets the attention far more than a rigid deduction. Another ground of assurance has been stated in chap. ii. 2: keeping the behests of Christ, of which (as we have seen) love is the most prominent. "The brothers" means all the members of the human family: the love of Christ which, in verse 16, we are bidden to imitate, was for the whole world of sinners. (Comp. Matt. v. 44; 1 Cor. iv. 12.)

Passed from death unto life.—This dates from the beginning of the new birth, the dawn of eternal life in the converted heart. And just as the perfect Christian love embraces all other Christian virtues, so not only does actual hatred, but the absence of love, indicate absolute spiritual deadness.

(4 *e.*) (15) Regarding the absence of love as of one class with the presence of hatred, St. John here puts more prominently forward the active member of the class than the quiescent. The statement is intended as an illustration of the fact that where no love is there can neither be eternal life. The full argument would be "Where love is not, there is hatred; where hatred is, there is murder; where murder is, there can be no eternal life." (Comp. Matt. v. 21—26.)

(4 *f.*) (16) **Hereby perceive we the love of God.**—Rather, *Hereby know we the true love;* meaning, of course, that perfection of love which is God Himself. Christ, the Word made flesh, is regarded as identical with this love, so only the pronoun is used. The highest proof of love is the sacrifice of that which is most precious: nothing could be more precious than the life of the Word made flesh. (Comp. John x. 11, 15, 17, 18; xiii. 37, 38; xv. 13; Gal. ii. 20; Eph. v. 2, 25.)

For us.—Rather, *on our behalf.* (See Rom. v. 8.)

And we ought.—The reason of this consequence is that we are to be like Christ in everything; as our being is orbed in His, so whatever was His spirit will be ours: even His unparallelled act of self-sacrifice must be reproduced in us, at however great a distance. For the good of our fellows we must be even ready to die. (Comp. John xiii. 34; xv. 12, 13; Rom. ix. 3; xvi. 3, 4.)

(4 *g.*) **But** implies a progress from the greater duty to the less; if the less is neglected, far more completely is the command disobeyed.

Good.—Rather, *sustenance*, or "necessaries of life."

World is not here used in a bad sense, but merely of such elements of existence as are not spiritual.

The word "see" is strong, and implies calm and attentive contemplation.

The word translated "bowels of compassion" is used in the LXX. (Prov. xii. 10) for "tender mercies." It is used in the New Testament as we use "heart," and has nothing to do with bowels. It should be translated "compassion."

How abideth.—In verse 15 it was eternal life; here St. John thinks of our love to God as one of the two chief signs and products of eternal life: eternal life bringing into activity its relation to its source.

(18) The words "My little children," are, as usual, a mark of a sudden access of warmth, tenderness, and earnestness. "Word," of course, is antithetical to "deed," "tongue" to "truth." The construction of the first pair (which is different from that of the second) implies merely the instruments of the love; that of the second implies its whole condition. St. John hints that there is some danger of this conventionality amongst his friends, and earnestly exhorts them to genuineness. He forbids all the traitorous babble of heartless insincerity, and urges that just, active, straightforward, all-embracing affection which was complete in Christ alone. (Comp. Rom. xii. 9; Eph. iv. 15; Jas. ii. 15—17; 1 Pet. i. 22; 2 John, verse 1; 3 John, verse 1.)

(5) THE GLORIOUS RESULTS OF GOD'S LOVE REALISED THROUGH THE SONSHIP (verses 19—24).

(*a*) *The comfort of assurance* (verses 19—21).
(*b*) *The grant of our requests* (verse 22).
(*c*) *The presence of God* (verse 23).
(*d*) *The gift of the Spirit* (verse 24).

Chap. iii. 19—24. Glorious results of sonship: Chap. iii. 19—21. (*a*) Assurance.

hereby we know that we are of the
truth, and shall assure[1]
our hearts before him.
(20) For if our heart con-
demn us, God is greater
than our heart, and knoweth all things.
(21) Beloved, if our heart condemn us
not, *then* have we confidence toward
God. (22) And whatsoever we ask, we
receive of him, because we keep his
commandments, and do those things
that are pleasing in his
sight. (23) And this is his
commandment, That we
should believe on the name of his Son
Jesus Christ, and love one another, as
he gave us commandment. (24) And
he that keepeth his com-
mandments dwelleth in
him, and he in him. And

Chap. iii. 22. (*b*) Grant of requests.

Chap. iii. 24. (*c*) Presence of God; (*d*) and gift of the Spirit.

1 Gr. *persuade.*

The style of St. John is so much the opposite of rhetorical, that the transitions are very gradual, and the paragraphs melt one into another. Here the reality and sincerity of the brotherly love which he has been urging reminds him of one happy consequence of it: that it convinces us of the truth of our profession and of the deep security of our relation to God. If we love as God loves, then our hearts need not fear. This immediately suggests, by way of contrast, the wholesome thought that, if our heart does condemn us, we ought very seriously to repent, because God is a far more accurate and searching judge. Moving on, however, from the idea of confidence, St. John next dwells on the happy consequence of keeping God's commandments and doing what is pleasing in His sight, as we can do when we are really His sons: and that is, the certainty that, in one way or another, according to His will; all our prayers will be answered. Then, lest there should be any mistake about the nature of God's commandments, he puts them in their simplest form: belief in the revealer of His will for theory, brotherly love for practice. This brings forward another result of being enabled to keep His commandments: the presence of God in the Christian, and the life of the Christian in God. Lastly, if we ask how we are to be sure of this presence, we are led to what may be regarded as the fourth consequence of sonship: the demonstrable transformation of all our aims and thoughts by the silent working of the Divine Spirit. Thus, although St. John did not set out intending to lay down these four results, they stand out evident from the rest of the train of thought.

(5 *a.*) (19) **Hereby** refers to what precedes in verse 18. "And" is best omitted. For "we know" read *shall we know.*

Are of the truth.—That we have our foundation in, and draw our life from, the truth—that we belong to its kingdom. "The truth" means all of the eternal nature, purpose, and will of God which it concerns us to know—revealed in Christ, brought home by the Spirit, exemplified in Christian lives. "The heart" means the affections (comp. John xiv. 1, 27; xvi. 6, 22); the seat of the moral feelings, as distinct from the intellect; the emotional side of the moral nature, of which the intellectual side was called by St. Paul "the conscience." (Comp. Acts xxiv. 16; Rom. ii. 15; ix. 1; xiii. 5; 1 Cor. viii. 7; 2 Cor. v. 11.) The construction here is more disputed than that of any other passage in the Epistle. There are five ways of taking it:—

(i.) Shall assure our hearts before Him; because, if our heart condemn us, it is because God is greater than our heart, and knoweth all things.

(ii.) Shall assure our hearts before Him, whereinsoever our hearts condemn us; for God is greater than our heart, and knoweth all things.

(iii.) Shall persuade our hearts before Him that, if our heart condemn us, God is greater than our heart, and knoweth all things.

(iv.) Shall assure our hearts before him; for, if our heart condemn us, God, since He is greater than our heart, knows all things.

(v.) As in the text.

The fifth makes the best sense, and is far more like St. John's usual style, with the statement, the contrast, and the statement repeated in a stronger form; but it is obliged to consider one of the words—the second "that" or the second "because," as in (i.)—a redundant repetition. The bias of the reader will probably be turned to one or other of these renderings, according as he holds "greater" to mean "more searching" or "more merciful." The former is necessary if we consider verse 20 a contrast, after the manner of St. John.

(5 *b.*) *The grant of requests the second result of this near relation to God* (verses 22, 23).

(22) **Whatsoever we ask.**—If this sounds unlimited, we should remember that it is said of us in our character as children of God; as far as that is true of us, we cannot ask anything contrary to His will. (Comp. John xvi. 23, 24.) Our prayers are heard through the merits of Christ; but if we do not keep the commands of God, if (still more positively) we make no attempt to do what is pleasing in his sight, prayer must be fruitless. The fact is that, unless there is such a moral result in ourselves, our faith has not laid hold of Christ's merits, is dead, and is no true faith at all.

(23) **And this . . .**—The sum of God's commandments, and the compendium of the life that pleases Him, is stated shortly in two spiritual facts indissolubly connected—(*a*) belief on the Name; (*b*) brotherly love. Belief is the root of the matter, because the recognition of Jesus as Messiah is the essential foundation of the Christian fellowship. (Comp. Gal. v. 6—14; and 1 Tim. i. 5.)

(5 *c.*) *The mutual indwelling of the Father and His redeemed sons the third result of the Adoption.* (Comp. chaps. i. 3; ii. 6, 24, 28; iv. 13.) St. John is not thinking specially of any Person of the Deity.

(5 *d.*) *The solid proof of the indwelling, and therefore the Sonship, is the demonstrable presence of the Spirit* (end of verse 24).

Hitherto the thoughts have been chiefly about the Father and the Son where any direct reference was made to Persons in the Trinity. Here the Divine Spirit comes into prominence; formerly He had only been alluded to in the anointing (chap. ii. 20, 26; comp. Rom. viii. 15; xv. 19; 1 Cor. ii. 4; Gal. iv. 6; 1 Thess. i. 5).

The mention of faith in verse 23 suggests to St. John the necessity of a still further discussion of truth and error, lest it should be thought that all

hereby we know that he abideth in us, by the Spirit which he hath given us.

CHAPTER IV.—(1) Beloved, believe not every spirit, but try the spirits whether they are of God: because many false prophets are gone out into the world. (2) Hereby know ye the Spirit of God: Every spirit that confesseth that Jesus Christ is come in the flesh is

Chap. iv. 1—6. Duty of trying the spirits.

After A.D. 90.

of God: (3) and every spirit that confesseth not that Jesus Christ is come in the flesh is not of God: and this is that *spirit* of antichrist, whereof ye have heard that it should come; and even now already is it in the world. (4) Ye are of God, little children, and have overcome them: because greater is he that is in you, than he that is in the world. (5) They are of the world: therefore speak they of the world, and the world heareth them. (6) We are of God:

---

religious fervour is of the truth. The mention of the Spirit enables him to make the transition distinctly, and he treats of the various phases of religious life, true and false, under the corresponding name of spirits.

IV.

(6) Not all Spirits are the Result of the Sonship: Necessity of Examining them (chap. iv. 1—6).

(*a*) *The difference among spirits* (verse 1).
(*b*) *The measure* (verses 2, 3).
(*c*) *The encouragement* (verse 4).
(*d*) *The condemnation* (verse 5).
(*e*) *Inference and conclusion* (verse 6).

The mention of faith in chap. iii. 23 had reminded St. John of the danger of intellectual, as well as of moral error. The mention of God's Spirit at the conclusion of the last paragraph gave him a form in which to clothe the discussion of truth and falsehood in its human manifestations. By "spirits" he means those tendencies towards good and evil (here especially with regard to thought and opinion) which may be considered as coming from the supreme power of God, on the one hand, and from the inferior power of the devil, on the other. Into the question what these influences are, whether, like the Holy Spirit, they are personal or not, he does not enter. Where one quality, or opinion, shows itself in different individuals, he identifies it and calls it a spirit. Religious fervour might take a form quite antagonistic to the real will and law of God. For Christians there was but one standard by which to measure all claims on their religious allegiance: confession that the man Christ Jesus was the Word. All that demurred to that plain fact, and the loyalty implied by it, belonged to the spirit of antichrist. His hearers, however, if he understood them rightly, need not fear. By virtue of their adherence to the truth, God was in them. In Him they had conquered the spirits of the world, and had but to claim their victory. The false teachers might be known, and must be condemned by the savour of the world that was in their method and their message, and by their popularity with what was opposed to God. The Apostles and those who taught with them could confidently before God put forward the grand claim that theirs was the spirit that came from Him, because they had held undeviatingly to the truth as manifested in Jesus.

(6 *a.*) (1) **Beloved.**—Whenever St. John uses this word, he has a strong and earnest exhortation in hand. (Comp. chap. iii. 2—21; verse 7.)

Try the spirits.—Comp. 1 Cor. x. 15; xi. 13; xii. 10; Eph. v. 10; 1 Thess. v. 21. It is most important to notice that this examination of truth and error is inculcated on all alike, not merely on an ordained and materially separate class.

Prophets, in the New Testament, preach rather than predict. (Comp. 1 Cor. xiv. 1—4, 24; Eph. iv. 11.)

Are gone out into the world, either "from us," or else "have appeared in order to give their message." (Comp. John vi. 14; xvi. 28; xviii. 37.)

(6 *b.*) Comp. 1 Cor. xii. 3. The real humanity of the Saviour is the truth here specially emphasised.

(2) **Jesus Christ** is taken to imply all His history. (Comp. chap. iii. 23, and verse 6.)

Come is used of Christ in St. John's language for His mission and manifestation. (Comp. John v. 43; vi. 14; vii. 28, 29; viii. 42; xvi. 28; xviii. 37.)

(3) **Every spirit that confesseth not.**—There is a curious old reading mentioned by Socrates, the historian, viz., "every spirit that destroyeth" (or, *dissolveth*) "Jesus Christ." It is, however, evidently a gloss, written against the Gnostics, which crept into the text. It is clear that this verse presupposes an evangelistic presentation of Christ before refusal to confess His historical person could be made. (Comp. chap. ii. 18.)

(6 *c.*) This consolation is in the same manner as that in chap. ii. 12, and is introduced by the same endearing phrase. He is sure they have held to the truth, and have the Sonship. (Comp. chap. iii. 1, 2, 13, 14.) God is in them, and therefore the victory is already theirs. Although they may still have to struggle, they have only to claim Christ's strength, and they have won. In making their choice between light and darkness, love and hate, good and evil, God and the devil, they became of the victorious party.

(4) **Them**—*i.e.*, the antichrists, the false prophets, the spirits that are not of God. (Comp. chap. ii. 13, 14.)

He that is in the world—*i.e.*, "the prince of this world," the devil.

(6 *d.*) As usual, a contrast. The reason of their success is at once their distinguishing mark and their condemnation. (Comp. John viii. 37, 43, 47; xviii. 37.)

(5) **Hearing them.**—This implies listening with attention and pleasure.

(6 *e.*) (6) **We are of God.**—The first side of the antithesis repeated, after St. John's manner, with a difference, *we* being substituted for *ye*, and meaning "the Apostles and those who taught with them." St. John feels the grave duty, in condemnation of Cerinthus and other opponents, to assert the genuine truth and divine authority of the apostolic gospel. There could be no spiritual pride in this; it was a conscientious obligation. God spoke in them, and their loyalty forbade alike disclaimer and accommodation. (Comp.

he that knoweth God heareth us; he that is not of God heareth not us. Hereby know we the spirit of truth, and the spirit of error. (7) Beloved, let us love one another: for love is of God; and every one that loveth is born of God, and knoweth God. (8) He that loveth not knoweth not God; for God is love. (9) In this was manifested the love of God toward us, because that God sent his only begotten Son into the world, that we might live through him. (10) Herein is love, not that we loved God, but that he loved us, and sent his Son *to be* the propitiation for our sins. (11) Be-

Chap. iv. 7—21. The test seen in love. Treatise on love.

John xviii. 37.) When heretics said, "Christ ought to have said this or that," the Apostles had only to reply, "But He did not say it."

Hereby know we.—The criterion here is much the same as in verses 2 and 3, but regarded from a different point of view: attention to false innovators, or faithful adherence to the Jesus Christ of history.

(7) THE PERFECT LOVE THE SUREST TEST (chap. iv. 7—21).

(*a*) *Fraternal love the necessary product of the true knowledge of God, because God is love* (verses 7, 8).
(*b*) *The grand recent historical exhibition of God's love* (verses 9, 10).
(*c*) *Our consequent duty* (verse 11).
(*d*) *God's abode in us, the perfecting of His love in us, and the proof of His presence through the Spirit, are the equivalent for seeing Him* (verses 12, 13).
(*e*) *All this is grounded on the strong, undeniable truth of the Apostolic witness to Christ* (verses 14, 15, 16).
(*f*) *The fearlessness which is the result of perfect love* (verses 17, 18).
(*g*) *The cause of our love to God, and the necessary connection of that love with love to our fellows* (verses 19, 20, 21).

This may be considered the central portion of the second half of the Epistle. Nothing could be more significant of St. John's teaching. Here many trains of thought which have occurred before are gathered together in one grand treatise on love, divine and human—the complement of the thirteenth chapter of the First Epistle to the Corinthians. The thought of (*a*) was suggested, though not in so complete and concise a form, in chaps. iii. 10, 11, 23, ii. 4, and iii. 6; that of (*b*) in chaps. iii. 16, and ii. 2; that of (*c*) also in chap. iii. 16; that of (*d*) in chaps. ii. 5, and iii. 24; that of (*e*) in chap. i. 1, 2; that of (*f*) in chap. ii. 28; that of (*g*) in chaps. ii. 4, and iii. 17. The connection with the paragraph on the trial of the spirits is very obvious: "every one that loveth is born of God;" so that the quality and quantity of our affection will be the best gauge whether we have the spirit of truth or of error. The absence of love is ignorance of God, for real knowledge of Him imparts His nature. And if any ask how we know of His love, the answer is that it was seen in His Son. In sending Him, He loved us without any love on our part. Our relation to God reminds us that we must have the same love to each other. The fact that God cannot be seen is an additional reason for mutual affection among us; for brotherly love is the demonstrable proof of His presence, and of the growing completeness of the work wrought by His love in us. The Spirit Himself, through whom our love would come, confirms the reality of God's indwelling. And these spiritual emotions and developments are not illusory, for they are guaranteed by the ocular and oral evidence of the Apostles to the historical Person of Christ. So the result of all this will be perfect and fearless confidence. To sum up (verse 19): our love to God springs from His to us; hatred of our brother (or the absence of love for him) is the denial of all love for God; and for this duty we rest not on our own deductions only, however true, but on His plain command.

(7 *a.*) (7) **One another.**—As God loved the world, so we are to love mankind, not merely Christians. (Comp. chap. iii. 13.)

For love is of God.—He who is truly alive shares the life of God, which is love. All true love is part of His being.

(8) **Knoweth not.**—Rather, *never knew.* Real knowledge of God has a convincing practical effect; without such an effect it is not knowledge, but a mere mental deception.

God is love.—In the early part of the Epistle St. John had defined God as light, and the thoughts had been grouped round and in relation to that central idea. It would of course be impossible ever to exhaust all the definitions of God; but just as our nature may be roughly classified as intellectual and moral, mind and heart, thought and emotion, so, when we have thought of God as Light (embracing all such attributes as truth, knowledge, purity, health, power, and justice), we shall not have traversed in outline all that we can know of His nature, or all that concerns us to know, until we have also thought of Him as Love, the author and source of all true affection, kindness, pity, friendliness, rejoicing in the creation of infinite life for the sake of its infinite happiness, and offering eternal bliss to all His human family, that He may be for ever surrounded by inexhaustible illustrations of the joy and glory of perfection.

(7 *b.*) (9) **In this was manifested.**—St. John echoes his beloved Lord (from John iii. 16).

In us.—(Comp. John ix. 3.) "In our case."

Only begotten.—In contrast to us, His adopted sons.

That we might live.—Human life is regarded as no true living, but a mere existence, until "Christ be formed in the heart" and we become "partakers of the divine nature."

(10) **Herein is love.**—What love is this, that, distasteful, uncongenial, unloving, unlovely as we must have been in His sight, He did this great thing for us! (Comp. John xv. 16; Rom. v. 8, 10; Tit. iii. 4.) On *Propitiation*, see chaps. ii. 2, and iii. 16.

(7 *c.*) (11) **Beloved.**—An impulse moves St. John's mind corresponding to that in verse 7.

We ought.—As God has bestowed his affection so gratuitously on us, and we benefit by it in such an inconceivable degree, and can make Him no return, we can only *pay the debt* by bestowing our poor equivalent

loved, if God so loved us, we ought
also to love one another. (12) No
man hath seen God at
any time. If we love
one another, God dwelleth
in us, and his love is perfected in
us. (13) Hereby know we that we
dwell in him, and he in us, because
he hath given us of his Spirit.
(14) And we have seen and do testify
that the Father sent the
Son *to be* the Saviour of
the world. (15) Whosoever shall confess
that Jesus is the Son of God, God
dwelleth in him, and he in God.
(16) And we have known and believed
the love that God hath to us. God is
love; and he that dwelleth in love
dwelleth in God, and God in him.
(17) Herein is our love[1] made perfect,
that we may have boldness
in the day of judgment:
because as he is, so are
we in this world. (18) There is no fear
in love; but perfect love casteth out
fear: because fear hath torment. He
that feareth is not made perfect in love.
(19) We love him, because he first loved

Chap. iv. 12, 13. Equivalent for seeing God.

Chap. iv. 14—16. The ground.

1 Gr. *love with us.*

Chap. iv. 17, 18. The consequence.

---

on our fellow men. Although our happiness depends strictly on God, still He has allowed us to be stewards for Him in some small degree for the happiness of those about us.

(7 *d.*) (12) **No man . . .**—St. John quotes his Gospel (chap. i. 18). This is simply the general proposition, "God is invisible," and has no reference to spiritual sight. (Comp. Ex. xxxiii. 20; John vi. 46; 1 Tim. vi. 16.) The appearances of God to Abraham or Moses would be like the Shechinah in the Temple, but no material glimpse of Him who is a Spirit. St. John mentions the fact as an admission of the limits of human nature and the condition of faith, but only in order to state the richness of the substitute, which is the presence of God within the soul, verified and substantiated by the historical Person of Christ.

His love is perfected in us.—Its operation in us has full scope and sway.

(13) **Hereby know we.**—Comp. chap. iii. 24.

(7 *e.*) A second antithesis to the opening words of verse 12. The Apostolic witness to the person of Christ is again and again insisted on as the foundation of Christian theology. (Comp. chap. i. 1—3; John i. 14; Acts iv. 20; xxii. 15; xxvi. 16.)

(14) **Saviour of the world.**—Comp. chap. ii. 2.

(15) **Whosoever shall confess**—*i.e.,* receives the Apostolic witness as beyond dispute. (Comp. chap. ii. 23, and verse 6; Rom. x. 9.) The noble width of this declaration is most remarkable, in opposition to human inventions of narrow and sectarian communions.

Son of God, in the sense of "only begotten," as in verse 9.

(16) **And we have known and believed.**—This has the effect of a reflective repetition of verse 14, "Yes, we have known and believed." This time, however, the "we" includes those who have heard and accepted the testimony of the eye-witnesses.

God is love.—In this meditative recapitulation St. John cannot help summing up everything again in the boundless formula of verse 8. Knowledge is here the process that leads to conviction; belief, the result of conviction.

He that dwelleth in love.—St. John's whole purpose is none other than to raise man to his highest possible development by demonstrating the reality and nature of fellowship with the Divine. Here he arrives at the very central position of all: that as God is Love itself, so he that allows nothing to trouble that atmosphere of pure love (here neither specially towards God or man) which God would enable him to breathe, if his own wilfulness did not turn him away from it, will be bathed in the light of God, animated with His life, and one with Him. It is a combination of verses 8 and 15.

Us has the same width as verse 15.

(7 *f.*) (17) **Herein is our love made perfect.**—Rather, *In this love is perfected with us.* "Love," as in verse 16, is the disposition to be attracted towards what is worthy of sympathy, whether it be God or man.

That we may have boldness.—The day of judgment, whether near or remote, is regarded as so certain that it is a present fact influencing our conduct. Love will be more or less perfect in us in proportion as it gives us more or less just and reasonable grounds for confidence were we suddenly placed before the great white throne. (Comp. chap. ii. 28.)

Because as he is, so are we in this world.—If we live in this serene atmosphere of pure sympathy with God and man, Christ is in us and we in Him, because God is Love itself. Sharing His nature, therefore, we must be like Him, and the more completely we allow this Divine love towards our Father and our brothers to transform our whole being, the more we shall be like our Judge, and the less cause we shall have for dread.

In this world merely indicates our present place of habitation.

(18) **There is no fear.**—The more perfect this disposition of serene sympathy becomes, the less share can any form of anxiety have in it. Even if regarded as directed to an earthly object, if it be pure and divine in its character, not even want of reciprocity can disturb its equanimity. Where it is a well-grounded sympathy with a perfect being, its serenity is all the more complete in proportion to its sincerity. When love is perfect, fear dwindles to nothing, is absolutely expelled. Love, seeking to be perfect, and finding fear alongside of it, will diligently seek out the cause of the fear, perfect itself by getting rid of the cause, and so get rid of the fear. Fear in such a connection implies some ground for alarm, and suffers punishment (not "torment") by anticipation. The presence of such a ground for alarm would imply a proportionate imperfection of love. (Comp. chap. iii. 19—21.)

(7 *g.*) *The cause of our love to God, and the necessary connection of that love with love to our fellows* (verses 19—21).

(19) **We love him, because he first loved us.**—God's loving us made it possible for us to love Him: otherwise we should not have known Him, or had the faculty of loving Him even had we known Him. To

Chap. iv. 19—21. The cause of love to God and the brother.

us. (20) If a man say, I love God, and
hateth his brother, he is
a liar: for he that loveth
not his brother whom he
hath seen, how can he love
God whom he hath not
seen? (21) And this commandment have
we from him, That he who loveth God
love his brother also.

CHAPTER V.—(1) Whosoever be-

After A.D. 90.

Chap. v. 1—12. The test: Power of faith (1—5).

lieveth that Jesus is the Christ is born
of God: and every one
that loveth him that begat
loveth him also that is be-
gotten of him. (2) By this we know that
we love the children of God, when we
love God, and keep his commandments.
(3) For this is the love of God, that we
keep his commandments: and his com-
mandments are not grievous. (4) For
whatsoever is born of God overcometh

---

suppose that St. John is putting a mere case of gratitude is to rob him of the dignity and depth of his meaning.

(20) These last three verses are a recapitulation, in a vivid form, of the truth and the duty contained in verses 10, 11. God made it possible for us to love Him, and the very first result of our feeling this power within us, and allowing it to put itself into force will be seen in pure and devout sympathy for all whom we can help. As usual, hating, and not loving, are put as interchangeable members of the class of malevolence. St. John argues on the ground that it is much easier for human nature to be interested by what comes before its eyes than by that about which it has to think. Gregory the Great says, "In love the eyes are guides;" and Œcumenius, "Sight leads on to love." (Comp. chaps. ii. 4; iii. 17; and verse 12.)

(21) However this may be, there is a still stronger position: the simple command of God in Christ. (Comp. Luke x. 27; John xiii. 34, 35; xiv. 21; xv. 9. 10, 12.)

V.

(8.) Faith the Test of Love (chap. v. 1—12).
 (*a*) *Its power* (verses 1—5).
 (*b*) *The evidence on which it rests* (verses 6—10).
 (*c*) *What it contains* (verses 11, 12).

(8 *a.*) St. John has been setting love in the supreme place which it held in our Lord's teaching and in St. Paul's. But there is another faculty which has to regulate, purify, direct, and stir up our weak and imperfect loving powers, and that is, faith. Without faith we cannot be certain about the quality of our love. He begins very simply with a position already laid down: genuine faith in Christ is the genuine birth from God. From that faith, through that birth, will come the proper love, as in a family: the love of our spiritual brothers and sisters. (This is specially sympathy with real Christians; but it does not exclude the more general love before inculcated.) If we are doubtful about the quality of our love, or are not sure whether any earthly elements may be mingled with it, we have only to ask ourselves whether we are loving God and keeping His commandments: the true work of faith. The love of God does, indeed, actually consist in keeping His commandments (and none can complain that they are tyrannical, vexatious, or capricious). The very object of the divine birth is the conquest of all that is opposed to God and to His commandments, and the instrument of the conquest is faith. There can be no victory over these elements that are opposed to God, and, consequently, no pure, true, God-like love, except through faith.

(8 *b.*) Having left the discussion about the effect of faith on love with the same thought which began it—belief in Jesus Christ—he is led to state the grounds on which that faith rests. These are here stated to be three: water, or Christ's baptism, symbolising the complete fulfilment of the Law in His own perfect purity, and thus appealing to the Old Testament; blood, or His meritorious cross and passion, symbolising His own special work of atonement and reconciliation; and the Spirit, embracing all those demonstrable proofs of His kingdom which were from day to day forcing themselves on the attention of believers. If we accept human testimony on proper grounds, far more should we receive this divine testimony of God to His Son—the witness of the Old Testament, of the work of Christ, and of the Spirit. This witness is not far to seek, for it is actually within the true believer.

(8 *c.*) The contents of the record which God has thus given us are at once most simple and most comprehensive: the gift of eternal life in His Son. The presence of the Word of God in the heart is the sole condition of life.

(8 *a.*) (1) **Whosoever believeth . . .**—What may be the works of God among those who have not heard of His Son we do not here inquire. Enough that those who have this privilege are sons if they accept the message.

Begotten.—Of those who have the new birth, in a general sense: quite distinct from "only-begotten."

(2) **By this we know . . .**—Love and obedience to God will assure us of the truth of our love to others. In chaps. ii. 3 and iv. 20, 21, obedience to God and love to our fellows were the signs of knowledge of God and love to Him. The two are really inseparable. If love of God is absent, then our love of our fellows is not genuine—is earthly, is a mockery. If love of our fellows is absent, then we have no love for God. All friendship must be tested by loyalty to God; all love to Him must be tested by charity.

(3) **For this is . . .**—These words are introduced to show that what were treated as two separate qualities in the last verse are in reality the same thing.

And his commandments are not grievous.—A transitional thought, introduced for encouragement, and forming a bridge to the next statement. (Comp. Matt. xi. 30.) God has commanded us nothing for His own sake, but everything for our own highest profit and happiness. Were we perfect, we should not find them commands at all, for they would be our natural impulses. The more sincerely we serve God, the more enjoyment we shall derive from them. Only to those whose inclinations are distorted, perverted, and corrupted by sin can God's laws seem irksome.

(4) The difficulty experienced by some in keeping God's commands arises from the influence of all that is opposed to Him in our surroundings. But he who is

the world: and this is the victory that
overcometh the world, *even* our faith.
(5) Who is he that overcometh the world,
but he that believeth that Jesus is the
Son of God? (6) This is he that came
Chap. v. 6—10. Evidence. by water and blood, *even*
Jesus Christ; not by water
only, but by water and blood. And
it is the Spirit that beareth witness,
because the Spirit is truth. (7) For
there are three that bear record in
heaven, the Father, the Word, and the
Holy Ghost: and these three are one.
(8) And there are three that bear wit-
ness in earth, the spirit, and the water,
and the blood: and these three agree
in one. (9) If we receive the witness of
men, the witness of God is greater: for

---

born of God—the true child of God—fights with this only as a conqueror, because, as far as he is born again, God is in him. God overcame the world in Christ, and is still ever conquering through Him in His sons: so that to such the commands are congenial. (Comp. chaps. iii. 9; iv. 4; John xvi. 33.)

And this is the victory . . .—A new thought, suitable to the tenor of the passage, which lays down that faith is the measure of love. As the conquest that is overcoming the world is wrought by human instruments, its agent may be regarded as our faith, which appropriates Christ's work, and carries it out for Him and through Him. (Comp. chaps. ii. 13, 14, 23; iv. 4; 1 Cor. xv. 55—57.)

(5) **Who is he that overcometh?**—An appeal to the consciousness of Christians. If there be any besides the disciples of Jesus who have vanquished all that is opposed to God, where are they? God has declared that He will not harshly judge the Pagan world (Rom. ii. 13, 15); but salvation by uncovenanted mercies is a very different thing from the glories of the illuminated and victorious Christian heart. Where are they? Not Socrates, with his want of the sense of sin and his tolerance of evil; not Cicero, with his tormenting vanity; not the Gnostics, with their questionable lives: only those in whom had dawned the bright and morning Star.

(8 *b*.) (6) **This is he that came by water and blood, even Jesus Christ.**—"Water" and "blood" are referred to as two of the three great witnesses, or sets of evidence, for Christ. They are symbols, and look back to two of the most characteristic and significant acts of His personal history. The one is His baptism, the other His cross. Why His baptism? The baptism of John was the seal of the Law. It was the outward sign by which those who repented at his preaching showed their determination to keep the Law no longer in the letter only, but also in the spirit. Jesus, too, showed this determination. Baptism in water was His outward sign and seal to the Old Testament: that He had not come to destroy but to fulfil the Law; not to supersede the prophecies, but to claim them. It was to show that in Him the righteousness and purification which the Law intended was to be a reality, and through Him to be the law of His kingdom. Thus it pointed to all the evidence which the Old Testament could possibly afford Him; and, through the Old Testament, it pointed to the dispensation of the Father. Thus, when this most symbolic act was complete, the Almighty Giver of the old Law or covenant was heard saying, "This is My beloved Son, in whom I am well pleased."

"Blood," in the same way, refers to the special work of Christ Himself—the work of reconciliation and atonement by His death and passion, the realisation of all that the sacrifices and types of the former state of religion had meant. That He was the true sacrifice was proved by the perfection of His life, by the signs and wonders with which He had attracted and convinced His followers, by the fulfilment of prophecy, by the marvels of His teaching, by the amazing events which had happened at the different crises of His life, by His resurrection and ascension, and by the confession of all who knew Him well that He was the Word made flesh, full of grace and truth, and with the glory as of the only-begotten of the Father.

Not by water only.—John the Baptist might have been said to come by water only: he came preaching the washing away of the personal results of sin through turning again to the truth and spirit of the Law; Jesus came by blood also, for His sacrifice atoned for sin as rebellion against God.

And it is the Spirit that beareth witness.—The Holy Spirit had descended on Jesus at His baptism, had proved Him to be the Son of God in every word and act of His life, had raised Him up on the third day, and glorified His body till it could no longer be seen on earth. He had made new men of His disciples on the Day of Pentecost, had laid far and wide the foundations of the new kingdom, and was daily demonstrating Himself in the renewed life in all parts of the world. (Comp. Matt. iii. 16; John i. 32, 33; iii. 34; Rom. i. 4; 1 Tim. iii. 16; 1 Pet. iii. 18.)

Because the Spirit is truth.—Rather, *the truth;* the sum and substance of God's revelation in all its fulness, regarded as personally proceeding from the divine throne, teaching the prophets their message, accompanying the Son on His human pilgrimage, and bringing all things afterwards to the remembrance of His disciples.

(7) For the reasons why this verse cannot be retained in the text, see the *Introduction.*

(8) The text of this verse is properly, *For there are three that bear witness; the Spirit, and the water, and the blood.* It is a repetition of verse 6 for the purpose of emphasis. The fact that the three that bear witness are in the masculine gender bears out the interpretation given of verse 6; that they imply the Holy Spirit, the author of the Law, and the author of Redemption. It also explains how verse 7 crept in as a gloss.

And these three agree in one.—Literally, *make for the one.* The old dispensation, of which the Baptist's preaching was the last message, had no other meaning than the preparation for the Messiah; the sacrifice of Calvary was the consummation of the Messiah's mission; the kingdom of the Spirit, starting from that mission, was the seal of it. The three witnesses to Christ have their counterparts in the Christian soul: "baptism, not the putting away of the filth of the flesh, but the answer of a good conscience toward God;" "the blood of Christ purging our conscience from dead works to serve the living God;" and "the baptism with the Holy Ghost and with fire."

(9) **If we receive the witness of men.**—Any human testimony, provided it is logically binding on

this is the witness of God which he hath testified of his Son. (10) He that believeth on the Son of God hath the witness in himself: he that believeth not God hath made him a liar; because he believeth not the record that God gave of his Son. (11) And this is the record, that God hath given to us eternal life, and this life is in his Son. (12) He that hath the Son hath life; *and* he that hath not the Son of God hath not life. (13) These things have I written unto you that believe on the

Chap. v. 11, 12. The contents of faith.

---

our understandings, to establish common facts or to prove opinions. (Comp. Deut. xvii. 6; xix. 15; Matt. xviii. 16; 2 Cor. xiii. 1; Heb. x. 28, 29.)

The witness of God is greater.—Any message that clearly comes from God is to be accepted by us with a readiness infinitely greater than in the case of mere human testimony. St. John considers the three-fold witness from God to convey a certainty which no human evidence could claim.

For this is the witness of God which he hath testified of his Son.—Such witness from God there is: for this three-fold testimony is what He has said to us about His Son. If any should doubt whether the carpenter, Jesus of Nazareth, was in reality God, St. John would refer them to the righteousness and predictions of the Law and the prophets all fulfilled, to the life and death of Christ which spoke for themselves, and to manifest inauguration of the reign of the Spirit. Under these three heads would come all possible evidence for Christian truth.

(10) **He that believeth on the Son of God hath the witness in himself.**—To the real believer the three-fold testimony of God no longer remains merely an outward object of thought to be contemplated and grasped: it has become part of his own nature. The three separate messages have each produced their proper result in him, and he can no more doubt them than he can doubt himself. The water has assured him that he is no longer under the Law, but under grace, and has taught him the necessity of the new birth unto righteousness (John iii. 5; Tit. iii. 5). The blood has shown him that he cannot face God unless his sins are forgiven; and it has enabled him to feel that they are forgiven, that he is being daily cleansed, and that he has in himself the beginnings of eternal life (chaps. i. 7; ii. 2; John vi. 53). And the Spirit, which has had part in both these, is daily making him grow in grace (Gal. v. 22; Eph. v. 9).

He that believeth not God hath made him a liar.—The negative contrast, as usual, to strengthen the affirmative. St. John regards the evidence as so certain, that he to whom it is brought and who rejects it seems as if he was boldly asserting that what God had said was false. The sceptical reply that the message did not really come from God at all it is not St. John's purpose to consider; his object is to warn his friends of the real light in which they ought to regard the opponents of the truth. There should be no complacent condoning; from the point of view of the Christians themselves, such unbelievers were throwing the truth back in God's face.

(8 *c.*) *What Faith contains* (verses 11, 12).

(11) **This is the record.**—This is the substance of the witness of God. The Christian creed is here reduced to a very small compass: the gift of eternal life and the dependance of that life upon His Son. Eternal life does not here mean the mere continuance of life after death, whether for good or evil; it is the expression used throughout St. John's writings for that life in God, thought of without reference to time, which can have no end, which implies heaven and every possible variety of blessedness, and which consists in believing in God the Father and in His Son. Its opposite is not annihilation, but the second death: existence in exclusion from God. (Comp. chap. ii. 25; John xvii. 3; 2 Tim. i. 10.)

(12) **He that hath the Son hath life.**—The emphatic word here is "hath." As this sentence is addressed to the faithful, there is no need to say "the Son of God." "Having the Son" is His dwelling in the heart by faith: a conscious difference to human life which transforms its whole character. "Having life" is the birth of the new man within which can never die.

He that hath not the Son of God hath not life.—As this is contemplating unbelievers, the words "of God" are added, to show them what they have lost.

[4. **The Conclusion** (chap. v. 13—21).

(1) Fresh Statement of the Purpose of Writing, equivalent to that at the beginning of the Epistle, but differing from it (verse 13).

(2) What can be done for those who do not come up to the Standard assumed throughout the Epistle (verses 14—17).

(3) Some Practical Points recapitulated (verses 18—20).

(*a*) *God's sons do not sin* (verse 18);

(*b*) *Personal assurance that we are God's sons* (verse 19);

(*c*) *Personal assurance that Christ is come, of the gift of the spiritual sense, and of abiding in the God of Truth through His Son* (verse 20).

(4) Last Warning (verse 21).]

St. John, thinking perhaps of the close of his Gospel, where he states the same purpose (John xx. 31), and reminded by verse 11 of the supreme importance of having eternal life, and of the necessity of finding this in the Son, sums up the object of his Letter in these two ideas. He tells his friends again that he writes to them because they believe on the name of the Son of God, and explains his wish to be that, by the thoughts which he has put before them, they may feel certain that the eternal life which ought to be theirs is theirs already, and that their belief may not cease, but may be really vital. Thinking then of those who would be deceiving themselves if they pretended to any such hopeful assurance, he reminds the faithful of the power of prayer. Beginning with the general statement that confidence in God means that He hears us, he goes on to show that hearing must imply that our petitions are granted; and next, that it would be a petition quite in accordance with God's will, and therefore likely to be heard, if a believer were to pray for a sinning brother. At the same time it must be recollected that there is

Chap. v. 13—21. The conclusion and recapitulation.

name of the Son of God; that ye may
know that ye have eternal
life, and that ye may be-
lieve on the name of the
Son of God. (14) And this
is the confidence that we have in him,[1]
that, if we ask any thing according to
his will, he heareth us: (15) and if we
know that he hear us, whatsoever we ask,
we know that we have the petitions that
we desired of him. (16) If any man see his
brother sin a sin *which is* not unto
death, he shall ask, and he shall give
him life for them that sin not unto
death. There is a sin unto death: I
do not say that he shall pray for it.
(17) All unrighteousness is sin: and there
is a sin not unto death. (18) We know
that whosoever is born of God sinneth
not; but he that is begotten of God
keepeth himself, and that wicked one
toucheth him not. (19) *And* we know

1 Or, *concerning him.*

---

such a state of wilful, hard-hearted rebellion that it is past praying for. Meantime they must remember again that as far as they were born of God they could not wilfully sin; that if they were what St. John thought them they had ample proofs that they were of God, and must not forget that the whole world was corrupted; and that there could not be any doubt that the Son of God was come, and had given them the spiritual sense necessary to discerning the true God. In that true God they were, through His Son. The God of whom the Son had spoken was that true God, and to know Him as such in His Son was eternal life. The last request was, that they should strictly guard themselves against any appearance or tendency whatsoever which might claim their sympathy or allegiance apart from God.

(1) Fresh Statement of Purpose (verse 13).

(13) Comp. John xx. 31. The expression here is more positive than in the Gospel: there, "that ye might believe, and that believing ye might have life;" here, "that ye may know that ye have." He wishes to produce in them a good hope. The specific object at the beginning of the Epistle was the communication of joy through fellowship with the Apostles; the knowledge of possessing eternal life and the continuance of their faith would be precisely that joy.

(2) What can be done for those who do not come up to the Standard assumed (verses 14—17).

(14) **And this is the confidence.**—The assurance intended in verse 13 implies confidence, and confidence means the conviction that God is not deaf to our prayers. But these must not be contrary to His will. The Lord's Prayer reminds us that the Person referred to here is the Father.

(15) **That we have the petitions.**—The goodness of God as Light and Love is so fully established that if our petitions are according to His will it follows necessarily that He grants them.

(16) **If any man see his brother sin a sin which is not unto death.**—Here are meant such stumblings as do not imply any distinct, wilful, deliberate severance from the faith of Christ. To divide sins, on the authority of this passage, into venial and mortal is to misunderstand the whole argument of the Epistle and to seduce the conscience. St. John only means that though prayer can do much for an erring brother, there is a wilfulness against which it would be powerless: for even prayer is not stronger than freewill. (Comp. chap. ii. 1; Luke xxii. 31, 32; John xvii. 9; Heb. vii. 25.)

And he shall give.—The interceding Christian is regarded as gaining life for the erring brother and handing it on to him.

There is a sin unto death.—The limit of intercession is now given: such conscious and determined sin as shows a loss of all hold on Christ. Such a state would be a sign of spiritual death. Hardened obstinacy would be invincible; and as it would not be according to the will of God that prayers, by the nature of the case in vain, should be offered to Him, St. John thinks that intercession ought to stop here. At the same time, he is careful not categorically to forbid it; he only says that in such cases he does not recommend intercessory prayer. (Comp. Matt. xii. 31, 32; Mark iii. 29; Heb. vi. 4, 6; x. 26, 27.) "His brother" is here, of course, a nominal Christian.

(17) **All unrighteousness is sin.**—Here St. John reminds them that all Christians might, at one time or another, stand in need of intercessory prayer, even those who, on the whole, might be considered as "sinning not" (because their permanent will was against sin, and for holiness), because every declension from the perfect righteousness of God is error or sin. Nothing that was not hopelessly deliberate need be considered a sign of absolute spiritual death. (Comp. chap. iii. 4.)

(3) Some Practical Points recapitulated (verses 18—21).

(*a*) *God's sons do not sin* (verse 18).

St. John refers back to "that ye may know" in verse 13, and sums up three points from former portions of the Epistle, describing the true consciousness of the Christian. Each begins with "We know."

(18) **Sinneth not.**—There is no reason to supply "unto death." (Comp. the Note on chap. iii. 9.) St. John means strongly to insist, in this the solemn close of his Letter, that the true ideal Christian frame is the absence of wilful sin. Stumbles there may be, even such as need the prayers of friends, but intentional lawlessness there cannot be.

But he that is begotten of God keepeth himself.—Rather, *he that is begotten of God keepeth him:* that is, the Son of God preserves him. (Comp. John vi. 39; x. 28; xvii. 12, 15.)

And that wicked one toucheth him not.—The last mention of the devil was in chap. iii. 10. The devil and his angels attack, but cannot influence so long as the Christian abides in Christ. (Comp. 1 Pet. v. 8; Eph. vi. 11; Rev. iii. 10.)

(3 *b.*) *Personal assurance that we are God's sons* (verse 19).

Next after the cardinal point that righteousness is the characteristic of the new birth comes the necessity that the Christian should make up his mind that he has been, or is being, born again, and is really different

that we are of God, and the whole world lieth in wickedness. (20) And we know that the Son of God is come, and hath given us an understanding, that we may know him that is true, and we are in him that is true, *even* in his Son Jesus Christ. This is the true God, and eternal life. (21) Little children, keep yourselves from idols. Amen.

---

from the world. The proofs would be seen in chaps. i. 6; ii. 3, 5, 29; iii. 9, 14, 19, 24; iv. 7, 13, 15; v. 1, 10.

(19) **The whole world lieth in wickedness.**—Rather, *the wicked one.* There is a constant danger lest Christians should forget this. (Comp. Gal. i. 4.)

(3 c.) *Personal assurance of the Incarnation, of the gift of the spiritual sense, and of abiding in the God of Truth through His Son* (verse 20).

The series ends with a climax: the Son is indeed come; He gave us the faculty of seeing the true God; and in that Almighty Being we actually are, through the Son. The greatest fact of all to St. John's mind is that his Friend and Master of sixty years ago was the very Word made flesh. (Comp. chaps. i. 1, 2; ii. 13, 22, 23; iii. 5, 8, 16, 23; iv. 2, 9, 10; v. 1, 5, 9, 11.)

(20) **And hath given us an understanding.**—Comp. Acts xxvi. 18; 1 Cor. ii. 12—15; Eph. i. 18. This spiritual faculty of discernment was one of the gifts of that Spirit which Christ was to send. (Comp. chap. ii. 20, 27; John xiv. 26; xvi. 13.)

Him that is true.—The personality of God. Amid all the deceptions and fluctuations of the world, St. John felt, with the most absolute and penetrating and thankful conviction, that the followers of Christ were rooted and grounded in perfect, unshakable, unassailable truth. This could not be unless they were resting on the living Son and holding fast to Him.

This is the true God, and eternal life.—A most solemn and emphatic crown to the whole Epistle. "This God, *as seen in His Son,* is the true God." If the Word had not been God, God could not have been seen in Him. "And God, seen in His Son, is eternal life." This is only another way of putting John xvii. 3. (Comp. verses 11, 12, and 13.) To make "this is the true God" refer only to the Son is equally admissible by grammar, but hardly suits the argument so well.

(4) Last Warning (verse 21).

(21) **Little children, keep yourselves from idols.**—This parting word is suggested by the thought of "the true God." Every scheme of thought, every object of affection, which is not of Him, is a rival of His empire, a false god, a delusive appearance only, without solidity or truth. We cannot conclude better than in the words of Ebrard: "This idea is a general and very comprehensive one: it embraces all things and everything which may be opposed to the God revealed in Christ and to His worship in spirit and in truth. Pre-eminently, therefore, it embraces the delusive and vain idols of the Corinthian Gnosticism, whether ancient or modern; but it includes also the idols and false mediators of superstition, to whom the confidence is transferred which is due only to God in Christ—be their name Madonna, or saints, or Pope, or priesthood, or good works, or pictures, or office, or church, or sacraments. The One Being in whom we have 'the life eternal' is *Christ.* . . . . And this Christ we possess through the *Spirit of God,* whose marks and tokens are not priestly vestments, but faith and love. In this meaning, the Apostle's cry sounds forth through all the ages, in the ears of all Christians, 'Little Children, keep yourselves from Idols!' The holiest things may become a snare if their letter is regarded and not their spirit. Every Christian Church has a tendency to worship its own brazen serpents. Happy are they who have a Hezekiah to call them Nehushtan!"

INTRODUCTION

TO

THE SECOND AND THIRD EPISTLES OF

JOHN

I. Who wrote them.
II. Date.
III. Character and Scope.
IV. Where were they written.
V. Literature.

I. Who wrote them?—It is difficult to imagine why any should suppose these two Epistles to be by different hands. Was this author the Apostle?

(1) *External Evidence.*—This is not nearly so strong as for the First. It is natural that it should be so, for the two Epistles seem to have been regarded as of far less general interest; and, therefore, there was less obvious propriety in placing them in a collection of important Apostolical literature, and little reason why they should be quoted at all. The main argument for them is, indeed, their unaffected, inartificial kinship to the First. The oldest authority for the Second is the Muratorian Canon, composed before A.D. 170. Origen speaks of St. John's Epistles in the plural, and his disciple, Dionysius, cites the Third by name. The Muratorian Canon speaks of two Epistles of John, apparently distinct from the First. The Muratorian writer explains the principle of his arrangement of the Canon distinctly: saying that the Epistles of Paul to Philemon and Timothy, although addressed only to individuals, were placed in the Canon on account of their character. And even if the two Epistles of John mentioned were the First and Second, the fact that the Epistle to Philemon has precedence of those to Timothy (and Titus), probably because it is addressed also to Apphia and Archippus and the church in Philemon's house, makes it very easy to understand that the Second Epistle of John (early supposed to be addressed to a church under the symbolic form of a lady) would be received into a canon, while the Third, addressed to an unknown individual, and dealing with special circumstances, might not be considered sufficiently general for such a position. In early days there must have been many fugitive writings of the Apostles; and the discretion of the churches in selecting from them for an authorised collection would be guided probably more by usage than by deliberate valuation. Clement of Alexandria (A.D. 190—220), says, "The Second Epistle of John, written to the Virgins, is of the simplest character; it is written to a certain Babylonian, called Electa, but that means the election of the holy Church" (*Opera*, p. 1011, ed. Potter). Origen, in addition to what has been quoted from him above, is alleged by Eusebius (*Eccl. Hist.* vi. 25) to have said, "Not all consider these Epistles to be genuine," without endorsing the doubt himself. Dionysius of Alexandria, pupil and successor of Origen, makes use of the Second and Third Epistle to illustrate St. John's diction; he says that they were generally received as St. John's by tradition. Irenæus, disciple of Polycarp and of Papias, (he died A.D. 202) quotes 2 John, verse 7, by a mistake of memory, as belonging to the First Epistle; the words of 2 John, verse 11, he cites as by John the disciple of the Lord. Ephrem the Syrian knew both Epistles, but it is easy to understand why two small fragments of such a private character were not translated in early days, and therefore did not appear in the Peschito version; for that contains only three general Epistles (James, 1 Peter, 1 John). Cyprian shows that the Second Epistle was received as Apostolical and Canonical in the North African Church, by the fact that he mentions a quotation of the tenth verse by Aurelius, Bishop of Chullabis. Eusebius by speaking of St. John's Epistles in the plural number (*Demonstratio Evangelica*, iii. 5) shows that he himself recognised some other Epistles as well as the First; but, as from their shortness and small range there had been very slight occasion to quote them, he put them among the highest class of those writings which were not placed by absolutely universal consent in the authoritative Canon, and were therefore called Antilegomena. Jerome gives the "opinion of several writers," not as his own, that they were by the traditional John the Presbyter; a view rejected by Oecumenius and Bede. In the Middle Ages they were received without question as the Apostle's; then Erasmus took up the opinion mentioned by Jerome, and was followed by Grotius. Most modern commentators recognise them as Apostolic. The Tübingen writers are, of course, obliged to consider them as later, referring them to Montanistic, or at any rate, sub-apostolic times.

(2) *Internal Evidence.*—The term "elder": The fact that St. John does not give his name is in favour of authenticity. As in the Gospel and the First Epistle, he prefers to retain a dignified incognito, intelligible to all whom it concerned. Even if the messengers did not know whose letters they were carrying, even if the correspondents did not know the handwriting, they would be perfectly aware from the style and matter, and the promise of a visit. It is doubtful whether by "elder" he meant "aged," or an official position. In classical Greek these words would have a different form, but St. John's Greek is that of a man who had become accustomed to a provincial form of the language late in life, and quite admits of slight irregularities. If he means an office, there is nothing to show that all the Apostles always used the apostolic title. St. Peter called himself "fellow-presbyter"

(1 Pet. v. 1), and Eusebius called the Apostles Presbyters (*Eccl. Hist.* iii. 39). The Apostles and "Overseers" were, in fact, only a specially responsible and important branch of the Presbyterate. As the last remaining Apostle, St. John might prefer not to insist on a designation now unique; or, as the name "elder" was originally adopted with reference to mature age, he may have used it as a hint of his own advanced years; or the dangers of the times may have made it advisable for him, for his messenger, and for his correspondents, to drop the higher title.

The only authority for the existence of another John at Ephesus, at the same time as the Apostle, called "the elder," and "the disciple of the Lord," is Papias, quoted by Eusebius. Is it not possible, that, as Eusebius says that he was "very small in mind," there may be some confusion in some of these details? May not even the confusion itself have arisen from these anonymous Epistles being misunderstood by the unintelligent? But, even admitting the existence of such a second John, it is too much to ask us to believe that he resembled the Apostle not only in name and history, but also in style, character, and thought. And where it was extremely reasonable that the Apostle should leave out his name, it becomes most improbable that this alternative John should have left it out.

The Second and Third Epistles are full of peculiar forms, common also to the First. Notice 2 John verse 1, "knowing the truth"; verse 2, "abide in"; verse 3, "in truth and love"; verse 4, "walking in"; verse 5, "the commandment which we had from the beginning" (1 John ii. 7); verse 6, "this is love, that"; "as ye heard from the beginning" (1 John iii. 11, 23); verse 7, "deceivers are gone forth" (1 John ii. 18); "confessing not Jesus Christ coming in the flesh" (1 John iv. 1, 2); "the antichrist"; verse 9, "abideth not in the doctrine, hath not God" (1 John ii. 23); "hath the Son and the Father"; verse 12, "that our joy may be full" (1 John i. 4); 3 John, verse 1, "in truth"; verses 3, 4, "walkest in truth"; verse 11, "is of God, hath not seen God" (1 John iii. 6, 10; iv. 8). There are five or six expressions in the two Epistles which do not occur elsewhere in St. John's writings, but it would be in the highest degree absurd to confine any writer exclusively to the language used in a former production. Additional reason for variety here would be found in the simple colloquial character of the writings.

Accordingly, while there is every reason to hold that the Second and Third Epistles are by the author of the First, and the First by the Author of the Gospel, it is difficult to find any valid reason to the contrary.

II. Date.—In the absence of all evidence to the contrary it seems probable that the circumstances and time were not very dissimilar in all three Epistles.

III. Character and Scope.—In the Second, the Apostle, who is probably staying at the same place as some of his correspondent's children, writes to a mother and her other children to express his sympathy and delight at the faith of the family, and to warn them against admitting false teachers to their circle. It contains noticeable definitions of love, antichrist, and of true and false believers. It also has a general lesson on the treatment of wilful depravers of divine truth.

In the Third, he recounts how some missionaries had been badly received by Diotrephes, who had ambitiously obtained for himself the chief influence in a certain church, but notwithstanding Gaius had been courageous and kind enough to entertain them hospitably. Gaius is exhorted to help them still further. The Letter gives us an idea of the high importance of hospitality at the time as a Christian virtue; and brings out the fact that St. John's authority was no less disputed in certain cases than St. Paul's. It is probable that the church of Diotrephes had not been founded by St. John; that St. John had special claim to be obeyed; and that ecclesiastical influence seems to have by this time become vested in a single head.

IV. Where were they written?—Probably at Ephesus, before a tour of inspection. Had they been written in Patmos, some notice of the captivity might be expected.

V. Literature.—To the authorities mentioned in the First Epistle, add the Articles in Smith's *Dictionary of the Bible*, and a paper by Professor Salmon on the Third Epistle in the *Christian Observer*, April, 1877. I should mention again my obligations to Dr. Karl Braune.

THE SECOND EPISTLE OF

JOHN

(1) THE elder unto the elect lady and her children, whom I love in the truth; and not I only, but also all they that have known the truth; (2) for the truth's sake, which dwelleth in us, and shall be with us for ever. (3) Grace be with you, mercy, *and* peace, from God the Father, and from the Lord Jesus Christ, the Son of

Verses 1, 2. The person addressed.

After A.D. 90.

Verse 3. Greeting.

[1. **Address.** (verses 1—3).

(*a*) CHARACTER OF THE PERSON ADDRESSED: her adherence to the truth (verses 1, 2).

(*b*) SALUTATION (verse 3).

2. **Exhortation** (verses 4—11).

(*a*) STATEMENT ABOUT CERTAIN OF HER CHILDREN (verse 4).

(*b*) MAIN MESSAGE: Appeal to mutual love (verse 5).

(*c*) DEFINITION OF LOVE (verse 6).

(*d*) FIXITY OF GOSPEL TEACHING (verse 6).

(*e*) THE DECEIVERS AND ANTICHRISTS (verse 7).

(*f*) DANGER (verse 8).

(*g*) FALSE PROGRESS A TEST (verse 9).

(*h*) THOSE WHO HAVE NOT THE CARDINAL DOCTRINE OF CHRISTIANITY NOT TO BE ENTERTAINED BY HER (verses 10, 11).

3. **Conclusion** (verses 12, 13).

(*a*) PURPOSE OF COMING SHORTLY (verse 12).

(*b*) MESSAGE FROM HER SISTER'S CHILDREN (verse 13).]

(1) A man so well-known to his correspondent that he only calls himself "the old man," or, "the elder," writes to a mother, whose name is possibly Kyria, and to her children. Her sister's children are in the same place as the writer. The two mothers are both honoured with the religious title "elect." The writer (we assume from the introduction that he is the Apostle John) loves the family with true Christian love. All who are in the way of truth have the same feelings for them, for the truth is a bond of union between all such. He wishes them grace, mercy, and peace from the Father and the Son, in all their thoughts and all their affections (verses 1—3).

(1 *a.*) (1) **The elder.**—The word is used with reference to age in 1 Tim. v. 2; 1 Pet. v. 5; with reference to office, Acts xi. 30; xiv. 23; xv. 4, 6, 23; xvi. 4; xx. 17; 1 Tim. v. 1, 17, 19; Tit. i. 5; Jas. v. 14; 1 Pet. v. 1.

Unto the elect lady.—St. Paul uses "elect" in exactly the same way (Rom. xvi. 13). (Comp. also 1 Pet. i. 1, 2.) The use of the epithet for the sister in verse 13 shows that it is impossible that the word should be the correspondent's name. The Greek word, however, for "lady," (*Kuria*, or *Kyria*) was a proper name; so that those who think that St. John addresses "the elect Kyria" are at liberty to do so. The absence of the article would not be more surprising in that case than it would be if we translate "lady," for "elect" would evidently be in such familiar use that the article would be easily omitted.

If the name of the matron is not given, it is not absurd to suppose that the dangers of the times, or family persecution, may have made it advisable that both her name and that of the writer should be withheld. The messenger would supply both deficiencies.

The term "lady" would not imply anything about her social station. Epictetus says that all women above fourteen were addressed by men in this term.

And her children.—Those of them who were with their mother. St. John seems to have seen some of the family later.

Whom I love in the truth.—Rather, *in truth; i.e.,* with true Christian love, with all the sincerity, purity, and respect, which the true love which springs from God requires. (See Notes on 1 John iii. 18, 19.)

And not I only . . .—St. John disclaims any special peculiarity in his affection for the family. All Christians who had been brought or should be brought into relation with them would have the same feeling; because the character of all of them was based on the truth as it is in Christ, and moulded on it.

(2) **For the truth's sake, which dwelleth in us, and shall be with us for ever.**—The personal form of this sentence irresistibly reminds us of John xv. 6, "I am the way, the truth, and the life." If Christ is once in our hearts, He will not leave us unless we deliberately leave Him. The expression is therefore equivalent to saying, "We will not let Him go."

(1 *b.*) (3) **Grace be with you, mercy, and peace.**—(Comp. 1 Tim. i. 2; 2 Tim. i. 21.) "Grace" is the favour of God conveying fully every spiritual blessing (Rom. iii. 4; Eph. ii. 4—10); "mercy" is the pitifulness which sympathises with man, is longing to forgive his sins, and is more ready to hear than he to pray (Luke x. 30—37; Ps. ciii. 3—18): "peace" is the result of the reception of these two gifts in the heart, the untroubled calm of a conscience void of offence before God and men (John xiv. 27; Rom. v. 1; Phil. iv. 4; Col. iii. 15).

From God the Father, and from the Lord Jesus Christ, the Son of the Father.—The perfect independence, parallel equality, and mutual connection of the two Persons is noticeable.

In truth and love.—To be joined with "grace mercy and peace." Truth was to absorb and regulate all their intellectual faculties; love, all their emotional.

the Father, in truth and love. (4) I re-
Verses 4—11. Exhortation. joiced greatly that I found
of thy children walking in
truth, as we have received a commandment from the Father. (5) And now I beseech thee, lady, not as though I wrote a new commandment unto thee, but that which we had from the beginning, that
we love one another. (6) And this is love,
that we walk after his commandments. This is the commandment, That, as ye have heard from the beginning, ye should walk in it. (7) For many deceivers are entered into the world, who confess not that Jesus Christ is come in the flesh. This is a deceiver and an
antichrist. (8) Look to yourselves, that
we lose not those things which we have wrought,[1] but that we receive a full
reward. (9) Whosoever transgresseth,
and abideth not in the doctrine of Christ, hath not God. He that abideth in the doctrine of Christ, he hath both
the Father and the Son. (10) If there

1 Or, *gained*: Some copies read, *which ye have gained, but that ye receive, &c.*

---

(2) St. John had lately had opportunity of observing how some of the matron's children proved their adherence to the truth by their daily conduct. Having congratulated her about this, he states the chief thing which he desires of her: the pure Christian love which implies every other grace and virtue; in other words, walking after the divine commandments. That this love should be pure, that these commandments should be unimpaired, it was necessary to remember that nothing new could be added to the original message of Christ. This warning was timely, because many errors had already appeared, especially that greatest error which denied the Incarnation. The family must, therefore, be on its guard, lest it should be cheated of its reward. The test was very simple: any advance beyond the doctrine of Christ. It would be better for the family not to entertain in their house any who had committed themselves to these doctrines of development (verses 4—11).

(2 *a.*) (4) **I rejoiced . . .**—Comp. Rom. i. 8; 1 Cor. i. 4; 2 Cor. i. 3; Eph. i. 3; Phil. i. 3; Col. i. 3.

Of thy children.—Probably those met at home.

Walking in truth.—Comp. John viii. 12; 1 John i. 6, 7; ii. 6; 3 John, verses 3, 4.

As we have received a commandment.—That is, walking according to the revelation of God's will in Christ Jesus.

(2 *b.*) (5) Love is the Christian's moral disposition of mind, which embraces all other virtues and graces. It implies faith, because it is founded on Christian principle, and can only be tested by a right belief. It implies purity, because it is modelled on the love of God, and has abjured the old man. It implies unselfishness, because it desires the good of the other for his own sake and God's. It implies humility, because it distrusts itself, relies on God, and thinks more of the other than of itself. (Comp. John xiii. 14; xv. 12; 1 Cor. xiii.; Eph. v. 2; 1 Pet. iv. 8; 1 John iii. 11, 23; iv. 7, 21.)

Not as though.—See the Notes on 1 John ii. 7, 8, and iii. 11.

(2 *c.*) (6) The attitude of love in general, whether towards God or man, is best defined and described as "walking after God's commandments." It might have been thought that love would be a vague immeasurable feeling, differing chiefly in intensity; but the Christian disposition which is described as love is that practical and enlightened result of faith which naturally acts and expresses itself by following God's will in all things. (Comp. 1 John iv. 7, 16.)

(2 *d.*) **This is the commandment.**—The sum of all God's commandments for us is this: that we should be doers of the word which we have heard since first Christ began to fulfil the Law and the Prophets, and not of any other. All development from what He said, or from what we have repeated from Him is disobedience and error. (Comp. 1 John ii. 24.)

(2 *e.*) *The appearance of deceivers is the reason for this warning against false progress* (verse 7).

The ground of his love for the matron and her family was that they held to the truth. He is proportionately anxious that they should not go beyond it through evil influences.

(7) **Deceivers.**—"Those who cause others to wander." (Comp. 1 John ii. 26; iv. 1—6; 1 Tim. iv. 1.)

Entered into the world.—Comp. 1 John ii. 19; iv. 1.

Confess not that Jesus Christ is come in the flesh.—Rather, *confess not Jesus Christ coming in flesh.* The Greek implies the idea only, without reference to time. (Comp. 1 John iv. 2, 3.) The expression would include both those who denied that Jesus was the Messiah, and those who, for Gnostic theories, held Him to be only a phantom, declaring the Incarnation to be an impossibility.

This is . . .—Rather, *the deceiver, and the antichrist —i.e.,* among all the human errors by which the influence of the Evil One is manifested, this is the most destructive. Those who adopt such errors are the most fatal deceivers and opponents of Christ and truth.

(2 *f.*) *The warning* (verse 8).

(8) **Look to yourselves.**—For the triple "we" in this verse, read "ye." The result of the error would be loss of the fellowship with the Father and the Son in truth and love. (Comp. Gal. iii. 1—4; iv. 11.)

Which we (or, *ye*) **have wrought.**—Their faith, hope, love, and the growth of the Christian graces.

A full reward.—The diminution of the reward would be in proportion to the gravity of the error. The reward would be the peace of God which passeth all understanding, the blessed stability, firmness, and joy which truth and love communicate. (Comp. Col. iii. 24; Gal. iv. 2.)

(2 *g.*) *The test* (verse 9).

Progression beyond Christ's teaching, a sign of the absence of God; refusal to go beyond His lines a proof of the presence of Father and Son.

(9) **Transgresseth.**—Rather, *goeth beyond.* (Comp. Matt. xxi. 9; 1 Tim. i. 18; v. 24; 2 Tim. iii. 7, 14; Tit. i. 9.)

The doctrine of Christ.—That which Christ taught. (Comp. Matt. vii. 28; xvi. 12; xxii. 33; Mark i. 22; iv. 2; xii. 38; John viii. 31; Acts ii. 42; v. 28.)

Hath not God.—Comp. 1 John ii. 23; v. 12.

(2 *h.*) *Practical direction* (verses 10, 11).

Although it would be possible to love unbelievers, in the sense of earnestly desiring that they might come to

come any unto you, and bring not
this doctrine, receive him not into
your house, neither bid him God
speed: (11) for he that biddeth him
God speed is partaker of his evil
deeds. (12) Having many things to
write unto you, I would not *write* with
paper and ink: but I trust
to come unto you, and
speak face to face,[1] that our joy may
be full. (13) The children of thy elect
sister greet thee. Amen.

Verses 12, 13. Conclusion.

[1] Gr. *mouth to mouth.*

---

a knowledge of the truth, it would be wrong—for sincere Christians it would be impossible—to hold out to them the right hand of fellowship. Especially dangerous would it be for the matron and her family. (Comp. 2 Tim. iii. 6.)

(10) **If there come.**—The construction implies that it was the case. St. John was dealing with facts. St. Paul held the same view (Rom. xvi. 17; Gal. i. 8, 9; Tit. iii. 10, 11; and, in regard to morals, 1 Cor. v. 11; xvi. 22).

This doctrine.—See verse 9. He is not speaking of those who had never heard or been instructed in the doctrine of Christ; they would be less dangerous. He means those who deliberately altered the Apostolic teaching. And his reason is evidently chiefly the religious welfare of the matron and her family. The case supplies an important instruction in the theory of Christian social conduct.

Receive him not into your house, neither bid him God speed.—These are no terms of ordinary politeness, which the Apostle does not forbid, but terms of close Christian intimacy and spiritual communion, the deliberate cultivation of personal acquaintance, fraternal intercourse. The highest sort of Christian brotherly love—love, that is, in its fulness and truth—can only find reciprocity in the same atmosphere of Christ, on the same basis, and in the same characteristics. (Comp. 2 Cor. vi. 16.)

(11) **Is partaker of his evil deeds.**—Condones his false doctrine; puts himself in a position to accept it; shares the guilt of his disloyalty by sympathising with him; and in this way lowers his whole moral standard, doing an injury to "God, Christ, the Church, the truth, individual communities, and his own soul." If any interpret the exhortations to love in the Epistles of St. John too liberally, or by too low a measure, this passage is a wholesome corrective. In applying this teaching to modern times we should remember (1) that St. John is only speaking of those who deliberately deprave the doctrine of Christ in its great outlines; (2) that there may be much in ourselves, in our systems, in our quarrels, in our incrustations of divine truth, in our want of the sense of proportion in dealing with divine things, which may have hindered others from receiving Christ.

(3) Conclusion (verses 12, 13).

(12) **Having many things to write unto you.**—This verse shows that the Letter to the matron and her family was not a mere accompaniment of a copy of the First Epistle. His heart is full of things to write, but he hopes soon to have unlimited conversation.

Paper.—The Egyptian *papyrus.*

Ink.—A mixture of soot, water, and gum. The papyrus-tree grows in the swamps of the Nile to the height of ten feet and more. Paper was prepared from the thin coats that surround the plant. Pliny describes the method (xiii. 23). The different pieces were joined together by the turbid Nile water, as it has a kind of glutinous property. One layer of papyrus was laid flat on a board, and a cross layer put over it; these were pressed, and afterwards dried in the sun. The sheets were then fastened or pasted together. There were never more than twenty of these sheets fastened together in a roll; but of course the length could be increased to any extent. The writing was in columns, with a blank slip between them; it was only on one side. When the work was finished, it was rolled on a staff, and sometimes wrapped in a parchment case (Smith, *Dictionary of Greek and Roman Antiquities,* p. 567).

Of the ink used by the Romans, Pliny says that it was made of soot in various ways, with burnt resin or pitch. "For this purpose they have built furnaces which do not allow the smoke to escape. The kind most commended is made in this way from pine-wood: it is mixed with soot from the furnaces or baths; and this they use for writing on rolls. Some also make a kind of ink by boiling and straining the lees of wine." The black matter of the cuttle-fish was also sometimes used for writing (Smith, *Dictionary of Greek and Roman Antiquities,* p. 110).

The pen was a reed, sharpened with a knife, and split like a quill-pen.

The Jews seem to have used lamp-black dissolved in gall-juice, or lamp-black and vitriol, for ink. The modern scribes "have an apparatus consisting of a metal or ebony tube for their reed-pens, with a cup or bulb of the same material attached to the upper end for ink. This they thrust through the girdle, and carry with them at all times" (Thomson, *The Land and the Book,* p. 131; Smith's *Dictionary of the Bible,* p. 1802).

Speak face to face.—Not that there was any oral tradition which he would not write down. His Gospel and First Epistle would contain the outline of all his teaching. But on this occasion there was no need for writing. (Comp. 1 Cor. xiii. 12.)

That our joy may be full.—Comp. 1 John i. 4. It would be the deep satisfaction of the interchange of spiritual thoughts and aspirations without the limitations of a monologue or of writing materials.

(13) **The children of thy elect sister.**—He may have been staying at this second matron's house; at any rate, the family knew he was writing. The simplicity of the great Apostle, the personal friend of the risen Lord, the last of the great pillars of the Church of Christ—in transmitting this familiar message, makes a most instructive finish to what is throughout a beautiful picture.

THE THIRD EPISTLE OF
JOHN

Verse 1. Address.

(1) THE elder unto the wellbeloved
Gaius, whom I love in
the truth.[1] (2) Beloved, I
wish[2] above all things that
thou mayest prosper and be in health,

Verses 2—12. Substance of the Epistle.

even as thy soul pros-
pereth. (3) For I rejoiced
greatly, when the brethren
came and testified of the truth that
is in thee, even as thou walkest in
the truth. (4) I have no greater joy
than to hear that my children walk in
truth. (5) Beloved, thou doest faithfully
whatsoever thou doest to the brethren,
and to strangers; (6) which have borne
witness of thy charity before the church:

After A.D. 90.

1 Or, *truly*.

2 Or, *pray*.

[1. **Address** (verse 1).

2. **Substance** (verses 2—12).
   (*a*) GOOD WISHES FOR BODILY HEALTH (verse 2).
   (*b*) HIGH CHARACTER OF GAIUS FOR (*a*) CONSISTENCY (verses 3, 4); (*b*) HOSPITALITY (verses 5, 6, 7).
   (*c*) GENERAL DUTY OF RECEIVING CHRISTIAN TRAVELLERS (verse 8).
   (*d*) OPPOSITION OF DIOTREPHES TO THE APOSTLE (verses 9, 10).
   (*e*) EXHORTATION TO GAIUS NOT TO FOLLOW SUCH AN EVIL EXAMPLE (verse 11).
   (*f*) GENERAL TRUTH: contrast between the followers of good and of evil (verse 12).
   (*g*) COMMENDATION OF DEMETRIUS, AND APPEAL TO CONFIDENCE (verse 12).

3. **Conclusion** (verses 13, 14).]

(1) **The elder.**—See the *Introduction*, and 2 John, verse 1.

Gaius.—The common Roman name Caius. A Caius is mentioned in Acts xix. 29; xx. 4; Rom. xvi. 23; 1 Cor. i. 14. The difference in date between these and St. John's correspondent would alone be sufficient reason against any attempt at identification. There is nothing to show whether he was a presbyter or not.

Whom I love in the truth.—Or, *in truth*. (See 2 John, verse 1.)

(2 *a*.) (2) **Beloved.**—St. John's affection is founded on the high merits of Caius as a Christian.

Above all things.—This may mean "*in* all things."

Be in health.—An ascetic would be surprised that one of the greatest of the Apostles should be so earnest on such a point. But the better a man's health, the more thoroughly he can do the work of God. Sickness may be allowed to chasten the erring or rebellious heart, but a Christian whose faith is firm and character established, can ill afford to despise the inestimable blessing of a sound body. Functional and organic disorder or enervation proportionately lessen the capacity for thought, resolution, and activity.

Even as thy soul prospereth.—The word "prospereth" is literally *makes good way*, and so links on to the idea of walking, in verses 3 and 4. The health of the soul came first in the Apostle's mind: when there is that, he can wish for bodily health to support it.

(2 *b*.) (3) **I rejoiced greatly.**—Compare 2 John, verse 4. "For" introduces the reason of the high praise in verse 2.

The truth that is in thee.—The inward presence of Christ, manifested by the Christian life and consistency of Caius.

Even as thou walkest in the truth.—This is an additional evidence from the brethren to show that the presence of the truth in Caius had been practically tested.

Thou is emphatic in the Greek, showing that there were others, like Diotrephes, of whom this could not be said.

(4) **I have no greater joy.**—This is a general statement arising out of the particular instance. The comparative is double—a comparative formed on a comparative; it may be only irregular, an evidence that the writer was not a classical Greek scholar, or it may be for intensity. There is a similar comparative in Eph. iii. 8, where the force is evidently intensive.

My children means the members of the churches specially under the care of St. John.

(5) **Thou doest faithfully**—*i.e.*, worthily of a faithful man, consistently with the Christian character. It may be translated, "Thou doest a faithful work in whatsoever . . . ."

Whatsoever thou doest.—Done from right motives, as unto Christ. Whatever form (it is hinted that the form would be various) the activity of Caius might take, so high was the Apostle's opinion of his character, that he was sure it would be done wisely and well.

And to strangers.—According to another reading it is, "And that, strangers," as in 1 Cor. vi. 6, Eph. ii. 8, Phil. i. 28. Either way, the strangers would be Christians; but, according to the reading in the text, the brethren would be more or less acquaintances of their host. The duty of entertaining Christians on their travels was of peculiar importance in early times, (1) from the length of time which travelling required, (2) from the poverty of the Christians, (3) from the kind of society they would meet at public inns. The duty is enforced in Rom. xii. 13; 1 Tim. iii. 2; Tit. i. 8; Heb. xiii. 2; 1 Pet. iv. 9.

(6) **Charity** might be translated "love."

Before the church.—That where the Apostle then was, and from which they had probably been sent forth as

whom if thou bring forward on their journey after a godly sort, thou shalt do well: (7) because that for his name's sake they went forth, taking nothing of the Gentiles. (8) We therefore ought to receive such, that we might be fellow-helpers to the truth. (9) I wrote unto the church: but Diotrephes, who loveth to have the preeminence among them, receiveth us not. (10) Wherefore, if I come, I will remember his deeds which he doeth, prating against us with malicious words: and not content therewith, neither doth he himself receive the brethren, and forbiddeth them that would, and casteth *them* out of the church. (11) Beloved, follow not that which is evil, but that which is good. He that doeth good is of God: but he that doeth evil hath not seen God. (12) Demetrius hath good report of all *men,* and of the

---

missionaries, or, at any rate, with some definite religious object.

Whom if thou bring forward.—Perhaps while they were still staying with Caius, the emissaries sent back a report to the church whence they came. St. John seems to imply that there was still something which Caius could do for them. "If thou bring forward" is in the Greek in the past; "when thou hast sent them on, it will be a good work."

After a godly sort.—Rather, *worthily of God.* (Comp. Tit. iii. 13, 1 Cor. xvi. 11.) It would imply journey money, provisions, love, care, encouragement, prayer, a humble and reasonable imitation of God's providence to Caius, proportional to his means, the occasion, and the recipients.

(7) **Because that for his name's sake they went forth.**—Their object was the highest possible—the glory of God's name. Hence there must have been some kind of missionary character in their journey. (Comp. Acts v. 41; xv. 40; Rom. i. 6; Jas. ii. 7.)

Of the Gentiles.—Probably the heathens among whom they were preaching. From settled churches, or wealthy Christians of long standing, there would be nothing inimical to the interests of the message in receiving material support. Among those who were hearing for the first time, it would be highly prejudicial if there were any appearance of selling the truth. (Comp. 1 Cor. ix. 18; 2 Cor. xi. 7; xii. 16; 1 Thess. ii. 9.)

(2 *c.*) (8) **We therefore.**—In contrast to the heathens.

To receive.—In the original there is a play with the word "receiving" in verse 8. (Comp. Matt. x. 40.)

That we might be fellowhelpers to the truth.—Fellow-helpers with them. The principle of co-operation was one of the earliest and leading ideas of the kingdom of Christ. Those who try to work alone lose the mighty force of sympathy, are sure to make mistakes, cannot help arousing opposition, and run the risk of nursing in their own souls an unsuspected spirit of self-will, self-confidence, and spiritual pride. Those who do not care to help the good works of others are at best cold Christians, feeble believers; they fail in the great critical testing virtue of Christian love; they limit the operation of God, who has chosen to work by human means; they hinder the spread of the gospel, and delay the second coming of Christ. (Comp. 2 Cor. viii. 23; Phil. i. 27; Col. iv. 11; 1 Thess. iii. 2.)

(2 *d.*) (9) **I wrote unto the church.**—"I wrote somewhat unto the Church." This may either have been a copy of his Gospel or his First Epistle, or a lost letter of no special importance. The Church was that of the place where Caius and Diotrephes lived. Nothing whatever can be said of Diotrephes, except that his personal ambition led him into the grievous sin of rejecting the authority of the bosom friend of the Saviour; that he talked malignantly against St. John and his friends; that he refused to entertain the emissaries of the Church in which St. John was residing; and that he actually went so far as to eject from the local congregation those who were willing to entertain them. We may conjecture that, on account of the loyalty of Caius to St. John, there was so little intercourse between him and Diotrephes, that he would not even hear that St. John had written; that the greater part of the people of the place adhered for the present to Diotrephes, so that in addressing Caius St. John calls them "the church," and "them;" and, from verse 11, that even now St. John did not think it superfluous to urge Caius not to follow the example of Diotrephes or submit to his influence.

Loveth to have the preeminence.—Makes it his evil aim to have the whole influence of the community in his own hands.

(10) **If I come.**—Comp. 1 John ii. 28. St. John was evidently expecting in both Letters to set out on the same journey.

Prating.—Idle slander; the moths that are always attracted to "the fierce light that beats about a throne." The intense spiritual affectionateness of the Apostle of love might be easily misunderstood by an unconverted pretender; but it is needless to imagine the groundless babble of a tyrannical upstart.

Casteth them out.—Not necessarily formal excommunication; but Diotrephes had so far succeeded in his object that he was able to exclude these better disposed persons from the Christian society of the place.

(2 *e.*) (11) **Follow not that which is evil.**—One of those simple exhortations so characteristic of St. John, which derive an intense meaning from the circumstances and the context. There was probably every reason why Caius should follow Diotrephes: peace, good-fellowship, the dislike of singularity, popular example, and the indolent indifference which ordinary men feel for truth and right. But the difference between right and wrong is eternal and irreconcilable. The conduct of Diotrephes was of the devil; and mighty moral consequences might follow if Caius gave way from good-natured pliability. (Comp. John v. 29; xviii. 23; Eph. v. 1; 2 Thess. iii. 7, 9; Heb. xiii. 7; 1 Pet. iii. 10, 11; 1 John iii. 12.)

(2 *f.*) **He that doeth good is of God.**—Comp. 1 John iii. 10. "Doeth good" includes all practical virtue. (Comp. 1 Pet. ii. 14, 15, 20; iii. 6, 17.)

He that doeth evil hath not seen God.—Comp. 1 John ii. 3; iii. 6, 10; iv. 2, 3, 4, 6, 8; v. 19.

(2 *g.*) (12) **Demetrius** may very likely be the bearer of the Epistle.

Good report.—Rather, *the witness.*

Of all men.—All Christians who knew him.

truth itself: yea, and we *also* bear record; and ye know that our record is true.
Verses 13, 14. Conclusion. (13) I had many things to write, but I will not with ink and pen write unto thee: (14) but I trust I shall shortly see thee, and we shall speak face to face.[1] Peace *be* to thee. *Our* friends salute thee. Greet the friends by name.

[1] Gr. *mouth to mouth.*

Of the truth itself.—Christ dwelling in him manifested His presence as the Way, the Truth, and the Life in new virtues for every circumstance that arose in the career of Demetrius. His walk, agreeing with the revealed truth of God, showed that God was with him. (Comp. Acts iv. 13.)

And we also.—St. John adds his own independent testimony as a third, in the most emphatic manner possible.

And ye know that our record is true.—There is no arrogance or egotism in this: it is solely the appeal to the loyal fidelity of Caius—to the simplicity of Christ's gospel as set forth by John in accordance with the other Apostles. The personal experience of believers would convince them of the truth of the last of the Apostles. (Comp. John xix. 25; xxi. 24.)

(3) (13) **I had many things to write.**—Rather, *There were many things which I wished to write.*

But I will not.—Comp. 2 John, verse 12.

(14) **Peace be to thee.**—The best wish which the Apostle can form, instead of the usual Greek ending, "Be strong," or "Farewell!" It was our Lord's resurrection greeting; the internal peace of a good conscience, the external peace of universal friendship, the heavenly peace of future glory begun even in this life. (Comp. John xx. 19, 26; Rom. v. 33; Gal. vi. 16; Eph. vi. 23; 2 Thess. iii. 16; 1 Pet. v. 14.)

Our friends salute thee.—Rather, *The friends.* By this appellation, uncommon in the New Testament, St. John recalls our Lord's words in John xv. 13, 14, 15.

Greet the friends by name.—Each friend was to receive a personal message from the Apostle, and Caius would know who they were as well as if St. John wrote them down. In a short private Letter it would be unsuitable to have a long list of special messages as in a Pauline Epistle, especially as the Apostle hoped shortly to see them. John perhaps thinks of his Master's ideal in John x. 3.

INTRODUCTION

TO

THE GENERAL EPISTLE OF

JUDE

I. **The Author.**—Whatever may be our opinion with regard to 2 Peter, sober criticism requires us to believe that this Epistle was written by the man whose name it bears. To suppose that Jude is an assumed name is gratuitous. It remains to determine who the Jude is who addresses us.

He tells us that he is a "servant of Jesus Christ" and "brother of James." Had he been an Apostle he would probably have said so. (Comp. Rom. i. 1; Titus i. 1; 2 Pet. i. 1.) Had he been an Apostle he would not have claimed attention by calling himself "the brother of James," when he possessed so very much stronger a claim. The fact that (verse 17) the writer appeals to the words of Apostles proves nothing; an Apostle might do so. But at least such an appeal is more natural in one who is not an Apostle: there being no reason why he should keep his Apostleship in the background if he possessed it. Our Jude, then, is the Judas of Matt. xiii. 55, and the Juda of Mark vi. 3; *not* the Judas of Luke vi. 16 and Acts i. 13, where "*brother* of James" should more probably be "*son* of James." The author of this Epistle is rightly described as the *brother* of James, "brother" being expressed in the Greek. The James indicated is James "the Just," the brother of the Lord, and first Bishop of Jerusalem, who, though not an Apostle, was nevertheless a person of such dignity as quite to account for this writer thinking it worth while to mention his near relationship to him. The present question is mixed up with the vexed question as to the brethren of our Lord. The view here taken is that they were not the sons of Alphæus—*i.e.*, cousins—but in some real sense brethren: either the children of Joseph and Mary, or of Joseph by a former wife, or by a levirate marriage, or by adoption. Which of these four alternatives is the right one will probably never be determined. Jerome's theory, that they were our Lord's cousins, children of Alphæus, is contradicted by John vii. 5. (See Note there and on Matt. xii. 46.) It owes its prevalence in the West mainly to Jerome's influence. The identification of James the Lord's brother with James the son of Alphæus, which it involves, has never prevailed in the Eastern Church. Our author, then, together with his better known brother, James, were in some sense our Lord's "brethren," and not Apostles. If it be asked, Would not Jude in this case have appealed to his relationship to Christ rather than to his relationship to James? we may securely answer "No." As the author of the *Adumbrationes* centuries ago remarked, religious feeling would deter him, as it did his brother James in his Epistle, from mentioning this fact. The Ascension had altered all Christ's human relationships, and His brethren would shrink from claiming kinship after the flesh with His glorified Body. This conjecture is supported by facts. Nowhere in primitive Christian literature is any authority claimed or attributed on the basis of nearness of kin to the Redeemer. He Himself had taught Christians that the lowliest among them might rise above the closest of such earthly ties (Luke xi. 27, 28); to be spiritually "the servant of Jesus Christ" was much more than being His actual brother.

Of this Jude very little is known. Unless he was an exception to the statement in John vii. 5 (of which there is no intimation), he did not at first believe on Christ, but joined the Apostles after the convincing fact of the Resurrection (Acts i. 14). That, like his brothers (see Note on 1 Cor. ix. 5), he was married appears from Hegesippus, who tells us (Eus. *H. E.*, III. xx.) that two grandsons of Jude were brought before Domitian as descendants of a royal house, and therefore dangerous persons; but on their proving their poverty, and explaining that Christ's kingdom was not of this world, they were contemptuously dismissed. This story almost implies that the relationship to Christ was very close; for Hegesippus remarks, by way of explanation, that Domitian was afraid of Christ, just as Herod was. Statements of St. Jude's preaching in various parts of the world rest upon late and untrustworthy evidence. That he was an Evangelist, is implied in his writing this Epistle; but nothing is known respecting his labours.

II. **Authenticity.**—The authenticity of the Epistle has been questioned by some from very early times, but without sufficient reason. The evidence against it is mainly this. *External.*—The Epistle is not contained in the Peschito or ancient Syriac version; Eusebius classes it among the disputed books (III. xxv. 3; II. xxiii. 25); Theodore of Mopsuestia seems to have rejected it; few references to it are found in early writers. *Internal.*—It cites apocryphal books; has a suspicious relationship to Romans and 2 Peter; is difficult in style. Against this we may urge that Ephrem Syrus seems to have recognised it; the Muratorian Fragment (*circ.* A.D. 170) contains it; the old Latin version contains it; Tertullian (*De Cult. Fem.* I. iii.) accepts it as genuine and Apostolic; Clement of Alexandria quotes it as Scripture (*Strom.* III. ii.; *Paed.* III. viii.); Origen, though he knew of doubts about it (*Comm.* on Matt. xxii. 23) fully accepted it (on Matt. xiii. 55; xviii. 10, *et al.*); Jerome (*Scrip. Eccles.* iv.) says that many rejected it because it quoted apocryphal books, but that it ought to be reckoned among the Scriptures; the Councils of Laodicea (*circ.* A.D 360) and of Hippo (A.D. 393) formally included it in the Canon. The doubts about it are very intelligible: it was not by an Apostle, and therefore seemed wanting in authority, and it quoted apocryphal works. Its brevity fully accounts for its not being often quoted. It is too insignificant to be a forgery; a forger would have said more, and would have selected some well-known name, and not that of one but little known, to give authority to his production. Respecting the apocryphal books quoted, see Notes on verses 9 and 14 and the *Excursus*. The difficult style is natural enough in a Jew writing Greek well, but not with ease. As already stated in reference to 2 Peter, a theory that these two Epistles (2 Peter and Jude) are translations from Aramaic originals has recently been advocated (*Did St. Peter write in Greek?* by E. G. King, Cambridge, 1871). It would be presumption on the part of one who is ignorant of Hebrew to pronounce an opinion on the arguments used; but the *number* of them seems to be insufficient. Mere internal evidence of this kind ought to be very strong to counterbalance the entire absence of external evidence. Jerome would certainly give information on this point, if he possessed any, when he makes his own suggestion that St. Peter used different "interpreters" to write his two Epistles. (See Note on 2 Pet. ii. 17.)

III. The Place and Time.—As to the place we have no evidence, either external or internal. The Epistle contains some indications of time. (1) The fact that the destruction of Jerusalem and consequent ruin of the Jewish nation is not mentioned among the instances of divine vengeance (verses 5—7) is a strong reason for believing that the Epistle was written before A.D. 70. (2) The fact that such libertines as are here described are allowed to remain members of the Christian community points to a time when Church discipline is in its very infancy. The evils are very similar to those which St. Paul has to condemn in the Church of Corinth (1 Cor. v. 1, 2; vi. 8—18; xi. 17—22). (3) It seems to be implied (verse 17) that some of those addressed had heard Apostles. As to the bearing of the quotation from the *Book of Enoch* on this question, see *Excursus*.

IV. Object and Contents.—The object is plainly stated (verses 3, 4)—to urge his readers to contend earnestly for the faith which was being caricatured and denied by the libertinism and practical infidelity of certain members of the community. In what Church or Churches this evil prevailed we are not told; but it would be more likely to arise among converts from heathenism than from Judaism. The plan of the Epistle, short as it is, is evidently laid with considerable care; and the writer betrays a fondness for three-fold divisions which is quite remarkable. It would scarcely be an exaggeration to say that wherever a group of three is possible he makes one. One or two of the triplets may be accidental, but the majority of them can hardly be so; and this fact may be worth remembering in discussing the question of priority between this Epistle and 2 Peter. There are ten (or possibly twelve) groups of three in this short Epistle of 25 verses: viz. (1 and 2) verse 1; (3) verse 2; (4) verse 4; (5) verses 5—7; (6) verse 8; (7) verse 11; (8) verses 12—15, 16—18, 19; (9) verse 19; (10) verses 20, 21; (11) verses 22, 23; (12) verse 25. Of these (4) and (10) are perhaps doubtful; but there can be no question about the rest, although the last two are obscured in the English version, owing to our translators having followed a defective Greek text.

(1) INTRODUCTION.
- (a) *Three-fold address and three-fold greeting* (verses 1, 2).
- (b) *Purpose of the Epistle* (verse 3).
- (c) *Occasion of the Epistle* (verse 4).

(2) WARNING AND DENUNCIATION.
- (a) *Three instances of God's vengeance* (verses 5—7), *and application of these three instances to the libertines who are now provoking God* (verses 8—10).
- (b) *Three examples of similar wickedness* (verse 11).
- (c) *Three-fold description corresponding to these three examples* (verses 12—15; 16—18; 19).

(3) EXHORTATION—
- (a) *To strengthen themselves in the faith by prayer, godliness, and hope* (verses 20, 21).
- (b) *To treat these libertines with discrimination, making three classes* (verses 22, 23).
- (c) *Concluding doxology* (verses 24, 25).

V. The relation of Jude to 2 Peter.—The similarity both in substance and wording between a considerable portion of these two Epistles is so great that only two alternatives are possible; either one has borrowed from the other, or both have borrowed from a common source. The second alternative is rarely if ever advocated; it does not explain the facts very satisfactorily, and critics are agreed in rejecting it. But here agreement ends. On the further question, as to which writer is prior, there is very great diversity of opinion. One thing, therefore, is certain; that whichever writer has borrowed, he is no ordinary borrower. He knows how to assimilate foreign material so as to make it thoroughly his own. He remains original even while he appropriates the words and thoughts of another. He controls them; not they him. Were this not so, there would be little doubt about the matter. In any ordinary case of appropriation, if both the original and copy are forthcoming, critics do not doubt long as to which is the original. It is when the copy itself is a masterpiece, as in the case of Holbein's Madonna, that criticism is baffled. Such would seem to be the case here. The present writer is free to confess his own uncertainty. A superficial acquaintance with the subject inclined him to believe in the priority of Jude: further study disposes him to think that the balance is decidedly in favour of the priority of 2 Peter, although the balance is considerably short of proof. The question cannot be kept distinct from that of the authenticity of St. Peter. Every argument in favour of the authenticity of 2 Peter is something in favour of its priority, and *vice versâ*; although many arguments bear more upon one point than the other. If, then, the genuineness of 2 Peter is accepted as probable, this will add additional weight to the considerations now to be urged in favour of the priority of 2 Peter; and they in turn will strengthen the arguments for its genuineness.

This question as to the relation between these two Epistles seems to be one in which the old-fashioned view is not so far wrong after all. And some value may fairly be allowed to the old-fashioned arguments for it: (1) that the account of evil-doers in 2 Peter is in the main a prophecy, whereas St. Jude speaks of them as present; the inference being that St. Jude recognised in what he saw the mischief which St. Peter had foretold; and added weight to his own denunciations by framing them in the very words of the Apostle; (2) that St. Jude's warning, "remember the words which were spoken before by the Apostles . . . how that they told you there shall be mockers in the last time walking after their own ungodly lusts" (verses 17, 18), is an obvious reference to St. Peter's prediction, "there shall come in the last days scoffers, walking after their own lusts" (2 Pet. iii. 3). Of course a forger, with St. Jude's words before him, might frame his own words to fit them; but in that case we have still to account for St. Jude's warning, "remember the words which were spoken before by the Apostles," &c. They may refer to such passages as Acts xx. 29; 2 Tim. iii. 1; or (as some who insist on "how that they *told* you," or "*used to tell* you," prefer) to warnings given orally by the Apostles; still 2 Pet. iii. 3 is the most obvious reference.

No doubt it is antecedently more probable that a small Epistle should be republished with much additional matter, than that one-third of a longer Epistle should be republished with very little additional matter: but what has been said above about 2 Peter being a prophecy, of which St. Jude saw the fulfilment, is an answer to this. Besides which, we may urge that it is antecedently improbable that a forger should take so much from an Epistle that was not only known, but regarded with suspicion in some quarters, because of its quoting apocryphal books. That St. Jude is quoted by one or two writers who seem not to know or to reject 2 Peter (Tertullian, Clement of Alexandria, Origen) may be allowed some weight; but this could easily be accounted for, and in itself is not very convincing.

One argument used for the priority of Jude seems to the present writer to tell strongly for the priority of 2 Peter. It is this: that the evil-doers denounced by St. Jude are much more distinctly portrayed than those denounced in 2 Peter. We know from history that the errors indicated increased rapidly from the apostolic age onwards. The later writer, therefore, would have the clearer picture *before his eyes.* Would not the clearer *description,* then, be likely to be his? (See above on *the False Teachers and Scoffers: Introduction to 2 Pet.*) In connexion with this point it is worth considering whether the careful directions which St. Jude gives as to the way in which different classes of the ungodly men are to be treated does not point to a later stage of the evil (see Notes on Jude, verses 22, 23). Again, the rather fanciful arrangement into triplets, which prevails in St. Jude's Epistle, looks more like a second writer working up old material, than a first writer working under no influence from a predecessor.

Of the numerous minute arguments drawn from the wording of parallel passages only one or two specimens can be given here: others are considered in the Notes. Jude, verse 6 contains a telling piece of irony in the double use of "kept," which is wanting in 2 Pet. ii. 4; Jude, verse 10 contains a striking antithesis, very epigrammatically stated, which is wanting in 2 Pet. ii. 12; Jude, verses 12, 13 contains some fine similes, especially the one of "wandering stars," which would have fitted the "false teachers" admirably; yet most of them are absent from 2 Peter. Would a writer who is quite willing to borrow anything that will serve his purpose (this is evident, whichever is the borrower) have wilfully rejected all these good things? If they are improvements added by St. Jude, all is natural enough. It is worth mentioning in conclusion, that the arguments urged for an Aramaic original tell decidedly in favour of the priority of 2 Peter.

While admitting, therefore, that the case is by no means proved, we may be content to retain the priority as well as the authenticity of 2 Peter, as at least *the best working hypothesis.*

THE GENERAL EPISTLE OF

JUDE

(1) JUDE, the servant of Jesus Christ,
Verses 1, 2. Greeting. and brother of James, to them that are sanctified
by God the Father, and preserved in
Jesus Christ, *and* called: (2) mercy unto
you, and peace, and love, be multiplied.
(3) Beloved, when I gave all diligence
to write unto you of the common

A.D. cir. 66.

(1, 2) Address and greeting.

(1) **Jude.**—As to the Jude who here addresses us see *Introduction*, I.

The servant of Jesus Christ.—Better, *a servant of Jesus Christ.* There is nothing to show that these words indicate an evangelist, although it is more than probable that he was one: his writing this Epistle is evidence of the fact. The words may have a side reference to the ungodly men against whom he writes, who are *not* "servants of Jesus Christ." As he does not say that he is an Apostle, the inference is that he is not one. Contrast Rom. i. 1 (where see Note on "servant"); 1 Cor. i. 1; 2 Cor. i. 1; Gal. i. 1; Eph. i. 1; Col. i. 1; 1 Tim. i. 1; 2 Tim. i. 1; 1 Pet. i. 1 (where "Apostle" is used without "servant"); and Tit. i. 1; 2 Pet. i. 1 (where "Apostle" is added to "servant"). Excepting St. John, whose characteristic reserve accounts for it, Apostles proclaim themselves to be such in stating their credentials. Hebrews and the Epistle of St. James must be set aside as doubtful, or be admitted as illustrations of the rule. Phil. i. 1; 1 Thess. i. 1; and 2 Thess. i. 1 are not exceptions: St. Paul is there combined with others who are not Apostles. The same may be said of Philem. verse 1. Moreover, there St. Paul naturally avoids stating credentials: he wishes to appeal to Philemon's affection (Philem. verses 8, 9), not to his own authority.

And brother of James.—This is added not merely to explain who he is, but his claim to be heard. It is almost incredible that an Apostle should have urged such a claim, and yet not have stated the much higher claim of his own office: the inference again is that the writer is not an Apostle. Only one James can be meant. After the death of James the brother of John, only one James appears in the Acts (chaps. xii. 17; xv. 13; xxi. 18)—James the Just, brother of our Lord (Matt. xiii. 55), and first Bishop of Jerusalem. (See *Introduction*, I.) The brother of so saintly a man, one of the "pillars" of the Church (Gal. ii. 9), and holding so high an office, might claim the attention of Christians.

To them that are sanctified.—A reading of very great authority compels us to substitute *beloved* for "sanctified"; and the whole should probably run thus: *to those who are called, beloved in God the Father, and preserved for Jesus Christ.* Some prefer to take "in God the Father" with both participles: *beloved, and preserved for Jesus Christ, in God the Father.* The love is such as has existed from the beginning and still continues.

Here, in the first verse, we have a couple of triplets: a three-fold designation of the writer himself, as "Jude, the servant of Jesus Christ, and brother of James;" and a three-fold designation of his readers, as "called, beloved, preserved." In the next verse we have another triplet.

By God the Father.—Better, *in God the Father.* He is the sphere in which the love is displayed: it is in God that Christians love and are loved. The expression, "beloved in God," is unique in the New Testament. St. Paul sometimes writes "God *our* Father" (Rom. i. 7; 1 Cor. i. 3, *et al.*), and at first this was the more common expression; sometimes "God *the* Father" (Gal. i. 1, 3, *et al.*).

And preserved in Jesus Christ.—Better, *preserved for Jesus Christ: i.e.,* preserved to be His in His kingdom. This preservation has gone on from the first, and continues (John xvii. 2, 12, 24).

Called.—The word is used, in St. Paul's sense, for all Christians—all who have been called to a knowledge of God and of the gospel. (Comp. Rom. i. 7; and see Note on 1 Cor. i. 24.)

(2) **Mercy unto you, and peace, and love.**—Another triplet, which possibly looks back to the one just preceding: called by God's mercy, preserved in peace, beloved in love. The addition "and love" is peculiar to this Epistle. "Mercy" and "peace" occur in the opening greetings of 1 and 2 Timothy, Titus, and 2 John. The three are in logical order here: mercy from God to man; hence peace between God and man; hence love of all towards all.

Be multiplied.—By God. The word, as used in salutations, is peculiar to 1 and 2 Peter, and Jude.

(3, 4) The purpose and occasion of the Letter.

(3) **Beloved.**—Very unusual at the beginning of an Epistle; 3 John, verse 2, is the only other example. It indicates, possibly, the writer's wish to be brief and get to his subject at once; and, as his subject is a very unpleasing one, he hastens to assure his readers of affection for them, to prevent his strong language from offending them.

When I gave all diligence.—Better, *in giving all diligence: i.e.,* in having it much at heart. Wiclif and Rheims are nearly right. The expression is unique in the New Testament—2 Pet. i. 5 is similar, but the

Verses 3, 4. Purpose of the Epistle.

salvation, it was needful for me to write unto you, and exhort *you* that ye should earnestly contend for the faith which was once delivered unto the saints. (4) For there are certain men crept in unawares, who were before of old ordained to this condemnation, ungodly men, turning the grace of our God into lasciviousness, and denying the only Lord God, and our Lord Jesus Christ. (5) I will therefore put you in remembrance, though ye once knew this, how that the Lord, having saved the people out of the land

Verses 5—10. God's punishments a warning to sinners.

Greek for "giving" differs in verb and tense from the word used here.

Of the common salvation.—The best MSS. insert "our"—*of our common salvation: i.e.,* of those things which pertain to the salvation of us all. (Comp. Tit. i. 4.) Some would take these words after "it was needful for me to write unto you." The Authorised version is better.

It was needful for me to write unto you.—Better, *I found it necessary to write at once to you,* St. Jude had intended to write on general grounds; then the circumstances stated in verse 4 made him write immediately for the special purpose of warning them against a pressing danger. The "at once" comes from the tense, which is present in the first clause, aorist in the second. That St. Jude had intended to write a *longer* letter is pure conjecture, for which there is no evidence.

Contend for.—The word is a graphic one, implying standing over a thing to fight in its defence. You must fight as well as build (Neh. iv. 16, 18).

The faith—*i.e.,* that which is believed by Christians: not the expression of the doctrine, nor the holding of it, but the substance of it.

Once delivered.—Rather, *once for all delivered.* No change in it is possible. (Comp. Gal. i. 8, 9.) By "the saints" are meant all Christians; comp. Acts ix. 13 (where see Note), 32, 41. The word is used advisedly here, in marked contrast to the libertines now to be denounced.

(4) **Certain men crept in unawares**—viz., into the Church. The "certain" shows that these men are a decided minority, and has a tinge of depreciation, as in Gal. ii. 12. "Crept in unawares" is analogous to "unawares brought in, who came in privily" (Gal. ii. 4, where see Note), and to "privily bring in" (2 Pet. ii. 1). It is this insidious invasion which constitutes the necessity for writing stated in verse 3. Unfaithful Christians are sometimes regarded as an emergence from within, rather than an invasion from without (1 John ii. 19).

Close similarity to 2 Peter begins here and continues down to verse 18; the Notes on the parallel passages in 2 Pet. ii. should be compared throughout. In this Epistle the first three and last seven verses are the only portions not intimately related to 2 Peter.

Who were before of old ordained to this condemnation.—Literally, *who have been of old written down beforehand for this sentence*; or, perhaps, "written *up*"; for the metaphor may come from the practice of posting up the names of those who had to appear in court for trial. The text is a favourite one with Calvinists; but it gives no countenance to extreme predestinarian views. "Of old" cannot refer to the eternal purposes of God, but to something in history. On the other hand, it is doubtful whether it can refer to the recent warnings of St. Paul and St. Peter that false teachers should arise: otherwise one would be tempted to refer it to 2 Pet. ii. Something more remote from the writer's own day seems to be required: either the Old Testament prophets, or the *Book of Enoch,* quoted below. The Greek word here rendered "before ordained" is in Rom. xv. 4 rendered "written aforetime." (Comp. Eph. iii. 3.)

To this condemnation.—Literally, *to this sentence,* or *judgment*; but the context shows that the judgment is an adverse one. "*This* condemnation," viz., the one stated in the denunciations which follow, and illustrated by the fate of those mentioned in verses 5—7. Note the three-fold description of the men thus written down for judgment: they are ungodly; they pervert God's grace; they deny Christ.

Turning the grace of our God into lasciviousness.—Turning Christian liberty into unchristian license. "*Our* God," not theirs; they are "without God in the world." "Wantonness" would be better than "lasciviousness" here, as in 2 Pet. ii. 18. The Greek word expresses license generally, not merely sins of impurity.

Denying the only Lord God, and our Lord Jesus Christ.—Rather, *denying the only Master, and our Lord Jesus Christ.* "God" is an addition to the original text, and must be omitted. "Lord" represents two words in the Greek quite different one from the other. The Genevan version is right all but the insertion of "God;" the Rhemish quite right—having "Dominator," however, for "Master." We are once more in doubt whether one or two Persons of the Trinity are mentioned here. (Comp. 2 Pet. i. 1.) Certainly 2 Pet. ii. 1 countenances our taking "the only Master" as meaning Christ; and the fact that the article is not repeated with "Lord" is in favour of only one Person being meant. But Luke ii. 29, Acts iv. 24, Rev. vi. 10 countenance our understanding these words as meaning the Father; and the absence of the article before "Lord" is not conclusive. The insertion of "God" is, perhaps, a gloss to insist on this latter interpretation. If it be right, the clause is closely parallel to 1 John ii. 22: "He is Antichrist that *denieth the Father and the Son.*" Note the emphatic insertion of "our" once more: they will not have Him for *their* Lord; His divine authority was precisely what they denied.

(5—7) We now enter upon the main body of the Epistle. Three instances of God's vengeance: the unbelievers in the wilderness; the impure angels; Sodom and Gomorrha.

(5) **I will therefore put you in remembrance.**—Or, *But I wish to remind you.* The "but" indicates opposition to the impiety of those just mentioned.

Though ye once knew this.—The best MSS. and versions compel us to substitute "all things" for "this," and we must translate, *because ye have once for all* (as in verse 3) *known all things.* You have once for all been taught all that I want to say to you; so that I need only remind you, there is no need to instruct. (Comp. Rom. xv. 14, 15, where see Notes; 2 Pet. i. 12; 1 John ii. 21.) "All things" probably

of Egypt, afterward destroyed them
that believed not. (6) And the angels
which kept not their first estate,[1] but
left their own habitation, he hath
reserved in everlasting chains under
darkness unto the judgment of the
great day. (7) Even as Sodom and
Gomorrha, and the cities about them
in like manner, giving themselves
over to fornication, and going after

1 Or, *principality.*

has special reference to Old Testament history, as what follows seems to show.

How that the Lord.—"How that" depends upon "remind," not upon "have known." There is very strong evidence in favour of substituting "Jesus" for "the Lord;" a most remarkable reading, showing how, in Christian language, the Man Jesus had become identified with the Eternal Son. The use of "Christ" in 1 Cor. x. 4, though less striking, is similar.

Having saved the people.—Or, perhaps, *having saved a people.* A whole nation was rescued. The order of the three examples of signal punishment is in 2 Peter chronological: impure angels, flood, Sodom and Gomorrha; here not. But the order here is quite intelligible. St. Jude's main object is to warn his readers against that party in the Christian community who, by its abuse of Christian liberty, transformed the gospel of purity into a gospel of wantonness, and to give them a safeguard against such. And the safeguard is this: to hold fast the faith once for all delivered to them, and to remember the consequences of being unbelieving. For this purpose, no warning could be more apposite than the fate of Jude's own nation in the wilderness. This palmary instance given, two others follow, probably suggested by 2 Peter.

Afterward destroyed.—Better, *secondly destroyed.* Wiclif, "the secunde tyme"; Rheims, "secondly." The Lord twice manifested His power on Israel: (1) in mercy; (2) in judgment. The reference is almost certainly to Num. xiv. 35; Deut. i. 35, &c. The destruction of Jerusalem can scarcely be meant, whatever date we assign to the Epistle, although the striking reading, "Jesus" for "the Lord," gives some countenance to such an interpretation. The most obvious meaning is, that the people destroyed were those who, in the first instance, were saved. Had the destruction of Jerusalem been intended, the reference would probably have been more clear.

(6) **And the angels which kept not.**—Rather, *because they kept not.* The construction is similar to that in Matt. xviii. 25, "Forasmuch as he had not to pay." (See Note on verse 8.) This second instance of the impure angels has nothing to do with the original rebellion of Satan, or "fall of the angels." The reference is either to Gen. vi. 2, or (more probably), to passages in the *Book of Enoch.* (See *Excursus* at the end of this Epistle.)

Their first estate.—The Greek word has two meanings: (1) beginning, which our translators have adopted here; (2) rule or power, which would be better. Wiclif has "prinshood;" Rheims, "principalitie." The word is translated "rule" (1 Cor. xv. 24) and "principality" (Rom. viii. 38; Eph. i. 21; iii. 10; vi. 12; Col. i. 16; ii. 10, 15; Titus iii. 1). The term belongs to the Jewish classification of angels, and here refers rather to their *power* over things earthly than to the *beginning* of their state. The two meanings are but two views of the same fact: their power or dignity *was* their first estate. Some explain the word of the power of God over the angels; but both wording and context are against this.

Their own habitation.—*Their proper home.* By leaving heaven and coming down to earth, they lost their power over the earth. (Comp. Milton's *Paradise Lost*, Book v.)

He hath reserved.—Better, *He hath kept*, in ironical contrast to "which kept not" just above: the same Greek word is used in both cases. This ironical contrast does not exist in the parallel passage, 2 Pet. ii. 4. Would a writer, quite willing to copy, have failed to copy this? On the other hand, what more natural than that St. Jude should add a forcible touch?

In everlasting chains.—Speculations as to how this and 2 Pet. ii. 4 are to be reconciled with such texts as Luke xxii. 31, 1 Pet. v. 8, which speak plainly of the freedom and activity of Satan, and Eph. vi. 12, Rom. viii. 38, Col. ii. 15, which imply numerous agents akin to him, are not very profitable. The reality of powers of evil may be inferred, apart from Scripture, from their effects. That some of these powers are personal, some not, some free, some not, and that all are to be defeated at last, seems to be implied in Scripture; but its silence is a rebuke to curious speculation. Enough is told us for our comfort, warning, and assurance. It consoles us to know that much of the evil of which we are conscious in ourselves is not our own, but comes from without. It puts us on our guard to know that we have such powers arrayed against us. It gives us confidence to know that we have abundant means of victory even over them.

Under darkness.—The Greek word occurs only here, verse 13, 2 Pet. ii. 4, 17, and possibly Heb. xii. 18. A separate English word, such as "gloom," is desirable for these passages.

The great day.—So called Rev. vi. 17 (comp. xvi. 14), and nowhere else in the New Testament. Perhaps it comes from Joel ii. 31; Mal. iv. 5. St. John's expression is the "last day" (John vi. 39, 40, 44, 54; xi. 24; xii. 48; and nowhere else). "The day of judgment," "that day," and "the day of the Lord," are other common expressions.

(7) **Even as.**—Or, possibly, *how*, like "how that" in verse 5, depending upon "put you in remembrance." Sodom and Gomorrha are typical instances of divine vengeance both in the Old and New Testament (Isa. xiii. 19; Jer. l. 40; Rom. ix. 29).

And the cities about them.—Adma and Zeboim (Deut. xxix. 23; Hos. xi. 8).

In like manner.—We must read, *in like manner to these*, and arrange the sentence thus: *Even as Sodom and Gomorrha, and the cities about them, giving themselves over to fornication in like manner to these.* Who are meant by "these"? Not the ungodly men of verse 4, which would anticipate verse 8; nor the inhabitants of Sodom and Gomorrha, which would be somewhat clumsy in the Greek; but the angels of verse 6. The reference is again to the impurity of certain angels in having intercourse with the daughters of men, of which there is so much in the *Book of Enoch.* This sin of the angels was strictly analogous to that of the people of Sodom.

Going after strange flesh.—Strictly, *going astray after other flesh—i.e.*, other than is allowed; leaving natural for unnatural uses.

Are set forth for an example, suffering the vengeance of eternal fire.—It would be possible

strange[1] flesh, are set forth for an example, suffering the vengeance of eternal fire.
(8) Likewise also these *filthy* dreamers defile the flesh, despise dominion, and speak evil of dignities.
(9) Yet Michael the archangel, when contending with the devil he disputed about the body of Moses, durst not bring against him a railing accusation, but said, The Lord rebuke thee.[a]
(10) But these speak evil of those things which they know not: but what they know naturally, as brute beasts, in those things they corrupt themselves.

1 Gr. *other.*

a Zech. 3. 2.

---

to take "of eternal fire" after "example," thus: *are set forth as an example of eternal fire in undergoing punishment.* (Comp. Wisd. x. 7.) The punishment of the submerged cities is perpetual; moreover, there are appearances as of volcanic fire under them. The Greek for "undergoing" occurs here only in the New Testament; but comp. 2 Macc. iv. 48.

(8–10) Application of these three instances to the libertines who are now provoking God.

(8) **Likewise also.**—Rather, *Yet in like manner: i.e.,* in spite of these warnings. These ungodly men were like the unbelievers in the wilderness in denying Christ and scoffing at His promises; they were like the impure angels in leaving that "constitution which is in heaven" (Phil. iii. 20) for the base pleasures of earth; they were like the people of Sodom in seeking even these base pleasures by unnatural courses.

These filthy dreamers.—We must add *also.* "Filthy" is not in the original Greek, nor in any previous English version, but is supplied from the next clause; not rightly, for "dreamers" goes with all three clauses, not with "defile the flesh" only. This being admitted, a number of painful interpretations are at once excluded. "These dreamers *also*" means these ungodly men, who are deep in the slumber of sin (see Note on Rom. xiii. 11), as well as the three classes of sinners just mentioned. Excepting in Acts ii. 17, which is a quotation from Joel ii. 28, the word for "dreamer" occurs nowhere else in the New Testament, but is found in the LXX. version of Isa. lvi. 10, of dogs that dream and make a noise in their sleep. St. Jude perhaps has this passage in his mind. (See below, second Note on verse 12.) "Dreamers" may perhaps refer to the empty speculations of these men.

Defile the flesh.—Like the inhabitants of the cities of the plain. Some of the earliest forms of Gnosticism, on its antinomian as distinct from its ascetic side, exhibit the licentiousness inveighed against here; *e.g.,* the Simonians, Nicolaitanes, Cainites, Carpocratians.

Despise dominion.— Like the impure angels. Insert "and" before "despise." The "dominion," or *lordship,* is that of Almighty God. *Set aside,* or *reject* (Mark vii. 9; Luke vii. 30; John xii. 48), would be better than "despise," to mark the difference between this and 2 Pet. ii. 10.

Speak evil of dignities.—Like the murmurers in the wilderness. By "dignities," or *glories,* are meant unseen powers worthy of reverence. The Greek word is rare in the New Testament; only here, 2 Pet. ii. 10, and 1 Pet. i. 11. Earthly dignities, whether ecclesiastical or civil, are not included. (Comp. the doctrine of Menander, Irenæus, I. xxiii. 5.)

(9) **Yet Michael the archangel.**—These libertines allow themselves to use language against celestial beings which even an archangel did not venture to use against Satan. In the Old Testament Michael appears as the guardian angel of the people of Israel, Dan. x. 21; xii. 1; in the New Testament he is mentioned only here and in Rev. xii. 7. In the *Book of Enoch* his meekness is spoken of; he is "the merciful, *the patient,* the holy Michael," xl. 8.

He disputed about the body of Moses.—To be understood quite literally: to make "the body of Moses" into a metaphor for the people of Israel, or the Mosaic law, is most unnatural. This passage is the only evidence extant of any such incident or tradition. The nearest approach to it is the Targum of Jonathan on Deut. xxxiv. 6, which says that Michael was the appointed guardian of Moses' grave. According to Origen (*De Princip.* III. ii. 1) the source of it is a book called the *Ascension,* or *Assumption of Moses.* Evidently it is something supposed to be well known to those whom St. Jude is addressing, and it appears to be given as a fact which he believes, though we cannot be sure of this. In any case it does not follow that we are to believe in it as an historical fact. Reverent, and therefore cautious, theories of inspiration need not exclude the possibility of an unhistorical incident being cited as an illustration or a warning. St. Paul makes use of the Jewish legend of the rock following the Israelites in the wilderness as an illustration (1 Cor. x. 4). The strange question, "What did the devil want with the body of Moses?" has been asked, and answered in more ways than one:—(1) to make it an object of idolatry, as the Israelites would be very likely to worship it; (2) to keep it as his own, as that of a murderer, because Moses killed the Egyptian (Ex. ii. 12).

Durst not . . .—Out of respect to Satan's original angelic nature. (Comp. 1 Cor. vi. 1.)

A railing accusation.—More literally, *a sentence savouring of evil-speaking.* Wiclif, "doom"; Tyndale and Cranmer, "sentence"; Rheims, "judgment." Michael brought no sentence against the devil, but left all judgment to God.

The Lord rebuke thee.—The same rebuke is administered to Satan by the angel of Jehovah, when Satan appears as the adversary of Joshua the high priest, the restorer of the temple and of the daily sacrifice, and one of the Old Testament types of Christ (Zech. iii. 2). It is probable that the tradition here given by St. Jude is derived from this passage in Zechariah, or from a source common to both. We have another reminiscence of Zech. iii. 2 in verse 23.

(10) **But these . . .**—In strong contrast to the scrupulous reverence of the archangel. "Fools rush in where angels fear to tread."

Those things which they know not.—The "dignities" of verse 8. This shows that unseen spiritual powers are there meant: these men would know earthly rulers. It is on the unseen that they show their irreverence.

What they know naturally.—The means of gratifying their desires. The two halves of the verse are in emphatic contrast. What they do not know, and cannot know, they abuse by gross irreverence: what they know, and cannot help knowing, they abuse by gross licentiousness. If this Epistle is prior to 2 Peter

(11) Woe unto them! for they have gone in the way of Cain, and ran greedily after the error of Balaam for reward, and perished in the gainsaying of Core. (12) These are spots in your feasts of charity, when they feast with you, feeding themselves without fear: clouds *they are* without water, carried about of winds; trees whose fruit withereth,

Verses 11—19. The sins of Cain, Balaam, and Korah.

it is strange that the author of the latter should have neglected so telling an antithesis, and should (from a literary point of view) have so spoiled the passage by his mode of adaptation (chap. ii. 12). If 2 Peter is prior there is nothing strange in St. Jude improving upon the mode of expression. The word for "know" is not the same in both clauses. The word used in "which they know not" is the most general and common word of the kind in Greek, expressing mere perception, and occurring about three hundred times in the New Testament; that used in "what they know naturally" is more definite, and expresses practical experience productive of skill and science; it occurs fourteen times in the New Testament, mostly in the Acts. (Comp. "Paul I know," Acts xix. 15.)

They corrupt themselves.—Or, perhaps, *they work their own ruin.* Note the tense; not future, but present. The corruption, or *ruin,* is not a judgment hanging over them; it is already going on.

(11) Three examples of similar wickedness: Cain, Balaam, Korah.

Woe unto them!—An echo of Christ's denunciations in the first three Gospels, whereby the description of these evil-doers takes for the moment a denunciatory form. The past tenses immediately following are owing to the writer's placing himself in thought at the moment when these men reap the consequences of their sins: their punishment is so certain, that he regards it as having come.

In the way of Cain.—The first great criminal; the first to outrage the laws of nature. Explanations to the effect that these libertines followed Cain by murdering men's *souls* by their corrupt doctrine, or by persecuting believers, and other suggestions still more curious, are needlessly far-fetched. John viii. 44, and 1 John iii. 15, are not strictly apposite: these ungodly men may have hated and persecuted the righteous, but St. Jude does not tell us so. Sensuality is always selfish, but by no means always ill-natured or malignant.

Ran greedily after the error of Balaam for reward.—The Greek for "ran greedily" literally means "they were poured out in streams;" the Greek for "error" may also mean "deception." Hence three renderings are possible: (1) as the Authorised version; (2) "they ran greedily after the deception of Balaam's reward;" (3) "they were undone by the deception of Balaam's reward." The first is best. "Reward" in the Greek is the genitive of *price.* Comp. "the *rewards* of divination" (Num. xxii. 7); "they *hired* against thee Balaam" (Deut. xxiii. 4; Neh. xiii. 2). Here, again, far-fetched explanations may be avoided. The allusion lies on the surface—running counter to God's will from interested motives. Possibly, there may also be some allusion to Balaam's causing the Israelites to be seduced into licentiousness (Rev. ii. 14).

Perished in the gainsaying of Core—*i.e.,* through gainsaying like that of Korah; referring to his *speaking against* Moses in the revolutionary opposition which he headed. These libertines, like Korah; treated sacred ordinances with contempt.

The triplet in this verse, like that in verse 8, is parallel to the three examples of God's vengeance, verses 5—7. Cain, like the inhabitants of Sodom and Gomorrha, outraged the laws of nature; Balaam, like the impure angels, despised the sovereignty of God; Korah, like those who disbelieved the report of the spies, spoke evil of dignities.

(12—19) Three-fold description of the ungodly, corresponding to the three examples just given. The divisions are clearly marked, each section beginning with "These are" (verses 12, 16, 19).

(12—15) Description corresponding to Cain.

(12) **These are spots in your feasts of charity, when they feast with you.**—Rather, *These are the rocks in your feasts of charity, banqueting with you fearlessly* (see next Note); or, *These are they who banquet together fearlessly, rocks in your feasts of charity.* The former is preferable. But in any case we must probably read *rocks*—*i.e.,* that on which those who meet them at your love-feasts will be wrecked (see Notes on 1 Cor. xi. 20—22)—not "spots," which is borrowed from 2 Pet. ii. 13. But it is just possible that as *spiloi,* St. Peter's word, may mean either "spots" or "rocks" (though most commonly the former), so St. Jude's word (*spilades*) may mean either "spots" or "rocks" (though almost invariably the latter). In an Orphic poem of the fourth century, *spilades* means "spots"; but this is rather late authority for its use in the first century. Here "rocks" is the safer translation. St. Peter is dwelling on the sensuality of these sinners, and for him "spots" is the more obvious metaphor. St. Jude, in tracing an analogy between them and Cain, would be more likely to select "rocks." These libertines, like Cain, turned the ordinances of religion into selfishness and sin: both, like sunken rocks, destroyed those who unsuspectingly approached them. On the difference of reading respecting the word for "feasts of charity," or "love-feasts," see Note on 2 Pet. ii. 13. Possibly the name *Agapæ* for such feasts comes from this passage. Had it been common when St. Paul wrote 1 Cor. xi., he would probably have made a point of it; love-feasts in which there was no love. (Comp. 1 Pet. v. 14.)

Feeding themselves without fear.—"Without fear" goes better with "feasting with you"; but the Greek admits of either construction. "Feeding themselves" instead of the poorer members of the flock; whereas feeding the poor was one great object of the love-feasts. Others explain, "feeding themselves" (literally, *pasturing themselves*) instead of waiting to be tended by the shepherds. The former is better, the scandal being similar to that described in 1 Cor. xi. 21. (Comp. Isa. lvi. 11, which St. Jude may possibly have had in his mind; and see above, second Note on verse 8.)

Clouds without water.—Comp. Prov. xxv. 14. The meaning is not that these men bring much food to the love-feasts and give nothing away: there is no longer any allusion to the love-feasts. Rather, these men are ostentatious generally, and yet do no good: inflated and empty. (See on 2 Pet. ii. 17.)

without fruit, twice dead, plucked up
by the roots; (13) raging waves of the
sea, foaming out their own shame;
wandering stars, to whom is reserved
the blackness of darkness for ever.
(14) And Enoch also, the seventh from
Adam, prophesied of these, saying,
Behold, the Lord cometh with ten
thousands of his saints, (15) to execute
judgment upon all, and to convince all
that are ungodly among them of all
their ungodly deeds which they have
ungodly committed, and of all their
hard *speeches* which ungodly sinners
have spoken against him. (16) These
are murmurers, complainers, walking
after their own lusts; and their mouth
speaketh great swelling *words*, having
men's persons in admiration because of
advantage. (17) But, beloved, remember

Carried about of winds.—More literally, *borne past* (without giving any rain) *by winds*; or, perhaps, *driven out of their course* (and so showing their flimsiness) *by winds*.

Trees whose fruit withereth, without fruit.—There is no such strange contradiction in the Greek, nor in any of the earlier English versions. The meaning rather is, *autumn trees* (which ought to be full of fruit, and yet are) *without fruit*; in allusion, probably, to the barren fig-tree. Others, less simply, explain "trees in *late* autumn"—*i.e.*, stripped and bare. But for this we should expect "winter trees" rather than "autumn trees."

Twice dead.—Utterly dead, and hence "plucked up by the roots." Spiritually these men were "twice dead" in having returned, after baptism, to the death of sin. The writer piles up metaphor on metaphor and epithet on epithet in the effort to express his indignation and abhorrence. The epithets here are in logical order: in autumn, fruitless, dead, rooted up.

(13) **Foaming out their own shame.**—More literally, *shames*; their shameful acts. Isa. lvii. 20 is probably in St. Jude's mind: "The wicked are like the troubled sea, whose waters cast up mire and dirt."

Wandering stars.—Nothing is gained by understanding comets, which have their orbits, and do not wander, in St. Jude's sense, any more than planets do. The image is that of stars leaving their place in the heavens, where they are beautiful and useful, and wandering away (to the utter confusion of every one who directs his course by them) into sunless gloom, where their light is extinguished, and whence they cannot return. This simile suits the "false teachers" of 2 Peter better than the "ungodly" of Jude. Would the writer of 2 Peter have neglected to avail himself of it?

(14) **And Enoch also.**—On the *Book of Enoch*, and this famous quotation from it, see *Excursus* at the end of the Epistle. The following passage from Irenæus (IV. xvi. 2) shows that he was acquainted with the book, and throws light on St. Jude's use of it:—"Enoch also, pleasing God without circumcision, was God's ambassador to the angels, although he was a man, and was raised to heaven, and is preserved even until now as a witness of the just judgment of God. For the angels by transgression fell to earth for judgment, while a man, by pleasing God, was raised to heaven for salvation." The mission of Enoch to the fallen angels is narrated in the *Book of Enoch*, xii.—xvi.

The seventh from Adam.—This is not inserted without special meaning. It was scarcely needed to distinguish the son of Jared from the son of Cain; in that case it would have been more simple to say, "the son of Jared." It either points to the extreme antiquity of the prophecy, or else to the mystical and sabbatical number seven. Enoch (see preceding Note) was a type of perfected humanity, and hence the notion of "divine completion and rest" is perhaps suggested here. Thus, Augustine, in his reply to Faustus the Manichæan (XII. xiv.):—"Enoch, *the seventh from Adam*, pleased God and was translated, as there is to be a *seventh day of rest*, in which all will be translated who during the sixth day of the world's history are created anew by the incarnate Word." Several of the numbers connected with Enoch in Genesis seem to be symmetrical, and intended to convey a meaning.

With ten thousands of his saints.—Or, *among His holy myriads*—*i.e.*, encircled by them. (Comp. Deut. xxxiii. 2; Heb. xii. 22.)

(15) **To execute judgment.**—The Greek phrase occurs only here and John v. 27.

To convince.—Better, *to convict*. (Comp. John viii. 46, and see Notes on John xvi. 8, and on 1 Cor. xiv. 24.) The words "among them" must be omitted, as wanting in authority.

Hard speeches.—Comp. John vi. 60, the only other place where this epithet is applied to words. The meaning is somewhat similar in each case: harsh, repulsive, inhuman. It does not mean "hard to understand." Nabal (1 Sam. xxv. 3) has this epithet with the LXX., where the Authorised version has "churlish." In the Ethiopic version of the *Book of Enoch* there appears to be nothing to represent "hard speeches . . . spoken" in this passage.

(16—18) Description corresponding to Balaam.

(16) **Complainers.**—Literally, *discontented with their lot*. Men who "shape their course according to their own lusts" can never be content, for (1) the means of gratifying them are not always present, and (2) the lusts are insatiable. Such was eminently the case with Balaam, in his cupidity and his chafing against the restraints which prevented him from gratifying it. There is a possible reference to this verse in the *Shepherd* of Hermas (*Sim.* IX. xix. 3).

Great swelling words.—See Note on 2 Pet. ii. 18.

Having men's persons in admiration.—More simply, *admiring persons* (so the Rhemish version)—*i.e.*, having regard to people of distinction, as Balaam to Balak. These ungodly men were courtiers, flatterers, and parasites.

Because of advantage.—*For the sake of advantage*—*i.e.*, to gain something by it: like "for reward" (verse 11). Exactly Balaam's case. Note that each half of the verse falls into an irregular triplet.

(17) **But, beloved.**—Better, as in verse 20, *But ye, beloved*. "Ye" is emphatic in both cases: "ye," in contrast to these impious men. All previous English versions insert the "ye." While taking the form of an exhortation, the passage still remains virtually

ye the words which were spoken before
of the apostles of our Lord Jesus Christ;
(18) how that they told you there should
be mockers in the last time, who should
walk after their own ungodly lusts.
(19) These be they who separate them-
selves, sensual, having not the Spirit.
(20) But ye, beloved, build-
ing up yourselves on your
most holy faith, praying

Verses 20—23. Final exhortations.

---

descriptive. "Be not ye deceived by their impudent boasting and interested pandering, for these are the scoffing sensualists against whom the Apostles warned you."

Spoken before of the apostles.—The old use of "of" for "by," like "carried about of winds" (verse 12). (Comp. 2 Pet. ii. 19.) St. Jude implies that this warning of the Apostles is well known to those whom he addresses. This appeal to the authority of Apostles would be more naturally made by one who was not an Apostle, but cannot be regarded as decisive. See *Introduction*, I., and Note on 2 Pet. iii. 2, to which, however, this is not quite parallel, for the writer there has already declared himself to be an Apostle (2 Pet. i. 1). There is nothing to show that the author of our Epistle regards the Apostles as considerably removed in time from himself. "In the last time" is *their* expression, not his; and by it *they* did not mean any age remote from themselves. (Comp. 1 John ii. 18; 2 Tim. iii. 1, 2, 6; Heb. i. 2; 1 Pet. i. 20.)

(18) **How that they told you.**—Or, perhaps, *used to tell you:* but we cannot infer from this that oral teaching exclusively is meant. This, again, leaves the question of the writer's position open. Had St. Jude written "how that they told *us*," it would have been decisive against his being an Apostle.

There should be mockers.—Better, *that there shall be scoffers.* The quotation is direct, and is introduced formally by a word which in Greek commonly precedes a direct quotation. This, however, scarcely amounts to proof that the quotation is from a written document. The word for "mockers" here is the same as that translated "scoffers" in 2 Pet. iii. 3. The translation should be the same in both passages.

In the last time.—These words had better come first: *that in the last time there shall be scoffers.*

Who should walk after their own ungodly lusts.—Better, *walking according to their own lusts of impieties.* The force of the genitive may be merely adjectival, as the Authorised version renders it: but as it may indicate the things lusted for, it is better to keep a literal rendering of it.

(19) Description corresponding to Korah.

(19) **These be they.**—Better, *These are they*—for the sake of making the openings of verses 12, 16, and 19 exactly alike, as they are in the Greek.

Who separate themselves.—"Themselves" must be omitted, the evidence against it being overwhelming. "Who separate:" who are creating a schism, like Korah and his company; claiming to be the chief and most enlightened members in the community to which they still profess to belong, though they turn upside down its fundamental principles. The context rather leads us to suppose that these libertines claimed to be the only "spiritual" Christians, inasmuch as they said that to their exalted spiritual natures the things of sense were purely indifferent, and might be indulged in without loss or risk; while they taunted other Christians, who regulated their conduct carefully with regard to such things, with being *psychic* or "sensuous." Note the three-fold division of the verse.

Sensual.—The Greek word is *psychic,* and has no English equivalent; "sensuous" would perhaps be best. The LXX. do not use it, but it occurs six times in the New Testament. Four times (1 Cor. ii. 14; xv. 44, 46) it is translated "natural" (see Note on 1 Cor. ii. 14); once (Jas. iii. 15), "sensual," with "natural" in the margin; and here simply "sensual." In 1 Cor. xv. 44, 46, the moral meaning is in the background; in the other three passages the moral meaning is prominent and is distinctly bad. *Psychic* is the middle term of a triplet of terms, "carnal, *psychic,* spiritual." "Carnal" and "spiritual" speak for themselves—the one bad, the other good. *Psychic,* which comes between, is much closer to "carnal," and with it is opposed to "spiritual." This is more clearly seen in the Latin equivalents—*carnalis, animalis, spiritalis.* The carnal man is ruled by his passions, and rises little above the level of the brutes. The psychic man is ruled by human reasoning, and human affections, and does not rise above the world of sense. The spiritual man is ruled by his spirit—the noblest part of his nature—and this is ruled by the Spirit of God. He rises to and lives among those things which can only be "spiritually discerned." Our Christian psychology is seriously affected by the absence of any English word for *psychic*—the part of man's nature which it represents is often lost sight of.

Having not the Spirit.—Or, perhaps, *because they have no spirit.* The Holy Spirit may be meant, although the Greek word has no article; but more probably spiritual power and insight is what is meant. These men had allowed the spiritual part of their nature, of which they talked so much, to become so buried in the mire of sensual indulgence and human self-sufficiency, that it was utterly inoperative and practically non-existent. The form of negative used in the Greek seems to imply that their "having no spirit" is the reason why they are justly called "sensuous."

Each of these three descriptions (verses 12—15, 16—18, and 19) is shorter than the preceding one. The writer hurries through an unpalatable subject to the more pleasing duty of exhorting those faithful Christians for whose sake he is writing.

(20, 21) Exhortation to strengthen themselves in the faith by prayer, godliness, and hope.

(20) **But ye, beloved.**—Exactly as in verse 17: "ye" in emphatic contrast to these sensuous and unspiritual men.

Building up yourselves.—Making yourselves firm on the sure foundation of faith, in contradistinction to those "who separate," and fancy themselves firm in their impious conceits. The notion is not so much that of increasing and completing an edifice as of strengthening its foundations. Faith and its object are here almost identified. To have faith as one's foundation is the same as having Christ as one's foundation. "*Your* faith," that which has been "once for all delivered" to you (verse 4). "*Most holy* faith," as opposed to the most unholy quicksands of the doctrines condemned in this Epistle.

in the Holy Ghost, (21) keep yourselves in
the love of God, looking for the mercy
of our Lord Jesus Christ unto eternal
life. (22) And of some have compassion,
making a difference: (23) and others save
with fear, pulling *them* out of the fire;
hating even the garment spotted by
the flesh. (24) Now unto him that is able
to keep you from falling, Verses 24, 25.
and to present *you* faultless Doxology.
before the presence of his glory with ex-
ceeding joy, (25) to the only wise God our
Saviour, *be* glory and majesty, dominion
and power, both now and ever. Amen.

Praying in the Holy Ghost.—Only in this way can Christians make firm their foundation. The Greek admits of "in the Holy Ghost" being taken with the previous clause; but our version is better. The expression "praying in the Holy Ghost" is not found elsewhere. It means that we pray in His strength and wisdom: He moves our hearts and directs our petitions. (See Notes on Rom. viii. 26.)

(21) **Keep yourselves in the love of God.**—Not our love of God, but His love of us. Consequently it is not the case that the three great Christian virtues—Faith, Hope, and Charity—are inculcated here, although at first sight we are tempted to think so. God's love is the region in which those who are built up on faith, and supported by prayer, may continually dwell.

The mercy of our Lord Jesus Christ.—The mercy which He will show as Judge at the Last Day. By prayer in the Spirit we are kept in the love of the Father for the mercy of the Son.

Unto eternal life.—These words may be taken either with "keep yourselves," or with "looking," or with "mercy": best with "keep yourselves."

(22, 23) Exhortation to treat these libertines with discrimination, making three classes.

(22) **And of some have compassion, making a difference.**—The evidence is very strong in favour of a widely different reading: *And some indeed convict* (verse 15) *when they are in doubt* (Matt. xxi. 21; Acts x. 20; xi. 12; Rom. iv. 20; xiv. 23; Jas. i. 6); or, *when they contend with you* (verse 9; Acts xi. 2); or, *when they separate from you.* The first seems best, though the second also makes excellent sense, and has verse 9 in its favour. This, then, is the first and least hopeless class—those who are still in doubt, though inclined the wrong way. They may still be remonstrated with, convicted of error, and reclaimed (Matt. xviii. 15; Titus i. 13; Jas. v. 20). Some would make this first class the worst and most hopeless—those who are to be argued down in disputation, but without much chance of success. Such interpreters make the third class the best: those who can probably be saved by gentle means. The Greek here is so ambiguous that we cannot be certain of the meaning. But the addition of "in fear" and "hating even the garment spotted by the flesh" to the directions respecting the third class, seems to indicate that that class is the worst.

(23) **And others save with fear.**—"With fear" must certainly be omitted, as no part of the true text. "Save" should perhaps be *try to save.* It is the present imperative, not the aorist.

Pulling them out of the fire.—Better, *snatching them out of the fire.* We have here another reminiscence of Zech. iii. 1—3: we had one in verse 9. (Comp. Amos iv. 11.) The fire of the judgment to come is probably not meant; rather the imminent danger (as of one who is asleep in a burning house) in which the fire of their sins keeps them. This is the second class: those who can still be rescued, but by strong measures.

After the words "out of the fire" we must insert another clause omitted from the inferior Greek texts used by our translators: "and on others have compassion in fear." Wiclif and the Rhemish version, following the Vulgate, have this clause. This is the third and worst class: those on whom profound pity is all that we dare bestow, and that in fear and trembling, lest by contact with them we may be brought within the influence of the deadly contamination that clings to all their surroundings. Abhorrence must be shown to the very externals of pollution. (Comp. 1 Cor. v. 11; 1 Tim. v. 22; Titus iii. 10, 11; 1 John v. 16; 2 John, verses 10, 11.)

(24, 25) Concluding Doxology.

(24) **Now unto him that is able.**—Comp. the conclusion Rom. xvi. 25. It would be rash to infer from the similarity that St. Jude must have known the Epistle to the Romans; although there is nothing incredible in the supposition that he was acquainted with it. The Epistle had been in circulation probably for some ten years before St. Jude wrote. Doxologies no doubt became elastic formulas almost from the first.

To keep you from falling.—Better, *to keep you unfallen.* From his own warnings, denunciations, and exhortations, which have been severe and sombre throughout, St. Jude turns in joyous, exulting confidence to Him who alone can make them effectual. "Keep you," or, *guard you:* not the more general word translated "preserved" in verse 1, but another more in harmony with the present context, as indicating *protection* against the great perils just pointed out. A reading of much authority has "them" for "you"—*to keep them unfallen.* If it be correct, it may be explained as being in thought, though not in form, addressed to God, so that those to whom he is writing are spoken of in the third person.

Before the presence of his glory.—The glory that shall be revealed at the day of judgment. The meaning is, "Who can bring it to pass that you stand blameless before the judgment-seat" (Col. i. 22; 1 Thess. iii. 13).

(25) **To the only wise God our Saviour.**—The coupling of "Saviour" with "God" is common in the Pastoral Epistles (1 Tim. i. 1; ii. 3; Titus i. 3; ii. 10; iii. 4). "Wise" must be omitted as wanting in authority. (See Note on Rom. xvi. 27.) Doxologies became well-known forms with many variations: changes to something more familiar to the copyist might easily be made in transcribing.

After "Saviour" must be inserted, on the highest MS. authority, "through Jesus Christ our Lord." Wiclif and the Rhemish have the missing clause.

Glory and majesty, dominion and power.—Omit the first "and." "Glory" and "dominion" are frequent in the New Testament doxologies: the Greek words represented by "majesty" and "power" occur here only. After "power" we must supply, on overwhelming authority, "before all time." Consequently "is" may be substituted for "be" before "glory;" but no verb is needed.

Both now and ever.—Better, *and now and to all the ages;* so that the whole will run thus: *To the only God our Saviour, through Jesus Christ our Lord, glory, majesty, dominion, and power, before all time, and now, and to all the ages.* Thus we have a most comprehensive phrase for eternity—before time, time, after time—and thus the three-fold arrangement runs through to the very end.

Amen.—Common ending of a doxology. (Rom. i. 25; 1 Pet. iv. 11; 2 Pet. iii. 18.) These ungodly men may "despise dominion, and speak evil of dignities," may utter "great swelling words" about their own knowledge and liberty, and scoff at those who walk not with them; but still, ages before they were born, and ages after they have ceased to be, glory, majesty, dominion, and power belong to Him who saves us, and would save even them, through Jesus Christ our Lord.

EXCURSUS ON NOTES TO JUDE

ON THE BOOK OF ENOCH.

THE precise place in history to which this intensely interesting relic belongs is a riddle of which the answer is as yet only very partially known. But the results of investigations during the nineteenth century have shown that the attention paid to the *Book of Enoch* in the second, third, and fourth centuries was fully justified. It is strange that such a book should have been allowed to pass out of sight. The canonical Book of Revelation inspired Christians, just as the Book of Daniel inspired Jews, with a love of revelations, visions, and prophecies, which was at times insatiable, and which has produced a mass of literature of which we could spare a great deal in exchange for something more solid. Men were so busy divining the future that they forgot to record the present and the past.

And yet a book so eminently in harmony with this taste was suffered to perish. This is all the more strange because judgment, hell, and heaven are among the main subjects of the book, and the end of the world was precisely the favourite subject of speculation among Christians from the fourth to the tenth century. Moreover, there was the passage in Jude, to say nothing of notices in the Fathers, to keep the book from being forgotten. Perhaps the reason was that just the two *data* by which men expected to determine the approach of the end of the world—the downfall of Rome and the coming of Antichrist—are not hinted at in the *Book of Enoch.* Be this as it may, the fact remains that from the fourth to the eighteenth century the book was entirely lost in Western Europe. Some fragments preserved in Greek in the *Chronographia* of Georgius Syncellus (circ. A.D. 800) show that the book was known in Eastern Christendom much later than in the West; but after that we lose all trace of it. Early in the seventeenth century it was rumoured that an Ethiopic version of it existed in Abyssinia. These rumours ended in disappointment. But in 1773 James Bruce brought back from Abyssinia three MSS. of the Ethiopic version. Silvestre de Sacy published a Latin translation of some of the early chapters in 1800; and in 1821 Archbishop Lawrence published an English translation of the whole, followed by the Ethiopic text in 1838. Since then the study of the book has been almost confined to Germany, where Hofmann, Gfrörer, Lützelberger, Lücke, Dillmann, Ewald, Köstlin, Hilgenfeld, Weisse, Volkmar, and Philippi, have all contributed to the subject; Dillmann far the most. The results are anything but harmonious; but something has been ascertained on which reliance can be placed.

The Ethiopic is a translation from the Greek, and the Greek (of which only the portion preserved by Georgius Syncellus is known) is probably a translation from the Aramaic. A Hebrew *Book of Enoch* was in existence as late as the thirteenth century, but we have no certainty that it was identical with the existing work. A more secure ground for believing in an Aramaic original is the fact that many of the proper names come from Aramaic roots. The Ethiopic version is both redundant and defective: redundant in containing repetitions which can scarcely be intentional; defective inasmuch as not even all that Georgius Syncellus has preserved is contained in it. The repetitions may possibly be the result of unintelligent copying, different recensions being clumsily strung together.

All are agreed that the book is not all by one hand. In the main it probably is so; but the author seems to have incorporated portions of other works; and it is suspected that the volume, as thus formed, has since been interpolated. To distinguish the earlier fragments and the later additions from the main body of the work, and to assign dates to each, is the great problem that still remains to be worked out. Very wide differences of opinion exist on the subject, but there is considerable agreement in assigning the main body of the book to B.C. 150—110. Lücke at first believed that the book was composed after the Christian era; but in the second edition of his *Einleitung in die Offenbarung Johannis* (Bonn, 1852) he abandoned this view, and placed the first and last parts in the Maccabæan period, and assigned the central part—*i.e.,* the parables—to about B.C. 40. Hofmann, Weisse, and Philippi have since taken up the theory of a post-Christian origin, but it has not met with much favour. Volkmar seems to stand alone in maintaining that the book was the work of disciples of the great Rabbi Akiba, and was written to incite people to join the standard of the impostor, Bar-Cochba, in his revolt against Hadrian, A.D. 132. Information on the subject for English readers is best derived from Lawrence's translation and preliminary dissertation, the article by Westcott in the *Dictionary of the Bible,* and that by Lipsius in the *Dictionary of Christian Biography*, from which sources much of the above is taken. See also Westcott's *Introduction to the Gospels*, p. 93.

The essentially Jewish character of the whole book is manifest, although it may contain Christian interpolations. There is no doctrine of the Trinity, and nothing distinctly Christian. Of the Incarnation, the name Jesus, the life on earth, the Crucifixion, the Resurrection, the Ascension, of Baptism, and the Eucharist, there is not a trace. The Messiah is the Son of Man (*passim*), the Son of woman (lxi. 9), the Elect (*passim*), whom the Lord of spirits seats on the throne of His glory to judge "in the word of the name of the Lord of spirits" (lx. 10, 11; lxviii. 39); but he is not the Word, he is not God.

These facts suffice to show that the book as a whole is Jewish and not Christian. On the other hand, the absence of antagonism to Christianity seems to show that the book was not written after the Christian era. Volkmar's theory, that it was written in the interests of the false Messiah, Bar-Cochba, is rendered at once improbable by the fact that constant reference to the *Book of Enoch* is made in the *Testaments of the Twelve Patriarchs*. This work was known to Origen, and perhaps to Tertullian, and therefore cannot be *later* than A.D. 150—200. But it was probably written *before* A.D. 135, *i.e.*, before that obliteration of the very walls and name of Jerusalem which was the immediate result of Bar-Cochba's revolt. The author, a Jewish Christian, attacks the idea that Jewish ceremonial is still binding; and is perpetually reminding the Jews that the Messiah is not only a King but a Priest, and a Priest to whom the Aaronic priesthood must resign. This idea does not at all suit the half century following Hadrian's destruction of Jerusalem; for that event put an end to the danger of Jewish ceremonial overgrowing Christianity. Whereas before that event the danger of a relapse into Judaism was, for the church in Palestine, a very real one. The *Testaments of the Twelve Patriarchs* may be placed A.D. 100—135; and consequently the *Book of Enoch* must be placed earlier still. (Comp. Dorner's *Person of Christ*, i., pp. 152, 417, 420.)

It is well worth while to read the whole of Lawrence's translation. Those who do so cannot fail to be often struck with the dignity and beauty even of this translation of a translation. Not unfrequently they will come upon something which reminds them of 2 Peter or Jude. The resemblance is often of the faintest—a couple of words in altogether different context, or a similar thought very differently expressed. It would be strange if all these resemblances were purely accidental; and an opportunity of forming an opinion on this question is given in the following pages, where specimens of these resemblances are tabulated.

The impression which this fact conveys is that the writers of these Epistles, or at least one of them, was well acquainted with the *Book of Enoch*, and that it suggested sometimes a thought, sometimes a phrase to him. It is possible, however, that all three writers may have derived material from a common source. These questions can scarcely be settled finally until a Greek copy of the book comes to light, an event by no means to be despaired of in an age in which so many literary treasures have been recovered.

The book is evidently the work of a man of the most earnest convictions: one who believes in God and fears Him, and is appalled at the practical infidelity and utter godlessness which he finds around him. There are two things on which he is never tired of insisting: (1) that God's rule extends everywhere, over men and angels no less than over winds and stars; (2) that this rule is a moral one, for He bounteously rewards righteousness and fearfully punishes sin. Nothing, therefore, could well be more in harmony with the spirit and purpose of St. Jude; and it ought not to surprise us that he makes use of such a work. Whether or no he was aware of the apocryphal nature of the book, we have no means of determining. Neither alternative need startle us—that he should have been mistaken on such a point, or should knowingly have quoted an uncanonical book. St. Paul was not afraid to quote heathen poets.

It may reassure us in any case to remember that, in spite of the quotation in St. Jude, the mind of Christ's Church has never wavered as to the true nature of the *Book of Enoch*. It is one of the many eccentricities of Tertullian that he upholds its authority; but he is alone in doing so. His argument is so curious as to be worth summarising:—"I am quite aware that some reject the book, and that it is not in the Jewish canon. I suppose people think that it could never have survived the deluge. But might not Noah have heard and remembered it all? or have been inspired to repeat it, just as Ezra is believed to have restored the Jewish literature lost in the destruction of Jerusalem? Nothing must be rejected which really concerns us; and we read that every Scripture suitable for edification is divinely inspired. The Jews reject it, as they reject other things, because it tells of Christ" (*De Cultu Fem.*, I. iii.).

It is not quite certain whether Justin Martyr knew it or not. In *Apol.* II., v., he gives in few words an account of the fall of the angels, and the consequences of it, very similar to that in the *Book of Enoch*, vi.—xvi. Justin and the author of the book may have got this from a common source; but, in any case, Justin's accepting the account is no proof that he accepted the book as of any authority. Origen and Augustine distinctly mark it as apocryphal, and it is included in no list of the Scriptures, whether Jewish or Christian.

The question still remains—*does* St. Jude quote this book? More than one critic answers in the negative, maintaining that he merely quotes a traditional saying of Enoch, which the author of the *Book of Enoch* inserted. Of course this is possible; but, as the book was in existence when St. Jude wrote, was probably well known, and contains the passage quoted, the more reasonable view is that St. Jude quotes from the book.

JUDE.

TABULATED SPECIMENS OF PARALLELS BETWEEN THE BOOK OF ENOCH AND THE SECOND EPISTLE OF ST. PETER AND THE EPISTLE OF ST. JUDE.

Enoch.	2 Peter.	Jude.
ii. Behold, He comes with ten thousands of His saints, to execute judgment upon them, and destroy the wicked and reprove all the carnal, for every thing which the sinful and ungodly have done and committed against Him.	- - - - -	14, 15. Behold, the Lord cometh with ten thousands of His saints, to execute judgment upon all, and to convince all that are ungodly among them of all their ungodly deeds which they have ungodly committed and of all their hard speeches which ungodly sinners have spoken against Him.
i. 8. *The splendour of the Godhead* shall illuminate them.	i. 17. *The excellent glory.*	
v. *The earth is scorched up with fervid heat.*	iii. 10. The elements shall be dissolved *with fervent heat, the earth also.*	
vi. 4, 5. You *calumniate* [*His*] *greatness*; and malignant are the words in your polluted mouths against His majesty. Ye *withered in heart, no peace shall be unto you.*	ii. 10. They are not afraid to *speak evil of dignities.*	8. Despise dominion, and *speak evil of dignities.* 10. But these speak evil of those things which they know not. 12. Without fruit, *twice dead, plucked up by the roots.*
vii. 1, 2. It happened, after the sons of men had multiplied in those days, that daughters were born to them, elegant and beautiful. And when *the angels, the sons of heaven,* beheld them, they became enamoured of them, saying to each other; Come, let us select for ourselves wives from the progeny of men, and let us beget children.	ii. 4. For if God spared not *the angels that sinned.*	6. And *the angels which kept not their first estate,* but left their own habitation.
x. 26. Then shall *the children of the earth be righteous.* (Comp. l. 5: *The earth shall rejoice; the righteous shall inhabit it,* and the elect possess it.)	iii. 13. We look for new heavens and *a new earth, wherein dwelleth righteousness.*	
xiv. 9. *Clouds* and a *mist* invited me; *agitated stars* . . . pressed me forwards.	ii. 17. *Mists* that are driven with the storm-wind.	12. *Clouds* they are without water. 13. *Wandering stars.*
xv. 7. Therefore I made not wives for you [angels], because, being spiritual, *your dwelling is in heaven.*	- - - - -	6. The *angels* which kept not their first estate, but *left their own habitation.*
xviii. 16. Therefore *was He offended with them* [the angels], and *bound them, until the period of the consummation of their crimes* in the secret year. (Comp. xxi. 2, 3: I beheld . . . a desolate spot, prepared, and terrific. There too I beheld seven stars of heaven [angels] *bound in it together.* . . . These are those of *the stars which have transgressed* the commandment of the most high God; and are here bound, until the infinite number of the days of their crimes be completed. Comp. lxxxvii. 2, 3.)	ii. 4. If *God spared not the angels that sinned,* but cast them down to hell, and *delivered them into chains of darkness, to be reserved unto judgment.*	6. *He hath reserved in everlasting chains* under darkness *unto the judgment* of the great day.
xl. 8. The merciful, *the patient,* the holy Michael.	- - - - -	9. Michael . . . durst not bring against him a railing accusation, but said, The Lord rebuke thee.

JUDE.

Enoch.	2 Peter.	Jude.
xli. 1. The sinners *who denied the Lord of glory*.	ii. 1. Even *denying the Lord* that bought them.	4. *Denying the only Lord*, and our Lord Jesus Christ.
xlv. 2. Sinners *who deny the name of the Lord* of spirits. (Comp. xlvii. 11; lxvi. 12.)		
xlv. 4, 5. I will *change the face of heaven*. . . . I will also *change the face of the earth*; will bless it; and *cause those whom I have elected to dwell upon it*.	iii. 13. We look for *new heavens* and a *new earth, wherein dwelleth righteousness*.	
liii. 8—10. All the waters, which are in the heavens and above them, shall be mixed together. The water which is above heaven shall be the agent; and the water which is under the earth shall be the recipient; and all shall be destroyed who dwell upon earth.	iii. 5, 6. By the word of God the heavens were of old, and the earth consisting out of water and through water: whereby the world that then was, being overflowed with water, perished.	
lviii. 4. Hitherto has existed the day of mercy; and He has been merciful and *long-suffering towards all who dwell on the earth*.	iii. 9. The Lord is not slack concerning His promise, as some men count slackness; but *is longsuffering to us-ward*, not willing that any should perish, but that all should come to repentance.	
lxvi. 6. The valley of the angels, who had been guilty of seduction, *burned underneath its soil*. 15. The waters will be changed, and become *a fire which shall blaze for ever*.	- - - - -	7. Sodom and Gomorrha . . . giving themselves over to fornication, and going after strange flesh, are set forth for an example, *suffering the vengeance of eternal fire*.
lxviii. 39. Those who seduced them *shall be bound with chains for ever*.	ii. 4. God spared not the angels that sinned, but . . . *delivered them into chains* of darkness.	6. The angels which kept not their first estate . . . *He hath reserved in everlasting chains*
lxxxii. 4—6. I saw in a vision *heaven purifying and snatched away*. . . . I saw *likewise the earth absorbed by a great abyss*, and mountains suspended over mountains. Hills were sinking upon hills, lofty trees were gliding off from their trunks and were . . . sinking into the abyss.	iii. 10. *The heavens shall pass away with a rushing noise*, and the elements shall be dissolved with fervent heat, *the earth also*; and shall the works thereof be found?	
xcii. 17, 18. *The former heaven shall depart and pass away*; a *new heaven* shall appear. . . . Afterwards likewise shall there be many weeks, which shall externally *exist in goodness and righteousness*. Neither shall sin be named there for ever.	iii. 10. *The heavens shall pass away*. 13. We look for *new heavens and a new earth, wherein dwelleth righteousness*.	
xcvi. 25. To them there shall be no peace; but *they shall surely die suddenly*.	ii. 1. *Shall bring upon themselves swift destruction*.	
xcvii. 1. Woe to them who act impiously, who laud and honour the word of falsehood.	- - - - -	11. Woe unto them! for they have gone in the way of Cain, and ran greedily after the error of Balaam for reward.
cii. 7. You have been satiated with meat and drink, with human plunder and rapine, with sin, with the acquisition of wealth, and with the sight of good days.	ii. 13. As they that count it pleasure to riot in the day-time. Spots they are and blemishes, sporting themselves with their own deceivings while they feast with you.	12. These are spots in your feasts of charity, when they feast with you, feeding themselves without fear. 16. Having men's persons in admiration because of advantage.
cv. 13, 14. Behold *they committed crimes; laid aside their class*, and intermingled with women. With them also they transgressed; married with them, and begot children. A *great destruction therefore shall come upon the earth; a deluge*, a great destruction, shall take place in one year.	ii. 4, 5. God spared not *the angels that sinned*, but cast them down to hell, and delivered them into chains of darkness, to be reserved unto judgment; and *spared not the old world . . . bringing in the flood upon the world* of the ungodly.	6. *The angels which kept not their first estate, but left their own habitation*, He hath reserved in everlasting chains.

THE REVELATION

OF

ST. JOHN THE DIVINE

INTRODUCTION

TO

THE REVELATION

OF

ST. JOHN THE DIVINE

I. The Author.— The general opinion of the Church of Christ has accepted the Apocalypse as the work of John the Apostle, but this general opinion has been called in question. Our space can only allow us to lay before our readers a brief *resumé* of the reasons which have been urged on either side. For convenience it will be as well to ask the following questions:—

(1) *Was the Writer's name John?*—At first sight it would seem that there could be but one answer to this question. The book announces itself as written by a person whose name was John. Four times over does the name occur (Rev. i. 1, 4, 9; xxii. 8).

Is there any reason for questioning the witness thus given by the book itself? It has been asserted that the writer does not claim to be John, but only "gives a report of a revelation which John had received" (Scholten). It is perfectly true that a writer might thus dramatically represent the Apostle John as the seer of the revelation; but such possibility is no proof that it was so, and certainly cannot be entertained in the total absence of all proof. The reiteration of the name four times is out of harmony with this conjecture; and the theory would not, as Gebhardt has remarked, be applied to any other book of the New Testament. Would any serious reply be "thought necessary should it occur to some one to reject the First Epistle to the Corinthians, because from such passages as 1 Cor. i. 13, it does not follow that the author identifies himself with Paul, but gives (1 Cor. i. 1, 2), after the manner of an introduction, a report of an Epistle which the Apostle wrote?"

We may assume, then, that the writer's name was John.

(2) *Was the Writer John the Apostle.*—It is round this question that we meet the most serious conflict.

(*a*) It is admitted on all hands, even by those who oppose the apostolic authorship of the book, that the great consensus of early opinion regarded the writer as St. John the Apostle. "From the time of Justin Martyr to that of Irenæus and the great Fathers, the Apocalypse was recognised as a production of the Apostle." Such is the opinion of Keim (*Jesu v. Nazara*). "We find the Revelation unhesitatingly attributed to him (St. John) by the Fathers from the middle of the second century downwards; by Justin Martyr, Irenæus, Clement of Alexandria, Tertullian, and others" (Bleek). The opinion of the third century was the same. Origen, whose opposition to millenarianism adds value to his testimony, Cyprian, Lactantius, and others, acknowledge the Apocalypse as the work of St. John.

Setting aside the opinion of Marcion, and of the unimportant sect of the Alogi (see *Introduction to the First Epistle to St. John*), doubts respecting the apostolic authorship seem to have commenced with Dionysius of Alexandria; these doubts, which were echoed hesitatingly by Eusebius, were based not on historical or critical, so much as upon doctrinal grounds: the dread of millenarianism created a wish to discredit the book which appeared to lend such weight to the disliked doctrine. It is needless to follow the history of this controversy; it is enough to notice that the first breach of this continuous early opinion in favour of the apostolic authorship grew out of doctrinal prejudice rather than candid examination.

(*b*) In later years, the controversy has been fought from different bases of operation. The conflict respecting the authorship of the Fourth Gospel (see *Introduction to St. John's Gospel*) has complicated the dispute. It seemed to some impossible to believe that the Fourth Gospel and the Apocalypse proceeded from the same pen. The divergence in style and language was, in their view, too great to admit of their being written by the same man, even though that man were an Apostle. If the Gospel was the work of St. John, the Apocalypse could not be. The generally accepted opinion that St. John wrote the Apocalypse was assailed by those who, in their wish to preserve their faith in the apostolic authorship of the Fourth Gospel, were ready to sacrifice the Book of Revelation. This was substantially the view adopted by Neander, Lücke, Ewald, Bleek, Düsterdieck, and others. In opposition to these, others were ready to adopt the other hypothesis: they accepted the view that the two books could not have been the work of one and the same writer; but they preferred to sacrifice the Gospel: the Apocalypse was the work of St. John; the Gospel, therefore, could not be. Such was the view of those who, like Baur, aimed at discrediting the Fourth Gospel, or who wished to support the theory of a designed antagonism between the school of St. John and that of St. Paul. Neither of these parties—those who would sacrifice the Apocalypse to the Gospel, and those who would sacrifice the Gospel to the Apocalypse—represent the most recent phase of the controversy. Another class of thinkers arose who felt that the witness which the Fourth Gospel and the Revelation alike gave to the Person of Christ was too strong to be allowed the authority of an Apostle by those who had formed other and lower conceptions of the Jesus of the Gospels. They saw no glimpses of His heavenly glory and majesty in the synoptical Gospels. They found that the Book of Revelation was full of them.

The Christ of the Apocalypse was the Word of God, the King of Kings; the Christ of the Gospels was One who came not to be ministered to, but to minister. The portrait given in the Gospels of "the loving and amiable Son of Man," as the Divine Son of God was patronisingly styled, was not to be found in the Apocalypse; such a book could not have been written by one who personally knew the gentle and self-sacrificing Prophet of Galilee—least of all, perhaps, by the beloved disciple. Such is the view of more recent critics, and advanced with varying power and arguments by Volkmar, Hoekstra, and Scholten. The book was a forgery, or at best the composition of some other John —not of John the Apostle. Besides, it was urged, the Apostle could not have been the author, for it is clear that the writer lived in Asia Minor, whereas the Apostle John never was in Asia Minor at all.

Such is, perhaps, the most recent phase of the controversy.

(*c*) We have not space to do more than touch but briefly, and only upon a few of the arguments advanced against the apostolic authorship of the book. It will, perhaps, be best to specify three or four.

(i.) St. John the Apostle, it is said, never resided in Asia Minor; he could not, therefore, have been the author of a book which is undoubtedly the work of one resident there.

It is proverbially difficult to prove a negative: it is increasingly difficult when only negative evidence can be adduced, and this is all that can be appealed to. The argument, if argument it can be called, runs thus: the residence of St. John in Asia Minor is not mentioned by those whom we might have expected to mention it: therefore, St. John did not reside there. To use the words of a modern critic (Mr. Matthew Arnold), "But there is the rigorous and vigorous theory of Prof. Scholten, that John never was at Ephesus at all. If he had been, Papias and Hegesippus must have mentioned it: if they had mentioned it, Irenæus and Eusebius must have quoted them to that effect. As if the very notoriety of John's residence at Ephesus would not have disproved Irenæus and Eusebius from advancing formal testimony to it, and made them refer to it just in the way they do. Here, again, we may be sure that no one judging evidence in a plain fashion would ever have arrived at Dr. Scholten's conclusion; above all, no one of Dr. Scholten's great learning and ability" (*Contemporary Review*, vol. xxv., p. 988).

To this also we may add Gebhardt's words:—"No one in the second century could believe that the Apostle John was the author of the Apocalypse, without at the same time believing that he lived in Asia Minor; and in like manner, the acknowledgment of the Apocalypse as the Apostle's from the time of Justin Martyr downwards, made prominent by Keim, is an acknowledgment of his residence in Asia Minor, and inferentially at Ephesus."

(ii.) There are, it is stated, traces of non-apostolic authorship in the book.

(*a*) The manner in which the Apostles are spoken of (see chaps. xviii. 20 and xxi. 14) is thought to be inconsistent with the opinion that the Apostle wrote it. The Apostles are mentioned with a degree of objectivity, and are assigned a prominence which is unlikely if an Apostle were the writer. But with regard to the last, if St. John describes the foundations of the heavenly Jerusalem as bearing the names of the twelve Apostles, St. Paul speaks of the Church being built upon the foundation of the Apostles and Prophets (Eph. ii. 20). The imagery is distinctly apostolic; and if the Apostles are mentioned with "objectivity" in the Apocalypse, are they not mentioned with an equal, if not greater, degree of objectivity by St. Matthew? (Matt. x. 2—4.)

(*β*) But, it is argued, there is no hint given throughout the book that the writer is an Apostle. If St. John were the writer, would he not betray himself somewhere as the beloved disciple? Should we not have some allusion to his intimacy with his Master, or to some circumstance connected with the life and ministry of Christ? In reply, it is enough to remark that the nature of the book would not lead us to expect such allusions. He writes as a Prophet, not as an Apostle. It would be as idle to expect some allusion to the circumstances of Milton's political life in the *Paradise Lost*. "The Apocalypse declares itself not to be the work of an Apostle in the same sense as Schiller's poetry declares itself not to be the work of a professor at Jena" (Gebhardt).

But it may be further urged that there are not wanting certain characteristic allusions which reveal the writer. The allusions to the piercing of the Saviour's side (chap. i. 7; comp. John xix. 34), and to the washing, or cleansing (chaps. i. 5; vii. 13, 14; xxii. 14—see Note there—John xiii. 8—10), are not to be overlooked; and more than these may be detected by a careful student.

(*γ*) There is no trace of Apostolic *authority*.

If we are not to expect personal reminiscences, we surely should expect the air of official authority. But the answer is, Do we not find this? The language is surely that of one who does not doubt that his name will carry a guarantee with the book. (Comp. Prof. Davidson's article in Kitto's *Biblical Cyclopædia*.)

(iii.) The Christology of the book is described as non-apostolic. The picture which the Apocalypse gives of Jesus Christ is not that of the Gospels. In the Gospels we have the loving and gentle Son of Man; in the Apocalypse we have the Word of God, whose eyes are as a flame of fire, and whose mouth a sharp sword, &c. Is not the whole conception of the kingly Christ thus portrayed the product of a later age? "The picture of Christ which here comes before us seems to presuppose a conception so perfectly free, that it can only belong to a later Christianity" (Scholten). "The apotheosis of Christ is too strong to be ascribed to a contemporary and disciple of Jesus" (quoted in Gebhardt).

Such objections as these arise from a fundamental misconception of the character and work of Jesus Christ. The Christ of the Gospels is not the colourless creation which has been evolved out of the thought of men living eighteen centuries afterwards. The Christology of the Apocalypse is distinct enough, but it does not differ from the Christology of St. Paul; and it is in complete harmony with the lofty and divine utterances of our Lord Himself even in the synoptical Gospels. Time and space would fail us in illustrating this position; it will suffice to refer to two or three passages, which might be multiplied: Matt. xxv. 31; xxvi. 13; Luke v. 20; vii. 8, 9, 23, 35; ix. 41; x. 16 —20.

(iv.) The divergence in style between the Revelation and the Fourth Gospel demands a few words. We have spoken of those critics, who, in their desire to preserve the authority of the Gospel, have been willing to throw overboard the apostolic authorship of the Apocalypse. Is it necessary to do this? It has been shown that the external evidence is in favour of the apostolic authorship. In the language of Prof. Davidson, "With the limited stock of early ecclesiastical literature that survives the wreck of time we should despair of proving the authenticity of any New Testament book by the help of early witnesses if that of the Apocalypse be rejected as insufficiently attested." Is there any reason in the internal character of the book sufficient to reverse this verdict? Or, in other words, assuming (and the stormy controversy has rather increased than diminished the right to the assumption; see *Introduction to St. John's Gospel*) the apostolic authorship of the Fourth Gospel, is there any ground for believing that the Apocalypse could not have proceeded from the same writer? There are no doubt strongly marked differences. We have not space to touch on the whole question. One or two points call for notice. There are differences of language; there are "anomalies," "awkward dispositions of words," "peculiar constructions;" "the Greek is moulded by the Hebrew tendencies of the writer." This is no doubt largely the case; but there has been often a want of appreciativeness at the root of some criticisms like these: some violations of grammatical construction have been set down to ignorance on the part of the writer, when it is clear that they were intentional. Notably, the language of Rev. i. 4 is beyond all doubt designedly ungrammatical; indeed, as Bishop Lightfoot has pointed out, were it not so, the writer would not have possessed sufficient literary power to construct a single sentence. Nor has sufficient weight been allowed to the different characters of the two books, or the interval of time which elapsed between their writing. The highly wrought rapture of the seer, when beholding the visions of the Apocalypse indicates a mental state in which volitional control is at the minimum, and the automatic action of the mind is left free. At such a time the images and associations which have been originally imbedded in the memory are those which rise uppermost to clothe the thoughts. Thus the strong Hebrew colouring is precisely what we should expect from one who, of ardent temperament, has spent the whole of his earlier life in Palestine, and among those who were constantly talking over Messianic hopes and prophecies. (Comp. John i. 38—41.) The force of this is not invalidated by saying that the seer did not write the visions as he saw them, but recorded them afterwards. In the first place, it is merely an assumption to affirm this; in the next, even were it true, the man who records such visions must recall the whole mental condition in which he was at the time of vision, and would preserve in his record the characteristics of such a state of mind. Nor can much stress be laid upon the fact that the writer was not young. The visions of God are given to the old as well as to the young. The loftiest revealings were given to Moses when he had passed fourscore years: and, even from a merely human point of view, it is possible for a man of sixty to retain the fire and warm imagination of youth. Even in modern life, when the faculties are too often drudged into imbecility by forced and premature development, and deprived of their full and ultimate power by being made reproductive when they ought to be remaining receptive, we may find the powers of imagination survive the strain and incessancy of toil; indeed, in some cases the imaginative powers have gathered force till the line of the threescore years has been passed. Edmund Burke was sixty when he wrote his *Reflections on the Revolution in France*, and none will condemn him for deficiency in imagination. It was not in the ardour of youth that Dante wrote the *Divine Comedy*. The conditions of ancient and Eastern life were probably much more favourable to the preservation and quiet ripening of the powers of thought and imagination. The truth is that there is nothing so deceptive as the comparison between the ages and powers of different writers; there is no standard which can be fairly used as a measure. Some men of sixty are, in mental force, more nearly allied to men of forty than to those of their own age; and the addition of twenty or five-and-twenty years brings them to the mellow and quiet autumn-time of their life.

The Apocalypse may be "sensuous," full of "creative fancy," "objective," and "concrete;" the Gospel may be "calm," "mystic," "spiritual," and delighting in "speculative depth"; but differences equally great may be found in the works of other writers. Literature supplies numberless instances of such varieties. "It is strange," wrote Lord Macaulay, "It is strange that the *Essay on the Sublime and Beautiful*, and the *Letter to a Noble Lord* should be the productions of one man;" yet no one has been found to doubt that they were both written by Edmund Burke. The writings of De Quincey supply examples. Let any one compare the *Autobiographic Sketches*, or *The Confessions of an Opium Eater*, with one of the little flights of fancy—such as the *Daughter of Lebanon*—written under different conditions, and he will find how much diversity may be found in the works of the same writer. And, not to go beyond the Gospels, might it not be said that there is a great separation in tone and thought between our Lord's discourses in Matt. xxiii.—xxv. and the Sermon on the Mount? We have, then, in the two books—the Gospel and the Apocalypse — different subject - matter, vision instead of history; a wide interval of time—some twenty or twenty-five years; and, with this interval of time, a changed atmosphere of associations and influences, Greek instead of Hebrew: these in themselves would account for divergences greater even than we find.

If we can thus account for the differences we meet with, we have to remember that there are resemblances in the two books which can scarcely be accidental, and which, found in two independent books, would have suggested to some shrewd critic the theory of a common authorship. There is a strong resemblance in language and imagery: both books delight in the words "witness" (*martyr*), "to overcome," "to keep" (the word of God), "sign" (*sémeion*), "dwell," or *tabernacle* (in this last case the coincidence is lost sight of in the English version, because the word "dwell" is used instead of *tabernacle*, or "tent"), "true" (*alethinos*), (John i. 9; xix. 35; Rev. iii. 14; xix. 9).

There is a similarity in the terms used to describe our Lord. He is the *Word* (John i. 1—3; Rev. xix. 13); the *Lamb* (John i. 29; Rev. v. 6); the *Shepherd* (John x. throughout; Rev. vii. 17); the *Bridegroom* (John iii. 29; Rev. xix. 7; xxi. 2); similar images are used—the *Living Water* (John iv. 10; vii. 38; and Rev. vii. 17; xxi. 6; xxii. 17); the *Hidden Food*, bread, or manna (John vi. 32—58; Rev. ii. 17); the *Harvest* (John iv. 34, 38; Rev. xiv. 15). The same incident—the piercing of our Lord's side—is referred to; and the word employed, both in the Gospel and in the Apocalypse, is singularly not the word used in the LXX. version of the prophet Zechariah. There is, besides, a similar disposition towards a seven-fold arrangement of subjects in the Gospel and the Revelation. (See *Introduction to St. John's Gospel*.)

Further resemblances might be pointed out. These, however, will suffice to show that Prof. Davidson, in his candid, impartial, and valuable article (see above), says no more than truth when he writes: "After every reasonable deduction, enough remains to prove that the correspondences between the Apocalpyse and the Fourth Gospel are not accidental. They either betray one author, or show that the writer of the one was acquainted with the other. These cognate phenomena have not been allowed their full force by Lücke, Ewald, De Wette, and Düsterdieck."

To conclude. The author represents himself as John in a way, and at a time, that would naturally suggest that he either was John the Apostle and Evangelist, or wished to pass as such. The general consensus of early opinion believed that the Apostle was the writer. The doubts grew out of doctrinal prejudice; there is no reasonable ground for disputing the residence of the Apostle in Asia Minor. There are not wanting traces of personal reminiscences such as the beloved disciple would have cherished. The portrait of Jesus Christ is in complete harmony with apostolic teaching; and the difficulties which beset the theory that there were two Johns—one who wrote the Gospel, and the other the Apocalypse—are greater than those which surround the theory of a common authorship.

It is only necessary to add the attesting language of various and independent critics. "The apostolic origin of the Apocalypse is as well attested as that of any other book in the New Testament" (Davidson). "The testimony has been pronounced more absolutely convincing than can be adduced in favour of the apostolic authorship of any of the books of the New Testament" (*Edinburgh Review*, October, 1874).

II. The Date and Time of Writing.—The evidence for determining the date of the Apocalypse is in many respects conflicting. Any conclusion on the matter should be given with caution and hesitation, and with the full admission that the arguments which can be brought on the other side are entitled to consideration. It has been too much the practice among the supporters of different theories to insist with unwise positiveness upon their own view. Briefly, there are practically only two opinions, between which the reader must decide. The book was either written about the year A.D. 68 or 69, or about a quarter of a century later (A.D. 96), in the reign of Domitian.

The later date was that which was accepted almost uniformly by the older theologians. In favour of this early tradition has been appealed to. The most important witness (in some respects) is Irenæus, who says that "the Apocalypse was seen not long ago, but almost in our own age, towards the end of the reign of Domitian." Other writers have been claimed as giving a support to this view by their mention of Patmos as the place of St. John's banishment; and it is plain from the way in which Eusebius quotes the mention of the Patmos exile by Clement of Alexandria, that he associated it with the reign of Domitian. On the other hand, it must be remembered that neither Clement of Alexandria, Tertullian, Origen, or Jerome, state that the banishment took place in the reign of Domitian. Tertullian, indeed, represents Domitian as *recalling* the exiles; and other writers affirm that the banishment took place much earlier. Theophylact, for example, declares that the Apostle was in Patmos thirty-two years after the Ascension; and the preface to the Syriac version of the Apocalypse affirms that the revelation was given to St. John in Patmos, whither he was banished by the Emperor Nero. Another tradition assigns the writing to the reign of Trajan. Epiphanius, in a passage of doubtful value, places the exile in the reign of Claudius.

On the whole, then, there is not any very certain conclusion to be drawn from the external evidence. The exile in Patmos receives ample support, but the date of the exile is hardly settled by early tradition.

Will the internal evidence help?

The advocates of the later date rely much upon the degenerate state of the Asiatic churches, as described in the Epistles to the Seven Churches. The Epistles to the Ephesians, Colossians, and Philemon were written during the captivity of St. Paul at Rome, about the year A.D. 63. If, then, the Apocalypse was written in A.D. 69 or 70, we have only an interval of six or seven years to account for a striking change in the spiritual condition of the Asiatic churches. Can we believe that a Church which is so forward in love as that of Ephesus (Eph. iii. 18) can have in so short a time left its first love? Can it be believed that the Laodicean Church—whose spiritual condition in A.D. 63 can be inferred from that of Colossæ (Col. i. 3, 4)—can have, in six brief years, forsaken their "faith in Christ Jesus, and their love to all the saints," and become the "lukewarm" church (Rev. iii. 15, 16) of the Apocalypse?

It may be noticed, in passing, that the above argument assumes that the (so-called) Epistle to the Ephesians was really addressed to the Church at Ephesus; and this is by no means certain: the weight of evidence appears to incline the other way. But allowing this to pass, and, for the purpose of argument, assuming that the Epistles to the Ephesians and Colossians afford indications of the spiritual condition of these and kindred Asiatic churches, it does not seem to the writer that the above argument can be sustained. The two propositions on which its force depends are the following:—

(1) It is impossible that churches could change much for the worse in six years.

(2) A comparison between the Apocalypse and the Letters of St. Paul show a great change for the worse.

From these two propositions it is inferred that the interval must have been more than six years: a generation at least being required to account for such degeneracy. "It bespeaks a change of persons, the arrival of a new generation" (Hengstenberg).

It is believed that neither of the two propositions mentioned above can be sustained. (1) It needs no long time for the first ardour of young converts' zeal to cool. The New Testament gives us examples of such rapid changes: the "evil eye" of a perverted teaching bewitched the Galatians (Gal. iii. 1), so that the Apostle marvelled that the disciples were so rapidly turning away to another gospel (Gal. i. 6). Changes quick and real soon sweep over a religious community, especially in districts where the natural temperament is warm, impressible, and vivacious. It is not impossible that six years may make changes in the religious condition of churches.

But (2) it is more important to consider the second proposition, and to ask whether it is so certain that any such great change had taken place in the instances before us. A comparison of the Epistle to the Colossians and that to Laodicea rather leads to an opposite conclusion. Professor (now Bishop) Lightfoot has shown that the same truths need enforcing (comp. Col. i. 15—18, and Rev. iii. 14), the same practical duties are taught (Col. iii. 1, and Rev. iii. 21), the same lukewarmness is the subject of caution (Col. iv. 17, and Rev. iii. 19). the same denunciations are heard against the pride of life, in wealth or intellect (Col. ii. 8, 18, 23, and Rev. iii. 17, 18). "The message communicated by

St. John to Laodicea prolongs the note which was struck by St. Paul in the letters to Colossæ. An interval of a very few years has not materially altered the character of these churches. Obviously the same temper prevails, the same errors are rife, the same correction must be applied" (Bishop Lightfoot, *Epistle to the Colossians*, pp. 41—44).

A similar comparison might be made between the two Ephesian Epistles. The impression left from a perusal of St. Paul's Letter to the Ephesians, whether addressed to that church or not, is that he was not without a fear that the warm love which prevailed among the Christians addressed might soon change: it is a love above the accidents of time and the powers of change which he desires may be theirs (Eph. vi. 24; Rev. ii. 4). The area of comparison between this Epistle to the Ephesians and the Epistles to the Seven Churches becomes much wider when we regard it, in harmony with probability, as a circular letter addressed to the Asiatic churches: then the resemblances become more plain, and the so-called great change in spiritual condition disappears. It will be sufficient to mention the following: Eph. i. 18, Rev. iii. 18; Eph. ii. 6, Rev. iii. 21; Eph. iii. 8, Rev. ii. 9; Eph. iii. 17—19, Rev. ii. 4.

Enough has been said to show that the argument from the spiritual condition of the churches lends little, or no support to the later date, but fairly strengthens the earlier.

The advocates of the earlier date adduce other internal evidence. They lay great weight upon inferences drawn from chaps. xi., xiii., and xvii. They argue that the measuring of the Temple and the treading down of the Holy City, described in chap. xi. 1, 2, is a token that Jerusalem had not yet fallen. This argument does not seem to the present writer satisfactory. The measuring of the Temple is symbolical, and it is unsafe to ground an argument upon it. The aim of the vision seems to us to point out the safety of the germ-Church during the times of desolation. The external framework, the old Jewish polity, might be swept away (chap. xi. 2; comp. Heb. viii. 13): the true spiritual germ would never die, but spring forth in fuller and freer vigour. Such a vision might indeed have preceded the fall of Jerusalem; but it might also have been given as a consolation and an instruction afterwards.

Hardly more convincing is the argument from chaps. xiii. and xvii. In the account of the seven-headed wild beast we read of seven kings, five of whom are fallen. The seven kings are said to be the emperors of Rome. The five fallen are Augustus, Tiberius, Caius, Claudius, Nero; the one that is, is Galba. The force of this depends upon the truth of the interpretation. If the seer meant the seven kings to represent seven emperors of Rome, then the date of the Apocalypse is fixed to the age of Galba; or to that of Nero if we begin to reckon with Julius Cæsar. The former is the most correct method of reckoning. To make the sixth head Vespasian, as some would do, is, as Dr. Davidson has remarked, quite arbitrary. There is no reason for omitting Galba, Otho, and Vitellius from the reckoning. But the force of the argument for the date here depends upon the truth of the interpretation; and the foundation passages in the prophecy of Daniel, from which the Apocalyptic seer drew so much of his imagery, describe under the emblem of the wild beasts, kingdoms, or world-powers, rather than individual monarchs. Still, of course, it is possible that there may be a double interpretation—one more local, the other more general—here as well as elsewhere. But the requisite interpretation does not seem to be sufficiently clear for the purpose of argument.

Nor can the argument from silence be accepted. There is no allusion to the fall of Jerusalem in the book; but it is scarcely safe to infer that the book was therefore earlier than that catastrophe.

One other internal (so called) argument respecting date may be noticed here. Lücke cites chap. xviii. 20, where the Apostles and prophets are invited to rejoice because they have been avenged on Babylon, to prove that St. John the Apostle was dead when the book was written. This is one of those prosaic errors into which even the most learned and trustworthy of literary experts are betrayed by their own acuteness.

There yet remains another class of evidence: that of language and style. Assuming the common authorship of the Fourth Gospel and the Apocalypse (see *Introduction* to the Gospel, and section on the Author above), we shall have very little doubt that the general probability is in favour of the Apocalypse having been written first. Not only is the Gospel marked by the sententiousness of age, and the Apocalypse by the warm colouring of earlier life, but the influence of Jewish associations is more strongly marked in the latter; while Greek influences are more distinctly traceable in the former.

The evidence on this head inclines to the earlier date, but it is not absolutely conclusive: the prevalence of Hebraic influences noticeable in the Apocalypse might well fit in with the later date. The influences of youth often re-assert themselves with startling vigour in declining years: the provincialisms and accent of boyhood have been resumed by men in the evening of life, after having been kept long in abeyance by the joint powers of control and culture. Illustrations of this will occur to the reader. But, in the instance before us, the probability seems to lie the other way: in the Apostle's case the Hebraic influences did prevail during the early life; the Greek influences were present during his later life; and we may well believe that the Apocalypse "marks the Hebraic period of St. John's life which was spent in the East, and among Aramaic speaking populations"; and that the Gospel was written twenty or thirty years afterwards, at the "close of the Hellenic period during which St. John lived in Ephesus, the great centre of Greek civilisation." (See Bishop Lightfoot's Article on "Supernatural Religion," *Contemporary Review*, vol. xxv., p. 859.)

To conclude this brief summary, we may say that the general weight of evidence is in favour of the earlier date, and certainly this supposition fits in best with all the circumstances of the case.

III. Schools and Principles of Interpretation.—Before entering upon the general meaning of the book, it is desirable to lay before the reader a brief account of the different schools of Apocalyptic interpretation.

(1) *Schools of Interpretation.*—It is well known that there are three main systems of interpretation: these are called, from their special tendencies of thought, the Præterist, the Futurist, and the Historical.

The Præterist in general maintains that the visions of the Apocalypse relate to events and circumstances which are past: the prophecies of the book—at least in their primary intention—have been fulfilled. Among the advocates of this view may be reckoned the names of Grotius and Hammond, the learned and eloquent Bossuet, Eichhorn, Ewald, De Wette, Lücke, Düsterdieck, Professor Moses Stuart of America, and in this country the late lamented Professor Maurice, Professor Davidson, and Mr. Desprez.

The Futurist is at the opposite pole of interpretation, and maintains that the fulfilment of the book is still future, when our Lord will come again. Professor Davidson has separated the Futurists into two classes —the simple Futurist and the extreme Futurist: the difference between these classes being that the simple Futurist believes that the prophecies of the book are future in fulfilment, while the extreme Futurist holds that even the first three chapters are prophetic. Among those who have maintained the more moderate Futurist view may be mentioned De Burgh, Maitland, Benjamin Newton, Todd, and the devout Isaac Williams. The extreme Futurist view has been supported chiefly by some Irish expositors.

The Historical school holds a sort of middle place between the Præterist and Futurist. Its advocates believe that in the Apocalypse we have a continuous prophecy, exhibiting to us the main features of the world's history: the visions therefore are partly fulfilled, partly they are in course of fulfilment, and a portion still remains unfulfilled. This view has been sustained by men of conspicuous ability. It was the interpretation which commended itself to many of the Reformers, and was favoured by Wiclif, Bullinger, Bale, and others. It was upheld with more systematic power by such distinguished writers as Mede, Vitringa, Daubuz, Sir Isaac Newton, Whiston, Bengel, and Bishop Newton: more recently it has been advocated by Hengstenberg, Ebrard, Auberlen, by Elliott and Faber, by Bishop Wordsworth and the late Dean Alford, by Barnes, Lord, and Glasgow.

It is, of course, to be understood that there are many varieties of interpretation even among those who belong to the same school of interpreters: but it would quite exceed the limits at our disposal to speak of these varieties.

Against these three schools of interpretations it is not difficult to find objections. It is hard to believe, with the Præterist, that the counselling voice of prophecy should have spoken only of immediate dangers, and left the Church for fifteen centuries unwarned; or, with the Futurist, to believe that eighteen centuries of the eventful history of the Church are passed over in silence, and that the whole weight of inspired warning was reserved for the few closing years of the dispensation. Nor, on the other hand, can we be thoroughly satisfied with the Historical school, however ably and learnedly represented. There is a certain nakedness about the interpretations often advocated by this school: the interpreter is too readily caught by external resemblances, and pays too little heed to inner spiritual and ethical principles. A mistake into which this system falls is that of bringing into prominence the idea of *time*. According to them, the visions of the book are pictures of occurrences to take place at a certain fixed date. Now it must never be forgotten that the question of *time*—the time when this or that was to happen—was one which our Lord steadily put on one side. It was not for His disciples to know the times and the seasons. The knowledge of the time of an event is insignificant compared with the knowledge of the forces, elements, and laws which combine to produce it. This seems to be our Master's teaching to His followers all through time. Our study is to know what are the foes we have to contend against, what combinations they are likely to make, in what power they are to be confronted, what difficulties are likely to arise, what certainty there is that all difficulties will be surmounted and every foe overthrown. It matters not for us to know when these things shall be: it may be at the first watch, or midnight, or at the cock-crowing: the time is a matter of no ethical importance. It is thus St. Peter treats it: "One day is with the Lord as a thousand years, and a thousand years as one day." It is but the echo of His Lord's warning. It may take a long time or a short time for the moral laws and moral forces at work in the world to bring forth a crisis period. To take St. Peter's words as laying down a kind of prophetical "time-measure" is to fall into that fatal source of error, the conversion of poetry into prose. We are not, then, to look for any indications of *time* in the visions of the Apocalypse; and what might have made this very plain is the employment of proportional numbers to denote the prophetic epochs in the book. These carefully-selected numbers, always bearing a relationship to one another, and so selected that a literal interpretation of them is almost precluded, are beyond doubt symbolical, and thus in harmony with the whole character of the book. "Most numbers in the Revelation should not be taken arithmetically, but indefinitely, because they are part of the poetic costume borrowed from the Old Testament" (Davidson). The anxiety respecting the "times and seasons" has led many interpreters into voluminous errors, and has created a Thessalonian restlessness of spirit in many quarters. Infinitely more important is it to notice the moral and spiritual aspects of the book, the evil and the good principles which are described in conflict, and the features which in different ages the combat will assume.

But, though the time-interpretation of the book is thus to be placed in the background, it must not be so done as to imply that the book has no reference to occurrences which will happen in time. If some of the Historical school of interpreters have so forced the question of time into prominence as to ignore the more important ethical bearings of the book, it is no less true that critics on the other side have erred in removing the application of the book wholly out of the sphere of history, and giving it only the force of a fairy tale with a possible and doubtful moral. This is to set aside the value of the book to the Church of Christ as she moves across the vexed and stormy sea of this world's history. The visions of the book do find counterparts in the occurrences of human history: they have had these, and they yet will have these, fulfilments; and these fulfilments belong neither wholly to the past, nor wholly to the future: the prophecies of God are written in a language which can be read by more than one generation: what was read here helped the early Christian to whom imperial Rome was the great Babylon which absorbed to herself the wealth, and the wickedness, the power and persecuting spirit of the world, to whom the emperor may have seemed as a wild beast, savage and relentless, rising out of the tumults of peoples and nations, fickle and ruthless as the sea. No less have the visions of this book consoled the mediæval saint or poet, who felt that the most influential seat of the Church had become the metropolis of worldliness when "the Prince of the New Pharisees" was seated in St. Peter's chair, and when out of a professedly Christianised society had arisen a power aspiring to some religious culture, but fierce, wild, and wanton as the wild beast of ancient days. (Comp. Dante, *Inf.* xxvii. 85; and Rosetti's *Antipapal Spirit of the Italian Poets—passim*). Nor is the force of the consolation exhausted: in the future, the visions of this book, showing the certain triumph of all that is good and true, in the final consummation of Christ's kingdom, may hereafter serve to console men and women groaning under a tyranny of ungodliness more terrible and more specious than any which have preceded it, because built up of a pride which worships physical laws, while it treads under foot all moral laws, and spurns contemptuously all spiritual laws. In the past, the book has had its meaning: in the future, its meaning may grow fuller and clearer; but in the present also there is no doubt that it has its practical value for all who will reverently and patiently hear and keep the sayings of this book.

We are disposed to view the Apocalypse as the pictorial unfolding of great principles in constant conflict, though under various forms. The Præterist may, then, be right in finding early fulfilments, and the Futurist in expecting undeveloped ones, and the Historical interpreter is unquestionably right in looking for them along the whole line of history; for the words of God mean more than one man, or one school of thought, can compass. There are depths of truth unexplored which sleep beneath the simplest sentences. Just as we are wont to say that history repeats itself, so the predictions of the Bible are not exhausted in one or even in many fulfilments. Each prophecy is a single key which unlocks many doors, and the grand and stately drama of the Apocalypse has been played out perchance in one age to be repeated in the next. Its majestic and mysterious teachings indicate the features of a struggle which, be the stage the human soul, with its fluctuations of doubt and fear, of hope and love—or the progress of kingdoms—or the destinies of the world, is the same struggle in all.

(2) *The Principles of Interpretation.*—It will have been seen that the writer does not feel at home under the leadership of any of the three great schools of prophetical interpretation. The Church of Christ owes much to all of them, though the cause of truth has suffered much from many who have sought to be prophets when at the most they could aspire to be interpreters; but the result even of the errors of interpreters has been the slow formation of sounder views, and therefore an advance towards a clearer, because a more modest, system. There are certain principles which seem to be now very generally accepted as essential to a right understanding of the book. It is not, indeed, to be supposed that the acceptance of these principles will enable the student to unlock every mystery, or expound every symbol; but it will certainly save him from following "wandering fires." Of these principles the chief seem to be the following:—(1) the root passages in the Old Testament prophecies must be considered; (2) the historical surroundings of the writer are to be remembered; (3) the fact that the book is symbolical must never be forgotten; (4) the obvious aim of the book to be a witness to the triumph and coming (*parousia*) of Jesus Christ must be recognised. These principles are simple enough, but their neglect has been only too fatally evident. The difficulty, indeed, lies rather in the application of these principles than in their acceptance. It is, perhaps, not too much to say that the Præterist school has been apt to ignore the first of these principles; the Historical school has not adequately recognised the second; and the Futurist school is in constant danger of forgetting the third; while partial views in all schools have violated or weakened the value of the last principle.

The "coming of Christ," viewed from the human side, is a phrase which is not always to be held to one meaning: it is, in this aspect, analogous to the "kingdom of God." "Holy Scripture, beyond all doubt, recognises potential and spiritual, as well as personal, 'comings' of the Lord." * "There are many comings of Christ. Christ came in the flesh as a mediatorial Presence. Christ came at the destruction of Jerusalem. Christ came, a spiritual Presence, when the Holy Ghost was given. Christ comes now in every signal manifestation of redeeming power. Any great reformation of morals and religion is a coming of Christ. A great revolution, like a thunderstorm, violently sweeping away evil to make way for the good, is a coming of Christ" (Robertson, *Sermons*, Fourth Series, p. 73). It is thus that the sacred writers speak as of Christ's coming always at hand: "The judge standeth at the door;" "The coming of the Lord draweth nigh." "So, also, our Lord speaks: "I will not leave you comfortless; I will come to you." Thus, viewed from one aspect, the "coming of Christ" has various applications; but viewed from another aspect, it will be seen to be a phrase expressive of a simple thought, and free from all perplexing ambiguity. The coming of Christ, viewed from the divine side, is as a single act, in which all subordinate applications are included. There is no past or future with God. All that is being done, is, in one sense, done. God's dealings, as seen by human eyes, are, as it were, projections on the page of history. An illustration may help. A telegraph cable, whether cut straight through or on the slope, will present to view exactly the same combination of copper and iron wire, gutta-percha, and tarred yarn; but in the elliptical section the elements will appear in more extended order than in the circular section: so the same features which to us appear separate and successive, when viewed from the higher level of heavenly thought, may be seen as forming parts of one act. The various advents of Christ may thus be viewed as forming elements in one Advent, which is progressive from one side, but complete from another. The morning spreads itself in every direction over the forehead of the sky, and yet is but one morning. All the varying scenes from the First Advent to the Second are but the beatings of the wings of God's new day. "It is," as the prophet expressed it in language of glorious paradox, "It is one day, known to the Lord, neither clear nor dark, but one day, at whose eventide it shall be light."

If this be true, there is no necessity for leaping to the conclusion that, when the sacred writers warned their hearers that the coming of the Lord was near, they were mistaken, or that they sought to sustain the fainting hopes of the early Church by expectations which have proved false. Doubtless some did not understand the full and deep meaning of the words

---

* The whole note from Bishop Waldegrave's *Bampton Lectures* is worth quoting. "Holy Scripture, beyond all doubt, recognises (1) potential and spiritual, as well as personal, 'comings' of the Lord. See, for potential 'comings,' Matt. x. 23; John xxi. 22, 23; Rev. ii. 5, 15, 16, 22—25; iii. 3, 10. . . . See, for spiritual 'comings,' Ps. ci. 2; John xiv. 18, 21—24; Rev. iii. 20. In like manner Holy Scripture recognises (2) a potential and spiritual, as distinct from a personal, 'presence' of Christ with His people. See Matt. xviii. 20; xxviii. 20; Mark xvi. 20; 2 Tim. iv. 17. Now such potential and spiritual comings and presence will naturally, when translated, if I may so speak, into the language of imagery, assume the outward appearance of a personal and visible coming and presence. And this fact will abundantly account for the use of language (expressive of potential and spiritual comings) like that in Ps. cii. 13—16; Isa. xix. 1, 16, 19—21; xl. 10; lix. 20; Zech. ii. 10—12: (expressive of potential and spiritual presence) like that in Ps. cxxxv. 21; Isa. xii. 6; xxiv. 23; lx. 13; Ezek. xxxiv. 23, 24; xli. 22; xliii. 1—9; xliv. 1, 2; Joel ii. 27; iii. 17, 20, 21; Micah iv. 7; Zeph. iii. 14, 15; Zech. vi. 12, 13; viii. 3, without expecting a personal reign of Christ upon earth as its only adequate counterpart."

employed: doubtless many still clung to their carnal conceptions: but the apostolic language, whether from the pen of a St. Paul, St. Peter, or St. John, expresses the wider and truer thoughts of the coming of Christ. We find them anxious to remind those to whom they wrote that the idea of an immediate visible personal coming of Christ must not be allowed to gain possession of the mind. There were forces at work which must have their way before the end would come: seeds had been planted, and these must grow: the sowing and the harvest are linked together as one in the law of growth, and are yet separate. Thus the spirit of wilfulness and impatience is rebuked when men grasp the true thoughts of God. Yet it must not be supposed that the waiting Church of Christ will be disappointed of her hope, or that the heavenly Bridegroom will not come. He will come again; and all the preliminary and subordinate advents in judgment and in comfort will then be seen to have been earnests of the fulness of His coming. The interpreters are as men who stand upon a plain to watch the sunrise. When the first veil of night is withdrawn, and the starlight is somewhat paled, the more ardent than the rest will cry, "The dawn!" but the rest answer, "Not yet." Then when the mountain peaks begin to flame, another will cry, "The dawn!" and the rest will still reply, "Not yet." And when the landscape around catches its true colours, another will cry, "The dawn!" but only when the great and glorious orb leaps into view will all be one in crying, "The dawn! the dawn!" So is the coming of Christ. Some look upon the faint lightening in the moral atmosphere, and say, "Christ comes!" Others look to the reflected lights of truth proclaimed in the high places of the world, and say, "Christ comes!" Others look to the general diffusion of knowledge, and say, "Christ comes!" They are right, and they are wrong: right, for it is indeed Christ who is thus enlightening the world; they are wrong, for there is a coming greater than these when He will, in fuller manifestation of Himself, tabernacle with His people as their everlasting light.

IV. General Scope of this Book.

(1) *Its Aim.*—What is the aim of this book? The answers given, though various, have much in common. Some see in it a prediction of the overthrow of Paganism; others carry it further, and see the destruction of Papal Rome; others read in it the rise and fall of some future Antichrist. Thus far the opinions vary; but in one respect there is agreement: the Revelation aims at assuring the Church of the advent of her Lord: it is the book of the Coming One. Every school of interpretation will admit this. Some indeed will say that the expectation raised was never fulfilled, but all appear to unite in regarding the Apocalypse as the book of the advent. We may take this as a key to its meaning; it proclaims Christ's coming and victory. But is it the victory of Christ over Paganism, or over degenerate forms of Christianity, or over some final and future antichristian power or person? The true answer appears to be, It is the victory of Christ over all wrong-thoughtedness, wrong-heartedness, and wrong-spiritedness; the pictures given in the visions find their counterpart not in one age only, but gather their *full-fil*ment as the ages advance: the fall of Paganism is included in the visions, as the downfall of the world-power of Imperial Rome is included; but the picture-prophecy is not exhausted, and will not be till every form of evil of which Pagan and Imperial Rome, of which the wild beast and Babylon are types, has been overthrown. The ages are seen in perspective; the incidents separated from one another in historical sequence are gathered into one prophetical scene, and the Apocalypse presents us with a variety of these prophetical scenes, which depict the salient features of the conquest of evil, the triumph and advent of Christ —"He comes" is the key. He comes when Paganism falls; He comes when brute world force is cast down; He comes when worldliness falls—He comes, and His coming is spreading ever over the world, shining more and more unto the perfect day. Clouds may gather, and make the epochs which are nearest the full day darker than those which preceded them, but still in every epoch leading up to the golden day; the line of conflict may advance and recede from time to time, but it is a triumphant battle-field which is pictured. It is thus the book of the advent and victory of Christ.

But is it a book affording false hopes? Is it an echo of the wish of the early Christian Church, or is it a revelation from Christ to the waiting and perhaps impatient Church? I believe it is the latter. So far from the book giving colour to the expectation of an immediate personal coming of Jesus Christ, it seems distinctly to caution the early Christians against cherishing mistaken notions: "that day shall not come except there come a falling away first," was the caution of St. Paul; the caution of St. John, though expressed in pictorial form, is none the less emphatic. Let any one bear in mind the eager impatience of suffering Christians in early days, and let them then read the Apocalypse, and they will learn that its undertone is "Not yet, not yet," but still surely is He coming—not as you think, but as He thinks well, so is He coming. Let the seals furnish an illustration: the first shows an ideal conqueror; Christ, or the gospel of Christ goes forth to conquer—it is the picture of the Church's hope; the vision tells her that her hope is right, Christ will conquer; but it is the prelude of visions which tell her that her expectation is wrong if she expects that the kingdom of Christ will be established without conflict, pain, suffering and revolution. The succeeding seals are the pictures of the things which must needs be: the wars, the persecutions, the sorrows which will afflict the world because she will not accept her King: the parable of Luke xix. 11—27, and the emphatic warning language of Christ Jesus in Matt. xxiv. 4—14, are not forgotten in the Apocalypse. In it we are bidden to remember that though the victory is sure, the victory is through suffering; we are shown scenes which betoken the prolonged sorrows of the faithful, the obstinate tenacity of evil, its subtle transformations. and the concealed powers by which it is sustained: we are thus, as it were, shown the world's drama from a heavenly view-point, not in continuous historical succession, but in its various essential features, it is in this dramatic—that it does not tell its story right on, but groups its episodes round convenient centres, bringing into special prominence successively the principles of God's world-government. It is thus an apocalypse unfolding in symbolical forms the characteristic features of the struggle between good and evil, when the power of the gospel enters the field; it is the revelation of the coming (*parousia*) of Christ, because it shows not only that He will come, but that He does come; that He who has been revealed, is being revealed, and will yet be revealed.

(2) *The Form.*—It is the symbolical form which hinders many in the right understanding of the book, "I am a man of the earth," wrote Goëthe; "I am a man of the earth, earthy; to me the parables of the

unjust steward, the prodigal son, the sower, the pearl, the lost piece of money, &c., are more divine (if aught divine there be about the matter), than the seven messengers, candlesticks, seals, stars, and woes." This is only saying that symbolism employed in the one case was simpler than that employed in the latter—simpler, that is to say, to Western minds; for it may perhaps be doubted whether the symbolism which to the Teutonic mind seemed so strange, may not have been simple enough to those who were accustomed to Hebrew symbolism. But however this may be, the general symbols of the book are not so difficult as might appear. There is not space at our disposal to enter upon a discussion of this in detail. Certain features, however, are worthy of notice. The geographical imagery needs attention: Jerusalem stands as the type of the good cause, Babylon as the type of the metropolis of the world-power: Jerusalem is thus the Church of Christ (this symbolism is in complete harmony with St. Paul and other apostolic writers (comp. Gal. iv. 24—31; Heb. xii. 22, 23. Babylon is the emblem of Pagan Rome, but not only of Pagan Rome, for the Babylon type remains to this day: there are inspiring powers on the side of the heavenly Jerusalem —God is with her; she shall not be moved; the metropolis of evil has the assistance of evil powers: the dragon, the wild beast, and the false prophet are for a time with her. The family of evil bears a marked parallel to the family of good throughout the book: there is a trinity of evil powers on the side of Babylon the harlot, as the blessed Trinity are, with the bride, the heavenly Jerusalem. (See *Excursus B: The Wild Beast*.) The scenes in the great conflict range themselves round the members of these families of good and evil. The general features and elements of this struggle are depicted. There are numerical symbols: seven is the number of perfection, six of man's worldly perfection without God, four of the universe, three and a half of a limited period. There are seals, trumpets, and vials; the seals of the book which could only be opened by Christ betoken that the direction of earth's history and its explanation can be found only in Christ; the trumpets are the symbols of God's war against all forms of evil; the vials are the tokens of the retribution which falls upon those who turn not at the divine summons to righteousness. The strong symbolism of the book has a two-fold advantage: when the application of the visions are not to be exhausted in one age, the pictorial form is the most convenient to embrace the manifold fulfilments. Again, the author has clothed his thoughts in the "variously limiting, but reverential and only suitable drapery of ancient sacred language and symbolism, in the conviction that the reader would penetrate the veil and reach the sense" (Gebhardt).

(3) *The General Structure.*—The majority of critics see a seven-fold structure in the book. The commentators differ, as might be expected, as to the way in which this seven-foldedness of structure shows itself; but most of them arrange the different parts of the book in a seven-fold fashion. This is worthy of note, as the Fourth Gospel (see *Introduction to St. John's Gospel*) has been shown to have a similar seven-fold arrangement. When we notice the fondness of the seer for such an arrangement in the subordinate visions, it is not to be wondered at that the whole book should fall into seven groups; but we must be careful not to be carried away by our love of symmetry. The charts and maps of Apocalyptic interpretation are often very Procrustean. The general structure of the book, however, may be noted.

There are:—

1. The Preliminary Chapters.—Christ and His Church.

(1) THE VISION OF THE CHRIST (chap. i.).

(2) THE MESSAGES TO THE CHURCHES (chaps. ii., iii.).

2. The Visions.

(1) THE VISION OF THE THRONED ONE (chap. iv.).

(2) THE VISIONS OF THE CONFLICT, in two main sections.

(*a*) *The conflict seen from the world side* (chaps. vi.—xi.):

(α) The seven seals (chaps. vi.—viii. 1).

(β) The seven trumpets (chaps. viii. 2—xi.).

(*b*) *The conflict seen from the heavenly side* (chaps. xii.—xx.):

(α) The spiritual foes (chaps. xii.—xiv.).

(β) The seven vials of retribution (chaps. xv., xvi.).

(γ) The fall of foes (chaps. xvii.—xx.).

(3) THE VISIONS OF PEACE (chaps. xxi., xxii. 1—6).

3. The Epilogue (chap. xxii. 6—21).

It will be seen that there is a moving onward from the more external to the deeper and more spiritual aspects of earth's story. The earlier visions (the seals, for example) show the ordinary phenomena of the world's story—war, famine, death, revolution. The next series (the trumpets) show us that there is another, even a spiritual war, going forward in the world, and that changes and revolutions are often tokens of the inner spiritual battle in life. These visions, however, are, so to speak, all in the sphere of earth: in the next series we are shown that the war carried on here is one which has its heavenly counterpart. The conflict is not simply between good men and bad, but between principalities and powers. (See an interesting article on "The Ideal Incarnation," by Dr. S. Cox, in the *Expositor*, Vol. II., p. 405.) There is a heavenly view-point of all things on earth: there are spiritual forces, the ideal Church, the unseen strength of God, and the hidden inspirations of evil. In this struggle all evil will be vanquished. The earthly manifestations of evil, as well as the unearthly inspirations of it, will fall; the great and arch-enemy will be overthrown; the true spiritual, eternal rest be reached, and the golden age be realised. We are thus taught, in this ever-deepening spirituality of the book, to look beneath the phenomena, to trace the subtle and unmasked principles which are at work, to separate between the false and the true, to believe in *ideals* which are not mere ideas, but the true thoughts of God, which will one day be made real in the eyes of men, and which are even now real to the eye of faith Thus does the Book of Revelation become the unfolding of a dream which is from God. In it are painted the scenes of earth's history: the thirst of a nation's life and its passing groan; the tears and prayers of the unreckoned holy ones of earth; the agony of half-despair which even the best have felt in the night of conflict, that has so often been the eve of triumph; the sustaining faith which has transfigured the weakling into a hero, and nerved the heart of solitary saintship to do battle alone against a degenerate Church or a persecuting world; the silent victory of truth, or the unperceived growth of worldliness and falsehood. The book is thus a help and stay—not as yielding fruit to curiosity. It is not a manual of tiresome details: it is not meant to be a treasure-house of marvels for the prophetical archæologist: it is a book of living principles. It exhibits the force and fortune of truth as it acts upon the great mass of human society: it shows the revolutions which are the result. It shows the decay of the outward form, the release of the true germ, which will spring up in better harvests. It shows us how the corn of wheat may fall and die, and so bring forth much fruit. It shows us how evermore, from first to last, Christ is with us—encouraging, consoling, warning, helping, and leading us onward through conflict to rest.

V. Literature of the Apocalypse.—It is perfectly hopeless to touch so vast a subject as this. The mere list of works on the Apocalypse given in Darling's *Cyclopædia Bibliographica*, published in 1859, occupies fifty-two columns. A history of various interpretations is given in Lücke, *Einleitung in die Offenbarung Johannis*; a similar sketch is given by Bleek, *Lectures on the Apocalypse*; and Elliott (*Horæ Apocalypticæ*, vol. iv.) has presented us with an exhaustive and impartial account, *History of Apocalyptic Interpretations*, followed by *A Critical Examination and Refutation of the Three Chief Counter-schemes of Apocalyptic Interpretation; and also of Dr. Arnold's General Prophetic Counter-theory.* Dean Alford's article (*Greek Test.*) on "Systems of Interpretation," is lucid and compact.

Of Commentaries, leaving unnoticed earlier expositions, those of Vitringa, De Wette, Ewald, Bleek, Hengstenberg, Meyer, Ebrard, Auberlen, and Düsterdieck; of Hammond, Bishop Newton, Elliott, Alford, Bishop Wordsworth, Cunningham, Woodhouse, Moses Stuart, De Burgh, I. Williams, besides the works of Faber, Maitland, and Prof. Birks, are well known; and Dr. Currey's Notes on Revelation, in the *Christian Knowledge Society's Commentary* add much to the value of a really useful work.

Of lectures, F. D. Maurice's *Lectures* are full of thought and interest; and many students are indebted to Dr. Vaughan for his *Lectures on the Revelation of St. John*, which are models of what expository lectures ought to be. Gebhardt's *Lehrbegriff der Apokalypse*, now accessible to English readers in Clarke's Foreign Translation Library—(Gebhardt's *Doctrine of the Apocalypse*) is a valuable addition to the literature of the subject; it contains a close and careful comparison between the doctrine of the Apocalypse and that of the Gospel and Epistles of St. John. Of other books may be mentioned—Rev. S. Garratt's *Commentary on the Revelation of St. John, considered as the Divine Book of History; Prophetical Landmarks*, by Rev. H. Bonar; Dr. J. H. Todd's *Donnellan Lectures*; and Bishop Wordsworth's *Hulsean Lectures*. *The Apocalypse*, by Rev. Charles B. Waller; *The Parousia, a Critical Inquiry into the New Testament Doctrine of our Lord's Second Coming; The Life and Writings of St. John*, by Dr. J. M. Macdonald, of Princetown. On special points the following works may be noted:—On the Epistles to the Seven Churches, in addition to Archbishop Trench's indispensable work, and to Stier's well-known one, a valuable contribution has been given by Prof. Plumptre. On the Millennium: Bishop Waldegrave's "New Testament Millennarianism" (*Bampton Lectures*), and the Rev. Dr. Brown's work entitled *Christ's Second Coming: will it be pre-Millennial?* On the Babylon of the Apocalypse: Bishop Wordsworth's *Rome, the Babylon of the Apocalypse.* On the types and symbols: Fairbairn's *Typology of Scripture*; Rev. Malcolm White's *Symbolical Numbers of Scripture*; and the essay on "The Formal Elements of Apocalyptics" prefixed to Lange's *Commentary on Revelation.* Of this last book, which has not been mentioned above, it is to be regretted that, with much that is most valuable, it should be disfigured by pedantry of style.

THE REVELATION

OF

ST. JOHN THE DIVINE

CHAPTER I.—(1) The Revelation of
Chap. i. 1—4. Jesus Christ, which God
Preface. gave unto him, to shew
unto his servants things which must
shortly come to pass; and he sent and

A.D. 96.

signified *it* by his angel unto his servant
John: (2) who bare record of the word
of God, and of the testimony of Jesus
Christ, and of all things that he saw.
(3) Blessed *is* he that readeth, and they

(1) **The Revelation of Jesus Christ.**—The book is a revelation of the things which are and the things which shall be. "John is the writer, but Jesus Christ is the author," says Grotius; and consistently with this the action of Christ is seen throughout. It is Christ who bids John write to the seven churches; it is Christ who opens the seven seals (chap. vi. 1), who reveals the sufferings of the Church (chap. vi. 9), who offers the prayers of the saints (chap. viii. 3), and delivers the little book to John (chap. x. 1—11). Thus it is seen that though the rise and fall of earth's history is included in the revelation, it is a revelation also of a living person; it is not the dull, dead onward flow of circumstances, but the lives of men and nations seen in the light of Him who is the light of every man and the life of all history; and thus we learn that "only a living person can be the Alpha and Omega, the starting-point of creation and its final rest." The testimony of Jesus is the spirit of this prophecy, as of all others. The Father gives this to the Son whom He loves, and shows Him all things that Himself doeth.

Shortly.—On this word much controversy has turned. Its force, "speedily," affords a groundwork, and, it must be admitted, a plausible one, to the præterist school of interpreters, who hold that the whole range of Apocalyptic predictions was fulfilled within a comparatively short time after the Apostle wrote. The truth, however, seems to be that the words of God are of perpetual fulfilment: they are not only to be fulfilled; they have not only been fulfilled; but they have been and they are being fulfilled; and they yet will be fulfilled; and the principles which are enunciated by the Prophet, though "shortly" fulfilled, are not exhausted in the immediate fulfilment, but carry still lessons for the succeeding generations of mankind.

John—*i.e.*, the Apostle and Evangelist. The arguments in support of this identification are admitted even by the most captious critics to be conclusive. "The Apocalypse, if any book can be traced to him, must be ascribed to the Apostle John" (*Supernatural Religion*). (See *Excursus A.*) To many it will seem natural that John, the beloved disciple, should be the recipient of this revelation. Those who have been nearest to God learn most of His will. Such are friends, not servants, for the servant knoweth not what his Lord doeth; and thus, as in the Old Testament to Abraham, the friend of God, and to Daniel, a man greatly beloved, so in the New Testament to the disciple who leaned on Jesus' bosom, are shown the things which God was about to do. "Mysteries are revealed unto the meek. The pure in heart shall see God. A pure heart penetrateth heaven and hell" (Thomas à-Kempis).

> "More bounteous aspects on me beam,
> Me mightier transports move and thrill;
> So keep I fair through faith and prayer,
> A virgin heart in work and will."—*Sir Galahad.*

(2) **Who bare record.**—Elsewhere as well as here. And he tells us of what he bore record—of the Word of God. The writer declares that the substance of his testimony and witness had been this Word of God. We have here an indication of what the general character of his teaching had been. It evidently had been a teaching laying stress on that aspect of truth which is so forcibly set before us in the Fourth Gospel and the Epistles bearing the name of John. (Comp. chap. xix. 11; John i. 1, 14; 1 John i. 1, *et al.* Note also that the words "record," "testimony," "witness," found in this verse, recur in the Gospel and Epistles. Comp. John v. 31—40; xix. 35; xxi. 24.)

(3) **Blessed is he that readeth . . . . prophecy.**—Any declaration of the principles of the divine government, with indications of their exemplification in coming history, is a prophecy. Sometimes the history which exemplifies these principles is immediate, sometimes more remote; in other cases (as, I venture to believe, is the case with the predictions of this book) the events are both immediate and remote. The prophecy gives us the rule, with some typical application illustrative of its method of working; after-history affords us the working out of various examples. We, then, as living actors in the world, have not only to read and hear, but to keep—keep in mind and action those principles which preside over the development of all human history (Jas. i. 22). The word "keep" is in itself a proof to me that the whole fulfilment of the Apocalypse could not have been exhausted in the earliest times, nor reserved to the latest times of the Church's history, but that its predictions are applicable in all eras.

The time is at hand.—In the apostolic mind this was always true, though the restless idleness of the Thessalonians was blamed (2 Thess. ii. 2, and iii. 11, 12). The spirit of vigilance and of ever readiness

that hear the words of this prophecy, and keep those things which are written therein: for the time *is* at hand.

a Ex. 3. 14.

(4) JOHN to the seven churches which are in Asia: Grace *be* unto you, and peace, from him which is,[a]

Chap. i. 4—8. Salutation to the seven churches. Christ the key of history.

---

for both the providential advents and the final advent of the Christ was enjoined. (Comp. Rom. xiii. 12; Jas. v. 9; 2 Pet. iii. 8, 9.)

(4) **JOHN to the seven churches** (or, *congregations*) **which are in Asia.**—It is needless to observe that the Asia here is not to be regarded as co-extensive with what we know as Asia Minor. It is the province of Asia (comp. Acts ii. 9, 10; xvi. 6, 7), which was under a Roman proconsul, and embraced the western portion of Asia Minor. In St. John's time it consisted of a strip of sea-board, some 100 square miles in extent. Its boundaries varied at different periods; but roughly, and for the present purpose, they may be regarded as the Caycus on the north, the Mæander on the south, the Phrygian Hills on the east, and the Mediterranean on the west.

Seven churches.—It has been maintained by some (notably by Vitringa) that the epistles to the seven churches are prophetic, and set forth the condition of the Church in the successive epochs of its after-history. The growth of error, the development of schisms, the gloom of superstition, the darkness of mediæval times, the dawn of the Reformation, the convulsions of after-revolutions, have been discovered in these brief and forcible epistles. Such a view needs no formal refutation. The anxiety for circumstantial and limited fulfilments of prophecy has been at the root of such attempts. When we read God's words as wider than our thoughts we stand in no need of such desperate efforts at symmetrical interpretations; for the truth then is seen to be that words addressed to one age have their fitness for all; and that these epistles are the heritage of the Church in every epoch. In this sense the churches are types and representatives of the whole family of God. Every community may find its likeness here. This much is admitted by the best commentators of all schools. "The seven churches," says St. Chrysostom, "are all churches by reason of the seven Spirits." "By the seven," writes St. Augustine, "is signified the perfection of the Church universal, and by writing to the seven he shows the fulness of one." And the words, "He that hath an ear, let him hear what the Spirit saith unto the churches," are, as has been well observed, a direct intimation that some universal application of their teaching was intended.

Grace be unto you, and peace.—Three apostles, St. Peter, St. Paul, and St. John, adopt the same salutation. Not only is this a kind of link of Christian fellowship between them, but its adoption by St. John, after St. Paul had first used it, is a slight token that the Apocalypse cannot be regarded (as some recent critics would have it) as an anti-Pauline treatise. As the Christian greeting, it transcends while it embraces the Greek and Hebrew salutations. There is no tinge of the sadness of separation; it is the greeting of hope and repose, grounded on the only true foundation of either, the grace of God, which is the well-spring of life and love.

From him which is, and which was, and which is to come (or, *which cometh*).—The phrase presents a remarkable violation of grammar; but the violation is clearly intentional. It is not the blunder of an illiterate writer; it is the deliberate putting in emphatic form the "Name of Names." "Should not," says Professor Lightfoot, "this remarkable feature be preserved in an English Bible? If in Ex. iii. 14 the words run, 'I AM hath sent me unto you,' may we not also be allowed to read here, from 'HE THAT IS, AND THAT WAS, AND THAT IS TO COME?'" The expression must not be separated from what follows. The greeting is triple: from Him which is, and which was, and which cometh; from the seven Spirits; and from Jesus Christ—*i.e.*, from the Triune God. The first phrase would therefore seem to designate God the Father, the self-existing, eternal One, the fount and origin of all existence. Professor Plumptre suggests that the phrase used here may be used in allusion and contrast to the inscription spoken of by Plutarch, on the Temple of Isis, at Sais: "I am all that has come into being, and that which is, and that which shall be; and no man hath lifted my vail." The heathen inscription identifies God with the universe, making Him, not an ever-being, but an ever-becoming, from whom personality is excluded: the Christian description is of the personal, everlasting, self-revealing God—who is, who was, and who *cometh*. We should have expected after "is" and "was" "will be;" but there is no "will be" with an eternal God. With Him all *is;* so the word "cometh" is used, hinting His constant manifestations in history, and the final coming in judgment. This allusion to the Second Coming is denied by Professor Plumptre, but as he admits that the words, "He that cometh," used in the Gospels, and applied by the Jews to the Messiah, may be designedly employed here by the Apostle, it is difficult to see how the Advent idea can be excluded. The word appears to imply that we are to be always looking for Him whose "comings" recur in all history as the earnests of the fuller and final Advent.

From the seven Spirits.—The interpretation which would understand these seven Spirits to be the seven chief angels, though supported by names of great weight, is plainly untenable. The context makes it impossible to admit any other meaning than that the greeting which comes from the Father and the Son comes also from the Holy Spirit sevenfold in His operations, whose gifts are diffused among all the churches, and who divides to every man severally as He will. For corresponding thoughts in the Old Testament, compare the seven lamps and seven eyes of Zechariah (chaps. iii. 9; iv. 2, 10), "the symbols of eternal light and all embracing knowledge." It may not be inappropriate to note that Philo speaks of the number seven in its mystical import as identical with unity, as unity developed in diversity, and yet remaining one. This unity in diversity is the thought St. Paul seems anxious to keep before the minds of the Corinthians, lest their gifts should become the source of division. All work that one and self-same spirit (1 Cor. xii. 11). The after-recurrence in this book of the number seven is, I think, selected to support this thought of completeness and variety; the dramatic unity is preserved, though the scenes which are unfolded are amply diversified; and the seven seals, seven trumpets, and seven vials, are not three successive periods, but three aspects of one complete period presided over by that one Spirit whose guidance may be seen in all ages, and in diverse ways. The Spirits are before the throne. This reference to the throne gives a touch of authority

and which was, and which is to come; and
from the seven Spirits which are before
his throne; (5) and from Jesus Christ,
who is the faithful witness, *and* the
first begotten of the dead,[a] and the
prince of the kings of the earth. Unto
him that loved us, and washed us from
our sins in his own blood,[b] (6) and hath
made us kings and priests unto God
and his Father;[c] to him *be* glory and
dominion for ever and ever. Amen.
(7) Behold, he cometh with clouds;[d] and
every eye shall see him, and they *also*
which pierced him:[e] and all kindreds
of the earth shall wail because of him.
Even so, Amen. (8) I am Alpha and
Omega, the beginning and the ending,
saith the Lord, which is, and which was,
and which is to come, the Almighty.
(9) I John, who also am your
brother, and companion in
tribulation, and in the
kingdom and patience of Jesus Christ,
was in the isle that is called Patmos,

Chap. i. 9—11. The occasion of the vision.

a 1 Cor. 15. 20; Col. 1. 18.
b Heb. 9. 14.
c 1 Pet. 2. 5.
d Matt. 24. 30.
e Zech. 12. 10; John 19. 37.

---

to the description. The Holy Spirit who pleads with men is the Spirit from God's Throne.

(5) **From Jesus Christ, who is the faithful witness, and the first begotten** (or, *firstborn*) **of the dead, and the prince** (or, *ruler*) **of the kings of the earth.**—The triple title applied to Christ corresponds to the three ideas of this book. Christ the Revealing Prophet, the Life-giving High Priest, and the real Ruler of mankind.

The faithful witness.—There may be a reference here, it has been suggested by Prof. Plumptre, to the bow in the cloud, which is described in Ps. lxxxix. 37 as the faithful witness. The coincidence of expression is remarkable: "I will make him my firstborn, higher than the kings of the earth; he shall stand fast as the sun before me, and as the faithful witness in heaven." The idea of testimony and witness is a favourite one with St. John, who records its use by our Lord Himself. (Comp. John iii. 32; v. 36; xviii. 37. See also Rev. xix. 10; xxii. 18. Comp. also the work of the Only Begotten as stated in John i. 18.)

The prince (or *ruler*) **of the kings of the earth.**—The message does not come from One who will be, but who *is* the true ruler of all earthly potentates. The disposition to dwell on the future and more visibly recognised reign of Christ hereafter has tended to obscure the truth of His present reign. It is instructive to notice that this book, which describes so vividly the manifestations of Christ's kingdom (chaps. xi. 15; xii. 10), claims for Him at the outset the place of the real King of kings. Such was the Apostle's faith. "Above all emperors and kings, above all armies and multitudes, he thought of the Crucified as ruling and directing the course of history, and certain in His own due time to manifest His sovereignty" (Prof. Plumptre). "What are we to see in the simple Anno Domini of our dates and superscriptions, but that for some reason the great world-history has been bending itself to the lowly person of Jesus" (Bushnell). "A handful read the philosophers; myriads would die for Christ; they in their popularity could barely found a school; Christ from His cross rules the world" (Farrar, *Witness of History*). Such is a real kingship.

Unto him that loved us, and washed us.—Instead of "washed us," some MSS. read, "loosed us." There is only one letter's difference in the two words in Greek. The general tone of thought would lead us to prefer "washed" as the true reading. On a solemn occasion, which St. John remembered clearly, our Lord had said, "If I wash thee not, thou hast no part with Me." The thought of the "cleansing blood," intensified by the recollection of the water and blood which he had seen flowing from Christ's pierced side, often recurred to his mind (chap. vii. 13, 14; 1 John i. 7; v. 6—8).

(6) **And hath made us kings and priests unto God and his Father; to him be glory and dominion for ever** (or, *unto the ages*).—The symbol of washing in the last verse naturally leads on to the thought of consecration, accompanied by blood-sprinkling, to the work of the priest (Ex. xix. 6, 10; xxiv. 8; Heb. ix. 21). The book will declare the kingship and priesthood of the children of God—a sovereignty over human fears and sufferings—their priesthood in their lives of consecration, and their offering of themselves even unto death.

> "And all thy saints do overcome
> By Thy blood and their martyrdom."

The doxology here is two-fold: glory and dominion. The doxologies in which the Redeemed Church takes part grow in strength in the earlier chapters of this book. It is three-fold in chap. iv. 9—11; four-fold in chap. v. 13; and it reaches the climax of seven-fold in chap. vii. 12.

(7) **Behold, he cometh with clouds.**—Better, *with the clouds.* The reference to Christ's words (Mark xiv. 62), is undoubted. In the "clouds" St. Augustine sees the emblem of the saints of the Church, which is His body, who spread as a vast fertilising cloud over the whole world.

Every eye shall see him, and they also which (*they were who* = "whosoever") **pierced him.**—Here again is a reference to the incident of the piercing of Christ's side (John xix. 34), recorded only by St. John.

Shall wail because of him.—Or, *shall wail over Him.* The prophecy in Zech. xii. 10, is the suggesting one of this. But the passage in Zechariah describes the mourning of grief over the dead; the passage here is the mourning towards one who was dead, and is alive. He towards whom they now direct their sorrow is the One over whom they should have wailed when He was laid in His tomb.

(8) **The beginning and the ending.**—These words are of doubtful authority; they are in all probability taken from chap. xxii. 13, and interpolated here. The description of the verse applies, with little doubt, to our Lord, and the words are a strong declaration of His divinity.

The Almighty.—The word thus rendered is, with one exception (2 Cor. vi. 18), peculiar to this book in the New Testament.

(9) **I John, who also am your brother . . .**—More literally, *I, John, your brother and fellow partner in the tribulation and kingdom and patience in Jesus, ... because of the word of God and the testimony of Jesus.* He was a fellow-sharer of tribulation with them, and he shares that patience which brings

for the word of God, and for the testi-
mony of Jesus Christ. (10) I was in the
Spirit on the Lord's day, and heard be-
hind me a great voice, as of a trumpet,
(11) saying, I am Alpha and Omega,
the first and the last: and, What
thou seest, write in a book, and send *it*
unto the seven churches which are in
Asia; unto Ephesus, and unto Smyrna,
and unto Pergamos, and unto Thyatira,
and unto Sardis, and unto
Philadelphia, and unto
Laodicea. (12) And I turned
to see the voice that spake

Chap. i. 12—20. The vision of the Revealer Himself.

experience, because it is a patience in Jesus. It is not patience for Christ, like 2 Thess. iii. 5, nor patience of Christ, but rather patience which draws its life and energy of endurance from Him.

Patmos.—Professor Plumptre notices how little the scenery of Patmos colours the Apocalypse. "The vision that follows is all but unaffected by the external surroundings of the seer. At the farthest, we can but think of the blue waters of the Mediterranean—now purple as wine, now green as emerald, flushing and flashing in the light as the hues on the plumage of a dove." The position of the Apostle in Patmos was probably that of an exile, free to roam where he would within the limits of the island. There was at any rate no limit of chains or guard, as in the case of St. Paul (Acts xxviii. 16, 20). He tells us what was the cause of his exile. It was his faithfulness in proclaiming, as we know he loved to do, *the word of God and the testimony of Jesus.* "St. John, proclaiming the Word of God, who was before all worlds, who had been made flesh and dwelt among men, who was the King of kings and Lord of lords, struck a blow at the worship as well as the polity of the Roman empire. He opposed the God-man to the man-god" (*Maurice on the Revel.*, p. 20). The contest is incessantly the same. False creeds ever aim to deify man. "Ye shall be as gods" is their motto and their bible. "Emmanuel," is the motto of the true faith—

> "The Lord was God, and came as man; the Pope
> Is man, and comes as God."—*Harold.*

The crucified, suffering Saviour, God in Christ, very God, and one with man in sorrow, was the stumbling-block in the past, and is the ideal which offends many now. (See Bp. Alexander's *Bampton Lectures*, p. 30, *et seq.*) The terms of the conflict remain unchanged through the ages. (Comp. chap. vi. 9.)

(10) **I was** (or, *I became*) **in the Spirit.**—The mind, drawn onward by the contemplation of things spiritual, is abstracted from the immediate consciousness of outward earthly forms of life. In great natures this power is usually strong. Socrates is related to have stood rapt in thought for hours, and even days, unconscious of the midday heat, or the mocking wonder of his comrades. To high-souled men, set upon the spiritual welfare of the race, this power of detaching themselves from the influence of the outward is the result of their earnestness; the things spiritual are to them the real; the things seen are temporal. It is the Holy Spirit alone which can give the power of this spiritual abstraction; but it is through the ordinary use of means that this power is bestowed. In St. John's case it was on the Lord's Day that this spiritual rapture was vouchsafed.

The Lord's day.—There is no ground whatever for the futurist interpretation that this expression refers to the "Day of the Lord," as in 2 Thess. ii. 2. The phrase in this latter passage is totally different. The phrase here is, *en te kuriake hemera.* The adjective is applied by St. Paul (perhaps coined by him for the purpose) to the Lord's Supper: from the Supper it came to be applied to the day on which Christians met for the breaking of bread. The day is still called κυριακὴ (*kuriake*) in the Levant. On the Lord's Day the vision came to the Apostle. It was the hour of sweetest, closest communion, when the memories of Christ risen, and the fellowship he had enjoyed at Ephesus, would work on his spirit, and aid in raising him in highest adoration, like St. Paul (2 Cor. xii. 2—4). When so rapt, he heard a voice, strong, clear, and resonant as a trumpet. The Apostle's voice could not be heard among his beloved flock at Ephesus; but there was a voice which would reach from the exile at Patmos, not to Ephesus and its sister churches, but to all churches and throughout all time. The mouth which persecution closes God opens, and bids it speak to the world. So St. Paul, through the Epistles of his Captivity, still speaks. Luther, by his translation of the Bible, spoke from his confinement at Wartburg; and Bunyan, by his divine allegory, shows how feeble were the walls of his cell at Bedford to silence the voice of God. If speech be silvern and silence golden, it is also true in the history of the Church that from the captivity of her teachers she has received her most abiding treasures.

(11) **I am Alpha and Omega.**—In this verse we pass from St. John to Him who was the Word, of whom St. John gave testimony. He who is the faithful witness now speaks. "What thou seest, write," &c. The previous words, "I am Alpha," &c., are not found in the best MSS. The words "which are in Asia," are also omitted.

The seven churches.—There were more than seven churches in Asia Minor; but the number selected indicates completeness. Thus, though having special reference to the conditions of those churches, the epistles may be regarded as epistles conveying ever appropriate lessons to the churches of succeeding ages. The names of the seven churches are enumerated, as they would naturally be by a person writing from Patmos. "First, Ephesus is addressed, as the Asiatic metropolis, and as the nearest church to Patmos; then the other churches on the western coast of Asia; then those in the interior" (Wordsworth).

(12) **Seven golden candlesticks.**—Comp. the vision in Zech. iv. 2—11. It has been observed that there is a difference in the two visions. In Zech., as in Ex. xxv. 31, 32, the seven branches are united, so as to form one candlestick; here there are said to be seven candlesticks; and from this supposed difference it is argued that we have a hint of the variety of the Christian churches, as distinguished from the singleness of the Jewish church. But is it not more probable that what St. John saw was the old familiar seven-branched candlestick, identical in form with that which has been rendered familiar to all by the Arch of Titus, but that as the mention of the seven churches was then fresh in his mind, his eye fell rather upon the seven limbs and seven lights than on the whole candlestand, especially if, as Prof. Plumptre suggests,

with me. And being turned, I saw
seven golden candlesticks; (13) and in
the midst of the seven candlesticks *one*
like unto the Son of man, clothed with
a garment down to the foot, and girt
about the paps with a golden girdle.
(14) His head and *his* hairs *were* white
like wool, as white as snow; and his
eyes *were* as a flame of fire; (15) and his
feet like unto fine brass, as if they
burned in a furnace; and his voice as
the sound of many waters. (16) And he
had in his right hand seven stars: and
out of his mouth went a sharp two-

the figure of the Christ concealed part of the main stem? Thus to his view the separate individuality of the churches, and their real union in Him who was the Light, would rather be symbolised. Thus, too, the external teachings of the earlier symbols are not disturbed: the new revelation illumines the types and shadows of the older. "These symbols were intended to raise them out of symbols; the truths were to throw light on the parables, rather than the parables on the truths. Men were to study the visions of an earlier day by the revelations of that day" (Maurice, *Apocalypse*, p. 22).

(13) **In the midst of the seven candlesticks** (the word "seven" is omitted in some of the best MSS.) **one like unto the Son of man.**—"He who kindled the light to be a witness of Himself and of His own presence with men was indeed present." He was present the same as He had been known on earth, yet different—the same, for He is seen as Son of Man; the same as He had been seen on the Resurrection evening; the same as He appeared to Stephen; the same Jesus, caring for, helping and counselling His people: yet different, for He is arrayed in the apparel of kingly and priestly dignity. He is robed to the foot with the long garment of the high priest. St. John uses the same word which is used in the LXX. version of Ex. xxviii. 31, to describe the robe of the Ephod. (Comp. Zech. iii. 4.) It has been understood by some, however, to indicate the "ample robe of judicial and kingly power." There is in the vision a combination of both thoughts. He is the King-Priest who is seen by the Evangelist, the Melchisedec whom the Epistle to the Hebrews had so gloriously set forth (Heb. v. 9, 10; vi. 20; especially vii. 1—17). He is girt about the breasts with a golden girdle. The girdle is not around the loins, as though ready for action and toil (Luke xii. 35), but it is worn as by one who rests from toil in the "repose of sovereignty." So, according to Josephus (*Ant.* iii. 7, § 2), the Levitical priests were girdled. The girdle is of gold; not interwoven with gold, as was the high priest's girdle (Ex. xxviii. 8), but pure gold, the emblem of a royal presence. (Comp. Isa. xi. 5; Dan. x. 5; Eph. vi. 14.)

(14) **His head and his hairs were white like wool, as white as snow.**—The whiteness here is thought by some to be the token of the transfiguration in light of the glorified person of the Redeemer. "It is the glorious white which is the colour and livery of heaven." This doubtless is true; but it appears to me a mistake to say that there is no hint here of age. It is argued that the white hair of age is a token of decay, and that no such token would have place here; but surely this is straining a point, and making a mere emblem an argument. Age and youth alike have their glories; the glory of young men is their strength; the hoary head, too, the token of experience, dignity, authority, is the glory of age. Physically, white hair may be a sign of decay; typically it never is, else the effort to produce the appearance of it in the persons of monarchs and judges would never have been made. The white head is never in public sentiment other than the venerable sign of ripe knowledge, mature judgment, and solid wisdom; and as such it well betokens that full wisdom and authority which is wielded by the Ancient of Days, who, though always the same in the fresh dew of youth, is yet *from* everlasting, the captain of salvation, perfect through suffering, radiant in the glorious youthhood of heaven, venerable in that eternal wisdom and glory which He had with the Father before the world. (Comp. Dan. vii. 9.) "He was one," Saadias Gaon beautifully says, "with the appearance of an old man, and like an old man full of mercies. His white hair, His white garments, indicated the pure, kind intentions He had to purify His people from their sins."

His eyes were as a flame of fire.—Comp. chap. xix. 12; Dan. x. 6. The eyes of the Lord, which are in every place, beholding the evil and the good, are here described as like unto fire, to express not merely indignation (He had looked once on the Jewish rulers in indignation) against evil, but determination to consume it; for our God is a consuming fire, purging away sin from those who forsake sin, and consuming in their sin those who refuse to be separated from it. (See chap. xx. 9; Dan. vii. 9, 10; Jude, verse 7.)

(15) **His feet like unto fine brass.**—The feet, like the feet of the ministering priests of Israel, were bare, and appeared like *chalcolibanus* (fine brass). The exact meaning of this word (used only here) is not certain. The most trustworthy authors incline to take it as a hybrid word, half Greek, half Hebrew—*chalcos*, brass, and *labân*, white, to whiten—and understand it to signify brass which has attained in the furnace a white heat. "Such technical words were likely enough to be current in a population like that of Ephesus, consisting largely of workers in metal, some of whom—if we may judge from the case of Alexander the coppersmith (Acts xix. 34; 2 Tim. iv. 14)—were, without doubt, Jews. I believe the word in question to have belonged to this technical vocabulary. It is at any rate used by St. John as familiar and intelligible to those for whom he wrote" (Prof. Plumptre in the *Epistles to Seven Churches, in loco*).

His voice as the sound (better, *voice*, as the same word—*phoné*—is used twice, and translated first "voice" and then "sound" in our English version) **of many waters.**—Daniel described the voice of the Ancient of Days as the voice of a multitude (Dan. x. 6); but the voice of the multitude was in earlier Hebrew writings compared to the sound of the waves of the sea, which the voice of the Lord alone could subdue (Ps. lxv. 7; xciii. 4). This image the Evangelist adopts to describe the voice of Christ—strong and majestic, amid the Babel-sounds of earth. That voice, whose word stilled the sea, sounds as the waves of the sea, which St. John heard Him rebuke.

(16) **And he had** (or, *having*) **in his right hand seven stars.**—The stars are explained later on (verse 20) to be the emblems of the angels of the

edged sword: and his countenance *was* as the sun shineth in his strength.
(17) And when I saw him, I fell at his feet as dead. And he laid his right hand upon me, saying unto me, Fear not; I am the first and the last:[a]
(18) *I am* he that liveth, and was dead; and, behold, I am alive for evermore,

[a] Isa. 41. 4. & 44. 6.

---

seven churches; they are described as stars in His right hand; they, perhaps, appeared as a wreath, or as a royal and star-adorned diadem in His hand. (See Isa. lxii. 3.) It expresses their preciousness in Christ's sight, and the care He takes of them. A similar emblem is used of Coniah (Jer. xxii. 24), where he is compared to the signet upon God's right hand.

And out of his mouth went a sharp two-edged sword.—There need be no doubt about the meaning here: the imagery of the Bible elsewhere is too explicit to be mistaken; it is the sword of the Spirit, even the word of God, which is here described; it is that word which is sharper than any two-edged sword, and which lays bare the thoughts and intents of the soul (Eph. vi. 17; Heb. iv. 12. Comp. Isa. xlix. 2). This is the weapon with which Christ will subdue His enemies; no carnal weapon is needed (2 Cor. x. 4). Those that take any other sword in hand than this to advance His kingdom will perish with the weapon to which they have appealed (chap. xiii. 10; Matt. xxvi. 52), but those who arm themselves with this will find it mighty through God. With this weapon of His word He Himself fights against His adversaries (chaps. ii. 12, 16; xix. 15, 21); with this He lays bare the hidden hypocrisies of men, cuts off the diseased members, and wounds that He may heal.

> "The sword wherewith Thou dost command,
> Is in Thy mouth and not Thy hand."

It is a *two-edged* sword; it has the double edge of the Old Testament and the New; "the Old Testament, cutting externally our *carnal;* the New Testament, internally our *spiritual* sins" (Richard of St. Victor). It has the double edge of its power to rebuke sin and self-righteousness; the evil of wrong-doing and the evil motives which wait on right-doing; the two edges of which will cut off sin from man, or else man in his sin. (Comp. Isa. xi. 4, and 2 Thess. ii. 8.) The Greek word here rendered "sword" is used six times in this book, and only once (Luke ii. 35) elsewhere in the New Testament.

His countenance was as the sun shineth in his strength.—It is the spiritual truth which gives the splendour to such descriptions as these. The dazzling glory of Him who is the Sun of Righteousness is intolerable to human eyes. There is no marvel in this when we remember that He is the brightness of His Father's glory, and that the Father dwells "in that light which no man can approach unto; whom no man hath seen, nor can see" (1 Tim. vi. 16). It is the lustre of holiness and righteousness which is here signified, and which "the eye of sinful man may not see," but of which saints and angel messengers may catch a faint reflection; so that the angel's face may look like lightning (Matt. xxviii. 3), and "the righteous shine forth as the sun in the kingdom of their Father" (Matt. xiii. 43). (Comp. the shining of Moses' face, Ex. xxxiv. 29.)

(17) **I fell at his feet as dead.**—At the sight of Him, the Evangelist fell as one dead. "Was this He whom upon earth St. John had known so familiarly? Was this He in whose bosom He had lain at that Last Supper, and said, 'Lord, which is he that betrayeth Thee?' When I saw Him thus transformed, thus glorified, I fell at His feet as one dead. Well might such be the effect, even upon the spirit of a just man made perfect—and St. John was still in the body—of such an open revelation of the risen glory of Christ" (Dr. Vaughan). It was pity, and the pang felt at the severity of retribution which overtook sin, which made Dánte fall as a dead body falls (*Inferno,* v.); it is the felt consciousness of unworthiness which seems to have overcome the Evangelist. This consciousness has its witness outside the Bible as well as in it. "Semele must perish if Jupiter reveals himself to her in his glory, being consumed in the brightness of that glory." (Comp. Ex. xxxiii. 18, 20, "Thou canst not see My face; for there shall no man see Me and live.") For every man it is a dreadful thing to stand face to face with God. Yet the consciousness of this unworthiness to behold God, or to receive a near revelation of His presence, is a sign of faith, and is welcomed as such. Of him who said, "Lord, I am not worthy that Thou shouldest come under my roof," Christ said, "I have not found so great faith, no, not in Israel" (Matt. viii. 8—10).

He laid his right hand upon me, saying unto me, Fear not.—The words "unto me" should be omitted. The gesture is designed to give the assurance of comfort; the hand which was raised up to bless (Luke xxiv. 51), which was reached forth to heal the leper, to raise the sinking Peter (Matt. xiv. 31), and to touch the wounded ear of Malchus, is now stretched out to reassure His servant; and the words, like those which John had heard upon the Mount of Transfiguration, and when toiling against the waves of Galilee, bid him not to be afraid. (Comp. Dan. x. 10.)

I am the first and the last.—The "last" must not be taken here to mean the least and lowest, as though it referred to our Lord's humiliation; the last points forwards, as the *first* points backwards. He was before all things, and so the *first;* and though all things change, folded up as a vesture, yet His years shall not fail, and so He is the *last.* "The *first* because all things are from Me; the last because to Me are all things" (Richard of St. Victor). (Comp. Col. i. 16—18; Heb. i. 11, 12.) This pre-eminence of first and last is thrice claimed for the Lord Jehovah in Isaiah (chaps. xli. 4; xliv. 6; xlviii. 12), and thrice for the Lord Jesus in this book (in this passage, in chap. ii. 8, and chap. xxii. 13).

(18) **I am he that liveth, and was dead.**—Better, *and the living One* (omit the words "I am"); *and I became dead; and, behold, I am alive* (or, *I am living*) *unto the ages of ages* (or, *for evermore*). "Amen" is omitted in the best MSS. This verse must be carefully kept in connection with the preceding, as the description should go on without pause. He is the living One—not merely one who once was alive, or is now alive—but the One who has "life in Himself, and the fountain and source of life to others, John i. 4; xiv. 6; the One who hath immortality," 1 Tim. vi. 16 (Trench). Yet He became dead. There are two wonders here: the living One becomes dead, and the dead One is alive for evermore. It is another form of the glorious truth and paradox of which the Apostles were so fond (Phil. ii

Amen; and have the keys of hell and of death. (19) Write the things which thou hast seen, and the things which are, and the things which shall be hereafter; (20) the mystery of the seven stars which thou sawest in my right hand, and the seven golden candlesticks. The seven stars are the angels of the seven churches: and the seven candlesticks which thou sawest are the seven churches.

A.D. 96.

CHAPTER II.—(1) Unto the angel of the church of Ephesus write; These things saith he that holdeth the seven stars in his right hand, who walketh in the midst of the seven golden

Chap. ii. 1—7. Epistle to Church in Ephesus.

8, 9; Heb. ii. 9). Comp. Christ's words, Luke ix. 24, and xiii. 43, which contain promises which He only could make who could say, "I have the keys of death and of Hades." The order of these words has been transposed in our English version. The true order is the more appropriate order, "For Hades is the vast unseen realm into which men are ushered by death; dark and mysterious as that realm was, and dreaded as was its monarch, our risen Lord has both under His power. The keys are the emblems of His right and authority." (Comp. chap. iii. 7, 8.) It is not of the second death that He speaks; our Lord is here seen as the conqueror of that clouded region, and that resistless foe which man dreaded. (Comp. John xi. 25; Heb. ii. 15.) Comp. Henry Vaughan's quaint poem "An Easter Hymn"—

> "Death and darkness get you packing,
> Nothing now to man is lacking;
> All your triumphs now are ended,
> And what Adam marred is mended;
> Graves are beds now for the weary,
> Death a nap to wake more merry."

Christ had spoken before of the *gates* of hell (Matt. xvi. 18), and of the keys. (Comp. also 1 Pet. iii. 19.) The key of the grave was one of the four keys which the Eternal King committed to no ministering angel, but reserved for himself (so Targum and Talmud). The whole verse affirms the undying power and inalienable authority of our Master, and is a fitting prelude to a book which is to show the inherent divine tenacity of Christianity. The Church lives on because Christ its Head lives on (John xiv. 19). The resurrection power which the Lord showed is to be reflected in the history of His Church. "The greatest honour is due to Christianity," says Goethe, "for continually proving its pure and noble origin by coming forth again, after the great aberrations into which human perversity has led it, more speedily than was expected, with its primitive special charm as a mission . . . . . for the relief of human necessity."

(19) **Write the things which thou hast seen** (better, *sawest*).—It is well to notice the small connecting word "then," which has been omitted in the English. It gives the practical thought to the whole of the previous vision. This vision is to be described for the benefit of the Church of Christ, that she may never forget Him who is the foundation on which she rests; the true fountain of her life; and in whom she will find the source of that renewing power to which the last Note alludes. In the history of the faith it will be always true that they who wait on the Lord shall renew their strength (Isa. xl. 28—31). Lest, then, at any time the saints of God should be tempted to cry that "their judgment was passed over from their God," the Evangelist is bidden first to detail this vision of Him who is the Life and Captain of His people. He is also to write *the things which are*—those eternal principles and truths which underlie all the phenomena of human history; or the things which concern the present state of the churches—*and the things which are about to be after these things*—those great and wondrous scenes of the fortunes of the Church and of the world which will be unfolded.

(20) **The mystery of the seven stars which thou sawest in my right hand.**—Having bidden him write the meaning of this mystery, or *secret*, He gives to St. John an explanatory key: "The seven stars are angels of seven churches (or *congregations*): and the seven candlesticks" (omit the words "which thou sawest") "are seven churches." The angels have been understood by some to be guardian angels; but it is difficult to reconcile words of warning and reproof (as in chap. ii. 4, 5), and of promise and encouragement (as in chap. ii. 10), with such a view. More probable is the view which takes the angel to be the ideal embodiment (so to speak) of the Church. The more generally adopted view is that the angel is the chief pastor or bishop of the Church. The description of them as stars favours this view. Similar imagery is applied elsewhere to teachers, true and false (Dan. xii. 3; Jude 13. Comp. Rev. viii. 10, and xii. 4). It is stated that the word "angel" was applied to the president in the Jewish synagogue. See, however, *Excursus A.*

II.

(1) **Unto the angel of the church of** (literally, *in*) **Ephesus.**—On the word "angel," see Note on chap. i. 20, and *Excursus A*. Adopting the view that the angel represents the chief pastor or bishop of the Church, it would be interesting to know who was its presiding minister at this time; but this must be determined by another question, viz., the date of the Apocalypse. Accepting the earlier date—*i.e.*, the reign of Nero, or (with Gebhardt) of Galba—the angel is no other than Timothy. Some striking coincidences favour this view. Labour, work, endurance, are what St. Paul acknowledges in Timothy, and which he exhorts him to cultivate more and more (2 Tim. ii. 6, 15; iv. 5). Again, against false teachers he warns him (1 Tim i. 7). Further, there is "a latent tone of anxiety" in the Epistles to Timothy. The nature with which he had to do was emotional even to tears, ascetic, devout; but there was in it a tendency to lack of energy and sustained enthusiasm. "He urges him to stand up, to rekindle the grace of God, just as here there is a hint of a first love left." (See Prof. Plumptre, *Ep. to Seven Churches.*)

Ephesus.—The chief city of Ionia, and at this time the most important city in Asia. It possessed advantages commercial, geographical, and ecclesiastical, and, in addition, great Christian privileges. It was a wealthy focus for trade; it reached out one hand to the East, while with the other it grasped Greek culture. Its magnificent temple was one of the seven wonders of the world; the skill of Praxiteles had contributed to its beauty. The fragments of its richly-sculptured columns, now to be seen in the British

candlesticks; (2) I know thy works, and thy labour, and thy patience, and how thou canst not bear them which are evil: and thou hast tried them which say they are apostles, and are not, and hast found them liars: (3) and hast borne, and hast patience, and for my name's sake hast laboured, and hast not fainted. (4) Nevertheless I have *somewhat* against thee, because thou hast left thy first love. (5) Remember therefore from whence thou art fallen, and repent, and do the first works; or else I will come unto thee quickly, and will remove thy

---

Museum, will convey some idea of its gigantic proportions and splendid decorations. But the religious tone induced by its pagan worship was of the lowest order. Degrading superstitions were upheld by a mercenary priesthood; the commercial instinct and the fanatical spirit had joined hands in support of a soul-enslaving creed, and in defence of a sanctuary which none but those devoid of taste could contemplate without admiration. But its spiritual opportunities were proportioned to its needs. It had been the scene of three years' labour of St. Paul (Acts xx. 31), of the captivating and convincing eloquence of Apollos (Acts xviii. 24), of the persistent labours of Aquila and Priscilla (Acts xviii. 26); Tychicus, the beloved and faithful, had been minister there (Eph. vi. 21); Timothy was its chief pastor.

These things saith he . . . .—The titles by which Christ is described at the opening of the seven epistles are mainly drawn from chap. i. The vision is found to supply features appropriate to the needs of the several churches. The message comes in this epistle from One who "*holdeth*" firmly in His grasp (a stronger word than "He that hath" of chap. i. 16), and walketh in the midst of the seven golden candlesticks. The Church at Ephesus needed to remember their Lord as such. The first love had gone out of their religion; there was a tendency to fall into a mechanical faith, strong against heresy, but tolerant of conventionalism. Their temptations did not arise from the prevalence of error, or the bitterness of persecution, but from a disposition to fall backward and again do the dead works of the past. There was not so much need to take heed unto their doctrine, but there was great need that they should take heed unto themselves (1 Tim. iv. 16). But when there is danger because earnestness in the holy cause is dying out, and the very decorum of religion has become a snare, what more fitting than to be reminded of Him whose hand can strengthen and uphold them, and who walks among the candlesticks, to supply them with the oil of fresh love? (Comp. Zech. iv. 2, 3; Matt. xxv. 3, 4.)

(2) **I know thy works.**—This phrase is probably common to all the epistles. See, however, Note on verse 9. It expresses the way in which all actions are naked and open before the eyes—those flame-like eyes (chap i. 14)—of Him with whom we have to do (Pss. xi. 4, 5; cxxxix. 11, 12; Heb. iv. 13). The veneer of a formal faith might impose on the world, but it would not escape His scrutiny (Acts i. 24). He knows, too, and lovingly accepts, the unmarked and unrequited acts of true love (Matt. x. 42; xxvi. 13), and appreciates, amid all its failures, genuine loyalty to Him (John xxi. 17).

And thy labour (or, *toil*), **and thy patience.**—The same things which St. Paul had pressed on Timothy (2 Tim. ii. 25, 26). The first word signifies labour carried on unto weariness. The "patience" is more than passive endurance; it is, as Archbishop Trench says, a beautiful word, expressing the brave and persistent endurance of the Christian. But though thus possessed of endurance, He commends them that they could not endure evil men. In one sense, the lingering of this grace among them is the green leaf betokening better things; they have not lost the power of hating evil. (Comp. Rom. xii. 9.) No man loves God truly who cannot hate evil (Ps. ci. 3).

And thou hast tried (literally, *didst try*) **them . . . and hast found them liars.**—St. Paul had warned the Ephesian elders of the appearance of false teachers (Acts xx. 28—31). Zeal for pure doctrine characterised the Ephesian Church. It is commended by Ignatius in his epistle (*ad Eph.* vi.). The false apostles here spoken of are not, I think, to be identified with the Nicolaitanes of verse 6; that verse is introduced as a further ground of commendation, mitigating the censure of verses 4 and 5. The claims to be considered apostles, which the Ephesian Church had disposed of, affords additional evidence of the early date of the Apocalypse. Such a claim could hardly have been put forward at a later date. But at the earlier periods such troublers of the Church were only too common (2 Cor ii. 17; xi. 14, 15; Gal. i. 7; ii. 4; Phil. iii. 2, 3).

(3) **And hast borne.**—This verse needs some change to bring it into harmony with the best MSS. It should stand, *And hast* (or, *hadst*) *patience, and didst bear for My name's sake, and didst not weary.* In this last word there is a recurrence to the word (*kopos*) translated labour or toil in verse 2. They had toiled on to very weariness without wearying of their toil (Gal. vi. 9), just as they could not *bear* the evil and yet had *borne* reproaches for Christ's sake. "There is toil, and patience, and abhorrence of evil, and discernment, and again patience, and endurance, and unwearied exertion. What can be wanting here?" (Dr. Vaughan.)

(4) **Nevertheless I have somewhat against thee.**—Better, *I have against thee that thou didst let go.* This is the fault, and it is no trifle which is blamed, as the word "somewhat" (which is not to be found in the original) might be taken to imply; for the decay of love is the decay of that without which all other graces are as nothing (1 Cor. xiii. 1—3), since "all religion is summed up in one word, Love. God asks this; we cannot give more; He cannot take less" (Norman Macleod, *Life*, i., p. 324). Great as the fault is, it is the fault which Love alone would have detected. "Can any one more touchingly rebuke *than* by commencing, 'Thou no longer lovest me enough?'" It is the regretful cry of the heavenly Bridegroom, recalling the early days of His Bride's love, the kindness of her youth, the love of her espousals (Jer. ii. 2. Comp. Hos. ii. 15). It is impossible not to see some reference in this to the language of St. Paul (which must have been familiar to the Ephesian Christians) in Eph. v. 23—33, where human love is made a type of the divine.

(5) **Remember therefore from whence thou art fallen, . . . and do the first works.**—It is argued that we have here evidence that the later, or Domitian, date of the Apocalypse is the true one, since it describes a fall in spiritual life which might have

candlestick out of his place, except thou
repent. (6) But this thou hast, that
thou hatest the deeds of the Nicolai-
tanes, which I also hate. (7) He that
hath an ear, let him hear what the
Spirit saith unto the churches; To
him that overcometh will I give to
eat of the tree of life, which is in
the midst of the para-
dise of God. (8) And unto
the angel of the church
in Smyrna write; These

Chap. ii. 8—11. The Epistle to the Church in Smyrna.

occurred in thirty years, but would hardly have taken place in the few years—ten at the utmost—which elapsed between the visit of St. Paul (Acts xx. 29, 30) and the reign of Nero. But greater changes than a decay of this kind have passed over communities in equally short periods. We have seen nations pass from imperialism to republicanism, from the fever-heat of radicalism to the lethargy of conservatism, in shorter space. Has not the past decade shown marvellously rapid movements in the Church of our own land! The change, moreover, in the Ephesian Church was not so great as the advocates of the later apocalyptic date would describe. There is at present little outward sign of decay; they have resisted evil and false teachers; they have shown toil and endurance; but the great Searcher of hearts detects the almost imperceptible symptoms of an incipient decay. He alone can tell the moment when love of truth is passing into a noisy, Pharisaic zealotism; when men are "settling down into a lower state of spiritual life than that which they once aimed at and once knew." Such a backsliding is "gentle, unmarked, unnoticed in its course." Further, it must not be forgotten that the Apostle did express his presentiments of coming danger, and specially warned the elders (Acts xx. 28) to take heed unto *themselves;* and in his Epistle (Eph. vi. 24) he gives in his closing words the covert caution that their love to Christ should be an incorruptible, unchanging love: "Grace be with all them that love our Lord Jesus Christ in *incorruption*" ("sincerity," English version). The advice now given is, "Repent, and do the first works." The advice is three-fold: remember, repent, reform. Remember the love of the past peaceful hours. "How sweet their memory still!" "There are ever goads," says Archbishop Trench, "in the memory of a better and a nobler past, goading him who has taken up with meaner things and lower, and urging him to make what he has lost once more his own." (Comp. Luke xv. 17, and Heb. x. 32.) So Ulysses urges his crew to further exertions.

> "Call to mind from whence ye sprung:
> Ye were not formed to live as brutes,
> But virtue to pursue and knowledge high."
> —*Inf.* xxvi.

Remember, but also repent, and repent in true practical fashion; for Love will recognise no repentance but that which is confirmed in the doing of the first works. It must be a repentance whereby we forsake sin. "Christ does not say, 'Feel thy first feelings,' but, 'Do the first works.'" "An ounce of reality," says a modern novelist, "is worth a pound of romance."

Or else I will come . . .—Better, *Or else I am coming unto* (or, *for thee, in a way which concerns*) *thee, and* (omit "quickly," which is wanting in the oldest MSS.) *will remove thy candlestick out of its place, unless thou shalt have repented—i.e.,* unless the change shall have come before the day of visitation. The "now they are hid from thine eyes," is not yet spoken for Ephesus.

(6) **But this thou hast, that thou hatest the deeds** (better, *works*) **of the Nicolaitanes.**—The Nicolaitanes were, as has been expressed, the Antinomians of the Asiatic Church. The life and conduct were little thought of, and the faith professed was everything. Some have thought that they were a sect who derived their name, under some colourable pretext, from Nicolas the Proselyte; others hold that the name is purely symbolical, signifying "destroyer of the people," and that it is no more than the Greek form of Balaam. (See Notes on verses 14, 15, below.) The existence of a sect called Nicolaitanes in the second century is attested by Irenæus, Tertullian, and Clement of Alexandria.

(7) **He that hath an ear . . .**—Or, *Let him that hath an ear, hear.* These words—an echo from the Gospels—recur in all the seven epistles. In the first three, however, they are placed before the promise; in the remaining four they follow it. The heart which is hardened is the precursor of the ear that is deaf (Jer. vi. 10, and John xii. 37—40). The "spiritual truth" needs a spiritual organ for its discernment. These are truths, then, only heard

> "When the soul seeks to hear; when all is hushed,
> And the *heart* listens."—Coleridge, *Reflection.*

To him that overcometh (or, *conquereth*) **will I give to eat of the tree of life, which is in the midst of the paradise of God.**—The reference to conquering is a prominent feature of St. John's other writings. The word—used but once in the three Gospels (Luke xi. 22), and but once by St. Paul (Rom. xii. 21)—is found in John xvi. 33; 1 John ii. 13, 14; v. 4, 5; and occurs in all these epistles to the churches. The promise of the tree of life is appropriate (1) to the virtue commended: those who had not indulged in the license of Nicolaitanes shall eat of the tree of life; (2) to the special weakness of the Ephesians: to those who had fallen, and lost the paradise of first loving communion and fellowship with God (comp. Gen. iii. 8, and 1 John i. 3), is held out the promise of a restored paradise and participation in the tree of life. (Comp. chap. xxii. 2, 14; Gen. iii. 22.) This boon of immortality is the gift of Christ—I will *give.* It is tasted in knowledge of God and of His Son (John xvii. 3); it is enjoyed in their presence (chap. xxii. 3, 4).

(8) **Smyrna,** the modern *Ismir,* now possessing a population of about 150,000. Its mercantile prosperity may be measured by its trade. In 1852 the export trade amounted to £1,766,653—about half of this being with England. The imports in the same year were £1,357,339. It has always been considered one of the most beautiful cities in Asia. It was situated in the ancient province of Ionia, a little north of Ephesus—next it, as Archbishop Trench says, in natural order, and also in spiritual. Its position was favourable for commerce. In olden times, as now, it commanded the trade of the Levant, besides being the natural outlet for the produce of the Hermus valley. The neighbourhood was peculiarly fertile; the vines are said to have been so productive as to have yielded two crops. There are indications that intemperance was very prevalent among the inhabitants. Servility and flattery may be added, for the people of Smyrna seem to have been astutely fickle, and to have been keen in pre-

things saith the first and the last, which
was dead, and is alive; (9) I know thy
works, and tribulation, and poverty,
(but thou art rich) and *I know* the blas-
phemy of them which say they are Jews,
and are not, but *are* the synagogue of
Satan. (10) Fear none of those things
which thou shalt suffer: behold, the
devil shall cast *some* of you into prison,
that ye may be tried; and ye shall have
tribulation ten days: be thou faithful
unto death, and I will give thee a crown

---

serving the patronage of the ruling powers. In one of their temples the inscription declared Nero to be "the Saviour of the whole human race." The city was specially famed for its worship of Dionysos. Games and mysteries were held yearly in his honour. Its public buildings were handsome, and its streets regular. One of its edifices used as a museum proclaimed, in its consecration to Homer, that Smyrna contested with six or seven other cities the honour of being the birthplace of the poet.

The angel of the church in Smyrna.—We have no means of determining certainly who was the person here addressed. Many who accept the Domitian date of the Apocalypse argue that Polycarp was at this time the bishop or presiding minister at Smyrna. Even on the supposition that this is the true date, it seems exceedingly doubtful that this was the case. It can only be true on the supposition that the episcopate of Polycarp extended over sixty years. Polycarp was martyred A.D. 156. We know from Ignatius, who addresses him in A.D. 108 as Bishop of Smyrna, that his ministry lasted nearly fifty years. It seems too much to assume that his episcopate commenced eight or ten years before. Of course, if we adopt the earlier date of the Apocalypse, the Epistle must have been written before Polycarp's conversion—probably before his birth. But though we are thus constrained to reject the identification which we would willingly adopt, it is well to remember that Polycarp is the living example of the language of the epistle, and that, as Professor Plumptre has said, "In his long conflict for the faith, his stedfast endurance, his estimate of the fire that can never be quenched, we find a character on which the promise to him that overcometh had been indelibly stamped."

The first and the last, which was dead, and is alive.—Or better, *who became dead, and lived again.* From chap. i. 17, 18, we have selected the title most fitted to console a church whose trial was persecution. In all vicissitudes, the unchanging One (Heb. vii. 3 and xiii. 8), who had truly tasted death, and conquered it even in seeming to fail, was their Saviour and King. Some have seen in these words, "dead and lived again," an allusion to the story of the death and return to life of Dionysos—a legend, of course, familiar to Smyrna.

(9) **I know thy works.**—Some would omit the word "works;" but the phrase "I know thy works" is admitted to be genuine in five out of the seven epistles; and it certainly seems natural to conclude that it was intended to be common to all, and to remind the Christian communities that whatever their state it was known to Him whose eyes were as a flame of fire. "We go from one hour to another, from one day and year to another, and what is once fairly past in our doing and omitting and suffering is scarcely regarded by us any more; it is like water that has flowed away. But into the omniscience of Christ all things are taken up" (Bengel).

Tribulation.—If persecution brought upon them poverty, it was the means also of unfolding to view their possession of the "true riches;" they were rich in honour, in that they were counted worthy to suffer; they would also grow rich in the graces which sufferings bring (Rom. v. 3—5; Jas. i. 2—4).

Blasphemy.—They had to endure reviling as well as tribulation and poverty; and, harder still, to hear some who blasphemed that worthy name by which they were called.

Jews.—The Jews were foremost in this. "It was in the synagogue that they heard words which reproached them as Nazarenes, Galileans, Christians, Disciples of the Crucified" (Plumptre). Comp. Jas. ii. 7. It is interesting to notice that this characteristic hostility of the Jews was illustrated in the martyrdom of Polycarp. The Jews, "as was their wont," were foremost in bringing logs for the pile.

Synagogue of Satan.—The word "synagogue" is only once used to describe the Christian assembly (Jas. ii. 2); and even there it is called "*your* synagogue," not the "synagogue of God." In all other instances the "word is abandoned by the Jews." With the "synagogue of Satan" here, compare "the throne of Satan" (chap. ii. 13), "the depths of Satan" (chap. ii. 24).

(10) **Fear none of those things.**—Though Christ proclaimed His yoke to be easy, He also said that His followers must expect tribulation (John xvi. 33). He never conceals the difficulties or dangers of His service. (See Matt. x. 16—31; Acts ix. 16.) So here He proclaims, "Behold, the devil shall cast some . . . ."

The devil.—The LXX. translation gives this name to Satan, regarding him as the "accuser." (See Job i. 6; Zech. iii. 1, 2; and comp. Rev. xii. 10, where he is described as the "accuser of the brethren.")

Tried.—On the part of the adversary, the intention was that they might be *tempted* from their allegiance to Christ. The real effect would be that they who endured would come forth tested and approved. The suffering would be for "ten days." This is variously explained. Some think it applies to the periods of persecution; others understand it to mean a long persecution of ten years; others take it literally; others again view it as expressing completeness: the test would be thorough. The exhortation, "Be thou faithful (even) unto death," seems to favour this last; while the mention of "ten days" was, perhaps, designed to remind them that the period of trial was limited by Him who knew what they could bear, and would be but a little while when compared with the life with which they would be crowned.

A crown of life.—Rather, *the crown of life.* A crown was given to the priest who presided at the Dionysian Mysteries, which were celebrated with great pomp at Smyrna. A crown was also given at the Olympian Games, which were held at Smyrna. If there is any allusion to either of these, the latter would be the most natural. Some hold, however, the crown—though the word is *stephanos*, not *diadema*—is rather that of royalty than of victory. It is interesting to note that the narrative which tells of the death of Polycarp closes with words which it is difficult not to believe to be an allusion to this promise—"By his patience he over-

of life. (11) He that hath an ear, let
him hear what the Spirit saith unto
the churches; He that overcometh
shall not be hurt of the second death.
(12) And to the angel of
the church in Pergamos
write; These things saith
he which hath the sharp
sword with two edges;[a] (13) I know
thy works, and where thou dwellest,
even where Satan's seat *is*: and
thou holdest fast my name, and hast
not denied my faith, even in those
days wherein Antipas *was* my faithful
martyr, who was slain among you, where
Satan dwelleth. (14) But I have a few
things against thee, because thou hast
there them that hold the doctrine of
Balaam,[b] who taught Balac to cast a
stumblingblock before the children of
Israel, to eat things sacrificed unto
idols, and to commit fornication. (15) So
hast thou also them that hold the doc-
trine of the Nicolaitanes, which thing I
hate. (16) Repent; or else I will come
unto thee quickly, and will fight against

Chap. ii. 12—17. The Epistle to the Church in Pergamos.

b Num. 24. 14; 25. 1; and 31. 16.

a Isa. 11. 4; 49. 2; Eph. 6. 17.

came the unrighteous ruler, and received the crown of immortality" (*Smyrn. Ep.*).

(11) **He that overcometh** (or *conquereth*) **shall not be hurt.**—The words used are precise, and give certainty to the promise.

The second death.—This phrase is a new one in Bible language. It is said that Jews were familiar with it through its use in the Chaldee Paraphrase. It clearly points to a death which is other than that of the body; it stands in contrast with the crown of *life*. The expressions of chaps. xx. 14, and xxi. 8, exclude the idea that a cessation of conscious existence is intended. The life of the spirit is the knowledge of God (John xvii. 3); the death of the spirit, or the second death, is the decay or paralysis of the powers by which such a knowledge was possible, and the experience of the awfulness of a life which is "without God."

(12) **Pergamos.**—Unlike Ephesus and Smyrna, Pergamos was not distinguished as a commercial city. Its importance was due to other causes. A striking cone-shaped hill rose from the plain which bordered the northern banks of the Caicus. The hill was considered sacred. Its value as a strong natural fortress was early recognised, and it was used as a keep and treasury where local chieftains deposited their wealth. Its greatness as a city dated from Eumenes II., who was given by the Romans a large surrounding territory, and who fixed Pergamos as his royal residence. Under his auspices a splendid city—rich in public buildings, temples, art galleries, and with a library which rivalled that of Alexandria—rose into being. It has been described as a city of temples, "a sort of union of a pagan cathedral city, an university town, and a royal residence." It retained its splendour even after it passed by bequest to the Roman Republic, and was declared by Pliny to be a city unrivalled in the province of Asia.

Sharp sword with two edges.—See Note on chap. i. 16. The appropriateness of this language to the state of the church in Pergamos will best appear afterwards. (See Note on verses 15, 16.)

(13) **I know thy works.**—Here, as in verse 9, some MSS. omit "thy works," and read, "I know where thou dwellest—even where Satan's *seat* is." The word is translated elsewhere "throne," and should be here, "Where the throne of Satan is." But why should this pre-eminence in evil be assigned to Pergamos? The answer is difficult. Some leave it unsolved, saying that in the absence of any historical notice, it must remain one of the unsolved riddles of these epistles. Prof. Plumptre suggests that the general character of the city, its worship and customs, in addition to the persecutions which the Christians had encountered, may well account for the description. Æsculapius was worshipped as the "Preserver," or "Saviour." The symbol of the serpent must have been conspicuous among the objects of adoration in his temple. Curious arts were practised; lying wonders were claimed; persecution had extended to death. Such evil in such a city may have led to its being regarded as the very head-quarters of the enemy.

Hast not denied.—Better, *Thou didst not deny My faith in the days in which Antipas My faithful witness, was slain*, &c.

Antipas.—Short for Antipater. (Comp. Lucas and Silas, short for Lucanus and Silvanus.) Nothing is known of Antipas. There are later traditions respecting him, but these are probably fancy-drawn.

(14) **But I have a few things against thee.**—The word "few" is not to be taken as though the ground of rebuke was a trifling one. The little leaven might leaven the whole lump; and those who had been brave unto death in the days of persecution had been less temptation-proof against more seductive influences. The church tolerated without remonstrance men holding [the word is the same as that used in commendation (verse 13), "Thou holdest (fast) My name"] "the teaching of Balaam, who taught Balak to put a stumbling-block before the sons of Israel; (namely) to eat things sacrified to idols, and to commit fornication." Israel could not be cursed, but they might be made to bring a curse upon themselves by yielding to sin; so the counsel of Balaam was to tempt them through the women of Midian, and "Behold, these caused the children of Israel to commit trespass against the Lord in the matter of Peor, and there was a plague among the congregation of the Lord" (Num. xxxi. 16). A similar temptation was endangering the Pergamene Church.

(15) **So hast thou also them that hold the doctrine of the Nicolaitanes**—*i.e.*, thou, as well as those of old, hast such teachers. There is little doubt that this is the connection between the verses, but opinions are divided whether we are on this account to identify the Balaamites with the Nicolaitanes, and to suppose that both names point to the same sect. The simplest meaning of the passage seems to be that the temptation to which the Israelites were exposed, is used to illustrate the temptations of the Pergamene Church, through the teaching of the Nicolaitanes. Both temptations lead in the same Antinomian direction. Such a tendency was early seen (comp. Rom. vi. 4; Gal. v. 13; Jude 4), and is not extinct now. "Is there not," writes Dr. Vaughan, "a vague, unavowed, unrealised idea that the Atonement has made sin less fatal, that even sin indulged and persisted in, may yet not work

them with the sword of my mouth.
(17) He that hath an ear, let him hear what the Spirit saith unto the churches; To him that overcometh will I give to eat of the hidden manna, and will give him a white stone, and in the stone a new name written, which no man knoweth saving he that receiveth *it*.
(18) And unto the angel of the church in Thyatira write; These things saith the Son of God, who hath his eyes like unto a flame of fire, and his feet *are* like fine brass;
(19) I know thy works, and charity, and service, and faith, and thy patience,

Chap. ii. 18—29. The Epistle to the Church in Thyatira.

---

death?" To such and all who countenance them the warning is, "Repent; but if not, I am coming for thee, and will war with thee (note the change of person and number) with (literally, *in—i.e.*, armed with) the sword of My mouth."

(17) **To him that overcometh.**—The promise should run thus:—*To him that conquereth will I give of the hidden manna, and I will give him a white stone, and upon the stone a new name graven, which no man knoweth, but he who receiveth it.* On this promise we may notice (1) that it is appropriate: those who refused to indulge the fleshly appetite are promised gratifications far higher, and hidden from the gaze of sense; (2) the allusions are not all easy to understand. That to the *manna* is indeed obvious. Israel ate manna in the wilderness, and died; the Father gives the true bread from heaven that a man may eat thereof and not die. The Son is that Bread of Life. He that eateth Him, even he shall live by Him (John vi. 35, 48, 57)—live, even though like Antipas he die; for a man's life consists not in the abundance of things which he possesses, but in the moral qualities which go to make up his character; and spiritual gifts are the food of these moral qualities, and these gifts are through Christ. But the promise is of *hidden* manna. Is the allusion to the pot of manna which had been laid up in the ark? There is no doubt that the Jews long cherished the belief that the ark and sacred treasures of the Temple had not perished. There was a fondly-held tradition that they had been buried by Jeremiah in a safe and secret spot on "the mountain where Moses climbed and saw the heritage of God, until the time that God shall gather His people again together, and show them His mercy" (2 Macc. ii. 4, 7). This "hidden manna," so longed for by an afflicted race, may have suggested the use of the word "hidden"; but the sacred writer would become anxious to bring out the spiritual truth that the fountains of Christian life are hidden (Col. iii. 3), the world knoweth us not. Like the fire in the Interpreter's house, men may try to quench it, but a hidden hand pours in secretly the food of the fuel. More difficult is the meaning of the white stone, graven with the new name. Some see in it an allusion to the Urim and Thummim; and therefore take it to indicate the "priestly dignity of the victorious Christian." In favour of this, it may be noted that it gives unity to the blessing. Manna and the precious stones worn by the high-priest are both wilderness and Jewish illustrations. Against it, however, must be set the fact that the word here rendered "stone" is never so applied, a different word being used both in the LXX. and in this book to denote a precious stone. Another suggestion, which is, perhaps, less encumbered with difficulty, is that the reference is to the stone or pebble of friendship, called *tessera hospitalis*, graven with some legend or device; and which gave to its possessor a claim of hospitality from him who gave it. Some such tickets admitted those invited into the heathen temples on festival days, when the meat which had been offered as a sacrifice formed part of the feast. The stone is called *white;* but the word does not imply that it is a stone of white colour, but that it is shining, glistering white. On the stone is graven a new name. The giving of new names is not uncommon in the Bible: for example, Abraham, Israel, Boanerges, Peter. The new name expressed the step which had been taken into a higher, truer life, and the change of heart and the elevation of character consequent upon it. Such are known in the world by their daily life, their business, their character; they are known above by the place they hold, and the work (the real character of which is quite unknown to the world) they are doing in the great war against evil. No man knoweth the characteristics of the growth of the character, the spiritual conflict in which the work is done, and the features of that change which has been, and is being wrought, except he who experiences the love, the grace, and the tribulation by which his spirit-life has grown.

(18) **Thyatira** was situated between Pergamos and Sardis, a little off the main road which connected these two cities. It was a Macedonian colony, founded by Alexander the Great after the overthrow of the Persian empire. The Macedonian colonists appear to have introduced the worship of Apollo, honoured as the Sun-god, under the name of Tyrimnas. It has been thought by some that the description here given of Christ—"the eyes of flame"—was selected in allusion to this worship of the Sun-god, under the form of some dazzlingly ornamented image. Certainly close commercial intercourse connected the daughter colony with its mother city. There seem to have been various mercantile guilds in the colony—bakers, potters, tanners, weavers, and dyers. The dye-trade was, perhaps, the most important. Lydia, the seller of purple, was in all likelihood connected with the guild of dyers; and her appearance in Philippi is an illustration of the trade relations of Macedonia and Thyatira. To her the Christian community at Thyatira may have owed its beginning. "She who had gone forth for a while, to buy and sell, and get gain, when she returned home may have brought home with her richer merchandise than any she had looked to obtain" (Trench). The population was of a mixed character, and included, besides Asiatics, Macedonians, Italians, and Chaldeans. The message which is sent to the Christians dwelling among them is from "*the Son of God.*" This is noteworthy, when we remember how persistently the other term, "*Son of Man,*" is used throughout the Book of Revelation, and that here only is the phrase "Son of God" used; but it suits, as does the whole description, the message which breathes the language of sovereignty and righteous sternness. The "eyes of flame" will search the reins and the hearts (verse 23); the "feet of fine brass" will tread down the enemies, and smooth the path before them, who will have power over the nations.

(19) **Thy works, and charity.**—In the words of commendation we find two pairs. We have the

and thy works; and the last *to be* more
than the first. (20) Notwithstanding I
have a few things against thee, because
thou sufferest that woman Jezebel,[a]
which calleth herself a prophetess, to
teach and to seduce my servants to
commit fornication, and to eat things
sacrificed unto idols. (21) And I gave
her space to repent of her fornication;
and she repented not. (22) Behold, I
will cast her into a bed, and them that
commit adultery with her into great
tribulation, except they repent of their
deeds. (23) And I will kill her children
with death; and all the churches shall
know that I am he which searcheth
the reins and hearts:[b] and I will give
unto every one of you according to your
works. (24) But unto you I say, and
unto the rest in Thyatira, as many as
have not this doctrine, and which have
not known the depths of Satan, as they
speak; I will put upon you none other
burden. (25) But that which ye have
already hold fast till I come. (26) And
he that overcometh, and keepeth my
works unto the end, to him will I give
power over the nations: (27) and he shall
rule them with a rod of iron;[c] as the
vessels of a potter shall they be broken
to shivers: even as I received of my
Father. (28) And I will give him the

b Jer. 11. 20, and 17. 10.

a 1 Kings 16. 31; Rom. 2. 4; 2 Pet. iii. 9.

c ch. 22. 16; Num. 24. 17; Ps. 2. 9; Matt. 2. 2; Luke 1. 78.

Christian community commended for charity and service, the outward ministrations which manifest the inner principle of love; their *labour* of love, or their work and *love* (Heb. vi. 10) in general. In the second pair, faith and patience; the patience is the token of the faith (Rom. ii. 7; Heb. xi. 27).

And the last . . .—Read, *and thy last works more than the first.* Besides their faith and love, they are commended for their progress in good works—the last are more than the first.

(20) **A few things.**—The Sinaitic MS. has "I have much against thee;" but the reading, *I have against thee that thou lettest alone, &c.*, is to be preferred.

Jezebel.—Some adopt the reading, "thy wife Jezebel." From these words it has been thought that there was some personal influence at work for evil in Thyatira. Whether in the household of the "angel" or not is at least doubtful. The sin alleged against her is the same for which the Nicolaitanes are condemned—fornication, and the eating of things sacrificed to idols. If the above view be right, the leader of the exorcists is a woman—regarded by her followers as a prophetess, as one with a real message from God; but viewed by the Lord of the churches as a very Jezebel, teaching and seducing the servants of God. For letting her alone, for being timid, paying too much deference to her spiritual pretensions, for failing to see and to show that the so-called "deep things" of these teachers were depths of Satan, the chief minister is rebuked. A large number of respectable critics regard Jezebel as a name applied to a faction, not as belonging to an individual. It seems best to view the name as symbolical, always remembering that the Jezebel spirit of proud, self-constituted authority, vaunting claims of superior holiness, or higher knowledge, linked with a disregard of—and perhaps a proud contempt for—"legalism," and followed by open immorality, has again and again run riot in the churches of God.

(21) **And I gave her space.**—Read, *And I gave her time to repent, and she will not* (or, *is not willing to*) *repent of her fornication*, or, *to repent out of*—*i.e.*, so as to forsake her fornication. Here, as before, we are reminded that true repentance is a repentance whereby we forsake sin. (Comp. chaps. ii. 5 and iii. 2.)

(22) **I will cast her into a bed.**—The chamber of voluptuousness will become the chamber of sickness. The spot of the sin shall be the scene of punishment. (Comp. 1 Kings xxi. 19.)

(23) **Her children.**—This is to be understood of her followers. The so-called prophetess led the way in looseness of morals, under the pretence of some deeper knowledge. She had her associates and their disciples; the evil and the evil consequences would grow; the disciples outrun their teachers, and more than tribulation—death—is their penalty.

(24) **But unto you I say** (omit "and unto") **the rest,** &c.

The depths.—Or, *the deep things.* These teachers, as was the case with the Gnostics, professed to have a deeper insight into mysteries, the deep things of God. They may have garnished their speech with this very phrase, borrowed—in sound though not in sense—from 1 Cor. ii. 10, and may have even boasted of their knowledge of Satan. But such knowledge was purchased too dearly. Better off were they who were simple concerning evil; they have a burden, but it is not the burden of judicial tribulation: it is the burden only of resisting the evils of those troublers of the Church. The allusion may be to the decree of Acts xv. 28; the same word for "burden" is used. They must not abandon their duty of witnessing for purity, and so for Christ; this burden they must take up, and hold fast till He come.

(26, 27) **Power** (or, *authority*) **over the nations: and he shall rule them** (or, *shepherd them*) **with a rod of iron; as the vessels of a potter shall they be broken to shivers.**—The promise is of authority ("the might of right, not the right of might") to share in the shepherd-like sovereignty of the anointed King. (Comp. the Messianic prophecy of Ps. ii.) Those who refused to stoop to the customs around them, and to gain influence by crushing or ignoring their convictions—those who, like their Master, refused to win power by doing homage to wrong (Matt. iv. 8—10), would share the nobler sway which He now established. Wherever the Church has illegitimately grasped at power, she has lost it. "The wretched power which she had wrenched and stolen from the nations has been turned against her; she has been obliged to crouch to them, and beg their help, and they have justly spurned her. She has chosen to exalt herself like Lucifer, and she has fallen like Lucifer. If she had trusted her Lord, He would have given her the morning star. She would have derived from Him what she claimed independently of Him. She would have dispensed light to the world."

(28) **The morning star.**—The pledge of the coming day, both for the waiting witnesses, and for the ungodly.

morning star. (29) He that hath an ear, let him hear what the Spirit saith unto the churches.

CHAPTER III.—(1) And unto the angel of the church in Sardis write; These things saith he that hath the seven Spirits of God, and the seven stars; I know thy works, that thou hast a name that thou livest, and art dead. (2) Be watchful, and strengthen the things which remain, that are ready to die: for I have not found thy works perfect before God. (3) Remember therefore how thou hast received and heard, and hold fast, and repent. If therefore thou shalt not watch,[a] I will come on thee as a thief, and thou shalt not

Chap. iii. 1–6. The Epistle to the Church in Sardis.

A.D. 96.

[a] 1 Thess. 5. 2; 2 Pet. 3. 10.

who loved darkness because their deeds were evil: the earnest of the sovereignty of light over darkness, when the children of the day would be manifest, and shine as the stars for ever and ever (Dan. xii. 3).

III.

(1) **Sardis.**—The modern *Sart*—now a mere village of paltry huts—once the capital of the old Lydian monarchy, and associated with the names of Crœsus, Cyrus, and Alexander. It was the great *entrepôt* of dyed woollen fabrics, the sheep of "many-flocked" Phrygia supplying the raw material. The art of dyeing is said to have been invented here; and many-coloured carpets or mats found in the houses of the wealthy were manufactured here. The metal known as electrum, a kind of bronze, was the produce of Sardis; and in early times gold-dust was found in the sand of the Pactolus, the little stream which passed through the Agora of Sardis, and washed the walls of the Temple of Cybele. It is said that gold and silver coins were first minted at Sardis, and that resident merchants first became a class there. An earthquake laid it waste in the reign of Tiberius; a pestilence followed, but the city seems to have recovered its prosperity before the date of this epistle. The worship of Cybele was the prevailing one; its rites, like those of Dionysos and Aphrodite, encouraged impurity.

The writer is described in words similar to those in chap. i. 4, as the one who hath the seven spirits of God, and the seven stars; but there is a difference. There Christ was seen holding the stars in His right hand; here it is said He *hath* the seven Spirits and also the seven stars. In this language it is difficult to overlook the unhesitating way in which Christ is spoken of as owning or possessing that Holy Spirit who alone can make angels of His Church to shine as stars. The Holy Spirit is the Spirit of Christ (Rom. viii. 9, 11). His promise is, "I will send the Comforter unto you" (John xv. 26), as possessing all power in heaven and earth. "He is able," to use the language of Professor Plumptre, "to bring together the gifts of life, and the ministry for which those gifts are needed. If those who minister are without gifts; it is because they have not asked for them." This the angel of the Sardian Church had not done; his faith and the faith of the Church around him had sunk into a superficial, though perhaps ostentatious, state. Here, then, lies the appropriateness of the description given of Christ, as the source of life and light to His Church.

A name that thou livest.—It is only needful to mention, and to dismiss the fanciful conjecture, that the name of the angel was Zosimos, or some parallel name, signifying life-bearing or living. It is the reputation for piety possessed by the Church of Sardis which is referred to. Living with the credit of superior piety, it was easy to grow satisfied with the reputation, and to forget to keep open the channels through which grace and life could flow, and to fail to realise that the adoption of habits of life higher than those around them, or those who lived before them, was no guarantee of real spiritual life; for "the real virtues of one age become the spurious ones of the next . . . The belief of the Pharisees, the religious practice of the Pharisees, was an improvement upon the life of the sensual and idolatrous Jews whom the prophets denounced. But those who used both the doctrinal and moral improvements as the fulcrum of a selfish power and earthly rank, were the same men after all as their fathers, only accommodated to a new age" (Mozley). Self-satisfaction, which springs up when a certain reputation has been acquired, is the very road to self-deception. The remedy is progress—forgetting the things behind, lest looking with complacency upon the past, moral and spiritual stagnation should set in, and spiritual death should follow.

(2) **Be watchful.**—Rather, *become wakeful.* It will not do simply to rouse and sleepily grasp at their spiritual weapons, or even to stand for once at arms; you must become of wakeful habit. Strengthen the remaining things which were (when I roused you) about to die; for I have not found thy (or, *any of thy*) works perfect—completed or fulfilled, fully done in weight and tale and measure—before *my* God.

(3) **Remember therefore how** (or, *after what sort*) **thou hast received and heard** (or, *didst hear*—the tense changes).—Remembering that the words are addressed primarily to the angel himself, the change of tense may have been designed to point him back to some particular period of his life, such as the time when he was set apart to his ministerial work. The further expectation is to hold fast, or keep—*i.e.*, as an abiding habit. It has been noticed that this counsel is identical with that given to Timothy to "keep the good thing which had been committed to his charge" (2 Tim. i. 14; comp. also 2 Tim. ii. 2). "Repent" is the closing word; combined with the exhortation to hold fast, it reminds us that formal tenacity of truth and a fruitless inactive regret are alike useless. There must be the sorrow for the past, and a sorrow which shows itself in action—a repentance whereby sin is forsaken. (Comp. chap. ii. 5, 21.)

If therefore thou shalt not watch.—Better, *If thou shalt not watch* (or, *have been awake*), *I will come* (omit "on thee") *as a thief, and thou shalt not know what hour I will come upon thee.* The warning is an echo from the Gospels (Matt. xxiv. 42, 43; Luke xii. 39, 40). The coming of Christ to judge His Church would be in an hour unlooked for. What kind of hour He would so come was unknown; the sound of His approaching footsteps unheard. Shod with wool, according to the ancient proverb, stealthily as a thief, the Judge would be at the door. Yet they

know what hour I will come upon thee.
(4) Thou hast a few names even in Sardis which have not defiled their garments; and they shall walk with me in white: for they are worthy.
(5) He that overcometh, the same shall be clothed in white raiment; and I will not blot out his name out of the book of life,[a] but I will confess his name before my Father, and before his angels. (6) He that hath an ear, let him hear what the Spirit saith unto the churches.

Chap. iii. 7—13. The Epistle to the Church in Philadelphia.

(7) And to the angel of the church in Philadelphia write; These things saith

[a] ch. 13. 8; 20. 12; 21. 27; Phil. 4. 3.

---

could not plead that they had been in darkness (1 Thess. v. 4).

(4) The best MSS. commence this verse with "But," or "Nevertheless." The case of the Sardian Church was bad, yet the loving eyes of the faithful witness would not ignore the good. There were a few who had not defiled their garments. These had not succumbed to the oppressive moral atmosphere around them. The words cannot, of course, be understood of absolute purity. Their praise is that, in the deathlike, self-complacent lethargy around, they had kept earnest in the pursuit of holiness, and had not forgotten Him who could cleanse and revive. (Comp. chap. vii. 14.)

They shall walk with me in white.—This "white" is not the white of the undefiled robe; it is the lustrous white of glory, as in the promise in the following verse. (Comp. also chap. ii. 17.)

(5) **He that overcometh.**—The promise is repeated to all who overcome; all, not who have never fallen, or failed, but who conquer, shall be clothed in glistening white raiment. On this glistering appearance comp. Dante's words, "robed in hue of living flame," and the description so frequent in the *Pilgrim's Progress*—"the shining ones." Trench, who reminds us that this glistening white is found in the symbolism of heathen antiquity, says: "The glorified body, defecated of all its dregs and impurities, whatever remained of those having been *precipitated* in death, and now transformed and transfigured into the likeness of Christ's body (Phil. iii. 31), this, with its robe, atmosphere, and effluence of light, is itself, I believe, the white raiment which Christ here promises to His redeemed." Professor Lightfoot thinks (see his *Epistle to Col.* p. 22) that there may be a reference to the purple dyes for which Sardis, as well as Thyatira, was celebrated.

I will not blot out . . .—The negative is emphatic, "I will in no wise blot out." This figure of speech—a book and the blotting out—was ancient. (See Deut. xxxii. 32; Ps. lxix. 21; Dan. xii. 1; comp. also Luke x. 20; Phil. iv. 3.) The name shall not be erased from the roll or register of the citizens of heaven. "A process of erasure is ever going on, besides the process of entering. When the soul has finally taken its choice for evil, when Christ is utterly denied on earth and trodden under foot, when the defilement of sin has become inveterate and indelible, then the pen is drawn through the guilty name, then the inverted style smears the wax over the unworthy characters; and when the owner of that name applies afterwards for admittance, the answer is, 'I know thee not; depart hence, thou willing worker and lover of iniquity'" (Dr. Vaughan).

But I will confess his name.—Another echo of Christ's words on earth (Matt. x. 32, 33; Luke xii. 8, 9).

(7) **Philadelphia.**—The town of Philadelphia derived its name from Attalus Philadelphus, the king of Pergamos, who died B.C. 138. It was situated on the slopes of Mount Tmolus, in the midst of a district the soil of which was favourable to the cultivation of the vine. On the coins of the town are to be found the head of Bacchus. The town was built on high ground—upwards of 900 feet above the sea-level. The whole region, however, was volcanic, and few cities suffered more from earthquakes; the frequent recurrence of these considerably reduced the population. But its favourable situation and fertile soil preserved it from entire desertion. And of all the seven churches, it had the longest life as a Christian city. "Philadelphia alone has been saved . . . ; among the Greek colonies and churches of Asia, Philadelphia is still erect, a column in a scene of ruins." Such is the language of Gibbon, referring to its later history. As a light in the world at the present day, we must look to no Eastern Philadelphia; the hand of William Penn kindled a light in its great namesake of the West.

These things saith he that is holy . . . .—Better, *These things saith the Holy, the True, He that hath the key of David, that openeth, and no man shall shut, and He shutteth, and no one shall open.*

Holy.—The main idea of the word here used is that of consecration. It is used of what is set apart to God; it does not assert the possession of personal holiness, but it implies it as a duty. It becomes, therefore, pre-eminently appropriate to Him who was not only consecrate, but holy, harmless, undefiled, and separate from sinners. Prof. Plumptre thinks there may be a reference here to the confession made by St. Peter (John vi. 69), where the right reading is, "Thou art the Christ, the *holy One* of God."

True.—A favourite word with St. John, and expressing more than the opposite of "false." It implies that which is perfect in contrast with the imperfect; the reality in contrast with the shadow; the antitype in contrast with the type; the ideal which is the only real in contrast with the real which is only ideal;—

> "The flower upon the spiritual side,
> Substantial, archetypal, all aglow
> With blossoming causes"

in contrast with the flower that fadeth here. Christ, then, in calling Himself the True, declares that "all titles and names given to Him are realised in Him; the idea and the fact in Him are, what they can never be in any other, absolutely commensurate" (Trench). In some MSS. the order of these words, "the Holy," "the True," is inverted.

The key of David.—Some early commentators saw in this key the key of knowledge which the scribes had taken away (Luke xi. 52), and understood this expression here as implying that Christ alone could unloose the seals of Scripture, and reveal its hidden truth to men. In support of this they referred to chap. v. 7—9. The fault of the interpretation is that it is too limited; it is only a corner of the full meaning. He who is "the True" alone can unlock the hidden treasures of truth. But the use of the word "David," and the

he that is holy, he that is true, he that hath the key of David, he that openeth, and no man shutteth; and shutteth, and no man openeth;
(8) I know thy works: behold, I have set before thee an open door, and no man can shut it: for thou hast a little strength, and hast kept my word, and hast not denied my name.
(9) Behold, I will make them of the synagogue of Satan, which say they are Jews, and are not, but do lie; behold, I will make them to come and worship before thy feet, and to know that I have loved thee.
(10) Because thou hast kept the word of my patience, I also will keep thee from the hour of temptation, which shall come upon all the world, to try them that dwell upon the earth.
(11) Behold, I come quickly: hold that fast which thou hast, that no man take thy crown.
(12) Him that overcometh will I make a pillar in the temple of my God, and he shall go no more out: and I will write upon him the name of

---

obvious derivation of the latter part of this verse from Isa. xxii. 22, points to a wider meaning. Jesus Christ is the true Steward of the house of David. (Comp. Heb. iii. 2, 5, 6.) The faulty, self-seeking stewards, the Shebnas of Jerusalem and Philadelphia, vainly claimed a right of exclusion from synagogue or church, where Jesus, the God-fixed nail in the sure place, upon which the bundle of earth's sorrows and sins might securely be suspended (Isa. xxii. 23—25), the Eliakim of a greater Zion, had the key of the sacred and royal house. In this, the chamber of truth was one treasure, as the chamber of holiness, the chamber of rest, the chamber of spiritual privileges, were others. In other words, though in a sense the keys of spiritual advantages are in the hands of His servants, "He still retains the highest administration of them in His own hands." The power of the keys entrusted to Apostles gave them no right to alter the "essentials of the gospel, or the fundamental principles of morality." The absolution given by them can only be conditional, unless the giver of it possesses the infallible discerning of spirits. The reader of Dante will remember how the cases of Guido di Montefeltro (*Inf.* xxvii.) and of his son Buonconte (*Purg.* v.) illustrate the belief which sustained so many illustrious spirits (John Huss, Savanarola, Dante), and in times of unjust oppression, tyrannical ecclesiasticism, and which this passage sanctions, that

> "Nought but repentance ever can absolve;
> And that though sins be horrible; yet so wide arms
> Hath goodness infinite, that it receives
> All who turn to it."

(8) **I know thy works: behold, I have set** (better, *given*) **before thee an open door** (better, *a door opened*).—A reference to the passages (Acts xiv. 27; 1 Cor. xvi. 8, 9; 2 Cor. ii. 12, 13; Col. iv. 3) in which a similar expression is used reminds us that the open door was not simply a way of escape from difficulties, but an opening for preaching the gospel, an opportunity of doing good, as well as an abundant entrance into the kingdom.

For thou hast a little strength, and hast kept my word, and hast not denied my name.—The tenses used point back to some epoch in the history of this Church when some heavy trial or persecution arose, which tested the sincerity, fidelity, or Christian love of the faithful. "The reward then of a little strength is a door opened" (Dr. Vaughan).

(9) **Behold, I will make.**—Better, *Behold, I give some.* There is no word to express this in the original, but as a word must be supplied to complete the sense, it is better to adopt "some" than the "them" of the Authorised version, as it is not a promise that all of the synagogue of Satan should come.

Of the synagogue of Satan.—We have here a re-appearance of the same troubles which afflicted the Church of Smyrna: the fixed and contemptuous exclusiveness of the Judaising party was their trial. But there was a time coming (perhaps the hour of temptation spoken of in the next verse) when these faithful ones, now abused and excommunicated by the fanatical synagogue, would be courted, acknowledged—nay, their aid invoked.

I will make them to come and worship before my feet, and to know that I have loved thee.—Some see in this a hint that the power of a large-hearted party to protect the Judaisers would be derived from the influence of the Gentiles, whose presence in the Church had been a stumbling-block to the Jewish party. This may have been, and doubtless was, often the case. But the promise seems to have a higher fulfilment. The course of events would show that the so-called latitudinarian was the nearest to Christ; time would transform the suspected into the respected. The Amorites would come, and the disinherited Jephthahs would be brought to be head of Gilead. In days of such trouble their strongest opponents would become their warmest supporters. An illustration of this will occur to the mind of the reader in the marvellous support which has been given to the growth of Christianity by Jews with the tongue, with the pen, with the harp and organ. Let the names of Neander, Rossini, and Mendelssohn stand for hundreds more.

(10) **Because thou hast kept** (better, *didst keep*) **the word of my patience.**—The one who keeps God's word is kept. Such is "the *benigna talio* of the kingdom of God," as Archbishop Trench calls it. The promise does not mean the being kept away from, but the being kept out from the tribulation. The head should be kept above the waters; they should not be ashamed, because they had kept the word of patience. It is through *patience*, as well as comfort of the Scripture that we have the hope which maketh not ashamed. (Comp. Rom. xv. 5, and verses 3—5.)

(11) **Behold, I come.**—Omit "Behold." Better, *I am coming quickly; hold fast; continue your race as those who are striving for a garland* (1 Cor. ix. 24).

(12) **Will I make a pillar.**—A pillar, and an unshaken one. There may be reference to the frequent earthquakes which had shaken down buildings in their city. Those who overcome will prove real supports to the great Christian temple. (Comp. Gal. ii. 9.)

Write upon him.—Or, *grave upon it.* On the sides of the four marble pillars which survive as ruins of Philadelphia inscriptions are to be found. The writing would be the name of God, the name of the heavenly Jerusalem and (omit the repetition, "I will write upon my God, and the name of the city of my God, *which is* new Jerusalem, which cometh down out of heaven from my God: and *I will write upon him* my new name. (13) He that hath an ear, let him hear what the Spirit saith unto the churches. (14) And unto the angel of the church of the Laodiceans[1] write; These things saith the Amen, the faithful and true witness, the beginning of the creation of God; (15) I know thy works, that thou art neither cold nor hot: I would thou wert cold or hot. (16) So then because thou art lukewarm,

Chap. iii. 14—22. The Epistle to the Laodiceans.

[1] Or, *in Laodicea.*

---

him") the new, unknown name of Christ Himself. The allusion is to the golden frontlet inscribed with the name of Jehovah. (Comp. chap. xxii. 4.) He will reflect the likeness of God; and not only so, he will bear the tokens—now seen in all clearness—of his heavenly citizenship (Phil. iii. 20; Heb. xii. 22, 23). And a further promise implies that in the day of the last triumph, as there will be new revealings of Christ's power, there will be unfolded to the faithful and victorious new and higher possibilities of purity. Thus does Scripture refuse to recognise any finality which is not a beginning as well as an end—a landing-stage in the great law of continuity. (See chaps. ii. 17, and xix. 12.)

(14) **Laodicea.**—Situated half way between Philadelphia and Colossæ, and not far from Hierapolis. It received its name from Laodice, wife of Antiochus the second king of Syria, by whom it was rebuilt and beautified. It had borne in earlier times the names of Diospolis and afterwards Rhoas. It shared with Thyatira and Sardis in the dye trade; the woods grown in the neighbourhood were famous for their quality and the rich blackness of their colour. Prosperity in trade had so enriched the population that when their city suffered in the great earthquake (A.D. 60) they were able to carry on the work of rebuilding without applying, as many of the neighbouring towns were compelled to do, to the Imperial Treasury for aid. The language of St. Paul (Col. i. 5—8) suggests that the churches of Colossæ and the neighbourhood first received Christianity from the preaching of Epaphras, though it seems strange that so important a city, lying hard upon the great Roman road from Ephesus to the east, should have been passed over by St. Paul in his journeyings throughout Phrygia (see Acts xvi. 6 and xviii. 23); yet, on the other hand, Phrygia was a vague term, and the language of Col. ii. 1 is most generally understood to imply that the Apostle had never personally visited either Colossæ or Laodicea. (See Note on Col. ii. 1.) But it was a Church in which St. Paul took the deepest possible interest; the believers there were constantly in his mind. He knew their special temptations to the worship of inferior mediators, and to spiritual paralysis springing from wordly prosperity and intellectual pride. He had great heart-conflict for those of Laodicea (Col. iii. 1), and in proof of his earnest solicitude he addressed a letter to them (Col. iv. 61), in all probability the epistle we call the Epistle to the Ephesians. From the Epistle to the Colossians we may gather that when St. Paul wrote the Christians at Laodicea assembled for worship in the house of Nymphas (Col. iv. 15) probably under the presidency of Archippus (verse 17).

Unto the angel of the church (or, *congregation*) **of the Laodiceans.**—Better, *in Laodicea.* By the angel we understand the presiding pastor. There is some ground for identifying him with Archippus. It is too much to dismiss this as a baseless supposition. (See Note in Trench.) It is a well-supported view which understands the passage (Col. iv. 17) to mean that Archippus was a minister or office-bearer in the Church at Laodicea.

These things saith the Amen, the faithful and true witness.—The "Amen," used only here as a personal name. It is the Hebrew word for verily, and may have some reference to Isa. lxv. 16; but more certainly it seems chosen to recall the frequent use of it by our Lord Himself. He who so often prefaced His solemn utterance by "Verily, verily," now reveals Himself as the source of all certainty and truth. In Him is Yea, and in Him Amen (2 Cor. i. 20). In Him there is no conjecture, or guess-work; for He is (and the Greek equivalents of the Hebrew Amen are used following) the faithful and true witness, who speaks what He *knows*, and testifies what He has *seen* (John iii. 11). "Faithful" is to be taken here as meaning trustworthy. The word sometimes means trustful (John xx. 27; Acts xiv. 1), at other times, trustworthy (2 Tim. ii. 22; 1 Thess. v. 24). In the Arian controversy, the application of the word to Christ was used as an argument against His divinity; it was enough to show in reply that the same word was applied to God, and expressed His faithfulness to His word and promise (1 Thess. v. 24). "True"—He is not only trustworthy as a witness, but He combines in Himself all those qualifications which a witness ought to possess. The same word is used here as in verse 7, where see Note. Trench suggests the three things necessary to constitute a true witness. He must have been an eye-witness of what He relates, possess competence to relate what He has seen, and be willing to do so.

The beginning (better, *the origination*) **of the creation of God.**—This title of our Lord does not occur in the Epistles to the other churches, but very closely resembles the language used by St. Paul in writing to the Colossians (chap. i. 15—18). The "beginning," not meaning that Christ was the first among the created, but that He was the origination, or *primary source* of all creation. By Him were all things made (John i. 1—3: comp. Col. i. 15, 18), not *with* Him, but *by* Him creation began. In short, the word "beginning" (like the word "faithful") must be understood in an active sense. He has originating power (Acts iii. 14) as well as priority of existence. The appropriateness of its use will be seen when we remember that the Laodicean Church was exposed to the temptation of worshipping inferior principalities. (See Col. i. 16; ii. 15, where the plural of the word here rendered "beginning," or *origin*, is used, and is translated "principalities.")

(15, 16) **Neither cold nor hot.**—The "heat" here is the glowing, fervent zeal and devotion which is commended and commanded elsewhere (Rom. xii. 11). It is not, however, the self-conscious, galvanised earnestness which, in days of senile pietism, passes for zeal. It is an earnestness which does not know itself earnest, being all too absorbed in its work. It is self-forgetful, and so self-sacrificing, rather than ambitious of self-sacrifice. It is, in short, kindled of God, and sustained by

and neither cold nor hot, I will spue
thee out of my mouth. (17) Because
thou sayest, I am rich, and increased
with goods, and have need of nothing;
and knowest not that thou art wretched,
and miserable, and poor, and blind, and
naked: (18) I counsel thee to buy of me
gold tried in the fire, that thou mayest
be rich; and white raiment, that thou
mayest be clothed, and *that* the shame
of thy nakedness do not appear; and
anoint thine eyes with eyesalve, that
thou mayest see. (19) As many as I
love, I rebuke and chasten:[a] be zealous

a Prov. 3. 11: Heb. 12. 5.

converse with the Divine One (Luke xxiv. 32), and restored by intercourse with Him (see verse 20; comp. 1 John iv. 15—20). The "cold" describes the state of those who are as yet untouched by the Gospel of Love. An intermediate state between these is the "lukewarm"; such are neither earnest for God nor utterly indifferent to religion. They are, perhaps, best described as those who take an interest in religion, but whose worship of their idol of good taste, or good form, leads them to regard enthusiasm as ill-bred, and disturbing; and who have never put themselves to any inconvenience, braved any reproach, or abandoned any comfort for Christ's sake, but hoped to keep well with the world, while they flattered themselves that they stood well with God; who were in danger of betraying their Master, Judas-like, with a kiss. With the denunciation of "lukewarmness" here we may compare the exhortation to greater ministerial earnestness addressed to Archippus (Col. iv. 17).

I would . . . .—The wish is not that they might grow cold rather than remain in this lukewarm state, it is more a regret that they are among those who are in a condition which is so liable to self-deception; such a state is "both to God displeasing and to His foes." And this is expressed in startling language, "I *am about* (such is the force of the words) to spue thee . . . ."

(17) **I am rich.**—The verse means, more literally, *Because thou sayest, I am rich, and have grown rich, and in nothing have need, and knowest not that thou art the wretched* (such is the emphasis) *one, and the pitiable one, and beggarly, and blind, and naked.* Thou art "the type, the embodiment of wretchedness." The words should, I think, be taken as an amplification of the reason for their rejection. Christ was about to reject them for being in that tepid state which, beginning with self-satisfaction, led on to self-deception. They were rich in worldly goods (unlike the Church in Smyrna), but their very wealth led them into a quiet unaggressive kind of religion; they were proud also of their intellectual wealth; self-complacent because in comfortable worldly circumstances, and became puffed up with a vain philosophy, they learned to be satisfied with their spiritual state, and to believe the best of themselves, and then to believe in themselves. Hypocrites they were, who did not know they were hypocrites. They thought themselves good; and this self-deception was their danger. "For," to use Prof. Mozley's words, "why should a man repent of his goodness? He may well repent, indeed, of his falsehood; but unhappily the falsehood of it is just the thing he does not see, and which he cannot see by the very law of his character. The Pharisee did not know he *was* a Pharisee. If he had known it, he would not have been a Pharisee. The victim of passion, then, may be converted—the gay, the thoughtless, or the ambitious; he whom human glory has intoxicated; he whom the show of life has ensnared; he whom the pleasures of sense have captivated—they may be converted any one of these; but who is to convert the hypocrite? He does not know he is a hypocrite; he cannot upon the very basis of his character; he must think himself sincere; and the more he is in the shackles of his own character, *i.e.*, the greater hypocrite he is, the more sincere he must think himself" (*University Sermons*, p. 34).

(18) **I counsel thee to buy.**—There is, perhaps, a touch of irony here. How could the poor and naked buy? But the irony has no sting, for the counsel but recalled the invitation of the prophet to buy "without money and without price" (Isa. lv. 1).

Gold—*i.e.*, golden coin, "tried," or, *fired out of fire*, and so free from alloy or dross. Trench suggests that "gold" here stands for *faith.* Does not, however, the self-deceiving state of this Church rather point to love as the missing grace? The Laodiceans were as those who had many graces in appearance; they were not unlike one who had gifts, tongues, understanding, liberality, but lacked that fervent love without which all was as nothing (1 Cor. xiii. 1—3); or, to use Trench's own image, they were lacking in the only grace accepted as currency in the kingdom of God.

> "O merchantman at heaven's mart for heavenly ware,
> Love is the only coin which passes there."

But the possession of this love would bring their zeal out of the tepid into the fervent state. Such love, pure and fervent, could only spring from God, who would shed abroad His love in their hearts (Rom. v. 5).

White raiment.—The putting on of apparel and the stripping of it off were tokens of honour and humiliation. (See 2 Sam. x. 1; Isa. lxvii. 2, 3; Hos. ii. 3, 9; Zech. iii. 3—5; Rev. xvi. 15; Luke xv. 22.) The wedding-feast was at hand. The unclad would then be put to shame (Matt. xxii. 11—13). Let them be prepared against this by putting on Christ (Col. iii. 10—14) and His righteousness (Phil. iii. 9), that the shame of their nakedness do not appear—or, much better, *be not made manifest.*

Eyesalve.—They were blind; they were proud of their intellectual wealth; they boasted of their enlightenment. (Comp. Col. ii. 8.) Self-deceived, they thought, like the Pharisees, that they saw. (Comp. John ix. 40, 41.) Better would it be for them that they should receive the anointing of the Holy One (1 John ii. 20), which would teach them all things, and especially reveal to them their self-ignorance. This anointing might be painful, but "the eyes of their understanding would be enlightened" (such is the remarkably parallel thought in the Epistle to the Ephesians), and they would be enabled to see and appreciate things spiritual. (Comp. John ix. 7, 25; 1 Cor. ii. 10—14; Eph. i. 18; v. 19.)

(19) **I rebuke and chasten.**—The first word is that used in the work of the Holy Spirit (John xvi. 8), and signifies to bring conviction; it is not empty censure. The second word signifies to educate by means of correction. The pronoun is emphatic, "I," and calls attention to the fidelity of Christ's love in comparison with the weak partiality seen in human love. (Comp. Heb. xii. 6.)

therefore, and repent. (20) Behold, I
stand at the door, and knock: if any
man hear my voice, and open the door,
I will come in to him, and will sup with
him, and he with me. (21) To him that
overcometh will I grant to sit with me
in my throne, even as I also overcame, and
am set down with my Father in his throne.
(22) He that hath an ear, let him hear
what the Spirit saith unto the churches.

A.D. 96.

CHAPTER IV.—(1) After this I
looked, and, behold, a door
was opened in heaven: and
the first voice which I heard
was as it were of a trumpet
talking with me; which said, Come up
hither, and I will shew thee things which
must be hereafter. (2) And immediately I
was in the spirit: and, behold, a throne
was set in heaven, and *one* sat on the

Chap. iv. 1—11. The vision of the throne of God in heaven.

Be zealous.—Or, be in a constant zealous state; and now, once for all, repent.

(20) **Behold, I stand at the door, and knock.**—It is difficult not to see an allusion in this image to Cant. v. 2—6. Perhaps, also, the memory of the first night spent by St. John with his Master and Friend (John i. 39) may have been strong in his mind. Indeed, the life of Christ on earth teems with illustrations which may well have suggested the image (Luke x. 38; xix. 5, 6; xxii. 11—13; xxiv. 29, 30).

(21) **To him that overcometh . . . .**—He will share Christ's throne as Christ shared His Father's throne. Here are two thrones mentioned. My throne, saith Christ: this is the condition of glorified saints who sit with Christ in His throne. "But My Father's (*i.e.*, God's) throne is the power of divine majesty." Herein none may sit but God, and the God-man Jesus Christ. The promise of sharing the throne is the climax of an ascending series of glorious promises, which carry the thought from the Garden of Eden (chap. ii. 7) through the wilderness (chap. ii. 17), the temple (chap. iii. 12), to the throne. The promise bears marked resemblance to the language of St. Paul to the Ephesians (chap. ii. 6). This crowning promise is made to the most unpleasing of the churches. But it is well that thus the despondency which often succeeds the sudden collapse of self-satisfied imaginations should be met by so bright a prospect. Though their religion has been proved an empty thing, there is a hope which may well drive away despair. "The highest place is within the reach of the lowest; the faintest spark of grace may be fanned into the mightiest flame of divine love."

IV.

In this chapter we pass from the sufferings and temptations of the churches below to the unsullied glory above. The vision of the Almighty here described is thought to be interposed here to remind us that all decrees respecting the future "rest with God, and come from Him through Jesus Christ." This is no doubt true; but there is another reason. From the world below, and the struggling churches, we are brought to see the Eternal who is ruling over all. A vision like this must dwarf our sense of life's sorrows and temptations, and is a fit preparation for the scenes of conflict, failure, and persecution, which are about to be unfolded. Whatever painful sights the seer is called upon to behold, this vision of Him who rules "over all from the beginning" will remain in the background as the constant witness that in all the changes and chances of this mortal life, in all the vicissitudes of the Church's history, God is her refuge; therefore she will not be moved though the earth be removed. It is the vision of eternal strength so often vouchsafed to the sad. As to Ezekiel "among the captives by the river of Chebar" (Ezek. i. 1), and to Isaiah mourning over the gloom which was settling on Judah (Isa. vi. 1); so now to the exile in Patmos, and through him to all who, in their life-conflict, need "everlasting consolation and good hope." "You see how distress and solitude and sorrow favour communications between a man and his God."

(1) **After this** (better, *these things*) **I looked** (literally, *I saw*; not "I looked," as though the prophet turned his gaze then towards it), **and, behold a door was opened** (or, *set open*) **in heaven.**—He did not look and see a door opening; he saw, and lo! the door stood open. There are differences as well as similarities between this vision and others where glimpses into heaven were given to prophets and saints. In Ezekiel's vision, and in the scene of Matt. iii. 16 (comp. also Acts vii. 56, and x. 11) the heavens divide; in this a door stands open. The way into the presence of God lies open (Heb. x. 19, 20); all who have faith may enter; in the minds of such the thoughts of the heavenly will mingle with the sorrows of the earthly, and the calm of security will be theirs (Ps. xlvi. 5). But the scenes of earth's troubles will always be dispiriting to those who cannot reach the heavenly view-point.

And the first voice (or, *behold, the first voice*) **which I heard was as it were of a trumpet talking with me;** (even one) **which said, Come up hither, and I will shew thee** (*the*) **things which must be hereafter.**—The *first* voice here spoken of is the voice which the Apostle had heard in the opening vision (chap. i. 10); he heard, and recognised that trumpet-like voice again. It is strange that any should have maintained that this is not the voice of Christ. It is admitted that it must be the same as the voice of chap. i. 10; but it is said that the voice of Christ is heard afterwards (chap. i. 15), not as a trumpet, but as the voice of many waters. The answer is simple; the voice of Christ has many tones; and the voice like a trumpet said, "I am Alpha and Omega, the first and the last." (See chap. i. 10—13.)

(2) **And immediately I was in the spirit.**—Comp. chap. i. 10. The mind and soul were absorbed in the vision of things celestial. (See 2 Cor. xii. 1—4.)

> "Words may not tell of that transhuman change;
> . . . .
> If I were only what Thou didst create,
> Then newly, Love! by whom the heaven is ruled,
> Thou know'st, who by Thy light didst bear me up."
> —*Paradiso*, i. 68—73.

And, behold, a throne was set (*i.e.*, not that the seer saw the throne being set, but when he saw it was already set) **in heaven, and one sat on the throne.**—Comp. Micaiah's speech (1 Kings xxii. 19). The enthroned One is not named. Have we here a touch of the Jewish reluctance to name Jehovah? or is it that the descriptive phrase, "He that sat on the throne" is used here, and kept before us in the whole book to remind us that the great world drama moves

throne. (3) And he that sat was to look upon like a jasper and a sardine stone: and *there was* a rainbow round about the throne, in sight like unto an emerald. (4) And round about the throne *were* four and twenty seats: and upon the seats I saw four and twenty elders sitting, clothed in white raiment; and they had on their heads crowns of gold. (5) And out of the throne proceeded lightnings and thunderings and voices: and *there were* seven lamps of fire burning before the throne, which are the seven Spirits of God. (6) And before the throne *there was* a sea of glass like unto crystal: and in the midst of the throne, and round about the throne, *were* four beasts full of eyes

---

forward ever under the eyes of the ruling One. (Comp. chaps. v. 1, 7; vi. 15; xx. 11; xxi. 5.)

(3) **And he that sat was to look upon like a jasper and a sardine stone.**—In determining the significance of these emblems we must be guided partly by the analogy of Bible imagery elsewhere, and partly by our knowledge of precious stones. The sardian, or sardine, is admitted to be a stone of fiery-red colour; the emerald, to which the bow round the throne is compared, is almost certainly a bright green; the hue of the jasper is the difficulty. The jasper—the last stone in the high-priest's breastplate, and first of the twelve foundations of the New Jerusalem (Ex. xxviii. 20, and Rev. xxi. 19)—is described by the best authorities as a dark, opaque green. Such a colour is quite in harmony with the colours of the other stones in the breastplate, and particularly with the foundation stones, which seem to be arranged in shades of colour (see Notes on chap. xxi. 19 *et seq.*); but the dark opaque green would be an ill combination with the red sardius and the green emerald in the vision of the present chapter. Is there no further light? We have a jasper stone spoken of in chap. xxi. 11, 18, with the descriptive phrase, "clear as crystal!" Does not this point to a stone somewhat different in appearance from that spoken of simply as jasper? Such a clear crystal stone would be the most natural companion to the sardine, and the combination of the sparkling brightness and fiery red suits the union of brightness and flame which appears elsewhere in the Bible (comp. chaps. i. 14; xi. 1; Ezek. i. 4; viii. 2; Dan. vii. 9), and is best understood of the holiness and righteousness of God. The latter half of this verse shows us these surrounded by the emerald-coloured bow, the evident symbol of the divine mercy. The allusion to the bow in the cloud (Gen. ix. 12—16) is obvious; the bow completely encircled the throne, as mercy encompassing judgment. It was a covenant token, bearing witness to God's faithfulness in dark times, God's care for the ark of His Church, and His mercy shining forth after storm.

(4) **And round about the throne were four and twenty seats** (or, *thrones*), **and upon the seats** (or, *thrones*) **I saw four and twenty elders sitting, clothed in white raiment; and they had on their heads crowns of gold.**—Perhaps the wish to give its due pre-eminence to the thought of Him who sat on the throne caused our translators to describe the elders as sitting on seats; but the same word *throne* is used of both, and those who are now seated on thrones are called (chap. v. 10) kings and priests. In the similar vision in Ezekiel no human beings are seen; their appearance here is significant. They are the representatives of Christ's Church and people, of those whom Christ calls His friends, and who are admitted to know what their Lord doeth (John xv. 15). Various reasons have been suggested why they should be described as twenty-four in number; they are the twelve tribes doubled, to signify the union of the Gentile with the Jewish Church; they are the two sets of twelve, to represent the two Testaments; they are the twelve Patriarchs cojoined with the twelve Apostles. It will be seen that these were all different forms of the same thought, that the twenty-four elders represent the complete Church of God in the past and in the future, in the Jewish and Gentile worlds; and as such the true spiritual successors, as priests to God, of those twenty-four courses (1 Chron. xxiv. 1—19) arranged by David, and which some have thought gave rise to the use of the number twenty-four in this passage. It is the great united Church. The same thought is touched upon in the double song of Moses and the Lamb (chap. xv. 3), and in the gates and foundations of the New Jerusalem (chap. xxi. 12, 14).

(5) **And out of the throne proceeded** (rather, *proceed;* there is a change in the tense used) **lightnings and thunderings and voices.**—These are viewed by some as the indications of approaching judgments. Perhaps it is better to view them as the tokens of God's power of judgment than as hints of immediately approaching judgments. The scene at Sinai (Ex. xix. 16) was no doubt in the prophet's mind. There the clouds and lightnings were not so much tokens of coming judgment as the symbols of that righteous power which can show itself in judgment. "Clouds and darkness are round about Him; righteousness and judgment are the habitation of His throne" (Ps. xcvii. 2). They are the constant tokens of that power of God

> "Which makes the darkness and the light,
> And dwells not in the light alone,
> But in the darkness and the cloud
> As over Sinai's peaks of old."

And there were seven lamps (or, *torches*) **of fire burning before the throne, which are the seven Spirits of God.**—See chap. iii. 1. The Spirit of God in His manifold powers is thus described under emblems of fire. Not merely as a fire of judgment. The baptism of the Holy Spirit is a baptism of fire (Matt. iii. 11, 12). The flaming presence purges the spirit from sin. The Holy Spirit consumes evil. It is an unquenchable fire against all evils, whether in men's hearts or in men's lives, or in the world. (Comp. 1 Cor. iii. 13, and Heb. xii. 29.) May there not be allusion to the covenant with Abraham, which was ratified by fire? Lamps, or torches, of fire (*lampades puros*, LXX., same as in this passage) went between the divided pieces of the heifer and the she-goat. If this be correct, the vision of this chapter reminds us that God is ever mindful of His covenant. The rainbow, the token of the covenant with Noah; the flaming torches, tokens of the covenant with Abraham; and the thunderings and lightnings, the tokens of the covenant at Sinai, are ever with Him. (Comp. also Ezek. i. 4.)

(6) **And before the throne there was a sea of glass like unto crystal.**—There is a sea before the throne of God. The woman apparelled in purple splendour sits upon many waters (chap. xvii. 1). The

before and behind. (7) And the first
beast *was* like a lion, and the second
beast like a calf, and the third beast
had a face as a man, and the fourth
beast *was* like a flying eagle. (8) And
the four beasts had each of them six
wings about *him*; and *they were* full of
eyes within: and they rest not[1] day
and night, saying, Holy,[a] holy, holy,
Lord God Almighty, which was, and is,
and is to come. (9) And when those
beasts give glory and honour and thanks
to him that sat on the throne, who
liveth for ever and ever, (10) the four
and twenty elders fall down before him
that sat on the throne, and worship him
that liveth for ever and ever, and cast
their crowns before the throne, saying,

1 Gr. *they have no rest.*

a ch. i. 4. 8; Isa. 6. 3.

---

waters are explained (chap. xvii. 15) to be "peoples, and multitudes, and nations, and tongues." Her throne rests on the fickle and stormy sea of world-opinion, fashion, and passion. The waters represent the unguided, unreasoning, and unprincipled thoughts of men. By analogy, the calm glass-like sea, which is never in storm, but only interfused with flame (chap. xv. 2), represents the counsels of God, those purposes of righteousness and love, often fathomless, but never obscure; always the same, though sometimes glowing with holy anger (chap. xv. 1). (Comp. the Psalmist's words, "Thy judgments are like the great deep," Ps. xxxvi. 6, Prayer Book version. See also Ps. lxxvii. 19, and Rom. xi. 33—36.) The position of the crystal sea is analogous to that of the molten sea in front of Solomon's Temple (2 Chron. iv. 9, 10).

And in the midst of the throne—*i.e.*, between the seer and the throne. The Apostle saw the crystal sea, and beyond it the living creatures encircling the throne—four living creatures (or, *living beings*) full of (or, *teeming with*) eyes before and behind.

(7) **And the first beast** (better, in each case, *living being*) **was like a lion, and the second beast like a calf** (comp. Ezek. i. 7, 10), **and the third beast had a face as a man** (or, *its countenance as of a man*), **and the fourth beast was like a flying eagle.**—These are *living beings*, not "beasts," as in the Authorised version. The rendering "beasts" introduces confusion of thought, and violates the laws of Apocalyptic, indeed of Bible imagery. The evil powers are described under the emblem of wild beasts; for thus brute force, and unrestrained passion, and self-will, &c., are symbolised. (See chaps. xi. 7; xiii. 1, 2; xvi. 2; xvii. 3, 7; xix. 19, 20; xx. 10.) But these "living beings" do not represent the evil element in the world. They are representative of animated nature. They are four in number—as there are four beings which hold a primacy in the world: among created beings, man; among birds, the eagle; among cattle, the ox; among untamed animals, the lion. The characteristics of these four chiefs of creation unite to make a perfect picture of the spirit of true service, which should be brave as the lion, patient as the ox, aspiring as the eagle, intelligent as man. It may here be noted that the number "four" in the Apocalypse is almost always associated with the earth. (See chap. vii. 1.) We need only call to mind the four quarters, four elements, four seasons, to see its fitness. (Comp. chap. xxi. 13, 16.) The living creatures are "full of eyes." This strong expression is used again in the next verse. Twice used, its meaning must be significant. The same idea is found in the later prophets of the Old Testament. The wheels of Ezekiel and their tires (Ezek. i. 18, and x. 12) were full of eyes. The stone of Zechariah had seven (the perfect number) eyes (Zech. iii. 9). The thought is emphasised again in chap. v. 6, where the Lamb is said to have seven eyes. Multiplicity of eyes may symbolise vitality and vigilance. Some have thought, inappropriately enough, that it signifies the unceasing praise of God's works. A better interpretation is given by Dr. Currey. "The power of nature is no blind force, it is employed in the service of God's providence, and all over it the stamp of reason is impressed." (See Speaker's *Commentary* on Ezek. i. 18). May we not add that the force of nature is always observant of God's will? Its myriad eyes are fixed on Him, as the eyes of a servant on his master (Ps. cxxiii. 2); doing His commandment, hearkening unto the voice of His word (Ps. ciii. 20, 21); the eyes too of all creation wait on God, who gives them meat in due season (Ps. civ. 27, Prayer Book version)—

> "His state
> Is kingly; thousands at His bidding speed
> And post o'er land and ocean without rest;
> They also serve who only stand and wait."

(8) **And the four beasts** (or, *living beings*) **had each of them** (literally, *one by one of them*) **six wings about him; and they were full of** (or, *teeming with*) **eyes.**—The last verse spoke of the living beings teeming with eyes; this tells us that neither the dropping nor the raising of their wings hindered their view.

And they rest not day and night, saying, Holy, holy, holy, Lord God Almightly, which was, and is, and is to come.—The resemblance to Isaiah's vision (chap. vi. 1—4) may remind us that the voice of God's creation has in every age proclaimed His eternal holiness. The word "holy" is repeated eight times in the Sinaitic version. The "six wings" are taken to express reverence, for with twain (Isa. vi. 2) he covered his face; humility, for with twain he covered his feet; and obedience, for with twain he did fly. Some have understood these living beings to betoken rather the creative power of God than the actual creation. There is much to be said for this; but the analogy of the passage suits better the view here adopted. The twenty-four elders represent, not the regenerating power of God, but the regenerate Church. The new creation in Christ Jesus join in praise with all created things. The doxology in verse 11 favours the interpretation, "Thou hast created all things."

(9, 10) **And when those beasts . . .**—Better, *And whensoever the living beings shall give* (the future is used) *glory and honour and thanks to Him who sitteth upon the throne, to Him who liveth to the ages of ages, the four-and-twenty elders shall* (as is their wont) *fall down before Him who sitteth on the throne, and worship Him that liveth unto the ages of ages, and shall* (as is their wont) *cast their crowns before the throne, saying* . . . It is not to Him who sat upon the throne, but to Him who sitteth there, as he liveth to the ages of ages, that this homage is paid. The future tense (*shall give glory, &c.*) implies the eternal repetition of the act. The connection between the praise given by creation, and the consequent homage of the twenty-four elders, expresses a truth. The Church of Christ does not

(11) Thou art worthy,[a] O Lord, to receive glory and honour and power: for thou hast created all things, and for thy pleasure they are and were created.

CHAPTER V.—(1) And I saw in the right hand of him that sat on the throne a book written within and on the backside,[b] sealed with seven seals. (2) And I saw a strong angel proclaiming with a loud voice, Who is worthy to open the book, and to loose the seals thereof? (3) And no man in heaven, nor in earth, neither under the earth, was able to

a ch. 5. 12.
b Isa. 29. 11; Ezek. 2. 9, 10; 32. 15; Dan. 12. 4.

A.D. 96.

Chaps. v. 1—vi. 17. The sealed book opened by the Lamb.

always hear the voice of praise from created things. Often the creation groaneth and travaileth; but her chorus of praise rises when she perceives that "every thing that hath breath praiseth the Lord." The converse of this thought—the earth bringeth forth her fruit when the people praise God—is hinted in Ps. lxvii. 5, 6, "the earth ceases her travail when the sons of God are made manifest (Rom. viii. 19—21).

Crowns.—The crowns are not royal crowns, but the crowns of conquerors. These are laid down before the throne by those who overcame, not in their own might, but through the blood of the Lamb (chap. xii. 11; comp. chap. vii. 14).

(11) The doxology is three-fold. (See Note on chap. i. 6.) It should run—

> "Worthy art Thou, O Lord, and our God,
> To receive the glory, and the honour, and the power,
> Because Thou didst create all things,
> And through (or, *owing to—i.e.*, because of) Thy will they *were* (not 'are') and were created."

The existence of all things was owing to the will of God, as also was the creation of all things, which was the realisation or manifestation of that will.

V.

THE SEALED ROLL.—The vision of the previous chapter remains. The scenery does not shift, but the attention of the seer is now directed to one feature—the book, or roll, which was on the hand of the Throned One. This roll none in heaven, earth, or under the earth could open; but the Lamb takes the roll to open it, or to unfold its purport to the waiting world and Church; the Church and world praise Him who is the Light, revealing to them all they need to know.

(1) **And I saw in the right hand . . .**—Better, *And I saw on* (not "in;" the roll lay on the open palm of the hand) *the right hand of Him that sitteth upon the throne a book written within and behind, fast sealed with seven seals.* The book is, of course, in the form of a roll; it lies on the open hand of the Throned One; it was not His will that the book should be kept from any. It is written, not on the inside only, as was the usual way, but, like the roll of the book which Ezekiel saw (Ezek. ii. 9, 10), it was written within and without. Some have thought that there are two divisions of predictions—those written within the roll, and those written on the outer side. This is merely fanciful; the passage in Ezekiel which supplies a guidance to the meaning might have shown the erroneousness of the thought. Clearly the "lamentation and mourning and woe" inscribed all over Ezekiel's roll indicate the filling up of sorrows: here the same overflowing writing indicates the completeness of the contents; there was no room for addition to that which was written therein. But what is meant by the book? Numberless interpretations have been offered: it is the Old Testament; it is the whole Bible; it is the title-deed of man's inheritance; it is the book containing the sentence of judgment on the foes of the faith; it is the Apocalypse; it is part of the Apocalypse; it is the book of God's purposes and providence. There is a truth underlying most of these interpretations, but most of them narrow the force of the vision. If we say it is the book which unfolds the principles of God's government—in a wide sense, the book of salvation (comp. Rom. xvi. 25, 26)—the interpretation of life, which Christ alone can bestow (see verses 3—6), we shall include, probably, the practical truths which underlie each of these interpretations; for all—Old Testament and New, man's heritage and destiny, God's purposes and providence—are dark, till He who is the Light unfolds those truths which shed a light on all. Such a book becomes one "which contains and interprets human history," and claims the kingdoms of the earth for God. The aim of all literature has been said by a distinguished critic to be little more than the criticism of life; the book which Christ unfolds is the key to the true meaning of life. The roll is not the Apocalypse so much as the book of those truths which are exemplified in the Apocalypse, as in a vast chamber of imagery. The roll was fast sealed, so that even those who were wise and learned enough to read it had it been unrolled could not do so (See Isa. xxix. 11.) There are things which are hidden from the wise and prudent, but revealed unto babes.

(2) **And I saw a strong** (better, *mighty*) **angel proclaiming with** (or, *in*) **a loud voice, Who is worthy . . .**—We must not let the word "worthy" pass as though it were simply equivalent to "strong enough." It seems to imply moral fitness (comp. Rom. i. 4), which is the true strength in the heavenly world. It was not lack of intellectual capacity so much as the taint of moral unworthiness which hindered the reading of the book. This is in harmony with what we have noticed before. "To commune with God, there is need of no subtle thought, no foreign tongue, no newest philosophy: 'the pure in heart shall see Him:' and Fox and Bunyan can more truly make Him known than 'masters of sentences' and 'angelic doctors.'" Those who are willing to do God's will know of God's doctrine. This thought corresponds, too, with the stress which is laid (in verse 5) on the victory of Christ. It is not simply as divine Son of God, but also as victorious Saviour and King of His people, that He opens the book: His worthiness has been established in conflict and temptation (John xiv. 30; Heb. ii. 9; iv. 15).

(3) **And no man . . . .**—Or, better, *no one* (for it is of more than mankind that the Apostle speaks) *was able, in the heaven, nor on the earth, nor under the earth, nor even* (still less?) *to look thereon.* The looking on the book is usually understood of the look cast on the book of one who would read the contents. If so, the thought is, none could open, still less read, the roll. It may, however, be that all who attempted to take the book were unable to face the glory in which it lay. When Christ revealed Himself to Saul he could not see for the glory of that light.

open the book, neither to look thereon.
(4) And I wept much, because no man
was found worthy to open and to read
the book, neither to look thereon.
(5) And one of the elders saith unto me,
Weep not: behold, the Lion of the tribe
of Juda,[a] the Root of David,[b] hath prevailed to open the book, and to loose
the seven seals thereof. (6) And I beheld, and, lo, in the midst of the throne
and of the four beasts, and in the midst
of the elders, stood a Lamb as it had
been slain, having seven horns and
seven eyes, which are the seven Spirits

a Gen. 49. 9; Heb. 7. 14.
b Isa. 11. 1, 10; 53. 2; Zech. 6. 12.

(4) **And I wept much, because no man** (better, *no one*) **was found worthy to open . . . the book** (omit, "and to read").—The Apostle is not ashamed to call attention to his tears. I, indeed, for my part (the "I" is emphatic) wept much. It was not a failure of faith; it was the outburst of an earnest heart, to which the knowledge of God and the destinies of his fellow-men were very dear. Those who have longed to see the end of oppression, fraud, and sorrow on the earth, to know something of the laws which govern the present, and of their issue in the future, will understand these tears. "The words, 'I wept much,' can only be understood by those who have lived in great catastrophes of the Church, and entered with the fullest sympathy into her sufferings. . . . . Without tears the Revelation was not written, neither can it without tears be understood."

(5) **And one of the elders . . .**—Better, *And one from among the elders saith unto me, Weep not; behold, the Lion, which is of the tribe of Judah, the Root of David, conquered (so as) to open the roll, and the seven seals thereof.* The position of the word "conquered" is emphatic, and should receive greater prominence. The verse has been translated, "Behold, one conquered, (even) the Lion . . ." The right to open the roll is thus made to turn, as we noticed before, not merely on the divine Sonship of our Lord, but upon His victory: He conquered, and so opens the secret purposes of God to His Church. The thought is exactly parallel with other scriptures which give emphasis to the work of redemption. It is "for the suffering of death" that Christ is clothed "with glory and honour" (Heb. ii. 9). Similarly St. Paul traces the exaltation of Christ as the outcome of His humiliation, "*wherefore* (*i.e.*, in consequence of His humiliation) God also hath highly exalted Him" (Phil. ii. 9). Thus Christ, who in conquest is seen to be the power of God, in revealing the true philosophy of history is seen to be the wisdom of God.

The Lion of the tribe of Juda.—The lion was the ancient symbol of the tribe of Judah. Jacob described his son as "a lion's whelp" (Gen. xlix. 9); the standard of Judah in the Israelitish encampment is said to have been a lion. It was the symbol of strength, courage, and sovereignty.

The Root of David.—The Lion is also the representative of the royal house of David. "Christ cometh of the seed of David" (comp. Mark xii. 35 with John viii. 42); the prophets have described Him as the Branch, which would spring from the ancient stock (Isa. xi. 1; Zech. vi. 12). But there seems also a reference to the deeper thought that He who is the Branch is also the Root (comp. Isa. xi. 10); He is the one who was David's Lord (Matt. xxii. 41—45), and "the true source and ground of all power" to David and David's tribe, and of all who looked to Him, and not to themselves, for strength.

(6) **And I beheld, and lo . . .**—Better, *And I saw* (omit "and lo") *in the midst of the throne and of the four living beings, and in the midst of the elders, a Lamb* (or, *a little Lamb*), *standing as if having been slain.* The position of the Lamb is described from the seer's point of view: the Lamb is not on the throne, but in the middle front of it, and so apparently between the living creatures, and in the midst of the circle formed by the twenty-four elders. The passage is most striking. The Evangelist is told of the *Lion* which will open the seals: he looks, and lo, it is a Lamb! yes, a little Lamb—for the word is diminutive. There is deep significance in this. When we read of the Lion, we think of power and majesty, and we are right; all power in heaven and earth is Christ's, but it is power manifested in seeming weakness. The waters of Shiloah are mightier than the Euphrates (Isa. viii. 6—8); righteousness and purity, meekness and gentleness, are greater than carnal weapons (comp. 2 Cor. vi. 6, 7; Eph. vi. 11, *et al.*); the Lamb mightier than the roaring lion which goeth about seeking whom he may devour (1 Pet. v. 8). But it is a Lamb as if it had been slain. The wound-marks are there, but it is not dead; it is standing, for it represents Him who though He died is alive for evermore; but the signs of suffering and death are visible, for it is not the Lamb, but the suffering Lamb, which is exalted; it is not the Christ, but the Christ crucified, which is the power of God; the Christ lifted up from the earth draws all men unto Him (John xii. 32; 1 Cor. i. 23, 24); the corn of wheat which dies brings forth fruit (John xii. 24). As such He is the worship of the Church and the world which He has redeemed. (See verses 8, 9; comp. chap. vii. 14.) The reference to earlier Scriptures (Ex. xii. 46; Isa. liii. 7; John i. 29, 36; 1 Cor. v. 7, 8) is not to be overlooked. From the tokens of suffering the seer passes to the tokens of strength and wisdom which he saw in the Lamb. He describes it as "having seven horns, and seven eyes, which are the seven spirits of God sent forth (or, *which are being sent forth*) into all the earth." The horn is the strength of the animal which carries it. It is so used in the blessing of Joseph: "His horns are like the horns of a wild bull" ("unicorns" in Authorised version); "with them shall he push the people together," &c. (Deut. xxxiii. 17; comp. Pss. lxxxix. 24; cxlviii. 14). The seven horns denote completeness or fulness of strength. The seven eyes, like the seven lamps (chap. iv. 5), represent the Holy Spirit in His manifold gifts of grace; but as they are described as eyes of the Lamb, they betoken His omniscience who is in heaven and yet, by His Spirit, everywhere (Matt. xxviii. 20); whose eye is on all events, great and small; whose eyes behold the children of men. Note, also, that the seven spirits are ascribed to the Son as well as to the Father. (Comp. John xiv. 26; xv. 26.) The seven spirits are said to be "sent"; the word is from the same root as the word "apostle." There is an apostolate of the Spirit as well as an apostolate of the Church; and, if we adopt the version here which gives the present participle, this spiritual apostolate is being continually exerted; the seven spirits are in process of being sent out by Him who says to this one "Go," and he goeth; to the twelve, "Go ye into

of God sent forth into all the earth.
(7) And he came and took the book out
of the right hand of him that sat upon
the throne. (8) And when he had taken
the book, the four beasts and four *and*
twenty elders fell down before the
Lamb, having every one of them harps,
and golden vials full of odours,[1] which
are the prayers of saints. (9) And they
sung a new song, saying, Thou art
worthy to take the book, and to open
the seals thereof: for thou wast slain,
and hast redeemed us to God by thy
blood out of every kindred, and tongue,
and people, and nation; (10) and hast
made us unto our God kings and priests:

[1] Or, *incense.*

all the world," and sends His Spirit to confer on His people grace according to the measure of the gift of Christ.

(7) **And he came . . .**—Better, *And He came, and He has taken* (omit the words "the book," and supply) *it* (*i.e.*, the roll) *out of the right hand of Him that sitteth upon the throne.* There is a change of tense ("came," "has taken"), which seems to be due to the rapt attention of the seer, whose narrative trembles with his own intensity of feeling. He wept awhile ago; now he need not weep. The Lamb conquered; He came; He has taken the roll. He is the wisdom of the Church; among all pre-eminent; all things will be reconciled in Him; the purpose and meaning of all life's mysteries and sorrows will be made plain in Him. (Comp. 1 Cor. i. 24; Eph. i. 9, 10; Col. i. 18.)

(8) **And when he had taken . . .**—Better, *And when He took the roll, the four living beings and the twenty-four elders fell before the Lamb, having each a harp, and golden vials* (or, *censers*) *full of incense, which are the prayers of the saints* (or, *the holy ones*). It is not the Church alone which is interested in the revelation which will throw light on life's mysteries and the delay of the kingdom: the whole creation groaneth, waiting for the reign of righteousness; and therefore the four living beings, who represent creation, join with the elders, who represent the Church, in the adoration of the Lamb who holds the secret of life's meaning in His hand. The vials (which seem to be censers, as they hold the incense) and the harps, it is perhaps more natural to suppose, were in the hands of the four-and-twenty elders, and not of the living creatures. Here, then, we have the praises (represented by the harps), and the prayers (represented by the censers) of the world-wide and age-long Church of Christ. The comparison of prayer with incense is in strict accordance with Old Testament language. "Let my prayer be set forth before Thee as incense" (Ps. cxli. 2). The incense held a conspicuous place in the ritual of the Temple. The greatest care was to be taken in the composition of the incense, and the same compound was not to be used anywhere but in the sanctuary. These precautions suggest its typical character. The true odours are the heart-prayers of God's children. "Of these three sweet ingredient perfumes," says Archbishop Leighton, alluding to the composition of the Temple-incense, "namely, petition, confession, thanksgiving, is the incense of prayer, and by the divine fire of love it ascends unto God, the heart and all with it; and when the hearts of the saints unite in joint prayer, the pillar of sweet smoke goes up the greater and the fuller." Every prayer which broke out in sob from an agonising heart, every sigh of the solitary and struggling Christian, every groan of those groping Godward, mingles here with the songs of the happy and triumphant.

(9, 10) **And they sung a new song, saying . . .**—Better, *And they sing a new song, saying.* The use of the present ("sing") is another example of that intensity of interest of which the change of tense in the last verse afforded an instance. As he records his vision, he sees it anew; he describes the action as though it were even now taking place, and he still hears the notes of praise. He who knows what it is to have the strains of some rich melody haunt him for days will understand how the prophet would hear the glad chorus burst forth afresh in his ears when he recalled the vision. The new song; the chorus of the redeemed—

"Worthy art Thou to take the roll,
And to open the seals thereof;
For Thou wast slain,
And didst buy to God in Thy blood
Out of every tribe, and tongue, and people, and nation,
And didst make them a kingdom and priests,
And they reign upon the earth."

The English version, "hast redeemed," and "hast made," weakens the reference to the completed character of Christ's redeeming work. It is the great victory in suffering and death which inspires the song, and makes them sing, "Thou art worthy;" and so they speak of that work of Christ as a *work truly* done: "Thou didst buy (omit "us") out of every tribe, &c., and *didst* make them," &c. The suffering Saviour has died, has broken the bond of the oppressor, has claimed, by right of purchase, mankind as His own; and the price was His blood. It is well to notice the harmony between this passage and the statements of other Apostles: "Ye are not your own;" "bought with a price." (See 1 Cor. vi. 20; vii. 23; 1 Pet. i. 18, 19; 2 Pet. ii. 1.) Observe, also, the *four* terms (tribe, tongue, people, nation), employed as if to give emphasis to the universality of redemption, for four is the number of extension in all directions. With this compare Rom. v. 15—19; Col. iii. 11; Heb. ii. 9. We have a right to teach all to say, "He redeemed me and all mankind." It is instructive to dwell on the climax "they reign," in contrast with "Thou wast slain." It is like an anticipation of the now familiar words—

"Thine the sharp thorns, and mine the golden crown;
Mine the life won, and Thine the life laid down."

"Didst make them a kingdom and priests." (See chap. i. 6.) This kingdom and reign is the outcome of Christ's work. "Every precept of Christianity is quickened by the power of the death and resurrection of Christ. It is by the presence of this power that they are Christians, and it is as Christians that they conquer the world" (Westcott). "They reign on the earth." Such is the best reading; the tense is present. It is not, I think, to be explained away as a vivid realisation of the future; it is a simple statement, which is as true as that the followers of Christ are "a kingdom and priests." They reign with and in Christ, but they also reign on the earth. Christ gives them a kingship, even sovereignty over themselves—the first, best, and most philanthropic of all kingships. He gives them, too, a kingship on the earth among men, for they are exerting those influences, promoting those principles, and dispensing those laws of righteousness,

and we shall reign on the earth. (11) And
I beheld, and I heard the voice of many
angels round about the throne and the
beasts and the elders: and the number
of them was ten thousand times ten
thousand,[a] and thousands of thousands;
(12) saying with a loud voice, Worthy is
the Lamb that was slain to receive
power, and riches, and wisdom, and
strength, and honour, and glory, and
blessing. (13) And every creature which
is in heaven, and on the earth, and
under the earth, and such as are in the
sea, and all that are in them, heard I
saying, Blessing, and honour, and glory,
and power, *be* unto him that sitteth
upon the throne, and unto the Lamb
for ever and ever. (14) And the four

a Dan. 7. 10; Heb. 12. 23.

---

holiness, and peace which in reality rule all the best developments of life and history. All who traverse these laws are intruders, transitory tyrants, exerting only a phantom power. They are not kings: they may govern, they do not reign. (Comp. 1 Cor. iii. 21—23; Eph. ii. 6.)

(11) **And I beheld . . .**—More literally, *And I saw, and I heard a voice of many angels around the throne, and the living beings, and the elders; and the number of them was myriads of myriads, and thousands of thousands.* The chorus of the redeemed is followed by a chorus of angels; for "that which is the highest act of love, towards whatever persons it was manifested, from whatever calamities it saved them, must be the highest manifestation of the divine character and will; therefore must be the cause of delight to all creatures, fallen or unfallen. If the Revelation is true, there can be no breach in the sympathies of any part of God's voluntary and intelligent universe." It is needless to observe that the numbers are not to be taken literally; they are simply employed to express the countless throng of that "innumerable company of angels" (Heb. xii. 22) which raised the song—

"Loud as from numbers without number, sweet
As from blest voices, uttering joy."
—*Paradise Lost*, iii. 346, 347.

(12) **Saying with a loud voice . . .**—The second chorus: the chorus of angels—

"Worthy is the Lamb,
That hath been slain,
To receive the power,
And riches, and wisdom, and might,
And honour, and glory, and blessing."

The doxology is seven-fold. We have noticed (chap. i. 6) the increasing strength of the doxologies in which the redeemed take part. This, though a *seven-fold* one, does not interrupt that advance of praise; for in this chorus the redeemed do not take part. The definite article is prefixed to the word "power" only; in the doxologies of chaps. iv. 11 and vii. 12 it stands before each word. This has led some to view the single article as prefixed to all that follows, and to regard all the words as though they formed one word. May it not, however, be used to give emphasis to the "power"? None, above or below, was "able" (same word as "power" here) to open the book (verse 3); but the Lamb has conquered to open it, and the chorus proclaims the Lamb worthy of that power. Some have thought that the seven terms of the doxology refer to the seven seals which the Lamb is about to open. This seems strained. The notion of completeness is common to this seven-fold blessing and the seven seals; this is the only connection between them.

(13) **And every creature . . .**—The third chorus: the chorus of the universe. The song of the redeemed, echoed by the hosts of angels, is now merged in the utterance of all. "Every creature which is in the heaven, and upon the earth, and beneath the earth, and upon the sea, and all the things that are in them, heard I saying—

"To Him that sitteth upon the throne,
And to the Lamb,
(Be) the blessing, and the honour,
And the glory, and the might,
To the ages of the ages."

The song of praise rises from all quarters, and from all forms of creation. The whole universe, animate and inanimate, joins in this glad acclaim. To limit it to either rational or animate creation is to enfeeble the climax which this third chorus forms to the two preceding ones, and is to denude the passage of its fulness and of its poetry. The Hebrew mind delighted in representing every bird and every grass-blade as joining in God's praise. "Mountains and all hills, fruitful trees and all cedars, beasts and all cattle, creeping things and flying fowl," as well as kings of the earth and all people, were called on to bless the name of the Lord. Christian poets have told us that "Earth with her thousand voices praises God."

"Nature, attend! join every living soul,
Beneath the spacious temple of the sky,
In adoration join'd; and, ardent, raise
One general song! To Him, ye vocal gales,
Breathe soft, whose Spirit in your freshness breathes.
* * * And thou, majestic main,
A secret world of wonders in thyself,
Sound His stupendous praise, whose greater voice
Or bids you roar, or bids your roaring fall.
Soft roll your incense, herbs, and fruits, and flowers,
In mingled clouds to Him whose sun exalts,
Whose breath perfumes you, and whose pencil paints."
—Thomson, *Hymn to Seasons.*

The Apostle who pictured all creation as waiting in eager expectation for the full redemption—the redemption of "the body" (Rom. viii. 23), looked forward to the time when "the whole universe, whether animate or inanimate, would bend the knee in homage and raise its voice in praise" (Phil. ii. 10). The doxology which thus rises from the universe is appropriately four-fold: the definite article (omitted in the English version) must be supplied before each word ("*The* blessing," &c.). The two preceding songs were in honour of the Lamb; in this last the praise is addressed to the Throned One and to the Lamb. This linking of the Lamb with God as the Throned One is common throughout the book. Here they are linked in praise; in chap. vi. 16 they are linked in wrath; in chap. vii. 17 they are linked in ministering consolation; in chap. xix. 6, 7, they are linked in triumph. In the final vision of the book the Lord God and the Lamb are the temple (chap. xxi. 22) and the light (chap. xxi. 23), the refreshment (chap. xxii. 1) and sovereignty (chap. xxii. 3), of the celestial city.

(14) **And the four beasts . . .**—Better, *And the four living beings said, Amen* (or, *the Amen*). *And the elders* (omit "four and twenty") *fell down and worshipped.* The remaining words of this verse are wanting in some of the best MSS., and they spoil the

beasts said, Amen. And the four *and* twenty elders fell down and worshipped him that liveth for ever and ever.

A.D. 96.

CHAPTER VI.—(1) And I saw when the Lamb opened one of the seals, and I heard, as it were the noise of

Chap. vi. 1, 2. The first seal opened.

graphic force of the description. The "Amen" rises from universal nature; the Church of Christ falls down in silent adoration. Thought and feeling assert themselves above all language. There are times when silence is the most eloquent applause; there are times when it is also the most real worship. "Let thy prayers be without words, rather than thy words, without prayer" was a wise precept of an old divine. An English and an Italian poet have given expression to the same feeling of the weakness of words. "O speech!" sang Dante, when telling his final vision—

> "How feeble and how faint art thou to give
> Conception birth."
> —*Parad.* xxxiii.

Thomson takes refuge in silence from the overwhelming thoughts of the divine glory:—

> "I lose
> Myself in Him, in light ineffable.
> Come, then, expressive silence, muse His praise."

Here the inspired seer describes the chorus of praise as dying into a silence born of awe and gratefulness and love.

VI.

The Vision of the Seals.—The relation of Christianity to great universal evils. The extinction of war, disease, death, persecution will not be immediate; the mission of Christianity is not to abolish them at once and by compulsion, but to undermine them; for her work is not coercion, but conviction, and is primarily to individuals, and only secondarily and indirectly to nations.

It is at this chapter that our most difficult work commences. We now enter upon the vexed sea of multitudinous interpretations. In the *Introduction* will be found a brief account of the principal schools of apocalyptic interpretation. It will be sufficient here to indicate the general view which appears the most simple and freest from difficulties. The seals which are opened by the Lamb seem to speak a double message. To the world they say, "When the Son of Man cometh, shall He find faith on the earth?" To the Church they say, "In the world ye shall have tribulation; but be of good cheer, I have overcome the world." There are two lines of thought in the Bible, and these give rise to two apparently contradictory sets of pictures. There are the pictures of what would be the state of the world were the principles of Christ fully and universally accepted; and there are the pictures of the world as it will be because men do not fully accept them. The first set are the ideal, and include the abolition of war, social injustice, poverty, when the golden age and reign of righteousness shall dawn. When, however, we speak of this as ideal, we do not imply that it is visionary; it is the sober statement of what would actually take place were the rule of Christ admitted in the hearts and lives of men, and what will take place whenever they do so. But between this grand possibility and its realisation stands the wayward, and tortuous, and weakened human will, which either rejects or fatally but half adopts the teachings of God. This will of man, seen in a world which is directly hostile to Christ, and in a Church which is but half faithful to him, must be convinced ere the true ideal of Christ shall be attained, and the fulness of His kingdom made manifest. Thus the ideal pictures are postponed, and the world, which might have been saved by love speaking in gentleness, must be saved by love speaking so as by fire. Now in the earlier Christian times the hope of an ideal kingdom, soon to be realised in the immediate establishment of Christ's kingdom, was very strong. The first disciples yearned to see it immediately set up. "Wilt thou at this time restore the kingdom?" The golden light of hope lingered long in their minds; they lived in the memory of those prophecies which foretold the cessation of war, sorrow, pain, and death. They thought, now that Christ had come, the Messianic kingdom in its utter gladness must immediately appear. They forgot the Prince's visit to the far country; they forgot the citizens who hated Him, and rejected His rule; they forgot the session at God's right hand till His enemies were made His footstool. They thought the day of the Lord, in the sense of the perfecting of His reign, was at hand; they forgot that the Heavenly Bridegroom must gird His sword upon His thigh, and that His arrows must be sharp in the heart of the King's enemies (Ps. xlv. 3, 5). The vision of these seven seals is the repetition of the warning against such forgetfulness. The ideal Kingdom might come if mankind would receive it, but it must be established by conviction, not by coercion; and so the actual history of the growth of the Kingdom would be different from the ideal; the Church, like her Master, must be made perfect through sufferings; where He was, His servant must be; through much tribulation the Kingdom must be entered. The seals unfold, then, the general aspects of the world's history after Christ's ascension. Certain features would continue; war, famine, disease, death would remain. They might, indeed, have been abolished had Christ's own received Him; but as it was, the face of the world's will being in opposition to God's will opposed the manifestation of the peaceful Kingdom. Thus the scenes which the seals unfold are but the pictorial statement of Christ's own utterances in Matt. xxiv. 6, 7, "Ye shall hear of wars; there shall be famines and pestilences." It will be seen, then, that the seals tell the seer that these troubles will exist till the times of the end. The Church through him is warned to prepare for her mission of suffering; and in this way the vision stretches on till the close of earth's history.

But this is not all. The visions of the book may have preliminary applications, because the principles on which they are constructed are eternal ones. Our Lord's own language in Matt. xxiv. is our guarantee that we may look for such preliminary applications. The story of the overthrow of many a nation presents these features of war, famine, misery, convulsion. The fall of Jerusalem, as well as that of the Roman empire, was preceded by such. On this principle, other interpretations of the vision have a truth in them, as long as they are confined to broad, general principles; the mischievous affection for trivial details has been the bane of more than one school of interpreters.

thunder, one of the four beasts saying,
Come and see. (2) And I saw, and behold
a white horse: and he that sat on him
had a bow; and a crown was given unto
him: and he went forth conquering,
and to conquer. (3) And when he had
opened the second seal, I heard the
second beast say, Come and
see. (4) And there went out
another horse *that was* red:[a]
and *power* was given to him that sat
thereon to take peace from the earth,

a Zech. 1. 8; 6. 2.

Chap. vi. 3, 4. The second seal opened.

It is perhaps worthy of notice that these seals are not to be regarded as being fulfilled one after another: in point of fact, the horseman of war and the horseman of pestilence have often ridden together. Yet it is true that there is a tendency in one to produce the other; war does lead to famine, famine does produce pestilence. There is, perhaps, also an application of these seals to the history of the Church. Her first era is that of purity and conquest; her next is that of controversy—the war of opinions; the age of controversy gives rise to the age of spiritual scarcity, for men intent upon controversy forget the true Bread, which came down from heaven, and a famine of the word of God succeeds; and out of this there emerges the pale horse of spiritual death, the parody of the victorious rider—the form of godliness without the power, the age of irreligious ritualism: the hidden ones of Christ may then be revealed, crying "How long?" and finally the age of revolution comes to overthrow the old order and give birth to the new.

(1) **And I saw when the Lamb** (the diminutive form of Lamb is still used) . . .—The words "and see" are doubtful. They are found in some MSS. and omitted in others: the authority for their omission and for their retention is about equally divided. Under these circumstances we may fairly be guided by the context. To whom is the summons addressed? Who is bidden to come? If it was taken to be addressed to the seer, we can understand why some copyist should add the words "and see." But are they addressed to the seer? It seems difficult to see the purpose of such a command. He was near already. He had seen the Lamb opening the seal. There was no object in his drawing near. Are the words, then, addressed, as Alford supposes, to Christ? It is difficult to believe that the living creature would thus cry to the Lamb, who was opening the scroll. The simplest way of answering the question is to ask another: Who did come in obedience to the voice? There is but one answer—the horseman. The living beings cry "Come," and their cry is responded to by the appearance of the several riders. What is the spiritual meaning of this? The living beings represent, as we have seen, animated nature—that nature and creation of God which groans and travails in pain, waiting for the manifestation of the sons of God. These summon the emblems of war and pestilence to come on the scene, for these things must needs be, and through these lies the way for the final coming of God's Christ, for whom creation longs. They bid the pains and troubles come, because they recognise them as the precursors of creation's true King. Thus their voice has in it an undertone which sighs for the advent of the Prince of Peace, who is *to come.*

(2) **Conquering, and to conquer.**—Better, *conquering, and that he might conquer.* One version has, "and he conquered." All commentators seem to be agreed that this rider represents victory. The emblems —the crown and white horse—are obviously those of victory. The crown (*stephanos*) is the crown of triumph. The horses used in Roman triumphs were white. On the white horse of triumph the crowned rider goes forth conquering, and that he might conquer. But who or what is here represented? Some take it to be a mere emblem of conquest, or victory, as the next rider represents war. There is then a harmony of interpretation: the horsemen reveal to the seer that the after-history will be marked by conquests, wars, famines, pestilences. The description, however, seems to demand something more: the expression, "that he might conquer," carries our thoughts beyond a mere transient conqueror. The vision, moreover, was surely designed to convey an assured happy feeling to the mind of the seer. No picture of mere Roman conquests or world-victory would have conveyed this. Is not the vision the reflex of the hopes of early Christian thought? It is the symbol of Christian victory. It was thus their hopes saw Christ: though ascended He went forth in spiritual power conquering. They were right in their faith, and wrong in their expectation. Right in their faith: He went forth conquering, and He would conquer. Wrong in their expectation: the visions of war, famine, death must intervene. It was through these that the conqueror would be proved more than conqueror. It is, perhaps, significant of this intervening period of trouble and suffering that the rider is armed with a *bow.* The arrows of His judgments (war, famine) would be sharp among those who refused the sword of His word. For those who will not turn He hath bent His bow and made it ready. His arrows are ordained against the persecutors.

(3, 4) **And when he had opened** . . .—Better, *And when he opened the second seal, I heard the second living being, saying, Come. And there came forth another horse, red; and to him that sat on him was given to take peace from the earth, and that they* (i.e., the inhabitants of the earth) *shall kill one another, and there was given to him a great sword.* This seal is the distinct and unmistakable declaration to the Church that they must look for wars, even after the Prince of Peace has come. The advent of the highest good does not work peace, but only because the hindrance is in man. Man's resistance to good turns the gospel of peace into an occasion for the sword. So our Lord declares, "I came not to send peace, but a sword." The reign of peace, the beating of swords into ploughshares, is not yet. The vision may help to fix the Christian position about war. It is to be expected; it is an evil, but often an inevitable evil. Those who take part in war are not condemned: those who occasion offences are. It is as much a mistake to condemn soldiering as a profession as it is to deny that Christianity aims at the suppression of war. She admits the soldier to be a soldier of Christ, even while she keeps before her the ideal age when nations shall learn war no more. We expect wars, even while we believe that the day will come when war will be reckoned as absurd as duelling is now. The vision says, "It must needs be that wars will come;" and war, even when roused by the passions of men, is a judgment of God, for God's judgments are mostly formed

and that they should kill one another:
and there was given unto him a great
sword. (5) And when he had opened
the third seal, I heard the
third beast say, Come and
see. And I beheld, and
lo a black horse; and he that sat on
him had a pair of balances in his hand.
(6) And I heard a voice in the midst of
the four beasts say, A measure[1] of
wheat for a penny,[a] and three measures
of barley for a penny; and *see* thou hurt
not the oil and the wine. (7) And when
he had opened the fourth
seal, I heard the voice of
the fourth beast say, Come
and see. (8) And I looked, and behold
a pale horse: and his name that sat on
him was Death, and Hell followed with
him. And power was given unto them[2]
over the fourth part of the earth, to kill
with sword, and with hunger, and with

Chap. vi. 5, 6. The third seal opened.

Chap. vi. 7, 8. The fourth seal opened.

1 The word *chœnix* signifieth a measure containing one wine quart, and the twelfth part of a quart.

a Gen. 41. 57: Lev. 26. 26; Ezek. 4. 10, 16.

2 Or, *to him.*

---

out of man's vices. The seal puts in pictorial form the warning of Christ that wars and rumours of wars would be heard of. How true the warning the after history shows—wars in the empire, wars among nations, controversies, and often fratricidal wars in the Church of Christ.

(5, 6) **When He had opened.**—Better, *When he opened.* The words "and see" are to be omitted here, as in the other seals. *And I saw, and behold a horse, black, and he that sat on him having a balance in his hand. And I heard as it were a voice in the midst of the four living beings, saying, A chœnix of wheat for a denarius* (penny), *and three chœnixes of barley for a denarius* (penny), *and the oil and the wine do thou not hurt.* "Balance:" There is scarcely a doubt that a balance, or pair of scales, is intended (the Greek word also means a yoke); but the whole imagery of the seal harmonises with the balance, and the passage from Ezekiel (Ezek. xlv. 10), cited by Alford, in which there is a "righteous balance" (the LXX. using the same Greek word as here) seems conclusive. It is the emblem of scarcity: food is not weighed out thus in times of abundance. (Comp. Ezek. iv. 16, "Behold I will break the staff of bread in Jerusalem, and they shall eat bread by weight and with care.") The chœnix ("measure" in English version) was the amount of food sufficient to support a man for a day. "A chœnix is the daily maintenance" (Suidas, quoted by Alford). The denarius ("penny" of English version, here and in Matt. xviii. 28, and Mark xii. 37) amounted to between sixpence and sevenpence of our money, and was the usual daily pay of the labourer, and of the soldier. (See especially Note on Matt. xx. 2.) It is difficult to speak of this as other than terribly high prices for food. The whole of a man's pay goes for food, and even the coarser bread is so expensive that it takes a whole day's wages to supply food for three adults. It has been thought that the voice calls to the rider to check his devastations, lest the growing famine should exterminate the whole human race. This may be, but the check is at a point which has already wrought the highest misery. The extent of the misery may be imagined by imagining what wretchedness would be entailed were a man obliged to pay three or four shillings for bread sufficient to keep him nourished for a day. Or we may measure it by the estimate of the disciples (Mark vi. 37) that two hundred pennyworth of bread would give a short meal to upwards of five thousand people. At the price in this seal, the cost of bread would have so risen that the two hundred pennyworth of bread would not suffice to feed one thousand. But what is meant by the words, "the oil and wine do not thou hurt"? They were not, like the bread, necessary to life, but among its luxuries and superfluities. There is a kind of irony in times of straitness, when the necessaries are scarcely to be had, and the luxuries remain comparatively low in price. The splendours and comforts of life are held cheap, when hunger is showing that the life is more than the dainty meat, and the body than raiment. The seal then tells the seer that in the ages the Church of Christ must expect to see famines and distress in the world, and luxuries abounding in the midst of straitness. Is it not true that the contrast, which is so ugly, between pampered opulence and indolent pauperism, is the result of the prevalence of world-principles? Wealth, self-indulgent and heartless, and poverty, reckless and self-willed, are sure tokens that the golden rule of Christ is not understood and obeyed. There is a similar experience in the history of the Church. The red horse of controversy is followed by the black horse of spiritual starvation. In the heat of polemical pride and passion for theological conquest is developed that love of barren dogmatics which forgets the milk of the word and the bread of life, which are the needed food of souls.

(7, 8) **The fourth seal.**—*And when He opened the fourth seal, I heard the voice of the fourth living being, saying, Come. And I saw, and behold, a horse, pallid* (or, *livid*), *and he that sat upon him his name was Death, and Hades was following with him; and there was given to them power over the fourth part of the earth to kill with sword, and with famine, and with death, and by the wild beasts of the earth.* The colour pallid, or *livid*, is that deadly greenish hue, which is the unmistakable token of the approach of death. The rider is Death—not a particular form of death, but Death himself. Attending him, ready to gather up the slain, is Hades. The fourth seal is the darkest and most terrible. Single forms of death (war and famine) were revealed in the earlier seals; now the great King of Terrors himself appears, and in his hand are gathered all forms of death—war, famine, pestilence (for the second time the word "death" is used: it must be taken in a subordinate sense, as a particular form of death, such as plague, or pestilence; we may compare the use of the word "death" thus applied to some special disease, in the case of The Death, or Black Death), and wild beasts. These forms of death correspond with God's four sore judgments—the sword, and famine, and pestilence, and the noisome beasts of Ezek. xiv. 21. The seal, therefore, gathers up into one all the awfulness of the past seals. It is the central seal, and it is the darkest. It is the midnight of sorrows, where all seems given up to the sovereignty of death. The middle things of life are often dark. Midway between the wicket-gate and golden city Bunyan placed his valley of the shadow of death, following the hint of the Psalmist, who placed it midway between the pasture and the house of the Lord (Ps. xxiii.). Dante, perhaps working from the same

death, and with the beasts of the earth.
(9) And when he had opened the fifth
seal, I saw under the altar
the souls of them that
were slain for the word of
God, and for the testimony which they
held:[a] (10) and they cried with a loud
voice, saying, How long, O Lord, holy
and true, dost thou not judge and
avenge our blood on them that dwell on
the earth? (11) And white robes were
given unto every one of them; and it
was said unto them, that they should
rest yet for a little season, until their
fellowservants also and their brethren,
that should be killed as they *were*,

Chap. vi. 9—11. The fifth seal opened.

a Gen. 4. 10; Phil. 3. 10; Col. 1. 24; 1 Pet. 4. 13.

---

hint, found his obscure wood and wanderings midway along the road of life:—

> "In the midway of this our mortal life
> I found me in a gloomy wood, astray."

The darkest periods of the Church's history were those we call the Middle Ages. By this, however, it is not meant that there is any chronological signification in the seal. The vision deepens in its central scene, like the horror of darkness in the dream of Abraham. The history of the Church has not unfrequently presented a sort of parallel. The age which follows the ages of barren dogmatism and of spiritual starvation is often an age of sham spiritual life. The pale horse of death is the parody of the white horse of victory: the form of godliness remains, the power is gone.

(9—11) **The fifth seal** differs from the four earlier seals. It is not introduced by the voice of the living beings, and the cry "Come." The voice which is now heard is not the cry of the groaning world, but of the oppressed and troubled Church. In the fourth seal the climax of world-sorrow seemed to be reached in the accumulation of war, famine, pestilence, and noisome beasts. It declared to the evangelist that there were evils which would continue and even increase in the world. "Ye shall hear of wars; nation shall rise against nation." Social troubles, war, poverty, and privation would still exist; religious troubles, evil men and seducers would wax worse and worse. Worldly policy, selfishness, and the untamed passions of mankind would still trouble humanity. Then if such troubles and disorders remain, what has the Church been doing? Where is the promise of that early vision of victory? The answer is given in the fifth seal. The Church has been following her Lord. As the vision of Bethlehem and the angel-song of "peace on earth" passed, and made way for the agony of Gethsemane, the cross of Calvary, and the cry "My God, why hast Thou forsaken Me?" so the glowing dream of a quick conquest over all evil passes away, and the picture of an agonising, persecuted Church takes its place, and the voice of its anguish is heard, "How long, O Lord!" The Church has her Bethlehem, her Nazareth, her Gethsemane, her Calvary, her Easter morn; for Christ said, "Where I am there shall also My servant be" (John xii. 26). The seals, then, are not merely visions of war, famine, &c., they are the tokens that the victory of Christ's Church must, like her Lord's, be a victory through apparent failure and certain death. The four seals proclaim her apparent failure; she has not brought peace and social and political harmony to the world. The fifth seal shows her suffering, the witness of the servants of Christ has been rejected; in the world they have tribulation (John xvi. 33).

(9) **I saw under the altar . . .**—Read, *when He opened*, and, instead of "were slain," &c., *had been slain because of the Word of God, and* (*because of*) *the testimony which they held.* The seal indicates that the mission of the Christian Church can only be carried out in suffering. An altar is seen, and at its foot tokens of the martyrs who had laid down their lives upon it. The word "souls" is to be taken as the equivalent of "lives"; the vision tells that their lives had been sacrificed. The blood of the victims was in the temple service poured out at the foot of the altar. St. Paul makes use of the same imagery—"I am now ready to be *poured out*" ("offered" in English version). In union with Christ Christians are called upon to suffer with Him, even to carry on to its great end the work of Christ in the world, and so fill up that which is lacking of the sufferings of Christ (Col. i. 24). The word "souls" has been made a resting-place for an argument respecting the intermediate state. There is no ground for this: it is quite beside the object of the seal, which simply exhibits the sufferings of Christ's people as the necessary accompaniment of the progress of the gospel. These sufferings are because of the Word of God and the testimony which they held. It was because of the Word of God and the testimony that the sacred seer himself suffered (chap. i. 9). The words here remind us that the same issue which St. John fought, the suffering ones of after ages would be fighting. Their witness and his was the God-man; to this testimony they clung. They were not ashamed of Christ, or of His words, and they suffered for their courage and fidelity.

(10) **How long . . .?**—Better, *Until when, O Master* (the word is the correlative of "servant," see verse 10) *the Holy and True, dost Thou not judge and avenge our blood from* (*on*) *those who dwell on the earth?* By a dramatic figure the persecuted and slain ones are represented as crying for retribution on their oppressors. It is not the Christians themselves (Luke xxiii. 34; and Acts vii. 60) who cry for vengeance, any more than it was Abel himself who cried from the ground to God: it was the blood of Abel (Gen. iv. 10), the earth disclosed her blood, and refused to cover her slain. The forgotten or ignored wrongs of generations come forth from oblivion and cry for vengeance. It is a poetical description, but it is not fiction. The righteous blood shed does fall upon the world in retribution: the laws of God avenge themselves, though the victims do not live to behold the reward of the ungodly. On the epithets *Holy* and *True*, see Notes on chap. iii. 7.

(11) **And white robes were given . . .**—The victims, however, are not forgotten. *There was given to them* (*each*) *a white robe.* The white robes, the glistening apparel of the saints (comp. chap. iii. 4, 5), shall be theirs; each shall receive it. They are robes of righteousness (chap. xix. 8); they are robes of honour (chap. iv. 4), for those who wear them are like God, seeing Him as He is, reflecting His image; they are acknowledged to be His, as they have acknowledged Him to be their God. Persecuted on earth, they are honoured in heaven. There is also a sense in which a white robe is given to them in the eyes of men: those whose names have been cast out as evil have been honoured by a repentant posterity with the robe of tardy praise; after-generations garnish the sepulchres of the righteous whom their fathers slew. The

should be fulfilled. (12) And I beheld
Chap. vi. 12—17. The sixth seal opened.
when he had opened the
sixth seal, and, lo, there
was a great earthquake;
and the sun became black as sackcloth
of hair, and the moon became as blood;
(13) and the stars of heaven fell unto the
earth, even as a fig tree casteth her un-
timely figs,[1] when she is shaken of a
mighty wind. (14) And the heaven
departed as a scroll when it is rolled
together;[a] and every mountain and
island were moved out of their places.
(15) And the kings of the earth, and the

1 Or, *green figs.*

a Isa. 34. 4.

---

excommunicated in one age are often the canonised of the next, for the dull world learns slowly, and its purest honours are posthumous. But however this may be, for the suffering saints there is the heavenly robe and the heavenly rest.

It was said unto them, that they should rest yet for a little season, until their fellow-servants also and their brethren, that should be killed (better, *who are to be slain*) **as they were, should be fulfilled** (or, *shall have fulfilled their course*).—They are to "rest." This does not mean that they are to cease their cry for vengeance, for the saints have never cried for this; but they are to rest, as the souls of the faithful after they are delivered from the burden of the flesh, in joy and felicity. But this rest is yet a waiting for a little while till fellow-servants and fellow-sufferers have achieved their work also. To every disciple a work is given in service and suffering, and till these have borne their witness and fulfilled their course (comp. 2 Tim. iv. 7, 8, and Acts xiii. 25) the departed must wait for their perfect consummation and bliss both in body and soul.

(12—17) **The sixth seal.**—The seals follow the lines laid down by our Lord in Matt. xxiv. There He tells His disciples that wars (verse 6), famines and pestilences (verse 7), and persecutions (verse 9) are to be expected; these are necessary features in the history of the world. But these features are described by our Master as preliminary to His Coming and the end of the world (Matt. xxiv. 3), and that when these had wrought their work then the Coming of the Son of Man would take place (verses 29—31). With this guide, it is impossible for us to deny that the opening of this sixth seal has reference to the Coming of the Son of Man, and finds its final and ultimate fulfilment in the day when He will come to gather His elect from the four winds. But it is not to be forgotten that our Lord wished us to regard certain great culminating epochs as in a secondary sense His advents. The eagles which swept down upon the carcase of any corrupt nationality were proofs of His reign and true shadows of His coming. The features indicated in the seals have a sequence which has been reproduced in the history of nations and churches. The promise of good; the breaking forth of the spirit of violence; the time of social misery, want, disease; the oppression of the good; revolution—these have repeated themselves in Jewish, Roman, French, and other histories; and the prophecy is not exhausted yet.

(12—14) **And I beheld . . .**—Better, *And I saw when He opened the sixth seal, and* (omit "lo!") *a great shaking took place, and the sun became black as sackcloth of hair, and the moon all became as blood, and the stars of the heaven fell to the earth, as a fig-tree casts its winter figs when shaken by a great wind, and the heaven departed like a scroll being rolled up, and every mountain and island were moved out of their places.* It is well to keep in mind the parallel imagery of the Old Testament. The *shaking* ("earthquake" is hardly an adequate rendering, as the shaking extends to heaven as well as earth) was spoken of by Haggai: "Yet once for all" (not "once more," as in the English version) "shake I not the earth only, but also the heavens. And this word 'Once for all' signifieth the removing of those things that are shaken" (Hag. ii. 6, and Heb. xii. 26, 27). *Sun black as sackcloth:* Joel has a similar thought —"the sun shall be turned into darkness" (Joel ii. 30, 31); and Isaiah, "I clothe the heavens with blackness, and I make sackcloth their covering" (Isa. l. 3). *The moon as blood* is repeated from Joel ii. 30, 31. The *falling of the stars of heaven* has its parallel in Isa. xxxiv. 3, 4, "All the host of heaven shall be dissolved." *As a fig-tree* is an echo of Isa. xxxiv. 4. It will be seen by these passages how closely the writer of the Apocalypse has kept to Old Testament imagery; and that events, such as great calamities, changes, and revolutions in the world's history, are described by emblems similar to those used here. St. Peter, for example, illustrates the great spiritual revolution of the Day of Pentecost by the passage from Joel, "The sun turned into darkness and the moon into blood." Hence it seems right to regard the language here as figurative, and to bear in mind that, though its fullest application belongs to the final advent, there may be many anticipatory advents. The judgment is often rehearsed before the day of judgment; the ages of oppression end in a day of catastrophe and confusion in which the righteous laws of a righteous King avenge themselves on the law breakers; the old lights and landmarks are for a time obliterated, and feeble, but pretentious, religionists are swept off as autumn figs from the fig-tree, and the proud and mighty are dismayed; things come to a crisis, and men "are proven by the hour" of that judgment; the unripe or untimely fruit drops off, as those who have no root in themselves fall away, and as the feebly-founded house fell in the tempest (Matt. vii. 26, 27). If this be so in the minor and preliminary crisis of the world, how much more so in the final crisis, which will try all? "Let him that thinketh he standeth take heed lest he fall." The *untimely* figs, or unripe figs, are the *grossos*, or winter figs, which grow under the leaves, and do not ripen at the proper season, but hang upon the trees till the winter. They are a fit emblem of those who have not used the opportunity and season to ripen for God. Like the unwise virgins, they have not replenished their lamps with oil; or, to use the unique expression of St. Luke, they bring no fruit to perfection (Luke viii. 14). The crisis thus puts the feeble, timid, and negligent to the test, and also proves the vanity of those who make any world-power their confidence. As the day of the Lord of which Isaiah spoke was upon every one that was proud and lifted up, upon the cedars and oaks, upon the towers and fenced walls, upon the loftiness and haughtiness of men, so does the Apocalyptic seer behold the dismay which falls upon every form of vaingloriousness, pretence, and pride.

(15—17) **And the kings . . .**—Translate, *And the kings of the earth, and the magnates, and the commanders of hosts, and the wealthy, and the strong, and every man, bond and free, hid themselves* (going) *into*

great men, and the rich men, and the
chief captains, and the mighty men,
and every bondman, and every free man,
hid themselves in the dens and in the
rocks of the mountains; (16) and said to
the mountains and rocks, Fall on us,[a]
and hide us from the face of him that
sitteth on the throne, and from the
wrath of the Lamb: (17) for the great
day of his wrath is come; and who shall
be able to stand?

A.D. 96.

a Luke 23. 30.

CHAPTER VII.—(1) And after these
things I saw four angels standing on the
four corners of the

Chap. vii. 1—17. The two assuring visions: the vision of security (1—8);

the caves and into the rocks of the mountains; and say to the mountains and to the rocks, Fall on us, and hide us from the face of Him that sitteth upon the throne, and from the wrath of the Lamb: for the day, the great (day) of His wrath came (or, *is come*); *and who is able to stand?* In the list of the great ones here we may notice the descending order—kings, magnates or statesmen, generals, rich men, strong men, bond and free men. The terror strikes into every class: monarchs and their advisers, the statesmen and diplomatists, the commanders of troops, the merchant princes, the men of ability, as well as the obscurer orders of society. Neither royalty, nor rank, nor force of arms, nor opulence, nor talent, nor strength, either of intellect or frame, avail in that crisis; neither does insignificance escape in that day when God brings to light the hidden things. The tests of God are spiritual, as the weapons of God's war are not carnal. Men who have relied upon wealth, rank, or power, have prepared themselves against one form of trial, but find themselves unarmed in the day of spiritual testing. Like Macbeth, they are unable to fight with the unexpected shape which haunts them. They would rather meet the bodily foe, "who would dare them to the desert with a sword."

Thus in the final day of judgment the revealing of the spiritual order of all life will confound men whose minds have been blinded by their entire absorption in world-splendours and world-powers. Nor is it merely the unveiling of the forgotten spiritual order which will confound them. The advent is of a Person. It is more than the manifestation of the kingdom of Him who all this while had been King on His throne, and whom they had forgotten—it is the revealing of God's Son from heaven. It is not without significance that He is described as the Lamb. In that day of His wrath, it is not as a Judge who has laid aside the tokens of His humiliation and suffering: it is as the Lamb. He whom they now shrink from is He who came meek as a lamb, gentle, pure, and suffering on their behalf. He whom they now behold with dismay is He whom they treated with neglect, and whose love they spurned.

(17) **Who shall be** (or, *is*) **able to stand?**—The thought is derived from Mal. iii. 2, which spoke of a coming of the Lord. Every advent of Christ is the advent of One whose fan is in His hand, and who will thoroughly purge His floor. Whether it be His advent in the flesh, He tested men; or whether one of His advents in Providence—such as the fall of Jerusalem, the overthrow of Pagan Rome, the convulsions of the Reformation and Revolution epochs of history—He still tests men whether they are able to abide in faith and love the day of His coming; and much more, then, in the closing personal advent, when these visions will receive their fullest illustration, will He try men. "Who is able to stand?" It is the question of questions. Christ's answer is: "Apart from Me ye can do nothing." "Let your loins be girt about and your lights burning, and ye yourselves like to men that wait for their Lord's coming." And parallel is St. Paul's advice: "Wherefore take unto you, (not the weapons on which men rely, but) the whole armour of God, that ye may be able to withstand in the evil day, and, having done all, to stand." This anxiety that his converts should be ready for the day of testing is continually appearing in his Epistles. Comp. the recurrence of "the day of Christ" in Phil. i. 6, 10, and the Apostle's wish that the Philippians might be sincere and without offence till the day of Christ; and St. John's desire that Christians should not "be ashamed before Him at His coming," and "may have boldness in the day of judgment" (1 John ii. 28, and iv. 17). "Who is able to stand?" The question is answered in the next chapter. They shall stand who are sealed with the seal of the living God.

The sixth seal does not give us a completed picture. We see the great and awe-inspiring movements which are heralds of the day of wrath. The whole world is stirred and startled at the tread of the approaching Christ, and then the vision melts away; we see no more, but we have seen enough to be sure that the close of the age is at hand. Yet we are anxious to know something of those who have been faithful, pure, and chivalrous witnesses for truth and right, for Christ and God. In that day, that awful day, the whole population of the world seems to be smitten with dismay; the trees, shaken with that terrible tempest, seem to be shedding all their fruit; the trembling of all created things seems to be about to shake down every building. Are all to go? Are none strong enough to survive? We heard that there were seven seals attached to the mystic book which the Lion of the tribe of Judah was opening; but this sixth seal presents us with the picture of universal desolation: what is there left for the seventh seal to tell us? The answer to these questions is given in the seventh chapter, which introduces scenes which may either be taken as dissolving views, presented in the course of the sixth seal, or as complementary visions. And those scenes show us in pictorial form that the Lord knoweth how to deliver the godly out of temptation: that in the midst of the time of the shaking of all things, when all might, majesty, strength, and genius of men is laid low, and every mere earth-born kingdom is overthrown, there is a kingdom which cannot be shaken. The germ of life was indestructible, and ready to break forth in fruit again: an ark, which sheltered all that was good, moved ever secure over the desolating floods:—

"I looked: aside the dust-cloud rolled,
The waster seemed the builder too;
Upspringing from the ruined old
I saw the new.

"'Twas but the ruin of the bad—
The wasting of the wrong and ill;
Whate'er of *good the old time had*
Was living still."

VII.

(1) **And after these things . . .**—Better, *And after this I saw four angels standing at the four corners of the earth, holding fast the four winds of the earth,*

earth, holding the four winds of the earth, that the wind should not blow on the earth, nor on the sea, nor on any tree.
(2) And I saw another angel ascending from the east, having the seal of the living God: and he cried with a loud voice to the four angels, to whom it was given to hurt the earth and the sea,
(3) saying, Hurt not the earth, neither the sea, nor the trees, till we have sealed the

that there might not blow a wind upon the earth, nor upon the sea, nor upon any tree. In the sixth seal the winds had blown, and had shaken violently the fig-tree, causing its untimely figs to drop off: the untimely or winter figs represented those whose religious life was unequal to the strain of trial, and who failed in the crisis to which they were exposed. But is all the fruit shaken off? No; Christ had said that "if a man abide not in Me, he is cast forth as a branch;" but that those who abode in Him, purged by their trials, would bring forth more fruit, and the fruit which these bore was not a fruit easily shaken off, but fruit that should remain (John xv. 6, 5, 16). They would not be as winter figs, easily torn from the boughs, for their strength was in God: before the stormy winds of manifold trials had blown they had been sealed with the seal of the living God. This is the scene which is brought before us in this chapter. In it the care of God, who restrains from violence the winds, that they should not shake too soon the immature fruit, the tokens by which the sealed are known and the meaning of their sealing are set forth. The chapter, in fact, answers the solemn question of the last chapter: "Who is able to stand?" The winds are clearly emblems of days of trouble or judgment; as the winds sweep away the chaff and clear the atmosphere, so do judgments try the ungodly, who are like the chaff which the wind driveth away: the storm of God's judgments shakes the mountains and the wilderness, and strips the oaks of the forest. (Comp. Ps. xxix.) These winds of judgment are ready to blow from all quarters (four corners of the earth), but they are restrained till the servants of God are sealed. For passages where winds are used as emblems of judgment, see especially Jer. xlix. 36, 37, "Upon Elam I will bring the four winds from the four quarters of heaven. And I will bring evil upon them, even My fierce anger, saith the Lord." Comp. also Dan. vii. 2, "I saw in my vision by night, and, behold, the four winds of the heaven strove upon the great sea." But those tempests would not arise or shake a single leaf till the securing of God's servants was accomplished.

(2) **And I saw another angel . . .**—Translate, *And I saw another angel going up from the rising of the sun, having a seal of the living God, and he was crying with a great voice to the four angels to whom it was given to injure the earth and the sea, saying, Injure ye not the earth, nor the sea, nor the trees, until we have sealed the servants of our God upon their foreheads.* The angels appear as carrying out the purposes of God. This angel rises into view from the door of the dawn. In the midst of the dark symptoms of coming storm and judgment there springs up a light for the righteous and joyful gladness for such as are true-hearted: they need not be afraid of evil tidings whose hearts stand fast believing in the Lord. This angel carries a seal of the living God. The seal is the emblem of security. The seal was placed on our Lord's sepulchre to keep the tomb safe from invasion; the king's seal was, in the same way, placed on the stone which was laid at the mouth of the den in which Daniel was imprisoned: "the king sealed it with his own signet" (Dan. vi. 17). The intrusting of the seal into the hands of others was the token that royal authority had been for the time delegated to man. So Jezebel "wrote letters in Ahab's name, and sealed them with his seal" (1 Kings xxi. 8). Esther obtained the use of the king's seal to protect her countrymen from the mischief devised by Haman: "for the writing which is written in the king's name, and sealed with the king's ring, may no man reverse" (Esth. viii. 8). There is also a seal of the living God. St. Paul tells us that this seal bears two legends. "The foundation of God standeth sure, having this seal, 'The Lord knoweth them that are his,' and, 'Let every one that nameth the name of Christ depart from iniquity'" (2 Tim. ii. 19). On the one side, it is dependence on and communion with God; on the other side, it is holiness of life. The sealed are found in Christ, not having their own righteousness, but the righteousness which is of God by faith (Phil. iii. 9). For this is the righteousness which will endure to the end, and which is found in them who are "sealed with the Holy Spirit of promise, which is the earnest of our inheritance" (Eph. i. 13, 14). God's image and superscription is impressed on such; just as afterwards we are told of all the servants of God, "His name shall be in their foreheads" (chap. xxii. 4). This token is a true safe-guard and talisman; as the sprinkled blood on the lintel protected the house from the destroying angel at the first Passover. It is a token also of those who have not conformed to the evil world; they are like those whom Ezekiel saw in Jerusalem, when the Lord sent the man with the inkhorn "to set a mark upon the foreheads of the men that sigh and that cry for all the abominations that be done" (Ezek. ix. 4). There has been much misapprehension respecting this act of sealing. It has been said that it implies security, and assures God's servants of protection in the coming judgments: this is, in a sense, true; but the sealing, as will have been seen by the passages quoted above, is that sealing of the Spirit, that root of heavenly life in the soul, which is the pledge of the soul's union with God; and the terms of the charter of their protection are, Who is he that will harm you, if ye be followers of that which is good? In the Bible idea, sin, or moral defilement, is the only real evil: all other things work together for good. The breastplate which turns aside the fiery darts is the breastplate of righteousness: those who, escaping the corruptions which are in the world through lust, become partakers of the divine nature are in consequence victorious over all the evil. They are not exempt from the vicissitudes and tribulation of life: the winds are let loose to blow, but they are sealed, and they cannot be shaken; for what and who can separate them from the love of Christ? They are sealed by the Holy Spirit; they have an earnest of that Spirit in their hearts (Eph. iv. 30, and 2 Cor. i. 22), and the pledge of His power in their lives. St. John gives the same two-fold test as St. Paul (2 Tim. ii. 9): (1) "Hereby know we that we dwell in him, and he in us, because he hath given us of his Spirit" (1 John iv. 13); and (2) "Hereby we do know that we know him, if we keep his commandments" (1 John ii. 3). The sealing is on the forehead: it is God's mark, but it is where all may see it. "By their fruits ye shall know

servants of our God in their foreheads.
(4) And I heard the number of them
which were sealed: *and there were* sealed
an hundred *and* forty *and* four thousand
of all the tribes of the children of
Israel. (5) Of the tribe of Juda *were*
sealed twelve thousand. Of the tribe
of Reuben *were* sealed twelve thousand.
Of the tribe of Gad *were* sealed twelve
thousand. (6) Of the tribe of Aser *were*
sealed twelve thousand. Of the tribe of
Nepthalim *were* sealed twelve thousand.
Of the tribe of Manasses *were* sealed
twelve thousand. (7) Of the tribe of
Simeon *were* sealed twelve thousand.
Of the tribe of Levi *were* sealed twelve
thousand. Of the tribe of Issachar
were sealed twelve thousand. (8) Of the
tribe of Zabulon *were* sealed twelve
thousand. Of the tribe of Joseph *were*
sealed twelve thousand. Of the tribe of
Benjamin *were* sealed twelve thousand.

---

them." The cry of the angel is, Injure not the sea nor the trees. Doubtless the sea and trees are mentioned as these are the objects which would be most disturbed and injured by a storm of wind. Trees are used as emblems of real and of pretended religionism. The true-hearted in faith are described as trees planted by the waterside, whose fruit does not wither; and it is singular that St. Jude, who pictures the Antinomian teachers of his day under the image of autumn trees (not trees whose fruit withereth, as in English version) without fruit, immediately adds an expression which almost suggests the sudden uprising of a testing storm: the fruitless trees are "plucked up by the roots" (Jude, verse 12).

(4) **And I heard the number of them . . .**—Translate, *And I heard the number of the sealed: there were a hundred and forty and four thousand sealed out of every tribe of the sons of Israel.* There are two or three questions which these verses suggest. What are we to understand by the number twelve thousand from each tribe? Who are these who are drawn from the tribes of Israel? Why is there a change of the order and name of the tribes? It may help us to clearer thoughts to take the second of these questions first. (1) Who are these one hundred and forty-four thousand? An answer to this has been partly anticipated in our previous comments; but perhaps a fuller consideration is needed. Some have thought that the sealed ones must be Jewish Christians: *i.e.,* they are disposed to take the twelve tribes literally. The scope of the previous verses seems decisive against this view. The time of judgment and trial is drawing near; we have seen the tokens of the coming storm in the opening of the sixth seal; our wish is to know the lot of the saints of God; this chapter answers this wish: they are safe, having the seal of God. Now, to limit the answer to the Israelitish Christians is to break in abruptly upon the general flow of thought with a bold literalism. The sealed ones are explained to be the servants of God; the description which follows proclaims them to be the "Israel of God." It would be a strange leap away from the subject to introduce a sudden limitation of thought. Nor is there any necessity for doing so. Israelitish and Jewish names are freely adopted by the sacred writers, and used in a spiritual sense without any explanation of such usage; and the Apostle most emphatically laid down the principle that "he is not a Jew which is one outwardly, neither is that circumcision which is outward in the flesh, but he is a Jew which is one inwardly, and circumcision is that of the heart, in the spirit and not in the letter" (Rom. ii. 28, 29); and the principle he applies by affirming that in Christ "there is neither Jew nor Greek" (Gal. iii. 28). The Christian Church absorbs the Jewish, inherits her privileges, and adopts, with wider and nobler meaning, her phraseology. She has her Jerusalem, but it is a heavenly Jerusalem (Heb. xii. 22): a Jerusalem from above (Gal. iv. 26): a new Jerusalem (Rev. xxi. 2; see chap. iii. 12); and to that Jerusalem of God the true Israel of God, the chosen generation and royal priesthood of every age, turn the eye of faith. It is needless to say that this view does not rob, as it has been said, the Jew of God's promises; it only intensifies those promises by showing the growth of that Church in which the Jew may yet find the truest consummation of his holiest and highest hopes, and into which God is yet able to graff them in again (Rom. xi. 23, 25, 26), and in which he may yet play a part loftier than men dream of. (2) How are we to understand the numbers? As we cannot adopt the literal interpretation of the tribes of Israel, still less can we admit a literal interpretation of the numbers here mentioned; but they are not on this ground to be looked upon as meaningless numbers: there is an appropriate symbolism in the numbers of the Apocalypse. Twelve is used as the number of those who in every age have been called out to witness for some truth which the world needed. Thus the twelve tribes of Israel were the appointed witnesses of a pure theology and a pure morality in the days of idolatry and license; and later, the twelve Apostles became the inheritors of a similar, though higher, spiritual work in the world. The number twelve, then, stands for a world-witness of divine truth; and the fruits of this world-witness is a wide and sustained success: the twelve multiplied by the twelve a thousand-fold—"the native and not degenerate progeny of the Apostles apostolically multiplied" (Mede, quoted by Dr. Currey). The skeleton organisation is twelve, the college of the Apostles; the one hundred and forty-four thousand represent the growth into full numbers of the choice ones of God. (3) Does the change in the order and names of the tribes symbolise anything? The alterations are not without significance. They are briefly these: The tribe of Dan is omitted, and the name of Ephraim does not appear, but the number is made up to twelve by two representatives of Joseph: Manasseh, who stands sixth in order, and Joseph (superseding the name, but representing the tribe of Ephraim), who is placed eleventh on the list. The number twelve is maintained to show that in all changes God's purposes stand. The omission of one tribe and the changed name of another are designed to show that in the Church, as in Israel, the most splendid opportunities may be lost. Dan, once a tribe, and not an insignificant tribe, which had reared its heroes, gradually lapsed into idolatry and immorality, dwindled in numbers and importance, and at length disappeared, and as a tribe became extinct. Its omission in this list is a silent but emphatic comment on the sacred warnings: "Let him that thinketh he standeth take heed lest he fall."

(9) After this I beheld, and, lo, a great multitude, which no man could number, of all nations, and kindreds, and people, and tongues, stood before the throne, and before the Lamb, clothed with white robes, and palms in their hands; (10) and cried with a loud voice, saying, Salvation to our God which sitteth upon the throne, and unto the

Chap. vii. 9—17. the vision of victorious rest.

"Begin not to say we have Abraham to our father: God is able of these stones to raise up children unto Abraham." Similarly, Ephraim, as has been suggested by a thoughtful writer, who exalted himself in Israel, is now lost in the greater name of Joseph. (Comp. Hos. xiii. 1; x. 11; Luke xviii. 14.) The order of the names is altered. Reuben no longer stands first: Judah has taken the firstborn's place; and Levi, though named, does not occupy the third, the place of his birthright, but the eighth place. Here, again, the changes have their teachings. The unstable Reuben, with all his splendid advantages—the firstborn, the excellency of dignity and the excellency of power—failed to hold his own among his brethren; the fatal instability of his character accompanied his history, and weakened his otherwise pre-eminent powers; yet weak and erring, the type of the brilliant and vacillating, he is not an outcast altogether, but finds place, and high place, among the servants of God. Judah, lion-like, resolute, and strong, wins the foremost place; from him springs the true Ruler, the Lion of the tribe of Judah, to unfold the counsels of God, and to rule the world with a righteous sceptre. Levi's subordinate position is thought to be due to the fact that the Mosaic ritual and Levitical priesthood are at an end. This may be so; the changes are the result of the actual history of the tribes, and illustrate how in the Christian Church, as in the Jewish, privileges may be lost, opportunities seized or cast away, offices and functions used for a time, and then laid aside when their work is accomplished; but in all and through all changes, God's unchanging purpose runs onward to its certain close. The grouping of the tribes is, as has been pointed out, in the order of closest kinship: "We find not one violent separation of those who are naturally united, where both are truly members of the Israel of God" (Rev. C. H. Waller, *Names on Gates of Pearl*).

(9) **After this I beheld . . .**—Better, *After these things I saw, and behold! a great multitude which no one was able to number, out of every nation, and* (*all*) *tribes, and peoples, and tongues, standing before the throne, and before the Lamb, clothed in white robes, and palm branches in their hands.* "A great multitude:" We have just had the picture of the sealing of a multitude which could be numbered: now we have the picture of a countless throng. Who are these? Are they the same as the one hundred and forty-four thousand, or are they others? Our answer must be that this vision gives the climax of the previous one. The sealing represented the Passover of the Church: this vision represents its Feast of Tabernacles. The sealing assured us that in the midst of the severe times of testing there would be those who, wearing God's armour, would come forth unscathed: this vision shows us the fruition of their labour and their rest after conflict. The sealing assured us that God's hidden ones would be safe in trouble: this tells us that they have come safe out of it—they are those who have come out of the great tribulation (verse 14). But how can the numbered of the one vision be the same as the numberless of the next? They are numbered in the first vision, as it is one of the assurances of their safety. In that vision the idea of their security in trial and danger is the main one. The servants of God are safe, for they are sealed and numbered; they are among those sheep of Christ whom He calls by name, whose very hairs are numbered; they are those whose reliance is not on self, but on their shepherd; and the sealing is the echo of Christ's words, "they shall never perish;" they are the servants of God, known by Him and recognised by Him. But in the next vision, the expanding prospects of the Church and her final repose are shown to us. The idea of victory and peace, not so much safety in danger as freedom from it, is set forth; and then countless multitudes are seen; the numbered are found to be numberless; countless as the sand by the sea and as the stars in heaven, they are yet in the reckoning and knowledge of Him who "telleth the number of the stars and calleth them all by their names." The numbering must not be understood to imply limitation. We have seen that it is a number which symbolises expansive energy and extensive success; it implies the real security and wide-spread growth of the Church of God; it has no limits; it gathers from every nation, and people; it welcomes all; where there is neither Jew, nor Greek, barbarian, Scythian, bond, nor free; its gates are open all night and all day to every quarter of the world—

> "From earth's wide bounds, from ocean's farthest coast,
> Through gates of pearl stream in the countless host,
> Singing to Father, Son, and Holy Ghost. Alleluia."

The multitude are clothed with white robes, and carry palm branches in their hands. It has been thought that these are the emblems of victory; they doubtless are tokens of a triumph: it is the sacred rejoicing of the Israel of God. The imagery is drawn from the Feast of Tabernacles: just as the sealing reminded us of the protecting sign on the lintels of the houses of Israel in Egypt, so do these palm branches and songs of joy recall the ceremonies of the later feast. No imagery would be more natural to the sacred seer, and none more appropriate to his subject. The Feast of Tabernacles commemorated God's care over them in the wilderness, and their gratitude for the harvest. The people forsook the houses, and dwelt in booths; the streets were full of glad multitudes who carried branches of palm, and olive, and myrtle; everywhere the sounds of rejoicing and singing were heard; "there was very great gladness" (Ex. xxiii. 16; Lev. xxiii. 43; Neh. viii. 14—17). The vision here shows us a far greater feast. "The troubles of the wilderness are ended, the harvest-home of the Church is come," and God tabernacles (verse 15) among His servants.

(10) **And cried with a loud voice . . .**—Better, *And they cry with a loud voice, saying, The salvation to our God who sitteth upon the throne, and to the Lamb.* Their cry, uttered with a loud voice, is the acknowledgment that their salvation—the salvation which they now taste—is due not to themselves, but to their God and to the Lamb. The salvation here must, I think, be taken in its most comprehensive sense, including every deliverance—from the curse of law, from the power of sin, and from the perils of life. The explanation in

Lamb. (11) And all the angels stood round about the throne, and *about* the elders and the four beasts, and fell before the throne on their faces, and worshipped God, (12) saying, Amen: Blessing, and glory, and wisdom, and thanksgiving, and honour, and power, and might, *be* unto our God for ever and ever. Amen. (13) And one of the elders answered, saying unto me, What are these which are arrayed in white robes? and whence came they? (14) And I said unto him, Sir, thou knowest. And he said to me, These are they which came out of great tribulation, and have washed their robes, and made them white in the blood of the Lamb. (15) Therefore are they before the throne of God, and serve him day and night in his temple: and he that sitteth on the throne shall dwell

---

verse 14 confirms this. (Comp. Gal. iii. 13; Phil. iii. 9.) This is "the voice of rejoicing and salvation which is in the tabernacles of the righteous," when the Lord, who is their strength and song, "has become their salvation" (Ps. cxviii. 14). Note the recurrence of "the Lamb." They are before the throne and before the Lamb; their salvation is ascribed to God and to the Lamb.

(11) **And all the angels . . .**—Translate, *And all the angels were standing round the throne, and the elders, and the four living beings . . . saying, Amen.* The great concourse of angels—those among whom there has been joy in heaven when a sinner has repented—now add their "Amen" to the cry of the redeemed, and then raise the seven-fold ascription of praise—

"Amen!
The blessing, and the glory, and the wisdom,
And the thanksgiving,
And the honour, and the power, and the strength,
(Is) unto our God
Unto the ages of the ages.
Amen!"

The seven-fold form of the doxology, which implies a divine completeness, is appropriate to this vision, which shows us the close of the Church's agony, and is in itself a slight indication that the view which would limit the seals to some short period of Church history is incorrect, as it is assuredly inadequate.

(13) **And one of the elders answered, saying unto me.**—The seer had asked no question, but the elder answers the wondering thoughts and questionings which fill his mind. Perhaps this scene was in Dante's mind when he described himself in Paradise:

"Silent was I, yet desire
Was painted in my looks; and thus I spake
My wish more earnestly than language could."
—*Paradiso*, iv. 10—12.

The elder asks the question which he knows St. John would fain ask. *These who are clothed in white robes, who are they, and whence came they?* The question brings *the white* robes into prominence. Is it, as has been suggested, that the wonder of the seer is excited more by the emblem of holiness and innocence than anything else? He recognises the multitudes as men and women out of every nation and tribe of sinful humanity, and he sees them clothed in the garb of holiness. Who are these countless throngs of holy ones?

(14) **And I said unto him . . .**—The form in which the answer of the seer is given shows how completely the elder had anticipated his thoughts; for he describes his reply as instantaneous. *And I have said, My Lord*—the language is that of reverent regard, but not of worship (see chaps. xix. 10 and xxii. 8, 9)—*thou knowest—i.e.*, it is for thee to tell me: thy knowledge and thy view-point is higher than mine; thou knowest: it is thine to speak, and mine to hearken.

And he said to me . . .—Read, *And he said to me, These are they who come* (the present tense is used: *these are those coming*) *out of* the *great tribulation.* They are those who come, not all at once, but gradually. The saints of God are continually passing into the unseen world, and taking their place among the spirits of just men made perfect. They come out of *the* great tribulation. Are we to limit the expression to the special and peculiar afflictions of the last great trial? There is no doubt about the emphasis which the definite article (unfortunately, ignored in our English version) gives: it is *the* great tribulation; but while there may yet be in store for the Church of Christ trials so great that they may be called, in comparison with those which went before, *the* great tribulation, it yet seems out of harmony with the spirit of the Apocalypse and the complexion of this vision to limit the phrase to some special season of trial. Is not the great tribulation the tribulation which those must encounter who are on the side of Christ and righteousness, and refuse to receive the mark of worldliness and sin on their heart, conscience, and life? In all ages it is true that we must through much tribulation enter the Kingdom of God; and the vision here is surely not of those who will come safe out of some particular trials, but of the great multitude from every age and every race who waged war against sin, and who, in the midst of that protracted conflict, endured the great tribulation which is to continue until Christ's return. *And they washed* (not "have washed," for the washing was done during their earthly life) *their robes, and made them white in the blood of the Lamb.* The imagery is to be found in the Gospel and in the Epistle (John xiii. 8—11; and 1 John i. 7); its use here and in chap. i. 5 (if the reading *washed* is to be preferred to *loosed*) points to a common authorship: the emblem of the *blood which washes white*, or cleanses, is not used with such distinctness elsewhere in the New Testament. It is, in St. John's lips, but a following out of the twice-repeated words which he quotes from John the Baptist at the opening of the Gospel, when he proclaimed Christ to be "the Lamb of God, which taketh away the sin of the world." In that Lamb of God those who came out of great tribulation found the forgiveness and the spiritual power which gave them confidence and hope in the midst of life's war and life's weariness; for the man who knows that he is forgiven and that he is being helped to holiness is the man who thinks no fiery trial strange, but rejoices in the knowledge that his salvation is of God.

(15) **Therefore are they before the throne . . .**—Better, *On this account are they before the throne of God—i.e.*, because they so washed their robes, and made them white in the blood of the Lamb. (Comp. chap. xxii. 14, where a well-supported reading is, "Blessed are they that wash their robes, that they may have right to the

among them.[a] (16) They shall hunger no more,[b] neither thirst any more; neither shall the sun light on them, nor any heat. (17) For the Lamb which is in the midst of the throne shall feed them, and shall lead them unto living fountains of waters: and God shall wipe away all tears from their eyes.[c]

a Isa. 4. 5, 6; ch. 21. 3.
b Isa. 49. 10.
c ch. 21. 4.

tree of life," &c.) They are before the throne: they are like Him, for they see Him as He is (1 John iii. 2), and *serve Him day and night in His temple, and He that sitteth upon the throne shall tabernacle over them.* The life is not simply one of joy or safety, it is one also of service. (Comp. chap. xxii. 3.) Those who were made priests to God here carry on their service in His temple; yet it is to be remembered that this can only be figurative language, for in the heavenly city there is no temple (chap. xxi. 22). It serves to teach us that the servant will find his fitting work of service there as well as here. *He that sitteth upon the throne shall tabernacle over them.* It is worth noticing how persistently St. John keeps up the phrase, "He that sitteth upon the throne" (chaps. iv. 2; v. 1, 7, 13; vii. 10). *Tabernacle,* or dwell as in a tent: The rendering "shall dwell" among them does not do justice to this word, and at the same time obscures the allusion which the seer has in his mind. The allusion is to the Shechinah, the symbol of the Divine Presence, which rested over the mercy seat. "The idea that the Shechinah, the σκηνή (*skéné*), the glory which betokened the Divine Presence in the Holy of Holies, and which was wanting to the sacred temple, would be restored once more in Messiah's days was a cherished hope of the Jewish doctors during and after the Apostolic ages." The expected and wished-for glory would be seen among God's saints. God's tabernacle shall be with them (chap. xxi. 3), and with them so as to stretch over them: He will tabernacle over (or, *upon*) them. With this we may compare St. Paul's expression in 2 Cor. xii. 9 ("that the power of Christ may tabernacle"—"rest" in the English version—"upon me"), where Professor Lightfoot (whose words have just been quoted) thinks that there is a similar reference to the symbol of the Divine Presence in the Holy of Holies. (Comp. Isa. iv. 5, 6; Ezek. xxxvii. 27; and John i. 14.) There seems also to be a carrying on of the imagery derived from the Feast of Tabernacles: as there were the palm branches of the harvest joy, so there will be the booth, or tabernacle, of God's presence among them. He shall be their pavilion, their shelter. "There shall be a tabernacle for a shadow in the day-time from the heat, and for a place of refuge and for a covert from storm and from rain."

(16) **They shall hunger no more . . .**—Better, *They shall not hunger any more, nor yet thirst any more; neither at all shall the sun light upon them, nor any heat.* The negatives are emphatic, and rise in force as the verse proceeds. None of the privations which they have endured for Christ's sake shall trouble them; none of the dissatisfactions and weariness of life shall afflict them; for hunger, thirst, and fatigue will be no more, for the former things are passed away (chap. xxi. 3, 4). And then, too, shall that blessed hunger and thirst—the hunger and thirst for righteousness—be appeased. Christ's benediction will then be realised in its fulness: Blessed are they who so hunger, for they shall be filled. And as they will receive inward strength and satisfaction, so also will they be kept from the outward trials which wear down the strength of the strongest. The sun shall not light on them: The Eastern sun, in its fierce and overpowering intensity, was a fit emblem of those trials which dry up the springs of strength. The sun, risen with a burning heat, devoured the beauty of the flower (Jas. i. 11); the rootless growth on the stony ground was scorched when the sun was up (Matt. xiii. 5, 6). Man's beauty of wealth and talent, man's resolutions of better things, all fade away before the testing beams of this sun; but the time of trial is past, the pains and temptations of life are over, the sun in that land will not scorch, for there is no longer need of these burning beams; the city has no need of the sun, for the glory of God lightens it, and the Lamb is the light thereof (chap. xxi. 23). No sun, and no heat, no burning hot wind like the sirocco, will spread withering influence there.

(17) **For the Lamb . . .**—Translate, *Because the Lamb which is in the midst of the throne shall tend them, and shall lead them to fountains of waters of life* (or, *life-springs of waters*); *and God shall wipe away every tear from their eyes.* The Lamb is described as "the Lamb in the midst of the throne." The writer told in chap. v. 6 that he had seen a Lamb in the midst of the throne. When he looked towards the throne, he saw the Lamb as the central object immediately in front of it. He who would draw near to the throne must pass the Lamb. The position which the Lamb held was one of significance, and is therefore repeated here. The Lamb will tend His people as a *shepherd* tends his flock (the word translated "feed" has this force), and will lead them to the springs of the water of life. The twenty-third Psalm rises at once to our minds. The Lord who was David's shepherd (Ps. xxiii. 2), who was the Good Shepherd who sought and brought home the lost for whom He died (Luke xv. 4; John x. 11), does not forget the shepherd's work in heaven. He who made His people to drink of the brook in the way (Ps. cx. 7), who gave to those who came to Him the water which alone would quench their thirst (John iv. 13, 14, and vii. 37—39), leads them now to the springs of the living water, and makes them drink of the river of His pleasures (Ps. xxxvi. 8). Significantly enough the springs of this living water are in the throne itself (chap. xxii. 1). Ezekiel saw the stream issuing forth from the Temple (Ezek. xlviii. 1), but in the city where there is no temple we are carried to the very throne of God, to find the well-spring of every gladness. In this emblem of the water we have another allusion to the Feast of Tabernacles. Among the ceremonies observed at the feast was that of the drawing water; the priest drew a vessel of water from the brook of Siloam, and poured it out in the temple-court by the altar of burnt offering, and the people sang the words, "With joy shall ye draw water out of the wells of salvation" (Isa. xii. 3). Here the Lamb, who is also the High Priest, leads His people to the springs of the water of life. Joy, too, is theirs; for God shall wipe away every tear from (or, *out of*) their eyes (Isa. xxv. 8; Rev. xxi. 4). In Isaiah it is said God shall wipe away tears from off all faces: here it is every tear. Thus shall all sorrow be removed from all: no tears shall gather in any eye, for the sources of sorrow will be cut off in the land where there is no more sin. None can weep again when it is God who wiped away their tears. Blessed are they that mourn, said Christ—blessed indeed in this, that God becomes their comforter. Only those who have wept can enjoy this consolation. Who would not shed life's tears to have God's hand to wipe them away!

CHAPTER VIII.—(1) And when he had opened the seventh seal, there was silence in heaven about the space of half an hour. (2) And I saw the seven angels which

Chap. viii. 1. The seventh seal opened.

A.D. 96.

Chap. viii. 2—6. The vision of the seven trumpet angels.

VIII.

(1) **And when he had opened the seventh seal . . .**—Translate, *And when he opened the seventh seal there took place a silence in heaven as it were for half an hour.* It is greatly to be regretted that this verse should have been prefixed to this chapter. The section of the book with which it is connected is that which goes before, not that which follows. The second verse of this eighth chapter introduces a new series of visions: the first verse gives the close of the visions which follow the opening of the seals. But what is the meaning of this verse which describes a half-hour's silence in heaven? It is a disputed point whether the book, or *roll*, fastened with the seven seals (chap. v. 1, 2) is ever really unrolled to view. Some have thought that as each seal is opened a portion of the roll is displayed, unfolding the vision of the seal: others have regarded the visions as mere accompaniments of the opening of the seals, and quite distinct from the writing on the roll; those who take this view are disposed to think that the roll never is read, for that when the last seal is broken, and all are expecting to hear what is written in the book, no reading takes place, but only a silence ensues. It does not seem to me that this latter view is altogether tenable. It appears a singularly harsh interpretation to say that the contents of the roll are never disclosed. The book of God's purposes was seen in the hand of Him who sat on the throne. The Evangelist longed to know something of its contents; vain efforts were made to open it; the Evangelist wept with disappointment; he was then comforted in his sorrow by hearing that the Lion of the tribe of Judah had conquered to open the book; but then, after all this, not a line or word of the book, it is said, is ever revealed. The servant is waiting to hear the divine word; the seer is waiting to record what is unfolded; but though the seals are opened, we are told that the words he waits for never came. St. John himself gives no hint of so disappointing a conclusion. Later on (chap. x. 4) he is told not to record the utterances of the seven thunders, but there the concealing of the utterances is clearly commanded. Here he evidently associates the visions of the seals with the contents of the roll. It is only a spirit in bondage to foolish literalisms which will ask how the visions can be the writing in the roll. The book represents God's purposes and principles of His government in relation to the world - history; the seals show us some typical scenes in that world-history, and if not seen on the parchment of the roll, are yet unfoldings of principles and truths in the book. But it does not follow that all that is in the roll is ever unfolded. Such portions are made manifest as the seer could hear, and as the Church of Christ needed; and thus it may well be that the half-hour's silence is significant that all God's purposes and revelations are not exhausted—that there is something behind which it is not well that we should know—that prophecy as well as knowledge is partial. But the stillness of this half hour, if it reminds us of what is yet untold, yet proclaims to us a time of deep, unbroken tranquillity, when the cries and groans of the earth, and even the grateful doxologies of heaven are hushed into calm. It is the silence which tells us that sorrow is ended, and eloquently tells us of heart peace. It is the rest of the troubled on the breast of God. All the earth, with her strife of tongues is still; all the cries of men (chap. vi. 15), of trafficker and warrior, of struggling wise, and suffering good, are stilled; all flesh keeps silence before Him; He gives His people peace.

> "O earth, so full of dreary noises!
> O men with wailing in your voices!
> O delvëd gold, the wailer's heap!
> O strife, O curse, that o'er it fall!
> God strikes a silence through you all,
> And giveth His beloved sleep."

Only those who have been carried away by an over-refined philosophy or morbid sentimentalism can see anything selfish in longing, out of earth's cares and injustices, for such a rest as this. It is surely not ignoble to pray—

> "Vouchsafe us such a half-hour's hush alone,
> In compensation for our stormy years;
> As heaven has paused from song, let earth from moan."

(2) THE VISIONS INTRODUCED BY THE SOUNDING OF SEVEN TRUMPETS.—The series of visions which is now introduced extend to the close of the eleventh chapter. There are some features which may be noticed here. There is a marked correspondence of arrangement between these and the visions of the seals. As there, so here, there are introduced two subordinate visions towards the end of the series. The sixth seal was followed by the vision of the one hundred and forty-four thousand and the countless multitude: the sixth trumpet is followed by the vision of the little book and the seven thunders and the measurement of the temple of God (chaps. x. and xi. 1—14). The general intention of these interposed visions is similar. In both cases they seem designed to give us an insight of the life within the life of Christ's Church. The main visions give us more external aspects; the interposed visions show the inner and more spiritual aspects. Thus the seals show the great outer features of world and Church history—the war, controversies, the famine and barren dogmatism, the death, and deathlike externalism, the persecutions and sorrows and revolutions of on-coming history; the interposed visions of chap. vii. show us the calm and strength and the victory of the children of God. So also with these visions of the trumpets. The main visions give us the trumpet-voices of God's manifold providences summoning the world to surrender to Him; the subsidiary visions point to the witness and work of the true children of God in this world, and the more secret growth of the Church of Christ. Another similarity between the seals and the trumpets is to be found in the separation between the first four and the last three. The first four trumpets, like the first four seals, are grouped together. The first four seals are introduced by the cry "Come"; the first four trumpets are followed by judgments on natural objects—the earth, the sea, the rivers, the lights of heaven—while the last three have been described as *woe trumpets*, being introduced by the thrice repeated cry of "Woe" (see verse 13). There is thus a correspondence of arrangement in the two series of visions; but their general import is very different. We reach in the seventh seal the eternal quiet of God's presence. Through a series of visions we have been shown that the way to rest is not easy, that we must be prepared to see the great features of earth's

stood before God; and to them were given seven trumpets. (3) And another angel came and stood at the altar, having a golden censer; and there was given unto him much incense, that he should offer *it* with the prayers[1] of

[1] Or, *add* it *to the prayers.*

troubles remain till the close, and that the children of God must through tribulation and even persecution enter into the kingdom of God's peace. The seals answer the question, "Lord, wilt thou at this time restore the kingdom?" But the kingdom will be restored. The Church may find her way a way of difficulty, delay, danger; but it will be a way to triumph. The kingdoms of the world will become the kingdoms of the Lord. Let the people of God go forward; let their prayers be set forth as incense; let them blow the trumpet, and summon men to repentance; they are not alone; the Lord still fights for His Israel. This is the assurance which we gather from the trumpets. In all the wondrous providences which the history of the world discloses we may hear the trumpet-voice which heralds the kingdom of Christ, to which the Church is bearing constant and sufficient witness (chap. xi. 3, 4). The seals close with peace; the trumpets close appropriately with victory (chap. xi. 15). The visions are not scenes of events which chronologically succeed one another. The one set shows us the way through trouble to rest; the other shows the way through conflict to triumph: the one set shows us the troubles which befall the Church because of the world; the other shows us the troubles which fall on the world because the Church advances to the conquest of the world, as Israel to the possession of the land of promise.

And I saw the seven angels . . .—Better, *And I saw the seven angels which stand* (not "stood") *before God; and there were given to them seven trumpets.* "The seven angels:" Who are these? The usual answer is that they are seven angels (or, according to some, *archangels*) distinguished among the myriads round the throne. The passages referred to in support of this view are two—one from the Apocryphal Book of Tobit, "I am Raphael, one of the seven holy angels which present the prayers of the saints, and which go in and out before the glory of the Holy One" (Tobit xii. 15); the other, the well-known passage from St. Luke, "I am Gabriel, that stand in the presence of God" (Luke i. 19). This may be true, and the emphatic article (*the* seven angels) gives the view some support, but seeing that the number seven is to be taken throughout the book as symbolical, and not literal, it is perhaps better to view the seven angels as representatives of the power of God over the world. They are the seven, the complete circle of God's power in judgment; for as we do not take the seven spirits to be literally seven spirits, but symbols of the complete and manifest influence of the one Holy Spirit, the third person in the glorious Trinity, so neither need we infer from the mention of the seven angels here that they are literally seven preeminent angelic personages, but rather regard them as symbols of that complete and varied messenger-force which God evermore commands.

Seven trumpets.—It will help our understanding of the symbol here employed to recall the occasions on which the trumpet was used. It was used to summon the people together, whether for worship, or festival, or war, "for the calling of the assembly, and for the journeying of the camps." "When they shall blow with them (the trumpets), all the assembly shall assemble themselves to thee (Moses) at the door of the tabernacle of the congregation" (Num. x. 4—8). For journeying an alarm was to be blown (Num. x. 6). "And if ye go to war in your land against the enemy that oppresseth you, then ye shall blow an alarm with the trumpets; and ye shall be remembered before the Lord your God, and ye shall be saved from your enemies" (verse 9). And as for war, so also on festival days the trumpets were blown: "Also in the day of your gladness, and in your solemn days, and in the beginnings of your months, ye shall blow with the trumpets over your burnt offerings, and over the sacrifices of your peace offerings; that they may be to you for a memorial before your God: I am the Lord your God." The reader will remember other illustrations. When the people were assembled to hear the Ten Commandments the voice of the trumpet sounded long, and waxed louder and louder (Ex. xix. 19). The feast held on the first day of the seventh month was "a day of blowing the trumpets" (Num. xxix. 1) among the people who would blow up the trumpet in the new moon, in the time appointed, on their solemn feast day (Ps. lxxxi. 3). At the siege of Jericho seven priests bore before the ark seven trumpets of rams' horns, and on the seventh day the priests blew with the trumpets (Josh. vi. 4, 5). For assembling, for journeying, for war, the sound of the trumpets was heard. The judgments which follow the blowing of the trumpets in this series of visions are the trumpet-toned calls of God, summoning mankind to assemble to the true tabernacle, bidding His people go forward, and announcing the overthrow of His adversaries. Every judgment, on earth, or sea, or river, by war, or by invasion, is a call which bids men listen to the still small voice, which they have neglected, perhaps resisted. Every judgment should rouse the true servant to greater vigilance and further advance: it is an alarm sounded on the great battle-field of life. Miracles have been called the alarm bells of the universe; no less are the strange and startling events of the world's history the alarm notes blown by God's angels across the world, to remind us of the war in which every citadel of evil must inevitably fall. It is mainly, then, as an alarm of war that these angel-trumpets are sounded. The land of promise is to be rescued from the tribes and peoples who corrupt it. As the Canaanites of old were swept away lest their wickedness, increasing beyond measure, should spread abroad a moral death, so are the judgments of these trumpets sent to undermine, purge away, and finally to destroy all evil powers which destroy the earth (chap. xi. 18). We may hear, then, in "each blast of the symbolical trumpet a promise and instalment of the victory" for which the groaning and travailing creation yearns, and which will be the banishment of earth's destroyers, and the manifestation of the sons of God.

(3) **And another angel came and stood at** (or, *over*) **the altar, having a golden censer.**—The appearance of this other angel has given rise to some questioning, and some strained explanations. Some have thought that by this other angel we are to understand Christ Himself. This is very doubtful: the designation "another angel" (see chap. vii. 2) is against this view. There is really no need to ask who the several angels are: the book is symbolical. The angels are not particular personages, but symbolical

all saints upon the golden altar which was before the throne. (4) And the smoke of the incense, *which came* with the prayers of the saints, ascended up before God out of the angel's hand.

(5) And the angel took the censer, and filled it with fire of the altar, and cast *it* into[1] the earth: and there were voices, and thunderings, and lightnings, and an earthquake. (6) And the seven angels

1 Or, *upon*.

---

of those agencies—whether personal, or natural, or supernatural—which are employed by Him who sitteth on the throne. The angel stood at the altar. The altar mentioned in chap. vi. 2 corresponded with the altar of burnt sacrifice, which stood in the open court in front of the tabernacle or temple. The symbolism of the Apocalypse being so largely built up out of Jewish materials, we need not be surprised to find the altar of incense introduced here. This altar was of gold, and was situated in the holy place. Here the priest was wont to burn incense, while the people outside were praying. We have an example of the custom in the history of Zecharias (Luke i. 8—11). The scene described by St. Luke bears a close resemblance to this, and gives a key to the symbolism. The prayers of the people and the smoke of the incense are ascending together. The angel has a golden censer. The word here rendered censer is used sometimes for the incense, but the epithet "golden" shows that it is the vessel to hold the incense which is intended. The censer is of gold, as was the altar, and as are so many things in the Apocalypse. (See chaps. iv. 4; v. 8; xv. 6, 7, and xxi. 15, 21.)

And there was given unto him much incense . . .—Literally, *And there was given to him much incense that he might* (not "offer it with," as English version, but) *give it to the prayers of all the saints upon the golden altar which was before the throne.* The incense was to be mingled with the prayers of the saints. The incense was added to give a fragrance to the prayers of the saints, and render them acceptable before God. The action of the angel has been spoken of as though it might give countenance to the erroneous doctrine of the mediatorship of saints and angels. It is only when we persist in viewing symbols as literal facts that there is any danger of such an inference. Dogmas, whose only foundation is in the incidental symbolism of a prophetic book, are ill-grounded. It is a safe canon that doctrinal inferences from metaphors are always to be suspected. The angel here is a mere symbol of a divinely-appointed agency. No personal angel actually ever did what is described here: how could incense mix with prayers? The whole is symbolical of the truth that the prayers of all the saints need to be rendered acceptable by the infusion of some divine element. The best prayers of the best saints are weak, and polluted and imperfect at the best. The incense which is added to the prayers is not supplied by the angel: it is first given to him, and he then mingles it with the prayers of all saints. It is hard to forget here Him whose offering and sacrifice became a savour of sweet smell (Eph. v. 1, 2). The altar is described as the golden altar—*i.e.*, the altar of incense, as noted above. It is well for us to remember Dean Alford's caution that we must not attempt to force the details of any of these visions into accordance with the arrangements of the tabernacle. "A general analogy in the use and character of the heavenly furniture is all that we can look for" (Alford, *in loco*).

(4) **And the smoke of . . .**—Better, *And there went up the smoke of the incense for* (or *to*, *i.e.*, designed for, and to give fragrance to) *the prayers of the saints, out of the hand of the angel, before God.* The emblem of the rising column of smoke, in which incense and prayer now mingled, is the token that the prayers of the saints, now rendered acceptable, and no longer premature, are about to be answered. These prayers of God's people, weak and imperfect as they are, are yet invincible weapons in the hands of Christ's soldiers, and will be found mightier than any carnal weapons. As Jericho fell without Israel needing to strike a blow, so now the Israel of God will be seen to be omnipotent through true and faithful prayer. The charter of the Church's power is in the words of Christ: "If ye abide in Me, and My words abide in you, ye shall ask what ye will, and it shall be done unto you" (John xv. 7). The judgments that follow are not indeed specifically prayed for by the Church of Christ, but they are the results of their prayers, and prove the might of all prayer.

(5) **And the angel . . .**—Translate, *And the angel has taken* (or, *took*) *the censer, and he filled it from the fire of the altar, and cast it* (*i.e.*, the fire or hot ashes which filled the censer) *upon the earth.* The prayers have gone up, and the sprinkling of the ashes earthward is the symbol of the answer descending from heaven. We may recall the similar action of Moses before Pharaoh, when he took ashes of the furnace and sprinkled it towards heaven, but it descended towards earth, as a symbol of the plague about to fall upon the land (Ex. ix. 8—10). The hot ashes are the tokens of the coming judgments. As in the parallel vision in Ezekiel (chap. x. 2), when the man clothed with linen is bidden to "go in between the wheels, even under the cherub, and fill his hand with coals of fire from between the cherubims, and scatter them over the doomed city;" so here the ashes fall—the judgments are at hand.

And there were voices . . .—Or, *And there took place thunders, and voices, and lightnings, and an earthquake.* There is some variety among the MSS. in the order of the words here used. Some place "lightnings" before "voices." These signs and sounds herald the approach of judgments. God has arisen in answer to the cry of His people. "The earth shook and trembled. There went up a smoke and a fire: coals were kindled at it. At the brightness that was before Him His thick clouds passed, hailstones and coals of fire. The Lord also thundered in the heavens, and the Highest gave His voice, hailstones and coals of fire. Yea, He sent out His arrows, and scattered them: He shot out lightnings and discomfited them . . . He delivered me from my strong enemy" (Ps. xviii. 4—19). It is a solemn thought that we may send up prayers, and the answer may come down a judgment; for often it is only through judgment that true loving-kindness can make her way.

(6) **And the seven angels . . .**—Translate, *And the seven angels who had the seven trumpets prepared themselves that they might sound.* The angels raised their trumpets to their mouths, ready to blow. The sounding of the trumpets introduced the series of startling events (or providences, as we sometimes call them) which serve to arrest men's attention, and remind them that there is a kingdom which cannot

which had the seven trumpets prepared themselves to sound. (7) The first angel sounded, and there followed hail and fire mingled with blood, and they were cast upon the earth: and the third part of trees was burnt up, and all green grass was burnt up. (8) And the second angel sounded, and as it were a great mountain burning with fire was cast into the sea: and the third part of the sea became blood; (9) and the third part of the creatures

Chap. viii. 7—12. The first group of trumpet-visions. Four angels sound their trumpets.

be shaken. Such events are landing-stages in the great advancing progress of Christ's kingdom. It may be well to remind those who are desirous of actual and limited historical fulfilments which correspond with the features of the several visions, that the aim of the visions seems to be to give the seer, and through him the Church at large, some idea of the general kind of events which ever mark the decay of the kingdom of wrong and the growth of the kingdom of our Lord. It is to this consummation the visions of the trumpets lead us. We are to see the destruction of those who destroy the earth, and the establishment of the kingdom of Him who will reign in righteousness (chap. xi. 15—18). This great consummation is to be achieved by slow and painful steps. "Wilt thou at this time restore the kingdom?" is the question answered by the seals. "How wilt thou restore the kingdom?" is the question answered by the trumpets. In both cases the answer is similar. These great results are not and cannot be attained in the quick ways human impatience would suggest. The history of the world is not to be folded up in a hurry, for that history is a development and a discipline; it is not only the consummation which is to be desired: the steps to that end are salutary, though painful. The chastisement which is not joyous but grievous may be the best means of bringing to the world the peaceable fruits of righteousness;—

> "And man, unfriended, faltering on the way,
> Must learn to weep before he learns to pray."

And this wholesome lesson of tears must be taught the world, in the slow and bitter progress of a human history marked not by one judgment but by many. The fulfilment, then, of these prophetic visions is not exhausted in one event, however nearly its features may correspond with the character of the vision.

(7) **The first angel . . .**—Better, *And the first sounded, and there took place hail, and fire mingled in blood, and it was cast upon the earth; and the third part of the earth was burnt up, and the third part of the trees was burnt up, and all green grass was burnt up.* The reference to the Egyptian plagues is obvious: "There was hail, and fire mingled with the hail, very grievous . . . and the hail smote every herb of the field, and brake every tree of the field" (Ex. ix. 23—25). This resemblance to the history of Israel in Egypt gives us the hint of the true meaning. It carries us back to the past, and asks us to remember the mighty works of God in old times. It reminds us that He who bade Joshua cause the trumpets to be sounded by the walls of Jericho, and who delivered His people from the tyranny of Pharaoh, is the same God, mighty to save His people, to break the fetters of ignorance, and to cast down the high walls of pride and sin. But it is needful to observe the variation as well as the resemblance. This plague differs from the Egyptian in the introduction of *blood.* This variation carries it out of the possibility of literal interpretations. We begin to think of the strongly figurative language of Joel: "the blood, and fire, and pillars of smoke" (Joel ii. 30); and we call to mind that St. Peter announced that the fulfilment of this prophecy of Joel commenced with the Pentecostal effusion of the Holy Spirit. Then the war trumpet of deliverance had been sounded; then the process of the earth's emancipation had begun; then commenced the series of sorrows and judgments which the obstinate love of men for darkness rather than light would bring upon themselves; and through the operation of these the kingdom of Christ would be established. The first judgment falls upon the trees and grass. Beneath its touch the grass withereth, the flower fadeth. Thus the day of the Lord is upon the cedars of Lebanon that are high and lifted up, and upon all the oaks of Bashan; upon every one that is proud and lofty (Isa. ii. 12, 13; and 1 Pet. i. 24). It matters little in what way this humbling of human pride takes place. The world is full of illustrations. The loftiness of Jerusalem was lowered when the weakness of her self-sufficient religiousness was revealed and her Pharisaic pride was exposed; the loftiness of Rome was humbled when the Gothic invaders, like a storm of hail (so they were described by Claudian), devastated the empire. These are illustrations; but the prophecy is for all time, for the day of the Lord is upon "all that are proud." We must not press the phrase "the third part" too closely: it clearly is designed to remind us that in wrath God remembers mercy, and that while He humbles all He does not utterly destroy. (Comp. Zech. xiii. 8.) Is this the baptism of fire which withers the florid, pretentious, but fruitless religions of mankind?

(8, 9) **And the second angel . . .**—Translate, *And the second angel sounded, and as it were a great mountain burning with fire was cast into the sea; and the third part of the sea became blood; and the third part of the creatures that were in the sea died, those which have lives; and the third part of the ships were destroyed.* The sea becoming blood reminds us again of the plagues in Egypt (Ex. vii. 20, 21); but we must once more note the variation. It is not an uplifted rod like that of Moses which produces this result: it is the casting into the sea of a huge mass, as it were a great mountain, burning with fire. Professor Stuart calls this image appropriate or peculiar to St. John. The prophet Jeremiah, however, in a chapter which in many particulars is parallel to this and the following chapter (comp. Rev. xi. 18), makes use of a very similar image: "Behold, I am against thee, O destroying mountain, saith the Lord, which destroyest all the earth; and I will stretch out mine hand upon thee, and roll thee down from the rocks, and will make thee a burnt mountain" (Jer. li. 25). The mountain was the emblem, in Jeremiah's prophecy, of the strong consolidated power and institutions of Babylon. Not only must the loftiness of man be brought low, but the mountains which they made so strong for themselves. The power of God's advancing cause would hurl the rooted mountains from their base. The power of faith, Christ declared, would suffice to do this (Matt. xxi. 21); and it is at least a singular coincidence that this

which were in the sea, and had life, died; and the third part of the ships were destroyed. (10) And the third angel sounded, and there fell a great star from heaven, burning as it were a lamp, and it fell upon the third part of the rivers, and upon the fountains of waters; (11) and the name of the star is called Wormwood: and the third part of the waters became wormwood; and many men died of the waters, because they were made bitter. (12) And the fourth angel sounded, and the third part of the sun was smitten, and the third part of the moon, and the third part of the stars; so as the third part of them was darkened, and the day shone not for a third part of it, and the night

---

saying of the Lord's respecting the overthrow of a mountain should occur in His own comment on the destruction of the fig-tree, just as, in this chapter, the vision of the mountain overthrown follows that of the destruction of tree and grass life. Our Lord encourages the faith of His disciples: "Your power will not only expose the pretentious religionisms of the world, as My word has shown the worthlessness of this tree, but you will overthrow also the long established usages and evil customs of nations which corrupt the world." The powers which seemed strong as the great mountains would be seen to be but evil powers, burning, poisoning, destroying; but its power to destroy is checked: it is cast into the sea. Yet no great institution, or nationality, or evil principle is overthrown without some corresponding disadvantages. The falling mountain carries evil even in its fall, the sea becomes blood, the ships are destroyed. The fall of a great nation—a Babylon—is always fraught with unavoidable miseries to the world and its nations. Doubtless, the interests of commerce and shipping suffer; but this is not, it seems to me, the point of the vision. The symbolism is only weakened by supposing an allegorical mountain to fall into a literal sea and to destroy literal ships. The force of the vision is that certain gigantic forms of evil will be overthrown, but the overthrow will be accompanied with the development of new evils: the advance is made, but the step forward unveils the subtle force of evil. Every corrupt institution is destroyed with the risk of the evil elements diffusing themselves elsewhere; just as the political victory of Christianity was followed by the infusion of certain Pagan elements into the Church. The vanquished always manage to impose some laws on the victor. Even the advance of the Church is accompanied by some such experience.

(10) **And the third angel . . .**—Translate, *And the third angel sounded, and there fell out of the heaven a great star burning* (or, *kindled*—the light is not inherent, but borrowed) *as a torch* (or, *lamp*—same word as in chap. iv. 5), *and it fell upon the third part of the rivers, and upon the springs of the waters.* The flaming star seems to symbolise the fall of a potentate; the trumpet-blast proclaims that the mighty who have been, as luminaries, admired, and perhaps worshipped, will fall. The advancing progress of Christianity is to be marked by many such a fall. The rulers of earth, burning with lust of conquest or with pride of fanaticism, will be plucked from their seat among the stars (Obad. verse 4); but their fall is accompanied, as in the last instance, with miseries. The fountains and rivers are smitten, the sources of health and joy, the streams of prosperity, are injured.

(11) **And the name of the star . . .**—Translate, *And the name of the star is called Wormwood: and the third part of the waters became wormwood; and many of mankind died from the waters, because they were embittered.* The bitter, nauseous plant known as wormwood (*apsinthos*) is used to represent troubles and calamities. In Jer. ix. 15 we have an example of this: "Behold, I will feed them, even this people, with wormwood, and give them water of gall to drink." It is worth noticing that the Israelites are warned against idolatry as "a root that beareth gall and wormwood" (Deut. xxix. 18); and we may recall the symbolical act of Moses, who ground the golden calf to powder, cast the powder in the brook, and made the children of Israel drink (Ex. xxxii. 20). Some have thought that this falling star signified some false teacher, whose evil influence poisoned the pure currents of the gospel, and perverted the minds of men of original genius, who are represented here as fountains. The passages cited above favour the thought, and it may be included in the general meaning of the vision; but the main point seems to be to give us hints of those stages which will mark the advance of Christianity. The fall of the great men, the rulers and leaders, will take place, and their fall will bring misery to mankind. Doubtless the appearance of false teachers in the Church is one of the evidences and an unavoidable accompaniment of a progressing faith (Matt. xiii. 26). But all such false lights shall fall before Him who is the true Light and Morning Star, and who will heal all embittered waters of life. (Comp. Ex. xv. 23, and 2 Kings ii. 19.)

(12) **And the fourth angel . . .**—Translate, *And the fourth angel sounded, and there was smitten the third part of the sun, and the third part of the moon, and the third part of the stars; that the third part of them might be darkened, and the day might not appear as to its third part, and the night in like manner.* The dimness which thus falls on the lights of heaven carries us back to the plague of darkness (Ex. x. 21—23); but yet there is this difference: there the children of Israel had light in their dwellings while all the rest of the land suffered the darkness that might be felt; here, however, the darkness is only such as results from the withdrawal of the third part of the light of the sun by day, and of the moon and the stars (so much more brilliant and needful in Eastern lands than in our own) by night. It is a day of the Lord in which the light is not clear nor dark—not day nor night (Zech. xiv. 6, 7). There will be periods in which the lights which guide men will give forth uncertain glimmers; upon the earth there will be distress of nations, men's hearts failing them for fear, and for looking after those things which are coming on the earth, for the powers of heaven shall be shaken (Luke xxi. 25, 26). Such times of darkness and sorrow must be. It is through seasons such as these, when the lights of human wisdom and of spiritual guidance seem alike obscured, that the Church must go forward. The chaos precedes creation, and it is through chaos again that the Church of Christ must pass to the new heaven and new earth. These trumpet-visions, if read by the side of the story of Genesis, seem like the

likewise. (13) And I beheld, and heard
an angel flying through
the midst of heaven, saying
with a loud voice, Woe,
woe, woe, to the inhabiters of the earth
by reason of the other voices of the
trumpet of the three angels, which are
yet to sound!

Chap. viii. 13. The eagle of warning.

A.D. 96.

CHAPTER IX.—(1) And the fifth angel
sounded, and I saw a star
fall from heaven unto the
earth: and to him was
given the key of the bot-
tomless pit. (2) And he opened the
bottomless pit; and there arose a
smoke out of the pit, as the smoke

Chap. ix. 1—12. The fifth trumpet. First woe.

---

undoing of creation: the vegetation is smitten, the earth and sea are intermingled, the lights of the heavens are darkened, the living things in seas and streams are destroyed; but

> "Fresher life the world shall draw
> From their decay."

The pulling down must precede the building up; the removing of the degenerate is one step in the way to the regeneration.

INTRODUCTION TO THE LAST THREE, OR WOE, TRUMPETS. AN EAGLE UTTERS THE THREE-FOLD WOE.

(13) **And I beheld . . .**—Better, *And I saw, and I heard a single eagle* (not "angel," as in English version) *flying in mid-heaven, saying with a mighty voice, Woe, woe, woe, to those that dwell upon the earth by reason of the remaining voices of the trumpet of the three angels who are about to sound!* The best MS. authority is against the reading "angel," and in favour of *eagle.* It is, then, an eagle, a solitary eagle, that moves across the heaven, and utters the warning Woe! It flies through the meridian sky, and is thus visible to the very horizon. It was an appropriate emblem: high-soaring as the spirit of the seer, the eagle-glance scanned the borders of the earth, and caught sight of the coming troubles, and gave warning; swift and strong as the judgments of God, its very form gave emphasis to the warnings of its voice (Deut. xxviii. 49; Hos. viii. 1; and Matt. xxiv. 28). And yet the emblem must bring to the minds of God's children the care of Him who led Israel, instructed him, and kept him as the apple of His eye, and cherished him as "an eagle stirreth up her nest, fluttereth over her young, spreadeth abroad her wings, taketh them, and beareth them on her wings" (Deut. xxxii. 11). Is it not also a precursor of those eagle-like judgments which fall upon the carcase of dead nations or a dead society?

IX.

The resemblance in arrangement of the visions of the trumpets and the visions of the seals has already been noticed; but the warning cry, Woe, woe, woe! has no parallel in the seals. The trumpets which follow are fraught with woe and judgment to the dwellers upon the earth.

(1) **And the fifth angel . . .**—Translate, *And the fifth angel sounded, and I saw a star out of the heaven fallen* (not "fall," as in English version; the seer saw not a falling, but a fallen, star) *upon the earth.* The emblem of a fallen star is used elsewhere in the Bible. Isaiah (chap. xiv. 12) speaks of Lucifer fallen from heaven. Christ described Satan as lightning falling from heaven. Some great power or ruler is represented, then, by this fallen star. He is, moreover, said to have fallen from heaven, and he is represented as having been given the key of the abyss. Does not this lead us to expect the working of some evil spirit and diabolical agency? The 11th verse confirms our expectation. We may compare chap. xii. 8—12, where Satan is described as defeated, cast down to the earth, and filled with wrath. To understand this fallen star as the representative of a good angel seems hardly possible.

And to him was given . . .—Literally, *and there was given to him* (*i.e.*, to the being represented as a fallen star) *the key of* (not "the bottomless pit") *the pit of the abyss.* The abyss is the same word rendered "the deep," in Luke viii. 31, where the demons besought our Lord not to send them into the abyss, or deep. It is the word which describes the abode of the evil spirits. The verse before us suggests the picture of a vast depth approached by a pit or shaft, whose top, or mouth, is covered. Dante's *Inferno,* with its narrowing circles winding down to the central shaft, is somewhat similar. The abyss is the lowest spring of evil, whence the worst dangers arise. (Comp. chaps. xi. 7; xvii. 8; xx. 1—3.)

(2) **And he opened . . .**—Translate, *And he opened the pit of the abyss; and there went up smoke out of the pit, as the smoke of a great furnace; and the sun was darkened, and the air, by reason of the smoke of the pit.* The first result of the opening of the pit is the diffusion of such a dense smoke that light and atmosphere are darkened. In the previous vision there was an obscuration of light arising from the smiting of the luminaries; in this the obscuration arises from causes external to the luminaries. In that the light-giving power was enfeebled; in this the light is not enfeebled, but hindered. This must be remembered. The interpretation of these visions is most difficult; but we must bear in mind that they are descriptive of that great war which the Church is waging with the world, which good is waging with evil, but the end of which, we are assured, is the victory of good. The kingdoms of this world become the kingdoms of the Lord, and of His Christ (chap. xi. 15); but during the progress of the war the issue will often appear doubtful: nay, even the triumph may seem to be in the hand of the enemy; but faith disregards the back-flowing waves, for she knows the tide is coming in. We have seen that the advance of Christianity is marked by the manifestation of evils as well as the establishment of good. Christianity does not create evils, but the very intense honesty of her principles reveals the hidden force of unsuspected corruption. Thus the faith of Christ is come to give light unto the world, but in her progress many lights fall—the false lights of world-power, world-wisdom, false religionism, and heresies. The enemy, too, is at work, and seeks to obscure her light by the diffusion of dark and low-born thoughts. The smoke of the pit blackens the light and confuses the atmosphere. Now, this obscuration is surely the diffusion on earth of evil thoughts and ideas, the spirit of falsehood and hate, hostility to truth, and enmity against God and man. The bright, clear air made

of a great furnace; and the sun and
the air were darkened by reason of
the smoke of the pit. (3) And there
came out of the smoke locusts upon
the earth: and unto them was given
power, as the scorpions of the earth
have power. (4) And it was commanded them that they should not hurt
the grass of the earth, neither any
green thing, neither any tree; but only
those men which have not the seal of
God in their foreheads. (5) And to
them it was given that they should not
kill them, but that they should be tormented five months: and their torment
was as the torment of a scorpion, when
he striketh a man. (6) And in those
days shall men seek death, and shall
not find it; and shall desire to die, and
death shall flee from them. (7) And

gladsome by the sun is darkened; "all forms that once appeared beautiful become hideous."

(3) **And there came . . .**—Better, *And out of the smoke there came forth locusts upon the earth; and there was given to them power, as the scorpions of the earth* (? land-scorpions) *have power.* The outcome of the gloom is the power of devastation and pain. We still have reference to the Egyptian plagues—this time to the locusts (Ex. x. 12—15): "They covered the face of the whole earth, so that the land was darkened." Similarly, Joel describes the darkening of the land through the plague of locusts (Joel ii. 3—10): "The sun and the moon shall be dark, and the stars shall withdraw their shining." But the locusts of our vision are armed with the power of scorpions, to sting and to torture (verse 5): the scorpions are called scorpions of the earth. Some have thought that this expression is equivalent to land-scorpions, in contradistinction from so-called sea-scorpions. This hardly seems likely or necessary. Their power to torment men is the prominent idea. The locusts are not literal locusts: this scorpion-like power given to them is enough to convince us of this, even if the next verse did not clearly show it. The scorpion-like power seems to depict a malicious energy, as the locusts depict a devastating multitude.

(4) **And it was commanded . . .**—Translate, *And it was commanded them that they shall not injure the grass of the earth, nor yet any green thing, nor yet any tree; but only* (or, *except*) *the men whosoever have not the seal of God on their foreheads.* The locusts which are sent not to injure the vegetation are clearly not literal locusts, and the security of those who have the seal of God in their foreheads (those who were described as sealed, and so assured of safety against the tempest blast: see chap. vii. 1—3, *et seq.*) may confirm us in this view. Whatever the plague be, it is one which cannot injure God's children. "Nothing," Christ has said, "shall by any means hurt you. I give you power to tread on serpents and scorpions, and over all the power of the enemy" (Luke x. 19). It is interesting and suggestive to notice that this promise of our Lord was given immediately after the saying, "I beheld Satan as lightning fall from heaven," as the safety of the sealed ones is mentioned here after the vision of the star fallen from heaven. The coincidence is hardly undesigned; at least, the sense in which we understand the danger from which Christ promised His disciples protection may afford us a guiding meaning here. Now, none have maintained that Christ promised His disciples entire freedom from danger, pain, and death. He said, "They shall persecute you and kill you; ye shall be hated of all men for My name's sake, but he that endureth to the end shall be saved." No real injury can happen to them; pain and death might be encountered, but all things work together for their higher good. They have a joy which no pain or peril can take away; they have a joy in this (it is the same chapter as above—Luke x.), that their "names are written in heaven." For such, death has no sting, the grave no victory. They meet famine and nakedness, and peril and sword; but in these they are more than conquerors. No plague can hurt those who have the seal of God in their foreheads. A plague from which those whose way is through tribulation are exempt can hardly be a physical one.

(5) **And to them . . .**—Better, *And it was given to them that they should not kill them* (*i.e.*, those who had not the seal of God in their foreheads), *but that they should be tortured five months.* The general period of a locust plague is about five months: "as the natural locusts commit their ravages only for five months, so the ravages of these symbolical ones will be only for a short period" (Stuart). Their power is to inflict torment, and not death. The next verse tells us that men would consider death preferable to this torment; but the relief of the grave is denied them.

And their torment . . .—Literally, *and the torture of them* (*i.e.*, the torture inflicted by them) *is as the torture of a scorpion when it has stricken a man.* The wound of a scorpion occasions intense suffering: we have in it the symbol of the malicious cruelty of the merciless. The emblem is used in Ezekiel: the rebellious and malicious opponents of the prophet being compared to scorpions (Ezek. ii. 6). We may compare the similar imagery of the bee for the Assyrian power (Isa. vii. 18), and the Psalmist's complaint that his enemies came about him like bees—a swarm, irritating him with wing and sting. The tenth verse tells us the way in which the injury was inflicted: there were stings in their tails.

(6) **And in those days . . .**—Translate, *And in those days men shall seek death, and shall not find it; and they shall yearn to die, and death flees from them.* The change of tense from the future ("shall seek—shall yearn") to the present ("death flees") gives graphic force to the description. Men will seek for death in vain; they will long to die, and lo! death is seen fleeing from them. We can see an age in which death will be regarded as a sweet respite from the tormenting trials of life: men will stretch out their hands to death as to a welcome deliverer; but behold! death is seen fleeing from them. The word translated "desire" in our English version is a strong word; it has been rendered *vehemently desire:* it is a passionate longing, as the yearning of the soul after one we love. There have been ages in which men have thus pined for death, in which light and life seem but mockeries to the miserable, and men "long for death, but it cometh not; and dig for it more than for hid treasures" (Job iii. 20, 21). Such times are those which have been well called reigns of terror.

(7) **And the shapes . . .**—Translate, *And the shapes* (or, *forms*) *of the locusts were like horses made*

the shapes of the locusts *were* like unto horses prepared unto battle; and on their heads *were* as it were crowns like gold, and their faces *were* as the faces of men. (8) And they had hair as the hair of women, and their teeth were as *the teeth* of lions. (9) And they had breastplates, as it were breastplates of iron; and the sound of their wings *was* as the sound of chariots of many horses running to battle. (10) And they had tails like unto scorpions, and there were

---

ready for war. The resemblance of the locust to the horse (especially in the head) has been remarked upon by travellers, and has found expression in the Italian and German names *cavalletta* and *heupferd.* The resemblance is more distinct when the horses are made ready for battle: the hard shell or scales of the locust having the appearance of armour. Hence it has been thought that the sacred writer here alludes to this horse-like appearance of the locust. It seems a little doubtful that this is the case, or that in this or any of the descriptions here there is any reference to the anatomical features of the locust. (See Note on verse 10.)

And on their heads were as it were crowns like gold, and their faces were as the faces of men.—Here again there has been a desire to find some physical appearance in the locust to suggest the crown of gold: the antennæ, the rugged elevation in the middle of the thorax, have been imagined to have some resemblance to a crown; and the face of the locust, it has actually been said, bears under ordinary circumstances a distant (the adjective is most needful) resemblance to the human countenance.

(8) **And they had hair . . .**—Translate, *And they had hair as the hair of women, and their teeth were as the teeth of lions, and they had breastplates as iron breastplates; and the sound of their wings was as the sound of chariots of* (having, *i.e.,* drawn by) *many horses, running to war.* The hair: It is said that some locusts are hairy, and the passage in Jeremiah (chap. li. 27) has been quoted as evidence (the rough caterpillars here spoken of being said to be "locusts bristling with hair"), but the application of the passage is uncertain: the rough caterpillar may be the locust in the third stage, when the wings are still enveloped in rough horny cases which stick upon their backs. Others think the idea of the woman-like hair has its basis in the antlers of the locust. The teeth like those of the lion is a description the origin of which is found in the prophet Joel, in his prediction of the locust plague: "a nation cometh upon my land, strong, and without number, whose teeth are the teeth of a lion, and he hath the cheek-teeth (or, *grinding-teeth*) of a great lion." The terrible destructiveness of the locusts, and their strong, ceaseless, and resistless voracity, were thus described. Their breastplates are taken as descriptive of their thoraxes, which in the vision seemed strong as iron. The comparison of the sound of the wings to the thunderous sound of chariots and horses rushing into battle is repeated from Joel ii.

(10) **And they had tails . . .**—Better, *And they have tails like to scorpions, and stings, and in their tails is their power to hurt men five months.* In this verse the secret of their power is mentioned: they have tails like scorpions' tails, and stings which wound and so cause agony to men. On the period of five months, see verse 5. In the exposition of this passage it is utterly vain to look for features of the ordinary natural locust corresponding to the several particulars set forth by the sacred seer: this is admitted even by those who seem anxious to find such counterparts. "We must regard the comparison as rather belonging to the supernatural portion of our description." The rule is a good one. Like the description of the Divine Presence in chap. 4, most of the visions of the book are incapable of pictorial realisation without incongruities which would be grotesque and profane; nor need we be surprised, since the principles and truths are the main points with the writer. This general rule must be kept in mind if we would avoid the danger of dwelling too much on the bearing of details. It is not in the locust that we shall find even the suggestive basis of the details in the description here. The smoke rises from the pit of the abyss; the heaven is darkened, and out of the smoke emerges the pitchy cloud of locusts. The seer then adds certain characteristics of this locust plague, partly drawn from the earlier prophets, but, as his custom is, with some original additions. They are locusts, but they have the malice of scorpions; they advance like horse-soldiers to battle; they wear crowns; they bear a resemblance to men; there is something womanlike also in their appearance, and in their voracity they are as lions. The exigencies of the symbolism are quite beyond the features of the ordinary locust: the sacred writer shows us a plague in which devastation, malice, kinglike authority, intelligence, seductiveness, fierceness, strength, meet together under one directing spirit, to torment men. Some parts may be purely graphic, as Alford says, but surely the vision shows us a great symbolical army multitudinous as locusts, malicious as scorpions, ruling as kings, intelligent as men, wily as womanhood, bold and fierce as lions, resistless as those clad in iron armour. The symbolism of course must not be pressed too closely, but its meaning must be allowed to widen as new elements are added, especially when those elements are not suggested by anything in the locust itself, but are additions clearly designed to give force to the symbol employed. The locust-like army has characteristics partly human, partly diabolical, partly civilised, partly barbarous. They have been variously interpreted: the historical school have seen in them the Saracens under Mohammed, who gave to them a religion which was "essentially a military system;" others are inclined to refer them to "the hordes of Goths and others whose unkempt locks and savage ferocity" resemble this locust host. There is a good ground for taking the vision to prefigure the hosts of a fierce invading army. Even those who believe that Joel's prophecy foretold a plague of literal locusts, yet acknowledge that these "may in a subsidiary manner" represent "the northern, or Assyrian enemies of Judah" (Introduction to Joel, *Speaker's Commentary*). But, as the writer there says, these were "themselves types of still future scourges;" so may we see here a vision which neither the history of the Zealots, nor that of Gothic hordes, nor of Saracens, have exhausted, but one which draws our thoughts mainly to its spiritual and moral bearing, and teaches us that in the history of advancing truth there will come times when confused ideas will darken simple truth and right, and out of the darkness will emerge strange and mongrel teachings, with a certain enforced unity, but without moral harmony, a medley of fair and hideous,

stings in their tails: and their power
was to hurt men five months. (11) And
they had a king over them, *which is* the
angel of the bottomless pit, whose name
in the Hebrew tongue *is* Abaddon, but
in the Greek tongue hath *his* name
Apollyon.[1] (12) One woe is past; *and,*
behold, there come two
woes more hereafter.
(13) And the sixth angel

[1] That is to say, *A destroyer.*

Chap. ix. 13—21. The sixth trumpet. Second woe.

reasonable and barbarous, dignified and debased, which enslave and torment mankind. The outcome of these teachings is oftentimes war and tyrannous oppression; but the sacred seer teaches us distinctly that those who hold fast by the seal of God are those who cannot be injured, for he would have us remember that the true sting of false conceptions is not in the havoc of open war, but in the wounded soul and conscience. Nor is it altogether out of place to notice (by way of one example) that the power of Mohammed was more in a divided and debased Christendom than in his own creed or sword; the smoke of ill-regulated opinions and erroneous teachings preceded the scourge. Here, as in other parts of the book, we may notice that subtle, plausible errors pave the way for dire troubles and often sanguinary revolutions. Falsehoods and false worships that have been diffused over the world become "the forerunners and foretellers of a conflict between the powers of good and evil." Yet as the trumpet sounds we know that every battle is a step towards the end of a victorious war.

(11) **And they had a king . . .**—Better, *They have over them as king* (not "*the* angel," as in English version) *an angel of the abyss; his name* (is) *in Hebrew Abaddon, and in the Greek he has a name, Apollyon.* There is more than one point in which the seer wishes us to mark the contrast between these symbolical and the natural locusts. Locusts have no sting; these have. Locusts have no king (Prov. xxx. 27); these have a king. The movements of the invading locusts are conducted with wonderful precision and order, yet no presiding monarch arranges their march; but here there is a directing and controlling head. The great movement is no mere undesigned or instinctive one, but the offspring of a hidden, spiritual force. The great battle is not on the surface only, the invasions, revolutions, tyrannies, which try and trouble mankind, involve spiritual principles, and are but tokens of the great conflict between the spirit of destruction and the spirit of salvation, between Christ and Belial, God and Mammon, the Prince of this world and the Prince of the kings of the earth. The king of these locust hordes is named in Hebrew Abaddon, or Perdition, a name sometimes given to the place or abode of destruction (Job xxvi. 6). "Destruction (Abaddon) hath no covering"—*i.e.,* before God. (Comp. Prov. xv. 11). In Greek his name is Apollyon, or Destroyer: The spirit of the destroyer is the spirit that inspires these hosts. It is a great movement, but its end is destruction, as its inspiring genius is from beneath, from an angel of the nether world. It is not necessary for us to seek some great historical personage for the fulfilment of this portion of the prophecy, any more than we ought to accept any great historical event as an exhaustive fulfilment of the vision. The picture is vivid and forcible, and its full and certain meaning will be plain hereafter; but it at least should draw our minds from the curiosity which seeks for historical or personal counterparts to the self-vigilance which fears lest our own spirit should be injured by the prevalence of any form of evil. It should teach us to remember always the vehement, earnest way in which the sacred writers describe the subtle, venomous power of all sin, and the merciless destructiveness of its work. It is not of any invading hosts, or signal and special forms of evil, but of the terrible and usual influence of all sin, that the Apostle St. Paul writes when he describes the world-wide devastations of sin in language partly borrowed from the Old Testament, but singularly reminding us of the vision before us. "There is none that doeth good; no, not one. Their throat is an open sepulchre; the poison of asps is upon their lips; their feet are swift to shed blood; destruction and misery are in their ways; and the way of peace have they not known; there is no fear of God before their eyes" (Rom. iii. 12—18). It is perhaps well to notice that at this fifth trumpet the unseen spiritual powers of darkness appear taking part in the conflict. There is a time when the obstinate resistance of mankind (yes, and of individual men and women also) to better things becomes fortified by an evil spirit, and they are no longer passive resisters of good, but they become active antagonists of good, hating and obscuring the light of truth, and wounding the spirits and consciences of men. Alas! many walk of whom the Apostle could only say with tears, "they are the enemies of the cross of Christ" (the emblem of salvation), "and whose end is destruction" (Phil. iii. 18, 19).

(12) **One woe is passed . . .**—Better, *The one woe has passed; behold there cometh* (the verb is in the singular) *yet two woes after these things.* Here is the patience and faith of the saints. The troubles which pass only yield place to more, the rest and the victory are not yet; the powers of evil have not exhausted themselves, the iniquity of the social and spiritual Amorites is not yet full.

(13) THE SIXTH TRUMPET—THE SECOND WOE TRUMPET.—The first point which will strike the reader is that the plague under this trumpet resembles the last, though it is one of much more aggravated nature. Again we have vast hosts, with the powers of the horse, the lion, and the viper, at command, but the destructive elements are increased, the multitudes are more numerous, the horses' heads grow lion-like. With the mouth breathing forth threatening and slaughter, as well as with the tail armed with deadly fangs, they can deal forth, not torment only, as in the last vision, but death itself, to a vast proportion of the human race. To aid in this new desolation new forces are released: the four angels bound near the Euphrates are loosed. The next point to notice is that, even more directly than before, we are reminded that the moral and spiritual aspect of these visions should claim our thought. The aim of the plague is to exhibit the death-working power of false thoughts, false customs, false beliefs, and to rouse men to forsake the false worships, worldliness, and self-indulgence into which they had fallen (verses 20, 21). The Psalmist has told us that great plagues remain for the ungodly. Here, whatever special interpretations we may adopt, is an illustration of the Psalmist's words. The enemy against whom these foes are gathered is the great world lost in false thoughts, luxurious ways, dishonest customs; that world which in the very essential genius of its nature is hostile to goodness and the God of

sounded, and I heard a voice from the four horns of the golden altar which is before God, (14) saying to the sixth angel which had the trumpet, Loose the four angels which are bound in the great river Euphrates.

goodness. But the hosts which come against this sin-drowned world are not merely plagues, as famine and pestilence, they are plagues which are the results of the world-spirit, and are to a great extent, therefore, the creation of those who suffer. For there are evils which are loosed upon the world by the natural action of sin and sinful customs. As the evil spirit mingled for the first time in the plague of the fifth trumpet, so from all quarters (typified by the *four* angels) new powers of misery arise. Nor must another feature be overlooked: the historical basis of the Apocalypse is the past history of the chosen people; God's dealings with men always follow the same lines. The Apocalypse shows us the same principles working in higher levels and in wider arena. The Israel of God, the Church of Christ, with its grand opportunities, takes the place of the national Israel. Its advance is against the world, and the trumpets of war are sounded. Its progress is, like Israel's, at first a success; it gains its footing in the world, but the world-spirit which infects it is its worst and bitterest foe; it becomes timid, and seeks false alliances; it has its Hezekiahs, men of astonishing faith in hours of real peril, and of astonishing timidity in times of comparative safety, who can defy a real foe, but fall before a pretended ally, and who in mistaken friendliness lay the foundation of more terrible dangers (2 Kings xx. 12—19). The people who are victorious by faith at Jericho lay themselves open by their timid worldliness to the dangers of a Babylonish foe. The plague which falls on the spirit of worldliness does not spare the worldliness in the Church. The overthrow of corrupted systems bearing the Christian name is not a victory of the world over the Church, but of the Church over the world. He who mistakes the husk for the grain, and the shell for the kernel, will despair for Christianity when organisations disappear; but he who remembers that God is able to raise up even of the stones children to Abraham, will never be confounded; he knows the vision may linger, but it cannot come too late (Heb. ii. 3). With all this section the prophecy of Habakkuk should be compared, especially chaps. i. 6—11, 14, 15; ii. 1—14; iii. 17—19. The history of Israel is in much the key to the history of the world.

And the sixth angel . . . .—Translate, *And the sixth angel sounded: and I heard a* (single) *voice out of the* (four) *horns of the golden altar, which is before God, saying to the sixth angel, him who had the trumpet* (or, *O thou, who hast the trumpet*), *Loose the four angels which are bound at the great river Euphrates.* There are one or two verbal points worthy of notice. The Sinaitic MS. omits the words "single" and "out of the four horns," and thus reads, "I heard a voice out of the golden altar." It was the same altar from which the incense ascended mingled with the prayers of the saints. (See chap. viii. 3.) Where the prayers were, thence the voice comes. It reminds us that the prayers are not ineffectual, that still they are heard, though the way of answering may be in strange and painful judgments. The voice is heard as a single voice out of the midst of the horns of the altar. It is very doubtful whether the word "four" ought to be retained. The voice is represented as rising from the surface of the altar, at the corners of which were the four projections known as horns. The command is to loose the four angels bound at the Euphrates. What are these? Their number—*four*—represents powers influencing all quarters. They are angels (that is, *messengers*, or *agencies*) employed for the purpose. They are at or near the river Euphrates—that is, the spot whence the forces would arise. What is meant by the Euphrates? Are we to understand it literally? This can hardly be, unless we are prepared to take Babylon and Jerusalem literally also, and to deny all mystical meaning; but this is what only few will be disposed to do. The two cities, Babylon and Jerusalem, are the types of two radically different sets of ideas, two totally antagonistic views of life; and the meaning and mystical import of the River Euphrates must be determined by its relation to these two cities. It has been, indeed, argued that we are not bound to take the name Euphrates mystically because the remainder of the vision is mystical, since in Scripture we often find the literal and the allegorical intermingled. For example, there is an allegory in Ps. lxxx. 8 and 11, "Thou hast brought a vine out of Egypt," &c. It is quite plain that the vine is used mystically to represent Israel; but the word Egypt is not mystical—it indicates the literal fact that out of Egypt Israel was brought. This is no doubt true, but it hardly meets the question here. No one will dispute that a distinct, literal fact or name may be introduced in a passage otherwise allegorical; but do we ever meet with a passage in which names of places are introduced, some of which were to be taken literally and some mystically? And such would be the case here. The whole tenor of the Apocalypse keeps before us Jerusalem, the temple, and its surroundings (chap. xi. 1, 8), and Babylon, with its might and opulence, as two opposing cities; and it is out of all scriptural analogy to interpret Jerusalem allegorically, and Babylon allegorically, and then to claim the privilege of understanding Euphrates literally. In fact, the inconsistency and arbitrariness of interpreters is tested by these three names, Babylon, Jerusalem, Euphrates. Some will have Jerusalem to be literal, and Babylon and Euphrates mystical; others will have Babylon mystical, and Jerusalem and Euphrates literal. Surely those who hold all three to be literal are more consistent. But if Babylon be mystical and Jerusalem mystical, it is hard to see why Euphrates should not be so also. I am far from denying that those who consistently hold all three to be literal may not be right. There are not wanting tokens that a revival of the East may change the whole political centre of gravity of the world; but no such literal fulfilment would annul the infinitely more important mystical aspect of the Apocalypse. The conflict between a literal Babylon and a literal Jerusalem either in the past or the future can never vie in interest with the prolonged and wide-spread conflict between the spirit of Christ and the spirit of Belial, between God and Mammon, which is waged along the whole line of history over the arena of the whole world, and plants its battle-ground in every human heart. In every man, and in the whole world, the war is waged, as the carnal and spiritual contend with one another. It is in this war between the mystical Jerusalem and the mystical Babylon that the great river Euphrates is to play an important part.

(15) And the four angels were loosed, which were prepared for[1] an hour, and a day, and a month, and a year, for to slay the third part of men.
(16) And the number of the army of the horsemen *were* two hundred thousand thousand: and I heard the number of them.
(17) And thus I saw the horses in the vision, and them that sat on them, having breastplates of fire, and of jacinth, and brimstone: and the heads of the horses *were* as the heads of

[1] Or, *at*.

Twice (here and in chap. xvi. 12) the river Euphrates appears, and each time in connection with some warlike demonstration or invasion. The basis of interpretation, as with Jerusalem and Babylon, must be sought in the history of Judah and Israel. Babylon is the great foe of Israel, and the Euphrates was the great river or flood which formed a natural boundary between them. "The other side of the flood" (*i.e.*, Euphrates) was the phrase which pointed back to the early life of Abraham before he had entered upon the life of pilgrimage and faith; the Euphrates was the rubicon of his spiritual history. The Euphrates was the great military barrier also between the northern and southern nations; it occupied a place similar to the Rhine and the Danube in modern history. The advance of the Egyptian army to the banks of the Euphrates threatened the integrity of the Assyrian empire (2 Kings xxiii. 29). The battle of Carchemish established the supremacy of the Chaldean power to the west of the Euphrates (2 Kings xxiv. 7); such a preponderance of Babylonish influence threatened the safety of Jerusalem. The loosing of the four angels (or, *powers*) bound at the Euphrates can only signify changes analogous to disturbances on the great frontier line, as the drying up of the Euphrates signifies the annihilation of the protecting boundary. Such a frontier line between the spiritual city and the world city does in practice exist. There is a vast stretch of intervening territory which neither the Church nor the world really possesses, but over which each desires to possess power. There is a great neutral zone of public opinion, civilised habits, general morality, which is hardly Christian, hardly anti-Christian. When Christianised sentiments prevail in this, there is comparative peace, but when this becomes saturated with anti-Christian ideas, the Church suffers; and it is out of this that the worst aspects of trouble and danger arise; for out of it arise those forces which bring into acute form the great war between the world spirit and the spirit of Christ. The loosing of these four angels, then, seems to indicate that the issues at stake have become more distinct; that the conflict which has gone on under veiled forms begins to assume wider proportions and to be fought on clearer issues. The issues have been somewhat confused: the world spirit has crept into the Church, and against the world spirit, wherever found, the trumpet blast declares war.

(15) **And the four angels . . .**—Better, *And there were loosed the four angels who had been made ready unto* (or *for*, *i.e.*, ready for) *the* (not "an hour," but *the*) *hour, and day, and month, and year, that they should slay the third part of mankind.* The English version reads as though the hour, day, month and year were to be understood as the length of time over which this plague of war should last. This idea has been adopted by many of the historical school of interpreters, and great ingenuity has been exercised to find some period which exactly corresponds with this, and during which disastrous wars prevailed. But the expression ("made ready unto the hour," &c.) is not to be taken to imply that such was the duration of the plague; it implies that the loosing of the angels would take place at a definite period, the year, month, day and hour of which were known; the expression corresponds somewhat with our Lord's words, "Of that day and hour knoweth no man." It reminds us that there is a period—an unknown period, but nevertheless a certain period—at which the latent powers of retribution wake and begin to avenge themselves, at which the restraints which have withheld the long-deserved scourges are removed. Men and nations little think of this. Peace they cry, where there is no peace, for they have been by their sins mining the ground under their feet, or dwelling in that abode of false security which Bunyan might have called the city of Meanwell, and that abode is built on the sands; and when the angels of judgment are loosed, and the restraining influences of public opinion broken, the tempest is abroad, the frail house of formal religion falls, and the time of testing leaves its inmates unsheltered. Happy only are they who are ready for the hour of the Lord's return. The angels are made ready that they should kill the third part of mankind. The way in which this slaughter is to take place is explained in verses 17, 18: it is a wide and devastating slaughter carrying away a large portion of the human race.

(16) **And the number . . .**—Translate, *And the number of the armies of the cavalry was two myriads of myriads. I heard the number of them.* The writer heard, perhaps from some herald angel, the number of this vast army of horsemen; it was twice ten-thousand times ten thousand—*i.e.*, two hundred millions. The number is like an echo from Ps. lxviii. 17—"The chariots of God are twenty thousand (*two myriads*), even thousands (or, *thousands of thousands*) of angels." This utterly bewildering number might have been sufficient to keep interpreters from looking for some slavishly literal fulfilment: it simply stands for an immense host, and may serve to point out the prolific powers of retribution—the harvest of sin is misery, multiplied thirty, sixty, one hundred-fold.

(17) **And thus I saw . . .**—Better, *And after this manner saw I the horses in the vision, and those who sat upon them, having breastplates fiery and jacinth-like, and brimstone-like, and the heads of the horses were as heads of lions; and out of their mouths goeth forth fire and smoke and brimstone.* The seer proceeds to describe the general appearance of the horses and horsemen. After this fashion were they: the horses and horsemen were armed with breastplates of triple hue (corresponding to the three-fold destructive stream which goes forth from their mouth), the hues of flame, and dark purple (jacinth), and brimstone. The jacinth colour seems to be the dark purple or blue so often seen in smoke. The Poet Laureate uses the word "azure" to describe the colour of ascending columns of smoke ("azure pillars of the hearth arise to thee"): the colour here would be darker, the smoke not arising from peaceful dwellings, but generated among death-giving elements. The army is mainly of horsemen, and they are described as resolute and relentless: we are reminded of somewhat similar features in the Chaldean armies spoken of by Habakkuk, "I raise up the Chaldeans, that bitter and hasty nation: they are

lions; and out of their mouths issued
fire and smoke and brimstone. (18) By
these three was the third part of men
killed, by the fire, and by the smoke,
and by the brimstone, which issued out
of their mouths. (19) For their power
is in their mouth, and in their tails:
for their tails *were* like unto serpents,
and had heads, and with them they do
hurt. (20) And the rest of the men
which were not killed by these plagues
yet repented not of the works of their
hands, that they should not worship
devils, and idols of gold,[a] and silver,
and brass, and stone, and of wood:
which neither can see, nor hear, nor
walk: (21) neither repented they of
their murders, nor of their sorceries,
nor of their fornication, nor of their
thefts.

[a] Ps. 115. 4; & 135. 15; Isa. 46. 7; Jer. 10. 5; Dan. 5. 23.

---

terrible and dreadful: their horses also are swifter than leopards," &c. (Habak. i. 6—10).

(18) **By these three . . .**—Better, *From these three plagues were the third part of mankind slain, by the fire and the smoke and the brimstone which goeth forth out of their mouths. For the power of the horse is in their mouth, and in their tails, for their tails were like serpents, having heads, and with them they hurt* (or, *injure*). The destructive power in this vision is in mouth and tail, in the last trumpet-vision it was in the tail only (verse 10). The devastating power is increased; the foes come swift as horsemen, strong as lions, venomous as serpents, breathing forth elements that blind and burn with deadly power. We have, then, forces which are mighty, malicious, and relentless, and which are bidden forth against mankind for their sins of worldliness. (See verses 20, 21.) It is not once only in the history of the world that such powers have been let loose. The desolations wrought by invading hordes—the force and ferocity of Turkish power establishing itself in Europe and threatening the power of Christendom—the widespread terror and slaughter promoted by the outbreak of the spirit of unrestrained violence in France, followed by reckless war, may illustrate such a vision as the present; but the main teaching of it is the never-failing truth that the spirit of worldliness provokes its own punishment, wherever it may exist, and its retribution is in a form which serves to reveal what latent power of destruction lurks behind every sin, and what hidden spiritual foes there are to intensify human passions and to increase human misery.

(20, 21) **And the rest . . .**—Translate, *And the rest of mankind who were not slain in these plagues did not even repent of* (or, *out of*—*i.e.*, so as to forsake) *the works of their hands, that they should not worship the demons* (evil spirits), *and the idols of gold, and of silver, and of brass, and of stone, and of wood; which can neither see, nor hear, nor walk: and they did not repent of* (or, *out of*) *their murders, nor of* (or, *out of*) *their sorceries, nor out of their fornication, nor out of their thefts.* These verses make one or two points clear. First, they show us that, whatever the nature of the plagues might be, they were afflictions designed to bring about repentance, and to rouse men, whether nominally Christian or not, from the lethargy into which long indulged sin had plunged them. Those terrible revolutions which are the growth of years, and which startle men with their apparent suddenness and violence, are the great appeals of God, asking men to see the meaning of sin; they are the trumpet blasts calling to repentance. But we are told more: the remainder of the godless did not repent. We are not, indeed, told that they did not feel terror, or remorse, or momentary qualms and misgivings, but that they did not show that which alone is regarded as genuine repentance, the repentance out of sin, the repentance which turns away from sin. We need always that wholesome caution. We need it most in times when hysterical and emotional religionism is fashionable, and it is forgotten that true repentance is a repentance whereby we forsake sins. These men repented not out of their sin. And their sins are enumerated, and the enumeration again takes us back to the history of Israel as to the historical basis which the sacred seer enlarged and vivified; for the sins are just those against which Israel was warned and into which Israel fell (Deut. iv. 28; Ps. cvi. 34—40; Acts vii. 41). The sins are demon-worship and idolatry: "They served idols; they sacrificed their sons and their daughters unto devils." (Comp. 1 Cor. x. 20; 1 Tim. iv. 1.) It is needful to trace these sins in the history of Israel, as it has been argued that these are heathen sins, and that therefore these plagues must be plagues which fall on those who are literally heathens. But if we bear in mind that the series of visions describe features which will accompany the advance of Christianity in the world, we shall remember that it is against worldliness, wherever found, idolatries, of whatever kind, murders and thefts, called by whatever name, that the true genius of Christianity makes war. Christ is king, and king of righteousness, and in righteousness does He make war, and the heathenisms which are called Christianity are as much the objects of His displeasure as the most obvious Paganism. It is needful to remember that Jews are addressed as if they were heathen, aye, very *habitués* of Sodom (Isa. i. 10), and that the Christian Church is warned against sins which are little else than idolatries. Covetousness, the very essence of worldliness, is by St. Paul twice over called idolatry (Col. iii. 5, and Eph. v. 5). It seems, therefore, to be foreign to the purpose to try and limit these plagues only to the non-Christian world. To do this is to get a narrow, improbable (may we not say an impossible?) interpretation; for the greatest strength of the world-power would be left untouched. It is true that the visions are not showing us the plagues which fall on apostasy and fornication within the Church; but it is true that we are beholding visions which show how terribly the world-spirit avenges itself on all who harbour it, whether called Christian or not. Gross sins, gigantic frauds, complacent familiarity with crime, followed by blunted moral sense, are heathenish, whether found in Pagan or Christian society. Heavy woes must inevitably await the society which tolerates such works; but the worst omen of the coming doom is seen when society has lost the power to repent because it has lost the power to hate evil. Such an incapacity is invariably significant of advanced moral decay. It is the climax in the growth of sin which the Psalmist noticed where men lose the sacred abhorrence of evil (Ps. xxxvi. 4). To such repentance is becoming impossible.

CHAPTER X.—(1) And I saw another mighty angel come down from heaven, clothed with a cloud: and a rainbow *was* upon his head, and his face *was* as it were the sun, and his feet as pillars of fire: (2) and he had in his hand a little book open: and he set his right

Chap. x. 1—11. The little book.

A.D. 96.

X.

THE INTERPOSED VISIONS. THE WITNESS AGAINST EVIL (chaps. x. 1—xi. 14.) — As between the opening of the sixth and seventh seals there was interposed a two-fold vision — the sealing of the hundred and forty-four thousand and the glimpse of the great multitude (chap. vii.)—so is a two-fold vision interposed here between the sounding of the sixth and seventh trumpets. The similarity of situation of these interposed visions (episodes, as they have not very accurately been called) suggests that there must be some corresponding value in their interpretation. This appears to be found in the answer to the question which rises spontaneously as the visions of the seals and of the trumpets draw to a close. We see the scenes which the seals disclose, and we learn how war, pestilence, death, persecution, revolution, are to continue, and we ask, What becomes of the Church, the bride of Christ? Where are the true servants of God during these trials? We are answered by the interposed visions of the seventh chapter that they are sealed, and they will be safe. Similarly, the scenes disclosed by the trumpets are spread before us, and we see the features which mark the advance of Christianity in the world; we see the pain, the confusion, the devastations and slaughters, the bringing to light of hidden evils, which are the necessary accompaniments of this prolonged war; we see, as it were, amid smoke and flame and sword, the advancing and receding line of battle, and we learn that the powers of evil are subtle and self-multiplying, and, like the dragon in the den of error, leap into new and multiform life, though smitten by the sword of the Red Cross Knight. And amid these confusions of war we almost lose sight of the Church, or gain only a few hints which show that she is not unharmed in the conflict; and again the question is forced from us, What becomes of the Church, the bride of Christ? Where is her work and the tokens of her advance? To this the interposed visions of the present section are designed to give an answer; and that answer is again a reminder to us that the work of God in the world is not work on the surface of history merely: the waves catch the eye, and men measure progress by the force of these, but the ebb of the tide is unseen. So also is there a work of God which is more potent than the conspicuous work on which men love to look. The work of the Church is not to be measured by results now. It does achieve results, but her best work is the work of which she knows not now but will know afterwards; and there is a Church within the Church which is carrying on this work. There are witnesses of God against the beast-power and the world-power, who, though persecuted, are faithful—though dying, live—though chastened, are not killed; who, through evil report and good report, triumph over faithlessness and fear.

The interposed vision is two-fold. In the first part, contained in chap. x., another mighty angel descends with a little book open in his hand. This book the sacred seer, as the type of all those who will witness truly for God in the world, is commanded to eat; from sweetness it turns to bitterness, in token that the very fidelity and love he had to God would be the occasion of sorrow, for he would have to be the witness of unpalatable truths to the potentates of the earth; but he has heard celestial thunders, and he knows that the end and victory are near. Such is the preparation of him who will be a true witness for Christ when many false witnesses and false Christs are abroad. The second part expands the same thought under different imagery. There is a holy of holies in the Church, where the true witnesses are lightened with celestial fire for their work of noble peril.

FIRST SCENE OF THE INTERPOSED VISION.

(1, 2) **And I saw . . .**—Translate, *And I saw another mighty angel descending out of the heaven, clothed with a cloud, and the* (not "a") *rainbow upon his head, and his face as the sun, and his feet as pillars of fire, and having in his hand a little book* (or, *roll*) *open.* Many have thought that this angel can be none other than Christ Himself. It must be acknowledged that the description is such that we might well hesitate to apply it to any but our Lord; but, nevertheless, the words, "*another* mighty angel," afford serious difficulty. Our Lord might indeed appear as an angel, but it is scarcely conceivable that He would be called "*another* mighty angel:" an expression which seems to associate this angel with those others who have taken part in these visions. Remembering this, we must separate from our thoughts the idea of personal angelic beings. Such are employed by God, but in the mechanism of these visions the angels are not necessarily such, any more than the stars are literal stars: they are typical, representative angels, as we speak of the Angel of Peace, the Angel of War; so we have the Angels of Time, of Death, of Life, as in the Apocalypse. The angel here, even if he does not represent Christ Himself, descends with the evidences of Christ's power. He comes to remind the secret ones of God that Christ is with them always, and that He will not hide His commandments from those who are living as strangers and pilgrims upon earth (Ps. cxix. 19; 1 Pet. ii. 11); for he bears a little book open in his hand. The value of this vision is best seen by calling to mind the vision of the Fifth Trumpet. There, for the first time, the plagues seemed to gather supernatural power: the key of the abyss was given to the star that fell, and the locust host were led by the angel of the abyss. As an answer to this comes this angel, bearing the witnesses of Christ's power. When the troubles come that darken and confuse, the messenger from heaven will come to give light, teaching, and strength to the faithful—so does this angel first give assurance of the power of Christ. He comes clothed with a cloud, the token always of the Divine Presence (Ex. xiii. 21; Ezek. i. 4; Matt. xvii. 5; Acts i. 9). *The,* not "a" rainbow, but the rainbow (*i.e.*, the rainbow of chap. iv. 3), the token of covenant and of love, glowed round his head; his face, like Moses', had caught the unutterable light, the sun-like light of Christ's presence (chap. i. 16); and his feet were like pillars of fire to tread the earth, strong in the power of purification and judgment. Some call this the Angel of Time, because of his utterance in verse 6; but is it not rather the typical representative of the Angel of the New Testament, coming with the tokens of covenant truth, and power and love? He had in his hand a little book open. Our

foot upon the sea, and *his* left *foot* on
the earth, (3) and cried with a loud
voice, as *when* a lion roareth: and when
he had cried, seven thunders uttered
their voices. (4) And when the seven
thunders had uttered their voices, I
was about to write: and I heard a voice
from heaven saying unto me, Seal up
those things which the seven thunders
uttered, and write them not. (5) And

memories are carried back to the other book, or roll, displayed in chap. v. 1—5, and two contrasts strike us: that roll, or book, was sealed, and none were found worthy to open it; this book is open—that book was larger; this one being described as a small book. Do these contrasts help us to the meaning? One thing they seem to tell us: the book contains none of those secret things which were the contents of the former book. The closed, sealed book pointed to the hidden springs of future history; this points to what is open to all. That book was comparatively large, and filled with writing, as the visions of oncoming history were great; this book is small, and contains what all may master. These considerations forbid the idea that the book is a repetition in brief of what was in the sealed book, "or that it was the revelation of some remaining prophecies," or of some "portion or section of prophecy." The vision is a representation that he who comes armed with the witnesses of Christ's presence comes also with that ever open proclamation of God's love and righteousness. The little open book is that gospel which is the sword of the Spirit, the weapon of the Church, that Word of God open to all, hidden only from those whom the god of this world hath blinded. The fallen powers may bear the key and let loose darkening clouds of confused thought and unworthy teaching; the outer courts of the Church may be overcast: but unto the upright there ariseth light in the darkness, and God's Word has risen with new light and power upon the bewilderments and glooms of the age. "Three books are associated in the Apocalypse. The first is the book of the course of this world (chap. v. 1); . . . the last is the Book of Life (chaps. xx. 15; xxi. 27) . . . : between these two comes" another book, which is the link between the other two, the ever open book of God's promises and the witness of God's righteousness and power. Elliott regarded this little roll as the Bible opened anew to mankind at the period of the Reformation. The period affords many magnificent illustrations of the vision, but it does not exhaust its truth, since in every age the reverent study of the Word of God has given freshness and strength to forgotten truths, and has saved men from the bondage of traditional notions. From among such students have arisen God's witnesses.

And he set . . .—The attitude of the angel, with one fiery foot planted on the sea and the other on the land, is that of a conqueror taking possession of the whole world. There is a power, then, by which the Church and children of God may possess the earth. It is not the power of pride or worldliness. The true weapons are not carnal: the sword of the Spirit is the word of God, and the meek-spirited (meek to be taught and meek in life) shall possess the earth.

(3) **And cried with a loud voice . . .**—Better, *and he cried with a loud voice, even as a lion roareth.* Another token of the presence of Christ with the Church. The voice is the voice of a courage and strength derived from Him who is the "Lion of the tribe of Judah."

And when he had cried . . .—Translate, *and when he cried, the seven thunders* (notice, not "seven thunders," but "*the* seven thunders") *spake their own voices.* The thunders are called the seven thunders to bring them before us as another order of sevens, and into harmony with the seven seals, the seven trumpets, the seven vials. Thus we have four sets of sevens. It was not a seven-fold peal of thunder, but seven thunders, which spake forth distinctly their own voices. This marked language brings the seven thunders, though their utterances are never revealed, into prominence as a portion of the Apocalyptic system. But what were these thunders? Were they more terrible judgments still? and did the sealing of them signify the shortening of the days of judgment, as Christ had said (Matt. xxiv. 22)? It may be so. One thing seems certain—the guesses which have been hazarded (such as that they are identical with the trumpets; that they are the seven crusades) can hardly be admitted. Whatever they were, they were perfectly intelligible to the Evangelist. He was on the point of writing down their utterances. Will this fact help us to understand the general object of their introduction here?

(4) **And when the seven . . .**—Translate, *And when the seven thunders spoke, I was about to write: and I heard a voice out of the heaven, saying, Seal up the things which the seven thunders spoke, and write them not.* He could have written down their utterances. It was no mere thunder-like sound he heard: the thunders spoke; and he would have continued his writing as he had been commanded (chap. i. 11) had not the voice out of heaven forbidden him. The utterances, then, are for those who hear them; they are not to be made generally known. Is it not the solemn, sacred, divine voice not to be known by all, but by those who have ears to hear when "the God of glory thundereth?" "Lo! He doth send forth His voice, yea, and that a mighty voice" (Ps. lxviii. 33). Mankind may hear the thunder; only those whose ears God has opened can hear the utterances and the inspiriting messages which they bring. So was it once in our Lord's life. The people said it thundered; some thought an angel spake; but there were articulate words which He who came to do God's will, in whose heart was God's law, heard, and to Him that thunder-like voice promised to "glorify His name" (John xii. 28, 29). Similarly here, the Evangelist (who is in this but a type of the true witnesses for God), who is to prophecy before peoples and kings (verse 11), hears words spoken by the divine voice which make him strong for his mission. It is so evermore. Dull ears there are who hear thunder, but never God's voice; dim eyes there are which see no trace of the divine craftsman in all nature, though

> "Earth 's crammed with God,
> And every common bush aglow with Him."

The thunders are not to be written down; they are for those who have ears to hear.

(5—7) **And the angel . . .**—Translate, *And the angel whom I saw standing upon the sea and upon the earth lifted his right hand to the heaven, and sware in* (or *by*) *Him who liveth unto the ages of the ages, who created the heaven, and the things in it, and the earth, and the*

the angel which I saw stand upon the
sea and upon the earth lifted up his
hand to heaven, (6) and sware by him
that liveth for ever and ever, who
created heaven, and the things that
therein are, and the earth, and the
things that therein are, and the sea,
and the things which are therein, that
there should be time no longer: (7) but
in the days of the voice of the seventh
angel, when he shall begin to sound,
the mystery of God should be finished,
as he hath declared to his servants the
prophets. (8) And the voice which I heard
from heaven spake unto me again, and
said, Go *and* take the little book which is
open in the hand of the angel which
standeth upon the sea and upon the
earth. (9) And I went unto the angel,
and said unto him, Give me the little
book. And he said unto me, Take *it*,[a]
and eat it up; and it shall make thy
belly bitter, but it shall be in thy mouth
sweet as honey. (10) And I took the

[a] Ezek. 2. 8, & 3. 3.

---

things in it, and the sea, and the things in it, that time (*i.e.*, delay, or postponement) *should no longer be: but in the days of the voice of the seventh angel, whenever he is about to sound* (his trumpet) *was finished the mystery of God, as he evangelised his servants the prophets.* There is a change of tense which sounds strange: he says, then (not "will be," but) *was* finished. In thought he hurries on to the end, and sees the close no longer in the dim future, but as, with the eye of God, an accomplished fact. The certainty is guaranteed with an oath. The gesture of the uplifted hand to give emphasis to the oath is of ancient date. Thus Abraham expressed his resolution to take none of the spoils of the conquered kings: "I have lift up mine hand unto the Lord . . . that I will not take from a thread to a shoelatchet" (Gen. xiv. 22; comp. Ex. vi. 8, margin). So, too, does the man clothed in linen (Dan. xii. 6—9, a passage which, in much, is the foundation of the one before us) lift up both hands and sware that there shall be a fixed period for the accomplishment of the scattering of the power of the holy people. The oath in the passage under consideration is to the effect (not that time should cease and eternity begin, but) that there shall be no longer any delay. The suffering saints had cried, "How long?" (chap. vi. 9—11), and they had been bidden to wait a little time. Now the close of all such waiting time is announced: when the seventh trumpet shall have blown the mystery of God will be finished. "'The mystery of God' does not mean something which cannot be understood or explained. It is never applied to such matters, for example, as the origin of evil, or the doctrine of the Trinity in Unity. It does mean a secret; but then a secret may be told, and when told is no mystery. The mystery, or secret, of God means, therefore, the whole of His plan and of His counsel concerning this earth in its present state of discipline and of imperfection; all that God means to do upon it and towards it, even till that which we read of as the time of the end (Dan. xii. 4—9), the close of this last dispensation, and the introduction of that new heavens and new earth wherein dwelleth righteousness" (Dr. Vaughan). No wonder, as he announced this fast approaching close of the ages of suffering and trial, he should add, "According as He (not "declared"—an utterly inadequate word—but) *evangelised*—*i.e.*, according to the glad tidings which He had ever proclaimed to and by His servants the prophets."

A somewhat remarkable parallelism between this passage and 1 Cor. xv. 51, 52, has been pointed out. In both passages there is reference to the *mystery*, the *glad tidings*, and the *last* (the seventh trumpet is also the last) *trumpet*. This harmony of reference—taken in connection with St. Paul's statement, "We shall not all sleep, but we shall all be changed"—is full of interest, if it were for nothing more than to notice the union of thought between the two Apostles; but it may also throw light upon the teaching respecting the first resurrection (chap. xx. 5, 6; but see Note there).

(8, 9) **And the voice . . .**—Translate, *And the voice which I heard out of the heaven* (I heard it) *again talking with me* (it is not the angel that speaks, but the voice which had bidden him seal up the thunders is heard again speaking), *and saying, Go, take the roll* (or, *the little roll*; there is a difference in the MSS.) *which is opened in the hand of the angel who stands upon the sea and upon the earth. And I went away to the angel, telling him to give me the little book. And he saith to me, Take and eat it up; and it shall make bitter thy belly, but in thy mouth it shall be sweet as honey.* The image of eating the roll is derived from the Old Testament. We meet with it in Ezekiel (chap. iii. 1—3) and Jeremiah (chap. xv. 16). The passage in Ezekiel is probably the basis of the present passage, and the chapter in which it occurs gives us the meaning of the symbol: the eating of the roll, or the words of the roll, is the complete mastering of the contents of the book—the digesting, as we say, its meaning, till the principles and truths are thoroughly familiar and loved. "All my words" (so runs the explanatory verse, Ezek. iii. 10) "that I shall speak unto thee receive in thine heart and hear with thine ears." It is similar to the Psalmist's practice: "Thy words have I hid within my heart;" he made himself so familiar with them that they were no longer a code of laws, but a constant instinct, a second nature to him. Thus preeminently should he be familiar with his Master's words and heart, saturated with his Master's principles, who is to be a witness and a prophet for his Lord. "He who would carry God's words to another must first be impressed and penetrated with them himself. He must not only hear, read, mark, and learn, but also (according to the Scriptural figure) inwardly digest them."

(10) **And I took . . .**—The Evangelist takes the roll, as he was bidden, out of the angel's hand, eats it up, and finds it, as he was told, "in his mouth as honey, sweet." In this his experience resembles that of Ezekiel, who found the roll in his mouth as honey for sweetness (Ezek. iii. 3). So the Psalmist could rejoice in God's words and God's law as sweet, sweeter than honey and the honeycomb (Pss. cxix. 103, and xix. 10). He who is ready to endure bitterness in his fidelity to God must not only be interpenetrated by divine teaching; he must have also realised its sweetness, or else, however pleasant his words may sound, they will lack the sweetness which is as needful to the words of the teacher as to the songs of the poet. But the after effect of the sweet-tasting roll is bitterness. Ezekiel makes no

little book out of the angel's hand, and
ate it up; and it was in my mouth
sweet as honey: and as soon as I
had eaten it, my belly was bitter.
(11) And he said unto me, Thou
must prophesy again before many
peoples, and nations, and tongues, and
kings.

A.D. 96.

CHAPTER XI.—(1) And there was
given me a reed like unto
a rod: and the angel

Chap. xi. 1—14. The witnesses.

mention of this bitterness; yet we know how much his fidelity to the words he loved so well must have cost him when he was bidden to arm himself with a flinty determination (Ezek. iii. 9—14, and ii. 6, 7), and the patient courage of one whose lot was among thorns and briars and scorpions. It must always be so. The love of Christ may constrain men, but the very ardour of their affections must bring them through tribulation, and may make them as outcasts, defamed, persecuted, slain. The flaming zeal to emancipate mankind from thraldoms, follies, and ruinous sins may stir the soul with a holy joy; but there come moments when men are almost tempted to turn back, and to think that they have undertaken a hopeless task, when they find how slow is their progress, and what new and unexpected difficulties arise. Such was the bitterness which Moses felt: "Why is it that Thou hast sent me? For since I came to Pharaoh to speak in Thy name, he hath done evil to this people; neither hast Thou delivered thy people at all." The most enthusiastic souls who love their fellow-men, and who feel how sweet and high is their calling, perhaps feel most of this bitterness. Their very love makes all failure very bitter to bear; yet is it through this martyrdom of failure that the noblest victories are won.

(11) **And he . . .**—Better, *And they* (not "he," as in the English version, but *they say*: an equivalent for "It was said,") *say to me, Thou must again prophesy concerning* (or, *with regard to*) *peoples, and nations, and tongues, and kings many.* He is told that the bitterness will arise in connection with his prophecies with regard to peoples and kings. This carries us on to the vision in the next chapter, where the two witnesses stand so solitary, and prophesy so mightily, yet so vainly, among men. He will have to tell the story of churches and peoples, priests and princes, unmindful of their high calling and their allegiance to their true king, and of their hatred of God's mightiest and purest witnesses. The end, indeed, will come. The Church will be victorious. The kingdoms of this world will become the kingdoms of Christ: but it will be through persecutions, apostacies, judgments. This is the sad vision he must describe. The interposed visions will answer the question, "What has the Church been doing?" but it will show how she has done that work, distressed by heresies, crippled by worldliness, trodden down by enemies, and, worse than enemies, foes veiled as friends. But this very vision will lead to the unfolding of the more truly spiritual aspects of the Church's work, and of that conflict in which she contends with the multiform spirit and power of evil. Thus will he prophesy of peoples and kings many.

XI.

The Second Part of the Interposed Vision. The Measuring of the Temple; the Two Witnesses; the Earthquake.

The Measuring of the Temple.—We enter upon the second part of the interposed vision. The Temple proper is secured. The measuring signifies its protection from profanation; the outer court given to the Gentiles indicates that practical heathenism and corruption have invaded the Church; against corruptions and profanities, witnesses, who draw their strength from divine help, are raised up to protest. Their power is great, though their witness is disregarded; for their influence outlasts their life, and their words avenge themselves on their adversaries; rejected reformation re-appears as revolution. The vision therefore declares that, whatever corruptions invade the Church, the kernel of the Church will never be destroyed, but out of it will arise those who will be true to the Master's commission, and whose words will never be void of power.

Such seems to be the general drift of this chapter. It is stated thus briefly and simply that it may be kept in mind as a leading idea in the comments which follow, and because the chapter is generally regarded as one of the most difficult in the book. On the relation between the allusions to the Temple in this chapter and the date of the book, see *Introduction.* It is perhaps well to remember that, as we have taken Jerusalem and Babylon as symbolical names, and not necessarily the literal Jerusalem and the literal Babylon, so the Temple and the court of the Temple are to be understood as symbols. The gospel has elevated the history and places of the past into a grand allegory, and breathed into their dead names the life of an ever-applicable symbolism. (See *Introduction, On the General Meaning and Practical Value of the Book.*)

(1) **And there was . . .**—Translate, *And there was given to me a reed like a rod* (we must omit the words "and the angel stood"), *saying.* It is not said by whom the reed was given, nor are we told who speaks the command. The whole transaction is impersonal. The reed, like a measuring rod, is given him, and at the same time the command is given to arise and measure the Temple, and the altar, and them that worship in the Temple. Here, again, we find the basis of the vision in the Old Testament. Ezekiel was brought, in vision, to a high mountain, and saw a man with a line of flax (for measuring long distances) and a measuring line (for shorter distances). But, more probably, the vision of Zechariah was in the seer's mind (Zech. ii. 1, 2), for the vision there of the man with the measuring rod to measure Jerusalem is followed, in the fourth chapter (Zech. iv. 1—6), by the vision of the two olive-trees, which are distinctly identified with the two witnesses in the present chapter (see verses 3, 4). The Temple, altar, and worshippers are to be measured. The measuring implies the protecting of, or the token of a resolve to protect, a portion of the sacred enclosure from desecration. The measuring, like the sealing of chap. vii., is a sign of preservation during impending dangers. To understand what is thus measured out for protection we must remember that there are two Greek words which are rendered Temple: the one (*hieron*) signifies "the whole compass of the sacred enclosure, including the outer courts, porches, porticoes, and other buildings subordinated to the Temple itself;" the other (*naos*) is the Temple itself, the house of God, the Holy

stood, saying, Rise, and measure the temple of God, and the altar, and them that worship therein. (2) But the court which is without the temple leave out,[1] and measure it not; for it is given unto the Gentiles: and the holy city shall they tread under foot forty *and* two months. (3) And I will

1 Gr. *cast out.*

---

and Holy of Holies. When it is said that Christ taught the people in the Temple, the first of these words is used; and it may be supposed that in one of the porches or courts of the sanctuary our Lord carried on His teaching. But when Zacharias is described as going into the Temple, the word is the second (*naos*), for he went into the Temple proper, and left the people in the outer court, or court where the brazen altar stood. It is the second of these words which is used here: the Temple proper, the *naos*, the house of God, is measured, together with the altar. We are not told which altar is intended. It is at least too hasty to say that it must be the altar of incense, as this alone was in the Temple proper; for the explicit direction to measure the altar sounds like an extension of the measured area, and may perhaps mean that some portion of the court reserved for Israel is to be included in the measurement. The next verse, however, seems to imply that every spot outside the Temple proper was given up to the Gentiles, and was not to be measured. It is perhaps wisest, therefore, not to settle too definitely. The gist of the measurement is the preservation of the true, invisible Church, the Church within the Church; and everything necessary to the worship—Temple, altar, worshippers—all are reserved. There will always be the real and the conventional—the true and the formal Christian; always those who profess and call themselves Christians, and those who hold the faith in unity of spirit, in the bond of peace, and in righteousness of life. These last are the called and chosen and faithful (Rev. xvii. 14), the sealed who dwell in the secret place of the Most High, and find therefore their safe lodging in the night of danger under the shadow of the Almighty (Ps. xci. 1; comp. also the whole Psalm, especially verses 4, 5, and 9—13).

(2) **But the court . . .**—Translate, *And the court which is outside the Temple cast out, and measure not it; because it was given to the nations* (Gentiles)*: and they shall tread down the holy city forty and two months.* The outer court—meaning, perhaps, all that lies outside the Temple itself—is to be omitted. A strong word is used; the words "leave out" are far too weak. He is not only not to measure it, but he is, in a sort, to pass it over, as though reckoned profane. The reason of this is that it was given to the Gentiles. Our Lord had said that Jerusalem should be trodden down of the Gentiles (Luke xxi. 24); the sacred seer catches the thought and the deeper significance. There is a treading down worse than that of the conqueror. It is the treading under of sacred things when the beast-power, or the world-power in men, tramples, like the swine, the pearls of grace under their feet, and turns fiercely upon those who gave them. Such an experience must the Church of Christ undergo. The shrine shall be safe, but the spirit of the nations, though nominally Christian, will be the spirit of Gentilism, worldliness, and even of violence. In the outer court of Church life there will be "the ebbing and flowing mass," who "sit in the way of knowledge," who "stand idle in the market-place," who have no oil in their lamps, and who indirectly pave the way for utter worldliness and practical heathenism. But there is a limit to this desecration: forty and two months it is to last. The same length of time is expressed in different forms throughout the book. Sometimes we have twelve hundred and sixty days, as in verse 3 and in chap. xii. 6; at another time forty-two months, as here and in chap. xiii. 5. A similar period seems to be meant in chap. xii. 14, where a time, times, and half a time is probably a way of expressing three years and a half; all three forms describe periods of the same length—not, of course, necessarily the same period. The idea is taken from Daniel, who uses such and similar expressions (Dan. vii. 25, and xii. 7, 11). This incorporation of the expressions used by Daniel is one of those hints which remind us that the laws and principles of God's government are the same in all ages: so that the principles which receive illustration in one set of historical events are likely to receive similar illustrations in after times; and that the prophecies of one era may contain seeds of fulfilments which spring to fruit in more than one age. Thus the words of Daniel were not exhausted in the age of Antiochus, nor the visions of the Apocalypse in the overthrow of any one nation or the corruptions of any one Church. So much may this constantly-recurring period of three years and a half, or forty-two months, or twelve hundred and sixty days, teach us. It is not needful, then, to take the period as an exact literal period. It is true that there have been some remarkable historical periods of this length, which various schools of interpreters have pointed out as the fulfilment of these prophecies; but there have been also remarkable blunders on the part of those who, forgetful of Christ's own warning, have tried to predict the year when certain prophecies will receive their accomplishments. It is true, also, that the future may bring us further light, and enable us to understand these descriptions of time better; but for the present, the period of forty and two months, the equivalent of three years and a half (the half of seven, the complete and divine number), is the symbol of a period limited in length, and under the control of Him who holds the seven stars and lives through the ages. It is the pilgrimage period of the Church, the period of the world's power, during which it seems to triumph; but the period of sackcloth (see verse 3) and of suffering will not last for ever.

(3—14) THE TWO WITNESSES.—It is the opinion of one able and pre-eminently painstaking commentator that "no solution has ever been given of this portion of the prophecy." I quote this that none may be disappointed when no satisfactory solution is given here; further light in the knowledge of the Bible, and the light of history, and, above all, the aid of the Holy Spirit, may show what the real solution is. At present it is best to lay down the lines which seem to lead in the direction of such a solution. First, the aim of the present vision must be kept in mind; and secondly, the vision in Zechariah (chap. iv., all), on which this is professedly built, must be remembered. Now the aim of our present vision seems to be to explain that in the great progress towards victory the Church itself will suffer through corruptions and worldliness, but that the true Temple—the kernel, so to speak, of the Church—will be unharmed and kept safe in her Master's hands. But the position of this hidden and enshrined Church will not be one of idle security; in that Temple will be reared in secret, as the rightful

give *power* unto my two witnesses, and
they shall prophesy[1] a thousand two
hundred *and* threescore days, clothed
in sackcloth. (4) These are the two
olive trees,[a] and the two candlesticks
standing before the God of the earth.

[1] Or, *I will give unto my two witnesses that they may prophesy.*
[a] Zech. 4. 3, 11, 14.

king Josiah was, those who will witness undaunted and undefiled for their Lord; throughout the whole of that chequered period of profanation and pain there will never be wanting true witnesses for righteousness and faith. To assure the sacred seer that this would be the case, to exhibit the nature of their work and its results, is the apparent aim of the vision. If this be so, the witnesses can scarcely be literal individual men, though it is true that many literal individual men have played the part of these witnesses. Turning to the foundation vision in Zechariah, we find that the vision there is designed to encourage the weak and restored exiles in their work of rebuilding the Temple; they are shown that, weak as they are, there is a hidden strength, like a sacred stream of oil, which can make them triumph over all their difficulties: not by might or power, but by God's Spirit, the mountain would become a plain (Zech. iv. 6, 7), and "Grace! Grace!" would be the triumphant shout when the headstone of the Temple was raised. In both visions, then, our minds are turned to the hidden sources of divine strength; there is a safe and secret place measured off by God, where He gives His children strength—not of ordinary might or power, but strength of grace. This is the grace which made Zerubbabel and Joshua strong to achieve their work; this is the grace which can make the two witnesses strong to do their part in the building of that more glorious spiritual temple which is built on the foundation of Apostles and prophets, Jesus Christ Himself being the chief corner-stone. The witnesses, then, stand as the typical representatives of those who, in the strength of God, have, through the long ages, borne witness for Christ against all wrong and falsehood, against a world in arms or a Church in error, or against a nominal Christianity in danger of becoming as corrupt and as cruel as heathenism. Such witnesses stand, like the two columns Jachin and Boaz, before the true Temple of God.

(3) **And I will give . . .**—Translate, *And I will give* (omit "power") *to my two witnesses, and they shall* . . . These are the words of God Himself; the omission of the words "and the angel stood" from verse 1 prevents any confusion of thought on this point. Two witnesses were required for competent evidence (Deut. xvii. 6; xix. 15, *et al.*), and there has constantly been a sending forth of God's chosen messengers in pairs—Moses and Aaron, Elijah and Elisha, besides Joshua and Zerubbabel, alluded to by Zechariah; and in New Testament times our Lord sent forth His disciples "two and two," as afterwards Paul and Barnabas, or Paul and Silas, went forth to preach. There is, besides the mere mutual support which two can give, a need for the association of two different characters in the same sort of work: the energy and the sympathy, the elucidator of doctrines and the messenger to the conscience, the apologist and the evangelist, the man of thought and the man of action, the Son of Thunder and the Son of Consolation; it is well that in a world-wide work this duality of power should be brought into play. The witnesses *prophesy*: the word prophesy must surely be allowed a much wider meaning than merely to predict or foretell future events. The compass of their work, as described afterwards, embraces much more than this (see verses 5—7): they work wonders, showing tokens that remind us of the days of Moses and Aaron; their words are mighty; their life is a testimony.

Their prophesying, or witnessing, extends over forty and two months: a symbolical period, as we have seen, but a period corresponding to that during which other witnesses had witnessed for God. Thus long did Elijah bear witness, under rainless heavens, against the idolatries of Israel; thus long did a greater than Elijah offer the water of life to the Jews, and witness against the hard, unspiritual, worldly religionism of the Pharisee and Sadducee; thus, too, must the witnesses for God bear testimony during the period that the world-power seems dominant. They are clad in sackcloth—the emblem of mourning (2 Kings vi. 30; Jon. iii. 4) adopted by the prophets, whose God-taught hearts saw reasons for mourning where shallower minds saw none (Isa. xx. 2, and Zech. xiii. 2). Compare the garb of Elijah and John the Baptist (2 Kings i. 8, and Matt. iii. 4), whose very apparel and appearance were designed to testify against the evils they saw. "The special witnesses of God, in a luxurious and self-pleasing age, are often marked out from the world by signs of self-denial, of austerity, and even of isolation" (Dr. Vaughan).

(4) **These are . . .**—Translate, *These are the two olive trees and the two candlesticks which stand before the Lord of the earth.* This is the verse which refers us to the vision of Zechariah for the basis of our present vision. There, as here, we have the two olive trees, which are explained to be "the two anointed ones which stand before the Lord of the whole earth." The explanation is supposed to refer to Zerubbabel and Joshua, or, as others think, to Zechariah and Haggai. At that time these men were the witnesses for God in their land and among their people. But the answer of the angel is general: "the olive trees are the two anointed ones which stand," &c. For the vision is general and age-long; it reminds us of the returned Jewish exiles, and of those who were then among them, as anointed witnesses, but it shows us that such witnesses are to be found in more than one era; for it is not Zerubbabel and Joshua who can exhaust the fulness of a vision which is the representation of the eternal truth that the oil of gladness and strength from God will rest on those who rely, not on might or power, but on God's Spirit. The fact that the witnesses are two is brought more prominently forward here than in Zechariah. There, though the olive trees are two, the candlestick is but one, with seven lamps; here there are two candlesticks spoken of as well as two olive trees. This amplification of the original vision is, perhaps, designed to remind us of the greater latitude of diversity in the new dispensation. Just as in the early chapters of this book we had seven golden candlesticks, which, though one in Christ, yet are spoken of as separate, so here the double aspect, the diverse though united efforts of the two witnesses, are brought into prominence. It may serve to remind us that the witnesses are to be expected to keep their individuality and to use freely their diverse powers. It is not from one class or with one mode of action that the witnesses come: they may be of the statesman class, like Moses and Zerubbabel; of the prophetic or priestly, like Zechariah and Haggai, like Aaron and the later Joshua (Zech. iii. 1); for men may witness for God, according as the evils of their time and age require it, in the State as well as in the Church. The work of

(5) And if any man will hurt them, fire
proceedeth out of their mouth, and
devoureth their enemies: and if any
man will hurt them, he must in this
manner be killed. (6) These have power
to shut heaven, that it rain not in the
days of their prophecy: and have power
over waters to turn them to blood, and
to smite the earth with all plagues, as
often as they will. (7) And when they
shall have finished their testimony, the
beast that ascendeth out of the bottom-
less pit shall make war against them,
and shall overcome them, and kill them.
(8) And their dead bodies *shall lie* in
the street of the great city, which
spiritually is called Sodom and Egypt,
where also our Lord was crucified.
(9) And they of the people and kindreds
and tongues and nations shall see their

Wilberforce, Clarkson, and Howard is a work and a witness for God as well as the work of Chrysostom, Athanasius, and Luther; for the witnesses are raised up to speak against the neglect of humanity as well as against errors in divinity; against a heartless as well as against a creedless Christianity, for both lead back to heathenism. These witnesses are burning and shining lights; in them is centred the light of their age; in them is found the token that the grace of God never fails, but as the Church's day so shall her strength be. Here, too, we have the pledge that from Him who is both Priest and King the civil rulers as well as the ecclesiastical rulers may draw grace according to their gifts; and from Him, too, all who are made kings as well as priests to God may derive the power to give the double witness of a life anointed by the Spirit of consecration and ruled by the sceptre of righteousness.

(5) **And if any man . . .**—Better, *And if any one wills to injure them, fire goeth forth out of their mouths, and devoureth their enemies: and if any one wills to injure them, thus must he be slain. These have power to shut the heaven that the rain may not moisten* (the earth) *during the days of their prophesying; and they have power over the waters to turn them into blood, and to smite the earth with every plague as often as they will.* Again the Old Testament basis becomes evident; the histories of Elijah and Moses supply the illustration. The fire devouring their foes seems to allude to 2 Kings i. 10; like Elijah, they can close the heaven (1 Kings xvii. 1); like Moses, they can turn water into blood and summon down every plague (Ex. vii. 20, *et seq.*). These last characteristics remind us of the spirit and power of Moses and Elias, but we must not forget what has gone before: the witnesses are like olive trees and lights. In them is concentrated grace, light, and power; their witness recalls the great features of various Old Testament teachers and leaders; they display the light of truth, and men may not oppose or injure them with impunity; they wield a power which it is not safe to provoke. As from the mouths of the great Sixth Trumpet host there went forth fire and smoke and brimstone to kill the third part of mankind, so out of the mouths of these witnesses there goes forth a purer, but mightier flame. (Comp. Ps. xviii. 8.) We may compare the sword out of the mouth of Christ (chap. i. 16), and the promise to Jeremiah (chap. v. 14), "Behold I will make my words in thy mouth fire and this people wood, and it shall devour them." The word which is like a sword to lay bare man to himself may become a consuming fire to those who resist or oppose it. The witnesses for God are thus armed with a spiritual might; for that word which, when accepted and lived by, brings peace, when rejected causes pain and danger. Thus often do the things which might have been for men's peace become an occasion for falling; the stone which, used and built into the life, becomes a precious corner-stone and immovable foundation, grinds to powder those upon whom it falls. Thus is it with these witnesses: they come to witness for principles which go to make the world a Paradise once more. The world, which casts away their words, will find them come back with scorching force; just as the breath of God gives life and beauty to the world, and power to men's hearts and lives (Ps. civ. 30; John xx. 22), yet with that same breath of His lips does He slay the wicked (Isa. xi. 4). Some have thought that there will be a time when witnesses for God will be raised up who will work literal wonders such as these. It is not for us to say that this will not be the case: all prophecy may take a sharper and clearer meaning as the times of the end draw near; but, meanwhile, it is needful for us to remember that the very power of truth is such that, when rejected, it can and does avenge itself by shutting heaven over our head, and making all the fresh rivulets of life's purest pleasures loathsome as blood to the sensualised and perverted heart.

(7) **And when . . .**—Better, *And when they shall have finished their testimony, the wild beast that goeth up out of the abyss shall make war with them, and conquer them, and kill them.* Only when their work is done has the wild beast power over them. To every one there are the symbolical twelve hours in which his life's work must be achieved; to every one there is the time secured when he may accomplish for God what God sent him to fulfil: then, but not till then, cometh the night, when none can work. *The wild beast:* We shall hear much of this wild beast later on. Here we are told distinctly that the wild beast will have his hour of triumph; he rises out of the abyss, as the locust horde did (chap. ix. 1, 2). There is, then, a beast-spirit which is in utter hostility to the Christ-spirit. We shall be able to study the features of this power in a future chapter (chap. xiii. 1); here he is seen to be a spirit of irreconcilable antagonism to Christ. The image here is not new; Daniel made use of it (Dan. vii.), though in a much more limited sense. This beast-power vanquishes the witnesses. If the witnesses are those who have taught the principles of a spiritual and social religion, the death of the witnesses following their overthrow signifies the triumph of opposing principles, the silencing of those who have withstood the growing current of evil. Men can silence, can conquer, can slay the witness for a higher, purer, nobler life. They have done so. The history of the world is often the history of the postponement of moral and social advancement for centuries through the wild outbreak of some brutal, irrational, selfish spirit. The Reformers, the best friends of the Church and of the world, have been silenced and slain, and their death has often been little more than the triumph of the ignorance and selfishness of a practical heathenism.

(8–10) **And their dead bodies . . .**—Better, *And their corpse* (*is*) *upon the street of the great city, which*

dead bodies three days and an half, and
shall not suffer their dead bodies to be
put in graves. (10) And they that dwell
upon the earth shall rejoice over them,
and make merry, and shall send gifts
one to another; because these two
prophets tormented them that dwelt
on the earth. (11) And after three days
and an half the Spirit of life from God
entered into them, and they stood upon
their feet; and great fear fell upon
them which saw them. (12) And they
heard a great voice from heaven saying
unto them, Come up hither. And they
ascended up to heaven in a cloud; and
their enemies beheld them. (13) And
the same hour was there a great earth-
quake, and the tenth part of the city
fell, and in the earthquake were slain of
men[1] seven thousand: and the remnant

[1] Gr. *names of men.*

---

is called spiritually Sodom and Egypt, where their Lord also was crucified. And some from among the peoples and tribes and tongues and nations look upon their corpse three days and a half, and do not suffer their corpses to be put into a tomb. And they that dwell upon the earth rejoice over them, and make merry, and shall send gifts one to another; because these two prophets tormented them that dwelt upon the earth. Their corpses remain unburied, while congratulations and rejoicings go on; harmony and concord prevail, as when Pilate and Herod were made friends; it is the millennium of evil, the paradise of fools who make a mock at sin; but the forms of the witnesses, though silenced, still in silence witness against evil. At no time are they hid away out of sight. Even in an age of religious and social anarchy the silent tokens of a better order remain, as when in mockery and profanation the harlot was enthroned within Notre Dame, the very sanctuary walls, which no longer echoed to the psalm of Christian life, yet bore silent testimony to the higher genius of the past. They are said to lie in "the street of the great city." The city is described as the great city (comp. chap. xvi. 19), and also as Sodom, Egypt, and Jerusalem. Do not passages like this show conclusively that to deny the mystical or allegorical sense of the Apocalypse is to keep the husk and cast away the seed? The city is great, for it is all-important in the eyes of the inhabitants, as public opinion is all-important to the weak or the worldly; it is Sodom, for it is the place where, through pleasure and luxuriousness (fulness of bread), the worst forms of immorality take root; it is Egypt, for it is the house of bondage, where the wages of sin become tyrannous; it is Jerusalem, for it is the apostate place where the presence of Christ is hated. The same spirit which slew their Lord is alive to persecute His servants. "It cannot be that a prophet perish out of Jerusalem. If they have called the master of the house Beelzebub, how much more them of his household;" and the reason of this hatred is told—the words of the witnesses "tormented them." "The reproof of their gospel and the reproof of their example . . . had been a torture to them; there was a voice in them which echoed its voice—the voice of a convicting conscience, and the voice of an anticipated judgment."

(11) **And after three days . . .**—Better, *And after the three days and a half* (not simply "three days and a half,") *a Spirit of life out of* (*from*) *God entered into* (or, *in; i.e.,* so as to be in) *them, and they stood upon their feet; and a great fear fell upon those who beheld them.* The vision of the dry bones will be remembered; in part, the very wording of it is employed here—*e.g.,* "they stood upon their feet" (Ezek. xxxvii. 1—10); and a yet more sacred remembrance—the three days of our Master's death-sleep—will be traced here. "Where I am there shall also My servant be" (John xii. 26). "If we suffer with Him, we shall also be glorified together" (Rom. viii. 17). There is a resurrection power in even rejected truth; the strength of it is undying. If it be of God, men cannot overthrow it. "The corn of wheat that dies brings forth much fruit." The cause that seemed dead is found to be possessed of a renewed power and life. "There is an end of resistance to the Papal rule and religion; opposers exist no more!" cried the orator of the Lateran Council in 1514; but within three years and a half the hand of Luther nailed up his theses at Wittenberg. It is one illustration among many.

(12) **And they heard . . .**—Translate, *And they heard* (or, *I heard;* the MS. authority is divided, though the balance inclines to the first) *a great voice out of the heaven saying to them, Come up hither. And they went up into the heaven in the cloud, and their enemies beheld them.* The resurrection of the witnesses is followed by their ascension. It is the token that in this too they shall have a portion with their Lord; rejected and slain, there is welcome and honour for them; they take their place with those who through faith and patience inherit the promises; they rest from their labours. But this is not all. Like Elijah (2 Kings ii. 11), they are taken up gloriously, but not, like Elijah, in comparative secret; their enemies see their exaltation. As for the witnesses themselves there is the welcome rest of heaven, so there is the visible recognition of their work and power on earth; the cause which seemed dead revives, and with its revival comes the recognition of those who laboured for it; the martyred are seen transfigured, they become glorious in the eyes of men:

> "Persecution dragged them into fame,
> And chased them up to heaven."

They went up in *the* cloud: There is here, perhaps, a touch of recollection. St. John remembers the cloud which received his Lord out of sight. Since then the cloud mingles with his every thought of ascension or descending from heaven. (Comp. chap. i. 7; Acts i. 9.) The witnesses, like their Master, disappeared in the cloud.

(13) **And the same hour . . .**—Better, *And in that hour there was* (took place) *a great earthquake, and the tenth part of the city fell, and there were slain in the earthquake names of men seven thousand: and the rest became affrighted, and gave glory to the God of the heaven.* The hour of their triumph is the hour of a retributive warning on the city where they were slain: convulsion, with the overthrow of dwellings and the death of seven thousand men. Is it accidental that the number is the same as the number of those who had not bowed to Baal? (1 Kings xix. 18.) Rejected reformation avenges itself in revolution, and the city which might have been purified by the word is purged by the spirit of judgment (Isa. iv. 4); good is effected, even through fear; some are saved though as by fire; and, unlike those who repented not (chap. ix. 21), they give

were affrighted, and gave glory to
the God of heaven. (14) The second
woe is past; *and*, behold, the third
woe cometh quickly. (15) And the
seventh angel sounded;
and there were great voices
in heaven, saying, The
kingdoms of this world are become *the*
kingdoms of our Lord, and of his Christ;
and he shall reign for ever and ever.
(16) And the four and twenty elders,
which sat before God on their seats, fell
upon their faces, and worshipped God,
(17) saying, We give thee thanks, O Lord
God Almighty, which art, and wast, and
art to come; because thou hast taken to

Chap. xi. 15—19. The seventh trumpet. Third woe.

---

glory to the God of heaven. The visible Church of Christ is stirred; there is a reaction from the spirit of worldliness.

(14) **The second woe . . .**—Translate, *The second woe is past.* (Omit the word "and," which weakens the proclamation.) The eagle flying in mid-heaven had announced the three woe trumpets. A voice now reminds us that two of these had passed, just as at the close of the fifth trumpet a voice proclaimed that the first woe was past. We must remember, too, that the angel which descended from heaven declared that the end should not be delayed beyond the sounding of the seventh trumpet; the last woe trumpet, therefore, is the trumpet which will usher in the closing woe and the finishing of the mystery of God. Whatever view we adopt concerning the interpretation of the Apocalypse must be governed by the plainly declared fact that the seventh trumpet brings us to the very end. The next verse only serves to make this plainer.

THE SEVENTH TRUMPET—THE LAST WOE TRUMPET.

(15) **And the seventh angel . . .**—Better, *And the seventh angel sounded; and there were great voices in the heaven* (*persons*) *saying, The kingdom of the world is become* (*the possession*) *of our Lord, and of His Christ, and He shall reign to the ages of ages.* The literal translation is, *The kingdom of the world is become our Lord's, and of His Christ.* As far as the expression "our Lord's" is concerned, there is no need that any word, such as kingdom or possession, should be supplied, but the additional phrase "of His Christ" creates an awkwardness, and the word "possession," or *inheritance*, may not inappropriately be used from the Psalm which foretells this final establishment of the kingdom of the anointed Messiah, the Christ of God. "Ask of me, and I shall give thee the heathen for thine inheritance, and the uttermost parts of the earth for thy possession" (Ps. ii. 8). It is the kingdom—not, as in the English version, "the kingdoms"—of the world which has become Christ's possession. The contest is not for the kingdoms, the separate nationalities: the varying political systems might exist, as far as mere organisation is concerned, under the rule of Christ; the contest is for the kingdom of the world. Satan was willing to surrender the kingdoms of the world to our Lord on condition of a homage which would have left him still in possession of the kingdom of the world. But now the close of the contest is the overthrow of the kingdom of evil, the establishment of the kingdom of good: that is, of God; *and He shall reign for ever and ever.* Dean Alford pointed out that our familiarity with the "Hallelujah Chorus" tempted us to put an emphasis on the word *He* which is not sanctioned by the Greek; it is the *reign* of the Lord which is the prominent thought. The reign is unto the ages of ages. Surely this means *always.* We are not told whose voices sing this chorus; it is just the tumultuous sound of heavenly voices, growing into natural and irresistible chorus as the trumpet heralds the approach of the glorious end.

(16) **And the four . . .**—Translate, *And the four-and-twenty elders, who before God were seated upon their thrones* (not "seats"), *fell upon their faces, and worshipped God.* The four-and-twenty elders represent the Church of God in all ages; they sit with Christ in heavenly places, even while they are toiling and sorrowing on earth; every one of the true children of the kingdom appear before God, and their angels behold the presence of their Father who is in heaven. They were seated on *thrones*, not "seats" (comp. chap. iv. 4), as in English version; the word used is the same which is translated "throne" when it refers to our Lord. It is the same word which is rendered "seat" (chaps. ii. 13, and xvi. 10) when it refers to Satan; but it is better rendered *throne* throughout, for by this variation of translation, as "Archbishop Trench has pointed out, two great ideas which run through this book, and, indeed, we may say through the whole of the New Testament, are obliterated: the one, that the true servants of Christ are crowned with Him and share His sovereignty; the other, that the antagonism of the Prince of Darkness to the Prince of Light develops itself in the hellish parody of the heavenly kingdom" (Prof. Lightfoot, *Revision of New Testament*, p. 41). It is specially desirable that this thought should be kept before us in this passage, which proclaims that the kingdom and throne and power of the wicked one have passed away, and the hour has come when the victorious saints may sit down with Christ in His throne (chap. iii. 21).

THE CHORUS OF THE CHURCH OF GOD.

(17) **Saying, We give thee thanks . . .**—Better,

"We thank Thee, O Lord,
The God, the Almighty,
He that is, and He that was,
Because Thou hast taken Thy great power
and didst reign.
And the nations were angry,
And then came Thine anger
And the season of the dead to be judged,
And to give their rewards to Thy servants the prophets, and to
the saints,
And to them that fear Thy name, the small and the great,
And to destroy them that destroy the earth."

On the expression "He that is and He that was," comp. chap. i. 8 and the Note there. We can catch the echo of the Second Psalm throughout this chorus of grateful praise. The prayers of the groaning Church (chap. v. 10, and Luke xviii. 7, 8) and the cries of travailing creation (Rom. viii. 19) have been heard; though the heathen raged and the people imagined a vain thing, their counsel against the Lord and His anointed, His Christ (compare verse 16), came to nought; the joy of their triumph was short-lived; the kingdom of evil was but for a moment; the kings were assembled, they passed by, they saw, they were troubled, they hasted away (Ps. xlviii. 4, 5); never did the real sovereignty of the Lord cease (Ps. ii. 6); but the nations would not believe in His rule; they were not wise; they turned from the kiss of reconciliation, which was life (Ps. ii. 10—12); then came His anger, and the season of judgment and the season of reward. The prophets, the saints, and

thee thy great power, and hast reigned.
(18) And the nations were angry, and
thy wrath is come, and the time of the
dead, that they should be judged, and
that thou shouldest give reward unto
thy servants the prophets, and to the
saints, and them that fear thy name,
small and great; and shouldest destroy
them which destroy[1] the earth. (19) And
the temple of God was opened in heaven,
and there was seen in his temple the
ark of his testament: and there were
lightnings, and voices, and thunderings,
and an earthquake, and great hail.

A.D. 96.

2 Or, *sign.*

1 Or, *corrupt.*

CHAPTER XII.—(1) And there ap-
peared a great wonder[2] in
heaven; a woman clothed
with the sun, and the
moon under her feet, and

Chap. xii. 1—6. The hostility of the arch-enemy.

those that fear God's name, the small and the great—every class and rank of the true servants of the King are included here; none are forgotten; not a cup of cold water, given in His name, shall miss its reward; for not alone the pre-eminent in Christian power and in Christian holiness, but the weak, the struggling, the obscure, the small as well as the great, are remembered: "Unto the God of gods appeareth every one of them in Zion" (Ps. lxxxiv. 7; Prayer Book version). Nor is the gladness only for this blessing; there is a joy at the overthrow of those who destroy the earth. The reign of evil is the destruction of the earth. The judgments of God are in mercy to stay the spread of destructive powers and principles. The tender mercies of the wicked are cruel; the very judgments of God are merciful. (See Note on chap. viii. 2.)

But where, we may be disposed to ask, is the "woe" in all this? We are led to expect that the seventh trumpet as a woe trumpet will bring in some period of pain and trouble, as the others have done; but all we hear is the chorus of glad voices uttering praise: we see no token of woe. The answer is that we must not overlook all that this song of rejoicing implies. The chorus we hear is the thanksgiving to God that the hour has come for the overthrow of the kingdom of evil, the manifestation of the sons of God, and the acknowledgment throughout the world of the sovereignty of the Lord and of His Christ. The overthrow of that evil kingdom, which is now to take place, brings with it woe to those who have supported it; for the time of the judgment of the dead, and of those whose lives have marred God's world, has come. It is, then, woe on all those who have misused God's gifts and those beautiful things which He gave us liberally to enjoy. It is a woe on those who have defiled those bodies, which are the temples of the Holy Ghost, profaned the earth, which is God's footstool, or darkened by their evil deeds the heaven, which is His throne. Those who thus defile (or, *destroy:* the word is so in the margin, and is the same as that which follows) God's temple anywhere, God will destroy (1 Cor. vi. 19, and iii. 17).

(19) **And the temple of God . . .**—Translate, *And the temple of God was opened in the heaven, and the ark of His covenant was seen in His temple: and there were lightnings, and voices, and thunders, and an earthquake, and a great hail.* At the beginning of the chapter we noticed the distinction between the two words (*naos* and *hieron*) applied to the Temple; the Temple building proper (the *naos*) was measured off. Now this (*naos*) Temple is opened, yes, to its very inmost recesses; for not the holy place alone is disclosed, but the holiest of all, the shrine of shrines, into which the high priest alone—and he only once a year—entered, is opened, as though anew the veil of the Temple had been rent in twain, and there the ark of the covenant of God is seen. The meaning of this, when read by the light of the measuring of the Temple, seems to be that now the secret abode of the safe-guarded children of God was revealed. In the hour of apostasies and worldliness the faithful had found their strength and protection in the shadow of the Almighty; they were regarded by God as His true living Temple, and in them He dwelt, as they, too, found their defence in Him. But now that the end has come there is no need that these should be hidden any more. The children of God, who are the Temple of God, are made manifest; and at the same time the secret spot of their shelter in troublous days is made plain, and in it is seen the token of that everlasting covenant which was the sheet-anchor of their hopes in the day of their trouble (Heb. vi. 19). The ark of God's covenant is seen; the ark which contained the tables of the law, the rod of Aaron, and the manna is unveiled; and now is known whence they derived that hidden manna, that bread of heaven which strengthened their hearts in the days of temptation; now is known how it was that the rod of Christ's power flourished and blossomed in spite of oft-repeated rejection; now, too, are known those high and holy principles by which the lives of the saints of God were ruled, even that law which the divine Spirit had written in their hearts (Heb. x. 16, and 2 Cor. iii. 2). Then, too, with the ark of God's covenant, is brought into view the mercy-seat, that throne of grace to which the weary and heavy-laden children of God had so often gone, and where they had never failed to receive grace to help in every time of need (Heb. iv. 16). The Temple of God was opened, and the secret springs of power which sustained the patience and faith of the saints are found to be in God. And out of the opened Temple, or round about it, as round the sacred peak of Sinai, the lightnings are seen and voices and thunders are heard: the tokens of that holy law which the power of the world had defied are made manifest; for God's righteousness has not lost its strength, and that which is a power of help to those who seek their shelter in God becomes a power of destruction to those who turn from Him. The habitation of God is an open sanctuary to faith; it is a clouded and lightning-crowned Sinai to faithlessness. (Comp. Heb. xii. 18—24.) The spirit of evil, of selfishness, of luxuriousness, of profanity, which rejects its birthright of better thoughts and holy things, leads to "the mount that burned with fire, and unto blackness and darkness and tempest, and the sound of a trumpet, and the voice of words;" the Spirit of God leads to "the city of the living God, the heavenly Jerusalem, and to an innumerable company of angels, to the general assembly and Church of the first-born which are written in heaven."

XII.

We now enter upon the third group of visions (or, the fourth section of the book, if we include the epistles

upon her head a crown of twelve stars; (2) and she being with child cried, travailing in birth, and pained to be delivered.

(3) And there appeared another wonder[1] in heaven; and behold a great red dragon, having seven heads and ten

1 Or, *sign.*

---

to the seven churches), which occupy chapters xii., xiii., and xiv., and close with the solemn scene of the harvest and the vintage (chap. xiv. 14—20). The close of each series of visions is in harmony with their general intention, and, as such, affords a key to their meaning. The seals end in peace; the trumpets end in victory; the present visions end in harvest. We have been shown that toil and trouble shall end in rest and conflict in triumph; now we are to be shown that there is to be a harvest at the end of the world, when the fruits of the conflicting principles of life will have ripened, and when whatsoever a man hath sown that shall he also reap: and men will be seen as they are. This set of visions accordingly moves in a different plane from the earlier groups; starting from the same point as the others, it reviews the ground with a different purpose. It deals with the spiritual conditions of the great war between evil and good; it disrobes the false appearances which deceive men; it makes manifest the thoughts of men's hearts; it shows that the great war is not merely a war between evil and good, but between an evil spirit and the Spirit of God: and that, therefore, the question is not only one between right and wrong conduct, but between true and false spiritual dispositions. Men look at the world, and they acknowledge a kind of conflict between evil and good; their sympathies are vaguely on the side of good; they admire much in Christianity; they are willing to think the martyred witnesses of the Church heroes; they think the reformers of past ages worthy of honour; they would not be averse to a Christianity without Christ or a Christianity without spirituality. They do not realise that the war which is raging round them is not a war between men morally good and men morally bad, but between spiritual powers, and that what the Gospel asks is not merely a moral life, but a life lived by faith in the Son of God, a life in which the spiritual dispositions are Godward and Christward. The Apocalypse, in this set of visions, unveils the spiritual aspects of the conflict, that we may know that the issue is not between Christianity and un-Christianity, but between Christianity and anti-Christianity. Hitherto we have seen the more outward aspects of the great war. Now we are to see its hidden, secret, spiritual—yes, supernatural aspects—that we may understand what immeasurably divergent and antagonistic principles are in conflict under various and specious aspects in the history of the world. Accordingly, we are shown the child encountered by the dragon, the woman in conflict with the dragon, the wild beast as the adversary of the lamb. We see no longer the battle under human forms, as the struggle for the possession of the Temple; but we see clearly and unmistakably the real issue which is being fought out, and we see the real spiritual work which the Church is designed to accomplish in the world. The motto of this section might well be, "He that is not with me is against me"—"He that gathereth not with me scattereth;" for only those who are truly with Christ will avoid falling under the yoke of one of the three enemies of Christ—the dragon and the two wild beasts animated and inspired by him.

(1) **And there appeared . . .**—Better, *And a great sign was seen in the heaven.* The word *sign* is preferable to "wonder," both in this verse and in verse 3. It is the same word which is rendered sign in chap. xv. 1. It is a sign which is seen: not a mere wonder, but something which has a meaning; it is not "a surprise ending with itself," but a signal to arrest attention, and possessing significance; there is "an idea concealed behind it." (Comp. Note on John ii. 11.)

A woman clothed with the sun, and the moon under her feet, and upon her head a crown of twelve stars.—All the lights of heaven are brought together here for a description which cannot fail to remind us of the picture of the Shulamite in the Canticles (vi. 10): 'Who is she that looketh forth as the morning, fair as the moon, clear as the sun, and terrible as an army with banners (or, *the heavenly host*)?" It is the picture of the bride, the Church. The beams of the divine glory clothe her; she has caught—like Moses—the radiance of her Lord, whose countenance was as the sun (chap. i. 16); the moon is beneath her feet; she rises superior to all change, and lays all lesser lights of knowledge under tribute; she is crowned with a crown of twelve stars: the illustrious members of the Church (twelve being the representative number in Old Testament as well as New Testament times) form her crown of rejoicing in the day of Christ.

(2) **And she . . .**—Better, *And being with child, she crieth, travailing, and tormented to bring forth.* All life dawns in anguish, according to the ancient fiat (Gen. iii. 16); but this is not all. There is an anguish of the Church which Christ laid upon her; it is the law of her life that she must bring forth Christ to the world; it is not simply that she must encounter pain, but that she cannot work deliverance without knowing suffering. Thus the Apostles felt: the love of Christ constrained them; woe it would be to them if they did not preach the Gospel; necessity was laid upon them; they spoke of themselves as travailing in birth over their children till Christ was formed in them. This, then, is the picture, the Church fulfilling her destiny even in pain. The work was to bring forth Christ to men, and never to be satisfied till Christ was formed in them, *i.e.*, till the spirit of Christ, and the teaching of Christ, and the example of Christ were received, loved, and obeyed, and men transformed to the same image, even as by the Spirit of the Lord.

But there was to be opposition; the enemy is on the watch to destroy the likeness of Christ wherever it was seen.

(3) **And there appeared . . .**—Better, *And another sign was seen in the heaven; and behold a great red dragon.* This, too, is a sign, and has a meaning. The dragon stands for some dread and hostile power. "The dragon is that fabulous monster of whom ancient poets told, as large in size, coiled like a snake, blood red in colour . . . insatiable in voracity, and ever athirst for human blood"—a fit emblem of him whom our Lord declared to be a murderer from the beginning; for the dragon is intended here to describe him who, in verse 9, is also said to be that old serpent, called the Devil and Satan. The red colour is the colour of flame and blood, and the symbol of destruction and slaughter. The dragon is the emblem of the evil spirit, the devil, the perpetual antagonist of good, the persecutor of the Church in all ages (comp. Ps. lxxiv. 13): just as the dragon is sometimes employed to represent the Egyptian power, the ancient foe of Israel (Isa. li. 9; Ezek. xxix. 3).

horns, and seven crowns upon his heads.
(4) And his tail drew the third part of the stars of heaven, and did cast them to the earth: and the dragon stood before the woman which was ready to be delivered, for to devour her child as soon as it was born.
(5) And she brought forth a man child, who was to rule all nations with a rod of iron: and her child was caught up unto God, and *to* his throne.
(6) And the woman fled into the wilderness, where she hath a place prepared of God, that they should feed her there a thousand two hundred

---

Having seven heads and ten horns, and seven crowns (*diadems*) **upon his heads.**—This is the further description of the dragon. He is one, yet diverse; one, as an evil spirit; diverse, in the varieties of his power. The woman is but one: but her foe is multiform; she has one trust to keep, one work to do, and can but fulfil it in her Master's way: evil is bound by no law, regards no scruple, and exerts its power through any channel and by every means. Is there not also an assumption of divine similitude here in the use of the number seven? It is at least the representation of the great and world-wide power which he exercises as the prince of this world, whose kingdom is in much a parody of the true kingdom. The whole description should be compared with the account given of the beast in chap. xvii. 3, 7, 10, 12. There the seven heads are explained as seven kings, and the heads here are crowned; the ten horns are also explained as ten kings. The sevenfold kingship and the tenfold power of the world are thus described as belonging to the dragon. The picture here, as the picture of the wild beast in chap. xvii., represents, as concentrated into a single hostile form, all the varying forces and successive empires which have opposed or oppressed the people of God, and sought to destroy their efforts for good: for all evil has its root in a spirit at enmity with God. Hence the dragon appears armed with all the insignia of those sovereignties and powers which have been animated by this spirit.

(4) **And his tail . . .**—Translate, *And his tail drags* (or, *sweeps*) *away the third part of the stars of the heaven, and casts them to the earth.* The stars are the light-bearers, the illustrious of earth, who were given by God high place that they might be burning and shining lights for Him. A large proportion of these are drawn away in the train of evil; they are cast down from their high position of noble opportunities of good work and great work; they are dragged down from the height of the grandest possibilities of good to the low level of a life enslaved to evil.

And the dragon.—Translate, *And the dragon stands* (not "stood") *before the woman who is about to bring forth, that whenever she has brought forth he may devour her child.* The spirit of evil is represented as ever on the watch to destroy the first tokens of better things. Our minds go back to the hatred and fear of Pharaoh, setting a watch for the off-spring of Israel and ordering their destruction; and even more are we reminded of the jealous hatred of Herod seeking the life of the infant Christ. It seems clear that it is on this last incident that the present vision is primarily built up; but its meaning is much wider than this. It shows us that evermore, as Herod waited to destroy Christ, the devil, the old spirit whose malignity wrought through the fears of Pharaoh and of Herod, is on the watch to destroy every token of good and every resemblance to Christ in the world. The mission of the Church is to bring forth in her members this life of Christ before men: the aim of the wicked spirit is to destroy that life. The same hostility which was shown to the infant Christ is active against His children: "If they have persecuted Me, they will also persecute you."

(5) **And she brought forth . . .**—Translate, *And she brought forth a man child, who is to shepherd all the nations with* (it is, literally, *in*) *a rod of iron.* There can be no doubt that this man child is Christ. The combination of features is too distinct to admit of doubt. It is the one who will feed His flock like a shepherd (Isa. xl. 12), who is to have, not His own people, but all nations as His inheritance (Ps. ii. 7—9), and whose rule over them is to be supreme and irresistible. But the fact that this child is Christ must not cause us to limit the meaning of the vision to the efforts of the evil one to destroy the infant Jesus; for it is also the Christ in the Church which the wicked one hates: and wherever Christ dwells in any heart by faith, and wherever the preachers of the gospel in earnest travail for their Master, seek to lift up Christ, there will the foe be found, like the fowls of the air, ready to carry away the good seed. Though the basis of the vision is in the historical fact, the power of the vision reaches over a wider area, and forcibly reminds us that as there are irreconcileable principles at work in the world, so all these, when traced to their original forms, are the Spirit of Christ and the spirit of the devil.

And her child was caught up unto God, and to his throne.—The efforts of the evil one to destroy are thwarted; the child is snatched away and placed out of the range of the dragon's power. The prince of this world might instigate Israel to take Jesus Christ and with wicked hands crucify and kill Him, but the eternal divine life of Him who had power to lay down His life and take it again, and whose years were for ever and ever, was beyond the reach of every hostile power; and after death and resurrection, Christ ascended up where He was before. But the vision is designed to assure us that, precisely because of this, so all life in Christ is beyond the power of the evil one, and that the forces hostile to good are powerless against that life which is hid with Christ in God. The Church may be as a weak, oppressed, and persecuted woman, but her faith rises up as a song from the lips of its members. "God hath raised us up together, and made us sit together in heavenly places in Christ Jesus." The contest is between the man child and the dragon; and those who in heart and mind ascend to where Christ is know that the contest is not one of mere ideas, but a conflict between the Christ, who is with them always, though He has ascended, and all the powers of evil, which will be smitten down by the rod of His power.

(6) **And the woman fled . . .**—Translate, *And the woman fled into the wilderness, where she hath there a place prepared from God, that there they may nourish her for a thousand two hundred and sixty days.* The flight of the woman into the wilderness, and her fortunes there, are more fully described in verse 13. This verse simply tells us that the woman fled; we read afterwards that it was persecution which drove her into the wilderness. As long as the evil one can be called the prince of this world: as long, that is, as the world

and threescore days. (7) And there was
war in heaven: Michael
and his angels fought
against the dragon; and
the dragon fought and his
angels, (8) and prevailed not; neither was
their place found any more in heaven.
(9) And the great dragon was cast out,
that old serpent, called the Devil, and
Satan, which deceiveth the whole world:
he was cast out into the earth, and his
angels were cast out with him. (10) And
I heard a loud voice saying in heaven,
Now is come salvation, and strength,
and the kingdom of our God, and the
power of his Christ: for the accuser

Chap. xii. 7—12. The heavenly victory over the arch-enemy.

refuses to recognise her true Prince, and pays homage to worldliness, and baseness, and falseness in heart, mind, or life, so long must the Church, in so far as she is faithful to Him who is true, dwell as an exile in the wilderness. This feeling it was—not any hostility to life as life, or to life's duties—which led the Apostle to speak of Christians as strangers and pilgrims, and of the Church as another Israel, whom a greater than Moses or Joshua was conducting to a land of better promise (Heb. iv. 8, 9). The woman, the representative of the Church, has a place prepared by God for her in the wilderness; she is not altogether uncared for; she has a place prepared, and nourishment. God provides her with a tabernacle of safety (Ps. xc. 1), and with the true Bread "which came down from heaven" (Ex. xvi. 15; Ps. lxxviii. 24, 25; John vi. 49, 50), and with the living water from the Rock (John iv. 14, vii. 37—39; 1 Cor. x. 3, 4). The time of the sojourn in the wilderness is twelve hundred and sixty days, a period corresponding in length to the forty-two months during which the witnesses prophesied; it is the period of the Church's witness against predominant evil. Driven forth, her voice, though but as the voice of one crying in the wilderness, is lifted up on behalf of righteousness and truth.

The War in Heaven.

(7) **And there was war . . .**—Translate, *And there was war in heaven: Michael and his angels to war with the dragon; and the dragon warred and his angels.* This is one of those passages which has ever been regarded as more or less perplexing. It has afforded material for many poetic fancies, and has been the occasion of much speculative interpretation. We shall fail to catch the spirit of its meaning if we insist upon detaching the passage from its context; and the more so that the structure of the chapter seems to give an express warning against doing so. The narrative of the woman's flight into the wilderness is suspended that this passage may be inserted. Could we have a clearer indication of the anxiety of the sacred writer to connect this war in heaven with the birth and rapture of the man child? The man child is born; born a conqueror. The dragon is His foe, and the powers of the foe are not confined to the material and historical world: he is a power in the world spiritual; but the man child is to be entirely a conqueror. His rapture into heaven is the announcement that there, in the very highest, He is acknowledged victor; and His victory is won over the power of the dragon, the old serpent, whose head is now bruised. "The prince of this world cometh," said Jesus Christ, "and hath nothing in Me." "Now is the judgment of this world; now is the prince of this world cast out. And I, if I be lifted up, will draw all men unto Me." Do we need more? There is mystery—unexplained mystery, perhaps—about this war in heaven, but there need be none about the general occasion referred to; it is the overthrow of the evil one by Christ: the death-blow given by the Lord of Life to him who had the power of death; it is the victory of Bethlehem, Calvary, and Olivet which is commemorated, and the effects of which are seen to transcend the sphere of the things seen. But why have we Michael and his angels introduced? This may be one of those unexplained mysteries referred to above. Some, indeed, think that this Michael is a designation of our Lord Himself, and of Him alone; but a consideration of the other passages in which Michael is mentioned (notably, Dan. x. 13, where Michael is called "one of the chief princes") leaves this limited meaning doubtful, and almost suggests conflict among the spiritual hierarchies. It may, however, be the case that the name *Michael*—the meaning of which is, "who is like unto God"—is a general name applied to any who for the moment represent the cause of God in the great conflict against evil. It may thus belong, not to any one angel being, but be a kind of type-name used for the champion and prince of God's people, and so employed in this passage to denote Him who is the Captain of our salvation.

(8) **And prevailed not . . .**—Better, *And their power failed them, and not even was place for them found any more in the heaven.* The result of the war was the dragon's defeat. The whole power of the evil hosts failed them. There is an inherent weakness in evil: a spot which may be touched whereupon all its vaunted strength withers. So complete was the overthrow, that even their place knew them no more. "I went by, and, lo! he was gone; I sought him, but he could nowhere be found."

(9) **And the great dragon . . .**—Better, *And he was thrown down, the great dragon, the ancient serpent, he that is called the Devil and Satan: he who deceives the whole world was thrown to the earth, and his angels were thrown with him.* Thus the victory of Christ is marked by the overthrow of the great adversary. The stronger than the strong one has come, and taken away his armour (Luke xi. 21, 22). The death-blow is given. The prince of this world (who found nothing in Christ) is judged (John xvi. 11). The adversary is described as the dragon, the fierce and cruel foe who is ever ready to devour (1 Pet. v. 8). *The ancient serpent.* The serpent was used as an emblem of the evil principle. (Comp. Gen. iii. 1). But the head of the ancient foe of man is now bruised: he is the devil, the accuser and calumniator. He is called the accuser of the brethren in the next verse; he is Satan, the adversary, and he is the seducer, the deceiver, as he is a liar, and the father of it (John viii. 44).

(10) **And I heard a loud voice . . .**—Better, *And I heard a great voice in the heavens saying, Now is come the salvation, and the might, and the kingdom of our God, and the power of his Christ.* The definite article is placed before the words "salvation" and "might." The words of this doxology are like an echo of the close of the Lord's Prayer. The prayer "Thy kingdom

of our brethren is cast down, which accused them before our God day and night.
(11) And they overcame him by the blood of the Lamb, and by the word of their testimony; and they loved not their lives unto the death.
(12) Therefore rejoice, *ye* heavens, and ye that dwell in them. Woe to the inhabiters of the earth and of the sea! for the devil is come down unto you, having great wrath, because he knoweth that he hath but a short time.
(13) And when the dragon saw that he was cast unto the earth, he persecuted the woman which brought forth the man *child*.
(14) And to the woman were given two wings of a great eagle, that

Chap. xii. 13—17. The persecution of the Church.

---

come" seems answered. Now is come the kingdom. But it is not the full establishment of the kingdom which is here described; it is rather the manifestation of it. Since our Master passed into the heavens—and His victory is achieved, we know Him to be *King*, and even while we pray "Thy kingdom come" we yet confess "Thine is the kingdom"—the salvation so anxiously looked for (1 Pet. i. 10); the power so much needed by weak and sinful men (1 Pet. i. 5 and 1 Cor. i. 24); and the kingdom which cannot be shaken (Heb. xii. 28). The accuser of the brethren is cast down. This is another reason for joy and another feature of the salvation. The habit of the accuser is expressed by the use of the present tense. We should read not "who accused," but "who *accuseth*." Night and day he accused. (Comp. Zech. iii. 1, and Job i. 9, and ii. 5.) In Jewish writings, Michael is called "the advocate" (*sunegor*), and stands in opposition to the accuser (*kategor*); but now the accuser is cast down; for who shall lay anything to the charge of God's elect, when it is God that justifieth, when it is Christ that died? (Rom. viii. 33, 34.)

(11) **And they overcame him . . .**—Better, *And they conquered him* (not "by," but) *on account of the blood of the Lamb, and on account of the word of their testimony*, &c. They overcame him—*i.e.*, the accuser, the devil: their victory over him is "owing to" the blood of the Lamb. Who is he that condemneth, when Christ hath died? What power can the accusations of the adversary have when the Lamb of God hath taken away the sin of the world (John i. 29), and when we have boldness to enter into the holiest by the blood of Jesus? (Heb. x. 19.) Dean Alford mentions the tradition that Satan accuses men all days of the year except on the Day of Atonement. But their victory is also in virtue of the *word of their testimony*: in virtue of the word to which they bore witness; not simply, I think, because they had a word of God to which they could bear witness, but because they had a word of God and did bear witness to it. The Christian victory is a victory of dependence and of obedience: of dependence on Him without whom they can do nothing; and of obedience to Him: it is in keeping of His commandments there is great reward: and in bearing testimony that the testimony becomes a power and a treasure. So it was the man who did Christ's commandments who was like the man whose house was founded on the rock. Theoretical religion relaxes the energy of faith, even though it may brace the intellect; practical religion invigorates faith, gives it its force, and moulds the heroism of those who, in their love of Christ, "love not their lives even unto death." It is thought that these last words imply that the martyred saints alone are spoken of. This seems to me a mistake. It is true that in the martyr we have the fullest practical token of that spirit of devotion to Christ which loves Him more than life itself; but the spirit of such devotion and such love has breathed in thousands who have never died the martyr's death, but who have devoted their lives to Him they loved. The martyr spirit needs not death to show itself; many lose their lives for Christ's sake who have never been called to lay down their lives for Him, and these, as truly as those who have passed away in the shroud of flame, have loved not their lives unto the death. "He may bid us die for Him: He does bid us live for Him. If we do not the one—the less—we may be quite sure that we shall never rise to the other—the higher and the more glorious" (Dr. Vaughan).

(12) **Therefore rejoice . . .**—Better, *For this cause rejoice, ye heavens, and ye that tabernacle in them.* The words "for this cause" must be taken to refer to the overthrow of the evil one. This is the cause of joy to the heavens, and to them that tabernacle (not "dwell") in them. The word is (as in chaps. vii. 15, xiii. 6, xxi. 3) "tabernacle." This allusion to the tabernacle where the glory of God and the mercy-seat were to be found, is not without force. The sacred imagery of the tabernacle of witness calls to mind the safe dwelling which the sanctuary of God afforded to those whose testimony was given in the wilderness of sorrow. Those who tabernacled in the secret place of the Most High could rejoice with joy unspeakable.

Woe to the inhabiters . . .—Translate, *Woe to the earth and the sea!* (the words "to the inhabiters of" are not found in the best MSS.) *because the devil is gone down to you, having great wrath, knowing* (or, *because he knoweth*: his knowledge that his season of power is short is the reason of his great wrath) *that he hath* (*but*) *a short season*. The painful consciousness of defeat has roused a deeper and more obstinate rage. Sin, which blunts the conscience, blinds the reason, and drives men madly to attempt the impossible, or to rouse

> "the unconquerable will
> And study of revenge, immortal hate,
> And courage never to submit or yield."

The *woe* to the sea and earth is simply a warning voice to all that, though the foe is overcome and death smitten, yet that he has power, quickened by defeat and fear, for a last struggle; and that therefore they need to be sober and vigilant against the adversary. His season is short. He may be active, sowing tares among the wheat and animating various hostile powers, such as the wild beasts of chap. xiii.; but he has only a season: there is a limit to his power and the time of his power. "A little while" was the word our Lord used to denote His time of absence (John xvi. 16—22): "Behold, He comes quickly!"

(13) **And when the dragon . . .**—The wrath of the defeated dragon is manifested in persecution of the woman. The present verse explains the reason of the flight into the wilderness mentioned in verse 6.

(14) **And to the woman . . .**—Better, *And there*

she might fly into the wilderness, into
her place, where she is nourished for a
time, and times, and half a time, from the
face of the serpent.
(15) And the serpent
cast out of his mouth water as a flood
after the woman, that he might cause
her to be carried away of the flood.
(16) And the earth helped the woman,
and the earth opened her mouth, and
swallowed up the flood which the dragon
cast out of his mouth.
(17) And the
dragon was wroth with the woman, and

---

were given to the woman (*the*) *two wings of the great eagle* (the definite article is used before "great eagle"), *that she might fly into the wilderness, unto her place, where she is nourished there for a season, and seasons, and half a season, from the face of the serpent.* The woman is persecuted and driven into the wilderness: yet it is with the eagle wings given her by her Lord that she flies; the serpent drives her into the wilderness: yet it is in the wilderness that her place is prepared by God. The way that seems hard is the way that is most blest. The opposition of the dragon brings her blessings that she never would have received except in persecution; neither the eagle power nor the heavenly sustenance had been hers without the serpent's hate. Thus is the trial of faith precious in bringing us to know the priceless blessings of heavenly help and heavenly food. She is given eagle's wings. God had spoken of the deliverance of Israel under a similar emblem, "Ye have seen . . . how I bare you on eagles' wings and brought you unto myself" (Ex. xix. 4; comp. Deut. xxxii. 10—12). There is a difference as well as a resemblance in the emblem here. In Exodus God is said to have borne Israel on eagles' wings: here the wings are given to the woman. The strength of the earlier dispensation is a strength often used for, rather than in, the people of God; the strength of the latter is a strength in them: "They mount up with wings as eagles" (Isa. xl. 31). The place is not a chance spot: it is prepared of God; it is in the wilderness, but still it is the place God prepared for her. It is always a delight to faith to mark how the ordering of God works in and through the wilfulness and wickedness of the enemy: the Son of man goeth, as it was written, though there is a "woe" against the man by whom He is betrayed. The wicked one can never drive us from God's place, but only to it, unless we are enemies to ourselves. She is nourished in the wilderness. (See Notes on verse 6.) The length of her sojourn is here called a season, seasons, and half a season; it was called twelve hundred and sixty days in verse 6. The period is in both cases the same in length, viz., three years and a half—*i.e.*, the season (one year), the seasons (two years), and the half season (half a year). This is the period of the Church's trouble and persecution. It is not to be sought by any effort to find some historical period of persecution corresponding in length to this, lasting three years and a half, or twelve hundred and sixty days or years. No such attempt has hitherto been crowned with success. The period is symbolical of the broken time (the half of the seven, the perfect number) of the tribulation of God's people. There may be some future period in which the vision may receive even more vivid fulfilment than it has hitherto received; but the woman has been nourished in the wilderness in the ages that are gone, and her sustenance there by God is an experience of the past, and will be in the future. It is not only in one age, but in every age, that God gives His children bread in the day of adversity, during the season that the pit is being dug for the ungodly. In many an era the servant of God can exclaim: "Thou preparedst a table before me in the presence of mine enemies."

(15) **And the serpent . . .**—Translate, *And the serpent cast out of his mouth after the woman water as a river, that he might make her to be carried away by the river.* The foe of the woman was described as a dragon for his cruelty and fierceness—as a serpent for his subtlety. The first attack on the woman is pictured as persecution by the dragon: from this she escapes by flight; but the subtlety of the enemy finds another device: the foe (now described as a serpent) pours forth water as a river to sweep away the woman. The emblem is not uncommon in the Bible. Invasion is described as "an overflowing flood" (Jer. xlvi. 7, 8; xlvii. 2; comp. Isa. viii. 7, 8). The same emblem is used in Ps. lxxiv. 2—6 to describe the uprising of a people's ill-will. The floods, the rivers, the waves of the sea, are employed to express popular movements. The woman that cannot be destroyed by positive persecution may be swept away by a hostile public opinion. It is not the rulers alone who stand up against the Lord and His Church: an infuriated populace may be stirred up against them. The temper of the mob occasioned as much suffering and as many deaths in early Christian days as did the political authorities. Ill-regulated popular impulses, leading to violence and unwise action, whether nominally for Christianity or against it, have done enough of the devil's work in the world.

(16) **And the earth . . .**—Translate, *And the earth helped the woman, and the earth opened her mouth, and drank up the river, &c.* This is generally understood of some earthly power which is raised up to protect the Church against persecution. Just as Persia was raised up to aid Israel after they had been swept away by the flood of Babylonish conquest, so does help come to the persecuted Church through the cultured Roman world, or through some other worldly power, "barbarian and godless in its beginning, but destined in due time to embrace, in name at least, the faith once abhorred, and to introduce that new order of things which should make a nominal Christianity the religion of states and nations, and secure it for ever against the risk of a repetition of bygone persecutions" (Dr. Vaughan). The passage seems to want a wider interpretation. By the flood or river we understand all great popular movements against Christianity: the earth swallows up these; they diffuse themselves for a time, but mother earth absorbs them all, for the earth is the Lord's and the fulness thereof, and no movement hostile to truth can permanently succeed: the eternal laws of truth and right are ultimately found stronger than all the half truths, whole falsehoods, and selfishness which give force to such movements. In a mysterious way, every devil-born flood of opinion, or violence, or sentiment, will sink beneath the surface; they rise like a river, they are tasted, and then rejected. The laws of the earth are against their permanent success. The finest epic of the world might have for its motto: "The earth helped the woman." Creation is ultimately a witness for righteousness and truth. It is not one nation, one age, which is represented here; it is an eternal law.

(17) **And the dragon . . .**—Translate, *And the dragon was wroth with the woman, and departed* (not

went to make war with the remnant of her seed, which keep the commandments of God, and have the testimony of Jesus Christ.

CHAPTER XIII.— (1) And I stood upon the sand of the sea, and saw a beast rise up out of the sea, having seven heads and ten horns, and upon his horns ten crowns, and upon his heads the name[1] of blasphemy. (2) And

Chap. xiii. 1—10. The great world-power. The first beast-like foe.

1 Or, *names.*

A.D. 96.

---

merely "went," but *departed*, as one baffled in his attempt to carry the woman away by the river) *to make war with the rest of her seed, who keep the commandments of God, and have the testimony of Jesus.* Omit the word Christ. The attempt to sweep away the Christian Church is vain. The wrath of man has always been found to turn to God's praise; the earth has always helped the woman; out of a thousand seeming defeats the Church of Christ has arisen; the banner of the Lord has been lifted up over every flood. But the foe will not give up his attacks. He can make war upon individual Christians; he may cease to assail the collective Church of Christ, but he can assail Christians by a thousand discomforts, by petty opposition, by undermining their morals, by making them unpopular, not as Christians, but as "very particular" Christians: for those thus assailed are they who "keep the commandments of God and the testimony of Jesus." It is the old combination of a holy life and a fidelity to their Master which is the test of true loyalty. They take heed to themselves; they abide in Christ; they take heed to the teaching, that Christ's word may abide in them. They keep His word, and they witness to Him in lip and life.

XIII.

This chapter describes the rise of two foes of Christ and His people. They are described as "wild beasts" in opposition to Him who is the Lamb. They are distinct from the dragon; yet they are inspired, as it were, by him. He gives them power (verse 4); his voice speaks through them (verse 11). They are forces and powers utilised by him in hostility to the cause of righteousness and truth. On the whole of this section the parallel vision in Dan. vii. ought to be read.

(1) **And I . . .**—Better, *And he* (not "I stood," as in English version, but *he, i.e.*, the dragon) *stood upon the sand of the sea.* Some make this sentence a separate verse, and insert it as the closing verse of chap. xii. It is true that the sentence has a connection with that chapter, but it is also closely linked with what follows. The way in which the dragon carries out his plan of war is described. Like Milton's "superior fiend," he stands upon the shore and summons his legions (*Par. Lost*, Book I.) to another form of war. Two monsters, one distinguished by more brutal, the other by more subtle power, rise at his bidding.

And saw . . .—Translate, *And I saw a wild beast rising out of the sea, having ten horns and seven heads, and upon his horns ten diadems, and upon his heads names of blasphemy.*—The wild beast rises out of the sea. In the vision of Daniel (chap. vii.) the beasts rose out of the sea upon which the four winds strove. The sea represents the great, restless mass of human kind; or, as it is expressed in chap. xvii. 15, "peoples and multitudes." St. James represented an undecided man as a wave driven by the wind (Jas. i. 6). The individuals, like larger and smaller waves, make up this great ocean-like mass of men, swayed by impulse or passion. Out of the sea rises a wild beast. The word is not the same as that used in chap. iv. 7 (see Note there), but is a word which implies the predominance of the beast nature. Whatever power rises is one which rules not by love or right, but by fear and wilfulness. It is the great force of the world-power, which in every age has been antagonistic to the power of right. The wild beast is always the figure of the kingdoms of this world—*i.e.*, the kingdoms which are founded on passion or selfishness. They are seven in number, as the beast had seven heads. We read afterwards of seven mountains. These world-powers are spoken of as mountains for their strength and stability; as heads of the wild beast because, though separate, they are inspired by the dragon spirit, the spirit of utter enmity to the rule of the Righteous King. The seven kingdoms, or heads of the wild beast, are more distinctly explained in chap. xvii. 10. There we read that five are fallen, one was in possession of power, and the seventh had not yet arisen. The key is thus placed in our hands. The sixth head is imperial Rome, the successor of those great world-powers which were, one and all, founded in unrighteousness—*i.e.*, in violation of the law of brotherly kindness and faith. The heads carry the names of blasphemy. The spirit of arrogant self-sufficiency characterised all the world-powers. Illustrations would be too numerous for our space. It is enough to refer to the spirit in Babylon: "Is not this great Babylon, that I have built for the house of the kingdom by the might of my power, and for the honour of my majesty?" The words were Nebuchadnezzar's (Dan. iv. 30). He became a beast in uttering them; but the spirit of them went through all the world-powers, from the days of Lamech (Gen. iv. 23, 24) and Babel (Gen. xi. 4) to the days when Roman poets prostituted their pens in abject flattery of emperors, and a degraded people welcomed them as gods, and put those to death who refused to offer frankincense and wine to the images of those who wore the purple.

Ten horns.—The beast has, besides seven heads, ten horns, which are explained further on (chap. xvii. 12) as "the kings which have received no kingdom as yet," but which, when they rise, will draw their strength from the dragon and be members of the wild beast.

(2) **And the beast . . .**—The wild beast combined the features of three wild animals: the leopard, the bear, the lion. In Daniel's vision (Dan. vii. 4) the kingdoms were described: the first, like a lion; the second, like a bear; the third, like a leopard or panther. Here all these features are combined, because the wild beast is a representative of all forms of world-power, which have been swift to shed blood: like a leopard leaping on the prey, tenacious and relentless as a bear, and all devouring (their throat is an open sepulchre) as a lion. The reader will remember the wild beasts which in vision hindered Dante when he sought to ascend the "pleasant mount"—the "cause and source of all delight." The leopard, the lion, the wolf were symbols of luxuriousness, cruel ambition, and hungry and heartless avarice, which oppose men and nations when they seek the Holy Hill, where the light of God ever rests. (Comp. *Inferno*, i. 10—74.)

the beast which I saw was like unto a leopard, and his feet were as *the feet* of a bear, and his mouth as the mouth of a lion: and the dragon gave him his power, and his seat, and great authority.
(3) And I saw one of his heads as it were wounded[1] to death; and his deadly wound was healed: and all the world wondered after the beast. (4) And they worshipped the dragon which gave power unto the beast: and they worshipped the beast, saying, Who *is* like unto the beast? who is able to make war with him? (5) And there was given unto him a mouth speaking great things and blasphemies; and power was given unto him to continue[2] forty *and* two months.
(6) And he opened his mouth in blasphemy against God, to blaspheme his name, and his tabernacle, and them that dwell in heaven. (7) And it was given unto him to make war with the saints, and to overcome them: and power was given him over all kindreds, and tongues, and nations. (8) And all that dwell upon the earth shall worship him, whose names are not written in the book of life of the Lamb slain from

[1] Gr. *slain.*

[2] Or, *to make war.*

And the dragon.—Read, *And the dragon gave him his power and his throne* (not his "seat," as in the English version; it is the royal seat, the throne, which is meant). (See Notes on chap. xi. 16 and chap. iv. 4.)

And great authority.—It is through this succession of world-powers that the dragon carries on his war. The wild beast becomes the vicegerent, so to speak, of the prince of this world.

(3) **And I saw . . .**—Translate, *And* (*I saw*) *one from among his heads as if having been slain* [the expression is the same as that applied to the Lamb in chap. v. 6: the wound marks are there when the vision rises] *unto death; and the stroke of his death was healed.* When the wild beast rose from the sea, the seer saw the deadly wound on the head: the wound was really unto death; the beast which had waged war against the true kingdom of righteousness and faith has received his death-blow. This is the historical point from which the vision starts. This being so, the death-blow is that which has just been dealt: the seed of the woman has bruised the serpent's head. The blow which casts down the dragon inflicts a deadly wound upon the wild beast, which is his agent. When Christ overthrew the wicked one He gave the death-blow to the world-power—to all systems founded on passion, or self-sufficiency, or inhumanity. But the death-blow is apparently healed. What is this but telling the Church of Christ that the fruits of Christ's victory will not be seen without delay? The world-power is smitten unto death; but the actual death does not follow immediately. The power of evil, contrary to all expectation, rises with new vigour. This revived power showed itself, with more or less force, in the way in which the spirit of the wild beast broke forth when Christianity seemed to have put fetters on the Roman empire.

(3, 4) **And all the world wondered . . .**—Literally, *And the whole earth wondered after the wild beast, and worshipped the dragon, because he gave the authority and worshipped the wild beast, saying, Who is like unto the wild beast? and who is able to war with him?* The healing of the death-blow causes wonder to all. Their wonder leads to worship. The spirit of the wild beast is adored wherever worldliness prevails. There is nothing so successful as success, and the homage of men is more often paid to power than to principle. "Who is like unto the beast?" The words are a parody, and a blasphemous parody, on the ascription of praise to God which the name Michael imported. (See chap. xii. 7; comp. Ps. cxii., Mic. vii. 18.) "Who is like unto God?" is the legend of the saints: the opposing cry is, "Who is like unto the beast?"

"Can you not hear the words coming across the centuries from the lips of two Roman youths talking with each other, as they lounge together in the Forum?" (Maurice.) Can we not hear the echo of the words in the Champs Elysées, in Piccadilly, in the Broadway, or Unter Den Linden, from the lips of young men who have taken fashion, rank, wealth, world-power in any shape, as their god?

(5) **And there was given . . .**—In these verses the words and the works of the wild beast are described. The 5th verse tells us that the liberty to speak and work *was given* to him. There is consolation in the words: he has no power beyond what is given; behind his reckless and apparently irresistible power there stands the veiled but real power of God. "Thou couldest have no power" (the saints may take up their Lord's words) "against me, except it were given thee from above." He speaks great things, and blasphemy. *And there was given him authority to act* (literally, *to do*) *forty-two months.* Again the familiar period, the limited time of the world-power.

(6) **And he opened his mouth . . .**—Translate, *And he opened his mouth unto blasphemies against God, to blaspheme His name, and His tabernacle, and them that tabernacle in the heaven.* Much of the beauty of the thought is lost by the translation "them that dwell;" the word is *tabernacle.* The saints, to whom the name of the Lord is a strong tower, and who have a tabernacle of witness in this wilderness world, can yet tabernacle their spirits where their treasure is, in the heaven, according to that word: "our citizenship is even now in heaven" (Phil. iii. 20). Against these the world-power blasphemes: who has not taken the Lord for his strength, God is not his might; his might is his god. (Comp. Hab. i. 11: "He passes over and is guilty, he whose might is his god.")

(7) **And it was given . . .**—Better, *He makes war with the saints, and conquers them.* This, too, is said to be "given him." The conquest is not a conquest of their fidelity; it is rather that the beast so far succeeds that they must suffer or submit. The saints seem to be single handed; for *there was given him authority over every tribe, and people, and tongues, and nations.* Nor does his success end here; the next verse shows us how completely earth is at his feet.

(8) **And all that dwell . . .**—Better, *And all they that dwell on the earth shall worship him* (*every one*) *whose name has not been written in the book of life of the Lamb that has been slain from the foundation of the world.* This is the climax of his triumph: he, or it, is worshipped; but the saints, though conquered, conquer;

the foundation of the world. (9) If any
man have an ear, let him hear. (10) He
that leadeth into captivity shall go
into captivity: he that killeth with the
sword must be killed with the sword.
Here is the patience and the faith of
the saints. (11) And I beheld another
beast coming up out of
the earth; and he had two
horns like a lamb, and he

Chap. xiii. 11—18. The second beast-like foe.

they do not worship after the fashion of the deluded or self-seeking. A stronger tie binds them to a better allegiance; their names are in the Lamb's Book of Life. There is some doubt about the connection of the words "from the foundation of the world." Some connect them with the word "written": this would express that the names were written "from the foundation of the world" in the book. Others connect them with the word "slain": this expresses that the Lamb was slain from the foundation of the world. For the former view, the similar passage in chap. xvii. 8 is cited; but, on the other hand, the phrase "from the foundation of the world" is connected in other parts of the Bible with certain aspects of the work of Christ (1 Pet. i. 19, 20, and John xvii. 24), and it seems more natural to take the words in their simple order. Whatever view we take, the verse proclaims that the security of God's saints is based on the eternal love of God. "An eternal deliverer is the only refuge from this great world-tyranny;" the strength of the tempted is in Him who is the same in love and righteousness through all the ages.

(9) This verse—an echo of his Master's words from the lips of the beloved disciple—calls marked attention to the warning words of the next verse.

(10) This verse may read: *If any one (is) for captivity, into captivity he goeth; if any one to be killed by the sword, he should by the sword be killed.*. If we read the verse thus, it is generally understood to be a caution to the suffering saints that there is nothing for them but to endure, just as Jeremiah told his countrymen that those who were for death must go out to meet it, and those who were for sword or captivity must face them (Jer. xv. 2). But is not this a warning to them that the way of the Church's victory lay through suffering captivity and meeting sword, and that the temptation to take the sword or seize the weapons of their foes would be fatal to their true success? The spirit of the words reminds them that their weapons are the weapons of faith and patience, of truth and righteousness; and they must accept the tribulation, as their Lord did His cross, because thus it must be. At the same time, their very doing so is a witness to their foes that "all those who take the sword will perish with the sword;" and that the sword, from which the saints do not shrink, will assuredly turn against those who use it. *Here* (*i.e.*, in the enduring of these persecutions, and amid so many temptations, not seizing easy, world-like methods of saving themselves) *is the endurance and faith of the saints.*

THE APPEARANCE OF THE SECOND WILD BEAST.

For the understanding of this portion of the vision we must notice the contrasts and resemblances between this and the former wild beast. They are both wild beasts: they both have horns: they both have a dragon-like inspiration (verse 11): they both tyrannise over men; but, on the other hand, the second beast is less monstrous in appearance: we read only of two horns, and we hear nothing of seven heads. He somewhat resembles a lamb; he rises from the earth, and not from the sea; his power lies in deception (verses 13, 14) as well as violence; he seems to possess more supernatural power: yet the whole of his work is directed to magnifying the first beast (verse 12). Do not these features lead to the conclusion that the principles which the second wild beast supports are the same as those on which the former wild beast acted, but that he supports them with more subtlety, intelligence, and culture? But for all the deception he employs, his work, when stripped of its specious drapery and seen in its naked ugliness, is to promote the honour of the first wild beast. Because of this seductiveness, and of his efforts to support his mission with higher sanctions (verse 13), he is called in later chapters (chaps. xvi. 13; xix. 20; xx. 10) the False Prophet; the force and appropriateness of this designation becomes more apparent when we notice that the features which are assumed bear a deceptive resemblance to those of a lamb. The advancing intelligence of the world, its increase in knowledge and wisdom, the wider diffusion of culture and thought, produce a change in the general fashion of life, but the spirit which animates society is unchanged. The second wild beast is that change which is a change of mode, but not of spirit—a change of manners, but not of heart; there is more refinement, more civilisation, more mind, but it is still the world-power which is worshipped; it is the self-seeking adoration of pleasures, honours, occupations, influences which spring from earth and end in earth—the pursuit of powers which are worldly. Some see in this second wild beast the Pagan priesthood aiding the imperial power, the embodiment of the first wild beast; others see in it the Papal sacerdotal power, the heir of Pagan rites; others, again, would combine the two, and view this second wild beast as the sacerdotal persecuting power, Pagan and Christian. I believe that, though there is truth in these views, they are too narrow. It is true that priesthoods—Pagan and Christian—have often devoted their influence to the upholding of the great world-power; it is true that men called to be Christian teachers forgot their function, and used their knowledge and power to bolster up the power of the beast and to make men worship the world, as though there were nothing higher for men to worship than this world could afford; it is true that they used, in later days, their powers to aggrandize the Church rather than to reform the world and regenerate men: in so far as they did this they acted like the second wild beast; but the stretch of the vision embraces more than these. All who use their knowledge, their culture, their wisdom, to teach men that there is nothing worthy of worship save what they can see, and touch, and taste, are acting the part of the second wild beast; and be they apostles of science, or apostles of culture, or apostles of logical immorality, or apostles of what is called materialism, if their teaching leads men to limit their worship to the visible and the tangible, they are making men worship the beast who is the adversary of the servants of the Lamb.

(11) **And I beheld . . .** Better, *And I saw another wild beast rising out of the earth.* Both wild beasts rise from beneath. The sea, out of which the first rises, represents the tumultuous impulses and passions of mankind; the earth, the more fixed element of human thought and wisdom, or society consolidated and dis-

spake as a dragon. (12) And he exer-
ciseth all the power of the first beast
before him, and causeth the earth and
them which dwell therein to worship
the first beast, whose deadly wound
was healed. (13) And he doeth great
wonders, so that he maketh fire come
down from heaven on the earth in the
sight of men, (14) and deceiveth them
that dwell on the earth by *the means of*
those miracles which he had power
to do in the sight of the beast; saying
to them that dwell on the earth, that
they should make an image to the beast,
which had the wound by a sword, and
did live. (15) And he had power to give
life[1] unto the image of the beast, that
the image of the beast should both
speak, and cause that as many as would
not worship the image of the beast
should be killed. (16) And he causeth
all, both small and great, rich and poor,
free and bond, to receive[2] a mark in
their right hand, or in their foreheads:

1 Gr. *breath.*

2 Gr. *to give.*

---

ciplined by intelligence and culture: the wisdom, however, which guides this wild beast is not divine wisdom, but that wisdom which a sacred writer described as earthly, sensual, devilish (Jas. iii. 17).

He had two horns like (*those of*) **a lamb.**—There is an appearance of gentleness about him, but he spake as a dragon; the voice betrayeth him. He that is of the earth is earthly, and speaketh of the earth. The spirit of the adversary is in him (John iii. 31; viii. 44).

(12) **And he exerciseth . . .**—Better, *And he works,* or *exercises* (literally, *does*), *all the authority* (or, *power*) *of the first wild beast in his presence.* It will be seen by this that we must not look upon the second wild beast as a successor, but rather as a supporter, of the first. The intellectual force of an earthly wisdom is practically subservient to the spirit of unmitigated worldliness.

(12, 13) **And causeth the earth . . .**—Literally, *and he makes the earth and them that dwell in it that they shall worship the first wild beast, the stroke of whose death was healed; and he does signs great, so that he even makes fire to descend out of the heaven to the earth in the sight of men.* This descent of fire is the counterpart of the work of the two witnesses (chap. xi. 5), and of Elijah in Old Testament days. It is one of the features of that deceivableness of unrighteousness which misleads man. There is a holy fire which inspires the lips and hearts of the holy; there is an unhallowed fire, a fire of mere power, which the worldly spirit is tempted to worship.

(14) **And deceiveth them . . .**—Better, *And he leads astray those who dwell on the earth because of the signs which were given him to do in the presence of the wild beast; saying to those who dwell on the earth, to make an image to the wild beast that has the stroke of the sword and lived.* He leads astray: this is the key to his success, he deifies the spirit of worldliness; but he does it by deception and subtlety: there is an appearance of wonderful power: he can work lying wonders. When men lose the sense of duty,—the will to ask, "Is it right?"—they become an easy prey to some specious deception. This is the reason that, both in the old and new dispensations, a caution against "immoral marvels" is entered (see Deut. xiii. 1—3; Matt. xxiv. 24; and 2 Thess. ii. 9); mere greatness, either of achievement or of miracle, is no guarantee of a good cause. The motto "Might is right" is the motto of worldliness; "Right is might" is the motto of faith, and those who hold it cannot worship the beast, even though the stroke of his death-wound is healed. Men have appealed to lying miracles on behalf of a death-wounded creed: the cleverness of self-interested partizanship is seldom barren of imposing expedients.

(15) **And he had power . . .**—Better, *And it was given to him to give breath to the image of the wild beast, that the image of the wild beast should both speak, and cause that as many as do not worship the image of the wild beast shall be slain.* The image to the wild beast is an image also of the wild beast: and the image of the monster is endued with apparent vitality. Wisdom can give a semblance of life to the most doomed cause; and the bulk of mankind read only with their eyes, and not at all with their thoughts. The image of the Roman emperor was, in ancient days, made an object of worship. Christians suffered rather than by such an act of worship prove disloyal to Christ: like their spiritual ancestors, they refused to worship the image which the world-power had set up; they were willing to render to Cæsar the things that were Cæsar's, but the homage which belonged to God they refused to any but their God. These are but types of those who have refused, though tempted by specious eloquence and sagacious subtlety, to offer homage to any mere world-power; for the golden image is ever set up upon the plains of this world: its glitter and its vitality survive the storm and the conflict of the ages: it speaks, and men hear and adore, for they walk by sight, not by faith; and it needs no imperial or papal edict to doom to social death and failure those who refuse to shape their conduct by considerations of self-interest, and who are sure to be treated as fanatics because they follow right and conscience and Christ.

(16, 17) **And he causeth . . .**—Better, *And he* [*i.e.,* probably, the second wild beast, and not the image, as in the latter clause of the last verse] *makes all men, the small and the great, and the rich and the poor, and the free and the slaves, that they should give them a mark upon their right hand or upon their forehead:* (*and*) *that no one should be able to buy or to sell but he who has the mark, the name of the wild beast, or the number of his name.* We have read of the sealing of the servants of God in their foreheads (chap. vii. 3): we shall hear of it again (chap. xxii. 4); the power of evil also has its mark or stamp. As slaves received a brand or mark in their flesh, betokening to whom they belonged, so in the spiritual conflict there is on the side of good and of evil a brand or mark. St. Paul spoke of such marks in his own body that proved him a slave of Jesus Christ (Gal. vi. 17). In the same way the subtle false prophet, the abettor of world-power, seeks to impress a mark on all, on the penalty of complete social exclusion. It is utterly unnecessary to take this brand of evil literally, any more than we took the seal of Christ literally. That seal we understood as spiritual, in the faith and in the character; this evil brand we must interpret in like manner. It surely means the acquiescence in character and action to the principles of this tyrannical world-

(17) and that no man might buy or sell,
save he that had the mark, or the name
of the beast, or the number of his name.
(18) Here is wisdom. Let him that hath
understanding count the number of the
beast: for it is the number of a man;
and his number *is* Six hundred three-
score *and* six.

A.D. 96.

CHAPTER XIV.—(1) And I looked,

power: the right hand is the symbol of toil and social intercourse; the forehead is the symbol of character, as time is ever writing its awful tale upon men's brows. There have been days when men's faith has been read only too plainly by a hostile world, and when their simple trust in Christ caused Christians to be suspected, and when "men cast out their name as evil," and when the mark of the beast was worn and gloried in everywhere. We might cite from the history of the past numberless such epochs. But are we sure that the days are gone? Are we sure that it is easy for simple, unaffected goodness and genuine faith to gain all it might gain? Are we sure that honesty, guilelessness, utter and strenuous truthfulness are not weighted in the race of life? The days of the future may bring intenser forms of this tyranny, as the days of the past have shown them; but the days of the present may afford us illustrations of how readily men may lose, lose much and lose terribly, rather than succumb to fashions which violate honour and dishonour Christ. But we read of more than a mark here: we read of a "name," and the "number of a name." What are we to understand by these?

(18) **Here is wisdom . . .**—Translate, *Hither is wisdom.* This most difficult verse is introduced by this word of preface. Wisdom—indeed, the highest wisdom—is needed for those who would understand it. Two or three points ought to be noticed. (1) The verse surely implies that the understanding of this name and number is attainable; it warns us that *wisdom* and *understanding* are needed, but it as certainly leads us to believe that to wisdom and understanding a solution of the problem will be granted. (2) There is a variation in the MSS. respecting the number. Some MSS. read six hundred and sixteen; but the probability is in favour of the reading six hundred and sixty-six. In an excursus (*Excursus B*) will be found a short account of the various interpretations which have been given. (3) The clause "It is the number of a man," has been rendered "For number is of man." The number, then, is the combination of three sixes; there is a wisdom and understanding which may grasp its import, and that import is to be guided by the principle that it is the number of a man, or that number is of man—is, that is to say, a method of computation which is used by man, and used by God in order to symbolise something made thus more intelligible to man. Is the wisdom which is to solve this, then, the mere cleverness which can guess an acrostic or an enigma? or is it rather that the true heavenly wisdom, which is moral rather than intellectual, is needed to unite itself with understanding to solve the problem? Surely the dignity of the Apocalypse is sacrificed when we search for its meaning like children playing with conundrums rather than like men being guided by its principles. There is a wisdom which brings its sevenfold beam of heavenly light to the children of men—a wisdom pure, peaceable, gentle, full of mercy, without partiality, without hypocrisy—and when this wisdom rests on men in the fulness of its seven-fold perfection they may read the number of the beast, and see that, with all its vaunted strength, it is but weak; with all its vaunted perfection, it is imperfect; that though it vaunts itself as rich, increased in goods and needing nothing, it still lacks that "one needful thing"—faith in God, or the love by which faith works. Without this it will never attain even the appearance of that perfect heavenly number symbolised by seven; it may multiply itself in earthly strength—the power of worldliness into the power of worldly wisdom, and this again by the power of a hundred-fold satanic subtlety—but it will remain still short of the tokens of the kingdom of God; and the number when read will be, however godlike it looks, but the number of a man after all.

I am disposed, therefore, to interpret this "six hundred and sixty-six" as a symbolical number, expressing all that it is possible for human wisdom, and human power, when directed by an evil spirit, to achieve, and indicating a state of marvellous earthly perfection, when the beast-power has reached its highest development, when culture, civilisation, art, song, science and reason have combined to produce an age so nearly resembling perfection—an age of gold, if not a golden age—that men will begin to say that faith in God is an impertinence, and the hope of a future life a libel upon the happiness of the present. Then will the world-power have reached the zenith of his influence; then will only a wisdom descended from above be able to detect the infinite difference between a world with faith and a world without faith, and the great gulf which the want of a little heaven-born love can fix between an age and an age.

At the same time, I feel bound to place here, as well as in the *Excursus*, two other views—one because it has recently been advanced with conspicuous ability; the other because it is perhaps the most generally adopted, as it is certainly the most ancient, view. Both these interpretations are based upon the theory that the letters of the name, when added together, according to their numerical value, will make up six hundred and sixty-six. The first of these alluded to finds the word in Nero Cæsar. The second, and more ancient, finds it in Lateinos: this last was mentioned by Irenæus. It will be seen that both these solutions are at one in making the number point to the great Roman Power; and this was the great embodiment of the terrible spirit of self-sufficiency, tyranny, and utter godless worldliness with which St. John was familiar. These interpretations are interpretations in example, and as such probably true; but they are only types, as it seems to me, of that fuller and deeper view which takes the number as symbolical of that power which, whether directed by Nero, or inspired by Emperor or Pope, or false teacher, or military tyrant, has dazzled mankind by a fictitious glory, a fictitious civilisation, and a fictitious religion, or deceived them by holding out the promise of splendour and happiness without the knowledge and obedience of God, without law, without faith, and therefore without true joy. (Comp. Note of the "Three Frogs," chap. xvi. 13, 14.)

XIV.

We have had before us the terrible foes which the cause of Christ and His righteousness must encounter in the world. We have seen the subtle spirit of the Evil One defeated, yet plotting new

Chap. xiv. 1—5. The camp of the Lamb.

and, lo, a Lamb stood on the mount
Sion, and with him an hun-
dred forty *and* four thou-
sand, having his Father's
name written in their foreheads. (2) And
I heard a voice from heaven, as the
voice of many waters, and as the voice
of a great thunder: and I heard the
voice of harpers harping with their
harps: (3) and they sung as it were a
new song before the throne, and before
the four beasts, and the elders: and no
man could learn that song but the
hundred *and* forty *and* four thousand,
which were redeemed from the earth.
(4) These are they which were not de-
filed with women; for they are virgins.
These are they which follow the Lamb
whithersoever he goeth. These were
redeemed[1] from among men, *being* the

1 Gr. *were bought.*

---

methods of assault, and utilising the powers of the world, its sheer force and its culture, to crush holiness and to destroy spiritual religion. The whole vision reminds us that our conflict is not with flesh and blood, but against the principalities, against the powers, and the world-rulers of this darkness (Eph. vi. 12). We have seen the spiritual issues which are at stake. In all the outward forms which the conflict may assume there is but one inward spiritual antagonism—the spirit of evil against the spirit of good, the god of this world against the Christ of God. We have seen this power of evil rise to its blasphemous climax. But what has the Church of Christ been doing? The sealed ones of God have suffered; but have they done more than suffer? Has theirs been only a passive endurance of evils? Have they wielded no weapons against these foes, and used no counter-influence for good? The chapter before us will answer. In it the sacred seer takes us from our survey of the powers of evil, and shows us the powers of good. We have seen the strength of the wild beast: we may now see the followers of the Lamb. In the chapter there are seven messengers, or agents, employed, who prepare for or complete the harvest: the angel of good news (ver. 6, 7); the angel proclaiming the doom of the great world city (ver. 8); the angel who warns men against the mark of the wild beast (ver. 9—12); the angel of comfort (ver. 13); the angel of the wheat harvest (ver. 14—16); the angel of the vintage (ver. 17—20); the angel of fire (ver. 18). But before these we are shown a vision of the servants of the Lamb.

The Citadel of the Saints and the Servants of the Lamb.

(1) **And I looked . . .**—Better, *And I saw, and behold, the Lamb* (not "a Lamb:" it is *the* Lamb, the true Lamb of God, against whom the wild beast wages savage and subtle war) *standing on the Mount Sion.* The Saviour, the Lamb, in whose blood the saints have found their victory, is seen standing on the citadel of the heavenly city. Babylon is to be introduced (verse 8). In contrast, Zion, the chosen abode of God (Ps. cxxxii. 13—18), the type of the spiritual city whose citizens are true to the King (comp. Ps. ii. 6, lxxiv. 2; Heb. xii. 22—24), is introduced. There are to be seen the Lamb, set as King upon the holy hill of Zion, and with Him the sealed ones, His faithful soldiers and servants. They are described as 144,000 in number: a number which represents the full growth of the choice ones of God, the true Israel of God. (See Note on chap. vii. 4.) These have their Father's name on their foreheads: they can be recognised as children of God, (Comp. Note on chap. vii. 2, 3, and chap. xxii. 4.)

(2) **And I heard a voice . . .**—Translate, *And I heard a voice out of the heaven.* The saints stand with their Lord, the Lamb, on Mount Zion, and just as of old a voice came from heaven bearing witness to Christ, so round the abode of the saints heavenly voices are heard, full of majesty, terribleness, and sweetness, as though the sounds of sea and thunder blended with the music of heavenly harps. We call to mind the magnificent 29th Psalm; there the saints, secure in Zion, hear all around them the voice of God in the thunder and in the sea, while in His safe sanctuary the saints can sing of His honour.

(3) **And they . . .**—Translate, *And they* (*i.e.,* the heavenly harpers) *sing a new song* (the words "as it were" ought, perhaps, to be omitted) *before the throne, and before the living creatures, and the elders* (*i.e.,* in the presence of God Himself, and creation, and the Church), *and no one was able to learn the song except the hundred and forty-four thousand who were purchased from the earth.* It is a heavenly song, and no spirit dulled by earthly desires can learn it. The Spirit of the Lord can open the dull ear to hear and to rejoice in the songs of God's saints. Amid the world-noises of Babylon men can neither hear nor sing aright the Lord's song (Ps. cxxxvii. 4); but the redeemed (the purchased from the earth) of the Lord can come with singing unto Zion (Isa. li. 11).

(4, 5) **These are they . . .**—The characteristics of the servants of the Lamb are given in this verse and the following. The first is *purity:* they are virgins. The expression can hardly be limited to the unmarried, as the 144,000 represent the wide society of the choice ones of God. They are those whose hearts have been made as the hearts of little children (Matt. xviii. 1—4), who have that purity of heart which Christ declared to be blessed, and which St. James declared to be the first mark of heavenly wisdom (Matt. v. 8, and Jas. iii. 17). The next is *implicit obedience:* they follow the Lamb whithersoever He goeth. Some, indeed, take this to be a kind of heavenly reward: they shall be the nearer companions of the Lamb. But it is better to take it as describing their complete consecration to Christ. They are those who are with Christ, who have tasted the cup that their Lord tasted, and have taken up their cross and followed Him (Matt. xx. 22; Luke xiv. 27; John xii. 24—26). It is well to weigh these words; it is in the "wheresoever" that we may test the reality of our Christian life. Here lies the cross that Christ bids us take up. Here is the echo of Christ's words, "Whosoever forsaketh not all he hath cannot be My disciple." The third mark is *separation,* or unworldliness: they were purchased from among men, as a firstfruit to God and to the Lamb. They were a chosen generation, a peculiar people (Tit. ii. 14; 1 Pet. ii. 9), as the Israel of God (Deut vii. 6). The fourth feature is *utter truthfulness:* in their mouth no guile or no falsehood. (Comp. Ps. xiv. and Deut. xxxii. 1, 2.) The verse emphatically ends with "They are blameless." The words "before

firstfruits unto God and to the Lamb.
(5) And in their mouth was found no
guile: for they are without fault before
the throne of God. (6) And I saw another
angel fly in the midst of
heaven, having the ever-
lasting gospel to preach
unto them that dwell on the earth, and to
every nation, and kindred, and tongue,
and people, (7) saying with a loud voice,
Fear God, and give glory to him; for
the hour of his judgment is come: and
worship him that made heaven, and
earth, and the sea, and the fountains of
waters.[a] (8) And there followed another
angel, saying, Babylon is fallen, is
fallen,[b] that great city, because she
made all nations drink of the wine
of the wrath of her fornication.
(9) And the third angel followed them,
saying with a loud voice, If any
man worship the beast and his image,
and receive *his* mark in his fore-
head, or in his hand, (10) the same shall
drink of the wine of the wrath of God,
which is poured out without mixture
into the cup of his indignation; and he
shall be tormented with fire and brim-
stone in the presence of the holy angels,
and in the presence of the Lamb: (11) and
the smoke of their torment ascendeth
up for ever and ever: and they have no

Chap. xiv. 6–13. The four celestial voices.

a Ps. 146. 5; Acts 14. 15.

b Isa. 21. 9; Jer. 5. 8; ch. 18. 2.

---

the throne of God" must be omitted. (Comp. chap. vii. 14, 15; Eph. v. 27; and Col. i. 22.)

We have seen the servants of God; we have marked their character; we are now to see the weapon which is to be employed in the conflict against the enemies of Christ.

(6) **And I saw . . .**—Better, *And I saw another angel flying in mid-heaven, having an everlasting gospel, to declare glad tidings over them that sit on the earth, and over every nation, and tribe, and tongue, and people.* In view of the world the gospel is proclaimed; this is the good news that God loves the world, has redeemed mankind, that they belong to Him. This word of God is the sword of the Spirit, and the weapon (not carnal) which the Church uses against her foes. It is represented as in the hand of an angel rising in view of all nations: "The sound has gone out unto all lands."

(7) **Saying . . .**—These words declare what ought to be the effect of the gospel. Those to whom it is preached are sitting inactive on the earth. They must be roused to fear God and give Him glory. They must not fear the powers of evil, the wild beasts, &c., or be afraid of their terror (1 Pet. iii. 14, 15). They must realise that there is an hour of judgment at hand, which will discriminate between the worshippers of the world and of God. Let them learn to worship the Creator of all, and to turn from the worship of lesser and lower.

If we ask when this gospel angel appeared, our answer must be that the whole cycle of the gospel preaching is included in the vision, though doubtless there have been ages when the light of the glad tidings of God has gone forth with revived lustre, and when the warnings against easy acquiescence in evil have been given with unmistakable distinctness.

(8) **And there followed . . .**—The gospel angel is followed by the angel that proclaims the downfall of Babylon. Better, *And another, a second, angel followed, saying, Fallen, fallen is Babylon the great, who has given all the nations to drink of,* &c. The second angel follows on the first: the doom of the world-city, the metropolis of the empire of the world-power, follows the proclamation of the gospel. The principles of Christ's gospel must undermine the world-power; the fall of some Babylon principle has almost always succeeded the age of spiritual revival. Pagan Rome goes down before the gospel. Civil freedom follows the wake of religious freedom, for Babylon belongs not to one age. Pagan Rome was Babylon to St. John; papal Rome was often Babylon to a later age. Dante, Savonarola, Tauler, Luther, felt her to be so in the days when their eyes were enlightened; but Babylon was not on the Euphrates alone: she has reared palaces on the Seine, and on the Thames, Tiber, and on the Bosphorus. She may yet erect her power in more imposing form; but faith in that gospel which is the power of God, will cast her down along with everything that exalts itself against the knowledge of God. The influence of Babylon is declared in this: that she has given all nations to drink of deadly wine—the wine alike of her sin and of her doom, of her fornication and of the wrath which will overtake it. Babylon, then, is clearly an emblem of some principles which have been more or less accepted by all nations, and which will more or less involve all in the consequences of her fall. (Comp. chaps. xvi. 19, and xvii., where the features of this Babylon are more fully developed.)

(9) **And the third angel . .**—Better, *And another angel, a third, followed them, saying in a loud voice, If any man worship the wild beast and his image, and a mark upon his forehead or upon his hand, he also himself shall drink of the wine of the wrath of God, which is mingled pure* (in full strength, undiluted, *e.g.,* "He shall have judgment without mercy that hath showed no mercy," Jas. ii. 13) *in the cup of his indignation, and shall be tormented in fire,* &c., &c. This third angel naturally follows the other two, which describe the powers which are in conflict: the word of God, and the Babylon of the world; the gospel will triumph; Babylon is doomed; hence comes the warning that men should not identify themselves with the city of worldliness, falsehood, and sin. The reference to the wild beast, the image, and the mark, carries us back to the last chapter, and shows us that Babylon is only another aspect of the work of God's enemies: it is the city of the world-power. The warning not to receive the mark is a declaration that man, individual man, is responsible: there is no necessity for his receiving the mark, the hall-mark of a cowardly connivance at wrong-doing, or for setting his judgments by the fashions of the world.

(11) **For ever and ever.**—Or, *unto ages of ages.* The imagery of the smoke going up reminds us of the overthrow of Sodom and Gomorrah (Gen. xix. 28; comp. Isa. xxxiv. 10). *They have not rest by day and by night, who worship the wild beast,* &c. Sin, which is first embraced as a delight, becomes soon an inexorable tyrant, by an awful

rest day nor night, who worship the
beast and his image, and whosoever
receiveth the mark of his name. (12) Here
is the patience of the saints: here *are*
they that keep the commandments of
God, and the faith of Jesus. (13) And
I heard a voice from heaven saying unto
me, Write, Blessed *are* the dead which
die in the Lord from henceforth: Yea,
saith the Spirit,[1] that they may rest
from their labours; and their works do
follow them. (14) And I looked, and
Chap. xiv. 14—16. The harvest. behold a white cloud, and
upon the cloud *one* sat
like unto the Son of man, having on
his head a golden crown, and in his
hand a sharp sickle. (15) And another
angel came out of the temple, crying
with a loud voice to him that sat on the
cloud, Thrust in thy sickle, and reap:
for the time is come for thee to reap;
for the harvest of the earth is ripe.[2][a]
(16) And he that sat on the cloud thrust
in his sickle on the earth; and the earth
was reaped. (17) And another angel came
out of the temple which is
Chap. xiv. 17—20. The vintage. in heaven, he also having
a sharp sickle. (18) And another angel

2 Or, *dried.*
a Joel 3. 13.

1 Or, *from henceforth saith the Spirit, Yea.*

---

retribution compelling men along the routine of the evil habits which they loathe while they long for, and long for even while they loathe them: there is a destiny of unrest in all sin. "The wicked are like the troubled sea, which cannot rest." It is well that solemn words like these should be read by the light of the most certain of all truths—the power sin has of stamping its indelible features upon the human character, and giving to habit the force of a destiny.

(12) **Here is the patience . . .**—Translate, *Here is the patience of the saints* (not "here are they," but) *who keep,* &c. In this readiness to wait, to endure through much tribulation to the end, is the patience of the saints seen. There is a patient waiting for Christ shown by those who keep God's commandments, who cleave to righteousness in spite of much temptation, and who refuse to pay homage to the god of this world because firm in the faith that Jesus is King.

(13) **And I heard a voice . . .**—Translate, *And I heard a voice out of the heaven, saying, Write, Blessed are the dead who die in the Lord from henceforth; Yea, saith the Spirit, in that they shall rest from their labours; for their works follow with them.* We are not told whose voice speaks, but it proclaims a blessing on (not only martyrs, but) those who die in the Lord, in happy union and fellowship with Him (John xv. 2—5; 1 John i. 3); such are happy, for they rest from toil, and their works of faith and labours of love (even if only the giving a cup of cold water in the name of Christ) follow with them into the presence of their Lord (Matt. x. 41, 42; Heb. vi. 10). The words "from henceforth" form a difficulty; the reason for their introduction is to be found in the state of trouble which the last verses describe: the righteous are happy in being taken away from the evil to come. Or may it be that the words are designed to console the mourners in an age when dark unbelief robs away the sweet resurrection trust, and writes over its graves, "Farewell for ever"? If the climax of world-power should be bitter scorn of the idea of a life to come, and complacent satisfaction with a portion in this world, then words of faith, proclaiming that the dead are happy and restful, and that their work is not in vain in the Lord, may find new force to sustain a fainting courage or a wavering trust.

THE HARVEST.

(14) **And I looked . . .**—Better, *And I saw, and behold a white cloud, and upon the cloud one seated like to a son of man, having upon his head a golden crown, and in his hand a sharp sickle.* There can be little doubt that Christ Himself is here intended: the "cloud" (Matt. xxiv. 30; Acts i. 9), the expression "Son of man" (comp. John v. 27 and Dan. vii. 13), the "crown," the general resemblance to the vision in chap. i. (see chap. i. 7—13), indicate as much. The "crown" is the crown of victory; the hour of conquest is at hand. The sickle shows that the harvest has come. (Comp. Joel iii. 12—14 and Mark iv. 26—29.)

(15) **And another angel . . .**—Translate, *And another angel came forth out of the temple,* &c. It has been asked, "What harvest is this?" It is the gathering of the good seed, the full corn in the ear, into the celestial garner (Mark iv. 26—29). The angel who announces that the harvest is ready comes forth from the Temple, the inner shrine, the holy place which was measured off in the sanctuary of the faithful (chap. xi. 1); whereas the angel who calls for the vintage comes forth from the altar (verse 18).

The angel cries—*Put forth* (or, *send*) *thy sickle and reap, because the hour is come to reap, because the harvest of the earth is ripe* (or, *dried*); the wheat stalks are dry, and the fields white for harvest (John iv. 35). The sickle was put in: the earth was reaped.

THE VINTAGE.

There must be some difference between the vintage and the harvest. There is an autumn gladness about the harvest: there are tokens of judgment in the vintage. It is not the sharp sickle alone which is required: the winepress, the winepress of God's wrath, is called into use. An angel from the Temple calls to the Son of man to reap the harvest: an angel from the altar calls to an angel from the Temple to gather in the vintage. The vintage symbolises a harvest of judgment; do not the words respecting Babylon (the wine of the wrath of her fornication, verse 8) come to the mind and confirm this? The angel rises from the altar, beneath which the murdered saints had cried, "How long?" and proclaims, "The vintage, the hour of vengeance, has come!" And it is not without significance that the angel to whom this cry is addressed comes forth out of the Temple, the safe sanctuary of God's faithful ones, as one who has witnessed their secret sorrows and their sufferings, and is fitted "to recompense tribulation to the troublers of Israel" (2 Thess. i. 6).

(17) **And another angel . . .**—Translate, *And another angel, . . . having himself also* (as well as the Son of man, verse 14) *a sharp sickle.*

(18) **And another angel . . .**—Translate, *And another angel, . . . he who hath authority over the fire.* The two scenes—one in chap. vi. 9, 10 (the souls crying beneath the altar), the other in chap. viii. 5 (the angel

came out from the altar, which had
power over fire; and cried with a loud
cry to him that had the sharp sickle,
saying, Thrust in thy sharp sickle, and
gather the clusters of the vine of the
earth; for her grapes are fully ripe.
(19) And the angel thrust in his sickle
into the earth, and gathered the vine
of the earth, and cast *it* into the great
winepress of the wrath of God. (20) And
the winepress was trodden without the
city, and blood came out of the wine-
press, even unto the horse bridles, by
the space of a thousand *and* six hundred
furlongs.

A.D. 96.

CHAPTER XV. — (1) And I saw
another sign in heaven,
great and marvellous, seven
angels having the seven
last plagues; for in them
is filled up the wrath of God. (2) And
I saw as it were a sea of glass mingled
with fire: and them that had gotten
the victory over the beast, and over
his image, and over his mark, *and* over

Chap. xv. 1–8. In preparation for the plagues, the Temple of God is closed.

---

mingling incense with the prayers of the saints)—must be remembered. The angel who had charge of the altar fire, and flung the ashes betokening judgments towards the earth, calls with a loud cry, *Send thy sharp sickle, and gather the bunches of the vine of the earth, because her grapes are ripe.*

(19, 20) **And the angel . . .**—The vine (*i.e.*, the vintage of the vine), when gathered, is cast into *the winepress of the wrath of God, the great* (*winepress*). *And the winepress was trodden without the city, and there came forth blood out of the winepress as far as the bridles of the horses, from a thousand six hundred furlongs* (stadii). The outflow of the blood of the grapes pressed reached over a distance of sixteen hundred stadii. The treading of the winepress was a figure representing vengeance; the red juice of the grape strongly suggested the shedding of blood. (Comp. Isa. lxiii. 2—4.) The winepresses stood usually outside the city: it is so represented here, not without an allusion to those who fall under the weight of this judgment because they have refused the defence of the true city and sanctuary. (Comp. verse 1 and Ps. cxxxii. 17, 18.) The distance (sixteen hundred stadii), *i.e.*, four multiplied into itself and then multiplied by a hundred, is symbolical (such seems the most probable meaning) of a judgment complete and full, and reaching to all corners of the earth—"the whole world, of which Satan is called the prince, is judged, and condemned, and punished" (Dr. Currey). In the vintage and harvest is a piercing discrimination between the faithful fruit-bearing children of the King and the cowardly or selfish, whose hearts are for self and not for Christ, but who yield themselves servants to sin.

XV.

(1) **And I saw another sign in (*the*) heaven.**—The sign is, as we noticed before (chap. xii. 1), a token, not a mere empty wonder. This sign is called "great and marvellous;" it introduces a new set of scenes; the same characters will reappear, but we must start with fresh attention.

The seer sees *seven angels* (not "the seven angels;" it is perfectly needless to ask what angels, or to try and identify them with the trumpet angels) *having seven plagues, the last, because in them is completed the wrath of God.* The statement that these are the *last* plagues seems to show that the set of visions now commencing carry us down to the end of the age; there are no other plagues after these: they are the last plagues; the vials, like the seals and the trumpets, run up to the final consummation. They are plagues; the word carries us back to Egypt: on Egypt fell the ten plagues which showed forth God's righteous power, and exposed the hollow pretensions of the magicians and their gods; the wild beast-power and the false prophet-power of that day was crippled and exposed. In like manner upon the wild beast-power of later ages the plagues of God fall. They are plagues, because they are sent forth, not like the trumpets to warn men to repent, but upon those who have obstinately refused to return; they are not goads to the wavering, but they are strokes upon the wilful and hardened; they are directed against those who are deliberately hostile.

(2) **And I saw as it were a sea of glass mingled with fire.**—The wild beast rose out of the sea (chap. xiii. 1); the evil-hearted woman sits upon many waters (chap. xvii. 1); they draw strength from the wild, and ungoverned, and short-sighted impulses of human passion; in opposition to this near the throne of God is the calm and translucent sea of God's counsels of righteousness and love, now clear as crystal, now ruddy with the fire of righteous indignation, the expression of His eternal will against sin. Such is the appearance of this glass-like sea now that the angels of the plagues are going forth.

But the seer saw more than this fire-flushed sea. He saw also those that are victorious over the wild beast. These he describes (such is the literal translation) as *those who conquer out of the wild beast, &c.*; they come off conquerors out of the struggle, and they escape from the temptation to worship his image and wear the badge of his service: they "escape victorious from" his image and from his mark. When he sees these, they are *standing upon* (*i.e.*, on the shore of) *the sea of glass, holding harps of God.* We have had the harps mentioned previously (chaps. v. 8, and xiv. 2); it is appropriate. The life which has been a discord to the world rises into true music before God; those who will make their life a melody must take it first as a conflict. The harps they hold are called harps of God, not merely because they are dedicated to Him, but because they are truly God's. All the most glorious and noble things in nature were named God's: the lofty trees were "trees of God"; the high-piled mountains were "mountains of God"; so also the harps which strike forth the richest music are "harps of God." Nor is this a mere phrase to be considered as equivalent to very great or very glorious; great and glorious the trees, hills, and harps are, but only a prosaic or a profane mind can be satisfied with such a naked equivalent. The godly saw the hand of God in these things; and St. John knows that the noblest melody in the ears of God is the noble life of faith, suffering, and love. The

the number of his name, stand on the
sea of glass, having the harps of God.
(3) And they sing the song of Moses
the servant of God,[a] and the song of
the Lamb, saying, Great and marvellous
are thy works, Lord God Almighty;
just and true *are* thy ways, thou King
of saints. (4) Who shall not fear
thee, O Lord, and glorify thy name?[b]
for *thou* only *art* holy: for all nations shall come and worship before thee; for thy judgments are made manifest.
(5) And after that I looked, and, behold, the temple of the tabernacle of the testimony in heaven was opened:
(6) and the seven angels came out of the temple, having the seven plagues, clothed in pure and white

a Ex. 15. 1.

b Ps. 145. 17.

---

power of such a life is in God, not in itself (John xv. 5; Gal. ii. 20), and the music of such a life is music which God makes (2 Cor. iv. 7—10), drawing the sweetest tones from the strings which are smitten with pain and sorrow; and as its life's music is God-taught, so does its song of triumph sound from a harp not its own, but God's. If our power to sing in trial here a song worthy of God is only found in God, so will the songs of heaven be sweet only in Him, for those who dwell there shall be all taught of Him.

(3) **And they sing the song of Moses the servant of God, and the song of the Lamb.**—They join their voices to the music of their harps. The song of Moses was a pæan of victory over Pharaoh and his hosts (Ex. xiv. 26—31, and xv. 1—21). Israel stood on the margin of the Red Sea and saw the tokens of the overthrow of the great world-power of that day; so these saints stand by the border of the fire-blent sea of glass, and sing the song of triumph over the doom of the great world-powers of every age. The cases are parallel, the songs are alike; and it would not be out of place were the words of that other song of Moses, the man of God, to be heard from those who are made glad according to the days of their affliction, and who are clothed with the beauty of the Lord their God (Ps. xc. 1, 15, 17). They also sing the song of the Lamb. The Apocalypse is full of Christ; the Lamb is the axis on which the world of its scenery moves; He is the key of earth's history; the victory of the saints is in Him (chap. xii. 11); their song of triumph is of Him who put a new song in their mouth and in whom all things are reconciled (Eph. i. 10; Phil. ii. 10, 11).

(3, 4) **Great and marvellous are thy works . . .**—The *song* is better thus translated:—

"Great and marvellous are Thy works,
Lord God Almighty.
Just and true are Thy ways,
Thou King of the nations.
Who will not fear, O Lord, and glorify Thy name?
Because Thou only art holy:
Because all the nations shall come and worship
in Thy presence:
Because Thy judgments were manifested."

The works are called "great;" the "ways" are called just and true. It is not mere marvel which calls forth the song of praise, but righteousness, truth, and holiness. The Almighty is the righteous ruler. The English version has "King of saints;" the reading should be "King of *the nations*," or else, perhaps, "King of *the ages*." The latter reading harmonises well with the immediate context and with the other passages, which link the thought of "the ages" with the "righteous dealings" of God. "Thy righteousness is an everlasting righteousness, and thy law is the truth" (Ps. cxix. 142; comp. also verses 144, 151, 152, 160). But the former is to be preferred; it is appropriate in a song which celebrates a victory over those who vaunted themselves as the princes of this world, and which proclaims the submission of the nations to God; and it seems to have been transplanted here from Jeremiah (x. 7): "Who would not fear thee, thou King of the nations?" The song celebrates the noble acts of the Lord; it declares them to be great; but it is not their greatness, it is their righteousness and faithfulness which calls forth the grateful praise. The long days of oppression, and the seeming silence of the Almighty, when the prayer and cry "How long?" has risen from perplexed and suffering saints, have brought the temptation of the psalmist: "I have cleansed my heart in vain" (Ps. lxxiii. 3—13). But now the righteous acts of the Lord are manifested; now it is acknowledged that "verily there is a reward for the righteous; verily He is a God that judgeth in the earth" (Ps. viii. 11). Though clouds and darkness have sometimes been round about Him, it is now beyond doubt that "righteousness and judgment are the habitation of His throne" (Ps. xcvii. 2).

(4) **Who shall not fear . . .**—Rather, *Who will not fear,* &c. (the word "Thee" should be omitted, *because Thou art holy.* The word rendered "holy" is not that which is usually employed when the holiness of God is spoken of; it is a word which, when applied to men, denotes one who reverences the sacred obligations of natural and moral order, apart from the thought of mere law or custom. The word is applied here, and in chap. xvi. 5, to God, and denotes the recognition of those sacred obligations which the character of God, if I may say so with reverence, imposes upon Himself. It is the remembrance that God will, as Judge of all the earth, do right, and will vindicate the expectations of those who stay themselves upon His character, which generates a holy fear of Him.

All nations shall come and worship . . .—Translate, *All the nations worship, because Thy judgments* (or, *righteous acts*) *are manifested.* The song is one in anticipation. The angels of judgment are going forth; the righteous dealings of God will be seen; but these things are spoken of as though accomplished: their completion is a divine certainty.

(5) **And after that . . .**—Better, *And after these things I saw, and there was opened the temple of the tabernacle of the testimony* (or, *witness*) *in the heaven.* This temple is called the temple of the tabernacle of the testimony; the expression sounds cumbrous, but it is nevertheless suitable. St. Stephen spoke of "the tabernacle of witness" in the wilderness, which was made after the pattern showed in the mount (Acts vii. 44). The tabernacle was well called the tabernacle of witness, for it contained the ark of the testimony with the Law of God, and was a perpetual witness of God's presence among His people. The temple of the tabernacle then is the shrine, or inner sanctuary, of the heavenly true tabernacle, after the pattern of which the tabernacle of Moses was fashioned, which is now opened.

(6) **And the seven angels . . .**—Better, *And there came out the seven angels who had the seven plagues*

linen, and having their breasts girded
with golden girdles. (7) And one of the
four beasts gave unto the seven angels
seven golden vials full of the wrath of
God, who liveth for ever and ever.
(8) And the temple was filled with smoke
from the glory of God, and from
his power; and no man was able
to enter into the temple, till the
seven plagues of the seven angels were
fulfilled.

A.D. 96.

CHAPTER XVI.—(1) And I heard a
great voice out of the temple saying to
the seven angels, Go your ways, and
pour out the vials of the wrath of God
upon the earth. (2) And the first went
and poured out his vial
upon the earth; and there
fell a noisome and grievous sore upon
the men which had the mark of the
beast, and *upon* them which worshipped
his image. (3) And the second angel

Chap. xvi. 2. The first vial.

from the temple, clothed in linen, pure, glistening, and girt about their breasts with golden girdles. The temple is the inner shrine, or sanctuary; it was this which was measured (chap. xi. 1); it was out of this that the angel with the sharp sickle came for the vintage of the earth (chap. xiv. 7); out of this now came the seven angels with the seven plagues. It is well to remember this, for these plagues are not, like the judgments of the trumpet, calls to repentance; they are plagues on those who have refused to return, who have rejected the sanctuary, the tabernacle of witness, which the Lord pitched among men, and who have refused, like obstinate builders, the stone which has become the head of the corner. Out of the rejected temple the angels of wrath come; it is ever true that out of rejected mercies the heaviest of plagues are forged. The angels are clad in a garb resembling that of Christ (chap. i. 13); they are come forth to do His bidding; they are clothed in raiment which indicates their righteous errand. (Comp. chap. xix. 8; Acts i. 10, and x. 30.) Instead of *linen*, some MSS. have "a stone:" the angels, according to this, were "clad in a stone, pure, brilliant." There is a parallel thought in Ezekiel, who describes the splendour of the King of Tyre: "Thou hast been in Eden the garden of God; every precious stone was thy covering, the sardius, topaz, and the diamond," &c. (chap. xxviii. 13).

(7) **And one of the four . . .**—Better, *And one from among the four living beings gave to the seven angels seven golden vials* (or, *bowls*) *full*, &c. The vials are the shallow bowls which were used for incense. They are filled with the wrath of God, and that wrath is now to be poured out "upon the kingdoms that have not called upon God's name" (Ps. lxxix. 6). These vials are given by one of the living creatures who represent creation; it is thus through creation that the wrath of God can visit the rebellious; that wrath of God is simply the operation of God's righteous law against sin. His statutes are eternally righteous. He has given to all things a law which cannot be broken; that law is adverse to evil, and will in the end root it out, for it does the bidding of God, who lives unto the ages of the ages.

(8) **And the temple . . .**—Translate, *And the temple* (the same word—*naos*—is used as in chap. xi. 1) *was filled with smoke from the glory of God, and from his might; and no one was able to enter into the temple until the seven plagues of the seven angels should be finished.* As in the wilderness (Ex. xl. 34, 35), and as at the dedication of Solomon's temple (1 Kings viii. 10, 11), the tokens of God's presence filled the temple, so it is now, but with a difference: it is smoke, not cloud, which is the symbol of God's presence. But the vision which perhaps, under all circumstances, most nearly corresponds with the present is that of Isaiah (chap. vi.); there the prophet beheld the vision of God. His train filled the temple, and the house was filled with smoke, and a message of judgment was given to the prophet; that message declared that the sin of the people had reached a climax: they had trifled with convictions, and henceforward the words of God's servants would harden rather than awaken them. "Make the heart of this people fat, and make their ears heavy, and shut their eyes," &c. (Isa. vi. 9, 10), till the desolating judgments had fallen. The general drift of the present vision is similar; the days of warning are over: the plagues which now fall will fall on those who have trifled with convictions: the sanctuary which was opened as a refuge is now closed: none can enter till the plagues have descended. The time has come when the judgments of God fail to stir the conscience which has been deadened by sin; the day when the gracious influences towards repentance was felt has passed. The word that has been spoken is about to descend in judgment (John vii. 48). "Who shall not pray, with an agony of earnestness, From hardness of heart and contempt of Thy word and commandment, good Lord, deliver us?" (Dr. Vaughan).

XVI.

The Seven Vials.

(1) **And I heard . . .**—A great voice is heard out of the temple; it bids the angels pour out their vials "into the earth;" later on (verse 17) the voice is heard saying, "It is done." The voice is then said to come from the throne; it seems likely that the voice of the first verse is the same—the divine voice from the throne itself.

(2) **And the first . . .**—Translate, *And the first went forth*, &c. The angel which receives the command departs and pours forth his vial upon the earth. All the vials are poured forth "into the earth" (verse 1) generally; the first angel pours his vial forth upon the earth, that is, the dry land. *And there came an evil and painful sore upon the men* (*i.e.*, upon that part of the human race) *who*, &c. The plague falls on those who carry the mark of the beast, and who worship it. Like the plagues of Egypt, *they* are directed against those who aid the oppressor. The plague here described resembles the sixth of the Egyptian plagues, the plague of boils (comp. Ex. ix. 8—12; Deut. xxviii. 27). Egypt is one type of the world-power; and the plagues are used as types also, and are not to be understood literally. The plague of the "evil sore" denotes some throbbing and hateful sore, perhaps spiritual or mental, which distracts attention and disturbs the personal serenity and self-complacency of the worshippers of the world-power.

(3) **And the second angel . . .**—Better, *And the second* (*angel*) *poured out his vial on the sea, and it became blood as of a dead man, and every*

poured out his vial upon the sea; and it became as the blood of a dead *man:* and every living soul died in the sea.

Chap. xvi. 3. The second vial.

(4) And the third angel poured out his vial upon the rivers and fountains of waters; and they became blood. (5) And I heard the angel of the waters say, Thou art righteous, O Lord, which art, and wast, and shalt be, because thou hast judged thus. (6) For they have shed the blood of saints and prophets, and thou hast given them blood to drink; for they are worthy. (7) And I heard another out of the altar say, Even so, Lord God Almighty, true and righteous *are* thy judgments.

Chap. xvi. 4—7. The third vial.

(8) And the fourth angel poured out his vial upon the sun; and power was

Chap. xvi. 8, 9. The fourth vial.

---

soul of life died (*even*) *the things that were in the sea.* The reference to the first of the Egyptian plagues is clear (Ex. vii. 20; comp. chap. viii. 8, 9). It has been remarked that "the Egyptian plagues stood in a very close connection with the natural state and circumstances of Egypt. The Nile, which was their strength, became worse than useless when its waters were turned to blood." There is a similar feature here. The sea, out of which the wild beast rose, from which the world-power drew strength, is turned to blood, the blood as of a dead man, corrupt and loathsome. The sea represented the tumultuous impulses and passions of the masses; there is a certain healthy force in these, but under certain conditions, when devoted to selfishness and earthliness, they become corrupt and deadly. Ruled by God and by right, the voice of multitudes is melodious as the voice of the sea, and the free movement of peoples, like the ocean, a health-giving moral environment to nations; but swayed by impulse, or directed by worldliness, they become an element of corruption, killing every token of better life.

(4) **And the third angel . . .**—The third vial resembles the second in its effects. As it is poured out on the rivers and springs of waters, they become blood. It is not only the great sea which becomes blood, but all the merry streams and babbling brooks which carry their tribute of water seawards also turn corrupt. And this plague is acknowledged by heavenly voices as a just retribution (verses 5—7). The streams and rivers feed the sea; they are the powers and influences which go to the making up of the great popular sentiment; these are smitten by the same corruption. Men cannot worship worldliness or earthliness without degrading even those who contribute to their instruction, their recreations, and their joys, to the same level. When the public taste grows corrupt, the literature will, for example, become so in a more or less degree; the up-flowing tide will colour the down-coming stream. "The morality of a nation's art," writes a modern critic, "always rises to the level of morality in a nation's manners. Morality takes care of itself, and always revenges any outrage which art may put upon its laws by either lowering the art that so offends, or extinguishing it" (Dallas, *Gay Science,* Vol. II., 16). It is true in even a wider sense. The loftier powers of imagination, the range of poetical elevation, are cramped and killed in a base, world-worshipping age. The streams of life grow putrid, the fresh and bright gifts of God are polluted, when the ocean of public thought is unwholesome.

(5—7) But this state of things is declared to be a just retribution, and reasonably so; for the corruption arises because the true power of life has been rejected: it is the refusal of the good, the want of the life-giving element, which is the secret of all death, physical, moral, spiritual. "'Tis life we want when breath is scant." The world-power and its worshippers have driven away goodness and faith, the elements of the higher life of man; they have slain the just and the righteous, who were the salt of the earth; they have rejected Christ, who is the life of men; how can they reap anything but decay and death? They slay the righteous; the death of righteousness leaves them nothing but the lifeless blood behind; they can no longer drink moral life from the good; there is but the legacy of death. "Blood of saints and prophets did they pour out; and blood didst Thou give them to drink."

(5) **And I heard the angel of the waters . . .**—That is, the angel who was set over the waters, or the angel who is, on the heavenly side, representative of the waters. (See *Excursus A: On the Angels.*) The angel acknowledges God's righteousness. *Thou art righteous . . . because Thou didst judge these things*—*i.e.,* because of the righteous law which these judgments manifested.

(6) **For they have shed . . .**—Better, *Because they shed* (not, "have shed," but *did shed,* or *pour out*), *and blood didst Thou give them; they are worthy.* "For" is to be omitted; the sentence has a startling force without it. They—*i.e.,* those enemies of all righteousness—are worthy; they receive the due reward of their deeds.

(7) **And I heard . . .**—Translate, *And I heard* (not "another out of the altar," but) *the altar saying, Even so, Lord God the Almighty, true and righteous are Thy judgments.* The altar beneath which the souls of the martyrs cried, and on which the prayers of saints were offered, is represented as confirming the testimony to the just dealings of God.

(8, 9) **And the fourth . . .**—Better, *And the fourth* (*angel*) *poured out his vial upon the sun; and it was given to it* (the "sun," not the "angel;" the rendering of the English version "unto him" is misleading) *to scorch men with fire. And men* (*i.e.,* those who were worshippers of the wild beast) *were scorched . . . and did not repent to give him glory.* The sun, the great source of light and warmth, whose beams call forth the flowers of the earth, becomes a power to blast, not to bless. This is another example of the way in which the things full of beneficence are turned into powers of sorrow to those who follow evil. Not only the pleasant gifts and influences, which, like streams, were made to gladden men, grow corrupt, but the very source of light and knowledge becomes a power to destroy. We may contrast this influence of the sun with the beneficent beams of the Sun of Righteousness. Christ rose as the light and sun upon the world, because He diffused the knowledge which gave life to men; but here we have a light and sun which scorches. There is a knowledge which withers while it illumines; there is a teaching which does not warm the heart, but

given unto him to scorch men with
fire. (9) And men were scorched[1] with
great heat, and blasphemed the name
of God, which hath power over these
plagues: and they repented not to give
him glory. (10) And the fifth angel
poured out his vial upon
the seat of the beast; and
his kingdom was full of
darkness; and they gnawed their tongues
for pain, (11) and blasphemed the God of
heaven because of their pains and their
sores, and repented not of their deeds.
(12) And the sixth angel poured out his
vial upon the great river
Euphrates; and the water
thereof was dried up, that
the way of the kings of the east might be
prepared. (13) And I saw three unclean
spirits like frogs *come* out of the mouth
of the dragon, and out of the mouth of
the beast, and out of the mouth of the
false prophet. (14) For they are the
spirits of devils, working miracles,

Chap. xvi. 10, 11. The fifth vial.

Chap. xvi. 12–16. The sixth vial.

[1] Or, *burned.*

dries both heart and conscience, and brings but pain. The result, painful as it is, does not work repentance. Suffering, without grace and humility, does not bless men; they grow angry; the fire hardens instead of purifying. The whole series of these judgments illustrate the awful truth that there is a stage in personal life, and in national and world life also, in which suffering loses its remedial force, because the character has become set, and even an occasional desire after higher things is no longer felt.

> "When we in our viciousness
> Grow hard, the wise gods seal our eyes,
> In our own slime drop our clear judgments,
> Make us adore our errors, and thus
> We strut to our destruction."

(10) **And the fifth . . .**—Better, *The fifth angel poured out his vial upon the throne* (not "the seat:" see Notes on chaps. iv. 10 and xiii. 2) *of the wild beast.* The vials of judgment gradually dissolve the integrity and organisation of the kingdom of the wild beast. The result of the principles on which it has been based begin to show themselves: first, moral disease in individuals; then a corrupt tone of national morals spreading into the higher orders of society; then the fierce pride of vaunted light which scorches. Where these are, disorganisation is not far off; evil goes out a murderer and comes home a suicide. The retribution comes home; the throne of the world-power, the very head and centre of its authority, is smitten.

And his kingdom was full of darkness.—*And his kingdom was darkened.* We have the counterpart of the Egyptian plague (Ex. x. 21—23); there was a typical force in that ancient plague: the kingdom which boasted itself so full of light becomes darkened. When men shut out the higher light, the smoke of their own candles will soon obscure the whole heaven. When moral evil is linked with intellectual light, the moral evil will be found the stronger; for we cannot have a sunbeam without the sun. "Take heed," said Christ, "that the light that is in thee be not darkness." There is a light that is darkness; the progress of evil bringing about its own retribution proves this conclusively.

(10, 11) But even the failure of their own light does not work repentance: *they gnawed their tongues from their pain.* Here is remorse and suffering. They are "unto themselves" (as the Book of Wisdom describes the Egyptians) "more grievous than the darkness" (Wisd. xvii. 21); but there is no softening or humbling of themselves, no turning to God. They still love what God hates, and hate what He loves, for they blasphemed God, &c., *and repented not of their works.* Such is the wretched state of the world-power in the day when retributive evil overtakes it—darkness, pain, and inability to repent. Is it not a picture of the ultimate state of all sin? It is not a vast world-power alone which exhibits pain and confusion like this. It is to be seen over and over again in men and nations. The power of evil comes home and robs men of their accustomed guides. They are brought into darkness and trouble; the throne where the master-power of worldliness sat is cast down; the evil passion which was the unifying power of their life is deprived of the field of its power; then follows exasperation, anger at defeat, readiness to accuse others, but no blame of self, no repentance.

(12) **And the sixth . . .**—Better, *The sixth* (*angel*) *poured out his vial on the great river Euphrates; and its water was dried that the way of the kings who are from the rising of the sun might be prepared.* The symbolical meaning of the Euphrates has been touched upon before. (See Notes on chap. ix. 14.) In the great age-long struggle between the kingdoms of Christ and the world the Euphrates represents the great separating boundary between the two kingdoms, as the literal Euphrates formed the barrier between Israel and the hostile northern and eastern kingdoms. It is the great impediment to war. It is true that there is a great interposed boundary of public opinion, which restrains evil from breaking forth in its ruder and more violent forms. Men may be hostile to spiritual religion, yet they scarcely like to shock public sentiment, or to incur the charge of depraving public morals; but there may come a time, after false principles have been taught, corrupt manners tolerated, and the light of better things darkened, when the public sentiment loses all sense of shame, and the decorums of life, which have acted as a breakwater against the tide of outrageous evil, are swept away: then is the Euphrates dried, and then may the hostile powers of evil, unrestrained by any considerations, unchecked by the popular conscience, cross boldly over and invade the whole sacred soil of human life. There have been times like this when shameless sin has walked forth, secure of public favour, to desecrate every sanctuary of purity and faith—when the most barbarous manners and the most unscrupulous violations of public faith and morals have been not only tolerated, but applauded. The "kings of the east" (or *of the sun-rising*) represent the forces of rude and open evil which have been long restrained. As the four barbarian and tyrant kings (Gen. xiv. 1—24) from the East invaded the land of promise in Abraham's days, so the leaders of open and violent hate of right, purity, and Christ, have the way of their advance prepared. But certain agencies go forth to bring about this uprising of rude revolt against every sanctity of life.

(13, 14) **And I saw . . .**—Better, *And I saw out of the*

which go forth unto the kings of the
earth and of the whole world, to gather
them to the battle of that great day of
God Almighty. (15) Behold, I come as a
thief.[a] Blessed *is* he that watcheth,
and keepeth his garments, lest he walk
naked, and they see his shame. (16) And
he gathered them together into a place
called in the Hebrew tongue Armageddon.
(17) And the seventh angel
poured out his vial into
the air; and there came
a great voice out of the
temple of heaven, from the throne,

[a] Matt. 24. 43.

Chap. xvi. 17—21. The seventh vial.

mouth of the dragon, and out of the mouth of the wild beast, and out of the mouth of the false prophet, three unclean spirits, as it were frogs. For they are spirits of demons, doing signs, which go forth upon the kings of the whole world, to gather them together to the war of the great day of God the Almighty. Some have thought that the kings of the East are the representatives of the Christian powers, and that the drying up of the Euphrates is the preparation for their entrance into the land of promise. The general drift of the chapter seems to me to be adverse to this view. The two hostile kingdoms are being brought slowly into open antagonism; the great issues are to be brought to a decisive test; the time comes when a decision must be made: "If God be God, follow Him; if Baal, then follow him." The situation becomes so strained that it is useless to keep up the appearance of a respectable neutrality, for forces have been at work which are gradually bringing all powers into the conflict. The forces which are at work preparing for this issue are evil forces; "unclean spirits," little frogs, spirits of demons go forth to gather every world-power to the struggle. All this points to the final mobilisation of the hosts of evil for an attack upon the kingdom of Christ. Every impediment is removed, and the Euphrates is dried. The kings may advance: like the hosts of Pharaoh they may enter the dried-up sea in hot haste of their hatred of all righteousness. Evil is reckless now, and moves to its destruction; but it cannot so move without working upon men. Three evil spirits go forth for this purpose. There are three radical foes of Christ and His righteousness: the dragon, representing the hate of evil spirits; the wild beast, representing the hostility of world-power; the false prophet, representing the antagonism of world-culture and intellectualism—these three send forth each their emissary, appealing to the pride and passions of men. What are we to understand by them? We must consider their origin. The world-power would have us worship the things seen. It sends forth the spirit of earthliness, the spirit which works in the voluptuary, the ambitious, and the avaricious, the spirit which makes earthly things its end (Phil. iii. 19). The world-culture sends forth its spirit of intellectualism, which denies the spiritual nature of man, and substitutes taste and culture for spirituality. The dragon sends forth the spirit of egotism, of proud, self-sufficient independence, which culminates in an utter hatred of the Creator. The three spirits combined make up that wisdom which St. James described as earthly, sensual (unspiritual, psychical), devilish (Jas. iii. 15). We may compare the three foes in the "Red Cross Knight:" Sansloy (without law), Sansfoy (without faith), and Sansjoy (without joy)—Spenser's *Faerie Queene.* They are like frogs: here is a reference again to the Egyptian plagues.

These spirits gather all earthly powers to the war (not "battle") of the great day of God the Almighty. The day which will test the power of combined evil, the day which, beginning in rash pride, will end in bitter defeat. to this the evil spirits lure their followers, as the false prophets lured Ahab to his overthrow at Ramoth-Gilead (1 Kings xxii. 20): such is one of the final aspects of evil. The voice of inclination is listened to as though it were prophetic. The suggestions of sinful desire are not only obeyed, but reverenced as oracles. The wicked hath an oracle of transgression in his heart (Ps. xxxvi. 1 *et seq.*).

(15) **Behold, I come . . .**—Translate, *Behold, I come as a thief.* It is the oft-repeated Scripture warning (chap. iii. 3; 1 Thess. v. 2, 3; 2 Pet. iii. 10. Comp. Luke xii. 35—40). It reminds us not only that our Lord may come unexpectedly, but that He may even come and we be unaware. There is one day when He will come, and every eye will behold Him; but He comes in various ways and forms to bless and to test man. Blessed are they who are ready, watching. But vigilance is not enough: the garments must be kept. The powers of evil are abroad. Sloth and pleasure may counsel ease, and tempt the watcher to lay aside his garments and take rest and sleep. The earnest watcher desires, like St. Paul, to be found in Christ, clad in the true righteousness of faith (Phil. iii. 9).

(16) **And he gathered . . .**—Better, *He gathered them together to the place which is called in Hebrew Armageddon.* Armageddon is the mountain of Megiddo. It is the high table-land surrounded by hills which was the great battle-field of the Holy Land. There the fortunes of dynasties and kingdoms have been decided; there the cause of liberty has triumphed; there kings fought and fell; there Gideon and Barak were victorious; there Ahaziah and Josiah were slain. The old battle-ground becomes the symbol of the decisive struggle. It is raised in meaning: it is a type, not a locality. The war of principles, the war of morals, the war of fashion culminates in an Armageddon. The progress of the spiritual struggle in individual men must lead in the same way to a mountain of decision, where the long-wavering heart must take sides, and the set of the character be determined. "There is no waving of banners and no prancing of horses' hoofs; the warfare is spiritual, so that there is in sight neither camp nor foe." It is that conflict which emerges out of various opinions and diverse principles: "the religious tendencies of the times" are (as we have been reminded) powers marshalling themselves for the battle of Armageddon. We must not look for great and startling signs: the kingdom and the conflict of the kingdom is within and around us (Luke xvii. 20, 21).

(17) **And the seventh . . .**—Translate, *And the seventh (angel) poured out his vial upon the air, and there came forth a voice out of the temple, from the throne, saying, It is done.* The results of the outpouring of this vial are described in the following verses; but before these are seen, the voice from the throne—God's own voice (see verse 1)—proclaims, as though rejoicing in the near approach of the happy end, "It is done." The close of these scenes of sin and

saying, It is done. (18) And there were
voices, and thunders, and lightnings;
and there was a great earthquake, such
as was not since men were upon the
earth, so mighty an earthquake, *and* so
great. (19) And the great city was
divided into three parts, and the cities
of the nations fell: and great Babylon
came in remembrance before God, to
give unto her the cup of the wine of
the fierceness of his wrath.[a] (20) And
every island fled away, and the moun-
tains were not found. (21) And there
fell upon men a great hail out of
heaven, *every stone* about the weight of
a talent: and men blasphemed God
because of the plague of the hail; for
the plague thereof was exceeding great.

A.D. 96.

a Jer. 25. 15

CHAPTER XVII.— (1) And there
came one of the seven
angels which had the seven
vials, and talked with me,
saying unto me, Come

Chap. xvii. 1—6. The vision of the scarlet-clad woman, Babylon.

---

suffering is now at hand, for the last of the last plagues has been sent forth.

(18) **And there were voices . . .**—There is some variety in the order of the words in different MSS. *There were lightnings, and voices, and thunders* (comp. chaps. viii. 5 and xi. 19); *there was a great earthquake, such as was not from the time there was a man upon the earth.* The earthquake, which is the shaking down of the kingdom of evil (comp. Heb. xii. 26—29), completes the overthrow of which the earlier judgments have been precursors. The throne of the wild beast has been visited, the centre of his power smitten; now the metropolis of his empire is about to fall. *And the great city* (*i.e.*, Babylon, the symbol of the world-power's capital) *became into three parts.* It lost its power of cohesion. The three evil spirits endeavoured to unite all powers in one grand assault, but there is no natural cohesion among those whose only bond is hatred of good. The first convulsion shakes them to pieces, and the cities of the nations fall. Every subordinate power in which the earthly element was mingled (comp. Dan. ii. 41—44) is overthrown in the earthquake, even as every tree which the "Heavenly Father hath not planted shall be rooted up" (Matt. xv. 13); and great Babylon was remembered before God, &c. The features of the overthrow of Babylon are described more fully later on (chaps. xvii., xviii.), where the various aspects of evil in the great metropolis of the world-power are dealt with (chaps. xvii. 1—7, and xviii. 1—3). The fall of Pagan Rome is but one illustration of the overthrow of Babylon.

(20) **And every island fled.**—So wide-spread are the effects of the earthquake; the convulsion tests every spot; there is only one kingdom which cannot be shaken. (Comp. Dan. ii. 44; vi. 26; Heb. x. 28.)

(21) **And there fell . . .**—*And a great hail, as of a talent in weight, descends from the heaven on men.* There is again a reference to the Egyptian plagues. But we may also call to mind the great defeat of the enemies of Israel at Beth-horon (Josh. x. 1—11), when "the Lord cast down great stones from heaven." Such an overthrow awaits every confederacy that sets itself in array against the kingdom of the righteous King. The discomfiture and the plague works no repentance; the men blaspheme God because of the hail, *for great is its plague exceedingly.* The proud, hard spirit which still hates the good remains: thus is sin its own worst penalty. As an illustration of this hard, unsubdued spirit, we may call to mind Capaneus, in Dante's *Inferno*, and the words in which Virgil addresses him:—

> "Thou art more punished, in that this thy pride
> Lives yet unquenched; no torment save thy rage
> Were to thy fury pain proportioned full.

The unrepentant state of those upon whom the vials are poured is to be contrasted with the different result of the earthquake in chap. xi. 13, when men gave glory to the God of heaven.

XVII.

This chapter and the following give the more minute account of great Babylon. We have had mention of her before in general terms (chaps. xiv. 8; xvi. 9) as the metropolis of the wild beast's empire, the great city hostile to Jerusalem, the city of the saints. The Evangelist is now told more particularly her character, crimes, power, and position. She is seen clothed in splendour, intoxicated with her own power and cruelty, supported by the wild beast, and hostile to the cause of the righteous King; but doomed to fall, amidst the wonder of the world and the rejoicing of the saints (chap. xviii. 17—21).

(1) **And there came . . .**—One of the vial-bearing angels summons the seer, saying, *Hither I will show thee the judgment of the great harlot that sitteth upon many waters* (or, *the many waters*—comp. verse 15). *The kings of the earth have committed fornication with her, and they who inhabit the earth were made drunken* (lost their reason and self-control) *from the wine, the delicious and delirious draught of her fornication.* Before we go further, it is well to make sure of our ground. Babylon was the great city, whose splendour dazzled, and whose power destroyed Jerusalem (Isa. xxxix. 1—8; xiii. 19; xiv. 4, 13, 14; xlvii. 5—8). Against Babylon the voices of the prophets were lifted up (Isa. xxi. 9; Jer. li. 25); she seemed to them the embodiment of splendid vice and resistless power; "the glory of kingdoms,". "the golden city," "who exalted her throne above the stars of God," "who sat as a lady given to pleasures, and flattering herself that she would see no sorrow." In her greatness and her hostility to Jerusalem she became a type of later world-powers; and, in St. John's vision, Babylon, in her purple and her pomp, in her luxuriousness and her tyranny, takes her place. And it is explained in the vision that Babylon is no longer the literal Babylon, but the power which has taken her place of pride and empire. That power was Rome. Rome was in St. John's day just what Babylon had been in the days of the prophets—"the hammer of the whole earth," the "golden cup that made all the earth drunken" (Jer. l. 23; li. 7; comp. verse 2 of this chapter). At the same time, the way in which the Evangelist transfers to the Rome of his day the prophetic language which earlier prophets applied to ancient Babylon (compare these chapters, xvii. and xviii., with Isa. xlvii., Jer. li. 6—14) ought to be sufficient

hither; I will shew unto thee the judgment of the great whore that sitteth upon many waters: (2) with whom the kings of the earth have committed fornication, and the inhabitants of the earth have been made drunk with the wine of her fornication. (3) So he carried me away in the spirit into the wilderness: and I saw a woman sit upon a scarlet coloured beast, full of names of blasphemy, having seven heads and ten horns. (4) And the woman was arrayed in purple and scarlet colour, and decked[1] with gold and precious stones and pearls, having a golden cup in her hand full of abominations and filthiness of her fornication: (5) and upon her forehead *was* a name written, MYSTERY, BABYLON THE GREAT, THE MOTHER OF HARLOTS[2] AND ABOMINATIONS OF THE EARTH. (6) And I saw the woman drunken with the blood of the saints, and with the blood of the martyrs of Jesus: and

1 Or, *gilded.*

2 Or, *fornications.*

---

to warn us against limited and local interpretations, even if the seven-headed wild beast did not show us that the world-power, like the moral principles of which Babylon and Rome were examples, is not confined to one age. If we remember this, we shall see that the Babylon of the Apocalypse, while, undoubtedly, Pagan Rome, cannot be limited to it. Is it, then, the question must be asked, Papal Rome? The answer is: In so far as Papal Rome has wielded tyrant power, turned persecutor, stood between the spirits of men and Christ, depraved men's consciences, withheld the truth, connived at viciousness, sought aggrandisement, and been a political engine rather than a witness for the righteous King, she has inherited the features of Babylon. The recognition of these features led Dante to apply this very passage in the Apocalypse to Rome under the rule of worldly and tyrant popes, when he exclaimed to the shade of Nicholas III. (*Il compiuto*):—

> "Of shepherds like to you the Evangelist
> Was ware, when her who sits upon the waves
> With kings in filthy whoredom he beheld:
> She who with seven heads tower'd at her birth,
> And from ten horns her proof of glory drew
> Long as her spouse in virtue took delight.
> Of gold and silver ye have made your god,
> Differing wherein from the idolater,
> But that he worships one, a hundred ye!"
> —*Inferno*, Cant. xix, 109–117.

(3) **So he carried . . . .**—Better, *And he carried me away into a wilderness in spirit: and I saw a woman sitting upon a wild beast of scarlet colour, teeming with names of blasphemy, having seven heads and ten horns.* We recognise the wild beast as that described in chap. xiii. Now the wild beast carries the woman; for she draws her support from the great world-power. The scene is the wilderness. The contrast between the desolation around her and the splendour of her appearance is striking and suggestive. The woman clothed with the sun (chap. xii. 1), persecuted by the dragon, finds a home in the wilderness into which she is driven. She is persecuted, but not forsaken; she can joy in tribulation. The scarlet-clad woman, amid all her dazzling surroundings, is still in a wilderness. The runagates continue in scarceness. Sansjoy is the brother of Sansloy. The wild beast is scarlet in colour. The dragon was red (chap. xii. 3); the woman is clothed in scarlet. Is it the emblem of lawlessness ending in violence? (Comp. Isa. i. 18). It has also a show of sovereignty.

Full of names.—*Teeming with names, &c.*—The living creatures (chap. iv. 8) *teemed* (the same word as here) with eyes, the tokens of ready obedience and true intelligence. The wild beast teems with tokens of lawlessness and self-sufficiency.

(4) **And the woman was arrayed . . .**—Better, *arrayed* (or, *clad*) *in purple* (the colour of the robe which was in mockery put on our Lord—John xix. 2) *and scarlet, gilded* (not "decked") *with gold, &c.* Her appearance is one of imperial splendour. (Comp. the description of Tyre in Ezekiel, chap. xxviii. 13.)

Having a golden cup in her hand . . .—Translate, *Having a golden cup in her hand teeming with abominations and with the unclean things of the fornication of the earth.* Jeremiah (chap. li. 7) called Babylon a "golden cup in the hand of the Lord." The cup had made all the earth drunken; the cup of intoxication, splendid and attractive, was full of an evil power, which robbed men's senses and degraded them. The great city of the world ever holds out such a glittering cup, which

> "Most do taste through fond intemperate desire.
> Soon as the potion works, their human countenance,
> Th' express resemblance of the gods, is changed
> Into some brutish form. . . . . .
> —*Comus*, 68–77.

(5) **And upon her forehead . . .**—It was usual with harlots to wear their name on the forehead; but the name here is more than a name. Like the name impressed upon the foreheads of the saints, it is "the expression of her nature"—

"MYSTERY,
BABYLON THE GREAT,
THE MOTHER OF THE HARLOTS AND OF THE ABOMINATIONS OF THE EARTH."

The word "mystery" is, perhaps, part of the name; it is, at any rate, a prefix which tells us that the name is not literal, but symbolical. Something lies behind, which will be made manifest in due time. (Comp. 2 Thess. ii. 7.) She is mother of harlots. Others, in smaller spheres, will follow her example; but she is the origin and type of all.

(6) **And I saw the woman drunken with the blood of the saints.**—It is said later (chap. xviii. 24) that in her was found the blood of prophets, and saints, and of all that have been slain upon the earth. The cruel spirit of persecution marked old Pagan Rome. She was drunk with their blood. It is not literally true that "all the blood shed on the earth" would be found in Rome, either Pagan or Papal; but it is spiritually true. Just as all the blood from righteous Abel to Zacharias was required of Jerusalem, so also of Babylon; for the spirit is the same spirit of hatred of holiness and love of worldliness. To slay one is to slay all, as to be guilty in one point of the Law is to be guilty of all; for it is not to mere acts, but also to the spirit and drift of men's conduct, that the Scriptures look. It is the Babylon spirit, whether dominant in Rome or in London, that kills the good. Wherever the spirit of worldliness (in its widest sense) is to be

when I saw her, I wondered with great admiration. (7) And the angel said unto me, Wherefore didst thou marvel? I will tell thee the mystery of the woman, and of the beast that carrieth her, which hath the seven heads and ten horns. (8) The beast that thou sawest was, and is not; and shall ascend out of the bottomless pit, and go into perdition: and they that dwell on the earth shall wonder, whose names were not written in the book of life from the foundation of the world, when they behold the beast that was, and is not, and yet is. (9) And here *is* the mind which hath wisdom. The seven heads are seven mountains, on which the woman sitteth. (10) And there are seven kings: five are fallen, and one is, *and*

Chap. xvii. 7—17. The vision explained.

---

found, there is the spirit at enmity with God and good, and there is the Babylon which has slain the saints.

And when I saw her, I wondered . . .—Rather, *And I wondered when I saw her with great wonder* (not "admiration" in our modern sense). Why did St. John wonder? Was it at the splendour or the blasphemous names? Hardly these; for he was familiar with the former in descriptions of Babylon given by the prophets, and with the latter from his own vision in chap. xiii. The wonder probably rose from the strange alliance of the woman with the wild beast. It was not wonderful to see the vision of a wild beast or monster dealing out death and slaughter, but to see a woman allied with the monster and drunken with the blood of the holy provoked astonishment. The woman, too, was a harlot. The prophets had spoken of Israel and Judah as harlots, where they had allied themselves with the world and its dark idolatries (comp. Isa. i. 21; Jer. ii. 20; Ezek. xvi. 15; Hos. ii. 5). Did he read in the form of the vision the hint that in the lapse of years the Church of Christ, like Israel of old, might fall from her high calling and become the ally of the world-power? The hint of it slumbered in the vision.

(7) **And the angel said unto me, Wherefore didst thou marvel?**—Better, *Wherefore didst thou wonder?* The angel explains the mystery or hidden meaning. In doing so he identifies the wild beast which carries the woman with the wild beast of chap. xiii. In that chapter the wild beast was seen wounded to death; the same thought is expressed in this chapter. *The wild beast was and is not.* It has received its death wound: the dying and risen Lord has given the death-blow to the world-power, as He has cast down Satan (chap. xii. 9), put limits to his power (chap. xx. 2), and destroyed him that had the power of death (Heb. ii. 14). In the victory of Christ the wild beast *that was* (*i.e.*, that had in successive ages been seen in the great world-powers) is slain, or, as the angel expresses it, *is not.* But though he is not, though he is to be reckoned as doomed, yet he will show signs of vitality: he will rise into temporary power. *He shall come up out of the abyss.* But the march of his power is only a march to the grave. He *goes to destruction.* Yet this transient revival and apparent recovery from its death-wound will be viewed (as was said in chap. xiii. 3: "all the earth wondered after the wild beast") as a marvel by those whose spirits are not heaven-taught, and whose minds are set upon earthly things. *They that dwell upon the earth shall wonder, whose name is not written on the book of life from the foundation of the world, seeing the wild beast that he was, and is not, and shall be present* (*i.e.*, shall come again).

(9) **And here is the mind . . .**—Better, *Here* (omit "and") *is the mind, &c.* Attention is asked to the fuller explanation which follows. It needs true wisdom to behold many incidents of the world's history and not find stumbling-blocks in them (Pss. lxxiii. 2, 3, and cxix. 165). *The seven heads are seven mountains where the woman sitteth upon them.* The description seems to be drawn from Rome, the seven-hilled city. This keeps the reference to Rome before us, but at the same time the further explanation (in verse 10) widens our thoughts, and shows us that the literalism on which the imagery is based is used to convey a broader symbolical meaning. *The seven heads are seven mountains, &c., and they* (the seven heads; the words "There are seven kings" in the English version are confusing) *are seven kings:* the woman rides on the seven-headed beast; even so Rome dwells on her seven hills, and so also the world-city, seen in vision, sits among the various empires which have risen, like great mountains, in the history of the world.

(10) **And there are seven kings . . . .**—Better, *They are seven kings: five* (not "are fallen," but) *fell, the one is, the other is not yet come; and when he shall come, he must continue a short time.* It has been debated whether these kings are individual sovereigns, or forms of government, or kingdoms. The last view is the one adopted in this Commentary. The wild beast belongs to no one age, but is a power which has risen in every age; the seven heads represent the successive culminations of the world-power. Our space is insufficient to discuss here the whole question. But the language here used and the passages in the earlier prophets, which may be called the parent passages of the present vision, favour the interpretation that great world-kingdoms are intended. The language favours this view. It is said that the "kings fell." The word is the one which has been used for political catastrophe: the cities of the nations fell (chap. xvi. 19); Babylon, it is cried, has fallen (chap. xiv. 8). It suits the overthrow of empires, and is so used in the LXX.; to apply it to individual kings is to ask that it shall be equivalent to "they died." It is to be noticed that the four beasts of Daniel (Dan. vii. 3—8) are declared to be four kings (verse 17), but these kings are not individual kings, but represent kingdoms. (See Dan. vii. 23). This brings us to the drift of the parent passage. Daniel saw four wild beasts rise from the sea; they represented the then great world-power Babylon, and its three successors, Persia, Greece, and Rome. This is a guide to us here, as most commentators admit; but two great world-powers had preceded Babylon, viz., Egypt and Assyria: these figure in the ancient prophecies as forces hostile to the righteous King. St. John, whose visions took the range of the world's drama, could not see the representative of the ever rising spirit of worldly hostility to God's chosen without seeing Egypt and Assyria included. The voices of Moses and Isaiah

the other is not yet come; and when he
cometh, he must continue a short space.
(11) And the beast that was, and is not,
even he is the eighth, and is of the
seven, and goeth into perdition. (12) And
the ten horns which thou sawest are
ten kings, which have received no king-
dom as yet; but receive power as kings
one hour with the beast. (13) These
have one mind, and shall give their
power and strength unto the beast.
(14) These shall make war with the
Lamb, and the Lamb shall overcome
them: for he is Lord of lords, and
King of kings:[a] and they that are with
him *are* called, and chosen, and faithful.
(15) And he saith unto me, The waters
which thou sawest, where the whore

a 1 Tim. 6. 15.

called to him across the centuries that in these the world principle of their day found its clearest and strongest manifestation. In various empires the world-power showed itself: in Egypt, the house of bondage (Ex. xx. 2); in Assyria, that exalted herself against God (Isa. xxxvii. 23); in Babylon, the hammer of the whole earth (Jer. l. 23); in Persia, and in Greece; and in succession these kingdoms fell, only to be succeeded by another—Rome. Five fell; the one is. But what is the seventh, the other who is not yet come? We must recall the appearance of the wild beast. It had seven heads and ten horns. Where were these ten horns? It seems generally admitted that they were all on the seventh head. The seventh head, which represents the seventh kingdom, or manifestation of the world principle which is described as not yet come, then, was different in appearance from the others. It was ten-horned. It had not the same unity of appearance as the others. Now the ten horns are explained as ten kings or minor powers (verse 12). The conclusion, therefore, is that the seventh head must be rather an aggregation of monarchies than a single universal empire. This agrees with Daniel's prophecy that out of the fourth kingdom, which corresponds, as we have seen, with the sixth head of the wild beast here, ten kings should arise (Dan. vii. 7, 23, 24).

The seventh kingdom (the ten-horned head) it is said will, when it arises, continue a "short time." The short time is probably the same as the "one hour" in ver. 12, where the ten kingdoms, represented by the ten horns, receive power one hour with the wild beast.

(11) **And the beast. . .**—Better, *And the wild beast which was, and is not, even he himself is the eighth, and is of the seven, and goeth into destruction.* The wild beast himself, forming as it were an eighth, has to be reckoned with. There are seven heads; when these fall no eighth head will rise, but the wild beast, whose vitality has been seen in these successive heads, forms, as it were, an eighth, which is "out of the seven"—not one of them, but one rising out of them; no eighth empire shall rise, but the wild beast, now smitten in all the seven heads of his power, will, in the convulsive death-throe, seem an eighth power, in which the ebbing life of all the seven finds expression. The wild beast linked itself with seven great empires in succession: these all fell; the wild beast is left, as an eighth: then "the wild beast goes into destruction." As an illustration, we may recall her whom the seven brothers had as wife; last of all the woman, the eighth, which was of the seven, died also. It has been noticed that the wild beast does not "fall," like the others, "but goes into destruction;" there are no more world-powers like those who have fallen, but the wild beast is left, a last power reserved for destruction, a final antichrist, the lawless one whom the Lord will destroy with the brightness of His coming (2 Thess. ii. 3). This fierce and last flickering up of the doomed power of evil is dwelt on again in chap. xx. 7—10.

(12) **And the ten horns . . .**—The explanation of the ten horns. They are the kings, not necessarily, as we have seen, personal kings, but rather kingdoms or nationalities, who received not a kingdom as yet; as they are on the seventh head, the hour of their power is not yet, but comes at the fall of the sixth head: then they receive power one hour. (Comp. "short time" in verse 10.) But though these are sundered powers, they are one in their subjection to the wild beast. They have one mind or judgment, and their power and authority they give to the wild beast. The universal empire idea may disappear, but the spirit and principle of mere earthliness will remain; it needs no vast power like Rome to illustrate its spirit. The ten horns are united in one mind; they move as the wild beast directs; their work and tendency of their power is hostile to Christ. They shall make war with the Lamb; and the Lamb shall conquer them because He is Lord of lords, and King of kings. When do these powers make war with the Lamb? The answer is, they make war when the direction of their policy and morals is in favour of oppression, wrong, worldliness; whenever nations or peoples allow the secular spirit to breathe through all they do, they are not with Christ, they are against Him. There are hints that some "special outbreak" of hostility may take place on the eve of the full manifestation of the righteous King and His kingdom (chap. xix. 16—19); busy evil spirits, lawless utterances, unbrotherly federations, unspiritual conceptions, may pave the way for such; the great crisis will then come, when the issue will be secularity and spirituality. It is not necessary to define the ten kings; the number does not need to be pressed as literal; for in Hebrew, "when a whole was to be divided into parts, ten was the number commonly adopted" (Bähr, quoted by Dr. Currey). The war of the ten kings against the Lamb is brought out more fully in chap. xix. There the King of kings is seen victorious; in His victory they who are with Him, the *called, and chosen, and faithful,* shall share. This threefold description is a brief summary of the Christian life. This is the only place where St. John employs the word translated "called." (Comp. Matt. xx. 16.)

(15) **And he said unto me . . .**—Better, *And he* (*i.e.*, the angel mentioned in ver. 1) *saith, &c.* The waters on which the harlot sits are explained as "multitudes." We have thus a key to the imagery employed here and elsewhere (chap. xiii. 1). The wild beast and the harlot both draw much of their power from the people. The easily-moved passions of the fickle crowd, its generous, unreasoning impulses, are used by subtle and seductive enemies. "Men never so much need to be theocratic as when they are most democratic," said De Tocqueville. They need to recognise God as their

sitteth, are peoples, and multitudes, and
nations, and tongues. (16) And the ten
horns which thou sawest upon the
beast, these shall hate the whore, and
shall make her desolate and naked, and
shall eat her flesh, and burn her with
fire. (17) For God hath put in their
hearts to fulfil his will, and to agree,
and give their kingdom unto the
beast, until the words of God shall
be fulfilled. (18) And the woman
which thou sawest is that great city,
which reigneth over the kings of the
earth.

A.D. 96.

a ch. 14. 8.

CHAPTER XVIII.—(1) And after
these things I saw another
angel come down from
heaven, having great power;
and the earth was lightened with his
glory. (2) And he cried
mightily with a strong
voice, saying, Babylon [a]
the great is fallen, is fallen, and is

Chap. xviii. 1—24. The fall of Babylon.

Chap. xviii. 2—3. Her demoralisation.

King, then, most when their new discovered strength is likely to be made the tool of unscrupulous ambition.

(16) **And the ten horns. . .**—Translate, *And the ten horns which thou sawest* (not, as in English version, "on the beast," but), *and the wild beast, these shall hate the harlot.* The harlot was seen in splendid apparel riding on the wild beast; now the wild beast, in the day of the seventh head, turns with the ten horns of his power upon her, makes her deserted, strips her of her adornments, consumes the spoil—for this is what is meant by " eating her flesh"—and burns her with fire. The woman in the days of the Evangelist was Rome (verse 18), but great and resistless as her power seemed, it was doomed; the day would come when other kingdoms would rise who would hate her for her tyranny, envy her splendour, and covet her wealth. Then the great Babylon would fall, like Jezebel of old; he painted cheek, the pencilled eyebrow, and the amorous glance have lost their fascination; those who have pandered to her vices would turn against her, and cast her out to be trampled under foot. So did the Babylon of St. John's day fall—perishing in the blood that she had spilt, or left "childless and crownless in her voiceless woe."

(17) **For God hath put. . .**—Better, *For God gave it into their hearts to do his mind, and* (*to do*) *one mind, and to give their kingdom, &c.* The kings give their kingdom to the wild beast; their authority and might is used for him, whether in making war upon the Lamb (verse 14) or in casting down the harlot. In these enterprises they act unitedly; there is given to them to make "one mind." But they are only carrying out the righteous will of God; God wills that the harlot shall fall; and even in their war upon the Lamb, they are but preparing for the crisis when the foes of the righteous King shall fall (chap. xix. 19). Thus does the wrath of man ever turn to God's praise.

(18) **And the woman which thou sawest . . .**—Read, *And the woman whom thou sawest is* (not "that," but) *the great city, which has a kingdom over the kings of the earth.* With these words the angel's explanation of "the mystery of the woman" (see verse 7) ends. The harlot is a city; the Babylon of the past lives again in Rome; the woman is Rome, the goddess of lands and peoples."

"She who was named Eternal, and arrayed
Her warriors but to conquer—she who veiled
Earth with her haughty shadow and displayed
Until the o'er canopied horizon failed
Her rushing wings—Oh! she who was Almighty hailed."

XVIII.

THE FALL OF BABYLON.—In the commencement of the last chapter the angel (one of the vial-bearing angels) had promised to show the seer the judgment of the harlot (verse 1); he was accordingly shown first the vision of the scarlet-clad woman seated on the wild beast. The seer was filled with wonder, and the angel entered into explanation of the mystery of the woman, touching on her relation to the beast, and her ultimate doom, and revealing to him who she was. But though the angel has proclaimed her overthrow in his explanatory statement, the judgment of the harlot has not been seen in the vision; we must, in fact, regard the portion of the last chapter, from verse 7 to the end, as a kind of parenthesis, a pause in the drama of vision, the action of which is resumed in chap. xviii. Yet though the dramatic action is taken up, we are not shown in vision her actual overthrow; but we gather it from the four agencies which are put forward—the angel which proclaims her moral fall (verses 1—3); the voice from the heaven which gives the vivid description of her sudden overthrow, and of the marvellous sensation it occasioned (verses 4—20); the angel which tells the irremediable character of her overthrow (verses 21—24); and finally, the chorus of the heavenly multitude rejoicing over her fall (chap. xix. 1—4).

(1) **And after these things . . .**—Or, better, *After these things* (omit "and") *I saw another angel coming down, having great power* (or, *authority*—entrusted to him for the work against Babylon); *and the earth was illumined by* (literally, *out of*) *his glory.* The light which shines from the heavenly messenger shines like day upon the tawdry splendour of Babylon, and shows that what was admired was but worthless and corrupt. In his brief, but rousing call, he proclaims it to be so.

(2) **And he cried . . .**—We must omit "mightily," and render, *And he cried in a mighty voice, saying, Fallen, fallen is Babylon the great, and is become an habitation of demons, and a prison of every unclean spirit, and a prison of every unclean and hated bird.* Those who walk in darkness, and whose eyes the god of this world hath blinded through their lusts, look only on the material side, upon prosperous times, large revenues, rapidly developing resources. The great city of the world looks fair and glorious in their eyes, and even the godly are dazzled by her beauty; but when the light of heaven shines, her fall is seen to be inevitable, for she is seen to be hateful; her palaces are seen to be prisons, her highest wisdom little more than low cunning, her most exalted intelligence base-born, her sweetest songs discordant cries; the evil spirit, welcomed back, has come in seven-fold power; for the dry places afford no rest to those who still love sin and the pleasures of sin. The description in this verse is drawn largely from Isa. xiii. 21, 22; it is a picture of desolation and degradation, but it has its moral counterpart.

become the habitation of devils, and the
hold of every foul spirit, and the cage of
every unclean and hateful bird. (3) For
all nations have drunk of the wine of the
wrath of her fornication, and the kings
of the earth have committed fornication
with her, and the merchants of the
earth are waxed rich through the abun-
dance[1] of her delicacies. (4) And I heard
another voice from heaven,
saying, Come out of her,
my people, that ye be not
partakers of her sins, and that ye re-
ceive not of her plagues. (5) For her
sins have reached unto heaven, and God
hath remembered her iniquities. (6) Re-
ward her even as she rewarded you,
and double unto her double according
to her works: in the cup which she hath
filled fill to her double. (7) How much
she hath glorified herself, and lived de-
liciously, so much torment and sorrow
give her: for she saith in her heart, I
sit a queen, and am no widow,[a] and
shall see no sorrow. (8) Therefore shall
her plagues come in one day, death, and
mourning, and famine; and she shall
be utterly burned with fire: for strong
is the Lord God who judgeth her.
(9) And the kings of the earth, who

Chap. xviii. 4—20. The dirge of doom.

1 Or, *power.*
a Isa. 47. 8.

---

(3) **For all nations have drunk . . .**—Better, *Because by the wrath of her fornication* (comp. chap. xiv. 8, and Note there) *all the nations have drunk* (or, according to another reading, *have fallen;* the readings are akin: the drinking of it leads to their degradation and fall), *and the kings of the earth committed* (not "have committed") *fornication with her, and the merchants of the earth waxed rich out of the strength of her luxury.* She has been an enemy to mankind viewed in three great aspects: nations, kings, and merchants. She has brought delirium upon nations; she has reduced kings; she has bribed merchants: her sins are strong sins; with both hands earnestly has she sinned.

(4—20) The voice out of heaven warns the faithful to leave her, and describes her fall.

(4) **Voice from heaven . . .**—Read, *Voice out of heaven, saying, Come forth out of her, my people, that ye partake not in her sins, and that of her plagues ye receive not.* The voice is not said to be that of another angel. It is not necessary to say whose voice it is; that it is a voice of divine love giving warning is enough. The coming forth is not to be understood of a bodily exodus from Rome. It is rather the warning which is so needful in every corrupt state of society, to have no fellowship with the unfruitful works of darkness; to practise that separation from the spirit of the world which is essential lest we should be entangled in the meshes of its sinful habits. This duty of separation may sometimes lead to a literal exodus, and even under the pressure of overwhelming necessity to secession from a world-corrupted church; but the jeopardy lies in attachment to the world-spirit (1 John ii. 15). The parallel warnings in Jer. li. 6, 45, and Zech. ii. 6, 7, should be read; but the story of Lot in Sodom best illustrates the spirit of the passage (Gen. xix.), for it is participation in sin which is to be primarily guarded against.

(5) **For her sins have reached . . .**—Better, *For her sins have reached as far as heaven.* The idea is of a great heap firmly fastened, and towering, like another Babel, as far as heaven. (Comp. 2 Chron. xxviii. 9, and Ezra ix. 6.) The idea is more than that of the cry of sin reaching heaven, as in the case of Sodom (Gen. xviii. 20, 21); the sins themselves, many and imperial, have touched the face of heaven. God hath remembered her. (Comp. chap. xvi. 19). Sometimes the oppressed have thought that God had forgotten the voice of the enemy (Ps. lxxiv. 10—23); but the long-suffering of the Lord is salvation (2 Pet. iii. 8—15).

(6) **Reward her even as she rewarded . . .**—The same voice which bids the people of God come forth, summons the agents of vengeance. Chap. xvii. 16 tells whence these may arise. Read, *Give back to her, as she herself also gave back* (the word "you" should be omitted; it is not the saints, or those who have suffered from her, that are called to repay her), *and double* (the) *double according to her works; in the cup in which she mingled, mingle for her double.* Many Old Testament parallels will suggest themselves (Jer. li. 18; Ps. lxxix. 12; cxxxvii. 8; and Isa. xl. 2). The "double" must not be taken to mean double her sins; her sins are themselves called double, and her judgment is according to her sins. She is double-stained in wickedness, and "the law of retribution fiercely works" in her. The cup of her luxuriousness becomes the cup of vengeance. (Comp. chap. xiv. 8; xvii. 4; and verse 3.) The flowery path "has led to the broad gate and the great fire."

(7) The thought of retribution is carried on in this verse. It should not read, "How much . . .," but, *In as many things as she glorified herself and luxuriated, so much give to her torment and grief; because in her heart she saith* (comp. Ps. xlix. 11; Luke xiv. 30), *I sit a queen, and am not a widow, and shall never see sorrow.* The words are echoes of prophecies against old Babylon (Isa. xlvii. 7—9) and Tyre (Ezek. xxviii. 2).

(8) **Therefore shall her plagues come . . .**—Read, *For this cause in one day shall come her plagues, death and mourning . . . and* with *fire shall she be burnt, for strong is the Lord God who judged her.* God, the mighty God, has passed sentence. She thought herself strong; she forgot the strength of the Almighty. Her plagues are four-fold, as though from every quarter her trouble came: "death for her scorn of the prospect of widowhood; mourning, for her inordinate revelling; famine, for her abundance;" and fire, the punishment of her fornication (Lev. xx. 14; xxi. 9). (Comp. the series of contrasts in Isa. iii. 24—26.)

THE LAMENT OF THE KINGS (verses 9, 10).—(Their words of lament are given in verse 10.)

(9) **And the kings of the earth . . . .**—Read, *And there shall weep and mourn over her the kings of the earth, who with her committed fornication and luxuriated, when they see the smoke of her burning, standing afar off because of the fear of her torment, saying, Woe, woe, the great city, Babylon the strong city; because in one hour is come thy judgment.* Kings, merchants (verses 11—17), shippers (verses 17—19)

have committed fornication and lived deliciously with her, shall bewail her, and lament for her, when they shall see the smoke of her burning, (10) standing afar off for the fear of her torment, saying, Alas, alas that great city Babylon, that mighty city! for in one hour is thy judgment come. (11) And the merchants of the earth shall weep and mourn over her; for no man buyeth their merchandise any more: (12) the merchandise of gold, and silver, and precious stones, and of pearls, and fine linen, and purple, and silk, and scarlet, and all thyine[1] wood, and all manner vessels of ivory, and all manner vessels of most precious wood, and of brass, and iron, and marble, (13) and cinnamon,[a] and odours, and ointments, and frankincense, and wine, and oil, and fine flour, and wheat, and beasts, and sheep, and horses, and chariots, and slaves,[2]

1 Or, *sweet.*

a Ex. 30. 23; Prov. 7. 17; Cant. 4. 14.

2 Or, *bodies.*

---

join in lamenting the overthrow of the great city; all stand afar off, as though fearing to be involved in her ruin; all cry, "Woe" (or, *Alas!*) at the beginning of their lament; and at the close the words, "in one hour," telling the suddenness of the great city's overthrow, recur (verses 10, 17, 19) with the monotony of a passing bell heard at intervals amid the strains of sad music. The parallel passages in Ezek. xxvi. 15, 16; xxvii. 35, should be compared. The grief described is the result of fear mingled with selfishness; the mourners remember with a regret, only tempered with terror, the voluptuous life, the quick-growing profits, and the varied commercial advantages which they have lost in her overthrow.

THE LAMENT OF THE MERCHANTS (verses 11—17).—The lament proper, that is, the actual words put in the mouths of the merchants, is contained in verses 16, 17. The immediately preceding verses describe the various kinds of merchandise which were dealt in.

(11—13) **And the merchants of the earth . . .**—Better, *The merchants of the earth weep and mourn* (not "shall weep;" the vividness of the description is intensified by the use of the present tense) *over her; because their cargo no one buyeth any longer*—the cargo of gold, &c. The list of the cargoes and merchandise is not without arrangement. The various goods are placed in groups. The *treasures* come first—gold, silver, precious stones, and pearls. The *soft goods* used for raiment are placed next—fine linen, purple, silk and scarlet; in the description of Dives, clothed in purple and fine linen (*Byssus*, the same word as here), we have a suggestive resemblance. Materials used in giving splendour to the furnishing of houses come next. Thyine wood, and every article (vessel, as in the English version, is hardly wide enough in meaning) of ivory, costly wood, brass, iron, and marble. The thyine wood was derived probably from a kind of citron-tree of African growth; the wood was sweet-scented, and was a favourite wood for doors, panels, and ceilings; its rich brown hue was often relieved by inlaid ivory. To articles used in furniture aromatics succeed. Cinnamon, amomum (this is omitted in the English version, but authority is in favour of its insertion), odours, ointments, and frankincense. Cinnamon, on its use, comp. Ex. xxx. 2, 3; it was one of the perfumes employed to enhance the delight of the voluptuary (Prov. vii. 17). It is doubtful whether it is the same as our modern cinnamon. Amomum, a kind of sweet-scented shrub, yielding an ointment much used for the hair. Odours, employed in incense. Next come articles of food—wine, oil, fine meal, wheat, cattle, and sheep. Then come the equipages—horses and chariots. The chariot (*rheda*) was a vehicle much used in Rome by the wealthy classes. Lastly, the traffic in human beings closes the list. Slaves (literally, *bodies*, and souls of men. There is perhaps an allusion specially to those slaves who were attached to the chariots or litters used by the rich. The traffic in slaves ("persons of men") is mentioned as part of the commerce of Tyre (Ezek. xxvii. 13). The number of slaves in Rome was enormous. "Souls of men." The climax of wicked worldliness is reached in this last; it gives the finishing touch to the picture of society wholly engrossed in pleasure and indolence and selfishness, which lays every market under tribute to add to its luxuriousness, and sacrifices not only the happiness, but the lives and liberties of their fellow-creatures, to their own enjoyment. It has been said that the general description here does not suit Rome, as Rome never was, and never could be, a commercial centre; but the picture is designed to show the corrupt luxury and voluptuousness of society in great Babylon, not necessarily the accumulated merchandize of a great commercial city. The various wares are "for her use and consumption," not for her to sell. All the avenues from every distant spot of the earth found their focus in Rome; her existence, her political supremacy, and her luxuriousness of living, created and sustained all the commercial activity here described; with her fall, the hope of their gains passed from the merchants of the earth. Compare the language of Gibbon:—"The most remote countries of the ancient world were ransacked to supply the pomp and delicacy of Rome. The forests of Scythia afforded some valuable furs; amber was brought from the shores of the Baltic and the Danube; and the barbarians were astonished at the price which they received for so useless a commodity. There was a considerable demand for Babylonian carpets and other manufactures of the East; but the most important and unpopular branch of foreign trade was carried on with Arabia and India. Every year, about the time of the summer solstice, a fleet of an hundred and twenty vessels sailed from Myos-hormos, a port of Egypt on the Red Sea. The coast of Malabar or the island of Ceylon was the usual term of their navigation, and it was in those markets that the merchants from the more remote countries of Asia expected their arrival. The return of the fleet was fixed to the months of December or January; and as soon as their rich cargo had been transported on the backs of camels, from the Red Sea to the Nile, and had descended that river as far as Alexandria, it was poured without delay into the capital of the Empire. The objects of Oriental traffic were splendid and trifling: silk, a pound of which was esteemed in value not inferior to a pound of gold; precious stones also, among which the pearl claimed the first rank after the diamond, and a variety of aromatics that were con-

and souls of men. (14) And the fruits
that thy soul lusted after are departed
from thee, and all things which were
dainty and goodly are departed from
thee, and thou shalt find them no more
at all. (15) The merchants of these
things, which were made rich by her,
shall stand afar off for the fear of her
torment, weeping and wailing. (16) And
saying, Alas, alas that great city, that
was clothed in fine linen, and purple,
and scarlet, and decked with gold, and
precious stones, and pearls! (17) For in
one hour so great riches is come to
nought. And every shipmaster, and all
the company in ships, and sailors, and
as many as trade by sea, stood afar off,
(18) and cried when they saw the smoke
of her burning, saying, What *city is*
like unto this great city! (19) And they
cast dust on their heads, and cried,
weeping and wailing, saying, Alas, alas
that great city, wherein were made rich
all that had ships in the sea by reason
of her costliness! for in one hour is she
made desolate. (20) Rejoice over her,
thou heaven, and *ye* holy apostles and
prophets; for God hath avenged you on

---

sumed in religious worship and the pomp of funerals. The labour and risk of the voyage was rewarded with almost incredible profits; but the profits were made upon Roman subjects, and a few individuals were enriched at the expense of the public" (Gibbon's *Decline and Fall*, vol. i., chap. ii.).

(14) Directly addressed to Babylon herself.

And the fruits that thy soul . . .—Rather, *And the fruits* (or, *the harvest*) *of the desire of thy soul* (that, namely, which thy soul lusteth after) *departed* (not "are departed:" the word expresses the thought that these things "departed once for all") *from thee, and all things that are rich and that are glorious perish from thee, and thou shalt not find them any more.* The descriptive passage is interrupted by this verse, in which Babylon herself is addressed. It is in harmony with the fervour of the whole chapter that the descriptive tone should for a moment give place to this apostrophe. The fruits to which the eye of desire had looked so longingly as to a harvest of delight departed. The desire of the wicked has perished.

(15—17) **The merchants of these things . . .**—The description is resumed. The merchants stand like the kings (see verse 10) afar off, because of the fear of her torment, saying, "Woe! woe! (or, alas! alas!) the great city, because in one hour so great wealth was desolated." The words of this lamentation are parallel to the lament of the kings, the only difference is characteristic—they bewail the sudden decay of the *wealth.* On the fine linen and purple, comp. verse 12, and Luke xvi. 19.

The Lament of the Shipmasters (verses 17—19).—On the whole passage read Ezek. xxvii. 32, &c.

(17, 18) **And every shipmaster . . . .**—Or, better, *And every shipmaster, and every one who sails for a place, and sailors, and all who work the sea, stood afar off, and cried when they saw the smoke of her burning, saying, Who is like the great city?* With this expression compare the similar one applied to the beast (chap. xiii. 4). It is the outcry of those who call to mind, with pain, a glory that was great, but now is gone. It is not to be taken as meaning "what city has suffered as she has?" but rather is it the recollection of her former splendour—"how great she was." This lingering of the mind over delights now vanished is one subtle element of misery. So the hapless Francesca thought—

"There is no greater woe,
Than to remember days of happiness
Amid affliction."—*Inf.* v. 121—3.

(19) **And they cast dust . . .**—Comp. Ezek. xxvii. 30. The casting of dust or earth on the head is a token of sorrow and humiliation; it bears relation to the sitting in the dust. The one upon whom the sorrow had fallen sat in the dust or ashes. The attitude expressed that he had been brought very low, even to the ground. The mourning friends who came round him cast dust on their heads to express that they shared his sorrow. Thus it is related of Job: Job sat in the ashes (Job ii. 8); the friends who came to comfort him sprinkled dust upon their heads towards heaven (verse 12). So in this place, Babylon has been brought low (comp. Isa. xlvii. 1); the mourners, whose gains sink with her fall, throw dust upon their heads.

(19) **Alas! alas! that great city . . .**—The lament is parallel with the laments of the kings and the merchants; the difference is the appropriate reference to the destruction of the shipping interests. *Woe! woe!* (or, *Alas! alas!*) *the great city, in which all who had their vessels on the sea grew rich out of her costliness.* By her "costliness" we are to understand her extravagances of living, and the splendour of her palaces, which drew materials from all ports of the world. The lament ends with the repeated cry, "in one hour." *Because in one hour she was desolated.*

The Call to the Holy to Rejoice.

(20) **Rejoice over her . . . .**—Better, *Rejoice over her, O heaven, and the saints, and the apostles, and the prophets, because God has judged your judgment on* (or, *out of*) *her.* The second portion of the chapter closes with this invitation to the saints to rejoice: they are summoned to rejoice because the law of retribution has worked on her. Your judgment (it is said to the saints) is judged on her. This does not mean a judgment which the saints have decreed, but the judgment which Babylon wrought on the holy is now exacted from her (comp. verse 6, and chaps. vi. 10, and xiii. 10). Heaven, and every class of those whose citizenship has been in heaven, are bidden by the heavenly voice to rejoice. The covetous and the worldly mourn; their minds were set upon a material glory, which has slipped away from their grasp. All saintly souls, whose affections have been towards righteousness and the righteous King, can rejoice; for the wealth of holiness is imperishable, and the fall of Babylon is the removal of one vast hindrance to holiness. It has been argued that the verse represents the Apostles to be in heaven, and from this it has been inferred that the twelve must have all died before the Apocalypse was written, and, if so, St. John was not the writer. The verse, however,

her. (21) And a mighty angel took up a
stone like a great millstone,
and cast *it* into the sea,
saying, Thus with violence
shall that great city Babylon be thrown
down, and shall be found no more at all.
(22) And the voice of harpers, and musicians, and of pipers, and trumpeters,
shall be heard no more at all in thee;
and no craftsman, of whatsoever craft
he be, shall be found any more in thee;
and the sound of a millstone shall be
heard no more at all in thee; (23) and
the light of a candle shall shine no
more at all in thee; and the voice of
the bridegroom and of the bride shall
be heard no more at all in thee: for
thy merchants were the great men of
the earth; for by thy sorceries were all
nations deceived. (24) And in her was
found the blood of prophets, and of
saints, and of all that were slain upon
the earth.

Chap. xviii. 21—24. Her fall is final.

A.D. 96.

CHAPTER XIX.—(1) And after
these things I heard a great
voice of much people in
heaven, saying, Alleluia;
Salvation, and glory, and
honour, and power, unto the Lord our
God: (2) for true and righteous *are* his
judgments: for he hath judged the great

Chap. xix. 1—4. The joy of the heavenly multitude.

---

has no reference whatever to the question: it is not meant to state who have passed into heaven and who have not: it is simply a summons to all who have fought on the side of their Lord to rejoice at the removal of one of the great obstacles to the manifestation of Christ's kingdom. Thus do all holy men, whether on earth or heaven, joy when any giant evil is swept away.

THE IRREMEDIABLE OVERTHROW OF BABYLON SYMBOLICALLY DECLARED.

(21) **And a mighty angel . . .**—The taking up of the stone and casting it into the waters is a symbol drawn from Jeremiah (chap. li.). Jeremiah enjoined Seraiah to bind the prophetic roll to a great stone, and cast them together into the Euphrates. The meaning of the act was explained—"Thus shall Babylon sink and shall not rise," &c. (Jer. li. 63, 64). The great dead mass, sinking helplessly by the law of its own weight, signified a fall past recovery. So Pharaoh and his host sank like lead in the mighty waters. It is the doom Christ foreshadowed as awaiting those who caused His children to fall (Matt. xviii. 6). The mighty angel, strong to lift the ponderous stone, throws it into the sea, saying, Thus with violence (or, *with a bound*) shall Babylon, the great city, be thrown, and shall not be found any more. At one bound, without a single resting-stage in its downward career, without chance or power of recovery, the vast world-city would fall. She who sat as a queen upon many waters, sinks as a stone in the mighty waters. She will not be found any more. The words "any more," or "no more," are repeated in these verses no less than six times, like a funeral knell over the departed greatness which is described.

(22, 23) **And the voice of harpers . . .**—Better, *the sound* . . . The sounds of mirth and triumph, &c., cease: *the sound of harpers, and musicians, and flute-players, and trumpeters, shall not be heard in thee* ANY MORE: the power of wealth has gone; her own right hand has forgotten her cunning: *every craftsman of every craft shall not be found in thee* ANY MORE: the sound of grinding the corn is at an end: *the sound of millstone shall not be heard in thee* ANY MORE: the cheerful lamps of home and feast are extinguished: *light of lamp shall not shine in thee* ANY MORE: the sounds of domestic joy are silenced: *voice of bridegroom and of bride shall not be heard in thee* ANY MORE. The words are an echo of earlier prophecy: "I destroy from them the voice of mirth, and the voice of gladness, the voice of the bridegroom and the voice of the bride, the sound of the millstones, and the light of the candle." It was thus Jeremiah warned Jerusalem of her coming doom (chap. xxv. 10). Now the same judgments are pronounced against the foe of the true Jerusalem.

(23) **For thy merchants were the great . . .**—The judgment does not fall because the merchants were great: it is the sorcery of the next clause which is the true cause of her fall: the merchants are those who traded with her, as well as those who dwelt in her: by "her sorceries" we must understand her artful policy, her attractiveness, and the seductions by which she drew into the meshes of her worldliness and sin the nations around. "In thy sorcery were all the nations led astray" (chap. xiii. 14).

(24) **And in her was found . . .**—It is not by seductiveness only that her guilt is measured: her hands are defiled with blood: the blood of prophets, who had witnessed against her: of saints, whose holy lives were a protest against her sins, and so hateful to her; and "*of all who have been slain on the earth.*" (Comp. chap. xvii. 6, and Note there.) It is not meant that literally all the blood shed by violence had been shed by Rome, or any other single city of which Babylon is type: all that is meant is that Babylon, the world city, is founded on those principles, the logical outcome of which is violence, bloodshed, and hostility to the highest right: those who die by her hands, few or many, are the evidence that the whole tendency of her power is against holiness and truth. In the earthly view, we are guilty of the acts we do: in the heavenly view, we are guilty of all that the spirit and sin of our conduct tends to do. The spirit of transgression is seen in one act as well as in many, and as it is the attitude of the spirit that God looks upon, so in a single act may be gathered up the transgression of the whole law. (Comp. chap. xvii. 6, and Note there; see also Jas. ii. 10). It is the fatal failure to perceive this which leads man to make light of sin, and to undervalue the Cross of Christ.

XIX.

THE CHORUS OF THE HEAVENLY MULTITUDE REJOICING OVER HER FALL.

(1—3) **And after these things I heard . . .**—Or, *I heard, as it were, a mighty voice of a great multitude in the heaven, saying.* The saints who were bidden in the last chapter to rejoice are now heard

whore, which did corrupt the earth with
her fornication, and hath avenged the
blood of his servants at her hand.
(3) And again they said, Alleluia. And
her smoke rose up for ever and ever.
(4) And the four and twenty elders and
the four beasts fell down and worshipped
God that sat on the throne, saying,
Amen; Alleluia. (5) And a voice came
out of the throne, saying, Praise our
God, all ye his servants, and ye that
fear him, both small and great. (6) And
I heard as it were the voice of a great
multitude, and as the voice of many
waters, and as the voice of mighty
thunderings, saying, Alleluia: for the
Lord God omnipotent reigneth. (7) Let
us be glad and rejoice, and give honour
to him: for the marriage of the Lamb
is come, and his wife hath made herself
ready. (8) And to her was granted that
she should be arrayed in fine linen,
clean and white: for the fine linen is
the righteousness of saints. (9) And he

---

raising their songs as in one great voice of praise. The song is as follows :—

Alleluia!
The salvation, and the glory, and the power
Are our God's,
Because true and righteous are His judgments,
Because He judged the great harlot, who corrupted the earth in her fornication,
And avenged the blood of His servants out of her hand,
Alleluia.

This last "Alleluia" clearly belongs to the song or chorus. It is separated from the body of it by the descriptive words (verse 3), *And again they said, Alleluia;* or better, *and a second time they have said.* The Evangelist, as he writes, seems to hear once more the strains of the anthem: he writes down the words, and, as the final "Alleluia" bursts forth after a musical pause, he writes, "once more they have said Alleluia." The word Alleluia occurs in this passage no less than four times (verses 1, 3, 4, 6): it is nowhere else used in the New Testament; but it is familiar to us in the Psalms, as fifteen of them begin or end with "Praise ye the Lord," or "Hallelujah;" and the genius of Handel has enshrined the word in imperishable music. The song here does not begin with ascribing "salvation, &c.," to God, as the English version suggests: it rather affirms the fact: the salvation, &c., is God's. It is the echo of the ancient utterance—"Salvation belongeth unto God." It is the triumphant affirmation of the truth by which the Church and children of God had sustained their struggling petitions, as they closed the prayer which Christ Himself had taught them, saying, when too often it seemed to be otherwise, "Thine is the kingdom, and the power, and the glory." So here they give a threefold praise: the salvation, and the glory, and the power are all God's. The manifestation of His power is in the deliverance of His children from the evil, from the great harlot, and in the avenging the blood of His servants out of her hand, "forcing, as it were, out of her hand the price of their blood."

(4) **And the four and twenty . . .**—The twenty-four elders, the representatives of the Church, and the four living beings, the representatives of nature, fell down and worshipped God who sitteth (not "sat," as in the English version) on the throne. These, too, join in the chorus of praise.

(5–7) **And a voice came.**—From the direction of the throne there came a voice bidding all God's servants rejoice. We are not told whose voice it is. Some have assumed that it is Christ's: it is better to leave it indefinite. In response to the bidding, the voice of praise is heard (like the voice spoken of in chap. xiv. 2), as it were, the voice of a great multitude; and, as it were, the voice of many waters; and, as it were, the voice of mighty thunders. All nature's tones seem mingled in this voice of praise: it is human, it is majestic as the sea, and glorious as the thunder.

The Anthem.

Alleluia!
For the Lord reigned,
The God, the Almighty.
Let us rejoice and exult,
And we will give the glory to Him,
Because the marriage of the Lamb is come,
And His wife hath made herself ready.

In this anthem the word for "reigneth" is not in the present tense, as in the English version; but, though it is translated here "reigned," we must not understand it of the past only: it expresses the exultation of the servants of God that the Kingship of their God is manifested, and vindicated against those who denied, or hated His rule. His reign never ceased; and He has showed that His was a real sovereignty. Their joy rises also from the prospect of the nearer union between the Lamb and His Bride. This close union is more fully spoken of later: here the glorious close is for a moment anticipated: the morning glow announces the coming day: it is near even at the doors. The image of the marriage is familiar. It entered into our Lord's parable (Matt. xxii. 2—10; xxv. 1—10): we catch it in the Psalms and in the Epistles (Ps. xlv., and Eph. v. 23, 30; 2 Cor. xi. 2.)

(8) **And to her was granted . . .**—Better, *And it was given to her that she should be clothed in fine linen, bright, pure; for the fine linen is the righteousness* (or, *righteousnesses;* the word is plural) *of the saints.* This verse is not to be taken as part of the song. The song closes with the announcement that the Lamb's wife has made herself ready. Then follows the explanation of this readiness: she is adorned in fine linen. Her apparel is in contrast to the harlot: it is not purple and scarlet (chaps. xvii. 4 and xviii. 16), but pure white. The symbol is explained: "the fine linen is the righteousness (or, *righteousnesses*) of the saints." The raiment is that which strikes the eye: it has its character, and it indicates the character of the wearer. The harlot attracts by ostentatious colours, the tokens of qualities more conspicuous than abiding, more dazzling than helpful; the Lamb's wife is robed in pure and stainless white, the token of those high, moral, spiritual qualities by which she has been known. The source of these righteousnesses is divine: it is given to her to be so arrayed. It is no fictitious righteousness: it is real, it is hers, though it would never have been hers but for Him without whom she can do nothing (comp. John xv. 4, 5, and Phil. iii. 8—10): and it is through the wearing of this white flower of a blameless life that she has borne witness for her Lord, and against the spirit of harlotry and sin (Matt. vii. 16—18).

(9) **And he saith unto me . . .**—Who is the

saith unto me, Write, Blessed *are* they
which are called unto the marriage sup-
per of the Lamb.[a] And he saith unto
me, These are the true sayings of God.
(10) And I fell at his feet to worship him.
And he said unto me, See *thou do it*
not: I am thy fellowservant, and of thy
brethren that have the testimony of
Jesus: worship God:[b] for the testimony
of Jesus is the spirit of prophecy. (11) And
I saw heaven opened, and behold a white
horse; and he that sat upon him *was* called
Faithful and True, and in righteousness
he doth judge and make war. (12) His
eyes *were* as a flame of fire, and on his
head *were* many crowns; and he had a
name written, that no man knew, but he
himself. (13) And he *was* clothed with a

a Matt. 22. 2.

b ch. 22. 9.

---

speaker? The general and simplest opinion is that it is the angel mentioned in chap. xvii. 1 who speaks. The speaker bids the seer *write:* "Blessed are they who are bidden to the supper of the marriage of the Lamb." This is one of the six benedictions of the Apocalypse (comp. chaps. i. 3; xiv. 13; xx. 6; xxii. 7, 14): it is founded on our Lord's parables (Matt. xxii. 1 and xxv. 1; comp. also chap. iii. 20): the blessing of the call to the marriage supper is more clearly realised now that the day of joy is at hand. We must not draw too sharp distinctions, as some have done, between the bride and the guests: the imagery is varied to give fulness and force to the truths which no emblems can adequately express. The Church of Christ will rest, and feast, and reign with her Lord; and in all the peace, gladness, and triumph of that joy-time God's servants will share. A solemn confirmation of this follows, as in chaps. xxi. 5 and xxii. 6: "these words are true (sayings) of God."

(10) **And I fell at his feet . . .**—The impulse to worship the messenger who had unfolded such visions was not unnatural: the immediate checking of it here and in chap. xxii. 8, 9, on the part of the angel, supplies an indirect evidence of the genuineness of the whole book, and gives it a moral tone immeasurably superior to the vision-books of pretended revelations. *And he saith to me, See* (or, *take heed*) *not* (i.e., *to do it*); *I am a fellow-servant of thee and of thy brethren who have the testimony of Jesus: worship God; for the testimony of Jesus is the spirit of prophecy.* One bond of service unites angels and men: to be servants of God is the highest title they can attain; worship is for God alone. The words "worship God" are most emphatic: "to God give thy worship, and not to me, who am but thy fellow-servant." The angel is his fellow-servant, and at that time he was emphatically so, as he and the Apostle were engaged in one common work—"the testimony of Jesus." The Apostle's work in the world was the testimony of Jesus (chap. i. 2, 9), and the Spirit of prophecy which moved (2 Pet. i. 21) the angel was likewise the testimony of Jesus. One work and one worship belong to both. He whom Apostles worshipped unrebuked (Matt. xxviii. 9, 17) was the one whom all the angels of God were bidden to worship (Ps. xcvii. 7; Heb. i. 6). It is wonderful, with this emphatic witness to our Lord Jesus Christ, any should have undervalued this book of Revelation, as one which failed to honour Him.

(11) **And I saw heaven opened . . .**—Better, *And I saw the heaven opened* (not "opening," but set open, already opened, as in chap. iv. 1), *and behold a white horse, and* (*behold*) *one that sitteth upon him called Faithful and True, and in righteousness He judgeth and warreth.* The description reminds us of the opening of the first seal. Again we have the white horse, and the rider. That early vision of a conquering Christ had been first a hope and then a despair, as age after age interposed its obstacles to the manifestation of the sons of God; but now, with added splendour, the vision is renewed: the hopes of the waiting shall not perish for ever. Once more the victorious rider appears, and His name dispels all fear, though the vision has been long in tarrying. At the end it speaks and does not tarry (Habak. ii. 1—4), for He who rides upon the heavens, as it were upon a horse, has His name Faithful and True (Heb. x. 23, and 36—38). This name combines two characteristics: fidelity to promises, trustworthiness; and the power to satisfy every legitimate desire which has been awakened in the hearts of His people; for in Him all hopes find repose, and every ideal is realised. He is further pictured as a warrior. This warrior bridegroom carries us back to Ps. xlv., where a similar combination of marriage joy and martial triumph is found. Righteousness marks His progress in war, as faithfulness is manifested towards those who trust Him (Isa. xi. 4, 5). Here is comfort on the threshold of a vision of deliverance. The book has shown us war, conflict, confusion: the passions of men surging against one another, and dashing like vain waves against God's immutable laws; the world history is written in blood. We blame men for these cruel and desolating wars; but another question rises imperiously, Why does an all-good ruler allow these heart-breaking scenes? If earth's groans pain and trouble us, do they not grieve Him? Where is He that He permits all this? The answer is, "In righteousness He judges and makes war." The worked-out history of the world will make this plain. The righteousness of God is being revealed: all will see it one day; but now the just must live by faith in Him who is faithful and true, and who preserves the germ of all divine life in the history of the world.

(12, 13) **His eyes were as a flame . . .**—Or, rather, *And His eyes are* (*as*) *a flame of fire, and upon His head many diadems*—(*He*) *having names written, and a name written which no one knows but He Himself—and clothed in a vesture dipped in blood, and His name is called The Word of God.* On the description here and in verse 5, comp. Notes on chap. i. 14—16. There is no doubt who is before us in this vision. These *flame-like eyes* have been fixed upon the moving scenes of human life, and have been reading the hearts of men, and the true meaning of all events and actions. All things have been naked and open to the eyes of Him with Whom we have to do" (Heb. iv. 13). He wears many *crowns*—diadems—crowns rather of royalty than of victory. Some have thought that the crowns He wears are crowns taken from the heads of the kings who have made war with Him (chap. xvii. 12, 13, and 19). It is needless to suppose this; their crowns were His before they were discrowned. The diadems He wears proclaim that not only over a world-wide empire He is king, but of all nations He is truly king. He is not as an emperor among kings, the head of a federation of princedoms; but He is truly King—King of history, King of life, King of human hearts,

vesture dipped in blood:[a] and his name
is called The Word of God. (14) And the
armies *which were* in heaven followed
him upon white horses, clothed in fine
linen, white and clean. (15) And out of
his mouth goeth a sharp sword, that
with it he should smite the nations: and
he shall rule them with a rod of iron:
and he treadeth the winepress of the
fierceness and wrath of Almighty God.
(16) And he hath on *his* vesture and on

a Isa. 63. 2.
b ch. 17. 14

his thigh a name written, KING OF
KINGS, AND LORD OF LORDS.[b]
(17) And I saw an angel standing in the
sun; and he cried with a
loud voice, saying to all the
fowls that fly in the midst
of heaven, Come and gather
yourselves together unto the supper of the
great God; (18) that ye may eat the flesh
of kings, and the flesh of captains, and
the flesh of mighty men, and the flesh

Chap. xix. 17—21. The wild beast and false prophet overthrown.

King everywhere, over each realm and over all realms, King of kings, and Lord of lords. He has *names written, and a name.* The clause having "names written" is omitted in the English version. The authority for its insertion is not entirely satisfactory; but perhaps the balance of evidence is in its favour. He has many names which may be understood, besides a name which no one knows. This is fitting in One who is known to men as Shepherd, Redeemer, Saviour, Prince of Life, but the fulness of Whose love and power none can exhaust, and the depth of Whose wisdom none can fathom. "He knows our names. Thanks be to God, we cannot fathom the depths of His." There is more yet to be known of Him in the world to which we go. His vesture is dipped in blood. The prophet Isaiah (chap. lxiii. 2) probably supplied the foundation of this description. (Comp. verse 15.) The blood-red vesture is a fit token of the work. He comes to destroy those that destroy the earth—to tread the winepress of the wrath of God; but we cannot forget that He who comes for this came first to shed His own blood. He is, too, "The Word of God." Again we hear this name; it is a name which is, besides other things, significant of Christ's mediating work. He is the Word who was with God, who was God, and who declares God to man. (Comp. John i. 1—4; iii. 13; xiv. 9.) The title the Word, the Word of God—used here and in the Gospel of St. John (chap. i. 2; John i. 1; 1 John i. 1)—is a token of their common authorship. (See *Introduction* and *Excursus A: The Doctrine of the Word,* in Commentary on the Gospel.)

(14) **And the armies . . .**—The words "which were" should be omitted. *The armies in heaven followed Him.* Some would limit these to angels. The apparel which they wear—the fine linen (*byssus*) "which is the righteousness of saints" (see verse 8)—is conclusive against this limited view. The saints who have fought the good fight here, and who loved not their lives unto the death, will share the triumph of their king. (Comp. also chap. xvii. 14.) The horses upon which they are seated are *white.* The raiment they wear is *white, pure.* (Comp. verse 8, and chaps. iii. 4; vii. 14.) The hue of triumph is here, but it is the triumph of righteousness. (Comp. also Ezek. xxxviii. 4.)

(15) **And out of his mouth . . .**—Translate, *And out of His mouth goeth a sharp sword, that with* (literally, *in*) *it He may smite the nations: and He* (*Himself*) *shall shepherd them with* (literally, *in*) *a rod of iron: and He* (*Himself*) *treadeth the winepress of the wine of the wrath of the anger of God the All ruler.* The sharp sword is the same that we have read of before (chap. i. 16); there it was called the two-edged sword. The omission of the epithet in this passage, which describes the Word of God as the conqueror and the judge, is not without significance. The sword is now wielded for but one work—the *word* that Christ spoke will judge men at the last day (John xii. 48). The power of this word found an illustration in the falling back of the hostile band which came to take Him in the day of His humiliation (John xviii. 5); yet more gloriously will the power of His word be felt (comp. Isa. xi. 4; Jer. xxiii. 29; 2 Thess. ii. 8) when He will slay the wicked with the word of His mouth. The passage in Ps. ii. 9 must be borne in mind. Christ comes as King; His is a rule in righteousness; those who oppose this kingdom of righteousness find the shepherd's staff as a rod of iron; the stone rejected falls upon the builders, and grinds them to powder. It is thus that the winepress of God's wrath is set up, and the righteous King appears as one who treads it out. (Comp. Isa. lxiii. 1—3.) *He* Himself (the emphasis lies here) treads it. We have again the figure of the vintage made use of. (Comp. chap. xiv. 20.) It is the harvest of retribution; the wicked are filled with the fruit of their own doings; so is the work seen to be the work of the All-Ruler.

(16) **And he hath on his vesture . . .**—The King rides at the head of His host. On His robe, where it spreads out from the waist, His title is inscribed; it proclaims Him to be the one who is the true supreme King of all. Inscriptions on the outer garments were sometimes used by distinguished personages. The title anticipates the final victory; His power is irresistible, his Kingship is universal.

Overthrow of the Wild Beast and of the False Prophet.—The birds of prey gather beforehand (verses 17, 18). The beast, and the kings of the earth hostile to the King of kings, gather for war (verse 20). Their defeat and fate (verses 21, 22).

(17, 18) **And I saw an angel . . .**—Better, *And I saw an* (literally, *one*) *angel standing in the sun; and he cried with a great voice, Hither be gathered together to the great supper of God, that ye may eat flesh of kings, and flesh of captains of thousands, and flesh of mighty men, and flesh of horses, and of them that are seated on them, and flesh of all, of free and of bond, and of small and of great.* The angel stands in the sun—the central spot to summon the birds, and the spot where he stands bathed in the sunlight, the symbol of the divine presence. (Comp. chaps. i. 16; x. 1; xii. 1.) The birds of prey are assembled beforehand; the adversaries of the righteous King have a name to live, but the eagles and vultures are gathered together as though the carcase had already fallen (Matt. xxiv. 28; comp. Ezek. xxxix. 17—20). The supper or banquet is the chief meal in the day, the meal to which guests would be invited. The banquet or supper here is in

of horses, and of them that sit on them,
and the flesh of all *men, both* free and
bond, both small and great. (19) And I
saw the beast, and the kings of the earth,
and their armies, gathered together to
make war against him that sat on the
horse, and against his army. (20) And
the beast was taken, and with him the
false prophet that wrought miracles be-
fore him, with which he deceived them
that had received the mark of the beast,
and them that worshipped his image.
These both were cast alive into a lake of
fire burning with brimstone. (21) And
the remnant were slain with the sword
of him that sat upon the horse, which
sword proceeded out of his mouth:
and all the fowls were filled with their
flesh.

A.D. 96.

CHAPTER XX.—(1) And I saw an
angel come down from
heaven, having the key of
the bottomless pit and a

Chap. xx. 1—3. The Millennium. Binding of Satan.

contrast with the marriage supper of the Lamb (verse 9), and with the great supper (Luke xiv. 16—24) from which the invited guests turned away. All classes—the great and small, the master and slave—are mentioned. Those who follow the world-power, and array themselves in hostility to the true King, belong not to one class, but may be found among all. The war is not between class and class, but between righteousness and unrighteousness, truth and falsehood, Christ and Belial. We must remember that the vision is a great figurative representation of the defeat of the anti-Christian powers and principles in the world; this will save us from misapprehending its purpose, and from a bondaged literalism.

(19) **And I saw the beast, and the kings . . .**—Rather, *I saw the wild beast.* The wild beast and the kings are gathered to make or wage not merely "war," but "*the* war" (the definite article is used; comp. chaps. xvi. 14; xvii. 14) against the King of kings. It has been noticed that the true King is followed by His army—one army, united by one bond, and under one King. The wild beast is supported by diverse armies, owning allegiance to diverse kings, and united only in hostility to good.

(20) **And the beast was taken . . .**—Or, *And the wild beast was taken, and with him the false prophet who did the signs in his presence . . .* Again the definite article ("*the* signs" or "miracles") recalls to our minds what was before described (chap. xiii. 13); the false prophet is the second wild beast of chap. xiii. He succeeded in deceiving those who received the mark. See Notes on chap. xiii., where their work of deception is described; here our thoughts are fixed upon their doom. *Alive they were cast, the two, into the lake of the fire which burns with brimstone.* The two—the wild beast and the false prophet—who are the anti-Christian leaders are cast into the fiery lake. These leaders are not to be, as we have seen, regarded as particular individuals. It has, indeed, often happened, and will doubtless again happen, that an individual personage places himself at the head of a great anti-Christian movement; yet, in the eye of the seer, such would be but subordinate leaders. The wild beast and the false prophet, directed by the dragon, are the true spiritual chiefs of all such movements. The world-power, whether coarse, ignorant and brutal, or cultured and intellectual, is seized, and consigned to the lake of fire. The imagery here is based upon the Old Testament: the lake, the fire, and the brimstone bring back the geography and the incidents attending the overthrow of Sodom and Gomorrha. (Comp. Num. xvi. 32—34; Isa. v. 14.) The lake of fire is mentioned here for the first time; we hear of it more frequently afterwards (chaps. xx. 10, 14, 15; xxi. 8). The flames and brimstone, smoke, and other volcanic forces indicating the existence of subterranean fire, might well lead the ancients to place their Tartarus and Gehenna in the under-world. (See Note in Moses Stuart on Rev. xiv. 10.) These supplied the imagery which has become crystallised in the language of after-generations.

(21) **And the remnant were slain . . .**—Better, *And the rest were slain with* (literally, *in*) *the sword of Him who is seated on the horse, which* (*sword*) *proceeded out of His mouth; and all the birds were filled with their flesh.* The rest (*i.e.*, the human beings, the kings and the great and small, who have been led away by the world-powers) were slain with the sword of the King. No human being is described here as being cast into the lake of fire—only the two great leaders, the ideal representatives of evil principles, receive that punishment. The sword which goes out of the King's mouth (comp. verse 15 and chap. i. 16) slays the human allies of evil. That word which is quick and powerful (Heb. iv. 12), that word which Christ spoke in the days of His humiliation, that word which is mighty and life-giving (Jas. i. 18) as well as death-giving, wins at the last. The birds devour the flesh. The pride and beauty of men, their apparent strength, the confederations and systems which they have made so strong for themselves, when their heart was fat as brawn, are proved to be worthless and strengthless; all the men whose hands were mighty find nothing (Ps. lxxvi. 5, 6). Thus, while all flesh is seen to be but grass, and all the goodliness and pride of it but as the flower thereof, the righteous word of the Lord stands for ever, and at the last rises up as a sword to smite down and to slay its enemies. "They were killed," says Bengel, "with the destroying sword of Christ, which is not of steel or iron, but goes out of His mouth, and so is a spiritual weapon of resistless might."

XX.

THE MILLENNIUM.—Some few introductory words on this most difficult chapter are needful. The outline of incidents described is very simple. An angel descends, lays hold upon the dragon, binds him, and imprisons him in the abyss, where he remains for a thousand years, after which he is loosed for a short time. During this thousand years the martyrs, and those who had not received the mark of the beast, live and reign with Christ. At the close of this period the dragon is loosed; the nations are once more deceived; the camp of the saints is threatened by the dragon, and those whom he has reduced to his service; but the fire from heaven destroys the adversaries, and the dragon is cast into the lake of fire. The general judgment follows. Simple as the vision appears, every interpretation is

great chain in his hand. (2) And he laid
hold on the dragon, that old serpent,
which is the Devil, and Satan, and
bound him a thousand years, (3) and
cast him into the bottomless pit, and
shut him up, and set a seal upon
him, that he should deceive the nations no more, till the thousand years
should be fulfilled: and after that he
must be loosed a little season. (4) And

---

beset with difficulties. These difficulties are too numerous to be treated of here. Our space will only allow us to indicate the view adopted, though with the greatest hesitation, in this Commentary. (1) The millennium vision is, like so many of the apostolic visions, an ideal picture; it exhibits a state of things which is possible to mankind at any time; for, to use the language of Hengstenberg, "If the earth were to watch and pray for a thousand years, Satan would have nothing on it." Like the vision of the first seal, it shows us that the victory of Christ was a real victory, and has put into man's hand the promise of security against the wicked one's devices. The defeat of Satan (inflicted by redemption) is described as "a fall from heaven" (Luke x. 18), as "a casting out" (John xii. 31), as "a judgment past," "the Prince of this world has been judged" (John xvi. 11). The ideal picture corresponds. "Satan is chained in the abyss, as the angels said by St. Peter to have been delivered into chains of darkness" (2 Pet. ii. 4). (2) But the rejection of Christ's power and victory postpones the realisation of this picture; the sullen refusing of the King's Son, "We will not have this man to reign over us," interposes a barrier against an immediate fulfilment of the vision. But the fulfilment is not utterly lost; the vision is for an appointed time; it will have its realisation, though man's waywardness and unbelief occasion its delay. (3) The vision has its approximate fulfilment as the Church of Christ, in the faith of the reality of her Lord's victory, carries on her warfare against the prince of this world and spiritual wickedness in high places. That this approximate fulfilment is not unreal may be seen in the fact that Christendom has replaced heathendom, Christ has taken the throne of the world, the prince of this world has been judged, the ascendency of Christian thought and Christian principles has marvellously humanised and purified the world. To an Irenæus, a Polycarp, a Justin Martyr, a Tertullian, the picture of the world during the Christian centuries would have the aspect of a millennium, when contrasted with the age of Pagan domination and Pagan persecution. In their eyes, accustomed to the darkness of heathenism, the world as influenced by a widely diffused Christianity would seem to be a world in which Christ ruled. They would see in the acknowledgment of apostles and martyrs and confessors the wondrous resurrection power of God's truth; they would see how those who fell for Christ had stepped from their forgotten graves to sit down with Christ in His throne. The apostles, the martyrs, the faithful do reign with Christ. The sovereignty of the world belongs far more to St. Paul and St. John than to Nero and Galba. But though thus the saints rise and reign with Christ over Christendom, we can see that this is only an approximate realisation, and falls short of the ideal picture. Christendom established and heathendom overthrown would be a millennium in the eyes of an Ignatius; but the Church of to-day looks for a further and higher fulfilment. Is she justified in this expectation? If the principles laid down elsewhere (see Note on chap. vi.) be correct, the Church is justified in looking for the full realisation of the vision in a future age. She can accept the first-fruits of God's promises, but she will not mistake them for the harvest; she can rejoice in the growth of her Lord's kingdom, but she looks for the day when the powers of evil will be more effectually curbed, and the gospel will have freer course. Then the fulness of Christ's victory will be more clearly seen.

THE BINDING OF SATAN.

(1) **And I saw an angel come down . . .**—Rather, *And I saw an angel descending out of the heaven, having the key of the abyss, and a great chain on* (not merely in his hand, but hanging from it as it would do when on) *his hand.* It is needless to settle who is represented by this angel. It is enough that in the vision he manifests by the key and the chain which he carries that there is power in Him, who has the keys of death and of Hades (chap. i. 18), to bind, as He has death-wounded, him that had the power of death. The bottomless pit is the abyss, as we have had elsewhere (chaps. ix. 1; xi. 7; and xvii. 8. Comp. Luke viii. 31); it is figuratively the abode of the devil and his associate angels (Matt. xxv. 41).

(2) **And he laid hold on the dragon . . .**—Or, *And he laid hold of the dragon, the ancient serpent, who is the devil and Satan, and bound him a thousand years.* The four words are thus used to describe the archenemy; they are the same as those used for the same purpose in chap. xii. 9. Over the world he has exercised in every quarter his power as prince of this world, and he has been found fierce as the dragon, subtle as the serpent, the slanderer of God and His people, and the adversary of all righteousness. He is bound as Christ declared (Matt. xii. 29; comp. Col. ii. 15). A thousand years was the length at which Rabbis fixed the duration of Messiah's kingdom. The period is not to be understood literally (see next verse).

(3) **And cast him into the bottomless pit . . .**—Rather, *and cast him into the abyss* (same word as in verse 1), *and locked and sealed* (*the door or mouth*) *above him, that he may not deceive the nations any more until the thousand years shall have been finished; after these things he must be loosed for a little time.* The sealing reminds us of the sealing employed when the wicked one had power through man's agency to imprison God's messengers. (Comp. Dan. vi. 17, and Matt. xxvii. 66.) Of the exact moment when this binding and imprisoning took place it is not needful to inquire too curiously. That which in the vision is described as the work of a moment may in the fact and fulfilment be a very gradual work; or rather, the full manifestation of its accomplishment may be only gradually made clear. To fix it, therefore, to any incident (for example, as Hengstenberg is disposed to do to the coronation of Charlemagne), is to fall into the "vicious realism" against which he rightly protests. The same applies to the duration of the imprisonment; it is not to be understood literally any more than the other numbers in the book; it symbolises a lengthened period. This period is followed by the loosing again of the devil for a short time. (See Note on verse 7.)

THE MILLENNIAL REIGN.

(4) **And I saw thrones, and they sat . . .**—There is a prominence given to the *thrones,* because

Chap. xx. 4–6. The millennial reign.

I saw thrones, and they sat upon them, and judgment was given unto them: and *I saw* the souls of them that were beheaded for the witness of Jesus, and for the word of God, and which had not worshipped the beast, neither his image, neither had received *his* mark upon their foreheads, or in their hands; and they lived and reigned with Christ a thousand years. (5) But the rest of the dead lived not again until the thousand years were finished. This *is* the first resurrection. (6) Blessed and holy *is* he that hath part in the first resurrection: on such the second death hath no power, but they shall be priests

---

the thought of the reign of the saints is uppermost in the mind of the seer. The thrones are seen, and those who sat on them. It has been asked, "By whom are the thrones occupied?" The answer is supplied in the latter part of the verse. Those who are in the latter part said to reign with Christ are clearly those who sit upon the thrones which first caught the prophet's eye; these are all the real servants of God. They appear before the seer in two great classes:—First, the martyrs who have been faithful unto death; for he speaks first of seeing *the souls of those who have been beheaded* (strictly, "slain with the axe," but clearly the special class of beheaded martyrs is to be taken as representing all), *because of the testimony of Jesus, and because of the word of God.* The number of the martyrs is now complete (comp. chap. vi. 11); these form the first class mentioned. Secondly, those who have been faithful in life occupy these thrones. The prophet sees these, even *whosoever did not worship* (during life) *the wild beast, nor yet his image, and did not receive the mark* (comp. chap. xiii. 10) *on their forehead and upon their hand.* The triumph and sovereignty, whatever they be, are shared by all the faithful. These things are stated as constituting their privileges. They lived, whereas the rest of the dead lived not; they reigned, and judgment was given them. This last has been felt to be a difficulty. What sort of judgment is intended? The passage in Daniel (chap. vii. 22) is clearly suggestive of the present one. The phrase (judgment was given) is not there to be understood as meaning that right was done them (see Note in *Speaker's Commentary* on Daniel), neither must it be so understood here. Judicial powers are given to the saints as to those who occupy thrones; "the chief power in governing" (Gebhardt) is given them (comp. Matt. xix. 28, and 1 Cor. vi. 2, 3); they reign, they judge, they live; the true and full powers of life are seen to be theirs. And is not this the case always? Who, next to Him who knows the secrets of our hearts, exercises judicial powers over men? Do not those whose lives, as we read them, rebuke our own? Truly, those who lived for God, and refused the mark of earthliness, reign and judge us in our worldliness and weakness. This is their sovereign honour here, besides the glad reign in the unseen world.

(5) **But the rest of the dead lived not again . . .**—Rather, *The rest of the dead lived not* (we must omit the word "*again*") *until the thousand years be finished. This is the first resurrection.* In those words we meet one of the keys to the controversy respecting the millennium. What is this resurrection? Is it the resurrection at which the saints shall assume the glorified bodies, and their perfect consummation and bliss? It has been argued that the word must be understood literally as of a bodily resurrection. It is further said that the contrasting words ("the rest of the dead lived not") necessitate this literal interpretation. But there is no reason for restricting the word Resurrection to a literal meaning. The sacred writers frequently use the idea figuratively. They speak of a resurrection which is spiritual; the dead in sin are summoned to rise from the dead that Christ might give them light (comp. Eph. ii. 1, and v. 14); indeed, the figure often underlies the language and arguments of New Testament writers (John v. 24, 25; Rom. vi. 5; 2 Cor. v. 15; Col. ii. 12). But do the words, "the rest of the dead lived not," force upon us so sharp a contrast that we must understand the first resurrection literally? Undoubtedly the words are in contrast. If the words "lived not" necessarily mean that the rest of the dead did not enjoy physical life on earth, then the living with Christ of the saints and the first resurrection must be understood as giving physical life on earth to the saints. But are we bound to thus understand literally the "lived" of verse 4 and the "lived not" of verse 5? There are two or three considerations which will be enough to show that they need not be understood thus. (1) The word "to *live*" is used about sixteen times in the Apocalypse. On nine of these it is applied to the eternal life of God the Father or God the Son; it is twice used in the passage before us (verses 4, 5). Of the remaining five occasions where the word is used, it is four times employed in what can scarcely be other than a figurative sense (chaps. iii. 1; vii. 17; xiii. 14; xix. 20—some *might* doubt the figurative use in this last passage), but only once is it employed in a sense which can fairly be defended as literal (chap. xvi. 3). (2) There will be faithless people during the millennium—the nations to be *deceived* (verse 8). Are we then to picture saints with glorified resurrection bodies living on the earth, which at the same time is tenanted by men and women still in the natural body? (3) There is a resurrection, which surely is the second resurrection, described in verses 12, 13: this last is a general resurrection of the dead, small and great. There seems no adequate reason to affirm that this first resurrection, then, *must* be physical. Our notions of life and death are so circumscribed by the geography of earth, that we seldom give to the word "life" in our thoughts its true richness and fulness of meaning. We fail to remember that the faithful ones who live, because Christ lives, have the promise of the life that now is, as well as that which is to come; we forget that God is not God of the dead, but of the living.

(6) **Blessed and holy is he that hath . . . .**—This is one of the benedictions of the Apocalypse. The blessing on those who have part or share in the first resurrection has this definite feature. On these the second death has not power (or authority). The second death stands in contrast with the first resurrection. The second death is not the mere physical dying; it is rather that more awful death which lies outside the region of the things seen and temporal. Whatever it means, and whatever the conditions which surround it, it is spiritual rather than physical. It is not the life of the body which protects the life of the spirit; it is the living and believing in God which

of God and of Christ, and shall reign
with him a thousand years. (7) And
Chap. xx. 7—10. The loosing and final overthrow of Satan. when the thousand years
are expired, Satan shall be
loosed out of his prison,
(8) and shall go out to deceive the
nations which are in the four quarters
of the earth, Gog and Magog,[a] to gather
them together to battle: the number of
whom *is* as the sand of the sea. (9) And
they went up on the breadth of the
earth, and compassed the camp of
the saints about, and the beloved city:
and fire came down from God out of

a Ezek. 38. 2; 39. 1.

---

protects from the second death; according to Christ's word of such, "they shall never die" (John xi. 26; comp. John x. 27, 28). Blessed, too, are such in being priests and kings (they shall reign). Theirs is the priesthood of life who have offered themselves a living sacrifice to God (Rom. xii. 1). The kingship of life is theirs, who have overcome the world-powers in the word of God and in the blood of the Lamb; these truly reign. (Comp. Note on chap. v. 10.)

THE LOOSING OF SATAN AND HIS FINAL OVERTHROW.

(7) **And when the thousand years are expired.**—Rather, *And when the thousand years have been finished.* The binding of Satan implied restraint put upon his power and freedom of action; the loosing means the removing of these restraints. The reign of Christ with His saints has been a witness to the power of our Master over the wicked one. This witness has been an opportunity also to the world. It was the earthly approximation to the ideal picture. It testified how completely "all power in heaven and in earth was given to Christ," and how there lay, therefore, within the reach of men the power of Him who would tread down their true enemies, and turn His hand against their adversaries (Ps. lxxxi. 13, 14). But the time of opportunity must end. "O that Israel would have hearkened," is a cry that might have its counterpart over the history of earth's lost opportunities. Christendom is planted in the world to be a framework of regenerating power to mankind, just as the Law and its adjuncts were designed to be in Israel. But, as there the old idolatrous influences broke in upon the rule of God's covenant, so here do we find the vision picturing to us how Christendom will be invaded by the influences of the evil one, when mankind has let slip this splendid opportunity of a really golden age.

(8) **And shall go out to deceive the nations.**—Perhaps better, *shall come out,* as the earth is the view-point. The nations deceived and led astray are designated as Gog and Magog. The names are derived from Ezekiel (chaps. xxxviii. and xxxix.). In rabbinical books the names were used to describe the nations who would rise against the reign of the Messiah. The names are to be understood figuratively. No particular nation could be well spoken of as "the nations in the four corners of the earth." The origin of the figure is not difficult. In Ezekiel, Gog is called the chief prince of Meshech and Tubal; or, adopting another rendering, the prince of Rosh, Meshech, and Tubal. Magog is mentioned in Gen. x. 2 as one of the sons of Japheth. The name is there associated with Gomer, Madai, and Meshech. Gomer is thought to correspond with the Cimmerians, Madai with the Medes, and Meshech with the Muscovites. Mr. Smith, in his history of Assurbanipal from cuneiform inscriptions, thinks that a certain chief of the Saka (Scythians), named Gaagi, is the same as Gog. The sons of this Gaagi are mentioned in connection with Birighudri, a chief of Madai (Medes). Josephus also identifies Magog with the Scythians. The remembrance of the Scythian invasion lingered long in the minds of Asiatic nations; and the names of those northern nations were adopted as representative of the great and undefined enemies who would in after ages assail the Messiah's kingdom, or wage unprovoked war against the true Israel of God. Ezekiel's language in chap. xxxviii. 17 seems to imply as much. The Evangelist here accepts the names employed by the earlier prophet. Gog and Magog stand for the great hosts of the nations, and their leaders, who would break forth into uncalled-for hostility against the people of the Lord. It must be remembered that the imagery is derived from the history of Israel. Jerusalem, the beloved city of the true Israel of God, looks out upon her foes. They are Babylon, Egypt, or they may come from the far northern regions, the abode of Gog and Magog, whence the wild and relentless invaders had poured upon the land. Gog and Magog are thus used as typical names. Under the auspices of such, the great gathering of turbulent and reckless enemies of the faith would take place. The hosts of the foes of Jerusalem are described as innumerable as the sand of the sea. This great concourse of countless hosts is moved by hostility to the faith of Christ. The nations, thus multitudinous, have been restrained during the millennial reign. Evil and unbelief have been held in check, but they have not been extinguished. The millennial reign is clearly, therefore, not a period in which the rule of Christ is universally and sincerely accepted. There are powers at work which compete for human affections and interests; but the general acceptance of Christian principles keeps the evil forces in abeyance, and the gracious strength of God limits the power of the arch-enemy. But when the restraints are removed, the long-suppressed evil breaks forth, and the reluctantly submissive nations are gathered together to *the war*—not to battle, as in our version, but to the war—*i.e.*, to the war which has been before spoken of in chaps. xvi. and xix. All the restraints which Christ and Christian teaching had supplied to the world are gradually removed. The Euphrates is dried, the Devil is loosed, the unclean spirits have gone forth, the last phase of the long war between good and evil, between Christ and Belial, has been entered.

(9) **And they went up on the breadth of the earth.**—The hostile multitudes spread like swarms over the earth, and surrounded the camp of the saints and the beloved city. Jerusalem is the beloved city—in it was the Mount Zion which God loved (Ps. lxxviii. 68). It is the figure of the true spiritual Zion and Jerusalem which has been faithful to her king. The beloved city has its camp; it is ready for war. It has waged its spiritual warfare against all forms of evil, Its citizens, like the returned exiles (Neh. iv. 17, 18), could never lay down the sword (comp. Eph. vi. 10; John ii. 14; v. 4); but the hostile demonstration is arrested by divine intervention. *There came down fire out of the heaven* (the words "from God" are of

heaven, and devoured them. (10) And
the devil that deceived them was cast
into the lake of fire and brimstone, where
the beast and the false prophet *are*, and
shall be tormented day and night for
ever and ever. (11) And I saw a great
Chap. xx. 11—15. The judgment of the world. white throne, and him that
sat on it, from whose face
the earth and the heaven
fled away; and there was found no place
for them. (12) And I saw the dead, small
and great, stand before God; and the
books were opened: and another book[a]
was opened, which is *the book* of life: and
the dead were judged out of those things
which were written in the books, according
to their works. (13) And the sea gave
up the dead which were in it; and death

a ch. 3. 5.

doubtful authority) *and devoured them.* The Shechinah light tabernacled over the holy city. Its light was also a flame ready to break forth upon the wicked. (Comp. chaps. i. 14; vii. 15, Note; Heb. xii. 29; 2 Thess. i. 6—10.) There may be allusion to the overthrow of the cities of the plains (Gen. xix. 24), but other incidents may have been in the prophet's mind: the fire which fell from heaven upon the enemies of an earlier prophet, Elijah (2 Kings i. 9—14), and the fire which broke forth from the tabernacle in the wilderness upon those who defied the laws of the God of Israel (Num. xvi. 16, 17, 35; Lev. x. 1, 2). It must be remembered that, in the passage before us, the prophet is using the incidents and actions of the past as imagery, and that the present vision is figurative, though of course not mere empty figure: for Christ will thoroughly purge His floor (Matt. iii. 12).

(10) **And the devil that deceived them . . .**—Better, *And the devil that deceiveth them, or was deceiving them, was cast into the lake of fire and brimstone, where are also the wild beasts and the false prophet; and they shall be tormented by day and by night unto the ages of the ages.* The devil cast from heaven (chap. xii. 9), bound in the abyss (chap. xx. 3), is now flung into the flaming lake. There *they* (*i.e.*, the devil, the wild beast, and the false prophet) are tormented unto the ages of ages. (Comp. chap. xiv. 10, 11; and Note on chap. xix. 20.)

The Judgment of the World.—The three enemies have been overthrown and driven forth from the earth which they have sought to destroy (chap. xi. 18). The judgment of human beings must follow.

(11) **And I saw a great white throne . . .**—Or, *And I saw a great white throne, and Him that was seated thereon, from whose face fled the earth and the heaven, and place was not found for them.* The throne is described as great and white, to set it in strong contrast to other thrones mentioned in the book, *e.g.*, chaps. iv. 4 and xx. 4. It is a white throne, in token of the purity of the judgment which follows. He who sits upon it is of purer eyes than to behold iniquity. It is asked, Who is He that is seated here? Throughout the book God is called "Him that sitteth upon the throne" (chaps. iv. 3 and v. 1); but we must not understand this as excluding the Son of God, who sits with His Father on His throne (chap. iii. 21), and who, as Son of Man, declared that He would sit upon the throne of His glory and divide "all the nations" as a shepherd divideth the sheep from the goats (Matt. xxv. 31, 32; comp. also chaps. vi. 16 and xi. 15—18). At the face of Him who sits upon the throne the heaven and earth flee. Hengstenberg interprets this of the putting out of the way "all of the irrational creation which had been pressed into the service of sin." Gebhardt interprets it of "the *destruction* of the whole *present* visible *world.*" A comparison, however, of the imagery employed in chaps. vi. 12—14 and xvi. 19, 20, should make us cautious of asserting that any great physical catastrophe is described here. Doubtless revolution must precede renewal (chap. xxi. 1); but it is never safe to ground our expectations of the nature of such changes upon language which is confessedly poetical in form. Some physical revolutions do in all probability await our earth, but the eye of the prophet looks more to the moral and spiritual regeneration of the world—more to the spiritual well-being of mankind, than to any physical changes which may synchronise with the culmination of the world's moral history.

(12, 13) **And I saw the dead, small and great . . .**—Or rather, *And I saw the dead, the great and the small, standing before* (not "God," as in text, but) *the throne, and books* (or, *rolls*) *were opened; and another book* (or, *roll*) *was opened, which is* (*the book*) *of life; and the dead were judged out of the things which had been written in the books* (or, *rolls*) *according to their works. And the sea gave forth the dead that were in it; and death and Hades gave forth the dead who were in them; and they were judged each according to their works.* The latter of these verses is added to assure us that the dead, in whatever quarter, must appear before the judgment throne. Death and Hades—"the grave world," and "the great watery grave"—the sea, "the universal hidden region of the dead," give up its prey; for there is One who sits upon the throne who has the keys of death and Hades (chap. i. 18). It has been said by some that the dead here spoken of as coming forth from the grave are not all the dead, but only "the rest of the dead" mentioned in chap. xx. 5. Those who believe that the first resurrection there mentioned is a literal physical resurrection are compelled to limit the resurrection here to the resurrection only of the remainder of the dead. But the verses before us suggest no limitation, and the language most assuredly tends to the idea that saints and faithful servants of God take part in this later resurrection. If all the saints and righteous men of old are raised prior to the millennium, and take no part in this last judgment scene, then only the faithless and wicked are left to be judged before the great white throne, and as none of these can be found written in the book of life, the bringing forth of that book becomes meaningless. This is one result of vicious literalism of interpretations. The real significance of the scene lies in the vivid picturing of that great and solemn truth that we must all stand before the judgment-seat of Christ, and that before Him there is nothing hidden which shall not be revealed (Matt. x. 26; comp. 1 Cor. iv. 5). Then shall every human life appear in its true light, stripped of all the deceptive adornments which have given a fictitious respectability to ingenious fraud, and a fatal popularity to adroit wickedness and splendid vice. Then shall men be judged, not by rank, or success, or achievement, but according to their works, as it is twice stated here, and according to whether

and hell[1] delivered up the dead which were in them: and they were judged every man according to their works.
(14) And death and hell were cast into the lake of fire. This is the second death.
(15) And whosoever was not found written in the book of life was cast into the lake of fire.

1 Or, *the grave.*

A.D. 96.

CHAPTER XXI.—(1) And I saw a

they have any life towards God. The works and the life towards God must be combined. A man may have, from the activities of his Christian works, a name to live, and yet be dead: the life-book and the work-book combine to mark the real servant of Christ. If he labours more abundantly than all, it is Christ who works in him, for his life is a life by the faith of the Son of God. (Comp. Gal. ii. 20; 1 Cor. xv. 10; Jas. ii. 14—26.)

(14, 15) **And death and hell were cast . . .**—Better, *And death and Hades were cast into the lake of fire.* The latter part of the verse contains, according to the best MS. authority, the additional words "the lake of fire." We then read, not "This is the second death"—as though the reference were to what went before—but, *This is the second death, the lake of fire.* The last verse then follows, *And if any was not found written in the book* (or, *roll*) *of life, he was cast into the lake of fire.* Thus, three times in these two short verses, like a refrain at the close of each clause, we have the terrible words "the lake of fire." Into this lake of fire Death and Hades are thrown. It is clearly figurative language, implying that Death, the last enemy (1 Cor. xv. 26) is destroyed, together with Hades, who was personified as Death's escort (chap. vi. 8). So we read in the next chapter (chap. xxi. 4) "there shall be no more death." The lake of fire into which Death is thrown is the second death! We have read of this before in this book (chaps. ii. 11; xx. 6). It is a death of which the first death—the physical death, now destroyed—was but a faint figure. It is a condition which needs no coarse exaggeration, or vulgar literalisation of the prophetic imagery, to heighten the horror of. Very awful is that spiritual death, which knows not and loves not God, and from which Christ has come to arouse us; more awful must be that second death, in which the spirit, no longer the sinning victim of hereditary evil, has become the victim of habitual choice of wrong, loving darkness rather than light, and choosing alienation rather than reconciliation —the husks of the swine rather than the Father's house. Of the full meaning of the words in their true and *future* force we can have little conception. It is enough for us to remember two things: they are figurative, but they are figurative of *something.*

XXI.

THE FINAL REGENERATION.—ALL THINGS NEW: NEW HEAVENS; NEW EARTH; NEW JERUSALEM (chaps. xxi. 1—xxii. 5).

THE NEW HEAVENS AND NEW EARTH.

(1) **And I saw a new heaven . . .**—The hope of the renewal and restitution of all things had been long cherished. Earlier prophets had sanctioned the hope: Isaiah had told of new heavens and new earth (Isa. lxv. 17); Ezekiel had closed his prophecy with the splendid vision of a renewed land of promise (Ezek. xl.—xlviii.); Christ Himself had spoken of the era which He inaugurated as the regeneration (Matt. xix. 28); His followers soon caught the truth that the outcome of the gospel age would be the realisation of all those marvellous visions with which prophets had sustained the fainting hopes of the people of God. The hope was not to be for ever receding as new height after height was surmounted. It will not always be said, "The days are prolonged, and every vision faileth" (Ezek. xii. 22). The fulfilment may seem to tarry; the unbelieving might doubt or scoff (Matt. xxiv. 43; 1 Thess. v. 2; 2 Pet. iii. 4); but those who felt that the gospel was a power of spiritual regeneration, making all things new (2 Cor. v. 17), learned to look forward to the widest and fullest restoration, and to expect new heavens and a new earth wherein dwelleth righteousness (2 Pet. iii. 13). The characteristic word which runs throughout the description is the word "*new.*" All things are to be made *new:* the heavens and earth are *new;* the Jerusalem is *new.* There are two words which are translated *new* in our English version: one of these (*neos*) relates to time; the other (*kainos*) relates to quality. The one would be applied to what had recently come into existence; the other to what showed fresh features. The tomb, for example, in which our Lord's body was laid was new, not in the sense that it had been recently hewn out of the rock, but in the sense that it had never been used before; it may have been long made, but it was one wherein never man was yet laid. To describe it the second word (*kainos*) is used (Matt. xxvii. 60 and John xix. 41). In the same way, the wine-skins (called "bottles" in our English version) required for the new wine were not necessarily wine-skins only just prepared for service, but they were skins which had not grown withered, but retained their freshness and elasticity. Here, again, the second word (*kainos*) is employed to describe them. Now, it is this latter word which is used throughout this chapter, and, indeed, throughout the book of Revelation. The newness which is pictured is the newness of freshness: the old, decaying, enfeebling, and corrupting elements are swept away. The aspects and features which will surround the inhabitants of that new earth will be full of novelty to satisfy the progressive instincts of our nature; but the imagery no less conveys the assurance that the conservative instinct, which clings to what is old, and finds sanctity in the past, will not be disregarded. All things may be new, full of fresh and fair beauty; but all things will not be *strange;* there must be some correspondency between the old and the new, when the new things are called new *heavens,* new *earth,* new *Jerusalem.* The description is figurative, but the spirit of it implies that in the restitution age the sweetness of things loved and familiar will blend with the charm of all that is fresh and new.

And there was no more sea.—Or, better, *And the sea is* (*exists*) *not any more.* Among the more detailed features of the new earth, this obliteration of the sea stands first. It is strange that so many commentators should vacillate between literal and figurative interpretations of the chapter; the ornaments and decorations of the new Jerusalem (verses 10—21) are treated as symbolical; the annihilation of the sea is considered as literal. It is wiser to leave the literal meaning to the future, and to grasp the spiritual teachings, which are of infinite and present interest. The

new heaven and a new earth:[a] for the
Chap. xxi. 1—8. The new heavens and new earth.
first heaven and the first
earth were passed away;
and there was no more
sea. (2) And I John saw the holy city,
new Jerusalem, coming down from God
out of heaven, prepared as a bride
adorned for her husband. (3) And I
Chap. xxi. 3, 4. The voice from the throne.
heard a great voice out of
heaven saying, Behold, the
tabernacle of God *is* with
men, and he will dwell with them,

a Isa. 65. 17; 2 Pet. 3. 13.

b ch. 7. 17.

c 2 Cor. 5. 17.

and they shall be his people, and God
himself shall be with them, *and be*
their God. (4) And God shall wipe away
all tears from their eyes;[b] and there
shall be no more death, neither sorrow,
nor crying, neither shall there be any
more pain: for the former things are
passed away. (5) And he that sat upon
the throne said, Behold, I
make all things new.[c] And
he said unto me, Write:
for these words are true and
Chap. xxi. 5—8. The voice from Him who is seated on the throne.

---

sea has played an important part in the symbolism of the book: out of the sea rose the wild beast (chap. xiii. 1); the purple-clad Babylon sat enthroned upon many waters (chap. xvii. 1); the restless, tumultuous ocean, now discordant with its clamorous waves, now flooding the earth in confederate force; the troubled sea of evil, which cannot rest, and casts up but mire and dirt (Isa. lvii. 21), is no more to be found on the face of that earth, or near that city whose peace is as a river, and whose righteousness as the waves of the sea (Isa. xlviii. 18), and whose inhabitants are delivered from "the waves of this troublesome world."

(2) **And I John saw the holy city . . .**—Better, *And the holy city, new Jerusalem, I saw coming down out of the heaven from God, prepared . . .* The name John is omitted in the best MSS. The new Jerusalem is more fully described later on (verse 10 *et seq.*). The city is also the bride (comp. verses 9, 10). Both images—the "city" and the "bride"—are familiar to the Bible student. The sacred city appears linked to God by a sacred bond. (Comp. Ps. xlv. 13, 14; Isa. lxi. 10; lxii. 4, 5; Gal. iv. 26; Eph. v. 25—27.) The city-bride is now adorned for her Husband. We know what her ornaments are, now that He is about to present her to Himself a glorious Church: the meekness and gentleness of Christ, and her loving obedience to Him (1 Pet. iii. 4), are her jewels. She is seen, not rising from earth or sea, like the foes of righteousness (chap. xiii. 1, 11), but coming down from heaven. The world will never evolve a golden age or ideal state. The new Jerusalem must descend from God. The true pattern, which alone will realise man's highest wishes, is the pattern in the mount of God (Acts vii. 44).

THE FIRST VOICE.—The voice out of the throne (verses 3, 4.)

(3) **And I heard a great voice out of heaven . . . .**—According to the best MSS. the voice now heard was heard "*out of the throne,*" saying, *Behold, the tabernacle of God is with men, and He will tabernacle with them.* Here, as in chap. vii. 15, the translation, "shall dwell," weakens the force of the allusion. The tent, or tabernacle, is in the seer's mind. There is a difference in the prepositions used here and in chap. vii.: in the latter, God was spoken of as tabernacling *over* them; here He tabernacles with them. He not only stretches His cloud-shelter over them, but He is with them. *They shall be His people, and He shall be God with them, their God.* The introduction of the words in italics ("and be") in our version is a weakness; the force of the thought is spoiled. *They* are God's people, and He is their Emmanuel—God with them, their God. The prophet Ezekiel supplies parallel thoughts (Ezek. xxxvii. 27, 28; comp. also Lev. xxvi. 11, 12).

(4) **And God shall wipe away all tears . . .**—Instead of "all tears" we should translate "every tear," and so possess the promise in its true and tender form. The first, or former, things are passed away: *death shall not be any longer; neither shall mourning, nor crying, nor pain, be any longer.* The splendid array of negatives come as heralds of the positive peace of the new Jerusalem: no sea, no tears, no death, no mourning, no crying, no pain; with the former things these six shadows pass away from life. "The *mourning* is that grief which so takes possession of the whole being that it cannot be hid" (Abp. Trench). It is the same word that is rendered "wailing" in our English version (chap. xviii. 15). It is used of mourning for the dead. *Crying* is the voice of despair and dismay, as well as sorrow; it is the loud outcry which is the witness that "the times are out of joint." *Pain* includes painful labour and weariness. With the passing away of these there must depart the ground for the often-repeated cry of "Vanity of vanities!" The sad minor of the poet's song will cease, for—

"Time with a gift of tears,
Grief with a glass that ran,"

together with "travail and heavy sorrow," shall be no more. On the whole passage, comp. Isa. xxv. 8; lxv. 19.

THE SECOND VOICE.—The voice of Him who sitteth on the Throne (verses 5—8).

(5) **And he that sat upon the throne . . .**—Better, *And he who sitteth on the throne said, Behold, I am making all things new. And he saith* (the words "unto me" should be omitted) *write; because these words are faithful and true.* It is the Throned one, the One who rules over all things from the beginning, and who has presided over all the changing scenes of earth's history, who speaks; it is He who makes even the wrath of man to praise Him, and who causes all things to work together for good to them that love Him, who gives this heart-helping assurance. "I am making all things new." In spite of the moral disorder, the pain and grief, the dark shadows of life and history, the new creation is being prepared, and will rise, like the early creation, out of chaos. The analogy between the old and new creation is the reason why the first chapter of Genesis and the earlier verses of this chapter are appointed as the morning lessons for Septuagesima Sunday; as out of an earth without form and void rose the world of order and beauty, which God pronounced very good, so out of the world, so full of distress and tears, and overshadowed by so many clouds

faithful. (6) And he said unto me, It is
done. I am Alpha and Omega, the
beginning and the end.[a] I will give
unto him that is athirst of the fountain
of the water of life freely.[b] (7) He that
overcometh shall inherit all things; and
I will be his God, and he shall be my
son. (8) But the fearful, and unbelieving,
and the abominable, and murderers, and
whoremongers, and sorcerers, and idolaters, and all liars, shall have their part
in the lake which burneth with fire and
brimstone: which is the second death.
(9) And there came unto me one of the

a ch. 1. 8; 22. 13.

b Isa. 55. 1.

of sin, will emerge the glad new world, wherein dwelleth righteousness. The closing words of the verse, perhaps an instruction from the angel, but more probably still the voice of Him that sits on the throne, adds the further assurance, "These words are true and faithful."

(6) **And he said unto me, It is done.**—Or, rather, *They* (the things promised) *have come to pass.* He spake, and it was done. The assurance is made trebly sure. "I am making all things new." "These words are true." "They are fulfilled." "Twice," says Bengel, "twice it is said in this book 'It is done.' First at the completion of the wrath of God in chap. xvi. 17, and here again at the making of all things new."

I am Alpha and Omega, the beginning and the end . . .—The definite article must be placed before Alpha and Omega. *I am the Alpha and the Omega, the beginning and the end.* He is the Alpha and Omega, whose words are faithful and true, and He is the beginning and the end, who is before all things and by whom all things consist (Col. i. 17; John i. 1). He finishes as well as begins. He who begins the good work will perform it (Phil. i. 6; Col. i. 20); all grace flows from Him; and all love flows back to Him, who is Love, who is the cause and end of all, who first makes us, and lastly makes us rest in Him. All the unsatisfied yearnings of the heart may find satisfaction in Him. Hence, perhaps, this promise, *I to him that thirsteth will give out of the spring of the water of life freely.* No promise shall fail—the needy and thirsty so often invited to Him may find fresh springs of life in Him. (Comp. Isa. lv. 1; John iv. 10—14; vii. 37, 38.) The blessing is promised freely, as an unbought gift, without money and without price. This is the genius of the good news of God—the gift is free to all. He who understands this will not be afraid to say, "Nothing in my hand I bring;" and he who says this will be he who will also say, "What things were gain to me, those I counted loss for Christ," so that he who brings everything brings nothing; and he who brings nothing brings everything, knowing that all is nothing.

(7) **He that overcometh shall inherit all things . . .**—Rather, *He that conquereth shall inherit these things; and I will be to him God, and he shall be to me a son.* The general promise of verse 3 is in part repeated, and this time more individually. Again we catch, as it were, the echo of the promises to the Seven Churches, the blessing is for him that conquereth. The idea of the war and the conquest is a favourite one with St. John. (John xvi. 33, and 1 John ii. 13, 14; v. 4, 5; see also Note on chap. ii. 7.) The source and weapon of victory have been before stated: the blood of the Lamb, the word of their testimony (chap. xii. 11), and the victory of faith (1 John v. 4).

(8) **But the fearful, and unbelieving, and the abominable . . .**—Better, *But for the cowardly and unfaithful* (or, *unbelieving*) *and defiled with abominations, and murderers, and fornicators, and sorcerers, and idolaters, and for all the false, their part* (*is*) *in the lake that burneth with fire and brimstone; which thing is the second death.* The list here given points to those classes of character which cannot find a place in the Holy City. Nothing that defileth shall enter in. The less glaring faults stand first, the *cowardly* and *unbelieving.* There is a high and holy fear in which the Christian passes the time of his sojourn here (1 Pet. i. 17); but there is a base and selfish fear, a fear of man, which brings a snare; those who have faith enter boldly the strife, following the Lamb whithersoever He goeth, and conquering by faith. The cowardly sink into companionship with the faithless and unbelieving, with the workers of iniquity. The abominations spoken of here have reference to those mentioned in chap. xvii. 4. The characters, it has been thought, form four pairs. Fear and unbelief go hand in hand (Deut. xx. 1—8; Matt viii. 26); the workers of abomination and the murderers, the fornicators and the sorcerers are united as those who sin in secret; the idolaters and the false, as those who change God's truth into a lie. (Comp. Eph. v. 5; Col. iii. 5; Phil. iii. 19.) These who are thus shut out from the heavenly city stand in contrast to those who are admitted; yet among those admitted are such who have sinned through fear, faithlessness, and fleshliness. Sin indeed excludes from the city, but it is sin loved, sin unrepented of, which alone can close the gate of the city whose gates lie open day and night.

THE HEAVENLY JERUSALEM DESCRIBED (9—xxii. 5).—Before entering upon this section it is wise to recall once more that the descriptions here given are figurative, and are not to be understood literally. "There is nothing in it as it seems saving the King." This remark may well be thought needless; but the misconceptions and misrepresentations of the Christian's hope have been many and reckless; and, even were this not the case, there is always a certain proportion of people who seem incapable of understanding figurative language. Half the errors of the Church have been due to prosaic-minded men who could not discern the difference between figure and fact; and men of unpoetical and vehement temperament have blundered over these descriptions, and their blunders have discredited the whole Apocalypse in the eyes of some. The following are the features of the heavenly city, which the description seems designed to enforce upon our thoughts. The great and holy community will be one which draws its glory from God (chaps. xxi. 11, 23; xxii. 5). Its blessings are not for a few, but open to all, for its gates lie open to all quarters (chap. xxi. 12, 13). The heavenly and the earthly will be at one; angels, apostles, and patriarchs are there (chap. xxi. 12, 14). Diverse characters will find entrance there; the gates bear the names of the twelve tribes. The door of admission is alike for all, though diverse characters from diverse quarters will enter in (chap. xxi. 21). It will be the abode of all that is fair and good, and no disproportions will mar its loveliness (chap. xxi. 17, 18). The ancient truths, spoken by various lips, will be found

Chaps. xxi. 9—xxii. 5. The heavenly Jerusalem described.

seven angels which had the seven vials
full of the seven last plagues,
and talked with me, saying,
Come hither, I will shew
thee the bride, the Lamb's
wife. (10) And he carried me away in
the spirit to a great and high mountain,
and shewed me that great city, the holy
Jerusalem, descending out of heaven
from God, (11) having the glory of
God: and her light *was* like unto a
stone most precious, even like a jasper
stone, clear as crystal; (12) and had a
wall great and high, *and* had twelve
gates, and at the gates twelve angels,
and names written thereon, which are
the names of the twelve tribes of the
children of Israel: (13) on the east three
gates; on the north three gates; on
the south three gates; and on the west
three gates. (14) And the wall of the
city had twelve foundations, and in them

---

to be eternal truths, full of varied but consistent beauty (chap. xxi. 14, 19, 20). The forms and helps which were needful here will not be needful there (chap. xxi. 22, 23); all that the servants of God have righteously hungered and thirsted for here will be supplied there (chap. xxii. 1, 2). There will be blessings, various, continuous, eternal; new fields of labour and new possibilities of service will be opened there (chap. xxii. 3, 4).

(9) **And there came unto me one of the seven angels . . .**—The words "unto me" should be omitted. One of the seven angels which had the seven vials of wrath had shown to the seer the scarlet-clad harlot, the great and guilty Babylon: so here does one of the same company of angels show him the pure Bride of the Lamb, the new and holy Jerusalem.

(10) **And he carried me away in the spirit . . .**—Better, *He carried me away in spirit on to a mountain, great and high.* It is not merely that the height gives a fine view-ground, the symbolism carries us further. The glimpse of God's coming glories is best gained from the consecrated heights of self-surrender and prayer. On a mountain apart—the mountain of supplication and separation from the world—is the light and glory of God best seen. There are Beulah heights and transfiguration heights from which we may gain glimpses of the city and the glory of the Lord of the city. (Comp. Matt. xvii. 1—4.) The angel carried away the seer to a mountain great and high, and showed him (not "that great city," but) *the holy city Jerusalem descending out of the heaven from* (having its origin from) *God.* The tempter showed to our Lord the kingdoms of the world and the glory of them; the comforting angel shows to our Lord's prophet the city that hath the foundations, and the glory of it—the city that is of God, its builder and maker. (Comp. Heb. xi. 10, where the right rendering is not "a city," but *the city which hath the foundations.*)

(11) **Having the glory of God . . .**—The glory of God is the glorious presence of God, the true Shechinah, of which we have read before (chap. xv. 8, and see verse 23). The light of the city is described: *And her light* (or, *brightness*: it is the light which she gives; the same word is used as that employed in the LXX., Gen. i. 17, for the heavenly bodies) *is like a stone most precious, as it were a jasper stone crystallising.* On the meaning and appearance of this stone, see Note on chap. iv. 3. It is in all probability a stone transparent and clear as the crystal, but retaining the greenish hue belonging to the jasper. The general brightness of the city was lustrous as the diamond but shot with the green tint of the emerald bow which swept the throne. (Comp. chap. iv. 3.)

(12, 13) **And had a wall great and high . . .**—Or, better (for the construction is continued), *Having a wall great and high, and having twelve gate-towers, and at the gate-towers twelve angels, and names inscribed which are* (*names*) *of the twelve tribes of the sons of Israel: from the sun-rising* (*i.e.*, facing east) *three gate-towers; from the north three gate-towers, from the south three gate-towers; from the sun-setting three gate-towers.* On this arrangement of gates Num. ii., Ezek. xlviii., and Rev. vii. should be compared. In the encampment in the wilderness (Num. ii.) the tribes were arranged as follows: on the east, Judah, Issachar, Zebulun; on the south, Reuben, Simeon, Gad; on the west, Ephraim, Manasseh, Benjamin; on the north, Dan, Asher, Naphtali. There is perhaps allusion in the present passage to this wilderness encampment, and to the re-adjustment of the order of the tribes in Ezekiel (chap. xlviii.); but there is more than order here: the gates lie open to all quarters; there is no refusal of admission to any people. The representatives of all nations, and kindreds, and people, and tongues, are (chap. vii. 9) in the city of Christ; in Him there is neither barbarian, Scythian, bond nor free, but all are one. The diversities of human nationality and character, of age and race, and climate, are brought into one communion and fellowship. (Comp. Note on chap. vii. 4.) "The wall great and high" is mentioned to assure us of the security and peace of that city where no foe "or thief approacheth" (Isa. xxvi. 1; Zech. ii. 5).

(14) **And the wall of the city had . . .**—Or, rather, *And the wall of the city having twelve foundations, and on them twelve names of the twelve Apostles of the Lamb.* There were twelve large stones forming the basement of the wall, the names of the Apostles were inscribed on these. The whole Old and New Testament Church is represented in the appearance of the city; but the work of the Apostles receives its special recognition; it is on their teaching and witness for Christ that the great spiritual Jerusalem is built. There is complete harmony of thought here between St. Paul and St. John. St. Paul described the Church as built upon the foundation of the Apostles and Prophets, Jesus Christ Himself being the chief corner-stone (Eph. ii. 20). We may compare the same illustration used by our Lord (Matt. xvi. 18) and afterwards by St. Peter (1 Pet. ii. 4—6). The argument that St. John could not be the writer of the Apocalypse because he speaks of the Apostles (and so includes himself) as the foundation-stones of the celestial city, might be applied with equal wisdom against the Pauline authorship of the Epistle to the Ephesians; it is, moreover, a class of argument which betrays a tendency to confusion of thought, and to misapprehension of the meaning and value of symbols. Historically and doctrinally the Church of Christ is built upon the foundations here described; our creeds declare an acknowledgment of a catholic and *apostolic* Church. Note the recurrence

the names of the twelve apostles of the
Lamb. (15) And he that talked with
me had a golden reed to
measure the city, and the
gates thereof, and the wall
thereof. (16) And the city lieth four-
square, and the length is as large as the
breadth: and he measured the city with
the reed, twelve thousand furlongs. The
length and the breadth and the height
of it are equal. (17) And he measured

Chap. xxi. 15—17. The measurement of the city.

the wall thereof, an hundred *and* forty
and four cubits, *according to* the measure
of a man, that is, of the angel. (18) And
the building of the wall
of it was *of* jasper: and
the city *was* pure gold, like
unto clear glass. (19) And the founda-
tions of the wall of the city *were*
garnished with all manner of precious
stones. The first foundation *was* jasper;
the second, sapphire; the third, a

Chap. xxi. 18—21. The precious stones.

---

of the name, the *Lamb*, to describe our Lord. He is still the Lamb; the writer lingers over the well and early known image. (Comp. John i. 29, 36.)

THE MEASUREMENT OF THE CITY.

(15) **And he that talked with me . . .**—Or, better, *And he who was talking with me had a golden reed . . .* The allusion here is to the angel mentioned in Ezekiel (Ezek. xv. 3); the reed, or measuring rod, is of gold, that used in chap. xi. 1 was not said to be of gold; the measurement there was the symbol of preservation amid impending danger; the measuring here is more glorious—it is measuring which exhibits the beauty and proportion of the city which is now dwelling at peace. Gold is one of the features of the city; the street is gold (verses 18, 21); it may stand as a token of the wealth (Ps. lxxii. 15; 1 Kings x. 14—21) of the royal city; but the wealth of that city is love. (Comp. Note on chap. iii. 18.)

(16) **And the city lieth foursquare . . .**—The city is foursquare, because the length and breadth are equal; but it is added that the height also is equal to the length and breadth, the city thus presents the symbol of perfect symmetry; this is all that is needed. Many interpreters are nervously anxious about the monstrous appearance of a city whose walls measured three thousand stadii (the word rendered "furlongs" is properly *stadii*); but there is no need to be nervous about the symbols; the city is not designed, any more than the vision of chap. iv., or the vision of Ezekiel (chap. i.) to be represented by painting to the eye: the attempt to do so only ends in the production of grotesque and profane pictures. It is not needful, however, in this case to suppose the actual wall to have been 3,000 stadii in height; the city is placed on a hill, the foundations are upon the holy hill, and the deep strong mountain foundations may be included in the measurement. The main thought, however, is to realise the harmony and proportion of that community, in which broad and low and high will meet, and in which no truth will be exaggerated or distorted; in which no disproportioned adjustments will mar its social order; in which all those who are inbuilt as living stones will be measured, not by the false estimates of worldly thoughts (comp. Jas. ii. 4), but by the golden reed of the sanctuary.

(17) **And he measured the wall thereof . . .**—Better, *And he measured its wall by an hundred and forty-four cubits* (*i.e.*, in height), *man's measure, which is angel's.* The measurement is in man's measure, but the reed was handled by an angel; the measure is true for men and true for angels; it may mean that the angel used the ordinary human measure, but may it not imply that the vision is true for all, for the earthly and for the heavenly? it is man's measure, it is angel's measure; the human will not find the picture untrue, though the city is not literal: it is figurative, but not mere figure. The recurrence of the number hundred and forty-four recalls us to the figurative character of the description. (Comp. Note on chap. vii. 4.)

THE BUILDING OR MATERIAL OF THE CITY.

(18) **And the building of the wall . . .**—Or, *And the building-work* (or, *the masonry*, so Alford) *of the wall of it was jasper, and the city was pure gold, like pure glass.* The general aspect of the city was jasper-like, because the material of the wall was of the jasper stone. On this stone, see Note on chap. iv. 3, and on verse 11 above. The city was gold. On the meaning of the gold see Note on verse 15 and on chap. iii. 18. To what has been said may be added the following:—"Gold has an inalienable reference to the sun itself, consequently, to the symbol of the face of God, or Christ, *i.e.*, to the manifestation of God's love" (Lange).

The wealth of heaven *is* love; love is the circulating medium of all holy activity and of all holy work: all who dwell within the heavenly city are encompassed by it; all who tread the streets of that city move along the ways of love; no dimness or obscuring motives of self-interest mar its lustre—the gold is clear as pure glass.

(19) **And the foundations of the wall . . .**—Better, *The foundations of the wall of the city* (*were*) *adorned with every precious stone.* We may compare the adornment of the harlot (chap. xvii. 4). Her robe was decked with gold, and precious stones, and pearls. The Bride, the Lamb's wife, has her beautiful ornaments, richer and rarer than those which adorned the world-mistress. The comparison reminds us, in a vivid and figurative way, of our Master's often-repeated teaching. He that saveth his life, loseth it; he that loseth, saveth it; he that is content to pass by the dazzling attractions of the world, refusing splendour from the outstretched hand of Babylon, will win the true spiritual riches. There is no man that has turned away for Christ's sake from the attractions of the world-spirit, that hath forsaken houses and lands for Christ's sake and the gospel, but shall receive manifold more, &c. (Mark x. 28—31). The "jewels of right celestial worth" are part of the heritage of him who can nobly hold cheap the degrading hire of the world. (Comp. Isa. liv. 12.)

The foundations are various. There were in the foundation of the Church diversities of gifts and administrations, but the same Lord and the same spirit. In the heavenly city we have harmony, not monotony; variety, not sameness; unity, not uniformity. The stones are not arranged in the order of

chalcedony; the fourth, an emerald;
(20) the fifth, sardonyx; the sixth,
sardius; the seventh, chrysolyte; the
eighth, beryl; the ninth, a topaz; the
tenth, a chrysoprasus; the eleventh, a
jacinth; the twelfth, an amethyst.
(21) And the twelve gates *were* twelve
pearls; every several gate was of one
pearl: and the street of the city *was*
pure gold, as it were transparent
glass. (22) And I saw no temple there-
in: for the Lord God Almighty and
the Lamb are the temple of it.
(23) And the city had no need of the
sun, neither of the moon, to shine in
it:[a] for the glory of God did lighten it,
and the Lamb *is* the light thereof.
(24) And the nations of them which are
saved shall walk in the light of it:[b] and
the kings of the earth do bring their

a Isa. 60. 19.

b Isa. 60. 3.

---

the high priest's breastplate, but according to their various shades of colour, beginning from the foundation.

1. *Jaspis*, dark opaque green.
2. *Sapphirus*, Lapis-lazuli, opaque blue.
3. *Chalcedon*, an Emerald of a greenish hue.
4. *Smaragdus*, bright transparent green.
5. *Sardonyx*, white and red.
6. *Sardius*, bright red.
7. *Chrysolite*, our Topaz, bright yellow.
8. *Beryl*, bluish green.
9. *Topazion*, or Peridot, yellowish green.
10. *Chrysoprasus*, a darker shade of the same colour.
11. *Hyacinthus*, Sapphire, sky blue.
12. *Amethystus*, violet.

"Chrysoprasus is probably an error for Chrysopaston, a dark blue stone, studded with gold, by which substitution all the shades of blue will follow each other." (See King, *On Gems*.)

With this blended harmony of colour the foundation-stones would encircle the heavenly city as with a rainbow belt. In the seer's view the light of the heavenly city would shine with hues that betoken the advent of the morning. The varying tints would glow like pledges of a dayspring from on high.

> "Along the tingling desert of the sky,
> Beyond the circle of the conscious hills
> Were laid in jasper-stone as clear as glass
> The first foundations of that new, near Day,
> Which should be builded out of heaven to God.
> . . . . . Jasper first, I said;
> And second, sapphire; third, chalcedony;
> The rest in order;—last, an amethyst."

The foundation-stones are twelve. "As twelve, they indicate their numerical completeness (chaps. vii. and xiv.); as shining with a common lustre, their unity; as stones of different hues, their manifoldness; as brilliant stones, the glorification of this earthly life through the light of Heaven" (Lange).

(21) **And the twelve gates . . .**—Or, *gate-towers*. Each gate was of one pearl—*i.e.*, made out of one pearl. The foundations are diverse; the gates are alike. There is one way, though there are many roads; one mode of entrance, through twelve gates. All find entrance through one new and living Way (John xiv. 6; Acts iv. 11, 12; 1 Cor. iii. 11; Heb. x. 20). The pearl was esteemed of the greatest value among the ancients; it is an appropriate emblem of the highest truth, and so of Him who is the Truth as well as the Way of Life. Lord Bacon compared truth to a pearl "that showeth best by day." Another feature may be added. It is the only precious stone which the art and skill of man cannot improve. The tools of the artificer may give fresh lustre to the emerald and the sapphire; but he must lift no tool upon the pearl. So is it with the truth, which sets men free (1 Cor. iii. 10). Through truth, and Him who is Truth, we enter the city; and *the street of the city was gold. pure as transparent glass*. (See Note on verse 18.)

(22) **And I saw no temple therein . . .**—Rather, *And temple I saw not in it, for the Lord God the Almighty is her temple, and the Lamb.* In Ezekiel's vision the vast and splendid proportions of the Temple formed a conspicuous part: its gigantic proportions declared it to be figurative (Ezek. xlviii. 8—20); but the present vision passes on to a higher state of things. "I saw no temple:" Ezekiel's vision declared that the literal temple would be replaced by a far more glorious spiritual temple. The age of the Christian Church succeeds the age of the Jewish temple-worship; the age of the Church triumphing will succeed the age of the Church toiling; and there the external organisations, helps, and instrumentalities required for the edifying of the body of Christ will no longer be needed. Tongues, prophecies, knowledge, may pass away (1 Cor. xiii. 9; Eph. iv. 11—13); churches will disappear, absorbed in the one glorious Church; ministries, missionary organisations, helps, governments, may cease. *There* God is all. The Lord is there—the temple, the sanctuary, the dwelling-place of His people. (Comp. Ezek. xlviii. 35.) Every merely local aspect of worship is at an end (John iv. 21—24).

(23) **And the city had no need of the sun . . .**—Rather, *And the city hath not need of the sun, nor of the moon that they should shine on* (or, *for*) *her; for the glory of God enlightened her, and her lamp is the Lamb.* The Shechinah is again alluded to. Light is the emblem of knowledge and holiness. God is light, and in Him is no darkness at all (1 John i. 5). Christ the Lamb, came as the Light of the World. Now in the heavenly Jerusalem is the light seen as a lamp that burneth. The imagery is drawn from Isaiah. "The sun shall be no more thy light by day; neither for brightness shall the moon give light unto thee; but the Lord shall be unto thee an everlasting light, and thy God thy glory" (Isa. lx. 19). No more will there be needed subsidiary or intermediate luminaries. He who makes the righteous to shine like stars, and causes His churches to shine like lights in the world, will be Himself the Light and Sun of His people: they shall see Him as He is. It is again to be noticed that the emblem of the Lamb is used to describe our Lord in this verse, and in the last, as it was also in verse 14. The memory of Christ's work on earth is never obliterated: still in the intense splendour and joy of that city of light the remembrance of Him who was led as a lamb to the slaughter gives depth and fulness to its joy.

(24) **And the nations of them which are saved . . .**—We must omit, with the best MSS., the words "of them which are saved," and read, *And the nations shall walk by means of its light, and the kings of the*

glory and honour into it. (25) And the
gates of it shall not be shut at all by
day:[a] for there shall be no night there.
(26) And they shall bring the glory and
honour of the nations into it. (27) And
there shall in no wise enter into it any
thing that defileth, neither *whatsoever*
worketh abomination, or *maketh* a lie:
but they which are written in the
Lamb's book of life.

A.D. 96.

a Isa. 60. 11.

CHAPTER XXII.—(1) And he shewed
me a pure river of water of life, clear as
crystal, proceeding out of the throne of
God and of the Lamb. (2) In the midst
of the street of it, and on either side of
the river, *was there* the tree of life,
which bare twelve *manner of* fruits, *and*
yielded her fruit every month: and the
leaves of the tree *were* for the healing
of the nations. (3) And there shall be

---

earth carry their glory into her. The outlook of the prophet is from the loneliness and depression of the then persecuted and despised churches; but in the vision he sees her beautiful and enlarged and honoured. All nations and peoples flock within the walls: it is the echo of the ancient prophecies. "All kings shall fall down before Him: all nations shall serve Him." The Church and kingdom of Christ increase without end; and all will cast their glory at His feet, and call Him blessed in whom all have been blessed (Ps. lxxii. 11, 17).

(25, 26) **And the gates of it . . .**—Better, *And the gates* (or, *gate-towers*) *shall never be shut by day, for night shall not be there.* The gates shall never be shut: all day they shall be open, and that day shall be for ever, for there shall be no night there. All that darkens—the sin that brings night on the soul; the sorrow that brings night on the heart—shall be banished for ever. In peace by day, the city gates will be open; nor can there be night when God the Almighty is the Sun. (Comp. Isa. lx. 11; Ezek. xxxviii. 11.) Through its open gates *they* (i.e., *men*) *will bring the glory and honour of the nations into her.* As men find that every good gift and every perfect gift is from above, and that their strength is in Christ, without whom they can do nothing, so will their lives bring back to Him the lustre of all their achievements.

(27) **And there shall in no wise enter into . . .**—Better, *And there shall never enter into her anything unclean, and he that worketh abomination and falsehood, but only* (or, *except*) *they that have been written in the book of life of the Lamb.* The gates stand open always, but no evil thing may find a home there. The emphatic repetition here (see verse 8) of the idea that all sin is excluded, is in harmony with all other Scripture: no unholiness can dwell in the presence of God. The allusion is to the care of the Jews to exclude all things unclean from the precincts of the sanctuary. The legal and ceremonial defilement had its spiritual significance, which the Apostles utilised elsewhere. (Comp. 2 Cor. vi. 17, 18; vii. 1; Rev. xviii. 4. On the "book of life," see chap. xx. 12.)

XXII.

The Restored Paradise (verses 1—5).—These five verses complete the description of the new heavens and new earth. The features of this last section reflect those of the first and forfeited paradise: the tree of life and the river that flows by the trees are here, and the happy and willing service of God is restored (verses 3, 4), and the curse has disappeared.

(1) **And he shewed me a pure river . . .**—The adjective "pure" must be omitted, as it is wanting in the best MSS. The river is full of water, and that water is the emblem of life: it is the beautiful symbol of life in its gladness, purity, activity, and fulness. The garden of Eden (Gen. ii. 10) had its river. Even in the wilderness Israel had from the smitten rock the water which gushed out like a river (Ps. cv. 41). Prophets, in their pictures of the ages of blessing, almost invariably introduced the river, or broad stream. Joel saw a fountain out of the house of the Lord (Joel iii. 18). Zechariah spoke of living waters from Jerusalem (Zech. xiv. 8); but Ezekiel had the fullest vision when he beheld the stream which deepened and broadened in its onward progress from under the threshold of the house of God, and carried life in its train: everything lived whither the water came (Ezek. xlvii. 9); thus did all prophets speak of the river of God's pleasures (Ps. xxxvi. 8). The teaching of our Lord threw new light on the prophetic imagery; the pure delights of spiritual joy and communion with God were vouchsafed to men by the presence of the Holy Spirit, the Giver of Life. In the bestowal of that spirit of life did Christ give true satisfaction to the thirsting souls of men. (Comp. John iv. 10—14; vii. 37—39.) The source of the river is in the *throne.* Ezekiel's river took rise in the temple; but in our vision there is no temple (chap. xxi. 22). We are brought nearer, even to the throne: it is the throne (not "thrones")—one throne of God and the Lamb. (Comp. chap. iii. 21.)

(2) **In the midst of the street of it . . .**—Or rather, *In the midst of the street of it, and of the river, on one side and on the other* (*was*) *a tree of life, yielding twelve fruits, according to each month giving its fruit; and the leaves of the tree are for healing of the nations.* The hunger as well as the thirst of the spirit is to be satisfied (Matt. v. 6). The tree of life, as well as the river of life, is to be found in the new and better Eden (Gen. ii. 9; iii. 22). The vision of Ezekiel is exactly parallel to the present: "On the border of the river there was wood very much, on both sides: every kind of tree; its leaf withers not, and its fruit ceases not; all months does it ripen; its fruit serves for food, and its leaf for healing" (Ezek. xlvii. 7—12). The twelve manner of fruit: The recurrence of the number—twelve—is to be noticed, for here, too, as well as in the foundations and gates of the city, we have variety allied with unity. Diverse and seasonable fruits, and yet one tree of life. Thus does the Almighty wisdom feed His people with food convenient for them (Prov. xxx. 8), though, in one sense there is but one food for all (John vi. 31); for true divine wisdom is a tree of life to them that lay hold upon her (Prov. iii. 18). That wisdom is not the mere knowledge of things (the tree of the knowledge of good and evil has no place in new Eden); but it is rather the knowledge of life which makes the knowledge of things available to the highest good. (Comp. 1 Cor. i. 22—24, 30; Jas. iii. 17; Prov. viii.)

(3) **And there shall be no more curse . . .**—Better, *And every curse, or accursed thing, shall not be*

no more curse: but the throne of God
and of the Lamb shall be in it; and his
servants shall serve him: (4) and they
shall see his face; and his name *shall*
be in their foreheads. (5) And there
shall be no night there; and they need
no candle, neither light of the sun;[a]
for the Lord God giveth them light:
and they shall reign for ever and ever.
(6) And he said unto me, These sayings
are faithful and true: and
the Lord God of the holy
prophets sent his angel
to shew unto his servants the things
which must shortly be done. (7) Behold,
I come quickly: blessed *is* he that

Chap. xxii. 6–15. Words of confirmation.

a ch. 21. 23.

any longer. There may be an allusion to Josh. vii. 12; there is certainly a borrowing of language from Zechariah (Zech. xiv. 11). All accursed things are removed, and with them passes the curse. The blessing of God's presence, and the blessing of God's rule take the place of the ascendancy of evil over the groaning creation (Rom. viii. 22). "The throne of God and the Lamb shall be in it." The song of the Psalmist receives new force: "the Lord reigneth: let the earth rejoice; let the multitudes of the isles be glad thereof;" the accursed things, even all things that offend, are gathered out of the kingdom (Matt. xiii. 41).

(3, 4) **And his servants shall serve him . . .**—We turn from the city to the inhabitants. They are described as serving Him, seeing Him, and resembling Him. They shall serve Him: they shall offer Him the service of the priesthood—the word employed is that used of temple service. The word translated "servants" is the word which the Apostles used when they spoke of themselves as *slaves* of Jesus Christ, owned as well as employed by Him (Phil. i. 1; 2 Pet. ii. 1; Jude, verse 1). Their service here was discharged in the midst of discouragements and in difficulty; and they walked by faith, not by sight. Now the servants shall serve without hindrance or opposition, and they shall be encouraged by His immediate presence. "They *shall see his face;*" they shall know even as they are known (1 Cor. xiii. 12); they shall see Him as He is. No wonder, then, that he should add (and observe that the thought is exactly that which occurs in the First Epistle of St. John (1 John iii. 2): "His name shall be in (or, *on*) their foreheads." The *name* stands for what God is in holiness and righteousness, purity and love. The name on the forehead indicates their resemblance to their Master. On earth the servants of God are changed from glory to glory into the same image (2 Cor. iii. 18). They aim to be perfect, as their Father in heaven is perfect (Matt. v. 48); but when they see God as He is they shall be like Him. His name is on their foreheads, for they behold His face: they wake up after His likeness, and they are satisfied (Ps. xvii. 15). There is a divine paradox in the double truth: those who are like God see Him, and those who see Him are like Him (Matt. v. 8). "There will come a time when the service of God shall be the beholding of Him; and though in these stormy seas, where we are now driven up and down, His Spirit is dimly seen on the face of the waters, and we are left to cast anchors out of the stern and wish for the day, that day will come, when, with the evangelist on the crystal and stable sea, all the creatures of God shall be full of eyes within, and there shall be no more curse, but His servants shall serve Him, and shall see His face" (Ruskin).

(5) **And there shall be no night there . . .**—Rather, *And night shall not be any more, and* (*they shall not have*) *need of the light of lamp, and of light of sun, because the Lord God shall give light upon them, and they shall reign unto the ages of ages.* There shall be no night. Twice is it said (chap xxi. 25) that all darkness shall cease; the darkness in which the saints and sorrowing walked shall be dispelled, when God gives them light. No artificial light is needed, since He who is Light is their light. Those who were children of light now dwell in the light of God's countenance; and they reign who were made kings and priests to God (chap. i. 6). With this utterance the visions of the Apocalypse close. The saints of God have been seen in the bitterness and toilfulness of their struggle and pilgrimage towards the Holy City; but from point to point they have made progress. They have gone from strength to strength, unto the God of gods appeareth every one of them in Zion. The Lord God is their sun and shield. He has given grace; He now gives glory. No good thing has been withheld; light, life, and love are theirs. "O Lord God of Hosts, blessed is the man that trusteth in Thee" (Ps. lxxxiv. 11, 12).

(6–21) These verses contain the concluding words. It is the Epilogue of the Book; it deals with practical exhortations, warnings, and blessings.

Words of Confirmation and Warning.

(6) **And he said unto me . . .**—It is the angel who speaks. (Comp. chap. xxi. and verse 9 of this chapter.) In verse 7 we hear the words of Christ Himself. *These sayings* (or, *words*) *are faithful and true.* The reference is to the whole book. The book contains the Revelation of the faithful and true witness (chap. iii. 14), whose words are faithful, trustworthy, and fulfilling the desire of them that fear Him. Nor is there reason to doubt this; for "*the Lord, the God of the spirits of the Prophets*—the God whose spirit moved the holy men of old to speak (2 Pet. i. 21)—*sent His angel to show to His servants things which must come to pass shortly.*" (Comp. Note on chap. i. 1.)

(7) **Behold, I come quickly.**—The words of Christ Himself follow (perhaps quoted by the angel), to confirm the declaration of the last verse. These confirming words are an embodiment of the spirit of the whole Apocalypse. *And behold I am coming quickly!* The Apocalypse is the revelation of the coming One; it reveals the dealings of Him who came, who comes, and is to come. (Comp. Note on chap. i. 4.) The blessing given in chap. i. 3 is in part repeated here, but it is a benediction emphatically on those who keep the words of the book. *Blessed is he who keepeth the words of the prophecy of this book.* It is not in reading, or wondering, or talking, but in keeping, that the blessing comes. He that loves Christ will keep His commandments (John xiv. 15), even as Christ loved His Father, and kept His commandments (John xv. 10). Those who so keep the sayings or words of Christ in this book will stand firm as those who have built upon the rock (Matt. vii. 24, 25). The blessing of Christ to such was victory over death. "If a man keep My saying, he shall never see death" (John viii. 51).

keepeth the sayings of the prophecy of
this book. (8) And I John saw these
things, and heard *them.* And when I
had heard and seen, I fell down to
worship before the feet of the angel
which shewed me these things. (9) Then
saith he unto me, See *thou do it* not:[a]
for I am thy fellowservant, and of thy
brethren the prophets, and of them
which keep the sayings of this book:
worship God. (10) And he saith unto
me, Seal not the sayings of the prophecy
of this book: for the time is at hand.
(11) He that is unjust, let him be unjust
still: and he which is filthy, let him be
filthy still: and he that is righteous, let
him be righteous still: and he that is
holy, let him be holy still. (12) And,
behold, I come quickly; and my reward
is with me, to give every man according
as his work shall be.[b] (13) I am Alpha
and Omega, the beginning and the end,
the first and the last.[c] (14) Blessed *are*
they that do his commandments, that

[a] ch. 19. 10.

[b] Rom. 2. 6.

[c] Isa. 41. 4; 44. 6.

---

(8) **And I John saw these things . . .**—Or rather, *And I John am he who hears and sees these things.* The words of the angel are confirmed by the words of Christ. Now we have the confirmatory testimony of the seer to the truth of the vision. The declaration reminds us of the opening of the Epistle of St. John: "That which we have seen and heard declare we unto you" (1 John i. 1—3). It is no mere dream or ingenious fancy of his own that he has recorded; it is a veritable revelation.

And when I had heard . . .—Or better, *When I heard and saw, I fell down to worship before the feet of the angel who was showing me these things.* Wonder and awe took possession of the seer, and for the second time he was about to offer unlawful homage to the angel-minister. (Comp. chap. xix. 10.) This twice offered and twice refused worship is full of teaching. To render to all their due is wise and seemly and Christlike; to offer exaggerated homage to any is to invert God's order, and to degrade by pretending to exalt man, whose true glory is that he is God's creation.

(9) **Then saith he unto me . . .**—Better, *And he saith to me, See* (or, *Take heed*) *not. I am a fellow servant of thee and of thy brethren the prophets, and of those who keep the words of this book; worship God* (or, *to God give worship*). This rebuke is similar to that given in chap. xix. It is a wide affirmation of the truth that all—whether angels, or prophets, or simple faithful followers of Christ—are united in a grand bond of common devotion and common service to the same Lord.

(10) **And he saith to me . . .**—The angel, in contrast to the injunctions given to Daniel (Dan. xii. 9—13), bids the prophet "Seal not the words of the prophecy": the reason is added, "for the time is near." "Such is ever the difference between the prophecy of the old, and the prophecy of the new dispensation. The one belonged to a preliminary and prefatory state; the other to a completive and final condition. However long the gospel age may have lasted, or may yet continue, *it is the last time* (1 John ii. 18): after it there is none other: then shall the end come" (Matt. xxiv. 14), (Dean Vaughan).

(11) **He that is unjust, let him be unjust . . .**—Better, *Let him that is unjust, do injustice still; and let the foul pollute himself still; and let the righteous do righteousness still; and let the holy sanctify himself still.* Two pairs are selected to stand as representatives of the good and of the bad: in these four are included all classes of godly and ungodly: those who sin against society, and those who sin against themselves: those who act honourably, and those who keep themselves pure. But what does the verse mean? Does it mean that the time is so short that it is hardly sufficient to allow of men reforming themselves, so as to be ready for their Lord, and that therefore the lesson is, let those who would be ready for Him remember that *now* is the day of salvation? This is the view adopted by some: it contains a truth, but the meaning of the verse seems more general. Is it not the declaration of the ever terrible truth, that men are building up their destiny by the actions and habits of their lives? "Sow an act—reap a habit: sow a habit—reap a character: sow a character—reap a destiny." The righteous become righteous: the godly become godly.

> "Thus, all characters
> Must shrink or widen, as our wine-skins do,
> For more or less that we can pass in them:
> And added years give ever a new key
> To fixed prediction."

So, slowly, but surely, may the power of being masters of our fate pass out of our hands. It is in this law of our nature that the key to many of the darkest problems of the future may lie; and not without a solemn declaration of this law does the Book of Revelation close.

(12) **And, behold, I come quickly . . .**—Rather, *Behold, I am coming quickly, and My reward is with Me to give back to each one as his work is.* To give back to each: here we have the truth declared by St. Paul uttered in words borrowed from Isaiah (Isa. xl. 10). "Whatsoever a man soweth, that shall he also reap," wrote St. Paul (Gal. vi. 7, 8): "God gives back to each one his work," says St. John.

(13) **I am Alpha . . .**—Here (as in chap. xxi. 6) we should render, *I am the Alpha and the Omega, the first and the last, the beginning and the end.* (See Note as above, and comp. John i. 1; Isa. xliv. 6.) The repetition of these glorious titles is not a mere idle repetition, or designed to give a rhetorical fulness to the peroration of the book: it is closely allied with the preceding thought. The warning has been given that men by continuing in sin (verse 11) are inviting against themselves the law by which act ripens to habit, and habit makes character, and character forms destiny. The moral laws set going by sin work thus:—Retribution is no dream: it is a terrible fact: it is written large over nature. But the eternal laws of God, though righteously ordered, are not God: the refuge from the eternal laws which we invoke against ourselves by our sin is to be found in the Eternal God: "I am the Alpha and the Omega, the first and the last, the beginning and the end." For those hunted by the wickedness of their own doings, God himself provides a refuge: underneath all laws are the everlasting arms (Deut. xxxiii. 27). The next verses set the way of refuge and safety before us.

(14) **Blessed are they that do his commandments . . .**—The reading of two of the best MSS. is, "Blessed are they that wash their robes." If we adopt, as we probably ought, this reading, the line

they may have right to the tree of life, and may enter in through the gates into the city. (15) For without *are* dogs, and sorcerers, and whoremongers, and murderers, and idolaters, and whosoever loveth and maketh a lie. (16) I Jesus have sent mine angel to testify unto you these things in the churches. I am the root and the offspring of David, *and* the bright and morning star. (17) And the Spirit and the bride say, Come. And let him that heareth say, Come. And let him that is athirst come. And whosoever will, let him take the water of life freely.[a] (18) For I testify unto every man that heareth the words of the prophecy of this book, If any man shall add unto these things, God shall add unto him the plagues that are written in this book:[b] (19) and if any man shall take away from the words of the book of this prophecy, God shall take away his part out of the book of life, and out of the holy city, and *from* the things which are written in this book. (20) He which testifieth these

Chap. xxii. 17. The final invitation.

Chap. xxii. 18, 19. The final warning.

a Isa. 55. 1.

b Deut. 4. 2; Prov. 30. 6.

---

of thought suggested above is helped forward: there is in Him who is the First and the Last, refuge from the power of sin and law against which such solemn warning has been given. The blood of Jesus Christ cleanseth from all sin: the best who have striven and conquered were victors not by their own might, but by the blood of the Lamb (chap. xii. 11). If, however, we follow the Received text, we have a benediction which echoes the blessing promised to obedience in verses 7, 9: this echoing of promises from point to point is in harmony with the spirit of the whole epilogue. (Comp. verses 7, 9; and 7, 12.) The special blessing held out to those who wash their robes (or do His commandments) is the right or authority over the tree of life. *Blessed are they . . . that they may have* (and continue to have) *authority over the tree of life, and that they may enter in by the gates into the city.* Admission into the city by the gate, which is of one pearl, and the continuous access to the tree of life, are the privileges of the faithful; and these privileges are free to all, for warnings do not forfeit privileges, but rather do they urge us to use them.

(15) **For without are dogs and sorcerers . . .**—Better, *Outside are the dogs, and the sorcerers, and the fornicators, and the murderers, and the idolators, and every one loving and doing falsehood.* The language is again an echo of earlier words. (See chap. xxi. 8.) The allusion to the dogs outside the city is hardly appreciated by Westerns. In the East, however, "troops of hungry and semi-wild dogs used to wander about the fields and streets of the cities, devouring dead bodies and other offal (1 Kings xiv. 11; xvi. 4; xxi. 19; xxii. 38; 2 Kings ix. 10, 36; Jer. xv. 3; Ps. lix. 6), and thus became such objects of dislike that fierce and cruel enemies are poetically styled *dogs* in Ps. xxii. 16, 20." The dog, moreover, was an unclean animal; dogs, therefore, are represented as outside the city, because nothing unclean is allowed to enter. The sins enumerated here are similar to those mentioned in the last chapter (verse 8); it is the reiteration, therefore, of the warning that those who would enter in must break off their sins by righteousness.

(16) **I Jesus have sent mine angel . . .**—The warning is followed by the voice of our Lord Himself testifying to the truth of the revelation made, *I Jesus sent* (not "have sent," as in the English version) *my angel to testify to you these things to the churches.* But it is not merely a message, or the confirmation of a message that we have—we have also stated what Christ is—the root and pledge of hope to all. *I am the root and offspring of David, and the star, the bright, the morning* (*star*). He is David's Lord and David's Son, possessing David's throne (Matt. xxii. 42—45; Luke i. 32); He is the bright star which leads up the dawn of everlasting day (Mal. iv. 2; 2 Pet. i. 19).

(17) **And the Spirit and the bride say, Come . . .**—The cry of all creation is for its true Lord; the cry of the Spirit in prophecies and in the hearts of God's people is for the coming Lord—the bride waiting for the bridegroom cries "Come." The Apocalypse is the book of the coming One; it ends with the cry that the coming One would come (comp. verse 20); but let those who thirst for His coming come to Him. We may draw near to Him, who is drawing near to us: *let him that thirsteth, come; let him that will take the water of life freely.* (Comp. John vii. 37.) "The power of the whole gospel," says Bengel, "concentrates itself in this, that one should be able to respond to this Come, and repeat it from the heart."

(18—19) **I testify unto every man that heareth.**—Omit "For," and read, *I testify to every one that hears . . .* The "I" is emphatic; it introduces the final warning; the revelation must not be tampered with. *If any one shall have added to them, God shall add to him the plagues which are written in this book; and if any one shall have taken away from the words of the book of this prophecy, God shall take away his portion from the tree of life, and out of the holy city which are written* (or printed) *in this book.* We may compare Deut. iv. 2, and xii. 32. The words are a solemn protest against the spirit which handles rashly or deceitfully the word of God; which adds its own thoughts, or makes its wishes the parent of its interpretations; which dilutes the force of its warnings, or impoverishes the fulness of its promises. The right of continual access to the tree of life was the promise of verse 14; this right or freedom is forfeited by those who deal falsely or faithlessly by the words of Christ here. In a minor degree, it is true that those who leave this book unstudied and unprayed over, lose much spiritual sustenance and comfort. How much more do they lose who trifle with it, ignore its spiritual teachings, and sin against the laws of that kingdom whose progress it so vividly portrays.

(20) **He which testifieth these things . . .**—Better, *He saith, who testifieth these things, Yea, I am coming quickly.* We have here the final witness; it is in the words of the faithful and true witness Himself. It is the answer to the repeated cry, "Come;" it is the warning to those who forget Him; it is introduced with the emphatic yea! "Yea, I am coming quickly." The answer breaks forth in prayer from the prophet's lips—*Amen.* (We must omit "even so") *Come, Lord Jesus.* The prophet is the mouthpiece of the Church;

Chap. xxii. 20. The final witness.

things saith, Surely I come
quickly. Amen. Even so,
come, Lord Jesus. (21) The
grace of our Lord Jesus
Christ *be* with you all.
Amen.

Chap. xxii. 21. The final blessing.

his desire is one with the desire of all who love Christ's appearing.

(21) **The grace of our Lord Jesus Christ . . .**—There is some variety of reading among the MSS. We ought probably to read, *The grace of the Lord Jesus Christ be with all* (or else, following the Sinaitic MS., *be with the saints*). *Amen.* In any case, it is the grace or free pardon of the Lord Jesus which is the last word left in our ears. It reminds us that whatever be the dangers or difficulties, the afflictions or persecutions which have been pictured in the book, there is strength and love in the Lord; it reminds us that whether we are readers or interpreters of this book, or whether we are trying to carry out its teachings practically in daily life, our power and wisdom must come from Him. The testimony of Jesus is the spirit of prophecy. Without Him it had not been written; without Him it cannot be understood; without Him it cannot be obeyed. This grace of Christ our Lord, for mind and heart and life, the writer prays may rest with those who read this Commentary, that they may be led into deeper knowledge of Him who is our life. The writer asks the reader to pray that this grace of Christ may rest in forgiveness and love upon him who has now finished his task of commenting on this book, whose hidden meanings must far transcend our knowledge and our expectations. May He (He alone can) open our eyes to see the shining towers of the Heavenly Jerusalem; may He unseal our ears to hear the heavenly music to which it is being built; may He bind us by His love to that sweet service and citizenship which is perfect freedom, and bring us to that spiritual city which is full of divine enchantments—

> "For there is nothing in it as it seems
> Saving the King; though some there be that hold
> The King a shadow, and the city real;
> Yet take thou heed of Him, for, so thou pass
> Beneath this archway, then wilt thou become
> A thrall to His enchantments, for the King
> Will bind thee by such vows as is a shame
> A man should not be bound by, yet the which
> No man can keep; but so thou dread to swear,
> Pass not beneath this gateway, but abide
> Without among the cattle of the field.
> For, an ye heard a music, like enow
> They are building still, seeing the city is built
> To music, therefore never built at all,
> And therefore built for ever."

EXCURSUS ON NOTES TO REVELATION.

EXCURSUS A: THE ANGELS OF THE CHURCHES.

THE most usual interpretation regards the angels of the churches as the chief ministers or presiding elders of the congregations. This interpretation is so very widely adopted that it has been mentioned in the Notes; but the reader will have perceived that it is not a view which can be considered altogether satisfactory. In the first place, whatever date we accept for the Apocalypse, it is at least strange to find the titles, "elders" or "bishops," which were in common use exchanged for the doubtful one of "angel." A common explanation is that the term is derived from the synagogue staff, where the messenger or "angel of the synagogue" was a recognised office; but the transference of such a title to any office in the Christian Church is at least doubtful, and as the officer so styled was only a subordinate in the synagogue, a "clerk" or "precentor" to conduct the devotions of the worshippers, it becomes very improbable that such a term or title would have been employed to describe the presiding elder of a Christian Church. Turning to the Old Testament, it is true that the word "angel" is used in a higher sense (Hagg. i. 13; Mal. ii. 7), being employed to describe the messengers of God; but the usage here is different. "It is conceivable, indeed, that a bishop or chief pastor should be called an angel, or messenger of God, or of Christ, but he would hardly be styled an angel of the church over which he presides." (Lightfoot, *Epistle to the Philippians*, p. 197, note.) Thus the interpretation under consideration appears scarcely satisfactory.

Others have thought the word "angel" is not to be applied to the individual presiding elder, but to the whole ministry of the Church, treated as one. This view, though in some senses approaching nearer to the truth, can hardly be sustained without considerable modification. Others, again, fall back upon Jewish authorities, and see in the angels the guardian angels of the churches. "In Daniel every nation has its ruling angel; and, according to the Rabbins, an angel is placed over every people." The angel, then, would be a literal, real angel, who has the guardianship of the church in question. In popular thought, then, the angel would be one of the good angelic beings whose special duty it was to bear up the church during its trials, by such providential ministries as were needed and ordered. There are some difficulties in accepting this interpretation. In particular the language of rebuke which is addressed directly to the angel himself—the threatening to remove his candlestick, for example—sounds meaningless.

But here it is that we may inquire whether the angel of a particular community, nation, or people is to be understood always of a good and powerful being sent forth by the Almighty to love and watch over it. It is believed that this view does not satisfy the case. It is certain that Daniel represents the guardian angels of nations as opposed to each other, and not co-operating always for the same great and good end. "The prince (*guardian angel*) of the kingdom of Persia withstood me," is the language addressed to Daniel by him whose face was like lightning (Dan. x. 13). (Compare also verses 20, 21, and Dr. Currey's Notes in the *Speaker's Commentary* on these passages.) Such passages seem to suggest that the "angels" are the powers in the spiritual sphere corresponding to the peoples or communities in the earthly; and these may be on the side of evil or of good. Next, it may be noticed that the action of these angels in the spiritual sphere seems to be the reflection of the action of the community or people in the earthly. If the church at Ephesus has left its first love, the angel is spoken of as sharing the same fault. The influences seen on the spiritual side correspond with those at work in the actual earthly community. The angel of the church or of the individual thus becomes their manifestation in the heavenly sphere. For all our life is thus double; our actions have an earthly meaning, and also a heavenly; what they touch of worldly interests gives them their earthly meaning, what they touch of spiritual welfare is their heavenly meaning. Like the planets, we lie half in shadow and half in light: from the earthly side the world-meaning of our actions lies in the light, and their spiritual value or force is only dimly seen, as it lies in at least partial shadow; but seen from the heavenly side the position is reversed, the worldly significance of human actions is cast into comparative shade, the actual spiritual influences of them are brought into clear light; and it is the spiritual significance of our actions which reveals what we are; in this is concentrated the true force which we are exerting. Seen from the heavenly side, the angel of our life mingles in the great spiritual war, and takes its part as a combatant there; while, on the earthly side, we are seen carrying on our daily occupations. Measured on the earthly side the balance is not struck; there is inconsistency in us; we are partly good and partly bad, sometimes helping, sometimes hindering the work of God on earth, as we judge; but the actual resultant of these inconsistent powers is seen in the heavenly sphere, either helping or thwarting the cause of good. Thus are we double combatants—in the world, for our livelihood, for our ease, for our advancement; in the heavenly, for good or for evil. And it is on the spiritual side that we lie open to spiritual influences; here, where our true self is seen more clearly than anywhere else, are the appeals to our better nature, as we say, most powerful; here, He who holds the stars in His right hand, makes His voice to be heard when He addresses, not merely the church or the individual, but the angel of the church; here, He calls them to see that there is a war in heaven, in which all are combatants, but in which He is the Captain of our salvation. Here too, on the heavenly side, are the wounds of the spiritual and better nature more plainly seen; the offence or blow given to the little one of

Christ is not noticed on the earthly side, but the inner nature is wounded, and the wound is seen in its real dimensions in the presence of God, for the angel nature beholds God's face. It is this thought which gives force and solemnity to our Lord's warning (Matt. xviii. 10).

The angel of the church, then, would be the spiritual personification of the church; but it must not be concluded from this, as Züllig does, that these angels are in "the mind of the poet himself nothing more than imaginary existences," or reduce the angel to be "just the community or church itself." It is no more the church itself than the "star" is the same as the candlestick. "The star is the supra-sensual counterpart, the heavenly representative; the lamp, the earthly realisation, the outward embodiment" (Lightfoot, *Epistle to the Philippians*, p. 198). The angel is the church seen in its heavenly representative, and seen, therefore, in the light of those splendid possibilities which are hers if she holds fast by Him who holds fast the seven stars.

Space forbids any treatment of the wider questions on the ministry of angels, or the nature of angelic beings. That such are recognised in Scripture there can be no doubt, and nothing written above is designed to militate against such a belief; but it seems well to remember that where we are dealing with a symbolical book, it is more in harmony with its character to treat symbols as symbols. The forces of nature are God's messengers, and we may regard them as truly such, and feel that the expressions "the angel of the waters," "the angel of fire," "the angel of the abyss," and so forth, are designed to remind us that all things serve Him, and are the ministers of Him, to do His pleasure; we may even believe that the various forces of nature, so little really understood by us, are under the guardianship of special personal messengers of God; but there is nothing in the imagery of the book which necessarily demands such a belief. It is, moreover, surely not inappropriate in our own day to reassert with some pertinacity the lofty thoughts of ancient belief that winds and storms, ocean and fire, do in truth belong to Him round whom are the clouds and darkness, whose is the sea, and whose hands prepared the dry land.

On the literature of this subject see Godet's *Studies on the New Testament;* Schaff, *History of the Apostolic Church;* Lightfoot's article on "The Christian Ministry" in the *Epistle to the Philippians*, pp. 193—199; Hengstenberg's lengthy note on Rev. i. 20; Professor Milligan's article, "The Candlestick and the Star," in the *Expositor* of September, 1878; Gebhardt, *Der Lehrbegriff der Apokalypse*, article "Die Engel," p. 37, or p. 36 in the English translation (*The Doctrine of the Apocalypse*) published by Messrs. Clark in the Foreign Theological Library. Also "Excursus on Angelology" in the *Speaker's Commentary* on Daniel, p. 348; article "Angels" in Smith's *Dictionary*.

EXCURSUS B: THE WILD BEAST.

It is to be noticed that the interpretation of the whole Apocalypse is coloured by the interpretation given to the wild beast. The book, as we have seen (see *Introduction*), is one of hope, but it is also one of warning; not without a struggle would the foe be driven from the earth where he had usurped power for so long. The devil is cast down—in the higher, heavenly sphere he is regarded as a fallen and defeated enemy; but this conflict has its counterpart on the arena of the world. The Apocalypse gives us in symbol some features of this conflict. It shows *four* powers of evil: the dragon, the first and second wild beasts, and Babylon the harlot. It is with the beast that we are now concerned, but one or two remarks on this family of evil will not be out of place.

I. The Family of Evil.

(1) The four antagonists of good are related to one another. The resemblance between the dragon and the wild beast (comp. Rev. xii. 3; xiii. 1; xvii. 3, 7, 10) is too obvious to be passed over; it seems designed to show us that the same principle and spirit of evil is at work in both. Again, the way in which the first wild beast gives place to the second wild beast, or false prophet (comp. chaps. xiii. 11, 12; xvi. 13; xix. 20; xx. 10), and yet retains its ascendency (comp. chap. xiii. 14—17) makes plain the close connection between them; and, lastly, the appearance of the harlot, riding on the scarlet-coloured beast (chap. xvii. 3), completes the chain of association between them. The same principles and spirit of evil make themselves manifest in different spheres.

(2) The four antagonists of good are arranged to meet the four corresponding manifestations of good. For every power of good there is an analogous power of evil. If on the side of good we have the three Persons of the blessed Trinity—the Throned One, the Lamb, and the Holy Spirit—besides the Church, the bride, the Lamb's wife, the heavenly Jerusalem; we have on the side of evil—the dragon, the beast, the false prophet, as a sort of trinity of evil—besides the harlot, Babylon. The dragon being a kind of anti-God; the wild beast, an anti-Christ; the false prophet, an anti-Spirit; the Babylon, an anti-Church. The minor features in the same way correspond: the true Christ died and rose again; the anti-Christ, the wild beast, was wounded unto death, but his deadly wound was healed. The crucified Christ was exalted to be Prince and Saviour, and the outpoured Spirit upon the Church glorified Him by taking of the things of Christ and showing them to the disciples, and by convincing the world of sin because Christ went to the Father; the second beast, or false prophet, works wonders, causes an image of the first wild beast to be made and worshipped. The followers of the Lamb are sealed with the Holy Spirit of Promise; the worshippers of the wild beast receive from the false prophet the mark of the beast. (See chap. xiii. throughout.) It is desirable to keep these lines of parody and correspondent antagonism in mind.

II. The Wild Beast—or Antichrist.—It is with the beast that we are concerned in this *Excursus;* but we cannot altogether dissociate the first beast from the second, though their work is diverse.

(1) The first wild beast is clearly to be connected with the vision of Dan. vii. 2—7; the identification of the beast described by Daniel with four great empires is unquestionable: it is hardly our purpose to inquire whether the four empires are Babylonia, Medo-Persia, Macedonia, and Rome; or Babylonia, Media, Persia, and Greece: the former, which is the more ancient opinion, appears the more probable; but it is enough to remember that these four beasts represent four great world-powers. St. John saw rising out of

the sea (comp. Dan. vii. 2), not seven diverse beasts, but one seven-headed beast. Now it is perfectly true that to the early Christians Pagan and Imperial Rome was the one great world-power whose shadow darkened the earth, and that a seven-headed monster might well depict this Pagan Rome, as a four-headed beast had represented to Daniel an earlier empire (Greece or Persia); and the wild beast of Rev. xiii. from one aspect undoubtedly represents this great tyrant power; but it seems to the present writer that the genius of the Apocalypse is concentration; that which to earlier prophets was seen in detail is to the Christian seer grouped. Daniel saw four beasts rising one after another; St. John saw one wild beast, uniting in himself all the early, present, and future manifestations of that world-empire which has ever been hostile to the spiritual kingdom. Two reasons may be noticed; one from the Book of Daniel, the other from Revelation. This concentration of different world-powers into one representative body was not foreign to the thought of the earlier prophet. Daniel relates the vision in which the diverse monarchies of the world were represented as one huge human figure cast out of gold, silver, brass, and iron (Dan ii. 31—49); the diverse powers were thus seen as one, and the little stone, which represented the true spiritual kingdom, in smiting upon one, caused the whole image to fall. The world-kingdoms were thus seen in prophetic vision as one great age-long world-power, which must be smitten by Christ's kingdom. The Book of Revelation also gives us a hint that the seven-fold aspect of the wild beast must not be given too limited or too local an interpretation. The wild beast, with seven heads and ten crowns, is in these features reproducing the appearance of the red dragon, who is also represented as having seven heads and ten horns. (Comp. Rev. xii. 3; xiii. 1.) Now the dragon is surely the type of the great arch-enemy the Devil—the Anti-God; the seven heads and ten horns denote that he is the prince of this world, who has more or less animated the successive great world-powers by hostility to righteousness; the empires of the world have been his in so far as they have been founded on force, or fraud, oppression, or unholiness. When, then, the seven-headed wild beast rises from the sea, must we not see in the seven heads the counterpart of those which the dragon bore? The dragon carries those seven heads as he is the great spiritual prince of this world, the one who is practically worshipped in all mere world-made empires. The wild beast carries these seven heads because he is the great representative of all these world-powers themselves, and what may give almost certainty to this interpretation is the fact that the wild beast unites in himself the appearances of leopard, bear, and lion, which were the emblems employed by Daniel to represent earlier monarchies. Actually at the moment St. John saw the vision the wild beast was to him Rome, because through Rome the great world-empire was then working. The seven heads might also look like types of successive emperors; but the more important, because age-long reading of the vision sets before us the concentration in one great monstrous wild beast of all those powers. Powers which were diverse and even politically hostile were yet ethically *one* power opposed to the fundamental principles of righteousness and peace, of purity and true godliness. The first wild beast, then, becomes the symbol of confederated and age-long world-powers.

(2) The second wild beast is allied with the first. His origin is not of God, he is of the earth: he is more peaceable in his appearance than the first beast, but his speech bewrays him; the dragon-voice is his, and he revives the worship of the first wild beast. In him, therefore, are combined the powers of the dragon and the first wild beast. Yet he yields homage to existing order: unlike the first wild beast, which rises out of an ocean of disorder and tumult, he springs out of the earth. He assumes in part, also, a Christian appearance: he is as a lamb. These features would lead us to expect a power not wholly irreligious—indeed, in some features Christian, yet practically Pagan: observing order, yet arrogant; a second power resembling the first, yet possessing a more specious appearance to mankind. It is on this second wild beast that the seer bids us fasten our more marked attention. It is this second wild beast who deceives by false wonders and false worship, and introduces a great and grinding tyranny. It is this second wild beast to whom is attributed the mysterious number 666. It is well now to turn back to earlier writings. In Dan. vii. we read of a "little horn," and in the description there we find much that is parallel with the description here. (Comp. Dan. vii. 8 with Rev. xiii. 5; Dan. vii. 21 with Rev. xiii. 7.) This "little horn" of Daniel has been identified (comp. *Excursus on Interpretation of* 2 Thess. ii. 3—12) with the "Man of Sin" spoken of by St. Paul (2 Thess. ii. 3). Some think that the little horn of Dan. vii. is identical with the horn of chap. viii. Into this question we have not space to enter: it will be enough here to keep in mind that St. Paul looked for the manifestation of an Antichrist, a Man of Sin, whose type in all likelihood he found in the little horn of Dan. vii.; and that the picture of the Antichrist painted by St. Paul is that of a power not professedly irreligious, but yet claiming from mankind the homage due to God (2 Thess. ii. 4). This seems quite in harmony with the characteristics of the second wild beast, who, it is to be remembered, is described (Rev. xvi. 13; xix. 20; xx. 10) as the "false prophet." We may, then, take the second wild beast as the picture of a power, cultured, quasi-religious, borrowing much from Christianity, yet built upon anti-Christian principles, and animated by an anti-Christian spirit.

(3) *The identification of the Wild Beast, False Prophet, or Antichrist.*—"Ye have heard that Antichrist shall come" (1 John ii. 18). This is St. John's acknowledgment of the wide-spread belief that a great falling away should precede the coming of Christ. Here he is at one with St. Paul, but it is consistent with the spirit of St. John's thought that he should remind his hearers that the spirit of Antichrist was abroad already, and that in a present antagonism to this spirit lay true Christian duty: accordingly, he indicates in more than one place what were some features of the anti-Christian spirit (1 John ii. 22; iv. 1—3). It is also significant that he uses the phrase "false prophet," reminding us of the Apocalypse, which identifies, as we have seen, the wild beast, or Antichrist, with the false prophet St. John thus appears to regard the spirits and false prophets abroad in his day as at least anticipations of the great future Antichrist and false prophet. Actually there were Antichrists then in the world; but in the prophetic ideal all these were as *one* great Antichrist. In the Apocalyptic vision the scattered spirits grew into one great representative opponent—the wild beast, the false prophet. Is there, then, no personal Antichrist? It has been ably argued (see *Excursus on Prophecy of* 2 Thess. ii.) that the Man of Sin must be an individual. There are certain expressions which seem to point to a single person—notably the remarkable use of the masculine gender when the wild

beast is referred to (see Rev. xiii. 5): but it seems more consonant with the symbolism of the Apocalypse to regard the wild beast as the figurative embodiment of the false, seductive, anti-Christian principle and spirit, which belongs to more ages than one, which reveals itself in diverse aspects, and yet always manifests the same hostility to the Divine Spirit. It must not, however, be supposed that this view denies a personal Antichrist. On the contrary, it is perfectly in harmony with this view to note that the wild-beast spirit has often culminated in an individual: the typical forecasts of Antichrist have often been individuals. Antiochus Epiphanes, Herod, Nero, might fairly be regarded as the incarnation of the ungodly spirit. Similarly, in later ages, it is not to be wondered at that holy, Christ-taught men, groaning for the sorrows of the world and the corruptions of Christianity, saw in many who occupied the Papal chair the very representatives of the false prophet, the Antichrist. Not more need it surprise us to find the same thought passing through men's minds when pretensions, which would be ridiculous if they were not blasphemous, have been advanced on behalf of the Roman pontiff, till the Church becomes a parody rather than a witness of divine truths. It follows that the view here maintained does not exclude the possibility of a future personal Antichrist, in whom the typical features shall yet find clearer and fuller manifestation than in any previous age. But though all this may be, and though godly men tell us that all these things must be, it appears to the writer infinitely more important to notice the principles which may constitute the Antichrist in every age: the denial of the Father and the Son (1 John ii. 22), the denial of the Mediator and Incarnate God (1 John iv. 2, 3), the arrogant claim of divine honours, the specious resemblance to Him who is the Lamb of God, the disregard of sacred ties (2 Thess. ii. 10; 1 Tim. iv. 3), the possession of wonderful power and culture (Rev. xiii. 11—14). The spirit which is depicted is one which might well develop out of the elements around us. It would not be impossible to imagine the rankest materialism allying itself with a gorgeous ritual—to see the high priests of science acquiescing in the most elaborate of ecclesiasticisms, and the agnostic in creed becoming a ceremonialist in worship, till the satire should be only too sadly true, "I found plenty of worshippers, but no God." We should then have every element in human nature allowed its nutriment—for the mind, science; for the emotions, worship; for the conduct, direction. The tripartite nature of man would be thus provided for, but the unity of his manhood would be at an end—for the worship would be unintelligent, the moral tone lifeless, because deprived of the vital sense of personal responsibility, and the intellect uninspired, because godless. Such an age would be the reign of that climax of anti-Christian spirit which is the perfection of man's powers without God, foreshadowed by the mysterious number 666, which is seeming exaltation of all human powers, but which is in truth their degradation and their discord.

III. **The Number of the Beast.**—It would serve but little purpose to recapitulate the various solutions of the number of the Beast. An account of them will be found in Elliott (vol. iii.). The chief solutions are those mentioned in the Notes. The most ancient, and perhaps most general, solution sees in the number the equivalent of *Lateinos*. Others see in it the numerical equivalent of one of the Roman emperors; Nero, advocated by Renan; Otho, advocated by an Italian writer, who accounts for the reading, "616" instead of "666," by the alteration made by a copyist to suit the name of another emperor, Caligula: *Γαιος καισαρ* = 616. None of these numerical solutions appears to the writer adequate to the whole depth of the seer's meaning, though they may be included in the significance of the symbol.